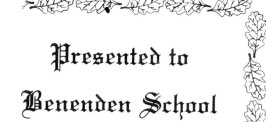

Presented to
Benenden School

by   Alexander Stiller

February 2008

The English Year

The English Year

*A month-by-month guide to
the nation's customs and festivals,
from May Day to Mischief Night*

STEVE ROUD

PENGUIN BOOKS

PENGUIN BOOKS

Published by the Penguin Group
Penguin Books Ltd, 80 Strand, London WC2R ORL, England
Penguin Group (USA) Inc., 375 Hudson Street, New York, New York 10014, USA
Penguin Group (Canada), 90 Eglinton Avenue East, Suite 700, Toronto, Ontario, Canada M4P 2Y3
(a division of Pearson Penguin Canada Inc.)
Penguin Ireland, 25 St Stephen's Green, Dublin 2, Ireland
(a division of Penguin Books Ltd)
Penguin Group (Australia), 250 Camberwell Road, Camberwell, Victoria 3124, Australia
(a division of Pearson Australia Group Pty Ltd)
Penguin Books India Pvt Ltd, 11 Community Centre, Panchsheel Park, New Delhi – 110 017, India
Penguin Group (NZ), cnr Airborne and Rosedale Roads, Albany, Auckland 1310, New Zealand
(a division of Pearson New Zealand Ltd)
Penguin Books (South Africa) (Pty) Ltd, 24 Sturdee Avenue, Rosebank, Johannesburg 2196, South Africa

Penguin Books Ltd, Registered Offices: 80 Strand, London WC2R ORL, England

www.penguin.com

First published 2006
1

Set in 8.5/12.8 pt TheAntiqua B5
Typeset by Andrew Barker
Printed in England by Clays Ltd, St Ives plc

ISBN-13: 978–0–140–51554–1
ISBN-10: 0–140–51554–2

For Jacqueline and Stephanie

Contents

List of Illustrations

Acknowledgements

Thanks to the numerous local studies library staff across the country who have welcomed me to their domains and have answered my somewhat bizarre questions with professionalism and good grace. Thanks particularly to my friends and colleagues at Croydon Local Studies Library, Chris C., Chris B., and Lizzie, for their help and cheerful forbearance; thanks also to what is left of the staff of the LSU section at Croydon for assistance with obscure inter-library loan requests, the library staff at the Folklore Society and the Vaughan Williams Memorial Library, and, most of all, the London Library for simply being a wonderful place for would-be scholars like me.

Thanks also to my fellow Penguin folklore authors Jacqueline Simpson and Jennifer Chandler; to Nigel Wilcockson, late of this parish; the many folklore writers and researchers who have helped with general guidance and specific pieces of information, including Peter Robson, Roy Palmer, Brian Shuel, Derek Schofield, Christine Bloxham, Bob and Jackie Patten; and to Kate Faulkner for preparing the index.

Thanks also to Countryside Books of Newbury, for permission to reprint the extract on Christmas puddings from their *Surrey Within Living Memory*; Persephone Books of London for recipes from their edition of Florence White's *Good Things in England*; and Lillian Barlow for her memories of Whit Walks from the *Have Your Say Magazine* website.

Introduction

The English Year concentrates on 'traditional' customs and festivals that take place within communities and are organized by members of that community, and have been around long enough to have been passed on to successive generations. The focus of the book is mainly historical, and for those customs that still exist, only a brief description of what now takes place is given, followed by a longer discussion of their history and development. In part, this is simply a reflection of my own particular interest in the subject, but it is also because this history has been so poorly served in recent years. Many books and websites describe what goes on nowadays at traditional events, but few give the history of these customs any real attention beyond reiterating standard popular explanations, which, as will be seen, are often spurious. It will also be seen that although we in England often pride ourselves on our love of tradition, numerous customs that were previously popular items in the calendar have simply disappeared, and the ones that have survived are but a small percentage of those of which past eras could boast.

Even with the relatively narrow focus on traditional customs, the events included in this book are too many and various to admit of any one overarching theory of origin, function, purpose, or meaning, except at the most superficial level. In the rare cases where we have solid information about origins, it seems that some customs were simply carried out for fun, others for the preservation of rights. Some function to foster social solidarity and to include members of the community, or to exclude outsiders, and many have religious overtones or origins. Some are parodies or burlesques, others are pious or deadly serious, and some start as one and end up as the other. Many customs had an economic basis, in that participants expected to collect money, food, or drink. Some are genuinely old, while others are surprisingly recent. New events are nowadays regularly created, usually as fun activities designed to

raise money for charity, and a sample of these has been included. But it remains to be seen how many will last long enough to become 'traditional' in their own right, handed on from generation to generation. Numerous pieces of conscious official pageantry at national and local level still exist, and a representative sample, such as the Lord Mayor's Show and the Royal Maundy distribution, is also included. Organized sport is not covered, although some of the most common traditional games are described.

It has to be said that any attempt to portray a single 'year', relevant to every English person, is doomed to failure, as the whole notion of time in this context is highly subjective. Historically speaking, the calendrical year is a complete mess. The adoption of the Gregorian calendar in 1752, eminently sensible from an astronomical point of view, introduced widespread uncertainty and confusion with regard to the timing of traditional events and customs, and the fact that the most important religious festivals (Shrovetide, Easter, Whitsun, etc.) float about from year to year plays havoc with any idea of a regular, ordered sequence of events. But an individual person's 'year' is not necessarily made up of official high days and holidays. The lives of many people in the past were dominated by the agricultural cycle, and this varied considerably depending on whether the main farming activity was arable or pastoral, and on local weather conditions. At the national level, the inexorable secularization of society has now stripped most saints' days of their special character, and surviving public customs have tended to drift from holy days towards secular bank holidays. But while the official religion has been seriously weakened, there is now a much wider variety of religions and sects in English society, each of which has its own calendar of special times and events, and for devout followers, this is the 'year' that really matters.

Apart from agriculture and religion, there are other

factors that dictate a person's year. Many occupations, for example, have long had a seasonal rhythm of their own, and for those who work in education, the year still begins in the autumn. International days of this, and national days of that, are now spread throughout the year, and most of the bigger charities use the idea of 'a day' to focus attention on their cause and raise money. But nowadays, it is personal hobby and leisure interests that influence the way many people see the year, and the sporting calendar dominates many people's lives.

The historical approach adopted in this book means that, with two exceptions, the customs of newer immigrant communities have not been included. The customs of new communities are already 'English' in the sense of taking place in this country, but if they have been simply imported from elsewhere they need time to become naturalized. Again, once they are passed on to second and third generations, and once they break out of the host community to become more widely known, they will become 'English' in every sense, whatever their origin. The Chinese New Year and the Notting Hill Carnival are included for precisely this reason. They are both public celebrations of the traditions of the communities that initially fostered them, but they now have a resonance on a much wider scale.

The loss of many of the customs of yesteryear has already been indicated. We may bemoan this loss of local colour and national heritage, but in many cases it was not necessarily a bad thing. The treatment of animals in many of our ancestors' games was barbaric, and few would like to see cockfighting or bear-baiting returned to the traditional calendar. Other mass gatherings were indeed excuses for drinking and fighting, just as the moralists of the time claimed, and the struggle over these activities made it clear that just because a pastime is old and customary does not make it acceptable or guarantee its survival. Many customs simply went out of fashion or faded away from lack of interest, but the headline grabbers were those that were forcibly suppressed, often after a bitter local struggle.

When matters of change, suppression, or revival are concerned, the central point to be considered is who owns the custom, and who therefore has the right to take action for or against it. This may seem a fatuous question, with a very simple answer – 'the community', or 'everybody' – but this does not adequately address a surprisingly complex matter. In any community there are different groups and factions, including those who carry out the custom and those to whom it is done. The bonfire boys of Victorian Lewes who wished to continue their riotous behaviour on 5 November shared their community with the shopkeepers, councillors, and clergymen who opposed them, and both sides believed they had the right to dictate the future of the event. On closer inspection, many a community has little real social cohesion, and breaks up into ever smaller groups before our eyes. Many older customs were performed and perpetuated by a small definable group, linked by the particular area in which they lived, by family ties, or by their occupation, and while these people could be fiercely protective of their own traditions, they were often prone to internal dissension, which resulted in acrimonious splits. There are two 'Osses at Padstow and three morris sides at Bampton, for example.

It has been largely the fashion since the 1970s for social historians to view the battle over the control of traditional customs in the nineteenth century in terms of class conflict, and such writers are almost always in sympathy with the workers. In case after case, the records of nineteenth-century public events show that they were firmly in the hands of the lower or working classes of the area, with active opposition coming from the middle- and upper-class residents. Increasingly during the nineteenth century, mass working-class customs were seen as harmful, distasteful, even dangerous, and those in authority began to condemn them and then actively interfere. In many cases, such as the celebrations surrounding May Day, their interference took the form of remodelling – cleaning up and constructing safe, child-based events. In other cases, however, where the customs were unsuitable for such accommodation, they were usually opposed outright and suppressed. National legislation provided assistance, by outlawing games involving cruelty to animals, forbidding the lighting of fires or discharging of guns in the street, and allowing fairs that had existed for centuries to be phased out or moved from town centres. Countless fairs, games of street football, bonfire night celebrations, and raucous mock-mayor ceremonies were banned by local authorities and broken up by the police. A few survived by cleaning up their act, or by chance circumstance, but most simply disappeared from the local scene.

The idea that we all have the right to control other people's leisure pursuits has not gone away, and, indeed, appears to be on the rise again. Some customs, such as Padstow's Darkie Day, and Cliffe's annual burning of the Pope at Lewes, cause widespread concern, but those involved claim the right to do as they please, as they have always done, citing notions of liberty and 'tradition' to justify their arguments. Meanwhile, other customs, such as the cheese-rolling at Cooper's Hill, fall foul of local government health and safety regulations, and, on another level, there were interminable arguments in the twentieth-century morris dance revival about whether women should be 'allowed' to take part. However, the most interesting recent example of control imposed by outsiders was the successful campaign to ban hunting with dogs – a traditional pastime with a long history, enjoyed by a particular group but condemned and bitterly opposed by others. Although the hunters' contention that it was a town-versus-country issue was simplistic, it contained more than a grain of truth, and there is no doubt that class antagonism played an important role, this time in an interesting case of role reversal.

In the past, it was not just high-profile mass events that came under fire: many small-scale customs also felt the cold disapproving eye of certain sections of society. Up to about the First World War, for example, it was generally accepted that people who performed traditional customs could collect money for themselves. But from about this time such activity was increasingly redefined as begging, and a general resistance began to build in the public mind. This disapproval was even extended to children's customs. An example is provided by Rose Gamble in her autobiography, *Chelsea Child*, concerning her early years in London in the 1920s. In this instance, Rose's older sister Lu had constructed a 'grotto' and had installed it, with Rose beside it, on a doorstep to sing the song she had been taught, 'Please remember the grotto . . .', to gather some pennies to go swimming. Some passers-by gave money, but others clearly disapproved:

Then a man in his shirtsleeves came out of a door next to my step and stood glaring down at me, so I *started to sing. 'You with anyone?'; I went on singing. 'And hold that bloody noise,' he shouted. 'Who's with you?' 'My sister, over there.' 'You'd better clear off,' he shouted, turning round to Lu. 'You're begging you are, and you'll get locked up!' 'No we ain't,' cried Lu indignantly, hurrying the pram across the road. 'We got something. We made something for them to look at!'*

Seventy years later, the loud protests that greeted the fad of American-style house-visiting (trick or treating) at Hallowe'en, which involved youngsters roaming the streets and knocking on doors, demanding money with threats, showed that children's customs still have the power to raise adult hackles.

However, the history of traditional customs is not simply a tale of opposition and decline and, indeed, the future for most of our surviving public events looks positively rosy. The biggest change in calendar customs in recent years has been that the communities have quite suddenly become proud of their local traditions, and even those who are not directly involved often view their customs as a way of celebrating distinctiveness and community tradition. In sharp contrast to their nineteenth-century counterparts, many local authorities are also taking an active interest, as they recognize the potential of traditional customs for fostering local pride and attracting tourists. Many give grants, include details of customs on their websites and in their tourist publicity, and provide venues and stewards. But this support comes at a price. Councils and other official bodies have agendas of their own, and the desire to reshape and control what they are supporting is often too strong to resist. The Greater London Authority, for example, in their perfectly understandable desire to champion London's cultural diversity and grassroots vitality, have seen the Notting Hill Carnival and the Chinese New Year celebrations as just the sort of thing that should be encouraged and supported. But this always means imposing changes, and the usual questions arise: Wouldn't it be better if the celebrations were moved out of the narrow streets? Why don't we extend this part because the crowd loves it, but that bit is rather boring? What about a prize for the best costume? Even without official 'support', there is often pressure at local level to 'improve' things. These impulses come from within the community and are therefore part of a custom's natural growth or development, and it cannot be said too often that communities have every right to do what they will with their traditions, whatever outsiders like me may think. However, these impulses also bring with them dangers, and the very distinctiveness that the community wishes to champion can be at risk from a creeping homogeneity: the custom may involve more and more participants, to 'make a day of it', or 'a better show'; ways are found to get children involved; people start dressing up in pseudo-historical Merrie England costume; and every custom becomes a pageant, with supplementary morris dancers.

Popularity itself brings problems and changes things. In the 1971 edition of his book *Padstow's Obby Oss*, for example, local writer Donald Rawe commented:

> *Modern publicity brings vast crowds, which impede the Mayers, tend to discourage dancing, and make it difficult for the singers to follow the leader's words. The night singing is more apt to begin in a general hubbub than the expectant silence of former years during which the church clock could be heard to strike twelve.*

And in the 1982 edition, he added the following postscript:

> *Today ... we are faced by what may be termed the Publicity Problem. Until 1970 or so, Padstow had never been loth to publicise its Great Day ... but television and the folk movement changed all that. Within a few years hordes of people were to descend on the little town: many behaved well and were genuinely interested, but others of somewhat dubious character apparently came here to drink themselves insensible, lying across our streets and quaysides, sleeping rough in Stile Field or in public shelters ... A reaction was sure to follow, and in 1975 television camera crews were told they were not welcome. Since then no one in Padstow has talked to radio or television interviewers or the press.*

Again there is a reversal: nowadays the onlookers misbehave, rather than the participants.

Almost without exception, the communities that possess the traditional customs included in this book also have 'historical' stories to explain how and when the custom originated. Some communities have more than one story, but one version usually becomes the dominant, orthodox explanation, and is taught to local children and told to any stranger who asks, appearing in local newspapers, booklets, and websites. These tales are a fascinating study in themselves, as interesting examples of narrative folklore, but they should never be taken at face value as real history. They are in fact legends, which for present purposes can be defined as traditional stories told as true but not supported by evidence. Nor should it be assumed that all legends have a kernel of truth in them. They very rarely do, and the vast majority are simply fictitious tales that have been repeated often enough to take on the veneer of accredited fact. They are believed because they function well as stories, they are neat and plausible, and people like them. They seem to correspond to what we think we know of the past, and we often hear them from respected informants. Like all traditional narratives, they come in all shapes and sizes, and they evolve and adapt, but their basic credibility relies on the dubious authenticity of oral tradition, and on internal corroborative details that support and seem to prove the basic story. However, these very details generally indicate that the story has been fabricated, often quite recently, to explain a custom that already exists.

An example of this is the name of the object that the Haxey Hood players strive to get to their goal – 'the Hood'. The prevailing story relates that the game was founded to commemorate the time when one Lady de Mowbray lost her hood in the wind, and local men tried to catch it for her. Once they had caught it, the Lady called one of the men a 'fool' and another a 'lord', which is said to explain why two characters in the game have these names. Similar *post facto* tales are found elsewhere. At Tichborne, in Hampshire, a story involving crawling has been invented to explain the name of a field, 'The Crawls'; and at Biddenden, in Kent, a story about conjoined twins is given to explain the image that is now printed on a commemorative biscuit, given as part of an annual dole there.

To the practised eye, these legends can be easily spotted and deconstructed in various ways. Because they are of quite recent origin themselves, their historicity is often decidedly shaky. I was recently told by a local resident in Croydon, Surrey, that a 1960s block of flats is called Cromwell House because Cromwell beat the French army on nearby Duppas Hill. This is a facetious example, but stories are usually based on the contemporary popular idea of what life was like in the past, rather than how it really was. Origin legends also regularly include motifs which occur in other stories and which are, in themselves, traditional. The explanation for the Penny Hedge custom at Whitby, for example, includes the motif of a hermit defying and being attacked by angry noble huntsmen. This same story is told of numerous saints and hermits across Europe.

The details woven into these stories necessarily chime well with the modern form of the customs, but this implies that every detail of the current version of a custom was present from the beginning. The one thing we know for sure about traditional customs is that they change over time, often quite dramatically. The neater the story, and the more complete its explanation of current detail, the more dubious it is. Alarm bells also sound when a story claims an origin far more remote than any independent evidence can support. Thus, if a custom that can only be traced back to the nineteenth century has an origin story set in the time of the Crusades, the story itself is insufficient evidence of the custom's earlier existence. Lastly, the details themselves rarely bear close examination. The idea that bedridden and dying Lady Tichborne could crawl around twenty-three acres of land, while holding a burning brand in one hand, is ludicrous. If you do not believe me, try it.

Understandably, those who like and believe the stories themselves do not take well to this type of deconstruction, and many people clearly believe that any legend is better than none. Talk of interchangeable motifs and historical accuracy is no match for romance, and folklorists and historians are regularly portrayed as inveterate wet blankets and wanton killjoys. To this charge we must plead guilty, especially as we cannot often offer any clear explanations to replace the stories we are so keen to debunk. Our only defence is the plea that there is no reason why fact and fiction cannot exist happily side by side, and there is nothing wrong with a legend as long as we take it for what it is. We can still enjoy a John Wayne film (well, some of us can), even though we know that he himself was not a real cowboy, and that the film is not a true historical portrait of cowboy life.

We do not have to believe that hobbits really exist to enjoy *Lord of the Rings*, and our children can believe in Father Christmas and are not permanently damaged when they learn the brutal truth.

One problem with accepting legends as truth is that it stops us enquiring further, and we thereby miss the opportunity to investigate how these customs originated. By accepting the historical legend of Lady Mowbray, which makes the Haxey Hood game seem unique, we forget to notice the similarities with other seasonal contests, usually known as 'football', at Ashbourne, Atherstone, and dozens of other places.

But the cold hard stare of the unromantic folklorist is not the real threat to the traditional 'historical' legends. The real danger is from a far more virulent virus – the idea that all customs, indeed all superstitions, nursery rhymes, and anything that smacks of 'folkiness', are direct survivals of ancient pagan fertility rites, and are concerned with the appeasement of gods and spirits. Although the suggestion of an ancient origin for our folklore was the central tenet of the Victorian and Edwardian pioneers of folklore collection, this notion has only become generally known in the last forty years or so, and has taken hold with astonishing rapidity; the majority of the population now carry the virus in some form or other, while some are very badly infected. The problem here is not simply that these theories are unsupported by any evidence, but that their blanket similarity destroys any individuality. All customs will soon end up with the same story.

Legends aside, there is no evidence that our customs have pre-Christian origins. Not one single custom can be proved to have such ancient roots, and there is usually a thousand years and more separating the nominal conversion of the English in the seventh century from the first evidence of a custom's existence; the idea that such customs formed part of a secret underground alternative religion is therefore risible. The whole panoply of vegetation spirits, earth goddesses, and the like has been invented in recent years, with no factual support, to provide a simplistic romantic and mystical backstory suited to the needs of the late twentieth and early twenty-first century. As a rule of thumb, apart from academic treatises, any description of the origin of a specific traditional English custom that uses the words 'pagan', 'fertility', or 'Celt' should be treated with extreme caution, and any description that uses the words 'sacrifice', 'Druid', 'earth goddess', or 'vegetation spirit' as complete nonsense.

A book entitled *The English Year*, which focuses on traditional customs, is bound to be drawn into the current debate on what constitutes *Englishness*. For a variety of reasons, including devolution elsewhere in the United Kingdom, the European Union, immigration, and the increasing influence of the USA, many sections of the population have started to fret about the potential loss of our national character. Leaving aside the ambiguity of the word 'English' in the context of this debate – does it mean found in England, originated in England, or invented by the English? – it has already been noted that the traditional customs listed here are too various to provide any meaningful summary.

On the national level, it is often stated that a 'love of tradition' is one of the strongest characteristics of the English, but this too is questionable, and it could easily be argued that the English have never been particularly good at preserving their traditions. As already indicated, countless customs have ceased to be performed, and not just because the powers-that-be have suppressed them: in numerous cases, the 'ordinary folk' were no longer interested. Other countries have plenty of similar customs and take them far more seriously. Indeed, there is probably very little mileage in calendar custom for the seeker after Englishness.

However, if traditional customs have little clear intrinsic meaning at national level, they certainly have more meaning on the smaller scale. The flourishing condition of the Padstow Hobby Horse, for example, may not tell us anything about being English, but it certainly says something about being Padstonian, and, perhaps, about being Cornish. It is on this more personal level that people's pride is evidenced, and feelings of belonging and continuity are fostered. Such feelings are a complex mixture of pride and nostalgia, and it is often said that Padstonians who are away from home on May Day, will sing the 'Obby 'Oss song to themselves to remind themselves of home.

Nevertheless, there is still something to be said about the attitude of the English to folk customs on a national scale. Historically, many countries have needed their folklore and traditions to help forge a national identity, either for political unification or in defence against a culturally dominant neighbour. But English culture has for so long been the dominant, even predator, culture in the neighbourhood that it has never needed to bolster national pride by drawing on traditional roots, and, because it has never needed it, the notion took hold that England had no valuable traditional culture; hence the almost total absence of academic support for the collection and study of folklore or cultural traditions in England, in stark contrast to the USA and most European countries. There is a School of Scottish Studies, a Welsh Folk Museum, a Department of Irish Folklore, but no official centre for specifically English folklore, and it has largely been left to amateur scholars and bodies like the Folklore Society to collect and document our traditions.

Yet, paradoxically, the result is not all bad. While English folklore has definitely been neglected, ignored, even derided, much of it has, in essence, been left alone. Scotland, Ireland, and Wales may have gained immeasurably from their thriving folk arts, and have each used their folklore to create and support a vibrant national identity, but they have also had to suffer the indignity of the ersatz and fake: the music hall 'stage Irish', the rampant shamrockery, the tourist leprechauns, the Chieftains; the White Heather Club, and pipe-bands perpetually playing *Amazing Grace*. It is symptomatic of this state of affairs that England does not have that arch-symbol of official fakelore, a 'national costume'. Nor have we ever taken much notice of St George's Day, much to the annoyance of patriots of various hues, and I, for one, am proud of that.

How to Use This Book

Anyone who attempts to render the English year in a single straightforward and logical sequence immediately faces three fundamental problems: what to do with the moveable feasts linked to Easter; how to deal with customs and events that are not really geared to the calendar at all; and, less obviously, how to accommodate the customs that have not been fixed to one particular day since time immemorial, but have actually shifted from year to year, as circumstances dictate. There is no completely satisfactory solution to these questions, and all one can do is to explain the decisions made in each category.

As regards the moveable feasts (tinted green), I have placed them in the position in which they fall in 2007. Fortunately, in that year Easter happens to fall on 8 April, which is roughly in the middle of its possible span. To help any reader interested in pinning down the actual festive calendar of any particular year, a table of dates for Easter Sunday for the next decade or so is provided on page 433.

In the absence of any logical or systematic way of ordering the non-calendar items such as bull-baiting and wife-selling, I have simply placed them where they seem to fit best, and readers must rely on the built-in cross-references and index to guide them to specific entries.

Similarly, there is little that can be done about the fact that many custom organizers and participants have proved pragmatic rather than romantic when choosing the day on which they hold their event, but I have placed most entries on the nominally 'correct' day. If anyone wishes to visit one of the many surviving public customs, they are cautioned *always* to check the date first. Most customs now have websites that announce the dates in advance, and local libraries or Tourist Information Centres should also be able to help.

The Calendar

There is little doubt that most of us take the structure of the calendar completely for granted, which is exactly how it should be. A universally agreed, regular, well-ordered system of time management is all we ask. We may occasionally wonder why there are twelve months of unequal length, or who decided that we needed an extra day every fourth year, but on the whole we are confident that the calendar has been worked out scientifically for us. Christmas will always fall in the middle of winter, and any diary we buy will agree with all the others on sale.

The history of the human race's attempts to understand and regulate time, and of the calendars which have been devised over the centuries, is extremely complex and fraught with false dawns, bitter controversies, and wasted opportunities. It has not been simply the inexorable march of the human intellect, based on an increasingly sophisticated understanding of the universe and the natural world, and backed by better methods of measurement, calculation, and recording. The real long-term struggle has been to wrest control of the calendar from the hands of religious leaders and move it into the secular sphere. In most cases, this has been a question of jettisoning lunar thinking and replacing it with solar.

In the following account, only the major events which have contributed to the development of the modern calendar as we know it in England receive attention, and the four key players in this story are the ancient Egyptians, the Roman Empire, the Catholic Church, and the Protestant Church. The fact that other civilizations, such as the Chinese and the Mayans, had sophisticated calendar traditions is largely ignored. It was the Romans, under Julius Caesar, that gave us the basis of the modern calendar, although they borrowed the idea from the Egyptians.

First it is necessary to understand something of the factual basis of time measurement as we understand it today. The earth's orbit round the sun takes 365.24219 mean solar days (365 days, 5 hours, 48 minutes, and 45 seconds), slightly more than the 365 days in our nominal year; hence we need an extra day every four years to prevent an accumulated disjunction between the physical solar year and our human year. The 'leap year', which includes this extra day, is normally any year whose number is exactly divisible by four, with the occasional exception. One extra day every four years is not quite accurate enough, as it overshoots the target, so the last year of each century is not a leap year unless it is divisible by 400 (1800 and 1900 were not leap years, but 2000 was).

There are four key points in the earth's annual journey round the sun: the two solstices and the two equinoxes. The solstice is the point at which the sun reaches its greatest distance from the equator, north or south, and appears to stand still for a few days (Latin *sol* means 'sun'; *sistere*, 'to stand still'). The summer solstice, which occurs around 21 June, is the longest day in the year, and the winter solstice, around 22 December, is the shortest. The two equinoxes, vernal (around 20 March) and autumnal (around 22 September), are the points at which the sun crosses the equator, when day and night are equal (Latin *equi* means 'equal'; *nox*, 'night').

To modern western eyes, the cycles of the sun are more important in terms of determining seasons, the weather, agricultural practices, and so on, but to early man it was the moon, with its cycles of waxing and waning, that seemed the more obvious candidate for time measurement. All the earliest known calendars are lunar, based on the phases of the moon, which is why we use the word 'month' to describe each of the twelve periods into which the year is divided. But this is where most of our problems start, because it takes long and complicated calculations to correlate the moon with the sun. A lunar month (the time from new moon to new moon) is 29.5306 days, so a twelve-month lunar year is just over 354 days long and thus runs almost 11 days out of step with the solar year. If the lunar year were followed, it would take only sixteen years or so for the seasons to be completely reversed. Whatever the religious investment in lunar phenomena may have been, it must have been obvious from an early date that the moon has little physical effect on nature or human life, but that the sun does. It is the sun's phases that bring the seasons, and determine when crops should be sown and when harvested, or when the weather is good enough to set sail. For centuries, the authorities attempted to keep their traditional lunar calendars while tinkering with them to bring them into line with the sun's movements. Centuries before the birth of Christ, the Babylonians tried to combine lunar and solar by intercalating extra months, the Greeks added ninety days every eight years but not always systematically, and the ancient Jewish calendar added one month every three years and another month every now and then to straighten things up. None of these amendments was sufficient, and all were immensely complex and open to corruption. As early as 4000 BC, the Egyptians were the first to calculate the solar year at 365 days, which gave them 12 months of 30 days each, plus 5 days, and they later calculated that the year was actually 365¼ days long.

The Romans had originally used a ten-month lunar year of approximately 304 days, but around 700 BC they added two more months, bringing the year to 355 days. Priests were in charge of inserting extra months periodically, but they performed this task in such an inconsistent and corrupt way that by Julius Caesar's time the calendar was seriously awry. Caesar learned of the solar calendar from the Egyptians – at a party thrown in his honour by Cleopatra, so legend has it – and in 45 BC he introduced the Julian calendar, based on the 365-day year, with an extra day every four years. Each year had twelve months, with thirty or thirty-one days (except February), and 1 January was confirmed as the beginning of the year.

Although not a perfect system, the introduction of the Julian calendar was by far the biggest step forward in the history of the calendar, and only the leader of the greatest empire on earth could have had the power to impose uniformity on such a grand scale. The month of Quintilius was later renamed 'Julius' in Caesar's honour, and after some small modifications became necessary in the year AD 8 under Emperor Augustus, the month Sextilis was renamed after him.

The calendar as we know it today was now more or less in place – regular, secular, based on the real movements of the sun, with an extra day every four years to take up the slack, and the year divided into twelve roughly equal months. The only real difference between the calendar then and now was the lack of seven-day weeks; instead, the Romans reckoned days before or after fixed points called 'kalends' (the 1st of each month), 'nones' (the 5th or the 7th), and 'ides' (the 13th or the 15th). The accepted calculation of 365¼ days for the length of the year was still not quite correct, and would cause problems centuries later, but for the time it was a brilliant achievement.

If only it were plain sailing for the calendar from this point, but this is far from the case. Emperor Constantine (d. AD 377) imposed Christianity as the official religion of the Empire, introducing the seven-day week, and Sunday as a regular holy day. Unfortunately, he also put the design of the calendar back into the hands of religious groups still wedded to traditional lunar movements for their major festival, Easter, and they could not even agree on how to calculate that. Constantine summoned Christian leaders from all quarters to their first major council at Nicaea in year 325 with the express purpose of settling differences and creating a credible, unified Church. In most areas they were largely successful, but their failure to agree a basic formula for the calculation of Easter laid the foundations for division and bitter dispute for centuries.

After the collapse of the Roman Empire and the spread of the 'barbarian hordes' across Europe, the Christian Church was the nearest thing to an international controlling body, but there were still major disputes and schisms, and the West entered a long dark period in which scientific enquiry was frowned upon. Apart from the complex calculations needed to fix the date of Easter every year, religious leaders regarded any enquiry into the calendar as at best unorthodox and at worst downright heresy, and this state of affairs lasted well into the early modern period.

By the sixteenth century, the western world was

sufficiently stable for new attempts to be made to reform the calendar. The small errors in the Julian system had now become noticeable and annoying, and in 1582 Pope Gregory finally announced changes in the calendar to correct these faults and to prevent them happening again, including the 400-year rule for leap years already described. He introduced what became known as the Gregorian Calendar, and ordained that 5 October be named 15 October to bring the calendar back into line with the physical world. This was a much-needed and sensible move, but with two major problems. The secular calendar may have been put on to a sounder footing, but Easter was still to be calculated on the basis of new moons; moreover, newly Protestant countries such as Britain labelled the reforms a Popish plot designed to undermine their credibility, and refused to join in. For more than a century following this change, half of Europe was ten days ahead of the other half.

Over the succeeding years, although other Protestant countries gradually surrendered to reform, Britain held out until 1752, by which time it had to correct by eleven days to bring it back in line. The eventual adoption of the Gregorian reforms in Britain was initiated by Philip Stanhope, fourth Earl of Chesterfield, who introduced a Bill to correct the 'inconvenient and disgraceful errors of our present calendar', which was finally signed into law by George II on 22 May 1752. 'Chesterfield's Act' decreed that Wednesday, 2 September 1752 was to be followed immediately by Thursday, 14 September 1752, and also that the New Year was to start officially on 1 January (for more on the timing of the New Year, see below).

For a long time it has been believed that there were widespread riots in Britain under the slogan of 'Give us back our eleven days', initiated by people who were too stupid to understand that the reforms were simply nominal and did not actually shorten their lives. The existence of these riots has been seriously questioned by modern scholarship, but there is no doubt that the reforms were misunderstood and unpopular in some quarters. Many people believed that the customary days of the calendar, and particularly the major religious festivals, were inextricably linked to the physical days on which they were held, and they used such spurious arguments as the alleged blossoming of the 'Holy Thorn' on Christmas Day to show that the

reforms were against God's pattern. Many people stubbornly continued to celebrate 'Old Christmas Day' right up to the late nineteenth century.

One of the problems for the historian of customs and festivals is that a double standard was created, which throws a shadow of doubt over much subsequent evidence. For example, Abbotsbury Garland Day, which now takes place on 13 May (1 May Old Style), appears to be a May Day custom which was moved when the calendar was reformed. But we have no evidence that the Abbotsbury custom even existed in 1752 (the earliest reference is 1867), and it is only by comparison with other garland customs that we expect it to have any connection with May Day. It might conceivably have been a custom that took place on 13 May from its inception, whenever that was.

The other major problem is that in the past the official calendar was only one of several ways in which time was viewed and regulated, and the further back in time one looks, the harder it is to discern any coherent pattern. The disjunctions and disagreements between religious and civil calendars have already been indicated, but it is clear that for many in the past it was the physical year of days and seasons, of sun, rain, and frost, which really mattered. However in thrall the farmer may have been to saints' days for visiting fairs, attending markets, and paying rents and wages (for more on saints' days, see below), the fact of the matter is that lambs are born when they are ready, and corn does not ripen on a set day. The agricultural year helped to set the educational year, with the long holiday timed to enable children to help with the all-important harvest, and a new year starting soon afterwards. Parliamentary sessions also start in the autumn, traditionally the time when gentlemen could be spared from their country estates. The legal profession had its own calendar, the fashionable set its seasons, the horse-racing fraternity its high and low points, and many trades their own peculiar annual rhythms.

Which New Year?

The idea that the New Year commences on 1 January is so deeply entrenched in our psyche that it will be a surprise to many modern readers that there should be any doubt about it, or that it ever took place on a different day. In fact, the question of when the New Year starts is enormously complex and in the past caused a great deal of debate and confusion. Echoes of this confusion still resonate whenever an English person wonders why the financial year runs till the end of March, or the tax year begins on 6 April.

In the ancient pre-Julian Roman calendar, there were ten months and the New Year started on 1 March (which is why the names of the months September to December derive from the words 'seven' to 'ten'). It was Julius Caesar, when introducing what became known as the Julian calendar, who changed it to 1 January. This was the accepted 'international standard' when Christianity was being formed, but when the new religion began making headway, many followers thought that a specifically Christian view of the calendar should be adopted, and once the Nativity of Christ had been set at 25 December, many naturally argued that this day should be regarded as the beginning of the year. Others, counting nine months back from Christmas Day, argued that the Feast of the Annunciation, the conception of Christ (25 March), should really mark the beginning of the Christian year. The supporters of 25 March won the day, and devout Christians celebrated that day as New Year. A dual system of New Years was thus created, which persisted for centuries, and as so much of civil administration was in the hands of monks and clerics, the religious definition was long adopted as the norm.

Pope Gregory, however, when ordering the introduction of the calendar system named after him in 1582, decreed that from that moment the official New Year would be 1 January. This detail had nothing to do with the reform of the Julian calendar per se, but was an added bonus for those who wished to introduce an international common calendar. As mentioned previously, half the western world followed suit, but those Protestant countries that held aloof from the calendar change also ignored the instruction about the New Year, although Scotland, while rejecting the main reform, adopted 1 January as its New Year in 1600.

England rejected the whole Gregorian reform, including the January New Year, and thus perpetuated a bizarre double standard, consigning the country to a further 200 years of confusion. Despite the fact that 25 March was the official start of the year, 1 January had been *called* New Year's Day by people high and low, from at least the thirteenth century. Henry III, for example, received New Year gifts in January 1249, and in the following 500 years there are numerous examples of letters, diaries, and other documents that name 1 January as 'New Year's Day'. However, and this is the really strange point, the people who wrote these documents did not change the number of the year in January, but in March, in line with official practice. Thus Samuel Pepys, in his famous *Diary*, regularly refers to 1 January as New Year's Day but only changes the year, without comment, on 25 March. Historians have long had to deal with this dating anomaly, and the practice of referring to the first three months of the year in the form of, for example, '1663/4' has been adopted to improve precision.

This state of affairs lasted until 1752, when the reform of the English calendar and the adoption of the Gregorian standard, was finally enacted. The first of January had finally received official recognition as 'New Year's Day', for most purposes. Unfortunately for those who value simplicity, the Exchequer decided not to change, and opted to continue the old New Year formula, although this was compounded by the loss of the eleven days occasioned by the change of calendar. The start of the tax year therefore became 6 April.

Almanacs

Almanacs were a hugely popular form of publication which could be found in nearly every household in the land. They were churned out in their hundreds of thousands every year, and they easily outsold any other form of printed works. They were paper-covered, pocket-sized, and cheap enough for almost anyone to afford. The first examples were produced soon after printing was invented, and from the mid fifteenth century, as their circulation grew in leaps and bounds, they were a major feature of the new printing trade. Exact figures are hard to come by, but it is clear that they were enormous; as historian Keith Thomas comments, 'The figure of 3 to 4 million which is sometimes suggested as the total production of almanacs in the seventeenth century, is a distinct underestimate; the ten years after November 1663 alone nearly reached that total. Not even the Bible sold at this rate.' Many different series existed over the years, including a number that became household names: *Zadkiel's*, *Old Moore's*, *Poor Robin's*, and *Raphael's*; others went for more fancy-sounding titles such as *Vox Stellarum* or *Merlinus Liberatus*.

Between about 1640 and 1700, almanac writers entered enthusiastically into the raging religious and political controversies of the day, but mostly their sights were set on much lower things. We can distinguish three different types of information in the typical almanac, although in reality they were not as distinct as these categories imply. The one that principally concerns us here was a full calendar of the year, which marked the saints' days and other festivals, with the major ones printed in red (hence 'red-letter days'). As so much of the rural year was organized by the veneration of saints, this was an essential aide-memoire for both farmer and farmworker. The second section included a rather miscellaneous collection of 'useful facts', such as tide tables, lists of kings and queens, birthdays of the current royal family, and a historical chronology of the world starting with 'the Creation'. It is impossible to know whether this information was valued or not by the average almanac reader, but the third section certainly was. The latter took up much of the publication and contained simplified astronomical tables, details of eclipses, phases of the moon, and their accompanying astrological meanings, along with other prophecies and predictions of a generalized political and social nature. The fact that much of this planetary material was couched in such pseudo-scientific language probably added to its attraction. An extract taken at random from the *Speculum Anni, or Season of the Seasons* for 1799, on the subject of the tails of comets, reads as follows:

> *We see this fluid rises from the earth into the atmosphere, and is probably going off from thence, when it appears in the Aurora Borealis: And as this electric matter, from its vast subtilty and velocity, seems capable of making great excursions from the planetary system, the several comets in their long excursions from the sun, in all directions, may overtake this matter, and, attracting it to themselves, may come back replete with it.*

The information about the phases of the moon was also vital to the farmer. It was very widely believed that the moon had a direct effect on various aspects of agriculture and needed to be carefully monitored. From at least the sixteenth to the nineteenth centuries, few farmers would willingly kill a pig when the moon was on the wane, as they believed that the meat would be sure to shrink in the cooking if they did so, and some were equally convinced that certain crops should always be planted on the waxing of the moon, and others when it was on the wane.

However useful the calendar and the other tables could be, it was the diet of popular astrology, prophecy, and prediction which gave the almanac a bad name with the more educated section of the population. The old radical William Cobbett, for example, writing in 1813, was scathing about the hold that almanacs seemed to have on the minds of semi-literate rural workers:

> *His standard book will, in all likelihood, be* Moore's Almanack, *that universal companion of the farmers and labourers of England. Here we will find a perpetual spring of knowledge; a daily supply, besides an extra portion monthly. Here are signs and wonders and prophesies, in all which he will believe as implicitly as he does in the first chapter of Genesis . . . To keep a people in a state of profound ignorance, to make them superstitious and slavish, there needs little more than the general reading of this single book.*

Saints' Days: Real and Invented

In rural areas especially, everybody had a good working knowledge of the saints' days and church festivals throughout the year, and for those who were unsure of the dates, many homes had a copy of the year's almanac to guide them. Despite the fact that the reformed English Church refused to recognize the power of saints, it is clear that for most of the population these days were far more important than those of the official calendar. In the mid seventeenth century, for example, Henry Best, gentleman-farmer of Elmswell in the East Riding of Yorkshire, noted down in his manuscript account of farming practice (published by the Surtees Society as *Rural Economy in Yorkshire in 1641*) all the fairs in his locality, over two dozen in all. In every case,

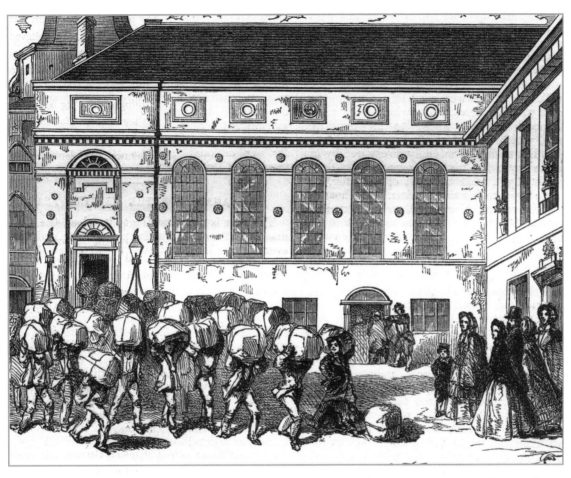

Almanac Day: the busiest day in the book trade, when the new almanacs arrived (Robert Chambers, *The Book of Days*, 1864)

he named the fair-day in terms of its nearest religious festival or saint's day, and only sometimes gave the calendar date as secondary information:

> On St. Peters day there is a fair at Frodingham . . .
> Malton horse fair begins now of late three days
> before St. Mathew Day . . . On St. Luke day there is a
> fair at Hunmanby . . .

Saints' days were so central to the popular notion of calendrical time that people made up their own to describe a particular day, often facetiously: St Distaff's Day (7 January) was the day that women went back to their spinning; St Monday was the extended weekend regularly taken by workers in the shoe trade (*see* p. 424); and Mother Shipton's Day was celebrated by washerwomen in Cambridge (*see* p. 196). Some of them entered everyday language. 'St Monday' was often used

to describe any unauthorized holiday, and another fictitious character, St Tibb, only existed in such phrases as 'You'll get your money on St Tibb's Day', which meant 'never'. Any far or mythical time could be referred to as St Tibb's Eve or St Tibb's Day, and sometimes it even meant what one hopes is the most distant day of all, the evening of the last day, or the Day of Judgement.

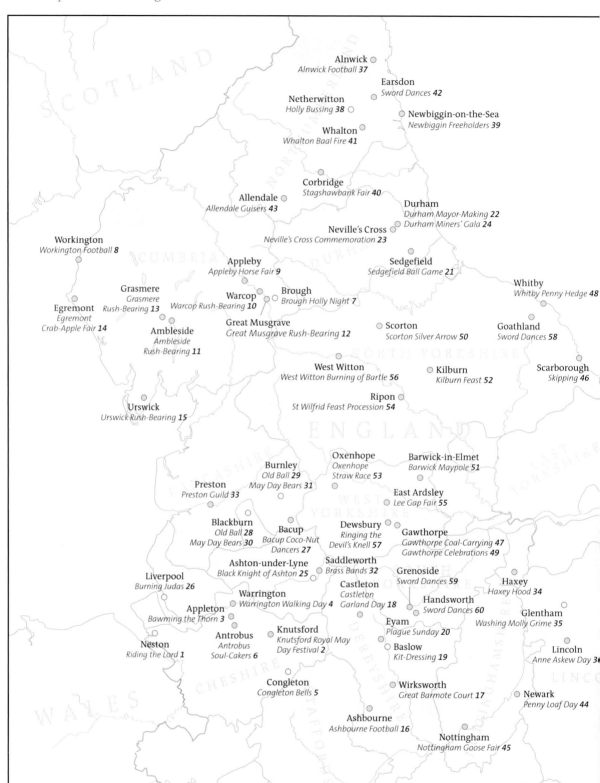

Alnwick
Alnwick Football **37**

Earsdon
Sword Dances **42**

Netherwitton
Holly Bussing **38**

Newbiggin-on-the-Sea
Newbiggin Freeholders **39**

Whalton
Whalton Baal Fire **41**

Corbridge
Stagshawbank Fair **40**

Allendale
Allendale Guisers **43**

Durham
Durham Mayor-Making **22**
Durham Miners' Gala **24**

Neville's Cross
Neville's Cross Commemoration **23**

Workington
Workington Football **8**

Appleby
Appleby Horse Fair **9**

Sedgefield
Sedgefield Ball Game **21**

Whitby
Whitby Penny Hedge **48**

Grasmere
Grasmere Rush-Bearing **13**

Warcop
Warcop Rush-Bearing **10**

Brough
Brough Holly Night **7**

Egremont
Egremont Crab-Apple Fair **14**

Great Musgrave
Great Musgrave Rush-Bearing **12**

Scorton
Scorton Silver Arrow **50**

Goathland
Sword Dances **58**

Ambleside
Ambleside Rush-Bearing **11**

West Witton
West Witton Burning of Bartle **56**

Kilburn
Kilburn Feast **52**

Scarborough
Skipping **46**

Urswick
Urswick Rush-Bearing **15**

Ripon
St Wilfrid Feast Procession **54**

Oxenhope
Oxenhope Straw Race **53**

Barwick-in-Elmet
Barwick Maypole **51**

Burnley
Old Ball **29**
May Day Bears **31**

Preston
Preston Guild **33**

East Ardsley
Lee Gap Fair **55**

Blackburn
Old Ball **28**
May Day Bears **30**

Bacup
Bacup Coco-Nut Dancers **27**

Dewsbury
Ringing the Devil's Knell **57**

Gawthorpe
Gawthorpe Coal-Carrying **47**
Gawthorpe Celebrations **49**

Ashton-under-Lyne
Black Knight of Ashton **25**

Saddleworth
Brass Bands **32**

Grenoside
Sword Dances **59**

Liverpool
Burning Judas **26**

Castleton
Castleton Garland Day **18**

Handsworth
Sword Dances **60**

Haxey
Haxey Hood **34**

Warrington
Warrington Walking Day **4**

Appleton
Bawming the Thorn **3**

Eyam
Plague Sunday **20**

Glentham
Washing Molly Grime **35**

Neston
Riding the Lord **1**

Antrobus
Antrobus Soul-Cakers **6**

Knutsford
Knutsford Royal May Day Festival **2**

Baslow
Kit-Dressing **19**

Lincoln
Anne Askew Day **3**

Congleton
Congleton Bells **5**

Wirksworth
Great Barmote Court **17**

Newark
Penny Loaf Day **44**

Ashbourne
Ashbourne Football **16**

Nottingham
Nottingham Goose Fair **45**

Key

○ Events still held
○ Events no longer held

Dates of Events

CHESHIRE
1 Easter
2 First Saturday in May
3 29 June
4 First Friday in July
5 12 August
6 31 October

CUMBRIA
7 6 January
8 Good Friday
9 First week in June
10 29 June
11 First Saturday in July
12 First Saturday in July
13 5 August
14 Third Saturday in September
15 29 September
Note: Friday following Ash Wednesday – Pully Lug Day (Cumbria) – no longer held, Pace Egg Plays (Cumbria)

DERBYSHIRE
16 Shrove Tuesday
17 April
18 29 May
19 4 August
20 Last Sunday in August
Note: Christmas – Old Horse (Derbyshire) – no longer held, Christmas – Old Tup (Derbyshire) – no longer held

DURHAM
21 Shrove Tuesday
22 Mid May
23 29 May
24 Second/Third Saturday in July

LANCASHIRE
25 Easter Monday
26 Good Friday
27 Easter Saturday
28 Easter
29 Easter
30 May Day
31 May Day

32 Whit Friday
33 29 August
Note: Pace Egging (Lancashire), Pace Egg Plays (Lancashire), 31 October – Mischief Night (Lancashire)

LINCOLNSHIRE
34 6 January
35 Good Friday
36 16 July
Note: Plough Plays (Lincolnshire), Straw Bears (Lincolnshire),

NORTHUMBERLAND
37 Shrove Tuesday
38 Easter Tuesday
39 18 May
40 4 July
41 4 July
42 Christmas
43 31 December

NOTTINGHAMSHIRE
44 11 March
45 First Wednesday in October

YORKSHIRE
46 Shrove Tuesday
47 Easter Monday
48 Ascension Eve
49 First Saturday in May
50 Mid to late May
51 Spring Bank Holiday
52 6 July
53 Sunday in early July
54 July/August
55 17 August
56 24 August
57 Christmas Eve
58 Christmas
59 Christmas
60 Christmas
Note: Pace Egging (Yorkshire), 31 October – Mischief Night (Yorkshire), Easter Monday – Legging Day (Yorkshire) – no longer held

LNSHIRE

NORFOLK

Dates of Events

BEDFORDSHIRE
1 Rogation

BERKSHIRE
2 Hocktide
3 March
4 Whitsun
5 30 November
6 13 December

BRISTOL
7 Easter Tuesday
8 Whitsun
9 A Sunday in October

BUCKINGHAMSHIRE
10 Shrove Tuesday
11 May
12 11 November

CAMBRIDGESHIRE
13 Whit Tuesday
14 14 September

CORNWALL
15 3 February
16 Shrove Tuesday
17 May Day
18 8 May
19 7 July
20 25 July
21 Boxing Day
Note: May Day – Ducking or Dipping Day (Cornwall) – no longer held

DEVON
22 Spring Bank Holiday
23 Spring Bank Holiday
24 Late May
25 Second Wednesday in July
26 August Bank Holiday
27 Second Wednesday in October

28 Last Thursday in October
29 5 November
30 5 November
31 Second Saturday in November
32 Fourth Tuesday in November
Note: May Day – Ducking or Dipping Day (Devon) – no longer held

DORSET
33 Shrove Tuesday
34 13 May (Old May Day)
35 14 September
36 10 October

ESSEX
37 New Year
38 Easter Monday
39 Third Thursday in May
40 Early July
41 Early September
42 20 October

GLOUCESTERSHIRE
43 May Day
44 Second Saturday in May
45 Whitsun
46 Spring Bank Holiday
47 Spring Bank Holiday
48 19 September
49 Boxing Day

HAMPSHIRE
50 25 March
51 First Wednesday in August
52 10 October
53 21 October

HERTFORDSHIRE
54 May Day
55 2 October

KENT
56 Easter
57 First Saturday in July
58 25 July
59 24 August
Note: Christmas – Hooden Horse (North Kent Coast)

LEICESTERSHIRE
60 Shrove Tuesday
61 Easter Monday
62 Easter Monday

LINCOLNSHIRE
63 13 November

NORFOLK
64 Third Thursday in September
Note: Norfolk Shrovetide Cookeels (or Coquilles) – no longer held

NORTHAMPTONSHIRE
65 May

OXFORDSHIRE
66 14 January
67 10 February
68 May Day
69 May Day
70 Ascension Day
71 Spring Bank Holiday
72 20 June
73 24 June
74 June/July
75 6 July

SHROPSHIRE
76 Shrove Tuesday
77 Last Sunday in May

Key

◉ Events still held
○ Events no longer held

Aston-on-Clun
Arbor Day 77

Kidderminster
Brecknell Bequest 102

Ludlow
Ludlow Rope-Pulling 76

St Briavels
St Briavels Bread and Cheese Dole 45

Randwick
Randwick Cheese-Rolling 43
Randwick Wap 44

Marshfield
Marshfield Paper Boys 49

Bristol
Tuppenny Starvers 7
St Mary Redcliffe Rush Sunday 8
Redcliffe Pipe Walk 9

Bridgwater
Bridgwater Carnival 83

Stoke St Gregory
Egg Shackling 78

Combe Martin
Hunting the Earl of Rone 22

Minehead
Minehead Hobby Horse 81

Tatworth
Tatworth Candle Auction 80

Shepton Beauchamp
Egg Shackling 79

Bampton
Bampton Fair 28

Shebbear
Devil's Stone 29

Sherborne
Pack Monday Fair 36

Holsworthy
Pretty Maid's Charity 25

Hatherleigh
Hatherleigh Carnival 31

Ottery St Mary
Ottery St Mary 30

Hinton St George
Punkie Night 82

Padstow
Padstow Hobby Horse 17
Padstow Mummers' (Darkie) Day 21

Tavistock
Tavistock Goosie Fair 27

Kingsteignton
Kingsteignton Ram-Roasting 23

Abbotsbury
Abbotsbury Garland Day 34

Bodmin
Bodmin Riding 19

Ashburton
Ashburton Court Leet 32

Marldon
Marldon Apple Pie Fair 26

St Columb
St Columb Hurling 16

St Ives
St Ives Hurling 15
John Knill Charity 20

Brixham
Blessing of the Sea 24

Helston
Helston Flora Day 18

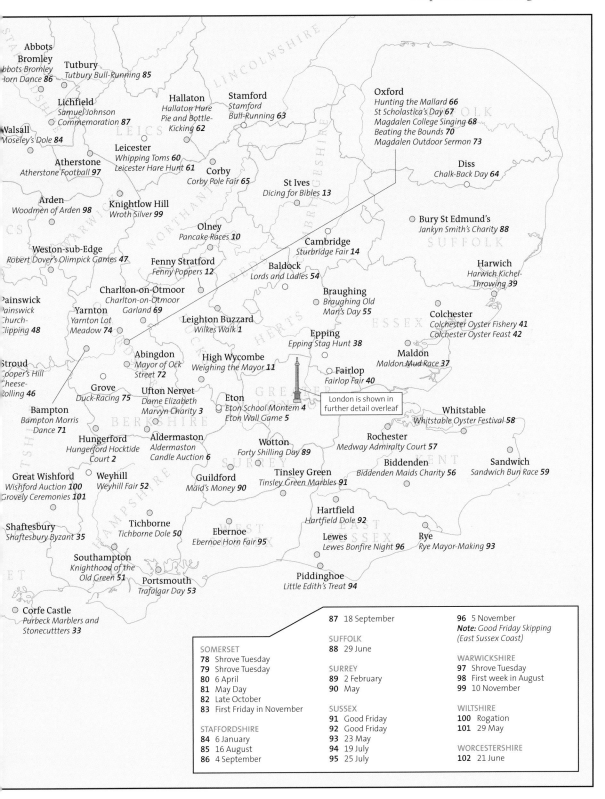

Abbots Bromley
Abbots Bromley Horn Dance 86

Tutbury
Tutbury Bull-Running 85

Lichfield
Samuel Johnson Commemoration 87

Hallaton
Hallaton Hare Pie and Bottle-Kicking 62

Stamford
Stamford Bull-Running 63

Oxford
Hunting the Mallard 66
St Scholastica's Day 67
Magdalen College Singing 68
Beating the Bounds 70
Magdalen Outdoor Sermon 73

Walsall
Moseley's Dole 84

Leicester
Whipping Toms 60
Leicester Hare Hunt 61

Corby
Corby Pole Fair 65

St Ives
Dicing for Bibles 13

Diss
Chalk-Back Day 64

Atherstone
Atherstone Football 97

Arden
Woodmen of Arden 98

Knightlow Hill
Wroth Silver 99

Olney
Pancake Races 10

Cambridge
Sturbridge Fair 14

Bury St Edmund's
Jankyn Smith's Charity 88

Weston-sub-Edge
Robert Dover's Olimpick Games 47

Fenny Stratford
Fenny Poppers 12

Baldock
Lords and Ladies 54

Harwich
Harwich Kichel-Throwing 39

Painswick
Painswick Church-Clipping 48

Yarnton
Yarnton Lot Meadow 74

Charlton-on-Otmoor
Charlton-on-Otmoor Garland 69

Leighton Buzzard
Wilkes Walk 1

Braughing
Braughing Old Man's Day 55

Colchester
Colchester Oyster Fishery 41
Colchester Oyster Feast 42

Epping
Epping Stag Hunt 38

Maldon
Maldon Mud Race 37

Stroud
Cooper's Hill Cheese-Rolling 46

Abingdon
Mayor of Ock Street 72

High Wycombe
Weighing the Mayor 11

Fairlop
Fairlop Fair 40

Grove
Duck-Racing 75

Ufton Nervet
Dame Elizabeth Marvyn Charity 3

Eton
Eton School Montem 4
Eton Wall Game 5

London is shown in further detail overleaf

Whitstable
Whitstable Oyster Festival 58

Bampton
Bampton Morris Dance 71

Hungerford
Hungerford Hocktide Court 2

Aldermaston
Aldermaston Candle Auction 6

Wotton
Forty Shilling Day 89

Rochester
Medway Admiralty Court 57

Great Wishford
Wishford Auction 100
Grovely Ceremonies 101

Weyhill
Weyhill Fair 52

Guildford
Maid's Money 90

Tinsley Green
Tinsley Green Marbles 91

Biddenden
Biddenden Maids Charity 56

Sandwich
Sandwich Bun Race 59

Shaftesbury
Shaftesbury Byzant 35

Tichborne
Tichborne Dole 50

Ebernoe
Ebernoe Horn Fair 95

Hartfield
Hartfield Dole 92

Lewes
Lewes Bonfire Night 96

Rye
Rye Mayor-Making 93

Southampton
Knighthood of the Old Green 51

Portsmouth
Trafalgar Day 53

Piddinghoe
Little Edith's Treat 94

Corfe Castle
Purbeck Marblers and Stonecuttters 33

87   18 September

SUFFOLK
88   29 June

SURREY
89   2 February
90   May

SUSSEX
91   Good Friday
92   Good Friday
93   23 May
94   19 July
95   25 July

96   5 November
Note: Good Friday Skipping (East Sussex Coast)

WARWICKSHIRE
97   Shrove Tuesday
98   First week in August
99   10 November

WILTSHIRE
100   Rogation
101   29 May

WORCESTERSHIRE
102   21 June

SOMERSET
78   Shrove Tuesday
79   Shrove Tuesday
80   6 April
81   May Day
82   Late October
83   First Friday in November

STAFFORDSHIRE
84   6 January
85   16 August
86   4 September

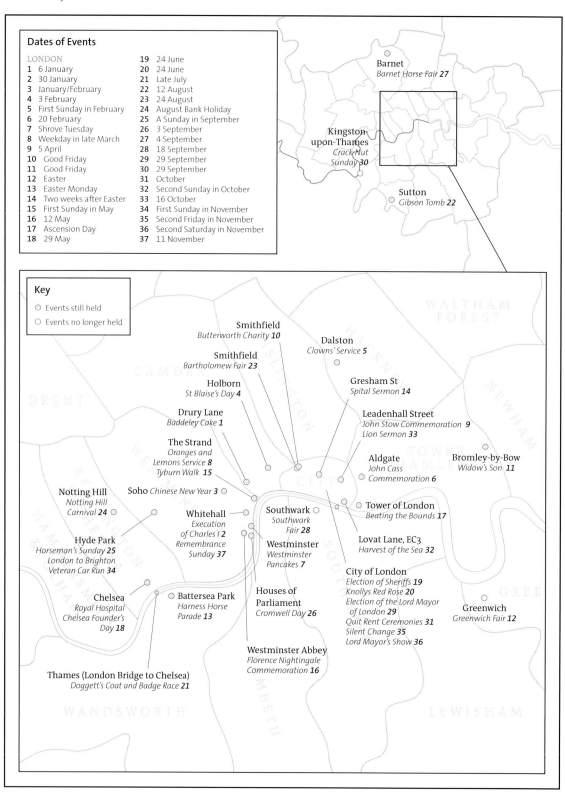

Dates of Events

LONDON
1 6 January
2 30 January
3 January/February
4 3 February
5 First Sunday in February
6 20 February
7 Shrove Tuesday
8 Weekday in late March
9 5 April
10 Good Friday
11 Good Friday
12 Easter
13 Easter Monday
14 Two weeks after Easter
15 First Sunday in May
16 12 May
17 Ascension Day
18 29 May

19 24 June
20 24 June
21 Late July
22 12 August
23 24 August
24 August Bank Holiday
25 A Sunday in September
26 3 September
27 4 September
28 18 September
29 29 September
30 29 September
31 October
32 Second Sunday in October
33 16 October
34 First Sunday in November
35 Second Friday in November
36 Second Saturday in November
37 11 November

Barnet
Barnet Horse Fair 27

Kingston-upon-Thames
Crack Nut Sunday 30

Sutton
Gibson Tomb 22

Key

⊙ Events still held
○ Events no longer held

Smithfield
Butterworth Charity 10

Dalston
Clowns' Service 5

Smithfield
Bartholomew Fair 23

Gresham St
Spital Sermon 14

Holborn
St Blaise's Day 4

Drury Lane
Baddeley Cake 1

Leadenhall Street
John Stow Commemoration 9
Lion Sermon 33

The Strand
Oranges and Lemons Service 8
Tyburn Walk 15

Aldgate
John Cass Commemoration 6

Bromley-by-Bow
Widow's Son 11

Notting Hill
Notting Hill Carnival 24

Soho *Chinese New Year 3*

Tower of London
Beating the Bounds 17

Whitehall
Execution of Charles I 2
Remembrance Sunday 37

Southwark
Southwark Fair 28

Lovat Lane, EC3
Harvest of the Sea 32

Hyde Park
Horseman's Sunday 25
London to Brighton Veteran Car Run 34

Westminster
Westminster Pancakes 7

City of London
Election of Sheriffs 19
Knollys Red Rose 20
Election of the Lord Mayor of London 29
Quit Rent Ceremonies 31
Silent Change 35
Lord Mayor's Show 36

Chelsea
Royal Hospital Chelsea Founder's Day 18

Battersea Park
Harness Horse Parade 13

Houses of Parliament
Cromwell Day 26

Greenwich
Greenwich Fair 12

Westminster Abbey
Florence Nightingale Commemoration 16

Thames (London Bridge to Chelsea)
Doggett's Coat and Badge Race 21

The English Year

January

Trapball/Knurr and Spell

1

NEW YEAR'S DAY
Burning the Bush
Cream of the Well
First-Footing and Letting In
Mad Maldon Mud Race
Pop (Pope) Ladies

2

3

8

PLOUGH MONDAY
Plough Plays
Ploughboys and Maids

9

**PLOUGH MONDAY/
PLOUGH TUESDAY**
Straw Bears

10

Shuttlecock

15

16

17

OLD TWELFTH NIGHT

Tipcat

Pell-Mell

22

ST VINCENT'S DAY

23

24

**EVE OF CONVERSION OF
ST PAUL**

Stoolball

29

30

Execution of Charles I

31

*Moveable events have been placed
on the date they fall in 2007.*

Camping

4	5	6	7
		EPIPHANY **OLD CHRISTMAS DAY** **TWELFTH NIGHT** Baddeley Cake Brough Holly Night Haxey Hood Moseley's Dole Twelfth Night Fires	**ST DISTAFF'S DAY OR ROCK DAY** **PLOUGH SUNDAY**

11	12	13	14
		ST HILARY'S DAY	Hunting the Mallard

18	19	20	21
	ST WULFSTAN'S DAY	**ST AGNES' EVE**	**ST AGNES' DAY**

25	26	27	28
ST PAUL'S DAY			

JANUARY/FEBRUARY
Chinese New Year

Lamb's Wool

NEW YEAR CUSTOMS AND SUPERSTITIONS

New Year's Day has always been rife with meaning for the superstitious person, and the potential problems start the moment the clock has struck midnight. One of the key underlying principles of superstition is that the *beginning* of any enterprise, journey, or period of time is of vital importance and largely determines future success or failure. Good or bad luck can therefore be predicted and influenced by ensuring that one does the right things and avoids the wrong things at the start. This principle can influence people's actions at a variety of levels: how one gets out of bed in the morning to start the day, how the first steps of a journey proceed, how good the first sale of the day is, what to do when one sees a new moon or hears the first cuckoo, and so on. Many wedding superstitions are based on the same principle, as the day marks the beginning of the couple's new life.

New Year's Day is the most obvious starting point of all, and most of us still have a vague feeling that what happens on the day is somehow predictive, as recorded by Jonathan Couch in his *History of Polperro* (1871):

> The character of the coming twelve months, for good or bad fortune, is foretold by the appearance of things on the morning of the new year. A trivial mishap, or the slightest instance of good luck, has now more than its usual significance, inasmuch as it predicts, in a general way, the course of events through the coming year.

One of the widespread ways in which a glimpse of the future could be obtained was by 'dipping' into the Bible for guidance, either late on New Year's Eve, or first thing on New Year's morning. A contributor to the *Folk-Lore Journal* of 1886 reported:

> Parties are general in Cornwall on New Year's Eve to watch in the New Year and wish friends health and happiness; but I know of no peculiar customs, except that before retiring to rest the old women opened their Bibles at haphazard to find out their luck for the coming year. The text on which the forefinger of the right hand rested was supposed to foretell the future.

Obviously, the randomly selected verse needed some interpretation, and it was quite common for people to discuss its symbolic meanings among themselves during the day. Any religious scruples about fortune-telling were allayed by the knowledge that the Holy Bible could not mislead you, and respectable people, including clergymen's families, were known to indulge in the practice. But there was also a long tradition of using other books opened at random for similar divinatory purposes, although not necessarily at New Year. There is some indication that this was regarded as an acceptable substitute for those who were worried about using the Bible. Oddly enough, the works of Virgil are often quoted in this context, and the use of poetry as a divinatory tool has an even longer history. In their *Dictionary of Superstitions* (1989), Iona Opie and Moira Tatem provide a quotation from St Augustine of Hippo's *Confessions* (*c.* AD 397):

> When a man by hap-hazard opens the pages of some poet, who sang and thought of something wholly different, a verse sometimes fell out, wonderfully agreeable to the present business.

Not content with simply observing or predicting the coming year, many people in the past took active steps to ensure their short-term prosperity. A number of customs and beliefs were based on the notion of luck potentially flowing *into* or *out of* the house in the coming year, luck that could be influenced by symbolic activity on New Year's Day. Householders were therefore keen to ensure that the predominant activity on the day was inward, and this is most clearly seen in the widespread custom of **first-footing** (*see* p. 8). Most were content with ensuring that the first *movement* was inward, as Llewellyn Jewitt recorded in 1853:

> On this day it is considered unlucky to remove anything from a house until something has been brought in; and therefore each member of the family carries some trifling thing in early in the morning. In the neighbourhood of Newark [in Nottinghamshire] I have heard the rhyme:
>
> > Take out, take in
> > Bad luck is sure to begin
> > Take in and take out
> > Good luck will come about.

But there were also many who believed that nothing – not even the ashes from the fire or the waste from the kitchen – should leave the house on New Year's Day.

The one thing that no superstitious nineteenth-century householder would allow to leave the house under any circumstances at this time of year was fire. At any other time they would be quite happy to let a neighbour or stranger take a live coal or taper to light their lantern or house fire, but not at New Year. For many, this ban was also in force throughout the Christmas period (*see* **Christmas: Superstitions** for another example), while for others it was only on New Year's morning. A correspondent to *Notes & Queries* wrote in 1862:

> *My maid, who comes from the neighbourhood of Pendle* [in Lancashire]*, informs me that an unlucky old woman in her native village, having allowed her fire to go out on New Year's Eve, had to wait till one o'clock on the following day before any neighbour would supply her with a light.*

On symbolically charged days such as New Year's Day, a number of everyday activities could take on additional meanings, and as superstition is primarily negative, these were to be avoided on the day, as here in Devon in 1896:

> *On New Year's Day one of our maidens (not a Devonshire one) was going to do the family washing, when our West-Country girl exclaimed in horror: 'Pray don't 'ee wash on New Year's Day, Or you'll wash one of the family away'. On inquiry I find the belief widely spread hereabouts, that if the year commences in domestic circles with a washing day, one of the occupants of the house is washed out (i.e. dies) during the year.*

The same was said about Good Friday, Holy Innocents' Day (*see* **28 December**), and occasionally Ascension Day, and for obvious reasons this superstition was particularly strong in fishing and other seafaring families.

See also **31 December: New Year's Eve**.

Bank Holiday

English people of middle age and over will remember that New Year's Day was only designated a bank holiday in 1974. Before that date, people still celebrated New Year's Eve, but most workplaces exhibited a decidedly sorry workforce on 1 January every year.

Burning the Bush

In December 1877, the Revd Francis Kilvert, who had just taken up the living of Bredwardine in Herefordshire, stayed up to see in the New Year, and then retired:

> *After I had gone to bed I saw from where I lay a bright blaze sprung up in the fields beyond the river and I knew at once that they were keeping up the old custom of Burning the Bush on New Year's Day in the morning . . . the whole valley can be seen early on New Year's morning alight with fires.*

This custom of 'Burning the Bush' seems to have been unique to Herefordshire, and was only reported from the second half of the nineteenth to the early twentieth centuries, when it was clearly on its last legs. Local folklore-collector Ella M. Leather provided a description in 1912:

> *This custom was generally kept up all over Herefordshire until about forty years ago, and survives here and there, in the Leominster and Kington districts. The 'bush' is a globe made of hawthorn, which is hung up in the kitchen of the farmhouse, with the mistletoe, after the bush-burning ceremony each New Year's morning; it hangs there till the day comes round again, when it is taken out to be burnt and a new one made. Mistletoe is never brought into the house before New Year's Day; to do so would be most unlucky.*
>
> *At five o'clock in the morning the workmen fetch the old 'bush' . . . It is carried to the earliest sown wheat field, where a large fire is lighted, of straw and bushes, in which it is burnt. While it is burning a new one is made; in making it, the ends of the branches are scorched in the fire. An old man, who had lived all his life in the Pembridge district, told me that at Shobdon, in his time, they poured cider over it afterwards, 'to varnish and darken the bush like' he said.*

Mrs Leather also gives further examples, on similar lines. This is clearly allied to the Twelfth Night fires (*see* **6 January: Twelfth Night Fires**), which were lighted in the fields elsewhere in the same region, and also connected with wassailing (*see* **Christmas: Wassailing**).

Cream of the Well

In line with the widespread superstitious principle that everyday things take on a special significance at the beginning of a key time-cycle, water drawn soon after midnight on New Year's Eve had a similar reputation to the dew that fell on May Day morning (*see* **1 May: May Dew**). In 1912, Ella M. Leather recorded:

> It was formerly the custom in Herefordshire farm-
> houses for the servants to sit up to see the New Year
> in, and at midnight to rush for the 'Cream o' the
> well', the first water drawn from the well in the year,
> which was thought to be beautifying and lucky. The
> maid who succeeded in getting it would take it to the
> bedroom of her mistress, who would give a present
> for it. 'My missus always had the cream o' the well to
> wash in on New Year's morning', said Mrs. M., 'and she
> always put a shilling under the basin for me, too'.

This first water went by various local names, such as the cream, flower, crop, or ream of the well, and although the idea was widely reported in the north of England and Scotland, the earliest definite reference is from Herefordshire in 1804.

First-Footing and Letting In the New Year

The idea that the first person over the threshold on New Year's Day brings luck to the household is regarded as particularly Scottish, but it was in fact widely practised all over England in the nineteenth and twentieth centuries. Nevertheless, there is no doubt that it was more common, and taken more seriously, the closer one approached Scotland. 'There can be few, if any, houses in our district where the custom of first-footing is not respected,' wrote Rosalie Bosanquet about the village of Cambo, Northumberland, in 1929.

The modern standard of 'a dark-haired man' bringing luck has effectively erased a wide range of local variations. Many early reports did not mention the hair colour of the first-footer and occasionally a fair-haired

person was preferred, but in the vast majority of cases a male was acceptable and a female was not. In 1895, C. J. Billson recorded:

> Mrs. Billson, native of country near Bagworth [in
> Leicestershire], assures me that she has a vivid
> recollection of her mother and her grandmother not
> permitting anyone to cross their threshold on New
> Year's morning until a dark man had first entered the
> house. They regarded it as particularly unlucky for a
> woman to be the first visitor.

It was similarly unusual for both sexes to have a role, although in Lincolnshire in 1908 Mrs Gutch and Mabel Peacock recorded:

> You must see first of all on a New Year's morning,
> one of the opposite sex (not a member of your own
> family). Boys go round and wish the women a Happy
> New Year, adding, 'and I've brought you a bit of
> stick'. Girls do the same to the men, and both expect
> rewards in the shape of current coin.

Not only does the first-footer need lucky characteristics himself, but he must also carry certain items, or perform certain tasks, to ensure the luck. First-footers often carry symbolic items into the house, such as coal, bread, or whisky; they might say something symbolic – wish luck and joy; or do symbolic things – stir the fire, cut a cake, and so on. The details vary considerably from house to house, but the principles of luck-bringing are the same almost everywhere.

Other superstitions based on the same principle also existed, such as who one first met in the morning or when going to work or when starting on a journey, and these are also classed as first-foot beliefs. They have been identified from at least the fourteenth century, but the earliest record of first-footing at Christmas or New Year is surprisingly late, and is not from Scotland, or even the north of England, but from Herefordshire in 1804:

> On Christmas Day it is deemed an omen of ill fortune
> … when a female first enters the house in the morning.

A number of other relatively low-key activities performed at this season were designed to welcome the New Year physically into the house and to allow the Old Year to depart. In Herefordshire in 1912:

THE FIRST FOOT.

ENTER MR. PUNCH, WHO WISHES EVERYONE "A MERRY CHRISTMAS AND A HAPPY NEW YEAR!"

"The first foot in a house brings good or ill-luck for the year."—*Old Belief.*

First-footing, as portrayed by *Punch*, 1897

As the clock struck twelve it was customary to open the back door to let the old year out, and then the front door to let-in the new year.

This was sometimes combined with the first-foot, so that the first-footer entered by the front door and left by the back. This, incidentally, broke the widespread rule that held for the rest of the year that it was extremely unlucky for someone to enter and leave a house by a different door.

Gifts

Long before Christmas presents were invented, people were accustomed to exchange gifts at New Year. This tradition was widespread across Europe, and the ancient Romans also indulged in it. Numerous records survive from Tudor times of sumptuous gifts presented to the ruling monarch by the nobility, higher clerics, members of the court and the royal household, and the sovereign reciprocated, mostly with money. Outside the court, other important people could expect gifts from their subordinates, and similar arrangements existed further down the social scale. Indeed, throughout the documentary record until the later eighteenth century there is a definite air of currying favour, if not actual bribery, in the custom. Samuel Pepys, for example, mentions New Year gifts many times in his diary between 1660 and 1669, in a number of contexts, including between him and his wife and friends. But even he was astonished at the number of 'gifts' he was expected to pay out for in his work at the Navy office.

There were many unwritten rules and traditions on the subject. Country tenants were expected to give a capon to their landlord every year. In the eighteenth century, the rector and antiquarian John Brand printed an extract from an untitled volume in the British Library, of the time of Queen Anne (1707–14), which indicates that the tendency for gifts to be given to superiors extended right down the age range:

On the first day of [January] *will be given many more gifts than will be kindly received or gratefully rewarded. Children to their inexpressible joy, will be drest in their best bibs and aprons, and may be seen handed along streets, some bearing Kentish pippins,*

others oranges stuck with cloves, in order to crave a blessing of their godfathers and godmothers.

Apart from money and jewellery, gifts ranged from the useful, such as gloves or papers of pins, to the ornamental gilt nutmeg, and often included food of various kinds. Urban middle-class families were certainly exchanging small gifts among themselves, and to friends, throughout the Victorian era. There was a strong tradition for children to make the presents they gave to parents, but popular magazines also ran advertisements for New Year gifts and continued to do so right up to the turn of the twentieth century. But by that time, the new fashion for giving presents at Christmas had made serious inroads into the New Year custom, prompted by the arrival of Santa Claus and the Christmas stocking in the 1860s.

See also **Christmas: Father Christmas/Santa Claus; Christmas: Stockings**.

Mad Maldon Mud Race

Future folklorists and cultural researchers will need to create a new category of custom origin called 'it started with a discussion in the pub', as so many of our modern customs seem to have been born this way. A case in point is the Mad Maldon Mud Race in Essex, a 400-yard dash across the River Blackwater and back, at low tide, which started with a pub dare in the mid 1970s. The event is now organized by the local Lions and Rotary Clubs in conjunction with Maldon District Council, and raises thousands of pounds for charity each year. The 2005 event attracted 180 competitors and about 6,000 spectators, including many journalists and TV camera crews. Fancy dress is a standard feature of modern customs, and the Maldon competitors are suitably attired in a variety of costumes, although it matters little what they are wearing after a few seconds in the Blackwater mud. The day and time vary a little, according to tidal conditions.

Pop (Pope) Ladies

Pop (or Pope) Ladies were cakes, made and sold every year on New Year's Day, and apparently unique to St Albans in Hertfordshire. A contributor to the

An action shot from the 2006 Mad Maldon Mud Race. This is from early in the race . . .

This is somewhat later (the doctor's costume is already barely recognizable)

Gentleman's Magazine in 1820 reported:

> I happened to sleep at St Albans on the night of the
> 31st December [1819] and was awakened the next
> morning by a confused noise of boys and girls in the
> street crying for sale 'Popladys! Popladys!' ... a plain
> cake, like the cross-buns sold on Good Friday but,
> instead of being circular, was long and narrow rudely
> resembling the human figure, with two dried raisins
> or currants to represent eyes and another for the
> mouth, the lower part being formed rather like the
> outer case of an Egyptian mummy.

The custom is mentioned occasionally during the nineteenth century, but was said to be dying out in 1896
and does not seem to have survived much into the
twentieth century.

*

6 JANUARY

Epiphany

In the Christian calendar, 6 January is Epiphany, named
after the Greek word for 'manifestation'. It was originally
celebrated in the Eastern churches as the day of Christ's
baptism, but after it had been introduced into the West
in the fourth century AD it developed into the feast of
the manifestation of Christ to the Magi ('wise men').
On the Continent, the day was marked by dramatic
representations in church: clergy were dressed as the
three Magi, a large star was suspended from the rafters,
and a depiction of the nativity scene was revealed by
drawing a curtain as the Magi approached. These religious dramas also existed in pre-Reformation England,
although it is not clear how widely practised they
were here. The churchwardens' accounts for St Mary's,
Cambridge, for example, include the following entries
for 1557–8:

For make of a star	*20d.*
For painting and gilding the same star	*20d.*

As the Magi were later identified as kings, it was appropriate for real monarchs to take particular note of the
day; a royal offering of gold, frankincense and myrrh
is still made every year at Epiphany. The custom may
date back to the Norman kings, and until the reign

of George II the sovereign performed the duty in
person, but since that time it has been carried out by
proxy. Nowadays, the offering is made during Holy
Communion in the Chapel Royal, St James's Palace, by
two ushers to the Queen, escorted by the Queen's Body
Guard of the Yeoman of the Guard.

But 6 January is also **Twelfth Night** (*see below*), and
although kings did feature in the secular celebrations
of the day, they were play-acted rather than real ones.
The duration of the Christmas festival was officially set
at twelve days by the Council of Tours in AD 567, when
it was laid down that the whole period should be spent
in celebration and thanks, and that no one should be
made to work during that time.

Old Christmas Day

When the Gregorian calendar was introduced in
September 1752 (*see* p. xx), there was much grumbling
about the change, and also much confusion. Many
people refused to change the habits of generations, and
continued to celebrate major festivals on their equivalent Old Style dates. Most of these temporal anomalies
sorted themselves out over the following generations,
but the one date on which a significant minority of
traditionalists refused to budge was Christmas Day. In
1912, the folklore-collector Ella M. Leather recorded the
following words from a Herefordshire man:

> 'My grandfather always kept up Christmas on Old
> Christmas Day,' said W.P. of Peterchurch, 'none of
> your new Christmas for him; it must be the real
> Christmas, too, for the Holy Thorn blossoms, and
> the cattle go down on their knees at twelve o'clock
> in remembrance.' I have talked to many people who
> firmly believed this; though they have not seen it,
> their parents or grandparents have.

This tendency continued in some rural families right
up to the turn of the twentieth century, one hundred
and fifty years after the official change, and even then
some folk were still grumbling about it, although they
had finally been forced to hold their celebrations on
the New Style date.

A 'Merrie England' view of Twelfth Night (after Joseph Nash (1809–78))

Twelfth Night

Twelfth Night (or Twelfth Day), the secular aspect of **Epiphany** (*see above*), is one of the three really important festivals of past eras that have almost completely lost their meaning in the modern world (Shrovetide and Whitsun being the others). For centuries, Twelfth Night was a universal time for merrymaking and indulgence by rich and poor alike and was second only to Christmas Day. But with changing fashions, and the restructuring of Christmas carried out by the Victorians, the festival rapidly faded into the vague 'end of Christmas' feeling that is prevalent today. Even its position marking the end of Christmas is now being usurped by New Year's Day.

The very definition of Twelfth Night is problematic. In trying to document the older seasonal customs, there is the problem of Old and New Style dates, created by the change of the calendar in 1752 (*see* p. xx). The introduction of the New Style calendar removed eleven days from the calendar, and this was particularly confusing over the Christmas/New Year period, as the 'lost' eleven days almost coincided with the traditional twelve days of Christmas, and the Old Style Christmas Eve became entangled with the New Style Twelfth Night. Many people continued to celebrate Old Christmas Day on 6 January, and some diehards even celebrated Old Twelfth Night on 17/18 January. Given the general decline in Twelfth Night celebrations, this confusion is now only important to historians and folklorists, but a further dating difficulty is now apparent. In earlier times, 'Twelfth Night' meant 5 January, i.e. the *Eve* of Twelfth Day, in the same way as Christmas Eve precedes Christmas Day. But nowadays most people regard 'Twelfth Night' as meaning the evening of Twelfth Day (6 January).

For the aristocracy and nobility of Tudor England, Twelfth Night and Day were marked by elaborate masques, plays, pageants, and expensive gifts to and from each other, and for the members of the courts of Charles II to George II heavy gambling was the order of the night. Lower down the social scale, parties and family gatherings were the norm, and the two long-standing features were the Twelfth Night cake and games in which those present took on the fantasy roles of King and Queen. These roles were chosen at random by items placed in the cake; in earlier times a bean and a pea were used: whoever found the bean became the King and whoever found the pea, the Queen. The game was so common that 'King of the Bean' became a phrase used to denote any temporary or play-acted ruler. A clove was also used, and whoever found it in their slice was designated 'the Knave'. Other items that were sometimes used were coins, thimbles, and rings, and those present could be given other characters to play. From the moment they were appointed, the King and Queen presided over the rest of the evening's entertainment.

Samuel Pepys often mentioned Twelfth cakes in his diary. In 1666 he admitted to finding the clove, but he secretly put it into his neighbour's piece. Three years later he recorded a change in the way the characters were chosen:

> I did bring out my cake, and a noble cake, and there cut into pieces with wine and good drink, and, after a new fashion, to prevent spoiling the cake, did put so many titles into a hat and so draw cuts; and I was the Queen and The Turner, King; Creed [was] Sir Martin Marrall; and Betty [was] Mrs. Millicent. And so we were merry till it was night.

Marrall and Millicent were characters in John Dryden's *Sir Martin Marrall*, a popular comedy of the period. One hundred years later, things had not changed a great deal, according to the *Universal Magazine* (1774):

> I went to a friend's house in the country to partake of some of those innocent pleasures that constitute a merry Christmas; I did not return till I had been present at drawing King and Queen, and eaten a slice of the Twelfth Cake . . . A noble cake was produced, and two bowls, containing the fortunate chances

> for the different sexes. Our host filled up the tickets; the whole company, except the King and Queen, were to be ministers of state, maids of honour, or ladies of the bedchamber. Our kind host and hostess, whether by design or accident, became King and Queen. According to Twelfth Day law, each party is to support their character till midnight.

Neither Pepys nor this anonymous writer says who made their 'noble cake', but the tradition of cakes on this day was so strong that it was the bakers' and confectioners' busiest time of year, and it was a point of honour to rise to the challenge. William Hone's *Every-Day Book* (1827) describes the tradition at its height:

> In London, with every pastry-cook in the city, and at the west end of the town, it is 'high change' on Twelfth-day. From the taking down of the shutters in the morning, he, and his men, with additional assistants, male and female, are fully occupied by attending to the dressing out of the window, executing orders of the day before, receiving fresh ones, or supplying the wants of chance customers. Before dusk the important arrangement of the window is completed. Then the gas is turned on, with supernumerary argand-lamps and manifold wax-lights to illuminate countless cakes of all prices and dimensions, that stand in rows and piles on the counters and sideboards, and in the windows. The richest in flavour and heaviest in weight and price are placed on large and massy salvers; one, enormously superior to the rest in size, is the chief object of curiosity; and all are decorated with all imaginable images of things animate and inanimate. Stars, castles, kings, cottages, dragons, trees, fish, palaces, cats, dogs, churches, lions, milkmaids, knights, serpents, and innumerable other forms, in snow-white confectionery, painted with variegated colours, glittering by 'excess of light', reflected from mirrors against the walls, festooned with artificial 'wonders of Flora'.

However, as the people gathered round the windows to admire the confectioners' art, another traditional pastime came into play: boys and youths in the crowd took the opportunity to nail bystanders' clothes surreptitiously to the shop window-frames, or to pin them to their neighbours. A really successful prankster

Twelfth Night: the cast of *Jack and the Beanstalk* cut the Baddeley cake at the Theatre Royal, Drury Lane, 1936

could pin several people, male and female, in a chain of trapped humanity. This game could be played at any crowded gathering, and often took place at country fairs, but it was particularly popular in the earlier nineteenth century on Twelfth Night, and, as with all such behaviour, then and now, the joke was appreciated by perpetrators and onlookers but not by those on the receiving end.

By the second half of the nineteenth century, however, Twelfth Night was beginning to lose ground, and its popularity continued to wane as the new 'Victorian' Christmas began to take shape. The Twelfth cake was replaced by the Christmas cake, the coins and thimbles started turning up in the Christmas pudding, the post-Christmas parties began to take place on New Year's Eve and Day, and to most people

nowadays, Twelfth Night, while still marking the 'end of Christmas', is simply the day on which we take down the decorations.

See **Baddeley Cake** (*below*) for perhaps the last remnant of the Twelfth Night cake tradition. *See also* **Christmas: Wassailing** for another custom that regularly took place on Twelfth Night.

Baddeley Cake

As already noted, Twelfth Night was traditionally associated with fancy cakes (*see* p. 13); it is therefore perhaps unsurprising that the actor Robert Baddeley (1732–94), who had previously been a pastry cook, hit upon the idea of an annual cake in his name when thinking of something to do for his fellow-performers. When he

Lamb's Wool

Lamb's Wool is frequently mentioned since at least the sixteenth century as a drink for special occasions, particularly winter celebrations such as Christmas, Twelfth Night, New Year, and it was often offered by wassailers (*see* **Christmas: Wassailing**). Its ingredients vary, but its base was hot cider, ale, or more rarely wine. Sugar and spices such as nutmeg, ginger, or cinnamon were added, along with the essential element, apples; the latter were baked or roasted until their pulp fell apart in the liquid, giving the appearance of lamb's wool.

died while dressing for a part in Sheridan's *School for Scandal*, his will revealed a bequest for impoverished actors, together with £100 to finance a Twelfth Night cake and wine feast for the company of Drury Lane. They still keep up the tradition at the Theatre Royal by gathering after the performance on that evening, still in costume and make-up, for the Baddeley cake.

Brough Holly Night

This Twelfth Night custom, which involves a lighted tree, seems to have died out in the later nineteenth century but was formerly practised at Brough in Westmorland (now Cumbria). There are several references to the custom from the mid nineteenth century, the fullest being in William Hone's *Table Book* (1827), which also prints an illustration:

Formerly the 'Holly-tree' at Brough was really 'holly', but ash being abundant, the latter is now substituted. There are two head inns in the town, which provide for the ceremony alternately, though the good townspeople mostly lend their assistance in preparing the tree, to every branch of which they fasten a torch. About eight o'clock in the evening, it is taken to a convenient part of the town, where the torches are lighted, the town band accompanying and playing till all is completed, when it is removed to the lower end of the town; and, after divers salutes and huzzas from the spectators, is carried up and

down the town, in stately procession, usually by a person of renowned strength, named Joseph Ling. The band march behind it, playing their instruments, and stopping every time they reach the town bridge, and the cross, where the 'holly' is again greeted with shouts of applause. Many of the inhabitants carry lighted branches and flambeaus; and rockets, squibs, &c. are discharged on the joyful occasion. After the tree is thus carried, and the torches are sufficiently burnt, it is placed in the middle of the town, when it is again cheered by the surrounding populace, and is afterwards thrown among them. They eagerly watch for this opportunity; and, clinging to each end of the tree, endeavour to carry it away to the inn they are contending for, where they are allowed their usual quantum of ale and spirits, and pass a 'merry night' which seldom breaks up before two in the morning.

Haxey Hood

The village of Haxey, historically in Lincolnshire but now in Humberside, is found in the strange area of land called the 'Isle of Axholme', which was once surrounded by such wet land until it was drained by Dutch immigrants in the seventeenth century that it was almost an inland island. Haxey hosts the annual Haxey Hood, one of the best-known and most intriguing customs in England, and the locals are fiercely proud of it.

There are thirteen officials connected with the game: the Lord of the Hood, who is in charge, a Chief Boggin, ten other Boggins, and a Fool. The Fool is dressed in clothes covered in shreds and patches, and has a painted or blackened face; the rest wear red jackets or jumpers, and the Lord and Chief wear impressive hats that are decorated with flowers. The Lord carries a 'wand' made of thirteen willow sticks, which are four or five feet long and bound tightly together into a compact bundle. The 'Hood' itself, which is hotly contended for in the game, is a tightly rolled piece of leather about eighteen inches long and three inches in diameter. Ostensibly, the struggle is between the men of Haxey and the men of Westwoodside, and the two goals are the King's Arms and the Carpenter's Arms respectively. The two teams can be of any size.

On New Year's Eve, the thirteen officials meet to

retrieve the Hood from the safekeeping of the pub in which it had ended up the previous year. In the following week they visit numerous pubs and houses in neighbouring villages, sing their three traditional songs, 'Farmer's Boy', 'John Barleycorn', and 'Drink England Dry (Cannons)', pass a hat round, to help defray the costs of the game, and move on.

On Plough Monday itself, the Lord and the Boggins make one more round of the village pubs, settling down in one of them to paint the Fool's face, mostly in black and red. They then process towards the church, but on the way the Fool tries to escape and is caught and carried back, shoulder high, by the other Boggins, and he is finally placed on the mounting stone (the base of an old cross) in front of the church. From this vantage point, he makes his speech of welcome, but the Boggins light a fire of straw behind him, to 'smoke' him. When the flames or smoke get too much, the Fool finishes his speech with the traditional words:

> Hoose agen hoose
> Toon agen toon
> If a man meets a man
> Knock 'im doon
> But do'ant 'ot 'im [But don't hurt him]

This last line was probably added in the late 1920s. The crowd then follows the Fool up to Haxey Hill, where the game takes place. The first phase of the game is the 'Running Hood', in which the Lord throws up a series of twelve sacking Hoods, one at a time, and the players try to escape from the field with the Hood without being touched by one of the Boggins, who are strategically placed to stop them. About an hour before sunset, however, the main game begins when the real Leather Hood is thrown up. Whoever catches it is immediately surrounded by a heaving mass of people, the 'sway', as each side tries to force it towards their goal. The sway can include anything up to 300 people and at first can seem to the outsider to be immovable. But move it always does, either inching its way forward, or swinging and spiralling violently, occasionally collapsing in a tangled heap of bodies. Sometime during the evening it is clear which way the sway is going, and progress is made towards the winning pub in what local writer Jeremy Cooper describes as a 'triumphant trudge'. The game is officially over when the landlord of the relevant

pub touches the Hood. It is then kept safe behind the bar until needed again next year.

The origins of the custom are unknown, and the early history and development are still unclear. The local story tells how Lady de Mowbray – the wife or daughter of a powerful local landowner – was out riding one day when a sudden gust of wind blew off her red silk hood. Twelve or thirteen labourers working in the neighbouring fields attempted to catch the recalcitrant hood, but the wind kept thwarting their attempts. Lady de Mowbray was so amused by their antics that she granted land to the men to provide for a commemorative event every year. The story continues with details which were probably added later: it is said that she called one of the men a 'fool' because he was too shy to hand the retrieved hood to her, and another a 'lord' because he did so. She is even said to have used the word 'boggined', meaning 'trapped or bogged down', which explains the names of the Hood officers.

Thus, suspiciously, all the main words, characters, and actions are explained in a story which, although it has the charm of a fairy tale, is likely to have been invented to explain the 'Hood'. An alternative suggestion is that the game is held annually to keep up common rights, or rights of tenure to certain lands.

The earliest known description dates from 1815, and there are several other published references from the first half of the nineteenth century which confirm the game's existence and that it was roughly the same as it is now. It is difficult to be sure, but the earliest accounts appear to be describing the more open-style game, referred to above as the 'Running Hood' game, rather than the mass sway. Three important broad conclusions emerge from these early descriptions: firstly, that a similar game was also played at other nearby villages until at least the late nineteenth century; secondly, that the de Mowbrays were already being cited as the custom's founders in the earliest reference; and thirdly, that the Plough Bullocks, who also went round the village at this season (see **Plough Monday**, p. 19), were also called 'Boggins' and also took part in the Hood.

There are dozens of similar mass games, usually described as **football** (p. 53), but including other local names such as **hurling** (p. 42) and **camping** (see **Games and Sports**, p. 32). The common elements of these games are the unlimited or large teams, the

Haxey Hood, Lincolnshire, 2001

lack of detailed rules, and the great distance between goals, but, as examined in the entry for 'football', the key determinant for the style of play is whether the game takes place in the streets of the town, or in an open space. Apart from the shape of the Hood, which is apparently unique, what differentiates Haxey from other football games are the elaborate ceremonies which surround it (e.g. smoking the Fool), and the characters involved, but these may well have been part of a Plough Bullocking custom that was left behind when the latter faded away.

Moseley's Dole

Moseley's Dole, which formerly took place at Walsall in Staffordshire on Twelfth Night, provided every man, woman, and child in that town and some neighbouring villages (including visitors) with the gift of one penny. The legend which explains this charity tells how Thomas Moseley, owner of the local Bascote Estate during the fifteenth century, was walking through Walsall on Twelfth Night and heard a child crying for want of bread. His heart was troubled, and he immediately founded this charity to ensure that at least on this night of the year nobody in the area would be without even a loaf of bread. Moseley was real enough, but the actual origin of the charity lies most probably in the custom of distributing money to encourage people to attend church and pray for the souls of the departed, in this case for Thomas and his wife. By the early nineteenth century, penny loaves were distributed in lieu of cash, and in 1825 the dole was discontinued and the money put towards the maintenance of eleven almshouses.

See also **Doles**, p. 87.

Twelfth Night Fires

This custom, allied to the idea of wassailing the fruit trees, and sometimes even going by the same name, involved lighting fires out in the fields on Twelfth Night, or Eve, to bring luck to the crops in the coming year. It was reported a number of times from Gloucestershire, Herefordshire, and Worcestershire in the late eighteenth and nineteenth centuries, and although it was by all accounts quite common in those areas, it does not seem to have been known elsewhere. The *Gentleman's Magazine* of 1791 provides details of an example from Herefordshire:

> *At the approach of evening, on the vigil of Twelfth Day, the farmers, with their friends and servants, meet together, and about six o'clock walk out to a field where wheat is growing. In the highest part of the ground, twelve small fires and one large one, are lighted up. The attendants, headed by the master of the family, pledge the company freely in old cider, which circulates freely on these occasions. A circle is formed round the large fire, when a general shout and hallooing takes place, which you hear answered from all the adjacent villages and fields. Sometimes fifty or sixty of these fires may be all seen at once. This being finished, the company return home, where the housewife and her maids are preparing a good supper. A large cake is always provided.*

Twelve fires (or thirteen if the bigger one is counted) are usually specified, but it is not clear whether they represent the twelve days of Christmas, or the twelve Apostles, or even the twelve months of the year. In one account, one of the fires, representing Judas Iscariot, is stamped out early, while there are also hints that the nature of the coming year can be predicted by the behaviour of the twelve fires.

See **New Year Customs and Superstitions: Burning the Bush** for a similar fire-in-the-fields custom from Herefordshire; *see also* **Christmas: Wassailing**.

*

PLOUGH SUNDAY

The first Monday after 6 January was widely known as **Plough Monday** (*see below*), and there was a tendency for the name to spread to adjoining days to give us Plough Sunday and Plough Tuesday. Given the religious origin of most Plough Monday festivities, it is likely that in arable areas the church services on the day before would have included some direct reference to ploughs and farming, but there is little evidence that the Sunday was celebrated in any other way. Nevertheless, soon after the Second World War a deliberate combined attempt by members of the Royal Agricultural Society and leaders of the Church of England to revive what they thought of as the 'old Saxon feasts of Plough Sunday, Rogation Sunday, Lammas-tide, and Harvest Thanksgiving' resulted in a number of churches featuring plough blessings in their services. *The Times* (11 January 1954) reported the movement:

> *Plough Sunday was commemorated at several churches yesterday. At Heddenham, Norfolk, the rector blessed a plough which had been placed in the chancel, and offered prayers for all engaged in agriculture. In the City of London a ceremonial plough which 24 men and women who work in the fields of Dorset brought up with them from Springfield, near Dorchester, was blessed at St Helen's, Bishopsgate. After the service, 12 Dorset men dressed in traditional costume performed the plough dance play in the churchyard.*

These celebrations do not seem to have taken permanent hold, and few lasted beyond the 1950s.

*

PLOUGH MONDAY

Plough Monday was the first Monday after Twelfth Day, and in rural areas the effective start of the new agricultural year, as Thomas Tusser advised in 1580:

> *Plough Monday, next after that Twelfth tide is past*
> *Bids out with the plough, the worst husband is last*

The commonest early references to customary behaviour on Plough Monday are records from the fifteenth century onwards of 'plough lights' in local churches. These were candles that were kept burning in the church specifically to bring the Lord's blessing on the efforts of farmers and farmworkers. The 'common' or 'town' plough was also kept there, to be loaned out in turn to villagers who could not afford one of their own, and its presence presumably gave the opportunity for services based on blessing the plough and praying for success in the coming year. Some parishes had plough guilds, dedicated to raising money to maintain the lights, and by the early fifteenth century there is evidence of ploughs being moved around for symbolic or fund-raising purposes. *Dives and Pauper* (c.1405–10) complains of people 'Leading the plough

about the fire as for good beginning of the year', and in 1413, in Durham, there is a record of 4d being given 'to the people who were drawing a plough'. From the 1460s onwards there are numerous references to lights and to ploughs being taken round the parish to raise money for church purposes, but this custom seems to have been restricted geographically, being found only in the eastern midland counties of Lincolnshire, Northamptonshire, Cambridgeshire, Essex, Norfolk, and Suffolk, and not even in every church in these areas. With the Reformation, plough lights were banned along with other 'superstitious practices', and as the raising of money by celebratory and festival customs also began to lose favour, the plough perambulation on behalf of the church soon faded away.

Nevertheless, from the late eighteenth century onwards, there are again numerous references to ploughs being taken round the parish on Plough Monday, but this time the activity was on behalf of those in the party, and the whole affair was, by all accounts, far from godly. It is not entirely clear whether this new plough activity was a direct survival of the old practice, a conscious revival, or a 'new' idea, but the custom of taking a plough round the neighbourhood on Plough Monday was widely reported. Again the activity was concentrated in the eastern counties, but was also found in a wider area, including the neighbouring counties of Yorkshire, Derbyshire, and Northumberland. The men who carried out this custom went by a variety of names – Plough Stots, Plough Jags, Plough Witchers, and Plough Bullocks – and what they did also varied widely: some simply took a plough round the parish, some danced and sang, others performed an elaborate play (*see below*), and some even dispensed with the plough altogether. Recurrent features included Fools of various descriptions, men dressed as women, blackened or reddened faces, white shirts and coloured ribbons, and straw inside clothes, but the one constant aspect was the request for money. In his *Memorials of Godmanchester*, F. W. Bird remembered that around 1850:

> *Plough Monday was a great institution at Godmanchester* [in Huntingdonshire]. *Farming men, many of them dressed as women, and having their faces besmeared, paraded the streets. Not*

Plough Monday (from George Walker's *The Costume of Yorkshire*, 1814)

*content with assuming grotesque costumes, and
bedaubed faces, they stuffed bundles of straw
between their shoulders, which gave them a hunch-
back appearance ... They dragged a wooden plough
behind them, and men, all more or less hideously
attired, accompanied the procession with money
boxes. They halted at all the principal houses of the
town and asked for 'toll', pedestrians being solicited
as they were encountered. If nothing was forthcoming from a call, rumour said that the plough witchers
made no more ado but forthwith ploughed up the
front part of the houses and departed, but no such
damage was remembered in Godmanchester.*

The attitude of the people who were visited, or caught
passing by, also varied enormously, from the amused
tolerance of those who liked to see old customs perpetuated, to vociferous opposition on the part of those
who only saw the drunkenness and potential menace
of these visitors. Of all the house-visiting customs in

the traditional calendar in the nineteenth century,
the Plough Jags excited the most local controversy,
perhaps owing to the size of the gangs, which could
often exceed twenty, or because they were predominately young men. Even without overt threats of retri-
bution if nothing was forthcoming (which certainly
did happen), there was always the covert threat posed
by a group of young men in disguise who had already
had plenty to drink and wanted more. By the later nineteenth century, local newspapers, magistrates, police,
Anglican clergy, Nonconformist ministers, and many
other pillars of society began to object, and the Plough
Jags either cleaned up their act or were suppressed. The
custom survived well into the twentieth century in
some parts, but usually in relatively tame forms, as the
journal *Folk-Lore* reported from Bedfordshire in 1926:

*Plough Monday – All the boys and men at farm work
disguise themselves with odd costumes and masks
and patrol the streets singing and shaking tins and*

saying – 'Give poor ploughboy a halfpenny or a penny'. They knock at doors and, on being admitted, sing and sometimes dance, and expect money and beer or wine.

As mechanization and agricultural depressions drastically reduced the numbers of men working on the land, the Plough Jags' days were inevitably numbered.

Plough Plays

The most spectacular and highly developed entertainment provided by the ploughboys in their Plough Monday perambulations was the 'plough play' or 'wooing play', which is regarded by folklorists as one of the three main sub-genres of English traditional drama. This play, which could be performed at any time over the Christmas period, is distinguished from other types of play by a range of characters – the Fool, the Farmer's Man, Dame Jane, Lady Bright and Gay, the Ribboner, and the Recruiting Sergeant – and a longer, more complex storyline than the more basic hero-combat or St George type found elsewhere (*see* **Christmas: Mummers**). Much of the dialogue was clearly designed to be sung, and the basic plot involves the courting of a Lady by the Farmer's Man, who is persuaded to enlist by the Recruiting Sergeant when the Lady rejects him. The Lady then accepts the Fool's offer instead. In some versions, a character called Dame Jane appears, with a baby, and accuses the Fool of being the father, which he denies.

JANE: *Tommy, take your bastard.*
FOOL: *Bastard, Jinny? It's not like me and none of mine.*
JANE: *Its nose, eyes, and chin as much like you as ever it can grin.*
FOOL: *Who sent you here with it, Jinny?*
JANE: *The overseer of the parish, who said I was to bring it to the biggest fool I could find so I thought I'd bring it to you.*

There are also introductory verses, and lines requesting money at the end. A short, fairly typical 'hero-combat' play with fight, doctor, and cure is usually embedded in the plough-play action, although it seems to bear little or no relation to the rest of the play. An examination of plough-play texts reveals that they are a pastiche of elements from other parts of popular culture. There

are, in fact, two semi-distinct types of plough play: in one, the wooing sequence is central to the plot, and comprises a series of suitors who the Lady rejects in turn until she finally chooses the Fool; while in the more common type, there is what the play expert Peter Millington calls 'a three-way operatic scene between the Recruiting Sergeant, the Farmer's Man, and the Lady Bright and Gay'.

As with other traditional plays, the performers wore a range of costumes. Some dressed as near to character as they could – the Doctor in a top hat, the Recruiting Sergeant in red uniform – but others wore streamers or patches on their clothes, a style which is found across a whole range of traditional performances. As with all such plays, the female parts were played by men, and these 'females' always dressed in women's clothes, with the Lady Bright and Gay always better dressed than poor old Dame Jane.

Plough plays were found only in the East Midlands – Lincolnshire, Nottinghamshire, Leicestershire, and Rutland – and the earliest known versions only date from the 1820s. The inclusion of a wooing sequence excited some earlier folklorists enough to suggest an origin in an ancient fertility ritual, but as there is no evidence that the plays existed before the early nineteenth century, this is improbable. A glance at a typical plough-play text reveals no sense of ancient ritual, but is pure late eighteenth-century stage song:

LADY: *What care I for your gold and silver*
What care I for your house and land
What care I for your rings and diamonds
All I want is a handsome man.
FOOL: *A handsome man will not detain you*
For his beauty will decay
The finest flower that grows in the summer
In the winter fades away.

Historians Alun Howkins and Linda Merricks have argued persuasively that these plays emerged exactly when changes in farming practices were introducing large farms and 'high farming' to the areas where the plays have been reported. These farms needed a large workforce of young men who lived in, mainly in rough and ready conditions, and who formed a semi-distinct group with its own values and culture within the broader society. It is this group of young 'ploughboys' who made up the gangs who went round with the plough or with a play over the Christmas period, and it is to the culture of these men that we should look for questions of origin rather than to the remote but romantic past.

Ploughboys and Maids

Another Plough Monday custom had little to do with ploughs as such, but involved some horseplay between plough lads and farm maids. It was one of those game customs that highlighted the very different spheres allotted to men and women in farm work in the past, and playfully pitted the sexes against each other. In Northamptonshire in 1854, Ann Elizabeth Baker wrote:

> When the ploughman returned from his labours
> in the evening, the servant maid used to meet him
> with a jug of toast and ale; and if he could succeed in
> throwing his plough hatchet into the house before
> she reached the door, he was entitled to a cock to
> throw at the next Shrove-tide, but if she was able
> to present him with the toast and ale first, then she
> gained the cock.

And in Warwickshire in 1930, J. Harvey Bloom recorded:

> It was customary for the farm-girls to race from the
> house to the nearest furrow, snatch up a clod of earth
> and scamper back again, chased by the plough-boys
> with their whips. If the girls reached the farm in time
> to stick a few feathers in the clod of earth before the
> boys could place their whips upon the kitchen table,
> then the boys lost their ration of plum pudding.

Such games were reported from various parts of the country in the nineteenth century, but were also known in earlier periods. A version from Leicestershire is included in Thomas Tusser's rustic poetry of 1580, in which the maid had to get the kettle on to boil before being caught:

> If ploughman get hatchet or whip to the skreene
> Maid loseth their cock if no water be seene.

*

PLOUGH MONDAY/ PLOUGH TUESDAY

Straw Bears

The annual custom of the 'straw bear' seems to have been confined to the fenland area of Ramsey and Whittlesey in Cambridgeshire, and took place on Plough Monday or the day after. The following account from the journal *Folk-Lore* in 1909 clearly relates to street performances:

> When I was at Whittlesey (Cambridgeshire) yester-
> day (12 Jan 1909), I had the pleasure of meeting a
> 'straw bear', if not two, in the street. I had not been
> at Whittlesey on the day for nearly forty years, and
> feared the custom had died out. In my boyhood the
> straw-bear was a man completely covered in straw,
> led by a string by another, and made to dance in
> front of people's houses, in return for which money
> was expected. This always took place on the Tuesday
> following Plough-Monday. Yesterday the straw bear
> was a boy, and I saw no dancing; otherwise there was
> no change. I was told that two years ago a zealous
> inspector of police had forbidden straw bears as a
> form of cadging, and my informant said that he
> thought that in many places they had been stopped
> by the police.

However, in Sybil Marshall's *Fenland Chronicle* (1967), the well-known evocation of her parents' lives at Ramsey, her mother describes the bear being brought into houses, and capering about inside. The earliest references to the custom date from about the 1850s, and it seems to have faded away with the First World War. The straw bear was successfully revived at Whittlesey in 1980.

There is no indication that the straw-bear performance was anything other than a simple entertainment carried out, like so many other customs, simply to raise money for the performers, and based on the real dancing bears that toured the country every year until well into the twentieth century. Although straw features in other customs – it was the main ingredient of various effigies such as **Jack-a-Lent** (*see* p. 67), and was stuffed into clothes to make humpbacks for char-

A revived straw bear at Whittlesey, Cambridgeshire, c.2002

acters in plough plays; moreover, similar straw-clad figures also featured in customs in Ireland, Germany, and Austria – the closest analogy to the straw bear in Britain is not linked to straw but to bears. In certain parts of Lancashire, it was customary on May Day for a boy to dress up in a sack and be led by other boys, from house to house, pretending to be a dancing bear (*see* **1 May: Bears**).

*

7 JANUARY

St Distaff's Day or Rock Day

St Distaff's Day was traditionally the day on which women resumed their spinning after the Christmas period, and was the female equivalent of **Plough Monday** (*see* p. 19). In a custom which, like many others,

pitted the sexes against each other, on this day young men would try to steal the women's flax and tow, and burn it, while the women retaliated by soaking them with water. Robert Herrick's poem 'St Distaff's Day or the Morrow After Twelfth Day' (1648) details the tradition:

Partly work and partly play
Ye must on S. Distaff's day
From the plough soon free your team;
Then come home and fother them.
If the maids a spinning go,
Burn the flax, and fire the tow:
Scorch their plackets, but beware,
That ye singe no maiden-hair.
Bring in pails of water then,
Let the maids bewash the men.
Give S. Distaff all the right,
Then bid Christmas sport good night;

And next morrow, every one
To his own vocation.

It is not clear from existing records how widespread this custom really was, or even how long it lasted. Although it is mentioned by several of the leading nineteenth-century antiquarians, their accounts have a vagueness and an underlying similarity which suggests that they were all extrapolating from one source – presumably the Herrick poem.

The 'distaff' and the 'rock' were implements used to spin yarn before the invention of the spinning wheel and were so closely associated with women's work that the phrase 'distaff side' was widely used to describe the female sphere, as opposed to the 'spear side' of the male. The word 'spinster' took on a much wider meaning in the same way. St Distaff did not exist, but the name was formed as a sort of joke, on the same lines as other fictitious saints such as **St Monday** (*see* p. 424) and St Tibb (*see* p. xxiii).

*

13 JANUARY

St Hilary's Day

St Hilary (*c.*315–*c.*368) may have been Bishop of Poitiers, and he may have produced some influential theological writings, but he would hardly be remembered in England if not for the accident that his feast day occurred around the beginning of one of the four terms of the Law Courts and some older universities. This legal session has therefore been traditionally called Hilary Term.

St Hilary's Day is also reputed to be the coldest day of the year.

*

14 JANUARY

Hunting the Mallard

Few institutions can feel secure enough in their longevity to host a custom which takes place once every hundred years, but Oxford colleges can certainly do so. Hunting the Mallard, a custom which was formerly practised annually but now takes place once a century, takes place at All Soul's College, on 14 January. The Fellows, who are gathered for their Gaudy on that night, elect a Lord Mallard and six officers, who carry white staves and wear special medals on which the bird is depicted. Led by the officers, the whole company sets out at midnight on a torch-lit procession that proceeds to 'hunt the mallard', a mythical bird, all over the college (including the roof), a performance that can take several hours. They sing a special mallard song, of which the chorus runs:

O by the blood of King Edward
O by the blood of King Edward
It was a swapping, swapping mallard.

The age of the custom is not known, but it certainly existed as early as 1632 when it was mentioned in a letter written by Archbishop Abbott. After complaining of gross misconduct such as tearing down doors, the Archbishop writes, 'civil men should never so far forget themselves under pretence of a foolish mallard, as to do things barbarously unbecoming.' The connection between the bird and the college is explained by the legend that a mallard of great size was discovered when the foundations were laid in 1437, but it seems more likely that the custom stemmed from what originally had been a students' joke. The most recent hunt took place in 2001.

*

17 JANUARY

Old Twelfth Night

When the calendar changed in 1752 (*see* p. xx), many customs were wrenched from their traditionally sanctioned dates and were left dangling on apparently meaningless ones. Clearly, those who organized some events felt a strong attachment to the original night, and were determined to keep to it whatever the government said. So it was that at many farms around Exmoor, and probably elsewhere, wassailers did their rounds of the local orchards on 17 January, as their forebears had done on Twelfth Night (*see* **6 January: Twelfth Night**).

See also **Christmas: Wassailing**.

*

The Eve of St Agnes: interior at Knole, near Sevenoaks. A watercolour by Sir John Everett Millais

19 JANUARY

St Wulfstan's Day

Wulfstan (*c*.1008–95), appointed Bishop of Worcester in 1062, was one of the leaders of the Anglo-Saxon church at the time of the Norman Conquest, in 1066. Most unusually, he kept his position under the new Norman regime, and continued to serve until his death nearly thirty years later. He was buried in Worcester Cathedral, the rebuilding of which had been one of his favourite projects, and his fame was soon enhanced by news of the miraculous cures that took place at his tomb, leading to his canonization in 1203.

Wulfstan was a very popular saint in the Middle Ages, and King John thought enough of him to request to be buried between his and St Oswald's tomb, at Worcester; pilgrimages in his name persisted at least until the turn of the eighteenth century. His day is almost completely ignored today, apart from at Worcester, where he is remembered by a special memorial service every few years.

*

20 JANUARY

St Agnes' Eve

In English tradition, St Agnes' Eve was a very popular night for young women (and occasionally men) to try to predict or control their future marriage prospects. Such love divinations often took place at night, on the eve of the saint whose aid was being invoked – presumably because so many of them involved going to sleep and dreaming. *See* **21 January: St Agnes' Day** for further details.

*

21 JANUARY

St Agnes' Day

Agnes was a Christian martyr who died in Rome c.350. Very few facts are known about her life, but later legends describe her as a particularly good-looking thirteen-year-old girl who refused all talk of marriage because she wished to remain a virgin and dedicate her life to Christ. She confounded all attempts to persuade and intimidate her, and despite being placed in a brothel and thrown into roaring flames, she is said to have survived with her virginity intact. She was finally killed by a dagger through the throat. Stories of cures and miracles at her tomb, and visions in which she figured prominently, spread her fame across the Christian world, and she became one of the most popular 'virgin martyrs' of the Middle Ages. In religious pictures, she is often accompanied by a lamb, no doubt because her name resembles the Latin *agnus*, meaning 'lamb', and the animal is a widely accepted symbol for meekness and innocence. The Roman Catholic Church formerly included a ceremony on her day in which newly shorn wool was presented and blessed.

In England, at least from the seventeenth to the nineteenth centuries, Agnes was one of several female saints invoked by young women who wanted to predict or influence their future love life, and St Agnes' Eve was the traditional time for carrying out divinatory practices. It may seem strange that a person who was famous for preferring death to marriage was called upon in this way, and we may think it would be more effective to appeal to someone who had shown some success in this area by having numerous husbands, but superstition doesn't follow such logical patterns. This connection between love divination and St Agnes' Eve was proverbial for seventeenth-century writers, who often mention it, and it was still well known in Victorian times and into the twentieth century. Its popularity was given a distinct boost by the publication of John Keats' famous dramatic medieval poem 'The Eve of St. Agnes' in 1820, which has more than a touch of *Romeo and Juliet* about it. The dashing hero finds out that the object of his affection, whose family is at war with his, plans to carry out a divination ceremony:

They told her how, upon St Agnes' Eve,
Young virgins might have visions of delight,
And soft adorings from their loves receive
Upon the honey'd middle of the night,
If ceremonies due they did aright.

So he sneaks into her bedroom to make sure that she dreams of him. She wakes, and they elope.

Many different love divinations have been recorded as popular on St Agnes' Eve, including the well-known ones of making of the **dumb cake** (p. 220), and the sowing of hemp seed, which was thrown over the shoulder at midnight to conjure up the wraith of the future lover; however, these ceremonies could be undertaken on other nights, such as Hallowe'en, St Mark's Eve, or even Christmas Eve. Other procedures specifically invoked Agnes's name and were thus particular to her night. The following, from Derbyshire, was printed in the magazine *Long Ago* in 1874:

The girl who wished to test her future, on St Agnes'
Day, prepared herself by a twenty-four hours' fast,
beginning at midnight on the 20th and ending
at midnight on the 21st. During this time she took
nothing but pure water and she would not, on any
account, speak to anyone about the divination and
not even mention it aloud to herself. At midnight, on
the 21st, she retired to bed, without breaking her fast,
and rested on her left side, saying three times the
following lines:

    Saint Agnes is a friend to me
    In the gift I ask of thee
    Let me this night my husband see

Her dreams ought to be about her future husband. If she should dream of more than one man, she would marry an indefinite number of times; if she does not dream of a man, she will never marry. The divination was very popular.

*

22 JANUARY

St Vincent's Day

Little is known of Vincent of Saragossa apart from the fact that he was martyred for his faith in AD 304, but he was a widely popular saint across Europe and in Anglo-Saxon England. In English tradition, his day is only remembered in weather predictions, most of which agree that sunshine on the day augurs well for the year. A Northumberland version, quoted in 1904 by local folklorist Mrs Balfour, makes the point:

Remember on St. Vincent's Day,
if the sun his beams display
Be sure to mark the transient beam,
which through the casement sheds a gleam
For 'tis a token bright and clear
of prosperous weather all the year

*

24 JANUARY

Eve of Conversion of St Paul

As noted under **25 January**, St Paul has more than one feast day, and 24 January is the Eve of his Conversion to Christianity. Late January was not a popular time for traditional festivals, presumably because it was too soon after the Christmas/New Year period, but a range of related customs, each concerned in some way with broken crockery, was reported from Cornwall in 1886 by the *Folk-Lore Journal*, including the following:

St Paul's Eve is a holiday with the miners, and is called by them Paul Pitcher Day, from a custom they have of setting up a water-pitcher, which they pelt with stones until it is broken in pieces. A new one is afterwards bought and carried to a beer-shop to be filled with beer.

In other examples, but from a similar period, children roamed the streets throwing broken crockery at people's doors, or into their hallways. The *Western Antiquary* records:

On entering a house, I have, more than once, stumbled over the broken pieces of a 'Paul's pitcher'.

The motif of throwing broken crockery at doors, which has no obvious rational explanation, is more commonly recorded as a Shrove Tuesday custom (*see* **Shrove Tuesday: Shroving and Lent-Crocking**, p. 65).

*

25 JANUARY

St Paul's Day

St Paul was important enough in Church history to receive more than one feast day; **29 June** is his main day, which he shares with St Peter, while 25 January commemorates his conversion to Christianity on the road to Damascus.

In the secular sphere, it was said that the weather on this day was an excellent guide to the prevailing character of the coming year. In most cases, the prognostication simply refers to weather and harvest – 'If St Paul's is fair and bright the harvest will be good' – but some took the prediction into weightier realms, as in the following Cornish example recorded in the *Western Antiquary* in 1884:

If Paul's Fair be fair and clear
We shall have a happy year
But if it be both wind and rain
Dear will be all kinds of grain
If the winds do blow aloft
Then wars will trouble this realm full oft
If clouds or mist do dark the sky
Great store of birds and beasts shall die.

This predictive nature of St Paul's Day was already well known in the early seventeenth century, but no one has yet suggested any explanation for the day's reputation.

*

30 JANUARY

Execution of Charles I

The execution of Charles I in January 1649 sent shock waves through English society that continued to reverberate for centuries. Almost immediately after his death he was portrayed as a martyr, and the day of his execution was included in the calendar of saints' days in the Anglican Prayer Book from 1662; the special prayers that marked this day were only removed from the official service in 1859. A number of churches in England and abroad are dedicated to him, and it

An Eyewitness Representation of the Execution of Charles I, by John Weesop (*fl.* 1641–9)

was the custom in many places to commemorate his martyrdom with a muffled peal of bells.

The Society of King Charles the Martyr was founded in 1894, in part to protest against the removal of Charles's feast from the calendar of the Prayer Book, but also to 'work for the preservation and furtherance of the Catholic inheritance within the Church of England'. The Society is still very active, and holds commemorative events for Charles's birth (on or near 19 November) and the Restoration of Charles II (Saturday nearest 19 May), but its main celebration is on 30 January at the Banqueting Hall in Whitehall, London – the site of the execution – with laying of wreaths, prayers, and a special sermon. Other organizations that hold annual commemorative events include the Royal Martyr Church Union (founded 1906) and the Royal Stuart Society.

*

JANUARY/FEBRUARY

Chinese New Year

There have been small groups of Chinese-born residents in Britain for centuries, but the first identifiable communities became established in England in the early nineteenth century, when increasing numbers of Chinese nationals were employed on merchant ships. The first 'Chinatowns' were therefore found in major ports, particularly East London and Liverpool, as shops and other businesses catering for the immigrant seamen were created. British-Chinese residents continued to work largely in the merchant navy until the turn of the twentieth century, but the first Chinese laundry opened in 1901, and the first known Chinese restaurant in 1908. By 1921, over a quarter of the Chinese residents in Britain were employed in laundry-work.

Chinese communities in Britain continued to grow slowly until the Second World War, although it was only after the war that significant numbers of wives and children began to settle, and Chinatowns became truly viable communities. Chinese restaurants, in particular, rapidly became a major feature of mainstream British culture, and could soon be found in nearly every town in the country. The 2001 census revealed 247,403 Chinese people living in the UK.

By the 1960s, the focus for Chinese residents in London had shifted from the East End to Soho, and by the next decade Chinese communities across the country felt confident enough to begin to celebrate

Chinese New Year, 2002

their culture in the public arena. The famous Chinese New Year celebrations that take over the local streets started, on a small scale, c.1973, but in London especially they rapidly became an essential part of the local scene, drawing enthusiastic crowds from far and near. Dancing dragons and lions, firecrackers, music, and a range of colourful performers became the instantly recognizable trademark of the Chinese community. The organizing body is the London Chinatown Chinese Association (founded 1978), and at the recent instigation of the Greater London Authority, the celebrations are being drawn further into the orbit of the official London tourist trade, with wider participation, the movement of the public displays into Leicester Square and Trafalgar Square, and the inauguration of an annual China Week. Some locals fear, however, that what they gain in official backing and recognition they may lose in the authentic feel of a home-grown local event.

The Chinese calendar is primarily lunar and does not synchronize well with the purely solar Gregorian calendar of the West. The New Year, or Spring Festival, therefore falls on a different day each year, sometime between 21 January and 21 February. In traditional Chinese culture, the New Year season lasts fifteen days, and everyone is expected to visit their families and friends. As a concession to the western milieu, public celebrations in Britain usually take place on the nearest Sunday.

The one fact that all Westerners know about the Chinese calendar is that each year has an animal name and character. There are twelve of these, and a full Chinese astrological cycle takes sixty years, passing through each of the animal signs five times, although each has one 'golden' year in each cycle. The origin of the animal signs is obscure, but a number of simple fables explain how it came about:

> *Buddha, on the turn of a new year, summoned all the animals to come to him before his departure from earth. Only twelve came to bid him farewell, so Buddha honoured them each with a year. The order was taken from the sequence that they appeared to him: first the Rat, who is said to have ridden on the back of the Ox and jumped off in front of the Ox when they arrived, then the Ox, the Tiger, Rabbit, Dragon, Snake, Horse, Sheep, Monkey, Rooster, Dog, and Pig.*

Other versions of the story mention the Jade Emperor, ruler of the heavens; in one legend, he sent an aide down to earth to bring back the twelve most interesting animals; in another, he held a swimming race and told the animals that the first twelve across a fast-flowing river would each have a year of the zodiac named after them. The absence of the Cat is usually said to be due to the Rat's trickery, which explains those two animals' traditional antipathy. It is worth remembering that 'the year of' does not equate exactly with any particular western year, because of the moveable nature of the New Year.

*

Games and Sports

In the many possible definitions of the words 'play' and 'recreation', the essential element would seem to be 'choice'. While 'work' is what we have to do, 'play' is what we *want* to do. Play is non-utilitarian, amateur, for pleasure rather than gain. But on another level, we now know that play is necessary for both the individual and society at large. It is essential to our development and to our psychological, physical, and social well-being. Through play we learn teamwork, respect, and community spirit; and, depending on our personal choice, we keep fit, mentally agile, or at least out of mischief.

These theoretical concepts have been developed in relatively modern times, although there have always been a few enlightened individuals who understood the value of a release from the daily grind. 'All work and no play makes Jack a dull boy' has been a well-known proverb since at least the 1650s, although Samuel Smiles, the doyen of Victorian hard-work philosophy, added, 'but all play and no work makes him something greatly worse'. There were also those in a position of authority who were well aware that one way to oil the wheels of local community was to supply the wherewithal for the people's games or festivities. Many squires and local dignitaries made a habit of donating an occasional bull to be baited or an ox to be roasted, or granted the use of their park for an annual fête, or provided some prizes for the children's sports. Such paternalistic gestures were not resented but were seen on all sides as an essential function of the social hierarchy. Local publicans often made similar gestures, although with more commercial motives.

On the other hand, there was also a long tradition of opposition to traditional games, and sustained attempts to control what the people did in their spare time. The religious authorities, in particular, were never happy to let the masses organize their own leisure, and consistently sought to control it. At different times, religious qualms focused on drunkenness, violence, the unsupervised mixing of the sexes, gambling, and other moral dangers, and a long-running battle raged over what people were allowed to do on Sundays, a battle that has still not quite gone away. There were also many other, more utilitarian concerns exercising the minds of those in authority. If folk chose to play bowls instead of practising their archery, the defence of the realm could suffer; if they were injured playing football they might not be able to do the work needed to feed their families. Games were a distraction from more important activities, as in the following example quoted by L. A. Govett in his treatment of *The King's Book of Sports* (1618 and 1633), decrees that were in themselves attempts to defuse the growing concern over Sunday games:

> In the records of the county of Surrey it is stated that in 1671 a man was severely punished for bull-baiting, not on account of the cruelty of the sport, but because it was harvest-time, and he caused thereby 'divers labourers and other poor persons to leave their work'.

Attempts to reform popular leisure pursuits were battles for physical space as well as for morals. Modern sports normally take place in dedicated venues – sports centres and stadiums, playing fields, and so on – but this has only been the case for the past hundred years or so. In the earlier Middle Ages, games were played in the churchyard, or even in the church itself, and one of the first campaigns for control saw religious leaders successfully striving to move secular celebrations away from Church property, and to prevent clergy themselves from taking an active part. In rural areas, the games moved to the village green if there was one, or on to nearby common land, or even to any suitably broad stretches of highway. But in urban areas, fairs, bull-runnings, and mass gatherings for football or Guy Fawkes Night took place in the narrow streets of town centres. As the rural areas became enclosed, and land ownership more tightly controlled, and as the town centres developed important business, retail, and civic functions, traditional activities began to be squeezed out. Trespass, civic pride, the danger to property, the effect on trade and the town's reputation, all became factors in this new battle for control.

The history of popular recreation is therefore a chequered one – of attempted control on the one hand and a determination to remain uncontrolled on the other. The documentary evidence of this struggle is, however, potentially misleading. Over the centuries, the voices of the reformers and critics of popular recreation have often been recorded, while those of the ordinary people and their supporters usually have not. We must not be too hasty in assuming that the reformers had it all their own way. Indeed, broadly speaking, most attempts at control were largely unsuccessful, except during the mid seventeenth century when Puritan control was at its height. For the most part, the people continued to play their games, and hold their ales, feasts and fairs, often in spite of the disapproving looks and Sunday sermons of their social betters. Folklorist Christina Hole was quite categorical in her contention that the people had not been beaten:

> The favourite pastimes of a country are amongst the toughest plants in the national soil, as uprooting governments have constantly found to their cost. Legal enactments have been made from time to time to restrict or abolish various forms of amusement, yet many of the latter are still with us, and those which have not have quite as often fallen victim to changing public taste as to the power of the law.

This may have been true for earlier periods, but the whole scene began to change for good at the turn of the nineteenth century. That era saw a real sea change in the way traditional recreations were viewed, and they began to be criticized, challenged, and attacked with renewed vigour on a variety of new fronts. This latest climate of opposition was first aimed at the banning of animal sports such as throwing at cocks, bull-running, and bull-baiting, on the grounds of animal cruelty, but it soon graduated to other mass customs such as football, Bonfire Night celebrations, mock mayors, and fairs. After a short, often bitter, struggle, most were suppressed or altered beyond recognition.

A few sports survived in recognizably traditional forms. Regional forms of wrestling, for example, are still popular in Cumbria and Cornwall, and isolated versions of street football and hurling still take place each year. Others were taken in hand by middle-class supporters, cleaned up, codified, and turned into modern professional sports such as cricket and rugby, and in this way the brutal prizefighting was turned into the slightly-less-brutal boxing. Some, like stool-ball, have been revived, while others, such as cock-fighting and dog-fighting have never quite gone away, despite being illegal for over 150 years

Many of the major pastimes such as **football** (p. 53) and **bull-baiting** (p. 352) have their own entries in this book, but there are dozens of other games and sports that could be investigated if space permitted. What follows is a small sampling of these other, less well-known traditional games.

See also **Shrove Tuesday: Cock Throwing and Threshing**, p. 56; **Shrove Tuesday: Cockfighting**, p. 58; **Shrove Tuesday: Skipping**, p. 65; **Good Friday: Tinsley Green Marbles**, p. 112; **Baiting Bears and Other Animals**, p. 294; **Goose-Riding**, p. 310; **Hurling**, p. 42; **Sparrow-Mumbling**, p. 271.

Camping

One of several old-time games, roughly equivalent to the early mass football but apparently only found in the eastern counties of Norfolk, Suffolk, Essex, and Cambridgeshire. The earliest references to camping as a game date only from the fifteenth century, although 'camp' and 'kemp' are found in Old English and cognate languages such as Dutch and German, meaning 'to fight' or 'to contend', which neatly sums up the impression given of a particularly rough kind of ball game. Robert Forby's *Vocabulary of East Anglia* (1830) gives a good description:

Of the sport itself, however, two varieties are at present expressly recognised: rough-play and civil-play. In the latter, there is no boxing. But the following is a general description of it as it was of old, and in some places still continues. Two goals are pitched at a distance of 120 yards from each other. In a line with each are ranged the combatants; for such they truly are. The number on each side

is equal; not always the same, but very commonly twelve. They ought to be uniformly dressed in light flannel jackets, distinguished by colours. The ball is deposited exactly in the mid-way. The sign or word is given by an umpire. The two sides, as they are called, rush forward. The sturdiest and most active of each encounter those of the other. The contest for the ball begins, and never ends without black eyes and bloody noses, broken heads or shins, and some serious mischiefs. If the ball can be carried, kicked, or thrown to one of the goals, in spite of all the resistance of the other party, it is reckoned for one towards the game; which has sometimes been known to last two or three hours. But the exertion and fatigue of this is excessive. So the victory is not always decided by number of points, but the game is placed against time, as the phrase is. It is common to limit it to half an hour . . . The prizes are commonly hats, gloves, shoes, or small sums of money . . .

It seems clear that camping and the various mass football games have a common ancestry, but by the time written descriptions are available they were at least theoretically distinguishable. In 1892, S. Arnott, writing about the 1780s in *Notes & Queries*, stated quite categorically that 'camping is not football', although in 1823 Edward Moor wrote, 'At times a large football was used, and the game was then called "a kicking camp".' However, Arnott claims that the ball was about the size of a cricket ball, and if the size of the ball is a determining factor, camping should perhaps be compared to Cornish hurling rather than football. By the time of Forby's report, despite the fact that camping seems a very rough game still, the teams were restricted in number and equal to each other, and presumably some sense of order prevailed. In several eastern villages, a piece of land or area called 'Camping Close', or 'Camping Pightle' lived on in memory of the game.

Pell-Mell

Pell-Mell, or Pall-Mall, was a game introduced to England from France, probably during the reign of James I (1603–25), and was very popular with royalty and the nobility. It needed a long flat narrow avenue, along which wooden balls were propelled by hitting them with a mallet. At each end was a ring, suspended from a pole, and players had to hit their ball to the end and through the ring in as few strokes as possible. Samuel Pepys recorded his first encounter with the game in his diary on 2 April 1661:

> So I into St. James parke, where I saw the Duke of Yorke playing at Peslemesle – the first time that I ever saw that sport . . .

He also records a conversation with the Pell-Mell keeper on 15 May 1663. The street Pall Mall, in London, is named after the game.

Shuttlecock

The forerunner of the modern sport of badminton (codified in the 1870s), 'battledore and shuttlecock', or simply 'shuttlecock', was very popular in England in the seventeenth century. In February 1602/3, John Manningham's diary records its popularity at the time:

> The play at shuttlecocke is become soe much in request at Court, that the making shuttlecocks is almost growne to a trade in London.

'Battledore' was another name for a horn-book, much used in teaching children to read, and consisted of a flat board made of wood and horn with a handle, something like a squared modern table-tennis bat, with text affixed. It is easy to see how this may have been used as a bat, or given its name to something shaped like it. The word 'shuttlecock' goes back at least to the sixteenth century, as the poet John Skelton uses the phrase 'I trow all wyll be nought, Nat worth a shyttel cocke' in his *Why come ye nat to Courte?* of 1522, an invective against Thomas Wolsey; and in his *Sports and Pastimes of the People of England* (1801), Joseph Strutt reprints a scene of two boys playing the game from a fourteenth-century manuscript.

The game passed into the hands of children, although adults could be known to take part on occasion: in nineteenth-century Leicestershire and Yorkshire, for example, Shrove Tuesday was known as Shuttlecock Day, and both children and adults played it. In 1863, *Notes & Queries* recorded:

> On the day itself the streets in the lower part of the town (Leicester) literally swarms with juveniles, and even grown men and women, engaged in the pastime . . . Passing through a by-street the other day, I heard a little girl singing –
>
> > Shuttlecock, shuttlecock, tell me true
> > How many years have I to go through.

Stoolball

This ball game was first mentioned in 1475 and regularly reported from then onwards, often as a game played particularly by women, but also by young men, as evidenced by Thomas D'Urfey's *Don Quixote* (1694):

> Down in a vale on a summer's day
> All the lads and lasses meet to be merry
> A match for kisses at stool-ball to play
> And for cakes, and ale, and sider, and perry
> (Chorus) Come all, great small, short tall, away to stool-ball.

There are numerous literary references to the game in the seventeenth century, including in Robert Herrick's *Hesperides* (1648) and John Aubrey's *Natural History of Wiltshire* (1671). The latter writes that it is solely a west of England game, but this is not borne out by other references.

Stoolball is generally regarded as one of the precursors to cricket, although this was questioned by John Goulstone in *Sussex Archaeological Collections* in 1998 and elsewhere. There are wide variations in the equipment and method of play. In the basic, and presumably earliest, form, a milking stool was placed on the ground. A bowler threw a ball and tried to hit the stool, which was defended by another player, using his or her hand. If the bowler hit the stool, or caught the ball when hit by the defender, they changed places. The humble stool was eventually replaced by a purpose-made flat wooden board, mounted on a stake about four feet high, and the batter's hand by a flat round bat. The game then developed along the lines of

Knurr and Spell (George Walker, *The Costume of Yorkshire*, 1814)

cricket, with runs, fielders, and so on, but with a softer ball and under-arm bowling. Lowerson details how Major W. W. Grantham championed stoolball as useful for convalescent troops during the First World War, and attempted its revival as part of a **Merrie England** movement (p. 372). Meanwhile, the game was also being played by predominantly middle- and upper-class women, especially in Sussex and adjoining counties, and the two groups vied for control of the game throughout the interwar years.

Modern-day stoolball is still found mainly in Sussex, where there are dozens of active women's and mixed teams, and many people from the county believe that it originated there. This is not so, but Sussex has had this reputation for some considerable time, as shown by a comment in *Notes & Queries* (1867):

Stool-ball: This game, so often mentioned in old writers, is still played in almost every village in Sussex, and is for ladies and girls exactly what cricket is to men.

Major Grantham's Stoolball Association for Great Britain folded in 1942, but the current National Stoolball Association was formed in 1979.

Joseph Strutt also described a circular form of the game in his *Sports and Pastimes of the People of England* (1801):

... a certain number of stools are set up in a circular form, and at a distance from each other, and every one is occupied by a single player; when the ball is struck, which is done as before with the hand, every one of them is obliged to alter his situation, running in succession from stool to stool.

Tipcat

Tipcat was once an internationally popular game with children and adults alike, but is now largely forgotten in England. The 'cat' was a piece of wood, placed on the ground, so shaped at the ends that when a player hit it with their bat (or catstaff) it would fly into the air. As it came up, the player tried to hit it as far as they could. A large ring had been marked out, or agreed, and if the player failed to hit the cat out of the ring they were out. If they succeeded then a score was awarded, depending on the distance the cat had travelled. Variant names for the game are 'Cat', 'Trippet', 'Nipsy', 'Piggy' or 'Peggy'.

The earliest reference to the game so far discovered in Britain is in an Anglo-Latin lexicon of *c*.1440, but wooden 'tipcats' were found in the ruins of Rahan, Egypt, dating from about 2500 BC. In a variant form, a number of evenly spaced holes were made round the circumference of a circle, and a player was placed by each hole, armed with a stick. The cat was thrown to the nearest batsman and if they hit it the players ran on from hole to hole until the cat was retrieved, scoring a point for each hole reached.

Trapball / Knurr and Spell

Trapball was once a popular game, particularly associated with Shrovetide, which has never quite died out. A ball is placed in the bowl of a spoon-shaped piece of wood, on a stand – this is the 'trap'. It is so contrived that when the player hits the handle of the spoon, with their bat, it pivots and throws the ball into the air. The player then has to hit the ball. The other team tries to catch it or bowl the batsman out by throwing the ball and hitting the trap from where the ball has landed. William Hone reports regular games of trapball played at Shrovetide, Easter, and Whitsun, by twelve old women of Bury St Edmunds. In his *Sports and Pastimes of the People of England* (1801), Joseph Strutt prints an illustration from a fourteenth-century manuscript clearly showing an early version of the game, and Iona and Peter Opie give this and other illustrations of the game through the centuries. Young people in rural areas who could not afford to buy or make a trap had to be content with a hole in the ground and an ox bone or piece of wood as a lever.

Knurr and Spell (there are numerous variations on the spelling) is a very similar game, played mainly in the north of England, and first mentioned by name *c*.1760. The ball was usually made of wood, and in some areas the playing season started at Easter. Later versions of the trap included a spring, which helped to ensure that the ball was released in the same way each time. Frank Atkinson provides some good illustrations and distribution maps of the game in his article 'Knur and Spell and Allied Games' in the journal *Folk Life* (1963).

February

Trial of the Pyx

| 5 | 6 | 7 |

Whipping Toms

| 12 | 13 | **14**
ST VALENTINE'S DAY |

| **19**
HALL MONDAY | **20**
John Cass Commemoration
SHROVE TUESDAY
Cockfighting/Throwing
Egg Shackling
Ludlow Rope-Pulling
Pancakes
Shroving and Lent-Crocking
Skipping | **21**
ASH WEDNESDAY
Jack-a-Lent |

| 26 | 27 | 28 |

*Moveable events have been placed
on the date they fall in 2007.
Events dependent on the timing
of Easter are coloured green.*

1

ST BRIDGET/ST BRIDE'S DAY

2

CANDLEMAS (Purification of the Blessed Virgin Mary)
FORTY SHILLING DAY

3

ST BLAISE'S DAY
St Ives Hurling

4

FIRST SUNDAY IN FEBRUARY
Clowns' Service

8

9

10

ST SCHOLASTICA'S DAY

11

15

16

17

EGG SATURDAY

18

22

23

FRIDAY FOLLOWING ASH WEDNESDAY
Pully Lug Day

24

25

(29)

LEAP YEAR DAY

Trial of the Pyx

This annual custom, which originated with Henry II's currency reforms in the twelfth century, is designed to check the composition and weight of newly minted coins. The 'pyx' is the box which contains sample coins put aside throughout the year from the Royal Mint, and every February or March a party of freemen of the Goldsmith's Company meet at Goldsmith's Hall in Gutter Lane, London, to carry out the trial, which is followed by a banquet. The ceremony is not open to the public.

*

FIRST SUNDAY IN FEBRUARY

Clowns' Service

The annual Clowns' Service, held in Dalston's Holy Trinity church, east London, on the first Sunday in February, must have the most colourful congregation in the country. On this day, dozens of professional and amateur clowns, all dressed in their best costumes and make-up, gather to commemorate the life of Joseph Grimaldi (1779–1837), the comic actor who did much to create the modern clown tradition. Grimaldi's tomb is at St James's church, Pentonville Road, which is where the first commemoration service was held in 1946, but when that church was de-commissioned in 1956, the service moved to Holy Trinity. The service includes a prayer which starts, 'Dear Lord, I thank you for calling me to share with others your most precious gift of laughter. May I never forget that it is your gift, and my privilege.'

*

1 FEBRUARY

St Bridget/St Bride's Day

In Ireland, Brighid, who died around the year 525, is second only in popularity to St Patrick, and her feast is a day of widespread celebration. She was of humble origins, was baptized by St Patrick himself, and later became a nun and first abbess of Kildare. Little is known of her beyond this, but numerous legends about her pious acts and miracles spread her fame across Ireland and on to the Continent by the early Middle Ages. On her day, children in Ireland would go from house to house and display an effigy or doll that represented the saint. Brighid's Crosses, made from straw, would also be hung up to protect the house from evil in the coming year.

In England, her popularity in pre-Reformation times is evidenced by the nineteen ancient churches dedicated to her, including St Bride's in Fleet Street, London, as well as a number of places called 'Bridewell', most probably derived from wells dedicated to her. The most famous of these Bridewells was a palace built between Fleet Street and the River Thames for Henry VIII (r. 1509–47), which eventually became a house of correction; the word 'Bridewell' later became a generic term for a prison.

Nevertheless, except where people of Irish extraction have settled, this saint's day does not seem to have been celebrated much in England since the Reformation, and no widespread customs have been reported, although there are some indications of a belief that dew gathered on St Bride's Day was considered to be particularly good for the complexion (*see also* **1 May: May Dew**).

*

2 FEBRUARY

Candlemas (Purification of the Blessed Virgin Mary)

The second of February is dedicated to the Purification of the Virgin Mary (which in Jewish law had to take place forty days after a birth) and to her presentation of the infant Jesus in the temple at Bethlehem, as described in Luke 2:22–39. Celebration of the day was slow to spread across the Christian world, but in the early eighth century the Northumbrian cleric the Venerable Bede recorded that the day was being celebrated in Britain, and he calls it the 'Feast of St Mary'. The vernacular English name 'Candlemas' is not recorded until the year 1014. The day has always had something of a dual aspect, depending on whether the emphasis was placed on the purification of Mary, or the presentation of Christ, and those Christians who were

One of the congregation at the Clowns' Service, 1973

uncomfortable with the 'Jewish' notion of purification after a birth ('churching' in everyday English) naturally tended towards the latter interpretation.

The key element, which gives the day its popular name in English, was the preponderance of candles. These were blessed in the church and were carried in procession around the parish; they could also be seen blazing all around the building itself. This custom is based quite simply upon the idea of Christ lighting the way, shedding light on our darkness, and it is linked in particular to the words of Simeon, who held the baby Jesus and called him 'A light to lighten the Gentiles, and the glory of thy people Israel' (Luke 2:32).

The day was extremely popular in England in the Middle Ages, and ceremonies included dramatic presentations of the scene in the temple; however, Protestant reformers attempted to discredit the blessing of candles and the processions, and by the 1540s many churches had given up the festival. Nevertheless, candles could hardly be eradicated from churches completely, and a special connection between them and the day remained fixed in the popular mind. Despite the efforts of the reformers, the official line in former times that blessed candles banish Satan was widely interpreted by parishioners to mean that candles used in church had protective and magical powers against various illnesses, and thunder and lightning, or could be placed in the hands of the dying to protect their souls.

Apart from superstitions connected with candles, Candlemas did not last well in the festive calendar and there are hardly any recorded customs linked to the day in modern times. One notable exception is the 'cradle rocking' at Blidworth in Nottinghamshire, which takes place on the Sunday nearest to 2 February, but this is a special case as the parish church is dedicated to St Mary of the Purification and therefore has a particular interest in the day. During the afternoon service, a baby boy, born as near as possible to the previous Christmas Day, is laid in a cradle to symbolize the original presentation of the baby Jesus, and is rocked by the vicar while the thanksgiving is said by the congregation. A plaque in the church records the names of all the babies who have been so honoured since the custom was inaugurated in 1922. Many authorities state that this is a revival of an ancient practice, but they offer no evidence to support the claim.

In shoemaking and other indoor trades, Candlemas was deemed to be the day on which candles could be dispensed with during working hours until the autumn – 'At Candlemas throw candle and candle-stick away' was a widely known saying. From at least the mid seventeenth to the late ninteenth century, Candlemas was also considered the end of the Christmas period. Robert Herrick's poem 'Upon Candlemasse Day', published in the collection *Hesperides* in 1648, declares not only that greenery should be taken down but also that all feasting and fun should cease:

> *End now the white-loaf, and the pie*
> *And let all sports with Christmas die.*

In Scotland, Candlemas was a full quarter day, and in various parts of England, particularly Cheshire, Lancashire, and Cumbria, it was held as a day for commencing or terminating farm tenancies, and for settling accounts, well into the twentieth century.

Candlemas also had an important part to play in traditional weather-lore, and the most common view was that the prevailing weather of the day predicted the opposite to come, as in this somewhat contrived rhyme from Devon in 1900:

> *If Candlemas day be dry and fair*
> *The half of the winter is to come, and mair*
> *If Candlemas day be wet and foul*
> *The half of the winter is gone at yule.*

In another report from Huntingdonshire, recorded by the local historian C. F. Tebbutt, we seem to have a pre-echo of the American Groundhog Day:

> *Candlemas Day was also known as Badgers' Day, in the belief that the supposedly hibernating badger woke up and came to the entrance of his sett on that day. If he found that it was sunny, and he could see the shadow of his tail, he went back to sleep … There used to be a stuffed badger at the Chequers public house at Glatton, specially set up because Badgers' Day was also the landlord's birthday.*

Forty Shilling Day

The will of William Glanville the younger, dated 1717, provides for five poor boys under the age of sixteen from Wotton in Surrey to be given forty shillings each on the anniversary of his death, if they fulfil certain conditions. To qualify, they must stand by his white marble tomb, with both hands on the stone, and recite the Lord's Prayer, the Apostles' Creed, and the Ten Commandments, from memory. They must then read a chapter from the Bible, and write out a section of it. If insufficient boys can be found in Wotton, it is permitted to include those from neighbouring parishes. In the past, it was occasionally necessary to erect a tent over the tomb to shelter the boys from the February weather, and in particularly bad winters the whole event was moved to later in the year. The annual event ceased during the later twentieth century, and attempts to revive it failed to attract enough boys to take part.

*

3 FEBRUARY

St Blaise's Day

St Blaise (also Blaize, Blaze) was widely popular in Britain from the eighth century to beyond the Middle Ages, although nothing is known for certain of his life. He is believed to have been Bishop of Sebaste in fourth-century Armenia (and he is still regularly referred to as 'Bishop', rather than 'St', Blaise), but stories of his martyrdom and miracles are later inventions. According to these stories, while hiding from persecutors in a cave he healed sick people and animals and, in particular, saved the life of a boy who had a fishbone stuck in his throat. He was also said to have been tortured by being torn with iron combs, and these combs became his recognized symbol.

In English tradition, Blaise was adopted as the patron saint of woolcombers – an important and widespread occupation before machinery wiped it out. Every year on or around his feast day, the woolcombers organized a trade procession, which even in small towns was an impressive event, and in larger centres of the wool industry these processions became truly spectacular affairs. The following description, recorded in the Suffolk volume of the Folk-Lore Society's *County Folklore* series, is typical:

[3 February 1777] *This day, Munday, being the anni-*

St Blaise Curing a Sick Child, by Jacques Stella (1596–1657)

versary of Bishop Blaze, the same was observed in this town in a manner far surpassing anything of the kind ever seen. The cavalcade consisting of between 2 and 300 woolcombers, upon horses in uniforms, properly decorated. Bishop Blaze, Jason, Castor and Pollux, a band of musick, drums, colours, and everything necessary to render the procession suitable to the greatness of the woollen manufactory. The following lines were spoken by the Orators:

> *With boundless gratitude, illustrious Blaze*
> *Again we celebrate, and speak thy praise, etc.*

The diarist Parson Woodforde recorded a trip to Norwich on 24 March 1793 especially to see the parade there, and even copied out details from the printed leaflet produced on the occasion. These processions presented a curious pastiche of a romanticized Bishop

Blaize and characters drawn from the Greek story of Jason and the Golden Fleece, combined with local pride and national patriotism. As the trade disappeared into the factories, the processions gradually faded from the local scene.

Blaise is still remembered, however, for his aid in cases of throat ailments, and in some Catholic churches one can get one's throat blessed on 3 February. The priest holds two lighted candles, tied with ribbon to form a cross, to the throat of the sufferer, and says a blessing along the lines of 'May the Lord deliver you from the evil of the throat, and from every other harm.' The most famous example of this annual blessing takes place at St Etheldreda's church in Holborn, London, where it has been a regular event since 1876.

St Ives Hurling

St Ives, in the far west of Cornwall, maintains one of only two surviving traditional **hurling** games (*see right*). The key feature of hurling is that it is played with a ball about the size of a cricket ball, made of wood or cork, with a silver coating, which is thrown or carried, but not kicked. In the other surviving game, at the Cornish town of St Columb, play takes place in the streets, but in St Ives it is played on the beach, and children and young people are now usually the main participants. The two goals are basketball nets. As is usual with this type of game, the two teams have traditionally been drawn from different parts of the town – 'uplong' and 'downlong' – although there is a local story that formerly one team was composed of men named Tom, Will, or John, and one of men with other names.

During the rest of the year, the ball is in the keeping of the mayor. On the Feast Monday (the day after the nearest Sunday to 3 February) at 9.30 a.m., the mayor carries the ball to the well of St Ia at Porthmeor, where it is blessed, then back to the churchyard, where he throws it from the wall to the players on the sands below, to the accompaniment of the game's motto, 'fair play is good play'. The game ceases at noon when the ball is returned to the mayor. Coins are later thrown from the balcony of the Guildhall for the waiting children.

See also **Shrove Tuesday: St Columb Hurling**, p. 64.

*

Hurling

Hurling is a fast-moving game played with a small, hand-held ball, made of cork or wood with a silver or occasionally gilt coating. It seems to be unique to Cornwall, although similar games are found elsewhere under different names, and it used to be played throughout the county but now only takes place regularly at St Columb at Shrovetide, and at St Ives on their Feast Monday (the day after the nearest Sunday to 3 February).

In Richard Carew's *Survey of Cornwall* (1602), we are fortunate to have what must be the most detailed explanation of any game in the period. He distinguished two forms of the game – 'to goals' and 'to the country' – and whereas the former was relatively civilized, the latter was an inter-parish match with few restrictions for as many as wanted to play. Carew wrote that hurling 'to goals' took place mostly at weddings, and other accounts mention the game being played at other gatherings, such as at Helston after beating the bounds in 1851 (*see* **Rogationtide**, p. 176, for a description of this custom). In Carew's description, the game was surprisingly well organized. The two teams, of fifteen, twenty, or thirty players, were evenly matched, and they lined up against each other at the start of the game so that individual players knew who they were to mark on the other side; two players were not allowed to set on the same opponent at the same time. Players could not pass the ball forwards, nor could they 'butt or hand-fast under the girdle' (presumably striking or grabbing below the belt).

10 FEBRUARY

St Scholastica's Day

St Scholastica (*c.*480–*c.*543) established a convent at Plombariola in Italy and was the sister of Benedict, the founder of the Benedictine monastic order. Brother and sister met regularly to discuss spiritual topics, and it is said that when Benedict wanted to go home after

Hurling to the country was 'more diffuse and confuse' and followed few rules. The goals could be two or three miles apart, and there was no matching of teams:

. . . a silver ball is cast up, and that company which can catch and carry it by force or sleight to their place assigned, gaineth the ball and victory. Whosoever getteth seizure of this ball findeth himself generally pursued by the adverse party, neither will they leave till (without all respects) he be laid flat on God's dear earth.

By all accounts, hurling was a pretty rough game, but no worse than any of the street-football-type games played elsewhere. Carew's final judgement was somewhat ambivalent:

The ball in this play may be compared to an infernal spirit, for whosoever catcheth it fareth straightways like a madman, struggling and fighting with those that go about to hold him, and no sooner is the ball gone from him but he resigneth this fury to the next receiver, and himself becometh peaceable as before. I cannot well resolve whether I should more commend this game for the manhood and exercise, or condemn it for the boisterousness and harms which it begetteth.

However, later writers, especially those from outside the West Country, were more decided in their opinion, and used their distaste for the game to dismiss Cornish society in general. Daniel Defoe, in his *Tour through the Whole Island of Great Britain* (1724–6), writes for example:

The game called the Hurlers, is a thing the Cornish men value themselves much upon; I confess, I see nothing in it, but that it is a rude violent play among the boors, or country people; brutish and furious, and a sort of an evidence that they were, once, a kind of barbarians.

Even before Carew's account, we have an unusual number of references to the game, which in combination show that it was already well known in the 1580s. 'The Hurlers' is a group of standing stones arranged in circles on Bodmin Moor, near the village of Minnions. Thirty-nine of the stones still survive, and they are the subject of two traditions, versions of which are told of standing stones all over the country. One tradition is that they cannot be counted; the second, which gives the stones their name, is that they were originally people who were turned to stone for hurling on a Sunday. This latter tradition was already in circulation *c.*1584, when the antiquarian John Norden first described the stones. A silver ball is also mentioned three times in 1594 and 1595 in the book of parish accounts called the *St. Columb Green Book*.

The *Oxford English Dictionary* explains that 'hurling' did not only mean 'throwing', but back in 1528 it also meant 'struggling' or 'conflicting'. 'Hurling' was also the name of a hockey-type game in Ireland, first recorded in 1527.

See also **3 February: St Ives Hurling**; **Shrove Tuesday: St Columb Hurling**, p. 64; *compare* **Football**, p. 53; **Games and Sports: Camping**, p. 32.

one such meeting, Scholastica successfully prayed for a storm to prevent his leaving. Her power over storms has meant that she has been invoked against them by her followers ever since. Her name, and her penchant for intellectual debate, ensured that she was remembered by the academic community, and there are numerous schools and colleges named after her. Her festival was traditionally remembered at Oxford, where long-standing rivalry between 'town' and 'gown'

exploded into violence on St Scholastica's Day in 1354. In February that year, some students objected to being served 'bad wine' in the Swindlestock tavern by breaking the vessel over the landlord's head. The landlord (who happened to be the town mayor at the time) summoned help from neighbours, the students mobilized their forces, and a pitched battle raged for several days. The townsmen were victorious, ransacking the university buildings and killing over sixty students.

The King expressed his wrath by depriving the town of various privileges, such as control over the price and quality of bread, ale, and wine sold in the neighbourhood, and jurisdiction over both criminal and civil cases where students were involved, bestowing them instead upon the university. He also forced the citizens to acknowledge their guilt by processing to the university for a service of penitence every 10 February, and paying an annual fine of sixty-three pence (one for every student killed in the riot). This continued until 1825, when university and town agreed to drop the custom.

*

14 FEBRUARY

St Valentine's Day

St Valentine's Day is one of the few festivals which have increased in popularity in recent decades, and it shows no sign of going out of fashion. Despite having an undisputed history spanning at least 600 years, the origins of the festival are still obscure, and the only certainty is that it has nothing to do with the saint from which it gets its name. The dominant feature has always been, as today, the giving of gifts, letters, or cards to a lover, but there have been wide variations within the basic framework. There have also been other customs on the day: children visited their neighbours and sang special rhymes in exchange for pennies; special buns were made and sold; and, not surprisingly, Valentine's Day was one of the times when love-divination procedures were thought particularly effective.

St Valentine and the Romans

There were numerous Valentines who achieved sainthood in the early years of Christianity, but the two who were famous enough to be widely known in late medieval England were a bishop from Terni and a priest from Rome. According to the popular books of saints' lives compiled centuries after these events, they were both martyred by beheading during the reign of the Emperor Claudius sometime around AD 269–73; however, their true histories will probably never be known. The key point for present purposes is that in neither case does the saint's legend offer the slightest hint of a connection with love and romance, or spring, or birds, or anything related to the later customs and beliefs. The only conclusion we can draw is that the martyrs happen to have been assigned a date that, falling in the period traditionally viewed as the start, or precursor, of spring, provided later writers with a convenient day on which to place their new notions of the romantic consonance between nature and the ideal of courtly love.

Although it is also common to explain the origin of Valentine's Day by citing the annual festival of Lupercalia in ancient Rome, which took place on 15 February, again there is no basis for this assumed connection. The Lupercalia was primarily a purification festival and, apart from the coincidence of the date, bore no relationship to any of the later Valentine customs. It seems to have been the Revd Alban Butler who, in his enthusiasm for classical antecedents, first claimed a connection between Valentine and the Lupercalia, in his *Lives of the Saints* (1756). Many writers have followed suit, and have gradually convinced themselves that the Lupercalia was really a love festival in disguise, and that St Valentine was a fertility figure. Some go even further and claim that the Romans chose future partners by lot at this festival, but this detail is not included in any classical writings, and seems to have been invented by the antiquarian Francis Douce, in his influential *Illustrations of Shakespeare* (1807), simply to claim a direct line of descent from the ancient world to the modern custom.

The fourteenth century

The record really begins with Geoffrey Chaucer and his contemporaries in the fourteenth century, although precise dating in this period is not possible and clear precedence cannot therefore be set. Chaucer's 700-line poem *Parlement of the Foules*, written some time between 1376 and 1382, relates how birds choose their mates on St Valentine's Day every year. His friend, John Gower, used the same theme in his *Cinkante Ballades*, written in French, possibly as early as 1374, as did the author of *The Cuckoo and the Nightingale* (probably Sir John Clanvowe, who died in 1391), and the Savoyard soldier-poet, Oton de Grandson, who spent much of the 1370s in England. These writers were almost

The Morning of St Valentine, by John Callcott Horsley (1817–1903)

certainly working within an existing tradition that held Valentine's Day to be the first day of spring, but it is not clear whether they invented the idea of birds mating on that day. Their key achievement was therefore simply in cementing the connection between this particular day and love and romance, albeit in the avian sphere. Most tellingly, however, they did not extend the mating motif in their poems from birds to people, and this negative evidence is the strongest indication we have that they were unaware of any connection between St Valentine and human romance. It is therefore most unlikely to have existed before their time.

The connection with humans was soon made, however, in both France and England, and John Lydgate's poem 'A Valentine to her that Excelleth All' (*c*.1440) includes several verses that describe people choosing their loves on this day. It commences:

Saint Valentine, of custom year by year
Men have an usaunce [usage] *in this region*
To look and search Cupid's calendar
And choose their choice by great affection
Such as been pricked by Cupid's motion
Taking their choice, as their sort [lot] *doth fall*
But I love one which excelleth all.

Development of the custom

From that time on, the connection between St Valentine and human romance was a commonplace for poets and playwrights, including Shakespeare, Ben Jonson, John Donne, Michael Drayton, and Robert Herrick, although many of them still emphasized the connection with birds. Moreover, there is plenty of evidence that Valentine's Day was not merely a literary conceit but had a place in real people's lives. The famous series of letters belonging to the Paston family, now in the British Library, includes three letters from Dame Elizabeth Brews to John Paston in February 1477 in which she calls him her 'ryght welebeloved Voluntyne' and also refers to birds choosing their mates on the 14th. A year later, the two were married. Nearly two hundred years later, on 19 February 1654, 27-year-old Dorothy Osborne wrote to her absent sweetheart, Sir William Temple:

> *I'll tell you something that you don't know, which is, that I am your Valentine and you are mine. I did not think of drawing any, but Mrs. Goldsmith and Jane would need make me write some for them and myself; so I writ down our three names, and for the men, Mr. Fish, James B., and you. I cut them all equal and made them up myself before they saw them, and because I would owe it wholly to my good fortune, if I were pleased, I made both them choose first that had never seen what was in them, and they left me you. Then I made them choose again for theirs, and my name was left. You cannot imagine how I was delighted with this little accident . . . I was not half so pleased with my encounter next morning. I was up early, but with no design of getting another Valentine and going out to walk in my night-clothes and night-gown, I met Mr. Fish going hunting, I think he was; but he stayed to tell me I was his Valentine . . .*

Dorothy and William were married on Christmas Day the same year.

From about the same period come the deservedly well-known and oft-quoted entries in Samuel Pepys's diaries. Pepys mentions the custom at least twenty-four times between 1660 and 1669, and his descriptions provide the most detailed picture of the custom available before the modern period. The picture that emerges from these early references is of a custom which already had several strands. The theme was romantic love, but in stark contrast to the modern way, the choice of partner was left to fate and the whole thing was treated as an elaborate game. At a party or family gathering, names were written on pieces of paper, which were drawn at random, and people were thus paired up, to play at being lovers. Even married people like Samuel and Elizabeth Pepys took part and

had their 'valentines', and they were expected to pay each of them little compliments for the next few days, while the men were required to buy presents. Pepys's entries often display a characteristic concern with how much the whole business would cost him, and he usually bought gifts for his valentine (for example, six pairs of plain and one of embroidered gloves) and for his wife. The higher up the social scale, the more lavish the gift. In February 1556, for example, Queen Mary's Secretary of State, Sir William Petre, gave a present of six yards of black satin (worth 60 shillings) to his valentine, Lady Bulkeley, even though he took no further part in the game, asking his wife to buy the material for him. Adults also sometimes made pretend valentine arrangements with their friends' children.

Fate could dictate your choice of valentine in another way, as it was widely believed that the first eligible person you saw in the morning was the one for you. This notion prompted Elizabeth Pepys to keep her eyes covered for much of the morning in February 1662, in order to avoid seeing the painters working in the house.

The play-acting could, of course, be taken more seriously if the participants wished. Real lovers like Dorothy Osborne were pleased when fate confirmed their choice, and there is some evidence that the result of pairing by lot or chance was regarded as genuinely predictive of future romance between the individuals involved, as expressed by Ben Jonson in Act I, scene 1 of his *Tale of a Tub* (1640):

> *Last night did draw him for her valentine;*
> *Which chance, it hath so taken her father, and mother,*
> *(Because themselves drew so on Valentine's Eve*
> *Was thirty yeare) as they will have her married*
> *Today by any meanes.*

It should also be noted that Samuel Pepys appears to use the valentine custom as a euphemism for some of his extra-marital affairs (see, for example, the entries for March and April 1668).

Letters and cards

Valentine letters were presumably a feature of the day from quite early on, but commercially produced valentine cards did not appear until the early nineteenth century. They rapidly became the norm for potential

Valentine's Day (George Cruickshank, *Comic Almanac*, 1837)

lovers, and they ranged from simple and unpretentious engravings or lithographs, to expensive handmade concoctions involving embossed card, real silk, feathers, and lace, which feature strongly in many extant collections. They often had spaces for hand-written messages, and the sender who could not compose his or her own verses could fall back on the many traditional verses of the 'roses are red' variety, or one could buy 'valentine writers', small books of suggested rhymes, suitable for all occasions. However, the commercial cards sowed the seeds of their own downfall by providing an all-too-easy means of insulting someone with humorous or offensive parodies of traditional greetings, and despite the huge popularity of card-sending in mid Victorian times, the custom declined markedly as the twentieth century drew near. Many writers in the 1890s took it for granted that valentine-sending was almost dead: on 17 February 1894, the *Graphic* records, 'St. Valentine's Day … attracts very little attention nowa-

days in England, but across the Atlantic the Saint is still honoured', while in 1896 the *Ludgate Illustrated News* remarks, 'Take the undeniable fact that St. Valentine's Day is a day of usages almost wholly neglected.' Many commentators blamed the widespread use of the offensive anti-valentines, although these had already been available for some decades. But the custom did not die, and it struggled on into the twentieth century, albeit a mere shadow of its former self.

After the Second World War, it underwent a major revival, under heavy influence from the USA and the watchful eye of the commercial card manufacturers. There is certainly no stopping it now, and, apart from cards, devotees can choose from a range of staple items such as chocolates, roses, romantic dinners, sexy underwear, and any and everything that can be represented in the shape of a heart or coloured red. One of the developments c.1980, which seems destined to become permanent, is the newspaper-column messages on the day.

Visiting customs

Cards and gifts were not the only traditions for which Valentine's Day was notable for previous generations. Several other customs existed, mostly in rural areas, such as a widespread visiting custom, undertaken mainly by children. This was recorded from most parts of the country but was apparently most popular in the eastern counties, particularly Norfolk. Anne Elizabeth Baker included a valentine song in her Northamptonshire glossary of 1854:

> *Valentining: Children going from house to house, the morning of St. Valentine's Day, soliciting small gratuities. The children of the villages go in parties, sometimes in considerable numbers, repeating at each house one or other of the following salutations, which vary in different districts:*
>
> > *Good morrow, Valentine!*
> > *First it's yours, and then it's mine,*
> > *So please give me a valentine.*
> > *Morrow, morrow, Valentine!*
> > *First 'tis yours, and then 'tis mine,*
> > *So please to give me a valentine,*
> > *Holly and ivy tickle my toe,*
> > *Give me red apple and then let me go.*
> > *Good morrow, Valentine!*
> > *Parsley grows by savoury,*
> > *Savoury grows by thyme,*
> > *A new pair of gloves on Easter day,*
> > *Good morrow, Valentine!*

The same author also reported a family custom, whereby the first child to say 'Good morrow, Valentine' on the morning of the 14th could claim a small present from their parents. The children's visiting custom could also include elements of scrambling for coins and eatables (for **Scrambling Customs**, *see* p. 128).

The majority of references to these visiting customs come from the nineteenth and twentieth centuries, but proof of its existence before 1800 can be found in the diary of Parson James Woodforde, of Weston Longeville, Norfolk. Woodforde recorded giving a penny to every child under fourteen in the parish who could say 'Good morrow, Valentine', on 14 February almost every year between 1777 and 1802, although when it fell on a Sunday, the children came the following day.

A few nineteenth-century sources, from Leicestershire, Rutland, and Northamptonshire, record that special cakes were made for the day, and called valentine buns or 'plum shuttles'. The latter (pronounced 'shittles') were named after the weaver's shuttle, which they resembled in shape, but further details are not given.

A combination of the visiting custom and gift-giving was also reported in the nineteenth century, in which anonymous gifts were left on the doorstep (although again, the cruel and vindictive could leave empty or worthless parcels). In 1832, the Northamptonshire poet John Clare wrote:

> *Young girls grow eager as the day retires*
> *& smile & whisper round their cottage fires*
> *Listning for noises in the dusky street*
> *For tinkling latches & for passing feet*
> *The prophecys of coming joys to hark*
> *Of wandring lovers stealing thro' the dark*
> *Dropping their valentines at beautys door*
> *With hearts & darts & love knots littered oer.*

Love divination

Last but not least of valentine traditions, the day (or its eve) was considered one of the key dates in the year on which love-divination procedures could properly be carried out. Many of these divinations were well known, such as sowing the hemp seed, in which unmarried girls threw hemp seed over their shoulders at midnight in hopes of seeing the forms of their future lovers following them. The following, as published by James Orchard Halliwell in 1849, is less common, but it is typical of the style for the day:

> *On Valentine's day, take two bay leaves, sprinkle them with rose water and place them on your pillow, in the evening. When you go to bed, put on a clean night-gown turned inside out and, lying down, say softly:*
>
> > *Good Valentine, be kind to me*
> > *In dreams let me my true love see.*
>
> *Then go to sleep as soon as you can, in expectation of seeing your future husband in a dream.*

*

20 FEBRUARY

John Cass Commemoration

Sir John Cass (1666–1718) was a London merchant and one-time alderman, sheriff, and Member of Parliament for the City. He is remembered as a major benefactor of east London, in particular in the educational sphere. He founded the Sir John Cass School in Aldgate – one of three educational institutions that now bear his name – and the pupils and staff of the school attend a founder's day service at nearby St Botolph's church every year on or near 20 February. Those attending the service carry or wear red feathers in his memory, supposedly because Sir John suffered a major haemorrhage as he sat writing his will and the quill pen he was holding was dyed red with his blood; it is more likely, however, that the red feathers are a reference to the one that is featured in his coat of arms.

*

SHROVETIDE AND LENT

The period of Lent comprises the forty days immediately preceding Easter (excluding Sundays), starting on Ash Wednesday and finishing on Holy (Easter) Saturday. Ash Wednesday can therefore fall anywhere between 4 February and 11 March. This period was decreed by the early Church as a season of strict fasting, penance, and piety, in preparation for the major festival of the year which culminated in the Resurrection of Christ, although the exact number of days of fasting has varied considerably since that time. During Lent, all meat, eggs, cooking fat, and cheese were strictly forbidden, as were marriage ceremonies and sexual intercourse, and solemn rituals took place in parish churches in which all images, and even parts of the churches themselves, were covered with veils.

In 1538, as leader of the new English Church, Henry VIII softened the official line by allowing dairy products to be eaten; somewhat surprisingly, subsequent Protestant monarchs did not abolish Lent completely but kept the ban on meat-eating in place and continued to enforce the fast. Nevertheless, the official explanation for the fast became increasingly secular and centred on the idea that eating fish supported the fishing industry, which in turn bolstered shipping and thus supported the Royal Navy. Lent was abolished by the Puritans in the 1640s, was reinstated by Charles II in 1664 but never really enforced, and began to fade from English society. By Victorian times, Lent had lost most of its power, as the local historian John Fisher recorded in 1865 in this example from Yorkshire:

At the beginning of Lent the most inveterate of card-players (and their number was legion) used to lay aside their packs of cards, and would not on any account so much as touch them during the whole season of Lent; but now, however, the practice is very different.

In the twenty-first century, only Roman Catholics and particularly devout Anglicans take any real notice of Lent, and even they are usually expected to do little more than give something up during the period.

In terms of the traditional calendar, the most lasting effect of Lent was the concentration of games and customs at Shrovetide, the days just before the season of Lent commenced. It is difficult for us nowadays to understand the almost desperate merrymaking that took place, in the face of six weeks of enforced restricted diet and best behaviour. In England, celebrations did not seem to coalesce into the extended bacchanalia that took place in many European cities, where the whole period between Christmas and Shrove could be devoted to feasting, drinking, and playing, in one long street festival, but there was still plenty of scope for extra food – particularly in the form of pancakes, eggs, and meat – and the playing of vigorous sports such as football, cockfighting, and throwing at cocks.

The former importance of Shrovetide in the traditional calendar is demonstrated by the huge range of customs that are recorded for the time, and the main examples, past and present, are each considered separately below.

See also **Games and Sports**, p. 30.

*

EGG SATURDAY

The Saturday preceding Shrove Tuesday; *see* **Shrove Tuesday: Egg Shackling**, p. 60.

*

HALL MONDAY

See **Shrove Tuesday: Shroving and Lent-Crocking**, p. 65.

*

SHROVE TUESDAY

Shrove Tuesday, the last day before the start of Lent, was named after the 'shriving' (confession and absolution) necessary on the day. Most of the secular festivities of Shrovetide also took place on this day, but the preceding days had their own traditions, which were mainly concerned with food. Collop Monday, for example, the day before Shrove Tuesday, was so called because of the custom of eating 'collops', a word that varies in meaning from place to place but usually means 'slices of meat', or what we would call 'eggs and bacon' or even 'ham and eggs'.

From medieval times onwards, the most enthusiastic of the Shrovetide revellers were apprentices and schoolchildren, and they are the ones who are often named as taking part in the street football, and other seasonal games. In 1890, John Nicholson records in his *Folk Lore of East Yorkshire*:

> . . . the children expect to be able to leave school, and
> have a half holiday, in which to play games with ball.
> As 'keppin' (catching) balls is the favourite game, the
> day is called Keppin Day.

Apprentices also had a tradition of wrecking any brothels in the neighbourhood, as described in *Pasquils Palinodia* (1619):

> It was the day, of all days in the year,
> That unto Bacchus hath his dedication,
> When mad brained prentices, that no men fear,
> O'rethrow the dens of bawdy recreation.

It is not clear why they should have done this; as a group they are not normally known for their moralistic beliefs or behaviour. More modern apprentices may not have vented their animosity on particular targets, but the feeling that the day should be a holiday survived into surprisingly recent times. As late as March 1954, *The Times* reported this as a potential problem:

> The custom of apprentices taking the afternoon off
> on Shrove Tuesday is dying, but some still carry it
> on. When all but twenty-five of those at Chadderton,
> Manchester, left as soon as they had clocked on
> yesterday morning, the firm felt that they must check
> a tendency to establish a full day's holiday.

See also **Shrovetide and Lent**, p. 49.

Alnwick Football

Alnwick, in Northumberland, keeps alive one of the few Shrovetide football games, which has survived mainly as a result of a willingness to compromise, but also because it had a powerful ally in the Duke of Northumberland. In 1884, the *Folk-Lore Journal* recorded:

> Before the Alnwick Improvement Act came into
> operation, over fifty years ago, the game was played
> in the streets of the town, a custom which resulted
> in much damage to windows, etc., the reparation of
> which was defrayed by the lord of the manor. The
> magistrates, after the passing of the Act, prohibited
> the playing of the game in the streets, and in conse-
> quence the Duke of Northumberland instituted an
> annual match between the married and unmar-
> ried freemen, also a match for the townspeople,
> and this custom went on until 1847, when the Duke
> of Northumberland died at Alnwick Castle in the
> month of February, and no game was played the
> following year. Subsequently, however, the game
> was resuscitated, the players to be the parishioners
> of St Michael's v. the parishioners of St Paul's. And
> so it has continued until now, on Shrove Tuesday, in
> the 'Pasture' or north demesne, by permission of his
> Grace the Duke of Northumberland.

Nowadays, the ball is brought from Alnwick Castle, in a procession headed by the Duke's piper, and thrown

Football at Alnwick, Northumberland, 1987

up at 2 p.m. Unlike other traditional games, the ball is kicked, not carried or thrown, and the goals, which used to be 400 yards apart, are now set at 200 yards. The teams are also much smaller than the 150-a-side that used to be common. The winning team has to score three goals (called 'hales'), and the wooden goals vaguely resemble soccer goals but are only 4 feet 6 inches wide and are decorated with an arch of greenery. After the game, whoever manages to get the ball off the pitch and over the River Aln keeps it.

Tradition has it that the game started after some bloody altercation with the Northumbrians' neighbours, as the jubilant Englishmen kicked a Scotsman's head around. This was said of many other football games, although it is more often a marauding Dane who unwillingly supplied the ball. The earliest known reference to football at Alnwick is in 1762, but there were many other football games in the area and it is probably much older than that.

See also **Football**, p. 53.

Ashbourne Football

Ashbourne Royal Shrovetide Football in Derbyshire is one of a handful of matches that preserve something of the flavour of the medieval game. Like the less well-known game at Atherstone in Warwickshire (*see* p. 56), the play takes place mainly in the town rather than in an open space, but at Ashbourne there are at least teams and goals which give it some semblance of an organized game. The teams, however, can be of any size, and are traditionally comprised of those born to the north of the River Henmore (the Up'ards), and those born to the south (the Down'ards).

The game is played on Shrove Tuesday and Ash

Ashbourne football, Derbyshire, in the 1930s

Wednesday, and starts each day at about 2 p.m., when the ball is turned up at Shaw Croft by a local dignitary. If a goal is scored before 5 p.m., a new ball is turned up to start a new game. The centre of town is well boarded up and protected, and only unsuspecting tourists park their cars anywhere nearby. There are few rules, although play cannot continue after midnight (introduced in 1955), and transport of the ball in a vehicle has not been allowed since 1957. The special balls are made in the town and are slightly bigger than a normal football. They are made of leather, with ground cork inside, and are attractively painted. Whoever scores a goal keeps the ball.

The two goals are three miles apart, at Shurston Mill and Clifton Mill. When the mills were still going concerns, the ball had to touch the mill wheel, but now there are purpose-built concrete goals, with a board on which the ball must be tapped three times. The ball is rarely kicked but can be thrown or run with, although often the players have little chance to do so. Most of the time the ball is in the middle of the 'hug' – a huge mass scrum (similar to the 'sway' at Haxey; see **6 January: Haxey Hood**), which inches its way in one direction or another, literally steaming in the cold February air. The ball, and the more intrepid players, always goes into Henmore Brook.

Games like this have been widespread in England since medieval times (see **Football**, *right*), but the first specific mention of the game at Ashbourne is in 1821. It is likely to be much older, but, unfortunately, earlier references do not make it clear whether they are referring to Ashbourne or nearby Derby, which also had a

Continues on page 56 >

Football

Football – whether Association or Rugby – is so much part of everyday life that we often forget that in the codified and structured forms we now know the game it is less than 150 years old, and for centuries before that time, 'football' meant something completely different. The early history of traditional 'football' games is clear enough in outline, but it is confused by the lack of precision in the early sources, and there are recurrent problems of definition. Most of the earlier writers only mention the game to rail against its violence and ungodliness, or to report on attempts to suppress it altogether.

The earliest mention of such a game is in William Fitz Stephen's account of London, written *c.*1180, but it is ambiguous, speaking of a 'game of ball', although the other details make it very likely that 'football' is being described:

Moreover, each year upon the day called Carnival . . . [he describes cockfighting in the morning]. After dinner all the youth of the City goes out into the fields to a much-frequented game of ball. The scholars of each school have their own ball and almost all the workers of each trade have theirs also in their hands. Elder men and fathers and rich citizens come on horse-back to watch the contests of their juniors, and after their fashion are young again with the young; and it seems that the motion of their natural heat is kindled by the contemplation of such violent motion and by their partaking in the joys of untrammelled youth.

It is clear from this description that this ball game was already a well-established custom at the time. The next reference is also unclear, primarily because it was written in the Anglo-French of the time and is therefore open to questions of translation. It occurs in the *Writ for Preserving the Peace According to the Articles of the Statute of Winchester*, issued on 13 April 1314, in the reign of Edward II, and designed to ban unruly behaviour in the city. The document uses the term *grosses pelotes de pee*, which some have translated as 'foot balls':

And because of the great disturbance in the city by some players of large foot balls thrown in the meadows [or crowds] of the people, from which many evils might arise . . .

We have to wait until the fifteenth century for the first clear use of the word 'football'. In Scotland in 1424 it was decreed that 'The Kinge forbiddes that na man play at the fut balle under the payne of iiiid [i.e. fourpence].'

From then on, references come thick and fast, although detail is rarely given, presumably because the game was so common and everyone knew all about it. Sir Thomas Elyot's sparse comment is typical of many from the sixteenth to seventeenth centuries: 'Foote balle wherin is nothing but beastly furie and exstreme violence'; although the vociferous Puritan Philip Stubbes can be relied upon, as usual, to give a fuller account (*see* p. 55).

Apart from the violence – which almost all writers emphasize – the picture that emerges is of games with few if any rules, large unrestricted teams of players, and based upon territories (one parish versus another, or the 'uppies and downies' of a town) or played specifically by apprentices or schoolboys. Games could be played in city streets, or in open fields, and the goals could be hundreds of yards or even a couple of miles apart. In the early periods, Shrovetide was clearly the most common time for such games, but they were by no means confined solely to that season.

The annual football at Derby achieved something of a national fame in its time, and in most features was typical of the game in the first half of the nineteenth century. It was described by Stephen Glover in his history of Derbyshire of 1829:

In the town of Derby the contest lies between the parishes of St. Peter and All Saints, and the goals to which the ball is to be taken are Nun's mill for the latter, and Gallow's balk on the Normanton Road for the former. None of the other parishes in the borough take any direct part in the contest, but the inhabitants of all join in the sport, together with persons from all parts of the adjacent country.

The players are young men from eighteen to thirty or upwards, married as well as single ... The game commences in the market-place, where the partisans of each parish are drawn up on each side; and, about noon, a large ball is tossed up in the midst of them. This is seized upon by some of the strongest and most active men of each party. The rest of the players immediately close in upon them, and a solid mass is formed. It then becomes the object of each party to impel the course of the crowd towards their particular goal. The struggle to obtain the ball, which is carried in the arms of those who have possessed themselves of it, is then violent, and the motion of this human tide heaving to and fro, without the least regard to consequences, is tremendous. Broken shins, broken heads, torn coats and lost hats, are among the minor accidents of this fearful contest, and it frequently happens that persons fall in consequence of the intensity of the pressure, fainting and bleeding beneath the feet of the surrounding mob. But it would be difficult to give an adequate idea of this ruthless sport: a Frenchman passing through Derby remarked, that if Englishmen called this playing, it would be impossible to say what they called fighting.

Some Frenchmen would not have been so surprised, however, as such games were not unique to Britain. Many European countries had similar pastimes, including, for example, the game of *soule* in northern France and *calcio* in northern Italy. Indeed, it is often suggested that the game was introduced into Britain from France, presumably by the Normans, although there is no documentary evidence to support this idea.

Local names for the sport – **camping** in the Eastern counties (*see* p. 32), or **hurling** in Cornwall (*see* p. 42) – may reflect different rules, but on present evidence there seems to be little intrinsic difference between these games. Nevertheless, some local factors must have made a real difference to the method of play: a game in a field is more likely to develop 'open' play than one held in the confines of a town, and a small, hard ball the size of a cricket ball is better for throwing distances than a pig's bladder filled with air.

It is appropriate that the first mention of the word 'football' in 1424 appears in an attempt to ban it, as the whole history of the game is littered with attempts at national and local level, mostly unsuccessful, to suppress the game entirely. As with many other mass working-class customs, it was in the mid nineteenth century that its opponents began to succeed in stamping it out. The traditional game at Beverley in Yorkshire was suppressed in the nineteenth century by the local authorities, aided by the militia, after the town's mayor was accidentally caught in the middle of the melee and trampled by the players. **Alnwick football**, in Northumberland (p. 50), is an excellent example of how the game survived by adaptation rather than confrontation, although in this case it helped tremendously that it had the active support of the Duke of Northumberland. The game there was played through the streets and was banned by local magistrates, but was saved from extinction by the grant of a nearby field by the Duke, and a redefinition of the rules.

At the same time as mass football was being suppressed by local authorities, developments in the major public schools were beginning the process of turning street football into modern rugby and soccer. By the early nineteenth century, some kind of football was being played in most of the biggest schools in the country, and from the 1820s to the 1840s there were various moves to codify rules of play within each school, and eventually to reach a national standard. Rugby School was the most influential in this movement, and gave its name to the emerging sport, especially after 1845, when its own rules were codified. But the oft-quoted story that rugby was founded in 1823 when a pupil at Rugby School, William Webb Ellis, astonished his teammates by picking up the ball and running with it must be apocryphal. The story depends for effect on the idea that the 'football' was previously always kicked, but in any village game of the time the ball would have been handled and run with as well as kicked. The year 1863 saw the beginning of the separation between rugby and soccer, when, in a dispute of rules, certain clubs formed a Football Association; the Rugby Football Union was founded in 1871.

Attempts to suppress the traditional games continued well into modern times. The successful campaign against the game at Chester-le-Street in County Durham, for example, where the game took place at Shrovetide between the Up-streeters and Down-streeters, followed the same pattern of opposition from tradespeople and the local authority that was familiar in the nineteenth century, although apparently without the same level of violent confrontation. On 10 February 1932, *The Times* reported:

> The old custom of playing football in the main thoroughfare of Chester-le-Street, Co. Durham, was observed yesterday, but with less enthusiasm than in former years. For 600 years the game has been played in the town on Shrove Tuesday, necessitating tradesmen barricading their shop fronts. Two years ago they unsuccessfully appealed to the town council for assistance, and finally sought police protection. Last year only a few shops were barricaded and the police seized any ball that was thrown into the street. This year not a single shop front in the mile-long main street was barricaded …The tradesmen feel that this old custom should be abolished in view of the thousands of pounds vested in their modern shop fronts.

Games which have something of the flavour of traditional football have survived in a handful of places on Shrove Tuesday, including the Alnwick football in Northumberland, the **Ashbourne football** in Derbyshire (p. 51), the **Atherstone football** in Warwickshire (p. 56), and the **Sedgefield ball game** in County Durham (p. 64), while other customs, such as the Haxey Hood in Lincolnshire (*see* **6 January: Haxey Hood**), the St Ives Hurling (*see* **3 February: St Ives Hurling**), the **St Columb Hurling** (p. 64) and the bottle-kicking at Hallaton in Leicestershire (*see* **Easter Monday: Hallaton Hare Pie and Bottle-Kicking**, p. 126), are clearly derived from the same roots. *See also* **Good Friday: Workington Football**, p. 113.

'Playing at football upon the Sabbath and other Days in England' by Philip Stubbes (1595)

Any exercise, which withdraweth us from godliness, either upon the Sabbath Day, or and other day else, is wicked and to be forbidden. Now, who is so grossly blind, that seeth not, that these aforesaid exercises not only withdraw us from godliness and virtue but also hale and allure us to wickedness and sin: for as concerning football playing, I protest unto you, it may rather be called a friendly fight, than a play or recreation. A bloody and murdering practice, than a fellowly sport or pastime. For, doth not every one lie in wait for his adversary, seeking to overthrow him, and to pick him on his nose, though it be upon hard stones, in ditch or dale, in valley or hole, or what place soever it be, he careth not so he have him down. And he that can serve the most of this fashion he is counted the only fellow, and who but he? So that by this means, sometimes their necks are broken, sometimes their backs, sometimes their legs, sometime their arms, sometime one part thrust out of joint, sometime another, sometimes their noses gush out with blood, sometimes their eyes start out of their heads, and sometimes hurt in one place, sometimes in another. But who soever scapeth away the best, goeth not scot free, but is either sore crushed and bruised, so as he dyeth of it, or else scapeth very hardly. And no marvel for they have sleights to meet one betwixt two, to dash him against the heart with their elbows, to hit him under the short ribs with their gripped fists, and with their knees to catch him upon the hip, and to pick him on his neck, with an hundred such murdering devices: and hereof groweth envy, malice, rancour, chollour, hatred[,] displeasure, enmity, and what not else? And sometimes, fighting, brawling, contention, quarrel picking, murder, homicide, and great effusion of blood, as experience daily teacheth. Is this murdering play now an exercise for the Sabbath Day? Is this a Christian dealing, for one brother to maim and hurt another, and that upon prepensed malice, or set purpose? If this to do to another, as we would wish another to do to us, God make us more careful over the bodies of our brethren.

long-standing and widely known street-football game. There have been many times in its history when the game has been under threat from reformers, who wished to move it out of the town streets, and abolitionists, who wished to suppress it altogether, usually on grounds of public safety and civic pride. The game got its 'Royal' epithet in 1928, when the then Prince of Wales (later Edward VIII) turned up the ball, and Prince Charles did the same honour in 2003.

Atherstone Football

The 'football' game at Atherstone, in North Warwickshire, preserves many of the reported features of medieval Shrovetide games. The whole play takes place in the town streets, there are no teams, no goals, virtually no rules, and the purpose of the game seems to be simply to get hold of the ball and to be holding it when the game finishes.

The ball, made by Gilbert of Rugby, is much bigger than an ordinary football, being twenty-seven inches in diameter and weighing four pounds. It is made of leather, and filled with water – allegedly to prevent it being kicked very far. The players gather in Long Street, the main shopping street of the town, and the game commences at about 2 p.m., when an invited celebrity throws the ball into the crowd from an upstairs window. All the shopkeepers wisely board up their windows and doors, as up to a thousand people will throng the street during the game, which stays in Long Street and does not spill into other parts of the town. The game finishes at about 5 p.m. when the klaxon sounds.

Attached to the ball are four ribbons – red, blue, white, and gold – and anyone who is in possession of one of these ribbons at the end of the game wins a small amount of money and an inscribed ribbon, but the real winner is the one who is holding the ball when the klaxon sounds, and he gets to keep the ball.

Newspaper cuttings in Warwickshire county libraries reveal that in the 1930s and 1940s the real winning trick was to smuggle the ball out of the street, and it was often stabbed to deflate it and make it easier to conceal.

Websites, newspapers, and local publications proudly state that the game has been played here in an unbroken tradition for over 800 years, but this cannot be proved. The assumption is based on the story that in the twelfth century King John put up a bag of gold for a football game between the lads of Warwickshire and the lads of Leicestershire, but this is unlikely to be true. Moreover, there is no evidence that it became an annual event, or that it was played at Atherstone all those years. Nevertheless, the game is certainly alive and well, and engenders fierce loyalty in its supporters. Some of the townspeople dislike the potential violence of the game, saying that it smacks of mob rule and is out of place in a modern town, but these are exactly the arguments that have been made against street football all over the country for at least 700 years. It seems that even if the game at Atherstone cannot claim its existence for that length of time, the opposition certainly can.

See also **Football**, p. 53.

Cock Throwing and Threshing

Shrovetide was a particularly bad time for cockerels. It is not clear why, but several of the games played on the day involved cocks being maimed or killed, whether by each other in a cockfight or by being beaten to death with flails or sticks thrown at them. 'Throwing at cocks' was a hugely popular pastime, found in urban and rural settings alike all over the country from at least the fifteenth century and probably a good deal longer. Several foreign visitors mentioned it in their journals, including the Dutchman William Schellinks. On Shrove Tuesday 1662, he wrote:

Their entertainment then is to throw at the cock. In London one sees in every street, wherever one goes, many apprentice boys running with, under their arms, a cock with a string on its foot, on which is a spike, which they push firmly into the ground between the stones. They always look for an open space and, for a penny, let people throw their cudgel from a good distance at the cock, and he who kills the cock, gets it. In the country or with countryfolk they bury a cock with only its head above ground, and blindfold a person and turn him two or three times round himself, and he then tries to hit the cock with a flail.

As described here, the usual game was to tether a live

Shrove Tuesday throwing at cocks (William Hone, *The Every-Day Book*, 1827)

bird and charge onlookers for the privilege of throwing pieces of wood at it, to kill or maim it. In some cases, a rule was followed whereby if the thrower who knocked a bird down could run and grab it before it regained its feet, he could claim it, while in others one simply had to kill the cockerel outright to win it. There were many other variations on the game, such as the one mentioned by Schellinks, usually called 'cock threshing', in which the cock was buried, and another in which the live bird was tied to someone's back and the threshers were again blindfolded.

Throwing at cocks was the first popular blood sport to fall victim to the inexorable changes in public taste that led to the suppression of animal baiting and fighting. Whereas cockfighting, although barbaric, could always be explained in sporting terms of a 'natural' fight between equals, so that it enjoyed support from many in the higher classes, throwing at cocks became a symbol of popular pastimes that were based on gratuitous cruelty and violence. There had been sporadic condemnations on both moral and public order grounds since Tudor times, but a sustained campaign began to take shape in the 1730s, with letters to the local and national press calling for its suppression. For the rest of the eighteenth century, suppression was piecemeal, as magistrates, encouraged by local reformers, began to ban the game in their areas. The following example from the *Warwick & Warwickshire Advertiser* of 19 February 1814 was typical:

All our readers, whose breasts are not utterly inaccessible to every just feeling of humanity towards

Cockfighting in a barn (George Walker, *The Costume of Yorkshire*, 1814)

the inferior creation, will rejoice to hear that the
Magistrates of this county have determined to
suppress the base and brutal custom of throwing at
game cocks on Shrove Tuesday. We earnestly hope
that the magistrates of other counties will follow
such a commendable an example by exerting their
authority to prevent at once this cruel oppression
of the brutish, and this shocking degradation of the
human species.

By the end of the eighteenth century, the game
was definitely on the wane, and the last place in
which it was reported as taking place was Quainton,
Buckinghamshire, in 1844. A pale imitation of the
pastime survived for much longer in a fairground
game, still called 'throwing at cocks', in which people
threw sticks at lead figures.

Cockfighting

Cockfighting could take place at any time of year, but in
the medieval and early modern period it was especially
popular at Shrovetide. Oddly enough to modern eyes,
the sport was particularly associated with schoolchildren and young people, and it was written into the rules
of some schools that pupils must pay their schoolmaster a regular sum – termed a 'cock-penny' – to provide
the birds for the traditional game on Shrove Tuesday.
The earliest reference to cockfighting in England, written by William Fitz Stephen *c.*1180, makes this connection clear:

Each year upon the day called Carnival – to begin
with the sports of boys (for we were all boys once)
– boys from the schools bring fighting-cocks to their
master, and the whole forenoon is given up to boyish
sport for they have a holiday in the schools that they
may watch their cocks do battle.

Although this is the first written evidence of cockfighting in this country, it was well known in ancient Greece and Rome, and may even have been introduced to Britain by the Romans.

Cockfighting developed into a well-organized professional sport, with well-defined rules and traditions, and a literature and terminology all of its own. Fighting birds were carefully bred and documented; beaks were sharpened, tails clipped, silver or steel spurs attached to their legs, alcohol was placed in their feed, and all the care and attention lavished on them that one would expect for a potentially valuable commodity. Cockfights at local level took place in barns, inns, or fairgrounds, but in London and other major centres there were purpose-built cockpits at which well-advertised professional meetings took place. Dutch visitor William Schellinks visited one in June 1662:

In the afternoon we went to the cockpit and saw there several cock fights. There a great deal of money is won and lost by betting. The place is well laid out for the purpose, a circle with a table or round stage in the middle is covered with mats, with the devotees sitting around it, with the seats rising up so they can see above each other.

Like horse-racing and prizefighting, cockfighting brought together men from all the social classes, from the roughest to the highest, each having their part to play. The rich subsidized the sport by organizing the events, providing funds and premises, owning the cocks, and betting heavily on games, with huge sums of money regularly changing hands. But there was also a strong working-class tradition of cockfighting all over the country, particularly among certain occupational groups such as miners.

Samuel Pepys recorded two visits to cockfights, and both times commented on the 'rabble' he encountered. On 21 December 1663 he recorded:

Did go to Shoe Lane to see a cock-fighting at a new pit there – a sport I was never at in my life. But Lord, to see the strange variety of people, from Parliament-man . . . to the poorest prentices, bakers, brewers, butchers, draymen, and what not; and all this fellows one with another in swearing, cursing and betting. I soon had enough of it.

Pepys and Schellinks were recording their thoughts at a time when cockfighting was enjoying a resurgence of popularity after the Restoration of the monarchy. Cockfighting had, in fact, been banned only nine years before, by the *Ordinance for prohibiting cock-matches* (31 March 1654). This order was not concerned with cruelty to animals but with the question of public order and private morality:

[They] *tend many times to the disturbance of the public peace, and are commonly accompanied with gaming, drinking, swearing, quarrelling, and other dissolute practices, to the dishonour of God, and do often produce the ruin of persons and their families . . .*

It is unlikely that this made much difference, as the people involved were hardly likely to be bothered about their immortal souls, but it drove the sport underground for a short while and explains its sudden high profile in Pepys's time. The sport's popularity continued unabated until the turn of the nineteenth century, when public opinion turned decisively against such activities. In the 1830s, intense opposition emerged when the RSPCA initiated a strenuous campaign for abolition. It was finally made illegal in 1849.

Nevertheless, cockfighting still takes place, on the quiet, all over the country. A joint raid by police and RSPCA officers at a disused warehouse in Lancaster in 2001 found a fight in progress and evidence of others having taken place. As reported in the *Guardian* on 29 May of that year, the RSPCA claimed not only that cockfighting is popular with the travelling community and in mining areas, but also that 'anyone you care to think of can be involved, regardless of wealth, job, or social status'.

Cookeels (or Coquilles)

This was a localized seasonal food, popular in Norfolk and the surrounding area at Shrovetide. It is described in nineteenth-century sources as akin to what we would now call a hot cross bun, but without the cross. There is no agreement as to spelling, and cookeels, coquilles, cockerells, and others were used indiscriminately. The most likely derivation is from 'cockerel', because these birds were so widely connected with Shrovetide for centuries, in the form of **cock throwing and threshing** (p. 56) and **cockfighting** (p. 58). All the written references to the buns stem from the nineteenth century, and there is no indication how old the custom of selling cookeels may have been.

Dough-Nut Day

Dough-Nut Day was a local name for Shrove Tuesday, reported in the nineteenth century from Baldock, Hertfordshire. Here, instead or perhaps as well as, the more usual pancakes, William Hone records in his *Year-Book* (1832) that mothers 'make a good store of small cakes fried in hog's lard, placed over the fire in a brass kettle or skillet, called "dough-nuts"'.

Egg Shackling

One of the staples of everyday diet that was banned during Lent was eggs, and it is no surprise that these feature in customs and food traditions of the Shrovetide season. The Saturday preceding Shrove Tuesday was sometimes called Egg Saturday, because of the number of eggs eaten on the day, and during Shrovetide there were also egg-based customs that mirror those carried out at Easter, as described in Marianne Dacombe's collection of material from Women's Institutes in Dorset, published in 1935:

> In the 19th century at Powerstock there was a curious Shrovetide custom called 'egg shackling' which took place in the school. The children elected a committee and a judge, and there were prizes for the whitest, the brownest, the biggest, and the smallest eggs. Then all the eggs were gently shaken in a sieve. As each egg got a little crack, it was taken out, until the strongest one remained – and this one received the biggest prize.

Egg shackling still takes place at two schools in Somerset – at Stoke St Gregory and Shepton Beauchamp.

Compare **Easter Day: Eggs**, p. 115.

Ludlow Rope-Pulling

This Shrovetide competition formerly took place at Ludlow in Shropshire and involved an immense tug-of-war. According to an account of the custom in 1826, published by William Hone, the 36-yard rope was supplied by the corporation and passed out of the Market Hall window at four o'clock on Shrove Tuesday. The two contesting parties were made up of different halves of the town, and nearly 2,000 people could take part. It was traditional for the losing side to make a collection and buy back the rope for a second contest, and sometimes a third. The overall victors would sell the rope and use the money to entertain themselves. The event began to get out of hand with so many people taking part, and it was suppressed in 1851. Two theories of origin were current: the first was that the corporation knew how the custom started but were keeping it secret; the second was that it commemorated the struggles between the respective supporters of Henry VI and the Duke of York, whose base was at Ludlow Castle, in the Wars of the Roses during the fifteenth century.

The old custom was the inspiration for an annual tug-of-war contest started in the early 1980s between customers of two Ludlow pubs, The Bull and The Feathers, which takes place on Boxing Day (or the day after if Boxing Day falls on a Sunday).

Pancakes

It is somehow appropriate that the last surviving Shrovetide custom for most of us is that we still try to eat pancakes on this day. The connection between Shrove Tuesday and the pancake is a genuinely old one, and *Pasquils Palinodia* (1619) shows that the fun of tossing was well understood from early times:

> It was the day whereon both rich and poor
> Are chiefly feasted with the self same dish,
> Where every paunch, till it can hold no more,
> Is fritter-filled, as well as heart can wish;
> And every man and maid do take their turn,
> And toss their pancakes up for fear they burn;
> And all the kitchen doth with laughter sound,
> To see the pancakes fall upon the ground.

Three hundred years later, essentially the same scene was repeated in cottages up and down the country. In *A Kind of Magic*, Mollie Harris remembered a telling incident from her Oxfordshire childhood in the 1920s:

> The excitement of pancake day in our house had to be seen to be believed, for no other day in the year

Pancakes on Shrove Tuesday (George Cruickshank, *Comic Almanac*, 1837)

could afford such luxuries. The fun began as soon as our mother brought her big wash-stand jug from the bedroom and set it on the kitchen table. Into it went a quart of skimmed milk that one of us fetched from Sarah Clarke's, and several eggs from our own hens, all whipped up together with plenty of plain flour into a creamy frothy mixture. A new frying pan – another annual event for the great day – and a pound of best lard to cook the pancakes in, and we were all set to begin. Our mother's face was flushed and happy, her hair untidily wispy as she bent over her task. The fire burnt fiercely, so that she had to hold the pan above the flames. As each pancake was cooked it was doled out to the members of the family in turn, according to one's age, the eldest first.

The room was filled with squealing and laughing as our mother skilfully tossed each pancake high in the air. Blue smoke rose from the boiling fat and there was a strong smell of lemon as she slipped the long-awaited treat on to each plate. At last, it was Ben's turn, he was last-but-one on the list. He had waited patiently for almost an hour, and as she tossed the pancake mother cried, 'Whose turn is it this time?' 'Mine,' Ben shouted excitedly, and he rushed forward, plate in hand and tried to catch it as it came down – our mother tried to do the same thing. She gave him a quick shove, and he went backside first into a bucket of water and she herself, slightly off balance, stumbled a couple of steps sideways onto the sleeping cat. The hot pancake landed right on top of the squealing animal who made a bee-line for the door. Someone rushed to open it

Pancake race at Olney, Buckinghamshire, 1980

*and the cat streaked out, completely enveloped in
the cooked batter. 'That's yours boy, go and get it,'
Mother yelled to him above the din as Ben heaved
himself up from the bucket; with water dripping
from his trousers he rushed out into the garden.
Minutes later he came back, stuffing lumps of fluff-
covered pancake into his mouth, having cornered his
quarry in the wash-house.*

The midday bell which, before the Reformation, had
called the faithful to be 'shriven' on **Shrove Tuesday**
(p. 50) continued to be rung in many places, and was
popularly called the 'pancake bell', being regarded as
a signal for the housewife to get the pan on the fire,
and schoolchildren and apprentices to stop work for
the day. In 1950, the journal *Folk-Lore* recorded that in
Bedfordshire:

*The 'pancake bell' is still rung, from 11.50 till noon,
and the local schoolchildren run to nearby Conger*

*Hill to put their ear to the ground to 'hear the old
lady frying her pancakes' underground.*

As with all feast foods, it was held by many to be
inadvisable to neglect the custom. Robert Forby's
Vocabulary of East Anglia (1830) contains the advice:
'Shrove Tuesday: Ill luck betides the family in which
pancakes are not served up on that day.'

There seems to be no deep symbolic reason why
pancakes should have been so firmly connected with
Shrovetide, and the practical reason that it used up the
remaining milk, eggs, and fat before the Lenten fast
makes perfect sense. The words 'pancake' and 'fritter'
(the latter from the French and related to the word 'fry')
are both first recorded in the mid fifteenth century, but
there is no reason to believe that the delicacy itself was
new at that time.

Pancake Races

All over the country, in the dull days of February, one of the standard ways that come to mind when a quick charity or fun event is needed is a pancake race. One place can claim to be the originator of this custom: the town of Olney in Buckinghamshire. For many years, in unbroken tradition, the women of Olney have run in their annual Shrove Tuesday race, tossing pancakes as they go, and since 1950 have even competed with the town of Liberal in Kansas for the world title. Competitors at Olney must be over eighteen and residents of the town. For the race they must wear the traditional 'housewife' costume of skirt, apron, and headscarf or hat, although this dress code still leaves plenty of scope for parody and/or fancy dress. The race route has changed a little over time, and now starts from the Bull Hotel, in the market square, and runs alongside rather than through the churchyard, but the length remains at the original 415 yards and the fastest time stands at 58.5 seconds.

The modern race was founded in 1948 by the Revd R. W. Collins, newly appointed vicar of the church of Sts Peter and Paul. He set the course, laid down the rules, and was the presiding presence for many years, an involvement that set the pattern for a strong church element in the custom. But Revd Collins always claimed that he revived the custom, rather than invented it, and he presented as evidence some cuttings from the 1920s that show women (hatted and aproned and holding frying pans) posing with the vicar and the sexton. However, in Graham Lenton's recent book on the custom, local resident Mrs Ivy Perkins remembers that in the 1920s there was no race, and states that they simply walked to the church with their pancakes. An article in *The Times* on 22 February 1939 is the first to describe the race, and claimed that it had been revived fourteen years previously but had recently lapsed.

Despite this confusion, it seems on present evidence that a church-based custom – not necessarily a race – was invented in the 1920s, which was embellished into a race before the Second World War and revived again soon after it. A further search of the local newspapers of the time would probably provide the details. This is very different to the widely accepted story, which claims that the race dates back to 1445 when a harassed housewife heard the Shrove bell and rushed to the church still holding her frying pan. Others have embellished the tale, stating that housewives tried to bribe the churchwarden with pancakes to ring the bell so that the Shrovetide festivities could begin earlier. However, these stories, interesting though they are as traditional tales, are not supported by the documentary evidence. As Graham Lenton points out, standard histories of the area and other pre-twentieth-century writers from the village make no mention of the custom, and nor does anyone anywhere else.

Westminster Pancakes

A custom which is unique to Westminster School in London but which combines the traditional Shrove Tuesday elements of **pancakes** (p. 60) and rough **scrambling customs** (p. 128) is the 'Pancake greaze'. The latter word is also apparently unique to the school, meaning a 'scrum' or 'crowd'. On Shrove Tuesday morning, the school cook is brought in procession to the middle of the old schoolroom, carrying a frying pan that contains an oversized pancake, which he tosses, straight from the pan, over a high metal bar that runs across the middle of the room, to the waiting boys on the other side. Margaret Brentnall, in her *Old Customs and Ceremonies of London* (1975), writes:

> Then, suddenly, the frying pan was swung and up soared the pancake – up and (good throw!) over the bar. At once pandemonium broke loose and the boys became a scrambling mass of bodies where the pancake fell. Then, from the whirl of legs and arms, several triumphant figures emerged, each clutching a piece of mangled pancake. These were duly weighed and the winner, overcome with glory, was presented with the award.

The boy who gets the biggest piece is presented with a sovereign by the Dean of Westminster.

The game was first mentioned as an established event in the 1750s, and since then it has undergone only two changes: in 1885 the participation was restricted to a representative of each form rather than the whole school, and in the late twentieth century fancy dress for the players was introduced.

Purbeck Marblers and Stonecutters

The Company of Marblers and Stonecutters was probably formed in medieval times, to protect the monopoly rights of workers in the lucrative Purbeck marble industry in Dorset. The rules that regulate the Company were laid down in 1651, but they were already then described as 'ancient'. The Company meets annually on Shrove Tuesday at Corfe Town Hall and, although fewer in number than in former times, it continues to regulate the business of the trade, which is still in the hands of certain local families. The members are summoned by the tolling of a bell to meet at noon. After a short service, various ceremonies are carried out, including the induction of apprentices, who, having reached the age of twenty-one, are accepted as freemen on payment of 33 pence (6s. 8d.), one penny loaf, and two pots of beer. In addition, the last married man in the Company brings a football, which is kicked along the streets from Corfe Castle to Owre, to preserve the right of way, essential in the past for getting the stone to the quay.

St Columb Hurling

The Cornish town of St Columb is one of only two places that have retained an annual hurling match, a game that was formerly very widespread in the county. The game here is still played in the streets, and begins at 4.30 p.m. in the market square on Shrove Tuesday and again on the following Saturday. Local traders barricade their premises for protection, as the game can involve hundreds of players and there are few rules to control them.

Hurling (p. 42) is played with a silver ball, about the size of an orange, made of wood or cork and coated in silver. The game begins when the ball is thrown up by last year's winner, or a local celebrity, standing on a stepladder in the market square, with the cry of the game's motto, 'Town and country do your best. But in this parish I must rest.' The ball can be thrown or carried but is rarely kicked, and while sometimes it is lost in a scrum, at other times the play moves fast through the streets with the ball frequently changing hands. For the first hour of the game, play traditionally stays in the streets around the town centre, but after that it can break in any direction. The game is ostensi-bly between town and country, and each goal is about two miles apart. Each team tries to get the ball to their goal, or to carry it across the parish boundary in any direction. The first to do either of these feats wins the game and is carried shoulder-high back to the square. Play often pauses as the ball is deliberately passed to an elderly or disabled person, or even into one of the adjoining properties, and before women started joining in it was not unknown for young men to try to gain the ball to impress the young women, as recorded in 1972 by A. Rabey, author of an informative booklet on the game:

> Many a young hurler has endeavoured to find favour with the young lady of his choice by obtaining the ball for her, often at great personal risk to life and limb, or so it appears, which when handed to the fair one, causes the great mass of hurlers to stand gallantly back as she re-starts the game by throwing the ball back to her would-be sweetheart.

The winner may keep the ball, which is made locally in a traditional manner, but she or he must pay for a replacement.

St Columb can claim to be the home of Cornish hurling in the sense that the earliest written record of the game that can be assigned to a particular place is found in the *St. Columb Green Book*, which includes references to silver balls in 1594–5.

See also **3 February: St Ives Hurling**.

Sedgefield Ball Game

The annual ball game at Sedgefield in County Durham is one of the survivors of the old Shrove Tuesday football, played in this case with a ball about the size of a cricket ball, which can be kicked, carried, or thrown. At the start and finish of the game, the ball is passed through the metal bull-ring on the village green. Traditionally, the game was played between the tradesmen and the countrymen, as in this account from 1884:

> The ball was put through the bull-ring in the middle of the village green exactly at 1pm on Tuesday . . . and was then in for play. Both sides were determined to win or die, as it were, and more reckless play we have not witnessed. No rules were adhered to, and scraped shins became the order of the day. After play lasting

three hours and fifteen minutes, the tradesmen were declared the victors, they having succeeded in passing the ball over the pond.

In the modern game there are still no real rules and play is fairly rough, but the action stops occasionally to let a child or pensioner in the crowd have a lucky kick at the ball.

It is not clear how old the Sedgefield game is, as records only go back to the nineteenth century, but confident assertions of 900 years or more, regularly made in the local press, can be discounted.

See also **Football**, p. 53.

Shroving and Lent-Crocking

Shrove Tuesday was one of several days in the year on which parties of children or young people went from house to house, recited a rhyme, and expected gifts of food or money from the householder. The custom went under various names: 'shroving' was the usual term, but Lent-crocking, Nickanan Night, Lansherd Night, and others were also recorded. The rhyme also varied considerably, but it always included a request for gifts, as here from Oxfordshire in 1903:

Pit-a-pat! the pan's hot,
I be come a-Shroving;
A bit of bread, a bit of cheese
Or a cold apple dumpling
Up with the kettle! Down with the pan!
Give me a penny, and I'll be on.

In some cases, however, there could be retaliation if they were not satisfied. The shrovers carried broken crockery or stones, which they threw, or at least threatened to throw, at the doors of anyone who refused to contribute. In other instances, the visitors did not request largesse at all, but simply went round at night and threw the sherds or stones at the door of anyone who had displeased them in recent months, or who they thought needed punishing for some reason. It is not entirely clear whether these two forms are facets of the same custom, or were distinct customs that happened to share some characteristics. Two experts on the subject, Peter Robson and Ronald Hutton, both argue for two separate customs, but the matter is not yet closed.

In some reports, there is more than a hint of what is elsewhere called Mischief Night (*see* **31 October: Mischief Night**). In 1871, the physician and author Jonathan Couch recorded the following example from Polperro in Cornwall:

On the day termed 'Hall' Monday, which precedes Shrove Tuesday, about the dusk of the evening, it is the custom for boys, and in some cases for those above the age of boys, to prowl about the streets with short clubs, and to knock loudly at every door, running off to escape detection on the slightest sign of a motion within. If, however, no attention be excited, and if any article be discovered negligently exposed, or carelessly guarded, then the things are carried away; and on the following morning are seen displayed in some conspicuous place, to expose the disgraceful want of vigilance supposed to characterise the owner. The time when this is practised is called 'Nicky-Nan-Night'.

Like many other house-visiting customs, shroving appears to have been restricted to certain areas of the country, in this case the South and West; the custom has been reported from Hertfordshire, Buckinghamshire, Oxfordshire, Berkshire, Wiltshire, Hampshire, the Isle of Wight, and especially all the counties of the West Country. The earliest references to shroving customs come from the turn of the nineteenth century, although Hutton quotes a similar stone-throwing custom on the Scilly Isles in the 1740s.

See also **24 January: Eve of Conversion of St Paul** for another variation on the 'crockery-throwing' theme.

Skipping

Several places in the country had an annual long-rope skipping custom on **Good Friday** (*see* p. 111), but at Scarborough in Yorkshire it was, and still is, carried out on Shrove Tuesday. Hundreds of people turn out with their old washing lines and skipping ropes and, weather permitting, spend the afternoon on the foreshore, which is closed to traffic. With someone at each end doing the turning, and others of all ages and abilities doing the jumping, a lively and energetic afternoon is spent in the seaside air. The mayor rings a bell at noon to signal the start of the session. This official sanction is not a new thing, according to the *Dalesman* (April 1994):

> [A previous article] *brought back memories of the 1920s and 30s, in particular of Johnny Jackson, a gents tailor and outfitter whose shop was at the bottom of Queen Street. A small dapper man in morning suit, homburgh hat, military moustache and spats who during his term as mayor rang the starting bell and then skipped in every rope from the Spa to sand-side.*

As at Brighton in Sussex, tradition links the skipping with the local fishing industry, who, it is claimed, finished their line-fishing season at this time of year and after sorting out their ropes gave any worn-out ones to local children.

Mass skipping is a well-entrenched local custom at Scarborough and needs no ancient legend to keep it going. However, theories that it is an ancient magical rite to make the crops grow are not helped by the fact that it cannot be proven that it was carried out here before 1903.

Whipping Toms

An apparently unique custom took place in Leicester every Shrove Tuesday until suppressed in 1846. At the annual fair that was held in the area of the town called the Newarke, various traditional sports such as **cock throwing** (p. 56), shinty (akin to hockey), and **football** (p. 53) were played, but later in the day the 'Whipping Toms' appeared, who claimed the right to use a cart-whip on anyone still in the area. This licensed attack was not without rules, however. The Toms wore a blind-fold over one eye, and they were not allowed to whip above the knee, or anyone who was kneeling down or who was willing to pay a small fine. When the Toms appeared, most of the people who remained in the Newarke did so specifically to play the game of dodg-ing the whips, and they wore stout boots and carried sticks to help in their defence. Nevertheless, as often happened with such customs in the mid nineteenth century, many local worthies objected to the rough play and in 1846 they sponsored a private Act of Parliament that banned playing at 'Whipping Toms, shindy, football, or any other game' on the Newarke on

Shrove Tuesday. Attempts by the locals to continue the custom in 1847 were thwarted by the police.

*

ASH WEDNESDAY

Compared to the wild abandon and activity of **Shrove Tuesday** customs (p. 50), Ash Wednesday was a universal day of penitence, and the first day of Lent. Its date depends on the timing of Easter, and it can fall anywhere between 4 February and 11 March. Ash Wednesday gets its name from the pre-Reformation rite that was carried out on the day, in which a priest would bless ashes (sometimes made from burning the 'palms' used in the previous year's Palm Sunday service), sprinkle them with holy water, and place some on the foreheads of the kneeling congregation. Words were intoned while this was carried out, which can be translated as 'Remember, man, that thou art dust and to dust thou shalt return.' The use of ashes was abolished in England in 1548 as one of Edward VI's Protestant reforms, but the name 'Ash Wednesday' has lived on in popular parlance to the present day and it is given in the *Book of Common Prayer* as a subtitle for the First Day of Lent.

At least a memory of the old Ash Wednesday survived into the Victorian era and beyond, in the form of which foods were deemed suitable for the day. In 1865, John Fisher recorded in his *History and Antiquities of Masham and Mashamshire* (Yorkshire):

> *On Ash Wednesday the good people of Masham certainly do not put on sack-cloth and ashes. Our fathers and grandfathers used so far to observe this day as to dine upon salt-fish; but we, of the present generation, dine on what we like best or rather upon what some of us can get, and the day is not now otherwise observed.*

And the journal *Folk-Lore* reported in 1929 that in Cumberland:

> *On Ash Wednesday, many folks mek tatie ash, tul t'dinner' (i.e. meat, potatoes, and an onion stewed together).*

Jack-a-Lent

One of the most fascinating, but elusive, figures of this season was Jack-a-Lent, sometimes spelled 'Jack o' Lent', who was particularly associated with Ash Wednesday:

An old custom, now quite defunct, was observed here not long since in the beginning of Lent. A figure made up of straw and cast-off clothes was drawn or carried round the town, amid much noise and merriment, after which it was either burnt, shot at, or brought to some other ignominious end. The image was called Jack o'Lent, and was, doubtless, intended to represent Judas Iscariot. A dirty slovenly fellow is often termed a Jack o' Lent.

This appearance in Cornwall in 1871 is a very late example of a figure that had existed in England since at least the 1550s, and was clearly a proverbial character by the seventeenth century, when poets and playwrights often used the name to signify a worthless, empty person, or someone who was attracting universal opprobrium, as in Francis Quarles's *Shepheards' Oracles* (1646):

How like a Jack a Lent
He stands, for boys to spend their Shrovetide throws,
Or like a puppit made to frighten crows.

The Jack figure was made of wood and straw and dressed in old clothes, and could be hung up in public for the duration of Lent, for all and sundry to throw things at ('three throws a penny', according to a line in Act IV, scene 2 of Ben Jonson's play *Tale of a Tub* (1640)), or he could be paraded around the town streets and then attacked and destroyed. Either way, he was there simply to be mistreated – pelted with sticks, stones and filth, shot at, torn apart, and finally burnt.

As in the Cornish example quoted above, some writers thought that our Jack represented Judas Iscariot, but this seems to have been a later idea. It was more widely assumed that he was the target of people's aggression because he signified Lent. Although there is little evidence that English people indulged in the extended bacchanalian festival of Carnival so well known in medieval times on the Continent and portrayed in paintings like *The Fight Between Carnival and Lent* (1559) by Peter Bruegel the Elder, the Jack-a-Lent figure certainly provides some cross-channel parallels. Among other

---

Scambling Days

In most parts of the country, to 'scamble' signified the action of indulging in a makeshift meal; hence the term 'Scambling Days', which were the Mondays and Saturdays in Lent. On these days, no regular meals were prepared, and people had to make whatever shift they could to keep from going hungry. 'Scambling' (often spelled 'skambling') has an interesting history. It pre-dates the word 'scrambling', to which it is closely related, and meant both 'to scatter', and 'to struggle', often in the sense of contesting for money, sweets, or food thrown to a crowd, as the *Oxford English Dictionary* puts it, 'in an indecorous and rapacious manner'.

---

things, the continental festival usually involved street theatre with personifications of Carnival and Lent, and the earliest reference to Jack-a-Lent in England indicates at least the germ of a dramatic representation. Henry Machyn recorded a sheriff of London's parade in his diary on 17 March 1552/3, which involved numerous characters, including minstrels, giants, hobby horses, morris dancers, and a priest shriving a Jack-of-Lent. He was followed by Jack-of-Lent's wife, who was offering a thousand pounds to a physician to save Jack's life.

In later years, the English traditional calendar included a number of very similar customs where a figure was mistreated, reviled, and destroyed, although they had no recorded connection with Lent (*see* **Rough Music**, p. 74; **Easter Day: Riding the Lord**, p. 122; **Easter Monday: Black Knight of Ashton**, p. 124; **24 August: West Witton Burning of Bartle**; and **5 November: Guy Fawkes Night**). A detailed study of these 'stuffed figure' customs may possibly help to illuminate the nature of Jack-a-Lent himself, and vice versa.

*

FRIDAY FOLLOWING ASH WEDNESDAY

Pully Lug Day

Two reported customs involve the belief that, at certain sanctioned times, one can pull another's ears with impunity. In nineteenth-century Cumberland and Westmorland, the Friday following Ash Wednesday was Pully Lug Day or Nippy Lug Day for schoolchildren, at least until midday. A correspondent to *Notes & Queries* wrote in 1878:

> I have a recollection . . . of one of the day-scholars coming up to me one day, and, exclaiming 'Pully-lug day', forthwith proceeding to pull my 'lugs'.

But in Carlisle, and possibly elsewhere, there existed the idea that one could pull ears on mayor-making day, which in Carlisle was held on 9 November. This is a localized example of a belief that between the retirement of the outgoing mayor and the installation of the new one, normal laws and social conventions do not apply (*see* **Lawless Hours and Days**, p. 303).

*

29 FEBRUARY

Leap Year Day

The concept of the leap year was introduced by Julius Caesar in his reform of the calendar in 45 BC, in order to correct a small but irritating discrepancy in calculating the length of the solar year, which is 365 days and 6 hours rather than a conveniently round figure. An extra day every four years brings us more or less back in line. But even this is not really accurate enough, which is why centennial years are only leap years if they are divisible by 400 (e.g. the year 1900 was not a leap year, but 2000 was).

By far the most widespread feature of the leap year in British tradition has long been that it is only in that year that women are allowed to propose marriage, and some even go so far as to argue that this 'ladies' privilege' only existed on Leap Year Day itself. It is often confidently asserted that this notion was enshrined in Scottish law at the time of Queen Margaret, in 1288 (or 1228 in other versions), and that if a man did not accept the proposal, the penalty was a fine of one hundred pounds (although some versions say 'one pound'). But this in itself is a myth, and no one has yet produced any evidence of such a law's actual existence. It is also declared, with a similar lack of evidence, that in England a man who refused such an offer could only redeem himself by buying his proposer a new silk gown. The woman herself had to wear a red petticoat when making the proposal. If this were true, every unmarried woman throughout history could have had a wardrobe full of silk gowns simply for the asking and for the price of one cheap petticoat.

The real origin of the 'ladies' privilege' idea is not known, and its early history is not easy to pin down. It was certainly in existence by 1606, when it was described in the book *Courtship, Love and Matrimony*, but a couplet attributed to Chaucer by Vincent Stuckey Lean in his mammoth *Collectanea* (1905) has so far proved impossible to verify:

> In Leap Year they have power to chuse
> The men no charter to refuse

Nevertheless, in the legendary sphere, a well-known story explains that the leap-year privilege is an early example of feminist agitation for reform of a patriarchal society. The right was reluctantly conceded by St Patrick, in answer to St Bridget's complaint that it was unfair that women were not allowed to propose. Patrick made the offer of allowing women to propose once in seven years, but Bridget bargained him down to once every four years. But the face of matrimony, and relations between the sexes, have changed so much in the last few decades that if the newspapers did not make a feature of the belief every four years, it is unlikely that many of today's young women would know that there ever had been any objection to their initiating a proposal.

There have probably been other notions about the leap year which have not survived. For example, a glimpse of how things were seen over a thousand years ago was provided by R. T. Hampson in 1841, who included the following extract from a 'Saxon document' in his book on the medieval calendar:

Some priests assert that the bissextus [Leap Year Day]
comes through this, that Joshua prayed to God that
the sun might stand still for one day's length when
he swept the heathens from the land, as God granted
him.

The incident in question is detailed in Joshua 10:12–14. The natural world apparently cares little about human proposals, but is nevertheless well aware of the existence of the leap year. It was widely thought that broad beans, and other plants, 'grow the wrong way' in a leap year . This idea is still regularly mentioned in gardening circles, although nobody seems to know exactly what the 'wrong way' actually means in this context.

March

Rough Music

5

ST PIRAN'S DAY

6

7

12

ST GREGORY'S DAY
SECOND MONDAY IN
   MARCH
Commonwealth Day

13

14

Wiggs

19

ST JOSEPH'S DAY

20

21

ST BENEDICT'S DAY

Doles

Pudding-Pies

26

27

28

Moveable events have been placed
on the date they fall in 2007.
Events dependent on the timing
of Easter are coloured green.

1
ST DAVID'S DAY

2
ST CHAD'S DAY

3
ST WINWALOE'S DAY

4

8

9
ST CONSTANTINE'S DAY

10

11
PENNY LOAF DAY

15

16
ST PATRICK'S DAY

17

18
BRAGGOT SUNDAY
MOTHERING SUNDAY
MOTHER'S DAY

22
WEEKDAY IN LATE
   MARCH
Oranges and Lemons Service

23

24

25
ANNUNCIATION/LADY
   DAY
Tichborne Dole
CARE OR CARLING
   SUNDAY

29

30

31

Dame Elizabeth Marvyn Charity

This annual dole emanates from the will of Dame Elizabeth Marvyn, who died in 1581. She was buried at St Peter's church in Ufton Nervet, Berkshire, and a tablet there gives the following details:

> Lady Marvin in 1581, gave 10 bushels of Wheat to be made into good household bread, 12½ ells of canvass at 1s per ell for shirts and smocks, and also 12½ yards of narrow blue cloth at 1s 3d per yard for coats and cassocks. She did by her will charge divers lands and hereditaments at Ufton and elsewhere with the payment of a sufficient sum of money to purchase the said wheat, canvass and blue cloth. To be annually distributed about the middle of Lent.

A loaf of bread is now given to local people from a window of Ufton Court, in March. The linen has been transmuted into a pair of sheets given to each of nine old-age pensioners who must have lived in the parish at least ten years.

*

1 MARCH

St David's Day

St Dewi, anglicized as St David, was a sixth-century monk and bishop. He was the only Welsh saint to be officially recognized in the wider Christian community, and was adopted as patron saint of Wales in the twelfth century. Little is known for certain about his life. As Wales's patron saint, his legendary exploits, and customs of his feast day, are largely the province of Welsh folklore, and perhaps this is why St David's Day seems to have had a very low profile in English lore, except insofar as it is reflected in relations between the two neighbouring nations.

There are several recorded instances in the seventeenth century of members of the royal court, including the monarch himself, wearing leeks on St David's Day. At a more popular level, however, traditional antipathy and derision have been more evident, most famously described by Shakespeare in *Henry V* (1599), in which the English braggart Pistol makes fun of the Welsh captain Fluellen's wearing of a leek on St David's Day, and is forced to eat the vegetable, skin and all (Act V, scene 1). Here, it is the English captain, Gower, who supports his Welsh colleague and berates Pistol for mocking 'an ancient tradition, begun upon an honourable respect and worn as a memorable trophy of predeceased valour'. Nevertheless, there was also a custom of hanging Welshmen in effigy on their day, as recorded by Samuel Pepys in his diary for 1 March 1667, and also by visiting Dutchman William Schellinks in his journal in 1662:

> . . . being St. David's Day, the day of the patron saint of Wales, when according to ancient tradition, all people born in that principality put a leek in the band of their hats. That is supposed to be in memory of a battle fought and won by them on St. David's Day, in which they wore them in a mark to distinguish themselves from their enemies. So his Majesty and many great Lords and gentlemen, common people, and even lackeys, coachmen. porters, and all kinds of riff-raff and layabouts wear one in their hats.. We saw some countryfolk carry such large leeks on their hats that their heads hung almost sideways because of them. And so on this day the Welshmen are greatly teased by the English, not only by calling after them Taffey, Taffey, or David, David, but also by hanging out all kinds of dolls and scarecrows with leeks on their heads, and as they celebrate the day with heavy boozing, and both sides, from the ale, strong beer, sack and claret, become short-tempered, obstinate and wild, so it is not often that this day goes by without mishaps, and without one or the other getting into an argument or a blood fight. It happened this year that near Westminster a Welsh nobleman stabbed an Englishman. So too an English cook who, for fun, stuck a leek on his hat and addressed, as a fellow countryman, a great lord, a Welshman, who passed by with his suite, who responded in Welsh, which is as different from English as French is from Dutch. When the cook replied sneeringly in English, the lord went for him, the cook fled into his shop and grabbed a spit from the fire and with this attacked the Welshman, who, supported by his servants with their rapiers, all turned against the cook, who was immediately helped by all sorts of rabble, throwing dirt and

other things, so that in the end he was compelled to retreat, and the furore getting greater, he was forced to take to the water, and, although he had got help, the mob, fighting furiously, got into the boat, and if his Majesty had not sent help quickly by water, they could easily have been killed . . .

Nearly one hundred years later, the *Poor Robin's Almanack* for 1757 confirmed that the custom still continued: 'But it would make the stranger laugh / To see th' English hang poor Taff'; and English bakers offered gingerbread figures for sale, fixed on skewers and called 'taffies'.

The connection between St David's Day and the leek has never been satisfactorily explained, although the most often quoted story is that St David prompted his countrymen to wear the plant in their hats while in battle with the invading Saxons, in order to distinguish themselves from the enemy, a story that imbues the leek with a defiantly anti-English symbolism. But another legend, also referred to by Shakespeare in *Henry V*, held that Welsh archers, doing service alongside their English brethren at Crécy in 1346 or Poitiers in 1356, started the fashion.

The only other relatively widespread English tradition about St David's Day, reported from late Victorian times, was the warning to housewives that this was the day that fleas appeared, to plague humans for the rest of the year, as in the following example from Devon *c.*1890:

A house-maid advised Mrs. Hewett not to open her bedroom window on 1st of March, and said that she had heard that the black army always come down Exeter Hill, in swarms, on that day.

The arrival of the 'black army' was sometimes said to be the work of Satan; in a common saying, 'The Devil shakes a bag of fleas at everybody's door on 1st March.'

On a different note, the well-known weather proverb 'March comes in like a lion and goes out like a lamb', has been a commonplace since at least the second half of the seventeenth century, when several writers included it in their books. But some proverb authorities since that time have reported different versions with rather obscure imagery, which have never been properly explained. These sayings preface the well-known words 'comes in like a lion' with phrases such as 'March black ham' or 'March hack ham'. The only version that seems to make any sense is 'March black ram', which some have seen as a reference to the astrological ram of Aries, although the case remains open.

For a rhyme about the weather in the first three days of March, *see* **3 March: St Winwaloe's Day**.

*

2 MARCH

St Chad's Day

Ceadda or Chad (died 672) was the first bishop of the newly converted kingdom of Mercia, and he made his seat at Lichfield. No major customs seem to have been attached to his feast day, although there were a fair number of churches dedicated to his name, and he achieved lasting fame in the sphere of medicinal wells. A number of wells with a healing reputation bore his name, including one in Lichfield which was claimed in the eighteenth century to be the very one in which the saint himself had bathed. A more famous one in Gray's Inn Road near King's Cross, London, developed into a popular spa and then a pleasure garden; it lasted until 1860, when it was swept away during the building of the Metropolitan Railway.

According to the Venerable Bede, Chad's reputation for healing emerged immediately after his death, and his first wooden shrine had an aperture into which the devout could put their hands to gather pinches of dust to drop into water in order to make medicinal drinks for sick men and beasts.

*

3 MARCH

St Winwaloe's Day

A somewhat obscure Breton saint of the sixth century; so obscure, in fact, that even the spelling of his name is uncertain: Winwaloe, Winneral, Winnold and Winnal are just some of the variations. His cult was quite popular in medieval England, particularly in Cornwall and East Anglia, and his day was regularly listed in almanacs. But except for the few places where churches

Continues on page 77 >

Rough Music

'Rough music' customs were an unmistakable way for a community to condemn the behaviour or moral failings of particular individuals in their midst. They usually took place after dark and could involve scores of protesters, mostly men but including some women and even children, who processed around the locality and then mounted a prolonged demonstration outside the home of the object of their disapproval. These demonstrations took various forms across the country, but a constant feature was the deafening cacophony of noise: cooking pots were banged with spoons; stones were rattled in tins; shovels were beaten with hammers; horns, rattles, and drums were used; and people shouted, screamed, and bayed. 'Rough music' is thus a useful generic term for the basic element of the custom, but in reality the activity had a wide number of local names, including 'lew-balling', 'skimmington (skimmity) riding', 'riding the stang', 'ran-tanning', and 'stag-hunting'.

A well-organized rough music usually included lifelike effigies of the guilty parties, which were mounted on a pole (a 'stang'), a cart, or a donkey (facing its tail) and paraded around the neighbourhood. The climax involved the mistreatment and destruction of these figures, which could be torn to pieces, shot at, burnt, or thrown in the river. If the crowd could get hold of the real victims, male or female, they were very roughly handled, forced to take part in the procession, thrown in a pond, and almost murdered, but most accounts stress the symbolic, rather than the actual, violence.

The demonstrators followed some informal rules, which they believed made their activities perfectly legal. In the majority of cases, the affair lasted for three nights, and there was a set-piece verbal accusation, or 'nominy', which was often in rhyme and was shouted out as part of the proceedings. Many believed that anything could be said in the nominy as long as the actual names of the accused were not mentioned, so the declaration often started with an anonymous formula, as in this one from Effingham, Surrey, in 1869:

> *There is a man lives in this place*
> *He brought his servant to disgrace*
> *He beat her black, he beat her blue*
> *And beat her till her bones came through.*

It is clear that local police rarely took any action to prevent rough-music demonstrations. They made themselves scarce while it was going on, or sometimes maintained a discreet presence in the background, as if to ensure that the proceedings did not get out of hand. But this very presence gave the demonstrators a veneer of legitimacy. Rough music could be adapted to suit any sort of community disapproval, but the overwhelming number of documented cases focus on sexual or marital behaviour. Adultery, illegitimacy, overtly 'loose' sexual behaviour, ill-matched marriages, such as a young person marrying an old one, or a widow(er) marrying too soon, were regular motives, as in a case from Croydon in 1881:

> *A thrice married man has been getting it warm in*
> *the Leslie Park Road, where he lives. It is said that he*
> *has married his third wife six weeks after the death*
> *of the second, and his neighbours and friends have*
> *thought fit to demonstrate their disapproval of this*
> *proceeding in a very marked manner. They have*
> *smashed his windows, discharged fireworks outside*
> *his house, treated him and his bride to rough music,*
> *and indulged in various other manifestations of*
> *ill-feeling.*

Men who beat their wives or neglected their families, women who beat or henpecked their husbands, and habitual scolds were all potential targets. A correspondent contributed a note to the *Folk-Lore Journal* in 1884 on the subject:

> *A few months ago, in a village not far from*
> *Stratford-on-Avon, I noticed a quantity of chaff*
> *before a house door; on my return home I*
> *mentioned that I supposed so-and-so was moving;*
> *when I was at once met with the reply, 'Because of*
> *the chaff at his door? Oh no, that is the way our*
> *people show their feelings for wife-beaters.*

The chaff announced publicly that the man had been 'threshing' his wife.

Rough music: riding the stang (George Walker, *The Costume of Yorkshire*, 1814)

Among the numerous published accounts of rough music, there are few written by participants, and this makes the diary entries of George James Dew, a young carpenter from Lower Heyford in Oxfordshire, particularly interesting. Dew was twenty-one when he recorded his impressions of a 'lew-belling' in his neighbourhood in 1867. Most of the usual elements – the discordant noise, the effigies, the general popular support, and the escalation over three nights – are present in his account. Dew is quite enthusiastic about the affair, but he does at least have second thoughts about the effects of his actions on any innocent parties involved. His account, edited by the historian Pamela Horn, is worth quoting in full:

[14 February 1867] *'Rough music' was heard tonight although not an organised band, on account of some misdeeds in the train between a married woman of Aston and George Coggins, baker, of Lower Heyford . . . the man in question is a drunkard.*

[15 February 1867] *This evening there was a regular organised band both at Aston and Heyford of 'rough music'. The Heyford party went down to George Coggins', and the Aston party following them. Afterwards they came back together and the rattle was most noisy; all the old tin and iron utensils I should think to be found in both parishes were rattling. George Coggins went to Banbury and came back by the last train. The musical party was awaiting his arrival at the station, but he popped into the waiting room, and they did not know he was there, else he would have had the honour (or rather the disgrace) of having a vast number of musicians to play to him in that strain which would have been suitable for the occasion – This has been the practice, in all occasions of known adultery or a man beating his wife. The punishment to the offenders must I am sure be very sharp. I somehow approve of it because it is a manifestation of the hatred of the public to such acts. They call it a 'skimmington' or 'lewbelling' . . .*

[16 February 1867] *A most tremendously noisy lew-belling tonight again for George Coggins. Our Heyford chaps went to Aston and played all round there, and then both came to Heyford to play. They had effigies of Mrs. Thomas and George Coggins; she with a large crinoline and bonnet, and he a stout fellow with his baking apron on. They were mounted on poles and were kissing each other at every short interval. They shot at these effigies when they got to the Bell Inn, and again as they passed George Coggins' house, but when they returned to here again they were both in flames and they burnt them, throwing about the flaming crinoline and apron and making such a rattle for the offender to hear as one would not easily forget. The place was swarmed with people and the old kettles rattled to a high pitch. I enjoyed it very much, because I never saw one carried out so well before – To look at the other side of the affair, although the discordant music was cheering and pleasing, is somewhat sad. This George Coggins, baker, has a wife faithful in every respect and such as a wife ought to be, but how dreadfully annoying must this disturbance be to her.*

There is no doubt that such activities had widespread popular support and were based on a feeling that they could reach those parts of community life that the law could not, and this underlying approval has been reaffirmed in the writing of many modern social historians. But the custom carried such a potential for sheer vindictiveness and moral fascism that a close reading reveals rough-music events to be as potentially dangerous and morally dubious as any other manifestation of mob rule. They were certainly open to a charge of hypocrisy. One wonders how many men in the rough-music band also knocked their wives around, or how many had committed adultery, or would do so, given half the chance. One wonders also how often the actions were prompted by inaccurate or spiteful rumour. A modern analogy might be drawn with those who recently attacked a paediatrician because they thought the word meant 'paedophile'. In many cases of rough music, it is implied that the crimes attracted attention because they were habitual, but in some instances, where we have unusually detailed information, there are indications of other underlying motives, such as disputes over money or property, and suggestions that the events were expressions of malice and naked aggression rather than pure moral indignation.

A particularly pointed version of rough music, called the 'Stag Hunt', existed in Devon and Somerset. In this, one of the villagers was chosen to be the 'stag', and dressed accordingly, complete with horns, if some could be procured. The others in the crowd acted as huntsmen and hounds, and 'pursued' the stag all around the town, accompanied by the usual rough-music sounds as well as a cacophony of hunting horns and baying dog noises. The chase studiously avoided approaching too close to the home of the victim until the climax of the affair, when he was finally 'caught' on the very doorstep and a bladderful of blood spilled. The symbolism of the Stag Hunt appears to be even more horrific than the usual rough-music antics of skimmingtons and stang-ridings elsewhere.

There are numerous historical accounts of rough-music events. Real-life examples occur in the diaries and memoirs of people such as Henry Machyn (for example on 22 February 1562/3) and Samuel Pepys (on 10 June 1667), as well as court records and newspaper reports from the seventeenth to twentieth centuries and folklore and local history publications from the mid nineteenth to the mid twentieth centuries. They were regularly mentioned in plays and poems of the sixteenth and seventeenth centuries, and well-known fictional treatments can be found in Hogarth's *Hudibras Encounters the Skimmington* (1726), and Thomas Hardy's *Mayor of Casterbridge* (1886).

were dedicated to him, or fairs held on his day, any lasting fame rested on the fact that his feast came third in the widespread rhyme which predicts stormy weather in the first days in March:

First comes David, then comes Chad,
And then comes Winneral as though he was mad.

*

5 MARCH

St Piran's Day

One of Cornwall's most popular saints, and also known in Brittany and Wales, Piran (or Perran) probably originated from Ireland and died in Cornwall sometime around the year 480. Details of his life are decidedly sketchy, mainly because of the mistaken identification of him as the Irish saint Ciaran, which has all but destroyed any facts that might have otherwise survived. Piran was claimed as the patron saint of Cornish tin-miners, and they regularly took this day off work in his honour, although the only detail that has survived of their celebrations is that they always got roundly drunk.

*

6 MARCH

See **14 December: St Tibba's Day**.

*

9 MARCH

St Constantine's Day

Tradition has it that St Constantine was a Cornish chieftain, of uncertain date, who later became a monk, but the name is so common in early Britain that it is impossible to disentangle one figure from another. There is even some doubt about whether his feast day should be 9 or 11 March. One legend told of him (and of others) is that he was out stag-hunting when the chase drove the quarry into the vicinity of a holy hermit, who took the animal under his protection. When Constantine moved to strike the hermit in anger,

Constantine became frozen to the spot and was unable to move a muscle until the holy man's prayers released him. Constantine was naturally so impressed that he immediately converted to Christianity.

A chapel dedicated to him existed at St Merran, and his feast day was celebrated with a game of **hurling** (p. 42). A holy well nearby had the useful attribute of allowing anyone to bring rain if they drew water from it and poured it out on the stone.

*

10 MARCH

In many collections of traditional lore, the character of the days of middle and late March predict the weather for the rest of the year, although the sayings are often contradictory. At the turn of the twentieth century, for example, Sarah Hewett recorded in her *Peasant Speech of Devon* that 'If it does not freeze on the 10th of March, a fertile year may be expected.' But the *Shepherd's Kalendar* of *c*.1680 maintained that 'Mists or hoar frosts on the 10th of March betoken a plentiful year.' Perhaps we can blame the change of calendar in 1752 for the discrepancy (*see* p. xx).

*

11 MARCH

Penny Loaf Day

During the English Civil War, when the Nottinghamshire town of Newark was under siege from Parliamentary forces, local merchant and alderman Hercules Clay dreamt on three separate nights that his house was on fire. He took this as a warning and moved his family out, and, sure enough, his house was destroyed by artillery fire soon afterwards. Hercules was so impressed that he left money to the town corporation and the vicar to commemorate his escape with a special sermon and the distribution of penny loaves to the poor every year on 11 March, the very day of his deliverance. Clay died soon afterwards, in December 1644, and at least part of his bequest is still carried out.

By the late nineteenth century, the distribution of penny loaves was so popular with locals that the police

Commonwealth Day at Westminster Abbey, 1997

were put under severe strain trying to keep order. Nottinghamshire writer J. Potter Briscoe recorded in 1876 that the distribution was then carried out at the town hall, and applicants had to enter in single file and were then locked in until the ceremony was over, to stop people coming up more than once for a loaf. In 1894, 2,000 children turned up, many of them from villages outside the town, and the trustees began to think of alternative ways to help the poor in the spirit of Clay's bequest. In 1899, instead of a general handout of loaves, poor local children were given boots, through the schools. The special service and sermon still continues each year at Newark parish church, attended by the mayor and members of the corporation, and a small loaf is now given to each of the members of the choir in remembrance of their benefactor.

For St Constantine's Day, *see* **9 March: St Constantine's Day**.

*

SECOND MONDAY IN MARCH

Commonwealth Day

Empire Day was inaugurated in 1901 and celebrated on 24 May, to mark the achievements of the British Empire. It was a day of popular festivity, but as the empire gradually disintegrated during the twentieth century, the patriotic fervour of the day became increasingly anachronistic. In 1958, it was renamed Commonwealth Day, and in 1977 the Commonwealth nations chose a new day for the celebrations – the second Monday in March – which is now celebrated in each country of the Commonwealth. The way in which the day is celebrated is deliberately left to each country to decide, although common themes are education, the benefits of democracy, and international links and cooperation. The Queen gives a special Commonwealth Day speech.

See also **24 May: Empire Day**.

*

St Patrick's Day Parade, Huddersfield

12 MARCH

St Gregory's Day

Pope Gregory the Great (*c*.540–604) holds a key position in the history of Christianity in England, as it was he who sent Augustine to convert the Anglo-Saxons. His feast day was thus given a high profile and celebrated in the early English Church, but this popularity does not seem to have translated into secular regard, and no known traditional customs took place on his day. Nevertheless, in the late 1930s, A. R. Wright and T. E. Lones reported from Lancashire:

> *The farmer and the cottager deem it necessary, in order to obtain a good crop of onions, to sow the seed on St. Gregory's day, which is called 'Gregory-gret onion'.*

*

17 MARCH

St Patrick's Day

St Patrick (*c*.390–*c*.461), the patron saint of Ireland, is enthusiastically celebrated wherever Irish people have settled. He was formerly famous all over the English-speaking world for bringing Christianity to Ireland, although the heroic, almost single-handed nature of his ministry has been greatly exaggerated and his two most famous exploits – banning all snakes from Ireland, and using the shamrock to explain the doctrine of the Trinity to doubting heathens – are much later accretions to his legend.

The key feature of his day has long been the wearing of the symbols of Irishness: the shamrock, the harp, the colour green, and, previously, a St Patrick's cross. The first mention of the shamrock as a national symbol is found in the early 1680s. The same source also describes the wearing of crosses on St Patrick's Day,

Pudding-Pies

A number of different special or festive dishes went by the local name 'pudding-pies' in various parts of the country. In 1869, for example, *Notes & Queries* recorded that at Deddington Fair in Oxfordshire, principally a livestock mart held on St Cecilia's Day (22 November):

... woe betides the farmer when he gets home from the gathering, if he has not brought home some 'pudding-pies' ... These are made by setting up a crust composed of flour mixed with milk or water, and mutton suet melted and poured into it hot. These crusts, which are set up like meat pie-crusts, are then placed in the sun for a day or two to stiffen. They vary in size from about three to four inches in diameter, and are about one inch deep. When thoroughly hard they are filled with the same materials as plum puddings are made of, and when baked are sold at twopence, threepence and fourpence each.

But in Kent in 1912, pudding-pies were quite different:

Throughout Lent the shops at Gravesend (Kent) sell 'pudding pies' (tartlets containing custard sprinkled with currants), and some people call the first Sunday in Lent 'Pudding-pie Sunday'. But I have been told that the pudding-pies should be eaten on the Sunday nearest the middle of Lent, i.e. Mothering Sunday.

Many other sources state that 'pudding-pies' were appropriate to Lent.

and for centuries the two symbols existed side by side. Jonathan Swift, for example, wrote to his 'Stella' (Esther Johnson) from London in 1713:

The Irish folks were disappointed that the Parliament did not meet today, because it was St. Patrick's day; and the Mall was so full of crosses that I thought all the world was Irish.

The sight of Irish children wearing crosses made of coloured paper or card, decorated with silks and ribbons, on this day was a regular occurrence until the early twentieth century. However, shamrocks and harps eventually took over. In her *Lincolnshire Calendar*, Maureen Sutton records that in the 1940s:

My grandmother would send my brothers and I a little Irish harp made from cardboard and covered in green, white and gold silk, it was lovely. We wore it to school on the day, or a bunch of shamrock pinned to our coat.

Today, in urban areas with large Irish populations, grand St Patrick's Day dances are held, although even in Ireland these major celebrations of St Patrick's Day appear to be a relatively recent phenomenon.

Beyond these celebrations by Irish communities, the day does not seem to have been marked by any other traditional customs in England. Indeed, John Brand's *Popular Antiquities* (1849) and A. R. Wright and T. E. Lones's *British Calendar Customs: England* (1936–40), which are the key texts for customs research, list no English events for the day at all. Perhaps the 'Irish' nature of the day was simply too strong to warrant any competition. Nevertheless, as with the wearing of Welsh leeks on **1 March**, donning the Irish national emblem in England has frequently caused friction by bringing local tensions to the fore, and latent anti-Irish feelings, one of the least-attractive traits of English society, can often be seen below the surface. On 17 March 1944, two English women working in a munitions factory in Croydon recorded in their diary:

St. Patrick's Day today and a great many Irish melodies on Music While You Work [a BBC radio programme]. Poor Moroney says that since the banning of travel to Ireland the people in the factory who don't like him make his life a burden to him by jibing at Ireland and the Irish.

In an unrelated tradition, recorded in Robert Chambers' *Book of Days*, it was reported that 'The early English calendars pretend that on the 17th of March Noah entered the Ark (*introitus Noae in arcam*) and they add, under 29th of April, *Egressus Noae de arca*' (Noah left the Ark).

*

Wiggs

'Wiggs' is a dialect word for a cake or bun, known virtually all over the country but meaning quite different things in each area. Correspondence on the subject published in *Notes & Queries* in 1874 includes descriptions as diverse as: an ordinary tea-cake (Durham and Northumberland); an elongated bun with carraway seeds (Lincolnshire); a plum bun (Lincolnshire); an oval cake with honey in the middle (Hampshire); and a plain half-penny bun (Bristol). The word has a long and respectable lineage, with the *OED* providing citations from 1376, including one from Good Friday (8 April) 1664, when Samuel Pepys ate a Lenten supper of 'wiggs and ale'.

BRAGGOT SUNDAY

'Braggot Sunday' is a colloquial name for Mid-Lent or **Mothering Sunday** (*see below*), in recognition of one of the popular drinks of the day, variously spelled 'braggot', 'bragget', and 'bracket'. The precise composition of the drink varied, but it usually consisted of fermented honey and ale, and was therefore akin to mead or metheglin, and a byword for sweetness; in *The Miller's Tale*, Chaucer wrote 'Hir mouth was swete as bragot or the meeth.'

*

MOTHERING SUNDAY

Mothering Sunday occurs on the fourth Sunday in Lent, otherwise known as Mid-Lent Sunday, and can fall anywhere between 1 March and 4 April. It was one of the few vernacular customs which was universally regarded as a good thing, and which therefore attracted no reformers who wanted it abolished. On this day, young people (usually women) who were working away from home would try to get back to visit their families, and, typically, bring them presents and share a family meal.

The two earliest references show that the custom was already well established in the mid seventeenth century. The first is from the diary of Richard Symonds, published in 1644:

Every mid-Lent Sunday is a great day in Worcester, when all the children and god-children meet at the head and chief of the family and have a feast. They call it the Mothering-day.

The second is from *Hesperides* (1648), the well-known collection of poems by Robert Herrick:

I'll to thee a simnell bring
Gainst thou go'st a mothering.

These and almost all the other references to Mothering Sunday come from either the western counties of England, or from Wales, and it seems likely that it was a regional custom that gradually spread across the rest of the country; however, it was apparently never universal, as a correspondent to the *Gentleman's Magazine* of 1784 commented:

I happened to reside last year near Chepstow in Monmouthshire, and there for the first time heard of Mothering Sunday.

In its traditional form, it just about lasted into the twentieth century. The folklore collector Ella M. Leather commented that in Herefordshire in 1912:

The pretty custom of going a-mothering on Mid-Lent Sunday was generally kept up until a few years by the country people, and is now by no means forgotten, but declining. The confectioners' shops in Hereford are well stocked with Simnel cakes during Lent; they have an inscription in sugar icing, 'For my dear mother', or 'Mother'. Formerly these cakes were always made by the donors.

Various special foods have been recorded as traditional Mothering Sunday fare, including veal, rice pudding, and **frumenty** (p. 390), but by far the most common delicacy was the simnel cake, mentioned by Herrick in 1648 and again by Mrs Leather in 1912. Unfortunately, there seems to be no agreement on what constitutes a proper simnel, and Shrewsbury, Devizes, and Bury each claimed to have the *real* one. Folklorist Charlotte

Mothering Sunday at St Jude's, Southwark, March 1936

Burne described one version from her own experience in Shropshire in 1883:

> They are very rich plum-cakes, encased in a crust of flour-and-water, coloured with saffron. They are made round, and rather flat, with a curiously-scalloped upper edge, and are first boiled for several hours, then brushed over with egg, and baked. Simnels are made in other towns besides Shrewsbury – notably Bury, in Lancashire – but the curious saffron crust and the singular manner of preparing the cake seem to be peculiar to our county.

She reprinted her grandmother's recipe for Bury simnels in the journal *Folk-Lore* in 1909:

> To 3 lbs of flour add 3 lbs of currants, ½ lb of butter rubbed into the flour, 2 oz of candied lemon, 1½ oz of bitter almonds, ½ oz of cinnamon, ¾ lb of loaf sugar,

the rinds of 2 large lemons, ½ lb of yeast, 5 eggs, the whites and yokes beaten separately, and a pint of cream. Mix it together and make it up immediately into simnels (i.e. in the shape described above). Let them stand to rise well on the tins, and bake in a moderate oven.

The word 'simnel' is attested in English at least from about 1300, coming to us from the French, but ultimately deriving from the Latin *simila* or 'fine flour'. Nevertheless, the traditional tale which explains the name is more colourful, as in this version from Shropshire, printed in Robert Chambers' *Book of Days* in 1864:

> Long ago there lived an honest old couple, boasting the names of Simon and Nelly, but their surnames are not known. It was their custom at Easter to gather their children about them, and thus meet

together once a year under the old homestead. The fasting season of Lent was just ending, but they had still left some of the unleavened dough which had been from time to time converted into bread during the forty days. Nelly was a careful woman, and it grieved her to waste anything, so she suggested that they should use the remains of the Lenten dough for the basis of a bake to regale the assembled family. Simon readily agreed to the proposal and further reminded his partner that there were still some remains of their Christmas plum pudding hoarded up in the cupboard, and that this might form the interior, and be an agreeable surprise to the young people when they made their way through the less tasty crust. So far, all things went on harmoniously; but when the cake was made, a subject of violent discord arose, Sim insisting that it should be boiled, while Nell no less obstinately contended that it should be baked. The dispute ran from words to blows, for Nell, not choosing to let her province in the household be thus interfered with, jumped up and threw the stool she was sitting on at Sim, who on his part seized a besom, and applied it with right good will to the head and shoulders of his spouse. She now seized the broom, and the battle became so warm, that it might have had a very serious result, had not Nell proposed as a compromise that the cake should be boiled first, and afterwards baked. This Sim acceded to, for he had no wish for further acquaintance with the heavy end of the broom. Accordingly, the big pot was set on the fire, and the stool broken up and thrown on to boil it, whilst the besom and broom furnished fuel for the oven. Some eggs, which had been broken in the scuffle, were used to coat the outside of the pudding when boiled, which gave it the shining gloss it possesses as a cake. This new and remarkable production in the art of confectionary became known by the name of the cake of Simon and Nelly, but soon only the first half of each name was alone preserved and joined together, and it has ever since been known as the cake of Sim-Nel, or Simnel.

The festival of Mothering Sunday was somewhat hijacked by Christian writers who declared, on no evidence other than the word 'mother', that the day had originally been the day on which people went home to visit their 'mother' church. Nevertheless, it is the churches that have kept its memory alive into recent times. In post-war Britain, child- and mother-centred services became customary, as a letter to *The Times* (4 April 1954) makes clear:

> *I should like to point out that Mothering Sunday in our village has not died out, but is a great occasion for the children. The older children go as a family to Holy Communion in the early morning, and in the afternoon the Sunday School children take their mothers to the Parish Church. Each takes its mother to the altar to receive a posy. A large iced cake made especially for the occasion by young wives of the church is blessed and a piece given to each parent. The Mid-Lent service is a red-letter day for the children.*

But in the same timeframe, for non church-goers, Mothering Sunday has been almost completely eclipsed by the imported **Mother's Day** (*see below*).

See also **Shrovetide and Lent**, p. 49; **Braggot Sunday**, p. 81.

*

MOTHER'S DAY

Mother's Day was first suggested in 1907 by Miss Anna Jarvis, a schoolteacher in Philadelphia, who wished to do something to commemorate her own mother and, by extension, mothers everywhere. As a direct result of her energetic lobbying, Congress recognized the new day in 1913 and set it at the second Sunday in May.

In 1916, there were attempts by Mr J. A. Whitehead of Richmond, director of Whitehead Aircraft Ltd, and his friends, to introduce a similar day in Britain. The idea was enthusiastically supported by many celebrities of the day, including the Queen, the Bishop of London, and Lady Haig, and for a few years *The Times* made an annual announcement of the chosen date, in early August. There is little doubt that the new initiative was a symptom of the rise in national sentiment occasioned by involvement in the First World War, and little is heard of the idea after 1920. However, it appeared again in Britain soon after the Second World War, probably as a result of a similar upsurge in feeling and the influence of American servicemen. Its real success this time was due to commercial interests in the following decades, when the opportunity was taken to create a new market for cards and other gift items. In Britain, the new Mother's Day got tangled up with the existing **Mothering Sunday** (*see above*), which was also undergoing a strong revival at the time, encouraged by the Church of England, and for decades the two existed side by side. But Mother's Day rapidly gained the upper hand, and it is probably true to say that except in church-going families, where Mothering Sunday is still enthusiastically kept up, Mothering Sunday is forgotten. If the wording on the cards available in shops is anything to go by, Mother's Day wins hands-down.

*

19 MARCH

St Joseph's Day

As the husband of the Virgin Mary, St Joseph has naturally featured in numerous legends, and he has had plenty of devotees over the centuries; however, his day does not seem to have attracted any widespread traditional lore in England. Nevertheless, in her *Lincolnshire Calendar* (1997), Maureen Sutton did report the following advice: 'On St. Joseph's Day throw away the warming pan.'

*

21 MARCH

St Benedict's Day

Benedict, founder of the influential Benedictine monastic order, was born around the year 480 and died on 21 March, around 550. His feast was therefore traditionally celebrated on the day of his death, but in the Roman Catholic Church it has been moved to 11 July. As with the other saints whose feast days fall at this time of year, Benedict's name is usually invoked in regard to weather and crops. The *Transactions of the Devonshire Association* (1973) recorded:

> *Where the wind is on 21 March it will prevail for the summer.*

And in John Ray's *English Proverbs* (1670):

> *Saint Benedick*
> *Sow thy pease or keep them in thy rick.*

*

WEEKDAY IN LATE MARCH

Oranges and Lemons Service

The church of St Clement Danes, which sits on a traffic island in the middle of the Strand in London, was built by Sir Christopher Wren in 1682, although the tower and spire were added by others at a later date. The first church on the site was believed to have been built by Danes, who settled nearby; hence the church's name. The church was very badly damaged by bombing in the Second World War, and when restored in the 1950s it became the official RAF church, dedicated to the memory of Allied airmen killed serving their country.

St Clement Danes has laid strong claim to be the church mentioned in the famous 'Oranges and Lemons' nursery rhyme, and a carillon that was installed in 1920 plays the tune every day at 9 a.m., 12 noon, 3 p.m. and 6 p.m., for all to enjoy. An annual children's service began that same year, and this still takes place in late March, attended by the pupils of St Clement Danes Primary School, which is itself over 300 years old. At the end of the service, the children are each given an orange and a lemon.

The 'Oranges and Lemons' rhyme is first recorded *c.*1744, but it is not unique, being simply the best known of several rhymes based on local church bells reported in various parts of the country. There is no way of knowing whether St Clement Danes is the one mentioned in the rhyme, as there is another London church dedicated to the same saint not far away in Eastcheap.

See also **23 November: St Clement's Day**.

*

25 MARCH

Annunciation/Lady Day

This feast, commonly called Lady Day, celebrates the day on which the Angel Gabriel visited Mary and announced the conception of Christ (as related in Luke 1:26–38). Once the birth of Christ had been fixed at 25 December, it was a simple matter to count back nine months to set the date of the conception. For early

Oranges and Lemons service at St Clement Danes church, London, *c.*1998

Christians, the Annunciation, rather than the Nativity, was seen as the start of the Christian era, and 25 March was therefore viewed as the real New Year's Day. This had serious long-term repercussions on the way the calendar developed in England (*see* p. xx).

Since at least late medieval times, Lady Day has been regarded as one of the key 'rent days' in the year – the time when rents and other legal payments were due, contracts were made, and periods of employment began or ended; although not always counted as one of the official 'quarter days', it retained this feature in many communities up and down the country. It was also a particularly popular time for **hiring fairs** (p. 345) and the merrymaking associated with such gatherings. In 1926, the *Transactions of the Devonshire Association* recorded:

Although servants are hired from Lady Day, they would not think of going to a new place until after the following Tuesday, which is known as 'Burgening

[Bargaining] day'. On that day they go to Bideford market [in Devon]*, meet each other and, if they have not already done so, make their 'burgens' with their future employers.*

Tichborne Dole

One of the most famous surviving charity doles in the country takes place every year at Tichborne in Hampshire. Each year, on Lady Day, the inhabitants of Tichborne and Cheriton, near Winchester, are entitled to visit the big house at Tichborne Park to collect a gallon of flour for each adult (half a gallon for children), provided by the descendants of the Tichborne family, who have been prominent in village affairs since at least 1166. The flour is first blessed, and a short prayer said to remember Lady Mabella, the supposed originator of the dole. The flour is then dispensed from a large wooden hopper into the sacks and pillowcases brought by the locals.

The Tichborne Dole, by Gillis van Tilborgh, 1671

Doles like these were common in England in the past, and many villages had similar distributions, but few have survived. Like the similar custom in Biddenden in Kent (*see* **Easter Monday: Biddenden Maids Charity**, p. 122), the Tichborne Dole is particularly memorable because of the unique, and suitably romantic, story of its origin.

In the time of Henry II (1154–89), as the much-loved Lady Mabella lay on her deathbed, she piously requested that her husband, Sir Roger Tichborne, should inaugurate an annual distribution of flour in her name to the poor. We know that he was not pleased with the suggestion, but we are not told the reason for his extreme response. He pulled a burning brand from the fire, and said that she could have as much land for her charity as she could walk around before the brand went out. As she was bedridden, this must have seemed a safe bet, but she called her servants to carry her outside and she managed to crawl round twenty-three acres before the flame went out. This land was thereafter known as 'The Crawls'. But Mabella was not finished yet. Not trusting her husband to keep his promise, she laid a curse on anyone who interfered with the annual dole, stating that if they did so, there would be a generation of seven

sons, followed by one of seven daughters, the family would die out, and the house would fall down.

Needless to say, effective as this story is, it is almost certainly a fabrication and was quite possibly invented to explain why the fields were called 'The Crawls'. No serious discussion can begin until some basic questions are asked: when was the dole itself, the Lady Mabella story, and the field name 'The Crawls' first recorded? It would also be interesting to know if an alternative origin was recorded before this story became current. At present the Mabella story cannot be shown to go back very far. It was already in circulation by 1855, when Francis Baigent published his article on Mabella's genealogy, 'On the Family of de Lymerston', in the *Journal of the British Archaeological Association*, where he rightly calls the story 'the traditionary legend', but no earlier written version has yet come to light. Nevertheless, there is evidence that the dole itself is much earlier, as the painting of the event carried out by the Flemish painter Gillis van Tilborgh in 1671 shows the family dispensing basket-loads of loaves.

There is another aspect of Tichborne history that has a strong bearing on the survival of this dole, and it explains why this little village in Hampshire was very much a household name in the middle years of Victoria's reign. In 1862, when the current baronet, Sir James Tichborne, died, the search began for his son and heir, Roger, who had travelled abroad nine years before. Roger's mother refused to believe him dead, advertised for information, and employed investigators in Australia to find him. In 1866, a man appeared who claimed to be the missing Roger, and although he had some supporters, and Lady Tichborne herself seemed to believe him, civil court proceedings were commenced to prove the claim, followed by criminal court proceedings against the claimant, which lasted until 1874. The man was revealed as a complete impostor – he was actually a man named Arthur Orton – and he was sentenced to fourteen years for perjury. The story of 'the Tichborne Claimant', or, after a while, simply 'the Claimant', was hugely popular in newspapers and magazines of the time, and was one of the most celebrated stories of the late nineteenth century. Countless articles, pamphlets, books, stories, and even songs were written about the case, and everybody in the country knew all the intimate details of the affair. In their search for something interesting to say about the village, journalists of the time also printed the story of the charity and its supposed origin with Sir Roger and Mabella in the twelfth century, thus ensuring that this explanation for this dole gained widespread publicity. *See also* **Doles**, *right*.

*

CARE OR CARLING SUNDAY

Care or Carling Sunday is the fifth Sunday in Lent, also known as Passion Sunday. The name 'Carling Sunday' is derived from the custom most often reported for this day, the eating of 'carlings', as in the following record from Yorkshire in 1810:

> *The rustics go to the public house and spend each their carling-groat in drink, for their carlings are provided for them gratis.*

'Carlings' were usually grey peas steeped overnight in water, then fried in butter the next day and seasoned with pepper, although at least one account describes them as being served with sugar and rum, a more

Continues on page 90 >

Doles

Charity has always been a Christian obligation, and there have always been people who took this duty very seriously. Although there were particular days when charity was expected from the living (*see*, for example, **21 December: St Thomas's Day**), there was also a strong and long-lasting tradition for people of means to make wills in which they left money or provisions to the local poor or some other deserving group. Most of these bequests consisted of a single donation, but some people opted to set up a long-term 'dole' in which something – money, food, clothes, or fuel – was distributed to local people on a regular basis, usually annually. Most doles were set up with a mixture of motives, but often the testator wished simply to be remembered. None of us like to think that we will be forgotten after death, and in a belief system that incorporated the idea that souls lingered in Purgatory instead of going straight to Heaven, the thought was particularly frightening. Souls could be helped on their way by the masses and prayers of the living, and much ingenuity was therefore spent in devising ways to ensure that the deceased was brought to people's minds at least once a year, for evermore. Nevertheless, it would be too cynical to imply that the testators' motives were always purely selfish and only concerned with the fate of their own soul. Bequests such as money, food, coal, and blankets made a real difference to the poor, and although a penny loaf a year does not sound much to modern ears, if there were several such doles in a parish, the cumulative effect could be impressive. For those living close to subsistence level, a little goes a long way.

After the Reformation, masses and obits were banned, and in many cases they were replaced by commemorative sermons. A graveside dole is a particularly effective way of ensuring that the recipients connect the gifts with the name of the donor (*see*, for example, **Maundy Thursday: Henry Travice Charity** (p. 101) and **Good Friday: Hartfield Dole** (p. 109)), while other benefactors requested that the first charge on the charity be the cleaning and repair of their tomb. However, those who wished to set up such a charity had to ensure that there remained sufficient money to cover both the dole itself and the costs of its administration over a long period. Some simply left a sum of money to be invested, so that the profits could be used to support the charity, but a safer method was to leave land that could be rented out year after year, and the rent used to support the purposes of the charity. Generally, the only institution that existed to serve the whole community, and was likely to continue to do so in perpetuity, was the Church, and it was common for legacy-writers to name the local vicar as administrator or chief trustee.

The recipients of charity doles varied considerably, according to the whim of the deceased. Some simply stipulated 'the poor', but many named specific groups such as twelve widows, four old men, six women who had lost their husbands by drowning, those born in a particular street (*see* **21 June: Brecknell Bequest**), or the current cast at Drury Lane Theatre (*see* **6 January: Baddeley Cake**). Yet others sought to help the young by sponsoring apprenticeships, rewarding good behaviour in certain trades, or encouraging pious education; and some tried to provide a service to the community in the form of a field on which the rushes could be grown to be strewn in church, or money to repair the church, to provide new bell ropes, or to repair the town bridge.

Many thousands of these charities were created from the early modern period up to the early nineteenth century. Some were straightforward and sensible, others were eccentric, but over the generations they often evolved in peculiar ways, accumulating and losing details as circumstances changed. In many cases, the original documents were lost and the doles developed into traditional customs, acquiring legends to explain their origin.

But what looks like a completely random set of traditions can be seen on closer inspection to display recurrent details and patterns, which may help to chart the development of doles. One regular motif is the moving of a dole from the church to the church-yard, as religious sensibilities changed or the dole

became too rowdy. Sometimes the dole was moved off church premises entirely. Another common element is the distribution of items by throwing them to crowds of people, to be scrambled for (*see* **Scrambling Customs**, p. 128; **Easter Monday: Hallaton Hare Pie and Bottle-Kicking**, p. 126; and **Whit Sunday: St Briavels Bread and Cheese Dole**, p. 193). Charities so often specify bread and cheese as the fare to be distributed, that land set aside for such purposes often became known locally as 'Bread and Cheese Land', as at Biddenden in Kent (*see* **Easter Monday: Biddenden Maids Charity**. p. 122).

Many simply gave out bread or buns, without gimmicks; for surviving examples of these doles, *see* **March: Dame Elizabeth Marvyn Charity** at Ufton in Berkshire, **Easter Tuesday: Tuppenny Starvers** in Bristol (p. 132), and **24 August: Sandwich Bun Race** in Kent. In more than one instance, the local vicar was expected to provide food and drink on a particular day. At Drayton Beauchamp in Buckinghamshire, for example, a long-standing custom developed in which anyone who wished could present themselves at the rectory on St Stephen's Day (26 December) and consume as much bread, cheese, and ale as they wished, at the vicar's expense. When the custom began to get out of hand in the early nineteenth century, the incumbent replaced it with a money dole (which the locals called 'Stephening money'), which in turn was abused. No evidence could be found to explain how it had started or if there was any legal obligation involved, and the whole affair was stopped *c*.1827.

There is no doubt that some of the bequests were eccentric, even by the standards of the time. But some of the bizarre details make some sense on closer inspection. Thomas Gray, for example, who composed his will in 1691, left money to buy land at Castle Donnington, so that the profits of that property could be used:

. . . to lay out six nobles yearly to buy six waistcoats of grey cloth, edged with blue galloon lace, and 40s to buy three coats of grey cloth, to be faced with baize; and that four of the said waistcoats should be given yearly to four poor widows . . .

It is clear that he wished his recipients to be distinguished by wearing a kind of uniform, and he specified its basic colour as a pun on his name.

Not everyone was in favour of such charity. Even as early as the mid seventeenth century, Sir William Petty (1623–87) wrote in his will:

As for legacies to the poor, I am at a stand; as for beggars by trade and election, I give them nothing; as for impotents by the hand of God, the public ought to maintain them; as for those who have no calling or estate, they should be put upon their kindred; as for those who can get no work, the magistrates should cause them to be employed, which may be well done in Ireland, where is fifteen acres of improvable land for every head; prisoners for crimes, by the king; for debts, by their prosecutors; as for those who compassionate the sufferings of any object, let them relieve themselves by relieving such sufferers – that is, give them alms pro re nata, and for God's sake, relieve the several species above mentioned, if the above-mentioned obligees fail in their duties. Wherefore, I am contented that I have assisted all my poor relations, and put many in a way of getting their own bread, and have laboured in public works, and by inventions have sought out real objects of charity; and I do hereby conjure all who partake of my estate, from time to time, to do the same at their peril. Nevertheless, to answer custom, and to take the surer side, I give £20 to the most wanting of the parish, in which I may die.

By the late nineteenth century, many doles had disappeared. The money had run out, the trustees could not be bothered to administer them, or the original terms were forgotten; sometimes, more honourably, the money had been put to more relevant charitable causes. But enough doles survived for them to be regarded as major nuisances, and some even argued that they were counterproductive. A writer in *The Times* in 1889 complained of a woman who had received a sixpence dole in church and gone straight to a public house to spend it on gin. The problem that exercised Victorian minds – and one that can still be heard in the rhetoric of politicians today – is how to help the 'deserving poor' without subsidizing the idle and wicked. A correspondent to *The Times* in 1898 spoke for many on this point:

In the course of 30 years' ministry in a rural parish, overdone with dole charities, of 1300 souls, it has been my duty as trustee to take part in distributing no less a sum in the aggregate than £7000 in gratuitous doles of money, flour, and clothing, of which it may be affirmed that as far as the conferring of any substantial and permanent blessing on the beneficiaries is concerned, it would have been much better to have thrown this money into the sea; the only apparent result being to raise unduly cottage rents . . . I cannot recall in my long experience an instance of gratitude on the part of any receiver of a dole, which is invariably regarded as a due, while nothing develops more quickly than the latent suspicion that the poor are being robbed of their rights, or breeds more fruitfully mutual jealousy and uncharitableness than any effort which may be made to deal with those doles so that the deserving and thrifty may be assisted and the shiftless and undeserving excluded.

Only a handful of doles remain today. There is a daily dole at Winchester in Hampshire (*see* **Daily Customs: Wayfarers' Dole**, p. 421) and a weekly one at Woodbridge in Suffolk (*see* **Weekly Customs: John Sayer Charity**, p. 424). Some struggle to find enough recipients, while others such as the one at Biddenden in Kent and Tichborne in Hampshire (*see* **25 March: Tichborne Dole**) are nationally known, having become part of our folk heritage, and are in little danger of disappearing.

interesting variation. Eating carlings on this day was common across the northern counties of England and in lowland Scotland, but it does not seem to have been found south of Cheshire or Lancashire.

The serving of peas and beans during Lent is no surprise, as pulses were an important staple when meat was forbidden, and it is most likely that the name 'carling' is derived from 'care' and not, as many other writers have presumed, that 'care' is derived from 'carling'. As the period of Lent progressed towards Holy Week, leading up to Good Friday and the commemoration of the Crucifixion, it was a time of increasing gloom for devout Christians, and various days in the sequence took on the term 'care'; thus 'Care Friday' and 'Care Week', in addition to 'Care Sunday'. The derivation of the word has excited much debate, but it seems quite clear that it is ultimately derived from Germanic roots in which 'kar' signified 'mourning' and was strongly attached to Holy Week in the same way as 'Care' was in this country. In English, the meaning of the word 'care' has changed over the years, but in its older form it signified sorrow, trouble, and grief, and was thus appropriate for the season.

See also **Shrovetide and Lent**, p. 49.

*

MARCH/APRIL

Borrowed Days

A widespread traditional saying, reported from all quarters of the British Isles since at least the mid sixteenth century, maintains that March borrowed three days from April; the last three days in March are therefore called the 'Borrowed Days' or 'Borrowing Days'. There is much confusion about the precise nature of this interchange and its result, however. If March had borrowed days from April, it would seem logical for the last three days in March to be warmer and milder than they should be for that time of year, and for three days in April to be unseasonably cold. Indeed, some of the recorded examples are clearly based on this reading of the situation:

[North of Ireland, 1852] *Give me (says March) three days of warmth and sunshine for my poor young*

lambs whilst they are yet too tender to bear the roughness of my wind and rain, and you shall have them repaid when the wool is grown.

Another assessment of the relative mildness of the months in question, as quoted in *Notes & Queries* in 1852, has a similar positive outlook:

[c.1709] *The three last days of March are called 'the Borrowing Days' in Scotland, on account of their being generally attended with very blustering weather, which inclines people to say that they would wish to borrow three days from the month of April in exchange for the last days of the month of March.*

But these views of the March/April swap, which are perhaps down to wishful rewriting or simple misunderstanding, are completely out of step with the vast majority of recorded versions. Most state unequivocally that the three borrowed days bring bad weather, as in John Brockett's *Glossary of North Country Words* (1846):

March borrowed of April
Three days, and they were ill
The one was sleet, the other was snow
The third was the worst that e'er did blow.

An alternative version of the third day was that it 'froze the birds' legs to the trees'. In addition to being the commonest reading, the extreme nature of the three days is found in all the earliest known versions, from the *Complaynt of Scotland* of 1548, onwards, and it is most probably the original meaning.

A motive for this deal between the two months is not usually provided, but some versions state that it is to kill or frighten some sheep, as in another Scottish example from Chambers' *Book of Days* (1864):

March said to April
I see three hoggs [young sheep] *upon a hill*
And if you'll lend me days three
I'll find a way to make them dee.

In most cases a reason for the need to kill the sheep is not given, but occasionally it is implied that the sheep were the bribe in the deal between the months.

To complicate matters still further, some versions of the story say that March borrowed three days from

February, or even that February borrowed them from January. And in other accounts, it was not simply a question of bad weather on these days, as noted in R. T. Hampson's *Medii Aevi Kalendarium* (1841):

> They who are very superstitious will neither borrow
> nor lend on any of those days, and if any should
> propose to borrow from them, they would esteem
> it an evidence that the person wished to employ
> the article borrowed for the purposes of witchcraft
> against the lender.

Moreover, H. P. Whitcombe records in his *Bygone Days* (1874):

> The first three days in March were formerly called
> 'blind days', and the farmer considered them
> unlucky; they would never sow any seed at that
> time . . .

According to *Notes & Queries* of 1903, France and Spain have similar beliefs about Borrowed Days.

April

2
HOLY WEEK MONDAY
Bourne Running Auction

3

4

9
EASTER MONDAY
Biddenden Maids Charity
Black Knight of Ashton
Epping Stag Hunt
Gawthorpe Coal-Carrying
Hallaton Hare Pie and Bottle-
    Kicking
Harness Horse Parade

10
**EASTER MONDAY AND
    TUESDAY**
Lifting
EASTER TUESDAY
Holly Bussing
Tuppenny Starvers

11

16
HOCKTIDE

17
Hungerford Hocktide Court

18
**TWO WEEKS AFTER
    EASTER**
Spital Sermon

23
ST GEORGE'S DAY

24
ST MARK'S EVE

25
ST MARK'S DAY

30
MAY DAY EVE

*Moveable events have been placed
on the date they fall in 2007.
Events dependent on the timing
of Easter are coloured green.*

1
ALL FOOLS' DAY
PALM SUNDAY
Caistor Gad-Whip Ceremony
Martinsell Hill
Pax Cakes
Water

5
John Stow Commemoration
MAUNDY THURSDAY
Henry Travice Charity
Peter's Pence

6
Flitting Day
Tatworth Candle Auction
GOOD FRIDAY
Butterworth Charity
Hartfield Dole
Tinsley Green Marbles
Washing Molly Grime
Widow's Son

7
EASTER SATURDAY
Bacup Coco-Nut Dancers

8
EASTER DAY
Greenwich Fair
Old Ball
Pace-Egging
Pace-Egg Plays
Riding the Lord

12

13

14

15
LOW SUNDAY

19
PRIMROSE DAY

20

21
Queen Elizabeth II's Birthday

22

26

27

28

29

Sun Dancing

Candle Auctions

Great Barmote Court

Once a year, at the Moot Hall in Wirksworth, right in the centre of the Derbyshire lead-mining district, a court is held that is claimed to be the oldest surviving industrial court in Britain, possibly even the world. The Great Barmote Court, set up by Edward I in 1288, is the official body that regulates the previously lucrative lead-mining industry. Lead-mining had already been carried out for centuries when the lead-rich area of Derbyshire was granted to Edmund, first Earl of Lancaster, in 1265. To encourage exploitation of the natural resource, and make significant money for the Crown at the same time, it was decreed that any man might mine for lead, without hindrance, but a duty would be payable on the extracted ore. There were a few exceptions to the areas that could be mined – churchyards, gardens, orchards, and highways – but every other part of what was known as 'The King's Field', extending over some 115 square miles of the Peak District, was open to all-comers. Even landowners could not stop someone mining their land. The minerals under the ground belonged to the Crown, and only the Crown could forbid people from getting at it.

The Great Barmote Court had widespread powers over those in the industry and even acted as coroner in the event of a fatal accident in a mine; however, the industry began to decline in the late eighteenth century and never recovered its former glory. The court's jurisdiction is now confined to upholding regulations and collecting fees. Nevertheless, it is still regulated by a Barmaster and a Steward, appointed by the Chancellor of the Duchy of Lancaster, and both must be an experienced barrister or solicitor. These officials are aided by a jury of twelve members (previously twenty-four), who hold office until the next meeting. Before the business of the court is carried out, it is customary to provide beer, bread and cheese, clay pipes, and tobacco for those attending.

There were previously two Great Barmote Courts, one at Monyash for the High Peak, and the one at Wirksworth with jurisdiction over the Low Peak, but these are now combined and the one Great Court meets once a year, although Small Barmote Courts can be convened at any time, as necessary.

*

1 APRIL

All Fools' Day

The first of April is the day it is traditional to play tricks on people. Nowadays universally called April Fool's Day, in earlier sources it was almost always given as 'All Fools' Day', parodying the Christian Church's All Souls' Day and All Saints' Day. There have been various local names for those fooled, such as April gowk (cuckoo), or April noddy or noodle.

The origin and development of April Fool's Day remains a mystery. The earliest mention we can find is in John Aubrey's *Remaines of Gentilisme and Judaisme* manuscript (*c*.1686), where he simply states: 'Fooles Holy Day – We observe it on ye first of April . . . and so it is kept in Germany everywhere.' But the complete absence of references to the custom in the plays and poems of the sixteenth and seventeenth centuries, and in the diaries and letters of people like Samuel Pepys, suggests that it was introduced to Britain sometime in the late seventeenth century, not long before Aubrey was writing, and it probably came from France or Germany, where it is known to have existed earlier. However, the custom certainly caught on quickly enough, and it is recorded throughout the eighteenth century in terms which show that everyone was familiar with it.

By the late nineteenth century, writers were beginning to claim that the custom of fooling people was dying out, at least for adults, and since then its demise has been regularly predicted. The tradition was still vigorously followed by children in the 1950s when Iona and Peter Opie were researching their influential book *The Lore and Language of Schoolchildren*, and they give a number of direct quotes from children up and down the country detailing how much fun they could still get from simple traditional jokes. Adults, too, had not entirely given it up at that time, as recorded in the recently published diary of two women working in a wartime aircraft factory in Croydon, edited by Sue Bruley:

Thursday 1 April 1943 – April Fool's Day, which was driven home to us because we found on arrival that the night shift had coated all the handles of

April Fool's Day: the famous 'spaghetti trees' broadcast by the BBC in 1957

the machines with grease! A simple-minded not very funny joke. After this Nancy roamed round the shop, her eyes sparkling and sending about a dozen people, one after the other, on a fool's errand to the time office. She told each one so gravely that they were wanted in the time office, that everyone was taken in and there was quite a procession and the clerks in the time office got quite hysterical.

Nevertheless, local observance seems to have gradually faded in recent decades, and we can probably agree with Maureen Sutton, writing on calendar customs in Lincolnshire in 1997, that 'The custom now seems to be losing some favour, but is still a favourite with the national media.' Newspapers, local and national, do certainly seem keen to keep the game alive, and their seasonal jokes often spoof officialdom and bureauc-

racy. Examples taken at random from a huge file include: the *Guardian* of 1 April 1986, which carried a number of spoof job advertisements on their Public Appointments page for, among other things, a fundraiser for the charity 'Aid to the Ambiguous', a 'Senior Rhubarb Consultant' for West Midlands County Council, and four 'Assistant Generic Complaints Postulators' for South Yorkshire; and the *Croydon Post* of 1 April 1998, which carried a front-page story under the bold headline 'Colour Cars Face Green Ban', written by one April-Fay Solod, who reported that the local council had agreed a plan to alleviate town-centre traffic problems by decreeing that streets could be used on particular days only by cars of a certain colour. These media jokes are following their own tradition, perhaps started by the famous occasion in 1957 when the normally strait-laced BBC broadcasted a report about spaghetti growing on trees in the current affairs programme *Panorama*. Public hoaxes are not new, however. Robert Chambers' *Book of Days* (1864), for example, recorded the following incident:

> . . . *in March 1860, a vast multitude of people received through the post a card* [saying] . . . *'Tower of London – Admit the bearer and friend to view the annual ceremony of washing the white lions, on Sunday April 1st, 1860. Admitted only at the White Gate . . .' The trick is said to have been highly successful. Cabs were rattling about Tower Hill all that Sunday morning, vainly endeavouring to discover the White Gate.*

A correspondent to *Notes & Queries*, however, claimed that this story had been in the newspapers in the mid 1850s, and in his *The Rise and Fall of Merry England* (1996), Ronald Hutton claims that the story appeared in 1698. Certainly, 'Washing lions in the Tower' became something of a saying in its own right, meaning a hoax or wild goose chase.

Apprentices and newcomers in various occupations were particularly likely to be the butt of April Fool's jokes, and they could be sent to fetch items such as straight hooks, left-handed screwdrivers, striped paint, or whatever was relevant to their particular trade. An italic full-stop was popular in the print trade. When the 'fool' asked for each item, the trick was to treat the request seriously, claim not to have it, and to send him/her on to another old hand – 'to hunt the gowk another mile', as the Scots put it.

Since the first descriptions, the core of April foolery was usually this sending of people on fruitless, or sleeveless, errands ('sleeveless', meaning 'futile' and of uncertain origin, has been around since at least 1387, but has long been obsolete). Pigeon's milk, hen's teeth, and a book about Eve's mother are other traditional items that fools were regularly sent to find. The simpler tricks, such as gluing a coin to the floor, leaving a purse or parcel in the street with string attached, pulling coat-tails, and pinning signs or tails to backs, seem to have been a later development, perhaps from the mid nineteenth century onwards, although, as the Opies point out, jokes such as 'Your shoelace is untied!' or 'Your buckle's undone!' have a history of at least 200 years.

As with other children's customs, there is a strict rule that any trickery must cease at midday (*see*, for exam-

ple, **29 May: Royal Oak Day**), and anyone who fails to observe this time-limit is themselves the fool:

> *April first has gone and past*
> *And you're the biggest fool at last.*

This rule has been in place at least since the 1870s.

Over the years, there have been a number of interesting but groundless claims about the origin of April Fool's Day. It has been posited that 1 April was the one day of the year when lunatics were let out of their asylums; it has also been suggested that it was the day that Noah foolishly sent the dove on its fruitless search for dry land, and that it was the day the Romans fooled the Sabine men into bringing their women to town. Tricks are not, of course, restricted to 1 April. In some parts of northern England, May Day was the day for playing tricks (*see* **1 May: May Goslings**), while certain tricks, such as pinning people's clothes together, were traditional on particular days (*see* **6 January: Twelfth Night**). Mischief Night (*see* **31 October: Mischief Night**) also shared some characteristics with April Fool's Day.

*

PALM SUNDAY

Palm Sunday is the sixth Sunday in Lent, the start of Easter or Holy Week, and can fall anywhere between 15 March and 18 April. It commemorates Christ's triumphant entry into Jerusalem on the donkey, when, according to the Gospel of John (12:12–13), the people spontaneously gathered to welcome him, 'Took branches of palm trees, and went forth to meet him, and cried, "Hosanna: Blessed *is* the King of Israel that cometh in the name of the Lord."'

By the Middle Ages, the day was celebrated with elaborate ritual: 'palms' were gathered beforehand, blessed in church, and then waved or strewn in front of a procession of clergy, which could include a wooden donkey on wheels or a picture of Christ riding one. Churches were decorated, and the day was one of joyful celebration, which contrasted markedly with the congregation's deepening gloom as Good Friday approached. At the Reformation, Palm Sunday celebrations were so entrenched that they escaped the reformers' zeal for a while, and in the 1530s they were specifically named as one of the few ceremonies to be spared the axe; however, in 1549 they were suppressed under Edward VI, then reprieved by Mary, and banned again by Elizabeth in 1559. In Catholic countries, and in Catholic churches in Britain, Palm Sunday continued to be celebrated with palm-bearing processions, and this probably helped to keep the original attributes of the day in the public's mind even while the established Church took no official notice.

The key features of the many secular Palm Sunday customs reported from most parts of the country in the nineteenth and twentieth centuries were trips into the countryside, called 'going a-palming' or something similar, to collect catkins, flowers, or other plants, in order to decorate the house or church, make crosses out of them, and wear pieces in buttonholes for the day. The problem for English people, of course, has always been that palms do not grow here, and although some churches have imported the real thing from Spain, several other plants have traditionally been used instead. Box, cypress, hazel, yew, and willow are mentioned in early records as being gathered to decorate homes and churches, but, as Maureen Sutton's *Lincolnshire Calendar* (1997) makes clear, the plant that many held in particular affection was the 'pussy willow', with its attractive catkins:

> We always went out for our Sunday walk, the whole family. Mother liked to take home some pussy-willow, especially for Palm Sunday. Father used to tell us a little rhyme that went: 'I have a little pussy, Her coat is silver grey, I found her in the meadow, Not very far away, My little silver pussy, Will never be a cat, 'Cause she's a pussy-willow, Now what do you think of that?'

Fond memories of a similar custom were included in Flora Thompson's evocation of an Oxfordshire childhood in the 1880s, published as *Lark Rise* in 1939, but earlier accounts, such as the almanac *Time's Telescope* (1826), show that the event was not necessarily so innocent:

> [On the Saturday night] *several hundreds of the workers of East London go with their families to the Sluice House at Hornsey, where, and in the adjacent fields, they carouse till daybreak. Soon afterwards,*

> *they collect their 'palm branches' and, to the best of their ability, make their way home.*

Along the Welsh border, the day was called 'Flowering Sunday', after the custom of decorating graves of deceased friends and relatives with flowers on the day, described by Charlotte Burne in 1883:

> *Popularly, Palm Sunday appears to have been regarded as a sort of anticipatory Easter and [they] are both celebrated in the once (no doubt) common custom of strewing the graves of departed friends with sweet spring flowers. Albrighton churchyard yearly presents a touching sight on Palm Sunday, when all the graves are decked with daffodils and other flowers gathered in the woods and meadows about Boscabel and Whiteladies. I learn from an eye-witness that the display in 1879 was especially brilliant.*

In other places this was done on Easter Sunday. Superstitions gathered round the plants used on Palm Sunday, as they do at all traditional festivals. The plants strewn in the church processions, for example, were eagerly collected afterwards as they were reputed to preserve the house from thunder and lightning.

In the later twentieth century, while Catholic churches were simplifying their Palm Sunday rites, many Anglican churches were busy re-introducing palms into their celebrations for the day, and many church-going people still take note of Palm Sunday, although in a much more restrained way than in previous times.

Caistor Gad-Whip Ceremony

A very odd ceremony formerly took place at Caistor church in Lincolnshire every Palm Sunday. A sale document of 1845 relates how a man would bring a 'gad-whip' into church while the service was in progress:

> *The whip is taken every Palm Sunday by a man from Broughton to the parish of Caistor, who, while the minister is reading the first lesson, cracks it three distinct times in the porch, then folds it neatly up, and retires to a seat. At the commencement of the second lesson, he approaches the minister, and kneeling opposite to him with the whip in his hand, and*

[a] *purse at the end of it, held perpendicularly over his head, waves it thrice, and continues in a steadfast position throughout the whole of the chapter. The ceremony is then concluded. The whip has a leathern purse tied at the end of it, which ought to contain thirty pieces of silver.*

A 'gad-whip' was a heavy cart-whip, and the one used in Caistor was substantial: according to a contributor to *Notes & Queries* in 1901, the whip-stock was 5 feet and 8 inches long, with a heavy lash of white leather of 7 feet and 9 inches.

This custom was described and dissected by many antiquarians in the first half of the nineteenth century and by others since then, but has puzzled them all, particularly as there is no documentary evidence of its origin or early history – there is no sign of it in the property deeds of the manors concerned, and nobody seems to have mentioned it in print before the late eighteenth century. It appears to be a service owed by the Lords of the Manor of Broughton to the owners of Hundon, and presumably it was some sort of condition of tenure, but this is based on supposition. In the absence of any real information regarding its origin, there have been the usual attempts to explain it from internal evidence. One story is that the ceremony was imposed on some early lord of the manor as penance for killing a boy with a whip. Others point to connections between the money in the purse – which some accounts describe as 'thirty pence' – and the thirty pieces of silver paid to Judas in Matthew 26–7, which were the passages traditionally read in church on Palm Sunday, although the biblical verses make no mention of whips or anything similar. Other details are similarly treated, so, for example, the three cracks of the whip have been equated with Peter's three denials.

By the mid nineteenth century, the days of the gad-whip custom were clearly numbered. In 1836, Sir Culling Eardley Smith was Lord of the Manor of Broughton and therefore responsible for maintaining the custom. He petitioned the House of Lords and the Bishop of Lincoln for help in identifying why the custom took place and what would happen to him if he failed to carry it on, with the clear intention of discontinuing it. Moreover, local newspapers began to comment that such antics in church were disgusting and irreverent, although the publicity they gave the ceremony brought crowds to the church to see it. It seems to have faded away *c.*1850.

For another custom that probably owes its existence to manorial obligations, *see* **Ascension Eve: Whitby Penny Hedge**, p. 179.

Figs

Palm Sunday was one of the days also called 'Fig Sunday' in parts of the country, as recorded in the *Folk-Lore Journal* (1885):

This day is called 'Fig Sunday' in Northamptonshire. A girl from Syresham in that county, living in service in Shropshire, received a present of a box of figs and a box of sweets from her mother last Palm Sunday.

Similarly, in *Folk-Lore* (1929), in Oxfordshire:

Palm Sunday is called Fig Sunday and people make fig puddings, 'in remembrance of the barren fig-tree'. Miss Christian remembered one family where the children used to have bags of figs or dates given them on the morning of Palm Sunday.

See **Fig Sunday** (p. 100) for further examples.

Martinsell Hill

Any prominent hill near a village is likely to have been the site of a fair or other gathering, often on 1 May or another special spring day. Martinsell Hill, at the southern end of the Marlborough Downs, overlooking the Vale of Pewsey, was no exception. The site of an impressive 32-acre Iron Age hill fort, it had a fair that took place on Palm Sunday which, apart from fighting and other field sports, was affectionately remembered for the custom of rolling oranges down the slopes, sliding down the hill, and a game that involved hitting a ball up and down the hill with a hockey stick. The annual gathering faded away *c.*1860, and A. G. Bradley, a Wiltshire writer who was born in 1850, was just too late to remember it at first hand:

In the eighteenth and nineteenth centuries, great sports were held up here on Martinsell. The custom still, I believe, survives in picnics for children. But at the original function a part of the programme consisted in sliding down the almost perpendicular

Pax cakes, Hentland, Herefordshire, 1983

*face of the hill seated on the jawbones of horses ... I
can myself remember as a child the well-worn mark
of a slide traced down this three or four hundred
feet of precipitous turf ... All trace, however, of the
historic slide has long vanished. But within the
memory of men only elderly, the pugilists of the
neighbouring villages used to take advantage of
what was left of the ancient festival, and fight out
their battles on the top of Martinsell. These encounters were sometimes so ferocious that unsuccessful
efforts were made to stamp out the festival, which,
however, died a natural death.*

See also **Fairs, Feasts, Wakes, and Revels**, p. 249.

Pax Cakes

In three Herefordshire churches – those of Sellack,
Hentland, and King's Caple – a custom that may be
500 years old takes place every Palm Sunday. After the
normal service, round shortbread biscuits called pax
cakes are handed by the vicar to each of the congregation, with the spoken blessing, 'Peace and good neighbourhood'; these words are also stamped on the cakes,
along with an image of a lamb. The custom is said to
date from the will of Thomas More in 1484, or of Lady
Scudamore in 1570, or both, which provided for a feast
to be held in the church each year, to promote peace
and friendship. The feast may have dwindled to a
biscuit, but the principle is still the same.

See also **Doles**, p. 87.

Water

Palm Sunday was one of several days on which children
customarily collected water from a certain well in the
neighbourhood and mixed it with ingredients such as
sugar, broken sweets, or liquorice in order to make it
into a drink, as in Oxfordshire in 1929:

*On Palm Sunday, which is often referred to as
Spanish Sunday, an old custom still survives. Just over*

Fig Sunday

In many parts of the country, regional dishes with figs as the main ingredient were eaten in great quantities on Palm Sunday, which was often called 'Fig Sunday' as a result. The dishes were sometimes called 'fig-sue' and could be in the form of pies or puddings, varying considerably from place to place. *Notes & Queries* (1856) records that in Staffordshire:

> *The fig-pies are made of dry figs, sugar, treacle, spice, etc. They are rather too luscious for those who are not 'to the manner born'.*

The reasoning behind this custom is not entirely clear. Fig trees are not native to this country, but English people would have been long familiar with imported figs and the many mentions of the plant in the Bible: Adam and Eve used fig leaves to cover their nakedness, and in his parables Jesus speaks of cursing a fig tree which bore no fruit when he was hungry (Matthew 21:19–21) and of the barren tree which the gardener offered to save with manure (Luke 13:6–9). The most plausible explanation of the strong link between the fig and Palm Sunday is that, as related by Matthew, Christ had wanted to eat figs on his way into Jerusalem. Nevertheless, in many parts of the country, the customary day for indulging in figs was Mid-Lent Sunday or even Good Friday, so this explanation may not be as convincing as it first appears. According to C. F. Tebbutt, folklorist of Huntingdonshire, fig puddings were still popular in St Neots in 1950.

Traditional recipes for fig pie and fig pudding can be found in Florence White's *Good Things in England* (1932), which includes the following, entitled 'Mrs. Hart's Fig Pudding (Worcestershire)':

> *½ lb breadcrumbs; ½ lb figs; ½ lb moist sugar; 6 oz suet; ½ nutmeg; 2 eggs; wine sauce. Time to boil 4 hours. 1) Mince the figs very very small; 2) Mince the suet very very fine; 3) Mix bread-crumbs, figs, sugar, suet, nutmeg, all together very well; 4) Moisten with the eggs which should first be well beaten; 5) Put in a greased mould or basin, cover well with greased paper and steam, 4½ hours; 6) Turn out and serve with wine sauce.*

the boundary, in the parish of Wilcote, is an old well of beautiful clear water, surrounded by a wall, with stone steps going down to it. It is called the Lady's Well, and on Palm Sunday the girls go there and take bottles with Spanish juice (liquorice), fill the bottles, walk round the well, and drink.

See also **Easter Monday: Water** (p. 130) for further examples.

*

HOLY WEEK MONDAY

Bourne Running Auction

By the terms of Matthew William Clay's will of 1742, a piece of land in Bourne, Lincolnshire, was bequeathed to the town, the rent from which was to be used to buy bread for the local poor. The original land was swallowed up by the local Enclosure Award of 1770, but another field of just over an acre, now called Whitebread Meadow, just north of Bourne, was set aside to satisfy the terms of Clay's bequest. On the Monday before Easter, the auction for the grazing rights on the field is still held, at Queen's Bridge at the end of the Eastgate area of the town. It follows a rather unusual procedure, set down in the will: two boys (or, nowadays, girls) start to run a 200-yard race and the bidding commences; the last bid made before the first runner's return is the winner. The money raised is now given to charity and has not been used to buy loaves for distribution since the late 1960s.

Although the exact nature of this auction is peculiar, it was not unusual in the past for auctions to have definite ending points dictated by a semi-random occurrence. **Candle auctions** were particularly common (*see* p. 106), and at Wishford in Wiltshire the 'midsummer tithes' auction ends when the sun disappears over the horizon (*see* **Rogation Monday: Wishford Auction**, p. 179).

See also **Doles**, p. 87.

*

Royal Maundy, at Liverpool, April 2004

MAUNDY THURSDAY

Maundy Thursday, the day before Good Friday, was also known as Holy Thursday or Shere Thursday. 'Shere' was a technical term, now obsolete, used in the manufacture of coins, and signified 'the deviation from the standard weight of coins permitted by law' (*OED*); its use in this context probably refers to the special coins minted for the day.

On Maundy Thursday, the ruling monarch (or his/her representative if they are away) presents Maundy gifts to as many elderly people as there are years in their reign. The custom takes its origin from an incident in the life of Christ, recorded in the Gospel of John (13:4). Immediately after the Last Supper, Jesus laid aside his garments, girded himself with a towel, and, taking a basin of water, washed the feet of the Disciples. He delivered to them a command for his followers to

love one another, saying, 'I have given you an example that ye should do as I have done to you.' This command, or *mandatum*, is the origin of both the name and the custom of Maundy. Most branches of the Christian faith formerly carried out a foot-washing ceremony, and England was no exception. Indeed, foot-washing ceremonies were quite common in abbeys and cathedrals around the country from about the sixth century until the Dissolution of the Monasteries (1536–40), and could be performed at any time during the year, sometimes daily. It is not clear when ruling monarchs started taking a regular personal role in the Maundy ceremony, but the earliest definite reference relates to King John in 1210. The present custom is properly called the Royal Maundy because, at least in earlier days, other nobles and high-ranking churchmen also gave out Maundy doles.

In earliest times, the poor people who received the

foot-washing numbered twelve or thirteen, and it is not clear when the figure was increased to match the years in a monarch's reign. Somewhat sumptuous robes were given to the poor people as well, but Queen Elizabeth I stopped this custom and instituted the more practical gift of money instead; it was also customary to give food. The last king to perform the foot-washing himself was James II, in 1685. Until the mid eighteenth century, when the foot-washing was abolished, the Lord High Almoner then carried out this part of the ceremony, and he also sometimes gave out the money on the monarch's behalf.

A description of the ceremony in 1731:

On the 5th April, 1731, it being Maundy Thursday, the King then being in his 48th year, there was distributed at the Banqueting House, Whitehall, to 48 poor men and 48 poor women, boiled beef and shoulders of mutton, and small bowls of ale, which is called dinner; after that, large wooden platters of fish and loaves, viz, undressed, one large ling and one large dried cod; twelve red herrings and twelve white herrings; and four quartern loaves. Each person had one platter of this provision; after which was distributed to them, shoes, stockings, linen and woollen cloth, and leathern bags, with onepenny, twopenny, threepenny and fourpenny pieces of silver, and shillings, to each about £4 in value. His Grace The Lord archbishop of York, Lord High Almoner, also performed the annual ceremony of washing the feet of the poor in the Royal Chapel, Whitehall, as formerly done by the kings themselves.

The custom has changed a great deal over the years, and both the food and the clothes have long been commuted into money. Since 1971, the ceremony has taken place at a different cathedral each year, and the recipients are chosen from the surrounding area for their contributions to the local community.

See also **Doles**, p. 87.

Henry Travice Charity

This Maundy Thursday dole was founded by Henry Travice, who died in 1626. In his will, he stipulated that £10 from the annual rent charge on a property in Widnes, Manchester, should be distributed to forty poor parishioners, on or near his grave. The charity itself takes place in the place of his burial, St Mary's church in Leigh, by his pew. A brass plaque in the church reads (with spelling modernized):

Here near adjoineth the burial place belonging to the house of Mr. Henrie Travice late of Light Oaks, who departed this life the 7th of August Anno Doi 1626 aged 64 and give by his last will unto forty poor people of this parish five shillings apiece yearly to be delivered them near his gravestone hereunder placed, on Thursday in the Passion Week forever.

Recipients have to walk the length of Henry's pew to be eligible, and as £10 gives forty people very little worth having, the number of recipients has been reduced.

See also **Doles**, p. 87.

Peter's Pence

This was one of the many customs in which coins or food were thrown to children to be 'scrambled for'. James Cossins reported in his *Reminiscencs of Exeter Fifty Years Since* (1878) that in Devon in the 1830s:

At Exeter Cathedral on this day, after service, 'Peter's Pence' were given to children, distributed by the vergers, standing at the door under the north tower; the exit being the entrance near Southernhay, giving the alert ones time to come round again. The confusion and noise were so great, the vergers were desired to throw the pence in the yard for a general scramble. The custom ceased many years since.

No other information is given, but the interesting detail here is the name for the money. 'Peter's pence' was the vernacular name for a tax of one penny per household (in Latin, *denarii S. Petri*) that was sent to Rome specifically to support the Pope, instituted by King Offa in the eighth century and renewed after a lapse by William the Conqueror. The custom spread to Europe, but was abolished in England by Act of Parliament (25 Henry VIII cap. 21) in 1534. In later years, the phrase denoted a voluntary contribution to the clergy paid by Roman Catholics.

See also **Scrambling Customs**, p. 128.

*

5 APRIL

John Stow Commemoration

John Stow was born in London in 1525. The son of a tailor and apprenticed to his father's trade, he would hardly be remembered today if he had not branched out into a very different field. What set him apart from other master tradesmen of the time was that he somehow acquired a taste for books and historical scholarship, and he began to collect materials to support his interest in historical study. His first book, published in 1561, was *A Summarie of Englysh Chronicles*. Only one copy of the first edition survives, but the book was popular enough to go through eleven editions in his lifetime. Sometime in the early 1560s, Stow took the very bold step of giving up his tailoring business to concentrate on research and writing, a decision that resulted in his lasting fame but ensured that he himself suffered an old age dogged by poverty. He was even granted a licence to beg the year before he died.

Elizabethan England may have seen a flowering of literary talent, but it was also a period of political and religious intrigue, and anyone who spent their days with books was considered highly suspect. Stow was reported to the authorities as 'a suspicious person, with many dangerous and superstitious books in his possession', and was duly investigated by Edmund Grindal, the Bishop of London, who sent his henchmen to inspect Stow's library. He must have been exonerated, as he continued to amass historical materials, and his most famous publication, the *Survey of London*, was published in 1598, with a revised edition in 1603.

This immensely readable book was the first real study of London and is one of our best sources of information on Elizabethan life. One of the pleasures of the *Survey* is that Stow does not confine himself to the lives of the great and the good, or to buildings and institutions, but also notices the daily doings of the common people around him, and the book contains numerous vignettes of real Elizabethan life; he writes of maypoles, and streets decorated with evergreens for Christmas, and provides one of the first descriptions of **rough music** justice (*see* p. 74), writing of one John

John Stow memorial, St Andrew Undershaft, Leadenhall, London

Atwod, a draper of the parish of St Michael's, who one day discovered a priest paying amorous attentions to his wife. He describes how the priest was:

> . . . *on three market-days conveyed through the high streets and markets of the city with a paper on his head, wherein was written his trespass. The first day he rode in a carry, the second on a horse, his face to the horse tail, the third led betwixt twain, and every day rung with basons, and proclamations made of the fact at every turning of the street, and also*

Flitting Day (George Cruickshank, *Comic Almanac*, 1836)

before John Atwod's stall, and the church door of his service . . .

Stow's *Survey* is still in print today, over 400 years after its first publication.

When Stow died on 5 April 1605, he was buried in St Andrew Undershaft church on Leadenhall Street, and his wife erected a terracotta monument in his memory; this was replaced by a marble monument in 1905. This later monument includes an effigy depicting him in characteristic writing pose, and every year, on or near the date of his death, a commemorative service takes place. As befits the memory of the first chronicler of the capital city, the service is formally attended by the Lord Mayor or one of the aldermen. During the service, they place a new quill pen in the hand of the effigy, which remains there until the following year.

*

6 APRIL

Flitting Day

The sixth of April was one of several regular 'flitting days' recorded in various parts of the country. As farm and domestic workers were often employed by the year, a set pattern arose, agreed by long local custom, by which the coming and going of staff was regulated: a hiring fair, or set market day, would take place, during which employers and workers could meet and make a bargain (*see* **Hiring Fairs**, p. 345); on another day their old employment officially ended; on another, the new position started, and there was usually a few days of free time built into the system when the workers could have something of a holiday. For single people the whole procedure was relatively simple, as a tin trunk usually held most of their belongings, but for families living in tied accommodation it was quite an operation moving from one place to another.

For many, the term ended at Michaelmas (29 September) and moving day was therefore in early

October, but in those areas where the employment year ran to and from Lady Day (25 March), 6 April was the usual day for removal. It was a matter of fierce pride that you left the place in good order. In her *Lincolnshire Calendar* (1997), Maureen Sutton remembers that:

> We always had to move on 6th April. It was a big job for mother as she had to leave everything spick and span for the new family moving in. You had to leave the fire grate spotless, white-wash the walls, and leave the fire ready to light. It was also the day when you paid up the year's rent.

Another widespread term for Flitting Day was 'Pack Rag Day' (*see* **14 May**).

Tatworth Candle Auction

The Tatworth Candle Auction is one of several **candle auctions** (p. 106) that survive in England, whereby the right to use a piece of common land is auctioned off while an inch of candle burns. In the Somerset village of Tatworth, the auction takes place on the Saturday after 6 April (Old Style Lady Day); a short business meeting is held on the same day. The property in question is a six-acre field called Stowell Mead, which, being wasteland left over after the enclosure of land in the parish in 1819, is owned by the villagers. The procedure is as follows: a short candle is placed on a square board suspended by chains from the ceiling of a room in a local inn, and whoever is the highest bidder when the flame dies is the winner; anyone who leaves their seat while the candle is burning is fined, a rule designed to prevent anyone from interfering with the flame, and the whole procedure takes about twenty minutes. The annual money raised at the auction is divided among the sixty or so locals who have 'rights', or shares, in the meadow, after deductions are made for the traditional bread, cheese, and watercress supper.

*

EASTER

Easter is the oldest feast of the Christian Church, and although the celebration of Christmas now eclipses all other festivals, both religious and secular, the earlier Christian churches regarded Easter as by far the most important of the year. Easter celebrates the central mystical miracle of the faith, the death and resurrection of the Saviour Jesus Christ, an event that for Christians proves Christ's divinity; and it was this that was commemorated in church in complex ritual over the Easter period.

In the pre-Reformation Church, Easter was marked by a series of impressively dramatic and emotional set pieces of religious symbolism, which were popular with clergy and congregation alike. First, the cloths that had veiled parts of the church and the saints' images during Lent were removed. Then, on Good Friday, both clergy and parishioners crept barefoot and on their knees to kiss the foot of the crucifix, in a ceremony usually called 'creeping to the Cross'. A model sepulchre was built, usually from wood and canvas but of more substantial form in the larger institutions, to represent the cave in which Christ's body was laid, and an elaborate pyx, containing the Host, was placed inside, along with a crucifix. Some parishioners sat up all night to watch, in memory of the soldiers who guarded the original tomb, and to tend the candles that were kept burning around it. On Easter Sunday, the clergy approached the sepulchre in procession, and 'raised up' the host and crucifix, returning them to their proper places in the church. On Easter Saturday, all lights and fires had been extinguished, and a new fire kindled by the clergy, using flints, from which holy flame all candles and fires were relit. The church was then ablaze with light, including a very large candle called the Paschal candle. References in churchwardens' accounts show that some sort of performance often took place, presumably re-enacting the principal events of the Easter story. All these rituals were swept away with the Reformation, and for those who lived through these changes, the new Easter must have seemed bleak indeed.

Unfortunately, the Scriptures do not make it clear when the resurrection of Christ occurred, and arguments about the correct method of calculation led to some of the bitterest controversies that Christianity has ever seen. Unfortunately, too, the Church Fathers of yesteryear opted for a complex moveable festival, based on full moons and equinoxes rather than a fixed date, and this has caused havoc with the calendar ever since. The following explanation printed in *Whitaker's*

Candle Auctions

Although nowadays we assume that an auction continues until no one present will bid any further, there have been many other ways of organizing sales to bidders in the past. Several earlier methods were based on having a definable end-point at which the highest standing bid won the purchase, and the most widespread way of calling time on the auction was to light a candle and allow people to bid until the flame went out. Clearly, a short piece of candle was necessary, and it was customary to use an inch; hence the phrase 'selling by inch of candle'. It is not always easy to define the exact moment a flame goes out, and in a later refinement a pin was inserted into the candle one inch from the top, with the bidding continuing until the pin dropped out – a much more dramatic, and precise, method. In some cases the candle was hidden out of sight of the bidders.

There is plenty of evidence that auction by candle was an officially sanctioned way of organizing such affairs. The *Act for Settling the Trade to the East Indies* of 1698, for example, stipulated that goods be 'sold openly and publicly by inch of candle', and even redundant Navy ships were disposed of in the same way, as recorded in Samuel Pepys's diary entry for 3 September 1662:

> *After dinner by water to the office; and there we met and sold the Weymouth, Successe, and Fellowship hulks. Where pleasant to see how backward men are at first to bid; and yet when the candle is going out, how they bawl and dispute afterward who bid the most first. And here I observed one man cunninger than the rest, that was sure to bid the last man and to carry it; and enquiring the reason, he told me that just as the flame goes out the smoke descends, which is a thing I never observed before, and by that he doth know the instant when to bid last – which is very pretty.*

Nevertheless, candle auctions are slow and inefficient, and only useful for sales in which not more than a handful of large lots are on offer. For a modern-day sale in which hundreds of lots are rattled through, candle auctions would be completely inadequate, and it is not surprising that the candle method lost favour in the eighteenth century and was gradually replaced by the open-ended ascending bid system. However, candle auctions have survived in a handful of places, nearly always concerned with the letting of common land; *see*, for example, **6 April: Tatworth Candle Auction**; **13 December: Aldermaston Candle Auction**; and **Occasional Customs: Chedzoy Candle Auction**, p. 425. For other unusual surviving auctions, *see* **Holy Week Monday: Bourne Running Auction**, p. 100; and **Rogation Monday: Wishford Auction**, p. 179.

Almanack is about as simple as one can find on the subject:

> Easter Day is the first Sunday after the full moon which happens on, or next after, the 21st day of March; if the full moon happens on a Sunday, Easter Day is the Sunday after... The moon referred to is not the real moon of the heavens, but a hypothetical moon on whose 'full' the date of Easter depends, and the lunations of this 'calendar' moon consist of twenty-nine and thirty days alternately, with certain necessary modifications to make the date of its full agree as nearly as possible with that of the real moon, which is known as the Paschal Full Moon. At present, Easter falls on one of 35 days (22 March to 25 April).

Parliament took the bold step of passing a bill in 1928 that fixed Easter to the first Sunday after the second Saturday in April, but with the proviso that the churches agreed. They have not yet done so, and the act remains unimplemented.

English is unique in calling this festival 'Easter'; nearly all the other European languages use a word derived from the Latin *pasch*, as is to be expected of a Christian festival. The origin of the word 'Easter' is obscure, and is not helped by the ubiquitous uncritical acceptance of an otherwise unsupported comment by the Venerable Bede (673–735) in his *De Temporum Ratione*:

> *Eosturmonath has a name which is now translated 'Paschal month', and which was once called after a goddess of theirs named Eostre, in whose honour feasts were celebrated in that month. Now they designate that Paschal season by her name, calling the joys of the new rite by the time-honoured name of the old observance.*

He similarly offered a deity as a derivation for the Anglo-Saxon name for March, stating, 'Hrethmonath is named for their goddess Hretha.' However, there is no other evidence that either goddess existed, and we have to face the possibility that Bede was wrong. It is with due trepidation that one questions not only the scholarship of such a pivotal figure but also the host of etymologists since who have accepted his word, and it can indeed be argued that as Bede was writing so soon after the conversion of the Anglo-Saxons to Christianity, he should have known what he was talking about. Nevertheless, it seems quite possible that Bede, as a Latin speaker and writer, simply expected months to be named after mythological or historic figures, and, faced with unknown words, fell prey to what is nowadays an extremely common trait – the construction of word origins based on present-day expectations and assumptions rather than on real evidence from the past. It is distinctly odd that only the months of April and March are given divine names. All the other months are named for the activities that went on in them; so, for example, Blodmonath (November) is 'blood month', named after the slaughter of animals for winter, and Solmonath (February) is 'cake month'. What seems clear is that, goddess or not, the English word 'Easter' is derived from the word 'east', and therefore probably from 'dawn'.

The general holiness of the Easter season made it a favourite time for charitable **doles** (p. 87). The **Biddenden Maids Charity**, in Kent (*see* p. 122), still survives, but most have long since disappeared. It was common for food provided by such bequests to be consumed in the church itself, but this offended emerging Puritan sensibilities. The poor parishioners of Clunganford, Shropshire, for example, complained to Archbishop Laud in 1637 that they had been accustomed to eat their annual Easter feast of bread, cheese, and beer in the church, but it had been moved to the parsonage a few years ago, and now the parson wanted to do away with it altogether. However, in 1647, the Puritans specifically banned Easter:

> *An Ordinance for Abolishing of Festivals (8 June 1647). Forasmusch as the feasts of the Nativity of Christ, Easter, and Whitsuntide, and other festivals commonly called holy days, have been heretofore superstitiously used and observed. Be it ordained by the Lords and Commons in Parliament assembled, that the said* [feasts] *. . . be no longer observed as festivals or holy days within this kingdom.*

It never regained its former ritual glory in English churches, but by the nineteenth century the attractive custom of decorating churches with flowers at the season, which still continues, was widespread. A correspondent to *Notes & Queries* reported in 1850:

> *In the village of Berkley, near Frome, and on the borders of Wiltshire, the church is decorated on Easter Sunday with yew. Flowers in churches on that day are common, but I believe the use of yew to be unusual.*

Other mid-century reports from around the country show that the use of yew, box, and other evergreens was not so unusual as this correspondent thought.

*

GOOD FRIDAY

The Friday before Easter Saturday is the day on which Christians commemorate the crucifixion of Jesus Christ. It has been called 'Good Friday' in England since at least 1290, and it is usually assumed to be derived from 'God's Friday', but the citations given in the *Oxford English Dictionary* do not bear this out, and it seems that in earlier times 'good' was added to various other words to denote holiness. 'Holy Friday' and 'Long Friday' were among other recorded names, the latter probably referring to the long fasting required on the day. Whatever its derivation, the 'good' in the name has long perplexed believers and non-believers alike, who have never been quite sure why it should be 'good' at all.

Before the Bank Holiday legislation of 1871 (*see* **Bank Holidays**, p. 274), Christmas Day and Good Friday were the only holidays granted to most workers, and it is hardly surprising that they regarded the latter as an opportunity for fun and pleasure. But the Church dictated that it be a day of solemnity and fasting, a sort of super Sunday, on which no work should be done. It was a popular day for Christian charity, and many annual **doles** (p. 87) were distributed on the day. In the secular sphere, however, the popular ambivalence surrounding the day is demonstrated in various superstitions: many of these were concerned with everyday activities considered unlucky on the day, such as washing clothes, cutting hair and fingernails, and baking bread; while others suggested that bread baked, and eggs laid, on Good Friday had excellent medicinal and protective properties, and it was also supposed to be a particularly good day for planting in the garden. Game customs such as marble-playing and skipping were also common (*see separate entries, below*).

Bread and Eggs

An extremely widespread belief, found in every part of England throughout the nineteenth century, maintained that bread or buns baked on Good Friday would never grow mouldy. They were also believed to have curative powers for a range of complaints, including those of the stomach or digestive system. The usual way to preserve this Good Friday bread was to hang it by a string from the kitchen ceiling, and when needed a piece would be grated or soaked in water to be drunk by the patient (*see* **Good Friday: Widow's Son** (p. 113) for a surviving example).

A parallel superstition, less commonly reported but still widespread, held that eggs were similarly incorruptible, and a letter in *Notes & Queries* (1921) confirmed it:

Last Christmas, a lady told one of my nearest relations that if an egg, laid on Good Friday, is kept without being disturbed, it will generally be perfectly fresh at the time when the Christmas pudding is made. She stated that she had proved this. Out of

pure curiosity my relation placed, on Good Friday last (March 25) an egg, laid by one of her hens on that day, in an egg-cup and put it in a cupboard in her drawing-room, where it remained untouched until Dec. 1, when it was broken and used in the Christmas pudding. I can avouch that when the egg was broken there was no smell, except that of a fresh egg, which in all one could judge of, it appeared to be.

These superstitions appear to be very old, but cannot be traced earlier than the eighteenth century. They are in line with other beliefs that edibles associated with Christian ceremonies, such as the wine and wafers of communion, and the water used in baptism, also possess similar medicinal powers.

Burning Judas

An example of a custom that only seems to have existed in this country in one small area is that of burning the Judas on Good Friday. An excellent account published in the journal *Folk-Lore* in 1954 is worth quoting in full:

A custom that is peculiar to one part of Liverpool only is one that happens every Good Friday. For weeks before the children collect wood, paper, straw, shavings, etc., anything that will burn. The boys get one of their father's old suits and stuff it with straw, etc. They get a comic mask to complete the job and this dummy is carefully looked after till the Day. At the first sign of daylight on Good Friday morning, all the children of the neighbourhood congregate round the particular guy which they now call Judas. The children's ages range from five years up to twelve and fourteen, and being a densely populated area close to the docks there are many children. The fun starts as the sun rises and the leader hoists the Judas on a pole and knocks at the bedroom windows and all the children join in the chorus, 'Judas is a penny short of his breakfast and until you throw some coppers to them they won't give you any peace'. When they have combed the neighbourhood they begin the serious part of burning the Judas, and out come all the combustibles they have been collecting. For some reason the burning of the Judas must take place by 11 o'clock a.m. Now the police intervene as the fires are

*lit in the middle of the street, and scores of children
whooping for joy and throwing wood and straw on
it. To prevent accidents the police scatter the fires and
seize the Judases and take them to the police station
at Essex Street and destroy them there. It is comic
to see a policeman with two or more Judases under
his arm striding off to the Bridewell and thirty or
forty children of all ages crowding after him, shriek-
ing, 'Judas', and by this time the younger children
are thinking the policeman is Judas. By 12 noon the
excitement is all over. This custom only occurs at the
South End of Liverpool, never up North or anywhere
else along the eight miles of Dock Estate. I was told
the idea originated many years ago when the old
Spanish sailing ships docked and discharged their
cargoes of wine and citrus fruits in the South End
Docks.*

The idea that the children learned the custom from
continental sailors is quite feasible. An illustration
published in the *Graphic* on 15 April 1876, for example,
shows Portuguese sailors in Liverpool Docks involved
in hanging an effigy for the custom of 'flogging Judas',
a custom that was widely practised in Portugal, Spain,
and South America.

Butterworth Charity

This annual charity, carried out at the priory church
of St Bartholomew the Great, in Smithfield, the City of
London, is named after Joshua Butterworth, although
it was already in existence before he gave money in
1887 to perpetuate the custom. It is believed to have
been founded in 1686, but it is not known by whom.
Every Good Friday, money and hot cross buns (presumably bread was used in earlier times) was distributed
to poor widows of the parish, on a conveniently flat
tombstone in the churchyard. In 1973, no poor widows
presented themselves, which, while being bad for the
tradition, is a good thing for society as a whole, and the
children who were present were invited to eat the bun
instead. They were not reluctant to do so, and the tradition continues with this new audience, every Good
Friday, after the morning service.

See also **Doles**, p. 87.

Hartfield Dole

This graveside dole takes place every Good Friday at
Hartfield church in Sussex, at the tomb of Nicholas
Smith, who died in 1631. Smith left money to be
invested and the interest to be divided among the poor
of the parish. There is no reason to believe that there is
more to this than a straightforward alms bequest, but
a story explaining the dole tells how Smith was a rich
man from East Grinstead who went about dressed as
a beggar, asking for food and shelter, in order to test
the true character of the people of Sussex. At every
turn he met with contempt and refusal, until he came
to Hartfield, where he was treated with kindness and
generosity. He therefore asked to be buried at Hartfield,
and founded the charity in his name.

See also **Doles**, p. 87.

Hot Cross Buns

Two festive foods – pancakes on Shrove Tuesday and
hot cross buns on Good Friday – have survived into the
present day, even though most traditional aspects of
their special days have long ceased to have any widespread resonance. Although hot cross buns can be
bought in supermarkets all year round, many English
families try to eat them on Good Friday, and some
baker's shops still open specially on the day to serve
freshly baked buns.

The development of the 'cross bun' is not very clear,
as there were apparently various types of cake that
were special to Good Friday. Some nineteenth-century
sources refer to triangular cakes, and others to 'cakes' of
unspecified shape or size. However, the earliest specific
reference to a 'hot cross bun' occurs in *Poor Robin's
Almanack* (1733):

*Good Friday comes this month, the old woman runs
With one or two a penny hot cross buns.*

Further confusion arises as the marking of food with a
cross was not confined to Good Friday buns. Right up to
the early years of the twentieth century, it was normal
practice when baking bread to mark the dough with a
cross before putting it into the oven, and this practice
is well documented from the mid thirteenth century.
Indeed, in pre-Reformation England it would have

Hot-cross-bun seller (*Illustrated London News*, 1851)

been commonplace to make the sign of the cross over all food, in preparation and before eating.

Many festive foods, such as goose at Michaelmas and mince pies at Christmas, attract superstitions which maintain that good luck will accompany those who follow custom, but that bad luck will result from a failure to partake, and the hot cross bun is no exception. *The Testimony, Trial, Conviction, Condemnation, Confession, and Execution of William Smith,* an account detailing the story of a man who was executed in 1753 for murdering several people by giving them arsenic-laced cake, provides a good example:

> I am a butcher, and I have had dealings with Mr.
> Harper ... and he invited me to dine upon a Good
> Friday Cake as we call it; for he was a right good
> neighbourly man and he invited five other neigh-
> bours ... to eat of this cake ... We have a notion
> ... in our country, that if we do eat of a cake made
> purposely on Good Friday we shall never want money

> or victuals all the year round, which for as many
> years as I can remember has always fallen out true.

In recent times, the poor old hot cross bun has come under pressure from a variety of directions. On 17 March 2003, *The Times* reported that four local councils have decided to ban them from their schools, because they might offend children of other religions. However, the bun has attracted ingenious but nonsensical speculation about its ancient pagan origins, despite its bearing the overtly Christian symbol of a cross and being sold on the day of Christ's crucifixion, and this has prompted some devout Christians to refuse them. Perhaps the wildest fancy that seeks to prove the hot cross bun's remote origins is based on the similarity of the word 'bun' to the Ancient Greek word *boun*, which, we are told by the eighteenth-century antiquarian John Brand, was a cake with two horns, offered to the gods at Arkite temples every seventh day. In fact, 'bun' is of uncertain derivation and has only been recorded in English since 1371. As the *Oxford English Dictionary* explains, although the word has various shades of meaning in different parts of the country, a basic definition for usage in England is 'a sweet cake (usually round), not too large to be held in the hand while being eaten', which sums it up perfectly.

Skipping

In several parts of the country, people would gather in a convenient open space on Good Friday to take part in an orgy of communal skipping. This was not the solo skipping of the type still done by girls in the school playground, but the version with two people turning a long rope, which could accommodate several skippers at the same time. The best known examples of Good Friday skipping customs were at Cambridge and along the Sussex coast. A correspondent to *Notes & Queries* reported in 1863 that:

> In Brighton on this day the children in the back streets bring up ropes from the beach. One stands on the pavement on one side, and one on the other, while one skips in the middle of the street. Sometimes a pair (a boy and a girl) skip together, and sometimes a great fat bathing-woman will take her place, and skip as merrily as the grandsire danced in Goldsmith's Traveller. They call the day 'Long Rope Day'. This was done as lately as 1863.

Twenty years later, Brighton antiquarian Frederick Sawyer commented further:

> The custom continues to be observed with vigour, and burly navvies may also be seen skipping actively; whilst on the Level at Brighton on Good Friday, 1883, there were scores of skippers. Mr. Rolf says the name is 'Long Line Day'.

The custom continued at Brighton until the outbreak of the Second World War, but the closing of the beaches in anticipation of invasion finally killed it. Good Friday skipping was also reported from Hastings, Hove, Southwick, Patcham, Lewes, Alciston, and other Sussex locations.

At Cambridge, local people gathered with ropes and picnics on the open ground called Parker's Piece. In her *Cambridgeshire Customs and Folklore* (1969), Enid Porter records that:

> Until early in the evening the skipping went on, the men traditionally turning the ropes and the women jumping, although this . . . was not always strictly followed because children often skipped with the adults. Tradesmen selling sweets, ice-creams, toys, lemonade, etc., set up stalls along the Parkside.

The Cambridge skipping also faded away at the outbreak of the Second World War, but Porter's informants referred to similar activities in other nearby villages earlier in the twentieth century.

There have been sporadic revivals of Good Friday skipping in various places in Sussex, but the one place that has continued its skipping without need of revival is Scarborough, in Yorkshire, where it is done on Shrove Tuesday (*see* p. 65). Communal skipping was probably much more widespread in the past than present evidence indicates. There are isolated reports, for example, from London, Leamington in Warwickshire, Pontypool in Monmouthshire, and Guildford in Surrey, and further research will probably turn up many more examples. One such is the remarkable film made by the firm Mitchell and Kenyon, of Preston egg-rolling in 1901, published by the British Film Institute as *Electric Edwardians*. In the massed crowd scenes, it is difficult to see any egg-rolling taking place, but in among the throng there are at least a dozen long skipping ropes in action, with men, women, and children taking part.

The origins of communal skipping on Good Friday are still uncertain. Although skipping is nowadays regarded as an activity for young girls, in the past it was done by boys and by adults as well; however, it does not seem to be as old as is usually assumed. Child-lore experts Iona and Peter Opie have found no earlier reference to skipping with ropes before the seventeenth century, although skipping through hoops is a little older. In Sussex, local tradition links the custom with fishing families, saying that the ropes were supplied by the fishermen, which may be true at these locations but can hardly be relevant at inland places. Another widespread tradition is that the custom celebrates the death of that unpopular figure Judas Iscariot, with the skipping rope symbolizing the rope he used to hang himself; however, any Good Friday custom is likely to attract a Judas Iscariot story. The problem with all these explanations is that such communal skipping customs cannot be shown to be any older than the mid nineteenth century.

Tinsley Green Marbles

Every Good Friday, the Greyhound pub at Tinsley Green, near Gatwick Airport in Sussex, plays host to teams of marble-players from far and wide for the World Marbles Championship. Marble-playing has a venerable history, which is hardly surprising given the essential simplicity of rolling round items along the ground, and evidence from the ancient world shows that analogous games were played with fruit stones, nuts, and clay balls, while in later years marble, alabaster, glass, and metal were used to make more effective missiles.

The first evidence of the game in Britain appears surprisingly late, in the mid seventeenth century, with references to 'bowling-stones', but from that time on there are numerous descriptions and illustrations to prove its popularity. It is clear that the game was played by people of all ages until the earlier twentieth century, when it became essentially a children's game.

The organized annual championship matches that take place at Tinsley and other places in Britain date only from the 1930s and 1940s, although they seem to have started a little earlier in America, in the 1920s. Marble-players are famous for having their own language: tolleys, alleys, and taws are types of marbles, while fudging, fubbing, fulking, and fullocking are dialect terms for leaning forward too far, or otherwise trying to cheat. There are also numerous arcane rules and traditions. The order of play is traditionally determined at Tinsley by a 'nose-drop', whereby contestants hold a marble at nose height, and drop it. The owner of the marble that lands nearest to a line drawn on the floor goes first.

The game at Tinsley takes place on a well-sanded raised concrete circle, six feet in diameter, between two teams of six. Forty-nine marbles are placed at the centre (four for each player, plus one). The rules are relatively simple, but appear complex, even in the words of expert observer Iona Opie:

First player knuckles down at edge of ring and shoots

his tolley to knock one or more marbles right out of the ring. If he succeeds, and his tolley remains in the ring, he shoots again. If he fails, but his tolley remains in the ring, it stays there until his turn comes round again, when he shoots from wherever it happens to be. If in the meantime his tolley has been knocked out of the ring by his own or the opposing side, he is 'killed' and is out of the game.

In 2005, twenty-three teams took part, necessitating a series of heats leading up to the final. As the date of Good Friday varies from year to year, weather conditions and, in particular, the all-important light can vary considerably. The game itself may not have altered in the seventy-five years since its inception, but the event certainly has, and over twenty-five years ago there were worries about wider fame affecting the day: 'Some of the original atmosphere has been lost with the influx of TV crews, foreign tourists and the like,' wrote Sussex expert Tony Wales in 1979.

No self-respecting annual custom can exist without a historical legend to explain its origin, and at Tinsley it is said that the game originated when two young Elizabethans contended for the hand of a local maiden. This must be such a recently invented story that it may not be too late to pin down its actual origin with some in-depth local research. There is no reason to think that Sussex was particularly known for marble-playing in the remote past, but in recent years the county has certainly earned that reputation, and another well-known Good Friday match has taken place at Battle since it was revived in 1948.

Washing Molly Grime

A strange charity, which formerly took place at Glentham in Lincolnshire every Good Friday, was popularly known as 'washing Molly Grime'. A rent-charge laid on a local estate provided the annual sum of seven shillings, which was used to reward seven poor spinsters of the parish provided they fetch water from Newell Well (about two miles away) and duly wash a stone statue on one of the tombstones, which was called 'Molly Grime'. The origin of the custom is still unknown, but it lapsed in 1832 when the estate was sold, and no provision was made for the money to continue.

See also **Doles**, p. 87.

Widow's Son

The pub called the Widow's Son (sub-titled 'the Bun House') in Devons Road, Bromley-by-Bow, has a mass of blackened, dust- and cobweb-laden hot cross buns hanging from its ceiling. Every Good Friday they add another one. The story behind this custom tells how a widow lived in a cottage on the site. Her only son went to sea, and, expecting his return at Easter, she baked a hot cross bun for him as she had always done before. By next Easter, he still had not returned, but, ever hopeful, she baked another, and so on each year until she had quite a collection hanging from a beam in the kitchen. After she died, a pub was built on the site, and the proprietors continued the tradition of hanging up a new bun every Good Friday.

Oddly enough, the strangest part of the tale – the hanging of buns from kitchen ceilings at Easter – is the part of the custom that is the most commonplace. It was very widely believed, from at least the mid eighteenth century, that bread or buns baked on Good Friday would never go mouldy and possessed marked medicinal powers, for animals as well as humans. Pieces of 'Good Friday bread' that had hardened over the months, or years, were grated and put into food and drink to cure a wide variety of complaints, including stomach upsets and bowel problems. The accumulated bread was usually hung up in the cottage kitchen until needed. Less well known, but still widespread, was the idea that the bread was also 'protective', as recorded in William Hone's *Every-Day Book* (1827):

> In the houses of some ignorant people, a Good Friday bun is still kept 'for luck', and sometimes there hangs from the ceiling a hard biscuit-like cake of open cross-work, baked on a Good Friday, to remain there till displaced on the next Good Friday by one of similar make ... and [it is] affirmed that it preserves the house from fire, and 'no fire ever happened in a house that had one'.

Others maintained that the bread protected against shipwreck, which may be more relevant to the Widow's Son story. The pub has been called 'The Widow's Son' since at least 1851, but it is not known how far back the bun-hanging goes. It is tempting to assume that the pub is so named because of the existing story, but it is equally likely that the story was invented to explain the unusual pub name.

For many years, the new bun was hung up by a sailor, and while the locality remained linked to the docks, it was not difficult to find one, but the area has changed dramatically, and in recent years it has been the custom for a serving member of the Royal Navy to do the honours. The event is now officially sponsored and has gained something of the air of a publicity stunt, but it still continues.

See also **Good Friday: Bread and Eggs**, p. 108.

Workington Football

At Workington in Cumberland, they have a surviving example of the 'mass' football games that were previously widespread in the country but can now only be found in a handful of places. The game is played on three days over the Easter period – Good Friday, Easter Tuesday, and the following Saturday, although the Easter Tuesday game is claimed to be the original one, and local records show it has been in existence since at least 1779.

The game is played with a leather ball, slightly smaller than a regular football, and teams can be of any size. Ostensibly, the contest is now between the 'Uppies and Downies', defined by which part of the town the player lives in, but most accounts state that it was previously between sailors and miners. Each game starts in the evening, between six-thirty and seven o'clock, and can last well into the night. Play starts when the ball is thrown up on the bridge over the beck, roughly halfway between the two 'hails', or goals, which are situated at Workington Hall and the harbour, respectively, about a mile and a half apart.

As is the case in many of these mass football customs, the ball spends much of its time in a huge unwieldy 'scrum', and the players have the reputation of being no respecters of property, regularly tramping over allotments, gardens, and cricket pitches, and spilling into the town's streets; however, the game was certainly rougher in the past. At least two players have been drowned during a game (in 1882 and 1932), and numerous serious injuries were regularly recorded. As elsewhere in similar circumstances, there was a local belief that players could not be prosecuted for

Bacup Coco-Nut Dancer, Lancashire, 2005

anything that happened during the game (*see* **Lawless Hours and Days**, p. 303). Although the local police have traditionally tried to control the game and prevent its worst excesses, there does not seem to have been any serious attempts to suppress it outright.

See also **Football**, p. 53.

*

EASTER SATURDAY

Bacup Coco-Nut Dancers

Every Easter Saturday, the Britannia Coco-Nut Dancers spend all day touring the streets of the Lancashire mill town of Bacup, dancing to the sound of a silver band, which trudges along in their wake. To the outsider, the dancers' costumes are colourful and distinctive, although somewhat bizarre. They wear a black long-sleeved jumper, crossed diagonally by a white sash, black breeches, white socks, fancy black clogs, a short white 'kilt' with red and blue horizontal stripes, and white hats decorated with rosettes and a feather of red or blue. They also have blackened faces. Strapped to their hands, knees, and waist are round pieces of wood, the 'coconuts' that give the dance its name, and that are struck together in set rhythmic patterns during dancing. There are eight men in the team, including a leader who is called the 'Whipper-In'. He uses a whistle, to communicate when the other dancers should stop and start, and he carries a whip, with which he can theoretically control the crowd.

The dancers progress along the street in two files of four on each side, with a kind of running dance step, stopping every now and then to perform a static dance in single file. Each dancer bends forward to strike his hands against his waist and knees, stands up to strike hands with his neighbour, and turns on the spot. Then they continue down the street. At certain locations they stop to perform their 'garland dances', of which they are five variations. They form up in couples in a square formation, each pair carrying a hooped garland between them, and they perform simplified quadrille movements. These garland dances have their own tunes, but the rest of the time the band plays the same melody over and over again, which, like other traditional tunes played all day at public customs, is more hypnotic than monotonous.

As Theresa Buckland suggests, the origins of the custom may lay in other local customs that involved 'blacking up'. The blackening of faces was formerly found in various traditional customs all over England, including pace-egging and versions of the mumming play, but its origin and meaning is obscure. In some cases, it is almost certainly directly descended from the blackface minstrelsy that was hugely popular in Britain in the nineteenth century (*see*, for example, **26 December: Padstow Mummers' (Darkie) Day**), and this has led some modern commentators to condemn the practice outright, as racist. But in many cases this link seems inappropriate, and it has often been suggested that blacking the face was originally a form of disguise. It is certainly an effective camouflage, and there are plenty of references to those who have blackened their faces for precisely this reason when involved in social disturbances, or when performing mass customs under threat from the police.

*

EASTER DAY

Eggs

The egg seems to have been one of the most adaptable symbols in myth and ritual across Europe and Asia, and most religions have some egg symbolism or other. It is often connected with spring, and in the Christian festival of Easter an egg can symbolize new life, birth, regeneration, or other qualities, depending on the context required. The emergence of a chick from the egg can be symbolic of Christ rising from the tomb, or the egg can even be seen as the stone rolled away from the tomb. It is perhaps this symbolic versatility rather

than any intrinsic properties that has ensured the egg's enduring attraction to people looking for metaphor.

On a more prosaic level, eggs were an essential part of the staple diet of rich and poor alike, but were banned for the forty days of Lent. This enforced abstinence goes a long way to explaining why eggs should feature so widely in Shrovetide customs, just before Lent, and at Easter when the people celebrated their return. Eggs were often given as gifts, or as tribute, or as payment in kind for rent or service to a superior in a social hierarchy, such as a medieval manor. In farming communities, eggs acted as a minor currency, and, being under the control of the women of the household, provided a modest but steady income for the family, in addition to much-needed protein at mealtimes.

See also **Easter Day: Pace-Egging**, p. 118; *compare* **Shrovetide and Lent**, p. 49; **Shrove Tuesday: Egg Shackling**, p. 60.

Greenwich Fair

Greenwich Fair is an excellent example of a fair that had no founding charter or official standing, but just grew on the spot by sheer weight of visitor numbers. From at least the early eighteenth century, Londoners had been in the habit of going out to Greenwich for day trips in spring and summer, and by the 1760s the Easter and Whitsun holidays had become the favourite days for these excursions. Among other simple pleasures, it was traditional for young people to run down the grassy hill, hand-in-hand in couples, or in long linked lines, but wherever there are people in holiday mood, providers of food, drink, and entertainment are never far behind. The attractions on offer soon grew from one lone gingerbread-seller to an impressive annual gathering of stalls, booths, rides, and sideshows. Nationally famous travelling outfits such as Richardson's Circus and Wombwell's Menagerie started making regular appearances, and by the turn of the nineteenth century a full-blown pleasure fair was in operation every year on both holidays.

The fair attracted the attention of many of the London-based writers and artists of the day, and there are many good descriptions and pictures of the event in the first half of the nineteenth century. Most other fairs were burdened by the lingering feeling that they

People running down the hill at Greenwich (George Cruickshank, *Comic Almanac*, 1836)

were being held for more important business than fun, something that stemmed from the days when the buying and selling of sheep, horses, or cheese had been their *raison d'être*. But Greenwich had no such baggage, and was devoted entirely to pleasure. By all accounts, it was particularly popular with London servant girls and their young men, and the dancing booths, where couples paid a small sum for each dance they took part in, did very good business. One of the crazes, noted by the social commentator Nathaniel Hawthorne in the following account from 1863, reflected their holiday mood:

What immediately perplexed me was a sharp, angry sort of a rattle, far off and close at hand, and sometimes right at my back. By-and-by, I discovered that this strange noise was produced by a little instrument called 'The Fun of the Fair' – a sort of rattle, consisting of a wooden wheel, the cogs of which turn against a thin slip of wood, and so produce a rasping sound when drawn smartly against a person's back.

The ladies draw their rattles against the backs of their male friends (and everybody passes for a friend at Greenwich Fair) and the young men return the compliment on the broad British backs of the ladies; and all are bound by immemorial custom to take it in good part and be merry at the joke.

This description helpfully elucidates an obscure passage in Douglas Jerrold's immensely popular comic tales *Mrs. Caudle's Curtain Lectures*, first published in *Punch* in 1845. In one of the chapters of this series, Mrs Caudle berates her husband for sneaking off to Greenwich Fair, and one of her particular complaints was:

Then you must go in the thick of the fair, and have the girls scratching your coat with rattles ... Don't tell me people don't scratch coats unless they're encouraged to do it.

Probably the most famous description of the fair is by Charles Dickens, in his capacity as journalist rather than novelist. His lively account appeared in *Sketches by Boz*:

> *Half the private houses are turned into tea-shops, fiddles are in great request, every little fruit-shop displays its stall of gilt gingerbread and penny toys; turnpike men are in despair, horses won't go on, and wheels will come off; ladies in 'carawans' scream with fright at every fresh concussion, and their admirers find it necessary to sit remarkably close to them, by way of encouragement; servants-of-all-works, who are not allowed to have followers, and have got a holiday for the day, make the most of their time with the faithful admirer who waits for a stolen interview at the corner of the street every night, when they go to fetch the beer – apprentices grow sentimental, and straw-bonnet makers kind.*

Nevertheless, the fun sometimes got out of hand, and without the protection of any kind of official status the fair was vulnerable to the displeasure of the local authorities. After serious rioting took place at the Easter gathering in 1850, it was rapidly suppressed.

New Clothes

In these days of cheap imported clothes, it is easy to lose sight of the tremendous importance of *new* clothes for people on restricted budgets, and it is no surprise that they take on a symbolic meaning above and beyond their practical use. In Britain, there were several widespread superstitions about new clothes, and one feature of these beliefs was that on certain days one was expected to wear at least one item of new clothing, for luck and future prosperity. If one did not, it was said, the birds would mess on you. Whitsun and New Year were two of these key times, but the superstition was most widespread at Easter. In 1909, Hastings M. Neville recorded that in Northumberland:

> *Whether from respect for the chief Sunday in the year, or simply from the following of old custom, every woman and child who comes to church on Easter Day wears some new article of clothing.*

This idea was found in all parts of the British Isles, well into the twentieth century, but in England it was probably most widely known in the northern counties,

where other Easter customs were also concentrated. In *Cumbria Within Living Memory* (1994), it was reported that:

> *After leaving the Sunday School we then set out on our favourite part of the day, calling on all the houses in the village to show off our new outfits and receive yet more pasche eggs and oranges. Sometimes after being told how smart we looked we would be given a little pinch and told 'that's a nip for new!'*

The 'pinch for luck' was also widespread, and if done cruelly (as at school) could take much of the child's pleasure in their new clothes away; however, an alternative, kinder verbal benediction was available in the form of: 'Health to wear it, strength to tear it, and money to buy another.'

Given the importance of Easter in the religious calendar, the emphasis on looking your best probably goes back a long way. It was certainly proverbial in the sixteenth century, as noted in Thomas Lodge's *Wits Miserie* (1596): 'The farmer that was contented in times past with his russet frock and mockado sleeves, now sells a cow against Easter to buy him silken gear for his credit'; and in Act III, scene 1 of William Shakespeare's *Romeo & Juliet* (1597), 'Didst thou not fall out with tailor for wearing his new doublet before Easter'. Over half a century later, Samuel Pepys provides some nice examples of the idea:

> [9 February 1662] . . . *was all day in my chamber – talking with my wife about her laying out of £20; which I had long since promised her to lay out in clothes against Easter for herself . . .*

> [30 March 1662] *Easterday: Having my old black suit new-furbished, I was pretty neat in clothes today – and my boy, his old suit new-trimmed, very handsome.*

Pepys's diary entries also demonstrate that Easter had been formalized as the time of year when new fashions were set, at least for the gentry who had the means to worry about such things:

> [15 February 1667] *She did give me account of this wedding today, its being private being imputed to its being just before Lent, and so in vain to make new clothes till Easter, that they might see the fashions*

*as they are like to be this summer – which is reason
good enough.*
See also **Whitsun: Superstitions**, p. 190.

Old Ball

Old Ball was an Easter house-visiting custom, reported
only from the area around Blackburn and Burnley in
Lancashire. A real horse's skull, or a wooden replica,
was mounted on a pole, with glass bottle bottoms for
eyes, a jaw that could open and close, and nails for
teeth. The operator would bend forward and grasp the
pole in both hands, and was covered by an old sack or
cloth, which formed the horse's body. Lancashire folklorists John Harland and T. T. Wilkinson described Old
Ball's antics in 1867:

> *He runs first at one then at another, neighing like
> a horse, kicking, rising on his hind legs, performing
> all descriptions of gambols, and running after the
> crowd; the consequence is, the women scream, the
> children are frightened, and all is one scene of the
> most ridiculous and boisterous mirth . . . Sometimes
> a doggerel song is sung, while Ball prances about and
> snaps at the company. As soon as the song is finished,
> Ball plays his most boisterous pranks and frequently
> hurts some of the company by snapping their fingers
> between his teeth when they are defending them-
> selves from his attacks. The writer has seen ladies so
> alarmed as to faint and go into hysterics.*

This was a localized form of the 'mast' version of the
hobby horse, similar to others found elsewhere such
as the **Hooden Horse** of Kent and the **Old Tup** in
Derbyshire and Yorkshire (*see* **24 December**). There are
no records of Old Ball before the nineteenth century
and he did not survive into the twentieth. Harland and
Wilkinson imply that it was Ball's rough behaviour that
prompted his downfall and disappearance.
See also **Hobby Horses**, p. 164.

Pace-Egging

Until the modern era succeeded in wiping out nearly all
vestiges of regionalism in traditional culture, the strong
connection with eggs made Easter one of the times at
which the northern counties of England had more in
common with lowland Scotland than with midland or

southern England. The 'pace-egg' customs described
below were widely reported in Lancashire, Cheshire,
parts of Yorkshire, Cumbria, Northumberland, and
County Durham, and many were also recorded in
Scotland, but the standard nineteenth-century folklore
collections from elsewhere in England make little reference to eggs at Easter. Indeed, they hardly mention the
season at all as a time for traditional custom. In those
northern areas, a series of varied but overlapping
customs, concerned with collecting eggs and using
them in various ways, existed throughout the nineteenth and well into the twentieth century. They could
be rolled on the ground, bashed together like conkers, kept for show, made into special Easter cakes, or
simply eaten then and there. They might be decorated,
grandly or simply, by the donors or the recipients,
or they might feature, somewhat marginally, in an
Easter version of the mummers' play (*see* **Easter Day:
Pace-Egg Plays**, p. 120). Any of these customs could be
called 'pace-egging', although this was often rendered
as 'peace-egging', 'pash-egging', or 'paste-egging'. This
term is clearly derived from *pasch* (the Latin for Easter),
a word that would presumably have been familiar to
English people from church services, and it has been
used with this meaning in English since at least 1385.
The word 'pace-egg' does not appear until 200 years
later, in the *Beehive of the Romishe Churche* (1579), in
a context which shows that the author regarded them
as examples of popish superstition, to be derided and
discarded:

> *Fasting days, years of grace, differences and diversi-
> ties of days, of meats, of clothing, of candles, holy
> ashes, holy pace eggs, and flames, palms and palm
> boughs, staves, fools' hoods, shells and bells, paxes,
> licking of rotten bones, etc.*

However, there is no record of a secular visiting or
egg-decorating custom until 1778, when William
Hutchinson wrote in his *History of Northumberland*
that 'The children have dyed and gilded eggs given to
them, which are called "Paste eggs".' In its most basic
form, pace-egging resembled numerous other house-
visiting customs in which parties (usually children
or young people in this case) went from house to
house singing a song and asking for money or food.
Similar visiting customs took place at other seasons

and in other areas: *see* **2 November: All Souls' Day**, **23 November: St Clement's Day**, and **Christmas: Wassailing** for examples. The song regularly used in this form of pace-egging also usually accompanied the pace-egg play, and versions varied considerably. One collected in Westmorland in 1909 commences:

> *Here's two or three jolly boys all of one mind*
> *We've come a-pace-egging if you will prove kind*
> *If you will prove kind with your eggs and strong beer*
> *We'll come no more nigh you until the next year*
> *Fol de roodle di diddle dum day*
> *Fol de roodle di diddle dum day.*

There were also numerous variations on the basic house-visit theme, as indicated in the standard collection of Lancashire folklore by John Harland and T. T. Wilkinson in 1882:

> *Young men in groups varying in number from three to twenty, dressed in various fantastic garbs, and wearing masks – some of the groups accompanied by a player or two on the violin – go from house to house singing, dancing, and capering. At most places they are liberally treated with wine, punch or ale, dealt out to them by the host or hostess. The young men strive to disguise their walk and voice, and the persons whom they visit use their efforts on the other hand to discover who they are; in which mutual endeavour many and ludicrous mistakes are made. Here you will see Macbeth and a fox-hunter arm in arm; Richard III and a black footman in familiar converse; a quack doctor and a bishop smoking their pipes and quaffing their 'half and half'; a gentleman and an oyster-seller; an admiral and an Irish umbrella-mender; in short every variety of character, some exceedingly well-dressed, and the characters well sustained . . .*
>
> *Children, both male and female, with little baskets in their hands, dressed in all the tinsel-coloured paper, ribbons, and 'doll-rags', which they can command, go up and down from house to house; at some receiving eggs, at others gingerbread, some of which is called hot gingerbread, having in it a mixture of ginger and cayenne, causing the most ridiculous contortions of feature in the unfortunate being who partakes of it. Houses are literally besieged by these juvenile troops from morning till night. 'God's sake! A pace egg', is the continual cry.*

Something of the feeling of these customs survived well into the twentieth century, as recorded in the Lancashire Federation of Women's Institutes' *Lancashire Lore* (1971):

> *Around Easter, at Overton and Middleton in the 1930s, we would go pace-egging. I remember one year putting on a dress inside out and covering my face with flour – it was then the custom to go round knocking on doors and be given decorated hard boiled eggs. We used to take little milk cans round the hedges collecting gorse flowers for my mother to colour our own home-produced eggs.*

What the recipients did with the eggs varied enormously, but one recurrent feature was rolling them. In Northumberland in 1909, Hastings M. Neville related that:

> *The children all assemble in a field having a steep slope and bowl the eggs uphill with as much force as they can. The object is to try whose egg will hold out longest without breaking; and sometimes who can throw the egg furthest.*

This account is only unusual in that the eggs were rolled uphill. More usually they were rolled downhill, or along flat ground, and some suitable slopes gained a reputation that have lasted for generations. In 1880, a correspondent to *Notes & Queries* reported:

> *On Easter Monday, the singular custom of rolling oranges and dyed eggs down the slopes of Avenham Park, Preston, Lancashire, was adhered to by all the youngsters of the neighbourhood. The grounds . . . were covered by a dense multitude of people, who come annually in the vicinity to witness and take part in this unique festivity.*

While on 4 April 1988, *The Times* announced, 'This afternoon, up to 40,000 will take part in the ancient custom of Easter egg-rolling in Avenham Park, Preston.' Egg-rolling could also be done competitively, with the eggs deliberately aimed at each other, like bowls, and with broken or cracked eggs being claimed by those whose eggs stayed whole. This could also be done in single combat, like conkers, and this was called 'egg-dumping' or 'jarping'; antiquarian John Brand described the game in the mid nineteenth century:

Holding his egg in his hand, he challenges a companion to give blow for blow. One of the eggs is sure to be broken, and the shattered remains are the spoil of the conqueror, who is instantly invested with the title of a cock of 'one, two, three', etc, in proportion as it may have fractured his antagonists' eggs in the conflict. A successful egg in a contest with one which had previously gained honours adds to its number the reckoning of its vanquished foe. An egg which is the 'cock' of ten or a dozen is frequently challenged.

The Opies found that egg-rolling was still popular in Scotland, and in England 'north of the Trent', in the 1950s. They also reported that egg-decorating, as mentioned by Hutchinson in 1778, was still prevalent. In 1849, John Brand also commented on this custom:

In the North of England, it is still the custom to send reciprocal presents of eggs at Easter to the children of families respectively betwixt whom any intimacy exists. The eggs being immersed in hot water for a few moments, the end of a common tallow candle is made use of to inscribe the names of individuals, dates of particular events, etc. The warmth of the egg renders this a very easy process. Thus inscribed, the egg is placed in a pan of hot water, saturated with cochineal, or other dye-woods; the part over which the tallow has been passed is impervious to the operation of the dye; and consequently when the egg is removed from the pan, there appears no discoloration of the egg where the inscription has been traced, but the egg presents a white inscription on a coloured ground. The colour of course depends upon the taste of the person who prepared the egg; but usually much variety of colour is made use of. Another method of ornamenting 'pace eggs' is, however, much neater, although more laborious, than that with the tallow candle. The egg being dyed, it may be decorated in a very pretty manner, by means of a penknife, with which the dye may be scraped off, leaving the design white, on a coloured ground.

Many other natural dyes were used, including onion skins, saffron, and the afore-mentioned gorse flowers, while ribbons, tinsel, and other items glued to the shell could be used to make presentation pieces. In middle-class Victorian homes, egg-decorating was often a complex craft, if not actually high art, and in this way the custom finally broke free from its regional confines and spread across the rest of the country in the later nineteenth century. The story of the 'Easter Eggs and How the Girls Made Them', for example, published in the *Girls' Own Paper* of 12 March 1881, explains how three teenagers made a range of pretty presentation eggs for their families, including ones with painted and etched shells and some with little dolls or sweets inside. But although the girls 'knew of' the tradition of decorating eggs, they had to look up how to do it in books.

By this time, shops had begun to sell professionally decorated eggs, and in 1875 John Cadbury had launched the first commercial chocolate egg, which eventually revolutionized the connection between eggs and Easter. On 10 March 1894, *Chambers's Journal* noticed the trend:

Year by year the season of Easter has attained increased importance in our midst, giving an opportunity to those so inclined of displaying feelings and affections towards relatives and friends by the distribution of little presents in the various forms of 'Easter Eggs'.

See also **Easter Day: Eggs**, p. 115; *compare* **Shrovetide and Lent**, p. 49; **Shrove Tuesday: Egg Shackling**, p. 60.

Pace-Egg Plays

A number of customs that took place at Easter were called **pace-egging** (*see* p. 118), but one of the best-known was a version of the mummers' play (*see* **Christmas: Mummers**). As with many other egg customs, pace-egg plays were found only in Lancashire, Yorkshire, and Cumbria (where they were called 'Jolly Boys'). They were often performed by children rather than adults, and from the 1930s onwards there was a strong tradition of performances organized by local schools. The play performed annually at Midgley in West Yorkshire by teenagers from Calder Valley High School since 1932 is the best known and longest-lasting of these. School-based teams normally performed in the street, for everyone present, rather than acting privately during house visits, and this pattern has been continued by modern revival teams.

Most pace-egg versions are at heart a fairly typical 'hero-combat' play in which two 'heroes' (typically, the King or Saint George, and Bold Slasher) boast and fight; one is injured or killed and is revived by a doctor. On the whole, the text is similar to other mumming plays, as in the extract here from Greenodd, Lancashire, published in Alex Helm's *The English Mummers' Play* (1980):

> *In steps I, Prince of Paradise, black Morocco King*
> *My sword and buckle by my side and through the*
> * woods I ring*
> *And through the woods I ring*
> *I'm brave, lads, and that's what makes us good*
> *And through thy dearest body, George, I'll draw thy*
> * precious blood.*

However, small details are different: a calling-on song is included, for example, which introduces characters such as Tosspot, Lord Nelson, Paddy from Cork, and a female called Molly Masket (with eggs in her basket) or Dirty Bet:

> *So the first to come in is old Tosspot you see*
> *A jolly old fellow in every degree*
> *He wears a top hat and he wears a pigtail*
> *And all his delight is in drinking mulled ale.*

Those named in the song do not normally take part in the play itself, and these songs also often accompanied the 'pace-eggers' who did not perform a play but simply went from house to house begging money and/or eggs. In general, performers in pace-egg plays dress 'in character' (i.e. with some attempt to depict their character realistically), although in earlier sources they often wore little more than distinguishing sashes over their ordinary clothes.

The question of the role of print in the development and dissemination of mummers' plays is still a vexed one, but chapbook texts were certainly influential in the spread of pace-egg plays, although even here the full extent of that influence is open to debate. Chapbooks were small cheap booklets that provided the texts of the plays and rudimentary instructions for

A Midgley pace-egger, Lancashire, 1981

performance, and were available from travelling chapmen and in stationers' and toyshops a few weeks before Easter, from the mid eighteenth century up to the First World War; one edition was even reprinted in 1959. The typical chapbook, like its cousin the broadside, was decidedly at the lower end of the printing trade, and was roughly printed on cheap paper. Pace-egg plays, with titles such as *The Peace Egg, or St. George's Annual Play for the Amusement of Youth,* were printed mainly in the area where the plays were later collected by folklorists, but they were also printed as far afield as Glasgow. One of their major attractions for children was the inclusion of several crude but lively woodcuts depicting the characters.

Since the 1960s, many enthusiastic revival teams have been founded, a number of which, having acquired sufficient stability and longevity, can now claim to have founded new traditions in themselves.

Riding the Lord

A problematic description of a custom, written by George Gleave of Manchester in 1895, describes a unique custom at Neston in Cheshire:

The morning's interlude usually began with the hidden but grotesque custom of what was called 'Riding the Lord'...[which] consisted in a man such as 'Ned Fabb,' who was not over scrupulous with regard to his employment, riding for some small pecuniary consideration on a donkey from the top of what is now called High-street to Chester-lane; and, in his burlesque progress, encountering, not only the ribald jeers of the holiday spectators, but also the more formidable and unsavoury bespatterment of a continuous fusillade of rotten eggs.

The Local Studies librarian at Cheshire Record Office confirms that no other independent source seems to mention this custom at all, although many subsequent writers, including the influential folklorist Christina Hole, repeat Gleave's account, often without acknowledgement. This being so, it would normally be safest to discount the custom completely, except for the fact that it appears to share interesting connections with other customs in which a person or effigy is similarly mistreated, including widespread **rough music** (p. 74) and Guy Fawkes events (*see* **5 November**), and particularly those surrounding **Jack-a-Lent** (p. 67), the Riding of the Black Lad (*see* **Easter Monday: Black Knight of Ashton**, p. 124) and the Burning of Bartle (*see* **24 August: West Witton Burning of Bartle**).

*

EASTER MONDAY

Biddenden Maids Charity

One of the most widely known charity doles in the country is the annual distribution of bread and cheese at Biddenden in Kent, on Easter Monday. Recipients are handed a large loaf of bread, half a pound of cheese, two pounds of tea, and a commemorative 'cake', which is actually a hard, inedible biscuit. A colourful story explains the origin of the custom. The cake bears an embossed image of two women, standing very close together, and the words 'Elizabeth and Mary Chulkhurst'; on the dress of one is written 'A 34 Y', and on the other, 'IN 1100', which is usually taken to mean 'Aged 34 in the year 1100'. The story relates that Eliza and Mary Chulkhurst were conjoined twins, joined at shoulder and hip, who were born (or died) in 1100. They lived until the age of thirty-four, when one of them died. The other twin refused offers to attempt a surgical separation, saying that 'they had come into the world together, and they would leave it in the same way', and she died soon after. As was common in those days, the sisters left a legacy, in the form of twenty acres of land, sufficient to fund the annual distribution of bread, cheese, and ale to poor parishioners.

The story of the Chulkhurst sisters is central to the village's heritage. They are depicted on the sign in the centre of the village and on at least one other property nearby; there is also a new development called Chulkhurst Close, and the dole itself is officially called the 'Chulkhurst Charity'. However, there is a problem with the story. Although the dole has certainly existed for a long time, and the 'Bread and Cheese Land' is real enough, there is no evidence of when the legacy was founded, or who it was founded by, although 1100 is probably far too early. There is also no independent evidence that Eliza and Mary Chulkhurst even existed, let alone that they were responsible for the Biddenden dole. The whole story of the Siamese twins seems to have been invented to explain the illustration on the biscuit. The evidence to support this idea comes from two early written sources, and the key witness is Edward Hasted, whose *History of Kent* was published in 1790:

There is a vulgar tradition in these parts that the figures on the cake represent the donors of this gift, being two women, twins who were joined together in their bodies and lived together so, till they were between twenty and thirty years of age. But this seems to be without foundation. The truth seems to be that it was the gift of two maidens of the name of Preston, and that the print of the women on the cakes has taken place only within these fifty years, and was made to represent two poor widows as a general object of a charitable benefaction.

Hasted may be referring to the second edition of Dr Ducarel's *Repertory of the Endowments and Vicarages*

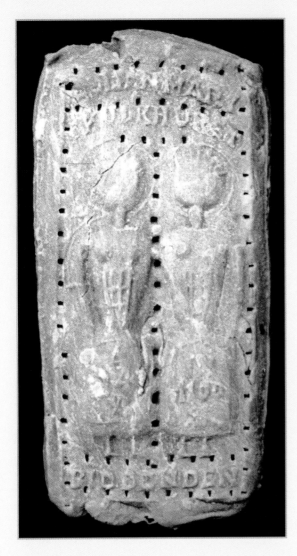

One of the Cakes annually Given at Biddenden Church on Easter Sunday.

Biddenden Maids Charity, Kent.
Left: the biscuit as it appeared in the 1950s;
above: the earliest known illustration of the maids, 1782

in the Dioceses of Canterbury and Rochester, published eight years before, in 1782. This short account mentions that the women were conjoined, and lists their age as twenty or thirty years, and Ducarel provides an engraving of the illustration on the cakes. In this picture, the two women do indeed seem to be joined at the arm, but although their dresses meet, they are clearly not joined 'at the hip'. The only word on the cakes is 'Biddenden', and there is none of the lettering on which the 'Chulkhurst' story is based.

We are also fortunate that in 1656, the rector of the parish, William Horner, attempted to prove that the Bread and Cheese Land formed part of his own glebe lands. He was unsuccessful, but his action resulted in

documentation of the charity being preserved in the parish records, which are now available in the Centre for Kentish Studies in Maidstone. As is the nature of such cases, the officials took evidence from elderly people in the parish, to establish what was known of the charity's history. In the surviving papers, the land is referred to throughout as the 'bread and cheese lands', and there are several mentions of the charity being instituted by 'two sisters', but there is no mention of the name Chulkhurst or any of the other colourful details of the modern story. Indeed, it seems that the names of the benefactors had already been forgotten in 1656, and how Edward Hasted came up with the name 'Preston' is at present unclear. Nevertheless, even if the story itself is full of holes, it is remarkable that the dole still continues each year.

The Biddenden dole is not unique, however, and in fact seems to be part of a long tradition of 'bread and cheese' charities, although the only other one still going is at St Briavels in Gloucestershire (*see* **Whit Sunday: St Briavels Bread and Cheese Dole**, p. 193), and that has taken a very different shape. A detailed comparison with these other doles may well shed some light on Biddenden's history. See, for example, the following piece taken from the Charity Commissioners' Reports:

> *Bread and cheese lands: the lands thus denominated are said to have been given by two maiden gentle-women, for the purpose of supplying the poor with a donation of bread and cheese on the Sunday before Christmas. Neither the names of the donors nor the date of the gift are known, but it is a very ancient one.*

Apart from the time of year, this description fits Biddenden exactly, but it was actually written about a custom that took place at Paddington, in London, until the mid nineteenth century. Similarly, a dole in which bread and cheese was thrown from a church tower existed at Twickenham, Middlesex, up to the turn of the nineteenth century. The custom had originally taken the form of breaking two large cakes in church on Easter Monday, but the Puritan parliament of 1645 decreed the cake to be superstitious and insisted it was replaced with bread and cheese for the poor. This is an excellent example of the way in which customs sometimes undergo abrupt alteration in response to changes in the prevailing religious or cultural atmosphere of the period, rather than being subject to the slow organic evolution that we often assume has always been the norm.

For another example of cakes being distributed in church, *see* **Palm Sunday: Pax Cakes**, p. 99. *See also* **Doles**, p. 87.

Black Knight of Ashton

The former celebrations at Ashton-under-Lyne in Lancashire are an excellent example of how a long-term local working-class custom can become a disreputable and discouraged event, but when taken by the ruling elite, and cleaned and prettied up, can be made the centrepiece of a new custom that celebrates and supports the town's prosperity and bolsters local pride.

Until late Victorian times, the inhabitants of Ashton-under-Lyne would be treated on Easter Monday to the spectacle of the Riding of the Black Lad (or Knight, or Boy). An effigy of a knight in black armour and black cloak was mounted on a horse, paraded around the town, and shouted and jeered at by the waiting crowds. At an appointed place, the Black Lad was dismounted, pelted with mud and stones, verbally insulted, and finally shot to pieces with any guns the townsfolk could muster. An eyewitness account from 1870 reveals the carnival nature of the proceedings:

> *It was easy to see that it was a gala day. In the market ground was the usual spectacle of a Lancashire fair. Once or twice we heard sounds of music in the distance and saw crowds hurrying off in search of the sounds which they knew heralded the approach of the Black Knight. We joined one of these parties and soon saw, marching down the middle of the street, a motley crowd. After the musicians came the figure of the Black Knight, in grotesque costume and mounted on some kind of a horse, followed by his retainers, who were busy collecting coppers from the crowd. The figure of the Black Knight, provided with a dragoon's helmet, a cuirass having the arm-holes stuffed with bunches of heather, and red trowsers apparently stuffed with sawdust, was held in place by a youth riding behind it. It turned out, however, that this was not the true Black Knight; we found that there were three Black Knights, so we paid to each.*

The tale that explains the Black Knight's fame tells of one Sir Ralph de Assheton, a fifteenth-century lord of the manor, who was exceptionally cruel to everybody in his power, including his wife, servants, and subjects. He pillaged and murdered at will, and had a habit of placing his victims in a spike-lined barrel and rolling them down a nearby hill. He also had a particular antipathy for those who allowed corn marigolds and other weeds to grow on his land. After murdering his wife, he was finally shot down in the street by one of her relatives, or by one of his disgruntled tenants. In a further incongruous detail, he (or his descendant) is reputed to have left money to fund the annual celebration of his life and death. Unsurprisingly, this story is not only historically inaccurate, with a mistaken chronology, but there is also no evidence that any of the Assheton family had a reputation for being cruel or despotic. The whole thing appears to have been invented simply to explain the *Black* in 'Black Knight', as that epithet, in popular parlance, refers to character as well as appearance.

The first known reference to the custom, in 1795, already cited Sir Ralph as the basis for the Black Lad, and this idea was developed by Dr Samuel Hibbert, of the Society of Scottish Antiquaries, in 1822. Hibbert's theory was recycled in William Hone's immensely influential *Every-Day Book* (1827), and from then on became the accepted story, accruing details along the way. Folklorists such as Christina Hole have offered a different interpretation, that the effigy, so reviled and mistreated, symbolized winter and was ritually destroyed each year to welcome the spring. Unfortunately for this explanation, however, there is no evidence that the custom even existed before the 1790s, or that it had a ritual basis.

A letter published by Hone in 1827 claimed 'it is the most thronged, and the most foolish, day the Ashtonians can boast of.' As indicated by William Axon in 1870, by his time there were several effigies parading the town, some more respectable than others, and the feeling grew that the 'real' custom had degenerated into a form of begging for money to spend on drink. It is a familiar story that was played out in towns all over the country, as such customs gradually lost the support of the important middle classes who increasingly ran local public affairs.

By the late nineteenth century, the old custom of Riding the Black Lad had virtually died out, unlamented by most of the respectable inhabitants of Ashton. By the time increasing prosperity and civic pride brought about the idea of a historical pageant to celebrate the town's heritage in 1910, the reality of the old celebrations was safely in the past, and the organizing committee chose the Black Knight of Ashton as the pageant's centrepiece. The unofficial historical story with which the figure had been associated became the official text, and was taught to schoolchildren and recounted in countless pageant programmes, local histories, town guides, and, nowadays, Internet sites. The Ashton pageant was on a large scale, and it became one of the best-known in the area. It included, over the years, all the usual waving dignitaries, trade floats, tableaux, marching children, banners, bands, collectors rattling tins, and individual and group efforts in fancy dress, in addition to, at various times, a May Queen, Rose Queen, Harvest Queen, Civic Queen, Pageant Queen, and Cotton Queen. The Rose Queen was prompted by the move of the pageant to Alexandra Rose Day, in 1928.

The real centrepiece, however, which the crowd waited eagerly to see, was always the Black Knight himself, an imposing figure on horseback, and usually dressed completely in black on a black horse. His costume changed over the years and was the subject of much comment and debate, but it always approximated the current idea of a knight, with helmet, cloak, and sword. He was attended by a large retinue, including wife, servants, and guards, all in period costume, and often some boys carrying a barrel with spikes inside.

The annual pageants increased in scale, complexity, and popularity for the next few years, but, as with many other celebratory events, the First World War put an end to it. Nevertheless, the Black Knight Pageant was successfully revived in 1928, lapsed in 1935, staged again in 1939, and 1947 (for the town's centenary celebrations), and finally lapsed in 1954. Over the years, the pageants provided immense pleasure for participants and onlookers, and raised significant amounts for local charities, particularly, in the early years, for the local hospital. In recent years, ideas for large-scale events in Ashton, as elsewhere, have taken the form of carnivals rather than pageants, and the Black Knight has lost his opportunity for an airing. But he has a new lease of life as emblem for the Arcades shopping centre in the middle of town, where his statue can be seen every day by the people of Ashton.

The Black Lad is not alone in English tradition. The mistreatment of an effigy or particular person is a motif that appears in a number of contexts, most widely as an essential element of **rough music** activities (p. 74), but also in other, specific customs: *see* **Easter Day: Riding the Lord**, p. 122; **Ash Wednesday: Jack-a-Lent**, p. 67; **Spring Bank Holiday: Hunting the Earl of Rone**, p. 206; and **24 August: West Witton Burning of Bartle**.

Epping Stag Hunt

An annual occasion at Epping, in Essex, until 1853 was a stag hunt held on Easter Monday, in which hundreds of Londoners joined, to their own peril and the chagrin of the real hunting fraternity in the area, who largely stayed away from the event. Later accounts stress the comic effect of hopelessly inexperienced men and women, gaudily dressed for the hunt, chasing an 'old fat one-eyed stag' released from a cart. Thomas Hood's comic poem 'The Epping Hunt' (written in the 1820s) sums it all up. It commences by introducing its 'hero' grocer:

> John Huggins was as bold a man
> As trade did ever know,
> A warehouse good he had, that stood
> Hard by the church of Bow.

And goes on to relate, in over a hundred verses dripping with puns, how Huggins and his co-hunters, in pursuit of the stag, get lost, thrown off their horses into ditches, and overturn their carts.

In previous times, however, the hunt had been much more respectable, with the Lord Mayor, aldermen, and the Corporation of London in attendance. It was reputedly inaugurated as long ago as 1226.

Gawthorpe Coal-Carrying

Gawthorpe, a small West Yorkshire village that lies between Dewsbury and Wakefield, hosts the World Coal-Carrying Championship. This annual race was started in 1963, apparently after a 'discussion' in the pub between two locals on the subject of how fit each one was. Contestants have to cover a course around the village of just over a thousand metres, carrying a sack of coal weighing fifty kilos across their shoulders. There is also a ladies' race, with competitors carrying twenty kilos. The current world record for men is four minutes and six seconds, while for women it is five minutes and five seconds. The winners receive money, vouchers, and so on, depending on the sponsor, which at present is the local brewery, H. B. Clarke & Co. The event has changed somewhat in its time, as the local coal-pits have closed and the racers are less likely to be local miners and more likely to be from outside the immediate area; but it still remains a well-loved event in the village, and raises money for local charities.

See also **First Saturday in May: Gawthorpe Celebrations**.

Hallaton Hare Pie and Bottle-Kicking

The Leicestershire village of Hallaton carries out an annual hare-pie scramble and bottle-kicking, which probably combines two previous customs joined into one – the first a traditional 'dole', and the second a form of mass 'football'. The two are now intertwined on Easter Monday, but either could quite logically stand alone.

The 'dole' part of the day involves the hare pie and some 'penny loaves', which are distributed to the people. After a church service at about 11 a.m. at St Michael's, the rector cuts up the hare pie, and distributes some pieces, but most of it is placed into sacks for later. In the afternoon, a procession takes place up to Hare Pie Bank, where the rest of the pie is flung to the crowd. The hare pie is not made of hares' meat, and as hares are out of season at Easter and have never been a popular food with English people, it possibly never was. It now contains beefsteak, although earlier sources mention mutton, veal, and bacon. Most **scrambling customs** (p. 128) involve hard or at least durable substances such as pennies, sweets, or oranges, and pieces of meat pie do not seem to be ideal for throwing to the crowds. It is often reported that people do not actually try to eat the pie, but photographer and author Brian Shuel commented in 1985 that '[t]he scramble was a token affair for the young, not taken very seriously. The pie was delicious, far from inedible like many early reports complain.'

The 'bottle-kicking' part of the day then takes place at Hare Pie Bank. The 'bottles' are actually three small wooden kegs, two of which contain beer, while one is empty. They are blessed in the morning church service, and are prominently carried in the procession by three men, each holding one at arm's length above his head. The contest then begins, and is between the people of Hallaton on one side and those of neighbouring Medbourne on the other, with any outsiders joining the latter team, which gives them a distinct advantage.

Bottle-kicking at Hallaton, Leicestershire

Each team tries to get the bottle to their goal, one of two streams, which are a mile apart.

As with other traditional games subsumed under the name **football** (p. 53), there is no limit to the number of players and virtually no rules, but because this game takes place in the fields rather than the village streets, the style of play is more open and more akin to a very rough rugby match than some other games are. Despite the name, the bottles are rarely kicked. The game begins when a bottle is thrown up three times, and play only starts when it lands after the third throw. Whoever first grabs it is immediately surrounded by a mass of players of both sides. John Morison and Peter Daisley write in their recently published book on the custom:

The scrum writhes and churns as combatants strive to get hold of the bottle. The whole throng struggles forward, backwards, and side to side in no clear pattern. The crowd presses all around until suddenly there is a break. A combatant emerges with the bottle. Scattering onlookers, he is oblivious to resistance and charges through such minor obstacles as barbed wire fences and hedges ... Such breaks rarely last long. Soon the man with the bottle is dragged down and becomes the nucleus of another scrum.

After a goal is scored, a second bottle is thrown up, and if there is a tie after the second game, the third is brought into play as a decider. The game changes character as the day wears on: participants become tired, some drop out, the scrums get smaller, and play becomes more open.

Certain aspects have been revived or introduced in recent years, as the usual tendency towards making an event a more family-friendly (or perhaps tourist-friendly) carnival or pageant has taken place. Many traditional customs were perfunctory and even dull for the outsider to watch, but a little imaginative tinkering can bring a sense of cohesion, as well as colour, to the

Scrambling Customs

A very common feature in a range of customs was to throw things to a waiting crowd to be 'scrambled for'. Coins were one of the staple items, but food such as buns, oranges, nuts, and even bread and cheese were regularly distributed in this way, and although in the twentieth century the scramblers were usually children, in previous times the method was also used with adults and even the elderly. The throwing could take place from any convenient vantage point, but balconies, upstairs windows, and even church towers were regularly used in this way.

Scrambling could form part of another custom (*see*, for example, **Easter Monday: Hallaton Hare Pie and Bottle-Kicking**, p. 126), or as the favoured method of distribution in a charity dole. It could also feature in well-to-do rural weddings, where the bridegroom might throw handfuls of coins to the village children, or it could provide the popular climax to a civic ceremony like a mayor-making. As late as 1956, a reporter in *The Times* took this civic connection for granted:

> It was truly reviving to the spirits to read of the aldermen and other civic dignitaries of Abingdon on the occasion of the Queen's visit, in accordance with their ancient custom, throwing buns ... As there were some 2000 buns, at least the enjoyment was not done for some while. In a short time on November 9 mayors in other boroughs will be throwing down hot coppers to children in the street, but there is about that gesture none of the fine venomous aiming that there can be with a bun.

At Harwich, Essex, where the bun-throwing is still part of the mayoral celebrations, there were worries about hygiene in the 1960s, and the decision was made to wrap the buns in cellophane first.

The whole idea might seem strange or even reprehensible to modern eyes, especially if perishable food is being flung, but there were two different trains of thought behind the procedure which were probably in action at different times. If children were the recipients, there was a definite emphasis on the 'fun' involved, not only for the children themselves, but also for the adult organizers and watchers. When coins were used, there was a strong tradition of heating them first, and there can be no other explanation for this procedure beyond the extra enjoyment it provided. But in cases where the scrambling was part of a charity dole, the throwing seems to have been a deliberate policy to ensure random distribution that showed no favour, and was therefore deemed to be 'fair'. There was also the added advantage that such a method needed little administration. It was only when the proceedings became too boisterous, or even riotous, that scramblings were replaced by more controlled methods of distribution. Oddly enough, however, there is some evidence that the scrambling element may not necessarily have been an original feature of any particular custom at all. In a case described by Daniel Lysons in his *Environs of*

day. There is now a children's parade in the morning, and some of the adults have recently started to dress up in medieval costume. The penny loaves have been re-introduced after having been dropped for many years, necessitating a 'bread lady' to carry the basket, and the carrying of a hare as a sort of standard in the procession revives an element mentioned in earlier descriptions, although nowadays it is a brass replica rather than a dead animal on the pole. Nevertheless, these improvements have made no difference to the bottle-kicking, which still remains one of the roughest, toughest customs in the English calendar.

It is nowadays suggested that the bottle-kicking aspect of the day developed from the scrambling custom. The argument is that the hare pie, penny loaves, and ale were all designed for distribution by scrambling, and that local youths, as is the nature of youths everywhere, were primarily interested in the drink, and banded together to ensure that they captured the prize. This idea is certainly supported by one of the earliest descriptions of the custom, found in a letter from John Tailby to local historian John Nichols in 1796 (reprinted in Morison & Daisley (2000)) that speaks of scrambling for the ale but not of any organ-

London (1792), it was introduced to replace much more sedate proceedings:

> There was an ancient custom at Twickenham, of dividing two great cakes in the church on Easter Day among the young people; but it being looked upon as a superstitious relic, it was ordered by Parliament, 1645, that the parishioners should forbear that custom and, instead thereof, buy loaves of bread for the poor of the parish with the money that should have bought the cakes. It appears that the sum of £1 per annum is still charged upon the vicarage for the purpose of buying penny loaves for poor children on the Thursday after Easter. Within the memory of man they were thrown from the church steeple to be scrambled for; a custom which prevailed also, some time ago, at Paddington, and is not yet totally demolished.

Scrambling customs still survive in a number of places.

See also **14 February: Valentine's Day**; **Shrove Tuesday: Westminster Pancakes**, p. 63; **Maundy Thursday: Peter's Pence**, p. 102; **Hocktide: Hungerford Hocktide Court**, p. 134; **Mid May: Durham Mayor-Making**; **Third Thursday in May: Harwich Kichel-Throwing**; **Ascension Day: Oxford Beating the Bounds**, p. 182; **23 May: Rye Mayor Making**; **Whit Sunday: St Briavels Bread and Cheese Dole**, p. 193; **29 September: Michaelmas/Feast of St Michael and All Angels**.

ized 'game'. But it is just as likely that the original dole was for food and drink – some of the food to be scrambled for, the rest distributed or consumed on the spot, and the ale would be in the latter category.

Much also has been made of the 'sacred' nature of hares for Ancient Britons, the ancient connection between hares and Easter, and a supposed pagan origin of the Hallaton custom, all of which are extremely dubious. The scrambling custom is clearly the result of a Christian dole that distributed food, a form of bequest common from medieval times onwards. The only mystery is why it is called a *hare* pie, and as we

only have second and third-hand reports of the nature and contents of the original bequest at present, which are already heavily coloured by later assumptions, this will only be solved if the original can be found.

See also **Doles**, p. 87.

Harness Horse Parade

The Harness Horse Parade takes place in London's Battersea Park every Easter Monday, although it was previously held in Regent's Park. The parade dates back to 1886, when it was inaugurated to encourage commercial horse owners to take a pride in their animals, but the current series came into being in 1965, when it amalgamated with the London Van Horse Parade. The event starts at 10 a.m. and attracts scores of entries, including a wide range of horses and vehicles.

For illustration, *see* p. 130.

Legging Day

The following report can be found in John Nicholson's *Folk Lore of East Yorkshire* (1890):

> At Easter, boys and girls try to catch each other by the ankles and trip one another up, or 'leg them down', as they say. Hence Easter Monday is known as 'Leggin Day', but if you trip any one up at any time, you offer as excuse 'It's leggin day ti-day!'

Unfortunately, no other information is forthcoming.

Leicester Hare Hunt

This former calendar custom, with civic overtones, took place in Leicester on Easter Monday until about 1767. The mayor, corporation, and officers would proceed to a piece of land called Black Annis' Bower Close, at the edge of Leicester Forest, to witness the annual 'hare hunt'. In this hunt, a dead cat that had been treated with aniseed water was trailed on a rope around the town, through streets and alleys, by a rider; the hounds and huntsmen were then let loose to follow the trail. The first documentary evidence for the custom occurs in the town records for 1668, but it was then described as an ancient custom, and it is more than likely that the hunt originally involved a real hare.

Harness Horse Parade, Battersea Park, London

Sun Dancing

One of the most widespread Easter beliefs, reported from all over England, and in Ireland and Wales as well, was the idea that the sun literally danced for joy at the Resurrection on Easter Monday morning. The notion was already proverbial in the mid seventeenth century, as it is included in John Suckling's 'Ballade Upon a Wedding' (1646):

> But oh! she dances such a way –
> No sun upon an Easter day
> Were half so fine a sight . . .

It was recorded several more times before 1700, and numerous times from then on. There were a few variations; in some families, for example, it was said that you could see a lamb in the sun as it rose on that morning.

Educated people usually smiled condescendingly when reporting the idea, but there is no doubt that many believed it literally. The majority presumably took it on trust from hearsay, but there were plenty who made an annual trip to the nearest high hill to try to see it, as with this gentleman in Devon in 1876:

> I was awoke at daylight by gravel being thrown against my window, and on lifting the blind found that it proceeded from old John, who had come to call me to see the 'sun dance' . . . On mounting the side of Corndon Torr old John would occasionally turn round toward 'sunrise' and remark how fortunate we were in having so favourable a morning for our observation. We did not follow his example, reserving ourselves for the coup d'oeil at the summit; and in a few moments we were amply repaid, for a scene of unparalleled splendour broke upon our view, through a cloudless sky and rare atmosphere. 'How long will this continue, John?', 'Why, maister, up along ten o'clock; but not so strong when the sun has more power. I saw it Good Friday morning preparing; but on this morning it is ordained to dance to remind us of the Saviour's rising from the grave. See how red it is at the edges!' And so the old man, with uplifted eyes, had his gaze fixed upon the now bright morning sun.

But the 'maister' reported only that 'there was the same flickering, radiating effect that is seen at sunrise from any high summit.' He clearly lacked sufficient faith, or perhaps it was the Devil at work, as was said in Sussex at a similar time:

> There is a tradition that the sun always dances on the morning of Holy Sunday, but nobody has ever seen it because the devil is so cunning that he always puts a hill in the way to hide it.

Compare **24 December: Cattle Kneeling; Christmas: Holy Thorn(s)**.

Water

A children's custom, which went under various local names, involved the collection of water from a specific well, and mixing it with sugar, broken sweets, peppermint, or liquorice, to make a special drink. A correspondent to *Notes & Queries* wrote in 1870:

> *Elecampane on Easter Monday: During a recent*
> *visit to the little village of Castleton in Derbyshire, I*
> *noticed every child without exception had a bottle*
> *of this mixture – the younger ones having one tied*
> *around their necks – all sucking away at this curious*
> *compound of Spanish juice, sugar and water, with*
> *great assiduity. I was informed by a very old man*
> *that this custom had always obtained in Castleton on*
> *Easter Monday as long as he could remember.*

The traditional day for this activity varied from place to place, but it usually took place on Easter Monday, Ascension Day, or Palm Sunday, and its names included Elecampane (a herb), Spanish Sunday, Sugar-Cupping Day, Sugar-and-Water Day, Rinsing Day, and Shakking Monday. Derbyshire seems to have been the centre of the custom, where it is frequently reported from *c.*1830 well into the twentieth century, but it does not seem to have been much known in England outside the Midlands.

See also **Palm Sunday: Water**, p. 99.

*

EASTER MONDAY AND TUESDAY

Lifting

This custom, also called 'heaving', was widely reported in eighteenth- and nineteenth-century sources from the western side of north and middle England (Lancashire, Cheshire, Shropshire, Staffordshire, Worcestershire, and Derbyshire) and the northern half of Wales. A Manchester correspondent to the *Gentleman's Magazine* of 1784 describes it in the following way:

> *The men lift the women on Easter Monday, and the*
> *women the men on Tuesday. One or more take hold*
> *of each leg, and one or more of each arm, near the*
> *body, and lift the person up, in a horizontal position,*
> *three times. It is a rude, indecent, and dangerous*
> *diversion, practised chiefly by the lower class of*
> *people. Our magistrates constantly prohibit it by the*
> *bellman, but it subsists at the end of the town; and*

> *the women have of late converted it into a money*
> *job. I believe it is chiefly confined to these northern*
> *counties.*

The basic procedure was very similar from place to place, although there were differences in detail. Charlotte Burne, for example, recorded that in part of Shropshire the men carried posies that were dipped in water to sprinkle on the feet of the women, and whereas men were usually lifted in the way described, women and elderly people were more often placed in a chair, which was usually decorated with ribbons and bows. There was also a wide variation in the amount of 'rough handling' allowed. Nearly all the descriptions stress that it was very much a working-class custom, and several say that women and timid men avoided going out on the day if they could. But staying at home was not always sufficient protection, as the *Folk-Lore Journal* (1883) indicates:

> *. . . a case heard before Norton Magistrates the*
> *other day. The prosecutor, William Pullen, charged*
> *Thomas Lawton for being in his house for an unlaw-*
> *ful purpose. Defendant entered Mr. Pullen's house,*
> *and said he had come to lift his wife, and two men*
> *followed defendant to the garden-gate. Prosecutor*
> *told defendant to get out, or he would kick him out.*
> *He would not allow any one to take such liberties.*
> *Defendant thereupon became very abusive. It was*
> *stated that defendant was endeavouring to carry out*
> *an old Cheshire custom. The men lifted the women*
> *on Easter Monday, and women lifted men on Easter*
> *Tuesday. The magistrates informed defendant he*
> *must apologise and pay the costs.*

On the other hand, an old bookseller, over eighty years of age in 1881, told Charlotte Burne, 'It was a very pretty, pleasant old game . . . and I never heard that there was any harm in it.'

Owing to the Easter setting, it has been assumed on all sides that the custom celebrated the resurrection of Christ, and one report mentions that the lifters sang, 'Jesus Christ is risen again.' It is possible that this is true, but there is no real evidence either way. Nor is it clear how old the custom might be. It was certainly widespread by the second half of the eighteenth century, but it seems to spring into being at that time fully formed. It is tempting to assume a direct development from the much earlier custom of Hocktide binding (*see* **Hocktide**, p. 133), which also involved men and women trapping each other on alternate days, and again this is a distinct possibility. Binding and lifting were done at different times, but only a week apart, and it is possible that as Hocktide had lost most of its meaning by the Restoration, a revival could have moved the custom to the previous week to bring it into the Easter holidays, and the alteration from binding to lifting made at the same time in reference to the Resurrection. Occasional examples involving both ropes and chairs, as here from Worcestershire in 1856, might be evidence of a direct link:

> At Kidderminster . . . the women decked themselves gaily for the occasion, dressed a chair with ribbons, and placed rope across the street; any man bold enough to come within yards of them was caught, placed in the chair, which was lifted up and turned round three times, and finally set down; the terms of release were then settled.

However, this is speculation, and one factor that can be used to argue against the theory is the geographical evidence. As stated, lifting was recorded almost exclusively in the western midland counties of England and in North Wales. Hocktide binding, on the other hand, was heavily concentrated in the South and East. Moreover, there were other variations on similar themes, less commonly reported, that pitted men against women on adjacent days, often concerned with shoes and hats. In 1865, in his *History and Antiquities of Masham and Mashamshire*, John Fisher recorded that in Yorkshire:

> On Easter Sunday, young men and boys, by prescriptive right, take the liberty of taking the shoes from off young women's feet, and of keeping them till redeemed by a payment of money; and on Easter Monday, the young women in exercise of the same right, possess themselves, as best they can, of the hats of the young men and retain them until they are redeemed by a like payment.

Lifting survived in a few places until the turn of the twentieth century, but faded away soon after.

*

EASTER TUESDAY

Holly Bussing

This Easter Tuesday practice was reported only from the Northumberland village of Netherwitton in the mid nineteenth century, although it was claimed to be a 'very ancient custom'. The young people of the village, accompanied by the parish clerk 'with his violin', gathered holly in the local woods and decorated a stone cross that stood in the village, after which they spent the rest of the day dancing.

Tuppenny Starvers

This annual dole takes place at the church of St Michael-on-the-Mount Without, in Bristol, on Easter Tuesday. After a children's service, those attending are given large buns called 'Tuppenny Starvers', although they were previously only given to children. The custom dates from at least 1739, when local inhabitants Peter and Mary Davis took steps to perpetuate it; they left a legacy to support it when they died in 1748. Incidentally, 'tuppenny' is the pre-decimal pronunciation of 'twopenny'.

See also **Doles**, p. 87.

*

LOW SUNDAY

Low Sunday is the first Sunday after Easter, and can fall anywhere between 29 March and 2 May. It goes by various names, including Little Easter Sunday, White Sunday, and Quasimodo Sunday. The latter refers directly to the first words of the Latin anthem chanted at the beginning of the mass for the day, 'Quasimodo geniti infantes' ('Like newborn babes'). Similarly, 'Low' is not intended to belittle the day in relation to Easter, but probably stems from *laudes*, 'praise'.

Few secular customs seem to have adhered to this day, perhaps because it was too close to the celebrations of Easter. But one apparently unique ceremony calls for special notice. The Cornish historian Richard Carew (1555–1620) provided an interesting description of an annual 'mock prince' ceremony at Lostwithiel, which in 1602 was 'only of late days discontinued':

Children with their Tuppenny Starvers, Bristol, 1984

There seems to be no direct parallel between this custom and any other, although it is tempting to link it to the numerous mock mayors found up and down the country (*see* **Mock Mayors and Courts**, p. 216). However, this comparison is not convincing: these mayors were invariably play-acted by the roughest elements in the community, with great parody and burlesque, whereas Carew's prince was drawn from the higher strata of society and treated with respect, even by the clergy.

*

HOCKTIDE

Hocktide is the Monday and Tuesday after Easter, and can therefore fall anywhere between 30/31 March and 3/4 May. Its origin is a real mystery, although it was already being cited as a quarter or term day by *c.*1175, and was often paired with Michaelmas to divide the year in two; from the early fifteenth century it was a minor church festival. Even the word 'Hocktide' has excited controversy, with the *Oxford English Dictionary* remarking, 'Few words have received so much etymological and historical investigation . . . but the origin has not yet been ascertained.' There is no trace of it in Old English or in other Germanic languages, although there have been numerous unsuccessful attempts to link it to words meaning 'high holiday' or even 'high wedding'.

By the early fifteenth century, Hocktide was almost synonymous with the custom of 'binding' that took place at the season, in which men and women tried to capture and bind each other with ropes that were only released on payment of a small fee. The men attempted to bind the women on one day, and the women tried to catch the men on another. The earliest sources to mention the custom – in London in 1406 and 1409 – condemn the practice, but by the 1450s church accounts begin to include regular entries for money raised in this way at Hocktide, and it is noteworthy that where the takings of two sexes are separately accounted, the women always gathered far more:

Upon little Easter Sunday the freeholders of the town and manor, by themselves or their deputies, did there assemble: amongst whom one (as it fell to his lot by turn) bravely apparelled, gallantly mounted, with a crown on his head, a sceptre in his hand, a sword borne before him, and dutifully attended by all the rest on horseback, rode through the principal street to the church; there the curate in his best beseen solemnly received him at the churchyard stile and conducted him to hear divine service, after which he repaired with the same pomp to a house foreprovided for that purpose, made a feast to his attendants, kept the table's end himself, and was served with kneeling, assay, and all other rites due to the estate of a prince: with which dinner the ceremony ended and every man returned home again.

St. Mary-at-Hill (London) parish accounts
1497
Gathered by the women on Hob Monday	*13s. 4d.*
By the men on Tuesday	*5s.*

It is clear from these records that the Hocktide games gathered significant sums of money for the Church, and there is also evidence that the participants were treated to a feast on the day, presumably to reward their efforts. But the later history of the custom is chequered, as it again fell foul of changing religious morality. It disappeared *c.*1549 under Edward VI, was revived under Mary, and continued into the reign of Elizabeth I, but gradually dwindled until it again disappeared with the Puritan rule of the mid seventeenth century. It is not clear how far Hocktide binding was revived after the Restoration, but by the eighteenth century it had been eclipsed by the custom of 'lifting' or 'heaving' at Easter, which also pitted men against women on alternate days (*see* **Easter Monday and Tuesday: Lifting**, p. 131).

As already indicated, the origins of both custom and festival remain a mystery. Popular explanations are that the binding custom commemorated the massacre of the Danes in 1002, or that it celebrated English freedom when the last Danish king, Hardicanute, died in 1042, and Edward the Confessor gained the throne. Neither of these explanations holds water, but the massacre story was already in circulation in the fifteenth and sixteenth centuries, and it is interesting to note that spurious historical explanations are not simply a modern manifestation.

Hungerford Hocktide Court

The people of Hungerford, in Berkshire, are probably the only ones in the country who still care about Hocktide. They have a unique surviving manorial court, with colourful characters and customs attached, which meets each year at this season. The owners of about one hundred properties in the High Street are commoners of the Court and have certain rights of common, and of fishing in the River Kennet, which were formerly economically significant and are still important to the local community. They were reputedly granted by John of Gaunt in 1364, although this cannot be proven as the supposed charter has been lost. Despite numerous attempts over the centuries to challenge these rights, they still exist and they are administered and upheld by the Court.

At 8 a.m. on Hock Tuesday, the commoners are called to attend the Hocktide Court by a man ringing a bell in the street and blowing a hunting horn from the balcony of the town hall; there is a fine for non-attendance. The Court sits at nine o'clock to consider business relating to the town's commons, and to elect officers, including the Constable (equivalent to a mayor), Portreeve, Bailiff, Water Bailiffs, Aletasters, and four Tithing men. Two of the latter are designated 'Tuttimen', and they set off along the High Street, ostensibly to collect dues from each inhabitant, but whereas the men have to pay in coin, the Tuttimen extract a kiss from the women. The Tuttimen wear top hats and morning dress, and carry poles decorated with ribbons and flowers. They are accompanied by the Orange Scrambler, who carries a bag of oranges to give in return for the kisses and to children they meet on the way. Their progress is traditionally impeded, rather than assisted, by the hospitality they receive in many houses. As the *Independent* reported in 1993:

> '*Basically all we do*', said one of the Tuttimen, '*is turn up, kiss a few girls, hand out a few coins, and get plastered.*'

Strangely enough, the word 'tutty' is in the *Oxford English Dictionary* and has a respectable lineage back to at least the sixteenth century, meaning 'a nosegay, a posy, a tuft or bunch of flowers'.

After the traditional luncheon following the Court's business, any newcomers are likely to be seized for the ceremony of 'Shoeing the Colt'. The Colt is grabbed by the Official Blacksmith and assistants, who commence to hammer a nail into his/her shoe, until s/he cries, 'Punch!' and thereby agrees to pay for more drinks.

The Hocktide Court is now a registered charitable trust, and those involved are fiercely proud of it. According to the same piece in the *Independent* from 1993:

> '*This is the sort of thing we English have gone to war to protect,*' said Andrew Sawyer, the local vicar . . . '*This, and the right to gather watercress from the marsh.*'

*

Hocktide at Hungerford, Berkshire, 1990

TWO WEEKS AFTER EASTER

Spital Sermon

'Spital' comes from the same root as 'hospital', but in late medieval times the word already meant a charitable institution dealing with beggars and those afflicted with 'foul diseases', and it never lost its low-class status. Annual sermons given in aid of these institutions were usually held outdoors, although visiting dignitaries would have shelters in which to sit. The sermon that now takes place at St Lawrence Jewry church in Gresham Street, London, has had a number of venues, and was originally held at the priory church of St Mary Spital, where the outdoor pulpit was destroyed in 1642.

After the Restoration, the sermons were held in other London churches until they settled at St Lawrence's after the Second World War. The Lord Mayor of London still attends in state, with his retinue, but the date of the sermon is sometimes rearranged to suit his/her busy schedule. Traditionally it occurs on the second Wednesday after Easter, but in 2006 it took place in March.

Another outdoor spital sermon takes place at Magdalen College, Oxford, in June every year (*see* **24 June: Magdalen Outdoor Sermon**).

*

19 APRIL

Primrose Day

The Primrose League was formed in 1883 to perpetuate the political ideals of Benjamin Disraeli (Prime Minister in 1868 and 1874–80), who died on 19 April 1881. Although nowhere near as strong as it used to be, the League was until recently still a presence in the modern Conservative Party, and sympathizers wear primroses, or primrose badges, on the day of Disraeli's death. It is clear that in the first half of the last century this was a popular feature of the day, and in her *Lincolnshire Calendar* (1997) Maureen Sutton includes reminiscences of several people who remember trips to the woods just before the day to gather primroses for sale to the general public.

It is usually stated that the spring flower was Disraeli's favourite, but Sutton also reports a tradition that this was a misunderstanding. She claims that Queen Victoria sent a wreath of primroses to Disraeli's funeral, with a note that read, 'His favourite flowers', by which she meant those of her late husband, Albert, but this was naturally taken to refer to Disraeli himself.

*

21 APRIL

Queen Elizabeth II's Birthday

Queen Elizabeth II's real birthday is on 21 April. The day is marked by gun salutes in Hyde Park at 12 noon, and at the Tower of London at 1 p.m.

See also **Second Saturday in June: Queen Elizabeth II's Official Birthday**.

*

23 APRIL

St George's Day

St George is the patron saint of England, but he has always proved something of a problem for the English. He may not even have existed at all, but it is possible that he was one of several candidates in early Christianity, none of whom had anything to do with England, dragons, or damsels in distress; these legends were not developed until the Middle Ages. Modern English people have proved notoriously unwilling to do anything to celebrate his day, despite periodic campaigns in the national press, and there are regular calls for his replacement by a home-grown real-life saint such as St Edmund, St Alban, or St Cuthbert.

The main contender for the real St George was a Christian, born in Cappadocia, who served with distinction in the Roman army. When Emperor Diocletian began his persecution of Christians, George publicly declared his faith, was tortured in just about every way imaginable, and finally beheaded in AD 303. The legend of his fight with a dragon was added in the thirteenth century, and was a masterstroke in public relations for the saint's image. It not only gave him a spectacular backstory, but also provided an instantly recognizable trademark, which made him a popular figure for all kinds of illustrations and effigies.

St George was introduced to Britain by returning Crusaders, who had come across his cult in their Middle Eastern campaigns. It was mainly his reputation as 'soldier saint' which attracted them, and he famously appeared in the sky to encourage the Christian troops at Antioch in 1098. St George's Day was officially recognized at the Synod of Oxford in 1222, and by the mid fourteenth century he had ousted Edward the Confessor as putative patron saint of England. George fitted well with the prevailing fashion for chivalry, and it is no accident that the most exclusive mock-chivalric institution of all, the Order of the Garter, was founded about the same time, with St George as patron.

George rapidly became widely popular with rich and poor alike. One of the most obvious manifestations of this popularity was the proliferation of guilds, or fraternities, dedicated to him, which existed in many areas as associations devoted to religious and charitable works. These guilds were particularly strong in Leicester, Norwich, Coventry, York, Stratford, and Chester, but not, it seems, in London, and their primary concern was to provide and maintain effigies of the saint in local churches; some were even wealthy enough to build chapels dedicated to him. The effigies were carried in procession around the parish every April – as near to St George's Day as possible – and these events became

A pre-Raphaelite St George, by Sir Edward Burne-Jones, 1868

one of the most spectacular and extravagant affairs in the local church calendar. Even more popular for the crowd than the saint himself was the figure of the dragon. This could be a small one made of wood and mounted on a pole (with snapping jaws worked by a string), or a more elaborate basket-work affair that men could carry from inside or wheel along. George also appeared in civic pageants, celebrating the election of a new mayor, for example, and 'riding St George' was an annual excuse for the local great and good to ride in state around the town.

Nevertheless, the adoration of saints came under severe attack in the reform of the church in the mid sixteenth century. Much to the surprise of many people, St George's status as national patron did not save him from the reformers' zeal. Effigies and statues of George, along with all the other saints, were destroyed, and most of the processions which featured him simply faded away or became purely secular events; the scene was set for the long period of official neglect of the national saint, which still continues. At any given time, at least since the restoration of the monarchy in 1660, St George's Day could have been declared a national holiday – for patriotic if not religious reasons – and there have been plenty of unsuccessful campaigns to bring this about.

There has been no shortage of debate about why the English take so little interest in their patron, but no definite conclusion is ever reached, and perhaps cannot be. The main argument of the pro-St George lobby is that neglect of the saint is evidence of a lamentable lack of patriotism on the part of the average English person, and that the English do not care enough about its great history and traditions. But this ignores the complexity of national identity. An apparent lack of interest can certainly be seen negatively, as apathy and indifference, but it can also be viewed positively, as inner strength and confidence. There is no doubt that the attitudes of many English people are based on assumptions of cultural supremacy, and many take an inverted pride in the fact that they do not need to make such a fuss to demonstrate their patriotism. In the words of an *Express* headline, 'If you're truly English, who needs St. George?' (6 April 1998). This trait, of course, is often seen as infuriating arrogance by England's neighbours, but it is a useful line of thought. It follows that the more fuss other nations make of their patriotic symbols, the more they show that they are trying too hard – always proving that they have something to prove.

At a more rarefied level, it can also be argued that the apparent disinterest in patriotic symbols is largely because the English have never felt particularly under threat as a nation (at least since 1066), and England has therefore never needed to assert its distinctiveness like many other nations have. Certainly, England has not been invaded or needed to tear itself away from another dominant nation, although the decline of international power and loss of empire in the last century certainly gave some patriots pause for thought. In the 1990s, plans for political devolution in Britain, and vague fears of being subsumed in a federal European Union, brought another upsurge of St George mania, which was fed by a new craze for supporters of England's sports teams to display St George flags on their houses and mini flagpoles on their cars. The broadsheet newspapers were full of articles debating concepts of 'Englishness', and the tabloids equated a love of St George with patriotism; in April 1997, the *Sun* gave away a 'cut-out-and-keep red and white flag of St. George', which they 'urged every Englishman and woman to wave with pride'.

The conspicuous display of the flag bearing the red cross of St George seems to be a relatively recent phenomenon, but there have been outbreaks of these flags before, as an integral part of attempts to 'bring back' St George's Day, for example at Kidderminster, Worcestershire, in 1914, and various places in 1936.

Nevertheless, a few scattered customs for St George's Day in latter years have been reported across the country. In 1997, the folklorist Maureen Sutton reported that some Lincolnshire people remembered school-based celebrations taking place on 23 April, and that some wore bluebells or other blue flowers to school on that day. One also commented, 'my mam used to say it was the day to pick dandelions to make your wine, but only if the sun was full on them.' And in his *Folklore of Gloucestershire* (1994), Roy Palmer describes a customary gift, made to successive sovereigns by the people of Gloucester, of a pie made from lampreys caught in the River Severn. The custom is reputed to have been started in the time of Henry I, and continued until 1917.

*

24 APRIL

St Mark's Eve

In English tradition, St Mark's Eve is one of the key nights on which to divine the future, but there is no clue as to why this particular date was chosen. Certainly, there seems to be nothing in the life or writings of the Evangelist St Mark that would deserve this reputation, but the idea was extremely widespread. Love divinations were the common forms of attempted prediction, and they come in a wide variety of forms, ranging from the relatively safe ('you will dream of your future lover') to the genuinely frightening ('the wraith of your future lover will be summoned to your side'). The most striking feature of St Mark's Eve divinations is that they frequently tend towards the scary end of this range. Girls would wash their chemises, in ritual silence, and hang them in front of the fire, waiting for their future husband to appear and turn them; or they would sit in the barn and wait for the figure to walk through at the stroke of midnight, or pluck grass from a grave at midnight and place it under their pillows to encourage prophetic dreams. The venue and timing combined with the prescribed actions to guarantee the frisson of trepidation that surrounded the whole proceedings. The climax nearly always occurred at midnight, when the house was still and silent, or was in a deserted barn, churchyard, or other scary place, as in the following Lincolnshire example from 1891:

> A youth or girl walks round the church, at dead of night . . . looking into each window in succession, in expectation of seeing, in the last window, the face of his or her partner in life.

'Porch-watching' was another very widespread custom, but this was designed to reveal more serious matters than who would marry whom. Anyone who wanted to know who would die in the parish in the coming year could stand in the church porch at midnight on St Mark's Eve, and they would see a ghostly procession of figures approaching and entering the church. Those who were destined to die would not come out again, while those who were to be seriously ill would leave the church after a short stay; in some versions, another procession, consisting of couples to be married, would also appear. In most cases, if the watcher fell asleep it was believed to be a sure sign that they would be one of the doomed, but occasionally they would simply sicken and die as a result of the shock of seeing themselves. It was also occasionally reported that anyone who 'watches' once must do it again every year, as for example in the following piece from Yorkshire, recorded by local writer Richard Blakeborough in 1898 (here translated from his colourful but almost unreadable attempt to render deep Yorkshire dialect on the page):

> I never watched myself, but one James How used to watch the dead go in and come out at Bon'iston church every St. Mark Eve as it come around. He had to; he was forced to it; he couldn't help himself . . . Aye, and he saw the spirits of all of them that were going to die that year, and all of them dressed in their natural clothes, or else how would he have known who they were? They all passed close to him, but none of them ever gave him a nod, or anything of that sort. But them as does it once have to do it. They can't hold themselves back. They're forced to go every time St. Mark's Eve comes round. Man! it's a desperate thing to have to do, because you have to go. Whah! at the last end you see yourself pass yourself and then you know your time's come and you'll be laid in the cold ground before that day twelvemonth.

The belief in porch-watching was reported from most parts of England, but it seems to have been particularly well known in East Anglia, the Midlands, and the northern counties. The earliest known reference is from Nottinghamshire in 1608, and the belief lasted well into the late nineteenth century, but became much rarer as the twentieth century advanced.

25 APRIL

St Mark's Day

St Mark's Day does not seem to have made any great impression on English tradition, and there are no widely reported customs special to the time – in marked contrast to the huge popularity of his eve for divinatory practices (*see* p. 139). Nevertheless, in places where the parish church was dedicated to the saint, there would certainly have been celebrations on the day.

One annual custom, which took place in Alnwick in Northumberland from at least *c*.1645 to the mid nineteenth century, was 'leaping the well', although 'scrambling through the pond' would have been a more appropriate name. Men who were to be made Freemen of the Borough assembled early on St Mark's Day and paraded the town on horseback. At a certain point in the day, they were obliged to dismount and make their way through the Freeman's Well, a large dirty pool about twenty yards long, as best they could. The background to this custom is unknown, but the local origin story includes the traditional motif, familiar from many other places, that King John found himself mired in the pond one dark night and set the freemen the task to punish them for neglecting to repair the town's roads.

At Morpeth, also in Northumberland, 25 April was the day for 'riding the boundaries of the common'. It was recorded in 1892 that:

> After meeting in the market place the corporation, on horseback, proceeded to the Common, the waits going first, then the serjeant carrying the purse on a staff, after him the Bailiffs, and lastly the mob; they passed round the boundaries of the Common till they reached a well, east of the road to the High House, when the younger ones raced up to the winning post. There was then a race for a silver cup.

The custom of riding the bounds of the common continued until 1974, when local government reorganization wiped it out. But the similar custom of riding the boundary of the whole borough is still practised every year, on or near to St Mark's Day. This is administered by a board of trustees, which means that the tradition should continue in the future.

George Dew, of Lower Heyford in Oxfordshire, recorded in his diary in 1866 a personal custom instituted by the local miller: Thomas Rose's Great Day. Rose kept it in commemoration of the day he won a lawsuit against Judge Page concerning the height of the water in the mill head. On his 'Great Day', his millers and other men dined at his house, business ceased,

and cakes or buns were distributed among the children. This is an excellent example of how people feel the need to mark particularly important days in their life, and the way that personal celebrations often took exactly the same form as traditional public ones.

*

29 APRIL

According to early English calendars, on 29 April, '*Egressus Noae de arca*' (Noah left the Ark), having entered it on 17 March.

*

30 APRIL

May Day Eve

Eves are often overshadowed by the activities of the days that follow them, and May Day Eve is no exception. In times when the predominant May Day custom was decorating buildings with greenery and flowers, many people spent much of 30 April out in the woods and fields gathering the materials for their celebrations (*see* **1 May**). Nevertheless, those living in Lancashire, Yorkshire, and neighbouring counties had at least one widely practised custom on the day, in the form of Mischief Night, when young people believed they had the traditional right to play tricks. In 1896, P. H. Ditchfield recorded in his *Old English Customs*:

> At Oldham, the Eve of May Day is known as Mischief Night when it was the custom for people to play tricks on their neighbours. My informant remembers seeing a thatched house, in a village near Oldham, adorned with mops, rakes and brushes, on the tops of which were stuck mugs, tubs, and pails.

Mischief Night itself has proved strangely schizophrenic. Not only did some people celebrate it on 4 November rather than 30 April, but sometime in the mid twentieth century it began to gravitate to Hallowe'en, which is when many young folk in Yorkshire now celebrate it (*see* **31 October: Mischief Night** for further details).

On a much grander scale, 30 April is also known in

Germanic countries as *Walpurgisnacht*. St Walburga, or Walpurgis, was an eighth-century Anglo-Saxon nun who was sent to Germany to help Boniface in his missionary work; she became abbess at the key religious centre of Heidenheim, and died there in AD 779. Her lasting fame, however, was prompted nearly a century later, when her remains were removed (to join the relics of her brother St Winnibald), and medicinal oil started to flow from her new tomb. Walburga's feast day is 25 February, but the eve of the date of her translation (1 May) became widely known as *Walpurgisnacht*, and in local tradition became the greatest night for witches to ride and meet. This tradition does not seem to have taken root in England, although the name has been familiar to literate Britons at least since the translation of Goethe's *Faust* in 1823, in which it featured.

Shakespeare set his play *Midsummer Night's Dream* on May Eve, and although one would expect to find the connection between the date and the fairy world to be evident in English folklore collections, this is not the case. If such a tradition existed, it has left only the faintest of echoes in occasional isolated examples, such as that recorded by Ella M. Leather in Herefordshire about the turn of the twentieth century:

> On the Eve of May Day, at Kingstone and Thruxton,
> folk used to put trays of moss outside their doors for
> the fairies to dance upon.

May

Milkmaids' Garland

Bears

Maids' Money

May Queens

Jack-in-the-Green

Hobby Horses

Corby Pole Fair

May Dolls

May Goslings

Weighing the Mayor

1

Charlton-on-Otmoor Garland
Ducking or Dipping Day
International Labour Day
Magdalen College Singing
Minehead Hobby Horse
Padstow Hobby Horse
Randwick Cheese-Rolling

2

7

8

HELSTON FLORA DAY

9

14

Pack Rag Day
ROGATIONTIDE
Beating the Bounds
ROGATION MONDAY
Wilkes Walk
Wishford Auction

15

MID MAY
Durham Mayor-Making
MID TO LATE MAY
Scorton Silver Arrow

16

ASCENSION EVE
Whitby Penny Hedge

21

22

23

Rye Mayor-Making

28

SPRING BANK HOLIDAY
Barwick Maypole
Cooper's Hill Cheese-Rolling
Hunting the Earl of Rone
Kingsteignton Ram-Roasting
Robert Dover's Olimpick
  Games

29

ROYAL OAK DAY
Castleton Garland Day
Grovely Ceremonies
Neville's Cross
  Commemoration
Royal Hospital Chelsea
  Founder's Day

30

*Moveable events have been placed
on the date they fall in 2007.
Events dependent on the timing
of Easter are coloured green.*

Maypoles

May Dew

Morris Dance

Blessing of the Sea

Church Ales

Fighting

3

THE DAY OF THE INVENTION OF THE HOLY CROSS

4

5

FIRST SATURDAY IN MAY
Gawthorpe Celebrations
Knutsford Royal May Day
   Festival

6

FIRST SUNDAY IN MAY
Tyburn Walk

10

11

12

Florence Nightingale
   Commemoration
The May
**SECOND SATURDAY IN
   MAY**
Randwick Wap

13

OLD MAY DAY
Abbotsbury Garland Day
Cowslips
Miners' Holiday
Rook Sunday

17

**THIRD THURSDAY IN
   MAY**
Harwich Kichel-Throwing
ASCENSION DAY
Oxford Beating the Bounds
Tower of London Beating the
   Bounds

18

Newbiggin Freeholders

19

ST DUNSTAN'S DAY

20

24

EMPIRE DAY

25

26

27

WHIT SUNDAY
St Briavels Bread and Cheese
   Dole
St Mary Redcliffe Rush Sunday
LAST SUNDAY IN MAY
Arbor Day

31

Horse Decorations

Eton School Montem

Whit Walks

Lords and Ladies

Corby Pole Fair

Two thousand people at Corby New Town, Northamptonshire, were clapped in the stocks yesterday, the day of the ancient village Pole Fair, which is held every 20 years. To be released from the stocks, a toll – a coin of the realm – had to be paid. The 'victims' did not go willingly but were taken by groups of men patrolling the streets, and carried to the stocks in a chair on a wooden pole. The money goes to charity.

The strange procedure described in this extract from *The Times* (12 June 1962) explains the name of 'Corby Pole Fair', which is indeed held only once in twenty years. It is not known why it is held so infrequently, or whether it previously occurred more often, as the town's charter, granted by Elizabeth I in 1585, does not mention a fair at all. It is claimed locally that the charter was granted in gratitude when Elizabeth was helped out of a bog by Corby people (although similar stories exist in many other places).

If townsfolk can only hold a fair once every two decades, it is inevitable that they will want to pack as much entertainment into the day as possible, and the 2002 programme included processions, bungee-jumping, a fireworks display, archery, tug-of-war, a pageant, maypole dancing, a Pole Fair Queen, and numerous other attractions, as well as the men with the pole. Although unusual at a fair, this pole activity is simply a version of the 'riding the stang' custom found in many other places, often in the context of **rough music** (p. 74).

Maids' Money

At Guildford in Surrey, local resident John Howe left money in his will, dated 27 January 1674, to buy land, the profits of which would pay for an annual gift to a deserving maidservant. The trustees should first find:

> *. . . two poor servant-maids, within the said town, of good report, who should have served masters or mistresses there two years together . . . and that no maid should be chosen that should live in any inn or alehouse . . .*

The two women then had to throw dice to decide who should get the money. The loser could try again for the following three years, but if she was still unsuccessful she had to retire from the field. The money was worth trying for – in 1900, the sum given was £12, less expenses. Nevertheless, many maids were happy to lose. It became the custom to use the income from another Guildford fund, John Parsons' charity, to give to the losing maid as a consolation prize. The Parsons' money formerly went to finance an apprenticeship, but there was often no suitable candidate. Ironically, this fund often generated a higher sum than the Howe charity, so the loser got more than the winner.

Remarkably, the ceremony is still carried out, every May, at the guildhall in Guildford, in the presence of the mayor. It forms part of the annual general meeting of the administering body, Guildford Poyle Charities, and the candidates, who are nowadays domestic helpers rather than live-in maids, still throw dice to win what now amounts to about £60 each year.

Weighing the Mayor

A unique civic custom takes place at the guildhall in High Wycombe High Street, Buckinghamshire, every May, when the newly elected mayor takes office. The new mayor is publicly weighed on a tall brass tripod balance fitted with a seat. His or her weight is then recorded, and the macebearer calls out the figure to the assembled crowd. A year later, the outgoing mayor is weighed again, but instead of the actual weight being announced, the macebearer declares the previous recorded weight, adding 'and some more' if it has increased, or 'and no more' if it has stayed the same or fallen. 'And no more' is greeted with cheers and applause, as it signifies that the incumbent has been diligent and active in pursuing mayoral duties, but the cry of 'and some more' is taken as evidence of too many civic dinners, and is greeted with good-natured jeers and barracking. The weighing-in ceremony can only be shown to date from Victorian times.

*

1 MAY

Judging by the range of traditional customs that took place on May Day, it was second only to Christmas in

Weighing the Mayor at High Wycombe, Buckinghamshire, *c.*2002

popularity with the English people. The day was cele-brated, in one way or another, all over the country, and a wide range of customs has evolved since the Middle Ages, which provide a complex pattern of interlocking custom and regional difference. It is therefore difficult to give a lucid chronological account in short order, except on a very simplistic level. We desperately need a full-scale historical study of the day in all its mani-festations.

The most obvious point to be made is that in a north-ern country like England, it is not at all surprising that previous generations thought the coming of spring and summer a cause for joy and celebration. Without being overly romantic or needing to invent ancient ritual origins, we can agree with folklorist Charlotte Burne's comment, made in 1883, that:

> We, with our coal fires, our plate-glass windows, our
> lamps and gas-lights, and all our many appliances
> for indoor comfort and amusement, can hardly
> appreciate the misery of the cold dark days of winter
> to our forefathers, their keen enjoyment of the light
> and warmth and freedom of summer, and the delight
> with which they greeted the returning spring . . .

If that was true in Victorian England, it is doubly so in the twenty-first century.

May celebrations took place at all levels of society, and evidence comes from a wide range of documen-tary sources, including royal, municipal, ecclesiastical, literary, antiquarian, and folkloric records. Kings and queens went maying; town corporations and guilds put on shows; the clergy took sides in supporting or vociferously condemning the people's activities; poets and playwrights, from Chaucer onwards, developed May Day into a potent arcadian symbol; nineteenth-century antiquarians and folklorists documented surviving customs in admiring or nostalgic detail; and twentieth-century enthusiasts revived and invented May customs with gay abandon. But there is confusion in this mass of information. Changing vocabularies and imprecise definitions often make it difficult to be sure what is going on. 'Going a-maying' and 'bringing in the May' originally meant going out of town or village into the countryside, to fetch greenery or flowers back for decoration, but either phrase was used in later times to cover any traditional May activity including, for example, bathing the face in May dew. A 'maypole' can be a seventy-foot pole set in the ground on the village green, or a portable six-foot pole for children to dance around, or a two-foot decorated stick carried from house to house by boys and girls accompanying their May garland. A 'garland' can be the pyramid of shiny metal carried on the head of a dancing milkmaid, a small nosegay sold in the street for luck, a huge wreath of flowers hung on a maypole, or a bell- or globe-shaped construction of greenery carried round the village by children or worn on the head of the King on Castleton Garland Day (see **29 May: Castleton Garland Day**).

May Day certainly roused strong feelings, for and against. In his *Survey of London* (2nd edn, 1603), John Stow writes:

> In the month of May, namely, on May-day in the
> morning, every man, except impediment, would
> walk into the sweet meadows and green woods, there
> to rejoice their spirits with the beauty and savour of
> sweet flowers, and with the harmony of birds, prais-
> ing God in their kind.

Compare Stow's sweet meadows with Philip Stubbes' famous diatribe against setting up maypoles, in which he claims that only a third of the maids who went a-maying came back 'undefiled' (see **1 May: Maypoles**). The earliest known reference to May Day customs, in 1240, is already a criticism – Robert Grosseteste, Bishop of Lincoln, complained of priests who took part in 'games which they call the bringing-in of May' – but by the fifteenth century, local authorities in Kent and Devon are recorded as giving money to people coming 'with their May', and in the following century even the royal family were involved. An oft-quoted account included in Edward Hall's *Chronicles* (1542) tells how King Henry VIII and Catherine of Aragon went a-maying in 1515 to Shooters Hill, and there played at being Robin Hood with a picnic banquet in flower-decked arbours.

This notion of going into the countryside and bring-ing back foliage was the core of May Day activity for centuries, even if only on a theoretical level, but what happened to the plants once they had been brought in varied widely. The earliest descriptions simply indi-cate that houses and public buildings were adorned with 'birch boughs' and the like, but by the nineteenth century there was a wide range of traditions, all based on the same simple principle. The following selection of extracts demonstrates something of this variety, but there were many more ways of using branches and flowers:

> [Lincolnshire, ?1820s] *A woman from the extreme north of Lincolnshire . . . said that when she was a girl at Winteringham, she and other girls always dressed the lugs (ears or handles) of their milk kits with leaves on May-day morning.*

> [Herefordshire, ?1850s] *When . . . I lived at Kington, no house was without its bough of green birch in the doorway.*

> [Derbyshire, 1860s] *When she was young, every house in Abney had a garland hung above its door on the first day of May. She had helped to make these garlands; they were round, like hoops, and made of bits of green things, Mary blobs, and so on. People would plod through snow to get flowers for them. The garlands were about a foot in diameter and were left hanging over doors till the flowers were withered.*

> [Leicestershire, 1895] *It hath been a custom, time out of mind, for children to scatter flowers before people's doors in towns, on May Day.*

> [Cheshire/Lancashire, 19th century] *It was formerly a custom . . . for young men to place birchen boughs on May-day over the doors of their mistresses, and mark the residence of a scold by an alder bough. There is an old rhyme which mentions peculiar boughs for various tempers, as an owler (alder) for a scolder, a nut for a slut, etc.*

If Puritan critics like Stubbes are to be believed, people also had a great deal of fun that had little to do with greenery while out in the woods overnight, and another characteristic feature of bringing in the May was noise. The returning Mayers announced their arrival with loud jubilant cheering, firing of guns, and, particularly, the blowing of horns.

Particular aspects of May customs – garlands, dolls, maypoles, and so on – are detailed below. Although the arrival of May Day itself was the catalyst for all these activities, it is clear that the celebrations spread into the rest of the month. This was particularly so after the Restoration, when Royal Oak Day was added to the calendar (*see* **29 May: Royal Oak Day**).

Bank Holiday

Normally quite consensual, the timing of bank holidays occasionally hits the headlines, especially when the idea of celebration or commemoration is mixed with that of 'holiday' pure and simple. August Bank Holiday causes no problems because it is simply an arbitrary late summer day, but the adoption of May Day as a new bank holiday in 1978, by the Labour Government of the day, created a major furore. The Conservative opposition claimed that May Day's international socialist nature made it an unsuitable choice, and *The Times* ran a suitably thunderous leader suggesting that the British public should use the day to commemorate innocent people murdered in the Soviet Union.

Many people countered by pointing out that much of the long history of May Day celebrations was devoid of any political content, but the Conservative politicians remembered the Labour Day rallies of the interwar and immediate postwar years, such as recollected by Jessica Mitford in her autobiography:

> *On May Day the entire community turned out, men, women, and children, home-made banners proclaiming slogans of the 'United Front against Fascism' waving alongside the official ones. The long march to Hyde Park started early in the morning, contingents of the Labour Party, the Co-ops, the Communist Party, the Independent Labour Party marching through the long day to join other thousands from all parts of London in the traditional May Day labour festival.*

When the Conservatives returned to power in 1979, they planned to scrap the May Day holiday and to replace it with a more patriotic 'Trafalgar Day' in October. This in turn was criticized, as it would disrupt manufacturing output in the important run-up to Christmas, and it met with a lukewarm response from the public who, not surprisingly, preferred a day off in early summer to one in late autumn. The plan was quietly shelved in 1993, but the principle of patriotism is still regularly cited when the question of the timing of new bank holidays is discussed, and many Conservative rank and file members still grumble about May Day every year. The edge is somewhat blunted by the fact that the holiday is now on the first Monday in May, which seldom falls on the first of the month.

Bears

A May Day custom that seems to have been restricted to the Burnley and Blackburn areas of Lancashire was a sort of mock dancing bear enacted by boys while the girls were out with their garlands and maypoles, as described in the *Burnley Express* (11 February 1983):

> One went to the grocer's shop and begged an old sugar sack. The boy chosen would have it put over his head, the position of his eyes and mouth located, and holes would be cut into the sack to allow him to see and breathe. Then the boys wanted a staff as the real bear man had. So a broom handle would be obtained … then a length of clothes line to keep the 'bear' at a safe distance from the public.

The 'bear' would dance, turn somersaults, and catch the pole, as instructed, just like a real dancing bear, and his attendants would keep up a constant chatter in imitation of the real bear-wards, who were normally Eastern or Southern Europeans, on the lines of 'Addy-om-pom-pay', or 'Addy-addy-on-kon-kay'.

The boys' bear was clearly well known within its restricted area from the First World War to the 1940s, but it is not clear whether it goes back any earlier. Real dancing bears were surprisingly common in late nineteenth-century England, and they could still be seen occasionally in both village and town streets in the 1920s.

Casting Clouts

The well-known phrase 'Cast ne'er a clout [or 'Ne'er cast a clout'] till May is out' cautions people not to cast off their winter clothes until they are sure that summer is with us. In recent years it has been commonly stated that the phrase does not refer to the month of May but rather to the blossoming of the hawthorn, which in many parts is referred to as 'may', but many earlier references to the phrase make it perfectly clear that the month is what is meant. The saying was often extended to include other months, as in a Devon version noted in

1932 – 'Till April is dead, change not a thread' – and a rhyme printed in *Notes & Queries* in 1870 but claimed to be current in Yorkshire a hundred years before:

> Don't change a clout
> Till May is out;
> If you change in June
> 'Twill be too soon.

The earliest known reference in English dates from 1732, but a Spanish version, which translates as 'Do not leave off your coat till May', was known at least a hundred years before that.

Charlton-on-Otmoor Garland

In the parish church of Charlton-on-Otmoor, dedicated to the Virgin Mary, there is a large image in the shape of a cross, or possibly of a person with outstretched arms, perched on top of the rood screen. The figure is made of wood, entirely covered with evergreens, and is therefore usually referred to as 'the garland', although some also call it 'the lady'. The garland greenery is replaced twice a year by the churchwardens, on 1 May and 19 September (the patronal festival), and on the first of these dates the local schoolchildren bring a long garland made of bunches of flowers joined together by a 'rope' of evergreens to the church for a special service. Others carry small crosses of wood or flowers, which are placed around the church, and the long garland is placed across the front of the screen. After the service, the children perform maypole and country dances to entertain the crowds who always flock to the church on this day. It is altogether a charming and relatively low-key community celebration.

This direct school involvement only dates back to 1963, and indeed the customs surrounding the 'garland' have undergone an astonishing degree of change, even within its 200-year recorded history. Our first reference is in fact an illustration, published in Dunkin's *History of Bicester* (1816), which shows two garlands of far more open construction than the present solid one, and although still basically cruciform in shape, looking more like John Wyndham's triffids than a person. A second illustration, from 1846, shows only one garland, of similar shape and still of openwork. We are told that in 1854 the local vicar, the Revd George

The garland at Charlton-on-Otmoor, Oxfordshire, 1984

Bliss, objected to the garland and had it removed, but it was restored as soon as he left the village. Up to about 1857, the garland(s) were carried in procession around the village on May Day, accompanied by music, morris dancing, and singing, and were taken to visit the principal houses of the area. By 1890, however, the custom had lapsed so far that nobody even bothered to replenish the greenery on the garland, and it took a deliberate effort on the part of local church officials to re-introduce it.

It is confidently stated by virtually all writers on the subject that the garlands are direct remnants of the statues that adorned parish churches before the 1540s. The view of folklorist Christina Hole in her *Dictionary of British Folk Customs* (1976) is typical:

> During the upheavals of the Reformation, the statues were destroyed, and the people of Charlton erected two green garlands in their place.

Certainly, prior to the Reformation, English churches were alive with saints. They were carved into the fabric, painted on walls and other flat surfaces, and stood as statues of painted wood or stone, often with their own candles burning and a small altar at their feet. The most impressive group of images was on the rood screen, with a huge crucifix, flanked by Mary and St John, which would have been in constant sight of the congregation. The removal of images did not happen overnight, but from the 1530s onwards saints gradually disappeared from the church, and all images, in every church and chapel, were ordered to be removed in February 1548, and again by Elizabeth I in 1559 after the reversal of policy during Mary's reign (1553–58).

To the average parishioner, little concerned with doctrinal niceties, the church must have seemed unbelievably bare and impersonal after the saints' removal, and we know that at least some images were hidden, or quietly spirited away to be stored in safety, in case they were ever allowed to return. In some places, there was violent opposition, but the reformers had all the power, and their orders were eventually carried out everywhere. The crucifixion scenes on roods were particularly disliked by reformers. If anything did escape their reforming zeal, it would certainly have been swept away by the further draconian Puritan repression of the seventeenth century.

The idea that the Charlton garlands are direct descendants of the rood screen group must therefore be regarded more as wishful thinking than serious reflection, based on the idea that the authorities did not mind, or somehow did not notice, the simple subterfuge. It is almost inconceivable that the garlands could have been tolerated for the next 300 years. Moreover, we do not have any indication that the garlands even existed before the early nineteenth century, and if they did so it is distinctly odd that no one thought them worthy of mention until 1816.

A possibly more fruitful avenue of investigation is to pursue the similarity between the Charlton garland and other garlands that were carried around on May Day. Oxfordshire had more than its fair share of garland customs, and they varied widely in detail, but mostly followed a similar overall pattern. They were nearly all made in a way similar to the Charlton garlands shown in the nineteenth-century illustrations, and they were all taken round the village and shown to local residents at the doors of their houses. Many included a doll, usually called 'my lady' or something similar. Admittedly, it was not usual for the perambulation of the village to be formalized into a procession with music and dancing, and nor was it common for the garland to be stored in the church, although garlands featured in other church-based customs. The case is therefore far from closed, but on present evidence it seems likely that rather than being a religious symbol that was later treated in a secular way, the Charlton garland is a secular May garland that later became incorporated into an ecclesiastical setting. Nevertheless, a possibly analogous custom took place at Bodmin, in Cornwall, which further research may show had relevance to the Charlton Garland. At Bodmin, a 'riding' or procession took place each year in July, and at least one account mentions the participants carrying flowers and decorated poles (*see* **7 July: Bodmin Riding**).

Children's Garlands

One of the prettiest and most characteristic of rural spring customs was the carrying of garlands around the village by children on May Day morning and singing or dancing at people's doors. By far the most famous account of May garlanding is the delightful description in Flora Thompson's *Lark Rise*, first published in 1939, which recalls her Oxfordshire childhood in the last decades of the nineteenth century, but there are many other detailed descriptions and May garlanding is one of the best documented of all calendar customs. The following was published in *Notes & Queries* in 1854:

> *In Huntingdonshire, the garland is of a pyramidal shape, in this respect resembling the old 'milk-maid's garland'... The crown of the garland is composed of tulips, anemones, cowslips, king-cups, meadow-orchids, wall-flowers, primroses, crown-imperials, lilacs, laburnums, and as many roses and bright flowers of all descriptions as can be pressed into the service. These, with the addition of green boughs, are made into a huge pyramidal nosegay; from the front of which a gaily dressed doll ... stares vacantly at her admirers. From the base of the nosegay hang ribbons, pieces of silk, handkerchiefs, and any other gay-coloured fabric that can be borrowed for the occasion. The garland is borne by the two maids-of-honour to the May Queen ... who place their hands beneath the nosegay, and allow the gay-coloured streamers to fall towards the ground. The garland is thus from four to five feet in height ... The sovereignty of the Queen o' the May is not hereditary, but elective; her majesty being annually chosen by her school-fellows in the morning ... Her chief symbol of sovereignty is a parasol, which she bears with grace and dignity. Moreover, she weareth white gloves, and carrieth a bag that displayeth a pocket-handkerchief. She has a white veil too; and around her bonnet is her crown, a coronal of flowers. In front of her dress is a bouquet ... You may be quite sure that her majesty is dressed in her very best, and has put on that white frock for the first time since last summer.*
>
> *Preceding the maids-of-honour, and followed by her attendants, both male and female, her majesty makes the tour of her native place, and, at the various homes of her subjects, exhibits the charms of Flora [the doll] and her garland. If, as is commonly the case, the regal procession is composed of school-children, they sing such songs as may have been taught them. It is then usual for loyal subjects to make a pecuniary present to the May Queen, which is deposited in her majesty's handkerchief-bag, and*

Children's May Day garland from Northamptonshire (William Hone, *The Every-Day Book*, 1827)

> *will be expended on the coronation banquet; a feast which will take place in the school-room, or some large-roomed cottage, as early as three o'clock in the afternoon, when her majesty will be graciously pleased to sit down in the midst of her subjects, and will probably quaff at least ten of those cups that cheer but not inebriate, and will consume plum-cake and bread-and-butter in proportion.*

Taken altogether, published accounts show a wide variety of detail, especially as regards the shapes and sizes of the garlands, but there is an overall similarity in what the children did at each door. In the journal *Folk-Lore* (1900), a correspondent wrote:

> *I was at Wilton [Wiltshire] on the first of May 1896. There I saw many parties of little girls, one of whom would carry a short stick, at the top of which was a garland or bunch of flowers. The girls would stand*

*at the doors of houses and sing a song, the last line
of which was, 'Please give a penny for the garland.'
Wilton is a small town and the garlands were numerous, so I suppose the house-to-house visitation was
soon done, as when I left, soon after nine a.m., the
girls were either wandering aimlessly about with
their garlands or sitting on doorsteps counting
their gains. I was told that the pence are collected in
order to be afterwards spent at Wilton Fair, which
is held on the first Monday in May. The same day I
reached Salisbury about eleven o'clock. Although it
is only three miles from Wilton, the fashion of the
May observance was different. The girls, instead of
being in parties of four or five, went about in couples,
each member of which held the end of a short stick,
to the middle of which the garland was tied, and
hung between the two girls as they walked along. The
garland (as I suppose I must call it) was in the form
of a crown, whose circlet and bows were covered with
flowers. I did not hear any singing, and the girls went
from shop to shop, within which they would wait
until they received either money or a dismissal.*

Children carrying portable maypoles almost always danced (*see* **1 May: Maypoles**), those with garlands usually sang, and the songs varied considerably from simple traditional ditties to somewhat trite poems taught to them by schoolteachers. But the main difference was the degree of adult involvement in the proceedings. Scholars have labelled the customs where the children acted on their own initiative as 'independent' garlanding, to distinguish them from those in which adults – usually the local school staff – took control of making the garland and organizing the children's activities. Even in so-called 'independ-ent' garlanding, it is unlikely that adults were ever completely excluded, but there is strong evidence that by about the 1880s adult involvement was increas-ing rapidly, with children still carrying the garlands but school, church, or parents taking on the essential planning and organizational roles. Adults oversaw the construction of the garland, taught the children more 'refined' songs, and even controlled how the money that the children collected was spent – often on a tea or other treat. Many took this patronage even further, and

sought to encourage the custom by offering prizes for the best garlands.

The most trustworthy writers on the subject, such as Roy Judge and Ronald Hutton, agree that children's garlanding customs increased strongly as the nine-teenth century progressed, especially in the south-east of England. Adult intervention is likely to be the main cause of this increase, and was often based on the fash-ionable ideas of a romantic **Merrie England** (p. 372) that were affecting traditional customs across the country. But not all places in England had children's May Day garlands, and the geographical pattern of the custom is puzzling. Numerous examples were documented in the South, South-East and Midlands, and along the southern coast of the West Country, but none in the North and few in East Anglia.

There is little evidence of children's garlanding before the early nineteenth century, but it certainly existed before that time. Gideon Mantell, for example, pioneer surgeon and geologist, was born in Lewes, East Sussex, in 1790, and he often noted in his journal the presence of garlands in the town on 1 May:

> [1819] *The garlands of this year are more beautiful
> and numerous than I ever remember;* [1821] *The
> annual custom of exhibiting garlands on this day
> was but partially observed;* [1829] *The garlands very
> numerous, but shabby in the extreme;* [1830] *But
> a sorry display of garlands, altho' flowers are very
> abundant; this, like every other cheerful innocent
> custom, is dwindling away;* [1846] *Went to Tunbridge
> Wells and returned in the evening . . . Children were
> carrying about garlands; the first I have seen since
> leaving Lewes. Well do I remember my childhood's
> garlands!*

These entries seem to indicate a tradition in decline, although this may simply be a facet of the diarist's increasing age. However, the last comment is particu-larly interesting, as it proves the existence of the garlanding custom in the area before 1800.

Ducking or Dipping Day

For some, 1 May (or 2 May in some accounts) was 'Ducking' or 'Dipping Day'. The Cornish historian Jonathan Couch recorded in 1871:

> On May morning the children, and even the adults, go out into the country, and fetch home branches of the narrow-leaved elm, or flowering boughs of the white-thorn, both of which are called 'May'. At a later hour, all the boys of the village sally forth with bucket, can, or other vessel, and avail themselves of a licence which the season confers, to 'dip', or well-nigh drown, without regard to person or circumstance, the passenger who has not the protection of a piece of 'May' conspicuously stuck in his dress, at the same time that they sing, 'the first of May is dipping day' … There is a great deal of fun on the occasion, for many an unfortunate body who has failed to comply with an ancient custom is seen slinking home like a drowned rat.

The custom seems to have been unique to Devon and Cornwall, but it has definite echoes of the more widely known Royal Oak Day, when anyone not wearing an oak leaf was punished (see **29 May: Royal Oak Day**). Naturally, not everybody found the custom a bit of harmless fun, as in the following example from Devon:

> In 1894 the practice resulted in the death of one Dr. Twining, when his horses were frightened by the water thrown over a fence by William John Luscombe (13) and Samuel George Hine (16), and in bolting overset his carriage. He sustained an injury to the ankle, which later necessitated amputation of his leg, from which he died. The boys were charged with manslaughter at Exeter Assizes, but were later discharged.

Fighting

People in the past seem to have taken their feeling of home territory very seriously, and to have readily used it as an excuse for a good punch-up. Even such a staid and decorous affair as 'beating the bounds' could result in fights if parties from one parish met another on their rounds (see **Rogationtide: Beating the Bounds**, p. 176). Yarleton Hill, in Gloucestershire, formed the intersection of several parishes, an opportunity too good to miss. In 1779, county historian Samuel Rudder described the events that occurred there:

> Annually, on the first day of May, there is a custom of assembling in bodies on the top of this hill, from the several parishes, to fight for the possession of it, upon which account it is sometimes called May-Hill.

A similar affray took place at another hilltop May fair every year at Wrekin Wakes, in Shropshire, according to folklorist Charlotte Burne in 1883. Here, the local colliers and countrymen fought for possession of the ground after the pleasure-seekers had enjoyed the sideshows and gingerbread stalls.

Such fierce territoriality existed in both town and country. Many urban working-class autobiographies touch upon the author's childhood fear of venturing into another area, or even down the wrong street, while Richard Jefferies, the immensely popular chronicler of the late Victorian rural scene, described a similar scenario in Wiltshire:

> Every hamlet used to have its representative fighting-man – often more than one – who visited the neighbouring villages on the feast days, when there was a good deal of liquor flowing, to vaunt their prowess before the local champions … There was a regular feud for many years between the Okebourne men and the Clipstone 'chaps'; and never did the stalwart labourers of those two villages meet without falling to fisticuffs with right goodwill.

The same pattern was repeated all over the country, and, as at Yarleton Hill, the rivalry could be formalized into a regular custom or even game. Many of the recorded mass football games, for example, were also ostensibly played between inhabitants of two different parishes, or parts of a town (see **Football**, p. 53).

See also **Palm Sunday: Martinsell Hill** (p. 98) for a similar affair.

Horse Decorations

The feeling that May Day should be celebrated with decoration and finery was not confined to rural areas, and there existed a strong tradition of decorating horses and vehicles, particularly in Manchester but also in towns in Lancashire, Yorkshire, and Cheshire, as well as in London. May Day decorations seem to have been first apparent in the coaching fraternity, and the earliest description so far unearthed occurs in the *Gentleman's Magazine* of 1754, although it is clear that it is a well-established custom even at that date:

> They took places in the waggon, and quitted London early on May morning; and it being the custom in this month for the passengers to give the waggoner at every inn a ribbon to adorn his team, she soon discovered the origin of the proverb, 'as fine as a horse', for, before they got to the end of their journey, the poor beasts were almost blinded by the tawdry party-coloured flowing honours of their heads.

By the time the coaching industry collapsed in the face of competition from railways, the custom was already entrenched in other horse-based occupations. Drivers of delivery vehicles, mail vans, cabs, and omnibuses all felt it their duty to put on a good show on the day. A correspondent described the scene in Manchester in the *Pall Mall Gazette* in 1880:

> There was on May-day the usual annual procession through the streets of Manchester of dray and cart horses, every trade, from machinery and cotton down to beer, being represented. The animals were literally covered with decorations of flowers, ribbons, garlands, flags, and small coloured balloons; the brass trappings shone like burnished gold, and the hoofs are first blacked, and then topped with white – to represent top-boots, I suppose. Many of these horses are simply perfection of their kind.

Perhaps inevitably, these spontaneous and individual forms of customary decoration soon became organized into parades and formal processions, with rules and prizes. In 1890, the *Stockport Advertiser* commented:

> Everything that went on wheels from a mourning coach to a doll's carriage was more or less ornamented ... [but] the display would have been infinitely better and more imposing had there been an organised competition and procession.

The same suggestions were also being made in other towns. The London Cart Horse Parade Society was set up in 1886 for just this purpose, while animal welfare pressure groups of the time openly used parades to improve the treatment of animals, by fostering pride in the animals' appearance.

For modern horse parades, *see* **Easter Monday: Harness Horse Parade**, p. 129; **A Sunday in September: Horseman's Sunday**, p. 288.

International Labour Day

The first of May was adopted as International Labour Day at the first congress of the Second Socialist International in Paris in 1889, to proclaim and celebrate the potential economic and political power of a united working class. It is often assumed that this was a deliberate move to take advantage of the long-standing traditional popularity of May Day across Europe, but it seems that the choice of day was largely fortuitous. In their eagerness to forge a truly international workers' movement, European organizers were keen to ally themselves with developments in the United States, where 1 May was already associated with strikes in support of the agitation for an eight-hour working day. But it was an inspired choice all the same, and the previous history of the day provided an immediate legitimacy to the new celebrations.

In the early days of the labour movement in Britain, and into the Edwardian era, a combination of socialism and romantic utopianism proved a heady mixture for an extremely wide range of individuals and organizations on the fringes of socialism and left-wing causes. Ideologies and projects as diverse as William Morris's Victorian medievalism, the Arts and Crafts movement, Garden Cities, folk song and dance, and countless brotherhood and utopian movements and experiments contributed to the new May Day. In retrospect, most of these smacked of well-meaning middle-class romanticism, and were a far cry from the realities of industrial toil, mass unemployment, and squalid urban living conditions, but the images conjured up by these movements had a powerful effect at the time. The iconography of labour publications often depicted a romantic view of May Day, harking back to a supposed utopian past, and a popular feature at labour gatherings was the presentation of maypole dances by the children of the local Socialist Sunday schools. As the *Oxford Chronicle* commented, in 1906:

> *The idea of a May-day festival took us a long way back, to the days when men and women led simpler and more natural lives, when the air was purer and food was unadulterated, when the people had a pride and pleasure in their work and felt glad to be alive.*

But all this changed after the First World War. Between the wars, May Day labour gatherings lost their romance and, particularly in large industrial towns, the day was celebrated with processions of bands, banners, and speeches, and demonstrations of class solidarity and strength, rather than maypole dancing. The soft edges of utopia had given way to the hard edges of interwar political struggles.

Jack-in-the-Green

Up to the turn of the twentieth century, a very odd-looking character called Jack-in-the-Green could be regularly seen dancing in the streets of certain towns every May Day. He was an integral part of the seasonal celebrations put on by chimney sweeps, and would play his part in collecting money to help see them through the summer, the lean period of the trade. A. R. Bennett, writing of his childhood in south London in the 1860s, provides a good description of the custom:

> *A lusty sweep – for strength and endurance were necessary for the due performance of the part – covered himself down to the boots with a circular wicker frame of bee-hive contour, carried on the shoulders, and terminating in a dome or pinnacle above his head. This frame was entirely concealed by green boughs and flowers. May blossoms preponderating if the season was propitious. A small window gave egress to his gaze, but was not very obvious from without, and one seldom caught a glimpse of the perspiring countenance within. Women and girls, one to each corner, and two or three men and youths, sometimes with sooty faces, mouth-organs and tambourines, formed his escort, the females being in short dresses, white stockings and gaudy shoes, like sorry May Queens. The verdure-clad sweep pranced, twirled, jumped and capered to the music while the others danced around.*

At this time, the Jack was just starting its slow decline, and thirty years later he had become a rarity. Because of this, he still had the power to surprise:

> *Walking along Jamaica Road I saw what looked like a big bush hopping from one side of the street to the other, and bobbing up and down . . . This being the first time I had seen a Jack-in-the-Green, it scared the life out of me.*

This was again in London, about 1900.

Jack-in-the-Green rarely appeared alone. He was first seen as an addition to the existing milkmaids' garland dancing (*see* **1 May: Milkmaids' Garland**), and although he himself would certainly need at least one musician and someone to collect the money, he invariably had other companions to increase the entertainment value of the performance. Early on these were sweeps' boys or apprentices, who played percussion on shovel and brush, but these went out of favour as the tide of indignation against the treatment of 'climbing boys' swept through the nation's conscience. A character dressed as a Lord, and another as a Lady – the latter sometimes a real woman and sometimes a male parody of one – as well as various kinds of clown, were his most common companions. They all danced and were no doubt very funny and charming, or tedious and grotesque, depending on their individual skill and the mood of the beholder.

There is a surprising amount of information on the Jack from the late eighteenth and nineteenth centuries, much of it pictorial, and we must be eternally grateful for the detective work of the late Roy Judge, whose study *The Jack-in-the-Green* (2nd edn, 2000) presents all the available evidence in a scholarly and accessible way; he commented that 'A reasonable conclusion from this evidence would seem to be that the Jack-in-the-Green appeared in the last thirty years of the eighteenth-century in the context of the May Day activity.' The mass of available evidence also shows that the custom was an urban one, found most often in London but also regularly in the southern counties of Hampshire, Sussex, and Kent, and in Buckinghamshire and Oxfordshire, and comparatively rarely outside this restricted area. Nevertheless, even with all this evidence, it is not totally clear how the Jack developed his distinctive leaf-clad garb. The most likely explana-

Jack-in-the-Green (George Cruickshank, *Comic Almanac*, 1835)

tion is that the costume is an extension of the May garland theme which, in the form that featured in the milkmaids' dance, was carried on the head, probably in combination with a costume that had greenery or ribbons attached to various parts of the body. But this, at present, is speculation.

Jack-in-the-Green has certainly proved popular with modern audiences, and he can be seen again in the streets taking part in many revived spring celebrations, such as the annual Rochester Sweeps Festival in Kent. However, his history and reputation have been sadly misrepresented. Despite the fact that Jack dates from the late eighteenth century, lasted for little more than 150 years, and was an urban rather than rural custom, he is routinely claimed as an ancient pagan tree-spirit, or as a personification of a vegetation god who dances to welcome the spring. He has also become inextricably tangled up in the complex modern persona of 'the Green Man', that powerful symbol used by the romantic wing of various eco-friendly and New Age groups. He has thus been absorbed into the amorphous blend of foliate heads (as the Green Man carvings in churches

were previously called), medieval wildmen, Robin Hood, Gawain and the Green Knight, and anything or anyone else 'green', who are all now equated with vegetation and nature spirits. Needless to say, there is not the slightest evidence that Jack-in-the-Green has any connections with these other characters, but it is probably impossible now to rescue him from such dubious company.

Lords and Ladies

A May Day calendar custom, apparently unique to the village of Baldock in Hertfordshire, was described by a correspondent to William Hone's *Year-Book* (1832). Female inhabitants in the poorer areas were in the habit of making effigies 'of rags, pasteboard, old masks, old canvas, straw, etc.', which they dressed up in their own and their husbands' clothes, and set on chairs by their front doors, with a hat to collect money from passers-by. The figures were called 'my lord and my lady', and were sometimes arranged as a domestic tableau beside a table with pipe, mug, newspaper, and so forth, and they were profusely decorated with flowers. The account is in the past tense, and the writer comments that he could not say whether the custom still continued.

Magdalen College Singing

Early on May Day morning, the choir of Magdalen College, Oxford, along with officials and invited guests, ascend to the top of the college's 144-foot tower, and sing a Latin anthem, *Te Deum Patrem Colimus*. Huge crowds of revellers have already gathered in the street at the base of the tower and on the river, and as soon as the songs (which are nowadays amplified) are over, the bells are rung and a noisy street party commences with jugglers, acrobats, morris dancers, sideshows, and fancy dress, to welcome in the month of May.

The ceremony on the tower is impressive in its simplicity, but even this relatively straightforward event has changed over the years, and, thanks to the thorough research of folklorist Roy Judge, we know a great deal about how and why these changes came about. What happened here can be taken as a model for changes imposed on numerous traditional calendar customs by reformers up and down the country in the nineteenth century.

The actual origin of the Magdalen singing is unknown, but the most likely explanation is that it commenced as a celebration of the tower's completion in 1509. Seventeenth-century sources describe it as a secular event, and the choir probably sang popular songs of the day, but from about 1800 it became widely believed that the singing had started as a requiem mass for the repose of the soul of Henry VII, probably because he had also died in 1509. This theory of origin dictated the way the custom was to change a few decades later. In the eyes of the college authorities, the occasion was clearly ripe for reform, and the key instigator of the reforms was Magdalen fellow Dr John Rouse Bloxam (1807–91), who first took note of the ceremony in the early 1840s. He found that it was:

> ... *more like a Baccanalian song than sacred hymn. The choirmen and choristers went up the Tower in their usual garb and kept their hats and caps on during the singing. The principal function of the choristers seemed to be to throw down rotten eggs on the people below.*

In other reports, those in the street below seemed mostly intent on drowning out the singing by blowing their traditional May Day tin trumpets, and the whole affair was viewed as an example of the long-standing antipathy between town and gown. Bloxam drastically reformed the occasion by introducing a new atmosphere of simple piety. He made the choir dress and behave appropriately, and insisted that the assembled crowd removed their hats. Most importantly, as Roy Judge commented, he made 'the ceremonial a self-conscious occasion, aware of its own tradition'.

Reformers such as Bloxam based their efforts on a combination of the currently accepted ideas of origin, which, as in this case, were usually spurious, and the preoccupations of the cultural milieu in which they themselves lived. What was in the air in mid-century Oxford was a heady combination of church reform (including the revival of ceremonials associated with the Oxford Movement) and a romantic medieval antiquarianism. Customs reformed in this way therefore possessed the dual power of contemporary resonance and an apparent historical legitimacy.

However, the story has another twist. In the 1870s, when scholars started looking at the documents preserved in Magdalen's archives, the Henry VII story was quickly discredited. But just as this new rigour in antiquarian research had finally laid Henry's soul to rest, a new explanation was being formulated that claimed – on no evidence – that the May Day singing must be a relic of pagan times. The Christian element, it was said, had been 'grafted on some pagan rite of the worshippers of nature', the custom being 'Druidical by origin and Christian by conversion'. The spread of this new orthodoxy was typified, and greatly assisted, by Holman Hunt's well-known painting *May Morning on Magdalen Tower* (1888–91) with its unashamedly romantic Druidism. Fortunately, this new interpretation, which is still rampant, has not yet been allowed to affect what happens on the tower, but it is quite feasible that it will one day, with the singers dressed in pseudo-Druidic robes and singing newly written anthems of sun worship.

The Magdalen singing gets all the headlines, but it is not unique, and there have been many other examples of tower-top singing, such as the event at Sidney Sussex College in Cambridge, detailed by Enid Porter in her *Cambridgeshire Customs and Folklore* (1969). Most of these are clearly copies of the Oxford event, but there are indications of a more complex history. Christine Bloxham, for example, relates how, in the early seventeenth century, singing on the New College tower was moved to Ascension Day precisely because the 'Magdalen College men and the rabble of the towns' dominated May Day morning.

May Dew

For at least 200 years, it was widely believed that bathing the face in dew early on May Day morning was excellent for the complexion, and in particular helped to whiten the skin and eradicate freckles. The most famous example of the belief is recorded in Samuel Pepys's diary:

> [28 May 1667] *After dinner my wife went down with Jane and W. Hewer to Woolwich in order to a little ayre, and to lie there tonight and so to gather May dew tomorrow morning, which Mrs. Turner hath taught her as the only thing in the world to wash her face with, and I am contented with it.*

Two years later, he was not so contented:

> [10 May 1669] *Troubled, about 3 in the morning, with my wife's calling her maid up, and rising herself, to go with her coach abroad to gather May-dew – which she did; and I troubled for it, for fear of any hurt, going abroad betimes, happening to her.*

But she returned safely before he was up. Elizabeth Pepys's morning jaunts are the first recorded examples of the belief in May dew, and the wording of the first extract seems to imply that the idea was new to her. It is quite possible that it was new to England at the time, perhaps introduced from the Continent. It is noteworthy that Elizabeth clearly believed that the efficacy of the dew lasted all the month of May, and not simply on 1 May; the latter date was most definitely the norm in later years.

The idea was still around in the twentieth century, but in some circles only just. In Gloucestershire, 1906:

> *I overheard this conversation between two Minchinhampton girls: 'They do say that if you wash your face in the May dew, early in the morning, you'll have a good complexion.' 'Oh, you silly, they only tell you that to make you get up early!'*

May dew was also occasionally reported as generally medicinal, especially for weak limbs, and some also claimed that you could 'make a wish' while gathering it.

May Dolls

Dolls were often included as an integral part of the May garlanding custom (*see* **1 May: Children's Garlands**), but sometimes the doll took the central role itself. 'May Dolls' and 'May Babies' were carried from door to door in exactly the same way as the 'vessel cup' visitors at Christmas (*see* **24 December: Vessel Cups**), except that spring flowers took the place of winter evergreens. A Miss Pinchard of Torquay, Devon, contributed the following description to the Devonshire Association in 1876:

> *At a very early hour every little cottage girl in whose family there is a doll is astir, completing preparations that have been begun days before. The doll, whether large or small, is dressed in her best, and laid in a long cardboard box. She is then decorated with the best flowers the little ones have been able to procure from field or garden . . . The doll herself is nearly hidden by flowers, and her bed and pillow also. She is then covered carefully over, and the owner, accompanied by a following of little sisters and friends, all neat and in their best, sallies forth. The little party call at every gentleman's house, with, 'Please to see the May doll?' as their appeal. Sometimes they succeed in getting them carried to the mistress, and sometimes not. It depends in part on whether the leaders are known to the family. I myself always now leave word with my servants whose dolls may be brought in; but in former days I used to be overwhelmed by their number. I have known as many as thirty carried to the bedside of a sick child, to whom the day was quite a delight. Of course the children expect, and receive, a few pence; and I am told that this is faithfully and equally divided between the seven or eight children who usually accompany each doll; the whole being collected in a little bag, and then shared at the close of the day.*

Enid Porter recorded that 'May Dolling' survived in Cambridgeshire until at least the 1960s.

May Goslings

Everybody knows that 1 April is the day for playing tricks, but in the northern counties of Cumbria, Lancashire, and parts of Yorkshire and Northumberland, people had a second chance to make fools of each other on 1 May. The victim was called a 'May gosling' or 'geslin' in the local pronunciation. Iona and Peter Opie found the custom alive and well in the 1950s, and reported that the traditional tricks were the same as those recorded for 1 April, and that the trickery had to stop at 12 noon:

May gosling's dead and gone
You're the fool for thinking on.

It is not clear how old the May gosling custom was. It was certainly widespread by the late eighteenth century, as the *Gentleman's Magazine* (April 1791) included a mention:

A May gosling on the 1st of May is made with as
much eagerness in the north of England, as an April
noddy (noodle) or fool, on the 1st of April.

But this is over a hundred years after the first mention of April Fool's Day.

May Queens

One of the most widespread elements of the modern May Day is the election and crowning of the May Queen, sometimes as a ceremony in its own right but more often as a key element in a larger event such as a village fête or procession. May Queen ceremonies vary considerably in complexity, but the core remains remarkably similar. A young woman or girl is chosen (elected or appointed) to personify the season or event and to be the Queen for the year. She is dressed in suitable garb, in which elements of royal, bridal, and fairy traditions combine, and is topped with flowers or a crown, and attended by a few similarly dressed companions. She rides in state in the procession, or sits in similar state at the village fête. The age of the May Queen varies considerably from place to place, but where she is old enough, she often acts as a minor

May Queen at Ickwell, Bedfordshire, 2001

celebrity throughout the year of her reign, appearing at a variety of local events. The popularity of the basic idea is demonstrated by the numerous variations on the theme, created to suit local circumstances, such as the Rose Queen, Harvest Queen, and Dairy Queen, but the principle is always the same.

Like the plaited maypole, the May Queen is so much part of England's accepted May Day iconography that we assume it to be an ancient institution, but it is, in fact, almost entirely another nineteenth-century invention, and was an integral part of the Victorian remodelling of May Day on Merrie England lines (*see also* **Merrie England** (p. 372) and **1 May: Maypoles**). A key feature of such nineteenth-century antiquarian innovations was that their creators invariably believed that they were bringing back the real spirit of a lost golden age, blithely billing their inventions as 'ancient traditions', and we have naturally inherited this notion.

The germ of the idea for a May Queen probably came from the May Lord and Lady characters who presided over Whitsun Ales (*see* **Church Ales**, p. 194) and other spring gatherings, but the genre was largely created from scratch by the usual suspects in the Merrie England movement – Washington Irving's *Sketch Book* (1820) and *Bracebridge Hall* (1822), articles in the *Examiner* and other campaigning periodicals by Leigh Hunt and others, and, most important of all, Tennyson's poem 'The May Queen' (1832), with its insistent refrain, 'For I'm to be queen o' the May', which provided the romantic literary backdrop to countless May Day re-creations. The interest in May Queens gathered pace throughout the century, and was given another huge boost with the foundation of the world-famous May Queen ceremony at Whitelands College, in London, inspired by John Ruskin in 1881.

There is no doubting the widespread popularity of the May Queen idea in communities across the country, or that it was entirely appropriate to the image of May Day that local event committees wished to create. But it was nearly always too tightly controlled and circumscribed by its romantic origin to become a true folk custom. Time and again in Victorian and Edwardian accounts of May Day, it is clear that the celebrations had been introduced, shaped, and organized by the local elite, including vicars, schoolteachers, stalwarts of temperance societies, and the Sunday school movement, all working to the same blueprint. As Charlotte Burne wrote in 1883:

At Albrighton, near Shiffnal [Shropshire]*, a May-day festival is yearly held under the superintendence of the venerable Vicar, whose custom it has been for many years past to gather the boys of his parish about him for a treat on the 5th of November, and the girls on the 1st of May, on which occasion a very pretty ceremony has gradually grown up. After morning service in church, almost the whole congregation go to the Vicarage, where presently the chosen May Queen, in pretty gala dress, her hair garlanded with flowers, is brought forth and mounted on a horse gaily caparisoned with wreaths of flowers and greenery. The Volunteers' band heads the procession, then come two little boys on horseback, as the Queen's herald and champion, and her page*

riding on a donkey, all gaily dressed in appropriate fancy costumes. Next follows her Majesty; the Vicar walking beside her, and four little girls as her maids of honour, holding a canopy over her head, while eight or ten others, all dressed alike in white frocks and coloured ribbons, follow two and two behind. The girls of the national schools come next, and the general company, wearing or carrying flowers, bring up the rear of the procession . . . They walk the whole length of the village, and then return to the Vicarage, where the Queen is enthroned beside a Maypole, and the children spend the afternoon in games and dancing.

May Queens and their Carnival and Rose sisters are still crowned in their hundreds every year, but there is a small but discernible shift in the general view of such events. In an increasing number of cases, girls and young women appear much less willing to be dressed in white satin and flowers, and paraded around billed as the 'prettiest girl' in town. They are less willing to volunteer or to feel it an honour, and it is quite possible that over the next fifty years the May Queen will become largely a thing of the past – and ripe for re-invention in the next century.

See also **First Saturday in May: Knutsford Royal May Day Festival**; **Rose Queens**, p. 242.

Maypoles

For most English people, mention of a maypole will conjure up a picture of schoolchildren dressed in white, dancing round a short pole, and holding ribbons that make pretty patterns as they weave in and out of each other. This type of 'ribbon dance' maypole has been around for little more than 170 years, however, having been introduced to this country by professional choreographers in numerous romantic theatrical pieces, organized fêtes, and revived or created May Day customs from about the 1830s. In the classic **Merrie England** mould (p. 372), it was immediately billed as an 'old English custom', despite its lack of historical roots. By the later nineteenth century, it was being disseminated through the English school system by enthusiastic schoolteachers, and although it can now claim to be 'traditional' in its own right, for many it will always have an air of official culture rather than genuine folk tradition, precisely because it is perpetuated by teachers rather than by the people themselves. It has little in common with the English maypole as it has existed since the late Middle Ages.

The older maypole tradition involved no plaited ribbons, although it was always the focal point of dancing. The pole could be anything up to one hundred feet tall, and was usually brightly painted and decorated with garlands, rosettes, and hanging ribbons, but there was nothing for the dancers to hold on to, except each other. Surviving illustrations of village celebrations almost invariably show adult dancers holding hands in a circle round the pole. If they remained in this linked circle, there would have been little else to do than go forward and back, and round to left or right. But if they let go their hands, they could thread in and out of each other, or undertake more complex movements, and more than one seventeenth-century maypole description refers to 'turning and kissing'. When dancing in couples became generally fashionable from the early nineteenth century, it is likely that most of the dances round the maypole became indistinguishable from dances round the village hall or ballroom.

Maypoles were almost always set up on the village green, or other appropriate open space, and became the true focal point for seasonal celebration. As Lincolnshire folklorist Ethel Rudkin recorded of the village of Hemswell in 1936:

Feast week was in Maytime (i.e. first week in May) and there used to be stalls in the street round the Maypole. There was 'good-stuff' stalls, and 'sweet-meat' stalls and 'aunt Sally' – a rare fine show it was! As a little 'un I remember it – and I'd 4d to spend, so I spent it all in halfpence – and I did buy a lot with that 4d! We danced at nighttime round the maypole, but only just ordinary round dances, none of these dances with ribbons attached to the pole – I never heard tell of that being done.

But there were other types of maypole around on May Day, especially in the hands of children. A variety of children's May customs included a portable maypole, or at least a decorated stick called by the same name, and, ever-resourceful, some twentieth-century children adapted the ribboned school model, as described by a contributor to the Opies' *Lore and Language of Schoolchildren* (1959):

On May 1, 1952, I visited the recent building estates in the Monkmoor area [of Shrewsbury] and found four separate groups of children performing a maypole dance ... The maypoles consisted of a pram wheel decorated with crepe paper and streamers set on top of a pole so that it would revolve. The pole (varying from about 3 to about 5 feet high) was held in position by the Queen seated upon a wooden stool. The number of dancers (all girls) varied from four to ten ... The performers seemed aged about 5–11 and were dressed in crepe paper finery, the queen usually wearing a crown of some sort.

The early development of the maypole is unclear. There is no evidence that the pole was a development of the pagan worship of trees, or was seen as a fertility-based phallic symbol. The first definite references are in the fourteenth century; one in a Welsh poem, although the word is in English, and the second in another poem, 'Chaunce of the Dice', a decade or so later. The latter concerns the permanent pole at Cornhill in London, reputedly taller than the steeple of the nearby church, which was generally known as St Andrew's *Undershaft* as a result. John Stow's *Survey of London* (1598) explains that this maypole was taken down for a while after 'Evil May Day' of 1517, when apprentices rioted against foreigners, and was finally attacked and chopped up by a zealous Protestant preacher in 1549. From this time onwards, the maypole had a chequered career, being used as a potent symbol by both sides in the protracted battle between religious reformers and conservative supporters of popular pastimes.

Real maypoles need regular replacement. The part that is underground quickly rots, and poles are regularly blown down or damaged in winter storms. The fetching and setting up of a new pole was always an occasion for celebration and merriment, and this was one of the grounds on which the reformers sought to ban the custom. The famous diatribe against maypoles, penned by Puritan Philip Stubbes in 1583, is worth quoting in full, as it not only demonstrates the depth of feeling against such events but also provides our best description of the custom at this period:

The manner of May games in England: . . . Against May day, Whitsunday, or some other time of the year, every parish, town, and village assemble themselves together, both men, women, and children, old and young, even all indifferently, and either going all together, or dividing themselves into companies, they go some into to the woods, and groves, some to the hills and mountains, some to one place, some to another, where they spend all night in pleasant pastimes, and in the morning they return bringing with them birch boughs, and branches of trees, to deck their assemblies withal. And no marvel, for there is a great Lord present amongst them, as super-intendent and lord over their pastimes and sports: namely, Satan Prince of Hell: But their chiefest jewel they bring from thence is the may-pole, which they bring home with great veneration, as thus: they have twenty, or forty yoke of oxen, every ox having a sweet nosegay of flowers tied on the tip of his horns, and these oxen draw home this May-pole (this stinking idol rather) which is covered all over with flowers and herbs, bound round about with strings from top to the bottom, and sometimes painted with variable colours, with two or three hundred men, women, and children following it, with great devotion. And thus being reared up, with handkerchiefs and flags streaming on the top, they strew the ground round about, bind green boughs about it, set up summer halls, bowers, and arbours hard by it. And then fall they to banquet and feast, to leap and dance about it, as the heathen people did, at the dedication of their idols, whereof this is a perfect pattern, or rather the thing itself. I have heard it credible reported (and that viva voce) by men of great gravity, credit, and reputation, that of forty, threescore, or a hundred maids, going to the wood overnight, there have scarcely the third part of them return home unde-filed. These be the fruits, which these cursed pastimes bring forth. Assuredly, I think neither Jews nor Turks, Saracens, nor Pagans, nor any other people how wicked, or barbarous soever, have ever used such devilish exercises as these; nay, they would have been ashamed once to have named them, much less to have used them. Yet we that would be Christian, think them not amiss. The Lord forgive us and remove them far from us.

Maypoles were banned by Parliament in 1644, and although some royalist centres were slow to comply, before long the country was devoid of maypoles for the first time in at least 300 years. Nevertheless, the symbolic nature of the maypole was again in evidence at the Restoration, as they sprang up all over the country in deliberate defiance of the Puritan rule of the Commonwealth. The one difference at this time, however, was that Royal Oak Day began to rival May Day as the time for celebration (*see* **29 May: Royal Oak Day**). Maypoles continued to be evident in English villages and towns through the next centuries, but after the peak of popularity at the Restoration, they gradu-ally faded away – this time from neglect and changing fashion rather than opposition. A few places still have maypoles on traditional lines, including: Barwick-in-Elmet in Yorkshire (*see* **Spring Bank Holiday: Barwick Maypole**, p. 204), Hemswell in Lincolnshire, Ickwell in Bedfordshire, and Padstow in Cornwall.

Milkmaids' Garland

[1 May 1667] *Thence to Westminster in the way meet-ing with many milk-maids with their garlands upon their pails, dancing with a fiddler before them.*

Samuel Pepys here shows no surprise about seeing milkmaids dancing, as it was a common sight in urban streets on May Day. The 'milkmaids' dance', or 'milk-maids' garland', was for many a symbol of spring, and there are numerous published approving descriptions and illustrations that demonstrate that the custom was a welcome diversion of the season. It should be explained that 'milkmaids' in this context are not necessarily those who milked the cows, but those who delivered the milk to urban houses. Ostensibly, the maids danced in the streets in front of their customers' houses, and collected money from them, but no doubt they solicited contributions from passers-by as well. On 2 May 1710, a correspondent to the *Tatler* reported:

I was looking out of the parlour window this morn-ing and receiving the honours which Margery, the milkmaid to our lane, was doing me by dancing before my door with the plate of half her customers on her head.

In Pepys's time, the 'garland' was usually the maid's

ordinary milk-pail, colourfully decorated with flowers and ribbons, and carried on her head, while she danced to the music of an accompanying fiddler. The poise and dexterity necessary to dance thus encumbered added to the charm of the scene. Later illustrations, however, indicate that the 'garland' developed rapidly through various stages to become a veritable pyramid of silver plate and utensils, borrowed or hired for the occasion, and heavy enough to need to be carried on the head of an attendant male, or even on a litter between two men, leaving the maid to dance more freely. The typical milkmaid's May Day entourage thus grew to include various supernumeraries, including even a policeman, or some other responsible person, to guard the valuable silverware on show.

There was also a bunters' garland, which parodied the milkmaids' custom. 'Bunters' were low female rag-pickers or, in some parlance, prostitutes, who danced accompanied by predominately brass garlands, rather than silver and gold. They were no doubt amusing or grotesque, according to the perspective of the beholder.

The heyday of the milkmaids' garland custom was the eighteenth century, and it seems to have faded away quite rapidly in the early nineteenth. By this time, the May Day streets were becoming quite crowded, as other trade groups also put on displays and collected money. The chimney sweeps and Jack-in-the-Greens (see p. 155), in particular, regarded this as their special day, and one that marked the end of the lucrative winter season, and illustrations show sweeps' boys and apprentices joining in the milkmaids' dance, providing percussion with the tools of their trade, the brush and shovel. The inherent ambiguity of this juxtaposition of summertime, milk-white, female grace, and winter soot-black male grotesquery was not lost on contemporary observers, and although it cannot be proved that the sweeps' involvement drove the milkmaids from the streets, the temporal coincidence of the decline of the one and the rise of the other is certainly suggestive.

Minehead Hobby Horse

The Minehead hobby horse, in Somerset, has the dubious distinction of always being compared unfavourably with the more widely known **Padstow Hobby Horse** (see below), but this is unfair. The two traditions are quite similar in outline, but whereas the Padstow 'Oss is predominately black, and it seems as if the whole town is celebrating the custom, the Minehead horse is colourful and mobile, playful and mischievous, and the undoubtedly charming festivities follow a simpler approach. The Minehead horse comes out briefly on the evening of 30 April, and then on the first three days of May. He tours the streets of the town and neighbouring area, to the music of accordions and drum. There are usually two or three horses at any given time, including, at present, the Sailors' Horse, which is generally regarded as the original, and the Town, or Show, Horse.

The basis of the horse is a boat-shaped wooden frame about eight feet long and three feet wide, supported on a man's shoulders. The frame is covered in a cloth, which hangs down to the ground and is decorated with coloured roundels and other shapes. Across the top are multicoloured ribbons, and the carrier is hidden by a mask and hood, which is also covered with ribbons. As with other hobby animals, the Minehead horse can run, dance, sway, or jump as the mood takes it, and, as Herbert W. Kille notes in his 1931 article on West Country hobby horses, it regularly pays 'obeisance to onlookers, especially if they be affluent-looking ones, or, if they be otherwise, flutters its hundreds of ribbons with a wicked shake and rushes affrightingly at them'.

The horse used to carry a ladle in its mouth to collect money, but nowadays this is done by attendants; its mouth could also be made to snap at people, but this too has been removed. If people refuse to give money they can be 'booted'. The victim is seized, held face down, and struck ten times on the posterior by the front of the horse (in previous times by a boot), to shouts of 'Oh one! Oh two! Oh three!', and so on. If anyone offends the horse it metes out a more summary punishment by suddenly whipping round and catching the unwary bystander with its rope tail.

Herbert Kille's account of the custom speaks of the horse being attended by fantastically dressed men known as 'gullivers', 'up to about fifty years ago' (i.e. about 1880), whose task was to collect money by knocking on doors and accosting passers-by. They were armed with clubs, and local legend maintains that

Hobby Horses

For many centuries, hobby animals have been a popular feature of a number of traditional customs, and although it is usually a horse that is impersonated, other animals, such as rams and bulls, are occasionally made on similar lines. The animals can appear on their own (*see* **24 December: Hooden Horse**) or as part of another custom (*see* **Whitsun: Morris Dance**, p. 188), and they come in a variety of guises. There are two basic forms of construction, dubbed the 'tourney' horse and the 'mast' horse, although the best-known existing hobby horse customs, at Padstow in Cornwall, and Minehead in Somerset (*see* **1 May: Minehead Hobby Horse**; **1 May: Padstow Hobby Horse**), are not typical, and are made on different lines.

For the tourney horse, a man stands inside an oval frame, which is fixed round his waist, usually by straps over the shoulders. The frame is covered with a cloth that hangs down all round, partly obscuring the rider's legs, and a small replica horse's head is fixed at the front, with a tail at the rear. The man appears to be riding the horse, and refinements such as reins for him to hold, and dummy rider's legs sewn on the horse's sides, greatly enhance the illusion. In skilled hands, a tourney horse can run, jump, skip, and dance; its rider can see perfectly well, and it is the most mobile of the hobby horse types under consideration.

The mast horse is decidedly more primitive-looking than the tourney horse. A real horse's skull, or a wooden replica, is mounted on a pole about three or four feet long. A man bends forward and grasps the pole near the top in both hands, and he and the pole are completely covered by a cloth fixed to the underside of the horse's head. The result is somewhat formless, and hardly horse-like at all, but it can be extremely effective, and frightening, in the right hands (*see*, for example, **24 December: Old Horse**).

Within these basic designs, either type of horse can have refinements. Particularly popular are snapping jaws worked by a string, bells, pieces of metal that jangle, and glass for reflective eyes. The tail might be realistically fashioned from horsehair or rope, which fetches the unwary onlooker a blow as the horse wheels round, or it can even be full of sharp tacks or fish hooks to make sure no bystanders try to catch hold of it.

The tourney horse has been known for many years as an accompaniment to the morris dance, but it has also featured in processions and other customs, such as the Horn Dance at Abbots Bromley (*see* **4 September: Abbots Bromley Horn Dance**). The mast horse has a much more varied history. He turns up as the Hooden Horse in Kent, the Wild Horse in the Cheshire version of the mummers' play (*see* **31 October: Antrobus Soul-Cakers**), in the plough plays of the East Midlands (*see* **Plough Monday**, p. 19), as the **Old Tup** and the **Old Horse** in the Midlands (*see* **24 December**), and in the well-known Welsh custom of the Mari Lwyd.

they were suppressed because they got involved in a fight with someone who would not contribute, and ended up killing him, but no evidence has yet been found to support this story. Numerous photographs of the custom in the twentieth century do not show any attendants, apart from musicians, but around 1970 one team re-introduced the gullivers, whose costume of ribbons and masks deliberately echoes that of the hobby horse itself.

The earliest known reference to the hobby horse custom is in James Savage's *History of the Hundred of Carhampton* (1830), but his comment that 'this custom has prevailed for ages' implies a much longer history that had gone unrecorded.

See also **Hobby Horses**, *above*.

Padstow Hobby Horse

Unite and unite and let us all unite
For summer is a-come unto day
And whither we are going we all will unite
In the merry morning of May.

The town of Padstow, on the north coast of Cornwall, has the most famous hobby horse in the country, and the

The earliest documentary evidence is found in a fourteenth-century Welsh poem by Gruffud Gryg, and a later Cornish play, *Beunas Meriasek* (1504). Although these were written in Welsh and Cornish respectively, in both the phrase 'hobby horse' appears in English. Sandwiched in time between these references is an entry in the churchwardens' accounts for St Andrew Hubbard in 1460/1: 'To Mayers child for dancing with the hobby horse'. From the early sixteenth century onwards, references to hobby horses abound, and a reasonable picture of its style and activities can be formed. Whenever contextual details can be found in these early references, it is clear that the hobby horse's primary task was the collection of money, often for the Church but also for other institutions, and it was probably used in this way because it was an immensely popular entertainment with the people. There is little doubt that the tourney horse, at least, owes its existence to its entertainment value rather than any supposed ritual or ceremonial function. But the real paradox for the hobby horse historian is that the apparently primitive mast-horse only starts to make an appearance in documentary records from the mid nineteenth century onwards.

This fact puts into serious doubt any supposed direct link between hobby horse customs and the prehistoric cave paintings found in some European sites, which appear to represent humans impersonating animals. The enormous gulf in time and geography between these primitive representations and our modern hobby horses make it impossible to draw any connections without a huge leap of faith. Similarly, the occasional prohibitions by early continental Church authorities against people dressing as animals, which themselves need re-analysis, are separated from our historical examples by over a thousand years.

The one comparison that might save our mast horses from the ignominy of being mere Victorian inventions is the Scandinavian evidence most recently presented by Terry Gunnell in his *Origins of Drama in Scandinavia* (1995). He describes a range of animals, including the widely known *Julebukk* or *Julegeit* (Christmas goat), which were found across most of Scandinavia, from the first known mention in Denmark in 1543, until the late nineteenth century. Apart from the fact that these creatures were decorated with fur and wore horns, they were constructed in a very similar way to our mast horses, and behaved in corresponding ways. They too were used primarily as part of a winter house-visiting custom, and could be found alone and with other dramatic forms. The British evidence has been ably collected by Dr E. C. Cawte in his *Ritual Animal Disguise* (1978), but thirty years later there is still much more work to be done on the subject.

See also **Easter Day: Old Ball**, p. 118; **24 June: Midsummer's Day/St John the Baptist's Day**.

---

locals are fiercely proud of their tradition. On 30 April the town is decorated with greenery, bunting, and flags in preparation for the big day, and on May morning the 'Oss emerges from his long sleep to spend the day dancing through the streets among the huge crowds of tourists and visitors, who outnumber the locals several to one. It is a mark of Padstow's independence that they not only still continue the tradition, but also do it on their own terms. Like other community customs, the celebrations at Padstow on May Day are so important to the community that those who live away try to get home for the day; and if they cannot, we are told, they make sure to sing the May Day song to themselves to compensate a little.

The 'Oss is difficult to describe adequately, but it comprises a circular frame, about five feet in diameter, which is carried on straps on the shoulders of a man inside. Covering the frame and hanging down all round, almost to the ground, is a black cloth. The carrier's head pokes up through a hole in the centre, and is covered with a tall conical hat and a grotesque mask. Attached to the front of the frame is a small stylized horse's head, and at the rear a tail. It is surprising how versatile and lifelike such a strange monster can be. It

Padstow 'Obby 'Oss, Cornwall, 1994

walks, sways, dances, swings, and swoops – not much like a horse, admittedly, but like a live creature all the same. There is a Teaser, previously called the Dancer, who holds a flat painted club and dances in front of the 'Oss, encouraging, leading, and teasing it, as well as musicians and drummers, lots of them nowadays, and young people, some of whom collect money from the onlookers, while others dance. The musicians play the same hypnotic tune all day, as the 'Oss dances all around the town, but every now and then it sinks to the ground, whether pretending to be dead, asleep, or from simple exhaustion is not clear. The music and song changes to a slow dirge, the dancers crouch, and those close enough might reach out and gently stroke the 'Oss, but as the slow verse ends, and with a triumphant cry of ''Oss 'Oss!' he springs back on to his feet and is off again.

There are two 'Osses at present, which to the untrained eye look identical, but their attendants are easily distinguished as they are dressed in either red or blue. There have been many 'Osses over the years, as reported to collector Doc Rowe:

> Well we had all sorts of Osses at one time. Old Baker had one and the . . . Lion had one; Albert Giddy had a horse called 'Princess Mary' . . . Didn't Sussex Langford have one? Then there was Rosie Walker's 'Oss . . . the striped one. We had a white 'Obby 'Oss for a year or two. Oh yes, I remember that one. It was all white.

The musicians and attendant singers, dancers, and collectors wear a white costume, but their hats, sashes, and ribbons are brightly coloured. The red team wear headscarves and sashes and look like stage pirates, while the blue team look more like stage sailors. The two 'Osses wend their separate ways around the town, and while you are following one it seems as if the other does not exist. But they both return to the middle of town for the evening climax, and sometimes they will dance together.

The red team claim that theirs is the original 'Oss, as

the blue one descends from an 'Oss that came out after the First World War, but although the respective lineage is well documented in the twentieth century, the earlier period is less clear, and some even say that the blue one is really the oldest. Hundreds of photographs, dating back to around the First World War, provide evidence for changing styles and fashions, although they do not reveal much about the actions of the 'Oss and the attendant dancing. In the earlier pictures there are far fewer onlookers, but also fewer musicians (only one or two melodeons, and one or two drums), fewer white costumes, and more hats decorated with flowers, like May Day customs elsewhere. The musicians and Teaser often seem to be in fancy dress, and the latter sometimes appears dressed as a woman.

The origin of the custom is not known. The popular historical story is that one day, when all the men were out fishing, a French ship appeared off Padstow and the women feared an invasion. So they dressed up as the 'Oss and the French were so perplexed at the sight that they promptly sailed away. The earliest known reference appears in the Revd R. Polwhele's *History of Cornwall* in 1803, but as he describes it as a 'man drest up in a stallion horse's skin', it is not clear whether he actually witnessed a performance. Two decades later, however, F. Hitchins and Samuel Drew's *History of Cornwall* (1824) refers to 'canvas being extended with hoops, and painted to resemble a horse', which is certainly akin to the present-day form.

The Padstow Mayers also have a night-visiting custom on 30 April, when they go round to selected houses singing their 'night song':

> *Arise up Mrs. ——, and gold be your ring*
> *For summer is acome unto day*
> *And give to us a cup of ale the merrier we shall sing*
> *In the merry morning of May.*

Other verses serenade the Mr and Miss ——, together with the 'young men', who are exhorted to go to the greenwood to fetch the May. Padstow also has a minstrel-inspired singing custom on Boxing Day (*see* **26 December: Padstow Mummers' (Darkie) Day**).

See also **1 May: Minehead Hobby Horse**; **Hobby Horses**, p. 164.

Randwick Cheese-Rolling

Randwick, near Stroud in Gloucestershire, was home to an apparently unique annual custom involving large, round cheeses. Unlike the other Gloucestershire cheese-rolling at Cooper's Hill, where they were chased down a hill (*see* **Spring Bank Holiday**, p. 204), at Randwick they were treated far more respectfully. William Hone records in his *Table Book* (1827) that:

> *Three large cheeses (Gloucestershire, of course), decked with the gayest flowers of this lovely season, are placed in litters, equally adorned with flowers, and boughs of trees waving at the corners. They are thus borne through the village, accompanied by a joyous throng, shouting and huzzaing with all their might and main, and usually accompanied by a little band of music.*

The cheeses were then rolled three times around the church, carried back through the village, and then cut up and distributed. This account is the first mention of the custom, and it was probably originally a dole, or the distribution of food as a result of a local bequest, which often featured seemingly bizarre characteristics (*see* **Doles**, p. 87).

The cheese-rolling was revived in 1972, and incorporated into the local festival called Randwick Wap (*see* **Second Saturday in May: Randwick Wap**).

*

3 MAY

The Day of the Invention of the Holy Cross

According to one version of the legend, St Helena, the mother of St Constantine, discovered the three crosses on which Christ and the two robbers had been crucified, in the Holy Land in the early fourth century AD. The day is sometimes called St Helena's, although her real feast day is 18 August, and to complicate things further, some early British writers confused matters by claiming her as English-born.

Presumably unrelated to these ecclesiastical connections, 3 May was known as 'Sting-Nettle Day' in Devon. In 1880, the Devonshire Association recorded:

The first of May is 'May-doll day'
The second of May is 'kissing day'
The third of May is 'sting-nettle day'.

On the 3rd of May this year I was passing through the village [Bovey Tracey] *and was struck with the peculiarity of all the children being provided with a nettle, or bunch of nettles, with which they were flogging each other. Having never seen the like before, Mr. B. thought there must be some meaning in this demonstration, and on enquiring of some of the children, he was informed that it was 'Sting-nettle Day'.*

This does not seem to be reported as a separate custom anywhere else in the country, although one of the common punishments for not wearing an oak leaf on Royal Oak Day (*see* **29 May: Royal Oak Day**) was to be attacked by nettle-wielding children.

∗

FIRST SATURDAY IN MAY

Gawthorpe Celebrations

Gawthorpe, the Yorkshire village famous for its World Coal-Carrying Championship contest every Easter Monday (*see* p. 126), also holds impressive May Day celebrations on the first Saturday in that month. A procession involving themed floats, bands, children in fancy dress, and the local May Queen takes place, and there is also plaited maypole dancing, of which Gawthorpe is particularly proud, performed by schoolgirls from the village. The event has been organized by the Maypole Committee since 1874, but this was merely a formalization of an older tradition of maypoles in the village.

Earlier May celebrations were not always so well disciplined as the current ones. In 1850, for example, inter-village rivalry got out of hand when men from nearby Chickenley undertook a raid and sawed partway through the pole; in the ensuing fight, one man died and many were injured. The wind finished off that particular pole not long after, but there have been others since.

Knutsford Royal May Day Festival

Knutsford, in Cheshire, offers one of the best-known and largest modern May Day celebrations; hundreds of people take part, and even more line the streets to watch and admire them. The main event is the procession through town, which manages to preserve a local homely feel by featuring local children dressed as 'figures from the pages of fable and history', as the local paper described them. There are also morris dancers, brass bands, a town crier, a Jack-in-the-Green, and a Chinese dragon, among others, as well as a May Queen and her court of attendants. Knutsford takes its May Queen very seriously, and her crown is a replica of Queen Elizabeth's. A new one is provided each year, because the May Queen is allowed to keep hers as a souvenir of the day.

The present series of celebrations commenced in 1864, which makes it probably the longest-running May Day in the country. It is an excellent example of how the Victorians remodelled May Day (as they did Christmas), to remove the less salubrious aspects and create a new, respectable, family-friendly festival that lasted for generations to come. The word 'Royal' was added to its title in 1887, in honour of a visit from the then Prince and Princess of Wales.

Knutsford also has a unique custom called 'sanding', in which coloured sand is used to decorate the pavements on May Day and in honour of other special occasions, and the town was the model for Mrs Gaskell's popular novel *Cranford* (1851–3).

∗

FIRST SUNDAY IN MAY

Tyburn Walk

A procession or pilgrimage takes place in London every year to commemorate Catholics martyred for their faith during the sixteenth and seventeenth centuries on Tyburn gallows. The route roughly follows that taken by prisoners from Newgate Prison to Tyburn, and it has been undertaken every year (including the War years) since its inauguration in 1910. The Walk was under severe threat in the year 2000 when pressure was put on the organizers to avoid busy shopping centres

Tyburn Walk, London, 1984

such as Oxford Street, but it has continued, albeit more informally and with fewer participants, and it now approaches its centenary. The Walk is normally now held on the first Sunday in May (except when this coincides with May Day Bank Holiday, in which case it is held on the second Sunday), and commences from the Church of the Holy Sepulchre, on the Strand (almost opposite the Old Bailey), at 2 or 2.30 p.m.

*

8 MAY

Helston Flora Day

The town of Helston, in Cornwall, maintains what must be the most famous traditional dance custom in Britain. Every May, the participants form up in couples and dance through the town, in and out of houses and shops, to a lively tune played by the town's silver band. The dance takes place four times during the day, each time involving a different section of the town's population.

In the case of most traditional customs, the earliest recorded references are vague and ambiguous, but we are lucky to have an unusually detailed account of the festivities at Helston in our first reference, which shows that all the essential elements of the day, as recently observed, were already in place in the late eighteenth century. The account was published in the *Gentleman's Magazine* of 1790 and signed by 'Durgan', and it is worth quoting in full:

> At Helstone [sic], *a genteel and populous borough town in Cornwall, it is customary to dedicate the 8th of May to revelry (festive mirth, not loose jollity). It is called the Furry-day, supposed Flora's day; not, I imagine, as many have thought, in remembrance of some festival instituted in honour of that goddess, but rather from the garlands commonly worn on that day. In the morning, very early, some trouble-some rogues go round the streets with drums, or other noisy instruments, disturbing their sober neighbours, and singing parts of a song, the whole of which nobody now recollects, and of which I know no more than that there is a mention in it of the 'grey goose quill' and of them going to the 'green*

> *wood to bring home the summer and the May-O' and, accordingly, hawthorn flowering branches are worn in hats . . . About the middle of the day they collect together to dance hand-in-hand round the streets, to the sound of the fiddle playing a particular tune, which they continue to do till it is dark. This is called a 'faddy'. In the afternoon, the gentility go to some farmhouse in the neighbourhood to drink tea, syllabub, etc., and return in a morris-dance to the town, where they form a faddy, and dance through the streets till it is dark, claiming the right of going through any person's house, in at one door and out at the other. And here it formerly used to end, and the company of all kinds to disperse quietly to their several habitations, but latterly, corruptions have in this, as in other matters, crept in by degrees.*

Already in 1790 he is writing of 'corruptions' creeping in, although the sum total of the changes that he mentions are that the 'gentility' go on to a ball, and faddy their way home at the end of the evening, while the 'mobility', as he calls the lower classes, have a similar evening's entertainment at the local pubs. Already, too, there is confusion over the name. It is clear that 'furry day' is the older term, and all serious researchers accept that it is derived from a Cornish or English dialect form of 'fair day'. This is supported by the fact that 8 May is St Michael's Day, to whom the parish church is dedicated, and therefore the logical day for a local fair or feast. The names 'floral' and 'flora' may well have been introduced by some eighteenth-century antiquarian in his quest for classical origins, but even if that is so, they have become so entrenched, and are used by both locals and outsiders, that there is no shifting them now. Indeed, 'Floral dance' fits the May-time scene so well that its acceptance was perhaps inevitable.

On Flora Day, the town is decorated with bunting, greenery, and blossoms, and people wear lily-of-the-valley buttonholes and other flowers. The streets are crammed with spectators, allowing only a narrow passageway for the dancers to make their way through. Nowadays, there are four dances, at seven, ten, noon and five in the afternoon. The first one, previously for servants and others who would be on duty later in the day, is mostly now for young people, the men wearing ties and white shirts, the women in smart summer dresses;

Helston Flora (Furry) Dance, Cornwall, 1995

the second is the children's dance (introduced in 1922), and the dancers are all in white. The most famous – probably because it photographs well – is the Principal Dance, which begins at noon at the guildhall. This dance used to be restricted to the gentry, but participation is now by invitation of the organizing committee. The men wear grey top hats and black tails and the women are in gaily coloured dresses and impressively wide-brimmed summer hats, which looks more like a scene from Ascot than one in a Cornish town. The last dance is a relative free-for-all, when anyone is allowed to join in. Each dance takes its own route, which can take over an hour to complete and is very tiring for participants. Douglas Kennedy, former long-time Director of the English Folk Dance and Song Society, described how he and his wife fared when they were invited to take part in the Principal Dance in 1957. The night before, they were schooled in dancing 'with gaiety combined with dignity', but on the day they faced the last stretch

up a steep hill to the town hall with decidedly flagging energy and stiff limbs.

One of the main reasons for the widespread fame of the event is the song 'The Floral Dance', composed in 1911 by a professional concert singer from London, Katie Moss, after she had visited the Helston Floral Dance that year. Her words, which are little short of twee, and her tune, which differs significantly from the way it has always been played in Helston, has been regularly performed as a pseudo-folk song by concert artists ever since. It was later arranged for brass band and became a staple of that repertoire all over the world. It is unfortunate that this later version is now more widely known than Helston's original, but it is encouraging that the people of Helston have remained resolutely unaffected by this.

Equally regrettable, but now firmly incorporated into the celebrations, is the 'enactment' of the 'Hal-an-Tow', the song that was sung by Durgan's 'troublesome rogues'. This part of the day was suppressed in the nineteenth century but was re-introduced in 1930, in suitably sanitized form, by the Helston Old Cornwall Society, when someone also decided that the song should not merely be sung but acted out in costume. The text is nothing if not eclectic, but it makes no real sense and speaks of Robin Hood and Little John, the Spaniards, St George, and Aunt Mary Moses in successive verses. However, its chorus makes perfect sense in the context of the day:

> *Hal-an-tow, jolly rumble O*
> *For we were up as soon as any day O*
> *And for to fetch the summer home*
> *The summer and the May O*
> *For summer is a-come O*
> *And winter is a-gone O.*

The phrase 'Hal-an-Tow' has generated a few fanciful derivations, but it probably means the dance 'Heel and toe'.

*

12 MAY

Florence Nightingale Commemoration

It takes a special kind of celebrity to become a lasting icon in the public's eye, but Florence Nightingale (1820–1910) fits that role perfectly. Nightingale was born to well-off parents, but at a relatively early age she decided to eschew the usual middle-class woman's path of marriage and family to dedicate herself to God's service. To this end, she decided to train as a nurse, and at the outbreak of the Crimean War in 1854 Nightingale used her connections, notably with Sidney Herbert, Secretary of War, to get permission to take a party of nurses to the front to care for wounded combatants. What she found there appalled her. The army offered the wounded no real care, and the hospitals were unhygienic and badly organized; above all, the military hierarchy seemed oblivious to the needs of sick and wounded soldiers. Nightingale was a formidable presence and completely reorganized hospital care, lobbying for improved conditions in health and welfare, and continuing to do so when back in Britain. She is credited with laying the foundations of modern nursing.

Florence Nightingale is still remembered at an annual service at Westminster Abbey, on or near her birthday, 12 May. Although her life and work is the focal point of the event, the service also celebrates nursing and healthcare work in general, and members of the different professions take an active part. Nightingale was famously dubbed 'the lady of the lamp', and the National Army Museum in Chelsea possesses one of the original lamps used in the Crimean hospital. In the Westminster Abbey service, the lamp is carried to the altar by a nurse, escorted by student nurses, and passed from hand to hand between representatives of the different branches of healthcare work and then to the officiating clergyman, who places it on the altar.

The May

Hastings Neville, writing of life in rural Northumberland just before the end of the nineteenth century, described the importance of 12 May to local families:

> *Our May Day is not the first of the month with its romance of maidens going forth to bathe their faces in the early dew, nor is it the 29th, the oak apple day of the South . . . We have no May Day of this sort . . . With us the 12th of the month is so important a crisis in the life of our agricultural families that it is always called by them 'The May'. It is well if that day dawns brightly and with good omens, for it is the great day which terminates and begins the annual term for which our farm workers are hired . . . above all it is the day of 'flitting' from farm to farm of those who for various reasons find it desirable to make a change of place and master . . . There they go, cart after cart, passing up the bank, as we call our hill, the furniture in one cart, piled to a dangerous height, with the grandfather clock lying lengthwise and risking its life on the top. The people themselves consider the flitting a sorrowful time.*

This day is, of course, close to Old May Day.

A different custom, reported in the early twentieth century in Lancashire, dictated that on this day children had to wear a particular flower. *Lancashire Lore*, published by the Lancashire Federation of Women's Institutes, recorded that the 'children wore a May gollen (marsh marigold) . . . Those without had their hair pulled.' *See* **29 May: Royal Oak Day** for a similar custom.

    See also **6 April: Flitting Day**; **14 May: Pack Rag Day.**

*

SECOND SATURDAY IN MAY

Randwick Wap

Randwick Wap is the local name for this Gloucestershire village's annual feast or revel, which was formerly held on Low Sunday (the Sunday after Easter), and which stood out from other such village festivals by featuring the election of a mock mayor. The *Gentleman's Magazine* of 1784 published the following account of the proceedings:

> *One of the parish is . . . elected mayor, and carried in great state, colours flying, drums beating, men, women, and children shouting, to a particular horsepond, in which his worship is placed, seated in his arm-chair; a song is then given out line by line by the clerk, and sung with great gravity by the surrounding crowd . . . The instant it is finished the mayor breaks the peace by throwing water in the face of his attendants. Upon this much confusion ensues.*

However, the ensuing horseplay – and the generally drunken nature of the goings-on – was enough to get the event suppressed in 1892. A medieval origin is claimed for these festivities, although printed records mentioning them can only be traced to *c.*1703. Nobody has yet come up with a convincing etymology for the word 'Wap' in this context.

    The event was revived in 1972, and is now held on the second Saturday in May every year. The focal point is a procession of villagers, all in costume, from the war memorial to the Mayor's Pool, led by a 'mop man' who carries a wet mop to clear the crowds out of the way. Various officials are elected for the day, including a mayor and mayoress, who are carried shoulder-high in the procession, and the mayor is dunked in the pool, as before. The afternoon is spent in the usual village fête manner. A cheese-rolling custom, formerly carried out

on 1 May (*see* **1 May: Randwick Cheese-Rolling**) is now incorporated into the revived Wap.

    See also **Mock Mayors and Courts**, p. 216.

*

SECOND SUNDAY IN MAY

Mother's Day (US)

In the USA, Mother's Day occurs on the second Sunday in May, but in Britain it is celebrated on Mid-Lent Sunday.

    See **Mothering Sunday**, p. 81; **Mother's Day**, p. 83.

*

13 MAY (OLD MAY DAY)

Abbotsbury Garland Day

In Abbotsbury, a small village on the coast of Dorset, the children have a May garland custom that has survived despite many changes in village life that would normally have wiped out such a thing years ago. Several villages along the Chesil coast previously had garlands in May, but all these traditions disappeared by 1950; at Abbotsbury, the custom has been kept going simply because the local people have been determined not to let it die. Flowers and greenery are fixed to a frame of wire, plastic, or wood, which is then mounted on a pole and carried between two children. The garlands are carried around the village and shown to each householder, and the children are usually given a small sum of money for their trouble.

    The custom is first mentioned in John Hutchins' *History of Dorset* (1867), and at that time it was in the hands of families involved in fishing. Each family made a garland, which was paraded around the town by the children, and a party was then held on the beach. Some of the garlands were rowed out to sea and thrown overboard, and the whole event was respectable enough to include a special church service. After the First World War, the garlands began to be placed on the village war memorial rather than being cast on the waves. The local fishing industry virtually disappeared after the Second World War, and the garland custom was kept

Abbotsbury Garland Day, Dorset, 1930s

alive by increasing school involvement. As the children in the village all went to the local school, they could be granted the day off on 'Garland Day'. Later, the older children were bussed to school in Weymouth, so the young ones took their garlands round during the day, and the older ones in the evening. However, the local school closed completely in 1981, and as the education authorities outside the area could hardly be expected to honour Garland Day in the same way, again there had to be changes. During these years, the number of garlands has gradually declined; eight was the norm in the 1920s, but there have been only two or three in recent years. For some time, it has been the custom to make one garland of wild flowers and one of garden flowers. In 2005, two garlands were made for the children to take round separately when they returned from school in the evening, but only eight children actually took part.

Cowslips

Some time in May, although at least one Victorian informant specified the 13th, country girls turned to the humble cowslip for a game and a marriage divination. Mollie Harris remembered doing so in Oxfordshire in the 1920s:

When spring had really come and the warm sun had brought out more meadow flowers, we would pick baskets of cowslips so that our mother might brew some home-made wine. We used to keep some of the best blooms ourselves to make what we called a 'tisty tosty ball'. Taking off the main stalk we would bunch up the thick flower-heads together, tying them in the middle with wool, and this made a lovely soft sweet-smelling ball. Then for hours we would play a game called 'Tell me true', each girl tossing a ball in the air, keeping in time with this jingle

> *Tisty tosty tell me true*
> *Who shall I be married to?*
> *Tisty tosty, cowslip ball*
> *At my sweetheart's name you'll fall.*

Each of us had our favourites where the boys were concerned and we'd chant them – Percy, Charlie, Jimmy, Tom, Billy, Frankie, Bob and Bert, and, strange as it seemed, the ball always managed to fall at the name we wanted it to.

Miners' Holiday

In the first third of the nineteenth century, Derbyshire miners had their own May Day celebration – on *old* May Day. In 1829, county historian Stephen Glover wrote:

> *On the 13th of May the miners dress their coves or cowes (the places in which they deposit the ore) with oak branches, garlands and other rural decorations. This is called the 'miners' holiday'. A dinner of beef, pudding and ale is provided on the occasion, and, when the weather is favourable, the festivities are conducted in the open air. The Bar-masters preside and music and old songs conclude the proceedings . . .*

Rook Sunday

According to Maureen Sutton, the nearest Sunday to 13 May was termed 'Rook Sunday' in parts of Lincolnshire well into the twentieth century, because rook pies were traditionally eaten on the day. The pies were made from baby rooks (called 'squabs'), which are easily obtained at that season and apparently taste like a cross between chicken and turkey. The outside edge of the pastry was marked with the rooks' feet, and although some informants commented that people would eat anything if they were hungry enough, it is clear that some regarded the rooks as a local delicacy. Florence White includes a traditional Nottinghamshire recipe for rook pie in her *Good Things in England* (1932).

*

14 MAY

Pack Rag Day

This day was one of the key dates in the farmworkers' calendar in Lincolnshire, as it was two days earlier in Northumberland (*see* **12 May: The May**). The folklore collectors Mrs Gutch and Mabel Peacock recorded in 1908 that:

> *Bank holidays pass almost unnoticed, but May 14th, or Pag-rag day, is a great event, when the single farm servants, male and female, leave their places, or at least take a week's holiday, and spend the time visiting their friends and going round to different markets. The married men decide whether they will remain with their masters at Candlemas; they have the privilege of attending what is called the labourer's market soon after that date, when they hire themselves again and leave their old places April 6th.*

See also **6 April: Flitting Day; Hiring Fairs**, p. 345.

*

MID MAY

Durham Mayor-Making

The Mayor of Durham is elected at the council's annual meeting, usually in mid May. After taking the oath of acceptance and being given the mayoral seal, he or she later appears on the town hall steps and throws a handful of coins (nowadays 5p pieces) to the waiting crowds. 'Scrambling' customs like these were not uncommon at mayor-making ceremonies, and similar actions still take place at Harwich in Essex (*see* **Third Thursday in May: Harwich Kichel-Throwing**) and at Rye in Sussex (*see* **23 May: Rye Mayor-Making**).

See also **Scrambling Customs**, p. 128

*

MID TO LATE MAY

Scorton Silver Arrow

The Society of Archers was formed in 1673, at a time when archery had already seen a long decline in popularity, as it changed from a military necessity to a sport. The first meeting of the new society took place at Scorton in Yorkshire on 14 May 1673 and, apart from understandable breaks during wartime, this annual meeting has taken place every year since, a feat that leads the society to claim it as 'The world's longest established and oldest recorded sporting event'. The modern meetings are always held in mid to late May, but the venue varies from year to year. The current rules state that it must take place in Yorkshire, although for a while it was allowed to wander into Lancashire on occasion.

As befits a sporting event with such a long history, there are plenty of strange rules and customs. The competitors clearly enjoy themselves, but the archery remains very serious indeed. Shooting takes place for two hours in morning and two hours in the afternoon, with a splendid lunch in between, followed by the Society's annual general meeting.

The targets are the standard four feet in diameter, and are one hundred yards apart, with shooting in both directions – alternating from one end to the other. The most coveted prize of the day, from which the event gets its name, is the Antient Scorton Silver Arrow, which is won by the first archer to hit the gold centre. In addition to the prestige of gaining the arrow, the winner becomes Captain of the Antient Scorton Silver Arrow for the year, and organizes the next meeting. The idea of a 'silver arrow' is itself traditional: it was the most common prize offered in early modern times when archery contests were common. There are also several other prizes, including a gold embroidered belt, a silver bugle, and a horn spoon.

*

15–18 MAY

These dates are sometimes known as 'Franklin Days' in Devon. *See* **19 May: St Dunstan's Day** for an explanation.

*

THIRD THURSDAY IN MAY

Harwich Kichel-Throwing

The throwing of coins by newly elected mayors, for people to 'scramble for', is a fairly regular motif across the country, but at Harwich in Essex they throw 'kichels' instead. These are small torpedo-shaped, spiced fruit buns, which are made specially by a local baker, and are eagerly sought by the waiting children. The throwing takes places about midday, from the window of the council chamber, in the guildhall.

See also **Scrambling Customs**, p. 128.

*

ROGATIONTIDE

Beating the Bounds

Rogationtide is the Monday, Tuesday, and Wednesday immediately preceding Ascension Day, the fortieth day after Easter Sunday, and can occur any time between 27/29 April and 31 May/2 June. It was traditionally the time for the faithful to go in procession around the parish, led by the clergy, carrying crosses and banners, giving thanks to God, and blessing the fields, crops, and animals. This three-day festival was inaugurated in Gaul, in the late fifth century, ostensibly as a direct response to a period of earthquakes, crop failures, and other disasters, and from there it spread to Rome and on to other parts of the Christian world. It was introduced to the English Church in 747, and came to be known as Rogation, from the Latin *rogare,* 'to ask or beseech'.

The division of the country into parishes also took place about this time, and, although it is not clear when it happened, the procession to bless the fields came to include the notion of checking the parish boundaries, and what is now called 'beating the bounds' was born. The latter is one of the longest-running festivals in the English calendar, although it has changed considerably over the years, and in particular the relative weight given to sacred and secular aspects of the custom has fluctuated widely. Checking parish boundaries was not an entirely secular activity, as local church finances (based on tithes, taxes, and rates) were calculated on a parish basis, and the clergy thus had a keen interest in preserving their rights. Nowadays the custom is universally called 'beating the bounds', but previous generations had a variety of names, such as ganging (=going), processioning, bannering, and crossing.

By the time of the Reformation, the overtly Catholic practices of carrying crosses and images and blessing the crops were banned, but the local clergy were instructed by decree of Elizabeth I to continue to be actively involved in the perambulations, to provide appropriate prayers, sermons, and the giving of thanks to God. In the absence of effective record-keeping, the extent to which local officials were forced to rely on the memories of old people for evidence in local matters and legal disputes cannot be overstated, and this was especially true in the area of custom and tradition. An example from Tudor Cheshire is included in a 'boundary roll' of a court leet at Congleton in 1593. The boundaries are described, followed by the testimony of three local men, each over eighty years old, which detail how things had been in the past and how they had changed in their lifetimes: watercourses and ditches had been altered; a barn had been built straddling the boundary; and people had been accustomed to cut turf on a certain common and had been responsible for repairing a certain road.

By the time of the Puritan revolution of the 1640s, there was little that even the strictest religious reformers could object to, and in most places the custom continued throughout the Interregnum. The secular importance of boundary-keeping is clear in the description preserved in the journal of visiting Dutchman William Schellinks, in 1662:

On the 16th [May], Ascension Day, we saw the minister taking procession, as is done in London every year as follows: The minister, the churchwardens, and all who depend on the parish inspect all the wards

Beating the Bounds. *Top*: at the Tower of London, 1987; *bottom*: illustration by George Cruickshank, *Comic Almanac*, 1837

of their parish to see whether any new houses or dwellings have been built, which should have been registered by them for the payment of tax and record these, and also renew the old markers, which are painted on the wall on many different corners and quarters, to mark the boundaries of the parishes. For this purpose all the youngsters of the parish, great and small, assemble, each with a stick or rod in his hand, and walk two and two ahead, and when a marker is put up or renewed with the date of the year they make a loud noise all together and then go on to the next. This is done to impress on the young memories of the children the extent of the parish, so that they preserve it in the future without loss, and everyone gets a loaf of white bread from the minister. If it happens that two such parties meet, a fight usually ensues.

In rural areas, the boundary markers were often stones, crosses, or prominent trees. On its way around the parish, the procession would stop at some of these key points, for a prayer, hymn, or sermon, and these activities often gave a lasting name for the locality. Many local maps still show a 'Vicar's Oak' or 'Gospel Oak' in memory of these customary points. In a detailed account of the two-day perambulation of Purton parish, in Wiltshire, in 1733, the regular phrase occurs, 'where a Gospel was read, and a cross made' and it is clear that crosses were cut into the trunks of trees.

The day was also one of community festivity: food and drink were provided at certain points in the perambulation, and many customs developed that were far from solemn. The wands carried by participants were often used to literally 'beat' the boundary markers, and other seemingly bizarre activities took place, designed to fix these locations in people's memories. Boys were turned upside down, bumped on stones, whipped, beaten, or otherwise mistreated, and items were thrown to be scrambled for. In Yorkshire in 1890:

At Beverley, 'Rammalation Day' is Rogation Monday. What a day of merriment it is to the boys! At certain places, money, nuts, and oranges are scrambled for, and, as ditches form the boundary here and there, great fun is caused by throwing the money and oranges into the water, the youngsters jumping in and splashing about in the water. He who knows the boundary stones will run on ahead; and, if found sitting there alone, receives a shilling.

There were also traditional ways of dealing with first-timers, although not all victims of this horseplay were willing ones, as the *Graphic* reported on 28 November 1874:

Mr. Checkley, a farmer, has recovered £10 as compensation for injuries he received at the hands of a party of officials, headed by the Mayor of Maidenhead, who, chancing to meet with him while they were beating the bounds of the borough, picked him up and bumped him against a post so severely that he was unable to go about his work for a week. One plea for the defence was that all the respectable members of the party, including the Mayor and Town Clerk, were bumped. The judge remarked that such horseplay was detestable.

Schellinks' comment about fighting, quoted above, is also borne out in many other descriptions, and however respectable most beating-the-bounds customs may have been, the underlying impulses of territoriality that inform them also had a much less civilized aspect, as here in Exeter in the 1830s, recorded by James Cossins in his *Reminiscences* in 1878:

If, by chance, any of the different parishes met in their perambulations, there was a desperate struggle to disarm each other; but the great event was to wait in the New London Inn Square, as the parishes of St. David's and St. Sidwell's generally finished the rounds at the same time at this point. Then commenced, not a sham fight, but an earnest one, many of the combatants being young men. The parishioners were at times obliged to interfere, there being no police to force them.

(*See also* **1 May: Fighting**.)

The nineteenth century saw a long, slow decline in boundary customs, mainly because more efficient mapping and record-keeping made them obsolete. But although the original *raison d'être* for beating the bounds has long disappeared, the custom is still carried out in some places and regularly revived in others, for a variety of reasons. Apart from the nostalgic notions of continuing ancient customs, perambulating the boundaries is often seen as an effective way of engendering local knowledge and community spirit, and is also used to raise money for church repairs or other charitable purposes, by combining the tradition with the more recent idea of 'sponsored walks'. In the 1990s, groups set up to safeguard dwindling common land and public open spaces deliberately encouraged boundary perambulations as a way of raising local consciousness on the subject.

However, even such a solidly Christian custom such as beating the bounds has not escaped the modern assumption that all traditional activities are pagan fertility rituals. Julia Smith reported in her *Fairs, Feasts and Frolics* (1989) that in Yorkshire:

> One vicar said there was no longer provision in the Church of England liturgy for such a service; the blessing was regarded as the remains of a pre-Christian ritual, and with modern maps it was no longer necessary for the people to be shown the physical boundaries. He dissociated the Church totally with any boundary walking that may still take place.

See also **Ascension Day: Oxford Beating the Bounds**, p. 182; **Ascension Day: Tower of London Beating the Bounds**, p. 183; **18 May: Newbiggin Freeholders**.

*

ROGATION MONDAY

Wilkes Walk

Edward Wilkes, who died in 1646, was a substantial benefactor to the Bedfordshire town of Leighton Buzzard, and among other projects founded the local almshouses. But it was his son, Matthew (who died in 1693), whose will stipulated a ceremony in his father's name that continues to this day. On the Monday of Rogationtide, at around midday, a procession including the charity's trustees, and the clergy, churchwardens, and choir of All Saints church, led by a garland-bearer, makes its way through the town to the almshouses in North Street. A short service takes place, and while an extract from Edward's will is read out, a member of the choir is stood on his or her head (on a cushion), 'in order that those watching may understand and retain the words better'. This detail clearly stems from the same idea as the bumping, suspending, and whipping that went on during beating-the-bounds perambulations, where the victims were meant to remember the location at which they were so dealt (*see* **Rogationtide: Beating the Bounds**, p. 176). But it could be seen to be counter-productive in the case of the Wilkes ceremony. It is quite likely that those watching are so amazed at what is happening to the poor upside-down youngster that they take no notice at all of what is being said at the time.

Matthew also left money to be given to residents of the almshouses and for refreshments at the end of the procession, but the latter had to be discontinued in the late nineteenth century because too many people used to turn up for them. They have now been re-introduced.

Wishford Auction

One of several unusual forms of auction in the country takes place every Rogation Monday at Wishford in Wiltshire. The auction is for the right to the summer grazing on two water-meadows, which is called the 'midsummer tithes' but runs from Rogationtide to old Lammas Day (12 August). Buyers are summoned by the church bell, about fifteen minutes before sunset, and the parish clerk walks up and down between the church porch and gate while the bidding takes place. As soon as the sun dips below the horizon, he strikes the church key on the gate, and the auction is over.

For other unusual auctions, *see* **Candle Auctions**, p. 106.

*

ASCENSION EVE

Whitby Penny Hedge

Early on the morning of the day before **Ascension Day** (p. 182), two local residents make their way across the mud on Whitby's upper harbour to construct the 'penny hedge' – in reality a mere apology for a fence of hazel and willow twigs – which must be strong enough to withstand three tides. When they have finished, a third man, who represents the Abbot of Whitby's steward, blows three blasts on an old horn and shouts, 'Out on ye! Out on ye! Out on ye!', which, we are told, means 'Shame on you!'

The custom itself is unique, impressively simple, and is carried out in such a matter-of-fact manner that onlookers are sometimes disappointed that there is not more to it. The temptation to jazz it up a bit must have been very strong in recent years. Indeed, Julia Smith reports that in 1982 the town council discussed the

Penny hedge at Whitby, Yorkshire, 1966

idea that the custom and accompanying legend should be annually re-enacted by actors or local schoolchildren. It is a tribute to the good sense of the people of Whitby that this suggestion was not accepted and the hedge is still constructed in the old way, without fuss, and without pseudo-historical costume. Long may it continue so.

Despite its simplicity, however, and the fact that numerous writers have spent considerable time analysing its history, the origin of the penny-hedge custom remains obscure. One problem is that commentators have not always succeeded in separating the custom, the accompanying legend, and the historical facts.

The legendary explanation relates that in 1159, in the reign of Henry II, a group of nobles, including one with the splendid name of Lord Ugglebardeby, were out boar-hunting in Eskdale Forest, which belonged to the Abbot of Whitby. They and their hounds were in full chase of a great wild boar, when the exhausted animal ran into an isolated hermitage. Some say the boar dropped dead at the hermit's feet, others say that the hermit barred the

door and refused to let the hunters in. Either way, the noblemen were so angry at being deprived of the best bit of the chase that they took their vengeance on the hermit by beating him almost to death. He only lived long enough to tell the Abbot to pardon the huntsmen if they agreed to pay penance every Ascension Eve by building the hedge (and, considering that he was dying, he went into impressively precise detail about the timing of the ceremony, where it should take place, and exactly how much wood they must cut – 'with a knife of one penny price'). According to early writer Lionel Charlton, this tale was already circulating in printed form before 1779, but while it may be no mere modern legend, it is clearly a romantic fiction. All the internal details of dates and names are incorrect, and very similar tales are told of other hermits in other woods.

All serious writers agree that the hedge-building custom is a survival of a medieval service, or obligation, called a *horngarth*, which was owed by tenants to the lord of the manor. In this case, the lord was the Abbot of Whitby, who was an immensely powerful figure in the local area. The abbey was founded by St Hilda in AD 651, destroyed by a Viking raid in 867, revived about the year 1078, and finally dissolved by Henry VIII in 1539. A great deal of evidence about the business affairs of the abbey has survived in two volumes of *Cartularies*, or registers of events and transactions, compiled in Latin by scribe monks, which cover the period from about 1170 to the early sixteenth century. The horngarth is mentioned many times in the *Cartularies* as a service owed to the Abbot of Whitby by holders of certain lands, and it was presumably important enough to warrant this continued reference, but its exact nature is never explained. The word *garth* is Anglo-Saxon for 'a fence or enclosure', but the *horn* element is open to debate. Most writers take it to mean 'cattle or oxen' (i.e. *horned* animals), but others assume that it signifies those who were responsible for constructing or repairing the *garth*, who were summoned by blasts of a horn. This has a spurious ring of authenticity only because the hermit tale and the later custom feature a horn.

Whatever its function, it is unlikely that the horngarth dates back to St Hilda's time, but it was definitely in existence by 1148. An important entry in the *Cartularies* of about 1315, reveals that the materials for the construction were taken from the Abbot's woods, and that 'Alexander's men' were taking too much and selling the surplus to people in the town. It was therefore decreed that the wood should be supplied by the Abbot's men rather than being collected by those about to use it. An even more detailed entry also exists, but its nature is highly ambiguous, being written on the flyleaf of the first volume, in a later hand. From internal evidence, this addition may possibly be as early as the 1540s (i.e. just after the dissolution of the abbey) but it could be much later. It presents a description of the horngarth service 'to be done on Holy Thursday even', saying that the men who were 'bound to this service' met at sunrise and, after cutting wood under supervision of the Abbot's bailiff, they carried it on their backs:

> . . . so coming to the water at the town end they made the hedge which should stand three tides, and then the officer did blow out upon they.

The crux of the matter is how much credence can be placed on this flyleaf addition.

It may, for example, be a contemporary agreement on the form of the custom now that the abbey had been dissolved, or it could simply be an addition by a later writer who was already familiar with the custom and the legend.

On balance, the most likely conclusion is that the horngarth service was indeed a commitment owed jointly to the lord of the manor, for erecting or maintaining a fence or other enclosure. There are verifiable examples of such obligations elsewhere in the country, for example in response to the annual need to erect a temporary fence to protect the land set aside from the open fields for the purpose of growing hay. It must be said, however, that the one major problem with this explanation is the riverside location, and the detail of the three tides, which are a prominent feature of the current custom, and were already in place when the flyleaf addition was made. This does not seem to fit with the idea of keeping farm animals in or out of a particular place, which has led some writers to propose that the horngarth was not an animal fence at all but something to do with the loading and unloading of boats – a jetty, for example, or a protective enclosure for goods in transit to and from the manor.

In theory, it is easy to see how a medieval obligation such as the horngarth could become an apparently 'meaningless' custom over time. There was a marked trend throughout the later medieval period for services to be commuted into cash payments. Given that several tenants were obliged to contribute their time and labour to the work, there may well have been a time when the majority had commuted to cash while a few continued to offer physical service. Even when changing circumstances had rendered the service itself unnecessary or superfluous, the tenants would be forced to continue to comply, because the custom of the manor dictated that failure to do so would result in a fine, loss of rights, or even loss of land. Similarly, it was in the lord of the manor's interest to hold the tenants to their obligation, in the expectation that they would eventually pay good money to be relieved of the burden.

For another bizarre custom, seemingly based on manorial obligations, *see* **Palm Sunday: Caistor Gad-Whip Ceremony**, p. 97.

*

ASCENSION DAY

Ascension Day commemorates the ascension of Christ into Heaven, forty days after he had risen from the dead, and is therefore held on the fifth Thursday after Easter, falling anywhere between 30 April and 3 June. Often referred to as Holy Thursday, it is one of the major festivals of the Christian Church and has been around in one form or another since at least the fourth century. In secular English tradition, the visual image of Christ ascending to the heavens resulted in a strong connection between the day and all things pertaining to the sky, such as clouds, rain, and birds. This underlying connection is manifested in a variety of customs, including **well-dressing** (p. 228) and beliefs in the medicinal properties of any rain that falls on the day. In 1882, the Folklore Society's journal *Folk-Lore Record* reported:

At daybreak on Ascension morning, two men, and a woman carrying a child, were seen hurrying towards the celebrated well at North Molton, each trying to outrun the others, so as to be the first to bathe, and to be cured of some ailment. Later in the day merry groups of children and picnic parties enlivened the glen in which the well is situated ... Every year pilgrims, full of faith in the miraculous power of the water, visit the spot for bathing; and jars of the water were carried by some of them to their homes; indeed, believers prize this water which they carry back with them, as much as ever did pilgrims of old value the leaden bottle of liquid obtained from Beckett's tomb at Canterbury.

More obscurely, but still based on the same principle:

[1584] *To hang an egg, laid on Ascension Day in the roof of the house, preserveth the same from all hurts.*

[In Worcestershire, 1909] *If you hang clothes out to dry on Holy Thursday there will be a death in the family, and the corpse will be laid out in some of the clothes.*

[In Devon, 1787] *Hailing the Lamb: It is the custom in many villages in the neighbourhood of Exeter 'to hail the lamb'. That the figure of a lamb actually appears in the east upon this morning is the popular persua-*

sion; and so deeply is it rooted that it had frequently resisted (even in intelligent minds) the force of the strongest argument.

The latter should be compared to the 'sun dancing' belief (*see* **Easter Monday**, p. 130).

Ascension Day follows Rogationtide, and there is often an overspill of beating-the-bounds ceremonies, sometimes even with the addition of a water feature, as in the following example from James Cossins' *Reminiscences of Exeter Fifty Years Since* (1878):

The parochial bounds were beaten on Ascension Day, by parishioners, accompanied by the clergymen, wardens, etc., who afterwards dined together at one of the hotels or inns in the parish. On this day it was considered lawful to throw water over any parties passing, and in many streets a pond would be made, and unless some pence were thrown in, the boys would splash the water over passers-by, and such dread was there of these customs that parties in the country would not come into the city on that day, unless necessity compelled.

Hunting the Earl of Rone

See **Spring Bank Holiday**, p. 206.

Oxford Beating the Bounds

Beating the bounds is still carried out in two adjoining parishes in Oxford on Ascension Day: St Michael in the Northgate, and St Mary the Virgin. At both events, there is a procession of the choir, various dignitaries, and numerous onlookers, led by the vicar. After a short service, they seek out the boundary markers, following a long-established route, mark them with chalk, and beat them with the long white canes that they carry. When thinking of beating-the-bounds ceremonies, most people probably imagine the typical rural scene of beaters locating boundary stones in fields and hedgerows, and being 'bumped on them', but in urban settings it is very different. The boundary markers in Oxford can be set into walls, high or low, or even into the floor, and can be down narrow alleys, in basements, and behind or inside buildings. The routes take in the college buildings within the parish as well as shops and pubs, much to the surprise of the people they meet on

Freeholders at Newbiggin, 1984

the way. They stop for refreshments at various loca-tions, and at one point students throw coins and sweets for the choristers to scramble for.

See also **Rogationtide: Beating the Bounds**, p. 176; **Scrambling Customs**, p. 128.

Tower of London Beating the Bounds

Most beating-the-bounds customs are concerned with ecclesiastical parishes, but the need to maintain boundaries is equally important for many other bodies. Every third year, in the evening of Ascension Day, the boundaries of the Liberty of the Tower of London are perambulated, and literally beaten. After a short service in the Chapel Royal of St Peter ad Vincula, a colourful procession forms up, led by the Tower's Chief Yeoman Warder, in full state dress and carrying his mace. Others include the Yeoman Gaoler, with his axe, two Yeoman Warders, the Resident Governor, and a group of children carrying willow wands.

There are thirty-one markers bearing the letters 'WD' (War Department), and as the procession reaches each one the Chief Yeoman Warder calls out, 'Cursed be he who removeth his neighbour's landmark – whack it, boys, whack it!', and they beat it to death with their wands. One innovation first tried in the 1980s in the interests of safety is that if a marker is situated on a busy road, the Chief points to it with his mace and shouts, 'Mark it well', and those in the procession answer loudly, 'Marked!' The perambulation is completed when the procession re-enters the Tower by the East Gate, and the National Anthem is sung on Tower Green. Refreshments are then served to the participants.

See also **Rogationtide: Beating the Bounds**, p. 176.

*

18 MAY

Newbiggin Freeholders

Newbiggin-on-the-sea, in Northumberland, was at one time a very important port, and to be a freeholder was a prized position, carrying the right, for example, of collecting tolls from ships loading and unloading in the harbour. Little of that right now remains, but the freeholders own Newbiggin Moor, from which they derive income from rent paid by a golf course, and others. On the Wednesday nearest to 18 May, the freeholders perambulate the boundaries of their land, distributing peanuts and collecting any monies due to them. If there is a new freeholder to initiate, they are lifted bodily and bumped gently ('dunted') on the dunting stone.

See also **Rogationtide: Beating the Bounds**, p. 176.

*

19 MAY

St Dunstan's Day

St Dunstan (909–88) took an extremely active part in the political and religious life of tenth-century England at the highest levels, serving as adviser, bishop, and archbishop to successive kings, including Eldred, Edgar, and Edward the Martyr. One of Dunstan's particular achievements was the revival of monastic life, and the introduction of the Benedictine rule, which lasted until the sixteenth century. After his death, he was credited with great wisdom and a number of miracles, and a nationwide cult grew up, which lasted for centuries. He was reputed to be an expert craftsman, and metalworkers such as goldsmiths, jewellers, and locksmiths adopted him as their patron saint. The most persistent of his legends, first recorded c.1120, tells how he was busy making a chalice when the Devil appeared, in the guise of a young woman, to tempt him. Dunstan grabbed the Devil's nose with his red-hot tongs, and kept him trapped for some considerable time. You can still see the very tongs at Mayfield in Sussex. (A similar story is told of St. Eligius; *see* **1 December**.)

Despite his popularity, no widespread customs or festivals on his day seem to have been recorded, although parish churches dedicated to him would have held celebrations in his honour. One calendar tradition, however, reported widely in Devon in the nineteenth and twentieth centuries, comes close to slandering his good name by implicating him in a shady business deal with the Devil. Three days in May, locally termed 'Franklin Days', were reputed to be prone to cold weather and sharp frosts. The particular days varied, but were often the 17th–19th, or the 19th–21st, and however they were counted, they usually included Dunstan's feast day. The story was told as follows in *Notes & Queries* (1861):

St. Dunstan bought a quantity of barley and therewith made beer. The Devil, knowing that the saint would naturally desire to get a good sale for the article which he had just brewed, went to him and said that if he would sell himself to him, the latter would go and blight all the apple trees; so that there would be no cider, and consequently there would be a greater demand for beer. St. Dunstan, wishing to drive a brisk trade . . . accepted the offer; but stipulated that the trees should be blighted in three days . . . 17th, 18th and 19th May, the last named date being St. Dunstan's Day . . . About the middle of May, consequently, as the three fatal days are approaching, many anxious allusions are made to St. Dunstan, and should a sharp frost nip the apple-blossoms, they believe they know who has been at the bottom of the mischief.

Sometimes the same story was told of a man named Franklin, or even of the anonymous and presumably infamous 'brewers from North Devon', but poor Dunstan was the most commonly cited villain of the piece.

One more aspect of the day was recorded in Yorkshire in the 1890s by Richard Blakeborough: 'No luck will follow a declaration of love if made on St. Dunstan's Day'; however, no explanation is given for this pronouncement.

In addition, the Society of King Charles the Martyr holds events on this day to commemorate the restoration of Charles II; *see* **30 January: Execution of Charles I**.

*

20–21 MAY

Reckoned by some people as two of the three 'Franklin Days'; *see* **19 May: St Dunstan's Day**.

*

Empire Day

23 MAY

Rye Mayor-Making

On or near 23 May, the town of Rye in East Sussex chooses its new mayor, and his or her first task in office is to throw pennies from the town hall window to the crowd of waiting children outside. Scrambling customs like this were formerly quite common, and just to add to the fun the pennies at Rye were heated before throwing.

The first of two stories told to explain the custom is that at one time the mayor was also the local Member of Parliament, and in the habit of bribing voters. The second says that Rye was previously the site of a mint, and once, when coins were in short supply, new pennies were brought still hot from the foundry. Neither of these explanations is true, or even neces-

sary, as throwing coins for scrambling was common at a variety of celebrations, including civic events such as mayor-making, weddings, and whenever someone rich enough to have coins to spare wanted the fun of seeing the children scramble.

See also **Scrambling Customs**, p. 128.

*

24 MAY

Empire Day

The idea for Empire Day originated in Ontario, Canada, where the Education Department there set aside a day in 1899 to celebrate the achievements and glory of the British Empire, and Canada's place in it. According to *The Times* on 20 March 1899:

The morning shall be devoted chiefly to familiar talk about Canada's relation to the Empire, and readings from Canadian and British authors, while patriotic recitations, songs, and speeches will occupy the afternoon.

The idea was soon being enthusiastically discussed in Britain, and after the death of Queen Victoria in 1901, Empire Day was formally adopted in 1903. It was also known as Victoria Day, because the date chosen was the late Queen's birthday. Following the Canadian precedent, it was mainly a school event, although in many villages there was also strong church involvement. The school day was given over to dressing up, processions, marching, speeches, tableaux, patriotic singing, and usually a tea or other festive gathering. One of the contributors to *East Kent Within Living Memory*, published by the East Kent Federation of W.I.s in 1993, reported that:

When I was at school at Cliftonville in the 1930s, we celebrated Empire Day every year. We practised for weeks before, then the day arrived. We started with the raising of the Union Jack and singing God Save the King. First came the top infants class, who danced, each representing the four corners of the British Isles, with a flag for each. They would finish by standing back-to-back, then a child would step up onto a chair holding a Union Jack. Next was the tableau. A senior pupil would come first and sit on the dais as Britannia, reciting a verse about Britain, followed by a girl in the costume of each country of the Empire, reciting a verse about each one and carrying produce they provided. I remember New Zealand carried a toy lamb and Australia a basket of apples. When the tableau was complete we all sang with gusto Land of Hope and Glory, Land of our Fathers, Londonderry Air, Jerusalem, and Ye Banks and Braes, ending with God Save the King and saluting the flag.

Such overtly imperial rhetoric was completely out of place in the postwar period, when the Empire was fast disintegrating, and in 1958 Empire Day was replaced by Commonwealth Day, on 12 June (Elizabeth II's official birthday), which was moved again in 1977 to the second Monday in March.

For many, 24 May is also Wesley Day, celebrating the lives of the Christian evangelists John Wesley (1703–91) and Charles Wesley (1707–88), with a special commemorative service at Lincoln Cathedral

See also **Second Monday in March: Commonwealth Day**.

*

WHITSUN

Whit Sunday is the seventh Sunday after Easter, and commemorates the descent of the Holy Spirit upon the disciples, in the form of tongues of fire, as promised by Christ before his ascent into Heaven. The official name for the festival is 'Pentecost', meaning 'fiftieth', and it is derived from an existing Jewish festival that celebrated the first fruits of the corn harvest, and the giving of the Law of Moses, fifty days after the Passover. It is still not entirely clear why the English call the festival 'Whitsun'. The most plausible explanation (though still not very convincing) is that it was named after the white clothes worn by people being baptized on the day. In the mid nineteenth century there was still vigorous debate about whether it should be written 'Whit Sunday' or 'Whitsun Day', but we now use both terms. Being tied to Easter, the actual date varies from year to year, but is always between mid May and mid June.

Whit Monday was officially recognized as a bank holiday in 1871, which gave a boost to its already considerable popularity, but it lost its status in 1971 when the **Spring Bank Holiday** (p. 203) was created. Some religious Whitsun events cling tenaciously to the real day, but most secular customs associated with the season have now moved to the bank holiday.

Whitsun's position in early summer made it one of the favourite times in the traditional calendar, and a range of open-air events took place on the day or during the following week. Whitsun ales and morris dancing in the South, and Whit walks and wakes in the North, were characteristic of the season, along with countless fêtes, fairs, club walks, pageants, parades, and excursions, all over the country. In many places, Whitsun was much more important than May Day. A poster advertising Whitsun attractions at Sunbury in Middlesex in 1758 gives a flavour of the season at the time:

*On Whit Monday, in the morning, will be a punting
match . . . The first boat that comes in to receive a
guinea . . . In the afternoon a gold-laced hat, value
30s. to be cudgell'd for . . . On Whit Tuesday, in the
morning, a fine holland smock and ribbons, value
one guinea, to be run for by girls and young women.
And in the afternoon six pairs of buckskin gloves to
be wrestled for.*

Nevertheless, in Victorian and Edwardian times, the
festivities of Whitsun were often decidedly less spontaneous than May Day, being organized by church or
chapel, school or club, or other worthy institution. Olive
M. Philpott records in the *Dorset Year Book* (1961/2) that
in Wiltshire, about 1910:

*Whit week, however, was the highlight of the whole
year. It was the Sunday School Anniversary at the
Chapel on Whit-Sunday when, dressed in our smart-
est summer frocks and suits, we gabbled our recitations and lustily sang our Anniversary hymns. That
was followed on Whit Monday by the excitement
of the Sunday School tea (what memories of slabs
of delicious plum cake, thin bread-and-butter and
sugary small cakes, washed down with sweet milky
tea). We thought this a cut above the Church children's lemonade and buns on the Rectory lawn. Tea
was followed by sports and games until sunset. But
all that excitement paled before Whit-Wednesday,
when we had the village Club-walking.*

In the newly industrialized towns of the Midlands and
the North, the tradition of the whole town closing down
for a week rapidly became a widespread feature, and
Whitsun was often the convenient time. John Harland
and T. T. Wilkinson report in their *Lancashire Folk-Lore*
(1882):

*It is customary for the cotton-mills, etc., to close
for Whitsuntide week to give the hands a holiday;
the men going to the races, etc., and the women
visiting Manchester on Whit-Saturday, thronging
the markets, the Royal Exchange, the Infirmary
Esplanade, and other public places; and gazing in at
the shop windows , whence this day is usually called
'Gaping Sunday'.*

See also **Easter Day: Greenwich Fair**, p. 115.

Eton School Montem

Eton School Montem was a well-known custom in its
day, perhaps based on the Boy Bishop ceremony (*see*
6 December: Boy Bishop), but with military rather than
ecclesiastical trappings. The day of the custom changed
over time, occurring in January, Whitsun, December,
sometimes once a year and sometimes every two years.
It was already well known in the seventeenth century,
when it was mentioned in John Aubrey's *Remaines of
Gentilisme and Judaisme* (1686).

The main event of the day was a procession by the
boys, who dressed as sumptuously as possible (many
hired costumes for the day). The senior boys were
given military rank for the occasion – Marshal, Captain,
Chaplain, Lieutenant, and Ensign, the latter carrying
the flag with the motto *Pro More et Monte* – and the
procession formed up in strict order. The younger boys
carried white poles and acted as servants. They marched
round the school and out to Salt Hill (*ad montem*,
meaning 'to the hill', gives its name to the custom), near
Slough, where the Chaplain led a service and speeches
were made. Some of the boys were designated as 'Salt
Collectors', whose job it was to collect money from the
boys and from any passers-by, visitors, or tourists. On
more than one occasion the visitors included royalty,
and the money collected, which could be a substantial
sum, went to the Head Boy. The Salt Collectors carried
bags of salt, either to exchange for the contribution,
as some sources specify, or to stuff into the mouths of
any enemies they might meet. The day ended with a
general feast. The ceremony was a mixture of serious
pomp and pointed parody, and could at times be rough.
Successive schoolmasters made attempts to tame it,
and it was finally suppressed *c*.1876.

Food

As with all the major festivals, Whitsun was associated with particular sorts of food. Tea and buns were
consumed at countless Whitsun gatherings, but other
foodstuffs varied from place to place. Earlier records
mention milk and cream products as being particularly linked to Whitsun, and there are references to
children going from house to house collecting these,
while several others mention gooseberries, as in the

following example from Enid Porter's *Cambridgeshire Customs and Folklore* (1969):

> *The village policeman of Manea said in 1936 that 'veal is always eaten here at Whitsun'. In many Cambridgeshire families Whitsunday is the day for eating the first gooseberry pie of the year with, if possible, the first home-grown new potatoes.*

On the question of seasonal cakes, many localities settled for a variation of the simnel, better-known elsewhere as Mid-Lent Sunday and Easter food (*see* **Mothering Sunday**, p. 81), and cheesecakes are also regularly mentioned. However, one unique example can be found in *Traditional Food East and West of the Pennines* (1991):

> *Goosnargh cakes can be bought at Goosnargh [Lancashire] Post Office and in surrounding towns. It was estimated that at one time over 50,000 were sold during Whitsuntide at one shilling per dozen. No one can agree on the origin of these distinctive biscuits, which resemble a shortbread, flavoured with caraway and coriander and with a thick sugary crust.*

Morris Dance

The morris dance is one of the most widely known forms of traditional display dance in England, and everybody knows roughly what morris dancers look like: usually male, they dress in white (or at least in a white shirt), with crossed baldrics, or rosettes and ribbons, and, most importantly, with pads of bells strapped to their shins, which ring loudly when they move. They wave white handkerchiefs or clash short sticks together as they dance, and we might expect them to be accompanied by a Fool with a bladder on the end of a stick, and a hobby horse. Many people picture a morris dance as taking place on a spring morning on the village green, with all the local folk gathered *en fête* around the maypole. However, while the costume of modern-day morris dancers certainly retains many features that were present as far back as the 1580s, and the village green was indeed one of the dance's natural habitats, the morris also existed in other contexts, many of them urban, for example in civic processions, at court, and in the theatre.

Our view of the morris dance has been heavily influ-enced by the wealth of material gathered by Edwardian folk-dance collectors when the traditional morris was on its last legs. Their evidence referred largely to the second half of the nineteenth century, and they presented a picture of numerous village teams, across the South Midlands, each with their own traditional dances, tunes, and steps, which varied from each other but clearly drew from a shared pool. These forms were labelled the 'Cotswold Morris', because of the area in which they were found, but further research identi-fied quite different styles of morris in other regions. 'North-West Morris', for example, found in Lancashire and Cheshire, features much larger teams, and dances designed for processional performance.

Over 300 years ago, the morris dance was popular with playwrights and poets, who used it as a symbol of simple rustic pleasures. It was clearly already prover-bial in Shakespeare's time: in Act II, scene 4 of *Henry V*, the Dauphin urges France to make war with England insouciantly:

> *And let us do it with no show of fear*
> *No, with no more than if we heard that England*
> *Were busied with a Whitsun morris dance.*

And in Act II, scene 2 of *All's Well That Ends Well*, a clown remarks, 'As a pancake for Shrove Tuesday, a morris for May Day'. At about the same time, Thomas Dekker also featured the morris in his plays *Shoemaker's Holiday* (1599/1600) and *Witch of Edmonton* (c.1623). Others, however, saw the morris as yet another example of the depravity of the peasantry's traditional pastimes, declaring that this ungodly behaviour should be reformed or suppressed outright. As is often the case, Philip Stubbes, the Puritan reformer, provides one of the earliest descriptions of the morris. It is included in his *Anatomie of Abuses* (1583), in the section on 'Lords of Misrule', by which he meant the May or Summer Lord appointed to oversee the spring celebrations:

> *Then every one of these his men, he investeth with his liveries of green, yellow, or some other light wanton colour. And as though that were not gaudy enough, I should say, they bedeck themselves with scarfs, ribbons and laces, hanged all over with gold rings, precious stones, and other jewels; this done, they tie about either leg twenty or forty bells, with rich handkerchiefs*

Bampton morris dancers, Oxfordshire, 1988

in their hands, and sometimes laid across their shoulders and necks, borrowed for the most part of their pretty Mopsies or loving Bessies, for bussing them in the dark. Thus all things set in order, then have they their hobby horses, their dragons, and other antiques, together with their bawdy pipers, and thundering drummers, to strike up the Devil's dance withal: Then march this heathen company towards the church and churchyard, their pipers piping, their drummers thundering, their stumps dancing, their bells jingling, their handkerchiefs fluttering about their heads like mad men, their hobby horses and other monsters skirmishing amongst the throng . . .

The early history of the morris dance is still under debate, but it is clear that it was already widely known in the second half of the fifteenth century. At least nine references are known from that period, with the two earliest dating from 1448.

Some of these early references refer to representations of morris dancers on fine art objects, such as silverware and tapestry, but there are others in contemporary account books that detail payments for actual performances. The spelling of the word varies considerably, including 'moryshh', 'morys', and 'moruske', and it is significant that these words had already been in circulation for at least a hundred years to describe 'Moorish' things. The etymological evidence seems to point quite conclusively to a connection with 'Moorish', but this only gets us part of the way. We do not know, for example, whether the dance was so called because it came from North Africa, or because people thought it looked like something that they would expect to see performed there. There are similar words, meaning both a dance and 'Moorish', in other European languages, so it is quite possible that the dance was introduced from another country – perhaps Spain, because of its close connection with Moorish culture, or the Low Countries – but if so, it is still not clear whether that country invented or inherited it. Despite the wealth of new material uncovered by the latest generation of morris-dance researchers, the origins of the dance still elude us, partly, perhaps, because we have been searching for one specific origin rather than several.

Various antiquarians and early folklorists showed some interest in the morris dance over the years, primarily because of its literary reputation, but it was not until the turn of the twentieth century that serious research got underway. A number of collectors were involved, but the leading light was undoubtedly Cecil Sharp (1859–1924), who deliberately set out to create a folk-dance revival, in which the morris was to play a central role. Sharp and his disciples were reasonably successful in spreading the word, and a number of morris-dance clubs were formed in the interwar years; however, the real explosion of interest came with the postwar folk revival in the 1960s, and there are still several hundred clubs in Britain.

See also: **Spring Bank Holiday: Bampton Morris Dance**, p. 203.

Superstitions

Whitsun does not seem to have engendered as many superstitions and beliefs as other festivals. The only one that was at all widespread was that it was one of the main times of year when new clothes were particularly prized (others were Easter and New Year), and, indeed, if one ventured out without wearing at least one new item, the birds would be sure to mess on you. New clothes were also a marked feature of those taking part in Whit Walks and Whit Sings (*see below*), and brought about their own traditions when children visited family and neighbours. In 1998, a member of the East Yorkshire Women's Institute remembered the custom in her childhood:

It was traditional on Whit Monday to go to grandma's and show her my new clothes. Nearly all children got some, if not all, new clothes at Whitsuntide. My cousins and I were all taken off to grandma's house in the morning, and on arrival we paraded and twirled before her and Auntie V.

See also **Easter Day: New Clothes**, p. 117.

Whit Walks

As indicated in the entry for **Whitsun** (p. 186), this festival was a favourite time for outdoor events, and particularly popular at this season was any type of walk, parade, or procession. In the South, it was common for local benefit clubs to choose this time of year for their

Cousins Florence and Mary Nutter, ready for their Whit Walk, Manchester, *c*.1905

annual parade and dinner, and for Sunday schools and church organizations to hold their treats. But further north, the real feature of the season was the Whit Walk, organized by the different churches and involving the whole clergy and congregation in an impressive procession through the town, with everyone in their best clothes, holding large banners and other symbols, and led by a brass band. These walks made a great feature of the children, who were usually dressed up in white for the occasion, and it was second only to Christmas as the high spot of the juvenile year. This focus on children was one of the earliest features of the walks, as they grew directly from the active Sunday school movement founded by Robert Raikes (1735–1811), which swept across the country in the early nineteenth century. In Manchester and other nearby towns, the Whit Walks quickly became large affairs and grew as the century progressed, with Anglican, Nonconformist, and Roman Catholic churches vying to put on the best show. In the mid twentieth century, they were still very popular events, as *The Times* of 7 June 1949 indicates:

> At Manchester, after a dull start, the weather brightened up for the 143rd Whit-walk. More than 12,000 children, representing 34 Church of England Sunday schools, were gaily dressed for the walk, which was led by the Bishop of Manchester, Dr. Greer, to the marching tunes of nearly 40 bands.

On the *Have Your Say Magazine* website recently, Lillian Barlow remembered the thrill of taking part in the Whit Procession in Manchester forty years ago, and her description highlights all the key points of the occasion: the chance to dress up in new clothes; the close connection between local pride, school, church, and community; the colour, banners, music, crowds, and noise; and a nostalgia for the simple pleasures of a bygone age:

> It was 1958, and I was 11 years old. In preparation for Whit Monday my sister and I had a bath, washed our hair, had our supper and were sent to bed early. We had to be up at 6am the following morning. I remember lying in bed feeling nervous and excited. My sister and I had both been confirmed that year, and this meant we would be walking with the banner representing our church. The Confirmation Banner

> always led the procession, behind the brass band, of course. The banner was huge, and had ten white ribbons hanging from it, five at the front and five at the back. Ten girls who'd been confirmed that year were chosen to walk with the banner, both my sister and I had been chosen.

> Mam had made our dresses. Though it was dark I could see the outline of them hung on the wardrobe door. The bodices were made of white satin and the skirts were ballerina length, made up of layers and layers of white net. They were lovely. Mam had made our head-dresses too. They were made in the same materials as our dresses, and were sort of a banana shape, rather like a headband but much more fancy. Our shoes were flat, white ballerina type and we had new white socks. And to complete the outfit a posy of flowers which had been made by my aunty. I closed my eyes and tried to imagine what we would look like. I finally drifted off to sleep.

> Morning came and the house was buzzing with excitement. I remember mam making toast which I couldn't eat because of the butterflies in my stomach. My sister and I were finally ready. Together with mam, dad, our younger brothers and sister, who were all dressed up in their best clothes, we made our way to St. James' Church, Collyhurst. It was a beautiful church. It was the church in which my mam and dad were married. It was the church where I was baptised, and it was the church in which I was confirmed . . .

> As we approached the church, I could see all the children assembled, dressed in their lovely outfits. The teachers from the school were trying to organise them. My sister and I were spotted by Mrs. Gaskell, one of the teachers from the school, and were ushered by her to the front of the procession. I remember my mam asking if my sister and I could walk at the back of the Confirmation Banner down to Albert Square. I wondered why. I realised later, if you walked at the back of the banner going down to Albert Square, you walked at the front of the banner coming back!

> Eventually we were organised and ready. My sister and I stood together holding the long white ribbons that draped from the back of this awesome banner. We spoke not one word to each other. The band struck up with Onward Christian Soldiers. To this day I will

never forget how overwhelmed I felt, I almost burst into tears. We followed the band down Rochdale Road making our way to Albert Square. The road was lined with people threefold. All my aunties, uncles, friends and neighbours were there, shouting and clapping as we walked by. 'Hold your Lily up,' they shouted. We reached Albert Square and my dad was there waiting to take us for a drink. The square was packed with children and adults from all the different churches in Manchester. I remember feeling intimidated and frightened and hoping I wouldn't get lost. I held onto my dad's hand tight. After our drink we found our way back to our assembly point and prepared for the walk back to church.

On the return journey, my sister and I walked in front of the banner, by this time the crowds were even greater. I remember seeing a mass of red, white and blue flags and shakers. Everyone was wearing red roses and there was red, white and blue bunting all along the roads and streets where we walked. The leader of the brass band periodically threw his stick up in the air and caught it, and everybody went wild, cheering and clapping him on. As the band marched on they played songs like There'll Always Be an England, Sons of the Sea, Pack Up Your Troubles in Your Old Kit Bag, and best of all Land of Hope and Glory. Now and again two or three women would come out of the crowd into the middle of the road in front of the brass band and dance and sing, kicking their legs in the air and waving their flags. It was a joy to see everyone so happy.

About twelve thirty in the afternoon we arrived back at the church. My mam, dad, brothers and sister were all there to meet us, we made our way back home chattering excitedly about the events of the morning. My nana would have a big potato pie ready for us at home. I was hungry now and look- ing forward to my potato pie. As we approached our house nana was on the veranda looking out for us. That was the last year I walked in the Whit Procession, but I continue to watch them every year. In fact I'm fifty now and I have not missed a Whit Monday yet.

Declining congregations in the later twentieth century caused the demise of many of the walks, but some still

survive, and usually take place now on Spring Bank Holiday. Other related customs have developed, like the Saddleworth Brass Band Competitions (see **Whit Friday: Brass Bands**, p. 196), and 'Whit Sings'. In 1996, a member of the West Yorkshire Federation of W.I.s remembered the 'Mollicar Sing':

> This annual event on Whit Sunday was first held in 1900. It was started by the Zion Chapel, Almondbury, later amalgamated with the Wesleyan Methodist church, and now simply the Methodist church. The walk always started at 7.30 am, mainly through the Mollicar . . . with the singing of hymns at allotted places through the walk. The woods were at their best, with new green foliage and birds in full song. The sing finished about 9 am, and in earlier years Mr. and Mrs. Gostridge of Farnley Hey boundary provided the breakfast – ham and eggs for the grown-ups and bantam eggs for the children.

Whitsun Ales

See **Church Ales**, p. 194.

*

WHIT SUNDAY

St Briavels Bread and Cheese Dole

In 1779, Gloucestershire historian Samuel Rudder wrote that at St Mary's church in the village of St Briavels in the Forest of Dean:

> They have a custom of distributing yearly upon Whitsunday, after divine service, pieces of bread and cheese to the congregation at church, to defray the cost of which, every householder in the parish pays a penny to the churchwardens; and this is said to be for the liberty of cutting and taking the wood in Hudnolls. The tradition is, that the privilege was obtained of some Earl of Hereford, then lord of the forest of Dean, at the instance of his lady, upon the same hard terms that Lady Godiva obtained the privileges for the citizens of Coventry.

No earlier record of the St Briavels custom has yet come to light, which is strange because one would expect a church-based custom to leave some evidence in church

Church Ales

In some areas of medieval and early modern England, before church rates and taxes were widely adopted, a common way of raising money for the upkeep of the parish church was to hold a fund-raising event called an 'ale'. As the name suggests, this was a day of merrymaking, with food, drink, dancing, and games. Ales were particularly common across the south of England and the South Midlands, but were only sporadically reported elsewhere in the country.

Many church ales took place at Whitsun or early May, taking the generic name 'Whitsun ales', but church ales could also be held at any time in the spring or summer, while some places held more than one in a year. Some became fixed annual events, but more often they were organized only when need arose. A group of neighbouring parishes might pool their resources and take it in turns to organize the event. In earlier reports, it is clear that the event took place in the church or churchyard, but changing notions of propriety forced it out of sacred ground and into the parish. Some parishes had a 'church-house' – the forerunner of the village hall – in which they could hold their festivities, while others made do with a barn or temporary building.

As they were organized by, and for, the Church, expenses for the ale were usually recorded in churchwardens' accounts, and a wealth of useful information has survived. The accounts for the parishes of Seal and Elstead in Surrey, transcribed by William Hart in the *Surrey Archaeological Collections*, vol. 2 (1864), are an excellent example. The accounts for 1592 include the following items:

3 bushels of wheat (14s.); 9 barrels of beer (40s.); Veal and lamb (22s. 9d.); A load of wood and the carriage (5s.); Spice and fruit (7s. 1d.); Butter, cream and milk (4s.); Cleats and nails to the smith (14d.); Gunpowder (4s.); More wheat (8s. 2d.); Paid to the musician for 5 days play (20s.); To the drummer (2s.); For more butter and cream (2s. 3d.); More spice and fruit (4s. 2d.); To Goodman Shrubbs' wife for helping all the time (12d.); Meat and beer for the musicians and other helpers (13s. 4d.).

It is interesting to note that they underestimated the butter, cream, spice and fruit, and had to order more, but the beer apparently lasted well enough. Four shillings' worth of gunpowder was presumably used for fireworks or some similar entertainment. The accounts for 1611 include similar items, including another payment to 'Shrubbs' wife' and payments to the musicians; however, one additional entry – 'paid the Vice, otherwise the Fool' – hints at a different form of entertainment.

Many church ales were discontinued in the early decades of the seventeenth century, while others

records. A further account published in 1807 adds the detail that the bread and cheese was cut into inch-square pieces and thrown to the congregation from the church gallery, resulting in a great 'tumult and uproar'. As a result, the annual distribution moved out of the church into the lane. Folklore writer Phyllis Crawford witnessed it in the 1930s:

So after Evensong is finished you may see them, a mixed crowd of country people, tourists, colliers from the Forest of Dean, farmers, small shopkeepers, maids. They gather in the lane by a high stone wall, from which, like a spasmodic shower of too, too solid snow, the pieces of bread float down. Everyone grabs for the same piece, fingers get scratched, arms get
bumped, hats get knocked askew. The polite apologise and get nothing, the eager snatch, hastily rejecting dry bits of bread for more succulent morsels of cheese. Finally with one devastating hurl the last fragments are flung to the crowd, the empty hamper overturned. Laughing and munching, the crowds slip away.

The bread and cheese is still thrown to the congregation every Whit Sunday, although the 'scrambling' is now more sedate. A local tradition holds that because the bread and cheese is blessed by the vicar before being distributed, it will not go bad and is particularly whole-some, which is a localized example of a previously widespread belief that bread baked on Good Friday, or the wafers and wine used in Holy Communion are

struggled on amid increasing calls for their suppression. They had long attracted the vociferous disapproval of the religious reformers, who seemed bent on eradicating all forms of enjoyment, but increasing opposition came from those who argued that such gatherings created too many opportunities for drunkenness and public disorder, and it is probably these latter concerns that prompted local magistrates to start taking action.

Nevertheless, ales had their supporters among those who cherished old customs and traditions or who were opposed to the new puritanical religion. Richard Carew, the Cornish historian, took an optimistic view of the benefits of social gatherings, in 1602:

> . . . *entertaining of Christian love, conforming of men's behaviour to a civil conversation, compounding of controversies, appeasing of quarrels, raising a store which might be converted partly to good and godly uses, as relieving all sorts of poor people, repairing of churches, building of bridges, amending of highways, and partly for the prince's service, by defraying at an instant such rates and taxes as the magistrates imposeth for a country's defence. Briefly, they tend to an instructing of the mind by amiable conference, and an enabling of the body by commendable exercises.*

And King James himself listed 'Whitsun ales' as suitable for Sunday entertainment in his *Book of Sports* of 1618 (*see* p. 262). However, once Parliament got the upper hand, church ales were specifically banned by the *Ordinance for the better observation of the Lords Day*, passed on 8 April 1644.

Some ales were revived after the Restoration, particularly in Oxfordshire, and continued into the nineteenth century, organized by publicans or other local individuals rather than the Church authorities. Eating, drinking, and dancing were still the main activities of the day. Published descriptions from the time show a remarkable similarity in how these later ales were organized. A Lord, Lady, and various attendants were elected to rule the festivities, which took place in a suitable barn or shed, or in a 'bower', which was created with greenery or tarpaulin. In an elaborate running joke, strangers were asked to name items displayed around the bower and were punished when they said the wrong thing. A wooden horse had to be referred to as 'my Lord's gelding', a stuffed owl as 'my Lady's canary', a flail as 'my Lord's nutcrackers', and so on. Offenders were forced to pay a forfeit of a shilling, and if they could not, they were manhandled and carried around the field on the wooden horse, or 'married' to 'his Lordship's cook', an ugly, dirty creature who wielded a dirty dishcloth and a sharp toasting fork.

similarly incorruptible (*see* **Good Friday: Bread and Eggs**, p. 108).

This would seem to be a simple example of a food dole, set up by a benefactor's bequest in aid of the poor, if it were not for the detail given by Rudder that all the householders paid money to finance the distribution. This strongly suggests the maintenance of a local right, and supports his assertion that the whole affair was linked to the liberty of cutting wood. Social historian Bob Bushaway draws parallels between the St Briavels custom and that of Great Wishford in Wiltshire, which was similarly concerned with wood rights (*see* **29 May: Grovely Ceremonies**).

See also **Doles**, p. 87; **Scrambling Customs**, p. 128.

St Mary Redcliffe Rush Sunday

The Rush Sunday service at St Mary Redcliffe church was instituted by the will of William Spenser, Mayor of Bristol, in 1493, and it originally commemorated an earlier mayor, William Canynge, who did much to rebuild and support the church, and even gave up his considerable wealth to become a priest. The Rush Service takes its name from the rushes and herbs strewn on the floor for the occasion, and as one of the official Civic Services of the year, it is attended by all the dignitaries of the City of Bristol in full regalia. The City can certainly put on a good show, and the procession to the church is led by the City Swordbearer, who carries the Pearl Sword and wears his Elizabethan Cap of Maintenance, followed by the Lord Mayor and Lady Mayoress, the city councillors and aldermen in their scarlet robes, and no less than eight macebearers carrying the City Maces. Everyone not carrying something else carries a posy of spring flowers in their hands. They enter the church to a fanfair of trumpets.

See also **Rush-Bearing**, p. 238.

*

WHIT TUESDAY

Dicing for Bibles

In a curious juxtaposition of the instruments of gambling and religion, the custom of dicing for Bibles takes place every Whit Tuesday in St Ives, Cambridgeshire, in accordance with the will of Dr Robert Wilde, who died in 1678. Wilde, who was a somewhat unconventional Puritan minister, left £50 to be invested in land to buy six Bibles, for which six boys and six girls (of good repute, over twelve years of age, and able to read) would contest by throwing dice. The land bought with the money became known as Bible Orchard. A report of an enquiry into the charity in 1879 reports that the vicar thought it a scandal that dice-playing should take place in church. The dicing was originally carried out on the altar of All Saints, but was moved to a table in the church *c*.1880, then to the local school, and then, in 1936, back into the church once more.

*

WHIT WEDNESDAY

Mother Shipton's Day

A former Cambridge resident, aged eighty-two in 1964, told folklorist Enid Porter that in her youth the washer-women in the many small laundries in the town used to drink rum in their tea on the Wednesday in Whitsun week. They called the day 'Mother Shipton's Holiday'. Another informant confirmed this description, and added that 'Mother Shipton was the patron saint of laundresses'.

'Mother Shipton' was a fictional character, given a spurious biography in a series of chapbook publications from 1641 onwards, which included her hugely famous prophecies. These prophecies have probably been in print in some form or other ever since, and new generations of prophecy lovers continue to find 'amazing' predictions therein. The best-known example of public credulity occurred following the publication of a new edition of her sayings, by Charles Hindley in 1862, which included not only a prediction of steam trains ('carriages without horses shall go') but also a prophecy that the world would end in 1881. These caused a great deal of consternation at the time, forcing Hindley to admit that he had simply fabricated them.

*

WHIT FRIDAY

Brass Bands

The Whit Friday brass band contests, which take place in the Pennine villages around Saddleworth, where Lancashire meets Yorkshire, are one of the high spots of the bandsman's year, and are quite unique in the musical calendar. Far from being a static competition, contests are held in various villages, and bands rush from one to another to compete in as many as they can. The Saddleworth contests grew directly from the bands' involvement in the Whit Walks, which were tremendously popular in the area (*see* p. 190). By the 1880s, so many churches and chapels wanted to hold a Whit Walk that bands were brought in from well outside the immediate area in order to satisfy demand. Alec Greenhalgh described the scene on a Whit morning in his book on the contests, published in 1992:

> *The Black Dyke Mills Band . . . were the first to arrive. They came by the train due at 7.42 am. There was a pretty large crowd assembled to welcome them and they marched away looking very smart in their Hussar uniform and playing a lively quickstep. The next train brought with it no less than six bands and by this time all the approaches to the station were besieged by the townsfolk and there was a very lively scene until the last of the bands had marched to its destination.*

The concentration of a number of bands in one area

led to inevitable fraternization between musicians and friendly rivalry between bands, and as the walks took place in the morning, the afternoons and evenings were free for musical pursuits. The year 1884 saw the first organized contest between bands, but the competitions stayed local and low key until an explosion of interest in the 1890s, as word of the contests spread and they took on a life of their own. At a local level, they still remained essentially an adjunct to the walks, but as the popularity of the walks began to decline, and the band contests continued to grow, the balance between the two gradually shifted. As with all public events, tensions sometimes occurred, as the *Stalybridge Reporter* (1926) commented:

> They [the churches] *take this one day in the year to have their processions, they spend combinedly hundreds of pounds in bringing the bands into the town, thereby making the band contest possible and then a certain number of people abuse the privilege of hearing good music by making it a day for drinking too much.*

The modern competitions start in the afternoon and are open to all-comers, so that local bands can compete against world-famous outfits; they are funded and organized by local volunteers in aid of charity. The contests now take place in twenty different locations and over a hundred bands take part. In most cases, each band plays two pieces at a contest, which is judged 'blind' (the adjudicator cannot see the bands), and then they move on swiftly by coach to the next venue, not knowing how well they have done until much later.

*

LATE MAY

Blessing of the Sea

'Blessing the Sea' or 'Blessing the Fleet' ceremonies take place in a number of locations around the coast, but many are one-off or short-lived events, prompted by one person's enthusiasm. The ceremony at Brixham in Devon, however, has managed to survive through several revivals, and is a good example of just such an event. The earliest reference we have to the ceremony is from 1926, when the Revd George Gordon, of St

Peter's church, conducted a special service at the pier on Rogation Sunday. It was particularly appropriate because at that time the congregation of St Peter's was mainly drawn from fishing families. Gordon led the choir and congregation in procession down to the pier, where they sang hymns, chanted Psalm 130, and offered special prayers for the blessing of the fishermen and fleet. Gordon left St Peter's in 1928, and it is unlikely that the special services continued as an annual event, but they certainly took place in 1937, 1947, and 1953, and throughout the 1980s. The service now takes place in late May, as part of the Brixham Heritage Festival, and features two local choirs and the town band.

The service held every May in Hastings is another example. An interdenominational service is organized by All Saints church, and includes the local Salvation Army band; the clergy addresses the congregation from the deck of the local lifeboat.

See also **25 July: Whitstable Oyster Festival**.

*

LAST SUNDAY IN MAY

Arbor Day

In the Shropshire village of Aston-on-Clun, close to the Welsh border, a unique annual tree-decorating custom is carried out on the last Sunday in May (but formerly on **Royal Oak Day**, for which *see below*). The tree, which stands prominently in the middle of the village, was once a large black poplar, reputed to be over 300 years old; however, this was blown down in 1995 and was replaced by a 28-year-old sapling.

The villagers decorate it with gaily coloured flags.

The story behind the custom tells how local landowner John Marston married Mary Carter in May 1786, and the tree was decorated to welcome the newlyweds to the village. Mary was so pleased with this gesture that she laid down the rule that the Marston family would provide the flags and manpower to decorate the tree every year on their anniversary. This explains why the tree is often called 'the Bride's Tree'. Nevertheless, some people argue that the villagers already had an old tree-decorating custom, or that they were simply celebrating Royal Oak Day, and young Mary Marston simply misunderstood and no one had the heart to tell her the truth. Nowadays, the tree is the focal point for a fête and a day of community celebrations, including a charming children's wedding pageant in eighteenth-century costume, but these cannot be proved to be any older than about 1912.

So the matter would rest, but unfortunately an idea has taken hold that the custom is linked to fertility rites, and the Arbor Tree Festival Committee's official website boldly states that it dates back to the Iron Age:

> ... a tree ... was decorated for the fertility rites practised by the pastoral shepherds living in the hills of Clun Forest ... These pastoral tribes worshipped Brigit, the Celtic Goddess of Fertility. Her shrine was a tree on which the tribal emblems and prayer flags were kept: fertility for the people and the land being invoked.

Needless to say, this is completely fanciful.

*

29 MAY

Royal Oak Day

29 May 1661 – This was the first anniversary appointed by Act of Parliament, to be observed as a day of general thanksgiving for the miraculous restoration of his Majesty; our vicar preaching on Psalm 118:24, requiring us to be thankful and rejoice, as indeed we had cause.

John Evelyn's diary here records the introduction of a new special day into the English calendar. When Charles II rode into London on his birthday, 29 May, in 1660, and restored the monarchy to England, the people were provided with a festival date which would continue to resonate for centuries and which, in a few isolated cases, is still celebrated today. As John Evelyn noted, the day was officially declared one of national joy and celebration, and was marked with the bonfires, bells, and special services common on such patriotic occasions. There was certainly no shortage of biblical references to provide religious legitimacy to the Restoration, and Samuel Pepys noted that in his church on that day the sermon was based on the phrase 'Nay, let him take all, since my Lord the King is returned'

(2 Samuel 19:30). Nevertheless, despite this religious backing, Royal Oak Day was part of the gradual trend of secularization that saw political and patriotic festivals (such as Guy Fawkes Night) replacing religious ones.

Three things ensured that Royal Oak Day was immediately accepted by the general populace. Firstly, the Restoration was genuinely popular and was seen as a welcome return of the 'merry England' that had been so harshly put down by the Puritan revolution. Secondly, the new king rapidly acquired a recognizable trademark – the oak leaf, which symbolized the story of his hiding in an oak tree after defeat at the Battle of Worcester had quashed any hopes of a royalist come-back in September 1651. Thirdly, the timing of the new celebration brought it into the ambit of existing May Day celebrations, which already had a tendency to spread through the month, and Royal Oak Day quickly rivalled May Day and Whitsun as the key day in early summer for time off work in pursuit of pleasure. Royal Oak Day even stole some of the main features of May Day, such as the erection of maypoles. Houses and churches were also decorated in the same way as at the beginning of the month, with the only real difference being the preponderance of oak boughs for the King's day. The habit of leaving boughs at people's doors also transferred from the 1st to the 29th, as in this account of customs in Charlbury, Oxfordshire, in the early twentieth century, published in *The Listener* in 1957:

> ... going round to the houses of the gentry very early on the morning of May 29 and decorating the knocker or lintel with oak-apple sprays. The decorators would call later on the day for a gift of money. If none were forthcoming, they would stand and chant:
>
> > Shig-shag – penny a rag
> > Bang his head in Cromwell's bag
> > Bad cess to this house come to stay
> > Before next twenty-ninth of May.

However, the dominant custom, which really came to symbolize the day, was the wearing of sprays of oak leaves (preferably with a gall or apple attached, and often gilded or otherwise enhanced) in lapels and hats, and by all accounts this was done by almost everybody, high and low, male and female, adult and child, throughout the eighteenth and early nineteenth centuries. John Byng (later Lord Torrington) recorded in his diary in 1789 that when passing through Barnet, in Hertfordshire, 'every horse, carriage and carter was adorned with oaken boughs and apples, in memory of this once-famous day'. Schoolchildren were given a day (or at least a half-day) off school, and all over the country it was reported that whoever did not wear such an emblem was attacked unmercifully by their school-fellows, and could be pinched, stung with nettles, kicked, or pelted with birds' eggs (sometimes rotten ones). 'These pinches are no common ones; they hurt pretty well and a kick is generally administered with it,' complained (Sir) Alfred Lyall, who was at Eton in 1845, and it was not only rough public-school boys you had to watch out for, as a correspondent to *Bye-Gones* (1889–90) showed:

> I was travelling from Crewe to Runcorn [Cheshire] *on the 29th of May. There were six girls in the carriage with me all wearing oak leaves and two of them carrying bunches of nettles. On being asked what the nettles were for, they said, 'To beat those who have no oak'.*

In common with several other children's customs (e.g. April Fool's Day, and 'pinch-punch' rituals), the persecution of non-participants usually had to end at noon, and indeed many removed their oak symbols at that hour. One completely unexplained development, however, was that in many villages the children substituted ash for their oak leaves and wore those in the afternoon.

Oak-wearing by adults was probably already declining when the special prayer of thanksgiving was removed from church services in 1859, and by Edwardian times many writers were mourning its demise. However, Iona and Peter Opie found it was still alive and well in the children's calendar in a number of places in the 1950s, particularly in midland and northern counties. It is certainly dead and forgotten now.

Numerous local dialect names for the day have been recorded, based on particular features of the custom, including: Oak Apple Day, Shick-Shack Day, Shig-Shag Day, Yak-Bob Day, Bobby-Ack Day, and Nettling Day.

Castleton Garland Day

The High Peak village of Castleton in Derbyshire plays host to a unique garland custom every 29 May. The famous garland is constructed on a heavy bell-shaped framework, large enough to envelop a man's body down to his waist, which is then completely covered in greenery and flowers. The man who 'wears' the garland is called the King, and he is seated on a horse, which must be led because his hands are busy supporting and controlling the garland. He is accompanied by a Queen, or Lady, also on horseback, and both are dressed in Stuart-style costumes. Before the garland is placed on his head, the King leads a procession, which includes a team of girl morris dancers dressed in white, a silver band, other attendants, and the Queen, who brings up the rear, around the village. The garland is then put into place, and the procession again tours the village, stopping at various places for the girls to dance. The King is then led to St Edmund's church, where the garland is hoisted by rope to the top of the church tower; it then remains on show for a few weeks until all the flowers have died. The special topknot of the garland, also called 'the Queen', is removed before the hoisting, and is laid on the village war memorial. The pubs in the village take it in turns to host the garland.

Until the early years of the twentieth century, the whole affair was the responsibility of the village bell-ringers, and had been so for some time; the earliest known reference to the custom is in the churchward-ens' accounts of 1749: 'paid for an iron rod to hang ye ringers garland in 8d.'.

The garland custom is deservedly well known, and very photogenic, so we are blessed with numerous descriptions and photographs from the post-Second World War period; however, we are doubly fortunate that Sheffield-based folklorist Sydney Oldall Addy visited Castleton in 1900 and published the results of his fieldwork in a detailed paper in the journal *Folk-Lore*, which remains a model for how to report on traditional customs. Addy's work is particularly important because he interviewed local people rather than just watching the event from the sidelines, and he took note of details that were often ignored by other collectors, such as the costumes worn and who was taking part. When Addy visited Castleton, he noted

Garland Day at Castleton, Derbyshire

the changes that had recently been made in the way the custom was carried out, and there have been many more alterations since his time. Although the essential parts of the custom – the two horseback figures, the garland on the man's head, the procession with dancers, the hoisting of the garland – have remained the same, almost all the details have undergone radical change: the dancers used to be men but are now young girls dressed in white; the 'Queen' was a man dressed as a woman, and is now a real woman; the 'Queen' part of the garland was given to a local dignitary, then to a recently married couple, and is now laid on the village war memorial; the costumes of the King and Queen have become more overtly historical; and the King and Queen themselves were previously simply known as the 'man' and the 'woman'.

The most important lesson to learn from these changes is the folly of basing explanations of a custom's origin on the details of the way it is now carried out. The origin and earlier history of the custom are very much open to speculation, and many theories have been put forward, including the idea that it developed from the story of Sir Gawain and the Green Knight, the Jack-in-the-Green (*see* **1 May: Jack-in-the-Green**), and foliate heads, or is linked to numerous spring gods and sacrificial beheadings. But May garlands of similar construction (although not of the same size) are common all over England, and even the hoisting of greenery to the top of the church tower is not unique, as a similar activity formerly took place at Membury, in Devon. On the current evidence, the custom appears to be the result of moving a May garland to Royal Oak Day and giving it 'royal' trappings in honour of Charles II (*see* **29 May: Royal Oak Day**, p. 198). Local folklorist Georgina Boyes, however, has suggested a connection with the custom of **rush-bearing** (*see* p. 238), which was particularly widespread in Derbyshire.

Grovely Ceremonies

In many traditional customs, details that seem strange to the modern eye might be the result of accretions over the years, or they might have been part of the conditions stipulated in bequests, charters, or other founding documents. Rarely do we have direct evidence either way, but in the case of Great Wishford's 'Grovely' Ceremonies in Wiltshire, we can see that some of the picturesque, even bizarre, details were laid down 400 years ago. In this case, the day's events are direct survivals of conditions stipulated in charters of 1597 and 1603, which confirm and delineate existing rights for villagers to gather wood in nearby Grovely Wood, a former royal forest. The charter specifically states that the inhabitants must go to the cathedral 'in a dance' and that they 'there made their claim to their customs in the Forest of Grovely in these words "Grovely! Grovely! And all Grovely!"'

In earlier times, the right to gather wood for fuel and other domestic uses was an extremely important one to the rural population, and it involved complex definitions of the type and size of wood that could be gathered, and the method of its taking, as well as strict regulations on who could demand access to woodlands and when access could take place. But there was also tension between villagers and landowners as the latter increasingly came to regard woodland as a commercial asset that required improved management and severely controlled access. The majority of the rural population lost any rights to gather wood centuries ago: most rights simply lapsed as they became unnecessary or meaningless, while others were legislated out of existence; however, the inhabitants of Great Wishford have managed to keep their rights alive, and are determined to continue to do so.

The celebrations that surround their declaration of rights used to take place in Whit week, but at some point they were moved to 29 May. It is not unusual to find customs gravitating to **Royal Oak Day** (*see* p. 198), and in this case the link between the 'oak' motif of the day and the wood-gathering theme of the custom make it a particularly logical development. This day is now the major festival day of the year for the village, organized by the Oak Apple Club, which was set up in 1892 to ensure the survival of the rights. At the crack of dawn there is a visit from the Tin Can band, who make a cacophonous noise to wake people up. Many people rise early to go in procession to the forest, dressed in old-fashioned clothes and bonnets, under a banner bearing the words 'Grovely! Grovely! And all Grovely!' along with their other motto, 'Unity is strength'. They return with branches to decorate houses, and a large bough to hoist to the top of the church tower. Representatives

Grovely celebrations at Wishford Magna, Wiltshire, 1982

go to Salisbury Cathedral to lay branches on the altar, and a dance is still performed, by four women wearing period costume, bonnets, and aprons. A village fête and other entertainments round off the day.

Neville's Cross Commemoration

On the Saturday nearest to 29 May every year, the choir of Durham Cathedral sing anthems from the top of the tower after evensong, facing east, south, and north. Tradition has it that they have done so almost every year since the mid fourteenth century, and that it has nothing to do with the month of May but commemorates a battle fought in October 1346. In that year, while King Edward was away besieging Calais, the Scots army, led by King David, took the opportunity to invade England. They were stopped and beaten back at the decisive battle of Neville's Cross, near Durham. The

Cathedral monks are said to have watched the battle from the tower and to have broken into a triumphant singing at its successful outcome. In a further legend, it is said that the Prior of Durham, John Fosser, had a dream the night before the battle that prompted him to go to the Cross and take with him as a banner the sacred cloth which St Cuthbert had used to cover the chalice while saying mass. The Prior and some of his monks did so, and this act was said to have provided the spiritual assitance necessary for the Scots' defeat. To this day, it is also said that if you walk nine times round the Cross, and then put your ear to the ground, you will hear the sounds of the fighting.

The connection between the tower singing and the battle has never been proved, and it is unlikely that the custom has survived in an unbroken line for nearly 700 years. Two alternative theories put forward the idea that the tower singing once formed part of a guild procession, or that the singing was started to celebrate deliverance from a great fire on 25 May 1429.

Royal Hospital Chelsea Founder's Day

The Royal Hospital Chelsea was founded by Charles II in 1682, as a retirement home for army veterans who had served for twenty years or who had been invalided out of the service. He borrowed the idea from a similar institution founded in France by Louis XIV in 1670. Residents wear a distinctive red coat and black tricorn hat, based on the army uniform worn in the time of the first Duke of Marlborough (1650–1722), and are known colloquially as Chelsea Pensioners.

It is appropriate that the Hospital's Founder's Day celebrations should take place on 29 May, Charles II's birthday and the anniversary of his Restoration in 1660, although they sometimes now take place in early June, for convenience. At present there are about 400 residents, termed 'in-pensioners', who occupy 'berths' within the building, and it is these men who parade in their best uniforms on Founder's Day. Since 1980 they have been inspected by a member of the royal family. The statue of Charles, which stands in the South or Figure Court, is draped with oak leaves, and all the participants also wear a sprig of the same. The grounds of the Hospital, and some of the buildings, are open to the public most of the year.

*

SPRING BANK HOLIDAY

Spring Bank Holiday (the last Monday in May) was created in 1971 to replace the moveable Whit Monday holiday, and formed part of the gradual shift from religious to secular holidays. For centuries, **Whitsun** (p. 186) had been a major marker of the onset of summer, and was thus a favourite day for outdoor events. Countless fairs, fêtes, walks and club feasts were held on the day, and it was natural that those that had survived into the 1970s should gravitate to the new day.

Bampton Morris Dance

At Bampton in Oxfordshire, every Spring Bank Holiday morning, one of the classic scenes of the English village idyll can be found, with the performance of the local morris dance. Of all the morris dancing that takes place in the country, the Bampton men have the strongest claim to being 'traditional', in the sense that they perform their local dances in their own style, and have performed every year since before the folk-dance revivals of the early twentieth century created a new nationwide interest in the subject. Nevertheless, it is certainly true that the interest created by these revivals has played a significant part in keeping the local tradition alive. Morris dancing was traditionally performed at Whitsun, but at Bampton, as elsewhere, it has gravitated to Spring Bank Holiday. The dancers perform all round the village and its environs on the day itself, but they also dance at other times of the year at special events, or when invited elsewhere.

Six dancers dressed in white, wearing black bowler hats decorated with flowers, bells round their legs, and holding handkerchiefs in their hands, go through the evolutions of the dances, to the sound of a fiddle or melodeon. There is also a Fool or clown to entertain the crowd with antics and banter, and a 'Cake-Bearer', who carries a whole fruitcake impaled on a sword. Pieces of this cake, which are considered lucky, are presented to members of the audience if they give a donation. Nowadays there are three sides, but they all use the same repertoire, and at its best the dancing is unhurried, almost perfunctory, but with the indefinable grace that revival teams never seem to be able to manage. It is no wonder that visiting romantics have thought they have seen pagan rituals to welcome the spring, or visions of a golden age of **Merrie England** (p. 372).

The first published account of morris dancing at Bampton is found in the Revd J. A. Giles's history of the village, published in 1847, but he was apparently not very keen on it:

> *Another season of festivity is Whitsuntide, when the Morris dancers exhibit their saltatory powers for the amusement of the people, and to gather a few shillings for their own private emolument. As these functionaries do nothing but dance, and thoroughly fatigue themselves before nightfall, they must be considered to have earned the hot suppers and mulled ale, which probably terminate the festival, but they have no farther claim to delay the progress of this history.*

This confirms that the dancing was already an established tradition by this date, and there has probably been an unbroken series of annual performance since that time, apart from during the First World War. Further research undertaken by dance historian Keith Chandler, based on the evidence of the continued involvement of particular local families, demonstrates that the local tradition can be traced back to the early nineteenth, or perhaps even late eighteenth, century. However, claims of a 600-year tradition – probably based on the fact that the earliest references to morris dancing in this country are from the fifteenth century – are groundless.

See also **Whitsun: Morris Dance**, p. 188. For illustration, *see* p. 189.

Barwick Maypole

Barwick-in-Elmet may not have the only traditional maypole in the country, or even in Yorkshire, but it does vie with other places for the tallest example, and once every three years it steals the limelight by taking the pole down – by hand – and putting it back up again a few weeks later.

The pole is taken down on Easter Monday, repainted, re-garlanded, and then re-erected on Spring Bank Holiday, amid much rejoicing. The whole operation was previously carried out through a combination of brute strength and skill, with ropes and ladders, and scores of men providing the muscle, all coordinated by an elected Pole Master shouting his orders. But modern safety rules now insist that cranes and hard hats are the order of the day, which is organized by the Barwick-in-Elmet Maypole Trust. Once down, the pole is transported to a field on the shoulders of a hundred volunteers, where the renovation is carried out: it is repainted white, with two parallel stripes, red and blue, spiralling around from top to bottom; a stainless-steel weathervane in the shape of a fox is fixed to the top; and the four large garlands are renewed. The latter are constructed by members of different local women's organizations and are fixed on the pole about fifty feet from the ground. Each garland weighs a hundredweight, and is decorated with coloured cloth rosettes (over 6,000 of them), artificial flowers, and ribbons of red, white, and blue that have little bells attached

to them. The garlands are paraded around the neighbouring villages before being hung. Every so often, the maypole needs to be completely replaced, as happened in 2005. The new pole is a Scots pine from Finland, ready spliced in two sections and nearly eighty-six feet tall.

Spring Bank Holiday in a maypole year is a major celebration for the villagers, especially for the children, and the day is taken up with a procession of floats and bands, maypole and morris dancing, and the crowning of the Maypole Queen. At about 6 o'clock in the evening, however, the climax of the day is the placing of the newly painted pole back in its hole and hauling it upright again. A local climbs up the pole to release the ropes and, if he is brave enough, he ascends to the top and gives the weathervane a swing.

Cooper's Hill Cheese-Rolling

Every Spring Bank Holiday, at Cooper's Hill, between Brockworth and Painswick in Gloucestershire, a large round Gloucester cheese, weighing about 8 lbs and specially made for the occasion, is set rolling down a hill. A dozen or so young men launch themselves headlong down the steep slope in pursuit, most of whom are sent sprawling, rolling, and tumbling within a few steps. They have little hope of catching the cheese, but the first to the bottom wins it. During the day there are three races for men, and one for women, and although there are numerous bruises, dislocations, concussions, and occasional broken bones, it is rare that anything more alarming occurs.

A description from the journal *Folk-Lore* in 1912 shows that little has changed:

The master of the ceremonies, Mr. W. Brookes, who has officiated in this capacity for thirty years, appeared wearing, as usual, a brown top-hat which his parents won in a dancing contest many years ago, and with a chemise over his coat. He stood by the maypole and repeatedly called to the crowd to form 'the alley' down the slope. The course being clear, the Vicar opened the ball by sending the first 'cheese' (a disc of wood wrapped in pink paper) rolling down the hill. Helter-skelter ran nine young men after it, and most of them pitch-poled. The first to

Cheese-rolling at Cooper's Hill, Gloucestershire in 2006

The 1968 winner of the Cooper's Hill cheese

secure the disc, stopped at the bottom by a hedge,
had to trudge uphill again, and there exchange it for
the prize cheese.

The 'cheese-rolling' custom is all that remains of the Cooper's Hill wake, which was once held on top of the hill every Whit Monday and included many other standard features of annual gatherings, such as wrestling, shin-kicking, girning, smock races, a maypole, and plenty to eat and drink. The cheese-rolling itself, far from being an ancient ritual, is therefore simply the sole survivor of an activity that routinely took place at fairs and wakes up and down the country – providing, of course, that they had a suitable hill nearby. Thomas Hughes mentions the custom in his *Scouring of the White Horse* (1859), stating that it was a feature of the fairs that took place at Uffington in Berkshire at the scouring of the chalk hill-figure there in the eighteenth and early nineteenth centuries. The cheese-rolling at Cooper's Hill certainly dates back at least to the early nineteenth century, but there is no record of it before that time.

In the early 1990s, the cheese-rolling custom came

under fire from the local authorities over fears of crowd and participant safety, and in 1999 it was even banned by Gloucestershire County Council, who own the land. A small group of stalwarts defied the ban and chased a cheese early on the day, and it was back the following year, at an earlier time of day (to try to ensure that the contestants were sober), and with some safety netting to protect the spectators from the bounding cheeses and runners. Oddly enough, this was just the time when the custom was becoming popular with the national press, who now report on it each year, usually accompanied by a piece on the eccentricities of the English. Now that its fame has spread, the event attracts entrants from far and wide, and seems in little danger of being allowed to lapse.

See also **Fairs, Feasts, Wakes, and Revels**, p. 249.

Hunting the Earl of Rone

On Spring Bank Holiday, the people of the North Devon coastal town of Combe Martin present their own unique ceremony, 'Hunting the Earl of Rone', a colourful revival and extension of a custom that was last performed in town around the time Queen Victoria came to the throne.

We have no accounts that date from when the original custom was active, but several good descriptions were published while it was still in living memory. It ceased *c*.1837, apparently suppressed because of the drunkenness and disorder that characterized the day. In these earlier accounts, the characters included: the Earl of Rone, who wore a grotesque mask, clothes stuffed with straw, and a string of twelve sea-biscuits around his neck; a hobby horse; a masked and gaudily dressed Fool; a donkey, decorated with flowers and another sea-biscuit necklace; and a troop of grenadiers, wearing tall hats covered with ribbons. The day for the full performance was **Ascension Day** (p. 182), but during the preceding fortnight the hobby horse and Fool had already toured the neighbourhood, collecting money to defray the costs of the custom. At 3 p.m. on Ascension Day, the grenadiers would march to nearby Lady's Wood, and after much searching, discover the Earl of Rone hidden there. They would fire a volley of shots and set the prisoner on the donkey, facing its tail. The hobby horse, Fool, and all the spectators would form up into procession to escort the prisoner back to town. At certain points, the grenadiers fired further volleys and the Earl fell from the donkey. The soldiers expressed their joy at this, but the hobby horse and Fool lamented the goings-on, and the latter would revive the Earl and set him back on the donkey. The procession halted at every pub and collected money from bystanders, but disbanded when it finally reached the sea.

Hunting the Earl of Rone provides a pleasant puzzle for would-be experts on traditional customs. Taken as a whole it is unique, but every single element, apart from the Earl himself perhaps, can be found in another custom. **Hobby horses** (p. 164) appear all over the country (most notably, for present purposes, in Minehead and Padstow), and Fools often accompany plough plays, morris and sword dancers, and many other performances. Guns fired in the air were a standard feature of a range of customs, including Guy Fawkes Night, the Padstow 'Obby 'Oss celebrations, and weddings, at least until the passing of the Firearms Act of 1835. A character placed backwards on a donkey was a regular feature of **rough music** activities (p. 74), and a character stuffed with straw appeared in several customs, including **Jack-a-Lent** (p. 67) and the Burning of Bartle (*see* **24 August: West Witton Burning of Bartle**). The grenadiers sound like South Country mummers, with their tall beribboned hats, and even the motif of someone falling down dead or wounded and then being revived is a commonplace of the mummers' play (*see* **Christmas: Mummers**). As for the Earl himself, most commentators, now and in the nineteenth century, have assumed that he is based upon the Irish 'outlaw' Hugh O'Neill, Earl of Tyrone (1540–1616), who fled to Rome in 1607. However, there is no evidence linking him with North Devon, or any of the other features of the custom, nor is there any indication that the story of his flight and adventures were well known enough at the time to influence any village customs.

The custom was researched and 'reconstructed' by local enthusiasts in the 1970s, and was performed as part of the town's carnival, but in 1978 the real revival came about, and the event has been staged successfully every year since. The 'Hunting' is now one of the most important features of Combe Martin's year, with scores of locals taking part, and hundreds of onlookers. All the known details of the old custom have been preserved, and a few additions have been made: more people are now allowed to take part, new features such as dancing and children's processions have extended the festivities, and many dress in old-fashioned costumes.

Kingsteignton Ram-Roasting

The ram-roasting fair at the Devonian village of Kingsteignton (a village billed on the parish council's website as the biggest in England), formerly took place on Whit Tuesday but is now held on Spring Bank Holiday Monday. It takes the usual form of a local fair, with stalls, bands, and May Queens, but a special feature is the roasting of a sheep on a spit, which is then shared out to the fair-goers. The event itself has not changed much since 1883, when a contributor to *Notes & Queries* described it in the following way:

> A lamb is drawn about the parish on Whitsun Monday in a cart covered with garlands of lilac, laburnum, and other flowers, when persons are requested to give something towards the animal and attendant expenses; on Tuesday it is killed and roasted whole in the middle of the village . . . The lamb is then sold in slices to the poor at a cheap rate.

However, the participants have not always behaved very respectably. Phyllis Crawford, who visited the fair *c*.1936 in preparation for her book *In England Still*, reported a conversation with the ninety-year-old widow of a former vicar, who explained how the custom had been tidied up and tamed:

> My husband started the procession, dear, and all the sports and fancy dresses; you see, before that when they had roasted the ram they used to go to the public houses and I am afraid they used to get drunk. Yes, my dear, it was very rough, you wouldn't have liked it at all. He let them go on with the ram-roasting, dear, they had always done that, but the rest he had to stop. And you see how nice it is now. Quite a fine old ceremony.

It has been said that the custom started at some remote period before Christianity was introduced to Devonshire when there was a terrible drought, and that a ram was sacrificed to the gods to bring a stream

Robert Dover's Olimpick Games (Robert Chambers, *The Book of Days*, 1864)

by the village – and so by rights the local river should be diverted and the ram roasted in the riverbed once more. However, there is no evidence that the custom is older than the nineteenth century, and it is standard fare for any custom involving dead animals to be linked to sacrifices. Rather more prosaically, it was once far from unusual for animals, usually sheep or oxen, to be roasted at local fairs and other gatherings, in order to feed the hundreds of people that attended them.

See also **Fairs, Feasts, Wakes, and Revels**, p. 249.

Robert Dover's Olimpick Games

Robert Dover (?1582–1652) was a lawyer who settled in the Cotswolds in 1611, and sometime soon afterwards organized the first of what became known as Robert Dover's Olimpick Games, on an open hillside called Kingcombe Plain (later renamed Dover's Hill), above Weston-sub-Edge in Gloucestershire. It is possible that he based his games on an existing local feast or ale, but it is equally possible that the idea was his own.

Dover seems to have been quite the extrovert and very skilled in self-promotion, and his Games soon achieved a much higher profile than most local events ever do. Based on contemporary publications, the early events included a range of activities, from horse-racing, hare-coursing, and hunting, to more modest field events such as running, jumping, throwing the sledgehammer, wrestling, fencing, dancing, and even board games such as chess. His Games were founded at the very time a national debate was raging over the propriety of such sports, and this can hardly be accidental. This controversy focused particularly on what should be allowed on Sundays, but an increasing number of Puritans wanted all such gatherings banned (*see **The King's Book of Sports** 1618 and 1633*, p. 262).

With the onset of the Civil War in 1642, Dover's Games ceased, but they were re-introduced after the Restoration by his grandsons John and Thomas Dover. The event continued to be held until 1852, when enclosure of the area again killed it. Dover's Hill became the property of the National Trust in 1929, and the Games were again held as a one-off event in May 1951 for the Festival of Britain. Meanwhile, at nearby Chipping Campden, a smaller Whitsun celebration occurred every year, known as the Scuttlebrook Wake. By the mid twentieth century, this event included all the usual May Queens, processions, fancy-dress competitions, and funfair rides expected of such affairs, and in 1966 Dover's Games were revived on Dover's Hill as part of the celebrations. The Games are now played on the Friday night and the Wake is celebrated on Saturday. At the Games, many of the traditional field sports of the earlier periods have been revived, coupled with spectacular events such as hot-air balloons, parachute jumps, and motorbike scrambling.

See also **Fairs, Feasts, Wakes, and Revels**, p. 249.

June

Dumb Cake

Appleby Horse Fair

Mock Mayors and Courts

| 4 | 5 | 6 |

| 11 | 12 | 13 |
| **ST BARNABAS' DAY** | | |

| 18 | 19 | 20 |
| | | Mayor of Ock Street |

| 25 | 26 | 27 |
| | **ST ANNE'S DAY** | |

*Moveable events have been placed
on the date they fall in 2007.
Events dependent on the timing
of Easter are coloured green.*

Well-Dressing

1

2

3

TRINITY SUNDAY

7

THURSDAY AFTER
   TRINITY SUNDAY
Corpus Christi

8

9

**SECOND SATURDAY IN
   JUNE**
Queen Elizabeth II's Official
Birthday

10

Duke of Edinburgh's Birthday

14

15

16

17

THIRD SUNDAY IN JUNE
Father's Day

21

Brecknell Bequest

22

23

**MIDSUMMER EVE/ST
   JOHN'S EVE**

24

**MIDSUMMER'S DAY/ST
   JOHN THE BAPTIST'S
   DAY**
Divination
Election of Sheriffs
Knollys Red Rose
Magdalen Outdoor Sermon
Midsummer Cushions

28

**ST PETER'S/ST PAUL'S
   EVE**

29

**ST PETER'S DAY/ST
   PAUL'S DAY**
Bawming the Thorn
Jankyn Smith's Charity
Warcop Rush-bearing

30

JUNE/JULY
Yarnton Lot Meadow

TRINITY SUNDAY

Trinity Sunday is celebrated eight weeks after Easter, the first Sunday after Whitsun, and can fall between 10 May and 20 June. The Christian doctrine of the Trinity, which developed in the earliest period of the Church's existence, caused a tremendous amount of discussion and dissension that rumbled on for centuries. By the Middle Ages, the idea of a special day devoted to the Holy Trinity existed in various parts of the Christian world, and it was particularly popular in England, probably because Thomas Becket, who was consecrated on that day in 1162, actively promoted its use. However, it was not fixed as a universal feast day until 1334. In Britain, after the Reformation, churches were widely dedicated to the Holy Trinity as a way of avoiding references to specific saints, and this tendency continued into the late nineteenth century. According to publisher William Chambers, writing in 1864, one-fifth of all new churches in his time were dedicated to the Trinity.

Nevertheless, the day does not seem to have attracted many traditional customs, and the few that are recorded are single local observances rather than widespread traditions. Seventeenth-century antiquarian John Aubrey described an apparently unique garland custom that took place at Newnton, in Wiltshire, in his time: a local girl would wear a garland round her neck, and then place it on a young man's neck, who returned it, with much saluting and kissing. Whenever possible during this custom, things were done three times (three knocks on the door, three kisses, and so on), in keeping with the day's name. This ceremony was reputed to commemorate the granting of some common land to the parish by King Athelstan, and the story goes that he had noticed their need for such land when he happened to be passing and met a milkmaid who was feeding her cow on the roadside verge.

Other customs are clearly linked to the dedication of the parish church, as at Old Clee in Lincolnshire, where they strew grass in the aisles of the Saxon church of the Holy Trinity and St Mary every Trinity Sunday. According to C. Ernest Watson, who wrote up the history of the area in 1901, stuffed chine and cheesecakes must be eaten on this day.

The time of year in which Trinity Sunday falls made it a favourite day for feasts, wakes, and other local gatherings. In the mid 1880s, Charlotte Burne described the Caradoc Wakes, which took place at the summit of one of the Stretton Hills and offered all the usual feast-day attractions, including stalls selling beer and food, gingerbread hawkers, foot-races, wrestling, rolling cakes down the side of the hill, fiddling, and dancing. This wake faded out in the mid nineteenth century, but in Burne's time parties of young people still spent at least some of Trinity Sunday on the hill.

See also **Fairs, Feasts, Wakes, and Revels**, p. 249.

*

THURSDAY AFTER TRINITY SUNDAY

Corpus Christi

This is one of several major Church festivals which were extremely important public events in their day, but are now virtually forgotten. Corpus Christi (meaning 'Body of Christ') was a relative latecomer to the festival calendar, being introduced by Pope Urban IV in 1264 and relaunched by Pope John XXII in 1317. It was created to honour the body of Christ, and to commemorate the central mystery of the Eucharist, in which Christ is believed to be truly present in the wine and bread of the mass.

The new feast was enthusiastically adopted by some English churches almost immediately, and in a very short time specialist guilds were being formed. By the middle of the fifteenth century, Corpus Christi guilds were so common as to be the third most popular subjects for such groups (after the Virgin and the Trinity), and their primary task was to organize processions of the host through the streets. These processions involved not only the Corpus Christi guild members but also the local clergy, officials of the town, and members of trade guilds, and by Tudor times the processions had grown into huge affairs, particularly in urban areas such as York, Shrewsbury, Durham, Coventry, and Lichfield, which could support lavish productions. Houses and churches were decorated, streets were strewn with rushes and flowers, and the members of the procession carried torches, banners,

Horse Fair at Appleby, Westmorland, 1999

crosses, garlands, pictures of saints, and even models of beasts. In pride of place at the front of the procession, the host, enshrined in a pyx of crystal, silver, or even gold, was carried on the shoulders of the clergy. Onlookers were required to kneel, bareheaded, as the procession passed.

As they developed in size and complexity, the processions began to include tableaux and pageants, which eventually turned into plays on biblical themes, enacted on carts both moving and stationary. It is generally agreed that these Corpus Christi plays performed an important role in the development of drama in Britain. An extract from a nineteenth-century description of proceedings in York, as presented by folklorists A. R. Wright and T. E. Lones, gives a flavour of the day:

On the day before and the morning of the day itself, thousands of spectators streamed into the city. On Corpus Christi morn, artisans and tradesmen rose early, spending an hour or two completing the arrangements of their large stages. At 9 a.m. the procession started, beginning to play first at the gates of the priory of the Holy Trinity; then it proceeded so every street had a pageant, 'all at one time playing together'. Scaffolds and stages were erected in the streets, in those places where they determined to play their pageants ... their Mystery Plays bearing titles such as, for example, 'Cain and Abel', 'Slaughter of the Innocents', and 'Deliverance of Souls from Hell'. In the year 1415, fifty-four distinct dramas were represented on fifty-four stages ... The Corpus Christi plays were kept up till 1584 at York.

It is no surprise that the ceremonial carrying of the host through the streets was abolished at the Reformation. In many places the processions also lapsed, but in others they simply took on a new secular role, and were transformed into trade guild affairs or town pageants, such as the Shrewsbury Show, which survived until the 1860s.

*

FIRST WEEK IN JUNE

Appleby Horse Fair

The fair at Appleby-in-Westmorland, twelve miles south-east of Penrith and now in Cumbria, is probably the best-known surviving horse fair in the country and – not coincidentally – also the best-known gathering of travellers and Gypsies in the year. Those who still travel in horse-drawn vans, and those who for generations have driven cars and lorries, still congregate at Appleby in the old-fashioned way.

Nominally restricted to the Fair Hill just outside the town, the trading spills over in all directions, and for horse lovers the fair is an exciting event. The running of horses through the crowded streets of the town has been banned by the local council for safety reasons, but there are plenty of other places where they can be put through their paces; in addition there is horse-racing, much voluble bargaining and trading, business for the farrier, fortune-telling, and stalls selling crafts and horse-related equipment. A set piece, most popular with photographers and tourists, is the riding of horses into the River Eden for a good wash (with washing-up liquid) and a swim. The banks of the river are lined with spectators, and if the weather is good it is hard to find a place to watch the free show. Many of the visitors do not trade in horses, and the number of tourists and would-be travellers grows each year, but of all groups in England, Gypsies are the ones who have resisted being turned into quaint tourist attractions, and Appleby retains much of its old atmosphere.

It is often claimed that Appleby Horse Fair was founded by a charter granted by James II in 1685; however, that charter was for a fair in April and was soon rescinded. The present fair has a more prosaic origin: by resolution of Appleby Borough, in 1750.

*

8 JUNE

In June, farmers are already anxiously looking forward to the harvest, and they could choose from any number of traditional weather predictions. In 1869, Richard Inwards recorded in his classic *Weather-Lore* collection:

> If on the 8th of June it rain
> It foretells a wet harvest, men sain'.

Let us hope its accuracy was more impressive than its poetry.

*

SECOND SATURDAY IN JUNE

Queen Elizabeth II's Official Birthday

It is not entirely clear when British sovereigns started to have two birthdays, but from at least the twentieth century it was the custom to name an 'official birthday' for each ruler in addition to their natural one. The reason is simple. Many of the celebrations that surround a monarch's birthday are held outdoors, and it is far more pleasant for those involved, and the crowds watching, if the events can take place on a summer's day. Until 1959, the Queen's official birthday was on the second Thursday in June, but it now takes place on the second Saturday in June. The day is celebrated by the Queen's Birthday Parade, which takes place on Horse Guards Parade, Whitehall, at 11 a.m., and by gun salutes in Hyde Park and the Tower of London.

See also **21 April: Queen Elizabeth II's Birthday**.

*

10 JUNE

Duke of Edinburgh's Birthday

The birthday of the Duke of Edinburgh is marked by gun salutes in Hyde Park and the Tower of London.

*

11 JUNE

St Barnabas' Day

Barnabas (martyred AD 71) was an early Christian disciple, but not one of the twelve Apostles. A one-time companion of St Paul, he was active in spreading the word of the new religion, especially in his native Cyprus. A dozen or so ancient churches in England were dedicated to him, which indicates that he was known here but was not particularly popular. Nevertheless, according to the evidence supplied by the church-wardens' accounts of St Mary-at-Hill, London, in the fifteenth and sixteenth centuries, St Barnabas' Day was an important feast day. Churches were decorated with garlands of roses, woodruff (a woodland herb with sweet-scented leaves and small white flowers), and lavender. Maidens went 'gathering' for church funds, and money was paid out for 'bread, wine and ale for the singers of the King's Chapel and for the clerks of the town'. Later periods show no evidence of such customs on the day. A possible clue to the basis of these activities is a rhyme, reported fairly regularly in later years:

> Barnaby bright, Barnaby bright,
> The longest day and the shortest night.

These words only make sense if account is taken of the adoption of the Gregorian Calendar in 1752 (*see* p. xx): old St Barnabas' Day fell eleven days later, so the customs could possibly be seen as celebrating midsummer. The midsummer date also made St Barnabas' Day a popular time for fairs.

*

THIRD SUNDAY IN JUNE

Father's Day

Father's Day was first suggested in 1909 by Sonora Dodd of Washington, in appreciation of her own father, and in direct imitation of the new Mother's Day, which was beginning to gain support at the time. It took much longer to catch on than Mother's Day had done, but was finally recognized by a joint resolution of Congress in 1956, and received Presidential support in 1966 and 1972. In the latter year it was officially set as the third Sunday in June. Father's Day entered British popular culture in the wake of Mother's Day sometime after the Second World War, not without opposition, and many still regard it as a 'card-day' too far.

*

20 JUNE

Mayor of Ock Street

One of the few surviving mock-mayor ceremonies in England, albeit in extremely attenuated form, is the election of the Mayor of Ock Street in Abingdon, Oxfordshire, each June. The mayor has no duties or powers, but serves as the squire of the local morris team.

In the nineteenth century, Ock Street was the proverbial 'rough end' of town, which is exactly the kind of place one would expect to find a mock-mayor custom, but the history of the ceremony has proved surprisingly difficult to chart with any certainty. Indeed, there is no record of a mock mayor before the 1860s, and its history is inextricably bound up with other, much older traditions: the local horse fair, which was formerly held each year in Ock Street on 20 June, until it was moved in 1876; and the local morris team, which claims to have been in existence for nearly 500 years. However, although there is a record of a payment for morris bells in the churchwardens' accounts for St Helen's church in Abingdon, in 1560, this does not prove the continuous existence of a morris team until the next evidence of one, in 1783. For much of its recorded history, the position of mayor has been held by members of the Hemmings family, who were also stalwarts of the morris team, and the holder of the office is now always a morris man. The modern morris side carries a pair of ox horns, mounted on a pole, on which is painted the date '1700', and this is often given as the date of foundation of both the dancing and the mayor-making. Keith Chandler, in his paper delivered at the Calendar Customs conference in 1984 (published in 1993), ably presents such conflicting and confusing evidence as is available.

See also **Mock Mayors and Courts**, p. 216.

*

21 JUNE

Brecknell Bequest

Charity doles often include seemingly bizarre details, which may once have had a rational basis or may simply have stemmed from the whim or sense of humour of the benefactor. The Brecknell bequest is an example of the latter, and is described in John Noake's *Guide to Worcestershire* (1868):

> [Kidderminster] *A bachelor named Brecknell, in 1778, bequeathed a farthing loaf and twopenny cake annually to every single person, born in Church*

Mock Mayors and Courts

In towns and villages up and down the country, the pomp and ceremony that surrounded local government and politics was deliberately parodied in raucous ceremonies which appointed a mock mayor, or occasionally a mock Member of Parliament or even a mock king. These burlesque officers often had traditional names that matched their sham status (for example the Mayor of Bartlemas (Newbury), the Lord Mayor of Pennyless Cove (Tenby), and the Mayor of Shamickshire (Bideford)), and were appointed in ways that poked pointed fun at the real dignitaries. Although many details varied widely, the basic structure of mock-mayor ceremonies was remarkably similar from place to place. He was invariably 'chaired' around the neighbourhood, or he rode a 'charger' (usually a donkey) around the town; he might carry a mace made of a cabbage stalk, in order to ridicule official regalia, and he often made preposterous speeches, promising food and drink for all, or gave out ludicrous summary judgments to punish imaginary transgressions by bystanders. He was often accompanied by his 'mayoress', a man dressed in women's clothes, which greatly increased the scope for ribald and coarse humour.

Before the passing of the 1836 Municipal Reform Act swept them away, there were indeed many civic and manorial customs and offices that had clearly outlived their usefulness and these were ripe for parody. A description of a real mayor-making in Exeter in the 1820s shows what the mock ones were satirizing:

The Mayors were nominated by the body, the free-men being nominally the electors. I never remember any opposition. On the day of the election, the members of the body and freemen assembled in the Guildhall; the intended Mayor was proposed, with the other officials; after taking the oath and duly signing the documents, on the cheering subsiding, the Hall echoed with the sound of various drawings of bottled wine corks ... A procession was then formed to perambulate the city walls, headed by the tradesmen's corps or constables, about twenty-four in number; then the staff and mace-bearers, sword-bearer, the Mayor elect walking uncovered, with his hat in hand; Aldermen, with scarlet robes and three-cornered hats, followed by members and officials; in the rear being three tradesmen's sons, named Mayor's stewards (the outside one called gutter steward), wearing long black robes, with tufts and three-cornered hats.

If this had survived to the present day we would cherish it as a piece of traditional pageantry, but at that time it must have struck a sour note with those who had no say in the way their community, or even their country, was governed. Nevertheless, the idea that mock mayors were an overt protest by a politically aware but disenfranchised underclass is hardly sustainable, although there must have been elements of this in some instances. Most of the evidence points to the parody as being just a bit of fun.

It is no surprise that Exeter had its own regular mock mayor. When china-dealer 'Sir Osborn China' was 'elected' and paraded round the town in the 1830s, he wore a chamberpot on his head, which he removed when ladies were present, and his election speech included something for everybody:

Street, who would apply for it on the 21st of June. The mere residents of that street, if not born there, are also entitled to a cake, but their claim is forfeited when they leave the street. The recipients make themselves truly 'jolly' on the night of the distribution.

For those born in the street, the right to this dole lasted for life, and tradition has it that it was once claimed by someone living in America. Bequests such as this would have done little to relieve real poverty, but if the purpose was primarily to perpetuate the benefactor's name, then this was duly achieved for a century or so.

See also **Doles**, p. 87.

*

*And that you may be enabled to have tea cheaper,
I will order a canal to be cut, that the largest ships
from China shall come close to your doors; your
mill stream shall be turned into milk, beer shall
be pumped from your wells, made from the finest
malt and hops that can be procured.*

Mock-mayor ceremonies could be held at any time
of year. Where there was a real mayor, the burlesque
usually took place on or near the day of the mayor-
making, but others gravitated to coincide with the
local feast, such as at Oswaldkirk, in North Yorkshire,
where the mock mayor presided over the annual
three-day fair in July. Some, like the famous one at
Garratt, in Wandworth, south London, were timed to
coincide with national elections.

In some places, the joke was extended, and a mock
corporation or mock court had a more permanent
existence. At Walton-Le-Dale in Lancashire, the mock
corporation grew from a Jacobite Club, founded in
1701, while the mock court of Halgavor in Cornwall,
as recorded by Richard Carew in 1602, had less
exalted aims:

*The youthlier sort of Bodmin townsmen use
sometimes to sport themselves by playing the box
with strangers, whom they summon to Halgavor.
The name signifieth the Goat's Moor, and such a
place it is, lying a little without the town, and full
of quagmires. When these mates meet with any
raw servingman or other young master who may
serve and deserve to make pastime, they cause
him to be solemnly arrested for his appearance
before the mayor of Halgavor, where he is charged
with wearing one spur, or going untrussed, or
wanting a girdle, or some such felony; and after*

*he hath been arraigned and tried with all requisite
circumstances, judgment is given in formal terms
and executed in some ungracious prank or other,
more to the scorn than hurt of the party concerned.
Hence is sprung the proverb, when we see one
slovenly apparelled, to say, 'He shall be presented in
Halgavor court'.*

Most mock-mayor customs had disappeared by the
late nineteenth century, although a few lasted until
the early twentieth, and one or two still survive
in one form or another. Civic pride was no doubt
piqued by these parodies, which must have played
a part in their demise, but in truth they were also
drunken and riotous affairs, openly organized or
supported by local publicans, and often shame-
lessly using 'dim-witted' locals to play the part of
mayor. There was also a local notion that normal
laws were suspended on mayor-making day,
when people believed they could get away with
anything (*see* **Lawless Hours and Days**, p. 303).
The 'ceremonies' were thus mostly attacked on
public order grounds, and put down by the police
– although suppression was not always a simple
matter, as demonstrated by the mayor-making
on the annual club day at Chipping, Lancashire, in
1881, reported by the *Antiquary*. Here, '[t]he police
interfered and summoned ten of the men before the
Clitheroe magistrates for being drunk', but the court
'dismissed all the cases, one of the justices remarking
that he approved of old customs being carried out'.

See also **Second Saturday in May: Randwick Wap**;
20 June: Mayor of Ock Street; **6 July: Kilburn Feast**;
26 July: Mace Monday.

23 JUNE

Midsummer Eve/St John's Eve

See **24 June: Midsummer's Day/St John the Baptist's
Day**.

*

24 JUNE

Midsummer's Day/St John the Baptist's Day

Midsummer was undoubtedly one of the high spots of
the festival year in medieval times, but the widespread

The Baal Fire at Whalton, Northumberland (Benjamin Stone, 1906)

modern idea that it was formerly regarded as one of the times of year when fairies and sprites were abroad is wrong. This notion is based solely on a literal reading of the title of Shakespeare's comedy *A Midsummer Night's Dream*, but the text makes clear that the play's action takes place on May Day Eve, which in European folklore is certainly the time when fairy and mortal worlds were believed to intermingle. In England, there is little folkloric evidence of a connection between midsummer and the supernatural, except in the limited sense that it was one of the favourite times for love **divination** (*see* p. 221). Another factor that has contributed to our mistaken view of midsummer is the unfounded belief that at this time of year Druids used to worship the rising sun at Stonehenge, for which a string of romantic antiquarians are at fault. As Stuart Piggott commented in his classic book on Druids, 'In [John] Aubrey's tentative association of Stonehenge and other prehistoric stone circles with the Druids is the germ of an idea which was to run like lunatic wildfire through all popular and much learned thought, and particularly emotive feeling, until modern times.' In fact, from the time of the earliest records, midsummer in England was celebrated with bonfires, processions and parades, and by decorating houses and churches with greenery.

By many accounts, it seems that the whole period between St John the Baptist's Eve (23 June) and St Peter's Day (29 June) was regarded as one festival, loosely termed 'midsummer', and many customs and celebrations could be found throughout that time. The flavour of the season is indicated in John Stow's famous description of midsummer in London in the 1590s:

In the months of June and July, on the vigils of festival days, and on the same festival days in the evening after the sun setting, there were usually made bonfires in the streets, every man bestowing wood or labour towards them; the wealthier sort also, before their doors near to the said bonfires, would set out tables on the vigils, furnished with sweet bread and good drink, and on the festival days with meats and drinks plentifully, whereunto they would invite their neighbours and passengers also to sit and be merry with them in great familiarity, praising God for His benefits bestowed on them. These were called bonfires as well of good amity amongst neighbours that being before at controversy, were there, by the labour of others, reconciled, and made of bitter enemies loving friends; and also for the virtue that a great fire hath to purge the infection of the air. On the vigil of St. John the Baptist, and on St. Peter and Paul the Apostles, every man's door being shadowed with green birch, long fennel, St. John's wort, orpin, white lilies, and such like, garnished upon with garlands of beautiful flowers, had also lamps of glass, with oil burning in them all the night; some hung out branches of iron curiously wrought, containing hundreds of lamps alight at once, which made a goodly show.

Churches, too, were bedecked with birch boughs. The records of St Mary-at-Hill church in London, for example, include many references to payments for 'birch at Midsummer' nearly every year throughout the fifteenth century, and it is interesting to note that they refer to the season by that secular name rather than St John's Day.

Stow rightly stressed the dual purpose of the bonfires – peace and good neighbourhood on the one hand, and on the other the belief that the smoke of bonfires was medicinal, and purified the air. For this reason, sixteenth-century religious reformers branded midsummer fires as 'superstitious' and they were finally suppressed. However, the impulse to build bonfires is too strong, especially on a summer's evening, to be laid aside to order. Even Henry Bourne, curate of All Hallows in Newcastle, and not usually one to tolerate any hint of popishness in popular custom, seemed loath to condemn the bonfire outright in his *Antiquitates Vulgares* (1725):

But whatever reason the heathens had for kindling these fires . . . it was certain that the custom was invented and practised by them; and because of the superstition attending the observation of it, was very justly forbidden by the Council. And undoubtedly was the making of such fires now attended with any such superstition, it would be equally criminal to observe them, but when they are only kindled as tokens of joy, to excite innocent mirth and diversion, and promote peace and good neighbourhood, they are lawful and innocent, and deserve no censure. And therefore when on Midsummer-Eve, St. Peter's Eve, and some other times, we make bonfires before shops and houses there would be no harm in doing so, was it not that some continue their diversion to too late hours, and others are guilty of excessive drinking.

Later folklorists found, or thought they found, lingering remnants of fire customs at midsummer in various parts, and the tradition of lighting bonfires seemed particularly tenacious in the West Country, but even these faded out until revived by the self-conscious inventions of the Old Cornwall Society in the 1930s. (For an event that retains the atmosphere of the communal fires of olden times, *see* **4 July: Whalton Baal Fire**.)

The other main feature of Midsummer was the processions. These had their ultimate origin in urban areas in the musters of the local watch, who were charged with policing the city at night, and were commanded to accompany the mayor and aldermen in procession on Midsummer and St Peter's Eve, as much as a show of strength as of civic dignity and pride. Trade guilds also had their parades, and in towns that could muster the necessary manpower and resources, these processions became spectacular torch-lit affairs, with giants, devils, hobby horses, drummers, trumpeters, armed mounted and marching companies, and tableaux depicting famous scenes. Something of the flavour of the late medieval midsummer processions can be gleaned from visiting the one processional giant to have survived – now safely housed in Salisbury Museum. This splendid giant belonged to the local Tailors' Guild, and was an essential feature of their annual midsummer processions until the Reformation declared such figures 'superstitious'. He may have been repaired, remade, reclothed, and repainted many times, but to all intents and purposes he is still the same giant.

Dumb Cake

One of the earliest descriptions of the dumb cake was included in an anonymous chapbook published in London in 1685, entitled *Mother Bunch's Closet Newly Broke Open*. Every page of this little book is devoted to ways in which young women can divine their future love life, and in particular how they can determine who their future husband will be. These divinatory procedures range from the simple to the complex, and one of the latter is to make what is here headed the 'Dutch Cake', although every other source calls it a 'dumb cake', on Midsummer Eve.

> *Three, or four, or more of you are to make a cake of half flour and half salt (no matter what flour it is) and some of every one of your own water, make this cake broad and thin, then every one of you either make a mark that you know or set the first two letters of your name on it with a pin or bodkin, but leave such distance that it may be cut; then set it before the fire to bake, but all this while speak not a word. Turn it every one of you once, then let it bake a little more, and then throw on every one a little salt, and she that turn'd it first let her turn it again, then the person to be*

> *her husband will cut out her name and break it in two and give her one half, and so the next, till the last. If there be any so unfortunate to hear a bell, I wish I had them to my bedfellows this night to prevent leading apes in hell . . .*

Although it is underplayed here, it is the wraith of her future husband who will appear and break the cake with the girl, not the real person, and it is this that gave the procedure the thrill of the supernatural. The key principle in this type of ceremony is that it has to be difficult, both as a test of the participant's resolve and as a way of ensuring that any perceived failure can be blamed on some tiny deviation from the rules rather than a failure of the underlying principle. The dumb cake therefore has to be made by several people in co-operation, in total silence from start to finish, and the ingredients are so unpleasant that it is a real trial to eat. The high concentration of salt, and the frequently recorded use of soot or urine, would certainly test anyone's determination. Mother Bunch does not actually stipulate that the girls must eat the cake, but in nearly all the other recorded versions they do, and this resulted in the participants making tiny, thimble-size cakes, which stuck to the letter of the rules but were far easier to cope with.

The Tailors' Guild had been chartered in 1447, and had been staging pageants and processions for many years before the Giant was first mentioned in its records in 1570, when they planned to 'sett goinge for the accustomed pageant of Mydsomer feaste, the Gyant, the thre black boyes, the bearer of the gyant and one person to play the Divell's part'. As the same entry speaks of making repairs to the Giant's coat, he was presumably not new at the time. St John the Baptist was the patron saint of tailors, so it was particularly appropriate for them to parade on 23 June, the eve of his feast. At some point, however, the giant became known as Christopher – presumably because that saint was the most famous giant in Christian legend, and many other processional giants were also associated with him in the popular mind.

When acquired by the museum in 1869, the Salisbury Giant was fourteen feet tall, but he was shortened a little to fit his new accommodation. His head is a piece of solid wood, but his body is a hollow open woodwork frame, light enough to be carried on the shoulders of one person hidden inside. He can therefore turn, sway, and tilt in a much more lifelike way than if he were simply wheeled along, although this brings the danger of accident, and in at least one photograph (from 1911) he can be seen lying flat on the ground. His attendants are called 'Whifflers' ('whiffler' is a name for an armed attendant in a procession, and dates back to at least the early sixteenth century), and carry his huge two-handed sword, and his 'mace', a rhomboid shape made of canvas on the end of a long pole. The museum also possesses Hob-nob, a hobby horse, which has accompanied the Giant on his outings since the sixteenth century. Morris dancers also featured regularly in the processions. From the eighteenth century onwards, the Salisbury Giant has only been brought out on special occasions, usually royal events such as coronations and jubilees, or to celebrate major military victories.

Finally, commenting on the weather around midsummer, Devon folklorist Sarah Hewett wrote in 1900, 'Before St John's Day we pray for rain, after that we get it anyhow.'

Divination

Midsummer's Day and Eve may not have been particularly well known for fairy activity, but they were regularly cited as times when particular divinations could be successfully carried out, such as watching in the church porch at midnight to see who in the parish would die in the coming year (*see* **24 April: St Mark's Eve**). Love divinations, such as sowing the hemp seed – whereby girls threw hemp seed over their shoulders, out of doors at night, in the hope of seeing the form of their future husband – and making a **dumb cake** (*opposite*), were also popularly carried out at this time, although they too could also be performed on other nights of the year. Two divinatory procedures, however, were only carried out at midsummer. The most widespread was a simple procedure called 'Midsummer Men', mentioned by John Aubrey in his *Remaines of Gentilisme and Judaisme* (1686) as being performed in Wiltshire in his day:

> *I remember, the maids (especially the cook-maids and dairy-maids) would stick up in some chinks of the joists, etc., Midsummer-men, which are slips of orpines. They placed them by pairs, one for such a man, the other for such a maid his sweetheart, and accordingly as the orpine did incline to, or recline from ye other, that there would be love, or aversion; if either did wither, death.*

The same procedure was being tried right into the twentieth century. Orpine was so often the plant used for this ceremony that it was called 'Midsummer men' in local dialects across the country. The other midsummer love-divination also involved plants, but this one needed better preparation, as described by Mrs Bray in Devon in 1838:

> *It is said here that if a young woman, blind-folded, plucks a full-blown rose, on Midsummer day, while the chimes are playing twelve, folds the rose up in a sheet of white paper and does not take out the rose until Christmas, it will be found fresh as when gathered. Then, if she places the rose on her bosom, the young man to whom she is to be married will come and snatch it away.*

Election of Sheriffs

The two Sheriffs of the City of London are elected by the City Livery Companies on 24 June, to serve for one year. They take office on 28 September, the day before the new Lord Mayor does so. The sheriffs' primary function is to support the Lord Mayor in carrying out his duties, which includes presenting petitions to Parliament and attending sessions at the Central Criminal Court. Candidates for Lord Mayor must have previously served as sheriff, and while the latter are mentioned as early as the seventh century, the title of Lord Mayor only came into being in 1189.

Knollys Red Rose

This ceremony, revived in 1924, involves the presentation of a red rose to the Lord Mayor of London every 24 June at the Mansion House in London. The story behind this custom tells of how Lady Constance, wife of Sir Robert Knollys, built a footbridge in 1381 connecting two of her properties in Seething Lane, London, without first obtaining the Lord Mayor's permission, for which she was fined one rose each year. That custom fell into disuse in the seventeenth century, and the present ceremony was revived by the Revd 'Tubby' Clayton (founder of the organization Toc H), who entrusted its continuance to the Company of Watermen and Lightermen.

Magdalen Outdoor Sermon

In medieval times, a 'spital' was a charity hospital that catered for the poorest people in society, and therefore usually had the reputation of being a foul and pestiferous place. One of the ways in which money was raised to support these institutions was for a special annual church service, with sermon, to be given, attended by

Open-air service at Magdalen College, Oxford, 1984

local dignitaries. Given the nature of these hospitals, however, it was traditional to hold these meetings out of doors. One surviving example, which lapsed in the nineteenth century, but was revived in 1896, is the sermon preached at Magdalen College, Oxford, on a Sunday morning near 24 June. The pulpit is built into the outside wall of the College, on the site of which the Hospital of St John the Baptist previously stood, and the congregation includes the President, Vice-Chancellor, and senior Proctors, seated in state on the lawn.

Another 'spital sermon' takes place two weeks after Easter at St Lawrence Jewry church, Gresham Street, in London, but this one is nowadays held indoors; *see* **Two weeks after Easter: Spital Sermon**, p. 135.

Midsummer Cushions

A picturesque custom, reported by M. A. Denham as common in northern England in the late eighteenth century but which had died out by his time in the 1850s, was the making and displaying of Midsummer Cushions:

> *The young lads and lasses of the town or village*
> *having procured a cushion . . . and covered it*
> *with calico, or silk of showy and attractive colour,*
> *proceeded to bedeck it with every variety of flower*
> *which they could procure out of their parents' and*
> *more wealthy neighbours' gardens, displaying them*
> *in such a manner so as to give it a most beautiful*
> *appearance. All this done, they placed themselves,*
> *with their cushion of Flora's choicest gems, in the*
> *most public place they conveniently could, solicit-*
> *ing of every passer-by a trifling present of pence,*
> *which in numerous cases was liberally and cheerfully*
> *bestowed . . . This custom prevailed from Midsummer*
> *Day to Magdalene Day [22 July], which latter has*
> *long been corrupted to 'Maudlin Day' . . .*

Unfortunately, Denham never managed to obtain the rhyme that accompanied this display custom. In 1778, John Hutchinson reported a similar custom from Northumberland, but explained that the cushions were made out of stools, with a layer of clay smeared on top, and flowers stuck into the clay. A similar custom of the same name was reported by the Northamptonshire poet John Clare: in preparing a manuscript collection of

his poems for publication in 1832, which he proposed to call *The Midsummer Cushion*, he wrote in explanation of the term, 'It is a very old custom among villagers in summer time to stick a piece of greensward full of field flowers & place it as an ornament in their cottages which ornaments are called Midsummer Cushions.'

*

26 JUNE

St Anne's Day

For many years, the rush-bearing custom at Ambleside in Westmorland was held on the nearest Saturday to St Anne's Day, but it now takes place at the beginning of July; *see* **First Saturday in July: Ambleside Rush-Bearing**.

*

28 JUNE

St Peter's Eve/St Paul's Eve

See **29 June: St Peter's Day/St Paul's Day**.

*

29 JUNE

St Peter's Day/St Paul's Day

Considering the pre-eminence of Sts Peter and Paul in early Christian history, and their continued popularity ever since, it might seem strange that no particular festivals and few customs have been recorded for this day. However, they were simply too close to St John's Eve and Day to acquire many customs of their own, and instead became incorporated into a midsummer festival season that lasted until the end of the month (*see* **24 June: Midsummer's Day/St John the Baptist's Day**).

In some areas it was said that the weather on St Peter's Day was crucial to the apple crop, as in this example from Herefordshire in 1886:

> *Unless the apples are christened on St. Peter's Day the*
> *crop will not be good; and there ought to be a shower*
> *of rain when the people will go through the orchards,*
> *but no one seems to know for what purpose exactly.*

Bawming the Thorn at Appleton, Cheshire, 1986

But similar things are also said of St Swithun's Day (*see* **15 July**), and sometimes of St James's Day (*see* **25 July**).

Bawming the Thorn

In the Cheshire village of Appleton, they have a seemingly unique custom called 'Bawming the Thorn', which is performed on or near 29 June each year. Local primary-school children decorate a hawthorn tree with ribbons, garlands, and flags, then dance round it singing their 'bawming song', and later have a tea, some sports, and a fancy-dress parade. The tree stands in the middle of the village, and is protected with railings; the present one dates from 1967, when its predecessor blew down. It is not known how many trees have come and gone on the site before, but the original is said to have been an offshoot of the famous Glastonbury thorn, and was brought to Appleton by Adam de Dutton, lord of the manor in the twelfth century. Local tradition maintains that the bawming custom also dates back to that time but was allowed to lapse in Victorian times and was revived in the 1930s – although there must have been other lapses, as the current series commenced in 1973. Some have stated that it goes back even further to times of pagan tree-worship.

The bawming song was composed by a local man named Rowland Eyles Egerton Warburton (1804–91), probably in the 1860s:

Up with fresh garlands this midsummer morn
Up with red ribbons on Appleton thorn
Come lasses and lads to the Thorn Tree today
To bawm it and shout as ye bawm it 'Hurray!'

The word 'bawm' is no help in tracing the custom's development. It is usually glossed simply as 'decorating', and is always assumed to be an ancient word, but the *Oxford English Dictionary* does not include it. Joseph Wright's *English Dialect Dictionary* does, and he gives several examples of its use, but all refer to the Appleton custom, except one later example from Cumberland, so we have no earlier use of the word than the custom itself. The earliest written description so far found is in Roger Wilbraham's *An Attempt at a Glossary of Some Words used in Cheshire* (1817), and this shows that the custom and name were already in existence in the early nineteenth century:

At Appleton it was the custom at the time of the Wake to clip and adorn an old hawthorn which till very lately stood in the middle of the town. The ceremony is called the Bawming of Appleton Thorn.

The real clue to the origin of the custom is Wilbraham's mention of the local wake, and in the absence of any other evidence it seems likely that the bawming is simply the survival of general village wake decorations (*see* **Fairs, Feasts, Wakes, and Revels**, p. 249). The dating of the tree to the twelfth century is highly questionable, and we can dismiss the tree-worship theory without hesitation. As regards the idea of the Glastonbury thorn, which nowadays seems to be said about nearly every plant-based custom in the country, it is interesting to note that although local author William Beament includes the story in his book *An Account of the Cheshire Township of Appleton Thorn* (1877), in his unpublished diary entry for 30 July 1844 he makes it clear that at that time he was in complete ignorance as to the origin of the custom.

A piece in the *Warrington Guardian* of 29 July 1912, shows that the 'Fête at Appleton Thorn' was alive and well at that time and that the celebrations then were much as they are now, except there is no mention of fancy dress. Children and officials paraded the village, led by a band, the children danced round the tree carrying bouquets and singing Warburton's song, and then hung their flowers on the fence. There was a tea, and then sports and games – including tug-of-war, climbing the greasy pole, and men's and women's slow bicycle races.

Jankyn Smith's Charity

Jankyn Smyth was a major benefactor to Bury St Edmunds in Suffolk, founding almshouses and building the town's guildhall. When he died, in 1481, he founded a charity that would ensure that he was remembered. He instructed that on the anniversary of his death a requiem mass should be said, for the benefit of his soul, attended by the town's officials and the residents of the almshouses. After the mass, the participants would be treated to cakes and ale. He could not have known, of course, that the Reformation was just around the corner, when masses for the dead would be abolished. Fortunately, the Bury officials substituted sermons for

Rush-bearing at Warcop, Cumbria, 1985

The wooden balls used to draw lots at Yarnton, Oxfordshire, 1985

the masses, and it continues to this day, attended by civic dignitaries and schoolchildren. It is said to be the oldest endowed service in England, and usually takes place on the Thursday before 29 June.

Warcop Rush-Bearing

Warcop is one of the five places in Cumbria that have existing rush-bearing ceremonies, and the distinctive feature of its celebrations is the ornate floral crown worn by each girl, as recorded in the *Cumbrian* magazine (1995):

> *The girls of the village wearing their best dresses are crowned with garlands made of rushes, ferns, mosses and flowers and the boys carry symbolic crosses made of rushes bound with red ribbon. To the sound of the brass band, all the villagers, young and old, walk from village to church where a special service is held to bless the rushes.*

The ornate crowns contrast well with the simple crosses. The procession takes place on St Peter's Day, although the church is dedicated to St Columba (whose feast day is on 9 June), and the clergy meet the children at the church gate, and lead them into the church, which is also decorated with flowers.

See also **Rush-Bearing**, p. 238.

*

JUNE/JULY

Yarnton Lot Meadow

In earlier forms of farming, villages often had open hayfields, held in common, in which various villagers had rights to a share of the yield. Rather than simply getting all the hay in and dividing it, complex systems usually evolved whereby parcels of land within the field were allotted to each individual. As the quality of the land and crop varied, lots were drawn to determine who got the hay from which plot. At Yarnton, four miles from Oxford, the three meadows of Pixey, Oxhay, and West Mead were formerly treated in this way, but only the latter remains. The field is divided into thirteen lots.

Continues on page 229 >

Well-Dressing

Without doubt the prettiest and most artistic of English customs, well-dressing is now found in many villages across the country; however, its real home is in Derbyshire, where it can be found in over eighty villages, including Youlgreave, Wirksworth, Tideswell, and, the most famous of them all, Tissington. Different villages undertake their dressing when convenient to themselves, at any time between May and August, but at Tissington it is usually carried out on Ascension Day. Many villages decorate a well or spring, but some bedeck another form of water feature, and a few decorate something that has no connection with water at all.

A simplified description of what is involved in well-dressing is as follows. One or more boards with a raised edge are prepared, depending on the size of the project. Hundreds of nails are driven into the board, to help keep the other materials in place, and it is then covered with a smooth layer of well-puddled clay, half an inch to an inch thick. The basic design has already been marked out on large sheets of paper, which are laid across the board, and the lines of the picture are pricked out through the paper on to the clay. The outlines of the design are then filled out, using hard objects such as small cones, berries, seeds, or pieces of wood. The full picture is then coloured in, painstakingly, using moss, leaves, and individual flower petals, all pressed into the clay by hand. The work is hugely labour-intensive, and requires patience, dexterity, and skill in equal measure. Many of the villages pride themselves on using nothing but natural organic materials.

The frames are then transported to the site, where they are set up, the largest often needing a scaffolding frame to keep them in position. Some consist of a simple flat screen, while others have side and top panels. Biblical scenes are by far the most common, but sometimes local scenes, or a topical reference to some national celebration, are depicted.

Most present-day well-dressings have a relatively short history, either originating in the last few

Well-dressing at Tissington, Derbyshire, 1981

decades, or being revivals of traditions from the nineteenth or early twentieth century. However, the earlier history of well-dressing is not at all easy to ascertain, and the picture is considerably distorted by extravagant claims that well-dressing has been carried out, in an unbroken tradition, for 600 or 700 years, or even that the custom stretches in an uninterrupted line back to pagan times. Certainly, archaeological evidence shows that some wells and other water features were the focus of attention or veneration at periods before the Christian era; however, the new Christian Church spent much time and effort both trying to suppress such 'superstitious veneration' and trying to promote its own holy wells, although not necessarily at the same time. Some 'pagan' sites were rededicated to Christian saints, and continued in use, but most, it seems, were not.

Be that as it may, early documentary references to 'decorated' wells refer to them as being adorned with rags, ribbons, garlands, and so on, which may have been personal relics left by those who had attended the well for a cure or to ask a favour, or they may have been decoration as celebration or veneration. With this possible ambiguity in mind, the earliest references to 'well-dressing' become less than clear; as, for example, the following extract, which appeared in the *Gentleman's Magazine* in 1794:

> *In the village of Tissington ... it has been the custom, time immemorial, on every Holy Thursday, to decorate the wells with boughs of trees, garlands of tulips and other flowers, placed in various fancied devices.*

Nevertheless, not long after this, in 1818, Ebenezer Rhodes provided a good description of the custom, which does follow the modern well-dressing form:

> *... newly-gathered flowers disposed in various boards ... cut to the figures intended to be represented, and covered with moist clay into which the stems of the flowers are inserted ...*

The first confirmatory picture appeared in *The Mirror* on 20 May 1837.

As the evidence stands, therefore, well-dressing as we know it today cannot be shown to have existed earlier than the late eighteenth century – over a thousand years after Christianity reached these shores. It is also noteworthy that all the pre-1820 evidence for well-dressing relates to the village of Tissington, making it possible that, far from being a widespread ancient custom, it was unique to Tissington and spread to other nearby villages in the early nineteenth century. Tissington is not one of those wells that contain archaeological proof of previous votive use.

An auction is first held to sell the rights to the hay, and those who have bought rights assemble at 8 a.m. on the meadow on the Monday after St Peter's Day, where the two Head Meadsmen are in charge of drawing the lots. The thirteen individual strips of meadow are marked with wooden pegs, and the Meadsmen draw small wooden balls from a bag to determine who gets which strips. The balls bear names such as Boat, Freeman, Gilbert, and Watery Molly, which were presumably the names of previous tenants. Once the hay is cut, those with rights can also graze cattle or horses on the field.

Previously, the hay was cut on one day, but this necessitated the influx of a large number of temporary workers, whose bad behaviour gave the event a bad name, and it was decided to spread the haymaking over three days so that local workers could manage it themselves. There were also celebrations after the haymaking, with decorated wagons, morris dancing, races, and a prize garland, but this too was suppressed in 1840 when the local vicar complained to the landlord.

See also **5 July: Old Midsummer's Day** for a similar open field procedure at Congresbury and Puxton in Somerset.

July

Dog Days

Fairlop Fair

2

3

4
Stagshawbank Fair
Whalton Baal Fire

9

10

11
**SECOND WEDNESDAY IN
JULY**
Pretty Maid's Charity

Ashburton Ale-Tasting

Swan-Upping

16
ANNE ASKEW DAY

17

18

Rush-Bearing

23

24

25
**ST CHRISTOPHER'S DAY
ST JAMES'S DAY**
Ebernoe Horn Fair
John Knill Charity
Whitstable Oyster Festival

30
MACE MONDAY

31

JULY/AUGUST
St Wilfrid Feast Procession

*Moveable events have been placed
on the date they fall in 2007.*

| | | | 1 |

5
OLD MIDSUMMER'S DAY

6
Duck-Racing
Kilburn Feast
FIRST FRIDAY IN JULY
Warrington Walking Day

7
Bodmin Riding
FIRST SATURDAY IN JULY
Ambleside Rush-Bearing
Great Musgrave Rush-Bearing
Medway Admiralty Court

8
SUNDAY IN EARLY JULY
Oxenhope Straw Race

12

13

14
SECOND/THIRD
 SATURDAY IN JULY
Durham Miners' Gala

15
ST SWITHUN'S DAY

19
ARMADA DAY
Little Edith's Treat

20
ST MARGARET'S DAY

21

22

26

27

28
OLD ST KENELM'S DAY

29

Fairlop oak, site of the Fairlop Fair (Robert Chambers, *The Book of Days*, 1864)

Ashburton Ale-Tasting

See **Fourth Tuesday in November: Ashburton Court Leet**.

*

EARLY JULY

Fairlop Fair

Fairlop Fair, an immensely popular haunt for visitors from east London and Essex, took place in early July around a huge oak tree in Hainault or Epping Forest (about ten miles out of London and two miles from Chigwell). The oak was reputed to be thirty-six feet in circumference, and was clearly centuries old. The fair was founded by Daniel Day (born 1683), block- and pump-maker, who used to visit the area every year to collect rent from land he owned there, and was in the habit of inviting his tenants and friends to an outdoor meal of bacon and beans under the tree. Others apparently started to join in, and before he knew it, a full-blown fair with stalls and sideshows had developed around him. He was well aware of his founding-father status, and revelled in the fair each year until his death in 1767. Day's coffin was made from a branch that had fallen from the tree, and he asked to be buried at its foot, but was actually laid to rest in nearby St Margaret's, Barking.

This story has the rounded contours of an oft-told, oft-copied account, and it may not be strictly true in all details. It is likely, for example, that such an impressive tree had already attracted al fresco gatherings before Day's time, and that he extended or formalized them. The tree continued to be the focal point of the fair, although it was damaged by a fire started by careless picnickers in 1805, until it was finally blown down in 1820. The wood was used to make the pulpit and reading desk of St Pancras church on Euston Road, London, and a number of other commemorative items, some of which still exist.

In its heyday, Fairlop attracted huge numbers of pleasure-seekers and was a regular feature of the Essex calendar, as reported in the *Illustrated London News* on 15 July 1843:

> According to ancient custom 'gay Fairlop' was held on 'the first Friday in July on the borders of Hainault or Epping Forest, and drew together an immense number of persons. The block-makers, sail-makers, mast-makers, as usual, proceeded to the forest at an early hour in their amphibious-looking 'frigates', mounted on carriages, rigged out like ships, and decorated with colours. Each of these vehicles was drawn by six horses, gaily dressed out, and the wives of the men in their holiday gear followed in open landaus. The booths and shows were not so numerous as on former occasions, and the restriction of the fair to one day by the Essex magistrates has sadly diminished the profits of those who cater for the public. The Gipsies were uncommonly numerous; but the thimble and pea-riggers were dispersed by the police, and quitted the fair amidst the hootings of the people ... The conduct of the assembled thousands was marked by the greatest good humour and decorum, and there was not a single police charge arising out of 'the first Friday in July'.

The detail of the trippers' 'frigates' is illustrated in Robert Chambers' *Book of Days* (1864), which shows a horse-drawn cart made up to look just like a sailing ship. The picturesque qualities of the old oak were also much appreciated by artists, and numerous illustrations and prints were produced. In common with many fairs, attempts at restriction and suppression continued through the Victorian era, but the Fairlop Fair struggled on until 1900, when it finally disappeared.

See also **Fairs, Feasts, Wakes, and Revels**, p. 249.

*

4 JULY

Stagshawbank Fair

Stagshawbank Fair, held annually at Corbridge in Northumberland, sixteen miles west of Newcastle, was one of the biggest and most popular fairs in the north of England for at least 700 years. It was originally held at midsummer, but 4 July (old Midsummer Eve) became the traditional date after the change of calendar in 1752 (*see* p. xx). The fair was certainly in existence in 1204, and possibly originated before the Norman Conquest.

As with other villages in the area, on both sides of the border, there was a perennial fear of attack by raiders, right up to the turn of the eighteenth century, but in more peaceful times the fair attracted crowds of buyers and sellers from Scotland as well as all over the north of England. During the Middle Ages, Stagshawbank was particularly known for metalwork products, and in 1314 the King's agent was present, buying up horseshoes and nails to equip the army in the Scottish wars. In later years, the fair became known primarily for the sale of livestock, especially sheep, but as with all big country fairs, the range of goods on sale was wide, as indicated by Robert Forster's description of the fair c.1850:

> Besides horses, sheep, cattle, and swine, various articles of merchandise were offered for sale consisting of men's hats, boots, and shoes, these articles generally filled several stalls, the former being mostly from Hexham, and a considerable quantity of the latter from Corbridge. Jewellery and hardware stalls were prominent; saddlery and farming goods, such as hay rakes, forks, etc., were always plentiful, and always a large supply of cooperage goods, such as tubs, barrel churns, etc. Webs of cloth coarse and fine were shown to advantage on the green carpet by the side of the pond. The far-famed gloves, known as 'Hexham Tans', suitable for all purposes and for all classes, always formed noticeable articles of sale ... At the south side of the Horse Fair, in the distance you saw a strong made man somewhat elevated, with a crowd around him offering articles for sale; on approaching, we observe that it is Mr. C., from the once famous Dog Bank, Newcastle, selling watches by auction being for the most part forfeited pledges, the auctioneer

Proclaiming Stagshawbank Fair, by Ralph Hedley, 1882

assuring the public that each watch he offered was far superior to the one just sold, as once belonging to some squire or gentleman whose name was well known in the neighbourhood.

The opening of the fair was accompanied by a certain degree of ceremony, as the officials of the lord of the manor, the Duke of Northumberland, rode out in procession from Corbridge and around the boundaries of the fair site, accompanied by the Duke's piper. A proclamation to declare the fair open was read before any trading was allowed to commence.

Stagshawbank Fair was finally abolished in 1927, under powers of the Fairs Act of 1871, but people still flock to Corbridge every Spring Bank Holiday for the County Agricultural Show, which is traditionally the first such show of the season in the region. Stagshawbank Fair is also still remembered in the title of a traditional tune, popular with pipers from the area.

See also **Fairs, Feasts, Wakes, and Revels**, p. 249.

Whalton Baal Fire

As detailed under **24 June**, one of the dominant features of the traditional midsummer festival was the communal bonfire, and the best modern example of a fire that retains the atmosphere of those old days is the annual 'Baal Fire' at Whalton in Northumberland, just over five miles from Morpeth. The fire takes place on old Midsummer Eve and is built on the village green, close to the local pub; older accounts describe the care with which the young men of the village built the fire each year, and the way locals danced round and jumped through the flames – as young people do with bonfires the world over. It is unlikely that the fire is a direct survival from medieval times, although it could be. The name 'Baal' has excited many writers to flights of ancient fancy, but its origin is still unknown.

For illustration, *see* p. 218.

*

5 JULY

Old Midsummer's Day

In the open field systems that existed before enclosure, much ingenuity was devoted to ensuring that everyone got their fair share of the land and its produce.

Fairness depended largely on allotting scattered parcels or strips of land to those local inhabitants who had rights to a share, and in particular on ensuring that nobody got the best, or the worst, land every year. A relatively well-documented survival of the old system existed in one area of Somerset until 1811, which provides a good example of how such things were managed and the seemingly bizarre local customs that grew up over time. A description published by the county historian the Revd John Collinson while the practice there was still in operation gives a good summary:

> In the parishes of Congresbury and Puxton are two
> large pieces of common land, called East and West
> Dolemoors, which are divided into single acres,
> each bearing a peculiar and different mark cut
> in the turf, such as a horn, four oxen and a mare,
> two oxen and a mare, pole-axe, cross, dung fork,
> oven, duck's nest, hand reel, and hare's tail. On the
> Saturday before Old-Midsummer, several proprietors
> of estates in the parishes of Congresbury, Puxton,
> and Week St. Lawrence, or their tenants, assemble
> on the commons. A number of apples are previ-
> ously prepared, marked in the same manner with
> the beforementioned acres, which are distributed
> by a young lad to each of the commoners from a
> bag or hat. At the close of distribution each person
> repairs to his allotment, as his apple directs him, and
> takes possession for the ensuing year. An adjourn-
> ment then takes place to the house of the overseer
> of Dolemoors (an officer annually elected from the
> tenants) where four acres, reserved for the purpose
> of paying expenses, are let by inch of candle, and
> the remainder of the day is spent in that sociabil-
> ity and hearty mirth, so congenial to the soul of a
> Somersetshire yeoman.

However, nothing was simple is these old field systems.

The acres, furlongs, and chains in which the land was measured were not standard sizes but local customary variations, the marks were symbolic rather than pictorial (the 'hare's tail' resembled a circle with a cross inside), and the number of tenants and plots seem to have had little direct relationship. The apples seem an unusually picturesque detail, but are strangely reminiscent of the situation at Yarnton, in Oxfordshire, where common land plots continue to be allotted each year by drawing wooden balls from a bag, each ball bearing a name that corresponds to a particular plot (*see* **June/July: Yarnton Lot Meadow**). Most of the detective work necessary to understand the situation has been recorded by Keith Gardner in *Bristol & Avon Archaeology*, to which article interested readers are directed.

See also **Candle Auctions**, p. 106

*

6 JULY

Duck-Racing

The custom of 'duck-racing' was traditionally carried out in the Oxfordshire (previously Berkshire) village of Grove on the first Saturday after 6 July, as the culmination of the traditional Grove Feast. The village brook was dammed, and a series of ducks released on to the water, one at a time. Contestants had to catch the duck with their bare hands, and the winner kept it as a prize. *John Bull* magazine (1955) reported the words of one competitor:

> 'Duck racing isn't as easy as it sounds', says Albert
> Cook, who one year won five out of six races, 'I've seen
> a dozen men take twenty minutes to catch a duck.'

There are many stories of spectators getting so excited that they jumped in the water fully clothed to join in the fun. According to local belief, the sport had been carried out in the village for over 200 years, which is such a modest figure in comparison with the claims of other customs that it may have been true. By the early 1960s, the RSPCA claimed that the sport was cruel to animals, and it was discontinued.

Kilburn Feast

Kilburn Feast, in North Yorkshire, is a mere shadow of what it used to be. In former times it was primarily a horse fair, with additional sideshows and village sports, although its origin is unclear, as the presumed charter, claimed to be of Charles II's time, is now lost.

The key feature of the present-day feast is the mock mayor and mayoress (the latter played by a man, of course), who are elected to direct proceedings. The couple are dressed in appropriate costumes, and they progress through the village in a handcart, fining people for ridiculous transgressions (in the manner of mock mayors everywhere) and thereby collecting money, food, and drink, which all go towards the feast. The first victim is the local landlord, who is fined a barrel of beer. Much of the fun is provided by the mayoress, who insists on kissing everyone 'she' can catch hold of, leaving bright-red lipstick traces on their faces. It is in the nature of traditional customs that they acquire and lose elements over the years. In the 1980s it was claimed that it was 'unlucky' for the identity of the mayoress to be guessed, but this can hardly have been a permanent feature – in July 1960, for example, the *Yorkshire Post* proudly announced 'her' identity as sixteen-year-old Peter Medhurst.

Locals are pleased to keep this a relatively low-key event. As one participant told author Julia Smith in the 1980s:

> Johnny Kirk, whose family had been connected with the mayor-making over the years, said they did not want to make a big production of it or turn it into a tourist attraction; they wanted to keep it as it was, a local event for local people.

See also **Mock Mayors and Courts**, p. 216.

*

FIRST FRIDAY IN JULY

Warrington Walking Day

Warrington, formerly located in Lancashire but now in Cheshire, is situated between Manchester and Liverpool. It hosts the biggest and best-known of the surviving walking days in the country, on the Friday of the first week in July each year. As with other such walks, church organizations together with groups such as the Guides and Scouts march proudly through the streets of the town, with banners, to the sound of various bands.

The Warrington Walk was reputedly started by local clergyman Revd Horace Powys, in 1834, as a counter-attraction to the local races, although Whit Walks in the Manchester area could have provided a model for it. Until 1857, only the Anglican churches took part, but the Roman Catholics, and, later, other denominations, then started to hold processions on the same day. Each denomination stuck to its own route until 1995, when a terrorist bomb brought a new feeling of solidarity to the local people and the churches started marching together. By tradition, local shops close while the walk is in progress, and although this is not so strictly observed now as it used to be, some still do. Nowadays, the walk attracts about 4,000 participants, from about thirty churches, but this is less than half the number who used to take part in its heyday before the Second World War.

See also **Whitsun: Whit Walks**, p. 190.

*

FIRST SATURDAY IN JULY

Ambleside Rush-Bearing

Of the five places in Cumbria that have existing rush-bearing ceremonies, Ambleside and Grasmere (*see* **5 August: Grasmere Rush-Bearing**) are the most famous and attract the most participants and onlookers. As elsewhere, at Ambleside the main part of the celebration is the procession with band, banners, and villagers carrying rushes, flowers, and 'burdens' of rushes made into symbolic shapes. They parade around the village and up to the church, where a special service takes place, and those taking part are traditionally rewarded with gingerbread. For many years, the ceremony was held on the Saturday nearest St Anne's Day (26 July), as the present St Mary's church replaced one dedicated to St Anne, but it is now held on the first Saturday in July.

Nowadays, the 'bearings' or 'burdens' are mostly made from natural flowers and rushes, but for a time in the past they were primarily made of wood covered with coloured paper. Margaret Nicholson, whose parents ran the local post office in the mid nineteenth century, wrote down her memories of the burdens in 1898, and extracts were included in the 1953 booklet on rush-bearing by E. F. Rawnsley:

> The 'burthens' were devices of every imaginable shape made by the carpenter for the great ladies, and by the skilful-handed ones at home during the winter months, covered with coloured papers and coloured flowers . . . Yards of tissue paper must have been used. Aye, we know about that, for we had to lay in a stock of blue and pink and yellow, and Mr. Harrison of Scale allowed us ten shillings to give away to the poor folk in sheets of tissue each year, and we used to cut it into frills for them for the making of rosettes and flowers.

Margaret's mother was in charge of making the collection to cover the cost of the gingerbread, and once they got 'refined' enough to replace the traditional fiddler with a proper band, for them too. The rush-bearing ceremony of half a century ago is depicted in a mural, twenty-six feet long, created by Gordon Ransom in 1944, which can be seen in St Mary's.

See also **Rush-Bearing**, p. 238.

Great Musgrave Rush-Bearing

Great Musgrave is one of the five places in Cumbria that have existing rush-bearing ceremonies. Theirs is less well known than similar customs at Grasmere (see **5 August: Grasmere Rush-Bearing**) or Ambleside (see above), and therefore preserves a more intimate village community feel. At two o'clock on the first Saturday in July, children form up behind the silver band and the village rush-bearing banner, while adult participants join in behind, and they all march from the village hall to St Theobold's church for a service that includes parts specially aimed at the children. The girls carry posies and wear floral crowns (made the day before to make sure they are still fresh), while the boys carry symbolic crosses made from green rushes bound at the centre and ends with red ribbon. These crowns and crosses are laid at the foot of the altar, but are removed on the following Monday when they are placed on special hooks in an arc above the west door, and there they stay till next year's rush-bearing. A tea is served in the village hall, and games are held in the neighbouring field to round off the day.

See also **Rush-Bearing**, p. 238.

Medway Admiralty Court

On the first Saturday in July, the Mayor of Medway assumes his or her other role as Admiral of the River Medway and in full regalia enters a gaily decorated barge moored on the river, to preside over the Medway Admiralty Court. This court regulates the fishery and oyster beds of the River Medway between Sheerness and Hawkwood Stone, near Snodland, in Kent, and takes its jurisdiction from a charter of Henry VI in 1446, which granted exclusive rights to the citizens of Rochester to take 'fish both great and small' from this part of the river. The court's powers were later codified in the Rochester Oyster Fishery Acts of 1729 and 1865. Daniel Defoe's Tour through the Whole Island of Great Britain (1724–6) described the court in the mid eighteenth century:

> There is in the River Medway, at Rochester, and in several of its creeks and branches within the jurisdiction of the City, an oyster-fishery, which is free to every one who has served seven years apprenticeship to any fisherman or dredger, who is free of the said fishery, and the Mayor and citizens of Rochester hold a Court, commonly called An Admiralty Court, once a year, or oftener, when occasions have required it, for the regulating of the said fishery, and to prevent abuses committed in it. In these courts they appoint from time to time, when oysters shall and shall not be dredged and taken, which they call 'opening and shutting the Grounds'; also the quantity each dredgerman shall take in a day, which is usually called 'Setting the Stint'. They have power to go on board, and enforce these orders.

The court is still made up of Aldermen of the City, and a jury of freemen, who are the only ones allowed to fish the river. The main qualification for freeman is the seven-year apprenticeship to another freeman described by Defoe. In 2004 there were twenty-two Freemen of the River, and that year also saw the first-ever female apprentice in fourteen-year-old Robyn Wadhams.

Continues on page 240 >

Rush-Bearing

Until 200 years ago, rushes strewn on the floors of buildings for warmth and comfort would have been a common enough sight in many rural areas, and before that in urban settings too. Floor rushes were used extensively in domestic settings, from cottage to royal palace, although there were vast differences in how they were treated. At the upper levels of society the rushes were changed frequently, and herbs and flowers were mixed with them to keep them sweet, but at the lower end, new rushes were simply thrown on top of the foetid mess that had become of the previous ones. In the better houses it was also the custom to honour guests by putting down new rushes; 'Is the supper ready, the house trimm'd, rushes strew'd, cobwebs swept?' asks Grumio in Act IV, scene 1 of Shakespeare's *Taming of the Shrew*, and many other dramatists and poets of the time have referred to the practice. Queen Elizabeth I was probably the last monarch to have her palaces regularly strewn with rushes, but in other circles rush floors could still be found in some areas in the nineteenth century.

Churches were also regularly strewn with rushes. In early modern times, there were no pews and the congregation stood, or knelt, on the floor for the whole service. In unheated churches with earth or stone floors, this could be a serious trial, and a layer of rushes could make all the difference. Provision of rushes was normally the responsibility of the churchwardens, and they were chargeable to the parish, so payments appear regularly in early parish accounts. It was quite common also for devout parishioners to bequeath money to pay for the rushes, or to leave parcels of land from which the rushes could be cut annually.

As churches gradually acquired decent floors, rushes became superfluous and in most cases simply faded from the local scene, but the speed at which these changes took place varied widely from parish to parish. In Lancashire alone, for example, Kirkham church was flagged in 1634, but Saddleworth was not paved until 1826, and the floor of Pilling church was covered with rushes until about 1868. By the nineteenth century, however, rushes on church floors were seen by many as decidedly unhygienic and unbelievably antiquated.

As often happens with church-based events, the annual rush-strewing took on a celebratory aspect, giving a devotional spin to a practical occasion, and bringing the rushes to the church, or 'rush-bearing', became a major festival in which the whole community could join. Again there was wide variety within the custom, but two relatively distinct ways of rush-bearing developed. In Cheshire and Lancashire, the rushes were brought with much celebration on highly decorated carts during the village wakes, accompanied by drummers, musicians, and morris dancers, as in the following memory from Lancashire in the 1830s:

> I remember going to stay at Radcliffe to see the rush-bearing . . . We stood out-of-doors to watch the procession coming up the road. The morris-dancers came along dancing, both men and women, and I think there was a clown. They were decked up with ribbons and things; the men had ribbons flying from their caps or hats and their shoulders. The cart (or I think it was a waggon) came after them. On the driving-seat, as I may call it, sat a man and a woman, Robin Hood and Maid Marian, in a green bower arching over their heads. Behind and above this was a tall erection, with straight sides and a pointed gable-ended top, all made of rushes, and against the flat front of it were hung large silver spoons and tankards, shining.

These rush-cart celebrations had taken shape by at least the 1720s, and had a carnival atmosphere. But in other places, the normal rush-bearing festival was a more controlled and dignified religious procession in which women and children took a prominent part, carrying flowers, token rushes, and symbolic devices in various shapes, such as crosses, harps, and crowns; it is this method of rush-bearing that has survived at places like Grasmere in Cumbria (*see* **5 August: Grasmere Rush-Bearing**). This form of celebration is probably nearer to the original than

Rush-bearing at Grasmere, 1985

the noisy extrovert festivities of the rush-carts, and James I's *Book of Sports* (1618), for example, which laid out the sports that were permissible on Sundays (*see* p. 262), specifically names rush-carrying as a female custom:

> And that women shall have leave to carry rushes to the church for the decoring of it, according to their old custom.

Similarly, a description of Grasmere in the eighteenth century:

> About the latter end of September, a number of young women and girls (generally the whole parish) go together to the tops of the hills to gather rushes. These they carry to the church, headed by one of the smartest girls in the company. She who leads the procession is styled the Queen, and carries in her hand a large garland, and the rest usually have nosegays. The Queen then goes and places her garland upon the pulpit, where it remains till after next Sunday, the rest then strew their rushes upon the bottom of the pews, and at the church door they are met by a fiddler, who plays before them to the public house, where the evening is spent in all kinds of rustic merriment.

This evidence also demonstrates that it is somewhat simplistic to believe that the routine practice of replacing the rushes on a church floor suddenly became a symbolic ritual once the practical necessity had disappeared. It is clear that the rush-bearing had taken on a range of festival trappings at many churches long before their new flooring made them obsolete. At Grasmere again, where the floor was paved in 1840, a visitor noted in 1818 that:

. . . every part of the church crammed with all sorts of tawdry and ridiculous things stuck upon sticks, hoops, and crosses, and made to stand upright. These sticks were . . . covered with coloured paper, red, green and yellow, flowers of all sorts.

Some further questions still remain, such as why the major rush-cart festival developed in such a restricted area and, indeed, how the transformation from practical to festive actually took place. Some have assumed that the change was planned by the Church authorities, as in an article in *Country Home* magazine in June 1909:

In their wisdom, clergymen and churchwardens turned a matter of necessity into a religious festival, and thus won the interest and co-operation of the laity, which likes to have a prosaic duty glorified into something higher and more attractive.

But in her analysis of rush-carts and wakes published in 1982, Theresa Buckland rightly stresses the community's involvement in the rush-bearing celebrations – the collection of money from the local gentry, the loan of silver items to decorate the cart, and the hours spent embroidering sheets, sewing on ribbons, and constructing 'bearings' to carry – and implies that this was a relatively secularized custom that had been grafted on to a religious base.

Children's rush-bearing processions survive at five Cumbrian villages, and the rush-carts have been revived in recent years at several places, including Saddleworth and Sowerby Bridge.

See also **Whit Sunday: St Mary Redcliffe Rush Sunday**, p. 195; **29 June: Warcop Rush-Bearing**; **First Saturday in July: Ambleside Rush-Bearing**; **First Saturday in July: Great Musgrave Rush-Bearing**; **5 August: Grasmere Rush-Bearing**; **24 August: St Bartholomew's Day**; **29 September: Urswick Rush-Bearing**.

For many years the Medway fisheries were in decline, but recent initiatives on conservation and water quality are showing results and fish stocks are improving rapidly. Unlike most of the courts that have survived from medieval times, the Admiralty Court still has a genuine function and real teeth: Medway Council and the Rochester Oyster and Floating Fishery continue to take action against poachers and unlawful fishing, and in 2003 they successfully prosecuted an Isle of Sheppey fisherman for encroaching on their stretch of the river.

*

SUNDAY IN EARLY JULY

Oxenhope Straw Race

The Oxenhope Straw Race is an excellent example of how a small fund-raising idea, hatched by individuals, can grow into a major community event. The Pennine village of Oxenhope, near Keighley, West Yorkshire, hosts an annual race that started with a few friends in 1975 but now attracts hundreds of contestants from all over the country, and has so far raised over £250,000 for local charities. Each team, of at least two people, has to follow a prescribed route of about two and a half miles around the village, taking in five pubs, carrying a bale of straw, and drinking a pint of beer at each pub. Serious athletes take part and try to get round in record time, but dozens of other teams also enter, often dressed in the most bizarre costumes imaginable: on skis, wearing underwater flippers, as a Chinese dragon, pushing prams, hospital beds, and so on. There is a prize for the best costume, and for various categories of participant, and the village caters for the huge influx of people by putting up marquees and providing bands, dances, and numerous other family activities.

*

7 JULY

Bodmin Riding

This day marks the translation of the relics of Thomas Becket (1118–70), Archbishop of Canterbury, to a new shrine in 1220. Thomas was famous for his long-running and bitter dispute with Henry II over the respective powers of Church and State, but is mostly remembered for his brutal murder in Canterbury Cathedral. Although he was well known enough across Europe during his life, his death brought him extreme celebrity, and numerous stories of miracles were soon in circulation, resulting in his canonization in 1173. His major feast day was celebrated on the day of his death, 29 December.

A well-known event took place on or near Thomas's feast day on 7 July, in Cornwall. Named the 'Bodmin Riding', it involved residents taking to the streets and processing around the town and into the countryside, and then gathering for sports and other entertainments. The earliest documentary evidence to anything called a 'riding' is found in the parish church rebuilding accounts of 1469–72. These accounts include details of money 'received of the stewards of the Riding Guilds', and list five such guilds – St Loy's, St Petroc's, St John's, St Anyan's, and St Martin's. There are indications elsewhere in the accounts that each guild was associated with a particular trade – smiths, skinners and glovers, shoemakers, and so on. No further details are given in these early accounts, but a later description is provided by a letter written by W. R. Gilbert of Bodmin Priory in July 1812, who claimed to have taken part within the previous twenty or thirty years:

> On Monday, a grand procession of the principal inhabitants, formed into classes with the emblems of their trades and professions, took place, preceded by music, drums, etc., and two men, one with a garland, the other a pole ornamented with flowers, ribbons, etc. etc. which they had previously deposited at the Priory.

Other descriptions vary considerably in detail, and although most writers have assumed that this later celebration was a direct survival of the medieval custom, there is a degree of confusion and misinformation in the documentary evidence, usefully gathered together by Pat Munn in her book *Bodmin Riding* (1975), that requires some careful historical interpretation – particularly as the word 'riding' can be interpreted in a number of ways, relating to several types of event that are all linked together by the idea of processing or parading, but not necessarily (although usually) on horseback. The pre-Reformation religious guilds

often called their annual procession around the parish, on which they carried images of their patron saint and other symbols, their 'riding' (*see* **23 April: St George's Day** for the example of the Riding of St George). Trade guilds, which were often closely connected to the Church, could also call their procession a 'riding', and in the civic sphere the annual procession by a town corporation, often at the investiture of a new mayor, could similarly be so named. A riding could also refer to the custom of 'beating the bounds' (*see* **Rogationtide**, p. 176), as in the 'common ridings' of some Scottish towns, and, last but not least, it could mean the parading of a particular effigy or character, such as the Riding of the Black Knight at Ashton-under-Lyne (*see* **Easter Monday**, p. 124).

It is not surprising that the earliest evidence of the Bodmin Riding reveals that trade guilds were involved in raising money for a church rebuilding fund, as support of the Church was one of the main reasons for the guilds' existence, and nor is it unusual that this was organized on a trade-by-trade basis; however, these religious guild-ridings should have disappeared with the Reformation, when they were expressly banned. The carrying of a garland in Gilbert's account is also worthy of note, although other descriptions simply mention that flowers were gathered. This garland brings Bodmin in line with another unexplained custom, which took place on May Day at Charlton-on-Otmoor in Oxfordshire, where a greenery-clad 'garland' was carried around the parish to principal houses (*see* **1 May: Charlton-on-Otmoor Garland**). Garlands on May Day were not unusual, but there is no evidence that the Bodmin Riding ever took place at that time of year. Indeed, it is not clear why the event took place on 7 July, apart from the reason that good weather could generally be expected on that day. The earliest account giving a firm dating of the custom is from 1700 – 'the two Mondays right after St. Becket's Day' – which is well before the confusion of the calendar change of 1752. However, it has also been suggested that the saint King Edgar was far more important to Bodmin than Thomas Becket, and his feast day is 8 July.

The exact relationship between the guild ridings of the fifteenth century and the 'ridings' of the nineteenth century at Bodmin has still to be determined, but it is most unlikely that a thinly disguised religious

Rose Queens

On 1 April 1989, the *Independent Magazine* recorded the following:

> *A vicar in Bury, Lancashire, has declared all-out war on superstition. The Rev. Ben Turner is the new Anglican incumbent of the Bury parish church, St. Stephen's. Until this year the local Rose Queen has been crowned in the church every May. The honour goes to the girl who has attended Sunday School most often. But it will not happen this year unless Mr. Turner relents. The Rose Queen is a heathen activity, he maintains, 'It is firmly rooted in pagan fertility rites, like dancing round a maypole . . . To continue such a practice, outwardly harmless and entertaining as it may be, shows poor theological understanding.'*

Unfortunately, the Revd Turner had fallen rather publicly into the trap of believing that all traditional customs must be extremely old, and are therefore linked to pagan activities. The Rose Queen was in fact a late Victorian invention encouraged, and perhaps even created, by clergy and respectable church-goers as a piece of safe and controlled pageantry, and it has continued largely in the same vein ever since.

Like the May Queen on which she is modelled, the Rose Queen is nearly always associated with other events, such as local fêtes, pageants, carnivals, and feasts, but unlike her predecessor, the Rose Queen seems to be a decidedly regional custom. It is very common across Cheshire and Lancashire, and some can be found over the border in Wales, but there are few elsewhere. It is probably no accident that these are the places where the 'Wakes Week' (*see* **Fairs, Feasts, Wakes, and Revels**, p. 249) is more important in the festival year than May Day, and it is likely that the Rose Queen tradition developed simply because it was the wrong time of year for a 'May' Queen. However, beyond the name, there is no discernible difference between the two, and sometimes they exist side by side.

The Rose Queen's main function is to act as a focal point (albeit a relatively inactive one) in the procession or fête to which she is linked, and in some cases to act as a temporary minor celebrity, gracing other local events with her presence during the year of her reign. She also has a more minor role the following year in the crowning of her successor. Most Rose Queens considered it a real honour to be chosen, and remember with pleasure the year they were crowned. Gatherings of 'past queens' in parades are always popular.

procession could have survived both the Reformation and the Puritan revolution of the seventeenth century. If there is a connection at all, it is more likely to have been one of revival than survival. The custom was certainly revived again in 1974, and the historical Riding is now used by local enthusiasts in the town as the basis of a popular 'medieval' festival, which is held each year in early July, organized by the Bodmin Riding and Heritage Committee.

*

10 JULY

An example of how the practices of the local farming year could dictate a rural community's calendar is provided by Northumbrian writer Hastings Neville, writing of the late nineteenth century:

Twice a year, 'Cheviot's mountain lone' is enlivened with a great gathering of the hill shepherds, and the bleating of many sheep. One meeting takes place on the very top of Cheviot on the 10th of July, the other on 10th November, lower down near the foot of the mountain. There are generally about 30 to 40 shepherds present, and sometimes 400 sheep to be exchanged. The day begins with sports, for our hill shepherd is a great lover of sport. The real purpose, however, of these meetings is to restore lost sheep to their proper owners. Many a stray sheep gets far away from its proper feeding ground to another where it does not belong, and these are looked after by each shepherd until the half-yearly exchange takes place.

*

Several local Rose Queen traditions have a similar foundation story, based on the spontaneous actions of a group of local girls whose idea was enthusiastically taken up by others, and although this may be true in some cases, it is more likely that the local fête committees made the first decision to have a Rose Queen, and the story has drifted from one location to another. *Lancashire Lore* (1971), which features contributions from the various Women's Institutes in the county, provides a prime example:

The crowning of a Rose Queen on field day is not a very old custom at Wrea Green [Lancashire]. Apparently, rather more than forty years ago, a group of young girls of the village having seen queens walk in procession in neighbouring towns, decided to have a queen of their own. They made their own dresses and had a lace curtain as a train. Then, dressed in their finery, they chose their queen and proceeded to walk round the Green. They carried a banner with 'Dr. Barnardo's Homes' written across it, for they were, in fact, collecting for that charity. A butcher from Ansdell watched them and was so thrilled with what he saw that he gave them half-a-crown. They then had their crowning ceremony in somebody's garden, followed by tea on the front lawn. The second-year children got a

length of cloth from the mill at Kirkham for their train. After that the field day committee incorporated the crowning of a Rose Queen into the field day festivities.

Many Rose Queen ceremonies were founded between the 1920s and 1950s, and many of these did not last very long, but a search of the Internet reveals that dozens of Rose Queens are still crowned each year. However, if the following report from the *This Is Lancashire* website (30 May 2000) is indicative of a general trend, their days may be numbered:

An unprecedented royal procession will be parading through the streets of Darcy Lever to mark the end of an era at a Bolton church. More than thirty 'de-throned' queens of the past will join the colourful parade to commemorate the last coronation at St. Stephen's and All Martyrs Church. The Rose Queen tradition has graced the church for more than half a century. But it comes to an end this year because of a lack of teenagers putting themselves forward for the honour. Where once teenage girls fought to be crowned Rose Queen, they no longer see the 'street cred' in the position, refusing to wear the frilly dresses.

See also **1 May: May Queens**.

SECOND WEDNESDAY IN JULY

Pretty Maid's Charity

Not all charities date from the distant past. In the North Devon town of Holsworthy, the Revd Thomas Meyrick founded what has become known as the Pretty Maid's Charity when he died in 1841 (Meyrick's brother, Owen, was Rector of Holsworthy at the time, which explains the charity's location). Thomas left money for government stock that would yield an annual interest of £3 10s, and of this, £2 10s was to be given to 'a young single woman resident in the parish being under 30 years of age, and generally esteemed by the young as the most deserving and most handsome, and most noted for her qualities and attendance at church'. He thought that by this example, 'rulers would learn that subjects are better directed and led by harmless amusement and judicious reward than by fear of punishment'. The other pound was to go to a spinster over sixty years old who had similar qualities, but this part of the charity has now been dropped and the whole amount is given to the young person. The identity of the recipient is kept secret until she walks out of St Peter's church door at twelve o'clock on the second Wednesday in July, the first day of the local fair, which she visits in her new official capacity.

*

SECOND/THIRD SATURDAY IN JULY

Durham Miners' Gala

Durham Miners' Gala, usually held on the second or third Saturday in July, was the biggest trade union gathering in Europe in its heyday, and even today is an impressive event. The Durham Gala was first held in 1871, organized by the Durham Miners' Association, and grew to outshine all other local galas in the North-East, soon becoming known as 'The Big Meeting'. The programme usually involves a grand procession of union lodges, each carrying their huge colourful banners and accompanied by brass bands, which march out to the city's racecourse. Speeches are then made by visiting unionists and politicians. The afternoon includes a large funfair and a variety of other entertainments, together with a memorial service at the cathedral. The procession then re-forms and marches back through the streets of the city.

The day has always been a major demonstration of worker solidarity and union pride, mixed with all the fun of a family summer outing. The Gala suffered as a result of the gradual wasting away of the coal-mining industry in the late twentieth century, and especially the rapid closure of pits in the 1990s, but in recent years a revival has begun, with the active help of trade unions in other industries. Saturday, 10 July 2004 saw the 120th Gala, and there is every sign that it will continue for many years to come.

*

15 JULY

St Swithun's Day

Swithun (or Swithin) was Bishop of Winchester in the ninth century, and a major player in the religious and political life of Wessex at a time when it was becoming the dominant force in the emergence of England as a nation. He died in 862 and would hardly have been remembered in the popular mind had it not been for the miracles that reportedly occurred when his remains were moved on 15 July 971. According to legend, he

had requested to be buried in the churchyard, but his remains were later brought into the church, as a matter of respect. Among other marvellous things that then occurred, it rained so hard for forty days that those in authority moved him outside again; hence the only fact that most people know about St Swithun's Day is the weather prediction:

> St Swithin's day, if thou dost rain,
> For forty days it will remain;
> St Swithin's day, if thou be fair,
> For forty days 'twill rain nae mair.

This idea was already current in the early fourteenth century, and has been proverbial ever since.

This connection between the saint and rain engendered other beliefs, including the idea commonly held all over the country till at least the early twentieth century that the day was crucial to the apple crop. In Warwickshire, folklorists A. R. Wright and T. E. Lones recorded that:

> You won't have the jam made till the apples are christened . . . We never eat or cut apples until St. Swithin has christened them.

Swithun was popular enough in medieval times for many ancient churches to have been dedicated to him, and in these parishes his day will have been marked with celebrations or other events. At Old Weston in Huntingdonshire, for example, a remnant of the annual hay-strewing (*see* **Rush-Bearing**, p. 238) on his day lasted well into the twentieth century. In the Roman Church, the day of his death, 2 July, was deemed his feast day, but in England it is 15 July.

*

16 JULY

Anne Askew Day

In the war that raged between Catholic and Protestant factions in Britain and elsewhere in the sixteenth century, both sides told and retold stories of their own martyrs, as evidence that they were in the right and their opponents in the wrong. Anne Askew, Protestant martyr, was born *c*.1520, and took on the Catholic establishment by daring to dispute publicly with Lincoln

The Spanish Armada (as portrayed in 1739), an enduring symbol for patriotic English people, celebrated on 19 July

Cathedral clergy. She was burnt at the stake for heresy in London in 1546, aged only twenty-five. Her case became a major *cause célèbre* in the growing Protestant agitation, and accounts of her 'examination' were published and widely read. She is commemorated by a service at Lincoln Cathedral every 16 July.

*

19 JULY

Armada Day

The defeat of the Spanish Armada in July and August 1588 is seen as one of the seminal events in the history of England, and is thus imbued with a considerable weight of nationalist, religious, military, and romantic symbolism that has outlasted its real historical significance. This is not to suggest that the threat of invasion was not very real at the time, but its memory, like that of the Gunpowder Plot of 1605, served a much wider purpose in national consciousness and rhetoric for a long time after the actual event.

The huge Spanish fleet sailed from Lisbon on 29 May 1588, planning to liaise with an army raised in Flanders by the Duke of Parma to invade and occupy England. The plan had been under discussion for several years, and all of Europe (including England) knew that it would soon be carried out. Despite Philip II's overtly religious rhetoric, which described the affair as a crusade to bring England back into the Catholic fold, backed by the Pope's cautious promise of financial aid if the campaign was successful, Philip clearly had ambitious political motives as well. He himself had a claim on the English throne, and there was a great deal for Spain to gain in terms of international influence, military supremacy, and trade. Both sides claimed that God was on their side, and when it was later discovered that an unseasonable storm had struck the decisive stroke against the Spanish, the victory was hailed in England, and other Protestant countries, as divine vindication of the Protestant religion. For centuries afterwards, the defeat of the Spanish Armada was used as a symbol to underpin Britain's claim to greatness.

News of the defeat was slow to circulate, and it was weeks before its decisive nature was fully realized by the English court. Nor was a straggling sea campaign conducive to engendering an official 'Armada Day', and celebrations in 1588 and ensuing years tended to be combined with the festivities that commemorated the accession of Elizabeth I on 19 November, which already had more than their fair share of patriotic and religious symbolism.

Any tributes that have sprung up since, such as those at Plymouth, where most of the English fleet was stationed to await the Armada's arrival, have usually settled on 19 July, as it was on this day that the Armada arrived off the Lizard and the English knew for sure that an invasion attempt was imminent. However, any time in late July would be equally appropriate.

Little Edith's Treat

Elizabeth Croft, a parishioner of Piddinghoe in East Sussex, left a bequest that funded annual gifts of coal, clothes, and money to the local poor, and money to respectable young people, in order to commemorate the lives of her husband, Hugh (d. 1866), and her son Gilmore (d. 1869). She also sought to perpetuate in the following way the memory of her only granddaughter, Edith, who was born on 19 July 1868 and died in October the same year:

> The interest arising from £100 of the said stock to be known as 'Little Edith's Treat' to be expended on the 19th of July in each year, in a treat to the children of the National School of the said Parish and in rewards, more especially to the girls who are skilled in plain needlework and to the boys and girls who are neat in their dress, clean in their habits, and regular in attendance at church and school.

These treats followed a regular pattern. On the afternoon of Edith's birthday (or the nearest school day), the schoolchildren were told the story of Little Edith and the bequest, and were then taken to the Hoe (the village open space) for games, races, and a splendid tea. The vicar usually threw a handful of coins into the air for the children to scramble for, and there were prizes and gifts distributed back at the school. After the local school closed in 1952, the treats became intermittent and were based around the Sunday school while it was in operation, sometimes taking the form of children's outings rather than treats. In 2000, some of the money

was used to provide a children's Christmas party. The fund is still active, and admirably fulfils the spirit of the original endowment even if actual circumstances have necessitated changes.

See also **Doles**, p. 87.

*

20 JULY

St Margaret's Day

Despite the fact that a historical Margaret of Antioch almost certainly never existed, St Margaret was extremely popular in the Middle Ages, and well over 200 ancient churches in England were dedicated to her. Her legend claims that she was the daughter of a pagan priest who threw her out of the house once she became a Christian, so she became a shepherdess. After converting numerous people to Christianity and stoutly refusing marriage, she underwent various tortures and was swallowed by a dragon, emerging unscathed when it burst asunder.

It was said that if pregnant women invoked her name, they would be spared the pain of childbirth, which naturally made her popular. Nevertheless, she does not seem to have had a lasting traditional impact, and no major festivals, customs, or superstitions are reported for her day, although it must have had local significance in parishes where the church was named after her.

In weather-lore, St Margaret's Day was often expected to be wet; if it was, it was termed 'Margaret's flood', or, somewhat confusingly, it was said that St Mary Magdalene (whose feast day was on 22 July) was washing her handkerchief to go to her cousin St James's Fair (25 July).

*

25 JULY

St Christopher's Day

The only thing that is known of Christopher is that he was martyred in the third century. His name means 'bearer of Christ', which explains the origin of the immensely popular story of his being instructed to help travellers across a river, and carrying the Christ child. As the patron saint of travellers, his popularity increased tenfold with the rise of mass transportation and tourism in the nineteenth and twentieth centuries, and the immediately recognizable emblem of a giant carrying a child can be found in countless cars, trains, and planes the Christian world over.

Less well known in modern times is the idea that St Christopher protected believers against sudden death, recorded by Samuel Rudder in his *New History of Gloucestershire* (1779):

> There was a colossal figure of St. Christopher painted against the wall of Bibury church, in pursuance of an opinion that prevailed in the ages of ignorance and superstition, that whosoever had seen the image of that saint, should not die of sudden or accidental death . . . Accordingly, this figure was opposite to the entrance at the south door of the church; but it hath lately been covered with whitewash, and nothing remains to be seen but the two following lines [in Latin, which translates as]

> Saint Christopher's fair figure who shall view
> Faintness nor feebleness that day shall rue.

Numerous other churches had similar images, but only a few survived the Reformation.

St James's Day

As befits his position as one of the Apostles, James the Great (martyred AD 44) was a very popular saint in England, with 400 ancient churches bearing his name. The idea that James preached in Spain before his death has now been exploded, but the claim that he is buried at Compostela made it Spain's most popular shrine and one of the best known in Europe, from the twelfth century onwards. So powerful was the connection between the saint and his shrine that his emblems became the hat and scallop shell associated with Spanish pilgrims.

In England, there are occasional printed references to apple trees being blessed on St James's Day, although this is more often said of St Swithun's Day (*see* **15 July**). The well-known proverb 'He who eats oysters on St James's Day will not want for money' is slightly puzzling because the English oyster season traditionally started on 4 August, but the proverb may be referring to Old St

James's Day (*see* **5 August: James I**). For another possible connection between St James and oysters, *see* **Early August: Grottoes**.

Ebernoe Horn Fair

This sparsely populated West Sussex village, about four miles from Petworth, is famous for its fair, which is more like a village fête, except that a whole sheep is roasted and eaten during the day. While the sheep is roasting, a cricket match is played between local teams, and the player on the winning side who scores the most runs is presented with the sheep's horns. A special Horn Fair song is sung during the presentation of the horns.

The origin of the fair is unknown. The only concrete date in its history is 1864, when, according to the local press, it was revived after a long lapse, but there is no evidence that it existed before that time. The Horn Fair song was 'discovered' in a nearby village in the early 1950s and enthusiastically taken up by the fair's organizers, but again there is no evidence that it was originally connected with Ebernoe, as its text contains no local allusions and the song is found elsewhere in the country. Nevertheless, after fifty years of singing it, the people of Ebernoe have made it their own. Versions vary, but the following was noted by Mervyn Plunkett from George Tompsett, of Cuckfield, Sussex, in the mid 1950s, with some gaps in his text filled from a version collected in Surrey by Ralph Vaughan Williams:

> As I was a walking one morning so fair
> So fresh was the lilies and cold blew the air
> I spied a fair damsel all on her grey mare
> And she was a-riding all unto Horn Fair.
> I asked this fair maid if I should ride by her side
> Oh no said this damsel my mammy would chide
> And besides my old daddy will beat me full sore
> He'll never let me ride on his grey mare no more.
> You charming fair creature why do you say so
> I can hear by your talk you are for a game of play
> I can hear by your talk you're for a game of play
> And if you don't make haste you won't get there today.
> If you would go unto Horn Fair you must walk on your
>   way
> I will not let you ride on my grey mare today
> You will rumple my muslin and uncurl my hair

Presentation of the sheep's horns at Ebernoe Horn Fair, Sussex, 1995

And leave me alone all unto Horn Fair.
You charming fair creature how can you say no
With you I intend to Horn Fair to go
We will join the best of company when we do get there
With horns on our heads as fine as our hair.
There's hook-d horns and crooked horns and horns of
*   every kind*
Like jolly cockle shells all in a row.

John Knill Charity

John Knill was a man apparently determined to be remembered. A St Ives worthy, customs and excise man for the district, and mayor in 1767, he first built a strange fifty-foot pyramid (called Knill's Steeple) on top of Worvas Hill to serve as his monument when he died, which also provided a useful landmark for ships off the Cornish coast. He then set up a detailed list of instructions about the celebrations that were to take place at his Steeple: little girls in white were to dance for at least fifteen minutes and then sing the Old Hundredth psalm, two widows were to oversee the proceedings, and prizes were to be given to the best pilchard packers, knitter of fishing nets, and apprentices. The first celebrations took place in 1801 while he was still alive, and he left money in trust for their continuation. Ironically, Knill is buried in London rather than on his hilltop, but the custom still takes place every five years, led by the current mayor and town officials, and little girls still dance around the monument as part of the celebrations. Naturally enough, some changes have had to be made, but on the whole the event remembers Knill as he wished. An early account of the proceedings, dated 1826, was published in William Hone's *Every-Day Book* (1827).

See also **Doles**, p. 87.

Whitstable Oyster Festival

Whitstable, a small town gathered around its harbour on the eastern coast of Kent, holds an annual nine-day festival in honour of its most famous product and staple of the local economy, the Whitstable native oyster. The festival usually starts on the Saturday nearest to 25 July, as the trade claims St James as its patron saint. The local oyster fishery was already an established trade in Norman times, but the grounds were leased from the Crown until 1793, when local people formed the Whitstable Oyster Company to buy them for themselves.

The festival is a modern version of the Whitstable

Continues on page 252 >

Fairs, Feasts, Wakes, and Revels

The English calendar is littered with local festive gatherings throughout the spring, summer, and autumn, which are almost indistinguishable from each other but have a bewildering variety of names – fairs, feasts, fêtes, wakes, revels, ales, treats, mops, and so on. In many cases, these names contain clues about the origins of the particular event, but this cannot be taken for granted because over time the words gradually came to mean simply 'annual festive gathering' and distinctions became blurred. Theoretically, the only one with a strict meaning is 'fair'. An official fair could only be granted by royal charter, which not only gave permission for the gathering to be held, but also assigned an 'owner' who possessed the very lucrative right to collect the tolls, dues, and fines generated by the event. The economic and social impact of a fair was greatly increased by the fact that while it was in operation all trading in the area fell under the jurisdiction of the owner, who in effect took over nearly all local power for the duration. The fair-owner even held his or her own court to try cases and settle disputes arising from the fair.

The economic value of fair-ownership was well understood in medieval times, and charters were often granted to religious and charitable institutions, as a way of giving them long-term funding. But as time went on, this situation almost inevitably led to power struggles with town or parish authorities who naturally resented being pushed aside every year at fair time.

Given that different rules applied while a fair was in operation, it was essential that everyone knew exactly when the fair opened and closed. Public ceremonies, such as the procession of worthies to the site, and the reading aloud of the charter, were therefore carried out, and a symbol was often hoisted aloft, such as the giant gloves at Honiton and Chester, which remained on show while the fair was in operation. Many fairs acquired quaint local names, either named after a saint, such as Barnaby Fair, or after some leading feature, such as gooseberry fair, ram fair, walnut fair, horn fair, pudding-pie fair, and pack Monday fair.

The architects of the calendar change of 1752 fully realized that fairs needed to be carefully handled, especially in cases where the timing of the fair was closely related to a particular produce or natural feature. It was therefore decreed that fairs should retain their place in the natural year by changing their nominal date. Unfortunately, this caused a good deal of confusion, and while some fairs immediately changed their date, others did not, and some even vacillated between the two. It took several years for a regular pattern to be established. By the nineteenth century, however, the trading basis for most fairs had been eroded to such an extent that they had outlived their commercial usefulness, and they continued to exist mainly as pleasure fairs. Some were inconveniently located in the crowded streets of a growing town or on prime building land, and they were increasingly seen as anachronistic, and an affront to local propriety and civic pride. Sometimes the possession of a royal charter made it difficult for local authorities to suppress them, and so the Fairs Act (1871) came into force, to remedy the situation:

Whereas certain of the fairs held in England and Wales are unnecessary, are the cause of grievous immorality, and are very injurious to the inhabitants of the towns in which such fairs are held, and it is therefore expedient to make provision to facilitate the abolition of such fairs.

Local authorities all over the country took the opportunity to close fairs down for good. Others were moved to more convenient open sites on the edge of town, and a stricter control of those that remained was introduced.

Feasts, on the other hand, were originally associated with the local church, and either occurred on the feast day of the saint to which the church was dedicated, or were celebrated on the anniversary of its consecration. Originally, they were therefore occasions of both piety and celebration and were at first held in the church and churchyard, but as the fun started to take precedence the ecclesiastical authorities tried to separate them from the holy ground by decreeing that they must be held elsewhere in the community. In many villages, the feast was the most enjoyable day of the year, but after the Reformation the link with saints, even if tenuous, became embarrassing, as any appearance of the veneration of saints could be construed as continuing outmoded popish habits. Henry VIII tried to bring feasts under control by decreeing that they were to be held on a Sunday in October, but this was widely ignored, and they continued to be held on dates to suit the community concerned.

Wakes were similarly linked to the church. Before the Reformation, the celebration of any major religious festival began the evening before, when the devout sat up in the church to watch through the night. The *Oxford English Dictionary* defines this sense of 'wake' as 'abstinence from sleep, watching, practised as a religious observance . . . a night spent in devout watching (on the eve of a festival . . .)'. Local festivals right across the Midlands and the north of the country were called 'wakes', and this same word was adopted in the early nineteenth century in newly industrialized towns when factory owners found it convenient to give all their workers time off at the same time. 'The Wakes' or 'Wakes Week' soon became generic terms for this annual holiday, even when it later began to last a fortnight.

Ales were organized specifically to raise money, usually for the church, but sometimes for other purposes (*see* **Church Ales**, p. 194).

Revel is the dialect word for an annual gathering in the south-west of the country, and this meaning of the word is recorded from the fourteenth century.

In our mobile modern world, where entertainment and company are available day and night, it is difficult to comprehend the importance of these gatherings in the lives of working people before the mid twentieth century. This was especially true of rural workers, whose opportunities for socializing were severely restricted by long hours and geographical isolation. When an opportunity did arise, they grasped it enthu-siastically, and perhaps uncritically. As late as 1909, Hastings Neville could say in his affectionate account of his fellow rural Northumbrians:

> They love a crowd. A crowd is their idea of success, whether the object be a bazaar, a missionary meeting, or a service in church or chapel. If they go away saying, 'What a people there was there!', you may know that your audience is satisfied.

Annual feasts and fairs were not simply seen as opportunities for time off work but also as chances for entertainment, shopping, lots of food and drink, meeting old friends, or old enemies, and as a rare opportunity to mingle with the opposite sex. The following example was printed in the journal *Folk-Lore* in 1912:

> A farmer's wife from Offord Cluny has given me the following information . . . The great day of the village year is Feast Sunday, the last Sunday in June, 'when all friends meet' and girls in service take a holiday. Scarce a house in the village but has been 'done up', papered or painted to be ready for the Feast. Plum puddings are made, and fillets of pork prepared. About two weeks beforehand part of the hind leg is put in salt water; these 'fillets' are stuffed and boiled, and everyone reckons to have new potatoes and green peas for the Feast. Things are very backward if they can't have them ready by Feast Sunday . . . On Feast Monday stalls are set up down the village street, and there is dancing in the evening . . . On Feast Tuesday the Sunday School children have their treat.

The standard fare of all these events was food and drink, music and dancing, stalls and sideshows, and sports and games, but another popular feature was a procession, and in later times they sometimes included carnivals, pageants, and May Queens. Memories of these times always loom large in the reminiscences of those who grew up before the First World War, as in the following account from Mrs Elie Hilda Williams, born in 1891, who was remembering Hay-on-Wye:

> For the children, at May Fair time, they had the

*ha'penny horses: that was a roundabout with
little horses and cockerels, and the man turned the
handle in the middle; that was for the tinies, and
then you graduated to the 'penny horses', and they
were bigger. Then there were coconut shies, and
boxing booths, and sideshows of all kinds: there
were always 'Fat Lady' shows if I remember rightly.*

And in 1966, a Yorkshire woman recalled:

*Our village church had a feast day in July when
the Sunday School scholars, followed by a large
congregation, walked behind the huge banner with
a picture of the Good Shepherd embroidered on it.
The village brass band led us to different points in
the village where hymns were sung. We always had
a new frock for this, the biggest day in our calendar.
Afterwards there was a tea in the Sunday School.*

However, the children may not have noticed everything that was happening in the adult world around
them. Nineteen-year-old George Dew, from Lower
Heyford in Oxfordshire, recorded in his diary on
Sunday, 27 August 1865:

*Heyford Feast – The drunkenness of this day has
been most abominable. Very few people at church;
but public houses full. It would be no loss if there
were no feasts.*

By all accounts, any of these events could have their
rough side, at least until Victorian reformers got
hold of them, but some had a particular reputation
for regular and almost ritualized fighting. There
seems to have been a particular liking for gatherings
on hills, which would often include fights between
different parishes (*see* **1 May: Fighting**, for examples).

More respectably, the rise of local friendly societies and mutual clubs in the nineteenth century
provided many communities with another opportunity for pleasure, in the form of the 'Club Feast'.
Members of these clubs were particularly fond of
ceremonial regalia and processions, which they took
very seriously. Arthur Wade, born in Rudston, East
Yorkshire, in 1900, remembered the Feast Days of
the Ancient Shepherds Friendly Society, in his young
days:

*Because you couldn't go in the Shepherds' proces-
sion on Club Feast Day without a staff and a sash
like these here. It was a green silk sash, with an
orange rosette or an orange and white one – there
was a few different kinds; and the officials used
to wear white sashes, wi' a white rosette . . . The
sashes went over one shoulder, and they fastened
wi' tapes; you'd be walking in twos, and one would
have it over one shoulder, and one over t'other, so
that they both slanted outwards – it looked better
that way. And if there was a lad, and he wanted to
walk wi' me, we had to change our sashes so they
both slanted out – you couldn't have 'em both
going one way. Then everybody would have a staff,
and that was green too . . . And we used to have a
very big banner, wi' Latin on it, and there'd be two
strong chaps carrying a pole at each end, and they
used to have white gloves on that carried 'em. And
they used to have two young lads to hold long tapes
from the banner, and when the wind got hold of
it, it used to nearly pull them kids off their feet,
because it was a terrible big banner.*

See also **Hiring Fairs**, p. 345.

Regatta, an annual gathering first recorded in the late eighteenth century, but is now a major spectacle that still manages to retain its local feel. It starts with the ceremonial landing of the first catch of the season, at Long Beach, followed by the 'oyster parade', which accompanies the horse-drawn cart that delivers the fresh oysters to restaurants and cafes in the town. The scene is then set for a week and a half of celebrations, including concerts, family events, and competitions, firework displays, workshops, Miss Whitstable and her entourage, sideshows, and demonstrations, many of which have a maritime theme, and all now organized by Canterbury City Council. The harbour is packed with boats of all kinds, many of which are historic or restored crafts, which gather for the 'Harbour Day'. One of the quieter moments is when a procession leaves St Peter's church for the 'blessing of the waters' service at Reeves Beach one evening during the festival.

See also **Late May: Blessing of the Sea**; **Early September: Colchester Oyster Fishery**; **20 October: Colchester Oyster Feast**.

*

26 JULY

Mace Monday

A mock-mayor ceremony formerly took place at Newbury, in Berkshire, on the first Monday after St Anne's Day, which apparently followed the normal pattern of such events (*see* **Mock Mayors and Courts**, p. 216). Mock mayors were usually associated with a particular public house – in this case the Bull and Dog, where a feast of bacon and beans was provided, and plenty to drink, as reported in William Hone's *Every-Day Book* (1827):

> In the course of the day a procession takes place. A cabbage is stuck on a pole and carried instead of a mace, accompanied by similar substitutes for the other emblems of civic dignity, and there is, of course, plenty of 'rough music'. A 'justice' is chosen at the same time, some other offices are filled up, and the day ends by all concerned getting comfortable 'how come ye so' [i.e. drunk].

This 'justice' was termed the Mayor of Bartlemas, and the day was called Mace Monday. It seems to have died out before the 1890s.

*

28 JULY

Old St Kenelm's Day

At Clent, in Worcestershire, the parish church is dedicated to St Kenelm, and presumably the local wake, or feast day, was formerly held on that saint's day (17 July), but slipped to 28 July following the introduction of the Gregorian calendar in 1752 (*see* p. xx). One bizarre feature of the festivities on this day, or on the Sunday following, was called 'crabbing the parson' and was reported by several writers as having taken place until the mid nineteenth century. In 1856, John Noake recorded:

> The custom of crabbing the parson was observed till lately at St. Kenelm's. It was the practice for the villagers and all who chose to arm themselves with crab apples on the wake Sunday, and as the parson approached the church the crabs were thrown at him, until he reached the church porch. The use of sticks and stones in place of crabs led to the suppression of the custom.

No sensible explanation for this custom has been put forward, and it is particularly unclear why the local clergy would put up with such behaviour, but the Clent custom was in fact far from unique. Almost exactly the same procedure was recorded in Victorian times at Hawkridge, Somerset, on Revel Sunday, the nearest Sunday to St Giles's Day (1 September), and at Mobberley, Cheshire, the Sunday after St Luke's Day (18 October). All that can be said is that this custom seems to be associated with the local saint's day rather than with a civic function such as mayor-making, which also attracted similar 'lawless' behaviour, such as throwing cabbage stalks at the officers of the new corporation (*see* **Lawless Hours and Days**, p. 303).

*

Doggett's badge, 1973

LATE JULY

Doggett's Coat and Badge Race

Thomas Doggett (*c.*1670–1721) was a popular actor, playwright, and theatre manager of his time, particularly celebrated for playing 'low comedy' parts. He was also a staunch Whig, and a particularly enthusiastic supporter of the new Hanoverian dynasty ushered in by the accession of George I in 1714. He inaugurated a boat race on the River Thames in the King's honour on the anniversary in 1715, which continues to this day. Doggett's political motives are quite clear, but another version of the race's origin was preferred by Dorothea Fisher OBE, born in 1890, who was steeped in river lore and so well known in the area that she was popularly called 'Mother Thames'. Her husband Billy had won the event in 1911, and the story she used to tell was reported in the *Guardian* in 1974:

Doggett was stranded on the wrong side of the river on a stormy night and the ferry wouldn't take him across. He was going to be late for the theatre. A young lighterman came to his rescue and rowed him over, thus earning gratitude and the first Doggett's coat and badge.

When Doggett died, he left money to the Fishmongers' Company to perpetuate the annual race, and it is still held over the same four-and-a-half-mile stretch of the Thames, from London Bridge to Chelsea.

Originally, the contestants had to row their ordinary wherries against the tide, which called for immense strength and stamina, and the race could take up to five hours. By the turn of the twentieth century, however, the decision had been made to row with the tide, and special racing skiffs were introduced in 1906; nowadays, the race takes about twenty-five minutes. There have been other minor changes: the coat is now red, rather than the original orange, and the race is held on a day in late July when the tide is right rather than the original 1 August. Holders of the coat and badge are expected to assist and officiate at future races and at ceremonial functions on the river.

Swan-Upping

Since its introduction to Britain in the thirteenth century, the swan has always been a royal bird. It could not be owned by anyone without express permission from the Crown – a right worth possessing when swans were a regular item on the banquet table. Permission to keep swans on the River Thames was granted to the worshipful Company of Vintners in 1473, and about the same time to the Dyers as well. These grants are still in force, and so any swans on the Thames belong to the sovereign or one of these two companies.

Once a year, in late July, the swan keepers for each of the companies meet the Royal Swan Keeper or Master, and together they journey down the river, from London Bridge to Henley, catching and examining around 600 birds. They mark the beaks of all the young birds they find – one nick for the Dyers, two for the Vintners – according to their parentage. Any brood of mixed parentage is split equally. The Queen's swans are left unmarked, on the principle that she owns *all* unmarked swans. This process, known as swan-upping,

Swan-upping (Benjamin Stone, 1906)

can take several days to complete, although in past times, when more birds were kept, it could take up to two weeks. The occasion is surrounded by a certain amount of colourful ceremony and pageantry as befits its royal purpose, but also calls for a great deal of skill and stamina.

*

JULY/AUGUST

Dog Days

Visited the old Merediths at the Bridge Gate. Mrs. Meredith said she was very ill. 'Tis the dog star,' she said, 'I shall not be better till Saturday when the dog days end. 'Tis an evil star.'

This entry in Francis Kilvert's *Diary* for 8 August 1878 refers to the 'dog days', the period in which the dog star rises coincidentally with the sun, which was believed to be the hottest, and therefore the most unwholesome, time of year. It was regarded as an evil time, when malign influences were abroad, dogs ran mad, and people became ill. The actual dates are difficult to pin down, as they can be calculated on the greater dog star (Sirius) or the lesser dog star (Procyon), and they differ considerably according to latitude. In ancient Rome, the days were calculated as falling between 3 July and 11 August, and many in the West keep to these dates, even if they are not correct for their own time or geographical position.

St Wilfrid Feast Procession

Wilfrid (c.633–709), Abbot of Ripon and Bishop of York, was one of the most influential figures in the early

English Church, and enjoyed a stormy relationship with sovereigns and fellow clergy, which resulted in two trips to Rome to gain the Pope's support. Wilfrid built Ripon's first church (St Peter's), in North Yorkshire, on the site of the present cathedral, which is now dedicated to him, and he founded numerous other churches and monasteries. His cult, which began soon after his death, was strongest at Ripon, and he is still very much part of the local scene. His feast day is 12 October, but his return from exile to the city at Lammas is celebrated by the people of Ripon on the Saturday before the first Monday in August. A man dressed as a bearded Bishop Wilfrid, in white robes and on a white horse, leads the procession of floats, bands, and morris dancers that ushers in the two weeks of celebration called the Wilfrid Feast. He is met at the cathedral door by the dean, the mayor, and the city council, and nominally presides over the feast. In her book on the customs of Yorkshire, published in 1989, Julia Smith reported that two feast delicacies bear the Saint's name: 'Wilfrid pies' – apple pies served with cheese, or with cheese cooked in them; and 'Wilfra tarts', which she describes as:

> *Shortcrust pastry base, but the filling consists of*
> *butter, ground almonds, sugar and grated rind of a*
> *lemon, together with breadcrumbs which*
> *have been soaked in hot milk, mixed together with a*
> *beaten egg.*

As Wilfrid was a popular local saint, his effigy would almost certainly have been carried through the streets on special occasions before the Reformation, and it is claimed that when effigies were banned, human representatives took their place. However, the notion that the custom at Ripon could have an unbroken lineage of over a thousand years is highly unlikely.

August

1

FIRST WEEK IN AUGUST
Woodmen of Arden

**LAMMAS/ST PETER AD
    VINCULA
MINDEN DAY
FIRST WEDNESDAY IN
    AUGUST**
Knighthood of the Old Green

6

7

8

Bank Holidays

The King's Book of Sports 1618 and 1633

13

14

15

20

21

22

27

AUGUST BANK HOLIDAY
Marldon Apple Pie Fair
Notting Hill Carnival

28

29
Preston Guild

*Moveable events have been placed
on the date they fall in 2007.*

Grottoes

2

3

4
Kit-Dressing

5
Grasmere Rush-Bearing
James I

9

10
ST LAWRENCE'S DAY

11

12
Congleton Bells
Gibson Tomb

16
ST ROCH'S DAY
Tutbury Bull-Running

17
Lee Gap Fair

18

19

23
ST BARTHOLOMEW'S EVE

24
ST BARTHOLOMEW'S DAY
Bartholomew Fair
Sandwich Bun Race
West Witton Burning of Bartle

25

26
LAST SUNDAY IN AUGUST
Plague Sunday

30

31

Sparrow-Mumbling

Grotto Day: notice the grotto on far left (*Illustrated London News*, 1851)

EARLY AUGUST

Grottoes

In nineteenth- and twentieth-century London, a common cry that greeted pedestrians in summer was 'Please Remember the Grotto!', as an urchin held out a shell or grubby hand in expectation of a small coin. The day on which this occurred was known as Grotto Day. An article in *The Times* (21 November 1957) remembers the Old Kent Road in the early 1900s:

> When was Grotto Day? It happened just once a year, but who whispered round Ruby Street that today was Grotter Day? It was a suggestion that sent some to the gasworks to collect clinker, one to the fishmonger to collect scallop shells, and some to beg or steal flowers. Then against the high gable at the end of the street we would build our grotto, clinker upon clinker, to form a mystic rockery with carefully spaced aper-

> tures in the fabric that would reveal the candlelight that was ultimately to shine inside. Two feet high and about as wide, the front elevation was finished with an arched doorway. A half-circle of stones for a forecourt, the whole decorated with flowers, mainly marigolds, and the edifice was finished. Then inside went the candles.

The children also chanted a traditional rhyme, which sounds more music hall than ancient folk song, as recalled by Rose Gamble in her autobiography *Chelsea Child* (1979):

> Please remember the grotto
> Me father has run off to sea
> Me mother's gone to fetch 'im back
> So please give a farthin' to me.

The custom was reported most regularly from London, but it was also found in places such as Essex, Norfolk, Hampshire, Sussex, and Swansea, and the time of year varies widely from report to report. Early August seems to be the most usual time, but it could be carried out in late July or early September. Nineteenth-century sources link the custom to the start of the oyster season in early August, and describe the grottoes as primarily built of oyster shells. Nowadays, oysters are hardly daily fare and their shells are not so easy to come by, but in earlier times the oyster was a poor person's food, often bought and eaten in the street, and vast quantities were sold. Henry Mayhew estimated in 1850 that 124 million oysters were sold each year in the streets of London alone. Later sources mention such grotto materials as clinker, stones, broken china and glass, beads, ribbons, flowers, and moss, and specify that there was nearly always a candle lit inside.

The earliest known mention of the custom is in the almanac *Time's Telescope* in 1823, and we have no evidence that it was any older than this. If it existed before that time, it certainly cannot have been as well known as it was soon to become, and by the 1840s and 1850s it was frequently mentioned in newspapers and magazines. The custom remained very widespread in the early twentieth century, and it lasted in some places into the post-Second World War period. The last was probably seen in Mitcham, in Surrey, in the 1960s.

Street customs such as these have long excited a range of adult reactions. A *Punch* cartoon of 15 August 1857, for example, urged people, 'Please do not remember the grotto', and seventy years later, in *The Times* of 1 September 1925:

> It was recently reported that the Justices of the Juvenile Offenders' Court at Tower Bridge had appealed to the Press to emphasise the nuisance caused by 'grottoes' made by children on the pavement at this time of the year, and by their appeals to 'remember the grotto'.

It is common for writers on the topic to assume a historical connection between the grotto custom and St James, whose symbol from the twelfth century onwards was the scallop shell associated with pilgrims visiting his shrine at Santiago de Compostela, in Spain. But this theory has its problems. St James's Day is 25 July, a little too early in the year for the core grotto season, which was most often reported as occurring in August. The native oyster season also often started in August, despite the traditional advice to only eat an oyster 'when there's an R in the month'. St James's feast day Old Style is 5 August, however, which brings it closer to the grotto season, but the theory is still not very convincing. Indeed, the late appearance of the custom in the documentary record, its variable date, and the close connection with the oyster season, make the St James connection appear to be simply a coincidence of timing, but further research is needed to verify or refute this idea.

*

FIRST WEDNESDAY IN AUGUST

Knighthood of the Old Green

Old Green in Southampton, Hampshire, is claimed to be the oldest bowling green in the world, having been reputedly in continuous use since 1299 (despite the fact that for some of that time bowling was illegal for ordinary folk; *see* **The *King's Book of Sports* 1618 and 1633**, p. 262). This particular tournament, however, known as the Knighthood of the Green, has been staged since 1776.

The winner of the tournament becomes a Knight of the Green and is forbidden to enter again, instead becoming one of the officers who organize and adjudicate the proceedings. The contest is open to all club members, who are referred to as 'Gentlemen Commoners' for the duration of the game, which can last several days. The rules differ from normal bowls. The jack, which has one flattened side so that it can be placed on a penny laid on the green, is placed by the Knights anywhere on the green. Contestants bowl two woods each and try to get as close to the jack as possible. As each wood is bowled, its distance from the jack is measured and recorded and it is then removed before the next wood is bowled. If the jack is knocked from its position, it is put back on the penny for the next contestant to aim at. When all have bowled, the winner of that 'end' is announced, the jack is placed somewhere else, and the contestants bowl from the jack's previous position. The first player to reach seven ends wins, and becomes a Knight. The Knights wear full morning dress, complete with black top hats.

For illustration, *see* p. 260.

*

Knighthood of the Old Green, Southampton, 1984

FIRST WEEK IN AUGUST

Woodmen of Arden

The Woodmen of Arden is an exclusive archery club, based at Meriden, in Warwickshire, which claims to be the exact centre of England. The Woodmen still use traditional longbows made of yew, and wooden arrows with silver tips, and they dress in an antiquated garb of green coat, buff waistcoat, green tie, and white trousers. They hold meetings, called Wardmotes, throughout the year, but their Grand Wardmote takes place over four days in the first week in August and comprises competitions, prizes, and business meetings. Club records date back to 1785, and it may well be even older than this.

*

1 AUGUST

Lammas/St Peter ad Vincula

The derivation of the word 'Lammas', and the ecclesiastical activity appropriate to the day, have exercised many antiquarians down the ages, resulting in some confusion. It was often assumed that the word meant 'lamb-mass', a false etymology that led to some parishes introducing services in which a lamb was brought to church for a blessing, as recorded by John Brand in 1849:

> On that day, the tenants who held lands of the cathedral church at York, which is dedicated to St. Peter ad Vincula [whose feast day is also 1 August] were bound by their tenure to bring a live lamb into the church at high mass.

However, the true derivation is from the Old English *hlafmaesse*, which means 'loaf-mass', and it is clear

A Woodman of Arden, Meriden, Warwickshire, 1984

from Anglo-Saxon records from the ninth century onwards that it was celebrated in the church as a festival of 'first fruits', with bread and wheat, to celebrate the corn harvest. Some Anglican churches still hold Lammas services in which loaves of bread feature prominently, but these are revivals or re-creations of the ancient festival, and were introduced in the 1940s. In 1945, for example, the Revd D. L. Couper, Chaplain to the Bishop of Chichester, working with groups such as the Young Farmers' Clubs and the Royal Agricultural Society, launched a campaign to revive 'the old Saxon festivals of Plough Sunday, Rogation-Sunday, Lammas-tide, and Harvest Thanksgiving' (*The Times*, 15 November 1948). He wrote new services for these days, and his ideas were enthusiastically adopted by many churches across the country.

Although not one of the official quarter days, Lammas was a regular day for paying rents, settling debts, and changing jobs and houses. Cumbrians, probably under Scottish influence, often divided the business year into two periods, rather than four, with settlements due at Candlemas (2 February) and Lammas. In an extension of this association with payment and the settlement of outstanding dues, the phrase 'the latter Lammas' was, from at least the mid sixteenth century, applied to the Day of Judgement, and by further extension it could mean 'never', as in the phrase 'I'll pay you at the latter Lammas!'

Its position in the year also contributed to its key role in the organization of rights to common lands. Where common or church land was rented out by the half-year, or where common strips of land were apportioned annually, Lammas was often the time that the business was carried out. In agricultural communities, these arrangements often involved important economic rights, and were jealously guarded and carefully administered. As A. R. Wright and T. E. Lones, the compilers of the classic *British Calendar Customs* volumes, recorded:

> *Certain lands were used by their owners for the growing of wheat and other crops, but on a date fixed by custom were thrown open for common pasture and other purposes . . . The lands remained open until the following spring. The custom was followed in or near Colchester, Coventry, Epping, Newbury, Staines, Ware, and Watford Fields.*

Lammas was also a very popular day for fairs, for example at Exeter and York, and local feasts and revels, as at Combe Martin in Devon, where the church is dedicated to St Peter ad Vincula. Given that temporary rules and regulations were in force during the time of a fair, it was essential that everybody knew when it opened and closed. Impressive civic processions and readings of proclamations were therefore often reported, along with the use of highly visible symbols, which could be displayed while the fair lasted. Local resident James Cossins remembered that in the 1820s the Lammas Fair at Exeter:

> *. . . was a pleasure fair, commencing on the Tuesday, by a procession starting from Westgate, consisting of the head constable, with a roll of parchment (tied with blue ribbons), containing the charter for holding the fair, which was read aloud by him at the site of the old gate. Two staff bearers accompanied him*

The King's Book of Sports 1618 and 1633

Before James I (VI in Scotland) had even arrived in London to take up the throne of England in 1617, he was embroiled in a controversy about games and pastimes.

Passing through Lancashire, he was presented with a petition from locals who claimed that they were being prevented from indulging in traditional games on Sundays by zealous clergy and magistrates. James's response was later codified in *The Kinges' Majesties Declaration Concerning Lawfull Sports*, commonly called *The King's Book of Sports*, printed and circulated in May 1618.

Certainly, James I liked his sport (by many accounts he was obsessed with stag-hunting), but *The King's Book of Sports* has to be seen primarily in terms of the religious controversies of the period. One of the main points at issue was the way in which Sunday should be celebrated, and, in particular, what the people at large were permitted and forbidden to do. Leaving aside the in-fighting over whether the 'Sabbath' meant Saturday (as in Judaism) or Sunday (as in Christianity), the growing Puritan faction in the English Church and establishment were increasingly able, at local level, to prevent games and sports taking place on what they regarded as the Lord's Day. It is not presuming too much to speculate that most of the people simply wanted to play games on the one day a week they were not at work, and no doubt wished that their sports had no religious or political significance.

The Sunday games – or at least the laissez-faire attitude that allowed them to take place – were associated in the religious reformers' mind with Catholicism, and it was a widespread conspiracy theory of the time that Catholics encouraged Sunday games specifically to undermine the Protestant church services. However, it was also argued, and believed by the King himself, that a certain measure of fun and relaxation could entice Catholics into the fold. It was no accident that the first decree was made for Lancashire, the county with a reputation for having the highest number of Catholics in England.

The King's Book of Sports explains that the declaration reiterated the decree that was made in response to the people in Lancashire, who had complained that they were being prevented from enjoying their:

> . . . lawful recreations, and honest exercises, after the afternoon sermon or service. We now find that two sorts of people, wherewith that country is much infected (we mean Papists and Puritans) have maliciously traduced and calumniated those Our just and honourable proceedings.

If sports were not allowed, the *Book of Sports* continues, there would be two regrettable 'inconveniences': firstly, as mentioned above, it would deter Catholics from converting to the Protestant Church; and secondly, healthy exercise makes people's bodies 'more able for war, when We, or Our successors, shall have occasion to use them'. The alternative was 'filthy tiplings and drunkenness, and breeds a number of idle and discontented speeches in their ale houses'. Some pastimes were therefore permitted, while others were banned:

> And as for Our good people's lawful recreation, Our pleasure likewise is, that, after the end of Divine Service, Our good people be not disturbed, letted, or discouraged from any lawful recreation, such as dancing, either of men or women, archery for men, leaping, vaulting, or any other such harmless recreation, nor from having of May Games, Whitsun Ales, and Morris-dances, and the setting

with their three-cornered hats, also two fifers and one drummer, followed by a man carrying a very long blue and white pole, surmounted by flowers and an immense stuffed white glove, and hundreds

of children following. After the perambulation, the glove was mounted on the highest part of the Guildhall, until the fair (which lasted three days) was over.

up of Maypoles, and other sports therewith used,
so as the same be had in due and convenient time,
without impediment or neglect of Divine Service:
and that women shall have leave to carry rushes to
the church for the decoring of it, according to their
old custom. But withal we do here account still as
prohibited all unlawful games to be used upon
Sundays only, as Bear and Bullbaitings, Interludes,
and at all times, in the meaner sort of people, by
law prohibited, bowling: and likewise we bar from
this benefit and liberty, all such known Recusants,
either men or women, as will abstain from coming
to church or Divine Service, that will not first
come to the church and serve God: prohibiting in
like sort, the said recreations to any that, though
conform in religion, are not present in the church
at the service of God, before their going to the said
recreations.

Modern readers might wonder why such an innocuous pastime as bowling should be ranked alongside bearbaiting and banned outright. However, bowling had become such a popular craze that working people were thought to be neglecting their ordinary labour in order to spend time playing, and so, for their own good and the good of the nation, it was believed that it had to be restrained. Notice that the declaration only bans bowling for 'the meaner sort'.

The *Book of Sports* was not well received by the religious reformers of the day, who denounced it roundly, although some magistrates were pleased to have a clear ruling on what was becoming a major focus of factional confrontation within their communities. The zealots took it as one more sign that the sovereign was not to be trusted in matters of religious policy, and they did not give up the fight. Charles I felt it necessary to reissue the book in 1633, but by this time the reformers had gained so much confidence that it was largely irrelevant, and only

eleven years later, not only were the provisions of the declaration rescinded by Parliament but the book itself was publicly burnt. The new statute, *An Ordinance for the better observation of the Lords Day* (8 April 1644) ran as follows:

And be it further ordained, that no person or
persons shall hereafter upon the Lords-day, use,
exercise, keep, maintain, or be present at any
wrastlings, shooting, bowling, ringing of bells for
pleasure or pastime, wake, otherwise called feasts,
church-ale, dancing, games, sport or pastime what-
soever; upon pain, that every person so offending
being above the age of fourteen years, shall lose,
and forfeit five shillings for every such offence . . .

And because the profanation of the Lords-day
hath been heretofore greatly occasioned by May-
poles (a heathenish vanity, generally abused
to superstition and wickedness), the Lords and
Commons do further order and ordain, that all and
singular May-poles, that are, or shall be erected,
shall be taken down and removed by the consta-
bles, borsholders, tything-men, petty constables,
and churchwardens of the parishes and place
where the same be: and that no May-pole shall be
hereafter set up, erected, or suffered to be within
this kingdom of England, or Dominion of Wales . . .

And it is further ordained by the said Lords and
Commons that the King's Declaration concerning
observing of wakes, and use of exercise and recrea-
tion upon the Lords-day; the Book intituled, The
Kings Majesties Declaration to his Subjects concern-
ing lawful sports to be used; and all other books
and pamphlets that have been, or shall be written,
printed, or published, against the morality of the
fourth Commandment, or of the Lords-day, or to
countenance the profanation thereof, be called
in, seized, suppressed and publicly burnt by the
Justices of Peace . . .

It is not entirely clear why a glove was the chosen symbol, but in other contexts a lord or other high-ranking individual would send an official or messenger with a glove as a token of his authority, and this is presumably an extension of this idea. The phrase 'The glove is up!' was often used to mean that the fair was open.

A further etymological puzzle surrounds 1 August, as in earlier records the day was referred to as 'the Gule of

August'. The *Oxford English Dictionary* states that the ulterior etymology of the word is unknown, but that it has been in use at least since 1300, and also existed in Old French and Medieval Latin. It has been suggested that it derives from the Welsh *gwyl*, or 'feast', but it is not clear why or how Norman English (or Old French) picked up such a word, and it is more likely that both the Welsh and English terms are derived from the Latin. It is very unlikely that the phrase meant 'the Yule of August', signifying that the festival was like a summer Christmas.

As already indicated, 1 August is also one of the feast days dedicated to St Peter. He shares his main feast day with St Paul on 29 June, but the feast on 1 August is called Peter Ad Vincula, or 'Peter in Chains', and commemorates the incident in the Acts of the Apostles (12:3–8) when an angel visited him in prison, 'and his chains fell off from his hands'. *See* **12 August: Congleton Bells** for a relevant custom.

See also **Fairs, Feasts, Wakes, and Revels**, p. 249.

Minden Day

Minden Day, important to British army personnel, veterans, and their families, commemorates the Battle of Minden in Germany, which took place on this day in 1759 during the Seven Years War. A column of British infantry, including men of six different British and three Hanovarian regiments, unexpectedly routed eleven squadrons of French cavalry and smashed through the French line, showing unbelievable bravery and coolness in the face of overwhelming odds. Each of the regiments involved (the Suffolk, the Royal Hampshire, the Lancashire Fusiliers, the Royal Welch Fusiliers, the King's Own Yorkshire Light Infantry, and the King's Own Scottish Borderers) still celebrates the day with parades and reunions, and serving and retired soldiers alike wear fresh 'Minden roses' in recognition of the story that while advancing towards the French line, the men passed through some gardens and plucked roses to decorate their hats. In August 2003, the florists Interflora sent 700 fresh red roses to the soldiers of the King's Own Scottish Borderers who were serving in Iraq at the time.

*

4 AUGUST

Kit-Dressing

Since at least the fourteenth century, the word 'kit' has been used in various parts of the country to mean a wooden vessel, with hooped staves and handles, of varying size, but often specifically to denote a milking pail, or receptacle for carrying produce such as butter or fish to customers or to market. In 1829, Stephen Glover wrote of a custom called 'kit-dressing' in his classic history of Derbyshire (1829):

> At Baslow the rural festive kit-dressing took place on the 4th of August, in 1829; the procession was attended by the Baslow band, and the decoration of the kits surpassed in beauty and taste any that had been seen before. On one of the kits was this inscription:
>
>> The farmer, the plough-boy, the fleece and the flail
>> Success to the milk-maid who carries the pail.
>
> A beautiful garland and a large pink flag were emblems carried in the procession. Twigs of willow were bent over the tops of the kits and entwined with flowers and ribbons. The garlands were formed upon a framework of woven willow twigs, and were adorned by means of silk, muslin, and trinkets of silver and gold.

As this is the only reference to the custom, it is not clear whether this was widely known or simply a local occurrence, but there is a reference to something similar in Lincolnshire in the 1820s (*see* **1 May**). The decorating of trade implements for celebration was not uncommon, and a close analogy to this custom was the milkmaids' dance (*see* **1 May: Milkmaids' Garland**), but the Baslow procession seems to have been larger and more organized. It is also a mystery why it took place on 4 August.

*

5 AUGUST

Grasmere Rush-Bearing

William and Dorothy Wordsworth lived and died in Grasmere, and the village is now one of the most popular literary shrines in England, besieged by tourists for much of the year. Given their romantic propensities, the Wordsworths were naturally very keen on local traditions, and they took a particular interest in the annual rush-bearing, which they regarded as the prettiest of summer celebrations. This interest helped to protect the custom when attendance was low, and ensured its survival into the twentieth century, when local traditions were appreciated and encouraged once more, as symbols of old-time community.

Grasmere rush-bearing remains justly famous, and is by far the best known of the five existing rush-bearing ceremonies in Cumbria. At present, the ceremony takes place on the Saturday nearest to St Oswald's Day (5 August), to whom the local church is dedicated, but the date seems to have varied over the years. As with other Cumbrian rush-bearings, the key part of the day is the procession, with marching band, banners, clergy, and the congregation, who carry flowers, rushes, and special 'bearings' – rush-covered wood and wire in symbolic shapes such as crosses, hearts, and harps, as well as wreaths, a pole with a serpent coiled round it, and appropriate biblical scenes, such as Moses in the bulrushes. The central focus of the procession is a group of six girls (the Rush-Maidens) dressed in green and white, with flowers in their hair, holding outspread between them a large embroidered sheet on which are placed a few token rushes, and carrying other rushes in their free hand. They all march to the church, where a special service is held, and the rest of the day is spent *en fête*, with wrestling and a dance in the evening.

Since at least the early nineteenth century it has been traditional to give all the participating children a piece of gingerbread and, from 1834, a small coin, which was introduced to encourage attendance after a particularly low point when only seven children turned up. There are numerous accounts of the celebrations from the nineteenth century onwards, which show that in essentials the day has changed little for nigh on 150 years. The following was published in *Notes & Queries* in 1875:

> I chanced to be in Grasmere . . . in July 1875 . . . As the children arrived with their standards they ranged themselves along the inside of the wall, resting their rush crosses, etc., on the wall, and holding them so. When more than a hundred of these pretty emblems,

> each held by a little child, were arranged on the wall, a more pleasing sight could hardly be seen . . . The church bells rang out a merry peal, and soon after six the children set off marching in procession two and two, headed by a band, through the village. The procession was very pretty . . . While the rush-bearers were assembling, a plate was handed round among spectators for the purpose of collecting a little money to pay the band, and to provide each of the children with twopence-worth of gingerbread . . . After marching through the village the children brought their rush standards back to the church where they were fixed upright on the edges of the pews; a nail driven through the wooden square at the foot of the standard seemed to be the mode of attachment. At morning service on Sunday the effect was extremely pretty, and the old church was filled with a most delightful perfume of flowers, ferns, and rushes. The service commenced with the singing of the . . . hymn which has been used for many years in Grasmere church, the Hymn for the Rush-Bearers.

Rush-bearing at Grasmere is first mentioned in the churchwardens' accounts of 1680, when a shilling was paid 'For ale bestowed on those who brought rushes and repaired the church', and similar entries appear regularly until 1841, when the church was paved. A painting of the Grasmere rush-bearing by local artist Frank Bramley, exhibited at the Royal Academy in 1905, now hangs in the village hall.

See also **Rush-Bearing**, p. 238.

James I

During the reign of James I (1603–25), 5 August was one of the days on which church bells across the nation were rung in his honour – in this case to commemorate his escape from the captivity imposed by Lord Gowrie in 1582–3 (known as 'the Gowrie conspiracy').

The fifth of August is also Old Style St James's Day, and regarded by some as the correct day to make grottoes in the street (*see* **Early August: Grottoes**).

*

St Lawrence being roasted, from a twelfth-century French Bible

10 AUGUST

St Lawrence's Day

St Lawrence, Deacon of Rome, was martyred in AD 258 and was an extremely popular saint across Europe; in pre-Reformation Britain, 228 churches were dedicated to him. No widespread customs seem to have taken place on his feast day, but its high summer date made it a popular time for fairs. The fair at Alvechurch, in Worcestershire, for example, included an ox-roasting, while a large gathering at Tan Hill, on the Wiltshire Downs near Devizes, was famous for its salt beef and beans. St Lawrence's is also the local feast day at Whitwell, in Derbyshire, and from 1879 until it lapsed in recent years, this included an open-air service of thanksgiving on the top of High Hill, where the stone for the church was believed to have been quarried.

As with many martyrs of the period, almost nothing is known of Lawrence's real life, but this did not stop the legend-makers, and various vivid stories are told about him. One in particular has been regarded by many as the origin of the term 'Lazy Lawrence', a phrase that was until recently, and possibly still is, regularly used in everyday speech. Legend has it that Lawrence was laid out on an iron griddle and slowly roasted over a fire. After a while, the saint taunted his tormentors and, exhibiting the power of Christian fortitude, asked them to turn him over, as he was quite done on that side. 'Lazy Lawrence' was thus a widespread term for anyone who showed signs of undue indolence. 'He has Lawrence on his back' or 'Lawrence has a hold of him' were similarly reported as meaning laziness personified, while 'St Lawrence weather' was used to describe hot sultry days. In truth, however, these phrases were derived from a popular seventeenth-century story, widely circulated in chapbooks, entitled 'The History of Lawrence Lazy'.

*

12 AUGUST

Congleton Bells

The feast of St Peter ad Vincula (St Peter in Chains) falls on 1 August, but an apparently unique custom that is clearly related to his festival took place at Congleton, in Cheshire, each year on 12 August, because of the eleven days lost at the change of calendar in 1752. The parish church there is dedicated to St Peter ad Vincula, and so the local feast or wake was held on his day. On the Wake Sunday, the following custom, described here by the *Monthly Packet* magazine, was also carried out:

On the Wake Sunday, from time immemorial until several years ago, an extraordinary musical perform-ance aroused the inhabitants from their sleep very early in the morning. The instruments were horse collars hung round with numerous bells of peculiar shape; these collars were placed on men's shoulders and, walking through the streets of the town, the men shake the collars vigorously and thus cause the bells to emit a loud noise. Formerly, a heavy chain was used; the bells were an innovation introduced a few generations ago.

Other accounts relate that the custom was still called 'the ringing of the chains' even when bells were used, and that the noise made was certainly not musical. It was suppressed in the late nineteenth century, apparently because it had long fallen into abuse and degradation. The ownership of the bells, and the right to perambulate the town with them, was said to be hereditary, and had for several generations been in the hands of a family of chimney sweeps named Stubbs. They had taken to profaning the occasion by getting drunk and descending into burlesque. Finally, when two branches of the family were disputing ownership of the bells, and both had been locked in the town gaol for fighting, the town clerk took the opportunity to buy the bells, and from then on they belonged to the town's corporation. They are now on display in the Congleton Museum, and can be seen on the museum's website. Although the symbolism of the chains or bells for the day is clear, it is not known how or when it started, and no reports of similar activities elsewhere have yet come to light.

Gibson Tomb

The eighteenth-century mausoleum of the Gibson family stands in the churchyard of St Nicholas church in Sutton (formerly Surrey but now a London borough) – although there is no evidence that the family, who came from Walthamstow, had any previous connection with Sutton. When Mary Gibson died in 1793, she left money to Christ's Hospital, on condition they ensured that the Rector of St Nicholas undertake an annual inspection of the tomb and carry out any necessary repairs, as well as preaching a memorial sermon. The sermon lapsed in the late nineteenth century, but the unlocking and inspecting of the tomb continues to this day every 12 August, although the exact form of the ceremony has changed several times in its 200-year history. As with other impressive tombs, the Gibson mausoleum has attracted its share of local beliefs and legends, including the idea that if one walks seven times around it, a ghost will emerge from an urn on its roof.

*

16 AUGUST

St Roch's Day

St Roch was born at Montpellier, France, c.1350, and spent his short life as a hermit and on repeated pilgrimages. On one of these religious trips he caught the plague and was kept alive in the woods by food that was brought to him by a dog. He died c.1380, but soon acquired the reputation for healing the disease. His fame was on the wane in the seventeenth century, but was revived in Europe in the nineteenth, as a result of widespread fears over cholera. Although antiquarian John Brand presented evidence in his *Observations on the Popular Antiquities of Great Britain* (1849) that St Roch's Day was celebrated in Britain in the seventeenth century under the name 'Rock Monday', it is not clear what was done on the day, or how widely known it was.

Tutbury Bull-Running

Bull-running was a 'sport' in which a bull was let loose and then chased through streets or fields by the people involved, and should therefore be sharply distinguished from the common **bull-baiting** (p. 352), in which dogs were set to attack a tethered animal. Only a handful of places in England are recorded as having bull-running customs, the most widely known being at Stamford, in Lincolnshire (*see* **13 November: St Brice's Day**).

At Stamford, the bull was forced to run through the streets, but at Tutbury, the chasers had to catch it on open land. In order to make this more difficult, the bull's horns were removed, its ears and tail cropped, and its body was smeared with soap. This latter detail makes it sound like a particularly difficult version of the well-known fairground game of catching the greasy pig. Pepper was blown into the bull's nose to make it angry. If the chasers could hold the bull long enough to cut off a piece of hair as proof, they could keep the animal, to sell, keep, or eat as they thought fit.

Originally, the bull-running was only a small part of the annual celebrations of the 'Court of Minstrels', a sort of trade guild for musicians, granted a charter by Richard II in 1380/1. The bull was originally supplied by the Prior of Tutbury, but after the Dissolution swept away the priory it was provided by the Duke of

Devonshire. In former times, only the minstrels did the chasing, but over the years the custom came to include enthusiastic participants from the town and further afield, which brought it into disrepute. It was abolished in 1778.

*

17 AUGUST

Lee Gap Fair

Lee Gap Fair, in the parish of Woodkirk, West Ardsley, near Leeds, is one of the surviving horse fairs that still attract a strong Gypsy presence, and its organizers claim it to be the oldest chartered fair in England. A charter from King Stephen in 1136, confirming an earlier one, does indeed grant two fairs to the parish of Woodkirk, in August and September, and there are still two Lee fairs: Lee Gap Fair on 17 August, and Latter Lee on 17 September.

See also **Fairs, Feasts, Wakes, and Revels**, p. 249.

*

23 AUGUST

St Bartholomew's Eve

John Stow, in his *Survey of London* (1598), recorded an interesting custom in which schoolboys pitted their learning against each other:

> I myself, in my youth, have yearly seen, on the eve of
> St. Bartholomew the Apostle, the scholars of divers
> grammar schools repair unto the churchyard of
> St. Bartholomew, the priory in Smithfield, where
> upon a bank boarded about under a tree, some one
> scholar hath stepped up, and there hath opposed
> and answered, till he were by some better scholar
> overcome and put down; and then the overcomer
> taking the place, did like as the first; and in the end
> the best opposers and answerers had rewards, which
> I observed not but it made both good schoolmasters,
> and also good scholars.

A contributor to William Hone's *Year-Book* (1832) commented that a similar custom prevailed in Yorkshire until the early eighteenth century at Lee Fair (*see* **17 August**).

*

24 AUGUST

St Bartholomew's Day

Despite being one of Christ's Apostles, nothing is known for sure about St Bartholomew's life, but according to legend he died after being flayed alive and then beheaded. He therefore became, somewhat pointedly, the patron saint of tanners and other workers with knives. In religious illustrations he is often shown holding a knife, or even with his own skin draped over his arm like a cloth. He was very popular in medieval England, and 165 ancient churches were dedicated to him, including Croyland Abbey, in Lincolnshire, where a custom of giving little knives to the congregation in his memory took place on this day until abolished in the fifteenth century. Although his popularity seems to have gradually waned, his day was a regular one for fairs, including Newbury Fair, in Berkshire, and Whittingham Fair, in Northumberland, as well as the famous **Bartholomew Fair**, in London (*see below*). There were also other outdoor gatherings on the day, and presumably the weather at this time of year contributed to their popularity. William Hone's *Year-Book* (1832) includes an example of one such event that took place 'some time ago' at the village of Donnington, in Lincolnshire:

> In the morning a number of maidens, clad in their
> best attire, went in procession to a small chapel, then
> standing in the parish, and strewed its floor with
> rushes, from whence they proceeded to a piece of
> land, called the 'Play Garths', where they were joined
> by most of the inhabitants of the place, who passed
> the remainder of the day in rural sports, such as
> foot-ball, wrestling, and other athletic exercises, with
> dancing, etc.

Apart from these, only a handful of disparate customs took place on this day (*see below*) each of which seem to have little or no connection with the saint, apart from being associated with an institution dedicated to him.

In the realm of weather-lore, according to Richard Inwards' classic collection on the subject, published in 1869, 'At St. Bartholomew, there comes cold dew.' But this seems more to do with the rhyme than any deep

One of the biscuits distributed at Sandwich, Kent, on St Bartholomew's Day, 1983

meteorological insight, because exactly the same was said of St Matthew's Day (21 September).

Bartholomew Fair

In its heyday, Bartholomew Fair was one of the four great fairs of England, and for centuries it was famous nationwide as a major place for entertainment of all kinds, high and low (but mainly low). Its charter was first granted in 1133 by Henry I, to the Prior of St Bartholomew's church and priory, Smithfield, but it was taken over by the City of London when the monasteries were dissolved. The fair commenced each year on St Bartholomew's Day, but its duration varied; in Charles II's time it was so popular that it was extended to fourteen days.

All the well-known writers and artists were familiar with it, and it became proverbial for summer fun, laughter, and a somewhat raffish pleasure – or for the depths of its iniquity, depending on your viewpoint. Numerous songs described its attractions or were set at the fair; Ben Jonson published a popular comedy, *Bartholomew Fair*, in 1614; and engravings of the fair appeared on a regular basis. All the major travelling play companies visited the fair every year, and it was famous for puppet plays and religious mystery plays as well as regular drama. In addition, there were numerous music and dance shows, spectaculars, acrobats, tightrope walkers, gingerbread sellers, a menagerie of animals, ballad-singers, bearded ladies, fat men, giants, dwarves, fortune-telling horses, mermaids, and, of course, card-sharps, pickpockets, prostitutes, pimps, and vagabonds.

Opposition came from many quarters, and there were repeated attempts at suppression in the late eighteenth and early nineteenth centuries, but the fair managed to struggle on till 1855, when it was proclaimed for the last time.

See also **Fairs, Feasts, Wakes, and Revels**, p. 249.

Sandwich Bun Race

Sandwich, one of the medieval cinque ports along the Kent and Sussex coast, has an 800-year-old almshouse called the Hospital of St Bartholomew. The exact date of its foundation is not known, but it was certainly in

The Burning of Bartle at West Witton, Yorkshire, in the 1950s

existence by 1287 and probably dates from the early thirteenth century. The hospital is still home to sixteen elderly 'brothers' and 'sisters', who live in cottages grouped around the equally ancient St Bartholomew's chapel. On St Bartholomew's Day each year, there is a special service at the chapel, attended by the residents and the Mayor and councillors of Sandwich. After the service, children race around the outside of the chapel and are then given buns. Adults are given a hard-baked biscuit stamped with the arms of the town. It has been suggested that the buns have replaced an earlier dole of bread, which is possible, and that this dole was itself a replacement of charity food given to pilgrims. However, the latter is said of every food custom within fifty miles of Canterbury, so is not likely to be accurate

See also **Doles**, p. 87.

West Witton Burning of Bartle

This unique custom takes place in the North Yorkshire village of West Witton. A few days before the Saturday

of the village feast, a larger-than-life effigy, stuffed with straw, with torches for eyes and named Bartle, is made by certain villagers. On the evening of the Saturday, Bartle is carried on the shoulders of two men and paraded through the village, stopping at houses and pubs, and being held up to peer in at cottage windows; the crowd grows as they proceed. Whenever the procession stops, a third man proclaims:

> *At Penhill Crags he tore his rags;*
> *At Hunter's Thorn he blew his horn;*
> *At Capplebank Stee he brake his knee;*
> *At Grisgill Beck he brake his neck;*
> *At Wadham's End he couldn't fend;*
> *At Grisgill End he made his end.*
> *Shout, lads, shout. Hooray!*

Everyone joins in the 'hooray'. Once the procession reaches Grass Gill End, Bartle is unceremoniously dowsed in paraffin and burnt, accompanied by the onlookers' cheers and jeers.

At first glance, the name and timing of the custom are easily explained. The parish church is dedicated to St Bartholomew, whose day is 24 August, and the local feast therefore took place at that time. However, it is unlikely that the figure represents the saint, as the mishandling and execution show a disrespect, or even hatred, that would hardly have been tolerated, so this may not be his original name. The dominant local legend is that Bartle was a swine thief who was hunted down and killed by outraged villagers, as detailed in the rhyme, which lists real local places on the moors above the village. Some, however, have claimed that Bartle was a local giant – in the days when giants were common enough – and that this explains why the effigy is usually larger than life. J. Fairfax-Blakeborough included a somewhat unpleasant story that detailed the life and death of 'The Wicked Giant of Penhill' in his book *The Hand of Glory* (1924), which was based on his father's extensive collection of Yorkshire lore. He does not give his giant a name, but the location and the fact that the giant's primary concern is care of his swine-herds indicate a connection with the Bartle. Unfortunately, Fairfax-Blakeborough's stories are usually so embellished as to preclude their being used as evidence of previous tradition, but they may well have influenced later perceptions.

Notwithstanding these legends, many writers have assumed that the custom has ancient origins, and have written of corn gods (because of the straw involved), scapegoats, and the usual fertility rituals, but any dispassionate examination of these theories is hampered by the fact that none of them ventures to say when the custom was first recorded, and so these theories are not supported by any factual evidence.

Although the Burning of Bartle appears to be unique, it does have connections with other customs. The most obvious common element is the production and destruction of an effigy in human form. Such figures are often found in 5 November proceedings, but were also used in a range of other traditions at different times of the year: *see*, for example, **Rough Music**, p. 74; **Ash Wednesday: Jack-a-Lent**, p. 67; **Good Friday: Burning Judas**, p. 108; and, most notably, **Easter Monday: Black Knight of Ashton**, p. 124.

*

Sparrow-Mumbling

One of the many sports or games in which our forebears indulged at fairs and other gatherings, but which to modern eyes seem cruel and senseless. Exact details vary, but in one version a live cock sparrow, with clipped wings, was placed into a hat, and participants, whose arms were tied behind them, tried to bite off the sparrow's head. The bird, of course, attempted to defend itself by pecking its assailant's face. In another version, to which nineteenth-century Cornish miners were apparently partial, a live sparrow was fastened to a man's teeth by a string, and he had to attempt to pluck the feathers off the unfortunate bird, using only his lips. Sparrow-mumbling dates back at least to George Chapman's *Andromeda Liberata* (1614), which includes the passage: "Twill be most ridiculous and pleasing to sit in a corner and spend your teeth to the stumps in mumbling an old sparrow till your lips bleed and your eyes water.'

LAST SUNDAY IN AUGUST

Plague Sunday

Few villages in Britain can claim genuine hero status, but Eyam (pronounced Eem) in Derbyshire is one. In September 1665, while the Great Plague was raging in London, the disease was brought to Eyam, probably in some infected cloth imported by the local tailor. The local rector, William Mompesson, supported by his wife Catherine and the previous incumbent Thomas Stanley (who had been ejected from the living at the Restoration) persuaded the villagers to impose a strict quarantine to contain the disease and prevent it spreading to neighbouring villages. The plan worked, and no cases were reported outside Eyam, but the village itself paid a heavy price. By November 1666, the disease had run its course, but few local families escaped its touch, and 260 of the original 350 inhabitants had perished. Many of their gravestones can still be seen. Since 1905, 'Plague Sunday' has been celebrated on the last Sunday

Plague Sunday commemoration at Eyam, Derbyshire, 1984

in August, to commemorate the villagers' sacrifice. A procession makes its way to Cucklet Delf, the spot where outdoor services had been held while the plague raged, and a memorial service, with special plague hymn, takes place.

On another note, although it is almost universally believed in Britain that the children's rhyme 'Ring a Ring o' Roses' commemorates the Great Plague of London, this is not supported by any evidence. Rather, it is the best-known example of the way in which modern groundless suppositions about traditional rhymes and customs are invented and take hold – indeed, becoming folklore themselves. The earliest printed reference to the rhyme that has been found to date is in an American source from the 1880s.

*

29 AUGUST

Preston Guild

In medieval times, in Britain and across Western Europe, a local guild merchant wielded a great deal of power over trade and commerce in the area of its jurisdiction, granting privileges to its members and severely circumscribing the commercial activities of outsiders. These restrictions amounted to a monopoly on most areas of commerce, and, apart from during a fair, no non-guild member could trade in the town without express permission, which was rarely granted. Guild court meetings at which new members were admitted and other business was transacted were held periodically, and these events became major celebrations in themselves, with trade processions, triumphal arches, dinners, speeches, balls, concerts, and all kinds of popular entertainment. Many guilds pre-dated the growth of effective local government and provided the basis of the latter when it finally evolved. As guilds also had close connections with the religious establishment, it was common for local business, civic, and religious elites to become inextricably intertwined.

The charter for Lancashire's Preston Guild, granted by Henry II, dates back to c.1179. Since 1562 the guild has met every twenty years (except in 1942), to confirm its powers and agree new freemen. Although gradually stripped of its power over the years, and losing all remaining vestiges of it by the Municipal Reform Act of 1835, the meetings are still held, and comprise general celebration and merrymaking in the town. To be elected Freeman of the Guild has no practical purpose any more, but it is still regarded as an honour; and the phrase 'once every Preston Guild', meaning 'not very often', is still current in Lancashire. The next Preston Guild will be held in 2012.

*

AUGUST BANK HOLIDAY

Marldon Apple Pie Fair

Marldon is a village near Paignton, in Devon, which holds an Apple Pie Fair every August Bank Holiday Monday. All the usual trappings of a popular village fête are present, including sideshows, craft tents, sports, demonstrations, and arena events, but the unique local feature is the entrance of a donkey pulling the apple pie cart, and the presence of the Apple Pie Princess. The following account was printed in the *Transactions of the Devonshire Association* in 1935 and is couched in the past tense, but it does not specify which year is being remembered:

> The Marldon Apple Pie, which was oval in shape, about the size of a kitchen table, and brought from Marldon to St. Marychurch in the apple season annually by a Marldon countryman who possessed an orchard. This man, George Hill by name, was in the habit of bringing into Torquay weekly a donkey laden with panniers full of apples, and returning home with panniers full of washing to be laundered. During the homeward journey, George was usually asleep, but the donkey would safely convey him home. The Marldon Apple Pie was driven all round St. Marychurch in a cart decorated with flowers and ribands, and drawn by two black donkeys wearing harness and reins decorated with plaited reed (i.e. straw). The pie was afterwards eaten, with cream if desired, by all who cared to pay for a slice, in a playing field by Cary Park, where a fair and sports were being held. The tale of poor George Hill's last days is a sad one. Once when asleep on his homeward journey, his goods were stolen. Not long after this calamity George was found dead, possibly from the effects of his shock.

Village tradition claims that the first fair was held in 1888, but it has certainly not had an unbroken run since that time. Cuttings from the *Western Morning News* show that the fair was revived in 1958 or 1959, after a 'lapse of 70 years'. Since then, however, it has been held every year, and now takes place in the Jubilee Meadow. For a while, the pie was a fake one containing hundreds of individual real pies, but about ten years ago it returned to its former glory and a very real apple pie is now made by a local baker in a stainless steel dish, about 2 feet 6 inches by 2 feet in size, which was donated to the village by the local postman. It is still brought to the fair in a donkey cart, and the Apple Pie Princess makes the first cut.

Notting Hill Carnival

London's Notting Hill Carnival, which takes place over the August Bank Holiday, is often billed as the biggest street party in Europe, or even the world, and attracts up to one and a half million people to its north London locality. From small local beginnings just over forty years ago, the event has grown to such huge proportions that its organization is a full-time operation, undertaken nowadays by the London Notting Hill Carnival Ltd.

Many events and activities are organized in the community in the preceding six weeks, and there are band competitions on the Saturday, and a shorter child-friendly family parade on the Sunday. However, the climax of the celebrations, and the event that steals all the headlines, is the big parade on the August Bank Holiday Monday, which covers a three-mile route around Great Western Road, Chepstow Road, Westbourne Grove, and Ladbroke Grove, and has to be experienced to be believed, consisting of a huge colourful orgy of loud music, dancing in the street, outrageous costumes – which would not disgrace carnival participants in Brazil – and much eating and drinking from the many stalls that line the route.

The Notting Hill Carnival grew from various ad hoc gatherings of immigrants, mainly from the Caribbean, who settled in the area in the 1950s and wished to bring something of their own culture to life in their new home. These events coalesced into a street carnival in 1964, and it has been held every year since, becom-

Bank Holidays

The current system of official bank holidays was created by the Bank Holidays Act of 1871, which was later incorporated into the Banking and Financial Dealings Act of 1971. The original Act provided for the Bank of England to be closed on certain days in the year, and, most importantly in legal terms, any bills or promissory notes that fell due on those days were payable on the following day without penalty. The days stipulated by the 1871 Act were Easter Monday, Whit Monday, the first Monday in August, and Boxing Day; Good Friday and Christmas Day were already accepted as common-law holidays by virtue of long tradition. It quickly became the norm for other institutions to close on these days, and employees in most sectors became accustomed to take them as holiday. Since that time, two have been added – New Year's Day (1974) and May Day (1978) – bringing the total number of bank holidays for England to eight per annum. In 1971, the moveable Whit Monday holiday was changed to the fixed Spring Bank Holiday, and August Bank Holiday moved from the first to the last Monday in August. There have also been a number of special bank holidays, such as one for the Royal Wedding in 1981 and for the Queen's Golden Jubilee in 2002. Contrary to widespread popular opinion, bank holidays are not 'statutory holidays', and employees are not permitted to refuse to work on those days.

Normally quite consensual, the timing of bank holidays occasionally hits the headlines of political debate, especially when the idea of celebration or commemoration is mixed with that of 'holiday' pure and simple. August Bank Holiday causes no problems because it is simply an arbitrary late summer day, but the adoption of May Day as a new bank holiday in 1978, by the Labour government of the day, created a major furore. The Conservative opposition claimed that May Day's international socialist nature made it an unsuitable choice, and *The Times* ran a suitably thunderous leader suggesting that the British public should use the day to commemorate innocent people murdered in the Soviet Union. When the Conservatives returned to power, they seriously planned to scrap the May Day holiday and to replace it with a more patriotic 'Trafalgar Day' in October (*see* **21 October**). This in turn was criticized, as it would disrupt manufacturing output in the important run-up to Christmas, and it met with a lukewarm response from the public, who, not surprisingly, preferred a day off in early summer to one in late autumn. The plan was quietly shelved in 1993, but the principle of patriotism is still regularly cited when the question of the timing of bank holidays is discussed.

A current campaign highlights the paucity of bank holidays in Britain, compared to many other European countries. A short paper by Michael Jacobs, published on the Fabian Society's website, shows that the Netherlands has seven bank holidays; Britain, Ireland, and Finland each have eight, while all the other major European countries have many more, with Italy and Iceland topping the chart with sixteen and fifteen bank holidays respectively.

ing bigger and more audacious every year. In earlier years there were some problems of violence in the crowds, but that is now long gone, and the main problems facing organizers nowadays are how to squeeze a million people safely into the narrow streets of this corner of north London, and provide enough facilities for them. Attempts by the Greater London Authority to spread the carnival into neighbouring areas and Hyde Park have so far met with resistance from local organizers, who fear that the event will lose its vital local base if it moves too far from its roots and becomes too closely identified with official local government tourism initiatives.

See also **First Friday in November: Bridgwater Carnival**.

Notting Hill Carnival, *c.2001*

September

Baiting Bears and Other Animals

Horseman's Sunday

Warden Pies

3

CROMWELL DAY
MERCHANT NAVY DAY

4

Abbots Bromley Horn Dance
Barnet Horse Fair

5

10

11

12

17

18

Samuel Johnson
    commemoration
Southwark Fair

19

Painswick Church-Clipping

24

25

26

*Moveable events have been placed
on the date they fall in 2007.*

Hop-Picking

Harvest Festivals

1

ST GILES'S DAY

2

6

7

8

9

13

THIRD THURSDAY IN SEPTEMBER

Chalk-Back Day

14

HOLY CROSS DAY/HOLY ROOD DAY

Shaftesbury Byzant

Sturbridge Fair

15

THIRD SATURDAY IN SEPTEMBER

Egremont Crab-Apple Fair

16

20

21

ST MATTHEW'S DAY

22

23

27

28

29

MICHAELMAS/FEAST OF ST MICHAEL AND ALL ANGELS

Blackberries

Crack-Nut Sunday

Election of the Lord Mayor of London

Urswick Rush-Bearing

30

Harvest Customs

The importance of the harvest in an agricultural economy can hardly be overstressed, and in England in past centuries the whole life of the nation depended on it. Even when the harvest had lost some of its economic edge, it still had a deep psychological impact on rural communities, as the Wiltshire writer Alfred Williams commented in 1912:

> *The in-gathering of the corn-harvest is by far the most important feature of the farm year, especially where there is much arable land, or perhaps it may be all corn in some places, as on the Downs, for instance. If the weather is wet in hay-time and the crop spoiled, that may not matter very much; but in the harvest, that is truly tragic! Who does not deeply grieve, apart from the monetary loss involved, to see all that is left of the beautiful corn blackening and rotting in the fields, under the dark rainy skies of October and November, as is sometimes the case, utterly useless for anything but litter and manure, and the ground too wet and sodden to admit of collecting it for that purpose even? It seems as though you have lived the year for nothing then; that all the bloom and sunshine of the spring and summer were mockery; that Nature brought forth her beautiful children but to destroy them.*

Of all the points of the farming year, it was the time when the farmer needed the full co-operation of his workers. The workers, too, knew that a successful harvest was essential to the economic well-being of the community, and that a bad one would affect their chances of employment the following year. They could also earn double their usual wage during the harvest, and the amount of work doubled too, so it was well within their own interest to make it a successful season. Embedded in the practical and physical arrangements necessary to 'win' the harvest, a number of customs and usages grew up over the years, which served to keep the workers amused, gain them some monetary advantage, or celebrate their achievements.

Whether a particular custom had its origin in a game, a practical response to a practical problem, or a superstitious impulse, remains to be discovered. However, the idea that harvest customs are direct survivals of belief in corn goddesses and vegetation spirits of pre-Christian times, which has been the ruling orthodoxy for many years, is not supported by the documentary record, and it is time it was discarded.

Farmworkers often tried to enhance their autonomy in their day-to-day work by organizing themselves: the sheep-shearers formed their own autonomous band, who contracted with the farmer for the job; the haymakers organized themselves under an elected captain and lieutenant; and so on. Rules were also created that helped the workers to take control of the process. A very widespread notion, for example, held that they could exact 'largesse' (i.e. money) from any stranger who set foot on the land on which they were working, or even who passed by on the footpath, and if the farmer himself appeared he could expect some rough handling. The following account was written in Northumberland in 1909, but refers to the second half of the nineteenth century:

> *A practical joke was played on the farmer if he dared to show himself in the field, and this he took good care as a rule not to do. It was called 'putting up the master'. If the farmer by any chance made his appearance, it was a custom for the hands, chiefly the women workers, to set on him, pull him off his horse, and 'grip' him, and toss him in the air, not only once, but three or four times, catching him as he fell … It says a great deal for the strength, nerve and dexterity of the harvest maidens of those days, that the farmer was always safely caught after his tossing and suffered no harm.*

The harvesters also called on tradesmen and others in the village who had dealings with the farm, and solicited contributions from them.

Many harvesters made a particular game out of cutting the last of the standing corn. A few stalks were left standing and tied together. The men then took it in turn to throw their sickles (sometimes blindfolded or backwards to make the game more difficult) to see who could cut them down. Others made even more of a ceremony of it. In 1903, the journal *Folk-Lore* reported:

> *A farm-worker from the East Riding of Yorkshire described a harvest custom of 'burning the old witch'. The harvesters twisted together the last few standing*

stalks of corn, making it into a little sheaf, and then
set fire to it. The last time he saw it done was about
1850, but he remembered it being referred to, as for
example when a co-worker said 'I think we'd better
burn it, if it would bring us better luck next time', as
late as the 1880s.

One regular procedure carried out upon the last sheaf, which was sometimes combined with the sickle-throwing, was called 'crying the neck', or something similar. It was most widespread in the West Country, but it existed elsewhere in the country too. This example, referring to Cornwall in 1839, was published in *Folk-Lore* in 1890:

Now, when all the corn was cut at Heligan, the farm-
ing men and women come in front of the house,
and bring with them a small sheaf of corn, the last
that has been cut, and this is adorned with ribbons
and flowers, and one part is tied quite tight, so as to
look like a neck. Then they cry out, 'Our/My side, my
side' as loud as they can; then the dairymaid gives
the neck to the head farming-man. He takes it and
says, very loudly three times, 'I have him, I have him,
I have him'. Then another farming-man shouts very
loudly, 'What have ye? what have ye? what have ye?',
'A neck, a neck, a neck'. And when he has said this, all
the people make a very great shouting. This they do
three times, and after one famous shout go away and
eat supper, and dance, and sing songs. The custom
passed away with the introduction of machines.

In other accounts, the ceremony was carried out in the field. The earliest, and fullest, description of this ceremony was contributed to William Hone's *Every-Day Book* in 1827 by a Devon correspondent.

A close examination of nineteenth- and twentieth-century descriptions shows that at that time the sickle-throwing, and probably also the 'crying of the neck', were simply games, and they may well have been nothing more than that. However, there may be relevant material in the regulations laid down on medieval manors to regulate the behaviour of the serfs in the harvest field – in particular, in the stipulations concerning the amount of free hay or corn the peasant could take from his lord's field after his labours there. The descriptions included in H. S. Bennett's excellent

Life on the English Manor 1150–1400 (1948) are at least suggestive of a connection with the later customs:

On certain Ramsey manors the peasants were
allowed to 'carry home so much hay or straw as they
could bind in a single bundle and lift upon their
sickle [or scythe] *handle, so that the handle touch*
not the ground. And, if perchance the handle break,
then he shall lose his straw or grass and be at the
lord abbot's mercy, and pay a fine, coming to the
best accord that he can with the abbot'... [another]
custom which allowed the serf to take from the
abbot's courtyard a bundle of as much straw as he
could carry, 'but, if the band break he shall lose his
straw'... In the west of England, on a manor of the
Abbot of Glastonbury, the size of the sheaf taken by
the peasant was measured in a strangely elaborate
manner: 'If any sheaf appears less than is right, it
ought to be put in the mud, and the hayward should
grasp his own hair above his ear, and the sheaf
should be drawn midway through his arm, and if this
can be done without defiling his garments or his hair,
then it is adjudged to be less than is right; but other-
wise it is judged sufficient.' In other manors the serfs
had the right to medkniche when they mowed the
lord's meadow. This was as much hay as the hayward
could lift with his little finger as high as his knees.

It takes no great stretch of the imagination to see these as possible precursors of the harvest games reported in the nineteenth century, and there are many more examples like these tucked away in medieval cartularies and other manorial documents. At present, evidence of a direct connection is hardly more than circumstantial and must be treated with due caution, but the hypothesis is certainly worth further investigation. Another 'game' related by Bennett was as follows:

In connection with the boon services at haymaking,
there was a widespread custom whereby the lord
released a sheep into the meadow. On some manors
it became the property of the serfs only if they could
catch it before it escaped out of the field; on other
manors it was handed over to them for their feast
as part of their reward... [Elsewhere] the ram was
brought to the centre of the field; if it remained
quietly grazing then the customary tenants claimed

it, but if it wandered out of the field they lost it and the abbess had it restored to her . . .

Once the corn was finally cut down, the last load was brought in with some considerable ceremony. The final cart itself was decorated with flowers, ribbons, greenery, and the like. Women and children would ride on top of the load, and sometimes a male and female were placed on the front of the waggon, to represent the king and queen of the harvest. These characters were not always what they seemed, as in a piece printed in *Folk-Lore* (1902) that referred to Oxfordshire in the 1830s:

On the last night of harvest, when the last load was to be carted, it was the custom to send down to the fields a number of band-boxes containing women's dresses and a good deal of finery for the men and horses. Four young men then dressed themselves up, two to represent women, and they sat in couples on the four horses that drew the load. Some of the village children sat on the top of the load (my inform-ant said that she and her sisters had often done so) and on reaching the house were treated to cakes, etc. . . . After this I believe the men had a supper.

Whatever else took place, there was always much shout-ing and cheering, as in this Devon example, also from *Folk-Lore* (1890):

At Kingsbridge, the following was formerly recited or sung (at the end of the harvest): 'we've a ploughed, and we've a sowed, we've a reaped, and we've a mowed, we've a sheaved, and we've a bound, and we'll a stood upon the ground'. At the end was 'Hip, hip, hip, hurrah!'

Several accounts of the last load mention that water was deliberately thrown over the jubilant harvesters:

The top of the last load was crowded with reapers – men, not children – who sang lustily as they came through the village 'Harvest home! Harvest home! We wants water and can't get none!' which certainly was not true in fact, as from every house they passed buckets of water were thrown on them . . .

This was from Oxfordshire in 1872, published in *Notes & Queries*, and a similar account in the same journal describes how, at a Rutland harvest, female servants waited concealed behind a hedge to attack the last load with buckets of water and apples.

The making of some sort of figure out of straw was extremely widespread in the British Isles, although it was not found, according to current evidence, in East Anglia, the south, or the south-east of the country. The figure went by a wide variety of names – 'kern', 'kirn', or 'churn', for example, from Yorkshire to Scotland – and was almost invariably referred to as a baby, or a female, such as 'maiden' or 'old hag'. This in itself has caused some confusion, as a historical account of, say, a 'harvest lady' could be describing a real person or a straw figure. The term 'corn dolly' was not used by farmworkers but was invented *c.*1940 by enthusiasts who developed straw-work into a new and complex craft.

The earliest probable reference to a straw figure comes from the writings of the German visitor Paul Hentzer, who met some harvest workers at Windsor, *c.*1598, and commented that their last load was deco-rated with flowers and 'an image richly dressed'. In later accounts, the nature of the figure, its size and complexity, what was done with it, and how it was treated, varied enormously and still needs to be fully documented. The figure might be made from the last stalks cut or from the 'best' straw; sometimes the figure consisted of a few stalks twisted together, usually in a cross or a crude human form, and sometimes it was skilfully made up to represent a small human figure, decorated with ribbons, and so on. However, if an elab-orate figure was fashioned, it must of necessity have been made some time in advance of the last load if it was to adorn the cart on its way back to the farmyard. In some accounts, it seems to have been simply decora-tive, but in others it was definitely symbolic and was hung up in the barn, on the principle that some part of that year's luck should be kept until the next year. This principle operated in other customs, such as the Yule Log, of which many householders were careful to keep a piece to be used to light next year's specimen (see **24 December: Yule Log**). The straw figure could also be used in a protective way, as in this Lincolnshire example from 1899:

No further back than last September, I saw a verita-ble 'kern baby' – a largish doll cunningly twisted out of barley straw, and perched up on a sheaf exactly facing the gate of the grand wheat-field in which it stood. I missed seeing the owner, a small freeholder, but mentioning the matter to an old dame (of whom a Marshman would say, 'them as knows all she knows hasn't no need to go to no school'). She made a reply which proves that, whatever else the Marshman has learnt of late to doubt, he still firmly believes in the Devil and his angels: 'Yes, she be there to fey away t' thunder an' lightnin' an' such-like. Prayers be good enough as far as they goes, but t' Almighty must be strange an' throng wi' so much corn to look after, an' in these here bad times we mustn't forget owd Providence. Happen it's best to keep in wi' both parties.'

Finally, it might even be sent to a neighbouring farmer who had not yet finished his harvest as a not-so-subtle jibe at his tardiness. This procedure was sometimes called 'the mare', but 'crying the mare' could also be achieved with a real horse. According to *The Times* (2 October 1934):

[An] *explanation was given me nearly 40 years ago by an old labourer in Staffordshire who remembered the days before the introduction of reaping and threshing machines. The first farmer to finish his harvest, he told me, would dress up one of his horses with ribbons, etc., and send it round in derision to his neighbours who were not so fortunate as himself. This mocking offer of help was, of course, always refused and the rider of the horse generally pelted. For this reason, said Old Dick, they generally put up on the mare the youngest boy on the farm. Such was the custom in Staffordshire in the first half of the nineteenth century.*

Gleaning

On most farms, by long-standing custom, local people were allowed on to the fields after harvest to 'glean' what crops had escaped the harvesters. Gleaning was an extremely important contribution to the domestic economy, and sufficient grain could sometimes be gathered to keep a family in flour for the whole winter. It had been allowed for time out of mind, and was regarded by many villagers as an inalienable right, although in reality it was at the discretion of the

farmer unless written into the agreement made with the harvesters.

Gleaning conduct was usually governed by well-understood local rules. Some farmers would leave a single sheaf in the field to signify that gleaning could not yet take place, and in many areas the church bell was tolled to signal the start and finish of the gleaning day. For local mothers gleaning was hard work, but it was not all bad for the children, as Edwin Grey described in his memories of rural Hertfordshire in the 1870s:

The gleaning season was made the most of by many of the cottage women, for the flour obtained as a result of this wheat gleaning was a great asset to the food supply of the household during the autumn and early winter. There were, of course, many women who, owing to home ties and duties, could not go out to glean, but the number who did so, together with the boys and girls, was quite considerable ... The gleaning of the harvest fields was much enjoyed by the youngsters, both boys and girls, for those who attended school were at this season of the year on holiday, and so were, as one might say, free; so that I and many others, though not compelled to glean, went more for the fun. As a rule the children did their bit at gleaning, but it was the games, the romping, and the searching of the hedgerows for nuts, skeggs (a large sloe) etc., which was the lure for most of us boys ... Mrs. Day was recognized as the head of our party. She it was who decided as to our route; to which farm and to which field we should go; the other women told of information obtained from their husbands as to the progress of the harvesting at the respective farms on which they worked, when such and such a field would probably be cleared and so on ...

I so well remember the lively cottager [Mrs Day], for although past middle age, she would sometime indulge in a step-dance for her own and our amusement. She generally wore a large straw hat with turned-down brim all round (mushroom shape, I think it was called) with a sort of frilled cap beneath it. To an outsider from town, these gleaning parties must have looked a queer company, for most wore their oldest clothes ... but although an odd-look-

ing lot of humanity, they were by no manner of means dejected or miserable, for they moved off to their destination with laughter, chatter, and many snatches of song. They carried their day's rations with them, generally bread, butter, cheese, or maybe some cold meat, or other homely fare, together with a bottle or two of cold tea, these provisions being either in baskets or wrapped in cloths or aprons. The two latter were used later to tie up the handfuls of wheat into bundles, which were then carried home on the head . . . It was an unwritten law that gleaning could not commence until the last shock was carried . . . When at length the time came to start gleaning, each donned his 'earbag'. This was made of any material, with strings or tapes at the top corners to tie round the waist; it was worn in front of the body, and had the appearance of a small apron nearly all pocket. Into this pocket during the gleaning were put the short or broken-off ears; we were told to pick up all of these short ears, and were assured that they were the best wheat. When the gleaning was finished for the day, the bunches of gleaned wheat were tied up into bundles in the cloths or aprons, large bundles for the adults and smaller ones for the youngsters; with those well-balanced on the head they started for home. I recollect the youngsters used to sing, or shout as they neared any cottage: 'Wheat, wheat, harvest home, see what great bundles we bring home.' On arriving at home, the wheat ears would be cut from the straw, the ears being put into a sack, or tied up into a bundle, the straw being either burnt or thrown into a neighbour's pigsty.

Harvest Suppers

Soon after the prolonged effort of getting in the harvest, most farmers treated their workers to a celebratory feast in the form of a harvest supper, although the exact name varied according to locality – harvest home, mell supper (in the northern counties), or horkey supper (in eastern England), for example. The event also varied considerably in scale, depending on the nature and size of the farm, the character of the farmer, and the social structure of the village, but most followed a relatively standard pattern. The successful harvest was a village-wide event, and it was common for key people in the village to be invited along to the supper. Some, like the squire, vicar, and doctor, were invited as a matter of courtesy because of their social position, while others, such as the blacksmith and wheelwright, were there as an acknowledgement of the part they played throughout the year in keeping the farm operational. Descriptions of harvest suppers often stress the class-less nature of the proceedings, with master and man attending on equal terms, but although this may have been the ideal, it can hardly ever have been the real situation. Not only was there a sharp division between farmer and worker, but within the farm workforce there was a strict hierarchy in which most workers were extremely jealous of their position. Nevertheless, the huge team effort needed to get the harvest in success-fully gave the harvest home at least a temporary foun-dation of brotherhood and common cause, assisted, no doubt, by the alcohol, which flowed freely.

It goes without saying that the real attraction for the workers was the feast itself. The opportunity to indulge in good food and drink, in large quantity, and at some-one else's expense, was too rare to be treated lightly, and there are many tales of the prodigious quantities some men could put away at this one sitting.

> [Norfolk, 1845] *Tomorrow the men have a harvest-home dinner, and the next day they put apart to get drunk; such being the invariable custom of the county. I proposed last year that they should get drunk on the day of the harvest dinner, but they scouted the idea – they would have a day for intoxi-cation entirely. Such was the custom. It was true that they would lose a day's wages, but they must do as their forefathers had always done before them.*

From a psychological perspective, this was not simply senseless gluttony. The harvest supper was the official end to an exceptionally gruelling time for most of the workers, who had been toiling hard, against the clock, for weeks on end. It was certainly an emotional and physical release as well as a free meal.

Harvest suppers usually took place in the barn, which had been cleaned up and decorated for the occasion. They tended to begin with the feast, then speeches and toasts would follow – particularly those thanking the farmer and his family – then singing, with contribu-tions from all and sundry. The singing might last for

Harvest home (*Illustrated London News*, 1843)

the rest of the evening, or it might be adjourned so that dancing could take place. In many cases, the farmer and his family would stay for the feast, the toasts, and the speeches, but would then withdraw, along with any other 'gentry', to let the workers enjoy themselves in their own way. However, there were many variations on this pattern, and games and other entertainments were sometimes included. The following is a Dorset version of the most widely reported harvest supper song, published in 1935:

> *Here's a health unto our Master, the founder of the feast*
> *I hope to God wi' all me heart his soul in heaven may rest*
> *And all his works may prosper, whatever he takes in hand*
> *For we are all his servants, and here at his command*
> *Then drink, boys, drink, and see you do not spill*
> *For if you do, you shall drink two, it is our Master's will.*
> *Here's a health unto our Master, our Mistress shan't go free*

> *For she's a good provider, provides as well as he*
> *For she's a good provider, and bids us all to come*
> *So take this cup and sup it up, for 'tis our harvest home*
> *Home boys home, home boys home*
> *Fill it up to the brim and drink it off clane*
> *For 'tis our harvest home.*

The theme of drinking was common in the songs, and in many of the games. In Yorkshire and Northumberland, young men wearing disguises might make a show of gatecrashing the event, as described by veteran folklorist Eliza Gutch in 1901:

> *Later in the evening a wild cry of fire! or an alarm of some kind would be sprung upon those within the barn. Whatever form the alarm given took, it had but one object in view, to induce those within to open the barn door. This having by some means been accomplished, the 'Guisers', a kind of sword dancers, attempted to force an entrance; and although it was the universal custom to make some show of keeping out these uninvited guests, they were always*

permitted to join the party, for great was the merriment they created.

The same book includes the text of a traditional
dialect playlet that was performed in the 1820s, which
comprised a sung dialogue between Polly and, in
succession, an old man, an old lady, and a squire; she
decides to marry the latter.

Other places had other traditions. In 1896, a
Lincolnshire contributor to *Notes & Queries* wrote:

> *In the first quarter of the present century 'the old sow'*
> *used to appear in that county at harvest suppers. To*
> *the critical eye this curious animal was nothing more*
> *nor less than two men dressed up in sacks to person-*
> *ate a traditional visitor to the feast. Its head was*
> *filled with cuttings from a furze-bush, and its habit*
> *was to prick everyone whom it honoured with its*
> *attentions. 'I used to be very much afraid of it when I*
> *was a child,' says my informant.*

Despite the show of égalité and fraternity to which the
harvest supper aspired, there were many in the nineteenth century who disapproved of the rough humour
and potential gluttony and drunkenness involved in
such affairs. Even before the suppers were killed by
mechanization and the reduction of the agricultural
workforce, there was pressure to clean them up. George
James Dew, of Lower Heyford, Oxford, recorded in his
diary a visit to a combined 'harvest home' for several
of the farms in his neighbourhood, in September 1864,
when he was eighteen. The event was clearly one of the
new-style, respectable affairs, with the vicar, and other
local worthies, presiding and giving speeches; entry was
by ticket. This was a far cry from the old homely private
gatherings of farmer and workers that were now being
castigated for their rough and drunken ways. Dew was
particularly impressed, as was the reporter from the
Oxford Chronicle (10 September 1864):

> *There could be no better proof of the good under-*
> *standing existing amongst the farmers of Lower*
> *Heyford than the unanimity and goodwill which*
> *existed among them on this first general gathering,*
> *for we believe that all joined in this demonstration*
> *with heartiness and goodwill which resulted in most*
> *complete success.*

Harvest Festivals

On 23 September 2000, the *Telegraph* reported:

> *Harvest festival is upon us again, a time when*
> *churches all over England welcome the fruitfulness*
> *of autumn by propping giant marrows against the*
> *rails of the altars and singing 'We plough the fields*
> *and scatter'.*

The harvest festival as we know it today was the single-
handed invention of one of the great eccentric clergymen of the nineteenth century, Robert Stephen Hawker
(1803–75), who was the vicar of Morwenstow parish in
north Cornwall for forty-one years. Despite the isolated
position of his parish, Hawker was well known in his
lifetime not only for his strange behaviour and colourful clothes, but also for his somewhat unorthodox religious beliefs, which culminated in his being baptized
into the Roman Catholic Church on his deathbed. He
was an enthusiastic antiquary, a published poet, and
intimately involved in the lives of his parishioners.
Stories of his antics abounded: he was said to have
rescued sailors from wrecks, fought drunken fishermen, smashed up the old pews in his church with an
axe, and regularly preached surrounded by ten cats.

Hawker announced the idea of a harvest thanksgiving to his congregation in 1843, and his notion obviously struck a chord with the times because within a
decade the idea had been taken up in churches all over
the country. Harvest festivals rapidly became widespread, and it became quite normal for churches to
be decorated with fruit, flowers, vegetables, and other
produce donated by the congregation, on a Sunday in
late September or early October. Even in the twentieth
century, the harvest festival had for many a slightly
unofficial feel about it, as if it belonged to the people
rather than the church itself, and it was certainly one of
the most popular events in the ecclesiastical calendar.

Hawker was very fond of early Church history, and
he almost certainly got the idea from reading about
Lammas (*see* **1 August**), which was probably celebrated
as a festival of 'first fruits' in the Anglo-Saxon Church.
Some authorities therefore write of him 'reviving'
rather than inventing the harvest thanksgiving, and he
may well have thought of it in this way himself.

Harvest festival at St Mary Redcliffe, Bristol

Hop-Picking

The use of hops for making beer was introduced into England from Holland in the early fifteenth century, and the new ingredient turned the traditional English ale into beer. The new bitter drink met with some opposition from traditionalists and gained acceptance only slowly, but hop-growing gradually became a major agricultural industry, so that by the mid seventeenth century hops were grown in fourteen counties in England. Kent claims to be the site of the earliest cultivation in Britain, and certainly it was the most famous of hop-growing areas, accounting for over a third of the national crop.

If left alone, hop bines will grow along the ground and twine around anything they meet, but cultivators soon learned to provide poles and wires for the hops to climb; if tied at regular intervals, they will grow over twenty feet high. The short picking season, and the labour-intensive task of hand-picking, made the use of migrant workers inevitable, and as the work of removing the hops from the bines was suitable for women and children, whole families could be involved, as Arthur Young's *Farmer's Kalendar* (1771) was well aware:

> Plenty of hands should, on all accounts, be provided for this important business; women do it as well as men; it is a work rather of care than of labour.

Hop-picking was thus very different from the usual pattern of predominately male migrant agricultural work, and whole families used to move into the area for the season, with the well-known annual exodus of working-class families from East London to go 'hopping down in Kent' mirrored in a smaller way in the Midlands and other hop-growing areas. Hopping was hard work and conditions were rough, but many urban families regarded it as a holiday with pay.

The local people viewed the annual invasion with ambivalence. Country folk have always distrusted townies, and the East London working-class families who descended on quiet Kent villages often seemed like a race of aliens to the locals, although as it happened every year both residents and visitors knew roughly what to expect. The influx brought colour, noise, and excitement, which pleased and frightened some locals in equal measure, but their townie habits were unfamiliar, and they behaved with a remarkable lack of restraint, as people on holiday often do. Country writer C. Henry Warren recorded his memories of village life in his *Boy in Kent* (1938), calling his chapter on hop-picking 'The Gay Invaders':

> These were all people from a world I knew nothing about. If I had been suddenly conveyed to the Bermudas, I could not have been more entranced than I was by these gay and vivacious people.

They brought welcome trade to the village, but this too came at a price. The following piece describes the scene in his father's village shop:

> In the shop itself the stir and bustle was just as frantic. First of all everything was cleared away until not so much as a jar of sweets or a tin of treacle was left within reach, and even in the windows there was nothing but a swept-up heap of dead wasps in a corner. Then, after the shop had been scrubbed from top to bottom, Horace, the odd-job man, would arrive with planks and poles and hammer and nails and begin erecting a high barricade round the counters. The place rattled with his vigorous hammerings . . . 'I think we could do with just a few more nails here, Horace', my father would say, 'or we shall have the hooligans all over us in a trice!'

Many pubs simply refused to serve them. But it was quite common for families to frequent the same farm every year, and in many cases a guarded respect or even friendship was built up over the generations. Many local families also welcomed the chance to earn extra money during the season, which helped with expenses such as winter fuel, or new coats and boots for the children, although locals and Londoners were usually kept apart in the fields. In *East Kent Within Living Memory* (1993), a villager is recorded saying:

> Our farm was a small, privately owned farm, where no Londoners were allowed; we were all 'respectable' local families.

The same villager also remembered the four-mile walk to and from the farm, the difficulty getting the brown stains and horrid taste off the hands, and the smell:

> The smell of the hops was really overpowering and

Hop-picking, *c.*1908

a few people, my mother and myself among them, were quite badly affected, feeling sick and faint for the first few days, after which we became immune to the smell.

It is easy to romanticize the old hand-picking days. The visiting pickers were often housed in appalling conditions, a state of affairs that lasted well into the twentieth century, and improvements were mainly the result of agitation by interested outsiders. Sending missionaries to the hop-fields was a popular activity for London churches, and even if the visiting philanthropists were overly concerned with the pickers' moral and spiritual shortcomings, they did sterling work in advertising and improving the degrading living conditions and lack of sanitation provided by the hop-growers.

Hop-picking naturally had its own traditional customs, modelled on those of other seasonal agricultural tasks, such as the hop-pickers' feast to celebrate the end of the season, and the election of a king and queen of the hop-fields. A traditional way of greeting a stranger, or punishing some minor transgression of hop-field etiquette, was by 'cribbing' them – bundling them into one of the hop bins.

By the middle of the twentieth century, the great days of hop-growing in Britain were definitely over, and as machines took over from hand-picking, a whole way of life simply faded away.

EARLY SEPTEMBER

Colchester Oyster Fishery

The River Colne and neighbouring estuaries on the Essex coast have been famous for oysters since Roman times and maybe even before. The industry of commercial oyster-growing needs to be carefully organized in order to avoid a local free-for-all, and this was recognized in the first municipal charter granted to the town of Colchester by Richard I in 1189, by which the corporation owns the fisheries, which are then rented out.

The oyster season traditionally opens in September,

and runs through to March – quite literally, as the proverb says, when there is an 'R' in the month. Early in September, the Mayor of Colchester, accompanied by other members and officials of the corporation, ventures out in a boat to dredge up the first oysters of the season. The charter is read out, and the company partakes of gin and gingerbread – nobody knows why – and samples the fresh oysters. They also send a loyal message to the Queen. The ceremony does not always go quite to plan, as *The Times* of 22 September 1928 reported:

> *The company were about to drink a toast in gin, in accordance with ancient custom, when the table containing the tiny glasses, filled with gin, overbalanced and fell, crashing to the deck, together with the small cakes of gingerbread provided for the occasion. Amid hearty laughter fresh supplies were soon forthcoming and the ceremony concluded in the time-honoured fashion.*

Later in the year, Colchester holds its annual Oyster Feast (*see* **20 October**).

Commercial oyster fishing is now concentrated in the Mersea Island area, due south of Colchester. According to the *Independent* (30 September 2005), Colchester native oysters are highly regarded abroad, and local producers have applied to the European Union for the delicacy to be granted Protected Geographical Indication (PGI) status, which would recognize its unique qualities and stipulate that it can only be produced in the designated area.

See also **25 July: Whitstable Oyster Festival**.

*

A SUNDAY IN SEPTEMBER

Horseman's Sunday

On a Sunday in September, horses and their riders gather outside the church of St John and St Michael, in Hyde Park Crescent, London, for a service and blessing conducted by the local vicar, who is also on horseback. The horses all receive commemorative rosettes, and they then parade around the park. The event was founded in 1968, by local resident Ross Nye, who was worried that if local riding stables were closed, horses

would disappear from the area. A similar event takes place in the same month on Epsom Downs.

For other horse parades, *see* **Easter Monday: Harness Horse Parade**, p. 129; **1 May: Horse Decorations**.

*

1 SEPTEMBER

St Giles's Day

Almost nothing is known of the real St Giles, who died about the year 710, except that he founded a monastery in Provence. This did not stop the medieval legend-makers, however, who provided a set of colourful incidents for his life story, including an explanation of how he was given the money for his great foundation. It was said that while he was living as a hermit he was accompanied by a pet doe, which provided milk for his nourishment. Unfortunately, the King's huntsmen loved to pursue this doe and eventually trapped her in the dense thicket in which Giles lived. The doe was protected from harm by Giles's prayers, but he himself was wounded by a huntsman's arrow. The King, on recognizing Giles's holiness, gave him many gifts, which he used to found the monastery. In other parts of the legend, Giles demonstrated remarkable healing powers, along with the ability to obtain pardon for people's sins, however great, simply by prayer.

These stories contributed to Giles's fame, and he was widely popular in medieval England, with many churches dedicated to him. His feast day was conveniently placed in the year for outdoor events, and was particularly popular for local fairs, feasts, and revels. Two of the most famous fairs in the country were held, at different periods, around St Giles's Day: one at Oxford, which still continues, and the other at Winchester. The Oxford fair was described by fairs historian R. W. Muncey in the 1930s:

> *Probably the greatest features of the fair are the steam roundabouts of various kinds, which are lit up at night by the brightest of electric lights, and stretch along for some considerable distance above the college in nearly one unbroken line and are usually crowded by numbers of visitors. The steam organs and instruments are continually playing and*

cause the greater part of the din which drowns every other softer sound. The fair occupies all the open space between St. Giles's Church and the Martyrs' Memorial. There are to be seen a circus, midgets, boxing exhibitions, freaks, people fat and people strong; while swings and sausage stalls occupy a place, together with shooting galleries and cocoa-nut shies. Smaller booths and stalls line the pavement of the street on both sides. Here you can buy toys, crockery and fancy articles of various kinds.

Strictly speaking, St Giles's Fair is not a proper fair at all, as it seems not to have been founded by charter but to have grown from a local 'wake', probably based on the feast day of the church (*see* **Fairs, Feasts, Wakes, and Revels**, p. 249). Nor is it nearly as ancient as many writers seem to think: the fashion at one time to describe it as 'eight hundred years old' seems to be based on the date of the foundation of St Giles's church. It is possible that an annual wake commenced at that time, but the earliest known documentary reference dates only from the 1620s, and the event only started to become widely known in the early nineteenth century. Its very shape proclaims its special nature. Not many large fairs now take place in city streets, and those that do are usually squashed into a central circle or square, but this fair stretches out along both sides of St Giles's church and into Woodstock and Banbury Roads.

As with most big fairs, St Giles's Fair came under pressure in Victorian times because of its drunkenness and rowdy behaviour, and came close to suppression at times, but it managed to survive and is still held on the first Monday and Tuesday in September, drawing large enthusiastic crowds. In direct contrast to its rowdy past, however, the Bishop of Oxford and the choir of St Giles's church nowadays open the fair with a blessing and some songs, delivered from one of the large roundabouts.

There is no doubt about the age of St Giles's Fair at Winchester, which flourished and died centuries before its Oxford counterpart. There is some disagreement about whether the oldest fairs in England were founded by the Romans or the Anglo-Saxons, but it was the Normans who were particularly energetic in the granting of charters for new fairs. Grants were often made to religious foundations as a convenient way of raising money for large building projects or the maintenance of monasteries and other institutions, and the great St Giles's Fair at Winchester was a good example of such a grant. It was founded by charter from William Rufus in 1079, primarily to raise money for rebuilding the cathedral, and although originally restricted to three days, it was so popular that in its heyday its term stretched to twenty-four days. The gathering took place on the top of St Giles's Hill, just outside the town, and the stalls on the site were so substantial, and laid out in regular streets, that it was likened to a 'wooden town', surrounded by a large fence to ensure that no traders got in or out without paying the required fees. The fair continued under the strict ownership and control of the Bishop, who opened it each year with much ceremony, and the city had no jurisdiction for the duration, which caused constant friction between the ecclesiastical and secular authorities. This fair attracted traders from all over Britain and Europe, and was one of the four major fairs in the country (the others were St Ives, Northampton, and Boston), but by the fifteenth century it was in decline. The citizens of Winchester petitioned for their own fair in 1449, and were granted a nine-day fair on St Swithun's Day (15 July); however, the days of St Giles's glory were past.

Many other smaller fairs and feasts took place on or around St Giles's Day, but one puzzling custom that is worthy of note took place at Hawkridge, in Somerset, on the Sunday nearest to St Giles's Day, which was their local Revel Sunday: on this day the rector was pelted with apples on his way from the rectory to the church. This bizarre custom was also reported from other places in the country at other times of the year (*see* **28 July: Old St Kenelm's Day**).

*

3 SEPTEMBER

Cromwell Day

The Cromwell Society exists to promote the study and understanding of the life and times of Oliver Cromwell (1599–1658). They commemorate the day of his death, 3 September, with an open-air service in front of his statue outside the Houses of Parliament, and lay a wreath there. The service is only allowed to be attended by members of the Cromwell Association, but the proceedings can be seen and heard from the public pavement.

Merchant Navy Day

In the year 2000, the Merchant Navy Association (founded 1989) declared 3 September as Merchant Navy Day, in commemoration of the sinking by U-boat of the unarmed merchant vessel the SS *Athenia* on this day in 1939 – the first day of the Second World War. All nineteen crew and ninety-three passengers were lost. Merchant seamen have long felt that their service's significant contribution to the war effort has been undervalued, and it is one of the aims of the Society to raise the profile of the Merchant Navy and celebrate its importance to Britain, past and present.

4 SEPTEMBER

Abbots Bromley Horn Dance

On the Monday following the local Wakes Sunday (i.e. the first Sunday after 4 September, or Old St Bartholomew's Day), the village and surroundings of Abbots Bromley in Staffordshire are visited by a unique set of dancers. The team comprises six men, each carrying a splendid pair of reindeer antlers, plus a Fool, a Maid Marian (played by a man), a hobby horse, a bowman (who twangs a bow), a musician and a triangle player.

Starting from the parish church at 8 a.m., the team perambulates the parish, visiting key houses, farms, and other places, at every stop forming up to perform their dance. Between visits, they often stroll along, as if 'off-duty', but when approaching any dancing place they fall into single file behind the leader, sometimes weaving in a serpentine form, or form a circle. At each 'station' they form up in two lines, advance and retire a few times, tilting their horns as they meet, and then cross over and repeat. During this dance, the horns are carried at chest height, and although they advance towards each other, they do not make any aggressive movements and they certainly do not clash them together, as some writers claim; nor is there any fancy

dance-step, but what has been variously described as an 'easy, matter-of-fact walk', or a 'steady rhythmical plod'. Round about 8 p.m. they return to the village and perform their final dance in the street.

Reliable eyewitness accounts from the earlier twentieth century all stress the unhurried and determinedly unspectacular manner of the whole affair, as in *The Times* of 7 September 1936:

> The whole thing is done unassumably and with a quiet purposefulness which is the keynote of the whole proceedings. One feels they are not dancing for joy or self-expression, but going quietly about a task which must be accomplished without unnecessary fuss.

Similarly, folklorist Evelyn Wells wrote in 1938:

> There was no audience, nor any expected. A small boy carried sandwiches and a flask. A horn dancer's wife straightened their costumes and sent them off . . . The costumes, which they hope soon to renew, were shabby; one or two chewed gum, and the hobby horse had an occasional cigarette. The tunes, a fast one and a slow one, were of a nameless variety.

The costumes worn today do not go back very far. A set of pseudo-medieval jerkins and knee-breeches was designed by Mrs Lowe, the local vicar's wife, in the 1880s, possibly based at some remove on those of the morris dancers shown in the famous early sixteenth-century painted window (usually called the Betley window, but now at Leigh Manor, Minsterley, in Shropshire). The costumes were renewed in 1904, and again in 1951, on similar lines, and this design has now become traditional in itself, but they remain as a warning to those who would take things at face value and extrapolate backwards to construct theories of origin. According to *The Times* (7 September 1936), 'The days are still remembered when the dancers wore only their workaday clothes with a few pink and white rosettes fastened to them for the occasion.'

The horns are kept in the church when not in use. They are genuine reindeer horns, mounted on wooden heads, with a handle protruding below to enable the dancers to carry them as they dance. They weigh between 16 and 25 lb, with a span ranging from 77 cm to 101 cm, and they seem to have always been painted

Abbots Bromley horn dancers, Staffordshire (Benjamin Stone, 1906)

three of one colour and three of another, although the colours have changed over the years – from red and white, to blue and white, and at present brown and off-white. One of the horns was carbon-dated in 1976, and the result was a mean date of AD 1065 +/- 80 years, although where they came from, and how they got to Abbots Bromley, remains unknown.

The earliest references are not quite as straightforward as one would like. Robert Plot, in his *Natural History of Staffordshire* (1686), mentions a 'hobby horse dance' accompanied by six men carrying 'rain deers heads', which was performed at Christmas, New Year, and Twelfth Night. Sir Simon Degge (1612–1704), who was brought up in the area, annotated his copy of Plot's book with the comment that he had often seen the dance before the Civil War, which probably takes us back to the 1620s. More recently, morris-dance historian Mike Heaney discovered an earlier reference,

which shows that the hobby horse already existed in the parish in 1532, but it does not mention the horns. In Plot's day the season for performance was midwinter, which is certainly the most common time for 'animal disguise' customs elsewhere in the country, and it was transferred to Wakes Week at some later date. Later sources also indicate that the dancers used to go out on several consecutive days.

There has naturally been a great deal of speculation about the origin of the custom, and many have connected it to a pagan fertility ritual, an ancient ceremony to ensure successful hunting, and the assertion of some common right or privilege in regard to the chase, but none of these is supported by any evidence. It may even be that the hobby horse is older than the horn dance. What is clear is that the hobby horse, as at other places, was used in the sixteenth century to collect taxes and dues owed to the lord of the manor (*see* **Hobby Horses**, p. 164); and Plot, straight after describing the dance, writes of money being collected for cakes and ale, and used to repair the church and keep the poor. Whether the horse did the collecting, or simply accompanied the money-collectors to sweeten the event by entertaining the people, is not known. But a significant proportion of early references indicate that this money-gathering was the horse's primary purpose.

On the question of dating, one confident but groundless assertion is that the horn dance was first performed at the founding of the local fair in 1226. This idea is now met with in so many sources that it is probably impossible to eradicate. It apparently started with speculation by Marcia Rice in her 1939 history of Abbots Bromley, and while it is true that Henry III granted a three-day fair for St Bartholomew's Day in 1226, there is no evidence that this had anything to do with the horn dancers.

Barnet Horse Fair

There is something romantic and slightly dangerous about a horse fair, which other livestock marts cannot hope to equal. Perhaps it is simply that Gypsies do not gather to exchange handfuls of money over sheep, or gentlemen wager their families' fortunes on a cow race. This fair was chartered in 1588, and for centuries was one of the busiest livestock marts in the region – although Barnet's real fame was for horse-racing, which drew large unruly crowds from north London until it ceased in 1870. The associated horse fair was similarly patronized by dealers and buyers from the capital, and was so well attended by street traders in mid Victorian times that it was known in some circles as the 'costermongers' carnival'. According to James Greenwood's *Unsentimental Journeys* (1867), it enjoyed an extremely raffish reputation:

> My first impression was my last, and still remains – viz, that Barnet Fair is a disgrace to civilisation. I have witnessed a Warwickshire 'mop' fair; I have some recollection of 'Bartlemy'; I was at Greenwich when, on account of its increasing abominations, the fair that so long afflicted that Kentish borough was held for the last time; but take all these, and skim them for their scum and precipitate them for

> their dregs, and even then, unless you throw in a very strong flavouring of the essence of Old Smithfield on a Friday, and a good armful of Colney Hatch and Earlswood sprigs, you will fail to make a brew equal to that at Barnet. It is appalling.

Given this kind of write-up, it is remarkable that Barnet Horse Fair survived at all, but while the races and the general livestock have long been forgotten, the horse fair persists to this day, albeit somewhat shakily. By the mid twentieth century, the glory days were well over, but it was still a significant date on the horse-lover's calendar, as William Addison indicates in his *English Fairs and Markets* (1953):

> Barnet Fair is still the most racy event of its kind near London. Even in 1952, 620 horses were sold, including 74 sturdy Welsh cobs from Glamorgan, most of which changed hands within a couple of hours.

However, the real threat to the fair came not from human opposition but the inexorable march of bricks and mortar, as the area rapidly developed from Hertfordshire countryside into a north London borough. The site of the fair changed many times in the interwar years, and it was increasingly seen as a historical relic. On 6 September 1954, *The Times* commented:

> In a 20-acre field which once afforded wider vistas, Barnet horse fair opened today, bringing its annual touch of medieval muddle to what tidy modern planners know as the South Hertfordshire conurbation. New facets of the fair's surroundings add point to the remarkable fact of its survival each year; since last September council flats have risen on waste ground close by and beyond the fairground stands the vitreous contemporary cube of a new school.

A mere shadow of its former self, Barnet Horse Fair is now held at Greengates Stables, on 4, 5, and 6 September, unless one of those dates is a Sunday, in which case it continues on the following day.

*

14 SEPTEMBER

Holy Rood or Holy Cross Day

This day, also known as the Exaltation of the Cross, has a somewhat confused ancestry. A much-revered relic of the True Cross was carried off by the Persians in the year 614, when they occupied Jerusalem, but it was recovered in the spring of 629 and lodged in Constantinople for safety; this event, however, is commemorated as a feast day on 14 September.

In English folk tradition, 14 September has long been known as 'the Devil's Nutting Day'; a phrase that draws together several strands of folklore dating back at least 450 years. Early connections between Holy Rood Day and nutting are shown in a tradition at Eton in 1560, recorded by antiquarian John Brand, in which the boys were allowed a half-holiday on the day to gather nuts, and in the line 'all the youth are now a-nutting gone', which occurs in *Grim the Collier of Croydon*, an anonymous play of the early seventeenth century. 'Going a-nutting' also crops up in songs and plays as a byword for seduction and sex, which gave the activity a particularly risqué air, and a well-known notion, current from at least the 1660s to the late twentieth century, claimed 'a good year for nuts, a good year for babies'. The Devil was also often coupled with the gathering of nuts. Country people were constantly warned not to go nutting on Sundays, as the Devil would be there, disguised as a gentleman, to pull down the upper branches for them. And going nutting on 14 September was believed to be particularly risky, as in the letter written by the Northamptonshire poet John Clare to William Hone, in 1825:

> On Holy Rood day it is faithfully and confidently believed both by old and young that the Devil goes a-nutting on that day and I have heard many people affirm that they once thought it a tale till they ventured to the woods on that day when they smelt such a strong smell of brimstone as nearly stifled them before they could escape out again.

There is also at least one legend (at Haselor, Warwickshire) that tells how a particular hill was formed when the Devil dropped his nutting bag in fright when he met the Virgin Mary on the road. In a few sources, 21 September is named as the 'Devil's Nutting Day'.

On a different note, passion flowers were traditionally associated with the crucifixion, and by extension with Holy Rood Day, when it was supposed most likely to flower. Believers saw symbolic analogies between parts of the flower and Christ's five wounds, the three nails used, and so on.

Shaftesbury Byzant

As it was built on a hill, the town of Shaftesbury in Dorset was without a water supply of its own, and inhabitants had to collect their water from wells at Enmore Green, in the neighbouring parish of Gillingham. In order to preserve their ancient right of access, the townsfolk processed to Enmore every year on Holy Cross Day, and there performed a dance and presented the monarch's bailiff with a penny loaf, a gallon of ale, a calf's head, and a pair of gloves. This annual excursion to Enmore had already developed into a general holiday by at least 1364, and the celebrations were further formalized by a new agreement between the Mayor of Shaftesbury and the Lord of Gillingham manor in 1662. This agreement also speaks of the procession being headed by a 'prize besome', decorated with feathers, gold, rings, and jewels – presumably the forerunner of the curious 'byzant', which is now in Shaftesbury Museum and has been described by researcher George Frampton as:

> . . . a trophy or mace about three feet in height . . . weighing around 40 lbs. Its frame is made of carved wood with gilded gesso, and is liberally decorated with gold coins, peacocks' feathers, and ribbons. In one year, this included a great variety of silver and gold medals, stone buckles, and garnet necklaces, and up the sides a number of diamond rings . . . and four pictures in miniature.

The annual processions continued until the custom lapsed in 1829, but it was revived, in varying degrees of fidelity to the original, on several occasions in the twentieth century.

Baiting Bears and Other Animals

Bull-baiting and bear-baiting were the two most popular 'sports' that pitted dogs against other animals for entertainment. **Bull-baiting** (p. 352) was more of an everyday occurrence and took place in pub yards and market-places for all and sundry to watch, but bear-baiting was more likely to be staged in more controlled surroundings, where admission could be charged. Both could be seen on a regular basis.

Bear-baiting has a long history. It is often stated that the sport was introduced to Britain from Italy in the twelfth century, and was first seen at Ashby-de-la-Zouche in Leicestershire, but it is likely to have been known here long before that time, as it was on the Continent. The first definite mention of the sport in England is in William Fitz Stephen's *Description of London* (c.1180; reprinted as *Norman London* in 1990), where he writes:

> In winter on almost every feast day . . . fat bulls with butting horns, or huge bears, do combat to the death against hounds let loose upon them.

Judging by the frequency with which bear-baiting appears in diaries and published accounts, it was a far from unusual spectacle in Britain from the sixteenth century onwards. Royalty was partial to the sport, and Henry VIII and Elizabeth I both kept their own stables of bears and mastiffs, as did several of the country's nobles in the same period. There were also regular venues, particularly in London, where the paying public could see baitings of various kinds; two of the most famous were the bear gardens at Bankside, Southwark, and Hockley-in-the-Hole, Clerkenwell. For the next 300 years, anyone who wished to attend a bear-baiting could usually find one somewhere in London most weeks of the year. The advertisements for these institutions make grim reading for modern eyes, as they often declared how fiercely the different animals would fight, and that the contests would be 'to the death!', as if the spectators felt cheated if no animal was actually killed.

In addition to the weekly spectacles in the big cities, some travelling dancing-bears were also available for 'baiting'. Gordon Home, in his fascinating history of Pickering, Yorkshire, quotes from a manuscript compiled in the early nineteenth century, which includes so many telling details that it is worth quoting in full.

> *Concerning a case of bear-baiting we have a most detailed account which Calvert heads with 'The Baiting of a Bear at Pickering, Tuesday, Aug 15th, 1809, which I did myself witness'. Then he begins: 'A week Wednesday senight there did with drum and panpipes parade publickly the streets of this town two mountebanks leading by a chain a monster brown bruin which, as well as it being a good dancer and handing of its pole, its master did acclaim it to be the master of any dog of no odds what be his breed and which they would match for a crown to come off conqueror if given fair play and a fifteen-foot chain. Now it happening that in these parts there be living several sporting men some of which be owners of bull dogs of good courage and nowther dog nor master ever shirking a fight more than one dog was entered to test its skill'.*

Sturbridge Fair

Sturbridge (sometimes Stourbridge) Fair was the greatest in the land in its heyday, but it began relatively humbly. In 1211, King John granted a charter to the lepers of the Hospital of St Mary Magdalen at Sturbridge to hold a fair on the vigil and feast of the Holy Cross; such a right was at that time a common way of ensuring that religious and charitable institutions had a regular income. By the end of that century the hospital had virtually ceased to function, but the town of Cambridge claimed the profits from the fair and continued to own it until its demise 700 years later. The University of Cambridge also claimed jurisdiction, which resulted in a long-running feud over their respective rights up to the mid sixteenth century.

In 1589, Sturbridge was described as by far the largest and most famous fair in all England, and it maintained

A day was fixed for the contests which were to take place in the castleyard, and soon the news was so handed from mouth to mouth that the demand for seats in the rough wooden stand, erected for those who chose to pay, was so great that another stand was built and the first one was enlarged.

On the appointed day a huge concourse including 'farmers, butchers, hucksters, badgers, cadgers, horse-jobbers, drovers, loafers, and scamps and raggels of all kinds' assembled in the castleyard. There were 'not a few young sparks and bespurred and beruffled bucks come thither from as far as Hull' who had brought with them certain over-dressed women.

The first dog matched against the bear was owned by one Castle Jack, 'a worthless waistrel'. The bear received the rush of the dog standing on his hind legs and gripped him in his forepaws, biting and crushing him to death. After this no one seemed inclined to let their dogs go to such certain death and the assemblage gradually became disorderly and many quarrels and fights took place before the crowd finally dispersed. Calvert says: 'and so when I did withdraw myself, the whole crowd seemed to be owther cursing, fighting, or loudly proffering for to fight any one. As I took my steps back to my uncle I could not help but consider that those of the Methodist holding, who did as we went towards the green beg and pray for us to be mindful of our sinful pleasures and of the wroth to come and who did pray for us to then turn from our sinful course, and though we who did pass them did so with scoffs and . . . gibes in some cases,

yet I could not help but in my own heart consider that they were fully in the right on't'.

This was at the time when the national campaign against animal-baiting was already underway, and would lead to its suppression in 1835, along with other blood sports. But the Pickering manuscript clearly describes a popular event, drawing eager spectators and would-be participants from a wide area, albeit largely from the disreputable end of the social spectrum. There was local opposition, but in the short term this seems ineffectual. The account, however, demonstrates why the attack on blood sports such as these could be made equally on moral and public order grounds, and also how their suppression could be portrayed, by later historians, as a class-based attack on the customs and pastimes of working people.

Before the watershed of the Cruelty to Animals Act of 1835, there seems to have been no limit to the ingenuity some people would use to cater for the public's lust for animal blood, and dog fights, baitings, and matches between various species were a common occurrence. Dogs were set on anything that could fight back, including horses and donkeys, or that could be made to participate in the 'game'. Badgers, for example, were often baited, and the principle there appears to have been to see how many times the dog would draw the badger from its box in a given time. Whereas bull- and bear-baiting are almost certainly extinct, dog-fighting, badger-baiting, and the like have proved more resilient and still continue clandestinely, although to what extent is impossible to say.

its pre-eminence well into the eighteenth century. The best description of the fair at the height of its fame was published by Daniel Defoe in his *Tour through the Whole Island of Great Britain* (1724–6). He was suitably impressed by its sheer size and the huge quantity of business carried out there:

It is kept in a large corn-field, near Casterton, extending from the side of the River Cam, towards the road,

for about half a mile square . . . The shops are placed in rows like streets, whereof one is call'd Cheapside; and here, as in several other streets, are all sorts of trades, who sell by retail, and who come principally from London with their goods; scarce any trades are omitted, goldsmiths, toyshops, brasiers, turners, milliners, haberdashers, hatters, mercers, drapers, pewterers, china-warehouses, and in a word all trades that can be named in London; with coffee-

houses, taverns, brandy-shops, and eating-houses, innumerable, and all in tents and booths.

Such an operation needed a great deal of preparation and organization. The fair traders had the right to enter the field on a set date, whether the farmers had finished their harvest or not, but by the same token the field reverted to the farmer on a set day after the fair, and he could 'throw down' any booths that had not been removed. Defoe commented that the huge quantity of dung, straw, and other litter and waste left behind was ample compensation to the farmer for the inconvenience of the fair, because when ploughed in it made excellent manure.

Defoe identified two staples of the trade there: wool and hops. The wool dealing was carried out in a special area called 'the Duddery', where £100,000 worth of trade was done in less than a week. Much of this was wholesale trade, with merchants using the fair as the main place to meet and restock their chapmen and agents, settle accounts, and place orders. The hop dealers also had their special part of the field, and the trade was so important that, as Defoe said, 'there is scarce any price fix'd for hops in England till they know how they sell at Sturbridge Fair.' In the last few days of the fair the emphasis was more on pleasure, and crowds flocked to the sideshows and entertainments, while a horse fair took place on the last day. The length of the fair fluctuated over the years, from the original two days up to thirty-five days at its peak.

Fairs like Sturbridge were so important to the country's economic well-being for so long because they provided regular and secure opportunities for wholesale dealing in commodities. The huge amount of money that changed hands was largely between manufacturer and the distributor, rather than between retailer and customer. But when the wholesalers found other methods of distributing their stock (by the newly developed railways, for example), the focus of the fair shifted, and while the retail trade was still large, it was not sufficient to maintain the fair on its former scale. While many famous fairs got out of hand and were suppressed, Sturbridge's fate was rather a long lingering decline throughout the nineteenth century. The *Victoria County History* for Cambridge recorded its final demise:

The fair was proclaimed for the last time in September 1933 to an audience of three. By Home Office order, confirming a resolution of the Town Council, it was abolished 5 July 1934.

See also **Fairs, Feasts, Wakes, and Revels**, p. 249.

*

THIRD THURSDAY IN SEPTEMBER

Chalk-Back Day

Chalk-Back Day was a little-known annual custom recorded in Diss, Norfolk, but with possible connections elsewhere. The earliest record of it goes back only to 1851, in *Notes & Queries*:

> *It is customary for the juvenile populace, on the Thursday before the third Friday in September ... to mark and disfigure each other's dress with white chalk, pleading a prescriptive right to be mischievous on 'chalk-back day'.*

This account is confirmed by later writers, who show that it was not simply a short-lived craze but survived until about 1900.

The local hiring fair was held on the same day, and this may be a clue to its meaning, as an account from Yorkshire in 1890 makes clear:

> *At Bridlington, on the Sunday night preceding the fair, which is held on the Monday before Whit Sunday, the boys used to assemble on the Church Green, where the fair was held, each armed with a lump of chalk, and each intent on chalking the backs of as many of the other boys as possible. This often led to quarrels, as the boys then had on their Sunday clothes.*

There is also a strange echo of this behaviour in reports of Greenwich Fair in mid Victorian times, where a local craze involved running wooden 'rattlers' down people's backs (*see* **Easter Day: Greenwich Fair**, p. 115). Another possible link comes from further afield: 'Chalk Sunday' (usually the first Sunday in Lent) was widely held in Ireland in the nineteenth century and up to about 1930. As at Diss, Irish children chalked people's backs on the day, but there it was specifically those who

Climbing the greasy pole at Egremont Crab Apple Fair, 1984

were unmarried, which could be a gentle joke or an unpleasant comment on the popularity, or otherwise, of the victim, depending on the circumstances. Further examples from England are needed before we can hope to speculate on its meaning or origin.

*

THIRD SATURDAY IN SEPTEMBER

Egremont Crab-Apple Fair

Egremont Fair, in Cumbria, consciously preserves many of the traditional games and pastimes of old-time country fairs, such as gurning (and Egremont is said to hold the World Championship competition), climbing the greasy pole, wrestling, tug-of-war, and children's races; but it has also introduced a number of others that are probably unique, including a pipe-smoking contest, ferret show, and the singing of hunting songs. The fine art of pole greasing was described by Egremont locals in *John Bull* magazine in 1955:

> We haven't been able to grease the pole properly since before the war . . . Nowadays, wagon grease is used . . . but really it should be soft soap covered by lard . . . A sheep's head or a leg of mutton trailing coloured ribbons is tied to the top of the pole and anyone who can bring down a ribbon wins the prize . . . The greasy pole is the bane of wives and mothers, and the delight of the outfitters.

The fair gets its name from the custom of throwing apples from a slow-moving lorry, to the waiting crowds, at midday. They used to be crab apples, but nowadays ordinary eating apples are thrown. Organizers claim that Egremont's fair has been held every year since its charter was granted in 1267 (except during the two world wars), and this could well be true.

For illustration, *see* p. 297.

*

17 SEPTEMBER

Latter Lee Fair

See **17 August: Lee Gap Fair**.

*

Samuel Johnson, commemorated at Lichfield, Staffordshire, on his birthday, 18 September

18 SEPTEMBER

Samuel Johnson Commemoration

Samuel Johnson (1709–84), journalist, critic, essayist, magazine editor, and, most famously, dictionary maker, was the leading figure in the literary world of his day and is still held in high regard. He is buried at Westminster Abbey, where an annual commemoration takes place each December. But on or near his birthday, 18 September, they hold a ceremony in his honour in Lichfield, Staffordshire, the place of his birth. The mayor and corporation, members of the Johnson Society, and pupils from Johnson's old school place a wreath on his statue, and later they hold a birthday supper and a commemoration service in the cathedral.

Warden Pies

Warden pies, made with Warden pears, were an autumn and winter delicacy in various parts of the country, up to Edwardian times at least. Sussex writer Lilian Candlin gave one example:

Wardens were not soft like the modern stewing pear. They were quite hard when cooked and needed good teeth to eat them . . . To make a Warden Pie: Peel the pears and quarter them, then simmer them in sweetened water for about two, to two and a half hours. By this time they should be tender and have turned a pale pink colour. Leave them to get cold. Meanwhile line the edge of a pie dish with thin pastry. Fill the dish with the pears, add a little lemon juice, and a wineglassful of claret or port wine. Top with pastry and bake. When serving lift the lid and gently spoon in two or three tablespoonsful of rich thick cream.

Warden pears were particularly prized in Bedfordshire, and hot baked Wardens were a delicacy of the Bedford Michaelmas (Old Style) Fair and were hawked in the streets throughout the season. The *Oxford English Dictionary* gives numerous literary references to Warden pies from the fifteenth century onwards, including one from Shakespeare's Clown in *The Winter's Tale*, who reminds himself in Act IV, scene 3, 'I must have saffron to colour the Warden pies.'

Southwark Fair

Southwark, or Lady, Fair was one of the big fairs of the London area, attracting huge crowds until the mid eighteenth century and second in importance only to Bartholomew Fair (*see* **24 August**). Southwark Fair was founded in 1462, by charter of Edward IV to the City of London, and was opened each year by the mayor and other officials, when they rode in state across London Bridge. Originally it ran from 7 to 9 September, but the change of calendar in 1752 (*see* p. xx) brought its start date to 18 September, and its original three days were regularly stretched to two weeks, much to the annoyance of the local inhabitants who often agitated to get the fair limited to its statutory duration.

Most ancient fairs followed the same historical pattern, beginning as essential gatherings for buying and selling goods, but gradually changing to those for pleasure only; and Southwark was particularly famous for its entertainments and show-booths, which drew enthusiastic playgoers from all levels of society in great numbers. The two great seventeenth-century diarists, John Evelyn and Samuel Pepys, both recorded visits, and both mentioned the spectacular tightrope walking and dancing (13 September 1660 and 21 September 1668, respectively). In 1720, John Strype's *Survey of the Cities of London and Westminster* commented that it was 'noted chiefly for shows, drolls, puppet-shows, rope-dancing, music booths and tippling houses', and it was particularly these show-booths that were guilty of staying longer than the official three days. By the mid eighteenth century, a combination of locals and reformers had become vociferous in their condemnation of the fair, claiming that it tended 'only to the destruction of youth of both sexes, and the encouragement of thieves and strollers', and they succeeded in getting it suppressed in 1762.

See also **Fairs, Feasts, Wakes, and Revels**, p. 249.

*

19 SEPTEMBER

Painswick Church-Clipping

On the Sunday nearest to 19 September, the parishioners of Painswick, Gloucestershire, gather to 'clip' their church. The church is dedicated to St Mary, and the patronal feast should therefore be on the Nativity of the Blessed Virgin (8 September), but owing to the reform of the calendar in 1752, 19 September is the Nativity Old Style, and the date of the village feast.

After a procession of the faithful to the church, the children (and some adults) join hands to completely encircle the building while the clipping hymn is sung. At the chorus they all walk three steps forward and back, swaying their arms, which some say represents the beating of angels' wings. The children are dressed in their best, and have flowers in their hair or in

Painswick church-clipping, Gloucestershire (Benjamin Stone, 1906)

buttonholes and posies, and there is a special church service. Participating children traditionally receive a bun and a small coin.

The modern ceremony at Painswick is a charming combination of simplicity, joyfulness, and solemnity, but its history and development is confused, and often misrepresented. The first confusion is over the name. 'Clipping' is an Old English word meaning 'clasping' or 'embracing', and has been used in that sense, in litera-ture and some local dialects, almost to the present day. However, because the Painswick ceremony occurs on the church's patronal festival, some earlier writers suggested that 'clipping' was derived from the Anglo-Saxon word *ycleping*, which meant 'naming', while others thought it was so named because of an allied custom of 'clipping' the churchyard yews for the day.

The survival of the custom is also a little confused. It is clear that it was revived in late Victorian times, by the Revd W. H. Seddon, having last been carried out around 1851. In addition, the Revd Percy Dearmer, while on

holiday duty at Painswick in 1908, claimed that he 'gave time to re-organizing the Clipping Service'. However, there is no evidence that it existed in Painswick before about 1820.

Other present-day churches occasionally hold clip-ping ceremonies, although Painswick rightly gets all the publicity. In past years the custom was by no means uncommon in England, and the list of places that are recorded as having church-clipping ceremo-nies in the nineteenth century includes: Cradley, Worcestershire; Burbage, Derbyshire; Guiseley, Yorkshire; Wellington and Ellesmere, Shropshire; Beckington and Rode, Somerset; Bradford-on-Avon, Wiltshire; and Sheepscombe, Gloucestershire. The majority of these took place on Shrove Tuesday, but some were held at Easter, and some on the day of the local church's dedication. There were local variations, of course. At Wellington, for example, the participants all carried toy trumpets, which they blew vigorously as they marched round the church, prompting some commentators to presume a connection with the story about the walls of Jericho.

The earliest reference to church-clipping, however, relates to Birmingham. A correspondent to William Hone's *Every-Day Book* (1827) remembered Easter Monday clipping there in his or her childhood, which probably therefore refers to the mid or late eighteenth century. Despite regular confident assertions of the ancient origins of church-clipping, there is thus no evidence at present that it existed earlier than a mere 250 years ago, and talk of direct survival from the Roman festival of Lupercalia must be regarded as nonsense. However, research into the early history and development of church-clipping would be welcome, and one element of that enquiry might be a possible connection between the circling of the church and the game-custom of dancing hand-in-hand through the streets, often called 'Thread the Needle'. An article in *Folk-Lore* in 1912 drew attention to several places where the two customs occurred together, and others where they were separate.

One further aspect of the Painswick Feast was mentioned in the magazine *John Bull* (24 September 1955):

> *'When I was a girl' says Lucy Hobbs, 'every family in Painswick made a puppy-dog pie for the Clipping.' Small china dogs were baked in meat and apple pies. The practice died out a few years ago, but Lucy Hobbs hopes to see it revived this year.*

These 'puppy-dog' or 'bow-wow' pies are variously described as containing meat, apple, or plum, or even as almond-paste cakes, but the china dog inside is the defining detail. There are several similar traditions regarding their origins. All the stories agree that visitors from a neighbouring town (usually Stroud), or some unwelcome and uncouth navvies, were given pies made out of dog meat – some say because the hosts had run out of proper meat, while others maintain that it was done deliberately to put the arrogant outsiders in their place. Either way, the relations between the two places were not improved by the occurrence, and the traditional rivalry of neighbours was given added point by the mere mention of puppy-dog pies by one side or the other.

*

21 SEPTEMBER

St Matthew's Day

This day was sometimes claimed to be the Devil's Nutting Day, but it was more commonly said of **14 September: Holy Cross Day/Holy Rood Day**. In weather terms, it was recorded by Richard Inwards in 1869 that 'St Matthew brings on the cold dew', but the same was also said of St Bartholomew's Day (24 August).

*

29 SEPTEMBER

Michaelmas/Feast of St Michael and All Angels

The Archangel Michael was extremely popular in England in the Middle Ages, and hundreds of early churches were dedicated to him. He was one of the figures portrayed killing a dragon, and his reputation as 'Captain of the heavenly host' in the biblical 'war in heaven' (Revelation 12:7–9) ensured his popularity with soldiers as well as with the general public.

The one feature of Michaelmas that affected almost everybody in the country but is now almost entirely forgotten was the custom of eating roast goose on the day. The Michaelmas goose tradition was once stronger than the modern traditions of eggs at Easter and turkey at Christmas combined, and as with most festival foods, there was a widespread idea that it was lucky to follow tradition, and unlucky not to. As Robert Forby's *Vocabulary of East Anglia* (1830) says, 'If you don't baste the goose on Michaelmas Day, you'll want money all the year', and Jane Austen was clearly aware of the superstition when she wrote to her sister Cassandra on 11/12 of October 1813 [i.e. Old Style Michaelmas Day], 'I dined upon goose yesterday – which I hope will secure a good sale of my 2nd edition.'

There has never been a satisfactory explanation for the goose-eating tradition, apart from the prosaic reason that geese are at their prime at that time. One widespread, but completely untrue, historical story makes it our patriotic duty to do so. It was said that Queen Elizabeth I was eating goose on Michaelmas

St Michael killing the dragon, by Josse Lieferinxe (*fl.* 1493–1508)

and ceremony. James Cossins described the scene in his youth in Exeter in the 1820s:

The election of Mayors for the City of Exeter, under the old Chamber, was about Michaelmas . . . On the day of the election, the members of the body and freemen assembled in the Guildhall; the intended Mayor was proposed, with the other officials; after taking the oath and duly signing the documents, on the cheering subsiding, the Hall echoed with the sound of various drawings of bottled wine corks, the liquor being freely passed around the table . . . A procession was then formed to perambulate the walls, headed by the tradesmen's corps of constables, about twenty-four in number, then the staff and mace-bearers, sword-bearers, the Mayor-elect walk-ing uncovered, with his hat in hand; Aldermen, with scarlet robes and three-cornered hats, followed by members and officials; in the rear being three trades-men's sons, named Mayor's stewards (the outside one being called gutter steward), wearing long black robes, with tufts and three-cornered hats, who had the privilege of dining at the Mayor's banquets. Some of the electors and inhabitants would accompany the procession, and give vent to their feelings by an occasional cheer. At two fixed points on the route . . . apples were thrown about for a general scramble, and at another wine was provided. The ceremony wound up in the evening with the good old English custom of dinner.

Day when she received the news that the Spanish Armada had been defeated, and she declared that henceforth all true English people should eat the same on that day, in thanks and remembrance for our national delivery. The romance of this story notwithstanding, there is evidence that the connec-tion between Michaelmas and the goose was already in place in the fifteenth century. It lasted into the early twentieth century, but then rapidly faded from the national consciousness.

As one of the four quarter days, Michaelmas was an important time in legal and economic affairs from at least medieval times to the late nineteenth century. It was often the day that local courts were held, rents were due, annual employment terms expired, and was one of the days locally called 'Pack Rag Day' because so many families were busy changing their accommoda-tion at the time (*see also* **14 May: Pack Rag Day**). In local government, it was a favourite day for new mayors to be elected (*see* **Election of the Lord Mayor of London**, *below*) or to take office, and was thus a day of civic pomp

A generation or two before this, Exeter's mayor-making, like many other places, was accompanied by rougher activities than scrambling for apples. It was traditional on these occasions for the incoming mayor to supply a bull to be baited in the street for the people's amusement, and there was a curious local belief that just before the new mayor took office there was a 'lawless hour' when normal laws and regulations had no effect. In Exeter, youths would dam up any streams or gutters to create pools of water with which they could soak passers-by if they were not paid a fee; but in Kidderminster, Worcestershire, the people threw cabbage stalks at each other, and then pelted the newly elected corporation with apples.

See also **Hiring Fairs**, p. 345; **Lawless Hours and Days**, p. 303.

Lawless Hours and Days

A minor thread running through many traditional customs is the belief that at certain times, or on certain days, normal laws are suspended, and everyone can do as they like without fear of reprisal. These are sometimes explicitly named as 'lawless' hours or days, meaning 'exempt from or outside the law' rather than simply 'illegal', a fine distinction. The times in question vary from place to place, and although some seem to be arbitrary, others are more specific. One regular time was on mayor-making day, apparently on the principle that there was an interregnum between departing and incoming mayor, which resulted in a temporary legal hiatus.

> According to the *Staffordshire Advertiser* of 5th February 1910, a woman from Alsager's Bank was summoned to the Newcastle-under-Lyme County Police Court for throwing liquid over a man at Silverdale, and pleaded that it was done on (the mayoral?) election day and that 'there is no law on election day; you may do whatever you like'. She was convicted and fined.

At other times, the lawlessness took a particular form, as recorded in the *Gentleman's Magazine* of 1790:

> At Kidderminster is a singular custom. On the election of a bailiff, the inhabitants assemble in the principal streets to throw cabbage-stalks at each other. The town-house bell gives signal for this affray. This is called 'lawless hour'. This done

(for it lasts an hour), the bailiff elect and corporation, in their robes, preceded by drums and fifes (for they have no waits), visit the old and new bailiff, constables, etc. attended by the mob. In the mean time, the most respectable families in the neighbourhood are invited to meet and fling apples at them on their entrance. I have known forty pots of apples expended at one house.

See **28 July: Old St Kenelm's Day** for another custom that involves throwing things at otherwise respected persons.

Another lawless day, similarly associated with the appointment of the mayor and civic officers, took place in Exeter, as described by a correspondent to William Hone's *Year-Book* (1832), remembering his time in the town 'more than a dozen years' earlier. He wrote of 'squads of the mischief-loving part of the mobility' taking to the streets on 29 May, damming up the kennels (watercourses) to make deep pools, and expecting passers-by to give money or be drenched with the none-too-clean water. The procedure was also described by James Cossins in his *Reminiscences of Exeter* (1878), but he places it on Ascension Day.

The belief also surfaced on certain days when locals believed they had the right to enter local woods to hunt small animals – sometimes specifically squirrels, but often any small game. Again, the day varied from place to place, including Good Friday, St Andrew's Day (*see* **30 November**), and Boxing Day (*see* **26 December: Hunting and Shooting**). For other nights that were widely considered to be lawless, *see* **31 October: Mischief Night** and **5 November: Guy Fawkes Night**.

See also **Mock Mayors and Courts**, p. 216.

Blackberries

An extremely widespread superstition, found all over the British Isles, maintained that blackberries were bad, or even poisonous, after a certain date. This date varied from place to place, ranging from Michaelmas to 10 or 11 October, and as the latter equates to 29 September before the change of calendar in 1752, it is clear that Michaelmas is the key day. The reason for the blackberries' sudden decline was that the Devil interfered on that day. In 1882, the *Western Antiquary* reported:

> The belief that it is unlucky to eat blackberries after Michaelmas Day, because 'His Royal Highness' then tampers with them, still lingers in Exeter and neighbourhood. Some time ago, whilst walking in

Incoming and outgoing Lord Mayor of London, 2003

the country round here, a young friend who was with me warned me against plucking any blackberries: 'Because,' said he, grimly, 'it's past Michaelmas Day and the Devil's been at 'em.'

In the polite versions of this superstition, the Devil puts his foot on the berries, or wipes his club or tail over them, but in more graphic versions he defiles them in more earthy ways. The belief certainly dates back to the early eighteenth century, but was particularly well known in the nineteenth, and can still be heard in some areas.

Crack-Nut Sunday

A peculiar custom, which prevailed at Kingston-upon-Thames church in Surrey until the early nineteenth century, involved the cracking of nuts during the service on the Sunday before St Michael's Day. This was not confined to children but was indulged in by all ages, and according to Edward Brayley's *Topographical History of Surrey* (1850), 'the cracking noise was often so powerful, that the minister was obliged to suspend his reading, or discourse, until greater quietness was obtained.' It was thought to be a remnant of a civic custom, having something to do with the choosing of the bailiffs and other members of the town corporation on Michaelmas Day, although it is difficult to understand quite how the two were connected, unless it had something to do with the idea of a 'lawless hour' (*see* **Lawless Hours and Days**, p. 303). The connection between nuts and Michaelmas, however, is shown by other references, such as Oliver Goldsmith's *Vicar of Wakefield* (1766):

They kept up the Christmas carol, sent true-love knots on Valentine morning, ate pan-cakes at Shrove-tide, shewed their wit on the first of April, and religiously cracked nuts on Michaelmas Eve.

Election of the Lord Mayor of London

The Lord Mayor of London is head of the Corporation of London, the local authority that governs the City of London – a position not to be confused with the Mayor of London, created in 2000, who is head of the Greater London Authority. The Lord Mayor's position is somewhat older, dating from about the year 1192.

The Lord Mayor is elected on 29 September, then presents himself to the Lord Chancellor at the House of Lords in October for royal approval, and finally takes office on the second Friday in November (*see* **Second Friday in November: Silent Change**). To be eligible, a candidate must be a serving alderman, and have served previously as a sheriff, of which there are always two at a time, elected annually from their own ranks by the aldermen. The Liverymen of the City put forward eligible names for Lord Mayor to the Court of Aldermen, who make the final decision at a meeting at the Guildhall.

The Lord Mayor of London is still an extremely important personage in the nation, and in many situations is second only in precedence to the sovereign. In addition to the numerous ceremonial tasks, the frequent entertaining of dignitaries, and the foreign trips to represent the City, the Lord Mayor chairs the Court of Aldermen and the Court of Common Council, and serves as Admiral of the Port of London, Chief Magistrate of the City, and Chancellor of City University.

As the Lord Mayor is drawn from the business and social elite of the capital, it is to be expected that the candidate has not always been at the cutting edge of societal change, but there have been numerous occasions when the City has quietly moved with the times. A minor ripple was caused in 1972 when the first Labour Lord Mayor, Lord Mais, was appointed, which occasioned *The Times* to comment, 'a Labour Lord Mayor of the City of London seems as rare as a vegetarian King of the Cannibals.' The first woman to hold the position was Lady Donaldson, in 1983.

Urswick Rush-Bearing

The pretty Lakeland village of Urswick has an annual rush-bearing ceremony that is similar to those of other Cumbrian villages such as Grasmere and Ambleside, but decidedly smaller in scale, local, and quietly religious. In Urswick, the event is organized by the church and the school, and rather than making a carnival day of it, they simply have a cup of tea and a piece of gingerbread after the procession and church service.

The procession starts at 1 p.m. from the school and walks round the village, with a brass band and banners, until it reaches the ancient church of St Mary and St Michael, where the service takes place. Participants carry rushes and flowers, and six children carry a white embroidered rush-sheet, as at Grasmere. There is a Rush Queen, along with her attendants, and on the banners are embroidered the names of all the girls that have served in that capacity.

The custom was revived, or perhaps introduced to Urswick, in 1905 by the Revd Thomas Postelthwaite, and they celebrated their centenary in 2005; however, survival for the next hundred years may not be guaranteed. It is clear that some parts of the ceremony are under threat from changes in the community and society at large, with girls reportedly less interested in being the Rush Queen and parading the village in a white dress. Links to such local community events have also weakened as the local school caters only for primary children, and the older ones have to travel to the nearest town.

See also **Rush-Bearing**, p. 238.

October

1

2
BRAUGHING OLD MAN'S DAY

3
FIRST WEDNESDAY IN OCTOBER
Nottingham Goose Fair

8

9

10
OLD MICHAELMAS DAY
Pack Monday Fair
Weyhill Fair
SECOND WEDNESDAY IN OCTOBER
Tavistock Goosie Fair

15

16
Lion Sermon

17

22

23

24

Punkie Night

29

30

31
HALLOWE'EN
Antrobus Soul-Cakers
Mischief Night

Moveable events have been placed on the date they fall in 2007.

Redcliffe Pipe Walk

Quit Rent Ceremonies

| 4 | 5 | 6 | 7 |

| **11** Blackberries | 12 | 13 | **14** **SECOND SUNDAY IN OCTOBER** Harvest of the Sea |

| **18** **ST LUKE'S DAY** | 19 | **20** Colchester Oyster Feast | **21** **APPLE DAY** **TRAFALGAR DAY** |

| **25** **ST CRISPIN'S DAY** **LAST THURSDAY IN OCTOBER** Bampton Fair | 26 | 27 | 28 |

Wife-Selling

Seed Cakes

Quit Rent Ceremonies

In feudal times, a quit rent was a payment or presentation made by tenants to the lord of the manor in order to excuse themselves from having to render customary services. Such payments were often nominal, or could involve customary obligations other than financial. Two of the latter survive in London, concerning two pieces of land, 'the Moors' in Eardington, Shropshire, and the Forge in St Clement Danes, London; they are carried out in October each year. The Comptroller of the City Corporation performs the ceremony at the Law Courts, in the presence of the Queen's Remembrancer. The former land is held by presentation, dating to the year 1211, of two knives, one of which has to be good enough to cut through a hazel stick. Thus, the comptroller brings a hatchet to court, with which he chops a bundle of hazel twigs. For the other land, in a procedure dating to 1295, six horseshoes and sixty-one horseshoe nails are presented and duly counted. There is nowadays much solemn ceremony involved, and the same hatchet, horseshoes, and nails are presented each year.

*

A SUNDAY IN OCTOBER

Redcliffe Pipe Walk

In a custom that superficially resembles a 'beating of the bounds', the vicar and churchwardens of St Mary Redcliffe church in Bristol, together with a surveyor, walk the mile-and-a-half course of a medieval water pipe, on a Sunday in October, usually accompanied by two or three dozen interested people. This early water supply for the area runs from the 'Rugewell' (probably meaning 'ridge well'), in Knowle, and was granted in 1190 by Lord Robert de Berkeley, whose tomb can be seen in the church. The pipe's course is marked by a series of stones (marked 'SMP') and manholes, down which the surveyor has to climb, and the walkers have right of way along its course. The water was stopped halfway along the course about fifty years ago, but it still feeds an ornate fountain, and the church authorities still have to make the complete inspection in order to retain certain endowments. A plaque on the outside wall of St Mary Redcliffe church, translated from the Latin, reads:

> For the health of the soul of Robert of Berkeley, who gave to God and the church of St. Mary Redcliffe and its ministers the Rugewell and conduit. AD 1190. Erected 1932.

*

2 OCTOBER

Braughing Old Man's Day

Matthew Wall was in his coffin, on his way to being buried in St Mary the Virgin's churchyard in the Hertfordshire town of Braughing, when one of the pall-bearers slipped, dropped the coffin, and jolted him awake. Matthew was naturally rather pleased with this outcome, and in his will, dated 1595, he left money to commemorate the event. Among other stipulations, he requested that the church bells be rung on 2 October (the day of his lucky escape), the sexton must look after his grave, and a poor man be paid a shilling to sweep the path up to the church gate.

And so it is that every 2 October, locally called 'Old Man's Day', children of the village gather with brooms and enthusiastically sweep Fleece Lane, while the funeral bell tolls. Brambles are placed on Matthew's grave, to keep the sheep off, and prayers are said at his graveside. Later, the church bells ring a wedding peal, as Matthew lived long enough to re-marry. The present ceremonies date back to a revival in the mid twentieth century, but it is not clear how long it had lapsed before that time.

*

FIRST WEDNESDAY IN OCTOBER

Nottingham Goose Fair

Various fairs up and down the country were famed for particular wares, reflected in their names, and several were known for the numbers of geese sold, usually because they were held around Michaelmas, the traditional time for goose-eating in England. Many goose

Braughing Old Man's Day, Hertfordshire, 1996

Nottingham Goose Fair, c.1910

fairs have faded from memory, but two that are still going strong, as pleasure fairs, are held in Nottingham and in Tavistock, Devon; both can claim considerable antiquity. A St Matthew Fair at Nottingham was still extant when the town was awarded a second fair in 1284, so it might well be Anglo-Saxon in origin. It was called a 'goose fair' at least as early as 1541, and in its heyday tens of thousands of geese were sold there each year. The change of calendar in 1752 forced the fair to move to 2 October, and continuing popularity brought much congestion to the city centre, where it took place each year. By 1927 it was becoming intolerably cramped, and new municipal building around the Market Square made a move desirable, although there were loud protests against this. It is now held at the Forest Recreation Ground about a mile away, and is one of the biggest pleasure fairs in the country. The actual days on which the Goose Fair is held can vary from year to year. For some time it was regularized as the first Thursday in October, and the following Friday and Saturday, but of late the fair has started on the Wednesday and run for four days.

See also **29 September: Michaelmas/Feast of St Michael and All Angels; Second Wednesday in October: Tavistock Goosie Fair; Fairs, Feasts, Revels, and Wakes**, p. 249.

*

Goose-Riding

Goose-riding was a 'sport', extant in Derbyshire and probably elsewhere in the 1790s, in which a live goose, its neck well greased to increase the difficulty, was suspended by its legs from a rope strung between two trees or posts. Participants rode at speed under the rope and attempted to pull the head off the goose as they passed; whoever succeeded won the goose.

SECOND SUNDAY
IN OCTOBER

Harvest of the Sea

The proximity of St Mary-at-Hill church in London's Lovat Lane to the ancient Billingsgate fish market has ensured that it has always had strong links with the fish industry, and the set piece of this historical connection is the Thanksgiving Service for the Harvest of the Sea, which takes place every October, usually on the second Sunday of the month. The church is decorated for the occasion with nets and other seagoing paraphernalia, and houses an intricate design made from a variety of fresh fish and seafood, still supplied by the Billingsgate traders. It is not clear how long this custom has been in operation at St Mary's, but *The Times* of 3 October 1922 described a very similar event at the church of St Magnus the Martyr, at London Bridge, where it had apparently taken place for the previous fifteen years.

*

Harvest of the Sea, St Mary-at-Hill, Lovat Lane, London

SECOND WEDNESDAY
IN OCTOBER

Tavistock Goosie Fair

Various fairs have come and gone in the history of Tavistock, in Devon. The earliest was granted to the Abbey of St Mary and St Rumon by charter of Henry I in the year 1116. But the famous Goosie Fair, held at Michaelmas, is of later foundation (probably the sixteenth century). The change of calendar in 1752 moved it from 29 September to 10 October, and this was later transferred to the second Wednesday in that month, where it still stands. The ubiquitous presence of roast goose on everybody's dinner table around Michaelmas is detailed under 29 September, and any livestock fair that took place at that time was likely to be termed a 'goose fair', even if other animals were sold in larger quantities. The move to October, the gradual decline in goose-eating, and the inexorable rise of the pleasure side of fairs at the expense of the commercial, all contributed to changes in the event, and by the twentieth century the occasional presence of real geese at the fair always prompted articles in the local and even national press. However, the fair retains its name and importance to the local community, and attracts numerous visitors. As it still takes place in the centre of town, Tavistock is closed to traffic on the day.

The fair also boasts its own song, 'Tavistock Goozey Vair', written by C. John Trythall in 1912, which commences:

> 'Tis just a month come Friday next, Bill Champerdown and me
> Us traipsed across old Darty moor, the Goosey Fair to see
> Us made ourselves quite fitting, us greased and oiled our hair
> Then off we goes in our Sunday clothes, behind old Bill's grey mare.

As with all such 'dialect' pieces, the song sounds fine when sung by locals, but can come across as excruciating stage-yokel in cold print or when sung by anyone else.

See also 29 **September: Michaelmas/Feast of St**

Michael and All Angels; **First Wednesday in October: Nottingham Goose Fair**; **Fairs, Feasts, Wakes, and Revels**, p. 249.

*

10 OCTOBER

Old Michaelmas Day

Dog-Whipping Day, a calendar custom apparently confined to Yorkshire, was variously given as occurring on either 10 October or 18 October (St Luke's Day). As folklore writer John Nicholson commented in 1890:

> So common was the practice at one time, that every little street arab considered it his bounden duty to prepare a whip for any unlucky dog that might be seen wandering in the streets on that day.

The custom was said to have originated when a dog swallowed the consecrated wafer during service in York Minster. It was suppressed, in Hull at least, by the police in 1853.

Stray dogs were a regular nuisance in past times, and a relatively humble, but no less useful, parish official was the dog-whipper (or dog-rapper) whose job it was to keep stray dogs out of church. The earliest reference known to us is in the Ludlow churchwardens' accounts for 1543, in Shropshire, when Thomas Payver was paid 8d for carrying out the task. Nine years later, Archbishop Holgate of York issued an injunction that the vergers should expel 'beggars, other light persons, and dogs' from the church during divine service. Payments to dog-whippers continue throughout the sixteenth to eighteenth centuries, but they fade out in the first two decades of the nineteenth.

This day was also one of several designated as the last day in the year to eat blackberries (*see* **29 September: Blackberries**).

Pack Monday Fair

Every year, starting on the Monday following 10 October (Old Michaelmas Day), the streets of Sherborne, in Dorset, are given over to Pack Monday Fair – previously an agricultural fair, but now devoted to stalls, sideshows, and a funfair. The second volume of William

Hone's *Every-Day Book* contains a lively description of the fair, written by a local man in 1826. It is worth quoting extensively, as an excellent example of the hustle and bustle of a nineteenth-century fair, its activities, and its attractions. The piece demonstrates the way the whole town is taken over by the event, the intermixing of business and pleasure, and of the classes and ages – farmers and farmworkers, tradesmen and customers, adults and children, from town and country:

> The fair is annually held on the first Monday after the 10th of October, and is a mart for the sale of horses, cows, fat and lean oxen, sheep, lambs, and pigs; cloth, earthenware, onions, wall and hazel nuts, apples, fruit, trees, and the usual nick nacks for children, toys, gingerbread, sweetmeats, sugar plums, etc., with drapery, hats, bonnets, caps, ribands, etc. for the country belles, of whom, when the weather is favourable, a great number is drawn together from the neighbouring villages . . . To the present time Pack Monday fair is annually announced three or four weeks previous by all the little urchins who can procure and blow a cow's horn, parading the streets in the evenings, and sending forth the different tones of their horny bugles, sometimes beating an old saucepan for a drum, to render the sweet sound more delicious . . .
>
> At four o'clock the great bell is rung for a quarter of an hour. From this time, the bustle commences by the preparations for the coming scene: stalls erecting, windows cleaning and decorating, shepherds and drovers going forth for their flocks and herds, which are depastured for the night in the neighbouring fields, and every individual seems on the alert. The business in the sheep and cattle fairs (which are held in different fields, nearly in the centre of the town, and well attended by the gentlemen farmers of Dorset, Somerset and Devon) takes precedence, and is generally concluded by twelve o'clock, when what is called the in-fair begins to wear the appearance of business-like activity, and from this time till three or four o'clock more business is transacted in the Ship counting house, parlour, hall, and kitchen, than at any other time of day, it being the custom of the tradespeople to have their yearly accounts settled about this time, and scarcely a draper, grocer, hatter,

ironmonger, bookseller, or other respectable trades-man, but is provided with an ample store of beef and home-brewed October [ale], for the welcome of their numerous customers . . . Now (according to an old saying) is the town alive. John takes Joan to see the shows – there he finds the giant – here the learned pig – the giantess and dwarf – the menagerie of wild beasts – the conjuror – and Mr. Merry Andrew crack-ing his jokes with his quondam master. Here it is – 'Walk up, walk up, ladies and gentlemen, we are now going to begin, be in time, the price is only twopence.' Here is Mr. Warr's merry round-about, with 'a horse or a coach for a halfpenny' – Here is Rebecca Swain with her black and red cock, and lucky-bag, who bawls out, 'Come my little lucky rogues, and try your fortune for a halfpenny, all prizes and no blanks, a faint heart never wins a fair lady.' – Here is pricking in the garter – Raffling for gingerbread, with the cry of 'One in, who makes two, the more the merrier.' – Here is the Sheffield hardwareman, sporting a worn-out wig and huge pair of spectacles, offering, in lots, a box of razors, knives, scissors, etc., each lot of which he modestly says, is worth seven shillings, but he'll not be too hard on the gaping crowd, he'll not take seven, nor six, nor five, nor four, nor three, nor two, but one shilling for the lot – going at one shilling – sold again and the money paid. – Here are two earthenware-men bawling their shilling's worth one against the other, and quaffing beer to each other's luck from that necessary and convenient chamber utensil that has modestly usurped the name of the great river Po. Here is poor Will, with a basket of gingerbread, crying 'toss or buy'. There is a smirking little lad pinning two girls together by their gowns, whilst his companion cracks a Waterloo bang-up [a cracker or firework] in their faces. Here stands John with his mouth wide open and Joan with her sloe-black ogles stretched to their extremity at a fine painted shawl, which Cheap John is offering for next to nothing; and here is a hundred other contrivances to draw the browns from the pockets of the unwary, and tickle the fancies of the curious; and sometimes the rogue of a pick-pocket extracting Farmer Anybody's watch or money from his pockets.

It is often claimed nowadays that the word 'pack' is here derived from the 'pacts' made between farmer and worker at the fair, but this is unlikely; 'pack' meaning 'pact' is included in some dialect dictionaries, but only from Scotland. On the dialect evidence from elsewhere in England, the word 'pack', which is very common, has two closely related meanings. The first, as in variations on 'Pack Rag Day', refers to the day on which the family packed up their belongings to move house at the end of the annual term of employment (*see* **14 May**). Indeed, 'Pack and Penny Day' was often found in Yorkshire and neighbouring counties as a term for the day after Old Michaelmas or Old Martinmas Day, and as these were two of the most common days for the annual move, and the former is exactly when Sherborne Fair occurs, this seems to be the most likely explanation. Nevertheless, 'pack' is also used all over the country to refer to itin-erant sellers and their wares, as in 'pack-man' (pedlar), 'pack-horse', and so on, which is equally apposite for an old-time fair.

An interesting custom that takes place the night before the fair is the perambulation of the town by Teddy Roe's (or Rowe's) Band, made up of the youth of the town, who make a great deal of noise with tin cans, horns, and whistles, in a similar way to **rough music** (p. 74) customs everywhere. The traditional story said to explain both this rough music and the fair's name relates that Teddy Roe was the foreman of some masons who were working on the great fan vault of Sherborne Abbey in 1490. They were given a day off to visit the fair, 'packed up' their tools, and marched in joyful noisy procession to the fairground.

This story is without foundation, however, and Teddy Roe's Band is not at all unusual, as many other fairs up and down the country were heralded by young people going in procession and making noise with toy trumpets and tin cans. The figure of Teddy Roe himself remains a mystery, although one account (*John Bull*, 8 October 1955) states that he was simply the leader of the band in the early nineteenth century. The custom has been associated with vandalism and violence on a number of occasions in the past, and the band has regularly been suppressed by the police, but it always seems to re-emerge.

See also **Fairs, Feasts, Wakes, and Revels**, p. 249.

Wife-Selling

Readers of Thomas Hardy's *Mayor of Casterbridge* (1886) will be familiar with the dramatic scene early in the book when Michael Henchard, in a morose drunken state, decides to sell his wife at a fair:

> 'For my part I don't see why men who have got wives and don't want 'em, shouldn't get rid of 'em as those gipsy fellows do their old horses,' said the man in the tent. 'Why shouldn't they put 'em up and sell 'em by auction to men who are in need of such articles? Hey? Why, begad, I'd sell mine this minute if anybody would buy her!'

Henchard's decision sets in motion much of the tragic action of the story, but the scene is not simply a novelist's clever trick: it is a fictionalized description of an occurrence that many people of the time would have regarded as nothing particularly unusual. Wife sales, if not exactly an everyday event, were certainly not unknown, and were often advertised in local newspapers, such as the *Windsor & Eton Express* of September 1815:

> On Friday last the common bellman gave notice in Staines market that the wife of —— Issey was then at the King's Head Inn, to be sold, with the consent of her husband, to any person inclined to buy her. There was a very numerous attendance to witness this singular sale, notwithstanding which only three shillings and fourpence were offered for the lot, no one choosing to contend with the bidder for the fair object, whose merits could only be appreciated by those who best knew them. This the purchaser could boast from a long and intimate acquaintance.

Hundreds of cases have been recorded over the past 500 years, and Sam Menefee, in the only full-length study of the custom, lists 387 known examples. The earliest definite case is recorded in the diary of London merchant tailor Henry Machyn: 'The 24th day of November [1553] did ride in a cart Cheken, parson of St. Nicholas Cold Abbey, about London, for he sold his wife to a butcher'; and there were several other instances in the sixteenth century, which indicate that this was not an isolated occurrence. Cases were still being reported into the 1920s.

There is no doubt that a wide section of the population genuinely believed that wife sales were not only permissible under law but also legally binding, providing, of course, that the sale was carried out properly. If the decision to sell was made on the spur of the moment, as in Thomas Hardy's novel, the sale will probably not have been recorded for posterity, but the majority of known cases were carefully given a semblance of regularity and legality. The sale often took place in a market or fair, where livestock was normally bought and sold, and the wife was presented with a halter round her neck and

Weyhill Fair

Weyhill was one of the big agricultural fairs that seemed to survive from habit and custom rather than from a solid legal basis. It had certainly been in existence a long time, as shown by the line in William Langland's *Piers Plowman*, of about 1377 – 'To Wy and to Wynchestre I wente to the feyre' (Passus V, line 201) – but no charter has ever been found. The position of the fair site, on a hillside a few miles from Andover, in Hampshire, is usually explained as the meeting point of several key ancient roads, but more pertinent is the fact that it straddled the boundaries of three parishes and three estates. This geographical ambiguity, coupled with the lack of a charter, made it particularly vulnerable to both legal challenge and more direct methods of takeover, by moving it on to neighbouring land. In the 1550s, for example, a long-running dispute broke out between the traditional owners of the fair and the citizens of the town of Andover, who claimed the fair, and its fees and tolls, for themselves. A similar dispute flared up in the 1670s. The town's claim was bolstered by a royal charter of 1559 that did indeed grant them the right to hold a fair at Weyhill, but the fair owners maintained that this did not apply to *their* fair, which had already been in existence long before.

displayed to potential buyers. The seller was careful to pay all regular tolls and to get a receipt. Most important of all, the sale was carried out in front of witnesses. The sums involved varied considerably, from fourpence and a pint of beer, to £50.

Occasionally, the sale was a way of sorting out a genuine marital problem, such as when the wife of a sailor had married again, believing him to have been drowned. The embarrassment caused by the man's unexpected return could be resolved by the new husband formally buying his wife from her first husband. Nor is all this necessarily an example of callous male brutality and enforced female submissiveness. There is plenty of evidence that in most cases the wife was pleased to be rid of her unwanted mate, the potential purchaser was known to her, and the whole thing agreed between them beforehand. The business of halters and bidding may have been degrading, but the women believed that this made the transaction legal, and no doubt many thought it was worth it. An example printed in *Notes & Queries* in 1951 makes this point clear:

> Brooks, auctioneer, Plymouth, put his wife up for sale [in 1822]. *The police interfered, but Mrs. B. told the magistrates she was anxious to be sold, had made arrangements with a gentleman that he should buy her, an innkeeper being instructed on his behalf to bid to £20. If the reserve was exceeded she was content to go to the highest bidder.*

Nevertheless, nobody seems to have thought that a wife could sell her husband.

Three hundred and eighty-seven cases in 500 years is not indicative of an epidemic of wife-selling, but it was enough to convince some that the English were at it all the time, as reported in Robert Chambers' *Book of Days* (1864):

> *Rather unfortunately, the occasional instances of wife-sale, while remarked by ourselves with little beyond a passing smile, have made a deep impression on our continental neighbours, who seriously believe that it is a habit of all classes of our people, and constantly cite it as an evidence of our low civilisation.*

Over forty years later, Sabine Baring-Gould agreed:

> *It is – so far as my experience goes – quite useless to assure a Frenchman that such transfer of wives is not a matter of everyday occurrence and is not legal: he replies with an expression of incredulity, that of course English people endeavour to make light of, or deny, a fact that is 'notorious'.*

It might go a little way to salvage our national pride to learn of a French case that took place at Maratz, near Lille, in 1865, and followed the same form as the English custom. The price was 126 francs, and, as reported in *Notes & Queries* in 1874, 'It appeared that neither buyer nor seller had any doubt of the legality of the transaction.'

Weyhill Fair survived these challenges and by the eighteenth century was one of the biggest in England, dominating the livestock trade in the South-West. It was particularly known for its sheep and horses, but hops and cheese were also traded in huge quantities, and a thriving pleasure fair also took place, with its sideshows, rides, freak shows, and boxing booths, along with a hiring fair. However, the nineteenth century saw a long slow decline in many of the country's big fairs. William Cobbett visited Weyhill on 11 October 1822, on one of the journeys that he later described in *Rural Rides*. He had first been to the fair about forty years previously and had fond memo-

ries of the trip, so he was shocked to find trade so depressed in the 1820s:

> *The 11th of October is the sheep-fair. About £300,000 used, some few years ago, to be carried home by the sheep-sellers. Today, less, perhaps, than £70,000, and yet the rents of these sheep-sellers are, perhaps, as high, on an average, as they were then. The countenances of the farmers were descriptive of their ruinous state. I never, in all my life, beheld a more mournful scene. There is a horse fair upon another part of the Down; and there I saw horses keeping pace in depression with the sheep.*

Cobbett was not a totally impartial observer – he had political reasons for painting a bad picture, as well as a generalized notion that things had been so much better in his youth – however, his rides took place at a time of real agricultural depression, in the difficult period between the revolution of enclosure and the drastic reorganization of agricultural practice and increased rural prosperity of later in the century. But even without the general agricultural depression, he would have noticed a marked change at Weyhill in the forty years since his first visit. Large-scale fairs all over the country were suffering from changes in economic structure and business practice that were gradually making them redundant as wholesale markets (*see* **14 September: Sturbridge Fair**).

Nevertheless, pleasure-seekers continued to attend Weyhill Fair, and, as with many other places, it was long famous for its burlesque initiation ceremony for newcomers (*see also* **Hocktide: Hungerford Hocktide Court**, p. 134; **Occasional Customs: Highgate Horns**, p. 428). Described in the Women's Institute book *It Happened in Hampshire*, the ceremony at Weyhill was called 'horning the colt':

> *The newcomer was seated in a chair, and a hat adorned with a pair of horns and a cup was placed on his head, and the following verses being sung:*
>
> > *So swift runs the fox, so cunning runs the fox*
> > *Why shouldn't this heifer grow up to be an ox?*
> > *And get his living among the briars and thorns*
> > *And drink like his daddy with a large pair of horns.*
> > > *Horns, boys, horns, boys, horns*
> > > *And drink like his daddy with a large pair of horns.*
>
> *The cup on his head had to be filled with ale. The newly initiated drank this, and paid for half a gallon, which was consumed by the company.*

The ceremony took place at several pubs in the area, and details varied from place to place, other versions of the song including 'So swift runs the hare' in the first line, and 'And die like his daddy' in the fourth. Weyhill also made an appearance in literature, as the model for the fair at which Michael Henchard sold his wife at the start of Thomas Hardy's novel *The Mayor of Casterbridge* (1886); *see* **Wife-Selling**, p. 314.

The dates on which Weyhill Fair was held changed over time. In the earliest records it was a Michaelmas fair, lasting for three days between 28 and 30 September, but it later moved to 8 October, running for six days, and then to 10 October. There were also other smaller fairs, for sheep, in April and July. Weyhill struggled on into the twentieth century, a mere shadow of its former self, and finally ceased in the 1950s.

See also **Fairs, Feasts, Feasts, and Revels**, p. 249; **Hiring Fairs**, p. 345.

*

11 OCTOBER

Blackberries

In 1909, the journal *Folk-Lore* reported that in Worcestershire:

> *All children who either gather or eat blackberries on or after the 11th of October will fall into great trouble. It is said that 'the Devil puts his paw on them' on that day.*

See **29 September: Blackberries** for further details.

*

16 OCTOBER

Lion Sermon

This annual sermon takes place at the church of St Katharine Cree, Leadenhall Street, London, on or near 16 October. It commemorates an incident in the life of Sir John Gayer, founder of the Levant Company and later Lord Mayor of London, who died in 1649. While abroad on a trading expedition he became separated from his companions in the desert and met a fierce lion. Praying for assistance, Gayer fell asleep and on being found in the morning he was surrounded by lion prints but had come to no harm. Back in London as a prosperous merchant, he made various charitable gifts, including a bequest for the poor of St Katharine's parish, and he is still commemorated with a special service at which the story is retold and a sermon is preached.

*

18 OCTOBER

St Luke's Day

Luke the evangelist, by tradition a Greek physician, was a disciple of St Paul and a key figure in the early development of the Christian Church. He became the patron saint of doctors, surgeons, and artists – the latter because of a tradition that he himself was one. In religious pictures he is sometimes shown painting, but the symbol that accompanies him in most images is an ox with horns, although it is not clear why. The good saint would have been horrified if he knew what connotations those very horns would have in later years, and what they would do to his feast day.

At Charlton, in Kent, where the parish church is dedicated to St Luke, a very famous fair took place each year, starting on 18 October. It was formerly held upon a green opposite the church but later moved to the other end of the village, and at some point became widely known as 'Charlton Horn Fair'; until suppressed in 1872, it was one of the most notorious fairs in the London region.

Horns were the theme of the fair and were ubiquitous on the day. Many of the people who frequented the fair wore or carried horns, the stalls specialized in items made of horn, and even the gingerbread men sported little horns on their heads. However, this was not simply a harmless gimmick; people found the wearing of horns immensely amusing because of their sexual connotations. From at least the mid fifteenth century onwards the phrase 'to wear the horns' referred to a cuckold (i.e. a man whose wife has been unfaithful to him), and anything to do with horns was replete with opportunities for ribald humour. If one held a hand to the forehead, with index and little finger extended, it would be taken as a gross personal insult, and numerous sexual slang phrases that included the word 'horn' traded on the same principle.

The popular story that explained the origin of the fair also traded on this sexual theme. It was said that one St Luke's Day, King John needed a rest while out hunting, and stepped into a nearby mill. The miller's attractive wife was home alone, so the King decided to make advances, and was just in the act of kissing her when the miller returned, drew his dagger, and threatened to kill them both. The King, however, granted him lordship over all the land between Charlton and the bend in the river beyond Rotherhithe, together with the right to hold a fair each year on that same day. The bend in the river bore the popular name of 'Cuckold's Point', and the German traveller Paul Hentzner, who was well aware of the connection between horns and cuckoldry, noted in his *Travels to England* (1598) that a long pole was sited there, with ram's horns affixed.

Although the custom probably began when someone carried a pair of St Luke's horns to open the fair, it soon degenerated into burlesque, with a procession of characters dressed as the King, the miller, and his wife, and hundreds of others wearing horns on their heads. The crowds who flocked to the fair in their thousands were also famous for their habit of cross-dressing (men as women, and vice versa), and as this annual gathering flaunted its ribaldry so openly, it hardly endeared itself to the authorities of Church and State. The idea of horned beings also added a 'devilish' tinge to the fair's reputation.

From the eighteenth century onwards, writers queued up to condemn the goings-on at Charlton. Kent county historian Edward Hasted commented in 1779 that it was 'infamous for rudeness and indecency', and Daniel Defoe described Charlton in the 1720s as:

> . . . a village famous, or rather infamous, for the yearly collected rabble of mad-people, at Horn Fair, the rudeness of which I cannot but think, is such as ought to be suppressed . . . The mob indeed at that time take all kinds of liberties, and the women are especially impudent for that day; as if it was a day that justified the giving themselves a loose to all manner of indecency and immodesty, without any reproach, or without suffering the censure which such behaviour would deserve.

This bad reputation continued into the nineteenth century, and it is remarkable that the fair lasted as long as it did. However, the Fairs Act of 1871 gave the local authorities the opportunity to get rid of it, which they promptly did.

There are some indications that St Luke's Day was also regarded as a day for love divination. A full description of a ceremony for the day appears in a chapbook printed in 1685 called *Mother Bunch's Closet Newly Broke Open*, in which Mother Bunch instructs young girls how to predict and control their matrimonial prospects. She tells them to take marigold flowers, marjoram, thyme, and wormwood, and then to mix, dry, and pound them to a powder, and simmer them with honey and vinegar over a slow fire. With this concoction, the girl should 'anoint [her] stomach, breast and lips lying down, and repeat these words thrice':

> St. Luke, St. Luke, be kind to me
> In dreams let me my true love see.

She should then go to sleep as fast as she can. This ceremony is so similar to those on other nights (*see*, for example, **20 January: St Agnes' Eve**) that it has been regarded as perhaps a literary fancy on the part of the chapbook author rather than evidence of a genuine popular tradition. Nevertheless, confirmation can be found in Act IV, scene 1 of George Chapman's play *Monsieur D'Olive* (1606), in which occurs the line 'St. Valentine's Day is fortunate to choose lovers, St. Luke's to choose husbands.'

Somewhat incongruously, St Luke's Day was also 'Dog-Whipping Day' in nineteenth-century York, when everybody carried whips with which to assault any dogs found running loose in the town (*see* **10 October: Old Michaelmas Day**). And on another note, according to folklorist Sidney Oldall Addy, writing in 1895, 'A fine autumn is known as a "St Luke's Summer".'

On Thursday, the Mayor, Aldermen, Assistants, and Common Council of this borough went in procession to proclaim the Fair of St. Denys. Proclamation was made according to the ancient custom at the door of the Town Hall, and repeated at the exchange. A liberal supply of oysters was furnished by the Colne Fishery Company, which, with wine and cake, the members of the corporate body partook of at the freeman's club in the evening.

*

20 OCTOBER

Colchester Oyster Feast

The annual Oyster Feast, held on or about 20 October, is a well-publicized feature in Colchester's municipal calendar. Originally, it was probably a simple civic luncheon, as found in some form or other in most corporations up and down the country, and took place in October because the local fair was on St Denys' Day (9 October, but moved to 20 October on the change of calendar in 1752). The fact that Colchester had a thriving local seafood industry added a unique touch, as reported by the *Essex Standard* of 21 October 1847:

The luncheon turned into a more grand affair by stages during the nineteenth century, as it was opened up to a wider clientele. One particularly extrovert mayor, who served at various times between 1845 and 1862, regularly invited 200 or 300 guests, at his own expense, and by the turn of the twentieth century, a special train from London had to be organized each year to bring all the important people who had been invited and were more than willing to come. Civic pride was well served by this lavish dinner, which helped to keep Colchester in the public eye.

However, owing to a combination of economics, occasional extreme weather, and pollution, the oyster fishery declined markedly in the twentieth century, and the industry no longer made a significant contribution to the town's economy. The feast, too, seemed increasingly anachronistic and fell on hard times, and between 1939 and 1950 it was not even held. When it

The death of Nelson on the lower deck of the *Victory*: a detail from Daniel MacLise's House of Commons fresco of 1863–5

was finally revived it became more of a gala evening, as befits the modern view of such affairs. No longer do trainloads of important people arrive from London, but it is still a large event, with celebrities from the world of entertainment, sport, and politics (especially those with local connections), and a number of tickets are available to local people by ballot. Not everyone in attendance eats oysters, which are still always included in the fare; however, the oyster fishery has also undergone a revival, and the sense of pride in a unique aspect of the town's heritage grows stronger every year.

See also **Early September: Colchester Oyster Fishery** for the annual ceremony that starts the oyster dredging season, and **25 July: Whitstable Oyster Festival**.

*

21 OCTOBER

Apple Day

This day was designated 'Apple Day' in 1990 by the environment and community charity Common Ground, who are based in Shaftesbury, Dorset. The day is designed as 'an annual celebration of apples, orchards, and local distinctiveness', and apple-related events take place up and down the country.

See also **First Weekend in December: Tree-Dressing Day** for another Common Ground initiative.

Trafalgar Day

A handful of military victories remain in public memory as symbols of national pride, while most are consigned to the history books. The one that appears to have the most resonance in this context is the Battle of Trafalgar of 1805, when the British fleet under Admiral Nelson destroyed the combined French and Spanish fleets in the decisive naval encounter of the Napoleonic Wars. A range of local Trafalgar Day celebrations take place each year on 21 October, particularly in places with strong naval ties, such as Gosport, Portsmouth, Plymouth, and Greenwich.

One of the best known is the annual service aboard the HMS *Victory* at Portsmouth Naval Base, but a more low-key ceremony takes place in Newcastle every October when the Lord Mayor lays a wreath at the foot of the statue of Admiral Lord Collingwood, who took command at Trafalgar when Nelson was killed.

The patriotic potential of Trafalgar Day makes it popular with those who wish to encourage English people to celebrate St George's Day (*see* **23 April**), and it is also the day that is favoured by many who dislike the connotations of May Day and wish to replace it with a different bank holiday later in the year (*see* **Bank Holidays**, p. 274). The year 2005 was the 200th anniversary of the battle, and numerous commemorative events were held around the country, along with the

St Crispin's Day: Shoemakers having a 'holiday' in honour of their patron saint (George Cruickshank, *Comic Almanac*, 1836)

publication of many books and articles, which brought the day to the notice of an even wider audience.

∗

25 OCTOBER

St Crispin's Day

If they existed at all, the brothers St Crispin and St Crispinian were Roman martyrs who died about the year AD 285, but their cult came to Britain much later via France, where they were reputed to have been buried. By tradition they were shoemakers who even lived for a time at Faversham, in Kent, and they were thus adopted as patron saints of cobblers and leather-workers in general. In some areas these workers held celebratory meetings and processions, as other trades did on their patron saints' days, and there are also traces of other customs that lasted into the mid nineteenth century, as recorded in *Notes & Queries* in 1852:

In the parishes of Cuckfield and Hurst-a-point in Sussex, it is still the custom to observe St. Crispin's Day, and it is kept with much rejoicing. The boys go round asking for money in the name of St. Crispin, bonfires are lighted, and it passes off very much in the same way as the fifth of November does.

However, the real lasting resonance for the day is patriotic rather than occupational, as it was the day that the Battle of Agincourt was fought in 1415, for ever encapsulated in the lines from Act IV, scene 3 of Shakespeare's *Henry V*:

This day is called the feast of Crispian.
He that outlives this day, and come safe home,
Will stand a tip-toe when this day is named,
And rouse him at the name of Crispian.
He that shall live this day, and see old age,
Will yearly on the vigil feast his neighbours,
And say, 'Tomorrow is Saint Crispian.'
Then will he strip his sleeve and show his scars,
And say 'These wounds I had on Crispin's day.'

∗

LAST THURSDAY IN OCTOBER

Bampton Fair

Six miles from Tiverton, on the edge of Exmoor National Park, lies the picturesque Devon village of Bampton, which for centuries was widely known in the region for its annual fair. It is not completely clear when Bampton Fair started. The first documentary record of the fair dates from 1212, but a sheep fair had probably existed there before then, and charters of 1258 and 1267 confirm the right to hold two annual fairs in the village. For most of its history, Bampton was primarily a sheep fair, held on St Luke's Day (18 October). It was one of the biggest in the West Country, and before its decline in the mid nineteenth century over 12,000 animals could be sold each year. There had also been a certain amount of trading in cattle and horses, but as the sheep trade declined, the horse trade increased, and the fair became famous for its Exmoor ponies.

As with nearly all horse fairs, the sale of animals dwindled to nothing in the late twentieth century, and the event seemed destined to survive, if at all, simply as a pleasure fair. However, in 2003 locals completely reorganized the event, and it now offers a street market, an arts and crafts fair, craft workshops, auctions, exhibitions, and a range of other activities, in addition to the funfair, and the event has taken on a heightened profile in the life of the community and as a popular tourist attraction. Pony sales and other related activities have also been re-introduced, and the future for the fair looks promising.

See also **Fairs, Feasts, Wakes, and Revels**, p. 249.

LATE OCTOBER

Punkie Night

It's Punky Night tonight
It's Punky Night tonight
Give us a candle, give us a light
It's Punky Night tonight.

Seed Cakes

It was the custom in certain areas, at the conclusion of the wheat-sowing season, to celebrate by making and distributing a special cake called a 'seed cake'. The 'seed' of the title thus refers to the occasion rather than the ingredients. Anne Baker, in her *Glossary of Northamptonshire Words and Phrases* (1854), referred to them as 'Siblet cakes' and wrote that the ploughmen received them, whereas William Hone, reporting a Bedfordshire example in 1831, called them 'Siblett cakes' and said they were made by farmers' wives and distributed to their friends and relations. In his *Five Hundred Points of Good Husbandry* (1580), Thomas Tusser does not make it clear who gets the cake, but confirms the custom's antiquity:

> *Wife, sometime this week, if ye weather hold clear,*
> *An end of wheat sowing we make for the year;*
> *Remember you therefore, though I do it not,*
> *The seed cake, the pasties, and furmety pot.*

Wheat-sowing in England often ended around All Souls' Day and the custom is therefore confused with, or related to, soul-cakes (*see* **2 November**).

This is one verse of the song chanted by children in certain Somerset villages, as they carry their 'punkies' around the village. A punkie is made from a mangold-wurzel, or a large turnip, on similar lines to the now-standard Hallowe'en pumpkin. The top is sliced off, the insides are scooped out, and designs are cut into the outer skin, leaving a thin membrane intact; a lighted candle is then placed inside to shine through the cuts. These designs vary considerably, and although scary faces are popular, much more imaginative scenes can also be found.

Although Punkie Nights have been reported from several Somerset villages, Hinton St George and Lopen both claim to be the originators of the custom. Various nights in late October have served, including the 28th or 29th, but Hinton St George eventually settled on the last Thursday in the month. It seems to have previously been a simple house-visiting custom, but was reorganized by members of the local Women's Institute in the mid twentieth century and is now celebrated with a procession of children carrying their punkies, and a party where prizes for the best designs are given, a Punkie King and Queen crowned, and money is raised for charity.

The local story usually told to explain the origin of the custom is given in *Notes & Queries* (1931), and is quite simple:

> *A party of men from Hinton and Lopen visited Chiselborough Fair – a noted cloth fair in years gone by – and did not return to their homes so early as promised. Their wives went in search of them, and the attractions of the fair apparently were so great that by the time they commenced their journey home their lamps were innocent of oil, and improvised lanterns, made from mangold-wurzels from the wayside fields, were utilised.*

In other versions the emphasis was slightly different, and it was said that the drunkenness of the men, and their inability to find their own way, meant that their wives had to improvise the lanterns so that they could go and bring the men home.

Nobody seems to have made any serious attempt to pin down the history and development of Punkie Night. Many simply assume that it is a localized version of the ubiquitous Hallowe'en (*see below*), or that it is in fact the original of the latter custom, which was exported to America and then re-imported to Britain. The key determining factor is therefore the age of Punkie Night, but despite the usual assumptions of ancient origins, none of the authorities consulted provide any evidence of its existence before the twentieth century.

*

31 OCTOBER

Hallowe'en

Hallowe'en is probably the most widely misunderstood and misrepresented day in the festival year, but so many now believe that it was originally a pagan festi-val of the dead that this belief is virtually impossible to shake. The facts, however, are very different, and are far more elusive and complex.

'Hallowe'en' means the Eve of Hallowtide (1 and 2 November), which was indeed designated as a time to commemorate the dead, but it was a Christian festival inaugurated in the medieval period. There is no evidence that this time of year was celebrated in in England before the Christian feast was created. In Ireland, 1 November was 'Samhain', the beginning of winter and of the year, and as such it was an important day of gathering and feasting, but not, it seems, of much religious or supernatural significance. Nor is there any evidence of the supernatural at Hallowe'en in early Welsh or Scottish material, except where Irish influence was strong. Most of the supernatural aura that supposedly surrounded the day in earlier times is an invention from the modern period that has now become entrenched in a way that is depressingly familiar throughout popular writing on folklore.

The modern Hallowe'en developed from the two closely linked Christian festivals of All Saints (**1 November**) and All Souls (**2 November**), which were both concerned in their way with the dead. The festival of All Saints, known in English as All-Hallows or Hallowmas ('hallow' from the Old English word for 'holy man' or 'saint'), was instituted to commemorate all the Christian saints and martyrs, known and unknown, who had been instrumental in forming and perpetuating the faith. It was originally celebrated in May, but was fixed at 1 November in the eighth century, and with this new date soon spread across the Christian west, including England.

The feast of All Souls, on 2 November, was added somewhat later, about the year 1000, and was created to commemorate the faithful departed who had gone before. For centuries there had been debate within the Church about whether Christian souls went straight to Heaven or were detained somewhere to undergo painful purgation to prepare them for eternal bliss; a particular problem was what happened to those who died suddenly without final rites, or who had no time to make proper preparation. It was clear that a halfway house on the way to Heaven was needed, but there was little agreement over the details of what it was, or how it worked. The existence of Purgatory was officially

Carved pumpkins for Hallowe'en

recognized in the Western Church at the Second General Council of Lyons, in 1274, along with the crucial notion that souls could be helped towards Heaven, and their sufferings relieved, by the actions of the living. All Souls thus took shape as an important feast at which special requiem masses were held, with candles and torches, and pious acts were encouraged, such as the giving of alms and offering prayers. For the laity, one of the most tangible methods of assisting souls was the ringing of church bells, and this was done so enthusiastically that the ringing went on for hour after hour at All Souls, and was one of the 'superstitious practices' vigorously attacked by the Protestant reformers of the sixteenth century. At the Reformation the whole idea of Purgatory, and the possibility of intercession on behalf of the dead, were rejected, and All Souls was excluded from the English religious calendar. The bells fell silent in 1559.

In Catholic countries, the festival continued to develop its connection with the supernatural, but in England it seems to have left little more than a vague notion that Hallowe'en was a time when the spirit world was particularly close to the everyday one. In Lincolnshire, as reported in 1908:

> On the Eve of All Saints Day, at 12 pm, twelve lights rise from the mound in All Hallows churchyard where the ancient church of Horsington stood (they are blue and rise slowly and do not jump about like jenny wisps), and then slowly proceed in threes toward the following villages – three to Horsington, three to Stixwould, three to Bucknall, and three to Wadingworth.

Even then it was not seen as necessarily the most potently supernatural day in the calendar, but one of several. Activities such as porch-watching, for example – staying up all night in the church porch to see the wraiths of all the local parishioners parade by, in order to determine who would die in the coming year – were far more likely to take place on St Mark's Eve (*see* **24 April**).

Two customs that may have been direct survivals of medieval practices were the house-visiting custom called souling (*see* **2 November: All Souls' Day**), reported in the nineteenth century, and the lighting of fires on Hallowe'en. One of the doctrinal notions about Purgatory was that the purgation of the souls was by holy fire, and the bonfires that were common throughout Hallowtide may be a memory of this connection, although bonfires in northern climes in late autumn or early winter are hardly remarkable, and the influence of the Guy Fawkes bonfires of 5 November cannot be ruled out.

Except for the areas in which souling customs took place, as the twentieth century approached, Hallowe'en had almost died out completely in most of England. The main folklore books of the closing quarter of the nineteenth century, and the early years of the twentieth, hardly mention Hallowe'en at all, except to quote Scottish examples, and the same is true of the mass of autobiographies that provide such telling details of life in England before the Second World War. It is hard to escape the conclusion that for most of the people of England, Hallowe'en passed without notice. When it *is* noticed, it is usually to describe the games and love divinations played on the day, as in John Brockett's *Glossary of North Country Words* (1825):

> The vigil of All Saints' Day, on which it is customary with young people in the North of England to dive for apples, or catch at them upon one end of a kind of hanging beam, at the other extremity of which is fixed a lighted candle, and that with their mouths only, their hands being tied behind their backs.

The games mentioned in these accounts have been remarkably stable over the years, utilizing nuts, or apples in buckets of water or hanging from strings, and the prevalence of these edibles does not seem to have any symbolic significance but simply reflects their availability at the time of year.

Hallowe'en was certainly one of the key nights of the year when young people (usually, but not always, girls) could discover who, when, and how they were going to marry, if at all, by following one of many tradi-

tional procedures. The *Transactions of the Devonshire Association* recorded:

> Mrs. Hook, of Chulmleigh [Devon], *aged 70, told me in May 1938, that in her young days it was the custom on All Hallowe'en to pare apples, then whirl the peel three times round the head and then throw it over the left shoulder to the floor. The letter formed on the floor by the apple peel would be the initial of the future husband or wife. Mrs. Hook assured me that her apple peel always formed the letter J., and she eventually married Jack Hook.*

As with the games, apples and nuts featured strongly in these divinations. Two nuts, for example, would be chosen to represent two potential lovers and placed side by side on the fire-shovel over the flames of a fire. The future romantic potential for the couple could be gauged by whether the heated nuts jumped apart or drew together. Alternatively, anyone brave enough could brush their hair in front of a mirror at midnight and it was said that they would see the face of their future spouse peering over their shoulder. A much less scary form of fortune-telling was recorded by folklorist Sidney Oldall Addy in the mid 1890s:

> In Derbyshire farmers carry a candle down the garden on All Hallow's Een, to see which way the wind blew. As the wind blew that night such would be the prevailing wind for the next three months.

In the mid twentieth century, however, the germs of the modern Hallowe'en were already visible. Iona and Peter Opie discovered that children in 1950s England celebrated either Hallowe'en or Guy Fawkes Night, depending on where they lived:

> When darkness closes in on the vigil of All Saints Day, Britain has the appearance of a land inhabited by two nations with completely different cultural backgrounds. While the young of one nation are employed upon their homework, the children of the other are wildly celebrating one of their major festivals.

The demarcation line between these two 'nations' ran from the mouth of the Humber on the east coast across to Knighton, near Stafford, and then southwards along the border with Wales down to the Bristol channel.

It was the children to the north and west of this line that enthusiastically celebrated Hallowe'en, by house-visiting in costume and carrying hollowed-out turnips. In some parts, Hallowe'en is also **Mischief Night** (*see below*), and misbehaviour on the day is sanctioned by tradition.

Then there was the explosion of interest in Hallowe'en in the 1970s and 1980s. Children all over England suddenly started dressing up as witches and ghosts, knocking on doors and expecting largesse, and using the words 'trick or treat'; and it is clear that this was largely imported directly from American films and television series, which regularly showed such scenes. The immensely popular film *ET* (1982), for example, provided a model for how to dress and what to do on the night. The newspapers were soon full of complaints about children demanding money with menaces, and reports of elderly people being confused and intimidated by this new custom. There is some evidence that the meteoric rise of Hallowe'en in the late twentieth century was deliberately encouraged by teachers trying to shift the attention from Guy Fawkes Night because of widespread criticism of the customs of that night, primarily because of fears over safety. But the teachers quickly found themselves in a different fire, as a howl of protest from fundamentalist Christians broke over their heads about the moral dangers of encouraging children to take an interest in supposed pagan matters and the occult. Dressing up as witches, and reading Harry Potter novels, is no mere game, we are told, but a sure way of endangering our immortal souls.

Hallowe'en parties, with guests dressed as witches and fiends, have been growing in popularity since the 1980s and although they too appear at first glance to have been influenced by American popular culture, they have, in fact, been around for a bit longer than that. In Nella Last's wartime diary, for example, she reflected on pre-war family occasions, and recorded for posterity the details of a family Hallowe'en party, presumably in the 1920s or early 1930s:

Tuesday 31 October 1939 – The wind howled and I could have howled like a banshee with it. Hallowe'en, and the house so straight and quiet, my towels all in a drawer and not in wet heaps in the garage where everybody would have been ducking for apples,

no smell of baking potatoes, no decorations – only memories. One year the boys received their guests in a novel way. Cliff painted a placard and put it on the door. It read 'Abandon hope all ye who enter here'. It was in old English lettering and had bats and owls drawn on the border . . . In the pitch-black the boys stood to welcome the guests. Arthur had a black bag over his head and Cliff's fiendishly grinning face, lit by a ghastly green electric bulb, was under his arm. A rubber glove filled with cold water was held out to the hand of each guest – it was a huge success!

Hallowe'en continues to grow in popularity, and the most recent development is the rise of fancy dress at parties for young adults; the day is undoubtedly the busiest time of the year for costume hire and joke shops.

See also **Late October: Punkie Night**.

Antrobus Soul-Cakers

Now ladies and gentlemen, light a fire and strike a
*   light*
For in this house there's going to be a dreadful fight
Between King George and the Black Prince
And I hope King George will win
Whether he wins, loses, fights or falls
We'll do our best to please you all

These are the first words (after the introductory song) of the soul-cakers, who perform in the pubs around Antrobus, in Cheshire, and neighbouring villages from Hallowe'en into the first weeks of November. Their souling play is one form of the ubiquitous mumming play (*see* **Christmas: Mummers**), and thus involves a sword-fight between King George and the Black Prince. The latter is killed, but revived by the Doctor. Other characters include Mary, Beelzebub, Derry Doubt, and the Letter-In, who speaks the introductory lines. Apart from the time of year it is performed, the key characteristic that distinguishes a souling play from other mumming plays is the presence of a man dressed up as the Wild Horse, and his Driver, who come in at the end of the play:

In comes Dick and all his men
He's come to see you once again
He was once alive, but now he's dead

He's nothing but a poor old horse's head
Stand around Dick, and show yourself!

As with other hobby horses across the country, Dick misbehaves, chases people, and causes havoc.

The Antrobus men dress, roughly, in costume depicting their character, and performances nowadays take place primarily in pubs, although in the past they would mainly perform in the local 'big houses' and other homes. It is perhaps because of the modern pub setting that performances nowadays include more ad-libbing and audience involvement than was previously the case.

In the late nineteenth and early twentieth century, there were many such souling teams in Cheshire, but at Antrobus regular performances ceased at the First World War, when some of the team were killed. Local enthusiast Major A. W. Boyd persuaded the local team to re-form, and as they have performed ever since, they are the only local team with a direct connection to the old tradition.

See also **2 November: All Souls' Day**; **Hobby Horses**, p. 164.

Mischief Night

For many young people in England, a highlight of the traditional year was Mischief Night, when they thought it their right to carry out a range of tricks on their elders and their property. In 1882, Lancashire folklorists John Harland and T. T. Wilkinson reported:

> *The evening before May Day is termed 'Mischief Night', by the young people of Burnley and the surrounding district. All kinds of mischief are then perpetrated. Formerly shopkeepers' sign-boards were exchanged; 'John Smith, grocer', finding his name and vocation changed, by the sign over his door, to 'Thomas Jones, tailor', and vice versa; but the police have put an end to these practical jokes.*

Earlier accounts of the mischief carried out are very similar to each other, and there was clearly a strong tradition of what could and could not be done. Gates and signs were the main targets, as they were easily removed, hidden, or swapped around. Front doors were also the focus of innumerable tricks based on knocking and running away, and tying neighbouring doors together, while tapping on windows and blocking up chimneys, were also popular. Anything not screwed down was fair game, and some tricksters were more inventive, as remembered by members of a local Women's Institute in the collection *Lancashire Lore* (1971):

> *Mischief Night in Blacko* [Lancashire] *was Hallowe'en ... On one occasion the mischief makers went to Lower Admergill Farm armed with a gun and a tin of blood collected from the slaughterhouse. When the farmer opened the door a shot was fired into the air, and simultaneously the blood was thrown over him. He staggered back, waving his arms and shouting, 'I've been shot.' Needless to say, no-one stayed to find out how long it took him to recover ...* [Another] *trick was sometimes played on patrons of the Moorcock Inn who left their 'transport' tied up outside. On leaving the inn, they would discover that their horse had been led into a nearby field, the gate closed, the cart still on the roadside, but hitched to the horse through the closed gate.*

The history of Mischief Night continues to puzzle folklorists, from several points of view, but most notably because there are three contenders for the correct day of the year. Most nineteenth-century reports name 30 April as Mischief Night (*see* **30 April: May Day Eve**), but by the 1950s this had changed to 4 November (Guy Fawkes Eve). Iona and Peter Opie, writing in the late 1950s, believed that the change from April to November had only taken place in the previous two decades. In some places in England, however, and throughout Scotland, Ireland, and the United States, Mischief Night has always fallen on Hallowe'en.

The geographical spread of the custom is more easily identified. From the nineteenth century to the 1950s, Mischief Night was regularly recorded in a broad swathe across the country, concentrated in Lancashire and Yorkshire but also found in northern parts of Cheshire, Derbyshire, Nottinghamshire, and Lincolnshire. Since that time, however, it seems to have gradually shrunk to remain in Yorkshire alone, where the tradition is tenaciously vigorous and called 'Miggy Night'. Every year the police in some towns are kept busy dealing with the mayhem caused by children and youths, and the local media bemoan the fact that Mischief Night has changed from relatively harmless fun to mind-less vandalism. One has to wonder, however, to what degree the custom is kept alive by the extensive press coverage.

It is certainly true that adults in areas where mischief traditions had been around since their own childhood were until recently relatively tolerant about the tricks played, as long as the children did not 'go too far'. Police, too, seem to have been philosophical about them. Without falling into the trap of believing that the past was a golden age, it is clear from the reminiscences of those involved, as well as press coverage, that today's Mischief Nighters see no difference between vandalism and tricks, and cause much more real damage to public property than previous generations dared – although it has always been widely reported that children who took part in mischievous activities firmly believed that the usual laws of the land did not apply on that night:

> When I was a kid I actually thought it was legal
> – 'coppers can't arrest you on Miggy Night.'

This idea is traditional in itself, and is shared with several other customs (*see* **Lawless Hours and Days**, p. 303).

Although Mischief Night itself was found in a restricted area of the country, children elsewhere enjoyed similar customs. In the West Country, for example, similar tricks were played on neighbours at Shrovetide, under such local names as Nickanan Night and Lansherd Night (*see* **Shrove Tuesday: Shroving and Lent-Crocking**, p. 65).

Some writers have assumed an ancient pagan origin for the custom, but there is no evidence that this is the case. Mischief Night itself only enters the documentary record in the 1830s, although some of the analogous 'tricking' customs may be older.

November

5
Devil's Stone
GUY FAWKES NIGHT
Lewes Bonfire Night
Ottery St Mary

6

7

12

13
ST BRICE'S DAY

14

Hiring Fairs

19

20

21

26

27
**FOURTH TUESDAY IN
NOVEMBER**
Ashburton Court Leet

28

*Moveable events have been placed
on the date they fall in 2007.*

1

ALL SAINTS' DAY

2

ALL SOULS' DAY
FIRST FRIDAY IN
NOVEMBER
Bridgwater Carnival

3

4

RINGING NIGHT
FIRST SUNDAY IN
NOVEMBER
London to Brighton Veteran
Car Run

8

9

PULLY LUG DAY
SECOND FRIDAY IN
NOVEMBER
Silent Change

10

ST MARTIN'S EVE
Wroth Silver
SECOND SATURDAY IN
NOVEMBER
Hatherleigh Carnival
Lord Mayor's Show

11

ST MARTIN'S DAY
Fenny Poppers
REMEMBRANCE SUNDAY

15

16

17

QUEEN ELIZABETH I/
ST HUGH'S DAY

18

22

ST CECILIA'S DAY

23

ST CLEMENT'S DAY

24

25

ST CATHERINE'S DAY
LATE NOVEMBER
Stir-Up Sunday

29

30

ST ANDREW'S DAY
Eton Wall Game

Parkin

Bull-Baiting

London to Brighton Veteran Car Run, 1986

FIRST SUNDAY IN NOVEMBER

London to Brighton Veteran Car Run

The London to Brighton Veteran Car Run, organized by the RAC (Royal Automobile Club) and affectionately known to many as 'the Old Crocks' Race', claims to be the world's longest running motoring event. Participants start at Hyde Park in central London, and then drive sixty miles down the A23 to Brighton. The event is open to vehicles manufactured before 1905, and attracts entrants from around the world. Around 300 entrants usually participate, although the 1996 centenary run attracted a record 680 cars.

The claim to be the longest running motoring event implies a continuous series of runs, but this is not quite the case. In November 1896, when the Act of Parliament was passed that raised the speed limit from 4 mph to 14 mph and abolished the regulation that vehicles must be preceded by a man with a red flag, thirty motorists took part in a semi-spontaneous run to Brighton (only fourteen actually got there). This run was re-enacted in 1927, and the event has taken place every year since, except during the Second World War and in 1947 when severe petrol rationing was in force.

*

1 NOVEMBER

All Saints' Day

The festival of All Saints, known previously as All-Hallows or Hallowmas ('hallow' from the Old English word for 'holy man' or 'saint'), was originally celebrated in May but moved to 1 November in the eighth century, reaching England soon afterwards. It is the day on which the faithful remember the lives and sacrifices of all saints and martyrs for the Church. In the more secular traditional calendar, however, little distinction seems to have been made between All Saints' Day and All Souls' Day (2 November), as both were concerned with commemorating the dead in one way or another, and similar customs were found on both days.

One of these customs was to make special soul-cakes. The antiquarian John Aubrey noted in 1686 that in Shropshire:

> There is set on the board a high heap of soul-cakes, lying one upon another like the picture of sew-bread in the old Bibles. They are about the bigness of 2d. cakes, and nearly all the visitants that day take one; and there is an old rhythm or saying,
>
> > A soul-cake, a soul-cake
> > Have mercy on all Christian souls for a soul-cake.

This custom of giving cakes seems to have been a useful double-sided coin: the act of charity helped the giver's soul, and at the same time, by commemorating the dead, consumption of the cake helped other peoples' souls to get out of Purgatory and into Heaven. Whenever charities such as this were on offer, house-visiting customs seem to have grown up around them, and in this case it was called 'souling': participants expected to be given cakes, apples, drink, or money at each house at which they called, in response to their singing a souling rhyme similar to that quoted by Aubrey (see **2 November: All Souls' Day**). By the nineteenth century, when this custom was adequately recorded, it was predominately carried out by children, but it had previously been a more serious affair, and was commonplace enough for Shakespeare to use the phrase 'to speak puling, like a beggar at Hallowmas' in Act II, scene 1 of *Two Gentlemen of Verona*.

*

2 NOVEMBER

All Souls' Day

The doctrine of Purgatory was slow to develop in the Christian Church, but was properly codified by the thirteenth century and seemed to answer the problem of what happened to the mass of people who were not good enough to go straight to Heaven, nor sufficiently bad to be consigned straight to Hell. Such souls, it was argued, stayed in Purgatory until they were purified by holy fire and went on to eternal bliss, and they could be helped on their journey by the prayers and other pious actions of the living. Thus, on All Souls' Day, it was the duty of all Christians to concentrate on assisting those souls, by attending special masses, offering special prayers, and making acts of charity. The parish church bells were also rung vigorously on the day, as this holy sound was believed to help.

The whole notion of the living being able to help the dead was rejected at the Reformation, when the 'superstitious' prayers and ringing of bells were condemned, but the basic connections between the time of year, charity, and the dead, lingered on in people's minds and were reflected in several secular customs. As indicated under **1 November**, most people seem in practice to have made little distinction between All Saints' Day and All Souls' Day, and these customs could occur at any time between Hallowe'en and the night of All Souls.

The most frequently documented example of the charity aspect of the season in the seventeenth century took the form of bread or 'soul-cakes' that were distributed either to the poor or to the whole congregation or community (see **1 November**). Bonfires were also popular, as in many other autumn and winter customs, but in this case they were directly relevant, echoing the purifying fires of Purgatory.

In later times, however, the main traditional activity for the season was a house-visiting custom in which groups of children knocked on doors, sang a song, and hoped for reward. A version from the Staffordshire/Cheshire border was included in *Note & Queries* (1868):

> Bands of children go from house to house, on the evening of All Souls' Day, begging for biscuits, nuts, apples, and the like – all of which they call 'soul-cakes' or 'sou'cakes' (pronounced 'sowl-cake' or 'sow'cake) in doggerel ballads such as these:
>
> > I hope you will prove kind with your apples and strong beer
> > And we'll come no more a-souling until this time next year.
> > One for Peter, one for Paul
> > One for Him as made us all

Up with your kettles, and down with your pans
Give us a sou'cake and we will be gone.

Souling was found elsewhere, but the available evidence shows that it was heavily concentrated in the midland counties of Cheshire, Staffordshire, and Lancashire, and it shared this area with two other almost identical visiting customs: clementing (*see* **23 November: St Clement's Day**) and catterning (*see* **25 November: St Catherine's Day**). It is only documented from the early nineteenth century onwards, but it lingered in some places until the 1950s.

A very different custom at this season also went by the name of 'souling' or 'soul-caking', in roughly the same geographical area. This was a local variation of the mummers' play, elsewhere played more commonly at Christmas; *see* **31 October: Antrobus Soul-Cakers** for further details.

*

FIRST FRIDAY IN NOVEMBER

Bridgwater Carnival

Bridgwater, in Somerset, bills itself as 'the home of carnival' and holds what is claimed to be the largest illuminated carnival in the world; it is certainly the biggest and brightest in the region. Crowds of 150,000 pack the town, around 150 entries take part in the procession of floats, and upwards of £24,000 is collected for charity along the way. Since 1909, the carnival had been held on the first Thursday in November, but in 2000 it was moved, after much local debate, to the first Friday, where it is at present.

The most noticeable features of the modern procession are the sheer size of the floats, decorated with thousands of light bulbs that provide stunning illuminated spectacles, the music, and the elaborately costumed 'living statues', which populate the tableaux. The themes vary widely, and an immense amount of thought and effort goes into their planning throughout the year by the carnival clubs (made up of volunteers from particular pubs or organizations), and there is keen competition between them for the numerous sponsored prizes that are awarded in a range of classes.

Many of the clubs take their floats to other illuminated carnivals in the region, and in recent years an official tie-up with Notting Hill Carnival (*see* **August Bank Holiday**) has resulted in some reciprocal visits. The procession itself is the climax of weeks of linked events, including a firework display on the evening before, and a series of concerts in late October, at which the clubs present their themes, in costume, on stage.

The organized carnival itself dates back to 1881, and developed directly from the more chaotic traditional 5 November celebrations, following a similar pattern to Lewes (*see* **5 November: Lewes Bonfire Night**), and other towns. At Bridgwater, two features of the modern carnival mark its origins in the old 'Fifth' celebrations. One is the relatively modest float that always leads the procession, which depicts the discovery of Guy Fawkes with his barrels of gunpowder, and the other is the display of synchronized 'squibbing' in the town centre. Over one hundred squibbers stand in lines, holding six-foot poles horizontally at arms' length above their heads. Fireworks fixed to each end of the pole are lit at a signal from the leader, and the result is a very impressive shower of sparks with ghostly figures in the middle. Nowadays, the squibbers wear hard hats and protective clothing, but in the nineteenth century they would run through the crowds, scattering sparks over everybody – just one example of the uncontrolled use of fireworks, blazing tar barrels, and street bonfires that gave the old celebrations such a bad name.

This cavalier attitude to crowd safety is demonstrated in a newspaper report of 1860, which also shows that the tendency for participants to use the event to comment on current affairs, both local and national, was already marked in the mid nineteenth century:

> *Men, boys and urchins paraded the streets decked out in their colourful costumes during the 1860 Guy Fawkes celebrations. Amongst the usual mix of characters was one young man who had the impudence to mimic 'to an alarming extent' the latest ladies' fashion – crinoline. But the young ladies of the day were able to get their own back by throwing lighted firecrackers at this display from the safety of their upstairs windows.*

In other years, the newspapers reported a fashion for aiming roman candles and rockets at open windows.

The year 1880 was the turning point in Bridgwater. 'The Fifth' had long been under threat of suppression from the local authorities, but in that year the celebrations turned nasty and a full-scale riot ensued, focused on the hapless members of the local fire brigade, who had been ordered to put out the bonfires. As a result, the old Fifth lost any remaining respectable support, and the participants faced the choice of complete suppression or the introduction of a relatively tame but properly organized and controlled event, which soon became the central feature of the town's calendar.

*

4 NOVEMBER

Ringing Night

In some nineteenth-century Cornish parishes, the ringers anticipated the celebratory peals of 5 November, by holding their own 'Ringing Night' on the evening of the 4th. Jonathan Couch described the custom in Polperro, Cornwall, in 1871:

'Ringing-Night' is on the fourth of November, the eve of gunpowder plot. The usual belfry rules, imposing fines on those who in a drunken or 'choleric' mood, should overturn a bell or 'by unskilful handling' mar a peal are, for the time, not rigidly enforced, and I fear that many cracked bells can date their ruin from this night.

Also in the West Country, an apparently unique custom, which also involved bell-ringers, was reported for this night, at East Budleigh, Devon, in 1885:

A very curious custom prevails here on the night of Nov. 4. The children are allowed to 'holloa for biscuits', as they call it. Seventeen shillings and sixpence is allowed by the parish for bell-ringing. Two and sixpence of this is spent in biscuits (i.e. farthing cakes). One shilling's worth of these are retained by the ringers; the remaining ones are given to the children, who formerly came into the churchyard and shouted, the biscuits being distributed from the porch. A few years since the people awoke to the fact that a churchyard was hardly a suitable place for holloaing, and the biscuits were distributed from the

church gate. For the last two years the biscuits have been given away at some distance from the sacred edifice. No one appears to know the origin of this custom.

In the northern half of the country, youngsters have had the pleasure of their own 'Mischief Night' for decades, when they believed that tricks could be played with impunity on the adult population. The night chosen for this mayhem varied, and although it was most commonly held on 30 April, Hallowe'en and 4 November were also cited as traditional Mischief Nights in some communities (*see* **31 October: Mischief Night** for further details.)

See also **5 November: Guy Fawkes Night** for other bell-ringing customs.

*

5 NOVEMBER

Devil's Stone

On the green just outside the church at Shebbear, between Great Torrington and Holsworthy, in Devon, lies a large boulder, about 6 foot by 4 foot in size, and reputed to weigh a ton. In geological terms it is an 'erratic', a large rock brought from elsewhere by glacial action. The locals call it the 'Shebbear Stone', but because of various stories it has also acquired the name 'Devil's Stone', and the village pub bears this name too. It is the self-inflicted task of the village bell-ringers to turn this boulder over every year on 5 November, or serious misfortune is said to follow. The bell-ringers gather in the church to ring the bells in the usual way, but just before 8 p.m. they give a short discordant jangling peal and then troop outside with torches and crowbars. The vicar says a short prayer, and the stone is duly turned. The actual ceremony is as perfunctory as a dozen men heaving on crowbars can be.

There are several legends that seek to explain the presence of the stone, although all of them are also told of other stones across the country: some say it was dropped by the Devil on his way to Hell, or thrown by him for some reason; while others, that it was chosen as the foundation stone for nearby Henscott church, but for several nights running it was mysteriously moved to Shebbear, so the locals decided it was best to leave it there. It is interesting that these stories explain the stone's presence, but not the custom of turning it over. The usual invented ancient pagan origins are also cited in some quarters, and one website claims it to be the 'oldest folk custom in Europe', but there is no evidence that the custom is older than the twentieth century. There is nothing unusual about bell-ringing on Guy Fawkes Night; indeed, it was formerly so common that 4 and 5 November were called 'Ringing Night' in various parts of the country, and the most likely explanation of the custom is that it began as a prank by the bell-ringers, or even that it was the result of a drunken conversation in the pub.

Guy Fawkes Night

Remember, remember, the fifth of November
Gunpowder, treason, and plot.

Guy Fawkes Night, Bonfire Night, Squib-Night, Plot Night, or simply 'the Fifth' are just some of the names that have been used to describe one of the most popular events of the traditional year for the last 400 years. People who nowadays flock to the safe and well-organized firework displays mounted by local councils and other respectable bodies will have little idea of the various stages that Guy Fawkes Night has been through since that unfortunate man and his associates tried to blow up the King and Parliament in November 1605. Those old enough will remember the cosy middle-class back-garden family firework parties of the mid twentieth century, which have not quite died out, or the more working-class annual ritual of children exhibiting a guy in the street from late October onwards, begging passers-by for 'a penny for the guy', which is close to extinction. But before these recent manifestations, 5 November had been such a rough and dangerous day that many respectable persons would not venture from their houses, and police fought an annual battle against bonfires and blazing tar barrels in the streets, torch-lit parades and processions, the indiscriminate throwing of fireworks, and the general notion that normal laws do not apply on this special night.

The enormity and astounding audacity of the plot to assassinate the sovereign and all the ruling elite of the country in one fell swoop was bound to mark the day as significant in the history of the nation. The fact that the plotters were Catholics gave the deed an added dimension, in an era when politics and religion were already inextricably mixed, and Parliament immediately decreed public celebrations to mark the miraculous deliverance. These took the normal form for that time – bell-ringing, bonfires, and special prayers and sermons – and a marked feature from the beginning was the notion that the events of that night must never be forgotten. The celebrations rapidly developed most of the features recognizable by later generations. The visiting Dutchman William Schellinks commented, for example, in 1662:

> On the 5th . . . in the evening the gunpowder plot, or the anniversary of the gunpowder treason of the year in the reign of King James, is celebrated in London: many bonfires are lit all over the town in celebration, and a great lot of fireworks are let off and thrown amongst the people.

However, the anti-Catholic nature of the celebrations was never far beneath the surface. As John Evelyn recorded in his diary on 5 November 1673, 'This night the youths of the city burnt the Pope in effigy after they had made procession with it in great triumph, displeased at the Duke for altering his religion, and now marrying an Italian lady', referring to the marriage of the Duke of York, Charles II's brother and soon to become James II, to the Catholic princess Mary D'Este of Modena.

Over the next 300 years, Guy Fawkes Night continued to develop as a mass working-class event, with the streets of most towns thronged every year with crowds, bonfires everywhere, fireworks thrown, and guns fired indiscriminately, along with spectacular practices such as the rolling of blazing tar barrels. But by the mid nineteenth century, these street celebrations were increasingly seen as dangerous drunken riots that should not be tolerated, and many towns across England, but particularly in the South, saw growing confrontations between the 'bonfire boys', who were determined to keep up their old traditions come what may, and town authorities, who were equally determined to put them down. Pitched battles and 'Guy riots' took place in many towns, including Guildford, Croydon, Exeter, and Worthing, between the police and the bonfire supporters, and it took many years for the authorities to finally gain control of the streets every November.

In the later Victorian period, celebrations then took two main directions. In some places, the bonfire enthusiasts compromised by organizing relatively tame processions, which culminated in a controlled bonfire and firework display on nearby open land, often sponsored by the council or local worthies. But the more respectable people largely withdrew from the public celebrations and started holding family parties in their own gardens. At this point, the next phase of 5 November came into play, and increasingly Guy Fawkes Night was seen either as a private family affair or as an organized community event. Nevertheless, the rough side of the celebration was never far away, and dark nights, bonfires, and fireworks were still a powerful concoction. On 28 November 1931, the *Hampshire Advertiser* reported an incident in Botley:

On the night of 5th November, a bonfire of wood, old motor tyres, and other kinds of rubbish was lighted, and two motor cars were pushed on to the fire and burnt in the presence of about a thousand people. Twenty-two young men were subsequently fined at Eastleigh Police Court for lighting a bonfire within fifty feet of the centre of the highway, and six of them were charged with stealing a motor car valued at £18 and destroying it by fire. In the course of the defence it was stated that 'for something like a hundred years Botley had been loyal to Guy Fawkes'; that the Square, the traditional site of the bonfire, 'was not treated as part of the highway' and that the owner of the £18 car 'stood in the crowd laughing while the car was being burned'. There was no case arising out of the burning of the second car.

Indeed, newspapers until as late as the 1950s and 1960s regularly reported riots in Oxford and Cambridge, and the centre of London on Guy Fawkes Night. Something of the old days can still be experienced at Lewes, in Sussex, and Ottery St Mary, in Devon (*see separate entries, below*). The later twentieth century saw a sharp decline in the back-garden style of celebration, primarily because of heightened fears about safety, and large organized events became more and more the norm, which still remains the case today.

Within this broad historical framework, there were numerous variations from place to place, and certain aspects of the Fifth are worth exploring in more detail, in part because they have interesting connections with other customs. As indicated, right from the beginning the official theme of remembrance was a defining feature of the Fifth. Church congregations were urged never to forget the enormity of Guy Fawkes' crime, and this continued to be a theme in the celebrations, as shown by the rhymes that were chanted as a kind of rallying cry of the 'bonfire boys' and by urchins in the streets to beg pennies. It must be noted, however, that the longevity of this theme was greatly assisted by the happy circumstance that 'remember' rhymes with 'November'. In 1903, the journal *Folk-Lore* recorded the following rhyme from 1890s Hastings, in Sussex:

Remember, remember, the fifth of November,
Gunpowder treason and plot;
I see no reason why Gunpowder Treason
Should ever be forgot.
A stick and a stake
For King George's sake,
Holla, boys! holla, boys! make the town ring!
Holla, boys! holla, boys! God save the King!
Hip, hip, hooray!

Another recurrent theme is the idea of licensed 'lawlessness'. As with many other public customs of long standing, there was a strong feeling in many communities that behaviour that would be prohibited at any other time of year was socially acceptable on this particular night, as in this memory of mid nineteenth-century Yorkshire:

In the days when there were no county police, if not wise enough to securely lock up your yard broom, of a certainty it would be stolen; and if ever you did see it again it would be in the evening of the fifth, soaked with tar, in the hands of some fellow rushing like a mad thing along the street with your property blazing in front of him. I have known scores of brooms which were stolen – aye, and stolen them myself – but I do not recollect an instance of the thief being prosecuted. No, if you did not secure your broom, it went, and that was very much the end of it. There was more fun running with a stolen broom than a bought one.

Indeed, many people seriously believed that normal

laws, especially game laws, did not apply on the Fifth. In the *York Herald*, on 15 November 1806, comes the following report:

> On Monday last, George Walkitt, farmer of Weaverthorpe, was convicted . . . in the penalty of £5 for destroying hares on that day. We insert this as a caution, as some people ignorantly conceive this to be a day free from all law.

(*See also* **26 December: Hunting and Shooting; Lawless Hours and Days**, p. 303.)

The making and parading of effigies is another widespread theme in English customs, and here, too, normal social rules were felt not to apply. It has a long history, stretching back at least a century before the Gunpowder Plot; as shown, for example, by the celebrations to commemorate the Accession of Elizabeth I (*see* **17 November**). Over the years, countless effigies of political and religious enemies (particularly of the Pope) have been mercilessly parodied and mistreated; social transgressors have found themselves treated in the same way as part of a **rough music** ceremony (p. 74); and other customs, from **Jack-a-Lent** (*see* p. 67) to the Burning of Bartle (*see* **24 August: West Witton Burning of Bartle**) have involved figures made specifically to be ridiculed and mistreated. Strangely, Guy Fawkes himself does not seem to have been singled out for this honour until the turn of the nineteenth century. Whereas nowadays, the word 'guy' is almost synonymous with effigy, the earliest reference to this meaning of the word in the *Oxford English Dictionary* only dates from 1806. Nineteenth-century illustrations usually show a life-size guy, seated upon a chair carried on poles, and paraded around the streets by children who are soliciting money from passers-by. By the early twentieth century, this had been replaced by the more static and individual 'penny for the guy' custom.

Apart from the Pope and Guy Fawkes, the tradition of burning effigies of real people has continued into the present-day, and public enemies such as the Prime Minister of the day, or a current bête noire of popular opinion, such as Saddam Hussein or Osama Bin Laden, are often chosen for this purpose (*see* **Lewes Bonfire Night**, *below*). It could be argued that these are fair game for a traditional form of popular protest, but things look very different when local vendettas or vigilante feelings are played out in this way, as in this example reported in the *Western Morning News* on 8 November 1960:

> The Devon village of Chulmleigh, for instance, was no place in which to court unpopularity in the old days. The inhabitants had the tradition of making effigies of people they did not like and then burning them. To make their disfavour as marked as possible they dressed their 'guys' in clothes similar to those worn by their victims, and then set them up for burning right outside the unpopular person's house. One record mentions 'evil doers' and 'evil livers' as people likely to be singled out for the unwelcome 'celebrity'.

Some members of the Bonfire Society of the Sussex village of Firle decided in 2003 to burn an effigy of a Gypsy caravan in protest against local travellers, but no doubt regretted their decision when their actions hit the national headlines and they were arrested under race relations legislation.

Running parallel to the mass community celebrations, there was also the persistent thread of child-centred activity, which was already in place at the turn of the nineteenth century. As the night approached, children all over the country could be seen ferreting about for materials for a bonfire, and trying to raise money for fireworks, and their own traditions naturally evolved. The penny-for-the-guy custom and the making of the guy for the garden bonfire are two widespread homely traditions that have largely disappeared, and numerous others have come and gone. Some families had special food for the evening – jacket potatoes cooked on the edge of the bonfire, or pieces of **parkin** (*see right*) munched as the rockets were set off. Derek Sheffield, describing his childhood in Kent in the early twentieth century, reported a family tradition of home-made fireworks that would make most modern parents go white at the very thought:

> There was a massive iron hook embedded in the giant oak beam that straddled the living room, and on which the whole house was supported. The hook had originally been used for hanging slaughtered pigs whilst burning the hairs off with tapers, but in my time it had another purpose; that was in the manufacture of fireworks, and Grandad was firework

maker par excellence. About a month before firework night, Grandad would be banging away in the shed producing lath frames on which to support various kinds of fireworks, and sawing five foot long sticks for his rockets. He also produced wooden blocks which were bored out to form a base for his bangers. The old house would become a hive of industry as we worked, under Grandad's guidance, on firework making. The main materials were wood, paper and string, and, of course, gunpowder, which was dried in the family oven. Grandad made all his own gunpowder, which would burn at different rates and in all sorts of magnificent colours depending on the mixtures and formulae that he used.

One further aspect of the Fifth that is largely missing from modern celebrations is the sound of bells. Ringing the church bells was part of the very first Guy Fawkes Night celebrations, and it was a standard part of national and patriotic celebrations for centuries. The Fifth (or its eve) was sometimes called 'Ringing Night' because of the enthusiasm with which ringers carried it out, as bell enthusiast John Camp wrote in 1988:

In some areas the custom of 'firing' the bells (the old method of alarm) is still used on Guy Fawkes Day and is known as 'shooting old Guy'. This also happens at Harlington, Bedfordshire, where the ringers are rewarded with pork pies and beer.

See also **4 November: Ringing Night**.

Lewes Bonfire Night

One of the most spectacular traditional events in the autumn calendar is Bonfire Night at Lewes in East Sussex. It is a direct descendant of the mass Guy Fawkes celebrations of the nineteenth century, and although it may now be safe enough for modern regulations, it still keeps its aura of spectacle and danger. Unlike the celebrations in Bridgwater in Somerset, where the Fifth has been transformed by the glare of thousands of electric light bulbs (*see* **First Friday in November**), at Lewes the light is supplied in the more elemental form of real flames carried on poles through the narrow streets.

Since at least the early nineteenth century, celebrations on the 5th in Lewes have been organized by particular groups, based on geographical territory, and

Parkin

In the northern counties of England, an oatmeal confection called 'parkin' has long been associated with Guy Fawkes Night. Charlotte Burne recorded her grandmother's recipe in the 1820s:

Another local dainty was 'parkin', or oatmeal gingerbread, which was made for the Fifth of November, and which my grandmother continued to have made within my own memory, long after she had moved away from Lancashire. This is the recipe she used: 3 lbs of sifted meal, 1 lb of butter, 1¾ lb of treacle, ¾ lb of brown sugar, 1 oz of ginger, a few caraway seeds, and a little candied lemon. Bake in a shallow tin, and, when cold, cut into narrow oblong pieces.

Dorothy Wordsworth, the poet's sister, recorded baking parkins in her Lakeland diary on 6 November 1800. Florence White gives several recipes in her classic cookery guide *Good Things in England* (1932).

these became the Bonfire Societies, the backbone of the event. Societies have come and gone over the years, but in 2004 there were five: Cliffe, Borough, Commercial Square, South Street, and Waterloo. Each society has a broadly similar way of doing things. They gather at their base in the late afternoon and hold processions around their territory, along with fancy-dress competitions for the children, the racing of tar barrels along the street, and visits to the war memorial. They join the Grand United Parade in the evening, and then return to their own sites for bonfires, firework displays, and effigy burning. Many of the small towns and villages in the Lewes area also have bonfire societies.

The Grand United Parade is the high spot for the visitor to the town, as most of the societies combine to provide a huge torch-lit, costumed, banner-carrying, band-playing procession. Some costumes are simple – such as the characteristic striped jerseys worn by many participants – but there is a strong tradition for the 'pioneers' (the group that leads each contingent in

Bonfire boys at Lewes, East Sussex, 2005

the procession) to be dressed more fantastically, and Zulu, Viking, and Red Indian costumes are a popular and traditional feature.

It is often asked why Lewes, of all the places that had mass Guy Fawkes celebrations in the nineteenth century, should be the one that has retained the spirit of the old Fifth in recognizable form. Taking their cue from the strong anti-Catholic elements of the celebrations, writers often assume a religious basis for this survival, and make reference to the so-called Lewes Martyrs – seventeen local Protestants who were burnt in the High Street in the 1550s during the Catholic backlash of Queen Mary's reign – or to the fact that Lewes always had strong Nonconformist traditions. But these explanations are too facile, and wide of the mark. The Nonconformists were not supporters of the celebrations, and were usually in the forefront of opposition to the event, primarily because of the drunkenness and

disorder that took place. In addition, the Lewes Martyrs were hardly mentioned until the end of the nineteenth century, and the erection of the Martyr's Memorial in May 1901 was the result of the long-running bonfire traditions, rather than the cause of them.

The real reason should be sought in the political rather than the religious sphere. When we look at what happened in other towns across southern England, we find the same broad pattern repeated. During the nineteenth century, mass street celebrations came under increasing fire from sections of the local establishment. Mayors, aldermen, councillors, magistrates, clergymen, police chiefs, schoolteachers, businessmen, and tradesmen all had their opinions, and condemned in turn the drunkenness, violence, and danger to property inherent in such events, along with their adverse effect on trade and prosperity. However, while the celebrations had supporters as well as enemies within these groups, they were relatively safe. Put crudely, in Lewes, as elsewhere, the supporters of traditions were on the Conservative wing of local politics, while the opponents were Liberals, but in other places a combination of changing notions of propriety, increasing civic pride, temperance campaigns, and a variety of other social changes gradually eroded that support. In Lewes, however, the particular balance of political power allowed the celebrations to survive long enough to become amenable to change rather than outright suppression.

Survival has also been the result of strategic compromises and retreats at key points on the part of the 'bonfire boys and girls' of the societies. When street fires in the centre of town were banned, the societies found their own fire sites; when 'Lewes Rousers' (large home-made squibs that shot across the ground) were banned, they adopted safer fireworks, and later agreed to abide by a rule of no fireworks in the crowded streets. As Jim Etherington, historian of the Fifth commented:

The bonfire societies transformed a night of riot into an organised and fairly disciplined street celebration. The most significant feature of this change was the introduction of the torchlit processions of costume-clad members carrying banners and accompanied by bands.

Even in recent years there has had to be further compromise as the standards for crowd control and safety have changed, and Lewes has continued to attract controversy over some of the elements of the celebrations that have survived relatively unchanged, in particular the overt anti-Catholic basis of the celebrationsand the marked propensity for using the event to comment on political and social issues of the day, in the form of effigies of unpopular figures. The real hardliners in the struggle to uphold tradition, against much criticism, are the Cliffe Bonfire Society, 150 years old in 2004, whose members regularly have to defend themselves against those who call for a toning down of the anti-Catholic elements in their activities. Cliffe still carry their traditional 'No Popery' banner along with seventeen fiery crosses to represent the Lewes Martyrs, and they are still addressed by mock bishops, and burn effigies of the Pope. However, this determination to perpetuate tradition has resulted in their being excluded from the Grand United Parade and, to a certain extent, their ostracism from the other societies, who have moved with the times to avoid trouble.

Ottery St Mary

Bonfire night at Ottery St. Mary, an otherwise sleepy little town twelve miles east of Exeter, is one of the most alarming experiences life has to offer, short of all-out war.

So wrote veteran customs photographer Brian Shuel in 1985. In the traditional calendar, Ottery St Mary in Devon is famous for its barrel-rolling custom, although this is far too pale a phrase to describe what really goes on. The wooden barrels are open-ended, with insides coated in tar, and they are then soaked in paraffin and set alight. They are carried through the crowded streets, one at a time, on the shoulders of the carriers, who wear crude protective gloves made of sacking but no other protection. The barrels are sponsored by the pubs of the town, and there are usually about seventeen barrels of various sizes. In the early part of the evening, there are children's barrels, and also some for women.

Each barrel is fired outside the sponsoring pub and then hoisted on to the shoulders of the first man, who runs off down the road with it. It is passed from one to another, and the carriers take it in turns until the barrel starts to disintegrate, when it is thrown down and left to burn out on the ground. As the evening wears on, the barrels and flames get bigger, and the crowds thicker, and the last one appears in the square about midnight. There is little crowd control, and the barrels pass close enough to the packed spectators to cause real alarm, screams, and rapid retreats, which is all part of the fun – although, as Brian Shuel comments, 'The sight of a large bearded weightlifter, bearing a huge flaming barrel, yelling at the top of his voice, coming at you like a runaway train, is not for the faint-hearted.'

Blazing tar barrels are mentioned as a feature in many descriptions of Guy Fawkes celebrations in the past, and, indeed, a few places still have them. They can be seen at Lewes in Sussex and Hatherleigh in Devon, where they are dragged through the streets, and at Allendale in Northumberland, where they are carried on people's heads, but nowhere else do the flames get

Blazing tar barrel at Ottery St Mary, Devon

so dangerously close to the onlookers. Nineteenth-century celebrations, where burning barrels were rolled and kicked about the streets, seem positively tame by comparison.

As ever, theories of pagan sun worship and fire sacrifice are frequently put forward to explain the origins of the custom, but none has the slightest evidence to support them. The earliest known references date from the 1850s, and there is no reason to think the custom in its present form is any older, although it could have developed from the more usual 5 November tar barrelling at any time over the last 300 years.

The barrel rolling is the most overtly spectacular part of Ottery's annual celebrations, but many other events also take place: a carnival is held a few days before, and on the Fifth itself there is a huge bonfire with guy on the banks of the River Otter, and a funfair going full tilt; there is also the firing of the 'rock cannons'. Before the Second World War, these were ancient muzzle-loading pistols, but the custom lapsed and when it was revived by local resident Nelson Owen in 1956 it was with newly designed and manufactured cannons, on the old principle. The modern rock cannon is made from an 1¼-inch steel bar, 16 inches long, bent in the middle to about 35 degrees, with a half-inch hole bored in one end to a depth of 3 inches, which is filled with well-rammed gunpowder. A cross-hole is drilled to take the percussion cap, which, when struck with a special hammer, sets off the powder with an almighty bang. There are ten or twelve of them, and they are fired three times every 5 November, at 5.30 a.m., 1 p.m., and 4 p.m., usually in rapid sequence, but sometimes all at once. The powder is usually that used for quarry blasting, called 'rock powder'; hence the name of the cannons. They are not quite unique: the Fenny Poppers at Fenny Stratford are quite similar in effect, if not in appearance (*see* **11 November: Fenny Poppers**).

Compare **5 November: Lewes Bonfire Night; Second Saturday in November: Hatherleigh Carnival; 31 December: Allendale Guisers.**

*

9 NOVEMBER

Pully Lug Day

See **Friday following Ash Wednesday: Pully Lug Day,** p. 68.

*

SECOND FRIDAY IN NOVEMBER

Silent Change

The new Lord Mayor of London, having been in waiting since his or her election on Michaelmas Day, is finally sworn in and takes office on the second Friday in November. At the Guildhall, the symbols of his office are passed to him – the sword, mace, crystal sceptre, seal, and City purse – and the old and new Lord Mayors exchange seats. Apart from a short declaration by the new incumbent, no words are spoken during the ceremony (hence its title), although nobody seems to know why.

See also **29 September: Election of the Lord Mayor of London**

*

SECOND SATURDAY IN NOVEMBER

Hatherleigh Carnival

The West Country is particularly proud of its carnivals, and the one that takes place at Hatherleigh in Devon is certainly as impressive as any. It started life as a fund-raising event for the local hospital, but later combined with the town's Guy Fawkes celebrations to form an impressive torch-lit procession, usually on the second Saturday in November. Other activities that take place over carnival weekend include decorated shop windows, a children's parade, a funfair, a grand disco, a bonfire, and the crowning of a carnival queen, prince, and princess.

In addition to these interesting, but controlled,

events, there is the more spectacular pastime of running blazing tar barrels through the streets early on the Saturday morning, and again in the evening after the main carnival. Three large open-ended tar-soaked barrels are placed on a sledge, set alight, and then dragged as fast as the men can run, round the town centre. Photographer Brian Shuel described the event in 1985:

> They came down the hill as the flames took hold. By the time they reached the George Hotel, from a bedroom window of which I was intrepidly recording events, the barrels were a raging inferno. With shouts of joy the men set off up High Street at full speed.

Compare **5 November: Ottery St Mary**.

Lord Mayor's Show

What is now called the Lord Mayor's Show is actually the procession that accompanies the new Lord Mayor of the City of London on a formal visit to the Law Courts to make a declaration of his or her fealty to the Crown. The new Lord Mayor is elected at or around Michaelmas (29 September) and the procession is his first official duty on taking office, as laid down by a charter granted to the City by King John in 1215. The Mayoralty itself dates to the 1190s, and in many City affairs the Lord Mayor is second only to the sovereign, thus holding a great deal of ceremonial power. The show has long been one of the major pieces of London pageantry, with the Lord Mayor travelling in a gilded horse-drawn coach, built in 1757, which can be seen in the Museum of London when not in use, and accompanied by a bodyguard of pikemen and musketeers, in period costume, and a panoply of military bands and decorated floats sponsored by organizations and companies connected with London. Although the Lord Mayor's visit to the Courts dates from the thirteenth century, the accompanying procession did not take on a high profile until the sixteenth century, when it replaced the older Midsummer Watch procession, which had lost official favour in a time of potential social and political unrest. Initially full of religious themes, after the Reformation the Lord Mayor's Show took on a more patriotic tone, and some elements of entertainment, such as acrobats, were introduced.

The day also includes a banquet, which Samuel Pepys recorded attending on 29 October 1663; however, he was not impressed by the affair, or the women there, and called the pageants 'very silly'. Nowadays, the procession is three miles long and can include 8,000 people. It attracts half a million spectators, plus many more who watch it live on television.

See also **29 September: Election of the Lord Mayor of London**.

*

10 NOVEMBER

St Martin's Eve

Martinmas (see **11 November: St Martin's Day**) was seen as a time of feasting and merrymaking, based on the habit of slaughtering animals at this time for salting down to last through the winter. But Northamptonshire poet John Clare singled out St Martin's Eve, in his poem of that name, which was written about 1830, as a time of indoor gatherings, where tales were told and games played, in defiance of the darkening nights and deteriorating weather of the autumn season:

> Now that the year grows wearisome with age
> And days grow short and nights excessive long
> No outdoor sports the village hinds engage
> Still is the meadow romp and harvest song.

See also **10 July** for a custom carried out by hill shepherds.

Wroth Silver

Whatever the weather, at daybreak on the eve of Martinmas, a number of people gather on Knightlow Hill near Rugby, in order to pay negligible sums of money to the Duke of Buccleuch's agent, for what rights or privileges nobody quite knows. With everybody gathered, and as soon as it is light enough to see, the agent commences:

> Wroth silver due to his Grace the Duke of Buccleuch and payable at Knightlow Cross on Martinmas Eve, 11th November . . . before sun-rising. Non-payment thereof forfeiture of 100 pence for every penny, or a white bull with red ears and red nose.

The Wroth Silver Ceremony at Knightlow Hill, near Rugby, Warwickshire, 1983

A list of twenty-five parishes is then read out – 'Arley, Astley, Birdingbury, Bourton and Draycote, Bramcote', and so on – with the amount due from each. As each parish representative places the money into a hole in a large square stone, which is all that is left of Knightlow Cross, he or she says, 'Wroth silver!' After the ceremony, everybody retires to a nearby pub – the Dun Cow at Dunchurch was for many years the favoured location – for a breakfast and the traditional glass of hot rum and milk. This breakfast was formerly open to anyone who wanted to go, but is now by ticket only.

The name 'Wroth silver' has puzzled commentators for some time. The *Oxford English Dictionary* reveals that *wroth* was simply an alternative spelling for 'wrath', and this has led some to assume that the payments are in recompense for some former transgression that angered a lord of the manor. An alternative derivation, however, is suggested by R. T. Simpson, who wrote a description of the custom in 1927. He commented that a seemingly similar payment, in the New Forest, Hampshire, was termed 'wrather' or

'rother' money, and this brings in the possibility that 'wroth' is derived from *rother*, which is an Old English word for 'ox' or 'cattle' that survived into the current era in some regional dialects. Wroth silver, therefore, may have been simply 'cattle money', given in payment for grazing rights or something similar.

*

11 NOVEMBER

St Martin's Day

Martin of Tours (*c*.316–97) was a soldier in the Roman army when he decided to convert to Christianity, and was imprisoned for his refusal to fight. He later became a monk, founded the first monastery in Gaul, and then became Bishop of Tours in 372, in which position he served till his death. His reputation for miracles, before and after his death, made him an extremely popular saint in France and neighbouring countries, including

Fenny Poppers at Fenny Stratford, Buckinghamshire, c.2002

Britain, throughout the Middle Ages, and numerous churches were dedicated to him.

The main aspect of this day in the traditional year, however, had little connection with the saint and his life, but everything to do with its position in the farming calendar. Martinmas (or sometimes Martlemas) was traditionally the time when animals were slaughtered to prepare for the coming winter months. It is because of this widespread activity that November was called 'blood-month' in the Anglo-Saxon calendar, and a vague superstition persisted until recent times, in Ireland at least, that something should be killed on this day 'for luck'. The slaughtered meat was salted or dried, and 'Martinmas beef' became a common term for meat preserved in this way. For much of the population, Martinmas itself was therefore one of the last opportunities in the year to eat fresh meat, and was known for food that was a by-product of the slaughter, such as black puddings and offal. The day therefore had something of a reputation for merrymaking.

St Martin's Day also took the place of Michaelmas (see **29 September**) as a 'settling day' in some parts of the country, particularly Cumbria and other parts of the North, although it was never one of the official English quarter days. In these areas it was the day when rents were due, annual terms of employment or occupancy started and finished, and house-moving took place. Across the whole country, one aspect that made it seem a pale reflection of Michaelmas was the popularity of roast goose for the dinner table.

A useful piece of advice was included by Richard Inwards in his collection of *Weather Lore*, first published in 1869: 'If the wind is in the south-west at Martinmas, it keeps there till after Candlemas [2 February].'

See also **Hiring Fairs**, *right*.

Fenny Poppers

Fenny Stratford parish church, St Martin's, in Buckinghamshire, was built by Browne Willis, the learned but eccentric local squire, in 1724, in memory of his grandfather Dr Thomas Willis who had lived in St Martin's Lane, London, and had died on St Martin's Day in 1675. Willis himself died in 1760, and left money for an annual sermon in his name. It is also assumed, but cannot be proved, that the 'Fenny Poppers' that are still fired today every St Martin's Day are part of his bequest.

The Poppers are six small cast-iron cannons, which are loaded with gunpowder and fired with the aid of a long iron rod with a red-hot tip. The result is six deafening bangs in quick succession, at 12 noon, 2 p.m., and 4 p.m. They used to be fired in the churchyard, but concern for the church's fabric prompted a move to nearby Leon recreation ground. The present Poppers were cast in 1859 because the originals were becoming dangerous, and they are sometimes fired on other special occasions, such as the death of Queen Victoria and the beginning of the new millennium. Odd as it may seem, the custom is not quite unique, as the rock cannons of Ottery St Mary in Devon are very similar (*see* **5 November: Ottery St Mary**).

Hiring Fairs

Until the turn of the twentieth century, and even later in some parts of the country, most agricultural workers and rural domestic workers were hired by the year. As the end of their term approached, they would enter into negotiation with their employers to decide whether they would be staying for another year or moving on. Those who wished to find a new place travelled to the nearest market town on a set day to attend a hiring fair, where they gathered at a particular spot sanctioned by long custom and waited for the farmer or his agent to come along and, they hoped, offer them a job. Employers would question likely workers about their experience, capabilities, and, most importantly, where they had previously worked, so that a 'character' or reference could be sought. On their side, the labourer or servant had the opportunity to ask about conditions – not only wages but also accommodation, food, and what sort of farm it was. The majority of unmarried year-term agricultural workers lived in, the women in the farmhouse and the men in dormitories in outhouses or above the stable. Living conditions for the latter could be extremely primitive even by contemporary standards, and working conditions harsh, but the advantages were job security and the knowledge that although they had little money in their pocket through the year, they had food and shelter for the foreseeable future, and they could look forward to a lump sum at the end of the year.

If a deal was made, the farmer handed over a small sum of money to seal the bargain. The amount varied from place to place, but was usually between a shilling and half a crown, and went by various local names, such as earnest money, arles, God's penny, fastening penny, and fes. The contract was then legally binding, although there was a strong tradition that the worker could change his or her mind if the money was returned within a specified period. Many places held a second fair a few weeks later, called a 'runaway mop' or something similar, at which those who had not found a place, or whose first choice had been disastrous, had another chance.

For those still out of a position, the insecurity of day-labouring was the chief option, although they could travel to another town that held a later fair if they wished. They rarely travelled too far, however, as employers were often suspicious of strangers.

Hiring fairs could be held at any time of year, according to local custom, but were usually conducted at slack times on the farm, for obvious reasons. Candlemas, 12 May, Michaelmas, Martinmas, or their Old Style equivalents, were particularly popular. The fairs also went under various local names, such as Statute, Statty, Mop fair, the Sittings, and the Hirings.

Throughout the eighteenth and nineteenth centuries, hiring fairs were an essential part of the rural scene, and there were numerous published accounts of what went on there. Thomas Hardy's description of a hiring fair in *Far from the Madding Crowd* (1874) is perhaps the best known, in which each farmworker wore a token of their specialism:

> Carters and waggoners were distinguished by having a piece of whip-cord twisted round their hats; thatchers wore a fragment of woven straw; shepherds held their sheep-crooks in their hand; and thus the situation required was known to the hirers at a glance.

However, this does not seem to have been the norm, as most eyewitness accounts of hirings describe a much simpler system, whereby those still for hire signified their availability in the same way – a straw in the mouth, a piece of whip-cord in the hatband, twisted straw in a buttonhole, and so on – which was removed as soon as they had found a place.

Once a new place was secured, and the earnest money given over, there were some chores to do before the fun began. Most had accounts to settle – for the year's washing, for the new pair of boots that had been necessary during the year, for next year's working clothes, and so on – and there were presents for parents and sweethearts to purchase. But wherever people gather in holiday mood, tradesmen, entertainers, and food and drink retailers are never far away, and many hiring fairs became large-scale festival events, attended by crowds who were not there to be hired. There were rides, sideshows, gingerbread stalls, and mountebanks, as well as the regular shops and pubs of the town, but there were also pickpockets, prostitutes, card-sharps, and recruiting parties to trap the inexperienced and unwary. It was considered essential to look one's best for the fair, and everyone tried to be as smart as possible, as there was also the rare chance of fraternizing with the opposite sex, and many workers eagerly seized the opportunity. It was a poor fair indeed that could not boast a few musicians and plenty of dancing. After the fair, workers would usually spend a few days with family or friends before starting at their new place.

However, not everybody was in favour of hiring fairs. For a number of vociferous Victorian reformers they were annual affairs of appalling debasement and debauchery, and vigorous campaigns were waged against them from the 1850s onwards. Some commentators were genuinely concerned to improve the bad conditions in which agricultural labourers had to live and work, and they set the need for the reform of annual contracts and hiring fairs in the context of general social improvement. Many argued that standing in the street waiting to be hired, like slaves or beasts, was degrading, especially for young women. There were numerous local attempts to provide indoor venues (away from the young men) where female servants could meet prospective employers in more decorous surroundings. In the long run, these proved popular with the women themselves, especially in bad weather, and became a fixture at many later nineteenth-century fairs. But mostly the reformers were exercised by what went on after the business of hiring had been carried out. To their mind, hordes of unsupervised young people, with money in their pockets, led to widespread drunkenness, fighting, and misbehaviour of all kinds. In November 1858, *The Times* commented:

Drunkenness is the curse to the labouring men of the present day, and love of dress to the young women of the same class. I cannot pretend that the 'mops' are the fountain-head from which these curses flow,

but I am sure, from my own observation, that they give great facility to the former and great encouragement to the latter. Instead of young men and women enjoying their holyday in a way that would really make them happy, they simply offer themselves up as victims to the tender mercies of the publican and the beerkeeper.

In particular, young men and women mixing freely, without the usual necessary constraints of their betters, was anathema to them. These are the same familiar strictures that were levied against all working-class leisure pursuits in mid Victorian times by the evangelical middle classes. The young rural workers themselves were determined to enjoy their scarce leisure time as they liked, and it is hardly surprising that their pleasures consisted largely of heavy drinking, eating, and flirting, which were denied them the rest of the year. But eyewitness accounts also show that fighting was endemic to the culture, and the level of violence played into the reformers' hands. By modern standards, the behaviour of many fair-goers was indeed pretty barbaric. 'Binge drinking' and 'yob culture' may be modern concepts, but they are not far off the mark for the way in which some groups regularly behaved. Beyond the practical measures of supplying separate indoor places to stand, however, it is unlikely that the reformers made much difference to the fairs. Their decline in the later nineteenth century was the result of changes in the economic basis of farming that removed their usefulness rather than any new moral climate among farmworkers.

Historians, too, are as divided as their Victorian ancestors on the question of the relative merits of the hiring-fair system. David Kerr Cameron, author of *The English Fair* (1998), writes:

They were days that changed destinies; days of heartbreak and misery for the vast numbers of young girls in domestic service and the men and boys who made up the labour force of the country's farms. Though they might change the milieu, the yearly statute fair offered them little but the opportunity to continue the same drudgery that had dogged their days since leaving school. Few would remember the old 'statty'

Ox Roasting, Stratford Mop.

Stratford Mop, Warwickshire, c.1908

fairs with affection; for most they were the bitterest of memories.

But Stephen Caunce, writing of East Yorkshire fairs, is much more positive:

The key to the success of the farm servant system was the ease with which lads changed jobs, and that was made possible by the hiring fairs ... In an age without advertisements, they brought together all the farmers and servants of a district and thereby encouraged the most efficient matching of the requirements of each and the maximum possible choice for both.

The ultimate origins of the hiring-fair system lay in the problems brought about by the acute shortage of labour in the wake of the Black Death. The Ordinance of Labourers (1349) and the Statute of Labourers (1351), passed respectively by Edward III and by Parliament, attempted to regulate the labour market by fixing wages and controlling conditions of employment on a national scale. Among other draconian stipulations, wages were pegged to pre-plague levels, labourers had to be employed by the year or other long term rather than by the day, and those seeking employment had to meet and deal with employers 'in a common place and not privy'. The desperate shortage of manpower, however, meant that these laws were widely ignored, and it was not until the reign of Elizabeth I that further attempts were made to regulate labour. The Statute of Artificers of 1562/3 went much further than previous statutes, and had a more permanent effect on labour relations. Wages were now to be assessed by local Justices of the Peace; all men between twelve and sixty were obliged to work unless they had other means to support themselves, and if they had no other trade or occupation they were forced to do agricultural work; while unmarried women were likewise instructed to undertake domestic service. Workers had to be engaged for a year at a time, and apprentices for seven years, and the working day was set at twelve hours in summer and daylight hours in winter. No one could leave their place without permission. A complex system of enforcement was brought into being, administered by constables, who were required to keep comprehensive lists of local workers and employers and present any who broke the rules to the Justices.

The Elizabethan statute remained the basis of all agricultural labour relations for centuries, but was showing increasing signs of breaking down at the turn of the eighteenth century, and was finally repealed in 1813. By that time, wages had begun to follow market forces, and it was increasingly left to individual workers and farmers to reach a satisfactory bargain. But even without legislative backing, the hiring fair was too essential an institution to be easily dispensed with, and it continued to be a major feature of the agricultural year for many years to come. Huge changes in agriculture and society at large finally made the fairs obsolete, and by the end of the Victorian era they were increasingly seen as anachronistic. Change occurred most rapidly in the south of the country, and new methods of finding work were in place well before the outbreak of the First World War, as recorded by Alfred Williams in Wiltshire in 1912:

> There is very little hiring done nowadays in this locality; the farmers generally advertise in the newspapers, or meet with the men on market-days, and make the necessary arrangements; and as for the fair, that is very nearly at an end.

However, the old system persisted in other parts, where local conditions were favourable, and hiring fairs, albeit mere shadows of their former selves, were still being held at some places in northern England between the wars, and a few even into the 1950s. Some hiring fairs continued as pleasure fairs, and it is now only the word 'mop' in their title that betrays their origins.

See also: **Fairs, Feasts, Wakes, and Revels**, p. 249.

Remembrance Sunday

They shall grow not old, as we that are left grow old:
Age shall not weary them, nor the years condemn.
At the going down of the sun and in the morning
We will remember them.

The poignant third verse of Lawrence Binyon's poem 'For the Fallen' (first published September 1914), engraved on war memorials and recited at countless ceremonies since 1919, neatly encapsulates the widespread postwar feeling that there was a national obligation to remember the fallen and their sacrifice. Other evocative quotations, such as Rudyard Kipling's 'Lest we forget', and 'Their name liveth for evermore', a line taken from Ecclesiasticus, were similarly incorporated into remembrance ceremonies and helped shape the way in which the First World War would be commemorated in Britain and throughout the Empire.

The unprecedented scale of the slaughter, and the fact that so many were volunteers and conscripts rather than regular soldiers, separated this conflict from all the wars that had gone before, and a new level of national response was clearly needed. Even while the fighting continued, there was much public debate about the form that commemoration should take, and a prevailing consensus quickly took hold that the tone must be one of sacrifice and redemption rather than exultation over victory; this has strongly influenced our view of the matter ever since. The Government, and other interested bodies, offered a stream of advice on the design of local memorials and appropriate wording for ceremonies, but many communities went their own way. There were those who wished to see money spent on practical memorials, such as hospital wings and village halls, rather than cenotaphs and churchyard crosses, and there was wide variation in the way different communities chose to honour their dead. However, Armistice Day, the day set aside for national commemoration, symbolically placed on 11 November, the anniversary of the day the armistice was signed, was devised as the official focus, and it rapidly became a major event in the national calendar. It soon acquired rituals and traditions of its own, which in turn have influenced the shape of later responses to other national crises and tragedies.

Remembrance Sunday, Whitehall, London, 2005

A temporary cenotaph, designed by Sir Edward Lutyens, was in place in Whitehall for the 1919 ceremony, and the real one in time for November 1920. The Tomb of the Unknown Warrior in Westminster Abbey was unveiled in 1920, and the sale of red poppies by the British Legion started in 1921. On the day, the central core of national commemoration takes place when the sovereign, accompanied by the nation's political and religious leaders, Commonwealth representatives, veterans, and serving military personnel, lay wreaths at the Cenotaph, followed by a two-minute silence at 11 a.m. There are numerous smaller ceremonies on similar lines at war memorials all over the country.

Once the rawness of both individual and national grief began to fade, and other societal problems such as mass unemployment took hold, Armistice Day began to lose some of its support, and drew particular criticism from the burgeoning peace movement. After 1945, the term 'Armistice Day' was thought too specific to the previous conflict, and 'Remembrance Day' became the official title, commemorating the sacrifices of both world wars, and all subsequent conflicts, on the nearest Sunday to 11 November.

Again, the commemoration gradually lost some of its immediacy over the years after the Second World War, and there were even calls for it to be phased out, but there were palpable increases in support for the ceremony when major anniversaries occurred, most notably the fiftieth and sixtieth anniversaries of the Second World War, in 1995 and 2005 respectively. The element that has perhaps attracted the most controversy is the two-minute silence, although largely for reasons far removed from the remembrance of the war dead.

There has been much debate about who first suggested the mass commemorative silence. Although Lord Milner suggested the idea to the government of the day, it is not known for certain who first suggested it to him, and South African Sir Percy Fitzpatrick and Australian journalist Edward George Honey are the main contenders for the honour. Either way, it was already in place in 1919, and has continued ever since, except during the years of the Second World War. Between the wars, the silence was literally imposed at 11 a.m. on 11 November. Police stopped traffic, public transport paused, and people in offices and schools were expected to conform, as the King's proclamation that announced the day decreed that 'All locomotion should cease, so that, in perfect stillness, the thoughts of everyone may be concentrated on reverent remembrance of the glorious dead.'

Moving the ceremony to a Sunday certainly blunted this effect, and there were many who complained that this downgraded the ceremony in national life. However, the real problem in recent years has been that 'silences' have become the standard response to tragedies, large and small, including terrorist attacks such as the New York 9/11 atrocity and the Bali, Madrid, and London bombings, the death of popular famous figures like Princess Diana and the Queen Mother, natural disasters such as the Asian Tsunami, local tragedies, and murders. Social commentator Patrick West has written on the subject: 'They are getting longer and we are having more of them, because we want to be seen to care – and increasingly are compelled to do so.'

West and other critics refer to 'silence inflation' and condemn mass silences as 'conspicuous compassion', which do nothing but make the participants feel superior. Others claim that these other 'silences' devalue the meaning of the original. It is the sacrifice of the fallen on our behalf that should be commemorated in this way, not the unfortunate but unknowing victims of tragedies both natural and man-made.

Nevertheless, these criticisms are strongly countered by those who claim that this method of focusing attention on tragedies or atrocities is one in which ordinary people can participate and demonstrate that they care, that the people involved are not alone, that the terrorists will not win, or whatever else is appropriate to the situation: not only do *I* care, but *we* care. There is no denying the emotional impact of a mass of people – a football crowd or a busy railway station – suddenly and impressively falling silent, in 'perfect stillness'.

As if to demonstrate how the customary calendar is in constant flux, as the above was being written, the Chancellor of the Exchequer and Prime Minister in waiting, Gordon Brown, suggested publicly that Remembrance Day could be developed into a 'British Day', on the lines of the American 4th of July. It remains to be seen whether this idea takes root.

*

13 NOVEMBER

St Brice's Day

Brice was Bishop of Tours, who died in AD 444 after a long and stormy period in office. He was soon accredited with saintly virtues, and his cult was popular in England until the Conquest, but his fame seems to have waned from about that time onwards.

The most well-known custom that took place on St Brice's Day was the annual bull-running at Stamford, Lincolnshire, which, although not quite unique, was famous countrywide and regarded by locals as an essential part of their town's identity. It was fiercely defended when it became the focus of the campaign to ban working-class blood sports, but by 1840 it had succumbed to the new reformers and was relegated to the town's history. To modern eyes, the custom was indeed barbaric, and it would certainly not be tolerated today, but in the context of the times it was no more cruel than many other so-called sports that involved animals.

The custom was believed to have been founded in the time of King John (1167–1216), when William, Earl of Warren, was said to have been standing on the battlements of his castle and saw two bulls fighting in the field below (later called the Bull Meadow). When butchers attempted to part them, the animals escaped into the town and caused uproar in the streets before they were finally recaptured. The Earl found this so entertaining that he decreed that it should be an annual event.

Every year, on 13 November (or the 14th when that day fell on a Sunday), the town was given over to the bull-running. A little before eleven in the morning, the church bells were rung, to warn the people to clear the streets, and at eleven a bull was released. Side streets and doorways were blocked off, to keep the bull in the town centre for a while, and shop windows were boarded up for safety, but upstairs windows, along with every other relatively safe vantage point, were crowded with spectators. By moving certain barriers, and goading the bull with noise, sticks, stones, and whips, the animal was induced to run a set route through the town, with the participants – the 'bullards'

– and their dogs, running and yelling before and after. The eventual idea was to 'bridge the bull', by getting it to cross the Welland river, and then the crowd closed in and together heaved it over the parapet into the water. The 'running' continued when it swam ashore in the nearby meadows, where it was finally killed, and later eaten. Sometimes a second bull was then started in the town.

The late eighteenth century saw a sharp rise in feeling against traditional sports that involved mass working-class participation, and also a new revulsion against cruelty to animals at all levels. The *Lincoln, Rutland & Stamford Mercury* of 18 November 1785 commented:

Monday last being our annual bull-running, the same was observed here with the usual celebrity – several men heated with liquor got tossed by the bull, and were most terribly hurt, while some others more sober had little better usage. What a pity it is so barbarous a custom is permitted to be continued, that has no one good purpose to recommend it, but is kept as an orgy of drunkenness and idleness to the manifest injury of many poor families, even tho' the men escape bodily hurt.

The Stamford Bull-Running became a *cause célèbre* for the reformers, but it proved remarkably resilient, and supporters managed to keep it going for many years, in the face of mounting opposition and pressure at both national and local levels. Although it was first banned in 1788, by order of the town's quarter sessions, the local authorities met so many difficulties attempting to suppress the custom in subsequent years that they eventually gave up trying. But time was against the running, and after a prolonged campaign by the Society for the Prevention of Cruelty to Animals (founded 1824), aided by the turning of respectable local opinion against the sport, the last bull-running took place in 1839. The suppression of the Stamford Bull-Running was the first major success for the new Society. For years afterwards, however, the cry of 'A bull! A bull!' could unite Stamfordians in feelings of local pride like no other could.

A similar sport existed at Tutbury, Staffordshire (*see* **16 August: Tutbury Bull-Running**). Bull-running is often confused with **bull-baiting** (p. 352), but beyond the cruelty to the animal, the two were very different.

*

Bull-Baiting

The spectacle of a bull being baited by dogs was a common enough sight in both rural and urban areas of England right up until the 1830s. Bear-baiting and other similar animal 'sports' were mostly staged at professional arenas, for the enjoyment of paying customers, but bull-baiting was usually carried out in the street, tavern yard, or market-place, free to all and sundry, including women and children. It was this very ordinariness and accessibility, as well as its obvious barbarity, that so incensed the emerging animal rights movement of the early nineteenth century, and made members so determined to rid society of such evil pastimes.

During a baiting, the bull was tethered by a rope attached to a stake driven into the ground or to a permanent metal bull-ring set into the road or a convenient wall. The points of the bull's horns were sawn off, presumably because they would otherwise have been too deadly. Dogs were released either singly or in groups, and were encouraged to attack the bull, which had two main means of defence: the use of its weight to trample them, and its horns, to toss them. The crowd particularly loved the latter, and there were many stories of dogs landing in ladies' laps, or on men's heads, and illustrations of the sport usually show dogs tossed high in the air. The dog owners carried long poles, which they cleverly placed at an angle to break the dogs' fall when they fell to earth. On their part, the dogs simply fastened on to the bull's flesh with their teeth, if possible going for a tender part such as face or throat, and hung on until the bull's own frantic movements shook them free, tearing the flesh off as they fell. The owners thus preferred breeds that would not only attack bravely but would hold on, come what may. After a while, the maddened bull was a mass of open bleeding wounds, and some of the dogs were trampled or had broken their necks from their fall. And the crowd loved it.

It is difficult for most of us in modern times to comprehend why so many people enjoyed spectacles in which animals were pitted against each other, but such 'sports' were almost everyday occurrences, and few before the early nineteenth century gave them much thought. It was genuinely believed that the meat of a bull was much more tender if it had been baited before being slaughtered, and some town councils had regulations insisting on the practice. Staging a bull-baiting was also a standard way of currying favour with the local populace. A candidate up for election, a new mayor who wanted to treat the townsfolk, a squire who wanted to celebrate his son's marriage, a publican who wished to draw a crowd to increase liquor sales – all these were likely to 'give a bull' to the people for baiting, in the sure knowledge that their generosity would be appreciated.

In the early nineteenth century, piecemeal opposition to bull-baiting began to grow into an organized movement determined to get all such blood sports banned, to alleviate the cruelty to the animals. But there were plenty of apologists for blood sports to be found, and many were in high places. Some argued that the sport was natural – both dogs and bull were simply being themselves – while many others, who cared little either way on the cruelty question, were determined to stop any legislation that prevented the individual from freely choosing his own leisure pursuits. Many were well aware that if they legislated against the blood sports of the lower classes, they were opening the way to abolition of their own hunting, shooting, and fishing lifestyles.

From 1800, there was a steady stream of anti-cruelty proposals put to Parliament, but until the breakthrough 1822 Act there was equally steady opposition from a group of determined MPs, led by the most vocal of them all, the Right Honourable William Windham (previously Secretary of State for War). Windham was the scourge of those who sought reform, and helped to scupper all attempts until his death in 1810. He spoke eloquently of liberty and freedom, claiming that such affairs were beneath the dignity of Parliament to discuss, and accusing anti-baiters of being a coalition of Methodists and Jacobins. The most successful of the early reformers was the eccentric Richard Martin, MP for Galway, who, though passionately opposed to the beating of horses, was himself an enthusiastic fox-hunter and was known to boast of the duels he had fought. In 1822, Martin finally managed to get an act passed that penalized anyone who had beaten, abused, or ill-treated a range of named species. However, this legislation failed to prevent bull-baiting because of a problem with the wording, and following a ruling that bulls were not included in the term 'other cattle', the baiters were permitted to continue with their old sport.

The Society for the Prevention of Cruelty to Animals was formed in June 1824, with Martin as one of its founder members; in 1840, Queen Victoria gave permission for the Society's 'Royal' accolade. Though small, the new Society provided a new focus for radical reform, and the 1835 Cruelty to Animals Act finally banned 'running, baiting or fighting any bull, bear, badger, dog, or other animal', and for good measure the Highways Act of the same year made it illegal to bait any animal on the public highway. It is a tribute to the determination of the early campaigners that within thirty years the whole climate of educated opinion had swung dramatically in their direction, and whereas the press of 1802 had derided the reformers as sentimental cranks, that of the 1830s were almost entirely on their side. It must be said, however, that many who supported the campaign against baiting cared little about the plight of animals, but were concerned with the potentially demoralizing effect of such blood sports on the working classes, which they believed encouraged drunkenness and the promiscuous mixing of the sexes, or were equally worried that gatherings of working-class revellers could too easily be used to foment political unrest and rioting. The successful campaign against popular blood sports was not simply a victory for animal-lovers but also for those who sought to control the masses by abolition or reform of their leisure pursuits.

See also **Baiting Bears and Other Animals**, p. 294.

17 NOVEMBER

Queen Elizabeth I/St Hugh's Day

Almost immediately after her death in 1603, the reign of Elizabeth I started to take on the aura of a golden age and she herself the mythic proportions of an unofficial patron saint. The day of her accession, 17 November, was widely celebrated well into the eighteenth century with sermons, bonfires, and bell-ringing. Indeed, by the 1630s, the enthusiastic bells on Elizabeth's day even aroused the jealousy of Charles I, who felt that his birthday, and that of his queen Henrietta Maria (on the 19 and 16 November respectively), were grudgingly and weakly marked. Much of the celebration was spontaneous and local rather than being nationally co-ordinated, but Elizabeth's status as icon of the Protestant revolution meant that the day was always available whenever the government wished to make an anti-Catholic point. The Pope and the Devil were regularly burnt in effigy on the day, as on 5 November.

*

19 NOVEMBER

The Society of King Charles the Martyr holds events on this day to celebrate the birthday of Charles I (*see* **30 January: Execution of Charles I**).

*

22 NOVEMBER

St Cecilia's Day

According to legend, first written in the fifth century and completely fictitious, Cecilia was a noble Roman Christian who converted Valerian, her new husband, to the faith by revealing that she was regularly visited by an angel. She insisted on remaining a virgin, and after Valerian and his brother were martyred, she too was condemned to death, first by roasting in her bath, which did not work, and then by beheading. Chaucer made her story famous in England by including it in his *Second Nun's Tale* of the *Canterbury Tales*.

As a line in the story referred to music at her

wedding, and claimed that she 'sang in her heart to the Lord', she was frequently portrayed as a lover of music and poetry and, somewhat incredibly, as the inventor of the organ. In paintings, she usually appears playing a musical instrument, and she was chosen as patroness of musicians by the Academy of Music in Rome, in 1584. In Britain, as elsewhere in Europe, she became popular with the likes of Henry Purcell, John Dryden, and Alexander Pope in the late seventeenth century, and concerts and odes were composed for her day.

St Cecilia's fame seems to have been largely confined to the poets and musicians of high art, and never to have reached the hearts and minds of the general public. Periodic revivals of interest in her have always had a slightly forced, refined quality. Writing about English festivals in 1947, Laurence Whistler commented:

> In 1945 it would have been fanciful to include St. Cecilia's Day among the English festivals. In 1947 it would be unimaginable to leave it out. If this charming day, twice cared for in England and twice almost forgotten, should come into public remembrance for a third time the year recorded in musical history will be 1946.

One major impetus for this postwar revival was the coincidence that 22 November was also the birthday of the influential English composer Benjamin Britten (1913–76), who dutifully revived the practice of composing odes for the day.

*

23 NOVEMBER

St Clement's Day

Clement is generally accepted as St Peter's third successor as Pope, and was venerated as a martyr in the early Christian Church, although his martyrdom cannot be proved. The legend of his death states that he was tied to an anchor and thrown into the sea; angels were then said to have built an ornate tomb for him on the seabed, which was miraculously uncovered by the sea every year on his day. The regular appearance of an anchor in pictures of the saint was enough to ensure his adoption as patron saint of seafarers, foundry-workers, and,

most famously, blacksmiths. In 1883, the journal of the Sussex Archaeological Society recorded:

> At Burwash a few years ago it was the custom to dress up a figure with a wig and a beard and pipe in his mouth, and set it up over the door of the inn where the blacksmiths feasted on St. Clement's Day. The figure was called 'Old Clem'.

One of the regular toasts at such gatherings was 'To the memory of Old Clem, and prosperity to all his descendants'. But the evidence for blacksmiths' particular interest in 'Old Clem' is surprisingly late, dating only from the early nineteenth century onwards. Much earlier material shows that St Clement was celebrated in the sixteenth century by fishermen, sailors, bakers, iron-founders, and other trades. This popularity was probably helped in the early modern period by the general belief that devotion to St Clement protected people from danger, specifically from water and fire, as mentioned in the sermon delivered by Bishop Wimbledon on St Clement's Day, 1388:

> For this blessed martyr our Lord God showeth many divers miracles, both by water and by land, and in special for peril of water and fire so far forth that who that prayeth devotedly to God and to this holy martyr Saint Clement is oft delivered from such.

Another custom of the day, probably unrelated to the 'Old Clem' activities of the blacksmiths but sometimes confused with it, was clementing. This was a house-visiting custom, primarily carried out by children, in which a rhyme was recited or sung, and money, food, or sweets were expected in return. A Warwickshire version from the 1870s was printed in *The Times* (10 December 1935):

> Clementing, clementing once a year
> Apples and pears are very good cheer
> One for Peter, two for Paul
> And three for Him who made us all
> Up with the hatchet and down with the shoe
> If you have no apples, money will do
> Money will do, money will do.

In some villages, exactly the same was done on St Catherine's Day (*see* **25 November**), and called 'cattering'; both in turn were closely related to the custom called 'souling' (*see* **2 November: All Souls' Day**). The earliest mention of clementing is in 1686, in wording which implies a much longer history.

For earlier blacksmith material, *see* **1 December: St Eligius' Day**.

*

25 NOVEMBER

St Catherine's Day

Stories of St Catherine of Alexandria's life began to circulate in the ninth century, and her cult was extremely popular in Britain, as elsewhere, from the medieval period onwards. She was reputed to have been tortured on a wheel (hence the term 'Catherine wheel'), before being beheaded. She was adopted by a variety of groups, as listed in David Farmer's *Oxford Dictionary of Saints* (1987):

Patron of young girls, students (and hence the clergy), especially philosophers and apologists, nurses (because milk instead of blood flowed from her severed head) and of craftsmen whose work was based on the wheel, such as wheelwrights, spinners, and millers.

A number of trades therefore celebrated her day, and there are various descriptions of processions and meetings of lacemakers, spinners, and ropemakers, which were presumably founded in late medieval times and continued until the mid nineteenth century before fading away. There seems to have been some confusion between St Catherine and Queen Catherine of Aragon: the latter was reputed to have saved lacemakers from acute distress when she learned of a decline in the trade, and encouraged ladies to burn their old lace and replace it with new.

St Catherine was also invoked in matters of matrimony. At a ruined Norman chapel that bore her name at Abbotsbury in Dorset, for example, folklorist J. S. Udal, writing in 1922, recorded that it had been the custom for women to go and say the following prayer:

A husband, St. Catherine;
A handsome one, St. Catherine;
A rich one, St. Catherine;

St Catherine of Alexandria, by Josse Lieferinxe (*fl.* 1493–1508)

A nice one, St. Catherine;
And soon, St. Catherine!

Any custom that took place on St Catherine's Day could be called 'catterning', but in the area where Worcestershire and Staffordshire meet, that name usually referred to a house-visiting custom whereby children sang or recited a rhyme and expected food or money to be given to them in return. This form of 'catterning' was first mentioned in 1730, but almost exactly the same activity, called 'clementing', took place on St Clement's Day (*see* **23 November**) in other villages in the area, and another very similar custom was 'souling' (*see* **2 November: All Souls' Day**); both clementing and souling are documented in earlier times.

*

FOURTH TUESDAY IN NOVEMBER

Ashburton Court Leet

A court leet was a manorial court that dealt with petty offences and nuisances in areas of communal interest such as highways and ditches, as well as the enforcement of regulations regarding the quality of staples such as ale and bread. It had the power to make by-laws, and to elect officers to enforce them. With successive reorganizations of local government, manorial courts were stripped of their powers, and those which remain are purely ceremonial.

Ashburton, on the edge of Dartmoor in Devon, is one place that preserves at least something of the old court. They still hold a meeting in November (on the fourth Tuesday), at St Lawrence's chapel, attended by freeholders of the town. They elect a portreeve (the equivalent of a mayor) to serve for the coming year, along with other officers including ale-tasters, bread-weighers, pig drivers, scavengers, and surveyors of markets and watercourses. The portreeve takes a leading role in community activities and celebrations, and in July the official ale-tasting and bread-weighing ceremonies take place, in which the local pubs and bakers are duly visited and their wares sampled and assessed. This ceremony is nowadays followed by a medieval fair. It is hardly surprising that such a task as ale-tasting is not taken too seriously these days.

*

LATE NOVEMBER

Stir-Up Sunday

This day, the Sunday before Advent and the twenty-fifth Sunday after Trinity, falling anywhere between 20 and 26 November, was widely known as 'Stir-up Sunday' from at least the 1830s into the mid twentieth century. The collect for the day commenced, 'Stir up, we beseech thee O Lord', but many in the congregation had their own version:

Stir up, we beseech thee, the pudding in the pot
Stir up, we beseech thee, and keep it all hot.

This was particularly apt, because it was generally acknowledged that this was the day to start making the Christmas pudding, and for local shops to ensure that they had all the necessary ingredients in stock.

*

30 NOVEMBER

St Andrew's Day

St Andrew, fisherman, Apostle (brother of Simon Peter), and martyr, became the patron saint of Scotland when his remains were reputed to have been brought to Fife by St Regulus (Rule) in the eighth century. As the Scottish patron, his day was obviously more celebrated north of the border, but in England several seemingly unrelated customs also took place on the day.

In Buckinghamshire and Northamptonshire, for example, he was considered the patron saint of lace-makers, and before machine-made lace devastated the cottage industry, those involved kept the day as a holiday, and met for what they termed their 'tandering feast' (*see also* **11 December: Old St Andrew's Day**). Indeed, customs that relate to the saint often seem to begin with 'T' in English folklore: some villagers in Bedfordshire ate 'tandry cakes' on the day, and there are also isolated reports of a special bell-ringing on the day, called the 'Tandrew' bell.

There was also a somewhat bizarre custom of going into the local woods, en masse, ostensibly to hunt squirrels; but while some accounts describe the serious attempts made to kill squirrels and small animals, others indicate that the main purpose of the jaunt was to make merry with as much noise and commotion as possible. 'Squirrel hunting' was apparently quite widespread in this form. In Kent and Sussex, it took place on St Andrew's Day, but in other parts of the country it was more common on some other day: in Suffolk on Christmas Day, in Hampshire on Boxing Day (*see* **26 December: Hunting and Shooting**), in Essex on Good Friday, and in Derbyshire in early November. There is some indication that this customary invasion may have been originally a way of preserving a right of access to enclosed and/or private woods, but as all the references so far found are from the late eighteenth and nineteenth century, further research would be necessary to test this theory.

St Andrew's Day was also one of the traditional days for schoolchildren to indulge in locking their teachers out of their schools (*see* **Barring Out**, p. 361). And one final tradition, not perhaps widely known, but reported in the *Church Times* on 22 June 1894, holds that wherever lilies of the valley grow wild, the parish church is dedicated to St Andrew.

Eton Wall Game

The famous Wall Game at Eton College in Buckinghamshire is played at various times in the year, but the big match is held on St Andrew's Day, between the Collegers (scholarship boys) and Oppidans (normal fee-payers). There are ten boys in each team: three 'walls', two 'seconds', three 'outsiders', and two 'behinds'. The leather ball is a bit smaller than a football but with two flattened sides – what Brian Shuel calls an 'oblate spheroid'. The wall against which the game is played is about 110 metres long, and has a vertical white line painted near each end; there are two goals: a door and a tree stump.

Each team tries to move the ball towards their opponents' end, and once past the white line a player tries to lift the ball against the wall with his foot. If he can achieve this, a teammate touches the ball with his hand and cries 'got it'. This scores one point, and the right to throw the ball at one of the goals. Goals score nine points, but are very rarely achieved. The game lasts about an hour and, as with most traditional 'football' games, the players spend much time in a scrum, here called the 'bully'. For the other rules (and arcane terminology), see the College website. The first recorded game was in 1766.

Wall Game, Eton College, Buckinghamshire, 1951

December

Wassailing

Frumenty *Bell-Ringing*

Barring Out

Vessel Cups

3

10

17

24

CHRISTMAS EVE
Ashen Faggot
Cattle Kneeling
Hooden Horse
Old Horse
Old Tup
Ringing the Devil's Knell

31

NEW YEAR'S EVE
Allendale Guisers
Bell-Ringing
Gatherings
Hogmanay

4

11

OLD ST ANDREW'S DAY

18

25

CHRISTMAS DAY
Father Christmas/Santa Claus
Geese Dancers
Guisers
Holy Thorn(s)
Sword Dance
Tree
Waits

5

12

19

26

**ST STEPHEN'S DAY/
BOXING DAY**
Bleeding Horses
Hunting and Shooting
Hunting the Wren
Marshfield Paper Boys
Padstow Mummers' (Darkie)
  Day

*Moveable events have been placed
on the date they fall in 2007.
Events dependent on Christmas
are coloured red.*

Pantomimes   *Mummers*   *Crackers*

Cards

Candles

Yule Log

Decorations

1

ST ELIGIUS' DAY

FIRST WEEKEND IN DECEMBER

Tree-Dressing Day

2

6

ST NICHOLAS' DAY

Boy Bishop

7

8

9

13

Aldermaston Candle Auction

SECOND THURSDAY BEFORE CHRISTMAS

Picrous Day

14

ST TIBBA'S DAY

15

16

Boar's Head

20

21

ST THOMAS'S DAY

22

23

27

28

HOLY INNOCENTS' DAY

29

30

Entertainments

Carol Singers

Merrie England

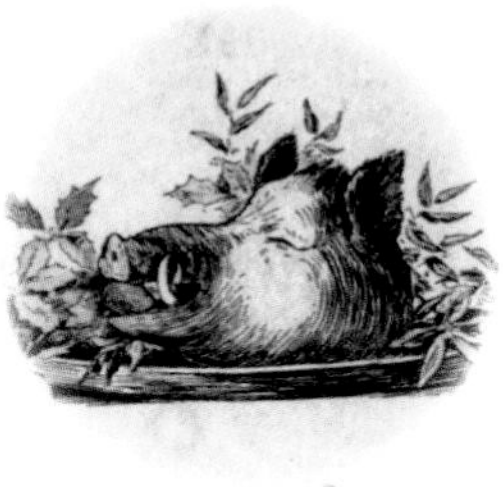

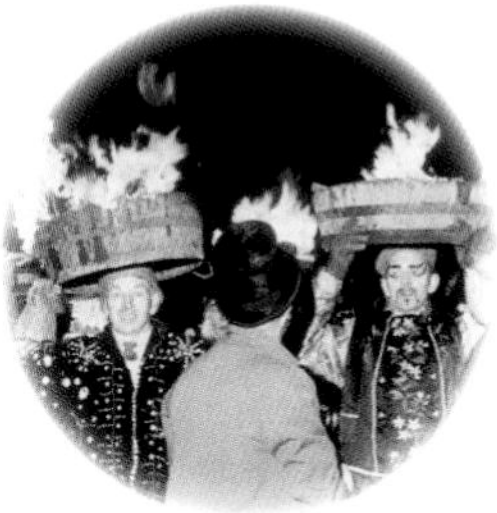

FIRST WEEKEND IN DECEMBER

Tree-Dressing Day

Since 1990, the environment and culture charity Common Ground has encouraged English people to take part in Tree-Dressing Day on the first weekend in December, as a 'celebration of trees in city and country, in the street, village green – anywhere in the public domain. It highlights our responsibility for looking after trees and reminds us of their enormous cultural and environmental importance.'

Common Ground also supports other traditional tree-based customs (*see* **Last Sunday in May: Arbor Day**; **29 June: Bawming the Thorn**; **Christmas: Wassailing**), along with their own Apple Day (**21 October: Apple Day**).

*

1 DECEMBER

St Eligius' Day

St Eligius (*c*.588–660), also Loy or Eloi, was a powerful figure in seventh-century France, acting as adviser to kings Clotaire II and Dagobert I, and the Bishop of Noyon and Tournai, as well as founding monasteries and building churches. He was famed for his piety, his miracles, and for being a skilled metalworker, and his most famous exploit occurred while he was shoeing a difficult horse, when he was said to have removed its leg, applied the shoe, and re-attached the leg. He was also reputed to have taken the Devil by the nose with his red-hot blacksmith's tongs (a story also told of St Dunstan; *see* **19 May**). He was quickly taken as patron saint by metalworkers in the Low Countries, and this soon spread to England, lasting until late medieval times at least, as the charter of the London company of Blacksmiths in 1434 makes clear:

Ordinance and articles and constitution ordained
and granted by the worshipful masters and wardens
in the worship of the brethren of Saint Loye at the

feast of Easter with all the whole Company of the
craft of the blacksmiths.

Despite being widely popular in medieval England, very few churches were named after him, and his fame waned so completely that by the nineteenth century blacksmiths were claiming St Clement ('Old Clem') as their patron saint (*see* **23 November**).

*

6 DECEMBER

St Nicholas' Day

Nicholas was Bishop of Myra, in south-western Turkey, in the fourth century, but little else is known of him. His lasting popularity is based entirely on the miraculous stories told about him, and the reputation he had for secret assistance to the needy; it was said that he possessed such a degree of holiness that he could work wonders at will. He was already immensely popular in the Eastern Church in the sixth century, and by the tenth century was equally widely known in the West, especially after his relics were transferred to Bari in 1087.

Most of the stories told of him, as recorded in the immensely influential book of saints' tales *The Golden Legend* (*c*.1260), relate how he intervened to save people in groups of three: he raised to life three boys who had been murdered, dismembered, and stored in a brine tub by a butcher; he freed three condemned men; saved three sailors and three princes; and delivered three girls from a fate worse than death:

At the time a certain fellow townsman of his, a
man of noble origin but very poor, was thinking of
prostituting his three virgin daughters in order to
make a living out of this vile transaction. When the
saint heard of this, abhorring the crime he wrapped
a quantity of gold in a cloth and, under cover of dark-
ness, threw it through a window of the other man's
house and withdrew unseen. Rising in the morning
the man found the gold, gave thanks to God and
celebrated the wedding of his eldest daughter.

He then did the same for the other two girls. As his miraculous acts concerned such a wide variety of

Barring Out

Barring out was a widespread custom particularly common in the northern counties of England, and also in Scotland and Ireland, from Tudor times onwards. It involved pupils taking possession of their school by locking out the staff, and keeping them out until certain demands were met, usually those relating to the perennial concerns of schoolchildren through the ages: holidays, playtimes, food, and the relaxation of corporal punishment. Barring out could take place at the end of any of the school terms, or at any other time if the scholars thought they had a major grievance, but was most common at Shrovetide and on St Nicholas' Day (6 December). Shrove Tuesday had a long history as a half-holiday for apprentices and schoolchildren, and schoolboys claimed Nicholas as their patron saint.

The custom survived into the late nineteenth century in a few places, as in this memory of Northumberland, written in 1929:

> We did it every year to Mr. Brown in the old school in the village hall on the shortest day of the year after dinner; he would go round and tap at the windows, and then he would go home, and we would go home too.

But it was not always that easy:

> There was a lot of big boys then, they went to school in winter, and worked out all the summer; they brought a lot of ropes to school that day, and there were a lot of forms, and they tied all three doors, and put forms in front. Mr. Brown got one door a little open, and broke a blade of his favourite penknife trying to cut the rope, and that made him very angry, and when he got in he did thrash them. I was frightened. I would be in the infants or standard I.

In earlier reports, the whole affair was more formalized and sanctioned by custom, and was even mentioned in some school rules. The pupils' demands were written out and passed ('through the keyhole') to the master outside, and it was sometimes stipulated that these be written in Latin. Many masters connived in planning the 'rebellion', and thereby exerted some degree of control, but in other instances there was serious violence as the master tried to force entry. Firearms could even be used in defence, and at the High School in Edinburgh in 1595 a local magistrate who had been brought in to help was killed by the 'schot of ane pistol on the forehead out of the scholl'. It is therefore hardly surprising that local authorities and teachers all over the country fought a sustained campaign to abolish the custom. Schoolchildren tried to keep it alive, but in most places by the nineteenth century it had become little more than a token gesture to mark the end of term, accompanied by a rhyme, which was a far cry from the glories of demands written in Latin:

> Pancake Tuesday [or other suitable day] is a very nice day
> If you don't give us a holiday, we'll all run away.

people, he was chosen as patron saint of numerous groups, including children, sailors, unmarried girls, merchants, pawnbrokers, apothecaries, and perfumiers. He was popular with the latter group because of the beautiful odour that was said to have emanated from his tomb until long after his death.

Despite his widespread popularity, few traditional customs seem to have been associated with his day in Britain. His connection with children made his day particularly appropriate for 'barring out' ceremonies, where schoolchildren tried to keep the master out of the school until he agreed to a holiday (see **Barring Out**, *above*), and also for the medieval custom of electing a **Boy Bishop** (*see below*), but otherwise his appearances in the traditional calendar are sporadic. Nevertheless, St Nicholas' real claim to fame in the modern world is his central role in the development of the Santa Claus figure (*see* **Christmas: Father Christmas/Santa Claus**).

The 'Boy Bishop' in Salisbury Cathedral

Boy Bishop

The Boy Bishop was a widespread ecclesiastical custom in which a boy – usually a chorister – was elected each year to act as bishop for a short period of time, supported by his fellow choirboys, while some of the normal juvenile tasks were carried out by the adult clergy. This role-reversal custom came to Britain from the Continent, and Ronald Hutton states that the roots of the Boy Bishop lie in the German Church, where there was already a tradition of lower clergy taking charge on certain days by the tenth century. It had reached England by the twelfth century, and it was at first centred on Holy Innocents' Day (28 December), a day on which other child-centred customs already existed, but it was soon influenced by the rapidly growing popularity of St Nicholas, the new patron saint of children. The two festivals of St Nicholas' Day and Holy Innocents' Day gave a natural beginning and end to the Boy Bishop's reign, and he was often elected on the former while his main ceremonial duties fell on the latter.

Almost all the cathedrals and other major religious centres in England had some version of the custom, although the details varied considerably. In essence, the boy was elected, either by his peers or by the real bishop's staff, and was invested with all the accoutrements of a real bishop. In this position he led processions, held services, delivered sermons, and performed all the duties of the normal clergy, except the mass itself. However, the 'role reversal' aspect of this tradition was strictly circumscribed, and only went so far. The boys were expected to behave themselves and were certainly not allowed to parody the services, or puncture the dignity of church officers or ritual. The most that was allowed was a little wry humour in the Boy Bishop's sermons, which were written by the adults. Even so, the Church authorities frequently found it necessary to lay down rules of conduct, and there was often trouble when the boys were out of sight of their masters. One of the most popular aspects of the Boy Bishop custom was when he, accompanied by a few other choristers, went round the parish over the Christmas period singing at people's houses, collecting money for the Church or, occasionally, for himself and his companions.

Sporadic attempts to create ceremonies in which girls were allowed to take on similar exalted positions were firmly stamped on by the Church authorities. Boys may have been allowed a little licence, as they would soon be men, but the idea of females stepping out of their assigned lot in life was too abhorrent to the medieval Church to be tolerated even for a short time.

Despite their apparent popularity, Henry VIII summarily banned Boy Bishops in 1541, on the grounds that they dented ecclesiastical dignity. They returned briefly under Queen Mary, only to be banned again by Elizabeth I. They were not to be seen again until the twentieth century, when periods of nostalgia and heritage consciousness led to the revival of various old church practices. Most such revivals come and go, but the strongest modern example is at Hereford Cathedral. Sometimes romanticism outweighs accuracy, and the revival mixes up traditions in interesting ways. In 1949, the journal *Folk-Lore* recorded that:

It was reported in the Daily Graphic (2 May 1949) that a Kentish vicar revived one May Day custom when, in a church packed with young people, the senior choirboy was proclaimed Boy Bishop. Later the Boy Bishop crowned the May Queen who watched a maypole dance outside the church from her floral throne.

*

11 DECEMBER

Old St Andrew's Day

Following the change of calendar in 1752 (*see* p. xx), some of the St Andrew's Day celebrations of 30 November were carried out by the more traditionally minded participants on the Old Style St Andrew's Day, eleven days later. Dialect collector Thomas Sternberg, for example, described the antics of the lacemakers on this day in his native Northamptonshire, which were still going strong in the mid nineteenth century:

'Tander' – Of all the numerous red-letter days which diversified the lives of our ancestors, this is the only one which has survived to our own times in anything like its pristine manner . . . Drinking and feasting prevail to a riotous extent. Towards evening the sober

villagers appear to have become suddenly smitten with a violent taste for masquerading. Women may be seen walking about in male attire, while men and boys have donned the female dress, and visit each other's cottages, drinking hot 'eldern wine', the staple beverage of the season.

*

13 DECEMBER

Aldermaston Candle Auction

One of the few surviving **candle auctions** (p. 106) takes place at Aldermaston, Berkshire, every three years on 13 December. The auction is for the lease of the land called Church Acre (although it is more than two acres in size), which was granted to the church there when the parish was enclosed in 1815. A nail is inserted into a lighted candle, about an inch from the top, and bidding continues until the nail falls to the table.

*

SECOND THURSDAY BEFORE CHRISTMAS

Picrous Day

Cornish tin-miners seem to have had a calendar all of their own, as their festivals were often different from those of the rest of the country. On the last Thursday before Christmas, they celebrated Picrous Day, which was reputedly named after the mythical man who discovered tin. Some called it Chewidden (White) Thursday, as tradition states that this was the day when 'white tin' (smelted tin) was first made or sold in Cornwall. Either way, the tinners claimed a holiday from work, and money to spend on drink.

See also **5 March: St Piran's Day**.

*

14 DECEMBER

St Tibba's Day

Tibba, and her cousin Eabba, lived in Rutland in the seventh century and were probably nieces of Penda, the King of Mercia. They were reputed to be fond of hunting, before becoming devout hermits, and were both made saints after their death. Because of her early liking for the chase, St Tibba was adopted as patroness of falconers and wildfowlers, but otherwise she is only remembered around Ryhall, where she lived and died, and where there is a well named after her. There is some disagreement about her feast day. Most sources give it as 14 December, but David Farmer's *Oxford Dictionary of Saints* (1987) gives it as 6 March.

*

16 DECEMBER

Boar's Head

The bringing in of the boar's head is a well-known feature of Christmas past, although few people can have seen it for themselves. In the standard description, the boar's head is served on a silver or gold platter, with some considerable ceremony, at a formal banquet in a university or great house. It is carried in by the butler or other servants, is liberally decorated with bay, rosemary, and laurel, and has a lemon, orange, or apple in its open mouth. Its entrance is heralded by music (often a trumpet fanfare), and one of the attendants sings the 'Boar's Head Carol' in Latin, or at least with a Latin refrain, supported by the company on the chorus. The ceremony almost certainly dates from medieval times, although the majority of descriptions emerged much later. William Husk, for example, printed seven versions of the song that accompanies the ceremony, dating from the fourteenth century onwards, but what is generally considered to be the earliest description of the custom must be taken on trust. It appears in Holinshed's *Chronicles* of 1577 (III, 76), and relates that in the year 1170, King Henry II served a boar's head to his son.

Only the very rich could afford such extravagant fare as boars' heads, dressed peacocks, and swans for dinner, and such dishes were designed as much to impress and inspire awe in their guests as cater for physical appetites. Down the years, there have been numerous descriptions of the ceremony at the substantial Christmas feasts of the royal court, the Inner Temple, and Oxford and Cambridge colleges, but all are suspiciously similar and seem to be more self-conscious and theatrical pieces of pageantry influenced by literary references rather than genuine traditions. Indeed, with its silver platters and Latin refrains, it is hard to escape the feeling that this has always been a pseudo-custom, and it was certainly one of the stock features of the Merrie England view of Christmas created in the nineteenth century and subsequently bequeathed to the twentieth as a component of a largely mythical English golden age (*see* **Merrie England**, p. 372). An early example of this tendency can be found in Washington Irving's best-selling *Sketch-Book* (1820), in which he describes Christmas dinner with a squire who was such a 'strenuous advocate for the revival of the old rural games and holiday observances'. It is no surprise that the squire was careful to re-enact the boar's head ceremony in his own 'baronial hall', with all the necessary trappings.

Nevertheless, this may be simply a jaundiced modern view. There are some indications that the ceremony had a more popular presence, and in his *Wonderful Yeare* (1603) Thomas Dekker reveals that at this time the custom was sufficiently well known to be used proverbially, writing about those who were overly cautious of catching the plague:

> *They went (most bitterly) miching and muffled up and down, with rue and wormwood stuft into their ears and nostrils, looking like so many boar's heads stuck with branches of rosemary, to be served in for brawn at Christmas.*

The boar's head ceremony is still carried out every year at Queen's College, Oxford, around 16 December, where, it is claimed, it has been performed continuously since the fourteenth century. A suitably academic story explains that the ceremony was founded to celebrate an exciting event: a university student was wandering about the Forest of Shotover one day, reading his

The bringing in of a boar's head, served on a platter, has been regarded by many as a traditional feature of Christmas past

copy of Aristotle, when he was suddenly confronted by a wild boar, which rushed at him. With no weapon to hand, but with great presence of mind, the student rammed his book into the open mouth of the beast and thus choked it to death.

*

21 DECEMBER

St Thomas's Day

By far the most widespread activity of 21 December was to go 'Thomasing' or 'gooding', a custom that clearly relied on the hospitality and charity that had been part of a traditional Christmas for centuries. On this day, poor women tramped round their neighbourhood, calling at the houses and farms of their better-off neighbours, expecting to receive doles of money or food in order to 'keep a good Christmas'. Local customary rules determined who was considered eligible and who gave what; some farmers, for example, gave quantities of wheat, which explains why the custom was called 'corning' in some areas. As Thomas Grey recorded in his memoirs of cottage life in Hertfordshire in the 1870s:

The women that I knew always called at the same houses and were evidently expected, for they told me they always got a 'something' at each place of call. One gentleman gave a new sixpence each year to every 'Thomaser' at his home. I asked what they said or did when calling at the houses. Said they: 'All we ses is please we've cum a-Thomasing, remember St. Thomas's Day.'

Most accounts state that the custom was almost entirely confined to women, often with the help of their children, although sometimes old men would take part.

'Gooding' is recorded as meaning 'begging' from as early as 1560, but there is no direct evidence that the custom of visiting neighbours on St Thomas's Day is any older than the late eighteenth century, although several writers indicate that it was already well established at that time. It was extremely widely practised until the late nineteenth century, when it started to decline. It is clear that these gooding or Thomasing customs could only work in a relatively small close-knit community, where everybody knew each other and understood the local informal rules by which the tradition operated. As rural communities began to change dramatically in the second half of the nineteenth century, many local charities fell by the wayside, or changed as the givers strove to keep a degree of control over what was given, and who should receive it. Charlotte Burne, the leading folklore collector for Shropshire, reported in 1883:

> It is in fact a custom very likely to be abused and to degenerate into a nuisance; the strongest, who could walk farthest, getting the greatest number of doles; several members of a family going to the same house at different times in the day, and thus getting an unfair share. In the year 1870, the farmers around Clun determined to put a stop to the begging, and instead of giving to all comers, they agreed to send their contributions of corn to the Town Hall, to be distributed under proper supervision to the deserving poor, in proportion to the size of their families . . .

However, in other places the distribution was put into the hands of the church.

See also **Doles**, p. 87.

*

24 DECEMBER

Christmas Eve

In many ways, Christmas Eve has never had much of a character of its own and has generally been seen as a prelude to the big day. Most of the customs and traditions that have taken place on Christmas Eve, including all the various visiting customs, could also be carried out at any time over the Christmas season. However, Christmas Eve was a particularly good time for traditional 'performers' to call, as they would be fairly sure to find someone at home, and the household was likely to be filled with that customary glow of Christmas spirit. In the nineteenth and early twentieth century, the old idea of charity and hospitality at Christmas had not yet died out completely, and even if money were not forthcoming, food and drink could be almost guaranteed. In nearly every part of the country at that time, therefore, you might be visited by the mummers or guisers, who would perform their traditional play, or wassailers, who called to wish good luck or to show you their yule baby. Carol singers or waits might serenade you, and in the

North-East you might see sword dancers, in Kent the Hooden Horse, or in Cornwall the guise dancers.

On farms, it was traditional to give extra food to the animals in the evening, partly to give them a Christmas treat but also in the hope that they would need less attention on Christmas Day. As indicated below (*see* **Christmas: Decorations**), the modern way of putting up decorations two weeks before Christmas would have been anathema to our great-grandparents. Most people believed it to be unlucky to decorate their home or church before Christmas Eve, and there would have been much to do to trim the tree and decorate the home with greenery. Similarly, in the days before freezers, there would have been an immense rush to get fresh and perishable food bought or delivered, and the shops would stay open very late on Christmas Eve. The yule log, ashen faggot, and Christmas candles needed to be prepared and lit, and then there was church to go to.

It is not surprising, therefore, that there was little time for other activities, but there are some reports of a few, as recorded in the *Gentleman's Magazine* of 1824:

> Christmas Eve is, in Yorkshire, celebrated in a peculiar manner. At eight o'clock in the evening, the bells greet 'old Father Christmas' with a merry peal, the children parade the streets with drums, trumpets, bells, or perhaps, in their absence, with the poker and shovel, taken from the humble cottage fire; the Yule candle is lighted.

As the midnight hour grew closer, nearly every church bell would be ringing (*see also* **Ringing the Devil's Knell**, *below*), and many people would open their door to 'welcome Christmas in'. The cattle in their stalls were said to kneel down in honour of the day at this time, and the bees to hum the Old Hundredth Psalm in their hives. In addition to these beliefs, treated separately below, Christmas Eve was also regarded as a good time for love divination, and there were various procedures, some simple, some complex, to help the enquirer find out who they were destined to marry. Sidney Oldall Addy recorded a relatively straightforward method from Derbyshire in the 1890s:

> If a girl walk backwards to a pear tree, on Christmas Eve, and walk round the tree three times, she will see an image of her future husband.

The burning of the ashen faggot, Dunster, Somerset, 1985

Christmas Eve was believed to be one of the safest times for divination, as ghosts and other spirits were said to be powerless on this night.

Ashen Faggot

A popular Christmas custom in Devon, and in neighbouring parts of Dorset and Somerset, was the burning of the ashen faggot, described here in *Bentley's Magazine* (1847):

> On Christmas Eve it is the custom in all the farmhouses of this neighbourhood to 'burn the ashen faggot'. All the labourers and servants are invited and a large fire is heaped up on to the wide hearth . . . We all sat round the hearth in a circle; the fire light deepening the shadows of the hard-featured mahogany countenances around, and setting off the peculiarities of each form. The ashen faggot which lay on the hearth consists of a long, immense log of ash, surrounded with smaller branches, which are bound to it with many withies, forming one large bundle; it filled the whole hearth, and as it burned, the roaring in the large chimney was tremendous. As the fire slowly catches, and consumes the withies, the sticks fly off, and kindle into a sudden blaze, and as each one after the other gives way, all present stand up and shout with might and main; the 'loving cup' of cider is handed round, and each drinks his fill. They then resume their seats, sing songs and crack jokes, till the bursting of another band, and the kindling of a fresh blaze demands renewed shouts, and another pull at the cider flagon. The merriment is allowed to go on till nearly midnight, before which hour the worthy giver of the feast likes to have her house clear, that the 'Holy Day' may begin in peace.

All the descriptions of the custom follow a similar pattern, although they differ in some details. Sometimes a central log, with sticks bound round it, was burned, while others describe a true faggot, or bundle of sticks. Some sources specify ash, but others talk of bands of willow, or other wood.

As is often the case, the antiquarian John Brand identified the earliest known reference – 'Christmas, a Poem', written by Romaine Joseph Thorn and published in 1795, which already mentions the essential features of the custom. It is already called the 'ashen faggot', has nine 'bandages', and as each breaks:

A mighty jug of sparkling cyder's brought
With brandy mixt, to elevate the guests.

It is quite possible that the ashen faggot is a localized offshoot of the more widely known and older **yule log** (*see below*), as they share the same principles of festive and ceremonial burning, but at present this cannot be proved either way. Some pubs in Devon still continue the tradition.

Cattle Kneeling

In former times, it was widely believed that at the stroke of midnight, as Christmas Eve becomes Christmas Day, the cattle in their stalls knelt down in honour of the occasion, and many said that they let out a groan as they did so.

An honest countryman, living on the edge of
St. Stephen's Down, near Launceston, Cornwall,
informed me, October 28th, 1790, that he once, with
some others, made trial of the truth of the above,
and watching several oxen in their stalls at the above
time, at twelve o'clock at night, they observed the
two oldest oxen only fall on their knees, and as he
expressed it, in the idiom of the country, make 'a
cruel moan like Christian creatures'. I could not but
with great difficulty keep my countenance: he saw
this, and seemed angry that I gave so little credit to
his tale, and walking off in a pettish humour seemed
to 'marvel at my unbelief'.

This description, from the 1849 edition of John Brand's *Observations on the Popular Antiquities of Great Britain*, is the first printed mention of this idea, but his wording suggests that it had already been in circulation for a while, and it was certainly extremely well known all over England in the nineteenth and early twentieth

centuries. Indeed, it may still be told to children in some families. Brand was also the first to suggest that many had been influenced by popular prints of the Nativity, which showed the cattle kneeling, which is certainly plausible. However, this is not the only belief that maintains that the natural world follows the Christian calendar: the sun dancing for joy as it rises on Easter Monday (*see* **Easter Monday: Sun Dancing**, p. 130) and the Holy Thorn blossoming on Christmas morning (*see* **Christmas: Holy Thorn(s)**) are based on the same idea. The faith of many in the truth of the Christian religion was therefore borne out in the idea that even the dumb beasts knew that Christmas was a special time.

People's faith in these date-related beliefs was severely tested, however, when the Gregorian calendar was introduced in 1752. Would nature follow the new rules, or stick to the old? We do not know whether the cattle-kneeling belief was around in 1752, but as late as 1847 it was still an issue, as reported in *Bentley's Magazine*:

It is said, as the morning of the day on which Christ
was born, the cattle in the stalls kneel down; and I
have heard it confidently asserted that, when the
new style came in, the younger cattle only knelt on
December 25, while the older bullocks preserved their
genuflections for Old Christmas Day, January 6.

Hooden Horse

In a number of East Kent villages, up to the early twentieth century, Christmas Eve was graced with a house-visiting custom called the Hooden Horse. The horse consisted of a wooden head (or possibly a real horse's skull), decorated with ribbons, brasses, and rosettes, and was mounted on a pole about four feet long. A man (the 'hoodener') bent over forwards to grasp the pole and was completely covered by a dark cloth. The jaws of the head were hinged, and could be opened and closed by the hoodener pulling a string. He was usually joined by the horse's groom or driver, who carried a whip and led him on a rope; a jockey; a character called Molly, played by a man, who carried a broom; and at least one musician. The team called at houses throughout the neighbourhood, where they would sing and play, the horse would play up and have to be restrained, and the jockey would try to ride him. They would then collect money, food, or drink, and move on.

Over thirty local versions of the Hooden Horse were recorded around the turn of the twentieth century, but all from a small restricted area of North and East Kent. Most of the teams came from areas along the coast, but a few were found in villages as far as fifteen miles inland. The tradition was fortunately well documented by Percy Maylam in his privately printed book *The Hooden Horse* (1909), but he was only just in time: the horse was then on its last legs, and there is hardly any evidence of its existence after that date.

The name has intrigued commentators on the custom, and there has been much speculation on its derivation. As far as we can tell, the locals called the custom 'oodening', and only educated writers added the initial 'h'. Nevertheless, the most likely derivation is from 'hood', because that best matches the details of the custom, although another possibility is that it is derived from 'wooden'. Two other suggestions can be dismissed out of hand: one theory is that the name is from Robin Hood (on the strength of the presence of Molly, who, it has been suggested, might represent Maid Marian), but least plausible of all is that it is a survival of the worship of the pagan god Woden, as it is quite improbable that a custom openly named after a pagan god could have survived over a thousand years of jealous Christianity.

The earliest known reference is a little ambiguous: Samuel Pegge defines 'Hooding' in his glossary of Kenticisms (1736) as

> ... a country masquerade at Christmas time, which in Derb[yshire] they call guising (I suppose a contraction of dis-guising), and in other places 'mumming' ...

This could conceivably be a simple custom involving disguises, but the next documentary sighting, in Ramsgate in 1807, quite clearly describes the horse, and there are several other accounts from the nineteenth century confirming that the custom had changed little in that time. In fact, apart from the name, the Hooden Horse custom is not really unique. It bears marked similarities to other 'animal disguise' customs, such as the 'Wild Horse' found in the souling version of the mummers' play in Cheshire (*see* **31 October: Antrobus Soul-Cakers**), the Mari Lwyd in Wales, and the **Old Horse** and **Old Tup** of the Midlands (*see below*).

The traditional Hooden Horse may have died out *c.*1910, but the postwar folk revival created many enthusiasts, and since then many revival teams have existed in Kent, no Christmas passing without the appearance of at least a few modern horses.

See also **Hobby Horses**, p. 164.

Old Horse

The Old Horse is both the name of a song and a dramatic Christmas house-visiting custom, similar to the **Old Tup** or Derby Ram (*see below*). In 1903, George Addy recorded the following version of the song that was sung during the visit:

> *It is a poor old horse*
> *And he's knocking at your door*
> *And if you choose to let him in*
> *He'll please you all I'm sure*
> *Poor old horse, let him in.*

The same writer also describes the scene in a Derbyshire farmhouse about the turn of the twentieth century:

> *What an eerie monster he looks! He opens his jaws*
> *and shuts them with a horrid metallic sort of a rattle.*
> *His painted eyeballs stare around with a kind of*
> *rigid deathlike smile. His lumpy hairy carcase moves*
> *uneasily on four legs – with trousers on. He is shod*
> *with collier's clogs. The more timid of the youngsters,*
> *on purpose to hearten each other, whisper, 'He's*
> *not real, you know.' Meanwhile the ponderous jaws*
> *and teeth of this mechanically arranged skeleton*
> *head clash and gibber weirdly, and snap at the leg of*
> *young Steeve, the farmer's boy. A score or so of young*
> *men have by this time trooped into the house and*
> *dressed up in rude theatrical attire and are almost*
> *beyond recognition.*

Young men such as these sang the 'Old Horse' song, and they were usually accompanied by one or two other characters, including a blacksmith, who tried to shoe the horse, which of course resisted. At another point in the song, the horse 'died' and then revived. As in all other visiting customs, the participants accepted food, drink, or money from the householders, and then moved on. The Old Horse custom was found in a very restricted area around Sheffield, where the counties of Derbyshire, Nottinghamshire, and Yorkshire meet, from the 1840s until the mid twentieth century.

See also **Hobby Horses**, p. 164.

Old Tup

The 'Old Tup', or 'Derby Ram', is a widely collected traditional song found in different versions all over the English-speaking world:

> As I was going to Derby
> 'Twas on a Derby day
> I saw the finest ram, sir
> That ever was fed on hay.

The song concerns a ram of such prodigious size that its horns reached to the moon and each foot covered an acre of land, and it tells how a butcher killed the ram and its parts were made into useful objects.

> And all the boys in Derby
> Came running for his eyes
> To make a pair of footballs
> For they were football size.

Around Sheffield, however, the song is the basis of a Christmas visiting custom, usually performed by children. They make the ram either by simply throwing a cloth over one of their number, or by fixing a pair of horns to a pole and covering the person who holds the pole in the cloth, in exactly the same way as many hobby horses are made (see **Hobby Horses**, p. 164). The participants sing the song, while the ram dances about, and then they enact the killing. The custom was common in the area from the mid nineteenth to the mid twentieth centuries, and is still not quite extinct.

Ringing the Devil's Knell

Many church towers resound to peals at midnight on Christmas Eve, but at All Saints, Dewsbury, in Yorkshire, the custom is given a unique twist. Here, they engage in 'tolling the Devil's knell', or ringing 't'owd lad's passin' bell'. The bell-ringers gather at around ten o'clock at night, and commence tolling the church's tenor bell – one stroke for every year since the birth of Christ. At the rate of one stroke every two seconds or so, the whole process takes about two hours and is carefully timed to end exactly at midnight. It has been known for one person to do the lot, but more usually a relay of ringers share the task. Someone is also employed to keep track of the number of strokes on specially prepared squared paper, in order to get the number of strokes exactly right.

The popular explanation of this custom is that the tenor bell used for the toll was presented to the church by local landowner Sir Thomas De Soothill, in the fifteenth century, as penance for murdering a servant; the bell is therefore colloquially called 'Black Tom' in his memory. A more theological explanation is that the toll is to remind parishioners that the Devil died when Christ was born and it is therefore appropriate to mark his demise by ringing a passing bell – as was routinely done for the death of more mortal souls in the parish.

It is unlikely that the Soothill story is true, and it is not clear when the tradition started, but it is generally accepted that the custom had fallen into abeyance and was revived in 1828 by the Revd John Buckworth. It is believed to have been carried out every year since, except when the bells were being recast, and during the Second World War, when all church bells were silent. The custom was depicted on a Christmas postage stamp in 1986.

Although Dewsbury is the only place to greet Christmas in this way nowadays, there is evidence that other places once had analogous, if not identical, customs. In 1866, William Henderson, for example, wrote that 'at Horbury, near Wakefield, and at Dewsbury . . . is tolled the 'Devil's Knell'; a hundred strokes, then a pause, then three strokes three, three strokes, and three strokes again.' Another example of a lengthy peal comes from Gloucestershire, and is recorded in A. R. Wright and T. E. Lones's *British Calendar Customs* (1940):

> The Rev. Anthony Sterry, Vicar of Lydney, gave, by deed, in 1599, a sum of 5s per annum . . . for ringing a peal on Christmas Eve, about midnight, for two hours, in commemoration of the Nativity.

Vessel Cups

The 'vessel cup' custom was one in which girls or women would go round houses on or just before Christmas Eve, displaying a doll or two in a decorated box and singing a carol or wassail song. 'Vessel' in this sense is certainly a dialect version of 'wassail', and 'cup' may perhaps indicate that this custom originated with the much more widely known wassail bowl. Another local term for the doll's receptacle was 'milly-box', presumably meaning 'my lady' box.

Vessel cups seem to have been restricted to the North-East. Most of the references to the custom are concentrated in Yorkshire, but one or two are from County Durham and as far south as Lincolnshire; however, none is earlier than the nineteenth century. As described in these sources, the custom was restricted to girls or elderly women, and it is likely that during these women's lives it had been an adult female custom, but had since degenerated into a children's activity. In 1898, local writer Richard Blakeborough documented the following version of the custom from Yorkshire:

> The 'vessel-cups'... still come round, with their doll in a box, decked out as the Virgin Mary, lying in pink cotton-wool and evergreens. Some of these vessel-cups are in their way quite little works of art. I remember, up to [five years ago] Lavinia Leather travelled every year all the way from the other side of Leeds, to sing the vessel-cup throughout that part of Cleveland ... There was no mistaking the advent of Christmas, when, after unceremoniously opening the door, the old lady commenced saying:
>
> > God bless the master of this hoos
> > An' t' mis-ter-ess also
> > An' all yer lahtle bonny bairns
> > 'At round yer table go!
> > For it is at this tahm
> > Straangers travel far an' near
> > Seea Ah wish ya a merry Kessamus
> > An' a happy New Year.

The decorations around the doll varied with the skill of the bearer, but usually included standard Christmas items such as holly, mistletoe, and tinsel, along with fruit and sweets. The vessel cup was therefore an almost exact equivalent of the May dolls custom, especially when in the hands of children, and it was the 'showing' of the box that particularly seemed to matter to them. The following was recorded in the journal *Folk-Lore* (1906):

> The children carrying a box never knock or ring, but open each house door and begin to sing, 'God rest you merry gentlemen.' If no notice is taken, they sing the piece over again, until someone goes to speak to them. They then ask if anyone would like to see the 'wassail box'. If no one cares to look at it, they go quietly away. They never uncover the box without first asking, 'Would you like to see the wassail box?'

Compare: **1 May: May Dolls**; **Christmas: Wassailing**.

Yule Log

The idea that a large log should be burning in the fireplace on Christmas Eve was almost universally acknowledged for at least 300 years. It went under various names, such as yule/Christmas log, block, clog, or brand, and could be found over most of the British Isles during that time. Those in towns may have had to make do with a token gesture, but any self-respecting country family would make the effort to obtain the real thing, as here in Herefordshire in 1886:

> A respectable middle-aged labourer (say 42 or 43) tells me that in his boyhood his father was always careful to provide a Christmas Yule-Log. On Christmas morning he would put a bit saved from last year's log on the fire, and lay the new log on top of it, so that it might be kindled from the last year's piece. Before the log was quite burnt out he took it off, extinguished it, and put it by to kindle the next log from.

The yule log was already well known in the seventeenth century, as both Robert Herrick, in his *Hesperides* (1648), and John Aubrey, in his *Remaines of Gentilisme and Judaisme* (1686), refer to it in familiar terms, and Herrick also shows that in his time the idea of saving a piece for next year was already in place:

> Come, bring with a noise,
> My merry, merry boys,

Continues on page 373 >

Merrie England

England was merry England, when
Old Christmas brought his sports again.

So said Walter Scott in his long poem *Marmion* (1808), setting the scene for a romantic view of the past that would have a profound influence on the way popular customs and traditions would be seen throughout the nineteenth and much of the twentieth centuries. Scott's phrase 'Merry England' has been adopted by historians and folklorists to describe the notion that there was a golden age in the English past, when society functioned without conflict, our rulers were just and kindly, our clergy attentive and understanding, everyone was adequately clothed, fed, and happy in their station, and contentment ruled the land. This is overstating the case a little, but it is not far off the mark for those writers who were disenchanted with the ways in which they saw the nineteenth and twentieth centuries progressing. Many hated the forces of urbanization and mechanization – in particular, the growth of factories, railways, and improved roads – which they saw gathering speed around them, and some even looked askance at education and increasing literacy, believing that these would somehow destroy the essential simplicity of the English peasant. When the present was compared to Merrie England, it was often found wanting. Washington Irving was a chief proponent of the Merrie England school:

> One of the least pleasing effects of modern refinement is the havoc it has made among the hearty old holiday customs. It has completely taken off the sharp touchings and spirited reliefs of these embellishments of life, and has worn down society into a more smooth and polished, but certainly a less characteristic, surface. Many of the games and ceremonials of Christmas have entirely disappeared . . . They flourished in times full of spirit and lustihood, when men enjoyed life roughly, but heartily and vigorously; times wild and picturesque . . . The world has become more worldly. There is more of dissipation, and less of enjoyment.

Needless to say, this golden age never really existed, as the non-romantic folklorist A. R. Wright commented in 1928:

> 'Ye Merrie England of ye Olden Time' of stage and story, with its folk chiefly engaged in dancing around the maypole on the village green or dragging the yule log into the baronial hall, according to the season of the year, is the creation of the romanticists and poets and painters of the nineteenth century.

In real historical terms, 'Merrie England' was somewhat loosely defined by its proponents, and could slide from era to era as the moment demanded. Feudal times were a contender, as they were considered an age when everyone knew their place and worked together for the common good, as part of an organic, interlinked society – although the small detail of the serfs' lack of freedom tarnished the era's image somewhat. At other times, the period of the Restoration was invoked as a golden age: the colourful monarchy had been returned to its rightful place, and Old Father Christmas and maypoles on the village green had replaced the joyless Puritan rule. But it was the reign of Elizabeth I, and the age of Shakespeare, that was generally considered to be the most golden of all golden ages.

Merrie Englandism is at the root of much popular historical writing from the nineteenth century onwards, but was particularly prevalent in the attitudes of those who sought to revive or recreate the customs of the past, and who tried to remodel local communities on supposedly traditional English lines. As the *Examiner* explained in 1817:

> Merry Old England died in the country a great while ago; and the sports, the pastimes, the holidays, the Christmas greens and gambols, the archeries, the May-mornings, the May-poles, the country dances, the masks, the harvest-homes, the new-year's gifts, the gallantries, the golden means, the poetries, the pleasures, the leisures, the real treasures – were all buried with her.

May Day and Christmas were the two festivals

most susceptible to this style of re-interpretation, although many other traditional activities, including morris dancing, rush-bearing, and well-dressing, received a similar treatment. Working with the raw data provided by the early antiquarians, a range of writers, including Walter Scott, Leigh Hunt, and Charles Dickens, sought to turn public opinion back to the past. The squire that features in Washington Irving's *Sketch-Book* (1819–20) and *Bracebridge Hall* (1822), and Mr Wardle of Dingley Dell, in Dickens's *Pickwick Papers* (1836–7), were classic creations in this mould. While their re-invention of Christmas worked directly on the middle-class families of the nation, their May Day ideas were filtered through countless organizers of local fêtes, pageants, and other gatherings. Choreographers introduced 'ancient morris dances' and maypole scenes to the stage, and artists joined in the movement, with a new genre of rustic paintings and engravings, starting with *May Day in the Reign of Queen Elizabeth* by Charles Leslie, which was exhibited at the Royal Academy in 1821.

A key characteristic of the genre was that the re-inventions were always billed as true English traditions, despite the fact that they had been concocted a short while before. The 'revivers' decided what was traditional and what was not, and it seemed that everyone was willing to be fooled. Although a few critics were not keen on all this rusticity, hardly anyone questioned its authenticity or cared to expose it, and there was no 'campaign for real traditions'. Little children dressed in white, demure May Queens, controlled processions, and tea on the village green were infinitely more acceptable than drunken morris men, or youths parading the streets throwing squibs, or farm labourers and maidservants mixing indiscriminately in unsupervised dancing booths or local pubs. Such activities were purged of their 'unsavoury' aspects, sanitized, and re-presented to a public eager for the rediscovery of its traditional heritage. In countless fêtes and May Day gatherings, and in our underlying notions of a 'real English Christmas', the spirit of the Merrie Englander lives on.

The Christmas log to the firing;
While my good dame, she
Bids ye all be free,
And drink to your heart's desiring.
With the last year's brand
Light the new block, and
For good success in his spending
On your psaltries play,
That sweet luck may
Come while the log is a-teending.

The idea behind keeping part of the wood was twofold: it not only ensured that the luck of the house continued from year to year, but was also believed to offer protection against fire and witchcraft. It was also widely maintained that the log had to burn for the whole of the night of Christmas Eve, and some said all of Christmas Day as well, or the luck would disperse.

Many late Victorian and twentieth-century books include illustrations of baronial halls with impossibly large 'yule logs' burning in huge fireplaces as depictions of 'old-time' Christmases, but it is clear that for the vast majority of families rather more modest logs sufficed to fill the domestic hearth. Nevertheless, there is a sense that size mattered, and where possible a larger than life trunk would be used. Folklorist Charlotte Burne recorded:

In 1845 I was at the Vessons Farmhouse [in Shropshire] *... The floor was of flags, an unusual thing in this part. Observing a sort of roadway through the kitchen, and the flags much broken, I enquired what caused it and was told it was from the horses' hoofs drawing in the 'Christmas Brand'.*

Along with many of the traditional features of Christmas, the yule log disappeared from most households during the twentieth century, but it lives on in spirit, and in chocolate form.

*

CHRISTMAS

In 1807, thirty years before Victoria came to the throne, the poet Robert Southey wrote:

> All persons say how differently this season was observed in their fathers' days, and speak of old ceremonies and old festivities as things which are obsolete. The cause is obvious. In large towns the population is continually shifting; a new settler neither continues the customs of his own province in a place where they would be strange, nor adopts those which he finds, because they are strange to him, and thus all local differences are wearing out.

This was the beginning of what could be termed the 'new seasonal nostalgia', when everyone agreed that Christmas was not what it was and that something should be done about it. Over the following decades, something was indeed done as, in modern terms, the season was rebranded and relaunched. To talk about our modern perceptions of the 'real Christmas', or to investigate the historical development of the festival, is thus to have a dialogue with the Victorians. They remodelled the season so thoroughly with their inventions, improvements, and importations that when we look at any Christmas custom our first question is what they did with it. Crackers and cards? They invented them. Christmas trees, stockings, Santa Claus? They imported them. Christmas presents, Christmas dinner, Father Christmas? They remodelled them.

The Christmas of old, to which so many nineteenth-century writers were constantly hearkening, was largely a figment of their romantic imaginations, however. It was sited in the mythical **Merrie England** (p. 372) rather than any real historical era, but it served its purpose. The golden age was evoked primarily to throw the contemporary festival into unflattering contrast, as a call to action, and it had many willing readers and followers. The real genius of the Victorians was to couple this nostalgia with a restless passion for progress, along with straightforward commercial instincts, and so lay the foundations for the mammoth spending sprees we experience nowadays. All those innovations had to be manufactured or grown, packaged, shipped, and bought by the householder, who was increasingly a town dweller. Business began to do very well out of Christmas.

Broadly speaking, the Victorian ideal of Christmas spread to all parts of society in the first half of the twentieth century. Since then, crackers may have got better and bigger, paper decorations may have been augmented with plastics, fairy lights may have proliferated, trees got bigger, and growing affluence resulted in growing piles of presents, but the overall trend has been for more of the same rather than any completely new customs. However, something important has indeed been happening. Whereas the Victorians made the family the focus of Christmas, the twentieth century saw this focus shift to the child. As the century progressed, the idea that Christmas was essentially a time for children pervaded our consciousness, until we took it for granted.

It is a truism to say that there have been huge changes in the last fifty years. The increase in the number and size of presents, and the colossal amount of money spent on them, has taken the season to new commercial heights. A poor Christmas for the retail sector has serious economic consequences for the nation. The television has almost wiped out home-made entertainments, and computer games are replacing board games. But small changes are also happening all the time, and these affect the way we celebrate the season, at least outwardly. In the last twenty years or so, charities have almost cornered the Christmas-card market, and now many office-workers circulate lists of those who would prefer to give money directly to charity instead of exchanging cards. Only a few years ago, a handful of people decorated the outside of their houses with lights, and many people thought it the height of bad taste, but each year more and more households have followed the trend, and the displays get bigger and brighter. Large plastic garden figures that glow, flash, and move are now readily available in the shops.

Many of us hold interesting double standards when it comes to Christmas: we love and hate it at the same time, holding the Dickensian ideal in our hearts and minds, but happily embracing changes, large and small, when convenient. Moreover, the child-friendly nature of the modern Christmas contains its own self-reinforcing gene. Because we believe that the season is a time for children, we constantly strive to recreate for our families the Christmases of our own past – not necessarily the physical realities, but the magical atmosphere, the fun, and the warmth and safety of the family; and although many bored teenagers can only be made to tolerate it because their friends are likewise trapped by their families, when they themselves become parents they will most likely start the cycle again.

Before examining the main individual features of the post-Victorian Christmas, two important elements in the history of the festival should be examined. The first is the antique word 'Yule', and how it relates to our idea of Christmas celebrations before the medieval period. The second is the vehement attack on Christmas launched by the Puritans in the seventeenth century, when they almost succeeded in completely eradicating the festival. Both Yule and 'the time they banned Christmas' have taken on heavy symbolic meaning in the popular view of the early history of our most popular festival.

Yule

The word 'Yule' is sometimes used as a semi-synonym for 'Christmas', but in current everyday language it has the slightly false ring of the deliberately antique. The word certainly pre-dates 'Christmas' in English, but its meaning has been so vague in earlier times that it can confuse even the experts. Variations of 'Yule' existed in most Germanic and Scandinavian languages, signifying an apparently loosely defined midwinter period, although there has been no consensus on its ultimate etymology. Bede reported that our Anglo-Saxon ancestors used the word to refer to both of the modern months of December and January, and it is clear that after the conversion to Christianity it was also used as the standard word for the festival of the Nativity. 'Christmas' only entered the language around the turn of the twelfth century.

The word 'Yule' seems to have simply gone out of fashion, as 'winter', 'midwinter', and 'Christmas' took its various meanings, but it lingered longer in the areas of Danish settlement and thus remained the normal alternative dialect word for Christmas in the northern counties, the East Midlands, and Scotland. It also survived in phrases such as 'yule log', 'yule candle', and 'yule baby'.

The perceived falseness of the word probably originated with the nineteenth-century writers who deliberately adopted it to conjure up the Christmas celebrations of an earlier and largely mythical Merrie England golden age. In more recent times, this tendency has led other popular writers to assume that 'Yule' referred to a pre-Christian midwinter festival, or a suitably muscular Anglo-Saxon Christianity, and to use it as a label for their own romantic inventions.

See also **24 December: Yule Log; Christmas: Candles; Christmas: Food**.

Christmas banned

The banning of Christmas by Parliament in the mid seventeenth century is well known, but is not always understood as the culmination of a long and bitter struggle for the soul of the festival, which had been in play since the Reformation. Sixteenth-century moralists had not been averse to taking shots at the way the people celebrated the birth of Christ, and Philip Stubbes's *Anatomie of Abuses* (1583) provides us with an excellent contemporary view of these celebrations, as well as his objections to them:

> But especially in Christmas time there is nothing else used but cards, dice, tables, masking, mumming, bowling, and such like fooleries. And the reason is, for that they think they have a commission and prerogative [at] that time, to do what they list, and to follow what vanity they will. But (alas) do they think that they are privileged at that time to do evil? . . . But what will they say? Is it not Christmas? must we not be merry? Truth it is, we ought both then, and at all times besides, to be merry in the Lord, but not otherwise, not to swill and gull in more than will suffice nature, nor to lavish forth more at that time than at other times. But the true celebration of the feast of Christmas is to meditate . . . upon the incarnation and birth of Jesus Christ, God and man.

These same problems have echoed down the ages, with folk being told to celebrate and be merry on one hand, and then being chastised for doing it the wrong way on the other. However, the real difference sixty years later was not simply that the Puritans were finally in charge and could take drastic action against the parts of the Christmas festivities that they disliked, but that they were against the festival of Christmas *per se*. On 8 June 1647, *An Ordinance for Abolishing of Festivals* was passed:

> *Forasmuch as the Feasts of the Nativity of Christ, Easter, and Whitsuntide, and other Festivals commonly called Holy-Days, have been heretofore superstitiously used and observed. Be it Ordained, by the Lords and Commons in Parliament assembled, that the said Feast of the Nativity of Christ, Easter and Whitsuntide, and all other Festival days, commonly called Holy-days, be no longer observed as Festivals or Holy-days within this Kingdom of England and Dominion of Wales.*

Five years later, on 24 December, they had to try again:

> *Resolved by the Parliament: That the markets be kept tomorrow, being the five-and-twentieth day of December . . . That all such persons as shall open their shops on that day be protected from wrong or violence, and the offenders punished. That no observation shall be had of the five-and-twentieth day of December, commonly called Christmas Day.*

The people were granted the second Tuesday in every month for recreation and relaxation, to compensate for the loss of their old holidays. Nevertheless, the reformers scored something of an own goal in their efforts to abolish the festival. The fate of Christmas became a rallying point for those opposed to the new reforms, and a symbolic personification of 'Old Father Christmas' became spokesman for the opposition. Numerous pamphlets and prints appeared that featured him and contrasted the miserable and gloomy piety of the Puritan outlook with the jolliness of the traditional festivities of 'the old days'. Opposition to the ban took many forms. Some refused to open their shops, some continued to eat roast meat and 'Christmas pies' on the day, and others, like the London diarist John Evelyn, went to semi-secret church services:

> [25 December 1657] *I went with my wife, etc. to London to celebrate Christmas Day. Mr. Gunning preaching in Exeter Chapel . . . as he was giving us the holy Sacrament, the chapel was surrounded with soldiers: all the communicants and assembly surprised and kept prisoners by them, some in the house, others carried away . . . These wretched miscreants held their muskets against us as we came up to receive the Sacred Elements, as if they would have shot us at the altar, but yet suffering us to finish the office of communion, as perhaps not in their instructions.*

All this was swept aside in England at the Restoration, and Old Father Christmas was triumphant. The Scottish Church, however, continued to frown on Christmas and the direct result was the sharp divergence between the ways the two neighbouring countries celebrated the season. Whereas the English celebrated Christmas as their major winter festival, the Scots opted for the secular New Year, and it is only in the last few decades that these national differences have finally begun to break down.

Candles

The pre-Reformation Church made a point of having plenty of candles ablaze for its Christmas services, as is fitting for a celebration in the darkest days of midwinter. In much later years, there was also a strong tradition of having a special Christmas candle in homes. The 'yule candle' was much larger than an average domestic candle, being about 18 inches tall, and was often presented as a gift to regular customers by grocers and other tradesmen. They were sometimes coloured or decorated with evergreens, and were put in a place of honour in the family home and treated with respect. Several of the superstitions that surrounded the yule log were also appropriated to the candle, in particular the idea of keeping a piece until next year, for luck. It was also considered bad luck if the candle would not light easily, or if it was moved while alight, and it was even more important that no one snuffed it out, as folklorist Sidney Oldall Addy reported from the Sheffield area in the 1890s:

> *A candle or lamp should be left burning all night on Christmas Eve. Unless this is done there will be a death in the house.*

The earliest description of a yule candle only dates

from 1817, but several others appeared in the following decades, showing that it was well known before Victoria came to the throne. However, all these nineteenth- and twentieth-century descriptions come from Yorkshire, or closely neighbouring areas, and it would appear that the custom was exclusive to that county, but for a single earlier reference from elsewhere. Parson James Woodforde, of Weston Longeville, in Norfolk, casually recorded in his diary on Christmas Day 1790, 'I lighted my large wax-candle being Xmas day during tea-time this afternoon for about an hour', so it seems that the idea of a special candle had some wider and older presence at that time, although as yet it is not clear just how much.

See also **24 December: Yule Log**.

Cards

The Christmas card is another example of how the new re-modelled Christmas, taking shape in the mid nineteenth century, stole bits and pieces from other festivals and recycled them into new customs (*see* **Christmas**, *above*). There had long been a tradition of sending New Year verses to friends and family, but by the mid nineteenth century Christmas was already starting to steal the limelight. The first identifiable Christmas card was designed by John Calcott Horsley, at the instigation of Henry Cole, in 1843. It presented three panels, the larger one in the middle depicting a family sitting round a well-stocked table, while the outer sections showed a man and a woman in the act of giving charity to the poor and needy. The centre panel also bore the legend 'A Merry Christmas and a Happy New Year to You'. The idea caught on relatively quickly, and by the 1860s a range of cheap cards was commercially available.

One superstition concerns the pictures that can be found on Christmas cards, and is linked to the formerly widespread belief that a wild bird entering one's house spells death for someone in the family – a belief that was extended by some to include birds depicted on wallpaper, crockery, and even seasonal cards. Whereas most of us are happy to see chirpy robins on the cards we receive, others are therefore horrified. In 1955, the journal *Folk-Lore* recorded that in Gloucestershire:

A young woman told me it was a death sign to

receive a Christmas card with a robin on it. This saying dashed me considerably at the time, as I had just had cards with robins printed. However, I sent them out in spite of the warning, and I am happy to say that there was no undue mortality amongst my friends that year.

The superstition was still being reported in the 1990s, so there are presumably still people who worry about such things.

Carol Singers

The mark of the astonishing success of the modern Christmas as a popular festival is that it can be all things to all people, and within its elastic parameters each person has plenty of room for individual choices. Christmas carols are just one seasonal element among many, but even here there are various ways in which we encounter them. We may sing them at school, hear them piped around the supermarket ad nauseam, or performed by a group in period costume at the shopping centre, in aid of charity, or in a splendid ecclesiastical setting. In his book *The English Folk Carol* (1967), Douglas Brice writes, 'One of the most wonderful experiences that can come the way of anyone living in the north-west of England is to be present in the Anglican cathedral in Liverpool for the annual Carol Service at Christmas time.'

However, we all know, in our Dickensian hearts, that carol singers should be heard through a cottage window on a clear cold frosty night in deepest rural England. This may be an unattainable dream for most of us nowadays, but it was indeed the reality only a hundred years ago, as shown by author Alison Uttley's memories of Derbyshire Christmases about 1890:

She hung her stocking at the foot of the bed and fell asleep. But soon singing roused her, and she sat up, bewildered. Yes, it was the carol-singers. Margaret came running upstairs and wrapped her in a blanket. She took her across the landing to her own room, and pulled up the linen blind. Outside under the stars she could see the group of men and women, with lanterns throwing beams across the paths and on to the stable door. One man stood apart beating time, another played a fiddle and another had a flute. The rest sang in four parts the Christmas hymns, 'While shepherds watched', 'Come all ye faithful', and 'Hark the herald angels sing' . . . They trooped, chattering and puffing out their cheeks, and clapping their arms round their bodies, to the front door. They were going into the parlour for elderberry wine and their collection money. A bright light flickered across the snow as the door was flung wide open. Then a bang, and Susan went back to bed.

The songs in today's basic carol repertoire are a pleasantly mixed hotchpotch of different periods and styles, although we like to think of them as timeless. A few are indeed traditional, in the sense that they originated before the mid nineteenth century and show signs of transmission over the generations by informal means, and usually their authors are not known; these include 'The Holly and the Ivy', 'God Rest Ye Merry, Gentlemen', 'As I Sat on a Sunny Bank', and 'The Cherry Tree Carol'. But most are the work of nineteenth-century enthusiasts. Some are American: 'We Three Kings of Orient Are' was written *c.*1857 by Dr John Henry Hopkins of Williamsport, and 'Away in a Manger' was first published in the American Lutheran collection *A Little Children's Book for Schools and Families*, in 1885. 'Silent Night' was written by parish priest Joseph Mohr and schoolteacher/organist Franz Gruber, of Hallein, Austria, in 1818, but 'While Shepherds Watched' is older, being written by Irish clergyman Nahum Tate and Nicholas Brady *c.*1700. While modern carols are written all the time, adding to the repertoire of choirs and professional singers, few new pieces have tunes that are sufficiently memorable to really catch on with the public.

Crackers

The Christmas cracker was invented by London confectioner Tom Smith, in 1847. He got the original idea from seeing *bon-bons* – sugared almonds sold in twists of tissue paper – on sale in Paris in 1840, and although he experimented with the idea for a few years, he was inspired to invent the essential 'snapper' after seeing a log crackling in the fire. The new Christmas novelty was an immediate success, and the firm of Tom Smith's was the leading cracker manufacturer in Britain for the next 150 years, with countless variations on the basic design.

Decorations

Until 150 years ago, the term 'Christmas decorations' simply meant evergreens and candles. Churchwardens' accounts throughout the sixteenth and the first half of the seventeenth century often include payments for plants at Christmas, and we know from John Stow's *Survey of London* (1598) that homes and streets were also decorated in the same way. All kinds of plants seem to have been used, including mistletoe, box, laurel, cypress, yew, rosemary, and bay, or, as Stow commented, 'whatsoever the season of the year afforded to be green'. However, holly and ivy were unquestionably the perennial favourites. Robert Herrick's oft-quoted poem 'Ceremonies for Candlemasse Eve' (1648) cautions readers to take decorations down on the day, and includes the usual items:

Down with the rosemary and the bays
Down with the mistletoe
In stead of holly, now up-raise
The greener box (for show).

And in 1827, a correspondent to the *Gentleman's Magazine* referred to decorations in Surrey:

Then may be seen the windows, the mantel-pieces, and the well-arranged kitchen shelves, clothed in the green holly with its scarlet berry, while in the hall of the hospitable mansion, in the farm house, and even in the humble labourer's cottage, the mystic mistletoe has its share of attraction – frequently suspended from the ceiling, in a large cluster of boughs rich in green leaves and white berries – the mirth-exciting challenger of youth, and the test of maiden coyness. Every kiss beneath it is entitled to the forfeiture of a berry fresh plucked from the bough; and it sometimes happens that ere the Christmas holidays are over the branches and the leaves are all that can be seen of the mistletoe.

It seems that there was little change from Herrick's time to the Victorian watershed, apart from during the Interregnum, when Christmas was banned. However, as in so many other spheres, the Victorians could leave nothing 'unimproved'. New tastes, new sensibilities, and new technology were brought to bear on decorations as on every other aspect of English culture. The

Girls Own Paper of Christmas 1887 recorded the changing mood:

> In this progressive nineteenth century Christmas decorations in churches have attained their highest perfection. Many of our readers may still remember the time when they simply consisted in garnishing the square, high-backed pews with small sprays of scarlet-berried holly, while large, clumsy boughs of box and laurels were distributed promiscuously over the sacred building, with no regard to fitness or symmetry.

Many houses held to the traditional ways for some time, but the scale of the operation had grown. J. S. Fletcher recalled his childhood Christmases in Yorkshire in the 1870s:

> On Christmas Eve they completed the decorations. Nowadays one never sees the decorations which everybody used to put up at that time. Every parlour and kitchen in the house was liberally ornamented with holly, ivy, laurel, box, and yew. The kitchens were like green bowers, for the men-servants and maid-servants gave all their spare time to decorating them for a week before Christmas. You may be quite certain that sprigs of mistletoe hung in every room and in every doorway. In those days they knew nothing of the new-fangled importation of German ideas about Christmas, from which we suffer nowadays.

However, for the first time choices were available. Hannah Cullwick, working as a servant in London about the same time as J. S. Fletcher was growing up in Yorkshire, recorded some Christmases in her diary, and occasionally mentioned the decorations. In the 1870s, she was working as general maidservant in a London house, along with a German girl called Clara:

> [24 December 1871] I wanted them both to come and see Clara's German way o' decorating for Christmas first thing in the morning . . . [25 December] Clara was up at 5 o'clock, hammering in the kitchen I could hear but we wasn't to come down afore 7 to see it all finish'd and ready. It was certainly very gay-looking and pretty. Colour'd paper cut and done in festoons all round the top o' the kitchen, and holly trimmings around the lower part [and on] one side o' the kitchen

> hung a picture of Jesus in the manger, Joseph and Mary and the wise men, and the oxen there too in the stall. Then under the picture was a table spread with presents for each of us, and nuts, biscuits and oranges too, and in the middle was the box o' music playing and a dozen colour'd candles burning. All very pleasing and gay to the senses, but with it all I felt afraid it was too much, too much for Missis to hear of, and Miss Margaret to see, for Missis wouldn't allow us 6d worth of holly and have none themselves.

Little of this would have seemed out of place in an English kitchen a few years later.

One aspect of Victorian Christmas decoration that is not so popular nowadays is the making of mottoes. Although many people still buy a banner, large or small, saying 'Merry Christmas', in the Victorian middle-class home, and church, one of the central features was a lovingly hand-crafted motto proclaiming a suitable text such as 'Peace and Goodwill to All'. These were made in a wide variety of ways, including the use of flower petals and leaves to spell out the words, and they were given pride of place in the room, or the church. On 25 December 1862, George James Dew of Lower Heyford, Oxford, recorded in his diary that:

> Heyford church is more neatly decorated this Christmas than it has been before in my recollection. As you enter the church over the porch doorway is 'Emmanuel' in large letters made of bay leaves. The front of the gallery has a border of evergreens with 'Unto us a Child is Born' made of variegated ivy; the word 'Child' is on the middle panel and larger than the rest which gives it an appearance of neatness and good style. On the chancel arch is 'Glory to God in the Highest' made in holly leaves . . . Taking it as a whole it is very prettily and neatly arranged.

Christmas decorations were being taken more seriously than ever before, and the pressure was on for more tasteful arrangements, brighter colours, and new materials. Developments can be traced through the issues of popular magazines, especially those aimed at women and girls, which started to run regular pieces on what and what not to do, and set the pattern for the countless articles that still appear every year. One of the many problems on which advice was regularly sought was how to manage in towns, where real evergreens were either hard to come by or not up to standard, for example when the holly for sale had no berries. However, the *Girls Own Paper* for 11 December 1880 had the answer:

> Ivy berries or dried peas dyed red (a sixpenny bottle of dye will be sufficient for a very large quantity); or, putty rolled into little balls and coloured either in the same way or in a solution of sealing wax mixed with spirits of wine; or red wax, to be bought at an oil shop, and shaped into berries after slightly softening before the fire. There are many different sorts of red berries to be had in the autumn, which, by soaking in strong salt and water, will keep till Christmas time, and may well pass for holly. And, lastly, easiest of all, artificial berries are sold in bunches very cheaply at most toy shops.

A number of superstitions clustered around Christmas decorations until relatively recent times, but the only real remnant is the question of when they should be taken down, and here again there has been a major sea change. As indicated in Herrick's poem, quoted above, in the mid seventeenth century Christmas decorations were expected to stay in place until Candlemas (2 February), and this remained the norm until the nineteenth century. This may seem a long time, but until the late nineteenth century it was usual to put up home and church decorations on Christmas Eve, and although offices and shops might steal a few days' march, nobody would have thought of putting them up before Christmas week. Nowadays, it is quite common to see home decorations in place two weeks before Christmas Day, and some shops even signal the start of the season in the last two weeks of November. During the Victorian era, however, the Christmas season was dramatically shortened, and people began to remove decorations in early January. It is now almost universally agreed that the day for removing the decorations is Twelfth Night, and that it is 'unlucky' to leave them any longer. But now that Twelfth Night has lost all other meaning, many people think that the Christmas decorations begin to look a bit sad after the New Year celebrations, and it is quite likely that the trend will develop towards removing them around 2 January.

There is little else to concern even the most superstitious among us today, but for the Victorians there was plenty to worry about in this sphere. In 1874, *Notes & Queries* recorded:

> It is still a prevailing idea, in some places, that if their decorations be not cleared out of the church by Candlemas Day (2 February), there will within the year, be a death in the family occupying the pew in which a berry or leaf is to be found on the later festival. Mr. Glyde, in his Norfolk Garland, quotes an East Anglian authority as follows: 'An old lady whom I knew was so persuaded of the truth of this superstition that she would not be contented to leave the clearing of her pew to the constituted authorities, but used to send her servant to see that her own seat, at any rate, was free from danger.'

Similarly, bringing holly into the house at any time except Christmas was believed to result in a death. It was also widely believed that the two common types of holly, prickly and smooth, were, respectively, male and female, and that whichever type of holly was brought into the house first determined who would be the master in the coming year. Some people were not keen on ivy, as it reminded them of cemeteries, and made sure it did not dominate in the house.

However, the burning question, quite literally, of the late nineteenth century was what to do with the evergreens when they were taken down. Some people held that they should be burnt, as soon and as completely as possible. But another camp recoiled in horror at this idea, and treated their old decorations with ceremony, even reverence. Some fed them to the farm animals to ensure that they shared in the household's luck, while others laid them carefully on the rubbish heap. It is reasonably clear from the documentary evidence that this is another of the changes that occurred in mid Victorian times. Up to the 1860s, it was commonplace to burn the decorations, and it is only from that point on that people started to worry about it.

One thing the Victorians did not invent was kissing under the mistletoe. Indeed, one of the worries expressed by traditionalists when the Christmas tree began to make inroads into British homes was that it would replace the traditional 'kissing bough'. The latter was the centrepiece of decoration in the early nineteenth century, made in various ways but usually

Mistletoe seller (*Illustrated London News*, 1853)

with two hoops set at right angles to make a globe, or a horizontal hoop with vertical semi-circles to make a 'crown'. This was then covered in greenery, with holly predominant, and a large bunch of mistletoe hanging in the centre, and the whole thing was suspended from the ceiling. As already shown, mistletoe formed part of the Christmas greenery since at least the sixteenth century, but we cannot find a mention of kissing underneath it before the 1813 edition of John Brand's *Observations on the Popular Antiquities of Great Britain* – although other references soon afterwards show it was already well known by that time. Charles Dickens gives a delightful picture of Christmas in a country farmhouse in his *Pickwick Papers* (1837), in which the branch of mistletoe hanging from the kitchen ceiling causes such a scene of 'struggling and confusion' and hiding in corners, as the men try to capture and kiss the women, and some maids indeed were so confused that they stood under the branch without realizing it.

Most people nowadays say that the kissing is 'for luck', but a number of ancillary beliefs accrued to the custom in the past. It was believed that any girl who was not kissed, for example, would not get married in the coming year, but that a maiden could dream of her future husband by putting some of the mistletoe under her pillow at night. In an echo of the controversy about burning decorations, some clinched the argument by asserting that 'If mistletoe be not burned all couples who have kissed beneath it will be foes before the end of the year.' It was also believed that mistletoe protected the house from being struck by lightning, but that power is also claimed of many other plants.

A word has to be said about the supposed 'pagan origins' of Christmas decorations. It is usually assumed that the pre-Christian inhabitants of what later became England celebrated the winter solstice by decorating their houses and temples with greenery, but there is no evidence that this was the case, and it is yet another example of a later assumption being used to colour in a past of which we know very little. Another groundless but persistent notion is that mistletoe was officially banned from Christian churches because of its pagan connotations. The idea stems from the well-known description by Pliny, *c.* AD 77, that speaks of Druids holding mistletoe sacred and harvesting it with a golden sickle. However, there is plenty of evidence that mistletoe was once used in Christian churches and homes, along with other evergreens, and it is quite clear that the question of the suitability of mistletoe has only been raised since antiquarians and learned clergymen started reading Pliny about 1,600 years after his time. Indeed, on closer inspection, it can be seen that the notion is based in any case on a series of assumptions: firstly, that Pliny was correct in his description; secondly, that what was written about Gaul was also true of England; thirdly, that the mistletoe ceremony lasted for another 500 years until Christianization, despite the huge upheavals of Romans leaving and Anglo-Saxons settling; fourthly, that the early English churches knew about the mistletoe ceremony and were sufficiently worried to ban this, and only this, plant from their churches; and finally that they did so without leaving any trace in any written laws or regulations. Nevertheless, groundless as it is, there are still occasional reports of local vicars trying to ban the plant from their churches on the grounds of its pagan connotations.

Entertainments

The cake and the nut-brown ale, the toast and the rich elder wine, are freely dispensed to every visitor, and the usual distinctions of rank are in a great degree forgotten amid the general hilarity of the season. It is the holiday of every class, and mirth and good-fellowship reign without control.

> *Gentleman's Magazine (1827)*

Aside from food and drink, the most commonly mentioned desirable for a proper Christmas has long been a good helping of 'mirth and good-fellowship', but with a degree of social conscience. Most of the nineteenth-century writers who bemoaned the Christmas festivities at that time harked back to a golden age of previous generations, focusing on universal hospitality and charity. To a certain extent, they were hankering for a romanticized **Merrie England** (p. 372), but it is true that a strong tradition of hospitality had existed since medieval times and still lingered into the Victorian era. Rural landowners often provided a communal feast for their tenants, farmers for their workers, and others entertained the poor. William

Dancing has been a key feature of the Christmas party for centuries (George Cruickshank, *Comic Almanac*, 1840)

Holland, parson of Overstowey, Somerset, from 1779 to 1819, entertained various people from the community in his rectory, and he often recorded his Christmas Day activities in his diary:

> [25 December 1799] *The kitchen was tolerably well lined with my poor neighbours, workmen, etc. Many of them staid till past ten o'clock and sang very melodiously. Sent half a crown to our church musicians who had serenaded the family this cold morning at five o'clock.*

Games played by the family have long been another feature of the season, and although the Victorians are rightly credited with making the family the focus of Christmas (*see* **Christmas**), there are indications that family games were played in some quarters well before their time, albeit to a lesser degree. Accounts of earlier festivities often mention what could be called 'parlour games', some of which are still recognizable, while others have gone completely out of fashion:

Round About Our Coal Fire (1740) lists 'Blind Man's Buff and Puss in the Corner, Questions and Commands, Hoop and Hide, cards and dice', while the *Gentleman's Magazine* of 1828 comments that 'Blind Man's Buff, Hunt the Slipper, the Game of Goose, Snap Dragon, Push Pin, and dancing, form the amusements of the younger part of the assemblage; whilst cards occupy the elders'.

Blind Man's Buff, also known under other names, including 'Hoodman Blind', has a particularly long history. It was first mentioned by name in the sixteenth century, but fourteenth-century illustrations in the Bodleian Library, first published by Joseph Strutt in his *Sports and Pastimes of the People of England* (1801), clearly depict the same game, and it has remained popular until the present day. Many writers have referred to it over the years, including Samuel Pepys, Oliver Goldsmith, Emily Tennyson, and Charles Dickens. In earlier times, the game was rougher than it tends to be nowadays; the word 'buff' means a blow, and the blindfolded player could be buffeted by the others, using their hoods or knotted scarves.

Snap Dragon was also mentioned frequently as a Christmas diversion, but it is unlikely that anyone plays it now, and certainly not if children are around. Raisins were placed in a dish of lighted brandy, and players had to snatch the fruit and eat it without getting burnt, which could only be done with quick decisive movements. Another perennial favourite for the season was cards, and even those who did not play cards during the rest of the year were often persuaded to play at Christmas.

Dancing was a key element of the Christmas party for centuries, which is one of the reasons why the Puritans disliked the festival so much. Thomas Hardy, writing in the 1870s of a previous Dorset generation to his own, provided a slightly romanticized but essentially accurate description of a Christmas party that tranter (horse and cart purveyor) Reuben Dewy and his wife Susan threw for their neighbours and friends, in *Under the Greenwood Tree* (1872). The evening is spent eating and drinking and being sociable, and after a while there is singing, too, and everyone performs their party piece. The young people are ready to dance at ten o'clock, but their elders insist that no 'jigging' take place until after the holy day itself has expired. At the stroke of midnight, the band strikes up, men remove their jackets, and for the next few hours country dances like the Triumph, and Step and Fetch Her, are performed with vigour or grace, depending on the skill and character of the individual dancer. They shortly reach a point where the movement, the music, and the heat seem to possess the cottage room:

> ... when the very fiddlers as well as the dancers get red in the face, the dancers having advanced further still towards incandescence, and entered the cadaverous phase; the fiddlers no longer sit down, but kick back their chairs and saw madly at the strings with legs firmly spread and eyes closed, regardless of the visible world.

Hardy was a fiddler himself, so he must have known all this from first-hand experience. Charles Dickens described a similar farmhouse scene in the *Pickwick Papers* (1837), but higher up the social scale dances will have been less vigorous, with waltzes and quadrilles, but no less enjoyable for the participants.

One element of Christmas past that has virtually disappeared is storytelling. From at least the eighteenth century onwards, there was a very strong tradition of the family gathering to tell stories round the fire which, at this season at least, was often a 'roaring' one. A Christmas storytelling session would almost always be dominated by stories of the supernatural – ghosts, witches, fairies, hobgoblins, and the Devil himself. These tales were all the more scary for the youngsters present because they usually referred to people and places in the immediate neighbourhood, so that many a listener dreaded going to bed, or worse, going outside, for the rest of the evening. They may have drawn some comfort from the widespread notion that Christmas Day was the one day of the year when evil was reputed to have been powerless. Storytelling has long been replaced by radio and television programmes, but the feeling that the time is appropriate for ghost stories still lingers in the media schedules, although it has now been eclipsed by Hallowe'en.

Nevertheless, Christmas was not all polite parlour games, dances, and stories. Some families had broader tastes, and although their entertainments were not usually recorded for posterity, we occasionally get a glimpse of them in a memoir, as in the following description by Derek Sheffield of his family gatherings in Kent in the 1930s:

> Most of the games were very physical and earthy in the extreme, but that was country humour; it made us laugh. All would be cleared away, the washing-up done, and the best table cloth laid in preparation for the next event of the day: my Uncle Bill's particular forte, an indoor firework display. A tin tray would be put on the table, and on it would be placed a tissue paper taken from one of the crackers with a map printed on it. One would place a lighted cigarette on the spot marked with an X, and it smouldered away and finally exploded with a sharp bang which would make everyone leap out of their skins. Things would get more interesting, with more adventurous and more revolting fireworks in the form of small pyramids which, when ignited, would give off dense clouds of smoke, splutter like a sparkler, and emit a

strange worm-like object that grew at an incredible rate and writhed all over the table, causing the ladies to scream with pretended horror and come over all faint. The pièce de résistance was a white statuette of a little boy about six inches high and made from plaster. He was in crouching position with his trousers down around his ankles, his shirt up over his back, and his bottom exposed for all to see. We waited with baited breath for what was to come – Uncle Bill, by this time laughing so much that he could hardly see, would poke a special indoor firework into the statuette's rear end and light it with a match, the result being that it would begin to blow smoke rings. It would then start to spark and splutter, which would make us weep with hysterics, and finally a large worm-like object would emerge and begin to crawl all over the table. The men would make all sorts of ribald remarks, much to the annoyance of the women. 'I reckon he's bin on one of mother's plum pies,' Grandad would say.

Father Christmas/Santa Claus

The Christmas festival had been personified in song, poetry, and drama centuries before the character of the modern Father Christmas emerged in the late Victorian period. There was a Sir Christmas, for example, in a mid fifteenth-century carol, and Lords of Misrule of the period, appointed to organize the season's festivities at the royal court and in other noble families, were sometimes given titles such as Captain or Prince Christmas. In the pamphlet war during the Puritan attack on the festival in the 1650s, Old Father Christmas emerged as the symbol and spokesman of the 'good old days' of feasting and good cheer, in stark contrast to the gloomy piety offered by the reformers, and from the Restoration to the mid nineteenth century this same character continued to be regarded as the presiding spirit of the festival. Nevertheless, he had a fairly low profile, and none of these pre-Victorian Christmas characters had any connection with presents, nocturnal visits to children, or any of the other trappings of the modern Father Christmas. By the early days of Victoria's reign, however, he had begun to take on a much more active role, as Christmas itself was remodelled (*see* **Christmas**). He started to appear regularly in

illustrated magazines, in a wide variety of costumes, but was almost always jolly-faced and bearded, and usually wore holly on his head. He was often surrounded with pictures of plentiful food and drink, and with images of people enjoying themselves. Yet this proto-Father Christmas was in for a great shock, as the figure of Santa Claus was about to appear on the scene.

The development of Santa Claus in America is well known, although some of the details still need to be pinned down. His main creator, Clement C. Moore (1779–1863), an Episcopal minister in New York, is not remembered for his life's work, the *Hebrew and English Lexicon*, but for a poem he composed for his children – 'The Visit of St. Nicholas', now universally known by the title based on its first line, 'The Night Before Christmas'. It was published in 1822, but, despite its immense success, Moore was not proud of his poem and refused to acknowledge authorship for over twenty years. Basing his invention on Dutch folklore, Moore gave to the world St Nicholas as a nocturnal Christmas gift-bringer, with sleigh, reindeer, and a sack of toys on his back, who entered the house via its chimney and filled children's stockings with toys and sweets. The verses imply that St Nicholas is small and elf-like, although he has a jolly rounded shape, and the sleigh is 'miniature' and the reindeer 'tiny'. However, Moore neglected to describe St Nicholas' costume, or even mention its colour, which led to great confusion over the following decades.

'St Nicholas' was soon shortened to Santa Claus, and as he featured in stories such as Susan Warner's *Carl Krinken; or the Christmas Stocking,* published in New York and London in 1854, the details of his visits on Christmas Eve became known to most American families. However, his physical appearance had not yet become fixed. Thomas Nast, illustrating an influential edition of Moore's poem in 1881, depicted Santa as white-bearded, fat, and jolly, and wearing a belted jacket similar to the one he is shown wearing today, but other artists of the time dressed him in a variety of costumes, and even in the early twentieth century he could be portrayed as wearing a green or blue outfit. The well-known Coca-Cola advertising campaign of 1931 put the seal of international mass media approval on the red costume.

Santa Claus seems to have reached England in the

Father Christmas, postcard, *c.*1910. It took many years for the Father Christmas costume to become fixed

1860s, at the time when many other Christmas innovations, such as stockings, crackers and cards, were being introduced, and slowly but surely Father Christmas took on Santa's attributes so that the two are now, to all intents and purposes, indistinguishable. Nevertheless, some English people still prefer their children to say 'Father Christmas' in preference to 'Santa', nearly 150 years after Santa's importation to England.

Attempts to trace Santa Claus back to shamans of Siberia, whose religious ecstasies were reputedly fuelled by magic mushrooms, are far-fetched and unnecessary.

Food

The one enduring feature of Christmas, since records began, has been the desire to eat well at the season. The wealthy would indulge in huge, lavish banquets during the festival, but they could do that at any time of year. For the vast majority of the population, Christmas was the one time when they could hope to have something special on the table, in sufficient quantity, and everyone tried hard to achieve at least some semblance of a feast. However, it should be remembered that before the mid twentieth century many people could not afford what the rest took for granted. For all the talk of turkeys and geese, many nineteenth-century families were delighted to get a couple of rabbits, or any meat at all, for their Christmas dinner. The strong tradition of charity at Christmas therefore played an important role in providing something special for the poor family's table, especially in rural areas. Farmers often gave a bird or joint to their workers as a sort of Christmas bonus, and paternalistic squires provided meals for poor tenants and workhouse residents. Local clergymen also did the same on a smaller scale, but the effectiveness of this type of charity was naturally patchy, and it only functioned properly in a stable hierarchical society. It also came with the price of expected servility and gratitude on the part of the 'deserving poor'.

Asked to name the staple foodstuffs of the modern Christmas season, most people would answer, 'Turkey, Christmas pudding, Christmas cake, and mince pies.' Even if we choose to ignore tradition and eat something completely different, we know that these four items will be on countless tables each year; and even though we, too, can eat them at any other time of year if we wish, many still feel that these four foodstuffs are an intrinsic part of the season. Each of these items has a long history, but numerous other festive foods, now completely forgotten, were just as popular on a national scale, and an even greater number were eaten at a regional or local level but were not known outside their own area. Add to this the class differences within society, and it is very difficult to summarize seasonal food adequately.

The main meat for the Christmas dinner has always had a high profile and has varied considerably over the past 500 years. The three most widely known staples were roast beef, goose, and turkey. Roast beef had long been the symbolic staple of English food, and until the nineteenth century it was by far the most often quoted symbol of good food at Christmas. As a character in the typical Hampshire mummers' play declaims:

Roast beef, plum pudding, and mince pie
Who likes that any better than I?

Although turkey and goose gradually replaced roast beef as the archetypal Christmas fare, many traditionalist families stuck firmly with beef throughout the Victorian period. Turkeys were already being bred and eaten in Britain in the mid sixteenth century and were quickly associated with Christmas in the more wealthy sections of the community. They joined the ranks of swans, peacocks, and other exotic birds that were regularly served at banquets, and they filtered down the social scale only very gradually. However, by the mid nineteenth century, broadly speaking, the middle classes were eating turkey and the poor ate goose, the turkey only achieving full dominance during the first half of the twentieth century. Geese were considerably cheaper than turkeys, but whatever meat was chosen for the Christmas dinner, it was usually out of the range of most working people's pockets, and one very useful Victorian invention for the working family was the 'goose club', in which members would pay a small sum each week to save up for their Christmas bird or joint of meat. Clubs were organized on a very local scale by pubs, provision dealers, or on an ad hoc basis between members, and they varied widely in what they offered in addition to the basic goose, with some managing to throw in a Christmas pudding or bottle of something in addition to the bird. One standard feature, however, was the drawing of lots to decide who got what. The geese, when delivered for distribution to club members, would vary in size and quality, and lots would be drawn by some impartial person, to ensure fairness. The meeting of the goose club was a convivial event in itself, and some reformers criticized the whole business as leading people to drink, but goose clubs served a very useful purpose, and the idea continued throughout the twentieth century in the form of various Christmas clubs offered by local shops and businesses.

The other convention which has now disappeared is the use of a communal oven to cook the dinner. Few ordinary families, in country or town, had ovens big enough to take a whole turkey or goose, and it was quite common for the whole community to take their main meat to the local baker's shop to be cooked. Around dinner time a procession of figures could be seen, often consisting of the older children of the family, carefully carrying the cloth-covered dinner back home; and woe betide anyone who dropped the precious burden on the way.

Mince pies, also called shred pies, were already associated with Christmas in the later sixteenth century, but they have changed dramatically since that time. Until the mid nineteenth century they contained real meat, but this was gradually replaced by the dried fruit and spices that we know today, when 'mince-meat' superseded 'minced meat'. Their shape has also changed. They were formerly oblong, and generally referred to as 'coffins', although it was popularly believed that the shape commemorated the manger in which the newborn Christ was laid.

In its earliest form, from at least the fifteenth century, the forerunner of the Christmas pudding also contained meat. It was generally known as 'plum pottage', and was made from chopped beef or mutton and onions, together with dried fruit, breadcrumbs, wine, herbs, and spices. The 'plum' in the name refers to the dried fruit – prunes, raisins, etc. – and the dish was much runnier than the modern pudding. The meat was gradually replaced by suet, and the classic spheroid shape was attained when the mixture became much thicker and boiling in a cloth became the norm. The nineteenth-century version was extremely dense and

had to be boiled for many hours; the trend in modern times has been for lighter mixtures.

Moving on to less familiar items, there was a wide range of delicacies that would surprise the modern Christmas diner. Haggis, for example, hardly sounds like an English Christmas dish, but in one form or another it was regularly eaten in the counties that border on Scotland, as recorded in John Brockett's *Glossary of North Country Words* (1825):

> *Haggis – A north country dish . . . It was, till lately, a common custom among the peasantry of the North of England, to have this fare to breakfast every Christmas-day; and some part of the family sat up all night to have it ready at an early hour. It is now used at dinner on the same day. Sold, savoury and hot, in the Newcastle market.*

It is clear from the numerous accounts that **frumenty** (p. 390) was also regarded as a particular delicacy at Christmas almost everywhere, although it was eaten at other times of the year as well. Another regular Christmas speciality, especially in Victorian northern England, was the 'yule dough' or 'yule baby', described by William Brockie in his collection of Durham superstitions and legends in 1886:

> *And when the child wakens in the morning, sure as fate, in the stocking is a Christmas pie – a yule dough, which is a bit of rich paste rolled out, cut, and baked in the shape of a little baby.*

Like a gingerbread man, the yule baby had currants for eyes and buttons, and sometimes the figure was of a mother holding a baby in her arms.

The Christmas cake as we know it today was simply transferred from Twelfth Night (*see* **6 January: Twelfth Night**), but many other sorts of cake were found in different parts of the country. In Cornwall in the 1870s, according to the *Folk-Lore Journal* (1886):

> *In some parts of the county it is customary for each household to make a batch of currant cakes on Christmas-eve. These cakes are made in the ordinary manner, coloured with saffron, as is the custom in those parts. On this occasion the peculiarity of the cakes is that a small portion of the dough in the centre of each top is pulled up and made into a form*

Subscribers collecting their birds from the local goose club (*Illustrated London News*)

which resembles a very small cake on the top of a large one, and this centre-piece is usually called 'the Christmas'. Each person in a house has his or her especial cake, and every person should taste a small piece of every other person's cake. Similar cakes are also bestowed on the hangers-on of the establishment, such as laundresses, sempstresses, charwomen, etc., and even some people who are in the receipt of weekly charity call, as a matter of course, for their Christmas cakes. The cakes must not be cut until Christmas-day, it being probably 'unlucky to eat them sooner'.

In East Anglia, there were kichels, as described in Edward Moor's dictionary of the Suffolk dialect in 1823:

A flat Christmas cake, of a triangular shape, with sugar and a few currants strowd over the top – differing only in shape, I believe, from a bun.

Many accounts of Christmas food in the past make special mention of meat pies, although there is some confusion here because what we now refer to as a

'mince pie' was, in its previous meat-filled incarnation, called a 'Christmas Pie'. Goose pies were particularly popular in the early nineteenth century, often made specifically from the giblets; John Brockett writes, 'At Christmas hardly any person, however poor, is without a giblet pie.' But sometimes it was the grand mixture of meats that made it so special. John Nicholson described the custom in his *Folk Lore of East Yorkshire* (1890):

In keeping with the hospitality of this season, hotels and inns provide a huge game pie for their customers, and none of the good things provided for this festive time are better than these pies, 'standing pies' they are called, being nearly a foot high, and filled with the choicest morsels of hare, rabbit, pheasant, etc.

One of the most obvious fundamental changes that have taken place in the past hundred years is the relative ease and convenience of modern cooking. In the past, the preparation of each item of the family's diet was not only a chore but also a ritual in itself. A Surrey member of the Women's Institute recalled her child-

Frumenty

Frumenty, or frumety, but often pronounced 'furmety', was both a staple and festive dish often mentioned but rarely described in detail, presumably because its very familiarity made it unnecessary. Its name is derived from the Latin *frumentum*, meaning 'corn'. The basic ingredient was wheat boiled in milk, but as it was made both for everyday use and for ceremonial and festival occasions (especially Christmas), it would have had several degrees of richness and tastiness, depending on the context. The following three descriptions indicate something of the range of variation:

> *The typical method of preparation was to parboil wholegrains of wheat in water, then strain off and boil in milk, sweeten the boiled product with sugar, and flavour with cinnamon and other spices.*

> *A receipt, three hundred years old, runs thus: 'Take clean wheat and bray it in a mortar till the hulls be all gone off, and seethe it till it burst, and take it up and let it cool; and take clean, fresh broth and sweet milk of almonds, or sweet milk of kine, and temper it all, and take yolks of eggs. Boil it a little and wet it down and mess it forth with fat venison or fresh mutton'.*

> *Somerset–Wiltshire: About forty years ago country women in shawls and sun bonnets used to come to the market at Weston-super-Mare in little carts carrying basins of new wheat boiled to a jelly, which was put into a large pot with milk, eggs and sultanas, and was lightly cooked; the resulting mixture was poured into pie-dishes and served on Mid-Lent Sunday and during the ensuing week. Frumenty is still prepared at Devizes for Mothering Sunday.*

It was frumenty (admittedly spiced with rum) that got Michael Henchard into such trouble in Thomas Hardy's novel *The Mayor of Casterbridge* (1886). Numerous references (and almost as many spellings) are given in Joseph Wright's *English Dialect Dictionary* (1900); and references in the *Oxford English Dictionary* commence in the fourteenth century. Folk cookery writer Florence White, who gives detailed instructions on its preparation in her *Good Things in England* (1932), commented, 'It does not seem as if there is any exaggerating in claiming frumenty as our oldest national dish.'

hood Christmases in the book *Surrey Within Living Memory* (1992):

> *Grandmama was less than five feet tall but she ruled her twelve children and 16 grandchildren with a rod of iron. It was she who organised the family preparations for Christmas and as we children became old enough to 'help', the weeks before 25th December became filled with excitement. Pudding making was an activity which involved every member of the family. Raisins, sultanas, prunes, cherries, and lumps of sticky dates had to be washed and laid out on large meat dishes to dry. They took days to reach the stage at which they could be handled. Armed with a sharp knife and a basin of hot water, Grandmama sat in her wing chair before a roaring fire and expertly removed the pips from every single fruit. We children were allowed to grate the suet which came from the butcher in huge lumps. Horrid stuff, suet – so much skin on it, but not on our fingers by the time we had finished. The more responsible of us were given the task of beating the dozens of fresh farm eggs into a foaming yellow mass. Eventually the day dawned for the mixing of all the ingredients. This was done in an earthenware crock normally used for the preserving of eggs. A whole bottle of brandy was added and all the family came together at a set time to stir the mixture and make a wish. If you could get the wooden spoon to stand up in the middle of the glorious-smelling mess then your wish was supposed to come true. I never did get the pony I wished for every time for years. Fourteen greased pudding basins, fourteen cloths, and a ball of string were used to make neat little parcels which were then placed*

in a scullery copper filled with hot water and kept boiling by means of a roaring fire underneath. The puddings were simmered for three days and nights, filling the house with a mouthwatering aroma and clouds of steam which floated about like a fog. I use my Grandmama's recipe today but my fruit and suet come from packets and I only use a small bottle of brandy. Somehow, my puddings do not taste like Grandmama's.

Geese Dancers

Geese-dancing was a well-known activity in Cornwall at Christmas time. The terms 'geese-dancing' or 'goose-dancing' have almost certainly been derived from a local pronunciation of the word 'guise', which in various local forms such as 'guiser' and 'guising' was found all over the country, signifying a custom in which people dressed up, or disguised themselves (*see* **Guisers**, *below*). Even in Cornwall there were wide variations in the custom, and its exact nature is difficult to pin down. Some geese-dancers performed a local variant of the mummers' play (*see* **Christmas: Mummers**), while others simply entered people's houses and engaged in licensed misbehaviour. Jonathan Couch wrote in his *History of Polperro* (1871):

In town, the family, flocking round the mock [yule log], *are interrupted by the cheerfully tolerated intrusion of the goosey-dancers. The boys and girls rifle their parents' wardrobe of old gowns and coats, and disguise themselves, their mien, and speech, so cleverly that it is impossible to identify them. They are allowed, and are not slow to take, the large amount of licence which the season warrants; for it is considered a mark of a churlish disposition to take offence at anything they do or say. Accordingly they enter without ceremony; dance, sing and carry on an extemporaneous dialogue well spiced with native wit. After tasting, unmasked perhaps, whatever may be on the table, they beg some money to make merry with. The children are much amused, and the mummers leave with a benediction.*

However, not everybody was amused by their antics, as recorded in the *Folk-Lore Journal* of 1886:

From Christmas to twelfth-tide parties of mummers

known as Goose or Geese-dancers, paraded the streets in all sorts of disguises, with masks on. They often behaved in such an unruly manner that women and children were afraid to venture out. If the houses were not locked they entered uninvited and stayed, playing all kinds of antics, until money was given to them to go away . . . These goose-dancers became such a terror to the respectable inhabitants of Penzance that the Corporation put them down about ten years since, and every Christmas Eve a notice is posted in conspicuous places forbidding their appearance in the streets, but they still perambulate the streets of St. Ives . . .

Guisers

One of the highlights of the Christmas season for many families in the nineteenth and earlier twentieth centuries was a visit from the 'guisers', although the exact nature of this visit varied considerably from place to place. The word has a long pedigree, and was used all over the country to describe any custom that featured people dressed up or disguised in some way. In Yorkshire, Northumberland, and lowland Scotland, for example, it was one of the regular names for the **mummers** (*see below*), while in Cornwall it was the root of the term **geese dancers** (*see above*). In many of these customs, the dressing-up simply took the form of wearing a costume, as in a play, but in some it was the disguise that played an integral part of the activity, as remembered by Alison Uttley from her Derbyshire childhood in the 1890s:

[After singing a song outside] *they pushed open the door and half entered.*

*God bless the master of this house,
And bless the mistress, too,
And call the little children
That round the table go.
And all your kin and kinsfolk,
That dwell both far and near,
I wish you a merry Christmas,
And a happy New Year.*

'Come in, come in,' shouted Tom, with his broad face wreathed in smiles. Half a dozen young men and a woman stamped their feet and entered, bringing

clots of snow and gusts of sweet icy air. Their faces
were masked and they disguised their voices, speak-
ing in gruff tones or high falsettos, which caused
much gay laughter. They stood in a row in front of
the dresser, and asked riddles of one another: 'How
many sticks go to the building of a crow's nest?'
– 'None, for they are all carried'; 'When is a man
thinner than a lath?' – 'When he's a-shaving'... 'I
know that voice,' returned Joshua, ' 'tis Jim Hodges
from Over Wood way.' 'You're right, Mester Taberner,'
said Jim, as he removed his mask and disclosed his
red cheeks. So the guessing went on, until all the
mummers were unmasked, Dick, Jolly, Tom Snow, Bob
Bird, Sam Roper, and Miriam Webster.

A very similar custom, called 'mummering', was
common in Newfoundland, where it had presumably
been taken by British settlers.

Holy Thorn(s)

In legendary terms, Glastonbury, in Somerset, is probably the most mystical place in England, with several
long-standing stories to its credit. This extraordinary
longevity must largely be attributed to the fact that
the legends themselves have developed with the times,
and have managed to satisfy the needs of successive
groups, so as always to be in vogue somewhere. As
each group has moved on or faded away, others have
taken its place. Over the centuries, Glastonbury devotees have included medieval monks and pilgrims,
eighteenth-century anti-Gregorians, 1960s hippies,
New Age travellers, modern pagans, King Arthur fans
throughout the ages, and nowadays the very fashionable Holy Grail hunters.

The legends themselves have been augmented by
new details over the years, but in their basic form they
tell of how Joseph of Arimathea came to Britain in AD 63
and founded the first Christian church in the country
at Glastonbury, and that King Arthur was buried there.
It is difficult to think of a more potent mix in the legend
stakes (it only lacks a Robin Hood connection to make
it perfect). Joseph appears in the Gospels as the man
who rescued Christ's body and placed it in the tomb,
and later additions showed him journeying to France,
and on to England, with a group of disciples. Some even
claimed that he was the Virgin Mary's uncle. However,

this Glastonbury connection was a blatant invention
by the monks of Glastonbury Abbey, as a clever gambit
in the incessant power struggles within the medieval
church. They were well aware that such stories gave the
abbey a distinct edge over rival religious houses, especially its claim to be the first Christian church in the
land, and they also encouraged the lucrative pilgrimage trade.

By the time the abbey was suppressed in 1539, the
stories had already taken on a life of their own, and
had long outlived their original purpose. Their fame
has ebbed and flowed over the subsequent centuries,
but they have enjoyed a marked renaissance in recent
decades. The ability of romantic legend to replace
prosaic history has been given a huge boost by the
invention of the Internet, and Glastonbury Abbey's
official website blithely claims it as the first Christian
sanctuary in the country, as do countless others.

The one element of this legend that concerns us from
a calendrical point of view is the Holy Thorn, which is
said to have sprung from Joseph's staff when he thrust
it into the ground on arrival at Glastonbury. This
Thorn is internationally famous for blossoming on
Christmas Day, and for 500 years has served the faithful as irrefutable proof of the truth of the Christian
religion. Innumerable people who have never been
near Glastonbury have taken its existence on trust, and
have been comforted and inspired by it. Local thorn
trees are first mentioned in the poem 'Lyfe of Joseph
of Arimathea' (1502), but the Christmas blossom is not
recorded until 1535, when it was apparently already
well known.

The alleged flowering on Christmas Day became a
major *cause célèbre* in the public disquiet after the
introduction of the Gregorian calendar in 1752. The idea
that there were extensive riots under the rallying cry of
'Give us back our eleven days' has now been exploded,
but there was definitely a great deal of concern around
the country for what seemed to be the wanton disre-
gard on the part of the Government for the real 'natural' days of the year. Many who had never taken much
notice of the custom before suddenly realized that a
plant which knew when it was Christmas Day could
be used as an 'objective' test of the new calendar, as
recorded in the *London Daily Advertiser* of 5 Jan 1753:

We hear from Quainton in Buckinghamshire, that upwards of two thousand people came on the 24th of December at night, with lanthorns and candles, to view a black thorn, which grows in that neighbourhood, and which was remembered (this year only) to be a slip from the famous Glastonbury Thorn, that it always budded on the 24th at night, was full blown the next day, and went off at night. But the people finding no buds, nor the appearance of any, it was agreed by all, that the 25th of December N.S. could not possibly be the right Christmas Day, and accordingly refused going to church.

Other holy thorns suddenly appeared elsewhere in the country and, in public hearsay at least, produced the same result. The oft-repeated tale was used to legitimate the anti-Gregorian sentiments of many sections of the population for years to come, and allowed the celebration of Old Christmas Day to continue as a deep-rooted tradition. Nevertheless, according to one published report, in the *Gloucester Journal* of 2 January 1753, the real Glastonbury Thorn was apparently on the Government's side:

To all tender consciences that are afraid of keeping Christmas Day according to the New Style. This is to certify that the Glastonbury Thorn is in full blossom this day, the 25th of December, New Style, as it was ever known to be on 25th of December Old Style.

A century later, anti-Gregorians had another widespread notion to support their dislike of the New Style Christmas, as by that time cattle were known to kneel down in their stalls on the stroke of midnight on Christmas Eve (*see* **24 December: Cattle Kneeling**).

As indicated, there were many other trees with similar attributes, and indeed, there is a marked tendency to claim any remarkable tree as a descendant of the Glastonbury thorn, as they have done at Appleton, in Cheshire (*see* **29 June: Bawming the Thorn**). In addition to the tree at Quainton, mentioned above, there were several in Herefordshire, one or two in Worcestershire, several in Somerset, and one at Kew Gardens, plus many more. The only partial truth in all this is that it is quite possible for a thorn to flower at Christmas. As Roy Vickery points out in his *Dictionary of Plant-Lore* (1995), *Crataegus monogyna* 'is a variety of common hawthorn which produces flowers in winter as well as at the usual time in early summer'; there is nothing supernatural about it.

Mummers

In comes I, Old Father Christmas
Am I welcome or am I not
I hope Old Father Christmas
Will never be forgot.

Probably the most widespread of calendar customs during the nineteenth century, and into the first decades of the twentieth, was the Christmas mummers, who performed their traditional play over and over again as they visited houses in the neighbourhood. They performed especially at the big houses, where they could be sure of a good fee, but sometimes also at the pub or other local venue. After the play, they entertained the company with a few songs, were given money and other Christmas fare, and then moved on, often walking over thirty miles in a day to visit as many places as possible. Their bizarre costumes and even more bizarre 'play' brought a touch of excitement, colour, and mystery to Christmas at many a country house, and the men could each earn as much as two weeks' normal wages over a couple of days.

Hundreds of villages had their set of mummers, in almost every part of the country; only Norfolk and Suffolk have no traces of the custom. Some teams lasted only a few years, while others continued in unbroken tradition for decades, and as is to be expected from a performance passed down through the generations, each team's version was a little different from the rest. But there were definite regional patterns in both text and characterization, and the similarities between versions across the country far outweigh the differences.

'Mummers' is the generic name used by folklorists and other writers, but most areas had a local dialect name for the custom, including tipteerers in Sussex and Surrey, Johnny Jacks in Hampshire, soul-cakers in Cheshire, pace-eggers in Lancashire, and guisers in Yorkshire. Christmas was the usual time for performance for many of the teams, but some performed at other times of year, most notably at Easter, Hallowe'en, and on Plough Monday.

Scholars have identified three main types of mummers' play: the hero-combat or St George play, the wooing play, and the sword-dance play. The most widely known is the basic hero-combat play, found in all areas and even sometimes embedded in some of the other types. The basic plot is simple, and highly stylized. A presenter introduces the play and says that the mummers are about to perform. A 'knight' appears, who strides about boasting of his martial prowess and challenges anyone who disagrees to a sword-fight. Another character appears, with similar boasts, and accepts the challenge. They fight, and one is wounded or killed. In some plays another knight enters and meets the same fate, and occasionally a third. A character, usually the Presenter, laments the death and calls for a doctor. The Doctor appears, boasts of his medical skill (usually in comic hyperbole or nonsense), bargains with the Presenter, and cures the fallen knight, usually with a drop from his bottle. A string of supernumeraries comes in, one by one, each with a short speech, and at least one of them asks the audience for money, food, and drink.

The pace-egg play, reported mainly from Lancashire and performed at Easter, is similar to the St George type but with different characters, and with a strong tradition of performance by children's teams. The wooing plays of the East Midlands, usually performed around Plough Monday, are longer and more involved and include sung dialogue sections of wooing between male and female characters. Sword-dance plays accompanied some of the traditional sword dances of the North-East. These other forms are described under Easter and Plough Monday, and the following is concerned with the St George hero-combat play only.

It is customary to use the language of theatrical plays to describe the mummers, but in many ways this is misleading. In a mummers' performance there was no stage, no wings, no real entering and exiting, few props, and little or no characterization. Most importantly, you did not go to see the mummers, they came to you. The performance space would vary from place to place, but it was usual for the men to stand in a shallow semicircle and to step forward into the centre to say their piece, then step back into line when finished.

The usual text is mock-heroic, in rhyming couplets, and characters often introduce themselves in formulaic manner:

> In comes I, King George
> That man of courage bold
> If his blood be hot
> I'll quickly fetch it cold . . .

And finish by introducing the next player:

> If you don't believe the words I say
> Step in Bold Slasher and clear the way.

Texts also often include bits and pieces from other sources. The standard doctor's speech, for example, formerly appeared in its own right in eighteenth-century broadsides, in skits parodying the quack doctors of the time, and some mumming plays include occasional fragments from plays performed in theatres.

The names of the characters vary considerably from version to version, and comparative discussion would be difficult if it was not for the fact that this variety masks a very limited number of roles within the play itself: Presenter, Combatants, Doctor, Doctor's Assistant, and Supernumeraries. The sections of the play are even more limited: Introduction, combat(s), cure, quête.

The 'Presenter' is often Father Christmas, although he sometimes has a functional name such as 'Roomer' (as his first words are 'Room, room, I pray'). The main 'hero' is usually the King or Saint George, and his adversary can vary – he is often a Turkish knight, but sometimes a bold soldier, or 'Bold Slasher'. The Doctor is sometimes called 'Doctor Brown' or 'Doctor Dodd', although this seems more to do with fitting the rhyme than anything else:

> In comes I Doctor Brown
> The best old doctor in this town.

In some regions, there is a 'female' character (always played by a man), called Molly, Betsy, or something similar. Of all the characters, the supernumeraries at the end vary most from region to region – Little Devil Doubt, Johnny Jack, and Billy Sweep, for example – although Beelzebub is sufficiently widespread to make us believe he might have been in the 'original' version:

Andover mummers, Hampshire, 1935

In comes I Beelzebub
Over my shoulder I carry me club
In me hand a dripping pan
Don't you think I'm a fine old man?

Contrary to popular impression, a dragon rarely appears as a character in the mummers' play, and where it does it can usually be taken as evidence of literary intervention.

Modern descriptions, and revivals, of mumming plays routinely misunderstand and misrepresent what the mummers did and how they did it, mostly by using inappropriate models such as amateur dramatics, pantomime, and melodrama. A traditional mummers' performance was not played for laughs (except for certain well-defined sections); they were not hammed up; the audiences were not expected to join in to cheer the hero or boo the villain; the plays were not ad-libbed; and the presence of St George was not used to engender overt patriotism or nationalism. What evidence there is about performance style all points the same way: little 'acting' was involved, and no attempt was made to portray character. The players' stance was woodenly upright, gestures were stylized, and speech was monotonously declamatory, especially in the boast and challenge sequences. The two characters involved in these sequences counter-marched across the stage, clashing their swords once each time they met and passed, declaiming their lines as they walked. When it was time for the 'fight', they simply met, clashed swords twice, and one fell, or even simply dropped to one knee. The section with the Doctor is the only part that was regularly played for comic effect, but even here it used verbal humour, using topsy-turvy language, for example, rather than physical:

I can cure the ips, the pips, the palsy and the gout
The pains within and the pains without
If a man has nineteen devils in his body
I can fetch twenty out.

However, this is not to argue that a visit from the

mummers was in any way dull. Kenneth Grahame, author of the children's classic *The Wind in the Willows* (1908), remembered the mummers of his Berkshire childhood in the 1860s in the following way:

> Twelfth Night had come and gone, and life next morning seemed a trifle flat and purposeless. But yester-eve, and the mummers were here! They had come striding into the old kitchen, powdering the red brick floor with snow from their barbaric bedizenments, and stamping, and crossing, and declaiming, till all was whirl and riot and shout. Harold was frankly afraid; unabashed, he buried himself in the cook's ample bosom. Edward feigned a manly superiority to illusion, and greeted these awful apparitions familiarly, as Dick and Harry and Joe. As for me, I was too big to run, too rapt to resist the magic and surprise. Whence came these outlanders, breaking in on us with song and ordered masque and a terrible clashing of wooden swords?

Costumes also varied from place to place. Many of the teams in the South, for example, wore a decidedly weird costume of long strips of wallpaper or rag sewn on to their clothes, which completely obscured their bodies, along with tall cardboard hats decorated with rosettes and tinsel, from which long streamers hung all round, even over their faces. In other areas, patches of material, rosettes, streamers, ribbons, and tassels were in evidence, and many teams blacked their faces. By the time the twentieth century dawned, some performers, and occasionally the whole team, were starting to dress in character – the Doctor in a frock coat and top hat, Father Christmas in red robes and white beard, and the 'knights' in vaguely military costume. It is noticeable that those characters who had easily identifiable costumes were the first to succumb to this modernizing tendency.

For the last fifty years or so, almost every writer on the mummers' play has assumed that it is a direct survival of a pre-Christian fertility ritual. The strange garb, the 'ritual' style of performance, and the elemental themes of death and resurrection are all taken as obvious indications of great age and ritual origin. Unfortunately, there is not the slightest evidence to support these notions, and the whole fabrication rests on the assumption that the plays are very, very old. The fact that they cannot be shown to have existed before the mid eighteenth century is the most telling indictment of a set of theories based entirely on romantic wishful thinking.

There are indeed some mysteries still to be solved, but they are more prosaic historical ones. It seems clear that the play stems from an original, presumably 'literary', form in the early eighteenth century. That form has not yet been identified, but the most likely candidate is some kind of mock-heroic puppet play, although it remains to be seen how that play could have spread so widely and how it was adapted into a village tradition. In some areas, such as Lancashire, chapbooks containing play texts were available in local shops, and we know they were used by performers; another possibility is that it was spread by travelling players or puppets. However, if the original 'play' was popular enough to have taken root across almost the whole country, why has it left so little direct evidence of its existence?

For many years, it was not surprising that these questions remained unanswered. The real problem with the 'pagan origins' theory is that it precludes any other serious enquiry. For generations, nobody thought to look anywhere but pre-history, and eighteenth-century puppet plays were ignored. But we now have a whole new generation of scholars who are desperately keen to find the missing link, as yet to no avail.

Up to the First World War, there were hundreds of local mummers' teams up and down the country, but in the interwar years the majority of them faded away, leaving perhaps a dozen to continue after the Second World War. In the 1960s, however, enthusiasts of the folk revival, and particularly members of morris dance teams, started taking an interest in the custom, and numerous sides started to perform the plays again. The relationship between these new teams and the old ones is still controversial, but any claim to be continuing the pre-war tradition is highly tenuous; one extreme view is that the only thing that connects the modern mummer with that of the pre-war period is a few pieces of text. Nevertheless, some argue, with considerable justification, that many postwar 'revival' teams have now existed for a long enough time to qualify for 'traditional' status, and that the differences between themselves and their predecessors proves that they are part of a living tradition. It is clear that, with each passing year, fewer and fewer people will remember the old style of mumming, and that the 'modern' way will gradually become the norm.

See also **Plough Monday: Plough Plays**, p. 21; **Easter Day: Pace-Egg Plays**, p. 120; **31 October: Antrobus Soul-Cakers; 2 November: All Souls' Day; Christmas: Geese Dancers; Christmas: Guisers; Christmas: Sword Dance; 26 December: Marshfield Paper Boys**.

Stockings

The Christmas stocking is one of several elements of the modern Christmas that still puzzles the historian, as it is not at all clear exactly when or how it came into vogue in Britain. Indeed, we are in the difficult position of doubting the word of two contemporary witnesses, including one who provides us with the earliest concrete reference, on the grounds that they assume the stocking had ancient roots. William Henderson, the best folklore collector of his generation, wrote in 1866:

> *The old custom of hanging up a stocking to receive Christmas presents, a custom which the pilgrim fathers carried to America and bequeathed, curiously enough, to their descendants, has not yet died out in the North of England . . . among my own personal friends [is] a family in which, without the excuse of a child to be surprised and pleased, each member duly and deliberately hangs out her stocking on Christmas Eve to receive the kindly gifts of mothers and sister.*

In fact, as there is no evidence that Old Father Christmas had a gift-giving function, or any of the trappings of nocturnal visits (*see* **Christmas: Father Christmas/ Santa Claus**), it is fairly unlikely that the Christmas stocking pre-dates the introduction of Santa Claus from America, around 1865–70 – although Yorkshire resident J. S. Fletcher, born 1863, who wrote of Christmases of his youth in his *Recollections of a Yorkshire Village* (1910), casts doubt on this interpretation:

> *Children knew nothing about Santa Claus or about Christmas trees – those are German innovations which should have been left to Germans. We believed that Old Father Christmas brought our Christmas presents and put them in our stockings, which we hung at the foot of our beds, and instead of the German Christmas tree we had the old-fashioned English mistletoe-bough.*

This puts the stocking in place before Santa Claus, but Fletcher was writing forty years after the event and his memory might have been confused. Even if the stocking were already making an appearance, it cannot have been widely known. In January 1879, for example, Edwin Lees, from Worcester, heard of a custom in Herefordshire and Worcestershire that clearly puzzled him, and he wrote to *Notes & Queries* to ask if anyone else knew of it:

> *On Christmas Eve, when the inmates of a house in the country retire to bed, all those desirous of a present place a stocking outside the door of their bedroom, with the expectation that some mythical being called Santiclaus will fill the stocking or place something within it before the morning. This is of course well known, and the master of the house does in reality place a Christmas gift secretly in each stocking; but the giggling girls in the morning, when bringing down their presents, affect to say that Santiclaus visited and filled the stockings in the night. From what region of the earth or air this benevolent Santiclaus takes flight I have not been able to ascertain . . . An Exeter resident tells me this custom prevails also in Devonshire.*

Sadly, no one answered his request for further information. Seven years later, another writer confirms the presence of stockings in County Durham, but was also having trouble with the new Christmas gift-giver's name:

> *On Christmas Eve, each child hangs up one of its stockings in a place where it can be easily reached, in order that Santa Cruz, the Holy Cross, may come into the bedroom during the night, and deposit some little present in it. And when the child wakens in the morning, sure as fate, in the stocking is a Christmas pie – a yule dough, which is a bit of rich paste rolled out, cut, and baked in the shape of a little baby, with currants for eyes – a packet of figs, raisins, bullets – an orange, a ball, a top, or some other article, brought by the mysterious nocturnal visitor, who has come with light and gentle step, when the children were fast asleep.*

By 1898, there is no question about its commonplace existence, as Richard Blakeborough could write of Yorkshire Christmases:

> *By and by the younger ones are packed off to bed, and with us, as the world over, their stockings are hung at the bed-foot to await the mysterious visit of Santa Claus.*

Although it seems likely that the Christmas stocking became widespread when the idea of Santa Claus was introduced from America, it is possible that the stocking custom had taken root in some families at an earlier date, and it may even have become a regional feature before going national. Certainly, many British people will have been familiar with the idea, at least, from books. In Clement C. Moore's poem 'The Visit of St. Nicholas' (usually known as 'The Night Before Christmas'), for example, which was written in 1821 and published the following year, the saint comes down the chimney and leaves presents in the stockings left hanging by the children. Similarly, in *Carl Krinken; or the Christmas Stocking*, the novel by the popular American children's author Susan Warner, published in New York and London in 1854, the author's comments have a surprisingly modern ring. After coming down the chimney, Santa Claus examines the family's stockings, which are already full to the brim, as 'they had to hold candy enough to make the child sick, and toys enough to make him unhappy because he did not know which to play with first.'

Superstitions

All the major festivals attracted superstitions, but Christmas seems to have had more than its fair share. Many focused on particular elements, such as **decorations** and **food**, and are discussed under those headings, but others applied more generally to the season. Many people had little rituals to welcome Christmas, as others did the New Year. In 1878, the journal *Folk-Lore Record* reported that in West Sussex:

> *It is lucky to be the first to open the house-door* [at] *Christmas . . . Saying 'Welcome, Old Father Christmas'.*

One of the key underlying motifs of Christmas/New Year superstitions was the fear of the luck of the house and family being lost, as this was believed to seriously affect the well-being of its inhabitants throughout the coming year. Many households up and down the country would not allow anything to leave the house at this period, while others restricted the ban to the symbolic staples of life – money, food, and fire. The prohibition against fire leaving the house was particularly widespread, and although this does not sound a particularly harsh rule by modern standards, before the invention of commercial 'lucifer' matches in the 1830s, it was extremely common for householders to borrow a light from a neighbour, and very inconvenient if one could not. The Shropshire folklore collector Charlotte Burne recorded that around 1805:

> *We were very good neighbours, willing to help each other in time of need; but there was one time of need when neither neighbour dared insult the other. Asking to borrow a bit of fire, or even to ask for a light to a candle, on Christmas Day or any day until after Old Twelfth Day, was the greatest insult we could offer to a neighbour, as nothing was so certain to cause bad luck to a family for the ensuing year, as to fetch fire from their house during Christmas-time. Consequently, it was no trifling undertaking on Christmas Eve to arrange the tinder box with all its implements in the art of striking a light; first to obtain a piece of old linen rag, and well burn it into a cinder; and then the flint and steel to be looked up and cleaned, or new ones bought in Shrewsbury market; next, the match-making – generally bits of small brown paper cut to sharp points at one end, then the brimstone melted in an old iron spoon, into which the bits of paper were dipped, and all carefully laid by in a dry place until Christmas morning. If each family attended to these precautions carefully, then we should be sure to be good neighbours all the year round.*

It was generally agreed that of all days in the year, Christmas Day was the luckiest to be born on, and it was also said that you would not be able to see ghosts or other spirits if you were born on that day. In addition, in Sussex, according to the *Folk-Lore Record* (1878), 'If you were born on Christmas Day you will neither be drowned nor hanged.' There was also a strong aversion to doing any work on the day, or, as in another example

Sword dancers, Flamborough, Yorkshire, 1986

from Charlotte Burne's *Shropshire Folk-Lore* (1883), at any time during the season:

> The horses might not go to plough during the whole twelve days; nor might any spinning be done; and the distaff, set aside, was not uncommonly dressed with flowers.

See also **New Year Customs and Superstitions**.

Sword Dance

The term 'sword dancers' will mean different things to different people. It might, for example, conjure up a picture of a Scotsman dancing over crossed swords laid on the floor, or the frantic whirling and clashing of real metal swords characteristic of visiting Cossack troupes. But the sword dance found in the counties of Yorkshire, Northumberland, and Durham, traditionally performed around the local neighbourhood over the Christmas/New Year period, is a very different matter. The 'swords' used in this custom are not real swords at all, but are either lathes of wood or metal about three feet long (in the 'longsword' tradition), or shorter ones made of pliable metal with swivelling wooden handles at each end (in the 'rapper' tradition). Mrs Keith, from Cambo in Northumberland, contributed this description to the book of local memories put together by the Women's Institute in 1929:

Almost the first thing I can remember was when we lived at the Dovecot, and sword dancers came at the New Year, in the dark, and danced the sword dance in the back yard by the light of lanterns, all dressed up – there was old Betty, and Nelson, and a doctor, and after they'd finished the dance one held up all the swords. They came from about Boghall. Yes, miners and the lads about. They used to come from Blaydon too. They were given ginger wine, and cake.

The dancers hold one end of a sword in each hand and are thus all linked in a circle, their movements circumscribed by what can be achieved in variations of this formation. The only time they let go of their swords is at the end of the dance when they interlace them to form a 'knot' or 'rose', which can be held aloft in triumph by one dancer. The two types of sword – longsword and rapper – give the dances a very different character, as dances using the rapper are much faster and more spectacular, but the linked circle remains the basic defining feature of the genre. Similar dances are found across most of Europe from the Middle Ages onwards, and while there are a few ambiguous references to such customs in Britain in the seventeenth century, the real bulk of evidence in this country comes from the second half of the eighteenth century onwards.

Sword dance performances often feature a calling-on song to introduce the dancers, and some versions have supernumerary characters, such as a Fool and a Bessie or Betty (always played by a man). These characters do not normally take part in the dance, and may be the remnant of a play which was formally an integral part of the custom and which scholars have identified as one of the three basic forms of English mumming play (*see* **Christmas: Mummers**). A marked feature of the sword play, which survives in some dances, is when the swords are linked around a character's neck, who is then 'killed' as the swords are smartly withdrawn. The term 'sword dance' is open to some confusion here, because in other customary performances, such as the plough play (*see* p. 21), the participants were locally called 'sword dancers'.

The sword dance is no longer a local house-visiting custom, but many teams still perform, including Handsworth and Grenoside, near Sheffield, Goathland, near Whitby, and Earsdon in Northumberland.

Tree

It is well known that the Christmas tree was directly imported from Germany in the 1840s by Queen Victoria's consort Prince Albert, but this is only partly true. Because of the close connections between the British and German royal families, decorated trees had in fact been a regular feature of court Christmases since at least the days of George III, who married Princess Charlotte of Mecklenburg-Strelitz in 1761. Christmas trees were also seen in other homes with German connections, and were already familiar to many English people. In 1829, for example, when Charles Greville, grandson of a duke, and secretary to the Privy Council, was staying at Pansanger, the Hertfordshire home of Earl Cowper, Greville recorded in his diary that on Christmas Day the Princess Lieven, wife of the Russian Ambassador, had:

. . . got up a little fête such as is customary all over Germany. Three large trees in large pots were put upon a long table covered with pink linen; each tree was illuminated with three circular tiers of coloured wax candles – blue, green, red and white. Before each tree was displayed a quantity of toys, gloves, pocket handkerchiefs, workboxes, books, and various articles – presents made to the owner of the tree. Here it was only for the children, in Germany the custom extends to persons of all ages.

However, it was certainly Victoria and Albert's homely Christmas tree in 1848 that caught the public's imagination and started the fashion in Britain. The famous engraving of the royal couple, with their five children admiring the bauble- and present-hung tree, appeared in the Christmas supplement of the *Illustrated London News*, and although it was there described as 'somewhat more of a German than an English custom', it struck a responsive chord with the British middle classes. By 1851, the same journal was running adverts for Christmas trees, and they were increasingly appearing as normal features in illustrations and articles. Not everybody was happy with the development, however. Remembering the Yorkshire of his childhood in the 1870s, J. S. Fletcher wrote:

Children knew nothing about Santa Claus or about

The picture of Victoria and Albert's tree that launched the craze for Christmas trees (*Illustrated London News*, 1848)

Christmas trees – those are German innovations which should have been left to Germans . . . Instead of the German Christmas tree we had the old-fashioned English mistletoe-bough.

But there was no stopping the new fashion, and it gradually filtered down through the layers of society to become one of the essential features of the twentieth-century Christmas. It still retains its important role both in practice and as a recognizable symbol of the season, and most families still have a tree of some sort, whether it is a token one on the sideboard, or as tall as the room will allow, one of the latest non-drop versions, or a synthetic one that plays a tune or changes colour.

Waits

Personal accounts of domestic life in the nineteenth and early twentieth centuries often mention that an essential part of the run-up to Christmas was the evening visits by musicians, called 'the waits'; however, these were just the tail-end of a very long musical tradition that originally was not confined to the festive season.

The word 'wait' is recorded from around 1300 with a variety of linked meanings, and comes from the same root as the word 'watch'. In its earliest sense it probably meant a military sentinel or watchman, who was furnished with a horn or trumpet for signalling, but not long after it was being used to mean a royal or municipal watchman, maintained at public charge, with musical instruments. A number of medieval towns maintained bodies of waits, York, Leicester, and Norwich among them, and those at Norwich were sufficiently famous to be commanded to accompany Edward IV to France in 1475, and Sir Francis Drake on his Lisbon campaign in 1588/9. At home, their duties included providing music at public events, such as dinners and civic gatherings, but their highest public profile came from their role as nightwatchmen – patrolling the streets at night, playing softly, and announcing the time, to reassure the populace that all was well.

The waits were paid for their services, as well as being supplied with instruments, badges of office, and suitable outdoor clothes, and no doubt it was a popular steady position for local musicians, but town records often document quite stormy relationships between employers and employed. In some towns, the waits survived until the early nineteenth century but were swept away by the Municipal Reform Act of 1836. The privatized band continued to function, however, and became particularly associated with Christmas. The word 'wait' therefore came to mean simply a band of musicians who came round at that season, just like the carol singers. In 1827, the *Gentleman's Magazine* recorded that:

About a week before Christmas Day it is the annual custom of the native minstrels in Holmsdale [Surrey] to serenade the inhabitants every morning at an early hour; then many a delusive dream is broken by 'the concord of sweet sounds'. The instrumental harmonists are welcomed from house to house, and hailed as the harbingers of joyous hours to come . . . I peeped through the chamber window and . . . there stood the venerable figure of Richard Dove, an established musician of the neighbourhood, fiddling with all his might, his head and foot beating time, while every string exulted aloud in 'The Downfall of Paris', and every note tingled in the ear, crying shame to the drowsy sleeper.

However, not everybody approved of the waits, or their choice of tune; a couple of years earlier, the same magazine reported:

Certain strolling minstrels still occasionally disturb our nocturnal slumbers for a few weeks previous to Christmas, calling themselves 'waites'; but alas! alack the day! instead of playing and singing the good old carol, our ears are saluted with 'Roy's Wife', 'St. Patrick's Day', or the latest quadrille tune.

Wassailing

Of all the traditional customs that are believed to be remnants of ancient luck-bringing rituals, wassailing is the only one with any reasonable claim to this description, as it is overtly concerned with wishing prosperity on those visited; however, even here there is no evidence for the prevailing notion that wassailing customs are pre-Christian, or even that they date back to before the late Middle Ages. The word itself is derived from the Old English *waes haell*, meaning 'be healthy', or, as we would perhaps say nowadays, 'Good

Wassailing in Carhampton, Somerset, 1984

health!', and was recorded as a general salutation and also as a drinking toast; the traditional reply was *drinc haell!* But before dreaming of marauding Anglo-Saxons carousing after sacking a British village or two, it is best to consider the linguistic evidence presented in the detailed entry in the *Oxford English Dictionary*. It is there revealed that *wassail* as a general salutation existed in Old Norse as well as in Old English, but that the use of the word as a drinking toast is not found in any of the Teutonic languages, and appears to be a peculiarly 'English' formation from the eleventh or twelfth century: 'It seems probable that this use arose among the Danish-speaking inhabitants of England . . . in the twelfth century it was regarded by Normans as markedly characteristic of Englishmen.' Later uses of the word, in the thirteenth to fifteenth centuries, show that it had undergone a considerable extension of meaning, with a 'wassail' meaning a party, or the drink

that was enjoyed there, or the words said when drinking, or even the songs that were sung. Like the word 'Yule', 'wassail' has long been used anachronistically by writers as a shorthand way to conjure up a popular romantic view of England in the Dark Ages (*see* **Merrie England**, p. 372). Indeed, the very first written evidence of the 'wassail-drinkhail' combination appears in Geoffrey of Monmouth's *History of the Kings of Britain* (VI:12), one of our first historical novels, written *c.*1140 but set in the fifth century.

In the sphere of more recent annual customs, there were two related but different forms of wassailing. The first was a domestic house-visiting custom, which could be done by men or women but was traditionally regarded as a predominately female custom, while the second was an agricultural custom carried out primarily in the orchard, in which one wassailed the trees, wishing a good crop and a prosperous coming year.

The key feature of the house-visiting custom was the good-luck drink offered to the householder, with an appropriate song, as in this example from Northamptonshire in 1853:

This friendly and neighbour-loving custom was observed by the young women of the village, who accustomed themselves to go about from door to door on new year's eve, neatly dressed for the occasion, and bearing a bowl richly decorated with evergreens and ribbands, and filled with a compound of ale, roasted apples, and toast, and seasoned with nutmeg and sugar. The bowl was offered to inmates, with the singing of the following amongst other verses:

> *Good master at your door*
> *Our wassail we begin*
> *We all are maidens poor*
> *So we pray you let us in*
> *And drink our wassail*
> *All hail wassail!*
> *Wassail, wassail!*
> *And drink our wassail!*

Traditions of seasonal goodwill notwithstanding, not everyone was pleased to see them, including John Selden, who wrote the following in his *Table-Talk* (1689):

The Pope in sending rellicks to princes, does as wenches do by their wassals at New-years-tide, they present you with a cup, and you must drink of a slabby stuff; but the meaning is you must give them moneys, ten times more than it is worth.

The whole custom was often referred to as 'the wassail bowl', or 'vessel cup', and the ingredients of the drink varied, but was typically mulled ale spiced with nutmeg, with the pulp from roasted apples – called in some areas **Lamb's Wool** (*see* p. 15). Domestic wassailing was also sometimes combined with the related custom of carrying of 'Christmas dolls' from house to house (*see* **24 December: Vessel Cups**). The earliest reference to a visiting wassail custom appears to be in the records of St Mary of Pré Priory at St Albans, Hertfordshire, between 1461 and 1493, which include payments to wassailers, harpers, and players, and so

on, as described in volume 4 of the *Victoria County History* for Hertfordshire. The orchard-visiting custom, which was more spectacular and survived well into the twentieth century, is nowadays probably better known than the house-visiting custom. Often thought to be a West Country custom, it was actually common in some form or other across the southern and western counties, and elsewhere. The exact day varied from place to place, and the custom could take place on Christmas Eve or Day, New Year, Twelfth Night, Plough Monday, or their Old Style equivalents, and in apple-growing areas a team of wassailers could be out on several nights.

Typically, the wassailing party would visit the farmhouse, and then go to the orchard and sing songs under the trees, beat them with sticks, and pour cider over their roots. A marked feature was noise – guns were fired, horns were blown, and there was much loud cheering. It is clear from the wassailers' songs that the purpose of the proceedings was to bring luck and encourage a good crop, and this must have been the case for some time, as in 1648 Robert Herrick included the following in his *Hesperides* collection:

> *Wassaile the trees, that they may beare*
> *You many a plum, and many a peare:*
> *For more or lesse fruits they will bring*
> *As you doe give them wassailing.*

The earliest clear reference to tree wassailing is surprisingly late, in Kent in 1585, as identified by Ronald Hutton in his seminal *Stations of the Sun* (1996).

Numerous versions of the wassailers' song were noted by nineteenth- and early twentieth-century folklorists, and although the songs bear a marked generic similarity, they vary considerably in detail. The first three verses of a version noted in Halse, Somerset, in 1894 are characteristic:

> *Wassail, wassail, all round the town*
> *The cider-cup is white, and the cider is brown*
> *Our cider is made from good apple trees*
> *And now, my fine fellows, we'll drink, if you please*
> *We'll drink your health with all our heart*
> *We'll drink to 'e all before we part.*
> *Here's one, and here's two*
> *And here's three before we go*
> *We're three jolly boys all in a row*

Wassailing in Devon in the 1930s

All in a row, boys, all in a row
And we're three jolly boys all in a row.
This is our wassail, our jolly wassail
And joy go with our jolly wassail
Hatfuls, capfuls, dree basket, basketfuls
And a littler heap under the stairs.

Wassailing was also well-reported in Sussex, where it was commonly called 'apple-howling', as recorded in the diary of the Revd Giles Moore, of Horsted Keynes, for 26 December 1670: 'I gave the howling boys 6d.' At least one unkind nineteenth-century commentator declared that the 'howling' referred to the style of singing, which was not always music to the ears of the educated.

Tree wassailing has long been popular with revivalists, and the sight of morris dancers among the apple trees is common at New Year. As with other revivals,

the temptation to 'improve' the proceedings by dressing up is sometimes too great to resist, as reported in the *Transactions of the Devonshire Association* (1954):

> *Apple wassailing . . . has been revived at Dunkeswell, Twelfth Night, 1954, after a lapse of twenty years . . . The only unusual feature was the presence of two evil spirits, dressed as witches, with tall hats and broomsticks, who squatted in the branches of an apple tree. When the guns were fired through the orchard, the spirits fell out of the tree and were chased away by the delighted crowd.*

See also **6 January: Twelfth Night Fires**

*

26 DECEMBER

St Stephen's Day/Boxing Day

Stephen was probably a Hellenistic Jew, appointed by the Apostles as Deacon in the emerging Christian Church. He was stoned to death by unbelievers c. AD 35, and as one of the first martyrs was given the day following Christ's birth as his feast. For most people in this country, however, 26 December is known as Boxing Day, a usage that was already widespread in the 1830s, but not recorded before that decade. There is little doubt that the name comes from the long-standing custom of giving and receiving 'Christmas boxes' on the day.

When first mentioned, in the 1620s, Christmas boxes were indeed the receptacles in which apprentices and servants collected their annual 'tips'. They were made of earthenware, with a slot for coins, and had to be broken to get the money out. The term 'Christmas box' later came to cover a variety of payments and presents, but the fundamental point is that these were not simply gifts, but gratuities for services rendered, and were therefore not transactions between social equals but between master or client and servant. Who got money from whom was a complex, and potentially expensive, affair. Anyone who served, looked after, or delivered goods to the public could expect a gratuity from each of their customers or clients. Parson James Woodforde in his Norfolk parish, for example, recorded the amount of money he gave each year on Boxing Day. In 1782 it was two shillings and sixpence to the bell-ringers, and a shilling each to the butcher's boy, the blacksmith's boy, and the maltster's man. The money went not to the tradesmen themselves, but to their workers, and the good parson never indicates any reluctance or complaint in his writing. But in towns there was a much wider range of potential recipients and the burden was much greater.

Eighty years after Woodforde, Hannah Cullwick, general maidservant in a London house, noted in her diary for 26 December 1863 how her mistress:

... gave me the money for the Christmas boxes to the men and boys same as last year and I give 'em as they came. I got a lot too – near £2 in all. They was sent to me ... I put mine in the bank wi' my wages – Mary says hern shall buy a new bonnet.

Hannah's money would have come from regular visitors to the house, and from tradespeople who supplied the family and who wished to keep their custom. Clearly, workers like Hannah were loath to part with a system that was, in effect, a Christmas bonus. But even by the eighteenth century there had been complaints about the number of people who expected a Christmas box, and the abuse and subtle blackmail inherent in the system. Periodicals of the earlier nineteenth century regularly printed letters and articles condemning the practice, and the satirical magazine *Punch* ran a piece on the topic at Christmas almost every year in the 1840s; the following example is from 1849:

Our postman ... who has all the year scarcely condescended to greet us with an odd nod, has ... been making a series of low bows, which for some time we thought were ironically meant, until we remembered the compliments of the season ... Our newspaper boy, instead of pitching our daily print into our area, as he has done since last Boxing-day, without even troubling himself to ring the bell, has begun to stand at our door, vociferating, in a sonorous tone of voice, the word 'Pa-per' ... The beadle, whom we have never seen since last Christmas and whom, during the year, we are accustomed to regard as a myth, has come across us, like a phantom, in his gold-laced coat, with crimson cape ... The milkman has begun for a while to put a little less of the pallida mors, or deadly whitewash, into his milkpails; and even the butcher boy is on his best behaviour, for he has only broken our bell-wire once a week for the last month, instead of every other day.

The reformers finally got their way, and by the early twentieth century the Christmas box was a mere shadow of its former self. Nevertheless, remnants of the custom still lingered in post-Second-World-War Britain, by which time the number of recipients had shrunk to a handful: postman, paperboy, milkman, and dustman. Indeed, some families still carry out the custom.

Bleeding Horses

The medical procedure of phlebotomy – blood-letting, or bleeding – is one of the oldest surgical practices known to man, and was a standard method in the treatment of both humans and animals in England until the modern era. For some reason, it was widely believed that the best day to bleed horses and cattle was St Stephen's Day, and most farms and other trades that used horses made sure that this was duly done. The practice was already in place in the late sixteenth century, when Suffolk writer Thomas Tusser compiled his book of agricultural advice, *Five Hundred Points of Good Husbandrie*:

> Ere Christmas be passed let horse be let blood,
> for many a purpose it doth them much good.
> The day of St. Stephen old fathers did use:
> if that do mislike thee some other day choose.

Tusser is uncharacteristically blasé about the choice of day, but few others would risk flouting what they regarded as age-old wisdom.

Hunting and Shooting

In various parts of the country, it was traditional for parties of men and boys to invade the local woods on a certain day of the year, to hunt and kill animals – sometimes specifically squirrels or birds, but any small game was apparently at their mercy. The proper day for this custom varied considerably from place to place.

In Suffolk, Hampshire and Essex, it took place on Christmas Day or Boxing Day, but elsewhere it was Good Friday, 5 November, or St Andrew's Day (*see* **30 November**). In all cases, the participants firmly believed that on that particular day the normal game and trespass laws were suspended, and their actions were therefore quite legal (*see* **Lawless Hours and Days**, p. 303). Another striking common element is the noise and general commotion in which they indulged, which were hardly conducive to a genuine desire to find game.

Robert Forby described one version of the custom in his *Vocabulary of East Anglia* (1830):

> In many parts of the country, particularly where there is much wood, the custom still prevails of hunt-ing squirrels on this day . . . On Christmas morning half the idle fellows and boys in a parish assemble in any wood, or plantation, where squirrels are known to harbour; and having started their game, pursue it with sticks and stones from tree to tree, hallooing and shouting with all their might, till the squirrel is killed . . . From the general discouragement shown to this sport, probably comes the common saying, 'Hunt squirrels and make no noise'.

The journal *Folk-Lore* (1903) included a Lincolnshire variant from about 1840:

> Mr. H., who is more than seventy, told me that when he was a lad, all the young men of Kirton-in-Lindsey, claimed the right of shooting over the whole parish on 5th November. 'When the sport was over,' he added, 'they met together in the market place to fire off their guns.' The belief that the people of a parish may legally shoot 'all over the lordship' on this day is not uncommon in North Lincolnshire.

It is possible that the custom preserves some right of common access to private woodland, but more research would be necessary before such a theory could be tested.

See also **Hunting the Wren** (*below*) for another possible line of enquiry.

Hunting the Wren

Hunting the Wren was a widespread custom in Ireland, Wales, and the Isle of Man, and took place at any time over the Christmas season, but mostly on 26 December. Parties of men and boys killed one or more wrens (or pretended to do so), which they placed in a garland-like 'bush' or special box, and perambulated the village singing, dancing, playing instruments, and collecting money. In many cases, the wren itself was almost forgotten. Some of the wrenboy teams could number up to twenty, and some performed a mummers' play (*see* **Christmas: Mummers**). The traditional song that accompanied the custom usually begins:

> The wren, the wren, the king of all birds
> St Stephen's Day was caught in the furze.

The idea that the tiny wren is the king of the birds is known all across Europe, and can be explained by the following folk tale, which portrays the wren as a trickster figure. In the competition to see who should be king of the birds, the eagle flew higher and faster than all the others. But just as he was proclaiming his victory, the wren, who had hidden in the eagle's feathers, popped out and flew a few inches higher, to claim the title. The eagle could do nothing to challenge this, but threw the wren to the ground in a temper – which explains the wren's short tail.

A different story explains why wrens should be hunted down. It seems that at some crucial point in the past, our people were about to ambush and annihilate the enemy, when a wren flew down and alerted them by pecking on a drum. The identity of the enemy changes in each version – for the Irish it can be 'the English', or King William's or Cromwell's army, but for others it is 'the Danes', who served as the archetypal enemy in many tales and traditions across Britain.

The custom was certainly known in England, but it was clearly not very widely known. The few definite references are scattered, and might well be sightings of groups of Irish or Welsh people perpetuating their own customs while living away from home. Edward Armstrong, whose *Folklore of Birds* (1958) is unfortunately influential in the subject, states boldly that 'Contrary to general belief the Hunting of the Wren was an English custom', and lists fifteen English counties in which traces of it have been found. His habit of paraphrasing unnamed sources makes the trail a little difficult to follow, but he appears to have reached this impressive total by uncritically conflating a series of references to two other wren-related traditions that may or may not be relevant.

The first is the simple song often called 'The Cutty Wren', which was widely collected across the British Isles and North America, and takes as its theme the exaggerated size and importance of the wren. A version noted from the singing of Bill Whiting of Longcot, Berkshire, by John Baldwin in 1967, is a good example:

> I'm goin' to the woods, said Richard to Robin
> I'm goin' to the woods, said Robin to Bobbin
> I'm goin' to the woods, said John alone
> I'm goin' to the woods, boys, ev'ryone.

Lines in successive verses include: 'What shall us do there?'; 'We'll shoot a wren'; 'How shall us get 'im up?';

'We must fetch a cart'; 'How shall us get 'im cooked?'; 'Put 'im i' th' oven'; 'We've 'ad a feast'; 'Let's 'ave some ale'. The tunes of different versions are usually simple, often described as more chant than song. The earliest version so far located is in a collection of nursery rhymes dating from around 1744, and although many writers assume that the song originated in some ancient ritual, it is more likely that it started life as a children's song'. It can also be assigned to a sub-genre of nonsense songs that could be termed 'hyperbolic animal songs' and includes 'The Derby Ram' and the 'The Wonderful Crocodile'.

The second tradition conflated by Armstrong does not always involve wrens. In various parts of the country there was a tradition that on a certain day of the year villagers were allowed to enter local woods to hunt 'game'. The quarry was often specifically named as squirrels, and although wrens were sometimes singled out, this is possibly because it is one of the smallest animals likely to be found. The day varied from place to place, including Good Friday, 5 November, and St Andrew's Day (*see* **30 November**), but Christmas Day or Boxing Day are marginally the most commonly cited (*see* **26 December: Hunting and Shooting** for further examples). The marked characteristic of the event in many reports was that it was hardly a serious hunt at all, and was accompanied by much shouting, hallooing, and crashing about, as if this noise was more important than actually bagging any game. Exactly the same commotion was reported of the Irish wrenboys trying to catch their birds, as in this example from County Cork in the 1840s, printed by Irish folklorist Kevin Danaher:

> In the hunt the utmost excitement prevails; shouting, screeching and rushing; all sorts of missiles are flung at the puny mark; and not unfrequently they light upon the head of some less innocent being. From bush to bush, from hedge to hedge is the wren pursued until bagged with as much pride and pleasure, as the cock of the woods by the more ambitious sportsman. The stranger is utterly at a loss to conceive the cause of this hubbub.

This was nothing new, as English antiquarian John Aubrey said of the Irish in 1686, 'You will see sometimes on holidays, a whole parish running like mad men from

Marshfield Paper Boys, Gloucestershire, 2005

hedge to hedge a wren-hunting.' This tradition of wren-hunting is particularly strange, in England at least, because at other times 'Jenny Wren' enjoyed considerable protection from being considered the robin's wife, and to kill a robin was one of the unluckiest things one could do:

> The robin red-breast and the wren
> Are God Almighty's cock and hen.

This belief was particularly widespread in England, but also known in other parts of the British Isles, from at least 1709 onwards.

To return, therefore, to Armstrong's fifteen English counties, once the song and the general Boxing Day hunting customs are removed from the account, there is little left to show that the Irish-style wren hunt was known in England, although William Henderson included a definite reference in his *Notes on the Folk Lore of the Northern Counties of England and the Border* (1866):

> At Christmas-tide, boys are accustomed in Essex to
> kill wrens and carry them about in furze-bushes,
> from house to house, asking a present in these words:
>
> > The wren, the wren, the king of the birds
> > St. Stephen's Day was killed in the furze
> > Although he be little, his honour is great
> > And so, good people, pray give us a treat.

In addition, a Boxing Day custom that existed in Devonport until the Second World War was reported in the *Transactions of the Devonshire Association* in 1972, in which participants with blackened faces and improvised costumes visited pubs, carrying a small tree or bush, and chanting a song which started with 'The ram, the ram, the king of the Jews', which, although it does not mention wrens, is clearly a garbled version of the usual wren song.

These references, and one or two others, are all that can be mustered, and the provisional conclusion must be that although wrens were hunted and killed in a customary manner, the perambulation of the village with a dead wren was probably not an English custom after all.

Marshfield Paper Boys

O yes! O yes! O yes! I have much pleasure in introducing the celebrated Marshfield Mummers, the old time Paper Boys. God save the Queen!

In the Cotswold village of Marshfield, Gloucestershire, twelve miles from Bristol, a team of men still performs the old mummers' play every Christmas, in the old-fashioned way. They call themselves the 'old-time Paper Boys' after their outlandish costume, which consists entirely of newspaper cut into strips and sewn on to their clothes and hats. The characters are: Father Christmas, King William, Little Man John, Doctor Phoenix, Saucy Jack, Tenpenny Nit, and Father Beelzebub. They are preceded by a top-hatted Town Crier, with handbell, who declaims the lines of introduction quoted above.

As with all 'hero-combat' mumming plays (*see* **Christmas: Mummers**), one character (King William) kills another (Little Man John) in a sword-fight, and the Doctor is summoned to revive him:

*I can cure the itch, the stitch, the palsy and the gout,
    all pains within and none without. Bring me an old
    woman seven years dead, seven years laid in her
    grave, take a pill from me, and this gallant boy will
    rise again.*
What's thy fee doctor?
*Ten pounds is my fee, but fifteen I'll take of thee, to set
    this man free.*

Apart from a few private performances, the play is acted outdoors, at set points around the village, every Boxing Day, and draws a large crowd from far and wide.

Like many other village customs across the country, the Marshfield play had lapsed in the 1880s, but it was revived in 1932 at the instigation of folklorist Violet Alford, whose brother was the local vicar. One of the new team had been in the play as a boy, and he provided the know-how to achieve a relatively faithful replication of the style in which the play was performed fifty years earlier. It is this direct connection with the previous tradition that makes the Marshfield 'revival' qualitatively different from other revivals that are created from scratch. The Marshfield Paper Boys are also most unusual in that they have resisted the temptation to dress in costume appropriate to each part, or to modernize the style of performance. They do not model themselves on pantomime or melodrama, but still conduct themselves with the serious demeanour of the old teams.

For illustration, *see* p. 409.

Ludlow Rope-Pulling

See **Shrove Tuesday: Ludlow Rope-Pulling**, p. 60.

Padstow Mummers' (Darkie) Day

A custom that has come under considerable fire recently is the 'Darkie Day' perambulations of Padstow, in Cornwall. Participants don top hats decorated with flowers, fancy waistcoats, chimney-sweep outfits, and other sorts of fancy dress, and go round local pubs and streets singing songs by Stephen Foster and others from the nineteenth-century minstrel days. But what gives 'Darkie Day' its name is that the singers and musicians black their faces.

Darkie Day is thus one of the last vestiges of the blackface minstrel craze of the nineteenth century. 'Nigger minstrels', as they were called then, were introduced to London in 1836, and became an immediate smash sensation, sweeping the country like wildfire. The simple catchy tunes, purporting to be real Negro folk songs but mostly written by white songwriters, were highly suitable for amateur musicians; every village had its minstrel troupe, and every local concert had somebody strumming a banjo and singing minstrel pieces. In London and the big provincial towns, there were semi-permanent minstrel troupes who put on lavish spectacular shows. These lasted into the twentieth century, but declined in the face of competition from new musical crazes. However, the form still had life in it, and survived on BBC television into the 1970s with the 'Black and White Minstrel Show'.

A photograph from *c.*1900 shows the Padstow Darkie Day troupe very smartly dressed in highly patterned suits and black top hats – very much as the big minstrel troupes of the day were dressed. But at the time of writing, the future of the custom is unclear. There are growing calls for its abolition, on the grounds that the blacked-up faces are racist, and police have taken a watching brief – quite literally, as they filmed it in 2005; although according to the *Observer* of 22 January 2006, the local MP has claimed that the blackened faces originated as a form of disguise rather than on the minstrel stage. In the meantime, the participants have renamed the event 'Mummers' Day'.

Pantomimes

The ultimate origins of that strange dramatic beast, the English pantomime, lie in the traditional Italian *commedia dell'arte*, which flourished from the sixteenth to the early eighteenth centuries. This highly stylized dramatic form, with stereotyped characters and plot outlines, but with largely improvised dialogue and action, also included music, dance, and clowning, and, unusually for the period, featured both male and female actors. The basic plot concerned two young lovers whose courtship was frustrated by the girl's aged father and his friend, but who were supported and assisted by comic servants, including the leading girl's maid. The most important stock character was Harlequin, and the plot always included a chase scene, with the lovers fleeing the old man's wrath. *Commedia*-type scenes were already familiar to British audiences by the turn of the eighteenth century, as Harlequin sequences had been included in a few home-grown comedies, but it was the impetus of French *commedia* troupes performing in this country that prompted the growth of the pantomime as a distinct form of entertainment.

The first real pantomime was *The Magician, or Harlequin a Director*, produced in 1721, with actor-manager John Rich as the first English Harlequin; he set the parameters of that character, which lasted for several generations. The 'director' of the title referred to the financial scandal known as the South Sea Bubble, which had burst a few months previously, and this started the trend for topical allusions in the pantomime that lasts to this day. For a while, pantomimes were staged as afterpieces to more conventional fare, but they proved so popular that they were soon extended to fill the whole evening. Indeed, the theatre-going public loved them so much that even those managers that had a distaste for such low-brow material were forced to stage them every year. Even at this time, they were an odd mixture of the romantic, serious, and comic, with song, dance, slapstick, and stunning special effects, and, as now, they were presented in the immediate post-Christmas period. It was quipped that theatres should dispense with their old repertoire of real plays and simply stage pantomimes all year.

The Harlequin created by John Rich was mute, relying on mime and special effects, and his dominance of the genre lasted for decades, but by the early nineteenth century the central role was taken by another comic character, the Clown. The success of this character was almost entirely due to Joseph Grimaldi (1778–1837), the most famous clown of all time, still annually commemorated in London (*see* **First Sunday in February: Clowns' Service**). Pantomime continued to develop, mainly by accretion, and was an integral part of the remodelled Christmas of the mid nineteenth century. Nevertheless, it seems that people have always either loved or hated the pantomime, with no position possible between these extremes. Charles Dickens was firmly in favour, stating in a piece in *Bentley's Miscellany* (1837):

> Let us at once confess to a fondness for pantomimes – to a gentle sympathy with clowns and pantaloons – to an unqualified admiration of Harlequins and Columbines – to a chaste delight in every action of their brief existence, varied and many-coloured as those actions are, and inconsistent though they occasionally be with those rigid and formal rules of propriety which regulate the proceedings of meaner and less comprehensive minds. We revel in pantomimes.

By later Victorian times, so much had been added to the performances that chaos reigned. Writing of the later nineteenth century, the *Oxford Companion to the Theatre* justly comments:

> With the importation of specialty acts from the music-halls, which held up the action but delighted the audiences, the show became such a hotchpotch of incongruous elements – slapstick, romance, topical songs, male and female impersonation, acrobatics, splendid settings and costumes, precision and ballet dancing, trick scenery and transformation scenes – that for a time the phrase 'a proper pantomime' was used outside the theatre in colloquial English to signify 'a state of confusion'.

Despite these strictures, and the constant lament of reviewers that 'pantomime is not what it used to be', the annual extravaganza still continues, and for many provincial theatres is the only sure-fire money-making venture of the year. Gerald Frow's history of the pantomime (1985) sums it all up:

> It all adds up to something refreshingly honest and utterly disarming. We all know the man's a woman; we all know the woman's a man; and anyone can see that the cow has got people in it. But isn't that the whole point?

*

28 DECEMBER

Holy Innocents' Day

Holy Innocents' Day, or Childermas, commemorates the day on which King Herod, in his desperate attempt to find the infant Jesus, ordered all children under the age of two in Bethlehem to be killed (Matthew 2:16). It therefore had two slightly conflicting traditional characteristics: the sadness and repentance of a tragic day, coupled with a particular regard for children. In church it was a day of fasting and penance, and the bells were rung in muffled tones. Children were not chastised on the day, and were allowed a certain degree of unaccustomed licence, as recorded by C. J. Billson, one of the editors of the Victorian *County Folklore Printed Extracts* series:

> When living in the parish Exton, Rutland, some 15 years ago [i.e. about 1880], I was told by an old lady that in her girlhood, in the very early years of this century, it was the custom for children to be allowed to play in church on 'Innocents Day'.

From the twelfth to the sixteenth centuries, Holy Innocents' Day was also the day on which the Boy Bishop reigned in many cathedrals and other religious institutions, although he was also often elected on the other holy day that was connected with children, St Nicholas' Day (*see* **6 December: Boy Bishop**).

The religious background to the day directly affected the way in which it was seen by the people. All over the country, at least until the early twentieth century, the day was regarded as particularly unlucky. This unluckiness was manifest in various ways – from the general idea that anything started on the day would not be finished, or be doomed to failure, to specific prohibitions against certain activities, such as doing the family washing ('you will wash one of the family away'). Workers in particularly dangerous occupations refused to work at all on the day, first recorded by Richard Carew in Cornwall in 1602:

> That proves as ominous to the fisherman as beginning a voyage on the day when Childermas day fell doth to the mariner.

It was still being said of lead-miners in Northumberland over 250 years later.

However, the unluckiness could affect more than the day itself, as reported by Charlotte Burne in 1883:

> Innocents' Day, sometimes called 'Cross day', is a day of ill omen. The ancient people of Pulverbatch [Shropshire] applied this name not only to Innocents' Day but throughout the year to the day of the week on which it had last fallen, such day of the week being believed to be an unlucky day for commencing any work or undertaking. A popular saying about any unfortunate enterprise was: 'It must have been begun on Cross day'.

On the same principle, Fridays throughout the year were widely regarded as unlucky, simply because the crucifixion took place on that day. There could therefore be two unlucky or 'cross' days every week.

In the northern counties of England, Holy Innocents' Day was also known as Dyzeman's Day, Dyzemas, or Dizimus Sunday (or variations thereon); the etymology of these names is unknown.

*

31 DECEMBER

New Year's Eve

Until quite recently, it was broadly the case that while people in Scotland heartily celebrated the New Year and ignored Christmas, in England people did the reverse. This situation held true for nigh on 300 years, but it would be a mistake to regard it as evidence of deep psychological differences between the two peoples. It was simply a result of different paths taken during the religious and political turmoil of seventeenth-century Britain. Christmas was banned in both countries by Puritan order, but was reinstated in England at the Restoration of the monarchy in 1660, when the people were positively encouraged to welcome 'Old Father Christmas' back into their lives. The Scottish Church, however, continued to frown on the festival, and their people thus put their festive energies into the secular New Year instead. It is only in recent years that these national differences have begun to break down.

In early Victorian England, New Year had a few traditions of its own which had been around for a long while, such as giving gifts and sending greetings messages (see **New Year Customs and Superstitions: Gifts**), but these were eventually usurped by the new-style Christmas being forged at the time. In 1864, William Chambers could write in his famous *Book of Days*:

> As a general statement, it may be asserted that neither the last evening of the old year nor the first day of the new one is much observed in England as an occasion of festivity. In some parts of the country, indeed, and more especially in the northern counties, various social merry-makings take place; but for the most part, the great annual holiday-time is now past.

New Year began to occupy an ambiguous position in the festive calendar. It fell awkwardly between Christmas Eve and Twelfth Night, which marked the beginning and end of the festive season, and New Year had no obvious role to play. Nor did New Year's Eve have many traditional customs of its own, and those that did occur at the season, such as wassailing and mumming, were not fixed to a particular night but could take place at any time over Christmas.

In recent years, however, New Year has quietly undergone a process of major change, which started when New Year's Day became a bank holiday in England in 1974. Increasingly it is seen as the end, not just of Christmas week, but effectively of the whole Christmas season. In this context it has completely eclipsed the old Twelfth Night and has become the new counterbalance to Christmas Day: many workers now get given the whole of Christmas week as holiday, and return to work after the New Year; couples might agree to see one

Allendale Guisers on New Year's Eve, Northumberland, 1972

set of parents at Christmas and the other at New Year; and young people who are required to spend Christmas in their parents' houses are often free to see their own friends at New Year.

Nevertheless, despite its lack of overt festivity, New Year has probably always had a quieter, deeper side, brought about by the symbolism inherent in the passing of one year into the next. It seems quite natural that it should be seen as a time of personal stocktaking, engendering those mixed feelings of nostalgia and hope, when even the least romantic of us feels compelled to think back on the past twelve months and make plans for the coming year. Many people who do not celebrate the night in any other way still feel they should stay up till midnight to 'see the New Year in'.

Allendale Guisers

Late in the evening of 31 December, the Northumbrian village of Allendale is quite literally lit up by the spectacular sight of forty fancy-dressed guisers, who parade the streets carrying blazing wooden barrels on their heads. The guisers are aided by a brass band and supported by most of the local population, and the climax is reached at midnight when they light the waiting bonfire in Market Place. In previous times they would dramatically throw their barrels on to the fire, but suitable barrels are not so easy to find these days, so they have to be more circumspect.

The barrels are the ends of ordinary wooden barrels cut down to about twelve inches deep and filled with rags and shavings, soaked in paraffin, although real tar was used in previous times. They can weigh up to 30 lbs, and take some carrying, even when not alight. The guisers take their responsibilities very seriously, and it is rare for a barrel to be dropped. The word 'guiser' is found in customs all over the country, especially in the northern counties, and signifies a character dressed up or 'disguised' (*see* **Christmas: Guisers**).

The wishful thinking that automatically assigns

ancient origins to traditional customs, repeated all over the country, has operated in Allendale, and the tar barrels have been confidently attributed to acts of ancient fire worship carried out by pagan Celts, Vikings, and Druids; however, the overwhelming evidence points to a far more prosaic explanation. It seems that the tar barrels were introduced in the second half of the nineteenth century as a form of illumination for the members of the local band, who always perambulated the village on New Year's Eve to play the old year out.

Nevertheless, a custom does not need to be ancient to be important to the local inhabitants, and in Allendale it has been preserved, and indeed extended, because it serves a community purpose – and fierce local pride will keep it going for a long time yet. Local determination is often only obvious to the outsider when a tradition is under threat, as many customs were during the Second World War. Venetia Newall's seminal article on the custom, published in 1974, recorded one of these moments:

> When war broke out and many of the guysers were called up for military service, blackout regulations enforced the cancellation of the bonfire. To maintain the continuity of the custom, Lancelot Bell, the local carpenter, designed a type of small tar barrel which he carried each New Year's Eve, unlit, along the usual route through the village to the Market Place. On the customary site of the bonfire, he placed it inside a tin trunk, set fire to it, and closed the lid. All the local people then danced around the trunk.

Blazing tar barrels have a long history, and feature in a number of other winter customs, usually on Guy Fawkes Night; *see*, for example **5 November: Ottery St Mary** and **Second Saturday in November: Hatherleigh Carnival**.

Bell-Ringing

The loud ringing of the church bells to honour special occasions has a very long history. On a national scale, military victories and royal events have been regularly marked in this way, and certain nights of the year, such as 5 November and Christmas Eve, have also acquired bell-ringing customs. The ringing of the old year out and the new year in on the night of New Year's Eve is still heard in many places, but in the past it was almost universal, and before the days of radio and television the New Year bell-ringing was for many not only the most evocative sound of the season but the eagerly awaited signal that the midnight hour had officially arrived. The moment inspired numerous poets, including Alfred Lord Tennyson, whose *In Memoriam* (1850) includes the famous verses:

> Ring out, wild bells, to the wild sky,
> The flying cloud, the frosty light;
> The year is dying in the night,
> Ring out, wild bells, and let him die.
> Ring out the old, ring in the new,
> Ring happy bells across the snow;
> The year is going, let him go,
> Ring out the false, ring in the true.

Many churches had their own ways of welcoming in the New Year, most commonly carried out with a combination of solemnity and joy, as in Nottinghamshire in 1853:

> On this night, in many parts of the county as well as in Derbyshire, a muffled peal is rung on the church bells until twelve o'clock, when the bandages are removed from the bells whilst the clock is striking, and a merry peal is instantly struck up; this is called 'ringing the old year out and the new year in'.

See also **4 November: Ringing Night**; **5 November: Guy Fawkes Night**; and **24 December: Ringing the Devil's Knell** for other bell-ringing customs.

Gatherings

The impetus to gather in some key public place on New Year's Eve seems to be fairly widespread, and most cities have a spot where this happens every year. In London, the earliest documented gathering occurred in 1878 when, according to the *Illustrated London News* for 2 January 1897, significant numbers collected outside St Paul's Cathedral to hear the newly installed bells ring in the New Year. The ringing was repeated for a few years, but the crowd became too large and 'uproarious', so the Cathedral authorities put a stop to it. Unfortunately, this did not stop the crowds gathering, and an illustration on the front page of the same issue of the *ILN*

Public gathering at St Paul's Cathedral on New Year's Eve, 1897 (*Illustrated London News*)

depicts two policemen in the middle of a huge festive crowd. Questions of public order and morality were regularly voiced, but the crowds continued to grow.

A letter to *The Times* in November 1935 summed up the feeling in many quarters that while there was nothing inherently bad about New Year gatherings, trouble might be avoided if they were better organized, and in particular that organized singing would be a good thing:

In England we seldom sing en masse, except at football matches. In this respect our shortcomings on New Year's Eve have been particularly deplorable. Alike in London and the provincial cities great crowds, obeying a good and natural emotion, forgather to greet the New Year. Their emotion finds no orderly outlet. Because they are leaderless they make no united musical effort. Instead, individuals and small groups sing. The strains of a dozen banal and tuneless ditties intermingle depressingly. Often the New Year breaks upon a scene of horseplay and alcoholic excess.

The Cathedral authorities did indeed provide community singing that year, along with a broadcast of the service to the crowds outside, which *The Times* declared a great success, but it was not repeated the following year. After the Second World War, the focus gradually shifted to Trafalgar Square, where it has stayed ever since.

Hogmanay

'Hogmanay', the standard Scottish word for New Year's Eve, was also used in Northumberland, Cumberland, Westmorland, and Yorkshire. In 1909, Northumbrian writer Hastings M. Neville recorded that:

Until about five-and-twenty years ago the custom of Hogmanay existed in our village. This took the form of a round of visits made by the children on Old New Year's Day. They would assemble at the front door, and, by way of greeting, sing with great gusto certain quaint catches, always including the following:

Get up, guid wife and shake your feathers
And dinna think that we are beggars
We're little children come to play

Please to give us our Hogmanay
May God bless all friends dear
A merry Christmas and happy New Year

. . . Each child went away pleased with a coin, an orange, and a kind word. The term Hogmanay is not only applied to this custom, but to any gift received at the New Year or at Christmas, and is practically what is called in the South a Christmas Box.

The word has puzzled scholars for many years, and even its spelling was once in dispute. A discussion in the *Gentleman's Magazine* in 1790, for example, gave it as 'hagman heigh' and 'Hagmenai', while others plumped for 'Hagmena' and 'Hogmena'; however, the *Oxford English Dictionary* gives the standard modern spelling and declares that it is from an Old French word:

Hogmanay . . . corresponds exactly in sense and use to Old French aguillanneuf, 'the last day of the year, new year's gift, the festival at which new year's gifts were asked with the shout of aguillanneuf!'

It is not at all clear how the word travelled from France to Scotland (or the north of England) and became attached to a home-grown custom, unless, of course, the custom accompanied the word. The earliest citation given in the *Oxford English Dictionary* for the word 'Hogmanay' in English or Scots is *c.*1680.

Daily Customs

Bainbridge Horn-Blower

Bainbridge in North Yorkshire is proud to possess a horn-blowing tradition, although it is not so well known as the horn-blowing at Ripon (see **Ripon Horn-Blower**, *below*). The current instrument is a buffalo horn, dating from 1864, and it is blown daily, at 9 p.m. but only between 28 September and Shrove Tuesday. The honour of being the horn-blower has been in the Metcalfe family for generations.

No one knows when it started, although there are various theories. One belief is that it is a survival from the Roman legions in the area; another is that it was originally used to guide benighted travellers through the surrounding Wensleydale Forest to safety. However, it is more plausible that it functioned as a curfew or a signal, as at Ripon, that the 'watch' was taking over for the night. All this is speculation, as the earliest definite reference to the custom only dates from the 1820s. In a relatively recent extension to the tradition, locals sometimes ask the horn-blower to attend weddings and other functions, 'for luck'.

Chime Hours

Several linked superstitions connect the time of day an individual is born to his/her ability to see ghosts or be otherwise supernaturally gifted. The best-known of these beliefs states that certain times are particularly potent. In 1916, *Notes & Queries* recorded:

> A recent experiment in clairvoyance that chanced to be successful evoked the comment from an observer in a Norfolk village that the experimentalist must have been 'born in chime hours'.

However, there is no general agreement on what exactly constituted the 'chime hours'. Nowadays, most people assume they are the quarters on which most chiming clocks strike, i.e. three, six, nine, and twelve, but some take it to mean eight in the evening, midnight, and four in the morning, which were the old monastic hours of prayer, marked by some churches with a bell. It is also unclear how close to the exact hour the birth has to be. But, as reported in *Notes & Queries* of 1862, all are agreed that the most potent hour of all is midnight:

> An old Kentish lady, while discussing hobgoblins last Christmas, said that she had never seen a ghost; though she had placed herself in spots visited by the departed, and had been present while others had seen an apparition. She then stated it as a fact, that people born at twelve o'clock at night, and only such, were gifted with this visionary power. An instance in point was, of course, adduced.

And the potency of midnight is said to be further increased if a child is born at that time on certain key dates such as Christmas Eve (good luck) or Hallowe'en (not so good).

Versions of these beliefs have been recorded in most parts of England and in Scotland. They sound like ancient beliefs, but they cannot be shown to have existed before the mid nineteenth century. The earliest known reference is in Charles Dickens's novel *David Copperfield* (1849), in which the hero introduces himself:

> I record that I was born (I have been informed and believe) on a Friday, at twelve o'clock at night . . . It was remarked that the clock began to strike, and I began to cry simultaneously. In consideration of the day and hour of my birth, it was declared by the nurse, and by some sage women in the neighbourhood . . . first, that I was destined to be unlucky in life, and, secondly, that I was privileged to see ghosts and spirits.

David Copperfield was probably believed to be destined

Ripon horn-blower, Yorkshire, 1981

for unluckiness because he was born on a Friday, but his supposed supernatural ability will have been the result of the midnight hour.

Lady Lee Monument, Aylesbury

In the church of St Mary the Virgin, Aylesbury, in Buckinghamshire, stands an alabaster monument of 1584, brought from the ruined and deserted church at Quarendon. It commemorates Lady Lee, wife of Sir Henry Lee, Queen's Champion to Elizabeth I. Lady Lee kneels on a tasselled cushion, wearing a full skirt and buttoned bodice, and a pleated ruff round her neck. Behind her kneels her daughter, Mary, and two baby boys, John and Henry, in swaddling clothes to show that they died in infancy. Part of the inscription, which is in pseudo-medieval verse and is reminiscent of Spenser's *Faerie Queene* (1590), runs:

Good frende, stick not to strew with crimson floures
This marble tombe wherin [sic] *her cinders rest,*
For sure her ghost lyes with the heavenly powers,
And guerdon [reward] *hathe of virtuous life possest.*

Because of this inscription it became the custom to place red flowers on the tomb, and this is still done. It is not known how long this has been going on, but a guide to the church published in 1908, and books on Buckinghamshire by Arthur Mee and Alison Uttley, published in 1940 and 1950 respectively, all mention it.

Ripon Horn-Blower

Ripon, in North Yorkshire, boasts what must be the only traditional public custom that takes place every day of the year, and has done so for centuries, although probably not for millennia as is sometimes claimed by the over-hopeful local council. Every night, the city's horn-blower dresses himself in his three-cornered hat and antiquated coat and proceeds to the market-place, where he blows three blasts of his horn at each of the four sides of the obelisk there.

This ceremony was originally designed to signify that the town was in the care of the Wakeman and his staff, who would patrol the streets until morning, keeping the inhabitants safe. The last Wakeman was Hugh

Ripley in 1604, who also became the first mayor when James I granted the town a charter, but the setting of the watch with the horn has, apparently, continued ever since. The horn used at present is a very impressive African ox horn, provided for the purpose in 1865, but the civic regalia also includes two previous horns – one dating from 1690, and one that is claimed to be the original charter horn given by King Alfred in the year 886. The latter claim is most unlikely, but it could be as old as the twelfth century. Plans for carbon-dating work on the old horn are underway.

Bainbridge, also in Yorkshire, has a similar horn-blowing custom every night in the winter months (*see* **Bainbridge Horn-Blower**, *above*).

Tower of London: Ceremony of the Keys

Every night, at precisely seven minutes to ten, the Chief Yeoman Warder of the Tower of London starts his rounds of the Tower's gates and ceremoniously locks them up until the morning. He is dressed in the formal and colourful Tudor garb so popular with tourists, and is accompanied by an escort of guards. Sentries at each gate 'salute the Queen's Keys' as they pass, and at the Bloody Tower the Warder is challenged and the traditional words are exchanged:

'Halt! Who goes there?'
'The Keys.'
'Whose keys?'
'Queen Elizabeth's Keys.'
'Pass, Queen Elizabeth's Keys, all's well.'

It is claimed that the ceremony has been carried out for 700 years. Tickets can be purchased to witness the ceremony.

Wayfarers' Dole

Most charitable doles are distributed annually to specific groups of people, but the Wayfarers' Dole at St Cross Hospital, Winchester, is given on any day to anyone who asks for it. The hospital's full name is the Hospital of St Cross and Almshouse of Noble Poverty, and as it was founded in the 1130s, it is probably the oldest continuing charitable institution in Britain. The impressive medieval buildings are home to a number of elderly 'brethren', who wear a traditional black gown and cap. Any passing stranger may ask at the porter's lodge for the Wayfarers' Dole, which consists of some beer (about a fifth of a pint nowadays) and a piece of bread.

See also **Doles**, p. 87.

Weekly Customs

Farthing Bundles

The Fern Street School Settlement in Bow, east London, was founded by Clara Grant in 1907 as one of the many philanthropic schemes of Victorian and Edwardian times designed to alleviate the endemic poverty and deprivation that characterized life in areas of England's cities; in this case the East End of London. One of the innovative ways in which the Settlement sought to reach the children of the area was the provision of 'farthing bundles' every Saturday. These bundles contained a variety of little things that would delight children who had little in the way of real toys or posses-sions, and included broken toys, bits of dolls, pieces of ribbon or coloured material, pencils, silver paper, cut-out pictures, beads, shells, and whistles. A farthing was charged (the smallest coin of the realm, worth only one quarter of an old penny), and when the bundles became too popular for the Settlement to cope, access was restricted to younger children by making them walk under a purpose-built portable wooden arch, which bore the words:

Enter now ye children small
None can come who are too tall

Only those who could walk under the arch without stooping were eligible, although the height of the arch had to be raised more than once, as growing prosperity resulted in taller children. Distribution of the bundles continued until well after the Second World War, now costing a penny, but changes in society, particularly in the East End, made them increasingly irrelevant, and the last regular distribution was in 1984. The custom is still occasionally revived on special occasions, such as the eightieth anniversary in 1987, and the Settlement still continues its good work in other spheres.

The wooden arch under which children walked in order to receive their farthing bundle at the Fern Street Settlement in Bow, east London, 1972

John Sayer Charity

This weekly dole is based on the will of John Sayer, who died in 1638. He left fifteen acres of land, the rent of which was to provide twopenny loaves every Sunday for the poor of Woodbridge in Suffolk. The charity has continued, but the land was sold in 1958 and the proceeds invested. A special wooden cage in the porch of St Mary's church, inscribed with John Sayer's name and the details of his will, holds nine small loaves every Saturday, to which certain locals help themselves.

See also **Doles**, p. 87.

St Monday

Countless people are familiar with that Monday-morning feeling of not wanting to go back to work, and one can therefore spare a thought for workers in the past, before the weekend was invented, who only had Sunday off each week. Nevertheless, many workers did manage to achieve their own unofficial weekend, by the simple expedient of declaring every Monday a day off, which they dedicated to an imaginary saint called 'St Monday'. Clearly, this could only happen in trades where the workers were largely self-employed and could survive on the proceeds of the work carried out on other days, and it was the shoemakers who were particularly prone to this self-indulgence. Monday was often called 'the shoemakers' holiday' in consequence, although some other workers managed to do something similar.

A spurious explanation for the origin of St Monday was printed in the *Folk-Lore Record* of 1878, from an undated newspaper cutting. It explained that when Cromwell's army was encamped outside Perth, one of his followers, named Monday, hanged himself. Cromwell offered a reward to the person who could compile the best verse on the subject, and was so pleased with one shoemaker's contribution that he declared that no one of that trade needed to work on Monday ever again. However, the tradition of St Monday was in place long before Cromwell's time: Thomas Dekker's earliest surviving play, for example, entitled *The Shoemaker's Holiday*, was published in the year 1600, and his play *If it be not good, the Divel is in it* (1612) contains the line, 'They say Monday's shoemaker's holiday, I'll fall to that trade.'

St Monday survived into the nineteenth century, but the whole idea was anathema to the type of Victorian social reformer who believed that workers should be either at work or at prayer. Those who claimed the St Monday privilege had a reputation for getting drunk and unruly, and were believed to set a bad example to other workers. When better working conditions, stricter time-keeping, and the half-day holiday on Saturday became the norm, St Monday faded away.

St Monday was also popular in Ireland and Scotland, and exactly the same tradition existed in France and Belgium, back to at least the sixteenth century, where the cobblers liked to *faire St Lundi*. Similar customs also existed in Spain, Germany, and elsewhere in Europe.

Occasional Customs

Abingdon Bun-Throwing

At Abingdon, in Oxfordshire, they have a long-standing custom of throwing buns to the waiting crowd on national and royal occasions. The earliest documented instance took place in 1809, to celebrate George III's recovery from illness, but records before 1838 simply refer to the buns being 'distributed'. In 1838, however, a thousand buns were recorded as being thrown to celebrate Victoria's coronation. In more recent times, buns were thrown at the end of the Second World War, in the year 2000 to mark the Millennium, and in 2002, to celebrate the anniversary of Queen Elizabeth's accession in 1952. June 2006 saw 4,000 buns thrown from the roof of the Market House (or county hall) by councillors and freemen to the crowds waiting in the market-square below, to celebrate the 450th anniversary of the granting of the borough charter to Abingdon.

Although it is unusual to find buns being thrown simply for special occasions, buns and other food such as bread and cheese were often thrown to people in other customs around the country, either as part of a charity dole or in mayor-making ceremonies, as at Harwich in Essex (*see* **Third Thursday in May: Harwich Kichel-Throwing**). Jackie Smith, Honorary Archivist for Abingdon Town Council, admitted in 2006 that bun-throwings have certainly become more frequent in Abingdon since the 1980s, and it is not clear whether this is due to an increase in notable occasions. A collection of the buns can be seen in Abingdon Museum.

See also **Scrambling Customs**, p. 128.

Bradshaw Memorial Dusting

Parish churches up and down the country contain thousands of grand memorials to local worthies who were thought important or good enough to be remembered for ever more. Many of the same individuals bequeathed money to the poor or other charitable causes, and sometimes also left instructions for activities that later became regular, and often seemingly eccentric, customs. The memorial to the successful London lawyer Anthonie Bradshaw, of Duffield in Derbyshire, is an interesting example of how a man could contrive to do good for the poor and ensure that his name was remembered after his death.

About 1600, fourteen years before his death, Bradshaw had a huge sandstone and alabaster memorial set against the wall of St Alkmund's church, commemorating himself, his two wives, and their twenty children (although he had three more before he died). He also founded an almshouse for four elderly women. One of the stipulations of Bradshaw's bequest was that the residents of the almshouse should regularly dust the memorial and keep it clean. The almshouse and the dusting disappeared in the 1880s and the monument fell into disrepair. However, it has now been carefully restored and is looked after by a charitable trust, the Friends of the Bradshaw Memorial.

See also **Doles**, p. 87.

Chedzoy Candle Auction

One of two surviving candle auctions in Somerset, the auction at Chedzoy is held once every twenty-one years to lease out Church Acre, which, as its name suggests, is a field that belongs to the parish church, St Mary the Virgin. All proceeds go towards the upkeep of the church. As usual with these affairs, the auction is 'by inch of candle', and the last bid made before the candle goes out is the winner. The auction is usually held at the Manor House Inn, and the next should take place in 2009.

See also **Candle Auctions**, p. 106.

Denby Dale Pie

The West Yorkshire town of Denby Dale is world-renowned for its giant pies. Once every thirty or forty years, the people of the town get the urge to make a huge pie, usually even bigger than the one before. The reasons behind these urges are various: in 1788, it was to celebrate the return to health of George III; in 1815, a 'Victory Pie' was made to mark the end of the Napoleonic threat; in 1846, the pie celebrated the repeal of the Corn Laws; in 1887, Queen Victoria's Golden Jubilee; in 1896, the jubilee of the repeal of the Corn Laws; in 1928, an 'Infirmary Pie' was made to support the local hospital; in 1964, a pie was made to raise money for a village hall; and in 1988, to celebrate 200 years of pie-making at Denby Dale.

The day the pie is unveiled and shared out has always been a major gala occasion, with speeches, processions, sideshows, funfairs and entertainments, but pie-making and eating has not always gone quite to plan. The 1846 event, to celebrate the repeal of the hated Corn Laws, was marred by a riot, which was probably organized by political opponents, and the pie was trampled underfoot. And in 1887, the pie was found to be rotten and the crowd got dangerously out of control, although the replacement 'Resurrection Pie', which was made a month later, was celebrated without any major hitch. Plans to make a pie to celebrate the end of the Second World War, and the coronation of Elizabeth II in 1953, were scuppered by rationing and food regulation.

The build-up to the 1964 effort was marked with tragi-comedy, and later real tragedy. In June, the specially made steel pie-dish, 18 feet long and 6 feet wide, was launched on to the Calder Navigation Canal at Mirfield, near Huddersfield, where it was to be floated to Denby. Unfortunately, however, it sank. The national press reported that teenagers were holding an impromptu party in the dish at the time of the accident – although it is not clear whether it was their fault – and the dish was duly salvaged by a local garage's rescue truck. The organizing committee revealed that the canal trip had been insured with Lloyd's, so the insurance would foot the bill. In August, however, four members of the organizing committee were killed in a road accident returning from a television interview.

Twentieth-century organizers had clearly got a better handle on crowd control than their Victorian predecessors, and all the events since 1896 have been major successes, attracting ever-increasing numbers of visitors, and with nearly everyone in the town making some contribution. The 1988 pie, organized by the Denby Dale Pie Trust, resulted in a pie that was 20 feet long, 7 feet wide, and 1 foot 6 inches deep, weighing nearly half a ton, but even this was surpassed in both size and technological achievement by the Millennium Pie in the year 2000. This one was baked in a dish that comprised twenty-four compartments, each with its own heating element, specially designed by the School of Engineering at the University of Huddersfield. The pie was 40 feet by 8 feet and nearly 4 foot deep, and contained 5,000 kg of beef, 2,000 kg of potatoes, and 1,000 kg of onions. It was brought in procession to the Pie Field on a lorry, and was blessed by the Bishop of Wakefield before being cut and distributed to the 30,000-strong crowd.

Denby Dale is not quite unique in the big-food stakes, as the village of Aughton, in Lancashire, had a giant-pudding custom. The Aughton feast was a plum pudding 20 feet long and 6 feet thick, weighing 1,000 lb, and was made every twenty-one years. The last one was made in 1886, but in the 1970s the field where the festivities had taken place was still known as 'the Pudding Field'.

Dunmow Flitch

Little Dunmow and Great Dunmow are Essex villages about twelve miles from Chelmsford, and are world famous for their ceremony of awarding a 'flitch of bacon' to couples who have been married for more than a year and a day and who have had neither a cross word nor a single thought regretting their married state during that time. In the modern version of the custom, claimants are brought up before a 'court', presided over by a judge, and complete with claimants' counsel, opposing counsel, a jury of twelve unmarried people (six men and six women), a clerk of the court, and an usher. It is not a competition between couples, as each claim is considered on its merits, and it is possible for them all to win. However, the opposing counsel always tries to demolish each case and persuade the jury to decide 'for the flitch' and against the claimants;

The Dunmow flitch , Essex, 1650, as imagined by R. Hillingford in 1864

and witnesses for and against can be called. Successful couples are carried in the Flitch Chair, shoulder high, to the market-place, and are obliged to take an oath:

You do swear by custom of confession,
That you ne'er made nuptial transgression
Nor since you were married man and wife
By household brawls or contentious strife
Or otherwise in bed or at board
Offended each other in deed or in word
Or in a twelve months and a day
Repented not in thought in any way
Or since the church clerk said amen
Wish't yourselves unmarried again
But continue true and desire
As when you joined hands in holy quire.

Nowadays, the event is held in a marquee every leap year, and is organized by a committee of volunteers. Judges and counsel often include well-known figures.

Unlike many customs, the Dunmow flitch is genuinely old, and was already well known over 600 years ago. It is mentioned in terms of general familiarity by both William Langland in his *Piers Plowman* (c.1377) and Chaucer in the *Wife of Bath's Tale* (c.1390), and not long after this, the earliest known awards of the bacon were recorded in the *Cartuleries* of Dunmow Priory, in 1445, 1467, and 1510. The first of these was to one Richard Wright, of Burburgh, near Norwich, which shows that even at this early date the flitch could be claimed by outsiders, and not simply by locals. In this period, the custom was in the province of the Priory of Little Dunmow, but at the Dissolution of the Monasteries in 1539, responsibility was given to the new lord of the manor. Successive lords kept it going until 1751, after which time they started to refuse all requests from prospective recipients, and it lapsed.

There was a tremendous revival of interest, however, after the publication of Harrison Ainsworth's *The Flitch* of Bacon, or the Custom of Dunmow in 1854. Ainsworth was an immensely popular historical novelist of the period, and he took the part of the judge in a well-publicized revival of the custom the following year. As with all such revivals, certain characteristics of the earlier form were maintained, others were dropped, and many were introduced for the first time. In this case, the custom was completely transformed by making it a public event. Whereas previously claim-ants would come forward of their own volition and would be vetted by the prior, the lord of the manor, or his steward, in private, in the revival version, a 'trial' would be announced and applications invited. After an initial vetting, the actual selection was made in a public mock 'court', with judge, jury, and barristers, and this brought scope for humour and burlesque. So the modern custom was born.

Despite the unusually rich documentary record, the origin of the ceremony is still not known. It is possible that the custom was created as a condition of a bequest to the priory by a benefactor; or perhaps it was some kind of manorial obligation by which land was held, or services rendered. Certainly, whimsical bequests are not unknown, and seemingly bizarre manorial customs were also common, but it is unclear why the prior or a mid sixteenth-century lord would keep up what must have been a potentially expensive custom unless they felt obliged to do so, and it is also unclear why there is no hint of a reason in the surviving priory or manor records.

The exact form of the earliest ceremonies is not known, but by the time of the records found in the Cartuleries, a fundamental element was the oath, taken by the applicants, testifying to the truth of everything they had stated. They took this oath while kneeling on uncomfortable (sometimes described as 'sharp') stones, and once the award had been given, the success-ful couple would be chaired around the vicinity. As far as we can tell, the award was taken seriously in the prior's time, and probably for most of the lord of the manor's jurisdiction as well, but it was not always taken very seriously by outsiders. The custom was regularly featured in novels, poems, ballad operas, and plays, and was also depicted in popular prints and engravings, and in many the flitch ceremony was treated either with broad humour or sentimental romance; a stand-

ard motif was the winning of the award by a couple who then argued noisily about how to take it home.

Surprisingly, the Dunmow flitch ceremony was not unique. In October 1714, a writer in the Spectator reported:

I find but two couples in this first century that were successful. The first was a sea captain and his wife, who since the day of their marriage had not seen each other till the day of the claim. The second was an honest pair in the neighbourhood. The husband was a man of plain good sense, and a peaceable temper. The woman was dumb.

This writer was in fact satirizing a very similar custom at Wychnor, in Staffordshire, which is reputed to have been first stipulated in the deed by which the Earl of Lancaster granted the manor to Sir Philip de Somerville, in the reign of Edward III, c.1336. Francis Steer, who wrote the standard history of the Dunmow custom in 1951, also identified other public flitches in Vienna and Brittany that were closely related to conju-gal contentment.

Highgate Horns

Highgate is now a suburb of north London, but in earlier times it was a village in Middlesex, high on a hill, strad-dling the main road north. Before the railways came, it was an important transport centre, and there were numerous inns catering for the coaching trade and the stream of horse-drawn traffic that passed through every day. An interesting custom grew up at Highgate, in which those who passed through the village for the first time were required to undergo a sort of initia-tion ceremony, which involved swearing an oath on a pair of horns. By the time the horns custom is first documented, it was carried out by the publicans of the neighbourhood with an eye to what we would now call the tourist trade, and each of the inns kept a pair of horns, mounted on a pole, ready for the purpose. The species from which the horns were taken seemed to matter little, as stag, ram, and bullock horns are mentioned. The burlesque ceremony usually involved the landlord dressing as a judge and administering an oath that included instructions on the lines of 'Never eat the brown bread if white is available, never kiss the

Swearing on the horns at Highgate, London (William Hone, *The Every-Day Book*, 1827)

maid if you can kiss the mistress, and if you see three pigs asleep in the gutter you may kick out the middle one and take its place.' The applicant had to kiss the horns and then buy drinks for the company or pay the landlord a fee.

The custom was clearly already well known in the mid eighteenth century. The earliest known mention is in the *Weekly Oracle* of 1737, and in 1742 the pantomime *Harlequin Teague* featured a song that already included the traditional jokes of brown bread and kisses. Francis Grose's *Classical Dictionary of the Vulgar Tongue* (1785) confirms the custom's widespread fame:

The proverb 'he has been sworn at Highgate' is more widely circulated than understood. In its ordinary signification it is applied to a 'knowing' fellow who is well acquainted with the 'good things', and always helps himself to the best; and it has its origin in an old usage still kept up at Highgate, in Middlesex.

As the custom is already fully-formed when it enters the documentary record, there is no indication that it was ever anything but burlesque, although some modern writers assume it had previously been a serious ceremony with an ancient lineage. Other customs involving horns existed, but none is quite the same. At Charlton Horn Fair, the horns almost certainly derive from the connection with St Luke (*see* **18 October: St Luke's Day**), but the closest analogy to the Highgate Horns was the custom of 'horning the colt' at Weyhill Fair, which was ostensibly an initiation ceremony probably started by cattle dealers (*see* **10 October: Weyhill Fair**). One sensible theory is therefore that the swearing was an in-joke of the cattle drovers who regularly passed through Highgate on their way to the northern markets, and this remains a possibility.

The custom finally lapsed in the late nineteenth century, but is revived, from time to time, at local pubs, including The Wrestlers, on North Road, and The Flask, on Highgate West Hill.

Oakham Horseshoes

Every peer of the realm who visits Oakham in Leicestershire (formerly in Rutland) for the first time is obliged by custom to present a horseshoe to the lord of the manor, or to pay a fine. Even royalty is not exempt and Queen Elizabeth II presented a shoe from one of her own racehorses in 1967, although the story that Elizabeth I did so is probably apocryphal. The shoes are exhibited on the walls of the great hall of Oakham Castle, and many of them are not real horseshoes but large, specially made presentation pieces, with the names and crests of the donors. Some have disappeared over the years – the official charged with putting them up often took down older ones to make room – but nearly 250 have survived and are still on show, including one from Edward IV (r. 1461–83). The shoes are all mounted with the prongs facing downwards, regarded as unlucky nowadays, but the general consensus over the orientation of a horseshoe is a relatively recent phenomenon and in the past either way would do.

The origin of the custom remains a mystery, but the first known written reference dates from 1521, and that document mentions the shoe presented by Edward IV, so it was clearly extant in his time. One plausible theory links the shoes to the family of Ferrers, who held the manor direct from the Crown from at least 1166 to 1252. The Ferrers were descended from the Norman Ferrières family, and as the name is clearly connected with iron-working, blacksmiths, and farriers, and the family arms comprise six black horseshoes on a silver background, there seems to be an obvious connection. The fact that the Great Hall was also built in the twelfth century adds circumstantial evidence, but there is no evidence that the arms pre-date the custom, or that either go back to before the fifteenth century.

Virgins' Crowns or Maidens' Garlands

A custom that was carried on for centuries in many parishes up and down the country, and still survives in one, involved the construction of a garland or crown to honour a deceased unmarried parishioner of unblemished character. The garland was carried before the coffin at the funeral and, if unchallenged within a certain period, hung high up in the church for all to see, where it remained until it fell to pieces with age. The construction of these garlands varied considerably, but one common basic form is made in the shape of a crown, with pliable twigs forming a horizontal hoop, and two vertical semicircles arching over it, at right angles to each other. The wood is then covered with cloth or coloured paper, and rosettes and artificial flowers are placed on it at intervals. Some had items hanging down inside, often gloves made of stiff paper, and many had verses from the Scriptures attached. Most had the name of the deceased and the date marked somewhere on the garland or on a small shield fixed to the wall nearby.

William Howitt, born 1792, is one of many writers who were impressed by the garlands in their youth:

Though I never saw a funeral in which so beautiful and appropriate a practice was retained, I well recollect seeing these gloves and garlands hanging in the church of my native village [Heanor] in Derbyshire, and I have heard my mother say, that in her younger days she has helped to cut and prepare them for the funeral of the young women of the place. The garlands were originally of actual flowers – lilies and roses – and the gloves of white kid. For these had been substituted simple white paper.

As the garlands were hung in the church, the custom was remembered by the congregation, even if new examples were only rarely made. In many cases, the poignant stories of the deceased recipients also lived on.

The custom was clearly known to Shakespeare, as the references to Ophelia's garlands and 'virgin crants' (crowns) in Act V, scene 1 of *Hamlet* demonstrate, and there are numerous descriptions throughout the eighteenth century. However, it is not clear whether the custom of mounting garlands was ever universal, although it was obviously widespread. A map provided by Gareth Spriggs in his comprehensive survey of garlands published in 1982 includes all known references to the custom, and shows that it was certainly found over most of the country, but was much more common in the Midlands and the North, particularly in Derbyshire and eastern Yorkshire. A fair number of southern examples are included, but there are none west of Hampshire. We will never know how many were swept away by nineteenth-century vicars, church improvers and restorers, but a few can still be seen around the country, and the one place that still keeps the custom alive is St Mary's church, Abbotts Ann, in Hampshire.

Dates for Easter Sunday 2007–20

2007	8 April
2008	23 March
2009	12 April
2010	4 April
2011	24 April
2012	8 April
2013	31 March
2014	20 April
2015	5 April
2016	27 March
2017	16 April
2018	1 April
2019	21 April
2020	12 April

Sources

Abbreviations

Devonshire Assoc.
Transactions of the Devonshire Association
EDD
English Dialect Dictionary
Gent. Mag.
Gentleman's Magazine
JEFDSS
Journal of the English Folk Dance & Song Society
N&Q
Notes & Queries
OED
Oxford English Dictionary
Sussex Arch. Colls.
Sussex Archaeological Collections
Wilts. Arch. & Nat. Hist. Mag.
Wiltshire Archaeological & Natural History Magazine

The Calendar

My mother will hardly: Opie & Tatem (1989) 53.
The figure of 3 to 4 million: Thomas (1971) 347–56.
His standard book: *Political Register*, 11 Dec. 1813, 751; quoted in Dyck (1992) 82.
On St Peters day: Surtees Society, *Rural Economy in Yorkshire in 1641* (1857) 112–14.
Capp (1979); Duncan (1998); Poole (1998); Roud (2003) 56.

January

NEW YEAR CUSTOMS AND SUPERSTITIONS
The character of the coming: Couch (1871) 151.
Parties are general: *Folk-Lore Journal* 4 (1886) 123.
When a man by hap-hazard: Opie & Tatem (1989) 35.
On this day: Jewitt (1853) 231.
My maid, who comes: N&Q 3S:2 (1862) 484.
On New Year's Day: N&Q 8S:9 (1896) 46.
Opie & Tatem (1989) 35–6; Roud (2003) 31.

Burning the Bush
This custom was generally: Leather (1912) 91-3.
Folk-Lore 12 (1901) 349–51.

Cream of the Well
It was formerly the custom: Leather (1912) 91.
Opie & Tatem (1989) 427–9; Roud (2003) 332–3.

First-Footing and Letting In
There can be few: Bosanquet (1929) 14.
Mrs. Billson: Billson (1895) 70.
You must see first of all: Gutch & Peacock (1908) 169.

On Christmas Day: Duncombe (1804) 210.
As the clock struck twelve: Leather (1912) 90.
Wright & Lones II (1938) 2–16; Opie & Tatem (1989) 159-61, 283–4; Roud (2003) 190–93, 334.

Gifts
On the first day: Brand I (1849) 11–12.
Brand I (1849) 10–20; Wright & Lones II (1938) 24–32.

Mad Maldon Mud Race
Kent (2005) 47–8; www.maldonlions.co.uk/events/mudrace.

Pop (Pope) Ladies
I happened to sleep: Gent. Mag. 90 (1820) 15.
N&Q 4S:11 (1873) 412; Wright & Lones I (1938) 29–30.

6 JANUARY

Epiphany
Brand I (1849) 21–34; Wright & Lones II (1938) 50–93; Metford (1991) 17–20, 40–42.

Old Christmas Day
My grandfather always kept: Leather (1912) 95.

Twelfth Night
I did bring out my cake: Samuel Pepys, *Diary*, 6 January 1669.
I went to a friend's house: Brand (1810) 228, quoting *Universal Magazine* (1774).
In London: Hone, *The Every-Day Book* I (1827) 24–5.
Hone, *The Every-Day Book* I (1827) 24–31; Brand I (1849) 21–34; Wright & Lones II (1938) 50–91; Hutton (1996) 15–18, 110–11.

Baddeley Cake
Brentnall (1975) 188; Shuel (1985) 127–8.

Brough Holly Night
Formerly the 'Holly-tree': Hone, *The Table Book* (1827) 13–14.
Wright & Lones II (1938) 68; Findler (1968) 47–9.

Haxey Hood
Newall (1980); Cooper (1993).

Moseley's Dole
Edwards (1842) 55–6; Wright & Lones II (1938) 68–74.

Twelfth Night Fires
At the approach of evening: Gent. Mag. (1791) 116.

PLOUGH SUNDAY
The Times, 11 Jan. 1954, 8.

PLOUGH MONDAY
Plough Monday, next after: Tusser (1580/1984) 177.
Leading the plough: *Dives and Pauper* (c.1405–10/1976/1980) 157.
Plough Monday was a great institution: Bird (1911) 39.
Plough Monday – All the boys: *Folk-Lore* 37 (1926) 76.
Gutch & Peacock (1908) 171–87; Wright & Lones II (1938) 93–103; Porter (1969) 96–103; Palmer (1985) 86–90; Howkins & Merricks (1991); Hutton (1996) 124–33.

Plough Plays
Baskervill (1924); Helm (1980); Howkins & Merricks (1991); Millington (1995); Cass & Roud (2002).

Ploughboys and Maids
When the ploughman returned: Baker II (1854) 123.
It was customary: Bloom (1930) 80.
If ploughman get hatchet: Tusser (1580/1984) 177.

PLOUGH MONDAY/PLOUGH TUESDAY

Straw Bears
When I was at Whittlesey: Folk-Lore 20 (1909) 202–3.
Marshall (1967) 199–201; Tebbutt (1984) 55–6; Frampton (1989).

7 JANUARY

St Distaff's Day
Partly work and partly play: Herrick (1648).
Chambers I (1864) 68–9; Wright & Lones III (1940) 91–2.

14 JANUARY

Hunting the Mallard
Hone, *The Year-Book* (1832) 44–6; Chambers I (1864) 113–14; Wright & Lones II (1938) 104–5; Hole (1976) 161–3.

17 JANUARY

Old Twelfth Night
Patten (1974) 6–8.

21 JANUARY

St Agnes' Day
The girl who wished: Long Ago 2 (1874) 80.
Wright & Lones II (1938) 106–110; Roud (2003) 386.

22 JANUARY

St Vincent's Day
Remember on St. Vincent's: Balfour (1904) 174.
Wright & Lones II (1938) 111.

24 JANUARY

Eve of Conversion of St Paul
St. Paul's Eve: Folk-Lore Journal 4 (1886) 127.
On entering a house: Western Antiquary 3 (1884) 67.

25 JANUARY

St Paul's Day
If Paul's Fair: Western Antiquary 3 (1884) 193.
Brand I (1849) 39–42; Chambers I (1864) 157–8; Wright & Lones II (1938) 112–15.

30 JANUARY

Execution of Charles I
Chambers I (1864) 189–92; Brentnall (1975) 174–6; Society of King Charles the Martyr website, www.skcm.org.

JANUARY/FEBRUARY

Chinese New Year
Buddha, on the turn of the year: www.chinatownchinese.com/rooster.htm.

Games and Sports
but all play and no work: Samuel Smiles, *Self Help* (1859), quoted in Flavell (1993) 144.
In the records: Govett (1890) 73.
The favourite pastimes: Hole (1949) 1.

Strutt (1801); Govett (1890); Hole (1949); Malcolmson (1973); Opie (1997a).

Camping
Of the sport itself: Forby (1830) 51.
camping is not football: N&Q 5S:2 (1892) 137.
At times a large football: Moor (1823) 65.
Moor (1823) 63–6; Forby (1830) 50–54; Porter (1969) 230–31.

Pell-Mell
Chambers I (1864) 465-6; Hazlitt (1905) 470–71.

Shuttlecock
The play at shuttlecocke: Manningham (1868), quoted in Hazlitt (1905) 33.
On the day itself: N&Q 3S:3 (1863) 87.
Gomme II (1894–8) 192-6; Wright & Lones I (1936) 28; Strutt (1801/1876) 400–401.

Stoolball
Stoolball: this game: N&Q 3S:11 (1867) 457–8.
a certain number: Strutt (1801/1876) 165.
Strutt (1801/1876) 165–6; Grantham (1931); Arlott (1975) 996–9; Lowerson (1995); Sussex Arch. Colls. 133 (1995) 263-74; Sussex Arch. Colls. 136 (1998) 204–5; National Stoolball Association website, www.stoolball.co.uk.

Tipcat
Strutt (1801/1876) 86; Hole (1949) 48; Opie (1997a) 316–21.

Trapball / Knurr and Spell
Strutt (1801/1876) 176-9; Hone, *The Every-Day Book* I (1827) 215; Hole (1949) 48–9; Atkinson (1963); Opie (1997a) 322–8.

February

Trial of the Pyx
Brentnall (1975) 42–7; www.thegoldsmiths.co.uk/company/trial.htm.

FIRST SUNDAY IN FEBRUARY

Clowns' Service
Shuel (1985) 79.

2 FEBRUARY

Candlemas (Purification of the Blessed Virgin Mary)
If Candlemas day be dry: Hewett (1900) 107.
Candlemas day was also known: Tebbutt (1984) 56–7.
Brand I (1849) 43–51; Wright & Lones II (1938) 118–29; Opie & Tatem (1989) 54–5; Metford (1991) 74–6; Duffy (1992) 15–22; Roud (2003) 56–9.

Forty Shilling Day
Kightly (1986) 117; information from the Revd Pam Robson of Holmbury St Mary church, Surrey, August 2005.

3 FEBRUARY

St Blaise's Day
This day, Munday: Gurdon (1893) 110.
Chambers I (1864) 219–20.

St Ives Hurling
Rabey (1972); Kightly (1986) 144-5; Williams (1987) 16–19.

Hurling
The game called the Hurlers: Defoe (1724–6) Letter IV: Cornwall.
Carew (1602/1969) 147–50; Rabey (1972); Williams (1987) 16–19, 20-1.

10 FEBRUARY

St Scholastica's Day
Dyer (1876) 97–8.

14 FEBRUARY

St Valentine's Day
I'll tell you something: Hart (1968) 167, citing Dorothy Osborne.
Valentining: Children going: Baker II (1854) 373–4.
Young girls grow eager: John Clare, *The Midsummer Cushion* (1832/1990)
On Valentine's day: Halliwell (1849) 219–20.

20 FEBRUARY

John Cass Commemoration
Brentnall (1975) 167–8.

SHROVETIDE AND LENT

At the beginning of Lent: Fisher (1865) 463.
Brand I (1849) 62–102; Chambers I (1864) 236–41; Wright & Lones I (1936) 1–42; Hutton (1996) 151–68.

SHROVE TUESDAY

the children expect: Nicholson (1890) 12
It was the day: Pasquils Palinodia (1619/1886) 29.
The custom of apprentices: The Times, 3 March 1954.

Alnwick Football
Before the Alnwick Improvement Act: Folk-Lore Journal 2 (1884) 123–4.
Independent, 11 Feb. 1989, 47.

Ashbourne Football
Porter (1992); Porter (1995); www.derbyshireuk.net/dcustom4. html.

Football
Moreover, each year: Fitz Stephen (c.1180/1990) 56–7.
And because of the great: N&Q 7S:2 (1886) 26-7.
The Kinge forbiddes: Sc. Act Jas. I c. 18.
Foote balle wherin is nothinge: The Boke named the Governour I (1531) xxvii.
In the town of Derby: Glover I (1829) 310.
The old custom: The Times, 10 Feb. 1932, 9.
Any exercise, which withdraweth us: Stubbes (1595/2002) 251–3.
Nicholson (1890) 34–9; Magoun (1938); Elias & Dunning (1971); Alexander (1986); Reid (1988).

Cock Throwing and Threshing
Their entertainment then: Schellinks (1993) 73.
Hone, *The Every-Day Book* II (1827) 123–9; Wright & Lones I (1936) 22–4; Malcolmson (1973) 48–9, 118–22.

Cockfighting
Each year upon the day: Fitz Stephen (c.1180/1990) 56.
In the afternoon we went: Schellinks (1993) 93.
Wright & Lones I (1936) 24–6; Malcolmson (1973) 49–50.

Cookeels (or Coquilles)
Forby (1830) 76; N&Q 1S:1 (1850) 293, 412–3.

Dough-Nut Day
Hone, *The Year-Book* (1832) 796.

Egg Shackling
In the 19th century: Dacombe (1935) 90.

Ludlow Rope-Pulling
Hone, *The Every-Day Book* II (1827) 128–9; Brand I (1849) 92; Wright & Lones I (1936) 29; Palmer (2004) 291–2.

Pancakes
It was the day: Pasquils Palinodia (1619/1866) 29.
The excitement of pancake day: Harris (1969) 149–51.
The 'pancake bell' is still rung: Folk-Lore 61 (1950) 167.
Shrove Tuesday: Ill-luck: Forby (1830) 242.

Pancake Races
Folk-Lore 60 (1949) 301–2; Lenton (2003).

Westminster Pancakes
Then, suddenly, the frying pan: Brentnall (1975) 158.
Brentnall (1975) 157–61; Shuel (1985) 151–2.

Purbeck Marblers and Stonecutters
www.uk-genealogy.org.uk/genuki/DOR/CorfeCastle/articles.html; Shuel (1985) 120; Kightly (1986) 156–7.

St Columb Hurling
Many a young hurler: Rabey (1972) 15.
Williams (1987) 20–21; Kightly (1986) 144–5.

Sedgefield Ball Game
The ball was put through: Folk-Lore Journal 2 (1884) 124.

Shroving and Lent-Crocking
Pit-a-pat! the pan's hot: Folk-Lore 14 (1903) 167–8.
On the day termed 'Hall Monday': Couch (1871) 151.
Wright & Lones I (1936) 16–20; Hutton (1996) 163–7; Robson (1996).

Skipping
brought back memories: Dalesman, Apr. 1994, 74–5.
Smith (1989) 3–8; Dalesman, Feb. 1994, 23–4.

Whipping Toms
Palmer (1985) 223–4.

ASH WEDNESDAY

On Ash Wednesday the good people: Fisher (1865) 463.
On Ash Wednesday, many folks: Folk-Lore 40 (1929) 283.

Jack-a-Lent
An old custom: Couch (1871) 152.
How like a Jack a Lent: Quarles (1646) 88.
Brand I (1849) 94–102; Wright & Lones I (1936) 39–42.

Scambling Days
Dyer (1876) 95; OED; EDD.

FRIDAY FOLLOWING ASH WEDNESDAY

Pully Lug Day
I have a recollection: N&Q 5S:10 (1878) 249.
N&Q 7S:2 (1886) 294. Wright, EDD IV (1898–1905) 644.

29 FEBRUARY

Leap Year Day
In Leap Year they have power: Lean I (1902–4) 468.
Some priests assert: Hampson II (1841) 31–2.
N&Q 4S:8 (1871) 505, citing Courtship, Love and Matrimony (1606).

March

Dame Elizabeth Marvyn Charity
Sykes (1977) 37.

1 MARCH

St David's Day
being St. David's Day: Schellinks (1993) 75.
A house-maid advised: Hewett (1892) 52.
The Devil shakes a bag: Bye-Gones (1899-1900) 344.

Lean I (1905) 357; for March coming in like a lion, *see* Inwards
    (1893) 19–20.

2 MARCH

St Chad's Day
Chambers I (1864) 320–21.

3 MARCH

St Winwaloe's Day
Wright & Lones II (1938) 159–62.

Rough Music
There is a man: Surrey Gazette, 9 Jan. 1869.
A thrice married man: Croydon Advertiser, 1 Oct. 1881, 5.
A few months ago: Folk-Lore Journal 2 (1884) 187–8.
'Rough music' was heard: Horn (1986) 52–3.
Ingram (1984); Thompson (1991).

5 MARCH

St Piran's Day
Wright & Lones II (1938) 162; Doble IV (1998) 3–30.

9 MARCH

St Constantine's Day
Wright & Lones II (1938) 163–4; Doble II (1997) 15–24.

10 MARCH

If it does not freeze: Hewett (1900) 109
Mists or hoar frosts: Thomas Passenger, *The Shepherd's Kalendar*
    (London, *c*.1680), quoted in *N&Q* 1S:8 (1853) 50.

11 MARCH

Penny Loaf Day
Newark Advertiser, 14 Mar. 1997, 36; J. Potter Briscoe,
    Nottinghamshire Facts and Fictions (1876), quoted in Wright &
    Lones II (1938) 164.

12 MARCH

St Gregory's Day
Wright & Lones II (1938) 164–5.

17 MARCH

St Patrick's Day
The Irish folks: Swift, *Journal to Stella* (1710–13) letter lxi.
My grandmother would send: Sutton (1997) 39.
St. Patrick's Day today: Bruley (2001) 173.
The early English calendars: Chambers I (1864) 385.

Pudding-Pies
Woe betide the farmer: *N&Q* 4S:4 (1869) 506–7.
Throughout Lent: Folk-Lore 23 (1912) 353.

Wiggs
N&Q 5S:1 (1874) 474; 5S:2 (1874) 138, 178–9; *EDD* VI (1905) 489.

BRAGGOT SUNDAY

Hir mouth was swete: Geoffrey Chaucer, *The Canterbury Tales: The
    Miller's Tale*, line 3261.

MOTHERING SUNDAY

Every mid-Lent Sunday: Symonds (1644/1909) 27.
I'll to thee a simnell bring: Herrick (1648) 'A Ceremonie in Gloster'.
I happened to reside: Gent. Mag. (1784) 343.
The pretty custom: Leather (1912) 97.
They are very rich plum-cakes: Burne (1883) 325
To 3lbs of flour: Folk-Lore 20 (1909) 203-4.
Long ago: Chambers II (1864) 337.
Chambers I (1864) 335–7; Wright & Lones I (1936) 42–51.

19 MARCH

St Joseph's Day
Sutton (1997) 35.

21 MARCH

St Benedict's Day
Where the wind is: Devonshire Assoc. 105 (1973) 214.
Saint Benedick: Ray (1670/1818) 30.
Wright & Lones II (1938) 165–6.

WEEKDAY IN LATE MARCH

Oranges and Lemons Service
Brentnall (1975) 171; Opie (1997b) 398–401.

25 MARCH

Annunciation/Lady Day
Although servants are hired: Devonshire Assoc. 57 (1926) 127.
Wright & Lones II (1938) 166–8.

Tichborne Dole
Baigent (1855); Shuel (1985) 127–9; James (1987); Westwood and
    Simpson (2005) 312.

Doles
to lay out six nobles: Edwards (1842) 112.
As for legacies: Chambers II (1864) 702-4.
In the course of 30 years' ministry: The Times, 12 Jan. 1898, 6.
Edwards (1842); Shuel (1985) 125–35; Kightly (1986) 58–9, 127–8.

CARE OR CARLING SUNDAY

The rustics go: Brand I (1810) 361–2.
Wright & Lones I (1936) 53.

MARCH/APRIL

Borrowed Days
Give me (says March): *N&Q* 1S:5 (1852) 342.
The three last days: *N&Q* 1S:5 (1852) 278–9.
March borrowed of April: Brockett (1846) 47.
March said to April: Chambers I (1864) 448.
They who are very superstitious: Hampson I (1841) 211.
The first three days in March: Whitcombe (1874) 7.
Brand II (1849) 41–4; Hampson I (1841) 210–11; Chambers I (1864)
    448; *N&Q* 9S:12 (1903) 23; Wright & Lones II (1938) 168–170.

April

Great Barmote Court
Porteous (1976) 12–13; www.duchyoflancaster.org.uk; www.
    en.wikipedia.org/wiki/Derbyshire_lead_mining_history.

1 APRIL

All Fools' Day
Fooles Holy Day: Aubrey (1686/1880) 10.
Thursday 1 April: Bruley (2001) 124.
in March 1860: Chambers I (1864) 462.
Hone, *The Every-Day Book* I (1827) 205–7; Brand I (1849) 131–41;
    Wright & Lones II (1938) 171–6; Opie (1959) 243–7; Hutton (1996)
    177–8; Sutton (1997) 82–3.

PALM SUNDAY

We always went out: Sutton (1997) 62.
several hundreds of the workers: Time's Telescope (1826) 66–7.
Popularly, Palm Sunday: Burne (1883) 330.

Brand I (1849) 118–31; Chambers I (1864) 395–8; Dyer (1876) 126–35;
    Wright & Lones I (1936) 54–61; Opie & Tatem (1989) 297;
    Metford (1991) 56–8.

Caistor Gad-Whip Ceremony
The whip is taken: Dyer (1876) 129, quoting a sale document of
    1845.
Dyer (1876) 128–32; Gomme (1883) 195–7; Andrews (1891) 91–104;
    N&Q 9S:7 (1901) 286; Sutton (1997) 63–5.

Figs
This day is called: *Folk-Lore Journal* 3 (1885) 283.
Palm Sunday is called: *Folk-Lore* 40 (1929) 82–3.

Martinsell Hill
In the eighteenth and nineteenth: Bradley (1913) 222.
Wilts. Arch. & Nat. Hist. Mag. 17 (1878) 289–90; Wright & Lones I
    (1936) 55; Whitlock (1976) 52.

Pax Cakes
Leather (1912) 97–8; Shuel (1985) 83–4; Palmer (2002) 64–5.

Water
On Palm Sunday: *Folk-Lore* 40 (1929) 381.

Fig Sunday
The fig-pies are made: *N&Q* 2S:1 (1856) 227.
½ lb breadcrumbs: White (1932) 335–6.
Hone, *The Year-Book* (1832) 797; Brand I (1849) 124; *EDD* II (1900)
    352; Wright & Lones I (1936) 58–9.

HOLY WEEK MONDAY

Bourne Running Auction
Sutton (1997) 80.

MAUNDY THURSDAY

On the 5th April: Ratcliffe & Wright (1960) 13–14, citing Edward
    Walford's *Old and New London* III (1890) 368.
Stone (1906) 52–4; Ratcliffe & Wright, (1960); Robinson (1992).

Henry Travice Charity
Sykes (1977) 39; Shuel (1985) 132; Kightly (1986) 127.

Peter's Pence
At Exeter Cathedral: Cossins (1878) 36.

5 APRIL

John Stow Commemoration
on three market-days: Stow (1603/1994)
Shuel (1985) 73; Kightly (1986) 82.

6 APRIL

Flitting Day
We always had to move: Sutton (1997) 83.

Tatworth Candle Auction
Independent, 14 Apr. 1994, 4; Kightly (1986) 65.

Candle Auctions
Learmount (1985); Kightly (1986) 65–6; *New Law Journal*, 23 Apr.
    1993, 598.

EASTER

Easter Day is the first Sunday: *Whitaker's Almanack* (1996 edn) 82.
Eosturmonath has a name: Wallis (1999) 54.
In the village of Berkley: *N&Q* 1:1 (1850) 294.
Brand I (1849) 157–84; Chambers I (1864) 423–31; Wright & Lones I
    (1936) 85–122; Duffy (1992); Hutton (1996) 198–213.

GOOD FRIDAY

Brand I (1849) 150–57; Metford (1991) 62–7; Roud (2003) 218–22.

Bread and Eggs
Last Christmas: *N&Q* 12S:9 (1921) 489.
Roud (2003) 219–20.

Burning Judas
A custom that is peculiar: *Folk-Lore* 65 (1954) 47.
Opie (1959) 248–9.

Butterworth Charity
Brentnall (1975) 184–5; Kightly (1986) 127.

Hartfield Dole
Sussex County Magazine 13 (1939) 282; 24 (1950) 138; 30 (1956) 197.

Hot Cross Buns
Good Friday comes this month: *Poor Robin's Almanack* (1733),
    quoted in Brand I (1849) 154.
I am a butcher: Gutch (1901) 243–4, citing *The Testimony, Trial,
    Conviction, Condemnation, Confession, and Execution of
    William Smith* (1753).
Brand I (1949) 155.

Skipping
In Brighton on this day: *N&Q* 3S:3 (1863) 444.
The custom continues: *Sussex Arch. Colls.* 33 (1883) 241–2.
Until early in the evening: Porter (1969) 107.
Wales (1990) 50–51; Porter (1969) 107–8; for skipping as a
    children's activity, *see* Opie (1997a) 160–306.

Tinsley Green Marbles
First player knuckles down: Opie (1997) 32–3.
Some of the original: Wales (1979) 30.
Wales (1990) 52–3; Opie (1997a); www.marblemuseum.org.

Washing Molly Grime
Edwards (1842) 100–101; Rudkin (1936) 44–5.

Widow's Son
In the houses of some: Hone, *The Every-Day Book* I (1827) 203.
Brentnall (1975) 192–3; *London Lore* 1:2 (Sept. 1978) 15–16; Shuel
    (1985) 16.

Workington Football
Cumbria, Mar. 1970, 647–8; Shuel (1985) 160–61; Murfin (1990)
    110–14.

EASTER SATURDAY

Bacup Coco-Nut Dancers
Buckland (1986).

EASTER DAY

Eggs
Newall (1971).

Greenwich Fair
What immediately perplexed me: Hawthorne (1863) 198.
Then you must go: Douglas Jerrold, 'Mrs. Caudle's Curtain
    Lectures', *Punch* (1845).
Half the private houses: Charles Dickens, *Sketches by Boz* (1836)
    chap. 12.
Grant (1838) chap. 9; Addison (1953) 100–105; Cameron (1998).

New Clothes
Whether from respect: Neville (1909) 8.
After leaving the Sunday School: Cumbrian Federation of Women's
    Institutes (1994) 234.
The farmer that was contented: Lodge (1596) 14.
Roud (2003) 100.

Old Ball
He runs first at one: Harland & Wilkinson (1867) 234–5.
Cawte (1978) 140–42.

Pace-Egging
Fasting days, years of grace: Beehive of the Romishe Churche (1579),
    quoted in Brand I (1849) 173.
The children have dyed: Hutchinson II (1778) Supp. p. 10.
Here's two or three jolly boys: Journal of Folk Song Society 5 (1915)
    214.
Young men in groups: Harland & Wilkinson (1882) 229–30.
Around Easter: Lancashire Federation of Women's Institutes (1997)
    205–6.
The children all assemble: Neville (1909) 8.
On Easter Monday: N&Q 6S:1 (1880) 337.
Holding his egg in his hand: Brand I (1849) 169.
In the North of England: Brand I (1849) 168.
Year by year: Chambers's Journal, 10 Mar. 1894, 159.
Brand I (1849) 168–76; Wright, *EDD* IV (1903) 399–400; Wright &
    Lones I (1936) 87–8; Opie (1959) 250–55; Newall (1971); Hutton
    (1996) 198–203.

Pace-Egg Plays
In steps I: Helm (1980) 67.
Cass (2001); Cass & Roud (2002).

Riding the Lord
The morning's interlude: Cheshire Sheaf, NS 1 (1895) 63–4.

EASTER MONDAY

Biddenden Maids Charity
There is a vulgar tradition: Hasted III (1790) 66.
Bread and cheese lands: Edwards (1842) 19–20.

Black Knight of Ashton
It was easy to see: Axon (1870) 20-5.
Hone, *The Every-Day Book* II (1827) 234–5; Axon (1870); Hole (1978)
    248-9; Williams & Williams (1998).

Epping Stag Hunt
Brand III (1849) 395; Wright & Lones I (1936) 106–7.

Gawthorpe Coal-Carrying
Smith (1989) 27–8; www.gawthorpe.ndo.co.uk/coal.htm.

Hallaton Hare Pie and Bottle-Kicking
[t]*he scramble was a token*: Shuel (1985) 165.
The scrum writhes: Morison & Daisley (2000) 12.
Morison & Daisley (2000).

  Scrambling Customs
It was truly reviving: The Times, 7 Nov. 1956, 11.
There was an ancient custom: Daniel Lysons, *Environs of London*
    (1792), quoted in Hone, *The Every-Day Book* II (1827) 225.

Harness Horse Parade
Shuel (1985) 60–61.

Legging Day
At Easter, boys and girls: Nicholson (1890) 12

Leicester Hare Hunt
Folk-Lore 3 (1892) 441–66; Billson (1895) 76–7.

Sun Dancing
I was awoke: Devonshire Assoc. 8 (1876) 57-8.
There is a tradition: Parish (1875) 57.
Roud (2003) 160–61.

Water
Elecampane on East Monday: N&Q 4S:5 (1870) 595.
Wright & Lones I (1936) 100–101, 112; Hole (1978) 285–6.

EASTER MONDAY AND TUESDAY

Lifting
The men lift the women: Gent. Mag. (1784:i) 96.
a case heard before: Folk-Lore Journal 1 (1883) 269–70.
It was a very pretty: Burne (1883) 336.
At Kidderminster: N&Q for Worcestershire (1856) 212.
On Easter Sunday: Fisher (1865) 463–4.
Wright & Lones I (1936) 107–10; Hutton (1996) 208–13; Palmer
    (2004) 296–8.

EASTER TUESDAY

Holly Bussing
N&Q 2S:3 (1857) 344.

Tuppenny Starvers
Shuel (1985) 84.

LOW SUNDAY
Upon little Easter Sunday: Carew (1602/2000) 164.

HOCKTIDE
Chambers I (1864) 498–9; Wright & Lones I (1936) 124–9; Hutton
    (1996) 207–14; MacLean (1996).

Hungerford Hocktide Court
Basically all we do: Independent, 23 Apr. 1993, 20.
Report of Charity Commissioners: Parish of Hungerford (Mar
    1906); Summers (1926); Pihlens (1983);

TWO WEEKS AFTER EASTER

Spital Sermon
Brentnall (1975) 185

19 APRIL

Primrose Day
Vickery (1995) 295; Sutton (1997) 84–5.

21 APRIL

Queen Elizabeth II's Birthday
www.royal.gov.uk.

23 APRIL

St George's Day
my mam used to say: Sutton (1997) 91–2.
Wright & Lones II (1938) 178–83; History Today 30 (Apr. 1980)
    17–22; Fox (1983); Palmer (1994) 290; Hutton (1996) 214–17.

24 APRIL

St Mark's Eve
 A youth or girl: Andrews (1891) 90.
I never watched myself: Blakeborough (1898) 80–81.
Wright & Lones II (1938) 183–92; Menefee (1989) 80–99; Roud
    (2003) 366–7.

25 APRIL

St Mark's Day
After meeting in the market place: History of Berwickshire
    Naturalists' Club 14 (1892–3) 135.
Horn (1986) 39; FLS News 48 (2006) 13–14.

29 APRIL
Chambers I (1864) 385.

30 APRIL

May Day Eve
At Oldham: Ditchfield (1896) 104–5.

On the Eve of May Day: Leather (1912) 44.
Wright & Lones II (1938) 195–9.

May

Corby Pole Fair
Two thousand people: *The Times*, 12 June 1962, 6.
www.polefair.com.

Maids' Money
Surrey Magazine 4 (1902) 119–20.

Weighing the Mayor
Shuel (1985) 104; Wycombe District Council website, www.
    wycombe.gov.uk.

1 MAY
We, with our coal fires: Burne (1883) 354.
In the month of May: Stow (1603/1994) 123
A woman from the extreme north: *Folk-Lore* 9 (1898) 365.
When … I lived at Kington: *Transactions of the Woolhope
    Naturalists' Field Club* (1877–80) 26.
When she was young: *Folk-Lore* 12 (1901) 426.
It hath been a custom: Billson (1895) 102.
It was formerly a custom: Harland & Wilkinson (1882) 238–40.

Bank Holiday
On May Day the entire: Mitford (1960) 145.

Bears
One went to the grocer's shop: *Burnley Express*, 11 Feb. 1983, 9.
Opie (1959) 261; *Burnley Express*, 1 Feb. 1983, 11 Feb. 1983.

Casting Clouts
Till April is dead: *Devonshire Assoc.* (1932).
Don't change a clout: *N&Q* 4S:6 (1870) 131.

Charlton-on-Otmoor Garland
During the upheavals: Hole (1976) 113.
Bloxham (2002) 81–9.

Children's Garlands
In Huntingdonshire: *N&Q* 1S:10 (1854) 91–2.
I was at Wilton: *Folk-Lore* 11 (1900) 210.
The garlands of this year: Mantell (1940).
Wright & Lones II (1938) 213–17; Thompson (1939) chap.13; *JEFDSS* 9
    (1961) 81–90; *Transactions of the Leicestershire Archaeological
    & Historical Society* 40 (1964/5) 69-84; Tebbutt (1984) 59–66;
    Judge (1987); Judge (1993); Hutton (1996) 237–41; Bloxham
    (2002) 63–136; *see* Bloxham in particular for excellent
    photographs of garlands.

Ducking or Dipping Day
On May morning the children: Couch (1871) 153–4.
In 1894 the practice: *Devonshire Assoc.* 27 (1895) 72–3.

Fighting
Annually, on the first of May: Rudder (1779) 533.
Every hamlet used: Jefferies (1880) 65-6.

Horse Decorations
They took places: *Gent. Mag.* (1754) 354.
There was on May-day: *Pall Mall Gazette* (1880), quoted in *N&Q*
    6S:1 (1929) 434–5.
Everything that went on wheels: *Stockport Advertiser*, 2 May 1890,
    8, quoted in Judge (1987) 132.

International Labour Day
The idea of a May-day festival: *Oxford Chronicle*, 4 May 1906, 2.
Judge (1987).

Jack-in-the-Green
A lusty sweep: Bennett (1924) 69–70.
Walking along Jamaica Road: Judge (2000) 126.
A reasonable conclusion: Judge (2000) 24.
Judge (2000).

Magdalen College Singing
more like a Baccanalian: Judge (1987) 425.
Hone (1832) 797; Porter (1969) 115; *Folklore* 97:1 (1986) 15–40; Judge
    (1987) 422–58; Bloxham (2002) 70–78;

May Dew
I overheard this conversation: *Folk-Lore* 23 (1912) 451.

May Dolls
At a very early hour: *Devonshire Assoc.* 8 (1876) 50
Porter (1969) 111–15.

May Goslings
A May gosling: *Gent Mag.* (Apr. 1791) 327.
Opie (1959) 255–7; Wright & Lones II (1938) 242.

May Queens
At Albrighton: Burne (1883) 361.
Wright & Lones II (1938) 223–8; Cole (1981); Judge (1993); Sutton
    (1997) 99–101.

Maypoles
Feast week was in Maytime: Rudkin (1936) 46.
On May 1, 1952: Opie (1959) 258.
The manner of May games: Stubbes (1583/2002).
Judge (1983); Judge (1987).

Milkmaids' Garland
Judge (2000); Phythian-Adams (1983).

Minehead Hobby Horse
obeisance to onlookers: Kille (1931) 67.
Kille (1931); Cawte (1978).

Hobby Horses
Maylam (1909); Alford (1978); Cawte (1978).

Padstow Hobby Horse
Well we had all sorts: Rowe (1982) 7.
man drest up: R. Polwhele, *History of Cornwall* (1803), quoted in
    Cawte (1978).
canvas being extended: F. Hitchins and Samuel Drew, *History of
    Cornwall*, quoted in Cawte (1978).
Arise up Mrs.——: Rawe (1982) 6.
Cawte (1978) 157–67; Rawe (1982); Rowe (1982).

Randwick Cheese-Rolling
Three large cheeses: Hone, *The Table Book* (1827) 277.

3 MAY

The Day of the Invention of the Holy Cross
The first of May: *Devonshire Assoc.* 12 (1880) 105–8.

FIRST SATURDAY IN MAY

Gawthorpe Celebrations
Smith (1989) 33–6; www.gawthorpe.ndo.co.uk/home.

Knutsford Royal May Day Festival
Strand Magazine, May 1892, 484–8; Shuel (1985) 34–9; www.
    virtual-knutsford.co.uk.

FIRST SUNDAY IN MAY

Tyburn Walk
London Tourist Board, *Traditional London* (1987) 56.

8 MAY

Helston Flora Day

At Helstone: Gent. Mag. 60:1 (1790) 520.

Toy (1936) 368–79; Kennedy (1964) 71–5; Newton (1978); Jones (1997).

12 MAY

The May

Our May Day is not: Neville (1909) 27–33.

children wore a May gollen: Lancashire Lore (1971) 74.

SECOND SATURDAY IN MAY

Randwick Wap

One of the parish is: Gent. Mag. (1784) 334–5.

Briggs (1974) 183–6; Palmer (1994) 295–7.

13 MAY (OLD MAY DAY)

Abbotsbury Garland Day

Robson (1993).

Cowslips

When spring had really come: Harris (1969) 138–9.

Miners' Holiday

On the 13th of May: Glover I (1829) 261.

Rook Sunday

White (1932) 202; Sutton (1997) 108–9.

14 MAY

Pack Rag Day

Bank holidays pass almost: Gutch & Peacock (1908) 205

MID TO LATE MAY

Scorton Silver Arrow

Hird (1972); Smith (1989) 65–72; www.scortonarrow.com.

ROGATIONTIDE

Beating the Bounds

Boundary roll from Tudor Cheshire: Head (1887) 119–23.

On the 16th [May]: Schellinks (1993) 85.

At Beverley: Nicholson (1890) 31–2.

Mr. Checkley, a farmer: The Graphic, 28 Nov. 1874, 527.

If, by chance: Cossins (1878) 11.

One vicar said: Smith (1989) 89–90.

Brand I (1849) 197–212; Wright & Lones I (1936) 129–38; Winchester (1990); Hutton (1996) 277–87; Bloxham (2002) 50–62.

ROGATION MONDAY

Wishford Auction

Whitlock (1976) 54–5.

ASCENSION EVE

Whitby Penny Hedge

Charlton (1779); Young (1817); Atkinson (1894); Turton (1909); Jeffrey (1923) 38–45; Smith (1989) 29–32.

ASCENSION DAY

At daybreak on Ascension: Folk-Lore Record 5 (1882) 160.

To hang an egg: Scot (1584/1972) Bk 12, chap. 18.

If you hang clothes: Folk-Lore 20 (1909) 345.

Hailing the Lamb: Devonshire Assoc. 68 (1936) 246, quoting Gent. Mag. 57 (1787) 718.

The parochial bounds: Cossins (1878) 34.

Wright & Lones I (1936) 129–48; Roud (2003) 10–12.

Tower of London Beating the Bounds

Brentnall (1975) 77, 79; Shuel (1985) 106.

18 MAY

Newbiggin Freeholders

Sykes (1977) 72–3; Shuel (1985) 114.

19 MAY

St Dunstan's Day

St. Dunstan bought: N&Q 2S:12 (1861) 303.

No luck will follow: Blakeborough (1898) 131.

N&Q 2S:12 (1861) 303; Westwood (1985) 95–7.

23 MAY

Rye Mayor-Making

Hogg (1971) 84–5; Simpson (1973) 119.

24 MAY

Empire Day

The morning shall be: The Times, 20 Mar. 1899, 8.

When I was at school: East Kent Federation of Women's Institutes (1993) 246.

For Wesley Day, see Sutton (1997) 116.

WHITSUN

On Whit Monday: Whitsun poster cited by Wright & Lones I (1936) 161.

Whit week, however: Philpott (1961/2) 173–4.

It is customary: Harland & Wilkinson (1882) 247.

Eton School Montem

Aubrey (1686/1880) 132; Wright & Lones I (1936) 167–9; Hazlitt (1905); N&Q 3S:12 (1867) 377–8; Chambers II (1864) 665–6.

Food

The village policeman: Porter (1969) 118.

Goosnargh cakes: Wilson (1991) 137.

Morris Dance

Then every one: Stubbes (1583/2002) 206–7.

The bibliography of the morris dance is voluminous. The following is a selection of the best recent treatments: Folklore 96:1 (1985) 29–37; Heaney (1985); Traditional Dance 5/6 (1988) 191–215; Folk Music Journal 6:2 (1991) 169–86; 7:3 (1997) 311–51; 8:4 (2004) 513–15; Chandler (1993a); Forrest (1999).

Superstitions

It was traditional: East Yorkshire Federation of Women's Institutes (1998) 203–4.

Whit Walks

At Manchester: The Times, 7 June 1949, 4.

It was 1958: www.haveyoursay.freeserve.co.uk/hys11/then1.htm Have Your Say Magazine (used by permission of Lillian Barlow).

This annual event: West Yorkshire Federation of Women's Institutes (1996) 29.

WHIT SUNDAY

St Briavels Bread and Cheese Dole

They have a custom: Rudder (1779) 307.

So after Evensong: Crawford (1938) 160–61.

Edwards (1842) 17–22; Bushaway (1982) 16–18; Palmer (1994) 298–9.

Church Ales

entertaining of Christian love: Carew (1602/2000) 141–2.

Hazlitt (1905) 631–2; Wright & Lones I (1936) 151–7; Chandler (1993a) 59–79; Hutton (1994); Hutton (1996) 244–61.

St Mary Redcliffe Rush Sunday
www.bristol-city.gov.uk/aboutbris/civic_services; www.
    stmaryredcliffe.co.uk

WHIT TUESDAY

Dicing for Bibles
N&Q 5S:12 (1879) 238; Hole (1975) 148; Kightly (1986) 101.

WHIT WEDNESDAY

Mother Shipton's Day
Porter (1969) 118–19; for Hindley's confession, *see* N&Q 4S:11 (1873)
    355.

WHIT FRIDAY

Brass Bands
The Black Dyke Mills band: Greenhalgh (1992) 18.
They [the churches] *take this day*: *Stalybridge Reporter* (1926),
    quoted in Greenhalgh (1992) 36.
Greenhalgh (1992).

LATE MAY

Blessing of the Sea
Brixham: Information supplied by Bridget Cusack, churchwarden
    and archivist of All Saints' Church, Lower Brixham. Hastings:
    Shuel (1985) 82. For a list of some other coastal blessings extant
    in the mid 1980s, *see* Kightly (1986) 55.

LAST SUNDAY IN MAY

Arbor Day
Shuel (1985) 39-40; Palmer (2004) 304; www.members.aol.com/
    arbortreefest.

29 MAY

Royal Oak Day
going round to the houses: *Listener*, 23 May 1957.
These pinches are: Durand (1913) 10.
I was travelling from Crewe: *Bye-Gones* (1889–90) 169.
Wright & Lones II (1938) 254–70; Opie (1959) 263–6; Cressy (1989).

Castleton Garland Day
Addy (1901); Boyes (1993); Membury example: *Devonshire Assoc.*
    102 (1970) 269.

Grovely Ceremonies
Bushaway (1982); Frampton (1992).

Neville's Cross Commemoration
Hole (1975) 132–3; Kightly (1986) 174.

Royal Hospital Chelsea Founder's Day
Brentnall (1975) 125–8; www.chelsea-pensioners.co.uk.

SPRING BANK HOLIDAY

Bampton Morris
Another season of festivity: Giles (1847) lxv.
Sharp and MacIlwaine (1924) 38–72; Chandler (1983); *Musical
    Traditions* 10 (1992) 18–24; Chandler (1993a).

Barwick Maypole
Smith (1989) 36–40; *Dalesman*, Jan. 1986, 849–50; www.hjsmith.
    clara.co.uk.

Cooper's Hill Cheese-Rolling
The master of the ceremonies: *Folk-Lore* 23 (1912) 351.
Folk-Lore 23 (1912) 351; Palmer (1994) 193–6; *Daily Telegraph*, 26
    May 1998, 3.

Hunting the Earl of Rone
Devonshire Assoc. 49 (1917) 71–5; Brown (1997).

Kingsteignton Ram-Roasting
A lamb is drawn: N&Q 6S:7 (1883) 345.
My husband started: Crawford (1938) 131–2.
Wright & Lones I (1936) 169–70.

Robert Dover's Olimpick Games
Burns (2000); Haddon (2004).

June

TRINITY SUNDAY
Burne (1883) 352; Sutton (1997) 127–8.

THURSDAY AFTER TRINITY SUNDAY

Corpus Christi
On the day before: Wright & Lones I (1936) 176–7.

8 JUNE

If on the 8th of June: Inwards (1869) 30.

11 JUNE

St Barnabas' Day
Brand I (1849) 293–4; Wright & Lones III (1940) 1–3.

20 JUNE

Mayor of Ock Street
Chandler (1993b)

21 JUNE

Brecknell Bequest
A bachelor named: Noake (1868) 218.

Mock Mayors and Courts
The Mayors were nominated: Cossins (1878) 9–10.
And that you may: Cossins (1878) 46–8.
The youthlier sort of Bodmin: Carew (1602/2000) 197–8.
[t]*he police interfered*: *Antiquary* 4 (1881) 80.
Chambers I (1864) 659–64; Gutch (1901) 325–31; N&Q 12S:12 (1923)
    194; Wright & Lones II (1938) 254; III (1940) 29–30, 94, 158–9;
    Shaw (1980).

24 JUNE

Midsummer's Day/St John the Baptist's Day
In [John] *Aubrey's*: Piggott (1968) 133.
In the months: Stow (1603/1994) 126–7.
*But whatever reaso*n: Bourne (1725) 214–15.
Before St John's Day: Hewett (1900) 112.
Stow (1603/1994) 125–9; Brand I (1849) 298–338; Wright & Lones III
    (1940) 6–23; Shortt (1988).

Dumb Cake
Opie & Tatem (1989) 127–8; Roud (2003) 156–7.

Divination
I remember, the maids: Aubrey (1686/1880) 25–6.
It is said here: Bray (1838) 287.
Wright & Lones III (1940) 12–19; Opie & Tatem (1989) 295, 332;
    Roud (2003) 247–8, 307–8, 383.

Election of Sheriffs
Brentnall (1975); www.cityoflondon.gov.uk.

Knollys Red Rose
Brentnall (1975) 47–9.

Magdalen Outdoor Sermon
Hole (1975) 81–2; Shuel (1985) 81–2.

Midsummer Cushions
The young lads and lasses: Denham II (1895) 1–2.

29 JUNE

St Peter's Day/St Paul's Day
Unless the apples: Folk-Lore Journal 4 (1886) 167.

Bawming the Thorn
Up with fresh garlands: Appleton Parish Council (1997) 11.
At Appleton it was the custom: Wilbraham (1826) 16.
Kightly (1986) 47; diary information supplied by Warrington Local
   Studies Library.

Jankyn Smith's Charity
Kightly (1986) 145; St Mary's Church Magazine (*View from Honey
   Hill*), June 1999.

Warcop Rush-Bearing
The girls of the village: Cumbrian, June 1995, 37–8.
The Globe, 30 June 1913; www.edenonline.net/pages/warcoprush.

JUNE/JULY

Yarnton Lot Meadow
Kightly (1986) 153–4; Bloxham (2002) 208–13.

Well-Dressing
In the village of Tissington: Gent. Mag. 64 (1794) 114–15.
newly-gathered flowers: Rhodes (1818).
Porteous (1949); Christian (1983); Rattue (1995); Naylor & Porter
   (2002).

July

EARLY JULY

Fairlop Fair
According to ancient custom: Illustrated London News, 15 July 1843,
   44.
Muncey (c.1935) 68–73; www.hainaultforest.co.uk/3Fairlop%20Fair

4 JULY

Stagshawbank Fair
Besides horses, sheep, cattle: Forster (1881) 65–6.
Forster (1881) 63–70; Muncey (c.1935) 147–52.

Whalton Baal Fire
Wright & Lones III (1940) 11; Shuel (1985) 183

5 JULY

Old Midsummer's Day
In the parishes: Collinson III (1791) 586.

6 JULY

Duck-Racing
Duck racing isn't as easy: John Bull, 9 July 1955, 41.
Reading Mercury, 5 Aug. 1961; Bloxham (2002) 214–15.

Kilburn Feast
Johnny Kirk, whose family: Smith (1989) 85–7.

FIRST FRIDAY IN JULY

Warrington Walking Day
www.shef.ac.uk/nfa/history/worlds_fair/articles/warrington.

FIRST SATURDAY IN JULY

Ambleside Rush-Bearing
The 'burthens' were devices: Rawnsley (1953) 26–8.
N&Q 5S:2 (1892) 141-2; Rawnsley (1953) 26–8.

Medway Admiralty Court
There is in the River Medway: Defoe (1724–6) Letter II: Kent.
Goodsall (1965); www.medway.gov.uk.

Rush-Bearing
I remember going: Folk-Lore 20 (1909) 204.
About the latter: Clarke (1789) 134.
every part of the church: Diary of Benjamin Newton, quoted by
   Rawnsley (1953) 10.
In their wisdom: Country Home, June 1909, 80.
Chambers I (1864) 505–7; Burton (1891); Buckland (1982); Rawnsley
   (1953); Helm (1970); Kightly (1986) 199–201; Brears (1989)
   178–203; Fletcher (1997/8).

SUNDAY IN EARLY JULY

Oxenhope Straw Race
Smith (1989) 92–5; www.strawrace.co.uk.

7 JULY

Bodmin Riding
On Monday, a grand procession: Munn (1975) 26.
the two Mondays right: Munn (1975) 20.
Munn (1975); Wright & Lones III (1940) 31–2.

Rose Queens
A vicar in Bury: Independent Magazine, 1 Apr. 1989, 9.
The crowning of a Rose Queen: Lancashire Lore (1971) 59.

10 JULY

Twice a year: Neville (1909) 72–3.

SECOND WEDNESDAY IN JULY

Pretty Maid's Charity
Sykes (1977) 108; Shuel (1985) 129–30; Kightly (1986) 190–91.

SECOND/THIRD SATURDAY IN JULY

Durham Miners' Gala
Richardson (2001).

15 JULY

St Swithun's Day
St. Swithin's Day: N&Q 11:4 (1911) 45.
You won't have the jam: Wright & Lones III (1940) 35.
Opie & Tatem (1989) 337–8.

16 JULY

Anne Askew Day
Sutton (1997) 146.

19 JULY

Little Edith's Treat
Information supplied by Valerie Mellor, historian of Piddinghoe.

25 JULY

St Christopher's Day
There was a colossal figure: Rudder (1779) 286.

Ebernoe Horn Fair
Sussex County Magazine 2 (1928) 331, 338; 29 (1955) 320–23, 403,
   501.

Song text: verse 4, line 3, and verse 5, lines 3 and 4, added from
    Vaughan Williams' manuscripts, as collected from Frederick
    Teal at Kingsfold, Surrey, 23 December 1904.

25 JULY

John Knill Charity
Hone, *The Every-Day Book* II (1827) 505–6; Shuel (1985) 129; Kightly
    (1986) 146–7.

Whitstable Oyster Festival
www.whitstableoysterfestival.co.uk.

Fairs, Feasts, Wakes, and Revels
They love a crowd: Neville (1909) 85–6.
A farmer's wife: *Folk-Lore* 23 (1912) 352.
For the children: Kightly (1986) 184–5.
Our village church: West Yorkshire Federation of Women's
    Institutes (1996) 211.
Heyford Feast: Horn (1986) 31.
Because you couldn't go: Kightly (1986) 182–3.
Walford (1883); Muncey (*c*.1935); Wright & Lones (1936–1940);
    Addison (1953); Cameron (1998).

26 JULY

Mace Monday
In the course of the day: Hone, *The Every-Day Book* II (1827) 523.
Ditchfield (1896) 246–7.

28 JULY

Old St Kenelm's Day
The custom of crabbing: John Noake, *N&Q for Worcestershire* (1856)
    206.
Wright & Lones III (1940) 38–9, 59–60, 99.

LATE JULY

Doggett's Coat and Badge Race
Doggett was stranded on the wrong side: *Guardian*, 19 July 1974.
Chambers II (1864) 157–8; Brentnall (1975) 94–9; Paget (1989) 56.

Swan-Upping
Stone (1906) 13–15; Hole (1975) 111–12; Kightly (1986) 213–14.

JULY/AUGUST

St Wilfrid Feast Procession
Shortcrust pastry base: Smith (1989) 107–8.

August

EARLY AUGUST

Grottoes
When was Grotto Day?: *The Times*, 21 Nov. 1957, 12.
Please remember the grotto: Gamble (1979) 107.
Opie (1959) 266–7; *Folklore* 88:2 (1977) 183–90.

FIRST WEDNESDAY IN AUGUST

Knighthood of the Old Green
Shuel (1985) 142–4; Southampton Old Bowling Green website,
    www.sobg.co.uk/ index.

The King's Book of Sports 1618 and 1633
Govett (1890).

FIRST WEEK IN AUGUST

Woodmen of Arden
Shuel (1985) 141–2.

1 AUGUST

Lammas/St Peter ad Vincula
On that day: Brand I (1849) 348.
Certain lands were used: Wright & Lones III (1940) 43.
was a pleasure fair: Cossins (1878) 20–21.
Brand I (1849) 347–9; Wright & Lones III (1940) 43–6; Hutton
    (1996) 327–31.

4 AUGUST

Kit-Dressing
At Baslow the rural: Glover I (1829) 261.

5 AUGUST

Grasmere Rush-Bearing
I chanced to be in Grasmere: *N&Q* 5S:4 (1875) 162–3.
Rawnsley (1953); Shuel (1985) 85–7; www.visitcumbria.com.

James I
Cressy (1989) 57–9.

10 AUGUST

St Lawrence's Day
For more on 'The History of Lawrence Lazy', see *Folklore* 107 (1996).

12 AUGUST

Congleton Bells
On the Wake Sunday: *Monthly Packet* 24 (1862) 660.
Head (1887) 203–4; Andrews (1895) 137–43; Congleton museum
    website, www. comcarenet.com/museum/default.

Gibson Tomb
FLS News 10 (1990) 11–12.

16 AUGUST

St Roch's Day
Brand I (1849) 350.

Tutbury Bull-Running
Raven (1978) 110-14; Bushaway (1993).

17 AUGUST

Lee Gap Fair
www.travellersinleeds.co.uk/_travellers/LeeGapFair.

23 AUGUST

St Bartholomew's Eve
I myself, in my youth: Stow (1603/1994) 100–101.

24 AUGUST

St Bartholomew's Day
In the morning a number of maidens: Hone, *The Year-Book* (1832)
    492.
At St. Bartholomew: Inwards (1869) 32.
Wright & Lones III (1940) 49–52.

Bartholomew Fair
Ward (1703/1927) 176–206; Hone, *The Every-Day Book* I (1827)
    583–626; Morley (1859).

Sandwich Bun Race
The Times, 24 Aug. 1953, 8; Kightly (1986) 202.

West Witton Burning of Bartle
Smith (1989) 119–22; *John Bull*, 27 Aug. 1955, 43.

Sparrow Mumbling
'Twill be most ridiculous: George Chapman, *Andromeda Liberata*
    (1614), cited in *N&Q* 4S:10 (1872) 184
All the Year Round, 3 June 1865.

29 AUGUST

Preston Guild
Crosby (1991).

AUGUST BANK HOLIDAY

Marldon Apple Pie Fair
The Marldon Apple Pie: Devonshire Assoc. 67 (1935) 377–8.

Notting Hill Carnival
www.london.gov.uk/mayor/carnival/index.jsp.

Bank Holidays
www.dti.gov.uk/er/bankhis; Michael Jacobs, 'More Bank Holidays!', www.fabian-society.org.uk

September

Harvest Customs
The in-gathering: Williams (1912) 116–17.
A practical joke: Neville (1909) 50–51.
A farm-worker from: *Folk-Lore* 14 (1903) 92–4.
Now, when all the corn: *Folk-Lore* 1 (1890) 280.
On certain Ramsey manors: Bennett (1948) 111–12.
On the last night of harvest: *Folk-Lore* 13 (1902) 180.
At Kingsbridge, the following: *Folk-Lore* 1 (1890) 280.
The top of the last load: *N&Q* 4S:10 (1872) 359.
No further back: Gutch & Peacock (1908) 209, quoting Heanley (1902) 11–12
[An] *explanation was given to me*: *The Times*, 2 Oct. 1934, 10.
Hone, *Every-Day Book* II (1827) 577–91; Jenkin (1934); Wright & Lones I (1936) 82–90; Evans (1969); Bushaway (1982) 107–66; Hutton (1996) 332–47; Main (1998–9).

Gleaning
The gleaning season: Grey (1934) 118–24.

Harvest Suppers
Tomorrow the men: *N&Q* 4S:10 (1872) 411.
Here's a health: Dacombe (1935) 93.
Later in the evening: Gutch (1901) 266.
In the first quarter: *N&Q* 8S:9 (1896) 128.
There could be no better: Horn (1986) 22, 86.

Harvest Festivals
Harvest festival is upon us again: *Daily Telegraph*, 23 Sept 2000, Weekend section, 5.

Hop-Picking
Plenty of hands: Arthur Young, *Farmer's Kalendar* (1771) quoted in Filmer (1982) 17.
These were all people and *In the shop*: Warren (1938) 18–35.
Our farm was a small and *The smell of the hops*: East Kent Federation of Women's Institutes (1993) 138.
Leather (1912) 105–6; Warren (1938) chap. 2; Filmer (1982); East Kent Federation of Women's Institutes (1993) 137–42; Heffernan (1996); Doel (2003) 59–66.

EARLY SEPTEMBER

Colchester Oyster Fishery
The company were about: *The Times*, 22 Sept. 1928, 15.
Victoria County History: Essex II (1907) 425–39.

1 SEPTEMBER

St Giles's Day
Probably the greatest: Muncey (c.1935) 100.

Victoria County History: Hampshire V (1912) 36–41; Muncey (c.1935) 79–85, 92–102; Wright & Lones III (1940) 59–60; *Victoria County History: Oxfordshire* IV (1979) 310–12.

3 SEPTEMBER

Cromwell Day
www.olivercromwell.org.

Merchant Navy Day
www.mna.org.uk.

4 SEPTEMBER

Abbots Bromley Horn Dance
There was no audience: *English Dance & Song* 3:2 (Nov. 1938) 27–8.
Sharp I (1911–13) 105–12; Cawte (1978) 65–79; Buckland (1980); Heaney (1987).

Barnet Horse Fair
My first impression: Greenwood (1867) 198.
Barnet Fair is still: Addison (1953) 147.
In a 20-acre field: *The Times*, 6 Sept. 1954, 2.
Daily Telegraph, 2 Sept. 1995, Weekend section, 10; www.barnet4u.co.uk/Barnet%20History/barnetfair

14 SEPTEMBER

Holy Rood or Holy Cross Day
On Holy Rood day: Clare (1993) 140.
Brand I (1849) 353; Cross (1957) 480; Metford (1991) 85; Vickery (1995) 276–7; Roud (2003) 343–4; Westwood & Simpson (2005) 750–51.

Shaftesbury Byzant
a trophy or mace: Frampton (1990) 155.

Sturbridge Fair
It is kept in a large corn-field: Defoe I (1724–6) 80.
The fair was proclaimed: *Victoria County History: Cambridge* III (1959) 95.
Walford (1883); Muncey (c.1935) 20–36; *Victoria County History: Cambridge* III (1959) 91–5.

Baiting Bears and Other Animals
In winter on almost every feast day: Fitz Stephen (c.1180/1990) 58.
Concerning a case: Home (1915) 224–6.
Chambers II (1864) 57–9; Porter (1969) 227–8; Malcolmson (1973); Richardson (2000).

THIRD THURSDAY IN SEPTEMBER

Chalk-Back Day
It is customary: *N&Q* 1S:4 (1851) 501–2.
At Bridlington: Nicholson (1890) 29.
Pursehouse (1966) 130–32; for Chalk Sunday in Ireland, *see* Danaher (1972) 47–8.

Egremont Crab-Apple Fair
We haven't been able: *John Bull*, 17 Sept. 1955.
Shuel (1985) 14–16; Kightly (1986) 98–9; www.egremontcrabfair.org.uk.

Warden Pies
Wardens were not soft: Candlin (1987) 73.

18 SEPTEMBER

Samuel Johnson Commemoration
www.lichfieldrambler.co.uk.

Southwark Fair
noted chiefly for shows: John Strype, *Survey of the Cities of London and Westminster*, quoted in Rosenfeld (1960) 71.

only to the destruction: Rosenfeld (1960) 74.
Rosenfeld (1960) 71–107; Muncey (*c.*1935) 54–8.

19 SEPTEMBER

Painswick Church-Clipping
gave time to re-organizing: *N&Q* 181 (1941) 36
'*When I was a girl*': *John Bull*, 24 Sept. 1955, 47.
Folk-Lore 23 (1912) 196–203.

21 SEPTEMBER

St Matthew's Day
Inwards (1869) 32–3.

29 SEPTEMBER

Michaelmas/Feast of St Michael and All Angels
If you don't baste: Forby (1830) 414.
I dined upon goose: Jane Austen, quoted in Le Faye (1995) 235.
The election of Mayors: Cossins (1878) 9.
Brand I (1849) 367–71; Wright & Lones III (1940) 80–90.

Lawless Hours and Days
According to the Staffordshire Advertiser: *Folk-Lore* 42 (1931) 466.
At Kidderminster is a singular: *Gent. Mag.* (1790), quoted in Burne (1883) 221–2.

Blackberries
The belief that it is unlucky: *Western Antiquary* 2 (1882) 137.
Opie & Tatem (1989) 29; Roud (2003) 39.

Crack-Nut Sunday
the cracking noise was: Edward Wedlake Brayley, *A Topographical History of Surrey* III (1850) 41–2.
They kept up the Christmas: Goldsmith (1766) chap. 4.

Election of the Lord Mayor of London
a Labour Lord Mayor: *The Times*, 30 September 1972.
Brentnall (1975) 19–53; Paget (1989) 15–18.

Urswick Rush-Bearing
Cumbrian Federation of Women's Institutes (1994) 240–42; information (May 2005) from Miss Joan Wood, Urswick resident of eighty-three years standing.

October

Quit Rent Ceremonies
Brentnall (1975) 153–6.

A SUNDAY IN OCTOBER

Redcliffe Pipe Walk
Shuel (1985) 106–7; www.members.lycos.co.uk/brisray/bristol/bstmary1.

2 OCTOBER

Braughing Old Man's Day
Jones-Baker (1977) 164; www.braughing.org.uk.

FIRST WEDNESDAY IN OCTOBER

Nottingham Goose Fair
Wilkes (1989); www.nottinghamgoosefair.co.uk

Goose-Riding
Hazlitt (1905) 284.

SECOND SUNDAY IN OCTOBER

Harvest of the Sea
Brentnall (1975) 183–4.

SECOND WEDNESDAY IN OCTOBER

Tavistock Goosie Fair
Gunnell (1978); Gerrish (2004).

10 OCTOBER

Old Michaelmas Day
So common was the practice: Nicholson (1890) 22.
Hone, *The Table Book* (1827) 838; *Wilts. Arch. & Nat. Hist. Mag.* 1 (1854) 89–91; Andrews (1900) 175–85; Hazlitt (1905) 377; Wright & Lones III (1940) 94, 100.

Pack Monday Fair
The fair is annually held: Hone, *The Every-Day Book* II (1827) 654–5.
Wright & Lones III (1940) 95–6; Hole (1976) 291–2.

Weyhill Fair
The 11th of October: Cobbett (1830) 'Through Hampshire . . .'
The newcomer was seated: Beddington & Christy (1936) 18.
Hampshire Field Club 3 (1894–7) 127–42; *Folk-Lore* 22 (1911) 300–302; *Victoria County History: Hampshire* IV (1911) 394–99; Beddington & Christy (1936) 17–19.

Wife-Selling
For my part I don't see: Hardy (1886) chap. 1.
On Friday last: *Windsor & Eton Express*, 10–17 Sept. 1815, quoted in *N&Q* 196 (1951) 82.
Brooks, auctioneer: *N&Q* 196 (1951) 460.
Rather unfortunately: Chambers I (1864) 487.
It is – so far as my experience: Baring-Gould (1908) 58.
Menefee (1981); Thompson (1991).

11 OCTOBER

Blackberries
All children who either gather: *Folk-Lore* 20 (1909) 343.

16 OCTOBER

Lion Sermon
N&Q 6S:1 (1880) 236, 303, 344; Brentnall (1975) 181–2.

18 OCTOBER

St Luke's Day
a village famous: Defoe (1724–6) Letter II: Kent.
A fine autumn is known: Addy (1895) 117.

20 OCTOBER

Colchester Oyster Feast
On Thursday, the Mayor: *Essex Standard*, 21 Oct. 1847, quoted in *Past & Present* 94 (1982) 112.
Cannadine (1982); Kightly (1986) 82.

21 OCTOBER

Apple Day
www.commonground.org.uk.

Trafalgar Day
Brentnall (1975) 114–16.

25 OCTOBER

St Crispin's Day
In the parishes: *N&Q* 1S:5 (1852) 30.
Wright & Lones III (1940) 102–4.

LAST THURSDAY IN OCTOBER

Bampton Fair
Gerrish (2004); www.bampton.org.uk/bampton_fair.

Seed Cakes

Wife, sometime this week: Tusser (1580/1984)
Hone, *The Year-Book* (1832) 798; Baker II (1854) 211.

LATE OCTOBER

Punkie Night

A party of men: N&Q 161 (1931) 372.
Opie (1959) 267–8; *Folklore* 83 (1972) 240–44; Palmer (1976) 105–7.

31 OCTOBER

Hallowe'en

On the Eve of All Saints Day: Gutch & Peacock (1908) 212.
The vigil of All Saints' Day: Brockett (1825) 145.
Mrs. Hook, of Chulmleigh: Devonshire Assoc. 70 (1938) 116.
In Derbyshire farmers: Addy (1895) 118.
When darkness closes in: Opie (1959) 268-75.
Tuesday 31 October: Last (1981) 21.

Antrobus Soul-Cakers

Helm (1968); *Lore & Language* 3 (1970) 9–11; 5 (1971) 11–15.

Mischief Night

The evening before May Day: Harland & Wilkinson (1882) 239.
Mischief Night in Blacko: Lancashire Lore (1971) 11.
When I was a kid: www.bbc.co.uk/northyorkshire/iloveny/2004/
    halloween/mischief_night.
Opie (1959) 255, 276–80.

November

FIRST SUNDAY IN NOVEMBER

London to Brighton Veteran Car Run

www.lvcr.com.

1 NOVEMBER

All Saints' Day

There is set on the board: Aubrey (1686/1880) 23.

2 NOVEMBER

All Souls' Day

Bands of children: N&Q 4S:2 (1868) 553.
Burne (1914); Wright & Lones III (1940) 121–45.

FIRST FRIDAY IN NOVEMBER

Bridgwater Carnival

Men, boys and urchins: Hocking (2004) 9.

4 NOVEMBER

Ringing Night

'Ringing-Night' is on the fourth: Couch (1871) 161.
A very curious custom: Gibbons (1885) 14.

5 NOVEMBER

Devil's Stone

Shuel (1985) 19.

Guy Fawkes Night

On the 5th: Schellinks (1993) 172.
On the night of 5th November: Hampshire Advertiser, 28 Nov. 1931,
    quoted in *Folk-Lore 42* (1931).
Remember, remember the fifth of November: Folk-Lore 14 (1903) 91.
In the days when there was no: Blakeborough (1898) 87.
On Monday last: York Herald, 15 Nov. 1806, quoted in Morsley
    (1979).

The Devon village of Chulmleigh: Western Morning News, 8 Nov.
    1960, quoted in *Devonshire Assoc.* 102 (1970) 270.
There was a massive: Sheffield (1993) 274–7.
In some areas: Camp (1988) 69.
Wright & Lones III (1940) 145–56; *History Today*, Nov. 1981, 5–9;
    Surrey Archaeological Collections 76 (1985) 61-8; *Folklore* 95:2
    (1984) 191–203; Cressy (1989); Buchanan *et al.* (2005); Sharpe
    (2005).

Parkin

Another local dainty: Folk-Lore 20 (1909) 204.

Lewes Bonfire Night

The bonfire societies: Etherington (1993) 23.
Shuel (1985) 186–7; Etherington (1993).

Ottery St Mary

Bonfire night at Ottery and *The sight of a large*: Shuel (1985) 187.
Owen (1984/5).

SECOND FRIDAY IN NOVEMBER

Silent Change

Brentnall (1975) 21–4; Paget (1989) 15–16.

SECOND SATURDAY IN NOVEMBER

Hatherleigh Carnival

They came down the hill: Shuel (1985) 189.
Shuel (1985) 188–9; www.hatherleigh.org.uk/carnival.

Lord Mayor's Show

Guildhall Miscellany 10 (1959) 3–18; Shuel (1985) 54–6; www.
    lordmayorsshow.org.

10 NOVEMBER

St Martin's Eve

Now that the year: Clare (1990) 112–17.

Wroth Silver

Chambers (1864) 571–2; Shuel (1985) 123–4; Waddilove & Eadon
    (1994).

11 NOVEMBER

St Martin's Day

If the wind: Inwards (1869) 33.
Brand I (1849) 399–404; Wright & Lones III (1940) 159–66.

Hiring Fairs

Carters and waggoners: Thomas Hardy, *Far from the Madding
    Crowd* (1874), chap. 6.
Drunkenness is the curse: The Times, 17 Nov. 1858, 8.
They were days: Cameron (1998) 120.
The key to the success: Caunce (1991) 54.
There is very little hiring: Williams (1912) 238–9.
Trotter (1919) 130–62; Catt (1986); Kightly (1986) 23–32; Roberts
    (1988); Caunce (1991) 54–73; Cameron (1998).

Remembrance Sunday

They are getting longer: West (2004) 19.
Bushaway (1992); West (2004) 19–22. For the contenders for the
    origin of the two-minute silence, see *The Times*, 14 Nov. 1930,
    14 and *N&Q* 162 (1932) 412. For 'British Day', see the *Guardian*, 14
    Jan. 2006.

13 NOVEMBER

St Brice's Day

Monday last being our annual: Lincoln, Rutland & Stamford
    Mercury, 18 Nov. 1785, quoted in Morsley (1979) 112.
Chambers II (1864) 574–6; Malcolmson (1973) 126–55.

Bull-Baiting
Turner (1964); Malcolmson (1973), *passim*.

17 NOVEMBER

Queen Elizabeth I/St Hugh's Day
Brand I (1849) 404–8; Cressy (1989), *passim*.

22 NOVEMBER

St Cecilia's Day
In 1945 it would have been: Whistler (1947) 213–18.

23 NOVEMBER

St Clement's Day
At Burwash a few years ago: Sussex Arch. Colls. 33 (1883) 252.
For this blessed martyr: N&Q 195 (1950) 531–2.
Clementing, clementing: The Times, 10 Dec. 1935, 17.
Folk-Lore Journal 2 (1884) 321–9; Folk-Lore 25 (1914) 285–99; Wright
    & Lones III (1940) 167–76; N&Q 195 (1950) 443–4, 530–32, 535–6.

25 NOVEMBER

St Catherine's Day
Patron of young girls: Farmer (1987) 77–8.
A husband, St. Catherine: Udal (1922) 102.
Folk-Lore 25 (1914) 285–99; Wright & Lones III (1940) 177–86.

FOURTH TUESDAY IN NOVEMBER

Ashburton Court Leet
Kightly (1986) 97; www.ashburton.org.

30 NOVEMBER

St Andrew's Day
Church Times, 22 June 1894, 689; Wright & Lones III (1940) 136–7,
    186–91, 261, 277.

Eton Wall Game
Shuel (1985) 167–8; www.etoncollege.com.

December

FIRST WEEKEND IN DECEMBER

Tree-Dressing Day
www.commonground.org.uk.

1 DECEMBER

St Eligius' Day
Ordinance and articles: N&Q 195 (1950) 532.

6 DECEMBER

St Nicholas
At the time a certain fellow: De Voragine (c.1260/1993) I, 21–7.

Barring Out
We did it every year and *There was a lot of big boys*: Bosanquet
    (1929/1989) 21.
schot of ane pistol: Quoted in Cathcart (1988) 51.
Pancake Tuesday: Folk-Lore 36 (1925) 256.
Hone, The Year-Book (1832) 653–4; Brand I (1849) 441–54; Chambers
    I (1864) 238–9; N&Q 187 (1944) 37, 83–4, 218–19; Thomas (1976);
    Cathcart (1988); History Today, Dec. 1988, 49–5.

Boy Bishop
It was reported: Folk-Lore 60 (1949) 302.
History Today 37 (1987) 10–16; Hutton (1996) 100–104.

11 DECEMBER

Old St Andrew's Day
Tander – Of all the numerous: Sternberg (1851) 183–5.

14 DECEMBER

St Tibba's Day
Hampson I (1841) 81–2; Palmer (1985) 31–2.

16 DECEMBER

Boar's Head
They went (most bitterly): Thomas Dekker, *Wonderful Yeare* (1603).
Brand I (1849) 484–6; Husk (1868) 115–27; Wright & Lones III (1940)
    252, 267, 279.

21 DECEMBER

St Thomas' Day
The women that I knew: Grey (1934) 195.
It is in fact a custom: Burne (1883) 393.

24 DECEMBER

Christmas Eve
Christmas Eve is: Gent. Mag. (1824:ii) 587–90.
If a girl walk: Addy (1895) 84.
Wright & Lones III (1940) 209–29.

Ashen Faggot
On Christmas Eve: Bentley's Magazine 21 (1847) 310.
Brand I (1849) 470; Wright & Lones III (1940) 213–14.

Cattle Kneeling
An honest countryman: Brand I (1849) 473–4.
It is said, as the morning: Devonshire Assoc. 70 (1938) 346, quoting
    Bentley's Magazine 21 (1847) 306.
Roud (2003) 7–8.

Hooden Horse
a country masquerade: Pegge (1736/1876), under *Hooding*.
Maylam (1909); Cawte (1978) 85–93.

Old Horse
What an eerie monster: Addy (1903) 3–6.
Cawte (1978) 117–24.

Ringing the Devil's Knell
at Horbury, near Wakefield: Henderson (1866) 40.
The Rev. Anthony Sterry: Wright & Lones III (1940) 219.
Colbeck (1983) 198–9; Smith (1989) 163–4.

Vessel Cups
The 'vessel-cups': Blakeborough (1898) 67–8.
The children carrying a box: Folk-Lore 17 (1906) 349–51 (includes a
    photograph of a 'wassail box' from Yorkshire).
Gent. Mag. (1832) 491–4; Brand I (1849) 454–5; Henderson (1879)
    64–6; Wright & Lones II (1938) 32–3; III (1940) 239–41.

Yule Log
A respectable middle-aged: Folk-Lore Journal 4 (1886) 167.
Come, bring with a noise: Herrick (1648), 'Ceremonies for
    Christmasse'.
In 1845 I was at: Burne (1883) 399.
Brand I (1849) 467–74; Wright & Lones III (1940) 210–13; Hutton
    (1996) 38–40.

Merrie England
England was merry England then: Walter Scott, *Marmion* (1808)
    canto VI.
One of the least pleasing effects: Irving (1819–20) 'Christmas'
    chapter.

Ye Merrie England of ye Olden Time: Wright (1928) 37.
Merry old England died: *Examiner*, 21 Dec. 1817, 801.

CHRISTMAS

All persons say: Robert Southey, *Letters from England*, ed. Jack Simmons (London: Cresset Press, 1951) 362.
But especially in Christmas: Stubbes (1595/2002) 238–9.
Durston (1985); Golby & Purdue (1986); Weightman & Humphries (1987); Davis (1990); Miller (1993); Dickens (1976), *passim*.

Candles
A candle or lamp: Addy (1895) 105.
Wright & Lones III (1940) 215; Opie & Tatem (1989) 75.

Cards
A young woman told me: *Folk-Lore* 66 (1955) 324.
Buday (1964); Higgs (1999).

Carol Singers
One of the most wonderful: Brice (1967) 1.
She hung her stocking: Uttley (1931) 119.
Poston (1965); Brice (1967); Poston (1970).

Crackers
A History of the Cracker, booklet issued by Tom Smith Group Ltd. (c.1997)
Kimpton (2004).

Decorations
Down with the rosemary: Herrick (1648).
Then may be seen: *Gent. Mag.* (1827:ii) 483–6.
In this progressive nineteenth century: *Girls Own Paper*, Christmas 1887, 32.
On Christmas Eve: Fletcher (1910) 152–3.
I wanted them both: Cullwick (1984) 184–5
Heyford Church is more neatly: Horn (1986) 6.
Ivy berries or dried peas: *Girls Own Paper*, 11 Dec. 1880, 170.
It is still a prevailing idea: *N&Q* 5S:2 (1874) 509.
If mistletoe be not burned: Igglesden (1932) 69–70.

Entertainments
The cake and the nut-brown ale: *Gent. Mag.* (1827:ii) 484–6.
The kitchen was tolerably: Ayres (1984) 23.
Blind Man's Buff: *Gent. Mag.* (1828) 506.
when the very fiddlers: Thomas Hardy, *Under the Greenwood Tree* (1872) chaps. 7–8.
Most of the games: Sheffield (1993) 269–70.

Food
Haggis – A north country: Brockett (1825) 144.
And when the child wakens: Brockie (1886/1974) 93, 99–100.
In some parts of the county: *Folk-Lore Journal* 4 (1886) 115.
A flat Christmas cake: Moor (1823) 192.
At Christmas hardly any: Brockett (1825) 132.
In keeping with the hospitality: Nicholson (1890) 19.
Grandmama was less: Surrey Federation of Women's Institutes (1992) 267–8.
Hone, *The Every-Day Book* I (1827) 819–20; Brand I (1849) 526–32; Davidson (2002) 221–2; 607.

Frumenty
The typical method: Wright and Lones I (1936) 50.
A receipt, three hundred years old: Esther Singleton, 'Ceremonial Dishes of England', *Cosmopolitan* 19 (1895) 51.
Somerset–Wiltshire: White (1932) 348.
It does not seem: White (1932) 363.
White (1932) 26–7, 341, 348, 361–5; Brears (1987) 172–4.

Geese Dancers
In town, the family: Couch (1871) 161-2.
From Christmas to twelfth-tide: *Folk-Lore Journal* 4 (1886) 118–19.

Guisers
they pushed open the door: Uttley (1931) 111–14.

Holy Thorn(s)
We hear from Quainton: *London Daily Advertiser*, 5 Jan. 1753, quoted in Mullan & Reid (2000) 214.
To all tender consciences: *Gloucester Journal*, 2 Jan. 1753.
Wright & Lones II (1938) 76–8 (for trees in Somerset); *The Times*, Jan. 1949 (for trees in Herefordshire); Vickery (1995) 184–8; Mullan & Reid (2000) 208-219; Westwood & Simpson (2005) 642–3;

Mummers
Twelfth Night had come: Grahame (1898) 121–2.
Cawte, Helm & Peacock (1967); Helm (1980); Cass (2001); Cass & Roud (2002).

Stockings
The old custom: Henderson (1866/1973) 50.
Children knew nothing: Fletcher (1910) 152–3.
On Christmas Eve, when the inmates: *N&Q* 5S:11 (1879) 66.
On Christmas Eve, each child: Brockie (1886/1974) 93.
By and by the younger ones: Blakeborough (1898) 67–9.
they had to hold candy: Warner (1854) 10.

Superstitions
It is lucky to be the first: *Folk-Lore Record* 1 (1878) 9.
We were very good neighbours: Burne (1883) 400.
If you were born: *Folk-Lore Record* 1 (1878) 9.
The horses might not go: Burne (1883) 403.

Sword Dance
Almost the first thing: Bosanquet (1929/1989) 23.
Sharp (1911–13); Helm (1980) 19–27; Shuel (1985) 47–9; Corrsin (1993); Corrsin (1997).

Tree
got up a little fête: Greville (2005) 27 December 1829.
Children knew nothing: Fletcher (1910) 152–3.

Waits
About a week before: *Gent. Mag.* (1827:ii) 483–6.
Certain strolling minstrels: *Gent. Mag.* (1824:ii) 587–90.
Stephen (1933); Wilshere (1970).

Wassailing
This friendly and neighbour-loving: Jewitt (1853) 230.
The Pope in sending: John Selden, *Table-Talk* (1689/1934) 86.
Wassaile the trees: Herrick (1648), 'Another [Christmasse Eve Ceremonie]'.
Wassail, wassail, all round the town: *Antiquary* 29 (1894) 122–4.
Apple wassailing: *Devonshire Assoc.* 86 (1954) 299.
Brand I (1849) 2–8; Wright & Lones III (1940) 223–4; Hutton (1996) 46; Sutton (1997) 13–14, 45–63;

26 DECEMBER

St Stephen's Day/Boxing Day
gave me the money: Cullwick (1984) 145, 261.
Our postman: *Punch* (1849) 237.
Brand I (1849) 532–4; Wright & Lones III (1940) 273; Hutton (1996) 23–4.

Bleeding Horses
Ere Christmas be past: Tusser (1580/1984) 57:2.
Brand I (1849) 532–4; Wright & Lones III (1940) 275.

Hunting and Shooting
In many parts of the country: Forby (1830) 420.
Mr. H., who is more: *Folk-Lore* 14 (1903) 89.

Hunting the Wren
I'm goin' to the woods: *Folk Music Journal* 1:5 (1969) 346.
In the hunt the utmost: Danaher (1972) 243.
You will see sometimes: Aubrey (1686/1880) 47–8.
The robin red-breast: Forby (1830) 409-10.
At Christmas-tide: Henderson (1866) 93.
Armstrong (1958) 141–66; Opie (1997b) 437–40; Roud (2003) 381–2,
    529–30; For Irish traditions, *see* Danaher (1972) 243–50; for
    Welsh traditions, *see* Owen (1987) 63–9; for traditions from the
    Isle of Man, *see* Moore (1891) 133–40.

Marshfield Paper Boys
Folklore 93 (1982) 105–11.

Pantomimes
Let us at once confess: Charles Dickens, *Bentley's Miscellany* (1837).
With the importation: Hartnoll (1983) 625.
It all adds up: Frow (1985) 186.
Wilson (1974); Frow (1985).

28 DECEMBER

Holy Innocents' Day
When living in the parish: Billson (1895) 96.
That proves as ominous: Carew (1602/2000) 32.
Innocents' Day, sometimes called: Burne (1883) 408-9.
Wright & Lones III (1940) 280–3; for lead-miners' refusal to work
    on the day, *see* N&Q 1:12 (1855) 201.

31 DECEMBER

New Year's Eve
As a general statement: Chambers II (1864) 787.
Brand I (1849) 1–10; Wright & Lones III (1940) 284–93.

Allendale Guisers
When war broke out: Newall (1974) 95.
Newall (1974); Shuel (1985) 190–91.

Bell-Ringing
On this night: Jewitt (1853) 230.
Wright & Lones II (1938) 18–21.

Gatherings
In England we seldom: *The Times*, 18 Nov. 1935, 15.
Wright & Lones II (1938) 16–18.

Hogmanay
Until about five-and-twenty: Neville (1909) 2.

Daily Customs

Bainbridge Horn-Blower
Kightly (1986) 141; Smith (1989) 142–5

Chime Hours
A recent experiment: N&Q 12S:1 (1916) 329.
An old Kentish lady: N&Q 3S:1 (1862) 223.
I record that I was born: Charles Dickens, *David Copperfield* (1849)
    chap. 1.
Opie & Tatem (1989) 71; Roud (2003) 36–7.

Lady Lee Monument, Aylesbury
Information from Jennifer Westwood (2006).

Tower of London: Ceremony of the Keys
Brentnall (1975) 77–9; Paget (1989) 22–3.

Wayfarers' Dole
Shuel (1985) 127; James (1987).

Weekly Customs

Farthing Bundles
Beer & Pickard (1987).

John Sayer Charity
Sykes (1977) 165.

St Monday
N&Q 8S:1 (1892) 88, 232–3, 252, 441, 523; Merceron (2002) 337–44.

Occasional Customs

Abingdon Bun-Throwing
Bloxham (2005) 124.

Bradshaw Memorial Dusting
Porteous (1976) 9; www.duffieldparishchurch.co.uk/bradshaw.

Chedzoy Candle Auction
Somerset & Avon Life, Apr. 1986, 85.

Denby Dale Pie
Bostwick (1987–8); Smith (1989) 125–9; for the Aughton plum
    pudding *see* N&Q 7S:2 (1886) 26.

Dunmow Flitch
I find but two couples: *Spectator*, 18 Oct. 1714.
Hackwood (1924) 67–9; Steer (1951); www.dunmowflitchtrials.
    co.uk.

Highgate Horns
The proverb 'he has been sworn at Highgate': Grose (1785).
Hone, *The Every-Day Book* II (1827) 40–44, 189; Bell (1866) 188–91;
    Thorne (1876) 346–7.

Oakham Horseshoes
Clough (1987).

Virgins' Crowns or Maidens' Garlands
Though I never saw: *Reliquary* 1 (1860–61) 8–9.
Chambers I (1864) 271–4; Brears (1982/3); Spriggs (1982/3).

Illustration Sources

Bibliography

Addison, William, *English Fairs and Markets* (London: Batsford, 1953).

Addy, George H., *Some Old Customs of Derbyshire* (London: London Society of Derbyshiremen, 1903).

Addy, Sidney Oldall, 'Garland Day at Castleton', *Folk-Lore* 12 (1901) 394–430.

——, *Folk Tales and Superstitions* (Wakefield: EP, 1973); previously published as *Household Tales with Other Traditional Remains* (1895).

Alexander, Matthew, 'Shrove Tuesday Football in Surrey', *Surrey Archaeological Collections* 77 (1986) 197–205.

Alford, Violet, *The Hobby Horse and other Animal Masks* (London: Merlin, 1978).

Andrews, William, *Bygone Lincolnshire* (Hull: A. Brown, 1891).

——, *Bygone Cheshire* (London: Simpkin Marshall, 1895).

——, *Old Church Life* (Hull: W. Andrews, 1900).

Appleton Parish Council, *A History of Appleton* (Appleton: Appleton Parish Council, 1997).

Arlott, John, *The Oxford Companion to Sports and Games* (Oxford: Oxford University Press, 1975).

Armstrong, Edward M., *The Folklore of Birds* (London: Collins, 1958).

Atkinson, Frank, 'Knur and Spell and Allied Games', *Folk Life* 1 (1963) 43–65; plus note by Ralph Merrifield in *Folk Life* 2 (1964) 116–17.

Atkinson, J. C., *Memorials of Old Whitby* (London: Macmillan, 1894).

Aubrey, John, *Remaines of Gentilisme and Judaisme* (1686); ed. James Britten (London: The Folklore Society, 1880).

Axon, William, *The Black Knights of Ashton* (Manchester: John Heywood, 1870).

Ayres, Jack (ed.), *Paupers and Pig Killers: The Diary of William Holland, a Somerset Parson, 1799–1818* (Gloucester: Alan Sutton, 1984).

Baigent, Francis Joseph, 'On the Family of de Lymerston', *Journal of the British Archaeological Association* 11 (1855) 277–302.

Baker, Anne Elizabeth, *Glossary of Northamptonshire Words and Phrases*, 2 vols. (London: Russell Smith, 1854).

Balfour, M. C., *County Folklore: Northumberland* (London: David Nutt, 1904).

Baring-Gould, S., *Devonshire Characters and Strange Events* (London: John Lane, 1908).

Baskervill, Charles Read, 'Mummers' Wooing Plays in England', *Modern Philology* 21 (1924) 225–72.

Beddington, Winifred G., and Christy, Elsa B., *It Happened in Hampshire* (Winchester: Hampshire Federation of Women's Institutes, 1936).

Bede, Venerable, *De Temporum Ratione*, in Wallis (1999).

Beer, R., and Pickard, C. A., *Eighty Years on Bow Common* (London: Fern Street Settlement, 1987).

Bell, Robert, *Ballads and Songs of the Peasantry of England* (London: Charles Griffin, 1866).

Bennett, A. R., *London and Londoners in the Eighteen-Fifties and Sixties* (London: Fisher Unwin, 1924).

Bennett, H. S., *Life on the English Manor: A Study of Peasant Conditions 1150–1400* (Cambridge: Cambridge University Press, 1948).

Billson, C. J., *County Folklore Printed Extracts 3: Leicestershire and Rutland* (London: The Folklore Society, 1895).

Bird, F. W., *Memorials of Godmanchester: Reminiscences of F. W. Bird* (Peterborough: Peterborough Advertiser, 1911).

Blakeborough, Richard, *Wit, Character, Folklore and Customs of the North Riding of Yorkshire* (London: Frowde, 1898).

Bloom, J. Harvey, *Folk Lore, Old Customs and Superstitions in Shakespeare Land* (London: Mitchell Hughes & Clarke, c.1930).

Bloxham, Christine, *May Day to Mummers: Folklore and Traditional Customs in Oxfordshire* (Charlbury: Wychwood Press, 2002).

——, *Folklore of Oxfordshire* (Stroud: Tempus, 2005).

Bosanquet, Rosalie E., *In the Troublesome Times* (Northumberland Press, 1929; reprinted Stocksfield: Spredden Press, 1989).

Bostwick, David, 'The Denby Dale Pies: An Illustrated Narrative History', *Folk Life* 26 (1987–8) 12–42.

Bourne, Henry, *Antiquitates Vulgares, or the Antiquities of the Common People* (Newcastle: privately printed, 1725).

Boyes, Georgina, 'Dressing the Part: The Role of Costume as an Indicator of Social Dynamics in the Castleton Garland Ceremony', in Buckland & Wood (1993) 105–18.

Bradley, A. G., *Round About Wiltshire* (1907; 3rd edn, London: Methuen, 1913).

Brand John, *Observations on Popular Antiquities* (London: Vernon, Bood & Sharpe, 1810).

Brand, John, *Observations on the Popular Antiquities of Great Britain*, new edn, ed. Henry Ellis, 3 vols. (London: Bohn, 1849).

Bray, Mrs A. E., *Traditions, Legends, Superstitions, and Sketches of Devonshire* (London: Murray, 1838).

Brears, Peter, *Traditional Food in Yorkshire* (Edinburgh: John Donald, 1987).

——, *North Country Folk Art* (Edinburgh: John Donald, 1989).

Brears, Peter C. D., 'Construction of a Maiden's Garland', *Folk Life* 21 (1982/83) 34–5.

Brentnall, Margaret, *Old Customs and Ceremonies of London* (London: Batsford, 1975).

Brice, Douglas, *The English Folk Carol* (London: Herbert Jenkins, 1967).

Briggs, Katharine M., *The Folklore of the Cotswolds* (London: Batsford, 1974).

British Film Institute, *Electric Edwardians: The Films of Mitchell and Kenyon*, DVD (London: BFI, 2005).

Brockett, John Trotter, *A Glossary of North Country Words* (Newcastle: Emerson Charnley, 1825; 3rd edn, 1846).

Brockie, William, *Legends and Superstitions of the County of Durham* (Sunderland, 1886; reprinted Wakefield: EP, 1974).

Brown, Tom, *The Hunting of the Earl of Rone*, revised edn (Combe Martin: Earl of Rone Council, 1997).

Bruley, Sue (ed.), *Working for Victory: A Diary of Life in a Second World War Factory* (Stroud: Sutton, 2001).

Buchanan, Brenda, *et al.*, *Gunpowder Plots* (London: Allen Lane, 2005).

Buckland, Theresa, 'The Reindeer Antlers of the Abbots Bromley Horn Dance: A Re-examination', *Lore and Language* 3:2 (1980) 1–8 (*see also* correspondence in vols. 3:7 (1982) 87; 4:1 (1985) 86–7; 5:2 (1986) 101).

——, 'Wakes and Rushbearing *c.* 1780–*c.* 1830: A Functional Analysis', *Lore & Language* 3:6 (1982) 29–44.

——, 'The Tunstead Mill Nutters of Rossendale, Lancashire', *Folk Music Journal* 5:2 (1986) 132–49.

Buckland, Theresa, and Wood, Juliette, *Aspects of British Calendar Customs* (Sheffield: Sheffield Academic Press, 1993).

Buday, George, *The History of the Christmas Card* (London: Spring Books, 1964).

Burne, Charlotte, *Shropshire Folk-Lore: A Sheaf of Gleanings* (London: Trübner, 1883).

——, 'Souling, Clementing, and Catterning: Three November Customs of the Western Midlands', *Folk-Lore* 25 (1914) 285–99.

Burns, Francis, *Heigh for Cotswold! A History of Robert Dover's Olimpick Games*, new edn (Chipping Campden: Robert Dover's Games Society, 2000).

Burton, Alfred, *Rush-Bearing* (Manchester: Brook & Chrystal, 1891).

Bushaway, Bob, *By Rite: Custom, Ceremony and Continuity in England 1700–1880* (London: Junction Books, 1982).

——, 'Name Upon Name: The Great War and Remembrance', in Porter (1992) 136–67.

——, 'Bulls, Ballads, Minstrels and Manors: Some Observations on the Defence of Custom in Eighteenth-Century England', in Buckland & Wood (1993) 75–93.

Bushaway, R. W., 'Grovely, Grovely, Grovely, and all Grovely: Custom, Crime and Conflict in the English Woodland', *History Today* 31 (March 1981) 37–43.

Byng, John, *The Torrington Diaries*, 4 vols. (London: Eyre & Spottiswoode, 1934–8).

Cameron, David Kerr, *The English Fair* (Stroud: Sutton, 1998).

Camp, John, *In Praise of Bells: The Folklore and Traditions of British Bells* (London: Robert Hale, 1988).

Candlin, Lilian, *Memories of Old Sussex* (Newbury: Countryside Books, 1987).

Cannadine, David, 'The Transformation of Civic Ritual in Modern Britain: The Colchester Oyster Feast', *Past & Present* 94 (1982) 107–30.

Capp, Bernard, *Astrology and the Popular Press: English Almanacs 1500–1800* (London: Faber, 1979).

Carew, Richard, *The Survey of Cornwall* (London: John Jaggard, 1602; reprinted Redruth: Tamar Books, 2000).

Cass, Eddie, *The Lancashire Pace-Egg Play: A Social History* (London: FLS Books, 2001).

Cass, Eddie, and Roud, Steve, *Room, Room, Ladies and Gentlemen: An Introduction to the English Mummers' Play* (London: English Folk Dance & Song Society, 2002).

Cathcart, Rex, 'Festive Capers? Barring-Out the Schoolmaster', *History Today* (Oct 1988) 49–53.

Catt, Jon, *Northern Hiring Fairs* (Chorley: Countryside Publications, 1986).

Caunce, Stephen, *Amongst Farm Horses: The Horselads of East Yorkshire* (Stroud: Alan Sutton, 1991).

Cawte, E. C., *Ritual Animal Disguise* (Cambridge: Brewer, 1978).

Cawte, E. C., Helm, Alex, and Peacock, Norman, *English Ritual Drama* (London: The Folklore Society, 1967).

Chambers, Robert, *The Book of Days: A Miscellany of Popular Antiquities*, 2 vols. (London: Chambers, 1864).

Chandler, Keith, *Morris Dancing at Bampton Until 1914* (Minster Lovell: privately printed, 1983).

——, *Ribbons, Bells and Squeaking Fiddles: The Social History of Morris Dancing in the English South Midlands, 1660–1900* (Enfield Lock: Hisarlik, 1993) [cited as 1993a].

——, 'The Abingdon Morris and the Election of the Mayor of Ock Street', in Buckland & Wood (1993) 119–36 [cited as 1993b].

Charlton, Lionel, *The History of Whitby and of Whitby Abbey* (York: A. Ward, 1779).

Christian, Roy, *Well-Dressing in Derbyshire* (Derby: Derbyshire Countryside, 1983).

Clare, John, *The Midsummer Cushion* (Manchester: Carcanet, 1990).

——, *Cottage Tales* (Manchester: Carcanet, 1993).

——, *The Midsummer Cushion*, in Eric Robinson, David Powell, and P. M. S. Dawson (eds.), *John Clare: Poems of the Middle Period* III (Oxford: Clarendon Press, 1998).

Clarke, James, *Survey of the Lakes of Cumberland, Westmorland, and Lancashire*, 2nd edn (London: privately printed, 1789).

Clough, T. H. McK., *The Horseshoes of Oakham Castle*, 2nd edn (Leicester: Leicestershire Museums, 1987).

Cobbett, William, *Rural Rides* (London: William Cobbett, 1830).

Colbeck, Maurice, *The Calendar Year: A Celebration of Events in the Yorkshire Television Region* (East Ardsley: EP, 1983).

Cole, Malcolm, *Whitelands College May Queen Festival 1881–1981* (London: Whitelands College, 1981).

Collinson, John, *The History and Antiquities of the County of Somerset*, 3 vols. (Bath: R. Cruttwell, 1791).

Cooper, Jeremy J., *A Fool's Game: The Ancient Tradition of Haxey Hood* (Haxey: Lord & Boggins of the Haxey Hood, 1993).

Corrsin, Stephen D., *Sword Dancing in Britain: An Annotated Bibliography* (London: English Folk Dance & Song Society, 1993).

——, *Sword Dancing in Europe: A History* (Enfield Lock: Hisarlik, 1997).

Cossins, James, *Reminiscences of Exeter Fifty Years Since* (Exeter: privately printed, 1878).

Couch, Jonathan, *The History of Polperro* (Truro: W. Lake, 1871).

Crawford, Phyllis, *In England Still* (London: Arrowsmith, 1938).

Cressy, David, *Bonfires and Bells: National Memory and the Protestant Calendar in Elizabethan and Stuart England* (London: Weidenfeld & Nicolson, 1989).

Crosby, Alan, *The History of the Preston Guild* (Preston: Lancashire County Books, 1991).

Cross, F. L., *The Oxford Dictionary of the Christian Church* (London: Oxford University Press, 1957).

Cullwick, Hannah, *The Diaries of Hannah Cullwick, Victorian Maidservant*, ed. Liz Stanley (London: Virago, 1984).

Cumbrian Federation of Women's Institutes, *Cumbria Within Living Memory* (Newbury: Countryside Books, 1994).

Dacombe, Marianne R. (ed.), *Dorset Up Along and Down Along* (Dorchester: Dorset Federation of Women's Institutes, 1935).

Danaher, Kevin, *The Year in Ireland: Irish Calendar Customs* (Cork: Mercier, 1972).

Davidson, Alan, *The Penguin Companion to Food* (London: Penguin, 2002).

Davis, Paul, *The Life and Times of Ebenezer Scrooge* (New Haven: Yale University Press, 1990).

De Carle, Donald, *British Time* (London: Crosby Lockwood, 1947).

De Voragine, Jacobus, *The Golden Legend: Readings on the Saints* (c.1260), trans. William Granger Ryan (Princeton: Princeton University Press, 1993).

Deane, Tony, and Shaw, Tony, *The Folklore of Cornwall* (London: Batsford, 1975).

Defoe, Daniel, *A Tour through the Whole Island of Great Britain* (1724–6; London: Dent, 1962).

Denham Tracts: A Collection of Folklore by Michael Aislabie Denham, ed. James Hardy, 2 vols. (London: The Folklore Society, 1892–5).

Dickens, Charles, *The Annotated Christmas Carol*, ed. Michael Patrick Hearn (New York: Clarkson N. Potter, 1976).

Ditchfield, P. H., *Old English Customs* (London: Methuen, 1896).

Dives and Pauper (c.1405–10; London: Early English Text Society, 1976/1980).

Doble, Gilbert H., *The Saints of Cornwall: Part 2, Saints of the Lizard District* (Felinfach: Llanerch, 1998).

Doel, Fran, and Doel, Geoff, *Folklore of Kent* (Stroud: Tempus, 2003).

Donoghue, Paul, and Capstick, Tony, *Appleby Horse Fair: A Collection of Stories, Poems, and Photographs* (Northallerton: Appleby Fair, 2002).

Dowden, John, *The Church Year and Kalendar* (Cambridge: Cambridge University Press, 1910).

Duffy, Eamon, *The Stripping of the Altars* (London: Yale University Press, 1992).

Duncan, David Ewing, *The Calendar* (London: Fourth Estate, 1998).

Duncomb, John, *Words Used in Herefordshire* (1804), in Walter W. Skeat, *Reprinted Glossaries, Series B* (London: English Dialect Society, 1874).

Durand, Mortimer, *The Life of the Rt. Hon. Sir Alfred Comyn Lyall* (London: Blackwood, 1913).

Durston, Chris, 'Lords of Misrule: The Puritan War on Christmas 1642–60', *History Today* (Dec. 1985) 7–14.

Dyck, Ian, *William Cobbett and Rural Popular Culture* (Cambridge: Cambridge University Press, 1992).

Dyer, T. F. Thiselton, *British Popular Customs, Past and Present* (London: George Bell, 1876).

East Kent Federation of Women's Institutes, *East Kent Within Living Memory* (Newbury: Countryside Books, 1993).

East Yorkshire Federation of Women's Institutes, *East Yorkshire Within Living Memory* (Newbury: Countryside Books, 1998).

Edwards, E., *A Collection of Old English Customs* (London: John Bower Nichols, 1842).

Elias, N., and Dunning, E., 'Folk Football in Medieval and Early Modern Britain', in E. Dunning, *The Sociology of Sport* (London: F. Cass, 1971).

Etherington, Jim, *Lewes Bonfire Night: A Short History of the Guy Fawkes Celebrations* (Seaford: S.B. Publications, 1993).

Evans, George Ewart, *The Farm and the Village* (London: Faber, 1969).

——, *Where Beards Wag All: The Relevance of the Oral Tradition* (London: Faber, 1972).

Evelyn, John, *The Diary of John Evelyn*, 3 vols. (London: Routledge/Thoemmes, 1996).

Farmer, David, *Oxford Dictionary of Saints*, 2nd edn (Oxford: Oxford University Press, 1987).

Filmer, Richard, *Hops and Hop Picking* (Princes Risborough: Shire, 1982).

Findler, Gerald, *Folk Lore of the Lake Counties* (Clapham: Dalesman, 1968).

Fisher, John, *The History and Antiquities of Masham and Mashamshire* (London: Simpkin Marshall, 1865).

Fitz Stephen, William, *Description of London* (c.1180; reprinted as *Norman London*, New York: Italica, 1990).

Flavell, Linda and Roger, *Dictionary of Proverbs and their Origins* (London: Kyle Cathie, 1993).

Fletcher, J. S., *Recollections of a Yorkshire Village* (London: Digby Long, 1910).

Fletcher, Linda, 'Strewings', *Folk Life* 36 (1997/8) 66–71.

Forby, Robert, *The Vocabulary of East Anglia* (London: Nichols, 1830).

Forrest, John, *The History of Morris Dancing 1458–1750* (Cambridge: James Clarke, 1999).

Forster, Robert, *History of Corbridge* (Newcastle: J. Beall, 1881).

Fox, David Scott, *Saint George: The Saint with Three Faces* (Windsor: Kensal Press, 1983).

Frampton, George, *Whittlesey Straw Bear* (Peterborough: Cambridgeshire Libraries, 1989).

——, 'The Shaftesbury Byzant: A South of England Morris?', *Folklore* 101:2 (1990) 152–61.

——, *Grovely! Grovely! Grovely! and All Grovely! The History of Oak Apple Day in Great Wishford* (York: Quacks Books, 1992).

Frow, Gerald, *Oh Yes It Is! A History of Pantomime* (London: BBC, 1985).

Fry, Lewis G., *Oxted, Limpsfield and Neighbourhood* (Oxted: privately printed, 1932).

Gamble, Rose, *Chelsea Child* (London: BBC, 1979).

Gardner, Keith, 'Apples in the Landscape: The Puxton Dolmoors', *Bristol and Avon Archaeology* 4 (1985) 13–20.

Gerould, Gordon Hall, *Saints' Legends* (Boston: Houghton Mifflin, 1916).

Gerrish, Tricia, *The Glove is Up! Devon's Historic Fairs* (unpublished typescript, West Country Studies Library, 2004) [unpaginated].

Gibbons, M. S., *We Donkeys in Devon* (Exeter: Eland, 1885).

Gibson, A. Craig, 'Ancient Customs and Superstitions in Cumberland', *Transactions of the Historical Society of Lancashire & Cheshire* 10 (1858) 96–110.

Giles, John A., *History of the Parish and Town of Bampton* (Oxford: J. H. Parker, 1847).

Glover, Stephen, *The History of the County of Derby*, 2 vols. (Derby: Henry Mozley, 1829).

Golby, J. M. and Purdue, A. W., *The Making of the Modern Christmas* (London: Batsford, 1986).

Golden Legend, see De Voragine.

Goldsmith, Oliver, *The Vicar of Wakefield* (London: F. Newbery, 1766).

Gomme, Alice Bertha, *The Traditional Games of England, Scotland and Ireland*, 2 vols. (London, David Nutt, 1894–8).

Gomme, G. L. (ed.), *The Gentleman's Magazine Library: Manners and Customs* (London: Eliot Stock, 1883).

Goodsall, Robert H., 'Oyster Fisheries on the North Kent Coast', *Archaeologia Cantiana* 80 (1965) 118–51.

Govett, L. A., *The King's Book of Sports* (London: Eliot Stock, 1890).

Grahame, Kenneth, *The Golden Age* (London: John Lane, 1898).

Grant, James, *Sketches in London* (London: W. S. Orr, 1838).

Grantham, W. W., *Stoolball and How to Play It*, 2nd edn (London: W. B. Tattershall, 1931).

Greenhalgh, Alec, *Hail Smiling Morn: Whit Friday Brass Band Contests, 1884–1991* (Oldham: Oldham Library, 1992).

Greenwood, James, *Unsentimental Journeys* (London: Lock & Tyler, 1867).

Greville, Charles, *The Diaries of Charles Greville*, ed. Edward Pearce (London: Pimlico, 2005).

Grey, Edwin, *Cottage Life in a Hertfordshire Village* (St Albans: Fisher, Knight & Co., 1934).

Grose, Francis, *Classical Dictionary of the Vulgar Tongue* (London: S. Hooper, 1785).

Gunnell, Clive, *To Tavistock Goosie Fair* (Bodmin: Bossiney, 1978).

Gunnell, Terry, *The Origins of Drama in Scandinavia* (Cambridge: Brewer, 1995).

Gurdon, E. C., *County Folk-Lore: Suffolk* (London: The Folklore Society, 1893).

Gutch, Mrs, *County Folk-Lore: North Riding of Yorkshire and the Ainsty* (London: David Nutt, 1901).

Gutch, Mrs and Peacock, Mabel, *County Folk-Lore Vol. 5: Lincolnshire* (London: David Nutt, 1908).

Hackwood, Frederick William, *Staffordshire Customs, Superstitions and Folklore* (Lichfield: Mercury Press, 1924).

Haddon, Celia, *The First Ever English Olimpick Games* (London: Hodder & Stoughton, 2004).

Halliwell, James Orchard, *The Popular Rhymes and Nursery Tales of England* (London: John Russell Smith, 1849).

Hampson, R. T., *Medii Aevi Kalendarium*, 2 vols. (London: Causton, 1841).

Hardy, Thomas, *The Mayor of Casterbridge* (London: Macmillan, 1886).

Harland, John, and Wilkinson, T. T., *Lancashire Legends, Traditions, Pageants and Sports* (London: Routledge, 1867).

——, *Lancashire Folk-Lore* (Manchester: Heywood, 1882).

Harris, Mollie, *A Kind of Magic: An Oxfordshire Childhood in the 1920s* (London: Chatto & Windus, 1969).

Harrison, Kenneth, *The Framework of Anglo-Saxon History to AD 900* (Cambridge: Cambridge University Press, 1967).

Hart, Kingsley, *The Letters of Dorothy Osborne to Sir William Temple 1652–54* (London: Folio Society, 1968).

Hartnoll, Phyllis, *The Oxford Companion to the Theatre*, 4th edn (Oxford: Oxford University Press, 1983).

Hasted, Edward, *History and Topographical Survey of the County of Kent*, 4 vols. (Canterbury: Simmons & Kirby, 1778–99).

Hawthorne, Nathaniel, *Our Old Home* (London: Smith Elder, 1863).

Hazlitt, W. C., *A Dictionary of Faiths and Folk-Lore* (London: Reeves & Turner, 1905).

Head, Robert, *Congleton Past and Present* (Congleton: privately printed, 1887).

Heaney, Michael, *An Introductory Bibliography on Morris Dancing* (London: English Folk Dance and Song Society, 1985).

——, 'New Evidence for the Abbots Bromley Hobby-Horse', *Folk Music Journal* 5:3 (1987) 359–60.

Heanley, R. M., 'The Vikings: Traces of their Folklore in Marshland', *Saga-Book* 3 (1902).

Heffernan, Hilary, *The Annual Hop London to Kent* (Stroud: Tempus, 1996).

Helm, Alex, *Cheshire Folk Drama* (Ibstock: Guizer Press, 1968).

——, 'Rushcarts of the North-West of England', *Folk Life* 8 (1970) 20–31.

——, *The English Mummers' Play* (Woodbridge: D.S. Brewer, 1980).

Henderson, William, *Notes on the Folk Lore of the Northern Counties of England and the Border* (London: Longmans Green, 1866; reprinted Wakefield: EP, 1973; 2nd edn, London: The Folklore Society, 1879).

Herrick, Robert, *Hesperides* (1648), in *The Poems of Robert Herrick* (London: Oxford University Press, 1965).

Hewett, Sarah, *The Peasant Speech of Devon*, 2nd edn (London: Elliot Stock, 1892).

——, *Nummits and Crummits: Devonshire Customs, Characteristics, and Folk-Lore* (London: Thomas Burleigh, 1900).

Higgs, Michelle, *Christmas Cards from the 1840s to the 1940s* (Princes Risborough: Shire, 1999).

Hird, Ben, *The Antient Scorton Silver Arrow* (London: Society of Archer-Antiquaries, 1972).

Hocking, Chris, *Remember, Remember: The Story of Bridgwater Guy Fawkes Carnival* (Bridgwater: privately printed, 2004).

Hogg, Garry, *Customs and Traditions of England* (Newton Abbot: David & Charles, 1971).

Hole, Christina, *English Sports and Pastimes* (London: Batsford, 1949).

——, *English Traditional Customs* (London: Batsford, 1975).

——, *Dictionary of British Folk Customs* (London: Hutchinson, 1976).

——, *A Dictionary of British Folk Customs* (London: Paladin, 1978).

Home, Gordon, *The Evolution of an English Town* (London: Dent, 1915).

Hone, William, *The Every-Day Book*, 2 vols. (London: Thomas Tegg, 1827).

——, *The Table Book* (London: Thomas Tegg, 1827).

——, *The Year-Book* (London: Thomas Tegg, 1832).

Horn, Pamela (ed.), *Oxfordshire Country Life in the 1860s: The Early Diaries of George James Dew (1846–1928) of Lower Heyford* (Sutton Courtenay: Beacon Publications, 1986).

Howkins, Alun, and Merricks, Linda, 'The Ploughboy and the Plough Play', *Folk Music Journal* 6:2 (1991) 187–208.

Hughes, Thomas, *The Scouring of the White Horse* (Cambridge, Macmillan, 1859).

Husk, William Henry, *Songs of the Nativity* (London: Hotten, 1868).

Hutchinson, W., *A View of Northumberland*, 2 vols. (Newcastle: T. Saint, 1778).

Hutton, Ronald, *The Rise and Fall of Merry England: The Ritual Year 1400–1700* (Oxford: Oxford University Press, 1994).

——, *Stations of the Sun: A History of the Ritual Year in Britain* (Oxford: Oxford University Press, 1996).

Hyett, F. A., *Glimpses of the History of Painswick* (Gloucester: British Publishing, 1957).

Igglesden, Charles, *Those Superstitions* (London: Jarrolds [1932]).

Ingram, Martin, 'Ridings, Rough Music and the Reform of Popular Culture in Early Modern England', *Past & Present* 105 (1984) 79–113.

Inwards, R., *Weather Lore* (London: W. Tweedie, 1869; new edn, London: Elliot Stock, 1893).

Irving, Washington, *The Sketch-Book of Geoffrey Crayon, Gent.* (1819–20; rev. edn, New York: Putnam, 1848).

——, *Bracebridge Hall* (London: John Murray, 1822).

James, Nicholas, 'The Survival of the Traditional Dole in Hampshire Today', *Lore Language* 6:1 (1987) 59–64.

Jefferies, Richard, *Round About a Great Estate* (London: Smith Elder, 1880).

Jeffrey, Percy Shaw, *Whitby Lore and Legend*, 2nd edn (Whitby: Horne, 1923).

Jenkin, A. K. Hamilton, *Cornish Homes and Customs* (London: Dent, 1934).

Jewitt, Llewellyn, 'On Ancient Customs and Sports of the County of Nottingham', *Journal of the British Archaeological Assoiation* 8 (1853) 229–40.

Jones, Kelvin I., *The Furry Dance: An Ancient Tradition* (Penzance: Oakmagic, 1997).

Jones-Baker, Doris, *The Folklore of Hertfordshire* (London: Batsford, 1977).

Judge, Roy, 'Tradition and the Plaited Maypole Dance', *Traditional Dance* 2 (1983) 1–22.

——, *Changing Attitudes to May Day 1844–1914* (unpublished Ph.D. thesis, University of Leeds, 1987).

——, 'Fact and Fancy in Tennyson's May Queen and Flora Thompson's May Day', in Buckland & Wood (1993) 167–83.

——, *The Jack-in-the-Green*, 2nd edn (London: FLS Books, 2000).

Kennedy, Douglas, *English Folk Dancing Today and Yesterday* (London: Bell, 1964).

Kent, Sylvia, *Folklore of Essex* (Stroud: Tempus, 2005).

Kightly, Charles, *The Customs and Ceremonies of Britain: An Encyclopaedia of Living Traditions* (London: Thames & Hudson, 1986).

Kille, Herbert W., 'West Country Hobby-Horses and Cognate Customs', *Proceedings of the Somerset Archaeological & Natural History Society*, 4th series, 17 (1931) 63–77.

Kilvert, Francis, *Kilvert's Diary*, ed. William Plomer, 4 vols. (London: Jonathan Cape, 1938–9).

Kimpton, Peter, *Tom Smith's Christmas Crackers: An Illustrated History* (Stroud: Tempus, 2004).

Kitchen, Fred, *Brother to the Ox: The Autobiography of a Farmer's Boy* (London: Dent, 1940).

Lancashire Federation of Women's Institutes, *Lancashire Within Living Memory* (Newbury: Countryside Books, 1997).

Lancashire Lore (Preston: Lancashire Federation of Women's Institutes, 1971).

Last, Nella, *Nella Last's War: A Mother's Diary*, ed. Richard Broad and Suzie Fleming (London: Falling Wall, 1981).

Le Faye, Deirdre, *Jane Austen's Letters*, new edn (Oxford: Oxford University Press, 1995).

Lean, Vincent Stuckey, *Lean's Collectanea*, 5 vols. (Bristol: Arrowsmith, 1902–4).

Learmount, Brian, *A History of the Auction* (Iver: Barnard & Larmount, 1985).

Leather, Ella Mary, *The Folk-Lore of Herefordshire* (London: Sidgwick and Jackson, 1912).

Leeds Mercury (4 Oct. 1879), 'Notes & Queries No. XL: Yorkshire Folk Lore' (contributed by Samuel Smith).

Lenton, Graham, *The Story of the Olney Pancake Race* (Whitney: gml art, 2003).

Lodge, Thomas, *Wit's Miserie* (London: Adam Islip, 1596).

Lowerson, John, 'Stoolball: Conflicting Values in the Revivals of a Traditional Sussex Game', *Sussex Archaeological Collections* 133 (1995) 263–74.

Machyn, Henry, *The Diary of Henry Machyn*, ed. John Gough Nichols (London: Camden Society, 1848).

MacLean, Sally-Beth, 'Hocktide: A Reassessment of a Popular Pre-Reformation Festival', in Twycross (1996) 233–41.

Magoun, F. P., *History of Football from the Beginnings to 1871* (Bochum-Langendreer: H. Poppinghaus, 1938).

Main, Veronica, 'Corn Dollies: Searching for the Seed of Truth', *Folk Life* 37 (1998–9) 44–63.

Malcolmson, Robert W., *Popular Recreations in English Society 1700–1850* (Cambridge: Cambridge University Press, 1973).

Manningham, John , *The Diary of John Manningham of the Middle Temple 1602–1603* (London: Camden Society, 1868).

Mantell, Gideon, *Journal of Gideon Mantell (Surgeon and Geologist)* (London: Curwen, 1940).

Marshall, Sybil, *Fenland Chronicle* (Cambridge: Cambridge University Press, 1967).

Maylam, Percy, *The Hooden Horse: An East Kent Christmas Custom* (Canterbury: privately printed, 1909).

Menefee, Samuel Pyeatt, *Wives for Sale* (Oxford: Blackwell, 1981).

——, 'Dead Reckoning: the Church Porch Watch in British Society', in Hilda Ellis Davidson (ed.), *The Seer in Celtic and Other Traditions* (Edinburgh: John Donald, 1989).

Merceron, Jacques E., *Dictionnaire des Saints Imaginaires et Facétieux* (Paris: Editions du Seuil, 2002).

Metford, J. C. J., *The Christian Year* (London: Thames & Hudson, 1991).

Miller, Dan (ed.), *Unwrapping Christmas* (Oxford: Clarendon Press, 1993).

Millington, Peter, 'The Ploughboy and the Plough Play', *Folk Music Journal* 7:1 (1995) 71–3.

Mitford, Jessica, *Hons and Rebels* (London: Gollancz, 1960).

Moor, Edward, *Suffolk Words and Phrases* (Woodbridge: Loder, 1823).

Moore, A. W., *The Folk-Lore of the Isle of Man* (London: D. Nutt, 1891).

Morison, John, and Daisley, Peter, *Hare Pie Scrambling & Bottle Kicking: Hallaton's Strange and Ancient Custom* (Hallaton: Hallaton Museum Press, 2000).

Morley, Henry, *Memoirs of Bartholomew Fair* (London: Chapman & Hall, 1859).

Morris, M. C. F., *Yorkshire Folk-Talk*, 2nd edn (London: A. Brown, 1911).

Morsley, Clifford, *News from the English Countryside 1750–1850* (London: Harrap, 1979).

Mullan, John, and Reid, Christopher, *Eighteenth-Century Popular Culture: A Selection* (Oxford: Oxford University Press, 2000).

Muncey, R. W., *Our Old English Fairs* (London: Sheldon Press [c.1935]).

Munn, Pat, *Bodmin Riding and Other Similar Celtic Customs* (Bodmin: Bodmin Books, 1975).

Murfin, Lyn, *Popular Leisure in the Lake Countries* (Manchester: Manchester University Press, 1990).

Naylor, Peter, and Porter, Lindsey, *Well Dressing* (Ashbourne: Landmark, 2002).

Neasham, George, *North-Country Sketches* (Durham: privately printed, 1893).

Neville, Hastings M., *A Corner in the North: Yesterday and Today with Border Folk* (Newcastle: Andrew Reid, 1909).

Newall, Venetia, *An Egg at Easter* (London: Routledge & Kegan Paul, 1971).

——, 'The Allendale Fire Festival in Relation to its Contemporary Social Setting', *Folklore* 85 (1974) 93–103.

——, 'Throwing the Hood at Haxey: A Lincolnshire Twelfth Night Custom', *Folk Life* 18 (1980) 7–23.

Newton, Jill, *Helston Flora Day* (Bodmin: Bossiney, 1978).

Nicholson, John, *Folk Lore of East Yorkshire* (London: Simpkin Marshall, 1890).

Noake, John, *Guide to Worcestershire* (London: Longman, 1868).

Opie, Iona and Peter, *The Lore and Language of Schoolchildren* (Oxford: Oxford University Press, 1959).

——, *Children's Games with Things* (Oxford: Oxford Univ. Press, 1997) [cited as 1997a].

——, *Oxford Dictionary of Nursery Rhymes* (2nd edn., Oxford: Oxford University Press, 1997) [cited as 1997b].

Opie, Iona, and Tatem, Moira, *A Dictionary of Superstitions* (Oxford: Oxford University Press, 1989).

Oruch, Jack, 'St. Valentine, Chaucer, and Spring in February', *Speculum* 56:3 (1981) 534–65.

Osborne, Dorothy, Letters of, in Hart (1968).

Owen, Nelson, 'Old Custom Goes with a Bang', *The Countryman* (Winter 1984/5) 70–74.

Owen, Trefor M., *Welsh Folk Customs*, new edn (Llandysul: Gomer, 1987).

Paget, Julian, *Discovering London Ceremonial and Traditions* (Princes Risborough: Shire, 1989).

Palmer, Kingsley, *The Folklore of Somerset* (London: Batsford, 1976).

Palmer, Roy, *The Folklore of Leicestershire and Rutland* (Wymondham: Sycamore Press, 1985).

——, *The Folklore of Gloucestershire* (Tiverton: Westcountry Books, 1994).

——, *Herefordshire Folklore* (Woonton Almeley: Logaston, 2002).

——, *The Folklore of Shropshire* (Almeley: Logaston Press, 2004).

Parish, W. D., *A Dictionary of the Sussex Dialect*, 2nd edn (Lewes: Farncombe, 1875).

Pasquils Palinodia and His Progress to the Taverne (London: Thomas Snodham, 1619); reprinted in J. Payne Collier, *Illustrations of Old English Literature* I (London: privately printed, 1866).

Patten, R.W., *Exmoor Custom and Song* (Dulverton: Exmoor Press, 1974).

Pegge, Samuel, *Glossary of Kenticisms* (1736); reprinted in English Dialect Society, *Original Glossaries* III (London: Trubner, 1876).

Philpott, Olive M., 'Whitsuntide in Our Village', *Dorset Year Book* (1961/2) 173–7.

Phythian-Adams, Charles, 'Milk and Soot: The Changing Vocabulary of a Popular Ritual in Stuart and Hanoverian London', in D. Fraser and A. Sutcliffe, *The Pursuit of Urban History* (London: Edward Arnold, 1983) 83–104.

Piggott, Stuart, *The Druids* (London: Thames & Hudson, 1968).

Pihlens, Hugh, *The Story of Hungerford* (Newbury: Local Heritage Books, 1983).

Pollard, A. F., 'New Year's Day and Leap Year in English History', *English Historical Review* 55 (1940) 177–93.

Poole, Robert, *Time's Alteration: Calendar Reform in Early Modern England* (London: UCL Press, 1998).

Porteous, Chrichton, *The Beauty and Mystery of Well-Dressing* (Derby: Pilgrim Press, 1949).

——, *The Ancient Customs of Derbyshire* (Derby: Derbyshire Countryside, 1976).

Porter, Enid, *Cambridgeshire Customs and Folklore* (London: Routledge & Kegan Paul, 1969).

Porter, Lindsey, *Ashbourne Royal Shrovetide Football: the Official History* (Ashbourne: Ashbourne Editions, 1992).

——, *Ashbourne Shrovetide Football: 100 Years in Photographs* (Ashbourne: Ashbourne Editions, 1995).

Poston, Elizabeth, *The Penguin Book of Christmas Carols* (Harmondsworth: Penguin, 1965).

——, *The Second Penguin Book of Christmas Carols* (Harmondsworth: Penguin, 1970).

Pursehouse, Eric, *Waveney Valley Studies: Gleanings from Local History* (Diss: Diss Publishing, 1966).

Quarles, Francis, *The Shepheards' Oracles* (London: printed for John & Richard Marriott, 1646).

Rabey, A. Ivan, *Hurling at St. Columb: and in Cornwall* (Padstow: Lodenek Press, 1972).

Ratcliffe, E. E., and Wright, Peter A., *The Royal Maundy: a Brief Outline of its History and Ceremonial*, 7th edn (London: Royal Almonry, 1960).

Rattue, James, *The Living Stream: Holy Wells in Historical Context* (Woodbridge: Boydell, 1995).

Raven, Jon, *The Folklore of Staffordshire* (London: Batsford, 1978).

Rawe, Donald R., *Padstow's Obby Oss*, enlarged edn (Padstow: Lodenek, 1982).

Rawnsley, E. F., *The Rushbearing in Grasmere and Ambleside* (booklet, no publisher, 1953).

Ray, John, *A Complete Collection of English Proverbs* (1670; London: Allman, 1818).

Reid, Douglas A., 'Folk-Football, the Aristocracy and Cultural Change', *International Journal of the History of Sport* 5 (1988) 224–38.

Rhodes, Ebenezer, *Peak Scenery* (London: privately printed, 1818).

Richardson, John, *The Annals of London* (London: Cassell, 2000).

Richardson, Michael, *The Durham Miners' Gala 1935–1960* (Derby: Breedon, 2001).

Roberts, Michael, 'Waiting Upon Chance: English Hiring Fairs and their Meanings from the 14th to the 20th Century', *Journal of Historical Sociology* 1:2 (1988) 119–60.

Robertson, John, *Uppies & Doonies: The Story of the Kirkwall Ba' Game* (Aberdeen: Aberdeen University Press, 1967).

Robinson, Brian, *Silver Pennies and Linen Towels: The Story of the Royal Maundy* (London: Spink, 1992).

Robson, Peter, 'Dorset Garland Days on the Chesil Coast', in Buckland & Wood (1993) 155–66.

——, 'Shrove-tide House-Visiting Customs in Dorset', *Lore & Language* 14:1 (1996) 31–47.

Rosenfeld, Sybil, *The Theatre of the London Fairs in the Eighteenth Century* (Cambridge: Cambridge University Press, 1960).

Roud, Steve, *The Penguin Guide to the Superstitions of Britain and Ireland* (London: Penguin, 2003).

Round About Our Coal Fire; or, Christmas Entertainments (London: J. Roberts, 1740; reprinted Whitstable: Pryor Publications, 1991).

Rowe, Doc, *We'll Call Once More Unto Your House* (Padstow: Padstow Echo, 1982).

Rudder, Samuel, *A New History of Gloucestershire* (Cirencester: privately printed, 1779).

Rudkin, E. M., *Lincolnshire Folklore* (Gainsborough, 1936).

Schellinks, William, *The Journal of William Schellinks' Travels in England 1661–1663* (London: Royal Historical Society, 1993).

Scot, Reginald, *The Discoverie of Witchcraft* (1584; reprinted New York: Dover, 1972).

Selden, John, *Table-Talk* (London: E. Smith, 1689); reprinted in James Thornton, *Table Talk from Ben Jonson to Leigh Hunt* (London: Dent, 1934).

Sharp, Cecil J., *The Sword Dances of Northern England*, 3 vols. (London: Novello, 1911–13).

Sharp, Cecil, and MacIlwaine, Herbert C., *The Morris Book*, Part III, 2nd edn (London: Novello, 1924).

Sharpe, James, *Remember Remember the Fifth of November: Guy Fawkes and the Gunpowder Plot* (London: Profile, 2005).

Shaw, Anthony, *The Mayor of Garratt* (Wandsworth: Wandsworth Borough Council, 1980).

Sheffield, Derek, *This Forgotten Place: a Kentish Chronicle* (Gillingham: Meresborough, 1993).

Shortt, Hugh, *The Giant and Hob-nob* (booklet, Salisbury and South Wiltshire Museum, 1988).

Shuel, Brian, *The National Trust Guide to the Traditional Customs of Britain* (Exeter: Webb & Bower, 1985).

Simpson, Jacqueline, *The Folklore of Sussex* (London: Batsford, 1973).

Smith, Julia, *Fairs, Feasts and Frolics: Customs and Traditions in Yorkshire* (Otley: Smith Settle, 1989).

Spriggs, Gareth, 'Maiden's Garlands', *Folk Life* 21 (1982/83) 12–32.

Steer, Francis W., *The History of the Dunmow Flitch Ceremony* (Chelmsford: Essex Record Office, 1951).

Stephen, George A., *The Waits of the City of Norwich* (Norwich: Goose, 1933).

Sternberg, Thomas, *The Dialect and Folk-Lore of Northamptonshire* (London: Russell Smith, 1851; reprinted East Ardsley: S. R. Publishers, 1971).

Stone, Benjamin, *Sir Benjamin Stone's Pictures* (London: Cassell, 1906).

Stow, John, *A Survey of London* (1598; 2nd edn, 1603; reprinted Stroud: Alan Sutton, 1994).

Strickland, Agnes, *Old Friends and New Acquaintances*, 2nd series (London, Simpkin Marshall, 1861).

Strutt, Joseph, *Glig-Gamena Angel-Deod, or The Sports and Pastimes of the People of England* (1801); later edition published as *The Sports and Pastimes of the People of England*, ed. William Hone (London: Chatto & Windus, 1876).

Stubbes, Philip, *The Anatomie of Abuses* (1583; 4th edn 1595), ed. Margaret Jane Kidnie (Tempe: Arizona Center for Medieval and Renaissance Studies, 2002).

Summers, W. H., *The Story of Hungerford in Berkshire* (London: Trustees of the Borough of Hungerford, 1926).

Surrey Federation of Women's Institutes, *Surrey Within Living Memory* (Newbury: Countryside Books, 1992).

Sutton, Maureen, *A Lincolnshire Calendar* (Stamford: Paul Watkins, 1997).

Swainson, C., *A Handbook of Weather Folk-Lore* (Edinburgh: Blackwood, 1873).

Swift, Jonathan, *Journal to Stella* (1710–13; Gloucester: Alan Sutton, 1984).

Sykes, Homer, *Once a Year: Some Traditional British Customs* (London: Gordon Fraser, 1977).

Symonds, Richard, *Diary of the Marches of the Royal Army during the Great Civil War* (1644; London: Camden Society, 1909).

Tebbutt, C. F., *Huntingdonshire Folklore* (St. Neots: Tomson & Lendrum, 1952).

——, *Huntingdonshire Folklore* (St Ives: Friends of Norris Museum, 1984).

Thomas, Keith, *Religion and the Decline of Magic* (London: Weidenfeld and Nicolson, 1971).

——, *Rule and Misrule in the Schools of Early Modern England* (Reading: University of Reading, 1976).

Thompson, E. P., *Customs in Common* (London: Merlin, 1991).

Thompson, Flora, *Lark Rise* (Oxford: Oxford University Press, 1939).

Thorne, James, *Handbook to the Environs of London* (London: J. Murray, 1876).

Toy, H. Spencer, *The History of Helston* (London: Oxford University Press, 1936).

Trotter, Eleanor, *Seventeenth-Century Life in the Country Parish* (Cambridge: Cambridge University Press, 1919).

Turner, E. S., *All Heaven in a Rage* (London: Michael Joseph, 1964).

Turton, Robert B., 'The Service of Horngarth', *Yorkshire Archaeological Journal* 20 (1909) 51–67.

Tusser, Thomas, *Five Hundred Points of Good Husbandry* (1580; Oxford: Oxford University Press, 1984).

Twycross, Meg (ed.), *Festive Drama* (Cambridge: Brewer, 1996).

Udal, J. S., *Dorsetshire Folk-Lore* (Hertford: Stephen Austin & Sons, 1922).

Uttley, Alison, *The Country Child* (London: Faber, 1931).

Vickery, Roy, *A Dictionary of Plant Lore* (Oxford: Oxford University Press, 1995).

Victoria County History: Cambridge III (London: Oxford University Press, 1959).

Victoria County History: Essex II, ed. William Page and J. Horace Round (London: Constable, 1907).

Victoria County History: Hampshire IV, ed. William Page (London: Constable, 1911).

Victoria County History: Hampshire V, ed. William Page (London: Constable, 1912).

Victoria County History: Hertfordshire IV, ed. William Page (London: Constable, 1914).

Victoria County History: Oxford IV, ed. Alan Crossley (London: Oxford University Press, 1979).

Waddilove, William, and Eadon, David, *Wroth Silver Today: An Ancient Warwickshire Custom* (Rugby: privately printed, 1994).

Wales, Tony, *A Sussex Garland* (Newbury: Countryside Books, 1979).

——, *Sussex Customs, Curiosities and Country Lore* (Southampton: Ensign, 1990).

Walford, Cornelius, *Fairs Past and Present: A Chapter in the History of Commerce* (London: Elliot Stock, 1883).

Wallis, Faith, *Bede: The Reckoning of Time* [English translation of Bede's *De Temporum Ratione*] (Liverpool: Liverpool University Press, 1999).

Ward, Ned, *The London Spy* (1703; London: Cassell, 1927).

Warner, Susan, *Carl Krinken; or the Christmas Stocking* (London: Routledge, 1854).

Warren, C. Henry, *A Boy in Kent* (London: G. Bles, 1938).

Weightman, Gavin, and Humphries, Steve, *Christmas Past* (London: Sidgwick & Jackson, 1987).

West, Patrick, *Conspicuous Compassion: Why Sometimes it Really is Cruel to be Kind* (London: Civitas, 2004).

West Yorkshire Federation of Women's Institutes, *West Yorkshire: Within Living Memory* (Newbury: Countryside Books, 1996).

Westwood, Jennifer, *Albion: A Guide to Legendary Britain* (London: Grafton, 1985).

Westwood, Jennifer, and Simpson, Jacqueline, *The Lore of the Land: A Guide to England's Legends* (London: Penguin, 2005).

Whistler, Laurence, *The English Festivals* (London: Heinemann, 1947).

Whitcombe, H. P., *Bygone Days* (London: R. Bentley, 1874).

White, Florence, *Good Things in England* (London: Jonathan Cape, 1932; reprinted London: Persephone, 1999).

Whitlock, Ralph, *The Folklore of Wiltshire* (London: Batsford, 1976).

Wilbraham, Roger, *An Attempt at a Glossary of Some Words used in Cheshire* (1817; London: T. Rodd, 1826).

Wilkes, Peter, *The Great Nottingham Goose Fair* (Burton-on-Trent: Trent Valley Publications, 1989).

Williams, Alfred, *A Wiltshire Village* (London: Duckworth, 1912).

Williams, Douglas, *Festivals of Cornwall* (Bodmin: Bossiney, 1987).

Williams, Philip Martin, and Williams, David L., *The Knight Rides Out* (Ashton-under-Lyne: History on Your Doorstep, 1998).

Wilshere, Jonathan E. O., *Leicester Towne Waytes* (Leicester: Leicester Research Services, 1970).

Wilson, A. E., *The Story of Pantomime* (1949; Wakefield: EP, 1974).

Wilson, C. Anne (ed.), *Traditional Food East and West of the Pennines* (Edinburgh: Edinburgh University Press, 1991).

Winchester, Angus, *Discovering Parish Boundaries* (Princes Risborough: Shire, 1990).

Woodforde, James, *The Diary of a Country Parson*, ed. John Beresford, 4 vols. (London: Oxford Univesity Press, 1924–9).

Woodman, William, 'Reminiscences and Desultory Notes of Morpeth Social Customs Now Obsolete', *History of the Berwickshire Naturalists' Club* 14 (1892–3) 125–38.

Wright, A. R., *English Folklore* (London: Benn, 1928).

Wright, A. R., and Lones, T. E., *British Calendar Customs: England*, 3 vols. (London: The Folklore Society, 1936–40).

Young, George, *A History of Whitby and Streoneshalh Abbey*, 2 vols. (Whitby: Clark & Medd, 1817).

Index

EQUATION SHEET

Ideal-gas law: $p = \rho RT$, $R_{\text{air}} = 287$ J/kg $\cdot$ K	Surface tension: $\Delta p = Y(R_1^{-1} + R_2^{-1})$
Hydrostatics, constant density: $$p_2 - p_1 = -\gamma(z_2 - z_1), \ \gamma = \rho g$$	Hydrostatic panel force: $F = \gamma h_{\text{CG}}A$, $\cdot \ y_{\text{CP}} = -I_{xx}\sin\theta/(h_{\text{CG}}A), \ x_{\text{CP}} = -I_{xy}\sin\theta/(h_{\text{CG}}A)$
Buoyant force: $$F_B = \gamma_{\text{fluid}}(\text{displaced volume})$$	CV mass: $d/dt(\int_{\text{cv}}\rho d\upsilon) + \Sigma(\rho AV)_{\text{out}}$ $$- \Sigma(\rho AV)_{\text{in}} = 0$$
CV momentum: $d/dt(\int_{\text{CV}}\rho\mathbf{V}d\upsilon)$ $$+ \Sigma[(\rho AV)\mathbf{V}]_{\text{out}} - \Sigma[(\rho AV)\mathbf{V}]_{\text{in}} = \Sigma\mathbf{F}$$	CV angular momentum: $d/dt(\int_{\text{cv}}\rho(\mathbf{r_0}\times\mathbf{V})d\upsilon)$ $$+ \Sigma\rho AV(\mathbf{r_0}\times\mathbf{V})_{\text{out}} - \Sigma\rho AV(\mathbf{r_0}\times\mathbf{V})_{\text{in}} = \Sigma\mathbf{M_0}$$
Steady flow energy: $(p/\gamma + \alpha V^2/2g + z)_{\text{in}} =$ $(p/\gamma + \alpha V^2/2g + z)_{\text{out}} + h_{\text{friction}} - h_{\text{pump}} + h_{\text{turbine}}$	Acceleration: $d\mathbf{V}/dt = \partial\mathbf{V}/\partial t$ $$+ u(\partial\mathbf{V}/\partial x) + v(\partial\mathbf{V}/\partial y) + w(\partial\mathbf{V}/\partial z)$$
Incompressible continuity: $\nabla \cdot \mathbf{V} = 0$	Navier-Stokes: $\rho(d\mathbf{V}/dt) = \rho\mathbf{g} - \nabla p + \mu\nabla^2\mathbf{V}$
Incompressible stream function $\psi(x,y)$: $$u = \partial\psi/\partial y; \quad v = -\partial\psi/\partial x$$	Velocity potential $\phi(x,y,z)$: $$u = \partial\phi/\partial x; v = \partial\phi/\partial y; w = \partial\phi/\partial z$$
Bernoulli unsteady irrotational flow: $$\partial\phi/\partial t + \int dp/\rho + V^2/2 + gz = \text{Const}$$	Turbulent friction factor: $1/\sqrt{f} =$ $$-2.0\log_{10}[\varepsilon/(3.7d) + 2.51/(\text{Re}_d\sqrt{f})]$$
Pipe head loss: $h_f = f(L/d)V^2/(2g)$ where f = Moody chart friction factor	Orifice, nozzle, venturi flow: $$Q = C_d A_{\text{throat}}[2\Delta p/\{\rho(1-\beta^4)\}]^{1/2}, \ \beta = d/D$$
Laminar flat plate flow: $\delta/x = 5.0/\text{Re}_x^{1/2}$, $$c_f = 0.664/\text{Re}_x^{1/2}, C_D = 1.328/\text{Re}_L^{1/2}$$	Turbulent flat plate flow: $\delta/x = 0.16/\text{Re}_x^{1/7}$, $$c_f = 0.027/\text{Re}_x^{1/7}, C_D = 0.031/\text{Re}_L^{1/7}$$
$C_D = \text{Drag}/(\frac{1}{2}\rho V^2 A); \ C_L = \text{Lift}/(\frac{1}{2}\rho V^2 A)$	2-D potential flow: $\nabla^2\phi = \nabla^2\psi = 0$
Isentropic flow: $T_0/T = 1 + \{(k-1)/2\}\text{Ma}^2$, $$\rho_0/\rho = (T_0/T)^{1/(k-1)}, \quad p_0/p = (T_0/T)^{k(k-1)}$$	One-dimensional isentropic area change: $$A/A^* = (1/\text{Ma})[1 + \{(k-1)/2\}\text{Ma}^2]^{(1/2)(k+1)/(k-1)}$$
Prandtl-Meyer expansion: $K = (k+1)/(k-1)$, $\omega = K^{1/2}\tan^{-1}[(\text{Ma}^2 - 1)/K]^{1/2} - \tan^{-1}(\text{Ma}^2 - 1)^{1/2}$	Uniform flow, Manning's n, SI units: $$V_0(\text{m/s}) = (1.0/n)[R_h(m)]^{2/3}S_0^{1/2}$$
Gradually varied channel flow: $$dy/dx = (S_0 - S)/(1 - \text{Fr}^2), \ \text{Fr} = V/V_{\text{crit}}$$	Euler turbine formula: $$\text{Power} = \rho Q(u_2 V_{t2} - u_1 V_{t1}), u = r\omega$$

Fluid Mechanics

Fluid Mechanics

Eighth Edition

Frank M. White
University of Rhode Island

Mc
Graw
Hill
Education

FLUID MECHANICS, EIGHTH EDITION

Published by McGraw-Hill Education, 2 Penn Plaza, New York, NY 10121. Copyright © 2016 by McGraw-Hill Education. All rights reserved. Printed in the United States of America. Previous editions © 2011, 2008, and 2003. No part of this publication may be reproduced or distributed in any form or by any means, or stored in a database or retrieval system, without the prior written consent of McGraw-Hill Education, including, but not limited to, in any network or other electronic storage or transmission, or broadcast for distance learning.

Some ancillaries, including electronic and print components, may not be available to customers outside the United States.

This book is printed on acid-free paper.

1 2 3 4 5 6 7 8 9 0 DOC/DOC 1 0 9 8 7 6 5

ISBN 978-0-07-339827-3
MHID 0-07-339827-6

Senior Vice President, Products & Markets: *Kurt L. Strand*
Vice President, General Manager, Products & Markets: *Marty Lange*
Vice President, Content Design & Delivery: *Kimberly Meriwether David*
Managing Director: *Thomas Timp*
Brand Manager: *Thomas Scaife*
Director, Product Development: *Rose Koos*
Product Developer: *Lorraine Buczek*
Marketing Manager: *Nick McFadden*
Director, Content Design & Delivery: *Linda Avenarius*
Program Manager: *Lora Neyens*
Content Project Manager: *Lisa Bruflodt*
Content Project Manager: *Tammy Juran*
Buyer: *Susan K. Culbertson*
Content Licensing Specialists: *Deanna Dausener*
Cover Image: Doug Sherman/Geofile
Compositor: *Aptara®, Inc.*
Printer: *R. R. Donnelley*

All credits appearing on page or at the end of the book are considered to be an extension of the copyright page.

Library of Congress Cataloging-in-Publication Data
White, Frank M.
   Fluid mechanics/Frank M. White, University of Rhode Island.—Eighth edition.
      pages cm
   Includes index.
   ISBN 978-0-07-339827-3 (alk. paper)—ISBN 0-07-339827-6 (alk. paper)
   1. Fluid mechanics. I. Title.
   TA357.W48 2016
   620.1'06—dc23
                                                          2014034259

100738049l
The Internet addresses listed in the text were accurate at the time of publication. The inclusion of a website does not indicate an endorsement by the authors or McGraw-Hill Education, and McGraw-Hill Education does not guarantee the accuracy of the information presented at these sites.

www.mhhe.com

About the Author

Frank M. White is Professor Emeritus of Mechanical and Ocean Engineering at the University of Rhode Island. He studied at Georgia Tech and M.I.T. In 1966 he helped found, at URI, the first department of ocean engineering in the country. Known primarily as a teacher and writer, he has received eight teaching awards and has written four textbooks on fluid mechanics and heat transfer.

From 1979 to 1990, he was editor-in-chief of the *ASME Journal of Fluids Engineering* and then served from 1991 to 1997 as chairman of the ASME Board of Editors and of the Publications Committee. He is a Fellow of ASME and in 1991 received the ASME Fluids Engineering Award. He lives with his wife, Jeanne, in Narragansett, Rhode Island.

To Jeanne

Contents

Preface

General Approach

The eighth edition of *Fluid Mechanics* sees some additions and deletions but no philosophical change. The basic outline of eleven chapters, plus appendices, remains the same. The triad of integral, differential, and experimental approaches is retained. Many problem exercises, and some fully worked examples, have been changed. The informal, student-oriented style is retained. A number of new photographs and figures have been added. Many new references have been added, for a total of 445. The writer is a firm believer in "further reading," especially in the postgraduate years.

Learning Tools

The total number of problem exercises continues to increase, from 1089 in the first edition, to 1683 in this eighth edition. There are approximately 20 new problems in each chapter. Most of these are basic end-of-chapter problems, classified according to topic. There are also Word Problems, multiple-choice Fundamentals of Engineering Problems, Comprehensive Problems, and Design Projects. The appendix lists approximately 700 Answers to Selected Problems.

The example problems are structured in the text to follow the sequence of recommended steps outlined in Section 1.7.

Most of the problems in this text can be solved with a hand calculator. Some can even be simply explained in words. A few problems, especially in Chapters 6, 9, and 10, involve solving complicated algebraic expressions, laborious for a hand calculator. Check to see if your institution has a license for equation-solving software. Here the writer solves complicated example problems by using the iterative power of Microsoft Office Excel, as illustrated, for example, in Example 6.5. For further use in your work, Excel also contains several hundred special mathematical functions for engineering and statistics. Another benefit: Excel is free.

Content Changes

There are some revisions in each chapter.

Chapter 1 has been substantially revised. The pre-reviewers felt, correctly, that it was too long, too detailed, and at too high a level for an introduction. Former Section 1.2, History of Fluid Mechanics, has been shortened and moved to the end of the chapter. Former Section 1.3, Problem-Solving Techniques, has been moved to appear just before Example 1.7, where these techniques are first used. Eulerian and Lagrangian descriptions have been moved to Chapter 4. A temperature-entropy chart for steam has been added, to illustrate when steam can and cannot be approximated as an ideal gas. Former Section 1.11, Flow Patterns, has been cut sharply and mostly moved to Chapter 4. Former Section 1.13, Uncertainty in Experimental Data, has been moved to a new Appendix E. No one teaches "uncertainty" in introductory fluid mechanics, but the writer feels it is extremely important in all engineering fields involving experimental or numerical data.

Chapter 2 adds a brief discussion of the fact that pressure is a thermodynamic property, not a *force*, has no direction, and is not a vector. The arrow, on a surface force caused by pressure, causes confusion for beginning students. The subsection of Section 2.8 entitled Stability Related to Waterline Area has been shortened to omit the complicated derivations. The final metacenter formula is retained; the writer does not think it is sufficient just to show a sketch of a floating body falling over. This book should have reference value.

Chapter 3 was substantially revised in the last edition, especially by moving Bernoulli's equation to follow the linear momentum section. This time the only changes are improvements in the example problems.

Chapter 4 now discusses the Eulerian and Lagrangian systems, moved from Chapter 1. The no-slip and no-temperature-jump boundary conditions are added, with problem assignments.

Chapter 5 explains a bit more about drag force before assigning dimensional analysis problems. It retains Ipsen's method as an interesting alternative which, of course, may be skipped by pi theorem adherents.

Chapter 6 downplays the Moody chart a bit, suggesting that students use either iteration or Excel. For rough walls, the chart is awkward to read, although it gives an approximation for use in iteration. The author's fancy rearrangement of pi groups to solve type 2, flow rate, and type 3, pipe diameter problems is removed from the main text and assigned as problems. For noncircular ducts, the hydraulic *radius* is omitted and moved to Chapter 10. There is a new Example 6.11, which solves for pipe diameter and determines if Schedule 40 pipe is strong enough. A general discussion of pipe strength is added. There is a new subsection on *laminar-flow* minor losses, appropriate for micro- and nano-tube flows.

Chapter 7 has more treatment of vehicle drag and rolling resistance, and a rolling resistance coefficient is defined. There is additional discussion of the Kline-Fogelman airfoil, extremely popular now for model aircraft.

Chapter 8 has backed off from extensive discussion of CFD methods, as proposed by the pre-reviewers. Only a few CFD examples are now given. The inviscid duct-expansion example and the implicit boundary layer method are now omitted, but the explicit method is retained. For airfoil theory, the writer considers thin-airfoil vortex-sheet theory to be obsolete and has deleted it.

Chapter 9 now has a better discussion of the normal shock wave. New supersonic wave photographs are added. The "new trend in aeronautics" is the Air Force X-35 Joint Strike Fighter.

Chapter 10 improves the definition of normal depth of a channel. There is a new subsection on the water-channel compressible flow analogy, and problems are assigned to find the oblique wave angle for supercritical water flow past a wedge.

Chapter 11 greatly expands the discussion of wind turbines, with examples and problems taken from the author's own experience.

Appendices B and D are unchanged. Appendix A adds a list of liquid kinematic viscosities to Table A.4. A few more conversion factors are added to Appendix C. There is a new Appendix E, Estimating Uncertainty in Experimental Data, which was moved from its inappropriate position in Chapter 1. The writer believes that "uncertainty" is vital to reporting measurements and always insisted upon it when he was an engineering journal editor.

Adaptive Online Learning Tools

McGraw-Hill LearnSmart® is available as a standalone product or an integrated feature of McGraw-Hill Connect Engineering. It is an adaptive learning system designed to help students learn faster, study more efficiently, and retain more knowledge for greater success. LearnSmart assesses a student's knowledge of course content through a series of adaptive questions. It pinpoints concepts the student does not understand and maps out a personalized study plan for success. This innovative study tool also has features that allow instructors to see exactly what students have accomplished and a built-in assessment tool for graded assignments. Visit the following site for a demonstration: www.LearnSmartAdvantage.com

SMARTBOOK®

Powered by the intelligent and adaptive LearnSmart engine, **SmartBook**™ is the first and only continuously adaptive reading experience available today. Distinguishing what students know from what they don't, and honing in on concepts they are most likely to forget, SmartBook personalizes the reading experience for each student. Reading is no longer a passive and linear experience but an engaging and dynamic one, where students are more likely to master and retain important concepts, coming to class better prepared. SmartBook includes powerful reports that identify specific topics and learning objectives students need to study. www.LearnSmartAdvantage.com

connect®
ENGINEERING

McGraw-Hill's Connect Engineering offers a number of powerful tools and features to make managing assignments easier, so you can spend more time teaching. Students engage with their coursework anytime from anywhere in a personalized way, making the learning process more accessible and efficient. Connect Engineering optimizes your time and energy, enabling you to focus on course content and learning outcomes, teaching, and student learning.

Online Supplements

A number of supplements are available to instructors at McGraw-Hill's Connect Engineering®. Instructors may obtain the text images in PowerPoint format and the full Solutions Manual in PDF format. The solutions manual provides complete and detailed solutions, including problem statements and artwork, to the end-of-chapter problems. Instructors can also obtain access to the Complete Online Solutions Manual Organization System (C.O.S.M.O.S.) for *Fluid Mechanics,* 8th edition. Instructors can use C.O.S.M.O.S. to create exams and assignments, to create custom content, and to edit supplied problems and solutions.

Acknowledgments

As usual, so many people have helped me that I may fail to list them all. Material help, in the form of photos, articles, and problems, came from Scott Larwood of the University of the Pacific; Sukanta Dash of the Indian Institute of Technology at Kharagpur; Mark Coffey of the Colorado School of Mines; Mac Stevens of Oregon State University; Stephen Carrington of Malvern Instruments; Carla Cioffi of NASA; Lisa Lee and Robert Pacquette of the Rhode Island Department of Environmental Management; Vanessa Blakeley and Samuel Schweighart of Terrafugia Inc.; Beric Skews of the University of the Witwatersrand, South Africa; Kelly Irene Knorr and John Merrill of the School of Oceanography at the University of Rhode Island; Adam Rein of Altaeros Energies Inc.; Dasari Abhinav of Anna University, India; Kris Allen of Transcanada Corporation; Bruce Findlayson of the University of Washington; Wendy Koch of USA Today; Liz Boardman of the South County Independent; Beth Darchi and Colin McAteer of the American Society of Mechanical Engineers; Catherine Hines of the William Beebe Web Site; Laura Garrison of York College of Pennsylvania.

The following pre-reviewers gave many excellent suggestions for improving the manuscript: Steve Baker, Naval Postgraduate School; Suresh Aggarwal, University of Illinois at Chicago; Edgar Caraballo, Miami University; Chang-Hwan Choi, Stevens Institute of Technology; Drazen Fabris, Santa Clara University; James Liburdy, Oregon State University; Daniel Maynes, Brigham Young University; Santosh Sahu, Indian Institute of Technology Indore; Brian Savilonis, Worcester Polytechnic Institute; Eric Savory, University of Western Ontario; Rick Sellens, Queen's University; Gordon Stubley, University of Waterloo.

Many others have supported me, throughout my revision efforts, with comments and suggestions: Gordon Holloway of the University of New Brunswick; David Taggart, Donna Meyer, Arun Shukla, and Richard Lessmann of the University of Rhode Island; Debendra K. Das of the University of Alaska–Fairbanks; Elizabeth Kenyon of Mathworks; Deborah V. Pence of Oregon State University; Sheldon Green of the University of British Columbia; Elena Bingham of the DuPont Corporation; Jane Bates of Broad Rock School; Kim Mather of West Kingston School; Nancy Dreier of Curtiss Corner School; Richard Kline, co-inventor of the Kline-Fogelman airfoil.

The McGraw-Hill staff was, as usual, very helpful. Thanks are due to Bill Stenquist, Katherine Neubauer, Lorraine Buczek, Samantha Donisi-Hamm, Raghu Srinivasan, Tammy Juran, Thomas Scaife, and Lisa Bruflodt.

Finally, I am thankful for the continuing support of my family, especially Jeanne, who remains in my heart, and my sister Sally White GNSH, my dog Jack, and my cats Cole and Kerry.

Fluid Mechanics

Falls on the Nesowadnehunk Stream in Baxter State Park, Maine, which is the northern terminus of the Appalachian Trail. Such flows, open to the atmosphere, are driven simply by gravity and do not depend much upon fluid properties such as density and viscosity. They are discussed later in Chap. 10. To the writer, one of the joys of fluid mechanics is that visualization of a fluid-flow process is simple and beautiful [*Photo Credit: Design Pics/Natural Selection Robert Cable*].

Chapter 1
Introduction

1.1 Preliminary Remarks

Fluid mechanics is the study of fluids either in motion (fluid *dynamics*) or at rest (fluid *statics*). Both gases and liquids are classified as fluids, and the number of fluid engineering applications is enormous: breathing, blood flow, swimming, pumps, fans, turbines, airplanes, ships, rivers, windmills, pipes, missiles, icebergs, engines, filters, jets, and sprinklers, to name a few. When you think about it, almost everything on this planet either is a fluid or moves within or near a fluid.

The essence of the subject of fluid flow is a judicious compromise between theory and experiment. Since fluid flow is a branch of mechanics, it satisfies a set of well-documented basic laws, and thus a great deal of theoretical treatment is available. However, the theory is often frustrating because it applies mainly to idealized situations, which may be invalid in practical problems. The two chief obstacles to a workable theory are geometry and viscosity. The basic equations of fluid motion (Chap. 4) are too difficult to enable the analyst to attack arbitrary geometric configurations. Thus most textbooks concentrate on flat plates, circular pipes, and other easy geometries. It is possible to apply numerical computer techniques to complex geometries, and specialized textbooks are now available to explain the new *computational fluid dynamics* (CFD) approximations and methods [1–4].[1] This book will present many theoretical results while keeping their limitations in mind.

The second obstacle to a workable theory is the action of viscosity, which can be neglected only in certain idealized flows (Chap. 8). First, viscosity increases the difficulty of the basic equations, although the boundary-layer approximation found by Ludwig Prandtl in 1904 (Chap. 7) has greatly simplified viscous-flow analyses. Second, viscosity has a destabilizing effect on all fluids, giving rise, at frustratingly small velocities, to a disorderly, random phenomenon called *turbulence*. The theory of turbulent flow is crude and heavily backed up by experiment (Chap. 6), yet it can be quite serviceable as an engineering estimate. This textbook only introduces the standard experimental correlations for turbulent time-mean flow. Meanwhile, there are advanced texts on both time-mean *turbulence and turbulence modeling* [5, 6] and on the newer, computer-intensive *direct numerical simulation* (DNS) of fluctuating turbulence [7, 8].

---

[1]Numbered references appear at the end of each chapter.

Thus there is theory available for fluid flow problems, but in all cases it should be backed up by experiment. Often the experimental data provide the main source of information about specific flows, such as the drag and lift of immersed bodies (Chap. 7). Fortunately, fluid mechanics is a highly visual subject, with good instrumentation [9–11], and the use of dimensional analysis and modeling concepts (Chap. 5) is widespread. Thus experimentation provides a natural and easy complement to the theory. You should keep in mind that theory and experiment should go hand in hand in all studies of fluid mechanics.

1.2 The Concept of a Fluid

From the point of view of fluid mechanics, all matter consists of only two states, fluid and solid. The difference between the two is perfectly obvious to the layperson, and it is an interesting exercise to ask a layperson to put this difference into words. The technical distinction lies with the reaction of the two to an applied shear or tangential stress. *A solid can resist a shear stress by a static deflection; a fluid cannot.* Any shear stress applied to a fluid, no matter how small, will result in motion of that fluid. The fluid moves and deforms continuously as long as the shear stress is applied. As a corollary, we can say that a fluid at rest must be in a state of zero shear stress, a state often called the hydrostatic stress condition in structural analysis. In this condition, Mohr's circle for stress reduces to a point, and there is no shear stress on any plane cut through the element under stress.

Given this definition of a fluid, every layperson also knows that there are two classes of fluids, *liquids* and *gases*. Again the distinction is a technical one concerning the effect of cohesive forces. A liquid, being composed of relatively close-packed molecules with strong cohesive forces, tends to retain its volume and will form a free surface in a gravitational field if unconfined from above. Free-surface flows are dominated by gravitational effects and are studied in Chaps. 5 and 10. Since gas molecules are widely spaced with negligible cohesive forces, a gas is free to expand until it encounters confining walls. A gas has no definite volume, and when left to itself without confinement, a gas forms an atmosphere that is essentially hydrostatic. The hydrostatic behavior of liquids and gases is taken up in Chap. 2. Gases cannot form a free surface, and thus gas flows are rarely concerned with gravitational effects other than buoyancy.

Figure 1.1 illustrates a solid block resting on a rigid plane and stressed by its own weight. The solid sags into a static deflection, shown as a highly exaggerated dashed line, resisting shear without flow. A free-body diagram of element A on the side of the block shows that there is shear in the block along a plane cut at an angle θ through A. Since the block sides are unsupported, element A has zero stress on the left and right sides and compression stress $\sigma = -p$ on the top and bottom. Mohr's circle does not reduce to a point, and there is nonzero shear stress in the block.

By contrast, the liquid and gas at rest in Fig. 1.1 require the supporting walls in order to eliminate shear stress. The walls exert a compression stress of $-p$ and reduce Mohr's circle to a point with zero shear everywhere—that is, the hydrostatic condition. The liquid retains its volume and forms a free surface in the container. If the walls are removed, shear develops in the liquid and a big splash results. If the container is tilted, shear again develops, waves form, and the free surface seeks a horizontal configuration, pouring out over the lip if necessary. Meanwhile, the gas is unrestrained

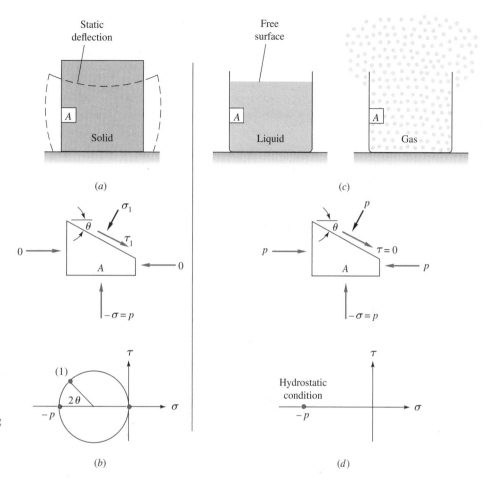

Fig. 1.1 A solid at rest can resist shear. (*a*) Static deflection of the solid; (*b*) equilibrium and Mohr's circle for solid element *A*. A fluid cannot resist shear. (*c*) Containing walls are needed; (*d*) equilibrium and Mohr's circle for fluid element *A*.

and expands out of the container, filling all available space. Element *A* in the gas is also hydrostatic and exerts a compression stress $-p$ on the walls.

In the previous discussion, clear decisions could be made about solids, liquids, and gases. Most engineering fluid mechanics problems deal with these clear cases—that is, the common liquids, such as water, oil, mercury, gasoline, and alcohol, and the common gases, such as air, helium, hydrogen, and steam, in their common temperature and pressure ranges. There are many borderline cases, however, of which you should be aware. Some apparently "solid" substances such as asphalt and lead resist shear stress for short periods but actually deform slowly and exhibit definite fluid behavior over long periods. Other substances, notably colloid and slurry mixtures, resist small shear stresses but "yield" at large stress and begin to flow as fluids do. Specialized textbooks are devoted to this study of more general deformation and flow, a field called *rheology* [16]. Also, liquids and gases can coexist in two-phase mixtures, such as steam–water mixtures or water with entrapped air bubbles. Specialized textbooks present the analysis of such *multiphase flows* [17]. Finally, in some situations the distinction between a liquid and a gas blurs. This is the case at temperatures and pressures above the so-called *critical point* of a substance, where only a single phase exists, primarily resembling a gas. As pressure increases far above the critical point, the gaslike substance becomes so dense that there is some resemblance to a liquid, and the usual thermodynamic approximations like the perfect-gas law become inaccurate. The critical temperature and pressure of water are $T_c = 647$ K and $p_c = 219$ atm (atmosphere)[2] so that typical problems involving water and steam are below the critical point. Air, being a mixture of gases, has no distinct critical point, but its principal component, nitrogen, has $T_c = 126$ K and $p_c = 34$ atm. Thus typical problems involving air are in the range of high temperature and low pressure where air is distinctly and definitely a gas. This text will be concerned solely with clearly identifiable liquids and gases, and the borderline cases just discussed will be beyond our scope.

1.3 The Fluid as a Continuum

We have already used technical terms such as *fluid pressure* and *density* without a rigorous discussion of their definition. As far as we know, fluids are aggregations of molecules, widely spaced for a gas, closely spaced for a liquid. The distance between molecules is very large compared with the molecular diameter. The molecules are not fixed in a lattice but move about freely relative to each other. Thus fluid density, or mass per unit volume, has no precise meaning because the number of molecules occupying a given volume continually changes. This effect becomes unimportant if the unit volume is large compared with, say, the cube of the molecular spacing, when the number of molecules within the volume will remain nearly constant in spite of the enormous interchange of particles across the boundaries. If, however, the chosen unit volume is too large, there could be a noticeable variation in the bulk aggregation of the particles. This situation is illustrated in Fig. 1.2, where the "density" as calculated from molecular mass δm within a given volume $\delta\mathcal{V}$ is plotted versus the size of the unit volume. There is a limiting volume $\delta\mathcal{V}^*$ below which molecular variations may be important and above which aggregate variations may be important. The *density* ρ of a fluid is best defined as

$$\rho = \lim_{\delta\mathcal{V} \to \delta\mathcal{V}^*} \frac{\delta m}{\delta\mathcal{V}} \tag{1.1}$$

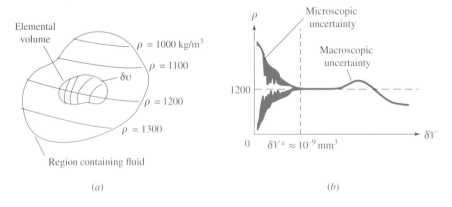

Fig. 1.2 The limit definition of continuum fluid density: (*a*) an elemental volume in a fluid region of variable continuum density; (*b*) calculated density versus size of the elemental volume.

Elemental volume

$\rho = 1000$ kg/m^3

$\rho = 1100$

$\delta\upsilon$

$\rho = 1200$

$\rho = 1300$

Region containing fluid

(*a*)

ρ

Microscopic uncertainty

Macroscopic uncertainty

1200

0    $\delta\mathcal{V}^* \approx 10^{-9}$ mm^3

$\delta\mathcal{V}$

(*b*)

[2]One atmosphere equals 2116 lbf/ft^2 = 101,300 Pa.

The limiting volume $\delta\mathcal{V}*$ is about 10^{-9} mm^3 for all liquids and for gases at atmospheric pressure. For example, 10^{-9} mm^3 of air at standard conditions contains approximately 3×10^7 molecules, which is sufficient to define a nearly constant density according to Eq. (1.1). Most engineering problems are concerned with physical dimensions much larger than this limiting volume, so that density is essentially a point function and fluid properties can be thought of as varying continually in space, as sketched in Fig. 1.2a. Such a fluid is called a *continuum*, which simply means that its variation in properties is so smooth that differential calculus can be used to analyze the substance. We shall assume that continuum calculus is valid for all the analyses in this book. Again there are borderline cases for gases at such low pressures that molecular spacing and mean free path[3] are comparable to, or larger than, the physical size of the system. This requires that the continuum approximation be dropped in favor of a molecular theory of rarefied gas flow [18]. In principle, all fluid mechanics problems can be attacked from the molecular viewpoint, but no such attempt will be made here. Note that the use of continuum calculus does not preclude the possibility of discontinuous jumps in fluid properties across a free surface or fluid interface or across a shock wave in a compressible fluid (Chap. 9). Our calculus in analyzing fluid flow must be flexible enough to handle discontinuous boundary conditions.

1.4 Dimensions and Units

A *dimension* is the measure by which a physical variable is expressed quantitatively. A *unit* is a particular way of attaching a number to the quantitative dimension. Thus length is a dimension associated with such variables as distance, displacement, width, deflection, and height, while centimeters and inches are both numerical units for expressing length. Dimension is a powerful concept about which a splendid tool called *dimensional analysis* has been developed (Chap. 5), while units are the numerical quantity that the customer wants as the final answer.

In 1872 an international meeting in France proposed a treaty called the Metric Convention, which was signed in 1875 by 17 countries including the United States. It was an improvement over British systems because its use of base 10 is the foundation of our number system, learned from childhood by all. Problems still remained because even the metric countries differed in their use of kiloponds instead of dynes or newtons, kilograms instead of grams, or calories instead of joules. To standardize the metric system, a General Conference of Weights and Measures, attended in 1960 by 40 countries, proposed the *International System of Units* (SI). We are now undergoing a painful period of transition to SI, an adjustment that may take many more years to complete. The professional societies have led the way. Since July 1, 1974, SI units have been required by all papers published by the American Society of Mechanical Engineers, and there is a textbook explaining the SI [19]. The present text will use SI units together with British gravitational (BG) units.

Primary Dimensions

In fluid mechanics there are only four *primary dimensions* from which all other dimensions can be derived: mass, length, time, and temperature.[4] These dimensions and

---

[3]The mean distance traveled by molecules between collisions (see Prob. P1.5).

[4]If electromagnetic effects are important, a fifth primary dimension must be included, electric current $\{I\}$, whose SI unit is the ampere (A).

Primary dimension	SI unit	BG unit	Conversion factor
Mass $\{M\}$	Kilogram (kg)	Slug	1 slug = 14.5939 kg
Length $\{L\}$	Meter (m)	Foot (ft)	1 ft = 0.3048 m
Time $\{T\}$	Second (s)	Second (s)	1 s = 1 s
Temperature $\{\Theta\}$	Kelvin (K)	Rankine (°R)	1 K = 1.8°R

their units in both systems are given in Table 1.1. Note that the Kelvin unit uses no degree symbol. The braces around a symbol like $\{M\}$ mean "the dimension" of mass. All other variables in fluid mechanics can be expressed in terms of $\{M\}$, $\{L\}$, $\{T\}$, and $\{\Theta\}$. For example, acceleration has the dimensions $\{LT^{-2}\}$. The most crucial of these secondary dimensions is force, which is directly related to mass, length, and time by Newton's second law. Force equals the time rate of change of momentum or, for constant mass,

$$\mathbf{F} = m\mathbf{a} \tag{1.2}$$

From this we see that, dimensionally, $\{F\} = \{MLT^{-2}\}$.

The International System (SI)

The use of a constant of proportionality in Newton's law, Eq. (1.2), is avoided by defining the force unit exactly in terms of the other basic units. In the SI system, the basic units are newtons $\{F\}$, kilograms $\{M\}$, meters $\{L\}$, and seconds $\{T\}$. We define

$$1 \text{ newton of force} = 1 \text{ N} = 1 \text{ kg} \cdot 1 \text{ m/s}^2$$

The newton is a relatively small force, about the weight of an apple (0.225 lbf). In addition, the basic unit of temperature $\{\Theta\}$ in the SI system is the degree Kelvin, K. Use of these SI units (N, kg, m, s, K) will require no conversion factors in our equations.

The British Gravitational (BG) System

In the BG system also, a constant of proportionality in Eq. (1.2) is avoided by defining the force unit exactly in terms of the other basic units. In the BG system, the basic units are pound-force $\{F\}$, slugs $\{M\}$, feet $\{L\}$, and seconds $\{T\}$. We define

$$1 \text{ pound of force} = 1 \text{ lbf} = 1 \text{ slug} \cdot 1 \text{ ft/s}^2$$

One lbf $\approx$ 4.4482 N and approximates the weight of four apples. We will use the abbreviation *lbf* for pound-force and *lbm* for pound-mass. The slug is a rather hefty mass, equal to 32.174 lbm. The basic unit of temperature $\{\Theta\}$ in the BG system is the degree Rankine, °R. Recall that a temperature difference 1 K = 1.8°R. Use of these BG units (lbf, slug, ft, s, °R) will require no conversion factors in our equations.

Other Unit Systems

There are other unit systems still in use. At least one needs no proportionality constant: the CGS system (dyne, gram, cm, s, K). However, CGS units are too small for most applications (1 dyne = 10^{-5} N) and will not be used here.

Table 1.2 Secondary Dimensions in Fluid Mechanics

Secondary dimension	SI unit	BG unit	Conversion factor
Area $\{L^2\}$	m^2	ft^2	1 m^2 = 10.764 ft^2
Volume $\{L^3\}$	m^3	ft^3	1 m^3 = 35.315 ft^3
Velocity $\{LT^{-1}\}$	m/s	ft/s	1 ft/s = 0.3048 m/s
Acceleration $\{LT^{-2}\}$	m/s^2	ft/s^2	1 ft/s^2 = 0.3048 m/s^2
Pressure or stress $\{ML^{-1}T^{-2}\}$	Pa = N/m^2	lbf/ft^2	1 lbf/ft^2 = 47.88 Pa
Angular velocity $\{T^{-1}\}$	s^{-1}	s^{-1}	1 s^{-1} = 1 s^{-1}
Energy, heat, work $\{ML^2T^{-2}\}$	J = N · m	ft · lbf	1 ft · lbf = 1.3558 J
Power $\{ML^2T^{-3}\}$	W = J/s	ft · lbf/s	1 ft · lbf/s = 1.3558 W
Density $\{ML^{-3}\}$	kg/m^3	slugs/ft^3	1 slug/ft^3 = 515.4 kg/m^3
Viscosity $\{ML^{-1}T^{-1}\}$	kg/(m · s)	slugs/(ft · s)	1 slug/(ft · s) = 47.88 kg/(m · s)
Specific heat $\{L^2T^{-2}\Theta^{-1}\}$	m^2/(s^2 · K)	ft^2/(s^2 · °R)	1 m^2/(s^2 · K) = 5.980 ft^2/(s^2 · °R)

In the USA, some still use the English Engineering system (lbf, lbm, ft, s, °R), where the basic mass unit is the *pound of mass*. Newton's law (1.2) must be rewritten:

$$\mathbf{F} = \frac{m\mathbf{a}}{g_c}, \text{ where } g_c = 32.174 \frac{\text{ft} \cdot \text{lbm}}{\text{lbf} \cdot \text{s}^2} \tag{1.3}$$

The constant of proportionality, g_c, has both dimensions and a numerical value not equal to 1.0. The present text uses only the SI and BG systems and will not solve problems or examples in the English Engineering system. Because Americans still use them, a few problems in the text will be stated in truly awkward units: acres, gallons, ounces, or miles. Your assignment will be to convert these and solve in the SI or BG systems.

The Principle of Dimensional Homogeneity

In engineering and science, *all* equations must be *dimensionally homogeneous,* that is, each additive term in an equation must have the same dimensions. For example, take Bernoulli's incompressible equation, to be studied and used throughout this text:

$$p + \frac{1}{2}\rho V^2 + \rho g Z = \text{constant}$$

Each and every term in this equation *must* have dimensions of pressure $\{ML^{-1}T^{-2}\}$. We will examine the dimensional homogeneity of this equation in detail in Example 1.3.

A list of some important secondary variables in fluid mechanics, with dimensions derived as combinations of the four primary dimensions, is given in Table 1.2. A more complete list of conversion factors is given in App. C.

EXAMPLE 1.1

A body weighs 1000 lbf when exposed to a standard earth gravity g = 32.174 ft/s^2. (*a*) What is its mass in kg? (*b*) What will the weight of this body be in N if it is exposed to the moon's standard acceleration g_{moon} = 1.62 m/s^2? (*c*) How fast will the body accelerate if a net force of 400 lbf is applied to it on the moon or on the earth?

Solution

We need to find the (*a*) mass; (*b*) weight on the moon; and (*c*) acceleration of this body. This is a fairly simple example of conversion factors for differing unit systems. No property data is needed. The example is too low-level for a sketch.

Part (a)   Newton's law (1.2) holds with known weight and gravitational acceleration. Solve for m:

$$F = W = 1000 \text{ lbf} = mg = (m)(32.174 \text{ ft/s}^2), \text{ or } m = \frac{1000 \text{ lbf}}{32.174 \text{ ft/s}^2} = 31.08 \text{ slugs}$$

Convert this to kilograms:

$$m = 31.08 \text{ slugs} = (31.08 \text{ slugs})(14.5939 \text{ kg/slug}) = 454 \text{ kg} \qquad \textit{Ans. (a)}$$

Part (b)   The mass of the body remains 454 kg regardless of its location. Equation (1.2) applies with a new gravitational acceleration and hence a new weight:

$$F = W_{\text{moon}} = mg_{\text{moon}} = (454 \text{ kg})(1.62 \text{ m/s}^2) = 735 \text{ N} = 165 \text{ lbf} \qquad \textit{Ans. (b)}$$

Part (c)   This part does not involve weight or gravity or location. It is simply an application of Newton's law with a known mass and known force:

$$F = 400 \text{ lbf} = ma = (31.08 \text{ slugs}) \, a$$

Solve for

$$a = \frac{400 \text{ lbf}}{31.08 \text{ slugs}} = 12.87 \, \frac{\text{ft}}{\text{s}^2} \left(0.3048 \, \frac{\text{m}}{\text{ft}} \right) = 3.92 \, \frac{\text{m}}{\text{s}^2} \qquad \textit{Ans. (c)}$$

Comment (c):   This acceleration would be the same on the earth or moon or anywhere.

Many data in the literature are reported in inconvenient or arcane units suitable only to some industry or specialty or country. The engineer should convert these data to the SI or BG system before using them. This requires the systematic application of conversion factors, as in the following example.

EXAMPLE 1.2

Industries involved in viscosity measurement [27, 29] continue to use the CGS system of units, since centimeters and grams yield convenient numbers for many fluids. The absolute viscosity (μ) unit is the *poise,* named after J. L. M. Poiseuille, a French physician who in 1840 performed pioneering experiments on water flow in pipes; 1 poise = 1 g/(cm-s). The kinematic viscosity (ν) unit is the *stokes,* named after G. G. Stokes, a British physicist who in 1845 helped develop the basic partial differential equations of fluid momentum; 1 stokes = 1 cm²/s. Water at 20°C has $\mu \approx 0.01$ poise and also $\nu \approx 0.01$ stokes. Express these results in (*a*) SI and (*b*) BG units.

Solution

Part (a)   • *Approach:*   Systematically change grams to kg or slugs and change centimeters to meters or feet.

- *Property values:* Given $\mu = 0.01$ g/(cm-s) and $\nu = 0.01$ cm²/s.
- *Solution steps:* (a) For conversion to SI units,

$$\mu = 0.01 \frac{g}{cm \cdot s} = 0.01 \frac{g(1 \text{ kg}/1000 \text{ g})}{cm(0.01 \text{ m}/cm)s} = 0.001 \frac{kg}{m \cdot s}$$

$$\nu = 0.01 \frac{cm^2}{s} = 0.01 \frac{cm^2(0.01 \text{ m}/cm)^2}{s} = 0.000001 \frac{m^2}{s} \qquad Ans. \ (a)$$

Part (b)

- For conversion to BG units

$$\mu = 0.01 \frac{g}{cm \cdot s} = 0.01 \frac{g(1 \text{ kg}/1000 \text{ g})(1 \text{ slug}/14.5939 \text{ kg})}{(0.01 \text{ m}/cm)(1 \text{ ft}/0.3048 \text{ m})s} = 0.0000209 \frac{slug}{ft \cdot s}$$

$$\nu = 0.01 \frac{cm^2}{s} = 0.01 \frac{cm^2(0.01 \text{ m}/cm)^2(1 \text{ ft}/0.3048 \text{ m})^2}{s} = 0.0000108 \frac{ft^2}{s} \qquad Ans. \ (b)$$

- *Comments:* This was a laborious conversion that could have been shortened by using the direct viscosity conversion factors in App. C or the inside front cover. For example, $\mu_{BG} = \mu_{SI}/47.88$.

We repeat our advice: Faced with data in unusual units, convert them immediately to either SI or BG units because (1) it is more professional and (2) theoretical equations in fluid mechanics are *dimensionally consistent* and require no further conversion factors when these two fundamental unit systems are used, as the following example shows.

EXAMPLE 1.3

A useful theoretical equation for computing the relation between pressure, velocity, and altitude in a steady flow of a nearly inviscid, nearly incompressible fluid with negligible heat transfer and shaft work[5] is the *Bernoulli relation,* named after Daniel Bernoulli, who published a hydrodynamics textbook in 1738:

$$p_0 = p + \tfrac{1}{2}\rho V^2 + \rho g Z \qquad (1)$$

where p_0 = stagnation pressure
$\quad\quad\ p$ = pressure in moving fluid
$\quad\quad\ V$ = velocity
$\quad\quad\ \rho$ = density
$\quad\quad\ Z$ = altitude
$\quad\quad\ g$ = gravitational acceleration

(a) Show that Eq. (1) satisfies the principle of dimensional homogeneity, which states that all additive terms in a physical equation must have the same dimensions. (b) Show that consistent units result without additional conversion factors in SI units. (c) Repeat (b) for BG units.

---

[5]That's an awful lot of assumptions, which need further study in Chap. 3.

Solution

Part (a)

We can express Eq. (1) dimensionally, using braces, by entering the dimensions of each term from Table 1.2:

$$\{ML^{-1}T^{-2}\} = \{ML^{-1}T^{-2}\} + \{ML^{-3}\}\{L^2T^{-2}\} + \{ML^{-3}\}\{LT^{-2}\}\{L\}$$

$$= \{ML^{-1}T^{-2}\} \text{ for all terms} \qquad\qquad Ans.\ (a)$$

Part (b)

Enter the SI units for each quantity from Table 1.2:

$$\{N/m^2\} = \{N/m^2\} + \{kg/m^3\}\{m^2/s^2\} + \{kg/m^3\}\{m/s^2\}\{m\}$$

$$= \{N/m^2\} + \{kg/(m \cdot s^2)\}$$

The right-hand side looks bad until we remember from Eq. (1.3) that 1 kg = 1 N · s²/m.

$$\{kg/(m \cdot s^2)\} = \frac{\{N \cdot s^2/m\}}{\{m \cdot s^2\}} = \{N/m^2\} \qquad\qquad Ans.\ (b)$$

Thus all terms in Bernoulli's equation will have units of pascals, or newtons per square meter, when SI units are used. No conversion factors are needed, which is true of all theoretical equations in fluid mechanics.

Part (c)

Introducing BG units for each term, we have

$$\{lbf/ft^2\} = \{lbf/ft^2\} + \{slugs/ft^3\}\{ft^2/s^2\} + \{slugs/ft^3\}\{ft/s^2\}\{ft\}$$

$$= \{lbf/ft^2\} + \{slugs/(ft \cdot s^2)\}$$

But, from Eq. (1.3), 1 slug = 1 lbf · s²/ft, so that

$$\{slugs/(ft \cdot s^2)\} = \frac{\{lbf \cdot s^2/ft\}}{\{ft \cdot s^2\}} = \{lbf/ft^2\} \qquad\qquad Ans.\ (c)$$

All terms have the unit of pounds-force per square foot. No conversion factors are needed in the BG system either.

There is still a tendency in English-speaking countries to use pound-force per square inch as a pressure unit because the numbers are more manageable. For example, standard atmospheric pressure is 14.7 lbf/in^2 = 2116 lbf/ft^2 = 101,300 Pa. The pascal is a small unit because the newton is less than $\frac{1}{4}$ lbf and a square meter is a very large area.

Consistent Units

Note that not only must all (fluid) mechanics equations be dimensionally homogeneous, one must also use *consistent units;* that is, each additive term must have the same units. There is no trouble doing this with the SI and BG systems, as in Example 1.3, but woe unto those who try to mix colloquial English units. For example, in Chap. 9, we often use the assumption of steady adiabatic compressible gas flow:

$$h + \tfrac{1}{2}V^2 = \text{constant}$$

where h is the fluid enthalpy and $V^2/2$ is its kinetic energy per unit mass. Colloquial thermodynamic tables might list h in units of British thermal units per pound mass (Btu/lb), whereas V is likely used in ft/s. It is completely erroneous to add Btu/lb to ft^2/s^2. The proper unit for h in this case is ft · lbf/slug, which is identical to ft^2/s^2. The conversion factor is 1 Btu/lb $\approx$ 25,040 ft^2/s^2 = 25,040 ft · lbf/slug.

Homogeneous versus Dimensionally Inconsistent Equations

All theoretical equations in mechanics (and in other physical sciences) are *dimensionally homogeneous;* that is, each additive term in the equation has the same dimensions. However, the reader should be warned that many empirical formulas in the engineering literature, arising primarily from correlations of data, are dimensionally inconsistent. Their units cannot be reconciled simply, and some terms may contain hidden variables. An example is the formula that pipe valve manufacturers cite for liquid volume flow rate Q (m^3/s) through a partially open valve:

$$Q = C_V\left(\frac{\Delta p}{SG}\right)^{1/2}$$

where Δp is the pressure drop across the valve and SG is the specific gravity of the liquid (the ratio of its density to that of water). The quantity C_V is the *valve flow coefficient,* which manufacturers tabulate in their valve brochures. Since SG is dimensionless {1}, we see that this formula is totally inconsistent, with one side being a flow rate $\{L^3/T\}$ and the other being the square root of a pressure drop $\{M^{1/2}/L^{1/2}T\}$. It follows that C_V must have dimensions, and rather odd ones at that: $\{L^{7/2}/M^{1/2}\}$. Nor is the resolution of this discrepancy clear, although one hint is that the values of C_V in the literature increase nearly as the square of the size of the valve. The presentation of experimental data in homogeneous form is the subject of *dimensional analysis* (Chap. 5). There we shall learn that a homogeneous form for the valve flow relation is

$$Q = C_d A_{\text{opening}}\left(\frac{\Delta p}{\rho}\right)^{1/2}$$

where ρ is the liquid density and A the area of the valve opening. The *discharge coefficient* C_d is dimensionless and changes only moderately with valve size. Please believe—until we establish the fact in Chap. 5—that this latter is a *much* better formulation of the data.

Meanwhile, we conclude that dimensionally inconsistent equations, though they occur in engineering practice, are misleading and vague and even dangerous, in the sense that they are often misused outside their range of applicability.

Table 1.3 Convenient Prefixes for Engineering Units

Multiplicative factor	Prefix	Symbol
10^{12}	tera	T
10^{9}	giga	G
10^{6}	mega	M
10^{3}	kilo	k
10^{2}	hecto	h
10	deka	da
10^{-1}	deci	d
10^{-2}	centi	c
10^{-3}	milli	m
10^{-6}	micro	μ
10^{-9}	nano	n
10^{-12}	pico	p
10^{-15}	femto	f
10^{-18}	atto	a

Convenient Prefixes in Powers of 10

Engineering results often are too small or too large for the common units, with too many zeros one way or the other. For example, to write p = 114,000,000 Pa is long and awkward. Using the prefix "M" to mean 10^6, we convert this to a concise p = 114 MPa (megapascals). Similarly, t = 0.000000003 s is a proofreader's nightmare compared to the equivalent t = 3 ns (nanoseconds). Such prefixes are common and convenient, in both the SI and BG systems. A complete list is given in Table 1.3.

EXAMPLE 1.4

In 1890 Robert Manning, an Irish engineer, proposed the following empirical formula for the average velocity V in uniform flow due to gravity down an open channel (BG units):

$$V = \frac{1.49}{n}R^{2/3}S^{1/2} \qquad (1)$$

where R = hydraulic radius of channel (Chaps. 6 and 10)
$\quad\quad S$ = channel slope (tangent of angle that bottom makes with horizontal)
$\quad\quad n$ = Manning's roughness factor (Chap. 10)

and n is a constant for a given surface condition for the walls and bottom of the channel. (*a*) Is Manning's formula dimensionally consistent? (*b*) Equation (1) is commonly taken to be valid in BG units with n taken as dimensionless. Rewrite it in SI form.

Solution

- *Assumption:*   The channel slope S is the tangent of an angle and is thus a dimensionless ratio with the dimensional notation $\{1\}$—that is, not containing M, L, or T.
- *Approach (a):*   Rewrite the dimensions of each term in Manning's equation, using brackets $\{\}$:

$$\{V\} = \left\{\frac{1.49}{n}\right\}\{R^{2/3}\}\,\{S^{1/2}\} \;\; \text{or} \;\; \left\{\frac{L}{T}\right\} = \left\{\frac{1.49}{n}\right\}\{L^{2/3}\}\{1\}$$

This formula is incompatible unless $\{1.49/n\} = \{L^{1/3}/T\}$. If n is dimensionless (and it is never listed with units in textbooks), the number 1.49 must carry the dimensions of $\{L^{1/3}/T\}$. *Ans.* (*a*)

- *Comment (a):*   Formulas whose numerical coefficients have units can be disastrous for engineers working in a different system or another fluid. Manning's formula, though popular, is inconsistent both dimensionally and physically and is valid only for water flow with certain wall roughnesses. The effects of water viscosity and density are hidden in the numerical value 1.49.
- *Approach (b):*   Part (*a*) showed that 1.49 has dimensions. If the formula is valid in BG units, then it must equal 1.49 $\text{ft}^{1/3}$/s. By using the SI conversion for length, we obtain

$$(1.49 \text{ ft}^{1/3}/\text{s})(0.3048 \text{ m/ft})^{1/3} = 1.00 \text{ m}^{1/3}/\text{s}$$

Therefore, Manning's inconsistent formula changes form when converted to the SI system:

$$\text{SI units:} \;\; V = \frac{1.0}{n}R^{2/3}S^{1/2} \qquad\qquad \textit{Ans.} \;(b)$$

with R in meters and V in meters per second.
- *Comment (b):*   Actually, we misled you: This is the way Manning, a metric user, first proposed the formula. It was later converted to BG units. Such dimensionally inconsistent formulas are dangerous and should either be reanalyzed or treated as having very limited application.

1.5 Properties of the Velocity Field

In a given flow situation, the determination, by experiment or theory, of the properties of the fluid as a function of position and time is considered to be the *solution* to the problem. In almost all cases, the emphasis is on the space–time distribution of the fluid properties. One rarely keeps track of the actual fate of the specific fluid particles. This treatment of properties as continuum-field functions distinguishes fluid mechanics from solid mechanics, where we are more likely to be interested in the trajectories of individual particles or systems.

The Velocity Field

Foremost among the properties of a flow is the velocity field $\mathbf{V}(x, y, z, t)$. In fact, determining the velocity is often tantamount to solving a flow problem, since other properties follow directly from the velocity field. Chapter 2 is devoted to the calculation of the pressure field once the velocity field is known. Books on heat transfer (for example, Ref. 20) are largely devoted to finding the temperature field from known velocity fields.

In general, velocity is a vector function of position and time and thus has three components u, v, and w, each a scalar field in itself:

$$\mathbf{V}(x, y, z, t) = \mathbf{i}u(x, y, z, t) + \mathbf{j}v(x, y, z, t) + \mathbf{k}w(x, y, z, t) \tag{1.4}$$

The use of u, v, and w instead of the more logical component notation V_x, V_y, and V_z is the result of an almost unbreakable custom in fluid mechanics. Much of this textbook, especially Chaps. 4, 7, 8, and 9, is concerned with finding the distribution of the velocity vector $\mathbf{V}$ for a variety of practical flows.

The Acceleration Field

The acceleration vector, $\mathbf{a} = d\mathbf{V}/dt$, occurs in Newton's law for a fluid and thus is very important. In order to follow a particle in the Eulerian frame of reference, the final result for acceleration is nonlinear and quite complicated. Here we only give the formula:

$$\mathbf{a} = \frac{d\mathbf{V}}{dt} = \frac{\partial \mathbf{V}}{\partial t} + u\frac{\partial \mathbf{V}}{\partial x} + v\frac{\partial \mathbf{V}}{\partial y} + w\frac{\partial \mathbf{V}}{\partial z} \tag{1.5}$$

where (u, v, w) are the velocity components from Eq. (1.4). We shall study this formula in detail in Chap. 4. The last three terms in Eq. (1.5) are nonlinear products and greatly complicate the analysis of general fluid motions, especially viscous flows.

1.6 Thermodynamic Properties of a Fluid

While the velocity field $\mathbf{V}$ is the most important fluid property, it interacts closely with the thermodynamic properties of the fluid. We have already introduced into the discussion the three most common such properties:

1. Pressure p
2. Density ρ
3. Temperature T

These three are constant companions of the velocity vector in flow analyses. Four other intensive thermodynamic properties become important when work, heat, and energy balances are treated (Chaps. 3 and 4):

4. Internal energy $\hat{u}$
5. Enthalpy $h = \hat{u} + p/\rho$
6. Entropy s
7. Specific heats c_p and c_v

In addition, friction and heat conduction effects are governed by the two so-called *transport properties:*

8. Coefficient of viscosity μ
9. Thermal conductivity k

All nine of these quantities are true thermodynamic properties that are determined by the thermodynamic condition or *state* of the fluid. For example, for a single-phase substance such as water or oxygen, two basic properties such as pressure and temperature are sufficient to fix the value of all the others:

$$\rho = \rho(p, T) \quad h = h(p, T) \quad \mu = \mu(p, T)$$

and so on for every quantity in the list. Note that the specific volume, so important in thermodynamic analyses, is omitted here in favor of its inverse, the density ρ.

Recall that thermodynamic properties describe the state of a *system*—that is, a collection of matter of fixed identity that interacts with its surroundings. In most cases here the system will be a small fluid element, and all properties will be assumed to be continuum properties of the flow field: $\rho = \rho(x, y, z, t)$, and so on.

Recall also that thermodynamics is normally concerned with *static* systems, whereas fluids are usually in variable motion with constantly changing properties. Do the properties retain their meaning in a fluid flow that is technically not in equilibrium? The answer is yes, from a statistical argument. In gases at normal pressure (and even more so for liquids), an enormous number of molecular collisions occur over a very short distance of the order of 1 μm, so that a fluid subjected to sudden changes rapidly adjusts itself toward equilibrium. We therefore assume that all the thermodynamic properties just listed exist as point functions in a flowing fluid and follow all the laws and state relations of ordinary equilibrium thermodynamics. There are, of course, important nonequilibrium effects such as chemical and nuclear reactions in flowing fluids, which are not treated in this text.

Pressure

Pressure is the (compression) stress at a point in a static fluid (Fig. 1.3). Next to velocity, the pressure p is the most dynamic variable in fluid mechanics. Differences or *gradients* in pressure often drive a fluid flow, especially in ducts. In low-speed flows, the actual magnitude of the pressure is often not important, unless it drops so low as to cause vapor bubbles to form in a liquid. For convenience, we set many such problem assignments at the level of 1 atm = 2116 lbf/ft^2 = 101,300 Pa. High-speed (compressible) gas flows (Chap. 9), however, are indeed sensitive to the magnitude of pressure.

Temperature

Temperature T is related to the internal energy level of a fluid. It may vary considerably during high-speed flow of a gas (Chap. 9). Although engineers often use Celsius or Fahrenheit scales for convenience, many applications in this text require *absolute* (Kelvin or Rankine) temperature scales:

$$°R = °F + 459.69$$
$$K = °C + 273.16$$

If temperature differences are strong, *heat transfer* may be important [20], but our concern here is mainly with dynamic effects.

Density

The density of a fluid, denoted by ρ (lowercase Greek rho), is its mass per unit volume. Density is highly variable in gases and increases nearly proportionally to the pressure level. Density in liquids is nearly constant; the density of water (about 1000 kg/m^3) increases only 1 percent if the pressure is increased by a factor of 220. Thus most liquid flows are treated analytically as nearly "incompressible."

In general, liquids are about three orders of magnitude more dense than gases at atmospheric pressure. The heaviest common liquid is mercury, and the lightest gas is hydrogen. Compare their densities at 20°C and 1 atm:

$$\text{Mercury: } \rho = 13{,}580 \text{ kg/m}^3 \qquad \text{Hydrogen: } \rho = 0.0838 \text{ kg/m}^3$$

They differ by a factor of 162,000! Thus, the physical parameters in various liquid and gas flows might vary considerably. The differences are often resolved by the use of *dimensional analysis* (Chap. 5). Other fluid densities are listed in Tables A.3 and A.4 (in App. A), and in Ref. 21.

Specific Weight

The *specific weight* of a fluid, denoted by γ (lowercase Greek gamma), is its weight per unit volume. Just as a mass has a weight $W = mg$, density and specific weight are simply related by gravity:

$$\gamma = \rho g \tag{1.6}$$

The units of γ are weight per unit volume, in lbf/ft^3 or N/m^3. In standard earth gravity, $g = 32.174$ ft/s^2 = 9.807 m/s^2. Thus, for example, the specific weights of air and water at 20°C and 1 atm are approximately

$$\gamma_{\text{air}} = (1.205 \text{ kg/m}^3)(9.807 \text{ m/s}^2) = 11.8 \text{ N/m}^3 = 0.0752 \text{ lbf/ft}^3$$

$$\gamma_{\text{water}} = (998 \text{ kg/m}^3)(9.807 \text{ m/s}^2) = 9790 \text{ N/m}^3 = 62.4 \text{ lbf/ft}^3$$

Specific weight is very useful in the hydrostatic pressure applications of Chap. 2. Specific weights of other fluids are given in Tables A.3 and A.4.

Specific Gravity

Specific gravity, denoted by SG, is the ratio of a fluid density to a standard reference fluid, usually water at 4°C (for liquids) and air (for gases):

$$SG_{\text{gas}} = \frac{\rho_{\text{gas}}}{\rho_{\text{air}}} = \frac{\rho_{\text{gas}}}{1.205 \text{ kg/m}^3} \tag{1.7}$$

$$SG_{\text{liquid}} = \frac{\rho_{\text{liquid}}}{\rho_{\text{water}}} = \frac{\rho_{\text{liquid}}}{1000 \text{ kg/m}^3}$$

For example, the specific gravity of mercury (Hg) is $SG_{Hg} = 13,580/1000 \approx 13.6$. Engineers find these dimensionless ratios easier to remember than the actual numerical values of density of a variety of fluids.

Potential and Kinetic Energies

In thermostatics the only energy in a substance is that stored in a system by molecular activity and molecular bonding forces. This is commonly denoted as *internal energy* $\hat{u}$. A commonly accepted adjustment to this static situation for fluid flow is to add two more energy terms that arise from newtonian mechanics: potential energy and kinetic energy.

The potential energy equals the work required to move the system of mass m from the origin to a position vector $\mathbf{r} = \mathbf{i}x + \mathbf{j}y + \mathbf{k}z$ against a gravity field $\mathbf{g}$. Its value is $-m\mathbf{g} \cdot \mathbf{r}$, or $-\mathbf{g} \cdot \mathbf{r}$ per unit mass. The kinetic energy equals the work required to change the speed of the mass from zero to velocity V. Its value is $\frac{1}{2}mV^2$ or $\frac{1}{2}V^2$ per unit mass. Then by common convention the total stored energy e per unit mass in fluid mechanics is the sum of three terms:

$$e = \hat{u} + \tfrac{1}{2}V^2 + (-\mathbf{g} \cdot \mathbf{r}) \tag{1.8}$$

Also, throughout this book we shall define z as upward, so that $\mathbf{g} = -g\mathbf{k}$ and $\mathbf{g} \cdot \mathbf{r} = -gz$. Then Eq. (1.8) becomes

$$e = \hat{u} + \tfrac{1}{2}V^2 + gz \tag{1.9}$$

The molecular internal energy $\hat{u}$ is a function of T and p for the single-phase pure substance, whereas the potential and kinetic energies are kinematic quantities.

State Relations for Gases

Thermodynamic properties are found both theoretically and experimentally to be related to each other by state relations that differ for each substance. As mentioned, we shall confine ourselves here to single-phase pure substances, such as water in its liquid phase. The second most common fluid, air, is a mixture of gases, but since the mixture ratios remain nearly constant between 160 and 2200 K, in this temperature range air can be considered to be a pure substance.

All gases at high temperatures and low pressures (relative to their critical point) are in good agreement with the *perfect-gas law*

$$\boxed{p = \rho RT \quad R = c_p - c_v = \text{gas constant}} \tag{1.10}$$

where the specific heats c_p and c_v are defined in Eqs. (1.14) and (1.15).

Since Eq. (1.10) is dimensionally consistent, R has the same dimensions as specific heat, $\{L^2T^{-2}\Theta^{-1}\}$, or velocity squared per temperature unit (kelvin or degree Rankine). Each gas has its own constant R, equal to a universal constant Λ divided by the molecular weight

$$R_{gas} = \frac{\Lambda}{M_{gas}} \tag{1.11}$$

where $\Lambda = 49,700$ ft-lbf/(slugmol · °R) = 8314 J/(kmol · K). Most applications in this book are for air, whose molecular weight is $M = 28.97$/mol:

$$R_{air} = \frac{49,700 \text{ ft} \cdot \text{lbf/(slugmol} \cdot \text{°R)}}{28.97/\text{mol}} = 1716 \frac{\text{ft} \cdot \text{lbf}}{\text{slug} \cdot \text{°R}} = 1716 \frac{\text{ft}^2}{\text{s}^2\text{°R}} = 287 \frac{\text{m}^2}{\text{s}^2 \cdot \text{K}} \quad (1.12)$$

Standard atmospheric pressure is 2116 lbf/ft² = 2116 slug/(ft · s²), and standard temperature is 60°F = 520°R. Thus standard air density is

$$\rho_{air} = \frac{2116 \text{ slug/(ft} \cdot \text{s}^2)}{[1716 \text{ ft}^2/(\text{s}^2 \cdot \text{°R})](520\text{°R})} = 0.00237 \text{ slug/ft}^3 = 1.22 \text{ kg/m}^3 \quad (1.13)$$

This is a nominal value suitable for problems. For other gases, see Table A.4.

Most of the common gases—oxygen, nitrogen, hydrogen, helium, argon—are nearly ideal. This is not so true for steam, whose simplified temperature-entropy chart is shown in Fig. 1.3. Unless you are sure that the steam temperature is "high" and the pressure "low," it is best to use the Steam Tables to make accurate calculations.

One proves in thermodynamics that Eq. (1.10) requires that the internal molecular energy $\hat{u}$ of a perfect gas vary only with temperature: $\hat{u} = \hat{u}(T)$. Therefore, the specific heat c_v also varies only with temperature:

$$c_v = \left(\frac{\partial \hat{u}}{\partial T}\right)_\rho = \frac{d\hat{u}}{dT} = c_v(T)$$

or

$$d\hat{u} = c_v(T)dT \quad (1.14)$$

In like manner h and c_p of a perfect gas also vary only with temperature:

$$h = \hat{u} + \frac{p}{\rho} = \hat{u} + RT = h(T)$$

$$c_p = \left(\frac{\partial h}{\partial T}\right)_p = \frac{dh}{dT} = c_p(T) \quad (1.15)$$

$$dh = c_p(T)dT$$

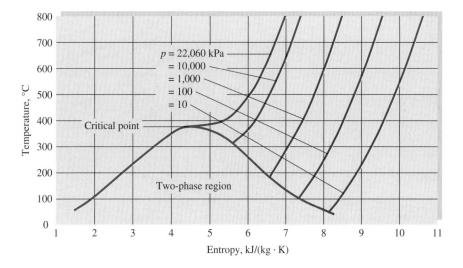

Fig. 1.3 Temperature-entropy chart for steam. The critical point is $p_c =$ 22,060 kPa, $T_c = 374$°C, $S_c =$ 4.41 kJ/(kg · K). Except near the critical point, the smooth isobars tempt one to assume, often incorrectly, that the ideal-gas law is valid for steam. It is *not*, except at low pressure and high temperature: the upper right of the graph.

The ratio of specific heats of a perfect gas is an important dimensionless parameter in compressible flow analysis (Chap. 9)

$$k = \frac{c_p}{c_v} = k(T) \geq 1 \tag{1.16}$$

As a first approximation in airflow analysis we commonly take c_p, c_v, and k to be constant:

$$k_{\text{air}} \approx 1.4$$

$$c_v = \frac{R}{k-1} \approx 4293 \text{ ft}^2/(\text{s}^2 \cdot {}^\circ\text{R}) = 718 \text{ m}^2/(\text{s}^2 \cdot \text{K}) \tag{1.17}$$

$$c_p = \frac{kR}{k-1} \approx 6010 \text{ ft}^2/(\text{s}^2 \cdot {}^\circ\text{R}) = 1005 \text{ m}^2/(\text{s}^2 \cdot \text{K})$$

Actually, for all gases, c_p and c_v increase gradually with temperature, and k decreases gradually. Experimental values of the specific-heat ratio for eight common gases are shown in Fig. 1.4. Nominal values are in Table A.4.

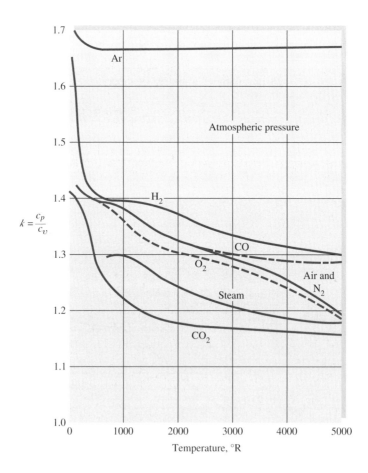

Fig. 1.4 Specific-heat ratio of eight common gases as a function of temperature. *(Data from Ref. 22.)*

Many flow problems involve steam. Typical steam operating conditions are often close to the critical point, so that the perfect-gas approximation is inaccurate. Then we must turn to the steam tables, either in tabular or CD-ROM form [23] or as online software [24]. Most online steam tables require a license fee, but the writer, in Example 1.5 that follows, suggests a free online source. Sometimes the error of using the perfect-gas law for steam can moderate, as the following example shows.

EXAMPLE 1.5

Estimate ρ and c_p of steam at 100 lbf/in^2 and 400°F, in English units, (a) by the perfect-gas approximation and (b) by the ASME Steam Tables [23].

Solution

- *Approach (a)—the perfect-gas law:* Although steam is not an ideal gas, we can estimate these properties with moderate accuracy from Eqs. (1.10) and (1.17). First convert pressure from 100 lbf/in^2 to 14,400 lbf/ft^2, and use absolute temperature, (400°F + 460) = 860°R. Then we need the gas constant for steam, in English units. From Table A.4, the molecular weight of H_2O is 18.02, whence

$$R_{\text{steam}} = \frac{\Lambda_{\text{English}}}{M_{H_2O}} = \frac{49{,}700 \text{ ft} \cdot \text{lbf/(slugmol °R)}}{18.02/\text{mol}} = 2758 \frac{\text{ft} \cdot \text{lbf}}{\text{slug °R}}$$

Then the density estimate follows from the perfect-gas law, Eq. (1.10):

$$\rho \approx \frac{p}{RT} = \frac{14{,}400 \text{ lbf/ft}^2}{[2758 \text{ ft} \cdot \text{lbf/(slug} \cdot \text{°R)}](860 \text{ °R})} \approx 0.00607 \frac{\text{slug}}{\text{ft}^3} \qquad \textit{Ans. (a)}$$

At 860°R, from Fig. 1.5, $k_{\text{steam}} = c_p/c_v \approx 1.30$. Then, from Eq. (1.17),

$$c_p \approx \frac{kR}{k-1} = \frac{(1.3)(2758 \text{ ft} \cdot \text{lbf/(slug °R))}}{(1.3-1)} \approx 12{,}000 \frac{\text{ft} \cdot \text{lbf}}{\text{slug °R}} \qquad \textit{Ans. (a)}$$

- *Approach (b)—tables or software:* One can either read the ASME Steam Tables [23] or use online software. Online software, such as [24], calculates the properties of steam without reading a table. Most of these require a license fee, which your institution may or may not possess. For work at home, the writer has found success with this free commercial online site:

www.spiraxsarco.com/esc/SH_Properties.aspx

The software calculates superheated steam properties, as required in this example. The Spirax Sarco Company makes many types of steam equipment: boilers, condensers, valves, pumps, regulators. This site provides many steam properties—density, specific heat, enthalpy, speed of sound—in many different unit systems. Here we need the density and specific heat of steam at 100 lbf/in^2 and 400°F. You enter these two inputs and it will calculate not only ρ and c_p but also many other properties of interest, in English or metric units. The software results are:

$$\rho(100 \text{ lbf/in}^2, 400°F) = 0.2027 \text{ lbm/ft}^3 = 3.247 \text{ kg/m}^3 \qquad \textit{Ans. (b)}$$

$$c_p(100 \text{ lbf/in}^2, 400°F) = 0.5289 \text{ Btu/(lbm-F)} = 2215 \text{ J/(kg-K)} \qquad \textit{Ans. (b)}$$

Comments: These are quite accurate and compare well to other steam tables. The perfect gas estimate of ρ is 4 percent low, and the estimate of c_p is 9 percent low. The chief reason for the discrepancy is that this temperature and pressure are rather close to the critical point and saturation line of steam. At higher temperatures and lower pressures, say, 800°F and 50 lbf/in^2, the perfect-gas law has an accuracy of about ±1 percent. See Fig. 1.3.

Again let us warn that English units (psia, lbm, Btu) are awkward and must be converted to SI or BG units in almost all fluid mechanics formulas.

State Relations for Liquids

The writer knows of no "perfect-liquid law" comparable to that for gases. Liquids are nearly incompressible and have a single, reasonably constant specific heat. Thus an idealized state relation for a liquid is

$$\rho \approx \text{const} \qquad c_p \approx c_v \approx \text{const} \qquad dh \approx c_p\, dT \tag{1.18}$$

Most of the flow problems in this book can be attacked with these simple assumptions. Water is normally taken to have a density of 998 kg/m^3 and a specific heat c_p = 4210 m^2/(s$^2 \cdot$ K). The steam tables may be used if more accuracy is required.

The density of a liquid usually decreases slightly with temperature and increases moderately with pressure. If we neglect the temperature effect, an empirical pressure–density relation for a liquid is

$$\frac{p}{p_a} \approx (B + 1)\left(\frac{\rho}{\rho_a}\right)^n - B \tag{1.19}$$

where B and n are dimensionless parameters that vary slightly with temperature and p_a and ρ_a are standard atmospheric values. Water can be fitted approximately to the values $B \approx 3000$ and $n \approx 7$.

Seawater is a variable mixture of water and salt and thus requires three thermodynamic properties to define its state. These are normally taken as pressure, temperature, and the *salinity* $\hat{S}$, defined as the weight of the dissolved salt divided by the weight of the mixture. The average salinity of seawater is 0.035, usually written as 35 parts per 1000, or 35 ‰. The average density of seawater is 2.00 slugs/ft$^3 \approx$ 1030 kg/m^3. Strictly speaking, seawater has three specific heats, all approximately equal to the value for pure water of 25,200 ft^2/(s$^2 \cdot$ °R) = 4210 m^2/(s$^2 \cdot$ K).

EXAMPLE 1.6

The pressure at the deepest part of the ocean is approximately 1100 atm. Estimate the density of seawater in slug/ft^3 at this pressure.

Solution

Equation (1.19) holds for either water or seawater. The ratio p/p_a is given as 1100:

$$1100 \approx (3001)\left(\frac{\rho}{\rho_a}\right)^7 - 3000$$

or
$$\frac{\rho}{\rho_a} = \left(\frac{4100}{3001}\right)^{1/7} = 1.046$$

Assuming an average surface seawater density $\rho_a = 2.00$ slugs/ft^3, we compute

$$\rho \approx 1.046(2.00) = 2.09 \text{ slugs/ft}^3 \qquad\qquad Ans.$$

Even at these immense pressures, the density increase is less than 5 percent, which justifies the treatment of a liquid flow as essentially incompressible.

1.7 Viscosity and Other Secondary Properties

The quantities such as pressure, temperature, and density discussed in the previous section are *primary* thermodynamic variables characteristic of any system. Certain secondary variables also characterize specific fluid mechanical behavior. The most important of these is viscosity, which relates the local stresses in a moving fluid to the strain rate of the fluid element.

Viscosity

Viscosity is a quantitative measure of a fluid's resistance to flow. More specifically, it determines the fluid strain rate that is generated by a given applied shear stress. We can easily move through air, which has very low viscosity. Movement is more difficult in water, which has 50 times higher viscosity. Still more resistance is found in SAE 30 oil, which is 300 times more viscous than water. Try to slide your hand through glycerin, which is five times more viscous than SAE 30 oil, or blackstrap molasses, another factor of five higher than glycerin. Fluids may have a vast range of viscosities.

Consider a fluid element sheared in one plane by a single shear stress τ, as in Fig. 1.5a. The shear strain angle $\delta\theta$ will continuously grow with time as long as the stress τ is maintained, the upper surface moving at speed δu larger than the lower. Such common fluids as water, oil, and air show a linear relation between applied shear and resulting strain rate:

$$\tau \propto \frac{\delta\theta}{\delta t} \tag{1.20}$$

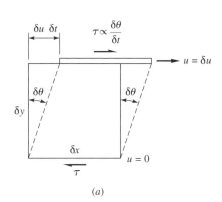

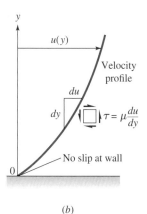

Fig. 1.5 Shear stress causes continuous shear deformation in a fluid: (*a*) a fluid element straining at a rate $\delta\theta/\delta t$; (*b*) newtonian shear distribution in a shear layer near a wall.

From the geometry of Fig. 1.5a, we see that

$$\tan \delta\theta = \frac{\delta u \, \delta t}{\delta y} \tag{1.21}$$

In the limit of infinitesimal changes, this becomes a relation between shear strain rate and velocity gradient:

$$\frac{d\theta}{dt} = \frac{du}{dy} \tag{1.22}$$

From Eq. (1.20), then, the applied shear is also proportional to the velocity gradient for the common linear fluids. The constant of proportionality is the viscosity coefficient μ:

$$\boxed{\tau = \mu\frac{d\theta}{dt} = \mu\frac{du}{dy}} \tag{1.23}$$

Equation (1.23) is dimensionally consistent; therefore μ has dimensions of stress–time: $\{FT/L^2\}$ or $\{M/(LT)\}$. The BG unit is slugs per foot-second, and the SI unit is kilograms per meter-second. The linear fluids that follow Eq. (1.23) are called *newtonian fluids,* after Sir Isaac Newton, who first postulated this resistance law in 1687.

We do not really care about the strain angle $\theta(t)$ in fluid mechanics, concentrating instead on the velocity distribution $u(y)$, as in Fig. 1.5b. We shall use Eq. (1.23) in Chap. 4 to derive a differential equation for finding the velocity distribution $u(y)$— and, more generally, $\mathbf{V}(x, y, z, t)$—in a viscous fluid. Figure 1.5b illustrates a shear layer, or *boundary layer,* near a solid wall. The shear stress is proportional to the slope of the velocity profile and is greatest at the wall. Further, at the wall, the velocity u is zero relative to the wall: This is called the *no-slip condition* and is characteristic of all viscous fluid flows.

The viscosity of newtonian fluids is a true thermodynamic property and varies with temperature and pressure. At a given state (p, T) there is a vast range of values among the common fluids. Table 1.4 lists the viscosity of eight fluids at standard pressure and temperature. There is a variation of six orders of magnitude from hydrogen up to glycerin. Thus there will be wide differences between fluids subjected to the same applied stresses.

Table 1.4 Viscosity and Kinematic Viscosity of Eight Fluids at 1 atm and 20°C

Fluid	μ, kg/(m · s)[†]	Ratio $\mu/\mu(H_2)$	ρ, kg/m³	ν m²/s[†]	Ratio $\nu/\nu(Hg)$
Hydrogen	9.0 E–6	1.0	0.084	1.05 E–4	910
Air	1.8 E–5	2.1	1.20	1.50 E–5	130
Gasoline	2.9 E–4	33	680	4.22 E–7	3.7
Water	1.0 E–3	114	998	1.01 E–6	8.7
Ethyl alcohol	1.2 E–3	135	789	1.52 E–6	13
Mercury	1.5 E–3	170	13,550	1.16 E–7	1.0
SAE 30 oil	0.29	33,000	891	3.25 E–4	2,850
Glycerin	1.5	170,000	1,260	1.18 E–3	10,300

[†] 1 kg/(m · s) = 0.0209 slug/(ft · s); 1 m²/s = 10.76 ft²/s.

Generally speaking, the viscosity of a fluid increases only weakly with pressure. For example, increasing p from 1 to 50 atm will increase μ of air only 10 percent. Temperature, however, has a strong effect, with μ increasing with T for gases and decreasing for liquids. Figure A.1 (in App. A) shows this temperature variation for various common fluids. It is customary in most engineering work to neglect the pressure variation.

The variation $\mu(p, T)$ for a typical fluid is nicely shown by Fig. 1.6, from Ref. 25, which normalizes the data with the *critical-point state* (μ_c, p_c, T_c). This behavior, called the *principle of corresponding states,* is characteristic of all fluids, but the actual numerical values are uncertain to ± 20 percent for any given fluid. For example, values of $\mu(T)$ for air at 1 atm, from Table A.2, fall about 8 percent low compared to the "low-density limit" in Fig. 1.6.

Note in Fig. 1.6 that changes with temperature occur very rapidly near the critical point. In general, critical-point measurements are extremely difficult and uncertain.

The Reynolds Number

The primary parameter correlating the viscous behavior of all newtonian fluids is the dimensionless *Reynolds number:*

$$\text{Re} = \frac{\rho V L}{\mu} = \frac{VL}{\nu} \tag{1.24}$$

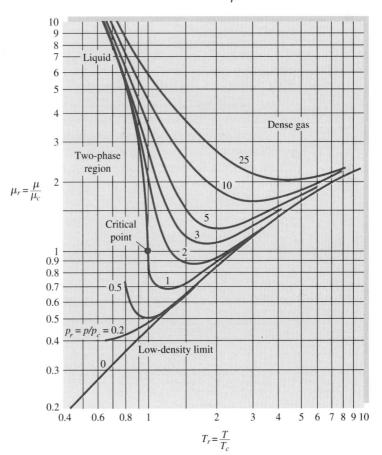

Fig. 1.6 Fluid viscosity nondimensionalized by critical-point properties. This generalized chart is characteristic of all fluids but is accurate only to ± 20 percent. *(From Ref. 25.)*

where V and L are characteristic velocity and length scales of the flow. The second form of Re illustrates that the ratio of μ to ρ has its own name, the *kinematic viscosity:*

$$\nu = \frac{\mu}{\rho} \qquad (1.25)$$

It is called kinematic because the mass units cancel, leaving only the dimensions $\{L^2/T\}$.

Generally, the first thing a fluids engineer should do is estimate the Reynolds number range of the flow under study. Very low Re indicates viscous *creeping* motion, where inertia effects are negligible. Moderate Re implies a smoothly varying *laminar* flow. High Re probably spells *turbulent* flow, which is slowly varying in the time-mean but has superimposed strong random high-frequency fluctuations. Explicit numerical values for low, moderate, and high Reynolds numbers cannot be stated here. They depend on flow geometry and will be discussed in Chaps. 5 through 7.

Table 1.4 also lists values of ν for the same eight fluids. The pecking order changes considerably, and mercury, the heaviest, has the smallest viscosity relative to its own weight. All gases have high ν relative to thin liquids such as gasoline, water, and alcohol. Oil and glycerin still have the highest ν, but the ratio is smaller. For given values of V and L in a flow, these fluids exhibit a spread of four orders of magnitude in the Reynolds number.

Flow between Plates

A classic problem is the flow induced between a fixed lower plate and an upper plate moving steadily at velocity V, as shown in Fig. 1.7. The clearance between plates is h, and the fluid is newtonian and does not slip at either plate. If the plates are large, this steady shearing motion will set up a velocity distribution $u(y)$, as shown, with $v = w = 0$. The fluid acceleration is zero everywhere.

With zero acceleration and assuming no pressure variation in the flow direction, you should show that a force balance on a small fluid element leads to the result that the shear stress is constant throughout the fluid. Then Eq. (1.23) becomes

$$\frac{du}{dy} = \frac{\tau}{\mu} = \text{const}$$

which we can integrate to obtain

$$u = a + by$$

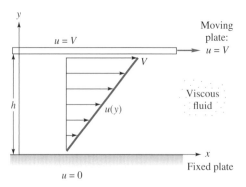

Fig. 1.7 Viscous flow induced by relative motion between two parallel plates.

The velocity distribution is linear, as shown in Fig. 1.7, and the constants a and b can be evaluated from the no-slip condition at the upper and lower walls:

$$u = \begin{cases} 0 = a + b\,(0) & \text{at } y = 0 \\ V = a + b\,(h) & \text{at } y = h \end{cases}$$

Hence $a = 0$ and $b = V/h$. Then the velocity profile between the plates is given by

$$u = V\frac{y}{h} \tag{1.26}$$

as indicated in Fig. 1.7. Turbulent flow (Chap. 6) does not have this shape.

Although viscosity has a profound effect on fluid motion, the actual viscous stresses are quite small in magnitude even for oils, as shown in the next example.

Problem-Solving Techniques

Fluid flow analysis is packed with problems to be solved. The present text has more than 1700 problem assignments. Solving a large number of these is a key to learning the subject. One must deal with equations, data, tables, assumptions, unit systems, and solution schemes. The degree of difficulty will vary, and we urge you to sample the whole spectrum of assignments, with or without the answers in the Appendix. Here are the recommended steps for problem solution:

1. Read the problem and restate it with your summary of the results desired.
2. From tables or charts, gather the needed property data: density, viscosity, etc.
3. Make sure you understand what is *asked*. Students are apt to answer the wrong question—for example, pressure instead of pressure gradient, lift force instead of drag force, or mass flow instead of volume flow. Read the problem carefully.
4. Make a detailed, *labeled* sketch of the system or control volume needed.
5. Think carefully and list your *assumptions*. You must decide if the flow is steady or unsteady, compressible or incompressible, viscous or inviscid, and whether a control volume or partial differential equations are needed.
6. Find an algebraic solution if possible. Then, if a numerical value is needed, use either the SI or BG unit systems reviewed in Sec. 1.4.
7. Report your solution, *labeled,* with the proper units and the proper number of significant figures (usually two or three) that the data uncertainty allows.

We shall follow these steps, where appropriate, in our example problems.

EXAMPLE 1.7

Suppose that the fluid being sheared in Fig. 1.7 is SAE 30 oil at 20°C. Compute the shear stress in the oil if $V = 3$ m/s and $h = 2$ cm.

Solution

• *System sketch:* This is shown earlier in Fig. 1.7.
• *Assumptions:* Linear velocity profile, laminar newtonian fluid, no slip at either plate surface.

- *Approach:*   The analysis of Fig. 1.7 leads to Eq. (1.26) for laminar flow.
- *Property values:*   From Table 1.4 for SAE 30 oil, the oil viscosity $\mu = 0.29$ kg/(m-s).
- *Solution steps:*   In Eq. (1.26), the only unknown is the fluid shear stress:

$$\tau = \mu \frac{V}{h} = \left(0.29 \, \frac{\text{kg}}{\text{m} \cdot \text{s}}\right) \frac{(3 \text{ m/s})}{(0.02 \text{ m})} = 43.5 \, \frac{\text{kg} \cdot \text{m/s}^2}{\text{m}^2} = 43.5 \, \frac{\text{N}}{\text{m}^2} \approx 44 \text{Pa} \qquad Ans.$$

- *Comments:*   Note the unit identities, 1 kg-m/s^2 $\equiv$ 1 N and 1 N/m^2 $\equiv$ 1 Pa. Although oil is very viscous, this shear stress is modest, about 2400 times less than atmospheric pressure. Viscous stresses in gases and thin (watery) liquids are even smaller.

Variation of Viscosity with Temperature

Temperature has a strong effect and pressure a moderate effect on viscosity. The viscosity of gases and most liquids increases slowly with pressure. Water is anomalous in showing a very slight decrease below 30°C. Since the change in viscosity is only a few percent up to 100 atm, we shall neglect pressure effects in this book.

Gas viscosity increases with temperature. Two common approximations are the power law and the Sutherland law:

$$\frac{\mu}{\mu_0} \approx \begin{cases} \left(\dfrac{T}{T_0}\right)^n & \text{power law} \\[2ex] \dfrac{(T/T_0)^{3/2}(T_0 + S)}{T + S} & \text{Sutherland law} \end{cases} \qquad (1.27)$$

where μ_0 is a known viscosity at a known absolute temperature T_0 (usually 273 K). The constants n and S are fit to the data, and both formulas are adequate over a wide range of temperatures. For air, $n \approx 0.7$ and $S \approx 110$ K $= 199$°R. Other values are given in Ref. 26.

Liquid viscosity decreases with temperature and is roughly exponential, $\mu \approx ae^{-bT}$; but a better fit is the empirical result that ln μ is quadratic in $1/T$, where T is absolute temperature:

$$\ln \frac{\mu}{\mu_0} \approx a + b\left(\frac{T_0}{T}\right) + c\left(\frac{T_0}{T}\right)^2 \qquad (1.28)$$

For water, with $T_0 = 273.16$ K, $\mu_0 = 0.001792$ kg/(m $\cdot$ s), suggested values are $a = -1.94$, $b = -4.80$, and $c = 6.74$, with accuracy about ± 1 percent. The viscosity of water is tabulated in Table A.1. For further viscosity data, see Refs. 21, 28, and 29.

Nonnewtonian Fluids

Fluids that do not follow the linear law of Eq. (1.23) are called *nonnewtonian* and are treated in books on *rheology* [16]. Figure 1.8a compares some examples to a newtonian fluid. For the nonlinear curves, the slope at any point is called the *apparent viscosity*.

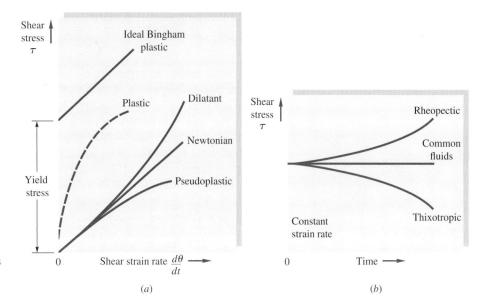

Fig. 1.8 Rheological behavior of various viscous materials: (*a*) stress versus strain rate; (*b*) effect of time on applied stress.

Fig. 1.9 A rotating parallel-disk rheometer (*Image of Kinexus rheometer, used with kind permission of Malvern Instruments*).

Rheometers

Dilatant.   This fluid is *shear-thickening,* increasing its resistance with increasing strain rate. Examples are suspensions of corn starch or sand in water. The classic case is *quicksand,* which stiffens up if one thrashes about.

Pseudoplastic.   A *shear-thinning* fluid is less resistant at higher strain rates. A very strong thinning is called *plastic.* Some of the many examples are polymer solutions, colloidal suspensions, paper pulp in water, latex paint, blood plasma, syrup, and molasses. The classic case is *paint,* which is thick when poured but thin when brushed at a high strain rate.

Bingham plastic.   The limiting case of a plastic substance is one that requires a finite yield stress before it begins to flow. Figure 1.8*a* shows yielding followed by linear behavior, but nonlinear flow can also occur. Some examples are clay suspensions, drilling mud, toothpaste, mayonnaise, chocolate, and mustard. The classic case is *catsup,* which will not come out of the bottle until you stress it by shaking.

A further complication of nonnewtonian behavior is the transient effect shown in Fig. 1.8*b.* Some fluids require a gradually increasing shear stress to maintain a constant strain rate and are called *rheopectic.* The opposite case of a fluid that thins out with time and requires decreasing stress is termed *thixotropic.* We neglect nonnewtonian effects in this book; see Ref. 16 for further study.

There are many commercial devices for measuring the shear stress versus strain rate behavior of both newtonian and nonnewtonian fluids. They are generically called *rheometers* and have various designs: parallel disks, cone-plate, rotating coaxial cylinders, torsion, extensional, and capillary tubes. Reference 29 gives a good discussion. A popular device is the parallel-disk rheometer, shown in Fig. 1.9. A thin layer of fluid is placed between the disks, one of which rotates. The resisting torque on the rotating disk is proportional to the viscosity of the fluid. A simplified theory for this device is given in Example 1.10.

Surface Tension

A liquid, being unable to expand freely, will form an *interface* with a second liquid or gas. The physical chemistry of such interfacial surfaces is quite complex, and whole textbooks are devoted to this specialty [30]. Molecules deep within the liquid repel each other because of their close packing. Molecules at the surface are less dense and attract each other. Since half of their neighbors are missing, the mechanical effect is that the surface is in tension. We can account adequately for surface effects in fluid mechanics with the concept of surface tension.

If a cut of length dL is made in an interfacial surface, equal and opposite forces of magnitude $Y\, dL$ are exposed normal to the cut and parallel to the surface, where Y is called the *coefficient of surface tension*. The dimensions of Y are $\{F/L\}$, with SI units of newtons per meter and BG units of pounds-force per foot. An alternate concept is to open up the cut to an area dA; this requires work to be done of amount $Y\, dA$. Thus the coefficient Y can also be regarded as the surface energy per unit area of the interface, in $N \cdot m/m^2$ or $ft \cdot lbf/ft^2$.

The two most common interfaces are water–air and mercury–air. For a clean surface at 20°C = 68°F, the measured surface tension is

$$Y = \begin{cases} 0.0050 \text{ lbf/ft} = 0.073 \text{ N/m} & \text{air–water} \\ 0.033 \text{ lbf/ft} = 0.48 \text{ N/m} & \text{air–mercury} \end{cases} \tag{1.29}$$

These are design values and can change considerably if the surface contains contaminants like detergents or slicks. Generally Y decreases with liquid temperature and is zero at the critical point. Values of Y for water are given in Fig. 1.10 and Table A.5.

If the interface is curved, a mechanical balance shows that there is a pressure difference across the interface, the pressure being higher on the concave side, as illustrated in Fig. 1.11. In Fig. 1.11*a*, the pressure increase in the interior of a liquid cylinder is balanced by two surface-tension forces:

$$2RL\, \Delta p = 2YL$$

or

$$\Delta p = \frac{Y}{R} \tag{1.30}$$

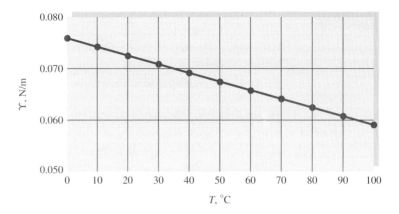

Fig. 1.10 Surface tension of a clean air–water interface. Data from Table A.5.

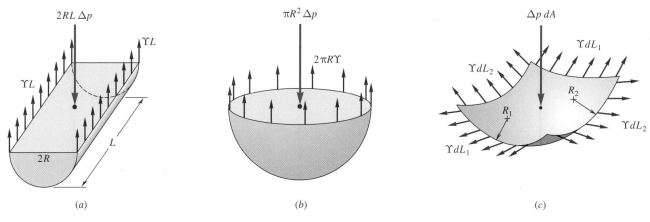

Fig. 1.11 Pressure change across a curved interface due to surface tension: (*a*) interior of a liquid cylinder; (*b*) interior of a spherical droplet; (*c*) general curved interface.

We are not considering the weight of the liquid in this calculation. In Fig. 1.11*b,* the pressure increase in the interior of a spherical droplet balances a ring of surface-tension force:

$$\pi R^2 \, \Delta p = 2\pi R \Upsilon$$

or

$$\Delta p = \frac{2\Upsilon}{R} \tag{1.31}$$

We can use this result to predict the pressure increase inside a soap bubble, which has *two* interfaces with air, an inner and outer surface of nearly the same radius *R*:

$$\Delta p_{\text{bubble}} \approx 2 \, \Delta p_{\text{droplet}} = \frac{4\Upsilon}{R} \tag{1.32}$$

Figure 1.11*c* shows the general case of an arbitrarily curved interface whose principal radii of curvature are R_1 and R_2. A force balance normal to the surface will show that the pressure increase on the concave side is

$$\Delta p = \Upsilon(R_1^{-1} + R_2^{-1}) \tag{1.33}$$

Equations (1.30) to (1.32) can all be derived from this general relation; for example, in Eq. (1.30), $R_1 = R$ and $R_2 = \infty$.

A second important surface effect is the *contact angle* θ, which appears when a liquid interface intersects with a solid surface, as in Fig. 1.12. The force balance would then involve both Υ and θ. If the contact angle is less than 90°, the liquid is said to *wet* the solid; if $\theta > 90°$, the liquid is termed *nonwetting.* For example, water wets soap but does not wet wax. Water is extremely wetting to a clean glass surface, with $\theta \approx 0°$. Like Υ, the contact angle θ is sensitive to the actual physicochemical conditions of the solid–liquid interface. For a clean mercury–air–glass interface, $\theta = 130°$.

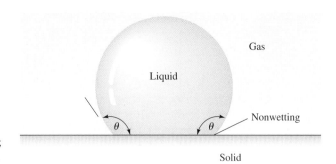

Fig. 1.12 Contact-angle effects at liquid–gas–solid interface. If $\theta < 90°$, the liquid "wets" the solid; if $\theta > 90°$, the liquid is nonwetting.

Example 1.8 illustrates how surface tension causes a fluid interface to rise or fall in a capillary tube.

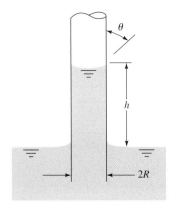

E1.8

EXAMPLE 1.8

Derive an expression for the change in height h in a circular tube of a liquid with surface tension Y and contact angle θ, as in Fig. E1.8.

Solution

The vertical component of the ring surface-tension force at the interface in the tube must balance the weight of the column of fluid of height h:

$$2\pi R Y \cos\theta = \gamma\pi R^2 h$$

Solving for h, we have the desired result:

$$h = \frac{2Y\cos\theta}{\gamma R} \qquad\qquad Ans.$$

Thus the capillary height increases inversely with tube radius R and is positive if $\theta < 90°$ (wetting liquid) and negative (capillary depression) if $\theta > 90°$.

Suppose that $R = 1$ mm. Then the capillary rise for a water–air–glass interface, $\theta \approx 0°$, $Y = 0.073$ N/m, and $\rho = 1000$ kg/m^3 is

$$h = \frac{2(0.073 \text{ N/m})(\cos 0°)}{(1000 \text{ kg/m}^3)(9.81 \text{ m/s}^2)(0.001 \text{ m})} = 0.015 \text{ (N}\cdot\text{s}^2)/\text{kg} = 0.015 \text{ m} = 1.5 \text{ cm}$$

For a mercury–air–glass interface, with $\theta = 130°$, $Y = 0.48$ N/m, and $\rho = 13,600$ kg/m^3, the capillary rise is

$$h = \frac{2(0.48)(\cos 130°)}{13,600(9.81)(0.001)} = -0.0046 \text{ m} = -0.46 \text{ cm}$$

When a small-diameter tube is used to make pressure measurements (Chap. 2), these capillary effects must be corrected for.

Vapor Pressure

Vapor pressure is the pressure at which a liquid boils and is in equilibrium with its own vapor. For example, the vapor pressure of water at 68°F is 49 lbf/ft^2, while that of mercury is only 0.0035 lbf/ft^2. If the liquid pressure is greater than the vapor pressure, the only exchange between liquid and vapor is evaporation at the interface. If, however, the liquid pressure falls below the vapor pressure, vapor bubbles begin to appear in the liquid. If water is heated to 212°F, its vapor pressure rises to 2116 lbf/ft^2, and thus water at normal atmospheric pressure will boil. When the liquid pressure is dropped below the vapor pressure due to a flow phenomenon, we call the process *cavitation*. If water is accelerated from rest to about 50 ft/s, its pressure drops by about 15 lbf/in^2, or 1 atm. This can cause cavitation [31].

The dimensionless parameter describing flow-induced boiling is the *cavitation number*

$$\text{Ca} = \frac{p_a - p_v}{\frac{1}{2}\rho V^2} \qquad (1.34)$$

where p_a = ambient pressure
$\quad\; p_v$ = vapor pressure
$\quad\; V$ = characteristic flow velocity
$\quad\; \rho$ = fluid density

Depending on the geometry, a given flow has a critical value of Ca below which the flow will begin to cavitate. Values of surface tension and vapor pressure of water are given in Table A.5. The vapor pressure of water is plotted in Fig. 1.13.

Figure 1.14*a* shows cavitation bubbles being formed on the low-pressure surfaces of a marine propeller. When these bubbles move into a higher-pressure region, they collapse implosively. Cavitation collapse can rapidly spall and erode metallic surfaces and eventually destroy them, as shown in Fig. 1.14*b*.

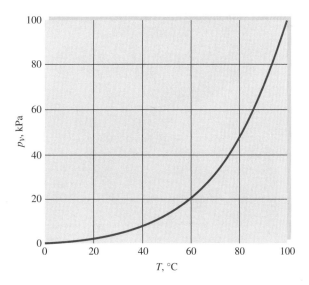

Fig. 1.13 Vapor pressure of water. Data from Table A.5.

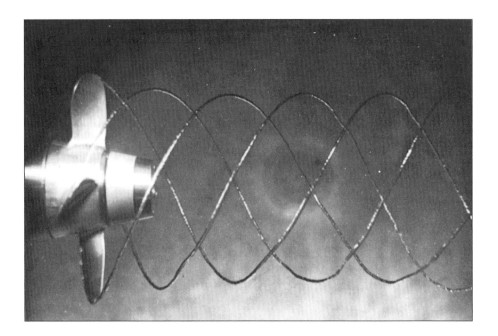

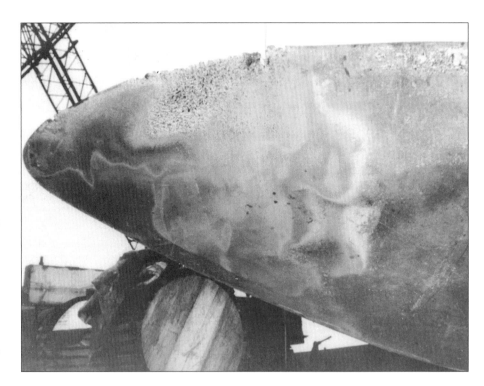

Fig. 1.14 Two aspects of cavitation bubble formation in liquid flows: (*a*) Beauty: spiral bubble sheets form from the surface of a marine propeller (*courtesy of the Garfield Thomas Water Tunnel, Pennsylvania State University*); (*b*) ugliness: collapsing bubbles erode a propeller surface (*courtesy of Thomas T. Huang, David Taylor Research Center*).

EXAMPLE 1.9

A certain torpedo, moving in fresh water at 10°C, has a minimum-pressure point given by the formula

$$p_{min} = p_0 - 0.35\, \rho V^2 \qquad (1)$$

where $p_0 = 115$ kPa, ρ is the water density, and V is the torpedo velocity. Estimate the velocity at which cavitation bubbles will form on the torpedo. The constant 0.35 is dimensionless.

Solution

- *Assumption:* Cavitation bubbles form when the minimum pressure equals the vapor pressure p_v.
- *Approach:* Solve Eq. (1) above, which is related to the Bernoulli equation from Example 1.3, for the velocity when $p_{min} = p_v$. Use SI units (m, N, kg, s).
- *Property values:* At 10°C, read Table A.1 for $\rho = 1000$ kg/m^3 and Table A.5 for $p_v = 1.227$ kPa.
- *Solution steps:* Insert the known data into Eq. (1) and solve for the velocity, using SI units:

$$p_{min} = p_v = 1227 \text{ Pa} = 115{,}000 \text{ Pa} - 0.35\left(1000\,\frac{\text{kg}}{\text{m}^3}\right)V^2, \text{ with } V \text{ in m/s}$$

$$\text{Solve } V^2 = \frac{(115{,}000 - 1227)}{0.35(1000)} = 325\,\frac{\text{m}^2}{\text{s}^2} \text{ or } V = \sqrt{325} \approx 18.0 \text{m/s} \qquad Ans.$$

- *Comments:* Note that the use of SI units requires no conversion factors, as discussed in Example 1.3*b*. Pressures must be entered in pascals, not kilopascals.

No-Slip and No-Temperature-Jump Conditions

When a fluid flow is bounded by a solid surface, molecular interactions cause the fluid in contact with the surface to seek momentum and energy equilibrium with that surface. All liquids essentially are in equilibrium with the surfaces they contact. All gases are, too, except under the most rarefied conditions [18]. Excluding rarefied gases, then, all fluids at a point of contact with a solid take on the velocity and temperature of that surface:

$$V_{\text{fluid}} \equiv V_{\text{wall}} \qquad T_{\text{fluid}} \equiv T_{\text{wall}} \qquad (1.35)$$

These are called the *no-slip* and *no-temperature-jump conditions,* respectively. They serve as *boundary conditions* for analysis of fluid flow past a solid surface. Figure 1.15 illustrates the no-slip condition for water flow past the top and bottom surfaces of a fixed thin plate. The flow past the upper surface is disorderly, or turbulent, while the lower surface flow is smooth, or laminar.[6] In both cases there is clearly no slip at the wall, where the water takes on the zero velocity of the fixed plate. The velocity profile is made visible by the discharge of a line of hydrogen bubbles from the wire shown stretched across the flow.

---

[6]Laminar and turbulent flows are studied in Chaps. 6 and 7.

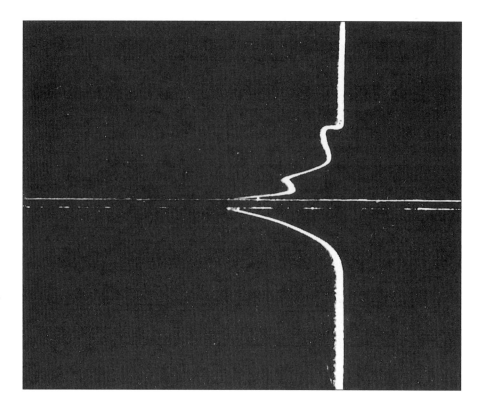

Fig. 1.15 The no-slip condition in water flow past a thin fixed plate. The upper flow is turbulent; the lower flow is laminar. The velocity profile is made visible by a line of hydrogen bubbles discharged from the wire across the flow. *(National Committee for Fluid Mechanics Films, Education Development Center, Inc., © 1972.)*

To decrease the mathematical difficulty, the no-slip condition is partially relaxed in the analysis of inviscid flow (Chap. 8). The flow is allowed to "slip" past the surface but not to permeate through the surface

$$V_{\text{normal}}(\text{fluid}) \equiv V_{\text{normal}}(\text{solid}) \tag{1.36}$$

while the tangential velocity V_t is allowed to be independent of the wall. The analysis is much simpler, but the flow patterns are highly idealized.

For high-viscosity newtonian fluids, the linear velocity assumption and the no-slip conditions can yield some sophisticated approximate analyses for two- and three-dimensional viscous flows. The following example, for a type of rotating-disk viscometer, will illustrate.

EXAMPLE 1.10

An oil film of viscosity μ and thickness $h \ll R$ lies between a solid wall and a circular disk, as in Fig. E1.10. The disk is rotated steadily at angular velocity Ω. Noting that both velocity and shear stress vary with radius r, derive a formula for the torque M required to rotate the disk. Neglect air drag.

Solution

• *System sketch:* Figure E1.10 shows a side view (*a*) and a top view (*b*) of the system.

(a)   (b)

E1.10

- *Assumptions:* Linear velocity profile, laminar flow, no-slip, local shear stress given by Eq. (1.23).
- *Approach:* Estimate the shear stress on a circular strip of width dr and area $dA = 2\pi r$ dr in Fig. E1.10b, then find the moment dM about the origin caused by this shear stress. Integrate over the entire disk to find the total moment M.
- *Property values:* Constant oil viscosity μ. In this steady flow, oil density is not relevant.
- *Solution steps:* At radius r, the velocity in the oil is tangential, varying from zero at the fixed wall (no-slip) to $u = \Omega r$ at the disk surface (also no-slip). The shear stress at this position is thus

$$\tau = \mu \frac{du}{dy} \approx \mu \frac{\Omega r}{h}$$

This shear stress is everywhere perpendicular to the radius from the origin (see Fig. E1.10b). Then the total moment about the disk origin, caused by shearing this circular strip, can be found and integrated:

$$dM = (\tau)(dA)r = \left(\frac{\mu\Omega r}{h}\right)(2\pi r\, dr)r, \quad M = \int dM = \frac{2\pi\mu\Omega}{h}\int_0^R r^3 dr = \frac{\pi\mu\Omega R^4}{2h} \quad Ans.$$

- *Comments:* This is a simplified engineering analysis, which neglects possible edge effects, air drag on the top of the disk, and the turbulence that might ensue if the disk rotates too fast.

Slip Flow in Gases

The "free slip" boundary condition, Eq. (1.36), is an unrealistic mathematical artifice to enable inviscid-flow solutions. However, actual, realistic wall slip occurs in rarefied gases, where there are too few molecules to establish momentum equilibrium with the wall. In 1879, the physicist James Clerk Maxwell used the kinetic theory of gases to predict a *slip velocity* at the wall:

$$\delta u_{\text{wall}} \approx \ell \frac{\partial u}{\partial y}\bigg|_{\text{wall}} \tag{1.37}$$

where ℓ is the mean free path of the gas, and u and x are along the wall. If ℓ is very small compared to the lateral scale L of the flow, the *Knudsen number*, Kn = ℓ/L, is small, and the slip velocity is near zero. We will assign a few slip problems, but the details of rarefied gas flow are left for further reading in Refs. 18 and 52.

Speed of Sound

In gas flow, one must be aware of *compressibility* effects (significant density changes caused by the flow). We shall see in Sec. 4.2 and in Chap. 9 that compressibility becomes important when the flow velocity reaches a significant fraction of the speed of sound of the fluid. The *speed of sound a* of a fluid is the rate of propagation of small-disturbance pressure pulses ("sound waves") through the fluid. In Chap. 9 we shall show, from momentum and thermodynamic arguments, that the speed of sound is defined by a pressure-density derivative proportional to the *isentropic bulk modulus*:

$$a^2 = \frac{\beta}{\rho} = \left(\frac{\partial p}{\partial \rho}\right)_s = k\left(\frac{\partial p}{\partial \rho}\right)_T, \quad k = \frac{c_p}{c_v}$$

where β = isentropic bulk modulus = $\rho\left(\dfrac{\partial p}{\partial \rho}\right)_s$.

This is true for either a liquid or a gas, but it is for *gases* that the problem of compressibility occurs. For an ideal gas, Eq. (1.10), we obtain the simple formula

$$a_{\text{ideal gas}} = (kRT)^{1/2} \tag{1.38}$$

where R is the gas constant, Eq. (1.11), and T the absolute temperature. For example, for air at 20°C, $a = \{(1.40)[287 \text{ m}^2/(\text{s}^2 \cdot \text{K})](293 \text{ K})\}^{1/2} \approx 343$ m/s (1126 ft/s = 768 mi/h). If, in this case, the air velocity reaches a significant fraction of a, say, 100 m/s, then we must account for compressibility effects (Chap. 9). Another way to state this is to account for compressibility when the *Mach number* Ma = V/a of the flow reaches about 0.3.

The speed of sound of water is tabulated in Table A.5. For near perfect gases, like air, the speed of sound is simply calculated by Eq. (1.38). Many liquids have their bulk modulus listed in Table A.3. Note, however, as discussed in Ref. 51, even a very small amount of dissolved gas in a liquid can reduce the mixture speed of sound by up to 80 percent.

EXAMPLE 1.11

A commercial airplane flies at 540 mi/h at a standard altitude of 30,000 ft. What is its Mach number?

Solution

• *Approach:* Find the "standard" speed of sound; divide it into the velocity, using proper units.
• *Property values:* From Table A.6, at 30,000 ft (9144 m), $a \approx 303$ m/s. Check this against the standard temperature, estimated from the table to be 229 K. From Eq. (1.38) for air,

$$a = [kR_{\text{air}}T]^{1/2} = [1.4(287)(229)]^{1/2} \approx 303 \text{ m/s}.$$

• *Solution steps:* Convert the airplane velocity to m/s:

$$V = (540 \text{ mi/h})[0.44704 \text{ m/s/(mi/h)}] \approx 241 \text{ m/s}.$$

Then the Mach number is given by

$$\text{Ma} = V/a = (241 \text{ m/s})/(303 \text{ m/s}) = 0.80 \qquad \textit{Ans.}$$

• *Comments:*   This value, Ma = 0.80, is typical of present-day commercial airliners.

1.8 Basic Flow Analysis Techniques

There are three basic ways to attack a fluid flow problem. They are equally important for a student learning the subject, and this book tries to give adequate coverage to each method:

1. Control-volume, or *integral* analysis (Chap. 3).
2. Infinitesimal system, or *differential* analysis (Chap. 4).
3. Experimental study, or *dimensional* analysis (Chap. 5).

In all cases, the flow must satisfy the three basic laws of mechanics plus a thermodynamic state relation and associated boundary conditions:

1. Conservation of mass (continuity).
2. Linear momentum (Newton's second law).
3. First law of thermodynamics (conservation of energy).
4. A state relation like $\rho = \rho(p, T)$.
5. Appropriate boundary conditions at solid surfaces, interfaces, inlets, and exits.

In integral and differential analyses, these five relations are modeled mathematically and solved by computational methods. In an experimental study, the fluid itself performs this task without the use of any mathematics. In other words, these laws are believed to be fundamental to physics, and no fluid flow is known to violate them.

1.9 Flow Patterns: Streamlines, Streaklines, and Pathlines

Fluid mechanics is a highly visual subject. The patterns of flow can be visualized in a dozen different ways, and you can view these sketches or photographs and learn a great deal qualitatively and often quantitatively about the flow.

Four basic types of line patterns are used to visualize flows:

1. A *streamline* is a line everywhere tangent to the velocity vector at a given instant.
2. A *pathline* is the actual path traversed by a given fluid particle.
3. A *streakline* is the locus of particles that have earlier passed through a prescribed point. [33]
4. A *timeline* is a set of fluid particles that form a line at a given instant.

The streamline is convenient to calculate mathematically, while the other three are easier to generate experimentally. Note that a streamline and a timeline are instantaneous lines, while the pathline and the streakline are generated by the passage of time. The velocity profile shown in Fig. 1.15 is really a timeline generated earlier by a single discharge of bubbles from the wire. A pathline can be found by a time exposure of a single marked particle moving through the flow. Streamlines are difficult to

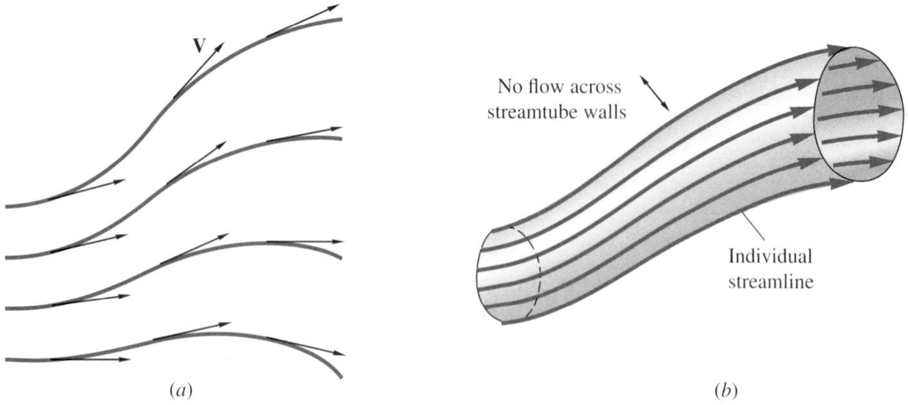

Fig. 1.16 The most common method of flow-pattern presentation: (*a*) Streamlines are everywhere tangent to the local velocity vector; (*b*) a streamtube is formed by a closed collection of streamlines.

No flow across streamtube walls

Individual streamline

(*a*)

(*b*)

generate experimentally in unsteady flow unless one marks a great many particles and notes their direction of motion during a very short time interval [32]. In steady flow, where velocity varies only with position, the situation simplifies greatly:

Streamlines, pathlines, and streaklines are identical in steady flow.

In fluid mechanics the most common mathematical result for visualization purposes is the streamline pattern. Figure 1.16*a* shows a typical set of streamlines, and Fig. 1.16*b* shows a closed pattern called a *streamtube*. By definition the fluid within a streamtube is confined there because it cannot cross the streamlines; thus the streamtube walls need not be solid but may be fluid surfaces.

Figure 1.17 shows an arbitrary velocity vector. If the elemental arc length dr of a streamline is to be parallel to **V**, their respective components must be in proportion:

Streamline:
$$\frac{dx}{u} = \frac{dy}{v} = \frac{dz}{w} = \frac{dr}{V} \tag{1.39}$$

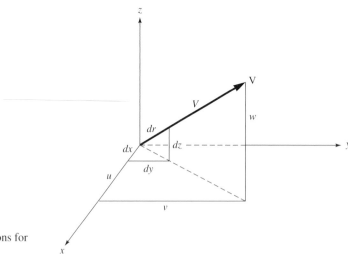

Fig. 1.17 Geometric relations for defining a streamline.

If the velocities (u, v, w) are known functions of position and time, Eq. (1.39) can be integrated to find the streamline passing through the initial point (x_0, y_0, z_0, t_0). The method is straightforward for steady flows but may be laborious for unsteady flow.

Flow Visualization

Clever experimentation can produce revealing images of a fluid flow pattern, as shown earlier in Figs. 1.14a and 1.15. For example, streaklines are produced by the continuous release of marked particles (dye, smoke, or bubbles) from a given point. If the flow is steady, the streaklines will be identical to the streamlines and pathlines of the flow.

Some methods of flow visualization include the following [34–36]:

1. Dye, smoke, or bubble discharges.
2. Surface powder or flakes on liquid flows.
3. Floating or neutral-density particles.
4. Optical techniques that detect density changes in gas flows: shadowgraph, schlieren, and interferometer.
5. Tufts of yarn attached to boundary surfaces.
6. Evaporative coatings on boundary surfaces.
7. Luminescent fluids, additives, or bioluminescence.
8. Particle image velocimetry (PIV).

Figures 1.14a and 1.15 were both visualized by bubble releases. Another example is the use of particles in Fig. 1.18 to visualize a flow negotiating a 180° turn in a serpentine channel [42].

Figure 1.18a is at a low, laminar Reynolds number of 1000. The flow is steady, and the particles form streaklines showing that the flow cannot make the sharp turn without separating away from the bottom wall.

Figure 1.18b is at a higher, turbulent Reynolds number of 30,000. The flow is unsteady, and the streaklines would be chaotic and smeared, unsuitable for visualization. The image is thus produced by the new technique of particle image velocimetry [37]. In PIV, hundreds of particles are tagged and photographed at two closely spaced times. Particle movements thus indicate local velocity vectors. These hundreds of vectors are then smoothed by repeated computer operations until the time-mean flow pattern in Fig. 1.18b is achieved. Modern flow experiments and numerical models use computers extensively to create their visualizations, as described in the text by Yang [38].

Mathematical details of streamline/streakline/pathline analysis are given in Ref. 33. References 39–41 are beautiful albums of flow photographs. References 34–36 are monographs on flow visualization techniques.

Fluid mechanics is a marvelous subject for visualization, not just for still (steady) patterns, but also for moving (unsteady) motion studies. An outstanding list of available flow movies and videotapes is given by Carr and Young [43].

(*a*)

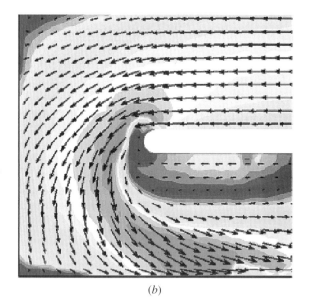

Fig. 1.18 Two visualizations of flow making a 180° turn in a serpentine channel: (*a*) particle streaklines at a Reynolds number of 1000; (*b*) time-mean particle image velocimetry (PIV) at a turbulent Reynolds number of 30,000. *(From Ref. 42, by permission of the American Society of Mechanical Engineers.)*

(*b*)

1.10 The Fundamentals of Engineering (FE) Examination

The road toward a professional engineer's license has a first stop, the Fundamentals of Engineering Examination, known as the FE exam. It was formerly known as the Engineer-in-Training (E-I-T) Examination. This eight-hour national test will probably soon be required of all engineering graduates, not just for licensure, but as a student assessment tool. The 120-problem, four-hour morning session covers many general studies:

Mathematics—15%	Ethics and business practices—7%	Material properties—7%
Engineering probability and statistics—7%	Engineering economics—8%	**Fluid mechanics—7%**
Chemistry—9%	Engineering mechanics—10%	Electricity and magnetism—9%
Computers—7%	Strength of materials—7%	Thermodynamics—7%

For the 60-problem, four-hour afternoon session you may choose one of seven modules: chemical, civil, electrical, environmental, industrial, mechanical, and other/general engineering. Note that fluid mechanics is an integral topic of the examination. Therefore, for practice, this text includes a number of end-of-chapter FE problems where appropriate.

The format for the FE exam questions is multiple-choice, usually with five selections, chosen carefully to tempt you with plausible answers if you used incorrect units, forgot to double or halve something, are missing a factor of π, or the like. In some cases, the selections are unintentionally ambiguous, such as the following example from a previous exam:

Transition from laminar to turbulent flow occurs at a Reynolds number of
(A) 900   (B) 1200   (C) 1500   (D) 2100   (E) 3000

The "correct" answer was graded as (D), Re = 2100. Clearly the examiner was thinking, but forgot to specify, Re_d for *flow in a smooth circular pipe,* since (see Chaps. 6 and 7) transition is highly dependent on geometry, surface roughness, and the length scale used in the definition of Re. The moral is not to get peevish about the exam but simply to go with the flow (pun intended) and decide which answer best fits an undergraduate training situation. Every effort has been made to keep the FE exam questions in this text unambiguous.

1.11 The History of Fluid Mechanics

Many distinguished workers have contributed to the development of fluid mechanics. If you are a student, however, this is probably not the time to be studying history. Later, during your career, you will enjoy reading about the history of, not just fluid mechanics, but all of science. Here are some names that will be mentioned as we encounter their contributions in the rest of this book.

Name	Important Contribution
Archimedes (285–212 BC)	Established laws of buoyancy and floating bodies.
Leonardo da Vinci (1452–1519)	Formulated the first equation of continuity.
Isaac Newton (1642–1727)	Postulated the law of linear viscous stresses.
Leonhard Euler (1707–1783)	Developed Bernoulli's equation by solving the basic equations.
L. M. H. Navier (1785–1836)	Formulated the basic differential equations of viscous flow.
Jean Louis Poiseuille (1799–1869)	Performed first experiments on laminar flow in tubes.
Osborne Reynolds (1842–1912)	Explained the phenomenon of transition to turbulence.
Ludwig Prandtl (1875–1953)	Formulated boundary layer theory, predicting flow separation.
Theodore von Kármán (1881–1963)	Major advances in aerodynamics and turbulence theory.

References [12] through [15] provide a comprehensive treatment of the history of fluid mechanics.

Summary

This chapter has discussed the behavior of a fluid—which, unlike a solid, must move if subjected to a shear stress—and the important fluid properties. The writer believes the most important property to be the velocity vector field $\mathbf{V}(x, y, z, t)$. Following closely are the pressure p, density ρ, and temperature T. Many secondary properties enter into various flow problems: viscosity μ, thermal conductivity k, specific weight γ, surface tension Y, speed of sound a, and vapor pressure p_v. You must learn to locate and use all these properties to become proficient in fluid mechanics.

There was a brief discussion of the five different kinds of mathematical relations we will use to solve flow problems—mass conservation, linear momentum, first law of thermodynamics, equations of state, and appropriate boundary conditions at walls and other boundaries.

Flow patterns are also discussed briefly. The most popular, and useful, scheme is to plot the field of streamlines, that is, lines everywhere parallel to the local velocity vector.

Since the earth is 75 percent covered with water and 100 percent covered with air, the scope of fluid mechanics is vast and touches nearly every human endeavor. The sciences of meteorology, physical oceanography, and hydrology are concerned with naturally occurring fluid flows, as are medical studies of breathing and blood circulation. All transportation problems involve fluid motion, with well-developed specialties in aerodynamics of aircraft and rockets and in naval hydrodynamics of ships and submarines. Almost all our electric energy is developed either from water flow, air flow through wind turbines, or from steam flow through turbine generators. All combustion problems involve fluid motion as do the more classic problems of irrigation, flood control, water supply, sewage disposal, projectile motion, and oil and gas pipelines. The aim of this book is to present enough fundamental concepts and practical applications in fluid mechanics to prepare you to move smoothly into any of these specialized fields of the science of flow—and then be prepared to move out again as new technologies develop.

Problems

Most of the problems herein are fairly straightforward. More diffi-cult or open-ended assignments are labeled with an asterisk as in Prob. 1.18. Problems labeled with a computer icon 📖 may require the use of a computer. The standard end-of-chapter problems 1.1 to 1.86 (categorized in the problem list below) are followed by funda-mentals of engineering (FE) exam problems FE1.1 to FE1.10 and comprehensive problems C1.1 to C1.12.

Problem Distribution

Section	Topic	Problems
1.1, 1.4, 1.5	Fluid continuum concept	1.1–1.4
1.6	Dimensions and units	1.5–1.23
1.8	Thermodynamic properties	1.24–1.37
1.9	Viscosity, no-slip condition	1.38–1.61
1.9	Surface tension	1.62–1.71
1.9	Vapor pressure; cavitation	1.72–1.74
1.9	Speed of sound, Mach number	1.75–1.80
1.11	Streamlines	1.81–1.83
1.2	History of fluid mechanics	1.84–1.85a–n
1.13	Experimental uncertainty	1.86–1.90

The concept of a fluid

P1.1 A gas at 20°C may be considered *rarefied,* deviating from the continuum concept, when it contains less than 10^{12} molecules per cubic millimeter. If Avogadro's number is 6.023 E23 molecules per mole, what absolute pressure (in Pa) for air does this represent?

P1.2 Table A.6 lists the density of the standard atmosphere as a function of altitude. Use these values to estimate, crudely—say, within a factor of 2—the number of molecules of air in the entire atmosphere of the earth.

P1.3 For the triangular element in Fig. P1.3, show that a *tilted* free liquid surface, in contact with an atmosphere at pres-sure p_a, must undergo shear stress and hence begin to flow. *Hint:* Account for the weight of the fluid and show that a no-shear condition will cause horizontal forces to be out of balance.

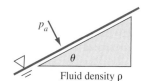

P1.3   Fluid density ρ

P1.4 Sand, and other granular materials, appear to *flow;* that is, you can pour them from a container or a hopper. There are whole textbooks on the "transport" of granular materials [54]. Therefore, is sand a *fluid*? Explain.

Dimensions and units

P1.5 The *mean free path* of a gas, l, is defined as the average distance traveled by molecules between collisions. A pro-posed formula for estimating l of an ideal gas is

$$l = 1.26 \frac{\mu}{\rho \sqrt{RT}}$$

What are the dimensions of the constant 1.26? Use the for-mula to estimate the mean free path of air at 20°C and 7 kPa. Would you consider air rarefied at this condition?

P1.6 Henri Darcy, a French engineer, proposed that the pressure drop Δp for flow at velocity V through a tube of length L could be correlated in the form

$$\frac{\Delta p}{\rho} = \alpha L V^2$$

If Darcy's formulation is consistent, what are the dimen-sions of the coefficient α?

P1.7 Convert the following inappropriate quantities into SI units: (*a*) 2.283 E7 U.S. gallons per day; (*b*) 4.5 furlongs per minute (racehorse speed); and (*c*) 72,800 avoirdupois ounces per acre.

P1.8 Suppose we know little about the strength of materials but are told that the bending stress σ in a beam is *proportional* to the beam half-thickness y and also depends on the bending moment M and the beam area moment of inertia I. We also learn that, for the particular case $M = 2900$ in · lbf, $y = 1.5$ in, and $I = 0.4$ in^4, the predicted stress is 75 MPa. Using this information and dimensional rea-soning only, find, to three significant figures, the only possible dimensionally homogeneous formula $\sigma = y\, f(M, I)$.

P1.9 A hemispherical container, 26 inches in diameter, is filled with a liquid at 20°C and weighed. The liquid weight is found to be 1617 ounces. (*a*) What is the density of the fluid, in kg/m^3? (*b*) What fluid might this be? Assume stan-dard gravity, $g = 9.807$ m/s^2.

P1.10 The Stokes-Oseen formula [33] for drag force F on a sphere of diameter D in a fluid stream of low velocity V, density ρ, and viscosity μ is

$$F = 3\pi\mu DV + \frac{9\pi}{16}\rho V^2 D^2$$

Is this formula dimensionally homogeneous?

P1.11 In English Engineering units, the specific heat c_p of air at room temperature is approximately 0.24 Btu/(lbm-°F). When working with kinetic energy relations, it is more ap-propriate to express c_p as a velocity-squared per absolute degree. Give the numerical value, in this form, of c_p for air in (*a*) SI units, and (*b*) BG units.

P1.12 For low-speed (laminar) steady flow through a circular pipe, as shown in Fig. P1.12, the velocity u varies with radius and takes the form

$$u = B\frac{\Delta p}{\mu}(r_0^2 - r^2)$$

where μ is the fluid viscosity and Δp is the pressure drop from entrance to exit. What are the dimensions of the constant B?

Pipe wall

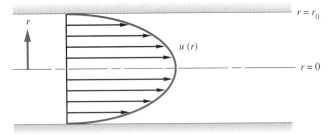

P1.12

P1.13 The efficiency η of a pump is defined as the (dimensionless) ratio of the power developed by the flow to the power required to drive the pump:

$$\eta = \frac{Q\Delta p}{\text{input power}}$$

where Q is the volume rate of flow and Δp is the pressure rise produced by the pump. Suppose that a certain pump develops a pressure rise of 35 lbf/in^2 when its flow rate is 40 L/s. If the input power is 16 hp, what is the efficiency?

*P1.14 Figure P1.14 shows the flow of water over a dam. The volume flow Q is known to depend only on crest width B, acceleration of gravity g, and upstream water height H above the dam crest. It is further known that Q is proportional to B. What is the form of the only possible dimensionally homogeneous relation for this flow rate?

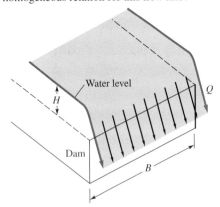

P1.14

P1.15 The height H that fluid rises in a liquid barometer tube depends upon the liquid density ρ, the barometric pressure p, and the acceleration of gravity g. (a) Arrange these four variables into a single dimensionless group. (b) Can you deduce (or guess) the numerical value of your group?

P1.16 Algebraic equations such as Bernoulli's relation, Eq. (1) of Example 1.3, are dimensionally consistent, but what about differential equations? Consider, for example, the boundary-layer x-momentum equation, first derived by Ludwig Prandtl in 1904:

$$\rho u\frac{\partial u}{\partial x} + \rho v\frac{\partial u}{\partial y} = -\frac{\partial p}{\partial x} + \rho g_x + \frac{\partial \tau}{\partial y}$$

where τ is the boundary-layer shear stress and g_x is the component of gravity in the x direction. Is this equation dimensionally consistent? Can you draw a general conclusion?

P1.17 The Hazen-Williams hydraulics formula for volume rate of flow Q through a pipe of diameter D and length L is given by

$$Q \approx 61.9\, D^{2.63}\left(\frac{\Delta p}{L}\right)^{0.54}$$

where Δp is the pressure drop required to drive the flow. What are the dimensions of the constant 61.9? Can this formula be used with confidence for various liquids and gases?

*P1.18 For small particles at low velocities, the first term in the Stokes-Oseen drag law, Prob. 1.10, is dominant; hence, $F \approx KV$, where K is a constant. Suppose a particle of mass m is constrained to move horizontally from the initial position $x = 0$ with initial velocity V_0. Show (a) that its velocity will decrease exponentially with time and (b) that it will stop after traveling a distance $x = mV_0/K$.

P1.19 In his study of the circular hydraulic jump formed by a faucet flowing into a sink, Watson [53] proposed a parameter combining volume flow rate Q, density ρ, and viscosity μ of the fluid, and depth h of the water in the sink. He claims that his grouping is dimensionless, with Q in the numerator. Can you verify this?

P1.20 Books on porous media and atomization claim that the viscosity μ and surface tension Y of a fluid can be combined with a characteristic velocity U to form an important dimensionless parameter. (a) Verify that this is so. (b) Evaluate this parameter for water at 20°C and a velocity of 3.5 cm/s. *Note:* You get extra credit if you know the name of this parameter.

P1.21 Aeronautical engineers measure the pitching moment M_0 of a wing and then write it in the following form for use in other cases:

$$M_0 = \beta V^2 AC\rho$$

where V is the wing velocity, A the wing area, C the wing chord length, and ρ the air density. What are the dimensions of the coefficient β?

P1.22 The *Ekman number*, Ek, arises in geophysical fluid dynamics. It is a dimensionless parameter combining seawater density ρ, a characteristic length L, seawater viscosity μ, and the Coriolis frequency $\Omega \sin\varphi$, where Ω is the rotation rate of the earth and φ is the latitude angle. Determine the correct form of Ek if the viscosity is in the numerator.

P1.23 During World War II, Sir Geoffrey Taylor, a British fluid dynamicist, used dimensional analysis to estimate the energy released by an atomic bomb explosion. He assumed that the energy released E, was a function of blast wave radius R, air density ρ, and time t. Arrange these variables into a single dimensionless group, which we may term the *blast wave number*.

Thermodynamic properties

P1.24 Air, assumed to be an ideal gas with $k = 1.40$, flows isentropically through a nozzle. At section 1, conditions are sea level standard (see Table A.6). At section 2, the temperature is −50°C. Estimate (a) the pressure, and (b) the density of the air at section 2.

P1.25 On a summer day in Narragansett, Rhode Island, the air temperature is 74°F and the barometric pressure is 14.5 lbf/in². Estimate the air density in kg/m³.

P1.26 When we in the United States say a car's tire is filled "to 32 lb," we mean that its internal pressure is 32 lbf/in² above the ambient atmosphere. If the tire is at sea level, has a volume of 3.0 ft³, and is at 75°F, estimate the total weight of air, in lbf, inside the tire.

P1.27 For steam at a pressure of 45 atm, some values of temperature and specific volume are as follows, from Ref. 23:

T, °F	500	600	700	800	900
v, ft³/lbm	0.7014	0.8464	0.9653	1.074	1.177

Find an average value of the predicted gas constant R in m²/(s² · K). Does this data reasonably approximate an ideal gas? If not, explain.

P1.28 Wet atmospheric air at 100 percent relative humidity contains saturated water vapor and, by Dalton's law of partial pressures,

$$p_{atm} = p_{dry\ air} + p_{water\ vapor}$$

Suppose this wet atmosphere is at 40°C and 1 atm. Calculate the density of this 100 percent humid air, and compare it with the density of dry air at the same conditions.

P1.29 A compressed-air tank holds 5 ft³ of air at 120 lbf/in² "gage," that is, above atmospheric pressure. Estimate the

energy, in ft-lbf, required to compress this air from the atmosphere, assuming an ideal isothermal process.

P1.30 Repeat Prob. 1.29 if the tank is filled with compressed *water* instead of air. Why is the result thousands of times less than the result of 215,000 ft · lbf in Prob. 1.29?

P1.31 One cubic foot of argon gas at 10°C and 1 atm is compressed isentropically to a pressure of 600 kPa. (a) What will be its new pressure and temperature? (b) If it is allowed to cool at this new volume back to 10°C, what will be the final pressure?

P1.32 A blimp is approximated by a prolate spheroid 90 m long and 30 m in diameter. Estimate the weight of 20°C gas within the blimp for (a) helium at 1.1 atm and (b) air at 1.0 atm. What might the *difference* between these two values represent (see Chap. 2)?

P1.33 A tank contains 9 kg of CO_2 at 20°C and 2.0 MPa. Estimate the volume of the tank, in m³.

P1.34 Consider steam at the following state near the saturation line: $(p_1, T_1) = (1.31 \text{ MPa}, 290°C)$. Calculate and compare, for an ideal gas (Table A.4) and the steam tables (a) the density ρ_1 and (b) the density ρ_2 if the steam expands isentropically to a new pressure of 414 kPa. Discuss your results.

P1.35 In Table A.4, most common gases (air, nitrogen, oxygen, hydrogen) have a specific heat ratio $k \approx 1.40$. Why do argon and helium have such high values? Why does NH_3 have such a low value? What is the lowest k for any gas that you know of?

P1.36 Experimental data [55] for the density of n-pentane liquid for high pressures, at 50°C, are listed as follows:

Pressure, kPa	100	10,230	20,700	34,310
Density, kg/m³	586.3	604.1	617.8	632.8

(a) Fit this data to reasonably accurate values of B and n from Eq. (1.19). (b) Evaluate ρ at 30 MPa.

P1.37 A near-ideal gas has a molecular weight of 44 and a specific heat $c_v = 610$ J/(kg · K). What are (a) its specific heat ratio, k, and (b) its speed of sound at 100°C?

Viscosity, no-slip condition

P1.38 In Fig. 1.7, if the fluid is glycerin at 20°C and the width between plates is 6 mm, what shear stress (in Pa) is required to move the upper plate at 5.5 m/s? What is the Reynolds number if L is taken to be the distance between plates?

P1.39 Knowing μ for air at 20°C from Table 1.4, estimate its viscosity at 500°C by (a) the power law and (b) the Sutherland law. Also make an estimate from (c) Fig. 1.6. Compare with the accepted value of $\mu \approx 3.58$ E-5 kg/m · s.

P1.40 Glycerin at 20°C fills the space between a hollow sleeve of diameter 12 cm and a fixed coaxial solid rod of diameter 11.8 cm. The outer sleeve is rotated at 120 rev/min. Assuming no temperature change, estimate the torque required, in N · m per meter of rod length, to hold the inner rod fixed.

P1.41 An aluminum cylinder weighing 30 N, 6 cm in diameter and 40 cm long, is falling concentrically through a long vertical sleeve of diameter 6.04 cm. The clearance is filled with SAE 50 oil at 20°C. Estimate the *terminal* (zero acceleration) fall velocity. Neglect air drag and assume a linear velocity distribution in the oil. *Hint:* You are given diameters, not radii.

P1.42 Helium at 20°C has a viscosity of 1.97 E-5 kg/(m · s). Use the data of Table A.4 to estimate the temperature, in °C, at which helium's viscosity will double.

P1.43 For the flow of gas between two parallel plates of Fig. 1.7, reanalyze for the case of *slip flow* at both walls. Use the simple slip condition, $\delta u_{wall} = \ell (du/dy)_{wall}$, where ℓ is the mean free path of the fluid. Sketch the expected velocity profile and find an expression for the shear stress at each wall.

P1.44 One type of viscometer is simply a long capillary tube. A commercial device is shown in Prob. C1.10. One measures the volume flow rate Q and the pressure drop Δp and, of course, the radius and length of the tube. The theoretical formula, which will be discussed in Chap. 6, is $\Delta p \approx 8\mu QL/(\pi R^4)$. For a capillary of diameter 4 mm and length 10 inches, the test fluid flows at 0.9 m³/h when the pressure drop is 58 lbf/in². Find the predicted viscosity in kg/m · s.

P1.45 A block of weight W slides down an inclined plane while lubricated by a thin film of oil, as in Fig. P1.45. The film contact area is A and its thickness is h. Assuming a linear velocity distribution in the film, derive an expression for the "terminal" (zero-acceleration) velocity V of the block. Find the terminal velocity of the block if the block mass is 6 kg, $A = 35$ cm², $\theta = 15°$, and the film is 1-mm-thick SAE 30 oil at 20°C.

P1.46 A simple and popular model for two nonnewtonian fluids in Fig. 1.8a is the *power-law*:

$$\tau \approx C\left(\frac{du}{dy}\right)^n$$

where C and n are constants fit to the fluid [16]. From Fig. 1.8a, deduce the values of the exponent n for which the fluid is (a) newtonian, (b) dilatant, and (c) pseudoplastic. Consider the specific model constant $C = 0.4$ N · s^n/m², with the fluid being sheared between two parallel plates as in Fig. 1.7. If the shear stress in the fluid is 1200 Pa, find the velocity V of the upper plate for the cases (d) $n = 1.0$, (e) $n = 1.2$, and (f) $n = 0.8$.

P1.47 Data for the apparent viscosity of average human blood, at normal body temperature of 37°C, varies with shear strain rate, as shown in the following table.

Strain rate, s^{-1}	1	10	100	1000
Apparent viscosity, kg/(m · s)	0.011	0.009	0.006	0.004

(a) Is blood a nonnewtonian fluid? (b) If so, what type of fluid is it? (c) How do these viscosities compare with plain water at 37°C?

P1.48 A thin plate is separated from two fixed plates by very viscous liquids μ_1 and μ_2, respectively, as in Fig. P1.48. The plate spacings h_1 and h_2 are unequal, as shown. The contact area is A between the center plate and each fluid. (a) Assuming a linear velocity distribution in each fluid, derive the force F required to pull the plate at velocity V. (b) Is there a necessary *relation* between the two viscosities, μ_1 and μ_2?

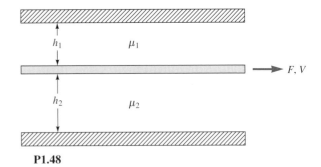

P1.48

P1.49 An amazing number of commercial and laboratory devices have been developed to measure fluid viscosity, as described in Refs. 29 and 49. Consider a concentric shaft, fixed axially and rotated inside the sleeve. Let the inner and outer cylinders have radii r_i and r_o, respectively, with total sleeve length L. Let the rotational rate be Ω (rad/s) and the

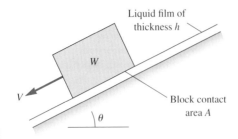

Liquid film of thickness h

W

V

Block contact area A

θ

P1.45

applied torque be M. Using these parameters, derive a theoretical relation for the viscosity μ of the fluid between the cylinders.

P1.50 A simple viscometer measures the time t for a solid sphere to fall a distance L through a test fluid of density ρ. The fluid viscosity μ is then given by

$$\mu \approx \frac{W_{net}t}{3\pi DL} \quad \text{if} \quad t \geq \frac{2\rho DL}{\mu}$$

where D is the sphere diameter and W_{net} is the sphere net weight in the fluid. (a) Prove that both of these formulas are dimensionally homogeneous. (b) Suppose that a 2.5 mm diameter aluminum sphere (density 2700 kg/m³) falls in an oil of density 875 kg/m³. If the time to fall 50 cm is 32 s, estimate the oil viscosity and verify that the inequality is valid.

P1.51 An approximation for the boundary-layer shape in Figs. 1.5b and P1.51 is the formula

$$u(y) \approx U \sin\left(\frac{\pi y}{2\delta}\right), \quad 0 \leq y \leq \delta$$

where U is the stream velocity far from the wall and δ is the boundary layer thickness, as in Fig. P1.51. If the fluid is helium at 20°C and 1 atm, and if $U = 10.8$ m/s and $\delta = 3$ cm, use the formula to (a) estimate the wall shear stress τ_w in Pa, and (b) find the position in the boundary layer where τ is one-half of τ_w.

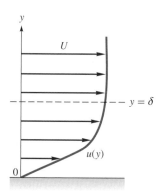

P1.51

P1.52 The belt in Fig. P1.52 moves at a steady velocity V and skims the top of a tank of oil of viscosity μ, as shown. Assuming a linear velocity profile in the oil, develop a simple formula for the required belt-drive power P as a function of (h, L, V, b, μ). What belt-drive power P, in watts, is required if the belt moves at 2.5 m/s over SAE 30W oil at 20°C, with $L = 2$ m, $b = 60$ cm, and $h = 3$ cm?

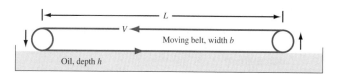

P1.52

*P1.53 A solid cone of angle 2θ, base r_0, and density ρ_c is rotating with initial angular velocity ω_0 inside a conical seat, as shown in Fig. P1.53. The clearance h is filled with oil of viscosity μ. Neglecting air drag, derive an analytical expression for the cone's angular velocity $\omega(t)$ if there is no applied torque.

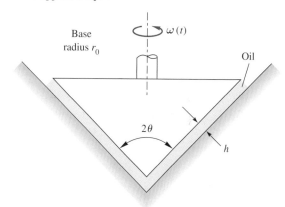

P1.53

*P1.54 A disk of radius R rotates at an angular velocity Ω inside a disk-shaped container filled with oil of viscosity μ, as shown in Fig. P1.54. Assuming a linear velocity profile and neglecting shear stress on the outer disk edges, derive a formula for the viscous torque on the disk.

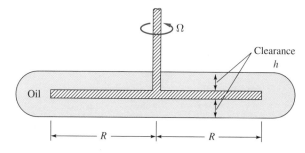

P1.54

P1.55 A block of weight W is being pulled over a table by another weight W_o, as shown in Fig. P1.55. Find an algebraic formula for the steady velocity U of the block if it slides on an oil film of thickness h and viscosity μ. The block bottom area A is in contact with the oil. Neglect the cord weight and the pulley friction. Assume a linear velocity profile in the oil film.

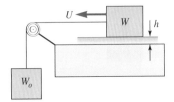

P1.55

*P1.56   The device in Fig. P1.56 is called a *cone-plate viscometer* [29]. The angle of the cone is very small, so that $\sin \theta \approx \theta$, and the gap is filled with the test liquid. The torque M to rotate the cone at a rate Ω is measured. Assuming a linear velocity profile in the fluid film, derive an expression for fluid viscosity μ as a function of (M, R, Ω, θ).

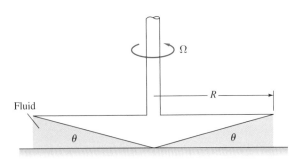

P1.56

P1.57   Extend the steady flow between a fixed lower plate and a moving upper plate, from Fig. 1.7, to the case of two immiscible liquids between the plates, as in Fig. P1.57.

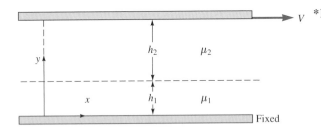

P1.57

(a) Sketch the expected no-slip velocity distribution $u(y)$ between the plates. (b) Find an analytic expression for the velocity U at the interface between the two liquid layers. (c) What is the result of (b) if the viscosities and layer thicknesses are equal?

*P1.58   The laminar pipe flow example of Prob. 1.12 can be used to design a *capillary viscometer* [29]. If Q is the volume flow rate, L is the pipe length, and Δp is the pressure drop from entrance to exit, the theory of Chap. 6 yields a formula for viscosity:

$$\mu = \frac{\pi r_0^4 \Delta p}{8LQ}$$

Pipe end effects are neglected [29]. Suppose our capillary has $r_0 = 2$ mm and $L = 25$ cm. The following flow rate and pressure drop data are obtained for a certain fluid:

Q, m³/h	0.36	0.72	1.08	1.44	1.80
Δp, kPa	159	318	477	1274	1851

What is the viscosity of the fluid? *Note:* Only the first three points give the proper viscosity. What is peculiar about the last two points, which were measured accurately?

P1.59   A solid cylinder of diameter D, length L, and density ρ_s falls due to gravity inside a tube of diameter D_0. The clearance, $D_0 - D \ll D$, is filled with fluid of density ρ and viscosity μ. Neglect the air above and below the cylinder. Derive a formula for the terminal fall velocity of the cylinder. Apply your formula to the case of a steel cylinder, $D = 2$ cm, $D_0 = 2.04$ cm, $L = 15$ cm, with a film of SAE 30 oil at 20°C.

P1.60   Pipelines are cleaned by pushing through them a close-fitting cylinder called a *pig*. The name comes from the squealing noise it makes sliding along. Reference 50 describes a new nontoxic pig, driven by compressed air, for cleaning cosmetic and beverage pipes. Suppose the pig diameter is 5-15/16 in and its length 26 in. It cleans a 6-in-diameter pipe at a speed of 1.2 m/s. If the clearance is filled with glycerin at 20°C, what pressure difference, in pascals, is needed to drive the pig? Assume a linear velocity profile in the oil and neglect air drag.

*P1.61   An air-hockey puck has a mass of 50 g and is 9 cm in diameter. When placed on the air table, a 20°C air film, of 0.12-mm thickness, forms under the puck. The puck is struck with an initial velocity of 10 m/s. Assuming a linear velocity distribution in the air film, how long will it take the puck to (a) slow down to 1 m/s and (b) stop completely? Also, (c) how far along this extremely long table will the puck have traveled for condition (a)?

Surface tension

P1.62   The hydrogen bubbles that produced the velocity profiles in Fig. 1.15 are quite small, $D \approx 0.01$ mm. If the hydrogen–water interface is comparable to air–water and the water temperature is 30°C, estimate the excess pressure within the bubble.

P1.63 Derive Eq. (1.33) by making a force balance on the fluid interface in Fig. 1.11c.

P1.64 Pressure in a water container can be measured by an open vertical tube—see Fig. P2.11 for a sketch. If the expected water rise is about 20 cm, what tube diameter is needed to ensure that the error due to capillarity will be less than 3 percent?

P1.65 The system in Fig. P1.65 is used to calculate the pressure p_1 in the tank by measuring the 15-cm height of liquid in the 1-mm-diameter tube. The fluid is at 60°C. Calculate the true fluid height in the tube and the percentage error due to capillarity if the fluid is (a) water or (b) mercury.

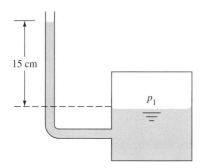

P1.65

P1.66 A thin wire ring, 3 cm in diameter, is lifted from a water surface at 20°C. Neglecting the wire weight, what is the force required to lift the ring? Is this a good way to measure surface tension? Should the wire be made of any particular material?

P1.67 A vertical concentric annulus, with outer radius r_o and inner radius r_i, is lowered into a fluid of surface tension Y and contact angle $\theta < 90°$. Derive an expression for the capillary rise h in the annular gap if the gap is very narrow.

*P1.68 Make an analysis of the shape $\eta(x)$ of the water–air interface near a plane wall, as in Fig. P1.68, assuming that the slope is small, $R^{-1} \approx d^2\eta/dx^2$. Also assume that the pressure difference across the interface is balanced by the specific weight and the interface height, $\Delta p \approx \rho g \eta$. The boundary conditions are a wetting contact angle θ at $x = 0$ and a horizontal surface $\eta = 0$ as $x \to \infty$. What is the maximum height h at the wall?

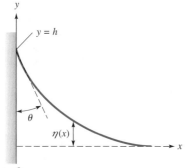

P1.68 $x = 0$

P1.69 A solid cylindrical needle of diameter d, length L, and density ρ_n may float in liquid of surface tension Y. Neglect buoyancy and assume a contact angle of 0°. Derive a formula for the maximum diameter d_{max} able to float in the liquid. Calculate d_{max} for a steel needle (SG = 7.84) in water at 20°C.

P1.70 Derive an expression for the capillary height change h for a fluid of surface tension Y and contact angle θ between two vertical parallel plates a distance W apart, as in Fig. P1.70. What will h be for water at 20°C if $W = 0.5$ mm?

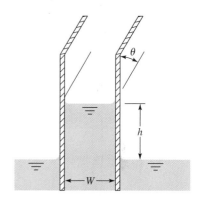

P1.70

*P1.71 A soap bubble of diameter D_1 coalesces with another bubble of diameter D_2 to form a single bubble D_3 with the same amount of air. Assuming an isothermal process, derive an expression for finding D_3 as a function of D_1, D_2, p_{atm}, and Y.

Vapor pressure

P1.72 Early mountaineers boiled water to estimate their altitude. If they reach the top and find that water boils at 84°C, approximately how high is the mountain?

P1.73 A small submersible moves at velocity V, in fresh water at 20°C, at a 2-m depth, where ambient pressure is 131 kPa. Its critical cavitation number is known to be $C_a = 0.25$. At what velocity will cavitation bubbles begin to form on the body? Will the body cavitate if $V = 30$ m/s and the water is cold (5°C)?

P1.74 Oil, with a vapor pressure of 20 kPa, is delivered through a pipeline by equally spaced pumps, each of which increases the oil pressure by 1.3 MPa. Friction losses in the pipe are 150 Pa per meter of pipe. What is the maximum possible pump spacing to avoid cavitation of the oil?

Speed of sound, Mach number

P1.75 An airplane flies at 555 mi/h. At what altitude in the standard atmosphere will the airplane's Mach number be exactly 0.8?

P1.76   Derive a formula for the bulk modulus of an ideal gas, with constant specific heats, and calculate it for steam at 300°C and 200 kPa. Compare your result to the steam tables.

P1.77   Assume that the n-pentane data of Prob. P1.36 represents isentropic conditions. Estimate the value of the speed of sound at a pressure of 30 MPa. [*Hint:* The data approximately fit Eq. (1.19) with $B = 260$ and $n = 11$.]

P1.78   Sir Isaac Newton measured the speed of sound by timing the difference between seeing a cannon's puff of smoke and hearing its boom. If the cannon is on a mountain 5.2 mi away, estimate the air temperature in degrees Celsius if the time difference is (a) 24.2 s and (b) 25.1 s.

P1.79   From Table A.3, the density of glycerin at standard conditions is about 1260 kg/m³. At a very high pressure of 8000 lb/in², its density increases to approximately 1275 kg/m³. Use this data to estimate the speed of sound of glycerin, in ft/s.

P1.80   In Problem P1.24, for the given data, the air velocity at section 2 is 1180 ft/s. What is the Mach number at that section?

Streamlines

P1.81   Use Eq. (1.39) to find and sketch the streamlines of the following flow field:

$$u = Kx; \quad v = -Ky; \quad w = 0, \text{ where } K \text{ is a constant.}$$

P1.82   A velocity field is given by $u = V\cos\theta$, $v = V\sin\theta$, and $w = 0$, where V and θ are constants. Derive a formula for the streamlines of this flow.

*P1.83   Use Eq. (1.39) to find and sketch the streamlines of the following flow field:

$$u = K(x^2 - y^2); \quad v = -2Kxy; \quad w = 0, \text{ where } K \text{ is a constant.}$$

Hint: This is a first-order *exact* differential equation.

Fundamentals of Engineering Exam Problems

FE1.1   The absolute viscosity μ of a fluid is primarily a function of
(a) Density, (b) Temperature, (c) Pressure, (d) Velocity, (e) Surface tension

FE1.2   Carbon dioxide, at 20°C and 1 atm, is compressed isentropically to 4 atm. Assume CO_2 is an ideal gas. The final temperature would be
(a) 130°C, (b) 162°C, (c) 171°C, (d) 237°C, (e) 313°C

FE1.3   Helium has a molecular weight of 4.003. What is the weight of 2 m³ of helium at 1 atm and 20°C?
(a) 3.3 N, (b) 6.5 N, (c) 11.8 N, (d) 23.5 N, (e) 94.2 N

FE1.4   An oil has a kinematic viscosity of 1.25 E-4 m²/s and a specific gravity of 0.80. What is its dynamic (absolute) viscosity in kg/(m · s)?
(a) 0.08, (b) 0.10, (c) 0.125, (d) 1.0, (e) 1.25

History of fluid mechanics

P1.84   In the early 1900s, the British chemist Sir Cyril Hinshelwood quipped that fluid dynamics study was divided into "workers who observed things they could not explain and workers who explained things they could not observe." To what historic situation was he referring?

P1.85   Do some reading and report to the class on the life and achievements, especially vis-à-vis fluid mechanics, of
(a) Evangelista Torricelli (1608–1647)
(b) Henri de Pitot (1695–1771)
(c) Antoine Chézy (1718–1798)
(d) Gotthilf Heinrich Ludwig Hagen (1797–1884)
(e) Julius Weisbach (1806–1871)
(f) George Gabriel Stokes (1819–1903)
(g) Moritz Weber (1871–1951)
(h) Theodor von Kármán (1881–1963)
(i) Paul Richard Heinrich Blasius (1883–1970)
(j) Ludwig Prandtl (1875–1953)
(k) Osborne Reynolds (1842–1912)
(l) John William Strutt, Lord Rayleigh (1842–1919)
(m) Daniel Bernoulli (1700–1782)
(n) Leonhard Euler (1707–1783)

Experimental uncertainty

P1.86   A right circular cylinder volume υ is to be calculated from the measured base radius R and height H. If the uncertainty in R is 2 percent and the uncertainty in H is 3 percent, estimate the overall uncertainty in the calculated volume. *Hint:* Read Appendix E.

FE1.5   Consider a soap bubble of diameter 3 mm. If the surface tension coefficient is 0.072 N/m and external pressure is 0 Pa gage, what is the bubble's internal gage pressure?
(a) −24 Pa, (b) +48 Pa, (c) +96 Pa, (d) +192 Pa, (e) −192 Pa

FE1.6   The only possible dimensionless group that combines velocity V, body size L, fluid density ρ, and surface tension coefficient σ is
(a) $L\rho\sigma/V$, (b) $\rho VL^2/\sigma$, (c) $\rho\sigma V^2/L$, (d) $\sigma LV^2/\rho$, (e) $\rho LV^2/\sigma$

FE1.7   Two parallel plates, one moving at 4 m/s and the other fixed, are separated by a 5-mm-thick layer of oil of specific gravity 0.80 and kinematic viscosity 1.25 E-4 m²/s. What is the average shear stress in the oil?
(a) 80 Pa, (b) 100 Pa, (c) 125 Pa, (d) 160 Pa, (e) 200 Pa

FE1.8 Carbon dioxide has a specific heat ratio of 1.30 and a gas constant of 189 J/(kg · °C). If its temperature rises from 20 to 45°C, what is its internal energy rise?

(a) 12.6 kJ/kg, (b) 15.8 kJ/kg, (c) 17.6 kJ/kg, (d) 20.5 kJ/kg, (e) 25.1 kJ/kg

FE1.9 A certain water flow at 20°C has a critical cavitation number, where bubbles form, $Ca \approx 0.25$, where $Ca = 2(p_a - p_{vap})/\rho V^2$. If $p_a = 1$ atm and the vapor pressure is 0.34 pounds per square inch absolute (psia), for what water velocity will bubbles form?

(a) 12 mi/h, (b) 28 mi/h, (c) 36 mi/h, (d) 55 mi/h, (e) 63 mi/h

FE1.10 Example 1.10 gave an analysis that predicted that the viscous moment on a rotating disk $M = \pi \mu \Omega R^4/(2h)$. If the uncertainty of each of the four variables (μ, Ω, R, h) is 1.0 percent, what is the estimated overall uncertainty of the moment M?

(a) 4.0 percent (b) 4.4 percent (c) 5.0 percent (d) 6.0 percent (e) 7.0 percent

Comprehensive Problems

C1.1 Sometimes we can develop equations and solve practical problems by knowing nothing more than the dimensions of the key parameters in the problem. For example, consider the heat loss through a window in a building. Window efficiency is rated in terms of "R value," which has units of $(ft^2 \cdot h \cdot °F)/Btu$. A certain manufacturer advertises a double-pane window with an R value of 2.5. The same company produces a triple-pane window with an R value of 3.4. In either case the window dimensions are 3 ft by 5 ft. On a given winter day, the temperature difference between the inside and outside of the building is 45°F.

(a) Develop an equation for the amount of heat lost in a given time period Δt, through a window of area A, with a given R value, and temperature difference ΔT. How much heat (in Btu) is lost through the double-pane window in one 24-h period?

(b) How much heat (in Btu) is lost through the triple-pane window in one 24-h period?

(c) Suppose the building is heated with propane gas, which costs $3.25 per gallon. The propane burner is 80 percent efficient. Propane has approximately 90,000 Btu of available energy per gallon. In that same 24-h period, how much money would a homeowner save per window by installing triple-pane rather than double-pane windows?

(d) Finally, suppose the homeowner buys 20 such triple-pane windows for the house. A typical winter has the equivalent of about 120 heating days at a temperature difference of 45°F. Each triple-pane window costs $85 more than the double-pane window. Ignoring interest and inflation, how many years will it take the homeowner to make up the additional cost of the triple-pane windows from heating bill savings?

C1.2 When a person ice skates, the surface of the ice actually melts beneath the blades, so that he or she skates on a thin sheet of water between the blade and the ice.

(a) Find an expression for total friction force on the bottom of the blade as a function of skater velocity V, blade length L, water thickness (between the blade and the ice) h, water viscosity μ, and blade width W.

(b) Suppose an ice skater of total mass m is skating along at a constant speed of V_0 when she suddenly stands stiff with her skates pointed directly forward, allowing herself to coast to a stop. Neglecting friction due to air resistance, how far will she travel before she comes to a stop? (Remember, she is coasting on *two* skate blades.) Give your answer for the total distance traveled, x, as a function of V_0, m, L, h, μ, and W.

(c) Find x for the case where $V_0 = 4.0$ m/s, m = 100 kg, L = 30 cm, W = 5.0 mm, and h = 0.10 mm. Do you think our assumption of negligible air resistance is a good one?

C1.3 Two thin flat plates, tilted at an angle α, are placed in a tank of liquid of known surface tension Y and contact angle θ, as shown in Fig. C1.3. At the free surface of the liquid in the tank, the two plates are a distance L apart and have width b into the page. The liquid rises a distance h between the plates, as shown.

(a) What is the total upward (z-directed) force, due to surface tension, acting on the liquid column between the plates?

(b) If the liquid density is ρ, find an expression for surface tension Y in terms of the other variables.

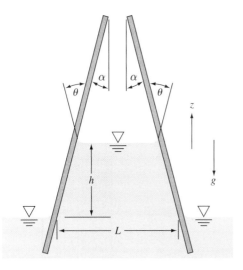

C1.3

C1.4   Oil of viscosity μ and density ρ drains steadily down the side of a tall, wide vertical plate, as shown in Fig. C1.4. In the region shown, *fully developed* conditions exist; that is, the velocity profile shape and the film thickness δ are independent of distance z along the plate. The vertical velocity w becomes a function only of x, and the shear resistance from the atmosphere is negligible.

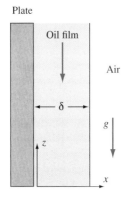

C1.4

(a) Sketch the approximate shape of the velocity profile $w(x)$, considering the boundary conditions at the wall and at the film surface.

(b) Suppose film thickness δ, and the slope of the velocity profile at the wall, $(dw/dx)_{\text{wall}}$, are measured by a laser Doppler anemometer (to be discussed in Chap. 6). Find an expression for the viscosity of the oil as a function of ρ, δ, $(dw/dx)_{\text{wall}}$, and the gravitational acceleration g. Note that, for the coordinate system given, both w and $(dw/dx)_{\text{wall}}$ are negative.

C1.5   Viscosity can be measured by flow through a thin-bore or *capillary* tube if the flow rate is low. For length L, (small) diameter $D \ll L$, pressure drop Δp, and (low) volume flow rate Q, the formula for viscosity is $\mu = D^4 \Delta p/(CLQ)$, where C is a constant.

(a) Verify that C is dimensionless. The following data are for water flowing through a 2-mm-diameter tube which is 1 meter long. The pressure drop is held constant at $\Delta p = 5$ kPa.

T, °C	10.0	40.0	70.0
Q, L/min	0.091	0.179	0.292

(b) Using proper SI units, determine an average value of C by accounting for the variation with temperature of the viscosity of water.

C1.6   The *rotating-cylinder viscometer* in Fig. C1.6 shears the fluid in a narrow clearance Δr, as shown. Assuming a linear velocity distribution in the gaps, if the driving torque M is measured, find an expression for μ by (a) neglecting and (b) including the bottom friction.

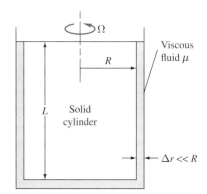

C1.6

C1.7   Make an analytical study of the transient behavior of the sliding block in Prob. 1.45. (a) Solve for $V(t)$ if the block starts from rest, $V = 0$ at $t = 0$. (b) Calculate the time t_1 when the block has reached 98 percent of its terminal velocity.

C1.8   A mechanical device that uses the rotating cylinder of Fig. C1.6 is the *Stormer viscometer* [29]. Instead of being driven at constant Ω, a cord is wrapped around the shaft and attached to a falling weight W. The time t to turn the shaft a given number of revolutions (usually five) is measured and correlated with viscosity. The formula is

$$t \approx \frac{A\mu}{W - B}$$

where A and B are constants that are determined by calibrating the device with a known fluid. Here are calibration data for a Stormer viscometer tested in glycerol, using a weight of 50 N:

μ, kg/(m-s)	0.23	0.34	0.57	0.84	1.15
t, sec	15	23	38	56	77

(a) Find reasonable values of A and B to fit this calibration data. *Hint:* The data are not very sensitive to the value of B.

(b) A more viscous fluid is tested with a 100 N weight and the measured time is 44 s. Estimate the viscosity of this fluid.

C1.9 The lever in Fig. C1.9 has a weight W at one end and is tied to a cylinder at the left end. The cylinder has negligible weight and buoyancy and slides upward through a film of heavy oil of viscosity μ. (a) If there is no acceleration (uniform lever rotation), derive a formula for the rate of fall V_2 of the weight. Neglect the lever weight. Assume a linear velocity profile in the oil film. (b) Estimate the fall velocity of the weight if $W = 20$ N, $L_1 = 75$ cm, $L_2 = 50$ cm, $D = 10$ cm, $L = 22$ cm, $\Delta R = 1$ mm, and the oil is glycerin at 20°C.

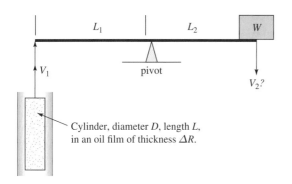

C1.9

C1.10 A popular gravity-driven instrument is the *Cannon-Ubbelohde viscometer,* shown in Fig. C1.10. The test liquid is drawn up above the bulb on the right side and allowed to drain by gravity through the capillary tube below the bulb. The time t for the meniscus to pass from upper to lower timing marks is recorded. The kinematic viscosity is computed by the simple formula:

$$v = Ct$$

where C is a calibration constant. For v in the range of 100–500 mm²/s, the recommended constant is $C = 0.50$ mm²/s², with an accuracy less than 0.5 percent.

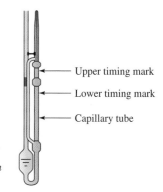

C1.10 The Cannon-Ubbelohde viscometer.
Source: Courtesy of Cannon Instrument Company.

(a) What liquids from Table A.3 are in this viscosity range? (b) Is the calibration formula dimensionally consistent? (c) What system properties might the constant C depend upon? (d) What problem in this chapter hints at a formula for estimating the viscosity?

C1.11 Mott [Ref. 49, p. 38] discusses a simple falling-ball viscometer, which we can analyze later in Chap. 7. A small ball of diameter D and density ρ_b falls through a tube of test liquid (ρ, μ). The fall velocity V is calculated by the time to fall a measured distance. The formula for calculating the viscosity of the fluid is

$$\mu = \frac{(\rho_b - \rho)gD^2}{18\,V}$$

This result is limited by the requirement that the Reynolds number $(\rho V D/\mu)$ be less than 1.0. Suppose a steel ball (SG = 7.87) of diameter 2.2 mm falls in SAE 25W oil (SG = 0.88) at 20°C. The measured fall velocity is 8.4 cm/s. (a) What is the viscosity of the oil, in kg/m-s? (b) Is the Reynolds number small enough for a valid estimate?

C1.12 A solid aluminum disk (SG = 2.7) is 2 in in diameter and 3/16 in thick. It slides steadily down a 14° incline that is coated with a castor oil (SG = 0.96) film one hundredth of an inch thick. The steady slide velocity is 2 cm/s. Using Figure A.1 and a linear oil velocity profile assumption, estimate the temperature of the castor oil.

References

1. T. J. Chung, *Computational Fluid Dynamics*, 2d ed., Cambridge University Press, New York, 2010.

2. J. D. Anderson, *Computational Fluid Dynamics: An Introduction*, 3d ed., Springer, New York, 2010.

3. H. Lomax, T. H. Pulliam, and D. W. Zingg, *Fundamentals of Computational Fluid Dynamics*, Springer, New York, 2011.

4. B. Andersson, L. Håkansson, and M. Mortensen, *Computational Fluid Dynamics for Engineers*, Cambridge University Press, New York, 2012.

5. D. C. Wilcox, *Turbulence Modeling for CFD*, 3d ed., DCW Industries, La Cañada, California, 2006.

6. P. S. Bernard and J. M. Wallace, *Turbulent Flow: Analysis, Measurement and Prediction*, Wiley, New York, 2002.

7. X. Jiang and C. H. Lai, *Numerical Techniques for Direct and Large-Eddy Simulations*, CRC Press, Boca Raton, Florida, 2009.

8. B. Geurts, *Elements of Direct and Large Eddy Simulation*, R. T. Edwards Inc., Flourtown, PA, 2003.

9. S. Tavoularis, *Measurement in Fluid Mechanics,* Cambridge University Press, New York, 2005.

10. R. C. Baker, *Introductory Guide to Flow Measurement,* Wiley, New York, 2002.

11. R. W. Miller, *Flow Measurement Engineering Handbook,* 3d ed., McGraw-Hill, New York, 1996.

12. H. Rouse and S. Ince, *History of Hydraulics,* Iowa Institute of Hydraulic Research, Univ. of Iowa, Iowa City, IA, 1957; reprinted by Dover, New York, 1963.

13. H. Rouse, *Hydraulics in the United States 1776–1976,* Iowa Institute of Hydraulic Research, Univ. of Iowa, Iowa City, IA, 1976.

14. G. A. Tokaty, *A History and Philosophy of Fluid Mechanics,* Dover Publications, New York, 1994.

15. Cambridge University Press, "Ludwig Prandtl—Father of Modern Fluid Mechanics," URL <www.fluidmech.net/msc/prandtl.htm>.

16. R. I. Tanner, *Engineering Rheology,* 2d ed., Oxford University Press, New York, 2000.

17. C. E. Brennen, *Fundamentals of Multiphase Flow*, Cambridge University Press, New York, 2009.

18. C. Shen, *Rarefied Gas Dynamics*, Springer, New York, 2010.

19. F. Carderelli and M. J. Shields, *Scientific Unit Conversion: A Practical Guide to Metrification,* 2d ed., Springer-Verlag, New York, 1999.

20. J. P. Holman, *Heat Transfer,* 10th ed., McGraw-Hill, New York, 2009.

21. B. E. Poling, J. M. Prausnitz, and J. P. O'Connell, *The Properties of Gases and Liquids,* 5th ed., McGraw-Hill, New York, 2000.

22. J. Hilsenrath et al., "Tables of Thermodynamic and Transport Properties," *U.S. Nat. Bur. Standards Circular 564,* 1955; reprinted by Pergamon, New York, 1960.

23. W. T. Parry, *ASME International Steam Tables for Industrial Use,* 2d ed., ASME Press, New York, 2009.

24. Steam Tables URL: http://www.steamtablesonline.com/

25. O. A. Hougen and K. M. Watson, *Chemical Process Principles Charts,* Wiley, New York, 1960.

26. F. M. White, *Viscous Fluid Flow,* 3d ed., McGraw-Hill, New York, 2005.

27. M. Bourne, *Food Texture and Viscosity: Concept and Measurement,* 2d ed., Academic Press, Salt Lake City, Utah, 2002.

28. *SAE Fuels and Lubricants Standards Manual,* Society of Automotive Engineers, Warrendale, PA, 2001.

29. C. L. Yaws, *Handbook of Viscosity,* 3 vols., Elsevier Science and Technology, New York, 1994.

30. A. W. Adamson and A. P. Gast, *Physical Chemistry of Surfaces,* Wiley, New York, 1999.

31. C. E. Brennen, *Fundamentals of Multiphase Flow*, Cambridge University Press, New York, 2009.

32. National Committee for Fluid Mechanics Films, *Illustrated Experiments in Fluid Mechanics,* M.I.T. Press, Cambridge, MA, 1972.

33. I. G. Currie, *Fundamental Mechanics of Fluids,* 3d ed., Marcel Dekker, New York, 2003.

34. W.-J. Yang (ed.), *Handbook of Flow Visualization,* 2d ed., Taylor and Francis, New York, 2001.

35. F. T. Nieuwstadt (ed.), *Flow Visualization and Image Analysis,* Springer, New York, 2007.

36. A. J. Smits and T. T. Lim, *Flow Visualization: Techniques and Examples,* 2d ed., Imperial College Press, London, 2011.

37. R. J. Adrian and J. Westerweel, *Particle Image Velocimetry,* Cambridge University Press, New York, 2010.

38. Wen-Jai Yang, *Computer-Assisted Flow Visualization,* Begell House, New York, 1994.

39. M. van Dyke, *An Album of Fluid Motion,* Parabolic Press, Stanford, CA, 1982.

40. Y. Nakayama and Y. Tanida (eds.), *Visualized Flow,* vol. 1, Elsevier, New York, 1993; vols. 2 and 3, CRC Press, Boca Raton, FL, 1996.

41. M. Samimy, K. S. Breuer, L. G. Leal, and P. H. Steen, *A Gallery of Fluid Motion,* Cambridge University Press, New York, 2003.

42. S. Y. Son et al., "Coolant Flow Field Measurements in a Two-Pass Channel Using Particle Image Velocimetry," 1999 Heat Transfer Gallery, *Journal of Heat Transfer,* vol. 121, August, 1999.

43. B. Carr and V. E. Young, "Videotapes and Movies on Fluid Dynamics and Fluid Machines," in *Handbook of Fluid Dynamics and Fluid Machinery,* vol. II, J. A. Schetz and A. E. Fuhs (eds.), Wiley, New York, 1996, pp. 1171–1189.

44. Online Steam Tables URL: http://www.spiraxsarco.com/esc/SH_Properties.aspx.

45. H. W. Coleman and W. G. Steele, *Experimentation and Uncertainty Analysis for Engineers,* 3d ed., Wiley, New York, 2009.

46. I. Hughes and T. Hase, *Measurements and Their Uncertainties*, Oxford University Press, New York, 2010.

47. A. Thom, "The Flow Past Circular Cylinders at Low Speeds," *Proc. Royal Society*, A141, London, 1933, pp. 651–666.

48. S. J. Kline and F. A. McClintock, "Describing Uncertainties in Single-Sample Experiments," *Mechanical Engineering,* January, 1953, pp. 3–9.

49. R. L. Mott, *Applied Fluid Mechanics,* Pearson Prentice-Hall, Upper Saddle River, NJ, 2006.

50. "Putting Porky to Work," Technology Focus, *Mechanical Engineering,* August 2002, p. 24.

51. R. M. Olson and S. J. Wright, *Essentials of Engineering Fluid Mechanics,* 5th ed., HarperCollins, New York, 1990.

52. B. Kirby, *Micro- and Nanoscale Fluid Mechanics*, Cambridge University Press, New York, 2010.

53. E. J. Watson, "The Spread of a Liquid Jet over a Horizontal Plane," *J. Fluid Mechanics*, vol. 20, 1964, pp. 481–499.

54. J. Dean and A. Reisinger, *Sands, Powders, and Grains: An Introduction to the Physics of Granular Materials*, Springer-Verlag, New York, 1999.

55. E. Kiran and Y. L. Sen, "High Pressure Density and Viscosity of n-alkanes," *Int. J. Thermophysics*, vol. 13, no. 3, 1992, pp. 411–442.

The bathyscaphe *Trieste* was built by explorers August and Jacques Picard in 1953. They made many deep-sea dives over the next five years. In 1958 the U.S. Navy purchased it and, in 1960, descended to the deepest part of the ocean, the Marianas Trench, near Guam. The recorded depth was 10,900 m, or nearly seven miles. The photo shows the vessel being lifted from the water. The pressure sphere is on the bottom, and the boat-shaped structure above is filled with gasoline, which provides buoyancy even at those depths. [*Image courtesy of the U.S. Navy.*]

Chapter 2
Pressure Distribution in a Fluid

Motivation. Many fluid problems do not involve motion. They concern the pressure distribution in a static fluid and its effect on solid surfaces and on floating and submerged bodies.

When the fluid velocity is zero, denoted as the *hydrostatic condition*, the pressure variation is due only to the weight of the fluid. Assuming a known fluid in a given gravity field, the pressure may easily be calculated by integration. Important applications in this chapter are (1) pressure distribution in the atmosphere and the oceans, (2) the design of manometer, mechanical, and electronic pressure instruments, (3) forces on submerged flat and curved surfaces, (4) buoyancy on a submerged body, and (5) the behavior of floating bodies. The last two result in Archimedes' principles.

If the fluid is moving in *rigid-body motion*, such as a tank of liquid that has been spinning for a long time, the pressure also can be easily calculated because the fluid is free of shear stress. We apply this idea here to simple rigid-body accelerations in Sec. 2.9. Pressure measurement instruments are discussed in Sec. 2.10. As a matter of fact, pressure also can be analyzed in arbitrary (nonrigid-body) motions $V(x, y, z, t)$, but we defer that subject to Chap. 4.

2.1 Pressure and Pressure Gradient

In Fig. 1.1 we saw that a fluid at rest cannot support shear stress and thus Mohr's circle reduces to a point. In other words, the normal stress on any plane through a fluid element at rest is a point property called the *fluid pressure p*, taken positive for compression by common convention. This is such an important concept that we shall review it with another approach.

First let us emphasize that pressure is a thermodynamic property of the fluid, like temperature or density. It is not a *force*. Pressure has no direction and is not a vector. The concept of force only arises when considering a surface immersed in fluid pressure. The pressure creates a force, due to fluid molecules bombarding the surface, and it is normal to that surface.

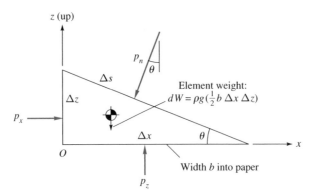

Fig. 2.1 Equilibrium of a small wedge of fluid at rest.

Figure 2.1 shows a small wedge of fluid at rest of size Δx by Δz by Δs and depth b into the paper. There is no shear by definition, but we postulate that the pressures p_x, p_z, and p_n may be different on each face. The weight of the element also may be important. The element is assumed to be small, so the pressure is constant on each face. Summation of forces must equal zero (no acceleration) in both the x and z directions.

$$\sum F_x = 0 = p_x b \, \Delta z - p_n b \, \Delta s \sin \theta$$

$$\sum F_z = 0 = p_z b \, \Delta x - p_n b \, \Delta s \cos \theta - \tfrac{1}{2}\rho g b \, \Delta x \, \Delta z \tag{2.1}$$

But the geometry of the wedge is such that

$$\Delta s \sin \theta = \Delta z \qquad \Delta s \cos \theta = \Delta x \tag{2.2}$$

Substitution into Eq. (2.1) and rearrangement give

$$p_x = p_n \qquad p_z = p_n + \tfrac{1}{2}\rho g \, \Delta z \tag{2.3}$$

These relations illustrate two important principles of the hydrostatic, or shear-free, condition: (1) There is no pressure change in the horizontal direction, and (2) there is a vertical change in pressure proportional to the density, gravity, and depth change. We shall exploit these results to the fullest, starting in Sec. 2.3.

In the limit as the fluid wedge shrinks to a "point," $\Delta z \rightarrow 0$ and Eq. (2.3) become

$$p_x = p_z = p_n = p \tag{2.4}$$

Since θ is arbitrary, we conclude that the pressure p in a static fluid is a point property, independent of orientation.

Pressure Force on a Fluid Element

Pressure (or any other stress, for that matter) causes a net force on a fluid element. To see this, consider the pressure acting on the two x faces in Fig. 2.2. Let the pressure vary arbitrarily

$$p = p(x, y, z, t)$$

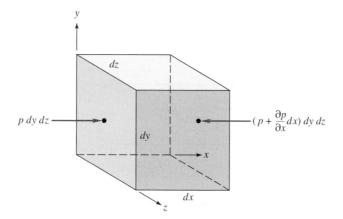

Fig. 2.2 Net x force on an element due to pressure variation.

The net force in the x direction on the element in Fig. 2.2 is given by

$$dF_x = p \, dy \, dz - \left(p + \frac{\partial p}{\partial x} dx \right) dy \, dz = -\frac{\partial p}{\partial x} dx \, dy \, dz$$

In like manner the net force dF_y involves $-\partial p/\partial y$, and the net force dF_z concerns $-\partial p/\partial z$. The total net-force vector on the element due to pressure is

$$d\mathbf{F}_{\text{press}} = \left(-\mathbf{i}\frac{\partial p}{\partial x} - \mathbf{j}\frac{\partial p}{\partial y} - \mathbf{k}\frac{\partial p}{\partial z} \right) dx \, dy \, dz \tag{2.5}$$

We recognize the term in parentheses as the negative vector gradient of p. Denoting $\mathbf{f}$ as the net force per unit element volume, we rewrite Eq. (2.5) as

$$\mathbf{f}_{\text{press}} = -\nabla p \tag{2.6}$$

where
$$\nabla = \text{gradient operator} = \mathbf{i}\frac{\partial}{\partial x} + \mathbf{j}\frac{\partial}{\partial y} + \mathbf{k}\frac{\partial}{\partial z}$$

Thus it is not the pressure but the pressure *gradient* causing a net force that must be balanced by gravity or acceleration or some other effect in the fluid.

2.2 Equilibrium of a Fluid Element

The pressure gradient is a *surface* force that acts on the sides of the element. There may also be a *body* force, due to electromagnetic or gravitational potentials, acting on the entire mass of the element. Here we consider only the gravity force, or weight of the element:

$$d\mathbf{F}_{\text{grav}} = \rho\mathbf{g} \, dx \, dy \, dz$$

or
$$\mathbf{f}_{\text{grav}} = \rho\mathbf{g} \tag{2.7}$$

In addition to gravity, a fluid in motion will have *surface* forces due to viscous stresses. By Newton's law, Eq. (1.2), the sum of these per-unit-volume forces equals the mass per unit volume (density) times the acceleration $\mathbf{a}$ of the fluid element:

$$\sum \mathbf{f} = \mathbf{f}_{\text{press}} + \mathbf{f}_{\text{grav}} + \mathbf{f}_{\text{visc}} = -\nabla p + \rho\mathbf{g} + \mathbf{f}_{\text{visc}} = \rho\mathbf{a} \tag{2.8}$$

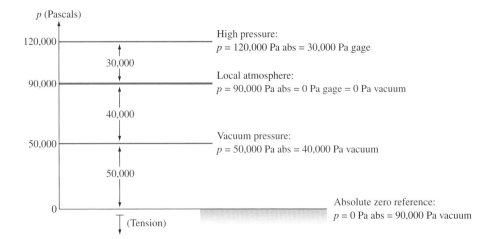

Fig. 2.3 Illustration of absolute, gage, and vacuum pressure readings.

This general equation will be studied in detail in Chap. 4. Note that Eq. (2.8) is a *vector* relation, and the acceleration may not be in the same vector direction as the velocity. For our present topic, *hydrostatics,* the viscous stresses and the acceleration are zero.

Gage Pressure and Vacuum Pressure: Relative Terms

Before embarking on examples, we should note that engineers are apt to specify pressures as (1) the *absolute* or total magnitude or (2) the value *relative* to the local ambient atmosphere. The second case occurs because many pressure instruments are of *differential* type and record, not an absolute magnitude, but the difference between the fluid pressure and the atmosphere. The measured pressure may be either higher or lower than the local atmosphere, and each case is given a name:

1. $p > p_a$ *Gage* pressure: $p(\text{gage}) = p - p_a$
2. $p < p_a$ *Vacuum* pressure: $p(\text{vacuum}) = p_a - p$

This is a convenient shorthand, and one later adds (or subtracts) atmospheric pressure to determine the absolute fluid pressure.

A typical situation is shown in Fig. 2.3. The local atmosphere is at, say, 90,000 Pa, which might reflect a storm condition in a sea-level location or normal conditions at an altitude of 1000 m. Thus, on this day, p_a = 90,000 Pa absolute = 0 Pa gage = 0 Pa vacuum. Suppose gage 1 in a laboratory reads p_1 = 120,000 Pa absolute. This value may be reported as a *gage* pressure, p_1 = 120,000 − 90,000 = 30,000 Pa *gage*. (One must also record the atmospheric pressure in the laboratory, since p_a changes gradually.) Suppose gage 2 reads p_2 = 50,000 Pa absolute. Locally, this is a *vacuum* pressure and might be reported as p_2 = 90,000 − 50,000 = 40,000 Pa *vacuum*. Occasionally, in the problems section, we will specify gage or vacuum pressure to keep you alert to this common engineering practice. If a pressure is listed without the modifier gage or vacuum, we assume it is absolute pressure.

2.3 Hydrostatic Pressure Distributions

If the fluid is at rest or at constant velocity, $\mathbf{a} = 0$ and $\mathbf{f}_{\text{visc}} = 0$. Equation (2.8) for the pressure distribution reduces to

$$\nabla p = \rho \mathbf{g} \qquad (2.9)$$

This is a *hydrostatic* distribution and is correct for all fluids at rest, regardless of their viscosity, because the viscous term vanishes identically.

Recall from vector analysis that the vector ∇p expresses the magnitude and direction of the maximum spatial rate of increase of the scalar property p. As a result, ∇p is perpendicular everywhere to surfaces of constant p. Thus Eq. (2.9) states that a fluid in hydrostatic equilibrium will align its constant-pressure surfaces everywhere normal to the local-gravity vector. The maximum pressure increase will be in the direction of gravity—that is, "down." If the fluid is a liquid, its free surface, being at atmospheric pressure, will be normal to local gravity, or "horizontal." You probably knew all this before, but Eq. (2.9) is the proof of it.

In our customary coordinate system z is "up." Thus the local-gravity vector for small-scale problems is

$$\mathbf{g} = -g\mathbf{k} \tag{2.10}$$

where g is the magnitude of local gravity, for example, 9.807 m/s^2. For these coordinates Eq. (2.9) has the components

$$\frac{\partial p}{\partial x} = 0 \qquad \frac{\partial p}{\partial y} = 0 \qquad \frac{\partial p}{\partial z} = -\rho g = -\gamma \tag{2.11}$$

the first two of which tell us that p is independent of x and y. Hence $\partial p / \partial z$ can be replaced by the total derivative dp/dz, and the hydrostatic condition reduces to

$$\frac{dp}{dz} = -\gamma$$

or

$$p_2 - p_1 = -\int_1^2 \gamma \, dz \tag{2.12}$$

Equation (2.12) is the solution to the hydrostatic problem. The integration requires an assumption about the density and gravity distribution. Gases and liquids are usually treated differently.

We state the following conclusions about a hydrostatic condition:

> Pressure in a continuously distributed uniform static fluid varies only with vertical distance and is independent of the shape of the container. The pressure is the same at all points on a given horizontal plane in the fluid. The pressure increases with depth in the fluid.

An illustration of this is shown in Fig. 2.4. The free surface of the container is atmospheric and forms a horizontal plane. Points a, b, c, and d are at equal depth in a horizontal plane and are interconnected by the same fluid, water; therefore, all points have the same pressure. The same is true of points A, B, and C on the bottom, which all have the same higher pressure than at a, b, c, and d. However, point D, although at the same depth as A, B, and C, has a different pressure because it lies beneath a different fluid, mercury.

Effect of Variable Gravity

For a spherical planet of uniform density, the acceleration of gravity varies inversely as the square of the radius from its center

$$g = g_0 \left(\frac{r_0}{r}\right)^2 \tag{2.13}$$

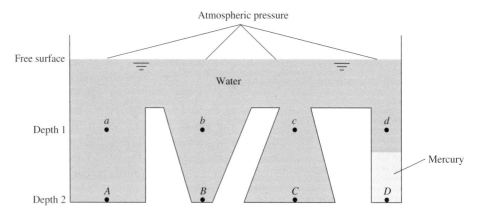

Fig. 2.4 Hydrostatic-pressure distribution. Points *a*, *b*, *c*, and *d* are at equal depths in water and therefore have identical pressures. Points *A*, *B*, and *C* are also at equal depths in water and have identical pressures higher than *a*, *b*, *c*, and *d*. Point *D* has a different pressure from *A*, *B*, and *C* because it is not connected to them by a water path.

where r_0 is the planet radius and g_0 is the surface value of g. For earth, $r_0 \approx 3960$ statute mi ≈ 6400 km. In typical engineering problems the deviation from r_0 extends from the deepest ocean, about 11 km, to the atmospheric height of supersonic transport operation, about 20 km. This gives a maximum variation in g of $(6400/6420)^2$, or 0.6 percent. We therefore neglect the variation of g in most problems.

Hydrostatic Pressure in Liquids

Liquids are so nearly incompressible that we can neglect their density variation in hydrostatics. In Example 1.6 we saw that water density increases only 4.6 percent at the deepest part of the ocean. Its effect on hydrostatics would be about half of this, or 2.3 percent. Thus we assume constant density in liquid hydrostatic calculations, for which Eq. (2.12) integrates to

$$\text{Liquids:} \qquad p_2 - p_1 = -\gamma\,(z_2 - z_1) \qquad (2.14)$$

$$\text{or} \qquad z_1 - z_2 = \frac{p_2}{\gamma} - \frac{p_1}{\gamma}$$

We use the first form in most problems. The quantity γ is called the *specific weight* of the fluid, with dimensions of weight per unit volume; some values are tabulated in Table 2.1. The quantity p/γ is a length called the *pressure head* of the fluid.

Table 2.1 Specific Weight of Some Common Fluids

Fluid	Specific weight γ at 68°F = 20°C	
	lbf/ft³	N/m³
Air (at 1 atm)	0.0752	11.8
Ethyl alcohol	49.2	7,733
SAE 30 oil	55.5	8,720
Water	62.4	9,790
Seawater	64.0	10,050
Glycerin	78.7	12,360
Carbon tetrachloride	99.1	15,570
Mercury	846	133,100

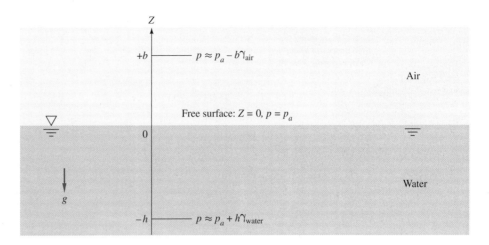

Fig. 2.5 Hydrostatic-pressure distribution in oceans and atmospheres.

For lakes and oceans, the coordinate system is usually chosen as in Fig. 2.5, with $z = 0$ at the free surface, where p equals the surface atmospheric pressure p_a. When we introduce the reference value $(p_1, z_1) = (p_a, 0)$, Eq. (2.14) becomes, for p at any (negative) depth z,

Lakes and oceans: $$p = p_a - \gamma z \qquad (2.15)$$

where γ is the average specific weight of the lake or ocean. As we shall see, Eq. (2.15) holds in the atmosphere also with an accuracy of 2 percent for heights z up to 1000 m.

EXAMPLE 2.1

Newfound Lake, a freshwater lake near Bristol, New Hampshire, has a maximum depth of 60 m, and the mean atmospheric pressure is 91 kPa. Estimate the absolute pressure in kPa at this maximum depth.

Solution

- *System sketch:* Imagine that Fig. 2.5 is Newfound Lake, with $h = 60$ m and $z = 0$ at the surface.
- *Property values:* From Table 2.1, $\gamma_{water} = 9790$ N/m^3. We are given that $p_{atmos} = 91$ kPa.
- *Solution steps:* Apply Eq. (2.15) to the deepest point. Use SI units, pascals, not kilopascals:

$$p_{max} = p_a - \gamma z = 91{,}000 \text{ Pa} - (9790 \, \frac{N}{m^3})(-60 \text{ m}) = 678{,}400 \text{ Pa} \approx 678 \text{ kPa} \qquad Ans.$$

- *Comments:* Kilopascals are awkward. Use pascals in the formula, then convert the answer.

The Mercury Barometer

The simplest practical application of the hydrostatic formula (2.14) is the barometer (Fig. 2.6), which measures atmospheric pressure. A tube is filled with mercury and inverted while submerged in a reservoir. This causes a near vacuum in the closed upper end because mercury has an extremely small vapor pressure at room temperatures

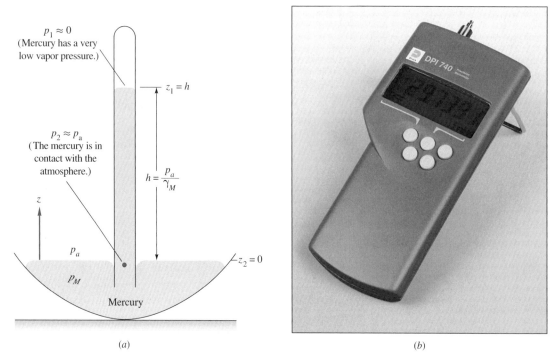

Fig. 2.6 A barometer measures local absolute atmospheric pressure: (*a*) the height of a mercury column is proportional to p_{atm}; (*b*) a modern portable barometer, with digital readout, uses the resonating silicon element of Fig. 2.28*c*. *(Courtesy of Paul Lupke, Druck, Inc.)*

(0.16 Pa at 20°C). Since atmospheric pressure forces a mercury column to rise a distance *h* into the tube, the upper mercury surface is at zero pressure.

From Fig. 2.6, Eq. (2.14) applies with $p_1 = 0$ at $z_1 = h$ and $p_2 = p_a$ at $z_2 = 0$:

$$p_a - 0 = -\gamma_M (0 - h)$$

or

$$h = \frac{p_a}{\gamma_M} \tag{2.16}$$

At sea-level standard, with $p_a = 101{,}350$ Pa and $\gamma_M = 133{,}100$ N/m³ from Table 2.1, the barometric height is $h = 101{,}350/133{,}100 = 0.761$ m or 761 mm. In the United States the weather service reports this as an atmospheric "pressure" of 29.96 inHg (inches of mercury). Mercury is used because it is the heaviest common liquid. A water barometer would be 34 ft high.

Hydrostatic Pressure in Gases

Gases are compressible, with density nearly proportional to pressure. Thus density must be considered as a variable in Eq. (2.12) if the integration carries over large pressure changes. It is sufficiently accurate to introduce the perfect-gas law $p = \rho RT$ in Eq. (2.12):

$$\frac{dp}{dz} = -\rho g = -\frac{p}{RT} g$$

Separate the variables and integrate between points 1 and 2:

$$\int_1^2 \frac{dp}{p} = \ln \frac{p_2}{p_1} = -\frac{g}{R} \int_1^2 \frac{dz}{T} \qquad (2.17)$$

The integral over z requires an assumption about the temperature variation $T(z)$. One common approximation is the *isothermal atmosphere*, where $T = T_0$:

$$p_2 = p_1 \exp \left[-\frac{g(z_2 - z_1)}{RT_0} \right] \qquad (2.18)$$

The quantity in brackets is dimensionless. (Think that over; it must be dimensionless, right?) Equation (2.18) is a fair approximation for earth, but actually the earth's mean atmospheric temperature drops off nearly linearly with z up to an altitude of about 36,000 ft (11,000 m):

$$T \approx T_0 - Bz \qquad (2.19)$$

Here T_0 is sea-level temperature (absolute) and B is the *lapse rate*, both of which vary somewhat from day to day.

The Standard Atmosphere

By international agreement [1] the following standard values are assumed to apply from 0 to 36,000 ft:

$$T_0 = 518.69°R = 288.16 \text{ K} = 15°C$$
$$B = 0.003566°R/ft = 0.00650 \text{ K/m}$$

This lower portion of the atmosphere is called the *troposphere*. Introducing Eq. (2.19) into Eq. (2.17) and integrating, we obtain the more accurate relation

$$p = p_a \left(1 - \frac{Bz}{T_0} \right)^{g/(RB)} \quad \text{where} \quad \frac{g}{RB} = 5.26 \text{ (air)}$$

$$\rho = \rho_o \left(1 - \frac{Bz}{T_o} \right)^{\frac{g}{RB} - 1} \quad \text{where} \quad \rho_o = 1.2255 \frac{kg}{m^3}, \quad p_o = 101,350 \, p_a \qquad (2.20)$$

in the troposphere, with $z = 0$ at sea level. The exponent $g/(RB)$ is dimensionless (again it must be) and has the standard value of 5.26 for air, with $R = 287 \text{ m}^2/(\text{s}^2 \cdot \text{K})$.

The U.S. standard atmosphere [1] is sketched in Fig. 2.7. The pressure is seen to be nearly zero at $z = 30$ km. For tabulated properties see Table A.6.

EXAMPLE 2.2

If sea-level pressure is 101,350 Pa, compute the standard pressure at an altitude of 5000 m, using (*a*) the exact formula and (*b*) an isothermal assumption at a standard sea-level temperature of 15°C. Is the isothermal approximation adequate?

Solution

Part (a)   Use absolute temperature in the exact formula, Eq. (2.20):

$$p = p_a \left[1 - \frac{(0.00650 \text{ K/m})(5000 \text{ m})}{288.16 \text{ K}} \right]^{5.26} = (101{,}350 \text{ Pa})(0.8872)^{5.26}$$

$$= 101{,}350(0.5328) = 54{,}000 \text{ Pa} \qquad \qquad \textit{Ans. (a)}$$

This is the standard-pressure result given at $z = 5000$ m in Table A.6.

Part (b)   If the atmosphere were isothermal at 288.16 K, Eq. (2.18) would apply:

$$p \approx p_a \exp\left(-\frac{gz}{RT} \right) = (101{,}350 \text{ Pa}) \exp\left\{ -\frac{(9.807 \text{ m/s}^2)(5000 \text{ m})}{[287 \text{ m}^2/(\text{s}^2 \cdot \text{K})](288.16 \text{ K})} \right\}$$

$$= (101{,}350 \text{ Pa}) \exp(-0.5929) \approx 56{,}000 \text{ Pa} \qquad \qquad \textit{Ans. (b)}$$

This is 4 percent higher than the exact result. The isothermal formula is inaccurate in the troposphere.

Is the Linear Formula Adequate for Gases?

The linear approximation from Eq. (2.14), $\delta p \approx -\rho g \, \delta z$, is satisfactory for liquids, which are nearly incompressible. For gases, it is inaccurate unless δz is rather small. Problem P2.26 asks you to show, by binomial expansion of Eq. (2.20), that the error in using constant gas density to estimate δp from Eq. (2.14) is small if

$$\delta z \ll \frac{2T_0}{(n-1)B} \qquad \qquad (2.21)$$

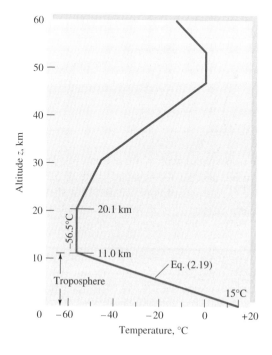

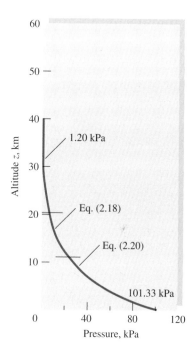

Fig. 2.7 Temperature and pressure distribution in the U.S. standard atmosphere.
Source: U.S. Standard Atmosphere, 1976, Government Printing Office, Washington DC, 1976.

where T_0 is the local absolute temperature, B is the lapse rate from Eq. (2.19), and $n = g/(RB)$ is the exponent in Eq. (2.20). The error is less than 1 percent if $\delta z < 200$ m.

2.4 Application to Manometry

From the hydrostatic formula (2.14), a change in elevation $z_2 - z_1$ of a liquid is equivalent to a change in pressure $(p_2 - p_1)/\gamma$. Thus a static column of one or more liquids or gases can be used to measure pressure differences between two points. Such a device is called a *manometer*. If multiple fluids are used, we must change the density in the formula as we move from one fluid to another. Figure 2.8 illustrates the use of the formula with a column of multiple fluids. The pressure change through each fluid is calculated separately. If we wish to know the total change $p_5 - p_1$, we add the successive changes $p_2 - p_1$, $p_3 - p_2$, $p_4 - p_3$, and $p_5 - p_4$. The intermediate values of p cancel, and we have, for the example of Fig. 2.8,

$$p_5 - p_1 = -\gamma_0(z_2 - z_1) - \gamma_w(z_3 - z_2) - \gamma_G(z_4 - z_3) - \gamma_M(z_5 - z_4) \qquad (2.22)$$

No additional simplification is possible on the right-hand side because of the different densities. Notice that we have placed the fluids in order from the lightest on top to the heaviest at bottom. This is the only stable configuration. If we attempt to layer them in any other manner, the fluids will overturn and seek the stable arrangement.

Pressure Increases Downward

The basic hydrostatic relation, Eq. (2.14), is mathematically correct but vexing to engineers because it combines two negative signs to have the pressure increase downward. When calculating hydrostatic pressure changes, engineers work instinctively by simply having the pressure increase downward and decrease upward. If point 2 is a distance h below point 1 in a uniform liquid, then $p_2 = p_1 + \rho g h$. In the meantime, Eq. (2.14) remains accurate and safe if used properly. For example, Eq. (2.22) is correct as shown, or it could be rewritten in the following "multiple downward increase" mode:

$$p_5 = p_1 + \gamma_0|z_1 - z_2| + \gamma_w|z_2 - z_3| + \gamma_G|z_3 - z_4| + \gamma_M|z_4 - z_5|$$

That is, keep adding on pressure increments as you move down through the layered fluid. A different application is a manometer, which involves both "up" and "down" calculations.

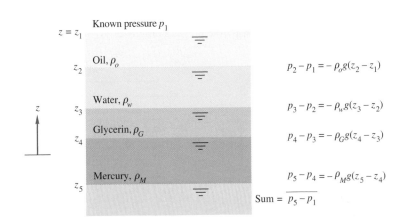

Fig. 2.8 Evaluating pressure changes through a column of multiple fluids.

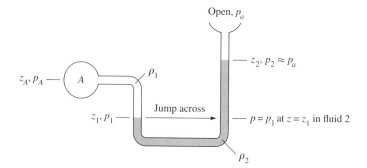

Fig. 2.9 Simple open manometer for measuring p_A relative to atmospheric pressure.

Application: A Simple Manometer

Figure 2.9 shows a simple U-tube open manometer that measures the *gage* pressure p_A relative to the atmosphere, p_a. The chamber fluid ρ_1 is separated from the atmosphere by a second, heavier fluid ρ_2, perhaps because fluid A is corrosive, or more likely because a heavier fluid ρ_2 will keep z_2 small and the open tube can be shorter.

We first apply the hydrostatic formula (2.14) from A down to z_1. Note that we can then go down to the bottom of the U-tube and back up on the right side to z_1, and the pressure will be the same, $p = p_1$. Thus we can "jump across" and then up to level z_2:

$$p_A + \gamma_1 |z_A - z_1| - \gamma_2 |z_1 - z_2| = p_2 \approx p_{\text{atm}} \qquad (2.23)$$

Another physical reason that we can "jump across" at section 1 is that a continuous length of the same fluid connects these two equal elevations. The hydrostatic relation (2.14) requires this equality as a form of Pascal's law:

> Any two points at the same elevation in a continuous mass of the same static fluid will be at the same pressure.

This idea of jumping across to equal pressures facilitates multiple-fluid problems. It will be inaccurate, however, if there are bubbles in the fluid.

EXAMPLE 2.3

The classic use of a manometer is when two U-tube legs are of equal length, as in Fig. E2.3, and the measurement involves a pressure difference across two horizontal points. The typical application is to measure pressure change across a flow device, as shown. Derive a formula for the pressure difference $p_a - p_b$ in terms of the system parameters in Fig. E2.3.

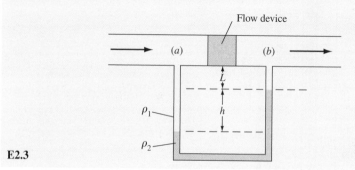

E2.3

Solution

Using Eq. (2.14), start at (a), evaluate pressure changes around the U-tube, and end up at (b):

$$p_a + \rho_1 gL + \rho_1 gh - \rho_2 gh - \rho_1 gL = p_b$$

or
$$p_a - p_b = (\rho_2 - \rho_1)gh \qquad\qquad\qquad \text{Ans.}$$

The measurement only includes h, the manometer reading. Terms involving L drop out. Note the appearance of the *difference* in densities between manometer fluid and working fluid. It is a common student error to fail to subtract out the working fluid density ρ_1—a serious error if both fluids are liquids and less disastrous numerically if fluid 1 is a gas. Academically, of course, such an error is always considered serious by fluid mechanics instructors.

Although Example 2.3, because of its popularity in engineering experiments, is sometimes considered to be the "manometer formula," it is best *not* to memorize it but rather to adapt Eq. (2.14) to each new multiple-fluid hydrostatics problem. For example, Fig. 2.10 illustrates a multiple-fluid manometer problem for finding the difference in pressure between two chambers A and B. We repeatedly apply Eq. (2.14), jumping across at equal pressures when we come to a continuous mass of the same fluid. Thus, in Fig. 2.10, we compute four pressure differences while making three jumps:

$$
\begin{aligned}
p_A - p_B &= (p_A - p_1) + (p_1 - p_2) + (p_2 - p_3) + (p_3 - p_B) \\
&= -\gamma_1(z_A - z_1) - \gamma_2(z_1 - z_2) - \gamma_3(z_2 - z_3) - \gamma_4(z_3 - z_B)
\end{aligned}
\tag{2.24}
$$

The intermediate pressures $p_{1,2,3}$ cancel. It looks complicated, but really it is merely *sequential*. One starts at A, goes down to 1, jumps across, goes up to 2, jumps across, goes down to 3, jumps across, and finally goes up to B.

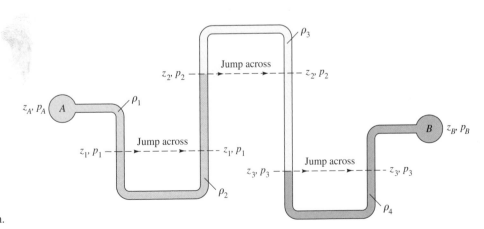

Fig. 2.10 A complicated multiple-fluid manometer to relate p_A to p_B. This system is not especially practical but makes a good homework or examination problem.

EXAMPLE 2.4

Pressure gage B is to measure the pressure at point A in a water flow. If the pressure at B is 87 kPa, estimate the pressure at A in kPa. Assume all fluids are at 20°C. See Fig. E2.4.

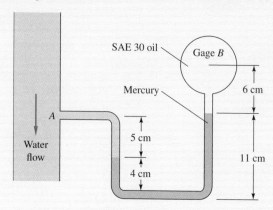

E2.4

Solution

- *System sketch:*   The system is shown in Fig. E2.4.
- *Assumptions:*   Hydrostatic fluids, no mixing, vertical "up" in Fig. E2.4.
- *Approach:*   Sequential use of Eq. (2.14) to go from A to B.
- *Property values:*   From Table 2.1 or Table A.3:

$$\gamma_{water} = 9790 \text{ N/m}^3; \quad \gamma_{mercury} = 133{,}100 \text{ N/m}^3; \quad \gamma_{oil} = 8720 \text{ N/m}^3$$

- *Solution steps:*   Proceed from A to B, "down" then "up," jumping across at the left mercury meniscus:

$$p_A + \rho_w \, |\Delta z|_w - \gamma_m \, |\Delta z_m| - \gamma_o \, |\Delta z|_o = p_B$$

or $p_A + (9790 \text{ N/m}^3)(0.05 \text{ m}) - (133{,}100 \text{ N/m}^3)(0.07 \text{ m}) - (8720 \text{ N/m}^3)(0.06 \text{ m}) = 87{,}000$

or $p_A + 490 - 9317 - 523 = 87{,}000$ Solve for $p_A = 96{,}350 \text{ N/m}^2 \approx 96.4 \text{ kPa}$ *Ans.*

- *Comments:*   Note that we abbreviated the units N/m^2 to pascals, or Pa. The intermediate five-figure result, $p_A = 96{,}350$ Pa, is unrealistic, since the data are known to only about three significant figures.

In making these manometer calculations we have neglected the capillary height changes due to surface tension, which were discussed in Example 1.8. These effects cancel if there is a fluid interface, or *meniscus,* between similar fluids on both sides of the U-tube. Otherwise, as in the right-hand U-tube of Fig. 2.10, a capillary correction can be made or the effect can be made negligible by using large-bore (≥ 1 cm) tubes.

2.5 Hydrostatic Forces on Plane Surfaces

The design of containment structures requires computation of the hydrostatic forces on various solid surfaces adjacent to the fluid. These forces relate to the weight of fluid bearing on the surface. For example, a container with a flat, horizontal bottom

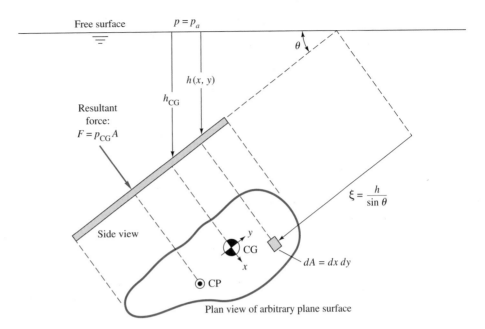

Fig. 2.11 Hydrostatic force and center of pressure on an arbitrary plane surface of area A inclined at an angle θ below the free surface.

of area A_b and water depth H will experience a downward bottom force $F_b = \gamma H A_b$. If the surface is not horizontal, additional computations are needed to find the horizontal components of the hydrostatic force.

If we neglect density changes in the fluid, Eq. (2.14) applies and the pressure on any submerged surface varies linearly with depth. For a plane surface, the linear stress distribution is exactly analogous to combined bending and compression of a beam in strength-of-materials theory. The hydrostatic problem thus reduces to simple formulas involving the centroid and moments of inertia of the plate cross-sectional area.

Figure 2.11 shows a plane panel of arbitrary shape completely submerged in a liquid. The panel plane makes an arbitrary angle θ with the horizontal free surface, so that the depth varies over the panel surface. If h is the depth to any element area dA of the plate, from Eq. (2.14) the pressure there is $p = p_a + \gamma h$.

To derive formulas involving the plate shape, establish an xy coordinate system in the plane of the plate with the origin at its centroid, plus a dummy coordinate ξ down from the surface in the plane of the plate. Then the total hydrostatic force on one side of the plate is given by

$$F = \int p\, dA = \int (p_a + \gamma h)\, dA = p_a A + \gamma \int h\, dA \qquad (2.25)$$

The remaining integral is evaluated by noticing from Fig. 2.11 that $h = \xi \sin \theta$ and, by definition, the centroidal slant distance from the surface to the plate is

$$\xi_{CG} = \frac{1}{A} \int \xi\, dA$$

Therefore, since θ is constant along the plate, Eq. (2.25) becomes

$$F = p_a A + \gamma \sin \theta \int \xi \, dA = p_a A + \gamma \sin \theta \, \xi_{CG} A$$

Finally, unravel this by noticing that $\xi_{CG} \sin \theta = h_{CG}$, the depth straight down from the surface to the plate centroid. Thus

$$F = p_a A + \gamma h_{CG} A = (p_a + \gamma h_{CG})A = p_{CG}A \qquad (2.26)$$

The force on one side of any plane submerged surface in a uniform fluid equals the pressure at the plate centroid times the plate area, independent of the shape of the plate or the angle θ at which it is slanted.

Equation (2.26) can be visualized physically in Fig. 2.12 as the resultant of a linear stress distribution over the plate area. This simulates combined compression and bending of a beam of the same cross section. It follows that the "bending" portion of the stress causes no force if its "neutral axis" passes through the plate centroid of area. Thus the remaining "compression" part must equal the centroid stress times the plate area. This is the result of Eq. (2.26).

However, to balance the bending-moment portion of the stress, the resultant force F acts not through the centroid but below it toward the high-pressure side. Its line of action passes through the *center of pressure* CP of the plate, as sketched in Fig. 2.11. To find the coordinates (x_{CP}, y_{CP}), we sum moments of the elemental force $p \, dA$ about the centroid and equate to the moment of the resultant F. To compute y_{CP}, we equate

$$F y_{CP} = \int yp \, dA = \int y(p_a + \gamma \xi \sin \theta) \, dA = \gamma \sin \theta \int y\xi \, dA$$

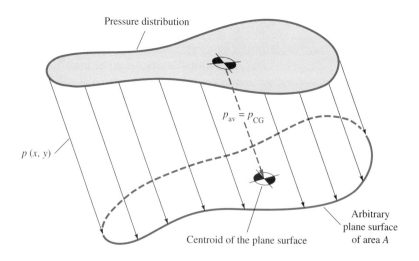

Fig. 2.12 The hydrostatic pressure force on a plane surface is equal, regardless of its shape, to the resultant of the three-dimensional linear pressure distribution on that surface $F = p_{CG}A$.

Pressure distribution

$p_{av} = p_{CG}$

$p(x, y)$

Arbitrary plane surface of area A

Centroid of the plane surface

The term $\int p_a y\, dA$ vanishes by definition of centroidal axes. Introducing $\xi = \xi_{CG} - y$, we obtain

$$Fy_{CP} = \gamma \sin\theta \left(\xi_{CG} \int y\, dA - \int y^2\, dA \right) = -\gamma \sin\theta\, I_{xx}$$

where again $\int y\, dA = 0$ and I_{xx} is the area moment of inertia of the plate area about its centroidal x axis, computed in the plane of the plate. Substituting for F gives the result

$$y_{CP} = -\gamma \sin\theta \frac{I_{xx}}{p_{CG}A} \tag{2.27}$$

The negative sign in Eq. (2.27) shows that y_{CP} is below the centroid at a deeper level and, unlike F, depends on angle θ. If we move the plate deeper, y_{CP} approaches the centroid because every term in Eq. (2.27) remains constant except p_{CG}, which increases.

The determination of x_{CP} is exactly similar:

$$Fx_{CP} = \int xp\, dA = \int x[p_a + \gamma(\xi_{CG} - y)\sin\theta]\, dA$$

$$= -\gamma \sin\theta \int xy\, dA = -\gamma \sin\theta\, I_{xy}$$

where I_{xy} is the product of inertia of the plate, again computed in the plane of the plate. Substituting for F gives

$$x_{CP} = -\gamma \sin\theta \frac{I_{xy}}{p_{CG}A} \tag{2.28}$$

For positive I_{xy}, x_{CP} is negative because the dominant pressure force acts in the third, or lower left, quadrant of the panel. If $I_{xy} = 0$, usually implying symmetry, $x_{CP} = 0$ and the center of pressure lies directly below the centroid on the y axis.

Gage Pressure Formulas

In most cases the ambient pressure p_a is neglected because it acts on both sides of the plate; for example, the other side of the plate is inside a ship or on the dry side of a gate or dam. In this case $p_{CG} = \gamma h_{CG}$, and the center of pressure becomes independent of specific weight:

$$F = \gamma h_{CG}A \qquad y_{CP} = -\frac{I_{xx}\sin\theta}{h_{CG}A} \qquad x_{CP} = -\frac{I_{xy}\sin\theta}{h_{CG}A} \tag{2.29}$$

Figure 2.13 gives the area and moments of inertia of several common cross sections for use with these formulas. Note that θ is the angle between the plate and the horizon.

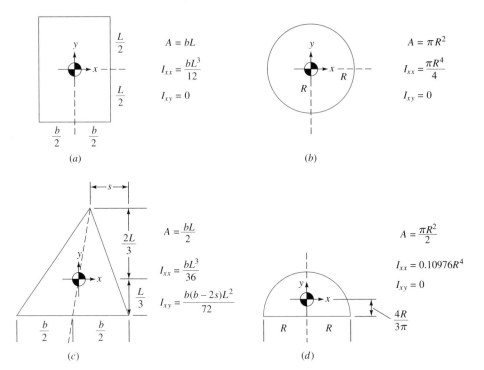

Fig. 2.13 Centroidal moments of inertia for various cross sections: (*a*) rectangle, (*b*) circle, (*c*) triangle, and (*d*) semicircle.

EXAMPLE 2.5

The gate in Fig. E2.5*a* is 5 ft wide, is hinged at point *B*, and rests against a smooth wall at point *A*. Compute (*a*) the force on the gate due to seawater pressure, (*b*) the horizontal force *P* exerted by the wall at point *A*, and (*c*) the reactions at the hinge *B*.

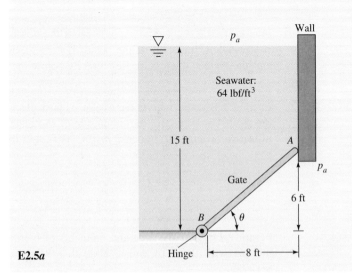

E2.5a

Solution

Part (a)

By geometry the gate is 10 ft long from A to B, and its centroid is halfway between, or at elevation 3 ft above point B. The depth h_{CG} is thus $15 - 3 = 12$ ft. The gate area is $5(10) = 50$ ft^2. Neglect p_a as acting on both sides of the gate. From Eq. (2.26) the hydrostatic force on the gate is

$$F = p_{CG}A = \gamma h_{CG}A = (64 \text{ lbf/ft}^3)(12 \text{ ft})(50 \text{ ft}^2) = 38{,}400 \text{ lbf} \qquad Ans. \ (a)$$

Part (b)

First we must find the center of pressure of F. A free-body diagram of the gate is shown in Fig. E2.5b. The gate is a rectangle, hence

$$I_{xy} = 0 \text{ and } I_{xx} = \frac{bL^3}{12} = \frac{(5 \text{ ft})(10 \text{ ft})^3}{12} = 417 \text{ ft}^4$$

The distance l from the CG to the CP is given by Eqs. (2.29) since p_a is neglected.

$$l = -y_{CP} = +\frac{I_{xx} \sin \theta}{h_{CG}A} = \frac{(417 \text{ ft}^4)(\frac{6}{10})}{(12 \text{ ft})(50 \text{ ft}^2)} = 0.417 \text{ ft}$$

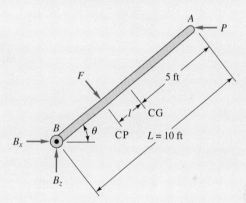

E2.5b

The distance from point B to force F is thus $10 - l - 5 = 4.583$ ft. Summing the moments counterclockwise about B gives

$$PL \sin \theta - F(5 - l) = P(6 \text{ ft}) - (38{,}400 \text{ lbf})(4.583 \text{ ft}) = 0$$

or

$$P = 29{,}300 \text{ lbf} \qquad Ans. \ (b)$$

Part (c)

With F and P known, the reactions B_x and B_z are found by summing forces on the gate:

$$\Sigma F_x = 0 = B_x + F \sin \theta - P = B_x + 38{,}400 \text{ lbf} (0.6) - 29{,}300 \text{ lbf}$$

or

$$B_x = 6300 \text{ lbf}$$

$$\Sigma F_z = 0 = B_z - F \cos \theta = B_z - 38{,}400 \text{ lbf} (0.8)$$

or

$$B_z = 30{,}700 \text{ lbf} \qquad Ans. \ (c)$$

This example should have reviewed your knowledge of statics.

The solution of Example 2.5 was achieved with the moment of inertia formulas, Eqs. (2.29). They simplify the calculations, but one loses a physical feeling for the forces. Let us repeat Parts (*a*) and (*b*) of Example 2.5 using a more visual approach.

EXAMPLE 2.6

Repeat Example 2.5 to sketch the pressure distribution on plate *AB*, and break this distribution into rectangular and triangular parts to solve for (*a*) the force on the plate and (*b*) the center of pressure.

Solution

Part (a)

Point *A* is 9 ft deep, hence $p_A = \gamma h_A = (64\ \text{lbf/ft}^3)(9\ \text{ft}) = 576\ \text{lbf/ft}^2$. Similarly, Point *B* is 15 ft deep, hence $p_B = \gamma h_B = (64\ \text{lbf/ft}^3)(15\ \text{ft}) = 960\ \text{lbf/ft}^2$. This defines the linear pressure distribution in Fig. E2.6. The rectangle is 576 by 10 ft by 5 ft into the paper. The triangle is $(960 - 576) = 384\ \text{lbf/ft}^2 \times 10$ ft by 5 ft. The centroid of the rectangle is 5 ft down the plate from *A*. The centroid of the triangle is 6.67 ft down from *A*. The total force is the rectangle force plus the triangle force:

$$F = \left(576\ \frac{\text{lbf}}{\text{ft}^2}\right)(10\ \text{ft})(5\ \text{ft}) + \left(\frac{384}{2}\ \frac{\text{lbf}}{\text{ft}^2}\right)(10\ \text{ft})(5\ \text{ft})$$

$$= 28{,}800\ \text{lbf} + 9600\ \text{lbf} = 38{,}400\ \text{lbf} \qquad\qquad Ans.\ (a)$$

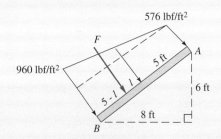

E2.6

Part (b)

The moments of these forces about point *A* are

$$\Sigma M_A = (28{,}800\ \text{lbf})(5\ \text{ft}) + (9600\ \text{lbf})(6.67\ \text{ft}) = 144{,}000 + 64{,}000 = 208{,}000\ \text{ft} \cdot \text{lbf}$$

Then $5\ \text{ft} + l = \dfrac{M_A}{F} = \dfrac{208{,}000\ \text{ft} \cdot \text{lbf}}{38{,}400\ \text{lbf}} = 5.417\ \text{ft}$ hence $l = 0.417\ \text{ft}$ *Ans.* (*b*)

Comment: We obtain the same force and center of pressure as in Example 2.5 but with more understanding. However, this approach is awkward and laborious if the plate is not a rectangle. It would be difficult to solve Example 2.7 with the pressure distribution alone because the plate is a triangle. Thus moments of inertia can be a useful simplification.

EXAMPLE 2.7

A tank of oil has a right-triangular panel near the bottom, as in Fig. E2.7. Omitting p_a, find the (*a*) hydrostatic force and (*b*) CP on the panel.

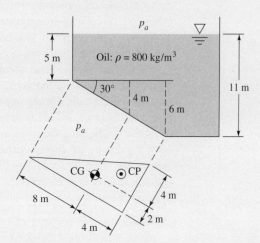

E2.7

Solution

Part (a)

The triangle has properties given in Fig. 2.13*c*. The centroid is one-third up (4 m) and one-third over (2 m) from the lower left corner, as shown. The area is

$$\tfrac{1}{2}(6 \text{ m})(12 \text{ m}) = 36 \text{ m}^2$$

The moments of inertia are

$$I_{xx} = \frac{bL^3}{36} = \frac{(6 \text{ m})(12 \text{ m})^3}{36} = 288 \text{ m}^4$$

and

$$I_{xy} = \frac{b(b - 2s)L^2}{72} = \frac{(6 \text{ m})[6 \text{ m} - 2(6 \text{ m})](12 \text{ m})^2}{72} = -72 \text{ m}^4$$

The depth to the centroid is $h_{CG} = 5 + 4 = 9$ m; thus the hydrostatic force from Eq. (2.26) is

$$F = \rho g h_{CG} A = (800 \text{ kg /m}^3)(9.807 \text{ m /s}^2)(9 \text{ m})(36 \text{ m}^2)$$

$$= 2.54 \times 10^6 \text{ (kg} \cdot \text{m)/s}^2 = 2.54 \times 10^6 \text{ N} = 2.54 \text{ MN} \qquad \textit{Ans. (a)}$$

Part (b)

The CP position is given by Eqs. (2.29):

$$y_{CP} = -\frac{I_{xx} \sin \theta}{h_{CG} A} = -\frac{(288 \text{ m}^4)(\sin 30°)}{(9 \text{ m})(36 \text{ m}^2)} = -0.444 \text{ m}$$

$$x_{CP} = -\frac{I_{xy} \sin \theta}{h_{CG} A} = -\frac{(-72 \text{ m}^4)(\sin 30°)}{(9 \text{ m})(36 \text{ m}^2)} = +0.111 \text{ m} \qquad \textit{Ans. (b)}$$

The resultant force $F = 2.54$ MN acts through this point, which is down and to the right of the centroid, as shown in Fig. E2.7.

2.6 Hydrostatic Forces on Curved Surfaces

The resultant pressure force on a curved surface is most easily computed by separating it into horizontal and vertical components. Consider the arbitrary curved surface sketched in Fig. 2.14a. The incremental pressure forces, being normal to the local area element, vary in direction along the surface and thus cannot be added numerically. We could sum the separate three components of these elemental pressure forces, but it turns out that we need not perform a laborious three-way integration.

Figure 2.14b shows a free-body diagram of the column of fluid contained in the vertical projection above the curved surface. The desired forces F_H and F_V are exerted by the surface on the fluid column. Other forces are shown due to fluid weight and horizontal pressure on the vertical sides of this column. The column of fluid must be in static equilibrium. On the upper part of the column $bcde$, the horizontal components F_1 exactly balance and are not relevant to the discussion. On the lower, irregular portion of fluid abc adjoining the surface, summation of horizontal forces shows that the desired force F_H due to the curved surface is exactly equal to the force F_H on the vertical left side of the fluid column. This left-side force can be computed by the plane surface formula, Eq. (2.26), based on a vertical projection of the area of the curved surface. This is a general rule and simplifies the analysis:

> The horizontal component of force on a curved surface equals the force on the plane area formed by the projection of the curved surface onto a vertical plane normal to the component.

If there are two horizontal components, both can be computed by this scheme. Summation of vertical forces on the fluid free body then shows that

$$F_V = W_1 + W_2 + W_{\text{air}} \tag{2.30}$$

We can state this in words as our second general rule:

> The vertical component of pressure force on a curved surface equals in magnitude and direction the weight of the entire column of fluid, both liquid and atmosphere, above the curved surface.

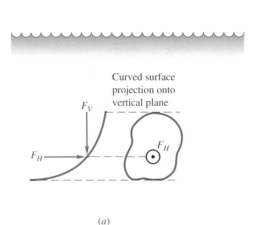

Fig. 2.14 Computation of hydrostatic force on a curved surface: (a) submerged curved surface; (b) free-body diagram of fluid above the curved surface.

(a)

(b)

Thus the calculation of F_V involves little more than finding centers of mass of a column of fluid—perhaps a little integration if the lower portion *abc* in Fig. 2.14*b* has a particularly vexing shape.

EXAMPLE 2.8

A dam has a parabolic shape $z/z_0 = (x/x_0)^2$ as shown in Fig. E2.8*a*, with $x_0 = 10$ ft and $z_0 = 24$ ft. The fluid is water, $\gamma = 62.4$ lbf/ft^3, and atmospheric pressure may be omitted. Compute the forces F_H and F_V on the dam and their line of action. The width of the dam is 50 ft.

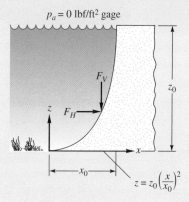

$p_a = 0$ lbf/ft^2 gage

$z = z_0 \left(\dfrac{x}{x_0}\right)^2$

E2.8*a*

Solution

- *System sketch:* Figure E2.8*b* shows the various dimensions. The dam width is $b = 50$ ft.
- *Approach:* Calculate F_H and its line of action from Eqs. (2.26) and (2.29). Calculate F_V and its line of action by finding the weight of fluid above the parabola and the centroid of this weight.
- *Solution steps for the horizontal component:* The vertical projection of the parabola lies along the z axis in Fig. E2.8*b* and is a rectangle 24 ft high and 50 ft wide. Its centroid is halfway down, or $h_{CG} = 24/2 = 12$ ft. Its area is $A_{proj} = (24 \text{ ft})(50 \text{ ft}) = 1200$ ft^2. Then, from Eq. (2.26),

$$F_H = \gamma h_{CG} A_{proj} = \left(62.4 \,\frac{\text{lbf}}{\text{ft}^3}\right)(12 \text{ ft})(1200 \text{ ft}^2) = 898{,}560 \text{ lbf} \approx 899 \times 10^3 \text{ lbf}$$

The line of action of F_H is below the centroid of A_{proj}, as given by Eq. (2.29):

$$y_{CP,\,proj} = -\frac{I_{xx} \sin \theta}{h_{CG} A_{proj}} = -\frac{(1/12)(50 \text{ ft})(24 \text{ ft})^3 \sin 90°}{(12 \text{ ft})(1200 \text{ ft}^2)} = -4 \text{ ft}$$

Thus F_H is $12 + 4 = 16$ ft, or two-thirds of the way down from the surface (8 ft up from the bottom).

- *Comments:* Note that you calculate F_H and its line of action from the *vertical projection* of the parabola, not from the parabola itself. Since this projection is *vertical*, its angle $\theta = 90°$.
- *Solution steps for the vertical component:* The vertical force F_V equals the weight of water above the parabola. Alas, a parabolic section is not in Fig. 2.13, so we had to look

it up in another book. The area and centroid are shown in Fig. E2.8b. The weight of this parabolic amount of water is

$$F_V = \gamma A_{section} b = \left(62.4 \frac{\text{lbf}}{\text{ft}^3} \right) \left[\frac{2}{3} (24 \text{ ft})(10 \text{ ft}) \right] (50 \text{ ft}) = 499{,}200 \text{ lbf} \approx 499 \times 10^3 \text{ lbf}$$

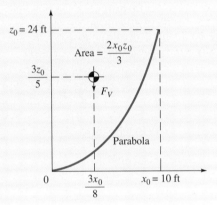

E2.8b

This force acts downward, through the centroid of the parabolic section, or at a distance $3x_0/8 = 3.75$ ft over from the origin, as shown in Figs. E2.8b,c. The resultant hydrostatic force on the dam is

$$F = (F_H^2 + F_V^2)^{1/2} = [(899\text{E3 lbf})^2 + (499\text{E3 lbf})^2]^{1/2} = 1028 \times 10^3 \text{ lbf at } 29° \quad Ans.$$

This resultant is shown in Fig. E2.8c and passes through a point 8 ft up and 3.75 ft over from the origin. It strikes the dam at a point 5.43 ft over and 7.07 ft up, as shown.
• *Comments:*   Note that entirely different formulas are used to calculate F_H and F_V. The concept of center of pressure CP is, in the writer's opinion, stretched too far when applied to curved surfaces.

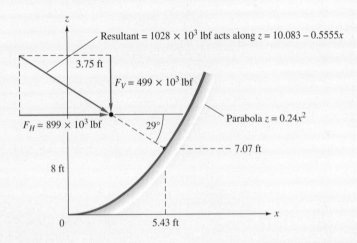

E2.8c

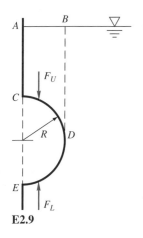

E2.9

EXAMPLE 2.9

Find an algebraic formula for the net vertical force F on the submerged semicircular project-ing structure CDE in Fig. E2.9. The structure has uniform width b into the paper. The liquid has specific weight γ.

Solution

The net force is the difference between the upward force F_L on the lower surface DE and the downward force F_U on the upper surface CD, as shown in Fig. E2.9. The force F_U equals γ times the volume $ABDC$ above surface CD. The force F_L equals γ times the volume $ABDEC$ above surface DE. The latter is clearly larger. The difference is γ times the volume of the structure itself. Thus the net upward fluid force on the semicylinder is

$$F = \gamma_{\text{fluid}} (\text{volume } CDE) = \gamma_{\text{fluid}} \frac{\pi}{2} R^2 b \qquad Ans.$$

This is the principle upon which the laws of buoyancy, Sec. 2.8, are founded. Note that the result is independent of the depth of the structure and depends upon the specific weight of the *fluid,* not the material within the structure.

2.7 Hydrostatic Forces in Layered Fluids

The formulas for plane and curved surfaces in Secs. 2.5 and 2.6 are valid only for a fluid of uniform density. If the fluid is layered with different densities, as in Fig. 2.15, a single formula cannot solve the problem because the slope of the linear pressure

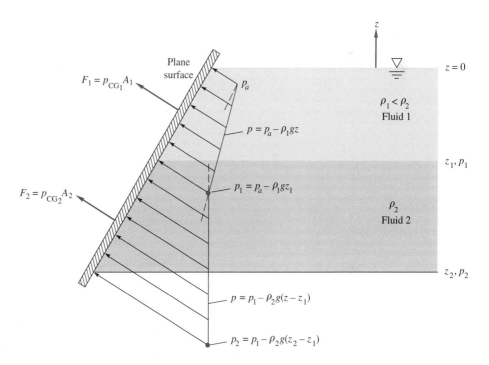

Fig. 2.15 Hydrostatic forces on a surface immersed in a layered fluid must be summed in separate pieces.

distribution changes between layers. However, the formulas apply separately to each layer, and thus the appropriate remedy is to compute and sum the separate layer forces and moments.

Consider the slanted plane surface immersed in a two-layer fluid in Fig. 2.15. The slope of the pressure distribution becomes steeper as we move down into the denser second layer. The total force on the plate does *not* equal the pressure at the centroid times the plate area, but the plate portion in each layer does satisfy the formula, so that we can sum forces to find the total:

$$F = \sum F_i = \sum p_{CG_i} A_i \qquad (2.31)$$

Similarly, the centroid of the plate portion in each layer can be used to locate the center of pressure on that portion:

$$y_{CP_i} = -\frac{\rho_i g \sin \theta_i I_{xx_i}}{p_{CG_i} A_i} \qquad x_{CP_i} = -\frac{\rho_i g \sin \theta_i I_{xy_i}}{p_{CG_i} A_i} \qquad (2.32)$$

These formulas locate the center of pressure of that particular F_i with respect to the centroid of that particular portion of plate in the layer, not with respect to the centroid of the entire plate. The center of pressure of the total force $F = \sum F_i$ can then be found by summing moments about some convenient point such as the surface. The following example will illustrate this.

EXAMPLE 2.10

A tank 20 ft deep and 7 ft wide is layered with 8 ft of oil, 6 ft of water, and 4 ft of mercury. Compute (*a*) the total hydrostatic force and (*b*) the resultant center of pressure of the fluid on the right-hand side of the tank.

Solution

Part (a) Divide the end panel into three parts as sketched in Fig. E2.10, and find the hydrostatic pressure at the centroid of each part, using the relation (2.26) in steps as in Fig. E2.10:

$$p_{CG_1} = (55.0 \text{ lbf/ft}^3)(4 \text{ ft}) = 220 \text{ lbf/ft}^2$$

$$p_{CG_2} = (55.0)(8) + 62.4(3) = 627 \text{ lbf/ft}^2$$

$$p_{CG_3} = (55.0)(8) + 62.4(6) + 846(2) = 2506 \text{ lbf/ft}^2$$

These pressures are then multiplied by the respective panel areas to find the force on each portion:

$$F_1 = p_{CG_1} A_1 = (220 \text{ lbf/ft}^2)(8 \text{ ft})(7 \text{ ft}) = 12{,}300 \text{ lbf}$$

$$F_2 = p_{CG_2} A_2 = 627(6)(7) = 26{,}300 \text{ lbf}$$

$$F_3 = p_{CG_3} A_3 = 2506(4)(7) = \underline{70{,}200 \text{ lbf}}$$

$$F = \sum F_i = 108{,}800 \text{ lbf} \qquad Ans. (a)$$

E2.10

Part (b)

Equations (2.32) can be used to locate the CP of each force F_i, noting that $\theta = 90°$ and $\sin \theta = 1$ for all parts. The moments of inertia are $I_{xx_1} = (7 \text{ ft})(8 \text{ ft})^3/12 = 298.7 \text{ ft}^4$, $I_{xx_2} = 7(6)^3/12 = 126.0 \text{ ft}^4$, and $I_{xx_3} = 7(4)^3/12 = 37.3 \text{ ft}^4$. The centers of pressure are thus at

$$y_{CP_1} = -\frac{\rho_1 g I_{xx_1}}{F_1} = -\frac{(55.0 \text{ lbf/ft}^3)(298.7 \text{ ft}^4)}{12,300 \text{ lbf}} = -1.33 \text{ ft}$$

$$y_{CP_2} = -\frac{62.4(126.0)}{26,300} = -0.30 \text{ ft} \qquad y_{CP_3} = -\frac{846(37.3)}{70,200} = -0.45 \text{ ft}$$

This locates $z_{CP_1} = -4 - 1.33 = -5.33$ ft, $z_{CP_2} = -11 - 0.30 = -11.30$ ft, and $z_{CP_3} = -16 - 0.45 = -16.45$ ft. Summing moments about the surface then gives

$$\Sigma F_i z_{CP_i} = F z_{CP}$$

or

$$12,300(-5.33) + 26,300(-11.30) + 70,200(-16.45) = 108,800 z_{CP}$$

or

$$z_{CP} = -\frac{1,518,000}{108,800} = -13.95 \text{ ft} \qquad\qquad Ans. (b)$$

The center of pressure of the total resultant force on the right side of the tank lies 13.95 ft below the surface.

2.8 Buoyancy and Stability

The same principles used to compute hydrostatic forces on surfaces can be applied to the net pressure force on a completely submerged or floating body. The results are the two laws of buoyancy discovered by Archimedes in the third century B.C.:

1. A body immersed in a fluid experiences a vertical buoyant force equal to the weight of the fluid it displaces.
2. A floating body displaces its own weight in the fluid in which it floats.

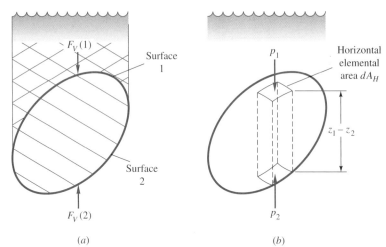

Fig. 2.16 Two different approaches to the buoyant force on an arbitrary immersed body: (*a*) forces on upper and lower curved surfaces; (*b*) summation of elemental vertical-pressure forces.

(*a*) (*b*)

Archimedes (287–212 B.C.) was born and lived in the Greek city-state of Syracuse, on what is now the island of Sicily. He was a brilliant mathematician and engineer, two millennia ahead of his time. He calculated an accurate value for pi and approximated areas and volumes of various bodies by summing elemental shapes. In other words, he invented the integral calculus. He developed levers, pulleys, catapults, and a screw pump. Archimedes was the first to write large numbers as powers of 10, avoiding Roman numerals. And he deduced the principles of buoyancy, which we study here, when he realized how light he was when sitting in a bathtub.

Archimedes' two laws are easily derived by referring to Fig. 2.16. In Fig. 2.16a, the body lies between an upper curved surface 1 and a lower curved surface 2. From Eq. (2.30) for vertical force, the body experiences a net upward force

$$
\begin{aligned}
F_B &= F_V(2) - F_V(1) \\
&= \text{(fluid weight above 2)} - \text{(fluid weight above 1)} \\
&= \text{weight of fluid equivalent to body volume} \quad (2.33)
\end{aligned}
$$

Alternatively, from Fig. 2.16b, we can sum the vertical forces on elemental vertical slices through the immersed body:

$$
F_B = \int_{\text{body}} (p_2 - p_1)\, dA_H = -\gamma \int (z_2 - z_1)\, dA_H = (\gamma)(\text{body volume}) \quad (2.34)
$$

These are identical results and equivalent to Archimedes' law 1.

Equation (2.34) assumes that the fluid has uniform specific weight. The line of action of the buoyant force passes through the center of volume of the displaced body; that is, its center of mass computed as if it had uniform density. This point through which F_B acts is called the *center of buoyancy*, commonly labeled B or CB on a drawing. Of course, the point B may or may not correspond to the actual center of mass of the body's own material, which may have variable density.

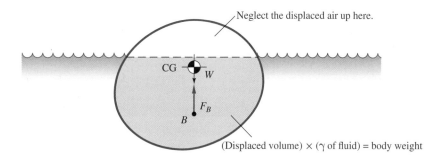

Neglect the displaced air up here.

CG — W

F_B

B

(Displaced volume) × (γ of fluid) = body weight

Fig. 2.17 Static equilibrium of a floating body.

Equation (2.34) can be generalized to a layered fluid (LF) by summing the weights of each layer of density ρ_i displaced by the immersed body:

$$(F_B)_{LF} = \sum \rho_i g(\text{displaced volume})_i \qquad (2.35)$$

Each displaced layer would have its own center of volume, and one would have to sum moments of the incremental buoyant forces to find the center of buoyancy of the immersed body.

Since liquids are relatively heavy, we are conscious of their buoyant forces, but gases also exert buoyancy on any body immersed in them. For example, human beings have an average specific weight of about 60 lbf/ft³. We may record the weight of a person as 180 lbf and thus estimate the person's total volume as 3.0 ft³. However, in so doing we are neglecting the buoyant force of the air surrounding the person. At standard conditions, the specific weight of air is 0.0763 lbf/ft³; hence the buoyant force is approximately 0.23 lbf. If measured in a vacuum, the person would weigh about 0.23 lbf more. For balloons and blimps the buoyant force of air, instead of being negligible, is the controlling factor in the design. Also, many flow phenomena, such as natural convection of heat and vertical mixing in the ocean, are strongly dependent on seemingly small buoyant forces.

Floating bodies are a special case; only a portion of the body is submerged, with the remainder poking up out of the free surface. This is illustrated in Fig. 2.17, where the shaded portion is the displaced volume. Equation (2.34) is modified to apply to this smaller volume:

$$F_B = (\gamma)(\text{displaced volume}) = \text{floating-body weight} \qquad (2.36)$$

Not only does the buoyant force equal the body weight, but also they are *collinear* since there can be no net moments for static equilibrium. Equation (2.36) is the mathematical equivalent of Archimedes' law 2, previously stated.

EXAMPLE 2.11

A block of concrete weighs 100 lbf in air and "weighs" only 60 lbf when immersed in fresh water (62.4 lbf/ft³). What is the average specific weight of the block?

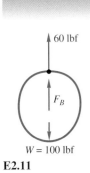

60 lbf

F_B

$W = 100$ lbf

E2.11

Solution

A free-body diagram of the submerged block (see Fig. E2.11) shows a balance between the apparent weight, the buoyant force, and the actual weight:

$$\Sigma F_z = 0 = 60 + F_B - 100$$

or
$$F_B = 40 \text{ lbf} = (62.4 \text{ lbf/ft}^3)(\text{block volume, ft}^3)$$

Solving gives the volume of the block as $40/62.4 = 0.641$ ft^3. Therefore, the specific weight of the block is

$$\gamma_{block} = \frac{100 \text{ lbf}}{0.641 \text{ ft}^3} = 156 \text{ lbf/ft}^3 \qquad\qquad Ans.$$

Occasionally, a body will have exactly the right weight and volume for its ratio to equal the specific weight of the fluid. If so, the body will be *neutrally buoyant* and will remain at rest at any point where it is immersed in the fluid. Small, neutrally buoyant particles are sometimes used in flow visualization, and a neutrally buoyant body called a *Swallow float* [2] is used to track oceanographic currents. A submarine can achieve positive, neutral, or negative buoyancy by pumping water into or out of its ballast tanks.

Stability

A floating body as in Fig. 2.17 may not approve of the position in which it is floating. If so, it will overturn at the first opportunity and is said to be statically *unstable*, like a pencil balanced on its point. The least disturbance will cause it to seek another equilibrium position that is stable. Engineers must design to avoid floating instability. The only way to tell for sure whether a floating position is stable is to "disturb" the body a slight amount mathematically and see whether it develops a restoring moment that will return it to its original position. If so, it is stable; if not, unstable. Such calculations for arbitrary floating bodies have been honed to a fine art by naval architects [3], but we can at least outline the basic principle of the static stability calculation. Figure 2.18 illustrates the computation for the usual case of a symmetric floating body. The steps are as follows:

1. The basic floating position is calculated from Eq. (2.36). The body's center of mass G and center of buoyancy B are computed.
2. The body is tilted a small angle $\Delta\theta$, and a new waterline is established for the body to float at this angle. The new position B' of the center of buoyancy is calculated. A vertical line drawn upward from B' intersects the line of symmetry at a point M, called the *metacenter*, which is independent of $\Delta\theta$ for small angles.
3. If point M is above G (that is, if the *metacentric height* $\overline{MG}$ is positive), a restoring moment is present and the original position is stable. If M is below G (negative $\overline{MG}$), the body is unstable and will overturn if disturbed. Stability increases with increasing $\overline{MG}$.

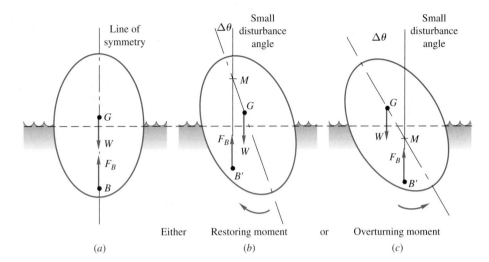

Fig. 2.18 Calculation of the metacenter M of the floating body shown in (*a*). Tilt the body a small angle $\Delta\theta$. Either (*b*) B' moves far out (point M above G denotes stability); or (*c*) B' moves slightly (point M below G denotes instability).

Thus the metacentric height is a property of the cross section for the given weight, and its value gives an indication of the stability of the body. For a body of varying cross section and draft, such as a ship, the computation of the metacenter can be very involved.

Stability Related to Waterline Area[1]

Naval architects [3] have developed the general stability concepts from Fig. 2.18 into a simple computation involving the area moment of inertia of the *waterline area* (as seen from above) about the axis of tilt. The derivation—see [3] for details—assumes that the body has a smooth shape variation (no discontinuities) near the waterline. Recall that M is the metacenter, B is the center of buoyancy, and G is the center of gravity. The final elegant formula relates the distances between these points:

$$\overline{MG} = \frac{I_O}{v_{\text{sub}}} - \overline{GB} \qquad (2.37)$$

Where I_O is the area moment of inertia of the waterline area about the tilt axis O and v_{sub} is the volume of the submerged portion of the floating body. It is desirable, of course, that $\overline{MG}$ be positive for the body to be stable.

The engineer locates G and B from the basic shape and design of the floating body and then calculates I_O and v_{sub} to determine if $\overline{MG}$ is positive.

Engineering design counts upon effective operation of the results. A stability analysis is useless if the floating body runs aground on rocks, as in Fig. 2.19.

[1]This section may be omitted without loss of continuity.

Fig. 2.19 The Italian liner *Costa Concordia* aground on January 14, 2012. Stability analysis may fail when operator mistakes occur (*Associated Press photo/Gregorio Borgia*).

EXAMPLE 2.12

A barge has a uniform rectangular cross section of width $2L$ and vertical draft of height H, as in Fig. E2.12. Determine (*a*) the metacentric height for a small tilt angle and (*b*) the range of ratio L/H for which the barge is statically stable if G is exactly at the waterline as shown.

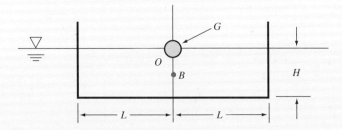

E2.12

Solution

If the barge has length b into the paper, the waterline area, relative to tilt axis O, has a base b and a height $2L$; therefore, $I_O = b(2L)^3/12$. Meanwhile, $\upsilon_{\text{sub}} = 2LbH$. Equation (2.37) predicts

$$\overline{MG} = \frac{I_o}{\upsilon_{\text{sub}}} - \overline{GB} = \frac{8bL^3/12}{2LbH} - \frac{H}{2} = \frac{L^2}{3H} - \frac{H}{2} \qquad \textit{Ans. (a)}$$

The barge can thus be stable only if

$$L^2 > 3H^2/2 \quad \text{or} \quad 2L > 2.45H \qquad \textit{Ans. (b)}$$

The wider the barge relative to its draft, the more stable it is. Lowering G would help also.

Fig. 2.20 A North Atlantic iceberg formed by calving from a Greenland glacier. These, and their even larger Antarctic sisters, are the largest floating bodies in the world. Note the evidence of further calving fractures on the front surface. *(© Corbis.)*

Even an expert will have difficulty determining the floating stability of a buoyant body of irregular shape. Such bodies may have two or more stable positions. For example, a ship may float the way we like it, so that we can sit on the deck, or it may float upside down (capsized). An interesting mathematical approach to floating stability is given in Ref. 11. The author of this reference points out that even simple shapes, such as a cube of uniform density, may have a great many stable floating orientations, not necessarily symmetric. Homogeneous circular cylinders can float with the axis of symmetry tilted from the vertical.

Floating instability occurs in nature. Fish generally swim with their planes of symmetry vertical. After death, this position is unstable and they float with their flat sides up. Giant icebergs may overturn after becoming unstable when their shapes change due to underwater melting. Iceberg overturning is a dramatic, rarely seen event.

Figure 2.20 shows a typical North Atlantic iceberg formed by calving from a Greenland glacier that protruded into the ocean. The exposed surface is rough, indicating that it has undergone further calving. Icebergs are frozen fresh, bubbly, glacial water of average density 900 kg/m^3. Thus, when an iceberg is floating in seawater, whose average density is 1025 kg/m^3, approximately 900/1025, or seven-eighths, of its volume lies below the water.

2.9 Pressure Distribution in Rigid-Body Motion

In rigid-body motion, all particles are in combined translation and rotation, and there is no relative motion between particles. With no relative motion, there are no strains or strain rates, so that the viscous term in Eq. (2.8) vanishes, leaving a balance between pressure, gravity, and particle acceleration:

$$\nabla p = \rho(\mathbf{g} - \mathbf{a}) \tag{2.38}$$

The pressure gradient acts in the direction $\mathbf{g} - \mathbf{a}$, and lines of constant pressure (including the free surface, if any) are perpendicular to this direction. The general case of combined translation and rotation of a rigid body is discussed in Chap. 3, Fig. 3.11.

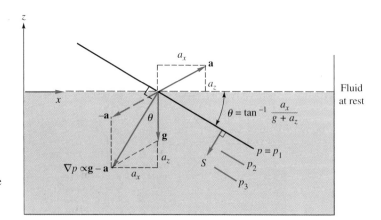

Fig. 2.21 Tilting of constant-pressure surfaces in a tank of liquid in rigid-body acceleration.

Fluids can rarely move in rigid-body motion unless restrained by confining walls for a long time. For example, suppose a tank of water is in a car that starts a constant acceleration. The water in the tank would begin to slosh about, and that sloshing would damp out very slowly until finally the particles of water would be in approximately rigid-body acceleration. This would take so long that the car would have reached hypersonic speeds. Nevertheless, we can at least discuss the pressure distribution in a tank of rigidly accelerating water.

Uniform Linear Acceleration

In the case of uniform rigid-body acceleration, Eq. (2.38) applies, **a** having the same magnitude and direction for all particles. With reference to Fig. 2.21, the parallelogram sum of **g** and $-\mathbf{a}$ gives the direction of the pressure gradient or greatest rate of increase of p. The surfaces of constant pressure must be perpendicular to this and are thus tilted at a downward angle θ such that

$$\theta = \tan^{-1}\frac{a_x}{g + a_z} \tag{2.39}$$

One of these tilted lines is the free surface, which is found by the requirement that the fluid retain its volume unless it spills out. The rate of increase of pressure in the direction $\mathbf{g} - \mathbf{a}$ is greater than in ordinary hydrostatics and is given by

$$\frac{dp}{ds} = \rho G \quad \text{where } G = [a_x^2 + (g + a_z)^2]^{1/2} \tag{2.40}$$

These results are independent of the size or shape of the container as long as the fluid is continuously connected throughout the container.

EXAMPLE 2.13

A drag racer rests her coffee mug on a horizontal tray while she accelerates at 7 m/s². The mug is 10 cm deep and 6 cm in diameter and contains coffee 7 cm deep at rest. (*a*) Assuming rigid-body acceleration of the coffee, determine whether it will spill out of the mug. (*b*) Calculate the gage pressure in the corner at point *A* if the density of coffee is 1010 kg/m³.

Solution

- *System sketch:* Figure E2.13 shows the coffee tilted during the acceleration.

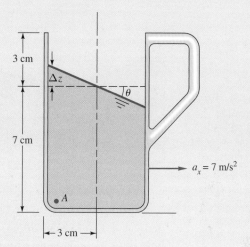

E2.13

- *Assumptions:* Rigid-body horizontal acceleration, $a_x = 7$ m/s^2. Symmetric coffee cup.
- *Property values:* Density of coffee given as 1010 kg/m^3.
- *Approach (a):* Determine the angle of tilt from the known acceleration, then find the height rise.
- *Solution steps:* From Eq. (2.39), the angle of tilt is given by

$$\theta = \tan^{-1}\frac{a_x}{g} = \tan^{-1}\frac{7.0 \text{ m/s}^2}{9.81 \text{ m/s}^2} = 35.5°$$

If the mug is symmetric, the tilted surface will pass through the center point of the rest position, as shown in Fig. E2.13. Then the rear side of the coffee free surface will rise an amount Δz given by

$$\Delta z = (3 \text{ cm})(\tan 35.5°) = 2.14 \text{ cm} < 3 \text{ cm} \quad \text{therefore no spilling} \qquad Ans. (a)$$

- *Comment (a):* This solution neglects sloshing, which might occur if the start-up is uneven.
- *Approach (b):* The pressure at A can be computed from Eq. (2.40), using the perpendicular distance Δs from the surface to A. When at rest, $p_A = \rho g h_{rest} = (1010 \text{ kg/m}^3)(9.81 \text{ m/s}^2)(0.07 \text{ m}) = 694$ Pa.

$$p_A = \rho G \, \Delta s = \left(1010\frac{\text{kg}}{\text{m}^3}\right)\left[\sqrt{(9.81)^2 + (7.0)^2}\right]\left[(0.07 + 0.0214)\cos 35.5°\right] \approx 906 \text{ Pa} \quad Ans. (b)$$

- *Comment (b):* The acceleration has increased the pressure at A by 31 percent. Think about this alternative: why does it work? Since $a_z = 0$, we may proceed vertically down the left side to compute

$$p_A = \rho g(z_{surf} - z_A) = (1010 \text{ kg/m}^3)(9.81 \text{ m/s}^2)(0.0214 \text{ m} + 0.07 \text{ m}) = 906 \text{ Pa}$$

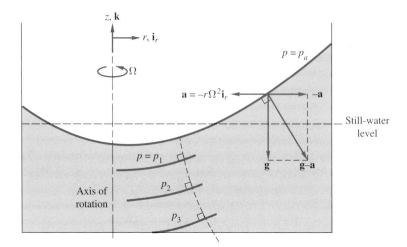

Fig. 2.22 Development of paraboloid constant-pressure surfaces in a fluid in rigid-body rotation. The dashed line along the direction of maximum pressure increase is an exponential curve.

Rigid-Body Rotation

As a second special case, consider rotation of the fluid about the z axis without any translation, as sketched in Fig. 2.22. We assume that the container has been rotating long enough at constant Ω for the fluid to have attained rigid-body rotation. The fluid acceleration will then be a centripetal term. In the coordinates of Fig. 2.22, the angular-velocity and position vectors are given by

$$\mathbf{\Omega} = \mathbf{k}\Omega \quad \mathbf{r_0} = \mathbf{i}_r r \tag{2.41}$$

Then the acceleration is given by

$$\mathbf{\Omega} \times (\mathbf{\Omega} \times \mathbf{r_0}) = -r\Omega^2 \mathbf{i}_r \tag{2.42}$$

as marked in the figure, and Eq. (2.38) for the force balance becomes

$$\nabla p = \mathbf{i}_r \frac{\partial p}{\partial r} + \mathbf{k} \frac{\partial p}{\partial z} = \rho(\mathbf{g} - \mathbf{a}) = \rho(-g\mathbf{k} + r\Omega^2 \mathbf{i}_r)$$

Equating like components, we find the pressure field by solving two first-order partial differential equations:

$$\frac{\partial p}{\partial r} = \rho r \Omega^2 \quad \frac{\partial p}{\partial z} = -\gamma \tag{2.43}$$

The right-hand sides of (2.43) are known functions of r and z. One can proceed as follows: Integrate the first equation "partially," holding z constant, with respect to r. The result is

$$p = \tfrac{1}{2}\rho r^2 \Omega^2 + f(z) \tag{2.44}$$

where the "constant" of integration is actually a function $f(z)$.[2] Now differentiate this with respect to z and compare with the second relation of (2.43):

$$\frac{\partial p}{\partial z} = 0 + f'(z) = -\gamma$$

---

[2]This is because $f(z)$ vanishes when differentiated with respect to r. If you don't see this, you should review your calculus.

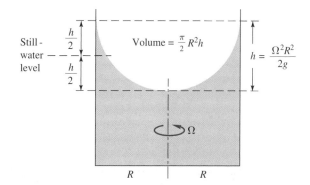

Fig. 2.23 Determining the free-surface position for rotation of a cylinder of fluid about its central axis.

or $$f(z) = -\gamma z + C$$

where C is a constant. Thus Eq. (2.44) now becomes

$$p = \text{const} - \gamma z + \tfrac{1}{2}\rho r^2 \Omega^2 \tag{2.45}$$

This is the pressure distribution in the fluid. The value of C is found by specifying the pressure at one point. If $p = p_0$ at $(r, z) = (0, 0)$, then $C = p_0$. The final desired distribution is

$$\boxed{p = p_0 - \gamma z + \tfrac{1}{2}\rho r^2 \Omega^2} \tag{2.46}$$

The pressure is linear in z and parabolic in r. If we wish to plot a constant-pressure surface, say, $p = p_1$, Eq. (2.45) becomes

$$z = \frac{p_0 - p_1}{\gamma} + \frac{r^2 \Omega^2}{2g} = a + br^2 \tag{2.47}$$

Thus the surfaces are paraboloids of revolution, concave upward, with their minimum points on the axis of rotation. Some examples are sketched in Fig. 2.22.

As in the previous example of linear acceleration, the position of the free surface is found by conserving the volume of fluid. For a noncircular container with the axis of rotation off-center, as in Fig. 2.22, a lot of laborious mensuration is required, and a single problem will take you all weekend. However, the calculation is easy for a cylinder rotating about its central axis, as in Fig. 2.23. Since the volume of a paraboloid is one-half the base area times its height, the still-water level is exactly halfway between the high and low points of the free surface. The center of the fluid drops an amount $h/2 = \Omega^2 R^2/(4g)$, and the edges rise an equal amount.

EXAMPLE 2.14

The coffee cup in Example 2.13 is removed from the drag racer, placed on a turntable, and rotated about its central axis until a rigid-body mode occurs. Find (a) the angular velocity that will cause the coffee to just reach the lip of the cup and (b) the gage pressure at point A for this condition.

Solution

Part (a)

The cup contains 7 cm of coffee. The remaining distance of 3 cm up to the lip must equal the distance $h/2$ in Fig. 2.23. Thus

$$\frac{h}{2} = 0.03 \text{ m} = \frac{\Omega^2 R^2}{4g} = \frac{\Omega^2 (0.03 \text{ m})^2}{4(9.81 \text{ m/s}^2)}$$

Solving, we obtain

$$\Omega^2 = 1308 \quad \text{or} \quad \Omega = 36.2 \text{ rad/s} = 345 \text{ r/min} \qquad \textit{Ans. (a)}$$

Part (b)

To compute the pressure, it is convenient to put the origin of coordinates r and z at the bottom of the free-surface depression, as shown in Fig. E2.14. The gage pressure here is $p_0 = 0$, and point A is at $(r, z) = (3 \text{ cm}, -4 \text{ cm})$. Equation (2.46) can then be evaluated:

$$p_A = 0 - (1010 \text{ kg/m}^3)(9.81 \text{ m/s}^2)(-0.04 \text{ m})$$
$$+ \tfrac{1}{2}(1010 \text{ kg/m}^3)(0.03 \text{ m})^2(1308 \text{ rad}^2/\text{s}^2)$$
$$= 396 \text{ N/m}^2 + 594 \text{ N/m}^2 = 990 \text{ Pa} \qquad \textit{Ans. (b)}$$

This is about 43 percent greater than the still-water pressure $p_A = 694$ Pa.

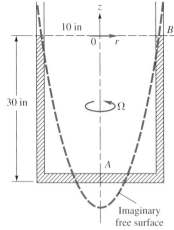

E2.14

Here, as in the linear acceleration case, it should be emphasized that the paraboloid pressure distribution (2.46) sets up in *any* fluid under rigid-body rotation, regardless of the shape or size of the container. The container may even be closed and filled with fluid. It is only necessary that the fluid be continuously interconnected throughout the container. The following example will illustrate a peculiar case in which one can visualize an imaginary free surface extending outside the walls of the container.

EXAMPLE 2.15

A U-tube with a radius of 10 in and containing mercury to a height of 30 in is rotated about its center at 180 r/min until a rigid-body mode is achieved. The diameter of the tubing is negligible. Atmospheric pressure is 2116 lbf/ft^2. Find the pressure at point A in the rotating condition. See Fig. E2.15.

Solution

Convert the angular velocity to radians per second:

$$\Omega = (180 \text{ r/min}) \frac{2\pi \text{ rad/r}}{60 \text{ s/min}} = 18.85 \text{ rad/s}$$

From Table 2.1 we find for mercury that $\gamma = 846$ lbf/ft^3 and hence $\rho = 846/32.2 = 26.3$ slugs/ft^3. At this high rotation rate, the free surface will slant upward at a fierce angle [about 84°; check this from Eq. (2.47)], but the tubing is so thin that the free surface will remain at approximately the same 30-in height, point B. Placing our origin of coordinates

E2.15

at this height, we can calculate the constant C in Eq. (2.45) from the condition $p_B = 2116$ lbf/ft^2 at $(r, z) = (10$ in, $0)$:

$$p_B = 2116 \text{ lbf/ft}^2 = C - 0 + \tfrac{1}{2}(26.3 \text{ slugs/ft}^3)(\tfrac{10}{12} \text{ ft})^2(18.85 \text{ rad/s})^2$$

or
$$C = 2116 - 3245 = -1129 \text{ lbf/ft}^2$$

We then obtain p_A by evaluating Eq. (2.46) at $(r, z) = (0, -30$ in$)$:

$$p_A = -1129 - (846 \text{ lbf/ft}^3)(-\tfrac{30}{12} \text{ ft}) = -1129 + 2115 = 986 \text{ lbf/ft}^2 \qquad Ans.$$

This is less than atmospheric pressure, and we can see why if we follow the free-surface paraboloid down from point B along the dashed line in the figure. It will cross the horizontal portion of the U-tube (where p will be atmospheric) and fall *below* point A. From Fig. 2.23 the actual drop from point B will be

$$h = \frac{\Omega^2 R^2}{2g} = \frac{(18.85)^2(\tfrac{10}{12})^2}{2(32.2)} = 3.83 \text{ ft} = 46 \text{ in}$$

Thus p_A is about 16 inHg below atmospheric pressure, or about $\tfrac{16}{12}(846) = 1128$ lbf/ft^2 below $p_a = 2116$ lbf/ft^2, which checks with the answer above. When the tube is at rest,

$$p_A = 2116 - 846(-\tfrac{30}{12}) = 4231 \text{ lbf/ft}^2$$

Hence rotation has reduced the pressure at point A by 77 percent. Further rotation can reduce p_A to near-zero pressure, and cavitation can occur.

An interesting by-product of this analysis for rigid-body rotation is that the lines everywhere parallel to the pressure gradient form a family of curved surfaces, as sketched in Fig. 2.22. They are everywhere orthogonal to the constant-pressure surfaces, and hence their slope is the negative inverse of the slope computed from Eq. (2.47):

$$\left.\frac{dz}{dr}\right|_{GL} = -\frac{1}{(dz/dr)_{p=\text{const}}} = -\frac{1}{r\Omega^2/g}$$

where GL stands for gradient line

or
$$\frac{dz}{dr} = -\frac{g}{r\Omega^2} \tag{2.48}$$

Separating the variables and integrating, we find the equation of the pressure-gradient surfaces:

$$r = C_1 \exp\left(-\frac{\Omega^2 z}{g}\right) \tag{2.49}$$

Notice that this result and Eq. (2.47) are independent of the density of the fluid. In the absence of friction and Coriolis effects, Eq. (2.49) defines the lines along which the apparent net gravitational field would act on a particle. Depending on its density, a small particle or bubble would tend to rise or fall in the fluid along these

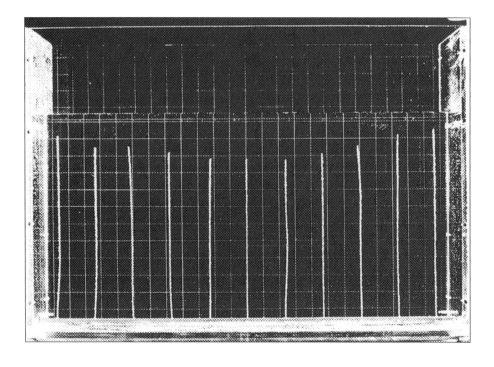

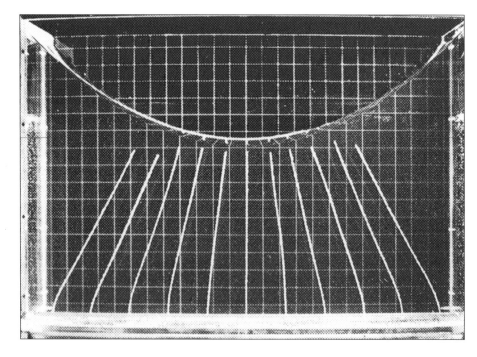

Fig. 2.24 Experimental demonstration with buoyant streamers of the fluid force field in rigid-body rotation: (*top*) fluid at rest (streamers hang vertically upward); (*bottom*) rigid-body rotation (streamers are aligned with the direction of maximum pressure gradient). (© *The American Association of Physics Teachers. Reprinted with permission from "The Apparent Field of Gravity in a Rotating Fluid System" by R. Ian Fletcher. American Journal of Physics vol. 40, pp. 959–965, July 1972.*)

exponential lines, as demonstrated experimentally in Ref. 5. Also, buoyant streamers would align themselves with these exponential lines, thus avoiding any stress other than pure tension. Figure 2.24 shows the configuration of such streamers before and during rotation.

2.10 Pressure Measurement

Pressure is a derived property. It is the force per unit area as related to fluid molecular bombardment of a surface. Thus most pressure instruments only *infer* the pressure by calibration with a primary device such as a deadweight piston tester. There are many such instruments, for both a static fluid and a moving stream. The instrumentation texts in Refs. 7 to 10, 12, 13, and 16–17 list over 20 designs for pressure measurement instruments. These instruments may be grouped into four categories:

1. *Gravity-based:* barometer, manometer, deadweight piston.
2. *Elastic deformation:* bourdon tube (metal and quartz), diaphragm, bellows, strain-gage, optical beam displacement.
3. *Gas behavior:* gas compression (McLeod gage), thermal conductance (Pirani gage), molecular impact (Knudsen gage), ionization, thermal conductivity, air piston.
4. *Electric output:* resistance (Bridgman wire gage), diffused strain gage, capacitative, piezoelectric, potentiometric, magnetic inductance, magnetic reluctance, linear variable differential transformer (LVDT), resonant frequency.
5. *Luminescent coatings* for surface pressures [15].

The gas-behavior gages are mostly special-purpose instruments used for certain scientific experiments. The deadweight tester is the instrument used most often for calibrations; for example, it is used by the U.S. National Institute for Standards and Technology (NIST). The barometer is described in Fig. 2.6.

The manometer, analyzed in Sec. 2.4, is a simple and inexpensive hydrostatic-principle device with no moving parts except the liquid column itself. Manometer measurements must not disturb the flow. The best way to do this is to take the measurement through a *static hole* in the wall of the flow, as illustrated in Fig. 2.25a. The hole should be normal to the wall, and burrs should be avoided. If the hole is small enough (typically 1-mm diameter), there will be no flow into the measuring tube once the pressure has adjusted to a steady value. Thus the flow is almost undisturbed. An oscillating flow pressure, however, can cause a large error due to possible dynamic response of the tubing. Other devices of smaller dimensions are used for dynamic-pressure measurements. The manometer in Fig. 2.25a measures the gage pressure p_1. The instrument in Fig. 2.25b is a digital *differential* manometer, which can measure the difference between two different points in the flow, with stated accuracy of 0.1 percent of full scale. The world of instrumentation is moving quickly toward digital readings.

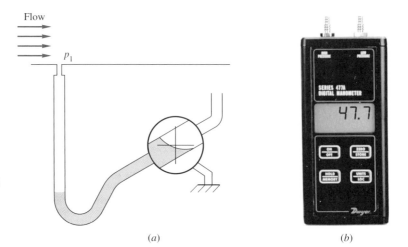

Fig. 2.25 Two types of accurate manometers for precise measurements: (*a*) tilted tube with eyepiece; (*b*) a capacitive-type digital manometer of rated accuracy ±0.1 percent. *(Courtesy of Dwyer Instruments, Inc.)*

(*a*)   (*b*)

In category 2, elastic-deformation instruments, a popular, inexpensive, and reliable device is the *bourdon tube,* sketched in Fig. 2.26. When pressurized internally, a curved tube with flattened cross section will deflect outward. The deflection can be measured by a linkage attached to a calibrated dial pointer, as shown. Or the deflection can be used to drive electric-output sensors, such as a variable transformer. Similarly, a membrane or *diaphragm* will deflect under pressure and can either be sensed directly or used to drive another sensor.

An interesting variation of Fig. 2.26 is the *fused-quartz, force-balanced bourdon tube,* shown in Fig. 2.27, whose spiral-tube deflection is sensed optically and returned to a zero reference state by a magnetic element whose output is proportional to the

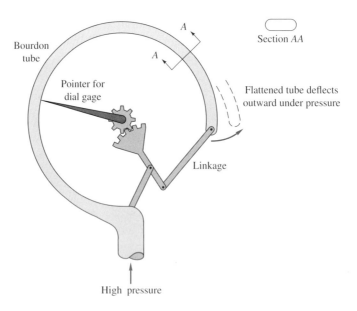

Fig. 2.26 Schematic of a bourdon-tube device for mechanical measurement of high pressures.

Fig. 2.27 The fused-quartz, force-balanced bourdon tube is the most accurate pressure sensor used in commercial applications today. *(Courtesy of Ruska Instrument Corporation, Houston, TX.)*

fluid pressure. The fused-quartz, force-balanced bourdon tube is reported to be one of the most accurate pressure sensors ever devised, with uncertainty on the order of ±0.003 percent.

The quartz gages, both the bourdon type and the resonant type, are expensive but extremely accurate, stable, and reliable [14]. They are often used for deep-ocean pressure measurements, which detect long waves and tsunami activity over extensive time periods.

The last category, *electric-output sensors,* is extremely important in engineering because the data can be stored on computers and freely manipulated, plotted, and analyzed. Three examples are shown in Fig. 2.28, the first being the *capacitive* sensor in Fig. 2.28*a*. The differential pressure deflects the silicon diaphragm and changes the capacitance of the liquid in the cavity. Note that the cavity has spherical end caps to prevent overpressure damage. In the second type, Fig. 2.28*b*, strain gages and other sensors are chemically diffused or etched onto a chip, which is stressed by the applied pressure. Finally, in Fig. 2.28*c*, a micromachined silicon sensor is arranged to deform under pressure such that its natural vibration frequency is proportional to the pressure. An oscillator excites the element's resonant frequency and converts it into appropriate pressure units.

Another kind of dynamic electric-output sensor is the *piezoelectric transducer,* shown in Fig. 2.29. The sensing elements are thin layers of quartz, which generate an electric charge when subjected to stress. The design in Fig. 2.29 is flush-mounted on a solid surface and can sense rapidly varying pressures, such as blast waves. Other designs are of the cavity type. This type of sensor primarily detects transient pressures, not steady stress, but if highly insulated can also be used for short-term static events. Note also that it measures *gage* pressure—that is, it detects only a change from ambient conditions.

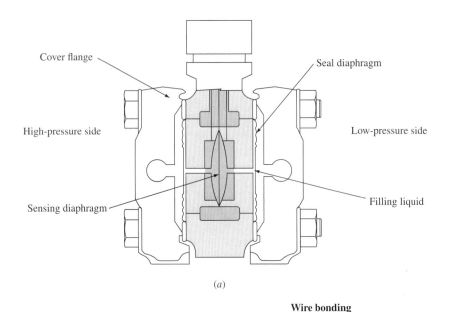

Cover flange

High-pressure side

Sensing diaphragm

Seal diaphragm

Low-pressure side

Filling liquid

(a)

Strain gages
Diffused into integrated
silicon chip

Wire bonding
Stitch bonded
connections from
chip to body plug

Etched cavity
Micromachined
silicon sensor

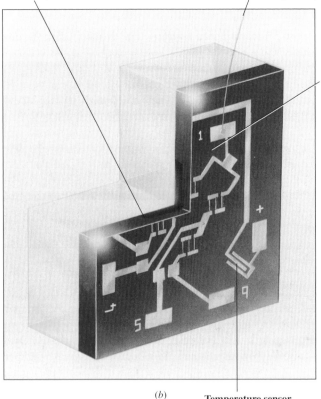

(b)

Temperature sensor
On-chip diode for
optimum temperature
performance

Fig. 2.28 Pressure sensors with
electric output: (*a*) a silicon
diaphragm whose deflection
changes the cavity capacitance
(*b*) a silicon strain gage that is
stressed by applied pressure; (*c*) a
micromachined silicon element
that resonates at a frequency
proportional to applied pressure.
*Source: (a) Courtesy of Yokogawa
Corporation of America. (b) and
(c) are courtesy of Druck, Inc.,
Fairfield, CT.*

0mm   1mm   2mm   3mm

(c)

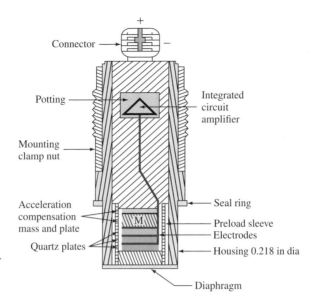

Fig. 2.29 A piezoelectric transducer measures rapidly changing pressures.
Source: Courtesy of PCB Piezorronics, Inc, Depew, New York.

Summary

This chapter has been devoted entirely to the computation of pressure distributions and the resulting forces and moments in a static fluid or a fluid with a known velocity field. All hydrostatic (Secs. 2.3 to 2.8) and rigid-body (Sec. 2.9) problems are solved in this manner and are classic cases that every student should understand. In arbitrary viscous flows, both pressure and velocity are unknowns and are solved together as a system of equations in the chapters that follow.

Problems

Most of the problems herein are fairly straightforward. More difficult or open-ended assignments are indicated with an asterisk, as in Prob. 2.9. Problems labeled with a computer icon 💻 may require the use of a computer. The standard end-of-chapter problems 2.1 to 2.161 (categorized in the problem distribution) are followed by word problems W2.1 to W2.9, fundamentals of engineering exam problems FE2.1 to FE2.10, comprehensive problems C2.1 to C2.9, and design projects D2.1 to D2.3.

Problem Distribution

Section	Topic	Problems
2.1, 2.2	Stresses; pressure gradient; gage pressure	2.1–2.6
2.3	Hydrostatic pressure; barometers	2.7–2.23
2.3	The atmosphere	2.24–2.29
2.4	Manometers; multiple fluids	2.30–2.47
2.5	Forces on plane surfaces	2.48–2.80
2.6	Forces on curved surfaces	2.81–2.100
2.7	Forces in layered fluids	2.101–2.102
2.8	Buoyancy; Archimedes' principles	2.103–2.126
2.8	Stability of floating bodies	2.127–2.136
2.9	Uniform acceleration	2.137–2.151
2.9	Rigid-body rotation	2.152–2.159
2.10	Pressure measurements	2.160–2.161

Stresses; pressure gradient; gage pressure

P2.1 For the two-dimensional stress field shown in Fig. P2.1 it is found that

$$\sigma_{xx} = 3000 \text{ lbf/ft}^2 \quad \sigma_{yy} = 2000 \text{ lbf/ft}^2 \quad \sigma_{xy} = 500 \text{ lbf/ft}^2$$

Find the shear and normal stresses (in lbf/ft^2) acting on plane AA cutting through the element at a 30° angle as shown.

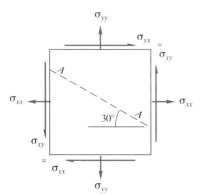

P2.1

P2.2   For the two-dimensional stress field shown in Fig. P2.1 suppose that

$$\sigma_{xx} = 2000 \text{ lbf/ft}^2 \quad \sigma_{yy} = 3000 \text{ lbf/ft}^2 \quad \sigma_n(AA) = 2500 \text{ lbf/ft}^2$$

Compute (*a*) the shear stress σ_{xy} and (*b*) the shear stress on plane *AA*.

P2.3   A vertical, clean, glass piezometer tube has an inside diameter of 1 mm. When pressure is applied, water at 20°C rises into the tube to a height of 25 cm. After correcting for surface tension, estimate the applied pressure in Pa.

P2.4   Pressure gages, such as the bourdon gage in Fig. P2.4, are calibrated with a deadweight piston. If the bourdon gage is designed to rotate the pointer 10 degrees for every 2 psig of internal pressure, how many degrees does the pointer rotate if the piston and weight together total 44 newtons?

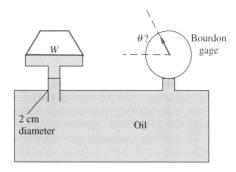

P2.4

P2.5   Quito, Ecuador, has an average altitude of 9350 ft. On a standard day, pressure gage A in a laboratory experiment reads 63 kPa and gage B reads 105 kPa. Express these readings in gage pressure or vacuum pressure, whichever is appropriate.

P2.6   Any pressure reading can be expressed as a length or *head,* $h = p/\rho g$. What is standard sea-level pressure expressed in (*a*) ft of glycerin, (*b*) inHg, (*c*) m of water, and (*d*) mm of ethanol? Assume all fluids are at 20°C.

Hydrostatic pressure; barometers

P2.7   La Paz, Bolivia, is at an altitude of approximately 12,000 ft. Assume a standard atmosphere. How high would the liquid rise in a *methanol* barometer, assumed at 20°C?
Hint: Don't forget the vapor pressure.

P2.8   Suppose, which is possible, that there is a half-mile deep lake of pure ethanol on the surface of Mars. Estimate the absolute pressure, in Pa, at the bottom of this speculative lake.

P2.9   A storage tank, 26 ft in diameter and 36 ft high, is filled with SAE 30W oil at 20°C. (*a*) What is the gage pressure, in lbf/in², at the bottom of the tank? (*b*) How does your result in (*a*) change if the tank diameter is reduced to 15 ft? (*c*) Repeat (*a*) if leakage has caused a layer of 5 ft of water to rest at the bottom of the (full) tank.

P2.10   A large open tank is open to sea-level atmosphere and filled with liquid, at 20°C, to a depth of 50 ft. The absolute pressure at the bottom of the tank is approximately 221.5 kPa. From Table A.3, what might this liquid be?

P2.11   In Fig. P2.11, pressure gage A reads 1.5 kPa (gage). The fluids are at 20°C. Determine the elevations *z*, in meters, of the liquid levels in the open piezometer tubes *B* and *C*.

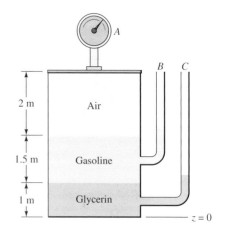

P2.11

P2.12   In Fig. P2.12 the tank contains water and immiscible oil at 20°C. What is *h* in cm if the density of the oil is 898 kg/m³?

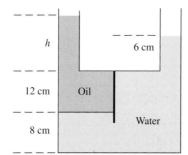

P2.12

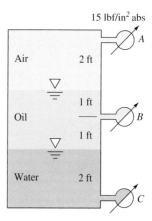

P2.15

P2.13 In Fig. P2.13 the 20°C water and gasoline surfaces are open to the atmosphere and at the same elevation. What is the height h of the third liquid in the right leg?

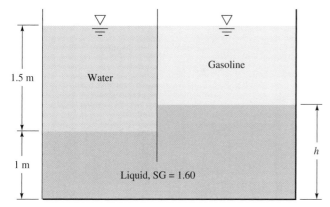

P2.13

P2.14 For the three-liquid system shown, compute h_1 and h_2. Neglect the air density.

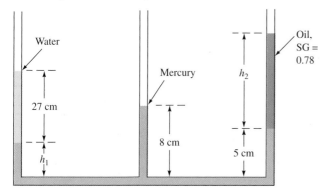

P2.14

P2.15 The air–oil–water system in Fig. P2.15 is at 20°C. Knowing that gage A reads 15 lbf/in² absolute and gage B reads 1.25 lbf/in² less than gage C, compute (a) the specific weight of the oil in lbf/ft³ and (b) the actual reading of gage C in lbf/in² absolute.

P2.16 If the absolute pressure at the interface between water and mercury in Fig. P2.16 is 93 kPa, what, in lbf/ft², is (a) the pressure at the surface and (b) the pressure at the bottom of the container?

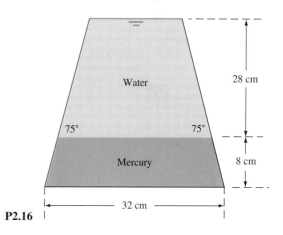

P2.16

P2.17 The system in Fig. P2.17 is at 20°C. Determine the height h of the water in the left side.

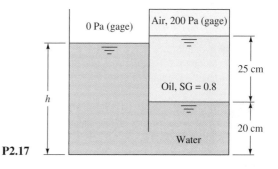

P2.17

P2.18 The system in Fig. P2.18 is at 20°C. If atmospheric pressure is 101.33 kPa and the pressure at the bottom of the tank is 242 kPa, what is the specific gravity of fluid X?

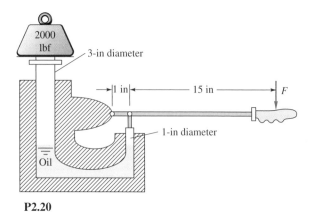

P2.20

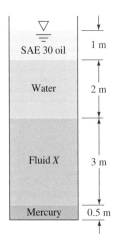

P2.18

P2.19 The U-tube in Fig. P2.19 has a 1-cm ID and contains mercury as shown. If 20 cm³ of water is poured into the right-hand leg, what will the free-surface height in each leg be after the sloshing has died down?

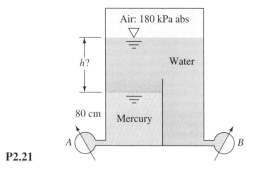

P2.21

P2.22 The fuel gage for a gasoline tank in a car reads proportional to the bottom gage pressure as in Fig. P2.22. If the tank is 30 cm deep and accidentally contains 2 cm of water plus gasoline, how many centimeters of air remain at the top when the gage erroneously reads "full"?

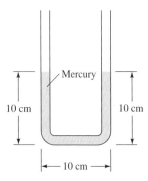

P2.19

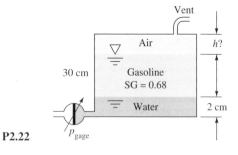

P2.22

P2.20 The hydraulic jack in Fig. P2.20 is filled with oil at 56 lbf/ft³. Neglecting the weight of the two pistons, what force F on the handle is required to support the 2000-lbf weight for this design?

P2.21 At 20°C gage A reads 350 kPa absolute. What is the height h of the water in cm? What should gage B read in kPa absolute? See Fig. P2.21.

P2.23 In Fig. P2.23 both fluids are at 20°C. If surface tension effects are negligible, what is the density of the oil, in kg/m³?

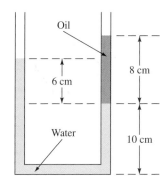

P2.23

The atmosphere

P2.24 In Prob. 1.2 we made a crude integration of the density distribution $\rho(z)$ in Table A.6 and estimated the mass of the earth's atmosphere to be $m \approx 6$ E18 kg. Can this result be used to estimate sea-level pressure on the earth? Conversely, can the actual sea-level pressure of 101.35 kPa be used to make a more accurate estimate of the atmospheric mass?

*P2.25 As measured by NASA's Viking landers, the atmosphere of Mars, where $g \approx 3.71$ m/s^2, is almost entirely carbon dioxide, and the surface pressure averages 700 Pa. The temperature is cold and drops off exponentially: $T \approx T_o\,e^{-Cz}$, where C = 1.3E-5 m^{-1} and T_o = 250 K. For example, at 20,000 m altitude, $T \approx 193$ K. (a) Find an analytic formula for the variation of pressure with altitude. (b) Find the altitude where pressure on Mars has dropped to 1 pascal.

P2.26 For gases that undergo large changes in height, the linear approximation, Eq. (2.14), is inaccurate. Expand the troposphere power-law, Eq. (2.20), into a power series, and show that the linear approximation $p \approx p_a - \rho_a\,gz$ is adequate when

$$\delta z \ll \frac{2T_0}{(n-1)B} \quad \text{where } n = \frac{g}{RB}$$

P2.27 Conduct an experiment to illustrate atmospheric pressure. *Note:* Do this over a sink or you may get wet! Find a drinking glass with a very smooth, uniform rim at the top. Fill the glass nearly full with water. Place a smooth, light, flat plate on top of the glass such that the entire rim of the glass is covered. A glossy postcard works best. A small index card or one flap of a greeting card will also work. See Fig. P2.27*a*.

(a) Hold the card against the rim of the glass and turn the glass upside down. Slowly release pressure on the card. Does the water fall out of the glass? Record your experimental observations. (b) Find an expression for the pressure at points 1 and 2 in Fig. P2.27*b*. Note that the glass is now inverted, so the original top rim of the glass is at the bottom of the picture, and the original bottom of the glass is at the top of the picture. The weight of the card can be neglected. (c) Estimate the theoretical maximum glass height at which this experiment could still work, such that the water would not fall out of the glass.

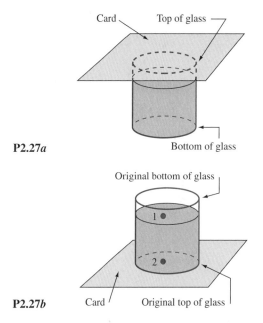

P2.27*a*

P2.27*b*

P2.28 A correlation of computational fluid dynamics results indicates that, all other things being equal, the distance traveled by a well-hit baseball varies inversely as the 0.36 power of the air density. If a home-run ball hit in Citi Field in New York travels 400 ft, estimate the distance it would travel in (a) Quito, Ecuador, and (b) Colorado Springs, CO.

P2.29 Follow up on Prob. P2.8 by estimating the altitude on Mars where the pressure has dropped to 20 percent of its surface value. Assume an *isothermal* atmosphere, not the exponential variation of P2.25.

Manometers; multiple fluids

P2.30 For the traditional equal-level manometer measurement in Fig. E2.3, water at 20°C flows through the plug device from *a* to *b*. The manometer fluid is mercury. If $L = 12$ cm and $h = 24$ cm, (a) what is the pressure drop through the device? (b) If the water flows through the pipe at a velocity $V = 18$ ft/s, what is the *dimensionless loss coefficient* of the device, defined by $K = \Delta p/(\rho V^2)$? We will study loss coefficients in Chap. 6.

P2.31　In Fig. P2.31 all fluids are at 20°C. Determine the pressure difference (Pa) between points A and B.

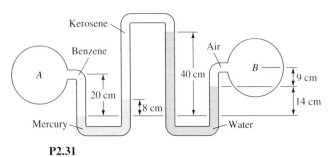

P2.31

P2.32　For the inverted manometer of Fig. P2.32, all fluids are at 20°C. If $p_B - p_A = 97$ kPa, what must the height H be in cm?

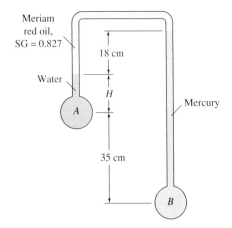

P2.32

P2.33　In Fig. P2.33 the pressure at point A is 25 lbf/in². All fluids are at 20°C. What is the air pressure in the closed chamber B, in Pa?

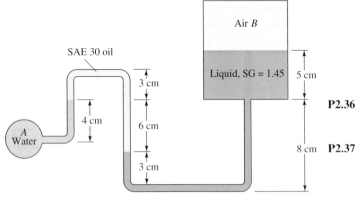

P2.33

*P2.34　Sometimes manometer dimensions have a significant effect. In Fig. P2.34 containers (a) and (b) are cylindrical and conditions are such that $p_a = p_b$. Derive a formula for the pressure difference $p_a - p_b$ when the oil–water interface on the right rises a distance $\Delta h < h$, for (a) $d \ll D$ and (b) $d = 0.15D$. What is the percentage change in the value of Δp?

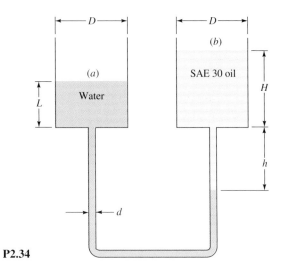

P2.34

P2.35　Water flows upward in a pipe slanted at 30°, as in Fig. P2.35. The mercury manometer reads $h = 12$ cm. Both fluids are at 20°C. What is the pressure difference $p_1 - p_2$ in the pipe?

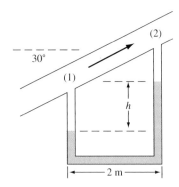

P2.35

P2.36　In Fig. P2.36 both the tank and the tube are open to the atmosphere. If $L = 2.13$ m, what is the angle of tilt θ of the tube?

P2.37　The inclined manometer in Fig. P2.37 contains Meriam red manometer oil, SG = 0.827. Assume that the reservoir is very large. If the inclined arm is fitted with graduations 1 in apart, what should the angle θ be if each graduation corresponds to 1 lbf/ft² gage pressure for p_A?

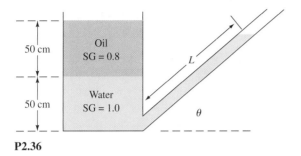

P2.36

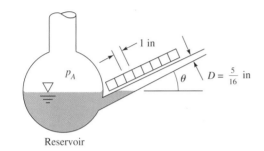

P2.37

P2.38 If the pressure in container A in Fig. P2.38 is 200 kPa, compute the pressure in container B.

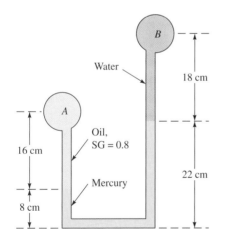

P2.38

P2.39 In Fig. P2.39 the right leg of the manometer is open to the atmosphere. Find the gage pressure, in Pa, in the air gap in the tank.

P2.40 In Fig. P2.40, if pressure gage A reads 20 lbf/in² absolute, find the pressure in the closed air space B. The manometer fluid is Meriam red oil, SG = 0.827.

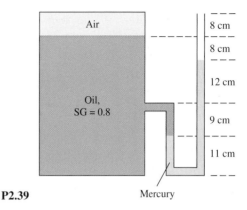

P2.39

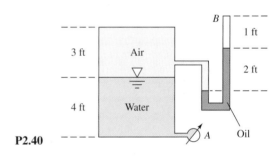

P2.40

P2.41 The system in Fig. P2.41 is at 20°C. Compute the pressure at point A in lbf/ft² absolute.

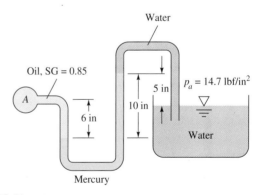

P2.41

P2.42 Very small pressure differences $p_A - p_B$ can be measured accurately by the two-fluid differential manometer in Fig. P2.42. Density ρ_2 is only slightly larger than that of the upper fluid ρ_1. Derive an expression for the proportionality between h and $p_A - p_B$ if the reservoirs are very large.

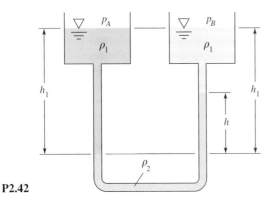

P2.42

P2.43 The traditional method of measuring blood pressure uses a *sphygmomanometer*, first recording the highest (*systolic*) and then the lowest (*diastolic*) pressure from which flowing "Korotkoff" sounds can be heard. Patients with dangerous hypertension can exhibit systolic pressures as high as 5 lbf/in^2. Normal levels, however, are 2.7 and 1.7 lbf/in^2, respectively, for systolic and diastolic pressures. The manometer uses mercury and air as fluids.
(*a*) How high in cm should the manometer tube be?
(*b*) Express normal systolic and diastolic blood pressure in millimeters of mercury.

P2.44 Water flows downward in a pipe at 45°, as shown in Fig. P2.44. The pressure drop $p_1 - p_2$ is partly due to gravity and partly due to friction. The mercury manometer reads a 6-in height difference. What is the total pressure drop $p_1 - p_2$ in lbf/in^2? What is the pressure drop due to friction only between 1 and 2 in lbf/in^2? Does the manometer reading correspond only to friction drop? Why?

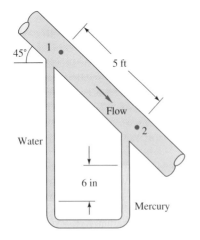

P2.44

P2.45 In Fig. P2.45, determine the gage pressure at point A in Pa. Is it higher or lower than atmospheric?

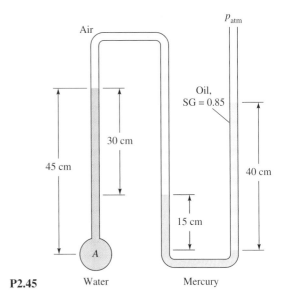

P2.45   Water   Mercury

P2.46 In Fig. P2.46 both ends of the manometer are open to the atmosphere. Estimate the specific gravity of fluid X.

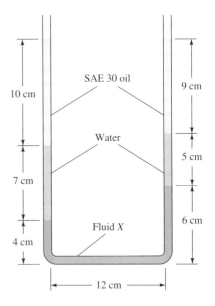

P2.46

P2.47 The cylindrical tank in Fig. P2.47 is being filled with water at 20°C by a pump developing an exit pressure of 175 kPa. At the instant shown, the air pressure is 110 kPa and $H = 35$ cm. The pump stops when it can no longer raise the water pressure. For isothermal air compression, estimate H at that time.

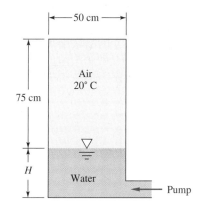

P2.47

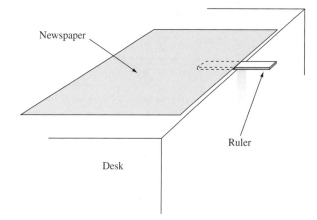

P2.49

P2.48 The system in Fig. P2.48 is open to 1 atm on the right side. (*a*) If *L* = 120 cm, what is the air pressure in container *A*? (*b*) Conversely, if p_A = 135 kPa, what is the length *L*?

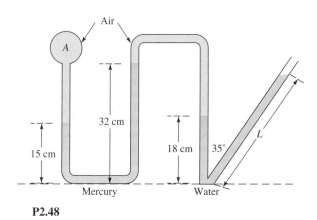

P2.48

Forces on plane surfaces

P2.49 Conduct the following experiment to illustrate air pressure. Find a thin wooden ruler (approximately 1 ft in length) or a thin wooden paint stirrer. Place it on the edge of a desk or table with a little less than half of it hanging over the edge lengthwise. Get two full-size sheets of newspaper; open them up and place them on top of the ruler, covering only the portion of the ruler resting on the desk as illustrated in Fig. P2.49. (*a*) Estimate the total force on top of the newspaper due to air pressure in the room. (*b*) *Careful!* To avoid potential injury, make sure nobody is standing directly in front of the desk. Perform a karate chop on the portion of the ruler sticking out over the edge of the desk. Record your results. (*c*) Explain your results.

P2.50 A small submarine, with a hatch door 30 in in diameter, is submerged in seawater. (*a*) If the water hydrostatic force on the hatch is 69,000 lbf, how deep is the sub? (*b*) If the sub is 350 ft deep, what is the hydrostatic force on the hatch?

P2.51 Gate *AB* in Fig. P2.51 is 1.2 m long and 0.8 m into the paper. Neglecting atmospheric pressure, compute the force *F* on the gate and its center-of-pressure position *X*.

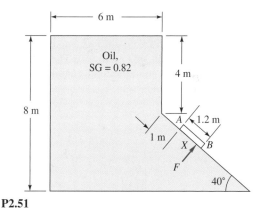

P2.51

P2.52 Example 2.5 calculated the force on plate *AB* and its line of action, using the moment-of-inertia approach. Some teachers say it is more instructive to calculate these by *direct integration* of the pressure forces. Using Figs. P2.52 and E2.5*a*, (*a*) find an expression for the pressure variation $p(\xi)$ along the plate; (*b*) integrate this expression to find the total force *F*; (*c*) integrate the moments about point *A* to find the position of the center of pressure.

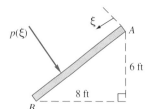

P2.52

P2.53   The Hoover Dam, in Arizona, encloses Lake Mead, which contains 10 trillion gallons of water. The dam is 1200 ft wide and the lake is 500 ft deep. (*a*) Estimate the hydrostatic force on the dam, in MN. (*b*) Explain how you might analyze the stress in the dam due to this hydrostatic force.

P2.54   In Fig. P2.54, the hydrostatic force *F* is the same on the bottom of all three containers, even though the weights of liquid above are quite different. The three bottom shapes and the fluids are the same. This is called the *hydrostatic paradox*. Explain why it is true and sketch a free body of each of the liquid columns.

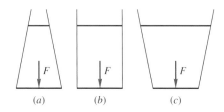

P2.54   (*a*)   (*b*)   (*c*)

P2.55   Gate *AB* in Fig. P2.55 is 5 ft wide into the paper, hinged at *A*, and restrained by a stop at *B*. The water is at 20°C. Compute (*a*) the force on stop *B* and (*b*) the reactions at *A* if the water depth *h* = 9.5 ft.

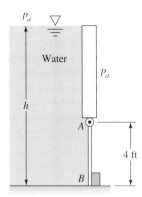

P2.55

P2.56   In Fig. P2.55, gate *AB* is 5 ft wide into the paper, and stop *B* will break if the water force on it equals 9200 lbf. For what water depth *h* is this condition reached?

P2.57   The square vertical panel *ABCD* in Fig. P2.57 is submerged in water at 20°C. Side *AB* is at least 1.7 m below the surface. Determine the difference between the hydrostatic forces on subpanels *ABD* and *BCD*.

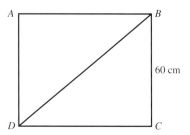

P2.57

P2.58   In Fig. P2.58, the cover gate *AB* closes a circular opening 80 cm in diameter. The gate is held closed by a 200-kg mass as shown. Assume standard gravity at 20°C. At what water level *h* will the gate be dislodged? Neglect the weight of the gate.

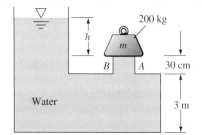

P2.58

*P2.59   Gate *AB* has length *L* and width *b* into the paper, is hinged at *B*, and has negligible weight. The liquid level *h* remains at the top of the gate for any angle *θ*. Find an analytic expression for the force *P*, perpendicular to *AB*, required to keep the gate in equilibrium in Fig. P2.59.

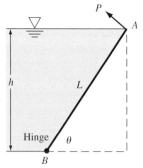

P2.59

P2.60   In Fig. P2.60, vertical, unsymmetrical trapezoidal panel *ABCD* is submerged in fresh water with side *AB* 12 ft below the surface. Since trapezoid formulas are complicated, (*a*) estimate, reasonably, the water force on the panel, in lbf, neglecting atmospheric pressure. For extra credit, (*b*) look up the formula and compute the exact force on the panel.

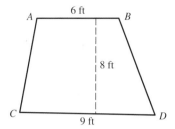

P2.60

*P2.61 Gate AB in Fig. P2.61 is a homogeneous mass of 180 kg, 1.2 m wide into the paper, hinged at A, and resting on a smooth bottom at B. All fluids are at 20°C. For what water depth h will the force at point B be zero?

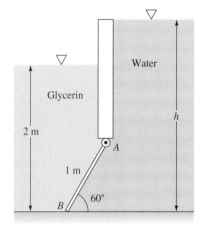

P2.61

P2.62 Gate AB in Fig. P2.62 is 15 ft long and 8 ft wide into the paper and is hinged at B with a stop at A. The water is at 20°C. The gate is 1-in-thick steel, SG = 7.85. Compute the water level h for which the gate will start to fall.

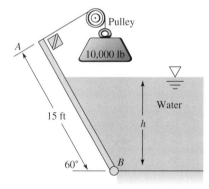

P2.62

P2.63 The tank in Fig. P2.63 has a 4-cm-diameter plug at the bottom on the right. All fluids are at 20°C. The plug will pop out if the hydrostatic force on it is 25 N. For this condition, what will be the reading h on the mercury manometer on the left side?

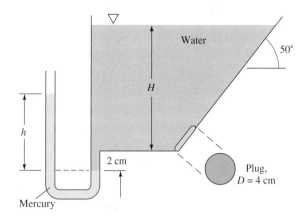

P2.63

*P2.64 Gate ABC in Fig. P2.64 has a fixed hinge line at B and is 2 m wide into the paper. The gate will open at A to release water if the water depth is high enough. Compute the depth h for which the gate will begin to open.

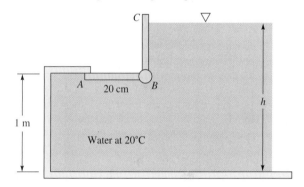

P2.64

*P2.65 Gate AB in Fig. P2.65 is semicircular, hinged at B, and held by a horizontal force P at A. What force P is required for equilibrium?

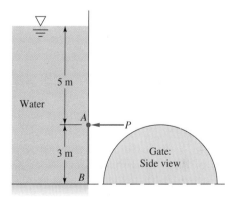

P2.65

P2.66 Dam *ABC* in Fig. P2.66 is 30 m wide into the paper and made of concrete (SG = 2.4). Find the hydrostatic force on surface *AB* and its moment about *C*. Assuming no seepage of water under the dam, could this force tip the dam over? How does your argument change if there is seepage under the dam?

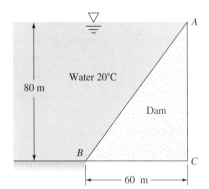

P2.66

*P2.67 Generalize Prob. P2.66 as follows. Denote length *AB* as *H*, length *BC* as *L*, and angle *ABC* as θ. Let the dam material have specific gravity SG. The width of the dam is *b*. Assume no seepage of water under the dam. Find an analytic relation between SG and the critical angle θ_c for which the dam will just tip over to the right. Use your relation to compute θ_c for the special case SG = 2.4 (concrete).

P2.68 Isosceles triangle gate *AB* in Fig. P2.68 is hinged at *A* and weighs 1500 N. What horizontal force *P* is required at point *B* for equilibrium?

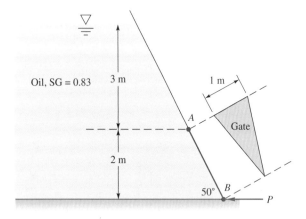

P2.68

P2.69 Consider the slanted plate *AB* of length *L* in Fig. P2.69. (*a*) Is the hydrostatic force *F* on the plate equal to the weight of the *missing water* above the plate? If not, correct this hypothesis. Neglect the atmosphere. (*b*) Can a "missing water" theory be generalized to *curved* surfaces of this type?

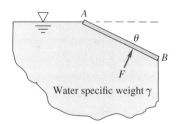

P2.69

P2.70 The swing-check valve in Fig. P2.70 covers a 22.86-cm diameter opening in the slanted wall. The hinge is 15 cm from the centerline, as shown. The valve will open when the hinge moment is 50 N · m. Find the value of *h* for the water to cause this condition.

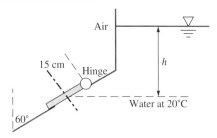

P2.70

*P2.71 In Fig. P2.71 gate *AB* is 3 m wide into the paper and is connected by a rod and pulley to a concrete sphere (SG = 2.40). What diameter of the sphere is just sufficient to keep the gate closed?

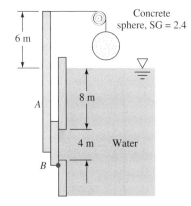

P2.71

P2.72 In Fig. P2.72, gate *AB* is circular. Find the moment of the hydrostatic force on this gate about axis *A*.

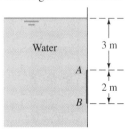

P2.72

P2.73 Gate *AB* is 5 ft wide into the paper and opens to let fresh water out when the ocean tide is dropping. The hinge at *A* is 2 ft above the freshwater level. At what ocean level *h* will the gate first open? Neglect the gate weight.

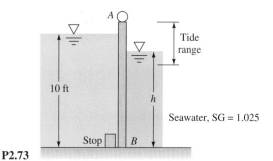

P2.73

P2.74 Find the height *H* in Fig. P2.74 for which the hydrostatic force on the rectangular panel is the same as the force on the semicircular panel below.

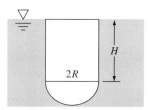

P2.74

P2.75 The cap at point B on the 5-cm-diameter tube in Fig. P2.75 will be dislodged when the hydrostatic force on its base reaches 22 lbf. For what water depth *h* does this occur?

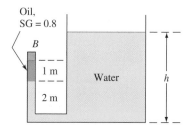

P2.75

P2.76 Panel *BC* in Fig. P2.76 is circular. Compute (*a*) the hydrostatic force of the water on the panel, (*b*) its center of pressure, and (*c*) the moment of this force about point *B*.

P2.77 The circular gate *ABC* in Fig. P2.77 has a 1-m radius and is hinged at *B*. Compute the force *P* just sufficient to keep the gate from opening when *h* = 8 m. Neglect atmospheric pressure.

P2.78 Panels AB and CD in Fig. P2.78 are each 120 cm wide into the paper. (*a*) Can you deduce, by inspection, which panel has the larger water force? (*b*) Even if your deduction is brilliant, calculate the panel forces anyway.

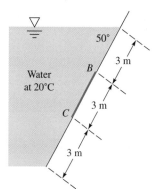

P2.76

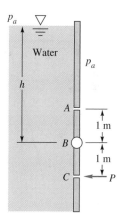

P2.77

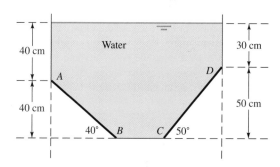

P2.78

P2.79 Gate *ABC* in Fig. P2.79 is 1 m square and is hinged at *B*. It will open automatically when the water level *h* becomes high enough. Determine the lowest height for which the gate will open. Neglect atmospheric pressure. Is this result independent of the liquid density?

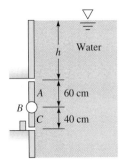

P2.79

*P2.80 A concrete dam (SG = 2.5) is made in the shape of an isosceles triangle, as in Fig. P2.80. Analyze this geometry to find the range of angles θ for which the hydrostatic force will tend to tip the dam over at point B. The width into the paper is b.

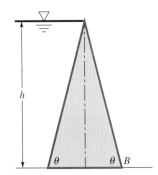

P2.80

Forces on curved surfaces

P2.81 For the semicircular cylinder CDE in Example 2.9, find the vertical hydrostatic force by integrating the vertical component of pressure around the surface from $\theta = 0$ to $\theta = \pi$.

*P2.82 The dam in Fig. P2.82 is a quarter circle 50 m wide into the paper. Determine the horizontal and vertical components of the hydrostatic force against the dam and the point CP where the resultant strikes the dam.

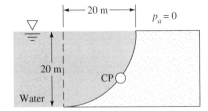

P2.82

*P2.83 Gate AB in Fig. P2.83 is a quarter circle 10 ft wide into the paper and hinged at B. Find the force F just sufficient to keep the gate from opening. The gate is uniform and weighs 3000 lbf.

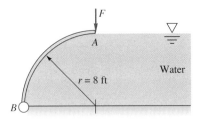

P2.83

P2.84 Panel AB in Fig. P2.84 is a parabola with its maximum at point A. It is 150 cm wide into the paper. Neglect atmospheric pressure. Find (a) the vertical and (b) the horizontal water forces on the panel.

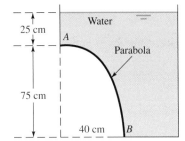

P2.84

P2.85 Compute the horizontal and vertical components of the hydrostatic force on the quarter-circle panel at the bottom of the water tank in Fig. P2.85.

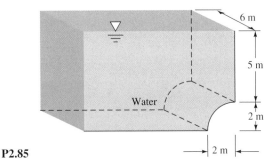

P2.85

P2.86 The quarter circle gate BC in Fig. P2.86 is hinged at C. Find the horizontal force P required to hold the gate stationary. Neglect the weight of the gate.

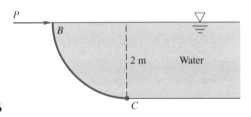

P2.86

P2.87   The bottle of champagne (SG = 0.96) in Fig. P2.87 is under pressure, as shown by the mercury-manometer reading. Compute the net force on the 2-in-radius hemispherical end cap at the bottom of the bottle.

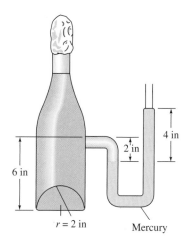

P2.87

*P2.88   Gate *ABC* is a circular arc, sometimes called a *Tainter gate*, which can be raised and lowered by pivoting about point *O*. See Fig. P2.88. For the position shown, determine (*a*) the hydrostatic force of the water on the gate and (*b*) its line of action. Does the force pass through point *O*?

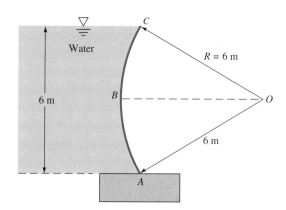

P2.88

P2.89   The tank in Fig. P2.89 contains benzene and is pressurized to 200 kPa (gage) in the air gap. Determine the vertical hydrostatic force on circular-arc section *AB* and its line of action.

P2.90   The tank in Fig. P2.90 is 120 cm long into the paper. Determine the horizontal and vertical hydrostatic forces on the quarter-circle panel *AB*. The fluid is water at 20°C. Neglect atmospheric pressure.

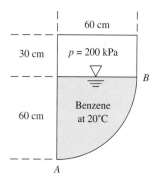

P2.89

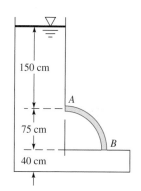

P2.90

P2.91   The hemispherical dome in Fig. P2.91 weighs 30 kN and is filled with water and attached to the floor by six equally spaced bolts. What is the force in each bolt required to hold down the dome?

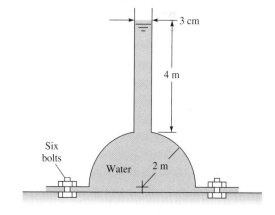

P2.91

P2.92   A 4-m-diameter water tank consists of two half cylinders, each weighing 4.5 kN/m, bolted together as shown in Fig. P2.92. If the support of the end caps is neglected, determine the force induced in each bolt.

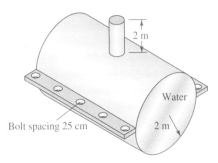

P2.92

*P2.93 In Fig. P2.93, a one-quadrant spherical shell of radius R is submerged in liquid of specific weight γ and depth $h > R$. Find an analytic expression for the resultant hydrostatic force, and its line of action, on the shell surface.

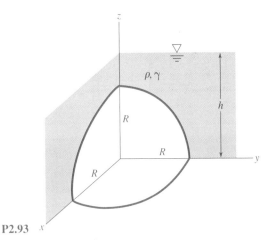

P2.93

P2.94 Find an analytic formula for the vertical and horizontal forces on each of the semicircular panels AB in Fig. P2.94. The width into the paper is b. Which force is larger? Why?

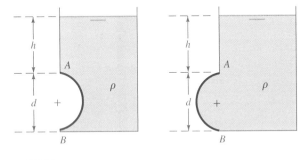

P2.94

*P2.95 The uniform body A in Fig. P2.95 has width b into the paper and is in static equilibrium when pivoted about hinge O. What is the specific gravity of this body if (a) $h = 0$ and (b) $h = R$?

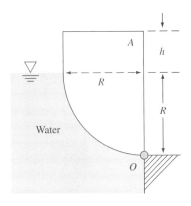

P2.95

P2.96 In Fig. P2.96, curved section AB is 5 m wide into the paper and is a 60° circular arc of radius 2 m. Neglecting atmospheric pressure, calculate the vertical and horizontal hydrostatic forces on arc AB.

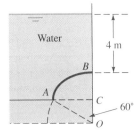

P2.96

P2.97 The contractor ran out of gunite mixture and finished the deep corner of a 5-m-wide swimming pool with a quarter-circle piece of PVC pipe, labeled AB in Fig. P2.97. Compute the horizontal and vertical water forces on the curved panel AB.

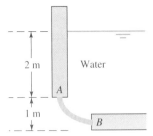

P2.97

P2.98 The curved surface in Fig. P2.98 consists of two quarter-spheres and a half cylinder. A side view and front view are shown. Calculate the horizontal and vertical forces on the surface.

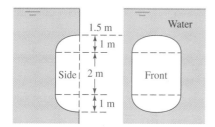

P2.98

P2.99 The mega-magnum cylinder in Fig. P2.99 has a hemispherical bottom and is pressurized with air to 75 kPa (gage) at the top. Determine (*a*) the horizontal and (*b*) the vertical hydrostatic forces on the hemisphere, in lbf.

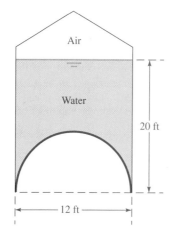

P2.99

P2.100 Pressurized water fills the tank in Fig. P2.100. Compute the net hydrostatic force on the conical surface *ABC*.

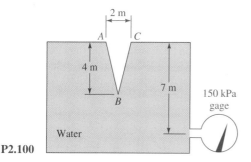

P2.100

Forces on layered surfaces

P2.101 The closed layered box in Fig. P2.101 has square horizontal cross sections everywhere. All fluids are at 20°C. Estimate the gage pressure of the air if (*a*) the hydrostatic force on panel *AB* is 48 kN or (*b*) the hydrostatic force on the bottom panel *BC* is 97 kN.

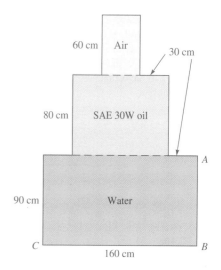

P2.101

P2.102 A cubical tank is 3 m × 3 m × 3 m and is layered with 1 meter of fluid of specific gravity 1.0, 1 meter of fluid with SG = 0.9, and 1 meter of fluid with SG = 0.8. Neglect atmospheric pressure. Find (*a*) the hydrostatic force on the bottom and (*b*) the force on a side panel.

Buoyancy; Archimedes' principles

P2.103 A solid block, of specific gravity 0.9, floats such that 75 percent of its volume is in water and 25 percent of its volume is in fluid *X*, which is layered above the water. What is the specific gravity of fluid *X*?

P2.104 The can in Fig. P2.104 floats in the position shown. What is its weight in N?

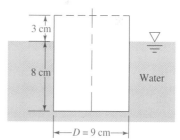

P2.104

P2.105 It is said that Archimedes discovered the buoyancy laws when asked by King Hiero of Syracuse to determine whether his new crown was pure gold (SG = 19.3). Archimedes measured the weight of the crown in air to be 11.8 N and its weight in water to be 10.9 N. Was it pure gold?

P2.106 A spherical helium balloon has a total mass of 3 kg. It settles in a calm standard atmosphere at an altitude of 5500 m. Estimate the diameter of the balloon.

P2.107 Repeat Prob. 2.62, assuming that the 10,000-lbf weight is aluminum (SG = 2.71) and is hanging submerged in the water.

P2.108 A 7-cm-diameter solid aluminum ball (SG = 2.7) and a solid brass ball (SG = 8.5) balance nicely when submerged in a liquid, as in Fig. P2.108. (*a*) If the fluid is water at 20°C, what is the diameter of the brass ball? (*b*) If the brass ball has a diameter of 3.8 cm, what is the density of the fluid?

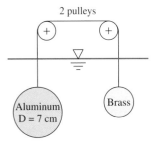

P2.108

P2.109 A *hydrometer* floats at a level that is a measure of the specific gravity of the liquid. The stem is of constant diameter *D*, and a weight in the bottom stabilizes the body to float vertically, as shown in Fig. P2.109. If the position $h = 0$ is pure water (SG = 1.0), derive a formula for *h* as a function of total weight *W*, *D*, SG, and the specific weight γ_0 of water.

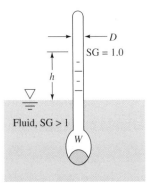

P2.109

P2.110 A solid sphere, of diameter 18 cm, floats in 20°C water with 1527 cubic centimeters exposed above the surface. (*a*) What are the weight and specific gravity of this sphere? (*b*) Will it float in 20°C gasoline? If so, how many cubic centimeters will be exposed?

P2.111 A solid wooden cone (SG = 0.729) floats in water. The cone is 30 cm high, its vertex angle is 90°, and it floats with vertex down. How much of the cone protrudes above the water?

P2.112 The uniform 5-m-long round wooden rod in Fig. P2.112 is tied to the bottom by a string. Determine (*a*) the tension in the string and (*b*) the specific gravity of the wood. Is it possible for the given information to determine the inclination angle θ? Explain.

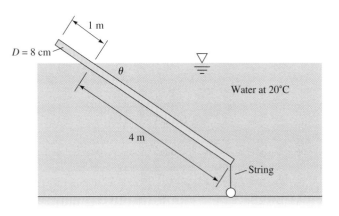

P2.112

P2.113 A *spar buoy* is a buoyant rod weighted to float and protrude vertically, as in Fig. P2.113. It can be used for measurements or markers. Suppose that the buoy is maple wood (SG = 0.6), 2 in by 2 in by 12 ft, floating in seawater (SG = 1.025). How many pounds of steel (SG = 7.85) should be added to the bottom end so that $h = 18$ in?

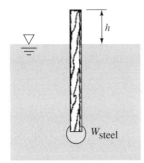

P2.113

P2.114 The uniform rod in Fig. P2.114 is hinged at point *B* on the waterline and is in static equilibrium as shown when 2 kg of lead (SG = 11.4) are attached to its end. What is the specific gravity of the rod material? What is peculiar about the rest angle $\theta = 30°$?

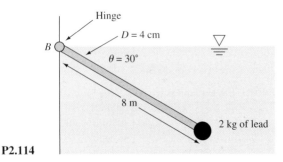

P2.114

P2.115 The 2-in by 2-in by 12-ft spar buoy from Fig. P2.113 has 5 lbm of steel attached and has gone aground on a rock, as in Fig. P2.115. Compute the angle θ at which the buoy will lean, assuming that the rock exerts no moments on the spar.

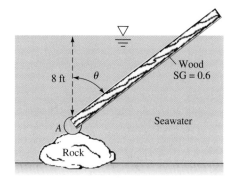

P2.115

P2.116 The bathysphere of the chapter-opener photo is steel, SG $\approx$ 7.85, with inside diameter 54 inches and wall thickness 1.5 inches. Will the empty sphere float in seawater?

P2.117 The solid sphere in Fig. P2.117 is iron (SG $\approx$ 7.9). The tension in the cable is 600 lbf. Estimate the diameter of the sphere, in cm.

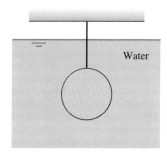

P2.117

P2.118 An intrepid treasure-salvage group has discovered a steel box, containing gold doubloons and other valuables, resting in 80 ft of seawater. They estimate the weight of the box and treasure (in air) at 7000 lbf. Their plan is to attach the box to a sturdy balloon, inflated with air to 3 atm pressure. The empty balloon weighs 250 lbf. The box is 2 ft wide, 5 ft long, and 18 in high. What is the proper diameter of the balloon to ensure an upward lift force on the box that is 20 percent more than required?

P2.119 When a 5-lbf weight is placed on the end of the uniform floating wooden beam in Fig. P2.119, the beam tilts at an angle θ with its upper right corner at the surface, as shown. Determine (*a*) the angle θ and (*b*) the specific gravity of the wood. *Hint:* Both the vertical forces and the moments about the beam centroid must be balanced.

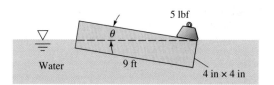

P2.119

P2.120 A uniform wooden beam (SG = 0.65) is 10 cm by 10 cm by 3 m and is hinged at A, as in Fig. P2.120. At what angle θ will the beam float in the 20°C water?

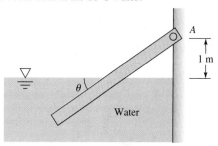

P2.120

P2.121 The uniform beam in Fig. P2.121, of size L by h by b and with specific weight γ_b, floats exactly on its diagonal when a heavy uniform sphere is tied to the left corner, as shown.

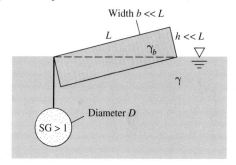

P2.121

Show that this can happen only (*a*) when $\gamma_b = \gamma/3$ and (*b*) when the sphere has size

$$D = \left[\frac{Lhb}{\pi(SG - 1)} \right]^{1/3}$$

P2.122 A uniform block of steel (SG = 7.85) will "float" at a mercury–water interface as in Fig. P2.122. What is the ratio of the distances a and b for this condition?

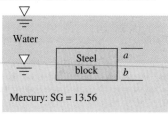

P2.122

P2.123 A barge has the trapezoidal shape shown in Fig. P2.123 and is 22 m long into the paper. If the total weight of barge and cargo is 350 tons, what is the draft H of the barge when floating in seawater?

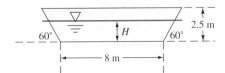

P2.123

P2.124 A balloon weighing 3.5 lbf is 6 ft in diameter. It is filled with hydrogen at 18 lbf/in^2 absolute and 60°F and is released. At what altitude in the U.S. standard atmosphere will this balloon be neutrally buoyant?

P2.125 A uniform cylindrical white oak log, $\rho = 710$ kg/m^3, floats lengthwise in fresh water at 20°C. Its diameter is 24 inches. What height of the log is visible above the surface?

P2.126 A block of wood (SG = 0.6) floats in fluid X in Fig. P2.126 such that 75 percent of its volume is submerged in fluid X. Estimate the vacuum pressure of the air in the tank.

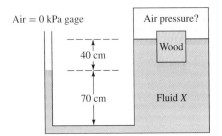

P2.126

Stability of floating bodies

*P2.127 Consider a cylinder of specific gravity $S < 1$ floating vertically in water ($S = 1$), as in Fig. P2.127. Derive a formula for the stable values of D/L as a function of S and apply it to the case $D/L = 1.2$.

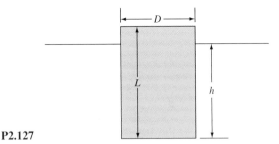

P2.127

P2.128 An iceberg can be idealized as a cube of side length L, as in Fig. P2.128. If seawater is denoted by $S = 1.0$, then glacier ice (which forms icebergs) has $S = 0.88$. Determine if this "cubic" iceberg is stable for the position shown in Fig. P2.128.

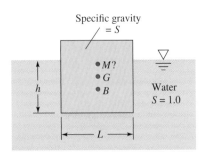

P2.128

P2.129 The iceberg idealization in Prob. P2.128 may become unstable if its sides melt and its height exceeds its width. In Fig. P2.128 suppose that the height is L and the depth into the paper is L, but the width in the plane of the paper is $H < L$. Assuming $S = 0.88$ for the iceberg, find the ratio H/L for which it becomes neutrally stable (about to overturn).

P2.130 Consider a wooden cylinder (SG = 0.6) 1 m in diameter and 0.8 m long. Would this cylinder be stable if placed to float with its axis vertical in oil (SG = 0.8)?

P2.131 A barge is 15 ft wide and 40 ft long and floats with a draft of 4 ft. It is piled so high with gravel that its center of gravity is 3 ft above the waterline. Is it stable?

P2.132 A solid right circular cone has SG = 0.99 and floats vertically as in Fig. P2.132. Is this a stable position for the cone?

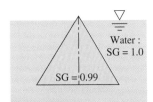

P2.132

P2.133 Consider a uniform right circular cone of specific gravity $S < 1$, floating with its vertex down in water ($S = 1$). The base radius is R and the cone height is H. Calculate and plot the stability MG of this cone, in dimensionless form, versus H/R for a range of $S < 1$.

P2.134 When floating in water (SG = 1.0), an equilateral triangular body (SG = 0.9) might take one of the two positions shown in Fig. P2.134. Which is the more stable position? Assume large width into the paper.

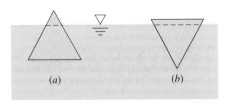

P2.134

P2.135 Consider a homogeneous right circular cylinder of length L, radius R, and specific gravity SG, floating in water (SG = 1). Show that the body will be stable with its axis vertical if

$$\frac{R}{L} > [2SG(1 - SG)]^{1/2}$$

P2.136 Consider a homogeneous right circular cylinder of length L, radius R, and specific gravity SG = 0.5, floating in water (SG = 1). Show that the body will be stable with its axis horizontal if $L/R > 2.0$.

Uniform acceleration

P2.137 A tank of water 4 m deep receives a constant upward acceleration a_z. Determine (a) the gage pressure at the tank bottom if $a_z = 5$ m²/s and (b) the value of a_z that causes the gage pressure at the tank bottom to be 1 atm.

P2.138 A 12-fl-oz glass, of 3-in diameter, partly full of water, is attached to the edge of an 8-ft-diameter merry-go-round, which is rotated at 12 r/min. How full can the glass be before water spills? *Hint:* Assume that the glass is much smaller than the radius of the merry-go-round.

P2.139 The tank of liquid in Fig. P2.139 accelerates to the right with the fluid in rigid-body motion. (a) Compute a_x in m/s². (b) Why doesn't the solution to part (a) depend on the density of the fluid? (c) Determine the gage pressure at point A if the fluid is glycerin at 20°C.

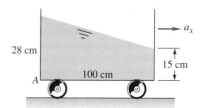

P2.139

P2.140 The U-tube in Fig. P2.140 is moving to the right with variable velocity. The water level in the left tube is 6 cm, and the level in the right tube is 16 cm. Determine the acceleration and its direction.

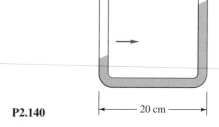

P2.140

P2.141 The same tank from Prob. P2.139 is now moving with constant acceleration up a 30° inclined plane, as in Fig. P2.141. Assuming rigid-body motion, compute (a) the value of the acceleration a, (b) whether the acceleration is up or down, and (c) the gage pressure at point A if the fluid is mercury at 20°C.

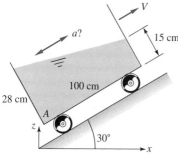

P2.141

P2.142 The tank of water in Fig. P2.142 is 12 cm wide into the paper. If the tank is accelerated to the right in rigid-body motion at 6.0 m/s², compute (a) the water depth on side AB and (b) the water-pressure force on panel AB. Assume no spilling.

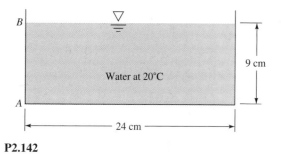

P2.142

P2.143 The tank of water in Fig. P2.143 is full and open to the atmosphere at point A. For what acceleration a_x in ft/s² will the pressure at point B be (a) atmospheric and (b) zero absolute?

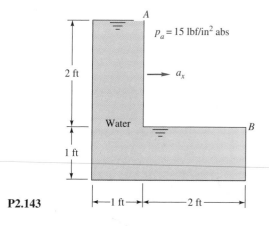

P2.143

P2.144 Consider a hollow cube of side length 22 cm, filled completely with water at 20°C. The top surface of the cube is horizontal. One top corner, point A, is open through a small hole to a pressure of 1 atm. Diagonally opposite to point A is top corner B. Determine and discuss the various rigid-body accelerations for which the water at point B begins to cavitate, for (a) horizontal motion and (b) vertical motion.

P2.145 A fish tank 14 in deep by 16 by 27 in is to be carried in a car that may experience accelerations as high as 6 m/s². What is the maximum water depth that will avoid spilling in rigid-body motion? What is the proper alignment of the tank with respect to the car motion?

P2.146 The tank in Fig. P2.146 is filled with water and has a vent hole at point A. The tank is 1 m wide into the paper. Inside the tank, a 10-cm balloon, filled with helium at 130 kPa, is tethered centrally by a string. If the tank accelerates to the right at 5 m/s² in rigid-body motion, at what angle will the balloon lean? Will it lean to the right or to the left?

P2.148 A child is holding a string onto which is attached a helium-filled balloon. (a) The child is standing still and suddenly accelerates forward. In a frame of reference moving with the child, which way will the balloon tilt, forward or backward? Explain. (b) The child is now sitting in a car that is stopped at a red light. The helium-filled balloon is not in contact with any part of the car (seats, ceiling, etc.) but is held in place by the string, which is in turn held by the child. All the windows in the car are closed. When the traffic light turns green, the car accelerates forward. In a frame of reference moving with the car and child, which way will the balloon tilt, forward or backward? Explain. (c) Purchase or borrow a helium-filled balloon. Conduct a scientific experiment to see if your predictions in parts (a) and (b) above are correct. If not, explain.

P2.149 The 6-ft-radius waterwheel in Fig. P2.149 is being used to lift water with its 1-ft-diameter half-cylinder blades. If the wheel rotates at 10 r/min and rigid-body motion is assumed, what is the water surface angle θ at position A?

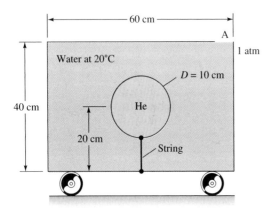

P2.146

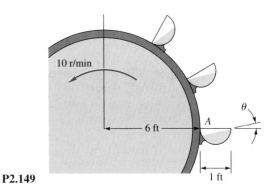

P2.149

P2.147 The tank of water in Fig. P2.147 accelerates uniformly by freely rolling down a 30° incline. If the wheels are frictionless, what is the angle θ? Can you explain this interesting result?

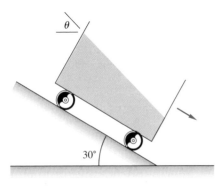

P2.147

P2.150 A cheap accelerometer, probably worth the price, can be made from a U-tube as in Fig. P2.150. If $L = 18$ cm and $D = 5$ mm, what will h be if $a_x = 6$ m/s²? Can the scale markings on the tube be linear multiples of a_x?

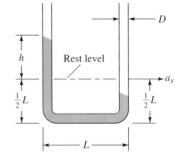

P2.150

P2.151 The U-tube in Fig. P2.151 is open at A and closed at D. If accelerated to the right at uniform a_x, what acceleration will cause the pressure at point *C* to be atmospheric? The fluid is water (SG = 1.0).

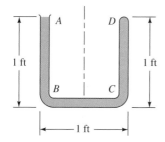

P2.151

Rigid-body rotation

P2.152 A 16-cm-diameter open cylinder 27 cm high is full of water. Compute the rigid-body rotation rate about its central axis, in r/min, (*a*) for which one-third of the water will spill out and (*b*) for which the bottom will be barely exposed.

P2.153 A tall cylindrical container, 14 in diameter, is used to make a mold for forming 14-in salad bowls. The bowls are to be 8 in deep. The cylinder is half-filled with molten plastic, $\mu = 1.6$ kg/(m-s), rotated steadily about the central axis, then cooled while rotating. What is the appropriate rotation rate, in r/min?

P2.154 A very tall 10-cm-diameter vase contains 1178 cm³ of water. When spun steadily to achieve rigid-body rotation, a 4-cm-diameter dry spot appears at the bottom of the vase. What is the rotation rate, in r/min, for this condition?

P2.155 For what uniform rotation rate in r/min about axis *C* will the U-tube in Fig. P2.155 take the configuration shown? The fluid is mercury at 20°C.

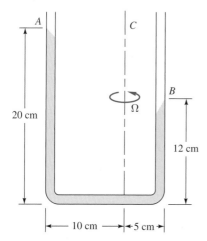

P2.155

P2.156 Suppose that the U-tube of Fig. P2.151 is rotated about axis *DC*. If the fluid is water at 122°F and atmospheric pressure is

2116 lbf/ft² absolute, at what rotation rate will the fluid within the tube begin to vaporize? At what point will this occur?

P2.157 The 45° V-tube in Fig. P2.157 contains water and is open at *A* and closed at *C*. What uniform rotation rate in r/min about axis *AB* will cause the pressure to be equal at points *B* and *C*? For this condition, at what point in leg *BC* will the pressure be a minimum?

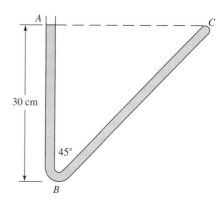

P2.157

*P2.158 It is desired to make a 3-m-diameter parabolic telescope mirror by rotating molten glass in rigid-body motion until the desired shape is achieved and then cooling the glass to a solid. The focus of the mirror is to be 4 m from the mirror, measured along the centerline. What is the proper mirror rotation rate, in r/min, for this task?

P2.159 The three-legged manometer in Fig. P2.159 is filled with water to a depth of 20 cm. All tubes are long and have equal small diameters. If the system spins at angular velocity Ω about the central tube, (*a*) derive a formula to find the change of height in the tubes; (*b*) find the height in cm in each tube if $\Omega = 120$ r/min. *Hint:* The central tube must supply water to *both* the outer legs.

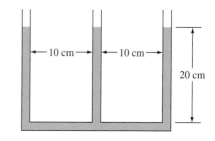

P2.159

Pressure measurements

P2.160 Figure P2.160 shows a gage for very low pressures, invented in 1874 by Herbert McLeod. (*a*) Can you deduce, from the figure, how it works? (*b*) If not, read about it and explain it to the class.

P2.160

P2.161 Figure P2.161 shows a sketch of a commercial pressure gage. (*a*) Can you deduce, from the figure, how it works?

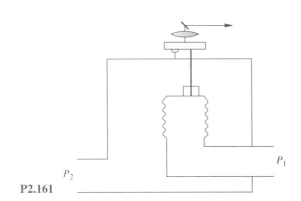

P2.161

Word Problems

W2.1 Consider a hollow cone with a vent hole in the vertex at the top, along with a hollow cylinder, open at the top, with the same base area as the cone. Fill both with water to the top. The *hydrostatic paradox* is that both containers have the same force on the bottom due to the water pressure, although the cone contains 67 percent less water. Can you explain the paradox?

W2.2 Can the temperature ever *rise* with altitude in the real atmosphere? Wouldn't this cause the air pressure to *increase* upward? Explain the physics of this situation.

W2.3 Consider a submerged curved surface that consists of a two-dimensional circular arc of arbitrary angle, arbitrary depth, and arbitrary orientation. Show that the resultant hydrostatic pressure force on this surface must pass through the center of curvature of the arc.

W2.4 Fill a glass approximately 80 percent with water, and add a large ice cube. Mark the water level. The ice cube, having SG ≈ 0.9, sticks up out of the water. Let the ice cube melt with negligible evaporation from the water surface. Will the water level be higher than, lower than, or the same as before?

W2.5 A ship, carrying a load of steel, is trapped while floating in a small closed lock. Members of the crew want to get out, but they can't quite reach the top wall of the lock. A crew member suggests throwing the steel overboard in the lock, claiming the ship will then rise and they can climb out. Will this plan work?

W2.6 Consider a balloon of mass m floating neutrally in the atmosphere, carrying a person/basket of mass $M > m$. Discuss the stability of this system to disturbances.

W2.7 Consider a helium balloon on a string tied to the seat of your stationary car. The windows are closed, so there is no air motion within the car. The car begins to accelerate forward. Which way will the balloon lean, forward or backward? *Hint:* The acceleration sets up a horizontal pressure gradient in the air within the car.

W2.8 Repeat your analysis of Prob. W2.7 to let the car move at constant velocity and go around a curve. Will the balloon lean in, toward the center of curvature, or out?

W2.9 The deep submersible vehicle ALVIN weighs approximately 36,000 lbf in air. It carries 800 lbm of steel weights on the sides. After a deep mission and return, two 400-lbm piles of steel are left on the ocean floor. Can you explain, in terms relevant to this chapter, how these steel weights are used?

Fundamentals of Engineering Exam Problems

FE2.1 A gage attached to a pressurized nitrogen tank reads a gage pressure of 28 in of mercury. If atmospheric pressure is 14.4 psia, what is the absolute pressure in the tank?
(*a*) 95 kPa, (*b*) 99 kPa, (*c*) 101 kPa, (*d*) 194 kPa,
(*e*) 203 kPa

FE2.2 On a sea-level standard day, a pressure gage, moored below the surface of the ocean (SG = 1.025), reads an absolute pressure of 1.4 MPa. How deep is the instrument?
(*a*) 4 m, (*b*) 129 m, (*c*) 133 m, (*d*) 140 m, (*e*) 2080 m

FE2.3 In Fig. FE2.3, if the oil in region B has SG = 0.8 and the absolute pressure at point A is 1 atm, what is the absolute pressure at point B?
(a) 5.6 kPa, (b) 10.9 kPa, (c) 107 kPa, (d) 112 kPa, (e) 157 kPa

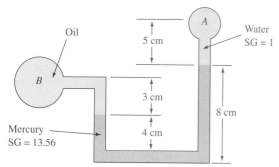

FE2.3

FE2.4 In Fig. FE2.3, if the oil in region B has SG = 0.8 and the absolute pressure at point B is 14 psia, what is the absolute pressure at point A?
(a) 11 kPa, (b) 41 kPa, (c) 86 kPa, (d) 91 kPa, (e) 101 kPa

FE2.5 A tank of water (SG = 1.0) has a gate in its vertical wall 5 m high and 3 m wide. The top edge of the gate is 2 m below the surface. What is the hydrostatic force on the gate?
(a) 147 kN, (b) 367 kN, (c) 490 kN, (d) 661 kN, (e) 1028 kN

FE2.6 In Prob. FE2.5, how far below the surface is the center of pressure of the hydrostatic force?
(a) 4.50 m, (b) 5.46 m, (c) 6.35 m, (d) 5.33 m, (e) 4.96 m

FE2.7 A solid 1-m-diameter sphere floats at the interface between water (SG = 1.0) and mercury (SG = 13.56) such that 40 percent is in the water. What is the specific gravity of the sphere?
(a) 6.02, (b) 7.28, (c) 7.78, (d) 8.54, (e) 12.56

FE2.8 A 5-m-diameter balloon contains helium at 125 kPa absolute and 15°C, moored in sea-level standard air. If the gas constant of helium is 2077 m^2/(s^2 · K) and balloon material weight is neglected, what is the net lifting force of the balloon?
(a) 67 N, (b) 134 N, (c) 522 N, (d) 653 N, (e) 787 N

FE2.9 A square wooden (SG = 0.6) rod, 5 cm by 5 cm by 10 m long, floats vertically in water at 20°C when 6 kg of steel (SG = 7.84) are attached to one end. How high above the water surface does the wooden end of the rod protrude?
(a) 0.6 m, (b) 1.6 m, (c) 1.9 m, (d) 2.4 m, (e) 4.0 m

FE2.10 A floating body will be stable when its
(a) center of gravity is above its center of buoyancy, (b) center of buoyancy is below the waterline, (c) center of buoyancy is above its metacenter, (d) metacenter is above its center of buoyancy, (e) metacenter is above its center of gravity.

Comprehensive Problems

C2.1 Some manometers are constructed as in Fig. C2.1, where one side is a large reservoir (diameter D) and the other side is a small tube of diameter d, open to the atmosphere. In such a case, the height of manometer liquid on the reservoir side does not change appreciably. This has the advantage that only one height needs to be measured rather than two. The manometer liquid has density ρ_m while the air has density ρ_a. Ignore the effects of surface tension. When there is no pressure difference across the manometer, the elevations on both sides are the same, as indicated by the dashed line. Height h is measured from the zero pressure level as shown. (a) When a high pressure is applied to the left side, the manometer liquid in the large reservoir goes down, while that in the tube at the right goes up to conserve mass. Write an exact expression for p_{1gage}, taking into account the movement of the surface of the reservoir. Your equation should give p_{1gage} as a function of h, ρ_m, and the physical parameters in the problem, h, d, D, and gravity constant g.
(b) Write an approximate expression for p_{1gage}, neglecting the change in elevation of the surface of the reservoir liquid.

(c) Suppose h = 0.26 m in a certain application. If p_a = 101,000 Pa and the manometer liquid has a density of 820 kg/m^3, estimate the ratio D/d required to keep the error of the approximation of part (b) within 1 percent of the exact measurement of part (a). Repeat for an error within 0.1 percent.

To pressure measurement location

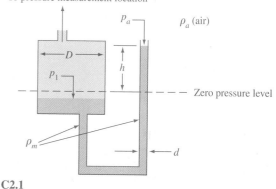

C2.1

C2.2 A prankster has added oil, of specific gravity SG_0, to the left leg of the manometer in Fig. C2.2. Nevertheless, the U-tube is still useful as a pressure-measuring device. It is attached to a pressurized tank as shown in the figure. (a) Find an expression for h as a function of H and other parameters in the problem. (b) Find the special case of your result in (a) when $p_{tank} = p_a$. (c) Suppose $H = 5.0$ cm, p_a is 101.2 kPa, p_{tank} is 1.82 kPa higher than p_a, and $SG_0 = 0.85$. Calculate h in cm, ignoring surface tension effects and neglecting air density effects.

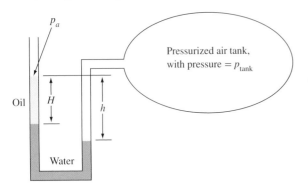

C2.2

C2.3 Professor F. Dynamics, riding the merry-go-round with his son, has brought along his U-tube manometer. (You never know when a manometer might come in handy.) As shown in Fig. C2.3, the merry-go-round spins at constant angular velocity and the manometer legs are 7 cm apart. The manometer center is 5.8 m from the axis of rotation. Determine the height difference h in two ways: (a) approximately, by assuming rigid-body translation with $\mathbf{a}$ equal to the average manometer acceleration; and (b) exactly, using rigid-body rotation theory. How good is the approximation?

C2.4 A student sneaks a glass of cola onto a roller coaster ride. The glass is cylindrical, twice as tall as it is wide, and filled to the brim. He wants to know what percent of the cola he should drink before the ride begins, so that none of it spills during the big drop, in which the roller coaster achieves

0.55-g acceleration at a 45° angle below the horizontal. Make the calculation for him, neglecting sloshing and assuming that the glass is vertical at all times.

C2.5 *Dry adiabatic lapse rate* (DALR) is defined as the negative value of atmospheric temperature gradient, dT/dz, when temperature and pressure vary in an isentropic fashion. Assuming air is an ideal gas, DALR $= -dT/dz$ when $T = T_0(p/p_0)^a$, where exponent $a = (k - 1)/k$, $k = c_p/c_v$ is the ratio of specific heats, and T_0 and p_0 are the temperature and pressure at sea level, respectively. (a) Assuming that hydrostatic conditions exist in the atmosphere, show that the dry adiabatic lapse rate is constant and is given by DALR $= g(k - 1)/(kR)$, where R is the ideal gas constant for air. (b) Calculate the numerical value of DALR for air in units of °C/km.

C2.6 In "soft" liquids (low bulk modulus β), it may be necessary to account for liquid compressibility in hydrostatic calculations. An approximate density relation would be

$$dp \approx \frac{\beta}{\rho}\, d\rho = a^2 d\rho \quad \text{or} \quad p \approx p_0 + a^2(\rho - \rho_0)$$

where a is the speed of sound and (p_0, ρ_0) are the conditions at the liquid surface $z = 0$. Use this approximation to show that the density variation with depth in a soft liquid is $\rho = \rho_0 e^{-gz/a^2}$ where g is the acceleration of gravity and z is positive upward. Then consider a vertical wall of width b, extending from the surface ($z = 0$) down to depth $z = -h$. Find an analytic expression for the hydrostatic force F on this wall, and compare it with the incompressible result $F = \rho_0 g h^2 b/2$. Would the center of pressure be below the incompressible position $z = -2h/3$?

C2.7 Venice, Italy, is slowly sinking, so now, especially in winter, plazas and walkways are flooded during storms. The proposed solution is the floating levee of Fig. C2.7. When filled with air, it rises to block off the sea. The levee is 30 m high, 5 m wide, and 20 m deep. Assume a uniform density of 300 kg/m³ when floating. For the 1-m sea–lagoon difference shown, estimate the angle at which the levee floats.

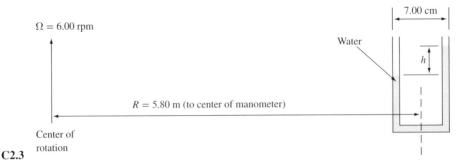

C2.3

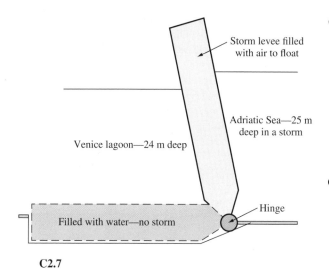

Storm levee filled with air to float

Adriatic Sea—25 m deep in a storm

Venice lagoon—24 m deep

Filled with water—no storm

Hinge

C2.7

C2.8 In the U.S. Standard Atmosphere, the lapse rate B may vary from day to day. It is not a fundamental quantity like, say, Planck's constant. Suppose that, on a certain day in Rhode Island, with $T_o = 288$ K, the following pressures are measured by weather balloons:

Altitude z, km	0	2	5	8
Pressure p, kPa	100	78	53	34

Estimate the best-fit value of B for this data. Explain any difficulties. [*Hint:* EES is recommended.]

C2.9 The ALVIN submersible vehicle has a passenger compartment which is a titanium sphere of inside diameter 78.08 in and thickness 1.93 in. If the vehicle is submerged to a depth of 3850 m in the ocean, estimate (*a*) the water pressure outside the sphere, (*b*) the maximum elastic stress in the sphere, in lbf/in^2, and (*c*) the factor of safety of the titanium alloy (6% aluminum, 4% vanadium).

Design Projects

D2.1 It is desired to have a bottom-moored, floating system that creates a nonlinear force in the mooring line as the water level rises. The design force F need only be accurate in the range of seawater depths h between 6 and 8 m, as shown in the accompanying table. Design a buoyant system that will provide this force distribution. The system should be practical (of inexpensive materials and simple construction).

h, m	F, N	h, m	F, N
6.00	400	7.25	554
6.25	437	7.50	573
6.50	471	7.75	589
6.75	502	8.00	600
7.00	530		

D2.2 A laboratory apparatus used in some universities is shown in Fig. D2.2. The purpose is to measure the hydrostatic force on the flat face of the circular-arc block and compare it with the theoretical value for given depth h. The counterweight is arranged so that the pivot arm is horizontal when the block is not submerged, whence the weight W can be correlated with the hydrostatic force when the submerged arm is again brought to horizontal. First show that the apparatus concept is valid in principle; then derive a formula for W as a function of h in terms of the system parameters. Finally, suggest some appropriate values of Y, L, and so on for a suitable apparatus and plot theoretical W versus h for these values.

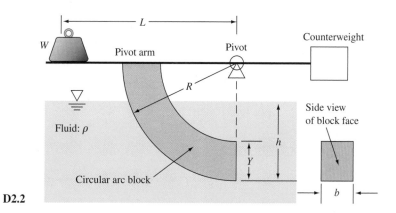

L

W

Pivot arm

Pivot

Counterweight

R

Fluid: ρ

Side view of block face

h

Y

Circular arc block

b

D2.2

D2.3   The Leary Engineering Company (see *Popular Science,* November 2000, p. 14) has proposed a ship hull with hinges that allow it to open into a flatter shape when entering shallow water. A simplified version is shown in Fig. D2.3. In deep water, the hull cross section would be triangular, with large draft. In shallow water, the hinges would open to an angle as high as $\theta = 45°$. The dashed line indicates that the bow and stern would be closed. Make a parametric study of this configuration for various θ, assuming a reasonable weight and center of gravity location. Show how the draft, the metacentric height, and the ship's stability vary as the hinges are opened. Comment on the effectiveness of this concept.

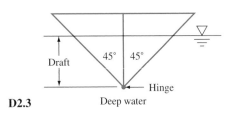 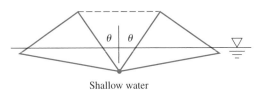

D2.3   Deep water   Shallow water

References

1. *U.S. Standard Atmosphere,* 1976, Government Printing Office, Washington, DC, 1976.
2. J. A. Knauss, *Introduction to Physical Oceanography*, 2d ed., Waveland Press, Long Grove, IL, 2005.
3. E. C. Tupper, *Introduction to Naval Architecture,* 4th ed., Elsevier, New York, 2004.
4. D. T. Greenwood, *Advanced Dynamics*, Cambridge University Press, New York, 2006.
5. R. I. Fletcher, "The Apparent Field of Gravity in a Rotating Fluid System," *Am. J. Phys.,* vol. 40, July 1972, pp. 959–965.
6. National Committee for Fluid Mechanics Films, *Illustrated Experiments in Fluid Mechanics,* M.I.T. Press, Cambridge, MA, 1972.
7. J. P. Holman, *Experimental Methods for Engineers,* 8th ed., McGraw-Hill, New York, 2011.
8. R. C. Baker, *Flow Measurement Handbook*, Cambridge University Press, New York, 2005.
9. T. G. Beckwith, R. G. Marangoni, and J. H. Lienhard V, *Mechanical Measurements*, 6th ed., Prentice-Hall, Upper Saddle River, NJ, 2006.
10. J. W. Dally, W. F. Riley, and K. G. McConnell, *Instrumentation for Engineering Measurements,* 2d ed., Wiley, New York, 1993.
11. E. N. Gilbert, "How Things Float," *Am. Math. Monthly,* vol. 98, no. 3, 1991, pp. 201–216.
12. R. J. Figliola and D. E. Beasley, *Theory and Design for Mechanical Measurements,* 4th ed., Wiley, New York, 2005.
13. R. W. Miller, *Flow Measurement Engineering Handbook,* 3d ed., McGraw-Hill, New York, 1996.
14. L. D. Clayton, E. P. EerNisse, R. W. Ward, and R. B. Wiggins, "Miniature Crystalline Quartz Electromechanical Structures," *Sensors and Actuators,* vol. 20, Nov. 15, 1989, pp. 171–177.
15. A. Kitai (ed.), *Luminescent Materials and Applications*, John Wiley, New York, 2008.
16. B. G. Liptak (ed.), *Instrument Engineer's Handbook: Process Measurement and Analysis,* 4th ed., vol. 1, CRC Press, Boca Raton, FL, 2003.
17. A. von Beckerath, *WIKA Handbook—Pressure and Temperature Measurement*, WIKA Instrument Corp., Lawrenceville, GA, 2008.

On July 16, 1969, a massive Saturn V rocket lifted *Apollo 11* from the NASA Kennedy Space Center, carrying astronauts Neil Armstrong, Michael Collins, and Edwin Aldrin to the first landing on the moon, four days later. The photo is filled with fluid momentum. In this chapter we learn how to analyze both the thrust of the rocket and the force of the exit jet on the solid surface. [*Photo credit: NASA*]

Chapter 3
Integral Relations
for a Control Volume

Motivation. In analyzing fluid motion, we might take one of two paths: (1) seeking to describe the detailed flow pattern at every point (x, y, z) in the field or (2) working with a finite region, making a balance of flow in versus flow out, and determining gross flow effects such as the force or torque on a body or the total energy exchange. The second is the "control volume" method and is the subject of this chapter. The first is the "differential" approach and is developed in Chap. 4.

We first develop the concept of the control volume, in nearly the same manner as one does in a thermodynamics course, and we find the rate of change of an arbitrary gross fluid property, a result called the *Reynolds transport theorem*. We then apply this theorem, in sequence, to mass, linear momentum, angular momentum, and energy, thus deriving the four basic control volume relations of fluid mechanics. There are many applications, of course. The chapter includes a special case of frictionless, shaft-work-free momentum and energy: the *Bernoulli equation*. The Bernoulli equation is a wonderful, historic relation, but it is extremely restrictive and should always be viewed with skepticism and care in applying it to a real (viscous) fluid motion.

3.1 Basic Physical Laws of Fluid Mechanics

It is time now to really get serious about flow problems. The fluid statics applications of Chap. 2 were more like fun than work, at least in this writer's opinion. Statics problems basically require only the density of the fluid and knowledge of the position of the free surface, but most flow problems require the analysis of an arbitrary state of variable fluid motion defined by the geometry, the boundary conditions, and the laws of mechanics. This chapter and the next two outline the three basic approaches to the analysis of arbitrary flow problems:

1. Control volume, or large-scale, analysis (Chap. 3).
2. Differential, or small-scale, analysis (Chap. 4).
3. Experimental, or dimensional, analysis (Chap. 5).

The three approaches are roughly equal in importance. Control volume analysis, the present topic, is accurate for any flow distribution but is often based on average or "one-dimensional" property values at the boundaries. It always gives useful "engineering" estimates. In principle, the differential equation approach of Chap. 4 can be applied to any problem. Only a few problems, such as straight pipe flow, yield to exact analytical solutions. But the differential equations can be modeled numerically, and the flourishing field of computational fluid dynamics (CFD)[8] can now be used to give good estimates for almost any geometry. Finally, the dimensional analysis of Chap. 5 applies to any problem, whether analytical, numerical, or experimental. It is particularly useful to reduce the cost of experimentation. Differential analysis of hydrodynamics began with Euler and d'Alembert in the late eighteenth century. Lord Rayleigh and E. Buckingham pioneered dimensional analysis at the end of the nineteenth century. The control volume was described in words, on an ad hoc one-case basis, by Daniel Bernoulli in 1753. Ludwig Prandtl, the celebrated founder of modern fluid mechanics, developed the control volume as a systematic tool in the early 1900s. The writer's teachers at M.I.T. introduced control volume analysis into American textbooks, for thermodynamics by Keenan in 1941 [10], and for fluids by Hunsaker and Rightmire in 1947 [11]. For a complete history of the control volume, see Vincenti [9].

Systems versus Control Volumes

All the laws of mechanics are written for a *system,* which is defined as an arbitrary quantity of mass of fixed identity. Everything external to this system is denoted by the term *surroundings,* and the system is separated from its surroundings by its *boundaries.* The laws of mechanics then state what happens when there is an interaction between the system and its surroundings.

First, the system is a fixed quantity of mass, denoted by m. Thus the mass of the system is conserved and does not change.[1] This is a law of mechanics and has a very simple mathematical form, called *conservation of mass:*

$$m_{syst} = \text{const}$$

or

$$\frac{dm}{dt} = 0 \tag{3.1}$$

This is so obvious in solid mechanics problems that we often forget about it. In fluid mechanics, we must pay a lot of attention to mass conservation, and it takes a little analysis to make it hold.

Second, if the surroundings exert a net force $\mathbf{F}$ on the system, Newton's second law states that the mass in the system will begin to accelerate:[2]

$$\mathbf{F} = m\mathbf{a} = m\frac{d\mathbf{V}}{dt} = \frac{d}{dt}(m\mathbf{V}) \tag{3.2}$$

In Eq. (2.8) we saw this relation applied to a differential element of viscous incompressible fluid. In fluid mechanics Newton's second law is called the linear momentum relation. Note that it is a vector law that implies the three scalar equations $F_x = ma_x$, $F_y = ma_y$, and $F_z = ma_z$.

---

[1]We are neglecting nuclear reactions, where mass can be changed to energy.
[2]We are neglecting relativistic effects, where Newton's law must be modified.

Third, if the surroundings exert a net moment **M** about the center of mass of the system, there will be a rotation effect

$$\mathbf{M} = \frac{d\mathbf{H}}{dt} \tag{3.3}$$

where $\mathbf{H} = \Sigma(\mathbf{r} \times \mathbf{V})\delta m$ is the angular momentum of the system about its center of mass. Here we call Eq. (3.3) the angular momentum relation. Note that it is also a vector equation implying three scalar equations such as $M_x = dH_x/dt$.

For an arbitrary mass and arbitrary moment, **H** is quite complicated and contains nine terms (see, for example, Ref. 1). In elementary dynamics we commonly treat only a rigid body rotating about a fixed x axis, for which Eq. (3.3) reduces to

$$M_x = I_x \frac{d}{dt}(\omega_x) \tag{3.4}$$

where ω_x is the angular velocity of the body and I_x is its mass moment of inertia about the x axis. Unfortunately, fluid systems are not rigid and rarely reduce to such a simple relation, as we shall see in Sec. 3.6.

Fourth, if heat δQ is added to the system or work δW is done by the system, the system energy dE must change according to the energy relation, or first law of thermodynamics:

$$\delta Q - \delta W = dE$$

or
$$\dot{Q} - \dot{W} = \frac{dE}{dt} \tag{3.5}$$

Like mass conservation, Eq. (3.1), this is a scalar relation having only a single component.

Finally, the second law of thermodynamics relates entropy change dS to heat added dQ and absolute temperature T:

$$dS \geq \frac{\delta Q}{T} \tag{3.6}$$

This is valid for a system and can be written in control volume form, but there are almost no practical applications in fluid mechanics except to analyze flow loss details (see Sec. 9.5).

All these laws involve thermodynamic properties, and thus we must supplement them with state relations $p = p(\rho, T)$ and $e = e(\rho, T)$ for the particular fluid being studied, as in Sec. 1.8. Although thermodynamics is not the main topic of this book, it is very important to the general study of fluid mechanics. Thermodynamics is crucial to compressible flow, Chap. 9. The student should review the first law and the state relations, as discussed in Refs. 6 and 7.

The purpose of this chapter is to put our four basic laws into the control volume form suitable for arbitrary regions in a flow:

1. Conservation of mass (Sec. 3.3).
2. The linear momentum relation (Sec. 3.4).
3. The angular momentum relation (Sec. 3.6).
4. The energy equation (Sec. 3.7).

Wherever necessary to complete the analysis we also introduce a state relation such as the perfect-gas law.

Equations (3.1) to (3.6) apply to either fluid or solid systems. They are ideal for solid mechanics, where we follow the same system forever because it represents the product we are designing and building. For example, we follow a beam as it deflects under load. We follow a piston as it oscillates. We follow a rocket system all the way to Mars.

But fluid systems do not demand this concentrated attention. It is rare that we wish to follow the ultimate path of a specific particle of fluid. Instead it is likely that the fluid forms the environment whose effect on our product we wish to know. For the three examples just cited, we wish to know the wind loads on the beam, the fluid pressures on the piston, and the drag and lift loads on the rocket. This requires that the basic laws be rewritten to apply to a specific *region* in the neighborhood of our product. In other words, where the fluid particles in the wind go after they leave the beam is of little interest to a beam designer. The user's point of view underlies the need for the control volume analysis of this chapter.

In analyzing a control volume, we convert the system laws to apply to a specific region, which the system may occupy for only an instant. The system passes on, and other systems come along, but no matter. The basic laws are reformulated to apply to this local region called a control volume. All we need to know is the flow field in this region, and often simple assumptions will be accurate enough (such as uniform inlet and/or outlet flows). The flow conditions away from the control volume are then irrelevant. The technique for making such localized analyses is the subject of this chapter.

Volume and Mass Rate of Flow

All the analyses in this chapter involve evaluation of the volume flow Q or mass flow $\dot{m}$ passing through a surface (imaginary) defined in the flow.

Suppose that the surface S in Fig. 3.1a is a sort of (imaginary) wire mesh through which the fluid passes without resistance. How much volume of fluid passes through S in unit time? If, typically, $\mathbf{V}$ varies with position, we must integrate over the elemental surface dA in Fig. 3.1a. Also, typically $\mathbf{V}$ may pass through dA at an angle θ off the normal. Let $\mathbf{n}$ be defined as the unit vector normal to dA. Then the amount of fluid swept through dA in time dt is the volume of the slanted parallelepiped in Fig. 3.1b:

$$d\mathcal{V} = V \, dt \, dA \cos \theta = (\mathbf{V} \cdot \mathbf{n}) \, dA \, dt$$

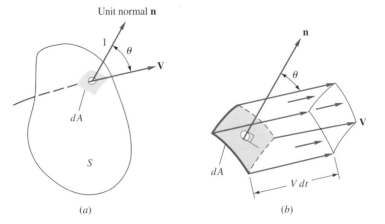

Fig. 3.1 Volume rate of flow through an arbitrary surface: (*a*) an elemental area *dA* on the surface; (*b*) the incremental volume swept through *dA* equals *V dt dA* cos *θ*.

The integral of $d\mathcal{V}/dt$ is the total volume rate of flow Q through the surface S:

$$Q = \int_s (\mathbf{V} \cdot \mathbf{n})\, dA = \int_s V_n\, dA \qquad (3.7)$$

We could replace $\mathbf{V} \cdot \mathbf{n}$ by its equivalent, V_n, the component of $\mathbf{V}$ normal to dA, but the use of the dot product allows Q to have a sign to distinguish between inflow and outflow. By convention throughout this book we consider $\mathbf{n}$ to be the *outward* normal unit vector. Therefore $\mathbf{V} \cdot \mathbf{n}$ denotes outflow if it is positive and inflow if negative. This will be an extremely useful housekeeping device when we are computing volume and mass flow in the basic control volume relations.

Volume flow can be multiplied by density to obtain the mass flow $\dot{m}$. If density varies over the surface, it must be part of the surface integral:

$$\dot{m} = \int_s \rho(\mathbf{V} \cdot \mathbf{n})\, dA = \int_s \rho V_n\, dA$$

If density and velocity are constant over the surface S, a simple expression results:

One-dimensional approximation: $\dot{m} = \rho Q = \rho A V$

Typical units for Q are m^3/s and for $\dot{m}$ kg/s.

3.2 The Reynolds Transport Theorem

To convert a system analysis to a control volume analysis, we must convert our mathematics to apply to a specific region rather than to individual masses. This conversion, called the *Reynolds transport theorem*, can be applied to all the basic laws. Examining the basic laws (3.1) to (3.3) and (3.5), we see that they are all concerned with the time derivative of fluid properties m, $\mathbf{V}$, $\mathbf{H}$, and E. Therefore what we need is to relate the time derivative of a system property to the rate of change of that property within a certain region.

The desired conversion formula differs slightly according to whether the control volume is fixed, moving, or deformable. Figure 3.2 illustrates these three cases. The fixed control volume in Fig. 3.2a encloses a stationary region of interest to a nozzle designer. The control surface is an abstract concept and does not hinder the flow in any way. It slices through the jet leaving the nozzle, encloses the surrounding atmosphere, and slices through the flange bolts and the fluid within the nozzle. This particular control volume exposes the stresses in the flange bolts,

Fig. 3.2 Fixed, moving, and deformable control volumes: (*a*) fixed control volume for nozzle stress analysis; (*b*) control volume moving at ship speed for drag force analysis; (*c*) control volume deforming within cylinder for transient pressure variation analysis.

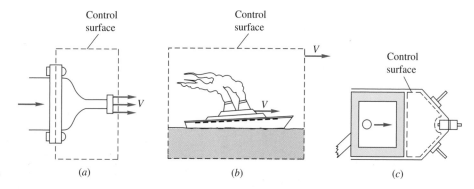

which contribute to applied forces in the momentum analysis. In this sense the control volume resembles the *free-body* concept, which is applied to systems in solid mechanics analyses.

Figure 3.2*b* illustrates a moving control volume. Here the ship is of interest, not the ocean, so that the control surface chases the ship at ship speed *V*. The control volume is of fixed volume, but the relative motion between water and ship must be considered. If *V* is constant, this relative motion is a steady flow pattern, which simplifies the analysis.[3] If *V* is variable, the relative motion is unsteady, so that the computed results are time-variable and certain terms enter the momentum analysis to reflect the noninertial (accelerating) frame of reference.

Figure 3.2*c* shows a deforming control volume. Varying relative motion at the boundaries becomes a factor, and the rate of change of shape of the control volume enters the analysis. We begin by deriving the fixed control volume case, and we consider the other cases as advanced topics. An interesting history of control volume analysis is given by Vincenti [9].

Arbitrary Fixed Control Volume Figure 3.3 shows a fixed control volume with an arbitrary flow pattern passing through. There are variable slivers of inflow and outflow of fluid all about the control surface. In general, each differential area *dA* of surface will have a different velocity **V** making a different angle θ with the local normal to *dA*. Some elemental areas will have

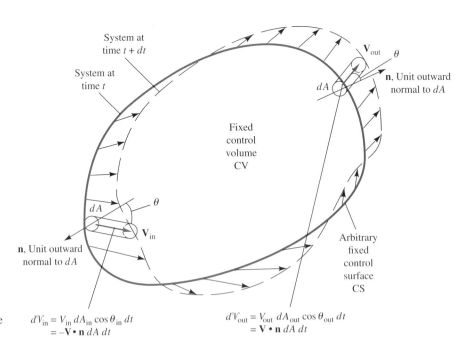

Fig. 3.3 An arbitrary control volume with an arbitrary flow pattern.

$$d\mathcal{V}_{\text{in}} = V_{\text{in}} \, dA_{\text{in}} \cos\theta_{\text{in}} \, dt$$
$$= -\mathbf{V} \cdot \mathbf{n} \, dA \, dt$$

$$d\mathcal{V}_{\text{out}} = V_{\text{out}} \, dA_{\text{out}} \cos\theta_{\text{out}} \, dt$$
$$= \mathbf{V} \cdot \mathbf{n} \, dA \, dt$$

[3]A *wind tunnel* uses a fixed model to simulate flow over a body moving through a fluid. A *tow tank* uses a moving model to simulate the same situation.

inflow volume $(VA \cos \theta)_{\text{in}} \, dt$, and others will have outflow volume $(VA \cos \theta)_{\text{out}} \, dt$, as seen in Fig. 3.3. Some surfaces might correspond to streamlines ($\theta = 90°$) or solid walls ($\mathbf{V} = 0$) with neither inflow nor outflow.

Let B be any property of the fluid (energy, momentum, enthalpy, etc.) and let $\beta = dB/dm$ be the *intensive* value, or the amount of B per unit mass in any small element of the fluid. The total amount of B in the control volume (the solid curve in Fig. 3.3) is thus

$$B_{\text{CV}} = \int_{\text{CV}} \beta \, dm = \int_{\text{CV}} \beta \rho \, d\mathcal{V} \quad \beta = \frac{dB}{dm} \tag{3.8}$$

Examining Fig. 3.3, we see three sources of changes in B relating to the control volume:

$$\text{A change within the control volume} \quad \frac{d}{dt}\left(\int_{\text{CV}} \beta \rho \, d\mathcal{V} \right)$$

$$\text{Outflow of } \beta \text{ from the control volume} \quad \int_{\text{CS}} \beta \rho V \cos \theta \, dA_{\text{out}} \tag{3.9}$$

$$\text{Inflow of } \beta \text{ to the control volume} \quad \int_{\text{CS}} \beta \rho V \cos \theta \, dA_{\text{in}}$$

The notations CV and CS refer to the control volume and control surface, respectively. Note, in Fig. 3.3, that the *system* has moved a bit. In the limit as $dt \to 0$, the instantaneous change of B in the system is the sum of the change within, plus the outflow, minus the inflow:

$$\boxed{\frac{d}{dt}(B_{\text{syst}}) = \frac{d}{dt}\left(\int_{\text{CV}} \beta \rho \, d\mathcal{V} \right) + \int_{\text{CS}} \beta \rho \mathbf{V} \cos \theta \, dA_{\text{out}} - \int_{\text{CS}} \beta \rho \mathbf{V} \cos \theta \, dA_{\text{in}}} \tag{3.10}$$

This is the *Reynolds transport theorem* for an arbitrary fixed control volume. By letting the property B be mass, momentum, angular momentum, or energy, we can rewrite all the basic laws in control volume form. Note that all three of the integrals are concerned with the intensive property β. Since the control volume is fixed in space, the elemental volumes $d\mathcal{V}$ do not vary with time, so that the time derivative of the volume integral vanishes unless either β or ρ varies with time (unsteady flow).

Equation (3.10) expresses the basic formula that a system derivative equals the rate of change of B within the control volume plus the flow of B out of the control surface minus the flow of B into the control surface. The quantity B (or β) may be any vector or scalar property of the fluid. Two alternate forms are possible for the flow terms. First we may notice that $V \cos \theta$ is the component of V normal to the area element of the control surface. Thus we can write

$$\text{Flow terms} = \int_{\text{CS}} \beta \rho V_n \, dA_{\text{out}} - \int_{\text{CS}} \beta \rho V_n \, dA_{\text{in}} = \int_{\text{CS}} \beta \, d\dot{m}_{\text{out}} - \int_{\text{CS}} \beta \, d\dot{m}_{\text{in}} \tag{3.10a}$$

where $d\dot{m} = \rho V_n \, dA$ is the differential mass flow through the surface. Form (3.10a) helps us visualize what is being calculated.

A second, alternative form offers elegance and compactness as advantages. If $\mathbf{n}$ is defined as the *outward* normal unit vector everywhere on the control surface, then $\mathbf{V} \cdot \mathbf{n} = V_n$ for outflow and $\mathbf{V} \cdot \mathbf{n} = -V_n$ for inflow. Therefore the flow terms can be represented by a single integral involving $\mathbf{V} \cdot \mathbf{n}$ that accounts for both positive outflow and negative inflow:

$$\text{Flow terms} = \int_{\text{CS}} \beta\rho(\mathbf{V} \cdot \mathbf{n})\, dA \tag{3.11}$$

The compact form of the Reynolds transport theorem is thus

$$\boxed{\frac{d}{dt}(B_{\text{syst}}) = \frac{d}{dt}\left(\int_{\text{CV}} \beta\rho\, d\mathcal{V}\right) + \int_{\text{CS}} \beta\rho(\mathbf{V} \cdot \mathbf{n})\, dA} \tag{3.12}$$

This is beautiful but only occasionally useful, when the coordinate system is ideally suited to the control volume selected. Otherwise the computations are easier when the flow of B out is added and the flow of B in is subtracted, according to Eqs. (3.10) or (3.11).

The time derivative term can be written in the equivalent form

$$\frac{d}{dt}\left(\int_{\text{CV}} \beta\rho\, d\mathcal{V}\right) = \int_{\text{CV}} \frac{\partial}{\partial t}(\beta\rho)\, d\mathcal{V} \tag{3.13}$$

for the fixed control volume since the volume elements do not vary.

Control Volume Moving at Constant Velocity

If the control volume is moving uniformly at velocity $\mathbf{V}_s$, as in Fig. 3.2b, an observer fixed to the control volume will see a relative velocity $\mathbf{V}_r$ of fluid crossing the control surface, defined by

$$\mathbf{V}_r = \mathbf{V} - \mathbf{V}_s \tag{3.14}$$

where $\mathbf{V}$ is the fluid velocity relative to the same coordinate system in which the control volume motion $\mathbf{V}_s$ is observed. Note that Eq. (3.14) is a vector subtraction. The flow terms will be proportional to $\mathbf{V}_r$, but the volume integral of Eq. (3.12) is unchanged because the control volume moves as a fixed shape without deforming. The Reynolds transport theorem for this case of a uniformly moving control volume is

$$\frac{d}{dt}(B_{\text{syst}}) = \frac{d}{dt}\left(\int_{\text{CV}} \beta\rho\, d\mathcal{V}\right) + \int_{\text{CS}} \beta\rho(\mathbf{V}_r \cdot \mathbf{n})\, dA \tag{3.15}$$

which reduces to Eq. (3.12) if $\mathbf{V}_s \equiv 0$.

Control Volume of Constant Shape but Variable Velocity[4]

If the control volume moves with a velocity $\mathbf{V}_s(t)$ that retains its shape, then the volume elements do not change with time, but the boundary relative velocity $\mathbf{V}_r = \mathbf{V}(\mathbf{r}, t) - \mathbf{V}_s(t)$ becomes a somewhat more complicated function. Equation (3.15) is unchanged in form, but the area integral may be more laborious to evaluate.

---

[4]This section may be omitted without loss of continuity.

Arbitrarily Moving and Deformable Control Volume[5]

The most general situation is when the control volume is both moving and deforming arbitrarily, as illustrated in Fig. 3.4. The flow of volume across the control surface is again proportional to the relative normal velocity component $\mathbf{V}_r \cdot \mathbf{n}$, as in Eq. (3.15). However, since the control surface has a deformation, its velocity $\mathbf{V}_s = \mathbf{V}_s(\mathbf{r}, t)$, so that the relative velocity $\mathbf{V}_r = \mathbf{V}(\mathbf{r}, t) - \mathbf{V}_s(\mathbf{r}, t)$ is or can be a complicated function, even though the flow integral is the same as in Eq. (3.15). Meanwhile, the volume integral in Eq. (3.15) must allow the volume elements to distort with time. Thus the time derivative must be applied *after* integration. For the deforming control volume, then, the transport theorem takes the form

$$\frac{d}{dt}(B_{\text{syst}}) = \frac{d}{dt}\left(\int_{\text{CV}} \beta\rho\, d\mathcal{V}\right) + \int_{\text{CS}} \beta\rho(\mathbf{V}_r \cdot \mathbf{n})\, dA \qquad (3.16)$$

This is the most general case, which we can compare with the equivalent form for a fixed control volume:

$$\frac{d}{dt}(B_{\text{syst}}) = \int_{\text{CV}} \frac{\partial}{\partial t}(\beta\rho)\, d\mathcal{V} + \int_{\text{CS}} \beta\rho(\mathbf{V} \cdot \mathbf{n})\, dA \qquad (3.17)$$

The moving and deforming control volume, Eq. (3.16), contains only two complications: (1) The time derivative of the first integral on the right must be taken outside, and (2) the second integral involves the *relative* velocity $\mathbf{V}_r$ between the fluid system and the control surface. These differences and mathematical subtleties are best shown by examples.

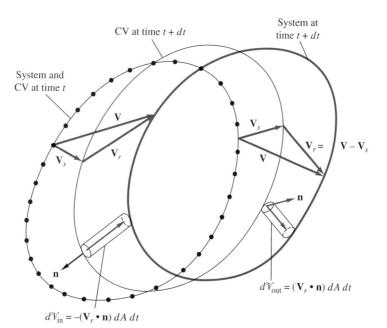

Fig. 3.4 Relative velocity effects between a system and a control volume when both move and deform. The system boundaries move at velocity $\mathbf{V}$, and the control surface moves at velocity $\mathbf{V}_s$.

[5]This section may be omitted without loss of continuity.

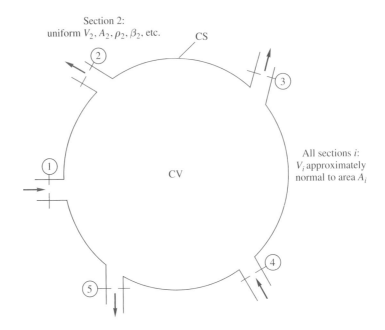

Fig. 3.5 A control volume with simplified one-dimensional inlets and exits.

One-Dimensional Flux Term Approximations

In many situations, the flow crosses the boundaries of the control surface only at simplified inlets and exits that are approximately *one-dimensional;* that is, flow properties are nearly uniform over the cross section. For a fixed control volume, the surface integral in Eq. (3.12) reduces to a sum of positive (outlet) and negative (inlet) product terms for each cross section:

$$\frac{d}{dt}(B_{\text{syst}}) = \frac{d}{dt}\left(\int_{\text{CV}} \beta \, dm\right) + \sum_{\text{outlets}} \beta_i \dot{m}_i \big|_{\text{out}} - \sum_{\text{inlets}} \beta_i \dot{m}_i \big|_{\text{in}} \quad \text{where } \dot{m}_i = \rho_i A_i V_i \quad (3.18)$$

To the writer, this is an attractive way to set up a control volume analysis without using the dot product notation. An example of multiple one-dimensional flows is shown in Fig. 3.5. There are inlet flows at sections 1 and 4 and outflows at sections 2, 3, and 5. Equation (3.18) becomes

$$\frac{d}{dt}(B_{\text{syst}}) = \frac{d}{dt}\left(\int_{\text{CV}} \beta \, dm\right) + \beta_2(\rho AV)_2 + \beta_3(\rho AV)_3 + \beta_5(\rho AV)_5$$
$$- \beta_1(\rho AV)_1 - \beta_4(\rho AV)_4 \quad (3.19)$$

with no contribution from any other portion of the control surface because there is no flow across the boundary.

EXAMPLE 3.1

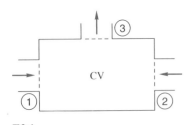

E3.1

A fixed control volume has three one-dimensional boundary sections, as shown in Fig. E3.1. The flow within the control volume is steady. The flow properties at each section are tabulated below. Find the rate of change of energy of the system that occupies the control volume at this instant.

Section	Type	ρ, kg/m^3	V, m/s	A, m^2	e, J/kg
1	Inlet	800	5.0	2.0	300
2	Inlet	800	8.0	3.0	100
3	Outlet	800	17.0	2.0	150

Solution

- *System sketch:* Figure E3.1 shows two inlet flows, 1 and 2, and a single outlet flow, 3.
- *Assumptions:* Steady flow, fixed control volume, one-dimensional inlet and exit flows.
- *Approach:* Apply Eq. (3.17) with *energy* as the property, where $B = E$ and $\beta = dE/dm = e$. Use the one-dimensional flow approximation and then insert the data from the table.
- *Solution steps:* Outlet 3 contributes a positive term, and inlets 1 and 2 are negative. The appropriate form of Eq. (3.12) is

$$\left(\frac{dE}{dt}\right)_{\text{syst}} = \frac{d}{dt}\left(\int_{\text{CV}} e\,\rho\,dv\right) + e_3\,\dot{m}_3 - e_1\,\dot{m}_1 - e_2\,\dot{m}_2$$

Since the flow is steady, the time-derivative volume integral term is zero. Introducing $(\rho AV)_i$ as the mass flow grouping, we obtain

$$\left(\frac{dE}{dt}\right)_{\text{syst}} = -e_1\rho_1 A_1 V_1 - e_2\rho_2 A_2 V_2 + e_3\rho_3 A_3 V_3$$

Introducing the numerical values from the table, we have

$$\left(\frac{dE}{dt}\right)_{\text{syst}} = -(300\ \text{J/kg})(800\ \text{kg/m}^3)(2\ \text{m}^2)(5\ \text{m/s}) - 100(800)(3)(8) + 150(800)(2)(17)$$

$$= (-2{,}400{,}000 - 1{,}920{,}000 + 4{,}080{,}000)\ \text{J/s}$$

$$= -240{,}000\ \text{J/s} = -0.24\ \text{MJ/s} \qquad\qquad Ans.$$

Thus the system is losing energy at the rate of 0.24 MJ/s = 0.24 MW. Since we have accounted for all fluid energy crossing the boundary, we conclude from the first law that there must be heat loss through the control surface, or the system must be doing work on the environment through some device not shown. Notice that the use of SI units leads to a consistent result in joules per second without any conversion factors. We promised in Chap. 1 that this would be the case.

- *Comments:* This problem involves energy, but suppose we check the balance of mass also. Then $B = $ mass m, and $\beta = dm/dm = $ unity. Again the volume integral vanishes for steady flow, and Eq. (3.17) reduces to

$$\left(\frac{dm}{dt}\right)_{\text{syst}} = \int_{\text{CS}} \rho(\mathbf{V}\cdot\mathbf{n})\,dA = -\rho_1 A_1 V_1 - \rho_2 A_2 V_2 + \rho_3 A_3 V_3$$

$$= -(800\ \text{kg/m}^3)(2\ \text{m}^2)(5\ \text{m/s}) - 800(3)(8) + 800(17)(2)$$

$$= (-8000 - 19{,}200 + 27{,}200)\ \text{kg/s} = 0\ \text{kg/s}$$

Thus the system mass does not change, which correctly expresses the law of conservation of system mass, Eq. (3.1).

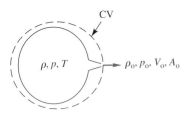

E3.2

EXAMPLE 3.2

Compressed air in a rigid tank of volume $\mathcal{V}$ exhausts through a small nozzle as in Fig. E3.2. Air properties change through the nozzle, and the flow exits at ρ_o, V_o, A_o. Find an expression for the rate of change of tank density.

Solution

- *System sketch:* Fig. E3.2 shows one exit, no inlets. The constant exit area is A_o.
- *Control volume:* As shown, we choose a CV that encircles the entire tank and nozzle.
- *Assumptions:* Unsteady flow (the tank mass decreases), one-dimensional exit flow.
- *Approach:* Apply Eq. (3.16) for mass, $B = m$ and $\beta = dm/dm =$ unity.
- *Solution steps:* Write out the Reynolds transport relation (3.16) for this problem:

$$\left(\frac{dm}{dt}\right)_{\text{syst}} = 0 = \frac{d}{dt}\left(\int_{\text{CV}} \rho\, d\mathcal{V}\right) + \int_{\text{CS}} \rho(\mathbf{V} \cdot \mathbf{n})\, dA = \mathcal{V}\frac{d\rho}{dt} + \rho_o V_o A_o$$

Solve for the rate of change of tank density:

$$\frac{d\rho}{dt} = -\frac{\rho_o V_o A_o}{\mathcal{V}} \qquad\qquad Ans.$$

- *Comments:* This is a first-order ordinary differential equation for the tank density. If we account for changes in ρ_o and V_o from the compressible-flow theories of Chap. 9, we can readily solve this equation for the tank density $\rho(t)$.

For advanced study, many more details of the analysis of deformable control volumes can be found in Hansen [4] and Potter et al. [5].

3.3 Conservation of Mass

The Reynolds transport theorem, Eq. (3.16) or (3.17), establishes a relation between system rates of change and control volume surface and volume integrals. But system derivatives are related to the basic laws of mechanics, Eqs. (3.1) to (3.5). Eliminating system derivatives between the two gives the control volume, or *integral,* forms of the laws of mechanics of fluids. The dummy variable B becomes, respectively, mass, linear momentum, angular momentum, and energy.

For conservation of mass, as discussed in Examples 3.1 and 3.2, $B = m$ and $\beta = dm/dm = 1$. Equation (3.1) becomes

$$\left(\frac{dm}{dt}\right)_{\text{syst}} = 0 = \frac{d}{dt}\left(\int_{\text{CV}} \rho\, d\mathcal{V}\right) + \int_{\text{CS}} \rho(\mathbf{V}_r \cdot \mathbf{n})\, dA \qquad (3.20)$$

This is the integral mass conservation law for a deformable control volume. For a fixed control volume, we have

$$\int_{\text{CV}} \frac{\partial \rho}{\partial t}\, d\mathcal{V} + \int_{\text{CS}} \rho(\mathbf{V} \cdot \mathbf{n})\, dA = 0 \qquad (3.21)$$

If the control volume has only a number of one-dimensional inlets and outlets, we can write

$$\int_{CV} \frac{\partial \rho}{\partial t} \, d\mathcal{V} + \sum_i (\rho_i A_i V_i)_{out} - \sum_i (\rho_i A_i V_i)_{in} = 0 \qquad (3.22)$$

Other special cases occur. Suppose that the flow within the control volume is steady; then $\partial \rho / \partial t \equiv 0$, and Eq. (3.21) reduces to

$$\int_{CS} \rho (\mathbf{V} \cdot \mathbf{n}) \, dA = 0 \qquad (3.23)$$

This states that in steady flow the mass flows entering and leaving the control volume must balance exactly.[6] If, further, the inlets and outlets are one-dimensional, we have for steady flow

$$\sum_i (\rho_i A_i V_i)_{in} = \sum_i (\rho_i A_i V_i)_{out} \qquad (3.24)$$

This simple approximation is widely used in engineering analyses. For example, referring to Fig. 3.5, we see that if the flow in that control volume is steady, the three outlet mass flows balance the two inlets:

$$Outflow = Inflow$$

$$\rho_2 A_2 V_2 + \rho_3 A_3 V_3 + \rho_5 A_5 V_5 = \rho_1 A_1 V_1 + \rho_4 A_4 V_4 \qquad (3.25)$$

The quantity ρAV is called the *mass flow* $\dot{m}$ passing through the one-dimensional cross section and has consistent units of kilograms per second (or slugs per second) for SI (or BG) units. Equation (3.25) can be rewritten in the short form

$$\dot{m}_2 + \dot{m}_3 + \dot{m}_5 = \dot{m}_1 + \dot{m}_4 \qquad (3.26)$$

and, in general, the steady-flow–mass-conservation relation (3.23) can be written as

$$\sum_i (\dot{m}_i)_{out} = \sum_i (\dot{m}_i)_{in} \qquad (3.27)$$

If the inlets and outlets are not one-dimensional, one has to compute $\dot{m}$ by integration over the section

$$\dot{m}_{cs} = \int_{cs} \rho (\mathbf{V} \cdot \mathbf{n}) \, dA \qquad (3.28)$$

where "cs" stands for cross section. An illustration of this is given in Example 3.4.

---

[6]Throughout this section we are neglecting *sources* or *sinks* of mass that might be embedded in the control volume. Equations (3.20) and (3.21) can readily be modified to add source and sink terms, but this is rarely necessary.

Incompressible Flow

Still further simplification is possible if the fluid is incompressible, which we may define as having density variations that are negligible in the mass conservation requirement.[7] As we saw in Chap. 1, all liquids are nearly incompressible, and gas flows can *behave* as if they were incompressible, particularly if the gas velocity is less than about 30 percent of the speed of sound of the gas.

Again consider the fixed control volume. For nearly incompressible flow, the term $\partial\rho/\partial t$ is small, so the time-derivative volume integral in Eq. (3.21) can be neglected. The constant density can then be removed from the surface integral for a nice simplification:

$$\frac{d}{dt}\left(\int_{CV} \frac{\partial\rho}{\partial t}\, dv\right) + \int_{CS} \rho(\mathbf{V}\cdot\mathbf{n})\, dA = 0 = \int_{CS} \rho(\mathbf{V}\cdot\mathbf{n})\, dA = \rho\int_{CS} (\mathbf{V}\cdot\mathbf{n})\, dA$$

or

$$\int_{CS} (\mathbf{V}\cdot\mathbf{n})\, dA = 0 \qquad (3.29)$$

If the inlets and outlets are one-dimensional, we have

$$\sum_i (V_i A_i)_{\text{out}} = \sum_i (V_i A_i)_{\text{in}} \qquad (3.30)$$

or

$$\sum Q_{\text{out}} = \sum Q_{\text{in}}$$

where $Q_i = V_i A_i$ is called the *volume flow* passing through the given cross section.

Again, if consistent units are used, $Q = VA$ will have units of cubic meters per second (SI) or cubic feet per second (BG). If the cross section is not one-dimensional, we have to integrate

$$Q_{CS} = \int_{CS} (\mathbf{V}\cdot\mathbf{n})\, dA \qquad (3.31)$$

Equation (3.31) allows us to define an *average velocity* V_{av} that, when multiplied by the section area, gives the correct volume flow:

$$V_{\text{av}} = \frac{Q}{A} = \frac{1}{A}\int (\mathbf{V}\cdot\mathbf{n})\, dA \qquad (3.32)$$

This could be called the *volume-average velocity*. If the density varies across the section, we can define an average density in the same manner:

$$\rho_{\text{av}} = \frac{1}{A}\int \rho\, dA \qquad (3.33)$$

But the mass flow would contain the product of density and velocity, and the average product $(\rho V)_{\text{av}}$ would in general have a different value from the product of the averages:

$$(\rho V)_{\text{av}} = \frac{1}{A}\int \rho(\mathbf{V}\cdot\mathbf{n})\, dA \approx \rho_{\text{av}} V_{\text{av}} \qquad (3.34)$$

[7]Be warned that there is subjectivity in specifying incompressibility. Oceanographers consider a 0.1 percent density variation very significant, while aerodynamicists may neglect density variations in highly compressible, even hypersonic, gas flows. Your task is to justify the incompressible approximation when you make it.

We illustrate average velocity in Example 3.4. We can often neglect the difference or, if necessary, use a correction factor between mass average and volume average.

EXAMPLE 3.3

Write the conservation-of-mass relation for steady flow through a streamtube (flow everywhere parallel to the walls) with a single one-dimensional inlet 1 and exit 2 (Fig. E3.3).

Solution

For steady flow Eq. (3.24) applies with the single inlet and exit:

$$\dot{m} = \rho_1 A_1 V_1 = \rho_2 A_2 V_2 = \text{const}$$

Thus, in a streamtube in steady flow, the mass flow is constant across every section of the tube. If the density is constant, then

$$Q = A_1 V_1 = A_2 V_2 = \text{const} \quad \text{or} \quad V_2 = \frac{A_1}{A_2} V_1$$

The volume flow is constant in the tube in steady incompressible flow, and the velocity increases as the section area decreases. This relation was derived by Leonardo da Vinci in 1500.

EXAMPLE 3.4

For steady viscous flow through a circular tube (Fig. E3.4), the axial velocity profile is given approximately by

$$u = U_0\left(1 - \frac{r}{R}\right)^m$$

so that u varies from zero at the wall ($r = R$), or no slip, up to a maximum $u = U_0$ at the centerline $r = 0$. For highly viscous (laminar) flow $m \approx \frac{1}{2}$, while for less viscous (turbulent) flow $m \approx \frac{1}{7}$. Compute the average velocity if the density is constant.

Solution

The average velocity is defined by Eq. (3.32). Here $\mathbf{V} = \mathbf{i}u$ and $\mathbf{n} = \mathbf{i}$, and thus $\mathbf{V} \cdot \mathbf{n} = u$. Since the flow is symmetric, the differential area can be taken as a circular strip $dA = 2\pi r\, dr$. Equation (3.32) becomes

$$V_{\text{av}} = \frac{1}{A}\int u\, dA = \frac{1}{\pi R^2}\int_0^R U_0\left(1 - \frac{r}{R}\right)^m 2\pi r\, dr$$

or
$$V_{\text{av}} = U_0 \frac{2}{(1 + m)(2 + m)} \qquad \text{Ans.}$$

E3.3

V · n = 0

V_1

V_2

Streamtube
control volume

①

②

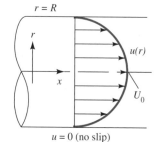

E3.4

$r = R$

r

$u(r)$

x

U_0

$u = 0$ (no slip)

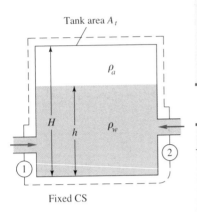

Tank area A_t

p_a

H h p_w

2

1

Fixed CS

E3.5

For the laminar flow approximation, $m \approx \frac{1}{2}$ and $V_{av} \approx 0.53U_0$. (The exact laminar theory in Chap. 6 gives $V_{av} = 0.50U_0$.) For turbulent flow, $m \approx \frac{1}{7}$ and $V_{av} \approx 0.82U_0$. (There is no exact turbulent theory, and so we accept this approximation.) The turbulent velocity profile is more uniform across the section, and thus the average velocity is only slightly less than maximum.

EXAMPLE 3.5

The tank in Fig. E3.5 is being filled with water by two one-dimensional inlets. Air is trapped at the top of the tank. The water height is h. (a) Find an expression for the change in water height dh/dt. (b) Compute dh/dt if $D_1 = 1$ in, $D_2 = 3$ in, $V_1 = 3$ ft/s, $V_2 = 2$ ft/s, and $A_t = 2$ ft^2, assuming water at 20°C.

Solution

Part (a)

A suggested control volume encircles the tank and cuts through the two inlets. The flow within is unsteady, and Eq. (3.22) applies with no outlets and two inlets:

$$\frac{d}{dt}\left(\int_{CV} \rho \, d\mathcal{V}\right) - \rho_1 A_1 V_1 - \rho_2 A_2 V_2 = 0 \tag{1}$$

Now if A_t is the tank cross-sectional area, the unsteady term can be evaluated as follows:

$$\frac{d}{dt}\left(\int_{CV} \rho \, d\mathcal{V}\right) = \frac{d}{dt}(\rho_w A_t h) + \frac{d}{dt}[\rho_a A_t(H-h)] = \rho_w A_t \frac{dh}{dt} \tag{2}$$

The ρ_a term vanishes because it is the rate of change of air mass and is zero because the air is trapped at the top. Substituting (2) into (1), we find the change of water height

$$\frac{dh}{dt} = \frac{\rho_1 A_1 V_1 + \rho_2 A_2 V_2}{\rho_w A_t} \qquad \text{Ans. (a)}$$

For water, $\rho_1 = \rho_2 = \rho_w$, and this result reduces to

$$\frac{dh}{dt} = \frac{A_1 V_1 + A_2 V_2}{A_t} = \frac{Q_1 + Q_2}{A_t} \tag{3}$$

Part (b)

The two inlet volume flows are

$$Q_1 = A_1 V_1 = \tfrac{1}{4}\pi(\tfrac{1}{12} \text{ ft})^2(3 \text{ ft/s}) = 0.016 \text{ ft}^3/\text{s}$$

$$Q_2 = A_2 V_2 = \tfrac{1}{4}\pi(\tfrac{3}{12} \text{ ft})^2(2 \text{ ft/s}) = 0.098 \text{ ft}^3/\text{s}$$

Then, from Eq. (3),

$$\frac{dh}{dt} = \frac{(0.016 + 0.098) \text{ ft}^3/\text{s}}{2 \text{ ft}^2} = 0.057 \text{ ft/s} \qquad \text{Ans. (b)}$$

Suggestion: Repeat this problem with the top of the tank open.

The control volume mass relations, Eq. (3.20) or (3.21), are fundamental to all fluid flow analyses. They involve only velocity and density. Vector directions are of no consequence except to determine the normal velocity at the surface and hence whether the flow is *in* or *out*. Although your specific analysis may concern forces or moments or energy, you must always make sure that mass is balanced as part of the analysis; otherwise the results will be unrealistic and probably incorrect. We shall see in the examples that follow how mass conservation is constantly checked in performing an analysis of other fluid properties.

3.4 The Linear Momentum Equation

In Newton's second law, Eq. (3.2), the property being differentiated is the linear momentum $m\mathbf{V}$. Therefore our dummy variable is $\mathbf{B} = m\mathbf{V}$ and $\beta = d\mathbf{B}/dm = \mathbf{V}$, and application of the Reynolds transport theorem gives the linear momentum relation for a deformable control volume:

$$\frac{d}{dt}(m\mathbf{V})_{\text{syst}} = \sum \mathbf{F} = \frac{d}{dt}\left(\int_{\text{CV}} \mathbf{V}\rho \, d\mathcal{V}\right) + \int_{\text{CS}} \mathbf{V}\rho(\mathbf{V}_r \cdot \mathbf{n}) \, dA \qquad (3.35)$$

The following points concerning this relation should be strongly emphasized:

1. The term $\mathbf{V}$ is the fluid velocity relative to an *inertial* (nonaccelerating) coordinate system; otherwise Newton's second law must be modified to include noninertial relative acceleration terms (see the end of this section).
2. The term $\Sigma \, \mathbf{F}$ is the *vector* sum of all forces acting on the system material considered as a free body; that is, it includes surface forces on all fluids and solids cut by the control surface plus all body forces (gravity and electromagnetic) acting on the masses within the control volume.
3. The entire equation is a vector relation; both the integrals are vectors due to the term $\mathbf{V}$ in the integrands. The equation thus has three components. If we want only, say, the x component, the equation reduces to

$$\sum F_x = \frac{d}{dt}\left(\int_{\text{CV}} u\rho \, d\mathcal{V}\right) + \int_{\text{CS}} u\rho(\mathbf{V}_r \cdot \mathbf{n}) \, dA \qquad (3.36)$$

and similarly, $\Sigma \, F_y$ and $\Sigma \, F_z$ would involve v and w, respectively. Failure to account for the vector nature of the linear momentum relation (3.35) is probably the greatest source of student error in control volume analyses.

For a fixed control volume, the relative velocity $\mathbf{V}_r \equiv \mathbf{V}$, and Eq. (3.35) becomes

$$\sum \mathbf{F} = \frac{d}{dt}\left(\int_{\text{CV}} \mathbf{V}\rho \, d\mathcal{V}\right) + \int_{\text{CS}} \mathbf{V}\rho(\mathbf{V} \cdot \mathbf{n}) \, dA \qquad (3.37)$$

Again we stress that this is a vector relation and that $\mathbf{V}$ must be an inertial-frame velocity. Most of the momentum analyses in this text are concerned with Eq. (3.37).

One-Dimensional Momentum Flux

By analogy with the term *mass flow* used in Eq. (3.28), the surface integral in Eq. (3.37) is called the *momentum flow term*. If we denote momentum by **M**, then

$$\dot{\mathbf{M}}_{CS} = \int_{sec} \mathbf{V}\rho(\mathbf{V} \cdot \mathbf{n}) \, dA \tag{3.38}$$

Because of the dot product, the result will be negative for inlet momentum flow and positive for outlet flow. If the cross section is one-dimensional, **V** and ρ are uniform over the area and the integrated result is

$$\dot{\mathbf{M}}_{seci} = \mathbf{V}_i(\rho_i V_{ni} A_i) = \dot{m}_i \mathbf{V}_i \tag{3.39}$$

for outlet flow and $-\dot{m}_i \mathbf{V}_i$ for inlet flow. Thus if the control volume has only one-dimensional inlets and outlets, Eq. (3.37) reduces to

$$\sum \mathbf{F} = \frac{d}{dt}\left(\int_{CV} \mathbf{V}\rho \, d\mathcal{V}\right) + \sum (\dot{m}_i \mathbf{V}_i)_{out} - \sum (\dot{m}_i \mathbf{V}_i)_{in} \tag{3.40}$$

This is a commonly used approximation in engineering analyses. It is crucial to realize that we are dealing with vector sums. Equation (3.40) states that the net vector force on a fixed control volume equals the rate of change of vector momentum within the control volume plus the vector sum of outlet momentum flows minus the vector sum of inlet flows.

Net Pressure Force on a Closed Control Surface

Generally speaking, the surface forces on a control volume are due to (1) forces exposed by cutting through solid bodies that protrude through the surface and (2) forces due to pressure and viscous stresses of the surrounding fluid. The computation of pressure force is relatively simple, as shown in Fig. 3.6. Recall from Chap. 2 that

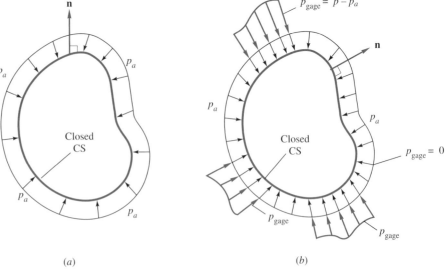

Fig. 3.6 Pressure force computation by subtracting a uniform distribution: (*a*) uniform pressure,

$$\mathbf{F} = -p_a \int \mathbf{n} \, dA \equiv 0;$$

(*b*) nonuniform pressure,

$$\mathbf{F} = -\int (p - p_a)\mathbf{n} \, dA.$$

(*a*)

(*b*)

the external pressure force on a surface is normal to the surface and *inward*. Since the unit vector **n** is defined as *outward*, one way to write the pressure force is

$$\mathbf{F}_{press} = \int_{CS} p(-\mathbf{n}) \, dA \tag{3.41}$$

Now if the pressure has a uniform value p_a all around the surface, as in Fig. 3.7a, the net pressure force is zero:

$$\mathbf{F}_{UP} = \int p_a(-\mathbf{n})dA = -p_a \int \mathbf{n} \, dA \equiv 0 \tag{3.42}$$

where the subscript UP stands for uniform pressure. This result is *independent of the shape of the surface*[8] as long as the surface is closed and all our control volumes are closed. Thus a seemingly complicated pressure force problem can be simplified by subtracting any convenient uniform pressure p_a and working only with the pieces of gage pressure that remain, as illustrated in Fig. 3.6b. So Eq. (3.41) is entirely equivalent to

$$F_{press} = \int_{CS} (p - p_a)(-\mathbf{n})dA = \int_{CS} p_{gage}(-\mathbf{n}) \, dA$$

This trick can mean quite a savings in computation.

EXAMPLE 3.6

A control volume of a nozzle section has surface pressures of 40 lbf/in^2 absolute at section 1 and atmospheric pressure of 15 lbf/in^2 absolute at section 2 and on the external rounded part of the nozzle, as in Fig. E3.6a. Compute the net pressure force if $D_1 = 3$ in and $D_2 = 1$ in.

Solution

- *System sketch:*   The control volume is the *outside* of the nozzle, plus the cut sections (1) and (2). There would also be *stresses* in the cut nozzle wall at section 1, which we are neglecting here. The pressures acting on the control volume are shown in Fig. E3.6a. Figure E3.6b shows the pressures after 15 lbf/in^2 has been subtracted from all sides. Here we compute the net pressure force only.

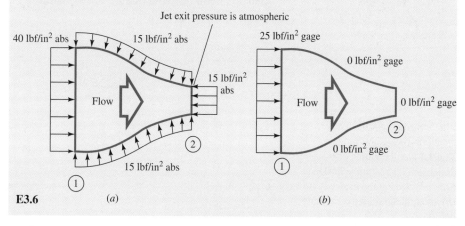

E3.6   (*a*)   (*b*)

---

[8]Can you prove this? It is a consequence of Gauss's theorem from vector analysis.

- *Assumptions:* Known pressures, as shown, on all surfaces of the control volume.
- *Approach:* Since three surfaces have $p = 15$ lbf/in^2, subtract this amount everywhere so that these three sides reduce to zero "gage pressure" for convenience. This is allowable because of Eq. (3.42).
- *Solution steps:* For the modified pressure distribution, Fig. E3.6b, only section 1 is needed:

$$\mathbf{F}_{press} = p_{gage,1}(-\mathbf{n})_1 A_1 = \left(25 \frac{\text{lbf}}{\text{in}^2}\right)\left[-(-\mathbf{i})\right]\left[\frac{\pi}{4}(3 \text{ in})^2\right] = 177\mathbf{i} \text{ lbf} \qquad Ans.$$

- *Comments:* This "uniform subtraction" artifice, which is entirely legal, has greatly simplified the calculation of pressure force. *Note:* We were a bit too informal when multiplying pressure in lbf/in^2 times area in square inches. We achieved lbf correctly, but it would be better practice to convert all data to standard BG units. *Further note:* In addition to $\mathbf{F}_{press}$, there are other forces involved in this flow, due to tension stresses in the cut nozzle wall and the fluid weight inside the control volume.

Pressure Condition at a Jet Exit

Figure E3.6 illustrates a pressure boundary condition commonly used for jet exit flow problems. When a fluid flow leaves a confined internal duct and exits into an ambient "atmosphere," its free surface is exposed to that atmosphere. Therefore the jet itself will essentially be at atmospheric pressure also. This condition was used at section 2 in Fig. E3.6.

Only two effects could maintain a pressure difference between the atmosphere and a free exit jet. The first is surface tension, Eq. (1.31), which is usually negligible. The second effect is a *supersonic* jet, which can separate itself from an atmosphere with expansion or compression waves (Chap. 9). For the majority of applications, therefore, we shall set the pressure in an exit jet as atmospheric.

EXAMPLE 3.7

A fixed control volume of a streamtube in steady flow has a uniform inlet flow (ρ_1, A_1, V_1) and a uniform exit flow (ρ_2, A_2, V_2), as shown in Fig. 3.7. Find an expression for the net force on the control volume.

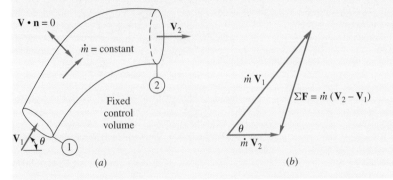

Fig. 3.7 Net force on a one-dimensional streamtube in steady flow: (*a*) streamtube in steady flow; (*b*) vector diagram for computing net force.

Solution

Equation (3.40) applies with one inlet and exit:

$$\sum \mathbf{F} = \dot{m}_2\mathbf{V}_2 - \dot{m}_1\mathbf{V}_1 = (\rho_2 A_2 V_2)\mathbf{V}_2 - (\rho_1 A_1 V_1)\mathbf{V}_1$$

The volume integral term vanishes for steady flow, but from conservation of mass in Example 3.3 we saw that

$$\dot{m}_1 = \dot{m}_2 = \dot{m} = \text{const}$$

Therefore a simple form for the desired result is

$$\sum \mathbf{F} = \dot{m}(\mathbf{V}_2 - \mathbf{V}_1) \qquad\qquad Ans.$$

This is a *vector* relation and is sketched in Fig. 3.7b. The term $\Sigma\,\mathbf{F}$ represents the net force acting on the control volume due to all causes; it is needed to balance the change in momentum of the fluid as it turns and decelerates while passing through the control volume.

EXAMPLE 3.8

As shown in Fig. 3.8a, a fixed vane turns a water jet of area A through an angle θ without changing its velocity magnitude. The flow is steady, pressure is p_a everywhere, and friction on the vane is negligible. (a) Find the components F_x and F_y of the applied vane force. (b) Find expressions for the force magnitude F and the angle ϕ between F and the horizontal; plot them versus θ.

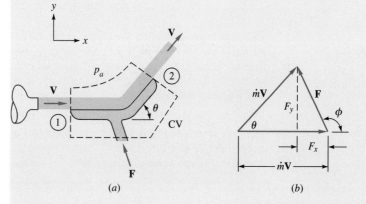

Fig. 3.8 Net applied force on a fixed jet-turning vane: (a) geometry of the vane turning the water jet; (b) vector diagram for the net force.

(a)   (b)

Solution

Part (a)

The control volume selected in Fig. 3.8a cuts through the inlet and exit of the jet and through the vane support, exposing the vane force $\mathbf{F}$. Since there is no cut along the vane–jet interface, vane friction is internally self-canceling. The pressure force is zero in the uniform atmosphere. We neglect the weight of fluid and the vane weight within the control volume. Then Eq. (3.40) reduces to

$$\mathbf{F}_{\text{vane}} = \dot{m}_2\mathbf{V}_2 - \dot{m}_1\mathbf{V}_1$$

But the magnitude $V_1 = V_2 = V$ as given, and conservation of mass for the streamtube requires $\dot{m}_1 = \dot{m}_2 = \dot{m} = \rho A V$. The vector diagram for force and momentum change becomes an isosceles triangle with legs $\dot{m}\mathbf{V}$ and base $\mathbf{F}$, as in Fig. 3.8b. We can readily find the force components from this diagram:

$$F_x = \dot{m}V(\cos\theta - 1) \quad F_y = \dot{m}V\sin\theta \qquad Ans. \ (a)$$

where $\dot{m}V = \rho A V^2$ for this case. This is the desired result.

Part (b)   The force magnitude is obtained from part (a):

$$F = (F_x^2 + F_y^2)^{1/2} = \dot{m}V[\sin^2\theta + (\cos\theta - 1)^2]^{1/2} = 2\dot{m}V\sin\frac{\theta}{2} \qquad Ans. \ (b)$$

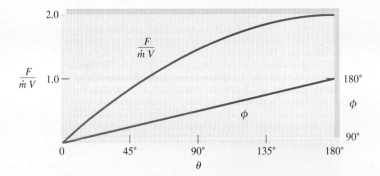

E3.8

From the geometry of Fig. 3.8b we obtain

$$\phi = 180° - \tan^{-1}\frac{F_y}{F_x} = 90° + \frac{\theta}{2} \qquad Ans. \ (b)$$

These can be plotted versus θ as shown in Fig. E3.8. Two special cases are of interest. First, the maximum force occurs at $\theta = 180°$—that is, when the jet is turned around and thrown back in the opposite direction with its momentum completely reversed. This force is $2\dot{m}V$ and acts to the *left*; that is, $\phi = 180°$. Second, at very small turning angles ($\theta < 10°$) we obtain approximately

$$F \approx \dot{m}V\theta \qquad \phi \approx 90°$$

The force is linearly proportional to the turning angle and acts nearly normal to the jet. This is the principle of a lifting vane, or airfoil, which causes a slight change in the oncoming flow direction and thereby creates a lift force normal to the basic flow.

EXAMPLE 3.9

A water jet of velocity V_j impinges normal to a flat plate that moves to the right at velocity V_c, as shown in Fig. 3.9a. Find the force required to keep the plate moving at constant velocity if the jet density is 1000 kg/m³, the jet area is 3 cm², and V_j and V_c are 20 and 15 m/s, respectively. Neglect the weight of the jet and plate, and assume steady flow with respect to the moving plate with the jet splitting into an equal upward and downward half-jet.

Solution

The suggested control volume in Fig. 3.9a cuts through the plate support to expose the desired forces R_x and R_y. This control volume moves at speed V_c and thus is fixed relative to the plate, as in Fig. 3.9b. We must satisfy both mass and momentum conservation for the assumed steady flow pattern in Fig. 3.9b. There are two outlets and one inlet, and Eq. (3.30) applies for mass conservation:

$$\dot{m}_{out} = \dot{m}_{in}$$

or
$$\rho_1 A_1 V_1 + \rho_2 A_2 V_2 = \rho_j A_j (V_j - V_c) \tag{1}$$

We assume that the water is incompressible $\rho_1 = \rho_2 = \rho_j$, and we are given that $A_1 = A_2 = \frac{1}{2} A_j$. Therefore Eq. (1) reduces to

$$V_1 + V_2 = 2(V_j - V_c) \tag{2}$$

Strictly speaking, this is all that mass conservation tells us. However, from the symmetry of the jet deflection and the neglect of gravity on the fluid trajectory, we conclude that the two velocities V_1 and V_2 must be equal, and hence Eq. (2) becomes

$$V_1 = V_2 = V_j - V_c \tag{3}$$

This equality can also be predicted by Bernoulli's equation in Sec. 3.5. For the given numerical values, we have

$$V_1 = V_2 = 20 - 15 = 5 \text{ m/s}$$

Now we can compute R_x and R_y from the two components of momentum conservation. Equation (3.40) applies with the unsteady term zero:

$$\sum F_x = R_x = \dot{m}_1 u_1 + \dot{m}_2 u_2 - \dot{m}_j u_j \tag{4}$$

where from the mass analysis, $\dot{m}_1 = \dot{m}_2 = \frac{1}{2} \dot{m}_j = \frac{1}{2} \rho_j A_j (V_j - V_c)$. Now check the flow directions at each section: $u_1 = u_2 = 0$, and $u_j = V_j - V_c = 5$ m/s. Thus Eq. (4) becomes

$$R_x = -\dot{m}_j u_j = -[\rho_j A_j (V_j - V_c)](V_j - V_c) \tag{5}$$

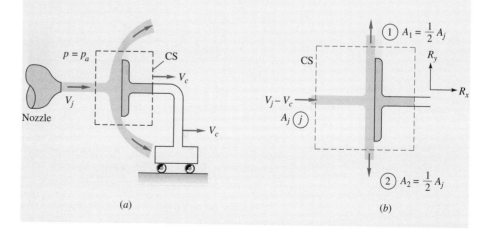

Fig. 3.9 Force on a plate moving at constant velocity: (a) jet striking a moving plate normally; (b) control volume fixed relative to the plate.

For the given numerical values we have

$$R_x = -(1000 \text{ kg/m}^3)(0.0003 \text{ m}^2)(5 \text{ m/s})^2 = -7.5 \text{ (kg} \cdot \text{m)/s}^2 = -7.5 \text{ N} \qquad \textit{Ans.}$$

This acts to the *left*; that is, it requires a restraining force to keep the plate from accelerating to the right due to the continuous impact of the jet. The vertical force is

$$F_y = R_y = \dot{m}_1 v_1 + \dot{m}_2 v_2 - \dot{m}_j v_j$$

Check directions again: $v_1 = V_1$, $v_2 = -V_2$, $v_j = 0$. Thus

$$R_y = \dot{m}_1(V_1) + \dot{m}_2(-V_2) = \tfrac{1}{2}\dot{m}_j(V_1 - V_2) \qquad (6)$$

But since we found earlier that $V_1 = V_2$, this means that $R_y = 0$, as we could expect from the symmetry of the jet deflection.[9] Two other results are of interest. First, the relative velocity at section 1 was found to be 5 m/s up, from Eq. (3). If we convert this to absolute motion by adding on the control-volume speed $V_c = 15$ m/s to the right, we find that the absolute velocity $\mathbf{V}_1 = 15\mathbf{i} + 5\mathbf{j}$ m/s, or 15.8 m/s at an angle of 18.4° upward, as indicated in Fig. 3.9a. Thus the absolute jet speed changes after hitting the plate. Second, the computed force R_x does not change if we assume the jet deflects in all radial directions along the plate surface rather than just up and down. Since the plate is normal to the x axis, there would still be zero outlet x-momentum flow when Eq. (4) was rewritten for a radial deflection condition.

EXAMPLE 3.10

The sluice gate in Fig. E3.10a controls flow in open channels. At sections 1 and 2, the flow is uniform and the pressure is hydrostatic. Neglecting bottom friction and atmospheric pressure, derive a formula for the horizontal force F required to hold the gate. Express your final formula in terms of the inlet velocity V_1, eliminating V_2.

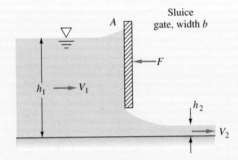

E3.10a

Solution

Choose a control volume, Fig. E3.10b, that cuts through known regions (section 1 and section 2 just above the bottom, and the atmosphere) and that cuts along regions where unknown information is desired (the gate, with its force F).

---

[9]Symmetry can be a powerful tool if used properly. Try to learn more about the uses and misuses of symmetry conditions.

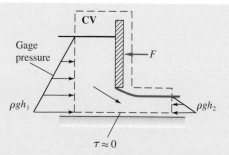

E3.10b

Assume steady incompressible flow with no variation across the width b. The inlet and outlet mass flows balance:

$$\dot{m} = \rho V_1 h_1 b = \rho V_2 h_2 b \quad \text{or} \quad V_2 = V_1(h_1/h_2)$$

We may use gage pressures for convenience because a uniform atmospheric pressure causes no force, as shown earlier in Fig. 3.6. With x positive to the right, equate the net horizontal force to the x-directed momentum change:

$$\Sigma F_x = -F_{\text{gate}} + \frac{\rho}{2}gh_1(h_1 b) - \frac{\rho}{2}gh_2(h_2 b) = \dot{m}(V_2 - V_1)$$
$$\dot{m} = \rho h_1 b V_1$$

Solve for F_{gate}, and eliminate V_2 using the mass flow relation. The desired result is:

$$F_{\text{gate}} = \frac{\rho}{2}gbh_1^2\left[1 - \left(\frac{h_2}{h_1}\right)^2\right] - \rho h_1 b V_1^2\left(\frac{h_1}{h_2} - 1\right) \qquad Ans.$$

This is a powerful result from a relatively simple analysis. Later, in Sec. 10.4, we will be able to calculate the actual flow rate from the water depths and the gate opening height.

EXAMPLE 3.11

Example 3.9 treated a plate at normal incidence to an oncoming flow. In Fig. 3.10 the plate is parallel to the flow. The stream is not a jet but a broad river, or *free stream*, of uniform velocity $\mathbf{V} = U_0\mathbf{i}$. The pressure is assumed uniform, and so it has no net force on the plate. The plate does not block the flow as in Fig. 3.9, so the only effect is due to boundary shear, which was neglected in the previous example. The no-slip condition at the wall brings the fluid there to a halt, and these slowly moving particles retard their neighbors above, so that at the end of the plate there is a significant retarded shear layer, or *boundary layer*, of thickness $y = \delta$. The viscous stresses along the wall can sum to a finite drag force on the plate. These effects are illustrated in Fig. 3.10. The problem is to make an integral analysis and find the drag force D in terms of the flow properties ρ, U_0, and δ and the plate dimensions L and b.[10]

Solution

Like most practical cases, this problem requires a combined mass and momentum balance. A proper selection of control volume is essential, and we select the four-sided region from

---

[10]The general analysis of such wall shear problems, called *boundary-layer theory,* is treated in Sec. 7.3.

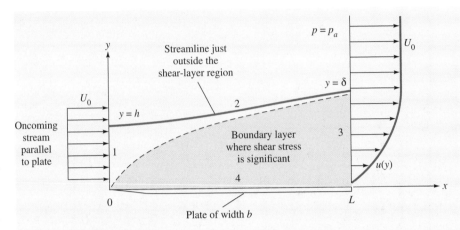

Fig. 3.10 Control volume analysis of drag force on a flat plate due to boundary shear. The control volume is bounded by sections 1, 2, 3, and 4.

0 to h to δ to L and back to the origin 0, as shown in Fig. 3.10. Had we chosen to cut across horizontally from left to right along the height $y = h$, we would have cut through the shear layer and exposed unknown shear stresses. Instead we follow the streamline passing through $(x, y) = (0, h)$, which is outside the shear layer and also has no mass flow across it. The four control volume sides are thus

1. From $(0, 0)$ to $(0, h)$: a one-dimensional inlet, $\mathbf{V} \cdot \mathbf{n} = -U_0$.
2. From $(0, h)$ to (L, δ): a streamline, no shear, $\mathbf{V} \cdot \mathbf{n} = 0$.
3. From (L, δ) to $(L, 0)$: a two-dimensional outlet, $\mathbf{V} \cdot \mathbf{n} = +u(y)$.
4. From $(L, 0)$ to $(0, 0)$: a streamline just above the plate surface, $\mathbf{V} \cdot \mathbf{n} = 0$, shear forces summing to the drag force $-D\mathbf{i}$ acting from the plate onto the retarded fluid.

The pressure is uniform, and so there is no net pressure force. Since the flow is assumed incompressible and steady, Eq. (3.37) applies with no unsteady term and flows only across sections 1 and 3:

$$\sum F_x = -D = \rho \int_1 u(0, y)(\mathbf{V} \cdot \mathbf{n})\, dA \;+\; \rho \int_3 u(L, y)\, (\mathbf{V} \cdot \mathbf{n})\, dA$$

$$= \rho \int_0^h U_0(-U_0)b\, dy + \rho \int_0^\delta u(L, y)[\,+u(L, y)\,]b\, dy$$

Evaluating the first integral and rearranging give

$$D = \rho U_0^2 bh - \rho b \int_0^\delta u^2 dy \mid_{x=L} \tag{1}$$

This could be considered the answer to the problem, but it is not useful because the height h is not known with respect to the shear layer thickness δ. This is found by applying mass conservation, since the control volume forms a streamtube:

$$\rho \int_{CS} (\mathbf{V} \cdot \mathbf{n})\, dA = 0 = \rho \int_0^h (-U_0)b\, dy + \rho \int_0^\delta ub\, dy \mid_{x=L}$$

or

$$U_0 h = \int_0^\delta u\, dy \mid_{x=L} \tag{2}$$

after canceling b and ρ and evaluating the first integral. Introduce this value of h into Eq. (1) for a much cleaner result:

$$D = \rho b \int_0^\delta u(U_0 - u) \, dy \,\big|_{x=L} \qquad\qquad Ans. \text{ (3)}$$

This result was first derived by Theodore von Kármán in 1921.[11] It relates the friction drag on one side of a flat plate to the integral of the *momentum deficit* $\rho u(U_0 - u)$ across the trailing cross section of the flow past the plate. Since $U_0 - u$ vanishes as y increases, the integral has a finite value. Equation (3) is an example of *momentum integral theory* for boundary layers, which is treated in Chap. 7.

Momentum Flux Correction Factor

For flow in a duct, the axial velocity is usually nonuniform, as in Example 3.4. For this case the simple momentum flow calculation $\int u\rho(\mathbf{V} \cdot \mathbf{n}) \, dA = \dot{m}V = \rho A V^2$ is somewhat in error and should be corrected to $\zeta \rho A V^2$, where ζ is the dimensionless momentum flow correction factor, $\zeta \geq 1$.

The factor ζ accounts for the variation of u^2 across the duct section. That is, we compute the exact flow and set it equal to a flow based on average velocity in the duct:

$$\rho \int u^2 dA = \zeta \dot{m} V_{av} = \zeta \rho A V_{av}^2$$

or
$$\zeta = \frac{1}{A} \int \left(\frac{u}{V_{av}}\right)^2 dA \qquad\qquad (3.43a)$$

Values of ζ can be computed based on typical duct velocity profiles similar to those in Example 3.4. The results are as follows:

Laminar flow:
$$u = U_0\left(1 - \frac{r^2}{R^2}\right) \quad \zeta = \frac{4}{3} \qquad\qquad (3.43b)$$

Turbulent flow:
$$u \approx U_0\left(1 - \frac{r}{R}\right)^m \quad \frac{1}{9} \leq m \leq \frac{1}{5}$$

$$\zeta = \frac{(1 + m)^2(2 + m)^2}{2(1 + 2m)(2 + 2m)} \qquad\qquad (3.43c)$$

The turbulent correction factors have the following range of values:

Turbulent flow:	m	$\frac{1}{5}$	$\frac{1}{6}$	$\frac{1}{7}$	$\frac{1}{8}$	$\frac{1}{9}$
	ζ	1.037	1.027	1.020	1.016	1.013

These are so close to unity that they are normally neglected. The laminar correction is often important.

---

[11]The autobiography of this great twentieth-century engineer and teacher [2] is recommended for its historical and scientific insight.

To illustrate a typical use of these correction factors, the solution to Example 3.8 for nonuniform velocities at sections 1 and 2 would be modified as

$$\sum \mathbf{F} = \dot{m}(\zeta_2 \mathbf{V}_2 - \zeta_1 \mathbf{V}_1) \tag{3.43d}$$

Note that the basic parameters and vector character of the result are not changed at all by this correction.

Linear Momentum Tips

The previous examples make it clear that the vector momentum equation is more difficult to handle than the scalar mass and energy equations. Here are some momentum tips to remember:

- The momentum relation is a *vector* equation. The forces and the momentum terms are directional and can have three components. A *sketch* of these vectors will be indispensable for the analysis.
- The momentum flow terms, such as $\int \mathbf{V}(\rho \mathbf{V} \cdot \mathbf{n})dA$, link *two* different sign conventions, so special care is needed. First, the vector coefficient $\mathbf{V}$ will have a sign depending on its direction. Second, the mass flow term $(\rho \mathbf{V} \cdot \mathbf{n})$ will have a sign $(+, -)$ depending on whether it is (out, in). For example, in Fig. 3.8, the x-components of $\mathbf{V}_2$ and $\mathbf{V}_1$, u_2 and u_1, are both positive; that is, they both act to the right. Meanwhile, the mass flow at (2) is positive (out) and at (1) is negative (in).
- The *one-dimensional approximation*, Eq. (3.40), is glorious, because non-uniform velocity distributions require laborious integration, as in Eq. (3.11). Thus the momentum flow correction factors ζ are very useful in avoiding this integration, especially for pipe flow.
- The applied forces $\Sigma \mathbf{F}$ act on *all the material in the control volume*—that is, the surfaces (pressure and shear stresses), the solid supports that are cut through, and the weight of the interior masses. Stresses on non-control-surface parts of the interior are self-canceling and should be ignored.
- If the fluid exits subsonically to an atmosphere, the fluid pressure there is *atmospheric*.
- Where possible, choose inlet and outlet surfaces *normal to the flow*, so that pressure is the dominant force and the normal velocity equals the actual velocity.

Clearly, with that many helpful tips, substantial practice is needed to achieve momentum skills.

Noninertial Reference Frame[12]

All previous derivations and examples in this section have assumed that the coordinate system is inertial—that is, at rest or moving at constant velocity. In this case the rate of change of velocity equals the absolute acceleration of the system, and Newton's law applies directly in the form of Eqs. (3.2) and (3.35).

In many cases it is convenient to use a *noninertial*, or accelerating, coordinate system. An example would be coordinates fixed to a rocket during takeoff. A second example is any flow on the earth's surface, which is accelerating relative to the fixed

---

[12]This section may be omitted without loss of continuity.

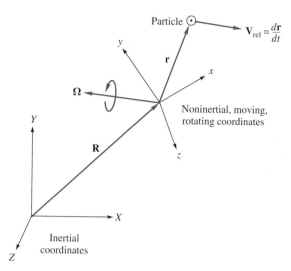

Fig. 3.11 Geometry of fixed versus accelerating coordinates.

stars because of the rotation of the earth. Atmospheric and oceanographic flows experience the so-called *Coriolis acceleration*, outlined next. It is typically less than $10^{-5}g$, where g is the acceleration of gravity, but its accumulated effect over distances of many kilometers can be dominant in geophysical flows. By contrast, the Coriolis acceleration is negligible in small-scale problems like pipe or airfoil flows.

Suppose that the fluid flow has velocity $\mathbf{V}$ relative to a noninertial *xyz* coordinate system, as shown in Fig. 3.11. Then $d\mathbf{V}/dt$ will represent a noninertial acceleration that must be added vectorially to a relative acceleration $\mathbf{a}_{rel}$ to give the absolute acceleration $\mathbf{a}_i$ relative to some inertial coordinate system *XYZ*, as in Fig. 3.11. Thus

$$\mathbf{a}_i = \frac{d\mathbf{V}}{dt} + \mathbf{a}_{rel} \tag{3.44}$$

Since Newton's law applies to the absolute acceleration,

$$\sum \mathbf{F} = m\mathbf{a}_i = m\left(\frac{d\mathbf{V}}{dt} + \mathbf{a}_{rel}\right)$$

or

$$\sum \mathbf{F} - m\mathbf{a}_{rel} = m\frac{d\mathbf{V}}{dt} \tag{3.45}$$

Thus Newton's law in noninertial coordinates *xyz* is analogous to adding more "force" terms $-m\mathbf{a}_{rel}$ to account for noninertial effects. In the most general case, sketched in Fig. 3.11, the term $\mathbf{a}_{rel}$ contains four parts, three of which account for the angular velocity $\Omega(t)$ of the inertial coordinates. By inspection of Fig. 3.11, the absolute displacement of a particle is

$$\mathbf{S}_i = \mathbf{r} + \mathbf{R} \tag{3.46}$$

Differentiation gives the absolute velocity

$$\mathbf{V}_i = \mathbf{V} + \frac{d\mathbf{R}}{dt} + \Omega \times \mathbf{r} \tag{3.47}$$

A second differentiation gives the absolute acceleration:

$$\mathbf{a}_i = \frac{d\mathbf{V}}{dt} + \frac{d^2\mathbf{R}}{dt^2} + \frac{d\mathbf{\Omega}}{dt} \times \mathbf{r} + 2\mathbf{\Omega} \times \mathbf{V} + \mathbf{\Omega} \times (\mathbf{\Omega} \times \mathbf{r}) \tag{3.48}$$

By comparison with Eq. (3.44), we see that the last four terms on the right represent the additional relative acceleration:

1. $d^2\mathbf{R}/dt^2$ is the acceleration of the noninertial origin of coordinates xyz.
2. $(d\mathbf{\Omega}/dt) \times \mathbf{r}$ is the angular acceleration effect.
3. $2\mathbf{\Omega} \times \mathbf{V}$ is the Coriolis acceleration.
4. $\mathbf{\Omega} \times (\mathbf{\Omega} \times \mathbf{r})$ is the centripetal acceleration, directed from the particle normal to the axis of rotation with magnitude $\Omega^2 L$, where L is the normal distance to the axis.[13]

Equation (3.45) differs from Eq. (3.2) only in the added inertial forces on the left-hand side. Thus the control volume formulation of linear momentum in noninertial coordinates merely adds inertial terms by integrating the added relative acceleration over each differential mass in the control volume:

$$\sum \mathbf{F} - \int_{\text{CV}} \mathbf{a}_{\text{rel}}\, dm = \frac{d}{dt}\left(\int_{\text{CV}} \mathbf{V}\rho\, d\mathcal{V}\right) + \int_{\text{CS}} \mathbf{V}\rho(\mathbf{V}_r \cdot \mathbf{n})\, dA \tag{3.49}$$

where

$$\mathbf{a}_{\text{rel}} = \frac{d^2\mathbf{R}}{dt^2} + \frac{d\mathbf{\Omega}}{dt} \times \mathbf{r} + 2\mathbf{\Omega} \times \mathbf{V} + \mathbf{\Omega} \times (\mathbf{\Omega} \times \mathbf{r})$$

This is the noninertial analog of the inertial form given in Eq. (3.35). To analyze such problems, one must know the displacement $\mathbf{R}$ and angular velocity $\mathbf{\Omega}$ of the noninertial coordinates.

If the control volume is fixed in a moving frame, Eq. (3.49) reduces to

$$\sum \mathbf{F} - \int_{\text{CV}} \mathbf{a}_{\text{rel}}\, dm = \frac{d}{dt}\left(\int_{\text{CV}} \mathbf{V}\rho\, d\mathcal{V}\right) + \int_{\text{CS}} \mathbf{V}\rho(\mathbf{V} \cdot \mathbf{n})\, dA \tag{3.50}$$

In other words, the right-hand side reduces to that of Eq. (3.37).

EXAMPLE 3.12

A classic example of an accelerating control volume is a rocket moving straight up, as in Fig. E3.12. Let the initial mass be M_0, and assume a steady exhaust mass flow $\dot{m}$ and exhaust velocity V_e relative to the rocket, as shown. If the flow pattern within the rocket motor is steady and air drag is neglected, derive the differential equation of vertical rocket motion $V(t)$ and integrate using the initial condition $V = 0$ at $t = 0$.

---

[13]A complete discussion of these noninertial coordinate terms is given, for example, in Ref. 4, pp. 49–51.

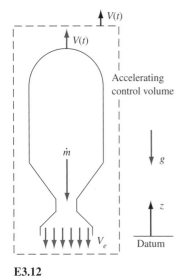

E3.12

Solution

The appropriate control volume in Fig. E3.12 encloses the rocket, cuts through the exit jet, and accelerates upward at rocket speed $V(t)$. The z-momentum Eq. (3.49) becomes

$$\sum F_z - \int a_{rel}\, dm = \frac{d}{dt}\left(\int_{CV} w\, d\dot{m}\right) + (\dot{m}w)_e$$

or

$$-mg - m\frac{dV}{dt} = 0 + \dot{m}(-V_e) \quad \text{with } m = m(t) = M_0 - \dot{m}t$$

The term $a_{rel} = dV/dt$ of the rocket. The control volume integral vanishes because of the steady rocket flow conditions. Separate the variables and integrate, assuming $V = 0$ at $t = 0$:

$$\int_0^V dV = \dot{m}\,V_e\int_0^t \frac{dt}{M_0 - \dot{m}t} - g\int_0^t dt \quad \text{or} \quad V(t) = -V_e\ln\left(1 - \frac{\dot{m}t}{M_0}\right) - gt \qquad Ans.$$

This is a classic approximate formula in rocket dynamics. The first term is positive and, if the fuel mass burned is a large fraction of initial mass, the final rocket velocity can exceed V_e.

3.5 Frictionless Flow: The Bernoulli Equation

A classic linear momentum analysis is a relation between pressure, velocity, and elevation in a frictionless flow, now called the *Bernoulli equation*. It was stated (vaguely) in words in 1738 in a textbook by Daniel Bernoulli. A complete derivation of the equation was given in 1755 by Leonhard Euler. The Bernoulli equation is very famous and very widely used, but one should be wary of its restrictions—all fluids are viscous and thus all flows have friction to some extent. To use the Bernoulli equation correctly, one must confine it to regions of the flow that are nearly frictionless. This section (and, in more detail, Chap. 8) will address the proper use of the Bernoulli relation.

Consider Fig. 3.12, which is an elemental fixed streamtube control volume of variable area $A(s)$ and length ds, where s is the streamline direction. The properties (ρ, V, p) may vary with s and time but are assumed to be uniform over the cross section A. The streamtube orientation θ is arbitrary, with an elevation change $dz = ds\sin\theta$. Friction on the streamtube walls is shown and then neglected—a very

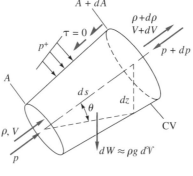

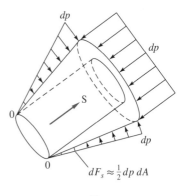

Fig. 3.12 The Bernoulli equation for frictionless flow along a streamline: (*a*) forces and flows; (*b*) net pressure force after uniform subtraction of p.

(*a*)　　　　　　(*b*)

restrictive assumption. Note that the limit of a vanishingly small area means that the streamtube is equivalent to a *streamline* of the flow. Bernoulli's equation is valid for both and is usually stated as holding "along a streamline" in frictionless flow.

Conservation of mass [Eq. (3.20)] for this elemental control volume yields

$$\frac{d}{dt}\left(\int_{CV} \rho \, d\mathcal{V}\right) + \dot{m}_{out} - \dot{m}_{in} = 0 \approx \frac{\partial \rho}{\partial t} \, d\mathcal{V} + d\dot{m}$$

where $\dot{m} = \rho A V$ and $d\mathcal{V} \approx A \, ds$. Then our desired form of mass conservation is

$$d\dot{m} = d(\rho A V) = -\frac{\partial \rho}{\partial t} A \, ds \tag{3.51}$$

This relation does not require an assumption of frictionless flow.

Now write the linear momentum relation [Eq. (3.37)] in the streamwise direction:

$$\sum dF_s = \frac{d}{dt}\left(\int_{CV} V\rho \, d\mathcal{V}\right) + (\dot{m}V)_{out} - (\dot{m}V)_{in} \approx \frac{\partial}{\partial t}(\rho V) A \, ds + d(\dot{m}V)$$

where $V_s = V$ itself because s is the streamline direction. If we neglect the shear force on the walls (frictionless flow), the forces are due to pressure and gravity. The streamwise gravity force is due to the weight component of the fluid within the control volume:

$$dF_{s,\text{grav}} = -dW \sin\theta = -\gamma A \, ds \sin\theta = -\gamma A \, dz$$

The pressure force is more easily visualized, in Fig. 3.12b, by first subtracting a uniform value p from all surfaces, remembering from Fig. 3.6 that the net force is not changed. The pressure along the slanted side of the streamtube has a streamwise component that acts not on A itself but on the outer ring of area increase dA. The net pressure force is thus

$$dF_{s,\text{press}} = \tfrac{1}{2} dp \, dA - dp(A + dA) \approx -A \, dp$$

to first order. Substitute these two force terms into the linear momentum relation:

$$\sum dF_s = -\gamma A \, dz - A \, dp = \frac{\partial}{\partial t}(\rho V) A \, ds + d(\dot{m}V)$$

$$= \frac{\partial \rho}{\partial t} VA \, ds + \frac{\partial V}{\partial t} \rho A \, ds + \dot{m} \, dV + V \, d\dot{m}$$

The first and last terms on the right cancel by virtue of the continuity relation [Eq. (3.51)]. Divide what remains by ρA and rearrange into the final desired relation:

$$\frac{\partial V}{\partial t} ds + \frac{dp}{\rho} + V \, dV + g \, dz = 0 \tag{3.52}$$

This is Bernoulli's equation for *unsteady frictionless flow along a streamline*. It is in differential form and can be integrated between any two points 1 and 2 on the streamline:

$$\boxed{\int_1^2 \frac{\partial V}{\partial t} ds + \int_1^2 \frac{dp}{\rho} + \frac{1}{2}(V_2^2 - V_1^2) + g(z_2 - z_1) = 0} \tag{3.53}$$

Steady Incompressible Flow

To evaluate the two remaining integrals, one must estimate the unsteady effect $\partial V/\partial t$ and the variation of density with pressure. At this time we consider only steady ($\partial V/\partial t = 0$) incompressible (constant-density) flow, for which Eq. (3.53) becomes

$$\frac{p_2 - p_1}{\rho} + \frac{1}{2}(V_2^2 - V_1^2) + g(z_2 - z_1) = 0$$

or

$$\frac{p_1}{\rho} + \frac{1}{2}V_1^2 + gz_1 = \frac{p_2}{\rho} + \frac{1}{2}V_2^2 + gz_2 = \text{const} \tag{3.54}$$

This is the Bernoulli equation for steady frictionless incompressible flow along a streamline.

Bernoulli Interpreted as an Energy Relation

The Bernoulli relation, Eq. (3.54), is a classic *momentum* result, Newton's law for a frictionless, incompressible fluid. It may also be interpreted, however, as an idealized *energy* relation. The changes from 1 to 2 in Eq. (3.54) represent reversible pressure work, kinetic energy change, and potential energy change. The fact that the total remains the same means that there is no energy exchange due to viscous dissipation, heat transfer, or shaft work. Section 3.7 will add these effects by making a control volume analysis of the first law of thermodynamics.

Restrictions on the Bernoulli Equation

The Bernoulli equation is a momentum-based force relation and was derived using the following restrictive assumptions:

1. *Steady flow:* a common situation, application to most flows in this text.
2. *Incompressible flow:* appropriate if the flow Mach number is less than 0.3. This restriction is removed in Chap. 9 by allowing for compressibility.
3. *Frictionless flow:* restrictive—solid walls and mixing introduce friction effects.
4. *Flow along a single streamline:* different streamlines may have different "Bernoulli constants" $w_o = p/\rho + V^2/2 + gz$, but this is rare. In most cases, as we shall prove in Chap. 4, a frictionless flow region is *irrotational*; that is, curl($\mathbf{V}$) = 0. For irrotational flow, the Bernoulli constant is the same everywhere.

The Bernoulli derivation does not account for possible energy exchange due to heat or work. These thermodynamic effects are accounted for in the steady flow energy equation. We are thus warned that the Bernoulli equation may be modified by such an energy exchange.

Figure 3.13 illustrates some practical limitations on the use of Bernoulli's equation (3.54). For the wind tunnel model test of Fig. 3.13*a*, the Bernoulli equation is valid in the core flow of the tunnel but not in the tunnel wall boundary layers, the model surface boundary layers, or the wake of the model, all of which are regions with high friction.

In the propeller flow of Fig. 3.13*b*, Bernoulli's equation is valid both upstream and downstream, but with a different constant $w_0 = p/\rho + V^2/2 + gz$, caused by the work addition of the propeller. The Bernoulli relation (3.54) is not valid near the propeller blades or in the helical vortices (not shown, see Fig. 1.14) shed downstream of the blade edges. Also, the Bernoulli constants are higher in the flowing "slipstream" than in the ambient atmosphere because of the slipstream kinetic energy.

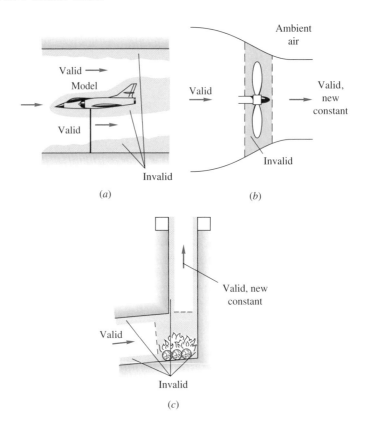

Fig. 3.13 Illustration of regions of validity and invalidity of the Bernoulli equation: (*a*) tunnel model, (*b*) propeller, (*c*) chimney.

For the chimney flow of Fig. 3.13*c*, Eq. (3.54) is valid before and after the fire, but with a change in Bernoulli constant that is caused by heat addition. The Bernoulli equation is not valid within the fire itself or in the chimney wall boundary layers.

Jet Exit Pressure Equals Atmospheric Pressure

When a subsonic jet of liquid or gas exits from a duct into the free atmosphere, it immediately takes on the pressure of that atmosphere. This is a very important boundary condition in solving Bernoulli problems, since the pressure at that point is known. The interior of the free jet will also be atmospheric, except for small effects due to surface tension and streamline curvature.

Stagnation, Static, and Dynamic Pressures

In many incompressible-flow Bernoulli analyses, elevation changes are negligible. Thus Eq. (3.54) reduces to a balance between pressure and kinetic energy. We can write this as

$$p_1 + \frac{1}{2}\rho V_1^2 = p_2 + \frac{1}{2}\rho V_2^2 = p_o = \text{constant}$$

The quantity p_o is the pressure at any point in the frictionless flow where the velocity is zero. It is called the *stagnation pressure* and is the highest pressure possible in the flow, if elevation changes are neglected. The place where zero-velocity occurs is called a *stagnation point*. For example, on a moving aircraft, the front nose and the wing leading edges are points of highest pressure. The pressures p_1 and p_2 are called *static* pressures, in the moving fluid. The grouping $(1/2)\rho V^2$ has dimensions of pressure and is called the *dynamic* pressure. A popular device called a *Pitot-static tube* (Fig. 6.30) measures $(p_o - p)$ and then calculates V from the dynamic pressure.

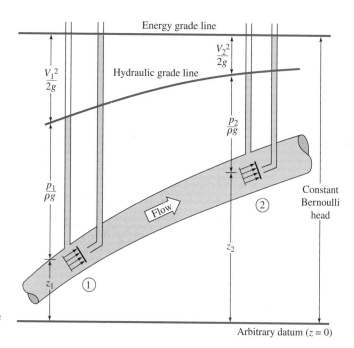

Fig. 3.14 Hydraulic and energy grade lines for frictionless flow in a duct.

Note, however, that one particular zero-velocity condition, no-slip flow along a fixed wall, does *not* result in stagnation pressure. The no-slip condition is a *frictional* effect, and the Bernoulli equation does not apply.

Hydraulic and Energy Grade Lines

A useful visual interpretation of Bernoulli's equation is to sketch two grade lines of a flow. The *energy grade line* (EGL) shows the height of the total Bernoulli constant $h_0 = z + p/\gamma + V^2/(2g)$. In frictionless flow with no work or heat transfer [Eq. (3.54)] the EGL has constant height. The *hydraulic grade line* (HGL) shows the height corresponding to elevation and pressure head $z + p/\gamma$—that is, the EGL minus the velocity head $V^2/(2g)$. The HGL is the height to which liquid would rise in a piezometer tube (see Prob. 2.11) attached to the flow. In an open-channel flow the HGL is identical to the free surface of the water.

Figure 3.14 illustrates the EGL and HGL for frictionless flow at sections 1 and 2 of a duct. The piezometer tubes measure the static pressure head $z + p/\gamma$ and thus outline the HGL. The pitot stagnation-velocity tubes measure the total head $z + p/\gamma + V^2/(2g)$, which corresponds to the EGL. In this particular case the EGL is constant, and the HGL rises due to a drop in velocity.

In more general flow conditions, the EGL will drop slowly due to friction losses and will drop sharply due to a substantial loss (a valve or obstruction) or due to work extraction (to a turbine). The EGL can rise only if there is work addition (as from a pump or propeller). The HGL generally follows the behavior of the EGL with respect to losses or work transfer, and it rises and/or falls if the velocity decreases and/or increases.

As mentioned before, no conversion factors are needed in computations with the Bernoulli equation if consistent SI or BG units are used, as the following examples will show.

In all Bernoulli-type problems in this text, we consistently take point 1 upstream and point 2 downstream.

EXAMPLE 3.13

Find a relation between nozzle discharge velocity V_2 and tank free surface height h as in Fig. E3.13. Assume steady frictionless flow.

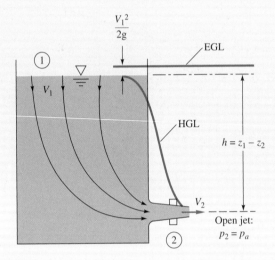

E3.13

Solution

As mentioned, we always choose point 1 upstream and point 2 downstream. Try to choose points 1 and 2 where maximum information is known or desired. Here we select point 1 as the tank free surface, where elevation and pressure are known, and point 2 as the nozzle exit, where again pressure and elevation are known. The two unknowns are V_1 and V_2.

Mass conservation is usually a vital part of Bernoulli analyses. If A_1 is the tank cross section and A_2 the nozzle area, this is approximately a one-dimensional flow with constant density, Eq. (3.30):

$$A_1 V_1 = A_2 V_2 \tag{1}$$

Bernoulli's equation (3.54) gives

$$\frac{p_1}{\rho} + \tfrac{1}{2}V_1^2 + gz_1 = \frac{p_2}{\rho} + \tfrac{1}{2}V_2^2 + gz_2$$

But since sections 1 and 2 are both exposed to atmospheric pressure $p_1 = p_2 = p_a$, the pressure terms cancel, leaving

$$V_2^2 - V_1^2 = 2g(z_1 - z_2) = 2gh \tag{2}$$

Eliminating V_1 between Eqs. (1) and (2), we obtain the desired result:

$$V_2^2 = \frac{2gh}{1 - A_2^2/A_1^2} \qquad\qquad Ans. \tag{3}$$

Generally the nozzle area A_2 is very much smaller than the tank area A_1, so that the ratio A_2^2/A_1^2 is doubly negligible, and an accurate approximation for the outlet velocity is

$$V_2 \approx (2gh)^{1/2} \qquad\qquad Ans. \tag{4}$$

This formula, discovered by Evangelista Torricelli in 1644, states that the discharge velocity equals the speed that a frictionless particle would attain if it fell freely from point 1 to point 2. In other words, the potential energy of the surface fluid is entirely converted to kinetic energy of efflux, which is consistent with the neglect of friction and the fact that no net pressure work is done. Note that Eq. (4) is independent of the fluid density, a characteristic of gravity-driven flows.

Except for the wall boundary layers, the streamlines from 1 to 2 all behave in the same way, and we can assume that the Bernoulli constant h_0 is the same for all the core flow. However, the outlet flow is likely to be nonuniform, not one-dimensional, so that the average velocity is only approximately equal to Torricelli's result. The engineer will then adjust the formula to include a dimensionless *discharge coefficient* c_d:

$$(V_2)_{av} = \frac{Q}{A_2} = c_d(2gh)^{1/2} \tag{5}$$

As discussed in Sec. 6.12, the discharge coefficient of a nozzle varies from about 0.6 to 1.0 as a function of (dimensionless) flow conditions and nozzle shape.

Surface Velocity Condition for a Large Tank

Many Bernoulli, and also steady flow energy, problems involve liquid flow from a large tank or reservoir, as in Example 3.13. If the outflow is small compared to the volume of the tank, the surface of the tank hardly moves. Therefore these problems are analyzed assuming *zero velocity* at the tank surface. The *pressure* at the top of the tank or reservoir is assumed to be atmospheric.

Before proceeding with more examples, we should note carefully that a solution by Bernoulli's equation (3.54) does *not* require a second control volume analysis, only a selection of two points 1 and 2 along a given streamline. The control volume was used to derive the differential relation (3.52), but the integrated form (3.54) is valid all along the streamline for frictionless flow with no heat transfer or shaft work, and a control volume is not necessary.

A classic Bernoulli application is the familiar process of siphoning a fluid from one container to another. No pump is involved; a hydrostatic pressure difference provides the motive force. We analyze this in the following example.

EXAMPLE 3.14

Consider the water siphon shown in Fig. E3.14. Assuming that Bernoulli's equation is valid, (*a*) find an expression for the velocity V_2 exiting the siphon tube. (*b*) If the tube is 1 cm in diameter and $z_1 = 60$ cm, $z_2 = -25$ cm, $z_3 = 90$ cm, and $z_4 = 35$ cm, estimate the flow rate in cm^3/s.

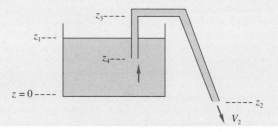

E3.14

Solution

- *Assumptions:*   Frictionless, steady, incompressible flow. Write Bernoulli's equation start- ing from where information is known (the surface, z_1) and proceeding to where informa- tion is desired (the tube exit, z_2).

$$\frac{p_1}{\rho} + \frac{\cancel{V_1^2}}{2} + gz_1 = \frac{p_2}{\rho} + \frac{V_2^2}{2} + gz_2$$

Note that the velocity is approximately zero at z_1, and a streamline goes from z_1 to z_2. Note further that p_1 and p_2 are both atmospheric, $p = p_{atm}$, and therefore cancel. (*a*) Solve for the exit velocity from the tube:

$$V_2 = \sqrt{2g(z_1 - z_2)} \qquad\qquad Ans.\ (a)$$

The velocity exiting the siphon increases as the tube exit is lowered below the tank surface. There is no siphon effect if the exit is at or above the tank surface. Note that z_3 and z_4 do not directly enter the analysis. However, z_3 should not be too high because the pressure there will be lower than atmospheric, and the liquid might vaporize. (*b*) For the given numerical information, we need only z_1 and z_2 and calculate, in SI units,

$$V_2 = \sqrt{2(9.81 \text{ m/s}^2)[0.6 \text{ m} - (-0.25) \text{ m}]} = 4.08 \text{ m/s}$$

$$Q = V_2 A_2 = (4.08 \text{ m/s})(\pi/4)(0.01 \text{ m})^2 = 321 \text{ E–6 m}^3/\text{s} = 321 \text{ cm}^3/\text{s} \quad Ans.\ (b)$$

- *Comments:*   Note that this result is independent of the density of the fluid. As an exercise, you may check that, for water (998 kg/m^3), p_3 is 11,300 Pa *below* atmospheric pressure. In Chap. 6 we will modify this example to include friction effects.

EXAMPLE 3.15

A constriction in a pipe will cause the velocity to rise and the pressure to fall at section 2 in the throat. The pressure difference is a measure of the flow rate through the pipe. The smoothly necked-down system shown in Fig. E3.15 is called a *venturi tube*. Find an expres- sion for the mass flow in the tube as a function of the pressure change.

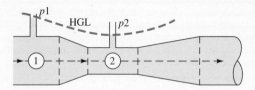

E3.15

Solution

Bernoulli's equation is assumed to hold along the center streamline:

$$\frac{p_1}{\rho} + \tfrac{1}{2} V_1^2 + gz_1 = \frac{p_2}{\rho} + \tfrac{1}{2} V_2^2 + gz_2$$

If the tube is horizontal, $z_1 = z_2$ and we can solve for V_2:

$$V_2^2 - V_1^2 = \frac{2\,\Delta p}{\rho} \qquad \Delta p = p_1 - p_2 \tag{1}$$

We relate the velocities from the incompressible continuity relation:

$$A_1 V_1 = A_2 V_2$$

or $\qquad\qquad\qquad V_1 = \beta^2 V_2 \qquad \beta = \dfrac{D_2}{D_1} \tag{2}$

Combining (1) and (2), we obtain a formula for the velocity in the throat:

$$V_2 = \left[\frac{2\,\Delta p}{\rho(1-\beta^4)}\right]^{1/2} \tag{3}$$

The mass flow is given by

$$\dot{m} = \rho A_2 V_2 = A_2\left(\frac{2\rho\,\Delta p}{1-\beta^4}\right)^{1/2} \tag{4}$$

This is the ideal frictionless mass flow. In practice, we measure $\dot{m}_{\text{actual}} = c_d \dot{m}_{\text{ideal}}$ and correlate the dimensionless discharge coefficient c_d.

EXAMPLE 3.16

A 10-cm fire hose with a 3-cm nozzle discharges 1.5 m³/min to the atmosphere. Assuming frictionless flow, find the force F_B exerted by the flange bolts to hold the nozzle on the hose.

Solution

We use Bernoulli's equation and continuity to find the pressure p_1 upstream of the nozzle, and then we use a control volume momentum analysis to compute the bolt force, as in Fig. E3.16.

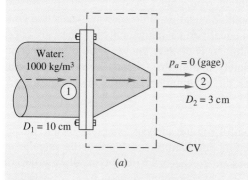
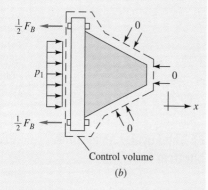

(a)   (b)

E3.16

The flow from 1 to 2 is a constriction exactly similar in effect to the venturi in Example 3.15, for which Eq. (1) gave

$$p_1 = p_2 + \tfrac{1}{2}\rho(V_2^2 - V_1^2) \tag{1}$$

The velocities are found from the known flow rate $Q = 1.5$ m³/min or 0.025 m³/s:

$$V_2 = \frac{Q}{A_2} = \frac{0.025 \text{ m}^3/\text{s}}{(\pi/4)(0.03 \text{ m})^2} = 35.4 \text{ m/s}$$

$$V_1 = \frac{Q}{A_1} = \frac{0.025 \text{ m}^3/\text{s}}{(\pi/4)(0.1 \text{ m})^2} = 3.2 \text{ m/s}$$

We are given $p_2 = p_a = 0$ gage pressure. Then Eq. (1) becomes

$$p_1 = \tfrac{1}{2}(1000 \text{ kg/m}^3)[(35.4^2 - 3.2^2)\text{m}^2/\text{s}^2]$$

$$= 620,000 \text{ kg/(m} \cdot \text{s}^2) = 620,000 \text{ Pa gage}$$

The control volume force balance is shown in Fig. E3.16b:

$$\sum F_x = -F_B + p_1 A_1$$

and the zero gage pressure on all other surfaces contributes no force. The x-momentum flow is $+\dot{m}V_2$ at the outlet and $-\dot{m}V_1$ at the inlet. The steady flow momentum relation (3.40) thus gives

$$-F_B + p_1 A_1 = \dot{m}(V_2 - V_1)$$

or

$$F_B = p_1 A_1 - \dot{m}(V_2 - V_1) \tag{2}$$

Substituting the given numerical values, we find

$$\dot{m} = \rho Q = (1000 \text{ kg/m}^3)(0.025 \text{ m}^3/\text{s}) = 25 \text{ kg/s}$$

$$A_1 = \frac{\pi}{4}D_1^2 = \frac{\pi}{4}(0.1 \text{ m})^2 = 0.00785 \text{ m}^2$$

$$F_B = (620,000 \text{ N/m}^2)(0.00785 \text{ m}^2) - (25 \text{ kg/s})[(35.4 - 3.2)\text{m/s}]$$

$$= 4872 \text{ N} - 805 \text{ (kg} \cdot \text{m)/s}^2 = 4067 \text{ N} \text{ (915 lbf)} \qquad Ans.$$

Notice from these examples that the solution of a typical problem involving Bernoulli's equation almost always leads to a consideration of the continuity equation as an equal partner in the analysis. The only exception is when the complete velocity distribution is already known from a previous or given analysis, but that means the continuity relation has already been used to obtain the given information. The point is that the continuity relation is always an important element in a flow analysis.

3.6 The Angular Momentum Theorem[14]

A control volume analysis can be applied to the angular momentum relation, Eq. (3.3), by letting our dummy variable **B** be the angular-momentum vector **H**. However, since the system considered here is typically a group of nonrigid fluid particles of variable velocity, the concept of mass moment of inertia is of no help, and we have to calculate

[14]This section may be omitted without loss of continuity.

the instantaneous angular momentum by integration over the elemental masses dm. If O is the point about which moments are desired, the angular momentum about O is given by

$$\mathbf{H}_o = \int_{\text{syst}} (\mathbf{r} \times \mathbf{V})\, dm \tag{3.55}$$

where $\mathbf{r}$ is the position vector from 0 to the elemental mass dm and $\mathbf{V}$ is the velocity of that element. The amount of angular momentum per unit mass is thus seen to be

$$\beta = \frac{d\mathbf{H}_o}{dm} = \mathbf{r} \times \mathbf{V}$$

The Reynolds transport theorem (3.16) then tells us that

$$\left. \frac{d\mathbf{H}_o}{dt} \right|_{\text{syst}} = \frac{d}{dt} \left[\int_{\text{CV}} (\mathbf{r} \times \mathbf{V})\rho\, d\mathcal{V} \right] + \int_{\text{CS}} (\mathbf{r} \times \mathbf{V})\rho(\mathbf{V}_r \cdot \mathbf{n})\, dA \tag{3.56}$$

for the most general case of a deformable control volume. But from the angular momentum theorem (3.3), this must equal the sum of all the moments about point O applied to the control volume

$$\frac{d\mathbf{H}_o}{dt} = \sum \mathbf{M}_o = \sum (\mathbf{r} \times \mathbf{F})_o$$

Note that the total moment equals the summation of moments of all applied forces about point O. Recall, however, that this law, like Newton's law (3.2), assumes that the particle velocity $\mathbf{V}$ is relative to an *inertial* coordinate system. If not, the moments about point O of the relative acceleration terms $\mathbf{a}_{\text{rel}}$ in Eq. (3.49) must also be included:

$$\sum \mathbf{M}_o = \sum (\mathbf{r} \times \mathbf{F})_o - \int_{\text{CV}} (\mathbf{r} \times \mathbf{a}_{\text{rel}})\, dm \tag{3.57}$$

where the four terms constituting $\mathbf{a}_{\text{rel}}$ are given in Eq. (3.49). Thus the most general case of the angular momentum theorem is for a deformable control volume associated with a noninertial coordinate system. We combine Eqs. (3.56) and (3.57) to obtain

$$\sum (\mathbf{r} \times \mathbf{F})_o - \int_{\text{CV}} (\mathbf{r} \times \mathbf{a}_{\text{rel}})\, dm = \frac{d}{dt} \left[\int_{\text{CV}} (\mathbf{r} \times \mathbf{V})\rho\, d9 \right] + \int_{\text{CS}} (\mathbf{r} \times \mathbf{V})\rho(\mathbf{V}_r \cdot \mathbf{n})\, dA \tag{3.58}$$

For a nondeformable inertial control volume, this reduces to

$$\boxed{\sum \mathbf{M}_0 = \frac{\partial}{\partial t} \left[\int_{\text{CV}} (\mathbf{r} \times \mathbf{V})\rho\, d\mathcal{V} \right] + \int_{\text{CS}} (\mathbf{r} \times \mathbf{V})\rho(\mathbf{V} \cdot \mathbf{n})\, dA} \tag{3.59}$$

Further, if there are only one-dimensional inlets and exits, the angular momentum flow terms evaluated on the control surface become

$$\int_{\text{CS}} (\mathbf{r} \times \mathbf{V})\rho(\mathbf{V} \cdot \mathbf{n})\, dA = \sum (\mathbf{r} \times \mathbf{V})_{\text{out}} \dot{m}_{\text{out}} - \sum (\mathbf{r} \times \mathbf{V})_{\text{in}} \dot{m}_{\text{in}} \tag{3.60}$$

Although at this stage the angular momentum theorem can be considered a supplementary topic, it has direct application to many important fluid flow problems involving torques or moments. A particularly important case is the analysis of rotating fluid flow devices, usually called *turbomachines* (Chap. 11).

EXAMPLE 3.17

As shown in Fig. E3.17a, a pipe bend is supported at point A and connected to a flow system by flexible couplings at sections 1 and 2. The fluid is incompressible, and ambient pressure p_a is zero. (a) Find an expression for the torque T that must be resisted by the support at A, in terms of the flow properties at sections 1 and 2 and the distances h_1 and h_2. (b) Compute this torque if $D_1 = D_2 = 3$ in, $p_1 = 100$ lbf/in² gage, $p_2 = 80$ lbf/in² gage, $V_1 = 40$ ft/s, $h_1 = 2$ in, $h_2 = 10$ in, and $\rho = 1.94$ slugs/ft³.

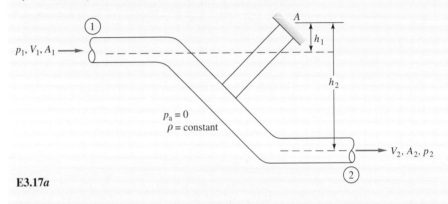

E3.17a

Solution

Part (a)

The control volume chosen in Fig. E3.17b cuts through sections 1 and 2 and through the support at A, where the torque T_A is desired. The flexible couplings description specifies that there is no torque at either section 1 or 2, and so the cuts there expose no moments. For the angular momentum terms $\mathbf{r} \times \mathbf{V}$, $\mathbf{r}$ should be taken from point A to sections 1 and 2. Note that the gage pressure forces $p_1 A_1$ and $p_2 A_2$ both have moments about A. Equation (3.59) with one-dimensional flow terms becomes

$$\sum \mathbf{M}_A = \mathbf{T}_A + \mathbf{r}_1 \times (-p_1 A_1 \mathbf{n}_1) + \mathbf{r}_2 \times (-p_2 A_2 \mathbf{n}_2)$$
$$= (\mathbf{r}_2 \times \mathbf{V}_2)(+\dot{m}_{out}) + (\mathbf{r}_1 \times \mathbf{V}_1)(-\dot{m}_{in}) \qquad (1)$$

Figure E3.17c shows that all the cross products are associated with either $r_1 \sin \theta_1 = h_1$ or $r_2 \sin \theta_2 = h_2$, the perpendicular distances from point A to the pipe axes at 1 and 2. Remember that $\dot{m}_{in} = \dot{m}_{out}$ from the steady flow continuity relation. In terms of counterclockwise moments, Eq. (1) then becomes

$$T_A + p_1 A_1 h_1 - p_2 A_2 h_2 = \dot{m}(h_2 V_2 - h_1 V_1) \qquad (2)$$

Rewriting this, we find the desired torque to be

$$T_A = h_2(p_2 A_2 + \dot{m} V_2) - h_1(p_1 A_1 + \dot{m} V_1) \qquad \textit{Ans. (a)} \ (3)$$

counterclockwise. The quantities p_1 and p_2 are gage pressures. Note that this result is independent of the shape of the pipe bend and varies only with the properties at sections 1 and 2 and the distances h_1 and h_2.[15]

---

[15]Indirectly, the pipe bend shape probably affects the pressure change from p_1 to p_2.

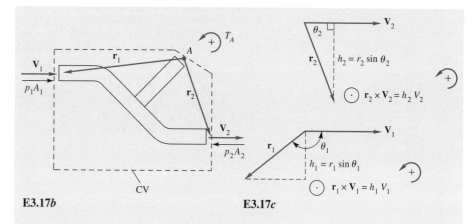

E3.17b   **E3.17c**

Part (b)   For the numerical example, convert all data to BG units:

$$D_1 = D_2 = 3 \text{ in} = 0.25 \text{ ft} \quad p_1 = 100 \frac{\text{lbf}}{\text{in}^2} = 14,400 \frac{\text{lbf}}{\text{ft}^2} \quad p_2 = 80 \frac{\text{lbf}}{\text{in}^2} = 11,520 \frac{\text{lbf}}{\text{ft}^2}$$

$$h_1 = 2 \text{ in} = \frac{2}{12} \text{ ft} \quad h_2 = 10 \text{ in} = \frac{10}{12} \text{ ft} \quad \rho = 1.94 \frac{\text{slug}}{\text{ft}^3}$$

The inlet and exit areas are the same, $A_1 = A_2 = (\pi/4)(0.25 \text{ ft})^2 = 0.0491 \text{ ft}^2$. Since the density is constant, we conclude from mass conservation, $\rho A_1 V_1 = \rho A_2 V_2$, that $V_1 = V_2 = 40$ ft/s. The mass flow is

$$\dot{m} = \rho A_1 V_1 = \left(1.94 \frac{\text{slug}}{\text{ft}^3}\right)(0.0491 \text{ ft}^2)\left(40 \frac{\text{ft}}{\text{s}}\right) = 3.81 \frac{\text{slug}}{\text{s}}$$

- *Evaluation of the torque:* The data can now be substituted into Eq. (3):

$$T_A = \left(\frac{10}{12} \text{ ft}\right)\left[\left(11,520 \frac{\text{lbf}}{\text{ft}^2}\right)(0.0491 \text{ ft}^2) + \left(3.81 \frac{\text{slug}}{\text{s}}\right)\left(40 \frac{\text{ft}}{\text{s}}\right)\right]$$

$$- \left(\frac{2}{12} \text{ ft}\right)\left[\left(14,400 \frac{\text{lbf}}{\text{ft}^2}\right)(0.0491 \text{ ft}^2) + \left(3.81 \frac{\text{slug}}{\text{s}}\right)\left(40 \frac{\text{ft}}{\text{s}}\right)\right]$$

$$= 598 \text{ ft} \cdot \text{lbf} - 143 \text{ ft} \cdot \text{lbf} = 455 \text{ ft} \cdot \text{lbf counterclockwise} \qquad Ans. (b)$$

- *Comments:* The use of standard BG units is crucial when combining dissimilar terms, such as pressure times area and mass flow times velocity, into proper additive units for a numerical solution.

EXAMPLE 3.18

Figure 3.15 shows a schematic of a centrifugal pump. The fluid enters axially and passes through the pump blades, which rotate at angular velocity ω; the velocity of the fluid is changed from V_1 to V_2 and its pressure from p_1 to p_2. (a) Find an expression for the torque T_o that must be applied to these blades to maintain this flow. (b) The power supplied to the pump would be $P = \omega T_o$. To illustrate numerically, suppose $r_1 = 0.2$ m, $r_2 = 0.5$ m, and

$b = 0.15$ m. Let the pump rotate at 600 r/min and deliver water at 2.5 m³/s with a density of 1000 kg/m³. Compute the torque and power supplied.

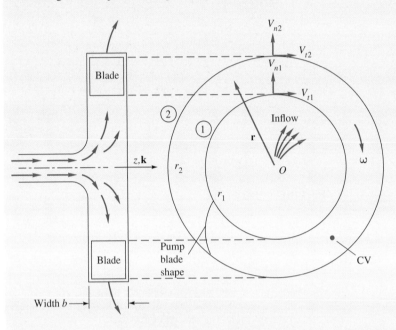

Fig. 3.15 Schematic of a simplified centrifugal pump.

Solution

Part (a)

The control volume is chosen to be the annular region between sections 1 and 2 where the flow passes through the pump blades (see Fig. 3.15). The flow is steady and assumed incompressible. The contribution of pressure to the torque about axis O is zero since the pressure forces at 1 and 2 act radially through O. Equation (3.59) becomes

$$\sum \mathbf{M}_o = \mathbf{T}_o = (\mathbf{r}_2 \times \mathbf{V}_2)\dot{m}_{\text{out}} - (\mathbf{r}_1 \times \mathbf{V}_1)\dot{m}_{\text{in}} \tag{1}$$

where steady flow continuity tells us that

$$\dot{m}_{\text{in}} = \rho V_{n1} 2\pi r_1 b = \dot{m}_{\text{out}} = \rho V_{n2} 2\pi r_2 b = \rho Q$$

The cross product $\mathbf{r} \times \mathbf{V}$ is found to be clockwise about O at both sections:

$$\mathbf{r}_2 \times \mathbf{V}_2 = r_2 V_{t2} \sin 90° \, \mathbf{k} = r_2 V_{t2}\mathbf{k} \quad \text{clockwise}$$
$$\mathbf{r}_1 \times \mathbf{V}_1 = r_1 V_{t1}\mathbf{k} \quad \text{clockwise}$$

Equation (1) thus becomes the desired formula for torque:

$$T_o = \rho Q (r_2 V_{t2} - r_1 V_{t1})\mathbf{k} \qquad \text{clockwise} \qquad \textit{Ans. (a) (2a)}$$

This relation is called *Euler's turbine formula*. In an idealized pump, the inlet and outlet tangential velocities would match the blade rotational speeds $V_{t1} = \omega r_1$ and $V_{t2} = \omega r_2$. Then the formula for torque supplied becomes

$$T_o = \rho Q \omega (r_2^2 - r_1^2) \quad \text{clockwise} \tag{2b}$$

Part (b)   Convert ω to $600(2\pi/60) = 62.8$ rad/s. The normal velocities are not needed here but follow from the flow rate

$$V_{n1} = \frac{Q}{2\pi r_1 b} = \frac{2.5 \text{ m}^3/\text{s}}{2\pi(0.2 \text{ m})(0.15 \text{ m})} = 13.3 \text{ m/s}$$

$$V_{n2} = \frac{Q}{2\pi r_2 b} = \frac{2.5}{2\pi(0.5)(0.15)} = 5.3 \text{ m/s}$$

For the idealized inlet and outlet, tangential velocity equals tip speed:

$$V_{t1} = \omega r_1 = (62.8 \text{ rad/s})(0.2 \text{ m}) = 12.6 \text{ m/s}$$

$$V_{t2} = \omega r_2 = 62.8(0.5) = 31.4 \text{ m/s}$$

Equation ($2a$) predicts the required torque to be

$$T_o = (1000 \text{ kg/m}^3)(2.5 \text{ m}^3/\text{s})[(0.5 \text{ m})(31.4 \text{ m/s}) - (0.2 \text{ m})(12.6 \text{ m/s})]$$

$$= 33,000 \text{ (kg} \cdot \text{m}^2)/\text{s}^2 = 33,000 \text{ N} \cdot \text{m} \qquad\qquad Ans.$$

The power required is

$$P = \omega T_o = (62.8 \text{ rad/s})(33,000 \text{ N} \cdot \text{m}) = 2,070,000 \text{ (N} \cdot \text{m)/s}$$

$$= 2.07 \text{ MW (2780 hp)} \qquad\qquad Ans.$$

In actual practice the tangential velocities are considerably less than the impeller-tip speeds, and the design power requirements for this pump may be only 1 MW or less.

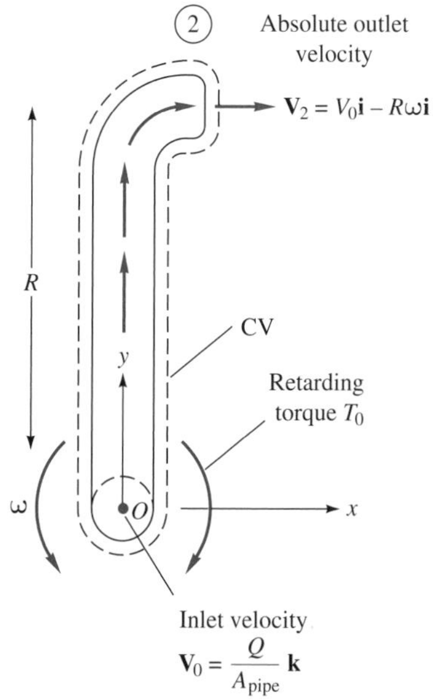

Fig. 3.16 View from above of a single arm of a rotating lawn sprinkler.

EXAMPLE 3.19

Figure 3.16 shows a lawn sprinkler arm viewed from above. The arm rotates about O at constant angular velocity ω. The volume flow entering the arm at O is Q, and the fluid is incompressible. There is a retarding torque at O, due to bearing friction, of amount $-T_o\mathbf{k}$. Find an expression for the rotation ω in terms of the arm and flow properties.

Solution

The entering velocity is $V_0\mathbf{k}$, where $V_0 = Q/A_{\text{pipe}}$. Equation (3.59) applies to the control volume sketched in Fig. 3.16 only if $\mathbf{V}$ is the absolute velocity relative to an inertial frame. Thus the exit velocity at section 2 is

$$\mathbf{V}_2 = V_0\mathbf{i} - R\omega\mathbf{i}$$

Equation (3.59) then predicts that, for steady flow,

$$\sum \mathbf{M}_o = -T_o\mathbf{k} = (\mathbf{r}_2 \times \mathbf{V}_2)\dot{m}_{\text{out}} - (\mathbf{r}_1 \times \mathbf{V}_1)\dot{m}_{\text{in}} \qquad (1)$$

where, from continuity, $\dot{m}_{\text{out}} = \dot{m}_{\text{in}} = \rho Q$. The cross products with reference to point O are

$$\mathbf{r}_2 \times \mathbf{V}_2 = R\mathbf{j} \times (V_0 - R\omega)\mathbf{i} = (R^2\omega - RV_0)\mathbf{k}$$

$$\mathbf{r}_1 \times \mathbf{V}_1 = 0\mathbf{j} \times V_0\mathbf{k} = 0$$

Equation (1) thus becomes

$$-T_o\mathbf{k} = \rho Q(R^2\omega - RV_0)\mathbf{k}$$

$$\omega = \frac{V_o}{R} - \frac{T_o}{\rho QR^2} \qquad \textit{Ans.}$$

The result may surprise you: Even if the retarding torque T_o is negligible, the arm rotational speed is limited to the value V_0/R imposed by the outlet speed and the arm length.

3.7 The Energy Equation[16]

As our fourth and final basic law, we apply the Reynolds transport theorem (3.12) to the first law of thermodynamics, Eq. (3.5). The dummy variable B becomes energy E, and the energy per unit mass is $\beta = dE/dm = e$. Equation (3.5) can then be written for a fixed control volume as follows:[17]

$$\frac{dQ}{dt} - \frac{dW}{dt} = \frac{dE}{dt} = \frac{d}{dt}\left(\int_{CV} e\rho \, d\mathcal{V}\right) + \int_{CS} e\rho(\mathbf{V} \cdot \mathbf{n}) \, dA \qquad (3.61)$$

Recall that positive Q denotes heat added to the system and positive W denotes work done by the system.

The system energy per unit mass e may be of several types:

$$e = e_{\text{internal}} + e_{\text{kinetic}} + e_{\text{potential}} + e_{\text{other}}$$

where e_{other} could encompass chemical reactions, nuclear reactions, and electrostatic or magnetic field effects. We neglect e_{other} here and consider only the first three terms as discussed in Eq. (1.9), with z defined as "up":

$$e = \hat{u} + \tfrac{1}{2}V^2 + gz \qquad (3.62)$$

The heat and work terms could be examined in detail. If this were a heat transfer book, dQ/dt would be broken down into conduction, convection, and radiation effects and whole chapters written on each (see, for example, Ref. 3). Here we leave the term untouched and consider it only occasionally.

Using for convenience the overdot to denote the time derivative, we divide the work term into three parts:

$$\dot{W} = \dot{W}_{\text{shaft}} + \dot{W}_{\text{press}} + \dot{W}_{\text{viscous stresses}} = \dot{W}_s + \dot{W}_p + \dot{W}_v$$

The work of gravitational forces has already been included as potential energy in Eq. (3.62). Other types of work, such as those due to electromagnetic forces, are excluded here.

The shaft work isolates the portion of the work that is deliberately done by a machine (pump impeller, fan blade, piston, or the like) protruding through the control surface into the control volume. No further specification other than $\dot{W}_s$ is desired at this point, but calculations of the work done by turbomachines will be performed in Chap. 11.

---

[16]This section should be read for information and enrichment even if you lack formal background in thermodynamics.

[17]The energy equation for a deformable control volume is rather complicated and is not discussed here. See Refs. 4 and 5 for further details.

The rate of work $\dot{W}_p$ done by pressure forces occurs at the surface only; all work on internal portions of the material in the control volume is by equal and opposite forces and is self-canceling. The pressure work equals the pressure force on a small surface element dA times the normal velocity component into the control volume:

$$dW_p = -(p\,dA)V_{n,\,\text{in}} = -p(-\mathbf{V}\cdot\mathbf{n})\,dA$$

The total pressure work is the integral over the control surface:

$$\dot{W}_p = \int_{CS} p(\mathbf{V}\cdot\mathbf{n})\,dA \tag{3.63}$$

A cautionary remark: If part of the control surface is the surface of a machine part, we prefer to delegate that portion of the pressure to the *shaft work* term $\dot{W}_s$, not to $\dot{W}_p$, which is primarily meant to isolate the fluid flow pressure work terms.

Finally, the shear work due to viscous stresses occurs at the control surface and consists of the product of each viscous stress (one normal and two tangential) and the respective velocity component:

$$d\dot{W}_v = -\boldsymbol{\tau}\cdot\mathbf{V}\,dA$$

or

$$\dot{W}_v = -\int_{CS}\boldsymbol{\tau}\cdot\mathbf{V}\,dA \tag{3.64}$$

where $\boldsymbol{\tau}$ is the stress vector on the elemental surface dA. This term may vanish or be negligible according to the particular type of surface at that part of the control volume:

Solid surface. For all parts of the control surface that are solid confining walls, $\mathbf{V} = 0$ from the viscous no-slip condition; hence $\dot{W}_v$ = zero identically.

Surface of a machine. Here the viscous work is contributed by the machine, and so we absorb this work in the term $\dot{W}_s$.

An inlet or outlet. At an inlet or outlet, the flow is approximately normal to the element dA; hence the only viscous work term comes from the normal stress $\tau_{nn}V_n\,dA$. Since viscous normal stresses are extremely small in all but rare cases, such as the interior of a shock wave, it is customary to neglect viscous work at inlets and outlets of the control volume.

Streamline surface. If the control surface is a streamline, such as the upper curve in the boundary layer analysis of Fig. 3.11, the viscous work term must be evaluated and retained if shear stresses are significant along this line. In the particular case of Fig. 3.11, the streamline is outside the boundary layer, and viscous work is negligible.

The net result of this discussion is that the rate-of-work term in Eq. (3.61) consists essentially of

$$\dot{W} = \dot{W}_s + \int_{CS} p(\mathbf{V}\cdot\mathbf{n})\,dA - \int_{CS}(\boldsymbol{\tau}\cdot\mathbf{V})_{ss}\,dA \tag{3.65}$$

where the subscript *SS* stands for stream surface. When we introduce (3.65) and (3.62) into (3.61), we find that the pressure work term can be combined with the energy flow term since both involve surface integrals of $\mathbf{V} \cdot \mathbf{n}$. The control volume energy equation thus becomes

$$\dot{Q} - \dot{W}_s - \dot{W}_v = \frac{\partial}{\partial t}\left(\int_{CV} e\rho \, d\mathcal{V} \right) + \int_{CS}\left(e + \frac{p}{\rho} \right)\rho(\mathbf{V} \cdot \mathbf{n}) \, dA \qquad (3.66)$$

Using e from (3.62), we see that the enthalpy $\hat{h} = \hat{u} + p/\rho$ occurs in the control surface integral. The final general form for the energy equation for a fixed control volume becomes

$$\dot{Q} - \dot{W}_s - \dot{W}_v = \frac{\partial}{\partial t}\left[\int_{CV}\left(\hat{u} + \tfrac{1}{2}V^2 + gz \right)\rho d\mathcal{V} \right] + \int_{CS}\left(\hat{h} + \tfrac{1}{2}V^2 + gz \right)\rho(\mathbf{V} \cdot \mathbf{n}) \, dA$$

$$(3.67)$$

As mentioned, the shear work term $\dot{W}_v$ is rarely important.

One-Dimensional Energy-Flux Terms

If the control volume has a series of one-dimensional inlets and outlets, as in Fig. 3.5, the surface integral in (3.67) reduces to a summation of outlet flows minus inlet flows:

$$\int_{CS}(\hat{h} + \tfrac{1}{2}V^2 + gz)\rho(\mathbf{V} \cdot \mathbf{n}) \, dA$$

$$= \sum (\hat{h} + \tfrac{1}{2}V^2 + gz)_{out}\dot{m}_{out} - \sum (\hat{h} + \tfrac{1}{2}V^2 + gz)_{in}\dot{m}_{in} \qquad (3.68)$$

where the values of $\hat{h}$, $\tfrac{1}{2}V^2$, and gz are taken to be averages over each cross section.

EXAMPLE 3.20

A steady flow machine (Fig. E3.20) takes in air at section 1 and discharges it at sections 2 and 3. The properties at each section are as follows:

Section	A, ft²	Q, ft³/s	T, °F	p, lbf/in² abs	z, ft
1	0.4	100	70	20	1.0
2	1.0	40	100	30	4.0
3	0.25	50	200	?	1.5

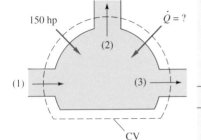

150 hp

(2)

$\dot{Q}$ = ?

(1)

(3)

CV

E3.20

Work is provided to the machine at the rate of 150 hp. Find the pressure p_3 in lbf/in² absolute and the heat transfer $\dot{Q}$ in Btu/s. Assume that air is a perfect gas with $R = 1716$ and $c_p = 6003$ ft-lbf/(slug · °R).

Solution

- *System sketch:* Figure E3.20 shows inlet 1 (negative flow) and outlets 2 and 3 (positive flows).
- *Assumptions:* Steady flow, one-dimensional inlets and outlets, ideal gas, negligible shear work. The flow is *not* incompressible. Note that $Q_1 \neq Q_2 + Q_3$ because the densities are different.

- *Approach:* Evaluate the velocities and densities and enthalpies and substitute into Eq. (3.67). Use BG units for all properties, including the pressures. With Q_i given, we evaluate $V_i = Q_i/A_i$:

$$V_1 = \frac{Q_1}{A_1} = \frac{100 \text{ ft}^3/\text{s}}{0.4 \text{ ft}^2} = 250 \frac{\text{ft}}{\text{s}} \qquad V_2 = \frac{40 \text{ ft}^3/\text{s}}{1.0 \text{ ft}^2} = 40 \frac{\text{ft}}{\text{s}} \qquad V_3 = \frac{50 \text{ ft}^3/\text{s}}{0.25 \text{ ft}^2} = 200 \frac{\text{ft}}{\text{s}}$$

The densities at sections 1 and 2 follow from the ideal-gas law:

$$\rho_1 = \frac{p_1}{RT_1} = \frac{(20 \times 144) \text{ lbf/ft}^2}{[1716 \text{ ft-lbf/(slug·°R)}][(70 + 460)°\text{R}]} = 0.00317 \frac{\text{slug}}{\text{ft}^3}$$

$$\rho_2 = \frac{(30 \times 144)}{(1716)(100 + 460)} = 0.00450 \frac{\text{slug}}{\text{ft}^3}$$

However, p_3 is unknown, so how do we find ρ_3? Use the steady flow continuity relation:

$$\dot{m}_1 = \dot{m}_2 + \dot{m}_3 \qquad \text{or} \qquad \rho_1 Q_1 = \rho_2 Q_2 + \rho_3 Q_3 \tag{1}$$

$$\left(0.00317 \frac{\text{slug}}{\text{ft}^3}\right)\left(100 \frac{\text{ft}^3}{\text{s}}\right) = 0.00450(40) + \rho_3(50) \quad \text{solve for } \rho_3 = 0.00274 \frac{\text{slug}}{\text{ft}^3}$$

Knowing ρ_3 enables us to find p_3 from the ideal-gas law:

$$p_3 = \rho_3 RT_3 = \left(0.00274 \frac{\text{slug}}{\text{ft}^3}\right)\left(1716 \frac{\text{ft-lbf}}{\text{slug °R}}\right)(200 + 460°\text{R}) = 3100 \frac{\text{lbf}}{\text{ft}^2} = 21.5 \frac{\text{lbf}}{\text{in}^2} \quad Ans.$$

- *Final solution steps:* For an ideal gas, simply approximate enthalpies as $h_i = c_p T_i$. The shaft work is *negative* (into the control volume) and viscous work is neglected for this solid-wall machine:

$$\dot{W}_v \approx 0 \qquad \dot{W}_s = (-150 \text{ hp})\left(550 \frac{\text{ft-lbf}}{\text{s-hp}}\right) = -82{,}500 \frac{\text{ft-lbf}}{\text{s}} \quad \text{(work } on \text{ the system)}$$

For steady flow, the volume integral in Eq. (3.67) vanishes, and the energy equation becomes

$$\dot{Q} - \dot{W}_s = -\dot{m}_1(c_p T_1 + \tfrac{1}{2}V_1^2 + gz_1) + \dot{m}_2(c_p T_2 + \tfrac{1}{2}V_2^2 + gz_2) + \dot{m}_3(c_p T_3 + \tfrac{1}{2}V_3^2 + gz_3) \tag{2}$$

From our continuity calculations in Eq. (1) above, the mass flows are

$$\dot{m}_1 = \rho_1 Q_1 = (0.00317)(100) = 0.317 \frac{\text{slug}}{\text{s}} \qquad \dot{m}_2 = \rho_2 Q_2 = 0.180 \frac{\text{slug}}{\text{s}}$$

$$\dot{m}_3 = \rho_3 Q_3 = 0.137 \frac{\text{slug}}{\text{s}}$$

It is instructive to separate the flow terms in the energy equation (2) for examination:

$$\text{Enthalpy flow} = c_p(-\dot{m}_1 T_1 + \dot{m}_2 T_2 + \dot{m}_3 T_3)$$
$$= (6003)[(-0.317)(530) + (0.180)(560) + (0.137)(660)]$$
$$= -1{,}009{,}000 + 605{,}000 + 543{,}000 \approx +139{,}000 \text{ ft-lbf/s}$$

$$\text{Kinetic energy flow} = \tfrac{1}{2}(-\dot{m}_1 V_1^2 + \dot{m}_2 V_2^2 + \dot{m}_3 V_3^2)$$
$$= \tfrac{1}{2}[-0.317(250)^2 + (0.180)(40)^2 + (0.137)(200)^2]$$
$$= -9900 + 140 + 2740 \approx -7000 \text{ ft-lbf/s}$$

$$\text{Potential energy flow} = g(-\dot{m}_1 z_1 + \dot{m}_2 z_2 + \dot{m}_3 z_3)$$
$$= (32.2)[-0.317(1.0) + 0.180(4.0) + 0.137(1.5)]$$
$$= -10 + 23 + 7 \approx +20 \text{ ft-lbf/s}$$

Equation (2) may now be evaluated for the heat transfer:

$$\dot{Q} - (-82,500) = 139,000 - 7,000 + 20$$

or $\qquad \dot{Q} \approx \left(+49,520 \, \frac{\text{ft-lbf}}{\text{s}} \right)\left(\frac{1 \text{ Btu}}{778.2 \text{ ft-lbf}} \right) = +64 \, \frac{\text{Btu}}{\text{s}}$ $\qquad\qquad$ *Ans.*

- *Comments:* The heat transfer is positive, which means *into* the control volume. It is typical of gas flows that potential energy flow is negligible, enthalpy flow is dominant, and kinetic energy flow is small unless the velocities are very high (that is, high subsonic or supersonic).

The Steady Flow Energy Equation

For steady flow with one inlet and one outlet, both assumed one-dimensional, Eq. (3.67) reduces to a celebrated relation used in many engineering analyses. Let section 1 be the inlet and section 2 the outlet. Then

$$\dot{Q} - \dot{W}_s - \dot{W}_v = -\dot{m}_1(\hat{h}_1 + \tfrac{1}{2}V_1^2 + gz_1) + \dot{m}_2(\hat{h}_2 + \tfrac{1}{2}V_2^2 + gz_2) \qquad (3.69)$$

But, from continuity, $\dot{m}_1 = \dot{m}_2 = \dot{m}$, we can rearrange (3.69) as follows:

$$\hat{h}_1 + \tfrac{1}{2}V_1^2 + gz_1 = (\hat{h}_2 + \tfrac{1}{2}V_2^2 + gz_2) - q + w_s + w_v \qquad (3.70)$$

where $q = \dot{Q}/\dot{m} = dQ/dm$, the heat transferred to the fluid per unit mass. Similarly, $w_s = \dot{W}_s/\dot{m} = dW_s/dm$ and $w_v = \dot{W}_v/\dot{m} = dW_v/dm$. Equation (3.70) is a general form of the *steady flow energy equation*, which states that the upstream *stagnation enthalpy* $H_1 = (h + \tfrac{1}{2}V^2 + gz)_1$ differs from the downstream value H_2 only if there is heat transfer, shaft work, or viscous work as the fluid passes between sections 1 and 2. Recall that q is positive if heat is added to the control volume and that w_s and w_v are positive if work is done by the fluid on the surroundings.

Each term in Eq. (3.70) has the dimensions of energy per unit mass, or velocity squared, which is a form commonly used by mechanical engineers. If we divide through by g, each term becomes a length, or head, which is a form preferred by civil engineers. The traditional symbol for head is h, which we do not wish to confuse with enthalpy. Therefore we use internal energy in rewriting the head form of the energy relation:

$$\frac{p_1}{\gamma} + \frac{\hat{u}_1}{g} + \frac{V_1^2}{2g} + z_1 = \frac{p_2}{\gamma} + \frac{\hat{u}_2}{g} + \frac{V_2^2}{2g} + z_2 - h_q + h_s + h_v \qquad (3.71)$$

where $h_q = q/g$, $h_s = w_s/g$, and $h_v = w_v/g$ are the head forms of the heat added, shaft work, and viscous work done, respectively. The term p/γ is called *pressure head,* and the term $V^2/2g$ is denoted as *velocity head.*

Friction and Shaft Work in Low-Speed Flow

A common application of the steady flow energy equation is for low-speed (incompressible) flow through a pipe or duct. A pump or turbine may be included in the pipe system. The pipe and machine walls are solid, so the viscous work is zero. Equation (3.71) may be written as

$$\left(\frac{p_1}{\gamma} + \frac{V_1^2}{2g} + z_1 \right) = \left(\frac{p_2}{\gamma} + \frac{V_2^2}{2g} + z_2 \right) + \frac{\hat{u}_2 - \hat{u}_1 - q}{g} \qquad (3.72)$$

Every term in this equation is a length, or *head*. The terms in parentheses are the upstream (1) and downstream (2) values of the useful or *available head* or *total head* of the flow, denoted by h_0. The last term on the right is the difference $(h_{01} - h_{02})$, which can include pump head input, turbine head extraction, and the friction head loss h_f, always *positive*. Thus, in incompressible flow with one inlet and one outlet, we may write

$$\left(\frac{p}{\gamma} + \frac{V^2}{2g} + z \right)_{\text{in}} = \left(\frac{p}{\gamma} + \frac{V^2}{2g} + z \right)_{\text{out}} + h_{\text{friction}} - h_{\text{pump}} + h_{\text{turbine}} \qquad (3.73)$$

Most of our internal flow problems will be solved with the aid of Eq. (3.73). The h terms are all positive; that is, friction loss is always positive in real (viscous) flows, a pump adds energy (increases the left-hand side), and a turbine extracts energy from the flow. If h_p and/or h_t are included, the pump and/or turbine must lie *between* points 1 and 2. In Chaps. 5 and 6 we shall develop methods of correlating h_f losses with flow parameters in pipes, valves, fittings, and other internal flow devices.

EXAMPLE 3.21

Gasoline at 20°C is pumped through a smooth 12-cm-diameter pipe 10 km long, at a flow rate of 75 m³/h (330 gal/min). The inlet is fed by a pump at an absolute pressure of 24 atm. The exit is at standard atmospheric pressure and is 150 m higher. Estimate the frictional head loss h_f, and compare it to the velocity head of the flow $V^2/(2g)$. (These numbers are quite realistic for liquid flow through long pipelines.)

Solution

- *Property values:* From Table A.3 for gasoline at 20°C, $\rho = 680$ kg/m³, or $\gamma = (680)(9.81) = 6670$ N/m³.
- *Assumptions:* Steady flow. No shaft work, thus $h_p = h_t = 0$. If $z_1 = 0$, then $z_2 = 150$ m.
- *Approach:* Find the velocity and the velocity head. These are needed for comparison. Then evaluate the friction loss from Eq. (3.73).
- *Solution steps:* Since the pipe diameter is constant, the average velocity is the same everywhere:

$$V_{\text{in}} = V_{\text{out}} = \frac{Q}{A} = \frac{Q}{(\pi/4)D^2} = \frac{(75 \text{ m}^3/\text{h})/(3600 \text{ s/h})}{(\pi/4)(0.12 \text{ m})^2} \approx 1.84 \frac{\text{m}}{\text{s}}$$

$$\text{Velocity head} = \frac{V^2}{2g} = \frac{(1.84 \text{ m/s})^2}{2(9.81 \text{ m/s}^2)} \approx 0.173 \text{ m}$$

Substitute into Eq. (3.73) and solve for the friction head loss. Use pascals for the pressures and note that the velocity heads cancel because of the constant-area pipe.

$$\frac{p_{\text{in}}}{\gamma} + \frac{V_{\text{in}}^2}{2g} + z_{\text{in}} = \frac{p_{\text{out}}}{\gamma} + \frac{V_{\text{out}}^2}{2g} + z_{\text{out}} + h_f$$

$$\frac{(24)(101{,}350 \text{ N/m}^2)}{6670 \text{ N/m}^3} + 0.173 \text{ m} + 0 \text{ m} = \frac{101{,}350 \text{ N/m}^2}{6670 \text{ N/m}^3} + 0.173 \text{ m} + 150 \text{ m} + h_f$$

or
$$h_f = 364.7 - 15.2 - 150 \approx 199 \text{ m} \qquad \qquad Ans.$$

The friction head is larger than the elevation change Δz, and the pump must drive the flow against both changes, hence the high inlet pressure. The ratio of friction to velocity head is

$$\frac{h_f}{V^2/(2g)} \approx \frac{199 \text{ m}}{0.173 \text{ m}} \approx 1150 \qquad\qquad Ans.$$

- *Comments:*   This high ratio is typical of long pipelines. (Note that we did not make direct use of the 10,000-m pipe length, whose effect is hidden within h_f.) In Chap. 6 we can state this problem in a more direct fashion: Given the flow rate, fluid, and pipe size, what inlet pressure is needed? Our correlations for h_f will lead to the estimate $p_{inlet} \approx 24$ atm, as stated here.

EXAMPLE 3.22

Air [$R = 1716$, $c_p = 6003$ ft · lbf/(slug · °R)] flows steadily, as shown in Fig. E3.22, through a turbine that produces 700 hp. For the inlet and exit conditions shown, estimate (*a*) the exit velocity V_2 and (*b*) the heat transferred Q in Btu/h.

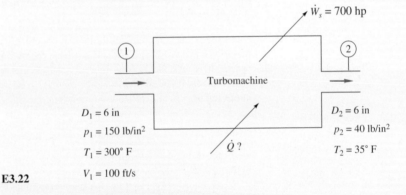

E3.22

Solution

Part (a)   The inlet and exit densities can be computed from the perfect-gas law:

$$\rho_1 = \frac{p_1}{RT_1} = \frac{150(144)}{1716(460 + 300)} = 0.0166 \text{ slug/ft}^3$$

$$\rho_2 = \frac{p_2}{RT_2} = \frac{40(144)}{1716(460 + 35)} = 0.00679 \text{ slug/ft}^3$$

The mass flow is determined by the inlet conditions

$$\dot{m} = \rho_1 A_1 V_1 = (0.0166)\frac{\pi}{4}\left(\frac{6}{12}\right)^2(100) = 0.325 \text{ slug/s}$$

Knowing mass flow, we compute the exit velocity

$$\dot{m} = 0.325 = \rho_2 A_2 V_2 = (0.00679)\frac{\pi}{4}\left(\frac{6}{12}\right)^2 V_2$$

or

$$V_2 = 244 \text{ ft/s} \qquad\qquad Ans. (a)$$

Part (b)

The steady flow energy equation (3.69) applies with $\dot{W}_v = 0$, $z_1 = z_2$, and $\hat{h} = c_pT$:

$$\dot{Q} - \dot{W}_s = \dot{m}(c_pT_2 + \tfrac{1}{2}V_2^2 - c_pT_1 - \tfrac{1}{2}V_1^2)$$

Convert the turbine work to foot-pounds-force per second with the conversion factor 1 hp = 550 ft · lbf/s. The turbine work $\dot{W}_s$ is positive

$$\dot{Q} - 700(550) = 0.325[6003(495) + \tfrac{1}{2}(244)^2 - 6003(760) - \tfrac{1}{2}(100)^2]$$

$$= -510{,}000 \text{ ft} \cdot \text{lbf/s}$$

or

$$\dot{Q} = -125{,}000 \text{ ft} \cdot \text{lbf/s}$$

Convert this to British thermal units as follows:

$$\dot{Q} = (-125{,}000 \text{ ft} \cdot \text{lbf/s}) \frac{3600 \text{ s/h}}{778.2 \text{ ft} \cdot \text{lbf/Btu}}$$

$$= -578{,}000 \text{ Btu/h} \qquad\qquad Ans.\ (b)$$

The negative sign indicates that this heat transfer is a *loss* from the control volume.

Kinetic Energy Correction Factor

Often the flow entering or leaving a port is not strictly one-dimensional. In particular, the velocity may vary over the cross section, as in Fig. E3.4. In this case the kinetic energy term in Eq. (3.68) for a given port should be modified by a dimensionless correction factor α so that the integral can be proportional to the square of the average velocity through the port:

$$\int_{port} (\tfrac{1}{2}V^2)\rho(\mathbf{V} \cdot \mathbf{n})\, dA \equiv \alpha(\tfrac{1}{2}V_{av}^2)\dot{m}$$

where

$$V_{av} = \frac{1}{A}\int u\, dA \qquad \text{for incompressible flow}$$

If the density is also variable, the integration is very cumbersome; we shall not treat this complication. By letting u be the velocity normal to the port, the first equation above becomes, for incompressible flow,

$$\tfrac{1}{2}\rho \int u^3 dA = \tfrac{1}{2}\rho\alpha V_{av}^3 A$$

or

$$\alpha = \frac{1}{A}\int \left(\frac{u}{V_{av}}\right)^3 dA \qquad (3.74)$$

The term α is the kinetic energy correction factor, having a value of about 2.0 for fully developed laminar pipe flow and from 1.04 to 1.11 for turbulent pipe flow. The complete incompressible steady flow energy equation (3.73), including pumps, turbines, and losses, would generalize to

$$\left(\frac{p}{\rho g} + \frac{\alpha}{2g}V^2 + z\right)_{in} = \left(\frac{p}{\rho g} + \frac{\alpha}{2g}V^2 + z\right)_{out} + h_{turbine} - h_{pump} + h_{friction} \qquad (3.75)$$

where the head terms on the right (h_t, h_p, h_f) are all numerically positive. All additive terms in Eq. (3.75) have dimensions of length $\{L\}$. In problems involving turbulent pipe flow, it is common to assume that $\alpha \approx 1.0$. To compute numerical values, we can use these approximations to be discussed in Chap. 6:

Laminar flow:
$$u = U_0\left[1 - \left(\frac{r}{R}\right)^2\right]$$

from which
$$V_{av} = 0.5U_0$$

and
$$\alpha = 2.0 \tag{3.76}$$

Turbulent flow:
$$u \approx U_0\left(1 - \frac{r}{R}\right)^m \qquad m \approx \frac{1}{7}$$

from which, in Example 3.4,
$$V_{av} = \frac{2U_0}{(1 + m)(2 + m)}$$

Substituting into Eq. (3.74) gives
$$\alpha = \frac{(1 + m)^3(2 + m)^3}{4(1 + 3m)(2 + 3m)} \tag{3.77}$$

and numerical values are as follows:

Turbulent flow:	m	$\frac{1}{5}$	$\frac{1}{6}$	$\frac{1}{7}$	$\frac{1}{8}$	$\frac{1}{9}$
	α	1.106	1.077	1.058	1.046	1.037

These values are only slightly different from unity and are often neglected in elementary turbulent flow analyses. However, α should never be neglected in laminar flow.

EXAMPLE 3.23

A hydroelectric power plant (Fig. E3.23) takes in 30 m³/s of water through its turbine and discharges it to the atmosphere at $V_2 = 2$ m/s. The head loss in the turbine and penstock system is $h_f = 20$ m. Assuming turbulent flow, $\alpha \approx 1.06$, estimate the power in MW extracted by the turbine.

Solution

We neglect viscous work and heat transfer and take section 1 at the reservoir surface (Fig. E3.23), where $V_1 \approx 0$, $p_1 = p_{atm}$, and $z_1 = 100$ m. Section 2 is at the turbine outlet.

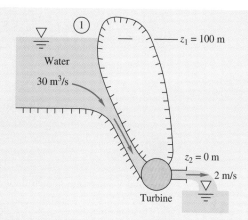

E3.23

The steady flow energy equation (3.75) becomes, in head form,

$$\frac{p_1}{\gamma} + \frac{\alpha_1 V_1^2}{2g} + z_1 = \frac{p_2}{\gamma} + \frac{\alpha_2 V_2^2}{2g} + z_2 + h_t + h_f$$

$$\frac{p_a}{\gamma} + \frac{1.06(0)^2}{2(9.81)} + 100 \text{ m} = \frac{p_a}{\gamma} + \frac{1.06(2.0 \text{ m/s})^2}{2(9.81 \text{ m/s}^2)} + 0 \text{ m} + h_t + 20 \text{ m}$$

The pressure terms cancel, and we may solve for the turbine head (which is positive):

$$h_t = 100 - 20 - 0.2 \approx 79.8 \text{ m}$$

The turbine extracts about 79.8 percent of the 100-m head available from the dam. The total power extracted may be evaluated from the water mass flow:

$$P = \dot{m}w_s = (\rho Q)(gh_t) = (998 \text{ kg/m}^3)(30 \text{ m}^3/\text{s})(9.81 \text{ m/s}^2)(79.8 \text{ m})$$

$$= 23.4 \text{ E6 kg} \cdot \text{m}^2/\text{s}^3 = 23.4 \text{ E6 N} \cdot \text{m/s} = 23.4 \text{ MW} \qquad \textit{Ans.}$$

The turbine drives an electric generator that probably has losses of about 15 percent, so the net power generated by this hydroelectric plant is about 20 MW.

EXAMPLE 3.24

The pump in Fig. E3.24 delivers water (62.4 lbf/ft^3) at 1.5 ft^3/s to a machine at section 2, which is 20 ft higher than the reservoir surface. The losses between 1 and 2 are given by

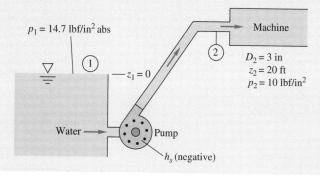

E3.24

$h_f = KV_2^2/(2g)$, where $K \approx 7.5$ is a dimensionless loss coefficient (see Sec. 6.7). Take $\alpha \approx 1.07$. Find the horsepower required for the pump if it is 80 percent efficient.

Solution

- *System sketch:* Figure E3.24 shows the proper selection for sections 1 and 2.
- *Assumptions:* Steady flow, negligible viscous work, large reservoir ($V_1 \approx 0$).
- *Approach:* First find the velocity V_2 at the exit, then apply the steady flow energy equation.
- *Solution steps:* Use BG units, $p_1 = 14.7(144) = 2117 \ \text{lbf/ft}^2$ and $p_2 = 10(144) = 1440 \ \text{lbf/ft}^2$.

Find V_2 from the known flow rate and the pipe diameter:

$$V_2 = \frac{Q}{A_2} = \frac{1.5 \ \text{ft}^3/\text{s}}{(\pi/4)(3/12 \ \text{ft})^2} = 30.6 \ \text{ft/s}$$

The steady flow energy equation (3.75), with a pump (no turbine) plus $z_1 \approx 0$ and $V_1 \approx 0$, becomes

$$\frac{p_1}{\gamma} + \frac{\alpha_1 V_1^2}{2g} + \cancel{z_1} = \frac{p_2}{\gamma} + \frac{\alpha_2 V_2^2}{2g} + z_2 - h_p + h_f, \quad h_f = K\frac{V_2^2}{2g}$$

or

$$h_p = \frac{p_2 - p_1}{\gamma} + z_2 + (\alpha_2 + K)\frac{V_2^2}{2g}$$

- *Comment:* The pump must balance four different effects: the pressure change, the elevation change, the exit jet kinetic energy, and the friction losses.
- *Final solution:* For the given data, we can evaluate the required pump head:

$$h_p = \frac{(1440 - 2117) \ \text{lbf/ft}^2}{62.4 \ \text{lbf/ft}^3} + 20 + (1.07 + 7.5)\frac{(30.6 \ \text{ft/s})^2}{2(32.2 \ \text{ft/s}^2)} = -11 + 20 + 124 = 133 \ \text{ft}$$

With the pump head known, the delivered pump power is computed similar to the turbine in Example 3.23:

$$P_{\text{pump}} = \dot{m}w_s = \gamma Q h_p = \left(62.4 \ \frac{\text{lbf}}{\text{ft}^3}\right)\left(1.5 \ \frac{\text{ft}^3}{\text{s}}\right)(133 \ \text{ft})$$

$$= 12450 \ \frac{\text{ft} - \text{lbf}}{\text{s}} = \frac{12{,}450 \ \text{ft-lbf/s}}{550 \ \text{ft-lbf/(s-hp)}} = 22.6 \ \text{hp}$$

If the pump is 80 percent efficient, then we divide by the efficiency to find the input power required:

$$P_{\text{input}} = \frac{P_{\text{pump}}}{\text{efficiency}} = \frac{22.6 \ \text{hp}}{0.80} = 28.3 \ \text{hp} \qquad\qquad Ans.$$

- *Comment:* The inclusion of the kinetic energy correction factor α in this case made a difference of about 1 percent in the result. The friction loss, not the exit jet, was the dominant parameter.

Summary

This chapter has analyzed the four basic equations of fluid mechanics: conservation of (1) mass, (2) linear momentum, (3) angular momentum, and (4) energy. The equations were attacked "in the large"—that is, applied to whole regions of a flow. As such, the typical analysis will involve an approximation of the flow field within the region, giving somewhat crude but always instructive quantitative results. However, the basic control volume relations are rigorous and correct and will give exact results if applied to the exact flow field.

There are two main points to a control volume analysis. The first is the selection of a proper, clever, workable control volume. There is no substitute for experience, but the following guidelines apply. The control volume should cut through the place where the information or solution is desired. It should cut through places where maximum information is already known. If the momentum equation is to be used, it should *not* cut through solid walls unless absolutely necessary, since this will expose possible unknown stresses and forces and moments that make the solution for the desired force difficult or impossible. Finally, every attempt should be made to place the control volume in a frame of reference where the flow is steady or quasi-steady, since the steady formulation is much simpler to evaluate.

The second main point to a control volume analysis is the reduction of the analysis to a case that applies to the problem at hand. The 24 examples in this chapter give only an introduction to the search for appropriate simplifying assumptions. You will need to solve 24 or 124 more examples to become truly experienced in simplifying the problem just enough and no more. In the meantime, it would be wise for the beginner to adopt a very general form of the control volume conservation laws and then make a series of simplifications to achieve the final analysis. Starting with the general form, one can ask a series of questions:

1. Is the control volume nondeforming or nonaccelerating?
2. Is the flow field steady? Can we change to a steady flow frame?
3. Can friction be neglected?
4. Is the fluid incompressible? If not, is the perfect-gas law applicable?
5. Are gravity or other body forces negligible?
6. Is there heat transfer, shaft work, or viscous work?
7. Are the inlet and outlet flows approximately one-dimensional?
8. Is atmospheric pressure important to the analysis? Is the pressure hydrostatic on any portions of the control surface?
9. Are there reservoir conditions that change so slowly that the velocity and time rates of change can be neglected?

In this way, by approving or rejecting a list of basic simplifications like these, one can avoid pulling Bernoulli's equation off the shelf when it does not apply.

Problems

Most of the problems herein are fairly straightforward. More difficult or open-ended assignments are labeled with an asterisk. Problems labeled with a computer icon 🖳 may require the use of a computer. The standard end-of-chapter problems P3.1 to P3.185 (categorized in the problem list here) are followed by word problems W3.1 to W3.7, fundamentals of engineering (FE) exam problems FE3.1 to FE3.10, comprehensive problems C3.1 to C3.5, and design project D3.1.

Problem Distribution

Basic physical laws; volume flow

P3.1 Discuss Newton's second law (the linear momentum relation) in these three forms:

$$\sum \mathbf{F} = m\mathbf{a} \qquad \sum \mathbf{F} = \frac{d}{dt}(m\mathbf{V})$$

$$\sum \mathbf{F} = \frac{d}{dt}\left(\int_{system} \mathbf{V}\rho \, d\mathcal{V} \right)$$

Are they all equally valid? Are they equivalent? Are some forms better for fluid mechanics as opposed to solid mechanics?

P3.2 Consider the angular momentum relation in the form

$$\sum \mathbf{M}_O = \frac{d}{dt}\left[\int_{system} (\mathbf{r} \times \mathbf{V})\rho \, d\mathcal{V} \right]$$

What does **r** mean in this relation? Is this relation valid in both solid and fluid mechanics? Is it related to the *linear* momentum equation (Prob. 3.1)? In what manner?

P3.3 For steady low-Reynolds-number (laminar) flow through a long tube (see Prob. 1.12), the axial velocity distribution is given by $u = C(R^2 - r^2)$, where R is the tube radius and $r \leq R$. Integrate $u(r)$ to find the total volume flow Q through the tube.

P3.4 Water at 20°C flows through a long elliptical duct 30 cm wide and 22 cm high. What average velocity, in m/s, would cause the weight flow to be 500 lbf/s?

P3.5 Water at 20°C flows through a 5-in-diameter smooth pipe at a high Reynolds number, for which the velocity profile is approximated by $u \approx U_0(y/R)^{1/8}$, where U_0 is the centerline velocity, R is the pipe radius, and y is the distance measured from the wall toward the centerline. If the centerline velocity is 25 ft/s, estimate the volume flow rate in gallons per minute.

The Reynolds transport theorem

P3.6 Water fills a cylindrical tank to depth h. The tank has diameter D. The water flows out at average velocity V_o from a hole in the bottom of area A_o. Use the Reynolds transport theorem to find an expression for the instantaneous depth change dh/dt.

P3.7 A spherical tank, of diameter 35 cm, is leaking air through a 5-mm-diameter hole in its side. The air exits the hole at 360 m/s and a density of 2.5 kg/m³. Assuming uniform mixing, (a) find a formula for the rate of change of average density in the tank and (b) calculate a numerical value for $(d\rho/dt)$ in the tank for the given data.

P3.8 Three pipes steadily deliver water at 20°C to a large exit pipe in Fig. P3.8. The velocity $V_2 = 5$ m/s, and the exit flow rate $Q_4 = 120$ m³/h. Find (a) V_1, (b) V_3, and (c) V_4 if it is known that increasing Q_3 by 20 percent would increase Q_4 by 10 percent.

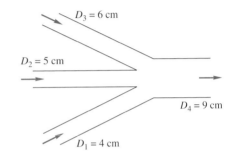

P3.8

P3.9 A laboratory test tank contains seawater of salinity S and density ρ. Water enters the tank at conditions (S_1, ρ_1, A_1, V_1) and is assumed to mix immediately in the tank. Tank water leaves through an outlet A_2 at velocity V_2. If salt is a "conservative" property (neither created nor destroyed), use the Reynolds transport theorem to find an expression for the rate of change of salt mass M_{salt} within the tank.

Conservation of mass

P3.10 Water flowing through an 8-cm-diameter pipe enters a porous section, as in Fig. P3.10, which allows a uniform radial velocity v_w through the wall surfaces for a distance of 1.2 m. If the entrance average velocity V_1 is 12 m/s, find the exit velocity V_2 if (a) $v_w = 15$ cm/s out of the pipe walls or (b) $v_w = 10$ cm/s into the pipe. (c) What value of v_w will make $V_2 = 9$ m/s?

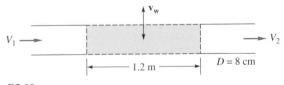

P3.10

P3.11 Water flows from a faucet into a sink at 3 U.S. gallons per minute. The stopper is closed, and the sink has two rectangular overflow drains, each $^3/_8$ in by 1¼ in. If the sink water level remains constant, estimate the average overflow velocity, in ft/s.

P3.12 The pipe flow in Fig. P3.12 fills a cylindrical surge tank as shown. At time $t = 0$, the water depth in the tank is 30 cm. Estimate the time required to fill the remainder of the tank.

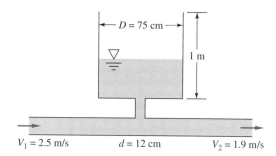

P3.12

P3.13 The cylindrical container in Fig. P3.13 is 20 cm in diameter and has a conical contraction at the bottom with an exit hole 3 cm in diameter. The tank contains fresh water at standard sea-level conditions. If the water surface is falling at the nearly steady rate $dh/dt \approx -0.072$ m/s, estimate the average velocity V out of the bottom exit.

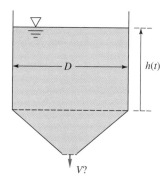

P3.13

P3.14 The open tank in Fig. P3.14 contains water at 20°C and is being filled through section 1. Assume incompressible flow. First derive an analytic expression for the water-level change dh/dt in terms of arbitrary volume flows (Q_1, Q_2, Q_3) and tank diameter d. Then, if the water level h is constant, determine the exit velocity V_2 for the given data $V_1 = 3$ m/s and $Q_3 = 0.01$ m³/s.

P3.15 Water, assumed incompressible, flows steadily through the round pipe in Fig. P3.15. The entrance velocity is constant, $u = U_0$, and the exit velocity approximates turbulent flow, $u = u_{max}(1 - r/R)^{1/7}$. Determine the ratio U_0/u_{max} for this flow.

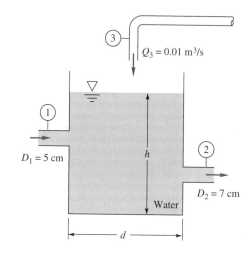

P3.14

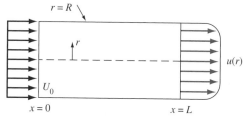

P3.15

P3.16 An incompressible fluid flows past an impermeable flat plate, as in Fig. P3.16, with a uniform inlet profile $u = U_0$ and a cubic polynomial exit profile

$$u \approx U_0 \left(\frac{3\eta - \eta^3}{2} \right) \quad \text{where } \eta = \frac{y}{\delta}$$

Compute the volume flow Q across the top surface of the control volume.

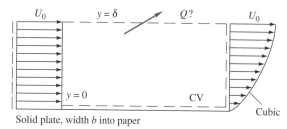

Solid plate, width b into paper

P3.16

P3.17 Incompressible steady flow in the inlet between parallel plates in Fig. P3.17 is uniform, $u = U_0 = 8$ cm/s, while downstream the flow develops into the parabolic laminar profile $u = az(z_0 - z)$, where a is a constant. If $z_0 = 4$ cm and the fluid is SAE 30 oil at 20°C, what is the value of u_{max} in cm/s?

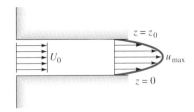

P3.17

P3.18   Gasoline enters section 1 in Fig. P3.18 at 0.5 m³/s. It leaves section 2 at an average velocity of 12 m/s. What is the average velocity at section 3? Is it in or out?

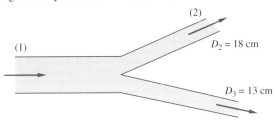

Fig. P3.18

P3.19   Water from a storm drain flows over an outfall onto a porous bed that absorbs the water at a uniform vertical velocity of 8 mm/s, as shown in Fig. P3.19. The system is 5 m deep into the paper. Find the length L of the bed that will completely absorb the storm water.

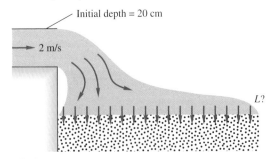

P3.19

P3.20   Oil (SG = 0.89) enters at section 1 in Fig. P3.20 at a weight flow of 250 N/h to lubricate a thrust bearing. The steady oil flow exits radially through the narrow clearance between thrust plates. Compute (a) the outlet volume flow in mL/s and (b) the average outlet velocity in cm/s.

P3.21   For the two-port tank of Fig. E3.5, assume D_1 = 4 cm, V_1 = 18 m/s, D_2 = 7 cm, and V_2 = 8 m/s. If the tank surface is rising at 17 mm/s, estimate the tank diameter.

P3.22   The converging–diverging nozzle shown in Fig. P3.22 expands and accelerates dry air to supersonic speeds at the exit, where p_2 = 8 kPa and T_2 = 240 K. At the throat, p_1 = 284 kPa, T_1 = 665 K, and V_1 = 517 m/s. For steady compressible flow of an ideal gas, estimate (a) the mass flow in kg/h, (b) the velocity V_2, and (c) the Mach number Ma_2.

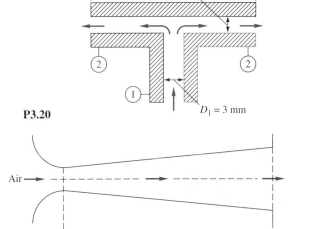

P3.20

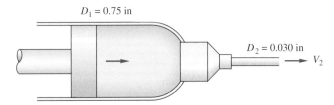

P3.22

P3.23   The hypodermic needle in Fig. P3.23 contains a liquid serum (SG = 1.05). If the serum is to be injected steadily at 6 cm³/s, how fast in in/s should the plunger be advanced (a) if leakage in the plunger clearance is neglected and (b) if leakage is 10 percent of the needle flow?

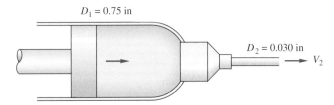

P3.23

*P3.24   Water enters the bottom of the cone in Fig. P3.24 at a uniformly increasing average velocity $V = Kt$. If d is very small, derive an analytic formula for the water surface rise $h(t)$ for the condition $h = 0$ at $t = 0$. Assume incompressible flow.

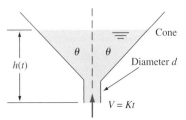

P3.24

P3.25 As will be discussed in Chaps. 7 and 8, the flow of a stream U_0 past a blunt flat plate creates a broad low-velocity *wake* behind the plate. A simple model is given in Fig. P3.25, with only half of the flow shown due to symmetry. The velocity profile behind the plate is idealized as "dead air" (near-zero velocity) behind the plate, plus a higher velocity, decaying vertically above the wake according to the variation $u \approx U_0 + \Delta U \, e2^{z/L}$, where L is the plate height and $z = 0$ is the top of the wake. Find ΔU as a function of stream speed U_0.

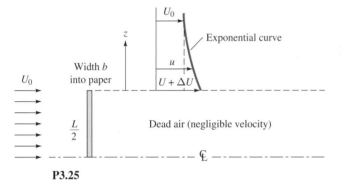

P3.25

P3.26 A thin layer of liquid, draining from an inclined plane, as in Fig. P3.26, will have a laminar velocity profile $u \approx U_0(2y/h - y^2/h^2)$, where U_0 is the surface velocity. If the plane has width b into the paper, determine the volume rate of flow in the film. Suppose that $h = 0.5$ in and the flow rate per foot of channel width is 1.25 gal/min. Estimate U_0 in ft/s.

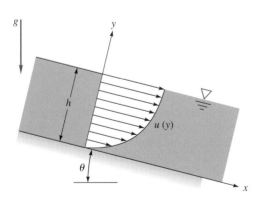

P3.26

P3.27 Consider a highly pressurized air tank at conditions (p_0, ρ_0, T_0) and volume v_0. In Chap. 9 we will learn that, if the tank is allowed to exhaust to the atmosphere through a well-designed converging nozzle of exit area A, the outgoing mass flow rate will be

$$\dot{m} = \frac{\alpha \, p_0 A}{\sqrt{RT_0}} \quad \text{where } \alpha \approx 0.685 \text{ for air}$$

This rate persists as long as p_0 is at least twice as large as the atmospheric pressure. Assuming constant T_0 and an ideal gas, (a) derive a formula for the change of density $\rho_0(t)$ within the tank. (b) Analyze the time Δt required for the density to decrease by 25 percent.

P3.28 Air, assumed to be a perfect gas from Table A.4, flows through a long, 2-cm-diameter insulated tube. At section 1, the pressure is 1.1 MPa and the temperature is 345 K. At section 2, 67 meters further downstream, the density is 1.34 kg/m³, the temperature 298 K, and the Mach number is 0.90. For one-dimensional flow, calculate (a) the mass flow; (b) p_2; (c) V_2; and (d) the change in entropy between 1 and 2. (e) How do you explain the entropy change?

P3.29 In elementary compressible flow theory (Chap. 9), compressed air will exhaust from a small hole in a tank at the mass flow rate $\dot{m} \approx C\rho$, where ρ is the air density in the tank and C is a constant. If ρ_0 is the initial density in a tank of volume $\mathscr{V}$, derive a formula for the density change $\rho(t)$ after the hole is opened. Apply your formula to the following case: a spherical tank of diameter 50 cm, with initial pressure 300 kPa and temperature 100°C, and a hole whose initial exhaust rate is 0.01 kg/s. Find the time required for the tank density to drop by 50 percent.

P3.30 For the nozzle of Fig. P3.22, consider the following data for air, $k = 1.4$. At the throat, $p_1 = 1000$ kPa, $V_1 = 491$ m/s, and $T_1 = 600$ K. At the exit, $p_2 = 28.14$ kPa. Assuming isentropic steady flow, compute (a) the Mach number Ma_1; (b) T_2; (c) the mass flow; and (d) V_2.

P3.31 A bellows may be modeled as a deforming wedge-shaped volume as in Fig. P3.31. The check valve on the left (pleated) end is closed during the stroke. If b is the bellows width into the paper, derive an expression for outlet mass flow $\dot{m}_0$ as a function of stroke $\theta(t)$.

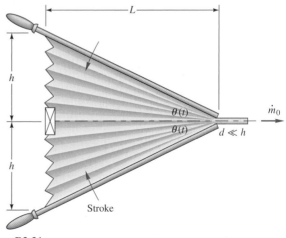

P3.31

P3.32 Water at 20°C flows steadily through the piping junction in Fig. P3.32, entering section 1 at 20 gal/min. The average velocity at section 2 is 2.5 m/s. A portion of the flow is diverted through the showerhead, which contains 100 holes of 1-mm diameter. Assuming uniform shower flow, estimate the exit velocity from the showerhead jets.

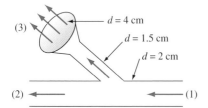

P3.32

P3.33 In some wind tunnels the test section is perforated to suck out fluid and provide a thin viscous boundary layer. The test section wall in Fig. P3.33 contains 1200 holes of 5-mm diameter each per square meter of wall area. The suction velocity through each hole is $V_s = 8$ m/s, and the test-section entrance velocity is $V_1 = 35$ m/s. Assuming incompressible steady flow of air at 20°C, compute (a) V_0, (b) V_2, and (c) V_f, in m/s.

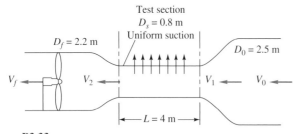

P3.33

P3.34 A rocket motor is operating steadily, as shown in Fig. P3.34. The products of combustion flowing out the exhaust nozzle approximate a perfect gas with a molecular weight of 28. For the given conditions calculate V_2 in ft/s.

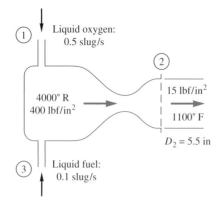

P3.34

P3.35 In contrast to the liquid rocket in Fig. P3.34, the solid-propellant rocket in Fig. P3.35 is self-contained and has no entrance ducts. Using a control volume analysis for the conditions shown in Fig. P3.35, compute the rate of mass loss of the propellant, assuming that the exit gas has a molecular weight of 28.

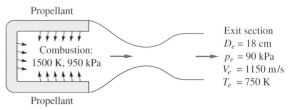

P3.35

P3.36 The jet pump in Fig. P3.36 injects water at $U_1 = 40$ m/s through a 3-in pipe and entrains a secondary flow of water $U_2 = 3$ m/s in the annular region around the small pipe. The two flows become fully mixed downstream, where U_3 is approximately constant. For steady incompressible flow, compute U_3 in m/s.

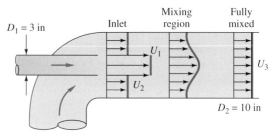

P3.36

P3.37 If the rectangular tank full of water in Fig. P3.37 has its right-hand wall lowered by an amount δ, as shown, water will flow out as it would over a weir or dam. In Prob. P1.14 we deduced that the outflow Q would be given by

$$Q = C b g^{1/2} \delta^{3/2}$$

where b is the tank width into the paper, g is the acceleration of gravity, and C is a dimensionless constant. Assume that the water surface is horizontal, not slightly curved as in the figure. Let the initial excess water level be δ_0. Derive a formula for the time required to reduce the excess water level to (a) $\delta_0/10$ and (b) zero.

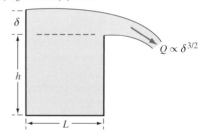

P3.37

P3.38 An incompressible fluid in Fig. P3.38 is being squeezed outward between two large circular disks by the uniform downward motion V_0 of the upper disk. Assuming one-dimensional radial outflow, use the control volume shown to derive an expression for $V(r)$.

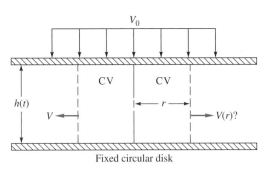

P3.38

The linear momentum equation

P3.39 A wedge splits a sheet of 20°C water, as shown in Fig. P3.39. Both wedge and sheet are very long into the paper. If the force required to hold the wedge stationary is $F =$ 124 N per meter of depth into the paper, what is the angle θ of the wedge?

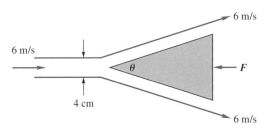

P3.39

P3.40 The water jet in Fig. P3.40 strikes normal to a fixed plate. Neglect gravity and friction, and compute the force F in newtons required to hold the plate fixed.

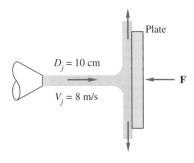

P3.40

P3.41 In Fig. P3.41 the vane turns the water jet completely around. Find an expression for the maximum jet velocity V_0 if the maximum possible support force is F_0.

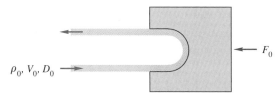

P3.41

P3.42 A liquid of density ρ flows through the sudden contraction in Fig. P3.42 and exits to the atmosphere. Assume uniform conditions (p_1, V_1, D_1) at section 1 and (p_2, V_2, D_2) at section 2. Find an expression for the force F exerted by the fluid on the contraction.

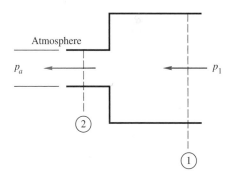

P3.42

P3.43 Water at 20°C flows through a 5-cm-diameter pipe that has a 180° vertical bend, as in Fig. P3.43. The total length of pipe between flanges 1 and 2 is 75 cm. When the weight flow rate is 230 N/s, $p_1 =$ 165 kPa and $p_2 =$ 134 kPa. Neglecting pipe weight, determine the total force that the flanges must withstand for this flow.

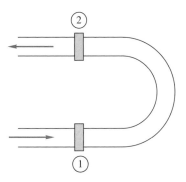

P3.43

*****P3.44** When a uniform stream flows past an immersed thick cylinder, a broad low-velocity wake is created downstream, idealized as a V shape in Fig. P3.44. Pressures p_1 and p_2 are approximately equal. If the flow is two-dimensional and incompressible, with width b into the paper, derive a formula for the drag force F on the cylinder. Rewrite your result in the form of a dimensionless *drag coefficient* based on body length $C_D = F/(\rho U^2 bL)$.

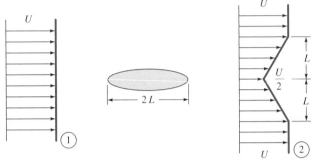

P3.44

P3.45 Water enters and leaves the 6-cm-diameter pipe bend in Fig. P3.45 at an average velocity of 8.5 m/s. The horizontal force to support the bend against momentum change is 300 N. Find (*a*) the angle ϕ; and (*b*) the vertical force on the bend.

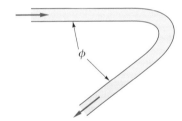

P3.45

P3.46 When a jet strikes an inclined fixed plate, as in Fig. P3.46, it breaks into two jets at 2 and 3 of equal velocity $V = V_{jet}$ but unequal flows αQ at 2 and $(1 - \alpha)Q$ at section 3, α being a fraction. The reason is that for frictionless flow the fluid can exert no tangential force F_t on the plate. The condition $F_t = 0$ enables us to solve for α. Perform this analysis, and find α as a function of the plate angle θ. Why doesn't the answer depend on the properties of the jet?

P3.47 A liquid jet of velocity V_j and diameter D_j strikes a fixed hollow cone, as in Fig. P3.47, and deflects back as a conical sheet at the same velocity. Find the cone angle θ for which the restraining force $F = \frac{3}{2}\rho A_j V_j^2$.

P3.48 The small boat in Fig. P3.48 is driven at a steady speed V_0 by a jet of compressed air issuing from a 3-cm-diameter hole at $V_e = 343$ m/s. Jet exit conditions are $p_e = 1$ atm and $T_e = 30°C$. Air drag is negligible, and the hull drag is kV_0^2, where $k \approx 19$ N $\cdot$ s^2/m^2. Estimate the boat speed V_0 in m/s.

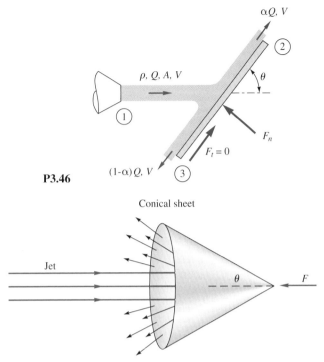

P3.46

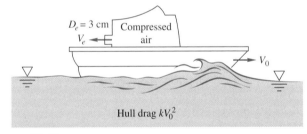

P3.47

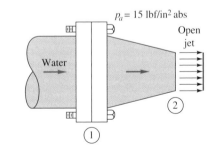

P3.48

P3.49 The horizontal nozzle in Fig. P3.49 has $D_1 = 12$ in and $D_2 = 6$ in, with inlet pressure $p_1 = 38$ lbf/in^2 absolute and $V_2 = 56$ ft/s. For water at 20°C, compute the horizontal force provided by the flange bolts to hold the nozzle fixed.

P3.49

P3.50 The jet engine on a test stand in Fig. P3.50 admits air at 20°C and 1 atm at section 1, where $A_1 = 0.5$ m^2 and $V_1 = 250$ m/s. The fuel-to-air ratio is 1:30. The air leaves section 2 at atmospheric pressure and higher temperature, where $V_2 = 900$ m/s and $A_2 = 0.4$ m^2. Compute the horizontal test stand reaction R_x needed to hold this engine fixed.

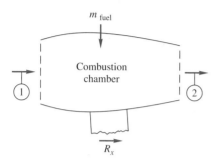

P3.50

P3.51 A liquid jet of velocity V_j and area A_j strikes a single 180° bucket on a turbine wheel rotating at angular velocity Ω, as in Fig. P3.51. Derive an expression for the power P delivered to this wheel at this instant as a function of the system parameters. At what angular velocity is the maximum power delivered? How would your analysis differ if there were many, many buckets on the wheel, so that the jet was continually striking at least one bucket?

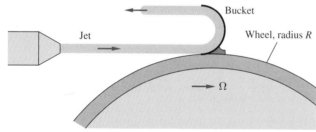

P3.51

P3.52 A large commercial power washer delivers 21 gal/min of water through a nozzle of exit diameter one-third of an inch. Estimate the force of the water jet on a wall normal to the jet.

P3.53 Consider incompressible flow in the entrance of a circular tube, as in Fig. P3.53. The inlet flow is uniform, $u_1 = U_0$. The flow at section 2 is developed pipe flow. Find the wall drag force F as a function of (p_1, p_2, ρ, U_0, R) if the flow at section 2 is

(a) Laminar: $u_2 = u_{max}\left(1 - \dfrac{r^2}{R^2}\right)$

(b) Turbulent: $u_2 \approx u_{max}\left(1 - \dfrac{r}{R}\right)^{1/7}$

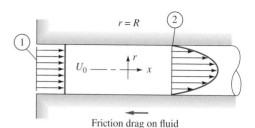

P3.53   Friction drag on fluid

P3.54 For the pipe-flow-reducing section of Fig. P3.54, $D_1 = 8$ cm, $D_2 = 5$ cm, and $p_2 = 1$ atm. All fluids are at 20°C. If $V_1 = 5$ m/s and the manometer reading is $h = 58$ cm, estimate the total force resisted by the flange bolts.

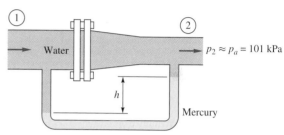

P3.54

P3.55 In Fig. P3.55 the jet strikes a vane that moves to the right at constant velocity V_c on a frictionless cart. Compute (a) the force F_x required to restrain the cart and (b) the power P delivered to the cart. Also find the cart velocity for which (c) the force F_x is a maximum and (d) the power P is a maximum.

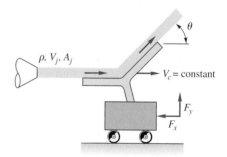

P3.55

P3.56 Water at 20°C flows steadily through the box in Fig. P3.56, entering station (1) at 2 m/s. Calculate the (a) horizontal and (b) vertical forces required to hold the box stationary against the flow momentum.

P3.57 Water flows through the duct in Fig. P3.57, which is 50 cm wide and 1 m deep into the paper. Gate BC completely closes the duct when $\beta = 90°$. Assuming one-dimensional flow, for what angle β will the force of the exit jet on the plate be 3 kN?

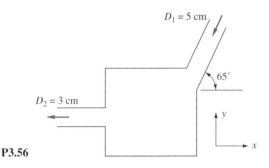

P3.56

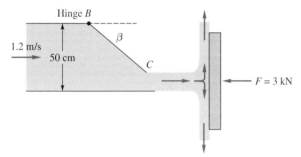

P3.57

P3.58 The water tank in Fig. P3.58 stands on a frictionless cart and feeds a jet of diameter 4 cm and velocity 8 m/s, which is deflected 60° by a vane. Compute the tension in the supporting cable.

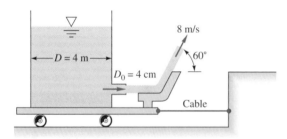

P3.58

P3.59 When a pipe flow suddenly expands from A_1 to A_2, as in Fig. P3.59, low-speed, low-friction eddies appear in the corners and the flow gradually expands to A_2 downstream. Using the suggested control volume for incompressible steady flow and assuming that $p \approx p_1$ on the corner annular ring as shown, show that the downstream pressure is given by

$$p_2 = p_1 + \rho V_1^2 \frac{A_1}{A_2}\left(1 - \frac{A_1}{A_2}\right)$$

Neglect wall friction.

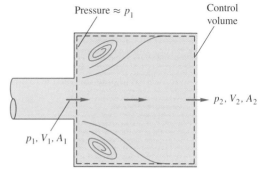

P3.59

P3.60 Water at 20°C flows through the elbow in Fig. P3.60 and exits to the atmosphere. The pipe diameter is $D_1 = 10$ cm, while $D_2 = 3$ cm. At a weight flow rate of 150 N/s, the pressure $p_1 = 2.3$ atm (gage). Neglecting the weight of water and elbow, estimate the force on the flange bolts at section 1.

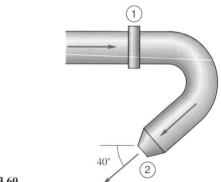

P3.60

P3.61 A 20°C water jet strikes a vane mounted on a tank with frictionless wheels, as in Fig. P3.61. The jet turns and falls into the tank without spilling out. If $\theta = 30°$, evaluate the horizontal force F required to hold the tank stationary.

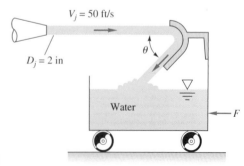

P3.61

P3.62 Water at 20°C exits to the standard sea-level atmosphere through the split nozzle in Fig. P3.62. Duct areas are $A_1 = 0.02$ m^2 and $A_2 = A_3 = 0.008$ m^2. If $p_1 = 135$ kPa (absolute) and the flow rate is $Q_2 = Q_3 = 275$ m^3/h, compute the force on the flange bolts at section 1.

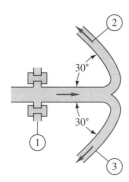

P3.62

P3.63 Water flows steadily through the box in Fig. P3.63. Average velocity at all ports is 7 m/s. The vertical momentum force on the box is 36 N. What is the inlet mass flow?

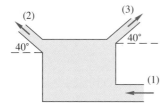

P3.63

P3.64 The 6-cm-diameter 20°C water jet in Fig. P3.64 strikes a plate containing a hole of 4-cm diameter. Part of the jet passes through the hole, and part is deflected. Determine the horizontal force required to hold the plate.

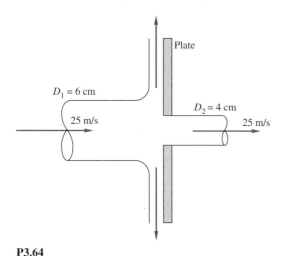

P3.64

P3.65 The box in Fig. P3.65 has three 0.5-in holes on the right side. The volume flows of 20°C water shown are steady, but the details of the interior are not known. Compute the force, if any, that this water flow causes on the box.

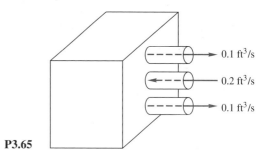

P3.65

P3.66 The tank in Fig. P3.66 weighs 500 N empty and contains 600 L of water at 20°C. Pipes 1 and 2 have equal diameters of 6 cm and equal steady volume flows of 300 m^3/h. What should the scale reading W be in N?

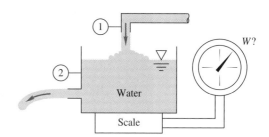

P3.66

P3.67 For the boundary layer of Fig. 3.10, for air, $\rho = 1.2$ kg/m^3, let $h = 7$ cm, $U_o = 12$ m/s, $b = 2$ m, and $L = 1$ m. Let the velocity at the exit, $x = L$, approximate a turbulent flow: $u/U_o \approx (y/\delta)^{1/7}$. Calculate (a) δ; and (b) the friction drag D.

P3.68 The rocket in Fig. P3.68 has a supersonic exhaust, and the exit pressure p_e is not necessarily equal to p_a. Show that the force F required to hold this rocket on the test stand is $F = \rho_e A_e V_e^2 + A_e(p_e - p_a)$. Is this force F what we term the *thrust* of the rocket?

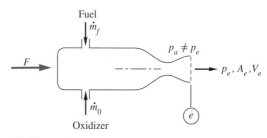

P3.68

P3.69 A uniform rectangular plate, 40 cm long and 30 cm deep into the paper, hangs in air from a hinge at its top (the 30-cm side). It is struck in its center by a horizontal 3-cm-diameter jet of water moving at 8 m/s. If the gate has a mass of 16 kg, estimate the angle at which the plate will hang from the vertical.

P3.70 The dredger in Fig. P3.70 is loading sand (SG = 2.6) onto a barge. The sand leaves the dredger pipe at 4 ft/s with a weight flow of 850 lbf/s. Estimate the tension on the mooring line caused by this loading process.

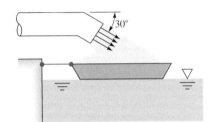

P3.70

P3.71 Suppose that a deflector is deployed at the exit of the jet engine of Prob. P3.50, as shown in Fig. P3.71. What will the reaction R_x on the test stand be now? Is this reaction sufficient to serve as a braking force during airplane landing?

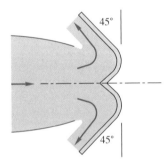

P3.71

*P3.72 When immersed in a uniform stream, a thick elliptical cylinder creates a broad downstream wake, as idealized in Fig. P3.72. The pressure at the upstream and downstream sections are approximately equal, and the fluid is water at 20°C. If $U_0 = 4$ m/s and $L = 80$ cm, estimate the drag force on the cylinder per unit width into the paper. Also compute the dimensionless drag coefficient $C_D = 2F/(\rho U_0^2 bL)$.

P3.73 A pump in a tank of water at 20°C directs a jet at 45 ft/s and 200 gal/min against a vane, as shown in Fig. P3.73. Compute the force F to hold the cart stationary if the jet follows (a) path A or (b) path B. The tank holds 550 gal of water at this instant.

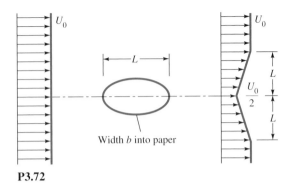

P3.72

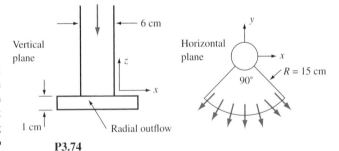

P3.73

P3.74 Water at 20°C flows down through a vertical, 6-cm-diameter tube at 300 gal/min, as in Fig. P3.74. The flow then turns horizontally and exits through a 90° radial duct segment 1 cm thick, as shown. If the radial outflow is uniform and steady, estimate the forces (F_x, F_y, F_z) required to support this system against fluid momentum changes.

P3.74

*P3.75 A jet of liquid of density ρ and area A strikes a block and splits into two jets, as in Fig. P3.75. Assume the same velocity V for all three jets. The upper jet exits at an angle θ and area αA. The lower jet is turned 90° downward. Neglecting fluid weight, (a) derive a formula for the forces (F_x, F_y) required to support the block against fluid momentum changes. (b) Show that $F_y = 0$ only if $\alpha \geq 0.5$. (c) Find the values of α and θ for which both F_x and F_y are zero.

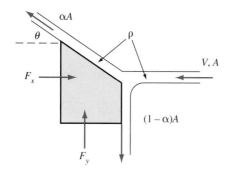

P3.75

P3.76 A two-dimensional sheet of water, 10 cm thick and moving at 7 m/s, strikes a fixed wall inclined at 20° with respect to the jet direction. Assuming frictionless flow, find (a) the normal force on the wall per meter of depth, and find the widths of the sheet deflected (b) upstream and (c) downstream along the wall.

P3.77 Water at 20°C flows steadily through a reducing pipe bend, as in Fig. P3.77. Known conditions are $p_1 = 350$ kPa, $D_1 = 25$ cm, $V_1 = 2.2$ m/s, $p_2 = 120$ kPa, and $D_2 = 8$ cm. Neglecting bend and water weight, estimate the total force that must be resisted by the flange bolts.

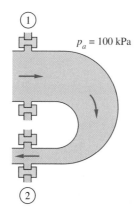

P3.77

P3.78 A fluid jet of diameter D_1 enters a cascade of moving blades at absolute velocity V_1 and angle β_1, and it leaves at absolute velocity V_2 and angle β_2, as in Fig. P3.78. The blades move at velocity u. Derive a formula for the power P delivered to the blades as a function of these parameters.

P3.79 The Saturn V rocket in the chapter opener photo was powered by five F-1 engines, each of which burned 3945 lbm/s of liquid oxygen and 1738 lbm of kerosene per second. The exit velocity of burned gases was approximately 8500 ft/s. In the spirit of Prob. P3.34, neglecting external pressure forces, estimate the total thrust of the rocket, in lbf.

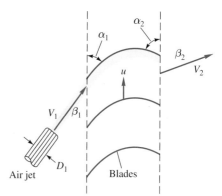

P3.78

P3.80 A river of width b and depth h_1 passes over a submerged obstacle, or "drowned weir," in Fig. P3.80, emerging at a new flow condition (V_2, h_2). Neglect atmospheric pressure, and assume that the water pressure is hydrostatic at both sections 1 and 2. Derive an expression for the force exerted by the river on the obstacle in terms of V_1, h_1, h_2, b, ρ, and g. Neglect water friction on the river bottom.

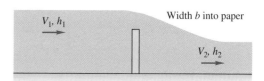

P3.80

P3.81 Torricelli's idealization of efflux from a hole in the side of a tank is $V = \sqrt{2\,gh}$, as shown in Fig. P3.81. The cylindrical tank weighs 150 N when empty and contains water at 20°C. The tank bottom is on very smooth ice (static friction coefficient $\zeta \approx 0.01$). The hole diameter is 9 cm. For what water depth h will the tank just begin to move to the right?

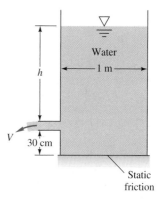

P3.81

*P3.82** The model car in Fig. P3.82 weighs 17 N and is to be accelerated from rest by a 1-cm-diameter water jet moving at 75 m/s. Neglecting air drag and wheel friction, estimate the velocity of the car after it has moved forward 1 m.

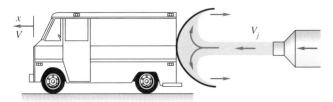

P3.82

P3.83 Gasoline at 20°C is flowing at $V_1 = 12$ m/s in a 5-cm-diameter pipe when it encounters a 1-m length of uniform radial wall suction. At the end of this suction region, the average fluid velocity has dropped to $V_2 = 10$ m/s. If $p_1 = 120$ kPa, estimate p_2 if the wall friction losses are neglected.

P3.84 Air at 20°C and 1 atm flows in a 25-cm-diameter duct at 15 m/s, as in Fig. P3.84. The exit is choked by a 90° cone, as shown. Estimate the force of the airflow on the cone.

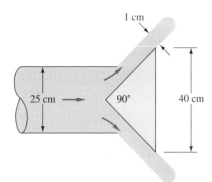

P3.84

P3.85 The thin-plate orifice in Fig. P3.85 causes a large pressure drop. For 20°C water flow at 500 gal/min, with pipe $D = 10$ cm and orifice $d = 6$ cm, $p_1 - p_2 \approx 145$ kPa. If the wall friction is negligible, estimate the force of the water on the orifice plate.

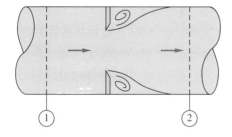

P3.85

P3.86 For the water jet pump of Prob. P3.36, add the following data: $p_1 = p_2 = 25$ lbf/in², and the distance between sections 1 and 3 is 80 in. If the average wall shear stress

between sections 1 and 3 is 7 lbf/ft², estimate the pressure p_3. Why is it higher than p_1?

P3.87 A vane turns a water jet through an angle α, as shown in Fig. P3.87. Neglect friction on the vane walls. (a) What is the angle α for the support force to be in pure compression? (b) Calculate this compression force if the water velocity is 22 ft/s and the jet cross section is 4 in².

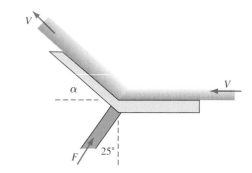

P3.87

P3.88 The boat in Fig. P3.88 is jet-propelled by a pump that develops a volume flow rate Q and ejects water out the stern at velocity V_j. If the boat drag force is $F = kV^2$, where k is a constant, develop a formula for the steady forward speed V of the boat.

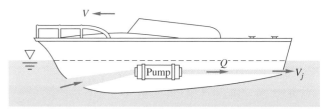

P3.88

P3.89 Consider Fig. P3.36 as a general problem for analysis of a mixing ejector pump. If all conditions (p, ρ, V) are known at sections 1 and 2 and if the wall friction is negligible, derive formulas for estimating (a) V_3 and (b) p_3.

P3.90 As shown in Fig. P3.90, a liquid column of height h is confined in a vertical tube of cross-sectional area A by a stopper. At $t = 0$ the stopper is suddenly removed, exposing the bottom of the liquid to atmospheric pressure. Using a control volume analysis of mass and vertical momentum, derive the differential equation for the downward motion $V(t)$ of the liquid. Assume one-dimensional, incompressible, frictionless flow.

P3.91 Extend Prob. P3.90 to include a linear (laminar) average wall shear stress resistance of the form $\tau \approx cV$, where c is a constant. Find the differential equation for dV/dt and then solve for $V(t)$, assuming for simplicity that the wall area remains constant.

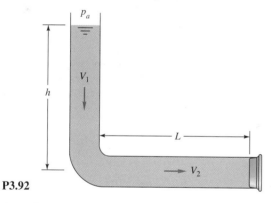

P3.90   Stopper

P3.92 A more involved version of Prob. P3.90 is the elbow-shaped tube in Fig. P3.92, with constant cross-sectional area A and diameter $D \ll h$, L. Assume incompressible flow, neglect friction, and derive a differential equation for dV/dt when the stopper is opened. *Hint:* Combine two control volumes, one for each leg of the tube.

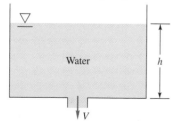

P3.92

P3.93 According to Torricelli's theorem, the velocity of a fluid draining from a hole in a tank is $V \approx (2gh)^{1/2}$, where h is the depth of water above the hole, as in Fig. P3.93. Let the hole have area A_o and the cylindrical tank have cross-section area $A_b \gg A_o$. Derive a formula for the time to drain the tank completely from an initial depth h_o.

P3.93

P3.94 A water jet 3 in in diameter strikes a concrete (SG = 2.3) slab which rests freely on a level floor. If the slab is 1 ft

wide into the paper, calculate the jet velocity which will just begin to tip the slab over.

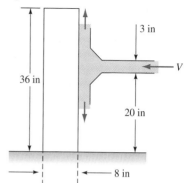

P3.94

P3.95 A tall water tank discharges through a well-rounded orifice, as in Fig. P3.95. Use the Torricelli formula of Prob. P3.81 to estimate the exit velocity. (*a*) If, at this instant, the force F required to hold the plate is 40 N, what is the depth h? (*b*) If the tank surface is dropping at the rate of 2.5 cm/s, what is the tank diameter D?

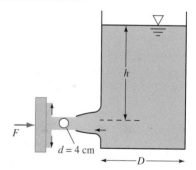

P3.95

P3.96 Extend Prob. P3.90 to the case of the liquid motion in a frictionless U-tube whose liquid column is displaced a distance Z upward and then released, as in Fig. P3.96.

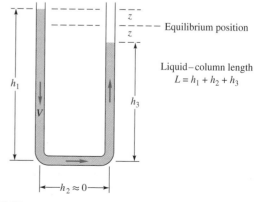

P3.96

Neglect the short horizontal leg, and combine control volume analyses for the left and right legs to derive a single differential equation for $V(t)$ of the liquid column.

*P3.97   Extend Prob. P3.96 to include a linear (laminar) average wall shear stress resistance of the form $\tau \approx 8\mu V/D$, where μ is the fluid viscosity. Find the differential equation for dV/dt and then solve for $V(t)$, assuming an initial displacement $z = z_0$, $V = 0$ at $t = 0$. The result should be a damped oscillation tending toward $z = 0$.

*P3.98   As an extension of Example 3.9, let the plate and its cart (see Fig. 3.9a) be unrestrained horizontally, with frictionless wheels. Derive (a) the equation of motion for cart velocity $V_c(t)$ and (b) a formula for the time required for the cart to accelerate from rest to 90 percent of the jet velocity (assuming the jet continues to strike the plate horizontally). (c) Compute numerical values for part (b) using the conditions of Example 3.9 and a cart mass of 2 kg.

P3.99   Let the rocket of Fig. E3.12 start at $z = 0$, with constant exit velocity and exit mass flow, and rise vertically with zero drag. (a) Show that, as long as fuel burning continues, the vertical height $S(t)$ reached is given by

$$S = \frac{V_e M_o}{\dot{m}}[\zeta\ln\zeta - \zeta + 1], \text{ where } \zeta = 1 - \frac{\dot{m}t}{M_o}$$

(b) Apply this to the case $V_e = 1500$ m/s and $M_o = 1000$ kg to find the height reached after a burn of 30 seconds, when the final rocket mass is 400 kg.

P3.100   Suppose that the solid-propellant rocket of Prob. P3.35 is built into a missile of diameter 70 cm and length 4 m. The system weighs 1800 N, which includes 700 N of propellant. Neglect air drag. If the missile is fired vertically from rest at sea level, estimate (a) its velocity and height at fuel burnout and (b) the maximum height it will attain.

P3.101   Water at 20°C flows steadily through the tank in Fig. P3.101. Known conditions are $D_1 = 8$ cm, $V_1 = 6$ m/s, and $D_2 = 4$ cm. A rightward force $F = 70$ N is required to keep the tank fixed. (a) What is the velocity leaving section 2? (b) If the tank cross section is 1.2 m², how fast is the water surface $h(t)$ rising or falling?

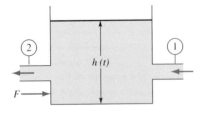

P3.101

P3.102   As can often be seen in a kitchen sink when the faucet is running, a high-speed channel flow (V_1, h_1) may "jump" to a low-speed, low-energy condition (V_2, h_2) as in Fig. P3.102.

The pressure at sections 1 and 2 is approximately hydrostatic, and wall friction is negligible. Use the continuity and momentum relations to find h_2 and V_2 in terms of (h_1, V_1).

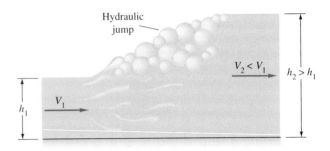

P3.102

*P3.103   Suppose that the solid-propellant rocket of Prob. P3.35 is mounted on a 1000-kg car to propel it up a long slope of 15°. The rocket motor weighs 900 N, which includes 500 N of propellant. If the car starts from rest when the rocket is fired, and if air drag and wheel friction are neglected, estimate the maximum distance that the car will travel up the hill.

P3.104   A rocket is attached to a rigid horizontal rod hinged at the origin as in Fig. P3.104. Its initial mass is M_0, and its exit properties are $\dot{m}$ and V_e relative to the rocket. Set up the differential equation for rocket motion, and solve for the angular velocity $\omega(t)$ of the rod. Neglect gravity, air drag, and the rod mass.

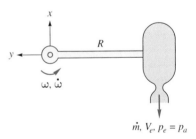

P3.104

P3.105   Extend Prob. P3.104 to the case where the rocket has a linear air drag force $F = cV$, where c is a constant. Assuming no burnout, solve for $\omega(t)$ and find the *terminal* angular velocity—that is, the final motion when the angular acceleration is zero. Apply to the case $M_0 = 6$ kg, $R = 3$ m, $\dot{m} = 0.05$ kg/s, $V_e = 1100$ m/s, and $c = 0.075$ N · s/m to find the angular velocity after 12 s of burning.

P3.106   Actual airflow past a parachute creates a variable distribution of velocities and directions. Let us model this as a circular air jet, of diameter half the parachute diameter, which is turned completely around by the parachute, as in Fig. P3.106. (a) Find the force F required to support the chute. (b) Express this force as a dimensionless *drag coefficient*, $C_D = F/[(\frac{1}{2})\rho V^2(\pi/4)D^2]$ and compare with Table 7.3.

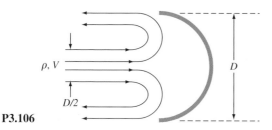

P3.106

P3.107 The cart in Fig. P3.107 moves at constant velocity $V_0 = 12$ m/s and takes on water with a scoop 80 cm wide that dips $h = 2.5$ cm into a pond. Neglect air drag and wheel friction. Estimate the force required to keep the cart moving.

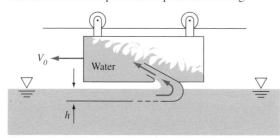

P3.107

*__P3.108__ A rocket sled of mass M is to be decelerated by a scoop, as in Fig. P3.108, which has width b into the paper and dips into the water a depth h, creating an upward jet at 60°. The rocket thrust is T to the left. Let the initial velocity be V_0, and neglect air drag and wheel friction. Find an expression for $V(t)$ of the sled for (a) $T = 0$ and (b) finite $T \neq 0$.

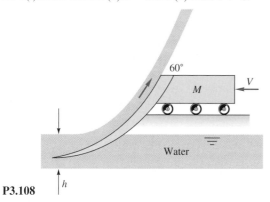

P3.108

P3.109 For the boundary layer flow in Fig. 3.10, let the exit velocity profile, at $x = L$, simulate turbulent flow, $u \approx U_0(y/\delta)^{1/7}$. (a) Find a relation between h and δ. (b) Find an expression for the drag force F on the plate between 0 and L.

The Bernoulli Equation

P3.110 Repeat Prob. P3.49 by assuming that p_1 is unknown and using Bernoulli's equation with no losses. Compute the new bolt force for this assumption. What is the head loss between 1 and 2 for the data of Prob. P3.49?

P3.111 As a simpler approach to Prob. P3.96, apply the unsteady Bernoulli equation between 1 and 2 to derive a differential equation for the motion $z(t)$. Neglect friction and compressibility.

P3.112 A jet of alcohol strikes the vertical plate in Fig. P3.112. A force $F \approx 425$ N is required to hold the plate stationary. Assuming there are no losses in the nozzle, estimate (a) the mass flow rate of alcohol and (b) the absolute pressure at section 1.

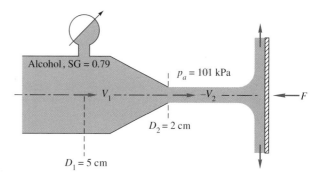

P3.112

P3.113 An airplane is flying at 300 mi/h at 4000 m standard altitude. As is typical, the air velocity relative to the upper surface of the wing, near its maximum thickness, is 26 percent higher than the plane's velocity. Using Bernoulli's equation, calculate the absolute pressure at this point on the wing. Neglect elevation changes and compressibility.

P3.114 Water flows through a circular nozzle, exits into the air as a jet, and strikes a plate, as shown in Fig. P3.114. The force required to hold the plate steady is 70 N. Assuming steady, frictionless, one-dimensional flow, estimate (a) the velocities at sections (1) and (2) and (b) the mercury manometer reading h.

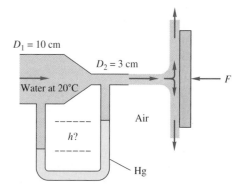

P3.114

P3.115 A free liquid jet, as in Fig. P3.115, has constant ambient pressure and small losses; hence from Bernoulli's equation $z + V^2/(2g)$ is constant along the jet. For the fire nozzle in the figure, what are (a) the minimum and (b) the maximum values of θ for which the water jet will clear the corner of the building? For which case will the jet velocity be higher when it strikes the roof of the building?

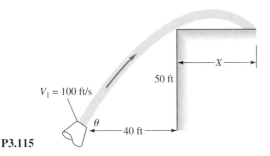

P3.115

P3.116 For the container of Fig. P3.116 use Bernoulli's equation to derive a formula for the distance X where the free jet leaving horizontally will strike the floor, as a function of h and H. For what ratio h/H will X be maximum? Sketch the three trajectories for $h/H = 0.25, 0.5,$ and 0.75.

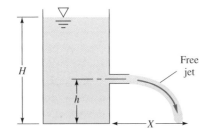

P3.116

P3.117 Water at 20°C, in the pressurized tank of Fig. P3.117, flows out and creates a vertical jet as shown. Assuming steady frictionless flow, determine the height H to which the jet rises.

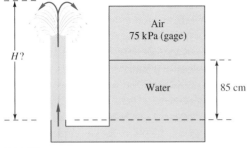

P3.117

P3.118 Bernoulli's 1738 treatise *Hydrodynamica* contains many excellent sketches of flow patterns related to his frictionless relation. One, however, redrawn here as Fig. P3.118, seems physically misleading. Can you explain what might be wrong with the figure?

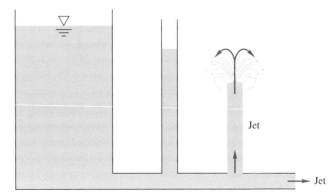

P3.118

P3.119 A long fixed tube with a rounded nose, aligned with an oncoming flow, can be used to measure velocity. Measurements are made of the pressure at (1) the front nose and (2) a hole in the side of the tube further along, where the pressure nearly equals stream pressure.
(a) Make a sketch of this device and show how the velocity is calculated. (b) For a particular sea-level airflow, the difference between nose pressure and side pressure is 1.5 lbf/in². What is the air velocity, in mi/h?

P3.120 The manometer fluid in Fig. P3.120 is mercury. Estimate the volume flow in the tube if the flowing fluid is (a) gasoline and (b) nitrogen, at 20°C and 1 atm.

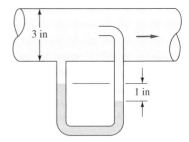

P3.120

P3.121 In Fig. P3.121 the flowing fluid is CO_2 at 20°C. Neglect losses. If $p_1 = 170$ kPa and the manometer fluid is Meriam red oil (SG = 0.827), estimate (a) p_2 and (b) the gas flow rate in m³/h.

P3.122 The cylindrical water tank in Fig. P3.122 is being filled at a volume flow $Q_1 = 1.0$ gal/min, while the water also drains from a bottom hole of diameter $d = 6$ mm. At time $t = 0$, $h = 0$. Find and plot the variation $h(t)$ and the eventual maximum water depth h_{max}. Assume that Bernoulli's steady-flow equation is valid.

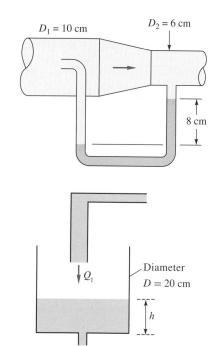

P3.121

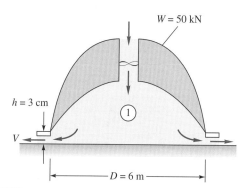

P3.122

P3.123 The air-cushion vehicle in Fig. P3.123 brings in sea-level standard air through a fan and discharges it at high velocity through an annular skirt of 3-cm clearance. If the vehicle weighs 50 kN, estimate (a) the required airflow rate and (b) the fan power in kW.

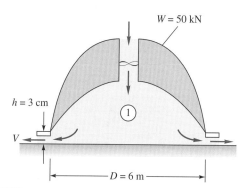

P3.123

P3.124 A necked-down section in a pipe flow, called a *venturi*, develops a low throat pressure that can aspirate fluid upward from a reservoir, as in Fig. P3.124. Using Bernoulli's equation with no losses, derive an expression for the velocity V_1 that is just sufficient to bring reservoir fluid into the throat.

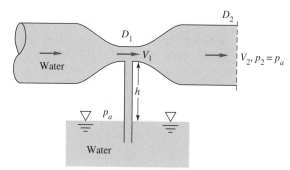

P3.124

P3.125 Suppose you are designing an air hockey table. The table is 3.0×6.0 ft in area, with $\frac{1}{16}$-in-diameter holes spaced every inch in a rectangular grid pattern (2592 holes total). The required jet speed from each hole is estimated to be 50 ft/s. Your job is to select an appropriate blower that will meet the requirements. Estimate the volumetric flow rate (in ft³/min) and pressure rise (in lb/in²) required of the blower. *Hint:* Assume that the air is stagnant in the large volume of the manifold under the table surface, and neglect any frictional losses.

P3.126 The liquid in Fig. P3.126 is kerosene at 20°C. Estimate the flow rate from the tank for (a) no losses and (b) pipe losses $h_f \approx 4.5V^2/(2g)$.

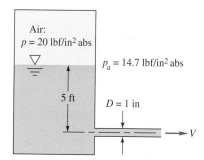

P3.126

P3.127 In Fig. P3.127 the open jet of water at 20°C exits a nozzle into sea-level air and strikes a stagnation tube as shown.

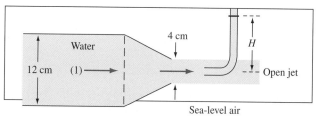

P3.127

If the pressure at the centerline at section 1 is 110 kPa, and losses are neglected, estimate (a) the mass flow in kg/s and (b) the height H of the fluid in the stagnation tube.

P3.128 A *venturi meter*, shown in Fig. P3.128, is a carefully designed constriction whose pressure difference is a measure of the flow rate in a pipe. Using Bernoulli's equation for steady incompressible flow with no losses, show that the flow rate Q is related to the manometer reading h by

$$ Q = \frac{A_2}{\sqrt{1 - (D_2/D_1)^4}} \sqrt{\frac{2gh(\rho_M - \rho)}{\rho}} $$

where ρ_M is the density of the manometer fluid.

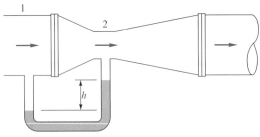

P3.128

P3.129 A water stream flows past a small circular cylinder at 23 ft/s, approaching the cylinder at 3000 lbf/ft². Measurements at low (laminar flow) Reynolds numbers indicate a maximum surface velocity 60 percent higher than the stream velocity at point B on the cylinder. Estimate the pressure at B.

P3.130 In Fig. P3.130 the fluid is gasoline at 20°C at a weight flow of 120 N/s. Assuming no losses, estimate the gage pressure at section 1.

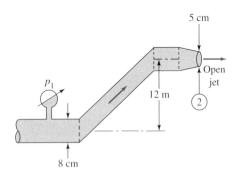

P3.130

P3.131 In Fig. P3.131 both fluids are at 20°C. If $V_1 = 1.7$ ft/s and losses are neglected, what should the manometer reading h ft be?

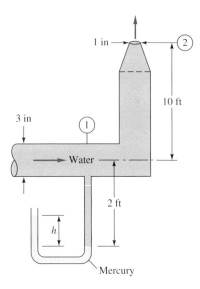

P3.131

P3.132 Extend the siphon analysis of Example 3.14 to account for friction in the tube, as follows. Let the friction head loss in the tube be correlated as $5.4(V_{tube})^2/(2g)$, which approximates turbulent flow in a 2-m-long tube. Calculate the exit velocity in m/s and the volume flow rate in cm³/s, and compare to Example 3.14.

P3.133 If losses are neglected in Fig. P3.133, for what water level h will the flow begin to form vapor cavities at the throat of the nozzle?

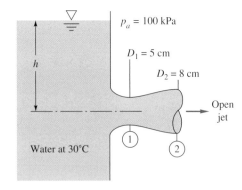

P3.133

*P3.134 For the 40°C water flow in Fig. P3.134, estimate the volume flow through the pipe, assuming no losses; then explain what is wrong with this seemingly innocent question. If the actual flow rate is $Q = 40$ m³/h, compute (a) the head loss in ft and (b) the constriction diameter D that causes cavitation, assuming that the throat divides the head loss equally and that changing the constriction causes no additional losses.

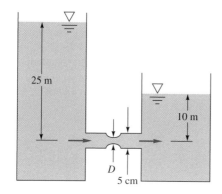

P3.134

25 m

10 m

D

5 cm

P3.135 The 35°C water flow of Fig. P3.135 discharges to sea-level standard atmosphere. Neglecting losses, for what nozzle diameter D will cavitation begin to occur? To avoid cavitation, should you increase or decrease D from this critical value?

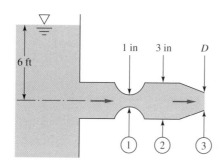

6 ft

1 in   3 in   D

(1)   (2)   (3)

P3.135

P3.136 Air, assumed frictionless, flows through a tube, exiting to sea-level atmosphere. Diameters at 1 and 3 are 5 cm, while $D_2 = 3$ cm. What mass flow of air is required to suck water up 10 cm into section 2 of Fig. P3.136?

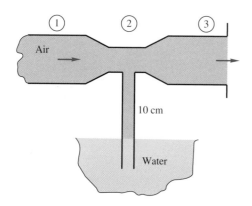

(1)   (2)   (3)

Air

10 cm

Water

P3.136

P3.137 In Fig. P3.137 the piston drives water at 20°C. Neglecting losses, estimate the exit velocity V_2 ft/s. If D_2 is further constricted, what is the limiting possible value of V_2?

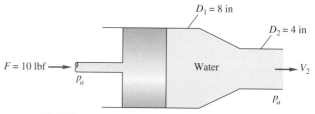

$D_1 = 8$ in

$D_2 = 4$ in

$F = 10$ lbf

p_a

Water

V_2

p_a

P3.137

P3.138 For the sluice gate flow of Example 3.10, use Bernoulli's equation, along the surface, to estimate the flow rate Q as a function of the two water depths. Assume constant width b.

P3.139 In the spillway flow of Fig. P3.139, the flow is assumed uniform and hydrostatic at sections 1 and 2. If losses are neglected, compute (a) V_2 and (b) the force per unit width of the water on the spillway.

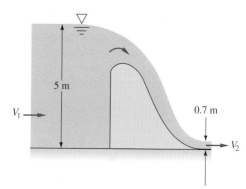

5 m

V_1

0.7 m

V_2

P3.139

P3.140 For the water channel flow of Fig. P3.140, $h_1 = 1.5$ m, $H = 4$ m, and $V_1 = 3$ m/s. Neglecting losses and assuming uniform flow at sections 1 and 2, find the downstream depth h_2, and show that *two* realistic solutions are possible.

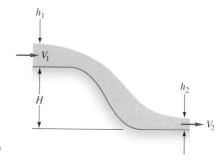

h_1

V_1

H

h_2

V_2

P3.140

P3.141 For the water channel flow of Fig. P3.141, $h_1 = 0.45$ ft, $H = 2.2$ ft, and $V_1 = 16$ ft/s. Neglecting losses and assuming uniform flow at sections 1 and 2, find the downstream depth h_2; show that *two* realistic solutions are possible.

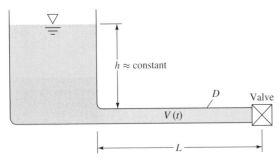

P3.141

*P3.142 A cylindrical tank of diameter D contains liquid to an initial height h_0. At time $t = 0$ a small stopper of diameter d is removed from the bottom. Using Bernoulli's equation with no losses, derive (a) a differential equation for the free-surface height $h(t)$ during draining and (b) an expression for the time t_0 to drain the entire tank.

*P3.143 The large tank of incompressible liquid in Fig. P3.143 is at rest when, at $t = 0$, the valve is opened to the atmosphere. Assuming $h \approx$ constant (negligible velocities and accelerations in the tank), use the unsteady frictionless Bernoulli equation to derive and solve a differential equation for $V(t)$ in the pipe.

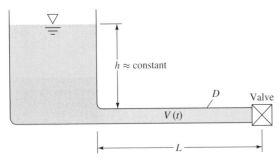

P3.143

P3.144 A fire hose, with a 2-in-diameter nozzle, delivers a water jet straight up against a ceiling 8 ft higher. The force on the ceiling, due to momentum change, is 25 lbf. Use Bernoulli's equation to estimate the hose flow rate, in gal/min. [*Hint:* The water jet area expands upward.]

P3.145 The incompressible flow form of Bernoulli's relation, Eq. (3.54), is accurate only for Mach numbers less than about 0.3. At higher speeds, variable density must be accounted for. The most common assumption for compressible fluids is *isentropic flow of an ideal gas,* or $p = C\rho^k$, where $k = c_p/c_v$. Substitute this relation into Eq. (3.52), integrate, and eliminate the constant C. Compare your compressible result with Eq. (3.54) and comment.

P3.146 The pump in Fig. P3.146 draws gasoline at 20°C from a reservoir. Pumps are in big trouble if the liquid vaporizes (cavitates) before it enters the pump. (a) Neglecting losses and assuming a flow rate of 65 gal/min, find the limitations on (x, y, z) for avoiding cavitation. (b) If pipe friction losses are included, what additional limitations might be important?

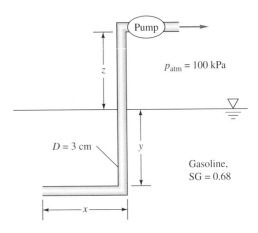

P3.146

P3.147 The very large water tank in Fig. P3.147 is discharging through a 4-in-diameter pipe. The pump is running, with a performance curve $h_p \approx 40 - 4Q^2$, with h_p in feet and Q in ft³/s. Estimate the discharge flow rate in ft³/s if the pipe friction loss is $1.5(V^2/2g)$.

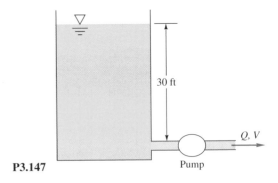

P3.147

P3.148 By neglecting friction, (a) use the Bernoulli equation between surfaces 1 and 2 to estimate the volume flow through the orifice, whose diameter is 3 cm. (b) Why is the result to part (a) absurd? (c) Suggest a way to resolve this paradox and find the true flow rate.

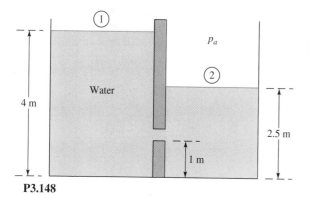

P3.148

The angular momentum theorem

P3.149 The horizontal lawn sprinkler in Fig. P3.149 has a water flow rate of 4.0 gal/min introduced vertically through the center. Estimate (a) the retarding torque required to keep the arms from rotating and (b) the rotation rate (r/min) if there is no retarding torque.

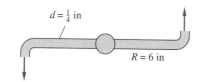

P3.149

P3.150 In Prob. P3.60 find the torque caused around flange 1 if the center point of exit 2 is 1.2 m directly below the flange center.

P3.151 The wye joint in Fig. P3.151 splits the pipe flow into equal amounts $Q/2$, which exit, as shown, a distance R_0 from the axis. Neglect gravity and friction. Find an expression for the torque T about the x axis required to keep the system rotating at angular velocity Ω.

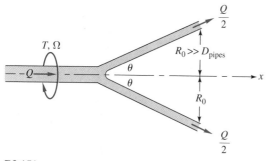

P3.151

P3.152 Modify Example 3.19 so that the arm starts from rest and spins up to its final rotation speed. The moment of inertia of the arm about O is I_0. Neglecting air drag, find $d\omega/dt$ and

integrate to determine the angular velocity $\omega(t)$, assuming $\omega = 0$ at $t = 0$.

P3.153 The three-arm lawn sprinkler of Fig. P3.153 receives 20°C water through the center at 2.7 m³/h. If collar friction is negligible, what is the steady rotation rate in r/min for (a) $\theta = 0°$ and (b) $\theta = 40°$?

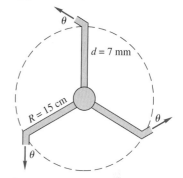

P3.153

P3.154 Water at 20°C flows at 30 gal/min through the 0.75-in-diameter double pipe bend of Fig. P3.154. The pressures are $p_1 = 30$ lbf/in² and $p_2 = 24$ lbf/in². Compute the torque T at point B necessary to keep the pipe from rotating.

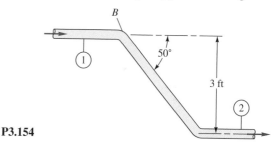

P3.154

P3.155 The centrifugal pump of Fig. P3.155 has a flow rate Q and exits the impeller at an angle θ_2 relative to the blades, as shown. The fluid enters axially at section 1. Assuming incompressible flow at shaft angular velocity ω, derive a formula for the power P required to drive the impeller.

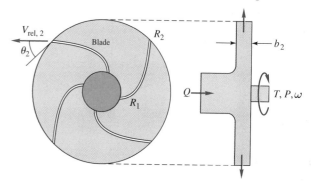

P3.155

P3.156 A simple turbomachine is constructed from a disk with two internal ducts that exit tangentially through square holes, as in Fig. P3.156. Water at 20°C enters normal to the disk at the center, as shown. The disk must drive, at 250 r/min, a small device whose retarding torque is 1.5 N · m. What is the proper mass flow of water, in kg/s?

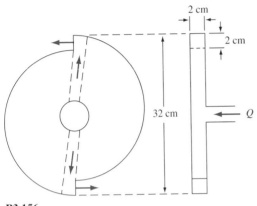

P3.156

P3.157 Reverse the flow in Fig. P3.155, so that the system operates as a radial-inflow *turbine*. Assuming that the outflow into section 1 has no tangential velocity, derive an expression for the power P extracted by the turbine.

P3.158 Revisit the turbine cascade system of Prob. P3.78, and derive a formula for the power P delivered, using the *angular* momentum theorem of Eq. (3.59).

P3.159 A centrifugal pump impeller delivers 4000 gal/min of water at 20°C with a shaft rotation rate of 1750 r/min. Neglect losses. If $r_1 = 6$ in, $r_2 = 14$ in, $b_1 = b_2 = 1.75$ in, $V_{t1} = 10$ ft/s, and $V_{t2} = 110$ ft/s, compute the absolute velocities (a) V_1 and (b) V_2 and (c) the horsepower required. (d) Compare with the ideal horsepower required.

P3.160 The pipe bend of Fig. P3.160 has $D_1 = 27$ cm and $D_2 = 13$ cm. When water at 20°C flows through the pipe at 4000 gal/min, $p_1 = 194$ kPa (gage). Compute the torque required at point B to hold the bend stationary.

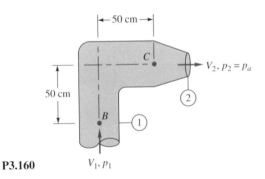

P3.160

*P3.161 Extend Prob. P3.46 to the problem of computing the center of pressure L of the normal face F_n, as in Fig. P3.161. (At the center of pressure, no moments are required to hold the plate at rest.) Neglect friction. Express your result in terms of the sheet thickness h_1 and the angle θ between the plate and the oncoming jet 1.

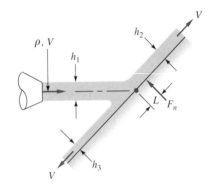

P3.161

P3.162 The waterwheel in Fig. P3.162 is being driven at 200 r/min by a 150-ft/s jet of water at 20°C. The jet diameter is 2.5 in. Assuming no losses, what is the horsepower developed by the wheel? For what speed Ω r/min will the horsepower developed be a maximum? Assume that there are many buckets on the waterwheel.

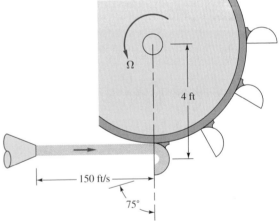

P3.162

P3.163 A rotating dishwasher arm delivers at 60°C to six nozzles, as in Fig. P3.163. The total flow rate is 3.0 gal/min. Each nozzle has a diameter of $\frac{3}{16}$ in. If the nozzle flows are equal and friction is neglected, estimate the steady rotation rate of the arm, in r/min.

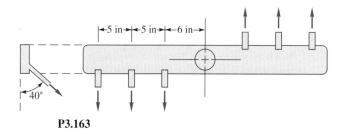

P3.163

*P3.164 A liquid of density ρ flows through a 90° bend as shown in Fig. P3.164 and issues vertically from a uniformly porous section of length L. Neglecting pipe and liquid weight, derive an expression for the torque M at point 0 required to hold the pipe stationary.

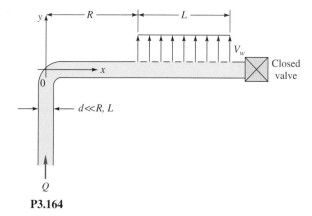

P3.164

The energy equation

P3.165 There is a steady isothermal flow of water at 20°C through the device in Fig. P3.165. Heat-transfer, gravity, and temperature effects are negligible. Known data are $D_1 = 9$ cm, $Q_1 = 220$ m³/h, $p_1 = 150$ kPa, $D_2 = 7$ cm, $Q_2 = 100$ m³/h, $p_2 = 225$ kPa, $D_3 = 4$ cm, and $p_3 = 265$ kPa. Compute the rate of shaft work done for this device and its direction.

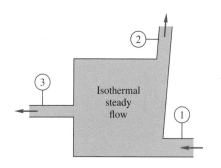

P3.165

P3.166 A power plant on a river, as in Fig. P3.166, must eliminate 55 MW of waste heat to the river. The river conditions

upstream are $Q_i = 2.5$ m³/s and $T_i = 18$°C. The river is 45 m wide and 2.7 m deep. If heat losses to the atmosphere and ground are negligible, estimate the downstream river conditions (Q_0, T_0).

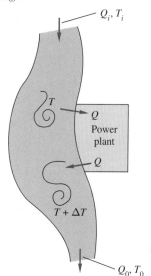

P3.166

P3.167 For the conditions of Prob. P3.166, if the power plant is to heat the nearby river water by no more than 12°C, what should be the minimum flow rate Q, in m³/s, through the plant heat exchanger? How will the value of Q affect the downstream conditions (Q_0, T_0)?

P3.168 Multnomah Falls in the Columbia River Gorge has a sheer drop of 543 ft. Using the steady flow energy equation, estimate the water temperature change in °F caused by this drop.

P3.169 When the pump in Fig. P3.169 draws 220 m³/h of water at 20°C from the reservoir, the total friction head loss is 5 m. The flow discharges through a nozzle to the atmosphere. Estimate the pump power in kW delivered to the water.

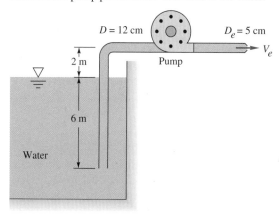

P3.169

P3.170 A steam turbine operates steadily under the following conditions. At the inlet, $p = 2.5$ MPa, $T = 450°C$, and $V = 40$ m/s. At the outlet, $p = 22$ kPa, $T = 70°C$, and $V = 225$ m/s. (a) If we neglect elevation changes and heat transfer, how much work is delivered to the turbine blades, in kJ/kg? (b) If the mass flow is 10 kg/s, how much total power is delivered? (c) Is the steam wet as it leaves the exit?

P3.171 Consider a turbine extracting energy from a penstock in a dam, as in Fig. P3.171. For turbulent pipe flow (Chap. 6), the friction head loss is approximately $h_f = CQ^2$, where the constant C depends on penstock dimensions and the properties of water. Show that, for a given penstock geometry and variable river flow Q, the maximum turbine power possible in this case is $P_{max} = 2\rho g H Q/3$ and occurs when the flow rate is $Q = \sqrt{H/(3C)}$.

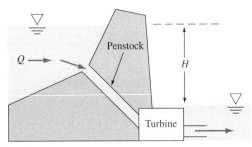

P3.171

P3.172 The long pipe in Fig. P3.172 is filled with water at 20°C. When valve A is closed, $p_1 - p_2 = 75$ kPa. When the valve is open and water flows at 500 m³/h, $p_1 - p_2 = 160$ kPa. What is the friction head loss between 1 and 2, in m, for the flowing condition?

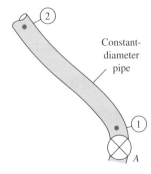

P3.172

P3.173 A 36-in-diameter pipeline carries oil (SG = 0.89) at 1 million barrels per day (bbl/day) (1 bbl = 42 U.S. gal). The friction head loss is 13 ft/1000 ft of pipe. It is planned to place pumping stations every 10 mi along the pipe. Estimate the horsepower that must be delivered to the oil by each pump.

P3.174 The *pump-turbine* system in Fig. P3.174 draws water from the upper reservoir in the daytime to produce power for a city. At night, it pumps water from lower to upper reservoirs to restore the situation. For a design flow rate of 15,000 gal/min in either direction, the friction head loss is 17 ft. Estimate the power in kW (a) extracted by the turbine and (b) delivered by the pump.

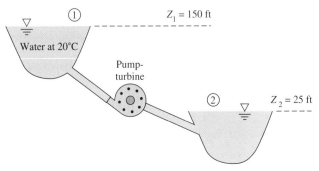

P3.174

P3.175 Water at 20°C is delivered from one reservoir to another through a long 8-cm-diameter pipe. The lower reservoir has a surface elevation $z_2 = 80$ m. The friction loss in the pipe is correlated by the formula $h_{loss} \approx 17.5(V^2/2g)$, where V is the average velocity in the pipe. If the steady flow rate through the pipe is 500 gallons per minute, estimate the surface elevation of the higher reservoir.

P3.176 A fireboat draws seawater (SG = 1.025) from a submerged pipe and discharges it through a nozzle, as in Fig. P3.176. The total head loss is 6.5 ft. If the pump efficiency is 75 percent, what horsepower motor is required to drive it?

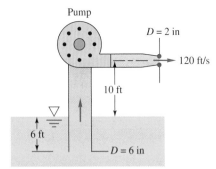

P3.176

P3.177 A device for measuring liquid viscosity is shown in Fig. P3.177. With the parameters (ρ, L, H, d) known, the flow rate Q is measured and the viscosity calculated, assuming a laminar-flow pipe loss from Chap. 6, $h_f = (32\mu LV)/(\rho g d^2)$. Heat transfer and all other losses are negligible. (a) Derive a formula for the viscosity μ of the fluid. (b) Calculate μ for the case $d = 2$ mm, $\rho = 800$ kg/m³, $L = 95$ cm, $H = 30$ cm, and $Q = 760$ cm^3/h. (*c*) What is your guess of the fluid in part (*b*)? (*d*) Verify that the Reynolds number Re$_d$ is less than 2000 (laminar pipe flow).

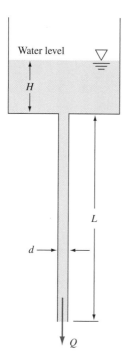

P3.177

P3.178 The horizontal pump in Fig. P3.178 discharges 20°C water at 57 m^3/h. Neglecting losses, what power in kW is delivered to the water by the pump?

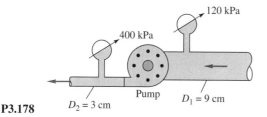

P3.178

P3.179 Steam enters a horizontal turbine at 350 lbf/in^2 absolute, 580°C, and 12 ft/s and is discharged at 110 ft/s and 25°C saturated conditions. The mass flow is 2.5 lbm/s, and the heat losses are 7 Btu/lb of steam. If head losses are negligible, how much horsepower does the turbine develop?

P3.180 Water at 20°C is pumped at 1500 gal/min from the lower to the upper reservoir, as in Fig. P3.180. Pipe friction losses are approximated by $h_f \approx 27V^2/(2g)$, where V is the average velocity in the pipe. If the pump is 75 percent efficient, what horsepower is needed to drive it?

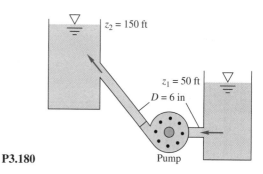

P3.180

P3.181 A typical pump has a head that, for a given shaft rotation rate, varies with the flow rate, resulting in a *pump performance curve* as in Fig. P3.181. Suppose that this pump is 75 percent efficient and is used for the system in Prob. 3.180. Estimate (*a*) the flow rate, in gal/min, and (*b*) the horsepower needed to drive the pump.

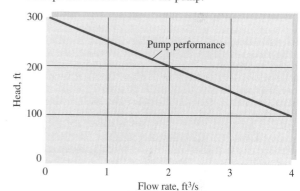

P3.181

P3.182 The insulated tank in Fig. P3.182 is to be filled from a high-pressure air supply. Initial conditions in the tank are $T = 20$°C and $p = 200$ kPa. When the valve is opened, the initial mass flow rate into the tank is 0.013 kg/s. Assuming an ideal gas, estimate the initial rate of temperature rise of the air in the tank.

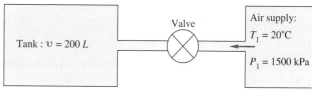

P3.182

P3.183 The pump in Fig. P3.183 creates a 20°C water jet oriented to travel a maximum horizontal distance. System friction head losses are 6.5 m. The jet may be approximated by the trajectory of frictionless particles. What power must be delivered by the pump?

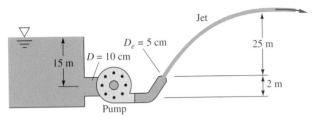

P3.183

P3.185 Kerosine at 20°C flows through the pump in Fig. P3.185 at 2.3 ft³/s. Head losses between 1 and 2 are 8 ft, and the pump delivers 8 hp to the flow. What should the mercury manometer reading h ft be?

P3.184 The large turbine in Fig. P3.184 diverts the river flow under a dam as shown. System friction losses are $h_f = 3.5V^2/(2g)$, where V is the average velocity in the supply pipe. For what river flow rate in m³/s will the power extracted be 25 MW? Which of the *two* possible solutions has a better "conversion efficiency"?

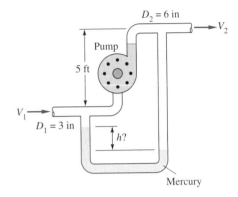

P3.185

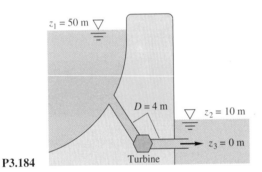

P3.184

Word Problems

W3.1 Derive a control volume form of the *second* law of thermodynamics. Suggest some practical uses for your relation in analyzing real fluid flows.

W3.2 Suppose that it is desired to estimate volume flow Q in a pipe by measuring the axial velocity $u(r)$ at specific points. For cost reasons only *three* measuring points are to be used. What are the best radii selections for these three points?

W3.3 Consider water flowing by gravity through a short pipe connecting two reservoirs whose surface levels differ by an amount Δz. Why does the incompressible frictionless Bernoulli equation lead to an absurdity when the flow rate through the pipe is computed? Does the paradox have something to do with the length of the short pipe? Does the paradox disappear if we round the entrance and exit edges of the pipe?

W3.4 Use the steady flow energy equation to analyze flow through a water faucet whose supply pressure is p_0. What physical mechanism causes the flow to vary continuously from zero to maximum as we open the faucet valve?

W3.5 Consider a long sewer pipe, half full of water, sloping downward at angle θ. Antoine Chézy in 1768 determined that the average velocity of such an open channel flow should be $V \approx C\sqrt{R \tan \theta}$, where R is the pipe radius and C is a constant. How does this famous formula relate to the steady flow energy equation applied to a length L of the channel?

W3.6 Put a table tennis ball in a funnel, and attach the small end of the funnel to an air supply. You probably won't be able to blow the ball either up or down out of the funnel. Explain why.

W3.7 How does a *siphon* work? Are there any limitations (such as how high or how low can you siphon water away from a tank)? Also, how far—could you use a flexible tube to siphon water from a tank to a point 100 ft away?

Fundamentals of Engineering Exam Problems

FE3.1 In Fig. FE3.1 water exits from a nozzle into atmospheric pressure of 101 kPa. If the flow rate is 160 gal/min, what is the average velocity at section 1?
(a) 2.6 m/s, (b) 0.81 m/s, (c) 93 m/s, (d) 23 m/s, (e) 1.62 m/s

FE3.2 In Fig. FE3.1 water exits from a nozzle into atmospheric pressure of 101 kPa. If the flow rate is 160 gal/min and friction is neglected, what is the gage pressure at section 1?
(a) 1.4 kPa, (b) 32 kPa, (c) 43 kPa, (d) 29 kPa, (e) 123 kPa

FE3.3 In Fig. FE3.1 water exits from a nozzle into atmospheric pressure of 101 kPa. If the exit velocity is $V_2 = 8$ m/s and friction is neglected, what is the axial flange force required to keep the nozzle attached to pipe 1?
(a) 11 N, (b) 56 N, (c) 83 N, (d) 123 N, (e) 110 N

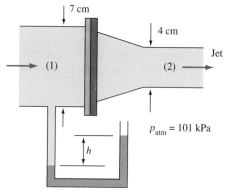

FE3.1

FE3.4 In Fig. FE3.1 water exits from a nozzle into atmospheric pressure of 101 kPa. If the manometer fluid has a specific gravity of 1.6 and $h = 66$ cm, with friction neglected, what is the average velocity at section 2?
(a) 4.55 m/s, (b) 2.4 m/s, (c) 2.95 m/s, (d) 5.55 m/s, (e) 3.4 m/s

FE3.5 A jet of water 3 cm in diameter strikes normal to a plate as in Fig. FE3.5. If the force required to hold the plate is 23 N, what is the jet velocity?
(a) 2.85 m/s, (b) 5.7 m/s, (c) 8.1 m/s, (d) 4.0 m/s, (e) 23 m/s

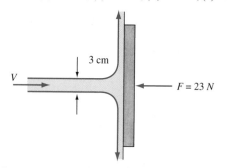

FE3.5

FE3.6 A fireboat pump delivers water to a vertical nozzle with a 3:1 diameter ratio, as in Fig. FE3.6. If friction is neglected and the flow rate is 500 gal/min, how high will the outlet water jet rise?
(a) 2.0 m, (b) 9.8 m, (c) 32 m, (d) 64 m, (e) 98 m

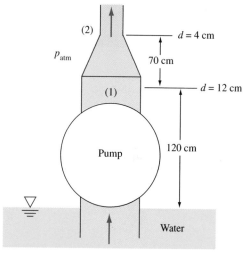

FE3.6

FE3.7 A fireboat pump delivers water to a vertical nozzle with a 3:1 diameter ratio, as in Fig. FE3.6. If friction is neglected and the pump increases the pressure at section 1 to 51 kPa (gage), what will be the resulting flow rate?
(a) 187 gal/min, (b) 199 gal/min, (c) 214 gal/min, (d) 359 gal/min, (e) 141 gal/min

FE3.8 A fireboat pump delivers water to a vertical nozzle with a 3:1 diameter ratio, as in Fig. FE3.6. If duct and nozzle friction are neglected and the pump provides 12.3 ft of head to the flow, what will be the outlet flow rate?
(a) 85 gal/min, (b) 120 gal/min, (c) 154 gal/min, (d) 217 gal/min, (e) 285 gal/min

FE3.9 Water flowing in a smooth 6-cm-diameter pipe enters a venturi contraction with a throat diameter of 3 cm. Upstream pressure is 120 kPa. If cavitation occurs in the throat at a flow rate of 155 gal/min, what is the estimated fluid vapor pressure, assuming ideal frictionless flow?
(a) 6 kPa, (b) 12 kPa, (c) 24 kPa, (d) 31 kPa, (e) 52 kPa

FE3.10 Water flowing in a smooth 6-cm-diameter pipe enters a venturi contraction with a throat diameter of 4 cm. Upstream pressure is 120 kPa. If the pressure in the throat is 50 kPa, what is the flow rate, assuming ideal frictionless flow?
(a) 7.5 gal/min, (b) 236 gal/min, (c) 263 gal/min, (d) 745 gal/min, (e) 1053 gal/min

Comprehensive Problems

C3.1   In a certain industrial process, oil of density ρ flows through the inclined pipe in Fig. C3.1. A U-tube manometer, with fluid density ρ_m, measures the pressure difference between points 1 and 2, as shown. The pipe flow is steady, so that the fluids in the manometer are stationary. (*a*) Find an analytic expression for $p_1 - p_2$ in terms of the system parameters. (*b*) Discuss the conditions on h necessary for there to be no flow in the pipe. (*c*) What about flow *up*, from 1 to 2? (*d*) What about flow *down*, from 2 to 1?

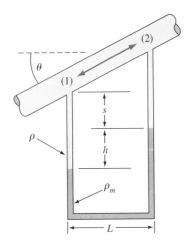

C3.1

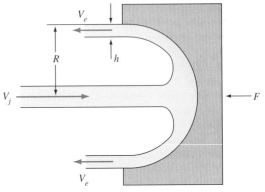

C3.3

C3.2   A rigid tank of volume $\mathcal{V} = 1.0 \text{ m}^3$ is initially filled with air at 20°C and $p_0 = 100$ kPa. At time $t = 0$, a vacuum pump is turned on and evacuates air at a constant volume flow rate $Q = 80$ L/min (regardless of the pressure). Assume an ideal gas and an isothermal process. (*a*) Set up a differential equation for this flow. (*b*) Solve this equation for t as a function of ($\mathcal{V}$, Q, p, p_0). (*c*) Compute the time in minutes to pump the tank down to $p = 20$ kPa. *Hint:* Your answer should lie between 15 and 25 min.

C3.3   Suppose the same steady water jet as in Prob. P3.40 (jet velocity 8 m/s and jet diameter 10 cm) impinges instead on a cup cavity as shown in Fig. C3.3. The water is turned 180° and exits, due to friction, at lower velocity, $V_e = 4$ m/s. (Looking from the left, the exit jet is a circular annulus of outer radius R and thickness h, flowing toward the viewer.) The cup has a radius of curvature of 25 cm. Find (*a*) the thickness h of the exit jet and (*b*) the force F required to hold the cupped object in place. (*c*) Compare part (*b*) to Prob. 3.40, where $F \approx 500$ N, and give a physical explanation as to why F has changed.

C3.4   The airflow underneath an air hockey puck is very complex, especially since the air jets from the air hockey table impinge on the underside of the puck at various points non-symmetrically. A reasonable approximation is that at any given time, the gage pressure on the bottom of the puck is halfway between zero (atmospheric pressure) and the stagnation pressure of the impinging jets. (Stagnation pressure is defined as $p_0 = \frac{1}{2}\rho V_{jet}^2$.) (*a*) Find the jet velocity V_{jet} required to support an air hockey puck of weight W and diameter d. Give your answer in terms of W, d, and the density ρ of the air. (*b*) For $W = 0.05$ lbf and $d = 2.5$ in, estimate the required jet velocity in ft/s.

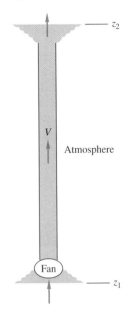

C3.5

C3.5   Neglecting friction sometimes leads to odd results. You are asked to analyze and discuss the following example in Fig. C3.5. A fan blows air through a duct from section 1 to section 2, as shown. Assume constant air density ρ.

Neglecting frictional losses, find a relation between the required fan head h_p and the flow rate and the elevation change. Then explain what may be an unexpected result.

Design Project

D3.1   Let us generalize Probs. P3.180 and P3.181, in which a pump performance curve was used to determine the flow rate between reservoirs. The particular pump in Fig. P3.181 is one of a family of pumps of similar shape, whose dimensionless performance is as follows:

Head:

$$\phi \approx 6.04 - 161\zeta \qquad \phi = \frac{gh}{n^2 D_p^2} \text{ and } \zeta = \frac{Q}{n D_p^3}$$

Efficiency:

$$\eta \approx 70\zeta - 91{,}500\zeta^3 \qquad \eta = \frac{\text{power to water}}{\text{power input}}$$

where h_p is the pump head (ft), n is the shaft rotation rate (r/s), and D_p is the impeller diameter (ft). The range of validity is $0 < \zeta < 0.027$. The pump of Fig. P3.181 had $D_p = 2$ ft in diameter and rotated at $n = 20$ r/s (1200 r/min). The solution to Prob. P3.181, namely, $Q \approx 2.57$ ft^3/s and $h_p \approx 172$ ft, corresponds to $\phi \approx 3.46$, $\zeta \approx 0.016$, $\eta \approx 0.75$ (or 75 percent), and power to the water $= \rho g Q h_p \approx 27{,}500$ ft · lbf/s (50 hp). Please check these numerical values before beginning this project.

Now revisit Prob. P3.181 and select a *low-cost* pump that rotates at a rate no slower than 600 r/min and delivers no less than 1.0 ft^3/s of water. Assume that the cost of the pump is linearly proportional to the power input required. Comment on any limitations to your results.

References

1. D. T. Greenwood, *Advanced Dynamics*, Cambridge University Press, New York, 2006.
2. T. von Kármán, *The Wind and Beyond*, Little, Brown, Boston, 1967.
3. J. P. Holman, *Heat Transfer*, 10th ed., McGraw-Hill, New York, 2009.
4. A. G. Hansen, *Fluid Mechanics*, Wiley, New York, 1967.
5. M. C. Potter, D. C. Wiggert, and M. Hondzo, *Mechanics of Fluids*, Brooks/Cole, Chicago, 2001.
6. S. Klein and G. Nellis, *Thermodynamics*, Cambridge University Press, New York, 2011.
7. Y. A. Cengel and M. A. Boles, *Thermodynamics: An Engineering Approach*, 7th ed., McGraw-Hill, New York, 2010.
8. J. F. Wendt, *Computational Fluid Dynamics: An Introduction*, Springer, 3d ed., New York, 2009.
9. W. G. Vincenti, "Control Volume Analysis: A Difference in Thinking between Engineering and Physics," *Technology and Culture,* vol. 23, no. 2, 1982, pp. 145–174.
10. J. Keenan, *Thermodynamics,* Wiley, New York, 1941.
11. J. Hunsaker and B. Rightmire, *Engineering Applications of Fluid Mechanics,* McGraw-Hill, New York, 1947.

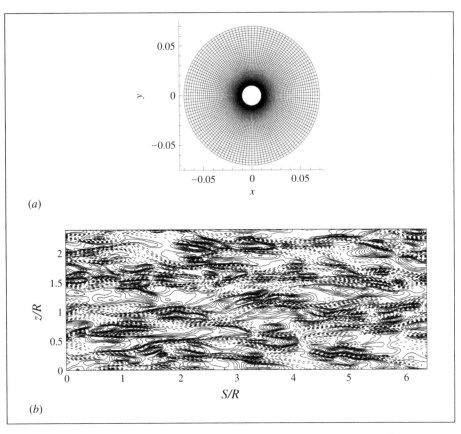

(a)

(b)

The differential equations to be studied in this chapter can be modeled numerically by computational fluid dynamics (CFD). This study, from Ref. 21, models turbulent flow near a rotating cylinder at a Reynolds number $\text{Re}_D \approx 8960$. The grid (a) contains 3.1 million nodes, very finely spaced near the cylinder. The results (b) show turbulent velocity fluctuations, obtained by direct numerical simulation (DNS), at $y^+ = 10$ away from the cylinder surface.

Source: From ASME J. Fluids Engineering, J-Y. Hwang, K-S. Yang, and K. Bremhorst, "Direct Numerical Simulation of Turbulent Flow Around a Rotating Circular Cylinder," Vol. 129, Jan. 2007, pp 40–47, by permission of the American Society of Mechanical Engineers.

Chapter 4
Differential Relations
for Fluid Flow

Motivation. In analyzing fluid motion, we might take one of two paths: (1) seeking an estimate of gross effects (mass flow, induced force, energy change) over a *finite* region or control volume or (2) seeking the point-by-point details of a flow pattern by analyzing an *infinitesimal* region of the flow. The former or gross-average viewpoint was the subject of Chap. 3.

This chapter treats the second in our trio of techniques for analyzing fluid motion: small-scale, or *differential,* analysis. That is, we apply our four basic conservation laws to an infinitesimally small control volume or, alternately, to an infinitesimal fluid system. In either case the results yield the basic *differential equations* of fluid motion. Appropriate *boundary conditions* are also developed.

In their most basic form, these differential equations of motion are quite difficult to solve, and very little is known about their general mathematical properties. However, certain things can be done that have great educational value. First, as shown in Chap. 5, the equations (even if unsolved) reveal the basic dimensionless parameters that govern fluid motion. Second, as shown in Chap. 6, a great number of useful solutions can be found if one makes two simplifying assumptions: (1) steady flow and (2) incompressible flow. A third and rather drastic simplification, frictionless flow, makes our old friend the Bernoulli equation valid and yields a wide variety of idealized, or *perfect-fluid,* possible solutions. These idealized flows are treated in Chap. 8, and we must be careful to ascertain whether such solutions are in fact realistic when compared with actual fluid motion. Finally, even the difficult general differential equations now yield to the approximating technique known as computational fluid dynamics (CFD) whereby the derivatives are simulated by algebraic relations between a finite number of grid points in the flow field, which are then solved on a computer. Reference 1 is an example of a textbook devoted entirely to numerical analysis of fluid motion.

4.1 The Acceleration Field of a Fluid

In Sec. 1.7 we established the cartesian vector form of a velocity field that varies in space and time:

$$\mathbf{V}(\mathbf{r}, t) = \mathbf{i}u(x, y, z, t) + \mathbf{j}\upsilon(x, y, z, t) + \mathbf{k}w(x, y, z, t) \qquad (1.4)$$

This is the most important variable in fluid mechanics: Knowledge of the velocity vector field is nearly equivalent to *solving* a fluid flow problem. Our coordinates are fixed in space, and we observe the fluid as it passes by—as if we had scribed a set of coordinate lines on a glass window in a wind tunnel. This is the *Eulerian* frame of reference, as opposed to the Lagrangian frame, which follows the moving position of individual particles.

The Eulerian system can be visualized as a window through which we watch a flow. The coordinates (x, y, z) are fixed, and the flow passes by. A fixed instrument placed in the flow takes an Eulerian measurement. In contrast, Lagrangian coordinates follow the moving particles and are common in solid mechanics. Almost all articles and books about fluid mechanics use the Eulerian system. Writers often use *traffic* as an example. A traffic engineer will remain fixed and will measure the flow of cars going by—an Eulerian viewpoint. Conversely, the police will follow specific cars as a function of time—a Lagrangian viewpoint.

To write Newton's second law for an infinitesimal fluid system, we need to calculate the acceleration vector field $\mathbf{a}$ of the flow. Thus, we compute the total time derivative of the velocity vector:

$$\mathbf{a} = \frac{d\mathbf{V}}{dt} = \mathbf{i}\frac{du}{dt} + \mathbf{j}\frac{d\upsilon}{dt} + \mathbf{k}\frac{dw}{dt}$$

Since each scalar component (u, υ, w) is a function of the four variables (x, y, z, t), we use the chain rule to obtain each scalar time derivative. For example,

$$\frac{du(x, y, z, t)}{dt} = \frac{\partial u}{\partial t} + \frac{\partial u}{\partial x}\frac{dx}{dt} + \frac{\partial u}{\partial y}\frac{dy}{dt} + \frac{\partial u}{\partial z}\frac{dz}{dt}$$

But, by definition, dx/dt is the local velocity component u, and $dy/dt = \upsilon$, and $dz/dt = w$. The total time derivative of u may thus be written as follows, with exactly similar expressions for the time derivatives of υ and w:

$$a_x = \frac{du}{dt} = \frac{\partial u}{\partial t} + u\frac{\partial u}{\partial x} + \upsilon\frac{\partial u}{\partial y} + w\frac{\partial u}{\partial z} = \frac{\partial u}{\partial t} + (\mathbf{V} \cdot \nabla)u$$

$$a_y = \frac{d\upsilon}{dt} = \frac{\partial \upsilon}{\partial t} + u\frac{\partial \upsilon}{\partial x} + \upsilon\frac{\partial \upsilon}{\partial y} + w\frac{\partial \upsilon}{\partial z} = \frac{\partial \upsilon}{\partial t} + (\mathbf{V} \cdot \nabla)\upsilon \qquad (4.1)$$

$$a_z = \frac{dw}{dt} = \frac{\partial w}{\partial t} + u\frac{\partial w}{\partial x} + \upsilon\frac{\partial w}{\partial y} + w\frac{\partial w}{\partial z} = \frac{\partial w}{\partial t} + (\mathbf{V} \cdot \nabla)w$$

Summing these into a vector, we obtain the total acceleration:

$$\mathbf{a} = \frac{d\mathbf{V}}{dt} = \underbrace{\frac{\partial \mathbf{V}}{\partial t}}_{\text{Local}} + \underbrace{\left(u\frac{\partial \mathbf{V}}{\partial x} + \upsilon\frac{\partial \mathbf{V}}{\partial y} + w\frac{\partial \mathbf{V}}{\partial z} \right)}_{\text{Convective}} = \frac{\partial \mathbf{V}}{\partial t} + (\mathbf{V} \cdot \nabla)\mathbf{V} \qquad (4.2)$$

The term $\partial \mathbf{V}/\partial t$ is called the *local acceleration,* which vanishes if the flow is steady—that is, independent of time. The three terms in parentheses are called the *convective acceleration,* which arises when the particle moves through regions of spatially varying velocity, as in a nozzle or diffuser. Flows that are nominally "steady" may have large accelerations due to the convective terms.

Note our use of the compact dot product involving $\mathbf{V}$ and the gradient operator ∇:

$$u\frac{\partial}{\partial x} + v\frac{\partial}{\partial y} + w\frac{\partial}{\partial z} = \mathbf{V} \cdot \nabla \qquad \text{where} \qquad \nabla = \mathbf{i}\frac{\partial}{\partial x} + \mathbf{j}\frac{\partial}{\partial y} + \mathbf{k}\frac{\partial}{\partial z}$$

The total time derivative—sometimes called the *substantial* or *material* derivative—concept may be applied to any variable, such as the pressure:

$$\frac{dp}{dt} = \frac{\partial p}{\partial t} + u\frac{\partial p}{\partial x} + v\frac{\partial p}{\partial y} + w\frac{\partial p}{\partial z} = \frac{\partial p}{\partial t} + (\mathbf{V} \cdot \nabla)p \tag{4.3}$$

Wherever convective effects occur in the basic laws involving mass, momentum, or energy, the basic differential equations become nonlinear and are usually more complicated than flows that do not involve convective changes.

We emphasize that this total time derivative follows a particle of fixed identity, making it convenient for expressing laws of particle mechanics in the eulerian fluid field description. The operator d/dt is sometimes assigned a special symbol such as D/Dt as a further reminder that it contains four terms and follows a fixed particle.

As another reminder of the special nature of d/dt, some writers give it the name *substantial* or *material derivative.*

EXAMPLE 4.1

Given the Eulerian velocity vector field

$$\mathbf{V} = 3t\mathbf{i} + xz\mathbf{j} + ty^2\mathbf{k}$$

find the total acceleration of a particle.

Solution

- *Assumptions:* Given three known unsteady velocity components, $u = 3t$, $v = xz$, and $w = ty^2$.
- *Approach:* Carry out all the required derivatives with respect to (x, y, z, t), substitute into the total acceleration vector, Eq. (4.2), and collect terms.
- *Solution step 1:* First work out the local acceleration $\partial \mathbf{V}/\partial t$:

$$\frac{\partial \mathbf{V}}{\partial t} = \mathbf{i}\frac{\partial u}{\partial t} + \mathbf{j}\frac{\partial v}{\partial t} + \mathbf{k}\frac{\partial w}{\partial t} = \mathbf{i}\frac{\partial}{\partial t}(3t) + \mathbf{j}\frac{\partial}{\partial t}(xz) + \mathbf{k}\frac{\partial}{\partial t}(ty^2) = 3\mathbf{i} + 0\mathbf{j} + y^2\mathbf{k}$$

- *Solution step 2:* In a similar manner, the convective acceleration terms, from Eq. (4.2), are

$$u\frac{\partial \mathbf{V}}{\partial x} = (3t)\frac{\partial}{\partial x}(3t\mathbf{i} + xz\mathbf{j} + ty^2\mathbf{k}) = (3t)(0\mathbf{i} + z\mathbf{j} + 0\mathbf{k}) = 3tz\,\mathbf{j}$$

$$v\frac{\partial \mathbf{V}}{\partial y} = (xz)\frac{\partial}{\partial y}(3t\mathbf{i} + xz\mathbf{j} + ty^2\mathbf{k}) = (xz)(0\mathbf{i} + 0\mathbf{j} + 2ty\mathbf{k}) = 2txyz\,\mathbf{k}$$

$$w\frac{\partial \mathbf{V}}{\partial z} = (ty^2)\frac{\partial}{\partial z}(3t\mathbf{i} + xz\mathbf{j} + ty^2\mathbf{k}) = (ty^2)(0\mathbf{i} + x\mathbf{j} + 0\mathbf{k}) = txy^2\,\mathbf{j}$$

- *Solution step 3:* Combine all four terms above into the single "total" or "substantial" derivative:

$$\frac{d\mathbf{V}}{dt} = \frac{\partial \mathbf{V}}{\partial t} + u\frac{\partial \mathbf{V}}{\partial x} + v\frac{\partial \mathbf{V}}{\partial y} + w\frac{\partial \mathbf{V}}{\partial z} = (3\mathbf{i} + y^2\mathbf{k}) + 3tz\mathbf{j} + 2txyz\mathbf{k} + txy^2\mathbf{j}$$

$$= 3\mathbf{i} + (3tz + txy^2)\mathbf{j} + (y^2 + 2txyz)\mathbf{k} \qquad Ans.$$

- *Comments:* Assuming that $\mathbf{V}$ is valid everywhere as given, this total acceleration vector $d\mathbf{V}/dt$ applies to all positions and times within the flow field.

4.2 The Differential Equation of Mass Conservation

Conservation of mass, often called the *continuity* relation, states that the fluid mass cannot change. We apply this concept to a very small region. All the basic differential equations can be derived by considering either an elemental control volume or an elemental system. We choose an infinitesimal fixed control volume (dx, dy, dz), as in Fig. 4.1, and use our basic control volume relations from Chap. 3. The flow through each side of the element is approximately one-dimensional, and so the appropriate mass conservation relation to use here is

$$\int_{CV} \frac{\partial \rho}{\partial t}\, d\mathcal{V} + \sum_i (\rho_i A_i V_i)_{\text{out}} - \sum_i (\rho_i A_i V_i)_{\text{in}} = 0 \qquad (3.22)$$

The element is so small that the volume integral simply reduces to a differential term:

$$\int_{CV} \frac{\partial \rho}{\partial t}\, d\mathcal{V} \approx \frac{\partial \rho}{\partial t}\, dx\, dy\, dz$$

The mass flow terms occur on all six faces, three inlets and three outlets. We make use of the field or continuum concept from Chap. 1, where all fluid properties are considered to be uniformly varying functions of time and position, such as $\rho = \rho(x, y, z, t)$. Thus, if T is the temperature on the left face of the element in Fig. 4.1, the right face will have a slightly different temperature $T + (\partial T/\partial x)\, dx$. For mass conservation, if ρu is known on the left face, the value of this product on the right face is $\rho u + (\partial \rho u/\partial x)\, dx$.

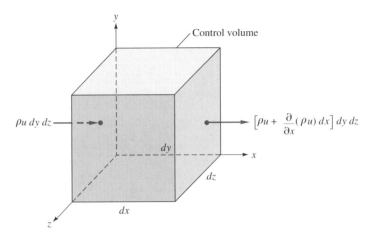

Fig. 4.1 Elemental cartesian fixed control volume showing the inlet and outlet mass flows on the x faces.

Figure 4.1 shows only the mass flows on the x or left and right faces. The flows on the y (bottom and top) and the z (back and front) faces have been omitted to avoid cluttering up the drawing. We can list all these six flows as follows:

Face	Inlet mass flow	Outlet mass flow
x	$\rho u \, dy \, dz$	$\left[\rho u + \dfrac{\partial}{\partial x} (\rho u) \, dx \right] dy \, dz$
y	$\rho v \, dx \, dz$	$\left[\rho v + \dfrac{\partial}{\partial y} (\rho v) \, dy \right] dx \, dz$
z	$\rho w \, dx \, dy$	$\left[\rho w + \dfrac{\partial}{\partial z} (\rho w) \, dz \right] dx \, dy$

Introduce these terms into Eq. (3.22) and we have

$$\frac{\partial \rho}{\partial t} dx \, dy \, dz + \frac{\partial}{\partial x} (\rho u) \, dx \, dy \, dz + \frac{\partial}{\partial y} (\rho v) \, dx \, dy \, dz + \frac{\partial}{\partial z} (\rho w) \, dx \, dy \, dz = 0$$

The element volume cancels out of all terms, leaving a partial differential equation involving the derivatives of density and velocity:

$$\frac{\partial \rho}{\partial t} + \frac{\partial}{\partial x} (\rho u) + \frac{\partial}{\partial y} (\rho v) + \frac{\partial}{\partial z} (\rho w) = 0 \qquad (4.4)$$

This is the desired result: conservation of mass for an infinitesimal control volume. It is often called the *equation of continuity* because it requires no assumptions except that the density and velocity are continuum functions. That is, the flow may be either steady or unsteady, viscous or frictionless, compressible or incompressible.[1] However, the equation does not allow for any source or sink singularities within the element.

The vector gradient operator

$$\nabla = \mathbf{i} \frac{\partial}{\partial x} + \mathbf{j} \frac{\partial}{\partial y} + \mathbf{k} \frac{\partial}{\partial z}$$

enables us to rewrite the equation of continuity in a compact form, not that it helps much in finding a solution. The last three terms of Eq. (4.4) are equivalent to the divergence of the vector $\rho \mathbf{V}$

$$\frac{\partial}{\partial x} (\rho u) + \frac{\partial}{\partial y} (\rho v) + \frac{\partial}{\partial z} (\rho w) \equiv \nabla \cdot (\rho \mathbf{V}) \qquad (4.5)$$

so the compact form of the continuity relation is

$$\frac{\partial \rho}{\partial t} + \nabla \cdot (\rho \mathbf{V}) = 0 \qquad (4.6)$$

In this vector form the equation is still quite general and can readily be converted to other coordinate systems.

---

[1] One case where Eq. (4.4) might need special care is *two-phase flow,* where the density is discontinuous between the phases. For further details on this case, see Ref. 2, for example.

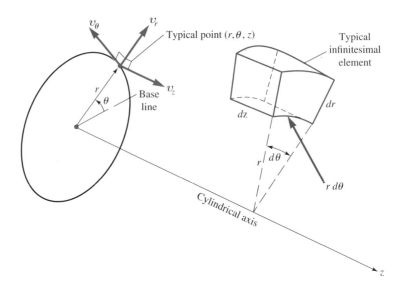

Fig. 4.2 Definition sketch for the cylindrical coordinate system.

Cylindrical Polar Coordinates

The most common alternative to the cartesian system is the *cylindrical polar* coordinate system, sketched in Fig. 4.2. An arbitrary point P is defined by a distance z along the axis, a radial distance r from the axis, and a rotation angle θ about the axis. The three independent orthogonal velocity components are an axial velocity v_z, a radial velocity v_r, and a circumferential velocity v_θ, which is positive counterclockwise—that is, in the direction of increasing θ. In general, all components, as well as pressure and density and other fluid properties, are continuous functions of r, θ, z, and t.

The divergence of any vector function $\mathbf{A}(r, \theta, z, t)$ is found by making the transformation of coordinates

$$r = (x^2 + y^2)^{1/2} \qquad \theta = \tan^{-1}\frac{y}{x} \qquad z = z \tag{4.7}$$

and the result is given here without proof[2]

$$\mathbf{\nabla} \cdot \mathbf{A} = \frac{1}{r}\frac{\partial}{\partial r}(rA_r) + \frac{1}{r}\frac{\partial}{\partial \theta}(A_\theta) + \frac{\partial}{\partial z}(A_z) \tag{4.8}$$

The general continuity equation (4.6) in cylindrical polar coordinates is thus

$$\frac{\partial \rho}{\partial t} + \frac{1}{r}\frac{\partial}{\partial r}(r\rho v_r) + \frac{1}{r}\frac{\partial}{\partial \theta}(\rho v_\theta) + \frac{\partial}{\partial z}(\rho v_z) = 0 \tag{4.9}$$

There are other orthogonal curvilinear coordinate systems, notably *spherical polar* coordinates, which occasionally merit use in a fluid mechanics problem. We shall not treat these systems here except in Prob. P4.12.

There are also other ways to derive the basic continuity equation (4.6) that are interesting and instructive. One example is the use of the divergence theorem. Ask your instructor about these alternative approaches.

[2]See, for example, Ref. 3.

Steady Compressible Flow

If the flow is steady, $\partial/\partial t \equiv 0$ and all properties are functions of position only. Equation (4.6) reduces to

Cartesian:
$$\frac{\partial}{\partial x}(\rho u) + \frac{\partial}{\partial y}(\rho v) + \frac{\partial}{\partial z}(\rho w) = 0$$

Cylindrical:
$$\frac{1}{r}\frac{\partial}{\partial r}(r\rho v_r) + \frac{1}{r}\frac{\partial}{\partial \theta}(\rho v_\theta) + \frac{\partial}{\partial z}(\rho v_z) = 0 \qquad (4.10)$$

Since density and velocity are both variables, these are still nonlinear and rather formidable, but a number of special-case solutions have been found.

Incompressible Flow

A special case that affords great simplification is incompressible flow, where the density changes are negligible. Then $\partial\rho/\partial t \approx 0$ regardless of whether the flow is steady or unsteady, and the density can be slipped out of the divergence in Eq. (4.6) and divided out. The result

$$\nabla \cdot \mathbf{V} = 0 \qquad (4.11)$$

is valid for steady or unsteady incompressible flow. The two coordinate forms are

Cartesian:
$$\frac{\partial u}{\partial x} + \frac{\partial v}{\partial y} + \frac{\partial w}{\partial z} = 0 \qquad (4.12a)$$

Cylindrical:
$$\frac{1}{r}\frac{\partial}{\partial r}(rv_r) + \frac{1}{r}\frac{\partial}{\partial \theta}(v_\theta) + \frac{\partial}{\partial z}(v_z) = 0 \qquad (4.12b)$$

These are *linear* differential equations, and a wide variety of solutions are known, as discussed in Chaps. 6 to 8. Since no author or instructor can resist a wide variety of solutions, it follows that a great deal of time is spent studying incompressible flows. Fortunately, this is exactly what should be done, because most practical engineering flows are approximately incompressible, the chief exception being the high-speed gas flows treated in Chap. 9.

When is a given flow approximately incompressible? We can derive a nice criterion by using some density approximations. In essence, we wish to slip the density out of the divergence in Eq. (4.6) and approximate a typical term such as

$$\frac{\partial}{\partial x}(\rho u) \approx \rho \frac{\partial u}{\partial x} \qquad (4.13)$$

This is equivalent to the strong inequality

$$\left| u \frac{\partial \rho}{\partial x} \right| \ll \left| \rho \frac{\partial u}{\partial x} \right|$$

or
$$\left| \frac{\delta\rho}{\rho} \right| \ll \left| \frac{\delta V}{V} \right| \qquad (4.14)$$

As shown in Eq. (1.38), the pressure change is approximately proportional to the density change and the square of the speed of sound a of the fluid:

$$\delta p \approx a^2 \, \delta\rho \qquad (4.15)$$

Meanwhile, if elevation changes are negligible, the pressure is related to the velocity change by Bernoulli's equation (3.52):

$$\delta p \approx -\rho V \, \delta V \qquad (4.16)$$

Combining Eqs. (4.14) to (4.16), we obtain an explicit criterion for incompressible flow:

$$\frac{V^2}{a^2} = \text{Ma}^2 \ll 1 \qquad (4.17)$$

where $\text{Ma} = V/a$ is the dimensionless *Mach number* of the flow. How small is small? The commonly accepted limit is

$$\text{Ma} \leq 0.3 \qquad (4.18)$$

For air at standard conditions, a flow can thus be considered incompressible if the velocity is less than about 100 m/s (330 ft/s). This encompasses a wide variety of airflows: automobile and train motions, light aircraft, landing and takeoff of high-speed aircraft, most pipe flows, and turbomachinery at moderate rotational speeds. Further, it is clear that almost all liquid flows are incompressible, since flow velocities are small and the speed of sound is very large.[3]

Before attempting to analyze the continuity equation, we shall proceed with the derivation of the momentum and energy equations, so that we can analyze them as a group. A very clever device called the *stream function* can often make short work of the continuity equation, but we shall save it until Sec. 4.7.

One further remark is appropriate: The continuity equation is always important and must always be satisfied for a rational analysis of a flow pattern. Any newly discovered momentum or energy "solution" will ultimately fail when subjected to critical analysis if it does not also satisfy the continuity equation.

EXAMPLE 4.2

Under what conditions does the velocity field

$$\mathbf{V} = (a_1 x + b_1 y + c_1 z)\mathbf{i} + (a_2 x + b_2 y + c_2 z)\mathbf{j} + (a_3 x + b_3 y + c_3 z)\mathbf{k}$$

where a_1, b_1, etc. = const, represent an incompressible flow that conserves mass?

Solution

Recalling that $\mathbf{V} = u\mathbf{i} + v\mathbf{j} + w\mathbf{k}$, we see that $u = (a_1 x + b_1 y + c_1 z)$, etc. Substituting into Eq. (4.12*a*) for incompressible continuity, we obtain

$$\frac{\partial}{\partial x}(a_1 x + b_1 y + c_1 z) + \frac{\partial}{\partial y}(a_2 x + b_2 y + c_2 z) + \frac{\partial}{\partial z}(a_3 x + b_3 y + c_3 z) = 0$$

or $\qquad\qquad\qquad\qquad\qquad a_1 + b_2 + c_3 = 0 \qquad\qquad\qquad\qquad\qquad$ *Ans.*

At least two of constants a_1, b_2, and c_3 must have opposite signs. Continuity imposes no restrictions whatever on constants b_1, c_1, a_2, c_2, a_3, and b_3, which do not contribute to a volume increase or decrease of a differential element.

---

[3]An exception occurs in geophysical flows, where a density change is imposed thermally or mechanically rather than by the flow conditions themselves. An example is fresh water layered upon saltwater or warm air layered upon cold air in the atmosphere. We say that the fluid is *stratified*, and we must account for vertical density changes in Eq. (4.6) even if the velocities are small.

EXAMPLE 4.3

An incompressible velocity field is given by

$$u = a(x^2 - y^2) \qquad v \text{ unknown} \qquad w = b$$

where a and b are constants. What must the form of the velocity component v be?

Solution

Again Eq. (4.12a) applies:

$$\frac{\partial}{\partial x}(ax^2 - ay^2) + \frac{\partial v}{\partial y} + \frac{\partial b}{\partial z} = 0$$

or
$$\frac{\partial v}{\partial y} = -2ax \qquad\qquad (1)$$

This is easily integrated partially with respect to y:

$$v(x, y, z, t) = -2axy + f(x, z, t) \qquad\qquad \textit{Ans.}$$

This is the only possible form for v that satisfies the incompressible continuity equation. The function of integration f is entirely arbitrary since it vanishes when v is differentiated with respect to y.[4]

EXAMPLE 4.4

A centrifugal impeller of 40-cm diameter is used to pump hydrogen at 15°C and 1-atm pressure. Estimate the maximum allowable impeller rotational speed to avoid compressibility effects at the blade tips.

Solution

- *Assumptions:* The maximum fluid velocity is approximately equal to the impeller tip speed:
$$V_{max} \approx \Omega r_{max} \qquad \text{where } r_{max} = D/2 = 0.20 \text{ m}$$

- *Approach:* Find the speed of sound of hydrogen and make sure that V_{max} is much less.
- *Property values:* From Table A.4 for hydrogen, $R = 4124 \text{ m}^2/(\text{s}^2 - \text{K})$ and $k = 1.41$. From Eq. (1.39) at 15°C = 288K, compute the speed of sound:

$$a_{H_2} = \sqrt{kRT} = \sqrt{1.41[4124 \text{ m}^2/(\text{s}^2 - \text{K})](288 \text{ K})} \approx 1294 \text{ m/s}$$

- *Final solution step:* Use our rule of thumb, Eq. (4.18), to estimate the maximum impeller speed:

$$V = \Omega r_{max} \le 0.3a \qquad \text{or} \qquad \Omega(0.2 \text{ m}) \le 0.3(1294 \text{ m/s})$$

$$\text{Solve for} \qquad \Omega \le 1940 \frac{\text{rad}}{\text{s}} \approx 18{,}500 \frac{\text{rev}}{\text{min}} \qquad\qquad \textit{Ans.}$$

- *Comments:* This is a high rate because the speed of sound of hydrogen, a light gas, is nearly four times greater than that of air. An impeller moving at this speed in air would create tip shock waves.

---

[4]This is a very realistic flow that simulates the turning of an inviscid fluid through a 60° angle; see Examples 4.7 and 4.9.

4.3 The Differential Equation of Linear Momentum

This section uses an elemental volume to derive Newton's law for a moving fluid. An alternate approach, which the reader might pursue, would be a force balance on an elemental moving particle. Having done it once in Sec. 4.2 for mass conservation, we can move along a little faster this time. We use the same elemental control volume as in Fig. 4.1, for which the appropriate form of the linear momentum relation is

$$\sum \mathbf{F} = \frac{\partial}{\partial t}\left(\int_{CV} \mathbf{V}\rho\, d\mathcal{V}\right) + \sum (\dot{m}_i\mathbf{V_i})_{\text{out}} - \sum (\dot{m}_i\mathbf{V_i})_{\text{in}} \qquad (3.40)$$

Again the element is so small that the volume integral simply reduces to a derivative term:

$$\frac{\partial}{\partial t}(\mathbf{V}\rho\, d\mathcal{V}) \approx \frac{\partial}{\partial t}(\rho\mathbf{V})\, dx\, dy\, dz \qquad (4.19)$$

The momentum fluxes occur on all six faces, three inlets and three outlets. Referring again to Fig. 4.1, we can form a table of momentum fluxes by exact analogy with the discussion that led up to the equation for net mass flux:

Faces	Inlet momentum flux	Outlet momentum flux
x	$\rho u\mathbf{V}\, dy\, dz$	$\left[\rho u\mathbf{V} + \dfrac{\partial}{\partial x}(\rho u\mathbf{V})\, dx\right] dy\, dz$
y	$\rho v\mathbf{V}\, dx\, dz$	$\left[\rho v\mathbf{V} + \dfrac{\partial}{\partial y}(\rho v\mathbf{V})\, dy\right] dx\, dz$
z	$\rho w\mathbf{V}\, dx\, dy$	$\left[\rho w\mathbf{V} + \dfrac{\partial}{\partial z}(\rho w\mathbf{V})\, dz\right] dx\, dy$

Introduce these terms and Eq. (4.19) into Eq. (3.40), and get this intermediate result:

$$\sum \mathbf{F} = dx\, dy\, dz\left[\frac{\partial}{\partial t}(\rho\mathbf{V}) + \frac{\partial}{\partial x}(\rho u\mathbf{V}) + \frac{\partial}{\partial y}(\rho v\mathbf{V}) + \frac{\partial}{\partial z}(\rho w\mathbf{V})\right] \qquad (4.20)$$

Note that this is a vector relation. A simplification occurs if we split up the term in brackets as follows:

$$\frac{\partial}{\partial t}(\rho\mathbf{V}) + \frac{\partial}{\partial x}(\rho u\mathbf{V}) + \frac{\partial}{\partial y}(\rho v\mathbf{V}) + \frac{\partial}{\partial z}(\rho w\mathbf{V})$$

$$= \mathbf{V}\left[\frac{\partial\rho}{\partial t} + \nabla\cdot(\rho\mathbf{V})\right] + \rho\left(\frac{\partial\mathbf{V}}{\partial t} + u\frac{\partial\mathbf{V}}{\partial x} + v\frac{\partial\mathbf{V}}{\partial y} + w\frac{\partial\mathbf{V}}{\partial z}\right) \qquad (4.21)$$

The term in brackets on the right-hand side is seen to be the equation of continuity, Eq. (4.6), which vanishes identically. The long term in parentheses on the right-hand side is seen from Eq. (4.2) to be the total acceleration of a particle that instantaneously occupies the control volume:

$$\frac{\partial\mathbf{V}}{\partial t} + u\frac{\partial\mathbf{V}}{\partial x} + v\frac{\partial\mathbf{V}}{\partial y} + w\frac{\partial\mathbf{V}}{\partial z} = \frac{d\mathbf{V}}{dt} \qquad (4.2)$$

Thus, we have now reduced Eq. (4.20) to

$$\sum \mathbf{F} = \rho\frac{d\mathbf{V}}{dt}\, dx\, dy\, dz \qquad (4.22)$$

It might be good for you to stop and rest now and think about what we have just done. What is the relation between Eqs. (4.22) and (3.40) for an infinitesimal control volume? Could we have *begun* the analysis at Eq. (4.22)?

Equation (4.22) points out that the net force on the control volume must be of differential size and proportional to the element volume. These forces are of two types, *body* forces and *surface* forces. Body forces are due to external fields (gravity, magnetism, electric potential) that act on the entire mass within the element. The only body force we shall consider in this book is gravity. The gravity force on the differential mass $\rho \, dx \, dy \, dz$ within the control volume is

$$d\mathbf{F}_{\text{grav}} = \rho \mathbf{g} \, dx \, dy \, dz \tag{4.23}$$

where $\mathbf{g}$ may in general have an arbitrary orientation with respect to the coordinate system. In many applications, such as Bernoulli's equation, we take z "up," and $\mathbf{g} = -g\mathbf{k}$.

The surface forces are due to the stresses on the sides of the control surface. These stresses are the sum of hydrostatic pressure plus viscous stresses τ_{ij} that arise from motion with velocity gradients:

$$\sigma_{ij} = \begin{vmatrix} -p + \tau_{xx} & \tau_{yx} & \tau_{zx} \\ \tau_{xy} & -p + \tau_{yy} & \tau_{zy} \\ \tau_{xz} & \tau_{yz} & -p + \tau_{zz} \end{vmatrix} \tag{4.24}$$

The subscript notation for stresses is given in Fig. 4.3. Unlike velocity $\mathbf{V}$, which is a three-component *vector*, stresses σ_{ij} and τ_{ij} and strain rates ε_{ij} are nine-component *tensors* and require two subscripts to define each component. For further study of *tensor analysis,* see Refs. 6, 11, or 13.

It is not these stresses but their *gradients,* or differences, that cause a net force on the differential control surface. This is seen by referring to Fig. 4.4, which shows only

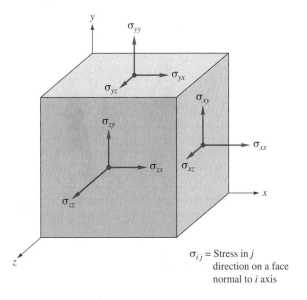

$$\sigma_{ij} = \text{Stress in } j$$
direction on a face
normal to i axis

Fig. 4.3 Notation for stresses.

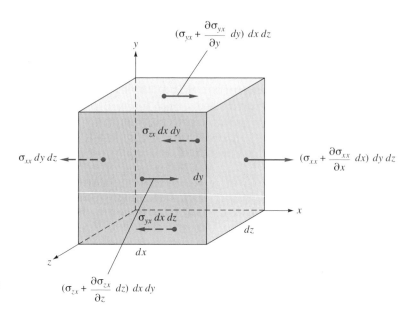

Fig. 4.4 Elemental cartesian fixed control volume showing the surface forces in the x direction only.

the x-directed stresses to avoid cluttering up the drawing. For example, the leftward force $\sigma_{xx}\, dy\, dz$ on the left face is balanced by the rightward force $\sigma_{xx}\, dy\, dz$ on the right face, leaving only the net rightward force $(\partial\sigma_{xx}/\partial x)\, dx\, dy\, dz$ on the right face. The same thing happens on the other four faces, so the net surface force in the x direction is given by

$$dF_{x,\text{surf}} = \left[\frac{\partial}{\partial x}(\sigma_{xx}) + \frac{\partial}{\partial y}(\sigma_{yx}) + \frac{\partial}{\partial z}(\sigma_{zx}) \right] dx\, dy\, dz \qquad (4.25)$$

We see that this force is proportional to the element volume. Notice that the stress terms are taken from the *top row* of the array in Eq. (4.24). Splitting this row into pressure plus viscous stresses, we can rewrite Eq. (4.25) as

$$\frac{dF_x}{d\mathcal{V}} = -\frac{\partial p}{\partial x} + \frac{\partial}{\partial x}(\tau_{xx}) + \frac{\partial}{\partial y}(\tau_{yx}) + \frac{\partial}{\partial z}(\tau_{zx}) \qquad (4.26)$$

where $d\mathcal{V} = dx\, dy\, dz$. In an exactly similar manner, we can derive the y and z forces per unit volume on the control surface:

$$\frac{dF_y}{d\mathcal{V}} = -\frac{\partial p}{\partial y} + \frac{\partial}{\partial x}(\tau_{xy}) + \frac{\partial}{\partial y}(\tau_{yy}) + \frac{\partial}{\partial z}(\tau_{zy})$$

$$\frac{dF_z}{d\mathcal{V}} = -\frac{\partial p}{\partial z} + \frac{\partial}{\partial x}(\tau_{xz}) + \frac{\partial}{\partial y}(\tau_{yz}) + \frac{\partial}{\partial z}(\tau_{zz}) \qquad (4.27)$$

Now we multiply Eqs. (4.26) and (4.27) by $\mathbf{i}$, $\mathbf{j}$, and $\mathbf{k}$, respectively, and add to obtain an expression for the net vector surface force:

$$\left(\frac{d\mathbf{F}}{d\mathcal{V}} \right)_{\text{surf}} = -\boldsymbol{\nabla}p + \left(\frac{d\mathbf{F}}{d\mathcal{V}} \right)_{\text{viscous}} \qquad (4.28)$$

where the viscous force has a total of nine terms:

$$\left(\frac{d\mathbf{F}}{d\mathcal{V}}\right)_{\text{viscous}} = \mathbf{i}\left(\frac{\partial \tau_{xx}}{\partial x} + \frac{\partial \tau_{yx}}{\partial y} + \frac{\partial \tau_{zx}}{\partial z}\right)$$
$$+ \mathbf{j}\left(\frac{\partial \tau_{xy}}{\partial x} + \frac{\partial \tau_{yy}}{\partial y} + \frac{\partial \tau_{zy}}{\partial z}\right)$$
$$+ \mathbf{k}\left(\frac{\partial \tau_{xz}}{\partial x} + \frac{\partial \tau_{yz}}{\partial y} + \frac{\partial \tau_{zz}}{\partial z}\right) \tag{4.29}$$

Since each term in parentheses in Eq. (4.29) represents the divergence of a stress component vector acting on the x, y, and z faces, respectively, Eq. (4.29) is sometimes expressed in divergence form:

$$\left(\frac{d\mathbf{F}}{d\mathcal{V}}\right)_{\text{viscous}} = \boldsymbol{\nabla} \cdot \boldsymbol{\tau}_{ij} \tag{4.30}$$

where

$$\tau_{ij} = \begin{bmatrix} \tau_{xx} & \tau_{yx} & \tau_{zx} \\ \tau_{xy} & \tau_{yy} & \tau_{zy} \\ \tau_{xz} & \tau_{yz} & \tau_{zz} \end{bmatrix} \tag{4.31}$$

is the viscous stress tensor acting on the element. The surface force is thus the sum of the *pressure gradient* vector and the divergence of the viscous stress tensor. Substituting into Eq. (4.22) and utilizing Eq. (4.23), we have the basic differential momentum equation for an infinitesimal element:

$$\rho\mathbf{g} - \boldsymbol{\nabla}p + \boldsymbol{\nabla} \cdot \boldsymbol{\tau}_{ij} = \rho\frac{d\mathbf{V}}{dt} \tag{4.32}$$

where

$$\frac{d\mathbf{V}}{dt} = \frac{\partial \mathbf{V}}{\partial t} + u\frac{\partial \mathbf{V}}{\partial x} + v\frac{\partial \mathbf{V}}{\partial y} + w\frac{\partial \mathbf{V}}{\partial z} \tag{4.33}$$

We can also express Eq. (4.32) in words:

Gravity force per unit volume + pressure force per unit volume
+ viscous force per unit volume = density × acceleration (4.34)

Equation (4.32) is so brief and compact that its inherent complexity is almost invisible. It is a *vector* equation, each of whose component equations contains nine terms. Let us therefore write out the component equations in full to illustrate the mathematical difficulties inherent in the momentum equation:

$$\rho g_x - \frac{\partial p}{\partial x} + \frac{\partial \tau_{xx}}{\partial x} + \frac{\partial \tau_{yx}}{\partial y} + \frac{\partial \tau_{zx}}{\partial z} = \rho\left(\frac{\partial u}{\partial t} + u\frac{\partial u}{\partial x} + v\frac{\partial u}{\partial y} + w\frac{\partial u}{\partial z}\right)$$

$$\rho g_y - \frac{\partial p}{\partial y} + \frac{\partial \tau_{xy}}{\partial x} + \frac{\partial \tau_{yy}}{\partial y} + \frac{\partial \tau_{zy}}{\partial z} = \rho\left(\frac{\partial v}{\partial t} + u\frac{\partial v}{\partial x} + v\frac{\partial v}{\partial y} + w\frac{\partial v}{\partial z}\right) \tag{4.35}$$

$$\rho g_z - \frac{\partial p}{\partial z} + \frac{\partial \tau_{xz}}{\partial x} + \frac{\partial \tau_{yz}}{\partial y} + \frac{\partial \tau_{zz}}{\partial z} = \rho\left(\frac{\partial w}{\partial t} + u\frac{\partial w}{\partial x} + v\frac{\partial w}{\partial y} + w\frac{\partial w}{\partial z}\right)$$

This is the differential momentum equation in its full glory, and it is valid for any fluid in any general motion, particular fluids being characterized by particular viscous stress terms. Note that the last three "convective" terms on the right-hand side of each component equation in (4.35) are nonlinear, which complicates the general mathematical analysis.

Inviscid Flow: Euler's Equation

Equation (4.35) is not ready to use until we write the viscous stresses in terms of velocity components. The simplest assumption is frictionless flow $\tau_{ij} = 0$, for which Eq. (4.32) reduces to

$$\rho \mathbf{g} - \nabla p = \rho \frac{d\mathbf{V}}{dt} \tag{4.36}$$

This is *Euler's equation* for inviscid flow. We show in Sec. 4.9 that Euler's equation can be integrated along a streamline to yield the frictionless Bernoulli equation, (3.52) or (3.54). The complete analysis of inviscid flow fields, using continuity and the Bernoulli relation, is given in Chap. 8.

Newtonian Fluid: Navier-Stokes Equations

For a newtonian fluid, as discussed in Sec. 1.9, the viscous stresses are proportional to the element strain rates and the coefficient of viscosity. For incompressible flow, the generalization of Eq. (1.23) to three-dimensional viscous flow is[5]

$$\tau_{xx} = 2\mu \frac{\partial u}{\partial x} \quad \tau_{yy} = 2\mu \frac{\partial v}{\partial y} \quad \tau_{zz} = 2\mu \frac{\partial w}{\partial z}$$

$$\tau_{xy} = \tau_{yx} = \mu \left(\frac{\partial u}{\partial y} + \frac{\partial v}{\partial x} \right) \quad \tau_{xz} = \tau_{zx} = \mu \left(\frac{\partial w}{\partial x} + \frac{\partial u}{\partial z} \right) \tag{4.37}$$

$$\tau_{yz} = \tau_{zy} = \mu \left(\frac{\partial v}{\partial z} + \frac{\partial w}{\partial y} \right)$$

where μ is the viscosity coefficient. Substitution into Eq. (4.35) gives the differential momentum equation for a newtonian fluid with constant density and viscosity:

$$\rho g_x - \frac{\partial p}{\partial x} + \mu \left(\frac{\partial^2 u}{\partial x^2} + \frac{\partial^2 u}{\partial y^2} + \frac{\partial^2 u}{\partial z^2} \right) = \rho \frac{du}{dt}$$

$$\rho g_y - \frac{\partial p}{\partial y} + \mu \left(\frac{\partial^2 v}{\partial x^2} + \frac{\partial^2 v}{\partial y^2} + \frac{\partial^2 v}{\partial z^2} \right) = \rho \frac{dv}{dt} \tag{4.38}$$

$$\rho g_z - \frac{\partial p}{\partial z} + \mu \left(\frac{\partial^2 w}{\partial x^2} + \frac{\partial^2 w}{\partial y^2} + \frac{\partial^2 w}{\partial z^2} \right) = \rho \frac{dw}{dt}$$

These are the incompressible flow *Navier-Stokes equations,* named after C. L. M. H. Navier (1785–1836) and Sir George G. Stokes (1819–1903), who are credited with

---

[5]When compressibility is significant, additional small terms arise containing the element volume expansion rate and a *second* coefficient of viscosity; see Refs. 4 and 5 for details.

their derivation. They are second-order nonlinear partial differential equations and are quite formidable, but solutions have been found to a variety of interesting viscous flow problems, some of which are discussed in Sec. 4.11 and in Chap. 6 (see also Refs. 4 and 5). For compressible flow, see Eq. (2.29) of Ref. 5.

Equations (4.38) have four unknowns: p, u, v, and w. They should be combined with the incompressible continuity relation [Eqs. (4.12)] to form four equations in these four unknowns. We shall discuss this again in Sec. 4.6, which presents the appropriate boundary conditions for these equations.

Even though the Navier-Stokes equations have only a limited number of known analytical solutions, they are amenable to fine-gridded computer modeling [1]. The field of CFD is maturing fast, with many commercial software tools available. It is possible now to achieve approximate, but realistic, CFD results for a wide variety of complex two- and three-dimensional viscous flows.

EXAMPLE 4.5

Take the velocity field of Example 4.3, with $b = 0$ for algebraic convenience

$$u = a(x^2 - y^2) \qquad v = -2axy \qquad w = 0$$

and determine under what conditions it is a solution to the Navier-Stokes momentum equations (4.38). Assuming that these conditions are met, determine the resulting pressure distribution when z is "up" ($g_x = 0$, $g_y = 0$, $g_z = -g$).

Solution

- *Assumptions:* Constant density and viscosity, steady flow (u and v independent of time).
- *Approach:* Substitute the known (u, v, w) into Eqs. (4.38) and solve for the pressure gradients. If a unique pressure function $p(x, y, z)$ can then be found, the given solution is exact.
- *Solution step 1:* Substitute (u, v, w) into Eqs. (4.38) in sequence:

$$\rho(0) - \frac{\partial p}{\partial x} + \mu(2a - 2a + 0) = \rho\left(u\frac{\partial u}{\partial x} + v\frac{\partial u}{\partial y}\right) = 2a^2\rho\,(x^3 + xy^2)$$

$$\rho(0) - \frac{\partial p}{\partial y} + \mu(0 + 0 + 0) = \rho\left(u\frac{\partial v}{\partial x} + v\frac{\partial v}{\partial y}\right) = 2a^2\rho(x^2y + y^3)$$

$$\rho(-g) - \frac{\partial p}{\partial z} + \mu(0 + 0 + 0) = \rho\left(u\frac{\partial w}{\partial x} + v\frac{\partial w}{\partial y}\right) = 0$$

Rearrange and solve for the three pressure gradients:

$$\frac{\partial p}{\partial x} = -2a^2\rho(x^3 + xy^2) \qquad \frac{\partial p}{\partial y} = -2a^2\rho(x^2y + y^3) \qquad \frac{\partial p}{\partial z} = -\rho g \tag{1}$$

- *Comment 1:* The vertical pressure gradient is *hydrostatic*. [Could you have predicted this by noting in Eqs. (4.38) that $w = 0$?] However, the pressure is velocity-dependent in the xy plane.

- *Solution step 2:*   To determine if the x and y gradients of pressure in Eq. (1) are compatible, evaluate the mixed derivative $(\partial^2 p/\partial x\ \partial y)$; that is, cross-differentiate these two equations:

$$\frac{\partial}{\partial y}\left(\frac{\partial p}{\partial x}\right) = \frac{\partial}{\partial y}\left[-2a^2\rho(x^3 + xy^2)\right] = -4a^2\rho xy$$

$$\frac{\partial}{\partial x}\left(\frac{\partial p}{\partial y}\right) = \frac{\partial}{\partial x}\left[-2a^2\rho(x^2y + y^3)\right] = -4a^2\rho xy$$

- *Comment 2:*   Since these are equal, the given velocity distribution is indeed an *exact* solution of the Navier-Stokes equations.
- *Solution step 3:*   To find the pressure, integrate Eqs. (1), collect, and compare. Start with $\partial p/\partial x$. The procedure requires care! Integrate *partially* with respect to x, holding y and z constant:

$$p = \int \frac{\partial p}{\partial x} \, dx\Big|_{y,z} = \int -2a^2\rho(x^3 + xy^2)\, dx\Big|_{y,z} = -2a^2\rho\left(\frac{x^4}{4} + \frac{x^2y^2}{2}\right) + f_1(y, z) \qquad (2)$$

Note that the "constant" of integration f_1 is a *function* of the variables that were not integrated. Now differentiate Eq. (2) with respect to y and compare with $\partial p/\partial y$ from Eq. (1):

$$\frac{\partial p}{\partial y}\Big|_{(2)} = -2a^2\rho\, x^2y + \frac{\partial f_1}{\partial y} = \frac{\partial p}{\partial y}\Big|_{(1)} = -2a^2\rho(x^2y + y^3)$$

$$\text{Compare:}\ \frac{\partial f_1}{\partial y} = -2a^2\rho\, y^3 \quad \text{or} \quad f_1 = \int \frac{\partial f_1}{\partial y}\, dy\Big|_z = -2a^2\rho\, \frac{y^4}{4} + f_2(z)$$

$$\text{Collect terms: So far} \quad p = -2a^2\rho\left(\frac{x^4}{4} + \frac{x^2y^2}{2} + \frac{y^4}{4}\right) + f_2(z) \qquad (3)$$

This time the "constant" of integration f_2 is a function of z only (the variable not integrated). Now differentiate Eq. (3) with respect to z and compare with $\partial p/\partial z$ from Eq. (1):

$$\frac{\partial p}{\partial z}\Big|_{(3)} = \frac{df_2}{dz} = \frac{\partial p}{\partial z}\Big|_{(1)} = -\rho g \qquad \text{or} \qquad f_2 = -\rho gz + C \qquad (4)$$

where C is a constant. This completes our three integrations. Combine Eqs. (3) and (4) to obtain the full expression for the pressure distribution in this flow:

$$p(x, y, z) = -\rho gz - \tfrac{1}{2}a^2\rho(x^4 + y^4 + 2x^2y^2) + C \qquad \text{Ans. (5)}$$

This is the desired solution. Do you recognize it? Not unless you go back to the beginning and square the velocity components:

$$u^2 + v^2 + w^2 = V^2 = a^2(x^4 + y^4 + 2x^2y^2) \qquad (6)$$

Comparing with Eq. (5), we can rewrite the pressure distribution as

$$p + \tfrac{1}{2}\rho V^2 + pgz = C \qquad (7)$$

- *Comment:*   This is Bernoulli's equation (3.54). That is no accident, because the velocity distribution given in this problem is one of a family of flows that are solutions to the Navier-Stokes equations and that satisfy Bernoulli's incompressible equation everywhere in the flow field. They are called *irrotational flows,* for which curl $\mathbf{V} = \nabla \times \mathbf{V} \equiv 0$. This subject is discussed again in Sec. 4.9.

4.4 The Differential Equation of Angular Momentum

Having now been through the same approach for both mass and linear momentum, we can go rapidly through a derivation of the differential angular momentum relation. The appropriate form of the integral angular momentum equation for a fixed control volume is

$$\sum \mathbf{M}_o = \frac{\partial}{\partial t}\left[\int_{CV} (\mathbf{r} \times \mathbf{V})\rho \, d\mathcal{V}\right] + \int_{CS} (\mathbf{r} \times \mathbf{V})\rho(\mathbf{V} \cdot \mathbf{n}) \, dA \qquad (3.59)$$

We shall confine ourselves to an axis through O that is parallel to the z axis and passes through the centroid of the elemental control volume. This is shown in Fig. 4.5. Let θ be the angle of rotation about O of the fluid within the control volume. The only stresses that have moments about O are the shear stresses τ_{xy} and τ_{yx}. We can evaluate the moments about O and the angular momentum terms about O. A lot of algebra is involved, and we give here only the result:

$$\left[\tau_{xy} - \tau_{yx} + \frac{1}{2}\frac{\partial}{\partial x}(\tau_{xy}) \, dx - \frac{1}{2}\frac{\partial}{\partial y}(\tau_{yx}) \, dy\right] dx \, dy \, dz$$
$$= \frac{1}{12}\rho(dx \, dy \, dz)(dx^2 + dy^2)\frac{d^2\theta}{dt^2} \qquad (4.39)$$

Assuming that the angular acceleration $d^2\theta/dt^2$ is not infinite, we can neglect all higher-order differential terms, which leaves a finite and interesting result:

$$\tau_{xy} \approx \tau_{yx} \qquad (4.40)$$

Had we summed moments about axes parallel to y or x, we would have obtained exactly analogous results:

$$\tau_{xz} \approx \tau_{zx} \qquad \tau_{yz} \approx \tau_{zy} \qquad (4.41)$$

There is *no* differential angular momentum equation. Application of the integral theorem to a differential element gives the result, well known to students of stress analysis or strength of materials, that the shear stresses are symmetric: $\tau_{ij} = \tau_{ji}$. This is the

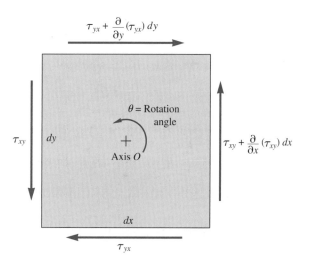

Fig. 4.5 Elemental cartesian fixed control volume showing shear stresses that may cause a net angular acceleration about axis O.

only result of this section.[6] There is no differential equation to remember, which leaves room in your brain for the next topic, the differential energy equation.

4.5 The Differential Equation of Energy[7]

We are now so used to this type of derivation that we can race through the energy equation at a bewildering pace. The appropriate integral relation for the fixed control volume of Fig. 4.1 is

$$\dot{Q} - \dot{W}_s - \dot{W}_v = \frac{\partial}{\partial t}\left(\int_{CV} e\rho \, d\mathcal{V}\right) + \int_{CS}\left(e + \frac{p}{\rho}\right)\rho(\mathbf{V} \cdot \mathbf{n}) \, dA \qquad (3.66)$$

where $\dot{W}_s = 0$ because there can be no infinitesimal shaft protruding into the control volume. By analogy with Eq. (4.20), the right-hand side becomes, for this tiny element,

$$\dot{Q} - \dot{W}_v = \left[\frac{\partial}{\partial t}(\rho e) + \frac{\partial}{\partial x}(\rho u \zeta) + \frac{\partial}{\partial y}(\rho v \zeta) + \frac{\partial}{\partial z}(\rho w \zeta)\right]dx \, dy \, dz$$

where $\zeta = e + p/\rho$. When we use the continuity equation by analogy with Eq. (4.21), this becomes

$$\dot{Q} - \dot{W}_v = \left(\rho\frac{de}{dt} + \mathbf{V} \cdot \nabla p + p\nabla \cdot \mathbf{V}\right)dx \, dy \, dz \qquad (4.42)$$

Thermal Conductivity; Fourier's Law

To evaluate $\dot{Q}$, we neglect radiation and consider only heat conduction through the sides of the element. Experiments for both fluids and solids show that the vector heat transfer per unit area, $\mathbf{q}$, is proportional to the vector gradient of temperature, ∇T. This proportionality is called *Fourier's law of conduction,* which is analogous to Newton's viscosity law:

$$\mathbf{q} = -k\nabla T$$

$$\text{or:} \quad q_x = -k\frac{\partial T}{\partial x}, \quad q_y = -k\frac{\partial T}{\partial y}, \quad q_z = -k\frac{\partial T}{\partial z} \qquad (4.43)$$

where k is called the *thermal conductivity,* a fluid property that varies with temperature and pressure in much the same way as viscosity. The minus sign satisfies the convention that heat flux is positive in the direction of decreasing temperature. Fourier's law is dimensionally consistent, and k has SI units of joules per (sec-meter-kelvin) and can be correlated with T in much the same way as Eqs. (1.27) and (1.28) for gases and liquids, respectively.

Figure 4.6 shows the heat flow passing through the x faces, the y and z heat flows being omitted for clarity. We can list these six heat flux terms:

---

[6]We are neglecting the possibility of a finite *couple* being applied to the element by some powerful external force field. See, for example, Ref. 6.

[7]This section may be omitted without loss of continuity.

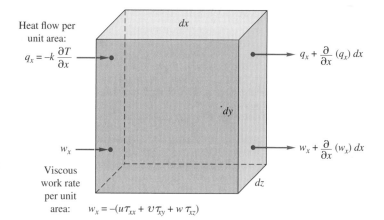

Heat flow per unit area:

$$q_x = -k \frac{\partial T}{\partial x}$$

$$q_x + \frac{\partial}{\partial x}(q_x)\,dx$$

$$w_x$$

$$w_x + \frac{\partial}{\partial x}(w_x)\,dx$$

Viscous work rate per unit area:

$$w_x = -(u\tau_{xx} + v\tau_{xy} + w\,\tau_{xz})$$

Fig. 4.6 Elemental cartesian control volume showing heat flow and viscous work rate terms in the x direction.

Faces	Inlet heat flux	Outlet heat flux
x	$q_x\,dy\,dz$	$\left[q_x + \dfrac{\partial}{\partial x}(q_x)\,dx\right]dy\,dz$
y	$q_y\,dx\,dz$	$\left[q_y + \dfrac{\partial}{\partial y}(q_y)\,dy\right]dx\,dz$
z	$q_z\,dx\,dy$	$\left[q_z + \dfrac{\partial}{\partial z}(q_z)\,dz\right]dx\,dy$

By adding the inlet terms and subtracting the outlet terms, we obtain the net heat added to the element:

$$\dot{Q} = -\left[\frac{\partial}{\partial x}(q_x) + \frac{\partial}{\partial y}(q_y) + \frac{\partial}{\partial z}(q_z)\right]dx\,dy\,dz = -\boldsymbol{\nabla}\cdot\mathbf{q}\,dx\,dy\,dz \quad (4.44)$$

As expected, the heat flux is proportional to the element volume. Introducing Fourier's law from Eq. (4.43), we have

$$\dot{Q} = \boldsymbol{\nabla}\cdot(k\boldsymbol{\nabla}T)\,dx\,dy\,dz \quad (4.45)$$

The rate of work done by viscous stresses equals the product of the stress component, its corresponding velocity component, and the area of the element face. Figure 4.6 shows the work rate on the left x face is

$$\dot{W}_{v,\text{LF}} = w_x\,dy\,dz \qquad \text{where } w_x = -(u\tau_{xx} + v\tau_{xy} + w\tau_{xz}) \quad (4.46)$$

(where the subscript LF stands for left face) and a slightly different work on the right face due to the gradient in w_x. These work fluxes could be tabulated in exactly the same manner as the heat fluxes in the previous table, with w_x replacing q_x, and so on. After outlet terms are subtracted from inlet terms, the net viscous work rate becomes

$$\dot{W}_v = -\left[\frac{\partial}{\partial x}(u\tau_{xx} + v\tau_{xy} + w\tau_{xz}) + \frac{\partial}{\partial y}(u\tau_{yx} + v\tau_{yy} + w\tau_{yz})\right.$$

$$\left. + \frac{\partial}{\partial z}(u\tau_{zx} + v\tau_{zy} + w\tau_{zz})\right]dx\,dy\,dz$$

$$= -\boldsymbol{\nabla}\cdot(\mathbf{V}\cdot\boldsymbol{\tau}_{ij})\,dx\,dy\,dz \quad (4.47)$$

We now substitute Eqs. (4.45) and (4.47) into Eq. (4.43) to obtain one form of the differential energy equation:

$$\rho \frac{de}{dt} + \mathbf{V} \cdot \nabla p + p\nabla \cdot \mathbf{V} = \nabla \cdot (k\nabla T) + \nabla \cdot (\mathbf{V} \cdot \boldsymbol{\tau}_{ij}) \tag{4.48}$$

where $e = \hat{u} + \frac{1}{2}V^2 + gz$

A more useful form is obtained if we split up the viscous work term:

$$\nabla \cdot (\mathbf{V} \cdot \boldsymbol{\tau}_{ij}) \equiv \mathbf{V} \cdot (\nabla \cdot \boldsymbol{\tau}_{ij}) + \Phi \tag{4.49}$$

where Φ is short for the *viscous-dissipation function*.[8] For a newtonian incompressible viscous fluid, this function has the form

$$\Phi = \mu \left[2\left(\frac{\partial u}{\partial x}\right)^2 + 2\left(\frac{\partial v}{\partial y}\right)^2 + 2\left(\frac{\partial w}{\partial z}\right)^2 + \left(\frac{\partial v}{\partial x} + \frac{\partial u}{\partial y}\right)^2 \right.$$
$$\left. + \left(\frac{\partial w}{\partial y} + \frac{\partial v}{\partial z}\right)^2 + \left(\frac{\partial u}{\partial z} + \frac{\partial w}{\partial x}\right)^2 \right] \tag{4.50}$$

Since all terms are quadratic, viscous dissipation is always positive, so a viscous flow always tends to lose its available energy due to dissipation, in accordance with the second law of thermodynamics.

Now substitute Eq. (4.49) into Eq. (4.48), using the linear momentum equation (4.32) to eliminate $\nabla \cdot \boldsymbol{\tau}_{ij}$. This will cause the kinetic and potential energies to cancel, leaving a more customary form of the general differential energy equation:

$$\boxed{\rho \frac{d\hat{u}}{dt} + p(\nabla \cdot \mathbf{V}) = \nabla \cdot (k\nabla T) + \Phi} \tag{4.51}$$

This equation is valid for a newtonian fluid under very general conditions of unsteady, compressible, viscous, heat-conducting flow, except that it neglects radiation heat transfer and internal *sources* of heat that might occur during a chemical or nuclear reaction.

Equation (4.51) is too difficult to analyze except on a digital computer [1]. It is customary to make the following approximations:

$$d\hat{u} \approx c_v\, dT \qquad c_v, \mu, k, \rho \approx \text{const} \tag{4.52}$$

Equation (4.51) then takes the simpler form, for $\nabla \cdot \mathbf{V} = 0$,

$$\rho c_v \frac{dT}{dt} = k\nabla^2 T + \Phi \tag{4.53}$$

which involves temperature T as the sole primary variable plus velocity as a secondary variable through the total time-derivative operator:

$$\frac{dT}{dt} = \frac{\partial T}{\partial t} + u\frac{\partial T}{\partial x} + v\frac{\partial T}{\partial y} + w\frac{\partial T}{\partial z} \tag{4.54}$$

[8]For further details, see, Ref. 5, p. 72.

A great many interesting solutions to Eq. (4.53) are known for various flow conditions, and extended treatments are given in advanced books on viscous flow [4, 5] and books on heat transfer [7, 8].

One well-known special case of Eq. (4.53) occurs when the fluid is at rest or has negligible velocity, where the dissipation Φ and convective terms become negligible:

$$\rho c_p \frac{\partial T}{\partial t} = k\nabla^2 T \tag{4.55}$$

The change from c_v to c_p is correct and justified by the fact that, when pressure terms are neglected from a gas flow energy equation [4, 5], what remains is approximately an enthalpy change, not an internal energy change. This is called the *heat conduction equation* in applied mathematics and is valid for solids and fluids at rest. The solution to Eq. (4.55) for various conditions is a large part of courses and books on heat transfer.

This completes the derivation of the basic differential equations of fluid motion.

4.6 Boundary Conditions for the Basic Equations

There are three basic differential equations of fluid motion, just derived. Let us summarize those here:

Continuity:
$$\frac{\partial \rho}{\partial t} + \nabla \cdot (\rho \mathbf{V}) = 0 \tag{4.56}$$

Momentum:
$$\rho \frac{d\mathbf{V}}{dt} = \rho \mathbf{g} - \nabla p + \nabla \cdot \boldsymbol{\tau}_{ij} \tag{4.57}$$

Energy:
$$\rho \frac{d\hat{u}}{dt} + p(\nabla \cdot \mathbf{V}) = \nabla \cdot (k\nabla T) + \Phi \tag{4.58}$$

where Φ is given by Eq. (4.50). In general, the density is variable, so these three equations contain five unknowns, ρ, V, p, $\hat{u}$, and T. Therefore, we need two additional relations to complete the system of equations. These are provided by data or algebraic expressions for the state relations of the thermodynamic properties:

$$\rho = \rho(p, T) \qquad \hat{u} = \hat{u}(p, T) \tag{4.59}$$

For example, for a perfect gas with constant specific heats, we complete the system with

$$\rho = \frac{p}{RT} \qquad \hat{u} = \int c_v \, dT \approx c_v T + \text{const} \tag{4.60}$$

It is shown in advanced books [4, 5] that this system of equations (4.56) to (4.59) is well posed and can be solved analytically or numerically, subject to the proper boundary conditions.

What are the proper boundary conditions? First, if the flow is unsteady, there must be an *initial condition* or initial spatial distribution known for each variable:

At $t = 0$: $\qquad\qquad \rho, V, p, \hat{u}, T = \text{known } f(x, y, z) \tag{4.61}$

Thereafter, for all times t to be analyzed, we must know something about the variables at each *boundary* enclosing the flow.

Figure 4.7 illustrates the three most common types of boundaries encountered in fluid flow analysis: a solid wall, an inlet or outlet, and a liquid–gas interface.

First, for a solid, impermeable wall, there can be slip and temperature jump in a viscous heat-conducting fluid:

No-slip: $\qquad\qquad\qquad \mathbf{V}_{\text{fluid}} = \mathbf{V}_{\text{wall}} \qquad\qquad T_{\text{fluid}} = T_{\text{wall}}$

Rarefied gas: $u_{\text{fluid}} - u_{\text{wall}} \approx \ell \dfrac{\partial u}{\partial n}\Big|_{\text{wall}} \quad T_{\text{fluid}} - T_{\text{wall}} \approx \left(\dfrac{2\zeta}{\zeta + 1}\right) \dfrac{k}{\mu c_p} \ell \dfrac{\partial T}{\partial n}\Big|_{\text{wall}}$ $\qquad$ (4.62)

where, for the rarefied gas, n is normal to the wall, u is parallel to the wall, ℓ is the mean free path of the gas [see Eq. (1.37)], and ζ denotes, just this one time, the specific heat ratio. The above so-called *temperature-jump relation* for gases is given here only for completeness and will not be studied (see page 48 of Ref. 5). A few velocity-jump assignments will be given.

Second, at any inlet or outlet section of the flow, the complete distribution of velocity, pressure, and temperature must be known for all times:

Inlet or outlet: $\qquad\qquad\qquad\qquad$ Known $\mathbf{V}, p, T$ $\qquad\qquad\qquad\qquad\qquad$ (4.63)

These inlet and outlet sections can be and often are at $\pm \infty$, simulating a body immersed in an infinite expanse of fluid.

Finally, the most complex conditions occur at a liquid–gas interface, or free surface, as sketched in Fig. 4.7. Let us denote the interface by

Interface: $\qquad\qquad\qquad\qquad\qquad z = \eta(x, y, t)$ $\qquad\qquad\qquad\qquad\qquad$ (4.64)

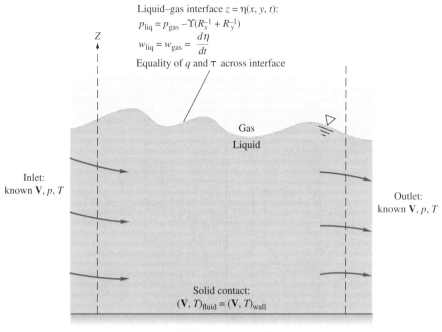

Fig. 4.7 Typical boundary conditions in a viscous heat-conducting fluid flow analysis.

Then there must be equality of vertical velocity across the interface, so that no holes appear between liquid and gas:

$$w_{\text{liq}} = w_{\text{gas}} = \frac{d\eta}{dt} = \frac{\partial \eta}{\partial t} + u \frac{\partial \eta}{\partial x} + v \frac{\partial \eta}{\partial y} \tag{4.65}$$

This is called the *kinematic boundary condition.*

There must be mechanical equilibrium across the interface. The viscous shear stresses must balance:

$$(\tau_{zy})_{\text{liq}} = (\tau_{zy})_{\text{gas}} \qquad (\tau_{zx})_{\text{liq}} = (\tau_{zx})_{\text{gas}} \tag{4.66}$$

Neglecting the viscous normal stresses, the pressures must balance at the interface except for surface tension effects:

$$p_{\text{liq}} = p_{\text{gas}} - Y(R_x^{-1} + R_y^{-1}) \tag{4.67}$$

which is equivalent to Eq. (1.33). The radii of curvature can be written in terms of the free surface position η:

$$
\begin{aligned}
R_x^{-1} + R_y^{-1} &= \frac{\partial}{\partial x}\left[\frac{\partial \eta/\partial x}{\sqrt{1 + (\partial \eta/\partial x)^2 + (\partial \eta/\partial y)^2}} \right] \\
&+ \frac{\partial}{\partial y}\left[\frac{\partial \eta/\partial y}{\sqrt{1 + (\partial \eta/\partial x)^2 + (\partial \eta/\partial y)^2}} \right]
\end{aligned}
\tag{4.68}
$$

Finally, the heat transfer must be the same on both sides of the interface, since no heat can be stored in the infinitesimally thin interface:

$$(q_z)_{\text{liq}} = (q_z)_{\text{gas}} \tag{4.69}$$

Neglecting radiation, this is equivalent to

$$\left(k \frac{\partial T}{\partial z}\right)_{\text{liq}} = \left(k \frac{\partial T}{\partial z}\right)_{\text{gas}} \tag{4.70}$$

This is as much detail as we wish to give at this level of exposition. Further and even more complicated details on fluid flow boundary conditions are given in Refs. 5 and 9.

Simplified Free Surface Conditions   In the introductory analyses given in this book, such as open-channel flows in Chap. 10, we shall back away from the exact conditions (4.65) to (4.69) and assume that the upper fluid is an "atmosphere" that merely exerts pressure on the lower fluid, with shear and heat conduction negligible. We also neglect nonlinear terms involving the slopes of the free surface. We then have a much simpler and linear set of conditions at the surface:

$$p_{\text{liq}} \approx p_{\text{gas}} - Y\left(\frac{\partial^2 \eta}{\partial x^2} + \frac{\partial^2 \eta}{\partial y^2}\right) \qquad w_{\text{liq}} \approx \frac{\partial \eta}{\partial t}$$

$$\left(\frac{\partial V}{\partial z}\right)_{\text{liq}} \approx 0 \qquad \left(\frac{\partial T}{z}\right)_{\text{liq}} \approx 0 \tag{4.71}$$

In many cases, such as open-channel flow, we can also neglect surface tension, so

$$p_{liq} \approx p_{atm} \tag{4.72}$$

These are the types of approximations that will be used in Chap. 10. The nondimensional forms of these conditions will also be useful in Chap. 5.

Incompressible Flow with Constant Properties

Flow with constant ρ, μ, and k is a basic simplification that will be used, for example, throughout Chap. 6. The basic equations of motion (4.56) to (4.58) reduce to

Continuity:
$$\mathbf{\nabla} \cdot \mathbf{V} = 0 \tag{4.73}$$

Momentum:
$$\rho \frac{d\mathbf{V}}{dt} = \rho \mathbf{g} - \mathbf{\nabla} p + \mu \nabla^2 \mathbf{V} \tag{4.74}$$

Energy:
$$\rho c_p \frac{dT}{dt} = k \nabla^2 T + \Phi \tag{4.75}$$

Since ρ is constant, there are only three unknowns: p, $\mathbf{V}$, and T. The system is closed.[9] Not only that, the system splits apart: Continuity and momentum are independent of T. Thus we can solve Eqs. (4.73) and (4.74) entirely separately for the pressure and velocity, using such boundary conditions as

Solid surface:
$$\mathbf{V} = \mathbf{V}_{wall} \tag{4.76}$$

Inlet or outlet:
$$\text{Known } \mathbf{V}, p \tag{4.77}$$

Free surface:
$$p \approx p_a \qquad w \approx \frac{\partial \eta}{\partial t} \tag{4.78}$$

Later, usually in another course,[10] we can solve for the temperature distribution from Eq. (4.75), which depends on velocity $\mathbf{V}$ through the dissipation Φ and the total time-derivative operator d/dt.

Inviscid Flow Approximations

Chapter 8 assumes inviscid flow throughout, for which the viscosity $\mu = 0$. The momentum equation (4.74) reduces to

$$\rho \frac{d\mathbf{V}}{dt} = \rho \mathbf{g} - \mathbf{\nabla} p \tag{4.79}$$

This is *Euler's equation;* it can be integrated along a streamline to obtain Bernoulli's equation (see Sec. 4.9). By neglecting viscosity we have lost the second-order derivative of $\mathbf{V}$ in Eq. (4.74); therefore, we must relax one boundary condition on velocity. The only mathematically sensible condition to drop is the no-slip condition at the wall. We let the flow slip parallel to the wall but do not allow it to flow into the wall. The proper inviscid condition is that the normal velocities must match at any solid surface:

Inviscid flow:
$$(V_n)_{fluid} = (V_n)_{wall} \tag{4.80}$$

---

[9]For this system, what are the thermodynamic equivalents to Eq. (4.59)?

[10]Since temperature is entirely *uncoupled* by this assumption, we may never get around to solving for it here and may ask you to wait until you take a course on heat transfer.

In most cases the wall is fixed; therefore, the proper inviscid flow condition is

$$V_n = 0 \tag{4.81}$$

There is *no* condition whatever on the tangential velocity component at the wall in inviscid flow. The tangential velocity will be part of the solution to an inviscid flow analysis (see Chap. 8).

EXAMPLE 4.6

For steady incompressible laminar flow through a long tube, the velocity distribution is given by

$$v_z = U\left(1 - \frac{r^2}{R^2}\right) \qquad v_r = v_\theta = 0$$

where U is the maximum, or centerline, velocity and R is the tube radius. If the wall temperature is constant at T_w and the temperature $T = T(r)$ only, find $T(r)$ for this flow.

Solution

With $T = T(r)$, Eq. (4.75) reduces for steady flow to

$$\rho c_p v_r \frac{dT}{dr} = \frac{k}{r}\frac{d}{dr}\left(r\frac{dT}{dr}\right) + \mu\left(\frac{dv_z}{dr}\right)^2 \tag{1}$$

But since $v_r = 0$ for this flow, the convective term on the left vanishes. Introduce v_z into Eq. (1) to obtain

$$\frac{k}{r}\frac{d}{dr}\left(r\frac{dT}{dr}\right) = -\mu\left(\frac{dv_z}{dr}\right)^2 = -\frac{4U^2\mu r^2}{R^4} \tag{2}$$

Multiply through by r/k and integrate once:

$$r\frac{dT}{dr} = -\frac{\mu U^2 r^4}{kR^4} + C_1 \tag{3}$$

Divide through by r and integrate once again:

$$T = -\frac{\mu U^2 r^4}{4kR^4} + C_1 \ln r + C_2 \tag{4}$$

Now we are in position to apply our boundary conditions to evaluate C_1 and C_2.

First, since the logarithm of zero is $-\infty$, the temperature at $r = 0$ will be infinite unless

$$C_1 = 0 \tag{5}$$

Thus, we eliminate the possibility of a logarithmic singularity. The same thing will happen if we apply the *symmetry* condition $dT/dr = 0$ at $r = 0$ to Eq. (3). The constant C_2 is then found by the wall-temperature condition at $r = R$:

$$T = T_w = -\frac{\mu U^2}{4k} + C_2$$

or
$$C_2 = T_w + \frac{\mu U^2}{4k} \tag{6}$$

The correct solution is thus

$$T(r) = T_w + \frac{\mu U^2}{4k}\left(1 - \frac{r^4}{R^4}\right) \qquad\qquad Ans.\ (7)$$

which is a fourth-order parabolic distribution with a maximum value $T_0 = T_w + \mu U^2/(4k)$ at the centerline.

4.7 The Stream Function

We have seen in Sec. 4.6 that even if the temperature is uncoupled from our system of equations of motion, we must solve the continuity and momentum equations simultaneously for pressure and velocity. The *stream function* ψ is a clever device that allows us to satisfy the continuity equation and then solve the momentum equation directly for the single variable ψ. Lines of constant ψ are streamlines of the flow.

The stream function idea works only if the continuity equation (4.56) can be reduced to *two* terms. In general, we have *four* terms:

Cartesian:
$$\frac{\partial \rho}{\partial t} + \frac{\partial}{\partial x}(\rho u) + \frac{\partial}{\partial y}(\rho v) + \frac{\partial}{\partial z}(\rho w) = 0 \tag{4.82a}$$

Cylindrical:
$$\frac{\partial \rho}{\partial t} + \frac{1}{r}\frac{\partial}{\partial r}(r\rho v_r) + \frac{1}{r}\frac{\partial}{\partial \theta}(\rho v_\theta) + \frac{\partial}{\partial z}(\rho v_z) = 0 \tag{4.82b}$$

First, let us eliminate unsteady flow, which is a peculiar and unrealistic application of the stream function idea. Reduce either of Eqs. (4.82) to any *two* terms. The most common application is incompressible flow in the xy plane:

$$\frac{\partial u}{\partial x} + \frac{\partial v}{\partial y} = 0 \tag{4.83}$$

This equation is satisfied *identically* if a function $\psi(x, y)$ is defined such that Eq. (4.83) becomes

$$\frac{\partial}{\partial x}\left(\frac{\partial \psi}{\partial y}\right) + \frac{\partial}{\partial y}\left(-\frac{\partial \psi}{\partial x}\right) \equiv 0 \tag{4.84}$$

Comparison of (4.83) and (4.84) shows that this new function ψ must be defined such that

$$\boxed{u = \frac{\partial \psi}{\partial y} \qquad v = -\frac{\partial \psi}{\partial x}} \tag{4.85}$$

or
$$\boxed{\mathbf{V} = \mathbf{i}\frac{\partial \psi}{\partial y} - \mathbf{j}\frac{\partial \psi}{\partial x}}$$

Is this legitimate? Yes, it is just a mathematical trick of replacing two variables (u and v) by a single higher-order function ψ. The vorticity[11] or curl $\mathbf{V}$ is an interesting function:

$$\text{curl } \mathbf{V} = -\mathbf{k}\nabla^2\psi \qquad \text{where} \qquad \nabla^2\psi = \frac{\partial^2\psi}{\partial x^2} + \frac{\partial^2\psi}{\partial y^2} \tag{4.86}$$

Thus, if we take the curl of the momentum equation (4.74) and utilize Eq. (4.86), we obtain a single equation for ψ for incompressible flow:

$$\frac{\partial\psi}{\partial y}\frac{\partial}{\partial x}(\nabla^2\psi) - \frac{\partial\psi}{\partial x}\frac{\partial}{\partial y}(\nabla^2\psi) = \nu\nabla^2(\nabla^2\psi) \tag{4.87}$$

where $\nu = \mu/\rho$ is the kinematic viscosity. This is partly a victory and partly a defeat: Eq. (4.87) is scalar and has only one variable, ψ, but it now contains *fourth*-order derivatives and probably will require computer analysis. There will be four boundary conditions required on ψ. For example, for the flow of a uniform stream in the x direction past a solid body, the four conditions would be

At infinity: $\qquad\qquad\qquad \dfrac{\partial\psi}{\partial y} = U_\infty \qquad \dfrac{\partial\psi}{\partial x} = 0$

At the body: $\qquad\qquad\qquad \dfrac{\partial\psi}{\partial y} = \dfrac{\partial\psi}{\partial x} = 0 \tag{4.88}$

Many examples of numerical solution of Eqs. (4.87) and (4.88) are given in Ref. 1.

One important application is inviscid, incompressible, *irrotational* flow[12] in the xy plane, where curl $\mathbf{V} \equiv 0$. Equations (4.86) and (4.87) reduce to

$$\nabla^2\psi = \frac{\partial^2\psi}{\partial x^2} + \frac{\partial^2\psi}{\partial y^2} = 0 \tag{4.89}$$

This is the second-order *Laplace equation* (Chap. 8), for which many solutions and analytical techniques are known. Also, boundary conditions like Eq. (4.88) reduce to

At infinity: $\qquad\qquad\qquad \psi = U_\infty y + \text{const} \tag{4.90}$

At the body: $\qquad\qquad\qquad \psi = \text{const}$

It is well within our capability to find some useful solutions to Eqs. (4.89) and (4.90), which we shall do in Chap. 8.

Geometric Interpretation of ψ

The fancy mathematics above would serve alone to make the stream function immortal and always useful to engineers. Even better, though, ψ has a beautiful geometric interpretation: Lines of constant ψ are *streamlines* of the flow. This can be shown as follows: From Eq. (1.41) the definition of a streamline in two-dimensional flow is

$$\frac{dx}{u} = \frac{dy}{v}$$

or $\qquad\qquad\qquad u\,dy - v\,dx = 0 \qquad \text{streamline} \tag{4.91}$

[11]See Section 4.8.
[12]See Section 4.8.

Introducing the stream function from Eq. (4.85), we have

$$\frac{\partial \psi}{\partial x} dx + \frac{\partial \psi}{\partial y} dy = 0 = d\psi \qquad (4.92)$$

Thus the change in ψ is zero along a streamline, or

$$\psi = \text{const along a streamline} \qquad (4.93)$$

Having found a given solution $\psi(x, y)$, we can plot lines of constant ψ to give the streamlines of the flow.

There is also a physical interpretation that relates ψ to volume flow. From Fig. 4.8, we can compute the volume flow dQ through an element ds of control surface of unit depth:

$$dQ = (\mathbf{V} \cdot \mathbf{n}) \, dA = \left(\mathbf{i} \frac{\partial \psi}{\partial y} - \mathbf{j} \frac{\partial \psi}{\partial x} \right) \cdot \left(\mathbf{i} \frac{dy}{ds} - \mathbf{j} \frac{dx}{ds} \right) ds(1)$$

$$= \frac{\partial \psi}{\partial x} dx + \frac{\partial \psi}{\partial y} dy = d\psi \qquad (4.94)$$

Thus the change in ψ across the element is numerically equal to the volume flow through the element. The volume flow between any two streamlines in the flow field is equal to the change in stream function between those streamlines:

$$Q_{1 \to 2} = \int_1^2 (\mathbf{V} \cdot \mathbf{n}) \, dA = \int_1^2 d\psi = \psi_2 - \psi_1 \qquad (4.95)$$

Further, the direction of the flow can be ascertained by noting whether ψ increases or decreases. As sketched in Fig. 4.9, the flow is to the right if ψ_U is greater than ψ_L, where the subscripts stand for upper and lower, as before; otherwise the flow is to the left.

Both the stream function and the velocity potential were invented by the French mathematician Joseph Louis Lagrange and published in his treatise on fluid mechanics in 1781.

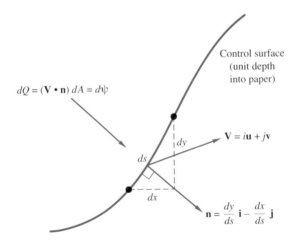

Fig. 4.8 Geometric interpretation of stream function: volume flow through a differential portion of a control surface.

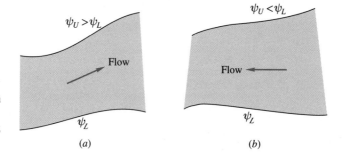

Fig. 4.9 Sign convention for flow in terms of change in stream function: (*a*) flow to the right if ψ_U is greater; (*b*) flow to the left if ψ_L is greater.

(*a*)   (*b*)

EXAMPLE 4.7

If a stream function exists for the velocity field of Example 4.5

$$u = a(x^2 - y^2) \quad v = -2axy \quad w = 0$$

find it, plot it, and interpret it.

Solution

- *Assumptions:* Incompressible, two-dimensional flow.
- *Approach:* Use the definition of stream function derivatives, Eqs. (4.85), to find $\psi(x, y)$.
- *Solution step 1:* Note that this velocity distribution was also examined in Example 4.3. It satisfies continuity, Eq. (4.83), but let's check that; otherwise ψ will not exist:

$$\frac{\partial u}{\partial x} + \frac{\partial v}{\partial y} = \frac{\partial}{\partial x}\left[a(x^2 - y^2)\right] + \frac{\partial}{\partial y}(-2axy) = 2ax + (-2ax) \equiv 0 \quad \text{checks}$$

Thus we are certain that a stream function exists.

- *Solution step 2:* To find ψ, write out Eqs. (4.85) and integrate:

$$u = \frac{\partial \psi}{\partial y} = ax^2 - ay^2 \tag{1}$$

$$v = -\frac{\partial \psi}{\partial x} = -2axy \tag{2}$$

and work from either one toward the other. Integrate (1) partially

$$\psi = ax^2 y - \frac{ay^3}{3} + f(x) \tag{3}$$

Differentiate (3) with respect to x and compare with (2)

$$\frac{\partial \psi}{\partial x} = 2axy + f'(x) = 2axy \tag{4}$$

Therefore $f'(x) = 0$, or $f = $ constant. The complete stream function is thus found:

$$\psi = a\left(x^2 y - \frac{y^3}{3}\right) + C \qquad \textit{Ans. (5)}$$

To plot this, set $C = 0$ for convenience and plot the function

$$3x^2y - y^3 = \frac{3\psi}{a} \qquad (6)$$

for constant values of ψ. The result is shown in Fig. E4.7a to be six 60° wedges of circulating motion, each with identical flow patterns except for the arrows. Once the streamlines are labeled, the flow directions follow from the sign convention of Fig. 4.9. How can the flow be interpreted? Since there is slip along all streamlines, no streamline can truly represent a solid surface in a viscous flow. However, the flow could represent the impingement of three incoming streams at 60, 180, and 300°. This would be a rather unrealistic yet exact solution to the Navier-Stokes equations, as we showed in Example 4.5.

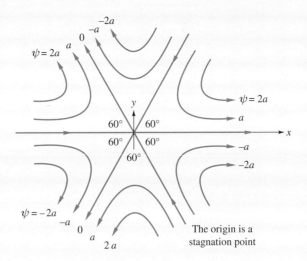

E4.7a

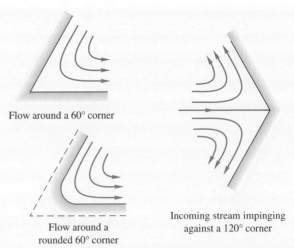

E4.7b

By allowing the flow to slip as a frictionless approximation, we could let any given streamline be a body shape. Some examples are shown in Fig. E4.7b.

A stream function also exists in a variety of other physical situations where only two coordinates are needed to define the flow. Three examples are illustrated here.

Steady Plane Compressible Flow

Suppose now that the density is variable but that $w = 0$, so that the flow is in the xy plane. Then the equation of continuity becomes

$$\frac{\partial}{\partial x}(\rho u) + \frac{\partial}{\partial y}(\rho v) = 0 \tag{4.96}$$

We see that this is in exactly the same form as Eq. (4.84). Therefore a compressible flow stream function can be defined such that

$$\rho u = \frac{\partial \psi}{\partial y} \qquad \rho v = -\frac{\partial \psi}{\partial x} \tag{4.97}$$

Again lines of constant ψ are streamlines of the flow, but the change in ψ is now equal to the *mass* flow, not the volume flow:

$$d\dot{m} = \rho(\mathbf{V} \cdot \mathbf{n}) \, dA = d\psi$$

or

$$\dot{m}_{1\to2} = \int_1^2 \rho(\mathbf{V} \cdot \mathbf{n}) \, dA = \psi_2 - \psi_1 \tag{4.98}$$

The sign convention on flow direction is the same as in Fig. 4.9. This particular stream function combines density with velocity and must be substituted into not only momentum but also the energy and state relations (4.58) and (4.59) with pressure and temperature as companion variables. Thus the compressible stream function is not a great victory, and further assumptions must be made to effect an analytical solution to a typical problem (see, for instance, Ref. 5, Chap. 7).

Incompressible Plane Flow in Polar Coordinates

Suppose that the important coordinates are r and θ, with $v_z = 0$, and that the density is constant. Then Eq. (4.82b) reduces to

$$\frac{1}{r}\frac{\partial}{\partial r}(rv_r) + \frac{1}{r}\frac{\partial}{\partial \theta}(v_\theta) = 0 \tag{4.99}$$

After multiplying through by r, we see that this is the analogous form of Eq. (4.84):

$$\frac{\partial}{\partial r}\left(\frac{\partial \psi}{\partial \theta}\right) + \frac{\partial}{\partial \theta}\left(-\frac{\partial \psi}{\partial r}\right) = 0 \tag{4.100}$$

By comparison of (4.99) and (4.100) we deduce the form of the incompressible polar coordinate stream function:

$$v_r = \frac{1}{r}\frac{\partial \psi}{\partial \theta} \qquad v_\theta = -\frac{\partial \psi}{\partial r} \tag{4.101}$$

Once again lines of constant ψ are streamlines, and the change in ψ is the *volume flow* $Q_{1\to2} = \psi_2 - \psi_1$. The sign convention is the same as in Fig. 4.9. This type of stream function is very useful in analyzing flows with cylinders, vortices, sources, and sinks (Chap. 8).

Incompressible Axisymmetric Flow

As a final example, suppose that the flow is three-dimensional (v_r, v_z) but with no circumferential variations, $v_\theta = \partial/\partial\theta = 0$ (see Fig. 4.2 for definition of coordinates). Such a flow is termed *axisymmetric*, and the flow pattern is the same when viewed on any meridional plane through the axis of revolution z. For incompressible flow, Eq. (4.82b) becomes

$$\frac{1}{r}\frac{\partial}{\partial r}(rv_r) + \frac{\partial}{\partial z}(v_z) = 0 \tag{4.102}$$

This doesn't seem to work: Can't we get rid of the one r outside? But when we realize that r and z are independent coordinates, Eq. (4.102) can be rewritten as

$$\frac{\partial}{\partial r}(rv_r) + \frac{\partial}{\partial z}(rv_z) = 0 \tag{4.103}$$

By analogy with Eq. (4.84), this has the form

$$\frac{\partial}{\partial r}\left(-\frac{\partial\psi}{\partial z}\right) + \frac{\partial}{\partial z}\left(\frac{\partial\psi}{\partial r}\right) = 0 \tag{4.104}$$

By comparing (4.103) and (4.104), we deduce the form of an incompressible axisymmetric stream function $\psi(r, z)$

$$v_r = -\frac{1}{r}\frac{\partial\psi}{\partial z} \qquad v_z = \frac{1}{r}\frac{\partial\psi}{\partial r} \tag{4.105}$$

Here again lines of constant ψ are streamlines, but there is a factor (2π) in the volume flow: $Q_{1\to2} = 2\pi(\psi_2 - \psi_1)$. The sign convention on flow is the same as in Fig. 4.9.

EXAMPLE 4.8

Investigate the stream function in polar coordinates

$$\psi = U \sin\theta\left(r - \frac{R^2}{r}\right) \tag{1}$$

where U and R are constants, a velocity and a length, respectively. Plot the streamlines. What does the flow represent? Is it a realistic solution to the basic equations?

Solution

The streamlines are lines of constant ψ, which has units of square meters per second. Note that $\psi/(UR)$ is dimensionless. Rewrite Eq. (1) in dimensionless form

$$\frac{\psi}{UR} = \sin\theta\left(\eta - \frac{1}{\eta}\right) \qquad \eta = \frac{r}{R} \tag{2}$$

Of particular interest is the special line $\psi = 0$. From Eq. (1) or (2) this occurs when (a) $\theta = 0$ or $180°$ and (b) $r = R$. Case (a) is the x axis, and case (b) is a circle of radius R, both of which are plotted in Fig. E4.8.

For any other nonzero value of ψ it is easiest to pick a value of r and solve for θ:

$$\sin \theta = \frac{\psi/(UR)}{r/R - R/r} \tag{3}$$

In general, there will be two solutions for θ because of the symmetry about the y axis. For example, take $\psi/(UR) = +1.0$:

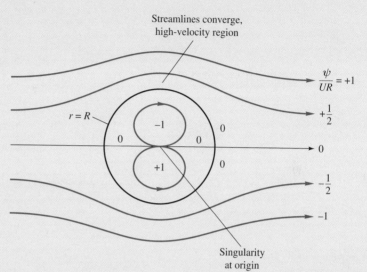

E4.8

Guess r/R	3.0	2.5	2.0	1.8	1.7	1.618
Compute θ	22°	28°	42°	53°	64°	90°
	158°	152°	138°	127°	116°	

This line is plotted in Fig. E4.8 and passes over the circle $r = R$. Be careful, though, because there is a second curve for $\psi/(UR) = +1.0$ for small $r < R$ below the x axis:

Guess r/R	0.618	0.6	0.5	0.4	0.3	0.2	0.1
Compute θ	−90°	−70°	−42°	−28°	−19°	−12°	−6°
		−110°	−138°	−152°	−161°	−168°	−174°

This second curve plots as a closed curve inside the circle $r = R$. There is a singularity of infinite velocity and indeterminate flow direction at the origin. Figure E4.8 shows the full pattern.

The given stream function, Eq. (1), is an exact and classic solution to the momentum equation (4.38) for frictionless flow. Outside the circle $r = R$ it represents two-dimensional inviscid flow of a uniform stream past a circular cylinder (Sec. 8.4). Inside the circle it represents a rather unrealistic trapped circulating motion of what is called a *line doublet*.

4.8 Vorticity and Irrotationality

The assumption of zero fluid angular velocity, or irrotationality, is a very useful simplification. Here we show that angular velocity is associated with the curl of the local velocity vector.

The differential relations for deformation of a fluid element can be derived by examining Fig. 4.10. Two fluid lines AB and BC, initially perpendicular at time t,

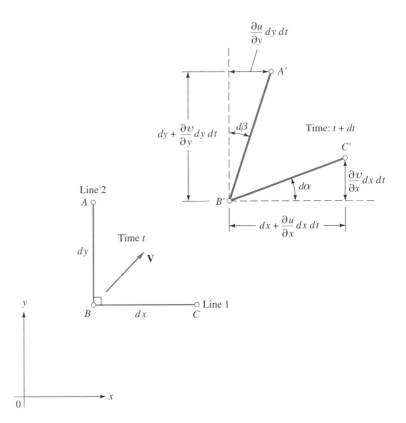

Fig. 4.10 Angular velocity and strain rate of two fluid lines deforming in the xy plane.

move and deform so that at $t + dt$ they have slightly different lengths $A'B'$ and $B'C'$ and are slightly off the perpendicular by angles $d\alpha$ and $d\beta$. Such deformation occurs kinematically because A, B, and C have slightly different velocities when the velocity field $\mathbf{V}$ has spatial gradients. All these differential changes in the motion of A, B, and C are noted in Fig. 4.10.

We define the angular velocity ω_z about the z axis as the average rate of counterclockwise turning of the two lines:

$$\omega_z = \frac{1}{2}\left(\frac{d\alpha}{dt} - \frac{d\beta}{dt}\right) \tag{4.106}$$

But from Fig. 4.10, $d\alpha$ and $d\beta$ are each directly related to velocity derivatives in the limit of small dt:

$$d\alpha = \lim_{dt \to 0}\left[\tan^{-1}\frac{(\partial v/\partial x)\,dx\,dt}{dx + (\partial u/\partial x)\,dx\,dt}\right] = \frac{\partial v}{\partial x}\,dt$$

$$d\beta = \lim_{dt \to 0}\left[\tan^{-1}\frac{(\partial u/\partial y)\,dy\,dt}{dy + (\partial v/\partial y)\,dy\,dt}\right] = \frac{\partial u}{\partial y}\,dt \tag{4.107}$$

Combining Eqs. (4.106) and (4.107) gives the desired result:

$$\omega_z = \frac{1}{2}\left(\frac{\partial v}{\partial x} - \frac{\partial u}{\partial y}\right) \tag{4.108}$$

In exactly similar manner we determine the other two rates:

$$\omega_x = \frac{1}{2}\left(\frac{\partial w}{\partial y} - \frac{\partial v}{\partial z}\right) \qquad \omega_y = \frac{1}{2}\left(\frac{\partial u}{\partial z} - \frac{\partial w}{\partial x}\right) \qquad (4.109)$$

The vector $\boldsymbol{\omega} = \mathbf{i}\omega_x + \mathbf{j}\omega_y + \mathbf{k}\omega_z$ is thus one-half the curl of the velocity vector

$$\boldsymbol{\omega} = \frac{1}{2}(\text{curl } \mathbf{V}) = \frac{1}{2}\begin{vmatrix} \mathbf{i} & \mathbf{j} & \mathbf{k} \\ \dfrac{\partial}{\partial x} & \dfrac{\partial}{\partial y} & \dfrac{\partial}{\partial z} \\ u & v & w \end{vmatrix} \qquad (4.110)$$

Since the factor of $\frac{1}{2}$ is annoying, many workers prefer to use a vector twice as large, called the *vorticity*:

$$\boldsymbol{\zeta} = 2\boldsymbol{\omega} = \text{curl } \mathbf{V} \qquad (4.111)$$

Many flows have negligible or zero vorticity and are called *irrotational*:

$$\text{curl } \mathbf{V} \equiv 0 \qquad (4.112)$$

The next section expands on this idea. Such flows can be incompressible or compressible, steady or unsteady.

We may also note that Fig. 4.10 demonstrates the *shear strain rate* of the element, which is defined as the rate of closure of the initially perpendicular lines:

$$\dot{\varepsilon}_{xy} = \frac{d\alpha}{dt} + \frac{d\beta}{dt} = \frac{\partial v}{\partial x} + \frac{\partial u}{\partial y} \qquad (4.113)$$

When multiplied by viscosity μ, this equals the shear stress τ_{xy} in a newtonian fluid, as discussed earlier in Eqs. (4.37). Appendix D lists strain rate and vorticity components in cylindrical coordinates.

4.9 Frictionless Irrotational Flows

When a flow is both frictionless and irrotational, pleasant things happen. First, the momentum equation (4.38) reduces to Euler's equation:

$$\rho \frac{d\mathbf{V}}{dt} = \rho \mathbf{g} - \nabla p \qquad (4.114)$$

Second, there is a great simplification in the acceleration term. Recall from Sec. 4.1 that acceleration has two terms:

$$\frac{d\mathbf{V}}{dt} = \frac{\partial \mathbf{V}}{\partial t} + (\mathbf{V} \cdot \nabla)\mathbf{V} \qquad (4.2)$$

A beautiful vector identity exists for the second term [11]:

$$(\mathbf{V} \cdot \nabla)\mathbf{V} \equiv \nabla(\tfrac{1}{2}V^2) + \boldsymbol{\zeta} \times \mathbf{V} \qquad (4.115)$$

where $\boldsymbol{\zeta} = \text{curl } \mathbf{V}$ from Eq. (4.111) is the fluid vorticity.

Now combine (4.114) and (4.115), divide by ρ, and rearrange on the left-hand side. Dot-product the entire equation into an arbitrary vector displacement $d\mathbf{r}$:

$$\left[\frac{\partial \mathbf{V}}{\partial t} + \boldsymbol{\nabla}\left(\frac{1}{2} V^2 \right) + \boldsymbol{\zeta} \times \mathbf{V} + \frac{1}{\rho} \boldsymbol{\nabla} p - \mathbf{g} \right] \cdot d\mathbf{r} = 0 \qquad (4.116)$$

Nothing works right unless we can get rid of the third term. We want

$$(\boldsymbol{\zeta} \times \mathbf{V}) \cdot (d\mathbf{r}) \equiv 0 \qquad (4.117)$$

This will be true under various conditions:

1. $\mathbf{V}$ is zero; trivial, no flow (hydrostatics).
2. $\boldsymbol{\zeta}$ is zero; irrotational flow.
3. $d\mathbf{r}$ is perpendicular to $\boldsymbol{\zeta} \times \mathbf{V}$; this is rather specialized and rare.
4. $d\mathbf{r}$ is parallel to $\mathbf{V}$; we integrate *along a streamline* (see Sec. 3.5).

Condition 4 is the common assumption. If we integrate along a streamline in frictionless compressible flow and take, for convenience, $\mathbf{g} = -g\mathbf{k}$, Eq. (4.116) reduces to

$$\frac{\partial \mathbf{V}}{\partial t} \cdot d\mathbf{r} + d\left(\frac{1}{2} V^2 \right) + \frac{dp}{\rho} + g\,dz = 0 \qquad (4.118)$$

Except for the first term, these are exact differentials. Integrate between any two points 1 and 2 along the streamline:

$$\int_1^2 \frac{\partial V}{\partial t}\,ds + \int_1^2 \frac{dp}{\rho} + \frac{1}{2}(V_2^2 - V_1^2) + g(z_2 - z_1) = 0 \qquad (4.119)$$

where ds is the arc length along the streamline. Equation (4.119) is Bernoulli's equation for frictionless unsteady flow along a streamline and is identical to Eq. (3.53). For incompressible steady flow, it reduces to

$$\frac{p}{\rho} + \frac{1}{2} V^2 + gz = \text{constant along streamline} \qquad (4.120)$$

The constant may vary from streamline to streamline unless the flow is also irrotational (assumption 2). For irrotational flow $\boldsymbol{\zeta} = 0$, the offending term Eq. (4.117) vanishes regardless of the direction of $d\mathbf{r}$, and Eq. (4.120) then holds all over the flow field with the same constant.

Velocity Potential

Irrotationality gives rise to a scalar function ϕ similar and complementary to the stream function ψ. From a theorem in vector analysis [11], a vector with zero curl must be the gradient of a scalar function

$$\text{If} \quad \boldsymbol{\nabla} \times \mathbf{V} \equiv 0 \quad \text{then} \quad \mathbf{V} = \boldsymbol{\nabla}\phi \qquad (4.121)$$

where $\phi = \phi(x, y, z, t)$ is called the *velocity potential function*. Knowledge of ϕ thus immediately gives the velocity components

$$\boxed{u = \frac{\partial \phi}{\partial x} \qquad v = \frac{\partial \phi}{\partial y} \qquad w = \frac{\partial \phi}{\partial z}} \qquad (4.122)$$

Lines of constant ϕ are called the *potential lines* of the flow.

Note that ϕ, unlike the stream function, is fully three-dimensional and is not limited to two coordinates. It reduces a velocity problem with three unknowns u, v, and w to a single unknown potential ϕ; many examples are given in Chap. 8. The velocity potential also simplifies the unsteady Bernoulli equation (4.118) because if ϕ exists, we obtain

$$\frac{\partial \mathbf{V}}{\partial t} \cdot d\mathbf{r} = \frac{\partial}{\partial t}(\nabla \phi) \cdot d\mathbf{r} = d\left(\frac{\partial \phi}{\partial t}\right) \tag{4.123}$$

along any arbitrary direction. Equation (4.118) then becomes a relation between ϕ and p:

$$\frac{\partial \phi}{\partial t} + \int \frac{dp}{\rho} + \frac{1}{2}|\nabla \phi|^2 + gz = \text{const} \tag{4.124}$$

This is the unsteady irrotational Bernoulli equation. It is very important in the analysis of accelerating flow fields (see Refs. 10 and 15), but the only application in this text will be in Sec. 9.3 for steady flow.

Orthogonality of Streamlines and Potential Lines

If a flow is both irrotational and described by only two coordinates, ψ and ϕ both exist, and the streamlines and potential lines are everywhere mutually perpendicular except at a stagnation point. For example, for incompressible flow in the xy plane, we would have

$$u = \frac{\partial \psi}{\partial y} = \frac{\partial \phi}{\partial x} \tag{4.125}$$

$$v = -\frac{\partial \psi}{\partial x} = \frac{\partial \phi}{\partial y} \tag{4.126}$$

Can you tell by inspection not only that these relations imply orthogonality but also that ϕ and ψ satisfy Laplace's equation?[13] A line of constant ϕ would be such that the change in ϕ is zero:

$$d\phi = \frac{\partial \phi}{\partial x}dx + \frac{\partial \phi}{\partial y}dy = 0 = u\,dx + v\,dy \tag{4.127}$$

Solving, we have

$$\left(\frac{dy}{dx}\right)_{\phi=\text{const}} = -\frac{u}{v} = -\frac{1}{(dy/dx)_{\psi=\text{const}}} \tag{4.128}$$

Equation (4.128) is the mathematical condition that lines of constant ϕ and ψ be mutually orthogonal. It may not be true at a stagnation point, where both u and v are zero, so their ratio in Eq. (4.128) is indeterminate.

---

[13]Equations (4.125) and (4.126) are called the *Cauchy-Riemann equations* and are studied in complex variable theory.

Generation of Rotationality[14]   This is the second time we have discussed Bernoulli's equation under different circumstances (the first was in Sec. 3.5). Such reinforcement is useful, since this is probably the most widely used equation in fluid mechanics. It requires frictionless flow with no shaft work or heat transfer between sections 1 and 2. The flow may or may not be irrotational, the former being an easier condition, allowing a universal Bernoulli constant.

The only remaining question is this: *When* is a flow irrotational? In other words, when does a flow have negligible angular velocity? The exact analysis of fluid rotationality under arbitrary conditions is a topic for advanced study (for example, Ref. 10, Sec. 8.5; Ref. 9, Sec. 5.2; and Ref. 5, Sec. 2.10). We shall simply state those results here without proof.

A fluid flow that is initially irrotational may become rotational if

1. There are significant viscous forces induced by jets, wakes, or solid boundaries. In this case Bernoulli's equation will not be valid in such viscous regions.
2. There are entropy gradients caused by curved shock waves (see Fig. 4.11*b*).
3. There are density gradients caused by *stratification* (uneven heating) rather than by pressure gradients.
4. There are significant *noninertial* effects such as the earth's rotation (the Coriolis acceleration).

In cases 2 to 4, Bernoulli's equation still holds along a streamline if friction is negligible. We shall not study cases 3 and 4 in this book. Case 2 will be treated briefly in Chap. 9 on gas dynamics. Primarily we are concerned with case 1, where rotation is induced by viscous stresses. This occurs near solid surfaces, where the no-slip condition creates a boundary layer through which the stream velocity drops to zero, and in jets and wakes, where streams of different velocities meet in a region of high shear.

Internal flows, such as pipes and ducts, are mostly viscous, and the wall layers grow to meet in the core of the duct. Bernoulli's equation does not hold in such flows unless it is modified for viscous losses.

External flows, such as a body immersed in a stream, are partly viscous and partly inviscid, the two regions being patched together at the edge of the shear layer or boundary layer. Two examples are shown in Fig. 4.11. Figure 4.11*a* shows a low-speed subsonic flow past a body. The approach stream is irrotational; that is, the curl of a constant is zero, but viscous stresses create a rotational shear layer beside and downstream of the body. Generally speaking (see Chap. 7), the shear layer is laminar, or smooth, near the front of the body and turbulent, or disorderly, toward the rear. A separated, or deadwater, region usually occurs near the trailing edge, followed by an unsteady turbulent wake extending far downstream. Some sort of laminar or turbulent viscous theory must be applied to these viscous regions; they are then patched onto the outer flow, which is frictionless and irrotational. If the stream Mach number is less than about 0.3, we can combine Eq. (4.122) with the incompressible continuity equation (4.73):

$$\nabla \cdot \mathbf{V} = \nabla \cdot (\nabla \phi) = 0$$

[14]This section may be omitted without loss of continuity.

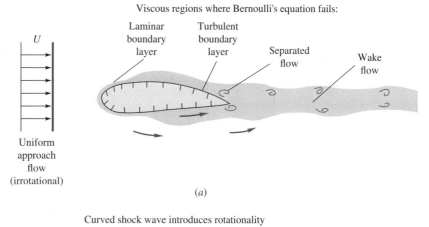

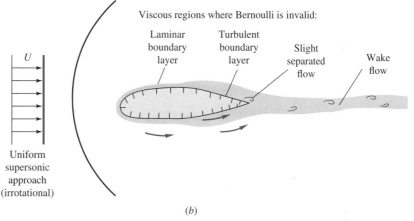

Fig. 4.11 Typical flow patterns illustrating viscous regions patched onto nearly frictionless regions: (*a*) low subsonic flow past a body ($U \ll a$); frictionless, irrotational potential flow outside the boundary layer (Bernoulli and Laplace equations valid); (*b*) supersonic flow past a body ($U > a$); frictionless, rotational flow outside the boundary layer (Bernoulli equation valid, potential flow invalid).

or

$$\nabla^2 \phi = 0 = \frac{\partial^2 \phi}{\partial x^2} + \frac{\partial^2 \phi}{\partial y^2} + \frac{\partial^2 \phi}{\partial z^2} \qquad (4.129)$$

This is Laplace's equation in three dimensions, there being no restraint on the number of coordinates in potential flow. A great deal of Chap. 8 will be concerned with solving Eq. (4.129) for practical engineering problems; it holds in the entire region of Fig. 4.11*a* outside the shear layer.

Figure 4.11*b* shows a supersonic flow past a round-nosed body. A curved shock wave generally forms in front, and the flow downstream is *rotational* due to entropy gradients (case 2). We can use Euler's equation (4.114) in this frictionless region but not potential theory. The shear layers have the same general character as in Fig. 4.11*a* except that the separation zone is slight or often absent and the wake is usually thinner. Theory of separated flow is presently qualitative, but we can make quantitative estimates of laminar and turbulent boundary layers and wakes.

EXAMPLE 4.9

If a velocity potential exists for the velocity field of Example 4.5

$$u = a(x^2 - y^2) \qquad v = -2axy \qquad w = 0$$

find it, plot it, and compare with Example 4.7.

Solution

Since $w = 0$, the curl of **V** has only one z component, and we must show that it is zero:

$$(\nabla \times \mathbf{V})_z = 2\omega_z = \frac{\partial v}{\partial x} - \frac{\partial u}{\partial y} = \frac{\partial}{\partial x}(-2axy) - \frac{\partial}{\partial y}(ax^2 - ay^2)$$

$$= -2ay + 2ay = 0 \qquad \text{checks} \qquad\qquad Ans.$$

The flow is indeed irrotational. A velocity potential exists.
   To find $\phi(x, y)$, set

$$u = \frac{\partial \phi}{\partial x} = ax^2 - ay^2 \tag{1}$$

$$v = \frac{\partial \phi}{\partial y} = -2axy \tag{2}$$

Integrate (1)

$$\phi = \frac{ax^3}{3} - axy^2 + f(y) \tag{3}$$

Differentiate (3) and compare with (2)

$$\frac{\partial \phi}{\partial y} = -2axy + f'(y) = -2axy \tag{4}$$

Therefore $f' = 0$, or $f =$ constant. The velocity potential is

$$\phi = \frac{ax^3}{3} - axy^2 + C \qquad\qquad Ans.$$

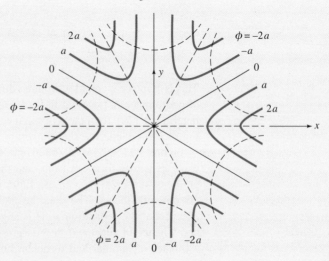

E4.9

Letting $C = 0$, we can plot the ϕ lines in the same fashion as in Example 4.7. The result is shown in Fig. E4.9 (no arrows on ϕ). For this particular problem, the ϕ lines form the same pattern as the ψ lines of Example 4.7 (which are shown here as dashed lines) but are displaced 30°. The ϕ and ψ lines are everywhere perpendicular except at the origin, a stagnation point, where they are 30° apart. We expected trouble at the stagnation point, and there is no general rule for determining the behavior of the lines at that point.

4.10 Some Illustrative Incompressible Viscous Flows

Inviscid flows do *not* satisfy the no-slip condition. They "slip" at the wall but do not flow through the wall. To look at fully viscous no-slip conditions, we must attack the complete Navier-Stokes equation (4.74), and the result is usually not at all irrotational, nor does a velocity potential exist. We look here at three cases: (1) flow between parallel plates due to a moving upper wall, (2) flow between parallel plates due to pressure gradient, and (3) flow between concentric cylinders when the inner one rotates. Other cases will be given as problem assignments or considered in Chap. 6. Extensive solutions for viscous flows are discussed in Refs. 4 and 5. All flows in this section are viscous and rotational.

Couette Flow between a Fixed and a Moving Plate

Consider two-dimensional incompressible plane ($\partial/\partial z = 0$) viscous flow between parallel plates a distance $2h$ apart, as shown in Fig. 4.12. We assume that the plates are very wide and very long, so the flow is essentially axial, $u \neq 0$ but $v = w = 0$. The present case is Fig. 4.12a, where the upper plate moves at velocity V but there is no pressure gradient. Neglect gravity effects. We learn from the continuity equation (4.73) that

$$\frac{\partial u}{\partial x} + \frac{\partial v}{\partial y} + \frac{\partial w}{\partial z} = 0 = \frac{\partial u}{\partial x} + 0 + 0 \qquad \text{or} \qquad u = u(y) \text{ only}$$

Thus there is a single nonzero axial velocity component that varies only across the channel. The flow is said to be *fully developed* (far downstream of the entrance).

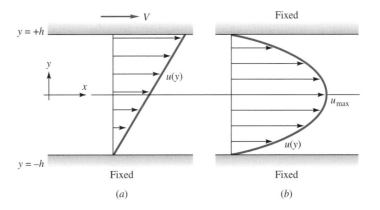

Fig. 4.12 Incompressible viscous flow between parallel plates: (*a*) no pressure gradient, upper plate moving; (*b*) pressure gradient $\partial p/\partial x$ with both plates fixed.

Substitute $u = u(y)$ into the x component of the Navier-Stokes momentum equation (4.74) for two-dimensional (x, y) flow:

$$\rho\left(u\frac{\partial u}{\partial x} + v\frac{\partial u}{\partial y}\right) = -\frac{\partial p}{\partial x} + \rho g_x + \mu\left(\frac{\partial^2 u}{\partial x^2} + \frac{\partial^2 u}{\partial y^2}\right)$$

or

$$\rho(0 + 0) = 0 + 0 + \mu\left(0 + \frac{d^2 u}{dy^2}\right) \tag{4.130}$$

Most of the terms drop out, and the momentum equation reduces to simply

$$\frac{d^2 u}{dy^2} = 0 \quad \text{or} \quad u = C_1 y + C_2$$

The two constants are found by applying the no-slip condition at the upper and lower plates:

At $y = +h$: $\qquad\qquad\qquad\qquad u = V = C_1 h + C_2$

At $y = -h$: $\qquad\qquad\qquad\qquad u = 0 = C_1(-h) + C_2$

or $\qquad\qquad\qquad\qquad C_1 = \dfrac{V}{2h} \quad \text{and} \quad C_2 = \dfrac{V}{2}$

Therefore the solution for this case (a), flow between plates with a moving upper wall, is

$$u = \frac{V}{2h}y + \frac{V}{2} \qquad -h \le y \le +h \tag{4.131}$$

This is *Couette flow* due to a moving wall: a linear velocity profile with no slip at each wall, as anticipated and sketched in Fig. 4.12a. Note that the origin has been placed in the center of the channel for convenience in case (b) which follows.

What we have just presented is a rigorous derivation of the more informally discussed flow of Fig. 1.7 (where y and h were defined differently).

Flow Due to Pressure Gradient between Two Fixed Plates

Case (b) is sketched in Fig. 4.12b. Both plates are fixed $(V = 0)$, but the pressure varies in the x direction. If $v = w = 0$, the continuity equation leads to the same conclusion as case (a)—namely, that $u = u(y)$ only. The x-momentum equation (4.130) changes only because the pressure is variable:

$$\mu\frac{d^2 u}{dy^2} = \frac{\partial p}{\partial x} \tag{4.132}$$

Also, since $v = w = 0$ and gravity is neglected, the y- and z-momentum equations lead to

$$\frac{\partial p}{\partial y} = 0 \quad \text{and} \quad \frac{\partial p}{\partial z} = 0 \quad \text{or} \quad p = p(x) \text{ only}$$

Thus the pressure gradient in Eq. (4.132) is the total and only gradient:

$$\mu\frac{d^2 u}{dy^2} = \frac{dp}{dx} = \text{const} < 0 \tag{4.133}$$

Why did we add the fact that dp/dx is *constant*? Recall a useful conclusion from the theory of separation of variables: If two quantities are equal and one varies only with y and the other varies only with x, then they must both equal the same constant. Otherwise they would not be independent of each other.

Why did we state that the constant is *negative*? Physically, the pressure must decrease in the flow direction in order to drive the flow against resisting wall shear stress. Thus the velocity profile $u(y)$ must have negative curvature everywhere, as anticipated and sketched in Fig. 4.12b.

The solution to Eq. (4.133) is accomplished by double integration:

$$u = \frac{1}{\mu}\frac{dp}{dx}\frac{y^2}{2} + C_1 y + C_2$$

The constants are found from the no-slip condition at each wall:

At $y = \pm h$: $\quad u = 0 \quad$ or $\quad C_1 = 0 \quad$ and $\quad C_2 = -\frac{dp}{dx}\frac{h^2}{2\mu}$

Thus the solution to case (b), flow in a channel due to pressure gradient, is

$$u = -\frac{dp}{dx}\frac{h^2}{2\mu}\left(1 - \frac{y^2}{h^2}\right) \tag{4.134}$$

The flow forms a *Poiseuille* parabola of constant negative curvature. The maximum velocity occurs at the centerline $y = 0$:

$$u_{\max} = -\frac{dp}{dx}\frac{h^2}{2\mu} \tag{4.135}$$

Other (laminar) flow parameters are computed in the following example.

EXAMPLE 4.10

For case (b) in Fig. 4.12b, flow between parallel plates due to the pressure gradient, compute (a) the wall shear stress, (b) the stream function, (c) the vorticity, (d) the velocity potential, and (e) the average velocity.

Solution

All parameters can be computed from the basic solution, Eq. (4.134), by mathematical manipulation.

Part (a)

The wall shear follows from the definition of a newtonian fluid, Eq. (4.37):

$$\tau_w = \tau_{xy\,\text{wall}} = \mu\left(\frac{\partial u}{\partial y} + \frac{\partial v}{\partial x}\right)\Bigg|_{y=\pm h} = \mu\frac{\partial}{\partial y}\left[\left(-\frac{dp}{dx}\right)\left(\frac{h^2}{2\mu}\right)\left(1 - \frac{y^2}{h^2}\right)\right]\Bigg|_{y=\pm h}$$

$$= \pm\frac{dp}{dx}h = \mp\frac{2\mu u_{\max}}{h} \qquad\qquad\qquad Ans.\ (a)$$

The wall shear has the same magnitude at each wall, but by our sign convention of Fig. 4.3, the upper wall has negative shear stress.

Part (b)   Since the flow is plane, steady, and incompressible, a stream function exists:

$$u = \frac{\partial \psi}{\partial y} = u_{max}\left(1 - \frac{y^2}{h^2}\right) \qquad v = -\frac{\partial \psi}{\partial x} = 0$$

Integrating and setting $\psi = 0$ at the centerline for convenience, we obtain

$$\psi = u_{max}\left(y - \frac{y^3}{3h^2}\right) \qquad\qquad \textit{Ans. (b)}$$

At the walls, $y = \pm h$ and $\psi = \pm 2u_{max}h/3$, respectively.

Part (c)   In plane flow, there is only a single nonzero vorticity component:

$$\zeta_z = (\text{curl } \mathbf{V})_z = \frac{\partial v}{\partial x} - \frac{\partial u}{\partial y} = \frac{2u_{max}}{h^2}y \qquad\qquad \textit{Ans. (c)}$$

The vorticity is highest at the wall and is positive (counterclockwise) in the upper half and negative (clockwise) in the lower half of the fluid. Viscous flows are typically full of vorticity and are not at all irrotational.

Part (d)   From part (c), the vorticity is finite. Therefore the flow is not irrotational, and the velocity potential *does not exist*. 　　　　　　　　　　　　　　　　　　　　　　　　　　　　*Ans. (d)*

Part (e)   The average velocity is defined as $V_{av} = Q/A$, where $Q = \int u \, dA$ over the cross section. For our particular distribution $u(y)$ from Eq. (4.134), we obtain

$$V_{av} = \frac{1}{A}\int u \, dA = \frac{1}{b(2h)}\int_{-h}^{+h} u_{max}\left(1 - \frac{y^2}{h^2}\right)b \, dy = \frac{2}{3}u_{max} \qquad \textit{Ans. (e)}$$

In plane Poiseuille flow between parallel plates, the average velocity is two-thirds of the maximum (or centerline) value. This result could also have been obtained from the stream function derived in part (b). From Eq. (4.95),

$$Q_{channel} = \psi_{upper} - \psi_{lower} = \frac{2u_{max}h}{3} - \left(-\frac{2u_{max}h}{3}\right) = \frac{4}{3}u_{max}h \text{ per unit width}$$

whence $V_{av} = Q/A_{b=1} = (4u_{max}h/3)/(2h) = 2u_{max}/3$, the same result.

This example illustrates a statement made earlier: Knowledge of the velocity vector $\mathbf{V}$ [as in Eq. (4.134)] is essentially the *solution* to a fluid mechanics problem, since all other flow properties can then be calculated.

Fully Developed Laminar Pipe Flow

Perhaps the most useful exact solution of the Navier-Stokes equation is for incompressible flow in a straight circular pipe of radius R, first studied experimentally by G. Hagen in 1839 and J. L. Poiseuille in 1840. By *fully developed* we mean that the region studied is far enough from the entrance that the flow is purely axial, $v_z \neq 0$, while v_r and v_θ are zero. We neglect gravity and also assume axial symmetry—that is, $\partial/\partial\theta = 0$. The equation of continuity in cylindrical coordinates, Eq. (4.12b), reduces to

$$\frac{\partial}{\partial z}(v_z) = 0 \qquad \text{or} \qquad v_z = v_z(r) \qquad \text{only}$$

The flow proceeds straight down the pipe without radial motion. The r-momentum equation in cylindrical coordinates, Eq. (D.5), simplifies to $\partial p / \partial r = 0$, or $p = p(z)$ only. The z-momentum equation in cylindrical coordinates, Eq. (D.7), reduces to

$$\rho v_z \frac{\partial v_z}{\partial z} = -\frac{dp}{dz} + \mu \nabla^2 v_z = -\frac{dp}{dz} + \frac{\mu}{r} \frac{d}{dr} \left(r \frac{dv_z}{dr} \right)$$

The convective acceleration term on the left vanishes because of the previously given continuity equation. Thus the momentum equation may be rearranged as follows:

$$\frac{\mu}{r} \frac{d}{dr} \left(r \frac{dv_z}{dr} \right) = \frac{dp}{dz} = \text{const} < 0 \qquad (4.136)$$

This is exactly the situation that occurred for flow between flat plates in Eq. (4.132). Again the "separation" constant is negative, and pipe flow will look much like the plate flow in Fig. 4.12b.

Equation (4.136) is linear and may be integrated twice, with the result

$$v_z = \frac{dp}{dz} \frac{r^2}{4\mu} + C_1 \ln(r) + C_2$$

where C_1 and C_2 are constants. The boundary conditions are no slip at the wall and finite velocity at the centerline:

$$\text{No slip at } r = R: \ v_z = 0 = \frac{dp}{dz} \frac{R^2}{4\mu} + C_1 \ln(R) + C_2$$

$$\text{Finite velocity at } r = 0: \ v_z = \text{finite} = 0 + C_1 \ln(0) + C_2$$

To avoid a logarithmic singularity, the centerline condition requires that $C_1 = 0$. Then, from no slip, $C_2 = (-dp/dz)(R^2/4\mu)$. The final, and famous, solution for fully developed *Hagen-Poiseuille flow* is

$$\boxed{v_z = \left(-\frac{dp}{dz} \right) \frac{1}{4\mu} (R^2 - r^2)} \qquad (4.137)$$

The velocity profile is a paraboloid with a maximum at the centerline. Just as in Example 4.10, knowledge of the velocity distribution enables other parameters to be calculated:

$$V_{\max} = v_z(r = 0) = \left(-\frac{dp}{dz} \right) \frac{R^2}{4\mu}$$

$$V_{\text{avg}} = \frac{1}{A} \int v_z \, dA = \frac{1}{\pi R^2} \int_0^R V_{\max} \left(1 - \frac{r^2}{R^2} \right) 2\pi r \, dr = \frac{V_{\max}}{2} = \left(-\frac{dp}{dz} \right) \frac{R^2}{8\mu}$$

$$Q = \int v_z \, dA = \int_0^R V_{\max} \left(1 - \frac{r^2}{R^2} \right) 2\pi r \, dr = \pi R^2 V_{\text{avg}} = \frac{\pi R^4}{8\mu} \left(-\frac{dp}{dz} \right) = \frac{\pi R^4 \Delta p}{8\mu L}$$

$$\tau_{\text{wall}} = \mu \left| \frac{\partial v_z}{\partial r} \right|_{r=R} = \frac{4\mu V_{\text{avg}}}{R} = \frac{R}{2} \left(-\frac{dp}{dz} \right) = \frac{R}{2} \frac{\Delta p}{L} \qquad (4.138)$$

Note that we have substituted the equality $(-dp/dz) = \Delta p/L$, where Δp is the pressure drop along the entire length L of the pipe.

These formulas are valid as long as the flow is *laminar*—that is, when the dimensionless Reynolds number of the flow, $\text{Re}_D = \rho V_{\text{avg}}(2R)/\mu$, is less than about 2100. Note also that the formulas do not depend on density, the reason being that the convective acceleration of this flow is zero.

EXAMPLE 4.11

SAE 10W oil at 20°C flows at 1.1 m³/h through a horizontal pipe with $d = 2$ cm and $L = 12$ m. Find (a) the average velocity, (b) the Reynolds number, (c) the pressure drop, and (d) the power required.

Solution

- *Assumptions:* Laminar, steady, Hagen-Poiseuille pipe flow.
- *Approach:* The formulas of Eqs. (4.138) are appropriate for this problem. Note that $R = 0.01$ m.
- *Property values:* From Table A.3 for SAE 10W oil, $\rho = 870$ kg/m³ and $\mu = 0.104$ kg/(m-s).
- *Solution steps:* The average velocity follows easily from the flow rate and the pipe area:

$$V_{\text{avg}} = \frac{Q}{\pi R^2} = \frac{(1.1/3600) \text{ m}^3/\text{s}}{\pi (0.01 \text{ m})^2} = 0.973 \ \frac{\text{m}}{\text{s}} \qquad \textit{Ans. (a)}$$

We had to convert Q to m³/s. The (diameter) Reynolds number follows from the average velocity:

$$\text{Re}_d = \frac{\rho V_{\text{avg}} d}{\mu} = \frac{(870 \text{ kg/m}^3)(0.973 \text{ m/s})(0.02 \text{ m})}{0.104 \text{ kg/(m-s)}} = 163 \qquad \textit{Ans. (b)}$$

This is less than the "transition" value of 2100; so the flow is indeed *laminar*, and the formulas are valid. The pressure drop is computed from the third of Eqs. (4.138):

$$Q = \frac{1.1}{3600} \frac{\text{m}^3}{\text{s}} = \frac{\pi R^4 \Delta p}{8 \mu L} = \frac{\pi (0.01 \text{ m})^4 \Delta p}{8(0.104 \text{ kg/(m-s)})(12 \text{ m})} \quad \text{solve for } \Delta p = 97{,}100 \text{ Pa} \quad \textit{Ans. (c)}$$

When using SI units, the answer returns in pascals; no conversion factors are needed. Finally, the power required is the product of flow rate and pressure drop:

$$\text{Power} = Q \Delta p = \left(\frac{1.1}{3600} \text{ m}^3/\text{s} \right) (97{,}100 \text{ N/m}^2) = 29.7 \ \frac{\text{N-m}}{\text{s}} = 29.7 \text{ W} \quad \textit{Ans. (d)}$$

- *Comments:* Pipe flow problems are straightforward algebraic exercises if the data are compatible. Note again that SI units can be used in the formulas without conversion factors.

Flow between Long Concentric Cylinders

Consider a fluid of constant (ρ, μ) between two concentric cylinders, as in Fig. 4.13. There is no axial motion or end effect $v_z = \partial/\partial z = 0$. Let the inner cylinder rotate at angular velocity Ω_i. Let the outer cylinder be fixed. There is circular symmetry, so the velocity does not vary with θ and varies only with r.

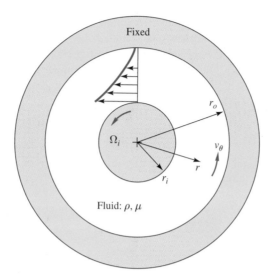

Fig. 4.13 Coordinate system for incompressible viscous flow between a fixed outer cylinder and a steadily rotating inner cylinder.

The continuity equation for this problem is Eq. (4.12b) with $v_z = 0$:

$$\frac{1}{r}\frac{\partial}{\partial r}(rv_r) + \frac{1}{r}\frac{\partial v_\theta}{\partial \theta} = 0 = \frac{1}{r}\frac{d}{dr}(rv_r) \quad \text{or} \quad rv_r = \text{const}$$

Note that v_θ does not vary with θ. Since $v_r = 0$ at both the inner and outer cylinders, it follows that $v_r = 0$ everywhere and the motion can only be purely circumferential, $v_\theta = v_\theta(r)$. The θ-momentum equation (D.6) becomes

$$\rho(\mathbf{V}\cdot\mathbf{\nabla})v_\theta + \frac{\rho v_r v_\theta}{r} = -\frac{1}{r}\frac{\partial p}{\partial \theta} + \rho g_\theta + \mu\left(\nabla^2 v_\theta - \frac{v_\theta}{r^2}\right)$$

For the conditions of the present problem, all terms are zero except the last. Therefore, the basic differential equation for flow between rotating cylinders is

$$\nabla^2 v_\theta = \frac{1}{r}\frac{d}{dr}\left(r\frac{dv_\theta}{dr}\right) = \frac{v_\theta}{r^2} \tag{4.139}$$

This is a linear second-order ordinary differential equation with the solution

$$v_\theta = C_1 r + \frac{C_2}{r}$$

The constants are found by the no-slip condition at the inner and outer cylinders:

Outer, at $r = r_o$: $\qquad\qquad v_\theta = 0 = C_1 r_o + \dfrac{C_2}{r_o}$

Inner, at $r = r_i$: $\qquad\qquad v_\theta = \Omega_i r_i = C_1 r_i + \dfrac{C_2}{r_i}$

The final solution for the velocity distribution is

Rotating inner cylinder: $\qquad v_\theta = \Omega_i r_i \dfrac{r_o/r - r/r_o}{r_o/r_i - r_i/r_o} \tag{4.140}$

The velocity profile closely resembles the sketch in Fig. 4.13. Variations of this case, such as a rotating outer cylinder, are given in the problem assignments.

Instability of Rotating Inner[15] Cylinder Flow

The classic *Couette flow* solution[16] of Eq. (4.140) describes a physically satisfying concave, two-dimensional, laminar flow velocity profile as in Fig. 4.13. The solution is mathematically exact for an incompressible fluid. However, it becomes unstable at a relatively low rate of rotation of the inner cylinder, as shown in 1923 in a classic paper by G. I. Taylor [17]. At a critical value of what is now called the dimensionless *Taylor number*, denoted Ta,

$$\text{Ta}_{\text{crit}} = \frac{r_i(r_o - r_i)^3\Omega_i^2}{\nu^2} \approx 1700 \tag{4.141}$$

the plane flow of Fig. 4.13 vanishes and is replaced by a laminar *three-dimensional* flow pattern consisting of rows of nearly square alternating toroidal vortices.

(a)

(b)

Fig. 4.14 Experimental verification of the instability of flow between a fixed outer and a rotating inner cylinder. (*a*) Toroidal Taylor vortices exist at 1.16 times the critical speed; (*b*) at 8.5 times the critical speed, the vortices are doubly periodic. (*Courtesy of Cambridge University Press— E.L. Koschmieder, "Turbulent Taylor Vortex Flow," Journal of Fluid Mechanics, vol. 93. pt. 3, 1979, pp. 515–527.*) This instability does not occur if only the outer cylinder rotates.

[15]This section may be omitted without loss of continuity.

[16]Named after M. Couette, whose pioneering paper in 1890 established rotating cylinders as a method, still used today, for measuring the viscosity of fluids.

An experimental demonstration of toroidal "Taylor vortices" is shown in Fig. 4.14a, measured at Ta $\approx$ 1.16 Ta$_{crit}$ by Koschmieder [18]. At higher Taylor numbers, the vortices also develop a circumferential periodicity but are still laminar, as illustrated in Fig. 4.14b. At still higher Ta, turbulence ensues. This interesting instability reminds us that the Navier-Stokes equations, being nonlinear, do admit to multiple (nonunique) laminar solutions in addition to the usual instabilities associated with turbulence and chaotic dynamic systems.

Summary

This chapter complements Chap. 3 by using an infinitesimal control volume to derive the basic partial differential equations of mass, momentum, and energy for a fluid. These equations, together with thermodynamic state relations for the fluid and appropriate boundary conditions, in principle can be solved for the complete flow field in any given fluid mechanics problem. Except for Chap. 9, in most of the problems to be studied here an incompressible fluid with constant viscosity is assumed.

In addition to deriving the basic equations of mass, momentum, and energy, this chapter introduced some supplementary ideas—the stream function, vorticity, irrotationality, and the velocity potential—which will be useful in coming chapters, especially Chap. 8. Temperature and density variations will be neglected except in Chap. 9, where compressibility is studied.

This chapter ended by discussing a few classic solutions for laminar viscous flows (Couette flow due to moving walls, Poiseuille duct flow due to pressure gradient, and flow between rotating cylinders). Whole books [4, 5, 9–11, 15] discuss classic approaches to fluid mechanics, and other texts [6, 12–14] extend these studies to the realm of continuum mechanics. This does not mean that all problems can be solved analytically. The new field of computational fluid dynamics [1] shows great promise of achieving approximate solutions to a wide variety of flow problems. In addition, when the geometry and boundary conditions are truly complex, experimentation (Chap. 5) is a preferred alternative.

Problems

Most of the problems herein are fairly straightforward. More difficult or open-ended assignments are labeled with an asterisk. Problems labeled with a computer icon 💻 may require the use of a computer. The standard end-of-chapter problems P4.1 to P4.99 (categorized in the problem list here) are followed by word problems W4.1 to W4.10, fundamentals of engineering exam problems FE4.1 to FE4.6, and comprehensive problems C4.1 and C4.2.

Problem Distribution

Section	Topic	Problems
4.1	The acceleration of a fluid	P4.1–P4.8
4.2	The continuity equation	P4.9–P4.25
4.3	Linear momentum: Navier-Stokes	P4.26–P4.38
4.4	Angular momentum: couple stresses	P4.39
4.5	The differential energy equation	P4.40–P4.41
4.6	Boundary conditions	P4.42–P4.46
4.7	Stream function	P4.47–P4.55
4.8 and 4.9	Velocity potential, vorticity	P4.56–P4.67
4.7 and 4.9	Stream function and velocity potential	P4.68–P4.78
4.10	Incompressible viscous flows	P4.79–P4.96
4.10	Slip flows	P4.97–P4.99

The acceleration of a fluid

P4.1 An idealized velocity field is given by the formula

$$\mathbf{V} = 4tx\mathbf{i} - 2t^2y\mathbf{j} + 4xz\mathbf{k}$$

Is this flow field steady or unsteady? Is it two- or three-dimensional? At the point $(x, y, z) = (-1, 1, 0)$, compute (a) the acceleration vector and (b) any unit vector normal to the acceleration.

P4.2 Flow through the converging nozzle in Fig. P4.2 can be approximated by the one-dimensional velocity distribution

$$u \approx V_0\left(1 + \frac{2x}{L}\right) \quad v \approx 0 \quad w \approx 0$$

(a) Find a general expression for the fluid acceleration in the nozzle. (b) For the specific case $V_0 = 10$ ft/s and $L = 6$ in, compute the acceleration, in g's, at the entrance and at the exit.

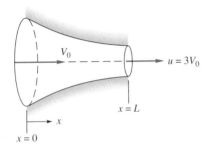

P4.2

P4.3 A two-dimensional velocity field is given by

$$\mathbf{V} = (x^2 - y^2 + x)\mathbf{i} - (2xy + y)\mathbf{j}$$

in arbitrary units. At $(x, y) = (1, 2)$, compute (a) the accelerations a_x and a_y, (b) the velocity component in the direction $\theta = 40°$, (c) the direction of maximum velocity, and (d) the direction of maximum acceleration.

P4.4 A simple flow model for a two-dimensional converging nozzle is the distribution

$$u = U_0\left(1 + \frac{x}{L}\right) \quad v = -U_0\frac{y}{L} \quad w = 0$$

(a) Sketch a few streamlines in the region $0 < x/L < 1$ and $0 < y/L < 1$, using the method of Sec. 1.11. (b) Find expressions for the horizontal and vertical accelerations. (c) Where is the largest resultant acceleration and its numerical value?

P4.5 The velocity field near a stagnation point may be written in the form

$$u = \frac{U_0 x}{L} \quad v = -\frac{U_0 y}{L} \quad U_0 \text{ and } L \text{ are constants}$$

(a) Show that the acceleration vector is purely radial. (b) For the particular case $L = 1.5$ m, if the acceleration at $(x, y) = (1 \text{ m}, 1 \text{ m})$ is 25 m/s², what is the value of U_0?

P4.6 In deriving the continuity equation, we assumed, for simplicity, that the mass flow per unit area on the left face was just ρu. In fact, ρu varies also with y and z, and thus it must be different on the four corners of the left face. Account for these variations, average the four corners, and determine how this might change the inlet mass flow from $\rho u \, dy \, dz$.

P4.7 Consider a sphere of radius R immersed in a uniform stream U_0, as shown in Fig. P4.7. According to the theory of Chap. 8, the fluid velocity along streamline AB is given by

$$\mathbf{V} = u\mathbf{i} = U_0\left(1 + \frac{R^3}{x^3}\right)\mathbf{i}$$

Find (a) the position of maximum fluid acceleration along AB and (b) the time required for a fluid particle to travel from A to B.

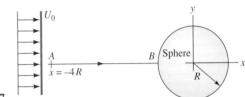

P4.7

P4.8 When a valve is opened, fluid flows in the expansion duct of Fig. P4.8 according to the approximation

$$\mathbf{V} = \mathbf{i}U\left(1 - \frac{x}{2L}\right)\tanh\frac{Ut}{L}$$

Find (a) the fluid acceleration at $(x, t) = (L, L/U)$ and (b) the time for which the fluid acceleration at $x = L$ is zero. Why does the fluid acceleration become negative after condition (b)?

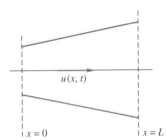

P4.8

The continuity equation

P4.9 An idealized incompressible flow has the proposed three-dimensional velocity distribution

$$\mathbf{V} = 4xy^2\mathbf{i} + f(y)\mathbf{j} - zy^2\mathbf{k}$$

Find the appropriate form of the function $f(y)$ that satisfies the continuity relation.

P4.10 A two-dimensional, incompressible flow has the velocity components $u = 4y$ and $v = 2x$. (a) Find the acceleration components. (b) Is the vector acceleration radial? (c) Sketch a few streamlines in the first quadrant and determine if any are straight lines.

P4.11 Derive Eq. (4.12b) for cylindrical coordinates by considering the flux of an incompressible fluid in and out of the elemental control volume in Fig. 4.2.

P4.12 Spherical polar coordinates (r, θ, ϕ) are defined in Fig. P4.12. The cartesian transformations are

$$x = r \sin \theta \cos \phi$$
$$y = r \sin \theta \sin \phi$$
$$z = r \cos \theta$$

Do not show that the cartesian incompressible continuity relation [Eq. (4.12a)] can be transformed to the spherical polar form

$$\frac{1}{r^2} \frac{\partial}{\partial r}(r^2 v_r) + \frac{1}{r \sin \theta} \frac{\partial}{\partial \theta}(v_\theta \sin \theta) + \frac{1}{r \sin \theta} \frac{\partial}{\partial \phi}(v_\phi) = 0$$

What is the most general form of v_r when the flow is purely radial—that is, v_θ and v_ϕ are zero?

P4.13 For an incompressible plane flow in polar coordinates, we are given

$$v_r = r^3 \cos \theta + r^2 \sin \theta$$

Find the appropriate form of circumferential velocity for which continuity is satisfied.

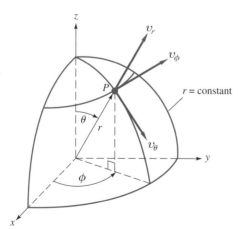

P4.12

P4.14 For incompressible polar coordinate flow, what is the most general form of a purely circulatory motion, $v_\theta = v_\theta(r, \theta, t)$ and $v_r = 0$, that satisfies continuity?

P4.15 What is the most general form of a purely radial polar coordinate incompressible flow pattern, $v_r = v_r(r, \theta, t)$ and $v_\theta = 0$, that satisfies continuity?

P4.16 Consider the plane polar coordinate velocity distribution

$$v_r = \frac{C}{r} \qquad v_\theta = \frac{K}{r} \qquad v_z = 0$$

where C and K are constants. (a) Determine if the equation of continuity is satisfied. (b) By sketching some velocity vector directions, plot a single streamline for $C = K$. What might this flow field simulate?

P4.17 An excellent approximation for the two-dimensional incompressible laminar boundary layer on the flat surface in Fig. P4.17 is

$$u \approx U\left(2\frac{y}{\delta} - 2\frac{y^3}{\delta^3} + \frac{y^4}{\delta^4}\right) \qquad \text{for } y \le \delta$$

$$\text{where } \delta = Cx^{1/2}, C = \text{const}$$

(a) Assuming a no-slip condition at the wall, find an expression for the velocity component $v(x, y)$ for $y \le \delta$. (b) Then find the maximum value of v at the station $x = 1$ m, for the particular case of airflow, when $U = 3$ m/s and $\delta = 1.1$ cm.

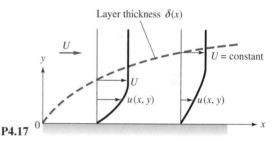

P4.17

P4.18 A piston compresses gas in a cylinder by moving at constant speed V, as in Fig. P4.18. Let the gas density and length at $t = 0$ be ρ_0 and L_0, respectively. Let the gas velocity vary linearly from $u = V$ at the piston face to $u = 0$ at $x = L$. If the gas density varies only with time, find an expression for $\rho(t)$.

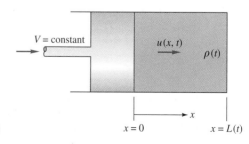

P4.18

P4.19 A proposed incompressible plane flow in polar coordinates is given by

$$v_r = 2r\cos(2\theta); \quad v_\theta = -2r\sin(2\theta)$$

(a) Determine if this flow satisfies the equation of continuity. (b) If so, sketch a possible streamline in the first quadrant by finding the velocity vectors at $(r, \theta) = (1.25, 20°)$, $(1.0, 45°)$, and $(1.25, 70°)$. (c) Speculate on what this flow might represent.

P4.20 A two-dimensional incompressible velocity field has $u = K(1 - e^{-ay})$, for $x \leq L$ and $0 \leq y \leq \infty$. What is the most general form of $v(x, y)$ for which continuity is satisfied and $v = v_0$ at $y = 0$? What are the proper dimensions for constants K and a?

P4.21 Air flows under steady, approximately one-dimensional conditions through the conical nozzle in Fig. P4.21. If the speed of sound is approximately 340 m/s, what is the minimum nozzle-diameter ratio D_e/D_0 for which we can safely neglect compressibility effects if $V_0 =$ (a) 10 m/s and (b) 30 m/s?

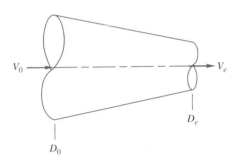

P4.21

P4.22 In an *axisymmetric* flow, nothing varies with θ, and the only nonzero velocities are v_r and v_z (see Fig. 4.2). If the flow is steady and incompressible and $v_z = Bz$, where B is constant, find the most general form of v_r which satisfies continuity.

P4.23 A tank volume $\mathcal{V}$ contains gas at conditions (ρ_0, p_0, T_0). At time $t = 0$ it is punctured by a small hole of area A. According to the theory of Chap. 9, the mass flow out of such a hole is approximately proportional to A and to the tank pressure. If the tank temperature is assumed constant and the gas is ideal, find an expression for the variation of density within the tank.

P4.24 For laminar flow between parallel plates (see Fig. 4.12b), the flow is two-dimensional ($v \neq 0$) if the walls are porous. A special case solution is $u = (A - Bx)(h^2 - y^2)$, where A and B are constants. (a) Find a general formula for velocity v if $v = 0$ at $y = 0$. (b) What is the value of the constant B if $v = v_w$ at $y = +h$?

P4.25 An incompressible flow in polar coordinates is given by

$$v_r = K\cos\theta\left(1 - \frac{b}{r^2}\right)$$

$$v_\theta = -K\sin\theta\left(1 + \frac{b}{r^2}\right)$$

Does this field satisfy continuity? For consistency, what should the dimensions of constants K and b be? Sketch the surface where $v_r = 0$ and interpret.

Linear momentum: Navier-Stokes

*P4.26 Curvilinear, or streamline, coordinates are defined in Fig. P4.26, where n is normal to the streamline in the plane of the radius of curvature R. Euler's frictionless momentum equation (4.36) in streamline coordinates becomes

$$\frac{\partial V}{\partial t} + V\frac{\partial V}{\partial s} = -\frac{1}{\rho}\frac{\partial p}{\partial s} + g_s \quad (1)$$

$$-V\frac{\partial\theta}{\partial t} - \frac{V^2}{R} = -\frac{1}{\rho}\frac{\partial p}{\partial n} + g_n \quad (2)$$

Show that the integral of Eq. (1) with respect to s is none other than our old friend Bernoulli's equation (3.54).

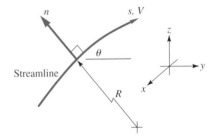

P4.26

P4.27 A frictionless, incompressible steady flow field is given by

$$\mathbf{V} = 2xy\mathbf{i} - y^2\mathbf{j}$$

in arbitrary units. Let the density be $\rho_0 =$ constant and neglect gravity. Find an expression for the pressure gradient in the x direction.

P4.28 For the velocity distribution of Prob. 4.10, (a) check continuity. (b) Are the Navier-Stokes equations valid? (c) If so, determine $p(x, y)$ if the pressure at the origin is p_0.

P4.29 Consider a steady, two-dimensional, incompressible flow of a newtonian fluid in which the velocity field is known: $u = -2xy$, $v = y^2 - x^2$, $w = 0$. (a) Does this flow satisfy conservation of mass? (b) Find the pressure field, $p(x, y)$ if the pressure at the point $(x = 0, y = 0)$ is equal to p_a.

P4.30 For the velocity distribution of Prob. P4.4, determine if (a) the equation of continuity and (b) the Navier-Stokes equation are satisfied. (c) If the latter is true, find the pressure distribution $p(x, y)$ when the pressure at the origin equals p_0.

P4.31 According to potential theory (Chap. 8) for the flow approaching a rounded two-dimensional body, as in Fig. P4.31, the velocity approaching the stagnation point is given by $u = U(1 - a^2/x^2)$, where a is the nose radius and U is the velocity far upstream. Compute the value and position of the maximum viscous normal stress along this streamline.

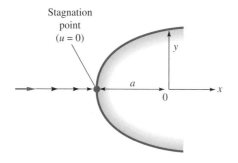

Stagnation point ($u = 0$)

P4.31

Is this also the position of maximum fluid deceleration? Evaluate the maximum viscous normal stress if the fluid is SAE 30 oil at 20°C, with $U = 2$ m/s and $a = 6$ cm.

P4.32 The answer to Prob. P4.14 is $v_\theta = f(r)$ only. Do not reveal this to your friends if they are still working on Prob. P4.14. Show that this flow field is an exact solution to the Navier-Stokes equations (4.38) for only two special cases of the function $f(r)$. Neglect gravity. Interpret these two cases physically.

P4.33 Consider incompressible flow at a volume rate Q toward a drain at the vertex of a 45° wedge of width b, as in Fig. P4.33. Neglect gravity and friction and assume purely radial inflow. (a) Find an expression for $v_r(r)$. (b) Show that the viscous term in the r-momentum equation is zero. (c) Find the pressure distribution $p(r)$ if $p = p_0$ at $r = R$.

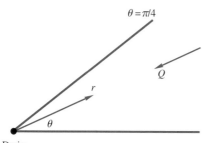

$\theta = \pi/4$

P4.33   Drain

P4.34 A proposed three-dimensional incompressible flow field has the following vector form:

$$\mathbf{V} = Kx\mathbf{i} + Ky\mathbf{j} - 2Kz\mathbf{k}$$

(a) Determine if this field is a valid solution to continuity and Navier-Stokes. (b) If $\mathbf{g} = -g\mathbf{k}$, find the pressure field $p(x, y, z)$. (c) Is the flow irrotational?

P4.35 From the Navier-Stokes equations for incompressible flow in polar coordinates (App. D for cylindrical coordinates), find the most general case of purely circulating motion $v_\theta(r)$, $v_r = v_z = 0$, for flow with no slip between two fixed concentric cylinders, as in Fig. P4.35.

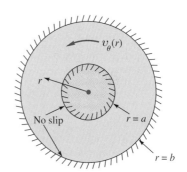

$v_\theta(r)$

No slip $r = a$

$r = b$

P4.35

P4.36 A constant-thickness film of viscous liquid flows in laminar motion down a plate inclined at angle θ, as in Fig. P4.36. The velocity profile is

$$u = Cy(2h - y) \quad v = w = 0$$

Find the constant C in terms of the specific weight and viscosity and the angle θ. Find the volume flux Q per unit width in terms of these parameters.

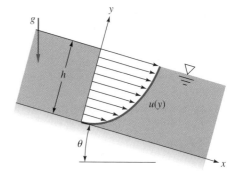

$u(y)$

P4.36

*P4.37 A viscous liquid of constant ρ and μ falls due to gravity between two plates a distance $2h$ apart, as in Fig. P4.37. The flow is fully developed, with a single velocity component

$w = w(x)$. There are no applied pressure gradients, only gravity. Solve the Navier-Stokes equation for the velocity profile between the plates.

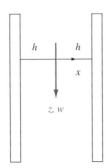

P4.37

P4.38　Show that the incompressible flow distribution, in cylindrical coordinates,

$$v_r = 0 \qquad v_\theta = Cr^n \qquad v_z = 0$$

where C is a constant, (a) satisfies the Navier-Stokes equation for only two values of n. Neglect gravity. (b) Knowing that $p = p(r)$ only, find the pressure distribution for each case, assuming that the pressure at $r = R$ is p_0. What might these two cases represent?

Angular momentum: couple stresses

P4.39　Reconsider the angular momentum balance of Fig. 4.5 by adding a concentrated *body couple* C_z about the z axis [6]. Determine a relation between the body couple and shear stress for equilibrium. What are the proper dimensions for C_z? (Body couples are important in continuous media with microstructure, such as granular materials.)

The differential energy equation

P4.40　For pressure-driven laminar flow between parallel plates (see Fig. 4.12b), the velocity components are $u = U(1 - y^2/h^2)$, $v = 0$, and $w = 0$, where U is the centerline velocity. In the spirit of Ex. 4.6, find the temperature distribution $T(y)$ for a constant wall temperature T_w.

P4.41　As mentioned in Sec. 4.10, the velocity profile for laminar flow between two plates, as in Fig. P4.41, is

$$u = \frac{4u_{max}y(h - y)}{h^2} \qquad v = w = 0$$

If the wall temperature is T_w at both walls, use the incompressible flow energy equation (4.75) to solve for the temperature distribution $T(y)$ between the walls for steady flow.

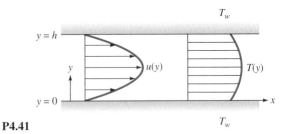

P4.41

Boundary conditions

P4.42　Suppose we wish to analyze the rotating, partly full cylinder of Fig. 2.23 as a *spin-up* problem, starting from rest and continuing until solid-body rotation is achieved. What are the appropriate boundary and initial conditions for this problem?

P4.43　For the draining liquid film of Fig. P4.36, what are the appropriate boundary conditions (a) at the bottom $y = 0$ and (b) at the surface $y = h$?

P4.44　Suppose that we wish to analyze the sudden pipe expansion flow of Fig. P3.59, using the full continuity and Navier-Stokes equations. What are the proper boundary conditions to handle this problem?

P4.45　For the sluice gate problem of Example 3.10, list all the boundary conditions needed to solve this flow exactly by, say, computational fluid dynamics.

P4.46　Fluid from a large reservoir at temperature T_0 flows into a circular pipe of radius R. The pipe walls are wound with an electric resistance coil that delivers heat to the fluid at a rate q_w (energy per unit wall area). If we wish to analyze this problem by using the full continuity, Navier-Stokes, and energy equations, what are the proper boundary conditions for the analysis?

Stream function

P4.47　A two-dimensional incompressible flow is given by the velocity field $\mathbf{V} = 3y\mathbf{i} + 2x\mathbf{j}$, in arbitrary units. Does this flow satisfy continuity? If so, find the stream function $\psi(x, y)$ and plot a few streamlines, with arrows.

P4.48　Consider the following two-dimensional incompressible flow, which clearly satisfies continuity:

$$u = U_0 = \text{constant}, \ v = V_0 = \text{constant}$$

Find the stream function $\psi(r, \theta)$ of this flow using *polar coordinates*.

P4.49　Investigate the stream function $\psi = K(x^2 - y^2)$, $K = $ constant. Plot the streamlines in the full xy plane, find any stagnation points, and interpret what the flow could represent.

P4.50 In 1851, George Stokes (of Navier-Stokes fame) solved the problem of steady incompressible low-Reynolds-number flow past a sphere, using *spherical polar* coordinates (r, θ) [Ref. 5, page 168]. In these coordinates, the equation of continuity is

$$\frac{\partial}{\partial r}(r^2 v_r \sin \theta) + \frac{\partial}{\partial \theta}(r v_\theta \sin \theta) = 0$$

(a) Does a stream function exist for these coordinates? (b) If so, find its form.

P4.51 The velocity profile for pressure-driven laminar flow between parallel plates (see Fig. 4.12b) has the form $u = C(h^2 - y^2)$, where C is a constant. (a) Determine if a stream function exists. (b) If so, find a formula for the stream function.

P4.52 A two-dimensional, incompressible, frictionless fluid is guided by wedge-shaped walls into a small slot at the origin, as in Fig. P4.52. The width into the paper is b,

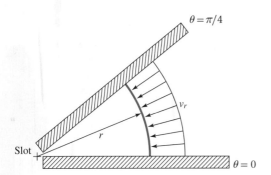

P4.52

and the volume flow rate is Q. At any given distance r from the slot, the flow is radial inward, with constant velocity. Find an expression for the polar coordinate stream function of this flow.

P4.53 For the fully developed laminar pipe flow solution of Eq. (4.137), find the axisymmetric stream function $\psi(r, z)$. Use this result to determine the average velocity $V = Q/A$ in the pipe as a ratio of u_{max}.

P4.54 An incompressible stream function is defined by

$$\psi(x, y) = \frac{U}{L^2}(3x^2y - y^3)$$

where U and L are (positive) constants. Where in this chapter are the streamlines of this flow plotted? Use this stream function to find the volume flow Q passing through the rectangular surface whose corners are defined by $(x, y, z) = (2L, 0, 0), (2L, 0, b), (0, L, b),$ and $(0, L, 0)$. Show the direction of Q.

P4.55 The proposed flow in Prob. P4.19 does indeed satisfy the equation of continuity. Determine the polar-coordinate stream function of this flow.

Velocity potential, vorticity

P4.56 Investigate the velocity potential $\phi = Kxy$, $K = $ constant. Sketch the potential lines in the full xy plane, find any stagnation points, and sketch in by eye the orthogonal streamlines. What could the flow represent?

P4.57 A two-dimensional incompressible flow field is defined by the velocity components

$$u = 2V\left(\frac{x}{L} - \frac{y}{L}\right) \qquad v = -2V\frac{y}{L}$$

where V and L are constants. If they exist, find the stream function and velocity potential.

P4.58 Show that the incompressible velocity potential in plane polar coordinates $\phi(r, \theta)$ is such that

$$v_r = \frac{\partial \phi}{\partial r} \qquad v_\theta = \frac{1}{r}\frac{\partial \phi}{\partial \theta}$$

Finally show that ϕ as defined here satisfies Laplace's equation in polar coordinates for incompressible flow.

P4.59 Consider the two-dimensional incompressible velocity potential $\phi = xy + x^2 - y^2$. (a) Is it true that $\nabla^2\phi = 0$, and, if so, what does this mean? (b) If it exists, find the stream function $\psi(x, y)$ of this flow. (c) Find the equation of the streamline that passes through $(x, y) = (2, 1)$.

P4.60 Liquid drains from a small hole in a tank, as shown in Fig. P4.60, such that the velocity field set up is given by $v_r \approx 0$, $v_z \approx 0$, $v_\theta = KR^2/r$, where $z = H$ is the depth of the water far from the hole. Is this flow pattern rotational or irrotational? Find the depth z_C of the water at the radius $r = R$.

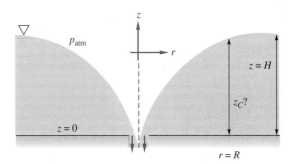

P4.60

P4.61   An incompressible stream function is given by $\psi = a\theta + br \sin\theta$. (*a*) Does this flow have a velocity potential? (*b*) If so, find it.

P4.62   Show that the linear Couette flow between plates in Fig. 1.7 has a stream function but no velocity potential. Why is this so?

P4.63   Find the two-dimensional velocity potential $\phi(r, \theta)$ for the polar coordinate flow pattern $v_r = Q/r$, $v_\theta = K/r$, where Q and K are constants.

P4.64   Show that the velocity potential $\phi(r, z)$ in axisymmetric cylindrical coordinates (see Fig. 4.2) is defined such that

$$v_r = \frac{\partial\phi}{\partial r} \qquad v_z = \frac{\partial\phi}{\partial z}$$

Further show that for incompressible flow this potential satisfies Laplace's equation in (r, z) coordinates.

P4.65   Consider the function $f = ay - by^3$. (*a*) Could this represent a realistic velocity potential? *Extra credit*: (*b*) Could it represent a stream function?

P4.66   A plane polar coordinate velocity potential is defined by

$$\phi = \frac{K \cos\theta}{r} \qquad K = \text{const}$$

Find the stream function for this flow, sketch some streamlines and potential lines, and interpret the flow pattern.

P4.67   A stream function for a plane, irrotational, polar coordinate flow is

$$\psi = C\theta - K \ln r \qquad C \text{ and } K = \text{const}$$

Find the velocity potential for this flow. Sketch some streamlines and potential lines, and interpret the flow pattern.

Stream function *and* velocity potential

P4.68   For the velocity distribution of Prob. P4.4, (*a*) determine if a velocity potential exists, and (*b*), if it does, find an expression for $\phi(x, y)$ and sketch the potential line which passes through the point $(x, y) = (L/2, L/2)$.

P4.69   A steady, two-dimensional flow has the following polar-coordinate velocity potential:

$$\phi = C r \cos\theta + K \ln r$$

where C and K are constants. Determine the stream function $\psi(r, \theta)$ for this flow. For extra credit, let C be a velocity scale U and let $K = UL$, sketch what the flow might represent.

P4.70   A CFD model of steady two-dimensional incompressible flow has printed out the values of stream function $\psi(x, y)$, in m²/s, at each of the four corners of a small 10-cm-by-10-cm cell, as shown in Fig. P4.70. Use these numbers to estimate

the resultant velocity in the center of the cell and its angle α with respect to the x axis.

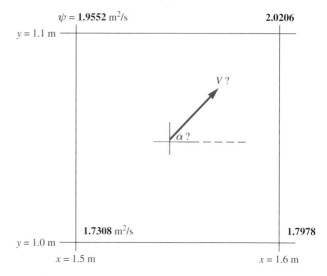

P4.70

P4.71   Consider the following two-dimensional function $f(x, y)$:

$$f = Ax^3 + Bxy^2 + Cx^2 + D \quad \text{where } A > 0$$

(*a*) Under what conditions, if any, on (A, B, C, D) can this function be a steady plane-flow velocity potential? (*b*) If you find a $\phi(x, y)$ to satisfy part (*a*), also find the associated stream function $\psi(x, y)$, if any, for this flow.

P4.72   Water flows through a two-dimensional narrowing wedge at 9.96 gal/min per meter of width into the paper (Fig. P4.72). If this inward flow is purely radial, find an expression, in SI units, for (*a*) the stream function and (*b*) the velocity potential of the flow. Assume one-dimensional flow. The included angle of the wedge is 45°.

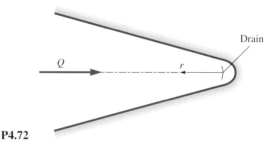

P4.72

P4.73   A CFD model of steady two-dimensional incompressible flow has printed out the values of velocity potential $\phi(x, y)$, in m²/s, at each of the four corners of a small 10-cm-by-10-cm cell, as shown in Fig. P4.73. Use these numbers to estimate the resultant velocity in the center of the cell and its angle α with respect to the x axis.

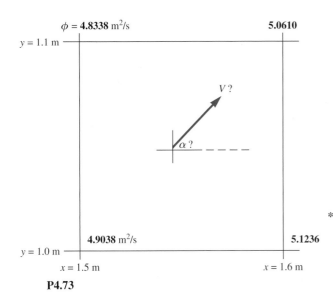

P4.73

P4.74 Consider the two-dimensional incompressible polar-coordinate velocity potential

$$\phi = Br \cos \theta + B L \theta$$

where B is a constant and L is a constant length scale. (a) What are the dimensions of B? (b) Locate the only stagnation point in this flow field. (c) Prove that a stream function exists and then find the function $\psi(r, \theta)$.

P4.75 Given the following steady *axisymmetric* stream function:

$$\psi = \frac{B}{2}\left(r^2 - \frac{r^4}{2R^2}\right) \quad \text{where } B \text{ and } R \text{ are constants}$$

valid in the region $0 \leqslant r \leqslant R$ and $0 \leqslant z \leqslant L$. (a) What are the dimensions of the constant B? (b) Show whether this flow possesses a velocity potential, and, if so, find it. (c) What might this flow represent? *Hint:* Examine the axial velocity v_z.

*P4.76 A two-dimensional incompressible flow has the velocity potential

$$\phi = K(x^2 - y^2) + C \ln(x^2 + y^2)$$

where K and C are constants. In this discussion, avoid the origin, which is a singularity (infinite velocity). (a) Find the sole stagnation point of this flow, which is somewhere

in the upper half plane. (b) Prove that a stream function exists, and then find $\psi(x, y)$, using the hint that $\int dx/(a^2 + x^2) = (1/a)\tan^{-1}(x/a)$.

P4.77 Outside an inner, intense-activity circle of radius R, a tropical storm can be simulated by a polar-coordinate velocity potential $\phi(r, \theta) = U_o R \theta$, where U_o is the wind velocity at radius R. (a) Determine the velocity components outside $r = R$. (b) If, at $R = 25$ mi, the velocity is 100 mi/h and the pressure 99 kPa, calculate the velocity and pressure at $r = 100$ mi.

P4.78 An incompressible, irrotational, two-dimensional flow has the following stream function in polar coordinates:

$$\psi = A r^n \sin (n\theta) \quad \text{where } A \text{ and } n \text{ are constants.}$$

Find an expression for the velocity potential of this flow.

Incompressible viscous flows

*P4.79 Study the combined effect of the two viscous flows in Fig. 4.12. That is, find $u(y)$ when the upper plate moves at speed V and there is also a constant pressure gradient (dp/dx). Is superposition possible? If so, explain why. Plot representative velocity profiles for (a) zero, (b) positive, and (c) negative pressure gradients for the same upper-wall speed V.

*P4.80 Oil, of density ρ and viscosity μ, drains steadily down the side of a vertical plate, as in Fig. P4.80. After a development region near the top of the plate, the oil film will become independent of z and of constant thickness δ. Assume that $w = w(x)$ only and that the atmosphere offers no shear resistance to the surface of the film. (a) Solve the Navier-Stokes equation for $w(x)$, and sketch its approximate shape. (b) Suppose that film thickness δ and the slope of the velocity profile at the wall $[\partial w/\partial x]_{\text{wall}}$ are measured with a laser-Doppler anemometer (Chap. 6). Find an expression for oil viscosity μ as a function of $(\rho, \delta, g, [\partial w/\partial x]_{\text{wall}})$.

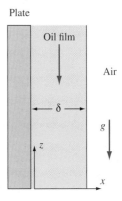

P4.80

P4.81 Modify the analysis of Fig. 4.13 to find the velocity u_θ when the inner cylinder is fixed and the outer cylinder rotates at angular velocity Ω_0. May this solution be *added* to Eq. (4.140) to represent the flow caused when both inner and outer cylinders rotate? Explain your conclusion.

*P4.82 A solid circular cylinder of radius R rotates at angular velocity Ω in a viscous incompressible fluid that is at rest far from the cylinder, as in Fig. P4.82. Make simplifying assumptions and derive the governing differential equation and boundary conditions for the velocity field v_θ in the fluid. Do not solve unless you are obsessed with this problem. What is the steady-state flow field for this problem?

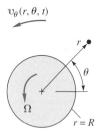

$v_\theta(r, \theta, t)$

P4.82

Ω

$r = R$

P4.83 The flow pattern in bearing lubrication can be illustrated by Fig. P4.83, where a viscous oil (ρ, μ) is forced into the gap $h(x)$ between a fixed slipper block and a wall moving at velocity U. If the gap is thin, $h \ll L$, it can be shown that the pressure and velocity distributions are of the form $p = p(x)$, $u = u(y)$, $v = w = 0$. Neglecting gravity, reduce the Navier-Stokes equations (4.38) to a single differential equation for $u(y)$. What are the proper boundary conditions? Integrate and show that

$$u = \frac{1}{2\mu}\frac{dp}{dx}(y^2 - yh) + U\left(1 - \frac{y}{h}\right)$$

where $h = h(x)$ may be an arbitrary, slowly varying gap width. (For further information on lubrication theory, see Ref. 16.)

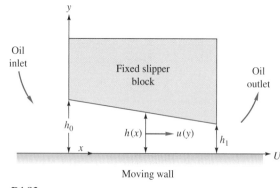

Oil inlet

Fixed slipper block

Oil outlet

h_0

$h(x)$ — $u(y)$

h_1

x

U

Moving wall

P4.83

*P4.84 Consider a viscous film of liquid draining uniformly down the side of a vertical rod of radius a, as in Fig. P4.84. At some distance down the rod the film will approach a terminal or *fully developed* draining flow of constant outer radius b, with $v_z = v_z(r)$, $v_\theta = v_r = 0$. Assume that the atmosphere offers no shear resistance to the film motion. Derive a differential equation for v_z, state the proper boundary conditions, and solve for the film velocity distribution. How does the film radius b relate to the total film volume flow rate Q?

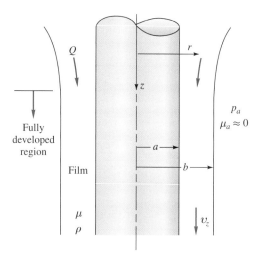

Q

r

z

p_a
$\mu_a \approx 0$

Fully developed region

a

Film

b

μ
ρ

v_z

P4.84

P4.85 A flat plate of essentially infinite width and breadth oscillates sinusoidally in its own plane beneath a viscous fluid, as in Fig. P4.85. The fluid is at rest far above the plate. Making as many simplifying assumptions as you can, set up the governing differential equation and boundary conditions for finding the velocity field u in the fluid. Do not solve (if you *can* solve it immediately, you might be able to get exempted from the balance of this course with credit).

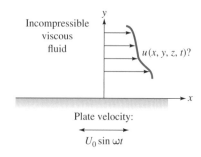

Incompressible viscous fluid

$u(x, y, z, t)$?

Plate velocity:

$U_0 \sin \omega t$

P4.85

P4.86 SAE 10 oil at 20°C flows between parallel plates 8 mm apart, as in Fig. P4.86. A mercury manometer, with wall pressure taps 1 m apart, registers a 6-cm height, as shown. Estimate the flow rate of oil for this condition.

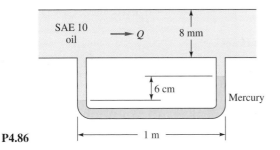

P4.86

P4.87 SAE 30W oil at 20°C flows through the 9-cm-diameter pipe in Fig. P4.87 at an average velocity of 4.3 m/s.

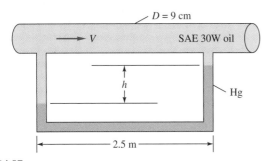

P4.87

(a) Verify that the flow is laminar. (b) Determine the volume flow rate in m^3/h. (c) Calculate the expected reading h of the mercury manometer, in cm.

P4.88 The viscous oil in Fig. P4.88 is set into steady motion by a concentric inner cylinder moving axially at velocity U inside a fixed outer cylinder. Assuming constant pressure and density and a purely axial fluid motion, solve Eqs. (4.38) for the fluid velocity distribution $v_z(r)$. What are the proper boundary conditions?

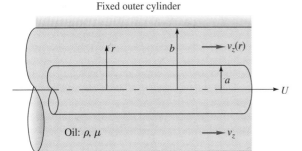

P4.88

P4.89 Oil flows steadily between two fixed plates that are 2 inches apart. When the pressure gradient is 3200 pascals per meter, the average velocity is 0.8 m/s. (a) What is the flow rate per meter of width? (b) What oil in Table A.4 fits this data? (c) Can we be sure that the flow is laminar?

P4.90 It is desired to pump ethanol at 20°C through 25 m of straight smooth tubing under laminar-flow conditions, $Re_d = \rho V d/\mu < 2300$. The available pressure drop is 10 kPa. (a) What is the maximum possible mass flow, in kg/h? (b) What is the appropriate diameter?

*P4.91 Analyze fully developed laminar pipe flow for a *power-law* fluid, $\tau = C(dv_z/dr)^n$, for $n \neq 1$, as in Prob. P1.46. (a) Derive an expression for $v_z(r)$. (b) For extra credit, plot the velocity profile shapes for $n = 0.5$, 1, and 2. [*Hint:* In Eq. (4.136), replace $\mu(dv_z/dr)$ with τ.]

P4.92 A tank of area A_0 is draining in laminar flow through a pipe of diameter D and length L, as shown in Fig. P4.92. Neglecting the exit jet kinetic energy and assuming the pipe flow is driven by the hydrostatic pressure at its entrance, derive a formula for the tank level $h(t)$ if its initial level is h_0.

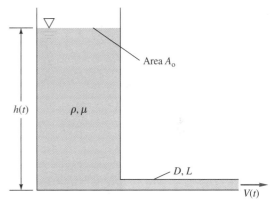

P4.92

P4.93 A number of straight 25-cm-long microtubes of diameter d are bundled together into a "honeycomb" whose total cross-sectional area is $0.0006 \ m^2$. The pressure drop from entrance to exit is 1.5 kPa. It is desired that the total volume flow rate be 5 m^3/h of water at 20°C. (a) What is the appropriate microtube diameter? (b) How many microtubes are in the bundle? (c) What is the Reynolds number of each microtube?

P4.94 A long, solid cylinder rotates steadily in a very viscous fluid, as in Fig. P4.94. Assuming laminar flow, solve the Navier-Stokes equation in polar coordinates to determine the resulting velocity distribution. The fluid is at rest far from the cylinder. [*Hint:* The cylinder does not induce any radial motion.]

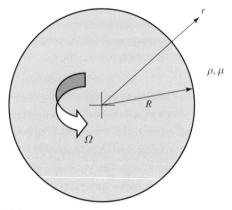

P4.94

*P4.95 Two immiscible liquids of equal thickness h are being sheared between a fixed and a moving plate, as in Fig. P4.95. Gravity is neglected, and there is no variation with x. Find an expression for (a) the velocity at the interface and (b) the shear stress in each fluid. Assume steady laminar flow.

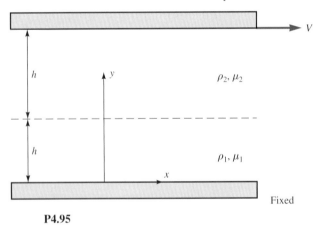

P4.95

P4.96 Use the data of Prob. P1.40, with the inner cylinder rotating and outer cylinder fixed, and calculate (a) the inner shear stress. (b) Determine whether this flow pattern is stable. [*Hint:* The shear stress in (r, θ) coordinates is *not* like plane flow.

Slip flows

P4.97 For Couette flow between a moving and a fixed plate, Fig. 4.12a, solve continuity and Navier-Stokes to find the velocity distribution when there is *slip* at both walls.

P4.98 For the pressure-gradient flow between two parallel plates of Fig. 4.12(b), reanalyze for the case of *slip flow* at both walls. Use the simple slip condition $u_{wall} = \ell(du/dy)_{wall}$, where ℓ is the mean free path of the fluid. (a) Sketch the expected velocity profile. (b) Find an expression for the shear stress at each wall. (c) Find the volume flow between the plates.

P4.99 For the pressure-gradient flow in a circular tube in Sec. 4.10, reanalyze for the case of *slip flow* at the wall. Use the simple slip condition $v_{z,wall} = \ell(dv_z/dr)_{wall}$, where ℓ is the mean free path of the fluid. (a) Sketch the expected velocity profile. (b) Find an expression for the shear stress at the wall. (c) Find the volume flow through the tube.

Word Problems

W4.1 The total acceleration of a fluid particle is given by Eq. (4.2) in the Eulerian[?] system, where $\mathbf{V}$ is a known function of space and time. Explain how we might evaluate particle acceleration in the Lagrangian[?] frame, where particle position $\mathbf{r}$ is a known function of time and initial position, $\mathbf{r} = fcn(\mathbf{r}_0, t)$. Can you give an illustrative example?

W4.2 Is it true that the continuity relation, Eq. (4.6), is valid for both viscous and inviscid, newtonian and nonnewtonian,

compressible and incompressible flow? If so, are there *any* limitations on this equation?

W4.3 Consider a CD (compact disc) rotating at angular velocity Ω. Does it have *vorticity* in the sense of this chapter? If so, how much vorticity?

W4.4 How much acceleration can fluids endure? Are fluids like astronauts, who feel that $5g$ is severe? Perhaps use the flow pattern of Example 4.8, at $r = R$, to make some estimates of fluid acceleration magnitudes.

W4.5   State the conditions (there are more than one) under which the analysis of temperature distribution in a flow field can be completely uncoupled, so that a separate analysis for velocity and pressure is possible. Can we do this for both laminar and turbulent flow?

W4.6   Consider liquid flow over a dam or weir. How might the boundary conditions and the flow pattern change when we compare water flow over a large prototype to SAE 30 oil flow over a tiny scale model?

W4.7   What is the difference between the stream function ψ and our method of finding the streamlines from Sec. 1.11? Or are they essentially the same?

W4.8   Under what conditions do both the stream function ψ and the velocity potential ϕ exist for a flow field? When does one exist but not the other?

W4.9   How might the remarkable three-dimensional Taylor instability of Fig. 4.14 be predicted? Discuss a general procedure for examining the stability of a given flow pattern.

W4.10   Consider an irrotational, incompressible, axisymmetric ($\partial/\partial\theta = 0$) flow in ($r$, z) coordinates. Does a stream function exist? If so, does it satisfy Laplace's equation? Are lines of constant ψ equal to the flow streamlines? Does a velocity potential exist? If so, does it satisfy Laplace's equation? Are lines of constant ϕ everywhere perpendicular to the ψ lines?

Fundamentals of Engineering Exam Problems

This chapter is not a favorite of the people who prepare the FE Exam. Probably not a single problem from this chapter will appear on the exam, but if some did, they might be like these.

FE4.1   Given the steady, incompressible velocity distribution $\mathbf{V} = 3x\mathbf{i} + Cy\mathbf{j} + 0\mathbf{k}$, where C is a constant, if conservation of mass is satisfied, the value of C should be
(*a*) 3,   (*b*) 3/2,   (*c*) 0,   (*d*) −3/2,   (*e*) −3

FE4.2   Given the steady velocity distribution $\mathbf{V} = 3x\mathbf{i} + 0\mathbf{j} + Cy\mathbf{k}$, where C is a constant, if the flow is irrotational, the value of C should be
(*a*) 3,   (*b*) 3/2,   (*c*) 0,   (*d*) −3/2,   (*e*) −3

FE4.3   Given the steady, incompressible velocity distribution $\mathbf{V} = 3x\mathbf{i} + Cy\mathbf{j} + 0\mathbf{k}$, where C is a constant, the shear stress τ_{xy} at the point (x, y, z) is given by
(*a*) 3μ,   (*b*) $(3x + Cy)\mu$,   (*c*) 0,   (*d*) $C\mu$,   (*e*) $(3 + C)\mu$

FE4.4   Given the steady, incompressible velocity distribution $u = Ax$, $v = By$, and $w = Cxy$, where (A, B, C) are constants. This flow satisfies the equation of continuity if A equals
(*a*) B,   (*b*) $B + C$, (*c*) $B - C$,   (*d*) $-B$,   (*e*) $-(B + C)$

FE4.5   For the velocity field in Prob. FE4.4, the convective acceleration in the x direction is
(*a*) Ax^2,   (*b*) A^2x,   (*c*) B^2y,   (*d*) By^2,   (*e*) Cx^2y

FE4.6   If, for laminar flow in a smooth, straight tube, the tube diameter and length both double, while everything else remains the same, the volume flow rate will increase by a factor of
(*a*) 2,   (*b*) 4,   (*c*) 8,   (*d*) 12,   (*e*) 16

Comprehensive Problems

C4.1   In a certain medical application, water at room temperature and pressure flows through a rectangular channel of length $L = 10$ cm, width $s = 1.0$ cm, and gap thickness $b = 0.30$ mm as in Fig. C4.1. The volume flow rate is sinusoidal with amplitude $\hat{Q} = 0.50$ mL/s and frequency $f = 20$ Hz, i.e., $Q = \hat{Q} \sin(2\pi ft)$.
(*a*) Calculate the maximum Reynolds number (Re = Vb/υ) based on maximum average velocity and gap thickness. Channel flow like this remains laminar for Re less than about 2000. If Re is greater than about 2000, the flow will be turbulent. Is this flow laminar or turbulent? (*b*) In this problem, the frequency is low enough that at any given time, the flow can be solved as if it were steady at the given flow rate. (This is called a *quasi-steady assumption.*) At any arbitrary instant of time, find an expression for streamwise velocity u as a function of y, μ, dp/dx, and b, where dp/dx is the pressure gradient required to push the flow through the channel at volume flow rate Q. In addition, estimate the maximum magnitude of velocity component u. (*c*) At any instant of time, find a relationship between volume flow rate Q and pressure gradient dp/dx. Your answer should be given as an expression for Q as a function of dp/dx, s, b, and viscosity μ. (*d*) Estimate the wall shear stress, τ_w as a function of $\hat{Q}$, f, μ, b, s, and time (t). (*e*) Finally, for the numbers given in the problem statement, estimate the amplitude of the wall shear stress, $\hat{\tau}_w$, in N/m^2.

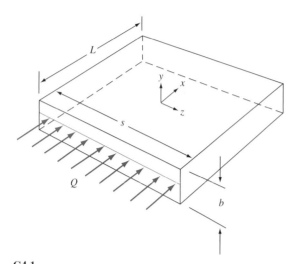

C4.1

average velocity V_{avg} in the film, and (c) the velocity V_c for which there is no net flow either up or down. (d) Sketch $v(x)$ for case (c).

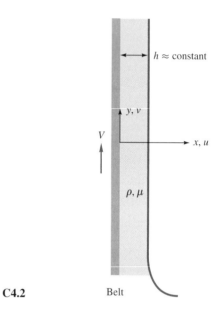

C4.2 Belt

C4.2 A belt moves upward at velocity V, dragging a film of viscous liquid of thickness h, as in Fig. C4.2. Near the belt, the film moves upward due to no slip. At its outer edge, the film moves downward due to gravity. Assuming that the only nonzero velocity is $v(x)$, with zero shear stress at the outer film edge, derive a formula for (a) $v(x)$, (b) the

References

1. J. D. Anderson, *Computational Fluid Dynamics: An Introduction*, 3d ed., Springer, New York, 2010.
2. C. E. Brennen, *Fundamentals of Multiphase Flow,* Cambridge University Press, New York, 2009. See also URL <http://caltechbook.library.caltech.edu/51/01/multiph.htm>
3. D. Zwillinger, *CRC Standard Mathematical Tables and Formulae*, 32d ed., CRC Press Inc., Cleveland, Ohio, 2011.
4. H. Schlichting and K. Gersten, *Boundary Layer Theory*, 8th ed., Springer, New York, 2000.
5. F. M. White, *Viscous Fluid Flow*, 3d ed., McGraw-Hill, New York, 2005.
6. E. B. Tadmor, R. E. Miller, and R. S. Elliott, *Continuum Mechanics and Thermodynamics*, Cambridge University Press, New York, 2012.
7. J. P. Holman, *Heat Transfer,* 10th ed., McGraw-Hill, New York, 2009.
8. W. M. Kays and M. E. Crawford, *Convective Heat and Mass Transfer,* 4th ed., McGraw-Hill, New York, 2004.
9. G. K. Batchelor, *An Introduction to Fluid Dynamics,* Cambridge University Press, Cambridge, England, 1967.
10. L. Prandtl and O. G. Tietjens, *Fundamentals of Hydro- and Aeromechanics,* Dover, New York, 1957.
11. D. Fleisch, *A Student's Guide to Vectors and Tensors*, Cambridge University Press, New York, 2011.
12. O. Gonzalez and A. M. Stuart, *A First Course in Continuum Mechanics*, Cambridge University Press, New York, 2008.
13. D. A. Danielson, *Vectors and Tensors in Engineering and Physics,* 2d ed., Westview (Perseus) Press, Boulder, CO, 2003.
14. R. I. Tanner, *Engineering Rheology,* 2d ed., Oxford University Press, New York, 2000.
15. H. Lamb, *Hydrodynamics,* 6th ed., Dover, New York, 1945.
16. J. P. Davin, *Tribology for Engineers: A Practical Guide*, Woodhead Publishing, Philadelphia, 2011.
17. G. I. Taylor, "Stability of a Viscous Liquid Contained between Two Rotating Cylinders," *Philos. Trans. Roy. Soc. London Ser. A,* vol. 223, 1923, pp. 289–343.
18. E. L. Koschmieder, "Turbulent Taylor Vortex Flow," *J. Fluid Mech.,* vol. 93, pt. 3, 1979, pp. 515–527.

19. M. T. Nair, T. K. Sengupta, and U. S. Chauhan, "Flow Past Rotating Cylinders at High Reynolds Numbers Using Higher Order Upwind Scheme," *Computers and Fluids,* vol. 27, no. 1, 1998, pp. 47–70.

20. M. Constanceau and C. Menard, "Influence of Rotation on the Near-Wake Development behind an Impulsively Started Circular Cylinder," *J. Fluid Mechanics,* vol. 1258, 1985, pp. 399–446.

21. J-Y. Hwang, K-S. Yang, and K. Bremhorst, "Direct Numerical Simulation of Turbulent Flow Around a Rotating Circular Cylinder." *Fluids Engineering*, vol. 129, Jan. 2007, pp. 40–47.

A full-scale NASA parachute, which helped lower the vehicle *Curiosity* to the Mars surface in 2012, was tested in the world's largest wind tunnel, at NASA Ames Research Center, Moffett Field, California. It is the largest disc-gap-band parachute [41] ever built, with a diameter of 51 feet. In the Mars atmosphere it will generate up to 65,000 lbf of drag, which leads to a problem assignment in Chapter 7. [*Image from NASA/JPL-Caltech.*]

Chapter 5
Dimensional Analysis and Similarity

Motivation. In this chapter we discuss the planning, presentation, and interpretation of experimental data. We shall try to convince you that such data are best presented in *dimensionless* form. Experiments that might result in tables of output, or even multiple volumes of tables, might be reduced to a single set of curves—or even a single curve—when suitably nondimensionalized. The technique for doing this is *dimensional analysis*. It is also effective in theoretical studies.

Chapter 3 presented large-scale control volume balances of mass, momentum, and energy, which led to global results: mass flow, force, torque, total work done, or heat transfer. Chapter 4 presented infinitesimal balances that led to the basic partial differential equations of fluid flow and some particular solutions for both inviscid and viscous (laminar) flow. These straight *analytical* techniques are limited to simple geometries and uniform boundary conditions. Only a fraction of engineering flow problems can be solved by direct analytical formulas.

Most practical fluid flow problems are too complex, both geometrically and physically, to be solved analytically. They must be tested by experiment or approximated by computational fluid dynamics (CFD) [2]. These results are typically reported as experimental or numerical data points and smoothed curves. Such data have much more generality if they are expressed in compact, economic form. This is the motivation for dimensional analysis. The technique is a mainstay of fluid mechanics and is also widely used in all engineering fields plus the physical, biological, medical, and social sciences. The present chapter shows how dimensional analysis improves the presentation of both data and theory.

5.1 Introduction

Basically, dimensional analysis is a method for reducing the number and complexity of experimental variables that affect a given physical phenomenon, by using a sort of compacting technique. If a phenomenon depends on n dimensional variables, dimensional analysis will reduce the problem to only k *dimensionless* variables, where the reduction

$n - k = 1, 2, 3,$ or 4, depending on the problem complexity. Generally $n - k$ equals the number of different dimensions (sometimes called basic or primary or fundamental dimensions) that govern the problem. In fluid mechanics, the four basic dimensions are usually taken to be mass M, length L, time T, and temperature Θ, or an $MLT\Theta$ system for short. Alternatively, one uses an $FLT\Theta$ system, with force F replacing mass.

Although its purpose is to reduce variables and group them in dimensionless form, dimensional analysis has several side benefits. The first is enormous savings in time and money. Suppose one knew that the force F on a particular body shape immersed in a stream of fluid depended only on the body length L, stream velocity V, fluid density ρ, and fluid viscosity μ; that is,

$$F = f(L, V, \rho, \mu) \tag{5.1}$$

Suppose further that the geometry and flow conditions are so complicated that our integral theories (Chap. 3) and differential equations (Chap. 4) fail to yield the solution for the force. Then we must find the function $f(L, V, \rho, \mu)$ experimentally or numerically.

Generally speaking, it takes about 10 points to define a curve. To find the effect of body length in Eq. (5.1), we have to run the experiment for 10 lengths L. For each L we need 10 values of V, 10 values of ρ, and 10 values of μ, making a grand total of 10^4, or 10,000, experiments. At \$100 per experiment—well, you see what we are getting into. However, with dimensional analysis, we can immediately reduce Eq. (5.1) to the equivalent form

$$\frac{F}{\rho V^2 L^2} = g\left(\frac{\rho VL}{\mu}\right)$$

or

$$C_F = g(\mathrm{Re}) \tag{5.2}$$

That is, the dimensionless *force coefficient* $F/(\rho V^2 L^2)$ is a function only of the dimensionless *Reynolds number* $\rho VL/\mu$. We shall learn exactly how to make this reduction in Secs. 5.2 and 5.3. Equation (5.2) will be useful in Chap. 7.

Note that Eq. (5.2) is just an *example,* not the full story, of forces caused by fluid flows. Some fluid forces have a very weak or negligible Reynolds number dependence in wide regions (Fig. 5.3a). Other groups may also be important. The force coefficient may depend, in high-speed gas flow, on the *Mach number*, $\mathrm{Ma} = V/a$, where a is the speed of sound. In free-surface flows, such as ship drag, C_F may depend upon *Froude number*, $\mathrm{Fr} = V^2/(gL)$, where g is the acceleration of gravity. In turbulent flow, force may depend upon the *roughness ratio*, ϵ/L, where ϵ is the roughness height of the surface.

The function g is different mathematically from the original function f, but it contains all the same information. Nothing is lost in a dimensional analysis. And think of the savings: We can establish g by running the experiment for only 10 values of the single variable called the Reynolds number. We do not have to vary L, V, ρ, or μ separately but only the *grouping* $\rho VL/\mu$. This we do merely by varying velocity V in, say, a wind tunnel or drop test or water channel, and there is no need to build 10 different bodies or find 100 different fluids with 10 densities and 10 viscosities. The cost is now about \$1000, maybe less.

A second side benefit of dimensional analysis is that it helps our thinking and planning for an experiment or theory. It suggests dimensionless ways of writing equations before we spend money on computer analysis to find solutions. It suggests variables that can be discarded; sometimes dimensional analysis will immediately reject variables, and at other times it groups them off to the side, where a few simple tests will show them to be unimportant. Finally, dimensional analysis will often give a great deal of insight into the form of the physical relationship we are trying to study.

A third benefit is that dimensional analysis provides *scaling laws* that can convert data from a cheap, small *model* to design information for an expensive, large *prototype*. We do not build a million-dollar airplane and see whether it has enough lift force. We measure the lift on a small model and use a scaling law to predict the lift on the full-scale prototype airplane. There are rules we shall explain for finding scaling laws. When the scaling law is valid, we say that a condition of *similarity* exists between the model and the prototype. In the simple case of Eq. (5.1), similarity is achieved if the Reynolds number is the same for the model and the prototype because the function g then requires the force coefficient to be the same also:

$$\text{If } \text{Re}_m = \text{Re}_p \quad \text{then} \quad C_{Fm} = C_{Fp} \tag{5.3}$$

where subscripts m and p mean model and prototype, respectively. From the definition of force coefficient, this means that

$$\frac{F_p}{F_m} = \frac{\rho_p}{\rho_m}\left(\frac{V_p}{V_m}\right)^2\left(\frac{L_p}{L_m}\right)^2 \tag{5.4}$$

for data taken where $\rho_p V_p L_p/\mu_p = \rho_m V_m L_m/\mu_m$. Equation (5.4) is a scaling law: If you measure the model force at the model Reynolds number, the prototype force at the same Reynolds number equals the model force times the density ratio times the velocity ratio squared times the length ratio squared. We shall give more examples later.

Do you understand these introductory explanations? Be careful; learning dimensional analysis is like learning to play tennis: There are levels of the game. We can establish some ground rules and do some fairly good work in this brief chapter, but dimensional analysis in the broad view has many subtleties and nuances that only time, practice, and maturity enable you to master. Although dimensional analysis has a firm physical and mathematical foundation, considerable art and skill are needed to use it effectively.

EXAMPLE 5.1

A copepod is a water crustacean approximately 1 mm in diameter. We want to know the drag force on the copepod when it moves slowly in fresh water. A scale model 100 times larger is made and tested in glycerin at $V = 30$ cm/s. The measured drag on the model is 1.3 N. For similar conditions, what are the velocity and drag of the actual copepod in water? Assume that Eq. (5.2) applies and the temperature is 20°C.

Solution

- *Property values:* From Table A.3, the densities and viscosities at 20°C are

Water (prototype):	$\mu_p = 0.001$ kg/(m-s)	$\rho_p = 998$ kg/m^3
Glycerin (model):	$\mu_m = 1.5$ kg/(m-s)	$\rho_m = 1263$ kg/m^3

- *Assumptions:* Equation (5.2) is appropriate and *similarity* is achieved; that is, the model and prototype have the same Reynolds number and, therefore, the same force coefficient.

• *Approach:*   The length scales are L_m = 100 mm and L_p = 1 mm. Calculate the Reynolds number and force coefficient of the model and set them equal to prototype values:

$$\mathrm{Re}_m = \frac{\rho_m V_m L_m}{\mu_m} = \frac{(1263 \text{ kg/m}^3)(0.3 \text{ m/s})(0.1 \text{ m})}{1.5 \text{ kg/(m-s)}} = 25.3 = \mathrm{Re}_p = \frac{(998 \text{ kg/m}^3) V_p (0.001 \text{ m})}{0.001 \text{ kg/(m-s)}}$$

$$\text{Solve for } V_p = 0.0253 \text{ m/s} = 2.53 \text{ cm/s} \qquad Ans.$$

In like manner, using the prototype velocity just found, equate the force coefficients:

$$C_{Fm} = \frac{F_m}{\rho_m V_m^2 L_m^2} = \frac{1.3 \text{ N}}{(1263 \text{ kg/m}^3)(0.3 \text{ m/s})^2(0.1 \text{ m})^2} = 1.14$$

$$= C_{Fp} = \frac{F_p}{(998 \text{ kg/m}^3)(0.0253 \text{ m/s})^2(0.001 \text{ m})^2}$$

$$\text{Solve for } F_p = 7.3\text{E-7 N} \qquad Ans.$$

• *Comments:*   Assuming we modeled the Reynolds number correctly, the model test is a very good idea, as it would obviously be difficult to measure such a tiny copepod drag force.

Historically, the first person to write extensively about units and dimensional reasoning in physical relations was Euler in 1765. Euler's ideas were far ahead of his time, as were those of Joseph Fourier, whose 1822 book *Analytical Theory of Heat* outlined what is now called the *principle of dimensional homogeneity* and even developed some similarity rules for heat flow. There were no further significant advances until Lord Rayleigh's book in 1877, *Theory of Sound,* which proposed a "method of dimensions" and gave several examples of dimensional analysis. The final breakthrough that established the method as we know it today is generally credited to E. Buckingham in 1914 [1], whose paper outlined what is now called the *Buckingham Pi Theorem* for describing dimensionless parameters (see Sec. 5.3). However, it is now known that a Frenchman, A. Vaschy, in 1892 and a Russian, D. Riabouchinsky, in 1911 had independently published papers reporting results equivalent to the pi theorem. Following Buckingham's paper, P. W. Bridgman published a classic book in 1922 [3], outlining the general theory of dimensional analysis.

Dimensional analysis is so valuable and subtle, with both skill and art involved, that it has spawned a wide variety of textbooks and treatises. The writer is aware of more than 30 books on the subject, of which his engineering favorites are listed here [3–10]. Dimensional analysis is not confined to fluid mechanics, or even to engineering. Specialized books have been published on the application of dimensional analysis to metrology [11], astrophysics [12], economics [13], chemistry [14], hydrology [15], medications [16], clinical medicine [17], chemical processing pilot plants [18], social sciences [19], biomedical sciences [20], pharmacy [21], fractal geometry [22], and even the growth of plants [23]. Clearly this is a subject well worth learning for many career paths.

5.2 The Principle of Dimensional Homogeneity

In making the remarkable jump from the five-variable Eq. (5.1) to the two-variable Eq. (5.2), we were exploiting a rule that is almost a self-evident axiom in physics. This rule, the *principle of dimensional homogeneity* (PDH), can be stated as follows:

> If an equation truly expresses a proper relationship between variables in a physical process, it will be *dimensionally homogeneous;* that is, each of its additive terms will have the same dimensions.

All the equations that are derived from the theory of mechanics are of this form. For example, consider the relation that expresses the displacement of a falling body:

$$S = S_0 + V_0 t + \tfrac{1}{2} g t^2 \tag{5.5}$$

Each term in this equation is a displacement, or length, and has dimensions $\{L\}$. The equation is dimensionally homogeneous. Note also that any consistent set of units can be used to calculate a result.

Consider Bernoulli's equation for incompressible flow:

$$\frac{p}{\rho} + \frac{1}{2} V^2 + gz = \text{const} \tag{5.6}$$

Each term, including the constant, has dimensions of velocity squared, or $\{L^2 T^{-2}\}$. The equation is dimensionally homogeneous and gives proper results for any consistent set of units.

Students count on dimensional homogeneity and use it to check themselves when they cannot quite remember an equation during an exam. For example, which is it:

$$S = \tfrac{1}{2} g t^2 ? \quad \text{or} \quad S = \tfrac{1}{2} g^2 t ? \tag{5.7}$$

By checking the dimensions, we reject the second form and back up our faulty memory. We are exploiting the principle of dimensional homogeneity, and this chapter simply exploits it further.

Variables and Constants

Equations (5.5) and (5.6) also illustrate some other factors that often enter into a dimensional analysis:

Dimensional variables are the quantities that actually vary during a given case and would be plotted against each other to show the data. In Eq. (5.5), they are S and t; in Eq. (5.6) they are p, V, and z. All have dimensions, and all can be nondimensionalized as a dimensional analysis technique.

Dimensional constants may vary from case to case but are held constant during a given run. In Eq. (5.5) they are S_0, V_0, and g, and in Eq. (5.6) they are ρ, g, and C. They all have dimensions and conceivably could be nondimensionalized, but they are normally used to help nondimensionalize the variables in the problem.

Pure constants have no dimensions and never did. They arise from mathematical manipulations. In both Eqs. (5.5) and (5.6) they are $\tfrac{1}{2}$ and the exponent 2, both of which came from an integration: $\int t\, dt = \tfrac{1}{2} t^2$, $\int V\, dV = \tfrac{1}{2} V^2$. Other common dimensionless constants are π and e. Also, the argument of any mathematical function, such as ln, exp, cos, or J_0, is dimensionless.

Angles and *revolutions* are dimensionless. The preferred unit for an angle is the radian, which makes it clear that an angle is a ratio. In like manner, a revolution is 2π radians.

Counting numbers are dimensionless. For example, if we triple the energy E to $3E$, the coefficient 3 is dimensionless.

Note that integration and differentiation of an equation may change the dimensions but not the homogeneity of the equation. For example, integrate or differentiate Eq. (5.5):

$$\int S \, dt = S_0 t + \tfrac{1}{2} V_0 t^2 + \tfrac{1}{6} g t^3 \tag{5.8a}$$

$$\frac{dS}{dt} = V_0 + gt \tag{5.8b}$$

In the integrated form (5.8a) every term has dimensions of $\{LT\}$, while in the derivative form (5.8b) every term is a velocity $\{LT^{-1}\}$.

Finally, some physical variables are naturally dimensionless by virtue of their definition as ratios of dimensional quantities. Some examples are strain (change in length per unit length), Poisson's ratio (ratio of transverse strain to longitudinal strain), and specific gravity (ratio of density to standard water density).

The motive behind dimensional analysis is that any dimensionally homogeneous equation can be written in an entirely equivalent nondimensional form that is more compact. Usually there are multiple methods of presenting one's dimensionless data or theory. Let us illustrate these concepts more thoroughly by using the falling-body relation (5.5) as an example.

Ambiguity: The Choice of Variables and Scaling Parameters[1]

Equation (5.5) is familiar and simple, yet it illustrates most of the concepts of dimensional analysis. It contains five terms (S, S_0, V_0, t, g), which we may divide, in our thinking, into variables and parameters. The *variables* are the things we wish to plot, the basic output of the experiment or theory: in this case, S versus t. The *parameters* are those quantities whose effect on the variables we wish to know: in this case S_0, V_0, and g. Almost any engineering study can be subdivided in this manner.

To nondimensionalize our results, we need to know how many dimensions are contained among our variables and parameters: in this case, only two, length $\{L\}$ and time $\{T\}$. Check each term to verify this:

$$\{S\} = \{S_0\} = \{L\} \qquad \{t\} = \{T\} \qquad \{V_0\} = \{LT^{-1}\} \qquad \{g\} = \{LT^{-2}\}$$

Among our parameters, we therefore select two to be *scaling parameters* (also called *repeating variables*), used to define dimensionless variables. What remains will be the "basic" parameter(s) whose effect we wish to show in our plot. These choices will not affect the content of our data, only the form of their presentation. Clearly there is ambiguity in these choices, something that often vexes the beginning experimenter. But the ambiguity is deliberate. Its purpose is to show a particular effect, and the choice is yours to make.

For the falling-body problem, we select any two of the three parameters to be scaling parameters. Thus, we have three options. Let us discuss and display them in turn.

---

[1]I am indebted to Prof. Jacques Lewalle of Syracuse University for suggesting, outlining, and clarifying this entire discussion.

Option 1: Scaling parameters S_0 and V_0: the effect of gravity g.

First use the scaling parameters (S_0, V_0) to define dimensionless (*) displacement and time. There is only one suitable definition for each:[2]

$$S^* = \frac{S}{S_0} \qquad t^* = \frac{V_0 t}{S_0} \tag{5.9}$$

Substitute these variables into Eq. (5.5) and clean everything up until each term is dimensionless. The result is our first option:

$$S^* = 1 + t^* + \frac{1}{2}\alpha t^{*2} \qquad \alpha = \frac{g S_0}{V_0^2} \tag{5.10}$$

This result is shown plotted in Fig. 5.1a. There is a single dimensionless parameter α, which shows here the effect of gravity. It cannot show the direct effects of S_0 and V_0, since these two are hidden in the ordinate and abscissa. We see that gravity increases the parabolic rate of fall for $t^* > 0$, but not the initial slope at $t^* = 0$. We would learn the same from falling-body data, and the plot, within experimental accuracy, would look like Fig. 5.1a.

Option 2: Scaling parameters V_0 and g: the effect of initial displacement S_0.

Now use the new scaling parameters (V_0, g) to define dimensionless (**) displacement and time. Again there is only one suitable definition:

$$S^{**} = \frac{Sg}{V_0^2} \qquad t^{**} = t\frac{g}{V_0} \tag{5.11}$$

Substitute these variables into Eq. (5.5) and clean everything up again. The result is our second option:

$$S^{**} = \alpha + t^{**} + \frac{1}{2}t^{**2} \qquad \alpha = \frac{g S_0}{V_0^2} \tag{5.12}$$

This result is plotted in Fig. 5.1b. The same single parameter α again appears and here shows the effect of initial *displacement,* which merely moves the curves upward without changing their shape.

Option 3: Scaling parameters S_0 and g: the effect of initial speed V_0.

Finally use the scaling parameters (S_0, g) to define dimensionless (***) displacement and time. Again there is only one suitable definition:

$$S^{***} = \frac{S}{S_0} \qquad t^{***} = t\left(\frac{g}{S_0}\right)^{1/2} \tag{5.13}$$

Substitute these variables into Eq. (5.5) and clean everything up as usual. The result is our third and final option:

$$S^{***} = 1 + \beta t^{***} + \frac{1}{2}t^{***2} \qquad \beta = \frac{1}{\sqrt{\alpha}} = \frac{V_0}{\sqrt{g S_0}} \tag{5.14}$$

---

[2]Make them *proportional* to S and t. Do not define dimensionless terms upside down: S_0/S or $S_0/(V_0 t)$. The plots will look funny, users of your data will be confused, and your supervisor will be angry. It is not a good idea.

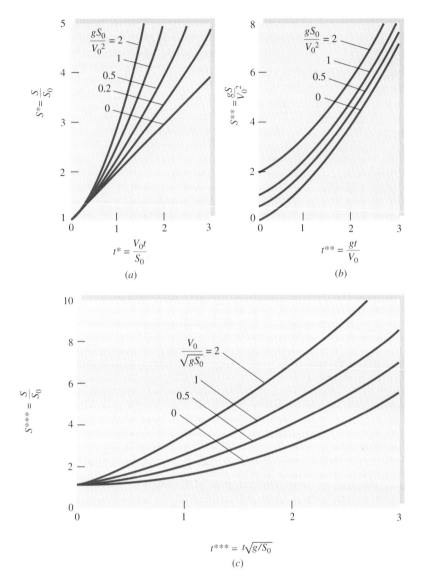

Fig. 5.1 Three entirely equivalent dimensionless presentations of the falling-body problem, Eq. (5.5): the effect of (a) gravity, (b) initial displacement, and (c) initial velocity. All plots contain the same information.

This final presentation is shown in Fig. 5.1c. Once again the parameter α appears, but we have redefined it upside down, $\beta = 1/\sqrt{\alpha}$, so that our display parameter V_0 is in the numerator and is linear. This is our free choice and simply improves the display. Figure 5.1c shows that initial *velocity* increases the falling displacement.

Note that, in all three options, the same parameter α appears but has a different meaning: dimensionless gravity, initial displacement, and initial velocity. The graphs, which contain exactly the same information, change their appearance to reflect these differences.

Whereas the original problem, Eq. (5.5), involved five quantities, the dimensionless presentations involve only three, having the form

$$S' = \mathrm{fcn}(t', \alpha) \qquad \alpha = \frac{gS_0}{V_0^2} \qquad (5.15)$$

The reduction $5 - 3 = 2$ should equal the number of fundamental dimensions involved in the problem $\{L, T\}$. This idea led to the pi theorem (Sec. 5.3).

Selection of Scaling (Repeating) Variables

The selection of scaling variables is left to the user, but there are some guidelines. In Eq. (5.2), it is now clear that the scaling variables were ρ, V, and L, since they appear in both force coefficient and Reynolds number. We could then interpret data from Eq. (5.2) as the variation of dimensionless *force* versus dimensionless *viscosity,* since each appears in only one dimensionless group. Similarly, in Eq. (5.5) the scaling variables were selected from (S_0, V_0, g), not (S, t), because we wished to plot S versus t in the final result.

The following are some guidelines for selecting scaling variables:

1. They must *not* form a dimensionless group among themselves, but adding one more variable *will* form a dimensionless quantity. For example, test powers of ρ, V, and L:

$$\rho^a V^b L^c = (ML^{-3})^a (L/T)^b (L)^c = M^0 L^0 T^0 \quad \text{only if } a = 0, b = 0, c = 0$$

In this case, we can see why this is so: Only ρ contains the dimension $\{M\}$, and only V contains the dimension $\{T\}$, so no cancellation is possible. If, now, we add μ to the scaling group, we will obtain the Reynolds number. If we add F to the group, we form the force coefficient.

2. Do not select output variables for your scaling parameters. In Eq. (5.1), certainly do not select F, which you wish to isolate for your plot. Nor was μ selected, for we wished to plot force versus viscosity.

3. If convenient, select *popular,* not obscure, scaling variables because they will appear in all of your dimensionless groups. Select density, not surface tension. Select body length, not surface roughness. Select stream velocity, not speed of sound.

The examples that follow will make this clear. Problem assignments might give hints.

Suppose we wish to study drag force versus *velocity*. Then we would not use V as a scaling parameter in Eq. (5.1). We would use (ρ, μ, L) instead, and the final dimensionless function would become

$$C_F' = \frac{\rho F}{\mu^2} = f(\text{Re}) \qquad \text{Re} = \frac{\rho V L}{\mu} \tag{5.16}$$

In plotting these data, we would not be able to discern the effect of ρ or μ, since they appear in both dimensionless groups. The grouping C_F' again would mean dimensionless force, and Re is now interpreted as either dimensionless velocity or size.[3] The plot would be quite different compared to Eq. (5.2), although it contains exactly the same information. The development of parameters such as C_F' and Re from the initial variables is the subject of the pi theorem (Sec. 5.3).

Some Peculiar Engineering Equations

The foundation of the dimensional analysis method rests on two assumptions: (1) The proposed physical relation is dimensionally homogeneous, and (2) all the relevant variables have been included in the proposed relation.

If a relevant variable is missing, dimensional analysis will fail, giving either algebraic difficulties or, worse, yielding a dimensionless formulation that does not resolve

---

[3]We were lucky to achieve a size effect because in this case L, a scaling parameter, did not appear in the drag coefficient.

the process. A typical case is Manning's open-channel formula, discussed in Example 1.4 and Chap. 10.

$$V = \frac{1.49}{n} R^{2/3} S^{1/2} \tag{1}$$

Since V is velocity, R is a radius, and n and S are dimensionless, the formula is not dimensionally homogeneous. This should be a warning that (1) the formula changes if the *units* of V and R change and (2) if valid, it represents a very special case. Equation (1) in Example 1.4 predates the dimensional analysis technique and is valid only for water in rough channels at moderate velocities and large radii in BG units.

Such dimensionally inhomogeneous formulas abound in the hydraulics literature. Another example is the Hazen-Williams formula [24] for volume flow of water through a straight smooth pipe:

$$Q = 61.9 D^{2.63} \left(\frac{dp}{dx} \right)^{0.54} \tag{5.17}$$

where D is diameter and dp/dx is the pressure gradient. Some of these formulas arise because numbers have been inserted for fluid properties and other physical data into perfectly legitimate homogeneous formulas. We shall not give the units of Eq. (5.17) to avoid encouraging its use.

On the other hand, some formulas are "constructs" that cannot be made dimensionally homogeneous. The "variables" they relate cannot be analyzed by the dimensional analysis technique. Most of these formulas are raw empiricisms convenient to a small group of specialists. Here are three examples:

$$B = \frac{25,000}{100 - R} \tag{5.18}$$

$$S = \frac{140}{130 + \text{API}} \tag{5.19}$$

$$0.0147 D_E - \frac{3.74}{D_E} = 0.26 t_R - \frac{172}{t_R} \tag{5.20}$$

Equation (5.18) relates the Brinell hardness B of a metal to its Rockwell hardness R. Equation (5.19) relates the specific gravity S of an oil to its density in degrees API. Equation (5.20) relates the viscosity of a liquid in D_E, or degrees Engler, to its viscosity t_R in Saybolt seconds. Such formulas have a certain usefulness when communicated between fellow specialists, but we cannot handle them here. Variables like Brinell hardness and Saybolt viscosity are not suited to an $MLT\Theta$ dimensional system.

5.3 The Pi Theorem

There are several methods of reducing a number of dimensional variables into a smaller number of dimensionless groups. The first scheme given here was proposed in 1914 by Buckingham [1] and is now called the *Buckingham Pi Theorem*. The name *pi* comes from the mathematical notation Π, meaning a product of variables. The dimensionless groups found from the theorem are power products denoted by Π_1, Π_2, Π_3, etc. The method allows the pi groups to be found in sequential order without resorting to free exponents.

The first part of the pi theorem explains what reduction in variables to expect:

> If a physical process satisfies the PDH and involves n dimensional variables, it can be reduced to a relation between k dimensionless variables or Πs. The reduction $j = n - k$ equals the maximum number of variables that do not form a pi among themselves and is always less than or equal to the number of dimensions describing the variables.

Take the specific case of force on an immersed body: Eq. (5.1) contains five variables F, L, U, ρ, and μ described by three dimensions $\{MLT\}$. Thus $n = 5$ and $j \leq 3$. Therefore it is a good guess that we can reduce the problem to k pi groups, with $k = n - j \geq 5 - 3 = 2$. And this is exactly what we obtained: two dimensionless variables $\Pi_1 = C_F$ and $\Pi_2 = \text{Re}$. On rare occasions it may take more pi groups than this minimum (see Example 5.5).

The second part of the theorem shows how to find the pi groups one at a time:

> Find the reduction j, then select j scaling variables that do not form a pi among themselves.[4] Each desired pi group will be a power product of these j variables plus one additional variable, which is assigned any convenient nonzero exponent. Each pi group thus found is independent.

To be specific, suppose the process involves five variables:

$$v_1 = f(v_2, v_3, v_4, v_5)$$

Suppose there are three dimensions $\{MLT\}$ and we search around and find that indeed $j = 3$. Then $k = 5 - 3 = 2$ and we expect, from the theorem, two and only two pi groups. Pick out three convenient variables that do *not* form a pi, and suppose these turn out to be v_2, v_3, and v_4. Then the two pi groups are formed by power products of these three plus one additional variable, either v_1 or v_5:

$$\Pi_1 = (v_2)^a(v_3)^b(v_4)^c v_1 = M^0 L^0 T^0 \quad \Pi_2 = (v_2)^a(v_3)^b(v_4)^c v_5 = M^0 L^0 T^0$$

Here we have arbitrarily chosen v_1 and v_5, the added variables, to have unit exponents. Equating exponents of the various dimensions is guaranteed by the theorem to give unique values of a, b, and c for each pi. And they are independent because only Π_1 contains v_1 and only Π_2 contains v_5. It is a very neat system once you get used to the procedure. We shall illustrate it with several examples.

Typically, six steps are involved:

1. List and count the n variables involved in the problem. If any important variables are missing, dimensional analysis will fail.
2. List the dimensions of each variable according to $\{MLT\Theta\}$ or $\{FLT\Theta\}$. A list is given in Table 5.1.
3. Find j. Initially guess j equal to the number of different dimensions present, and look for j variables that do not form a pi product. If no luck, reduce j by 1 and look again. With practice, you will find j rapidly.
4. Select j scaling parameters that do not form a pi product. Make sure they please you and have some generality if possible, because they will then appear

[4]Make a clever choice here because all pi groups will contain these j variables in various groupings.

Table 5.1 Dimensions of Fluid-Mechanics Properties

Quantity	Symbol	Dimensions $MLT\Theta$	Dimensions $FLT\Theta$
Length	L	L	L
Area	A	L^2	L^2
Volume	$\mathcal{V}$	L^3	L^3
Velocity	V	LT^{-1}	LT^{-1}
Acceleration	dV/dt	LT^{-2}	LT^{-2}
Speed of sound	a	LT^{-1}	LT^{-1}
Volume flow	Q	L^3T^{-1}	L^3T^{-1}
Mass flow	$\dot{m}$	MT^{-1}	FTL^{-1}
Pressure, stress	p, σ, τ	$ML^{-1}T^{-2}$	FL^{-2}
Strain rate	$\dot{\varepsilon}$	T^{-1}	T^{-1}
Angle	θ	None	None
Angular velocity	ω, Ω	T^{-1}	T^{-1}
Viscosity	μ	$ML^{-1}T^{-1}$	FTL^{-2}
Kinematic viscosity	ν	L^2T^{-1}	L^2T^{-1}
Surface tension	Υ	MT^{-2}	FL^{-1}
Force	F	MLT^{-2}	F
Moment, torque	M	ML^2T^{-2}	FL
Power	P	ML^2T^{-3}	FLT^{-1}
Work, energy	W, E	ML^2T^{-2}	FL
Density	ρ	ML^{-3}	FT^2L^{-4}
Temperature	T	Θ	Θ
Specific heat	c_p, c_v	$L^2T^{-2}\Theta^{-1}$	$L^2T^{-2}\Theta^{-1}$
Specific weight	γ	$ML^{-2}T^{-2}$	FL^{-3}
Thermal conductivity	k	$MLT^{-3}\Theta^{-1}$	$FT^{-1}\Theta^{-1}$
Thermal expansion coefficient	β	Θ^{-1}	Θ^{-1}

in every one of your pi groups. Pick density or velocity or length. Do not pick surface tension, for example, or you will form six different independent Weber-number parameters and thoroughly annoy your colleagues.

5. Add one additional variable to your j repeating variables, and form a power product. Algebraically find the exponents that make the product dimensionless. Try to arrange for your output or *dependent* variables (force, pressure drop, torque, power) to appear in the numerator, and your plots will look better. Do this sequentially, adding one new variable each time, and you will find all $n - j = k$ desired pi products.

6. Write the final dimensionless function, and check the terms to make sure all pi groups are dimensionless.

EXAMPLE 5.2

Repeat the development of Eq. (5.2) from Eq. (5.1), using the pi theorem.

Solution

Step 1 Write the function and count variables:

$$F = f(L, U, \rho, \mu) \quad \text{there are five variables } (n = 5)$$

Step 2 List dimensions of each variable. From Table 5.1

F	L	U	ρ	μ
$\{MLT^{-2}\}$	$\{L\}$	$\{LT^{-1}\}$	$\{ML^{-3}\}$	$\{ML^{-1}T^{-1}\}$

Step 3 Find j. No variable contains the dimension Θ, and so j is less than or equal to 3 (MLT). We inspect the list and see that L, U, and ρ cannot form a pi group because only ρ contains mass and only U contains time. Therefore j does equal 3, and $n - j = 5 - 3 = 2 = k$. The pi theorem guarantees for this problem that there will be exactly two independent dimensionless groups.

Step 4 Select repeating j variables. The group L, U, ρ we found in step 3 will do fine.

Step 5 Combine L, U, ρ with one additional variable, in sequence, to find the two pi products.

First add force to find Π_1. You may select *any* exponent on this additional term as you please, to place it in the numerator or denominator to any power. Since F is the output, or dependent, variable, we select it to appear to the first power in the numerator:

$$\Pi_1 = L^a U^b \rho^c F = (L)^a (LT^{-1})^b (ML^{-3})^c (MLT^{-2}) = M^0 L^0 T^0$$

Equate exponents:

Length: $\qquad\qquad\qquad\qquad\qquad a + b - 3c + 1 = 0$

Mass: $\qquad\qquad\qquad\qquad\qquad\qquad\quad c + 1 = 0$

Time: $\qquad\qquad\qquad\qquad\qquad\quad -b \qquad -2 = 0$

We can solve explicitly for

$$a = -2 \qquad b = -2 \qquad c = -1$$

Therefore $\qquad\qquad \Pi_1 = L^{-2} U^{-2} \rho^{-1} F = \dfrac{F}{\rho U^2 L^2} = C_F \qquad\qquad$ *Ans.*

This is exactly the right pi group as in Eq. (5.2). By varying the exponent on F, we could have found other equivalent groups such as $UL\rho^{1/2}/F^{1/2}$.

Finally, add viscosity to L, U, and ρ to find Π_2. Select any power you like for viscosity. By hindsight and custom, we select the power -1 to place it in the denominator:

$$\Pi_2 = L^a U^b \rho^c \mu^{-1} = L^a (LT^{-1})^b (ML^{-3})^c (ML^{-1}T^{-1})^{-1} = M^0 L^0 T^0$$

Equate exponents:

Length: $\qquad\qquad\qquad\qquad\qquad a + b - 3c + 1 = 0$

Mass: $\qquad\qquad\qquad\qquad\qquad\qquad\quad c - 1 = 0$

Time: $\qquad\qquad\qquad\qquad\qquad\quad -b \qquad + 1 = 0$

from which we find

$$a = b = c = 1$$

Therefore $\qquad\qquad \Pi_2 = L^1 U^1 \rho^1 \mu^{-1} = \dfrac{\rho U L}{\mu} = \text{Re} \qquad\qquad$ *Ans.*

Step 6   We know we are finished; this is the second and last pi group. The theorem guarantees that the functional relationship must be of the equivalent form

$$\frac{F}{\rho U^2 L^2} = g\left(\frac{\rho U L}{\mu}\right)$$ *Ans.*

which is exactly Eq. (5.2).

EXAMPLE 5.3

The power input P to a centrifugal pump is a function of the volume flow Q, impeller diameter D, rotational rate Ω, and the density ρ and viscosity μ of the fluid:

$$P = f(Q, D, \Omega, \rho, \mu)$$

Rewrite this as a dimensionless relationship. *Hint:* Use Ω, ρ, and D as repeating variables. We will revisit this problem in Chap. 11.

Solution

Step 1   Count the variables. There are six (don't forget the one on the left, P).

Step 2   List the dimensions of each variable from Table 5.1. Use the $\{FLT\Theta\}$ system:

P	Q	D	Ω	ρ	μ
$\{FLT^{-1}\}$	$\{L^3 T^{-1}\}$	$\{L\}$	$\{T^{-1}\}$	$\{FT^2 L^{-4}\}$	$\{FTL^{-2}\}$

Step 3   Find j. Lucky us, we were told to use (Ω, ρ, D) as repeating variables, so surely $j = 3$, the number of dimensions (FLT)? Check that these three do *not* form a pi group:

$$\Omega^a \rho^b D^c = (T^{-1})^a (FT^2 L^{-4})^b (L)^c = F^0 L^0 T^0 \quad \text{only if} \quad a = 0, b = 0, c = 0$$

Yes, $j = 3$. This was not as obvious as the scaling group (L, U, ρ) in Example 5.2, but it is true. We now know, from the theorem, that adding one more variable will indeed form a pi group.

Step 4a   Combine (Ω, ρ, D) with power P to find the first pi group:

$$\Pi_1 = \Omega^a \rho^b D^c P = (T^{-1})^a (FT^2 L^{-4})^b (L)^c (FLT^{-1}) = F^0 L^0 T^0$$

Equate exponents:

Force: $b \quad\quad + 1 = 0$

Length: $-4b + c + 1 = 0$

Time: $-a + 2b \quad -1 = 0$

Solve algebraically to obtain $a = -3$, $b = -1$, and $c = -5$. This first pi group, the output dimensionless variable, is called the *power coefficient* of a pump, C_P:

$$\Pi_1 = \Omega^{-3} \rho^{-1} D^{-5} P = \frac{P}{\rho \Omega^3 D^5} = C_P$$

Step 4b   Combine (Ω, ρ, D) with flow rate Q to find the second pi group:

$$\Pi_2 = \Omega^a \rho^b D^c Q = (T^{-1})^a (FT^2 L^{-4})^b (L)^c (L^3 T^{-1}) = F^0 L^0 T^0$$

After equating exponents, we now find $a = -1$, $b = 0$, and $c = -3$. This second pi group is called the *flow coefficient* of a pump, C_Q:

$$\Pi_2 = \Omega^{-1} \rho^0 D^{-3} Q = \frac{Q}{\Omega D^3} = C_Q$$

Step 4c   Combine (Ω, ρ, D) with viscosity μ to find the third and last pi group:

$$\Pi_3 = \Omega^a \rho^b D^c \mu = (T^{-1})^a (FT^2 L^{-4})^b (L)^c (FTL^{-2}) = F^0 L^0 T^0$$

This time, $a = -1$, $b = -1$, and $c = -2$; or $\Pi_3 = \mu/(\rho \Omega D^2)$, a sort of Reynolds number.

Step 5   The original relation between six variables is now reduced to three dimensionless groups:

$$\frac{P}{\rho \Omega^3 D^5} = f\left(\frac{Q}{\Omega D^3}, \frac{\mu}{\rho \Omega D^2}\right) \qquad\qquad Ans.$$

Comment: These three are the classical coefficients used to correlate pump power in Chap. 11.

EXAMPLE 5.4

At low velocities (laminar flow), the volume flow Q through a small-bore tube is a function only of the tube radius R, the fluid viscosity μ, and the pressure drop per unit tube length dp/dx. Using the pi theorem, find an appropriate dimensionless relationship.

Solution

Write the given relation and count variables:

$$Q = f\left(R, \mu, \frac{dp}{dx}\right) \qquad \text{four variables } (n = 4)$$

Make a list of the dimensions of these variables from Table 5.1 using the $\{MLT\}$ system:

Q	R	μ	dp/dx
$\{L^3 T^{-1}\}$	$\{L\}$	$\{ML^{-1} T^{-1}\}$	$\{ML^{-2} T^{-2}\}$

There are three primary dimensions (M, L, T), hence $j \leq 3$. By trial and error we determine that R, μ, and dp/dx cannot be combined into a pi group. Then $j = 3$, and $n - j = 4 - 3 = 1$. There is only *one* pi group, which we find by combining Q in a power product with the other three:

$$\Pi_1 = R^a \mu^b \left(\frac{dp}{dx}\right)^c Q^1 = (L)^a (ML^{-1} T^{-1})^b (ML^{-2} T^{-2})^c (L^3 T^{-1})$$
$$= M^0 L^0 T^0$$

Equate exponents:

Mass:
$$b + c = 0$$

Length:
$$a - b - 2c + 3 = 0$$

Time:
$$-b - 2c - 1 = 0$$

Solving simultaneously, we obtain $a = -4$, $b = 1$, and $c = -1$. Then

$$\Pi_1 = R^{-4}\mu^1\left(\frac{dp}{dx}\right)^{-1} Q$$

or
$$\Pi_1 = \frac{Q\mu}{R^4(dp/dx)} = \text{const} \qquad\qquad Ans.$$

Since there is only one pi group, it must equal a dimensionless constant. This is as far as dimensional analysis can take us. The laminar flow theory of Sec. 4.10 shows that the value of the constant is $-\frac{\pi}{8}$. This result is also useful in Chap. 6.

EXAMPLE 5.5

Assume that the tip deflection δ of a cantilever beam is a function of the tip load P, beam length L, area moment of inertia I, and material modulus of elasticity E; that is, $\delta = f(P, L, I, E)$. Rewrite this function in dimensionless form, and comment on its complexity and the peculiar value of j.

Solution

List the variables and their dimensions:

δ	P	L	I	E
$\{L\}$	$\{MLT^{-2}\}$	$\{L\}$	$\{L^4\}$	$\{ML^{-1}T^{-2}\}$

There are five variables ($n = 5$) and three primary dimensions (M, L, T), hence $j \leq 3$. But try as we may, we *cannot* find any combination of three variables that does not form a pi group. This is because $\{M\}$ and $\{T\}$ occur only in P and E and only in the same form, $\{MT^{-2}\}$. Thus we have encountered a special case of $j = 2$, which is less than the number of dimensions (M, L, T). To gain more insight into this peculiarity, you should rework the problem, using the (F, L, T) system of dimensions. You will find that only $\{F\}$ and $\{L\}$ occur in these variables, hence $j = 2$.

With $j = 2$, we select L and E as two variables that cannot form a pi group and then add other variables to form the three desired pis:

$$\Pi_1 = L^a E^b I^1 = (L)^a(ML^{-1}T^{-2})^b(L^4) = M^0 L^0 T^0$$

from which, after equating exponents, we find that $a = -4$, $b = 0$, or $\Pi_1 = I/L^4$. Then

$$\Pi_2 = L^a E^b P^1 = (L)^a(ML^{-1}T^{-2})^b(MLT^{-2}) = M^0 L^0 T^0$$

from which we find $a = -2$, $b = -1$, or $\Pi_2 = P/(EL^2)$, and

$$\Pi_3 = L^a E^b \delta^1 = (L)^a(ML^{-1}T^{-2})^b(L) = M^0 L^0 T^0$$

from which $a = -1$, $b = 0$, or $\Pi_3 = \delta/L$. The proper dimensionless function is $\Pi_3 = f(\Pi_2, \Pi_1)$, or

$$\frac{\delta}{L} = f\left(\frac{P}{EL^2}, \frac{I}{L^4}\right) \qquad Ans. (1)$$

This is a complex three-variable function, but dimensional analysis alone can take us no further.

Comments: We can "improve" Eq. (1) by taking advantage of some physical reasoning, as Langhaar points out [4, p. 91]. For small elastic deflections, δ is proportional to load P and inversely proportional to moment of inertia I. Since P and I occur separately in Eq. (1), this means that Π_3 must be proportional to Π_2 and inversely proportional to Π_1. Thus, for these conditions,

$$\frac{\delta}{L} = (\text{const}) \frac{P}{EL^2} \frac{L^4}{I}$$

or

$$\delta = (\text{const}) \frac{PL^3}{EI} \qquad (2)$$

This could not be predicted by a pure dimensional analysis. Strength-of-materials theory predicts that the value of the constant is $\frac{1}{3}$.

An Alternate Step-by-Step Method by Ipsen (1960)[5]

The pi theorem method, just explained and illustrated, is often called the *repeating variable method* of dimensional analysis. Select the repeating variables, add one more, and you get a pi group. The writer likes it. This method is straightforward and systematically reveals all the desired pi groups. However, there are drawbacks: (1) All pi groups contain the same repeating variables and might lack variety or effectiveness, and (2) one must (sometimes laboriously) check that the selected repeating variables do *not* form a pi group among themselves (see Prob. P5.21).

Ipsen [5] suggests an entirely different procedure, a step-by-step method that obtains all of the pi groups at once, without any counting or checking. One simply successively eliminates each dimension in the desired function by division or multiplication. Let us illustrate with the same classical drag function proposed in Eq. (5.1). Underneath the variables, write out the dimensions of each quantity.

$$F = \text{fcn}(L, \quad V, \quad \rho, \quad \mu) \qquad (5.1)$$
$$\{MLT^{-2}\} \quad \{L\} \quad \{LT^{-1}\} \quad \{ML^{-3}\} \quad \{ML^{-1}T^{-1}\}$$

There are three dimensions, $\{MLT\}$. Eliminate them successively by division or multiplication by a variable. Start with mass $\{M\}$. Pick a variable that contains mass and divide it into all the other variables with mass dimensions. We select ρ, divide, and rewrite the function (5.1):

$$\frac{F}{\rho} = \text{fcn}\left(L, \quad V, \quad \rho, \quad \frac{\mu}{\rho}\right) \qquad (5.1a)$$
$$\{L^4T^{-2}\} \quad \{L\} \quad \{LT^{-1}\} \quad \{L^2T^{-1}\}$$

[5]This method may be omitted without loss of continuity.

We did not divide into L or V, which do not contain $\{M\}$. Equation (5.1a) at first looks strange, but it contains five distinct variables and the same information as Eq. (5.1).

We see that ρ is no longer important. Thus *discard* ρ, and now there are only four variables. Next, eliminate time $\{T\}$ by dividing the time-containing variables by suitable powers of, say, V. The result is

$$\frac{F}{\rho V^2} = \text{fcn}\left(L, \quad \cancel{V,} \quad \frac{\mu}{\rho V}\right) \qquad (5.1b)$$
$$\{L^2\} \quad\quad \{L\} \quad\quad\quad\quad \{L\}$$

Now we see that V is no longer relevant. Finally, eliminate $\{L\}$ through division by, say, appropriate powers of L itself:

$$\frac{F}{\rho V^2 L^2} = \text{fcn}\left(\cancel{L,} \quad \frac{\mu}{\rho V L}\right) \qquad (5.1c)$$
$$\{1\} \quad\quad\quad \{1\}$$

Now L by itself is no longer relevant, and so discard it also. The result is equivalent to Eq. (5.2):

$$\frac{F}{\rho V^2 L^2} = \text{fcn}\left(\frac{\mu}{\rho V L}\right) \qquad (5.2)$$

In Ipsen's step-by-step method, we find the force coefficient is a function solely of the Reynolds number. We did no counting and did not find j. We just successively eliminated each primary dimension by division with the appropriate variables.

Recall Example 5.5, where we discovered, awkwardly, that the number of repeating variables was *less* than the number of primary dimensions. Ipsen's method avoids this preliminary check. Recall the beam-deflection problem proposed in Example 5.5 and the various dimensions:

$$\delta = f(P, \quad\quad L, \quad I, \quad\quad E)$$
$$\{L\} \quad \{MLT^{-2}\} \quad \{L\} \quad \{L^4\} \quad \{ML^{-1}T^{-2}\}$$

For the first step, let us eliminate $\{M\}$ by dividing by E. We only have to divide into P:

$$\delta = f\left(\frac{P}{E}, \quad L, \quad I, \quad \cancel{E}\right)$$
$$\{L\} \quad \{L^2\} \quad\quad \{L\} \quad \{L^4\}$$

We see that we may discard E as no longer relevant, and the dimension $\{T\}$ has vanished along with $\{M\}$. We need only eliminate $\{L\}$ by dividing by, say, powers of L itself:

$$\frac{\delta}{L} = \text{fcn}\left(\frac{P}{EL^2}, \quad \cancel{L,} \quad \frac{I}{L^4}\right)$$
$$\{1\} \quad\quad \{1\} \quad \{1\}$$

Discard L itself as now irrelevant, and we obtain *Answer* (1) to Example 5.5:

$$\frac{\delta}{L} = \text{fcn}\left(\frac{P}{EL^2}, \frac{I}{L^4}\right)$$

Ipsen's approach is again successful. The fact that $\{M\}$ and $\{T\}$ vanished in the same division is proof that there are only *two* repeating variables this time, not the three that would be inferred by the presence of $\{M\}$, $\{L\}$, and $\{T\}$.

EXAMPLE 5.6

The leading-edge aerodynamic moment M_{LE} on a supersonic airfoil is a function of its chord length C, angle of attack α, and several air parameters: approach velocity V, density ρ, speed of sound a, and specific heat ratio k (Fig. E5.6). There is a very weak effect of air viscosity, which is neglected here.

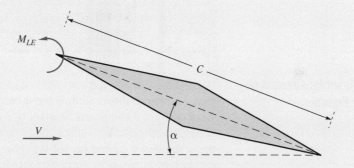

E5.6

Use Ipsen's method to rewrite this function in dimensionless form.

Solution

Write out the given function and list the variables' dimensions $\{MLT\}$ underneath:

$$M_{LE} \quad = \text{fcn}(C, \quad \alpha, \quad V, \quad \rho, \quad a, \quad k)$$
$$\{ML^2/T^2\} \quad \{L\} \quad \{1\} \quad \{L/T\} \quad \{M/L^3\} \quad \{L/T\} \quad \{1\}$$

Two of them, α and k, are already dimensionless. Leave them alone; they will be pi groups in the final function. You can eliminate any dimension. We choose mass $\{M\}$ and divide by ρ:

$$\frac{M_{LE}}{\rho} = \text{fcn}(C, \quad \alpha, \quad V, \quad \cancel{\rho}, \quad a, \quad k)$$
$$\{L^5/T^2\} \quad \{L\} \quad \{1\} \quad \{L/T\} \quad \{L/T\} \quad \{1\}$$

Recall Ipsen's rules: Only divide into variables containing mass, in this case only M_{LE}, and then discard the divisor, ρ. Now eliminate time $\{T\}$ by dividing by appropriate powers of a:

$$\frac{M_{LE}}{\rho a^2} = \text{fcn}\left(C, \quad \alpha, \quad \frac{V}{a}, \quad \cancel{a}, \quad k\right)$$
$$\{L^3\} \quad \{L\} \quad \{1\} \quad \{1\} \quad \{1\}$$

Finally, eliminate $\{L\}$ on the left side by dividing by C^3:

$$\frac{M_{LE}}{\rho a^2 C^3} = \text{fcn}\left(\frac{\rho}{},\ \alpha,\ \frac{V}{a},\ k\right)$$

$$\{1\} \qquad\qquad \{1\}\ \{1\}\ \{1\}$$

We end up with four pi groups and recognize V/a as the Mach number, Ma. In aerodynamics, the dimensionless moment is often called the *moment coefficient*, C_M. Thus our final result could be written in the compact form

$$C_M = \text{fcn}(\alpha, \text{Ma}, k) \qquad\qquad\qquad Ans.$$

Comments: Our analysis is fine, but experiment and theory and physical reasoning all indicate that M_{LE} varies more strongly with V than with a. Thus aerodynamicists commonly define the moment coefficient as $C_M = M_{LE}/(\rho V^2 C^3)$ or something similar. We will study the analysis of supersonic forces and moments in Chap. 9.

5.4 Nondimensionalization of the Basic Equations

We could use the pi theorem method of the previous section to analyze problem after problem after problem, finding the dimensionless parameters that govern in each case. Textbooks on dimensional analysis [for example, 5] do this. An alternative and very powerful technique is to attack the basic equations of flow from Chap. 4. Even though these equations cannot be solved in general, they will reveal basic dimensionless parameters, such as the Reynolds number, in their proper form and proper position, giving clues to when they are negligible. The boundary conditions must also be nondimensionalized.

Let us briefly apply this technique to the incompressible flow continuity and momentum equations with constant viscosity:

Continuity: $$\nabla \cdot \mathbf{V} = 0 \qquad\qquad (5.21a)$$

Navier-Stokes: $$\rho \frac{d\mathbf{V}}{dt} = \rho \mathbf{g} - \nabla p + \mu \nabla^2 \mathbf{V} \qquad\qquad (5.21b)$$

Typical boundary conditions for these two equations are (Sect. 4.6)

Fixed solid surface: $$\mathbf{V} = 0$$

Inlet or outlet: $$\text{Known } \mathbf{V}, p \qquad\qquad (5.22)$$

Free surface, $z = \eta$: $$w = \frac{d\eta}{dt} \qquad p = p_a - \Upsilon(R_x^{-1} + R_y^{-1})$$

We omit the energy equation (4.75) and assign its dimensionless form in the problems (Prob. P5.43).

Equations (5.21) and (5.22) contain the three basic dimensions M, L, and T. All variables p, $\mathbf{V}$, x, y, z, and t can be nondimensionalized by using density and two reference constants that might be characteristic of the particular fluid flow:

$$\text{Reference velocity} = U \qquad \text{Reference length} = L$$

For example, U may be the inlet or upstream velocity and L the diameter of a body immersed in the stream.

Now define all relevant dimensionless variables, denoting them by an asterisk:

$$\mathbf{V}^* = \frac{\mathbf{V}}{U} \qquad \boldsymbol{\nabla}^* = L\boldsymbol{\nabla}$$

$$x^* = \frac{x}{L} \quad y^* = \frac{y}{L} \quad z^* = \frac{z}{L} \quad R^* = \frac{R}{L} \tag{5.23}$$

$$t^* = \frac{tU}{L} \quad p^* = \frac{p + \rho gz}{\rho U^2}$$

All these are fairly obvious except for p^*, where we have introduced the piezometric pressure, assuming that z is up. This is a hindsight idea suggested by Bernoulli's equation (3.54).

Since ρ, U, and L are all constants, the derivatives in Eqs. (5.21) can all be handled in dimensionless form with dimensional coefficients. For example,

$$\frac{\partial u}{\partial x} = \frac{\partial(Uu^*)}{\partial(Lx^*)} = \frac{U}{L}\frac{\partial u^*}{\partial x^*}$$

Substitute the variables from Eqs. (5.23) into Eqs. (5.21) and (5.22) and divide through by the leading dimensional coefficient, in the same way as we handled Eq. (5.12). Here are the resulting dimensionless equations of motion:

Continuity:

$$\boxed{\boldsymbol{\nabla}^* \cdot \mathbf{V}^* = 0} \tag{5.24a}$$

Momentum:

$$\boxed{\frac{d\mathbf{V}^*}{dt^*} = -\boldsymbol{\nabla}^* p^* + \frac{\mu}{\rho UL}\boldsymbol{\nabla}^{*2}(\mathbf{V}^*)} \tag{5.24b}$$

The dimensionless boundary conditions are:

Fixed solid surface:

$$\boxed{\mathbf{V}^* = 0}$$

Inlet or outlet:

$$\boxed{\text{Known } \mathbf{V}^*, p^*}$$

Free surface, $z^* = \eta^*$:

$$\boxed{\begin{array}{c} w^* = \dfrac{d\eta^*}{dt^*} \\[2mm] p^* = \dfrac{p_a}{\rho U^2} + \dfrac{gL}{U^2}z^* - \dfrac{Y}{\rho U^2 L}(R_x^{*-1} + R_y^{*-1}) \end{array}} \tag{5.25}$$

These equations reveal a total of four dimensionless parameters, one in the Navier-Stokes equation and three in the free-surface-pressure boundary condition.

Dimensionless Parameters

In the continuity equation there are no parameters. The Navier-Stokes equation contains one, generally accepted as the most important parameter in fluid mechanics:

$$\text{Reynolds number Re} = \frac{\rho UL}{\mu}$$

It is named after Osborne Reynolds (1842–1912), a British engineer who first proposed it in 1883 (Ref. 4 of Chap. 6). The Reynolds number is always important, with or without a free surface, and can be neglected only in flow regions away from high-velocity gradients—for example, away from solid surfaces, jets, or wakes.

The no-slip and inlet-exit boundary conditions contain no parameters. The free-surface-pressure condition contains three:

$$\text{Euler number (pressure coefficient) Eu} = \frac{p_a}{\rho U^2}$$

This is named after Leonhard Euler (1707–1783) and is rarely important unless the pressure drops low enough to cause vapor formation (cavitation) in a liquid. The Euler number is often written in terms of pressure differences: $\text{Eu} = \Delta p/(\rho U^2)$. If Δp involves vapor pressure p_v, it is called the *cavitation number* $\text{Ca} = (p_a - p_v)/(\rho U^2)$. Cavitation problems are surprisingly common in many water flows.

The second free-surface parameter is much more important:

$$\text{Froude number Fr} = \frac{U^2}{gL}$$

It is named after William Froude (1810–1879), a British naval architect who, with his son Robert, developed the ship-model towing-tank concept and proposed similarity rules for free-surface flows (ship resistance, surface waves, open channels). The Froude number is the dominant effect in free-surface flows. It can also be important in *stratified flows*, where a strong density difference exists without a free surface. For example, see Ref. [42]. Chapter 10 investigates Froude number effects in detail.

The final free-surface parameter is

$$\text{Weber number We} = \frac{\rho U^2 L}{Y}$$

It is named after Moritz Weber (1871–1951) of the Polytechnic Institute of Berlin, who developed the laws of similitude in their modern form. It was Weber who named Re and Fr after Reynolds and Froude. The Weber number is important only if it is of order unity or less, which typically occurs when the surface curvature is comparable in size to the liquid depth, such as in droplets, capillary flows, ripple waves, and very small hydraulic models. If We is large, its effect may be neglected.

If there is no free surface, Fr, Eu, and We drop out entirely, except for the possibility of cavitation of a liquid at very small Eu. Thus, in low-speed viscous flows with no free surface, the Reynolds number is the only important dimensionless parameter.

Compressibility Parameters

In high-speed flow of a gas there are significant changes in pressure, density, and temperature that must be related by an equation of state such as the perfect-gas law, Eq. (1.10). These thermodynamic changes introduce two additional dimensionless parameters mentioned briefly in earlier chapters:

$$\text{Mach number Ma} = \frac{U}{a} \qquad \text{Specific-heat ratio } k = \frac{c_p}{c_v}$$

The Mach number is named after Ernst Mach (1838–1916), an Austrian physicist. The effect of k is only slight to moderate, but Ma exerts a strong effect on compressible flow properties if it is greater than about 0.3. These effects are studied in Chap. 9.

Oscillating Flows

If the flow pattern is oscillating, a seventh parameter enters through the inlet boundary condition. For example, suppose that the inlet stream is of the form

$$u = U \cos \omega t$$

Nondimensionalization of this relation results in

$$\frac{u}{U} = u^* = \cos\left(\frac{\omega L}{U}t^*\right)$$

The argument of the cosine contains the new parameter

$$\text{Strouhal number St} = \frac{\omega L}{U}$$

The dimensionless forces and moments, friction, and heat transfer, and so on of such an oscillating flow would be a function of both Reynolds and Strouhal numbers. This parameter is named after V. Strouhal, a German physicist who experimented in 1878 with wires singing in the wind.

Some flows that you might guess to be perfectly steady actually have an oscillatory pattern that is dependent on the Reynolds number. An example is the periodic vortex shedding behind a blunt body immersed in a steady stream of velocity U. Figure 5.2a shows an array of alternating vortices shed from a circular cylinder immersed in a steady crossflow. This regular, periodic shedding is called a *Kármán vortex street,* after T. von Kármán, who explained it theoretically in 1912. The shedding occurs in the range $10^2 < \text{Re} < 10^7$, with an average Strouhal number $\omega d/(2\pi U) \approx 0.21$. Figure 5.2$b$ shows measured shedding frequencies.

Resonance can occur if a vortex shedding frequency is near a body's structural vibration frequency. Electric transmission wires sing in the wind, undersea mooring lines gallop at certain current speeds, and slender structures flutter at critical wind or vehicle speeds. A striking example is the disastrous failure of the Tacoma Narrows suspension bridge in 1940, when wind-excited vortex shedding caused resonance with the natural torsional oscillations of the bridge. The problem was magnified by the bridge deck nonlinear stiffness, which occurred when the hangers went slack during the oscillation.

Other Dimensionless Parameters

We have discussed seven important parameters in fluid mechanics, and there are others. Four additional parameters arise from nondimensionalization of the energy equation (4.75) and its boundary conditions. These four (Prandtl number, Eckert number, Grashof number, and wall temperature ratio) are listed in Table 5.2 just in case you fail to solve Prob. P5.43. Another important and perhaps surprising parameter is the

(a)

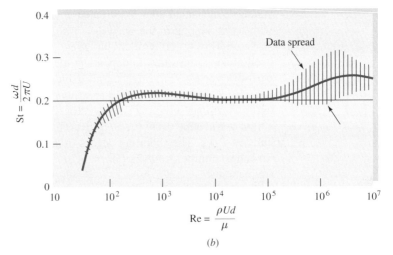

(b)

Fig. 5.2 Vortex shedding from a circular cylinder: (*a*) vortex street behind a circular cylinder *(Courtesy of U.S. Navy);* (*b*) experimental shedding frequencies *(data from Refs. 25 and 26).*

wall roughness ratio ε/L (in Table 5.2).[6] Slight changes in surface roughness have a striking effect in the turbulent flow or high-Reynolds-number range, as we shall see in Chap. 6 and in Fig. 5.3.

This book is primarily concerned with Reynolds-, Mach-, and Froude-number effects, which dominate most flows. Note that we discovered these parameters (except ε/L) simply by nondimensionalizing the basic equations without actually solving them.

---

[6]Roughness is easy to overlook because it is a slight geometric effect that does not appear in the equations of motion. It is a boundary condition that one might forget.

Table 5.2 Dimensionless Groups in Fluid Mechanics

Parameter	Definition	Qualitative ratio of effects	Importance
Reynolds number	$\mathrm{Re} = \dfrac{\rho U L}{\mu}$	$\dfrac{\text{Inertia}}{\text{Viscosity}}$	Almost always
Mach number	$\mathrm{Ma} = \dfrac{U}{a}$	$\dfrac{\text{Flow speed}}{\text{Sound speed}}$	Compressible flow
Froude number	$\mathrm{Fr} = \dfrac{U^2}{gL}$	$\dfrac{\text{Inertia}}{\text{Gravity}}$	Free-surface flow
Weber number	$\mathrm{We} = \dfrac{\rho U^2 L}{Y}$	$\dfrac{\text{Inertia}}{\text{Surface tension}}$	Free-surface flow
Rossby number	$\mathrm{Ro} = \dfrac{U}{\Omega_{\text{earth}} L}$	$\dfrac{\text{Flow velocity}}{\text{Coriolis effect}}$	Geophysical flows
Cavitation number (Euler number)	$\mathrm{Ca} = \dfrac{p - p_v}{\frac{1}{2}\rho U^2}$	$\dfrac{\text{Pressure}}{\text{Inertia}}$	Cavitation
Prandtl number	$\mathrm{Pr} = \dfrac{\mu c_p}{k}$	$\dfrac{\text{Dissipation}}{\text{Conduction}}$	Heat convection
Eckert number	$\mathrm{Ec} = \dfrac{U^2}{c_p T_0}$	$\dfrac{\text{Kinetic energy}}{\text{Enthalpy}}$	Dissipation
Specific-heat ratio	$k = \dfrac{c_p}{c_v}$	$\dfrac{\text{Enthalpy}}{\text{Internal energy}}$	Compressible flow
Strouhal number	$\mathrm{St} = \dfrac{\omega L}{U}$	$\dfrac{\text{Oscillation}}{\text{Mean speed}}$	Oscillating flow
Roughness ratio	$\dfrac{\varepsilon}{L}$	$\dfrac{\text{Wall roughness}}{\text{Body length}}$	Turbulent, rough walls
Grashof number	$\mathrm{Gr} = \dfrac{\beta \Delta T g L^3 \rho^2}{\mu^2}$	$\dfrac{\text{Buoyancy}}{\text{Viscosity}}$	Natural convection
Rayleigh number	$\mathrm{Ra} = \dfrac{\beta \Delta T g L^3 \rho^2 c_p}{\mu\, k}$	$\dfrac{\text{Buoyancy}}{\text{Viscosity}}$	Natural convection
Temperature ratio	$\dfrac{T_w}{T_0}$	$\dfrac{\text{Wall temperature}}{\text{Stream temperature}}$	Heat transfer
Pressure coefficient	$C_p = \dfrac{p - p_\infty}{\frac{1}{2}\rho U^2}$	$\dfrac{\text{Static pressure}}{\text{Dynamic pressure}}$	Aerodynamics, hydrodynamics
Lift coefficient	$C_L = \dfrac{L}{\frac{1}{2}\rho U^2 A}$	$\dfrac{\text{Lift force}}{\text{Dynamic force}}$	Aerodynamics, hydrodynamics
Drag coefficient	$C_D = \dfrac{D}{\frac{1}{2}\rho U^2 A}$	$\dfrac{\text{Drag force}}{\text{Dynamic force}}$	Aerodynamics, hydrodynamics
Friction factor	$f = \dfrac{h_f}{(V^2/2g)(L/d)}$	$\dfrac{\text{Friction head loss}}{\text{Velocity head}}$	Pipe flow
Skin friction coefficient	$c_f = \dfrac{\tau_{\text{wall}}}{\rho V^2/2}$	$\dfrac{\text{Wall shear stress}}{\text{Dynamic pressure}}$	Boundary layer flow

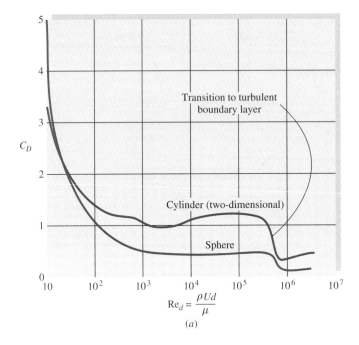
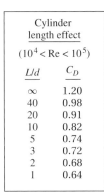

Cylinder length effect $(10^4 < Re < 10^5)$	
L/d	C_D
∞	1.20
40	0.98
20	0.91
10	0.82
5	0.74
3	0.72
2	0.68
1	0.64

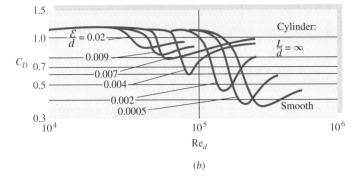

Fig. 5.3 The proof of practical dimensional analysis: drag coefficients of a cylinder and sphere: (*a*) drag coefficient of a smooth cylinder and sphere (data from many sources); (*b*) increased roughness causes earlier transition to a turbulent boundary layer.

If the reader is not satiated with the 19 parameters given in Table 5.2, Ref. 29 contains a list of over 1200 dimensionless parameters in use in engineering and science.

A Successful Application

Dimensional analysis is fun, but does it work? Yes, if all important variables are included in the proposed function, the dimensionless function found by dimensional analysis will collapse all the data onto a single curve or set of curves.

An example of the success of dimensional analysis is given in Fig. 5.3 for the measured drag on smooth cylinders and spheres. The flow is normal to the axis of the cylinder, which is extremely long, $L/d \rightarrow \infty$. The data are from many sources, for both liquids and gases, and include bodies from several meters in diameter down to fine wires and balls less than 1 mm in size. Both curves in Fig. 5.3*a* are entirely experimental; the analysis of immersed body drag is one of the weakest areas of modern fluid mechanics theory. Except for digital computer calculations, there is little theory for cylinder and sphere drag except *creeping flow*, $Re < 1$.

The concept of a fluid-caused *drag force* on bodies is covered extensively in Chap. 7. Drag is the fluid force parallel to the oncoming stream—see Fig. 7.10 for details.

The Reynolds number of both bodies is based on diameter, hence the notation Re_d. But the drag coefficients are defined differently:

$$C_D = \begin{cases} \dfrac{\text{drag}}{\frac{1}{2}\rho U^2 Ld} & \text{cylinder} \\[2ex] \dfrac{\text{drag}}{\frac{1}{2}\rho U^2 \frac{1}{4}\pi d^2} & \text{sphere} \end{cases} \tag{5.26}$$

They both have a factor $\frac{1}{2}$ because the term $\frac{1}{2}\rho U^2$ occurs in Bernoulli's equation, and both are based on the projected area—that is, the area one sees when looking toward the body from upstream. The usual definition of C_D is thus

$$C_D = \frac{\text{drag}}{\frac{1}{2}\rho U^2(\text{projected area})} \tag{5.27}$$

However, one should carefully check the definitions of C_D, Re, and the like before using data in the literature. Airfoils, for example, use the planform area.

Figure 5.3a is for long, smooth cylinders. If wall roughness and cylinder length are included as variables, we obtain from dimensional analysis a complex three-parameter function:

$$C_D = f\left(\mathrm{Re}_d, \frac{\varepsilon}{d}, \frac{L}{d}\right) \tag{5.28}$$

To describe this function completely would require 1000 or more experiments or CFD results. Therefore it is customary to explore the length and roughness effects separately to establish trends.

The table with Fig. 5.3a shows the length effect with zero wall roughness. As length decreases, the drag decreases by up to 50 percent. Physically, the pressure is "relieved" at the ends as the flow is allowed to skirt around the tips instead of deflecting over and under the body.

Figure 5.3b shows the effect of wall roughness for an infinitely long cylinder. The sharp drop in drag occurs at lower Re_d as roughness causes an earlier transition to a turbulent boundary layer on the surface of the body. Roughness has the same effect on sphere drag, a fact that is exploited in sports by deliberate dimpling of golf balls to give them less drag at their flight $\mathrm{Re}_d \approx 10^5$. See Fig. D5.2.

Figure 5.3 is a typical experimental study of a fluid mechanics problem, aided by dimensional analysis. As time and money and demand allow, the complete three-parameter relation (5.28) could be filled out by further experiments.

EXAMPLE 5.7

A smooth cylinder, 1 cm in diameter and 20 cm long, is tested in a wind tunnel for a crossflow of 45 m/s of air at 20°C and 1 atm. The measured drag is 2.2 ± 0.1 N. (a) Does this data point agree with the data in Fig. 5.3? (b) Can this data point be used to predict the drag of a chimney 1 m in diameter and 20 m high in winds at 20°C and 1 atm? If so, what is the recommended range of wind velocities and drag forces for this data point? (c) Why are the answers to part (b) always the same, regardless of the chimney height, as long as $L = 20d$?

Solution

(a) For air at 20°C and 1 atm, take $\rho = 1.2$ kg/m³ and $\mu = 1.8$ E-5 kg/(m-s). Since the test cylinder is short, $L/d = 20$, it should be compared with the tabulated value $C_D \approx 0.91$ in the table to the right of Fig. 5.3a. First calculate the Reynolds number of the test cylinder:

$$\text{Re}_d = \frac{\rho U d}{\mu} = \frac{(1.2 \text{ kg/m}^3)(45 \text{ m/s})(0.01 \text{ m})}{1.8\text{E}-5 \text{ kg/(m} - \text{s)}} = 30{,}000$$

Yes, this is in the range $10^4 < \text{Re} < 10^5$ listed in the table. Now calculate the test drag coefficient:

$$C_{D,\text{test}} = \frac{F}{(1/2)\rho U^2 L d} = \frac{2.2 \text{ N}}{(1/2)(1.2 \text{ kg/m}^3)(45 \text{ m/s})^2(0.2 \text{ m})(0.01 \text{ m})} = 0.905$$

Yes, this is close, and certainly within the range of ± 5 percent stated by the test results.

Ans. (a)

(b) Since the chimney has $L/d = 20$, we can use the data if the Reynolds number range is correct:

$$10^4 < \frac{(1.2 \text{ kg/m}^3)U_{\text{chimney}}(1 \text{ m})}{1.8 \text{ E}-5 \text{ kg/(m} \cdot \text{s)}} < 10^5 \quad \text{if} \quad 0.15\frac{\text{m}}{\text{s}} < U_{\text{chimney}} < 1.5\frac{\text{m}}{\text{s}}$$

These are negligible winds, so the test data point is not very useful   Ans. (b)
The drag forces in this range are also negligibly small:

$$F_{\text{min}} = C_D \frac{\rho}{2} U_{\text{min}}^2 L d = (0.91)\left(\frac{1.2 \text{ kg/m}^3}{2}\right)(0.15 \text{ m/s})^2(20 \text{ m})(1 \text{ m}) = 0.25 \text{ N}$$

$$F_{\text{max}} = C_D \frac{\rho}{2} U_{\text{max}}^2 L d = (0.91)\left(\frac{1.2 \text{ kg/m}^3}{2}\right)(1.5 \text{ m/s})^2(20 \text{ m})(1 \text{ m}) = 25 \text{ N}$$

(c) Try this yourself. Choose any 20:1 size for the chimney, even something silly like 20 mm:1 mm. You will get the same results for U and F as in part (b) above. This is because the product Ud occurs in Re_d and, if $L = 20d$, the same product occurs in the drag force. For example, for $\text{Re} = 10^4$,

$$Ud = 10^4 \frac{\mu}{\rho} \quad \text{then } F = C_D \frac{\rho}{2} U^2 L d = C_D \frac{\rho}{2} U^2(20d)d = 20C_D \frac{\rho}{2}(Ud)^2 = 20C_D \frac{\rho}{2}\left(\frac{10^4 \mu}{\rho}\right)^2$$

The answer is always $F_{\text{min}} = 0.25$ N. This is an algebraic quirk that seldom occurs.

EXAMPLE 5.8

Telephone wires are said to "sing" in the wind. Consider a wire of diameter 8 mm. At what sea-level wind velocity, if any, will the wire sing a middle C note?

Solution

For sea-level air take $\nu \approx 1.5\,E{-}5$ m^2/s. For nonmusical readers, middle C is 262 Hz. Measured shedding rates are plotted in Fig. 5.2b. Over a wide range, the Strouhal number is approximately 0.2, which we can take as a first guess. Note that $(\omega/2\pi) = f$, the shedding frequency. Thus

$$\text{St} = \frac{fd}{U} = \frac{(262\,\text{s}^{-1})(0.008\,\text{m})}{U} \approx 0.2$$

$$U \approx 10.5\ \frac{\text{m}}{\text{s}}$$

Now check the Reynolds number to see if we fall into the appropriate range:

$$\text{Re}_d = \frac{Ud}{\nu} = \frac{(10.5\,\text{m/s})(0.008\,\text{m})}{1.5\,E{-}5\,\text{m}^2/\text{s}} \approx 5600$$

In Fig. 5.2b, at Re = 5600, maybe St is a little higher, at about 0.21. Thus a slightly improved estimate is

$$U_{\text{wind}} = (262)(0.008)/(0.21) \approx 10.0\ \text{m/s} \qquad\qquad Ans.$$

5.5 Modeling and Similarity

So far we have learned about dimensional homogeneity and the pi theorem method, using power products, for converting a homogeneous physical relation to dimensionless form. This is straightforward mathematically, but certain engineering difficulties need to be discussed.

First, we have more or less taken for granted that the variables that affect the process can be listed and analyzed. Actually, selection of the important variables requires considerable judgment and experience. The engineer must decide, for example, whether viscosity can be neglected. Are there significant temperature effects? Is surface tension important? What about wall roughness? Each pi group that is retained increases the expense and effort required. Judgment in selecting variables will come through practice and maturity; this book should provide some of the necessary experience.

Once the variables are selected and the dimensional analysis is performed, the experimenter seeks to achieve *similarity* between the model tested and the prototype to be designed. With sufficient testing, the model data will reveal the desired dimensionless function between variables:

$$\Pi_1 = f(\Pi_2, \Pi_3, \ldots \Pi_k) \qquad\qquad (5.29)$$

With Eq. (5.29) available in chart, graphical, or analytical form, we are in a position to ensure complete similarity between model and prototype. A formal statement would be as follows:

> Flow conditions for a model test are completely similar if all relevant dimensionless parameters have the same corresponding values for the model and the prototype.

This follows mathematically from Eq. (5.29). If $\Pi_{2m} = \Pi_{2p}$, $\Pi_{3m} = \Pi_{3p}$, and so forth, Eq. (5.29) guarantees that the desired output Π_{1m} will equal Π_{1p}. But this is easier said than done, as we now discuss. There are specialized texts on model testing [30–32].

Instead of complete similarity, the engineering literature speaks of particular types of similarity, the most common being geometric, kinematic, dynamic, and thermal. Let us consider each separately.

Geometric Similarity

Geometric similarity concerns the length dimension $\{L\}$ and must be ensured before any sensible model testing can proceed. A formal definition is as follows:

> A model and prototype are *geometrically similar* if and only if all body dimensions in all three coordinates have the same linear scale ratio.

Note that *all* length scales must be the same. It is as if you took a photograph of the prototype and reduced it or enlarged it until it fitted the size of the model. If the model is to be made one-tenth the prototype size, its length, width, and height must each be one-tenth as large. Not only that, but also its entire shape must be one-tenth as large, and technically we speak of *homologous* points, which are points that have the same relative location. For example, the nose of the prototype is homologous to the nose of the model. The left wingtip of the prototype is homologous to the left wingtip of the model. Then geometric similarity requires that all homologous points be related by the same linear scale ratio. This applies to the fluid geometry as well as the model geometry.

> All angles are preserved in geometric similarity. All flow directions are preserved. The orientations of model and prototype with respect to the surroundings must be identical.

Figure 5.4 illustrates a prototype wing and a one-tenth-scale model. The model lengths are all one-tenth as large, but its angle of attack with respect to the free stream is the same for both model and prototype: 10° not 1°. All physical details on the model must be scaled, and some are rather subtle and sometimes overlooked:

1. The model nose radius must be one-tenth as large.
2. The model surface roughness must be one-tenth as large.

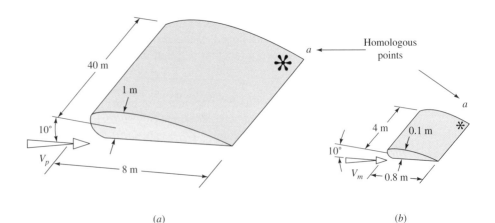

Fig. 5.4 Geometric similarity in model testing: (*a*) prototype; (*b*) one-tenth-scale model.

(*a*)

(*b*)

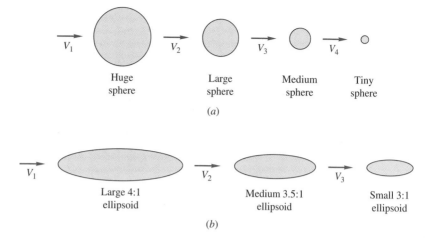

Fig. 5.5 Geometric similarity and dissimilarity of flows: (*a*) similar; (*b*) dissimilar.

V_1 Huge sphere

V_2 Large sphere

V_3 Medium sphere

V_4 Tiny sphere

(*a*)

V_1 Large 4:1 ellipsoid

V_2 Medium 3.5:1 ellipsoid

V_3 Small 3:1 ellipsoid

(*b*)

3. If the prototype has a 5-mm boundary layer trip wire 1.5 m from the leading edge, the model should have a 0.5-mm trip wire 0.15 m from its leading edge.

4. If the prototype is constructed with protruding fasteners, the model should have homologous protruding fasteners one-tenth as large.

And so on. Any departure from these details is a violation of geometric similarity and must be justified by experimental comparison to show that the prototype behavior was not significantly affected by the discrepancy.

Models that appear similar in shape but that clearly violate geometric similarity should not be compared except at your own risk. Figure 5.5 illustrates this point. The spheres in Fig. 5.5*a* are all geometrically similar and can be tested with a high expectation of success if the Reynolds number, Froude number, or the like is matched. But the ellipsoids in Fig. 5.5*b* merely *look* similar. They actually have different linear scale ratios and therefore cannot be compared in a rational manner, even though they may have identical Reynolds and Froude numbers and so on. The data will not be the same for these ellipsoids, and any attempt to "compare" them is a matter of rough engineering judgment.

Kinematic Similarity

Kinematic similarity requires that the model and prototype have the same length scale ratio and the same time scale ratio. The result is that the velocity scale ratio will be the same for both. As Langhaar [4] states it:

> The motions of two systems are kinematically similar if homologous particles lie at homologous points at homologous times.

Length scale equivalence simply implies geometric similarity, but time scale equivalence may require additional dynamic considerations such as equivalence of the Reynolds and Mach numbers.

One special case is incompressible frictionless flow with no free surface, as sketched in Fig. 5.6*a*. These perfect-fluid flows are kinematically similar with independent length and time scales, and no additional parameters are necessary (see Chap. 8 for further details).

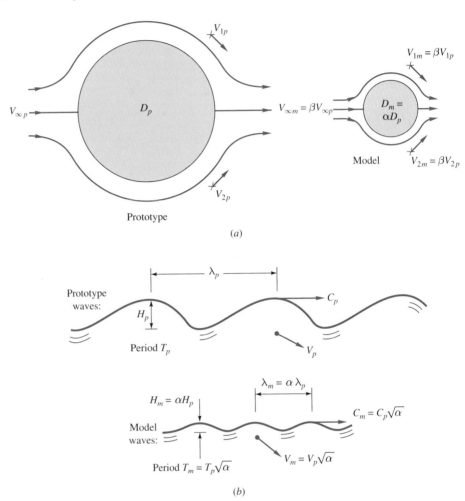

Fig. 5.6 Frictionless low-speed flows are kinematically similar: (*a*) Flows with no free surface are kinematically similar with independent length and time scale ratios; (*b*) free-surface flows are kinematically similar with length and time scales related by the Froude number.

Froude Scaling

Frictionless flows with a free surface, as in Fig. 5.6*b*, are kinematically similar if their Froude numbers are equal:

$$\text{Fr}_m = \frac{V_m^2}{gL_m} = \frac{V_p^2}{gL_p} = Fr_p \tag{5.30}$$

Note that the Froude number contains only length and time dimensions and hence is a purely kinematic parameter that fixes the relation between length and time. From Eq. (5.30), if the length scale is

$$L_m = \alpha L_p \tag{5.31}$$

where α is a dimensionless ratio, the velocity scale is

$$\frac{V_m}{V_p} = \left(\frac{L_m}{L_p}\right)^{1/2} = \sqrt{\alpha} \tag{5.32}$$

and the time scale is

$$\frac{T_m}{T_p} = \frac{L_m/V_m}{L_p/V_p} = \sqrt{\alpha} \qquad (5.33)$$

These Froude-scaling kinematic relations are illustrated in Fig. 5.6b for wave motion modeling. If the waves are related by the length scale α, then the wave period, propagation speed, and particle velocities are related by $\sqrt{\alpha}$.

If viscosity, surface tension, or compressibility is important, kinematic similarity depends on the achievement of dynamic similarity.

Dynamic Similarity

Dynamic similarity exists when the model and the prototype have the same length scale ratio, time scale ratio, and force scale (or mass scale) ratio. Again geometric similarity is a first requirement; without it, proceed no further. Then dynamic similarity exists, simultaneous with kinematic similarity, if the model and prototype force and pressure coefficients are identical. This is ensured if

1. For compressible flow, the model and prototype Reynolds number and Mach number and specific-heat ratio are correspondingly equal.
2. For incompressible flow
    a. With no free surface: model and prototype Reynolds numbers are equal.
    b. With a free surface: model and prototype Reynolds number, Froude number, and (if necessary) Weber number and cavitation number are correspondingly equal.

Mathematically, Newton's law for any fluid particle requires that the sum of the pressure force, gravity force, and friction force equal the acceleration term, or inertia force,

$$\mathbf{F}_p + \mathbf{F}_g + \mathbf{F}_f = \mathbf{F}_i$$

The dynamic similarity laws listed above ensure that each of these forces will be in the same ratio and have equivalent directions between model and prototype. Figure 5.7

Fig. 5.7 Dynamic similarity in sluice gate flow. Model and prototype yield identical homologous force polygons if the Reynolds and Froude numbers are the same corresponding values: (a) prototype; (b) model.

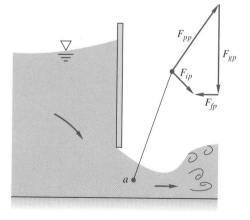

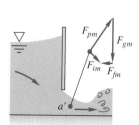

(a)   (b)

shows an example for flow through a sluice gate. The force polygons at homologous points have exactly the same shape if the Reynolds and Froude numbers are equal (neglecting surface tension and cavitation, of course). Kinematic similarity is also ensured by these model laws.

Discrepancies in Water and Air Testing

The perfect dynamic similarity shown in Fig. 5.7 is more of a dream than a reality because true equivalence of Reynolds and Froude numbers can be achieved only by dramatic changes in fluid properties, whereas in fact most model testing is simply done with water or air, the cheapest fluids available.

First consider hydraulic model testing with a free surface. Dynamic similarity requires equivalent Froude numbers, Eq. (5.30), *and* equivalent Reynolds numbers:

$$\frac{V_m L_m}{\nu_m} = \frac{V_p L_p}{\nu_p} \tag{5.34}$$

But both velocity and length are constrained by the Froude number, Eqs. (5.31) and (5.32). Therefore, for a given length scale ratio α, Eq. (5.34) is true only if

$$\frac{\nu_m}{\nu_p} = \frac{L_m}{L_p} \frac{V_m}{V_p} = \alpha\sqrt{\alpha} = \alpha^{3/2} \tag{5.35}$$

For example, for a one-tenth-scale model, $\alpha = 0.1$ and $\alpha^{3/2} = 0.032$. Since ν_p is undoubtedly water, we need a fluid with only 0.032 times the kinematic viscosity of water to achieve dynamic similarity. Referring to Table 1.4, we see that this is impossible: Even mercury has only one-ninth the kinematic viscosity of water, and a mercury hydraulic model would be expensive and bad for your health. In practice, water is used for both the model and the prototype, and the Reynolds number similarity (5.34) is unavoidably violated. The Froude number is held constant since it is the dominant parameter in free-surface flows. Typically the Reynolds number of the model flow is too small by a factor of 10 to 1000. As shown in Fig. 5.8, the low-Reynolds-number model data are used to estimate by extrapolation the desired high-Reynolds-number prototype data. As the figure indicates, there is obviously considerable uncertainty in using such an extrapolation, but there is no other practical alternative in hydraulic model testing.

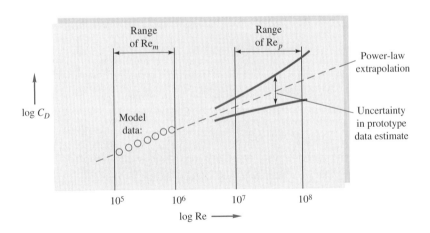

Fig. 5.8 Reynolds-number extrapolation, or scaling, of hydraulic data with equal Froude numbers.

Second, consider aerodynamic model testing in air with no free surface. The important parameters are the Reynolds number and the Mach number. Equation (5.34) should be satisfied, plus the compressibility criterion

$$\frac{V_m}{a_m} = \frac{V_p}{a_p} \tag{5.36}$$

Elimination of V_m/V_p between (5.34) and (5.36) gives

$$\frac{\nu_m}{\nu_p} = \frac{L_m}{L_p}\frac{a_m}{a_p} \tag{5.37}$$

Since the prototype is no doubt an air operation, we need a wind-tunnel fluid of low viscosity and high speed of sound. Hydrogen is the only practical example, but clearly it is too expensive and dangerous. Therefore, wind tunnels normally operate with air as the working fluid. Cooling and pressurizing the air will bring Eq. (5.37) into better agreement but not enough to satisfy a length scale reduction of, say, one-tenth. Therefore Reynolds number scaling is also commonly violated in aerodynamic testing, and an extrapolation like that in Fig. 5.8 is required here also.

There are specialized monographs devoted entirely to wind tunnel testing: low speed [38], high speed [39], and a detailed general discussion [40]. The following example illustrates modeling discrepancies in aeronautical testing.

EXAMPLE 5.9

A prototype airplane, with a chord length of 1.6 m, is to fly at Ma = 2 at 10 km standard altitude. A one-eighth scale model is to be tested in a helium wind tunnel at 100°C and 1 atm. Find the helium test section velocity that will match (*a*) the Mach number or (*b*) the Reynolds number of the prototype. In each case criticize the lack of dynamic similarity. (*c*) What high pressure in the helium tunnel will match *both* the Mach and Reynolds numbers? (*d*) Why does part (*c*) *still* not achieve dynamic similarity?

Solution

For helium, from Table A.4, $R = 2077$ m^2/(s^2-K), $k = 1.66$, and estimate $\mu_{He} \approx 2.32$ E-5 kg/(m · s) from the power-law, $n = 0.67$, in the table. (*a*) Calculate the helium speed of sound and velocity:

$$a_{He} = \sqrt{(kRT)_{He}} = \sqrt{(1.66)(2077 \text{ m}^2/\text{s}^2\text{K}) \times (373 \text{ K})} = 1134 \text{ m/s}$$

$$\text{Ma}_{air} = \text{Ma}_{He} = 2.0 = \frac{V_{He}}{a_{He}} = \frac{V_{He}}{1134 \text{ m/s}}$$

$$V_{He} = 2268 \frac{\text{m}}{\text{s}} \qquad\qquad Ans. (a)$$

For dynamic similarity, the Reynolds numbers should also be equal. From Table A.6 at an altitude of 10,000 m, read $\rho_{air} = 0.4125$ kg/m^3, $a_{air} = 299.5$ m/s, and estimate $\mu_{air} \approx 1.48$ E-5 kg/m · s from the power-law, $n = 0.7$, in Table A.4. The air velocity is $V_{air} = (\text{Ma})(a_{air}) = 2(299.5) = 599$ m/s. The model chord length is (1.6 m)/8 = 0.2 m. The helium density is $\rho_{He} = (p/RT)_{He} = (101{,}350\ \text{Pa})/[(2077\ \text{m}^2/\text{s}^2\ \text{K})(373\ \text{K})] = 0.131\ \text{kg/m}^3$. Now calculate the two Reynolds numbers:

$$\text{Re}_{C,air} = \frac{\rho VC}{\mu}\bigg|_{air} = \frac{(0.4125\ \text{kg/m}^3)(599\ \text{m/s})(1.6\ \text{m})}{1.48\ \text{E}{-}5\ \text{kg/(m} \cdot \text{s)}} = 26.6\ \text{E6}$$

$$\text{Re}_{C,He} = \frac{\rho VC}{\mu}\bigg|_{He} = \frac{(0.131\ \text{kg/m}^3)(2268\ \text{m/s})(0.2\ \text{m})}{2.32\ \text{E}{-}5\ \text{kg/(m} \cdot \text{s)}} = 2.56\ \text{E6}$$

The model Reynolds number is 10 times less than the prototype. This is typical when using small-scale models. The test results must be extrapolated for Reynolds number effects.
(b) Now ignore Mach number and let the model Reynolds number match the prototype:

$$\text{Re}_{He} = \text{Re}_{air} = 26.6\ \text{E6} = \frac{(0.131\ \text{kg/m}^3)V_{He}(0.2\ \text{m})}{2.32\ \text{E}{-}5\ \text{kg/(m} \cdot \text{s)}}$$

$$V_{He} = 23{,}600\ \frac{\text{m}}{\text{s}} \qquad\qquad Ans.\ (b)$$

This is ridiculous: a hypersonic Mach number of 21, suitable for escaping from the earth's gravity. One should match the Mach numbers and correct for a lower Reynolds number.
(c) Match both Reynolds and Mach numbers by increasing the helium density:
Ma matches if

$$V_{He} = 2268\ \frac{\text{m}}{\text{s}}$$

Then

$$\text{Re}_{He} = 26.6\ \text{E6} = \frac{\rho_{He}(2268\ \text{m/s})(0.2\ \text{m})}{2.32\ \text{E}{-}5\ \text{kg/(m} \cdot \text{s)}}$$

Solve for

$$\rho_{He} = 1.36\ \frac{\text{kg}}{\text{m}^3}\quad p_{He} = \rho RT|_{He} = (1.36)(2077)(373) = 1.05\ \text{E6 Pa} \qquad Ans.\ (c)$$

A match is possible if we increase the tunnel pressure by a factor of ten, a daunting task.
(d) Even with Ma and Re matched, we are *still* not dynamically similar because the two gases have different specific heat ratios: $k_{He} = 1.66$ and $k_{air} = 1.40$. This discrepancy will cause substantial differences in pressure, density, and temperature throughout supersonic flow.

Figure 5.9 shows a hydraulic model of the Bluestone Lake Dam in West Virginia. The model itself is located at the U.S. Army Waterways Experiment Station in Vicksburg, MS. The horizontal scale is 1:65, which is sufficient that the vertical scale can also be 1:65 without incurring significant surface tension (Weber number) effects. Velocities are scaled by the Froude number. However, the prototype Reynolds number, which is of order 1 E7, cannot be matched here. The engineers set the Reynolds number at about 2 E4, high enough for a reasonable approximation of prototype turbulent flow viscous effects. Note the intense turbulence below the dam. The downstream bed, or *apron,* of a dam must be strengthened structurally to avoid bed erosion.

Fig. 5.9 Hydraulic model of the Bluestone Lake Dam on the New River near Hinton, West Virginia. The model scale is 1:65 both vertically and horizontally, and the Reynolds number, though far below the prototype value, is set high enough for the flow to be turbulent. *(Courtesy of the U.S. Army Corps of Engineers Waterways Experiment Station.)*

For hydraulic models of larger scale, such as harbors, estuaries, and embayments, geometric similarity may be violated of necessity. The vertical scale will be distorted to avoid Weber number effects. For example, the horizontal scale may be 1:1000, while the vertical scale is only 1:100. Thus the model channel may be *deeper* relative to its horizontal dimensions. Since deeper passages flow more efficiently, the model channel bottom may be deliberately roughened to create the friction level expected in the prototype.

EXAMPLE 5.10

The pressure drop due to friction for flow in a long, smooth pipe is a function of average flow velocity, density, viscosity, and pipe length and diameter: $\Delta p = \text{fcn}(V, \rho, \mu, L, D)$. We wish to know how Δp varies with V. (*a*) Use the pi theorem to rewrite this function in dimensionless form. (b) Then plot this function, using the following data for three pipes and three fluids:

D, cm	L, m	Q, m³/h	Δp, Pa	ρ, kg/m³	μ, kg/(m · s)	V, m/s*
1.0	5.0	0.3	4,680	680†	2.92 E-4†	1.06
1.0	7.0	0.6	22,300	680†	2.92 E-4†	2.12
1.0	9.0	1.0	70,800	680†	2.92 E-4†	3.54
2.0	4.0	1.0	2,080	998‡	0.0010‡	0.88
2.0	6.0	2.0	10,500	998‡	0.0010‡	1.77
2.0	8.0	3.1	30,400	998‡	0.0010‡	2.74
3.0	3.0	0.5	540	13,550§	1.56 E-3§	0.20
3.0	4.0	1.0	2,480	13,550§	1.56 E-3§	0.39
3.0	5.0	1.7	9,600	13,550§	1.56 E-3§	0.67

*$V = Q/A$, $A = \pi D^2/4$.
†Gasoline.
‡Water.
§Mercury.

(c) Suppose it is further known that Δp is proportional to L (which is quite true for long pipes with well-rounded entrances). Use this information to simplify and improve the pi theorem formulation. Plot the dimensionless data in this improved manner and comment on the results.

Solution

There are six variables with three primary dimensions involved $\{MLT\}$. Therefore, we expect that $j = 6 - 3 = 3$ pi groups. We are correct, for we can find three variables that do not form a pi product (e.g., ρ, V, L). Carefully select three (j) repeating variables, but not including Δp or V, which we plan to plot versus each other. We select (ρ, μ, D), and the pi theorem guarantees that three independent power-product groups will occur:

$$\Pi_1 = \rho^a \mu^b D^c \, \Delta p \qquad \Pi_2 = \rho^d \mu^e D^f V \qquad \Pi_3 = \rho^g \mu^h D^i L$$

or
$$\Pi_1 = \frac{\rho D^2 \Delta p}{\mu^2} \qquad \Pi_2 = \frac{\rho V D}{\mu} \qquad \Pi_3 = \frac{L}{D}$$

We have omitted the algebra of finding (a, b, c, d, e, f, g, h, i) by setting all exponents to zero M^0, L^0, T^0. Therefore, we wish to plot the dimensionless relation

$$\frac{\rho D^2 \, \Delta p}{\mu^2} = \text{fcn}\left(\frac{\rho V D}{\mu}, \frac{L}{D}\right) \qquad\qquad Ans. \ (a)$$

We plot Π_1 versus Π_2 with Π_3 as a parameter. There will be nine data points. For example, the first row in the data here yields

$$\frac{\rho D^2 \, \Delta p}{\mu^2} = \frac{(680)(0.01)^2(4680)}{(2.92\,\text{E-4})^2} = 3.73\,\text{E9}$$

$$\frac{\rho V D}{\mu} = \frac{(680)(1.06)(0.01)}{2.92\,\text{E-4}} = 24{,}700 \qquad \frac{L}{D} = 500$$

The nine data points are plotted as the open circles in Fig. 5.10. The values of L/D are listed for each point, and we see a significant length effect. In fact, if we connect the only two points that have the same L/D (= 200), we could see (and cross-plot to verify) that Δp increases linearly with L, as stated in the last part of the problem. Since L occurs only in

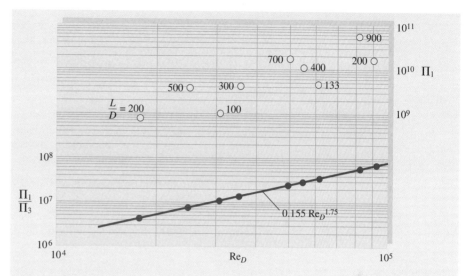

Fig. 5.10 Two different correlations of the data in Example 5.10: Open circles when plotting $\rho D^2\,\Delta p/\mu^2$ versus Re_D, L/D is a parameter; once it is known that Δp is proportional to L, a replot (solid circles) of $\rho D^3\,\Delta p/(L\mu^2)$ versus Re_D collapses into a single power-law curve.

$\Pi_3 = L/D$, the function $\Pi_1 = \mathrm{fcn}(\Pi_2, \Pi_3)$ must reduce to $\Pi_1 = (L/D)\,\mathrm{fcn}(\Pi_2)$, or simply a function involving only *two* parameters:

$$\frac{\rho D^3\,\Delta p}{L\mu^2} = \mathrm{fcn}\left(\frac{\rho VD}{\mu}\right) \qquad \text{flow in a long pipe} \qquad\qquad Ans.\ (c)$$

We now modify each data point in Fig. 5.10 by dividing it by its L/D value. For example, for the first row of data, $\rho D^3\,\Delta p/(L\mu^2) = (3.73\ \mathrm{E}9)/500 = 7.46\ \mathrm{E}6$. We replot these new data points as solid circles in Fig. 5.10. They correlate almost perfectly into a straight-line power-law function:

$$\frac{\rho D^3\,\Delta p}{L\mu^2} \approx 0.155\left(\frac{\rho VD}{\mu}\right)^{1.75} \qquad\qquad Ans.\ (c)$$

All newtonian smooth pipe flows should correlate in this manner. This example is a variation of the first completely successful dimensional analysis, pipe-flow friction, performed by Prandtl's student Paul Blasius, who published a related plot in 1911. For this range of (turbulent flow) Reynolds numbers, the pressure drop increases approximately as $V^{1.75}$.

EXAMPLE 5.11

The smooth sphere data plotted in Fig. 5.3a represent dimensionless drag versus dimensionless *viscosity*, since (ρ, V, d) were selected as scaling or repeating variables. (a) Replot these data to display the effect of dimensionless *velocity* on the drag. (b) Use your new figure to predict the terminal (zero-acceleration) velocity of a 1-cm-diameter steel ball (SG = 7.86) falling through water at 20°C.

Solution

- *Assumptions:*   Fig 5.3a is valid for any smooth sphere in that Reynolds number range.
- *Approach* (a):   Form pi groups from the function $F = \mathrm{fcn}(d, V, \rho, \mu)$ in such a way that F is plotted versus V. The answer was already given as Eq. (5.16), but let us review the

steps. The proper scaling variables are (ρ, μ, d), which do *not* form a pi. Therefore $j = 3$, and we expect $n - j = 5 - 3 = 2$ pi groups. Skipping the algebra, they arise as follows:

$$\Pi_1 = \rho^a \mu^b d^c F = \frac{\rho F}{\mu^2} \qquad \Pi_2 = \rho^a \mu^b d^c V = \frac{\rho V d}{\mu} \qquad Ans.\ (a)$$

We may replot the data of Fig. 5.3a in this new form, noting that $\Pi_1 \equiv (\pi/8)(C_D)(\text{Re})^2$. This replot is shown as Fig. 5.11. The drag increases rapidly with velocity up to transition, where there is a slight drop, after which it increases more than ever. If force is known, we may predict velocity from the figure, and vice versa.

- *Property values for part (b):* $\quad \rho_{\text{water}} = 998 \text{ kg/m}^3 \qquad \mu_{\text{water}} = 0.001 \text{ kg/(m-s)}$

$$\rho_{\text{steel}} = 7.86\rho_{\text{water}} = 7844 \text{ kg/m}^3.$$

- *Solution to part (b):* For terminal velocity, the drag force equals the net weight of the sphere in water:

$$F = W_{\text{net}} = (\rho_s - \rho_w)g\frac{\pi}{6}d^3 = (7840 - 998)(9.81)\left(\frac{\pi}{6}\right)(0.01)^3 = 0.0351 \text{ N}$$

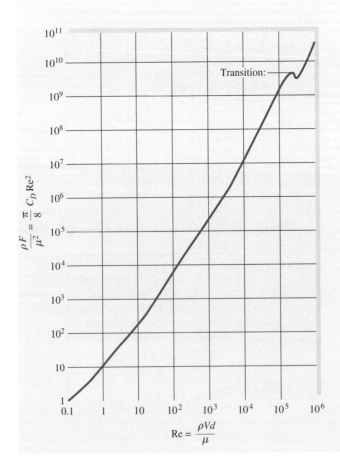

Fig. 5.11 Cross-plot of sphere drag data from Fig. 5.3a to show dimensionless force versus dimensionless velocity.

Therefore, the ordinate of Fig. 5.11 is known:

Falling steel sphere: $\dfrac{\rho F}{\mu^2} = \dfrac{(998 \text{ kg/m}^3)(0.0351 \text{ N})}{[0.001 \text{ kg/(m} \cdot \text{s)}]^2} \approx 3.5 \text{ E7}$

From Fig. 5.11, at $\rho F/\mu^2 \approx 3.5$ E7, a magnifying glass reveals that $\text{Re}_d \approx 2$ E4. Then a crude estimate of the terminal fall velocity is

$$\frac{\rho V d}{\mu} \approx 20,000 \quad \text{or} \quad V \approx \frac{20,000[0.001 \text{ kg/(m} \cdot \text{s)}]}{(998 \text{ kg/m}^3)(0.01 \text{ m})} \approx 2.0 \, \frac{\text{m}}{\text{s}} \quad Ans. \ (b)$$

- *Comments:*   Better accuracy could be obtained by expanding the scale of Fig. 5.11 in the region of the given force coefficient. However, there is considerable uncertainty in published drag data for spheres, so the predicted fall velocity is probably uncertain by at least ± 10 percent.

  Note that we found the answer directly from Fig. 5.11. We could use Fig. 5.3a also but would have to iterate between the ordinate and abscissa to obtain the final result, since V is contained in both plotted variables.

Summary

Chapters 3 and 4 presented integral and differential methods of mathematical analysis of fluid flow. This chapter introduces the third and final method: experimentation, as supplemented by the technique of dimensional analysis. Tests and experiments are used both to strengthen existing theories and to provide useful engineering results when theory is inadequate.

The chapter begins with a discussion of some familiar physical relations and how they can be recast in dimensionless form because they satisfy the principle of dimensional homogeneity. A general technique, the pi theorem, is then presented for systematically finding a set of dimensionless parameters by grouping a list of variables that govern any particular physical process. A second technique, Ipsen's method, is also described. Alternately, direct application of dimensional analysis to the basic equations of fluid mechanics yields the fundamental parameters governing flow patterns: Reynolds number, Froude number, Prandtl number, Mach number, and others.

It is shown that model testing in air and water often leads to scaling difficulties for which compromises must be made. Many model tests do not achieve true dynamic similarity. The chapter ends by pointing out that classic dimensionless charts and data can be manipulated and recast to provide direct solutions to problems that would otherwise be quite cumbersome and laboriously iterative.

Problems

Most of the problems herein are fairly straightforward. More difficult or open-ended assignments are labeled with an asterisk. Problems labeled with a computer icon 🖫 may require the use of a computer. The standard end-of-chapter problems P5.1 to P5.91 (categorized in the problem list here) are followed by word problems W5.1 to W5.10, fundamentals of engineering exam problems FE5.1 to FE5.12, comprehensive applied problems C5.1 to C5.5, and design projects D5.1 and D5.2.

Problem Distribution

Section	Topic	Problems
5.1	Introduction	P5.1–P5.9
5.2	The principle of dimensional homogeneity	P5.10–P5.13
5.3	The pi theorem; Ipsen's method	P5.14–P5.42
5.4	Nondimensionalizing the basic equations	P5.43–P5.47
5.4	Data for spheres, cylinders, other bodies	P5.48–P5.59
5.5	Scaling of model data	P5.60–P5.74
5.5	Froude and Mach number scaling	P5.75–P5.84
5.5	Inventive rescaling of the data	P5.85–P5.91

Introduction; dynamic similarity

P5.1 For axial flow through a circular tube, the Reynolds number for transition to turbulence is approximately 2300 [see Eq. (6.2)], based on the diameter and average velocity. If $d = 5$ cm and the fluid is kerosene at 20°C, find the volume flow rate in m^3/h that causes transition.

P5.2 A prototype automobile is designed for cold weather in Denver, CO (-10°C, 83 kPa). Its drag force is to be tested on a one-seventh-scale model in a wind tunnel at 150 mi/h, 20°C, and 1 atm. If the model and prototype are to satisfy dynamic similarity, what prototype velocity, in mi/h, needs to be matched? Comment on your result.

P5.3 The transfer of energy by viscous dissipation is dependent upon viscosity μ, thermal conductivity k, stream velocity U, and stream temperature T_0. Group these quantities, if possible, into the dimensionless *Brinkman number,* which is proportional to μ.

P5.4 When tested in water at 20°C flowing at 2 m/s, an 8-cm-diameter sphere has a measured drag of 5 N. What will be the velocity and drag force on a 1.5-m-diameter weather balloon moored in sea-level standard air under dynamically similar conditions?

P5.5 An automobile has a characteristic length and area of 8 ft and 60 ft^2, respectively. When tested in sea-level standard air, it has the following measured drag force versus speed:

V, mi/h	20	40	60
Drag, lbf	31	115	249

The same car travels in Colorado at 65 mi/h at an altitude of 3500 m. Using dimensional analysis, estimate (*a*) its drag force and (*b*) the horsepower required to overcome air drag.

P5.6 The disk-gap-band parachute in the chapter-opener photo had a drag of 1600 lbf when tested at 15 mi/h in air at 20°C and 1 atm. (*a*) What was its drag coefficient? (*b*) If, as stated, the drag on Mars is 65,000 lbf and the velocity is 375 mi/h in the thin Mars atmosphere, $\rho \approx 0.020$ kg/m^3, what is the drag coefficient on Mars? (*c*) Can you explain the difference between (*a*) and (*b*)?

P5.7 A body is dropped on the moon ($g = 1.62$ m/s^2) with an initial velocity of 12 m/s. By using option 2 variables, Eq. (5.11), the ground impact occurs at $t^{**} = 0.34$ and $S^{**} = 0.84$. Estimate (*a*) the initial displacement, (*b*) the final displacement, and (*c*) the time of impact.

P5.8 The Archimedes number, Ar, used in the flow of stratified fluids, is a dimensionless combination of gravity g, density difference $\Delta\rho$, fluid width L, and viscosity μ. Find the form of this number if it is proportional to g.

P5.9 The *Richardson number,* Ri, which correlates the production of turbulence by buoyancy, is a dimensionless combination of the acceleration of gravity g, the fluid temperature T_0, the local temperature gradient $\partial T/\partial z$, and the local velocity gradient $\partial u/\partial z$. Determine the form of the Richardson number if it is proportional to g.

The principle of dimensional homogeneity

P5.10 Determine the dimension $\{MLT\Theta\}$ of the following quantities:

$(a)\ \rho u \dfrac{\partial u}{\partial x}$ $(b)\ \displaystyle\int_1^2 (p - p_0)\, dA$ $(c)\ \rho c_p \dfrac{\partial^2 T}{\partial x\, \partial y}$

$(d)\ \displaystyle\iiint \rho \dfrac{\partial u}{\partial t}\, dx\, dy\, dz$

All quantities have their standard meanings; for example, ρ is density.

P5.11 During World War II, Sir Geoffrey Taylor, a British fluid dynamicist, used dimensional analysis to estimate the wave speed of an atomic bomb explosion. He assumed that the blast wave radius R was a function of energy released E, air density ρ, and time t. Use dimensional reasoning to show how wave radius must vary with time.

P5.12 The *Stokes number,* St, used in particle dynamics studies, is a dimensionless combination of *five* variables: acceleration of gravity g, viscosity μ, density ρ, particle velocity U, and particle diameter D. (*a*) If St is proportional to μ and inversely proportional to g, find its form. (*b*) Show that St is actually the quotient of two more traditional dimensionless groups.

P5.13 The speed of propagation C of a capillary wave in deep water is known to be a function only of density ρ, wavelength λ, and surface tension Y. Find the proper functional relationship, completing it with a dimensionless constant. For a given density and wavelength, how does the propagation speed change if the surface tension is doubled?

The pi theorem or Ipsen's method

P5.14 Flow in a pipe is often measured with an orifice plate, as in Fig. P5.14. The volume flow Q is a function of the pressure drop Δp across the plate, the fluid density ρ, the pipe diameter D, and the orifice diameter d. Rewrite this functional relationship in dimensionless form.

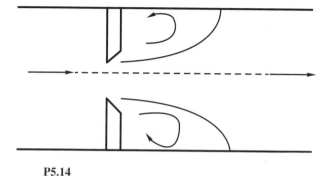

P5.14

P5.15 The wall shear stress τ_w in a boundary layer is assumed to be a function of stream velocity U, boundary layer thickness δ, local turbulence velocity u', density ρ, and local pressure gradient dp/dx. Using (ρ, U, δ) as repeating variables, rewrite this relationship as a dimensionless function.

P5.16 Convection heat transfer data are often reported as a *heat transfer coefficient* h, defined by

$$\dot{Q} = hA \, \Delta T$$

where $\dot{Q}$ = heat flow, J/s
A = surface area, m^2
ΔT = temperature difference, K

The dimensionless form of h, called the *Stanton number,* is a combination of h, fluid density ρ, specific heat c_p, and flow velocity V. Derive the Stanton number if it is proportional to h. What are the units of h?

P5.17 If you disturb a tank of length L and water depth h, the surface will oscillate back and forth at frequency Ω, assumed here to depend also upon water density ρ and the acceleration of gravity g. (*a*) Rewrite this as a dimensionless function. (*b*) If a tank of water sloshes at 2.0 Hz on earth, how fast would it oscillate on Mars ($g \approx 3.7$ m/s^2)?

P5.18 Under laminar conditions, the volume flow Q through a small triangular-section pore of side length b and length L is a function of viscosity μ, pressure drop per unit length $\Delta p/L$, and b. Using the pi theorem, rewrite this relation in dimensionless form. How does the volume flow change if the pore size b is doubled?

P5.19 The period of oscillation T of a water surface wave is assumed to be a function of density ρ, wavelength l, depth h, gravity g, and surface tension Y. Rewrite this relationship in dimensionless form. What results if Y is negligible? *Hint:* Take l, ρ, and g as repeating variables.

P5.20 A fixed cylinder of diameter D and length L, immersed in a stream flowing normal to its axis at velocity U, will experience zero average lift. However, if the cylinder is rotating at angular velocity Ω, a lift force F will arise. The fluid density ρ is important, but viscosity is secondary and can be neglected. Formulate this lift behavior as a dimensionless function.

P5.21 In Example 5.1 we used the pi theorem to develop Eq. (5.2) from Eq. (5.1). Instead of merely listing the primary dimensions of each variable, some workers list the *powers* of each primary dimension for each variable in an array:

$$\begin{array}{c} \\ M \\ L \\ T \end{array} \begin{array}{cccccc} F & L & U & \rho & \mu \\ \begin{bmatrix} 1 & 0 & 0 & 1 & 1 \\ 1 & 1 & 1 & -3 & -1 \\ -2 & 0 & -1 & 0 & -1 \end{bmatrix} \end{array}$$

This array of exponents is called the *dimensional matrix* for the given function. Show that the *rank* of this matrix (the size of the largest nonzero determinant) is equal to $j = n - k$, the desired reduction between original variables and the pi groups. This is a general property of dimensional matrices, as noted by Buckingham [1].

P5.22 As will be discussed in Chap. 11, the power P developed by a wind turbine is a function of diameter D, air density ρ, wind speed V, and rotation rate ω. Viscosity effects are negligible. Rewrite this relationship in dimensionless form.

P5.23 The period T of vibration of a beam is a function of its length L, area moment of inertia I, modulus of elasticity E, density ρ, and Poisson's ratio σ. Rewrite this relation in dimensionless form. What further reduction can we make if E and I can occur only in the product form EI? *Hint:* Take L, ρ, and E as repeating variables.

P5.24 The lift force F on a missile is a function of its length L, velocity V, diameter D, angle of attack α, density ρ, viscosity μ, and speed of sound a of the air. Write out the dimensional matrix of this function and determine its rank. (See Prob. P5.21 for an explanation of this concept.) Rewrite the function in terms of pi groups.

P5.25 The thrust F of a propeller is generally thought to be a function of its diameter D and angular velocity Ω, the forward speed V, and the density ρ and viscosity μ of the fluid. Rewrite this relationship as a dimensionless function.

P5.26 A pendulum has an oscillation period T which is assumed to depend on its length L, bob mass m, angle of swing θ, and the acceleration of gravity. A pendulum 1 m long, with a bob mass of 200 g, is tested on earth and found to have a period of 2.04 s when swinging at 20°. (*a*) What is its period when it swings at 45°? A similarly constructed pendulum, with $L = 30$ cm and $m = 100$ g, is to swing on the moon ($g = 1.62$ m/s^2) at $\theta = 20°$. (b) What will be its period?

P5.27 In studying sand transport by ocean waves, A. Shields in 1936 postulated that the threshold wave-induced bottom shear stress τ required to move particles depends on gravity g, particle size d and density ρ_p, and water density ρ and viscosity μ. Find suitable dimensionless groups of this problem, which resulted in 1936 in the celebrated Shields sand transport diagram.

P5.28 A simply supported beam of diameter D, length L, and modulus of elasticity E is subjected to a fluid crossflow of velocity V, density ρ, and viscosity μ. Its center deflection δ is assumed to be a function of all these variables. (a) Rewrite this proposed function in dimensionless form. (b) Suppose it is known that δ is independent of μ, inversely proportional to E, and dependent only on ρV^2, not ρ and V separately. Simplify the dimensionless function accordingly. *Hint:* Take L, ρ, and V as repeating variables.

P5.29 When fluid in a pipe is accelerated linearly from rest, it begins as laminar flow and then undergoes transition to turbulence at a time t_{tr} that depends on the pipe diameter D, fluid acceleration a, density ρ, and viscosity μ. Arrange this into a dimensionless relation between t_{tr} and D.

P5.30 When a large tank of high-pressure gas discharges through a nozzle, the exit mass flow $\dot{m}$ is a function of tank pressure p_0 and temperature T_0, gas constant R, specific heat c_p, and nozzle diameter D. Rewrite this as a dimensionless function. Check to see if you can use (p_0, T_0, R, D) as repeating variables.

P5.31 The pressure drop per unit length in horizontal pipe flow, $\Delta p/L$, depends on the fluid density ρ, viscosity μ, diameter D, and volume flow rate Q. Rewrite this function in terms of pi groups.

P5.32 A *weir* is an obstruction in a channel flow that can be calibrated to measure the flow rate, as in Fig. P5.32. The volume flow Q varies with gravity g, weir width b into the paper, and upstream water height H above the weir crest. If it is known that Q is proportional to b, use the pi theorem to find a unique functional relationship $Q(g, b, H)$.

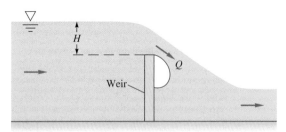

P5.32

P5.33 A spar buoy (see Prob. P2.113) has a period T of vertical (heave) oscillation that depends on the waterline cross-sectional area A, buoy mass m, and fluid specific weight γ. How does the period change due to doubling of (a) the mass and (b) the area? Instrument buoys should have long periods to avoid wave resonance. Sketch a possible long-period buoy design.

P5.34 To good approximation, the thermal conductivity k of a gas (see Ref. 21 of Chap. 1) depends only on the density ρ, mean free path l, gas constant R, and absolute temperature T. For air at 20°C and 1 atm, $k \approx 0.026$ W/(m · K) and $l \approx$ 6.5 E-8 m. Use this information to determine k for hydrogen at 20°C and 1 atm if $l \approx 1.2$ E-7 m.

P5.35 The torque M required to turn the cone-plate viscometer in Fig. P5.35 depends on the radius R, rotation rate Ω, fluid viscosity μ, and cone angle θ. Rewrite this relation in dimensionless form. How does the relation simplify it if it is known that M is proportional to θ?

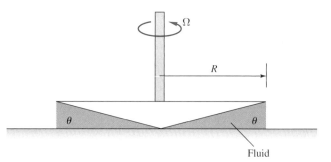

P5.35

P5.36 The rate of heat loss $\dot{Q}_{loss}$ through a window or wall is a function of the temperature difference between inside and outside ΔT, the window surface area A, and the R value of the window, which has units of (ft^2 · h · °F)/ Btu. (a) Using the Buckingham Pi Theorem, find an expression for rate of heat loss as a function of the other three parameters in the problem. (b) If the temperature difference ΔT doubles, by what factor does the rate of heat loss increase?

P5.37 The volume flow Q through an orifice plate is a function of pipe diameter D, pressure drop Δp across the orifice, fluid density ρ and viscosity μ, and orifice diameter d. Using D, ρ, and Δp as repeating variables, express this relationship in dimensionless form.

P5.38 The size d of droplets produced by a liquid spray nozzle is thought to depend on the nozzle diameter D, jet velocity U, and the properties of the liquid ρ, μ, and Y. Rewrite this relation in dimensionless form. *Hint:* Take D, ρ, and U as repeating variables.

P5.39 The volume flow Q over a certain dam is a function of dam width b, gravity g, and the upstream water depth H above the dam crest. It is known that Q is proportional to b. If $b = 120$ ft and $H = 15$ in., the flow rate is 600 ft^3/s. What will be the flow rate if $H = 3$ ft?

P5.40 The time t_d to drain a liquid from a hole in the bottom of a tank is a function of the hole diameter d, the initial fluid volume v_0, the initial liquid depth h_0, and the density ρ and viscosity μ of the fluid. Rewrite this relation as a dimensionless function, using Ipsen's method.

P5.41 A certain axial flow turbine has an output torque M that is proportional to the volume flow rate Q and also depends on the density ρ, rotor diameter D, and rotation rate Ω. How does the torque change due to a doubling of (a) D and (b) Ω?

P5.42 When disturbed, a floating buoy will bob up and down at frequency f. Assume that this frequency varies with buoy mass m, waterline diameter d, and the specific weight γ of the liquid. (a) Express this as a dimensionless function. (b) If d and γ are constant and the buoy mass is halved, how will the frequency change?

Nondimensionalizing the basic equations

P5.43 Nondimensionalize the energy equation (4.75) and its boundary conditions (4.62), (4.63), and (4.70) by defining $T^* = T/T_0$, where T_0 is the inlet temperature, assumed constant. Use other dimensionless variables as needed from Eqs. (5.23). Isolate all dimensionless parameters you find, and relate them to the list given in Table 5.2.

P5.44 The differential energy equation for incompressible two-dimensional flow through a "Darcy-type" porous medium is approximately

$$\rho c_p \frac{\sigma}{\mu} \frac{\partial p}{\partial x} \frac{\partial T}{\partial x} + \rho c_p \frac{\sigma}{\mu} \frac{\partial p}{\partial y} \frac{\partial T}{\partial y} + k \frac{\partial^2 T}{\partial y^2} = 0$$

where σ is the *permeability* of the porous medium. All other symbols have their usual meanings. (a) What are the appropriate dimensions for σ? (b) Nondimensionalize this equation, using (L, U, ρ, T_0) as scaling constants, and discuss any dimensionless parameters that arise.

P5.45 A model differential equation, for chemical reaction dynamics in a plug reactor, is as follows:

$$u \frac{\partial C}{\partial x} = D \frac{\partial^2 C}{\partial x^2} - kC - \frac{\partial C}{\partial t}$$

where u is the velocity, D is a diffusion coefficient, k is a reaction rate, x is distance along the reactor, and C is the (dimensionless) concentration of a given chemical in the reactor. (a) Determine the appropriate dimensions of D and k. (b) Using a characteristic length scale L and average velocity V as parameters, rewrite this equation in dimensionless form and comment on any pi groups appearing.

P5.46 If a vertical wall at temperature T_w is surrounded by a fluid at temperature T_0, a natural convection boundary layer flow will form. For laminar flow, the momentum equation is

$$\rho \left(u \frac{\partial u}{\partial x} + v \frac{\partial u}{\partial y} \right) = \rho \beta (T - T_0) g + \mu \frac{\partial^2 u}{\partial y^2}$$

to be solved, along with continuity and energy, for (u, v, T) with appropriate boundary conditions. The quantity β is the thermal expansion coefficient of the fluid. Use ρ, g, L, and $(T_w - T_0)$ to nondimensionalize this equation. Note that there is no "stream" velocity in this type of flow.

P5.47 The differential equation for small-amplitude vibrations $y(x, t)$ of a simple beam is given by

$$\rho A \frac{\partial^2 y}{\partial t^2} + EI \frac{\partial^4 y}{\partial x^4} = 0$$

where ρ = beam material density
A = cross-sectional area
I = area moment of inertia
E = Young's modulus

Use only the quantities ρ, E, and A to nondimensionalize y, x, and t, and rewrite the differential equation in dimensionless form. Do any parameters remain? Could they be removed by further manipulation of the variables?

Data for spheres, cylinders, other bodies

P5.48 A smooth steel (SG = 7.86) sphere is immersed in a stream of ethanol at 20°C moving at 1.5 m/s. Estimate its drag in N from Fig. 5.3a. What stream velocity would quadruple its drag? Take $D = 2.5$ cm.

P5.49 The sphere in Prob. P5.48 is dropped in gasoline at 20°C. Ignoring its acceleration phase, what will its terminal (constant) fall velocity be, from Fig. 5.3a?

P5.50 The parachute in the chapter-opener photo is, of course, meant to decelerate the payload on Mars. The wind tunnel test gave a drag coefficient of about 1.1, based upon the projected area of the parachute. Suppose it was falling on *earth* and, at an altitude of 1000 m, showed a steady descent rate of about 18 mi/h. Estimate the weight of the payload.

P5.51 A ship is towing a sonar array that approximates a submerged cylinder 1 ft in diameter and 30 ft long with its axis normal to the direction of tow. If the tow speed is 12 kn (1 kn = 1.69 ft/s), estimate the horsepower required to tow this cylinder. What will be the frequency of vortices shed from the cylinder? Use Figs. 5.2 and 5.3.

P5.52 When fluid in a long pipe starts up from rest at a uniform acceleration a, the initial flow is laminar. The flow undergoes transition to turbulence at a time t^* which depends, to first approximation, only upon a, ρ, and μ. Experiments by

P. J. Lefebvre, on water at 20°C starting from rest with 1-g acceleration in a 3-cm-diameter pipe, showed transition at $t^* = 1.02$ s. Use this data to estimate (a) the transition time and (b) the transition Reynolds number Re_D for water flow accelerating at 35 m/s^2 in a 5-cm-diameter pipe.

P5.53 Vortex shedding can be used to design a *vortex flowmeter* (Fig. 6.34). A blunt rod stretched across the pipe sheds vortices whose frequency is read by the sensor downstream. Suppose the pipe diameter is 5 cm and the rod is a cylinder of diameter 8 mm. If the sensor reads 5400 counts per minute, estimate the volume flow rate of water in m^3/h. How might the meter react to other liquids?

P5.54 A fishnet is made of 1-mm-diameter strings knotted into 2 × 2 cm squares. Estimate the horsepower required to tow 300 ft^2 of this netting at 3 kn in seawater at 20°C. The net plane is normal to the flow direction.

P5.55 The radio antenna on a car begins to vibrate wildly at 8 Hz when the car is driven at 45 mi/h over a rutted road that approximates a sine wave of amplitude 2 cm and wavelength $\lambda = 2.5$ m. The antenna diameter is 4 mm. Is the vibration due to the road or to vortex shedding?

P5.56 Flow past a long cylinder of square cross-section results in more drag than the comparable round cylinder. Here are data taken in a water tunnel for a square cylinder of side length $b = 2$ cm:

V, m/s	1.0	2.0	3.0	4.0
Drag, N/(m of depth)	21	85	191	335

(a) Use these data to predict the drag force per unit depth of wind blowing at 6 m/s, in air at 20°C, over a tall square chimney of side length $b = 55$ cm. (b) Is there any uncertainty in your estimate?

P5.57 The simply supported 1040 carbon-steel rod of Fig. P5.57 is subjected to a crossflow stream of air at 20°C and 1 atm. For what stream velocity U will the rod center deflection be approximately 1 cm?

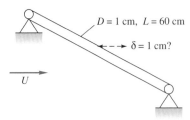

$D = 1$ cm, $L = 60$ cm

$\delta = 1$ cm?

U

P5.57

P5.58 For the steel rod of Prob. P5.57, at what airstream velocity U will the rod begin to vibrate laterally in resonance in its first mode (a half sine wave)? *Hint:* Consult a vibration text [34,35] under "lateral beam vibration."

P5.59 A long, slender, smooth 3-cm-diameter flagpole bends alarmingly in 20 mi/h sea-level winds, causing patriotic citizens to gasp. An engineer claims that the pole will bend less if its surface is deliberately roughened. Is she correct, at least qualitatively?

Scaling of model data

*P5.60 The thrust F of a free propeller, either aircraft or marine, depends upon density ρ, the rotation rate n in r/s, the diameter D, and the forward velocity V. Viscous effects are slight and neglected here. Tests of a 25-cm-diameter model aircraft propeller, in a sea-level wind tunnel, yield the following thrust data at a velocity of 20 m/s:

Rotation rate, r/min	4800	6000	8000
Measured thrust, N	6.1	19	47

(a) Use this data to make a crude but effective dimensionless plot. (b) Use the dimensionless data to predict the thrust, in newtons, of a similar 1.6-m-diameter prototype propeller when rotating at 3800 r/min and flying at 225 mi/h at 4000-m standard altitude.

P5.61 If viscosity is neglected, typical pump flow results from Example 5.3 are shown in Fig. P5.61 for a model pump tested in water. The pressure rise decreases and the power required increases with the dimensionless flow coefficient. Curve-fit expressions are given for the data. Suppose a similar pump of 12-cm diameter is built to move gasoline at 20°C and a flow rate of 25 m^3/h. If the pump rotation speed is 30 r/s, find (a) the pressure rise and (b) the power required.

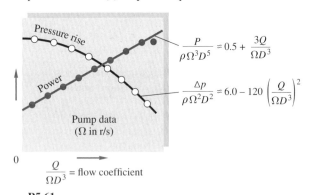

$$\frac{P}{\rho \Omega^3 D^5} = 0.5 + \frac{3Q}{\Omega D^3}$$

$$\frac{\Delta p}{\rho \Omega^2 D^2} = 6.0 - 120 \left(\frac{Q}{\Omega D^3}\right)^2$$

Pressure rise

Power

Pump data
(Ω in r/s)

$\dfrac{Q}{\Omega D^3}$ = flow coefficient

P5.61

P5.62 For the system of Prob. P5.22, assume that a small model wind turbine of diameter 90 cm, rotating at 1200 r/min, delivers 280 watts when subjected to a wind of 12 m/s. The data is to be used for a prototype of diameter 50 m and winds of 8 m/s. For dynamic similarity, estimate (a) the rotation rate, and (b) the power delivered by the prototype. Assume sea-level air density.

*P5.63 The Keystone Pipeline in the Chapter 6 opener photo has $D = 36$ in. and an oil flow rate $Q = 590,000$ barrels per day (1 barrel = 42 U.S. gallons). Its pressure drop per unit length, $\Delta p/L$, depends on the fluid density ρ, viscosity μ, diameter D, and flow rate Q. A water-flow model test, at $20°C$, uses a 5-cm-diameter pipe and yields $\Delta p/L \approx 4000$ Pa/m. For dynamic similarity, estimate $\Delta p/L$ of the pipeline. For the oil take $\rho = 860$ kg/m^3 and $\mu = 0.005$ kg/m · s.

P5.64 The natural frequency ω of vibration of a mass M attached to a rod, as in Fig. P5.64, depends only on M

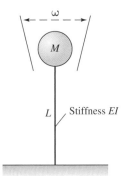

P5.64

and the stiffness EI and length L of the rod. Tests with a 2-kg mass attached to a 1040 carbon steel rod of diameter 12 mm and length 40 cm reveal a natural frequency of 0.9 Hz. Use these data to predict the natural frequency of a 1-kg mass attached to a 2024 aluminum alloy rod of the same size.

P5.65 In turbulent flow near a flat wall, the local velocity u varies only with distance y from the wall, wall shear stress τ_w, and fluid properties ρ and μ. The following data were taken in the University of Rhode Island wind tunnel for airflow, $\rho = 0.0023$ slug/ft^3, $\mu = 3.81$ E-7 slug/(ft · s), and $\tau_w = 0.029$ lbf/ft^2:

y, in	0.021	0.035	0.055	0.080	0.12	0.16
u, ft/s	50.6	54.2	57.6	59.7	63.5	65.9

(a) Plot these data in the form of dimensionless u versus dimensionless y, and suggest a suitable power-law curve fit. (b) Suppose that the tunnel speed is increased until $u = 90$ ft/s at $y = 0.11$ in. Estimate the new wall shear stress, in lbf/ft^2.

P5.66 A torpedo 8 m below the surface in $20°C$ seawater cavitates at a speed of 21 m/s when atmospheric pressure is 101 kPa. If Reynolds number and Froude number effects are negligible, at what speed will it cavitate when running at a depth of 20 m? At what depth should it be to avoid cavitation at 30 m/s?

P5.67 A student needs to measure the drag on a prototype of characteristic dimension d_p moving at velocity U_p in air at standard atmospheric conditions. He constructs a model of characteristic dimension d_m, such that the ratio d_p/d_m is some factor f. He then measures the drag on the model at dynamically similar conditions (also with air at standard atmospheric conditions). The student claims that the drag force on the prototype will be identical to that measured on the model. Is this claim correct? Explain.

P5.68 For the rotating-cylinder function of Prob. P5.20, if $L >> D$, the problem can be reduced to only two groups, $F/(\rho U^2 LD)$ versus $(\Omega D/U)$. Here are experimental data for a cylinder 30 cm in diameter and 2 m long, rotating in sea-level air, with $U = 25$ m/s.

Ω, rev/min	0	3000	6000	9000	12000	15000
F, N	0	850	2260	2900	3120	3300

(a) Reduce this data to the two dimensionless groups and make a plot. (b) Use this plot to predict the lift of a cylinder with $D = 5$ cm, $L = 80$ cm, rotating at 3800 rev/min in water at $U = 4$ m/s.

P5.69 A simple flow measurement device for streams and channels is a notch, of angle α, cut into the side of a dam, as shown in Fig. P5.69. The volume flow Q depends only on α, the acceleration of gravity g, and the height δ of the upstream water surface above the notch vertex. Tests of a model notch, of angle $\alpha = 55°$, yield the following flow rate data:

δ, cm	10	20	30	40
Q, m^3/h	8	47	126	263

(a) Find a dimensionless correlation for the data. (b) Use the model data to predict the flow rate of a prototype notch, also of angle $\alpha = 55°$, when the upstream height δ is 3.2 m.

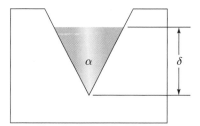

P5.69

P5.70 A diamond-shaped body, of characteristic length 9 in, has the following measured drag forces when placed in a wind tunnel at sea-level standard conditions:

V, ft/s	30	38	48	56	61
F, 1bf	1.25	1.95	3.02	4.05	4.81

Use these data to predict the drag force of a similar 15-in diamond placed at similar orientation in 20°C water flowing at 2.2 m/s.

P5.71 The pressure drop in a venturi meter (Fig. P3.128) varies only with the fluid density, pipe approach velocity, and diameter ratio of the meter. A model venturi meter tested in water at 20°C shows a 5-kPa drop when the approach velocity is 4 m/s. A geometrically similar prototype meter is used to measure gasoline at 20°C and a flow rate of 9 m^3/min. If the prototype pressure gage is most accurate at 15 kPa, what should the upstream pipe diameter be?

P5.72 A one-twelfth-scale model of a large commercial aircraft is tested in a wind tunnel at 20°C and 1 atm. The model chord length is 27 cm, and its wing area is 0.63 m^2. Test results for the drag of the model are as follows:

V, mi/h	50	75	100	125
Drag, N	15	32	53	80

In the spirit of Fig. 5.8, use this data to estimate the drag of the full-scale aircraft when flying at 550 mi/h, for the same angle of attack, at 32,800 ft standard altitude.

P5.73 The power P generated by a certain windmill design depends on its diameter D, the air density ρ, the wind velocity V, the rotation rate Ω, and the number of blades n. (a) Write this relationship in dimensionless form. A model windmill, of diameter 50 cm, develops 2.7 kW at sea level when $V = 40$ m/s and when rotating at 4800 r/min. (b) What power will be developed by a geometrically and dynamically similar prototype, of diameter 5 m, in winds of 12 m/s at 2000 m standard altitude? (c) What is the appropriate rotation rate of the prototype?

P5.74 A one-tenth-scale model of a supersonic wing tested at 700 m/s in air at 20°C and 1 atm shows a pitching moment of 0.25 kN · m. If Reynolds number effects are negligible, what will the pitching moment of the prototype wing be if it is flying at the same Mach number at 8-km standard altitude?

Froude and Mach number scaling

P5.75 According to the web site *USGS Daily Water Data for the Nation,* the mean flow rate in the New River near Hinton, WV, is 10,100 ft^3/s. If the hydraulic model in Fig. 5.9 is to match this condition with Froude number scaling, what is the proper model flow rate?

* **P5.76** A 2-ft-long model of a ship is tested in a freshwater tow tank. The measured drag may be split into "friction" drag (Reynolds scaling) and "wave" drag (Froude scaling). The model data are as follows:

Tow speed, ft/s	0.8	1.6	2.4	3.2	4.0	4.8
Friction drag, lbf	0.016	0.057	0.122	0.208	0.315	0.441
Wave drag, lbf	0.002	0.021	0.083	0.253	0.509	0.697

The prototype ship is 150 ft long. Estimate its total drag when cruising at 15 kn in seawater at 20°C.

P5.77 A dam 75 ft wide, with a nominal flow rate of 260 ft^3, is to be studied with a scale model 3 ft wide, using Froude scaling. (a) What is the expected flow rate for the model? (b) What is the danger of only using Froude scaling for this test? (c) Derive a formula for a force on the model as compared to a force on the prototype.

P5.78 A prototype spillway has a characteristic velocity of 3 m/s and a characteristic length of 10 m. A small model is constructed by using Froude scaling. What is the minimum scale ratio of the model that will ensure that its minimum Weber number is 100? Both flows use water at 20°C.

P5.79 An East Coast estuary has a tidal period of 12.42 h (the semidiurnal lunar tide) and tidal currents of approximately 80 cm/s. If a one-five-hundredth-scale model is constructed with tides driven by a pump and storage apparatus, what should the period of the model tides be and what model current speeds are expected?

P5.80 A prototype ship is 35 m long and designed to cruise at 11 m/s (about 21 kn). Its drag is to be simulated by a 1-m-long model pulled in a tow tank. For Froude scaling find (a) the tow speed, (b) the ratio of prototype to model drag, and (c) the ratio of prototype to model power.

P5.81 An airplane, of overall length 55 ft, is designed to fly at 680 m/s at 8000-m standard altitude. A one-thirtieth-scale model is to be tested in a pressurized helium wind tunnel at 20°C. What is the appropriate tunnel pressure in atm? Even at this (high) pressure, exact dynamic similarity is not achieved. Why?

P5.82 A one-fiftieth-scale model of a military airplane is tested at 1020 m/s in a wind tunnel at sea-level conditions. The model wing area is 180 cm^2. The angle of attack is 3°. If measured model lift is 860 N, what is the prototype lift, using Mach number scaling, when it flies at 10,000 m standard altitude under dynamically similar conditions? *Note:* Be careful with the area scaling.

P5.83 A one-fortieth-scale model of a ship's propeller is tested in a tow tank at 1200 r/min and exhibits a power output of 1.4 ft · lbf/s. According to Froude scaling laws, what should the revolutions per minute and horsepower output of the prototype propeller be under dynamically similar conditions?

P5.84 A prototype ocean platform piling is expected to encounter currents of 150 cm/s and waves of 12-s period and 3-m height. If a one-fifteenth-scale model is tested in a wave channel, what current speed, wave period, and wave height should be encountered by the model?

Inventive rescaling of the data

* **P5.85** As shown in Example 5.3, pump performance data can be nondimensionalized. Problem P5.61 gave typical

dimensionless data for centrifugal pump "head," $H = \Delta p/\rho g$, as follows:

$$\frac{gH}{n^2 D^2} \approx 6.0 - 120 \left(\frac{Q}{nD^3}\right)^2$$

where Q is the volume flow rate, n the rotation rate in r/s, and D the impeller diameter. This type of correlation allows one to compute H when (ρ, Q, D) are known. (a) Show how to rearrange these pi groups so that one can *size* the pump, that is, compute D directly when (Q, H, n) are known. (b) Make a crude but effective plot of your new function. (c) Apply part (b) to the following example: Find D when $H = 37$ m, $Q = 0.14$ m³/s, and $n = 35$ r/s. Find the pump diameter for this condition.

P5.86 Solve Prob. P5.49 for glycerin at 20°C, using the modified sphere-drag plot of Fig. 5.11.

P5.87 In Prob. P5.61 it would be difficult to solve for Ω because it appears in all three of the dimensionless pump coefficients. Suppose that, in Prob. 5.61, Ω is unknown but $D = 12$ cm and $Q = 25$ m³/h. The fluid is gasoline at 20°C. Rescale the coefficients, using the data of Prob. P5.61, to make a plot of dimensionless power versus dimensionless rotation speed. Enter this plot to find the maximum rotation speed Ω for which the power will not exceed 300 W.

P5.88 Modify Prob. P5.61 as follows: Let $\Omega = 32$ r/s and $Q = 24$ m³/h for a geometrically similar pump. What is the maximum diameter if the power is not to exceed 340 W? Solve this problem by rescaling the data of Fig. P5.61 to make a plot of dimensionless power versus dimensionless diameter. Enter this plot directly to find the desired diameter.

P5.89 Wall friction τ_w, for turbulent flow at velocity U in a pipe of diameter D, was correlated, in 1911, with a dimensionless correlation by Ludwig Prandtl's student H. Blasius:

$$\frac{\tau_w}{\rho U^2} \approx \frac{0.632}{(\rho U D/\mu)^{1/4}}$$

Suppose that (ρ, U, μ, τ_w) were all known and it was desired to find the unknown velocity U. Rearrange and rewrite the formula so that U can be immediately calculated.

P5.90 Knowing that Δp is proportional to L, rescale the data of Example 5.10 to plot dimensionless Δp versus dimensionless *viscosity*. Use this plot to find the viscosity required in the first row of data in Example 5.10 if the pressure drop is increased to 10 kPa for the same flow rate, length, and density.

*P5.91 The traditional "Moody-type" pipe friction correlation in Chap. 6 is of the form

$$f = \frac{2\Delta p D}{\rho V^2 L} = \text{fcn}\left(\frac{\rho V D}{\mu}, \frac{\varepsilon}{D}\right)$$

where D is the pipe diameter, L the pipe length, and ε the wall roughness. Note that pipe average velocity V is used on both sides. This form is meant to find Δp when V is known. (a) Suppose that Δp is known, and we wish to find V. Rearrange the above function so that V is isolated on the left-hand side. Use the following data, for $\varepsilon/D = 0.005$, to make a plot of your new function, with your velocity parameter as the ordinate of the plot.

f	0.0356	0.0316	0.0308	0.0305	0.0304
$\rho V D/\mu$	15,000	75,000	250,000	900,000	3,330,000

(b) Use your plot to determine V, in m/s, for the following pipe flow: $D = 5$ cm, $\varepsilon = 0.025$ cm, $L = 10$ m, for water flow at 20°C and 1 atm. The pressure drop Δp is 110 kPa.

Word Problems

W5.1 In 98 percent of data analysis cases, the "reducing factor" j, which lowers the number n of dimensional variables to $n - j$ dimensionless groups, exactly equals the number of relevant dimensions (M, L, T, Θ). In one case (Example 5.5) this was not so. Explain in words why this situation happens.

W5.2 Consider the following equation: 1 dollar bill ≈ 6 in. Is this relation dimensionally inconsistent? Does it satisfy the PDH? Why?

W5.3 In making a dimensional analysis, what rules do you follow for choosing your scaling variables?

W5.4 In an earlier edition, the writer asked the following question about Fig. 5.1: "Which of the three graphs is a more effective presentation?" Why was this a dumb question?

W5.5 This chapter discusses the difficulty of scaling Mach and Reynolds numbers together (an airplane) and Froude and Reynolds numbers together (a ship). Give an example of a flow that would combine Mach and Froude numbers. Would there be scaling problems for common fluids?

W5.6 What is different about a very *small* model of a weir or dam (Fig. P5.32) that would make the test results difficult to relate to the prototype?

W5.7 What else are you studying this term? Give an example of a popular equation or formula from another course (thermodynamics, strength of materials, or the like) that does not satisfy the principle of dimensional homogeneity. Explain what is wrong and whether it can be modified to be homogeneous.

W5.8 Some colleges (such as Colorado State University) have environmental wind tunnels that can be used to study phenomena like wind flow over city buildings. What details of scaling might be important in such studies?

W5.9   If the model scale ratio is $\alpha = L_m/L_p$, as in Eq. (5.31), and the Weber number is important, how must the model and prototype surface tension be related to α for dynamic similarity?

W5.10   For a typical incompressible velocity potential analysis in Chap. 8 we solve $\nabla^2\phi = 0$, subject to known values of $\partial\phi/\partial n$ on the boundaries. What dimensionless parameters govern this type of motion?

Fundamentals of Engineering Exam Problems

FE5.1   Given the parameters (U, L, g, ρ, μ) that affect a certain liquid flow problem, the ratio $V^2/(Lg)$ is usually known as the
(a) velocity head, (b) Bernoulli head, (c) Froude number, (d) kinetic energy, (e) impact energy

FE5.2   A ship 150 m long, designed to cruise at 18 kn, is to be tested in a tow tank with a model 3 m long. The appropriate tow velocity is
(a) 0.19 m/s, (b) 0.35 m/s, (c) 1.31 m/s, (d) 2.55 m/s, (e) 8.35 m/s

FE5.3   A ship 150 m long, designed to cruise at 18 kn, is to be tested in a tow tank with a model 3 m long. If the model wave drag is 2.2 N, the estimated full-size ship wave drag is
(a) 5500 N, (b) 8700 N, (c) 38,900 N, (d) 61,800 N, (e) 275,000 N

FE5.4   A tidal estuary is dominated by the semidiurnal lunar tide, with a period of 12.42 h. If a 1:500 model of the estuary is tested, what should be the model tidal period?
(a) 4.0 s, (b) 1.5 min, (c) 17 min, (d) 33 min, (e) 64 min

FE5.5   A football, meant to be thrown at 60 mi/h in sea-level air ($\rho = 1.22$ kg/m^3, $\mu = 1.78$ E-5 N · s/m^2), is to be tested using a one-quarter scale model in a water tunnel ($\rho = 998$ kg/m^3, $\mu = 0.0010$ N · s/m^2). For dynamic similarity, what is the proper model water velocity?
(a) 7.5 mi/h, (b) 15.0 mi/h, (c) 15.6 mi/h, (d) 16.5 mi/h, (e) 30 mi/h

FE5.6   A football, meant to be thrown at 60 mi/h in sea-level air ($\rho = 1.22$ kg/m^3, $\mu = 1.78$ E-5 N · m^2), is to be tested using a one-quarter scale model in a water tunnel ($\rho = 998$ kg/m^3, $\mu = 0.0010$ N · s/m^2). For dynamic similarity, what is the ratio of prototype force to model force?
(a) 3.86:1, (b) 16:1, (c) 32:1, (d) 56:1, (e) 64:1

FE5.7   Consider liquid flow of density ρ, viscosity μ, and velocity U over a very small model spillway of length scale L, such that the liquid surface tension coefficient Y is important. The quantity $\rho U^2 L/Y$ in this case is important and is called the
(a) capillary rise, (b) Froude number, (c) Prandtl number, (d) Weber number, (e) Bond number

FE5.8   If a stream flowing at velocity U past a body of length L causes a force F on the body that depends only on U, L, and fluid viscosity μ, then F must be proportional to
(a) $\rho UL/\mu$, (b) $\rho U^2 L^2$, (c) $\mu U/L$, (d) μUL, (e) UL/μ

FE5.9   In supersonic wind tunnel testing, if different gases are used, dynamic similarity requires that the model and prototype have the same Mach number and the same
(a) Euler number, (b) speed of sound, (c) stagnation enthalpy, (d) Froude number, (e) specific-heat ratio

FE5.10   The Reynolds number for a 1-ft-diameter sphere moving at 2.3 mi/h through seawater (specific gravity 1.027, viscosity 1.07 E-3 N · s/m^2) is approximately
(a) 300, (b) 3000, (c) 30,000, (d) 300,000, (e) 3,000,000

FE5.11   The Ekman number, important in physical oceanography, is a dimensionless combination of μ, L, ρ, and the earth's rotation rate Ω. If the Ekman number is proportional to Ω, it should take the form
(a) $\rho\Omega^2 L^2/\mu$, (b) $\mu\Omega L/\rho$, (c) $\rho\Omega L/\mu$, (d) $\rho\Omega L^2/\mu$, (e) $\rho\Omega/L\mu$

FE5.12   A valid, but probably useless, dimensionless group is given by $(\mu T_0 g)/(YL\alpha)$, where everything has its usual meaning, except α. What are the dimensions of α?
(a) $\Theta L^{-1}T^{-1}$, (b) $\Theta L^{-1}T^{-2}$, (c) ΘML^{-1}, (d) $\Theta^{-1}LT^{-1}$, (e) ΘLT^{-1}

Comprehensive Problems

C5.1   Estimating pipe wall friction is one of the most common tasks in fluids engineering. For long circular rough pipes in turbulent flow, wall shear τ_w is a function of density ρ, viscosity μ, average velocity V, pipe diameter d, and wall roughness height e. Thus, functionally, we can write $\tau_w = \text{fcn}(\rho, \mu, V, d, e)$. (a) Using dimensional analysis, rewrite this function in dimensionless form. (b) A certain pipe has $d = 5$ cm and $\varepsilon = 0.25$ mm. For flow of water at 20°C, measurements show the following values of wall shear stress:

Q, gal/min	1.5	3.0	6.0	9.0	12.0	14.0
τ_w, Pa	0.05	0.18	0.37	0.64	0.86	1.25

Plot these data using the dimensionless form obtained in part (a) and suggest a curve-fit formula. Does your plot reveal the entire functional relation obtained in part (a)?

C5.2 When the fluid exiting a nozzle, as in Fig. P3.49, is a gas, instead of water, compressibility may be important, especially if upstream pressure p_1 is large and exit diameter d_2 is small. In this case, the difference $p_1 - p_2$ is no longer controlling, and the gas mass flow $\dot{m}$ reaches a maximum value that depends on p_1 and d_2 and also on the absolute upstream temperature T_1 and the gas constant R. Thus, functionally, $\dot{m} = $ fcn(p_1, d_2, T_1, R). (a) Using dimensional analysis, rewrite this function in dimensionless form. (b) A certain pipe has $d_2 = 1$ cm. For flow of air, measurements show the following values of mass flow through the nozzle:

T_1, K	300	300	300	500	800
p_1, kPa	200	250	300	300	300
$\dot{m}$, kg/s	0.037	0.046	0.055	0.043	0.034

Plot these data in the dimensionless form obtained in part (a). Does your plot reveal the entire functional relation obtained in part (a)?

C5.3 Reconsider the fully developed draining vertical oil film problem (see Fig. P4.80) as an exercise in dimensional analysis. Let the vertical velocity be a function only of distance from the plate, fluid properties, gravity, and film thickness. That is, $w = $ fcn(x, ρ, μ, g, δ). (a) Use the pi theorem to rewrite this function in terms of

dimensionless parameters. (b) Verify that the exact solution from Prob. P4.80 is consistent with your result in part (a).

C5.4 The Taco Inc. model 4013 centrifugal pump has an impeller of diameter $D = 12.95$ in. When pumping 20°C water at $\Omega = 1160$ r/min, the measured flow rate Q and pressure rise Δp are given by the manufacturer as follows:

Q, gal/min	200	300	400	500	600	700
Δp, lb/in^2	36	35	34	32	29	23

(a) Assuming that $\Delta p = $ fcn(ρ, Q, D, Ω), use the pi theorem to rewrite this function in terms of dimensionless parameters and then plot the given data in dimensionless form. (b) It is desired to use the same pump, running at 900 r/min, to pump 20°C gasoline at 400 gal/min. According to your dimensionless correlation, what pressure rise Δp is expected, in lbf/in^2?

C5.5 Does an automobile radio antenna vibrate in resonance due to vortex shedding? Consider an antenna of length L and diameter D. According to beam vibration theory [see [34] or [35, p. 401]], the first mode natural frequency of a solid circular cantilever beam is $\omega_n = 3.516[EI/(\rho AL^4)]^{1/2}$, where E is the modulus of elasticity, I is the area moment of inertia, ρ is the beam material density, and A is the beam cross-section area. (a) Show that ω_n is proportional to the antenna radius R. (b) If the antenna is steel, with $L = 60$ cm and $D = 4$ mm, estimate the natural vibration frequency, in Hz. (c) Compare with the shedding frequency if the car moves at 65 mi/h.

Design Projects

D5.1 We are given laboratory data, taken by Prof. Robert Kirchhoff and his students at the University of Massachusetts, for the spin rate of a 2-cup anemometer. The anemometer was made of ping-pong balls ($d = 1.5$ in) split in half, facing in opposite directions, and glued to thin ($\frac{1}{4}$-in) rods pegged to a center axle. (See Fig. P7.91 for a sketch.) There were four rods, of lengths $l = 0.212, 0.322, 0.458,$ and 0.574 ft. The experimental data, for wind tunnel velocity U and rotation rate Ω, are as follows:

$l = 0.212$		$l = 0.322$		$l = 0.458$		$l = 0.574$	
U, ft/s	Ω, r/min	U, ft/s	Ω, r/min	U, ft/s	Ω, r/min	U, ft/s	Ω, r/min
18.95	435	18.95	225	20.10	140	23.21	115
22.20	545	23.19	290	26.77	215	27.60	145
25.90	650	29.15	370	31.37	260	32.07	175
29.94	760	32.79	425	36.05	295	36.05	195
38.45	970	38.45	495	39.03	327	39.60	215

Assume that the angular velocity Ω of the device is a function of wind speed U, air density ρ and viscosity μ, rod length l, and cup diameter d. For all data, assume air is at 1 atm and 20°C. Define appropriate pi groups for this problem, and plot the data in this dimensionless manner. Comment on the possible uncertainty of the results.

As a design application, suppose we are to use this anemometer geometry for a large-scale ($d = 30$ cm) airport wind anemometer. If wind speeds vary up to 25 m/s and we desire an average rotation rate $\Omega = 120$ r/min, what should be the proper rod length? What are possible limitations of your design? Predict the expected Ω (in r/min) of your design as affected by wind speeds from 0 to 25 m/s.

D5.2 By analogy with the cylinder drag data in Fig. 5.3b, spheres also show a strong roughness effect on drag, at least in the Reynolds number range 4 E4 < Re$_D$ < 3 E5, which accounts for the dimpling of golf balls to increase their distance traveled. Some experimental data for roughened spheres [33] are given in Fig. D5.2. The figure also shows typical golf ball data. We see that some roughened spheres are better than golf balls in some regions. For the present study, let us neglect the ball's *spin,* which causes the very important side-force or *Magnus effect* (see Fig. 8.15) and assume that the ball is hit without spin and follows the equations of motion for plane motion (x, z):

$$m\ddot{x} = -F \cos\theta \quad m\ddot{z} = -F \sin\theta - W$$

where

$$F = C_D \frac{\rho}{2} \frac{\pi}{4} D^2 (\dot{x}^2 + \dot{z}^2) \quad \theta = \tan^{-1}\frac{\dot{z}}{\dot{x}}$$

The ball has a particular $C_D(\text{Re}_D)$ curve from Fig. D5.2 and is struck with an initial velocity V_0 and angle θ_0. Take the ball's average mass to be 46 g and its diameter to be 4.3 cm. Assuming sea-level air and a modest but finite range of initial conditions, integrate the equations of motion to compare the trajectory of "roughened spheres" to actual golf ball calculations. Can the rough sphere outdrive a normal

golf ball for any conditions? What roughness-effect differences occur between a low-impact duffer and, say, Tiger Woods?

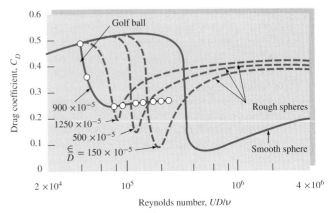

D5.2

References

1. E. Buckingham, "On Physically Similar Systems: Illustrations of the Use of Dimensional Equations," *Phys. Rev.,* vol. 4, no. 4, 1914, pp. 345–376.

2. J. D. Anderson, *Computational Fluid Dynamics: The Basics with Applications,* McGraw-Hill, New York, 1995.

3. P. W. Bridgman, *Dimensional Analysis,* Yale University Press, New Haven, CT, 1922, rev. ed., 1963.

4. H. L. Langhaar, *Dimensional Analysis and the Theory of Models,* Wiley, New York, 1951.

5. E. C. Ipsen, *Units, Dimensions, and Dimensionless Numbers,* McGraw-Hill, New York, 1960.

6. H. G. Hornung, *Dimensional Analysis: Examples of the Use of Symmetry,* Dover, New York, 2006.

7. E. S. Taylor, *Dimensional Analysis for Engineers,* Clarendon Press, Oxford, England, 1974.

8. G. I. Barenblatt, *Dimensional Analysis,* Gordon and Breach, New York, 1987.

9. A. C. Palmer, *Dimensional Analysis and Intelligent Experimentation,* World Scientific Publishing, Hackensack, NJ, 2008.

10. T. Szirtes, *Applied Dimensional Analysis and Modeling,* 2d ed., Butterworth-Heinemann, Burlington, MA, 2006.

11. R. Esnault-Pelterie, *Dimensional Analysis and Metrology,* F. Rouge, Lausanne, Switzerland, 1950.

12. R. Kurth, *Dimensional Analysis and Group Theory in Astrophysics,* Pergamon, New York, 1972.

13. R. Kimball and M. Ross, *The Data Warehouse Toolkit: The Complete Guide to Dimensional Modeling,* 2d ed., Wiley, New York, 2002.

14. R. Nakon, *Chemical Problem Solving Using Dimensional Analysis,* Prentice-Hall, Upper Saddle River, NJ, 1990.

15. D. R. Maidment (ed.), *Hydrologic and Hydraulic Modeling Support: With Geographic Information Systems,* Environmental Systems Research Institute, Redlands, CA, 2000.

16. A. M. Curren, *Dimensional Analysis for Meds,* 4th ed., Delmar Cengage Learning, Independence, KY, 2009.

17. G. P. Craig, *Clinical Calculations Made Easy: Solving Problems Using Dimensional Analysis,* 4th ed., Lippincott Williams and Wilkins, Baltimore, MD, 2008.

18. M. Zlokarnik, *Dimensional Analysis and Scale-Up in Chemical Engineering,* Springer-Verlag, New York, 1991.

19. W. G. Jacoby, *Data Theory and Dimensional Analysis,* Sage, Newbury Park, CA, 1991.

20. B. Schepartz, *Dimensional Analysis in the Biomedical Sciences,* Thomas, Springfield, IL, 1980.

21. T. Horntvedt, *Calculating Dosages Safely: A Dimensional Analysis Approach,* F. A. Davis Co., Philadelphia, PA, 2012.

22. J. B. Bassingthwaighte et al., *Fractal Physiology,* Oxford Univ. Press, New York, 1994.

23. K. J. Niklas, *Plant Allometry: The Scaling of Form and Process,* Univ. of Chicago Press, Chicago, 1994.

24. "*Flow of Fluids through Valves, Fittings, and Pipes,*" Crane Valve Group, Long Beach, CA, 1957 (now updated as a CD-ROM; see <http://www.cranevalves.com>).

25. A. Roshko, "On the Development of Turbulent Wakes from Vortex Streets," *NACA Rep.* 1191, 1954.

26. G. W. Jones, Jr., "Unsteady Lift Forces Generated by Vortex Shedding about a Large, Stationary, Oscillating Cylinder at High Reynolds Numbers," *ASME Symp. Unsteady Flow,* 1968.

27. O. M. Griffin and S. E. Ramberg, "The Vortex Street Wakes of Vibrating Cylinders," *J. Fluid Mech.,* vol. 66, pt. 3, 1974, pp. 553–576.

28. *Encyclopedia of Science and Technology,* 11th ed., McGraw-Hill, New York, 2012.

29. J. Kunes, *Dimensionless Physical Quantities in Science and Engineering*, Elsevier, New York, 2012.

30. V. P. Singh et al. (eds.), *Hydraulic Modeling,* Water Resources Publications LLC, Highlands Ranch, CO, 1999.

31. L. Armstrong, *Hydraulic Modeling and GIS*, ESRI Press, La Vergne, TN, 2011.

32. R. Ettema, *Hydraulic Modeling: Concepts and Practice,* American Society of Civil Engineers, Reston, VA, 2000.

33. R. D. Blevins, *Applied Fluid Dynamics Handbook,* van Nostrand Reinhold, New York, 1984.

34. W. J. Palm III, *Mechanical Vibration*, Wiley, New York, 2006.

35. S. S. Rao, *Mechanical Vibrations,* 5th ed., Prentice-Hall, Upper Saddle River, NJ, 2010.

36. G. I. Barenblatt, *Scaling,* Cambridge University Press, Cambridge, UK, 2003.

37. L. J. Fingersh, "Unsteady Aerodynamics Experiment," *Journal of Solar Energy Engineering,* vol. 123, Nov. 2001, p. 267.

38. J. B. Barlow, W. H. Rae, and A. Pope, *Low-Speed Wind Tunnel Testing,* Wiley, New York, 1999.

39. B. H. Goethert, *Transonic Wind Tunnel Testing,* Dover, New York, 2007.

40. American Institute of Aeronautics and Astronautics, *Recommended Practice: Wind Tunnel Testing,* 2 vols., Reston, VA, 2003.

41. P. N. Desai, J. T. Schofield, and M. E. Lisano, "Flight Reconstruction of the Mars Pathfinder Disk-Gap-Band Parachute Drag Coefficients," *J. Spacecraft and Rockets*, vol. 42, no. 4, July–August 2005, pp. 672–676.

42. K.-H. Kim, "Recent Advances in Cavitation Research," 14th International Symposium on Transport Phenomena, Honolulu, HI, March 2012.

This chapter is mostly about flow analysis. The photo shows the 36-inch-diameter Keystone Pipeline, which has been operating since July 2010. This pipeline delivers heavy and light blends of oil from Hardisty, Alberta, Canada, to refineries in Texas. The pipeline is completely buried and emerges occasionally at delivery or pump stations; it can currently deliver up to 700,000 barrels of oil per day. [*Image courtesy of TransCanada*]

Chapter 6
Viscous Flow in Ducts

Motivation. This chapter is completely devoted to an important practical fluids engineering problem: flow in ducts with various velocities, various fluids, and various duct shapes. Piping systems are encountered in almost every engineering design and thus have been studied extensively. There is a small amount of theory plus a large amount of experimentation.

The basic piping problem is this: Given the pipe geometry and its added components (such as fittings, valves, bends, and diffusers) plus the desired flow rate and fluid properties, what pressure drop is needed to drive the flow? Of course, it may be stated in alternative form: Given the pressure drop available from a pump, what flow rate will ensue? The correlations discussed in this chapter are adequate to solve most such piping problems.

This chapter is for incompressible flow; Chap. 9 treats compressible pipe flow.

6.1 Reynolds Number Regimes

Now that we have derived and studied the basic flow equations in Chap. 4, you would think that we could just whip off myriad beautiful solutions illustrating the full range of fluid behavior, of course expressing all these educational results in dimensionless form, using our new tool from Chap. 5, dimensional analysis.

The fact of the matter is that no general analysis of fluid motion yet exists. There are several dozen known particular solutions, there are many approximate digital computer solutions, and there are a great many experimental data. There is a lot of theory available if we neglect such important effects as viscosity and compressibility (Chap. 8), but there is no general theory and there may never be. The reason is that a profound and vexing change in fluid behavior occurs at moderate Reynolds numbers. The flow ceases being smooth and steady (*laminar*) and becomes fluctuating and agitated (*turbulent*). The changeover is called *transition* to turbulence. In Fig. 5.3a we saw that transition on the cylinder and sphere occurred at about $Re = 3 \times 10^5$, where the sharp drop in the drag coefficient appeared. Transition depends on many effects, such as wall roughness (Fig. 5.3b) or fluctuations in the inlet stream, but the primary parameter is the Reynolds number. There are a great many data on transition but only a small amount of theory [1 to 3].

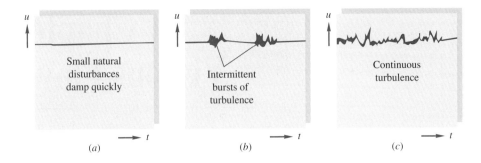

Fig. 6.1 The three regimes of viscous flow: (*a*) laminar flow at low Re; (*b*) transition at intermediate Re; (*c*) turbulent flow at high Re.

Turbulence can be detected from a measurement by a small, sensitive instrument such as a hot-wire anemometer (Fig. 6.29*e*) or a piezoelectric pressure transducer. The flow will appear steady on average but will reveal rapid, random fluctuations if turbulence is present, as sketched in Fig. 6.1. If the flow is laminar, there may be occasional natural disturbances that damp out quickly (Fig. 6.1*a*). If transition is occurring, there will be sharp bursts of intermittent turbulent fluctuation (Fig. 6.1*b*) as the increasing Reynolds number causes a breakdown or instability of laminar motion. At sufficiently large Re, the flow will fluctuate continually (Fig. 6.1*c*) and is termed *fully turbulent*. The fluctuations, typically ranging from 1 to 20 percent of the average velocity, are not strictly periodic but are random and encompass a continuous range, or spectrum, of frequencies. In a typical wind tunnel flow at high Re, the turbulent frequency ranges from 1 to 10,000 Hz, and the wavelength ranges from about 0.01 to 400 cm.

EXAMPLE 6.1

The accepted transition Reynolds number for flow in a circular pipe is $\mathrm{Re}_{d,\mathrm{crit}} \approx 2300$. For flow through a 5-cm-diameter pipe, at what velocity will this occur at 20°C for (*a*) airflow and (*b*) water flow?

Solution

Almost all pipe flow formulas are based on the *average* velocity $V = Q/A$, not centerline or any other point velocity. Thus transition is specified at $\rho V d / \mu \approx 2300$. With d known, we introduce the appropriate fluid properties at 20°C from Tables A.3 and A.4:

(*a*) Air: $\qquad \dfrac{\rho V d}{\mu} = \dfrac{(1.205 \text{ kg/m}^3) V (0.05 \text{ m})}{1.80 \text{ E-5 kg/(m} \cdot \text{s)}} = 2300 \qquad$ or $\qquad V \approx 0.7 \dfrac{\text{m}}{\text{s}}$

(*b*) Water: $\qquad \dfrac{\rho V d}{\mu} = \dfrac{(998 \text{ kg/m}^3) V (0.05 \text{ m})}{0.001 \text{ kg/(m} \cdot \text{s)}} = 2300 \qquad$ or $\qquad V = 0.046 \dfrac{\text{m}}{\text{s}}$

These are very low velocities, so most engineering air and water pipe flows are turbulent, not laminar. We might expect laminar duct flow with more viscous fluids such as lubricating oils or glycerin.

In free-surface flows, turbulence can be observed directly. Figure 6.2 shows liquid flow issuing from the open end of a tube. The low-Reynolds-number jet (Fig. 6.2*a*) is smooth and laminar, with the fast center motion and slower wall flow forming different trajectories

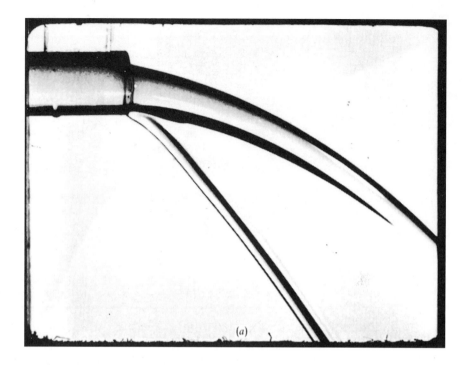

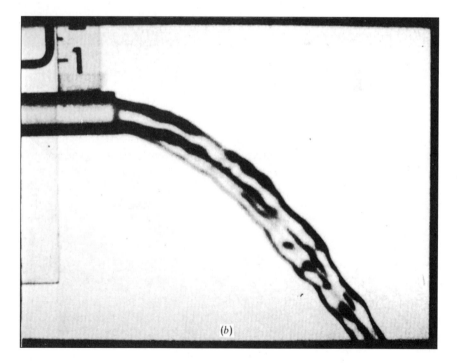

Fig. 6.2 Flow issuing at constant speed from a pipe: (*a*) high-viscosity, low-Reynolds-number, laminar flow; (*b*) low-viscosity, high-Reynolds-number, turbulent flow. Note the ragged, disorderly shape of the jet. *(National Committee for Fluid Mechanics Films, Education Development Center, Inc., © 1972.)*

Flow ⟶

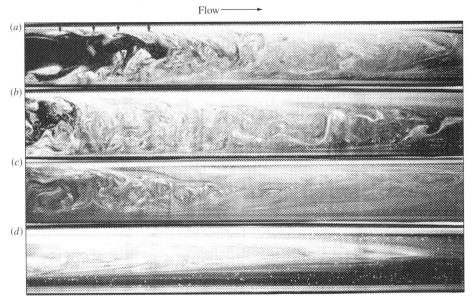

Fig. 6.3 Formation of a turbulent puff in pipe flow: (*a*) and (*b*) near the entrance; (*c*) somewhat downstream; (*d*) far downstream. *(Courtesy of Cambridge University Press–P. R. Bandyopadhyay, "Aspects of the Equilibrium Puff in Transitional Pipe Flow," Journal of Fluid Mechanics, vol. 163, 1986, pp. 439–458.)*

joined by a liquid sheet. The higher-Reynolds-number turbulent flow (Fig. 6.2b) is unsteady and irregular but, when averaged over time, is steady and predictable.

How did turbulence form inside the pipe? The laminar parabolic flow profile, which is similar to Eq. (4.137), became unstable and, at $Re_d \approx 2300$, began to form "slugs" or "puffs" of intense turbulence. A puff has a fast-moving front and a slow-moving rear and may be visualized by experimenting with glass tube flow. Figure 6.3 shows a puff as photographed by Bandyopadhyay [45]. Near the entrance (Fig. 6.3a and b) there is an irregular laminar–turbulent interface, and vortex roll-up is visible. Further downstream (Fig. 6.3c) the puff becomes fully turbulent and very active, with helical motions visible. Far downstream (Fig. 6.3d) the puff is cone-shaped and less active, with a fuzzy, ill-defined interface, sometimes called the "relaminarization" region.

A complete description of the statistical aspects of turbulence is given in Ref. 1, while theory and data on transition effects are given in Refs. 2 and 3. At this introductory level we merely point out that the primary parameter affecting transition is the Reynolds number. If $Re = UL/\nu$, where U is the average stream velocity and L is the "width," or transverse thickness, of the shear layer, the following approximate ranges occur:

$$0 < Re < \quad 1: \text{highly viscous laminar "creeping" motion}$$
$$1 < Re < 100: \text{laminar, strong Reynolds number dependence}$$
$$100 < Re < 10^3: \text{laminar, boundary layer theory useful}$$
$$10^3 < Re < 10^4: \text{transition to turbulence}$$
$$10^4 < Re < 10^6: \text{turbulent, moderate Reynolds number dependence}$$
$$10^6 < Re < \quad \infty: \text{turbulent, slight Reynolds number dependence}$$

These representative ranges vary somewhat with flow geometry, surface roughness, and the level of fluctuations in the inlet stream. The great majority of our analyses are concerned with laminar flow or with turbulent flow, and one should not normally design a flow operation in the transition region.

Historical Outline

Since turbulent flow is more prevalent than laminar flow, experimenters have observed turbulence for centuries without being aware of the details. Before 1930 flow instruments were too insensitive to record rapid fluctuations, and workers simply reported mean values of velocity, pressure, force, and so on. But turbulence can change the mean values dramatically, as with the sharp drop in drag coefficient in Fig. 5.3. A German engineer named G. H. L. Hagen first reported in 1839 that there might be *two* regimes of viscous flow. He measured water flow in long brass pipes and deduced a pressure-drop law:

$$\Delta p = (\text{const}) \frac{LQ}{R^4} + \text{entrance effect} \qquad (6.1)$$

This is exactly our laminar flow scaling law from Example 5.4, but Hagen did not realize that the constant was proportional to the fluid viscosity.

The formula broke down as Hagen increased Q beyond a certain limit—that is, past the critical Reynolds number—and he stated in his paper that there must be a second mode of flow characterized by "strong movements of water for which Δp varies as the second power of the discharge. . . ." He admitted that he could not clarify the reasons for the change.

A typical example of Hagen's data is shown in Fig. 6.4. The pressure drop varies linearly with $V = Q/A$ up to about 1.1 ft/s, where there is a sharp change. Above about

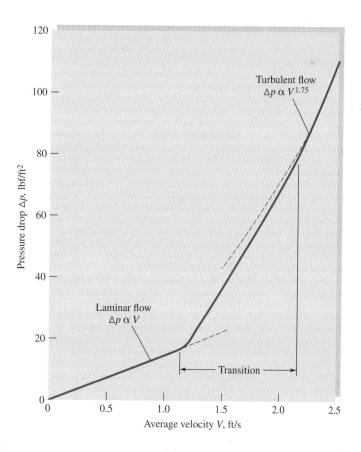

Fig. 6.4 Experimental evidence of transition for water flow in a $\frac{1}{4}$-in smooth pipe 10 ft long.

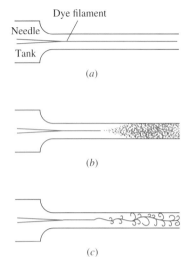

Fig. 6.5 Reynolds' sketches of pipe flow transition: (*a*) low-speed, laminar flow; (*b*) high-speed, turbulent flow; (*c*) spark photograph of condition (*b*).

Source: Reynolds, "An Experimental Investigation of the Circumstances which Determine Whether the Motion of Water Shall Be Direct or Sinuous and of the Law of Resistance in Parallel Channels," Phil. Trans. R. Soc., vol. 174, 1883, pp. 935–982.

$V = 2.2$ ft/s the pressure drop is nearly quadratic with V. The actual power $\Delta p \propto V^{1.75}$ seems impossible on dimensional grounds but is easily explained when the dimensionless pipe flow data (Fig. 5.10) are displayed.

In 1883 Osborne Reynolds, a British engineering professor, showed that the change depended on the parameter $\rho V d/\mu$, now named in his honor. By introducing a dye streak into a pipe flow, Reynolds could observe transition and turbulence. His sketches [4] of the flow behavior are shown in Fig. 6.5.

If we examine Hagen's data and compute the Reynolds number at $V = 1.1$ ft/s, we obtain $\mathrm{Re}_d = 2100$. The flow became fully turbulent, $V = 2.2$ ft/s, at $\mathrm{Re}_d = 4200$. The accepted design value for pipe flow transition is now taken to be

$$\mathrm{Re}_{d,\mathrm{crit}} \approx 2300 \tag{6.2}$$

This is accurate for commercial pipes (Fig. 6.13), although with special care in providing a rounded entrance, smooth walls, and a steady inlet stream, $\mathrm{Re}_{d,\mathrm{crit}}$ can be delayed until much higher values. The study of transition in pipe flow, both experimentally and theoretically, continues to be a fascinating topic for researchers, as discussed in a recent review article [55]. *Note:* The value of 2300 is for transition in *pipes*. Other geometries, such as plates, airfoils, cylinders, and spheres, have completely different transition Reynolds numbers.

Transition also occurs in external flows around bodies such as the sphere and cylinder in Fig. 5.3. Ludwig Prandtl, a German engineering professor, showed in 1914 that the thin boundary layer surrounding the body was undergoing transition from laminar to turbulent flow. Thereafter the force coefficient of a body was acknowledged to be a function of the Reynolds number [Eq. (5.2)].

There are now extensive theories and experiments of laminar flow instability that explain why a flow changes to turbulence. Reference 5 is an advanced textbook on this subject.

Laminar flow theory is now well developed, and many solutions are known [2, 3], but no analyses can simulate the fine-scale random fluctuations of turbulent flow.[1] Therefore most turbulent flow theory is semiempirical, based on dimensional analysis and physical reasoning; it is concerned with the mean flow properties only and the mean of the fluctuations, not their rapid variations. The turbulent flow "theory" presented here in Chaps. 6 and 7 is unbelievably crude yet surprisingly effective. We shall attempt a rational approach that places turbulent flow analysis on a firm physical basis.

6.2 Internal versus External Viscous Flows

Both laminar and turbulent flow may be either internal (that is, "bounded" by walls) or external and unbounded. This chapter treats internal flows, and Chap. 7 studies external flows.

An internal flow is constrained by the bounding walls, and the viscous effects will grow and meet and permeate the entire flow. Figure 6.6 shows an internal flow in a long duct. There is an *entrance region* where a nearly inviscid upstream flow converges and enters the tube. Viscous boundary layers grow downstream, retarding the

---

[1]However, direct numerical simulation (DNS) of low-Reynolds-number turbulence is now quite common [32].

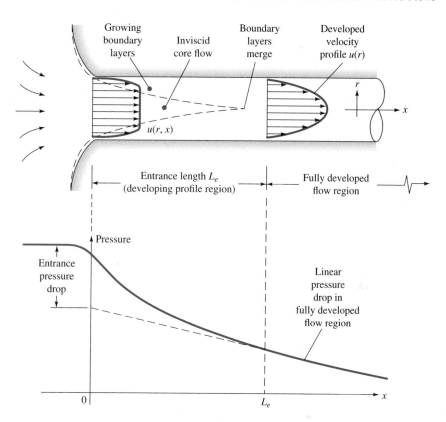

Fig. 6.6 Developing velocity profiles and pressure changes in the entrance of a duct flow.

axial flow $u(r, x)$ at the wall and thereby accelerating the center core flow to maintain the incompressible continuity requirement

$$Q = \int u\, dA = \text{const} \tag{6.3}$$

At a finite distance from the entrance, the boundary layers merge and the inviscid core disappears. The tube flow is then entirely viscous, and the axial velocity adjusts slightly further until at $x = L_e$ it no longer changes with x and is said to be *fully developed*, $u \approx u(r)$ only. Downstream of $x = L_e$ the velocity profile is constant, the wall shear is constant, and the pressure drops linearly with x, for either laminar or turbulent flow. All these details are shown in Fig. 6.6.

Dimensional analysis shows that the Reynolds number is the only parameter affecting entrance length. If

$$L_e = f(d, V, \rho, \mu) \qquad V = \frac{Q}{A}$$

then

$$\frac{L_e}{d} = g\left(\frac{\rho V d}{\mu}\right) = g(\text{Re}_d) \tag{6.4}$$

For laminar flow [2, 3], the accepted correlation is

$$\frac{L_e}{d} \approx 0.06\, \text{Re}_d \qquad \text{laminar} \tag{6.5}$$

The maximum laminar entrance length, at $\mathrm{Re}_{d,\mathrm{crit}} = 2300$, is $L_e = 138d$, which is the longest development length possible.

In turbulent flow, the boundary layers grow faster, and L_e is relatively shorter. For decades, the writer has favored a sixth-power-law estimate, $L_e/d \approx 4.4\,\mathrm{Re}_d^{1/6}$, but recent CFD results, communicated by Fabien Anselmet, and separately by Sukanta Dash, indicate that a better turbulent entrance-length correlation is

$$\frac{L_e}{d} \approx 1.6\,\mathrm{Re}_d^{1/4} \quad \text{for} \quad \mathrm{Re}_d \leq 10^7 \tag{6.6}$$

Some computed turbulent entrance-length estimates are thus

Re_d	4000	10^4	10^5	10^6	10^7
L_e/d	13	16	28	51	90

Now 90 diameters may seem "long," but typical pipe flow applications involve an L/d value of 1000 or more, in which case the entrance effect may be neglected and a simple analysis made for fully developed flow. This is possible for both laminar and turbulent flows, including rough walls and noncircular cross sections.

EXAMPLE 6.2

A $\frac{1}{2}$-in-diameter water pipe is 60 ft long and delivers water at 5 gal/min at 20°C. What fraction of this pipe is taken up by the entrance region?

Solution

Convert

$$Q = (5\ \text{gal/min})\,\frac{0.00223\ \text{ft}^3/\text{s}}{1\ \text{gal/min}} = 0.0111\ \text{ft}^3/\text{s}$$

The average velocity is

$$V = \frac{Q}{A} = \frac{0.0111\ \text{ft}^3/\text{s}}{(\pi/4)[(\frac{1}{2}/12)\ \text{ft}]^2} = 8.17\ \text{ft/s}$$

From Table 1.4 read for water $\nu = 1.01 \times 10^{-6}$ m²/s $= 1.09 \times 10^{-5}$ ft²/s. Then the pipe Reynolds number is

$$\mathrm{Re}_d = \frac{Vd}{\nu} = \frac{(8.17\ \text{ft/s})[(\frac{1}{2}/12)\ \text{ft}]}{1.09 \times 10^{-5}\ \text{ft}^2/\text{s}} = 31{,}300$$

This is greater than 4000; hence the flow is fully turbulent, and Eq. (6.6) applies for entrance length:

$$\frac{L_e}{d} \approx 1.6\,\mathrm{Re}_d^{1/4} = (1.6)(31{,}300)^{1/4} = 21$$

The actual pipe has $L/d = (60\ \text{ft})/[(\frac{1}{2}/12)\text{ft}] = 1440$. Hence the entrance region takes up the fraction

$$\frac{L_e}{L} = \frac{21}{1440} = 0.015 = 1.5\% \qquad\qquad Ans.$$

This is a very small percentage, so we can reasonably treat this pipe flow as essentially fully developed.

Shortness can be a virtue in duct flow if one wishes to maintain the inviscid core. For example, a "long" wind tunnel would be ridiculous, since the viscous core would invalidate the purpose of simulating free-flight conditions. A typical laboratory low-speed wind tunnel test section is 1 m in diameter and 5 m long, with $V = 30$ m/s. If we take $\nu_{air} = 1.51 \times 10^{-5}$ m²/s from Table 1.4, then $\mathrm{Re}_d = 1.99 \times 10^6$ and, from Eq. (6.6), $L_e/d \approx 49$. The test section has $L/d = 5$, which is much shorter than the development length. At the end of the section the wall boundary layers are only 10 cm thick, leaving 80 cm of inviscid core suitable for model testing.

An external flow has no restraining walls and is free to expand no matter how thick the viscous layers on the immersed body may become. Thus, far from the body the flow is nearly inviscid, and our analytical technique, treated in Chap. 7, is to patch an inviscid-flow solution onto a viscous boundary-layer solution computed for the wall region. There is no external equivalent of fully developed internal flow.

6.3 Head Loss—The Friction Factor

When applying pipe flow formulas to practical problems, it is customary to use a control volume analysis. Consider incompressible steady flow between sections 1 and 2 of the inclined constant-area pipe in Fig. 6.7. The one-dimensional continuity relation, Eq. (3.30), reduces to

$$Q_1 = Q_2 = \text{const} \quad \text{or} \quad V_1 = V_2 = V$$

since the pipe is of constant area. The steady flow energy equation (3.75) becomes

$$\left(\frac{p}{\rho g} + \alpha \frac{V^2}{2g} + z\right)_1 = \left(\frac{p}{\rho g} + \alpha \frac{V^2}{2g} + z\right)_2 + h_f \tag{6.7}$$

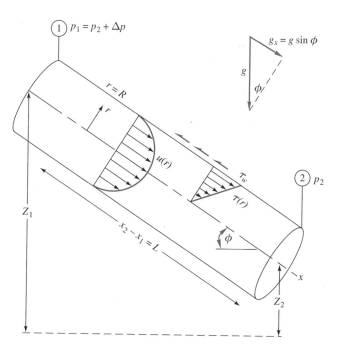

Fig. 6.7 Control volume, just inside the pipe wall, of steady, fully developed flow between two sections in an inclined pipe.

since there is no pump or turbine between 1 and 2. For fully developed flow, the velocity profile shape is the same at sections 1 and 2. Thus $\alpha_1 = \alpha_2$ and, since $V_1 = V_2$, Eq. (6.7) reduces to head loss versus pressure drop and elevation change:

$$h_f = (z_1 - z_2) + \left(\frac{p_1}{\rho g} - \frac{p_2}{\rho g}\right) = \Delta z + \frac{\Delta p}{\rho g} \tag{6.8}$$

The pipe head loss equals the change in the sum of pressure and gravity head—that is, the change in height of the hydraulic grade line (HGL).

Finally, apply the momentum relation (3.40) to the control volume in Fig. 6.7, accounting for applied x-directed forces due to pressure, gravity, and shear:

$$\sum F_x = \Delta p\,(\pi R^2) + \rho g(\pi R^2)L \sin \phi - \tau_w(2\pi R)L = \dot{m}(V_2 - V_1) = 0 \tag{6.9a}$$

Rearrange this and we find that the head loss is also related to wall shear stress:

$$\Delta z + \frac{\Delta p}{\rho g} = h_f = \frac{2\tau_w}{\rho g}\frac{L}{R} = \frac{4\tau_w}{\rho g}\frac{L}{d} \tag{6.9b}$$

where we have substituted $\Delta z = L \sin \phi$ from the geometry of Fig. 6.7. Note that, regardless of whether the pipe is horizontal or tilted, the head loss is proportional to the wall shear stress.

How should we correlate the head loss for pipe flow problems? The answer was given a century and a half ago by Julius Weisbach, a German professor who in 1850 published the first modern textbook on hydrodynamics. Equation (6.9b) shows that h_f is proportional to (L/d), and data such as Hagen's in Fig. 6.6 show that, for turbulent flow, h_f is approximately proportional to V^2. The proposed correlation, still as effective today as in 1850, is

$$h_f = f\frac{L}{d}\frac{V^2}{2g} \quad \text{where} \quad f = \text{fcn}(\text{Re}_d, \frac{\varepsilon}{d}, \text{duct shape}) \tag{6.10}$$

The dimensionless parameter f is called the *Darcy friction factor,* after Henry Darcy (1803–1858), a French engineer whose pipe flow experiments in 1857 first established the effect of roughness on pipe resistance. The quantity ε is the wall roughness height, which is important in turbulent (but not laminar) pipe flow. We added the "duct shape" effect in Eq. (6.10) to remind us that square and triangular and other noncircular ducts have a somewhat different friction factor than a circular pipe. Actual data and theory for friction factors will be discussed in the sections that follow.

By equating Eqs. (6.9) and (6.10) we find an alternative form for friction factor:

$$f = \frac{8\tau_w}{\rho V^2} \tag{6.11}$$

For noncircular ducts, we must interpret τ_w to be an average value around the duct perimeter. For this reason Eq. (6.10) is preferred as a unified definition of the Darcy friction factor.

6.4 Laminar Fully Developed Pipe Flow

Analytical solutions can be readily derived for laminar flows, either circular or non-circular. Consider fully developed *Poiseuille* flow in a round pipe of diameter d, radius R. Complete analytical results were given in Sec. 4.10. Let us review those formulas here:

$$u = u_{max}\left(1 - \frac{r^2}{R^2}\right) \quad \text{where} \quad u_{max} = \left(-\frac{dp}{dx}\right)\frac{R^2}{4\mu} \quad \text{and} \quad \left(-\frac{dp}{dx}\right) = \left(\frac{\Delta p + \rho g \Delta z}{L}\right)$$

$$V = \frac{Q}{A} = \frac{u_{max}}{2} = \left(\frac{\Delta p + \rho g \Delta z}{L}\right)\frac{R^2}{8\mu}$$

$$Q = \int u\,dA = \pi R^2 V = \frac{\pi R^4}{8\mu}\left(\frac{\Delta p + \rho g \Delta z}{L}\right) \tag{6.12}$$

$$\tau_w = \left|\mu\frac{du}{dr}\right|_{r=R} = \frac{4\mu V}{R} = \frac{8\mu V}{d} = \frac{R}{2}\left(\frac{\Delta p + \rho g \Delta z}{L}\right)$$

$$h_f = \frac{32\mu L V}{\rho g d^2} = \frac{128\mu L Q}{\pi \rho g d^4}$$

The paraboloid velocity profile has an average velocity V which is one-half of the maximum velocity. The quantity Δp is the pressure *drop* in a pipe of length L; that is, (dp/dx) is negative. These formulas are valid whenever the pipe Reynolds number, $Re_d = \rho V d/\mu$, is less than about 2300. Note that τ_w is proportional to V (see Fig. 6.6) and is independent of density because the fluid acceleration is zero. Neither of these is true in turbulent flow.

With wall shear stress known, the Poiseuille flow friction factor is easily determined:

$$f_{lam} = \frac{8\tau_{w,lam}}{\rho V^2} = \frac{8(8\mu V/d)}{\rho V^2} = \frac{64}{\rho V d/\mu} = \frac{64}{Re_d} \tag{6.13}$$

In laminar flow, the pipe friction factor decreases inversely with Reynolds number. This famous formula is effective, but often the algebraic relations of Eqs. (6.12) are more direct for problems.

EXAMPLE 6.3

An oil with $\rho = 900$ kg/m^3 and $\nu = 0.0002$ m^2/s flows upward through an inclined pipe as shown in Fig. E6.3. The pressure and elevation are known at sections 1 and 2, 10 m apart. Assuming steady laminar flow, (a) verify that the flow is up, (b) compute h_f between 1 and 2, and compute (c) Q, (d) V, and (e) Re_d. Is the flow really laminar?

Solution

Part (a)

For later use, calculate

$$\mu = \rho\nu = (900 \text{ kg/m}^3)(0.0002 \text{ m}^2/\text{s}) = 0.18 \text{ kg/(m}\cdot\text{s)}$$

$$z_2 = \Delta L \sin 40° = (10 \text{ m})(0.643) = 6.43 \text{ m}$$

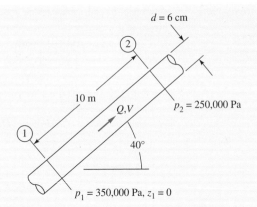

E6.3

The flow goes in the direction of falling HGL; therefore, compute the hydraulic grade-line height at each section:

$$HGL_1 = z_1 + \frac{p_1}{\rho g} = 0 + \frac{350,000}{900(9.807)} = 39.65 \text{ m}$$

$$HGL_2 = z_2 + \frac{p_2}{\rho g} = 6.43 + \frac{250,000}{900(9.807)} = 34.75 \text{ m}$$

The HGL is lower at section 2; hence the flow is up from 1 to 2 as assumed.   *Ans. (a)*

Part (b)   The head loss is the change in HGL:

$$h_f = HGL_1 - HGL_2 = 39.65 \text{ m} - 34.75 \text{ m} = 4.9 \text{ m}   \textit{Ans. (b)}$$

Half the length of the pipe is quite a large head loss.

Part (c)   We can compute Q from the various laminar flow formulas, notably Eq. (6.12):

$$Q = \frac{\pi \rho g d^4 h_f}{128 \mu L} = \frac{\pi(900)(9.807)(0.06)^4(4.9)}{128(0.18)(10)} = 0.0076 \text{ m}^3/\text{s}   \textit{Ans. (c)}$$

Part (d)   Divide Q by the pipe area to get the average velocity:

$$V = \frac{Q}{\pi R^2} = \frac{0.0076}{\pi(0.03)^2} = 2.7 \text{ m/s}   \textit{Ans. (d)}$$

Part (e)   With V known, the Reynolds number is

$$Re_d = \frac{Vd}{\nu} = \frac{2.7(0.06)}{0.0002} = 810   \textit{Ans. (e)}$$

This is well below the transition value $Re_d = 2300$, so we are fairly certain the flow is laminar. Notice that by sticking entirely to consistent SI units (meters, seconds, kilograms, newtons) for all variables we avoid the need for any conversion factors in the calculations.

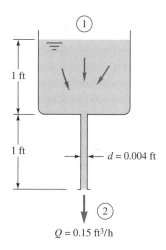

1 ft

1 ft

$d = 0.004$ ft

$Q = 0.15$ ft^3/h

E6.4

EXAMPLE 6.4

A liquid of specific weight $\rho g = 58$ lb$_f$/ft^3 flows by gravity through a 1-ft tank and a 1-ft capillary tube at a rate of 0.15 ft^3/h, as shown in Fig. E6.4. Sections 1 and 2 are at atmospheric pressure. Neglecting entrance effects and friction in the large tank, compute the viscosity of the liquid.

Solution

- *System sketch:* Figure E6.4 shows $L = 1$ ft, $d = 0.004$ ft, and $Q = 0.15$ ft^3/h.
- *Assumptions:* Laminar, fully developed, incompressible (Poiseuille) pipe flow. Atmospheric pressure at sections 1 and 2. Negligible velocity at surface, $V_1 \approx 0$.
- *Approach:* Use continuity and energy to find the head loss and thence the viscosity.
- *Property values:* Given $\rho g = 58$ lbf/ft^3, figure out $\rho = 58/32.2 = 1.80$ slug/ft^3 if needed.
- *Solution step 1:* From continuity and the known flow rate, determine V_2:

$$V_2 = \frac{Q}{A_2} = \frac{Q}{(\pi/4)d^2} = \frac{(0.15/3600)\text{ft}^3/\text{s}}{(\pi/4)(0.004 \text{ ft})^2} = 3.32 \text{ ft/s}$$

Write the energy equation between 1 and 2, canceling terms, and find the head loss:

$$\frac{p_1}{\rho g} + \frac{\alpha_1 V_1^2}{2g} + z_1 = \frac{p_2}{\rho g} + \frac{\alpha_2 V_2^2}{2g} + z_2 + h_f$$

or $\qquad h_f = z_1 - z_2 - \dfrac{\alpha_2 V_2^2}{2g} = 2.0 \text{ ft} - 0 \text{ ft} - \dfrac{(2.0)(3.32 \text{ ft/s})^2}{2(32.2 \text{ ft/s}^2)} = 1.66 \text{ ft}$

- *Comment:* We introduced $\alpha_2 = 2.0$ for laminar pipe flow from Eq. (3.76). If we forgot α_2, we would have calculated $h_f = 1.83$ ft, a 10 percent error.
- *Solution step 2:* With head loss known, the viscosity follows from the laminar formula in Eqs. (6.12):

$$h_f = 1.66 \text{ ft} = \frac{32 \mu LV}{(\rho g)d^2} = \frac{32\mu(1.0 \text{ ft})(3.32 \text{ ft/s})}{(58 \text{ lbf/ft}^3)(0.004 \text{ ft})^2} \quad \text{solve for } \mu = 1.45 \text{ E-5} \frac{\text{slug}}{\text{ft-s}} \quad Ans.$$

- *Comments:* We didn't need the value of ρ—the formula contains ρg, but who knew? Note also that L in this formula is the *pipe length* of 1 ft, not the total elevation change.
- *Final check:* Calculate the Reynolds number to see if it is less than 2300 for laminar flow:

$$\text{Re}_d = \frac{\rho V d}{\mu} = \frac{(1.80 \text{ slug/ft}^3)(3.32 \text{ ft/s})(0.004 \text{ ft})}{(1.45 \text{ E-5 slug/ft-s})} \approx 1650 \quad \text{Yes, laminar.}$$

- *Comments:* So we did need ρ after all to calculate Re_d.
- *Unexpected comment:* For this head loss, there is a *second* (turbulent) solution, as we shall see in Example 6.8.

6.5 Turbulence Modeling

Throughout this chapter we assume constant density and viscosity and no thermal interaction, so that only the continuity and momentum equations are to be solved for velocity and pressure

Continuity: $\qquad\qquad \dfrac{\partial u}{\partial x} + \dfrac{\partial v}{\partial y} + \dfrac{\partial w}{\partial z} = 0$

$$(6.14)$$

Momentum: $\qquad\qquad \rho \dfrac{d\mathbf{V}}{dt} = -\nabla p + \rho\mathbf{g} + \mu \nabla^2 \mathbf{V}$

subject to no slip at the walls and known inlet and exit conditions. (We shall save our free-surface solutions for Chap. 10.)

We will not work with the differential energy relation, Eq. (4.53), in this chapter, but it is very important, both for heat transfer calculations and for general understanding of duct flow processes. There is work being done by pressure forces to drive the fluid through the duct. Where does this energy go? There is no work done by the wall shear stresses, because the velocity at the wall is zero. The answer is that pressure work is balanced by viscous dissipation in the interior of the flow. The integral of the dissipation function Φ, from Eq. (4.50), over the flow field will equal the pressure work. An example of this fundamental viscous flow energy balance is given in Problem C6.7.

Both laminar and turbulent flows satisfy Eqs. (6.14). For laminar flow, where there are no random fluctuations, we go right to the attack and solve them for a variety of geometries [2, 3], leaving many more, of course, for the problems.

Reynolds' Time-Averaging Concept

For turbulent flow, because of the fluctuations, every velocity and pressure term in Eqs. (6.14) is a rapidly varying random function of time and space. At present our mathematics cannot handle such instantaneous fluctuating variables. No single pair of random functions $V(x, y, z, t)$ and $p(x, y, z, t)$ is known to be a solution to Eqs. (6.14). Moreover, our attention as engineers is toward the average or *mean* values of velocity, pressure, shear stress, and the like in a high-Reynolds-number (turbulent) flow. This approach led Osborne Reynolds in 1895 to rewrite Eqs. (6.14) in terms of mean or time-averaged turbulent variables.

The time mean $\bar{u}$ of a turbulent function $u(x, y, z, t)$ is defined by

$$\bar{u} = \frac{1}{T}\int_0^T u \, dt \tag{6.15}$$

where T is an averaging period taken to be longer than any significant period of the fluctuations themselves. The mean values of turbulent velocity and pressure are illustrated in Fig. 6.8. For turbulent gas and water flows, an averaging period $T \approx 5$ s is usually quite adequate.

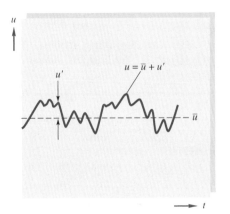

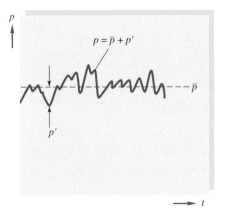

Fig. 6.8 Definition of mean and fluctuating turbulent variables: (*a*) velocity; (*b*) pressure.

(*a*)

(*b*)

The *fluctuation* u' is defined as the deviation of u from its average value

$$u' = u - \bar{u} \tag{6.16}$$

also shown in Fig. 6.8. It follows by definition that a fluctuation has zero mean value:

$$\overline{u'} = \frac{1}{T} \int_0^T (u - \bar{u}) \, dt = \bar{u} - \bar{u} = 0 \tag{6.17}$$

However, the mean square of a fluctuation is not zero and is a measure of the *intensity* of the turbulence:

$$\overline{u'^2} = \frac{1}{T} \int_0^T u'^2 \, dt \neq 0 \tag{6.18}$$

Nor in general are the mean fluctuation products such as $\overline{u'v'}$ and $\overline{u'p'}$ zero in a typical turbulent flow.

Reynolds' idea was to split each property into mean plus fluctuating variables:

$$u = \bar{u} + u' \quad v = \bar{v} + v' \quad w = \bar{w} + w' \quad p = \bar{p} + p' \tag{6.19}$$

Substitute these into Eqs. (6.14), and take the time mean of each equation. The continuity relation reduces to

$$\frac{\partial \bar{u}}{\partial x} + \frac{\partial \bar{v}}{\partial y} + \frac{\partial \bar{w}}{\partial z} = 0 \tag{6.20}$$

which is no different from a laminar continuity relation.

However, each component of the momentum equation (6.14b), after time averaging, will contain mean values plus three mean products, or *correlations,* of fluctuating velocities. The most important of these is the momentum relation in the mainstream, or x, direction, which takes the form

$$\rho \frac{d\bar{u}}{dt} = -\frac{\partial \bar{p}}{\partial x} + \rho g_x + \frac{\partial}{\partial x}\left(\mu \frac{\partial \bar{u}}{\partial x} - \rho \overline{u'^2}\right)$$
$$+ \frac{\partial}{\partial y}\left(\mu \frac{\partial \bar{u}}{\partial y} - \rho \overline{u'v'}\right) + \frac{\partial}{\partial z}\left(\mu \frac{\partial \bar{u}}{\partial z} - \rho \overline{u'w'}\right) \tag{6.21}$$

The three correlation terms $-\rho \overline{u'^2}$, $-\rho \overline{u'v'}$, and $-\rho \overline{u'w'}$ are called *turbulent stresses* because they have the same dimensions and occur right alongside the newtonian (laminar) stress terms $\mu(\partial \bar{u}/\partial x)$ and so on.

The turbulent stresses are unknown a priori and must be related by experiment to geometry and flow conditions, as detailed in Refs. 1 to 3. Fortunately, in duct and boundary layer flow, the stress $-\rho \overline{u'v'}$, associated with direction y normal to the wall is dominant, and we can approximate with excellent accuracy a simpler streamwise momentum equation

$$\rho \frac{d\bar{u}}{dt} \approx -\frac{\partial \bar{p}}{\partial x} + \rho g_x + \frac{\partial \tau}{\partial y} \tag{6.22}$$

where

$$\tau = \mu \frac{\partial \bar{u}}{\partial y} - \rho \overline{u'v'} = \tau_{\text{lam}} + \tau_{\text{turb}} \tag{6.23}$$

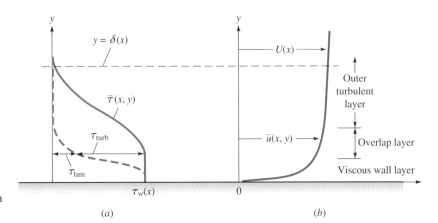

Fig. 6.9 Typical velocity and shear distributions in turbulent flow near a wall: (*a*) shear; (*b*) velocity.

(*a*)   (*b*)

Figure 6.9 shows the distribution of τ_{lam} and τ_{turb} from typical measurements across a turbulent shear layer near a wall. Laminar shear is dominant near the wall (the *wall layer*), and turbulent shear dominates in the *outer layer*. There is an intermediate region, called the *overlap layer,* where both laminar and turbulent shear are important. These three regions are labeled in Fig. 6.9.

In the outer layer τ_{turb} is two or three orders of magnitude greater than τ_{lam}, and vice versa in the wall layer. These experimental facts enable us to use a crude but very effective model for the velocity distribution $\bar{u}(y)$ across a turbulent wall layer.

The Logarithmic Overlap Law

We have seen in Fig. 6.9 that there are three regions in turbulent flow near a wall:

1. Wall layer: Viscous shear dominates.
2. Outer layer: Turbulent shear dominates.
3. Overlap layer: Both types of shear are important.

From now on let us agree to drop the overbar from velocity $\bar{u}$. Let τ_w be the wall shear stress, and let δ and U represent the thickness and velocity at the edge of the outer layer, $y = \delta$.

For the wall layer, Prandtl deduced in 1930 that u must be independent of the shear layer thickness:

$$u = f(\mu, \tau_w, \rho, y) \tag{6.24}$$

By dimensional analysis, this is equivalent to

$$u^+ = \frac{u}{u^*} = F\left(\frac{yu^*}{\nu}\right) \qquad u^* = \left(\frac{\tau_w}{\rho}\right)^{1/2} \tag{6.25}$$

Equation (6.25) is called the *law of the wall,* and the quantity u^* is termed the *friction velocity* because it has dimensions $\{LT^{-1}\}$, although it is not actually a flow velocity.

Subsequently, Kármán in 1933 deduced that u in the outer layer is independent of molecular viscosity, but its deviation from the stream velocity U must depend on the layer thickness δ and the other properties:

$$(U - u)_{outer} = g(\delta, \tau_w, \rho, y) \tag{6.26}$$

Again, by dimensional analysis we rewrite this as

$$\frac{U - u}{u^*} = G\left(\frac{y}{\delta}\right) \qquad (6.27)$$

where u^* has the same meaning as in Eq. (6.25). Equation (6.27) is called the *velocity-defect law* for the outer layer.

Both the wall law (6.25) and the defect law (6.27) are found to be accurate for a wide variety of experimental turbulent duct and boundary layer flows [Refs. 1 to 3]. They are different in form, yet they must overlap smoothly in the intermediate layer. In 1937 C. B. Millikan showed that this can be true only if the overlap layer velocity varies logarithmically with y:

$$\boxed{\frac{u}{u^*} = \frac{1}{\kappa} \ln \frac{yu^*}{\nu} + B \quad \text{overlap layer}} \qquad (6.28)$$

Over the full range of turbulent smooth wall flows, the dimensionless constants κ and B are found to have the approximate values $\kappa \approx 0.41$ and $B \approx 5.0$. Equation (6.28) is called the *logarithmic overlap layer*.

Thus by dimensional reasoning and physical insight we infer that a plot of u versus $\ln y$ in a turbulent shear layer will show a curved wall region, a curved outer region, and a straight-line logarithmic overlap. Figure 6.10 shows that this is exactly the case.

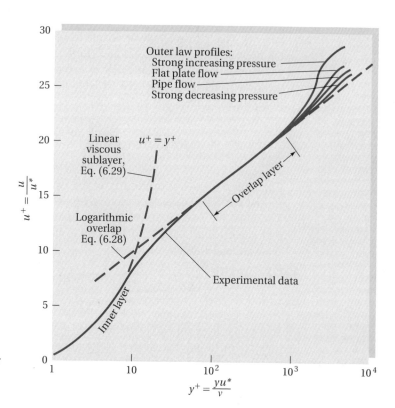

Fig. 6.10 Experimental verification of the inner, outer, and overlap layer laws relating velocity profiles in turbulent wall flow.

The four outer-law profiles shown all merge smoothly with the logarithmic overlap law but have different magnitudes because they vary in external pressure gradient. The wall law is unique and follows the linear viscous relation

$$u^+ = \frac{u}{u^*} = \frac{yu^*}{\nu} = y^+ \tag{6.29}$$

from the wall to about $y^+ = 5$, thereafter curving over to merge with the logarithmic law at about $y^+ = 30$.

Believe it or not, Fig. 6.10, which is nothing more than a shrewd correlation of velocity profiles, is the basis for most existing "theory" of turbulent shear flows. Notice that we have not solved any equations at all but have merely expressed the streamwise velocity in a neat form.

There is serendipity in Fig. 6.10: The logarithmic law (6.28), instead of just being a short overlapping link, actually approximates nearly the entire velocity profile, except for the outer law when the pressure is increasing strongly downstream (as in a diffuser). The inner wall law typically extends over less than 2 percent of the profile and can be neglected. Thus we can use Eq. (6.28) as an excellent approximation to solve nearly every turbulent flow problem presented in this and the next chapter. Many additional applications are given in Refs. 2 and 3.

Advanced Modeling Concepts

Turbulence modeling is a very active field. Scores of papers have been published to more accurately simulate the turbulent stresses in Eq. (6.21) and their y and z components. This research, now available in advanced texts [1, 13, 19], goes well beyond the present book, which is confined to the use of the logarithmic law (6.28) for pipe and boundary layer problems. For example, L. Prandtl, who invented boundary layer theory in 1904, later proposed an *eddy viscosity* model of the Reynolds stress term in Eq. (6.23):

$$-\rho\,\overline{u'v'} = \tau_{\text{turb}} \approx \mu_t \frac{du}{dy} \qquad \text{where} \qquad \mu_t \approx \rho\, l^2 \left|\frac{du}{dy}\right| \tag{6.30}$$

The term μ_t, which is a property of the *flow*, not the fluid, is called the *eddy viscosity* and can be modeled in various ways. The most popular form is Eq. (6.30), where l is called the *mixing length* of the turbulent eddies (analogous to mean free path in molecular theory). Near a solid wall, l is approximately proportional to distance from the wall, and Kármán suggested

$$l \approx \kappa y \quad \text{where} \quad \kappa = \text{Kármán's constant} \approx 0.41 \tag{6.31}$$

As a homework assignment, Prob. P6.40, you may show that Eqs. (6.30) and (6.31) lead to the logarithmic law (6.28) near a wall.

Modern turbulence models approximate three-dimensional turbulent flows and employ additional partial differential equations for such quantities as the turbulence kinetic energy, the turbulent dissipation, and the six Reynolds stresses. For details, see Refs. 1, 13, and 19.

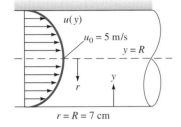

E6.5

EXAMPLE 6.5

Air at 20°C flows through a 14-cm-diameter tube under fully developed conditions. The centerline velocity is $u_0 = 5$ m/s. Estimate from Fig. 6.10 (*a*) the friction velocity u^* and (*b*) the wall shear stress τ_w.

Solution

- *System sketch:* Figure E6.5 shows turbulent pipe flow with $u_0 = 5$ m/s and $R = 7$ cm.
- *Assumptions:* Figure 6.10 shows that the logarithmic law, Eq. (6.28), is reasonable all the way to the center of the tube.
- *Approach:* Use Eq. (6.28) to estimate the unknown friction velocity u^*.
- *Property values:* For air at 20°C, $\rho = 1.205$ kg/m^3 and $\nu = 1.51$ E-5 m^2/s.
- *Solution step:* Insert all the given data into Eq. (6.28) at $y = R$ (the centerline). The only unknown is u^*:

$$\frac{u_0}{u^*} = \frac{1}{\kappa}\ln\left(\frac{Ru^*}{\nu}\right) + B \quad \text{or} \quad \frac{5.0 \text{ m/s}}{u^*} = \frac{1}{0.41}\ln\left[\frac{(0.07 \text{ m})u^*}{1.51 \text{ E-5 m}^2/\text{s}}\right] + 5$$

Although the logarithm makes it awkward, one can solve this either by hand or by Excel iteration. There is an automatic iteration procedure in Excel—File, Excel Options, Formulas, Enable iterative calculation—but here we simply show how to iterate by repeat calculations, copied and pasted downward. For a single unknown, in this case u^*, we only need two columns, one for the unknown and one for the equation. The writer hopes that the following copy-and-iterate procedure is clear:

	A	B
	Here place the first guess for u*:	Here place the equation that solves for u*:
1	1.0	=(5.0/(1/0.41*ln(0.07*a1/1.51E-5)+5))
2	=B1 (the number, not the equation)	Copy B1 equation and place here
3	Copy A2 here	Copy B2 here
4	Keep copying down…	Keep copying down until convergence

Note that B2 uses the *cell* location for u^*, A1, not the notation u^*. Here are the actual numbers, not instructions or equations, for this problem:

A	B
1.0000	0.1954
0.1954	0.2314
0.2314	0.2271
0.2271	0.2275
0.2275	0.2275

The solution for u^* has converged to 0.2275. To three decimal places,

$$u^* \approx 0.228 \text{ m/s} \qquad \qquad \textit{Ans. (a)}$$

$$\tau_w = \rho u^{*2} = (1.205)(0.228)^2 \approx 0.062 \text{ Pa} \qquad \textit{Ans. (b)}$$

- *Comments:* The logarithmic law solved everything! This is a powerful technique, using an experimental velocity correlation to approximate general turbulent flows. You may check that the Reynolds number Re_d is about 40,000, definitely turbulent flow.

6.6 Turbulent Pipe Flow

For turbulent pipe flow we need not solve a differential equation but instead proceed with the logarithmic law, as in Example 6.5. Assume that Eq. (6.28) correlates the local mean velocity $u(r)$ all the way across the pipe

$$\frac{u(r)}{u^*} \approx \frac{1}{\kappa} \ln \frac{(R-r)u^*}{\nu} + B \tag{6.32}$$

where we have replaced y with $R - r$. Compute the average velocity from this profile:

$$V = \frac{Q}{A} = \frac{1}{\pi R^2} \int_0^R u^* \left[\frac{1}{\kappa} \ln \frac{(R-r)u^*}{\nu} + B \right] 2\pi r \, dr$$

$$= \frac{1}{2} u^* \left(\frac{2}{\kappa} \ln \frac{Ru^*}{\nu} + 2B - \frac{3}{\kappa} \right) \tag{6.33}$$

Introducing $\kappa = 0.41$ and $B = 5.0$, we obtain, numerically,

$$\frac{V}{u^*} \approx 2.44 \ln \frac{Ru^*}{\nu} + 1.34 \tag{6.34}$$

This looks only marginally interesting until we realize that V/u^* is directly related to the Darcy friction factor:

$$\frac{V}{u^*} = \left(\frac{\rho V^2}{\tau_w} \right)^{1/2} = \left(\frac{8}{f} \right)^{1/2} \tag{6.35}$$

Moreover, the argument of the logarithm in (6.34) is equivalent to

$$\frac{Ru^*}{\nu} = \frac{\frac{1}{2}Vd}{\nu} \frac{u^*}{V} = \frac{1}{2} \text{Re}_d \left(\frac{f}{8} \right)^{1/2} \tag{6.36}$$

Introducing (6.35) and (6.36) into Eq. (6.34), changing to a base-10 logarithm, and rearranging, we obtain

$$\frac{1}{f^{1/2}} \approx 1.99 \log (\text{Re}_d f^{1/2}) - 1.02 \tag{6.37}$$

In other words, by simply computing the mean velocity from the logarithmic law correlation, we obtain a relation between the friction factor and Reynolds number for turbulent pipe flow. Prandtl derived Eq. (6.37) in 1935 and then adjusted the constants slightly to fit friction data better:

$$\frac{1}{f^{1/2}} = 2.0 \log (\text{Re}_d f^{1/2}) - 0.8 \tag{6.38}$$

This is the accepted formula for a smooth-walled pipe. Some numerical values may be listed as follows:

Re_d	4000	10^4	10^5	10^6	10^7	10^8
f	0.0399	0.0309	0.0180	0.0116	0.0081	0.0059

Thus f drops by only a factor of 5 over a 10,000-fold increase in Reynolds number. Equation (6.38) is cumbersome to solve if Re_d is known and f is wanted. There are many alternative approximations in the literature from which f can be computed explicitly from Re_d:

$$f = \begin{cases} 0.316 \, Re_d^{-1/4} & 4000 < Re_d < 10^5 \quad \text{H. Blasius (1911)} \\ \left(1.8 \log \dfrac{Re_d}{6.9}\right)^{-2} & \text{Ref. 9, Colebrook} \end{cases} \tag{6.39}$$

However, Eq. (6.38) the preferred formula, is easily solved by computer iteration.

Blasius, a student of Prandtl, presented his formula in the first correlation ever made of pipe friction versus Reynolds number. Although his formula has a limited range, it illustrates what was happening in Fig. 6.4 to Hagen's 1839 pressure-drop data. For a horizontal pipe, from Eq. (6.39),

$$h_f = \frac{\Delta p}{\rho g} = f \frac{L}{d} \frac{V^2}{2g} \approx 0.316 \left(\frac{\mu}{\rho V d}\right)^{1/4} \frac{L}{d} \frac{V^2}{2g}$$

or

$$\Delta p \approx 0.158 \, L \rho^{3/4} \mu^{1/4} d^{-5/4} V^{7/4} \tag{6.40}$$

at low turbulent Reynolds numbers. This explains why Hagen's data for pressure drop begin to increase as the 1.75 power of the velocity, in Fig. 6.4. Note that Δp varies only slightly with viscosity, which is characteristic of turbulent flow. Introducing $Q = \frac{1}{4}\pi d^2 V$ into Eq. (6.40), we obtain the alternative form

$$\Delta p \approx 0.241 L \rho^{3/4} \mu^{1/4} d^{-4.75} Q^{1.75} \tag{6.41}$$

For a given flow rate Q, the turbulent pressure drop decreases with diameter even more sharply than the laminar formula (6.12). Thus the quickest way to reduce required pumping pressure is to increase the pipe size, although, of course, the larger pipe is more expensive. Doubling the pipe size decreases Δp by a factor of about 27 for a given Q. Compare Eq. (6.40) with Example 5.7 and Fig. 5.10.

The maximum velocity in turbulent pipe flow is given by Eq. (6.32), evaluated at $r = 0$:

$$\frac{u_{max}}{u^*} \approx \frac{1}{\kappa} \ln \frac{R u^*}{\nu} + B \tag{6.42}$$

Combining this with Eq. (6.33), we obtain the formula relating mean velocity to maximum velocity:

$$\frac{V}{u_{max}} \approx (1 + 1.3\sqrt{f})^{-1} \tag{6.43}$$

Some numerical values are

Re_d	4000	10^4	10^5	10^6	10^7	10^8
V/u_{max}	0.794	0.814	0.852	0.877	0.895	0.909

The ratio varies with the Reynolds number and is much larger than the value of 0.5 predicted for all laminar pipe flow in Eq. (6.12). Thus a turbulent velocity profile, as shown in Fig. 6.11b, is very flat in the center and drops off sharply to zero at the wall.

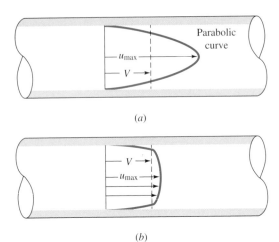

Fig. 6.11 Comparison of laminar and turbulent pipe flow velocity profiles for the same volume flow: (*a*) laminar flow; (*b*) turbulent flow.

Effect of Rough Walls

It was not known until experiments in 1800 by Coulomb [6] that surface roughness has an effect on friction resistance. It turns out that the effect is negligible for laminar pipe flow, and all the laminar formulas derived in this section are valid for rough walls also. But turbulent flow is strongly affected by roughness. In Fig. 6.10 the linear viscous sublayer extends out only to $y^+ = yu*/\nu = 5$. Thus, compared with the diameter, the sublayer thickness y_s is only

$$\frac{y_s}{d} = \frac{5\nu/u*}{d} = \frac{14.1}{\mathrm{Re}_d f^{1/2}} \tag{6.44}$$

For example, at $\mathrm{Re}_d = 10^5, f = 0.0180$, and $y_s/d = 0.001$, a wall roughness of about $0.001d$ will break up the sublayer and profoundly change the wall law in Fig. 6.10.

Measurements of $u(y)$ in turbulent rough-wall flow by Prandtl's student Nikuradse [7] show, as in Fig. 6.12*a*, that a roughness height ε will force the logarithm law profile outward on the abscissa by an amount approximately equal to $\ln \varepsilon^+$, where $\varepsilon^+ = \varepsilon u*/\nu$. The slope of the logarithm law remains the same, $1/\kappa$, but the shift outward causes the constant B to be less by an amount $\Delta B \approx (1/\kappa) \ln \varepsilon^+$.

Nikuradse [7] simulated roughness by gluing uniform sand grains onto the inner walls of the pipes. He then measured the pressure drops and flow rates and correlated friction factor versus Reynolds number in Fig. 6.12*b*. We see that laminar friction is unaffected, but turbulent friction, after an *onset* point, increases monotonically with the roughness ratio ε/d. For any given ε/d, the friction factor becomes constant (*fully rough*) at high Reynolds numbers. These points of change are certain values of $\varepsilon^+ = \varepsilon u*/\nu$:

$$\frac{\varepsilon u*}{\nu} < 5: \quad \textit{hydraulically smooth} \text{ walls, no effect of roughness on friction}$$

$$5 \le \frac{\varepsilon u*}{\nu} \le 70: \quad \textit{transitional} \text{ roughness, moderate Reynolds number effect}$$

$$\frac{\varepsilon u*}{\nu} > 70: \quad \textit{fully rough} \text{ flow, sublayer totally broken up and friction independent of Reynolds number}$$

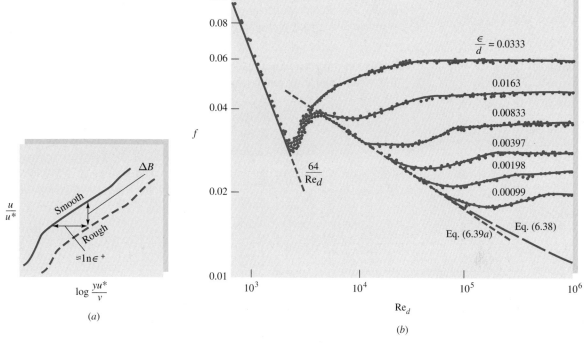

Fig. 6.12 Effect of wall roughness on turbulent pipe flow. (*a*) The logarithmic overlap velocity profile shifts down and to the right; (*b*) experiments with sand-grain roughness by Nikuradse [7] show a systematic increase of the turbulent friction factor with the roughness ratio.

For fully rough flow, $\varepsilon^+ > 70$, the log law downshift ΔB in Fig. 6.12*a* is

$$\Delta B \approx \frac{1}{\kappa} \ln \varepsilon^+ - 3.5 \tag{6.45}$$

and the logarithm law modified for roughness becomes

$$u^+ = \frac{1}{\kappa} \ln y^+ + B - \Delta B = \frac{1}{\kappa} \ln \frac{y}{\varepsilon} + 8.5 \tag{6.46}$$

The viscosity vanishes, and hence fully rough flow is independent of the Reynolds number. If we integrate Eq. (6.46) to obtain the average velocity in the pipe, we obtain

$$\frac{V}{u^*} = 2.44 \ln \frac{d}{\varepsilon} + 3.2$$

or $\qquad \dfrac{1}{f^{1/2}} = -2.0 \log \dfrac{\varepsilon/d}{3.7} \qquad$ fully rough flow $\qquad$ (6.47)

There is no Reynolds number effect; hence the head loss varies exactly as the square of the velocity in this case. Some numerical values of friction factor may be listed:

ε/d	0.00001	0.0001	0.001	0.01	0.05
f	0.00806	0.0120	0.0196	0.0379	0.0716

The friction factor increases by 9 times as the roughness increases by a factor of 5000. In the transitional roughness region, sand grains behave somewhat differently from commercially rough pipes, so Fig. 6.12b has now been replaced by the Moody chart.

The Moody Chart

In 1939 to cover the transitionally rough range, Colebrook [9] combined the smooth wall [Eq. (6.38)] and fully rough [Eq. (6.47)] relations into a clever interpolation formula:

$$\frac{1}{f^{1/2}} = -2.0 \log\left(\frac{\varepsilon/d}{3.7} + \frac{2.51}{\mathrm{Re}_d f^{1/2}}\right) \tag{6.48}$$

This is the accepted design formula for turbulent friction. It was plotted in 1944 by Moody [8] into what is now called the *Moody chart* for pipe friction (Fig. 6.13).

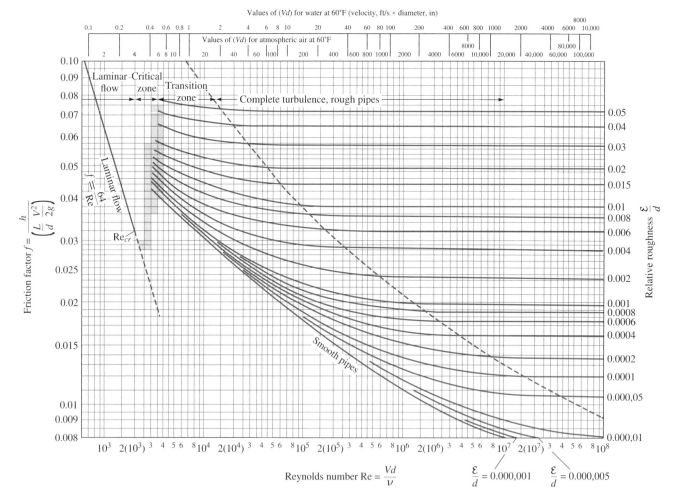

Fig. 6.13 The Moody chart for pipe friction with smooth and rough walls. This chart is identical to Eq. (6.48) for turbulent flow. *(From Ref. 8, Source: ASME.)*

Table 6.1 Recommended Roughness Values for Commercial Ducts

Material	Condition	ε ft	mm	Uncertainty, %
Steel	Sheet metal, new	0.00016	0.05	±60
	Stainless, new	0.000007	0.002	±50
	Commercial, new	0.00015	0.046	±30
	Riveted	0.01	3.0	±70
	Rusted	0.007	2.0	±50
Iron	Cast, new	0.00085	0.26	±50
	Wrought, new	0.00015	0.046	±20
	Galvanized, new	0.0005	0.15	±40
	Asphalted cast	0.0004	0.12	±50
Brass	Drawn, new	0.000007	0.002	±50
Plastic	Drawn tubing	0.000005	0.0015	±60
Glass	—	Smooth	Smooth	
Concrete	Smoothed	0.00013	0.04	±60
	Rough	0.007	2.0	±50
Rubber	Smoothed	0.000033	0.01	±60
Wood	Stave	0.0016	0.5	±40

The Moody chart is probably the most famous and useful figure in fluid mechanics. It is accurate to ±15 percent for design calculations over the full range shown in Fig. 6.13. It can be used for circular and noncircular (Sec. 6.6) pipe flows and for open-channel flows (Chap. 10). The data can even be adapted as an approximation to boundary layer flows (Chap. 7).

The Moody chart gives a good visual summary of laminar and turbulent pipe friction, including roughness effects. When the writer was in college, everyone solved problems by carefully reading this chart. Currently, though, Eq. (6.48), though implicit in f, is easily solved by iteration or a direct solver. If only a calculator is available, the clever explicit formula given by Haaland [33] as

$$\frac{1}{f^{1/2}} \approx -1.8 \log \left[\frac{6.9}{\text{Re}_d} + \left(\frac{\varepsilon/d}{3.7} \right)^{1.11} \right] \qquad (6.49)$$

varies less than 2 percent from Eq. (6.48).

The shaded area in the Moody chart indicates the range where transition from laminar to turbulent flow occurs. There are no reliable friction factors in this range, $2000 < \text{Re}_{d,} < 4000$. Notice that the roughness curves are nearly horizontal in the fully rough regime to the right of the dashed line.

From tests with commercial pipes, recommended values for average pipe roughness are listed in Table 6.1.

EXAMPLE 6.6[2]

Compute the loss of head and pressure drop in 200 ft of horizontal 6-in-diameter asphalted cast iron pipe carrying water with a mean velocity of 6 ft/s.

---

[2]This example was given by Moody in his 1944 paper [8].

Solution

- *System sketch:*   See Fig. 6.7 for a horizontal pipe, with $\Delta z = 0$ and h_f proportional to Δp.
- *Assumptions:*   Turbulent flow, asphalted horizontal cast iron pipe, $d = 0.5$ ft, $L = 200$ ft.
- *Approach:*   Find Re_d and ε/d; enter the Moody chart, Fig. 6.13; find f, then h_f and Δp.
- *Property values:*   From Table A.3 for water, converting to BG units, $\rho = 998/515.38 = 1.94$ slug/ft^3, $\mu = 0.001/47.88 = 2.09$ E-5 slug/(ft-s).
- *Solution step 1:*   Calculate Re_d and the roughness ratio. As a crutch, Moody provided water and air values of "Vd" at the top of Fig. 6.13 to find Re_d. Instead, let's calculate it ourselves:

$$Re_d = \frac{\rho V d}{\mu} = \frac{(1.94 \text{ slug/ft}^3)(6 \text{ ft/s})(0.5 \text{ ft})}{2.09 \text{ E-5 slug/(ft} \cdot \text{s)}} \approx 279{,}000 \quad \text{(turbulent)}$$

From Table 6.1, for asphalted cast iron, $\varepsilon = 0.0004$ ft. Then calculate

$$\varepsilon/d = (0.0004 \text{ ft})/(0.5 \text{ ft}) = 0.0008$$

- *Solution step 2:*   Find the friction factor from the Moody chart or from Eq. (6.48). If you use the Moody chart, Fig. 6.13, you need practice. Find the line on the right side for $\varepsilon/d = 0.0008$ and follow it back to the left until it hits the vertical line for $Re_d \approx 2.79$ E5. Read, approximately, $f \approx 0.02$ [or compute $f = 0.0198$ from Eq. (6.48).]
- *Solution step 3:*   Calculate h_f from Eq. (6.10) and Δp from Eq. (6.8) for a horizontal pipe:

$$h_f = f\frac{L}{d}\frac{V^2}{2g} = (0.02)\left(\frac{200 \text{ ft}}{0.5 \text{ ft}}\right)\frac{(6 \text{ ft/s})^2}{2(32.2 \text{ ft/s}^2)} \approx 4.5 \text{ ft} \qquad\qquad Ans.$$

$$\Delta p = \rho g h_f = (1.94 \text{ slug/ft}^3)(32.2 \text{ ft/s}^2)(4.5 \text{ ft}) \approx 280 \text{ lbf/ft}^2 \qquad\qquad Ans.$$

- *Comments:*   In giving this example, Moody [8] stated that this estimate, even for clean new pipe, can be considered accurate only to about ± 10 percent.

EXAMPLE 6.7

Oil, with $\rho = 900$ kg/m^3 and $\nu = 0.00001$ m^2/s, flows at 0.2 m^3/s through 500 m of 200-mm-diameter cast iron pipe. Determine (a) the head loss and (b) the pressure drop if the pipe slopes down at 10° in the flow direction.

Solution

First compute the velocity from the known flow rate:

$$V = \frac{Q}{\pi R^2} = \frac{0.2 \text{ m}^3/\text{s}}{\pi(0.1 \text{ m})^2} = 6.4 \text{ m/s}$$

Then the Reynolds number is

$$Re_d = \frac{Vd}{\nu} = \frac{(6.4 \text{ m/s})(0.2 \text{ m})}{0.00001 \text{ m}^2/\text{s}} = 128{,}000$$

From Table 6.1, $\varepsilon = 0.26$ mm for cast iron pipe. Then

$$\frac{\varepsilon}{d} = \frac{0.26 \text{ mm}}{200 \text{ mm}} = 0.0013$$

Enter the Moody chart on the right at $\varepsilon/d = 0.0013$ (you will have to interpolate), and move to the left to intersect with Re $= 128,000$. Read $f \approx 0.0225$ [from Eq. (6.48) for these values we could compute $f = 0.0227$]. Then the head loss is

$$h_f = f \frac{L}{d} \frac{V^2}{2g} = (0.0225) \frac{500 \text{ m}}{0.2 \text{ m}} \frac{(6.4 \text{ m/s})^2}{2(9.81 \text{ m/s}^2)} = 117 \text{ m} \qquad Ans. \ (a)$$

From Eq. (6.9) for the inclined pipe,

$$h_f = \frac{\Delta p}{\rho g} + z_1 - z_2 = \frac{\Delta p}{\rho g} + L \sin 10°$$

or $\quad \Delta p = \rho g[h_f - (500 \text{ m}) \sin 10°] = \rho g(117 \text{ m} - 87 \text{ m})$

$$= (900 \text{ kg/m}^3)(9.81 \text{ m/s}^2)(30 \text{ m}) = 265,000 \text{ kg/(m} \cdot \text{s}^2) = 265,000 \text{ Pa} \quad Ans. \ (b)$$

EXAMPLE 6.8

Repeat Example 6.4 to see whether there is any possible turbulent flow solution for a smooth-walled pipe.

Solution

In Example 6.4 we estimated a head loss $h_f \approx 1.66$ ft, assuming laminar exit flow ($\alpha \approx 2.0$). For this condition the friction factor is

$$f = h_f \frac{d}{L} \frac{2g}{V^2} = (1.66 \text{ ft}) \frac{(0.004 \text{ ft})(2)(32.2 \text{ ft/s}^2)}{(1.0 \text{ ft})(3.32 \text{ ft/s})^2} \approx 0.0388$$

For laminar flow, $\text{Re}_d = 64/f = 64/0.0388 \approx 1650$, as we showed in Example 6.4. However, from the Moody chart (Fig. 6.13), we see that $f = 0.0388$ also corresponds to a *turbulent* smooth-wall condition, at $\text{Re}_d \approx 4500$. If the flow actually were turbulent, we should change our kinetic energy factor to $\alpha \approx 1.06$ [Eq. (3.77)], whence the corrected $h_f \approx 1.82$ ft and $f \approx 0.0425$. With f known, we can estimate the Reynolds number from our formulas:

$$\text{Re}_d \approx 3250 \ [\text{Eq. (6.38)}] \qquad \text{or} \qquad \text{Re}_d \approx 3400 \ [\text{Eq. (6.39}b)]$$

So the flow *might* have been turbulent, in which case the viscosity of the fluid would have been

$$\mu = \frac{\rho V d}{\text{Re}_d} = \frac{1.80(3.32)(0.004)}{3300} = 7.2 \times 10^{-6} \text{ slug/(ft} \cdot \text{s)} \qquad Ans.$$

This is about 55 percent less than our laminar estimate in Example 6.4. The moral is to keep the capillary-flow Reynolds number below about 1000 to avoid such duplicate solutions.

6.7 Four Types of Pipe Flow Problems

The Moody chart (Fig. 6.13) can be used to solve almost any problem involving friction losses in long pipe flows. However, many such problems involve considerable iteration and repeated calculations using the chart because the standard Moody chart is essentially a *head loss chart*. One is supposed to know all other variables, compute Re_d, enter the chart, find f, and hence compute h_f. This is one of four fundamental problems which are commonly encountered in pipe flow calculations:

1. Given d, L, and V or Q, ρ, μ, and g, compute the head loss h_f (head loss problem).
2. Given d, L, h_f, ρ, μ, and g, compute the velocity V or flow rate Q (flow rate problem).
3. Given Q, L, h_f, ρ, μ, and g, compute the diameter d of the pipe (sizing problem).
4. Given Q, d, h_f, ρ, μ, and g, compute the pipe length L.

Problems 1 and 4 are well suited to the Moody chart. We have to iterate to compute velocity or diameter because both d and V are contained in the ordinate *and* the abscissa of the chart.

There are two alternatives to iteration for problems of type 2 and type 3: (*a*) preparation of a suitable new Moody-type formula (see Probs. P6.68 and P6.73); or (*b*) the use of *solver* software, like Excel. Examples 6.9 and 6.11 include the Excel approach to these problems.

Type 2 Problem: Find the Flow Rate

Even though velocity (or flow rate) appears in both the ordinate and the abscissa on the Moody chart, iteration for turbulent flow is nevertheless quite fast because f varies so slowly with Re_d. In earlier editions, the writer rescaled the Colebrook formula (6.48) into a relation where Q could be calculated directly. That idea is now downsized to Problem P6.68. Example 6.9, which follows, is illustrated both by iteration and by an Excel solution.

EXAMPLE 6.9

Oil, with $\rho = 950$ kg/m³ and $\nu = 2$ E-5 m²/s, flows through a 30-cm-diameter pipe 100 m long with a head loss of 8 m. The roughness ratio is $\varepsilon/d = 0.0002$. Find the average velocity and flow rate.

Iterative Solution

By definition, the friction factor is known except for V:

$$f = h_f \frac{d}{L} \frac{2g}{V^2} = (8 \text{ m}) \left(\frac{0.3 \text{ m}}{100 \text{ m}} \right) \left[\frac{2(9.81 \text{ m/s}^2)}{V^2} \right] \qquad \text{or} \qquad fV^2 \approx 0.471 \quad \text{(SI units)}$$

To get started, we only need to guess f, compute $V = \sqrt{0.471/f}$, then get Re_d, compute a better f from the Moody chart, and repeat. The process converges fairly rapidly. A good first guess is the "fully rough" value for $\varepsilon/d = 0.0002$, or $f \approx 0.014$ from Fig. 6.13. The iteration would be as follows:

Guess $f \approx 0.014$, then $V = \sqrt{0.471/0.014} = 5.80$ m/s and $Re_d = Vd/\nu \approx 87,000$.
At $Re_d = 87,000$ and $\varepsilon/d = 0.0002$, compute $f_{new} \approx 0.0195$ [Eq. (6.48)].

New $f \approx 0.0195$, $V = \sqrt{0.471/0.0195} = 4.91$ m/s and $\text{Re}_d = Vd/\nu = 73{,}700$. At $\text{Re}_d = 73{,}700$ and $\varepsilon/d = 0.0002$, compute $f_{new} \approx 0.0201$ [Eq. (6.48)].

Better $f \approx 0.0201$, $V = \sqrt{0.471/0.0201} = 4.84$ m/s and $\text{Re}_d \approx 72{,}600$. At $\text{Re}_d = 72{,}600$ and $\varepsilon/d = 0.0002$, compute $f_{new} \approx 0.0201$ [Eq. (6.48)].

We have converged to three significant figures. Thus our iterative solution is

$$V = 4.84 \text{ m/s}$$

$$Q = V\left(\frac{\pi}{4}\right)d^2 = (4.84)\left(\frac{\pi}{4}\right)(0.3)^2 \approx 0.342 \text{ m}^3/\text{s} \qquad Ans.$$

The iterative approach is straightforward and not too onerous, so it is routinely used by engineers. Obviously this repetitive procedure is ideal for a personal computer.

Solution by Iteration with Excel

To iterate by repeated copying in Excel, we need five columns: velocity, flow rate, Reynolds number, an initial guess for f, and a calculation of f from $(\varepsilon/d) = 0.0002$ and the current value of Re_d. We modify our guess for f, in the next row, with the new value of f and calculate again, as shown in the following table. Since f is a slowly varying function, the process converges rapidly.

	V(m/s) = $(0.471/E1)^{\wedge}0.5$	Q(m³/s) = $(\pi/4)A1*0.3^{\wedge}2$	Re_d = $A1*0.3/0.00002$	f(Eq. 6.48)	f-guess
	A	B	C	D	E
1	5.8002	0.4100	87004	0.02011	0.01400
2	4.8397	0.3421	72596	0.02011	0.02011
3	**4.8397**	**0.3421**	72596	0.02011	0.02011

As shown in the hand-iterated method, the proper solution is $V = 4.84$ m/s and $Q = 0.342$ m²/s.

Type 3 Problem: Find the Pipe Diameter

The Moody chart is especially awkward for finding the pipe size, since d occurs in all three parameters f, Re_d, and ε/d. Further, it depends on whether we know the velocity or the flow rate. We cannot know both, or else we could immediately compute $d = \sqrt{4Q/(\pi V)}$.

Let us assume that we know the flow rate Q. Note that this requires us to redefine the Reynolds number in terms of Q:

$$\text{Re}_d = \frac{Vd}{\nu} = \frac{4Q}{\pi d \nu} \qquad (6.50)$$

If, instead, we knew the velocity V, we could use the first form for the Reynolds number. The writer finds it convenient to solve the Darcy friction factor correlation, Eq. (6.10), by solving for f:

$$f = h_f \frac{d}{L} \frac{2g}{V^2} = \frac{\pi^2}{8} \frac{gh_f \, d^5}{LQ^2} \qquad (6.51)$$

The following two examples illustrate the iteration.

EXAMPLE 6.10

Work Example 6.9 backward, assuming that $Q = 0.342 \text{ m}^3/\text{s}$ and $\varepsilon = 0.06$ mm are known but that d (30 cm) is unknown. Recall $L = 100$ m, $\rho = 950 \text{ kg/m}^3$, $\nu = 2$ E-5 m^2/s, and $h_f = 8$ m.

Iterative Solution

First write the diameter in terms of the friction factor:

$$f = \frac{\pi^2}{8} \frac{(9.81 \text{ m/s}^2)(8 \text{ m})d^5}{(100 \text{ m})(0.342 \text{ m}^3/\text{s})^2} = 8.28d^5 \quad \text{or} \quad d \approx 0.655 f^{1/5} \tag{1}$$

in SI units. Also write the Reynolds number and roughness ratio in terms of the diameter:

$$\text{Re}_d = \frac{4(0.342 \text{ m}^3/\text{s})}{\pi(2 \text{ E-5 m}^2/\text{s})d} = \frac{21,800}{d} \tag{2}$$

$$\frac{\varepsilon}{d} = \frac{6 \text{ E-5 m}}{d} \tag{3}$$

Guess f, compute d from (1), then compute Re_d from (2) and ε/d from (3), and compute a better f from the Moody chart or Eq. (6.48). Repeat until (fairly rapid) convergence. Having no initial estimate for f, the writer guesses $f \approx 0.03$ (about in the middle of the turbulent portion of the Moody chart). The following calculations result:

$$f \approx 0.03 \quad d \approx 0.655(0.03)^{1/5} \approx 0.325 \text{ m}$$

$$\text{Re}_d \approx \frac{21,800}{0.325} \approx 67,000 \quad \frac{\varepsilon}{d} \approx 1.85 \text{ E-4}$$

Eq. (6.48): $\qquad f_{\text{new}} \approx 0.0203 \quad \text{then} \quad d_{\text{new}} \approx 0.301 \text{ m}$

$$\text{Re}_{d,\text{new}} \approx 72,500 \quad \frac{\varepsilon}{d} \approx 2.0 \text{ E-4}$$

Eq. (6.48): $\qquad f_{\text{better}} \approx 0.0201 \quad \text{and} \quad d = 0.300 \text{ m}$ *Ans.*

The procedure has converged to the correct diameter of 30 cm given in Example 6.9.

Solution by Iteration with Excel

To iterate by repeated copying in Excel, we need five columns: ε/d, friction factor, Reynolds number, diameter d, and an initial guess for f. With the guess for f, we calculate $d \approx 0.655 f^{1/5}$, $\text{Re}_d \approx 21,800/d$, and $\varepsilon/d = (0.00006 \text{ m})/d$. Replace the guessed f with the new f. Thus Excel is doing the work of our previous hand calculation:

	$\varepsilon/d =$ 0.00006/d	f – Eq. (6.48)	$Re_d =$ 21,800/d	d(meters) = 0.655f^0.2	f-guess
	A	**B**	**C**	**D**	**E**
1	0.000185	0.0196	67111	0.325	0.0300
2	0.000201	0.0201	73106	0.298	0.0196
3	0.000200	0.0201	72677	0.300	0.0201
4	0.000200	0.0201	72706	**0.300**	0.0201

As shown in our hand-iterated method, the proper solution is $d = 0.300$ m.

EXAMPLE 6.11

A smooth plastic pipe is to be designed to carry 8 ft³/s of water at 20°C through 1000 ft of horizontal pipe with an exit at 15 lbf/in². The pressure drop is to be approximately 250 lbf/in². Determine (a) the proper diameter for this pipe and (b) whether a Schedule 40 is suitable if the pipe material has an allowable stress of 8000 lbf/in².

Solution by Excel Iteration

Assumptions: Steady turbulent flow, smooth walls. For water, take $\rho = 1.94$ slug/ft³ and $\mu = 2.09$ E-5 slug/(ft · s). With d unknown, use Eq. (6.51):

$$f = \frac{\pi^2}{8} \frac{gh_f d^5}{LQ^2} = \frac{\pi^2}{8} \frac{\Delta p d^5}{\rho L Q^2} = \frac{\pi^2}{8} \frac{(250 \times 144 \text{ lbf/ft}^2) d^5}{(1.94 \text{ slug/ft}^3)(1000 \text{ ft})(8 \text{ ft}^3/\text{s})^2} = 0.358\, d^5 \quad (1)$$

We know neither d nor f, but they are related by the Prandtl formula, Eq. (6.38):

$$\frac{1}{f^{1/2}} \approx 2.0 \log(Re_d f^{1/2}) - 0.8, \quad Re_d = \frac{\rho V d}{\mu} = \frac{4\rho Q}{\pi \mu d} = \frac{4(1.94)(8)}{\pi(2.09 \text{ E} - 5)d} = \frac{945,500}{d} \quad (2)$$

Part (a)   Equations (1) and (2) can be solved simultaneously for f and d. Using Excel iteration, we have four columns: a guessed $f = 0.02$, d from Eq. (1), Re_d from Eq. (2), and a better f from Eq. (6.38). The pipe is smooth, so we don't need roughness:

	f – Eq. (6.38)	$Re_d = 945500/C2$	$d = (D2/0.358)^0.2$	f-guess
	A	**B**	**C**	**D**
1	0.01009	1683574	0.562	0.02000
2	0.01047	1930316	0.490	0.01009
3	0.01044	1916418	0.493	0.01047
4	**0.01045**	**1917156**	**0.493**	0.01044

The process converges rapidly to:

$$Re_d \approx 1.92\ E6; \quad f \approx 0.01045; \quad d \approx 0.493 \text{ ft}$$

Take the next highest Schedule 40 diameter in Table 6.2: $d \approx 0.5$ ft = **6 in**   *Ans. (a)*

Part (b)   Check to see if Schedule 40 is strong enough. The maximum pressure occurs at the pipe entrance: $p_{max} = p_{exit} + \Delta p = 15 + 250 = 265$ lb/in^2. The schedule number is thus

$$\text{Schedule number} = (1000)\frac{(\text{maximum pressure})}{(\text{allowable stress})} = (1000)\left(\frac{265 \text{ psi}}{8000 \text{ psi}}\right) \approx 33$$

Schedule 30 is too weak for this pressure, so choose a **Schedule 40 pipe**.   *Ans. (b)*

Commercial Pipe Sizes

In solving a problem to find the pipe diameter, we should note that commercial pipes are made only in certain sizes. Table 6.2 gives nominal and actual sizes of pipes in the United States. The term *Schedule 40* is a measure of the pipe thickness and its resistance to stress caused by internal fluid pressure. If P is the internal fluid pressure and S is the allowable stress of the pipe material, then the schedule number = (1000) (P/S). Commercial schedules vary from 5 to 160, but 40 and 80 are by far the most popular. Example 6.11 is a typical application.

Type 4 Problem:
Find the Pipe Length

In designing piping systems, it is desirable to estimate the appropriate pipe length for a given pipe diameter, pump power, and flow rate. The pump head will match the piping head loss. If minor losses, Sec. 6.9, are neglected, the (horizontal) pipe length follows from Darcy's formula (6.10):

$$h_{pump} = \frac{\text{Power}}{\rho g Q} = h_f = f\frac{L}{d}\frac{V^2}{2g} \tag{6.52}$$

With Q, d, and ε known, we may compute Re$_d$ and f, after which L is obtained from the formula. Note that pump efficiency varies strongly with flow rate (Chap. 11). Thus, it is important to match pipe length to the pump's region of maximum efficiency.

Table 6.2 Nominal and Actual Sizes of Schedule 40 Pipe

Nominal size, in	Actual ID, in	Wall thickness, in
1/8	0.269	0.068
1/4	0.364	0.088
3/8	0.493	0.091
1/2	0.622	0.109
3/4	0.824	0.113
1	1.049	0.133
1-1/2	1.610	0.145
2	2.067	0.154
2-1/2	2.469	0.203
3	3.068	0.216
4	4.026	0.237
5	5.047	0.258
6	6.065	0.280

EXAMPLE 6.12

A pump delivers 0.6 hp to water at 68°F, flowing in a 6-in-diameter asphalted cast iron horizontal pipe at $V = 6$ ft/s. What is the proper pipe length to match these conditions?

Solution

- *Approach:* Find h_f from the known power and find f from Re_d and ε/d. Then find L.
- *Water properties:* For water at 68°F, Table A.3, converting to BG units, $\rho = 1.94$ slug/ft^3 and $\mu = 2.09$ E-5 slug/(ft $-$ s).
- *Pipe roughness:* From Table 6.1 for asphalted cast iron, $\varepsilon = 0.0004$ ft.
- *Solution step 1:* Find the pump head from the flow rate and the pump power:

$$Q = AV = \frac{\pi}{4}(0.5 \text{ ft})^2\left(6\,\frac{\text{ft}}{\text{s}}\right) = 1.18\,\frac{\text{ft}^3}{\text{s}}$$

$$h_{\text{pump}} = \frac{\text{Power}}{\rho g Q} = \frac{(0.6 \text{ hp})[550(\text{ft} \cdot \text{lbf})/(\text{s} \cdot \text{hp})]}{(1.94 \text{ slug/ft}^3)(32.2 \text{ ft/s}^2)(1.18 \text{ ft}^3/\text{s})} = 4.48 \text{ ft}$$

- *Solution step 2:* Compute the friction factor from the Colebrook formula, Eq. (6.48):

$$Re_d = \frac{\rho V d}{\mu} = \frac{(1.94)(6)(0.5)}{2.09 \text{ E}-5} = 278{,}500 \qquad \frac{\varepsilon}{d} = \frac{0.0004 \text{ ft}}{0.5 \text{ ft}} = 0.0008$$

$$\frac{1}{\sqrt{f}} \approx -2.0 \log_{10}\left(\frac{\varepsilon/d}{3.7} + \frac{2.51}{Re_d\sqrt{f}}\right) \quad \text{yields} \quad f = 0.0198$$

- *Solution step 3:* Find the pipe length from the Darcy formula (6.10):

$$h_p = h_f = 4.48 \text{ ft} = f\frac{L}{d}\frac{V^2}{2g} = (0.0198)\left(\frac{L}{0.5 \text{ ft}}\right)\frac{(6 \text{ ft/s})^2}{2(32.2 \text{ ft/s}^2)}$$

$$\text{Solve for } L \approx 203 \text{ ft} \qquad \textit{Ans.}$$

- *Comment:* This is Moody's problem (Example 6.6) turned around so that the length is unknown.

6.8 Flow in Noncircular Ducts[3]

If the duct is noncircular, the analysis of fully developed flow follows that of the circular pipe but is more complicated algebraically. For laminar flow, one can solve the exact equations of continuity and momentum. For turbulent flow, the logarithm law velocity profile can be used, or (better and simpler) the hydraulic diameter is an excellent approximation.

The Hydraulic Diameter

For a noncircular duct, the control volume concept of Fig. 6.7 is still valid, but the cross-sectional area A does not equal πR^2 and the cross-sectional perimeter wetted by the shear stress $\mathcal{P}$ does not equal $2\pi R$. The momentum equation (6.9a) thus becomes

$$\Delta p\, A + \rho g A\, \Delta L \sin\phi - \bar{\tau}_w \mathcal{P} \Delta L = 0$$

or
$$h_f = \frac{\Delta p}{\rho g} + \Delta z = \frac{\bar{\tau}_w}{\rho g}\frac{\Delta L}{A/\mathcal{P}} \qquad (6.53)$$

[3]This section may be omitted without loss of continuity.

Comparing this to Eq. (6.9b), we see that $A/\mathcal{P}$ takes the place of one-fourth of the pipe diameter for a circular cross section. We define the friction factor in terms of average shear stress:

$$f_{NCD} = \frac{8\bar{\tau}_w}{\rho V^2} \tag{6.54}$$

where NCD stands for noncircular duct and $V = Q/A$ as usual, Eq. (6.53) becomes

$$h_f = f\frac{L}{D_h}\frac{V^2}{2g} \tag{6.55}$$

This is equivalent to Eq. (6.10) for pipe flow except that d is replaced by D_h. Therefore, we customarily define the *hydraulic diameter* as

$$\boxed{D_h = \frac{4A}{\mathcal{P}} = \frac{4 \times \text{area}}{\text{wetted perimeter}}} \tag{6.56}$$

We should stress that the wetted perimeter includes all surfaces acted upon by the shear stress. For example, in a circular annulus, both the outer and the inner perimeter should be added.

We would therefore expect by dimensional analysis that this friction factor f, based on hydraulic diameter as in Eq. (6.55), would correlate with the Reynolds number and roughness ratio based on the hydraulic diameter

$$f = F\left(\frac{VD_h}{\nu}, \frac{\varepsilon}{D_h}\right) \tag{6.57}$$

and this is the way the data are correlated. But we should not necessarily expect the Moody chart (Fig. 6.13) to hold exactly in terms of this new length scale. And it does not, but it is surprisingly accurate:

$$f \approx \begin{cases} \dfrac{64}{\mathrm{Re}_{D_h}} & \pm 40\% \quad \text{laminar flow} \\[3mm] f_{\text{Moody}}\left(\mathrm{Re}_{D_h}, \dfrac{\varepsilon}{D_h}\right) & \pm 15\% \quad \text{turbulent flow} \end{cases} \tag{6.58}$$

Now let us look at some particular cases.

Flow between Parallel Plates

Probably the simplest noncircular duct flow is fully developed flow between parallel plates a distance $2h$ apart, as in Fig. 6.14. As noted in the figure, the width $b \gg h$, so the flow is essentially two-dimensional; that is, $u = u(y)$ only. The hydraulic diameter is

$$D_h = \frac{4A}{\mathcal{P}} = \lim_{b \to \infty} \frac{4(2bh)}{2b + 4h} = 4h \tag{6.59}$$

that is, twice the distance between the plates. The pressure gradient is constant, $(-dp/dx) = \Delta p/L$, where L is the length of the channel along the x axis.

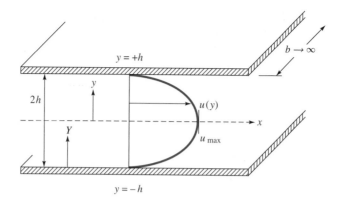

Fig. 6.14 Fully developed flow between parallel plates.

Laminar Flow Solution

The laminar solution was given in Sec. 4.10, in connection with Fig. 4.16b. Let us review those results here:

$$u = u_{max}\left(1 - \frac{y^2}{h^2}\right) \quad \text{where} \quad u_{max} = \frac{h^2}{2\mu}\frac{\Delta p}{L}$$

$$Q = \frac{2bh^3}{3\mu}\frac{\Delta p}{L}$$

$$V = \frac{Q}{A} = \frac{h^2}{3\mu}\frac{\Delta p}{L} = \frac{2}{3}u_{max} \tag{6.60}$$

$$\tau_w = \mu\left|\frac{du}{dy}\right|_{y=h} = h\frac{\Delta p}{L} = \frac{3\mu V}{h}$$

$$h_f = \frac{\Delta p}{\rho g} = \frac{3\mu L V}{\rho g h^2}$$

Now use the head loss to establish the laminar friction factor:

$$f_{lam} = \frac{h_f}{(L/D_h)(V^2/2g)} = \frac{96\mu}{\rho V(4h)} = \frac{96}{Re_{D_h}} \tag{6.61}$$

Thus, if we could not work out the laminar theory and chose to use the approximation $f \approx 64/Re_{D_h}$, we would be 33 percent low. The hydraulic-diameter approximation is relatively crude in laminar flow, as Eq. (6.58) states.

Just as in circular-pipe flow, the laminar solution above becomes unstable at about $Re_{D_h} \approx 2000$; transition occurs and turbulent flow results.

Turbulent Flow Solution

For turbulent flow between parallel plates, we can again use the logarithm law, Eq. (6.28), as an approximation across the entire channel, using not y but a wall coordinate Y, as shown in Fig. 6.14:

$$\frac{u(Y)}{u^*} \approx \frac{1}{\kappa}\ln\frac{Yu^*}{\nu} + B \qquad 0 < Y < h \tag{6.62}$$

This distribution looks very much like the flat turbulent profile for pipe flow in Fig. 6.11b, and the mean velocity is

$$V = \frac{1}{h}\int_0^h u\, dY = u^*\left(\frac{1}{\kappa}\ln\frac{hu^*}{\nu} + B - \frac{1}{\kappa}\right) \tag{6.63}$$

Recalling that $V/u^* = (8/f)^{1/2}$, we see that Eq. (6.63) is equivalent to a parallel-plate friction law. Rearranging and cleaning up the constant terms, we obtain

$$\frac{1}{f^{1/2}} \approx 2.0 \log{(\mathrm{Re}_{D_h} f^{1/2})} - 1.19 \qquad (6.64)$$

where we have introduced the hydraulic diameter $D_h = 4h$. This is remarkably close to the smooth-wall pipe friction law, Eq. (6.38). Therefore we conclude that the use of the hydraulic diameter in this turbulent case is quite successful. That turns out to be true for other noncircular turbulent flows also.

Equation (6.64) can be brought into exact agreement with the pipe law by rewriting it in the form

$$\frac{1}{f^{1/2}} = 2.0 \log{(0.64\,\mathrm{Re}_{D_h} f^{1/2})} - 0.8 \qquad (6.65)$$

Thus the turbulent friction is predicted most accurately when we use an effective diameter D_{eff} equal to 0.64 times the hydraulic diameter. The effect on f itself is much less, about 10 percent at most. We can compare with Eq. (6.66) for laminar flow, which predicted

Parallel plates:
$$D_{\mathrm{eff}} = \frac{64}{96}D_h = \frac{2}{3}D_h \qquad (6.66)$$

This close resemblance ($0.64D_h$ versus $0.667D_h$) occurs so often in noncircular duct flow that we take it to be a general rule for computing turbulent friction in ducts:

$$D_{\mathrm{eff}} = D_h = \frac{4A}{\mathcal{P}} \quad \text{reasonable accuracy}$$

$$D_{\mathrm{eff}} = D_h \frac{64}{(f\,\mathrm{Re}_{D_h})\text{laminar theory}} \quad \text{better accuracy} \qquad (6.67)$$

Jones [10] shows that the effective-laminar-diameter idea collapses all data for rectangular ducts of arbitrary height-to-width ratio onto the Moody chart for pipe flow. We recommend this idea for all noncircular ducts.

EXAMPLE 6.13

Fluid flows at an average velocity of 6 ft/s between horizontal parallel plates a distance of 2.4 in apart. Find the head loss and pressure drop for each 100 ft of length for $\rho = 1.9$ slugs/ft^3 and (a) $\nu = 0.00002$ ft^2/s and (b) $\nu = 0.002$ ft^2/s. Assume smooth walls.

Solution

Part (a)   The viscosity $\mu = \rho\nu = 3.8 \times 10^{-5}$ slug/(ft · s). The spacing is $2h = 2.4$ in $= 0.2$ ft, and $D_h = 4h = 0.4$ ft. The Reynolds number is

$$\mathrm{Re}_{D_h} = \frac{VD_h}{\nu} = \frac{(6.0 \text{ ft/s})(0.4 \text{ ft})}{0.00002 \text{ ft}^2/\text{s}} = 120,000$$

The flow is therefore turbulent. For reasonable accuracy, simply look on the Moody chart (Fig. 6.13) for smooth walls:

$$f \approx 0.0173 \quad h_f \approx f \frac{L}{D_h} \frac{V^2}{2g} = 0.0173 \frac{100}{0.4} \frac{(6.0)^2}{2(32.2)} \approx 2.42 \text{ ft} \qquad Ans. \ (a)$$

Since there is no change in elevation,

$$\Delta p = \rho g h_f = 1.9(32.2)(2.42) = 148 \text{ lbf/ft}^2 \qquad Ans. \ (a)$$

This is the head loss and pressure drop per 100 ft of channel. For more accuracy, take $D_{\text{eff}} = \frac{64}{96}D_h$ from laminar theory; then

$$\text{Re}_{\text{eff}} = \frac{64}{96}(120{,}000) = 80{,}000$$

and from the Moody chart read $f \approx 0.0189$ for smooth walls. Thus a better estimate is

$$h_f = 0.0189 \frac{100}{0.4} \frac{(6.0)^2}{2(32.2)} = 2.64 \text{ ft}$$

and

$$\Delta p = 1.9(32.2)(2.64) = 161 \text{ lbf/ft}^2 \qquad Better \ ans. \ (a)$$

The more accurate formula predicts friction about 9 percent higher.

Part (a)

Compute $\mu = \rho \nu = 0.0038$ slug/(ft · s). The Reynolds number is $6.0(0.4)/0.002 = 1200$; therefore the flow is laminar, since Re is less than 2300.

You could use the laminar flow friction factor, Eq. (6.61)

$$f_{\text{lam}} = \frac{96}{\text{Re}_{D_h}} = \frac{96}{1200} = 0.08$$

from which

$$h_f = 0.08 \frac{100}{0.4} \frac{(6.0)^2}{2(32.2)} = 11.2 \text{ ft}$$

and

$$\Delta p = 1.9(32.2)(11.2) = 684 \text{ lbf/ft}^2 \qquad Ans. \ (b)$$

Alternately you can finesse the Reynolds number and go directly to the appropriate laminar flow formula, Eq. (6.60):

$$V = \frac{h^2}{3\mu} \frac{\Delta p}{L}$$

or

$$\Delta p = \frac{3(6.0 \text{ ft/s})[0.0038 \text{ slug/(ft} \cdot \text{s})](100 \text{ ft})}{(0.1 \text{ ft})^2} = 684 \text{ slugs/(ft} \cdot \text{s}^2) = 684 \text{ lbf/ft}^2$$

and

$$h_f = \frac{\Delta p}{\rho g} = \frac{684}{1.9(32.2)} = 11.2 \text{ ft}$$

Flow through a Concentric Annulus

Consider steady axial laminar flow in the annular space between two concentric cylinders, as in Fig. 6.15. There is no slip at the inner ($r = b$) and outer radius ($r = a$). For $u = u(r)$ only, the governing relation is Eq. (D.7) in Appendix D:

$$\frac{d}{dr}\left(r\mu \frac{du}{dr}\right) = Kr \qquad K = \frac{d}{dx}(p + \rho gz) \qquad (6.68)$$

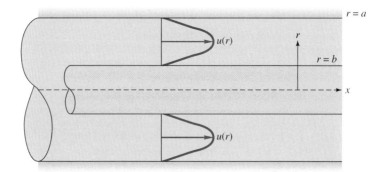

Fig. 6.15 Fully developed flow through a concentric annulus.

Integrate this twice:

$$u = \frac{1}{4}r^2\frac{K}{\mu} + C_1 \ln r + C_2$$

The constants are found from the two no-slip conditions:

$$u(r = a) = 0 = \frac{1}{4}a^2\frac{K}{\mu} + C_1 \ln a + C_2$$

$$u(r = b) = 0 = \frac{1}{4}b^2\frac{K}{\mu} + C_1 \ln b + C_2$$

The final solution for the velocity profile is

$$u = \frac{1}{4\mu}\left[-\frac{d}{dx}(p + \rho g z)\right]\left[a^2 - r^2 + \frac{a^2 - b^2}{\ln(b/a)}\ln\frac{a}{r}\right] \qquad (6.69)$$

The volume flow is given by

$$Q = \int_b^a u\,2\pi r\,dr = \frac{\pi}{8\mu}\left[-\frac{d}{dx}(p + \rho g z)\right]\left[a^4 - b^4 - \frac{(a^2 - b^2)^2}{\ln(a/b)}\right] \qquad (6.70)$$

The velocity profile $u(r)$ resembles a parabola wrapped around in a circle to form a split doughnut, as in Fig. 6.15.

It is confusing to base the friction factor on the wall shear because there are two shear stresses, the inner stress being greater than the outer. It is better to define f with respect to the head loss, as in Eq. (6.55),

$$f = h_f\frac{D_h}{L}\frac{2g}{V^2} \qquad \text{where } V = \frac{Q}{\pi(a^2 - b^2)} \qquad (6.71)$$

The hydraulic diameter for an annulus is

$$D_h = \frac{4\pi(a^2 - b^2)}{2\pi(a + b)} = 2(a - b) \qquad (6.72)$$

It is twice the clearance, rather like the parallel-plate result of twice the distance between plates [Eq. (6.59)].

Substituting h_f, D_h, and V into Eq. (6.71), we find that the friction factor for laminar flow in a concentric annulus is of the form

$$f = \frac{64\zeta}{\text{Re}_{D_h}} \qquad \zeta = \frac{(a - b)^2(a^2 - b^2)}{a^4 - b^4 - (a^2 - b^2)^2/\ln(a/b)} \qquad (6.73)$$

The dimensionless term ζ is a sort of correction factor for the hydraulic diameter. We could rewrite Eq. (6.73) as

Concentric annulus: $\qquad f = \dfrac{64}{\text{Re}_{\text{eff}}} \qquad \text{Re}_{\text{eff}} = \dfrac{1}{\zeta}\text{Re}_{D_h} \qquad (6.74)$

Some numerical values of $f\,\text{Re}_{D_h}$ and $D_{\text{eff}}/D_h = 1/\zeta$ are given in Table 6.3. Again, laminar annular flow becomes unstable at $\text{Re}_{D_h} \approx 2000$.

For turbulent flow through a concentric annulus, the analysis might proceed by patching together two logarithmic law profiles, one going out from the inner wall to meet the other coming in from the outer wall. We omit such a scheme here and proceed directly to the friction factor. According to the general rule proposed in Eq. (6.58), turbulent friction is predicted with excellent accuracy by replacing d in the Moody chart with $D_{\text{eff}} = 2(a - b)/\zeta$, with values listed in Table 6.3.[4] This idea includes roughness also (replace ε/d in the chart with $\varepsilon/D_{\text{eff}}$). For a quick design number with about 10 percent accuracy, one can simply use the hydraulic diameter $D_h = 2(a - b)$.

Table 6.3 Laminar Friction Factors for a Concentric Annulus

b/a	$f\,\text{Re}_{D_h}$	$D_{\text{eff}}/D_h = 1/\zeta$
0.0	64.0	1.000
0.00001	70.09	0.913
0.0001	71.78	0.892
0.001	74.68	0.857
0.01	80.11	0.799
0.05	86.27	0.742
0.1	89.37	0.716
0.2	92.35	0.693
0.4	94.71	0.676
0.6	95.59	0.670
0.8	95.92	0.667
1.0	96.0	0.667

EXAMPLE 6.14

What should the reservoir level h be to maintain a flow of 0.01 m³/s through the commercial steel annulus 30 m long shown in Fig. E6.14? Neglect entrance effects and take $\rho = 1000$ kg/m³ and $\nu = 1.02 \times 10^{-6}$ m²/s for water.

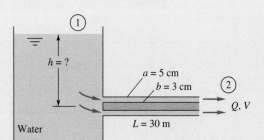

E6.14

Solution

- *Assumptions:* Fully developed annulus flow, minor losses neglected.
- *Approach:* Determine the Reynolds number, then find f and h_f and thence h.

---

[4]Jones and Leung [44] show that data for annular flow also satisfy the effective-laminar-diameter idea.

- *Property values:*   Given $\rho = 1000$ kg/m^3 and $\nu = 1.02$ E-6 m^2/s.
- *Solution step 1:*   Calculate the velocity, hydraulic diameter, and Reynolds number:

$$V = \frac{Q}{A} = \frac{0.01 \text{ m}^3/\text{s}}{\pi[(0.05 \text{ m})^2 - (0.03 \text{ m})^2]} = 1.99 \frac{\text{m}}{\text{s}}$$

$$D_h = 2(a - b) = 2(0.05 \text{ m} - 0.03 \text{ m}) = 0.04 \text{ m}$$

$$\text{Re}_{D_h} = \frac{VD_h}{\nu} = \frac{(1.99 \text{ m/s})(0.04 \text{ m})}{1.02 \text{ E-6 m}^2/\text{s}} = 78,000 \quad \text{(turbulent flow)}$$

- *Solution step 2:*   Apply the steady flow energy equation between sections 1 and 2:

$$\frac{p_1}{\rho g} + \frac{\alpha_1 V_1^2}{2g} + z_1 = \frac{p_2}{\rho g} + \frac{\alpha_2 V_2^2}{2g} + z_2 + h_f$$

or

$$h = \frac{\alpha_2 V_2^2}{2g} + h_f = \frac{V_2^2}{2g}\left(\alpha_2 + f\frac{L}{D_h}\right) \tag{1}$$

Note that $z_1 = h$. For turbulent flow, from Eq. (3.43c), we estimate $\alpha_2 \approx 1.03$

- *Solution step 3:*   Determine the roughness ratio and the friction factor. From Table 6.1, for (new) commercial steel pipe, $\varepsilon = 0.046$ mm. Then

$$\frac{\varepsilon}{D_h} = \frac{0.046 \text{ mm}}{40 \text{ mm}} = 0.00115$$

For a reasonable estimate, use Re_{D_h} to estimate the friction factor from Eq. (6.48):

$$\frac{1}{\sqrt{f}} \approx -2.0 \log_{10}\left(\frac{0.00115}{3.7} + \frac{2.51}{78,000\sqrt{f}}\right) \quad \text{solve for } f \approx 0.0232$$

For slightly better accuracy, we could use $D_{\text{eff}} = D_h/\zeta$. From Table 6.3, for $b/a = 3/5$, $1/\zeta = 0.67$. Then $D_{\text{eff}} = 0.67(40 \text{ mm}) = 26.8$ mm, whence $\text{Re}_{D_{\text{eff}}} = 52,300$, $\varepsilon/D_{\text{eff}} = 0.00172$, and $f_{\text{eff}} \approx 0.0257$. Using the latter estimate, we find the required reservoir level from Eq. (1):

$$h = \frac{V_2^2}{2g}\left(\alpha_2 + f_{\text{eff}}\frac{L}{D_h}\right) = \frac{(1.99 \text{ m/s})^2}{2(9.81 \text{ m/s})^2}\left[1.03 + 0.0257\frac{30 \text{ m}}{0.04 \text{ m}}\right] \approx 4.1 \text{ m} \quad \textit{Ans.}$$

- *Comments:*   Note that we do *not* replace D_h with D_{eff} in the head loss term fL/D_h, which comes from a momentum balance and *requires* hydraulic diameter. If we used the simpler friction estimate, $f \approx 0.0232$, we would obtain $h \approx 3.72$ m, or about 9 percent lower.

Other Noncircular Cross Sections

In principle, any duct cross section can be solved analytically for the laminar flow velocity distribution, volume flow, and friction factor. This is because any cross section can be mapped onto a circle by the methods of complex variables, and other powerful analytical techniques are also available. Many examples are given by White [3, pp. 112–115], Berker [11], and Olson [12]. Reference 34 is devoted entirely to laminar duct flow.

In general, however, most unusual duct sections have strictly academic and not commercial value. We list here only the rectangular and isosceles-triangular sections, in Table 6.4, leaving other cross sections for you to find in the references.

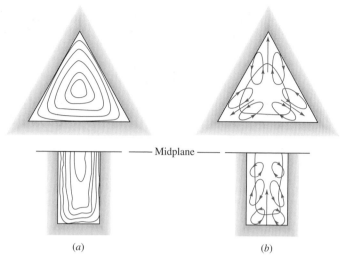

— Midplane —

(a)   (b)

Fig. 6.16 Illustration of secondary turbulent flow in noncircular ducts: (*a*) axial mean velocity contours; (*b*) secondary flow in-plane cellular motions. (*After J. Nikuradse, dissertation, Göttingen, 1926.*)

Table 6.4 Laminar Friction Constants fRe for Rectangular and Triangular Ducts

Rectangular		Isosceles triangle	
b/a	$f\,\mathrm{Re}_{D_h}$	θ, deg	$f\,\mathrm{Re}_{D_h}$
0.0	96.00	0	48.0
0.05	89.91	10	51.6
0.1	84.68	20	52.9
0.125	82.34	30	53.3
0.167	78.81	40	52.9
0.25	72.93	50	52.0
0.4	65.47	60	51.1
0.5	62.19	70	49.5
0.75	57.89	80	48.3
1.0	56.91	90	48.0

For turbulent flow in a duct of unusual cross section, one should replace d with D_h on the Moody chart if no laminar theory is available. If laminar results are known, such as Table 6.4, replace d with $D_{\text{eff}} = [64/(f\text{Re})]D_h$ for the particular geometry of the duct.

For laminar flow in rectangles and triangles, the wall friction varies greatly, being largest near the midpoints of the sides and zero in the corners. In turbulent flow through the same sections, the shear is nearly constant along the sides, dropping off sharply to zero in the corners. This is because of the phenomenon of turbulent *secondary flow*, in which there are nonzero mean velocities v and w in the plane of the cross section. Some measurements of axial velocity and secondary flow patterns are shown in Fig. 6.16, as sketched by Nikuradse in his 1926 dissertation. The secondary flow "cells" drive the mean flow toward the corners, so that the axial velocity contours are similar to the cross section and the wall shear is nearly constant. This is why the hydraulic-diameter concept is so successful for turbulent flow. Laminar flow in a straight noncircular duct has no secondary flow. An accurate theoretical prediction of turbulent secondary flow has yet to be achieved, although numerical models are often successful [36].

EXAMPLE 6.15

Air, with $\rho = 0.00237$ slug/ft^3 and $\nu = 0.000157$ ft^2/s, is forced through a horizontal square 9-by-9-in duct 100 ft long at 25 ft^3/s. Find the pressure drop if $\varepsilon = 0.0003$ ft.

Solution

Compute the mean velocity and hydraulic diameter:

$$V = \frac{25 \text{ ft}^3/\text{s}}{(0.75 \text{ ft})^2} = 44.4 \text{ ft/s}$$

$$D_h = \frac{4A}{\mathcal{P}} = \frac{4(81 \text{ in}^2)}{36 \text{ in}} = 9 \text{ in} = 0.75 \text{ ft}$$

From Table 6.4, for $b/a = 1.0$, the effective diameter is

$$D_{eff} = \frac{64}{56.91} D_h = 0.843 \text{ ft}$$

whence

$$Re_{eff} = \frac{V D_{eff}}{\nu} = \frac{44.4(0.843)}{0.000157} = 239,000$$

$$\frac{\varepsilon}{D_{eff}} = \frac{0.0003}{0.843} = 0.000356$$

From the Moody chart, read $f = 0.0177$. Then the pressure drop is

$$\Delta p = \rho g h_f = \rho g \left(f \frac{L}{D_h} \frac{V^2}{2g} \right) = 0.00237(32.2) \left[0.0177 \frac{100}{0.75} \frac{44.4^2}{2(32.2)} \right]$$

or

$$\Delta p = 5.5 \text{ lbf/ft}^2 \qquad\qquad Ans.$$

Pressure drop in air ducts is usually small because of the low density.

6.9 Minor or Local Losses in Pipe Systems

For any pipe system, in addition to the Moody-type friction loss computed for the length of pipe, there are additional so-called *minor losses* or *local losses* due to

1. Pipe entrance or exit.
2. Sudden expansion or contraction.
3. Bends, elbows, tees, and other fittings.
4. Valves, open or partially closed.
5. Gradual expansions or contractions.

The losses may not be so minor; for example, a partially closed valve can cause a greater pressure drop than a long pipe.

Since the flow pattern in fittings and valves is quite complex, the theory is very weak. The losses are commonly measured experimentally and correlated with the pipe flow parameters. The data, especially for valves, are somewhat dependent on the particular manufacturer's design, so that the values listed here must be taken as average design estimates [15, 16, 35, 43, 46].

The measured minor loss is usually given as a ratio of the head loss $h_m = \Delta p/(\rho g)$ through the device to the velocity head $V^2/(2g)$ of the associated piping system:

$$\text{Loss coefficient } K = \frac{h_m}{V^2/(2g)} = \frac{\Delta p}{\frac{1}{2}\rho V^2} \qquad (6.75)$$

Although K is dimensionless, it often is not correlated in the literature with the Reynolds number and roughness ratio but rather simply with the raw size of the pipe in, say, inches. Almost all data are reported for turbulent flow conditions.

A single pipe system may have many minor losses. Since all are correlated with $V^2/(2g)$, they can be summed into a single total system loss if the pipe has constant diameter:

$$\Delta h_{tot} = h_f + \Sigma h_m = \frac{V^2}{2g} \left(\frac{fL}{d} + \Sigma K \right) \qquad (6.76)$$

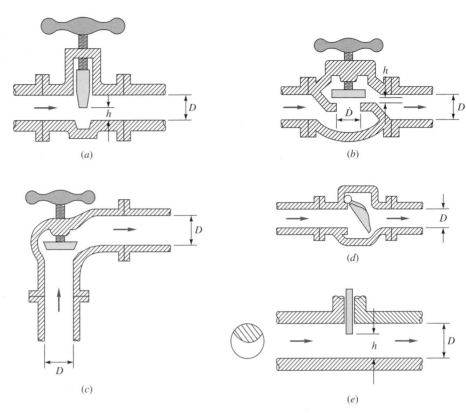

Fig. 6.17 Typical commercial valve geometries: (*a*) gate valve; (*b*) globe valve; (*c*) angle valve; (*d*) swing-check valve; (*e*) disk-type gate valve.

Note, however, that we must sum the losses separately if the pipe size changes so that V^2 changes. The length L in Eq. (6.76) is the total length of the pipe axis.

There are many different valve designs in commercial use. Figure 6.17 shows five typical designs: (*a*) the *gate,* which slides down across the section; (*b*) the *globe,* which closes a hole in a special insert; (*c*) the *angle,* similar to a globe but with a 90° turn; (*d*) the *swing-check* valve, which allows only one-way flow; and (*e*) the *disk,* which closes the section with a circular gate. The globe, with its tortuous flow path, has the highest losses when fully open. Many excellent details about these and other valves are given in the handbooks by Skousen [35] and Crane Co. [52].

Table 6.5 lists loss coefficients K for four types of valve, three angles of elbow fitting, and two tee connections. Fittings may be connected by either internal screws or flanges, hence the two listings. We see that K generally decreases with pipe size, which is consistent with the higher Reynolds number and decreased roughness ratio of large pipes. We stress that Table 6.5 represents losses *averaged among various manufacturers,* so there is an uncertainty as high as ±50 percent.

In addition, most of the data in Table 6.5 are relatively old [15, 16] and therefore based on fittings manufactured in the 1950s. Modern forged and molded fittings may yield somewhat different loss factors, often less than those listed in Table 6.5. An example, shown in Fig. 6.18*a*, gives recent data [48] for fairly short (bend-radius/elbow-diameter = 1.2) flanged 90° elbows. The elbow diameter was 1.69 in. Notice first that K is plotted versus Reynolds number, rather than versus the raw (dimensional) pipe

Table 6.5 Resistance Coefficients $K = h_m/[V^2/(2g)]$ for Open Valves, Elbows, and Tees

	Nominal diameter, in								
	Screwed				Flanged				
	$\frac{1}{2}$	1	2	4	1	2	4	8	20
Valves (fully open):									
Globe	14	8.2	6.9	5.7	13	8.5	6.0	5.8	5.5
Gate	0.30	0.24	0.16	0.11	0.80	0.35	0.16	0.07	0.03
Swing check	5.1	2.9	2.1	2.0	2.0	2.0	2.0	2.0	2.0
Angle	9.0	4.7	2.0	1.0	4.5	2.4	2.0	2.0	2.0
Elbows:									
45° regular	0.39	0.32	0.30	0.29					
45° long radius					0.21	0.20	0.19	0.16	0.14
90° regular	2.0	1.5	0.95	0.64	0.50	0.39	0.30	0.26	0.21
90° long radius	1.0	0.72	0.41	0.23	0.40	0.30	0.19	0.15	0.10
180° regular	2.0	1.5	0.95	0.64	0.41	0.35	0.30	0.25	0.20
180° long radius					0.40	0.30	0.21	0.15	0.10
Tees:									
Line flow	0.90	0.90	0.90	0.90	0.24	0.19	0.14	0.10	0.07
Branch flow	2.4	1.8	1.4	1.1	1.0	0.80	0.64	0.58	0.41

diameters in Table 6.5, and therefore Fig. 6.18a has more generality. Then notice that the K values of 0.23 ± 0.05 are significantly less than the values for 90° elbows in Table 6.5, indicating smoother walls and/or better design. One may conclude that (1) Table 6.5 data are probably conservative and (2) loss factors are highly dependent on actual design and manufacturing factors, with Table 6.5 serving only as a rough guide.

The valve losses in Table 6.5 are for the fully open condition. Losses can be much higher for a partially open valve. Figure 6.18b gives average losses for three valves

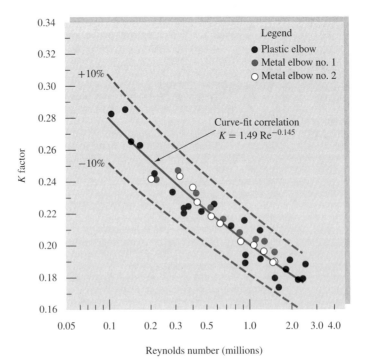

Fig. 6.18a Recent measured loss coefficients for 90° elbows. These values are less than those reported in Table 6.5. *(From Ref. 48, Source of Data R. D. Coffield.)*

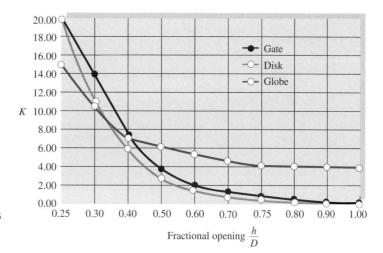

Fig. 6.18b Average loss coefficients for partially open valves (see sketches in Fig. 6.17).

(a)

Fig. 6.19 Performance of butterfly valves: (a) typical geometry (*Courtesy of Tyco Engineered Products and Services*); (b) loss coefficients for three different manufacturers.

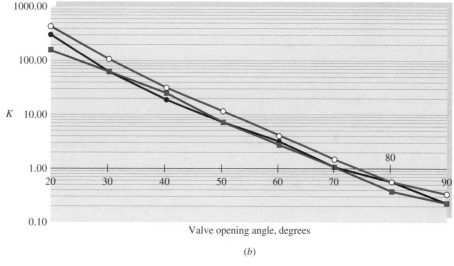

(b)

as a function of "percentage open," as defined by the opening-distance ratio h/D (see Fig. 6.17 for the geometries). Again we should warn of a possible uncertainty of ± 50 percent. Of all minor losses, valves, because of their complex geometry, are most sensitive to manufacturers' design details. For more accuracy, the particular design and manufacturer should be consulted [35].

The *butterfly* valve of Fig. 6.19a is a stem-mounted disk that, when closed, seats against an O-ring or compliant seal near the pipe surface. A single 90° turn opens the valve completely, hence the design is ideal for controllable quick-opening and quick-closing situations such as occur in fire protection and the electric power industry. However, considerable dynamic torque is needed to close these valves, and losses are high when the valves are nearly closed.

Figure 6.19b shows butterfly-valve loss coefficients as a function of the opening angle θ for turbulent flow conditions ($\theta = 0$ is closed). The losses are huge when the

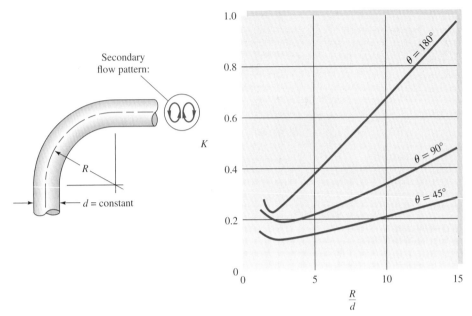

Fig. 6.20 Resistance coefficients for smooth-walled 45°, 90°, and 180° bends, at $\mathrm{Re}_d = 200{,}000$, after Ito [49].
Source: After H. Ito, "Pressure Losses in Smooth Pipe Bends," Journal of Basic Engineering, March 1960, pp. 131–143.

opening is small, and K drops off nearly exponentially with the opening angle. There is a factor of 2 spread among the various manufacturers. Note that K in Fig. 6.19*b* is, as usual, based on the average *pipe* velocity $V = Q/A$, not on the increased velocity of the flow as it passes through the narrow valve passage.

A bend or curve in a pipe, as in Fig. 6.20, always induces a loss larger than the simple straight-pipe Moody friction loss, due to flow separation on the curved walls and a swirling secondary flow arising from the centripetal acceleration. The smooth-wall loss coefficients K in Fig. 6.20, from the data of Ito [49], are for *total* loss, including Moody friction effects. The separation and secondary flow losses decrease with R/d, while the Moody losses increase because the bend length increases. The curves in Fig. 6.20 thus show a minimum where the two effects cross. Ito [49] gives a curve-fit formula for the 90° bend in turbulent flow:

$$90° \text{ bend: } K \approx 0.388\alpha \left(\frac{R}{d}\right)^{0.84} \mathrm{Re}_D^{-0.17} \quad \text{where } \alpha = 0.95 + 4.42\left(\frac{R}{d}\right)^{-1.96} \geq 1 \quad (6.80a)$$

The formula accounts for Reynolds number, which equals 200,000 in Fig. 6.20. Comprehensive reviews of curved-pipe flow, for both laminar and turbulent flow, are given by Berger et al. [53] and for 90° bends by Spedding et al. [54].

As shown in Fig. 6.21, entrance losses are highly dependent on entrance geometry, but exit losses are not. Sharp edges or protrusions in the entrance cause large zones of flow separation and large losses. A little rounding goes a long way, and a well-rounded entrance ($r = 0.2d$) has a nearly negligible loss $K = 0.05$. At a submerged exit, on the other hand, the flow simply passes out of the pipe into the large downstream reservoir and loses all its velocity head due to viscous dissipation. Therefore $K = 1.0$ for all *submerged exits,* no matter how well rounded.

If the entrance is from a finite reservoir, it is termed a *sudden contraction* (SC) between two sizes of pipe. If the exit is to finite-sized pipe, it is termed a *sudden expansion* (SE). The losses for both are graphed in Fig. 6.22. For the sudden expansion,

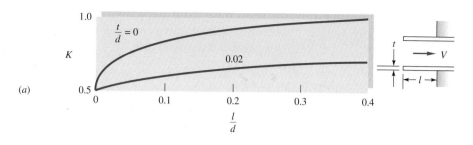

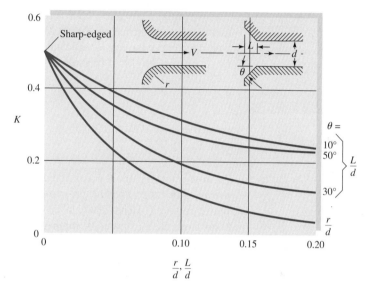

Fig. 6.21 Entrance and exit loss coefficients: (*a*) reentrant inlets; (*b*) rounded and beveled inlets. Exit losses are $K \approx 1.0$ for all shapes of exit (reentrant, sharp, beveled, or rounded).

Source: From ASHRAE Handbook-2012 Fundamentals, ASHRAE, Atlanta, GA, 2012.

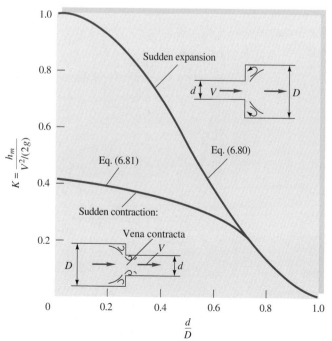

Fig. 6.22 Sudden expansion and contraction losses. Note that the loss is based on velocity head in the small pipe.

the shear stress in the corner separated flow, or deadwater region, is negligible, so that a control volume analysis between the expansion section and the end of the separation zone gives a theoretical loss:

$$K_{SE} = \left(1 - \frac{d^2}{D^2}\right)^2 = \frac{h_m}{V^2/(2g)}$$ (6.77)

Note that K is based on the velocity head in the small pipe. Equation (6.77) is in excellent agreement with experiment.

For the sudden contraction, however, flow separation in the downstream pipe causes the main stream to contract through a minimum diameter d_{min}, called the *vena contracta,* as sketched in Fig. 6.22. Because the theory of the vena contracta is not well developed, the loss coefficient in the figure for sudden contraction is experimental. It fits the empirical formula

$$K_{SC} \approx 0.42\left(1 - \frac{d^2}{D^2}\right)$$ (6.78)

up to the value $d/D = 0.76$, above which it merges into the sudden-expansion prediction, Eq. (6.77).

Gradual Expansion—The Diffuser   As flow enters a gradual expansion or *diffuser,* such as the conical geometry of Fig. 6.23, the velocity drops and the pressure rises. An efficient diffuser reduces the pumping power required. Head loss can be large, due to flow separation on the walls, if the cone angle is too great. A thinner entrance boundary layer, as in Fig. 6.6, causes

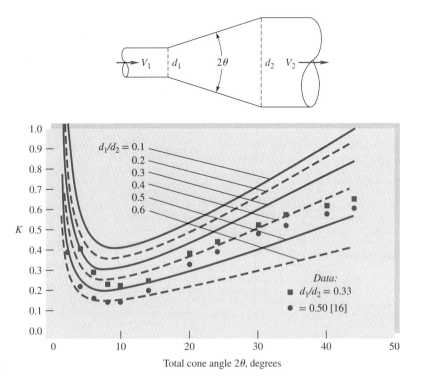

Fig. 6.23 Flow losses in a gradual conical expansion region, as calculated from Gibson's suggestion [15, 50], Eq. (6.79), for a smooth wall.

a slightly smaller loss than a fully developed inlet flow. The flow loss is a combination of nonideal pressure recovery plus wall friction. Some correlating curves are shown in Fig. 6.23. The loss coefficient K is based on the velocity head in the inlet (small) pipe and depends upon cone angle 2θ and the diffuser diameter ratio d_1/d_2. There is scatter in the reported data [15, 16]. The curves in Fig. 6.23 are based on a correlation by A. H. Gibson [50], cited in Ref. 15:

$$K_{\text{diffuser}} = \frac{h_m}{V_1^2/(2\,g)} \approx 2.61 \sin\theta \left(1 - \frac{d^2}{D^2}\right)^2 + f_{\text{avg}} \frac{L}{d_{\text{avg}}} \quad \text{for} \quad 2\theta \le 45° \quad (6.79)$$

For large angles, $2\theta > 45°$, drop the coefficient ($2.61 \sin\theta$), which leaves us with a loss equivalent to the sudden expansion of Eq. (6.77). As seen, the formula is in reasonable agreement with the data from Ref. 16. The minimum loss lies in the region $5° < 2\theta < 15°$, which is the best geometry for an efficient diffuser. For angles less than $5°$, the diffuser is too long and has too much friction. Angles greater than $15°$ cause flow separation, resulting in poor pressure recovery. Professor Gordon Holloway provided the writer a recent example, where an improved diffuser design reduced the power requirement of a wind tunnel by 40 percent (100 hp decrease!). We shall look again at diffusers in Sec. 6.11, using the data of Ref. 14.

For a gradual *contraction,* the loss is very small, as seen from the following experimental values [15]:

Contraction cone angle 2θ, deg	30	45	60
K for gradual contraction	0.02	0.04	0.07

References 15, 16, 43, and 46 contain additional data on minor losses.

EXAMPLE 6.16

Water, $\rho = 1.94$ slugs/ft^3 and $\nu = 0.000011$ ft^2/s, is pumped between two reservoirs at 0.2 ft^3/s through 400 ft of 2-in-diameter pipe and several minor losses, as shown in Fig. E6.16. The roughness ratio is $\epsilon/d = 0.001$. Compute the pump horsepower required.

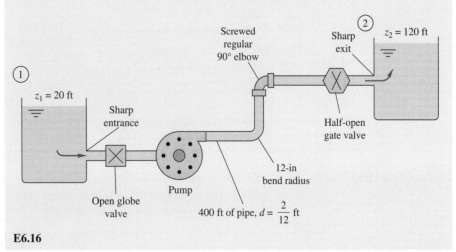

E6.16

Solution

Write the steady flow energy equation between sections 1 and 2, the two reservoir surfaces:

$$\frac{p_1}{\rho g} + \frac{V_1^2}{2g} + z_1 = \left(\frac{p_2}{\rho g} + \frac{V_2^2}{2g} + z_2\right) + h_f + \sum h_m - h_p$$

where h_p is the head increase across the pump. But since $p_1 = p_2$ and $V_1 = V_2 \approx 0$, solve for the pump head:

$$h_p = z_2 - z_1 + h_f + \sum h_m = 120 \text{ ft} - 20 \text{ ft} + \frac{V^2}{2g}\left(\frac{fL}{d} + \sum K\right) \qquad (1)$$

Now with the flow rate known, calculate

$$V = \frac{Q}{A} = \frac{0.2 \text{ ft}^3/\text{s}}{\frac{1}{4}\pi(\frac{2}{12}\text{ ft})^2} = 9.17 \text{ ft/s}$$

Now list and sum the minor loss coefficients:

Loss	K
Sharp entrance (Fig. 6.21)	0.5
Open globe valve (2 in, Table 6.5)	6.9
12-in bend (Fig. 6.20)	0.25
Regular 90° elbow (Table 6.5)	0.95
Half-closed gate valve (from Fig. 6.18b)	3.8
Sharp exit (Fig. 6.21)	1.0
	$\Sigma K = 13.4$

Calculate the Reynolds number and pipe friction factor:

$$\text{Re}_d = \frac{Vd}{\nu} = \frac{9.17(\frac{2}{12})}{0.000011} = 139{,}000$$

For $\varepsilon/d = 0.001$, from the Moody chart read $f = 0.0216$. Substitute into Eq. (1):

$$h_p = 100 \text{ ft} + \frac{(9.17 \text{ ft/s})^2}{2(32.2 \text{ ft/s}^2)}\left[\frac{0.0216(400)}{\frac{2}{12}} + 13.4\right]$$

$$= 100 \text{ ft} + 85 \text{ ft} = 185 \text{ ft pump head}$$

The pump must provide a power to the water of

$$P = \rho g Q h_p = [1.94(32.2) \text{ lbf/ft}^3](0.2 \text{ ft}^3/\text{s})(185 \text{ ft}) \approx 2300 \text{ ft} \cdot \text{lbf/s}$$

The conversion factor is 1 hp = 550 ft · lbf/s. Therefore

$$P = \frac{2300}{550} = 4.2 \text{ hp} \qquad\qquad Ans.$$

Allowing for an efficiency of 70 to 80 percent, a pump is needed with an input of about 6 hp.

Laminar Flow Minor Losses

The data in Table 6.5 are for *turbulent* flow in fittings. If the flow is laminar, a different form of loss occurs, which is proportional to V, not V^2. By analogy with Eqs. (6.12) for Poiseuille flow, the laminar minor loss takes the form

$$K_{\text{lam}} = \frac{\Delta p_{\text{loss}}\, d}{\mu V}$$

Laminar minor losses are just beginning to be studied, due to increased interest in micro- and nano-flows in tubes. They can be substantial, comparable to the Poiseuille loss. Professor Bruce Finlayson, of the University of Washington, kindly provided the writer with new data in the following table:

Laminar Minor Loss Coefficients K_{lam} in Tube Fittings for $1 \leq Re_d \leq 10$ [60]

Type of fitting	K_{lam}
45° bend, long radius	0.2
90° bend, short radius	0.5
90° bend, long radius	0.36
2:1 pipe contraction	7.3
3:1 pipe contraction	8.6
4:1 pipe contraction	9.0
2:1 pipe expansion	3.1
3:1 pipe expansion	4.1
4:1 pipe expansion	4.5

For the bends in the table, K_{lam} is the excess loss after calculating Poiseuille flow around the centerline of the bend. For the contractions and expansion, K_{lam} is based upon the velocity in the smaller section.

6.10 Multiple-Pipe Systems[5]

If you can solve the equations for one-pipe systems, you can solve them all; but when systems contain two or more pipes, certain basic rules make the calculations very smooth. Any resemblance between these rules and the rules for handling electric circuits is not coincidental.

Figure 6.24 shows three examples of multiple-pipe systems.

Pipes in Series

The first is a set of three (or more) pipes in series. Rule 1 is that the flow rate is the same in all pipes:

$$Q_1 = Q_2 = Q_3 = const \tag{6.80}$$

or

$$V_1 d_1^2 = V_2 d_2^2 = V_3 d_3^2 \tag{6.81}$$

Rule 2 is that the total head loss through the system equals the sum of the head loss in each pipe:

$$\Delta h_{A \to B} = \Delta h_1 + \Delta h_2 + \Delta h_3 \tag{6.82}$$

In terms of the friction and minor losses in each pipe, we could rewrite this as

$$\Delta h_{A \to B} = \frac{V_1^2}{2g}\left(\frac{f_1 L_1}{d_1} + \sum K_1\right) + \frac{V_2^2}{2g}\left(\frac{f_2 L_2}{d_2} + \sum K_2\right)$$
$$+ \frac{V_3^2}{2g}\left(\frac{f_3 L_3}{d_3} + \sum K_3\right) \tag{6.83}$$

and so on for any number of pipes in the series. Since V_2 and V_3 are proportional to V_1 from Eq. (6.81), Eq. (6.83) is of the form

$$\Delta h_{A \to B} = \frac{V_1^2}{2g}(\alpha_0 + \alpha_1 f_1 + \alpha_2 f_2 + \alpha_3 f_3) \tag{6.84}$$

[5]This section may be omitted without loss of continuity.

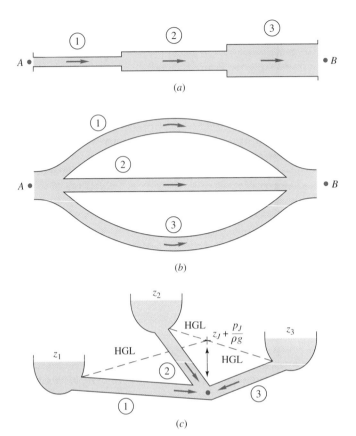

Fig. 6.24 Examples of multiple-pipe systems: (*a*) pipes in series; (*b*) pipes in parallel; (*c*) the three-reservoir junction problem.

where the α_i are dimensionless constants. If the flow rate is given, we can evaluate the right-hand side and hence the total head loss. If the head loss is given, a little iteration is needed, since f_1, f_2, and f_3 all depend on V_1 through the Reynolds number. Begin by calculating f_1, f_2, and f_3, assuming fully rough flow, and the solution for V_1 will converge with one or two iterations.

EXAMPLE 6.17

Given is a three-pipe series system, as in Fig. 6.24a. The total pressure drop is $p_A - p_B = 150,000$ Pa, and the elevation drop is $z_A - z_B = 5$ m. The pipe data are

Pipe	L, m	d, cm	ε, mm	ε/d
1	100	8	0.24	0.003
2	150	6	0.12	0.002
3	80	4	0.20	0.005

The fluid is water, $\rho = 1000$ kg/m^3 and $\nu = 1.02 \times 10^{-6}$ m^2/s. Calculate the flow rate Q in m^3/h through the system.

Solution

The total head loss across the system is

$$\Delta h_{A \to B} = \frac{p_A - p_B}{\rho g} + z_A - z_B = \frac{150{,}000}{1000(9.81)} + 5 \text{ m} = 20.3 \text{ m}$$

From the continuity relation (6.84) the velocities are

$$V_2 = \frac{d_1^2}{d_2^2} V_1 = \frac{16}{9} V_1 \qquad V_3 = \frac{d_1^2}{d_3^2} V_1 = 4 V_1$$

and

$$\text{Re}_2 = \frac{V_2 d_2}{V_1 d_1} \text{Re}_1 = \frac{4}{3} \text{Re}_1 \qquad \text{Re}_3 = 2 \text{Re}_1$$

Neglecting minor losses and substituting into Eq. (6.83), we obtain

$$\Delta h_{A \to B} = \frac{V_1^2}{2g} \left[1250 f_1 + 2500 \left(\frac{16}{9} \right)^2 f_2 + 2000(4)^2 f_3 \right]$$

or

$$20.3 \text{ m} = \frac{V_1^2}{2g} (1250 f_1 + 7900 f_2 + 32{,}000 f_3) \qquad (1)$$

This is the form that was hinted at in Eq. (6.84). It seems to be dominated by the third pipe loss $32{,}000 f_3$. Begin by estimating f_1, f_2, and f_3 from the Moody-chart fully rough regime:

$$f_1 = 0.0262 \qquad f_2 = 0.0234 \qquad f_3 = 0.0304$$

Substitute in Eq. (1) to find $V_1^2 \approx 2g(20.3)/(33 + 185 + 973)$. The first estimate thus is $V_1 = 0.58$ m/s, from which

$$\text{Re}_1 \approx 45{,}400 \qquad \text{Re}_2 = 60{,}500 \qquad \text{Re}_3 = 90{,}800$$

Hence, from the Moody chart,

$$f_1 = 0.0288 \qquad f_2 = 0.0260 \qquad f_3 = 0.0314$$

Substitution into Eq. (1) gives the better estimate

$$V_1 = 0.565 \text{ m/s} \qquad Q = \tfrac{1}{4} \pi d_1^2 V_1 = 2.84 \times 10^{-3} \text{ m}^3/\text{s}$$

or

$$Q = 10.2 \text{ m}^3/\text{h} \qquad \qquad Ans.$$

A second iteration gives $Q = 10.22$ m³/h, a negligible change.

Pipes in Parallel

The second multiple-pipe system is the *parallel* flow case shown in Fig. 6.24b. Here the pressure drop is the same in each pipe, and the total flow is the sum of the individual flows:

$$\Delta h_{A \to B} = \Delta h_1 = \Delta h_2 = \Delta h_3 \qquad (6.85a)$$
$$Q = Q_1 + Q_2 + Q_3 \qquad (6.85b)$$

If the total head loss is known, it is straightforward to solve for Q_i in each pipe and sum them, as will be seen in Example 6.18. The reverse problem, of determining ΣQ_i when h_f is known, requires iteration. Each pipe is related to h_f by the Moody relation $h_f = f(L/d)(V^2/2g) = f Q^2/C$, where $C = \pi^2 g d^5 / 8L$. Thus each pipe has nearly quadratic nonlinear parallel resistance, and head loss is related to total flow rate by

$$h_f = \frac{Q^2}{\left(\Sigma \sqrt{C_i / f_i} \right)^2} \qquad \text{where} \quad C_i = \frac{\pi^2 g d_i^5}{8 L_i} \qquad (6.86)$$

Since the f_i vary with Reynolds number and roughness ratio, one begins Eq. (6.86) by guessing values of f_i (fully rough values are recommended) and calculating a first estimate of h_f. Then each pipe yields a flow-rate estimate $Q_i \approx (C_i h_f/f_i)^{1/2}$ and hence a new Reynolds number and a better estimate of f_i. Then repeat Eq. (6.86) to convergence.

It should be noted that both of these parallel-pipe cases—finding either ΣQ or h_f—are easily solved by Excel if reasonable guesses are given.

EXAMPLE 6.18

Assume that the same three pipes in Example 6.17 are now in parallel with the same total head loss of 20.3 m. Compute the total flow rate Q, neglecting minor losses.

Solution

From Eq. (6.85a) we can solve for each V separately:

$$20.3 \text{ m} = \frac{V_1^2}{2g} 1250 f_1 = \frac{V_2^2}{2g} 2500 f_2 = \frac{V_3^2}{2g} 2000 f_3 \tag{1}$$

Guess fully rough flow in pipe 1: $f_1 = 0.0262$, $V_1 = 3.49$ m/s; hence $Re_1 = V_1 d_1/\nu = 273{,}000$. From the Moody chart read $f_1 = 0.0267$; recompute $V_1 = 3.46$ m/s, $Q_1 = 62.5$ m³/h.

Next guess for pipe 2: $f_2 \approx 0.0234$, $V_2 \approx 2.61$ m/s; then $Re_2 = 153{,}000$, and hence $f_2 = 0.0246$, $V_2 = 2.55$ m/s, $Q_2 = 25.9$ m³/h.

Finally guess for pipe 3: $f_3 \approx 0.0304$, $V_3 \approx 2.56$ m/s; then $Re_3 = 100{,}000$, and hence $f_3 = 0.0313$, $V_3 = 2.52$ m/s, $Q_3 = 11.4$ m³/h.

This is satisfactory convergence. The total flow rate is

$$Q = Q_1 + Q_2 + Q_3 = 62.5 + 25.9 + 11.4 = 99.8 \text{ m}^3/\text{h} \qquad Ans.$$

These three pipes carry 10 times more flow in parallel than they do in series.

This example may be solved by Excel iteration using the Colebrook-formula procedure outlined in Ex. 6.9. Each pipe is a separate iteration of friction factor, Reynolds number, and flow rate. The pipes are rough, so only one iteration is needed. Here are the Excel results:

	A	B	C	D	E	F
			Ex. 6.18 – Pipe 1			
	Re_1	$(\varepsilon/d)_1$	V_1 – m/s	Q_1 – m³/h	f_1	f_1-guess
1	313053	0.003	3.991	72.2	0.0267	0.0200
2	271100	0.003	3.457	**62.5**	0.0267	0.0267
			Ex. 6.18 – Pipe 2			
	Re_2	$(\varepsilon/d)_2$	V_2 – m/s	Q_2 – m³/h	f_2	f_2-guess
1	166021	0.002	2.822	28.7	0.0246	0.0200
2	149739	0.002	2.546	**25.9**	0.0246	0.0246
			Ex. 6.18 – Pipe 3			
	Re_3	$(\varepsilon/d)_3$	V_3 – m/s	Q_3 – m³/h	f_3	f_3-guess
1	123745	0.005	3.155	14.3	0.0313	0.0200
2	98891	0.005	2.522	**11.4**	0.0313	0.0313

Thus, as in the hand calculations, the total flow rate = 62.5 + 25.9 + 11.4 = **99.8** m³/h. *Ans.*

Three-Reservoir Junction

Consider the third example of a *three-reservoir pipe junction,* as in Fig. 6.24c. If all flows are considered positive toward the junction, then

$$Q_1 + Q_2 + Q_3 = 0 \qquad (6.87)$$

which obviously implies that one or two of the flows must be away from the junction. The pressure must change through each pipe so as to give the same static pressure p_J at the junction. In other words, let the HGL at the junction have the elevation

$$h_J = z_J + \frac{p_J}{\rho g}$$

where p_J is in gage pressure for simplicity. Then the head loss through each, assuming $p_1 = p_2 = p_3 = 0$ (gage) at each reservoir surface, must be such that

$$\Delta h_1 = \frac{V_1^2}{2g} \frac{f_1 L_1}{d_1} = z_1 - h_J$$

$$\Delta h_2 = \frac{V_2^2}{2g} \frac{f_2 L_2}{d_2} = z_2 - h_J \qquad (6.88)$$

$$\Delta h_3 = \frac{V_3^2}{2g} \frac{f_3 L_3}{d_3} = z_3 - h_J$$

We guess the position h_J and solve Eqs. (6.88) for V_1, V_2, and V_3 and hence Q_1, Q_2, and Q_3, iterating until the flow rates balance at the junction according to Eq. (6.87). If we guess h_J too *high,* the sum $Q_1 + Q_2 + Q_3$ will be *negative* and the remedy is to reduce h_J, and vice versa.

EXAMPLE 6.19

Take the same three pipes as in Example 6.17, and assume that they connect three reservoirs at these surface elevations

$$z_1 = 20 \text{ m} \quad z_2 = 100 \text{ m} \quad z_3 = 40 \text{ m}$$

Find the resulting flow rates in each pipe, neglecting minor losses.

Solution

As a first guess, take h_J equal to the middle reservoir height, $z_3 = h_J = 40$ m. This saves one calculation ($Q_3 = 0$) and enables us to get the lay of the land:

Reservoir	h_J, m	$z_i - h_J$, m	f_i	V_i, m/s	Q_i, m³/h	L_i/d_i
1	40	−20	0.0267	−3.43	−62.1	1250
2	40	60	0.0241	4.42	45.0	2500
3	40	0		0	0	2000
					$\Sigma Q = -17.1$	

Since the sum of the flow rates toward the junction is negative, we guessed h_J too high. Reduce h_J to 30 m and repeat:

Reservoir	h_J, m	$z_i - h_J$, m	f_i	V_i, m/s	Q_i, m³/h
1	30	−10	0.0269	−2.42	−43.7
2	30	70	0.0241	4.78	48.6
3	30	10	0.0317	1.76	8.0
					$\Sigma Q = 12.9$

This is positive ΣQ, and so we can linearly interpolate to get an accurate guess: $h_J \approx 34.3$ m. Make one final list:

Reservoir	h_J, m	$z_i - h_J$, m	f_i	V_i, m/s	Q_i, m³/h
1	34.3	−14.3	0.0268	−2.90	−52.4
2	34.3	65.7	0.0241	4.63	47.1
3	34.3	5.7	0.0321	1.32	6.0
					$\Sigma Q = 0.7$

This is close enough; hence we calculate that the flow rate is 52.4 m³/h toward reservoir 3, balanced by 47.1 m³/h away from reservoir 1 and 6.0 m³/h away from reservoir 3.

One further iteration with this problem would give $h_J = 34.53$ m, resulting in $Q_1 = -52.8$, $Q_2 = 47.0$, and $Q_3 = 5.8$ m³/h, so that $\Sigma Q = 0$ to three-place accuracy. Pedagogically speaking, we would then be exhausted.

Pipe Networks

The ultimate case of a multipipe system is the *piping network* illustrated in Fig. 6.25. This might represent a water supply system for an apartment or subdivision

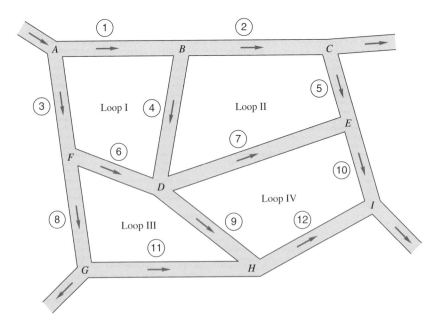

Fig. 6.25 Schematic of a piping network.

or even a city. This network is quite complex algebraically but follows the same basic rules:

1. The net flow into any junction must be zero.
2. The net pressure change around any closed loop must be zero. In other words, the HGL at each junction must have one and only one elevation.
3. All pressure changes must satisfy the Moody and minor-loss friction correlations.

By supplying these rules to each junction and independent loop in the network, one obtains a set of simultaneous equations for the flow rates in each pipe leg and the HGL (or pressure) at each junction. Solution may then be obtained by numerical iteration, as first developed in a hand calculation technique by Prof. Hardy Cross in 1936 [17]. Computer solution of pipe network problems is now quite common and is covered in at least one specialized text [18]. Network analysis is quite useful for real water distribution systems if well calibrated with the actual system head loss data.

6.11 Experimental Duct Flows: Diffuser Performance[6]

The Moody chart is such a great correlation for tubes of any cross section with any roughness or flow rate that we may be deluded into thinking that the world of internal flow prediction is at our feet. Not so. The theory is reliable only for ducts of constant cross section. As soon as the section varies, we must rely principally on experiment to determine the flow properties. As mentioned many times before, experimentation is a vital part of fluid mechanics.

Literally thousands of papers in the literature report experimental data for specific internal and external viscous flows. We have already seen several examples:

1. Vortex shedding from a cylinder (Fig. 5.2).
2. Drag of a sphere and a cylinder (Fig. 5.3).
3. Hydraulic model of a dam spillway (Fig. 5.9).
4. Rough-wall pipe flows (Fig. 6.12).
5. Secondary flow in ducts (Fig. 6.16).
6. Minor duct loss coefficients (Sec. 6.9).

Chapter 7 will treat a great many more external flow experiments, especially in Sec. 7.6. Here we shall show data for one type of internal flow, the diffuser.

Diffuser Performance

A diffuser, shown in Fig. 6.26a and b, is an expansion or area increase intended to reduce velocity in order to recover the pressure head of the flow. Rouse and Ince [6] relate that it may have been invented by customers of the early Roman (about 100 A.D.) water supply system, where water flowed continuously and was billed according to pipe size. The ingenious customers discovered that they could increase the flow rate at no extra cost by flaring the outlet section of the pipe.

Engineers have always designed diffusers to increase pressure and reduce kinetic energy of ducted flows, but until about 1950, diffuser design was a combination of art, luck, and vast amounts of empiricism. Small changes in design parameters caused large changes in performance. The Bernoulli equation seemed highly suspect as a useful tool.

---

[6]This section may be omitted without loss of continuity.

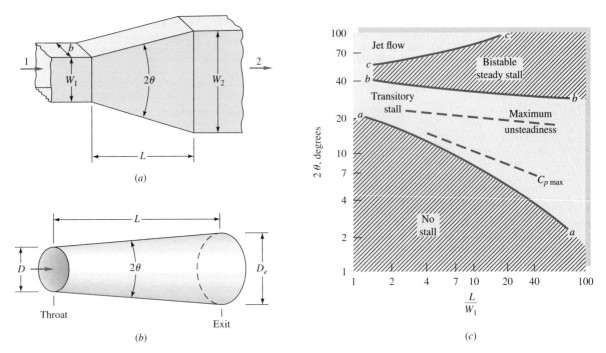

Fig. 6.26 Diffuser geometry and typical flow regimes: (*a*) geometry of a flat-walled diffuser; (*b*) geometry of a conical diffuser; (*c*) flat diffuser stability map. (*From Ref. 14, by permission of Creare, Inc.*)

Neglecting losses and gravity effects, the incompressible Bernoulli equation predicts that

$$p + \tfrac{1}{2}\rho V^2 = p_0 = \text{const} \tag{6.89}$$

where p_0 is the stagnation pressure the fluid would achieve if the fluid were slowed to rest ($V = 0$) without losses.

The basic output of a diffuser is the *pressure-recovery coefficient* C_p, defined as

$$C_p = \frac{p_e - p_t}{p_{0t} - p_t} \tag{6.90}$$

where subscripts e and t mean the exit and the throat (or inlet), respectively. Higher C_p means better performance.

Consider the flat-walled diffuser in Fig. 6.26a, where section 1 is the inlet and section 2 the exit. Application of Bernoulli's equation (6.89) to this diffuser predicts that

$$p_{01} = p_1 + \tfrac{1}{2}\rho V_1^2 = p_2 + \tfrac{1}{2}\rho V_2^2 = p_{02}$$

or

$$C_{p,\text{frictionless}} = 1 - \left(\frac{V_2}{V_1}\right)^2 \tag{6.91}$$

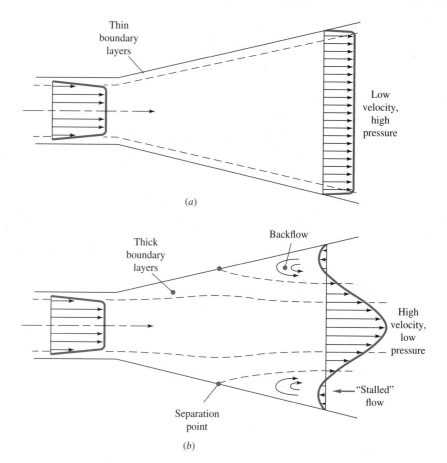

Thin
boundary
layers

Low
velocity,
high
pressure

(a)

Thick
boundary
layers

Backflow

High
velocity,
low
pressure

Separation
point

"Stalled"
flow

(b)

Fig. 6.27 Diffuser performance:
(a) ideal pattern with good
performance; (b) actual measured
pattern with boundary layer
separation and resultant poor
performance.

Meanwhile, steady one-dimensional continuity would require that

$$Q = V_1 A_1 = V_2 A_2 \tag{6.92}$$

Combining (6.91) and (6.92), we can write the performance in terms of the *area ratio*
$AR = A_2/A_1$, which is a basic parameter in diffuser design:

$$C_{p,\text{frictionless}} = 1 - (AR)^{-2} \tag{6.93}$$

A typical design would have $AR = 5:1$, for which Eq. (6.93) predicts $C_p = 0.96$, or
nearly full recovery. But, in fact, measured values of C_p for this area ratio [14] are
only as high as 0.86 and can be as low as 0.24.

The basic reason for the discrepancy is flow separation, as sketched in Fig. 6.27b.
The increasing pressure in the diffuser is an unfavorable gradient (Sec. 7.5), which
causes the viscous boundary layers to break away from the walls and greatly reduces
the performance. Computational fluid dynamics (CFD) can now predict this
behavior.

As an added complication to boundary layer separation, the flow patterns in a diffuser are highly variable and were considered mysterious and erratic until 1955, when Kline revealed the structure of these patterns with flow visualization techniques in a simple water channel.

A complete *stability map* of diffuser flow patterns was published in 1962 by Fox and Kline [21], as shown in Fig. 6.26c. There are four basic regions. Below line *aa* there is steady viscous flow, no separation, and moderately good performance. Note that even a very short diffuser will separate, or stall, if its half-angle is greater than 10°.

Between lines *aa* and *bb* is a transitory stall pattern with strongly unsteady flow. Best performance (highest C_p) occurs in this region. The third pattern, between *bb* and *cc*, is steady bistable stall from one wall only. The stall pattern may flip-flop from one wall to the other, and performance is poor.

The fourth pattern, above line *cc*, is *jet flow,* where the wall separation is so gross and pervasive that the mainstream ignores the walls and simply passes on through at nearly constant area. Performance is extremely poor in this region.

Dimensional analysis of a flat-walled or conical diffuser shows that C_p should depend on the following parameters:

1. Any two of the following geometric parameters:
   a. Area ratio AR $= A_2/A_1$ or $(D_e/D)^2$
   b. Divergence angle 2θ
   c. Slenderness L/W_1 or L/D
2. Inlet Reynolds number $Re_t = V_1 W_1/\nu$ or $Re_t = V_1 D/\nu$
3. Inlet Mach number $Ma_t = V_1/a_1$
4. Inlet boundary layer *blockage factor* $B_t = A_{BL}/A_1$, where A_{BL} is the wall area blocked, or displaced, by the retarded boundary layer flow in the inlet (typically B_t varies from 0.03 to 0.12)

A flat-walled diffuser would require an additional shape parameter to describe its cross section:

5. Aspect ratio AS $= b/W_1$

Even with this formidable list, we have omitted five possible important effects: inlet turbulence, inlet swirl, inlet profile vorticity, superimposed pulsations, and downstream obstruction, all of which occur in practical machinery applications.

The three most important parameters are AR, θ, and B. Typical performance maps for diffusers are shown in Fig. 6.28. For this case of 8 to 9 percent blockage, both the flat-walled and conical types give about the same maximum performance, $C_p = 0.70$, but at different divergence angles (9° flat versus 4.5° conical). Both types fall far short of the Bernoulli estimates of $C_p = 0.93$ (flat) and 0.99 (conical), primarily because of the blockage effect.

From the data of Ref. 14 we can determine that, in general, performance decreases with blockage and is approximately the same for both flat-walled and conical diffusers, as shown in Table 6.6. In all cases, the best conical diffuser is 10 to 80 percent longer than the best flat-walled design. Therefore, if length is limited in the design, the flat-walled design will give the better performance depending on duct cross section.

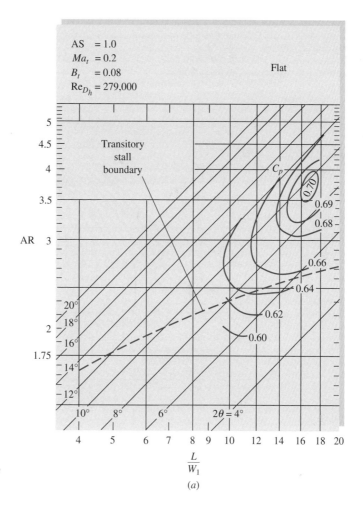

Fig. 6.28a Typical performance maps for flat-wall and conical diffusers at similar operating conditions: flat wall.

Source: From P. W. Runstadler, Jr., et al., "Diffuser Data Book," Crème Inc. Tech. Note 186, Hanover, NH, 1975., by permission of Creare, Inc.

The experimental design of a diffuser is an excellent example of a successful attempt to minimize the undesirable effects of adverse pressure gradient and flow separation.

Table 6.6 Maximum Diffuser Performance Data [14]

Source: From P. W. Runstadler, Jr., et al., "Diffuser Data Book," Crème Inc. Tech. Note 186, Hanover, NH, 1975.

Inlet blockage B_t	Flat-walled		Conical	
	C_p,max	L/W_1	C_p,max	L/d
0.02	0.86	18	0.83	20
0.04	0.80	18	0.78	22
0.06	0.75	19	0.74	24
0.08	0.70	20	0.71	26
0.10	0.66	18	0.68	28
0.12	0.63	16	0.65	30

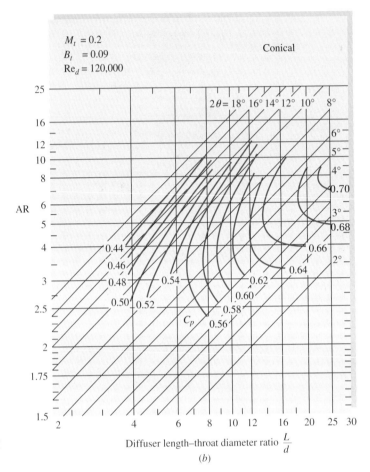

Fig. 6.28b Typical performance maps for flat-wall and conical diffusers at similar operating conditions: conical wall. *(From Ref. 14, by permission of Creare, Inc.)*

6.12 Fluid Meters

Almost all practical fluid engineering problems are associated with the need for an accurate flow measurement. There is a need to measure *local* properties (velocity, pressure, temperature, density, viscosity, turbulent intensity), *integrated* properties (mass flow and volume flow), and *global* properties (visualization of the entire flow field). We shall concentrate in this section on velocity and volume flow measurements.

We have discussed pressure measurement in Sec. 2.10. Measurement of other thermodynamic properties, such as density, temperature, and viscosity, is beyond the scope of this text and is treated in specialized books such as Refs. 22 and 23. Global visualization techniques were discussed in Sec. 1.11 for low-speed flows, and the special optical techniques used in high-speed flows are treated in Ref. 34 of Chap. 1. Flow measurement schemes suitable for open-channel and other free-surface flows are treated in Chap. 10.

Local Velocity Measurements

Velocity averaged over a small region, or point, can be measured by several different physical principles, listed in order of increasing complexity and sophistication:

1. Trajectory of floats or neutrally buoyant particles.
2. Rotating mechanical devices:
   a. Cup anemometer.
   b. Savonius rotor.
   c. Propeller meter.
   d. Turbine meter.
3. Pitot-static tube (Fig. 6.30).
4. Electromagnetic current meter.
5. Hot wires and hot films.
6. Laser-doppler anemometer (LDA).
7. Particle image velocimetry (PIV).

Some of these meters are sketched in Fig. 6.29.

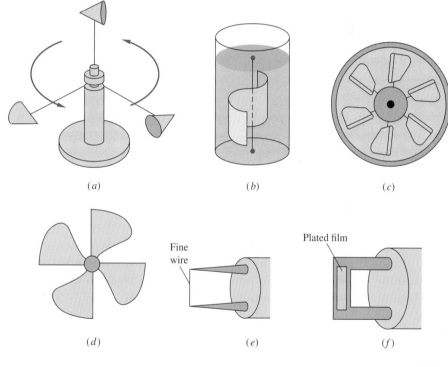

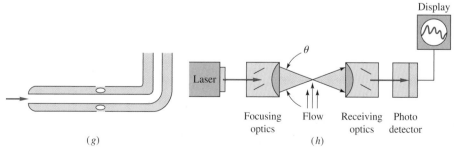

Fig. 6.29 Eight common velocity meters: (*a*) three-cup anemometer; (*b*) Savonius rotor; (*c*) turbine mounted in a duct; (*d*) free-propeller meter; (*e*) hot-wire anemometer; (*f*) hot-film anemometer; (*g*) pitot-static tube; (*h*) laser-doppler anemometer.

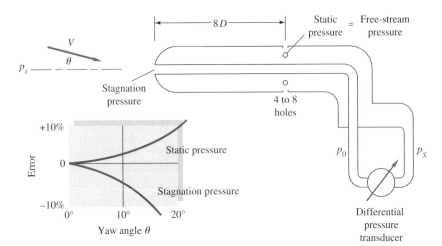

Fig. 6.30 Pitot-static tube for combined measurement of static and stagnation pressure in a moving stream.

Floats or Buoyant Particles.   A simple but effective estimate of flow velocity can be found from visible particles entrained in the flow. Examples include flakes on the surface of a channel flow, small neutrally buoyant spheres mixed with a liquid, or hydrogen bubbles. Sometimes gas flows can be estimated from the motion of entrained dust particles. One must establish whether the particle motion truly simulates the fluid motion. Floats are commonly used to track the movement of ocean waters and can be designed to move at the surface, along the bottom, or at any given depth [24]. Many official tidal current charts [25] were obtained by releasing and timing a floating spar attached to a length of string. One can release whole groups of spars to determine a flow pattern.

Rotating Sensors.   The rotating devices of Fig. 6.29a to d can be used in either gases or liquids, and their rotation rate is approximately proportional to the flow velocity. The cup anemometer (Fig. 6.29a) and Savonius rotor (Fig. 6.29b) always rotate the same way, regardless of flow direction. They are popular in atmospheric and oceanographic applications and can be fitted with a direction vane to align themselves with the flow. The ducted-propeller (Fig. 6.29c) and free-propeller (Fig. 6.29d) meters must be aligned with the flow parallel to their axis of rotation. They can sense reverse flow because they will then rotate in the opposite direction. All these rotating sensors can be attached to counters or sensed by electromagnetic or slip-ring devices for either a continuous or a digital reading of flow velocity. All have the disadvantage of being relatively large and thus not representing a "point."

Pitot-Static Tube.   A slender tube aligned with the flow (Figs. 6.29g and 6.30) can measure local velocity by means of a pressure difference. It has sidewall holes to measure the static pressure p_s in the moving stream and a hole in the front to measure the *stagnation* pressure p_0, where the stream is decelerated to zero velocity. Instead of measuring p_0 or p_s separately, it is customary to measure their difference with, say, a transducer, as in Fig. 6.30.

   If $\mathrm{Re}_D > 1000$, where D is the probe diameter, the flow around the probe is nearly frictionless and Bernoulli's relation, Eq. (3.54), applies with good accuracy. For incompressible flow

$$p_s + \tfrac{1}{2}\rho V^2 + \rho g z_s \approx p_0 + \tfrac{1}{2}\rho(0)^2 + \rho g z_0$$

Assuming that the elevation pressure difference $\rho g(z_s - z_0)$ is negligible, this reduces to

$$V \approx \left[2\frac{(p_0 - p_s)}{\rho} \right]^{1/2} \tag{6.94}$$

This is the *Pitot formula,* named after the French engineer, Henri de Pitot, who designed the device in 1732.

The primary disadvantage of the pitot tube is that it must be aligned with the flow direction, which may be unknown. For yaw angles greater than 5°, there are substantial errors in both the p_0 and p_s measurements, as shown in Fig. 6.30. The pitot-static tube is useful in liquids and gases; for gases a compressibility correction is necessary if the stream Mach number is high (Chap. 9). Because of the slow response of the fluid-filled tubes leading to the pressure sensors, it is not useful for unsteady flow measurements. It does resemble a point and can be made small enough to measure, for example, blood flow in arteries and veins. It is not suitable for low-velocity measurement in gases because of the small pressure differences developed. For example, if $V = 1$ ft/s in standard air, from Eq. (6.94) we compute $p_0 - p$ equal to only 0.001 lbf/ft^2 (0.048 Pa). This is beyond the resolution of most pressure gages.

Electromagnetic Meter. If a magnetic field is applied across a conducting fluid, the fluid motion will induce a voltage across two electrodes placed in or near the flow. The electrodes can be streamlined or built into the wall, and they cause little or no flow resistance. The output is very strong for highly conducting fluids such as liquid metals. Seawater also gives good output, and electromagnetic current meters are in common use in oceanography. Even low-conductivity fresh water can be measured by amplifying the output and insulating the electrodes. Commercial instruments are available for most liquid flows but are relatively costly. Electromagnetic flowmeters are treated in Ref. 26.

Hot-Wire Anemometer. A very fine wire ($d = 0.01$ mm or less) heated between two small probes, as in Fig. 6.29e, is ideally suited to measure rapidly fluctuating flows such as the turbulent boundary layer. The idea dates back to work by L. V. King in 1914 on heat loss from long, thin cylinders. If electric power is supplied to heat the cylinder, the loss varies with flow velocity across the cylinder according to *King's law*

$$q = I^2 R \approx a + b(\rho V)^n \tag{6.95}$$

where $n \approx \frac{1}{3}$ at very low Reynolds numbers and equals $\frac{1}{2}$ at high Reynolds numbers. The hot wire normally operates in the high-Reynolds-number range but should be calibrated in each situation to find the best-fit a, b, and n. The wire can be operated either at constant current I, so that resistance R is a measure of V, or at constant resistance R (constant temperature), with I a measure of velocity. In either case, the output is a nonlinear function of V, and the equipment should contain a *linearizer* to produce convenient velocity data. Many varieties of commercial hot-wire equipment are available, as are do-it-yourself designs [27]. Excellent detailed discussions of the hot wire are given in Ref. 28.

Because of its frailty, the hot wire is not suited to liquid flows, whose high density and entrained sediment will knock the wire right off. A more stable yet quite sensitive alternative for liquid flow measurement is the hot-film anemometer (Fig. 6.29f). A thin metallic film, usually platinum, is plated onto a relatively thick support, which can be a wedge, a cone, or a cylinder. The operation is similar to the hot wire. The cone gives best response but is liable to error when the flow is yawed to its axis.

Hot wires can easily be arranged in groups to measure two- and three-dimensional velocity components.

Laser-Doppler Anemometer. In the LDA a laser beam provides highly focused, coherent monochromatic light that is passed through the flow. When this light is scattered from a moving particle in the flow, a stationary observer can detect a change, or *doppler shift*, in the frequency of the scattered light. The shift Δf is proportional to the velocity of the particle. There is essentially zero disturbance of the flow by the laser.

Figure 6.29*h* shows the popular dual-beam mode of the LDA. A focusing device splits the laser into two beams, which cross the flow at an angle θ. Their intersection, which is the measuring volume or resolution of the measurement, resembles an ellipsoid about 0.5 mm wide and 0.1 mm in diameter. Particles passing through this measuring volume scatter the beams; they then pass through receiving optics to a photodetector, which converts the light to an electric signal. A signal processor then converts electric frequency to a voltage that can be either displayed or stored. If λ is the wavelength of the laser light, the measured velocity is given by

$$V = \frac{\lambda \, \Delta f}{2 \sin (\theta/2)} \tag{6.96}$$

Multiple components of velocity can be detected by using more than one photodetector and other operating modes. Either liquids or gases can be measured as long as scattering particles are present. In liquids, normal impurities serve as scatterers, but gases may have to be seeded. The particles may be as small as the wavelength of the light. Although the measuring volume is not as small as with a hot wire, the LDA is capable of measuring turbulent fluctuations.

The advantages of the LDA are as follows:

1. No disturbance of the flow.
2. High spatial resolution of the flow field.
3. Velocity data that are independent of the fluid thermodynamic properties.
4. An output voltage that is linear with velocity.
5. No need for calibration.

The disadvantages are that both the apparatus and the fluid must be transparent to light and that the cost is high (a basic system shown in Fig. 6.29*h* begins at about $50,000).

Once installed, an LDA can map the entire flow field in minutest detail. To truly appreciate the power of the LDA, one should examine, for instance, the amazingly detailed three-dimensional flow profiles measured by Eckardt [29] in a high-speed centrifugal compressor impeller. Extensive discussions of laser velocimetry are given in Refs. 38 and 39.

Particle Image Velocimetry. This popular new idea, called PIV for short, measures not just a single point but instead maps the entire field of flow. An illustration was shown in Fig. 1.18*b*. The flow is seeded with neutrally buoyant particles. A planar laser light sheet across the flow is pulsed twice and photographed twice. If $\Delta \mathbf{r}$ is the particle displacement vector over a short time Δt, an estimate of its velocity is $\mathbf{V} \approx \Delta \mathbf{r}/\Delta t$.

A dedicated computer applies this formula to a whole cloud of particles and thus maps the flow field. One can also use the data to calculate velocity gradient and vorticity fields. Since the particles all look alike, other cameras may be needed to identify them. Three-dimensional velocities can be measured by two cameras in a stereoscopic arrangement. The PIV method is not limited to stop-action. New high-speed cameras (up to 10,000 frames per second) can record movies of unsteady flow fields. For further details, see the monograph by M. Raffel [51].

EXAMPLE 6.20

The pitot-static tube of Fig. 6.30 uses mercury as a manometer fluid. When it is placed in a water flow, the manometer height reading is $h = 8.4$ in. Neglecting yaw and other errors, what is the flow velocity V in ft/s?

Solution

From the two-fluid manometer relation (2.23b), with $z_A = z_2$, the pressure difference is related to h by

$$p_0 - p_s = (\gamma_M - \gamma_w)h$$

Taking the specific weights of mercury and water from Table 2.1, we have

$$p_0 - p_s = (846 - 62.4 \text{ lbf/ft}^3) \frac{8.4}{12} \text{ft} = 549 \text{ lbf/ft}^2$$

The density of water is $62.4/32.2 = 1.94$ slugs/ft³. Introducing these values into the pitot-static formula (6.97), we obtain

$$V = \left[\frac{2(549 \text{ lbf/ft}^2)}{1.94 \text{ slugs/ft}^3} \right]^{1/2} = 23.8 \text{ ft/s} \qquad \textit{Ans.}$$

Since this is a low-speed flow, no compressibility correction is needed.

Volume Flow Measurements

It is often desirable to measure the integrated mass, or volume flow, passing through a duct. Accurate measurement of flow is vital in billing customers for a given amount of liquid or gas passing through a duct. The different devices available to make these measurements are discussed in great detail in the ASME text on fluid meters [30]. These devices split into two classes: mechanical instruments and head loss instruments.

The mechanical instruments measure actual mass or volume of fluid by trapping it and counting it. The various types of measurement are

1. Mass measurement
   a. Weighing tanks
   b. Tilting traps
2. Volume measurement
   a. Volume tanks
   b. Reciprocating pistons

    c.   Rotating slotted rings

    d.   Nutating disc

    e.   Sliding vanes

    f.   Gear or lobed impellers

    g.   Reciprocating bellows

    h.   Sealed-drum compartments

The last three of these are suitable for gas flow measurement.

    The head loss devices obstruct the flow and cause a pressure drop, which is a measure of flux:

1.   Bernoulli-type devices

    a.   Thin-plate orifice

    b.   Flow nozzle

    c.   Venturi tube

2.   Friction loss devices

    a.   Capillary tube

    b.   Porous plug

The friction loss meters cause a large nonrecoverable head loss and obstruct the flow too much to be generally useful.

    Six other widely used meters operate on different physical principles:

1.   Turbine meter

2.   Vortex meter

3.   Ultrasonic flowmeter

4.   Rotameter

5.   Coriolis mass flowmeter

6.   Laminar flow element

Nutating Disc Meter.   For measuring liquid *volumes,* as opposed to volume rates, the most common devices are the nutating disc and the turbine meter. Figure 6.31 shows

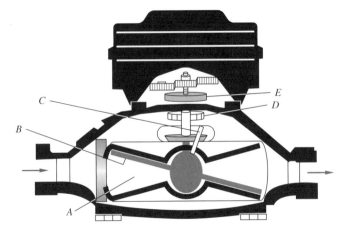

Fig. 6.31 Cutaway sketch of a nutating disc fluid meter. *A*: metered-volume chamber; *B*: nutating disc; *C*: rotating spindle; *D*: drive magnet; *E*: magnetic counter sensor.
Source: Courtesy of Badger Meter, Inc., Milwaukee, Wisconsin.

a cutaway sketch of *a nutating disc meter,* widely used in both water and gasoline delivery systems. The mechanism is clever and perhaps beyond the writer's capability to explain. The metering chamber is a slice of a sphere and contains a rotating disc set at an angle to the incoming flow. The fluid causes the disc to *nutate* (spin eccentrically), and one revolution corresponds to a certain fluid volume passing through. Total volume is obtained by counting the number of revolutions.

Turbine Meter. The turbine meter, sometimes called a *propeller meter,* is a freely rotating propeller that can be installed in a pipeline. A typical design is shown in Fig. 6.32a. There are flow straighteners upstream of the rotor, and the rotation is

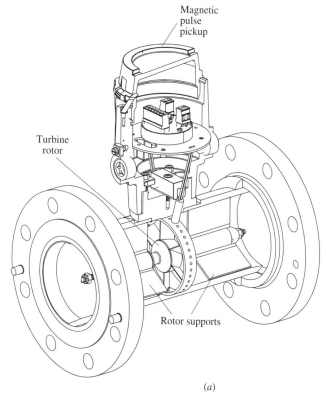

(*a*)

Fig. 6.32 The turbine meter widely used in the oil and gas industry: (*a*) basic design; (*b*) the linearity curve is the measure of variation in the signal output across the 10% to 100% nominal flow range of the meter. *(Daniel Measurement and Control, Houston, TX.)*

Source: (a) Daniel Industries of Fluke Calibration, Houston, TX.

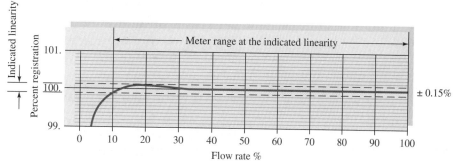

Fig. 6.33 A Commercial handheld wind velocity turbine meter. *(Courtesy of Nielsen-Kellerman Company.)*

measured by electric or magnetic pickup of pulses caused by passage of a point on the rotor. The rotor rotation is approximately proportional to the volume flow in the pipe.

Like the nutating disc, a major advantage of the turbine meter is that each pulse corresponds to a finite incremental volume of fluid, and the pulses are digital and can be summed easily. Liquid flow turbine meters have as few as two blades and produce a constant number of pulses per unit fluid volume over a 5:1 flow rate range with ±0.25 percent accuracy. Gas meters need many blades to produce sufficient torque and are accurate to ±1 percent.

Since turbine meters are very individualistic, flow calibration is an absolute necessity. A typical liquid meter calibration curve is shown in Fig. 6.32b. Researchers attempting to establish universal calibration curves have met with little practical success as a result of manufacturing variabilities.

Turbine meters can also be used in unconfined flow situations, such as winds or ocean currents. They can be compact, even microsize with two or three component directions. Figure 6.33 illustrates a handheld wind velocity meter that uses a seven-bladed turbine with a calibrated digital output. The accuracy of this device is quoted at ±2 percent.

Vortex Flowmeters. Recall from Fig. 5.2 that a bluff body placed in a uniform crossflow sheds alternating vortices at a nearly uniform Strouhal number St = fL/U, where U is the approach velocity and L is a characteristic body width. Since L and St are constant, this means that the shedding frequency is proportional to velocity:

$$f = (\text{const})(U) \tag{6.97}$$

The vortex meter introduces a shedding element across a pipe flow and picks up the shedding frequency downstream with a pressure, ultrasonic, or heat transfer type of sensor. A typical design is shown in Fig. 6.34.

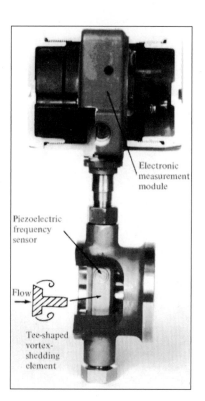

Fig. 6.34 A vortex flowmeter.
(Courtesy of Invensys p/c.)

The advantages of a vortex meter are as follows:

1. Absence of moving parts.
2. Accuracy to ± 1 percent over a wide flow rate range (up to 100:1).
3. Ability to handle very hot or very cold fluids.
4. Requirement of only a short pipe length.
5. Calibration insensitive to fluid density or viscosity.

For further details see Ref. 40.

Ultrasonic Flowmeters.   The sound-wave analog of the laser velocimeter of Fig. 6.29*h* is the ultrasonic flowmeter. Two examples are shown in Fig. 6.35. The pulse-type flowmeter is shown in Fig. 6.35*a*. Upstream piezoelectric transducer *A* is excited with a short sonic pulse that propagates across the flow to downstream transducer *B*. The arrival at *B* triggers another pulse to be created at *A*, resulting in a regular pulse frequency f_A. The same process is duplicated in the reverse direction from *B* to *A*, creating frequency f_B. The difference $f_A - f_B$ is proportional to the flow rate. Figure 6.35*b* shows a doppler-type arrangement, where sound waves from transmitter *T* are scattered by particles or contaminants in the flow to receiver *R*. Comparison of the two signals reveals a doppler frequency shift that is proportional to the flow rate. Ultrasonic meters are nonintrusive and can be directly attached to pipe flows in the

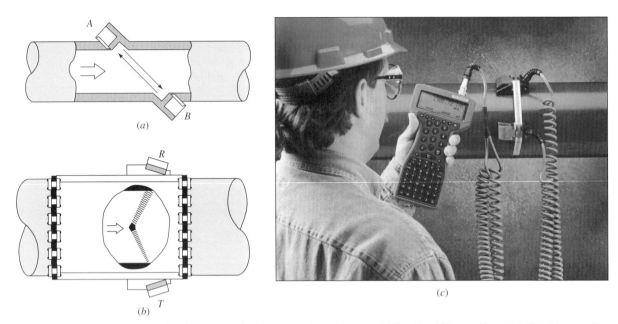

Fig. 6.35 Ultrasonic flowmeters: (*a*) pulse type; (*b*) doppler-shift type *(from Ref. 41)*; (*c*) a portable noninvasive installation *(Courtesy of Thermo Polysonics, Houston, TX.)*

field (Fig. 6.35*c*). Their quoted uncertainty of ± 1 to 2 percent can rise to ± 5 percent or more due to irregularities in velocity profile, fluid temperature, or Reynolds number. For further details see Ref. 41.

Rotameter. The variable-area transparent *rotameter* of Fig. 6.36 has a float that, under the action of flow, rises in the vertical tapered tube and takes a certain equilibrium position for any given flow rate. A student exercise for the forces on the float would yield the approximate relation

$$Q = C_d A_a \left(\frac{2W_{\text{net}}}{A_{\text{float}} \rho_{\text{fluid}}} \right)^{1/2} \tag{6.98}$$

where W_{net} is the float's net weight in the fluid, $A_a = A_{\text{tube}} - A_{\text{float}}$ is the annular area between the float and the tube, and C_d is a dimensionless discharge coefficient of order unity, for the annular constricted flow. For slightly tapered tubes, A_a varies nearly linearly with the float position, and the tube may be calibrated and marked with a flow rate scale, as in Fig. 6.36. The rotameter thus provides a readily visible measure of the flow rate. Capacity may be changed by using different-sized floats. Obviously the tube must be vertical, and the device does not give accurate readings for fluids containing high concentrations of bubbles or particles.

Coriolis Mass Flowmeter. Most commercial meters measure *volume* flow, with mass flow then computed by multiplying by the nominal fluid density. An attractive

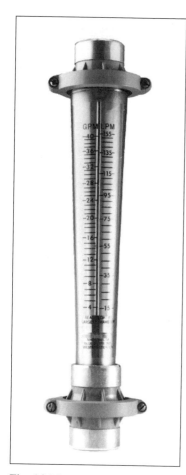

modern alternative is a *mass* flowmeter, which operates on the principle of the Coriolis acceleration associated with noninertial coordinates [recall Fig. 3.11 and the Coriolis term $2\Omega \times V$ in Eq. (3.48)]. The output of the meter is directly proportional to mass flow.

Figure 6.37 is a schematic of a Coriolis device, to be inserted into a piping system. The flow enters a loop arrangement, which is electromagnetically vibrated at a high natural frequency (amplitude < 1 mm and frequency > 100 Hz). The Coriolis effect induces a downward force on the loop entrance and an upward force on the loop exit, as shown. The loop twists, and the twist angle can be measured and is proportional to the mass flow through the tube. Accuracy is typically less than 1 percent of full scale.

Laminar Flow Element.   In many, perhaps most, commercial flowmeters, the flow through the meter is turbulent and the variation of flow rate with pressure drop is nonlinear. In laminar duct flow, however, Q is linearly proportional to Δp, as in Eq. (6.12): $Q = [\pi R^4/(8\mu L)] \Delta p$. Thus a *laminar* flow sensing element is attractive, since its calibration will be linear. To ensure laminar flow for what otherwise would be a turbulent condition, all or part of the fluid is directed into small passages, each of which has a low (laminar) Reynolds number. A honeycomb is a popular design.

Figure 6.38 uses axial flow through a narrow annulus to create laminar flow. The theory again predicts $Q \propto \Delta p$, as in Eq. (6.70). However, the flow is very sensitive to passage size; for example, halving the annulus clearance increases Δp more than eight times. Careful calibration is thus necessary. In Fig. 6.38 the laminar flow concept has been synthesized into a complete mass flow system, with temperature control, differential pressure measurement, and a microprocessor all self-contained. The accuracy of this device is rated at ±0.2 percent.

Fig. 6.36 A commercial rotameter. The float rises in the tapered tube to an equilibrium position, which is a measure of the fluid flow rate. (*Courtesy of Blue White Industries, Huntington Beach, CA.*)

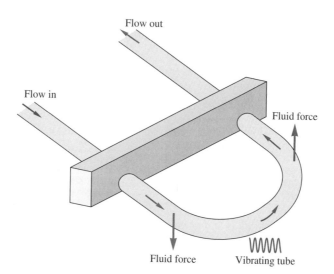

Fig. 6.37 Schematic of a Coriolis mass flowmeter.

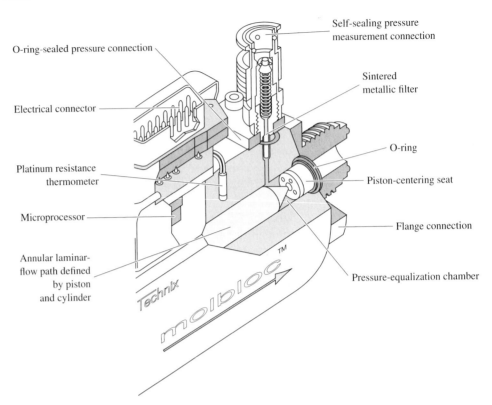

Fig. 6.38 A complete flowmeter system using a laminar flow element (in this case a narrow annulus). The flow rate is linearly proportional to the pressure drop.
Source: Courtesy of Martin Girard, DH Instruments, Inc.

Bernoulli Obstruction Theory. Consider the generalized flow obstruction shown in Fig. 6.39. The flow in the basic duct of diameter D is forced through an obstruction of diameter d; the β ratio of the device is a key parameter:

$$\beta = \frac{d}{D} \tag{6.99}$$

After leaving the obstruction, the flow may neck down even more through a vena contracta of diameter $D_2 < d$, as shown. Apply the Bernoulli and continuity equations for incompressible steady frictionless flow to estimate the pressure change:

Continuity:
$$Q = \frac{\pi}{4}D^2 V_1 = \frac{\pi}{4}D_2^2 V_2$$

Bernoulli:
$$p_0 = p_1 + \tfrac{1}{2}\rho V_1^2 = p_2 + \tfrac{1}{2}\rho V_2^2$$

Eliminating V_1, we solve these for V_2 or Q in terms of the pressure change $p_1 - p_2$:

$$\frac{Q}{A_2} = V_2 \approx \left[\frac{2(p_1 - p_2)}{\rho(1 - D_2^4/D^4)} \right]^{1/2} \tag{6.100}$$

But this is surely inaccurate because we have neglected friction in a duct flow, where we know friction will be very important. Nor do we want to get into the business of measuring vena contracta ratios D_2/d for use in (6.100). Therefore we assume that

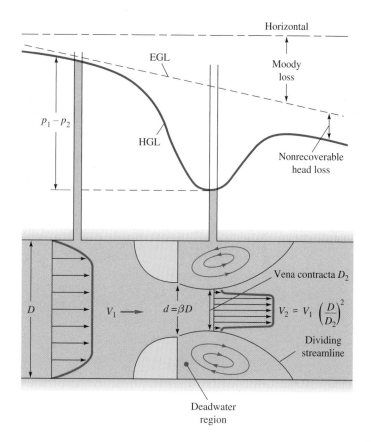

Fig. 6.39 Velocity and pressure change through a generalized Bernoulli obstruction meter.

$D_2/D \approx \beta$ and then calibrate the device to fit the relation

$$Q = A_t V_t = C_d A_t \left[\frac{2(p_1 - p_2)/\rho}{1 - \beta^4} \right]^{1/2} \qquad (6.101)$$

where subscript t denotes the throat of the obstruction. The dimensionless *discharge coefficient* C_d accounts for the discrepancies in the approximate analysis. By dimensional analysis for a given design we expect

$$C_d = f(\beta, \mathrm{Re}_D) \quad \text{where} \quad \mathrm{Re}_D = \frac{V_1 D}{\nu} \qquad (6.102)$$

The geometric factor involving β in (6.101) is called the *velocity-of-approach factor*:

$$E = (1 - \beta^4)^{-1/2} \qquad (6.103)$$

One can also group C_d and E in Eq. (6.101) to form the dimensionless *flow coefficient* α:

$$\alpha = C_d E = \frac{C_d}{(1 - \beta^4)^{1/2}} \qquad (6.104)$$

Thus Eq. (6.101) can be written in the equivalent form

$$Q = \alpha A_t \left[\frac{2(p_1 - p_2)}{\rho} \right]^{1/2} \tag{6.105}$$

Obviously the flow coefficient is correlated in the same manner:

$$\alpha = f(\beta, \text{Re}_D) \tag{6.106}$$

Occasionally one uses the throat Reynolds number instead of the approach Reynolds number:

$$\text{Re}_d = \frac{V_t d}{\nu} = \frac{\text{Re}_D}{\beta} \tag{6.107}$$

Since the design parameters are assumed known, the correlation of α from Eq. (6.106) or of C_d from Eq. (6.102) is the desired solution to the fluid metering problem.

The mass flow is related to Q by

$$\dot{m} = \rho Q \tag{6.108}$$

and is thus correlated by exactly the same formulas.

Figure 6.40 shows the three basic devices recommended for use by the International Organization for Standardization (ISO) [31]: the orifice, nozzle, and venturi tube.

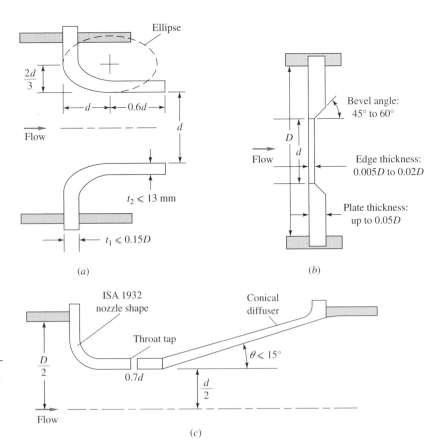

Fig. 6.40 Standard shapes for the three primary Bernoulli obstruction-type meters: (*a*) long-radius nozzle; (*b*) thin-plate orifice; (*c*) venturi nozzle. (*Based on data from the International Organization for Standardization.*)

Thin-Plate Orifice. The thin-plate orifice, Fig. 6.40b, can be made with β in the range of 0.2 to 0.8, except that the hole diameter d should not be less than 12.5 mm. To measure p_1 and p_2, three types of tappings are commonly used:

1. Corner taps where the plate meets the pipe wall.
2. $D: \frac{1}{2}D$ taps: pipe-wall taps at D upstream and $\frac{1}{2}D$ downstream.
3. Flange taps: 1 in (25 mm) upstream and 1 in (25 mm) downstream of the plate, regardless of the size D.

Types 1 and 2 approximate geometric similarity, but since the flange taps 3 do not, they must be correlated separately for every single size of pipe in which a flange-tap plate is used [30, 31].

Figure 6.41 shows the discharge coefficient of an orifice with $D: \frac{1}{2}D$ or type 2 taps in the Reynolds number range $\text{Re}_D = 10^4$ to 10^7 of normal use. Although detailed charts such as Fig. 6.41 are available for designers [30], the ASME recommends use of the curve-fit formulas developed by the ISO [31]. The basic form of the curve fit is [42]

$$C_d = f(\beta) + 91.71\beta^{2.5}\text{Re}_D^{-0.75} + \frac{0.09\beta^4}{1 - \beta^4} F_1 - 0.0337\beta^3 F_2 \qquad (6.109)$$

where

$$f(\beta) = 0.5959 + 0.0312\beta^{2.1} - 0.184\beta^8$$

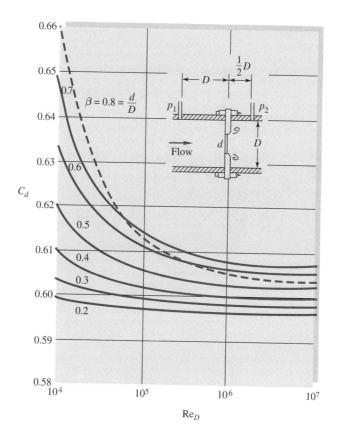

Fig. 6.41 Discharge coefficient for a thin-plate orifice with $D: \frac{1}{2}D$ taps, plotted from Eqs. (6.109) and (6.110b).

The correlation factors F_1 and F_2 vary with tap position:

Corner taps:

$$F_1 = 0 \quad F_2 = 0 \tag{6.110a}$$

$D: \frac{1}{2}D$ taps:

$$F_1 = 0.4333 \quad F_2 = 0.47 \tag{6.110b}$$

Flange taps:

$$F_2 = \frac{1}{D \text{ (in)}} \quad F_1 = \begin{cases} \dfrac{1}{D \text{ (in)}} & D > 2.3 \text{ in} \\ 0.4333 & 2.0 \le D \le 2.3 \text{ in} \end{cases} \tag{6.110c}$$

Note that the flange taps (6.110c), not being geometrically similar, use raw diameter in inches in the formula. The constants will change if other diameter units are used. We cautioned against such dimensional formulas in Example 1.4 and Eq. (5.17) and give Eq. (6.110c) only because flange taps are widely used in the United States.

Flow Nozzle. The flow nozzle comes in two types, a long-radius type shown in Fig. 6.40a and a short-radius type (not shown) called the ISA 1932 nozzle [30, 31]. The flow nozzle, with its smooth, rounded entrance convergence, practically eliminates the vena contracta and gives discharge coefficients near unity. The nonrecoverable loss is still large because there is no diffuser provided for gradual expansion. The ISO recommended correlation for long-radius-nozzle discharge coefficient is

$$C_d \approx 0.9965 - 0.00653\beta^{1/2}\left(\frac{10^6}{\text{Re}_D}\right)^{1/2} = 0.9965 - 0.00653\left(\frac{10^6}{\text{Re}_d}\right)^{1/2} \tag{6.111}$$

The second form is independent of the β ratio and is plotted in Fig. 6.42. A similar ISO correlation is recommended for the short-radius ISA 1932 flow nozzle:

$$C_d \approx 0.9900 - 0.2262\beta^{4.1}$$
$$+ (0.000215 - 0.001125\beta + 0.00249\beta^{4.7})\left(\frac{10^6}{\text{Re}_D}\right)^{1.15} \tag{6.112}$$

Flow nozzles may have β values between 0.2 and 0.8.

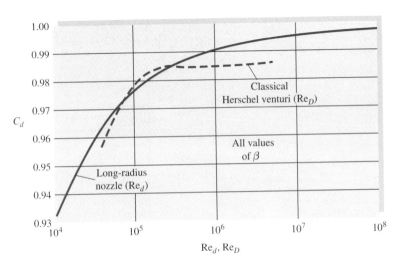

Fig. 6.42 Discharge coefficient for long-radius nozzle and classical Herschel-type venturi.

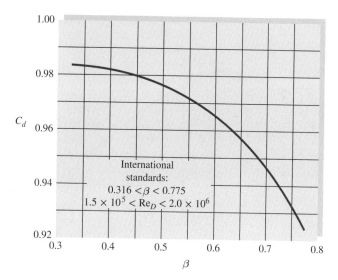

Fig. 6.43 Discharge coefficient for a venturi nozzle.

Venturi Meter. The third and final type of obstruction meter is the venturi, named in honor of Giovanni Venturi (1746–1822), an Italian physicist who first tested conical expansions and contractions. The original, or *classical,* venturi was invented by a U.S. engineer, Clemens Herschel, in 1898. It consisted of a 21° conical contraction, a straight throat of diameter d and length d, then a 7° to 15° conical expansion. The discharge coefficient is near unity, and the nonrecoverable loss is very small. Herschel venturis are seldom used now.

The modern venturi nozzle, Fig. 6.40c, consists of an ISA 1932 nozzle entrance and a conical expansion of half-angle no greater than 15°. It is intended to be operated in a narrow Reynolds number range of 1.5×10^5 to 2×10^6. Its discharge coefficient, shown in Fig. 6.43, is given by the ISO correlation formula

$$C_d \approx 0.9858 - 0.196\beta^{4.5} \tag{6.113}$$

It is independent of Re_D within the given range. The Herschel venturi discharge varies with Re_D but not with β, as shown in Fig. 6.42. Both have very low net losses.

The choice of meter depends on the loss and the cost and can be illustrated by the following table:

Type of meter	Net head loss	Cost
Orifice	Large	Small
Nozzle	Medium	Medium
Venturi	Small	Large

As so often happens, the product of inefficiency and initial cost is approximately constant.

The average nonrecoverable head losses for the three types of meters, expressed as a fraction of the throat velocity head $V_t^2/(2g)$, are shown in Fig. 6.44. The orifice has the greatest loss and the venturi the least, as discussed. The orifice and nozzle

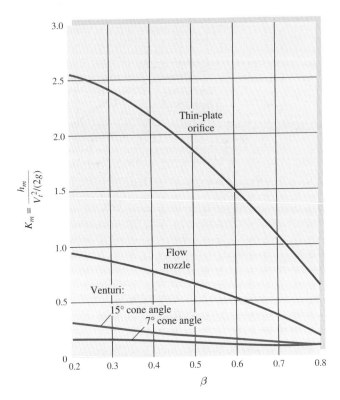

Fig. 6.44 Nonrecoverable head loss in Bernoulli obstruction meters. *(Adapted from Ref. 30.)*

simulate partially closed valves as in Fig. 6.18*b*, while the venturi is a very minor loss. When the loss is given as a fraction of the measured *pressure drop*, the orifice and nozzle have nearly equal losses, as Example 6.21 will illustrate.

The other types of instruments discussed earlier in this section can also serve as flowmeters if properly constructed. For example, a hot wire mounted in a tube can be calibrated to read volume flow rather than point velocity. Such hot-wire meters are commercially available, as are other meters modified to use velocity instruments. For further details see Ref. 30.

Compressible Gas Flow Correction Factor. The orifice/nozzle/venturi formulas in this section assume incompressible flow. If the fluid is a gas, and the pressure ratio (p_2/p_1) is not near unity, a compressibility correction is needed. Equation (6.101) is rewritten in terms of mass flow and the upstream density ρ_1:

$$\dot{m} = C_d \, Y \, A_t \sqrt{\frac{2\rho_1(p_1 - p_2)}{1 - \beta^4}} \quad \text{where} \quad \beta = \frac{d}{D} \tag{6.114}$$

The dimensionless *expansion factor* Y is a function of pressure ratio, β, and the type of meter. Some values are plotted in Fig. 6.45. The orifice, with its strong jet contraction, has a different factor from the venturi or the flow nozzle, which are designed to eliminate contraction.

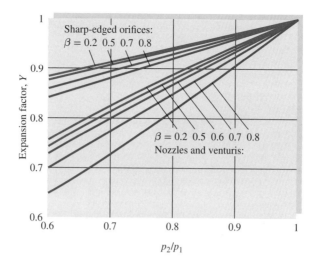

Fig. 6.45 Compressible flow expansion factor Y for flowmeters.

EXAMPLE 6.21

We want to meter the volume flow of water ($\rho = 1000$ kg/m³, $\nu = 1.02 \times 10^{-6}$ m²/s) moving through a 200-mm-diameter pipe at an average velocity of 2.0 m/s. If the differential pressure gage selected reads accurately at $p_1 - p_2 = 50{,}000$ Pa, what size meter should be selected for installing (a) an orifice with D: $\frac{1}{2}D$ taps, (b) a long-radius flow nozzle, or (c) a venturi nozzle? What would be the nonrecoverable head loss for each design?

Solution

Here the unknown is the β ratio of the meter. Since the discharge coefficient is a complicated function of β, iteration will be necessary. We are given $D = 0.2$ m and $V_1 = 2.0$ m/s. The pipe-approach Reynolds number is thus

$$\text{Re}_D = \frac{V_1 D}{\nu} = \frac{(2.0)(0.2)}{1.02 \times 10^{-6}} = 392{,}000$$

For all three cases [(a) to (c)] the generalized formula (6.105) holds:

$$V_t = \frac{V_1}{\beta^2} = \alpha\left[\frac{2(p_1 - p_2)}{\rho}\right]^{1/2} \qquad \alpha = \frac{C_d}{(1 - \beta^4)^{1/2}} \tag{1}$$

where the given data are $V_1 = 2.0$ m/s, $\rho = 1000$ kg/m³, and $\Delta p = 50{,}000$ Pa. Inserting these known values into Eq. (1) gives a relation between β and α:

$$\frac{2.0}{\beta^2} = \alpha\left[\frac{2(50{,}000)}{1000}\right]^{1/2} \qquad \text{or} \qquad \beta^2 = \frac{0.2}{\alpha} \tag{2}$$

The unknowns are β (or α) and C_d. Parts (a) to (c) depend on the particular chart or formula needed for $C_d = \text{fcn}(\text{Re}_D, \beta)$. We can make an initial guess $\beta \approx 0.5$ and iterate to convergence.

Part (a)   For the orifice with D: $\frac{1}{2}D$ taps, use Eq. (6.109) or Fig. 6.41. The iterative sequence is

$$\beta_1 \approx 0.5, \, C_{d1} \approx 0.604, \, \alpha_1 \approx 0.624, \, \beta_2 \approx 0.566, \, C_{d2} \approx 0.606, \, \alpha_2 \approx 0.640, \, \beta_3 = 0.559$$

We have converged to three figures. The proper orifice diameter is

$$d = \beta D = 112 \text{ mm} \qquad \text{Ans. } (a)$$

Part (b)

For the long-radius flow nozzle, use Eq. (6.111) or Fig. 6.42. The iterative sequence is

$$\beta_1 \approx 0.5, C_{d1} \approx 0.9891, \alpha_1 \approx 1.022, \beta_2 \approx 0.442, C_{d2} \approx 0.9896, \alpha_2 \approx 1.009, \beta_3 = 0.445$$

We have converged to three figures. The proper nozzle diameter is

$$d = \beta D = 89 \text{ mm} \qquad \text{Ans. } (b)$$

Part (c)

For the venturi nozzle, use Eq. (6.113) or Fig. 6.43. The iterative sequence is

$$\beta_1 \approx 0.5, C_{d1} \approx 0.977, \alpha_1 \approx 1.009, \beta_2 \approx 0.445, C_{d2} \approx 0.9807, \alpha_2 \approx 1.0004, \beta_3 = 0.447$$

We have converged to three figures. The proper venturi diameter is

$$d = \beta D = 89 \text{ mm} \qquad \text{Ans. } (c)$$

Comments: These meters are of similar size, but their head losses are not the same. From Fig. 6.44 for the three different shapes we may read the three K factors and compute

$$h_{m,\text{orifice}} \approx 3.5 \text{ m} \qquad h_{m,\text{nozzle}} \approx 3.6 \text{ m} \qquad h_{m,\text{venturi}} \approx 0.8 \text{ m}$$

The venturi loss is only about 22 percent of the orifice and nozzle losses.

Solution by Excel Iteration for the Flow Nozzle

Parts (*a, b, c*) were solved by hand, but Excel is ideal for these calculations. You may review this procedure from the instructions in Example 6.5. We need five columns: C_d, calculated from Eq. (6.111), throat velocity V_t calculated from Δp, α as calculated from Eq. (6.104), and β calculated from the velocity ratio (V/V_t). The fifth column is an initial guess for β, which is replaced in its next row by the newly computed β. Any initial $\beta < 1$ will do. Here we chose $\beta = 0.5$ as in part (*b*) for the flow nozzle. Remember to use *cell* names, not symbols: in row 1, $C_d = A1$, $V_t = B1$, $\alpha = C1$, and $\beta = D1$. The process converges rapidly, in only two or three iterations:

	C_d from Eq.(6.114)	$V_t = \alpha(2\Delta p/\rho)$	$\alpha = $ $C_d/(1 - \beta^4)^{0.5}$	$\beta = $ $(V/V_t)^{0.5}$	β-guess
	A	**B**	**C**	**D**	**E**
1	0.9891	10.216	1.0216	0.4425	0.5000
2	0.9896	10.091	1.0091	0.4452	0.4425
3	0.9895	10.096	1.0096	0.4451	0.4452
4	0.9895	10.096	1.0096	0.4451	0.4451

The final answers for the long-radius flow nozzle are:

$$\alpha = 1.0096 \qquad C_d = 0.9895 \qquad \beta = 0.4451 \qquad \text{Ans. } (b)$$

EXAMPLE 6.22

A long-radius nozzle of diameter 6 cm is used to meter airflow in a 10-cm-diameter pipe. Upstream conditions are $p_1 = 200$ kPa and $T_1 = 100°C$. If the pressure drop through the nozzle is 60 kPa, estimate the flow rate in m^3/s.

Solution

- *Assumptions:* The pressure drops 30 percent, so we need the compressibility factor Y, and Eq. (6.114) is applicable to this problem.
- *Approach:* Find ρ_1 and C_d and apply Eq. (6.114) with $\beta = 6/10 = 0.6$.
- *Property values:* Given p_1 and T_1, $\rho_1 = p_1/RT_1 = (200{,}000)/[287(100 + 273)] = 1.87$ kg/m^3. The downstream pressure is $p_2 = 200 - 60 = 140$ kPa, hence $p_2/p_1 = 0.7$. At 100°C, from Table A.2, the viscosity of air is 2.17 E-5 kg/m-s.
- *Solution steps:* Initially apply Eq. (6.114) by guessing, from Fig. 6.42, that $C_d \approx 0.98$. From Fig. 6.45, for a nozzle with $p_2/p_1 = 0.7$ and $\beta = 0.6$, read $Y \approx 0.80$. Then

$$\dot{m} = C_d\, Y A_t \sqrt{\frac{2\rho_1(p_1 - p_2)}{1 - \beta^4}} \approx (0.98)(0.80)\,\frac{\pi}{4}\,(0.06\text{ m})^2 \sqrt{\frac{2(1.87\text{ kg/m}^3)(60{,}000\text{ Pa})}{1 - (0.6)}}$$

$$\approx 1.13\,\frac{\text{kg}}{\text{s}}$$

Now estimate Re$_d$, putting it in the convenient mass flow form:

$$\text{Re}_d = \frac{\rho V d}{\mu} = \frac{4\,\dot{m}}{\pi \mu d} = \frac{4(1.13\text{ kg/s})}{\pi(2.17\text{ E-5 kg/m} - \text{s})(0.06\text{ m})} \approx 1.11\text{ E6}$$

Returning to Fig. 6.42, we could read a slightly better $C_d \approx 0.99$. Thus our final estimate is

$$\dot{m} \approx 1.14\text{ kg/s} \qquad\qquad\qquad Ans.$$

- *Comments:* Figure 6.45 is not just a "chart" for engineers to use casually. It is based on the compressible flow theory of Chap. 9. There, we may reassign this example as a *theory*.

Summary

This chapter has been concerned with internal pipe and duct flows, which are probably the most common problems encountered in engineering fluid mechanics. Such flows are very sensitive to the Reynolds number and change from laminar to transitional to turbulent flow as the Reynolds number increases.

The various Reynolds number regimes were outlined, and a semiempirical approach to turbulent flow modeling was presented. The chapter then made a detailed analysis of flow through a straight circular pipe, leading to the famous Moody chart (Fig. 6.13) for the friction factor. Possible uses of the Moody chart were discussed for flow rate and sizing problems, as well as the application of the Moody chart to noncircular ducts using an equivalent duct "diameter." The addition of minor losses due to valves, elbows, fittings, and other devices was presented in the form of loss coefficients to be incorporated along with Moody-type friction losses. Multiple-pipe systems were discussed briefly and were seen to be quite complex algebraically and appropriate for computer solution.

Diffusers are added to ducts to increase pressure recovery at the exit of a system. Their behavior was presented as experimental data, since the theory of real diffusers is still not well developed. The chapter ended with a discussion of flowmeters, especially the pitot-static tube and the Bernoulli obstruction type of meter. Flowmeters also require careful experimental calibration.

Problems

Most of the problems herein are fairly straightforward. More difficult or open-ended assignments are labeled with an asterisk. Problems labeled with a computer icon 🖳 may require the use of a computer. The standard end-of-chapter problems P6.1 to P6.163 (categorized in the problem list here) are followed by word problems W6.1 to W6.4, fundamentals of engineering exam problems FE6.1 to FE6.15, comprehensive problems C6.1 to C6.9, and design projects D6.1 and D6.2.

Problem Distribution

Section	Topic	Problems
6.1	Reynolds number regimes	P6.1–P6.5
6.2	Internal and external flow	P6.6–P6.8
6.3	Head loss—friction factor	P6.9–P6.11
6.4	Laminar pipe flow	P6.12–P6.33
6.5	Turbulence modeling	P6.34–P6.40
6.6	Turbulent pipe flow	P6.41–P6.62
6.7	Flow rate and sizing problems	P6.63–P6.85
6.8	Noncircular ducts	P6.86–P6.98
6.9	Minor or local losses	P6.99–P6.110
6.10	Series and parallel pipe systems	P6.111–P6.120
6.10	Three-reservoir and pipe network systems	P6.121–P6.130
6.11	Diffuser performance	P6.131–P6.134
6.12	The pitot-static tube	P6.135–P6.139
6.12	Flowmeters: the orifice plate	P6.140–P6.148
6.12	Flowmeters: the flow nozzle	P6.149–P6.153
6.12	Flowmeters: the venturi meter	P6.154–P6.159
6.12	Flowmeters: other designs	P6.160–P6.161
6.12	Flowmeters: compressibility correction	P6.162–P6.163

Reynolds number regimes

P6.1   An engineer claims that the flow of SAE 30W oil, at 20°C, through a 5-cm-diameter smooth pipe at 1 million N/h, is laminar. Do you agree? A million newtons is a lot, so this sounds like an awfully high flow rate.

P6.2   The present pumping rate of crude oil through the Alaska Pipeline, with an ID of 48 in, is 550,000 barrels per day (1 barrel = 42 U.S. gallons). (*a*) Is this a turbulent flow? (*b*) What would be the maximum rate if the flow were constrained to be laminar? Assume that Alaskan oil fits Fig. A.1 of the Appendix at 60°C.

P6.3   The Keystone Pipeline in the chapter opener photo has a maximum proposed flow rate of 1.3 million barrels of crude oil per day. Estimate the Reynolds number and whether the flow is laminar. Assume that Keystone crude oil fits Fig. A.1 of the Appendix at 40°C.

P6.4   For flow of SAE 30 oil through a 5-cm-diameter pipe, from Fig. A.1, for what flow rate in m³/h would we expect transition to turbulence at (*a*) 20°C and (*b*) 100°C?

P6.5   In flow past a body or wall, early transition to turbulence can be induced by placing a trip wire on the wall across the flow, as in Fig. P6.5. If the trip wire in Fig. P6.5 is placed where the local velocity is U, it will trigger turbulence if $Ud/\nu = 850$, where d is the wire diameter [3, p. 388]. If the sphere diameter is 20 cm and transition is observed at $Re_D = 90{,}000$, what is the diameter of the trip wire in mm?

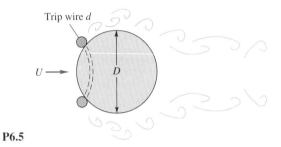

Trip wire d

$U \longrightarrow$ D

P6.5

Internal and external flow

P6.6   For flow of a uniform stream parallel to a sharp flat plate, transition to a turbulent boundary layer on the plate may occur at $Re_x = \rho U x / \mu \approx 1$ E6, where U is the approach velocity and x is distance along the plate. If $U = 2.5$ m/s, determine the distance x for the following fluids at 20°C and 1 atm: (*a*) hydrogen, (*b*) air, (*c*) gasoline, (*d*) water, (*e*) mercury, and (*f*) glycerin.

P6.7   SAE 10W30 oil at 20°C flows from a tank into a 2-cm-diameter tube 40 cm long. The flow rate is 1.1 m³/hr. Is the entrance length region a significant part of this tube flow?

P6.8   When water at 20°C is in steady turbulent flow through an 8-cm-diameter pipe, the wall shear stress is 72 Pa. What is the axial pressure gradient $(\partial p/\partial x)$ if the pipe is (*a*) horizontal and (*b*) vertical with the flow up?

Head loss—friction factor

P6.9   A light liquid ($\rho \approx 950$ kg/m³) flows at an average velocity of 10 m/s through a horizontal smooth tube of diameter 5 cm. The fluid pressure is measured at 1-m intervals along the pipe, as follows:

x, m	0	1	2	3	4	5	6
p, kPa	304	273	255	240	226	213	200

Estimate (*a*) the total head loss, in meters; (*b*) the wall shear stress in the fully developed section of the pipe; and (*c*) the overall friction factor.

P6.10 Water at 20°C flows through an inclined 8-cm-diameter pipe. At sections A and B the following data are taken: $p_A = 186$ kPa, $V_A = 3.2$ m/s, $z_A = 24.5$ m, and $p_B = 260$ kPa, $V_B = 3.2$ m/s, $z_B = 9.1$ m. Which way is the flow going? What is the head loss in meters?

P6.11 Water at 20°C flows upward at 4 m/s in a 6-cm-diameter pipe. The pipe length between points 1 and 2 is 5 m, and point 2 is 3 m higher. A mercury manometer, connected between 1 and 2, has a reading $h = 135$ mm, with p_1 higher. (a) What is the pressure change $(p_1 - p_2)$? (b) What is the head loss, in meters? (c) Is the manometer reading proportional to head loss? Explain. (d) What is the friction factor of the flow?

In Probs. 6.12 to 6.99, neglect minor losses.

Laminar pipe flow—no minor losses

P6.12 A 5-mm-diameter capillary tube is used as a viscometer for oils. When the flow rate is 0.071 m³/h, the measured pressure drop per unit length is 375 kPa/m. Estimate the viscosity of the fluid. Is the flow laminar? Can you also estimate the density of the fluid?

P6.13 A soda straw is 20 cm long and 2 mm in diameter. It delivers cold cola, approximated as water at 10°C, at a rate of 3 cm³/s. (a) What is the head loss through the straw? What is the axial pressure gradient $\partial p/\partial x$ if the flow is (b) vertically up or (c) horizontal? Can the human lung deliver this much flow?

P6.14 Water at 20°C is to be siphoned through a tube 1 m long and 2 mm in diameter, as in Fig. P6.14. Is there any height H for which the flow might not be laminar? What is the flow rate if $H = 50$ cm? Neglect the tube curvature.

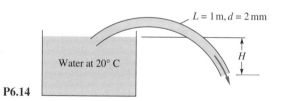

P6.14

P6.15 Professor Gordon Holloway and his students at the University of New Brunswick went to a fast-food emporium and tried to drink chocolate shakes ($\rho \approx 1200$ kg/m³, $\mu \approx 6$ kg/m-s) through fat straws 8 mm in diameter and 30 cm long. (a) Verify that their human lungs, which can develop approximately 3000 Pa of vacuum pressure, would be unable to drink the milkshake through the vertical straw. (b) A student cut 15 cm from his straw and proceeded to drink happily. What rate of milkshake flow was produced by this strategy?

P6.16 Fluid flows steadily, at volume rate Q, through a large pipe and then divides into two small pipes, the larger of which

has an inside diameter of 25 mm and carries three times the flow of the smaller pipe. Both small pipes have the same length and pressure drop. If all flows are laminar, estimate the diameter of the smaller pipe.

P6.17 A *capillary viscometer* measures the time required for a specified volume v of liquid to flow through a small-bore glass tube, as in Fig. P6.17. This transit time is then correlated with fluid viscosity. For the system shown, (a) derive an approximate formula for the time required, assuming laminar flow with no entrance and exit losses. (b) If $L = 12$ cm, $l = 2$ cm, $v = 8$ cm³, and the fluid is water at 20°C, what capillary diameter D will result in a transit time t of 6 seconds?

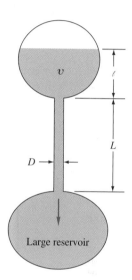

P6.17

P6.18 SAE 50W oil at 20°C flows from one tank to another through a tube 160 cm long and 5 cm in diameter. Estimate the flow rate in m³/hr if $z_1 = 2$ m and $z_2 = 0.8$ m.

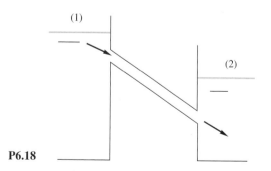

P6.18

P6.19 An oil (SG = 0.9) issues from the pipe in Fig. P6.19 at $Q = 35$ ft³/h. What is the kinematic viscosity of the oil in ft³/s? Is the flow laminar?

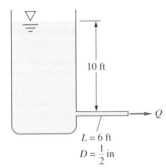

P6.19

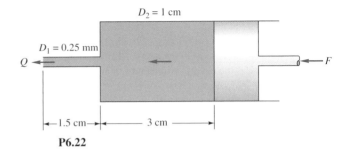

P6.22

P6.20 The oil tanks in Tinyland are only 160 cm high, and they discharge to the Tinyland oil truck through a smooth tube 4 mm in diameter and 55 cm long. The tube exit is open to the atmosphere and 145 cm below the tank surface. The fluid is medium fuel oil, $\rho = 850$ kg/m^3 and $\mu = 0.11$ kg/(m · s). Estimate the oil flow rate in cm^3/h.

P6.21 In Tinyland, houses are less than a foot high! The rainfall is laminar! The drainpipe in Fig. P6.21 is only 2 mm in diameter. (*a*) When the gutter is full, what is the rate of draining? (*b*) The gutter is designed for a sudden rainstorm of up to 5 mm per hour. For this condition, what is the maximum roof area that can be drained successfully? (*c*) What is Re$_d$?

P6.23 SAE 10 oil at 20°C flows in a vertical pipe of diameter 2.5 cm. It is found that the pressure is constant throughout the fluid. What is the oil flow rate in m^3/h? Is the flow up or down?

P6.24 Two tanks of water at 20°C are connected by a capillary tube 4 mm in diameter and 3.5 m long. The surface of tank 1 is 30 cm higher than the surface of tank 2. (*a*) Estimate the flow rate in m^3/h. Is the flow laminar? (*b*) For what tube diameter will Re$_d$ be 500?

P6.25 For the configuration shown in Fig. P6.25, the fluid is ethyl alcohol at 20°C, and the tanks are very wide. Find the flow rate which occurs in m^3/h. Is the flow laminar?

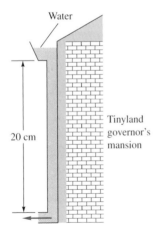

P6.21

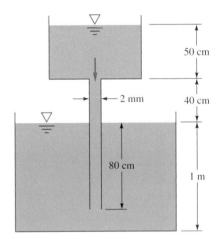

P6.25

P6.22 A steady push on the piston in Fig. P6.22 causes a flow rate $Q = 0.15$ cm^3/s through the needle. The fluid has $\rho = 900$ kg/m^3 and $\mu = 0.002$ kg/(m · s). What force F is required to maintain the flow?

P6.26 Two oil tanks are connected by two 9-m-long pipes, as in Fig. P6.26. Pipe 1 is 5 cm in diameter and is 6 m higher than pipe 2. It is found that the flow rate in pipe 2 is twice as large as the flow in pipe 1. (*a*) What is the diameter of pipe 2? (*b*) Are both pipe flows laminar? (*c*) What is the flow rate in pipe 2 (m^3/s)? Neglect minor losses.

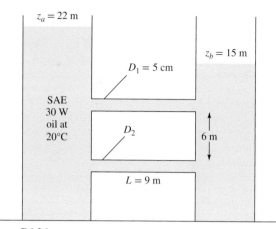

P6.26

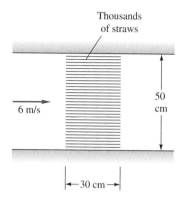

P6.28

*P6.27 Let us attack Prob. P6.25 in symbolic fashion, using Fig. P6.27. All parameters are constant except the upper tank depth $Z(t)$. Find an expression for the flow rate $Q(t)$ as a function of $Z(t)$. Set up a differential equation, and solve for the time t_0 to drain the upper tank completely. Assume quasi-steady laminar flow.

P6.29 SAE 30W oil at 20°C flows through a straight pipe 25 m long, with diameter 4 cm. The average velocity is 2 m/s. (a) Is the flow laminar? Calculate (b) the pressure drop and (c) the power required. (d) If the pipe diameter is doubled, for the same average velocity, by what percent does the required power increase?

P6.30 SAE 10 oil at 20°C flows through the 4-cm-diameter vertical pipe of Fig. P6.30. For the mercury manometer reading $h = 42$ cm shown, (a) calculate the volume flow rate in m^3/h and (b) state the direction of flow.

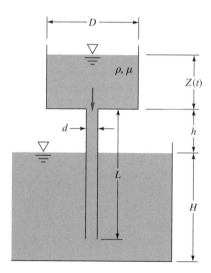

P6.27

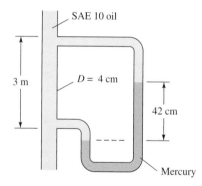

P6.30

P6.28 For straightening and smoothing an airflow in a 50-cm-diameter duct, the duct is packed with a "honeycomb" of thin straws of length 30 cm and diameter 4 mm, as in Fig. P6.28. The inlet flow is air at 110 kPa and 20°C, moving at an average velocity of 6 m/s. Estimate the pressure drop across the honeycomb.

P6.31 A *laminar flow element* (LFE) (Meriam Instrument Co.) measures low gas-flow rates with a bundle of capillary tubes or ducts packed inside a large outer tube. Consider oxygen at 20°C and 1 atm flowing at 84 ft^3/min in a 4-in-diameter pipe. (a) Is the flow turbulent when approaching the element? (b) If there are 1000 capillary tubes, $L = 4$ in, select a tube diameter to keep Re_d below 1500 and also to keep the tube pressure drop no greater than 0.5 lbf/in^2. (c) Do the tubes selected in part (b) fit nicely within the approach pipe?

P6.32 SAE 30 oil at 20°C flows in the 3-cm-diameter pipe in Fig. P6.32, which slopes at 37°. For the pressure measurements shown, determine (*a*) whether the flow is up or down and (*b*) the flow rate in m³/h.

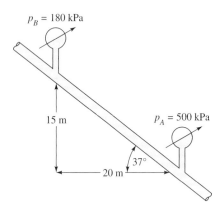

$p_B = 180$ kPa

15 m

$p_A = 500$ kPa

37°

20 m

P6.32

P6.33 Water at 20°C is pumped from a reservoir through a vertical tube 10 ft long and 1/16th in in diameter. The pump provides a pressure rise of 11 lbf/in² to the flow. Neglect entrance losses. (*a*) Calculate the exit velocity. (*b*) Approximately how high will the exit water jet rise? (*c*) Verify that the flow is laminar.

Turbulence modeling

P6.34 Derive the time-averaged *x*-momentum equation (6.21) by direct substitution of Eqs. (6.19) into the momentum equation (6.14). It is convenient to write the convective acceleration as

$$\frac{du}{dt} = \frac{\partial}{\partial x}(u^2) + \frac{\partial}{\partial y}(uv) + \frac{\partial}{\partial z}(uw)$$

which is valid because of the continuity relation, Eq. (6.14).

P6.35 In the overlap layer of Fig. 6.9a, turbulent shear is large. If we neglect viscosity, we can replace Eq. (6.24) with the approximate velocity-gradient function

$$\frac{du}{dy} = fcn(y, \tau_w, \rho)$$

Show by dimensional analysis that this leads to the logarithmic overlap relation (6.28).

P6.36 The following turbulent flow velocity data *u*(*y*), for air at 75°F and 1 atm near a smooth flat wall were taken in the University of Rhode Island wind tunnel:

y, in	0.025	0.035	0.047	0.055	0.065
u, ft/s	51.2	54.2	56.8	57.6	59.1

Estimate (*a*) the wall shear stress and (*b*) the velocity *u* at *y* = 0.22 in.

P6.37 Two infinite plates a distance *h* apart are parallel to the *xz* plane with the upper plate moving at speed *V*, as in Fig. P6.37. There is a fluid of viscosity *μ* and constant pressure between the plates. Neglecting gravity and assuming incompressible turbulent flow *u*(*y*) between the plates, use the logarithmic law and appropriate boundary conditions to derive a formula for dimensionless wall shear stress versus dimensionless plate velocity. Sketch a typical shape of the profile *u*(*y*).

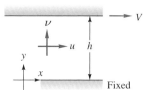

ν V

u h

y

x

P6.37   Fixed

P6.38 Suppose in Fig. P6.37 that *h* = 3 cm, the fluid in water at 20°C, and the flow is turbulent, so that the logarithmic law is valid. If the shear stress in the fluid is 15 Pa, what is *V* in m/s?

P6.39 By analogy with laminar shear, $\tau = \mu\, du/dy$, T. V. Boussinesq in 1877 postulated that turbulent shear could also be related to the mean velocity gradient $\tau_{turb} = \varepsilon\, du/dy$, where *ε* is called the *eddy viscosity* and is much larger than *μ*. If the logarithmic overlap law, Eq. (6.28), is valid with $\tau_{turb} \approx \tau_w$, show that $\varepsilon \approx \kappa \rho u^* y$.

P6.40 Theodore von Kármán in 1930 theorized that turbulent shear could be represented by $\tau_{turb} = \varepsilon\, du/dy$, where $\varepsilon = \rho\kappa^2 y^2 |du/dy|$ is called the *mixing-length eddy viscosity* and $\kappa \approx 0.41$ is Kármán's dimensionless *mixing-length constant* [2, 3]. Assuming that $\tau_{turb} \approx \tau_w$ near the wall, show that this expression can be integrated to yield the logarithmic overlap law, Eq. (6.28).

Turbulent pipe flow—no minor losses

P6.41 Two reservoirs, which differ in surface elevation by 40 m, are connected by 350 m of new pipe of diameter 8 cm. If the desired flow rate is at least 130 N/s of water at 20°C, can the pipe material be made of (*a*) galvanized iron, (*b*) commercial steel, or (*c*) cast iron? Neglect minor losses.

P6.42 Fluid flows steadily, at volume rate *Q*, through a large horizontal pipe and then divides into two small pipes, the larger of which has an inside diameter of 25 mm and carries three times the flow of the smaller pipe. Both small pipes have the same length and pressure drop. If all flows are turbulent, at Re_*D* near 10⁴, estimate the diameter of the smaller pipe.

P6.43 A reservoir supplies water through 100 m of 30-cm-diameter cast iron pipe to a turbine that extracts 80 hp from the flow. The water then exhausts to the atmosphere.

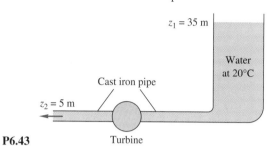

P6.43

Neglect minor losses. (a) Assuming that $f \approx 0.019$, find the flow rate (which results in a cubic polynomial). Explain why there are *two* legitimate solutions. (b) For extra credit, solve for the flow rates using the actual friction factors.

P6.44 Mercury at 20°C flows through 4 m of 7-mm-diameter glass tubing at an average velocity of 5 m/s. Estimate the head loss in m and the pressure drop in kPa.

P6.45 Oil, SG = 0.88 and ν = 4 E-5 m²/s, flows at 400 gal/min through a 6-in asphalted cast iron pipe. The pipe is 0.5 mi long and slopes upward at 8° in the flow direction. Compute the head loss in ft and the pressure change.

P6.46 The Keystone Pipeline in the chapter opener photo has a diameter of 36 inches and a design flow rate of 590,000 barrels per day of crude oil at 40°C. If the pipe material is new steel, estimate the pump horsepower required per mile of pipe.

P6.47 The gutter and smooth drainpipe in Fig. P6.47 remove rainwater from the roof of a building. The smooth drainpipe is 7 cm in diameter. (a) When the gutter is full, estimate the rate of draining. (b) The gutter is designed for a sudden rainstorm of up to 5 inches per hour. For this condition, what is the maximum roof area that can be drained successfully?

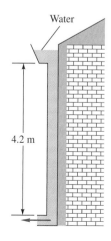

P6.47

P6.48 Follow up Prob. P6.46 with the following question. If the total Keystone pipeline length, from Alberta to Texas, is 2147 miles, how much flow, in barrels per minute, will result if the total available pumping power is 8,000 hp?

P6.49 The tank–pipe system of Fig. P6.49 is to deliver at least 11 m³/h of water at 20°C to the reservoir. What is the maximum roughness height ε allowable for the pipe?

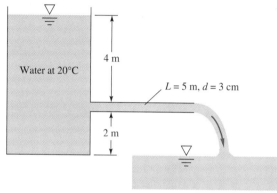

P6.49

P6.50 Ethanol at 20°C flows at 125 U.S. gal/min through a horizontal cast iron pipe with L = 12 m and d = 5 cm. Neglecting entrance effects, estimate (a) the pressure gradient dp/dx, (b) the wall shear stress τ_w, and (c) the percentage reduction in friction factor if the pipe walls are polished to a smooth surface.

P6.51 The viscous sublayer (Fig. 6.9) is normally less than 1 percent of the pipe diameter and therefore very difficult to probe with a finite-sized instrument. In an effort to generate a thick sublayer for probing, Pennsylvania State University in 1964 built a pipe with a flow of glycerin. Assume a smooth 12-in-diameter pipe with V = 60 ft/s and glycerin at 20°C. Compute the sublayer thickness in inches and the pumping horsepower required at 75 percent efficiency if L = 40 ft.

P6.52 The pipe flow in Fig. P6.52 is driven by pressurized air in the tank. What gage pressure p_1 is needed to provide a 20°C water flow rate Q = 60 m³/h?

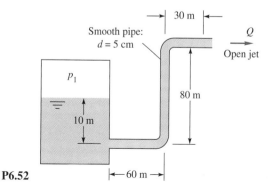

P6.52

P6.53 Water at 20°C flows by gravity through a smooth pipe from one reservoir to a lower one. The elevation difference is 60 m. The pipe is 360 m long, with a diameter of 12 cm. Calculate the expected flow rate in m^3/h. Neglect minor losses.

*P6.54 A swimming pool W by Y by h deep is to be emptied by gravity through the long pipe shown in Fig. P6.54. Assuming an average pipe friction factor f_{av} and neglecting minor losses, derive a formula for the time to empty the tank from an initial level h_o.

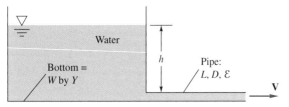

P6.54

P6.55 The reservoirs in Fig. P6.55 contain water at 20°C. If the pipe is smooth with $L = 4500$ m and $d = 4$ cm, what will the flow rate in m^3/h be for $\Delta z = 100$ m?

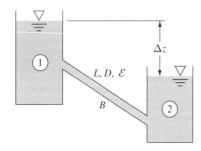

P6.55

P6.56 The Alaska Pipeline in the chapter opener photo has a design flow rate of 4.4 E7 gallons per day of crude oil at 60°C (see Fig. A.1). (a) Assuming a galvanized-iron wall, estimate the total pressure drop required for the 800-mile trip. (b) If there are nine equally spaced pumps, estimate the horsepower each pump must deliver.

P6.57 Apply the analysis of Prob. P6.54 to the following data. Let $W = 5$ m, $Y = 8$ m, $h_o = 2$ m, $L = 15$ m, $D = 5$ cm, and $\varepsilon = 0$. (a) By letting $h = 1.5$ m and 0.5 m as representative depths, estimate the average friction factor. Then (b) estimate the time to drain the pool.

P6.58 For the system in Prob. 6.53, a pump is used at night to drive water back to the upper reservoir. If the pump delivers 15,000 W to the water, estimate the flow rate.

P6.59 The following data were obtained for flow of 20°C water at 20 m^3/h through a badly corroded 5-cm-diameter pipe that slopes downward at an angle of 8°: $p_1 = 420$ kPa, $z_1 = 12$ m, $p_2 = 250$ kPa, $z_2 = 3$ m. Estimate (a) the roughness ratio of the pipe and (b) the percentage change in head loss if the pipe were smooth and the flow rate the same.

P6.60 In the spirit of Haaland's explicit pipe friction factor approximation, Eq. (6.49), Jeppson [20] proposed the following explicit formula:

$$\frac{1}{\sqrt{f}} \approx -2.0 \log_{10}\left(\frac{\varepsilon/d}{3.7} + \frac{5.74}{Re_d^{0.9}}\right)$$

(a) Is this identical to Haaland's formula with just a simple rearrangement? Explain. (b) Compare Jeppson's formula to Haaland's for a few representative values of (turbulent) Re_d and ε/d and their errors compared to the Colebrook formula (6.48). Discuss briefly.

P6.61 What level h must be maintained in Fig. P6.61 to deliver a flow rate of 0.015 ft^3/s through the $\frac{1}{2}$-in commercial steel pipe?

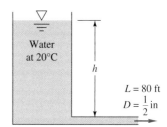

P6.61

P6.62 Water at 20°C is to be pumped through 2000 ft of pipe from reservoir 1 to 2 at a rate of 3 ft^3/s, as shown in Fig. P6.62. If the pipe is cast iron of diameter 6 in and the pump is 75 percent efficient, what horsepower pump is needed?

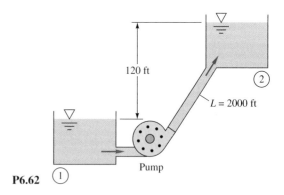

P6.62

Flow rate and sizing problems

P6.63 A tank contains 1 m^3 of water at 20°C and has a drawn-capillary outlet tube at the bottom, as in Fig. P6.63. Find the outlet volume flux Q in m^3/h at this instant.

P6.64 For the system in Fig. P6.63, solve for the flow rate in m^3/h if the fluid is SAE 10 oil at 20°C. Is the flow laminar or turbulent?

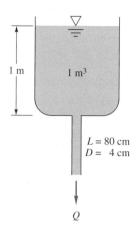

P6.63 Q

P6.65 In Prob. P6.63 the initial flow is turbulent. As the water drains out of the tank, will the flow revert to laminar motion as the tank becomes nearly empty? If so, at what tank depth? Estimate the time, in h, to drain the tank completely.

P6.66 Ethyl alcohol at 20°C flows through a 10-cm horizontal drawn tube 100 m long. The fully developed wall shear stress is 14 Pa. Estimate (a) the pressure drop, (b) the volume flow rate, and (c) the velocity u at $r = 1$ cm.

P6.67 A straight 10-cm commercial-steel pipe is 1 km long and is laid on a constant slope of 5°. Water at 20°C flows downward, due to gravity only. Estimate the flow rate in m³/h. What happens if the pipe length is 2 km?

*P6.68 The Moody chart cannot find V directly, since V appears in both ordinate and abscissa. (a) Arrange the variables (h_f, d, g, L, ν) into a single dimensionless group, with $h_f d^3$ in the numerator, denoted as ξ, which equals ($f\,Re_d^2/2$). (b) Rearrange the Colebrook formula (6.48) to solve for Re_d in terms of ξ. (c) For extra credit, solve Example 6.9 with this new formula.

P6.69 For Prob. P6.62 suppose the only pump available can deliver 80 hp to the fluid. What is the proper pipe size in inches to maintain the 3 ft³/s flow rate?

P6.70 Ethylene glycol at 20°C flows through 80 m of cast iron pipe of diameter 6 cm. The measured pressure drop is 250 kPa. Neglect minor losses. Using a noniterative formulation, estimate the flow rate in m³/h.

*P6.71 It is desired to solve Prob. 6.62 for the most economical pump and cast iron pipe system. If the pump costs $125 per horsepower delivered to the fluid and the pipe costs $7000 per inch of diameter, what are the minimum cost and the pipe and pump size to maintain the 3 ft³/s flow rate? Make some simplifying assumptions.

P6.72 Modify Prob. P6.57 by letting the diameter be unknown. Find the proper pipe diameter for which the pool will drain in about two hours flat.

P6.73 For 20°C water flow in a smooth, horizontal 10-cm pipe, with $\Delta p/L = 1000$ Pa/m, the writer computed a flow rate of 0.030 m³/s. (a) Verify, or disprove, the writer's answer. (b) If verified, use the power-law friction factor relation, Eq. (6.41), to estimate the pipe diameter that will triple this flow rate. (c) For extra credit, use the more exact friction factor relation, Eq. (6.38), to solve part (b).

P6.74 Two reservoirs, which differ in surface elevation by 40 m, are connected by a new commercial steel pipe of diameter 8 cm. If the desired flow rate is 200 N/s of water at 20°C, what is the proper length of the pipe?

P6.75 You wish to water your garden with 100 ft of $\frac{5}{8}$-in-diameter hose whose roughness is 0.011 in. What will be the delivery, in ft³/s, if the gage pressure at the faucet is 60 lbf/in²? If there is no nozzle (just an open hose exit), what is the maximum horizontal distance the exit jet will carry?

P6.76 The small turbine in Fig. P6.76 extracts 400 W of power from the water flow. Both pipes are wrought iron. Compute the flow rate Q in m³/h. Why are there two solutions? Which is better?

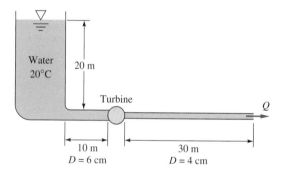

P6.76

*P6.77 Modify Prob. P6.76 into an economic analysis, as follows: Let the 40 m of wrought iron pipe have a uniform diameter d. Let the steady water flow available be $Q = 30$ m³/h. The cost of the turbine is $4 per watt developed, and the cost of the piping is $75 per centimeter of diameter. The power generated may be sold for $0.08 per kilowatt-hour. Find the proper pipe diameter for minimum *payback time*—that is, the minimum time for which the power sales will equal the initial cost of the system.

P6.78 In Fig. P6.78 the connecting pipe is commercial steel 6 cm in diameter. Estimate the flow rate, in m³/h, if the fluid is water at 20°C. Which way is the flow?

P6.79 A garden hose is to be used as the return line in a waterfall display at a mall. In order to select the proper pump, you need to know the roughness height inside the garden hose. Unfortunately, roughness information is not supplied by the hose manufacturer. So you devise a simple experiment to measure the roughness. The hose is attached to the drain of an above-ground swimming pool, the surface of which is 3.0 m above the hose outlet. You estimate the minor loss coefficient of the entrance region as 0.5, and the drain valve has a minor loss equivalent length of 200 diameters when fully open. Using a bucket and stopwatch, you open the valve and measure the flow rate to be 2.0×10^{-4} m³/s for a hose that is 10.0 m long and has an inside diameter of 1.50 cm. Estimate the roughness height in mm inside the hose.

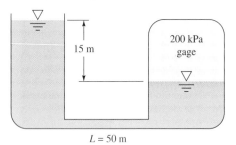

P6.78 $L = 50$ m

P6.80 The head-versus-flow-rate characteristics of a centrifugal
💻 pump are shown in Fig. P6.80. If this pump drives water at 20°C through 120 m of 30-cm-diameter cast iron pipe, what will be the resulting flow rate, in m³/s?

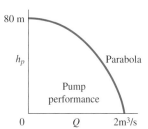

P6.80   0   Q   2m³/s

P6.81 The pump in Fig. P6.80 is used to deliver gasoline at 20°C through 350 m of 30-cm-diameter galvanized iron pipe. Estimate the resulting flow rate, in m³/s. (Note that the pump head is now in meters of gasoline.)

P6.82 Fluid at 20°C flows through a horizontal galvanized-iron pipe 20 m long and 8 cm in diameter. The wall shear stress is 90 Pa. Calculate the flow rate in m³/h if the fluid is (a) glycerin and (b) water.

P6.83 For the system of Fig. P6.55, let $\Delta z = 80$ m and $L = 185$ m of cast iron pipe. What is the pipe diameter for which the flow rate will be 7 m³/h?

P6.84 It is desired to deliver 60 m³/h of water at 20°C through a horizontal asphalted cast iron pipe. Estimate the pipe diameter that will cause the pressure drop to be exactly 40 kPa per 100 m of pipe length.

P6.85 For the system in Prob. P6.53, a pump, which delivers 15,000 W to the water, is used at night to refill the upper reservoir. The pipe diameter is increased from 12 cm to provide more flow. If the resultant flow rate is 90 m³/h, estimate the new pipe size.

Noncircular ducts

P6.86 SAE 10 oil at 20°C flows at an average velocity of 2 m/s between two smooth parallel horizontal plates 3 cm apart. Estimate (a) the centerline velocity, (b) the head loss per meter, and (c) the pressure drop per meter.

P6.87 A commercial steel annulus 40 ft long, with $a = 1$ in and $b = \frac{1}{2}$ in, connects two reservoirs that differ in surface height by 20 ft. Compute the flow rate in ft³/s through the annulus if the fluid is water at 20°C.

P6.88 An oil cooler consists of multiple parallel-plate passages, as shown in Fig. P6.88. The available pressure drop is 6 kPa, and the fluid is SAE 10W oil at 20°C. If the desired total flow rate is 900 m³/h, estimate the appropriate number of passages. The plate walls are hydraulically smooth.

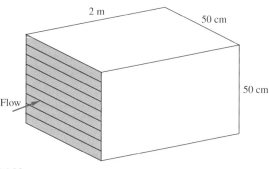

P6.88

P6.89 An annulus of narrow clearance causes a very large pressure drop and is useful as an accurate measurement of viscosity. If a smooth annulus 1 m long with $a = 50$ mm and $b = 49$ mm carries an oil flow at 0.001 m³/s, what is the oil viscosity if the pressure drop is 250 kPa?

P6.90 A rectangular sheet-metal duct is 200 ft long and has a fixed height $H = 6$ in. The width B, however, may vary from 6 to 36 in. A blower provides a pressure drop of 80 Pa of air at 20°C and 1 atm. What is the optimum width B that will provide the most airflow in ft³/s?

P6.91 Heat exchangers often consist of many triangular passages. Typical is Fig. P6.91, with $L = 60$ cm and an isosceles-triangle cross section of side length $a = 2$ cm and included angle $\beta = 80°$. If the average velocity is $V = 2$ m/s and the fluid is SAE 10 oil at 20°C, estimate the pressure drop.

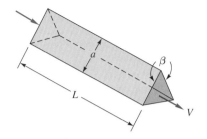

P6.91

P6.92 A large room uses a fan to draw in atmospheric air at 20°C through a 30-cm by 30-cm commercial-steel duct 12 m long, as in Fig. P6.92. Estimate (a) the airflow rate in m³/h if the room pressure is 10 Pa vacuum and (b) the room pressure if the flow rate is 1200 m³/h. Neglect minor losses.

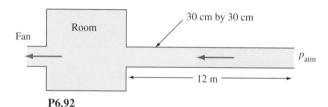

P6.92

P6.93 In Moody's Example 6.6, the 6-inch diameter, 200-ft-long asphalted cast iron pipe has a pressure drop of about 280 lbf/ft² when the average water velocity is 6 ft/s. Compare this to an *annular* cast iron pipe with an inner diameter of 6 in and the same annular average velocity of 6 ft/s. (a) What outer diameter would cause the flow to have the same pressure drop of 280 lbf/ft²? (b) How do the cross-section areas compare, and why? Use the hydraulic diameter approximation.

P6.94 Air at 20°C flows through a smooth duct of diameter 20 cm at an average velocity of 5 m/s. It then flows into a smooth square duct of side length a. Find the square duct size a for which the pressure drop per meter will be exactly the same as the circular duct.

P6.95 Although analytical solutions are available for laminar flow in many duct shapes [34], what do we do about ducts of arbitrary shape? Bahrami et al. [57] propose that a better approach to the pipe result, $f Re = 64$, is achieved by replacing the hydraulic diameter D_h with $\sqrt{A}$, where A is the area of the cross section. Test this idea for the isosceles triangles of Table 6.4. If time is short, at least try 10°, 50°, and 80°. What do you conclude about this idea?

P6.96 A fuel cell [59] consists of air (or oxygen) and hydrogen micro ducts, separated by a membrane that promotes proton exchange for an electric current, as in Fig. P6.96. Suppose that the air side, at 20°C and approximately 1 atm, has five 1 mm by 1 mm ducts, each 1 m long. The total flow rate is 1.5 E-4 kg/s. (a) Determine if the flow is laminar or turbulent. (b) Estimate the pressure drop. *(Problem courtesy of Dr. Pezhman Shirvanian.)*

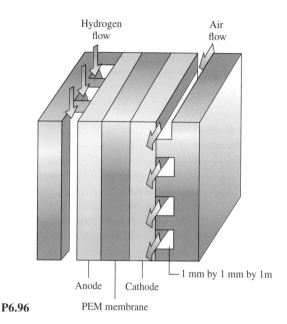

P6.96

P6.97 A heat exchanger consists of multiple parallel-plate passages, as shown in Fig. P6.97. The available pressure drop is 2 kPa, and the fluid is water at 20°C. If the desired total flow rate is 900 m³/h, estimate the appropriate number of passages. The plate walls are hydraulically smooth.

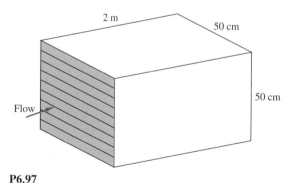

P6.97

P6.98 A rectangular heat exchanger is to be divided into smaller sections using sheets of commercial steel 0.4 mm thick, as sketched in Fig. P6.98. The flow rate is 20 kg/s of water at 20°C. Basic dimensions are $L = 1$ m, $W = 20$ cm, and $H = 10$ cm. What is the proper number of *square* sections if the overall pressure drop is to be no more than 1600 Pa?

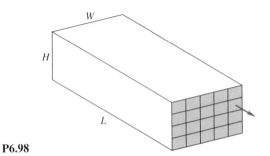

P6.98

Minor or local losses

P6.99 In Sec. 6.11 it was mentioned that Roman aqueduct customers obtained extra water by attaching a diffuser to their pipe exits. Fig. P6.99 shows a simulation: a smooth inlet pipe, with or without a 15° conical diffuser expanding to a 5-cm-diameter exit. The pipe entrance is sharp-edged. Calculate the flow rate (a) without and (b) with the diffuser.

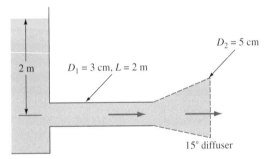

P6.99

*P6.100 Modify Prob. P6.55 as follows: Assume a pump can deliver 3 kW to pump the water back up to reservoir 1 from reservoir 2. Accounting for an open flanged globe valve and sharp-edged entrance and exit, estimate the predicted flow rate, in m^3/h.

P6.101 In Fig. P6.101 a thick filter is being tested for losses. The flow rate in the pipe is 7 m^3/min, and the upstream pressure is 120 kPa. The fluid is air at 20°C. Using the water manometer reading, estimate the loss coefficient K of the filter.

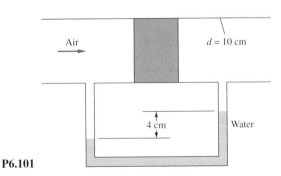

P6.101

*P6.102 A 70 percent efficient pump delivers water at 20°C from one reservoir to another 20 ft higher, as in Fig. P6.102. The piping system consists of 60 ft of galvanized iron 2-in pipe, a reentrant entrance, two screwed 90° long-radius elbows, a screwed-open gate valve, and a sharp exit. What is the input power required in horsepower with and without a 6° well-designed conical expansion added to the exit? The flow rate is 0.4 ft^3/s.

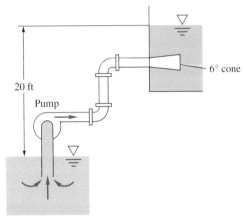

P6.102

P6.103 The reservoirs in Fig. P6.103 are connected by cast iron pipes joined abruptly, with sharp-edged entrance and exit. Including minor losses, estimate the flow of water at 20°C if the surface of reservoir 1 is 45 ft higher than that of reservoir 2.

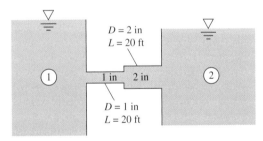

P6.103

P6.104 Consider a 20°C flow at 2 m/s through a smooth 3-mm diameter microtube which consists of a straight run of 10 cm, a long radius bend, and another straight run of 10 cm. Compute the total pressure drop if the fluid is (a) water; and (b) ethylene glycol.

P6.105 The system in Fig. P6.105 consists of 1200 m of 5 cm cast iron pipe, two 45° and four 90° flanged long-radius elbows, a fully open flanged globe valve, and a sharp exit into a reservoir. If the elevation at point 1 is 400 m, what gage pressure is required at point 1 to deliver 0.005 m^3/s of water at 20°C into the reservoir?

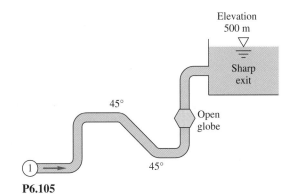

P6.105

P6.106 The water pipe in Fig. P6.106 slopes upward at 30°. The pipe has a 1-in diameter and is smooth. The flanged globe valve is fully open. If the mercury manometer shows a 7-in deflection, what is the flow rate in ft³/s?

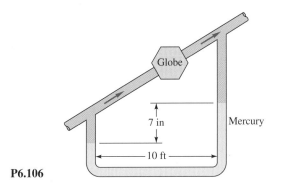

P6.106

*P6.107** A tank of water 4 m in diameter and 7 m deep is to be drained by a 5-cm-diameter exit pipe at the bottom, as in Fig. P6.107. In design (1), the pipe extends out for 1 m and into the tank for 10 cm. In design (2), the interior pipe is removed and the entrance beveled, Fig. 6.21, so that $K \approx 0.1$ in the entrance. (a) An engineer claims that design (2) will drain 25 percent faster than design (1). Is this claim true? (b) Estimate the time to drain of design (2), assuming $f \approx 0.020$.

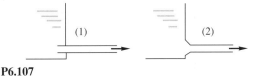

P6.107

P6.108 The water pump in Fig. P6.108 maintains a pressure of 6.5 psig at point 1. There is a filter, a half-open disk valve, and two regular screwed elbows. There are 80 ft of 4-in diameter commercial steel pipe. (a) If the flow rate is 0.4 ft³/s, what is the loss coefficient of the filter? (b) If the disk valve is wide open and $K_{filter} = 7$, what is the resulting flow rate?

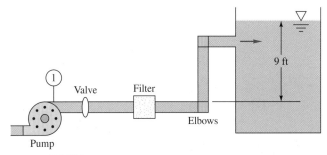

P6.108

P6.109 In Fig. P6.109 there are 125 ft of 2-in pipe, 75 ft of 6-in pipe, and 150 ft of 3-in pipe, all cast iron. There are three 90° elbows and an open globe valve, all flanged. If the exit elevation is zero, what horsepower is extracted by the turbine when the flow rate is 0.16 ft³/s of water at 20°C?

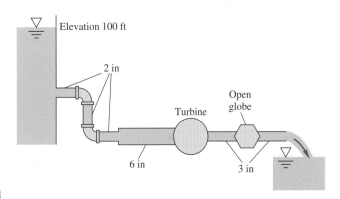

P6.109

P6.110 In Fig. P6.110 the pipe entrance is sharp-edged. If the flow rate is 0.004 m³/s, what power, in W, is extracted by the turbine?

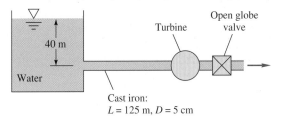

P6.110

Series and parallel pipe systems

P6.111 For the parallel-pipe system of Fig. P6.111, each pipe is cast iron, and the pressure drop $p_1 - p_2 = 3$ lbf/in². Compute the total flow rate between 1 and 2 if the fluid is SAE 10 oil at 20°C.

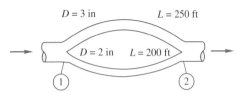

P6.111

P6.112 If the two pipes in Fig. P6.111 are instead laid in series with the same total pressure drop of 3 lbf/in², what will the flow rate be? The fluid is SAE 10 oil at 20°C.

P6.113 The parallel galvanized iron pipe system of Fig. P6.113 delivers water at 20°C with a total flow rate of 0.036 m³/s. If the pump is wide open and not running, with a loss coefficient $K = 1.5$, determine (a) the flow rate in each pipe and (b) the overall pressure drop.

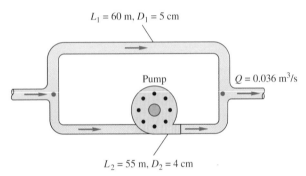

P6.113

*****P6.114** A blower supplies standard air to a plenum that feeds two horizontal square sheet-metal ducts with sharp-edged entrances. One duct is 100 ft long, with a cross-section 6 in by 6 in. The second duct is 200 ft long. Each duct exhausts to the atmosphere. When the plenum pressure is 5.0 lbf/ft² (gage) the volume flow in the longer duct is three times the flow in the shorter duct. Estimate both volume flows and the cross-section size of the longer duct.

P6.115 In Fig. P6.115 all pipes are 8-cm-diameter cast iron. Determine the flow rate from reservoir 1 if valve C is (a) closed and (b) open, $K = 0.5$.

P6.116 For the series-parallel system of Fig. P6.116, all pipes are 8-cm-diameter asphalted cast iron. If the total pressure drop $p_1 - p_2 = 750$ kPa, find the resulting flow rate Q m³/h for water at 20°C. Neglect minor losses.

P6.117 A blower delivers air at 3000 m³/h to the duct circuit in Fig. P6.117. Each duct is commercial steel and of square cross section, with side lengths $a_1 = a_3 = 20$ cm and $a_2 = a_4 = 12$ cm. Assuming sea-level air conditions, estimate the power required if the blower has an efficiency of 75 percent. Neglect minor losses.

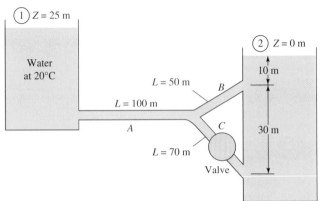

P6.115

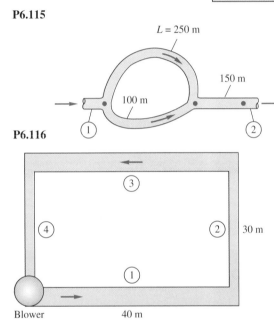

P6.116

P6.117

P6.118 For the piping system of Fig. P6.118, all pipes are concrete with a roughness of 0.04 in. Neglecting minor losses, compute the overall pressure drop $p_1 - p_2$ in lbf/in² if $Q = 20$ ft³/s. The fluid is water at 20°C.

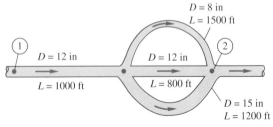

P6.118

P6.119 For the piping system of Prob. P6.111, let the fluid be gasoline at 20°C, with both pipes cast iron. If the flow rate in the 2-in pipe (b) is 1.2 ft³/min, estimate the flow rate in the 3-in pipe (a), in ft³/min.

P6.120 Three cast iron pipes are laid in parallel with these dimensions:

Pipe	Length, m	Diameter, cm
1	800	12
2	600	8
3	900	10

The total flow rate is 200 m³/h of water at 20°C. Determine (a) the flow rate in each pipe and (b) the pressure drop across the system.

Three-reservoir and pipe network systems

P6.121 Consider the three-reservoir system of Fig. P6.121 with the following data:

$$L_1 = 95m \quad L_2 = 125 \text{ m} \quad L_3 = 160 \text{ m}$$

$$z_1 = 25 \text{ m} \quad z_2 = 115 \text{ m} \quad z_3 = 85 \text{ m}$$

All pipes are 28-cm-diameter unfinished concrete ($\varepsilon = 1$ mm). Compute the steady flow rate in all pipes for water at 20°C.

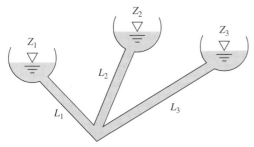

P6.121

P6.122 Modify Prob. P6.121 as follows: Reduce the diameter to 15 cm (with $\varepsilon = 1$ mm), and compute the flow rates for water at 20°C. These flow rates distribute in nearly the same manner as in Prob. P6.121 but are about 5.2 times lower. Can you explain this difference?

P6.123 Modify Prob. P6.121 as follows: All data are the same except that z_3 is unknown. Find the value of z_3 for which the flow rate in pipe 3 is 0.2 m³/s toward the junction. (This problem requires iteration and is best suited to a computer.)

P6.124 The three-reservoir system in Fig. P6.124 delivers water at 20°C. The system data are as follows:

$$D_1 = 8 \text{ in} \quad D_2 = 6 \text{ in} \quad D_3 = 9 \text{ in}$$

$$L_1 = 1800 \text{ ft} \quad L_2 = 1200 \text{ ft} \quad L_3 = 1600 \text{ ft}$$

All pipes are galvanized iron. Compute the flow rate in all pipes.

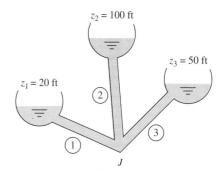

P6.124

P6.125 Suppose that the three cast iron pipes in Prob. P6.120 are instead connected to meet smoothly at a point B, as shown in Fig. P6.125. The inlet pressures in each pipe are

$$p_1 = 200 \text{ kPa} \quad p_2 = 160 \text{ kPa} \quad p_3 = 100 \text{ kPa}.$$

The fluid is water at 20°C. Neglect minor losses. Estimate the flow rate in each pipe and whether it is toward or away from point B.

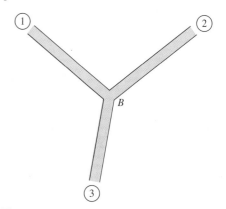

P6.125

P6.126 Modify Prob. P6.124 as follows: Let all data be the same except that pipe 1 is fitted with a butterfly valve (Fig. 6.19b). Estimate the proper valve opening angle (in degrees) for the flow rate through pipe 1 to be reduced to 1.5 ft³/s toward reservoir 1. (This problem requires iteration and is best suited to a computer.)

P6.127 In the five-pipe horizontal network of Fig. P6.127, assume that all pipes have a friction factor $f = 0.025$. For the given inlet and exit flow rate of 2 ft³/s of water at

20°C, determine the flow rate and direction in all pipes. If p_A = 120 lbf/in² gage, determine the pressures at points B, C, and D.

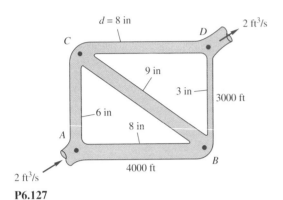

P6.127

P6.128 Modify Prob. P6.127 as follows: Let the inlet flow rate at A and the exit flow at D be unknown. Let $p_A - p_B$ = 100 lbf/in². Compute the flow rate in all five pipes.

P6.129 In Fig. P6.129 all four horizontal cast iron pipes are 45 m long and 8 cm in diameter and meet at junction a, delivering water at 20°C. The pressures are known at four points as shown:

$$p_1 = 950 \text{ kPa} \quad p_2 = 350 \text{ kPa}$$

$$p_3 = 675 \text{ kPa} \quad p_4 = 100 \text{ kPa}$$

Neglecting minor losses, determine the flow rate in each pipe.

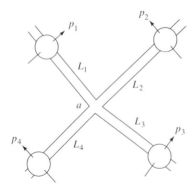

P6.129

P6.130 In Fig. P6.130 lengths AB and BD are 2000 and 1500 ft, respectively. The friction factor is 0.022 everywhere, and p_A = 90 lbf/in² gage. All pipes have a diameter of 6 in. For water at 20°C, determine the flow rate in all pipes and the pressures at points B, C, and D.

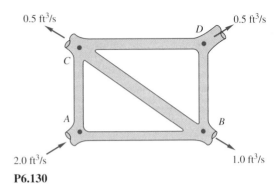

P6.130

Diffuser performance

P6.131 A water tunnel test section has a 1-m diameter and flow properties V = 20 m/s, p = 100 kPa, and T = 20°C. The boundary layer blockage at the end of the section is 9 percent. If a conical diffuser is to be added at the end of the section to achieve maximum pressure recovery, what should its angle, length, exit diameter, and exit pressure be?

P6.132 For Prob. P6.131 suppose we are limited by space to a total diffuser length of 10 m. What should the diffuser angle, exit diameter, and exit pressure be for maximum recovery?

P6.133 A wind tunnel test section is 3 ft square with flow properties V = 150 ft/s, p = 15 lbf/in² absolute, and T = 68°F. Boundary layer blockage at the end of the test section is 8 percent. Find the angle, length, exit height, and exit pressure of a flat-walled diffuser added onto the section to achieve maximum pressure recovery.

P6.134 For Prob. P6.133 suppose we are limited by space to a total diffuser length of 30 ft. What should the diffuser angle, exit height, and exit pressure be for maximum recovery?

The pitot-static tube

P6.135 An airplane uses a pitot-static tube as a velocimeter. The measurements, with their uncertainties, are a static temperature of (-11 ± 3)°C, a static pressure of 60 ± 2 kPa, and a pressure difference $(p_o - p_s)$ = 3200 ± 60 Pa. (a) Estimate the airplane's velocity and its uncertainty. (b) Is a compressibility correction needed?

P6.136 For the pitot-static pressure arrangement of Fig. P6.136, the manometer fluid is (colored) water at 20°C. Estimate (a) the centerline velocity, (b) the pipe volume flow, and (c) the (smooth) wall shear stress.

P6.137 For the 20°C water flow of Fig. P6.137, use the pitot-static arrangement to estimate (a) the centerline velocity and (b) the volume flow in the 5-in-diameter smooth pipe. (c) What error in flow rate is caused by neglecting the 1-ft elevation difference?

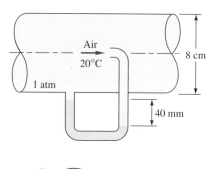

P6.136

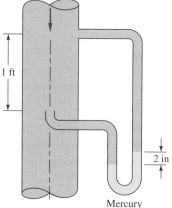

P6.137   Mercury

P6.138 An engineer who took college fluid mechanics on a pass–fail basis has placed the static pressure hole far upstream of the stagnation probe, as in Fig. P6.138, thus contaminating the pitot measurement ridiculously with pipe friction losses. If the pipe flow is air at 20°C and 1 atm and the manometer fluid is Meriam red oil (SG = 0.827), estimate the air centerline velocity for the given manometer reading of 16 cm. Assume a smooth-walled tube.

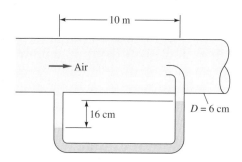

P6.138

P6.139 Professor Walter Tunnel needs to measure the flow velocity in a water tunnel. Due to budgetary restrictions, he cannot

afford a pitot-static probe, but instead inserts a total head probe and a static pressure probe, as shown in Fig. P6.139, a distance h_1 apart from each other. Both probes are in the main free stream of the water tunnel, unaffected by the thin boundary layers on the sidewalls. The two probes are connected as shown to a U-tube manometer. The densities and vertical distances are shown in Fig. P6.139. (a) Write an expression for velocity V in terms of the parameters in the problem. (b) Is it critical that distance h_1 be measured accurately? (c) How does the expression for velocity V differ from that which would be obtained if a pitot-static probe had been available and used with the same U-tube manometer?

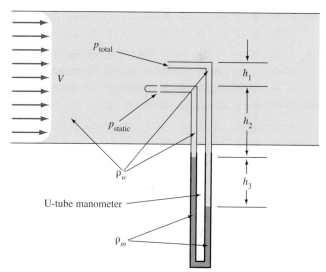

P6.139

Flowmeters: the orifice plate

P6.140 Gasoline at 20°C flows at 3 m³/h in a 6-cm-diameter pipe. A 4-cm-diameter thin-plate orifice with corner taps is installed. Estimate the measured pressure drop, in Pa.

P6.141 Gasoline at 20°C flows at 105 m³/h in a 10-cm-diameter pipe. We wish to meter the flow with a thin-plate orifice and a differential pressure transducer that reads best at about 55 kPa. What is the proper β ratio for the orifice?

P6.142 The shower head in Fig. P6.142 delivers water at 50°C. An orifice-type flow reducer is to be installed. The upstream pressure is constant at 400 kPa. What flow rate, in gal/min, results without the reducer? What reducer orifice diameter would decrease the flow by 40 percent?

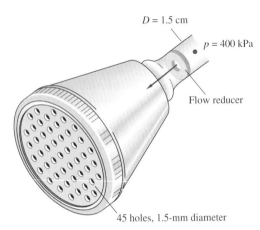

$D = 1.5$ cm

$p = 400$ kPa

Flow reducer

45 holes, 1.5-mm diameter

P6.142

P6.143 A 10-cm-diameter smooth pipe contains an orifice plate with $D: \frac{1}{2}D$ taps and $\beta = 0.5$. The measured orifice pressure drop is 75 kPa for water flow at 20°C. Estimate the flow rate, in m³/h. What is the nonrecoverable head loss?

*P6.144 Water at 20°C flows through the orifice in Fig. P6.154, which is monitored by a mercury manometer. If $d = 3$ cm, (a) what is h when the flow rate is 20 m³/h and (b) what is Q in m³/h when $h = 58$ cm?

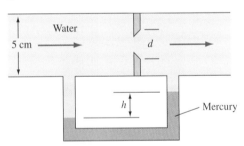

Water

5 cm

d

h

Mercury

P6.144

P6.145 The 1-m-diameter tank in Fig. P6.145 is initially filled with gasoline at 20°C. There is a 2-cm-diameter orifice in the bottom. If the orifice is suddenly opened, estimate the time for the fluid level $h(t)$ to drop from 2.0 to 1.6 m.

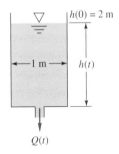

$h(0) = 2$ m

1 m

$h(t)$

P6.145

$Q(t)$

P6.146 A pipe connecting two reservoirs, as in Fig. P6.146, contains a thin-plate orifice. For water flow at 20°C, estimate (a) the volume flow through the pipe and (b) the pressure drop across the orifice plate.

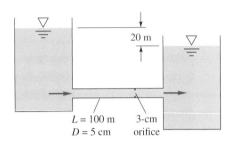

20 m

$L = 100$ m
$D = 5$ cm

3-cm
orifice

P6.146

P6.147 Air flows through a 6-cm-diameter smooth pipe that has a 2-m-long perforated section containing 500 holes (diameter 1 mm), as in Fig. P6.147. Pressure outside the pipe is sea-level standard air. If $p_1 = 105$ kPa and $Q_1 = 110$ m³/h, estimate p_2 and Q_2, assuming that the holes are approximated by thin-plate orifices. (*Hint:* A momentum control volume may be very useful.)

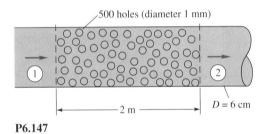

500 holes (diameter 1 mm)

1

2

2 m

$D = 6$ cm

P6.147

P6.148 A smooth pipe containing ethanol at 20°C flows at 7 m³/h through a Bernoulli obstruction, as in Fig. P6.148. Three piezometer tubes are installed, as shown. If the obstruction is a thin-plate orifice, estimate the piezometer levels (a) h_2 and (b) h_3.

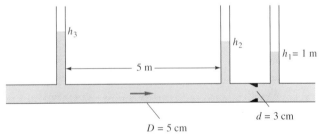

h_3

h_2

$h_1 = 1$ m

5 m

$d = 3$ cm

$D = 5$ cm

P6.148

Flowmeters: the flow nozzle

P6.149 In a laboratory experiment, air at 20°C flows from a large tank through a 2-cm-diameter smooth pipe into a sea-level atmosphere, as in Fig. P6.149. The flow is metered by a long-radius nozzle of 1-cm diameter, using a manometer with Meriam red oil (SG = 0.827). The pipe is 8 m long. The measurements of tank pressure and manometer height are as follows:

p_{tank}, Pa(gage):	60	320	1200	2050	2470	3500	4900
h_{mano}, mm:	6	38	160	295	380	575	820

Use these data to calculate the flow rates Q and Reynolds numbers Re_D and make a plot of measured flow rate versus tank pressure. Is the flow laminar or turbulent? Compare the data with theoretical results obtained from the Moody chart, including minor losses. Discuss.

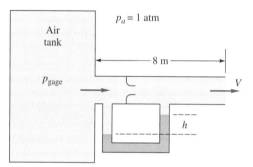

P6.149

P6.150 Gasoline at 20°C flows at 0.06 m³/s through a 15-cm pipe and is metered by a 9-cm long-radius flow nozzle (Fig. 6.40a). What is the expected pressure drop across the nozzle?

P6.151 An engineer needs to monitor a flow of 20°C gasoline at about 250 ± 25 gal/min through a 4-in-diameter smooth pipe. She can use an orifice plate, a long-radius flow nozzle, or a venturi nozzle, all with 2-in-diameter throats. The only differential pressure gage available is accurate in the range 6 to 10 lbf/in². Disregarding flow losses, which device is best?

P6.152 Kerosene at 20°C flows at 20 m³/h in an 8-cm-diameter pipe. The flow is to be metered by an ISA 1932 flow nozzle so that the pressure drop is 7000 Pa. What is the proper nozzle diameter?

P6.153 Two water tanks, each with base area of 1 ft², are connected by a 0.5-in-diameter long-radius nozzle as in Fig. P6.153. If $h = 1$ ft as shown for $t = 0$, estimate the time for $h(t)$ to drop to 0.25 ft.

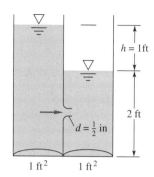

P6.153

Flowmeters: the venturi meter

P6.154 Gasoline at 20°C flows through a 6-cm-diameter pipe. It is metered by a modern venturi nozzle with $d = 4$ cm. The measured pressure drop is 8.5 kPa. Estimate the flow rate in gallons per minute.

P6.155 It is desired to meter methanol at 20°C flowing through a 5-in-diameter pipe. The expected flow rate is about 300 gal/min. Two flowmeters are available: a venturi nozzle and a thinplate orifice, each with $d = 2$ in. The differential pressure gage on hand is most accurate at about 12–15 lbs/in². Which meter is better for this job?

P6.156 Ethanol at 20°C flows down through a modern venturi nozzle as in Fig. P6.156. If the mercury manometer reading is 4 in, as shown, estimate the flow rate, in gal/min.

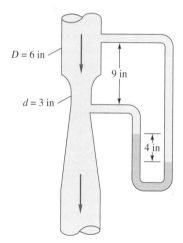

P6.156

P6.157 Modify Prob. P6.156 if the fluid is air at 20°C, entering the venturi at a pressure of 18 lbf/in². Should a compressibility correction be used?

P6.158 Water at 20°C flows in a long horizontal commercial steel 6-cm-diameter pipe that contains a classical Herschel venturi with a 4-cm throat. The venturi is connected to a mercury manometer whose reading is $h = 40$ cm. Estimate (*a*) the flow rate, in m³/h, and (*b*) the total pressure difference between points 50 cm upstream and 50 cm downstream of the venturi.

P6.159 A modern venturi nozzle is tested in a laboratory flow with water at 20°C. The pipe diameter is 5.5 cm, and the venturi throat diameter is 3.5 cm. The flow rate is measured by a weigh tank and the pressure drop by a water–mercury manometer. The mass flow rate and manometer readings are as follows:

$\dot{m}$, kg/s	0.95	1.98	2.99	5.06	8.15
h, mm	3.7	15.9	36.2	102.4	264.4

Use these data to plot a calibration curve of venturi discharge coefficient versus Reynolds number. Compare with the accepted correlation, Eq. (6.114).

Flowmeters: other designs

P6.160 An instrument popular in the beverage industry is the *target flowmeter* in Fig. P6.160. A small flat disk is mounted in the center of the pipe, supported by a strong but thin rod. (*a*) Explain how the flowmeter works. (*b*) If the bending moment M of the rod is measured at the wall, derive a formula for the estimated velocity of the flow. (*c*) List a few advantages and disadvantages of such an instrument.

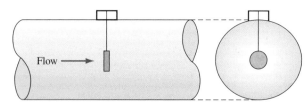

Flow →

P6.160

P6.161 An instrument popular in the water supply industry, sketched in Fig. P6.161, is the single jet water meter. (*a*) How does it work? (*b*) What do you think a typical calibration curve would look like? (*c*) Can you cite further details, for example, reliability, head loss, cost [58]?

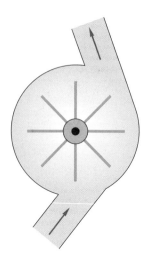

P6.161

Flowmeters: compressibility correction

P6.162 Air flows at high speed through a Herschel venturi monitored by a mercury manometer, as shown in Fig. P6.162. The upstream conditions are 150 kPa and 80°C. If $h = 37$ cm, estimate the mass flow in kg/s. (*Hint:* The flow is compressible.)

P6.163 Modify Prob. P6.162 as follows: Find the manometer reading h for which the mass flow through the venturi is approximately 0.4 kg/s. (*Hint:* The flow is compressible.)

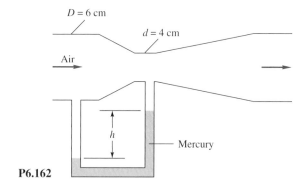

$D = 6$ cm

$d = 4$ cm

Air

h

Mercury

P6.162

Word Problems

W6.1 In fully developed straight-duct flow, the velocity profiles do not change (why?), but the pressure drops along the pipe axis. Thus there is pressure work done on the fluid. If, say, the pipe is insulated from heat loss, where does this energy go? Make a thermodynamic analysis of the pipe flow.

W6.2 From the Moody chart (Fig. 6.13), rough surfaces, such as sand grains or ragged machining, do not affect laminar flow.

Can you explain why? They *do* affect turbulent flow. Can you develop, or suggest, an analytical–physical model of turbulent flow near a rough surface that might be used to predict the known increase in pressure drop?

W6.3 Differentiation of the laminar pipe flow solution, Eq. (6.40), shows that the fluid shear stress $\tau(r)$ varies linearly from zero at the axis to τ_w at the wall. It is claimed that this is also true, at least in the time mean, for fully developed *turbulent* flow. Can you verify this claim analytically?

W6.4 A porous medium consists of many tiny tortuous passages, and Reynolds numbers based on pore size are usually very low, of order unity. In 1856 H. Darcy proposed that the pressure gradient in a porous medium was directly proportional to the volume-averaged velocity $\mathbf{V}$ of the fluid:

$$\nabla p = -\frac{\mu}{K}\mathbf{V}$$

where K is termed the *permeability* of the medium. This is now called *Darcy's law* of porous flow. Can you make a Poiseuille flow model of porous-media flow that verifies Darcy's law? Meanwhile, as the Reynolds number increases, so that $VK^{1/2}/\nu > 1$, the pressure drop becomes nonlinear, as was shown experimentally by P. H. Forscheimer as early as 1782. The flow is still decidedly laminar, yet the pressure gradient is quadratic:

$$\nabla p = -\frac{\mu}{K}\mathbf{V} - C|V|\mathbf{V} \quad \text{Darcy-Forscheimer law}$$

where C is an empirical constant. Can you explain the reason for this nonlinear behavior?

Fundamentals of Engineering Exam Problems

FE6.1 In flow through a straight, smooth pipe, the diameter Reynolds number for transition to turbulence is generally taken to be
(*a*) 1500, (*b*) 2300, (*c*) 4000, (*d*) 250,000, (*e*) 500,000

FE6.2 For flow of water at 20°C through a straight, smooth pipe at 0.06 m³/h, the pipe diameter for which transition to turbulence occurs is approximately
(*a*) 1.0 cm, (*b*) 1.5 cm, (*c*) 2.0 cm, (*d*) 2.5 cm, (*e*) 3.0 cm

FE6.3 For flow of oil [$\mu = 0.1$ kg/(m · s), SG = 0.9] through a long, straight, smooth 5-cm-diameter pipe at 14 m³/h, the pressure drop per meter is approximately
(*a*) 2200 Pa, (*b*) 2500 Pa, (*c*) 10,000 Pa, (*d*) 160 Pa, (*e*) 2800 Pa

FE6.4 For flow of water at a Reynolds number of 1.03 E6 through a 5-cm-diameter pipe of roughness height 0.5 mm, the approximate Moody friction factor is
(*a*) 0.012, (*b*) 0.018, (*c*) 0.038, (*d*) 0.049, (*e*) 0.102

FE6.5 Minor losses through valves, fittings, bends, contractions, and the like are commonly modeled as proportional to
(*a*) total head, (*b*) static head, (*c*) velocity head, (*d*) pressure drop, (*e*) velocity

FE6.6 A smooth 8-cm-diameter pipe, 200 m long, connects two reservoirs, containing water at 20°C, one of which has a surface elevation of 700 m and the other a surface elevation of 560 m. If minor losses are neglected, the expected flow rate through the pipe is
(*a*) 0.048 m³/h, (*b*) 2.87 m³/h, (*c*) 134 m³/h, (*d*) 172 m³/h, (*e*) 385 m³/h

FE6.7 If, in Prob. FE6.6 the pipe is rough and the actual flow rate is 90 m³/h, then the expected average roughness height of the pipe is approximately
(*a*) 1.0 mm, (*b*) 1.25 mm, (*c*) 1.5 mm, (*d*) 1.75 mm, (*e*) 2.0 mm

FE6.8 Suppose in Prob. FE6.6 the two reservoirs are connected, not by a pipe, but by a sharp-edged orifice of diameter 8 cm. Then the expected flow rate is approximately
(*a*) 90 m³/h, (*b*) 579 m³/h, (*c*) 748 m³/h, (*d*) 949 m³/h, (*e*) 1048 m³/h

FE6.9 Oil [$\mu = 0.1$ kg/(m · s), SG = 0.9] flows through a 50-m-long smooth 8-cm-diameter pipe. The maximum pressure drop for which laminar flow is expected is approximately
(*a*) 30 kPa, (*b*) 40 kPa, (*c*) 50 kPa, (*d*) 60 kPa, (*e*) 70 kPa

FE6.10 Air at 20°C and approximately 1 atm flows through a smooth 30-cm-square duct at 1500 ft³/min. The expected pressure drop per meter of duct length is
(*a*) 1.0 Pa, (*b*) 2.0 Pa, (*c*) 3.0 Pa, (*d*) 4.0 Pa, (*e*) 5.0 Pa

FE6.11 Water at 20°C flows at 3 m³/h through a sharp-edged 3-cm-diameter orifice in a 6-cm-diameter pipe. Estimate the expected pressure drop across the orifice.
(*a*) 440 Pa, (*b*) 680 Pa, (*c*) 875 Pa, (*d*) 1750 Pa, (*e*) 1870 Pa

FE6.12 Water flows through a straight 10-cm-diameter pipe at a diameter Reynolds number of 250,000. If the pipe roughness is 0.06 mm, what is the approximate Moody friction factor?
(*a*) 0.015, (*b*) 0.017, (*c*) 0.019, (*d*) 0.026, (*e*) 0.032

FE6.13 What is the hydraulic diameter of a rectangular air-ventilation duct whose cross section is 1 m by 25 cm?
(*a*) 25 cm, (*b*) 40 cm, (*c*) 50 cm, (*d*) 75 cm, (*e*) 100 cm

FE6.14 Water at 20°C flows through a pipe at 300 gal/min with a friction head loss of 45 ft. What is the power required to drive this flow?
(*a*) 0.16 kW, (*b*) 1.88 kW, (*c*) 2.54 kW, (*d*) 3.41 kW, (*e*) 4.24 kW

FE6.15 Water at 20°C flows at 200 gal/min through a pipe 150 m long and 8 cm in diameter. If the friction head loss is 12 m, what is the Moody friction factor?
(*a*) 0.010, (*b*) 0.015, (*c*) 0.020, (*d*) 0.025, (*e*) 0.030

Comprehensive Problems

C6.1   A pitot-static probe will be used to measure the velocity distribution in a water tunnel at 20°C. The two pressure lines from the probe will be connected to a U-tube manometer that uses a liquid of specific gravity 1.7. The maximum velocity expected in the water tunnel is 2.3 m/s. Your job is to select an appropriate U-tube from a manufacturer that supplies manometers of heights 8, 12, 16, 24, and 36 in. The cost increases significantly with manometer height. Which of these should you purchase?

*C6.2   A pump delivers a steady flow of water (ρ, μ) from a large tank to two other higher-elevation tanks, as shown in Fig. C6.2. The same pipe of diameter d and roughness ε is used throughout. All minor losses *except through the valve* are

neglected, and the partially closed valve has a loss coefficient K_{valve}. Turbulent flow may be assumed with all kinetic energy flux correction coefficients equal to 1.06. The pump net head H is a known function of Q_A and hence also of $V_A = Q_A/A_{pipe}$; for example, $H = a - bV_A^2$, where a and b are constants. Subscript J refers to the junction point at the tee where branch A splits into B and C. Pipe length L_C is much longer than L_B. It is desired to predict the pressure at J, the three pipe velocities and friction factors, and the pump head. Thus there are eight variables: H, V_A, V_B, V_C, f_A, f_B, f_C, p_J. Write down the eight equations needed to resolve this problem, but *do not solve,* since an elaborate iteration procedure would be required.

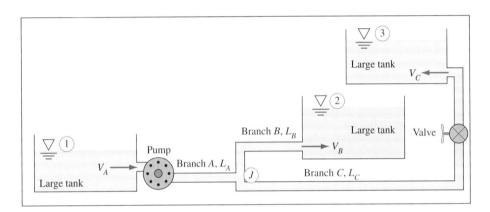

C6.2

C6.3   A small water slide is to be installed inside a swimming pool. See Fig. C6.3. The slide manufacturer recommends a continuous water flow rate Q of 1.39×10^{-3} m³/s (about 22 gal/min) down the slide, to ensure that the customers do not burn their bottoms. A pump is to be installed under the slide, with a 5.00-m-long, 4.00-cm-diameter hose supplying swimming pool water for the slide. The pump is 80 percent efficient and will rest fully submerged 1.00 m below the water surface. The roughness inside the hose is about 0.0080 cm. The hose discharges the water at the top of the slide as a free jet open to the atmosphere. The hose outlet is 4.00 m above the water surface. For fully developed turbulent pipe flow, the kinetic energy flux correction factor is about 1.06. Ignore any minor losses here. Assume that $\rho = 998$ kg/m³ and $v = 1.00 \times 10^{-6}$ m²/s for this water. Find the brake horsepower (that is, the actual shaft power in watts) required to drive the pump.

*C6.4   Suppose you build a rural house where you need to run a pipe to the nearest water supply, which is fortunately at an elevation of about 1000 m above that of your house.

The pipe will be 6.0 km long (the distance to the water supply), and the gage pressure at the water supply is 1000 kPa. You require a minimum of 3.0 gal/min of water when the end of your pipe is open to the atmosphere. To minimize cost, you want to buy the smallest-diameter pipe possible. The pipe you will use is extremely smooth. (a) Find the total head loss from the pipe inlet to its exit. Neglect any minor losses due to valves, elbows, entrance lengths, and so on, since the length is so long here and major losses dominate. Assume the outlet of the pipe is open to the atmosphere. (b) Which is more important in this problem, the head loss due to elevation difference or the head loss due to pressure drop in the pipe? (c) Find the minimum required pipe diameter.

C6.5   Water at room temperature flows at the *same* volume flow rate, $Q = 9.4 \times 10^{-4}$ m³/s, through two ducts, one a round pipe and one an annulus. The cross-sectional area A of the two ducts is identical, and all walls are made of commercial steel. Both ducts are the same length. In the cross sections shown in Fig. C6.5 $R = 15.0$ mm and $a = 25.0$ mm.

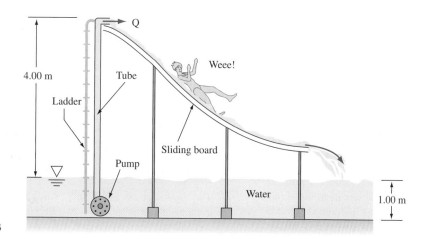

C6.3

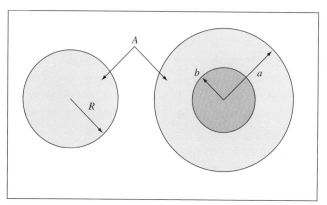

C6.5

(a) What is the radius b such that the cross-sectional areas of the two ducts are identical? (b) Compare the frictional head loss h_f per unit length of pipe for the two cases, assuming fully developed flow. For the annulus, do both a quick estimate (using the hydraulic diameter) and a more accurate estimate (using the effective diameter correction), and compare. (c) If the losses are different for the two cases, explain why. Which duct, if any, is more "efficient"?

C6.6 John Laufer (*NACA Tech Rep.* 1174, 1954) gave velocity data 20°C airflow in a smooth 24.7-cm-diameter pipe at Re ≈ 5 E5:

u/u_{CL}	1.0	0.997	0.988	0.959	0.908	0.847	0.818	0.771	0.690
r/R	0.0	0.102	0.206	0.412	0.617	0.784	0.846	0.907	0.963

Source: John Laufer (NASA Tech Rep. 1174, 1954)

The centerline velocity u_{CL} was 30.5 m/s. Determine (a) the average velocity by numerical integration and (b) the wall shear stress from the log law approximation. Compare with the Moody chart and with Eq. (6.43).

C6.7 Consider energy exchange in fully developed laminar flow between parallel plates, as in Eqs. (6.60). Let the pressure drop over a length L be Δp. Calculate the rate of work done by this pressure drop on the fluid in the region ($0 < x < L$, $-h < y < +h$) and compare with the integrated energy dissipated due to the viscous function Φ from Eq. (4.50) over this same region. The two should be equal. Explain why this is so. Can you relate the viscous drag force and the wall shear stress to this energy result?

C6.8 This text has presented the traditional correlations for the turbulent smooth-wall friction factor, Eq. (6.38), and the law of the wall, Eq. (6.28). Recently, groups at Princeton and Oregon [56] have made new friction measurements and suggest the following smooth-wall friction law:

$$\frac{1}{\sqrt{f}} = 1.930 \log_{10}(Re_D\sqrt{f}) - 0.537$$

In earlier work, they also report that better values for the constants κ and B in the log-law, Eq. (6.28), are $\kappa \approx 0.421 \pm 0.002$ and $B \approx 5.62 \pm 0.08$. (a) Calculate a few values of f in the range 1 E4 ⩽ Re_D ⩽ 1 E8 and see how the two formulas differ. (b) Read Ref. 56 and briefly check the five papers in its bibliography. Report to the class on the general results of this work.

C6.9 A pipeline has been proposed to carry natural gas 1715 miles from Alaska's North Slope to Calgary, Alberta, Canada. The (assumed smooth) pipe diameter will be 52 in. The gas will be at high pressure, averaging 2500 lbs/in². (a) Why? The proposed flow rate is 4 billion cubic feet per day at sea-level conditions. (b) What volume flow rate, at 20°C, would carry the same mass at the high pressure? (c) If natural gas is assumed to be methane (CH_4), what is the total pressure drop? (d) If each pumping station can deliver 12,000 hp to the flow, how many stations are needed?

Design Projects

D6.1 A hydroponic garden uses the 10-m-long perforated-pipe system in Fig. D6.1 to deliver water at 20°C. The pipe is 5 cm in diameter and contains a circular hole every 20 cm. A pump delivers water at 75 kPa (gage) at the entrance, while the other end of the pipe is closed. If you attempted, for example, Prob. P3.125, you know that the pressure near the closed end of a perforated "manifold" is surprisingly high, and there will be too much flow through the holes near that end. One remedy is to vary the hole size along the pipe axis. Make a design analysis, perhaps using a personal computer, to pick the optimum hole size distribution that will make the discharge flow rate as uniform as possible along the pipe axis. You are constrained to pick hole sizes that correspond only to commercial (numbered) metric drill-bit sizes available to the typical machine shop.

D6.2 It is desired to design a pump-piping system to keep a 1-million-gallon capacity water tank filled. The plan is to use a modified (in size and speed) version of the model 1206 centrifugal pump manufactured by Taco Inc., Cranston, Rhode Island. Test data have been provided to us by Taco Inc. for a small model of this pump: $D = 5.45$ in, $\Omega = 1760$ r/min, tested with water at 20°C:

Q, gal/min	0	5	10	15	20	25	30	35	40	45	50	55	60
H, ft	28	28	29	29	28	28	27	26	25	23	21	18	15
Efficiency, %	0	13	25	35	44	48	51	53	54	55	53	50	45

The tank is to be filled daily with rather chilly (10°C) groundwater from an aquifer, which is 0.8 mi from the tank and 150 ft lower than the tank. Estimated daily water use is 1.5 million gal/day. Filling time should not exceed 8 h per day. The piping system should have four "butterfly" valves

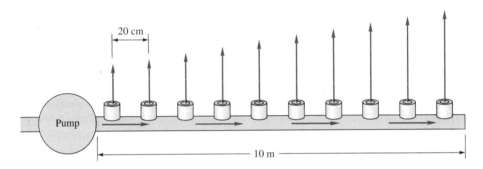

D6.1

with variable openings (see Fig. 6.19), 10 elbows of various angles, and galvanized iron pipe of a size to be selected in the design. The design should be economical—both in capital costs and operating expense. Taco Inc. has provided the following cost estimates for system components:

Pump and motor	$3500 plus $1500 per inch of impeller size
Pump speed	Between 900 and 1800 r/min
Valves	$300 + $200 per inch of pipe size
Elbows	$50 plus $50 per inch of pipe size
Pipes	$1 per inch of diameter per foot of length
Electricity cost	10¢ per kilowatt-hour

Your design task is to select an economical pipe size and pump impeller size and speed for this task, using the pump test data in nondimensional form (see Prob. P5.61) as design data. Write a brief report (five to six pages) showing your calculations and graphs.

References

1. P. S. Bernard and J. M. Wallace, *Turbulent Flow: Analysis, Measurement, and Prediction,* Wiley, New York, 2002.
2. H. Schlichting et al., *Boundary Layer Theory,* Springer, New York, 2000.
3. F. M. White, *Viscous Fluid Flow,* 3d ed., McGraw-Hill, New York, 2005.
4. O. Reynolds, "An Experimental Investigation of the Circumstances which Determine Whether the Motion of Water Shall Be Direct or Sinuous and of the Law of Resistance in Parallel Channels," *Phil. Trans. R. Soc.,* vol. 174, 1883, pp. 935–982.
5. P. G. Drazin and W. H. Reid, *Hydrodynamic Stability,* 2d ed., Cambridge University Press, New York, 2004.

6. H. Rouse and S. Ince, *History of Hydraulics,* Iowa Institute of Hydraulic Research, State University of Iowa, Iowa City, 1957.

7. J. Nikuradse, "Strömungsgesetze in Rauhen Rohren," *VDI Forschungsh.* 361, 1933; English trans., *NACA Tech. Mem.*1292.

8. L. F. Moody, "Friction Factors for Pipe Flow," *ASME Trans.,* vol. 66, pp. 671–684, 1944.

9. C. F. Colebrook, "Turbulent Flow in Pipes, with Particular Reference to the Transition between the Smooth and Rough Pipe Laws," *J. Inst. Civ. Eng. Lond.,* vol. 11, 1938–1939, pp. 133–156.

10. O. C. Jones, Jr., "An Improvement in the Calculations of Turbulent Friction in Rectangular Ducts," *J. Fluids Eng.,* June 1976, pp. 173–181.

11. R. Berker, *Handbuch der Physik,* vol. 7, no. 2, pp. 1–384, Springer-Verlag, Berlin, 1963.

12. R. M. Olson, *Essentials of Engineering Fluid Mechanics,* Literary Licensing LLC, Whitefish, MT, 2012.

13. P. A. Durbin and B. A. Pettersson, *Statistical Theory and Modeling for Turbulent Flows,* 2d ed., Wiley, New York, 2010.

14. P. W. Runstadler, Jr., et al., "Diffuser Data Book," *Creare Inc. Tech. Note* 186, Hanover, NH, 1975.

15. *"Flow of Fluids through Valves, Fittings, and Pipes,"* Tech. Paper 410, Crane Valve Group, Long Beach, CA, 1957 (now updated as a CD-ROM; see < http://www.cranevalves.com >).

16. E. F. Brater, H. W. King, J. E. Lindell, and C. Y. Wei, *Handbook of Hydraulics,* 7th ed., McGraw-Hill, New York, 1996.

17. H. Cross, "Analysis of Flow in Networks of Conduits or Conductors," *Univ. Ill. Bull.* 286, November 1936.

18. P. K. Swamee and A. K. Sharma, *Design of Water Supply Pipe Networks*, Wiley-Interscience, New York, 2008.

19. D. C. Wilcox, *Turbulence Modeling for CFD,* 3d ed., DCW Industries, La Cañada, CA, 2006.

20. R. W. Jeppson, *Analysis of Flow in Pipe Networks,* Butterworth-Heinemann, Woburn, MA, 1976.

21. R. W. Fox and S. J. Kline, "Flow Regime Data and Design Methods for Curved Subsonic Diffusers," *J. Basic Eng.,* vol. 84, 1962, pp. 303–312.

22. R. C. Baker, *Flow Measurement Handbook: Industrial Designs, Operating Principles, Performance, and Applications*, Cambridge University Press, New York, 2005.

23. R. W. Miller, *Flow Measurement Engineering Handbook,* 3d edition, McGraw-Hill, New York, 1997.

24. B. Warren and C. Wunsch (eds.), *Evolution of Physical Oceanography,* M.I.T. Press, Cambridge, MA, 1981.

25. U.S. Department of Commerce, *Tidal Current Tables,* National Oceanographic and Atmospheric Administration, Washington, DC, 1971.

26. J. A. Shercliff, *Electromagnetic Flow Measurement,* Cambridge University Press, New York, 1962.

27. J. A. Miller, "A Simple Linearized Hot-Wire Anemometer," *J. Fluids Eng.,* December 1976, pp. 749–752.

28. R. J. Goldstein (ed.), *Fluid Mechanics Measurements,* 2d ed., Hemisphere, New York, 1996.

29. D. Eckardt, "Detailed Flow Investigations within a High Speed Centrifugal Compressor Impeller," *J. Fluids Eng.,* September 1976, pp. 390–402.

30. H. S. Bean (ed.), *Fluid Meters: Their Theory and Application,* 6th ed., American Society of Mechanical Engineers, New York, 1971.

31. "Measurement of Fluid Flow by Means of Orifice Plates, Nozzles, and Venturi Tubes Inserted in Circular Cross Section Conduits Running Full," *Int. Organ. Stand. Rep.* DIS-5167, Geneva, April 1976.

32. P. Sagaut and C. Meneveau, *Large Eddy Simulation for Incompressible Flows: An Introduction*, 3d ed., Springer, New York, 2006.

33. S. E. Haaland, "Simple and Explicit Formulas for the Friction Factor in Turbulent Pipe Flow," *J. Fluids Eng.,* March 1983, pp. 89–90.

34. R. K. Shah and A. L. London, *Laminar Flow Forced Convection in Ducts,* Academic, New York, 1979.

35. P. L. Skousen, *Valve Handbook,* 3d ed. McGraw-Hill, New York, 2011.

36. W. Li, W.-X. Chen, and S.-Z. Xie, "Numerical Simulation of Stress-Induced Secondary Flows with Hybrid Finite Analytic Method," *Journal of Hydrodynamics,* vol. 14, no. 4, December 2002, pp. 24–30.

37. *ASHRAE Handbook—2012 Fundamentals,* ASHRAE, Atlanta, GA, 2012.

38. F. Durst, A. Melling, and J. H. Whitelaw, *Principles and Practice of Laser-Doppler Anemometry,* 2d ed., Academic, New York, 1981.

39. A. P. Lisitsyn et al., *Laser Doppler and Phase Doppler Measurement Techniques,* Springer-Verlag, New York, 2003.

40. J. E. Amadi-Echendu, H. Zhu, and E. H. Higham, "Analysis of Signals from Vortex Flowmeters," *Flow Measurement and Instrumentation,* vol. 4, no. 4, Oct. 1993, pp. 225–231.

41. G. Vass, "Ultrasonic Flowmeter Basics," *Sensors,* vol. 14, no. 10, Oct. 1997, pp. 73–78.

42. ASME Fluid Meters Research Committee, "The ISO-ASME Orifice Coefficient Equation," *Mech. Eng.* July 1981, pp. 44–45.

43. R. D. Blevins, *Applied Fluid Dynamics Handbook,* Van Nostrand Reinhold, New York, 1984.

44. O. C. Jones, Jr., and J. C. M. Leung, "An Improvement in the Calculation of Turbulent Friction in Smooth Concentric Annuli," *J. Fluids Eng.,* December 1981, pp. 615–623.

45. P. R. Bandyopadhyay, "Aspects of the Equilibrium Puff in Transitional Pipe Flow," *J. Fluid Mech.,* vol. 163, 1986, pp. 439–458.

46. I. E. Idelchik, *Handbook of Hydraulic Resistance,* 3d ed., CRC Press, Boca Raton, FL, 1993.

47. S. Klein and W. Beckman, *Engineering Equation Solver (EES),* University of Wisconsin, Madison, WI, 2014.

48. R. D. Coffield, P. T. McKeown, and R. B. Hammond, "Irrecoverable Pressure Loss Coefficients for Two Elbows in Series with Various Orientation Angles and Separation Distances," *Report WAPD-T-3117,* Bettis Atomic Power Laboratory, West Mifflin, PA, 1997.

49. H. Ito, "Pressure Losses in Smooth Pipe Bends," *Journal of Basic Engineering,* March 1960, pp. 131–143.

50. A. H. Gibson, "On the Flow of Water through Pipes and Passages," *Proc. Roy. Soc. London,* Ser. A, vol. 83, 1910, pp. 366–378.

51. M. Raffel et al., *Particle Image Velocimetry: A Practical Guide,* 2d ed., Springer, New York, 2007.

52. Crane Co., *Flow of Fluids through Valves, Fittings, and Pipe,* Crane, Stanford, CT, 2009.

53. S. A. Berger, L. Talbot, and L.-S. Yao, "Flow in Curved Pipes," *Annual Review of Fluid Mechanics,* vol. 15, 1983, pp. 461–512.

54. P. L. Spedding, E. Benard, and G. M. McNally, "Fluid Flow through 90° Bends," *Developments in Chemical Engineering and Mineral Processing,* vol. 12, nos. 1–2, 2004, pp. 107–128.

55. R. R. Kerswell, "Recent Progress in Understanding the Transition to Turbulence in a Pipe," *Nonlinearity,* vol. 18, 2005, pp. R17–R44.

56. B. J. McKeon et al., "Friction Factors for Smooth Pipe Flow," *J. Fluid Mech.,* vol. 511, 2004, pp. 41–44.

57. M. Bahrami, M. M. Yovanovich, and J. R. Culham, "Pressure Drop of Fully-Developed Laminar Flow in Microchannels of Arbitrary Cross-Section," *J. Fluids Engineering,* vol. 128, Sept. 2006, pp. 1036–1044.

58. G. S. Larraona, A. Rivas, and J. C. Ramos, "Computational Modeling and Simulation of a Single-Jet Water Meter," *J. Fluids Engineering,* vol. 130, May 2008, pp. 0511021–05110212.

59. C. Spiegel, *Designing and Building Fuel Cells,* McGraw-Hill, New York, 2007.

60. B. A. Finlayson et al., *Microcomponent Flow Characterization,* Chap. 8 of *Micro Instrumentation,* M. V. Koch (Ed.), John Wiley, Hoboken, NJ, 2007.

This chapter is devoted to lift and drag of various bodies immersed in an approaching stream of fluid. Pictured is the Swiss solar-powered aircraft, Solar Impulse, over the Golden Gate Bridge. Earlier solar aircraft needed to be towed aloft before flying and were not able to fly at night. The Solar Impulse is the first solar airplane to fly day and night, approaching the notion of perpetual flight. The long, high-aspect-ratio wings have more lift, and less drag, than a short wing of the same area. Its first international flight was from Switzerland to Brussels, on May 14, 2011. In the summer of 2013, as shown, it flew from San Francisco to New York City, in five legs. The pilots were Bertrand Piccard and André Borschberg.

Chapter 7
Flow Past
Immersed Bodies

Motivation. This chapter is devoted to "external" flows around bodies immersed in a fluid stream. Such a flow will have viscous (shear and no-slip) effects near the body surfaces and in its wake, but will typically be nearly inviscid far from the body. These are unconfined *boundary layer* flows.

Chapter 6 considered "internal" flows confined by the walls of a duct. In that case the viscous boundary layers grow from the sidewalls, meet downstream, and fill the entire duct. Viscous shear is the dominant effect. For example, the Moody chart of Fig. 6.13 is essentially a correlation of wall shear stress for long ducts of constant cross section.

External flows are unconfined, free to expand no matter how thick the viscous layers grow. Although boundary layer theory (Sec. 7.3) and computational fluid dynamics (CFD) [4] are helpful in understanding external flows, complex body geometries usually require experimental data on the forces and moments caused by the flow. Such immersed-body flows are commonly encountered in engineering studies: *aerodynamics* (airplanes, rockets, projectiles), *hydrodynamics* (ships, submarines, torpedos), *transportation* (automobiles, trucks, cycles), *wind engineering* (buildings, bridges, water towers, wind turbines), and *ocean engineering* (buoys, breakwaters, pilings, cables, moored instruments). This chapter provides data and analysis to assist in such studies.

7.1 Reynolds Number and Geometry Effects

The technique of boundary layer (BL) analysis can be used to compute viscous effects near solid walls and to "patch" these onto the outer inviscid motion. This patching is more successful as the body Reynolds number becomes larger, as shown in Fig. 7.1.

In Fig. 7.1 a uniform stream U moves parallel to a sharp flat plate of length L. If the Reynolds number UL/ν is low (Fig. 7.1a), the viscous region is very broad and extends far ahead and to the sides of the plate. The plate retards the oncoming stream greatly, and small changes in flow parameters cause large changes in the pressure

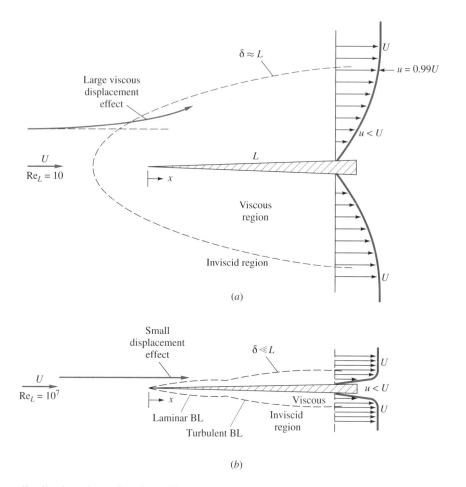

Fig. 7.1 Comparison of flow past a sharp flat plate at low and high Reynolds numbers: (*a*) laminar, low-Re flow; (*b*) high-Re flow.

distribution along the plate. Thus, although in principle it should be possible to patch the viscous and inviscid layers in a mathematical analysis, their interaction is strong and nonlinear [1 to 3]. There is no existing simple theory for external flow analysis at Reynolds numbers from 1 to about 1000. Such thick-shear-layer flows are typically studied by experiment or by numerical modeling of the flow field on a computer [4].

A high-Reynolds-number flow (Fig. 7.1*b*) is much more amenable to boundary layer patching, as first pointed out by Prandtl in 1904. The viscous layers, either laminar or turbulent, are very thin, thinner even than the drawing shows. We define the boundary layer thickness δ as the locus of points where the velocity u parallel to the plate reaches 99 percent of the external velocity U. As we shall see in Sec. 7.4, the accepted formulas for flat-plate flow, and their approximate ranges, are

$$\frac{\delta}{x} \approx \begin{cases} \dfrac{5.0}{\mathrm{Re}_x^{1/2}} & \text{laminar} \quad 10^3 < \mathrm{Re}_x < 10^6 \\[4mm] \dfrac{0.16}{\mathrm{Re}_x^{1/7}} & \text{turbulent} \quad 10^6 < \mathrm{Re}_x \end{cases}$$

$$(7.1a)$$

$$(7.1b)$$

where $\mathrm{Re}_x = Ux/\nu$ is called the *local Reynolds number* of the flow along the plate surface. The turbulent flow formula applies for Re_x greater than approximately 10^6.

Some computed values from Eq. (7.1) are

Re_x	10^4	10^5	10^6	10^7	10^8
$(\delta/x)_{\mathrm{lam}}$	0.050	0.016	0.005		
$(\delta/x)_{\mathrm{turb}}$			0.022	0.016	0.011

The blanks indicate that the formula is not applicable. In all cases these boundary layers are so thin that their displacement effect on the outer inviscid layer is negligible. Thus the pressure distribution along the plate can be computed from inviscid theory as if the boundary layer were not even there. This external pressure field then "drives" the boundary layer flow, acting as a forcing function in the momentum equation along the surface. We shall explain this boundary layer theory in Secs. 7.4 and 7.5.

For slender bodies, such as plates and airfoils parallel to the oncoming stream, we conclude that this assumption of negligible interaction between the boundary layer and the outer pressure distribution is an excellent approximation.

For a blunt-body flow, however, even at very high Reynolds numbers, there is a discrepancy in the viscous–inviscid patching concept. Figure 7.2 shows two

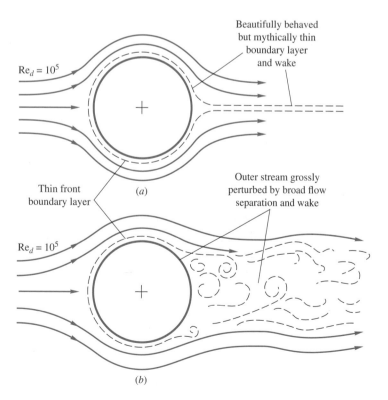

Fig. 7.2 Illustration of the strong interaction between viscous and inviscid regions in the rear of blunt-body flow: (*a*) idealized and definitely false picture of blunt-body flow; (*b*) actual picture of blunt-body flow.

sketches of flow past a two- or three-dimensional blunt body. In the idealized sketch (7.2a), there is a thin film of boundary layer about the body and a narrow sheet of viscous wake in the rear. The patching theory would be glorious for this picture, but it is false. In the actual flow (Fig. 7.2b), the boundary layer is thin on the front, or windward, side of the body, where the pressure decreases along the surface (*favorable* pressure gradient). But in the rear the boundary layer encounters increasing pressure (*adverse* pressure gradient) and breaks off, or separates, into a broad, pulsating wake. (See Fig. 5.2a for a photograph of a specific example.) The mainstream is deflected by this wake, so that the external flow is quite different from the prediction from inviscid theory with the addition of a thin boundary layer.

The theory of strong interaction between blunt-body viscous and inviscid layers is not well developed. Flows like that of Fig. 7.2b are normally studied experimentally or with CFD [4]. Reference 5 is an example of efforts to improve the theory of separated flows. Reference 6 is another textbook devoted to separated flow.

EXAMPLE 7.1

A long, thin, flat plate is placed parallel to a 20-ft/s stream of water at 68°F. At what distance x from the leading edge will the boundary layer thickness be 1 in?

Solution

- *Assumptions:* Flat-plate flow, with Eqs. (7.1) applying in their appropriate ranges.
- *Approach:* Guess laminar flow first. If contradictory, try turbulent flow.
- *Property values:* From Table A.1 for water at 68°F, $\nu \approx 1.082$ E-5 ft^2/s.
- *Solution step 1:* With $\delta = 1$ in $= 1/12$ ft, try laminar flow, Eq. (7.1a):

$$\frac{\delta}{x}\bigg|_{\text{lam}} = \frac{5}{(Ux/\nu)^{1/2}} \quad \text{or} \quad \frac{1/12 \text{ ft}}{x} = \frac{5}{\left[(20 \text{ ft/s})x/(1.082 \text{ E-5 ft}^2/\text{s})\right]^{1/2}}$$

$$\text{Solve for} \quad x \approx 513 \text{ ft}$$

Pretty long plate! This does not sound right. Check the local Reynolds number:

$$\text{Re}_x = \frac{Ux}{\nu} = \frac{(20 \text{ ft/s})(513 \text{ ft})}{1.082 \text{ E-5 ft}^2/\text{s}} = 9.5 \text{ E8} \quad (!)$$

This is impossible, since laminar boundary layer flow only persists up to about 10^6 (or, with special care to avoid disturbances, up to 3×10^6).
- *Solution step 2:* Try turbulent flow, Eq. (7.1b):

$$\frac{\delta}{x} = \frac{0.16}{(Ux/\nu)^{1/7}} \quad \text{or} \quad \frac{1/12 \text{ ft}}{x} = \frac{0.16}{\left[(20 \text{ ft/s})x/(1.082 \text{ ft}^2/\text{s})\right]^{1/7}}$$

$$\text{Solve for} \quad x \approx 5.17 \text{ ft} \qquad\qquad Ans.$$

Check $\text{Re}_x = (20 \text{ ft/s})(5.17 \text{ ft})/(1.082 \text{ E-5 ft}^2/\text{s}) = 9.6 \text{ E6} > 10^6$. OK, turbulent flow.
- *Comments:* The flow is turbulent, and the inherent ambiguity of the theory is resolved.

7.2 Momentum Integral Estimates

When we derived the momentum integral relation, Eq. (3.37), and applied it to a flat-plate boundary layer in Example 3.11, we promised to consider it further in Chap. 7. Well, here we are! Let us review the problem, using Fig. 7.3.

A shear layer of unknown thickness grows along the sharp flat plate in Fig. 7.3. The no-slip wall condition retards the flow, making it into a rounded profile $u(x, y)$, which merges into the external velocity $U =$ constant at a "thickness" $y = \delta(x)$. By utilizing the control volume of Fig. 3.11, we found (without making any assumptions about laminar versus turbulent flow) in Example 3.11 that the drag force on the plate is given by the following momentum integral across the exit plane:

$$D(x) = \rho b \int_0^{\delta(x)} u(U - u)\, dy \tag{7.2}$$

where b is the plate width into the paper and the integration is carried out along a vertical plane $x =$ constant. You should review the momentum integral relation (3.37) and its use in Example 3.11.

Kármán's Analysis of the Flat Plate

Equation (7.2) was derived in 1921 by Kármán [7], who wrote it in the convenient form of the *momentum thickness* θ:

$$D(x) = \rho b U^2 \theta \qquad \theta = \int_0^{\delta} \frac{u}{U}\left(1 - \frac{u}{U}\right) dy \tag{7.3}$$

Momentum thickness is thus a measure of total plate drag. Kármán then noted that the drag also equals the integrated wall shear stress along the plate:

$$D(x) = b \int_0^x \tau_w(x)\, dx$$

or
$$\frac{dD}{dx} = b\tau_w \tag{7.4}$$

Meanwhile, the derivative of Eq. (7.3), with $U =$ constant, is

$$\frac{dD}{dx} = \rho b U^2 \frac{d\theta}{dx}$$

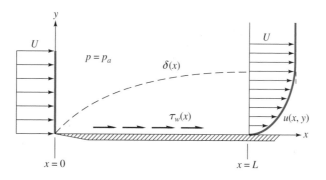

Fig. 7.3 Growth of a boundary layer on a flat plate. The thickness is exaggerated.

By comparing this with Eq. (7.4) Kármán arrived at what is now called the *momentum integral relation* for flat-plate boundary layer flow:

$$\tau_w = \rho U^2 \frac{d\theta}{dx} \tag{7.5}$$

It is valid for either laminar or turbulent flat-plate flow.

To get a numerical result for laminar flow, Kármán assumed that the velocity profiles had an approximately parabolic shape

$$u(x, y) \approx U\left(\frac{2y}{\delta} - \frac{y^2}{\delta^2}\right) \qquad 0 \le y \le \delta(x) \tag{7.6}$$

which makes it possible to estimate both momentum thickness and wall shear:

$$\theta = \int_0^\delta \left(\frac{2y}{\delta} - \frac{y^2}{\delta^2}\right)\left(1 - \frac{2y}{\delta} + \frac{y^2}{\delta^2}\right) dy \approx \frac{2}{15}\delta$$

$$\tau_w = \mu \frac{\partial u}{\partial y}\bigg|_{y=0} \approx \frac{2\mu U}{\delta} \tag{7.7}$$

By substituting (7.7) into (7.5) and rearranging, we obtain

$$\delta \, d\delta \approx 15 \frac{\nu}{U} dx \tag{7.8}$$

where $\nu = \mu/\rho$. We can integrate from 0 to x, assuming that $\delta = 0$ at $x = 0$, the leading edge:

$$\frac{1}{2}\delta^2 = \frac{15\nu x}{U}$$

or

$$\frac{\delta}{x} \approx 5.5\left(\frac{\nu}{Ux}\right)^{1/2} = \frac{5.5}{\mathrm{Re}_x^{1/2}} \tag{7.9}$$

This is the desired thickness estimate. It is all approximate, of course, part of Kármán's *momentum integral theory* [7], but it is startlingly accurate, being only 10 percent higher than the known accepted solution for laminar flat-plate flow, which we gave as Eq. (7.1a).

By combining Eqs. (7.9) and (7.7) we also obtain a shear stress estimate along the plate:

$$c_f = \frac{2\tau_w}{\rho U^2} \approx \left(\frac{\frac{8}{15}}{\mathrm{Re}_x}\right)^{1/2} = \frac{0.73}{\mathrm{Re}_x^{1/2}} \tag{7.10}$$

Again this estimate, in spite of the crudeness of the profile assumption [Eq. (7.6)] is only 10 percent higher than the known exact laminar-plate-flow solution $c_f = 0.664/\mathrm{Re}_x^{1/2}$, treated in Sec. 7.4. The dimensionless quantity c_f, called the *skin friction coefficient*, is analogous to the friction factor f in ducts.

A boundary layer can be judged as "thin" if, say, the ratio δ/x is less than about 0.1. This occurs at $\delta/x = 0.1 = 5.0/\mathrm{Re}_x^{1/2}$ or at $\mathrm{Re}_x = 2500$. For Re_x less than 2500 we can estimate that boundary layer theory fails because the thick layer has a significant effect on the outer inviscid flow. The upper limit on Re_x for laminar flow is about 3×10^6, where measurements on a smooth flat plate [8] show that the flow undergoes transition to a turbulent boundary layer. From 3×10^6 upward the turbulent Reynolds number may be arbitrarily large, and a practical limit at present is 5×10^{10} for oil supertankers.

Displacement Thickness

Another interesting effect of a boundary layer is its small but finite displacement of the outer streamlines. As shown in Fig. 7.4, outer streamlines must deflect outward a distance $\delta^*(x)$ to satisfy conservation of mass between the inlet and outlet:

$$\int_0^h \rho U b \, dy = \int_0^\delta \rho u b \, dy \qquad \delta = h + \delta^* \qquad (7.11)$$

The quantity δ^* is called the *displacement thickness* of the boundary layer. To relate it to $u(y)$, cancel ρ and b from Eq. (7.11), evaluate the left integral, and slyly add and subtract U from the right integrand:

$$Uh = \int_0^\delta (U + u - U) \, dy = U(h + \delta^*) + \int_0^\delta (u - U) \, dy$$

or

$$\delta^* = \int_0^\delta \left(1 - \frac{u}{U}\right) dy \qquad (7.12)$$

Thus the ratio of δ^*/δ varies only with the dimensionless velocity profile shape u/U.

Introducing our profile approximation (7.6) into (7.12), we obtain by integration this approximate result:

$$\delta^* \approx \frac{1}{3} \delta \qquad \frac{\delta^*}{x} \approx \frac{1.83}{Re_x^{1/2}} \qquad (7.13)$$

These estimates are only 6 percent away from the exact solutions for laminar flat-plate flow given in Sec. 7.4: $\delta^* = 0.344\delta = 1.721x/Re_x^{1/2}$. Since δ^* is much smaller than x for large Re_x and the outer streamline slope V/U is proportional to δ^*, we conclude that the velocity normal to the wall is much smaller than the velocity parallel to the wall. This is a key assumption in boundary layer theory (Sec. 7.3).

We also conclude from the success of these simple parabolic estimates that Kármán's momentum integral theory is effective and useful. Many details of this theory are given in Refs. 1 to 3.

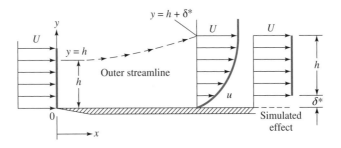

Fig. 7.4 Displacement effect of a boundary layer.

EXAMPLE 7.2

Are low-speed, small-scale air and water boundary layers really thin? Consider flow at $U = 1$ ft/s past a flat plate 1 ft long. Compute the boundary layer thickness at the trailing edge for (a) air and (b) water at 68°F.

Solution

Part (a)   From Table A.2, $\nu_{air} \approx 1.61$ E-4 ft^2/s. The trailing-edge Reynolds number thus is

$$\text{Re}_L = \frac{UL}{\nu} = \frac{(1 \text{ ft/s})(1 \text{ ft})}{1.61 \text{ E-4 ft}^2/\text{s}} = 6200$$

Since this is less than 10^6, the flow is presumed laminar, and since it is greater than 2500, the boundary layer is reasonably thin. From Eq. (7.1a), the predicted laminar thickness is

$$\frac{\delta}{x} = \frac{5.0}{\sqrt{6200}} = 0.0634$$

or, at $x = 1$ ft, $\delta = 0.0634$ ft ≈ 0.76 in   *Ans.* (a)

Part (b)   From Table A.1, $\nu_{water} \approx 1.08$ E-5 ft^2/s. The trailing-edge Reynolds number is

$$\text{Re}_L = \frac{(1 \text{ ft/s})(1 \text{ ft})}{1.08 \text{ E-5 ft}^2/\text{s}} \approx 92{,}600$$

This again satisfies the laminar and thinness conditions. The boundary layer thickness is

$$\frac{\delta}{x} \approx \frac{5.0}{\sqrt{92{,}600}} = 0.0164$$

or, at $x = 1$ ft, $\delta = 0.0164$ ft ≈ 0.20 in   *Ans.* (b)

Thus, even at such low velocities and short lengths, both airflows and water flows satisfy the boundary layer approximations.

7.3 The Boundary Layer Equations

In Chaps. 4 and 6 we learned that there are several dozen known analytical laminar flow solutions [1 to 3]. None are for external flow around immersed bodies, although this is one of the primary applications of fluid mechanics. No exact solutions are known for turbulent flow, whose analysis typically uses empirical modeling laws to relate time-mean variables.

There are presently three techniques used to study external flows: (1) numerical (computer) solutions, (2) experimentation, and (3) boundary layer theory.

Computational fluid dynamics is now well developed and described in advanced texts such as that by Anderson [4]. Thousands of computer solutions and models have been published; execution times, mesh sizes, and graphical presentations are improving each year. Both laminar and turbulent flow solutions have been published, and turbulence modeling is a current research topic [9]. Except for a brief discussion of computer analysis in Chap. 8, the topic of CFD is beyond our scope here.

Experimentation is the most common method of studying external flows. Chapter 5 outlined the technique of dimensional analysis, and we shall give many nondimensional experimental data for external flows in Sec. 7.6.

The third tool is boundary layer theory, first formulated by Ludwig Prandtl in 1904. We shall follow Prandtl's ideas here and make certain order-of-magnitude assumptions to greatly simplify the Navier-Stokes equations (4.38) into boundary layer equations that are solved relatively easily and patched onto the outer inviscid flow field.

One of the great achievements of boundary layer theory is its ability to predict the flow separation that occurs in adverse (positive) pressure gradients, as illustrated in Fig. 7.2b. Before 1904, when Prandtl published his pioneering paper, no one realized that such thin shear layers could cause such a gross effect as flow separation. Even today, however, boundary layer theory cannot accurately predict the behavior of the separated-flow region and its interaction with the outer flow. Modern research [4, 9] has focused on detailed CFD simulations of separated flow, and the resultant wakes, to gain further insight.

Derivation for Two-Dimensional Flow

We consider only steady two-dimensional incompressible viscous flow with the x direction along the wall and y normal to the wall, as in Fig. 7.3.[1] We neglect gravity, which is important only in boundary layers where fluid buoyancy is dominant [2, sec. 4.14]. From Chap. 4, the complete equations of motion consist of continuity and the x- and y-momentum relations:

$$\frac{\partial u}{\partial x} + \frac{\partial v}{\partial y} = 0 \tag{7.14a}$$

$$\rho\left(u\frac{\partial u}{\partial x} + v\frac{\partial u}{\partial y}\right) = -\frac{\partial p}{\partial x} + \mu\left(\frac{\partial^2 u}{\partial x^2} + \frac{\partial^2 u}{\partial y^2}\right) \tag{7.14b}$$

$$\rho\left(u\frac{\partial v}{\partial x} + v\frac{\partial v}{\partial y}\right) = -\frac{\partial p}{\partial y} + \mu\left(\frac{\partial^2 v}{\partial x^2} + \frac{\partial^2 v}{\partial y^2}\right) \tag{7.14c}$$

These should be solved for u, v, and p subject to typical no-slip, inlet, and exit boundary conditions, but in fact they are too difficult to handle for most external flows except with CFD.

In 1904 Prandtl correctly deduced that a shear layer must be very thin if the Reynolds number is large, so that the following approximations apply:

Velocities: $$v \ll u \tag{7.15a}$$

Rates of change: $$\frac{\partial u}{\partial x} \ll \frac{\partial u}{\partial y} \qquad \frac{\partial v}{\partial x} \ll \frac{\partial v}{\partial y} \tag{7.15b}$$

Reynolds number: $$\text{Re}_x = \frac{Ux}{\nu} \gg 1 \tag{7.15c}$$

[1]For a curved wall, x can represent the arc length along the wall and y can be everywhere normal to x with negligible change in the boundary layer equations as long as the radius of curvature of the wall is large compared with the boundary layer thickness [1 to 3].

Our discussion of displacement thickness in the previous section was intended to justify these assumptions.

Applying these approximations to Eq. (7.14c) results in a powerful simplification:

$$\rho\left(u\frac{\partial v}{\partial x}\right) + \rho\left(v\frac{\partial v}{\partial y}\right) = -\frac{\partial p}{\partial y} + \mu\left(\frac{\partial^2 v}{\partial x^2}\right) + \mu\left(\frac{\partial^2 v}{\partial y^2}\right)$$

$$\underset{\text{small}}{\qquad} \underset{\text{small}}{\qquad} \underset{\text{very small}}{\qquad} \underset{\text{small}}{\qquad}$$

$$\frac{\partial p}{\partial y} \approx 0 \quad \text{or} \quad p \approx p(x) \quad \text{only} \tag{7.16}$$

In other words, the y-momentum equation can be neglected entirely, and the pressure varies only *along* the boundary layer, not through it. The pressure gradient term in Eq. (7.14b) is assumed to be known in advance from Bernoulli's equation applied to the outer inviscid flow:

$$\frac{\partial p}{\partial x} = \frac{dp}{dx} = -\rho U \frac{dU}{dx} \tag{7.17}$$

Presumably we have already made the inviscid analysis and know the distribution of $U(x)$ along the wall (Chap. 8).

Meanwhile, one term in Eq. (7.14b) is negligible due to Eqs. (7.15):

$$\frac{\partial^2 u}{\partial x^2} \ll \frac{\partial^2 u}{\partial y^2} \tag{7.18}$$

However, neither term in the continuity relation (7.14a) can be neglected—another warning that continuity is always a vital part of any fluid flow analysis.

The net result is that the three full equations of motion (7.14) are reduced to Prandtl's two boundary layer equations for two-dimensional incompressible flow:

Continuity:
$$\frac{\partial u}{\partial x} + \frac{\partial v}{\partial y} = 0 \tag{7.19a}$$

Momentum along wall:
$$u\frac{\partial u}{\partial x} + v\frac{\partial u}{\partial y} \approx U\frac{dU}{dx} + \frac{1}{\rho}\frac{\partial \tau}{\partial y} \tag{7.19b}$$

where
$$\tau = \begin{cases} \mu\dfrac{\partial u}{\partial y} & \text{laminar flow} \\[2mm] \mu\dfrac{\partial u}{\partial y} - \overline{\rho u' v'} & \text{turbulent flow} \end{cases}$$

These are to be solved for $u(x, y)$ and $v(x, y)$, with $U(x)$ assumed to be a known function from the outer inviscid flow analysis. There are two boundary conditions on u and one on v:

At $y = 0$ (wall): $\qquad\qquad\qquad u = v = 0 \qquad$ (no slip) $\qquad$ (7.20a)

As $y = \delta(x)$ (other stream): $\qquad u = U(x) \qquad$ (patching) $\qquad$ (7.20b)

Unlike the Navier-Stokes equations (7.14), which are mathematically elliptic and must be solved simultaneously over the entire flow field, the boundary layer equations (7.19) are mathematically parabolic and are solved by beginning at the leading edge and marching downstream as far as you like, stopping at the separation point or earlier if you prefer.[2]

The boundary layer equations have been solved for scores of interesting cases of internal and external flow for both laminar and turbulent flow, utilizing the inviscid distribution $U(x)$ appropriate to each flow. Full details of boundary layer theory and results and comparison with experiment are given in Refs. 1 to 3. Here we shall confine ourselves primarily to flat-plate solutions (Sec. 7.4).

7.4 The Flat-Plate Boundary Layer

The classic and most often used solution of boundary layer theory is for flat-plate flow, as in Fig. 7.3, which can represent either laminar or turbulent flow.

Laminar Flow

For laminar flow past the plate, the boundary layer equations (7.19) can be solved exactly for u and v, assuming that the free-stream velocity U is constant ($dU/dx = 0$). The solution was given by Prandtl's student Blasius, in his 1908 dissertation from Göttingen. With an ingenious coordinate transformation, Blasius showed that the dimensionless velocity profile u/U is a function only of the single composite dimensionless variable $(y)[U/(\nu x)]^{1/2}$:

$$\frac{u}{U} = f'(\eta) \quad \eta = y\left(\frac{U}{\nu x}\right)^{1/2} \tag{7.21}$$

where the prime denotes differentiation with respect to η. Substitution of (7.21) into the boundary layer equations (7.19) reduces the problem, after much algebra, to a single third-order nonlinear ordinary differential equation for f [1–3]:

$$f''' + \tfrac{1}{2}ff'' = 0 \tag{7.22}$$

The boundary conditions (7.20) become

At $y = 0$: $\qquad\qquad f(0) = f'(0) = 0 \tag{7.23a}$

As $y \to \infty$: $\qquad\qquad f'(\infty) \to 1.0 \tag{7.23b}$

This is the *Blasius equation,* for which accurate solutions have been obtained only by numerical integration. Some tabulated values of the velocity profile shape $f'(\eta) = u/U$ are given in Table 7.1.

Since u/U approaches 1.0 only as $y \to \infty$, it is customary to select the boundary layer thickness δ as that point where $u/U = 0.99$. From the table, this occurs at $\eta \approx 5.0$:

$$\delta_{99\%}\left(\frac{U}{\nu x}\right)^{1/2} \approx 5.0$$

or
$$\boxed{\frac{\delta}{x} \approx \frac{5.0}{\mathrm{Re}_x^{1/2}} \quad \text{Blasius (1908)}} \tag{7.24}$$

[2]For further mathematical details, see Ref. 2, Sec. 2.8.

Table 7.1 The Blasius Velocity Profile [1 to 3]

$y[U/(vx)]^{1/2}$	u/U	$y[U/(vx)]^{1/2}$	u/U
0.0	0.0	2.8	0.81152
0.2	0.06641	3.0	0.84605
0.4	0.13277	3.2	0.87609
0.6	0.19894	3.4	0.90177
0.8	0.26471	3.6	0.92333
1.0	0.32979	3.8	0.94112
1.2	0.39378	4.0	0.95552
1.4	0.45627	4.2	0.96696
1.6	0.51676	4.4	0.97587
1.8	0.57477	4.6	0.98269
2.0	0.62977	4.8	0.98779
2.2	0.68132	5.0	0.99155
2.4	0.72899	∞	1.00000
2.6	0.77246		

With the profile known, Blasius, of course, could also compute the wall shear and displacement thickness:

$$c_f = \frac{0.664}{\mathrm{Re}_x^{1/2}} \qquad \frac{\delta^*}{x} = \frac{1.721}{\mathrm{Re}_x^{1/2}} \tag{7.25}$$

Notice how close these are to our integral estimates, Eqs. (7.9), (7.10), and (7.13). When c_f is converted to dimensional form, we have

$$\tau_w(x) = \frac{0.332\rho^{1/2}\mu^{1/2}U^{1.5}}{x^{1/2}}$$

The wall shear drops off with $x^{1/2}$ because of boundary layer growth and varies as velocity to the 1.5 power. This is in contrast to laminar pipe flow, where $\tau_w \propto U$ and is independent of x.

If $\tau_w(x)$ is substituted into Eq. (7.4), we compute the total drag force:

$$D(x) = b \int_0^x \tau_w(x)\,dx = 0.664b\rho^{1/2}\mu^{1/2}U^{1.5}x^{1/2} \tag{7.26}$$

The drag increases only as the square root of the plate length. The nondimensional *drag coefficient* is defined as

$$C_D = \frac{2D(L)}{\rho U^2 bL} = \frac{1.328}{\mathrm{Re}_L^{1/2}} = 2c_f(L) \tag{7.27}$$

Thus, for laminar plate flow, C_D equals twice the value of the skin friction coefficient at the trailing edge. This is the drag on one side of the plate.

Kármán pointed out that the drag could also be computed from the momentum relation (7.2). In dimensionless form, Eq. (7.2) becomes

$$C_D = \frac{2}{L} \int_0^\delta \frac{u}{U}\left(1 - \frac{u}{U}\right) dy \tag{7.28}$$

This can be rewritten in terms of the momentum thickness at the trailing edge:

$$C_D = \frac{2\theta(L)}{L} \tag{7.29}$$

Computation of θ from the profile u/U or from C_D gives

$$\frac{\theta}{x} = \frac{0.664}{\mathrm{Re}_x^{1/2}} \qquad \text{laminar flat plate} \tag{7.30}$$

Since δ is so ill defined, the momentum thickness, being definite, is often used to correlate data taken for a variety of boundary layers under differing conditions. The ratio of displacement to momentum thickness, called the dimensionless-profile *shape factor*, is also useful in integral theories. For laminar flat-plate flow

$$H = \frac{\delta^*}{\theta} = \frac{1.721}{0.664} = 2.59 \tag{7.31}$$

A large shape factor then implies that boundary layer separation is about to occur.

If we plot the Blasius velocity profile from Table 7.1 in the form of u/U versus y/δ, we can see why the simple integral theory guess, Eq. (7.6), was such a great success. This is done in Fig. 7.5. The simple parabolic approximation is not far from the true Blasius profile; hence its momentum thickness is within 10 percent of the true value. Also shown in Fig. 7.5 are three typical turbulent flat-plate velocity profiles. Notice how strikingly different in shape they are from the laminar profiles.

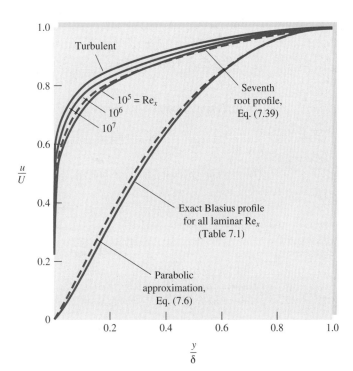

Fig. 7.5 Comparison of dimensionless laminar and turbulent flat-plate velocity profiles.

Instead of decreasing parabolically to zero, the turbulent profiles are very flat and then drop off sharply at the wall. As you might guess, they follow the logarithmic law shape and thus can be analyzed by momentum integral theory if this shape is properly represented.

Transition to Turbulence

The laminar flat-plate boundary layer eventually becomes turbulent, but there is no unique value for this change to occur. With care in polishing the wall and keeping the free stream quiet, one can delay the transition Reynolds number to $Re_{x,tr} \approx$ 3 E6 [8]. However, for typical commercial surfaces and gusty free streams, a more realistic value is

$$Re_{x,tr} \approx 5 \text{ E5}.$$

EXAMPLE 7.3

A sharp flat plate with $L = 50$ cm and $b = 3$ m is parallel to a stream of velocity 2.5 m/s. Find the drag on *one side* of the plate, and the boundary thickness δ at the trailing edge, for (a) air and (b) water at 20°C and 1 atm.

Solution

- *Assumptions:* Laminar flat-plate flow, but we should check the Reynolds numbers.
- *Approach:* Find the Reynolds number and use the appropriate boundary layer formulas.
- *Property values:* From Table A.2 for air at 20°C, $\rho = 1.2$ kg/m³, $\nu = 1.5$ E-5 m²/s. From Table A.1 for water at 20°C, $\rho = 998$ kg/m³, $\nu = 1.005$ E-6 m²/s.
- *(a) Solution for air:* Calculate the Reynolds number at the trailing edge:

$$Re_L = \frac{UL}{\nu_{air}} = \frac{(2.5 \text{ m/s})(0.5 \text{ m})}{1.5 \text{ E-5 m}^2/\text{s}} = 83{,}300 < 5 \text{ E5 therefore assuredly laminar}$$

The appropriate thickness relation is Eq. (7.24):

$$\frac{\delta}{L} = \frac{5}{Re_L^{1/2}} = \frac{5}{(83{,}300)^{1/2}} = 0.0173, \text{ or } \delta_{x=L} = 0.0173(0.5 \text{ m}) \cong 0.0087 \text{ m} \qquad Ans. (a)$$

The laminar boundary layer is only 8.7 mm thick. The drag coefficient follows from Eq. (7.27):

$$C_D = \frac{1.328}{Re_L^{1/2}} = \frac{1.328}{(83{,}300)^{1/2}} = 0.0046$$

$$\text{or } D_{one \ side} = C_D \frac{\rho}{2} U^2 bL = (0.0046) \frac{1.2 \text{ kg/m}^3}{2} (2.5 \text{ m/s})^2 (3 \text{ m})(0.5 \text{ m}) \approx 0.026 \text{ N} \quad Ans. (a)$$

- *Comment (a):* This is purely *friction* drag and is very small for gases at low velocities.
- *(b) Solution for water:* Again calculate the Reynolds number at the trailing edge:

$$Re_L = \frac{UL}{\nu_{water}} = \frac{(2.5 \text{ m/s})(0.5 \text{ m})}{1.005 \text{ E-6 m}^2/\text{s}} = 1.24 \text{ E6} > 5 \text{ E5 therefore it might be turbulent}$$

This is a quandary. If the plate is rough or encounters disturbances, the flow at the trailing edge will be turbulent. Let us assume a smooth, undisturbed plate, which will remain laminar. Then again the appropriate thickness relation is Eq. (7.24):

$$\frac{\delta}{L} = \frac{5}{Re_L^{1/2}} = \frac{5}{(1.24\ E6)^{1/2}} = 0.00448 \quad \text{or} \quad \delta_{x=L} = 0.00448(0.5\ \text{m}) \cong 0.0022\ \text{m} \quad \textit{Ans. (b)}$$

This is four times thinner than the air result in part (a), due to the high laminar Reynolds number. Again the drag coefficient follows from Eq. (7.27):

$$C_D = \frac{1.328}{Re_L^{1/2}} = \frac{1.328}{(1.24\ E6)^{1/2}} = 0.0012$$

$$\text{or} \quad D_{\text{one side}} = C_D \frac{\rho}{2} U^2 bL = (0.0012)\frac{998\ \text{kg/m}^3}{2}(2.5\ \text{m/s})^2(3\ \text{m})(0.5\ \text{m}) \approx 5.6\ \text{N} \quad \textit{Ans. (b)}$$

- Comment (b):   The drag is 215 times larger for water, although C_D is lower, reflecting that water is 56 times more viscous and 830 times denser than air. From Eq. (7.26), for the same U and x, the water drag should be $(56)^{1/2}(830)^{1/2} \approx 215$ times higher. Note: If transition to turbulence had occurred at $Re_x = 5\ E5$ (at about $x = 20$ cm), the drag would be about 2.5 times higher, and the trailing edge thickness about four times higher than for fully laminar flow.

Turbulent Flow

There is no exact theory for turbulent flat-plate flow, although there are many elegant computer solutions of the boundary layer equations using various empirical models for the turbulent eddy viscosity [9]. The most widely accepted result is simply an integral analysis similar to our study of the laminar profile approximation (7.6).

We begin with Eq. (7.5), which is valid for laminar or turbulent flow. We write it here for convenient reference:

$$\tau_w(x) = \rho U^2 \frac{d\theta}{dx} \tag{7.32}$$

From the definition of c_f, Eq. (7.10), this can be rewritten as

$$c_f = 2\frac{d\theta}{dx} \tag{7.33}$$

Now recall from Fig. 7.5 that the turbulent profiles are nowhere near parabolic. Going back to Fig. 6.10, we see that flat-plate flow is very nearly logarithmic, with a slight outer wake and a thin viscous sublayer. Therefore, just as in turbulent pipe flow, we assume that the logarithmic law (6.28) holds all the way across the boundary layer

$$\frac{u}{u^*} \approx \frac{1}{\kappa} \ln \frac{yu^*}{\nu} + B \qquad u^* = \left(\frac{\tau_w}{\rho}\right)^{1/2} \tag{7.34}$$

with, as usual, $\kappa = 0.41$ and $B = 5.0$. At the outer edge of the boundary layer, $y = \delta$ and $u = U$, and Eq. (7.34) becomes

$$\frac{U}{u^*} = \frac{1}{\kappa} \ln \frac{\delta u^*}{\nu} + B \tag{7.35}$$

But the definition of the skin friction coefficient, Eq. (7.10), is such that the following identities hold:

$$\frac{U}{u^*} \equiv \left(\frac{2}{c_f}\right)^{1/2} \qquad \frac{\delta u^*}{\nu} \equiv \mathrm{Re}_\delta \left(\frac{c_f}{2}\right)^{1/2} \tag{7.36}$$

Therefore, Eq. (7.35) is a *skin friction law* for turbulent flat-plate flow:

$$\left(\frac{2}{c_f}\right)^{1/2} \approx 2.44 \ln \left[\mathrm{Re}_\delta \left(\frac{c_f}{2}\right)^{1/2} \right] + 5.0 \tag{7.37}$$

It is a complicated law, but we can at least solve for a few values and list them:

Re_δ	10^4	10^5	10^6	10^7
c_f	0.00493	0.00315	0.00217	0.00158

Following a suggestion of Prandtl, we can forget the complex log friction law (7.37) and simply fit the numbers in the table to a power-law approximation:

$$c_f \approx 0.02 \, \mathrm{Re}_\delta^{-1/6} \tag{7.38}$$

This we shall use as the left-hand side of Eq. (7.33). For the right-hand side, we need an estimate for $\theta(x)$ in terms of $\delta(x)$. If we use the logarithmic law profile (7.34), we shall be up to our hips in logarithmic integrations for the momentum thickness. Instead we follow another suggestion of Prandtl, who pointed out that the turbulent profiles in Fig. 7.5 can be approximated by a one-seventh-power law:

$$\left(\frac{u}{U}\right)_{\mathrm{turb}} \approx \left(\frac{y}{\delta}\right)^{1/7} \tag{7.39}$$

This is shown as a dashed line in Fig. 7.5. It is an excellent fit to the low-Reynolds-number turbulent data, which were all that were available to Prandtl at the time. With this simple approximation, the momentum thickness (7.28) can easily be evaluated:

$$\theta \approx \int_0^\delta \left(\frac{y}{\delta}\right)^{1/7} \left[1 - \left(\frac{y}{\delta}\right)^{1/7} \right] dy = \frac{7}{72} \delta \tag{7.40}$$

We accept this result and substitute Eqs. (7.38) and (7.40) into Kármán's momentum law (7.33):

$$c_f = 0.02 \, \mathrm{Re}_\delta^{-1/6} = 2 \frac{d}{dx} \left(\frac{7}{72}\delta\right)$$

or

$$\mathrm{Re}_\delta^{-1/6} = 9.72 \frac{d\delta}{dx} = 9.72 \frac{d(\mathrm{Re}_\delta)}{d(\mathrm{Re}_x)} \tag{7.41}$$

Separate the variables and integrate, assuming $\delta = 0$ at $x = 0$:

$$\boxed{\mathrm{Re}_\delta \approx 0.16 \, \mathrm{Re}_x^{6/7} \qquad \text{or} \qquad \frac{\delta}{x} \approx \frac{0.16}{\mathrm{Re}_x^{1/7}}} \tag{7.42}$$

Thus the thickness of a turbulent boundary layer increases as $x^{6/7}$, far more rapidly than the laminar increase $x^{1/2}$. Equation (7.42) is the solution to the problem, because all other parameters are now available. For example, combining Eqs. (7.42) and (7.38), we obtain the friction variation

$$c_f \approx \frac{0.027}{\mathrm{Re}_x^{1/7}} \tag{7.43}$$

Writing this out in dimensional form, we have

$$\tau_{w,\mathrm{turb}} \approx \frac{0.0135 \mu^{1/7} \rho^{6/7} U^{13/7}}{x^{1/7}} \tag{7.44}$$

Turbulent plate friction drops slowly with x, increases nearly as ρ and U^2, and is rather insensitive to viscosity.

We can evaluate the drag coefficient by integrating the wall friction:

$$D = \int_0^L \tau_w b\, dx$$

or

$$C_D = \frac{2D}{\rho U^2 \, bL} = \int_0^1 c_f \, d\left(\frac{x}{L}\right)$$

$$C_D = \frac{0.031}{\mathrm{Re}_L^{1/7}} = \frac{7}{6} c_f\,(L) \tag{7.45}$$

Then C_D is only 16 percent greater than the trailing-edge skin friction coefficient [compare with Eq. (7.27) for laminar flow].

The displacement thickness can be estimated from the one-seventh-power law and Eq. (7.12):

$$\delta^* \approx \int_0^\delta \left[1 - \left(\frac{y}{\delta}\right)^{1/7} \right] dy = \frac{1}{8}\delta \tag{7.46}$$

The turbulent flat-plate shape factor is approximately

$$H = \frac{\delta^*}{\theta} = \frac{\frac{1}{8}}{\frac{7}{72}} = 1.3 \tag{7.47}$$

These are the basic results of turbulent flat-plate theory.

Figure 7.6 shows flat-plate drag coefficients for both laminar and turbulent flow conditions. The smooth-wall relations (7.27) and (7.45) are shown, along with the effect of wall roughness, which is quite strong. The proper roughness parameter here is x/ε or L/ε, by analogy with the pipe parameter ε/d. In the fully rough regime, C_D is independent of the Reynolds number, so that the drag varies exactly as U^2 and is independent of μ. Reference 2 presents a theory of rough flat-plate flow, and Ref. 1 gives a curve fit for skin friction and drag in the fully rough regime:

$$c_f \approx \left(2.87 + 1.58 \log \frac{x}{\varepsilon} \right)^{-2.5} \tag{7.48a}$$

$$C_D \approx \left(1.89 + 1.62 \log \frac{L}{\varepsilon} \right)^{-2.5} \tag{7.48b}$$

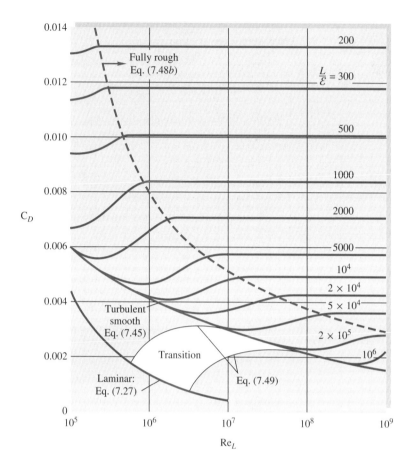

Fig. 7.6 Drag coefficient of laminar and turbulent boundary layers on smooth and rough flat plates. This chart is the flat-plate analog of the Moody diagram of Fig. 6.13.

Equation (7.48b) is plotted to the right of the dashed line in Fig. 7.6. The figure also shows the behavior of the drag coefficient in the transition region $5 \times 10^5 < \mathrm{Re}_L < 8 \times 10^7$, where the laminar drag at the leading edge is an appreciable fraction of the total drag. Schlichting [1] suggests the following curve fits for these transition drag curves, depending on the Reynolds number $\mathrm{Re}_{\mathrm{trans}}$ where transition begins:

$$C_D \approx \begin{cases} \dfrac{0.031}{\mathrm{Re}_L^{1/7}} - \dfrac{1440}{\mathrm{Re}_L} & \mathrm{Re}_{\mathrm{trans}} = 5 \times 10^5 \qquad (7.49a) \\[2ex] \dfrac{0.031}{\mathrm{Re}_L^{1/7}} - \dfrac{8700}{\mathrm{Re}_L} & \mathrm{Re}_{\mathrm{trans}} = 3 \times 10^6 \qquad (7.49b) \end{cases}$$

EXAMPLE 7.4

A hydrofoil 1.2 ft long and 6 ft wide is placed in a seawater flow of 40 ft/s, with $\rho = 1.99$ slugs/ft^3 and $\nu = 0.000011$ ft^2/s. (a) Estimate the boundary layer thickness at the end of the plate. Estimate the friction drag for (b) turbulent smooth-wall flow from the leading edge, (c) laminar turbulent flow with $Re_{trans} = 5 \times 10^5$, and (d) turbulent rough-wall flow with $\varepsilon = 0.0004$ ft.

Solution

Part (a)   The Reynolds number is

$$Re_L = \frac{UL}{\nu} = \frac{(40 \text{ ft/s})(1.2 \text{ ft})}{0.000011 \text{ ft}^2/\text{s}} = 4.36 \times 10^6$$

Thus the trailing-edge flow is certainly turbulent. The maximum boundary layer thickness would occur for turbulent flow starting at the leading edge. From Eq. (7.42),

$$\frac{\delta(L)}{L} = \frac{0.16}{(4.36 \times 10^6)^{1/7}} = 0.018$$

or

$$\delta = 0.018(1.2 \text{ ft}) = 0.0216 \text{ ft}$$ *Ans.* (a)

This is 7.5 times thicker than a fully laminar boundary layer at the same Reynolds number.

Part (b)   For fully turbulent smooth-wall flow, the drag coefficient on one side of the plate is, from Eq. (7.45),

$$C_D = \frac{0.031}{(4.36 \times 10^6)^{1/7}} = 0.00349$$

Then the drag on both sides of the foil is approximately

$$D = 2C_D(\tfrac{1}{2}\rho U^2)bL = 2(0.00349)(\tfrac{1}{2})(1.99)(40)^2(6.0)(1.2) = 80 \text{ lbf}$$ *Ans.* (b)

Part (c)   With a laminar leading edge and $Re_{trans} = 5 \times 10^5$, Eq. (7.49a) applies:

$$C_D = 0.00349 - \frac{1440}{4.36 \times 10^6} = 0.00316$$

The drag can be recomputed for this lower drag coefficient:

$$D = 2C_D(\tfrac{1}{2}\rho U^2)bL = 72 \text{ lbf}$$ *Ans.* (c)

Part (d)   Finally, for the rough wall, we calculate

$$\frac{L}{\varepsilon} = \frac{1.2 \text{ ft}}{0.0004 \text{ ft}} = 3000$$

From Fig. 7.6 at $Re_L = 4.36 \times 10^6$, this condition is just inside the fully rough regime. Equation (7.48b) applies:

$$C_D = (1.89 + 1.62 \log 3000)^{-2.5} = 0.00644$$

and the drag estimate is

$$D = 2C_D(\tfrac{1}{2}\rho U^2)bL = 148 \text{ lbf}$$ *Ans.* (d)

This small roughness nearly doubles the drag. It is probable that the total hydrofoil drag is still another factor of 2 larger because of trailing-edge flow separation effects.

7.5 Boundary Layers with Pressure Gradient[3]

The flat-plate analysis of the previous section should give us a good feeling for the behavior of both laminar and turbulent boundary layers, except for one important effect: flow separation. Prandtl showed that separation like that in Fig. 7.2b is caused by excessive momentum loss near the wall in a boundary layer trying to move downstream against increasing pressure, $dp/dx > 0$, which is called an *adverse pressure gradient*. The opposite case of decreasing pressure, $dp/dx < 0$, is called a *favorable gradient*, where flow separation can never occur. In a typical immersed-body flow, such as in Fig. 7.2b, the favorable gradient is on the front of the body and the adverse gradient is in the rear, as discussed in detail in Chap. 8.

We can explain flow separation with a geometric argument about the second derivative of velocity u at the wall. From the momentum equation (7.19b) at the wall, where $u = v = 0$, we obtain

$$\left.\frac{\partial \tau}{\partial y}\right|_{\text{wall}} = \mu \left.\frac{\partial^2 u}{\partial y^2}\right|_{\text{wall}} = -\rho U \frac{dU}{dx} = \frac{dp}{dx}$$

or

$$\left.\frac{\partial^2 u}{\partial y^2}\right|_{\text{wall}} = \frac{1}{\mu}\frac{dp}{dx} \tag{7.50}$$

for either laminar or turbulent flow. Thus in an adverse gradient the second derivative of velocity is positive at the wall; yet it must be negative at the outer layer ($y = \delta$) to merge smoothly with the mainstream flow $U(x)$. It follows that the second derivative must pass through zero somewhere in between, at a point of inflection, and any boundary layer profile in an adverse gradient must exhibit a characteristic S shape.

Figure 7.7 illustrates the general case. In a favorable gradient (Fig. 7.7a) the profile is very rounded, there is no point of inflection, there can be no separation, and laminar profiles of this type are very resistant to a transition to turbulence [1 to 3].

In a zero pressure gradient (Fig. 7.7b), such as a flat-plate flow, the point of inflection is at the wall itself. There can be no separation, and the flow will undergo transition at Re_x no greater than about 3×10^6, as discussed earlier.

In an adverse gradient (Fig. 7.7c to e), a point of inflection (PI) occurs in the boundary layer, its distance from the wall increasing with the strength of the adverse gradient. For a weak gradient (Fig. 7.7c) the flow does not actually separate, but it is vulnerable to transition to turbulence at Re_x as low as 10^5 [1, 2]. At a moderate gradient, a critical condition (Fig. 7.7d) is reached where the wall shear is exactly zero ($\partial u/\partial y = 0$). This is defined as the *separation point* ($\tau_w = 0$), because any stronger gradient will actually cause backflow at the wall (Fig. 7.7e): the boundary layer thickens greatly, and the main flow breaks away, or separates, from the wall (Fig. 7.2b).

The flow profiles of Fig. 7.7 usually occur in sequence as the boundary layer progresses along the wall of a body. For example, in Fig. 7.2a, a favorable gradient occurs on the front of the body, zero pressure gradient occurs just upstream of the shoulder, and an adverse gradient occurs successively as we move around the rear of the body.

---

[3]This section may be omitted without loss of continuity.

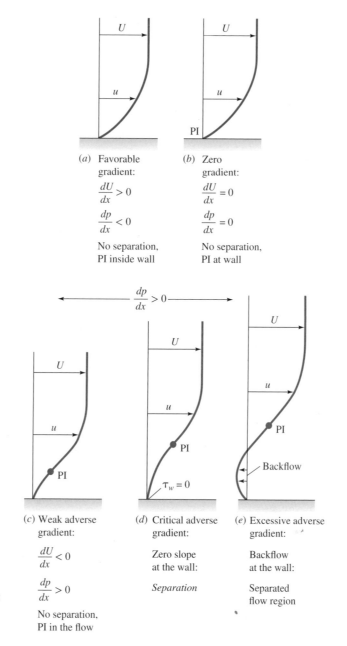

Fig. 7.7 Effect of pressure gradient on boundary layer profiles; PI = point of inflection.

(a) Favorable gradient:

$$\frac{dU}{dx} > 0$$

$$\frac{dp}{dx} < 0$$

No separation, PI inside wall

(b) Zero gradient:

$$\frac{dU}{dx} = 0$$

$$\frac{dp}{dx} = 0$$

No separation, PI at wall

$$\frac{dp}{dx} > 0$$

(c) Weak adverse gradient:

$$\frac{dU}{dx} < 0$$

$$\frac{dp}{dx} > 0$$

No separation, PI in the flow

(d) Critical adverse gradient:

Zero slope at the wall:

Separation

(e) Excessive adverse gradient:

Backflow at the wall:

Separated flow region

A second practical example is the flow in a duct consisting of a nozzle, throat, and diffuser, as in Fig. 7.8. The nozzle flow is a favorable gradient and never separates, nor does the throat flow where the pressure gradient is approximately zero. But the expanding-area diffuser produces low velocity and increasing pressure, an adverse gradient. If the diffuser angle is too large, the adverse gradient is excessive, and the boundary layer will separate at one or both walls, with backflow,

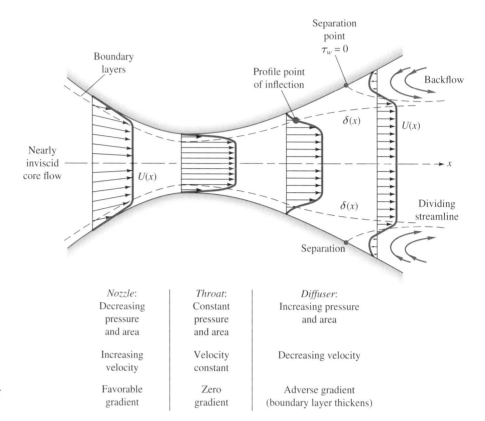

Fig. 7.8 Boundary layer growth and separation in a nozzle–diffuser configuration.

Nozzle: Decreasing pressure and area	*Throat*: Constant pressure and area	*Diffuser*: Increasing pressure and area
Increasing velocity	Velocity constant	Decreasing velocity
Favorable gradient	Zero gradient	Adverse gradient (boundary layer thickens)

increased losses, and poor pressure recovery. In the diffuser literature [10] this condition is called *diffuser stall,* a term used also in airfoil aerodynamics (Sec. 7.6) to denote airfoil boundary layer separation. Thus the boundary layer behavior explains why a large-angle diffuser has heavy flow losses (Fig. 6.23) and poor performance (Fig. 6.28).

Presently boundary layer theory can compute only up to the separation point, after which it is invalid. Techniques are now developed for analyzing the strong interaction effects caused by separated flows [5, 6].

Laminar Integral Theory[4]

Both laminar and turbulent theories can be developed from Kármán's general two-dimensional boundary layer integral relation [2, 7], which extends Eq. (7.33) to variable $U(x)$ by integration across the boundary layer:

$$\frac{\tau_w}{\rho U^2} = \frac{1}{2}c_f = \frac{d\theta}{dx} + (2 + H)\frac{\theta}{U}\frac{dU}{dx} \qquad (7.51)$$

[4]This section may be omitted without loss of continuity.

where $\theta(x)$ is the momentum thickness and $H(x) = \delta^*(x)/\theta(x)$ is the shape factor. From Eq. (7.17) negative dU/dx is equivalent to positive dp/dx—that is, an adverse gradient.

We can integrate Eq. (7.51) to determine $\theta(x)$ for a given $U(x)$ if we correlate c_f and H with the momentum thickness. This has been done by examining typical velocity profiles of laminar and turbulent boundary layer flows for various pressure gradients. Some examples are given in Fig. 7.9, showing that the shape factor H is a good indicator of the pressure gradient. The higher the H, the stronger the adverse gradient, and separation occurs approximately at

$$H \approx \begin{cases} 3.5 & \text{laminar flow} \\ 2.4 & \text{turbulent flow} \end{cases} \tag{7.52}$$

The laminar profiles (Fig. 7.9a) clearly exhibit the S shape and a point of inflection with an adverse gradient. But in the turbulent profiles (Fig. 7.9b) the points of inflection are typically buried deep within the thin viscous sublayer, which can hardly be seen on the scale of the figure.

There are scores of turbulent theories in the literature, but they are all complicated algebraically and will be omitted here. The reader is referred to advanced texts [1–3, 9].

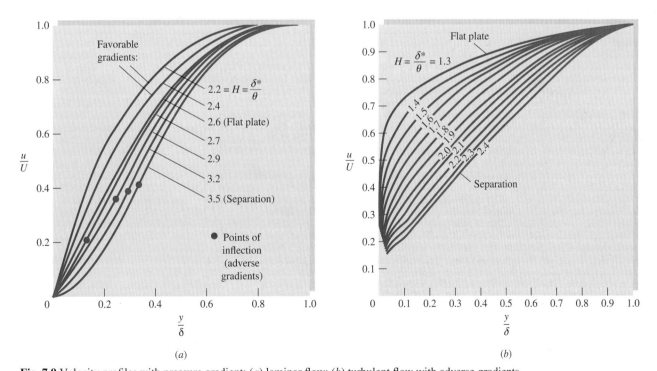

Fig. 7.9 Velocity profiles with pressure gradient: (a) laminar flow; (b) turbulent flow with adverse gradients.

For laminar flow, a simple and effective method was developed by Thwaites [11], who found that Eq. (7.51) can be correlated by a single dimensionless momentum thickness variable λ, defined as

$$\lambda = \frac{\theta^2}{\nu}\frac{dU}{dx} \tag{7.53}$$

Using a straight-line fit to his correlation, Thwaites was able to integrate Eq. (7.51) in closed form, with the result

$$\theta^2 = \theta_0^2 \left(\frac{U_0}{U}\right)^6 + \frac{0.45\nu}{U^6}\int_0^x U^5\, dx \tag{7.54}$$

where θ_0 is the momentum thickness at $x = 0$ (usually taken to be zero). Separation ($c_f = 0$) was found to occur at a particular value of λ:

Separation: $\qquad\qquad\qquad\qquad \lambda = -0.09 \tag{7.55}$

Finally, Thwaites correlated values of the dimensionless shear stress $S = \tau_w\theta/(\mu U)$ with λ, and his graphed result can be curve-fitted as follows:

$$S(\lambda) = \frac{\tau_w\theta}{\mu U} \approx (\lambda + 0.09)^{0.62} \tag{7.56}$$

This parameter is related to the skin friction by the identity

$$S \equiv \tfrac{1}{2}c_f\,\mathrm{Re}_\theta \tag{7.57}$$

Equations (7.54) to (7.56) constitute a complete theory for the laminar boundary layer with variable $U(x)$, with an accuracy of ± 10 percent compared with computer solutions of the laminar-boundary-layer equations (7.19). Complete details of Thwaites's and other laminar theories are given in Ref. 2.

As a demonstration of Thwaites's method, take a flat plate, where $U = $ constant, $\lambda = 0$, and $\theta_0 = 0$. Equation (7.54) integrates to

$$\theta^2 = \frac{0.45\nu x}{U}$$

or $\qquad\qquad\qquad\qquad \dfrac{\theta}{x} = \dfrac{0.671}{\mathrm{Re}_x^{1/2}} \tag{7.58}$

This is within 1 percent of Blasius's numerical solution, Eq. (7.30).

With $\lambda = 0$, Eq. (7.56) predicts the flat-plate shear to be

$$\frac{\tau_w\theta}{\mu U} = (0.09)^{0.62} = 0.225$$

or $\qquad\qquad\qquad\qquad c_f = \dfrac{2\tau_w}{\rho U^2} = \dfrac{0.671}{\mathrm{Re}_x^{1/2}} \tag{7.59}$

This is also within 1 percent of the Blasius result, Eq. (7.25). However, the general accuracy of this method is poorer than 1 percent because Thwaites actually "tuned" his correlation constants to make them agree with exact flat-plate theory.

We shall not compute any more boundary layer details here; but as we go along, investigating various immersed-body flows, especially in Chap. 8, we shall use Thwaites's method to make qualitative assessments of the boundary layer behavior.

EXAMPLE 7.5

In 1938 Howarth proposed a linearly decelerating external velocity distribution

$$U(x) = U_0\left(1 - \frac{x}{L}\right) \tag{1}$$

as a theoretical model for laminar-boundary-layer study. (a) Use Thwaites's method to compute the separation point x_{sep} for $\theta_0 = 0$, and compare with the exact computer solution $x_{sep}/L = 0.119863$ given by H. Wipperman in 1966. (b) Also compute the value of $c_f = 2\tau_w/(\rho U^2)$ at $x/L = 0.1$.

Solution

Part (a)

First note that $dU/dx = -U_0/L =$ constant: Velocity decreases, pressure increases, and the pressure gradient is adverse throughout. Now integrate Eq. (7.54):

$$\theta^2 = \frac{0.45\nu}{U_0^6(1 - x/L)^6}\int_0^x U_0^5\left(1 - \frac{x}{L}\right)^5 dx = 0.075\frac{\nu L}{U_0}\left[\left(1 - \frac{x}{L}\right)^{-6} - 1\right] \tag{2}$$

Then the dimensionless factor λ is given by

$$\lambda = \frac{\theta^2}{\nu}\frac{dU}{dx} = -\frac{\theta^2 U_0}{\nu L} = -0.075\left[\left(1 - \frac{x}{L}\right)^{-6} - 1\right] \tag{3}$$

From Eq. (7.55) we set this equal to -0.09 for separation:

$$\lambda_{sep} = -0.09 = -0.075\left[\left(1 - \frac{x_{sep}}{L}\right)^{-6} - 1\right]$$

or

$$\frac{x_{sep}}{L} = 1 - (2.2)^{-1/6} = 0.123 \qquad \qquad Ans. \ (a)$$

This is less than 3 percent higher than Wipperman's exact solution, and the computational effort is very modest.

Part (b)

To compute c_f at $x/L = 0.1$ (just before separation), we first compute λ at this point, using Eq. (3):

$$\lambda(x = 0.1L) = -0.075[(1 - 0.1)^{-6} - 1] = -0.0661$$

Then from Eq. (7.56) the shear parameter is

$$S(x = 0.1L) = (-0.0661 + 0.09)^{0.62} = 0.099 = \tfrac{1}{2}c_f \text{Re}_\theta \tag{4}$$

We can compute Re_θ in terms of Re_L from Eq. (2) or (3):

$$\frac{\theta^2}{L^2} = \frac{0.0661}{UL/\nu} = \frac{0.0661}{\text{Re}_L}$$

or

$$\text{Re}_\theta = 0.257\ \text{Re}_L^{1/2} \qquad \text{at } \frac{x}{L} = 0.1$$

Substitute into Eq. (4):

$$0.099 = \tfrac{1}{2}c_f(0.257 \, \mathrm{Re}_L^{1/2})$$

or $\qquad\qquad\qquad\qquad c_f = \dfrac{0.77}{\mathrm{Re}_L^{1/2}} \qquad \mathrm{Re}_L = \dfrac{UL}{\nu}$ $\qquad\qquad\qquad$ *Ans. (b)*

We cannot actually compute c_f without the value of, say, $U_0 L/\nu$.

7.6 Experimental External Flows

Boundary layer theory is very interesting and illuminating and gives us a great qualitative grasp of viscous flow behavior; but, because of flow separation, the theory does not generally allow a quantitative computation of the complete flow field. In particular, there is at present no satisfactory theory, except CFD results, for the forces on an arbitrary body immersed in a stream flowing at an arbitrary Reynolds number. Therefore, experimentation is the key to treating external flows.

Literally thousands of papers in the literature report experimental data on specific external viscous flows. This section gives a brief description of the following external flow problems:

1. Drag of two- and three-dimensional bodies:
    a. Blunt bodies.
    b. Streamlined shapes.
2. Performance of lifting bodies:
    a. Airfoils and aircraft.
    b. Projectiles and finned bodies.
    c. Birds and insects.

For further reading see the goldmine of data compiled in Hoerner [12]. In later chapters we shall study data on supersonic airfoils (Chap. 9), open-channel friction (Chap. 10), and turbomachinery performance (Chap. 11).

Drag of Immersed Bodies

Any body of any shape when immersed in a fluid stream will experience forces and moments from the flow. If the body has arbitrary shape and orientation, the flow will exert forces and moments about all three coordinate axes, as shown in Fig. 7.10. It is customary to choose one axis parallel to the free stream and positive downstream. The force on the body along this axis is called *drag,* and the moment about that axis the *rolling moment.* The drag is essentially a flow loss and must be overcome if the body is to move against the stream.

A second and very important force is perpendicular to the drag and usually performs a useful job, such as bearing the weight of the body. It is called the *lift.* The moment about the lift axis is called *yaw.*

The third component, neither a loss nor a gain, is the *side force,* and about this axis is the *pitching moment.* To deal with this three-dimensional force-moment situation is more properly the role of a textbook on aerodynamics [for example, 13]. We shall limit the discussion here to lift and drag.

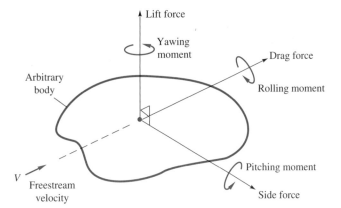

Fig. 7.10 Definition of forces and moments on a body immersed in a uniform flow.

When the body has symmetry about the lift–drag axis, as with airplanes, ships, and cars moving directly into a stream, the side force, yaw, and roll vanish, and the problem reduces to a two-dimensional case: two forces, lift and drag, and one moment, pitch.

A final simplification often occurs when the body has two planes of symmetry, as in Fig. 7.11. A wide variety of shapes such as cylinders, wings, and all bodies of revolution satisfy this requirement. If the free stream is parallel to the intersection of these two planes, called the *principal chord line of the body,* the body experiences drag only, with no lift, side force, or moments.[5] This type of degenerate one-force drag data is what is most commonly reported in the literature, but if the free stream is not parallel to the chord line, the body will have an unsymmetric orientation and all three forces and three moments can arise in principle.

In low-speed flow past geometrically similar bodies with identical orientation and relative roughness, the drag coefficient should be a function of the body Reynolds number:

$$C_D = f(\mathrm{Re}) \tag{7.60}$$

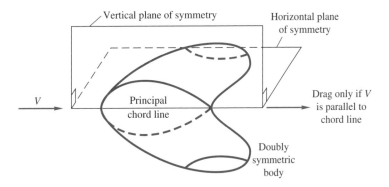

Fig. 7.11 Only the drag force occurs if the flow is parallel to both planes of symmetry.

---

[5]In bodies with shed vortices, such as the cylinder in Fig. 5.2, there may be *oscillating* lift, side force, and moments, but their mean value is zero.

The Reynolds number is based upon the free-stream velocity V and a characteristic length L of the body, usually the chord or body length parallel to the stream:

$$\mathrm{Re} = \frac{VL}{\nu} \tag{7.61}$$

For cylinders, spheres, and disks, the characteristic length is the diameter D.

Characteristic Area

Drag coefficients are defined by using a characteristic area A, which may differ depending on the body shape:

$$\boxed{C_D = \frac{\mathrm{drag}}{\frac{1}{2}\rho V^2 A}} \tag{7.62}$$

The factor $\frac{1}{2}$ is our traditional tribute to Euler and Bernoulli. The area A is usually one of three types:

1. *Frontal area,* the body as seen from the stream; suitable for thick, stubby bodies, such as spheres, cylinders, cars, trucks, missiles, projectiles, and torpedoes.
2. *Planform area,* the body area as seen from above; suitable for wide, flat bodies such as wings and hydrofoils.
3. *Wetted area,* customary for surface ships and barges.

In using drag or other fluid force data, it is important to note what length and area are being used to scale the measured coefficients.

Friction Drag and Pressure Drag

As we have mentioned, the theory of drag is weak and inadequate, except for the flat plate. This is because of flow separation. Boundary layer theory can predict the separation point but cannot accurately estimate the (usually low) pressure distribution in the separated region. The difference between the high pressure in the front stagnation region and the low pressure in the rear separated region causes a large drag contribution called *pressure drag.* This is added to the integrated shear stress or *friction drag* of the body, which it often exceeds:

$$C_D = C_{D,\mathrm{press}} + C_{D,\mathrm{fric}} \tag{7.63}$$

The relative contribution of friction and pressure drag depends upon the body's shape, especially its thickness. Figure 7.12 shows drag data for a streamlined cylinder of very large depth into the paper. At zero thickness the body is a flat plate and exhibits 100 percent friction drag. At thickness equal to the chord length, simulating a circular cylinder, the friction drag is only about 3 percent. Friction and pressure drag are about equal at thickness $t/c = 0.25$. Note that C_D in Fig. 7.12b looks quite different when based on frontal area instead of planform area, planform being the usual choice for this body shape. The two curves in Fig. 7.12b represent exactly the same drag data.

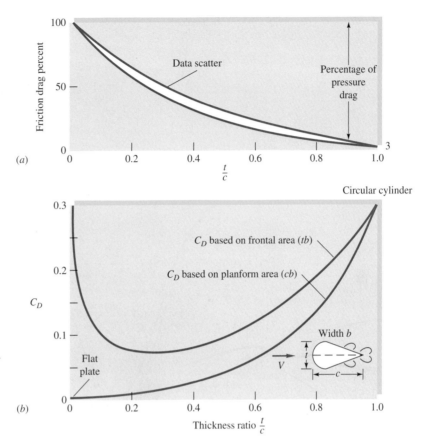

Fig. 7.12 Drag of a streamlined two-dimensional cylinder at $Re_c = 10^6$: (a) effect of thickness ratio on percentage of friction drag; (b) total drag versus thickness when based on two different areas.

Figure 7.13 illustrates the dramatic effect of separated flow and the subsequent failure of boundary layer theory. The theoretical inviscid pressure distribution on a circular cylinder (Chap. 8) is shown as the dashed line in Fig. 7.13c:

$$C_p = \frac{p - p_\infty}{\frac{1}{2}\rho V^2} = 1 - 4\sin^2\theta$$

where P_∞ and V are the pressure and velocity, respectively, in the free stream. The actual laminar and turbulent boundary layer pressure distributions in Fig. 7.13c are startlingly different from those predicted by theory. Laminar flow is very vulnerable to the adverse gradient on the rear of the cylinder, and separation occurs at $\theta = 82°$, which certainly could not have been predicted from inviscid theory. The broad wake and very low pressure in the separated laminar region cause the large drag $C_D = 1.2$.

The turbulent boundary layer in Fig. 7.13b is more resistant, and separation is delayed until $\theta = 120°$, with a resulting smaller wake, higher pressure on the rear, and 75 percent less drag, $C_D = 0.3$. This explains the sharp drop in drag at transition in Fig. 5.3.

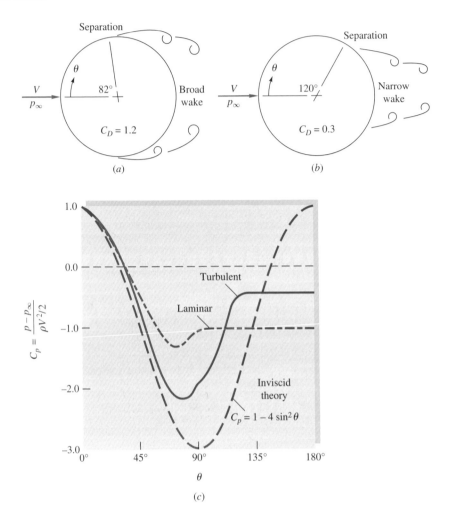

Fig. 7.13 Flow past a circular cylinder: (*a*) laminar separation; (*b*) turbulent separation; (*c*) theoretical and actual surface pressure distributions.

The same sharp difference between vulnerable laminar separation and resistant turbulent separation can be seen for a sphere in Fig. 7.14. The laminar flow (Fig. 7.14*a*) separates at about 80°, $C_D = 0.5$, while the turbulent flow (Fig. 7.14*b*) separates at 120°, $C_D = 0.2$. Here the Reynolds numbers are exactly the same, and the turbulent boundary layer is induced by a patch of sand roughness at the nose of the ball. Golf balls fly in this range of Reynolds numbers, which is why they are deliberately dimpled—to induce a turbulent boundary layer and lower drag. Again we would find the actual pressure distribution on the sphere to be quite different from that predicted by inviscid theory.

In general, we cannot overstress the importance of body streamlining to reduce drag at Reynolds numbers above about 100. This is illustrated in Fig. 7.15. The rectangular cylinder (Fig. 7.15*a*) has separation at all sharp corners and very high drag. Rounding its nose (Fig. 7.15*b*) reduces drag by about 45 percent, but C_D is still high. Streamlining its rear to a sharp trailing edge (Fig. 7.15*c*) reduces its drag another 85 percent to a practical minimum for the given thickness. As a dramatic contrast, the circular cylinder (Fig. 7.15*d*) has one-eighth the thickness and one-three-hundredth the cross

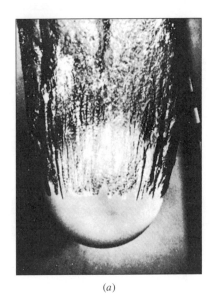 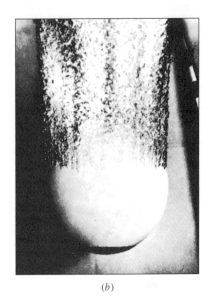

Fig. 7.14 Strong differences in laminar and turbulent separation on an 8.5-in bowling ball entering water at 25 ft/s: (*a*) smooth ball, laminar boundary layer; (*b*) same entry, turbulent flow induced by patch of nose-sand roughness. (*NAVAIR Weapons Division Historical Archives.*)

(*a*)   (*b*)

section (*c*) (Fig. 7.15*c*), yet it has the same drag. For high-performance vehicles and other moving bodies, the name of the game is drag reduction, for which intense research continues for both aerodynamic and hydrodynamic applications [20, 39].

Two-Dimensional Bodies

The drag of some representative wide-span (nearly two-dimensional) bodies is shown versus the Reynolds number in Fig. 7.16*a*. All bodies have high C_D at very low (*creeping flow*) Re ≤ 1.0, while they spread apart at high Reynolds numbers according to their degree of streamlining. All values of C_D are based on the planform area except the plate normal to the flow. The birds and the sailplane are, of course, not very two-dimensional, having only modest span length. Note that birds are not nearly as efficient as modern sailplanes or airfoils [14, 15].

Creeping Flow

In 1851 G. G. Stokes showed that, if the Reynolds number is very small, Re ≪ 1, the acceleration terms in the Navier-Stokes equations (7.14*b*, *c*) are negligible. The flow is termed *creeping flow*, or Stokes flow, and is a balance between pressure

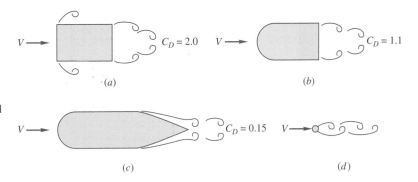

Fig. 7.15 The importance of streamlining in reducing drag of a body (C_D based on frontal area): (*a*) rectangular cylinder; (*b*) rounded nose; (*c*) rounded nose and streamlined sharp trailing edge; (*d*) circular cylinder with the same drag as case (*c*).

$V \rightarrow$ $C_D = 2.0$ $V \rightarrow$ $C_D = 1.1$
(*a*)   (*b*)

$V \rightarrow$ $C_D = 0.15$ $V \rightarrow$
(*c*)   (*d*)

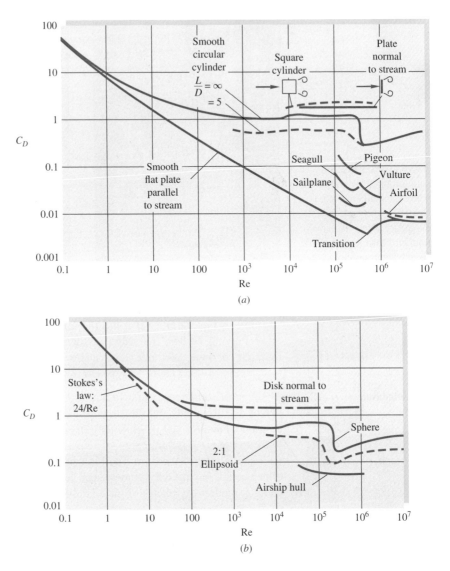

Fig. 7.16 Drag coefficients of smooth bodies at low Mach numbers: (*a*) two-dimensional bodies; (*b*) three-dimensional bodies. Note the Reynolds number independence of blunt bodies at high Re.

gradient and viscous stresses. Continuity and momentum reduce to two linear equations for velocity and pressure:

$$\text{Re} \ll 1: \quad \nabla \cdot \mathbf{V} = 0 \quad \text{and} \quad \nabla p \approx \mu \nabla^2 \mathbf{V}$$

If the geometry is simple (for example, a sphere or disk), closed-form solutions can be found and the body drag can be computed [2]. Stokes himself provided the sphere drag formula:

$$F_{\text{sphere}} = 3\pi \mu U d$$

or

$$C_D = \frac{F}{\frac{1}{2}\rho U^2 \frac{\pi}{4} d^2} = \frac{24}{\rho U d/\mu} = \frac{24}{\text{Re}_d} \tag{7.64}$$

This relation is plotted in Fig. 7.16*b* and is seen to be accurate for about $\text{Re}_d \lesssim 1$.

Table 7.2 gives a few data on drag, based on frontal area, of two-dimensional bodies of various cross section, at Re $\geq 10^4$. The sharp-edged bodies, which tend to cause flow separation regardless of the character of the boundary layer, are insensitive to the Reynolds number. The elliptic cylinders, being smoothly rounded, have the

Table 7.2 Drag of Two-Dimensional Bodies at Re $\geq 10^4$

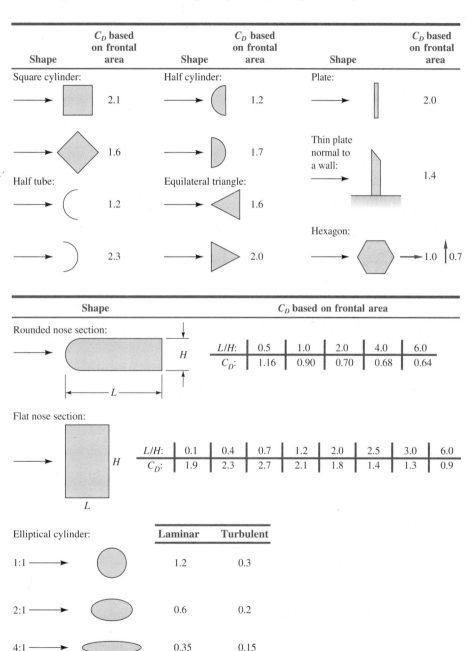

Shape	C_D based on frontal area	Shape	C_D based on frontal area	Shape	C_D based on frontal area
Square cylinder:	2.1	Half cylinder:	1.2	Plate:	2.0
	1.6		1.7	Thin plate normal to a wall:	1.4
Half tube:	1.2	Equilateral triangle:	1.6		
	2.3		2.0	Hexagon:	1.0 0.7

Shape	C_D based on frontal area				
Rounded nose section:					
	L/H:	0.5	1.0	2.0	4.0	6.0
	C_D:	1.16	0.90	0.70	0.68	0.64

	L/H:	0.1	0.4	0.7	1.2	2.0	2.5	3.0	6.0
Flat nose section:	C_D:	1.9	2.3	2.7	2.1	1.8	1.4	1.3	0.9

Elliptical cylinder:	Laminar	Turbulent
1:1	1.2	0.3
2:1	0.6	0.2
4:1	0.35	0.15
8:1	0.25	0.1

laminar-to-turbulent transition effect of Figs. 7.13 and 7.14 and are therefore quite sensitive to whether the boundary layer is laminar or turbulent.

EXAMPLE 7.6

A square 6-in piling is acted on by a water flow of 5 ft/s that is 20 ft deep, as shown in Fig. E7.6. Estimate the maximum bending exerted by the flow on the bottom of the piling.

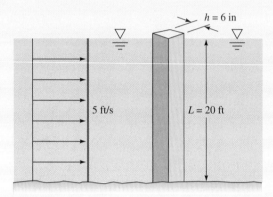

E7.6

Solution

Assume seawater with $\rho = 1.99$ slugs/ft^3 and kinematic viscosity $\nu = 0.000011$ ft^2/s. With a piling width of 0.5 ft, we have

$$\text{Re}_h = \frac{(5 \text{ ft/s})(0.5 \text{ ft})}{0.000011 \text{ ft}^2/\text{s}} = 2.3 \times 10^5$$

This is the range where Table 7.2 applies. The worst case occurs when the flow strikes the flat side of the piling, $C_D \approx 2.1$. The frontal area is $A = Lh = (20 \text{ ft})(0.5 \text{ ft}) = 10$ ft^2. The drag is estimated by

$$F = C_D(\tfrac{1}{2}\rho V^2 A) \approx 2.1(\tfrac{1}{2})(1.99 \text{ slugs/ft}^3)(5 \text{ ft/s})^2(10 \text{ ft}^2) = 522 \text{ lbf}$$

If the flow is uniform, the center of this force should be at approximately middepth. Therefore, the bottom bending moment is

$$M_0 \approx \frac{FL}{2} = 522(10) = 5220 \text{ ft} \cdot \text{lbf} \qquad\qquad Ans.$$

According to the flexure formula from strength of materials, the bending stress at the bottom would be

$$S = \frac{M_0 y}{I} = \frac{(5220 \text{ ft} \cdot \text{lb})(0.25 \text{ ft})}{\frac{1}{12}(0.5 \text{ ft})^4} = 251{,}000 \text{ lbf/ft}^2 = 1740 \text{ lbf/in}^2$$

to be multiplied, of course, by the stress concentration factor due to the built-in end conditions.

Three-Dimensional Bodies

Some drag coefficients of three-dimensional bodies are listed in Table 7.3 and Fig. 7.16b. Again we can conclude that sharp edges always cause flow separation and high drag

Table 7.3 Drag of Three-Dimensional Bodies at Re $\geq 10^4$

| Body | C_D based on frontal area | Body | C_D based on frontal area | | | | | | | |

Cube:

1.07

0.81

Cup:

1.4

0.4

Disk:

1.17

Parachute (Low porosity):

1.2

Streamlined train (approximately 5 cars):

$C_D A = 8.5 \text{ m}^2$

Bicycle:

Upright: $C_D A = 0.51 \text{ m}^2$; Racing: $C_D A = 0.30 \text{ m}^2$

Cone: [60]

θ:	10°	20°	30°	40°	60°	75°	90°
C_D:	0.30	0.40	0.55	0.65	0.80	1.05	1.15

Short cylinder, laminar flow:

L/D:	1	2	3	5	10	20	40	∞
C_D:	0.64	0.68	0.72	0.74	0.82	0.91	0.98	1.20

Porous parabolic dish [23]:

Porosity:	0	0.1	0.2	0.3	0.4	0.5
$\leftarrow C_D$:	1.42	1.33	1.20	1.05	0.95	0.82
$\rightarrow C_D$:	0.95	0.92	0.90	0.86	0.83	0.80

Average person:

$\rightarrow C_D A = 9 \text{ ft}^2$ $\uparrow C_D A = 1.2 \text{ ft}^2$

Pine and spruce trees [24]:

U, m/s:	10	20	30	40
C_D:	1.2 ± 0.2	1.0 ± 0.2	0.7 ± 0.2	0.5 ± 0.2

Tractor-trailer truck:

Without deflector: 0.96; with deflector: 0.76

Body	Ratio	C_D based on frontal area		Body	Ratio	C_D based on frontal area
Rectangular plate:	b/h 1	1.18		**Flat-faced cylinder:**		
	5	1.2			L/d 0.5	1.15
	10	1.3			1	0.90
	20	1.5			2	0.85
	∞	2.0			4	0.87
					8	0.99

Body	Ratio	Laminar	Turbulent	Body	Ratio	C_D based on frontal area
Ellipsoid:	L/d 0.75	0.5	0.2	**Buoyant rising sphere** [50],	$C_D \approx 0.95$	
	1	0.47	0.2	$135 < \text{Re}_d < 1\text{E}5$		
	2	0.27	0.13			
	4	0.25	0.1			
	8	0.2	0.08			

that is insensitive to the Reynolds number. Rounded bodies like the ellipsoid have drag that depends on the point of separation, so both the Reynolds number and the character of the boundary layer are important. Body length will generally decrease pressure drag by making the body relatively more slender, but sooner or later the friction drag will catch up. For the flat-faced cylinder in Table 7.3, pressure drag decreases with L/d but friction increases, so minimum drag occurs at about $L/d = 2$.

Buoyant Rising Light Spheres

The sphere data in Fig. 7.16b are for fixed models in wind tunnels and from falling sphere tests and indicate a drag coefficient of about 0.5 in the range 1 E3 < Re_d < 1 E5. It was pointed out [50] that this is *not* the case for a freely rising buoyant sphere or bubble. If the sphere is light, $\rho_{sphere} < 0.8\, \rho_{fluid}$, a wake instability arises in the range 135 < Re_d < 1 E5. The sphere then spirals upward at an angle of about 60° from the horizontal. The drag coefficient is approximately doubled, to an average value $C_D \approx$ 0.95, as listed in Table 7.3 [50]. For a heavier body, $\rho_{sphere} \approx \rho_{fluid}$, the buoyant sphere rises vertically and the drag coefficient follows the standard curve in Fig. 7.16b.

EXAMPLE 7.7

According to Ref. 12, the drag coefficient of a blimp, based on surface area, is approximately 0.006 if $Re_L > 10^6$. A certain blimp is 75 m long and has a surface area of 3400 m². Estimate the power required to propel this blimp at 18 m/s at a standard altitude of 1000 m.

Solution

- *Assumptions:* We hope the Reynolds number will be high enough that the given data are valid.
- *Approach:* Determine if $Re_L > 10^6$ and, if so, compute the drag and the power required.
- *Property values:* Table A.6 at $z = 1000$ m: $\rho = 1.112$ kg/m³, $T = 282$ K, thus $\mu \approx$ 1.75 E-5 kg/m · s.
- *Solution steps:* Determine the Reynolds number of the blimp:

$$Re_L = \frac{\rho U L}{\mu} = \frac{(1.112 \text{ kg/m}^3)(18 \text{ m/s})(75 \text{ m})}{1.75 \text{ E-5 kg/m} \cdot \text{s}} = 8.6 \text{ E7} > 10^6 \quad \text{OK}$$

The given drag coefficient is valid. Compute the blimp drag and the power = (drag) × (velocity):

$$F = C_D \frac{\rho}{2} U^2 A_{wet} = (0.006)\frac{1.112 \text{ kg/m}^3}{2}(18 \text{ m/s})^2 (3400 \text{ m}^2) = 3675 \text{ N}$$

$$\text{Power} = FV = (3675 \text{ N})(18 \text{ m/s}) = 66{,}000 \text{ W} \quad (89 \text{ hp}) \qquad Ans.$$

- *Comments:* These are nominal estimates. Drag is highly dependent on both shape and Reynolds number, and the coefficient $C_D = 0.006$ has considerable uncertainty.

Aerodynamic Forces on Road Vehicles

Automobiles and trucks are now the subject of much research on aerodynamic forces, both lift and drag [21]. At least one textbook is devoted to the subject [22]. A very readable description of race car drag is given by Katz [51]. Consumer, manufacturer, and government interest has cycled between high speed/high horsepower and lower speed/lower drag. Better streamlining of car shapes has resulted over the years in a large decrease in the automobile drag coefficient, as shown in Fig. 7.17a. Modern cars have an average drag coefficient of about 0.25, based on the frontal area. Since the frontal area has also decreased sharply, the actual raw drag *force* on cars has dropped even more than indicated in Fig. 7.17a. The theoretical minimum shown in the figure, $C_D \approx 0.15$, is about right for a commercial automobile, but lower values are possible for experimental vehicles; see Prob. P7.109. Note that basing C_D on the frontal area is awkward, since one would need an accurate drawing of the automobile to estimate its frontal area. For this reason, some technical articles simply report the raw drag in newtons or pound-force, or the product $C_D A$.

Many companies and laboratories have automotive wind tunnels, some full-scale and/or with moving floors to approximate actual kinematic similarity. The blunt shapes of most automobiles, together with their proximity to the ground, cause a wide variety of flow and geometric effects. Simple changes in part of the shape can have

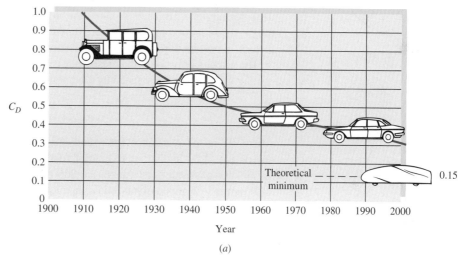

(a)

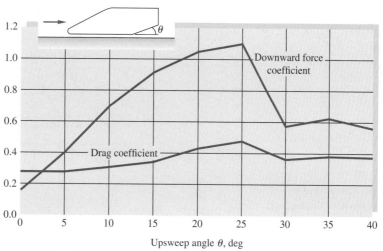

Fig. 7.17 Aerodynamics of automobiles: (*a*) the historical trend for drag coefficients (from Ref. 21); (*b*) effect of bottom rear upsweep angle on drag and downward lift force (from Ref. 25).

(b)

a large influence on aerodynamic forces. Figure 7.17b shows force data by Bearman et al. [25] for an idealized smooth automobile shape with upsweep in the rear of the bottom section. We see that by simply adding an upsweep angle of 25°, we can quadruple the downward force, gaining tire traction at the expense of doubling the drag. For this study, the effect of a moving floor was small—about a 10 percent increase in both drag and lift compared to a fixed floor.

It is difficult to quantify the exact effect of geometric changes on automotive forces, since, for example, changes in a windshield shape might interact with downstream flow over the roof and trunk. Nevertheless, based on correlation of many model and full-scale tests, Ref. 26 proposes a formula for automobile drag that adds separate effects such as front ends, cowls, fenders, windshield, roofs, and rear ends.

Figure 7.18a illustrates the power required to drive a typical tractor-trailer truck. An approximation is that the rolling resistance increases linearly and the drag quadratically with speed. The two are about equal at 55 mi/h. Figure 7.18b shows that air drag can be reduced by attaching a deflector to the top of the cab. When the deflector angle is adjusted to carry the flow smoothly over the top and sides of the trailer, the reduction in C_D is about 20 percent. This type of applied fluids engineering is very important for modern transportation problems [58].

The velocity effect on rolling resistance is mostly due to the engine-transmission-wheel-bearing system. The tires generally have a nearly constant *rolling resistance coefficient,*

$$C_{rr} = \frac{F_{rr}}{N}$$

where F_{rr} is the resistance force and N is the normal force on the tires [61]. This coefficient C_{rr} is analogous to a solid friction factor but is much smaller: about 0.01 to 0.04 for passenger car tires and 0.006 to 0.01 for truck tires.

Progress in computational fluid dynamics means that complicated vehicle flow fields can be predicted fairly well. Reference 42 compares one-equation and two-equation turbulence models [9] with NASA data for a simplified tractor-trailer model. Even with two million mesh points, the predicted vehicle drag is from 20 to 50 percent higher than the measurements. The turbulence models do not reproduce the pressures and wake

Fig. 7.18 Drag reduction of a tractor-trailer truck: (*a*) horsepower required to overcome resistance; (*b*) deflector added to cab reduces air drag by 20 percent.

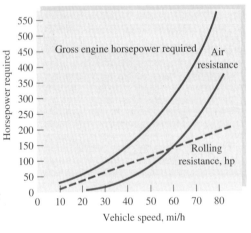

(*a*)

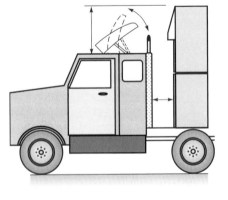

(*b*)

structure in the rear of the vehicle. Newer models, such as large eddy simulation (LES) and direct numerical simulation (DNS) will no doubt improve the calculations.

EXAMPLE 7.8

A high-speed car with $m = 2000$ kg, $C_D = 0.3$, and $A = 1$ m^2 deploys a 2-m parachute to slow down from an initial velocity of 100 m/s (Fig. E7.8). Assuming constant C_D, brakes free, and no rolling resistance, calculate the distance and velocity of the car after 1, 10, 100, and 1000 s. For air assume $\rho = 1.2$ kg/m^3, and neglect interference between the wake of the car and the parachute.

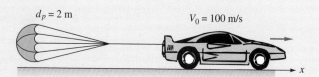

E7.8

Solution

Newton's law applied in the direction of motion gives

$$F_x = m\frac{dV}{dt} = -F_c - F_p = -\frac{1}{2}\rho V^2(C_{Dc}A_c + C_{Dp}A_p)$$

where subscript c denotes the car and subscript p the parachute. This is of the form

$$\frac{dV}{dt} = -\frac{K}{m}V^2 \qquad K = \sum C_D A\frac{\rho}{2}$$

Separate the variables and integrate:

$$\int_{v_0}^{v}\frac{dV}{V^2} = -\frac{K}{m}\int_0^t dt$$

or

$$V_0^{-1} - V^{-1} = -\frac{K}{m}t$$

Rearrange and solve for the velocity V:

$$V = \frac{V_0}{1 + (K/m)V_0 t} \qquad K = \frac{(C_{Dc}A_c + C_{Dp}A_p)\rho}{2} \qquad (1)$$

We can integrate this to find the distance traveled:

$$S = \frac{V_0}{\alpha}\ln(1 + \alpha t) \qquad \alpha = \frac{K}{m}V_0 \qquad (2)$$

Now work out some numbers. From Table 7.3, $C_{Dp} \approx 1.2$; hence

$$C_{Dc}A_c + C_{Dp}A_p = 0.3(1\text{ m}^2) + 1.2\frac{\pi}{4}(2\text{ m})^2 = 4.07\text{ m}^2$$

Then

$$\frac{K}{m}V_0 = \frac{\frac{1}{2}(4.07\text{ m}^2)(1.2\text{ kg/m}^3)(100\text{ m/s})}{2000\text{ kg}} = 0.122\text{ s}^{-1} = \alpha$$

Now make a table of the results for V and S from Eqs. (1) and (2):

t, s	1	10	100	1000
V, m/s	89	45	7.6	0.8
S, m	94	654	2110	3940

Air resistance alone will not stop a body completely. If you don't apply the brakes, you'll be halfway to the Yukon Territory and still going.

Other Methods of Drag Reduction

Sometimes drag is good, for example, when using a parachute. Do not jump out of an airplane holding a flat plate parallel to your motion (see Prob. P7.81). Mostly, though, drag is bad and should be reduced. The classical method of drag reduction is *streamlining* (Figs. 7.15 and 7.18). For example, nose fairings and body panels have produced motorcycles that can travel over 200 mi/h. More recent research has uncovered other methods that hold great promise, especially for turbulent flows.

1. Oil pipelines introduce an *annular strip* of water to reduce the pumping power [36]. The low-viscosity water rides the wall and reduces friction up to 60 percent.
2. Turbulent friction in liquid flows is reduced up to 60 percent by dissolving small amounts of a *high-molecular-weight polymer additive* [37]. Without changing pumps, the Trans-Alaska Pipeline System (TAPS) increased oil flow 50 percent by injecting small amounts of polymer dissolved in kerosene.
3. Stream-oriented surface *vee-groove microriblets* can reduce turbulent friction up to 8 percent [38]. Riblet heights are of order 1 mm and were used on the Stars and Stripes yacht hull in the Americas Cup races. Riblets are also effective on aircraft skins.
4. Small, near-wall *large-eddy breakup devices* (LEBUs) reduce local turbulent friction up to 10 percent [39]. However, one must add these small structures to the surface, and LEBU drag may be significant.
5. Air *microbubbles* injected at the wall of a water flow create a low-shear bubble blanket [40]. At high void fractions, drag reduction can be 80 percent.
6. Spanwise (transverse) *wall oscillation* may reduce turbulent friction up to 30 percent [41].
7. *Active flow control*, especially of turbulent flows, is the wave of the future, as reviewed in Ref. 47. These methods generally require expenditure of energy but can be worth it. For example, tangential blowing at the rear of an auto [48] evokes the *Coanda effect*, in which the separated near-wake flow attaches itself to the body surface and reduces auto drag up to 10 percent.

Drag reduction is presently an area of intense and fruitful research and applies to many types of airflows [39, 53] and water flows for both vehicles and conduits.

Drag of Surface Ships

The drag data given so far, such as Tables 7.2 and 7.3, are for bodies "fully immersed" in a free stream—that is, with no free surface. If, however, the body moves at or near a free liquid surface, *wave-making drag* becomes important and is dependent on both the Reynolds number and the Froude number. To move through a water surface, a ship must create waves on both sides. This implies putting energy into the water surface and requires a finite drag force to keep the ship moving, even in a frictionless fluid. The total drag of a ship can then be approximated as the sum of friction drag and wave-making drag:

$$F \approx F_{\text{fric}} + F_{\text{wave}} \qquad \text{or} \qquad C_D \approx C_{D,\text{fric}} + C_{D,\text{wave}}$$

The friction drag can be estimated by the (turbulent) flat-plate formula, Eq. (7.45), based on the below-water or *wetted area* of the ship.

Reference 27 is an interesting review of both theory and experiment for wake-making surface ship drag. Generally speaking, the bow of the ship creates a wave system whose wavelength is related to the ship speed but not necessarily to the ship length. If the stern of the ship is a wave *trough,* the ship is essentially climbing uphill and has high wave drag. If the stern is a wave crest, the ship is nearly level and has lower drag. The criterion for these two conditions results in certain approximate Froude numbers [27]:

$$\text{Fr} = \frac{V}{\sqrt{gL}} \approx \frac{0.53}{\sqrt{N}} \qquad \begin{array}{l} \text{high drag if } N = 1, 3, 5, 7, \ldots ; \\ \text{low drag if } N = 2, 4, 6, 8, \ldots \end{array} \qquad (7.65)$$

where V is the ship's speed, L is the ship's length along the centerline, and N is the number of half-lengths, from bow to stern, of the drag-making wave system. The wave drag will increase with the Froude number and oscillate between lower drag (Fr $\approx$ 0.38, 0.27, 0.22, . . .) and higher drag (Fr $\approx$ 0.53, 0.31, 0.24, . . .) with negligible variation for Fr $<$ 0.2. Thus it is best to design a ship to cruise at $N = 2, 4, 6, 8$. Shaping the bow and stern can further reduce wave-making drag.

Figure 7.19 shows the data of Inui [27] for a model ship. The main hull, curve *A,* shows peaks and valleys in wave drag at the appropriate Froude numbers $>$ 0.2. Introduction of a *bulb* protrusion on the bow, curve *B,* greatly reduces the drag. Adding a second bulb to the stern, curve *C,* is still better, and Inui recommends that the design speed of this two-bulb ship be at $N = 4$, Fr $\approx$ 0.27, which is a nearly "waveless" condition. In this figure $C_{D,\text{wave}}$ is defined as $2F_{\text{wave}}/(\rho V^2 L^2)$ instead of using the wetted area.

The solid curves in Fig. 7.19 are based on potential flow theory for the below-water hull shape. Chapter 8 is an introduction to potential flow theory. Modern computers can be programmed for numerical CFD solutions of potential flow over the hulls of ships, submarines, yachts, and sailboats, including boundary layer effects driven by the potential flow [28]. Thus theoretical prediction of flow past surface ships is now at a fairly high level. See also Ref. 15.

Body Drag at High Mach Numbers

All the data presented to this point are for nearly incompressible flows, with Mach numbers assumed less than about 0.3. Beyond this value compressibility can be very important, with $C_D = \text{fcn}(\text{Re}, \text{Ma})$. As the stream Mach number increases, at some subsonic value $M_{\text{crit}} < 1$ that depends on the body's bluntness and thickness, the local velocity at some point near the body surface will become sonic. If Ma increases beyond Ma_{crit}, shock waves form, intensify, and spread, raising surface

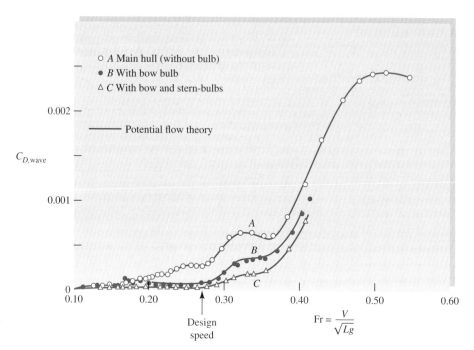

Fig. 7.19 Wave-making drag on a ship model. (*After Inui [27].*) *Note:* The drag coefficient is defined as $C_{DW} = 2F/(\rho V^2 L^2)$.

pressures near the front of the body and therefore increasing the pressure drag. The effect can be dramatic with C_D increasing tenfold, and 70 years ago this sharp increase was called the *sonic barrier*, implying that it could not be surmounted. Of course, it can be—the rise in C_D is finite, as supersonic bullets have proved for centuries.

Figure 7.20 shows the effect of the Mach number on the drag coefficient of various body shapes tested in air.[6] We see that compressibility affects blunt bodies earlier, with Ma_{crit} equal to 0.4 for cylinders, 0.6 for spheres, and 0.7 for airfoils and pointed projectiles. Also the Reynolds number (laminar versus turbulent boundary layer flow) has a large effect below Ma_{crit} for spheres and cylinders but becomes unimportant above $Ma \approx 1$. In contrast, the effect of the Reynolds number is small for airfoils and projectiles and is not shown in Fig. 7.20. A general statement might divide Reynolds and Mach number effects as follows:

$$Ma \leq 0.3: \text{Reynolds number important, Mach number unimportant}$$

$$0.3 < Ma < 1: \text{both Reynolds and Mach numbers important}$$

$$Ma > 1.0: \text{Reynolds number unimportant, Mach number important}$$

At supersonic speeds, a broad *bow shock wave* forms in front of the body (see Figs. 9.10*b* and 9.19), and the drag is mainly due to high shock-induced pressures on the front. Making the bow a sharp point can sharply reduce the drag (Fig. 9.28) but

---

[6]There is a slight effect of the specific-heat ratio k, which would appear if other gases were tested.

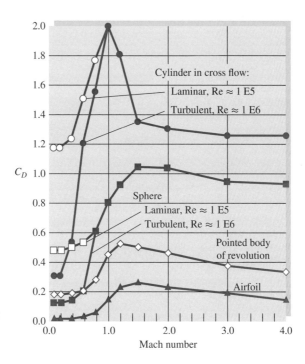

Fig. 7.20 Effect of the Mach number on the drag of various body shapes. (*Data from Refs. 23 and 29.*)

does not eliminate the bow shock. Chapter 9 gives a brief treatment of compressible flow. References 30 and 31 are more advanced textbooks devoted entirely to compressible flow.

Biological Drag Reduction

A great deal of engineering effort goes into designing immersed bodies to reduce their drag. Most such effort concentrates on rigid-body shapes. A different process occurs in nature, as organisms adapt to survive high winds or currents, as reported in a series of papers by S. Vogel [33, 34]. A good example is a tree, whose flexible structure allows it to reconfigure in high winds and thus reduce drag and damage. Tree root systems have evolved in several ways to resist wind-induced bending moments, and trunk cross sections have become resistant to bending but relatively easy to twist and reconfigure. We saw this in Table 7.3, where tree drag coefficients [24] reduced by 60 percent as wind velocity increased. The shape of the tree changes to offer less resistance.

The individual branches and leaves of a tree also curl and cluster to reduce drag. Figure 7.21 shows the results of wind tunnel experiments by Vogel [33]. A tulip tree leaf, Fig. 7.21*a*, broad and open in low wind, curls into a conical low-drag shape as wind increases. A compound black walnut leaf group, Fig. 7.21*b*, clusters into a low-drag shape at high wind speed. Although drag coefficients were reduced up to 50 percent by flexibility, Vogel points out that rigid structures are sometimes just as effective. An interesting recent symposium [35] was devoted entirely to the solid mechanics and fluid mechanics of biological organisms.

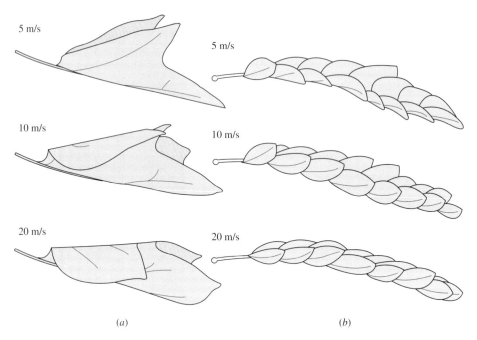

Fig. 7.21 Biological adaptation to wind forces: (*a*) a tulip tree leaf curls into a conical shape at high velocity; (*b*) black walnut leaves cluster into a low-drag shape as wind increases. (*From Vogel, Ref. 33.*)

(*a*)

(*b*)

Forces on Lifting Bodies

Lifting bodies (airfoils, hydrofoils, or vanes) are intended to provide a large force normal to the free stream and as little drag as possible. Conventional design practice has evolved a shape not unlike a bird's wing—that is, relatively thin ($t/c \leq 0.24$) with a rounded leading edge and a sharp trailing edge. A typical shape is sketched in Fig. 7.22.

For our purposes we consider the body to be symmetric, as in Fig. 7.11, with the free-stream velocity in the vertical plane. If the chord line between the leading and trailing edge is not a line of symmetry, the airfoil is said to be *cambered*. The camber line is the line midway between the upper and lower surfaces of the vane.

The angle between the free stream and the chord line is called the *angle of attack* α. The lift L and the drag D vary with this angle. The dimensionless forces are defined

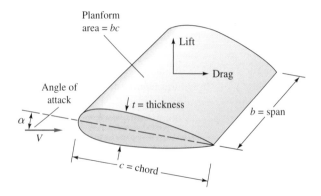

Fig. 7.22 Definition sketch for a lifting vane.

with respect to the planform area $A_p = bc$:

Lift coefficient:

$$C_L = \frac{L}{\frac{1}{2}\rho V^2 A_p}$$

(7.66a)

Drag coefficient:

$$C_D = \frac{D}{\frac{1}{2}\rho V^2 A_p}$$

(7.66b)

If the chord length is not constant, as in the tapered wings of modern aircraft, $A_p = \int c\, db$.

For low-speed flow with a given roughness ratio, C_L and C_D should vary with α and the chord Reynolds number:

$$C_L = f(\alpha, \text{Re}_c) \qquad \text{or} \qquad C_D = f(\alpha, \text{Re}_c)$$

where $\text{Re}_c = Vc/\nu$. The Reynolds numbers are commonly in the turbulent boundary layer range and have a modest effect.

The rounded leading edge prevents flow separation there, but the sharp trailing edge causes a tangential wake motion that generates the lift. Figure 7.23 shows what happens when a flow starts up past a lifting vane or an airfoil.

Just after start-up in Fig. 7.23a the streamline motion is irrotational and inviscid. The rear stagnation point, assuming a positive angle of attack, is on the upper surface, and there is no lift; but the flow cannot long negotiate the sharp turn at the trailing edge: it separates, and a *starting vortex* forms in Fig. 7.23b. This starting vortex is shed downstream in Figs. 7.23c and d, and a smooth streamline flow develops over the wing, leaving the foil in a direction approximately parallel to the chord line. Lift at this time is fully developed, and the starting vortex is gone. Should the flow now cease, a *stopping vortex* of opposite (clockwise) sense will form and be shed. During flight, increases or decreases in lift will cause incremental starting or stopping vortices,

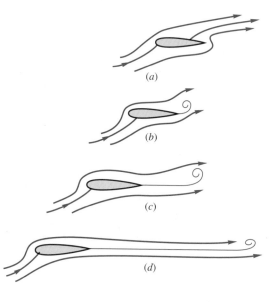

Fig. 7.23 Transient stages in the development of lift: (a) start-up: rear stagnation point on the upper surface: no lift; (b) sharp trailing edge induces separation, and a starting vortex forms: slight lift; (c) starting vortex is shed; and streamlines flow smoothly from trailing edge: lift is now 80 percent developed; (d) starting vortex now shed far behind, trailing edge now very smooth: lift fully developed.

always with the effect of maintaining a smooth parallel flow at the trailing edge. We pursue this idea mathematically in Chap. 8.

At a low angle of attack, the rear surfaces have an adverse pressure gradient but not enough to cause significant boundary layer separation. The flow pattern is smooth, as in Fig. 7.23d, and drag is small and lift excellent. As the angle of attack is increased, the upper-surface adverse gradient becomes stronger, and generally a *separation bubble* begins to creep forward on the upper surface.[7] At a certain angle $\alpha = 15$ to $20°$, the flow is separated completely from the upper surface, as in Fig. 7.24. The airfoil is said to be *stalled*: Lift drops off markedly, drag increases markedly, and the foil is no longer flyable.

Early airfoils were thin, modeled after birds' wings. The German engineer Otto Lilienthal (1848–1896) experimented with flat and cambered plates on a rotating arm. He and his brother Gustav flew the world's first glider in 1891. Horatio Frederick Phillips (1845–1912) built the first wind tunnel in 1884 and measured the lift and drag of cambered vanes. The first theory of lift was proposed by Frederick W. Lanchester shortly afterward. Modern airfoil theory dates from 1905, when the Russian hydrodynamicist N. E. Joukowsky (1847–1921) developed a circulation theorem (Chap. 8) for computing airfoil lift for arbitrary camber and thickness. With this basic theory, as extended and developed by Prandtl and Kármán and their students, it is now possible to design a low-speed airfoil to satisfy particular surface pressure distributions and

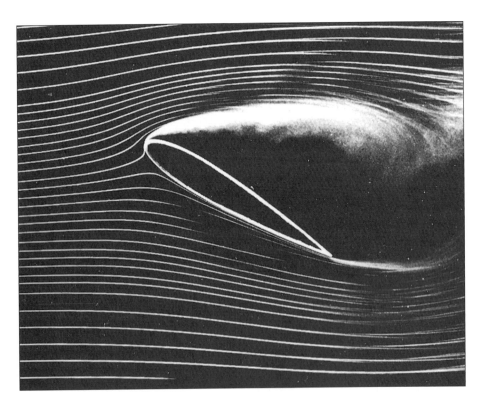

Fig. 7.24 At high angle of attack, smoke flow visualization shows stalled flow on the upper surface of a lifting vane. (*National Committee for Fluid Mechanics Films, Education Development Center, Inc.,* © *1972.*)

[7]For some airfoils the bubble leaps, not creeps, forward and stall occurs rapidly and dangerously.

boundary layer characteristics. There are whole families of airfoil designs, notably those developed in the United States under the sponsorship of the NACA (now NASA). Extensive theory and data on these airfoils are contained in Ref. 16. We shall discuss this further in Chap. 8. The history of aeronautics is a rich and engaging topic and highly recommended to the reader [43, 44].

Figure 7.25 shows the lift and drag on a symmetric airfoil denoted as the NACA 0009 foil, the last digit indicating the thickness of 9 percent. With no flap extended, this airfoil, as expected, has zero lift at zero angle of attack. Up to about 12° the lift coefficient increases linearly with a slope of 0.1 per degree, or 6.0 per radian. This is in agreement with the theory outlined in Chap. 8:

$$C_{L,\text{theory}} \approx 2\pi \sin\left(\alpha + \frac{2h}{c}\right) \tag{7.67}$$

where h/c is the maximum camber expressed as a fraction of the chord. The NACA 0009 has zero camber; hence $C_L = 2\pi \sin\alpha \approx 0.11\alpha$, where α is in degrees. This is excellent agreement.

The drag coefficient of the smooth-model airfoils in Fig. 7.25 is as low as 0.005, which is actually lower than both sides of a flat plate in turbulent flow. This is misleading inasmuch as a commercial foil will have roughness effects; for example, a paint job will double the drag coefficient.

The effect of increasing Reynolds number in Fig. 7.25 is to increase the maximum lift and stall angle (without changing the slope appreciably) and to reduce the drag coefficient. This is a salutary effect since the prototype will probably be at a higher Reynolds number than the model (10^7 or more).

For takeoff and landing, the lift is greatly increased by deflecting a split flap, as shown in Fig. 7.25. This makes the airfoil unsymmetric (or effectively cambered)

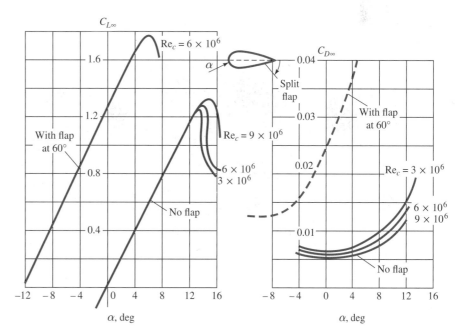

Fig. 7.25 Lift and drag of a symmetric NACA 0009 airfoil of infinite span, including effect of a split-flap deflection. Note that roughness can increase C_D from 100 to 300 percent.

and changes the zero-lift point to $\alpha = -12°$. The drag is also greatly increased by the flap, but the reduction in takeoff and landing distance is worth the extra power needed.

A lifting craft cruises at low angle of attack, where the lift is much larger than the drag. Maximum lift-to-drag ratios for the common airfoils lie between 20 and 50.

Some airfoils, such as the NACA 6 series, are shaped to provide favorable gradients over much of the upper surface at low angles. Thus separation is small, and transition to turbulence is delayed; the airfoil retains a good length of laminar flow even at high Reynolds numbers. The lift-drag *polar plot* in Fig. 7.26 shows the NACA 0009 data from Fig. 7.25 and a laminar flow airfoil, NACA 63-009, of the same thickness. The laminar flow airfoil has a low-drag bucket at small angles but also suffers lower stall angle and lower maximum lift coefficient. The drag is 30 percent less in the bucket, but the bucket disappears if there is significant surface roughness.

All the data in Figs. 7.25 and 7.26 are for infinite span—that is, a two-dimensional flow pattern about wings without tips. The effect of finite span can be correlated with the dimensionless slenderness, or *aspect ratio*, denoted (AR):

$$\text{AR} = \frac{b^2}{A_p} = \frac{b}{\bar{c}} \tag{7.68}$$

where $\bar{c}$ is the average chord length. Finite-span effects are shown in Fig. 7.27. The lift slope decreases, but the zero-lift angle is the same; and the drag increases, but the zero-lift drag is the same. The theory of finite-span airfoils [16] predicts that the effective angle of attack increases, as in Fig. 7.27, by the amount

$$\Delta\alpha \approx \frac{C_L}{\pi\text{AR}} \tag{7.69}$$

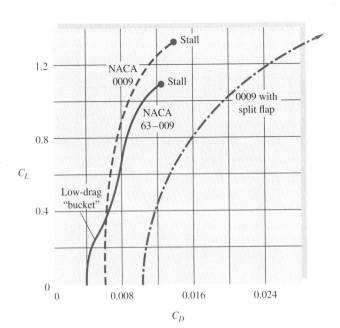

Fig. 7.26 Lift-drag polar plot for standard (0009) and a laminar flow (63-009) NACA airfoil.

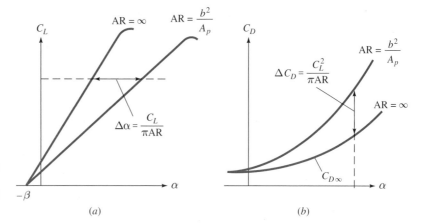

Fig. 7.27 Effect of finite aspect ratio on lift and drag of an airfoil: (*a*) effective angle increase; (*b*) induced drag increase.

When applied to Eq. (7.67), the finite-span lift becomes

$$C_L \approx \frac{2\pi \sin(\alpha + 2h/c)}{1 + 2/\text{AR}} \qquad (7.70)$$

The associated drag increase is $\Delta C_D \approx C_L \sin \Delta\alpha \approx C_L \Delta\alpha$, or

$$C_D \approx C_{D\infty} + \frac{C_L^2}{\pi\text{AR}} \qquad (7.71)$$

where $C_{D\infty}$ is the drag of the infinite-span airfoil, as sketched in Fig. 7.25. These correlations are in good agreement with experiments on finite-span wings [16].

The existence of a maximum lift coefficient implies the existence of a minimum speed, or *stall speed*, for a craft whose lift supports its weight:

$$L = W = C_{L,\text{max}}(\tfrac{1}{2}\rho V_s^2 A_p)$$

or
$$V_s = \left(\frac{2W}{C_{L,\text{max}}\rho A_p}\right)^{1/2} \qquad (7.72)$$

The stall speed of typical aircraft varies between 60 and 200 ft/s, depending on the weight and value of $C_{L,\text{max}}$. The pilot must hold the speed greater than about $1.2V_s$ to avoid the instability associated with complete stall.

The split flap in Fig. 7.25 is only one of many devices used to secure high lift at low speeds. Figure 7.28*a* shows six such devices whose lift performance is given in Fig. 7.28*b* along with a standard (*A*) and laminar flow (*B*) airfoil. The double-slotted flap achieves $C_{L,\text{max}} \approx 3.4$, and a combination of this plus a leading-edge slat can achieve $C_{L,\text{max}} \approx 4.0$. These are not scientific curiosities; for instance, the Boeing 727 commercial jet aircraft uses a triple-slotted flap plus a leading-edge slat during landing.

A violation of conventional aerodynamic wisdom is that military aircraft are beginning to fly, briefly, *above the stall point.* Fighter pilots are learning to make quick

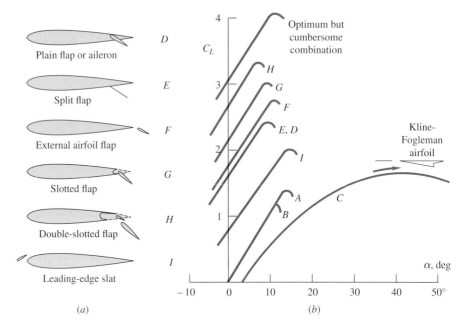

Fig. 7.28 Performance of airfoils with and without high-lift devices: A = NACA 0009; B = NACA 63-009; C = Kline-Fogleman airfoil (*from Ref. 17*); D to I shown in (*a*): (*a*) types of high-lift devices; (*b*) lift coefficients for various devices (Ref. 62).

maneuvers in the stalled region as detailed in Ref. 32. Some planes can even *fly continuously* while stalled—the Grumman X-29 experimental aircraft recently set a record by flying at $\alpha = 67°$.

The Kline-Fogelman Airfoil

Traditionally, an airfoil is a thin teardrop shape, with a rounded leading edge and a sharp trailing edge, Fig. 7.28*a*. It provides low drag but stalls at low $\alpha \approx 10$ to $15°$. In 1972 R. F. Kline and F. F. Fogelman designed an airfoil with a sharp leading edge and a rear cut-out [17]. When tested in a wind tunnel, Fig. 7.28*b*, it did not stall until $\alpha \approx 45°$, but the drag was very high. Fertis [55] rounded the leading edge and reduced the drag. Finaish and Witherspoon [56] made further improvements, but the drag is still too high for full-scale commercial applications. The KF airfoil, though, is extremely popular for radio-controlled model aircraft.

A Wing Inspired by the Humpback Whale

Biologists have long noticed the high maneuverability of the humpback whale when it seeks prey. Unlike most whales, the humpback has tubercles, or bumps, on the leading edge of its flippers. Miklosovic et al. [57] tested this idea, using a standard wing with periodic bumps glued to its leading edge, as in Fig. 7.29. They report a 40 percent increase in stall angle, compared to the same wing without bumps, plus higher lift and higher lift-to-drag ratios. The concept has promise for commercial applications such as wind turbine blades. Flow visualization shows that the bumps create energetic streamwise vortices along the wing surface, helping to delay separation.

Fig. 7.29 New experimental airfoils: plan view of a wing modeled on the humpback whale flipper [57]. *Source: D. S. Miklosovic et al., "Leading Edge Tubercles Delay Stall on Humpback Whale," Physics of Fluids, vol. 16, no. 5, May 2004, pp. L39–L42.*

A Combination Car and Airplane

Engineers have long dreamed of a viable car that can fly. Hop in at home, drive to the airport, fly somewhere, then drive to the motel. Designer efforts date back to the Glenn Curtiss 1917 Autoplane, with other projects in the 1930s and 1940s. Perhaps the most famous was Moulton Taylor's Aerocar in 1947. Only five Aerocars were built. The year 2008 seems to have been the Year of the Car-Plane, with at least five different companies working on designs. Engineers can now use lightweight materials, better engines, and guidance systems. The writer's favorite is the *Transition*®, made by Terrafugia, Inc., shown in Fig. 7.30.

The Transition® has wings that fold out to a span of 27.5 ft. The twin tails do not fold. The front canard wing doubles as a bumper for the highway. The 100-hp engine drives both the rear propeller for flight and also the front wheels for the highway. Gross takeoff weight is 1430 lbf. Operators need only a Light Sport Airplane license. The Transition® made a successful maiden flight on Mar. 5, 2009. This craft's data will clearly be useful for setting end-of-chapter problems.

Fig. 7.30 The Transition® car-plane in flight on March 23, 2012. It has a gross weight of 1,430 lbf and a cruise velocity of 105 mi/h. (*Image from Terrafugia, Inc.,* http:// www.terrafugia.com)

Further information on the performance of lifting craft can be found in Refs. 12, 13, and 16. We discuss this matter again briefly in Chap. 8.

EXAMPLE 7.9

An aircraft weighs 75,000 lbf, has a planform area of 2500 ft^2, and can deliver a constant thrust of 12,000 lb. It has an aspect ratio of 7, and $C_{D\infty} \approx 0.02$. Neglecting rolling resistance, estimate the takeoff distance at sea level if takeoff speed equals 1.2 times stall speed. Take $C_{L,max} = 2.0$.

Solution

The stall speed from Eq. (7.72), with sea-level density $\rho = 0.00237$ slug/ft^3, is

$$V_s = \left(\frac{2W}{C_{L,max}\rho A_p} \right)^{1/2} = \left[\frac{2(75,000)}{2.0(0.00237)(2500)} \right]^{1/2} = 112.5 \text{ ft/s}$$

Hence takeoff speed $V_0 = 1.2V_s = 135$ ft/s. The drag is estimated from Eq. (7.71) for AR = 7 as

$$C_D \approx 0.02 + \frac{C_L^2}{7\pi} = 0.02 + 0.0455C_L^2$$

A force balance in the direction of takeoff gives

$$F_s = m\frac{dV}{dt} = \text{thrust} - \text{drag} = T - kV^2 \qquad k = \tfrac{1}{2}C_D\rho A_p \qquad (1)$$

Since we are looking for distance, not time, we introduce $dV/dt = V\,dV/ds$ into Eq. (1), separate variables, and integrate:

$$\int_0^{s_0} dS = \frac{m}{2}\int_0^{V_0} \frac{d(V^2)}{T - kV^2} \qquad k \approx \text{const}$$

or

$$S_0 = \frac{m}{2k}\ln\frac{T}{T - kV_0^2} = \frac{m}{2k}\ln\frac{T}{T - D_0} \qquad (2)$$

where $D_0 = kV_0^2$ is the takeoff drag. Equation (2) is the desired theoretical relation for takeoff distance. For the particular numerical values, take

$$m = \frac{75,000}{32.2} = 2329 \text{ slugs}$$

$$C_{L_0} = \frac{W}{\frac{1}{2}\rho V_0^2 A_p} = \frac{75,000}{\frac{1}{2}(0.00237)(135)^2(2500)} = 1.39$$

$$C_{D_0} = 0.02 + 0.0455(C_{L_0})^2 = 0.108$$

$$k \approx \tfrac{1}{2}C_{D_0}\rho A_p = (\tfrac{1}{2})(0.108)(0.00237)(2500) = 0.319 \text{ slug/ft}$$

$$D_0 = kV_0^2 = 5820 \text{ lbf}$$

Then Eq. (2) predicts that

$$S_0 = \frac{2329 \text{ slugs}}{2(0.319 \text{ slug/ft})}\ln\frac{12,000}{12,000 - 5820} = 3650 \ln 1.94 = 2420 \text{ ft} \qquad Ans.$$

A more exact analysis accounting for variable k [13] gives the same result to within 1 percent.

EXAMPLE 7.10

For the aircraft of Example 7.9, if maximum thrust is applied during flight at 6000 m standard altitude, estimate the resulting velocity of the plane, in mi/h.

Solution

- *Assumptions:* Given $W = 75{,}000$ lbf, $A_p = 2500$ ft^2, $T = 12{,}000$ lbf, $AR = 7$, $C_{D\infty} = 0.02$.
- *Approach:* Set lift equal to weight and drag equal to thrust and solve for the velocity.
- *Property values:* From Table A.6, at $z = 6000$ m, $\rho = 0.6596$ kg/m^3 = 0.00128 slug/ft^3.
- *Solution steps:* Write out the formulas for lift and drag. The unknowns will be C_L and V.

$$W = 75{,}000 \text{ lbf} = \text{lift} = C_L \frac{\rho}{2} V^2 A_p = C_L \frac{0.00128 \text{ slug/ft}^3}{2} V^2 (2500 \text{ ft}^2)$$

$$T = 12{,}000 \text{ lbf} = \text{drag} = \left(C_{D\infty} + \frac{C_L^2}{\pi AR} \right) \frac{\rho}{2} V^2 A_p$$

$$= \left[0.02 + \frac{C_L^2}{\pi(7)} \right] \frac{0.00128 \text{ slug/ft}^3}{2} V^2 (2500 \text{ ft}^2)$$

Some clever manipulation (dividing W by T) would reveal a quadratic equation for C_L. The final solution is

$$C_L = 0.13 \qquad V \approx 600 \text{ ft/s} = 410 \text{ mi/h} \qquad\qquad \textit{Ans.}$$

- *Comments:* These are *preliminary design* estimates that do not depend on airfoil shape.

Summary

This chapter has dealt with viscous effects in external flow past bodies immersed in a stream. When the Reynolds number is large, viscous forces are confined to a thin boundary layer and wake in the vicinity of the body. Flow outside these "shear layers" is essentially inviscid and can be predicted by potential theory and Bernoulli's equation.

The chapter began with a discussion of the flat-plate boundary layer and the use of momentum integral estimates to predict the wall shear, friction drag, and thickness of such layers. These approximations suggest how to eliminate certain small terms in the Navier-Stokes equations, resulting in Prandtl's boundary layer equations for laminar and turbulent flow. Section 7.4 then solved the boundary layer equations to give very accurate formulas for flat-plate flow at high Reynolds numbers. Rough-wall effects were included, and Sec. 7.5 gave a brief introduction to pressure gradient effects. An adverse (decelerating) gradient was seen to cause flow separation, where the boundary layer breaks away from the surface and forms a broad, low-pressure wake.

Boundary layer theory fails in separated flows, which are commonly studied by experiment or CFD. Section 7.6 gave data on drag coefficients of various two- and three-dimensional body shapes. The chapter ended with a brief discussion of lift forces generated by lifting bodies such as airfoils and hydrofoils. Airfoils also suffer flow separation or *stall* at high angles of incidence.

Problems

Most of the problems herein are fairly straightforward. More diffi-cult or open-ended assignments are labeled with an asterisk. Prob-lems labeled with a computer icon may require the use of a computer. The standard end-of-chapter problems P7.1 to P7.127 (categorized in the problem list here) are followed by word prob-lems W7.1 to W7.12, fundamentals of engineering exam problems FE7.1 to FE7.10, comprehensive problems C7.1 to C7.5, and design project D7.1.

Problem Distribution

Section	Topic	Problems
7.1	Reynolds number and geometry	P7.1–P7.5
7.2	Momentum integral estimates	P7.6–P7.12
7.3	The boundary layer equations	P7.13–P7.15
7.4	Laminar flat-plate flow	P7.16–P7.29
7.4	Turbulent flat-plate flow	P7.30–P7.47
7.5	Boundary layers with pressure gradient	P7.48–P7.50
7.6	Drag of bodies	P7.51–P7.114
7.6	Lifting bodies—airfoils	P7.115–P7.127

Reynolds number and geometry

P7.1 An ideal gas, at 20°C and 1 atm, flows at 12 m/s past a thin flat plate. At a position 60 cm downstream of the leading edge, the boundary layer thickness is 5 mm. Which of the 13 gases in Table A.4 is this likely to be?

P7.2 A gas at 20°C and 1 atm flows at 6 ft/s past a thin flat plate. At $x = 3$ ft, the boundary layer thickness is 0.052 ft. Assuming laminar flow, which of the gases in Table A.4 is this likely to be?

P7.3 Equation (7.1b) assumes that the boundary layer on the plate is turbulent from the leading edge onward. Devise a scheme for determining the boundary layer thickness more accurately when the flow is laminar up to a point $Re_{x,crit}$ and turbulent thereafter. Apply this scheme to computation of the boundary layer thickness at $x = 1.5$ m in 40 m/s flow of air at 20°C and 1 atm past a flat plate. Compare your result with Eq. (7.1b). Assume $Re_{x,crit} \approx$ 1.2 E6.

P7.4 A smooth ceramic sphere (SG = 2.6) is immersed in a flow of water at 20°C and 25 cm/s. What is the sphere diameter if it is encountering (a) creeping motion, $Re_d = 1$ or (b) transition to turbulence, $Re_d = 250,000$?

P7.5 SAE 30 oil at 20°C flows at 1.8 ft³/s from a reservoir into a 6-in-diameter pipe. Use flat-plate theory to estimate the position x where the pipe wall boundary layers meet in the center. Compare with Eq. (6.5), and give some explana-tions for the discrepancy.

Momentum integral estimates

P7.6 For the laminar parabolic boundary layer profile of Eq. (7.6), compute the shape factor H and compare with the exact Blasius result, Eq. (7.31).

P7.7 Air at 20°C and 1 atm enters a 40-cm-square duct as in Fig. P7.7. Using the "displacement thickness" concept of Fig. 7.4, estimate (a) the mean velocity and (b) the mean pressure in the core of the flow at the position $x = 3$ m. (c) What is the average gradient, in Pa/m, in this section?

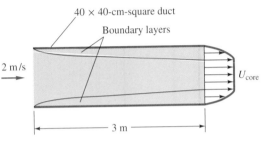

P7.7

P7.8 Air, $\rho = 1.2$ kg/m³ and $\mu = 1.8$ E-5 kg/(m · s), flows at 10 m/s past a flat plate. At the trailing edge of the plate, the following velocity profile data are measured:

y, mm	0	0.5	1.0	2.0	3.0	4.0	5.0	6.0
u, m/s	0	1.75	3.47	6.58	8.70	9.68	10.0	10.0

If the upper surface has an area of 0.6 m², estimate, using momentum concepts, the friction drag, in N, on the upper surface.

P7.9 Repeat the flat-plate momentum analysis of Sec. 7.2 by replacing Eq. (7.6) with the simple but unrealistic linear velocity profile suggested by Schlichting [1]:

$$\frac{u}{U} \approx \frac{y}{\delta} \quad \text{for} \quad 0 \leq y \leq \delta$$

Compute momentum–integral estimates of c_f, θ/x, δ^*/x, and H.

P7.10 Repeat Prob. P7.9, using a trigonometric profile approxi-mation:

$$\frac{u}{U} \approx \sin\left(\frac{\pi y}{2\delta}\right)$$

Does this profile satisfy the conditions of laminar flat-plate flow?

P7.11 Air at 20°C and 1 atm flows at 2 m/s past a sharp flat plate. Assuming that Kármán's parabolic-profile analysis, Eqs. (7.6–7.10), is accurate, estimate (a) the local velocity u and (b) the local shear stress τ at the position $(x, y) = (50$ cm, 5 mm).

P7.12 The velocity profile shape $u/U \approx 1 - \exp(-4.605y/\delta)$ is a smooth curve with $u = 0$ at $y = 0$ and $u = 0.99U$ at $y = \delta$ and thus would seem to be a reasonable substitute for the parabolic flat-plate profile of Eq. (7.3). Yet when this new profile is used in the integral analysis of Sec. 7.3, we get the lousy result $\delta/x \approx 9.2/\mathrm{Re}_x^{1/2}$, which is 80 percent high. What is the reason for the inaccuracy? [*Hint:* The answer lies in evaluating the laminar boundary layer momentum equation (7.19b) at the wall, $y = 0$.]

The boundary layer equations

P7.13 Derive modified forms of the laminar boundary layer equations (7.19) for the case of axisymmetric flow along the outside of a circular cylinder of constant radius R, as in Fig. P7.13. Consider the two special cases (a) $\delta \ll R$ and (b) $\delta \approx R$. What are the proper boundary conditions?

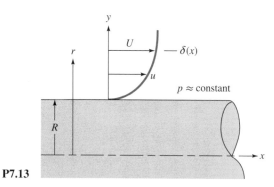

P7.13

P7.14 Show that the two-dimensional laminar flow pattern with $dp/dx = 0$

$$u = U_0(1 - e^{Cy}) \qquad v = v_0 < 0$$

is an exact solution to the boundary layer equations (7.19). Find the value of the constant C in terms of the flow parameters. Are the boundary conditions satisfied? What might this flow represent?

P7.15 Discuss whether fully developed laminar incompressible flow between parallel plates, Eq. (4.134) and Fig. 4.14b, represents an exact solution to the boundary layer equations (7.19) and the boundary conditions (7.20). In what sense, if any, are duct flows also boundary layer flows?

Laminar flat-plate flow

P7.16 A thin flat plate 55 by 110 cm is immersed in a 6-m/s stream of SAE 10 oil at 20°C. Compute the total friction drag if the stream is parallel to (a) the long side and (b) the short side.

P7.17 Consider laminar flow past a sharp flat plate of width b and length L. What percentage of the friction drag on the plate is carried by the rear half of the plate?

P7.18 Air at 20°C and 1 atm flows at 5 m/s past a flat plate. At $x = 60$ cm and $y = 2.95$ mm, use the Blasius solution, Table 7.1, to find (a) the velocity u; and (b) the wall shear stress. (c) For extra credit, find a Blasius formula for the shear stress away from the wall.

P7.19 Air at 20°C and 1 atm flows at 50 ft/s past a thin flat plate whose area (bL) is 24 ft². If the total friction drag is 0.3 lbf, what are the length and width of the plate?

P7.20 Air at 20°C and 1 atm flows at 20 m/s past the flat plate in Fig. P7.20. A pitot stagnation tube, placed 2 mm from the wall, develops a manometer head $h = 16$ mm of Meriam red oil, SG = 0.827. Use this information to estimate the downstream position x of the pitot tube. Assume laminar flow.

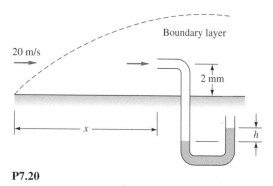

P7.20

P7.21 For the experimental setup of Fig. P7.20, suppose the stream velocity is unknown and the pitot stagnation tube is traversed across the boundary layer of air at 1 atm and 20°C. The manometer fluid is Meriam red oil, and the following readings are made:

y, mm	0.5	1.0	1.5	2.0	2.5	3.0	3.5	4.0	4.5	5.0
h, mm	1.2	4.6	9.8	15.8	21.2	25.3	27.8	29.0	29.7	29.7

Using these data only (not the Blasius theory) estimate (a) the stream velocity, (b) the boundary layer thickness, (c) the wall shear stress, and (d) the total friction drag between the leading edge and the position of the pitot tube.

P7.22 In the Blasius equation (7.22), f is a dimensionless plane stream function:

$$f(\eta) = \frac{\psi(x, y)}{\sqrt{\nu U x}}$$

Values of f are not given in Table 7.1, but one published value is $f(2.0) = 0.6500$. Consider airflow at 6 m/s, 20°C, and 1 atm past a flat plate. At $x = 1$ m, estimate (a) the height y; (b) the velocity, and (c) the stream function at $\eta = 2.0$.

P7.23 Suppose you buy a 4- by 8-ft sheet of plywood and put it on your roof rack. (See Fig. P7.23.) You drive home at 35 mi/h. (a) Assuming the board is perfectly aligned with the airflow, how thick is the boundary layer at the end of the board? (b) Estimate the drag on the sheet of plywood if the boundary layer remains laminar. (c) Estimate the drag on the sheet of plywood if the boundary layer is turbulent (assume the wood is smooth), and compare the result to that of the laminar boundary layer case.

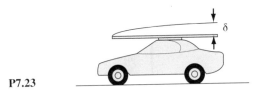

P7.23

*P7.24** Air at 20°C and 1 atm flows past the flat plate in Fig. P7.24 under laminar conditions. There are two equally spaced pitot stagnation tubes, each placed 2 mm from the wall. The manometer fluid is water at 20°C. If $U = 15$ m/s and $L = 50$ cm, determine the values of the manometer readings h_1 and h_2, in mm.

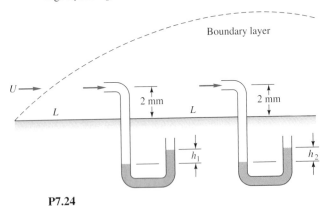

P7.24

P7.25 Consider the smooth square 10-cm-by-10-cm duct in Fig. P7.25. The fluid is air at 20°C and 1 atm, flowing at $V_{avg} = 24$ m/s. It is desired to increase the pressure drop over the 1-m length by adding sharp 8-mm-long flat plates across the duct, as shown. (a) Estimate the pressure drop if there are no plates. (b) Estimate how many plates are needed to generate an additional 100 Pa of pressure drop.

P7.26 Consider laminar boundary layer flow past the square-plate arrangements in Fig. P7.26. Compared to the friction drag of a single plate 1, how much larger is the drag of four plates together as in configurations (a) and (b)? Explain your results.

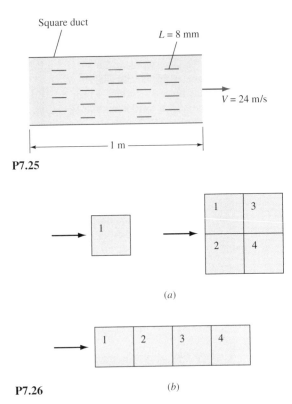

Square duct

$L = 8$ mm

$V = 24$ m/s

1 m

P7.25

(a)

(b)

P7.26

P7.27 Air at 20°C and 1 atm flows at 3 m/s past a sharp flat plate 2 m wide and 1 m long. (a) What is the wall shear stress at the end of the plate? (b) What is the air velocity at a point 4.5 mm normal to the end of the plate? (c) What is the total friction drag on the plate?

P7.28 Flow straighteners are arrays of narrow ducts placed in wind tunnels to remove swirl and other in-plane secondary velocities. They can be idealized as square boxes constructed by vertical and horizontal plates, as in Fig. P7.28. The cross section is a by a, and the box length is L. Assuming laminar flat-plate flow and an array of $N \times N$ boxes, derive a formula for (a) the total drag on the bundle of boxes and (b) the effective pressure drop across the bundle.

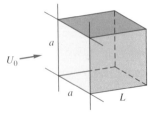

P7.28

P7.29 Let the flow straighteners in Fig. P7.28 form an array of 20×20 boxes of size $a = 4$ cm and $L = 25$ cm. If the approach velocity is $U_0 = 12$ m/s and the fluid is sea-level standard air, estimate (a) the total array drag and (b) the pressure drop across the array. Compare with Sec. 6.8.

Turbulent flat-plate flow

P7.30 In Ref. 56 of Chap. 6, McKeon et al. propose new, more accurate values for the turbulent log-law constants, $\kappa = 0.421$ and $B = 5.62$. Use these constants, and the one-seventh power-law, to repeat the analysis that led to the formula for turbulent boundary layer thickness, Eq. (7.42). By what percent is δ/x in your new formula different from that in Eq. (7.42)? Comment.

P7.31 The centerboard on a sailboat is 3 ft long parallel to the flow and protrudes 7 ft down below the hull into sea-water at 20°C. Using flat-plate theory for a smooth surface, estimate its drag if the boat moves at 10 knots. Assume $\text{Re}_{x,tr} = 5$ E5.

P7.32 A flat plate of length L and height δ is placed at a wall and is parallel to an approaching boundary layer, as in Fig. P7.32. Assume that the flow over the plate is fully turbulent and that the approaching flow is a one-seventh-power law:

$$u(y) = U_0 \left(\frac{y}{\delta}\right)^{1/7}$$

Using strip theory, derive a formula for the drag coefficient of this plate. Compare this result with the drag of the same plate immersed in a uniform stream U_0.

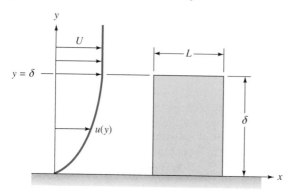

P7.32

P7.33 An alternate analysis of turbulent flat-plate flow was given by Prandtl in 1927, using a wall shear stress formula from pipe flow:

$$\tau_w = 0.0225\rho U^2 \left(\frac{\nu}{U\delta}\right)^{1/4}$$

Show that this formula can be combined with Eqs. (7.33) and (7.40) to derive the following relations for turbulent flat-plate flow:

$$\frac{\delta}{x} = \frac{0.37}{\text{Re}_x^{1/5}} \qquad c_f = \frac{0.0577}{\text{Re}_x^{1/5}} \qquad C_D = \frac{0.072}{\text{Re}_L^{1/5}}$$

These formulas are limited to Re_x between 5×10^5 and 10^7.

P7.34 Consider turbulent flow past a sharp, smooth flat plate of width b and length L. What percentage of the friction drag on the plate is carried by the rear half of the plate?

P7.35 Water at 20°C flows at 5 m/s past a 2-m-wide sharp flat plate. (a) Estimate the boundary layer thickness at $x = 1.2$ m. (b) If the total drag (on both sides of the plate) is 310 N, estimate the length of the plate using, for simplicity, Eq. (7.45).

P7.36 A ship is 125 m long and has a wetted area of 3500 m². Its propellers can deliver a maximum power of 1.1 MW to seawater at 20°C. If all drag is due to friction, estimate the maximum ship speed, in kn.

P7.37 Air at 20°C and 1 atm flows past a long flat plate, at the end of which is placed a narrow scoop, as shown in Fig. P7.37. (a) Estimate the height h of the scoop if it is to extract 4 kg/s per meter of width into the paper. (b) Find the drag on the plate up to the inlet of the scoop, per meter of width.

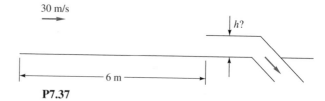

P7.37

P7.38 Atmospheric boundary layers are very thick but follow formulas very similar to those of flat-plate theory. Consider wind blowing at 10 m/s at a height of 80 m above a smooth beach. Estimate the wind shear stress, in Pa, on the beach if the air is standard sea-level conditions. What will the wind velocity striking your nose be if (a) you are standing up and your nose is 170 cm off the ground and (b) you are lying on the beach and your nose is 17 cm off the ground?

P7.39 A hydrofoil 50 cm long and 4 m wide moves at 28 kn in seawater at 20°C. Using flat-plate theory with $\text{Re}_{tr} = 5$ E5, estimate its drag, in N, for (a) a smooth wall and (b) a rough wall, $\varepsilon = 0.3$ mm.

P7.40 Hoerner [12, p. 3.25] states that the drag coefficient of a flag in winds, based on total wetted area $2bL$, is approximated by $C_D \approx 0.01 + 0.05L/b$, where L is the flag length in the flow direction. Test Reynolds numbers Re_L were 1 E6 or greater. (a) Explain why, for $L/b \geq 1$, these drag values are much higher than for a flat plate. Assuming sea-level standard air at 50 mi/h, with area $bL = 4$ m², find (b) the proper flag dimensions for which the total drag is approximately 400 N.

P7.41 Repeat Prob. P7.20 with the sole change that the pitot probe is now 10 mm from the wall (5 times higher). Show that the flow there cannot possibly be laminar, and use smooth-wall turbulent flow theory to estimate the position x of the probe, in m.

P7.42 A light aircraft flies at 30 m/s in air at 20°C and 1 atm. Its wing is an NACA 0009 airfoil, with a chord length of 150 cm and a very wide span (neglect aspect ratio effects). Estimate the drag of this wing, per unit span length, (a) by flat plate theory and (b) using the data from Fig. 7.25 for $\alpha = 0°$.

P7.43 In the flow of air at 20°C and 1 atm past a flat plate in Fig. P7.43, the wall shear is to be determined at position x by a *floating element* (a small area connected to a strain-gage force measurement). At $x = 2$ m, the element indicates a shear stress of 2.1 Pa. Assuming turbulent flow from the leading edge, estimate (a) the stream velocity U, (b) the boundary layer thickness δ at the element, and (c) the boundary layer velocity u, in m/s, at 5 mm above the element.

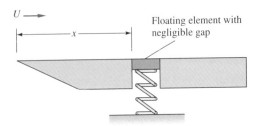

P7.43

P7.44 Extensive measurements of wall shear stress and local velocity for turbulent airflow on the flat surface of the University of Rhode Island wind tunnel have led to the following proposed correlation:

$$\frac{\rho y^2 \tau_w}{\mu^2} \approx 0.0207 \left(\frac{uy}{\nu}\right)^{1.77}$$

Thus, if y and $u(y)$ are known at a point in a flat-plate boundary layer, the wall shear may be computed directly. If the answer to part (c) of Prob. P7.43 is $u \approx 26.3$ m/s, determine the shear stress and compare with Prob. P7.43. Discuss.

P7.45 A thin sheet of fiberboard weighs 90 N and lies on a rooftop, as shown in Fig. P7.45. Assume ambient air at 20°C and 1 atm. If the coefficient of solid friction between board and roof is $\sigma \approx 0.12$, what wind velocity will generate enough fluid friction to dislodge the board?

P7.46 A ship is 150 m long and has a wetted area of 5000 m². If it is encrusted with barnacles, the ship requires 7000 hp to overcome friction drag when moving in seawater at

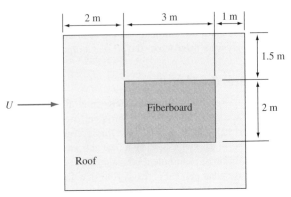

P7.45

15 kn and 20°C. What is the average roughness of the barnacles? How fast would the ship move with the same power if the surface were smooth? Neglect wave drag.

P7.47 Local boundary layer effects, such as shear stress and heat transfer, are best correlated with local variables, rather using distance x from the leading edge. The momentum thickness θ is often used as a length scale. Use the analysis of turbulent flat-plate flow to write local wall shear stress τ_w in terms of dimensionless θ and compare with the formula recommended by Schlichting [1]: $C_f \approx 0.033 \, \text{Re}_\theta^{-0.268}$.

Boundary layers with pressure gradient

P7.48 In 1957 H. Görtler proposed the adverse gradient test cases

$$U = \frac{U_0}{(1 + x/L)^n}$$

and computed separation for laminar flow at $n = 1$ to be $x_{\text{sep}}/L = 0.159$. Compare with Thwaites's method, assuming $\theta_0 = 0$.

P7.49 Based strictly on your understanding of flat-plate theory plus adverse and favorable pressure gradients, explain the direction (left or right) for which airflow past the slender airfoil shape in Fig. P7.49 will have lower total (friction + pressure) drag.

P7.49

P7.50 Consider the flat-walled diffuser in Fig. P7.50, which is similar to that of Fig. 6.26a with constant width b. If x is measured from the inlet and the wall boundary layers are thin, show that the core velocity $U(x)$ in the diffuser is given approximately by

$$U = \frac{U_0}{1 + (2x \tan \theta)/W}$$

where W is the inlet height. Use this velocity distribution with Thwaites's method to compute the wall angle θ for which laminar separation will occur in the exit plane when diffuser length $L = 2W$. Note that the result is independent of the Reynolds number.

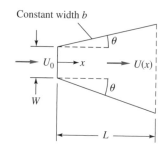

Constant width b

P7.50

Drag of bodies

P7.51 A 2-cm-diameter solid metal sphere falls steadily at about 1 m/s in 20°C fresh water. If we use Table 7.3 for a drag estimate, is the sphere made of steel, aluminum, or copper?

P7.52 Clift et al. [46] give the formula $F \approx (6\pi/5)(4 + a/b)\mu Ub$ for the drag of a prolate spheroid in *creeping motion*, as shown in Fig. P7.52. The half-thickness b is 4 mm. If the fluid is SAE 50W oil at 20°C, (a) check that $Re_b < 1$ and (b) estimate the spheroid length if the drag is 0.02 N.

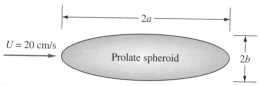

$U = 20$ cm/s

Prolate spheroid

$2a$

$2b$

P7.52

P7.53 From Table 7.2, the drag coefficient of a wide plate normal to a stream is approximately 2.0. Let the stream conditions be U_∞ and p_∞. If the average pressure on the front of the plate is approximately equal to the free-stream stagnation pressure, what is the average pressure on the rear?

*P7.54 If a missile takes off vertically from sea level and leaves the atmosphere, it has zero drag when it starts and zero drag when it finishes. It follows that the drag must be a maximum somewhere in between. To simplify the analysis, assume a constant drag coefficient, C_D, and a constant vertical acceleration, a. Let the density variation be modeled by the troposphere relation, Eq. (2.20). Find an expression for the altitude $z*$ where the drag is a maximum. Comment on your result.

P7.55 A ship tows a submerged cylinder, which is 1.5 m in diameter and 22 m long, at 5 m/s in fresh water at 20°C. Estimate the towing power, in kW, required if the cylinder is (a) parallel and (b) normal to the tow direction.

P7.56 A delivery vehicle carries a long sign on top, as in Fig. P7.56. If the sign is very thin and the vehicle moves at 65 mi/h, (a) estimate the force on the sign with no crosswind and (b) discuss the effect of a crosswind.

8 m

Phil's Pizza: 555-5748

60 cm

P7.56

P7.57 The main cross-cable between towers of a coastal suspension bridge is 60 cm in diameter and 90 m long. Estimate the total drag force on this cable in crosswinds of 50 mi/h. Are these laminar flow conditions?

*P7.58 Modify Prob. P7.54 to be more realistic by accounting for missile drag during ascent. Assume constant thrust T and missile weight W. Neglect the variation of g with altitude. Solve for the altitude $z*$ in the standard atmosphere where the drag is a maximum, for $T = 16,000$ N, $W = 8000$ N, and $C_D A = 0.4$ m^2. The writer does not believe an analytic solution is possible.

*P7.59 Joe can pedal his bike at 10 m/s on a straight level road with no wind. The rolling resistance of his bike is 0.80 N · s/m—that is, 0.80 N of force per m/s of speed. The drag area $(C_D A)$ of Joe and his bike is 0.422 m^2. Joe's mass is 80 kg and that of the bike is 15 kg. He now encounters a headwind of 5.0 m/s. (a) Develop an equation for the speed at which Joe can pedal into the wind. *Hint:* A cubic equation for V will result. (b) Solve for V; that is, how fast can Joe ride into the headwind? (c) Why is the result not simply $10 - 5.0 = 5.0$ m/s, as one might first suspect?

P7.60 A fishnet consists of 1-mm-diameter strings overlapped and knotted to form 1-by-1-cm squares. Estimate the drag of 1 m^2 of such a net when towed normal to its plane at 3 m/s in 20°C seawater. What horsepower is required to tow 400 ft^2 of this net?

P7.61 A filter may be idealized as an array of cylindrical fibers normal to the flow, as in Fig. P7.61. Assuming that the fibers are uniformly distributed and have drag coefficients given by Fig. 7.16a, derive an approximate expression for the pressure drop Δp through a filter of thickness L.

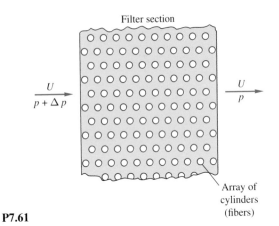

Filter section

U

$p + \Delta p$

U

p

Array of cylinders (fibers)

P7.61

P7.62   A sea-level smokestack is 52 m high and has a square cross section. Its supports can withstand a maximum side force of 90 kN. If the stack is to survive 90-mi/h hurricane winds, what is its maximum possible width?

P7.63   For those who think electric cars are sissy, Keio University in Japan has tested a 22-ft-long prototype whose eight electric motors generate a total of 590 horsepower. The "Kaz" cruises at 180 mi/h (see *Popular Science*, August 2001, p. 15). If the drag coefficient is 0.35 and the frontal area is 26 ft², what percentage of this power is expended against sea-level air drag?

P7.64   A parachutist jumps from a plane, using an 8.5-m-diameter chute in the standard atmosphere. The total mass of the chutist and the chute is 90 kg. Assuming an open chute and quasi-steady motion, estimate the time to fall from 2000- to 1000-m altitude.

P7.65   As soldiers get bigger and packs get heavier, a parachutist and load can weigh as much as 400 lbf. The standard 28-ft parachute may descend too fast for safety. For heavier loads, the U.S. Army Natick Center has developed a 28-ft, higher-drag, less porous XT-11 parachute (see <http://www.natick.army.mil>). This parachute has a sea-level descent speed of 16 ft/s with a 400-lbf load. (a) What is the drag coefficient of the XT-11? (b) How fast would the standard chute descend at sea level with such a load?

P7.66   A sphere of density ρ_s and diameter D is dropped from rest in a fluid of density ρ and viscosity μ. Assuming a constant drag coefficient C_{d_0}, derive a differential equation for the fall velocity $V(t)$ and show that the solution is

$$V = \left[\frac{4gD(S-1)}{3C_{d_0}} \right]^{1/2} \tanh Ct$$

$$C = \left[\frac{3gC_{d_0}(S-1)}{4S^2 D} \right]^{1/2}$$

where $S = \rho_s/\rho$ is the specific gravity of the sphere material.

P7.67   The Toyota Prius has a drag coefficient of 0.25, a frontal area of 23.4 ft², and an empty weight of 3042 lbf. Its rolling resistance coefficient is $C_{rr} = 0.03$, that is, the rolling resistance is 3 percent of the normal force on the tires. If rolling freely down a slope of 8° at an altitude of 500 m, calculate its maximum velocity, in mi/h.

P7.68   The Mars roving-laboratory parachute, in the Chap. 5 opener photo, is a 51-ft-diameter disk-gap-band chute, with a measured drag coefficient of 1.12 [59]. Mars has very low density, about 2.9 E-5 slug/ft³, and its gravity is only 38 percent of earth gravity. If the mass of payload and chute is 2400 kg, estimate the terminal fall velocity of the parachute.

P7.69   Two baseballs of diameter 7.35 cm are connected to a rod 7 mm in diameter and 56 cm long, as in Fig. P7.69. What power, in W, is required to keep the system spinning at 400 r/min? Include the drag of the rod, and assume sea-level standard air.

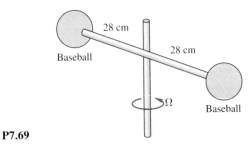

28 cm

Baseball

28 cm

Ω

Baseball

P7.69

P7.70   The Army's new ATPS personnel parachute is said to be able to bring a 400-lbf load, trooper plus pack, to ground at 16 ft/s in "mile-high" Denver, Colorado. If we assume that Table 7.3 is valid, what is the approximate diameter of this new parachute?

P7.71   The 2013 Toyota Camry has an empty weight of 3190 lbf, a frontal area of 22.06 ft², and a drag coefficient of 0.28. Its rolling resistance is $C_{rr} \approx 0.035$. Estimate the maximum velocity, in mi/h, this car can attain when rolling freely at sea level down a 4° slope.

P7.72   A settling tank for a municipal water supply is 2.5 m deep, and 20°C water flows through continuously at 35 cm/s. Estimate the minimum length of the tank that will ensure that all sediment (SG = 2.55) will fall to the bottom for particle diameters greater than (a) 1 mm and (b) 100 μm.

P7.73   A balloon is 4 m in diameter and contains helium at 125 kPa and 15°C. Balloon material and payload weigh 200 N, not including the helium. Estimate (a) the terminal ascent velocity in sea-level standard air, (b) the final standard altitude (neglecting winds) at which the balloon will come to rest, and (c) the minimum diameter (< 4 m) for which the balloon will just barely begin to rise in sea-level standard air.

P7.74 It is difficult to define the "frontal area" of a motorcycle due to its complex shape. One then measures the *drag area* (that is, $C_D A$) in area units. Hoerner [12] reports the drag area of a typical motorcycle, including the (upright) driver, as about 5.5 ft². Rolling friction is typically about 0.7 lbf per mi/h of speed. If that is the case, estimate the maximum sea-level speed (in mi/h) of the Harley-Davidson V-Rod™ cycle, whose liquid-cooled engine produces 115 hp.

P7.75 The helium-filled balloon in Fig. P7.75 is tethered at 20°C and 1 atm with a string of negligible weight and drag. The diameter is 50 cm, and the balloon material weighs 0.2 N, not including the helium. The helium pressure is 120 kPa. Estimate the tilt angle θ if the airstream velocity U is (*a*) 5 m/s or (*b*) 20 m/s.

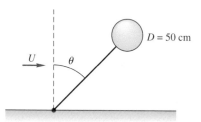

P7.75

P7.76 The movie *The World's Fastest Indian* tells the story of Burt Munro, a New Zealander who, in 1967, set a motorcycle record of 201 mi/h on the Bonneville Salt Flats. Using the data of Prob. P7.74, (*a*) estimate the horsepower needed to drive this fast. (*b*) What horsepower would have gotten Burt up to 250 mi/h?

P7.77 To measure the drag of an upright person, without violating human subject protocols, a life-sized mannequin is attached to the end of a 6-m rod and rotated at $\Omega = 80$ rev/min, as in Fig. P7.77. The power required to maintain the rotation is 60 kW. By including rod drag power, which is significant, estimate the drag area $C_D A$ of the mannequin, in m².

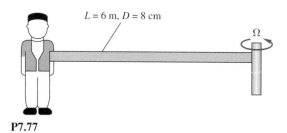

P7.77

P7.78 On April 24, 2007, a French bullet train set a new speed record, for rail-driven trains, of 357.2 mi/h, beating the old record by 12 percent. Using the data in Table 7.3, estimate the sea-level horsepower required to drive this train at such a speed.

P7.79 Assume that a radioactive dust particle approximates a sphere of density 2400 kg/m³. How long, in days, will it take such a particle to settle to sea level from an altitude of 12 km if the particle diameter is (*a*) 1 μm or (*b*) 20 μm?

P7.80 A heavy sphere attached to a string should hang at an angle θ when immersed in a stream of velocity U, as in Fig. P7.80. Derive an expression for θ as a function of the sphere and flow properties. What is θ if the sphere is steel (SG = 7.86) of diameter 3 cm and the flow is sea-level standard air at $U = 40$ m/s? Neglect the string drag.

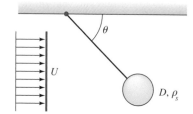

P7.80

P7.81 A typical U.S. Army parachute has a projected diameter of 28 ft. For a payload mass of 80 kg, (*a*) what terminal velocity will result at 1000-m standard altitude? For the same velocity and net payload, what size drag-producing "chute" is required if one uses a square flat plate held (*b*) vertically and (*c*) horizontally? (Neglect the fact that flat shapes are not dynamically stable in free fall.)

P7.82 Skydivers, flying over sea-level ground, typically jump at about 8000 ft altitude and free-fall spread-eagled until they open their chutes at about 2000 ft. They take about 10 s to reach terminal velocity. Estimate how many seconds of free-fall they enjoy if (*a*) they fall spread-eagled or (*b*) they fall feet first? Assume a total skydiver weight of 220 lbf.

P7.83 A blimp approximates a 4:1 spheroid that is 196 ft long. It is powered by two 150 hp ducted fans. Estimate the maximum speed attainable, in mi/h, at an altitude of 8200 ft.

P7.84 A Ping-Pong ball weighs 2.6 g and has a diameter of 3.8 cm. It can be supported by an air jet from a vacuum cleaner outlet, as in Fig. P7.84. For sea-level standard air, what jet velocity is required?

P7.84

P7.85 In this era of expensive fossil fuels, many alternatives have been pursued. One idea from SkySails, Inc., shown in Fig. P7.85, is the assisted propulsion of a ship by a large tethered kite. The tow force of the kite assists the ship's propeller and is said to reduce annual fuel consumption by 10–35 percent. For a typical example, let the ship be 120 m long, with a wetted area of 2800 m². The kite area is 330 m² and has a force coefficient of 0.8. The kite cable makes an angle of 25° with the horizontal. Let V_{wind} = 30 mi/h. Neglect ship wave drag. Estimate the ship speed (a) due to the kite only and (b) if the propeller delivers 1250 hp to the water. [*Hint:* The kite sees the *relative* velocity of the wind.]

P7.85 Ship propulsion assisted by a large kite. (*Courtesy of SkySails, Inc.*)

P7.86 Hoerner [Ref. 12, pp. 3–25] states that the drag coefficient of a flag of 2:1 aspect ratio is 0.11 based on planform area. The University of Rhode Island has an aluminum flagpole 25 m high and 14 cm in diameter. It flies equal-sized national and state flags together. If the fracture stress of aluminum is 210 MPa, what is the maximum flag size that can be used without breaking the flagpole in hurricane (75 mi/h) winds? (Neglect the drag of the flagpole.)

P7.87 A tractor-trailer truck has a drag area $C_D A = 8$ m² bare and 6.7 m² with an aerodynamic deflector (Fig. 7.18b). Its rolling resistance is 50 N for each mile per hour of speed. Calculate the total horsepower required at sea level with and without the deflector if the truck moves at (a) 55 mi/h and (b) 75 mi/h.

P7.88 A pickup truck has a clean drag area $C_D A$ of 35 ft². Estimate the horsepower required to drive the truck at 55 mi/h (a) clean and (b) with the 3- by 6-ft sign in Fig. P7.88 installed if the rolling resistance is 150 lbf at sea level.

P7.88

P7.89 The AMTRAK Acela train passes through Kingston, RI, at 130 mi/h, scaring all the villagers daily. Its total weight is 624 short tons, with a rolling resistance $C_{rr} \approx 0.0024$. Estimate the horsepower required to drive the train this fast.

P7.90 In the great hurricane of 1938, winds of 85 mi/h blew over a boxcar in Providence, Rhode Island. The boxcar was 10 ft high, 40 ft long, and 6 ft wide, with a 3-ft clearance above tracks 4.8 ft apart. What wind speed would topple a boxcar weighing 40,000 lbf?

*P7.91 A cup anemometer uses two 5-cm-diameter hollow hemispheres connected to 15-cm rods, as in Fig. P7.91. Rod drag is negligible, and the central bearing has a retarding torque of 0.004 N · m. Making simplifying assumptions to average out the time-varying geometry, estimate and plot the variation of anemometer rotation rate Ω with wind velocity U in the range $0 < U < 25$ m/s for sea-level standard air.

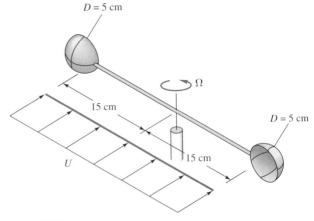

P7.91

P7.92 A 1500-kg automobile uses its drag area $C_D A = 0.4$ m², plus brakes and a parachute, to slow down from 50 m/s. Its brakes apply 5000 N of resistance. Assume sea-level standard air. If the automobile must stop in 8 s, what diameter parachute is appropriate?

P7.93 A hot-film probe is mounted on a cone-and-rod system in a sea-level airstream of 45 m/s, as in Fig. P7.93. Estimate the maximum cone vertex angle allowable if the flow-induced bending moment at the root of the rod is not to exceed 30 N · cm.

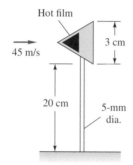

P7.93

P7.94 Baseball drag data from the University of Texas are shown in Fig. P7.94. A baseball weighs approximately 5.12 ounces and has a diameter of 2.91 in. Hall-of-Famer Nolan Ryan, in a 1974 game, threw the fastest pitch ever recorded: 108.1 mi/h. If it is 60 ft from Nolan's hand to the catcher's mitt, estimate the sea-level ball velocity which the catcher experiences for (a) a normal baseball, and (b) a perfectly smooth baseball.

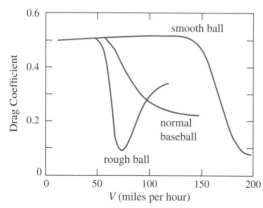

Fig. P7.94

P7.95 An airplane weighing 28 kN, with a drag area $C_D A \approx 5$ m², lands at sea level at 55 m/s and deploys a drag parachute 3 m in diameter. No other brakes are applied. (a) How long will it take the plane to slow down to 20 m/s? (b) How far will it have traveled in that time?

*P7.96 A Savonius rotor (Fig. 6.29b) can be approximated by the two open half-tubes in Fig. P7.96 mounted on a central axis. If the drag of each tube is similar to that in Table 7.2, derive an approximate formula for the rotation rate Ω as a function of U, D, L, and the fluid properties (ρ, μ).

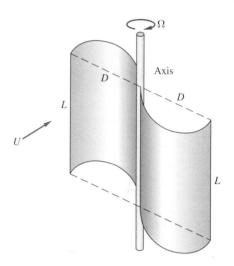

P7.96

P7.97 A simple measurement of automobile drag can be found by an unpowered *coastdown* on a level road with no wind. Assume rolling resistance proportional to velocity. For an automobile of mass 1500 kg and frontal area 2 m², the following velocity-versus-time data are obtained during a coastdown:

t, s	0	10	20	30	40
V, m/s	27.0	24.2	21.8	19.7	17.9

Estimate (a) the rolling resistance and (b) the drag coefficient. This problem is well suited for computer analysis but can be done by hand also.

*P7.98 A buoyant ball of specific gravity SG < 1 dropped into water at inlet velocity V_0 will penetrate a distance h and then pop out again, as in Fig. P7.98. Make a dynamic analysis of this problem, assuming a constant drag coefficient, and derive an expression for h as a function of the system properties. How far will a 5-cm-diameter ball with SG = 0.5 and $C_D \approx 0.47$ penetrate if it enters at 10 m/s?

P7.99 Two steel balls (SG = 7.86) are connected by a thin hinged rod of negligible weight and drag, as in Fig. P7.99. A stop prevents the rod from rotating counterclockwise. Estimate the sea-level air velocity U for which the rod will first begin to rotate clockwise.

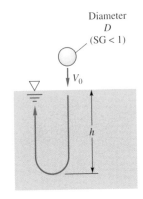

Diameter
D
(SG < 1)

V_0

h

P7.98

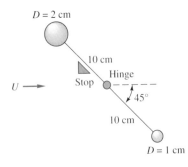

$D = 2$ cm

10 cm

Hinge

$U \longrightarrow$ Stop

45°

10 cm

$D = 1$ cm

P7.99

P7.100 A tractor-trailer truck is coasting freely, with no brakes, down an 8° slope at 1000-m standard altitude. Rolling resistance is 120 N for every m/s of speed. Its frontal area is 9 m², and the weight is 65 kN. Estimate the terminal coasting velocity, in mi/h, for (a) no deflector and (b) a deflector installed.

P7.101 Icebergs can be driven at substantial speeds by the wind. Let the iceberg be idealized as a large, flat cylinder, $D \gg L$, with one-eighth of its bulk exposed, as in Fig. P7.101. Let the seawater be at rest. If the upper and lower drag forces depend on relative velocities between the iceberg and the fluid, derive an approximate expression for the steady iceberg speed V when driven by wind velocity U.

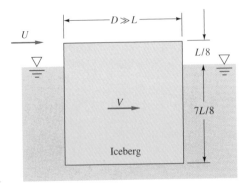

$U \longrightarrow$

$D \gg L$

$L/8$

V

$7L/8$

Iceberg

P7.101

P7.102 Sand particles (SG = 2.7), approximately spherical with diameters from 100 to 250 μm, are introduced into an upward-flowing stream of water at 20°C. What is the minimum water velocity that will carry all the sand particles *upward?*

P7.103 When immersed in a uniform stream V, a heavy rod hinged at A will hang at *Pode's angle* θ, after an analysis by L. Pode in 1951 (Fig. P7.103). Assume that the cylinder has normal drag coefficient C_{DN} and tangential coefficient C_{DT} that relate the drag forces to V_N and V_T, respectively. Derive an expression for Pode's angle as a function of the flow and rod parameters. Find θ for a steel rod, $L = 40$ cm, $D = 1$ cm, hanging in sea-level air at $V = 35$ m/s.

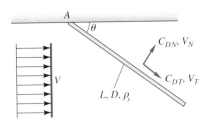

A

θ

C_{DN}, V_N

V

C_{DT}, V_T

L, D, ρ_s

P7.103

P7.104 The Russian Typhoon-class submarine is 170 m long, with a maximum diameter of 23 m. Its propulsor can deliver up to 80,000 hp to the seawater. Model the submarine as an 8:1 ellipsoid and estimate the maximum speed, in knots, of this ship.

P7.105 A ship 50 m long, with a wetted area of 800 m², has the hull shape tested in Fig. 7.19. There are no bow or stern bulbs. The total propulsive power available is 1 MW. For seawater at 20°C, plot the ship's velocity V kn versus power P for $0 < P < 1$ MW. What is the most efficient setting?

P7.106 For the kite-assisted ship of Prob. P7.85, again neglect wave drag and let the wind velocity be 30 mi/h. Estimate the kite area that would tow the ship, unaided by the propeller, at a ship speed of 8 knots.

P7.107 The largest flag in Rhode Island stands outside Herb Chambers' auto dealership, on the edge of Route I-95 in Providence. The flag is 50 ft long, 30 ft wide, weighs 250 lbf, and takes four strong people to raise it or lower it. Using Prob. P7.40 for input, estimate (a) the wind speed, in mi/h, for which the flag drag is 1000 lbf and (b) the flag drag when the wind is a low-end category 1 hurricane, 74 mi/h. [*Hint:* Providence is at sea level.]

P7.108 The data in Fig. P7.108 are for the lift and drag of a spinning sphere from Ref. 45. Suppose that a tennis ball ($W \approx 0.56$ N, $D \approx 6.35$ cm) is struck at sea level with initial velocity $V_0 = 30$ m/s and "topspin" (front of the ball rotating downward) of 120 r/s. If the initial height of the ball is 1.5 m, estimate the horizontal distance traveled before it strikes the ground.

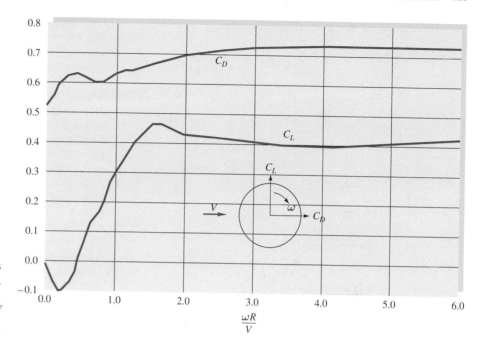

P7.108 Drag and lift coefficients for a rotating sphere at $Re_D \approx 10^5$, from Ref. 45. (*Reproduced by permission of the American Society of Mechanical Engineers.*)

P7.109 The world record for automobile mileage, 12,665 miles per gallon, was set in 2005 by the PAC-CAR II in Fig. P7.109, built by students at the Swiss Federal Institute of Technology in Zurich [52]. This little car, with an empty weight of 64 lbf and a height of only 2.5 ft, traveled a 21-km course at 30 km/h to set the record. It has a reported drag coefficient of 0.075 (comparable to an airfoil), based upon a frontal area of 3 ft^2. (*a*) What is the drag of this little car when on the course? (*b*) What horsepower is required to propel it? (*c*) Do a bit of research and explain why a value of miles per gallon is completely misleading in this particular case.

P7.110 A baseball pitcher throws a curveball with an initial velocity of 65 mi/h and a spin of 6500 r/min about a vertical axis. A baseball weighs 0.32 lbf and has a diameter of 2.9 in. Using the data of Fig. P7.108 for turbulent flow, estimate how far such a curveball will have deviated from its straight-line path when it reaches home plate 60.5 ft away.

*P7.111 A table tennis ball has a mass of 2.6 g and a diameter of 3.81 cm. It is struck horizontally at an initial velocity of 20 m/s while it is 50 cm above the table, as in Fig. P7.111. For sea-level air, what spin, in r/min, will cause the ball to strike the opposite edge of the table, 4 m away? Make an analytical estimate, using Fig. P7.108, and account for the fact that the ball decelerates during flight.

P7.112 A smooth wooden sphere (SG = 0.65) is connected by a thin rigid rod to a hinge in a wind tunnel, as in Fig. P7.112. Air at 20°C and 1 atm flows and levitates the sphere. (*a*) Plot the angle θ versus sphere diameter d in the range 1 cm $\leq d \leq$ 15 cm. (*b*) Comment on the feasibility of this configuration. Neglect rod drag.

P7.109 The world's best mileage set by PAC-Car II of ETH Zurich.

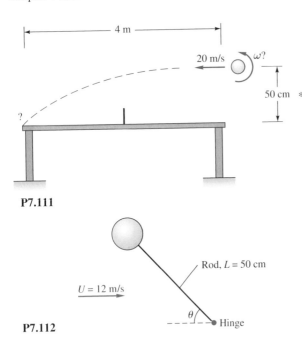

P7.111

P7.112

Rod, L = 50 cm

U = 12 m/s

θ

Hinge

P7.113 An automobile has a mass of 1000 kg and a drag area $C_D A = 0.7$ m². The rolling resistance of 70 N is approximately constant. The car is coasting without brakes at 90 km/h as it begins to climb a hill of 10 percent grade (slope = $\tan^{-1} 0.1 = 5.71°$). How far up the hill will the car come to a stop?

P7.114 The deep submergence vehicle ALVIN is 23 ft long and 8.5 ft wide. It weighs about 36,000 lbf in air and ascends (descends) in the seawater due to about 360 lbf of positive (negative) buoyancy. Noting that the front face of the ship is quite different for ascent and descent, (*a*) estimate the velocity for each direction, in meters per minute. (*b*) How long does it take to ascend from its maximum depth of 4500 m?

Lifting bodies—airfoils

P7.115 The Cessna Citation executive jet weighs 67 kN and has a wing area of 32 m². It cruises at 10 km standard altitude with a lift coefficient of 0.21 and a drag coefficient of 0.015. Estimate (*a*) the cruise speed in mi/h and (*b*) the horsepower required to maintain cruise velocity.

P7.116 An airplane weighs 180 kN and has a wing area of 160 m² and a mean chord of 4 m. The airfoil properties are given by Fig. 7.25. If the plane is designed to land at $V_0 = 1.2 V_{stall}$, using a split flap set at 60°, (*a*) what is the proper landing speed in mi/h? (*b*) What power is required for take-off at the same speed?

P7.117 The Transition® auto-car in Fig. 7.30 has a weight of 1200 lbf, a wingspan of 27.5 ft, and a wing area of 150 ft², with

a symmetrical airfoil, $C_{D\infty} \approx 0.02$. Assume that the fuselage and tail section have a drag-area comparable to the Toyota *Prius* [21], $C_D A \approx 6.24$ t². If the pusher propeller provides a thrust of 250 lbf, how fast, in mi/h, can this carplane fly at an altitude of 8200 ft?

*P7.118 Suppose that the airplane of Prob. P7.116 is fitted with all the best high-lift devices of Fig. 7.28. What is its minimum stall speed in mi/h? Estimate the stopping distance if the plane lands at $V_0 = 1.25 V_{stall}$ with constant $C_L = 3.0$ and $C_D = 0.2$ and the braking force is 20 percent of the weight on the wheels.

P7.119 A transport plane has a mass of 45,000 kg, a wing area of 160 m², and an aspect ratio of 7. Assume all lift and drag due to the wing alone, with $C_{D\infty} = 0.020$ and $C_{L,max} = 1.5$. If the aircraft flies at 9000 m standard altitude, make a plot of drag (in N) versus speed (from stall to 240 m/s) and determine the optimum cruise velocity (minimum drag per unit speed).

P7.120 Show that if Eqs. (7.70) and (7.71) are valid, the maximum lift-to-drag ratio occurs when $C_D = 2 C_{D\infty}$. What are $(L/D)_{max}$ and α for a symmetric wing when AR = 5 and $C_{D\infty} = 0.009$?

P7.121 In gliding (unpowered) flight, the lift and drag are in equilibrium with the weight. Show that if there is no wind, the aircraft sinks at an angle

$$\tan \theta \approx \frac{\text{drag}}{\text{lift}}$$

For a sailplane of mass 200 kg, wing area 12 m², and aspect ratio 11, with an NACA 0009 airfoil, estimate (*a*) the stall speed, (*b*) the minimum gliding angle, and (*c*) the maximum distance it can glide in still air when it is 1200 m above level ground.

P7.122 A boat of mass 2500 kg has two hydrofoils, each of chord 30 cm and span 1.5 m, with $C_{L,max} = 1.2$ and $C_{D\infty} = 0.08$. Its engine can deliver 130 kW to the water. For seawater at 20°C, estimate (*a*) the minimum speed for which the foils support the boat and (*b*) the maximum speed attainable.

P7.123 In prewar days there was a controversy, perhaps apocryphal, about whether the bumblebee has a legitimate aerodynamic right to fly. The average bumblebee (*Bombus terrestris*) weighs 0.88 g, with a wingspan of 1.73 cm and a wing area of 1.26 cm². It can indeed fly at 10 m/s. Using fixed-wing theory, what is the lift coefficient of the bee at this speed? Is this reasonable for typical airfoils?

*P7.124 The bumblebee can hover at zero speed by flapping its wings. Using the data of Prob. P7.123, devise a theory for flapping wings where the downstroke approximates a short flat plate normal to the flow (Table 7.3) and the upstroke is feathered at nearly zero drag. How many flaps per second of such a model wing are needed to support the bee's weight? (Actual measurements of bees show a flapping rate of 194 Hz.)

*P7.125 The Solar Impulse aircraft in the chapter-opener photo has a wingspan of 208 ft, a wing area of 2140 ft², and a weight of 1600 kgf. Its propellers deliver an average of 24 hp to the air at a cruising altitude of 8.5 km. Assuming an NACA 0009 airfoil, and neglecting the drag of the fuselage and tail, estimate (a) the wing aspect ratio, (b) the cruise speed, in mi/h, and (c) the wing angle of attack. [Hint: Simplify by using Fig. 7.25 to estimate lift and drag.]

P7.126 Using the data for the Transition® auto-car from Prob. P7.117, and a maximum lift coefficient of 1.3, estimate the distance for the vehicle to take off at a speed of $1.2V_{stall}$. Note that we have to add the car-body drag to the wing drag.

P7.127 The so-called Rocket Man, Yves Rossy, flew across the Alps in 2008, wearing a rocket-propelled wing-suit with the following data: thrust = 200 lbf, altitude = 8,200 ft, and wingspan = 8 ft (http://en.wikipedia.org/wiki/Yves_Rossy). Further assume a wing area of 12 ft², total weight of 280 lbf, $C_{D\infty} = 0.08$ for the wing, and a drag area of 1.7 ft² for Rocket Man. Estimate the maximum velocity possible for this condition, in mi/h.

Word Problems

W7.1 How do you *recognize* a boundary layer? Cite some physical properties and some measurements that reveal appropriate characteristics.

W7.2 In Chap. 6 the Reynolds number for transition to turbulence in pipe flow was about $Re_{tr} \approx 2300$, whereas in flat-plate flow $Re_{tr} \approx 1\ E6$, nearly three orders of magnitude higher. What accounts for the difference?

W7.3 Without writing any equations, give a verbal description of boundary layer displacement thickness.

W7.4 Describe, in words only, the basic ideas behind the "boundary layer approximations."

W7.5 What is an *adverse* pressure gradient? Give three examples of flow regimes where such gradients occur.

W7.6 What is a *favorable* pressure gradient? Give three examples of flow regimes where such gradients occur.

W7.7 The drag of an airfoil (Fig. 7.12) increases considerably if you turn the sharp edge around 180° to face the stream. Can you explain this?

W7.8 In Table 7.3, the drag coefficient of a spruce tree decreases sharply with wind velocity. Can you explain this?

W7.9 Thrust is required to propel an airplane at a finite forward velocity. Does this imply an energy loss to the system? Explain the concepts of thrust and drag in terms of the first law of thermodynamics.

W7.10 How does the concept of *drafting,* in automobile and bicycle racing, apply to the material studied in this chapter?

W7.11 The circular cylinder of Fig. 7.13 is doubly symmetric and therefore should have no lift. Yet a lift sensor would definitely reveal a finite root-mean-square value of lift. Can you explain this behavior?

W7.12 Explain in words why a thrown spinning ball moves in a curved trajectory. Give some physical reasons why a side force is developed in addition to the drag.

Fundamentals of Engineering Exam Problems

FE7.1 A smooth 12-cm-diameter sphere is immersed in a stream of 20°C water moving at 6 m/s. The appropriate Reynolds number of this sphere is approximately
(a) 2.3 E5, (b) 7.2 E5, (c) 2.3 E6, (d) 7.2 E6, (e) 7.2 E7

FE7.2 If, in Prob. FE7.1, the drag coefficient based on frontal area is 0.5, what is the drag force on the sphere?
(a) 17 N, (b) 51 N, (c) 102 N, (d) 130 N, (e) 203 N

FE7.3 If, in Prob. FE7.1, the drag coefficient based on frontal area is 0.5, at what terminal velocity will an aluminum sphere (SG = 2.7) fall in still water?
(a) 2.3 m/s, (b) 2.9 m/s, (c) 4.6 m/s, (d) 6.5 m/s, (e) 8.2 m/s

FE7.4 For flow of sea-level standard air at 4 m/s parallel to a thin flat plate, estimate the boundary layer thickness at $x = 60$ cm from the leading edge:
(a) 1.0 mm, (b) 2.6 mm, (c) 5.3 mm, (d) 7.5 mm, (e) 20.2 mm

FE7.5 In Prob. FE7.4, for the same flow conditions, what is the wall shear stress at $x = 60$ cm from the leading edge?
(a) 0.053 Pa, (b) 0.11 Pa, (c) 0.16 Pa, (d) 0.32 Pa, (e) 0.64 Pa

FE7.6 Wind at 20°C and 1 atm blows at 75 km/h past a flagpole 18 m high and 20 cm in diameter. The drag coefficient, based on frontal area, is 1.15. Estimate the wind-induced bending moment at the base of the pole.
(a) 9.7 kN · m, (b) 15.2 kN · m, (c) 19.4 kN · m, (d) 30.5 kN · m, (e) 61.0 kN · m

FE7.7 Consider wind at 20°C and 1 atm blowing past a chimney 30 m high and 80 cm in diameter. If the chimney may fracture at a base bending moment of 486 kN·m, and its drag coefficient based on frontal area is 0.5, what is the approximate maximum allowable wind velocity to avoid fracture?
(a) 50 mi/h, (b) 75 mi/h, (c) 100 mi/h, (d) 125 mi/h, (e) 150 mi/h

FE7.8 A dust particle of density 2600 kg/m^3, small enough to satisfy Stokes's drag law, settles at 1.5 mm/s in air at 20°C and 1 atm. What is its approximate diameter?
(*a*) 1.8 µm, (*b*) 2.9 µm, (*c*) 4.4 µm, (*d*) 16.8 µm, (*e*) 234 µm

FE7.9 An airplane has a mass of 19,550 kg, a wingspan of 20 m, and an average wing chord of 3 m. When flying in air of density 0.5 kg/m^3, its engines provide a thrust of 12 kN

against an overall drag coefficient of 0.025. What is its approximate velocity?
(*a*) 250 mi/h, (*b*) 300 mi/h, (*c*) 350 mi/h, (*d*) 400 mi/h, (*e*) 450 mi/h

FE7.10 For the flight conditions of the airplane in Prob. FE7.9 above, what is its approximate lift coefficient?
(*a*) 0.1, (*b*) 0.2, (*c*) 0.3, (*d*) 0.4, (*e*) 0.5

Comprehensive Problems

C7.1 Jane wants to estimate the drag coefficient of herself on her bicycle. She measures the projected frontal area to be 0.40 m^2 and the rolling resistance to be 0.80 N · s/m. The mass of the bike is 15 kg, while the mass of Jane is 80 kg. Jane

coasts down a long hill that has a constant 4° slope. (See Fig. C7.1.) She reaches a terminal (steady state) speed of 14 m/s down the hill. Estimate the aerodynamic drag coefficient C_D of the rider and bicycle combination.

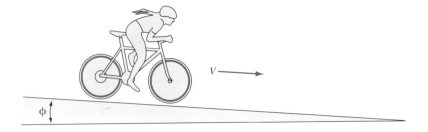

C7.1

C7.2 Air at 20°C and 1 atm flows at $V_{avg} = 5$ m/s between long, smooth parallel heat exchanger plates 10 cm apart, as in Fig. C7.2. It is proposed to add a number of widely spaced 1-cm-long interrupter plates to increase the heat transfer, as shown. Although the flow in the channel is turbulent, the boundary layers over the interrupter plates are essentially laminar. Assume all plates are 1 m wide into the paper. Find (*a*) the pressure drop in Pa/m without the small plates present. Then find (*b*) the number of small plates per meter of channel length that will cause the pressure drop to rise to 10.0 Pa/m.

C7.2

C7.3 A new pizza store is planning to open. It will, of course, offer free delivery, and therefore need a small delivery car with a large sign attached. The sign (a flat plate) is 1.5 ft high and 5 ft long. The boss (having no feel for fluid mechanics) mounts the sign bluntly facing the wind. One of his drivers is taking fluid mechanics and tells his boss he can save lots of money by mounting the sign parallel to the wind. (See Fig. C7.3.) (*a*) Calculate the drag (in lbf) on the *sign alone* at 40 mi/h (58.7 ft/s) in *both orientations*. (*b*) Suppose the car without any sign has a drag coefficient of 0.4 and a frontal area of 40 ft^2. For $V = 40$ mi/h, calculate the *total* drag of the car–sign combination for both orientations. (*c*) If the car has a rolling resistance of 40 lbf at 40 mi/h, calculate the horsepower required by the engine to drive the car at 40 mi/h in both orientations. (*d*) Finally, if the engine can deliver 10 hp for 1 h on a gallon of gasoline, calculate the fuel efficiency in mi/gal for both orientations at 40 mi/h.

C7.3

C7.4 Consider a pendulum with an unusual bob shape: a hemispherical cup of diameter D whose axis is in the plane of oscillation, as in Fig. C7.4. Neglect the mass and drag of

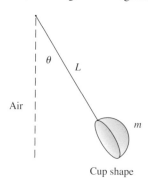

C7.4   Cup shape

the rod L. (a) Set up the differential equation for the oscillation $\theta(t)$, including different cup drag (air density ρ) in each direction, and (b) nondimensionalize this equation. (c) Determine the natural frequency of oscillation for small $\theta \ll 1$ rad. (d) For the special case $L = 1$ m, $D = 10$ cm, $m = 50$ g, and air at 20°C and 1 atm, with $\theta(0) = 30°$, find (numerically) the time required for the oscillation amplitude to drop to 1°.

C7.5 Program a method of numerical solution of the Blasius flat-plate relation, Eq. (7.22), subject to the conditions in Eqs. (7.23). You will find that you cannot get started without knowing the initial second derivative $f''(0)$, which lies between 0.2 and 0.5. Devise an iteration scheme that starts at $f''(0) \approx 0.2$ and converges to the correct value. Print out $u/U = f'(\eta)$ and compare with Table 7.1.

Design Project

D7.1 It is desired to design a cup anemometer for wind speed, similar to Fig. P7.91, with a more sophisticated approach than the "average-torque" method of Prob. P7.91. The design should achieve an approximately linear relation between wind velocity and rotation rate in the range $20 < U < 40$ mi/h, and the anemometer should rotate at about 6 r/s at $U = 30$ mi/h. All specifications—cup diameter D, rod length L, rod diameter d, the bearing type, and all materials—are to be selected through your analysis. Make suitable assumptions about the instantaneous drag of the cups and rods at any given angle $\theta(t)$ of the system. Compute the instantaneous torque $T(t)$, and find and integrate the instantaneous angular acceleration of the device. Develop a complete theory for rotation rate versus wind speed in the range $0 < U < 50$ mi/h. Try to include actual commercial bearing friction properties.

References

1. H. Schlichting and K. Gersten, *Boundary Layer Theory*, 8th ed., Springer, New York, 2000.
2. F. M. White, *Viscous Fluid Flow*, 3d ed., McGraw-Hill, New York, 2005.
3. J. Cousteix, *Modeling and Computation of Boundary-Layer Flows*, 2d ed., Springer-Verlag, New York, 2005.
4. J. D. Anderson, *Computational Fluid Dynamics: An Introduction*, 3d ed., Springer, New York, 2010.
5. V. V. Sychev et al., *Asymptotic Theory of Separated Flows*, Cambridge University Press, New York, 2008.
6. I. J. Sobey, *Introduction to Interactive Boundary Layer Theory*, Oxford University Press, New York, 2001.
7. T. von Kármán, "On Laminar and Turbulent Friction," *Z. Angew. Math. Mech.*, vol. 1, 1921, pp. 235–236.
8. G. B. Schubauer and H. K. Skramstad, "Laminar Boundary Layer Oscillations and Stability of Laminar Flow," *Natl. Bur. Stand. Res. Pap.* 1772, April 1943 (see also *J. Aero. Sci.*, vol. 14, 1947, pp. 69–78, and *NACA Rep.* 909, 1947).
9. P. S. Bernard and J. M. Wallace, *Turbulent Flow: Analysis, Measurement, and Prediction*, Wiley, New York, 2002.
10. P. W. Runstadler, Jr., et al., "Diffuser Data Book," Creare Inc., *Tech. Note* 186, Hanover, NH, May 1975.
11. B. Thwaites, "Approximate Calculation of the Laminar Boundary Layer," *Aeronaut. Q.*, vol. 1, 1949, pp. 245–280.
12. S. F. Hoerner, *Fluid Dynamic Drag*, published by the author, Midland Park, NJ, 1965.
13. J. D. Anderson, *Fundamentals of Aerodynamics*, 5th ed., McGraw-Hill, New York, 2010.
14. V. Tucker and G. C. Parrott, "Aerodynamics of Gliding Flight of Falcons and Other Birds," *J. Exp. Biol.*, vol. 52, 1970, pp. 345–368.
15. E. C. Tupper, *Introduction to Naval Architecture*, 5th ed., Butterworth-Heinemann, Burlington, MA, 2013.
16. I. H. Abbott and A. E. von Doenhoff, *Theory of Wing Sections*, Dover, New York, 1981.

17. R. L. Kline and F. F. Fogelman, "Airfoil for Aircraft," U. S. Patent 3,706,430, Dec. 19, 1972.

18. A. Azuma, *The Biokinetics of Swimming and Flying*, AIAA, Reston, VA, 2006.

19. National Committee for Fluid Mechanics Films, *Illustrated Experiments in Fluid Mechanics*, M.I.T. Press, Cambridge, MA, 1972.

20. D. M. Bushnell and J. Hefner (Eds.), *Viscous Drag Reduction in Boundary Layers*, American Institute of Aeronautics & Astronautics, Reston, VA, 1990.

21. "Automobile Drag Coefficient," URL <http://en.wikipedia.org/wiki/Automobile_drag_coefficients>.

22. R. H. Barnard, *Road Vehicle Aerodynamic Design*, 3d ed., Mechaero Publishing, St. Albans, U.K., 2010.

23. R. D. Blevins, *Applied Fluid Dynamics Handbook*, BBS, New York, 2009.

24. R. C. Johnson, Jr., G. E. Ramey, and D. S. O'Hagen, "Wind Induced Forces on Trees," *J. Fluids Eng.*, vol. 104, March 1983, pp. 25–30.

25. P. W. Bearman et al., "The Effect of a Moving Floor on Wind-Tunnel Simulation of Road Vehicles," Paper No. 880245, SAE Transactions, *J. Passenger Cars*, vol. 97, sec. 4, 1988, pp. 4.200–4.214.

26. *CRC Handbook of Tables for Applied Engineering Science*, 2d ed., CRC Press, Boca Raton, FL, 1973.

27. T. Inui, "Wavemaking Resistance of Ships," *Trans. Soc. Nav. Arch. Marine Engrs.*, vol. 70, 1962, pp. 283–326.

28. L. Larsson, "CFD in Ship Design—Prospects and Limitations," *Ship Technology Research*, vol. 44, no. 3, July 1997, pp. 133–154.

29. R. L. Street, G. Z. Watters, and J. K. Vennard, *Elementary Fluid Mechanics*, 7th ed., Wiley, New York, 1995.

30. J. D. Anderson, Jr., *Modern Compressible Flow: with Historical Perspective*, 3d ed., McGraw-Hill, New York, 2002.

31. J. D. Anderson, Jr., *Hypersonic and High Temperature Gas Dynamics*, AIAA, Reston, VA, 2000.

32. J. Rom, *High Angle of Attack Aerodynamics: Subsonic, Transonic, and Supersonic Flows*, Springer-Verlag, New York, 2011.

33. S. Vogel, "Drag and Reconfiguration of Broad Leaves in High Winds," *J. Exp. Bot.*, vol. 40, no. 217, August 1989, pp. 941–948.

34. S. Vogel, *Life in Moving Fluids*, Princeton University Press 2d ed., Princeton, NJ, 1996.

35. J. A. C. Humphrey (ed.), *Proceedings 2d International Symposium on Mechanics of Plants, Animals, and Their Environment*, Engineering Foundation, New York, January 2000.

36. D. D. Joseph, R. Bai, K. P. Chen, and Y. Y. Renardy, "Core-Annular Flows," *Annu. Rev. Fluid Mech.*, vol. 29, 1997, pp. 65–90.

37. J. W. Hoyt and R. H. J. Sellin, "Scale Effects in Polymer Solution Pipe Flow," *Experiments in Fluids*, vol. 15, no. 1, June 1993, pp. 70–74.

38. S. Nakao, "Application of V-Shape Riblets to Pipe Flows," *J. Fluids Eng.*, vol. 113, December 1991, pp. 587–590.

39. P. Thiede (ed.), *Aerodynamic Drag Reduction Technologies*, Springer, New York, 2001.

40. C. L. Merkle and S. Deutsch, "Microbubble Drag Reduction in Liquid Turbulent Boundary Layers," *Applied Mechanics Reviews*, vol. 45, no. 3 part 1, March 1992, pp. 103–127.

41. K. S. Choi and G. E. Karniadakis, "Mechanisms on Transverse Motions in Turbulent Wall Flows," *Annual Review of Fluid Mechanics*, vol. 35, 2003, pp. 45–62.

42. C. J. Roy, J. Payne, and M. McWherter-Payne, "RANS Simulations of a Simplified Tractor-Trailer Geometry," *J. Fluids Engineering*, vol. 128, Sept. 2006, pp. 1083–1089.

43. *Evolution of Flight*, Internet URL <http://www.flight100.org>.

44. J. D. Anderson, Jr., *A History of Aerodynamics*, Cambridge University Press, New York, 1999.

45. Y. Tsuji, Y. Morikawa, and O. Mizuno, "Experimental Measurement of the Magnus Force on a Rotating Sphere at Low Reynolds Numbers," *Journal of Fluids Engineering*, vol. 107, 1985, pp. 484–488.

46. R. Clift, J. R. Grace, and M. E. Weber, *Bubbles, Drops and Particles*, Dover, NY, 2005.

47. M. Gad-el-Hak, "Flow Control: The Future," *Journal of Aircraft*, vol. 38, no. 3, 2001, pp. 402–418.

48. D. Geropp and H. J. Odenthal, "Drag Reduction of Motor Vehicles by Active Flow Control Using the Coanda Effect," *Experiments in Fluids*, vol. 28, no. 1, 2000, pp. 74–85.

49. Z. Zapryanov and S. Tabakova, *Dynamics of Bubbles, Drops, and Rigid Particles*, Kluwer Academic Pub., New York, 1998.

50. D. G. Karamanev, and L. N. Nikolov, "Freely Rising Spheres Do Not Obey Newton's Law for Free Settling," *AIChE Journal*, vol. 38, no. 1, Nov. 1992, pp. 1843–1846.

51. Katz J., *Race-Car Aerodynamics*, Robert Bentley Inc., Cambridge, MA, 2003.

52. A. S. Brown, "More than 12,000 Miles to the Gallon," *Mechanical Engineering*, January 2006, p. 64.

53. D. M. Bushnell, "Aircraft Drag Reduction: A Review," *Proceedings of the Institution of Mechanical Engineers, Part G: Journal of Aerospace Engineering*, vol. 217, no. 1, 2003, pp. 1–18.

54. D. B. Spalding, "A Single Formula for the Law of the Wall," *J. Appl. Mechanics*, vol. 28, no. 3, 1961, pp. 444–458.

55. D. G. Fertis, "New Airfoil-Design Concept with Improved Aerodynamic Characteristics," *J. Aerospace Engineering*, vol. 7, no. 3, July 1994, pp. 328–339.

56. F. Finaish and S. Witherspoon, "Aerodynamic Performance of an Airfoil with Step-Induced Vortex for Lift Augmentation," *J. Aerospace Engineering*, vol. 11, no. 1, Jan. 1998, pp. 9–16.

57. D. S. Miklosovic et al., "Leading Edge Tubercles Delay Stall on Humpback Whale," *Physics of Fluids*, vol. 16, no. 5, May 2004, pp. L39–L42.

58. R. McCallen, J. Ross, and F. Browand, *The Aerodynamics of Heavy Vehicles: Trucks, Buses, and Trains*, Springer-Verlag, New York, 2005.

59. J. R. Cruz et al., "Wind Tunnel Testing of Various Disk-Gap-Band Parachutes," AIAA Paper 2003–2129, 17th AIAA Aerodynamic Decelerator Systems Conference, May 2003.

60. B. de Gomars, "Drag of Cones at Zero Incidence," URL http://perso.numericable.fr/fbouquetbe63/gomars/cx_cones.

61. National Highway Traffic Safety Administration, "NHTSA Tire Fuel Efficiency," Report DOT HS 811 154, August 2009.

62. J. F. Cahill, "Summary of Section Data on Trailing-Edge High-Lift Devices," National Advisory Committee for Aeronautics, Report 938, 1949.

Until they reach shallow water and feel the bottom, ocean waves are almost frictionless. Waves are created by winds, especially storms. Long waves—large distances between crests—travel the fastest and decay the slowest. Short waves decay more quickly but are still nearly frictionless. The pictured long waves, breaking on the beach in Narragansett, Rhode Island, might have been formed from a storm off the coast of Africa. The theory of ocean waves [21] is based almost entirely upon frictionless flow. *(Photo courtesy of Ellen Emerson White.)*

Chapter 8
Potential Flow
and Computational
Fluid Dynamics

Motivation. The basic partial differential equations of mass, momentum, and energy were discussed in Chap. 4. A few solutions were then given for incompressible *viscous* flow in Sec. 4.10. The viscous solutions were limited to simple geometries and unidirectional flows, where the difficult nonlinear convective terms were neglected. Potential flows are not limited by such nonlinear terms. Then, in Chap. 7, we found an approximation: patching *boundary layer flows* onto an outer inviscid flow pattern. For more complicated viscous flows, we found no theory or solutions, just experimental data or computer solutions.

The purposes of the present chapter are (1) to explore examples of potential theory and (2) to indicate some flows that can be approximated by computational fluid dynamics (CFD). The combination of these two gives us a good picture of incompressible-flow theory and its relation to experiment. One of the most important applications of potential-flow theory is to aerodynamics and marine hydrodynamics. First, however, we will review and extend the concepts of Chap. 4.

8.1 Introduction and Review

Figure 8.1 reminds us of the problems to be faced. A free stream approaches two closely spaced bodies, creating an "internal" flow between them and "external" flows above and below them. The fronts of the bodies are regions of favorable gradient (decreasing pressure along the surface), and the boundary layers will be attached and thin: Inviscid theory will give excellent results for the outer flow if $Re > 10^4$. For the internal flow between bodies, the boundary layers will grow and eventually meet, and the inviscid core vanishes. Inviscid theory works well in a "short" duct $L/D < 10$, such as the nozzle of a wind tunnel. For longer ducts we must estimate boundary layer growth and be cautious about using inviscid theory.

521

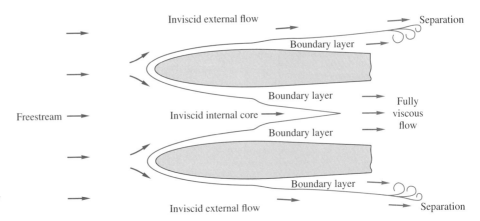

Fig. 8.1 Patching viscous and inviscid flow regions. Potential theory in this chapter does not apply to the boundary layer regions.

For the external flows above and below the bodies in Fig. 8.1, inviscid theory should work well for the outer flows, until the surface pressure gradient becomes adverse (increasing pressure) and the boundary layer separates or stalls. After the separation point, boundary layer theory becomes inaccurate, and the outer flow streamlines are deflected and have a strong interaction with the viscous near-wall regions. The theoretical analysis of separated-flow regions is an active research area at present.

Review of Velocity Potential Concepts

Recall from Sec. 4.9 that if viscous effects are neglected, low-speed flows are irrotational, $\nabla \times \mathbf{V} = 0$, and the velocity potential ϕ exists, such that

$$\mathbf{V} = \nabla\phi \quad \text{or} \quad u = \frac{\partial\phi}{\partial x} \quad v = \frac{\partial\phi}{\partial y} \quad w = \frac{\partial\phi}{\partial z} \tag{8.1}$$

The continuity equation (4.73), $\nabla \cdot \mathbf{V} = 0$, reduces to Laplace's equation for ϕ:

$$\nabla^2\phi = \frac{\partial^2\phi}{\partial x^2} + \frac{\partial^2\phi}{\partial y^2} + \frac{\partial^2\phi}{\partial z^2} = 0 \tag{8.2}$$

and the momentum equation (4.74) reduces to Bernoulli's equation:

$$\frac{\partial\phi}{\partial t} + \frac{p}{\rho} + \frac{1}{2}V^2 + gz = \text{const} \quad \text{where } V = |\nabla\phi| \tag{8.3}$$

Typical boundary conditions are known free-stream conditions

Outer boundaries: Known $\dfrac{\partial\phi}{\partial x}, \dfrac{\partial\phi}{\partial y}, \dfrac{\partial\phi}{\partial z}$ \hfill (8.4)

and no velocity normal to the boundary at the body surface:

Solid surfaces: $\dfrac{\partial\phi}{\partial n} = 0$ where n is perpendicular to body \hfill (8.5)

Unlike the no-slip condition in viscous flow, here there is *no* condition on the tangential surface velocity $V_s = \partial\phi/\partial s$, where s is the coordinate along the surface. This velocity is determined as part of the solution to the problem.

Occasionally the problem involves a free surface, for which the boundary pressure is known and equal to p_a, usually a constant. The Bernoulli equation (8.3) then supplies a relation at the surface between V and the elevation z of the surface. For steady flow,

Free surface: $$V^2 = |\boldsymbol{\nabla}\phi|^2 = \text{const} - 2gz_{\text{surf}} \qquad (8.6)$$

It should be clear to the reader that this use of Laplace's equation, with known values of the derivative of ϕ along the boundaries, is much easier than a direct attack using the fully viscous Navier-Stokes equations. The analysis of Laplace's equation is very well developed and is termed *potential theory,* with whole books written about its application to fluid mechanics [1 to 4]. There are many analytical techniques, including superposition of elementary functions, conformal mapping [4], numerical finite differences [5], numerical finite elements [6], numerical boundary elements [7], and electric or mechanical analogs [8] that are now outdated. Having found $\phi(x, y, z, t)$ from such an analysis, we then compute $\mathbf{V}$ by direct differentiation in Eq. (8.1), after which we compute p from Eq. (8.3). The procedure is quite straightforward, and many interesting albeit idealized results can be obtained. A beautiful collection of computer-generated potential flow sketches is given by Kirchhoff [43].

Review of Stream Function Concepts

Recall from Sec. 4.7 that if a flow is described by only two coordinates, the stream function ψ also exists as an alternate approach. For plane incompressible flow in xy coordinates, the correct form is

$$u = \frac{\partial\psi}{\partial y} \quad v = -\frac{\partial\psi}{\partial x} \qquad (8.7)$$

The condition of irrotationality reduces to Laplace's equation for ψ also:

$$2\omega_z = 0 = \frac{\partial v}{\partial x} - \frac{\partial u}{\partial y} = \frac{\partial}{\partial x}\left(-\frac{\partial\psi}{\partial x}\right) - \frac{\partial}{\partial y}\left(\frac{\partial\psi}{\partial y}\right)$$

or $$\boxed{\frac{\partial^2\psi}{\partial x^2} + \frac{\partial^2\psi}{\partial y^2} = 0} \qquad (8.8)$$

The boundary conditions again are known velocity in the stream and no flow through any solid surface:

Free stream: $$\text{Known } \frac{\partial\psi}{\partial x}, \frac{\partial\psi}{\partial y} \qquad (8.9a)$$

Solid surface: $$\psi_{\text{body}} = \text{const} \qquad (8.9b)$$

Equation (8.9b) is particularly interesting because *any* line of constant ψ in a flow can therefore be interpreted as a body shape and may lead to interesting applications.

For the applications in this chapter, we may compute either ϕ or ψ or both, and the solution will be an *orthogonal flow net* as in Fig. 8.2. Once found, either set of lines may be considered the ϕ lines, and the other set will be the ψ lines. Both sets of lines are laplacian and could be useful.

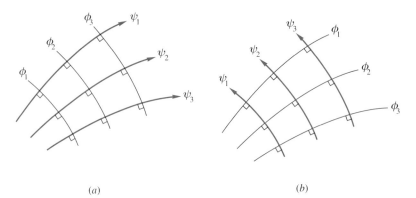

Fig. 8.2 Streamlines and potential lines are orthogonal and may reverse roles if results are useful: (*a*) typical inviscid flow pattern; (*b*) same as (*a*) with roles reversed.

(*a*) (*b*)

Plane Polar Coordinates

Many solutions in this chapter are conveniently expressed in polar coordinates (r, θ). Both the velocity components and the differential relations for ϕ and ψ are then changed, as follows:

$$v_r = \frac{\partial \phi}{\partial r} = \frac{1}{r}\frac{\partial \psi}{\partial \theta} \qquad v_\theta = \frac{1}{r}\frac{\partial \phi}{\partial \theta} = -\frac{\partial \psi}{\partial r} \tag{8.10}$$

Laplace's equation takes the form

$$\frac{1}{r}\frac{\partial}{\partial r}\left(r\frac{\partial \phi}{\partial r} \right) + \frac{1}{r^2}\frac{\partial^2 \phi}{\partial \theta^2} = 0 \tag{8.11}$$

Exactly the same equation holds for the polar-coordinate form of $\psi(r, \theta)$.

An intriguing facet of potential flow with no free surface is that the governing equations (8.2) and (8.8) contain no parameters, nor do the boundary conditions. Therefore, the solutions are purely geometric, depending only on the body shape, the freestream orientation, and—surprisingly—the position of the rear stagnation point.[1] There is no Reynolds, Froude, or Mach number to complicate the dynamic similarity. Inviscid flows are kinematically similar without additional parameters—recall Fig. 5.6a.

8.2 Elementary Plane Flow Solutions

The present chapter is a detailed introductory study of inviscid incompressible flows, especially those that possess both a stream function and a velocity potential. Many solutions make use of the superposition principle, so we begin with the three elementary building blocks illustrated in Fig. 8.3: (*a*) a uniform stream in the *x* direction, (*b*) a line source or sink at the origin, and (*c*) a line vortex at the origin.

Uniform Stream in the *x* Direction

A uniform stream $\mathbf{V} = \mathbf{i}U$, as in Fig. 8.3a, possesses both a stream function and a velocity potential, which may be found as follows:

$$u = U = \frac{\partial \phi}{\partial x} = \frac{\partial \psi}{\partial y} \qquad v = 0 = \frac{\partial \phi}{\partial y} = -\frac{\partial \psi}{\partial x}$$

---

[1]The rear stagnation condition establishes the net amount of "circulation" about the body, giving rise to a lift force. Otherwise the solution could not be unique. See Sec. 8.4.

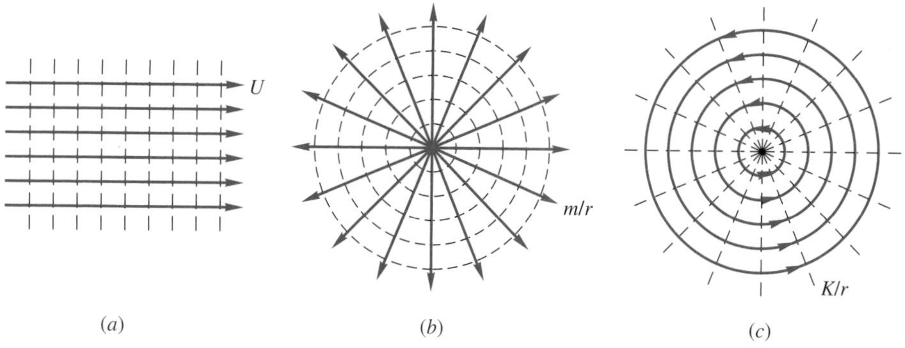

Fig. 8.3 Three elementary plane potential flows. Solid lines are streamlines; dashed lines are potential lines. (*a*) uniform stream; (*b*) line sink; (*c*) line vortex.

We may integrate each expression and discard the constants of integration, which do not affect the velocities in the flow. The results are

Uniform stream $\mathbf{i}U$:
$$\psi = Uy \qquad \phi = Ux \qquad (8.12)$$

The streamlines are horizontal straight lines ($y = $ const), and the potential lines are vertical ($x = $ const)—that is, orthogonal to the streamlines, as expected.

Line Source or Sink at the Origin

Suppose that the z axis were a sort of thin pipe manifold through which fluid issued at total rate Q uniformly along its length b. Looking at the xy plane, we would see a cylindrical radial outflow or *line source,* as sketched in Fig. 8.3*b*. Plane polar coordinates are appropriate (see Fig. 4.2), and there is no circumferential velocity. At any radius r, the velocity is

$$v_r = \frac{Q}{2\pi rb} = \frac{m}{r} = \frac{1}{r}\frac{\partial \psi}{\partial \theta} = \frac{\partial \phi}{\partial r} \qquad v_\theta = 0 = -\frac{\partial \psi}{\partial r} = \frac{1}{r}\frac{\partial \phi}{\partial \theta}$$

where we have used the polar coordinate forms of the stream function and the velocity potential. Integrating and again discarding the constants of integration, we obtain the proper functions for this simple radial flow:

Line source or sink:
$$\psi = m\theta \qquad \phi = m \ln r \qquad (8.13)$$

where $m = Q/(2\pi b)$ is a constant, positive for a source, negative for a sink. As shown in Fig. 8.3*b*, the streamlines are radial spokes (constant θ), and the potential lines are circles (constant r).

Line Irrotational Vortex

A (two-dimensional) line vortex is a purely circulating steady motion, $v_\theta = f(r)$ only, $v_r = 0$. This satisfies the continuity equation identically, as may be checked from Eq. (4.12*b*). We may also note that a variety of velocity distributions $v_\theta(r)$ satisfy the θ momentum equation of a viscous fluid, Eq. (D.6). We may show, as a problem exercise, that only one function $v_\theta(r)$ is *irrotational;* that is, curl $\mathbf{V} = 0$, and $v_\theta = K/r$, where K is a constant. This is sometimes called a *free vortex,* for which the stream function and velocity may be found:

$$v_r = 0 = \frac{1}{r}\frac{\partial \psi}{\partial \theta} = \frac{\partial \phi}{\partial r} \qquad v_\theta = \frac{K}{r} = -\frac{\partial \psi}{\partial r} = \frac{1}{r}\frac{\partial \phi}{\partial \theta}$$

We may again integrate to determine the appropriate functions:

$$\psi = -K \ln r \qquad \phi = K\theta \qquad (8.14)$$

where K is a constant called the *strength* of the vortex. As shown in Fig. 8.3c, the streamlines are circles (constant r), and the potential lines are radial spokes (constant θ). Note the similarity between Eqs. (8.13) and (8.14). A free vortex is a sort of reversed image of a source. The "bathtub vortex," formed when water drains through a bottom hole in a tank, is a good approximation to the free-vortex pattern.

Superposition: Source Plus an Equal Sink

Each of the three elementary flow patterns in Fig. 8.3 is an incompressible irrotational flow and therefore satisfies both plane "potential flow" equations $\nabla^2 \psi = 0$ and $\nabla^2 \phi = 0$. Since these are linear partial differential equations, any *sum* of such basic solutions is also a solution. Some of these composite solutions are quite interesting and useful.

For example, consider a source $+m$ at $(x, y) = (-a, 0)$, combined with a sink of equal strength $-m$, placed at $(+a, 0)$, as in Fig. 8.4. The resulting stream function is simply the sum of the two. In cartesian coordinates,

$$\psi = \psi_{\text{source}} + \psi_{\text{sink}} = m \tan^{-1} \frac{y}{x + a} - m \tan^{-1} \frac{y}{x - a}$$

Similarly, the composite velocity potential is

$$\phi = \phi_{\text{source}} + \phi_{\text{sink}} = \frac{1}{2} m \ln \left[(x + a)^2 + y^2 \right] - \frac{1}{2} m \ln \left[(x - a)^2 + y^2 \right]$$

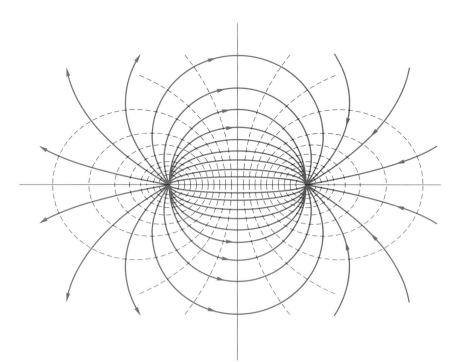

Fig. 8.4 Potential flow due to a line source plus an equal line sink, from Eq. (8.15). Solid lines are streamlines; dashed lines are potential lines.

By using trigonometric and logarithmic identities, these may be simplified to

Source plus sink:
$$\psi = -m \tan^{-1} \frac{2ay}{x^2 + y^2 - a^2}$$

$$\phi = \frac{1}{2} m \ln \frac{(x + a)^2 + y^2}{(x - a)^2 + y^2}$$

(8.15)

These lines are plotted in Fig. 8.4 and are seen to be two families of orthogonal circles, with the streamlines passing through the source and sink and the potential lines encircling them. They are harmonic (laplacian) functions that are exactly analogous in electromagnetic theory to the electric current and electric potential patterns of a magnet with poles at $(\pm a, 0)$.

Sink Plus a Vortex at the Origin

An interesting flow pattern, approximated in nature, occurs by superposition of a sink and a vortex, both centered at the origin. The composite stream function and velocity potential are

Sink plus vortex: $\psi = m\theta - K \ln r$ $\phi = m \ln r + K\theta$ (8.16)

When plotted, these form two orthogonal families of logarithmic spirals, as shown in Fig. 8.5. This is a fairly realistic simulation of a tornado (where the sink flow moves up the z axis into the atmosphere) or a rapidly draining bathtub vortex. At the center of a real (viscous) vortex, where Eq. (8.16) predicts infinite velocity, the actual circulating flow is highly *rotational* and approximates solid-body rotation $v_\theta \approx Cr$.

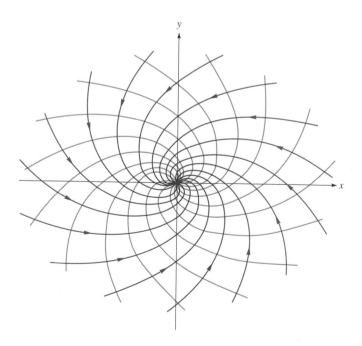

Fig. 8.5 Superposition of a sink plus a vortex, Eq. (8.16), simulates a tornado.

Uniform Stream Plus a Source at the Origin: The Rankine Half-Body

If we superimpose a uniform x-directed stream against an isolated source, a half-body shape appears. If the source is at the origin, the combined stream function is, in polar coordinates,

Uniform stream plus source: $\psi = Ur \sin \theta + m\theta$ (8.17)

We can set this equal to various constants and plot the streamlines, as shown in Fig. 8.6. A curved, roughly elliptical, *half-body* shape appears, which separates the source flow from the stream flow. The body shape, which is named after the Scottish engineer W. J. M. Rankine (1820–1872), is formed by the particular streamlines $\psi = \pm \pi m$. The half-width of the body far downstream is $\pi m/U$. The upper surface may be plotted from the relation

$$r = \frac{m(\pi - \theta)}{U \sin \theta}$$ (8.18)

It is not a true ellipse. The nose of the body, which is a "stagnation" point where $V = 0$, stands at $(x, y) = (-a, 0)$, where $a = m/U$. The streamline $\psi = 0$ also crosses this point—recall that streamlines can cross only at a stagnation point.

The cartesian velocity components are found by differentiation:

$$u = \frac{\partial \psi}{\partial y} = U + \frac{m}{r} \cos \theta \qquad v = -\frac{\partial \psi}{\partial x} = \frac{m}{r} \sin \theta$$ (8.19)

Setting $u = v = 0$, we find a single stagnation point at $\theta = 180°$ and $r = m/U$, or $(x, y) = (-m/U, 0)$, as stated. The resultant velocity at any point is

$$V^2 = u^2 + v^2 = U^2 \left(1 + \frac{a^2}{r^2} + \frac{2a}{r} \cos \theta \right)$$ (8.20)

where we have substituted $m = Ua$. If we evaluate the velocities along the upper surface $\psi = \pi m$, we find a maximum value $U_{s,\max} \approx 1.26U$ at $\theta = 63°$. This point is labeled in Fig. 8.6 and, by Bernoulli's equation, is the point of minimum pressure on the body surface. After this point, the surface flow decelerates, the pressure rises, and the viscous layer grows thicker and more susceptible to "flow separation," as we saw in Chap. 7.

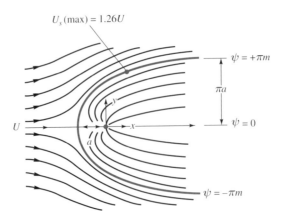

Fig. 8.6 Superposition of a source plus a uniform stream forms a Rankine half-body.

EXAMPLE 8.1

The bottom of a river has a 4-m-high bump that approximates a Rankine half-body, as in Fig. E8.1. The pressure at point B on the bottom is 130 kPa, and the river velocity is 2.5 m/s. Use inviscid theory to estimate the water pressure at point A on the bump, which is 2 m above point B.

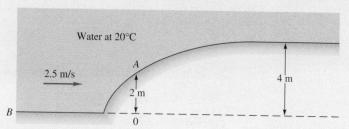

E8.1

Solution

As in all inviscid theories, we ignore the low-velocity boundary layers that form on solid surfaces due to the no-slip condition. From Eq. (8.18) and Fig. 8.6, the downstream bump half-height equals πa. Therefore, for our case, $a = (4 \text{ m})/\pi = 1.27$ m. We have to find the spot where the bump height is half that much, $h = 2 \text{ m} = \pi a/2$. From Eq. (8.18) we may compute

$$r = h_A = \frac{a(\pi - \theta)}{\sin \theta} = \frac{\pi}{2} a \qquad \text{or} \qquad \theta = \frac{\pi}{2} = 90°$$

Thus point A in Fig. E8.1 is directly above the (initially unknown) origin of coordinates (labeled O in Fig. E8.1) and is 1.27 m to the right of the nose of the bump. With $r = \pi a/2$ and $\theta = \pi/2$ known, we compute the velocity at point A from Eq. (8.20):

$$V_A^2 = U^2 \left[1 + \frac{a^2}{(\pi a/2)^2} + \frac{2a}{\pi a/2} \cos \frac{\pi}{2} \right] = 1.405 U^2$$

or $\qquad V_A \approx 1.185 U = 1.185(2.5 \text{ m/s}) = 2.96$ m/s

For water at 20°C, take $\rho = 998 \text{ kg/m}^2$ and $\gamma = 9790 \text{ N/m}^3$. Now, since the velocity and elevation are known at point A, we are in a position to use Bernoulli's inviscid, incompressible flow equation (4.120) to estimate p_A from the known properties at point B (on the same streamline):

$$\frac{p_A}{\gamma} + \frac{V_A^2}{2g} + z_A \approx \frac{p_B}{\gamma} + \frac{V_B^2}{2g} + z_B$$

or $\qquad \dfrac{p_A}{9790 \text{ N/m}^3} + \dfrac{(2.96 \text{ m/s})^2}{2(9.81 \text{ m/s}^2)} + 2 \text{ m} \approx \dfrac{130,000}{9790} + \dfrac{(2.5)^2}{2(9.81)} + 0$

Solving, we find

$$p_A = (13.60 - 2.45)(9790) \approx 109,200 \text{ Pa} \qquad \qquad \textit{Ans.}$$

If the approach velocity is uniform, this should be a pretty good approximation, since water is relatively inviscid and its boundary layers are thin.

Uniform Stream at an Angle α

If the uniform stream is written in plane polar coordinates, it becomes

Uniform stream iU: $\psi = Ur \sin \theta$ $\phi = Ur \cos \theta$ (8.21)

This makes it easier to superimpose, say, a stream and a source or vortex by using the same coordinates. If the uniform stream is moving at angle α with respect to the x axis—that is,

$$u = U \cos \alpha = \frac{\partial \psi}{\partial y} = \frac{\partial \phi}{\partial x} \qquad v = U \sin \alpha = -\frac{\partial \psi}{\partial x} = \frac{\partial \phi}{\partial y}$$

then by integration we obtain the correct functions for flow at an angle:

$$\psi = U(y \cos \alpha - x \sin \alpha) \qquad \phi = U(x \cos \alpha + y \sin \alpha) \qquad (8.22)$$

These expressions are useful in airfoil angle-of-attack problems (Sec. 8.7).

Circulation

The line vortex flow is irrotational everywhere except at the origin, where the vorticity $\nabla \times \mathbf{V}$ is infinite. This means that a certain line integral called the *fluid circulation* Γ does not vanish when taken around a vortex center.

With reference to Fig. 8.7, the circulation is defined as the counterclockwise line integral, around a closed curve C, of arc length ds times the velocity component tangent to the curve:

$$\Gamma = \oint_C V \cos \alpha \, ds = \int_C \mathbf{V} \cdot ds = \int_C (u \, dx + v \, dy + w \, dz) \qquad (8.23)$$

From the definition of ϕ, $\mathbf{V} \cdot ds = \nabla\phi \cdot ds = d\phi$ for an irrotational flow; hence normally Γ in an irrotational flow would equal the final value of ϕ minus the initial value of ϕ. Since we start and end at the same point, we compute $\Gamma = 0$, but not for vortex flow: With $\phi = K\theta$ from Eq. (8.14) there is a change in ϕ of amount $2\pi K$ as we make one complete circle:

Path enclosing a vortex: $\Gamma = 2\pi K$ (8.24)

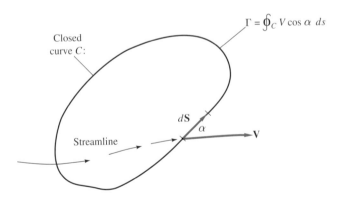

Fig. 8.7 Definition of the fluid circulation Γ.

Alternatively the calculation can be made by defining a circular path of radius r around the vortex center, from Eq. (8.23):

$$\Gamma = \int_C v_\theta \, ds = \int_0^{2\pi} \frac{K}{r} r \, d\theta = 2\pi K$$

In general, Γ denotes the net algebraic strength of all the vortex filaments contained within the closed curve. In the next section we shall see that a region of finite circulation within a flowing stream will be subjected to a lift force proportional to both U_∞ and Γ.

One can show, by using Eq. (8.23), that a source or sink creates no circulation. If there are no vortices present, the circulation will be zero for any path enclosing any number of sources and sinks.

8.3 Superposition of Plane Flow Solutions

We can now form a variety of interesting potential flows by summing the velocity potential and stream functions of a uniform stream, source or sink, and vortex. Most of the results are classic, of course, needing only a brief treatment here. Superposition is valid because the basic equations, (8.2) and (8.8), are linear.

Graphical Method of Superposition

A simple means of accomplishing $\psi_{tot} = \Sigma \, \psi_i$ graphically is to plot the individual stream functions separately and then look at their intersections. The value of ψ_{tot} at each intersection is the sum of the individual values ψ_i that cross there. Connecting intersections with the same value of ψ_{tot} creates the desired superimposed flow streamlines.

A simple example is shown in Fig. 8.8, summing two families of streamlines ψ_a and ψ_b. The individual components are plotted separately, and four typical intersections are shown. Dashed lines are then drawn through intersections representing the same sum of $\psi_a + \psi_b$. These dashed lines are the desired solution. Often this graphical method is a quick means of evaluating the proposed superposition before a full-blown numerical plot routine is executed.

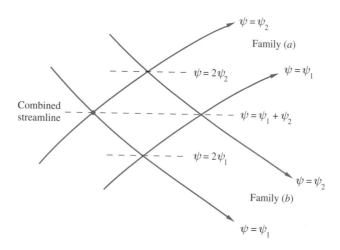

Fig. 8.8 Intersections of elementary streamlines can be joined to form a combined streamline.

Boundary Layer Separation on a Half-Body

Although the inviscid flow patterns seen in Figs. 8.9a and c are mirror images, their viscous (boundary layer) behavior is different. The body shape and the velocity along the surface are

$$V^2 = U_\infty^2 \left(1 + \frac{a^2}{r^2} + \frac{2a}{r} \cos \theta \right) \quad \text{along} \quad r = \frac{m(\pi - \theta)}{U_\infty \sin \theta} \quad (8.25)$$

The computed surface velocities are plotted along the half-body contours in Fig. 8.9b and d as a function of arc length s/a measured from the stagnation point. These plots are also mirror images. However, if the nose is in front, Fig. 8.9b, the pressure gradient there is *favorable* (decreasing pressure along the surface). In contrast, the pressure gradient is *adverse* (increasing pressure along the surface) when the nose is in the rear, Fig. 8.9d, and boundary layer separation may occur.

Application to Fig. 8.9b of Thwaites's laminar boundary method from Eqs. (7.54) and (7.56) reveals that separation does not occur on the front nose of the half-body. Therefore, Fig. 8.9a is a very realistic picture of streamlines past a half-body nose. In contrast, when applied to the tail, Fig. 8.9c, Thwaites's method predicts separation at about $s/a \approx -2.2$, or $\theta \approx 110°$. Thus, if a half-body is a solid surface, Fig. 8.9c is *not* realistic and a broad separated wake will form. However, if the half-body tail is a *fluid line* separating the sink-directed flow from the outer stream, as in Example 8.2, then Fig. 8.9c is quite realistic and useful. Computations for turbulent boundary layer theory would be similar: separation on the tail, no separation on the nose.

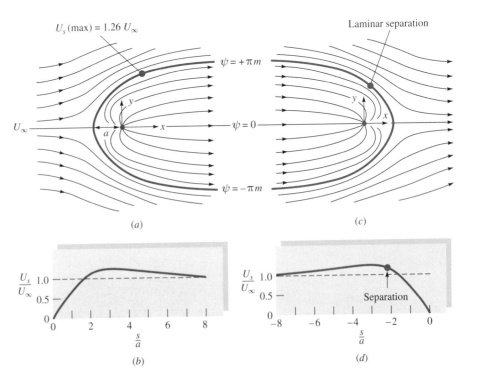

Fig. 8.9 The Rankine half-body; pattern (c) is not found in a real fluid because of boundary layer separation. (a) Uniform stream plus a source equals a half-body; stagnation point at $x = -a = -m/U_\infty$. (b) Slight adverse gradient for s/a greater than 3.0: no separation. (c) Uniform stream plus a sink equals the rear of a half-body; stagnation point at $x = a = m/U_\infty$. (d) Strong adverse gradient for $s/a > -3.0$: separation.

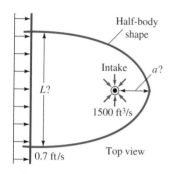

E8.2

EXAMPLE 8.2

An offshore power plant cooling-water intake sucks in 1500 ft³/s in water 30 ft deep, as in Fig. E8.2. If the tidal velocity approaching the intake is 0.7 ft/s, (a) how far downstream does the intake effect extend and (b) how much width L of tidal flow is entrained into the intake?

Solution

Recall from Eq. (8.13) that the sink strength m is related to the volume flow Q and the depth b into the paper:

$$m = \frac{Q}{2\pi b} = \frac{1500 \text{ ft}^3/\text{s}}{2\pi(30 \text{ ft})} = 7.96 \text{ ft}^2/\text{s}$$

Therefore from Fig. 8.9 the desired lengths a and L are

$$a = \frac{m}{U_\infty} = \frac{7.96 \text{ ft}^2/\text{s}}{0.7 \text{ ft/s}} = 11.4 \text{ ft} \qquad \textit{Ans. (a)}$$

$$L = 2\pi a = 2\pi(11.4 \text{ ft}) = 71 \text{ ft} \qquad \textit{Ans. (b)}$$

Flow Past a Vortex

Consider a uniform stream U_∞ in the x direction flowing past a vortex of strength K with center at the origin. By superposition the combined stream function is

$$\psi = \psi_{\text{stream}} + \psi_{\text{vortex}} = U_\infty r \sin\theta - K \ln r \qquad (8.26)$$

The velocity components are given by

$$v_r = \frac{1}{r}\frac{\partial\psi}{\partial\theta} = U_\infty \cos\theta \qquad v_\theta = -\frac{\partial\psi}{\partial r} = -U_\infty \sin\theta + \frac{K}{r} \qquad (8.27)$$

The streamlines are plotted in Fig. 8.10 by the graphical method, intersecting the circular streamlines of the vortex with the horizontal lines of the uniform stream.

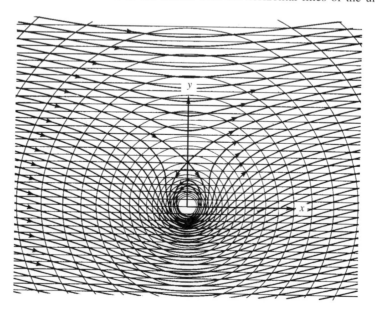

Fig. 8.10 Flow of a uniform stream past a vortex constructed by the graphical method.

By setting $v_r = v_\theta = 0$ from (8.27) we find a stagnation point at $\theta = 90°$, $r = a = K/U_\infty$, or $(x, y) = (0, a)$. This is where the counterclockwise vortex velocity K/r exactly cancels the stream velocity U_∞.

Probably the most interesting thing about this example is that there is a nonzero lift force normal to the stream on the surface of any region enclosing the vortex, but we postpone this discussion until the next section.

An Infinite Row of Vortices

Consider an infinite row of vortices of equal strength K and equal spacing a, as in Fig. 8.11a. This case is included here to illustrate the interesting concept of a *vortex sheet*.

From Eq. (8.14), the ith vortex in Fig. 8.11a has a stream function $\psi_i = -K \ln r_i$, so that the total infinite row has a combined stream function

$$\psi = -K \sum_{i=1}^{\infty} \ln r_i$$

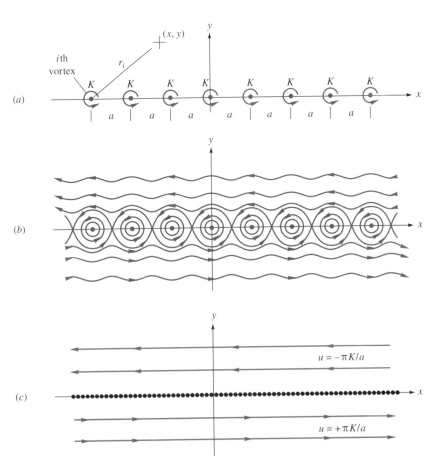

Fig. 8.11 Superposition of vortices: (*a*) an infinite row of equal strength; (*b*) streamline pattern for part (*a*); (*c*) vortex sheet: part (*b*) viewed from afar.

It can be shown [2, Sec. 4.51] that this infinite sum of logarithms is equivalent to a closed-form function:

$$\psi = -\tfrac{1}{2}K \ln\left[\frac{1}{2}\left(\cosh\frac{2\pi y}{a} - \cos\frac{2\pi x}{a}\right)\right] \tag{8.28}$$

Since the proof uses the complex variable $z = x + iy$, $i = (-1)^{1/2}$, we are not going to show the details here.

The streamlines from Eq. (8.28) are plotted in Fig. 8.11b, showing what is called a *cat's-eye* pattern of enclosed flow cells surrounding the individual vortices. Above the cat's eyes the flow is entirely to the left, and below the cat's eyes the flow is to the right. Moreover, these left and right flows are uniform if $|y| \gg a$, which follows by differentiating Eq. (8.28):

$$u = \left.\frac{\partial\psi}{\partial y}\right|_{|y|\gg a} = \pm\frac{\pi K}{a}$$

where the plus sign applies below the row and the minus sign above the row. This uniform left and right streaming is sketched in Fig. 8.11c. We stress that this effect is induced by the row of vortices: There is no uniform stream approaching the row in this example.

The Vortex Sheet

When Fig. 8.11b is viewed from afar, the streaming motion is uniform left above and uniform right below, as in Fig. 8.11c, and the vortices are packed so closely together that they are smudged into a continuous *vortex sheet*. The strength of the sheet is defined as

$$\gamma = \frac{2\pi K}{a} \tag{8.29}$$

and in the general case γ can vary with x. The circulation about any closed curve that encloses a short length dx of the sheet would be, from Eqs. (8.23) and (8.29),

$$d\Gamma = u_l\, dx - u_u\, dx = (u_l - u_u)\, dx = \frac{2\pi K}{a}\, dx = \gamma\, dx \tag{8.30}$$

where the subscripts l and u stand for lower and upper, respectively. Thus the sheet strength $\gamma = d\Gamma/dx$ is the circulation per unit length of the sheet. Thus when a vortex sheet is immersed in a uniform stream, γ is proportional to the lift per unit length of any surface enclosing the sheet.

Note that there is no velocity normal to the sheet at the sheet surface. Therefore a vortex sheet can simulate a thin-body shape, like a plate or thin airfoil. This is the basis of the thin airfoil theory mentioned in Sec. 8.7.

The Doublet

As we move far away from the source–sink pair of Fig. 8.4, the flow pattern begins to resemble a family of circles tangent to the origin, as in Fig. 8.12. This limit of vanishingly small distance a is called a *doublet*. To keep the flow strength large enough to exhibit decent velocities as a becomes small, we specify that the product

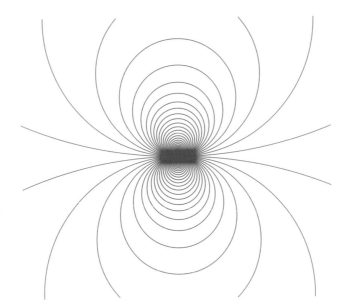

Fig. 8.12 A doublet, or source–sink pair, is the limiting case of Fig. 8.4 viewed from afar. Streamlines are circles tangent to the *x* axis at the origin. This figure was prepared using the *contour* feature of MATLAB [34, 35].

2*am* remain constant. Let us call this constant λ. Then the stream function of a doublet is

$$\psi = \lim_{\substack{a \to 0 \\ 2am = \lambda}} \left(-m \tan^{-1} \frac{2ay}{x^2 + y^2 - a^2} \right) = -\frac{2amy}{x^2 + y^2} = -\frac{\lambda y}{x^2 + y^2} \qquad (8.31)$$

We have used the fact that $\tan^{-1} \alpha \approx \alpha$ as α becomes small. The quantity λ is called the *strength* of the doublet.

Equation (8.31) can be rearranged to yield

$$x^2 + \left(y + \frac{\lambda}{2\psi} \right)^2 = \left(\frac{\lambda}{2\psi} \right)^2$$

so that, as advertised, the streamlines are circles tangent to the origin with centers on the *y* axis. This pattern is sketched in Fig. 8.12.

Although the author has in the past laboriously sketched streamlines by hand, this is no longer necessary. Figure 8.12 was computer-drawn, using the *contour* feature of the student version of MATLAB [34]. Simply set up a grid of points, spell out the stream function, and call for a contour. For Fig. 8.12, the actual statements were

    [X, Y] = meshgrid (−1 : .02 : 1);

    PSI = −Y. / (X. ^2 + Y. ^2);

    contour (X, Y, PSI, 100)

This would produce 100 contour lines of ψ from Eq. (8.31), with $\lambda = 1$ for convenience. The plot would include grid lines, scale markings, and a surrounding box, and the circles might look a bit elliptical. These blemishes can be eliminated with three statements of cosmetic improvement:

    axis square

    grid off

    axis off

The final plot, Fig. 8.12, has no markings but the streamlines themselves. MATLAB is thus a recommended tool and, in addition, has scores of other uses. All this chapter's problem assignments that call for "sketch the streamlines/potential lines" can be completed using this contour feature. For further details, consult Ref. 34.

In a similar manner the velocity potential of a doublet is found by taking the limit of Eq. (8.15) as $a \rightarrow 0$ and $2am = \lambda$:

$$\phi_{\text{doublet}} = \frac{\lambda x}{x^2 + y^2}$$

or
$$\left(x - \frac{\lambda}{2\phi} \right)^2 + y^2 = \left(\frac{\lambda}{2\phi} \right)^2 \tag{8.32}$$

The potential lines are circles tangent to the origin with centers on the x axis. Simply turn Fig. 8.12 clockwise $90°$ to visualize the ϕ lines, which are everywhere normal to the streamlines.

The doublet functions can also be written in polar coordinates:

$$\psi = -\frac{\lambda \sin \theta}{r} \qquad \phi = \frac{\lambda \cos \theta}{r} \tag{8.33}$$

These forms are convenient for the cylinder flows of the next section.

8.4 Plane Flow Past Closed-Body Shapes

A variety of closed-body external flows can be constructed by superimposing a uniform stream with sources, sinks, and vortices. The body shape will be closed only if the net source outflow equals the net sink inflow.

The Rankine Oval

A cylindrical shape called a *Rankine oval*, which is long compared with its height, is formed by a source–sink pair aligned parallel to a uniform stream, as in Fig. 8.13a.

From Eqs. (8.12) and (8.15) the combined stream function is

$$\psi = U_\infty y - m \tan^{-1} \frac{2ay}{x^2 + y^2 - a^2} = U_\infty r \sin \theta + m(\theta_1 - \theta_2) \tag{8.34}$$

When streamlines of constant ψ are plotted from Eq. (8.34), an oval body shape appears, as in Fig. 8.13b. The half-length L and half-height h of the oval depend on the relative strength of source and stream—that is, the ratio $m/(U_\infty a)$, which equals 1.0 in Fig. 8.13b. The circulating streamlines inside the oval are uninteresting and not usually shown. The oval is the line $\psi = 0$.

There are stagnation points at the front and rear, $x = \pm L$, and points of maximum velocity and minimum pressure at the shoulders, $y = \pm h$, of the oval. All these

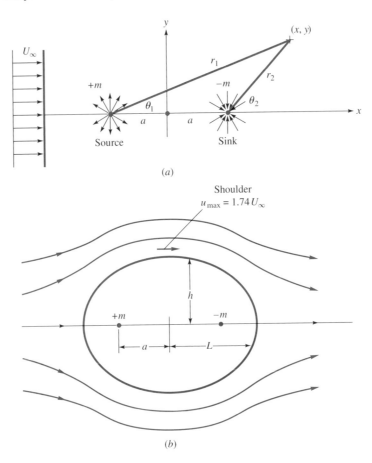

Fig. 8.13 Flow past a Rankine oval: (*a*) uniform stream plus a source–sink pair; (*b*) oval shape and streamlines for $m/(U_\infty a) = 1.0$.

parameters are a function of the basic dimensionless parameter $m/(U_\infty a)$, which we can determine from Eq. (8.34):

$$\frac{h}{a} = \cot\frac{h/a}{2m/(U_\infty a)} \qquad \frac{L}{a} = \left(1 + \frac{2m}{U_\infty a}\right)^{1/2}$$

$$\frac{u_{max}}{U_\infty} = 1 + \frac{2m/(U_\infty a)}{1 + h^2/a^2}$$

(8.35)

As we increase $m/(U_\infty a)$ from zero to large values, the oval shape increases in size and thickness from a flat plate of length $2a$ to a huge, nearly circular cylinder. This is shown in Table 8.1. In the limit as $m/(U_\infty a) \to \infty$, $L/h \to 1.0$ and $u_{max}/U_\infty \to 2.0$, which is equivalent to flow past a circular cylinder.

All the Rankine ovals except very thin ones have a large adverse pressure gradient on their leeward surface. Thus boundary layer separation will occur in the rear with a broad wake flow, and the inviscid pattern is unrealistic in that region.

Flow Past a Circular Cylinder with Circulation

From Table 8.1 at large source strength the Rankine oval becomes a large circle, much greater in diameter than the source–sink spacing $2a$. Viewed on the scale of the

Table 8.1 Rankine Oval Parameters from Eq. (8.30)

$m/(U_\infty a)$	h/a	L/a	L/h	u_{max}/U_∞
0.0	0.0	1.0	∞	1.0
0.01	0.031	1.010	32.79	1.020
0.1	0.263	1.095	4.169	1.187
1.0	1.307	1.732	1.326	1.739
10.0	4.435	4.583	1.033	1.968
100.0	14.130	14.177	1.003	1.997
∞	∞	∞	1.000	2.000

cylinder, this is equivalent to a uniform stream plus a doublet. We also throw in a vortex at the doublet center, which does not change the shape of the cylinder.

Thus the stream function for flow past a circular cylinder with circulation, centered at the origin, is a uniform stream plus a doublet plus a vortex:

$$\psi = U_\infty r \sin \theta - \frac{\lambda \sin \theta}{r} - K \ln r + \text{const} \tag{8.36}$$

The doublet strength λ has units of velocity times length squared. For convenience, let $\lambda = U_\infty a^2$, where a is a length, and let the arbitrary constant in Eq. (8.36) equal $K \ln a$. Then the stream function becomes

$$\psi = U_\infty \sin \theta \left(r - \frac{a^2}{r} \right) - K \ln \frac{r}{a} \tag{8.37}$$

The streamlines are plotted in Fig. 8.14 for four different values of the dimensionless vortex strength $K/(U_\infty a)$. For all cases the line $\psi = 0$ corresponds to the circle $r = a$—that is, the shape of the cylindrical body. As circulation $\Gamma = 2\pi K$ increases, the velocity becomes faster and faster below the cylinder and slower and slower above it. The velocity components in the flow are given by

$$v_r = \frac{1}{r} \frac{\partial \psi}{\partial \theta} = U_\infty \cos \theta \left(1 - \frac{a^2}{r^2} \right)$$

$$v_\theta = -\frac{\partial \psi}{\partial r} = -U_\infty \sin \theta \left(1 + \frac{a^2}{r^2} \right) + \frac{K}{r} \tag{8.38}$$

The velocity at the cylinder surface $r = a$ is purely tangential, as expected:

$$v_r(r = a) = 0 \quad v_\theta(r = a) = -2U_\infty \sin \theta + \frac{K}{a} \tag{8.39}$$

For small K, two stagnation points appear on the surface at angles θ_s where $v_\theta = 0$; or, from Eq. (8.39),

$$\sin \theta_s = \frac{K}{2U_\infty a} \tag{8.40}$$

Figure 8.14a is for $K = 0$, $\theta_s = 0$ and 180°, or doubly symmetric inviscid flow past a cylinder with no circulation. Figure 8.14b is for $K/(U_\infty a) = 1$, $\theta_s = 30$ and 150°; and Fig. 8.14c is the limiting case where the two stagnation points meet at the top, $K/(U_\infty a) = 2$, $\theta_s = 90°$.

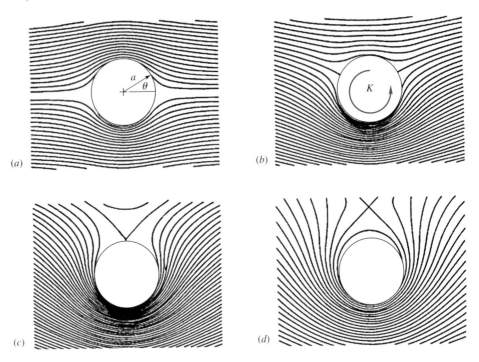

Fig. 8.14 Flow past a circular cylinder with circulation for values of $K/(U_\infty a)$ of (a) 0, (b) 1.0, (c) 2.0, and (d) 3.0.

For $K > 2U_\infty a$, Eq. (8.40) is invalid, and the single stagnation point is above the cylinder, as in Fig. 8.14d, at a point $y = h$ given by

$$\frac{h}{a} = \frac{1}{2}[\beta + (\beta^2 - 4)^{1/2}] \qquad \beta = \frac{K}{U_\infty a} > 2$$

In Fig. 8.14d, $K/(U_\infty a) = 3.0$, and $h/a = 2.6$.

The Kutta-Joukowski Lift Theorem

The cylinder flows with circulation, Figs. 8.14b to d, develop an inviscid downward *lift* normal to the free stream, called the *Magnus-Robins force*. This lift is proportional to stream velocity and vortex strength. Its discovery, by experiment, has long been attributed to the German physicist Gustav Magnus, who observed it in 1853. It is now known [40, 45] that the brilliant British engineer Benjamin Robins first reported a lift force on a spinning body in 1761. We see from the streamline patterns that the velocity on top of the cylinder is less, and, thus, from Bernoulli's equation, the pressure is higher. On the bottom, we see tightly packed streamlines, high velocity, and low pressure; viscosity is neglected. Inviscid theory predicts this force.

The surface velocity is given by Eq. (8.39). From Bernoulli's equation (8.3), neglecting gravity, the surface pressure p_s is given by

$$p_\infty + \frac{1}{2}\rho U_\infty^2 = p_s + \frac{1}{2}\rho\left(-2U_\infty \sin\theta + \frac{K}{a}\right)^2$$

or

$$p_s = p_\infty + \tfrac{1}{2}\rho U_\infty^2(1 - 4\sin^2\theta + 4\beta\sin\theta - \beta^2) \qquad (8.41)$$

where $\beta = K/(U_\infty a)$ and p_∞ is the free-stream pressure. If b is the cylinder depth into the paper, the drag D is the integral over the surface of the horizontal component of pressure force:

$$D = -\int_0^{2\pi} (p_s - p_\infty) \cos \theta \, ba \, d\theta$$

where $p_s - p_\infty$ is substituted from Eq. (8.41). But the integral of $\cos \theta$ times any power of $\sin \theta$ over a full cycle 2π is identically zero. Thus we obtain the (perhaps surprising) result

$$D(\text{cylinder with circulation}) = 0 \qquad (8.42)$$

This is a special case of d'Alembert's paradox, mentioned in Sec. 1.2:

> According to inviscid theory, the drag of any body of any shape immersed in a uniform stream is identically zero.

D'Alembert published this result in 1752 and pointed out himself that it did not square with the facts for real fluid flows. This unfortunate paradox caused everyone to over-react and reject all inviscid theory until 1904, when Prandtl first pointed out the profound effect of the thin viscous boundary layer on the flow pattern in the rear, as in Fig. 7.2b, for example.

The lift force L normal to the stream, taken positive upward, is given by summation of vertical pressure forces:

$$L = -\int_0^{2\pi} (p_s - p_\infty) \sin \theta \, ba \, d\theta$$

Since the integral over 2π of any odd power of $\sin \theta$ is zero, only the third term in the parentheses in Eq. (8.41) contributes to the lift:

$$L = -\frac{1}{2} \rho U_\infty^2 \frac{4K}{aU_\infty} ba \int_0^{2\pi} \sin^2 \theta \, d\theta = -\rho U_\infty (2\pi K) b$$

or

$$\boxed{\frac{L}{b} = -\rho U_\infty \Gamma} \qquad (8.43)$$

Notice that the lift seems independent of the radius a of the cylinder. Actually, though, as we shall see in Sec. 8.7, the circulation Γ depends on the body size and orientation through a physical requirement.

Equation (8.43) was generalized by W. M. Kutta in 1902 and independently by N. Joukowski in 1906 as follows:

> According to inviscid theory, the lift per unit depth of any cylinder of any shape immersed in a uniform stream equals $\rho u_\infty \Gamma$, where Γ is the total net circulation contained within the body shape. The direction of the lift is 90° from the stream direction, rotating opposite to the circulation.

The problem in airfoil analysis, Sec. 8.7, is thus to determine the circulation Γ as a function of airfoil shape and orientation.

Lift and Drag of Rotating Cylinders[2]

The flows in Fig. 8.14 are mathematical: a doublet plus a vortex plus a uniform stream. The physical realization could be a rotating cylinder in a free stream. The no-slip condition would cause the fluid in contact with the cylinder to move tangentially at velocity $v_\theta = a\omega$, setting up a net circulation Γ. Measurement of forces on a spinning cylinder is very difficult, and no reliable drag data are known to the author. However, Tokumaru and Dimotakis [22] used a clever auxiliary scheme to measure lift forces at $Re_D = 3800$.

Figure 8.15 shows lift and drag coefficients, based on frontal area ($2ab$), for a rotating cylinder at $Re_D = 3800$. The drag curve is from CFD calculations [41]. Reported CFD drag results, from several different authors, are quite controversial because they do not agree, even qualitatively. The writer feels that Ref. 41 gives the most reliable results. Note that the experimental C_L increases to a value of 15.3 at $a\omega/U_\infty = 10$. This contradicts an early theory of Prandtl, in 1926, that the maximum possible value of C_L would be $4\pi \approx 12.6$, corresponding to the flow conditions in Fig. 8.14c. The inviscid theory for lift would be:

$$C_L = \frac{L}{\frac{1}{2}\rho U_\infty^2 (2ba)} = \frac{2\pi\rho U_\infty K b}{\rho U_\infty^2 ba} = \frac{2\pi v_{\theta s}}{U_\infty} \tag{8.44}$$

where $v_{\theta s} = K/a$ is the peripheral speed of the cylinder.

Figure 8.15 shows that the theoretical lift from Eq. (8.44) is much too high, but the measured lift is quite respectable, much larger in fact than a typical airfoil of the same chord length, as in Fig. 7.25. Thus rotating cylinders have practical possibilities. The Flettner rotor ship built in Germany in 1924 employed rotating vertical cylinders that developed a thrust due to any winds blowing past the ship. The Flettner design did not gain any popularity, but such inventions may be more attractive in this era of high energy costs.

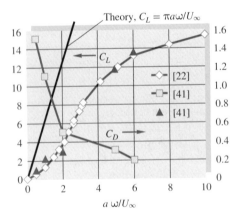

Fig. 8.15 Drag and lift of a rotating cylinder of large aspect ratio at $Re_D = 3800$, after Tokumaru and Dimotakis [22] and Sengupta et al. [41].

---

[2]The writer is indebted to Prof. T. K. Sengupta of I.I.T. Kanpur for data and discussion for this subsection.

EXAMPLE 8.3

The experimental Flettner rotor sailboat at the University of Rhode Island is shown in Fig. E8.3. The rotor is 2.5 ft in diameter and 10 ft long and rotates at 220 r/min. It is driven by a small lawnmower engine. If the wind is a steady 10 kn and boat relative motion is neglected, what is the maximum thrust expected for the rotor? Assume standard air and water density.

Solution

Convert the rotation rate to $\omega = 2\pi(220)/60 = 23.04$ rad/s. The wind velocity is 10 kn = 16.88 ft/s, so the velocity ratio is

$$\frac{a\omega}{U_\infty} = \frac{(1.25 \text{ ft})(23.04 \text{ rad/s})}{16.88 \text{ ft/s}} = 1.71$$

Using Fig. 8.15, we read $C_D \approx 0.7$ and $C_L \approx 2.5$. From Table A.6, standard air density in BG units is 0.00238 slug/ft^3. Then the estimated rotor lift and drag are

$$L = C_L \frac{1}{2} \rho U_\infty^2\, 2ba = (2.5)\frac{1}{2}\left(0.00238\,\frac{\text{slug}}{\text{ft}^3}\right)\left(16.88\,\frac{\text{ft}}{\text{s}}\right)^2 2(10 \text{ ft})(1.25 \text{ ft}) = 21.2 \text{ lbf}$$

$$D = C_D \frac{1}{2} \rho U_\infty^2\, 2ba = (0.7)\frac{1}{2}\left(0.00238\,\frac{\text{slug}}{\text{ft}^3}\right)\left(16.88\,\frac{\text{ft}}{\text{s}}\right)^2 2(10 \text{ ft})(1.25 \text{ ft}) = 5.9 \text{ lbf}$$

The maximum thrust available to the sailboat is the resultant of these two:

$$F = [(21.2)^2 + (5.9)^2] = 22.0 \text{ lbf} \qquad \textit{Ans.}$$

Note that water density did not enter into this calculation, which is a force due to *air*. If aligned along the boat's keel, this thrust will drive the boat through the water at a speed of about 4 kn.

E8.3   *(Courtesy of R. C. Lessmann, University of Rhode Island.)*

Comment: For the sake of a numerical example, we have done something improper here. We have used data for $Re_D = 3800$ to estimate forces when the rotor $Re_D \approx 260{,}000$. Do not do this in your real job after you graduate!

The Kelvin Oval

A family of body shapes taller than they are wide can be formed by letting a uniform stream flow normal to a vortex pair. If U_∞ is to the right, the negative vortex $-K$ is placed at $y = +a$ and the counterclockwise vortex $+K$ placed at $y = -a$, as in Fig. 8.16. The combined stream function is

$$\psi = U_\infty y - \frac{1}{2} K \ln \frac{x^2 + (y + a)^2}{x^2 + (y - a)^2} \tag{8.45}$$

The body shape is the line $\psi = 0$, and some of these shapes are shown in Fig. 8.16. For $K/(U_\infty a) > 10$ the shape is within 1 percent of a Rankine oval (Fig. 8.13) turned 90°, but for small $K/(U_\infty a)$ the waist becomes pinched in, and a figure-eight shape occurs at 0.5. For $K/(U_\infty a) < 0.5$ the stream blasts right between the vortices and isolates two more or less circular body shapes, one surrounding each vortex.

A closed body of practically any shape can be constructed by proper superposition of sources, sinks, and vortices. See the advanced work in Refs. 1 to 3 for further details. A summary of elementary potential flows is given in Table 8.2.

Potential Flow Analogs

For complicated potential flow geometries, one can resort to other methods than superposition of sources, sinks, and vortices. A variety of devices simulate solutions to Laplace's equation.

From 1897 to 1900 Hele-Shaw [9] developed a technique whereby laminar flow between very closely spaced parallel plates simulated potential flow when viewed

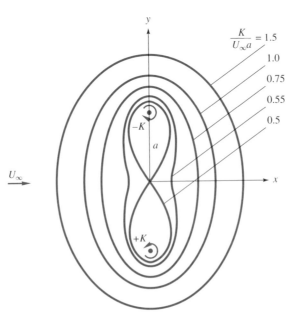

Fig. 8.16 Kelvin oval body shapes as a function of the vortex strength parameter $K/(U_\infty a)$; outer streamlines not shown.

Table 8.2 Summary of Plane Incompressible Potential Flows

Type of flow	Potential functions		Remarks
Stream iU	$\psi = Uy$	$\phi = Ux$	See Fig. 8.3a
Line source ($m > 0$) or sink ($m < 0$)	$\psi = m\theta$	$\phi = m \ln r$	See Fig. 8.3b
Line vortex	$\psi = -K \ln r$	$\phi = K\theta$	See Fig. 8.3c
Half-body	$\psi = Ur \sin \theta + m\theta$		
	$\phi = Ur \cos \theta + m \ln r$		See Fig. 8.9
Doublet	$\psi = \dfrac{-\lambda \sin \theta}{r}$	$\phi = \dfrac{\lambda \cos \theta}{r}$	See Fig. 8.12
Rankine oval	$\psi = Ur \sin \theta + m(\theta_1 - \theta_2)$		See Fig. 8.13
Cylinder with circulation	$\psi = U \sin \theta \left(r - \dfrac{a^2}{r} \right) - K \ln \dfrac{r}{a}$		See Fig. 8.14

from above the plates. Obstructions simulate body shapes, and dye streaks represent the streamlines. The Hele-Shaw apparatus makes an excellent laboratory demonstration of potential flow [10, pp. 197–198, 219–220]. Figure 8.17a illustrates Hele-Shaw (potential) flow through an array of cylinders, a flow pattern that would be difficult to analyze just using Laplace's equation. However beautiful this array pattern may be, it is not a good approximation to real (laminar viscous) array flow. Figure 8.17b shows experimental streakline patterns for a similar staggered-array flow at Re ≈ 6400. We see that the interacting wakes of the real flow (Fig. 8.17b) cause intensive mixing and transverse motion, not the smooth streaming passage of the potential flow model (Fig. 8.17a). The moral is that this is an internal flow with multiple bodies and, therefore, not a good candidate for a realistic potential flow model.

Other flow-mapping techniques are discussed in Ref. 8. Electromagnetic fields also satisfy Laplace's equation, with voltage analogous to velocity potential and current lines analogous to streamlines. At one time commercial analog field plotters were available, using thin conducting paper cut to the shape of the flow geometry. Potential lines (voltage contours) were plotted by probing the paper with a potentiometer pointer. Hand-sketching "curvilinear square" techniques were also popular. The availability and the simplicity of computer potential flow methods [5 to 7] have made analog models obsolete.

EXAMPLE 8.4

A Kelvin oval from Fig. 8.16 has $K/(U_\infty a) = 1.0$. Compute the velocity at the top shoulder of the oval in terms of U_∞.

Solution

We must locate the shoulder $y = h$ from Eq. (8.45) for $\psi = 0$ and then compute the velocity by differentiation. At $\psi = 0$ and $y = h$ and $x = 0$, Eq. (8.45) becomes

$$\frac{h}{a} = \frac{K}{U_\infty a} \ln \frac{h/a + 1}{h/a - 1}$$

With $K/(U_\infty a) = 1.0$ and the initial guess $h/a \approx 1.5$ from Fig. 8.16, we iterate and find the location $h/a = 1.5434$.

By inspection $v = 0$ at the shoulder because the streamline is horizontal. Therefore the shoulder velocity is, from Eq. (8.45),

$$u \bigg|_{y=h} = \frac{\partial \psi}{\partial y} \bigg|_{y=h} = U_\infty + \frac{K}{h-a} - \frac{K}{h+a}$$

Introducing $K = U_\infty a$ and $h = 1.5434a$, we obtain

$$u_{\text{shoulder}} = U_\infty(1.0 + 1.84 - 0.39) = 2.45U_\infty \qquad\qquad Ans.$$

Because they are short-waisted compared with a circular cylinder, all the Kelvin ovals have shoulder velocity greater than the cylinder result $2.0U_\infty$ from Eq. (8.39).

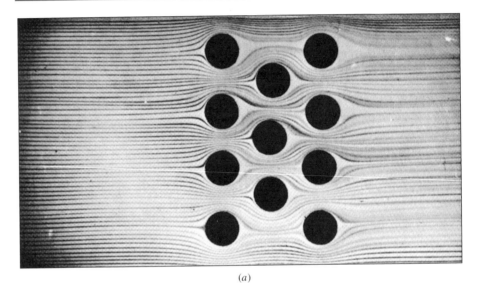

(a)

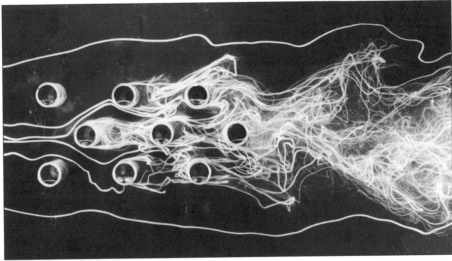

Fig. 8.17 Flow past a staggered array of cylinders: (a) potential flow model using the Hele-Shaw apparatus *(TQ Education and Training Ltd.)*; (b) experimental streaklines for actual staggered-array flow at $\text{Re}_D \approx 6400$. *(From Ref. 36, Courtesy of Jack Hoyt, with the permission of the American Society of Mechanical Engineers.)*

(b)

8.5 Other Plane Potential Flows[3]

References 2 to 4 treat many other potential flows of interest in addition to the cases presented in Secs. 8.3 and 8.4. In principle, any plane potential flow can be solved by the method of *conformal mapping,* by using the complex variable

$$z = x + iy \quad i = (-1)^{1/2}$$

It turns out that any arbitrary analytic function of this complex variable z has the remarkable property that both its real and its imaginary parts are solutions of Laplace's equation. If

$$f(z) = f(x + iy) = f_1(x, y) + i f_2(x, y)$$

then
$$\frac{\partial^2 f_1}{\partial x^2} + \frac{\partial^2 f_1}{\partial y^2} = 0 = \frac{\partial^2 f_2}{\partial x^2} + \frac{\partial^2 f_2}{\partial y^2} \tag{8.46}$$

We shall assign the proof of this as Prob. W8.4. Even more remarkable if you have never seen it before is that lines of constant f_1 will be everywhere perpendicular to lines of constant f_2:

$$\left(\frac{dy}{dx}\right)_{f_1 = C} = -\frac{1}{(dy/dx)_{f_2 = C}} \tag{8.47}$$

This is true for totally arbitrary $f(z)$ as long as this function is analytic; that is, it must have a unique derivative df/dz at every point in the region.

The net result of Eqs. (8.46) and (8.47) is that the functions f_1 and f_2 can be interpreted to be the potential lines and streamlines of an inviscid flow. By long custom we let the real part of $f(z)$ be the velocity potential and the imaginary part be the stream function:

$$f(z) = \phi(x, y) + i\psi(x, y) \tag{8.48}$$

We try various functions $f(z)$ and see whether any interesting flow pattern results. Of course, most of them have already been found, and we simply report on them here.

We shall not go into the details, but there are excellent treatments of this complex-variable technique on both an introductory [4] and a more advanced [2, 3] level. The method is less important now because of the popularity of computer techniques.

As a simple example, consider the linear function

$$f(z) = U_\infty z = U_\infty x + iU_\infty y$$

It follows from Eq. (8.48) that $\phi = U_\infty x$ and $\psi = U_\infty y$, which, we recall from Eq. (8.12), represents a uniform stream in the x direction. Once you get used to the complex variable, the solution practically falls in your lap.

To find the velocities, you may either separate ϕ and ψ from $f(z)$ and differentiate, or differentiate f directly:

$$\frac{df}{dz} = \frac{\partial \phi}{\partial x} + i\frac{\partial \psi}{\partial x} = -i\frac{\partial \phi}{\partial y} + \frac{\partial \psi}{\partial y} = u - iv \tag{8.49}$$

Thus the real part of df/dz equals $u(x, y)$, and the imaginary part equals $-v(x, y)$. To get a practical result, the derivative df/dz must exist and be unique, hence the requirement

---

[3]This section may be omitted without loss of continuity.

that f be an analytic function. For $f(z) = U_\infty z$, $df/dz = U_\infty = u$, since it is real, and $v = 0$, as expected.

Sometimes it is convenient to use the polar coordinate form of the complex variable

$$z = x + iy = re^{i\theta} = r\cos\theta + ir\sin\theta$$

where

$$r = (x^2 + y^2)^{1/2} \qquad \theta = \tan^{-1}\frac{y}{x}$$

This form is especially convenient when powers of z occur.

Uniform Stream at an Angle of Attack

All the elementary plane flows of Sec. 8.2 have a complex-variable formulation. The uniform stream U_∞ at an angle of attack α has the complex potential

$$f(z) = U_\infty z e^{-i\alpha} \tag{8.50}$$

Compare this form with Eq. (8.22).

Line Source at a Point z_0

Consider a line source of strength m placed off the origin at a point $z_0 = x_0 + iy_0$. Its complex potential is

$$f(z) = m\ln(z - z_0) \tag{8.51}$$

This can be compared with Eq. (8.13), which is valid only for the source at the origin. For a line sink, the strength m is negative.

Line Vortex at a Point z_0

If a line vortex of strength K is placed at point z_0, its complex potential is

$$f(z) = -iK\ln(z - z_0) \tag{8.52}$$

to be compared with Eq. (8.14). Also compare to Eq. (8.51) to see that we reverse the meaning of ϕ and ψ simply by multiplying the complex potential by $-i$.

Flow around a Corner of Arbitrary Angle

Corner flow is an example of a pattern that cannot be conveniently produced by superimposing sources, sinks, and vortices. It has a strikingly simple complex representation:

$$f(z) = Az^n = Ar^n e^{in\theta} = Ar^n\cos n\theta + iAr^n\sin n\theta$$

where A and n are constants.

It follows from Eq. (8.48) that for this pattern

$$\phi = Ar^n\cos n\theta \qquad \psi = Ar^n\sin n\theta \tag{8.53}$$

Streamlines from Eq. (8.53) are plotted in Fig. 8.18 for five different values of n. The flow is seen to represent a stream turning through an angle $\beta = \pi/n$. Patterns in Fig. 8.18d and e are not realistic on the downstream side of the corner, where separation will occur due to the adverse pressure gradient and sudden change of direction. In general, separation always occurs downstream of salient, or protruding corners, except in creeping flows at low Reynolds number Re < 1.

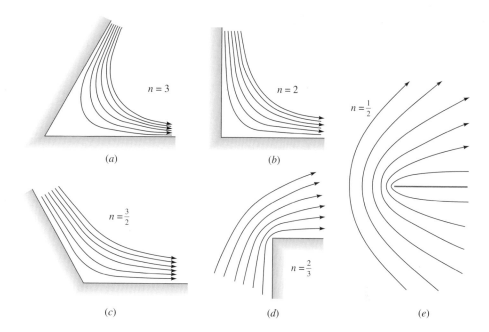

Fig. 8.18 Streamlines for corner flow, Eq. (8.53), for corner angle β of (a) 60°, (b) 90°, (c) 120°, (d) 270°, and (e) 360°.

Since $360° = 2\pi$ is the largest possible corner, the patterns for $n < \frac{1}{2}$ do not represent corner flow.

If we expand the plot of Fig. 8.18a to c to double size, we can represent stagnation flow toward a corner of angle $2\beta = 2\pi/n$. This is done in Fig. 8.19 for $n = 3$, 2, and 1.5. These are very realistic flows; although they slip at the wall, they can be patched to boundary layer theories very successfully. We took a brief look at corner flows before, in Examples 4.5 and 4.9 and in Probs. P4.49 to P4.51.

Flow Normal to a Flat Plate

We treat this case separately because the Kelvin ovals of Fig. 8.16 failed to degenerate into a flat plate as K became small. The flat plate normal to a uniform stream is an extreme case worthy of our attention.

Although the result is quite simple, the derivation is very complicated and is given, for example, in Ref. 2, Sec. 9.3. There are three changes of complex variable, or *mappings,* beginning with the basic cylinder flow solution of Fig. 8.14a. First the uniform stream is rotated to be vertical upward, then the cylinder is squeezed down into a plate shape, and finally the free stream is rotated back to the horizontal. The final result for complex potential is

$$f(z) = \phi + i\psi = U_\infty(z^2 + a^2)^{1/2} \tag{8.54}$$

where $2a$ is the height of the plate. To isolate ϕ or ψ, square both sides and separate real and imaginary parts:

$$\phi^2 - \psi^2 = U_\infty^2(x^2 - y^2 + a^2) \qquad \phi\psi = U_\infty^2 xy$$

We can solve for ψ to determine the streamlines

$$\psi^4 + \psi^2 U_\infty^2(x^2 - y^2 + a^2) = U_\infty^4 x^2 y^2 \tag{8.55}$$

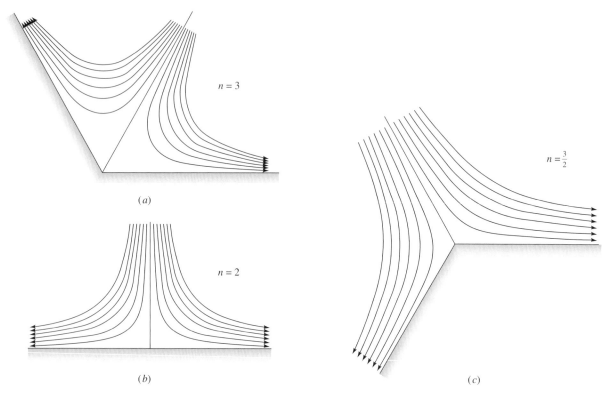

Fig. 8.19 Streamlines for stagnation flow from Eq. (8.53) for corner angle 2β of (*a*) 120°, (*b*) 180°, and (*c*) 240°.

Equation (8.55) is plotted in Fig. 8.20*a*, revealing a doubly symmetric pattern of streamlines that approach very closely to the plate and then deflect up and over, with very high velocities and low pressures near the plate tips.

The velocity v_s along the plate surface is found by computing df/dz from Eq. (8.54) and isolating the imaginary part:

$$\left.\frac{v_s}{U_\infty}\right|_{\text{plate surface}} = \frac{y/a}{(1 - y^2/a^2)^{1/2}} \tag{8.56}$$

Some values of surface velocity can be tabulated as follows:

y/a	0.0	0.2	0.4	0.6	0.707	0.8	0.9	1.0
v_s/U_∞	0.0	0.204	0.436	0.750	1.00	1.33	2.07	∞

The origin is a stagnation point; then the velocity grows linearly at first and very rapidly near the tip, with both velocity and acceleration being infinite at the tip.

As you might guess, Fig. 8.20*a* is not realistic. In a real flow the sharp salient edge causes separation, and a broad, low-pressure wake forms in the lee, as in Fig. 8.20*b*. Instead of being zero, the drag coefficient is very large, $C_D \approx 2.0$ from Table 7.2.

A discontinuous potential flow theory that accounts for flow separation was devised by Helmholtz in 1868 and Kirchhoff in 1869. This free-streamline solution is shown in Fig. 8.20*c*, with the streamline that breaks away from the tip having a constant

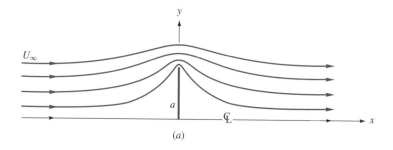

(a)

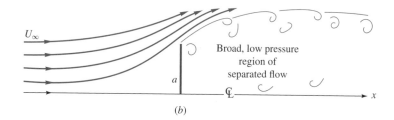

Broad, low pressure
region of
separated flow

(b)

Fig. 8.20 Streamlines in upper
half-plane for flow normal to a flat
plate of height 2a: (a) continuous
potential flow theory, Eq. (8.55);
(b) actual measured flow pattern;
(c) discontinuous potential theory
with $k \approx 1.5$.

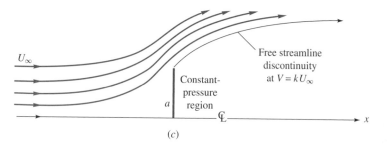

Free streamline
discontinuity
at $V = kU_\infty$

Constant-
pressure
region

(c)

velocity $V = kU_\infty$. From Bernoulli's equation the pressure in the dead-water region behind the plate will equal $p_r = p_\infty + \frac{1}{2}\rho U_\infty^2(1 - k^2)$ to match the pressure along the free streamline. For $k = 1.5$ this Helmholtz-Kirchoff theory predicts $p_r = p_\infty - 0.625\rho U_\infty^2$ and an average pressure on the front $p_f = p_\infty + 0.375\rho U_\infty^2$, giving an overall drag coefficient of 2.0, in agreement with experiment. However, the coefficient k is a priori unknown and must be tuned to experimental data, so free-streamline theory can be considered only a qualified success. For further details see Ref. 2, Sec. 11.2.

8.6 Images[4]

The previous solutions have all been for unbounded flows, such as a circular cylinder immersed in a broad expanse of uniformly streaming fluid, Fig. 8.14a. However, many practical problems involve a nearby rigid boundary constraining the flow, such as (1) groundwater flow near the bottom of a dam, (2) an airfoil near the ground, simulating landing or takeoff, or (3) a cylinder mounted in a wind tunnel with narrow

[4]This section may be omitted without loss of continuity.

walls. In such cases the basic unbounded potential flow solutions can be modified for wall effects by the method of *images*.

Consider a line source placed a distance a from a wall, as in Fig. 8.21a. To create the desired wall, an image source of identical strength is placed the same distance below the wall. By symmetry the two sources create a plane surface streamline between them, which is taken to be the wall.

In Fig. 8.21b a vortex near a wall requires an image vortex the same distance below but of *opposite* rotation. We have shaded in the wall, but of course the pattern could also be interpreted as the flow near a vortex pair in an unbounded fluid.

In Fig. 8.21c an airfoil in a uniform stream near the ground is created by an image airfoil below the ground of opposite circulation and lift. This looks easy, but actually it is not because the airfoils are so close together that they interact and distort each

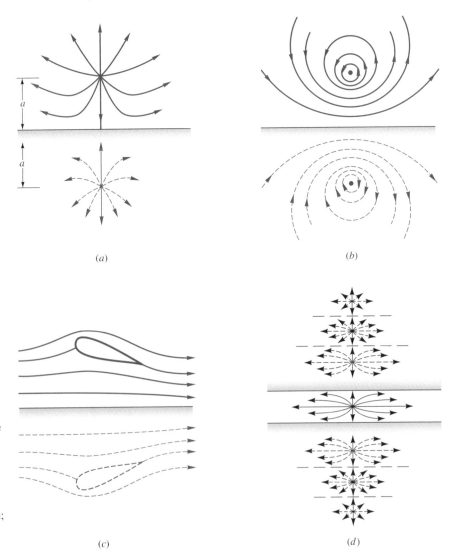

(a)

(b)

Fig. 8.21 Constraining walls can be created by image flows: (a) source near a wall with identical image source; (b) vortex near a wall with image vortex of opposite sense; (c) airfoil in ground effect with image airfoil of opposite circulation; (d) source between two walls requiring an infinite row of images.

(c)

(d)

other's shapes. A rule of thumb is that nonnegligible shape distortion occurs if the body shape is within two chord lengths of the wall. To eliminate distortion, a whole series of "corrective" images must be added to the flow to recapture the shape of the original isolated airfoil. Reference 2, Sec. 7.75, has a good discussion of this procedure, which usually requires computer summation of the multiple images needed.

Figure 8.21*d* shows a source constrained between two walls. One wall required only one image in Fig. 8.21*a*, but *two* walls require an infinite array of image sources above and below the desired pattern, as shown. Usually computer summation is necessary, but sometimes a closed-form summation can be achieved, as in the infinite vortex row of Eq. (8.28).

EXAMPLE 8.5

For the source near a wall as in Fig. 8.21*a*, the wall velocity is zero between the sources, rises to a maximum moving out along the wall, and then drops to zero far from the sources. If the source strength is 8 m²/s, how far from the wall should the source be to ensure that the maximum velocity along the wall will be 5 m/s?

Solution

At any point x along the wall, as in Fig. E8.5, each source induces a radial outward velocity $v_r = m/r$, which has a component $v_r \cos \theta$ along the wall. The total wall velocity is thus

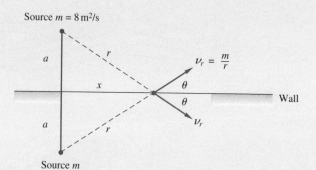

E8.5

$$u_{\text{wall}} = 2v_r \cos \theta$$

From the geometry of Fig. E8.5, $r = (x^2 + a^2)^{1/2}$ and $\cos \theta = x/r$. Then the total wall velocity can be expressed as

$$u = \frac{2mx}{x^2 + a^2}$$

This is zero at $x = 0$ and at $x \rightarrow \infty$. To find the maximum velocity, differentiate and set equal to zero:

$$\frac{du}{dx} = 0 \quad \text{at} \quad x = a \quad \text{and} \quad u_{\max} = \frac{m}{a}$$

We have omitted a bit of algebra in giving these results. For the given source strength and maximum velocity, the proper distance a is

$$a = \frac{m}{u_{max}} = \frac{8 \ m^2/s}{5 \ m/s} = 1.6 \ m \qquad \qquad Ans.$$

For $x > a$, there is an adverse pressure gradient along the wall, and boundary layer theory should be used to predict separation.

8.7 Airfoil Theory[5]

As mentioned in conjunction with the Kutta-Joukowski lift theorem, Eq. (8.43), the problem in airfoil theory is to determine the net circulation Γ as a function of airfoil shape and free-stream angle of attack α.

The Kutta Condition

Even if the airfoil shape and free-stream angle of attack are specified, the potential flow theory solution is nonunique: An infinite family of solutions can be found corresponding to different values of circulation Γ. Four examples of this nonuniqueness were shown for the cylinder flows in Fig. 8.14. The same is true of the airfoil, and Fig. 8.22 shows three mathematically acceptable "solutions" to a given airfoil flow for small (Fig. 8.22a), large (Fig. 8.22b), and medium (Fig. 8.22c) net circulation.

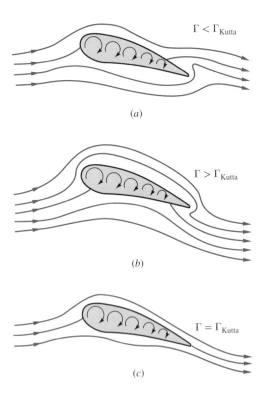

(a)

(b)

Fig. 8.22 The Kutta condition properly simulates the flow about an airfoil; (a) too little circulation, stagnation point on rear upper surface; (b) too much, stagnation point on rear lower surface; (c) just right, Kutta condition requires smooth flow at trailing edge.

(c)

[5]This section may be omitted without loss of continuity.

You can guess which case best simulates a real airfoil from the earlier discussion of transient lift development in Fig. 7.23. It is the case (Fig. 8.22c) where the upper and lower flows meet and leave the trailing edge smoothly. If the trailing edge is rounded slightly, there will be a stagnation point there. If the trailing edge is sharp, approximating most airfoil designs, the upper- and lower-surface flow velocities will be equal as they meet and leave the airfoil.

This statement of the physically proper value of Γ is generally attributed to W. M. Kutta, hence the name *Kutta condition,* although some texts give credit to Joukowski and/or Chaplygin. All airfoil theories use the Kutta condition, which is in good agreement with experiment. It turns out that the correct circulation Γ_{Kutta} depends on flow velocity, angle of attack, and airfoil shape.

Potential Theory for Thick Cambered Airfoils

The theory of thick cambered airfoils is covered in advanced texts [for example, 2 to 4]; Ref. 13 has a thorough and comprehensive review of both inviscid and viscous aspects of airfoil behavior.

Basically the theory uses a complex-variable mapping that transforms the flow about a cylinder with circulation in Fig. 8.14 into flow about a foil shape with circulation. The circulation is then adjusted to match the Kutta condition of smooth exit flow from the trailing edge.

Regardless of the exact airfoil shape, the inviscid mapping theory predicts that the correct circulation for any thick cambered airfoil is

$$\Gamma_{Kutta} = \pi C U_\infty \left(1 + 0.77\frac{t}{C} \right) \sin{(\alpha + \beta)} \qquad (8.57)$$

where $\beta = \tan^{-1}{(2h/C)}$ and h is the maximum camber, or maximum deviation of the airfoil midline from its chord line, as in Fig. 8.24a.

The lift coefficient of the infinite-span airfoil is thus

$$C_L = \frac{\rho U_\infty \Gamma}{\frac{1}{2}\rho U_\infty^2 bC} = 2\pi \left(1 + 0.77\frac{t}{C} \right) \sin{(\alpha + \beta)} \qquad (8.58)$$

Figure 8.23 shows that the thickness effect $1 + 0.77t/C$ is not verified by experiment. Some airfoils increase lift with thickness, others decrease, and none approach the theory very closely, the primary reason being the boundary layer growth on the upper surface affecting the airfoil "shape." Thus it is customary to drop the thickness effect from the theory:

$$\boxed{C_L \approx 2\pi \sin{(\alpha + \beta)}} \qquad (8.59)$$

The theory correctly predicts that a cambered airfoil will have finite lift at zero angle of attack and zero lift (ZL) at an angle

$$\alpha_{ZL} = -\beta = -\tan^{-1}{\frac{2h}{C}} \qquad (8.60)$$

Equation (8.60) overpredicts the measured zero-lift angle by 1° or so, as shown in Table 8.3. The measured values are essentially independent of thickness. The designation XX in the NACA series indicates the thickness in percent, and the other digits refer to camber and other details. For example, the 2415 airfoil has 2 percent maximum

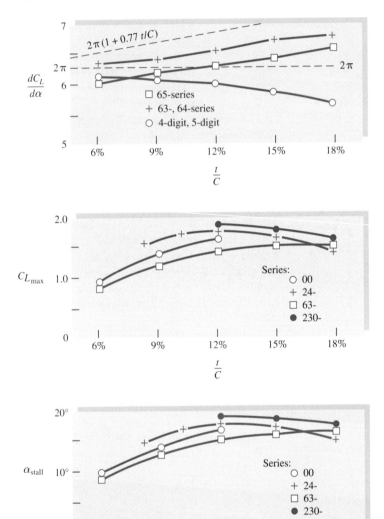

Fig. 8.23 Lift characteristics of smooth NACA airfoils as a function of thickness ratio, for infinite aspect ratio. *(From Ref. 12.)*

camber (the first digit) occurring at 40 percent chord (the second digit) with 15 percent maximum thickness (the last two digits). The maximum thickness need not occur at the same position as the maximum camber.

Table 8.3 Zero-Lift Angle of NACA Airfoils

Airfoil series	Camber h/C, %	Measured α_{ZL}, deg	Theory − β, deg
24XX	2.0	−2.1	−2.3
44XX	4.0	−4.0	−4.6
230XX	1.8	−1.3	−2.1
63-2XX	2.2	−1.8	−2.5
63-4XX	4.4	−3.1	−5.0
64-1XX	1.1	−0.8	−1.2

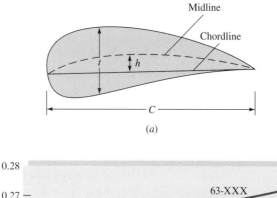

(a)

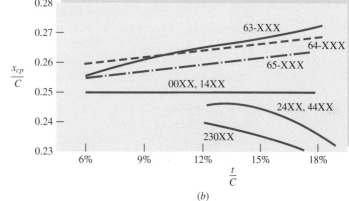

(b)

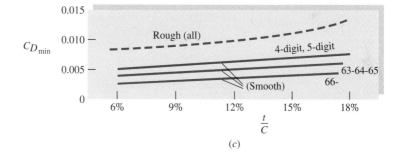

(c)

Fig. 8.24 Characteristics of NACA airfoils: (a) typical thick cambered airfoil; (b) center-of-pressure data; and (c) minimum drag coefficient.

Figure 8.24b shows the measured position of the center of pressure of the various NACA airfoils, both symmetric and cambered. In all cases x_{CP} is within 0.02 chord length of the theoretical quarter-chord point. The standard cambered airfoils (24, 44, and 230 series) lie slightly forward of $x/C = 0.25$ and the low-drag (60 series) foils slightly aft. The symmetric airfoils are at 0.25.

Figure 8.24c shows the minimum drag coefficient of NACA airfoils as a function of thickness. As mentioned earlier in conjunction with Fig. 7.25, these foils when smooth actually have less drag than turbulent flow parallel to a flat plate, especially the low-drag 60 series. However, for standard surface roughness all foils have about the same minimum drag, roughly 30 percent greater than that for a smooth flat plate.

Wings of Finite Span

The results of airfoil theory and experiment in the previous subsection were for two-dimensional, or infinite-span, wings. But all real wings have tips and are therefore of finite span or finite aspect ratio AR, defined by

$$\text{AR} = \frac{b^2}{A_p} = \frac{b}{C} \qquad (8.61)$$

where b is the span length from tip to tip and A_p is the planform area of the wing as seen from above. The lift and drag coefficients of a finite-aspect-ratio wing depend strongly on the aspect ratio and slightly on the planform shape of the wing.

Vortices cannot end in a fluid; they must either extend to the boundary or form a closed loop. Figure 8.25a shows how the vortices that provide the wing circulation bend downstream at finite wing tips and extend far behind the wing to join the starting vortex (Fig. 7.23) downstream. The strongest vortices are shed from the tips, but some are shed from the body of the wing, as sketched schematically in Fig. 8.25b. The effective circulation $\Gamma(y)$ of these trailing shed vortices is zero at the tips and usually a maximum at the center plane, or root, of the wing. In 1918 Prandtl successfully modeled this flow by replacing the wing with a single lifting line and a continuous sheet of semi-infinite trailing vortices of strength $\gamma(y) = d\Gamma/dy$, as in Fig. 8.25c. Each elemental piece of trailing sheet $\gamma(\eta)\,d\eta$ induces a downwash, or downward velocity, $dw(y)$, given by

$$dw(y) = \frac{\gamma(\eta)\,d\eta}{4\pi(y - \eta)}$$

at position y on the lifting line. Note the denominator term 4π rather than 2π because the trailing vortex extends only from 0 to ∞ rather than from $-\infty$ to $+\infty$.

The total downwash $w(y)$ induced by the entire trailing vortex system is thus

$$w(y) = \frac{1}{4\pi} \int_{-(1/2)b}^{(1/2)b} \frac{\gamma(\eta)\,d\eta}{y - \eta} \qquad (8.62)$$

When the downwash is vectorially added to the approaching free stream U_∞, the effective angle of attack at this section of the wing is reduced to

$$\alpha_{\text{eff}} = \alpha - \alpha_i \qquad \alpha_i = \tan^{-1} \frac{w}{U_\infty} \approx \frac{w}{U_\infty} \qquad (8.63)$$

where we have used a small-amplitude approximation $w \ll U_\infty$.

The final step is to assume that the local circulation $\Gamma(y)$ is equal to that of a two-dimensional wing of the same shape and same effective angle of attack. From thin-airfoil theory we have the estimate

$$C_L = \frac{\rho U_\infty \Gamma b}{\frac{1}{2}\rho U_\infty^2 bC} \approx 2\pi\alpha_{\text{eff}}$$

or

$$\Gamma \approx \pi C U_\infty \alpha_{\text{eff}} \qquad (8.64)$$

Combining Eqs. (8.62) and (8.64), we obtain Prandtl's lifting-line theory for a finite-span wing:

$$\Gamma(y) = \pi C(y) U_\infty \left[\alpha(y) - \frac{1}{4\pi U_\infty} \int_{-(1/2)b}^{(1/2)b} \frac{(d\Gamma/d\eta)\,d\eta}{y - \eta} \right] \qquad (8.65)$$

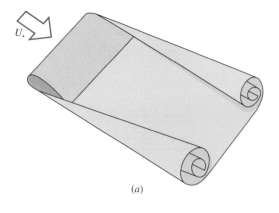

(a)

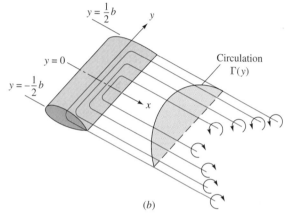

(b)

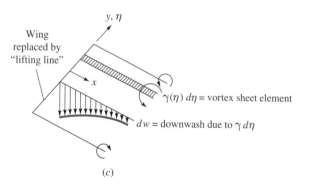

(c)

Fig. 8.25 Lifting-line theory for a finite wing: (a) actual trailing-vortex system behind a wing; (b) simulation by vortex system "bound" to the wing; (c) downwash on the wing due to an element of the trailing-vortex system.

This is an integrodifferential equation to be solved for $\Gamma(y)$ subject to the conditions $\Gamma(\frac{1}{2}b) = \Gamma(-\frac{1}{2}b) = 0$. Once it is solved, the total wing lift and induced drag are given by

$$L = \rho U_\infty \int_{-(1/2)b}^{(1/2)b} \Gamma(y) \, dy \qquad D_i = \rho U_\infty \int_{-(1/2)b}^{(1/2)b} \Gamma(y)\alpha_i(y) \, dy \qquad (8.66)$$

Here is a case where the drag is not zero in a frictionless theory because the downwash causes the lift to slant backward by angle α_i so that it has a drag component parallel to the free-stream direction, $dDi = dL \sin \alpha_i \approx dL\alpha_i$.

The complete solution to Eq. (8.65) for arbitrary wing planform $C(y)$ and arbitrary twist $\alpha(y)$ is treated in advanced texts [for example, 11]. It turns out that there is a simple representative solution for an untwisted wing of elliptical planform:

$$C(y) = C_0 \left[1 - \left(\frac{2y}{b} \right)^2 \right]^{1/2}$$

The area and aspect ratio of this wing are

$$A_p = \int_{-(1/2)b}^{(1/2)b} C \, dy = \frac{1}{4} \pi b C_0 \qquad \text{AR} = \frac{4b}{\pi C_0} \tag{8.67}$$

The solution to Eq. (8.65) for this $C(y)$ is an elliptical circulation distribution of exactly similar shape:

$$\Gamma(y) = \Gamma_0 \left[1 - \left(\frac{2y}{b} \right)^2 \right]^{1/2}$$

Substituting into Eq. (8.65) and integrating give a relation between Γ_0 and C_0:

$$\Gamma_0 = \frac{\pi C_0 U_\infty \alpha}{1 + 2/\text{AR}}$$

where α is assumed constant across the untwisted wing.

Substitution into Eq. (8.66) gives the elliptical wing lift:

$$L = \tfrac{1}{4} \pi^2 b C_0 \rho U_\infty^2 \alpha / (1 + 2/\text{AR})$$

or

$$C_L = \frac{2\pi\alpha}{1 + 2/\text{AR}} \tag{8.68}$$

If we generalize this to a thick cambered finite wing of approximately elliptical planform, we obtain

$$\boxed{C_L = \frac{2\pi \sin(\alpha + \beta)}{1 + 2/\text{AR}} = \frac{2L}{\rho U_\infty^2 A_p}} \tag{8.69}$$

This result was given without proof as Eq. (7.70). From Eq. (8.62) the computed downwash for the elliptical wing is constant:

$$w(y) = \frac{2U_\infty \alpha}{2 + \text{AR}} = \text{const} \tag{8.70}$$

Finally, the induced drag coefficient from Eq. (8.63) is

$$C_{Di} = C_L \frac{w}{U_\infty} = \frac{C_L^2}{\pi \text{AR}} \tag{8.71}$$

This was given without proof as Eq. (7.71).

Figure 8.26 shows the effectiveness of this theory when tested against a nonelliptical cambered wing by Prandtl in 1921 [14]. Figures 8.26a and b show the measured lift curves and drag polars for five different aspect ratios. Note the increase in stall angle and drag and the decrease in lift slope as the aspect ratio decreases.

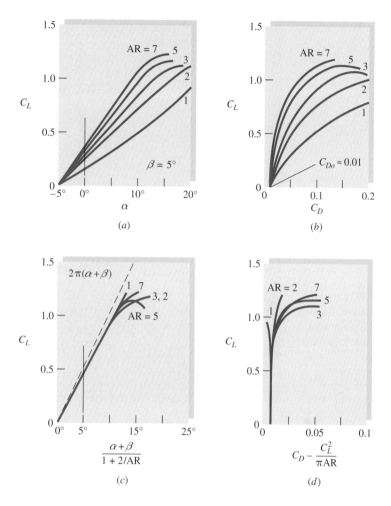

Fig. 8.26 Comparison of theory and experiment for a finite wing: (a) measured lift [14]; (b) measured drag polar [14]; (c) lift reduced to infinite aspect ratio; (d) drag polar reduced to infinite aspect ratio.

Figure 8.26c shows the lift data replotted against effective angle of attack $\alpha_{eff} = (\alpha + \beta)/(1 + 2/AR)$, as predicted by Eq. (8.69). These curves should be equivalent to an infinite-aspect-ratio wing, and they do collapse together except near stall. Their common slope $dC_L/d\alpha$ is about 10 percent less than the theoretical value 2π, but this is consistent with the thickness and shape effects noted in Fig. 8.23.

Figure 8.26d shows the drag data replotted with the theoretical induced drag $C_{Di} = C_L^2/(\pi AR)$ subtracted out. Again, except near stall, the data collapse onto a single line of nearly constant infinite-aspect-ratio drag $C_{D0} \approx 0.01$. We conclude that the finite-wing theory is very effective and may be used for design calculations.

Aircraft Trailing Vortices

The trailing vortices in Fig. 8.25a are real, not just mathematical abstractions. On commercial aircraft, such vortices are long, strong, and lingering. They can stretch for miles behind a large aircraft and endanger the following planes by inducing drastic rolling moments. The vortex persistence governs the separation distance between planes at an airport and thus determines airport capacity. An example of strong trailing

Fig. 8.27 Wingtip vortices from a smoke-visualization test of a Boeing 737. Vortices from large airplanes can be extremely dangerous to any following aircraft, especially small planes. This test was part of a research effort to alleviate these swirling wakes. *(NASA photo.)*

vortices is shown in Fig. 8.27. There is a continuing research effort to alleviate trailing vortices by breaking them up or otherwise causing them to decay. See the review article by Spalart [46].

8.8 Axisymmetric Potential Flow[6]

The same superposition technique that worked so well for plane flow in Sec. 8.3 is also successful for axisymmetric potential flow. We give some brief examples here.

Most of the basic results carry over from plane to axisymmetric flow with only slight changes owing to the geometric differences. Consider the following related flows:

Basic plane flow	Counterpart axisymmetric flow
Uniform stream	Uniform stream
Line source or sink	Point source or sink
Line doublet	Point doublet
Line vortex	No counterpart
Rankine half-body cylinder	Rankine half-body of revolution
Rankine oval cylinder	Rankine oval of revolution
Circular cylinder	Sphere
Symmetric airfoil	Tear-shaped body

---

[6]This section may be omitted without loss of continuity.

Since there is no such thing as a point vortex, we must forgo the pleasure of studying circulation effects in axisymmetric flow. However, as any smoker knows, there is an axisymmetric ring vortex, and there are also ring sources and ring sinks, which we leave to advanced texts [for example, 3].

Spherical Polar Coordinates

Axisymmetric potential flows are conveniently treated in the spherical polar coordinates of Fig. 8.28. There are only two coordinates (r, θ), and flow properties are constant on a circle of radius $r \sin \theta$ about the x axis.

The equation of continuity for incompressible flow in these coordinates is

$$\frac{\partial}{\partial r}(r^2 v_r \sin \theta) + \frac{\partial}{\partial \theta}(r v_\theta \sin \theta) = 0 \tag{8.72}$$

where v_r and v_θ are radial and tangential velocity as shown. Thus a spherical polar stream function[7] exists such that

$$v_r = -\frac{1}{r^2 \sin \theta}\frac{\partial \psi}{\partial \theta} \qquad v_\theta = \frac{1}{r \sin \theta}\frac{\partial \psi}{\partial r} \tag{8.73}$$

In like manner a velocity potential $\phi(r, \theta)$ exists such that

$$v_r = \frac{\partial \phi}{\partial r} \qquad v_\theta = \frac{1}{r}\frac{\partial \phi}{\partial \theta} \tag{8.74}$$

These formulas serve to deduce the ψ and ϕ functions for various elementary axisymmetric potential flows.

Uniform Stream in the x Direction

A stream U_∞ in the x direction has components

$$v_r = U_\infty \cos \theta \qquad v_\theta = -U_\infty \sin \theta$$

Substitution into Eqs. (8.73) and (8.74) and integrating give

Uniform stream: $\qquad \psi = -\tfrac{1}{2}U_\infty r^2 \sin^2 \theta \qquad \phi = U_\infty r \cos \theta \tag{8.75}$

As usual, arbitrary constants of integration have been neglected.

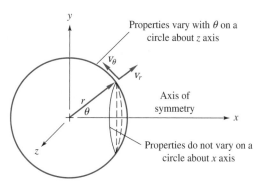

Fig. 8.28 Spherical polar coordinates for axisymmetric flow.

---

[7]It is often called *Stokes's stream function,* having been used in a paper Stokes wrote in 1851 on viscous sphere flow.

Point Source or Sink

Consider a volume flux Q issuing from a point source. The flow will spread out radially and at radius r will equal Q divided by the area $4\pi r^2$ of a sphere. Thus

$$v_r = \frac{Q}{4\pi r^2} = \frac{m}{r^2} \qquad v_\theta = 0 \tag{8.76}$$

with $m = Q/(4\pi)$ for convenience. Integrating (8.73) and (8.74) gives

Point source $\qquad\qquad \psi = m\cos\theta \qquad \phi = -\dfrac{m}{r}$ $\qquad\qquad$ (8.77)

For a point sink, change m to $-m$ in Eq. (8.77).

Point Doublet

Exactly as in Fig. 8.12, place a source at $(x, y) = (-a, 0)$ and an equal sink at $(+a, 0)$, taking the limit as a becomes small with the product $2am = \lambda$ held constant:

$$\psi_{\text{doublet}} = \lim_{\substack{a\to 0 \\ 2am=\lambda}} (m\cos\theta_{\text{source}} - m\cos\theta_{\text{sink}}) = \frac{\lambda\sin^2\theta}{r} \tag{8.78}$$

We leave the proof of this limit as a problem. The point-doublet velocity potential is

$$\phi_{\text{doublet}} = \lim_{\substack{a\to 0 \\ 2am=\lambda}} \left(-\frac{m}{r_{\text{source}}} + \frac{m}{r_{\text{sink}}} \right) = \frac{\lambda\cos\theta}{r^2} \tag{8.79}$$

The streamlines and potential lines are shown in Fig. 8.29. Unlike the plane doublet flow of Fig. 8.12, neither set of lines represents perfect circles.

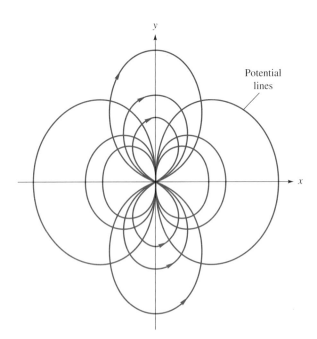

Fig. 8.29 Streamlines and potential lines due to a point doublet at the origin, from Eqs. (8.78) and (8.79).

Uniform Stream plus a Point Source

By combining Eqs. (8.75) and (8.77), we obtain the stream function for a uniform stream plus a point source at the origin:

$$\psi = -\tfrac{1}{2}U_\infty r^2 \sin^2 \theta + m \cos \theta \tag{8.80}$$

From Eq. (8.73) the velocity components are, by differentiation,

$$v_r = U_\infty \cos \theta + \frac{m}{r^2} \qquad v_\theta = -U_\infty \sin \theta \tag{8.81}$$

Setting these equal to zero reveals a stagnation point at $\theta = 180°$ and $r = a = (m/U_\infty)^{1/2}$, as shown in Fig. 8.30. If we let $m = U_\infty a^2$, the stream function can be rewritten as

$$\frac{\psi}{U_\infty a^2} = \cos \theta - \frac{1}{2}\left(\frac{r}{a}\right)^2 \sin^2 \theta \tag{8.82}$$

The stream surface that passes through the stagnation point $(r, \theta) = (a, \pi)$ has the value $\psi = -U_\infty a^2$ and forms a half-body of revolution enclosing the point source, as shown in Fig. 8.30. This half-body can be used to simulate a pitot tube. Far downstream the half-body approaches the constant radius $R = 2a$ about the x axis. The maximum velocity and minimum pressure along the half-body surface occur at $\theta = 70.5°$, $r = a\sqrt{3}$, $V_s = 1.155U_\infty$. Downstream of this point there is an adverse gradient as V_s slowly decelerates to U_∞, but boundary layer theory indicates no flow separation. Thus Eq. (8.82) is a very realistic simulation of a real half-body flow. But when the uniform stream is added to a sink to form a half-body rear surface, similar to Fig. 8.9c, separation is predicted and the rear inviscid pattern is not realistic.

Uniform Stream plus a Point Doublet

From Eqs. (8.75) and (8.78), combination of a uniform stream and a point doublet at the origin gives

$$\psi = -\frac{1}{2}U_\infty r^2 \sin^2 \theta + \frac{\lambda}{r}\sin^2 \theta \tag{8.83}$$

Examination of this relation reveals that the stream surface $\psi = 0$ corresponds to the sphere of radius

$$r = a = \left(\frac{2\lambda}{U_\infty}\right)^{1/3} \tag{8.84}$$

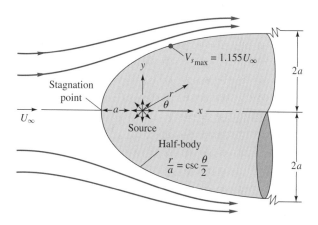

Fig. 8.30 Streamlines for a Rankine half-body of revolution.

This is exactly analogous to the cylinder flow of Fig. 8.14a formed by combining a uniform stream and a line doublet.

Letting $\lambda = \frac{1}{2}U_\infty a^3$ for convenience, we rewrite Eq. (8.83) as

$$\frac{\psi}{\frac{1}{2}U_\infty a^2} = -\sin^2 \theta \left(\frac{r^2}{a^2} - \frac{a}{r}\right) \qquad (8.85)$$

The streamlines for this sphere flow are plotted in Fig. 8.31. By differentiation from Eq. (8.73) the velocity components are

$$v_r = U_\infty \cos \theta \left(1 - \frac{a^3}{r^3}\right) \qquad v_\theta = -\frac{1}{2} U_\infty \sin \theta \left(2 + \frac{a^3}{r^3}\right) \qquad (8.86)$$

We see that the radial velocity vanishes at the sphere surface $r = a$, as expected. There is a stagnation point at the front (a, π) and the rear $(a, 0)$ of the sphere. The maximum velocity occurs at the shoulder $(a, \pm\frac{1}{2}\pi)$, where $v_r = 0$ and $v_\theta = \mp 1.5 U_\infty$. The surface velocity distribution is

$$V_s = -v_\theta|_{r=a} = \frac{3}{2} U_\infty \sin \theta \qquad (8.87)$$

Note the similarity to the cylinder surface velocity equal to $2U_\infty \sin \theta$ from Eq. (8.39) with zero circulation.

Equation (8.87) predicts, as expected, an adverse pressure gradient on the rear $(\theta < 90°)$ of the sphere. If we use this distribution with laminar boundary layer theory [for example, 15, p. 294], separation is computed to occur at about $\theta = 76°$, so that in the actual flow pattern of Fig. 7.14 a broad wake forms in the rear. This wake interacts with the free stream and causes Eq. (8.87) to be inaccurate even in the front of the sphere. The measured maximum surface velocity is equal only to about $1.3U_\infty$ and occurs at about $\theta = 107°$ (see Ref. 15, Sec. 4.10.4, for further details).

The Concept of Hydrodynamic Mass

When a body moves through a fluid, it must push a finite mass of fluid out of the way. If the body is accelerated, the surrounding fluid must also be accelerated. The body behaves as if it were heavier by an amount called the *hydrodynamic mass* (also

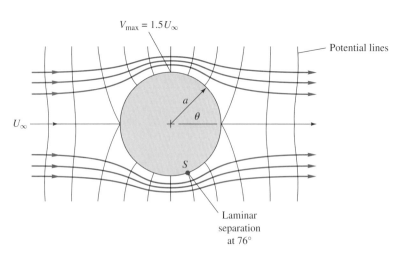

Fig. 8.31 Streamlines and potential lines for inviscid flow past a sphere.

called the *added* or *virtual mass*) of the fluid. If the instantaneous body velocity is $\mathbf{U}(t)$, the summation of forces must include this effect:

$$\Sigma \mathbf{F} = (m + m_h) \frac{d\mathbf{U}}{dt} \qquad (8.88)$$

where m_h, the hydrodynamic mass, is a function of body shape, the direction of motion, and (to a lesser extent) flow parameters such as the Reynolds number.

According to potential theory [2, Sec. 6.4; 3, Sec. 9.22], m_h depends only on the shape and direction of motion and can be computed by summing the total kinetic energy of the fluid relative to the body and setting this equal to an equivalent body energy:

$$KE_{fluid} = \int \tfrac{1}{2} dm \, V_{rel}^2 = \tfrac{1}{2} m_h U^2 \qquad (8.89)$$

The integration of fluid kinetic energy can also be accomplished by a body-surface integral involving the velocity potential [16, Sec. 11].

Consider the previous example of a sphere immersed in a uniform stream. By subtracting out the stream velocity we can replot the flow as in Fig. 8.32, showing the streamlines relative to the moving sphere. Note the similarity to the doublet flow in Fig. 8.29. The relative velocity components are found by subtracting U from Eqs. (8.86):

$$v_r = -\frac{Ua^3 \cos \theta}{r^3} \qquad v_\theta = -\frac{Ua^3 \sin \theta}{2r^3}$$

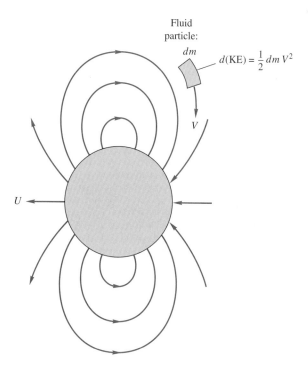

Fig. 8.32 Potential flow streamlines relative to a moving sphere. Compare with Figs. 8.29 and 8.31.

The element of fluid mass, in spherical polar coordinates, is

$$dm = \rho(2\pi r \sin\theta)r\, dr\, d\theta$$

When dm and $V_{rel}^2 = v_r^2 + v_\theta^2$ are substituted into Eq. (8.89), the integral can be evaluated:

$$\text{KE}_{\text{fluid}} = \tfrac{1}{3}\rho\pi a^3 U^2$$

or
$$m_h(\text{sphere}) = \tfrac{2}{3}\rho\pi a^3 \qquad (8.90)$$

Thus, according to potential theory, the hydrodynamic mass of a sphere equals one-half of its displaced mass, independent of the direction of motion.

A similar result for a cylinder moving normal to its axis can be computed from Eqs. (8.38) after subtracting out the stream velocity. The result is

$$m_h(\text{cylinder}) = \rho\pi a^2 L \qquad (8.91)$$

for a cylinder of length L, assuming two-dimensional motion. The cylinder's hydrodynamic mass equals its displaced mass.

Tables of hydrodynamic mass for various body shapes and directions of motion are given by Patton [17]. See also Ref. 21.

8.9 Numerical Analysis

When potential flow involves complicated geometries or unusual stream conditions, the classical superposition scheme of Secs. 8.3 and 8.4 becomes less attractive. Conformal mapping of body shapes, by using the complex-variable technique of Sec. 8.5, is no longer popular. Numerical analysis is the appropriate modern approach, and at least three different approaches are in use:

1. The finite element method (FEM) [6, 19]
2. The finite difference method (FDM) [5, 20, 23–26], or its close sibling, the finite volume method [27].
3. *a.* Integral methods with distributed singularities [18]
   b. The boundary element method (BEM) [7, 38]

Methods 3*a* and 3*b* are closely related, having first been developed on an ad hoc basis by aerodynamicists in the 1960s [18] and then generalized into a multipurpose applied mechanics technique in the 1970s [7].

Methods 1 (or FEM) and 2 (or FDM), though strikingly different in concept, are comparable in scope, mesh size, and general accuracy. We concentrate here on the latter method for illustration purposes.

All three of these methods—FEM, FDM, and BEM—are popular in present-day computational fluid dynamics. Although simplified online CFD codes are available—sometimes free—the writer believes that CFD, as a serious method of flow analysis, should wait until one studies the professional software available. This subject is more appropriate for advanced electives or graduate school. The discussion here will be brief and descriptive, with only nominal illustrations for an FDM method.

The Finite Element Method

The finite element method [19] is applicable to all types of linear and nonlinear partial differential equations in physics and engineering. The computational domain is divided into small regions, usually triangular or quadrilateral. These regions are delineated with a finite number of *nodes* where the field variables—temperature, velocity, pressure, stream function, and so on—are to be calculated. The solution in each region is approximated by an algebraic combination of local nodal values. Then the approximate functions are integrated over the region, and their error is minimized, often by using a weighting function. This process yields a set of N algebraic equations for the N unknown nodal values. The nodal equations are solved simultaneously, by matrix inversion or iteration. For further details see Ref. 6 or 19.

The Finite Difference Method

Although textbooks on numerical analysis [5, 20] apply finite difference techniques to many different problems, here we concentrate on potential flow. The idea of FDM is to approximate the partial derivatives in a physical equation by "differences" between nodal values spaced a finite distance apart—a sort of numerical calculus. The basic partial differential equation is thus replaced by a set of algebraic equations for the nodal values. For potential (inviscid) flow, these algebraic equations are linear, but they are generally nonlinear for viscous flows. The solution for nodal values is obtained by iteration or matrix inversion. Nodal spacings need not be equal.

Here we illustrate the two-dimensional Laplace equation, choosing for convenience the stream-function form

$$\frac{\partial^2 \psi}{\partial x^2} + \frac{\partial^2 \psi}{\partial y^2} = 0 \tag{8.92}$$

subject to known values of ψ along any body surface and known values of $\partial\psi/\partial x$ and $\partial\psi/\partial y$ in the free stream.

Our finite difference technique divides the flow field into equally spaced nodes, as shown in Fig. 8.33. To economize on the use of parentheses or functional notation,

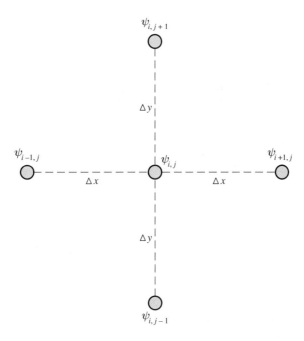

Fig. 8.33 Definition sketch for a two-dimensional rectangular finite difference grid.

subscripts i and j denote the position of an arbitrary, equally spaced node, and $\psi_{i,j}$ denotes the value of the stream function at that node:

$$\psi_{i,j} = \psi(x_0 + i\,\Delta x, y_0 + j\,\Delta y)$$

Thus $\psi_{i+1,j}$ is just to the right of $\psi_{i,j}$, and $\psi_{i,j+1}$ is just above.

An algebraic approximation for the derivative $\partial\psi/\partial x$ is

$$\frac{\partial\psi}{\partial x} \approx \frac{\psi(x + \Delta x, y) - \psi(x, y)}{\Delta x}$$

A similar approximation for the second derivative is

$$\frac{\partial^2\psi}{\partial x^2} \approx \frac{1}{\Delta x}\left[\frac{\psi(x + \Delta x, y) - \psi(x, y)}{\Delta x} - \frac{\psi(x, y) - \psi(x - \Delta x, y)}{\Delta x}\right]$$

The subscript notation makes these expressions more compact:

$$\frac{\partial\psi}{\partial x} \approx \frac{1}{\Delta x}(\psi_{i+1,j} - \psi_{i,j})$$

$$\frac{\partial^2\psi}{\partial x^2} \approx \frac{1}{\Delta x^2}(\psi_{i+1,j} - 2\psi_{i,j} + \psi_{i-1,j})$$

(8.93)

These formulas are exact in the calculus limit as $\Delta x \to 0$, but in numerical analysis we keep Δx and Δy finite, hence the term *finite differences*.

In an exactly similar manner we can derive the equivalent difference expressions for the y direction:

$$\frac{\partial\psi}{\partial y} \approx \frac{1}{\Delta y}(\psi_{i,j+1} - \psi_{i,j})$$

$$\frac{\partial^2\psi}{\partial y^2} \approx \frac{1}{\Delta y^2}(\psi_{i,j+1} - 2\psi_{i,j} + \psi_{i,j-1})$$

(8.94)

The use of subscript notation allows these expressions to be programmed directly into a scientific computer language.

When (8.93) and (8.94) are substituted into Laplace's equation (8.92), the result is the algebraic formula

$$2(1 + \beta)\psi_{i,j} \approx \psi_{i-1,j} + \psi_{i+1,j} + \beta(\psi_{i,j-1} + \psi_{i,j+1}) \tag{8.95}$$

where $\beta = (\Delta x/\Delta y)^2$ depends on the mesh size selected. This finite difference model of Laplace's equation states that every nodal stream-function value $\psi_{i,j}$ is a linear combination of its four nearest neighbors.

The most commonly programmed case is a square mesh ($\beta = 1$), for which Eq. (8.95) reduces to

$$\boxed{\psi_{i,j} \approx \tfrac{1}{4}(\psi_{i,j+1} + \psi_{i,j-1} + \psi_{i+1,j} + \psi_{i-1,j})} \tag{8.96}$$

Thus, for a square mesh, each nodal value equals the arithmetic average of the four neighbors shown in Fig. 8.33. The formula is easily remembered and easily programmed. The formula is applied in iterative fashion sweeping over each of the internal nodes (I, J), with known values of P specified at each of the surrounding boundary nodes. Any initial guesses can be specified for the internal nodes, and the iteration process will converge to the final algebraic solution in a finite number of sweeps. The numerical error, compared with the exact solution of Laplace's equation, is proportional to the square of the mesh size.

The Boundary Element Method

A relatively new technique for numerical solution of partial differential equations is the *boundary element method* (BEM). Reference 7 is an introductory textbook outlining the concepts of BEM. There are no interior elements. Rather, all nodes are placed on the boundary of the domain, as in Fig. 8.34. The "element" is a small piece of the boundary surrounding the node. The "strength" of the element can be either constant or variable.

For plane potential flow, the method takes advantage of the particular solution

$$\psi^* = \frac{1}{2\pi} \ln \frac{1}{r} \qquad (8.97)$$

which satisfies Laplace's equation, $\nabla^2 \psi = 0$. Each element i is assumed to have a different strength ψ_i. Then r represents the distance from that element to any other point in the flow field. Summing all these elemental effects, with proper boundary conditions, will give the total solution to the potential flow problem.

At each element of the boundary, we typically know either the value of ψ or the value of $\partial\psi/\partial n$, where n is normal to the boundary. (Mixed combinations of ψ and $\partial\psi/\partial n$ are also possible but are not discussed here.) The correct strengths ψ_i are such that these boundary conditions are satisfied at every element. Summing these effects over N elements requires integration by parts plus a careful evaluation of the (singular) effect of element i upon itself. The mathematical details are given in Ref. 7. The result is a set of N algebraic equations for the unknown boundary values. In the case of elements of constant strength, the final expression is

$$\frac{1}{2}\psi_i + \sum_{j=1}^{N} \psi_j \left(\int_j \frac{\partial\psi^*}{\partial n} \, ds \right) = \sum_{j=1}^{N} \left(\frac{\partial\psi}{\partial n} \right)_j \left(\int_j \psi^* \, ds \right) \qquad i = 1 \text{ to } N \qquad (8.98)$$

The integrals, which involve the logarithmic particular solution ψ^* from Eq. (8.97), are evaluated numerically for each element.

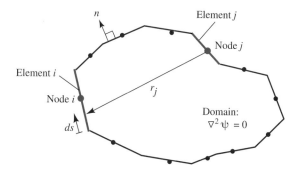

Fig. 8.34 Boundary elements of constant strength in plane potential flow.

Reference 7 is a general introduction to boundary elements, while Ref. 38 emphasizes programming methods. Meanwhile, research continues. Dargush and Grigoriev [42] have developed a multilevel boundary element method for steady Stokes or *creeping* flows (see Sec. 7.6) in irregular geometries. Their scheme avoids the heavy memory and CPU-time requirements of most boundary element methods. They estimate that CPU time is reduced by a factor of 700,000 and required memory is reduced by a factor of 16,000.

Viscous Flow Computer Models

Our previous finite difference model of Laplace's equation, as in Eq. (8.96), was very well behaved and converged nicely with or without overrelaxation. Much more care is needed to model the full Navier-Stokes equations. The challenges are quite different, and they have been met to a large extent, so there are now many textbooks [5, 20, 23 to 27] on (fully viscous) CFD. This is not a textbook on CFD, but we will address some of the issues in this section.

One-Dimensional Unsteady Flow

We consider a simplified problem, showing that even a single viscous term introduces new effects and possible instabilities. Recall (or review) Prob. P4.85, where a wall moves and drives a viscous fluid parallel to itself. Gravity is neglected. Let the wall be the plane $y = 0$, moving at a speed $U_0(t)$, as in Fig. 8.35. A uniform vertical grid, of spacing Δy, has nodes n at which the local velocity u_n^j is to be calculated, where superscript j denotes the time-step $j\Delta t$. The wall is $n = 1$. If $u = u(y, t)$ only and $v = w = 0$, continuity, $\nabla \cdot \mathbf{V} = 0$, is satisfied, and we need only solve the x-momentum Navier-Stokes equation:

$$\frac{\partial u}{\partial t} = \nu \frac{\partial^2 u}{\partial y^2} \tag{8.99}$$

where $\nu = \mu/\rho$. Utilizing the same finite difference approximations as in Eq. (8.93), we may model Eq. (8.99) algebraically as a forward time difference and a central spatial difference:

$$\frac{u_n^{j+1} - u_n^j}{\Delta t} \approx \nu \frac{u_{n+1}^j - 2u_n^j + u_{n-1}^j}{\Delta y^2}$$

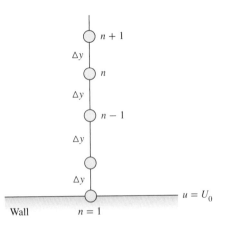

Fig. 8.35 An equally spaced finite difference mesh for one-dimensional viscous flow [Eq. (8.99)].

Rearrange and find that we can solve explicitly for u_n at the next time-step $j + 1$:

$$u_n^{j+1} \approx (1 - 2\sigma)\, u_n^j + \sigma(u_{n-1}^j + u_{n+1}^j) \qquad \sigma = \frac{\nu \Delta t}{\Delta y^2} \qquad (8.100)$$

Thus u at node n at the next time-step $j + 1$ is a weighted average of three previous values, similar to the "four-nearest-neighbors" average in the laplacian model of Eq. (8.96). Since the new velocity is calculated immediately, Eq. (8.100) is called an *explicit* model. It differs from the well-behaved laplacian model, however, because it may be *unstable*. The weighting coefficients in Eq. (8.100) must all be positive to avoid divergence. Now σ is positive, but $(1 - 2\sigma)$ may not be. Therefore, our explicit viscous flow model has a stability requirement:

$$\sigma = \frac{\nu \Delta t}{\Delta y^2} \le \frac{1}{2} \qquad (8.101)$$

Normally one would first set up the mesh size Δy in Fig. 8.35, after which Eq. (8.101) would limit the time-step Δt. The solutions for nodal values would then be stable, but not necessarily that accurate. The mesh sizes Δy and Δt could be reduced to increase accuracy, similar to the case of the potential flow laplacian model (8.96).

For example, to solve Prob. P4.85 numerically, one sets up a mesh with plenty of nodes (30 or more Δy within the expected viscous layer); selects Δt according to Eq. (8.101); and sets two boundary conditions[8] for all j: $u_1 = U_0 \sin \omega t$ and $u_N = 0$, where N is the outermost node. For initial conditions, perhaps assume the fluid initially at rest: $u_n^1 = 0$ for $2 \le n \le N - 1$. Sweeping the nodes $2 \le n \le N - 1$ using Eq. (8.100) (an Excel spreadsheet is excellent for this), one generates numerical values of u_n^j for as long as one desires. After an initial transient, the final "steady" fluid oscillation will approach the classical solution in viscous flow textbooks [15]. Try Prob. P8.115 to demonstrate this.

Steady Two-Dimensional Laminar Flow

The previous example, unsteady one-dimensional flow, had only one viscous term and no convective accelerations. Let us look briefly at incompressible two-dimensional steady flow, which has four of each type of term, plus a nontrivial continuity equation:

Continuity:
$$\frac{\partial u}{\partial x} + \frac{\partial v}{\partial y} = 0 \qquad (8.102a)$$

x momentum:
$$u\frac{\partial u}{\partial x} + v\frac{\partial u}{\partial y} = -\frac{1}{\rho}\frac{\partial p}{\partial x} + \nu\left(\frac{\partial^2 u}{\partial x^2} + \frac{\partial^2 u}{\partial y^2}\right) \qquad (8.102b)$$

y momentum:
$$u\frac{\partial v}{\partial x} + v\frac{\partial v}{\partial y} = -\frac{1}{\rho}\frac{\partial p}{\partial y} + \nu\left(\frac{\partial^2 v}{\partial x^2} + \frac{\partial^2 v}{\partial y^2}\right) \qquad (8.102c)$$

These equations, to be solved for (u, v, p) as functions of (x, y), are familiar to us from analytical solutions in Chaps. 4 and 6. However, to a numerical analyst, they are odd, because there is no *pressure equation*—that is, a differential equation for which the dominant derivatives involve p. This situation has led to several different

---

[8]Finite differences are not analytical; one must set U_0 and ω equal to numerical values.

"pressure adjustment" schemes in the literature [20, 23 to 27], most of which manipulate the continuity equation to insert a pressure correction.

A second difficulty in Eqs. (8.102b and c) is the presence of nonlinear convective accelerations such as $u(\partial u/\partial x)$, which creates asymmetry in viscous flows. Early attempts, which modeled such terms with a central difference, led to numerical instability. The remedy is to relate convection finite differences solely to the *upwind* flow entering the cell, ignoring the downwind cell. For example, the derivative $\partial u/\partial x$ could be modeled, for a given cell, as $(u_{\text{upwind}} - u_{\text{cell}})/\Delta x$. Such improvements have made fully viscous CFD an effective tool, with various commercial user-friendly codes available. For details beyond our scope, see Refs. 20 and 23 to 27.

Mesh generation and gridding have also become quite refined in modern CFD. Figure 8.36 illustrates a CFD solution of two-dimensional flow past an NACA

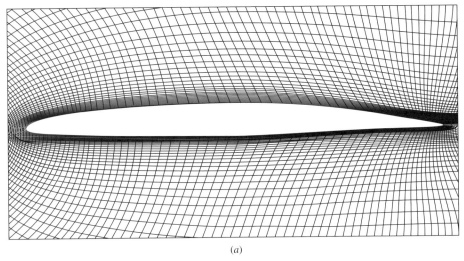

(a)

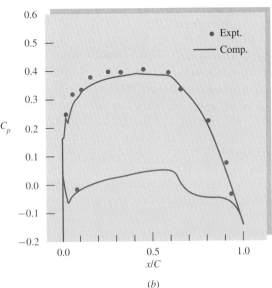

Fig. 8.36 CFD results for water flow past an NACA 66(MOD) hydrofoil *(from Ref. 28, with permission of the American Society of Mechanical Engineers)*: (a) C gridding, 262 by 91 nodes; (b) surface pressures at $\alpha = 1°$.

(b)

66(MOD) hydrofoil [28]. The gridding in Fig. 8.36*a* is of the C type, which wraps around the leading edge and trails off behind the foil, thus capturing the important near-wall and wake details without wasting nodes in front or to the sides. The grid size is 262 by 91.

The CFD model for this hydrofoil flow is also quite sophisticated: a full Navier-Stokes solver with turbulence modeling [29] and allowance for cavitation bubble formation when surface pressures drop below the local vapor pressure. Figure 8.36*b* compares computed and experimental surface pressure coefficients for an angle of attack of 1°. The dimensionless pressure coefficient is defined as $C_p = (p_{\text{surface}} - p_\infty)/(\rho V_\infty^2/2)$. The agreement is excellent, as indeed it is also for cases where the hydrofoil cavitates [28]. Clearly, when properly implemented for the proper flow cases, CFD can be an extremely effective tool for engineers.

Commercial CFD Codes

The arrival of the third millennium has seen an enormous emphasis on computer applications in nearly every field, fluid mechanics being a prime example. It is now possible, at least for moderately complex geometries and flow patterns, to model on a computer, approximately, the equations of motion of fluid flow, with dedicated CFD textbooks available [5, 20, 23 to 27]. The flow region is broken into a fine grid of elements and nodes, which algebraically simulate the basic partial differential equations of flow. While simple two-dimensional flow simulations have long been reported and can be programmed as student exercises, three-dimensional flows, involving thousands or even millions of grid points, are now solvable with the modern supercomputer.

Although elementary computer modeling was treated briefly here, the general topic of CFD is essentially for advanced study or professional practice. The big change over the past decade is that engineers, rather than laboriously programming CFD problems themselves, can now take advantage of any of several commercial CFD codes. These extensive software packages allow engineers to construct a geometry and boundary conditions to simulate a given viscous flow problem. The software then grids the flow region and attempts to compute flow properties at each grid element. The convenience is great; the danger is also great. That is, computations are not merely automatic, like when using a hand calculator, but rather require care and concern from the user. Convergence and accuracy are real problems for the modeler. Use of the codes requires some art and experience. In particular, when the flow Reynolds number, $\text{Re} = \rho VL/\mu$, goes from moderate (laminar flow) to high (turbulent flow), the accuracy of the simulation is no longer assured in any real sense. The reason is that turbulent flows are not completely resolved by the full equations of motion, and one resorts to using approximate turbulence models.

Turbulence models [29] are developed for particular geometries and flow conditions and may be inaccurate or unrealistic for others. This is discussed by Freitas [30], who compared eight different commercial code calculations (FLOW-3D, FLOTRAN, STAR-CD, N3S, CFD-ACE, FLUENT, CFDS-FLOW3D, and NISA/3D-FLUID) with experimental results for five benchmark flow experiments. Calculations were made by the vendors themselves. Freitas concludes that commercial codes, though promising in general, can be inaccurate for certain laminar and turbulent flow situations. Recent modifications to the standard turbulence models have improved their accuracy and reliability, as shown by Elkhoury [47].

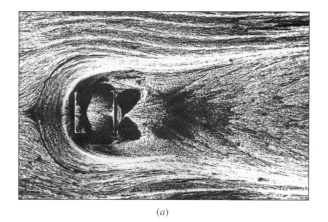

(a)

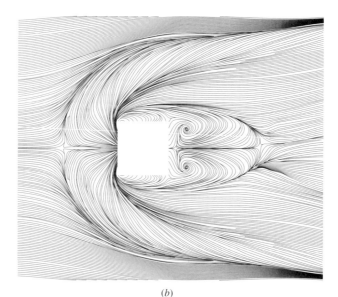

Fig. 8.37 Flow over a surface-mounted cube creates a complex and perhaps unexpected pattern: (a) experimental oil-streak visualization of surface flow at Re = 40,000 (based on cube height) (*Courtesy of Robert Martinuzzi with the permission of the American Society of Mechanical Engineers*); (b) computational large-eddy simulation of the surface flow in (a) (*from Ref. 32, courtesy of Kishan Shah, Stanford University*); and (c) a side view of the flow in (a) visualized by smoke generation and a laser light sheet (*Courtesy of Robert Martinuzzi with the permission of the American Society of Mechanical Engineers*).

(b)

(c)

An example of erratic CFD results has already been mentioned here, namely, the drag and lift of a rotating cylinder, Fig. 8.15. Perhaps because the flow itself is physically unstable [41, 44], results computed by different workers are strikingly different: Some predicted forces are high, some low, some increase, some decrease.

In spite of this warning to treat CFD codes with care, one should also realize that the results of a given CFD simulation can be spectacular. Figure 8.37 illustrates turbulent flow past a cube mounted on the floor of a channel whose clearance is twice the cube height. Compare Fig. 8.37a, a top view of the experimental surface flow [31] as visualized by oil streaks, with Fig. 8.37b, a CFD supercomputer result using the method of large-eddy simulation [32, 33]. The agreement is remarkable. The C-shaped flow pattern in front of the cube is caused by formation of a horseshoe vortex, as seen in a side view of the experiment [31] in Fig. 8.37c. Horseshoe vortices commonly result when surface shear flows meet an obstacle. We conclude that CFD has a tremendous potential for flow prediction.

Summary

This chapter has analyzed a highly idealized but very useful type of flow: inviscid, incompressible, irrotational flow, for which Laplace's equation holds for the velocity potential (8.1) and for the plane stream function (8.7). The mathematics is well developed, and solutions of potential flows can be obtained for practically any body shape.

Some solution techniques outlined here are (1) superposition of elementary line or point solutions in both plane and axisymmetric flow, (2) the analytic functions of a complex variable, and (3) numerical analysis on a computer. Potential theory is especially useful and accurate for thin bodies such as airfoils. The only requirement is that the boundary layer be thin—in other words, that the Reynolds number be large.

For blunt bodies or highly divergent flows, potential theory serves as a first approximation, to be used as input to a boundary layer analysis. The reader should consult the advanced texts [for example, 2 to 4, 11 to 13] for further applications of potential theory. Section 8.9 discussed computational methods for viscous (nonpotential) flows.

Problems

Most of the problems herein are fairly straightforward. More difficult or open-ended assignments are labeled with an asterisk. Problems labeled with a computer icon 💻 may require the use of a computer. The standard end-of-chapter problems P8.1 to P8.115 (categorized in the problem list here) are followed by word problems W8.1 to W8.7, comprehensive problems C8.1 to C8.7, and design projects D8.1 to D8.3.

Problem Distribution

Section	Topic	Problems
8.1	Introduction and review	P8.1–P8.7
8.2	Elementary plane flow solutions	P8.8–P8.17
8.3	Superposition of plane flows	P8.18–P8.34
8.4	Plane flow past closed-body shapes	P8.35–P8.59
8.5	The complex potential	P8.60–P8.71
8.6	Images	P8.72–P8.79
8.7	Airfoil theory: two-dimensional	P8.80–P8.84
8.7	Airfoil theory: finite-span wings	P8.85–P8.90
8.8	Axisymmetric potential flow	P8.91–P8.103
8.8	Hydrodynamic mass	P8.104–P8.105
8.9	Numerical methods	P8.106–P8.115

Introduction and review

P8.1 Prove that the streamlines $\psi(r, \theta)$ in polar coordinates from Eqs. (8.10) are orthogonal to the potential lines $\phi(r, \theta)$.

P8.2 The steady plane flow in Fig. P8.2 has the polar velocity components $v_\theta = \Omega r$ and $v_r = 0$. Determine the circulation Γ around the path shown.

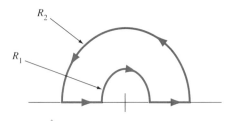

P8.2

P8.3 Using cartesian coordinates, show that each velocity component (u, v, w) of a potential flow satisfies Laplace's equation separately.

P8.4 Is the function $1/r$ a legitimate velocity potential in plane polar coordinates? If so, what is the associated stream function $\psi(r, \theta)$?

P8.5 A proposed harmonic function $F(x, y, z)$ is given by

$$F = 2x^2 + y^3 - 4xz + f(y)$$

(a) If possible, find a function $f(y)$ for which the laplacian of F is zero. If you do indeed solve part (a), can your final function F serve as (b) a velocity potential or (c) a stream function?

P8.6 An incompressible plane flow has the velocity potential $\phi = 2Kxy$, where B is a constant. Find the stream function of this flow, sketch a few streamlines, and interpret the flow pattern.

P8.7 Consider a flow with constant density and viscosity. If the flow possesses a velocity potential as defined by Eq. (8.1), show that it exactly satisfies the full Navier-Stokes equations (4.38). If this is so, why for inviscid theory do we back away from the full Navier-Stokes equations?

Elementary plane flow solutions

P8.8 For the velocity distribution $u = -By$, $v = +Bx$, $w = 0$, evaluate the circulation Γ about the rectangular closed curve defined by $(x, y) = (1,1), (3,1), (3,2),$ and $(1,2)$. Interpret your result, especially vis-à-vis the velocity potential.

P8.9 Consider the two-dimensional flow $u = -Ax$, $v = Ay$, where A is a constant. Evaluate the circulation Γ around the rectangular closed curve defined by $(x, y) = (1, 1), (4, 1), (4, 3),$ and $(1, 3)$. Interpret your result, especially vis-à-vis the velocity potential.

P8.10 A two-dimensional Rankine half-body, 8 cm thick, is placed in a water tunnel at 20°C. The water pressure far upstream along the body centerline is 105 kPa. What is the nose radius of the half-body? At what tunnel flow velocity will cavitation bubbles begin to form on the surface of the body?

P8.11 A power plant discharges cooling water through the manifold in Fig. P8.11, which is 55 cm in diameter and 8 m high and is perforated with 25,000 holes 1 cm in diameter. Does

this manifold simulate a line source? If so, what is the equivalent source strength m?

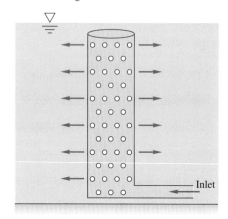

P8.11

P8.12 Consider the flow due to a vortex of strength K at the origin. Evaluate the circulation from Eq. (8.23) about the clockwise path from $(r, \theta) = (a, 0)$ to $(2a, 0)$ to $(2a, 3\pi/2)$ to $(a, 3\pi/2)$ and back to $(a, 0)$. Interpret the result.

P8.13 Starting at the stagnation point in Fig. 8.6, the fluid *acceleration* along the half-body surface rises to a maximum and eventually drops off to zero far downstream. (a) Does this maximum occur at the point in Fig. 8.6 where $U_{max} = 1.26U$? (b) If not, does the maximum acceleration occur before or after that point? Explain.

P8.14 A tornado may be modeled as the circulating flow shown in Fig. P8.14, with $v_r = v_z = 0$ and $v_\theta(r)$ such that

$$v_\theta = \begin{cases} \omega r & r \le R \\ \dfrac{\omega R^2}{r} & r > R \end{cases}$$

Determine whether this flow pattern is irrotational in either the inner or outer region. Using the r-momentum equation (D.5) of App. D, determine the pressure distribution $p(r)$ in the tornado, assuming $p = p_\infty$ as $r \to \infty$. Find the location and magnitude of the lowest pressure.

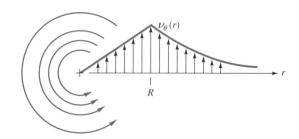

P8.14

P8.15 Hurricane Sandy, which hit the New Jersey coast on Oct. 29, 2012, was extremely broad, with wind velocities of 40 mi/h at 400 miles from its center. Its maximum velocity was 90 mi/h. Using the model of Fig. P8.14, at 20°C with a pressure of 100 kPa far from the center, estimate (a) the radius R of maximum velocity, in mi; and (b) the pressure at $r = R$.

P8.16 Air flows at 1.2 m/s along a flat surface when it encounters a jet of air issuing from the horizontal wall at point A, as in Fig. P8.16. The jet volume flow is 0.4 m^3/s per unit depth into the paper. If the jet is approximated as an inviscid line source, (a) locate the stagnation point S on the wall. (b) How far vertically will the jet flow extend into the stream?

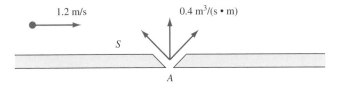

P8.16

P8.17 Find the position (x, y) on the upper surface of the half-body in Fig. 8.9a for which the local velocity equals the uniform stream velocity. What should be the pressure at this point?

Superposition of plane flows

P8.18 Plot the streamlines and potential lines of the flow due to a line source of strength m at $(a, 0)$ plus a source $3m$ at $(-a, 0)$. What is the flow pattern viewed from afar?

P8.19 Plot the streamlines and potential lines of the flow due to a line source of strength $3m$ at $(a, 0)$ plus a sink $-m$ at $(-a, 0)$. What is the pattern viewed from afar?

P8.20 Plot the streamlines of the flow due to a line vortex $+K$ at $(0, +a)$ and a vortex $-K$ at $(0, -a)$. What is the pattern viewed from afar?

P8.21 At point A in Fig. P8.21 is a clockwise line vortex of strength $K = 12$ m^2/s. At point B is a line source of strength $m = 25$ m^2/s. Determine the resultant velocity induced by these two at point C.

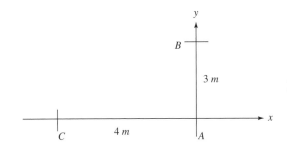

P8.21

P8.22 Consider inviscid stagnation flow, $\psi = Kxy$ (see Fig. 8.19b), superimposed with a source at the origin of strength m. Plot the resulting streamlines in the upper half-plane, using the length scale $a = (m/K)^{1/2}$. Give a physical interpretation of the flow pattern.

P8.23 Sources of strength $m = 10$ m^2/s are placed at points A and B in Fig. P8.23. At what height h should source B be placed so that the net induced horizontal velocity component at the origin is 8 m/s to the left?

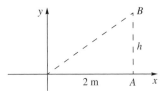

P8.23

P8.24 Line sources of equal strength $m = Ua$, where U is a reference velocity, are placed at $(x, y) = (0, a)$ and $(0, -a)$. Sketch the stream and potential lines in the upper half plane. Is $y = 0$ a "wall"? If so, sketch the pressure coefficient

$$C_p = \frac{p - p_0}{\frac{1}{2}\rho U^2}$$

along the wall, where p_0 is the pressure at $(0, 0)$. Find the minimum pressure point and indicate where flow separation might occur in the boundary layer.

P8.25 Let the vortex/sink flow of Eq. (8.16) simulate a tornado as in Fig. P8.25. Suppose that the circulation about the tornado is $\Gamma = 8500$ m^2/s and that the pressure at $r = 40$ m is 2200 Pa less than the far-field pressure. Assuming inviscid flow at sea-level density, estimate (a) the appropriate sink strength $-m$, (b) the pressure at $r = 15$ m, and (c) the angle β at which the streamlines cross the circle at $r = 40$ m (see Fig. P8.25).

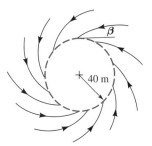

P8.25

P8.26 A coastal power plant takes in cooling water through a vertical perforated manifold, as in Fig. P8.26. The total volume flow intake is 110 m^3/s. Currents of 25 cm/s flow past the manifold, as shown. Estimate (a) how far downstream and (b) how far normal to the paper the effects of the intake are felt in the ambient 8-m-deep waters.

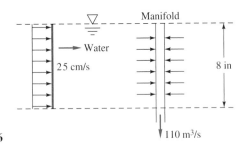

P8.26

P8.27   Water at 20°C flows past a half-body as shown in Fig. P8.27. Measured pressures at points A and B are 160 kPa and 90 kPa, respectively, with uncertainties of 3 kPa each. Estimate the stream velocity and its uncertainty.

P8.28   Sources of equal strength m are placed at the four symmetric positions $(x, y) = (a, a), (-a, a), (-a, -a)$, and $(a, -a)$. Sketch the streamline and potential line patterns. Do any plane "walls" appear?

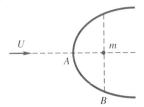

P8.27

P8.29   A uniform water stream, $U_\infty = 20$ m/s and $\rho = 998$ kg/m^3, combines with a source at the origin to form a half-body. At $(x, y) = (0, 1.2$ m$)$, the pressure is 12.5 kPa less than p_∞. (a) Is this point outside the body? Estimate (b) the appropriate source strength m and (c) the pressure at the nose of the body.

P8.30   A tornado is simulated by a line sink $m = -1000$ m^2/s plus a line vortex $K = 1600$ m^2/s. Find the angle between any streamline and a radial line, and show that it is independent of both r and θ. If this tornado forms in sea-level standard air, at what radius will the local pressure be equivalent to 29 inHg?

P8.31   A Rankine half-body is formed as shown in Fig. P8.31. For the stream velocity and body dimension shown, compute (a) the source strength m in m^2/s, (b) the distance a, (c) the distance h, and (d) the total velocity at point A.

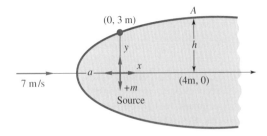

P8.31

P8.32   Line sources m_1 and m_2 are near point A, as in Fig. P8.32. If $m_1 = 30$ m^2/2, find the value of m_2 for which the resultant velocity at point A is exactly vertical.

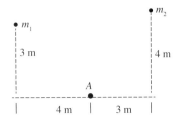

P8.32

P8.33   Sketch the streamlines, especially the body shape, due to equal line sources $+m$ at $(0, +a)$ and $(0, -a)$ plus a uniform stream $U_\infty = ma$.

P8.34   Consider three equally spaced sources of strength m placed at $(x, y) = (+a, 0), (0, 0)$, and $(-a, 0)$. Sketch the resulting streamlines, noting the position of any stagnation points. What would the pattern look like from afar?

Plane flow past closed-body shapes

P8.35   A uniform stream, $U_\infty = 4$ m/s, approaches a Rankine oval as in Fig. 8.13, with $a = 50$ cm. Find the strength m of the source–sink pair, in m^2/s, which will cause the total length of the oval to be 250 cm. What is the maximum width of this oval?

P8.36   When a line source–sink pair with $m = 2$ m^2/s is combined with a uniform stream, it forms a Rankine oval whose minimum dimension is 40 cm. If $a = 15$ cm, what are the stream velocity and the velocity at the shoulder? What is the maximum dimension?

P8.37   A Rankine oval 2 m long and 1 m high is immersed in a stream $U_\infty = 10$ m/s, as in Fig. P8.37. Estimate (a) the velocity at point A and (b) the location of point B where a particle approaching the stagnation point achieves its maximum deceleration.

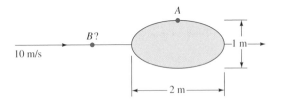

P8.37

P8.38   Consider potential flow of a uniform stream in the x direction plus two equal sources, one at $(x, y) = (0, +a)$ and the other at $(x, y) = (0, -a)$. Sketch your ideas of the body contours that would arise if the sources were (a) very weak and (b) very strong.

P8.39 A large Rankine oval, with $a = 1$ m and $h = 1$ m, is immersed in 20°C water flowing at 10 m/s. The upstream pressure on the oval centerline is 200 kPa. Calculate (a) the value of m; and (b) the pressure on the top of the oval (analogous to point A in Fig. P8.37).

P8.40 Modify the Rankine oval in Fig. P8.37 so that the stream velocity and body length are the same but the thickness is unknown (not 1 m). The fluid is water at 30°C and the pressure far upstream along the body centerline is 108 kPa. Find the body thickness for which cavitation will occur at point A.

P8.41 A Kelvin oval is formed by a line–vortex pair with $K = 9$ m^2/s, $a = 1$ m, and $U = 10$ m/s. What are the height, width, and shoulder velocity of this oval?

P8.42 The vertical keel of a sailboat approximates a Rankine oval 125 cm long and 30 cm thick. The boat sails in seawater in standard atmosphere at 14 knots, parallel to the keel. At a section 2 m below the surface, estimate the lowest pressure on the surface of the keel.

P8.43 Water at 20°C flows past a 1-m-diameter circular cylinder. The upstream centerline pressure is 128,500 Pa. If the lowest pressure on the cylinder surface is exactly the vapor pressure, estimate, by potential theory, the stream velocity.

P8.44 Suppose that circulation is added to the cylinder flow of Prob. P8.43 sufficient to place the stagnation points at θ equal to 35° and 145°. What is the required vortex strength K in m^2/s? Compute the resulting pressure and surface velocity at (a) the stagnation points and (b) the upper and lower shoulders. What will the lift per meter of cylinder width be?

P8.45 If circulation K is added to the cylinder flow in Prob. P8.43, (a) for what value of K will the flow begin to cavitate at the surface? (b) Where on the surface will cavitation begin? (c) For this condition, where will the stagnation points lie?

P8.46 A cylinder is formed by bolting two semicylindrical channels together on the inside, as shown in Fig. P8.46. There are 10 bolts per meter of width on each side, and the inside pressure is 50 kPa (gage). Using potential theory for the outside pressure, compute the tension force in each bolt if the fluid outside is sea-level air.

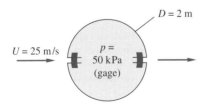

P8.46

P8.47 A circular cylinder is fitted with two surface-mounted pressure sensors, to measure p_a at $\theta = 180°$ and p_b at $\theta = 105°$. The intention is to use the cylinder as a stream velocimeter. Using inviscid theory, derive a formula for estimating U_∞ in terms of p_a, p_b, ρ, and the cylinder radius a.

*P8.48 Wind at U_∞ and p_∞ flows past a Quonset hut which is a half-cylinder of radius a and length L (Fig. P8.48). The internal pressure is p_i. Using inviscid theory, derive an expression for the upward force on the hut due to the difference between p_i and p_s.

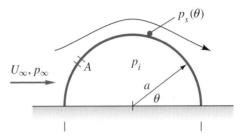

P8.48

P8.49 In strong winds the force in Prob. P8.48 can be quite large. Suppose that a hole is introduced in the hut roof at point A to make p_i equal to the surface pressure there. At what angle θ should hole A be placed to make the net wind force zero?

P8.50 It is desired to simulate flow past a two-dimensional ridge or bump by using a streamline that passes above the flow over a cylinder, as in Fig. P8.50. The bump is to be $a/2$ high, where a is the cylinder radius. What is the elevation h of this streamline? What is U_{max} on the bump compared with stream velocity U?

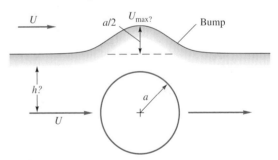

P8.50

P8.51 A hole is placed in the front of a cylinder to measure the stream velocity of sea-level fresh water. The measured pressure at the hole is 2840 lbf/ft^2. If the hole is misaligned by 12° from the stream, and misinterpreted as stagnation pressure, what is the error in velocity?

P8.52 The Flettner rotor sailboat in Fig. E8.3 has a water drag coefficient of 0.006 based on a wetted area of 45 ft^2. If the rotor spins at 220 r/min, find the maximum boat velocity that can be achieved in a 15-mi/h wind. What is the optimum angle between the boat and the wind?

P8.53 Modify Prob. P8.52 as follows. For the same sailboat data, find the wind velocity, in mi/h, that will drive the boat at an optimum speed of 8 kn parallel to its keel.

P8.54 The original Flettner rotor ship was approximately 100 ft long, displaced 800 tons, and had a wetted area of 3500 ft². As sketched in Fig. P8.54, it had two rotors 50 ft high and 9 ft in diameter rotating at 750 r/min, which is far outside the range of Fig. 8.15. The measured lift and drag coefficients for each rotor were about 10 and 4, respectively. If the ship is moored and subjected to a crosswind of 25 ft/s, as in Fig. P8.54, what will the wind force parallel and normal to the ship centerline be? Estimate the power required to drive the rotors.

P8.55 Assume that the Flettner rotor ship of Fig. P8.54 has a water resistance coefficient of 0.005. How fast will the ship sail in seawater at 20°C in a 20-ft/s wind if the keel aligns itself with the resultant force on the rotors? [*Hint:* This is a problem in relative velocities.]

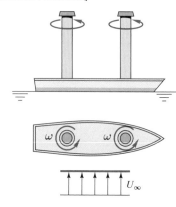

P8.54

P8.56 A proposed free-stream velocimeter would use a cylinder with pressure taps at $\theta = 180°$ and at $150°$. The pressure difference would be a measure of stream velocity U_∞. However, the cylinder must be aligned so that one tap exactly faces the free stream. Let the misalignment angle be δ; that is, the two taps are at $(180° + \delta)$ and $(150° + \delta)$. Make a plot of the percentage error in velocity measurement in the range $-20° < \delta < +20°$ and comment on the idea.

P8.57 In principle, it is possible to use rotating cylinders as aircraft wings. Consider a cylinder 30 cm in diameter, rotating at 2400 r/min. It is to lift a 55-kN airplane cruising at 100 m/s. What should the cylinder length be? How much power is required to maintain this speed? Neglect end effects on the rotating wing.

P8.58 Plot the streamlines due to the combined flow of a line sink $-m$ at the origin plus line sources $+m$ at $(a, 0)$ and $(4a, 0)$. [*Hint:* A cylinder of radius $2a$ will appear.]

P8.59 The Transition® car-plane in Fig. 7.30 has a gross weight of 1430 lbf. Suppose we replace the wing with a 1-ft-diameter rotating cylinder 20 ft long. (*a*) What rotation rate from Fig. 8.15, in r/min, would lift the plane at a take-off speed of 55 mi/h? (*b*) Estimate the cylinder drag at this rotation rate. Neglect fuselage lift and cylinder end effects.

The complex potential

P8.60 One of the corner flow patterns of Fig. 8.18 is given by the cartesian stream function $\psi = A(3yx^2 - y^3)$. Which one? Can the correspondence be proved from Eq. (8.53)?

P8.61 Plot the streamlines of Eq. (8.53) in the upper right quadrant for $n = 4$. How does the velocity increase with x outward along the x axis from the origin? For what corner angle and value of n would this increase be linear in x? For what corner angle and n would the increase be as x^5?

P8.62 Combine stagnation flow, Fig. 8.19*b*, with a source at the origin:

$$f(z) = Az^2 + m \ln z$$

Plot the streamlines for $m = AL^2$, where L is a length scale. Interpret.

P8.63 The superposition in Prob. P8.62 leads to stagnation flow near a curved bump, in contrast to the flat wall of Fig. 8.19*b*. Determine the maximum height H of the bump as a function of the constants A and m.

P8.64 Consider the polar-coordinate stream function $\psi = Br^{1.2} \sin(1.2\,\theta)$, with B equal, for convenience, to 1.0 ft$^{0.8}$/s. (*a*) Plot the streamline $\psi = 0$ in the upper half plane. (*b*) Plot the streamline $\psi = 1.0$ and interpret the flow pattern. (*c*) Find the locus of points above $\psi = 0$ for which the resultant velocity $= 1.2$ ft/s.

P8.65 Potential flow past a wedge of half-angle θ leads to an important application of laminar boundary layer theory called the *Falkner-Skan flows* [15, pp. 239–245]. Let x denote distance along the wedge wall, as in Fig. P8.65, and let $\theta = 10°$. Use Eq. (8.53) to find the variation of surface velocity $U(x)$ along the wall. Is the pressure gradient adverse or favorable?

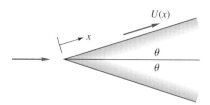

P8.65

*P8.66 The inviscid velocity along the wedge in Prob. P8.65 has the analytic form $U(x) = Cx^m$, where $m = n - 1$ and n is the exponent in Eq. (8.53). Show that, for any C and n, computation of the boundary layer by Thwaites's method, Eqs. (7.53) and (7.54), leads to a unique value of the Thwaites parameter λ. Thus wedge flows are called *similar* [15, p. 241].

P8.67 Investigate the complex potential function $f(z) = U_\infty(z + a^2/z)$ and interpret the flow pattern.

P8.68 Investigate the complex potential function $f(z) = U_\infty z + m \ln [(z + a)/(z-a)]$ and interpret the flow pattern.

P8.69 Investigate the complex potential $f(z) = A \cosh [\pi(z/a)]$, and plot the streamlines inside the region shown in Fig. P8.69. What hyphenated word (originally French) might describe such a flow pattern?

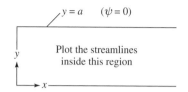

P8.69

P8.70 Show that the complex potential $f = U_\infty \{ z + \frac{1}{4}a \coth [\pi(z/a)] \}$ represents flow past an oval shape placed midway between two parallel walls $y = \pm\frac{1}{2}a$. What is a practical application?

P8.71 Figure P8.71 shows the streamlines and potential lines of flow over a thin-plate weir as computed by the complex potential method. Compare qualitatively with Fig. 10.16a. State the proper boundary conditions at all boundaries. The velocity potential has equally spaced values. Why do the flow-net "squares" become smaller in the overflow jet?

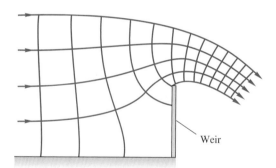

Weir

P8.71

Images

P8.72 Use the method of images to construct the flow pattern for a source $+m$ near two walls, as shown in Fig. P8.72. Sketch the velocity distribution along the lower wall ($y = 0$). Is there any danger of flow separation along this wall?

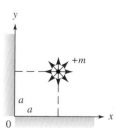

P8.72

P8.73 Set up an image system to compute the flow of a source at unequal distances from two walls, as in Fig. P8.73. Find the point of maximum velocity on the y axis.

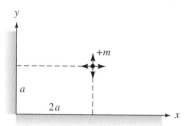

P8.73

P8.74 A positive line vortex K is trapped in a corner, as in Fig. P8.74. Compute the total induced velocity vector at point B, $(x, y) = (2a, a)$, and compare with the induced velocity when no walls are present.

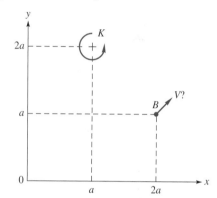

P8.74

P8.75 Using the four-source image pattern needed to construct the flow near a corner in Fig. P8.72, find the value of the source strength m that will induce a wall velocity of 4.0 m/s at the point $(x, y) = (a, 0)$ just below the source shown, if $a = 50$ cm.

P8.76 Use the method of images to approximate the flow pattern past a cylinder a distance $4a$ from a single wall, as in Fig. P8.76. To illustrate the effect of the wall, compute the velocities at corresponding points A, B, C, and D, comparing with a cylinder flow in an infinite expanse of fluid.

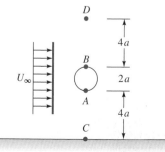

P8.76

P8.77 Discuss how the flow pattern of Prob. P8.58 might be interpreted to be an image system construction for circular walls. Why are there two images instead of one?

*P8.78 Indicate the system of images needed to construct the flow of a uniform stream past a Rankine half-body constrained between two parallel walls, as in Fig. P8.78. For the particular dimensions shown in this figure, estimate the position of the nose of the resulting half-body.

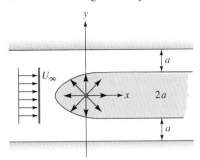

P8.78

P8.79 Explain the system of images needed to simulate the flow of a line source placed unsymmetrically between two parallel walls as in Fig. P8.79. Compute the velocity on the lower wall at $x = a$. How many images are needed to estimate this velocity within 1 percent?

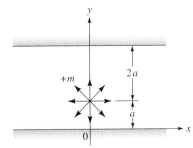

P8.79

Airfoil theory: two-dimensional

*P8.80 The beautiful expression for lift of a two-dimensional airfoil, Eq. (8.59), arose from applying the Joukowski transformation, $\zeta = z + a^2/z$, where $z = x + iy$ and $\zeta = \eta + i\beta$. The constant a is a length scale. The theory transforms a certain circle in the z plane into an airfoil in the ζ plane. Taking $a = 1$ unit for convenience, show that (a) a circle with center at the origin and radius > 1 will become an ellipse in the ζ plane and (b) a circle with center at $x = -\varepsilon \ll 1$, $y = 0$, and radius $(1 + \varepsilon)$ will become an airfoil shape in the ζ plane. [*Hint:* The Excel spreadsheet is excellent for solving this problem.]

*P8.81 Given an airplane of weight W, wing area A, aspect ratio AR, and flying at an altitude where the density is ρ. Assume all drag and lift is due to the wing, which has an infinite-span

drag coefficient $C_{D\infty}$. Further assume sufficient thrust to balance whatever drag is calculated. (a) Find an algebraic expression for the *best cruise velocity* V_b, which occurs when the ratio of drag to speed is a minimum. (b) Apply your formula to the data in Prob. P7.119 for which a laborious graphing procedure gave an answer $V_b \approx 180$ m/s.

P8.82 The ultralight plane *Gossamer Condor* in 1977 was the first to complete the Kremer Prize figure-eight course under human power. Its wingspan was 29 m, with $C_{av} = 2.3$ m and a total mass of 95 kg. The drag coefficient was approximately 0.05. The pilot was able to deliver $\frac{1}{4}$ hp to propel the plane. Assuming two-dimensional flow at sea level, estimate (a) the cruise speed attained, (b) the lift coefficient, and (c) the horsepower required to achieve a speed of 15 kn.

P8.83 The world's largest airplane, the Airbus A380, has a maximum weight of 1,200,000 lbf, wing area of 9100 ft², wingspan of 262 ft, and $C_{Do} = 0.026$. When cruising at maximum weight at 35,000 ft, the four engines each provide 70,000 lbf of thrust. Assuming all lift and drag are due to the wing, estimate the cruise velocity, in mi/h.

P8.84 Reference 12 contains inviscid theory calculations for the upper and lower surface velocity distributions $V(x)$ over an airfoil, where x is the chordwise coordinate. A typical result for small angle of attack is as follows:

x/c	V/U_∞(upper)	V/U_∞(lower)
0.0	0.0	0.0
0.025	0.97	0.82
0.05	1.23	0.98
0.1	1.28	1.05
0.2	1.29	1.13
0.3	1.29	1.16
0.4	1.24	1.16
0.6	1.14	1.08
0.8	0.99	0.95
1.0	0.82	0.82

Use these data, plus Bernoulli's equation, to estimate (a) the lift coefficient and (b) the angle of attack if the airfoil is symmetric.

Airfoil theory: finite-span wings

P8.85 A wing of 2 percent camber, 5-in chord, and 30-in span is tested at a certain angle of attack in a wind tunnel with sea-level standard air at 200 ft/s and is found to have lift of 30 lbf and drag of 1.5 lbf. Estimate from wing theory (a) the angle of attack, (b) the minimum drag of the wing and the angle of attack at which it occurs, and (c) the maximum lift-to-drag ratio.

P8.86 An airplane has a mass of 20,000 kg and flies at 175 m/s at 5000-m standard altitude. Its rectangular wing has a 3-m chord and a symmetric airfoil at 2.5° angle of attack. Estimate (a) the wing span, (b) the aspect ratio, and (c) the induced drag.

P8.87 A freshwater boat of mass 400 kg is supported by a rectangular hydrofoil of aspect ratio 8, 2 percent camber, and 12 percent thickness. If the boat travels at 7 m/s and $\alpha = 2.5°$, estimate (a) the chord length, (b) the power required if $C_{D_\infty} = 0.01$, and (c) the top speed if the boat is refitted with an engine that delivers 20 hp to the water.

P8.88 The Boeing 787-8 Dreamliner has a maximum weight of 502,500 lbf, a wingspan of 197 ft, a wing area of 3501 ft², and cruises at 567 mi/h at 35,000 ft altitude. When cruising, its overall drag coefficient is about 0.027. Estimate (a) the aspect ratio, (b) the lift coefficient, (c) the cruise Mach number, and (d) the engine thrust needed when cruising.

P8.89 The Beechcraft T-34C aircraft has a gross weight of 5500 lbf and a wing area of 60 ft² and flies at 322 mi/h at 10,000-ft standard altitude. It is driven by a propeller that delivers 300 hp to the air. Assume for this problem that its airfoil is the NACA 2412 section described in Figs. 8.23 and 8.24, and neglect all drag except the wing. What is the appropriate aspect ratio for the wing?

P8.90 NASA is developing a swing-wing airplane called the Bird of Prey [37]. As shown in Fig. P8.90, the wings pivot like a pocketknife blade: forward (a), straight (b), or backward (c). Discuss a possible advantage for each of these wing positions. If you can't think of one, read the article [37] and report to the class.

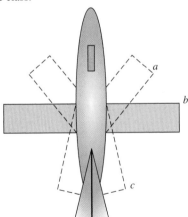

P8.90

Axisymmetric potential flow

P8.91 If $\phi(r, \theta)$ in axisymmetric flow is defined by Eq. (8.72) and the coordinates are given in Fig. 8.28, determine what partial differential equation is satisfied by ϕ.

P8.92 A point source with volume flow $Q = 30$ m³/s is immersed in a uniform stream of speed 4 m/s. A Rankine half-body of revolution results. Compute (a) the distance from source to

the stagnation point and (b) the two points (r, θ) on the body surface where the local velocity equals 4.5 m/s.

P8.93 The Rankine half-body of revolution (Fig. 8.30) could simulate the shape of a pitot-static tube (Fig. 6.30). According to inviscid theory, how far downstream from the nose should the static pressure holes be placed so that the local velocity is within ±0.5 percent of U_∞? Compare your answer with the recommendation $x \approx 8D$ in Fig. 6.30.

P8.94 Determine whether the Stokes streamlines from Eq. (8.73) are everywhere orthogonal to the Stokes potential lines from Eq. (8.74), as is the case for Cartesian and plane polar coordinates.

P8.95 Show that the axisymmetric potential flow formed by superposition of a point source $+m$ at $(x, y) = (-a, 0)$, a point sink $-m$ at $(+a, 0)$, and a stream U_∞ in the x direction forms a Rankine body of revolution as in Fig. P8.95. Find analytic expressions for determining the length $2L$ and maximum diameter $2R$ of the body in terms of m, U_∞, and a.

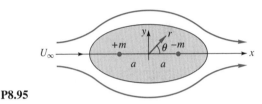

P8.95

P8.96 Consider inviscid flow along the streamline approaching the front stagnation point of a sphere, as in Fig. 8.31. Find (a) the maximum fluid deceleration along this streamline and (b) its position.

P8.97 The Rankine body of revolution in Fig. P8.97 is 60 cm long and 30 cm in diameter. When it is immersed in the low-pressure water tunnel as shown, cavitation may appear at point A. Compute the stream velocity U, neglecting surface wave formation, for which cavitation occurs.

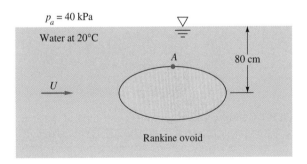

P8.97

P8.98 We have studied the point source (sink) and the line source (sink) of infinite depth into the paper. Does it make any sense to define a finite-length line sink (source) as in

Fig. P8.98? If so, how would you establish the mathematical properties of such a finite line sink? When combined with a uniform stream and a point source of equivalent strength as in Fig. P8.98, should a closed-body shape be formed? Make a guess and sketch some of these possible shapes for various values of the dimensionless parameter $m/(U_\infty L^2)$.

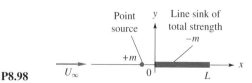

P8.98

*P8.99 Consider air flowing past a hemisphere resting on a flat surface, as in Fig. P8.99. If the internal pressure is p_i, find an expression for the pressure force on the hemisphere. By analogy with Prob. P8.49, at what point A on the hemisphere should a hole be cut so that the pressure force will be zero according to inviscid theory?

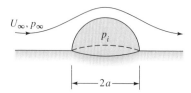

P8.99

P8.100 A 1-m-diameter sphere is being towed at speed V in fresh water at 20°C as shown in Fig. P8.100. Assuming inviscid theory with an undistorted free surface, estimate the speed V in m/s at which cavitation will first appear on the sphere surface. Where will cavitation appear? For this condition, what will be the pressure at point A on the sphere, which is 45° up from the direction of travel?

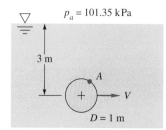

P8.100

P8.101 Consider a steel sphere (SG = 7.85) of diameter 2 cm, dropped from rest in water at 20°C. Assume a constant drag coefficient $C_D = 0.47$. Accounting for the sphere's hydrodynamic mass, estimate (a) its terminal velocity and (b) the time to reach 99 percent of terminal velocity. Compare these to the results when hydrodynamic mass is neglected, $V_{terminal} \approx 1.95$ m/s and $t_{99\%} \approx 0.605$ s, and discuss.

P8.102 A golf ball weighs 0.102 lbf and has a diameter of 1.7 in. A professional golfer strikes the ball at an initial velocity of 250 ft/s, an upward angle of 20°, and a backspin (front of the ball rotating upward). Assume that the lift coefficient on the ball (based on frontal area) follows Fig. P7.108. If the ground is level and drag is neglected, make a simple analysis to predict the impact point (a) without spin and (b) with backspin of 7500 r/min.

P8.103 Consider inviscid flow past a sphere, as in Fig. 8.31. Find (a) the point on the front surface where the fluid acceleration a_{max} is maximum and (b) the magnitude of a_{max}. (c) If the stream velocity is 1 m/s, find the sphere diameter for which a_{max} is 10 times the acceleration of gravity. Comment.

Hydrodynamic mass

P8.104 Consider a cylinder of radius a moving at speed U_∞ through a still fluid, as in Fig. P8.104. Plot the streamlines relative to the cylinder by modifying Eq. (8.32) to give the relative flow with $K = 0$. Integrate to find the total relative kinetic energy, and verify the hydrodynamic mass of a cylinder from Eq. (8.91).

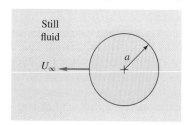

P8.104

P8.105 A 22-cm-diameter solid aluminum sphere (SG = 2.7) is accelerating at 12 m/s² in water at 20°C. (a) According to potential theory, what is the hydrodynamic mass of the sphere? (b) Estimate the force being applied to the sphere at this instant.

Numerical methods

P8.106 Laplace's equation in plane polar coordinates, Eq. (8.11), is complicated by the variable radius. Consider the finite difference mesh in Fig. P8.106, with nodes (i, j) equally spaced $\Delta\theta$ and Δr apart. Derive a finite difference model for Eq. (8.11) similar to the cartesian expression (8.96).

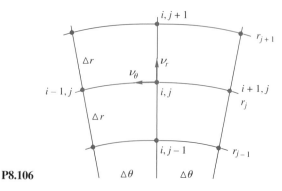

P8.106

P8.107 SAE 10W30 oil at 20°C is at rest near a wall when the wall suddenly begins moving at a constant 1 m/s. (*a*) Use $\Delta y = 1$ cm and $\Delta t = 0.2$ s and check the stability criterion (8.101). (*b*) Carry out Eq. (8.100) to $t = 2$ s and report the velocity u at $y = 4$ cm.

P8.108 Consider two-dimensional potential flow into a step contraction as in Fig. P8.108. The inlet velocity $U_1 = 7$ m/s, and the outlet velocity U_2 is uniform. The nodes (i, j) are labeled in the figure. Set up the complete finite difference algebraic relations for all nodes. Solve, if possible, on a computer and plot the streamlines in the flow.

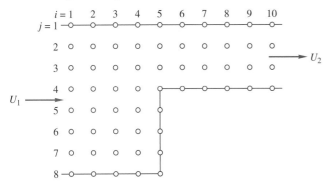

P8.108

P8.109 Consider inviscid flow through a two-dimensional 90° bend with a contraction, as in Fig. P8.109. Assume uniform flow at the entrance and exit. Make a finite difference computer analysis for small grid size (at least 150 nodes), determine the dimensionless pressure distribution along the walls, and sketch the streamlines. (You may use either square or rectangular grids.)

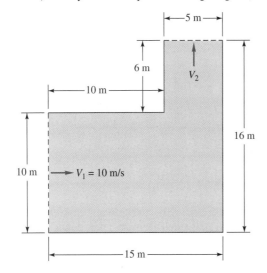

P8.109

P8.110 For fully developed laminar incompressible flow through a straight noncircular duct, as in Sec. 6.8, the Navier-Stokes equations (4.38) reduce to

$$\frac{\partial^2 u}{\partial y^2} + \frac{\partial^2 u}{\partial z^2} = \frac{1}{\mu}\frac{dp}{dx} = \text{const} < 0$$

where (y, z) is the plane of the duct cross section and x is along the duct axis. Gravity is neglected. Using a nonsquare rectangular grid $(\Delta x, \Delta y)$, develop a finite difference model for this equation, and indicate how it may be applied to solve for flow in a rectangular duct of side lengths a and b.

P8.111 Solve Prob. P8.110 numerically for a rectangular duct of side length b by $2b$, using at least 100 nodal points. Evaluate the volume flow rate and the friction factor, and compare with the results in Table 6.4:

$$Q \approx 0.1143\frac{b^4}{\mu}\left(-\frac{dp}{dx}\right) \qquad f\,\text{Re}_{D_h} \approx 62.19$$

where $D_h = 4A/P = 4b/3$ for this case. Comment on the possible truncation errors of your model.

P8.112 In CFD textbooks [5, 23–27], one often replaces the left-hand sides of Eqs. (8.102*b* and *c*) with the following two expressions, respectively:

$$\frac{\partial}{\partial x}(u^2) + \frac{\partial}{\partial y}(vu) \quad \text{and} \quad \frac{\partial}{\partial x}(uv) + \frac{\partial}{\partial y}(v^2)$$

Are these equivalent expressions, or are they merely simplified approximations? Either way, why might these forms be better for finite difference purposes?

P8.113 Formulate a numerical model for Eq. (8.99), which has no instability, by evaluating the second derivative at the *next* time step, $j + 1$. Solve for the center velocity at the next time step and comment on the result. This is called an *implicit model* and requires iteration.

P8.114 If your institution has an online potential flow boundary element computer code, consider flow past a symmetric airfoil, as in Fig. P8.114. The basic shape of an NACA symmetric airfoil is defined by the function [12]

$$\frac{2y}{t_{max}} \approx 1.4845\zeta^{1/2} - 0.63\zeta - 1.758\zeta^2$$
$$+ 1.4215\zeta^3 - 0.5075\zeta^4$$

where $\zeta = x/C$ and the maximum thickness t_{max} occurs at $\zeta = 0.3$. Use this shape as part of the lower boundary for zero angle of attack. Let the thickness be fairly large, say, $t_{max} = 0.12$, 0.15, or 0.18. Choose a generous number of nodes (≥ 60), and calculate and plot the velocity distribution V/U_∞ along the airfoil surface. Compare with the

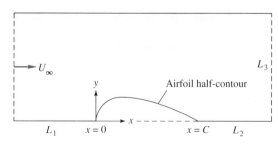

P8.114

theoretical results in Ref. 12 for NACA 0012, 0015, or 0018 airfoils. If time permits, investigate the effect of the boundary lengths L_1, L_2, and L_3, which can initially be set equal to the chord length C.

P8.115 Use the explicit method of Eq. (8.100) to solve Prob. P4.85 numerically for SAE 30 oil at 20°C with $U_0 = 1$ m/s and $\omega = M$ rad/s, where M is the number of letters in your surname. (This author will solve the problem for $M = 5$.) When steady oscillation is reached, plot the oil velocity versus time at $y = 2$ cm.

Word Problems

W8.1 What simplifications have been made, in the potential flow theory of this chapter, which result in the elimination of the Reynolds number, Froude number, and Mach number as important parameters?

W8.2 In this chapter we superimpose many basic solutions, a concept associated with *linear* equations. Yet Bernoulli's equation (8.3) is *nonlinear,* being proportional to the square of the velocity. How, then, do we justify the use of superposition in inviscid flow analysis?

W8.3 Give a physical explanation of circulation Γ as it relates to the lift force on an immersed body. If the line integral defined by Eq. (8.23) is zero, it means that the integrand is a perfect differential—but of what variable?

W8.4 Give a simple proof of Eq. (8.46)—namely, that both the real and imaginary parts of a function $f(z)$ are laplacian if $z = x + iy$. What is the secret of this remarkable behavior?

W8.5 Figure 8.18 contains five body corners. Without carrying out any calculations, explain physically what the value of the inviscid fluid velocity must be at each of these five corners. Is any flow separation expected?

W8.6 Explain the Kutta condition physically. Why is it necessary?

W8.7 We have briefly outlined finite difference and boundary element methods for potential flow but have neglected the *finite element* technique. Do some reading and write a brief essay on the use of the finite element method for potential flow problems.

Comprehensive Problems

C8.1 Did you know that you can solve simple fluid mechanics problems with Microsoft Excel? The successive relaxation technique for solving the Laplace equation for potential flow problems is easily set up on a spreadsheet, since the stream function at each interior cell is simply the average of its four neighbors. As an example, solve for the irrotational potential flow through a contraction, as given in Fig. C8.1. *Note:* To avoid the "circular reference" error, you must turn on the iteration option. Use the help index for more information. For full credit, attach a printout of your spreadsheet, with stream function converged and the value of the stream function at each node displayed to four digits of accuracy.

C8.2 Use an explicit method, similar to but not identical to Eq. (8.100), to solve the case of SAE 30 oil at 20°C starting from rest near a *fixed* wall. Far from the wall, the oil accelerates linearly; that is, $u_\infty = u_N = at$, where $a = 9$ m/s². At $t = 1$ s, determine (a) the oil velocity at $y = 1$ cm and (b) the instantaneous boundary layer thickness (where $u \approx 0.99\ u_\infty$). *Hint:* There is a nonzero pressure gradient in the outer (nearly shear-free) stream, $n = N$, which must be included in Eq. (8.99) and your explicit model.

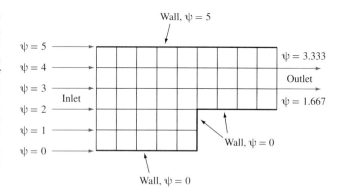

C8.1

C8.3 Consider plane inviscid flow through a symmetric diffuser, as in Fig. C8.3. Only the upper half is shown. The flow is to expand from inlet half-width h to exit half-width $2h$, as shown. The expansion angle θ is 18.5° ($L \approx 3h$). Set up a nonsquare potential flow mesh for this problem, and calculate and plot (*a*) the velocity distribution and (*b*) the pressure coefficient along the centerline. Assume uniform inlet and exit flows.

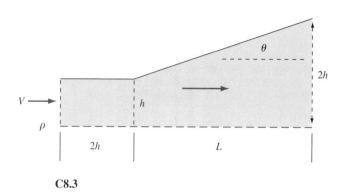

C8.3

C8.4 Use potential flow to approximate the flow of air being sucked up into a vacuum cleaner through a two-dimensional slit attachment, as in Fig. C8.4. In the *xy* plane through the centerline of the attachment, model the flow as a line sink of strength $(-m)$, with its axis in the *z* direction at height *a* above the floor. (*a*) Sketch the streamlines and locate any stagnation points in the flow. (*b*) Find the magnitude of velocity $V(x)$ along the floor in terms of the parameters *a* and *m*. (*c*) Let the pressure far away be p_∞, where velocity is zero. Define a velocity scale $U = m/a$. Determine the variation of dimensionless pressure coefficient, $C_p = (p - p_\infty)/(\rho U^2/2)$, along the floor. (*d*) The vacuum cleaner is most effective where C_p is a minimum—that is, where velocity is maximum. Find the locations of minimum pressure coefficient along the *x* axis. (*e*) At which points along the *x* axis do you expect the vacuum cleaner to work most effectively? Is it best at $x = 0$ directly beneath the slit, or at some other *x* location along the floor? Conduct a scientific experiment at home with a vacuum cleaner and some small pieces of dust or dirt to test your prediction. Report your results and discuss the agreement with prediction. Give reasons for any disagreements.

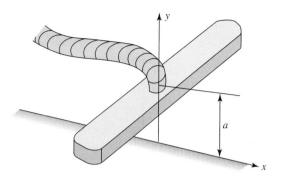

C8.4

C8.5 Consider a three-dimensional, incompressible, irrotational flow. Use the following two methods to prove that the viscous term in the Navier-Stokes equation is identically zero: (*a*) using vector notation; and (*b*) expanding out the scalar terms and substituting terms from the definition of irrotationality.

C8.6 Find, either on-line or in Ref. 12, lift-drag data for the NACA 4412 airfoil. (*a*) Draw the polar lift–drag plot and compare qualitatively with Fig. 7.26. (*b*) Find the maximum value of the lift-to-drag ratio. (*c*) Demonstrate a straight-line construction on the polar plot that will immediately yield the maximum *L/D* in (*b*). (*d*) If an aircraft could use this two-dimensional wing in actual flight (no induced drag) and had a perfect pilot, estimate how far (in miles) this aircraft could glide to a sea-level runway if it lost power at 25,000 ft altitude.

C8.7 Find a formula for the stream function for flow of a doublet of strength λ a distance *a* from a wall, as in Fig. C8.7. (*a*) Sketch the streamlines. (*b*) Are there any stagnation points? (*c*) Find the maximum velocity along the wall and its position.

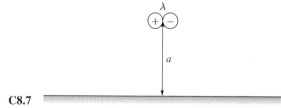

C8.7

Design Projects

D8.1 In 1927, Theodore von Kármán developed a scheme to use a uniform stream, plus a row of sources and sinks, to generate an arbitrary closed-body shape. A schematic of the idea is sketched in Fig. D8.1. The body is symmetric and at zero angle of attack. A total of *N* sources and sinks are distributed along the axis within the body, with strengths m_i at positions x_i, for $i = 1$ to *N*. The object is to find the correct distribution of strengths that approximates a given body shape $y(x)$ at a finite number of surface locations and then to compute the approximate surface velocity and pressure. The technique should work for either two-dimensional bodies (distributed line sources) or bodies of revolution (distributed point sources).

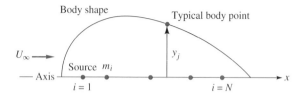

D8.1

For our body shape let us select the NACA 0018 airfoil, given by the formula in Prob. P8.114 with $t_{max} = 0.18$. Develop the ideas stated here into N simultaneous algebraic equations that can be used to solve for the N unknown line source/sink strengths. Then program your equations for a computer, with $N \geq 20$; solve for m_i; compute the surface velocities; and compare with the theoretical

velocities for this shape in Ref. 12. Your goal should be to achieve accuracy within ± 1 percent of the classic results. If necessary, you should adjust N and the locations of the sources.

D8.2 Modify Prob. D8.1 to solve for the point-source distribution that approximates an "0018" body-of-revolution shape. Since no theoretical results are published, simply make sure that your results converge to ± 1 percent.

D8.3 Consider water at 20°C flowing at 12 m/s in a water channel. A Rankine oval cylinder, 40 cm long, is to be placed parallel to the flow, where the water static pressure is 120 kPa. The oval's thickness is a design parameter. Prepare a plot of the minimum pressure on the oval's surface as a function of body thickness. Especially note the thicknesses where (a) the local pressure is 50 kPa and (b) cavitation first occurs on the surface.

References

1. J. Wermer, *Potential Theory*, Springer-Verlag, New York, 2008.
2. J. M. Robertson, *Hydrodynamics in Theory and Application*, Prentice-Hall, Englewood Cliffs, NJ, 1965.
3. L. M. Milne-Thomson, *Theoretical Hydrodynamics*, 4th ed., Dover, New York, 1996.
4. D. H. Armitage and S. J. Gardiner, *Classical Potential Theory*, Springer, New York, 2013.
5. J. Tu, G. H. Yeoh, and C. Liu, *Computational Fluid Dynamics: A Practical Approach*, 2d ed., Elsevier Science, New York, 2012.
6. O. C. Zienkiewicz, R. L. Taylor, and P. Nithiarasu, *The Finite Element Method for Fluid Dynamics*, vol. 3, 6th ed., Butterworth-Heinemann, Burlington, MA, 2005.
7. G. Beer, I. Smith, and C. Duenser, *The Boundary Element Method with Programming: For Engineers and Scientists*, Springer-Verlag, New York, 2010.
8. A. D. Moore, "Fields from Fluid Flow Mappers," *J. Appl. Phys.*, vol. 20, 1949, pp. 790–804.
9. H. J. S. Hele-Shaw, "Investigation of the Nature of the Surface Resistance of Water and of Streamline Motion under Certain Experimental Conditions," *Trans. Inst. Nav. Archit.*, vol. 40, 1898, p. 25.
10. S. W. Churchill, *Viscous Flows: The Practical Use of Theory*, Butterworth, Stoneham, MA, 1988.
11. J. D. Anderson, Jr., *Fundamentals of Aerodynamics*, 5th ed., McGraw-Hill, New York, 2010.
12. I. H. Abbott and A. E. von Doenhoff, *Theory of Wing Sections*, Dover, New York, 1981.
13. F. O. Smetana, *Introductory Aerodynamics and Hydrodynamics of Wings and Bodies: A Software-Based Approach*, AIAA, Reston, VA, 1997.
14. L. Prandtl, "Applications of Modern Hydrodynamics to Aeronautics," *NACA Rep. 116*, 1921.
15. F. M. White, *Viscous Fluid Flow*, 3d ed., McGraw-Hill, New York, 2005.
16. C. S. Yih, *Fluid Mechanics*, McGraw-Hill, New York, 1969.
17. K. T. Patton, "Tables of Hydrodynamic Mass Factors for Translational Motion," *ASME Winter Annual Meeting*, Paper 65-WA/UNT-2, 1965.
18. J. L. Hess and A. M. O. Smith, "Calculation of Nonlifting Potential Flow about Arbitrary Three-Dimensional Bodies," *J. Ship Res.*, vol. 8, 1964, pp. 22–44.
19. K. H. Huebner, *The Finite Element Method for Engineers*, 4th ed., Wiley, New York, 2001.
20. J. C. Tannehill, D. A. Anderson, and R. H. Pletcher, *Computational Fluid Mechanics and Heat Transfer*, 3d ed., Taylor and Francis, Bristol, PA, 2011.
21. J. N. Newman, *Marine Hydrodynamics*, M.I.T. Press, Cambridge, MA, 1977.
22. P. T. Tokumaru and P. E. Dimotakis, "The Lift of a Cylinder Executing Rotary Motions in a Uniform Flow," *J. Fluid Mechanics*, vol. 255, 1993, pp. 1–10.
23. J. H. Ferziger and M. Peric, *Computational Methods for Fluid Dynamics*, 3d ed. Springer-Verlag, New York, 2002.
24. P. J. Roache, *Fundamentals of Computational Fluid Dynamics*, Hermosa Pub., Albuquerque, NM, 1998.
25. B. A. Finlayson, *Introduction to Chemical Engineering Computing*, Wiley, New York, 2012.
26. B. Andersson, *Computational Fluid Dynamics*, Cambridge University Press, New York, 2012.
27. H. Versteeg and W. Malalasekera, *Computational Fluid Dynamics: The Finite Volume Method*, 2d ed., Prentice-Hall, Upper Saddle River, NJ, 2007.

28. M. Deshpande, J. Feng, and C. L. Merkle, "Numerical Modeling of the Thermodynamic Effects of Cavitation," *J. Fluids Eng.,* June 1997, pp. 420–427.

29. P. A. Durbin and R. B. A. Pettersson, *Statistical Theory and Modeling for Turbulent Flows,* Wiley, New York, 2001.

30. C. J. Freitas, "Perspective: Selected Benchmarks from Commercial CFD Codes," *J. Fluids Eng.,* vol. 117, June 1995, pp. 208–218.

31. R. Martinuzzi and C. Tropea, "The Flow around Surface-Mounted, Prismatic Obstacles in a Fully Developed Channel Flow," *J. Fluids Eng.,* vol. 115, March 1993, pp. 85–92.

32. K. B. Shah and J. H. Ferzier, "Fluid Mechanicians View of Wind Engineering: Large Eddy Simulation of Flow Past a Cubic Obstacle," *J. Wind Engineering and Industrial Aerodynamics,* vol. 67–68, 1997, pp. 221–224.

33. P. Sagaut, *Large Eddy Simulation for Incompressible Flows: An Introduction,* 3rd ed., Springer, New York, 2010.

34. W. J. Palm, *Introduction to MATLAB 7 for Engineers,* 3d ed. McGraw-Hill, New York, 2010.

35. A. Gilat, *MATLAB: An Introduction with Applications,* 4th ed., Wiley, New York, 2010.

36. J. W. Hoyt and R. H. J. Sellin, "Flow over Tube Banks—A Visualization Study," *J. Fluids Eng.,* vol. 119, June 1997, pp. 480–483.

37. S. Douglass, "Switchblade Fighter Bomber," *Popular Science,* Nov. 2000, pp. 52–55.

38. G. Beer, I. Smith, and C. Duenser, The Boundary Element Method with Programming: For Engineers and Scientists, Springer, New York, 2010.

39. J. D. Anderson, *A History of Aerodynamics and Its Impact on Flying Machines,* Cambridge University Press, Cambridge, UK, 1999.

40. B. Robins, *Mathematical Tracts 1 & 2,* J. Nourse, London, 1761.

41. T. K. Sengupta, A. Kasliwal, S. De, and M. Nair, "Temporal Flow Instability for Magnus-Robins Effect at High Rotation Rates," *J. Fluids and Structures,* vol. 17, 2003, pp. 941–953.

42. G. F. Dargush and M. M. Grigoriev, "Fast and Accurate Solutions of Steady Stokes Flows Using Multilevel Boundary Element Methods," *J. Fluids Eng.,* vol. 127, July 2005, pp. 640–646.

43. R. H. Kirchhoff, *Potential Flows: Computer Graphic Solutions,* Marcel Dekker, New York, 2001.

44. H. Werle, "Hydrodynamic Visualization of the Flow around a Streamlined Cylinder with Suction: Cousteau-Malavard Turbine Sail Model," *Le Recherche Aerospatiale,* vol. 4, 1984, pp. 29–38.

45. T. K. Sengupta and S. R. Talla, "Robins-Magnus Effect: A Continuing Saga," *Current Science,* vol. 86, no. 7, 2004, pp. 1033–1036.

46. P. R. Spalart, "Airplane Trailing Vortices," *Annual Review Fluid Mechanics,* vol. 30, 1998, pp. 107–138.

47. M. Elkhoury, "Assessment and Modification of One-Equation Models of Turbulence for Wall-Bounded Flows," *J. Fluids Eng.,* vol. 129, July 2007, pp. 921–928.

Ever since the demise of the Concorde, engineers have been working on the design of an overland supersonic airplane. For such airplanes to be practical, sonic booms must be reduced to an acceptable level. Theory, though useful, cannot solve this problem without extensive testing. Shown here is Boeing's *Lynx* design, being tested in NASA's Glenn Research Center in Cleveland. Sensors capture both the forces on the plane and the pressures far from the vehicle. The goal is to generate sonic booms so low that they barely register on the ground. [*Photo courtesy of NASA*]

Chapter 9
Compressible Flow

Motivation.   All eight of our previous chapters have been concerned with "low-speed" or "incompressible" flow, where the fluid velocity is much less than its speed of sound. In fact, we did not even develop an expression for the speed of sound of a fluid. That is done in this chapter.

When a fluid moves at speeds comparable to its speed of sound, density changes become significant and the flow is termed *compressible*. Such flows are difficult to obtain in liquids, since high pressures on the order of 1000 atm are needed to generate sonic velocities. In gases, however, a pressure ratio of only 2:1 will likely cause sonic flow. Thus compressible gas flow is quite common, and this subject is often called *gas dynamics*. The most important parameter is the Mach number.

Probably the two most important and distinctive effects of compressibility on flow are (1) *choking,* wherein the duct flow rate is sharply limited by the sonic condition, and (2) *shock waves,* which are nearly discontinuous property changes in a supersonic flow. The purpose of this chapter is to explain such striking phenomena and to familiarize the reader with engineering calculations of compressible flow.

Speaking of calculations, the present chapter can use the help of Excel. Compressible flow analysis is filled with scores of complicated algebraic equations, many of which are difficult to manipulate or invert. Consequently, for nearly a century, compressible flow textbooks have relied on extensive tables of Mach number relations (see App. B) for numerical work. With Excel, however, any equation in this chapter can be typed into a cell and iterated to solve for any variables—see part (b) of Example 9.13 for an especially intricate example. With such a tool, App. B serves only as a backup, for initial estimates, and may soon vanish from textbooks.

9.1 Introduction: Review of Thermodynamics

We took a brief look in Chap. 4 [Eqs. (4.13) to (4.17)] to see when we might safely neglect the compressibility inherent in every real fluid. We found that the proper criterion for a nearly incompressible flow was a small Mach number

$$\text{Ma} = \frac{V}{a} \ll 1$$

593

where V is the flow velocity and a is the speed of sound of the fluid. Under small Mach number conditions, changes in fluid density are everywhere small in the flow field. The energy equation becomes uncoupled, and temperature effects can be either ignored or put aside for later study. The equation of state degenerates into the simple statement that density is nearly constant. This means that an incompressible flow requires only a momentum and continuity analysis, as we showed with many examples in Chaps. 7 and 8.

This chapter treats compressible flows, which have Mach numbers greater than about 0.3 and thus exhibit nonnegligible density changes. If the density change is significant, it follows from the equation of state that the temperature and pressure changes are also substantial. Large temperature changes imply that the energy equation can no longer be neglected. Therefore, the work is doubled from two basic equations to four

1. Continuity equation
2. Momentum equation
3. Energy equation
4. Equation of state

to be solved simultaneously for four unknowns: pressure, density, temperature, and flow velocity (p, ρ, T, V). Thus the general theory of compressible flow is quite complicated, and we try here to make further simplifications, especially by assuming a reversible adiabatic or *isentropic* flow.

We note in passing that at least two flow patterns depend strongly on very small density differences, acoustics, and natural convection. Acoustics [7, 9] is the study of sound wave propagation, which is accompanied by extremely small changes in density, pressure, and temperature. Natural convection is the gentle circulating pattern set up by buoyancy forces in a fluid stratified by uneven heating or uneven concentration of dissolved materials. Here we are concerned only with steady compressible flow where the fluid velocity is of magnitude comparable to that of the speed of sound.

The Mach Number

The Mach number is the dominant parameter in compressible flow analysis, with different effects depending on its magnitude. Aerodynamicists especially make a distinction between the various ranges of Mach number, and the following rough classifications are commonly used:

Ma < 0.3:   *incompressible flow*, where density effects are negligible.

0.3 < Ma < 0.8:   *subsonic flow*, where density effects are important but no shock waves appear.

0.8 < Ma < 1.2:   *transonic flow*, where shock waves first appear, dividing subsonic and supersonic regions of the flow. Powered flight in the transonic region is difficult because of the mixed character of the flow field.

1.2 < Ma < 3.0:   *supersonic flow*, where shock waves are present but there are no subsonic regions.

3.0 < Ma: *hypersonic flow* [11], where shock waves and other flow changes are especially strong.

The numerical values listed are only rough guides. These five categories of flow are appropriate to external high-speed aerodynamics. For internal (duct) flows, the most important question is simply whether the flow is subsonic (Ma $<$ 1) or supersonic (Ma $>$ 1), because the effect of area changes reverses, as we show in Sec. 9.4. Since supersonic flow effects may go against intuition, you should study these differences carefully.

The Specific-Heat Ratio

In addition to geometry and Mach number, compressible flow calculations also depend on a second dimensionless parameter, the *specific-heat ratio* of the gas:

$$k = \frac{c_p}{c_v} \tag{9.1}$$

Earlier, in Chaps. 1 and 4, we used the same symbol k to denote the thermal conductivity of a fluid. We apologize for the duplication; thermal conductivity does not appear in these later chapters of the text.

Recall from Fig. 1.4 that k for the common gases decreases slowly with temperature and lies between 1.0 and 1.7. Variations in k have only a slight effect on compressible flow computations, and air, $k \approx 1.40$, is the dominant fluid of interest. Therefore, although we assign some problems involving other gases like steam and CO_2 and helium, the compressible flow tables in App. B are based solely on the single value $k = 1.40$ for air.

This text contains only a single chapter on compressible flow, but, as usual, whole books have been written on the subject. Here we list only certain recent or classic texts. References 1 to 4 are introductory or intermediate treatments, while Refs. 5 to 10 are advanced books. One can also become specialized within this specialty of compressible flow. Reference 11 concerns *hypersonic flow*—that is, at very high Mach numbers. Reference 12 explains the exciting new technique of direct simulation of gas flows with a *molecular dynamics model*. Compressible flow is also well suited for computational fluid dynamics (CFD), as described in Ref. 13. Finally, a short, thoroughly readable (no calculus) Ref. 14 describes the principles and promise of high-speed (supersonic) flight. From time to time we shall defer some specialized topic to these other texts.

The Perfect Gas

In principle, compressible flow calculations can be made for any fluid equation of state, and we shall assign a few problems involving the steam tables [15], the gas tables [16], and liquids [Eq. (1.19)]. But in fact most elementary treatments are confined to the perfect gas with constant specific heats:

$$p = \rho RT \quad R = c_p - c_v = \text{const} \quad k = \frac{c_p}{c_v} = \text{const} \tag{9.2}$$

For all real gases, c_p, c_v, and k vary with temperature but only moderately; for example, c_p of air increases 30 percent as temperature increases from 0 to 5000°F. Since we rarely deal with such large temperature changes, it is quite reasonable to assume constant specific heats.

Recall from Sec. 1.8 that the gas constant is related to a universal constant Λ divided by the gas molecular weight:

$$R_{gas} = \frac{\Lambda}{M_{gas}} \tag{9.3}$$

where $\qquad \Lambda = 49,720 \text{ ft-lbf/(lbmol} \cdot {}^{\circ}\text{R)} = 8314 \text{ J/(kmol} \cdot \text{K)}$

For air, $M = 28.97$, and we shall adopt the following property values for air throughout this chapter:

$$R = 1716 \text{ ft}^2/(\text{s}^2 \cdot {}^{\circ}\text{R}) = 287 \text{ m}^2/(\text{s}^2 \cdot \text{K}) \qquad k = 1.400$$

$$c_v = \frac{R}{k-1} = 4293 \text{ ft}^2/(\text{s}^2 \cdot {}^{\circ}\text{R}) = 718 \text{ m}^2/(\text{s}^2 \cdot \text{K}) \tag{9.4}$$

$$c_p = \frac{kR}{k-1} = 6009 \text{ ft}^2/(\text{s}^2 \cdot {}^{\circ}\text{R}) = 1005 \text{ m}^2/(\text{s}^2 \cdot \text{K})$$

Experimental values of k for eight common gases were shown in Fig. 1.4. From this figure and the molecular weight, the other properties can be computed, as in Eqs. (9.4).

The changes in the internal energy $\hat{u}$ and enthalpy h of a perfect gas are computed for constant specific heats as

$$\hat{u}_2 - \hat{u}_1 = c_v(T_2 - T_1) \qquad h_2 - h_1 = c_p(T_2 - T_1) \tag{9.5}$$

For variable specific heats one must integrate $\hat{u} = \int c_v dT$ and $h = \int c_p dT$ or use the gas tables [16]. Most modern thermodynamics texts now contain software for evaluating properties of nonideal gases [17].

Isentropic Process

The isentropic approximation is common in compressible flow theory. We compute the entropy change from the first and second laws of thermodynamics for a pure substance [17 or 18]:

$$T\,ds = dh - \frac{dp}{\rho} \tag{9.6}$$

Introducing $dh = c_p dT$ for a perfect gas and solving for ds, we substitute $\rho T = p/R$ from the perfect-gas law and obtain

$$\int_1^2 ds = \int_1^2 c_p \frac{dT}{T} - R \int_1^2 \frac{dp}{p} \tag{9.7}$$

If c_p is variable, the gas tables will be needed, but for constant c_p we obtain the analytic results

$$s_2 - s_1 = c_p \ln \frac{T_2}{T_1} - R \ln \frac{p_2}{p_1} = c_v \ln \frac{T_2}{T_1} - R \ln \frac{\rho_2}{\rho_1} \tag{9.8}$$

Equations (9.8) are used to compute the entropy change across a shock wave (Sec. 9.5), which is an irreversible process.

For isentropic flow, we set $s_2 = s_1$ and obtain these interesting power-law relations for an isentropic perfect gas:

$$\frac{p_2}{p_1} = \left(\frac{T_2}{T_1}\right)^{k/(k-1)} = \left(\frac{\rho_2}{\rho_1}\right)^k \qquad (9.9)$$

These relations are used in Sec. 9.3.

EXAMPLE 9.1

Argon flows through a tube such that its initial condition is $p_1 = 1.7$ MPa and $\rho_1 = 18$ kg/m^3 and its final condition is $p_2 = 248$ kPa and $T_2 = 400$ K. Estimate (a) the initial temperature, (b) the final density, (c) the change in enthalpy, and (d) the change in entropy of the gas.

Solution

From Table A.4 for argon, $R = 208$ m^2/(s$^2 \cdot$ K) and $k = 1.67$. Therefore estimate its specific heat at constant pressure from Eq. (9.4):

$$c_p = \frac{kR}{k-1} = \frac{1.67(208)}{1.67 - 1} \approx 519 \text{ m}^2/(\text{s}^2 \cdot \text{K})$$

The initial temperature and final density are estimated from the ideal-gas law, Eq. (9.2):

$$T_1 = \frac{p_1}{\rho_1 R} = \frac{1.7 \text{ E6 N/m}^2}{(18 \text{ kg/m}^3)[208 \text{ m}^2/(\text{s}^2 \cdot \text{K})]} = 454 \text{ K} \qquad Ans. \text{ (a)}$$

$$\rho_2 = \frac{p_2}{T_2 R} = \frac{248 \text{ E3 N/m}^2}{(400 \text{ K})[208 \text{ m}^2/(\text{s}^2 \cdot \text{K})]} = 2.98 \text{ kg/m}^3 \qquad Ans. \text{ (b)}$$

From Eq. (9.5) the enthalpy change is

$$h_2 - h_1 = c_p(T_2 - T_1) = 519(400 - 454) \approx -28{,}000 \text{ J/kg (or m}^2/\text{s}^2) \quad Ans. \text{ (c)}$$

The argon temperature and enthalpy decrease as we move down the tube. Actually, there may not be any external cooling; that is, the fluid enthalpy may be converted by friction to increased kinetic energy (Sec. 9.7).

Finally, the entropy change is computed from Eq. (9.8):

$$s_2 - s_1 = c_p \ln \frac{T_2}{T_1} - R \ln \frac{p_2}{p_1}$$

$$= 519 \ln \frac{400}{454} - 208 \ln \frac{0.248 \text{ E6}}{1.7 \text{ E6}}$$

$$= -66 + 400 \approx 334 \text{ m}^2/(\text{s}^2 \cdot \text{K}) \qquad Ans. \text{ (d)}$$

The fluid entropy has increased. If there is no heat transfer, this indicates an irreversible process. Note that entropy has the same units as the gas constant and specific heat.

This problem is not just arbitrary numbers. It correctly simulates the behavior of argon moving subsonically through a tube with large frictional effects (Sec. 9.7).

9.2 The Speed of Sound

The so-called speed of sound is the rate of propagation of a pressure pulse of infinitesimal strength through a still fluid. It is a thermodynamic property of a fluid. Let us analyze it by first considering a pulse of finite strength, as in Fig. 9.1. In Fig. 9.1a the pulse, or pressure wave, moves at speed C toward the still fluid (p, ρ, T, $V = 0$) at the left, leaving behind at the right a fluid of increased properties ($p + \Delta p$, $\rho + \Delta \rho$, $T + \Delta T$) and a fluid velocity ΔV toward the left following the wave but much slower. We can determine these effects by making a control volume analysis across the wave. To avoid the unsteady terms that would be necessary in Fig. 9.1a, we adopt instead the control volume of Fig. 9.1b, which moves at wave speed C to the left. The wave appears fixed from this viewpoint, and the fluid appears to have velocity C on the left and $C - \Delta V$ on the right. The thermodynamic properties p, ρ, and T are not affected by this change of viewpoint.

The flow in Fig. 9.1b is steady and one-dimensional across the wave. The continuity equation is thus, from Eq. (3.24),

$$\rho A C = (\rho + \Delta \rho)(A)(C - \Delta V)$$

or

$$\Delta V = C \frac{\Delta \rho}{\rho + \Delta \rho} \tag{9.10}$$

This proves our contention that the induced fluid velocity on the right is much smaller than the wave speed C. In the limit of infinitesimal wave strength (sound wave) this speed is itself infinitesimal.

Notice that there are no velocity gradients on either side of the wave. Therefore, even if fluid viscosity is large, frictional effects are confined to the interior of the wave. Advanced texts [for example, 9] show that the thickness of pressure waves in

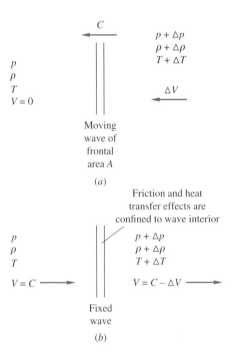

C

$p + \Delta p$
$\rho + \Delta \rho$
$T + \Delta T$

p
ρ
T
$V = 0$

ΔV

Moving
wave of
frontal
area A

(a)

Friction and heat
transfer effects are
confined to wave interior

p
ρ
T

$p + \Delta p$
$\rho + \Delta \rho$
$T + \Delta T$

$V = C$

$V = C - \Delta V$

Fixed
wave

(b)

Fig. 9.1 Control volume analysis of a finite-strength pressure wave: (a) control volume fixed to still fluid at left; (b) control volume moving left at wave speed C.

gases is of order 10^{-6} ft at atmospheric pressure. Thus we can safely neglect friction and apply the one-dimensional momentum equation (3.40) across the wave:

$$\sum F_{\text{right}} = \dot{m}(V_{\text{out}} - V_{\text{in}})$$

or
$$pA - (p + \Delta p)A = (\rho AC)(C - \Delta V - C) \tag{9.11}$$

Again the area cancels, and we can solve for the pressure change:

$$\Delta p = \rho C\, \Delta V \tag{9.12}$$

If the wave strength is very small, the pressure change is small.

Finally, combine Eqs. (9.10) and (9.12) to give an expression for the wave speed:

$$C^2 = \frac{\Delta p}{\Delta \rho}\left(1 + \frac{\Delta \rho}{\rho}\right) \tag{9.13}$$

The larger the strength $\Delta\rho/\rho$ of the wave, the faster the wave speed; that is, powerful explosion waves move much more quickly than sound waves. In the limit of infinitesimal strength $\Delta\rho \to 0$, we have what is defined to be the speed of sound a of a fluid:

$$a^2 = \frac{\partial p}{\partial \rho} \tag{9.14}$$

But the evaluation of the derivative requires knowledge of the thermodynamic process undergone by the fluid as the wave passes. Sir Isaac Newton in 1686 made a famous error by deriving a formula for sound speed that was equivalent to assuming an isothermal process, the result being 20 percent too low for air, for example. He rationalized the discrepancy as being due to the "crassitude" (dust particles and so on) in the air; the error is certainly understandable when we reflect that it was made 180 years before the proper basis was laid for the second law of thermodynamics.

We now see that the correct process must be *adiabatic* because there are no temperature gradients except inside the wave itself. For vanishing-strength sound waves we therefore have an infinitesimal adiabatic or isentropic process. The correct expression for the sound speed is

$$a = \left(\frac{\partial p}{\partial \rho}\bigg|_s\right)^{1/2} = \left(k\frac{\partial p}{\partial \rho}\bigg|_T\right)^{1/2} \tag{9.15}$$

for any fluid, gas or liquid. Even a solid has a sound speed.

For a perfect gas, from Eq. (9.2) or (9.9), we deduce that the speed of sound is

$$a = \left(\frac{kp}{\rho}\right)^{1/2} = (kRT)^{1/2} \tag{9.16}$$

The speed of sound increases as the square root of the absolute temperature. For air, with $k = 1.4$, an easily memorized dimensional formula is

$$a(\text{ft/s}) \approx 49[T(^\circ\text{R})]^{1/2}$$
$$a(\text{m/s}) \approx 20[T(\text{K})]^{1/2} \tag{9.17}$$

Table 9.1 Sound Speed of Various Materials at 60°F (15.5°C) and 1 atm

Material	a, ft/s	a, m/s
Gases:		
H_2	4,246	1,294
He	3,281	1,000
Air	1,117	340
Ar	1,040	317
CO_2	873	266
CH_4	607	185
$^{238}UF_6$	297	91
Liquids:		
Glycerin	6,100	1,860
Water	4,890	1,490
Mercury	4,760	1,450
Ethyl alcohol	3,940	1,200
Solids:*		
Aluminum	16,900	5,150
Steel	16,600	5,060
Hickory	13,200	4,020
Ice	10,500	3,200

*Plane waves. Solids also have a *shear-wave* speed.

At sea-level standard temperature, $60°F = 520°R$, $a = 1117$ ft/s. This decreases in the upper atmosphere, which is cooler; at 50,000-ft standard altitude, $T = -69.7°F = 389.9°R$ and $a = 49(389.9)^{1/2} = 968$ ft/s, or 13 percent less.

Some representative values of sound speed in various materials are given in Table 9.1. For liquids and solids it is common to define the *bulk modulus K* of the material:

$$K = -\mathcal{V}\frac{\partial p}{\partial \mathcal{V}}\bigg|_s = \rho\frac{\partial p}{\partial \rho}\bigg|_s \qquad (9.18)$$

In terms of bulk modulus, then, $a = (K/\rho)^{1/2}$. For example, at standard conditions, the bulk modulus of liquid carbon tetrachloride is 1.32 GPa absolute, and its density is 1590 kg/m³. Its speed of sound is therefore $a = (1.3\text{ E9 Pa}/1590\text{ kg/m}^3)^{1/2} = 911$ m/s = 2980 ft/s. Steel has a bulk modulus of about 2 E11 Pa and water about 2.2 E9 Pa (see Table A.3), or 90 times less than steel.

For solids, it is sometimes assumed that the bulk modulus is approximately equivalent to Young's modulus of elasticity E, but in fact their ratio depends on Poisson's ratio σ:

$$\frac{E}{K} = 3(1 - 2\sigma) \qquad (9.19)$$

The two are equal for $\sigma = \frac{1}{3}$, which is approximately the case for many common metals such as steel and aluminum.

EXAMPLE 9.2

Estimate the speed of sound of carbon monoxide at 200-kPa pressure and 300°C in m/s.

Solution

From Table A.4, for CO, the molecular weight is 28.01 and $k \approx 1.40$. Thus from Eq. (9.3) $R_{CO} = 8314/28.01 = 297$ m²/(s² · K), and the given temperature is 300°C + 273 = 573 K. Thus from Eq. (9.16) we estimate

$$a_{CO} = (kRT)^{1/2} = [1.40(297)(573)]^{1/2} = 488 \text{ m/s} \qquad Ans.$$

9.3 Adiabatic and Isentropic Steady Flow

As mentioned in Sec. 9.1, the isentropic approximation greatly simplifies a compressible flow calculation. So does the assumption of adiabatic flow, even if nonisentropic.

Consider high-speed flow of a gas past an insulated wall, as in Fig. 9.2. There is no shaft work delivered to any part of the fluid. Therefore, every streamtube in the flow satisfies the steady flow energy equation in the form of Eq. (3.70):

$$h_1 + \tfrac{1}{2}V_1^2 + gz_1 = h_2 + \tfrac{1}{2}V_2^2 + gz_2 - q + w_v \qquad (9.20)$$

where point 1 is upstream of point 2. You may wish to review the details of Eq. (3.70) and its development. We saw in Example 3.20 that potential energy changes of a

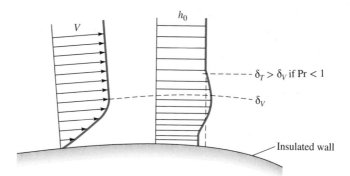

Fig. 9.2 Velocity and stagnation enthalpy distributions near an insulated wall in a typical high-speed gas flow.

gas are extremely small compared with kinetic energy and enthalpy terms. We shall neglect the terms gz_1 and gz_2 in all gas dynamic analyses.

Inside the thermal and velocity boundary layers in Fig. 9.2 the heat transfer and viscous work terms q and w_v are not zero. But outside the boundary layer q and w_v are zero by definition, so that the outer flow satisfies the simple relation

$$h_1 + \tfrac{1}{2}V_1^2 = h_2 + \tfrac{1}{2}V_2^2 = \text{const} \tag{9.21}$$

The constant in Eq. (9.21) is equal to the maximum enthalpy that the fluid would achieve if brought to rest adiabatically. We call this value h_0, the *stagnation enthalpy* of the flow. Thus we rewrite Eq. (9.21) in the form

$$h + \tfrac{1}{2}V^2 = h_0 = \text{const} \tag{9.22}$$

This should hold for steady adiabatic flow of any compressible fluid outside the boundary layer. The wall in Fig. 9.2 could be either the surface of an immersed body or the wall of a duct. We have shown the details of Fig. 9.2; typically the thermal layer thickness δ_T is greater than the velocity layer thickness δ_V because most gases have a dimensionless Prandtl number Pr less than unity (see, for example, Ref. 19, Sec. 4-3.2). Note that the stagnation enthalpy varies inside the thermal boundary layer, but its average value is the same as that at the outer layer due to the insulated wall.

For nonperfect gases we may have to use the steam tables [15] or the gas tables [16] to implement Eq. (9.22). But for a perfect gas $h = c_pT$, and Eq. (9.22) becomes

$$c_pT + \tfrac{1}{2}V^2 = c_pT_0 \tag{9.23}$$

This establishes the stagnation temperature T_0 of an adiabatic perfect-gas flow—that is, the temperature it achieves when decelerated to rest adiabatically.

An alternate interpretation of Eq. (9.22) occurs when the enthalpy and temperature drop to (absolute) zero, so the velocity achieves a maximum value:

$$V_{\text{max}} = (2h_0)^{1/2} = (2c_pT_0)^{1/2} \tag{9.24}$$

No higher flow velocity can occur unless additional energy is added to the fluid through shaft work or heat transfer (Sec. 9.8).

Mach Number Relations

The dimensionless form of Eq. (9.23) brings in the Mach number Ma as a parameter, by using Eq. (9.16) for the speed of sound of a perfect gas. Divide through by $c_p T$ to obtain

$$1 + \frac{V^2}{2c_p T} = \frac{T_0}{T} \qquad (9.25)$$

But, from the perfect-gas law, $c_p T = [kR/(k-1)]T = a^2/(k-1)$, so that Eq. (9.25) becomes

$$1 + \frac{(k-1)V^2}{2a^2} = \frac{T_0}{T}$$

or

$$\boxed{\frac{T_0}{T} = 1 + \frac{k-1}{2}\,\text{Ma}^2 \qquad \text{Ma} = \frac{V}{a}} \qquad (9.26)$$

This relation is plotted in Fig. 9.3 versus the Mach number for $k = 1.4$. At Ma = 5 the temperature has dropped to $\frac{1}{6}T_0$.

Since $a \propto T^{1/2}$, the ratio a_0/a is the square root of (9.26):

$$\frac{a_0}{a} = \left(\frac{T_0}{T}\right)^{1/2} = \left[1 + \frac{1}{2}(k-1)\text{Ma}^2\right]^{1/2} \qquad (9.27)$$

Equation (9.27) is also plotted in Fig. 9.3. At Ma = 5 the speed of sound has dropped to 41 percent of the stagnation value.

Isentropic Pressure and Density Relations

Note that Eqs. (9.26) and (9.27) require only adiabatic flow and hold even in the presence of irreversibilities such as friction losses or shock waves.

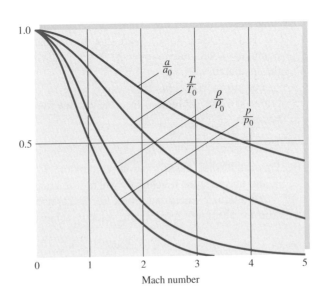

Fig. 9.3 Adiabatic (T/T_0 and a/a_0) and isentropic (p/p_0 and ρ/ρ_0) properties versus Mach number for $k = 1.4$.

If the flow is also *isentropic,* then for a perfect gas the pressure and density ratios can be computed from Eq. (9.9) as a power of the temperature ratio:

$$\frac{p_0}{p} = \left(\frac{T_0}{T}\right)^{k/(k-1)} = \left[1 + \frac{1}{2}(k-1)\text{Ma}^2\right]^{k/(k-1)} \tag{9.28a}$$

$$\frac{\rho_0}{\rho} = \left(\frac{T_0}{T}\right)^{1/(k-1)} = \left[1 + \frac{1}{2}(k-1)\text{Ma}^2\right]^{1/(k-1)} \tag{9.28b}$$

These relations are also plotted in Fig. 9.3; at Ma = 5 the density is 1.13 percent of its stagnation value, and the pressure is only 0.19 percent of stagnation pressure.

The quantities p_0 and ρ_0 are the isentropic stagnation pressure and density, respectively that is, the pressure and density that the flow would achieve if brought isentropically to rest. In an adiabatic nonisentropic flow p_0 and ρ_0 retain their local meaning, but they vary throughout the flow as the entropy changes due to friction or shock waves. The quantities h_0, T_0, and a_0 are constant in an adiabatic nonisentropic flow (see Sec. 9.7 for further details).

Relationship to Bernoulli's Equation

The isentropic assumptions (9.28) are effective, but are they realistic? Yes. To see why, take the differential of Eq. (9.22):

Adiabatic:
$$dh + V\,dV = 0 \tag{9.29}$$

Meanwhile, from Eq. (9.6), if $ds = 0$ (isentropic process),

$$dh = \frac{dp}{\rho} \tag{9.30}$$

Combining (9.29) and (9.30), we find that an isentropic streamtube flow must be

$$\frac{dp}{\rho} + V\,dV = 0 \tag{9.31}$$

But this is exactly the Bernoulli relation, Eq. (3.54), for steady frictionless flow with negligible gravity terms. Thus we see that the isentropic flow assumption is equivalent to use of the Bernoulli or streamline form of the frictionless momentum equation.

Critical Values at the Sonic Point

The stagnation values (a_0, T_0, p_0, ρ_0) are useful reference conditions in a compressible flow, but of comparable usefulness are the conditions where the flow is sonic, Ma = 1.0. These sonic, or *critical,* properties are denoted by asterisks: p^*, ρ^*, a^*, and T^*. They are certain ratios of the stagnation properties as given by Eqs. (9.26) to (9.28) when Ma = 1.0; for $k = 1.4$

$$\frac{p^*}{p_0} = \left(\frac{2}{k+1}\right)^{k/(k-1)} = 0.5283 \qquad \frac{\rho^*}{\rho_0} = \left(\frac{2}{k+1}\right)^{1/(k-1)} = 0.6339$$

$$\frac{T^*}{T_0} = \frac{2}{k+1} = 0.8333 \qquad \frac{a^*}{a_0} = \left(\frac{2}{k+1}\right)^{1/2} = 0.9129 \tag{9.32}$$

In all isentropic flow, all critical properties are constant; in adiabatic nonisentropic flow, a^* and T^* are constant, but p^* and ρ^* may vary.

The critical velocity V^* equals the sonic sound speed a^* by definition and is often used as a reference velocity in isentropic or adiabatic flow:

$$V^* = a^* = (kRT^*)^{1/2} = \left(\frac{2k}{k+1} RT_0\right)^{1/2} \tag{9.33}$$

The usefulness of these critical values will become clearer as we study compressible duct flow with friction or heat transfer later in this chapter.

Some Useful Numbers for Air

Since the great bulk of our practical calculations are for air, $k = 1.4$, the stagnation property ratios p/p_0 and so on from Eqs. (9.26) to (9.28) are tabulated for this value in Table B.1. The increments in Mach number are rather coarse in this table because the values are meant as only a guide; these equations are now a trivial matter to manipulate on a hand calculator. Thirty years ago every text had extensive compressible flow tables with Mach number spacings of about 0.01, so that accurate values could be interpolated. Even today, reference books are available [20, 21, 29] with tables and charts and computer programs for a wide variety of compressible flow situations. Reference 22 contains formulas and charts applying to the thermodynamics of *real* (nonperfect) gas flows.

For $k = 1.4$, the following numerical versions of the isentropic and adiabatic flow formulas are obtained:

$$\frac{T_0}{T} = 1 + 0.2\,\text{Ma}^2 \qquad \frac{\rho_0}{\rho} = (1 + 0.2\,\text{Ma}^2)^{2.5}$$

$$\frac{p_0}{p} = (1 + 0.2\,\text{Ma}^2)^{3.5} \tag{9.34}$$

Or, if we are given the properties, it is equally easy to solve for the Mach number (again with $k = 1.4$):

$$\text{Ma}^2 = 5\left(\frac{T_0}{T} - 1\right) = 5\left[\left(\frac{\rho_0}{\rho}\right)^{2/5} - 1\right] = 5\left[\left(\frac{p_0}{p}\right)^{2/7} - 1\right] \tag{9.35}$$

Note that these isentropic flow formulas serve as the equivalent of the frictionless adiabatic momentum and energy equations. They relate velocity to physical properties for a perfect gas, but they are *not* the "solution" to a gas dynamics problem. The complete solution is not obtained until the continuity equation has also been satisfied, for either one-dimensional (Sec. 9.4) or multidimensional (Sec. 9.9) flow.

One final note: These isentropic-ratio–versus–Mach-number formulas are seductive, tempting one to solve all problems by jumping right into the tables. Actually, many problems involving (dimensional) velocity and temperature can be solved more easily from the original raw dimensional energy equation (9.23) plus the perfect-gas law (9.2), as the next example will illustrate.

EXAMPLE 9.3

Air flows adiabatically through a duct. At point 1 the velocity is 240 m/s, with $T_1 = 320$ K and $p_1 = 170$ kPa. Compute (a) T_0, (b) p_0, (c) ρ_0, (d) Ma, (e) V_{max}, and (f) V^*. At point 2 further downstream $V_2 = 290$ m/s and $p_2 = 135$ kPa. (g) What is the stagnation pressure p_{02}?

Solution

- *Assumptions:* Let air be approximated as an ideal gas with constant k. The flow is adiabatic but *not* isentropic. Isentropic formulas are used *only* to compute local p_0 and ρ_0, which vary.
- *Approach:* Use adiabatic and isentropic formulas to find the various properties.
- *Ideal gas parameters:* For air, $R = 287$ m^2/(s$^2 \cdot$ K), $k = 1.40$, and $c_p = 1005$ m^2/(s$^2 \cdot$ K).
- *Solution steps (a, b, c, d):* With T_1, p_1, and V_1 known, other properties at point 1 follow:

$$T_{01} = T_1 + \frac{V_1^2}{2c_p} = 320 + \frac{(240 \text{ m/s})^2}{2[1005 \text{ m}^2/(\text{s}^2 \cdot \text{K})]} = 320 + 29 = 349 \text{ K} \qquad Ans. \text{ (a)}$$

Once the Mach number is found from Eq. (9.35), local stagnation pressure and density follow:

$$\text{Ma}_1 = \sqrt{5\left(\frac{T_{01}}{T_1} - 1\right)} = \sqrt{5\left(\frac{349 \text{ K}}{320 \text{ K}} - 1\right)} = \sqrt{0.448} = 0.67 \qquad Ans. \text{ (b)}$$

$$p_{01} = p_1(1 + 0.2 \text{ Ma}_1^2)^{3.5} = (170 \text{ kPa})[1 + 0.2(0.67)^2]^{3.5} = 230 \text{ kPa} \qquad Ans. \text{ (d)}$$

$$\rho_{01} = \frac{p_{01}}{RT_{01}} = \frac{230,000 \text{ N/m}^2}{[287 \text{ m}^2/(\text{s}^2 \cdot \text{K})](349 \text{ K})} = 2.29 \frac{\text{N} \cdot \text{s}^2/\text{m}}{\text{m}^3} = 2.29 \frac{\text{kg}}{\text{m}^3} \qquad Ans. \text{ (c)}$$

- *Comment:* Note that we used dimensional (non-Mach-number) formulas where convenient.
- *Solution steps (e, f):* Both V_{max} and V^* are directly related to stagnation temperature from Eqs. (9.24) and (9.33):

$$V_{max} = \sqrt{2c_p T_0} = \sqrt{2[1005 \text{ m}^2/(\text{s}^2 \cdot \text{K})](349 \text{ K})} = 837 \frac{\text{m}}{\text{s}} \qquad Ans. \text{ (e)}$$

$$V^* = \sqrt{\frac{2k}{k+1} RT_0} = \sqrt{\frac{2(1.4)}{(1.4+1)}\left(287 \frac{\text{m}^2}{\text{s}^2 \cdot \text{K}}\right)(349 \text{ K})} = 342 \frac{\text{m}}{\text{s}} \qquad Ans. \text{ (f)}$$

- At point 2 downstream, the temperature is unknown, but since the flow is adiabatic, the stagnation temperature is constant: $T_{01} = T_{02} = 349$ K. Thus, from Eq. (9.23),

$$T_2 = T_{02} - \frac{V_2^2}{2c_p} = 349 - \frac{(290 \text{ m/s})^2}{2[1005 \text{ m}^2/(\text{s}^2 \cdot \text{K})]} = 307 \text{ K}$$

Hence, from Eq. (9.28a), the isentropic stagnation pressure at point 2 is

$$p_{02} = p_2\left(\frac{T_{02}}{T_2}\right)^{k/(k-1)} = (135 \text{ kPa})\left(\frac{349 \text{ K}}{307 \text{ K}}\right)^{1.4/0.4} = 211 \text{ kPa} \qquad Ans. \text{ (g)}$$

- *Comments:*   Part (g), a ratio-type ideal-gas formula, is more direct than finding the Mach number, which turns out to be $Ma_2 = 0.83$, and using the Mach number formula, Eq. (9.34) for p_{02}. Note that p_{02} is 8 percent less than p_{01}. The flow is nonisentropic: Entropy rises downstream, and stagnation pressure and density drop, due in this case to frictional losses.

9.4 Isentropic Flow with Area Changes

By combining the isentropic and/or adiabatic flow relations with the equation of continuity we can study practical compressible flow problems. This section treats the one-dimensional flow approximation.

Figure 9.4 illustrates the one-dimensional flow assumption. A real flow, Fig. 9.4a, has no slip at the walls and a velocity profile $V(x, y)$ that varies across the duct section (compare with Fig. 7.8). If, however, the area change is small and the wall radius of curvature large

$$\frac{d\mathbf{b}}{dx} \ll 1 \qquad \mathbf{b}(x) \ll R(x) \tag{9.36}$$

then the flow is approximately one-dimensional, as in Fig. 9.4b, with $V \approx V(x)$ reacting to area change $A(x)$. Compressible flow nozzles and diffusers do not always satisfy conditions (9.36), but we use the one-dimensional theory anyway because of its simplicity.

For steady one-dimensional flow the equation of continuity is, from Eq. (3.24),

$$\rho(x)V(x)A(x) = \dot{m} = \text{const} \tag{9.37}$$

Before applying this to duct theory, we can learn a lot from the differential form of Eq. (9.37):

$$\frac{d\rho}{\rho} + \frac{dV}{V} + \frac{dA}{A} = 0 \tag{9.38}$$

The differential forms of the frictionless momentum equation (9.31) and the sound–speed relation (9.15) are recalled here for convenience:

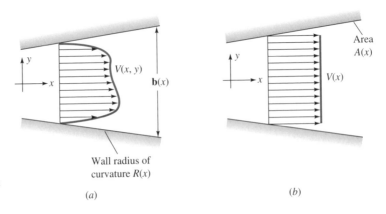

Fig. 9.4 Compressible flow through a duct: (a) real-fluid velocity profile; (b) one-dimensional approximation.

(a)

(b)

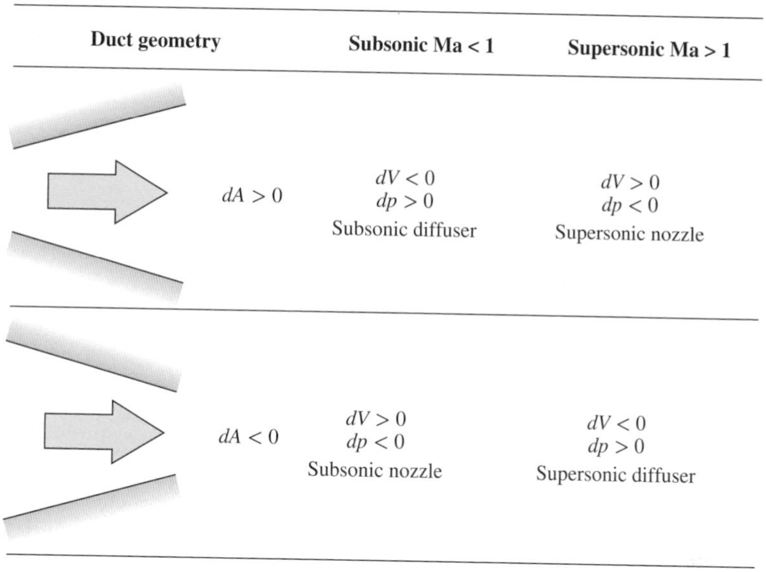

Duct geometry	Subsonic Ma < 1	Supersonic Ma > 1
$dA > 0$	$dV < 0$ $dp > 0$ Subsonic diffuser	$dV > 0$ $dp < 0$ Supersonic nozzle
$dA < 0$	$dV > 0$ $dp < 0$ Subsonic nozzle	$dV < 0$ $dp > 0$ Supersonic diffuser

Fig. 9.5 Effect of Mach number on property changes with area change in duct flow.

Momentum

$$\frac{dp}{\rho} + V\, dV = 0$$

(9.39)

Sound speed:

$$dp = a^2\, d\rho$$

Now eliminate dp and $d\rho$ between Eqs. (9.38) and (9.39) to obtain the following relation between velocity change and area change in isentropic duct flow:

$$\frac{dV}{V} = \frac{dA}{A}\frac{1}{\text{Ma}^2 - 1} = -\frac{dp}{\rho V^2}$$

(9.40)

Inspection of this equation, without actually solving it, reveals a fascinating aspect of compressible flow: Property changes are of opposite sign for subsonic and supersonic flow because of the term $\text{Ma}^2 - 1$. There are four combinations of area change and Mach number, summarized in Fig. 9.5.

From earlier chapters we are used to subsonic behavior (Ma < 1): When area increases, velocity decreases and pressure increases, which is denoted a subsonic diffuser. But in supersonic flow (Ma > 1), the velocity actually increases when the area increases, a supersonic nozzle. The same opposing behavior occurs for an area decrease, which speeds up a subsonic flow and slows down a supersonic flow.

What about the sonic point Ma = 1? Since infinite acceleration is physically impossible, Eq. (9.40) indicates that dV can be finite only when $dA = 0$—that is, a minimum area (throat) or a maximum area (bulge). In Fig. 9.6 we patch together a throat section and a bulge section, using the rules from Fig. 9.5. The throat or converging–diverging section can smoothly accelerate a subsonic flow through sonic to supersonic flow, as in Fig. 9.6a. This is the only way a supersonic flow can be created by expanding the gas from a stagnant reservoir. The bulge section fails; the bulge Mach number moves away from a sonic condition rather than toward it.

Although supersonic flow downstream of a nozzle requires a sonic throat, the opposite is not true: A compressible gas can pass through a throat section without becoming sonic.

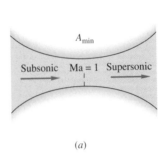

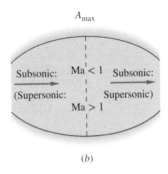

Fig. 9.6 From Eq. (9.40), in flow through a throat (*a*) the fluid can accelerate smoothly through sonic and supersonic flow. In flow through the bulge (*b*) the flow at the bulge cannot be sonic on physical grounds.

(*a*)

(*b*)

Perfect-Gas Area Change

We can use the perfect-gas and isentropic flow relations to convert the continuity relation (9.37) into an algebraic expression involving only area and Mach number, as follows. Equate the mass flow at any section to the mass flow under sonic conditions (which may not actually occur in the duct):

$$\rho V A = \rho^* V^* A^*$$

or
$$\frac{A}{A^*} = \frac{\rho^*}{\rho}\frac{V^*}{V} \tag{9.41}$$

Both terms on the right are functions only of Mach number for isentropic flow. From Eqs. (9.28) and (9.32)

$$\frac{\rho^*}{\rho} = \frac{\rho^*}{\rho_0}\frac{\rho_0}{\rho} = \left\{\frac{2}{k+1}\left[1 + \frac{1}{2}(k-1)\mathrm{Ma}^2\right]\right\}^{1/(k-1)} \tag{9.42}$$

From Eqs. (9.26) and (9.32) we obtain

$$\frac{V^*}{V} = \frac{(kRT^*)^{1/2}}{V} = \frac{(kRT)^{1/2}}{V}\left(\frac{T^*}{T_0}\right)^{1/2}\left(\frac{T_0}{T}\right)^{1/2}$$

$$= \frac{1}{\mathrm{Ma}}\left\{\frac{2}{k+1}\left[1 + \frac{1}{2}(k-1)\mathrm{Ma}^2\right]\right\}^{1/2} \tag{9.43}$$

Combining Eqs. (9.41) to (9.43), we get the desired result:

$$\boxed{\frac{A}{A^*} = \frac{1}{\mathrm{Ma}}\left[\frac{1 + \frac{1}{2}(k-1)\,\mathrm{Ma}^2}{\frac{1}{2}(k+1)}\right]^{(1/2)(k+1)/(k-1)}} \tag{9.44}$$

For $k = 1.4$, Eq. (9.44) takes the numerical form

$$\frac{A}{A^*} = \frac{1}{\mathrm{Ma}}\frac{(1 + 0.2\,\mathrm{Ma}^2)^3}{1.728} \tag{9.45}$$

which is plotted in Fig. 9.7. Equations (9.45) and (9.34) enable us to solve any one-dimensional isentropic airflow problem given, say, the shape of the duct $A(x)$ and the stagnation conditions and assuming that there are no shock waves in the duct.

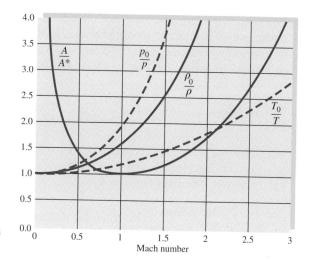

Fig. 9.7 Area ratio and fluid properties versus Mach number for isentropic flow of a perfect gas with $k = 1.4$.

Figure 9.7 shows that the minimum area that can occur in a given isentropic duct flow is the sonic, or critical, throat area. All other duct sections must have A greater than A^*. In many flows a critical sonic throat is not actually present, and the flow in the duct is either entirely subsonic or, more rarely, entirely supersonic.

Choking

From Eq. (9.41) the inverse ratio A^*/A equals $\rho V/(\rho^* V^*)$, the mass flow per unit area at any section compared with the critical mass flow per unit area. From Fig. 9.7 this inverse ratio rises from zero at $\text{Ma} = 0$ to unity at $\text{Ma} = 1$ and back down to zero at large Ma. Thus, for given stagnation conditions, the maximum possible mass flow passes through a duct when its throat is at the critical or sonic condition. The duct is then said to be *choked* and can carry no additional mass flow unless the throat is widened. If the throat is constricted further, the mass flow through the duct must decrease.

From Eqs. (9.32) and (9.33) the maximum mass flow is

$$\dot{m}_{\max} = \rho^* A^* V^* = \rho_0 \left(\frac{2}{k+1}\right)^{1/(k-1)} A^* \left(\frac{2k}{k+1} R T_0\right)^{1/2}$$

$$= k^{1/2} \left(\frac{2}{k+1}\right)^{(1/2)(k+1)/(k-1)} A^* \rho_0 (R T_0)^{1/2} \qquad (9.46a)$$

For $k = 1.4$ this reduces to

$$\boxed{\dot{m}_{\max} = 0.6847 A^* \rho_0 (R T_0)^{1/2} = \frac{0.6847 p_0 A^*}{(R T_0)^{1/2}}} \qquad (9.46b)$$

For isentropic flow through a duct, the maximum mass flow possible is proportional to the throat area and stagnation pressure and inversely proportional to the square root of the stagnation temperature. These are somewhat abstract facts, so let us illustrate with some examples.

The Local Mass Flow Function

Equations (9.46) give the *maximum* mass flow, which occurs at the choking condition (sonic exit). They can be modified to predict the actual (nonmaximum) mass flow at any section where local area A and pressure p are known.[1] The algebra is convoluted, so here we give only the final result, expressed in dimensionless form:

$$\text{Mass flow function} = \frac{\dot{m}}{A}\frac{\sqrt{RT_0}}{p_0} = \sqrt{\frac{2k}{k-1}\left(\frac{p}{p_0}\right)^{2/k}\left[1 - \left(\frac{p}{p_0}\right)^{(k-1)/k}\right]} \tag{9.47}$$

We stress that p and A in this relation are the *local* values at position x. As p/p_0 falls, this function rises rapidly and then levels out at the maximum of Eqs. (9.46). A few values may be tabulated here for $k = 1.4$:

p/p_0	1.0	0.98	0.95	0.9	0.8	0.7	0.6	$\leq$0.5283
Function	0.0	0.1978	0.3076	0.4226	0.5607	0.6383	0.6769	0.6847

Equation (9.47) is handy if stagnation conditions are known and the flow is not choked.

When A/A^* is known and the Mach number is unknown, no algebraic solution of Eq. (9.44) is known to the writer. One could interpolate in Table B.1 or simply iterate Eq. (9.44) with a calculator. But Excel can iterate Eq. (9.44) for subsonic flow in its direct form:

$$\text{Subsonic flow: Ma} = \frac{A^*}{A}\left[\frac{1 + 0.5(k-1)\text{Ma}^2}{0.5(k+1)}\right]^{0.5(k+1)/(k-1)} \tag{9.48}$$

Make a subsonic guess for Ma on the right side and then replace it with the value calculated on the left side. For example, suppose $A/A^* = 2.035$, corresponding to Ma $=$ 0.300. A poor guess of Ma $= 0.5$ in Eq. (9.44) leads to a better Ma $= 0.329$, then 0.303, then 0.300.

For supersonic flow, iteration of Eq. (9.44) diverges. Instead, simply try different Mach numbers in Eq. (9.44) until the proper area is achieved. For example, suppose $A/A^* = 3.183$, corresponding to Ma $= 2.70$. A poor guess of Ma $= 2.4$ yields $A/A^* = 2.403$, 24 percent low. Improve the guess to Ma $= 2.8$ to give $A/A^* = 3.500$, or 10 percent high. Interpolate to Ma $= 2.72$, $A/A^* = 3.244$, 2 percent high. Finally settle on Ma $= 2.70$, correct. These calculations simply require that you retype your guess for Ma, check the error, and convergence only depends upon your cleverness.

Note that two solutions are possible for a given A/A^*, one subsonic and one supersonic. The proper solution cannot be selected without further information, such as known pressure or temperature at the given duct section.

EXAMPLE 9.4

Air flows isentropically through a duct. At section 1 the area is 0.05 m^2 and $V_1 = 180$ m/s, $p_1 = 500$ kPa, and $T_1 = 470$ K. Compute (a) T_0, (b) Ma$_1$, (c) p_0, and (d) both A^* and $\dot{m}$. If at section 2 the area is 0.036 m^2, compute Ma$_2$ and p_2 if the flow is (e) subsonic or (f) supersonic. Assume $k = 1.4$.

---

[1]The author is indebted to Georges Aigret, of Chimay, Belgium, for suggesting this useful function.

Solution

Part (a)

A general sketch of the problem is shown in Fig. E9.4. With V_1 and T_1 known, the energy equation (9.23) gives

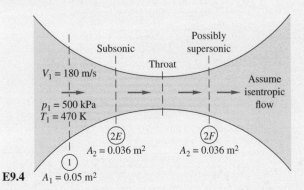

$V_1 = 180$ m/s
Subsonic
Throat
Possibly supersonic
$p_1 = 500$ kPa
$T_1 = 470$ K
Assume isentropic flow
2E
$A_2 = 0.036$ m^2
2F
$A_2 = 0.036$ m^2
1
E9.4 $A_1 = 0.05$ m^2

$$T_0 = T_1 + \frac{V_1^2}{2c_p} = 470 + \frac{(180)^2}{2(1005)} = 486 \text{ K} \qquad Ans.\ (a)$$

Part (b)

The local sound speed $a_1 = \sqrt{kRT_1} = [(1.4)(287)(470)]^{1/2} = 435$ m/s. Hence

$$\text{Ma}_1 = \frac{V_1}{a_1} = \frac{180}{435} = 0.414 \qquad Ans.\ (b)$$

Part (c)

With Ma_1 known, the stagnation pressure follows from Eq. (9.34):

$$p_0 = p_1(1 + 0.2\,\text{Ma}_1^2)^{3.5} = (500 \text{ kPa})[1 + 0.2(0.414)^2]^{3.5} = 563 \text{ kPa} \quad Ans.\ (c)$$

Part (d)

Similarly, from Eq. (9.45), the critical sonic throat area is

$$\frac{A_1}{A^*} = \frac{(1 + 0.2\,\text{Ma}_1^2)^3}{1.728\,\text{Ma}_1} = \frac{[1 + 0.2(0.414)^2]^3}{1.728(0.414)} = 1.547$$

or

$$A^* = \frac{A_1}{1.547} = \frac{0.05 \text{ m}^2}{1.547} = 0.0323 \text{ m}^2 \qquad Ans.\ (d)$$

This throat must *actually be present* in the duct if the flow is to become supersonic.

We now know A^*. So to compute the mass flow we can use Eqs. (9.46), which remain valid, based on the numerical value of A^*, whether or not a throat actually exists:

$$\dot{m} = 0.6847 \frac{p_0 A^*}{\sqrt{RT_0}} = 0.6847 \frac{(563{,}000)(0.0323)}{\sqrt{(287)(486)}} = 33.4 \text{ kg/s} \qquad Ans.\ (d)$$

Or we could fare equally well with our new "local mass flow" formula, Eq. (9.47), using, say, the pressure and area at section 1. Given $p_1/p_0 = 500/563 = 0.889$, Eq. (9.47) yields

$$\dot{m} \frac{\sqrt{287(486)}}{563{,}000(0.05)} = \sqrt{\frac{2(1.4)}{0.4}(0.889)^{2/1.4}[1 - (0.889)^{0.4/1.4}]} = 0.444 \quad \dot{m} = 33.4 \frac{\text{kg}}{\text{s}} \quad Ans.\ (d)$$

Part (e)

For subsonic flow upstream of the throat at section 2E, the area ratio is $A_2/A^* = 0.036/0.0323 = 1.115$, corresponding to the left side of Fig. 9.7 or the subsonic numbers in Table B.1, neither of which is very accurate. Guess Ma_2 at section $2E$, from Fig. 9.7, at about 0.70. Enter this guess into Eq. (9.48) and repeat. The Excel table is:

Ma – guess	Ma – Eq. (9.48)	A/A*
0.700	0.687	1.115
0.687	0.680	1.115
0.680	0.677	1.115
0.677	0.675	1.115
0.675	0.674	1.115
0.674	**0.674**	1.115

The (slowly) converged subsonic Mach number is

$$Ma_2 = 0.674 \qquad \qquad Ans.\ (e)$$

The pressure is given by the isentropic relation

$$p_2 = \frac{p_o}{[1 + 0.2(0.674)^2]^{3.5}} = \frac{563\ \text{kPa}}{1.356} = 415\ \text{kPa} \qquad Ans.\ (e)$$

Part (e) does not require a throat, sonic or otherwise; the flow could simply be contracting subsonically from A_1 to A_2.

Part (f)

For supersonic flow at section $2F$, again the area ratio is $0.036/0.0323 = 1.115$. On the right side of Fig. 9.7 we estimate $Ma_2 \approx 1.5$. The table from Eq. (9.44) is

Ma – guess	A/A* – Eq. (9.44)	A/A*
1.5000	1.1762	1.1150
1.4000	1.1149	1.1150
1.4001	**1.1150**	**1.1150**

We were lucky that this Mach number is easy to guess:

$$Ma_2 = 1.4001 \qquad \qquad Ans.\ (f)$$

Again the pressure is given by the isentropic relation at this new Mach number:

$$p_2 = \frac{p_o}{[1 + 0.2(1.4001)^2]^{3.5}} = \frac{563\ \text{kPa}}{3.183} = 177\ \text{kPa} \qquad Ans.\ (f)$$

Note that the supersonic-flow pressure level is much less than p_2 in part (e), and a sonic throat *must* have occurred between sections 1 and $2F$.

EXAMPLE 9.5

It is desired to expand air from $p_0 = 200$ kPa and $T_0 = 500$ K through a throat to an exit Mach number of 2.5. If the desired mass flow is 3 kg/s, compute (a) the throat area and the exit (b) pressure, (c) temperature, (d) velocity, and (e) area, assuming isentropic flow, with $k = 1.4$.

Solution

The throat area follows from Eq. (9.47), because the throat flow must be sonic to produce a supersonic exit:

$$A* = \frac{\dot{m}(RT_0)^{1/2}}{0.6847p_0} = \frac{3.0[287(500)]^{1/2}}{0.6847(200,000)} = 0.00830 \text{ m}^2 = \frac{1}{4}\pi D*^2$$

or
$$D_{\text{throat}} = 10.3 \text{ cm}$$ *Ans. (a)*

With the exit Mach number known, the isentropic flow relations give the pressure and temperature:

$$p_e = \frac{p_0}{[1 + 0.2(2.5)^2]^{3.5}} = \frac{200,000}{17.08} = 11,700 \text{ Pa}$$ *Ans. (b)*

$$T_e = \frac{T_0}{1 + 0.2(2.5)^2} = \frac{500}{2.25} = 222 \text{ K}$$ *Ans. (c)*

The exit velocity follows from the known Mach number and temperature:

$$V_e = \text{Ma}_e(kRT_e)^{1/2} = 2.5[1.4(287)(222)]^{1/2} = 2.5(299 \text{ m/s}) = 747 \text{ m/s}$$ *Ans. (d)*

The exit area follows from the known throat area and exit Mach number and Eq. (9.45):

$$\frac{A_e}{A*} = \frac{[1 + 0.2(2.5)^2]^3}{1.728(2.5)} = 2.64$$

or
$$A_e = 2.64A* = 2.64(0.0083 \text{ m}^2) = 0.0219 \text{ m}^2 = \tfrac{1}{4}\pi D_e^2$$

or
$$D_e = 16.7 \text{ cm}$$ *Ans. (e)*

One point might be noted: The computation of the throat area $A*$ did not depend in any way on the numerical value of the exit Mach number. The exit was supersonic; therefore the throat is sonic and choked, and no further information is needed.

9.5 The Normal Shock Wave

Shock waves are nearly discontinuous changes in a supersonic flow. They can occur due to a higher downstream pressure, a sudden change in flow direction, blockage by a downstream body, or the result of an explosion. The simplest algebraically is a one-dimensional change, or *normal shock wave*, shown in Fig. 9.8. We select a control volume just before and after the wave.

The analysis is identical to that of Fig. 9.1; that is, a shock wave is a fixed strong pressure wave. To compute all property changes rather than just the wave speed, we use all our basic one-dimensional steady flow relations, letting section 1 be upstream and section 2 be downstream:

Continuity: $\rho_1 V_1 = \rho_2 V_2 = G = \text{const}$ (9.49a)

Momentum: $p_1 - p_2 = \rho_2 V_2^2 - \rho_1 V_1^2$ (9.49b)

Energy: $h_1 + \tfrac{1}{2}V_1^2 = h_2 + \tfrac{1}{2}V_2^2 = h_0 = \text{const}$ (9.49c)

Perfect gas: $\dfrac{p_1}{\rho_1 T_1} = \dfrac{p_2}{\rho_2 T_2}$ (9.49d)

Constant c_p: $h = c_p T \qquad k = \text{const}$ (9.49e)

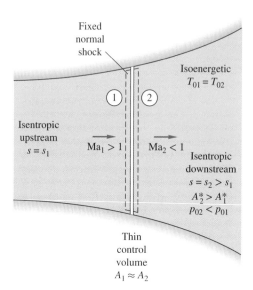

Fixed
normal
shock

Isoenergetic
$T_{01} = T_{02}$

(1) (2)

Isentropic
upstream
$s = s_1$

$Ma_1 > 1$ $Ma_2 < 1$

Isentropic
downstream
$s = s_2 > s_1$
$A_2^* > A_1^*$
$p_{02} < p_{01}$

Thin
control
volume
$A_1 \approx A_2$

Fig. 9.8 Flow through a fixed normal shock wave.

Note that we have canceled out the areas $A_1 \approx A_2$, which is justified even in a variable duct section because of the thinness of the wave. The first successful analyses of these normal shock relations are credited to W. J. M. Rankine (1870) and A. Hugoniot (1887), hence the modern term *Rankine-Hugoniot relations*. If we assume that the upstream conditions (p_1, V_1, ρ_1, h_1, T_1) are known, Eqs. (9.49) are five algebraic relations in the five unknowns (p_2, V_2, ρ_2, h_2, T_2). Because of the velocity-squared term, two solutions are found, and the correct one is determined from the second law of thermodynamics, which requires that $s_2 > s_1$.

The velocities V_1 and V_2 can be eliminated from Eqs. (9.49a) to (9.49c) to obtain the Rankine-Hugoniot relation:

$$h_2 - h_1 = \frac{1}{2}(p_2 - p_1)\left(\frac{1}{\rho_2} + \frac{1}{\rho_1}\right) \tag{9.50}$$

This contains only thermodynamic properties and is independent of the equation of state. Introducing the perfect-gas law $h = c_p T = kp/[(k-1)\rho]$, we can rewrite this as

$$\frac{\rho_2}{\rho_1} = \frac{1 + \beta p_2/p_1}{\beta + p_2/p_1} \qquad \beta = \frac{k+1}{k-1} \tag{9.51}$$

We can compare this with the isentropic flow relation for a very weak pressure wave in a perfect gas:

$$\frac{\rho_2}{\rho_1} = \left(\frac{p_2}{p_1}\right)^{1/k} \tag{9.52}$$

Also, the actual change in entropy across the shock can be computed from the perfect-gas relation:

$$\frac{s_2 - s_1}{c_v} = \ln\left[\frac{p_2}{p_1}\left(\frac{\rho_1}{\rho_2}\right)^k\right] \tag{9.53}$$

Assuming a given wave strength p_2/p_1, we can compute the density ratio and the entropy change and list them as follows for $k = 1.4$:

$\dfrac{p_2}{p_1}$	ρ_2/ρ_1		$\dfrac{s_2 - s_1}{c_v}$
	Eq. (9.51)	Isentropic	
0.5	0.6154	0.6095	−0.0134
0.9	0.9275	0.9275	−0.00005
1.0	1.0	1.0	0.0
1.1	1.00704	1.00705	0.00004
1.5	1.3333	1.3359	0.0027
2.0	1.6250	1.6407	0.0134

We see that the entropy change is negative if the pressure decreases across the shock, which violates the second law. Thus a rarefaction shock is impossible in a perfect gas.[2] We see also that weak shock waves ($p_2/p_1 \leq 2.0$) are very nearly isentropic.

Mach Number Relations

For a perfect gas all the property ratios across the normal shock are unique functions of k and the upstream Mach number Ma_1. For example, if we eliminate ρ_2 and V_2 from Eqs. (9.49a) to (9.49c) and introduce $h = kp/[(k - 1)\rho]$, we obtain

$$\frac{p_2}{p_1} = \frac{1}{k + 1} \left[\frac{2\rho_1 V_1^2}{p_1} - (k - 1) \right] \tag{9.54}$$

But for a perfect gas $\rho_1 V_1^2/p_1 = kV_1^2/(kRT_1) = k\,Ma_1^2$, so that Eq. (9.54) is equivalent to

$$\frac{p_2}{p_1} = \frac{1}{k + 1} \left[2k\,Ma_1^2 - (k - 1) \right] \tag{9.55}$$

From this equation we see that, for any k, $p_2 > p_1$ only if $Ma_1 > 1.0$. Thus for flow through a normal shock wave, the upstream Mach number must be supersonic to satisfy the second law of thermodynamics.

What about the downstream Mach number? From the perfect-gas identity $\rho V^2 = kp\,Ma^2$, we can rewrite Eq. (9.49b) as

$$\frac{p_2}{p_1} = \frac{1 + k\,Ma_1^2}{1 + k\,Ma_2^2} \tag{9.56}$$

which relates the pressure ratio to both Mach numbers. By equating Eqs. (9.55) and (9.56) we can solve for

$$Ma_2^2 = \frac{(k - 1)\,Ma_1^2 + 2}{2k\,Ma_1^2 - (k - 1)} \tag{9.57}$$

Since Ma_1 must be supersonic, this equation predicts for all $k > 1$ that Ma_2 must be subsonic. Thus a normal shock wave decelerates a flow almost discontinuously from supersonic to subsonic conditions.

[2]This is true also for most real gases; see Ref. 9, Sec. 7.3.

Further manipulation of the basic relations (9.49) for a perfect gas gives additional equations relating the change in properties across a normal shock wave in a perfect gas:

$$\frac{\rho_2}{\rho_1} = \frac{(k+1)\,\text{Ma}_1^2}{(k-1)\,\text{Ma}_1^2 + 2} = \frac{V_1}{V_2}$$

$$\frac{T_2}{T_1} = [2 + (k-1)\,\text{Ma}_1^2]\,\frac{2k\,\text{Ma}_1^2 - (k-1)}{(k+1)^2\,\text{Ma}_1^2} \qquad (9.58)$$

$$T_{02} = T_{01}$$

$$\frac{p_{02}}{p_{01}} = \frac{\rho_{02}}{\rho_{01}} = \left[\frac{(k+1)\,\text{Ma}_1^2}{2 + (k-1)\,\text{Ma}_1^2}\right]^{k/(k-1)} \left[\frac{k+1}{2k\,\text{Ma}_1^2 - (k-1)}\right]^{1/(k-1)}$$

Of additional interest is the fact that the critical, or sonic, throat area A^* in a duct increases across a normal shock:

$$\frac{A_2^*}{A_1^*} = \frac{\text{Ma}_2}{\text{Ma}_1}\left[\frac{2 + (k-1)\,\text{Ma}_1^2}{2 + (k-1)\,\text{Ma}_2^2}\right]^{(1/2)(k+1)/(k-1)} \qquad (9.59)$$

All these relations are given in Table B.2 and plotted versus upstream Mach number Ma_1 in Fig. 9.9 for $k = 1.4$. We see that pressure increases greatly while temperature and density increase moderately. The effective throat area A^* increases slowly at first and then rapidly. The failure of students to account for this change in A^* is a common source of error in shock calculations.

The stagnation temperature remains the same, but the stagnation pressure and density decrease in the same ratio; in other words, the flow across the shock is adiabatic but nonisentropic. Other basic principles governing the behavior of shock waves can

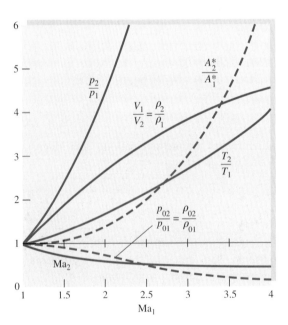

Fig. 9.9 Change in flow properties across a normal shock wave for $k = 1.4$.

be summarized as follows:

1. The upstream flow is supersonic, and the downstream flow is subsonic.
2. For perfect gases (and also for real fluids except under bizarre thermodynamic conditions) rarefaction shocks are impossible, and only a compression shock can exist.
3. The entropy increases across a shock with consequent decreases in stagnation pressure and stagnation density and an increase in the effective sonic throat area.
4. Weak shock waves are very nearly isentropic.

Normal shock waves form in ducts under transient conditions, such as in shock tubes, and in steady flow for certain ranges of the downstream pressure. Figure 9.10a shows a normal shock in a supersonic nozzle. Flow is from left to right. The oblique wave pattern to the left is formed by roughness elements on the nozzle walls and indicates

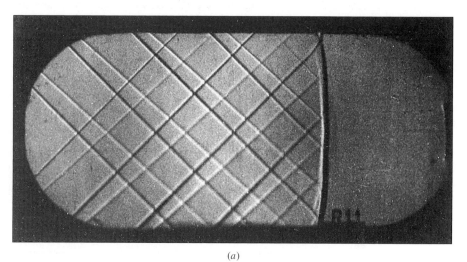

(a)

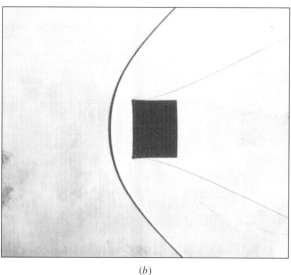

Fig. 9.10 Normal shocks form in both internal and external flows. (a) Normal shock in a duct; note the Mach wave pattern to the left (upstream), indicating supersonic flow. *(Courtesy of U.S. Air Force Arnold Engineering Development Center.)* (b) Supersonic flow past a blunt body creates a normal shock at the nose; the apparent shock thickness and body-corner curvature are optical distortions. *(Courtesy of U.S. Army Ballistic Research Laboratory, Aberdeen Proving Ground.)*

(b)

that the upstream flow is supersonic. Note the absence of these Mach waves (see Sec. 9.10) in the subsonic flow downstream.

Normal shock waves occur not only in supersonic duct flows but also in a variety of supersonic external flows. An example is the supersonic flow past a blunt body shown in Fig. 9.10b. The bow shock is curved, with a portion in front of the body that is essentially normal to the oncoming flow. This normal portion of the bow shock satisfies the property change conditions just as outlined in this section. The flow inside the shock near the body nose is thus subsonic and at relatively high temperature $T_2 > T_1$, and convective heat transfer is especially high in this region.

Each nonnormal portion of the bow shock in Fig. 9.10b satisfies the oblique shock relations to be outlined in Sec. 9.9. Note also the oblique recompression shock on the sides of the body. What has happened is that the subsonic nose flow has accelerated around the corners back to supersonic flow at low pressure, which must then pass through the second shock to match the higher downstream pressure conditions.

Note the fine-grained turbulent wake structure in the rear of the body in Fig. 9.10b. The turbulent boundary layer along the sides of the body is also clearly visible.

The analysis of a complex multidimensional supersonic flow such as in Fig. 9.10 is beyond the scope of this book. For further information see, for example, Ref. 9, Chap. 9, or Ref. 5, Chap. 16.

Moving Normal Shocks

The preceding analysis of the fixed shock applies equally well to the moving shock if we reverse the transformation used in Fig. 9.1. To make the upstream conditions simulate a still fluid, we move the shock of Fig. 9.8 to the left at speed V_1; that is, we fix our coordinates to a control volume moving with the shock. The downstream flow then appears to move to the left at a slower speed $V_1 - V_2$ following the shock. The thermodynamic properties are not changed by this transformation, so that all our Eqs. (9.50) to (9.59) are still valid.

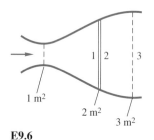

E9.6

EXAMPLE 9.6

Air flows from a reservoir where $p = 300$ kPa and $T = 500$ K through a throat to section 1 in Fig. E9.6, where there is a normal shock wave. Compute (a) p_1, (b) p_2, (c) p_{02}, (d) A_2^*, (e) p_{03}, (f) A_3^*, (g) p_3, and (h) T_{03}.

Solution

- *System sketch:*   This is shown in Fig. E9.6. Between sections 1 and 2 is a normal shock.
- *Assumptions:*   Isentropic flow before and after the shock. Lower p_0 and ρ_0 after the shock.
- *Approach:*   After first noting that the throat is *sonic*, work your way from 1 to 2 to 3.
- *Property values:*   For air, $R = 287$ m^2/(s$^2 \cdot$ K), $k = 1.40$, and $c_p = 1005$ m^2/(s$^2 \cdot$ K). The inlet stagnation pressure of 300 kPa is constant up to point 1.
- *Solution step (a):*   A shock wave cannot exist unless Ma_1 is supersonic. Therefore the throat is *sonic* and choked: $A_{\text{throat}} = A_1^* = 1$ m^2. The area ratio gives Ma_1 from Eq. (9.45) for $k = 1.4$:

$$\frac{A_1}{A_1^*} = \frac{2 \text{ m}^2}{1 \text{ m}^2} = 2.0 = \frac{1}{Ma_1} \frac{(1 + 0.2 \, Ma_1^2)^3}{1.728} \qquad \text{solve for} \qquad Ma_1 = 2.1972$$

Such four-decimal-place accuracy might require iteration or the use of Excel. Linear interpolation in Table B.1 would give $Ma_1 \approx 2.194$, quite good also. The pressure at section 1 then follows from the isentropic relation, Eq. (9.28):

$$p_1 = \frac{p_{01}}{(1 + 0.2Ma_1^2)^{3.5}} = \frac{300 \text{ kPa}}{\left[1 + 0.2(2.194)^2\right]^{3.5}} = 28.2 \text{ kPa} \qquad Ans. (a)$$

- *Steps (b, c, d):*   The pressure p_2 is found from the normal shock Eq. (9.55) or Table B.2:

$$p_2 = \frac{p_1}{k + 1}\left[2k\, Ma_1^2 - (k - 1)\right] = \frac{28.2 \text{ kPa}}{(1.4 + 1)}\left[2(1.4)(2.194)^2 - (1.4 - 1)\right] = 154 \text{ kPa} \quad Ans. (b)$$

Similarly, for $Ma_1 \approx 2.20$, Table B.2 gives $p_{02}/p_{01} \approx 0.628$ (Excel gives 0.6294) and $A_2^*/A_1^* \approx 1.592$ (Excel gives 1.5888). Thus, to good accuracy,

$$p_{02} \approx 0.628p_{01} = 0.628(300 \text{ kPa}) \approx 188 \text{ kPa} \qquad Ans. (c)$$

$$A_2^* = 1.59A_1^* = 1.59(1.0 \text{ m}^2) \approx 1.59 \text{ m}^2 \qquad Ans. (d)$$

- *Comment:*   To calculate A_2^* directly, without Table B.2, you would need to pause and calculate $Ma_2 \approx 0.547$ from Eq. (9.57), since Eq. (9.59) involves both Ma_1 and Ma_2.
- *Step (e, f):*   The flow from 2 to 3 is isentropic (but at higher entropy than upstream of the shock); therefore

$$p_{03} = p_{02} \approx 188 \text{ kPa} \qquad Ans. (e)$$

$$A_3^* = A_2^* \approx 1.59 \text{ m}^2 \qquad Ans. (f)$$

- *Steps (g, h):*   The flow is adiabatic throughout, so the stagnation temperature is constant:

$$T_{03} = T_{02} = T_{01} = 500 \text{ K} \qquad Ans. (h)$$

Next, the area ratio, using the *new* sonic area, gives the Mach number at section 3:

$$\frac{A_3}{A_3^*} = \frac{3 \text{ m}^2}{1.59 \text{ m}^2} = 1.89 = \frac{1}{Ma_3}\frac{(1 + 0.2\, Ma_3^2)^3}{1.728} \qquad \text{solve for} \quad Ma_3 \approx 0.33$$

Excel would yield $Ma_3 = 0.327$. Finally, with p_{02} known, Eq. (9.28) yields p_3:

$$p_3 = \frac{p_{02}}{(1 + 0.2\, Ma_3^2)^{3.5}} \approx \frac{188 \text{ kPa}}{\left[1 + 0.2(0.33)^2\right]^{3.5}} \approx 174 \text{ kPa} \qquad Ans. (g)$$

- *Comments:*   Excel would give $p_3 = 175$ kPa, so we see that Table B.2 is satisfactory for this type of problem. A duct flow with a normal shock wave requires straightforward application of algebraic perfect-gas relations, coupled with a little thought as to which formula is appropriate for the given property.

EXAMPLE 9.7

An explosion in air, $k = 1.4$, creates a spherical shock wave propagating radially into still air at standard conditions. At the instant shown in Fig. E9.7, the pressure just inside the shock is 200 lbf/in² absolute. Estimate (a) the shock speed C and (b) the air velocity V just inside the shock.

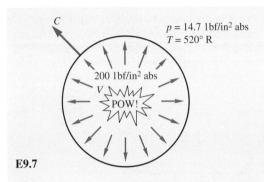

$p = 14.7$ lbf/in^2 abs
$T = 520°$ R

C

200 lbf/in^2 abs

V

POW!

E9.7

Solution

Part (a)

In spite of the spherical geometry, the flow across the shock moves normal to the spherical wave front; hence the normal shock relations (9.50) to (9.59) apply. Fixing our control volume to the moving shock, we find that the proper conditions to use in Fig. 9.8 are

$$C = V_1 \qquad p_1 = 14.7 \text{ lbf/in}^2 \text{ absolute} \qquad T_1 = 520°\text{R}$$

$$V = V_1 - V_2 \qquad p_2 = 200 \text{ lbf/in}^2 \text{ absolute}$$

The speed of sound outside the shock is $a_1 \approx 49T_1^{1/2} = 1117$ ft/s. We can find Ma$_1$ from the known pressure ratio across the shock:

$$\frac{p_2}{p_1} = \frac{200 \text{ lbf/in}^2 \text{ absolute}}{14.7 \text{ lbf/in}^2 \text{ absolute}} = 13.61$$

From Eq. (9.55) or Table B.2

$$13.61 = \frac{1}{2.4}(2.8 \text{ Ma}_1^2 - 0.4) \qquad \text{or} \qquad \text{Ma}_1 = 3.436$$

Then, by definition of the Mach number,

$$C = V_1 = \text{Ma}_1 \, a_1 = 3.436(1117 \text{ ft/s}) = 3840 \text{ ft/s} \qquad\qquad \textit{Ans. (a)}$$

Part (b)

To find V_2, we need the temperature or sound speed inside the shock. Since Ma$_1$ is known, from Eq. (9.58) or Table B.2 for Ma$_1 = 3.436$ we compute $T_2/T_1 = 3.228$. Then

$$T_2 = 3.228T_1 = 3.228(520°\text{R}) = 1679°\text{R}$$

At such a high temperature we should account for non-perfect-gas effects or at least use the gas tables [16], but we won't. Here just estimate from the perfect-gas energy equation (9.23) that

$$V_2^2 = 2c_p(T_1 - T_2) + V_1^2 = 2(6010)(520 - 1679) + (3840)^2 = 815,000$$

or $$V_2 \approx 903 \text{ ft/s}$$

Notice that we did this without bothering to compute Ma$_2$, which equals 0.454, or $a_2 \approx 49T_2^{1/2} = 2000$ ft/s.

Finally, the air velocity behind the shock is

$$V = V_1 - V_2 = 3840 - 903 \approx 2940 \text{ ft/s} \qquad \qquad \textit{Ans. (b)}$$

Thus a powerful explosion creates a brief but intense blast wind as it passes.[3]

9.6 Operation of Converging and Diverging Nozzles

By combining the isentropic flow and normal shock relations plus the concept of sonic throat choking, we can outline the characteristics of converging and diverging nozzles.

Converging Nozzle

First consider the converging nozzle sketched in Fig. 9.11a. There is an upstream reservoir at stagnation pressure p_0. The flow is induced by lowering the downstream outside, or *back*, pressure p_b below p_0, resulting in the sequence of states a to e shown in Figs. 9.11b and c.

For a moderate drop in p_b to states a and b, the throat pressure is higher than the critical value p^* that would make the throat sonic. The flow in the nozzle is subsonic throughout, and the jet exit pressure p_e equals the back pressure p_b. The mass flow is predicted by subsonic isentropic theory and is less than the critical value $\dot{m}_{max}$, as shown in Fig. 9.11c.

For condition c, the back pressure exactly equals the critical pressure p^* of the throat. The throat becomes sonic, the jet exit flow is sonic, $p_e = p_b$, and the mass flow equals its maximum value from Eqs. (9.46). The flow upstream of the throat is subsonic everywhere and predicted by isentropic theory based on the local area ratio $A(x)/A^*$ and Table B.1.

Finally, if p_b is lowered further to conditions d or e below p^*, the nozzle cannot respond further because it is choked at its maximum throat mass flow. The throat remains sonic with $p_e = p^*$, and the nozzle pressure distribution is the same as in state c, as sketched in Fig. 9.11b. The exit jet expands supersonically so that the jet pressure can be reduced from p^* down to p_b. The jet structure is complex and multidimensional and is not shown here. Being supersonic, the jet cannot send any signal upstream to influence the choked flow conditions in the nozzle.

If the stagnation plenum chamber is large or supplemented by a compressor, and if the discharge chamber is larger or supplemented by a vacuum pump, the converging nozzle flow will be steady or nearly so. Otherwise the nozzle will be blowing down, with p_0 decreasing and p_b increasing, and the flow states will be changing from, say, state e backward to state a. Blowdown calculations are usually made by a quasi-steady analysis based on isentropic steady flow theory for the instantaneous pressures $p_0(t)$ and $p_b(t)$.

---

[3]This is the principle of the *shock tube wind tunnel,* in which a controlled explosion creates a brief flow at very high Mach number, with data taken by fast-response instruments. See, for example, Ref. 5.

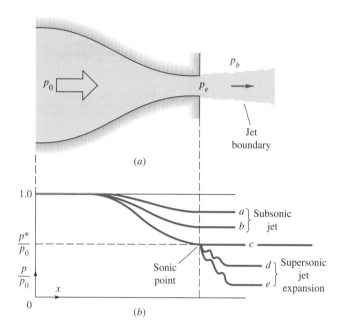

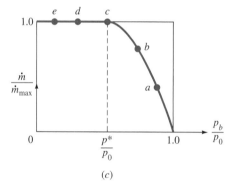

Fig. 9.11 Operation of a converging nozzle: (a) nozzle geometry showing characteristic pressures; (b) pressure distribution caused by various back pressures; (c) mass flow versus back pressure.

EXAMPLE 9.8

A converging nozzle has a throat area of 6 cm^2 and stagnation air conditions of 120 kPa and 400 K. Compute the exit pressure and mass flow if the back pressure is (a) 90 kPa and (b) 45 kPa. Assume $k = 1.4$.

Solution

From Eq. (9.32) for $k = 1.4$ the critical (sonic) throat pressure is

$$\frac{p^*}{p_0} = 0.5283 \quad \text{or} \quad p^* = (0.5283)(120 \text{ kPa}) = 63.4 \text{ kPa}$$

If the back pressure is less than this amount, the nozzle flow is choked.

Part (a)

For $p_b = 90$ kPa $> p^*$, the flow is subsonic, not choked. The exit pressure is $p_e = p_b$. The throat Mach number is found from the isentropic relation (9.35) or Table B.1:

$$\text{Ma}_e^2 = 5\left[\left(\frac{p_0}{p_e}\right)^{2/7} - 1\right] = 5\left[\left(\frac{120}{90}\right)^{2/7} - 1\right] = 0.4283 \quad \text{Ma}_e = 0.654$$

To find the mass flow, we could proceed with a serial attack on Ma_e, T_e, a_e, V_e, and ρ_e, hence to compute $\rho_e A_e V_e$. However, since the local pressure is known, this part is ideally suited for the dimensionless mass flow function in Eq. (9.47). With $p_e/p_0 = 90/120 = 0.75$, compute

$$\frac{\dot{m}\sqrt{RT_0}}{Ap_0} = \sqrt{\frac{2(1.4)}{0.4}(0.75)^{2/1.4}[1 - (0.75)^{0.4/1.4}]} = 0.6052$$

hence

$$\dot{m} = 0.6052\frac{(0.0006)(120{,}000)}{\sqrt{287(400)}} = 0.129 \text{ kg/s} \qquad \textit{Ans. (a)}$$

for

$$p_e = p_b = 90 \text{ kPa} \qquad \textit{Ans. (a)}$$

Part (b)

For $p_b = 45$ kPa $< p^*$, the flow is choked, similar to condition d in Fig. 9.11b. The exit pressure is sonic:

$$p_e = p^* = 63.4 \text{ kPa} \qquad \textit{Ans. (b)}$$

The (choked) mass flow is a maximum from Eq. (9.46b):

$$\dot{m} = \dot{m}_{\text{max}} = \frac{0.6847 p_0 A_e}{(RT_0)^{1/2}} = \frac{0.6847(120{,}000)(0.0006)}{[287(400)]^{1/2}} = 0.145 \text{ kg/s} \quad \textit{Ans. (b)}$$

Any back pressure less than 63.4 kPa would cause this same choked mass flow. Note that the 50 percent increase in exit Mach number, from 0.654 to 1.0, has increased the mass flow only 12 percent, from 0.128 to 0.145 kg/s.

Converging–Diverging Nozzle

Now consider the converging–diverging nozzle sketched in Fig. 9.12a. If the back pressure p_b is low enough, there will be supersonic flow in the diverging portion and a variety of shock wave conditions may occur, which are sketched in Fig. 9.12b. Let the back pressure be gradually decreased.

For curves A and B in Fig. 9.12b the back pressure is not low enough to induce sonic flow in the throat, and the flow in the nozzle is subsonic throughout. The pressure distribution is computed from subsonic isentropic area-change relations, such as in Table B.1. The exit pressure $p_e = p_b$, and the jet is subsonic.

For curve C the area ratio A_e/A_t exactly equals the critical ratio A_e/A^* for a subsonic Ma_e in Table B.1. The throat becomes sonic, and the mass flux reaches a maximum in Fig. 9.12c. The remainder of the nozzle flow is subsonic, including the exit jet, and $p_e = p_b$.

Now jump for a moment to curve H. Here p_b is such that p_b/p_0 exactly corresponds to the critical area ratio A_e/A^* for a *supersonic* Ma_e in Table B.1. The diverging flow is entirely supersonic, including the jet flow, and $p_e = p_b$. This is called the *design pressure ratio* of the nozzle and is the back pressure suitable for operating a supersonic wind tunnel or an efficient rocket exhaust.

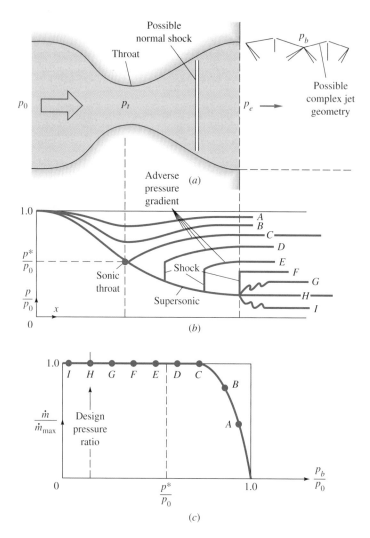

Fig. 9.12 Operation of a converging–diverging nozzle: (*a*) nozzle geometry with possible flow configurations; (*b*) pressure distribution caused by various back pressures; (*c*) mass flow versus back pressure.

Now back up and suppose that p_b lies between curves C and H, which is impossible according to purely isentropic flow calculations. Then back pressures D to F occur in Fig. 9.12*b*. The throat remains choked at the sonic value, and we can match $p_e = p_b$ by placing a normal shock at just the right place in the diverging section to cause a *subsonic diffuser* flow back to the back-pressure condition. The mass flow remains at maximum in Fig. 9.12*c*. At back pressure F the required normal shock stands in the duct exit. At back pressure G no single normal shock can do the job, and so the flow compresses outside the exit in a complex series of oblique shocks until it matches p_b.

Finally, at back pressure I, p_b is lower than the design pressure H, but the nozzle is choked and cannot respond. The exit flow expands in a complex series of supersonic wave motions until it matches the low back pressure. See, Ref. 7, Sec. 5.4, for further details of these off-design jet flow configurations.

Note that for p_b less than back pressure C, there is supersonic flow in the nozzle, and the throat can receive no signal from the exit behavior. The flow remains choked, and the throat has no idea what the exit conditions are.

Note also that the normal shock-patching idea is idealized. Downstream of the shock, the nozzle flow has an adverse pressure gradient, usually leading to wall boundary layer separation. Blockage by the greatly thickened separated layer interacts strongly with the core flow (recall Fig. 6.27) and usually induces a series of weak two-dimensional compression shocks rather than a single one-dimensional normal shock (see, Ref. 9, pp. 292 and 293, for further details).

EXAMPLE 9.9

A converging–diverging nozzle (Fig. 9.12a) has a throat area of 0.002 m^2 and an exit area of 0.008 m^2. Air stagnation conditions are $p_0 = 1000$ kPa and $T_0 = 500$ K. Compute the exit pressure and mass flow for (a) design condition and the exit pressure and mass flow if (b) $p_b \approx 300$ kPa and (c) $p_b \approx 900$ kPa. Assume $k = 1.4$.

Solution

Part (a)

The design condition corresponds to supersonic isentropic flow at the given area ratio $A_e/A_t = 0.008/0.002 = 4.0$. We can find the design Mach number by iteration of the area ratio formula (9.45):

$$\text{Ma}_{e,\text{design}} \approx 2.95$$

The design pressure ratio follows from Eq. (9.34):

$$\frac{p_0}{p_e} = [1 + 0.2(2.95)^2]^{3.5} = 34.1$$

or

$$p_{e,\text{design}} = \frac{1000 \text{ kPa}}{34.1} = 29.3 \text{ kPa} \qquad \textit{Ans. (a)}$$

Since the throat is clearly sonic at design conditions, Eq. (9.46b) applies:

$$\dot{m}_{\text{design}} = \dot{m}_{\text{max}} = \frac{0.6847 p_0 A_t}{(RT_0)^{1/2}} = \frac{0.6847(10^6 \text{ Pa})(0.002 \text{ m}^2)}{[287(500)]^{1/2}} \qquad \textit{Ans. (a)}$$

$$= 3.61 \text{ kg/s}$$

Part (b)

For $p_b = 300$ kPa we are definitely far below the subsonic isentropic condition C in Fig. 9.12b, but we may even be below condition F with a normal shock in the exit—that is, in condition G, where oblique shocks occur outside the exit plane. If it is condition G, then $p_e = p_{e,\text{design}} = 29.3$ kPa because no shock has yet occurred. To find out, compute condition F by assuming an exit normal shock with $\text{Ma}_1 = 2.95$—that is, the design Mach number just upstream of the shock. From Eq. (9.55)

$$\frac{p_2}{p_1} = \frac{1}{2.4}[2.8(2.95)^2 - 0.4] = 9.99$$

or

$$p_2 = 9.99 p_1 = 9.99 p_{e,\text{design}} = 293 \text{ kPa}$$

Since this is less than the given $p_b = 300$ kPa, there is a normal shock just upstream of the exit plane (condition E). The exit flow is subsonic and equals the back pressure:

$$p_e = p_b = 300 \text{ kPa} \qquad \qquad \textit{Ans. (b)}$$

Also
$$\dot{m} = \dot{m}_{\text{max}} = 3.61 \text{ kg/s} \qquad \qquad \textit{Ans. (b)}$$

The throat is still sonic and choked at its maximum mass flow.

Part (c)   Finally, for $p_b = 900$ kPa, which is up near condition C, we compute Ma_e and p_e for condition C as a comparison. Again $A_e/A_t = 4.0$ for this condition, with a subsonic Ma_e estimated from Eq. (9.48):

$$\text{Ma}_e(C) \approx 0.147 \qquad (\text{exact} = 0.14655)$$

Then the isentropic exit pressure ratio for this condition is

$$\frac{p_0}{p_e} = [1 + 0.2(0.147)^2]^{3.5} = 1.0152$$

or
$$p_e = \frac{1000}{1.0152} = 985 \text{ kPa}$$

The given back pressure of 900 kPa is less than this value, corresponding roughly to condition D in Fig. 9.12b. Thus for this case there is a normal shock just downstream of the throat, and the throat is choked:

$$p_e = p_b = 900 \text{ kPa} \qquad \dot{m} = \dot{m}_{\text{max}} = 3.61 \text{ kg/s} \qquad \qquad \textit{Ans. (c)}$$

For this large exit area ratio, the exit pressure would have to be larger than 985 kPa to cause a subsonic flow in the throat and a mass flow less than maximum.

9.7 Compressible Duct Flow with Friction[4]

Section 9.4 showed the effect of area change on a compressible flow while neglecting friction and heat transfer. We could now add friction and heat transfer to the area change and consider coupled effects, which is done in advanced texts [for example, Ref. 5, Chap. 8]. Instead, as an elementary introduction, this section treats only the effect of friction, neglecting area change and heat transfer. The basic assumptions are

1. Steady one-dimensional adiabatic flow.
2. Perfect gas with constant specific heats.
3. Constant-area straight duct.
4. Negligible shaft work and potential energy changes.
5. Wall shear stress correlated by a Darcy friction factor.

In effect, we are studying a Moody-type pipe friction problem but with large changes in kinetic energy, enthalpy, and pressure in the flow.

This type of duct flow—constant area, constant stagnation enthalpy, constant mass flow, but variable momentum (due to friction)—is often termed *Fanno flow*, after Gino

---

[4]This section may be omitted without loss of continuity.

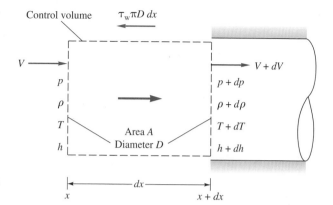

Fig. 9.13 Elemental control volume for flow in a constant-area duct with friction.

Fanno, an Italian engineer born in 1882, who first studied this flow. For a given mass flow and stagnation enthalpy, a plot of enthalpy versus entropy for all possible flow states, subsonic or supersonic, is called a *Fanno line*. See Probs. P9.94 and P9.111 for examples of a Fanno line.

Consider the elemental duct control volume of area A and length dx in Fig. 9.13. The area is constant, but other flow properties (p, ρ, T, h, V) may vary with x. Application of the three conservation laws to this control volume gives three differential equations:

Continuity:
$$\rho V = \frac{\dot{m}}{A} = G = \text{const}$$

or
$$\frac{d\rho}{\rho} + \frac{dV}{V} = 0 \tag{9.60a}$$

x momentum: $pA - (p + dp)A - \tau_w \pi D\, dx = \dot{m}(V + dV - V)$

or
$$dp + \frac{4\tau_w dx}{D} + \rho V\, dV = 0 \tag{9.60b}$$

Energy: $h + \tfrac{1}{2}V^2 = h_0 = c_p T_0 = c_p T + \tfrac{1}{2}V^2$

or
$$c_p\, dT + V\, dV = 0 \tag{9.60c}$$

Since these three equations have five unknowns—p, ρ, T, V, and τ_w—we need two additional relations. One is the perfect-gas law:

$$p = \rho RT \quad \text{or} \quad \frac{dp}{p} = \frac{d\rho}{\rho} + \frac{dT}{T} \tag{9.61}$$

To eliminate τ_w as an unknown, it is assumed that wall shear is correlated by a local Darcy friction factor f

$$\tau_w = \tfrac{1}{8} f\rho V^2 = \tfrac{1}{8} f kp\, \text{Ma}^2 \tag{9.62}$$

where the last form follows from the perfect-gas speed-of-sound expression $a^2 = kp/\rho$. In practice, f can be related to the local Reynolds number and wall roughness from, say, the Moody chart, Fig. 6.13.

Equations (9.60) and (9.61) are first-order differential equations and can be integrated, by using friction factor data, from any inlet section 1, where p_1, T_1, V_1, and so on are known, to determine $p(x)$, $T(x)$, and other properties along the duct. It is practically impossible to eliminate all but one variable to give, say, a single differential equation for $p(x)$, but all equations can be written in terms of the Mach number $\text{Ma}(x)$ and the friction factor, by using this definition of Mach number:

$$V^2 = \text{Ma}^2\, kRT$$

or

$$\frac{2\,dV}{V} = \frac{2\,d\,\text{Ma}}{\text{Ma}} + \frac{dT}{T} \tag{9.63}$$

Adiabatic Flow

By eliminating variables between Eqs. (9.60) to (9.63), we obtain the working relations

$$\frac{dp}{p} = -k\,\text{Ma}^2\,\frac{1 + (k-1)\,\text{Ma}^2}{2(1 - \text{Ma}^2)}\,f\frac{dx}{D} \tag{9.64a}$$

$$\frac{d\rho}{\rho} = -\frac{k\,\text{Ma}^2}{2(1 - \text{Ma}^2)}\,f\frac{dx}{D} = -\frac{dV}{V} \tag{9.64b}$$

$$\frac{dp_0}{p_0} = \frac{d\rho_0}{\rho_0} = -\frac{1}{2}\,k\,\text{Ma}^2\,f\frac{dx}{D} \tag{9.64c}$$

$$\frac{dT}{T} = -\frac{k(k-1)\,\text{Ma}^4}{2(1 - \text{Ma}^2)}\,f\frac{dx}{D} \tag{9.64d}$$

$$\frac{d\,\text{Ma}^2}{\text{Ma}^2} = k\,\text{Ma}^2\,\frac{1 + \frac{1}{2}(k-1)\,\text{Ma}^2}{1 - \text{Ma}^2}\,f\frac{dx}{D} \tag{9.64e}$$

All these except dp_0/p_0 have the factor $1 - \text{Ma}^2$ in the denominator, so that, like the area change formulas in Fig. 9.5, subsonic and supersonic flow have opposite effects:

Property	Subsonic	Supersonic
p	Decreases	Increases
ρ	Decreases	Increases
V	Increases	Decreases
$p_0,\ \rho_0$	Decreases	Decreases
T	Decreases	Increases
Ma	Increases	Decreases
Entropy	Increases	Increases

We have added to this list that entropy must increase along the duct for either subsonic or supersonic flow as a consequence of the second law for adiabatic flow. For the same reason, stagnation pressure and density must both decrease.

The key parameter in this discussion is the Mach number. Whether the inlet flow is subsonic or supersonic, the duct Mach number always tends downstream toward $\text{Ma} = 1$ because this is the path along which the entropy increases. If the pressure and density are computed from Eqs. (9.64a) and (9.64b) and the entropy from Eq. (9.53), the result can be plotted in Fig. 9.14 versus Mach number for $k = 1.4$.

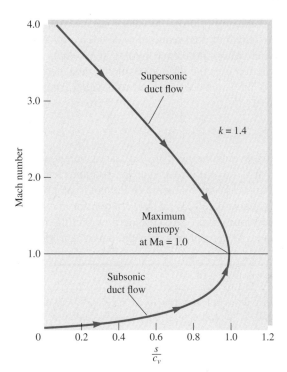

Fig. 9.14 Adiabatic frictional flow in a constant-area duct always approaches Ma = 1 to satisfy the second law of thermodynamics. The computed curve is independent of the value of the friction factor.

The maximum entropy occurs at Ma = 1, so the second law requires that the duct flow properties continually approach the sonic point. Since p_0 and ρ_0 continually decrease along the duct due to the frictional (nonisentropic) losses, they are not useful as reference properties. Instead, the sonic properties p^*, ρ^*, T^*, p_0^*, and ρ_0^* are the appropriate constant reference quantities in adiabatic duct flow. The theory then computes the ratios p/p^*, T/T^*, and so forth as a function of local Mach number and the integrated friction effect.

To derive working formulas, we first attack Eq. (9.64e), which relates the Mach number to friction. Separate the variables and integrate:

$$\int_0^{L^*} f\frac{dx}{D} = \int_{Ma^2}^{1.0} \frac{1 - Ma^2}{k\,Ma^4[1 + \frac{1}{2}(k-1)Ma^2]}\, d\,Ma^2 \tag{9.65}$$

The upper limit is the sonic point, whether or not it is actually reached in the duct flow. The lower limit is arbitrarily placed at the position $x = 0$, where the Mach number is Ma. The result of the integration is

$$\boxed{\frac{\bar{f}L^*}{D} = \frac{1 - Ma^2}{k\,Ma^2} + \frac{k+1}{2k}\ln\frac{(k+1)Ma^2}{2 + (k-1)Ma^2}} \tag{9.66}$$

where $\bar{f}$ is the average friction factor between 0 and L^*. In practice, an average f is always assumed, and no attempt is made to account for the slight changes in Reynolds number along the duct. For noncircular ducts, D is replaced by the hydraulic diameter $D_h = (4 \times \text{area})/\text{perimeter}$ as in Eq. 6.56.

Equation (9.66) is tabulated versus Mach number in Table B.3. The length L^* is the length of duct required to develop a duct flow from Mach number Ma to the sonic point. Many problems involve short ducts that never become sonic, for which the solution uses the differences in the tabulated "maximum," or sonic, length. For example, the length ΔL required to develop from Ma_1 to Ma_2 is given by

$$\bar{f}\frac{\Delta L}{D} = \left(\frac{\bar{f}L^*}{D}\right)_1 - \left(\frac{\bar{f}L^*}{D}\right)_2 \tag{9.67}$$

This avoids the need for separate tabulations for short ducts.

It is recommended that the friction factor $\bar{f}$ be estimated from the Moody chart (Fig. 6.13) for the average Reynolds number and wall roughness ratio of the duct. Available data [23] on duct friction for compressible flow show good agreement with the Moody chart for subsonic flow, but the measured data in supersonic duct flow are up to 50 percent less than the equivalent Moody friction factor.

EXAMPLE 9.10

Air flows subsonically in an adiabatic 2-cm-diameter duct. The average friction factor is 0.024. What length of duct is necessary to accelerate the flow from $Ma_1 = 0.1$ to $Ma_2 = 0.5$? What additional length will accelerate it to $Ma_3 = 1.0$? Assume $k = 1.4$.

Solution

Equation (9.67) applies with values of $\bar{f}L^*/D$ computed from Eq. (9.66) or read from Table B.3:

$$\bar{f}\frac{\Delta L}{D} = \frac{0.024\,\Delta L}{0.02\text{ m}} = \left(\frac{\bar{f}L^*}{D}\right)_{Ma=0.1} - \left(\frac{\bar{f}L^*}{D}\right)_{Ma=0.5}$$

$$= 66.9216 - 1.0691 = 65.8525$$

Thus
$$\Delta L = \frac{65.8525(0.02\text{ m})}{0.024} = 55\text{ m} \qquad \textit{Ans. (a)}$$

The additional length $\Delta L'$ to go from Ma = 0.5 to Ma = 1.0 is taken directly from Table B.2:

$$f\frac{\Delta L'}{D} = \left(\frac{fL^*}{D}\right)_{Ma=0.5} = 1.0691$$

or
$$\Delta L' = L^*_{Ma=0.5} = \frac{1.0691(0.02\text{ m})}{0.024} = 0.9\text{ m} \qquad \textit{Ans. (b)}$$

This is typical of these calculations: It takes 55 m to accelerate up to Ma = 0.5 and then only 0.9 m more to get all the way up to the sonic point.

Formulas for other flow properties along the duct can be derived from Eqs. (9.64). Equation (9.64e) can be used to eliminate $f\,dx/D$ from each of the other relations, giving, for example, dp/p as a function only of Ma and $d\,Ma^2/Ma^2$. For convenience in tabulating the results, each expression is then integrated all the way from (p, Ma)

to the sonic point (p^*, 1.0). The integrated results are

$$\frac{p}{p^*} = \frac{1}{\text{Ma}} \left[\frac{k+1}{2+(k-1)\text{Ma}^2} \right]^{1/2} \tag{9.68a}$$

$$\frac{\rho}{\rho^*} = \frac{V^*}{V} = \frac{1}{\text{Ma}} \left[\frac{2+(k-1)\text{Ma}^2}{k+1} \right]^{1/2} \tag{9.68b}$$

$$\frac{T}{T^*} = \frac{a^2}{a^{*2}} = \frac{k+1}{2+(k-1)\text{Ma}^2} \tag{9.68c}$$

$$\frac{p_0}{p_0^*} = \frac{\rho_0}{\rho_0^*} = \frac{1}{\text{Ma}} \left[\frac{2+(k-1)\text{Ma}^2}{k+1} \right]^{(1/2)(k+1)/(k-1)} \tag{9.68d}$$

All these ratios are also tabulated in Table B.3. For finding changes between points Ma_1 and Ma_2 that are not sonic, products of these ratios are used. For example,

$$\frac{p_2}{p_1} = \frac{p_2}{p^*} \frac{p^*}{p_1} \tag{9.69}$$

since p^* is a constant reference value for the flow.

EXAMPLE 9.11

For the duct flow of Example 9.10 assume that, at $\text{Ma}_1 = 0.1$, we have $p_1 = 600$ kPa and $T_1 = 450$ K. At section 2 farther downstream, $\text{Ma}_2 = 0.5$. Compute (a) p_2, (b) T_2, (c) V_2, and (d) p_{02}.

Solution

As preliminary information we can compute V_1 and p_{01} from the given data:

$$V_1 = \text{Ma}_1 \, a_1 = 0.1[(1.4)(287)(450)]^{1/2} = 0.1(425 \text{ m/s}) = 42.5 \text{ m/s}$$

$$p_{01} = p_1(1 + 0.2 \, \text{Ma}_1^2)^{3.5} = (600 \text{ kPa})[1 + 0.2(0.1)^2]^{3.5} = 604 \text{ kPa}$$

Now enter Table B.3 or Eqs. (9.68) to find the following property ratios:

Section	Ma	p/p^*	T/T^*	V/V^*	p_0/p_0^*
1	0.1	10.9435	1.1976	0.1094	5.8218
2	0.5	2.1381	1.1429	0.5345	1.3399

Use these ratios to compute all properties downstream:

$$p_2 = p_1 \frac{p_2/p^*}{p_1/p^*} = (600 \text{ kPa}) \frac{2.1381}{10.9435} = 117 \text{ kPa} \qquad \textit{Ans. (a)}$$

$$T_2 = T_1 \frac{T_2/T^*}{T_1/T^*} = (450 \text{ K}) \frac{1.1429}{1.1976} = 429 \text{ K} \qquad \textit{Ans. (b)}$$

$$V_2 = V_1 \frac{V_2/V^*}{V_1/V^*} = (42.5 \text{ m/s}) \frac{0.5345}{0.1094} = 208 \frac{\text{m}}{\text{s}} \qquad \textit{Ans. (c)}$$

$$p_{02} = p_{01} \frac{p_{02}/p_0^*}{p_{01}/p_0^*} = (604 \text{ kPa}) \frac{1.3399}{5.8218} = 139 \text{ kPa} \qquad \textit{Ans. (d)}$$

Note the 77 percent reduction in stagnation pressure due to friction. The formulas are seductive, so check your work by other means. For example, check $p_{02} = p_2(1 + 0.2 \, Ma_2^2)^{3.5}$.

Choking Due to Friction

The theory here predicts that for adiabatic frictional flow in a constant-area duct, no matter what the inlet Mach number Ma_1 is, the flow downstream tends toward the sonic point. There is a certain duct length $L^*(Ma_1)$ for which the exit Mach number will be exactly unity. The duct is then choked.

But what if the actual length L is greater than the predicted "maximum" length L^*? Then the flow conditions must change, and there are two classifications.

Subsonic Inlet. If $L > L^*(Ma_1)$, the flow slows down until an inlet Mach number Ma_2 is reached such that $L = L^*(Ma_2)$. The exit flow is sonic, and the mass flow has been reduced by *frictional choking*. Further increases in duct length will continue to decrease the inlet Ma and mass flow.

Supersonic Inlet. From Table B.3 we see that friction has a very large effect on supersonic duct flow. Even an infinite inlet Mach number will be reduced to sonic conditions in only 41 diameters for $\bar{f} = 0.02$. Some typical numerical values are shown in Fig. 9.15, assuming an inlet Ma = 3.0 and $\bar{f} = 0.02$. For this condition $L^* = 26$ diameters. If L is increased beyond $26D$, the flow will not choke but a normal shock will form at just the right place for the subsequent subsonic frictional flow to

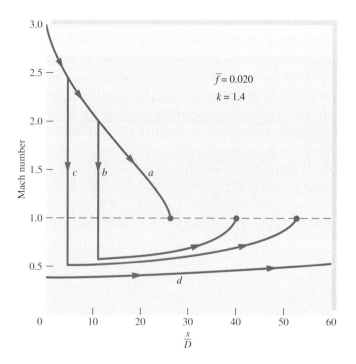

Fig. 9.15 Behavior of duct flow with a nominal supersonic inlet condition Ma = 3.0: (*a*) $L/D \leq 26$, flow is supersonic throughout duct; (*b*) $L/D = 40 > L^*/D$, normal shock at Ma = 2.0 with subsonic flow then accelerating to sonic exit point; (*c*) $L/D = 53$, shock must now occur at Ma = 2.5; (*d*) $L/D > 63$, flow must be entirely subsonic and choked at exit.

become sonic exactly at the exit. Figure 9.15 shows two examples, for $L/D = 40$ and 53. As the length increases, the required normal shock moves upstream until, for Fig. 9.15, the shock is at the inlet for $L/D = 63$. Further increase in L causes the shock to move upstream of the inlet into the supersonic nozzle feeding the duct. Yet the mass flow is still the same as for the very short duct, because presumably the feed nozzle still has a sonic throat. Eventually, a very long duct will cause the feed-nozzle throat to become choked, thus reducing the duct mass flow. Thus supersonic friction changes the flow pattern if $L > L^*$ but does not choke the flow until L is much larger than L^*.

EXAMPLE 9.12

Air enters a 3-cm-diameter duct at $p_0 = 200$ kPa, $T_0 = 500$ K, and $V_1 = 100$ m/s. The friction factor is 0.02. Compute (a) the maximum duct length for these conditions, (b) the mass flow if the duct length is 15 m, and (c) the reduced mass flow if $L = 30$ m.

Solution

Part (a)

First compute

$$T_1 = T_0 - \frac{\frac{1}{2}V_1^2}{c_p} = 500 - \frac{\frac{1}{2}(100 \text{ m(s)}^2}{1005 \text{ m}^2/\text{s}^2 \cdot \text{K}} = 500 - 5 = 495 \text{ K}$$

$$a_1 = (kRT_1)^{1/2} \approx 20(495)^{1/2} = 445 \text{ m/s}$$

Thus

$$\text{Ma}_1 = \frac{V_1}{a_1} = \frac{100}{445} = 0.225$$

For this Ma_1, from Eq. (9.66) or interpolation in Table B.3,

$$\frac{\bar{f}L^*}{D} = 11.0$$

The maximum duct length possible for these inlet conditions is

$$L^* = \frac{(\bar{f}L^*/D)D}{\bar{f}} = \frac{11.0(0.03 \text{ m})}{0.02} = 16.5 \text{ m} \qquad \textit{Ans. (a)}$$

Part (b)

The given $L = 15$ m is less than L^*, and so the duct is not choked and the mass flow follows from the inlet conditions:

$$\rho_{01} = \frac{p_{01}}{RT_0} = \frac{200,000 \text{ Pa}}{287(500 \text{ K})} = 1.394 \text{ kg/m}^3$$

$$\rho_1 = \frac{\rho_{01}}{[1 + 0.2(0.225)^2]^{2.5}} = \frac{1.394}{1.0255} = 1.359 \text{ kg/m}^3$$

whence

$$\dot{m} = \rho_1 A V_1 = (1.359 \text{ kg/m}^3)\left[\frac{\pi}{4}(0.03 \text{ m})^2\right](100 \text{ m/s})$$

$$= 0.0961 \text{ kg/s} \qquad \textit{Ans. (b)}$$

Part (c)   Since $L = 30$ m is greater than L^*, the duct must choke back until $L = L^*$, corresponding to a lower inlet Ma_1:

$$L^* = L = 30 \text{ m}$$

$$\frac{\bar{f}L^*}{D} = \frac{0.02(30 \text{ m})}{0.03 \text{ m}} = 20.0$$

Although it is difficult to interpolate in the coarse Table B.3 for $fL/D = 20$, it is a simple matter for Excel to iterate to find this subsonic Mach number. Program Eq. (9.66) into a cell, guess a subsonic Mach number, and calculate fL/D. Adjust Ma until you approximate $fL/D = 20$. The writer's effort took five guesses, as in the following Excel table:

	A	B
	Ma$_1$	**$(fL/D)_1$ – Eq. (9.66)**
1	0.2	14.533
2	0.15	27.932
3	0.17	21.115
4	0.175	19.772
5	**0.1741**	**20.005**

An accurate solution for Ma is thus $\text{Ma}_{\text{choked}} \approx 0.174$ (23 percent less)

$$T_{1,\text{new}} = \frac{T_0}{1 + 0.2(0.174)^2} = 497 \text{ K}$$

$$a_{1,\text{new}} \approx 20(497 \text{ K})^{1/2} = 446 \text{ m/s}$$

$$V_{1,\text{new}} = \text{Ma}_1 \, a_1 = 0.174(446) = 77.6 \text{ m/s}$$

$$\rho_{1,\text{new}} = \frac{\rho_{01}}{\left[1 + 0.2(0.174)^2\right]^{2.5}} = 1.373 \text{ kg/m}^3$$

$$\dot{m}_{\text{new}} = \rho_1 A V_1 = 1.373 \left[\frac{\pi}{4}(0.03)^2\right](77.6)$$

$$= 0.0753 \text{ kg/s} \quad (22 \text{ percent less}) \qquad\qquad\qquad Ans. \ (c)$$

Minor Losses in Compressible Flow

For incompressible pipe flow, as in Eq. (6.78), the loss coefficient K is the ratio of pressure head loss $(\Delta p/\rho g)$ to the velocity head $(V^2/2g)$ in the pipe. This is inappropriate in compressible pipe flow, where ρ and V are not constant. Benedict [24] suggests that the static pressure loss $(p_1 - p_2)$ be related to downstream conditions and a *static loss coefficient* K_s:

$$K_s = \frac{2(p_1 - p_2)}{\rho_2 V_2^2} \tag{9.70}$$

Benedict [24] gives examples of compressible losses in sudden contractions and expansions. If data are unavailable, a first approximation would be to use $K_s \approx K$ from Sec. 6.9.

Isothermal Flow with Friction: Long Pipelines

The adiabatic frictional flow assumption is appropriate to high-speed flow in short ducts. For flow in long ducts, such as natural gas pipelines, the gas state more closely approximates an isothermal flow. The analysis is the same except that the isoenergetic energy equation (9.60c) is replaced by the simple relation

$$T = \text{const} \quad dT = 0$$

Again it is possible to write all property changes in terms of the Mach number. Integration of the Mach number–friction relation yields

$$\frac{\bar{f} L_{max}}{D} = \frac{1 - k \, \text{Ma}^2}{k \, \text{Ma}^2} + \ln \, (k \, \text{Ma}^2) \tag{9.71}$$

which is the isothermal analog of Eq. (9.66) for adiabatic flow.

This friction relation has the interesting result that L_{max} becomes zero not at the sonic point but at $\text{Ma}_{crit} = 1/k^{1/2} = 0.845$ if $k = 1.4$. The inlet flow, whether subsonic or supersonic, tends downstream toward this limiting Mach number $1/k^{1/2}$. If the tube length L is greater than L_{max} from Eq. (9.71), a subsonic flow will choke back to a smaller Ma_1 and mass flow and a supersonic flow will experience a normal shock adjustment similar to Fig. 9.15.

The exit isothermal choked flow is not sonic, and so the use of the asterisk is inappropriate. Let p', ρ', and V' represent properties at the choking point $L = L_{max}$. Then the isothermal analysis leads to the following Mach number relations for the flow properties:

$$\frac{p}{p'} = \frac{1}{\text{Ma} \, k^{1/2}} \qquad \frac{V}{V'} = \frac{\rho'}{\rho} = \text{Ma} \, k^{1/2} \tag{9.72}$$

The complete analysis and some examples are given in advanced texts [for example, Ref. 5, Sec. 6.4].

Mass Flow for a Given Pressure Drop

An interesting by-product of the isothermal analysis is an explicit relation between the pressure drop and duct mass flow. This common problem requires numerical iteration for adiabatic flow, as outlined here. In isothermal flow, we may substitute $dV/V = -dp/p$ and $V^2 = G^2/[p/(RT)]^2$ in Eq. (9.63) to obtain

$$\frac{2p \, dp}{G^2 RT} + f \frac{dx}{D} - \frac{2 \, dp}{p} = 0$$

Since $G^2 RT$ is constant for isothermal flow, this may be integrated in closed form between $(x, p) = (0, p_1)$ and (L, p_2):

$$G^2 = \left(\frac{\dot{m}}{A}\right)^2 = \frac{p_1^2 - p_2^2}{RT \left[\bar{f} L/D + 2 \ln \, (p_1/p_2) \right]} \tag{9.73}$$

Thus mass flow follows directly from the known end pressures, without any use of Mach numbers or tables.

The writer does not know of any direct analogy to Eq. (9.73) for adiabatic flow. However, a useful adiabatic relation, involving velocities instead of pressures, is

$$V_1^2 = \frac{a_0^2 \left[1 - (V_1/V_2)^2 \right]}{k \bar{f} L/D + (k + 1) \ln \, (V_2/V_1)} \tag{9.74}$$

where $a_0 = (kRT_0)^{1/2}$ is the stagnation speed of sound, constant for adiabatic flow. This may be combined with continuity for constant duct area $V_1/V_2 = \rho_2/\rho_1$, plus the following combination of adiabatic energy and the perfect-gas relation:

$$\frac{V_1}{V_2} = \frac{p_2}{p_1}\frac{T_1}{T_2} = \frac{p_2}{p_1}\left[\frac{2a_0^2 - (k-1)V_1^2}{2a_0^2 - (k-1)V_2^2}\right] \tag{9.75}$$

If we are given the end pressures, neither V_1 nor V_2 will likely be known in advance. We suggest only the following simple procedure: Begin with $a_0 \approx a_1$ and the bracketed term in Eq. (9.75) approximately equal to 1.0. Solve Eq. (9.75) for a first estimate of V_1/V_2, and use this value in Eq. (9.74) to get a better estimate of V_1. Use V_1 to improve your estimate of a_0, and repeat the procedure. The process should converge in a few iterations.

Equations (9.73) and (9.74) have one flaw: With the Mach number eliminated, the frictional choking phenomenon is not directly evident. Therefore, assuming a subsonic inlet flow, one should check the exit Mach number Ma_2 to ensure that it is not greater than $1/k^{1/2}$ for isothermal flow or greater than 1.0 for adiabatic flow. We illustrate both adiabatic and isothermal flow with the following example.

EXAMPLE 9.13

Air enters a pipe of 1-cm diameter and 1.2-m length at $p_1 = 220$ kPa and $T_1 = 300$ K. If $\bar{f} = 0.025$ and the exit pressure is $p_2 = 140$ kPa, estimate the mass flow for (a) isothermal flow and (b) adiabatic flow.

Solution

Part (a)   For isothermal flow Eq. (9.73) applies without iteration:

$$\frac{\bar{f}L}{D} + 2\ln\frac{p_1}{p_2} = \frac{(0.025)(1.2\text{ m})}{0.01\text{ m}} + 2\ln\frac{220}{140} = 3.904$$

$$G^2 = \frac{(220{,}000\text{ Pa})^2 - (140{,}000\text{ Pa})^2}{[287\text{ m}^2/(\text{s}^2\cdot\text{K})](300\text{ K})(3.904)} = 85{,}700 \quad\text{or}\quad G = 293\text{ kg/(s}\cdot\text{m}^2)$$

Since $A = (\pi/4)(0.01\text{ m})^2 = 7.85$ E-5 m², the isothermal mass flow estimate is

$$\dot{m} = GA = (293)(7.85\text{ E-5}) \approx 0.0230\text{ kg/s} \qquad\qquad\text{Ans. (a)}$$

Check that the exit Mach number is not choked:

$$\rho_2 = \frac{p_2}{RT} = \frac{140{,}000}{(287)(300)} = 1.626\text{ kg/m}^3 \qquad V_2 = \frac{G}{\rho_2} = \frac{293}{1.626} = 180\text{ m/s}$$

or

$$Ma_2 = \frac{V_2}{\sqrt{kRT}} = \frac{180}{[1.4(287)(300)]^{1/2}} = \frac{180}{347} \approx 0.52$$

This is well below choking, and the isothermal solution is accurate.

Part (b)   For adiabatic flow, we can iterate by hand, in the time-honored fashion, using Eqs. (9.74) and (9.75), plus the definition of stagnation speed of sound, $a_o = (kRT_o)^{1/2}$. A few years ago the writer would have done just that, laboriously. However, these equations can be iterated and manipulated by Excel. First list the given data and requirements:

$$k = 1.4;\ p_1 = 220{,}000\ \text{Pa};\ p_2 = 140{,}000\ \text{Pa};\ T_1 = 300\text{K};\ \frac{\bar{f}\Delta L}{D} = \frac{(0.025)(1.2)}{0.01} = 3.0,\ p_1^* = p_2^*$$

Now use Excel to apply Eqs. (9.66), for $\bar{f}L/D$, and (9.68a), for p/p^*, to points 1 and 2 in the pipe. We are iterating to find the inlet Mach number for which (a) $\bar{f}\Delta L/D = 3.0$ and (b) $p_1^* = p_2^*$. Even with Excel doing all the work, the iteration is exasperating. We guess Ma_1 and adjust Ma_2 until $\Delta(fL/D) = 3.0$, after which we check for equal values of p^*. The tabulated results are below. It took four guesses of Ma_1 to arrive at $p^* \approx 67{,}900$ Pa.

	A	B	C	D	E	F	G	H	I
	Ma_1	$(fL/D)_1$	p_1/p^*	Ma_2	$(fL/D)_2$	p_2/p^*	$\Delta(fL/D)$	p_1^*	p_2^*
1	0.2	14.533	5.455	0.221	11.533	4.944	3.000	40327	28317
2	0.3	5.299	3.619	0.401	2.299	2.692	3.000	60789	51999
3	0.34	3.752	3.185	0.546	0.752	1.950	3.000	69068	71802
4	**0.3343**	**3.936**	**3.241**	**0.518**	**0.935**	**2.062**	**3.001**	**67884**	**67886**

The mass flow follows from the inlet Mach number and density and is quite close to part (a):

$$V_1 = \text{Ma}_1\sqrt{kRT_1} = (0.3343)\sqrt{1.4(287)(300)} = 116\ \text{m/s}$$

$$\rho_1 = p_1/(RT_1) = (220{,}000)/[287(300)] = 2.56\ \text{kg/m}^3$$

$$\dot{m} = \rho_1 A V_1 = (2.56)(\pi/4)(0.01)^2(116) = 0.0233\ \text{kg/s} \qquad \text{Ans. (}b\text{)}$$

9.8 Frictionless Duct Flow with Heat Transfer[5]

Heat addition or removal has an interesting effect on a compressible flow. Advanced texts [for example, Ref. 5, Chap. 8] consider the combined effect of heat transfer coupled with friction and area change in a duct. Here we confine the analysis to heat transfer with no friction in a constant-area duct.

This type of duct flow—constant area, constant momentum, constant mass flow, but variable stagnation enthalpy (due to heat transfer)—is often termed *Rayleigh flow* after John William Strutt, Lord Rayleigh (1842–1919), a famous physicist and engineer. For a given mass flow and momentum, a plot of enthalpy versus entropy for all possible flow states, subsonic or supersonic, forms a *Rayleigh line*. See Probs. P9.110 and P9.111 for examples of a Rayleigh line.

Consider the elemental duct control volume in Fig. 9.16. Between sections 1 and 2 an amount of heat δQ is added (or removed) to each incremental mass δm passing through. With no friction or area change, the control volume conservation relations are quite simple:

Continuity: $\qquad\qquad\qquad\qquad \rho_1 V_1 = \rho_2 V_2 = G = \text{const} \qquad\qquad (9.76a)$

x momentum: $\qquad\qquad\qquad\quad p_1 - p_2 = G(V_2 - V_1) \qquad\qquad\qquad (9.76b)$

Energy: $\qquad\qquad\qquad\quad \dot{Q} = \dot{m}(h_2 + \tfrac{1}{2}V_2^2 - h_1 - \tfrac{1}{2}V_1^2)$

or $\qquad\qquad\qquad\qquad\quad q = \dfrac{\dot{Q}}{\dot{m}} = \dfrac{\delta Q}{\delta m} = h_{02} - h_{01} \qquad\qquad (9.76c)$

[5]This section may be omitted without loss of continuity.

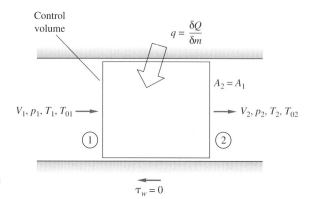

Fig. 9.16 Elemental control volume for frictionless flow in a constant-area duct with heat transfer. The length of the element is indeterminate in this simplified theory.

The heat transfer results in a change in stagnation enthalpy of the flow. We shall not specify exactly how the heat is transferred—combustion, nuclear reaction, evaporation, condensation, or wall heat exchange—but simply that it happened in amount q between 1 and 2. We remark, however, that wall heat exchange is not a good candidate for the theory because wall convection is inevitably coupled with wall friction, which we neglected.

To complete the analysis, we use the perfect-gas and Mach number relations:

$$\frac{p_2}{\rho_2 T_2} = \frac{p_1}{\rho_1 T_1} \qquad h_{02} - h_{01} = c_p(T_{02} - T_{01})$$

$$\frac{V_2}{V_1} = \frac{\mathrm{Ma}_2\, a_2}{\mathrm{Ma}_1\, a_1} = \frac{\mathrm{Ma}_2}{\mathrm{Ma}_1}\left(\frac{T_2}{T_1}\right)^{1/2} \tag{9.77}$$

For a given heat transfer $q = \delta Q/\delta m$ or, equivalently, a given change $h_{02} - h_{01}$, Eqs. (9.76) and (9.77) can be solved algebraically for the property ratios p_2/p_1, $\mathrm{Ma}_2/\mathrm{Ma}_1$, and so on between inlet and outlet. Note that because the heat transfer allows the entropy to either increase or decrease, the second law imposes no restrictions on these solutions.

Before writing down these property ratio functions, we illustrate the effect of heat transfer in Fig. 9.17, which shows T_0 and T versus Mach number in the duct. Heating

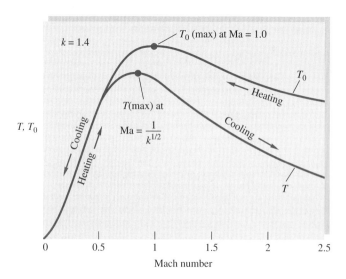

Fig. 9.17 Effect of heat transfer on Mach number.

increases T_0, and cooling decreases it. The maximum possible T_0 occurs at Ma = 1.0, and we see that heating, whether the inlet is subsonic or supersonic, drives the duct Mach number toward unity. This is analogous to the effect of friction in the previous section. The temperature of a perfect gas increases from Ma = 0 up to Ma = $1/k^{1/2}$ and then decreases. Thus there is a peculiar—or at least unexpected—region where heating (increasing T_0) actually decreases the gas temperature, the difference being reflected in a large increase of the gas kinetic energy. For $k = 1.4$ this peculiar area lies between Ma = 0.845 and Ma = 1.0 (interesting but not very useful information).

The complete list of the effects of simple T_0 change on duct flow properties is as follows:

	Heating		Cooling	
	Subsonic	Supersonic	Subsonic	Supersonic
T_0	Increases	Increases	Decreases	Decreases
Ma	Increases	Decreases	Decreases	Increases
p	Decreases	Increases	Increases	Decreases
ρ	Decreases	Increases	Increases	Decreases
V	Increases	Decreases	Decreases	Increases
p_0	Decreases	Decreases	Increases	Increases
s	Increases	Increases	Decreases	Decreases
T	*	Increases	†	Decreases

*Increases up to Ma = $1/k^{1/2}$ and decreases thereafter.
†Decreases up to Ma = $1/k^{1/2}$ and increases thereafter.

Probably the most significant item on this list is the stagnation pressure p_0, which always decreases during heating whether the flow is subsonic or supersonic. Thus heating does increase the Mach number of a flow but entails a loss in effective pressure recovery.

Mach Number Relations

Equations (9.76) and (9.77) can be rearranged in terms of the Mach number and the results tabulated. For convenience, we specify that the outlet section is sonic, Ma = 1, with reference properties T_0^*, T^*, p^*, ρ^*, V^*, and p_0^*. The inlet is assumed to be at arbitrary Mach number Ma. Equations (9.76) and (9.77) then take the following form:

$$\frac{T_0}{T_0^*} = \frac{(k + 1)\,\text{Ma}^2\,[2 + (k - 1)\text{Ma}^2]}{(1 + k\,\text{Ma}^2)^2} \tag{9.78a}$$

$$\frac{T}{T^*} = \frac{(k + 1)^2\,\text{Ma}^2}{(1 + k\,\text{Ma}^2)^2} \tag{9.78b}$$

$$\frac{p}{p^*} = \frac{k + 1}{1 + k\,\text{Ma}^2} \tag{9.78c}$$

$$\frac{V}{V^*} = \frac{\rho^*}{\rho} = \frac{(k + 1)\text{Ma}^2}{1 + k\,\text{Ma}^2} \tag{9.78d}$$

$$\frac{p_0}{p_0^*} = \frac{k + 1}{1 + k\,\text{Ma}^2}\left[\frac{2 + (k - 1)\,\text{Ma}^2}{k + 1}\right]^{k/(k-1)} \tag{9.78e}$$

These formulas are all tabulated versus Mach number in Table B.4. The tables are very convenient if inlet properties Ma_1, V_1, and the like are given but are somewhat cumbersome if the given information centers on T_{01} and T_{02}. Let us illustrate with an example.

EXAMPLE 9.14

A fuel–air mixture, approximated as air with $k = 1.4$, enters a duct combustion chamber at $V_1 = 75$ m/s, $p_1 = 150$ kPa, and $T_1 = 300$ K. The heat addition by combustion is 900 kJ/kg of mixture. Compute (a) the exit properties V_2, p_2, and T_2 and (b) the total heat addition that would have caused a sonic exit flow.

Solution

Part (a)

First compute $T_{01} = T_1 + V_1^2/(2c_p) = 300 + (75)^2/[2(1005)] = 303$ K. Then compute the change in stagnation temperature of the gas:

$$q = c_p(T_{02} - T_{01})$$

or
$$T_{02} = T_{01} + \frac{q}{c_p} = 303 \text{ K} + \frac{900,000 \text{ J/kg}}{1005 \text{ J/(kg} \cdot \text{K)}} = 1199 \text{ K}$$

We have enough information to compute the initial Mach number:

$$a_1 = \sqrt{kRT_1} = [1.4(287)(300)]^{1/2} = 347 \text{ m/s} \qquad Ma_1 = \frac{V_1}{a_1} = \frac{75}{347} = 0.216$$

For this Mach number, use Eq. (9.78a) or Table B.4 to find the sonic value T_0^*:

At $Ma_1 = 0.216$: $\qquad \dfrac{T_{01}}{T_0^*} \approx 0.1992 \qquad$ or $\qquad T_0^* = \dfrac{303 \text{ K}}{0.1992} \approx 1521 \text{ K}$

Then the stagnation temperature ratio at section 2 is $T_{02}/T_0^* = 1199/1521 = 0.788$, which corresponds in Table B.4 to a Mach number $Ma_2 \approx 0.573$.

Now use Eqs. (9.78) at Ma_1 and Ma_2 to tabulate the desired property ratios.

Section	Ma	V/V*	p/p*	T/T*
1	0.216	0.1051	2.2528	0.2368
2	0.573	0.5398	1.6442	0.8876

The exit properties are computed by using these ratios to find state 2 from state 1:

$$V_2 = V_1 \frac{V_2/V^*}{V_1/V^*} = (75 \text{ m/s}) \frac{0.5398}{0.1051} = 385 \text{ m/s} \qquad \textit{Ans. (a)}$$

$$p_2 = p_1 \frac{p_2/p^*}{p_1/p^*} = (150 \text{ kPa}) \frac{1.6442}{2.2528} = 109 \text{ kPa} \qquad \textit{Ans. (a)}$$

$$T_2 = T_1 \frac{T_2/T^*}{T_1/T^*} = (300 \text{ K}) \frac{0.8876}{0.2368} = 1124 \text{ K} \qquad \textit{Ans. (a)}$$

Part (b)

The maximum allowable heat addition would drive the exit Mach number to unity:

$$T_{02} = T_0^* = 1521 \text{ K}$$

$$q_{max} = c_p(T_0^* - T_{01}) = [1005 \text{ J/(kg} \cdot \text{K)}](1521 - 303 \text{ K}) \approx 1.22 \text{ E6 J/kg} \qquad \textit{Ans. (b)}$$

Choking Effects Due to Simple Heating

Equation (9.78a) and Table B.4 indicate that the maximum possible stagnation temperature in simple heating corresponds to T_0^*, or the sonic exit Mach number. Thus, for given inlet conditions, only a certain maximum amount of heat can be added to the flow—for example, 1.22 MJ/kg in Example 9.14. For a subsonic inlet there is no theoretical limit on heat addition: The flow chokes more and more as we add more heat, with the inlet velocity approaching zero. For supersonic flow, even if Ma_1 is infinite, there is a finite ratio $T_{01}/T_0^* = 0.4898$ for $k = 1.4$. Thus if heat is added without limit to a supersonic flow, a normal shock wave adjustment is required to accommodate the required property changes.

In subsonic flow there is no theoretical limit to the amount of cooling allowed: The exit flow just becomes slower and slower, and the temperature approaches zero. In supersonic flow only a finite amount of cooling can be allowed before the exit flow approaches infinite Mach number, with $T_{02}/T_0^* = 0.4898$ and the exit temperature equal to zero. There are very few practical applications for supersonic cooling.

EXAMPLE 9.15

What happens to the inlet flow in Example 9.14 if the heat addition is increased to 1400 kJ/kg and the inlet pressure and stagnation temperature are fixed? What will be the subsequent decrease in mass flow?

Solution

For $q = 1400$ kJ/kg, the exit will be choked at the stagnation temperature:

$$T_0^* = T_{01} + \frac{q}{c_p} = 303 + \frac{1.4 \text{ E6 J/kg}}{1005 \text{ J/(kg} \cdot \text{K)}} \approx 1696 \text{ K}$$

This is higher than the value $T_0^* = 1521$ K in Example 9.14, so we know that condition 1 will have to choke down to a lower Mach number. The proper value is found from the ratio $T_{01}/T_0^* = 303/1696 = 0.1787$. From Table B.4 or Eq. (9.78a) for this condition, we read the new, lowered entrance Mach number: $Ma_{1,\text{new}} \approx 0.203$. With T_{01} and p_1 known, the other inlet properties follow from this Mach number:

$$T_1 = \frac{T_{01}}{1 + 0.2 \, Ma_1^2} = \frac{303}{1 + 0.2(0.203)^2} = 301 \text{ K}$$

$$a_1 = \sqrt{kRT_1} = [1.4(287)(301)]^{1/2} = 348 \text{ m/s}$$

$$V_1 = Ma_1 a_1 = (0.203)(348 \text{ m/s}) = 71 \text{ m/s}$$

$$\rho_1 = \frac{p_1}{RT_1} = \frac{150,000}{(287)(301)} = 1.74 \text{ kg/m}^3$$

Finally, the new lowered mass flow per unit area is

$$\frac{\dot{m}_{\text{new}}}{A} = \rho_1 V_1 = (1.74 \text{ kg/m}^3)(71 \text{ m/s}) = 123 \text{ kg/(s} \cdot \text{m}^2)$$

This is 7 percent less than in Example 9.14, due to choking by excess heat addition.

**Relationship to the
Normal Shock Wave**

The normal shock wave relations of Sec. 9.5 actually lurk within the simple heating relations as a special case. From Table B.4 or Fig. 9.17 we see that for a given stagnation temperature less than T_0^* two flow states satisfy the simple heating relations, one subsonic and the other supersonic. These two states have (1) the same value of T_0, (2) the same mass flow per unit area, and (3) the same value of $p + \rho V^2$. Therefore these two states are exactly equivalent to the conditions on each side of a normal shock wave. The second law would again require that the upstream flow Ma_1 be supersonic.

To illustrate this point, take $Ma_1 = 3.0$ and from Table B.4 read $T_{01}/T_0^* = 0.6540$ and $p_1/p^* = 0.1765$. Now, for the same value $T_{02}/T_0^* = 0.6540$, use Table B.4 or Eq. (9.78a) to compute $Ma_2 = 0.4752$ and $p_2/p^* = 1.8235$. The value of Ma_2 is exactly what we read in the shock table, Table B.2, as the downstream Mach number when $Ma_1 = 3.0$. The pressure ratio for these two states is $p_2/p_1 = (p_2/p^*)/(p_1/p^*) = 1.8235/0.1765 = 10.33$, which again is just what we read in Table B.2 for $Ma_1 = 3.0$. This illustration is meant only to show the physical background of the simple heating relations; it would be silly to make a practice of computing normal shock waves in this manner.

9.9 Mach Waves and Oblique Shock Waves

Up to this point we have considered only one-dimensional compressible flow theories. This illustrated many important effects, but a one-dimensional world completely loses sight of the wave motions that are so characteristic of supersonic flow. The only "wave motion" we could muster in a one-dimensional theory was the normal shock wave, which amounted only to a flow discontinuity in the duct.

Mach Waves

When we add a second dimension to the flow, wave motions immediately become apparent if the flow is supersonic. Figure 9.18 shows a celebrated graphical construction that appears in every fluid mechanics textbook and was first presented by Ernst Mach in 1887. The figure shows the pattern of pressure disturbances (sound waves) sent out by a small particle moving at speed U through a still fluid whose sound velocity is a.

As the particle moves, it continually crashes against fluid particles and sends out spherical sound waves emanating from every point along its path. A few of these spherical disturbance fronts are shown in Fig. 9.18. The behavior of these fronts is quite different according to whether the particle speed is subsonic or supersonic.

In Fig. 9.18a, the particle moves subsonically, $U < a$, $Ma = U/a < 1$. The spherical disturbances move out in all directions and do not catch up with one another. They move well out in front of the particle also, because they travel a distance $a \, \delta t$ during the time interval δt in which the particle has moved only $U \, \delta t$. Therefore a subsonic body motion makes its presence felt everywhere in the flow field: You can "hear" or "feel" the pressure rise of an oncoming body before it reaches you. This is apparently why that pigeon in the road, without turning around to look at you, takes to the air and avoids being hit by your car.

At sonic speed, $U = a$, Fig. 9.18b, the pressure disturbances move at exactly the speed of the particle and thus pile up on the left at the position of the particle into a

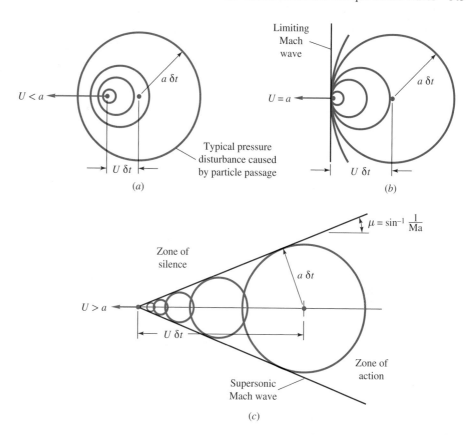

Fig. 9.18 Wave patterns set up by a particle moving at speed U into still fluid of sound velocity a: (*a*) subsonic, (*b*) sonic, and (*c*) supersonic motion.

sort of "front locus," which is now called a *Mach wave*, after Ernst Mach. No disturbance reaches beyond the particle. If you are stationed to the left of the particle, you cannot "hear" the oncoming motion. If the particle blew its horn, you couldn't hear that either: A sonic car can sneak up on a pigeon.

In supersonic motion, $U > a$, the lack of advance warning is even more pronounced. The disturbance spheres cannot catch up with the fast-moving particle that created them. They all trail behind the particle and are tangent to a conical locus called the *Mach cone*. From the geometry of Fig. 9.18*c* the angle of the Mach cone is seen to be

$$\mu = \sin^{-1} \frac{a \, \delta t}{U \, \delta t} = \sin^{-1} \frac{a}{U} = \sin^{-1} \frac{1}{\text{Ma}} \tag{9.79}$$

The higher the particle Mach number, the more slender the Mach cone; for example, μ is 30° at Ma = 2.0 and 11.5° at Ma = 5.0. For the limiting case of sonic flow, Ma = 1, $\mu = 90°$; the Mach cone becomes a plane front moving with the particle, in agreement with Fig. 9.18*b*.

You cannot "hear" the disturbance caused by the supersonic particle in Fig. 9.18*c* until you are in the *zone of action* inside the Mach cone. No warning can reach your ears if you are in the *zone of silence* outside the cone. Thus an observer on the ground beneath a supersonic airplane does not hear the *sonic boom* of the passing cone until the plane is well past.

Fig. 9.19 The wave pattern around a model of the X-15 fighter, moving at about Ma = 1.7. The heavy lines are oblique shock waves, caused by sharp turns, and the light lines are Mach waves, caused by gentle turns. [*Photo Courtesy of NASA*]

The Mach wave need not be a cone: Similar waves are formed by a small disturbance of any shape moving supersonically with respect to the ambient fluid. For example, the "particle" in Fig. 9.18c could be the leading edge of a sharp flat plate, which would form a Mach wedge of exactly the same angle μ. Mach waves are formed by small roughnesses or boundary layer irregularities in a supersonic wind tunnel or at the surface of a supersonic body. Look again at Fig. 9.10: Mach waves are clearly visible along the body surface downstream of the recompression shock, especially at the rear corner. Their angle is about 30°, indicating a Mach number of about 2.0 along this surface.

A more complicated system of waves, seen in Fig. 9.19, emanates from a model of the supersonic X-15 fighter plane, catapulted at Ma ≈ 1.7 through a wind tunnel. The Mach and shock waves are visualized by the knife-edge *schlieren* photographic technique [31]. Note the supersonic turbulent wake.

EXAMPLE 9.16

An observer on the ground does not hear the sonic boom caused by an airplane moving at 5-km altitude until it is 9 km past her. What is the approximate Mach number of the plane? Assume a small disturbance, and neglect the variation of sound speed with altitude.

Solution

A finite disturbance like an airplane will create a finite-strength oblique shock wave whose angle will be somewhat larger than the Mach wave angle μ and will curve downward due to the variation in atmospheric sound speed. If we neglect these effects, the altitude and distance are a measure of μ, as seen in Fig. E9.16.

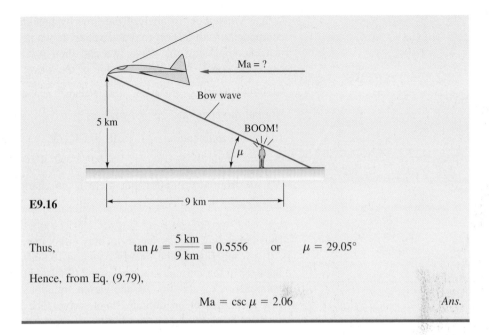

Thus, $\qquad\qquad \tan\mu = \dfrac{5\text{ km}}{9\text{ km}} = 0.5556 \qquad$ or $\qquad \mu = 29.05°$

Hence, from Eq. (9.79),

$$\text{Ma} = \csc\mu = 2.06 \qquad\qquad\qquad Ans.$$

The Oblique Shock Wave

Figures 9.10 and 9.19 and our earlier discussion all indicate that a shock wave can form at an oblique angle to the oncoming supersonic stream. Such a wave will deflect the stream through an angle θ, unlike the normal shock wave, for which the downstream flow is in the same direction. In essence, an oblique shock is caused by the necessity for a supersonic stream to turn through such an angle. Examples could be a finite wedge at the leading edge of a body and a ramp in the wall of a supersonic wind tunnel.

The flow geometry of an oblique shock is shown in Fig. 9.20. As for the normal shock of Fig. 9.8, state 1 denotes the upstream conditions and state 2 is downstream. The shock angle has an arbitrary value β, and the downstream flow V_2 turns at an angle θ which is a function of β and state 1 conditions. The upstream flow is always supersonic, but the downstream Mach number $\text{Ma}_2 = V_2/a_2$ may be subsonic, sonic, or supersonic, depending on the conditions.

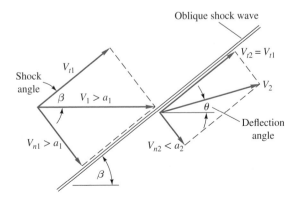

Fig. 9.20 Geometry of flow through an oblique shock wave.

It is convenient to analyze the flow by breaking it up into normal and tangential components with respect to the wave, as shown in Fig. 9.20. For a thin control volume just encompassing the wave, we can then derive the following integral relations, canceling out $A_1 = A_2$ on each side of the wave:

Continuity: $$\rho_1 V_{n1} = \rho_2 V_{n2} \tag{9.80a}$$

Normal momentum: $$p_1 - p_2 = \rho_2 V_{n2}^2 - \rho_1 V_{n1}^2 \tag{9.80b}$$

Tangential momentum: $$0 = \rho_1 V_{n1}(V_{t2} - V_{t1}) \tag{9.80c}$$

Energy: $$h_1 + \tfrac{1}{2}V_{n1}^2 + \tfrac{1}{2}V_{t1}^2 = h_2 + \tfrac{1}{2}V_{n2}^2 + \tfrac{1}{2}V_{t2}^2 = h_0 \tag{9.80d}$$

We see from Eq. (9.80c) that there is no change in tangential velocity across an oblique shock:

$$V_{t2} = V_{t1} = V_t = \text{const} \tag{9.81}$$

Thus tangential velocity has as its only effect the addition of a constant kinetic energy $\tfrac{1}{2}V_t^2$ to each side of the energy equation (9.80d). We conclude that Eqs. (9.80) are identical to the normal shock relations (9.49), with V_1 and V_2 replaced by the normal components V_{n1} and V_{n2}. All the various relations from Sec. 9.5 can be used to compute properties of an oblique shock wave. The trick is to use the "normal" Mach numbers in place of Ma_1 and Ma_2:

$$\boxed{Ma_{n1} = \frac{V_{n1}}{a_1} = Ma_1 \sin \beta}$$

$$\tag{9.82}$$

$$\boxed{Ma_{n2} = \frac{V_{n2}}{a_2} = Ma_2 \sin (\beta - \theta)}$$

Then, for a perfect gas with constant specific heats, the property ratios across the oblique shock are the analogs of Eqs. (9.55) to (9.58) with Ma_1 replaced by Ma_{n1}:

$$\frac{p_2}{p_1} = \frac{1}{k+1}\left[2k\,Ma_1^2 \sin^2 \beta - (k-1)\right] \tag{9.83a}$$

$$\frac{\rho_2}{\rho_1} = \frac{\tan \beta}{\tan (\beta - \theta)} = \frac{(k+1)\,Ma_1^2 \sin^2 \beta}{(k-1)\,Ma_1^2 \sin^2 \beta + 2} = \frac{V_{n1}}{V_{n2}} \tag{9.83b}$$

$$\frac{T_2}{T_1} = [2 + (k-1)\,Ma_1^2 \sin^2 \beta]\frac{2k\,Ma_1^2 \sin^2 \beta - (k-1)}{(k+1)^2\,Ma_1^2 \sin^2 \beta} \tag{9.83c}$$

$$T_{02} = T_{01} \tag{9.83d}$$

$$\frac{p_{02}}{p_{01}} = \left[\frac{(k+1)\,Ma_1^2 \sin^2 \beta}{2 + (k-1)\,Ma_1^2 \sin^2 \beta}\right]^{k/(k-1)} \left[\frac{k+1}{2k\,Ma_1^2 \sin^2 \beta - (k-1)}\right]^{1/(k-1)} \tag{9.83e}$$

$$Ma_{n2}^2 = \frac{(k-1)\,Ma_{n1}^2 + 2}{2k\,Ma_{n1}^2 - (k-1)} \tag{9.83f}$$

All these are tabulated in the normal shock Table B.2. If you wondered why that table listed the Mach numbers as Ma_{n1} and Ma_{n2}, it should be clear now that the table is also valid for the oblique shock wave.

Thinking all this over, we realize with hindsight that an oblique shock wave is the flow pattern one would observe by running along a normal shock wave (Fig. 9.8) at a constant tangential speed V_t. Thus the normal and oblique shocks are related by a galilean, or inertial, velocity transformation and therefore satisfy the same basic equations.

If we continue with this run-along-the-shock analogy, we find that the deflection angle θ increases with speed V_t up to a maximum and then decreases. From the geometry of Fig. 9.20, the deflection angle is given by

$$\theta = \tan^{-1}\frac{V_t}{V_{n2}} - \tan^{-1}\frac{V_t}{V_{n1}} \tag{9.84}$$

If we differentiate θ with respect to V_t and set the result equal to zero, we find that the maximum deflection occurs when $V_t/V_{n1} = (V_{n2}/V_{n1})^{1/2}$. We can substitute this back into Eq. (9.84) to compute

$$\theta_{max} = \tan^{-1}r^{1/2} - \tan^{-1}r^{-1/2} \qquad r = \frac{V_{n1}}{V_{n2}} \tag{9.85}$$

For example, if $Ma_{n1} = 3.0$, from Table B.2 we find that $V_{n1}/V_{n2} = 3.8571$, the square root of which is 1.9640. Then Eq. (9.85) predicts a maximum deflection of $\tan^{-1} 1.9640 - \tan^{-1} (1/1.9640) = 36.03°$. The deflection is quite limited even for infinite Ma_{n1}: From Table B.2 for this case $V_{n1}/V_{n2} = 6.0$, and we compute from Eq. (9.85) that $\theta_{max} = 45.58°$.

This limited-deflection idea and other facts become more evident if we plot some of the solutions of Eqs. (9.83). For given values of V_1 and a_1, assuming as usual that $k = 1.4$, we can plot all possible solutions for V_2 downstream of the shock. Figure 9.21 does this in velocity-component coordinates V_x and V_y, with x parallel to V_1. Such a plot is called a *hodograph*. The heavy dark line that looks like a fat airfoil is the locus, or *shock polar*, of all physically possible solutions for the given Ma_1. The two dashed-line fishtails are solutions that increase V_2; they are physically impossible because they violate the second law.

Examining the shock polar in Fig. 9.21, we see that a given deflection line of small angle θ crosses the polar at two possible solutions: the *strong* shock, which greatly decelerates the flow, and the *weak* shock, which causes a much milder deceleration.

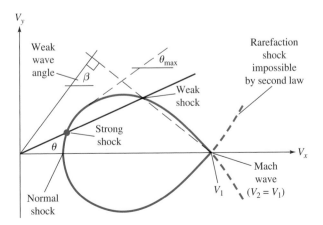

Fig. 9.21 The oblique shock polar hodograph, showing double solutions (strong and weak) for small deflection angle and no solutions at all for large deflection.

The flow downstream of the strong shock is always subsonic, while that of the weak shock is usually supersonic but occasionally subsonic if the deflection is large. Both types of shock occur in practice. The weak shock is more prevalent, but the strong shock will occur if there is a blockage or high-pressure condition downstream.

Since the shock polar is only of finite size, there is a maximum deflection θ_{max}, shown in Fig. 9.21, that just grazes the upper edge of the polar curve. This verifies the kinematic discussion that led to Eq. (9.85). What happens if a supersonic flow is forced to deflect through an angle greater than θ_{max}? The answer is illustrated in Fig. 9.22 for flow past a wedge-shaped body.

In Fig. 9.22a the wedge half-angle θ is less than θ_{max}, and thus an oblique shock forms at the nose of wave angle β just sufficient to cause the oncoming supersonic stream to deflect through the wedge angle θ. Except for the usually small effect of boundary layer growth (see, for example, Ref. 19, Sec. 7–5.2), the Mach number Ma_2 is constant along the wedge surface and is given by the solution of Eqs. (9.83). The pressure, density, and temperature along the surface are also nearly constant, as predicted by Eqs. (9.83). When the flow reaches the corner of the wedge, it expands to higher Mach number and forms a wake (not shown) similar to that in Fig. 9.10.

In Fig. 9.22b the wedge half-angle is greater than θ_{max}, and an attached oblique shock is impossible. The flow cannot deflect at once through the entire angle θ_{max}, yet somehow the flow must get around the wedge. A detached curve shock wave forms in front of the body, discontinuously deflecting the flow through angles smaller than θ_{max}. The flow then curves, expands, and deflects subsonically around the wedge, becoming sonic and then supersonic as it passes the corner region. The flow just inside each point on the curved shock exactly satisfies the oblique shock relations (9.83) for

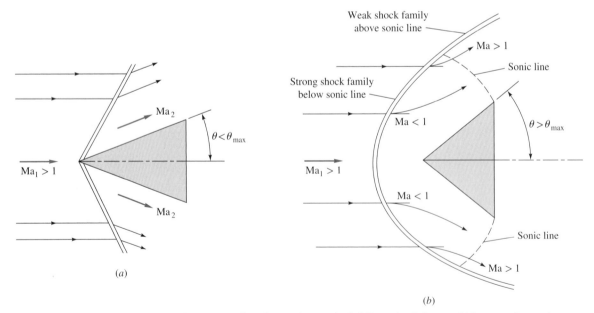

(a)

(b)

Fig. 9.22 Supersonic flow past a wedge: (a) small wedge angle, attached oblique shock forms; (b) large wedge angle, attached shock not possible, broad curved detached shock forms.

that particular value of β and the given Ma_1. Every condition along the curved shock is a point on the shock polar of Fig. 9.21. Points near the front of the wedge are in the strong shock family, and points aft of the sonic line are in the weak shock family. The analysis of detached shock waves is extremely complex [13], and experimentation is usually needed, such as the shadowgraph optical technique of Fig. 9.10.

The complete family of oblique shock solutions can be plotted or computed from Eqs. (9.83). For a given k, the wave angle β varies with Ma_1 and θ, from Eq. (9.83b). By using a trigonometric identity for $\tan(\beta - \theta)$ this can be rewritten in the more convenient form

$$\tan\theta = \frac{2\cot\beta\,(Ma_1^2\sin^2\beta - 1)}{Ma_1^2\,(k + \cos 2\beta) + 2} \tag{9.86}$$

All possible solutions of Eq. (9.86) for $k = 1.4$ are shown in Fig. 9.23. For deflections $\theta < \theta_{max}$ there are two solutions: a weak shock (small β) and a strong shock (large β), as expected. All points along the dash–dot line for θ_{max} satisfy Eq. (9.85). A dashed line has been added to show where Ma_2 is exactly sonic. We see that there is a narrow region near maximum deflection where the weak shock downstream flow is subsonic.

For zero deflections ($\theta = 0$) the weak shock family satisfies the wave angle relation

$$\beta = \mu = \sin^{-1}\frac{1}{Ma_1} \tag{9.87}$$

Thus weak shocks of vanishing deflection are equivalent to Mach waves. Meanwhile the strong shocks all converge at zero deflection to the normal shock condition $\beta = 90°$.

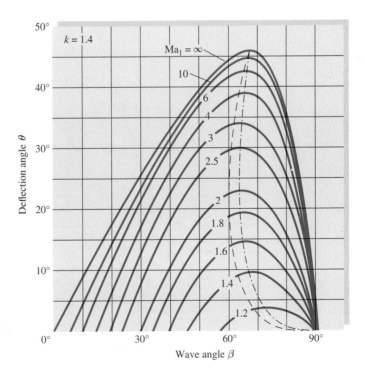

Fig. 9.23 Oblique shock deflection versus wave angle for various upstream Mach numbers, $k = 1.4$: dash–dot curve, locus of θ_{max}, divides strong (right) from weak (left) shocks; dashed curve, locus of sonic points, divides subsonic Ma_2 (right) from supersonic Ma_2 (left).

Two additional oblique shock charts are given in App. B for $k = 1.4$, where Fig. B.1 gives the downstream Mach number Ma_2 and Fig. B.2 the pressure ratio p_2/p_1, each plotted as a function of Ma_1 and θ. Additional graphs, tables, and computer programs are given in Refs. 20 and 21.

Very Weak Shock Waves

For any finite θ the wave angle β for a weak shock is greater than the Mach angle μ. For small θ Eq. (9.86) can be expanded in a power series in $\tan \theta$ with the following linearized result for the wave angle:

$$\sin \beta = \sin \mu + \frac{k + 1}{4 \cos \mu} \tan \theta + \cdots + \mathcal{O}(\tan^2 \theta) + \cdots \qquad (9.88)$$

For Ma_1 between 1.4 and 20.0 and deflections less than $6°$ this relation predicts β to within $1°$ for a weak shock. For larger deflections it can be used as a useful initial guess for iterative solution of Eq. (9.86).

Other property changes across the oblique shock can also be expanded in a power series for small deflection angles. Of particular interest is the pressure change from Eq. (9.83a), for which the linearized result for a weak shock is

$$\frac{p_2 - p_1}{p_1} = \frac{k\,Ma_1^2}{(Ma_1^2 - 1)^{1/2}} \tan \theta + \cdots + \mathcal{O}(\tan^2 \theta) + \cdots \qquad (9.89)$$

The differential form of this relation is used in the next section to develop a theory for supersonic expansion turns. Figure 9.24 shows the exact weak shock pressure jump

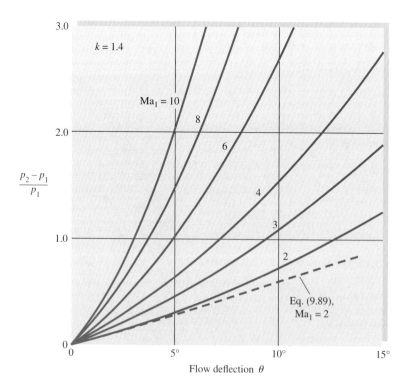

Fig. 9.24 Pressure jump across a weak oblique shock wave from Eq. (9.83a) for $k = 1.4$. For very small deflections Eq. (9.89) applies.

computed from Eq. (9.83*a*). At very small deflections the curves are linear with slopes given by Eq. (9.89).

Finally, it is educational to examine the entropy change across a very weak shock. Using the same power series expansion technique, we can obtain the following result for small flow deflections:

$$\frac{s_2 - s_1}{c_p} = \frac{(k^2 - 1)\text{Ma}_1^6}{12(\text{Ma}_1^2 - 1)^{3/2}} \tan^3 \theta + \cdots + \mathbb{O}(\tan^4 \theta) + \cdots \qquad (9.90)$$

The entropy change is cubic in the deflection angle θ. Thus weak shock waves are very nearly isentropic, a fact that is also used in the next section.

EXAMPLE 9.17

Air at Ma = 2.0 and $p = 10 \text{ lbf/in}^2$ absolute is forced to turn through 10° by a ramp at the body surface. A weak oblique shock forms as in Fig. E9.17. For $k = 1.4$ compute from exact oblique shock theory (*a*) the wave angle β, (*b*) Ma_2, and (*c*) p_2. Also use the linearized theory to estimate (*d*) β and (*e*) p_2.

Solution using Excel

With $\text{Ma}_1 = 2.0$ and $\theta = 10°$ known, we can estimate $\beta \approx 40° \pm 2°$ from Fig. 9.23. For more accuracy, we can set an Excel iteration, using improved guesses for β. Begin with a guess of 40° and zero in on the correct wave angle. The writer's guesses are as follows:

	A	B
	β – guess	θ – Eq. **(9.86)**
1	40.00	10.623
2	38.00	8.767
3	39.00	9.710
4	39.30	9.987
5	**39.32**	**10.006**

The iteration converges to $\beta = 39.32°$ *Ans.* (*a*)

The normal Mach number upstream is thus

$$\text{Ma}_{n1} = \text{Ma}_1 \sin \beta = 2.0 \sin 39.32° = 1.267$$

With Ma_{n1} we can use the normal shock relations (Table B.2) or Fig. 9.9 or Eqs. (9.56) to (9.58) to compute

$$\text{Ma}_{n2} = 0.8031 \qquad \frac{p_2}{p_1} = 1.707$$

Thus the downstream Mach number and pressure are

$$\text{Ma}_2 = \frac{\text{Ma}_{n2}}{\sin (\beta - \theta)} = \frac{0.8031}{\sin (39.32° - 10°)} = 1.64 \qquad Ans.\ (b)$$

$$p_2 = (10 \text{ lbf/in}^2 \text{ absolute})(1.707) = 17.07 \text{ lbf/in}^2 \text{ absolute} \qquad Ans.\ (c)$$

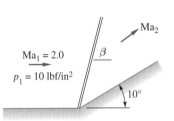

$\text{Ma}_1 = 2.0$
$p_1 = 10 \text{ lbf/in}^2$

β Ma_2

$10°$

E9.17

Notice that the computed pressure ratio agrees with Figs. 9.24 and B.2.

For the linearized theory the Mach angle is $\mu = \sin^{-1}(1/2.0) = 30°$. Equation (9.88) then estimates that

$$\sin \beta \approx \sin 30° + \frac{2.4 \tan 10°}{4 \cos 30°} = 0.622$$

or

$$\beta \approx 38.5° \qquad\qquad Ans.\ (d)$$

Equation (9.89) estimates that

$$\frac{p_2}{p_1} \approx 1 + \frac{1.4(2)^2 \tan 10°}{(2^2 - 1)^{1/2}} = 1.57$$

or

$$p_2 \approx 1.57(10 \text{ lbf/in}^2 \text{ absolute}) \approx 15.7 \text{ lbf/in}^2 \text{ absolute} \qquad Ans.\ (e)$$

These are reasonable estimates in spite of the fact that 10° is really not a "small" flow deflection.

9.10 Prandtl-Meyer Expansion Waves

The oblique shock solution of Sec. 9.9 is for a finite compressive deflection θ that obstructs a supersonic flow and thus decreases its Mach number and velocity. The present section treats gradual changes in flow angle that are primarily *expansive;* they widen the flow area and increase the Mach number and velocity. The property changes accumulate in infinitesimal increments, and the linearized relations (9.88) and (9.89) are used. The local flow deflections are infinitesimal, so the flow is nearly isentropic according to Eq. (9.90).

Figure 9.25 shows four examples, one of which (Fig. 9.25c) fails the test for gradual changes. The gradual compression of Fig. 9.25a is essentially isentropic, with a smooth increase in pressure along the surface, but the Mach angle increases along the surface and the waves tend to coalesce farther out into an oblique shock wave. The gradual expansion of Fig. 9.25b causes a smooth isentropic increase of Mach number and velocity along the surface, with diverging Mach waves formed.

The sudden compression of Fig. 9.25c cannot be accomplished by Mach waves: An oblique shock forms, and the flow is nonisentropic. This could be what you would see if you looked at Fig. 9.25a from far away. Finally, the sudden expansion of Fig. 9.25d is isentropic and forms a fan of centered Mach waves emanating from the corner. Note that the flow on any streamline passing through the fan changes smoothly to higher Mach number and velocity. In the limit as we near the corner the flow expands almost discontinuously at the surface. The cases in Figs. 9.25a, b, and d can all be handled by the Prandtl-Meyer supersonic wave theory of this section, first formulated by Ludwig Prandtl and his student Theodor Meyer in 1907 to 1908.

Note that none of this discussion makes sense if the upstream Mach number is subsonic, since Mach wave and shock wave patterns cannot exist in subsonic flow.

The Prandtl-Meyer Perfect-Gas Function

Consider a small, nearly infinitesimal flow deflection $d\theta$ such as occurs between the first two Mach waves in Fig. 9.25a. From Eqs. (9.88) and (9.89) we have, in

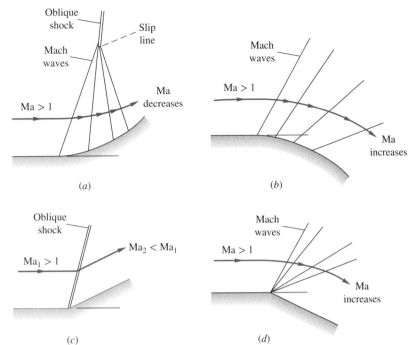

Fig. 9.25 Some examples of supersonic expansion and compression: (*a*) gradual isentropic compression on a concave surface, Mach waves coalesce farther out to form oblique shock; (*b*) gradual isentropic expansion on convex surface, Mach waves diverge; (*c*) sudden compression, nonisentropic shock forms; (*d*) sudden expansion, centered isentropic fan of Mach waves forms.

the limit,

$$\beta \approx \mu = \sin^{-1}\frac{1}{\text{Ma}} \tag{9.91a}$$

$$\frac{dp}{p} \approx \frac{k\,\text{Ma}^2}{(\text{Ma}^2 - 1)^{1/2}}\,d\theta \tag{9.91b}$$

Since the flow is nearly isentropic, we have the frictionless differential momentum equation for a perfect gas:

$$dp = -\rho V\,dV = -kp\,\text{Ma}^2\frac{dV}{V} \tag{9.92}$$

Combining Eqs. (9.91*a*) and (9.92) to eliminate *dp*, we obtain a relation between turning angle and velocity change:

$$d\theta = -(\text{Ma}^2 - 1)^{1/2}\frac{dV}{V} \tag{9.93}$$

This can be integrated into a functional relation for finite turning angles if we can relate *V* to Ma. We do this from the definition of Mach number:

$$V = \text{Ma}\,a$$

or

$$\frac{dV}{V} = \frac{d\,\text{Ma}}{\text{Ma}} + \frac{da}{a} \tag{9.94}$$

Finally, we can eliminate da/a because the flow is isentropic and hence a_0 is constant for a perfect gas:

$$a = a_0[1 + \tfrac{1}{2}(k - 1)\,\mathrm{Ma}^2]^{-1/2}$$

or

$$\frac{da}{a} = \frac{-\tfrac{1}{2}(k - 1)\,\mathrm{Ma}\,d\,\mathrm{Ma}}{1 + \tfrac{1}{2}(k - 1)\,\mathrm{Ma}^2} \tag{9.95}$$

Eliminating dV/V and da/a from Eqs. (9.93) to (9.95), we obtain a relation solely between turning angle and Mach number:

$$d\theta = -\frac{(\mathrm{Ma}^2 - 1)^{1/2}}{1 + \tfrac{1}{2}(k - 1)\,\mathrm{Ma}^2}\,\frac{d\,\mathrm{Ma}}{\mathrm{Ma}} \tag{9.96}$$

Before integrating this expression, we note that the primary application is to expansions: increasing Ma and decreasing θ. Therefore, for convenience, we define the Prandtl-Meyer angle $\omega(\mathrm{Ma})$, which increases when θ decreases and is zero at the sonic point:

$$d\omega = -d\theta \qquad \omega = 0 \quad \text{at} \quad \mathrm{Ma} = 1 \tag{9.97}$$

Thus we integrate Eq. (9.96) from the sonic point to any value of Ma:

$$\int_0^{\omega} d\omega = \int_1^{\mathrm{Ma}} \frac{(\mathrm{Ma}^2 - 1)^{1/2}}{1 + \tfrac{1}{2}(k - 1)\,\mathrm{Ma}^2}\,\frac{d\,\mathrm{Ma}}{\mathrm{Ma}} \tag{9.98}$$

The integrals are evaluated in closed form, with the result, in radians,

$$\boxed{\;\omega(\mathrm{Ma}) = K^{1/2}\,\tan^{-1}\left(\frac{\mathrm{Ma}^2 - 1}{K}\right)^{1/2} - \tan^{-1}(\mathrm{Ma}^2 - 1)^{1/2}\;} \tag{9.99}$$

where

$$\boxed{\;K = \frac{k + 1}{k - 1}\;}$$

This is the *Prandtl-Meyer supersonic expansion function,* which is plotted in Fig. 9.26 and tabulated in Table B.5 for $k = 1.4$, $K = 6$. The angle ω changes rapidly at first and then levels off at high Mach number to a limiting value as $\mathrm{Ma} \to \infty$:

$$\omega_{\max} = \frac{\pi}{2}(K^{1/2} - 1) = 130.45° \qquad \text{if} \qquad k = 1.4 \tag{9.100}$$

Thus a supersonic flow can expand only through a finite turning angle before it reaches infinite Mach number, maximum velocity, and zero temperature.

Gradual expansion or compression between finite Mach numbers Ma_1 and Ma_2, neither of which is unity, is computed by relating the turning angle $\Delta\omega$ to the difference in Prandtl-Meyer angles for the two conditions

$$\Delta\omega_{1\to2} = \omega(\mathrm{Ma}_2) - \omega(\mathrm{Ma}_1) \tag{9.101}$$

The change $\Delta\omega$ may be either positive (expansion) or negative (compression) as long as the end conditions lie in the supersonic range. Let us illustrate with an example.

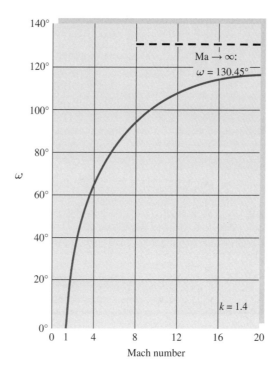

Fig. 9.26 The Prandtl-Meyer supersonic expansion from Eq. (9.99) for $k = 1.4$.

EXAMPLE 9.18

Air ($k = 1.4$) flows at $Ma_1 = 3.0$ and $p_1 = 200$ kPa. Compute the final downstream Mach number and pressure for (*a*) an expansion turn of $20°$ and (*b*) a gradual compression turn of $20°$.

Solution using Excel

Part (a)

The isentropic stagnation pressure is

$$p_0 = p_1[1 + 0.2(3.0)^2]^{3.5} = 7347 \text{ kPa}$$

and this will be the same at the downstream point. For $Ma_1 = 3.0$ we find from Table B.5 or Eq. (9.99) that $\omega_1 = 49.757°$. The flow expands to a new condition such that

$$\omega_2 = \omega_1 + \Delta\omega = 49.757° + 20° = 69.757°$$

Inversion of Eq. (9.99), to find Ma when ω is given, requires iteration, and Excel is well suited for this job. Hard to read, but Fig. 9.26 indicates $\omega \approx 4$. Make a guess of $\omega = 4$ and program Eq. (9.99) into an Excel cell. The writer's improved guesses are shown.

	A Ma – guess	B ω – Eq. (9.99)
1	4.00	65.78
2	4.20	68.33
3	4.30	69.54
4	**4.32**	**69.78**

The iteration converges to $\qquad\qquad\qquad$ $\text{Ma}_2 = 4.32$ $\qquad\qquad$ *Ans.* (*a*)

The isentropic pressure at this new condition is

$$p_2 = \frac{p_0}{[1 + 0.2(4.32)^2]^{3.5}} = \frac{7347}{230.1} = 31.9 \text{ kPa} \qquad\qquad Ans.\ (a)$$

Part (b)   The flow compresses to a lower Prandtl-Meyer angle:

$$\omega_2 = 49.757° - 20° = 29.757°$$

Again from Eq. (9.99), Table B.5, or Excel we compute that

$$\text{Ma}_2 = 2.125 \qquad\qquad\qquad\qquad\qquad\qquad Ans.\ (b)$$

$$p_2 = \frac{p_0}{[1 + 0.2(2.125)^2]^{3.5}} = \frac{7347}{9.51} = 773 \text{ kPa} \qquad\qquad Ans.\ (b)$$

Similarly, we compute density and temperature changes by noticing that T_0 and ρ_0 are constant for isentropic flow.

Application to Supersonic Airfoils

The oblique shock and Prandtl-Meyer expansion theories can be used to patch together a number of interesting and practical supersonic flow fields. This marriage, called *shock expansion theory,* is limited by two conditions: (1) Except in rare instances the flow must be supersonic throughout, and (2) the wave pattern must not suffer interference from waves formed in other parts of the flow field.

A very successful application of shock expansion theory is to supersonic airfoils. Figure 9.27 shows two examples, a flat plate and a diamond-shaped foil. In contrast to subsonic flow designs (Fig. 8.21), these airfoils must have sharp leading edges, which form attached oblique shocks or expansion fans. Rounded supersonic leading edges would cause detached bow shocks, as in Fig. 9.19 or 9.22*b*, greatly increasing the drag and lowering the lift.

In applying shock expansion theory, one examines each surface turning angle to see whether it is an expansion ("opening up") or compression (obstruction) to the surface flow. Figure 9.27*a* shows a flat-plate foil at an angle of attack. There is a leading-edge shock on the lower edge with flow deflection $\theta = \alpha$, while the upper edge has an expansion fan with increasing Prandtl-Meyer angle $\Delta\omega = \alpha$. We compute p_3 with expansion theory and p_2 with oblique shock theory. The force on the plate is thus $F = (p_2 - p_3)Cb$, where C is the chord length and b the span width (assuming no wingtip effects). This force is normal to the plate, and thus the lift force normal to the stream is $L = F \cos \alpha$, and the drag parallel to the stream is $D = F \sin \alpha$. The dimensionless coefficients C_L and C_D have the same definitions as in low-speed flow, Eqs. (7.66), except that the perfect-gas law identity $\frac{1}{2}\rho V^2 \equiv \frac{1}{2}kp \, \text{Ma}^2$ is very useful here:

$$C_L = \frac{L}{\frac{1}{2}kp_\infty \, \text{Ma}_\infty^2 \, bC} \qquad C_D = \frac{D}{\frac{1}{2}kp_\infty \, \text{Ma}_\infty^2 \, bC} \qquad (9.102)$$

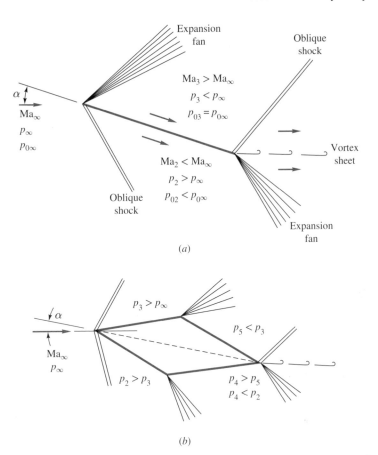

Fig. 9.27 Supersonic airfoils: (*a*) flat plate, higher pressure on lower surface, drag due to small downstream component of net pressure force; (*b*) diamond foil, higher pressures on both lower surfaces, additional drag due to body thickness.

The typical supersonic lift coefficient is much smaller than the subsonic value $C_L \approx 2\pi\alpha$, but the lift can be very large because of the large value of $\frac{1}{2}\rho V^2$ at supersonic speeds.

At the trailing edge in Fig. 9.27*a*, a shock and fan appear in reversed positions and bend the two flows back so that they are parallel in the wake and have the same pressure. They do not have quite the same velocity because of the unequal shock strengths on the upper and lower surfaces; hence a vortex sheet trails behind the wing. This is very interesting, but in the theory you ignore the trailing-edge pattern entirely, since it does not affect the surface pressures: The supersonic surface flow cannot "hear" the wake disturbances.

The diamond foil in Fig. 9.27*b* adds two more wave patterns to the flow. At this particular α less than the diamond half-angle, there are leading-edge shocks on both surfaces, the upper shock being much weaker. Then there are expansion fans on each shoulder of the diamond: The Prandtl-Meyer angle change $\Delta\omega$ equals the sum of the leading-edge and trailing-edge diamond half-angles. Finally, the trailing-edge pattern is similar to that of the flat plate (9.27*a*) and can be ignored in the calculation. Both lower-surface pressures p_2 and p_4 are greater than their upper counterparts, and the lift is nearly that of the flat plate. There is an additional drag due to thickness because p_4 and p_5 on the trailing surfaces are lower than their counterparts p_2 and p_3. The diamond drag is greater than the flat-plate drag, but this must be endured in practice to achieve a wing structure strong enough to support these forces.

The theory sketched in Fig. 9.27 is in good agreement with measured supersonic lift and drag as long as the Reynolds number is not too small (thick boundary layers) and the Mach number not too large (hypersonic flow). It turns out that for large Re_C and moderate supersonic Ma_∞ the boundary layers are thin and separation seldom occurs, so that the shock expansion theory, although frictionless, is quite successful. Let us look now at an example.

EXAMPLE 9.19

A flat-plate airfoil with $C = 2$ m is immersed at $\alpha = 8°$ in a stream with $Ma_\infty = 2.5$ and $p_\infty = 100$ kPa. Compute (a) C_L and (b) C_D, and compare with low-speed airfoils. Compute (c) lift and (d) drag in newtons per unit span width.

Solution

Instead of using a lot of space outlining the detailed oblique shock and Prandtl-Meyer expansion computations, we list all pertinent results in Fig. E9.19 on the upper and lower surfaces. Using the theories of Secs. 9.9 and 9.10, you should verify every single one of the calculations in Fig. E9.19 to make sure that all details of shock expansion theory are well understood.

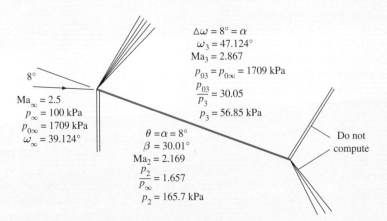

E9.19

The important final results are p_2 and p_3, from which the total force per unit width on the plate is

$$F = (p_2 - p_3)bC = (165.7 - 56.85)(\text{kPa})(1\text{ m})(2\text{ m}) = 218\text{ kN}$$

The lift and drag per meter width are thus

$$L = F \cos 8° = 216\text{ kN} \qquad \textit{Ans. (c)}$$
$$D = F \sin 8° = 30\text{ kN} \qquad \textit{Ans. (d)}$$

These are very large forces for only 2 m² of wing area.

From Eq. (9.102) the lift coefficient is

$$C_L = \frac{216\text{ kN}}{\frac{1}{2}(1.4)(100\text{ kPa})(2.5)^2(2\text{ m}^2)} = 0.246 \qquad \textit{Ans. (a)}$$

The comparable low-speed coefficient from Eq. (8.67) is $C_L = 2\pi \sin 8° = 0.874$, which is 3.5 times larger.

From Eq. (9.102) the drag coefficient is

$$C_D = \frac{30 \text{ kN}}{\frac{1}{2}(1.4)(100 \text{ kPa})(2.5)^2(2 \text{ m}^2)} = 0.035 \qquad \textit{Ans. (b)}$$

From Fig. 7.25 for the NACA 0009 airfoil, C_D at $\alpha = 8°$ is about 0.009, or about 4 times smaller.

Notice that this supersonic theory predicts a finite drag in spite of assuming frictionless flow with infinite wing aspect ratio. This is called *wave drag,* and we see that the d'Alembert paradox of zero body drag does not occur in supersonic flow.

Thin-Airfoil Theory

In spite of the simplicity of the flat-plate geometry, the calculations in Example 9.19 were laborious. In 1925 Ackeret [28] developed simple yet effective expressions for the lift, drag, and center of pressure of supersonic airfoils, assuming small thickness and angle of attack.

The theory is based on the linearized expression (9.89), where $\tan \theta \approx$ surface deflection relative to the free stream and condition 1 is the free stream, $\text{Ma}_1 = \text{Ma}_\infty$. For the flat-plate airfoil, the total force F is based on

$$\frac{p_2 - p_3}{p_\infty} = \frac{p_2 - p_\infty}{p_\infty} - \frac{p_3 - p_\infty}{p_\infty}$$

$$= \frac{k\,\text{Ma}_\infty^2}{(\text{Ma}_\infty^2 - 1)^{1/2}}[\alpha - (-\alpha)] \qquad (9.103)$$

Substitution into Eq. (9.102) gives the linearized lift coefficient for a supersonic flat-plate airfoil:

$$C_L \approx \frac{(p_2 - p_3)bC}{\frac{1}{2}kp_\infty \text{Ma}_\infty^2\, bC} \approx \frac{4\alpha}{(\text{Ma}_\infty^2 - 1)^{1/2}} \qquad (9.104)$$

Computations for diamond and other finite-thickness airfoils show no first-order effect of thickness on lift. Therefore, Eq. (9.104) is valid for any sharp-edged supersonic thin airfoil at a small angle of attack.

The flat-plate drag coefficient is

$$C_D = C_L \tan \alpha \approx C_L\alpha \approx \frac{4\alpha^2}{(\text{Ma}_\infty^2 - 1)^{1/2}} \qquad (9.105)$$

However, the thicker airfoils have additional thickness drag. Let the chord line of the airfoil be the x axis, and let the upper-surface shape be denoted by $y_u(x)$ and the lower profile by $y_l(x)$. Then the complete Ackeret drag theory (see Ref. 5, Sec. 14.6, for details) shows that the additional drag depends on the mean square of the slopes of the upper and lower surfaces, defined by

$$\overline{y'^2} = \frac{1}{C}\int_0^C \left(\frac{dy}{dx}\right)^2 dx \qquad (9.106)$$

The final expression for drag [5, p. 442] is

$$C_D \approx \frac{4}{(\text{Ma}_\infty^2 - 1)^{1/2}} \left[\alpha^2 + \frac{1}{2}(\overline{y_u'^2} + \overline{y_l'^2}) \right] \tag{9.107}$$

These are all in reasonable agreement with more exact computations, and their extreme simplicity makes them attractive alternatives to the laborious but accurate shock expansion theory. Consider the following example.

EXAMPLE 9.20

Repeat parts (a) and (b) of Example 9.19, using the linearized Ackeret theory.

Solution

From Eqs. (9.104) and (9.105) we have, for $\text{Ma}_\infty = 2.5$ and $\alpha = 8° = 0.1396$ rad,

$$C_L \approx \frac{4(0.1396)}{(2.5^2 - 1)^{1/2}} = 0.244 \qquad C_D = \frac{4(0.1396)^2}{(2.5^2 - 1)^{1/2}} = 0.034 \qquad Ans.$$

These are less than 3 percent lower than the more exact computations of Example 9.19.

A further result of the Ackeret linearized theory is an expression for the position x_{CP} of the center of pressure (CP) of the force distribution on the wing:

$$\frac{x_{CP}}{C} = 0.5 + \frac{S_u - S_l}{2\alpha C^2} \tag{9.108}$$

where S_u is the cross-sectional area between the upper surface and the chord and S_l is the area between the chord and the lower surface. For a symmetric airfoil ($S_l = S_u$) we obtain x_{CP} at the half-chord point, in contrast with the low-speed airfoil result, where x_{CP} is at the quarter-chord.

The difference in difficulty between the simple Ackeret theory and shock expansion theory is even greater for a thick airfoil, as the following example shows.

EXAMPLE 9.21

By analogy with Example 9.19 analyze a diamond, or double-wedge, airfoil of 2° half-angle and $C = 2$ m at $\alpha = 8°$ and $\text{Ma}_\infty = 2.5$. Compute C_L and C_D by (a) shock expansion theory and (b) Ackeret theory. Pinpoint the difference from Example 9.19.

Solution

Part (a)

Again we omit the details of shock expansion theory and simply list the properties computed on each of the four airfoil surfaces in Fig. E9.21. Assume $p_\infty = 100$ kPa. There are both a force F normal to the chord line and a force P parallel to the chord. For the normal force the pressure difference on the front half is $p_2 - p_3 = 186.4 - 65.9 = 120.5$ kPa, and on the rear half it is $p_4 - p_5 = 146.9 - 48.8 = 98.1$ kPa. The average pressure difference is $\frac{1}{2}(120.5 + 98.1) = 109.3$ kPa, so that the normal force is

$$F = (109.3 \text{ kPa})(2 \text{ m}^2) = 218.6 \text{ kN}$$

For the chordwise force P the pressure difference on the top half is $p_3 - p_5 = 65.9 - 48.8 = 17.1$ kPa, and on the bottom half it is $p_2 - p_4 = 186.4 - 146.9 = 39.5$ kPa. The average difference is $\frac{1}{2}(17.1 + 39.5) = 28.3$ kPa, which when multiplied by the frontal area (maximum thickness times 1-m width) gives

$$P = (28.3 \text{ kPa})(0.07 \text{ m})(1 \text{ m}) = 2.0 \text{ kN}$$

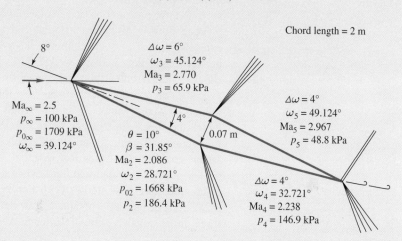

Chord length = 2 m

$8°$

$\Delta\omega = 6°$
$\omega_3 = 45.124°$
$Ma_3 = 2.770$
$p_3 = 65.9$ kPa

$\Delta\omega = 4°$
$\omega_5 = 49.124°$
$Ma_5 = 2.967$
$p_5 = 48.8$ kPa

$Ma_\infty = 2.5$
$p_\infty = 100$ kPa
$p_{0\infty} = 1709$ kPa
$\omega_\infty = 39.124°$

$4°$

0.07 m

$\theta = 10°$
$\beta = 31.85°$
$Ma_2 = 2.086$
$\omega_2 = 28.721°$
$p_{02} = 1668$ kPa
$p_2 = 186.4$ kPa

$\Delta\omega = 4°$
$\omega_4 = 32.721°$
$Ma_4 = 2.238$
$p_4 = 146.9$ kPa

E9.21

Both F and P have components in the lift and drag directions. The lift force normal to the free stream is

$$L = F \cos 8° - P \sin 8° = 216.2 \text{ kN}$$

and

$$D = F \sin 8° + P \cos 8° = 32.4 \text{ kN}$$

For computing the coefficients, the denominator of Eq. (9.102) is the same as in Example 9.19: $\frac{1}{2}kp_\infty Ma_\infty^2 bC = \frac{1}{2}(1.4)(100 \text{ kPa})(2.5)^2(2 \text{ m}^2) = 875$ kN. Thus, finally, shock expansion theory predicts

$$C_L = \frac{216.2 \text{ kN}}{875 \text{ kN}} = 0.247 \qquad C_D = \frac{32.4 \text{ kN}}{875 \text{ kN}} = 0.0370 \qquad \textit{Ans. (a)}$$

Part (b)

Meanwhile, by Ackeret theory, C_L is the same as in Example 9.20:

$$C_L = \frac{4(0.1396)}{(2.5^2 - 1)^{1/2}} = 0.244 \qquad \textit{Ans. (b)}$$

This is 1 percent less than the shock expansion result above. For the drag we need the mean-square slopes from Eq. (9.106):

$$\overline{y_u'^2} = \overline{y_l'^2} = \tan^2 2° = 0.00122$$

Then Eq. (9.107) predicts this linearized result:

$$C_D = \frac{4}{(2.5^2 - 1)^{1/2}}\left[(0.1396)^2 + \frac{1}{2}(0.00122 + 0.00122)\right] = 0.0362 \qquad \textit{Ans. (b)}$$

This is 2 percent lower than shock expansion theory predicts. We could judge Ackeret theory to be "satisfactory." Ackeret theory predicts $p_2 = 167$ kPa (-11 percent), $p_3 = 60$ kPa (-9 percent), $p_4 = 140$ kPa (-5 percent), and $p_5 = 33$ kPa (-6 percent).

Three-Dimensional Supersonic Flow

We have gone about as far as we can go in an introductory treatment of compressible flow. Of course, there is much more, and you are invited to study further in the references at the end of the chapter.

Three-dimensional supersonic flows are highly complex, especially if they concern blunt bodies, which therefore contain embedded regions of subsonic and transonic flow, as in Fig. 9.10. Some flows, however, yield to accurate theoretical treatment such as flow past a cone at zero incidence, as shown in Fig. 9.28. The exact theory of cone flow is discussed in advanced texts [for example, Ref. 5, Chap. 17], and extensive tables of such solutions have been published [25]. There are similarities between cone flow and the wedge flows illustrated in Fig. 9.22: an attached oblique shock, a thin turbulent boundary layer, and an expansion fan at the rear corner. However, the conical shock deflects the flow through an angle less than the cone half-angle, unlike the wedge shock. As in the wedge flow, there is a maximum cone angle above which the shock must detach, as in Fig. 9.22b. For $k = 1.4$ and $Ma_\infty = \infty$, the maximum cone half-angle for an attached shock is about 57°, compared with the maximum wedge angle of 45.6° (see Ref. 25).

The use of computational fluid dynamics (CFD) is now very popular and successful in compressible flow studies [13]. For example, a supersonic cone flow such as Fig. 9.28, even at an angle of attack, can be solved by numerical simulation of the full three-dimensional (viscous) Navier-Stokes equations [26].

Fig. 9.28 Shadowgraph of flow past an 8° half-angle cone at $Ma_\infty = 2.0$. The turbulent boundary layer is clearly visible. The Mach lines curve slightly, and the Mach number varies from 1.98 just inside the shock to 1.90 at the surface. *(Courtesy of U.S. Army Ballistic Research Laboratory, Aberdeen Proving Ground.)*

Fig. 9.29 Wind tunnel test of the Cobra P-530 supersonic interceptor. The surface flow patterns are visualized by the smearing of oil droplets. *(Courtesy of Northrop Grumman.)*

For more complicated body shapes one usually resorts to experimentation in a supersonic wind tunnel. Figure 9.29 shows a wind tunnel study of supersonic flow past a model of an interceptor aircraft. The many junctions and wingtips and shape changes make theoretical analysis very difficult. Here the surface flow patterns, which indicate boundary layer development and regions of flow separation, have been visualized by the smearing of oil drops placed on the model surface before the test.

As we shall see in the next chapter, there is an interesting analogy between gas dynamic shock waves and the surface water waves that form in an open-channel flow. Chapter 11 of Ref. 9 explains how a water channel can be used in an inexpensive simulation of supersonic flow experiments.

New Trends in Aeronautics

The previous edition of this text discussed NASA's proposed hypersonic scramjet aircraft, the X-43A [30], which set a new world speed record, in 2004, of Mach 9.6, or nearly 7000 miles per hour. This is hardly a design for a hypersonic airliner, though, since it has to be launched at high altitude from a B-52 bomber.

Also discussed earlier was the Air Force X-35 Joint Strike Fighter, whose wind tunnel test is shown here in Figure 9.19. This design is now operational, designated as the F-35, seen in Fig. 9.30, and it has been ordered by the U.S. military and also by Australia and seven NATO countries. A special version, for the U.S. Marine Corps, takes off and lands vertically. It reaches a speed of Mach 1.6 at 40,000 ft altitude. Its shortcomings are the present poor world economy and the fact that the price of one F-35 has risen to 220 million dollars.

Fig. 9.30 The F-35 Joint Strike Fighter is planned to become the standard supersonic fighter plane for the countries aligned with the United States. [*Lockheed Martin photo provided by F-35 Lightning II Program Office.*]

Summary

This chapter briefly introduced a very broad subject, compressible flow, sometimes called *gas dynamics*. The primary parameter is the Mach number Ma = V/a, which is large and causes the fluid density to vary significantly. This means that the continuity and momentum equations must be coupled to the energy relation and the equation of state to solve for the four unknowns (p, ρ, T, V).

The chapter reviewed the thermodynamic properties of an ideal gas and derived a formula for the speed of sound of a fluid. The analysis was then simplified to one-dimensional steady adiabatic flow without shaft work, for which the stagnation enthalpy of the gas is constant. A further simplification to isentropic flow enables formulas to be derived for high-speed gas flow in a variable-area duct. This reveals the phenomenon of sonic-flow *choking* (maximum mass flow) in the throat of a nozzle.

At supersonic velocities there is the possibility of a normal shock wave, where the gas discontinuously reverts to subsonic conditions. The normal shock explains the effect of back pressure on the performance of converging–diverging nozzles.

To illustrate nonisentropic flow conditions, the chapter briefly focused on constant-area duct flow with friction and with heat transfer, both of which lead to choking of the exit flow.

The chapter ended with a discussion of two-dimensional supersonic flow, where oblique shock waves and Prandtl-Meyer (isentropic) expansion waves appear. With a proper combination of shocks and expansions one can analyze supersonic airfoils.

Problems

Most of the problems herein are fairly straightforward. More difficult or open-ended assignments are labeled with an asterisk. Problems labeled with a computer icon 💻 may require the use of a computer. The standard end-of-chapter problems P9.1 to P9.157 (categorized in the problem list here) are followed by word problems W9.1 to W9.8, fundamentals of engineering exam problems FE9.1 to FE9.10, comprehensive problems C9.1 to C9.8, and design projects D9.1 and D9.2.

Problem Distribution

Section	Topic	Problems
9.1	Introduction	P9.1–P9.9
9.2	The speed of sound	P9.10–P9.18
9.3	Adiabatic and isentropic flow	P9.19–P9.33
9.4	Isentropic flow with area changes	P9.34–P9.53
9.5	The normal shock wave	P9.54–P9.62
9.6	Converging and diverging nozzles	P9.63–P9.85
9.7	Duct flow with friction	P9.86–P9.106
9.8	Frictionless duct flow with heat transfer	P9.107–P9.115
9.9	Mach waves	P9.116–P9.121
9.9	The oblique shock wave	P9.122–P9.139
9.10	Prandtl-Meyer expansion waves	P9.140–P9.148
9.10	Supersonic airfoils	P9.149–P9.157

Introduction

P9.1 An ideal gas flows adiabatically through a duct. At section 1, $p_1 = 140$ kPa, $T_1 = 260°C$, and $V_1 = 75$ m/s. Farther downstream, $p_2 = 30$ kPa and $T_2 = 207°C$. Calculate V_2 in m/s and $s_2 - s_1$ in J/(kg · K) if the gas is (a) air, $k = 1.4$, and (b) argon, $k = 1.67$.

P9.2 Solve Prob. P9.1 if the gas is steam. Use two approaches: (a) an ideal gas from Table A.4 and (b) real gas data from the steam tables [15].

P9.3 If 8 kg of oxygen in a closed tank at 200°C and 300 kPa is heated until the pressure rises to 400 kPa, calculate (a) the new temperature, (b) the total heat transfer, and (c) the change in entropy.

P9.4 Consider steady adiabatic airflow in a duct. At section B, the pressure is 600 kPa and the temperature is 177°C. At section D, the density is 1.13 kg/m³ and the temperature is 156°C. (a) Find the entropy change, if any. (b) Which way is the air flowing?

P9.5 Steam enters a nozzle at 377°C, 1.6 MPa, and a steady speed of 200 m/s and accelerates isentropically until it exits at saturation conditions. Estimate the exit velocity and temperature.

P9.6 Methane, approximated as a perfect gas, is compressed adiabatically from 101 kPa and 20°C to 300 kPa. Estimate (a) the final temperature, and (b) the final density.

P9.7 Air flows through a variable-area duct. At section 1, $A_1 = 20$ cm², $p_1 = 300$ kPa, $\rho_1 = 1.75$ kg/m³, and $V_1 = 122.5$ m/s. At section 2, the area is exactly the same, but the density is much lower: $\rho_2 = 0.266$ kg/m³ and $T_2 = 281$ K. There is no transfer of work or heat. Assume one-dimensional steady flow. (a) How can you reconcile these differences? (b) Find the mass flow at section 2. Calculate (c) V_2, (d) p_2, and (e) $s_2 - s_1$. [Hint: This problem requires the continuity equation.]

P9.8 Atmospheric air at 20°C enters and fills an insulated tank that is initially evacuated. Using a control volume analysis from Eq. (3.67), compute the tank air temperature when it is full.

P9.9 Liquid hydrogen and oxygen are burned in a combustion chamber and fed through a rocket nozzle that exhausts at $V_{exit} = 1600$ m/s to an ambient pressure of 54 kPa. The nozzle exit diameter is 45 cm, and the jet exit density is 0.15 kg/m³. If the exhaust gas has a molecular weight of 18, estimate (a) the exit gas temperature, (b) the mass flow, and (c) the thrust developed by the rocket.

The speed of sound

P9.10 A certain aircraft flies at 609 mi/h at standard sea level. (a) What is its Mach number? (b) If it flies at the same Mach number at 34,000 ft altitude, how much slower (or faster) is it flying, in mi/h?

P9.11 At 300°C and 1 atm, estimate the speed of sound of (a) nitrogen, (b) hydrogen, (c) helium, (d) steam, and (e) $^{238}UF_6$ ($k \approx 1.06$).

P9.12 Assume that water follows Eq. (1.19) with $n \approx 7$ and $B \approx 3000$. Compute the bulk modulus (in kPa) and the speed of sound (in m/s) at (a) 1 atm and (b) 1100 atm (the deepest part of the ocean). (c) Compute the speed of sound at 20°C and 9000 atm and compare with the measured value of 2650 m/s (A. H. Smith and A. W. Lawson, *J. Chem. Phys.*, vol. 22, 1954, p. 351).

P9.13 Consider steam at 500 K and 200 kPa. Estimate its speed of sound by two different methods: (a) assuming an ideal gas from Table B.4, or (b) using finite differences for isentropic densities between 210 kPa and 190 kPa.

P9.14 Benzene, listed in Table A.3, has a measured density of 57.75 lbm/ft^3 at a pressure of 700 bar. Use this data to estimate the speed of sound of benzene.

P9.15 The pressure-density relation for ethanol is approximated by Eq. (1.19) with $B = 1600$ and $n = 7$. Use this relation to estimate the speed of sound of ethanol at 2000 atmospheres.

P9.16 A weak pressure pulse Δp propagates through still air. Discuss the type of reflected pulse that occurs and the boundary conditions that must be satisfied when the wave strikes normal to, and is reflected from, (a) a solid wall and (b) a free liquid surface.

P9.17 A submarine at a depth of 800 m sends a sonar signal and receives the reflected wave back from a similar submerged object in 15 s. Using Prob. P9.12 as a guide, estimate the distance to the other object.

P9.18 Race cars at the Indianapolis Speedway average speeds of 185 mi/h. After determining the altitude of Indianapolis, find the Mach number of these cars and estimate whether compressibility might affect their aerodynamics.

Adiabatic and isentropic flow

P9.19 In 1976, the SR-71A, flying at 20 km standard altitude, set a jet-powered aircraft speed record of 3326 km/h. Estimate the temperature, in °C, at its front stagnation point. At what Mach number would it have a front stagnation-point temperature of 500°C?

P9.20 Air flows isentropically in a channel. Properties at section 1 are $V_1 = 250$ m/s, $T_1 = 330$ K, and $p_1 = 80$ kPa. At section 2 downstream, the temperature has dropped to 0°C. Find (a) the pressure, (b) velocity, and (c) Mach number at section 2.

P9.21 N_2O expands isentropically through a duct from $p_1 = 200$ kPa and $T_1 = 250$°C to a downstream section where $p_2 = 26$ kPa and $V_2 = 594$ m/s. Compute (a) T_2; (b) Ma_2; (c) T_o; (d) p_o; (e) V_1; and (f) Ma_1.

P9.22 Given the pitot stagnation temperature and pressure and the static pressure measurements in Fig. P9.22, estimate the air velocity V, assuming (a) incompressible flow and (b) compressible flow.

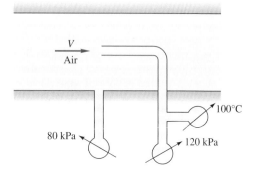

P9.22

P9.23 A gas, assumed ideal, flows isentropically from point 1, where the velocity is negligible, the pressure is 200 kPa, and the temperature is 300°C, to point 2, where the pressure is 40 kPa. What is the Mach number Ma_2 if the gas is (a) air, (b) argon, or (c) CH_4? (d) Can you tell, without calculating, which gas will be the coldest at point 2?

P9.24 For low-speed (nearly incompressible) gas flow, the stagnation pressure can be computed from Bernoulli's equation:

$$p_0 = p + \frac{1}{2}\rho V^2$$

(a) For higher subsonic speeds, show that the isentropic relation (9.28a) can be expanded in a power series as follows:

$$p_0 \approx p + \frac{1}{2}\rho V^2 \left(1 + \frac{1}{4}Ma^2 + \frac{2-k}{24}Ma^4 + \cdots\right)$$

(b) Suppose that a pitot-static tube in air measures the pressure difference $p_0 - p$ and uses the Bernoulli relation, with stagnation density, to estimate the gas velocity. At what Mach number will the error be 4 percent?

P9.25 If it is known that the air velocity in the duct is 750 ft/s, use the mercury manometer measurement in Fig. P9.25 to estimate the static pressure in the duct in lbf/in^2 absolute.

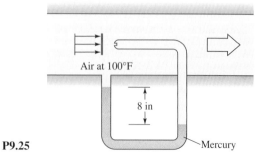

P9.25

P9.26 Show that for isentropic flow of a perfect gas if a pitot-static probe measures p_0, p, and T_0, the gas velocity can be calculated from

$$V^2 = 2c_pT_0\left[1 - \left(\frac{p}{p_0}\right)^{(k-1)/k}\right]$$

What would be a source of error if a shock wave were formed in front of the probe?

P9.27 A pitot tube, mounted on an airplane flying at 8000 m standard altitude, reads a stagnation pressure of 57 kPa. Estimate the plane's (a) velocity and (b) Mach number.

P9.28 Air flows isentropically through a duct. At section 1, the pressure and temperature are 250 kPa and 125°C, and the velocity is 200 m/s. At section 2, the area is 0.25 m² and the Mach number is 2.0. Determine (a) Ma_1; (b) T_2; (c) V_2; and (d) the mass flow.

P9.29 Steam from a large tank, where $T = 400°C$ and $p = 1$ MPa, expands isentropically through a nozzle until, at a section of 2-cm diameter, the pressure is 500 kPa. Using the steam tables [15], estimate (a) the temperature, (b) the velocity, and (c) the mass flow at this section. Is the flow subsonic?

P9.30 When does the incompressible-flow assumption begin to fail for pressures? Construct a graph of p_0/p for incompressible flow of a perfect gas as compared to Eq. (9.28a). Plot both versus Mach number for $0 \le \text{Ma} \le 0.6$ and decide for yourself where the deviation is too great.

P9.31 Air flows adiabatically through a duct. At one section $V_1 = 400$ ft/s, $T_1 = 200°F$, and $p_1 = 35$ lbf/in² absolute, while farther downstream $V_2 = 1100$ ft/s and $p_2 = 18$ lbf/in² absolute. Compute (a) Ma_2, (b) U_{max}, and (c) p_{02}/p_{01}.

P9.32 The large compressed-air tank in Fig. P9.32 exhausts from a nozzle at an exit velocity of 235 m/s. The mercury manometer reads $h = 30$ cm. Assuming isentropic flow, compute the pressure (a) in the tank and (b) in the atmosphere. (c) What is the exit Mach number?

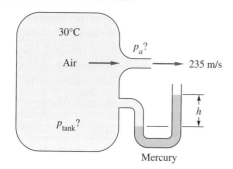

P9.32

P9.33 Air flows isentropically from a reservoir, where $p = 300$ kPa and $T = 500$ K, to section 1 in a duct, where $A_1 = 0.2$ m² and $V_1 = 550$ m/s. Compute (a) Ma_1, (b) T_1, (c) p_1, (d) $\dot{m}$, and (e) A^*. Is the flow choked?

Isentropic flow with area changes

P9.34 Air in a large tank, at 300°C and 400 kPa, flows through a converging-diverging nozzle with throat diameter 2 cm. It exits smoothly at a Mach number of 2.8. According to one-dimensional isentropic theory, what is (a) the exit diameter, and (b) the mass flow?

P9.35 Helium, at $T_0 = 400$ K, enters a nozzle isentropically. At section 1, where $A_1 = 0.1$ m², a pitot-static arrangement (see Fig. P9.25) measures stagnation pressure of 150 kPa and static pressure of 123 kPa. Estimate (a) Ma_1, (b) mass flow $\dot{m}$, (c) T_1, and (d) A^*.

P9.36 An air tank of volume 1.5 m³ is initially at 800 kPa and 20°C. At $t = 0$, it begins exhausting through a converging nozzle to sea-level conditions. The throat area is 0.75 cm². Estimate (a) the initial mass flow in kg/s, (b) the time required to blow down to 500 kPa, and (c) the time at which the nozzle ceases being choked.

P9.37 Make an exact control volume analysis of the blowdown process in Fig. P9.37, assuming an insulated tank with negligible kinetic and potential energy within. Assume critical flow at the exit, and show that both p_0 and T_0 decrease during blowdown. Set up first-order differential equations for $p_0(t)$ and $T_0(t)$, and reduce and solve as far as you can.

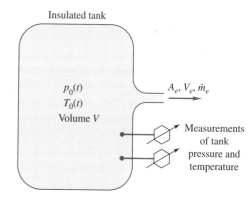

P9.37

P9.38 Prob. P9.37 makes an ideal senior project or combined laboratory and computer problem, as described in Ref. 27, Sec. 8.6. In Bober and Kenyon's lab experiment, the tank had a volume of 0.0352 ft³ and was initially filled with air at 50 lb/in² gage and 72°F. Atmospheric pressure was 14.5 lb/in² absolute, and the nozzle exit diameter was 0.05 in. After 2 s of blowdown, the measured tank pressure was 20 lb/in² gage and the tank temperature was −5°F. Compare these values with the theoretical analysis of Prob. P9.37.

P9.39 Consider isentropic flow in a channel of varying area, from section 1 to section 2. We know that $Ma_1 = 2.0$ and desire that the velocity ratio V_2/V_1 be 1.2. Estimate (a) Ma_2 and (b) A_2/A_1. (c) Sketch what this channel looks like. For example, does it converge or diverge? Is there a throat?

P9.40 Steam, in a tank at 300 kPa and 600 K, discharges isentropically to a low-pressure atmosphere through a converging nozzle with exit area 5 cm². (a) Using an ideal gas approximation from Table B.4, estimate the mass flow. (b) Without actual calculations, indicate how you would use real properties of steam to find the mass flow.

P9.41 Air, with a stagnation pressure of 100 kPa, flows through the nozzle in Fig. P9.41, which is 2 m long and has an area variation approximated by

$$A \approx 20 - 20x + 10x^2$$

with A in cm² and x in m. It is desired to plot the complete family of isentropic pressures $p(x)$ in this nozzle, for the range of inlet pressures $1 < p(0) < 100$ kPa. Indicate which inlet pressures are not physically possible and discuss briefly. If your computer has an online graphics routine, plot at least 15 pressure profiles; otherwise just hit the highlights and explain.

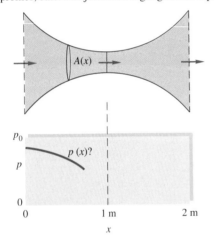

P9.41

P9.42 A bicycle tire is filled with air at an absolute pressure of 169.12 kPa, and the temperature inside is 30.0°C. Suppose the valve breaks, and air starts to exhaust out of the tire into the atmosphere ($p_a = 100$ kPa absolute and $T_a = 20.0°C$). The valve exit is 2.00 mm in diameter and is the smallest cross-sectional area of the entire system. Frictional losses can be ignored here; one-dimensional isentropic flow is a reasonable assumption. (a) Find the Mach number, velocity, and temperature at the exit plane of the valve (initially). (b) Find the initial mass flow rate out of the tire. (c) Estimate the velocity at the exit plane using the incompressible Bernoulli equation. How well does this estimate agree with the "exact" answer of part (a)? Explain.

P9.43 Air flows isentropically through a variable-area duct. At section 1, $A_1 = 20$ cm², $p_1 = 300$ kPa, $\rho_1 = 1.75$ kg/m³, and $Ma_1 = 0.25$. At section 2, the area is exactly the same, but the flow is much faster. Compute (a) V_2, (b) Ma_2, (c) T_2, and (d) the mass flow. (e) Is there a sonic throat between sections 1 and 2? If so, find its area.

P9.44 In Prob. P3.34 we knew nothing about compressible flow at the time, so we merely assumed exit conditions p_2 and T_2 and computed V_2 as an application of the continuity equation. Suppose that the throat diameter is 3 in. For the given stagnation conditions in the rocket chamber in Fig. P3.34 and assuming $k = 1.4$ and a molecular weight of 26, compute the actual exit velocity, pressure, and temperature according to one-dimensional theory. If $p_a = 14.7$ lbf/in² absolute, compute the thrust from the analysis of Prob. P3.68. This thrust is entirely independent of the stagnation temperature (check this by changing T_0 to 2000°R if you like). Why?

P9.45 It is desired to have an isentropic airflow achieve a velocity of 550 m/s at a 6-cm-diameter section where the pressure is 87 kPa and the density 1.3 kg/m³. (a) Is a sonic throat needed? (b) If so, estimate its diameter, and compute (c) the stagnation temperature and (d) the mass flow.

P9.46 A one-dimensional isentropic airflow has the following properties at one section where the area is 53 cm²: $p = 12$ kPa, $\rho = 0.182$ kg/m³, and $V = 760$ m/s. Determine (a) the throat area, (b) the stagnation temperature, and (c) the mass flow.

P9.47 In wind tunnel testing near Mach 1, a small area decrease caused by model blockage can be important. Suppose the test section area is 1 m², with unblocked test conditions Ma = 1.10 and $T = 20°C$. What model area will first cause the test section to choke? If the model cross section is 0.004 m² (0.4 percent blockage), what percentage change in test section velocity results?

P9.48 A force $F = 1100$ N pushes a piston of diameter 12 cm through an insulated cylinder containing air at 20°C, as in Fig. P9.48. The exit diameter is 3 mm, and $p_a = 1$ atm. Estimate (a) V_e, (b) V_p, and (c) $\dot{m}_e$.

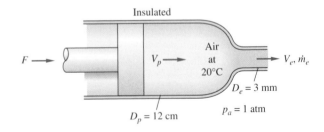

P9.48

P9.49 Consider the venturi nozzle of Fig. 6.40c, with $D = 5$ cm and $d = 3$ cm. Stagnation temperature is 300 K, and the upstream velocity $V_1 = 72$ m/s. If the throat pressure is 124 kPa, estimate, with isentropic flow theory, (a) p_1, (b) Ma_2, and (c) the mass flow.

P9.50 Methane is stored in a tank at 120 kPa and 330 K. It discharges to a second tank through a converging nozzle whose exit area is 5 cm². What is the initial mass flow rate if the second tank has a pressure of (a) 70 kPa or (b) 40 kPa?

P9.51 The scramjet engine is supersonic throughout. A sketch is shown in Fig. C9.8. Test the following design. The flow enters at Ma = 7 and air properties for 10,000 m altitude. Inlet area is 1 m², the minimum area is 0.1 m², and the exit area is 0.8 m². If there is no combustion, (a) will the flow still be supersonic in the throat? Also, determine (b) the exit Mach number, (c) exit velocity, and (d) exit pressure.

P9.52 A converging–diverging nozzle exits smoothly to sea-level standard atmosphere. It is supplied by a 40-m³ tank initially at 800 kPa and 100°C. Assuming isentropic flow in the nozzle, estimate (a) the throat area and (b) the tank pressure after 10 s of operation. The exit area is 10 cm².

P9.53 Air flows steadily from a reservoir at 20°C through a nozzle of exit area 20 cm² and strikes a vertical plate as in Fig. P9.53. The flow is subsonic throughout. A force of 135 N is required to hold the plate stationary. Compute (a) V_e, (b) Ma_e, and (c) p_0 if $p_a = 101$ kPa.

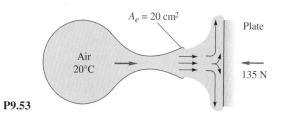

$A_e = 20$ cm²

Plate

Air 20°C

135 N

P9.53

The normal shock wave

P9.54 The airflow in Prob. P9.46 undergoes a normal shock just past the section where data was given. Determine the (a) Mach number, (b) pressure, and (c) velocity just downstream of the shock.

P9.55 Air, supplied by a reservoir at 450 kPa, flows through a converging–diverging nozzle whose throat area is 12 cm². A normal shock stands where $A_1 = 20$ cm². (a) Compute the pressure just downstream of this shock. Still farther downstream, at $A_3 = 30$ cm², estimate (b) p_3, (c) A_3^*, and (d) Ma_3.

P9.56 Air from a reservoir at 20°C and 500 kPa flows through a duct and forms a normal shock downstream of a throat of area 10 cm². By an odd coincidence it is found that the stagnation pressure downstream of this shock exactly equals the throat pressure. What is the area where the shock wave stands?

P9.57 Air flows from a tank through a nozzle into the standard atmosphere, as in Fig. P9.57. A normal shock stands in the exit of the nozzle, as shown. Estimate (a) the pressure in the tank and (b) the mass flow.

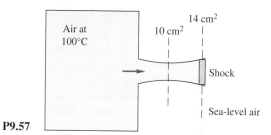

Air at 100°C   10 cm²   14 cm²

Shock

Sea-level air

P9.57

P9.58 Downstream of a normal shock wave, in airflow, the conditions are $T_2 = 603$ K, $V_2 = 222$ m/s, and $p_2 = 900$ kPa. Estimate the following conditions just upstream of the shock: (a) Ma_1; (b) T_1; (c) p_1; (d) p_{01}; and (e) T_{01}.

P9.59 Air, at stagnation conditions of 450 K and 250 kPa, flows through a nozzle. At section 1, where the area is 15 cm², there is a normal shock wave. If the mass flow is 0.4 kg/s, estimate (a) the Mach number and (b) the stagnation pressure just downstream of the shock.

P9.60 When a pitot tube such as in Fig. 6.30 is placed in a supersonic flow, a normal shock will stand in front of the probe. Suppose the probe reads $p_0 = 190$ kPa and $p = 150$ kPa. If the stagnation temperature is 400 K, estimate the (supersonic) Mach number and velocity upstream of the shock.

P9.61 Air flows from a large tank, where $T = 376$ K and $p = 360$ kPa, to a design condition where the pressure is 9800 Pa. The mass flow is 0.9 kg/s. However, there is a normal shock in the exit plane just after this condition is reached. Estimate (a) the throat area and, just downstream of the shock, (b) the Mach number, (c) the temperature, and (d) the pressure.

P9.62 An atomic explosion propagates into still air at 14.7 lbf/in² absolute and 520°R. The pressure just inside the shock is 5000 lbf/in² absolute. Assuming $k = 1.4$, what are the speed C of the shock and the velocity V just inside the shock?

Converging and diverging nozzles

P9.63 Sea-level standard air is sucked into a vacuum tank through a nozzle, as in Fig. P9.63. A normal shock stands where the nozzle area is 2 cm², as shown. Estimate (a) the pressure in the tank and (b) the mass flow.

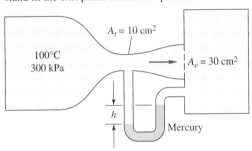

P9.63

P9.64 Air, from a reservoir at 350 K and 500 kPa, flows through a converging–diverging nozzle. The throat area is 3 cm². A normal shock appears, for which the downstream Mach number is 0.6405. (a) What is the area where the shock appears? Calculate (b) the pressure and (c) the temperature downstream of the shock.

P9.65 Air flows through a converging–diverging nozzle between two large reservoirs, as shown in Fig. P9.65. A mercury manometer between the throat and the downstream reservoir reads $h = 15$ cm. Estimate the downstream reservoir pressure. Is there a normal shock in the flow? If so, does it stand in the exit plane or farther upstream?

P9.65

P9.66 In Prob. P9.65 what would be the mercury manometer reading h if the nozzle were operating exactly at supersonic design conditions?

P9.67 A supply tank at 500 kPa and 400 K feeds air to a converging–diverging nozzle whose throat area is 9 cm². The exit area is 46 cm². State the conditions in the nozzle if the pressure outside the exit plane is (a) 400 kPa, (b) 120 kPa, and (c) 9 kPa. (d) In each of these cases, find the mass flow.

P9.68 Air in a tank at 120 kPa and 300 K exhausts to the atmosphere through a 5-cm²-throat converging nozzle at a rate of 0.12 kg/s. What is the atmospheric pressure? What is the maximum mass flow possible at low atmospheric pressure?

P9.69 With reference to Prob. P3.68, show that the thrust of a rocket engine exhausting into a vacuum is given by

$$F = \frac{p_0 A_e (1 + k\,\text{Ma}_e^2)}{\left(1 + \dfrac{k-1}{2}\,\text{Ma}_e^2\right)^{k/(k-1)}}$$

where A_e = exit area
Ma_e = exit Mach number
p_0 = stagnation pressure in combustion chamber

Note that stagnation temperature does not enter into the thrust.

P9.70 Air, with $p_0 = 500$ kPa and $T_0 = 600$ K, flows through a converging–diverging nozzle. The exit area is 51.2 cm², and mass flow is 0.825 kg/s. What is the highest possible back pressure that will still maintain supersonic flow inside the diverging section?

P9.71 A converging-diverging nozzle has a throat area of 10 cm² and an exit area of 28.96 cm². A normal shock stands in the exit when the back pressure is sea-level standard. If the upstream tank temperature is 400 K, estimate (a) the tank pressure and (b) the mass flow.

P9.72 A large tank at 500 K and 165 kPa feeds air to a converging nozzle. The back pressure outside the nozzle exit is sea-level standard. What is the appropriate exit diameter if the desired mass flow is 72 kg/h?

P9.73 Air flows isentropically in a converging–diverging nozzle with a throat area of 3 cm². At section 1, the pressure is 101 kPa, the temperature is 300 K, and the velocity is 868 m/s. (a) Is the nozzle choked? Determine (b) A_1 and (c) the mass flow. Suppose, without changing stagnation conditions or A_1, the (flexible) throat is reduced to 2 cm². Assuming shock-free flow, will there be any change in the gas properties at section 1? If so, compute new p_1, V_1, and T_1 and explain.

P9.74 Use your strategic ideas, from part (b) of Prob. P9.40, to actually carry out the calculations for mass flow of steam, with $p_0 = 300$ kPa and $T_0 = 600$ K, discharging through a converging nozzle of choked exit area 5 cm².

***P9.75** A double-tank system in Fig. P9.75 has two identical converging nozzles of 1-in² throat area. Tank 1 is very large, and tank 2 is small enough to be in steady-flow equilibrium with the jet from tank 1. Nozzle flow is isentropic, but entropy changes between 1 and 3 due to jet dissipation in tank 2. Compute the mass flow. (If you give up, Ref. 9, pp. 288–290, has a good discussion.)

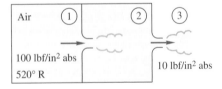

P9.75

P9.76 A large reservoir at 20°C and 800 kPa is used to fill a small insulated tank through a converging–diverging nozzle with 1-cm² throat area and 1.66-cm² exit area. The small tank has a volume of 1 m³ and is initially at 20°C and 100 kPa.

Estimate the elapsed time when (a) shock waves begin to appear inside the nozzle and (b) the mass flow begins to drop below its maximum value.

P9.77 A perfect gas (not air) expands isentropically through a supersonic nozzle with an exit area 5 times its throat area. The exit Mach number is 3.8. What is the specific-heat ratio of the gas? What might this gas be? If $p_0 = 300$ kPa, what is the exit pressure of the gas?

P9.78 The orientation of a hole can make a difference. Consider holes A and B in Fig. P9.78, which are identical but reversed. For the given air properties on either side, compute the mass flow through each hole and explain why they are different.

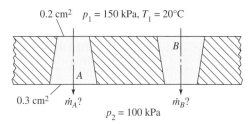

P9.78

P9.79 A large tank, at 400 kPa and 450 K, supplies air to a converging-diverging nozzle of throat area 4 cm^2 and exit area 5 cm^2. For what range of back pressures will the flow (a) be entirely subsonic; (b) have a shock wave inside the nozzle; (c) have oblique shocks outside the exit; and (d) have supersonic expansion waves outside the exit?

P9.80 A sea-level automobile tire is initially at 32 lbf/in^2 gage pressure and 75°F. When it is punctured with a hole that resembles a converging nozzle, its pressure drops to 15 lbf/in^2 gage in 12 min. Estimate the size of the hole, in thousandths of an inch. The tire volume is 2.5 ft^2.

P9.81 Air, at $p_0 = 160$ lbf/in^2 and $T_0 = 300$°F, flows isentropically through a converging–diverging nozzle. At section 1, where $A_1 = 288$ in^2, the velocity is $V_1 = 2068$ ft/s. Calculate (a) Ma$_1$, (b) A^*, (c) p_1, and (d) the mass flow, in slug/s.

P9.82 Air at 500 K flows through a converging–diverging nozzle with throat area of 1 cm^2 and exit area of 2.7 cm^2. When the mass flow is 182.2 kg/h, a pitot-static probe placed in the exit plane reads $p_0 = 250.6$ kPa and $p = 240.1$ kPa. Estimate the exit velocity. Is there a normal shock wave in the duct? If so, compute the Mach number just downstream of this shock.

P9.83 When operating at design conditions (smooth exit to sea-level pressure), a rocket engine has a thrust of 1 million lbf. The chamber pressure and temperature are 600 lbf/in^2 absolute and 4000°R, respectively. The exhaust gases approximate $k = 1.38$ with a molecular weight of 26. Estimate (a) the exit Mach number and (b) the throat diameter.

P9.84 Air flows through a duct as in Fig. P9.84, where $A_1 = 24$ cm^2, $A_2 = 18$ cm^2, and $A_3 = 32$ cm^2. A normal shock stands at section 2. Compute (a) the mass flow, (b) the Mach number, and (c) the stagnation pressure at section 3.

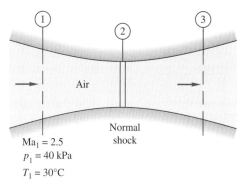

P9.84

P9.85 A typical carbon dioxide tank for a paintball gun holds about 12 oz of liquid CO$_2$. The tank is filled no more than one-third with liquid, which, at room temperature, maintains the gaseous phase at about 850 psia. (a) If a valve is opened that simulates a converging nozzle with an exit diameter of 0.050 in, what mass flow and exit velocity results? (b) Repeat the calculations for helium.

Duct flow with friction

P9.86 Air enters a 3-cm-diameter pipe 15 m long at $V_1 = 73$ m/s, $p_1 = 550$ kPa, and $T_1 = 60$°C. The friction factor is 0.018. Compute V_2, p_2, T_2, and p_{02} at the end of the pipe. How much additional pipe length would cause the exit flow to be sonic?

P9.87 Problem C6.9 gives data for a proposed Alaska-to-Canada natural gas (assume CH$_4$) pipeline. If the design flow rate is 890 kg/s and the entrance conditions are 2500 lbf/in^2 and 140°F, determine the maximum length of adiabatic pipe before choking occurs.

P9.88 Air flows adiabatically, with $\bar{f} = 0.024$, down a long 6-cm-diameter pipe. At section 1, conditions are $T_1 = 300$ K, $p_1 = 400$ kPa, and $V_1 = 104$ m/s. At section 2, $V_2 = 233$ m/s. (a) How far downstream is section 2? Estimate (b) Ma$_2$, (c) p_2, and (d) T_2.

P9.89 Carbon dioxide flows through an insulated pipe 25 m long and 8 cm in diameter. The friction factor is 0.025. At the entrance, $p = 300$ kPa and $T = 400$ K. The mass flow is 1.5 kg/s. Estimate the pressure drop by (a) compressible and (b) incompressible (Sec. 6.6) flow theory. (c) For what pipe length will the exit flow be choked?

P9.90 Air flows through a rough pipe 120 ft long and 3 in in diameter. Entrance conditions are $p = 90$ lbf/in^2, $T = 68°F$, and $V = 225$ ft/s. The flow chokes at the end of the pipe. (a) What is the average friction factor? (b) What is the pressure at the end of the pipe?

P9.91 Air flows steadily from a tank through the pipe in Fig. P9.91. There is a converging nozzle on the end. If the mass flow is 3 kg/s and the nozzle is choked, estimate (a) the Mach number at section 1 and (b) the pressure inside the tank.

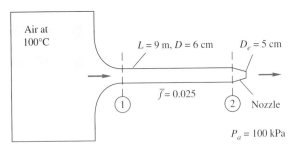

Air at 100°C
$L = 9$ m, $D = 6$ cm
$D_e = 5$ cm
$\bar{f} = 0.025$
① ② Nozzle
$P_a = 100$ kPa

P9.91

P9.92 Air enters a 5-cm-diameter pipe at 380 kPa, 3.3 kg/m^3, and 120 m/s. The friction factor is 0.017. Find the pipe length for which the velocity (a) doubles, (b) triples, and (c) quadruples.

P9.93 Air flows adiabatically in a 3-cm-diameter duct, with $\bar{f} = 0.018$. At the entrance, $T_1 = 323$ K, $p_1 = 200$ kPa, and $V_1 = 72$ m/s. (a) What is the mass flow? (b) For what tube length will the flow choke? (c) If the tube length is increased to 112 m, with the same inlet pressure and temperature, what will be the new mass flow?

P9.94 Compressible pipe flow with friction, Sec. 9.7, assumes constant stagnation enthalpy and mass flow but variable momentum. Such a flow is often called *Fanno flow,* and a line representing all possible property changes on a temperature–entropy chart is called a *Fanno line*. Assuming a perfect gas with $k = 1.4$ and the data of Prob. P9.86, draw a Fanno curve of the flow for a range of velocities from very low (Ma $\ll$ 1) to very high (Ma $\gg$ 1). Comment on the meaning of the maximum-entropy point on this curve.

P9.95 Helium (Table A.4) enters a 5-cm-diameter pipe at $p_1 = 550$ kPa, $V_1 = 312$ m/s, and $T_1 = 40°C$. The friction factor is 0.025. If the flow is choked, determine (a) the length of the duct and (b) the exit pressure.

P9.96 Methane (CH$_4$) flows through an insulated 15-cm-diameter pipe with $f = 0.023$. Entrance conditions are 600 kPa, 100°C, and a mass flow of 5 kg/s. What lengths of pipe will (a) choke the flow, (b) raise the velocity by 50 percent, or (c) decrease the pressure by 50 percent?

P9.97 By making a few algebraic substitutions, show that Eq. (9.74) may be written in the density form

$$\rho_1^2 = \rho_2^2 + \rho^{*2}\left(\frac{2k}{k+1}\frac{\bar{f}L}{D} + 2\ln\frac{\rho_1}{\rho_2}\right)$$

Why is this formula awkward if one is trying to solve for the mass flow when the pressures are given at sections 1 and 2?

P9.98 Compressible *laminar* flow, $f \approx 64/Re$, may occur in capillary tubes. Consider air, at stagnation conditions of 100°C and 200 kPa, entering a tube 3 cm long and 0.1 mm in diameter. If the receiver pressure is near vacuum, estimate (a) the average Reynolds number, (b) the Mach number at the entrance, and (c) the mass flow in kg/h.

P9.99 A compressor forces air through a smooth pipe 20 m long and 4 cm in diameter, as in Fig. P9.99. The air leaves at 101 kPa and 200°C. The compressor data for pressure rise versus mass flow are shown in the figure. Using the Moody chart to estimate $\bar{f}$, compute the resulting mass flow.

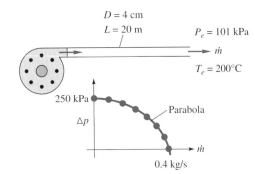

$D = 4$ cm
$L = 20$ m
$P_e = 101$ kPa
$\dot{m}$
$T_e = 200°C$
250 kPa
Δp
Parabola
$\dot{m}$
0.4 kg/s

P9.99

P9.100 Natural gas, approximated as CH$_4$, flows through a Schedule 40 six-inch pipe from Providence to Narragansett, RI, a distance of 31 miles. Gas companies use the *barg* as a pressure unit, meaning a bar of pressure *gage*, above ambient pressure. Assuming isothermal flow at 68°F, with $f \approx 0.019$, estimate the mass flow if the pressure is 5 bargs in Providence and 1 barg in Narragansett.

P9.101 How do the compressible pipe flow formulas behave for small pressure drops? Let air at 20°C enter a tube of diameter 1 cm and length 3 m. If $\bar{f} = 0.028$ with $p_1 = 102$ kPa and $p_2 = 100$ kPa, estimate the mass flow in kg/h for (a) isothermal flow, (b) adiabatic flow, and (c) incompressible flow (Chap. 6) at the entrance density.

P9.102 Air at 550 kPa and 100°C enters a smooth 1-m-long pipe and then passes through a second smooth pipe to a 30-kPa reservoir, as in Fig. P9.102. Using the Moody chart to compute $\bar{f}$, estimate the mass flow through this system. Is the flow choked?

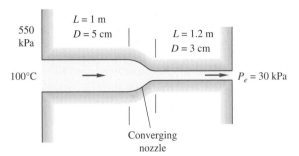

P9.102

P9.103 Natural gas, with $k \approx 1.3$ and a molecular weight of 16, is to be pumped through 100 km of 81-cm-diameter pipeline. The downstream pressure is 150 kPa. If the gas enters at 60°C, the mass flow is 20 kg/s, and $\bar{f} = 0.024$, estimate the required entrance pressure for (a) isothermal flow and (b) adiabatic flow.

P9.104 A tank of oxygen (Table A.4) at 20°C is to supply an astronaut through an umbilical tube 12 m long and 1.5 cm in diameter. The exit pressure in the tube is 40 kPa. If the desired mass flow is 90 kg/h and $\bar{f} = 0.025$, what should be the pressure in the tank?

P9.105 Modify Prob. P9.87 as follows: The pipeline will not be allowed to choke. It will have pumping stations about every 200 miles. (a) Find the length of pipe for which the pressure has dropped to 2000 lbf/in². (b) What is the temperature at that point?

P9.106 Air, from a 3 cubic meter tank initially at 300 kPa and 200°C, blows down adiabatically through a smooth pipe 1 cm in diameter and 2.5 m long. Estimate the time required to reduce the tank pressure to 200 kPa. For simplicity, assume constant tank temperature and $f \approx 0.020$.

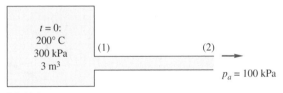

P9.106

Frictionless flow with heat transfer

P9.107 A fuel–air mixture, assumed equivalent to air, enters a duct combustion chamber at $V_1 = 104$ m/s and $T_1 = 300$ K. What amount of heat addition in kJ/kg will cause the exit flow to be choked? What will be the exit Mach number and temperature if 504 kJ/kg are added during combustion?

P9.108 What happens to the inlet flow of Prob. P9.107 if the combustion yields 1500 kJ/kg heat addition and p_{01} and T_{01} remain the same? How much is the mass flow reduced?

P9.109 A jet engine at 7000-m altitude takes in 45 kg/s of air and adds 550 kJ/kg in the combustion chamber. The chamber cross section is 0.5 m², and the air enters the chamber at 80 kPa and 5°C. After combustion the air expands through an isentropic converging nozzle to exit at atmospheric pressure. Estimate (a) the nozzle throat diameter, (b) the nozzle exit velocity, and (c) the thrust produced by the engine.

P9.110 Compressible pipe flow with heat addition, Sec. 9.8, assumes constant momentum ($p + \rho V^2$) and constant mass flow but variable stagnation enthalpy. Such a flow is often called *Rayleigh flow,* and a line representing all possible property changes on a temperature–entropy chart is called a *Rayleigh line.* Assuming air passing through the flow state $p_1 = 548$ kPa, $T_1 = 588$ K, $V_1 = 266$ m/s, and $A = 1$ m², draw a Rayleigh curve of the flow for a range of velocities from very low (Ma $\ll$ 1) to very high (Ma $\gg$ 1). Comment on the meaning of the maximum-entropy point on this curve.

P9.111 Add to your Rayleigh line of Prob. P9.110 a Fanno line (see Prob. P9.94) for stagnation enthalpy equal to the value associated with state 1 in Prob. P9.110. The two curves will intersect at state 1, which is subsonic, and at a certain state 2, which is supersonic. Interpret these two states vis-ã-vis Table B.2.

P9.112 Air enters a duct at $V_1 = 144$ m/s, $p_1 = 200$ kPa, and $T_1 = 323$ K. Assuming frictionless heat addition, estimate (a) the heat addition needed to raise the velocity to 372 m/s; and (b) the pressure at this new section 2.

P9.113 Air enters a constant-area duct at $p_1 = 90$ kPa, $V_1 = 520$ m/s, and $T_1 = 558$°C. It is then cooled with negligible friction until it exits at $p_2 = 160$ kPa. Estimate (a) V_2, (b) T_2, and (c) the total amount of cooling in kJ/kg.

P9.114 The scramjet of Fig. C9.8 operates with supersonic flow throughout. Assume that the heat addition of 500 kJ/kg, between sections 2 and 3, is frictionless and at constant area of 0.2 m². Given $Ma_2 = 4.0$, $p_2 = 260$ kPa, and $T_2 = 420$ K. Assume airflow at $k = 1.40$. At the combustion section exit, find (a) Ma_3, (b) p_3, and (c) T_3.

P9.115 Air enters a 5-cm-diameter pipe at 380 kPa, 3.3 kg/m³, and 120 m/s. Assume frictionless flow with heat addition. Find the amount of heat addition for which the velocity (a) doubles, (b) triples, and (c) quadruples.

Mach waves

P9.116 An observer at sea level does not hear an aircraft flying at 12,000-ft standard altitude until it is 5 (statute) mi past her. Estimate the aircraft speed in ft/s.

P9.117 A tiny scratch in the side of a supersonic wind tunnel creates a very weak wave of angle 17°, as shown in Fig. P9.117, after which a normal shock occurs. The air temperature in region (1) is 250 K. Estimate the temperature in region (2).

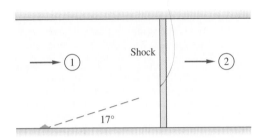

P9.117

P9.118 A particle moving at uniform velocity in sea-level standard air creates the two disturbance spheres shown in Fig. P9.118. Compute the particle velocity and Mach number.

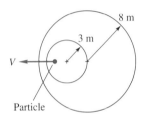

P9.118

P9.119 The particle in Fig. P9.119 is moving supersonically in sea-level standard air. From the two given disturbance spheres, compute the particle Mach number, velocity, and Mach angle.

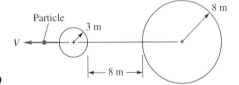

P9.119

P9.120 The particle in Fig. P9.120 is moving in sea-level standard air. From the two disturbance spheres shown, estimate (a) the position of the particle at this instant and (b) the temperature in °C at the front stagnation point of the particle.

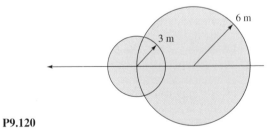

P9.120

P9.121 A thermistor probe, in the shape of a needle parallel to the flow, reads a static temperature of $-25°C$ when inserted into a supersonic airstream. A conical disturbance cone of half-angle $17°$ is created. Estimate (a) the Mach number, (b) the velocity, and (c) the stagnation temperature of the stream.

The oblique shock wave

P9.122 Supersonic air takes a $5°$ compression turn, as in Fig. P9.122. Compute the downstream pressure and Mach number and the wave angle, and compare with small-disturbance theory.

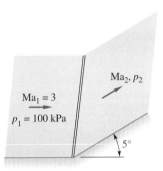

P9.122

P9.123 The $10°$ deflection in Example 9.17 caused a final Mach number of 1.641 and a pressure ratio of 1.707. Compare this with the case of the flow passing through two $5°$ deflections. Comment on the results and why they might be higher or lower in the second case.

P9.124 When a sea-level flow approaches a ramp of angle $20°$, an oblique shock wave forms as in Figure P9.124. Calculate (a) Ma_1, (b) p_2, (c) T_2, and (d) V_2.

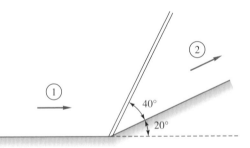

P9.124

P9.125 We saw in the text that, for $k = 1.40$, the maximum possible deflection caused by an oblique shock wave occurs at infinite approach Mach number and is $\theta_{max} = 45.58°$. Assuming an ideal gas, what is θ_{max} for (a) argon and (b) carbon dioxide?

P9.126 Airflow at Ma = 2.8, p = 80 kPa, and T = 280 K undergoes a 15° compression turn. Find the downstream values of (a) Mach number, (b) pressure, and (c) temperature.

P9.127 Do the Mach waves upstream of an oblique shock wave intersect with the shock? Assuming supersonic downstream flow, do the downstream Mach waves intersect the shock? Show that for small deflections the shock wave angle β lies halfway between μ_1 and $\mu_2 + \theta$ for any Mach number.

P9.128 Air flows past a two-dimensional wedge-nosed body as in Fig. P9.128. Determine the wedge half-angle δ for which the horizontal component of the total pressure force on the nose is 35 kN/m of depth into the paper.

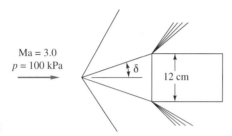

P9.128

P9.129 Air flows at supersonic speed toward a compression ramp, as in Fig. P9.129. A scratch on the wall at point a creates a wave of 30° angle, while the oblique shock created has a 50° angle. What is (a) the ramp angle θ and (b) the wave angle ϕ caused by a scratch at b?

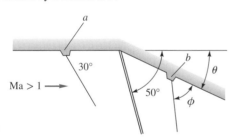

P9.129

P9.130 A supersonic airflow, at a temperature of 300 K, strikes a wedge and is deflected 12°. If the resulting shock wave is attached, and the temperature after the shock is 450 K, (a) estimate the approach Mach number and wave angle. (b) Why are there two solutions?

P9.131 The following formula has been suggested as an alternate to Eq. (9.86) to relate upstream Mach number to the oblique shock wave angle β and turning angle θ:

$$\sin^2 \beta = \frac{1}{Ma_1^2} + \frac{(k + 1) \sin \beta \sin \theta}{2 \cos (\beta - \theta)}$$

Can you prove or disprove this relation? If not, try a few numerical values and compare with the results from Eq. (9.86).

P9.132 Air flows at Ma = 3 and p = 10 lbf/in² absolute toward a wedge of 16° angle at zero incidence in Fig. P9.132. If the pointed edge is forward, what will be the pressure at point A? If the blunt edge is forward, what will be the pressure at point B?

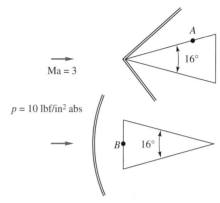

P9.132

P9.133 Air flows supersonically toward the double-wedge system in Fig. P9.133. The (x, y) coordinates of the tips are given. The shock wave of the forward wedge strikes the tip of the aft wedge. Both wedges have 15° deflection angles. What is the free-stream Mach number?

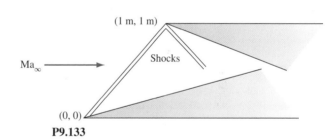

P9.133

P9.134 When an oblique shock strikes a solid wall, it reflects as a shock of sufficient strength to cause the exit flow Ma_3 to be parallel to the wall, as in Fig. P9.134. For airflow with Ma_1 = 2.5 and p_1 = 100 kPa, compute Ma_3, p_3, and the angle ϕ.

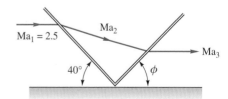

P9.134

P9.135 A bend in the bottom of a supersonic duct flow induces a shock wave that reflects from the upper wall, as in Fig. P9.135. Compute the Mach number and pressure in region 3.

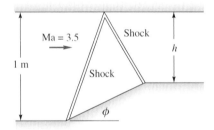

P9.135

P9.136 Figure P9.136 is a special application of Prob. P9.135. With careful design, one can orient the bend on the lower wall so that the reflected wave is exactly canceled by the return bend, as shown. This is a method of reducing the Mach number in a channel (a supersonic diffuser). If the bend angle is $\phi = 10°$, find (a) the downstream width h and (b) the downstream Mach number. Assume a weak shock wave.

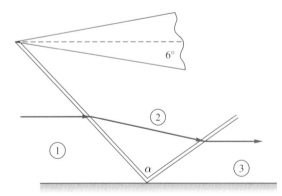

P9.136

P9.137 A 6° half-angle wedge creates the reflected shock system in Fig. P9.137. If $Ma_3 = 2.5$, find (a) Ma_1 and (b) the angle α.

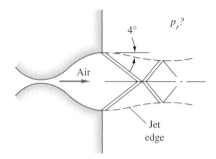

P9.138

P9.138 The supersonic nozzle of Fig. P9.138 is overexpanded (case G of Fig. 9.12b) with $A_e/A_t = 3.0$ and a stagnation pressure of 350 kPa. If the jet edge makes a 4° angle with the nozzle centerline, what is the back pressure p_r in kPa?

P9.139 Airflow at Ma = 2.2 takes a compression turn of 12° and then another turn of angle θ in Fig. P9.139. What is the maximum value of θ for the second shock to be attached? Will the two shocks intersect for any θ less than θ_{max}?

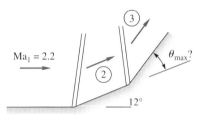

P9.139

Prandtl-Meyer expansion waves

P9.140 The solution to Prob. P9.122 is $Ma_2 = 2.750$ and $p_2 = 145.5$ kPa. Compare these results with an isentropic compression turn of 5°, using Prandtl-Meyer theory.

P9.141 Supersonic airflow takes a 5° expansion turn, as in Fig. P9.141. Compute the downstream Mach number and pressure, and compare with small-disturbance theory.

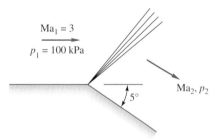

P9.141

P9.142 A supersonic airflow at $Ma_1 = 3.2$ and $p_1 = 50$ kPa undergoes a compression shock followed by an isentropic expansion turn. The flow deflection is 30° for each turn. Compute Ma_2 and p_2 if (a) the shock is followed by the expansion and (b) the expansion is followed by the shock.

P9.143 Airflow at Ma = 3.4 and 300 K encounters a 28° oblique shock turn. What subsequent isentropic expansion turn will bring the temperature back to 300 K?

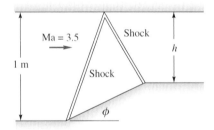 (P9.137 figure)

P9.137

P9.144 The 10° deflection in Example 9.17 caused the Mach number to drop to 1.64. (*a*) What turn angle will create a Prandtl-Meyer fan and bring the Mach number back up to 2.0? (*b*) What will be the final pressure?

P9.145 Air at $Ma_1 = 2.0$ and $p_1 = 100$ kPa undergoes an isentropic expansion to a downstream pressure of 50 kPa. What is the desired turn angle in degrees?

P9.146 Air flows supersonically over a surface that changes direction twice, as in Fig. P9.146. Calculate (*a*) Ma_2 and (*b*) p_3.

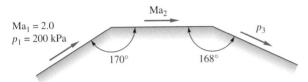

P9.146

P9.147 A converging–diverging nozzle with a 4:1 exit-area ratio and $p_0 = 500$ kPa operates in an underexpanded condition (case *I* of Fig. 9.12*b*) as in Fig. P9.147. The receiver pressure is $p_a = 10$ kPa, which is less than the exit pressure, so that expansion waves form outside the exit. For the given conditions, what will the Mach number Ma_2 and the angle ϕ of the edge of the jet be? Assume $k = 1.4$ as usual.

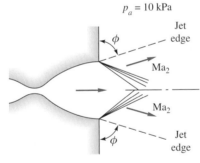

P9.147

P9.148 Air flows supersonically over a circular-arc surface as in Fig. P9.148. Estimate (*a*) the Mach number Ma_2 and (*b*) the pressure p_2 as the flow leaves the circular surface.

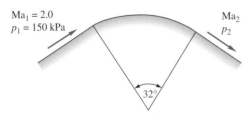

P9.148

Supersonic airfoils

P9.149 Air flows at $Ma_\infty = 3.0$ past a doubly symmetric diamond airfoil whose front and rear included angles are both 24°. For zero angle of attack, compute the drag coefficient obtained using shock-expansion theory and compare with Ackeret theory.

P9.150 A flat-plate airfoil with $C = 1.2$ m is to have a lift of 30 kN/m when flying at 5000-m standard altitude with $U_\infty = 641$ m/s. Using Ackeret theory, estimate (*a*) the angle of attack and (*b*) the drag force in N/m.

P9.151 Air flows at $Ma = 2.5$ past a half-wedge airfoil whose angles are 4°, as in Fig. P9.151. Compute the lift and drag coefficient at α equal to (*a*) 0° and (*b*) 6°.

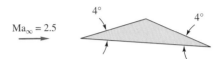

P9.151

P9.152 The X-43 model A scramjet aircraft in Fig. C9.8 is small $W = 3000$ lbf, and unmanned, only 12.33 ft long and 5.5 ft wide. The aerodynamics of a slender arrowhead-shaped hypersonic vehicle is beyond our scope. Instead, let us assume it is a flat plate airfoil of area 2.0 m². Let $Ma = 7$ at 12,000 m standard altitude. Estimate the drag, by shock-expansion theory. *Hint:* Use Ackeret theory to estimate the angle of attack.

P9.153 A supersonic transport has a mass of 65 Mg and cruises at 11-km standard altitude at a Mach number of 2.25. If the angle of attack is 2° and its wings can be approximated by flat plates, estimate (*a*) the required wing area in m² and (*b*) the thrust required in N.

P9.154 The F-22 supersonic fighter cruises at 11,000 m altitude, with a weight of 50,000 lbf and thrust of 10,000 lbf. Its wing area is 840 ft². Assume the wing is a 6-percent-thick diamond shape and provides all lift and thrust. Use Ackeret theory to estimate the resulting Mach number.

*P9.155 The F-35 airplane in Fig. 9.30 has a wingspan of 10 m and a wing area of 41.8 m². It cruises at about 10 km altitude with a gross weight of about 200 kN. At that altitude, the engine develops a thrust of about 50 kN. Assume the wing has a symmetric diamond airfoil with a thickness of 8 percent, and accounts for all lift and drag. Estimate the cruise Mach number of the airplane. For extra credit, explain why there are *two* solutions.

P9.156 Consider a flat-plate airfoil at an angle of attack of 6°. The Mach number is $Ma_\infty = 3.2$ and the stream pressure p_∞ is unspecified. Calculate the predicted lift and drag coefficients by (*a*) shock-expansion theory and (*b*) Ackeret theory.

P9.157 The Ackeret airfoil theory of Eq. (9.104) is meant for *moderate* supersonic speeds, $1.2 < Ma < 4$. How does it fare for *hypersonic* speeds? To illustrate, calculate (*a*) C_L and (*b*) C_D for a flat-plate airfoil at $a = 5°$ and $Ma_\infty = 8.0$, using shock-expansion theory, and compare with Ackeret theory. Comment.

Word Problems

W9.1 Notice from Table 9.1 that (*a*) water and mercury and (*b*) aluminum and steel have nearly the same speeds of sound, yet the second of each pair of materials is much denser. Can you account for this oddity? Can molecular theory explain it?

W9.2 When an object approaches you at Ma = 0.8, you can hear it, according to Fig. 9.18*a*. But would there be a Doppler shift? For example, would a musical tone seem to you to have a higher or a lower pitch?

W9.3 The subject of this chapter is commonly called *gas dynamics*. But can liquids not perform in this manner? Using water as an example, make a rule-of-thumb estimate of the pressure level needed to drive a water flow at velocities comparable to the sound speed.

W9.4 Suppose a gas is driven at compressible subsonic speeds by a large pressure drop, p_1 to p_2. Describe its behavior on an appropriately labeled Mollier chart for (*a*) frictionless flow in a converging nozzle and (*b*) flow with friction in a long duct.

W9.5 Describe physically what the "speed of sound" represents. What kind of pressure changes occur in air sound waves during ordinary conversation?

W9.6 Give a physical description of the phenomenon of choking in a converging-nozzle gas flow. Could choking happen even if wall friction were not negligible?

W9.7 Shock waves are treated as discontinuities here, but they actually have a very small finite thickness. After giving it some thought, sketch your idea of the distribution of gas velocity, pressure, temperature, and entropy through the inside of a shock wave.

W9.8 Describe how an observer, running along a normal shock wave at finite speed V, will see what appears to be an oblique shock wave. Is there any limit to the running speed?

Fundamentals of Engineering Exam Problems

One-dimensional compressible flow problems have become quite popular on the FE Exam, especially in the afternoon sessions. In the following problems, assume one-dimensional flow of ideal air, $R = 287$ J/(kg · K) and $k = 1.4$.

FE9.1 For steady isentropic flow, if the absolute temperature increases 50 percent, by what ratio does the static pressure increase?
(*a*) 1.12, (*b*) 1.22, (*c*) 2.25, (*d*) 2.76, (*e*) 4.13

FE9.2 For steady isentropic flow, if the density doubles, by what ratio does the static pressure increase?
(*a*) 1.22, (*b*) 1.32, (*c*) 1.44, (*d*) 2.64, (*e*) 5.66

FE9.3 A large tank, at 500 K and 200 kPa, supplies isentropic airflow to a nozzle. At section 1, the pressure is only 120 kPa. What is the Mach number at this section?
(*a*) 0.63, (*b*) 0.78, (*c*) 0.89, (*d*) 1.00, (*e*) 1.83

FE9.4 In Prob. FE9.3 what is the temperature at section 1?
(*a*) 300 K, (*b*) 408 K, (*c*) 417 K, (*d*) 432 K, (*e*) 500 K

FE9.5 In Prob. FE9.3, if the area at section 1 is 0.15 m², what is the mass flow?
(*a*) 38.1 kg/s, (*b*) 53.6 kg/s, (*c*) 57.8 kg/s, (*d*) 67.8 kg/s, (*e*) 77.2 kg/s

FE9.6 For steady isentropic flow, what is the maximum possible mass flow through the duct in Fig. FE9.6?
(*a*) 9.5 kg/s, (*b*) 15.1 kg/s, (*c*) 26.2 kg/s, (*d*) 30.3 kg/s, (*e*) 52.4 kg/s

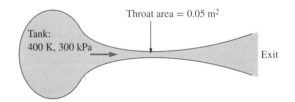

FE9.6

FE9.7 If the exit Mach number in Fig. FE9.6 is 2.2, what is the exit area?
(*a*) 0.10 m², (*b*) 0.12 m², (*c*) 0.15 m², (*d*) 0.18 m², (*e*) 0.22 m²

FE9.8 If there are no shock waves and the pressure at one duct section in Fig. FE9.6 is 55.5 kPa, what is the velocity at that section?
(*a*) 166 m/s, (*b*) 232 m/s, (*c*) 554 m/s, (*d*) 706 m/s, (*e*) 774 m/s

FE9.9 If, in Fig. FE9.6, there is a normal shock wave at a section where the area is 0.07 m², what is the air density just upstream of that shock?
(*a*) 0.48 kg/m³, (*b*) 0.78 kg/m³, (*c*) 1.35 kg/m³, (*d*) 1.61 kg/m³, (*e*) 2.61 kg/m³

FE9.10 In Prob. FE9.9, what is the Mach number just downstream of the shock wave?
(*a*) 0.42, (*b*) 0.55, (*c*) 0.63, (*d*) 1.00, (*e*) 1.76

Comprehensive Problems

C9.1   The converging–diverging nozzle sketched in Fig. C9.1 is designed to have a Mach number of 2.00 at the exit plane (assuming the flow remains nearly isentropic). The flow travels from tank a to tank b, where tank a is much larger than tank b. (*a*) Find the area at the exit A_e and the back pressure p_b that will allow the system to operate at design conditions. (*b*) As time goes on, the back pressure will grow, since the second tank slowly fills up with more air. Since tank a is huge, the flow in the nozzle will remain the same, however, until a normal shock wave appears at the exit plane. At what back pressure will this occur? (*c*) If tank b is held at constant temperature, $T = 20°C$, estimate how long it will take for the flow to go from design conditions to the condition of part (*b*)—that is, with a shock wave at the exit plane.

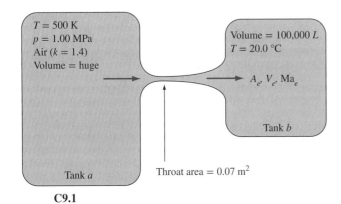

$T = 500$ K
$p = 1.00$ MPa
Air ($k = 1.4$)
Volume = huge

Volume = 100,000 L
$T = 20.0$ °C

A_e, V_e, Ma$_e$

Tank b

Tank a Throat area = 0.07 m^2

C9.1

C9.2   Two large air tanks, one at 400 K and 300 kPa and the other at 300 K and 100 kPa, are connected by a straight tube 6 m long and 5 cm in diameter. The average friction factor is 0.0225. Assuming adiabatic flow, estimate the mass flow through the tube.

*C9.3   Figure C9.3 shows the exit of a converging–diverging nozzle, where an oblique shock pattern is formed. In the exit plane, which has an area of 15 cm^2, the air pressure is 16 kPa and the temperature is 250 K. Just outside the exit shock, which makes an angle of 50° with the exit plane, the temperature is 430 K. Estimate (*a*) the mass flow, (*b*) the throat area, (*c*) the turning angle of the exit flow, and, in the tank supplying the air, (*d*) the pressure and (*e*) the temperature.

C9.4   The properties of a dense gas (high pressure and low temperature) are often approximated by van der Waals's equation of state [17, 18]:

$$p = \frac{\rho R T}{1 - b_1 \rho} - a_1 \rho^2$$

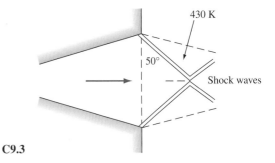

430 K

50°

Shock waves

C9.3

where constants a_1 and b_1 can be found from the critical temperature and pressure

$$a_1 = \frac{27 R^2 T_c^2}{64 p_c} = 9.0 \times 10^5 \text{ lbf} \cdot \text{ft}^4/\text{slug}^2$$

for air, and

$$b_1 = \frac{R T_c}{8 p_c} = 0.65 \text{ ft}^3/\text{slug}$$

for air. Find an analytic expression for the speed of sound of a van der Waals gas. Assuming $k = 1.4$, compute the speed of sound of air in ft/s at $-100°F$ and 20 atm for (*a*) a perfect gas and (*b*) a van der Waals gas. What percentage higher density does the van der Waals relation predict?

C9.5   Consider one-dimensional steady flow of a nonideal gas, steam, in a converging nozzle. Stagnation conditions are $p_0 = 100$ kPa and $T_0 = 200°C$. The nozzle exit diameter is 2 cm. (*a*) If the nozzle exit pressure is 70 kPa, calculate the mass flow and the exit temperature for real steam from the steam tables. (As a first estimate, assume steam to be an ideal gas from Table A.4.) Is the flow choked? (*b*) Find the nozzle exit pressure and mass flow for which the steam flow *is* choked, using the steam tables.

C9.6   Extend Prob. C9.5 as follows: Let the nozzle be converging–diverging, with an exit diameter of 3 cm. Assume isentropic flow. Find the exit Mach number, pressure, and temperature for an ideal gas from Table A.4. Does the mass flow agree with the value of 0.0452 kg/s in Prob. C9.5?

C9.7   Professor Gordon Holloway and his student, Jason Bettle, of the University of New Brunswick obtained the following tabulated data for blow-down airflow through a converging–diverging nozzle similar in shape to Fig. P3.22. The supply tank pressure and temperature were 29 psig and 74°F, respectively. Atmospheric pressure was 14.7 psia. Wall pressures and centerline stagnation pressures were measured in the expansion section, which was a frustrum of a cone. The nozzle throat is at $x = 0$.

x(cm)	0	1.5	3	4.5	6	7.5	9
Diameter (cm)	1.00	1.098	1.195	1.293	1.390	1.488	1.585
p_{wall} (psig)	7.7	−2.6	−4.9	−7.3	−6.5	−10.4	−7.4
$p_{stagnation}$ (psig)	29	26.5	22.5	18	16.5	14	10

Use the stagnation pressure data to estimate the local Mach number. Compare the measured Mach numbers and wall pressures with the predictions of one-dimensional theory. For $x > 9$ cm, the stagnation pressure data was not thought by Holloway and Bettle to be a valid measure of Mach number. What is the probable reason?

C9.8   Engineers call the supersonic combustion in a scramjet engine almost miraculous, "like lighting a match in a hurricane." Figure C9.8 is a crude idealization of the engine. Air enters, burns fuel in the narrow section, then exits, all at supersonic speeds. There are no shock waves. Assume areas of 1 m² at sections 1 and 4 and 0.2 m² at sections 2 and 3. Let the entrance conditions be $Ma_1 = 6$, at 10,000 m standard altitude. Assume isentropic flow from 1 to 2, frictionless heat transfer from 2 to 3 with $Q = 500$ kJ/kg, and isentropic flow from 3 to 4. Calculate the exit conditions and the thrust produced.

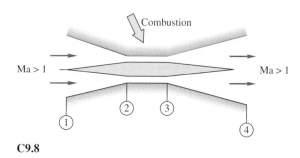

C9.8

Design Projects

D9.1   It is desired to select a rectangular wing for a fighter aircraft. The plane must be able (*a*) to take off and land on a 4500-ft-long sea-level runway and (*b*) to cruise supersonically at Ma = 2.3 at 28,000-ft altitude. For simplicity, assume a wing with zero sweepback. Let the aircraft maximum weight equal $(30 + n)(1000)$ lbf, where n is the number of letters in your surname. Let the available sea-level maximum thrust be one-third of the maximum weight, decreasing at altitude proportional to ambient density. Making suitable assumptions about the effect of finite aspect ratio on wing lift and drag for both subsonic and supersonic flight, select a wing of minimum area sufficient to perform these takeoff/landing and cruise requirements. Some thought should be given to analyzing the wingtips and wing roots in supersonic flight, where Mach cones form and the flow is not two-dimensional. If no satisfactory solution is possible, gradually increase the available thrust to converge to an acceptable design.

D9.2   Consider supersonic flow of air at sea-level conditions past a wedge of half-angle θ, as shown in Fig. D9.2. Assume that the pressure on the back of the wedge equals the fluid pressure as it exits the Prandtl-Meyer fan.

(*a*) Suppose $Ma_\infty = 3.0$. For what angle θ will the supersonic wave drag coefficient C_D, based on frontal area, be exactly 0.5? (*b*) Suppose that $\theta = 20°$. Is there a free-stream Mach number for which the wave drag coefficient C_D, based on frontal area, will be exactly 0.5? (*c*) Investigate the percentage increase in C_D from (*a*) and (*b*) due to including boundary layer friction drag in the calculation.

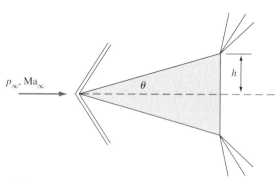

D9.2

References

1. J. E. A. John and T. G. Keith, *Gas Dynamics,* 3d ed., Pearson Education, Upper Saddle River, NJ, 2005.

2. B. K. Hodge and K. Koenig, *Compressible Fluid Dynamics: With Personal Computer Applications,* Pearson Prentice-Hall, Upper Saddle River, NJ, 1995.

3. R. D. Zucker and O. Biblarz, *Fundamentals of Gas Dynamics,* 2d ed., Wiley, New York, 2002.

4. J. D. Anderson, *Modern Compressible Flow: with Historical Perspective,* 3d ed., McGraw-Hill, New York, 2002.

5. A. H. Shapiro, *The Dynamics and Thermodynamics of Compressible Fluid Flow,* 2 vols., Wiley, New York, 1953.

6. C. Cercignani, *Rarefied Gas Dynamics,* Cambridge University Press, New York, 2000.

7. H. W. Liepmann and A. Roshko, *Elements of Gas Dynamics,* Dover, New York, 2001.

8. I. Straskraba, *Introduction to the Mathematical Theory of Compressible Flow,* Oxford University Press, New York, 2004.

9. P. A. Thompson, *Compressible Fluid Dynamics,* McGraw-Hill, New York, 1972.

10. P. H. Oosthuizen and W. E. Carscallen, *Compressible Fluid Flow,* McGraw-Hill, New York, 2003.

11. J. D. Anderson, *Hypersonic and High Temperature Gas Dynamics,* 2d ed., AIAA, Reston, VA, 2006.

12. G. A. Bird, *Molecular Gas Dynamics and the Direct Simulation of Gas Flows,* Clarendon Press, Oxford, 1994.

13. D. D. Knight, *Elements of Numerical Methods for Compressible Flows*, Cambridge University Press, New York, 2012.

14. L. W. Reithmaier, *Mach 1 and Beyond: The Illustrated Guide to High-Speed Flight,* McGraw-Hill, 1994.

15. W. T. Parry, *ASME International Steam Tables for Industrial Use,* 2d ed., ASME, New York, 2009.

16. J. H. Keenan et al., *Gas Tables: International Version,* Krieger Publishing, Melbourne, FL, 1992.

17. Y. A. Cengel and M. A. Boles, *Thermodynamics: An Engineering Approach,* 7th ed., McGraw-Hill, New York, 2010.

18. M. J. Moran and H. A. Shapiro, *Fundamentals of Engineering Thermodynamics,* 7th ed., Wiley, New York, 2010.

19. F. M. White, *Viscous Fluid Flow,* 3d ed., McGraw-Hill, New York, 2005.

20. J. Palmer, K. Ramsden, and E. Goodger, *Compressible Flow Tables for Engineers: With Appropriate Computer Programs,* Scholium Intl., Port Washington, NY, 1989.

21. M. R. Lindeburg, *Consolidated Gas Dynamics Tables,* Professional Publications, Inc., Belmont, CA, 1994.

22. A. M. Shektman, *Gasdynamic Functions of Real Gases,* Taylor and Francis, New York, 1991.

23. J. H. Keenan and E. P. Neumann, "Measurements of Friction in a Pipe for Subsonic and Supersonic Flow of Air," *J. Applied Mechanics,* vol. 13, no. 2, 1946, p. A-91.

24. R. P. Benedict, *Fundamentals of Pipe Flow,* John Wiley, New York, 1980.

25. J. L. Sims, *Tables for Supersonic Flow around Right Circular Cones at Zero Angle of Attack,* NASA SP-3004, 1964 (see also NASA SP-3007).

26. J. L. Thomas, "Reynolds Number Effects on Supersonic Asymmetrical Flows over a Cone," *J. Aircraft,* vol. 30, no. 4, 1993, pp. 488–495.

27. W. Bober and R. A. Kenyon, *Fluid Mechanics,* Wiley, New York, 1980.

28. J. Ackeret, "Air Forces on Airfoils Moving Faster than Sound Velocity," *NACA Tech. Memo.* 317, 1925.

29. W. B. Brower, *Theory, Tables and Data for Compressible Flow,* Taylor & Francis, New York, 1990.

30. M. Belfiore, "The Hypersonic Age is Near," *Popular Science,* January 2008, pp. 36–41.

31. G. S. Settles, *Schlieren and Shadowgraph Techniques: Visualizing Phenomena in Transparent Media*, Springer-Verlag, Berlin, 2001.

In March of 2010, the normally placid Saugatucket River, in South Kingstown, Rhode Island, was flooded by heavy rains. Instead of its usual gentle trickle over the Main Street dam, the flow rate was enormously increased and flooded the medical building in the background, ruining their offices and X-ray machines. The open-channel flow analysis methods in this chapter can handle both the trickle and the flood. [*Photo courtesy of Independent Newspapers*]

Chapter 10
Open-Channel Flow

Motivation. An *open-channel flow* denotes a flow with a free surface touching an atmosphere, like a river or a canal or a flume. Closed-duct flows (Chap. 6) are full of fluid, either liquid or gas, have no free surface within, and are driven by a pressure gradient along the duct axis. The open-channel flows here are driven by gravity alone, and the pressure gradient at the atmospheric interface is negligible. The basic force balance in an open channel is between gravity and friction.

Open-channel flows are an especially important mode of fluid mechanics for civil and environmental engineers. One needs to predict the flow rates and water depths that result from a given channel geometry, whether natural or artificial, and a given wet-surface roughness. Water is almost always the relevant fluid, and the channel size is usually large. Thus open-channel flows are generally turbulent, three-dimensional, sometimes unsteady, and often quite complex. This chapter presents some simple engineering theories and experimental correlations for steady flow in straight channels of regular geometry. We can borrow and use some concepts from duct flow analysis: hydraulic radius, friction factor, and head losses.

10.1 Introduction

Simply stated, open-channel flow is the flow of a liquid in a conduit with a free surface. There are many practical examples, both artificial (flumes, spillways, canals, weirs, drainage ditches, culverts) and natural (streams, rivers, estuaries, floodplains). This chapter introduces the elementary analysis of such flows, which are dominated by the effects of gravity.

The presence of the free surface, which is essentially at atmospheric pressure, both helps and hurts the analysis. It helps because the pressure can be taken as constant along the free surface, which therefore is equivalent to the *hydraulic grade line* (HGL) of the flow. Unlike flow in closed ducts, the pressure gradient is not a direct factor in open-channel flow, where the balance of forces is confined to gravity and friction.[1] But the free surface complicates the analysis because its shape is a priori unknown:

---

[1]Surface tension is rarely important because open channels are normally quite large and have a very large Weber number. Surface tension affects small models of large channels.

The depth profile changes with conditions and must be computed as part of the problem, especially in unsteady problems involving wave motion.

Before proceeding, we remark, as usual, that whole books have been written on open-channel hydraulics [1 to 7, 32]. There are also specialized texts devoted to wave motion [8 to 10] and to engineering aspects of coastal free-surface flows [11 to 13]. This chapter is only an introduction to broader and more detailed treatments. The writer recommends, as an occasional break from free-surface flow analysis, Ref. 31, which is an enchanting and spectacular gallery of ocean wave photographs.

The One-Dimensional Approximation

An open channel always has two sides and a bottom, where the flow satisfies the no-slip condition. Therefore, even a straight channel has a three-dimensional velocity distribution. Some measurements of straight-channel velocity contours are shown in Fig. 10.1. The profiles are quite complex, with maximum velocity typically occurring in the midplane about 20 percent below the surface. In very broad shallow channels the maximum velocity is near the surface, and the velocity profile is nearly logarithmic from the bottom to the free surface, as in Eq. (6.62). In noncircular channels there are also secondary motions similar to Fig. 6.16 for closed-duct flows. If the channel curves or meanders, the secondary motion intensifies due to centrifugal effects, with high velocity occurring near the outer radius of the bend. Curved natural channels are subject to strong bottom erosion and deposition effects.

With the advent of the supercomputer, it is possible to make numerical simulations of complex flow patterns such as those in Fig. 10.1 [27, 28]. However, the practical engineering approach, used here, is to make a one-dimensional flow approximation, as in Fig. 10.2. Since the liquid density is nearly constant, the steady flow continuity equation reduces to constant-volume flow Q along the channel

$$Q = V(x)A(x) = \text{const} \tag{10.1}$$

where V is average velocity and A the local cross-sectional area, as sketched in Fig. 10.2.

A second one-dimensional relation between velocity and channel geometry is the energy equation, including friction losses. If points 1 (upstream) and 2 (downstream) are on the free surface, $p_1 = p_2 = p_a$, and we have, for steady flow,

$$\frac{V_1^2}{2g} + z_1 = \frac{V_2^2}{2g} + z_2 + h_f \tag{10.2}$$

where z denotes the total elevation of the free surface, which includes the water depth y (see Fig. 10.2a) plus the height of the (sloping) bottom. The friction head loss h_f is analogous to head loss in duct flow from Eq. (6.10):

$$h_f \approx f \frac{x_2 - x_1}{D_h} \frac{V_{av}^2}{2g} \qquad D_h = \text{hydraulic diameter} = \frac{4A}{P} \tag{10.3}$$

where f is the average friction factor (Fig. 6.13) between sections 1 and 2. Since channels are irregular in shape, their "size" is taken to be the hydraulic *radius*:

$$\boxed{R_h = \frac{1}{4}D_h = \frac{A}{P}} \tag{10.4}$$

2.0
1.5
1.0
0.5
Triangular channel
1.5
2.0
1.0
0.5
Trapezoidal channel
2.5
2.0
1.5
1.0
0.5
Pipe
2.0
1.5
1.0
0.5
Shallow ditch
2.5
2.0
1.0
1.5
0.5
Natural irregular channel
2.5
2.0
1.5
1.0
0.5
Narrow rectangular section

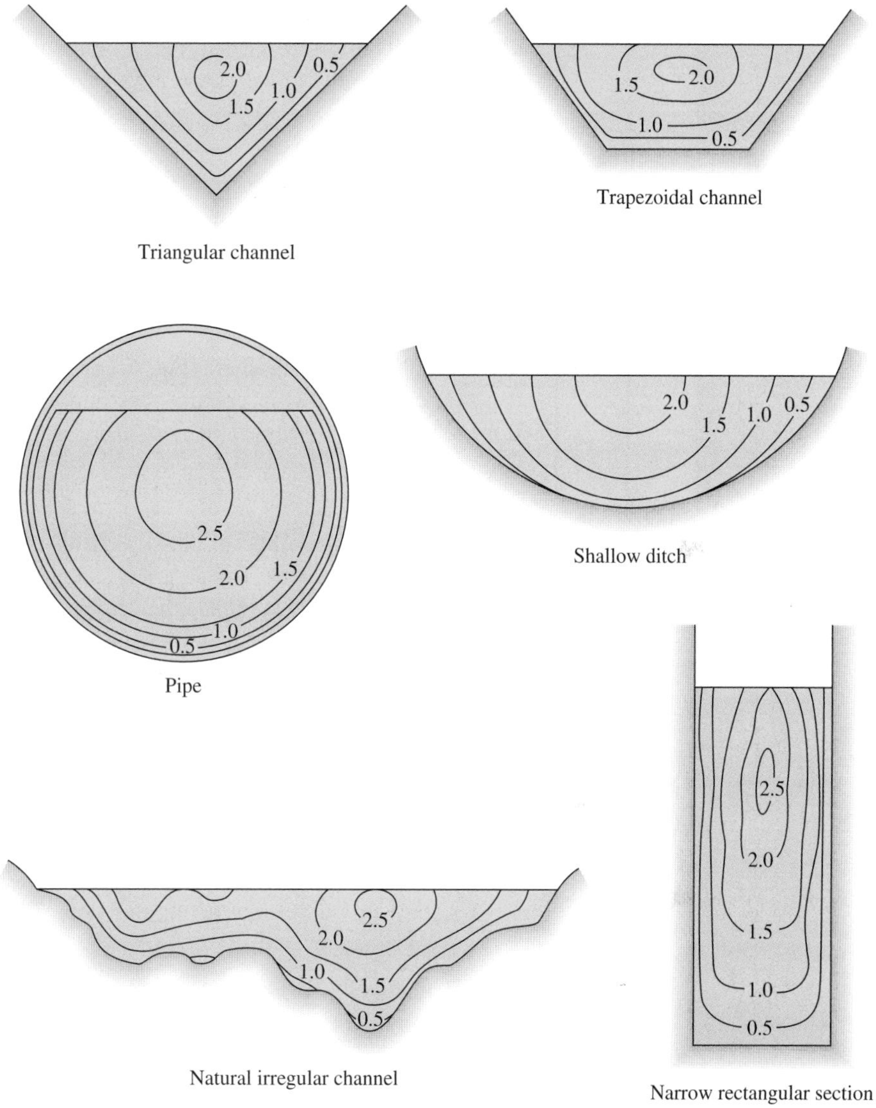

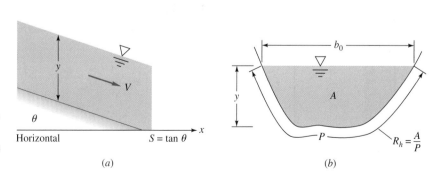

Fig. 10.1 Measured isovelocity contours in typical straight open-channel flows. *(From Ref. 2.)* *Source: From V. T. Chow, Open Channel Hydraulics, Blackburn Press, Caldwell, NJ, 2009.*

y
V
θ
Horizontal
S = tan θ
x
(a)
b0
y
A
P
Rh = A/P
(b)

Fig. 10.2 Geometry and notation for open-channel flow: (*a*) side view; (*b*) cross section. All these parameters are constant in uniform flow.

The local Reynolds number of the channel would be Re $= VR_h/\nu$, which is usually highly turbulent (>1 E5). The only commonly occurring laminar channel flows are the thin sheets that form as rainwater drains from crowned streets and airport runways.

The wetted perimeter P (see Fig. 10.2b) includes the sides and bottom of the channel but not the free surface and, of course, not the parts of the sides above the water level. For example, if a rectangular channel is b wide and h high and contains water to depth y, its wetted perimeter is

$$P = b + 2y$$

not $2b + 2h$.

Although the Moody chart (Fig. 6.13) would give a good estimate of the friction factor in channel flow, in practice it is seldom used. An alternative correlation due to Robert Manning, discussed in Sec. 10.2, is the formula of choice in open-channel hydraulics.

Flow Classification by Depth Variation

The most common method of classifying open-channel flows is by the rate of change of the free-surface depth. The simplest and most widely analyzed case is *uniform flow,* where the depth and area (hence the velocity in steady flow) remain constant. Uniform flow conditions are approximated by long, straight runs of constant-slope and constant-area channel. A channel in uniform flow is said to be moving at its *normal depth* y_n, which is an important design parameter.

If the channel slope or cross section changes or there is an obstruction in the flow, then the depth changes and the flow is said to be *varied*. The flow is *gradually varying* if the one-dimensional approximation is valid and *rapidly varying* if not. Some examples of this method of classification are shown in Fig. 10.3. The classes can be summarized as follows:

1. Uniform flow (constant depth and slope)
2. Varied flow:
   a. Gradually varied (one-dimensional)
   b. Rapidly varied (multidimensional)

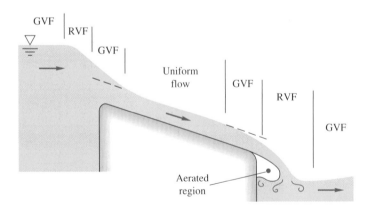

Fig. 10.3 Open-channel flow classified by regions of rapidly varying flow (RVF), gradually varying flow (GVF), and uniform flow depth profiles.

Typically uniform flow is separated from rapidly varying flow by a region of gradually varied flow. Gradually varied flow can be analyzed by a first-order differential equation (Sec. 10.6), but rapidly varying flow usually requires experimentation or three-dimensional computational fluid dynamics [14, 27, 28].

Flow Classification by Froude Number

A second and very useful classification of open-channel flow is by the dimensionless Froude number, Fr, which is the ratio of channel velocity to the speed of propagation of a small-disturbance wave in the channel. For a rectangular or very wide constant-depth channel, this takes the form

$$\text{Fr} = \frac{\text{flow velocity}}{\text{surface wave speed}} = \frac{V}{\sqrt{gy}} \tag{10.5}$$

where y is the water depth. The flow behaves differently depending on these three flow regimes:

$$
\begin{array}{lll}
\text{Fr} < 1.0 & \text{subcritical flow} & \\
\text{Fr} = 1.0 & \text{critical flow} & \qquad(10.6)\\
\text{Fr} > 1.0 & \text{supercritical flow} &
\end{array}
$$

The Froude number for irregular channels is defined in Sec. 10.4. As mentioned in Sec. 9.10, there is a strong analogy here with the three compressible flow regimes of the Mach number: subsonic (Ma < 1), sonic (Ma = 1), and supersonic (Ma > 1). We shall use the analogy in Secs. 10.4 and 10.5. The analogy is pursued in Ref. 21.

Surface Wave Speed

The Froude number denominator $(gy)^{1/2}$ is the speed of an infinitesimal shallow-water surface wave. We can derive this with reference to Fig. 10.4a, which shows a wave of height δy propagating at speed c into still liquid. To achieve a steady flow inertial frame of reference, we fix the coordinates on the wave as in Fig. 10.4b, so that the still water moves to the right at velocity c. Figure 10.4 is exactly analogous to Fig. 9.1, which analyzed the speed of sound in a fluid. It can be used to analyze tidal bores, Fig. P10.86, which are described by Chanson [34].

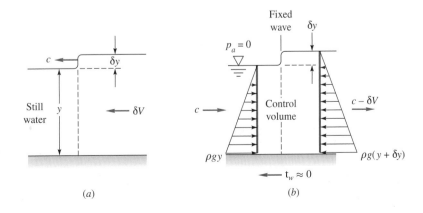

Fig. 10.4 Analysis of a small surface wave propagating into still shallow water; (a) moving wave, nonsteady frame; (b) fixed wave, inertial frame of reference.

For the control volume of Fig. 10.4*b*, the one-dimensional continuity relation is, for channel width *b*,

$$\rho c b y = \rho(c - \delta V)(y + \delta y)b$$

or
$$\delta V = c\,\frac{\delta y}{y + \delta y} \tag{10.7}$$

This is analogous to Eq. (9.10); the velocity change δV induced by a surface wave is small if the wave is "weak," $\delta y \ll y$. If we neglect bottom friction in the short distance across the wave in Fig. 10.4*b*, the momentum relation is a balance between the net hydrostatic pressure force and momentum:

$$-\tfrac{1}{2}\rho g b[(y + \delta y)^2 - y^2] = \rho c b y(c - \delta V - c)$$

or
$$g\left(1 + \frac{\tfrac{1}{2}\delta y}{y}\right)\delta y = c\,\delta V \tag{10.8}$$

This is analogous to Eq. (9.12). By eliminating δV between Eqs. (10.7) and (10.8) we obtain the desired expression for wave propagation speed:

$$c^2 = gy\left(1 + \frac{\delta y}{y}\right)\left(1 + \frac{\tfrac{1}{2}\delta y}{y}\right) \tag{10.9}$$

The "stronger" the wave height δy, the faster the wave speed c, by analogy with Eq. (9.13). In the limit of an infinitesimal wave height $\delta y \to 0$, the speed becomes

$$\boxed{c_0^2 = gy} \tag{10.10}$$

This is the surface-wave equivalent of fluid sound speed *a*, and thus the Froude number in channel flow $\mathrm{Fr} = V/c_0$ is the analog of the Mach number. For $y = 1$ m, $c_o = 3.1$ m/s.

As in gas dynamics, a channel flow can accelerate from subcritical to critical to supercritical flow and then return to subcritical flow through a sort of normal shock called a *hydraulic jump* (Sec. 10.5). This is illustrated in Fig. 10.5. The flow upstream of the sluice gate is subcritical. It then accelerates to critical and supercritical flow as it passes under the gate, which serves as a sort of "nozzle." Further downstream the

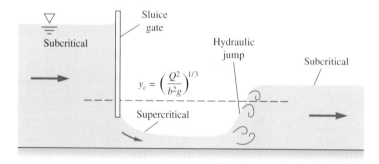

Fig. 10.5 Flow under a sluice gate accelerates from subcritical to critical to supercritical flow and then jumps back to subcritical flow.

flow "shocks" back to subcritical flow because the downstream "receiver" height is too high to maintain supercritical flow. Note the similarity with the nozzle gas flows of Fig. 9.12.

The critical depth $y_c = [Q^2/(b^2g)]^{1/3}$ is sketched as a dashed line in Fig. 10.5 for reference. Like the normal depth y_n, y_c is an important parameter in characterizing open-channel flow (see Sec. 10.4).

An excellent discussion of the various regimes of open-channel flow is given in Ref. 15.

10.2 Uniform Flow; The Chézy Formula

Uniform flow can occur in long, straight runs of constant slope and constant channel cross section. The water depth is constant at $y = y_n$, and the velocity is constant at $V = V_0$. Let the slope be $S_0 = \tan \theta$, where θ is the angle the bottom makes with the horizontal, considered positive for downhill flow. Then Eq. (10.2), with $V_1 = V_2 = V_0$, becomes

$$h_f = z_1 - z_2 = S_0 L \tag{10.11}$$

where L is the horizontal distance between sections 1 and 2. The head loss thus balances the loss in height of the channel. The flow is essentially fully developed, so the Darcy-Weisbach relation, Eq. (6.10), holds

$$h_f = f\frac{L}{D_h}\frac{V_0^2}{2g} \qquad D_h = 4R_h \tag{10.12}$$

with $D_h = 4A/P$ used to accommodate noncircular channels. The geometry and notation for open-channel flow analysis are shown in Fig. 10.2.

By combining Eqs. (10.11) and (10.12) we obtain an expression for flow velocity in uniform channel flow:

$$V_0 = \left(\frac{8g}{f}\right)^{1/2} R_h^{1/2} S_0^{1/2} \tag{10.13}$$

For a given channel shape and bottom roughness, the quantity $(8g/f)^{1/2}$ is constant and can be denoted by C. Equation (10.13) becomes

$$V_0 = C(R_h S_0)^{1/2} \qquad Q = CA(R_h S_0)^{1/2} \qquad \tau_{avg} = \rho g R_h S_0 \tag{10.14}$$

These are called the *Chézy formulas,* first developed by the French engineer Antoine Chézy in conjunction with his experiments on the Seine River and the Courpalet Canal in 1769. The quantity C, called the *Chézy coefficient,* varies from about 60 ft$^{1/2}$/s for small, rough channels to 160 ft$^{1/2}$/s for large, smooth channels (30 to 90 m$^{1/2}$/s in SI units).

Over the past century a great deal of hydraulics research [16] has been devoted to the correlation of the Chézy coefficient with the roughness, shape, and slope of various open channels. Correlations are due to Ganguillet and Kutter in 1869, Manning in 1889, Bazin in 1897, and Powell in 1950 [16]. All these formulations are discussed in delicious detail in Ref. 2, Chap. 5. Here we confine our treatment to Manning's correlation, the most popular.

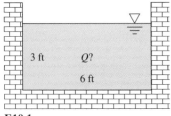

E10.1

EXAMPLE 10.1

A straight rectangular channel is 6 ft wide and 3 ft deep and laid on a slope of 2°. The friction factor is 0.022. Estimate the uniform flow rate in cubic feet per second.

Solution

- *System sketch:* The channel cross section is shown in Fig. E10.1.
- *Assumptions:* Steady, uniform channel flow with $\theta = 2°$.
- *Approach:* Evaluate the Chézy formula, Eq. (10.13) or (10.14).
- *Property values:* Please note that there are *no* fluid physical properties involved in the Chézy formula. Can you explain this?
- *Solution step:* Simply evaluate each term in the Chézy formula, Eq. (10.13):

$$C = \sqrt{\frac{8g}{f}} = \sqrt{\frac{8(32.2 \text{ ft/s}^2)}{0.022}} = 108 \frac{\text{ft}^{1/2}}{\text{s}} \qquad A = by = (6 \text{ ft})(3 \text{ ft}) = 18 \text{ ft}^2$$

$$R_h = \frac{A}{P_{\text{wet}}} = \frac{18 \text{ ft}^2}{(3 + 6 + 3) \text{ ft}} = 1.5 \text{ ft} \qquad S_0 = \tan(\theta) = \tan(2°)$$

$$\text{Then } Q = CAR_h^{1/2}S_0^{1/2} = \left(108 \frac{\text{ft}^{1/2}}{\text{s}}\right)(18 \text{ ft}^2)(1.5 \text{ ft})^{1/2}(\tan 2°)^{1/2} \approx 450 \text{ ft}^3/\text{s} \qquad Ans.$$

- *Comments:* Uniform flow estimates are straightforward if the geometry is simple. Results are independent of water density and viscosity because the flow is fully rough and driven by gravity. Note the high flow rate, larger than some rivers. Two degrees is a substantial channel slope.

The Manning Roughness Correlation

The most fundamentally sound approach to the Chézy formula is to use Eq. (10.13) with f estimated from the Moody friction factor chart, Fig. 6.13. Indeed, the open-channel research establishment [18] strongly recommends use of the friction factor in all calculations. Since typical channels are large and rough, we would generally use the fully rough turbulent flow limit of Eq. (6.48)

$$f \approx \left(2.0 \log \frac{14.8R_h}{\varepsilon}\right)^{-2} \tag{10.15}$$

where ε is the roughness height, with typical values listed in Table 10.1.

In spite of the attractiveness of this friction factor approach, most engineers prefer to use a simple (dimensional) correlation published in 1891 by Robert Manning [17], an Irish engineer. In tests with real channels, Manning found that the Chézy coefficient C increased approximately as the sixth root of the channel size. He proposed the simple formula

$$C = \left(\frac{8g}{f}\right)^{1/2} \approx \alpha \frac{R_h^{1/6}}{n} \tag{10.16}$$

where n is a roughness parameter. Since the formula is clearly not dimensionally consistent, it requires a conversion factor α that changes with the system of units used:

$$\alpha = 1.0 \quad \text{SI units} \qquad \alpha = 1.486 \quad \text{BG units} \tag{10.17}$$

Table 10.1 Experimental Values of Manning's n Factor*

	n	Average roughness height ε	
		ft	mm
Artificial lined channels:			
Glass	0.010 ± 0.002	0.0011	0.3
Brass	0.011 ± 0.002	0.0019	0.6
Steel, smooth	0.012 ± 0.002	0.0032	1.0
Painted	0.014 ± 0.003	0.0080	2.4
Riveted	0.015 ± 0.002	0.012	3.7
Cast iron	0.013 ± 0.003	0.0051	1.6
Concrete, finished	0.012 ± 0.002	0.0032	1.0
Unfinished	0.014 ± 0.002	0.0080	2.4
Planed wood	0.012 ± 0.002	0.0032	1.0
Clay tile	0.014 ± 0.003	0.0080	2.4
Brickwork	0.015 ± 0.002	0.012	3.7
Asphalt	0.016 ± 0.003	0.018	5.4
Corrugated metal	0.022 ± 0.005	0.12	37
Rubble masonry	0.025 ± 0.005	0.26	80
Excavated earth channels:			
Clean	0.022 ± 0.004	0.12	37
Gravelly	0.025 ± 0.005	0.26	80
Weedy	0.030 ± 0.005	0.8	240
Stony, cobbles	0.035 ± 0.010	1.5	500
Natural channels:			
Clean and straight	0.030 ± 0.005	0.8	240
Sluggish, deep pools	0.040 ± 0.010	3	900
Major rivers	0.035 ± 0.010	1.5	500
Floodplains:			
Pasture, farmland	0.035 ± 0.010	1.5	500
Light brush	0.05 ± 0.02	6	2000
Heavy brush	0.075 ± 0.025	15	5000
Trees	0.15 ± 0.05	?	?

*A more complete list is given in Ref. 2, pp. 110–113.

Recall that we warned about this awkwardness in Example 1.4. You may verify that α is the cube root of the conversion factor between the meter and your chosen length scale: In BG units, $\alpha = (3.2808 \text{ ft/m})^{1/3} = 1.486.$[2]

The Manning formula for uniform flow velocity is thus

$$V_0 \,(\text{m/s}) \approx \frac{1.0}{n} \left[R_h \,(\text{m}) \right]^{2/3} S_0^{1/2}$$

$$V_0 \,(\text{ft/s}) \approx \frac{1.486}{n} \left[R_h \,(\text{ft}) \right]^{2/3} S_0^{1/2}$$

(10.18)

[2]An interesting discussion of the history and "dimensionality" of Manning's formula is given in Ref. 2, pp. 98–99.

The channel slope S_0 is dimensionless, and n is taken to be the same in both systems. The volume flow rate simply multiplies this result by the area:

Uniform flow:

$$\boxed{Q = V_0 A \approx \frac{\alpha}{n} A R_h^{2/3} S_0^{1/2}}$$

(10.19)

Experimental values of n (and the corresponding roughness height) are listed in Table 10.1 for various channel surfaces. There is a factor-of-15 variation from a smooth glass surface ($n \approx 0.01$) to a tree-lined floodplain ($n \approx 0.15$). Due to the irregularity of typical channel shapes and roughness, the scatter bands in Table 10.1 should be taken seriously. For routine calculations, always use the average roughness in Table 10.1.

Since Manning's sixth-root size variation is not exact, real channels can have a variable n depending on the water depth. The Mississippi River near Memphis, Tennessee, has $n \approx 0.032$ at 40-ft flood depth, 0.030 at normal 20-ft depth, and 0.040 at 5-ft low-stage depth. Seasonal vegetative growth and factors such as bottom erosion can also affect the value of n. Even nearly identical man-made channels can vary. Brater et al. [19] report that U.S. Bureau of Reclamation tests, on large concrete-lined canals, yielded values of n ranging from 0.012 to 0.017.

EXAMPLE 10.2

Engineers find that the most efficient rectangular channel (maximum uniform flow for a given area) flows at a depth equal to half the bottom width. Consider a rectangular brickwork channel laid on a slope of 0.006. What is the best bottom width for a flow rate of 100 ft^3/s?

Solution

- *Assumptions:* Uniform flow in a straight channel of constant of slope $S = 0.006$.
- *Approach:* Use the Manning formula in English units, Eq. (10.19), to predict the flow rate.
- *Property values:* For brickwork, from Table 10.1, the roughness factor $n \approx 0.015$.
- *Solution:* For bottom width b, take the water depth to be $y = b/2$. Equation (10.19) becomes

$$A = by = b(b/2) = \frac{b^2}{2} \qquad R_h = \frac{A}{P} = \frac{by}{b + 2y} = \frac{b^2/2}{b + 2(b/2)} = \frac{b}{4}$$

$$Q = \frac{\alpha}{n} A R_h^{2/3} S^{1/2} = \frac{1.486}{0.015}\left(\frac{b^2}{2}\right)\left(\frac{b}{4}\right)^{2/3}(0.006)^{1/2} = 100 \frac{\text{ft}^3}{\text{s}}$$

Clean this up: $b^{8/3} = 65.7$ solve for $b \approx 4.8$ ft   *Ans.*

- *Comments:* The Manning approach is simple and effective. The Moody friction factor method, Eq. (10.14), requires laborious iteration and leads to a result $b \approx 4.81$ ft.

Normal Depth Estimates

With water depth y known, the computation of Q is quite straightforward. However, if Q is given, the computation of the normal depth y_n may require iteration. Since the normal depth is a characteristic flow parameter, this is an important type of problem.

The *normal depth*, y_n, is the depth, in uniform flow, of the water in a straight, constant-area, constant-slope channel. It varies with the flow rate and is a useful reference depth, calculated by solving Eq. (10.19) when Q is given.

EXAMPLE 10.3

The asphalt-lined trapezoidal channel in Fig. E10.3 carries 300 ft³/s of water under uniform flow conditions when $S = 0.0015$. What is the normal depth y_n?

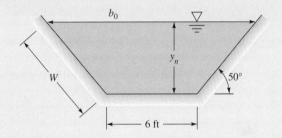

Note: See Fig. 10.7 for generalized trapezoid notation.

E10.3

Solution using Excel

From Table 10.1, for asphalt, $n \approx 0.016$. The area and hydraulic radius are functions of y_n, which is unknown:

$$b_0 = 6 \text{ ft} + 2y_n \cot 50° \qquad A = \tfrac{1}{2}(6 + b_0)y_n = 6y_n + y_n^2 \cot 50°$$

$$P = 6 + 2W = 6 + 2y_n \csc 50°$$

From Manning's formula (10.19) with a known $Q = 300$ ft³/s, we have

$$300 = \frac{1.49}{0.016}(6y_n + y_n^2 \cot 50°)\left(\frac{6y_n + y_n^2 \cot 50°}{6 + 2y_n \csc 50°}\right)^{2/3}(0.0015)^{1/2}$$

or

$$(6y_n + y_n^2 \cot 50°)^{5/3} = 83.2(6 + 2y_n \csc 50°)^{2/3} \qquad (1)$$

One can iterate Eq. (1) by hand laboriously and eventually find $y_n \approx 4.6$ ft. However, it is a good candidate for iteration in Excel. One could iterate the Chézy formula directly and find the value of y_n that gives a flow rate of 300 ft³/s. The writer chose to deal with the rearranged version, Eq. (1), guessing values of y_n until the left-hand side equals the right-hand side. The writer's first guess was $y_n = 10$ ft, which was much too deep. Four more guesses achieved quite accurate convergence, in the following table:

	y_n	Eq. (1) LHS	Eq. (1) RHS	LHS − RHS
	A	B	C	D
1	10	3952.01	840.49	3111.52
2	5	700.86	593.54	107.32
3	4	418.74	538.00	−119.26
4	4.6	576.83	571.65	5.18
5	**4.578**	**570.45**	**570.43**	0.02

At 300 ft³/s, the normal depth for this channel is $\qquad y_n = 4.578$ ft $\qquad$ *Ans.*

For later use, we might also list the other properties of this channel:

$$b_o = 13.68 \text{ ft}; \quad P = 17.95 \text{ ft}; \quad A = 45.05 \text{ ft}^2; \quad R_h = 2.51 \text{ ft}$$

Hand calculation is too cumbersome for open-channel problems where the depth is unknown.

Uniform Flow in a Partly Full Circular Pipe

Consider the partially full pipe of Fig. 10.6a in uniform flow. The maximum velocity and flow rate actually occur before the pipe is completely full. In terms of the pipe radius R and the angle θ up to the free surface, the geometric properties are

$$A = R^2\left(\theta - \frac{\sin 2\theta}{2}\right) \qquad P = 2R\theta \qquad R_h = \frac{R}{2}\left(1 - \frac{\sin 2\theta}{2\theta}\right)$$

The Manning formulas (10.19) predict a uniform flow as follows:

$$V_0 \approx \frac{\alpha}{n}\left[\frac{R}{2}\left(1 - \frac{\sin 2\theta}{2\theta}\right)\right]^{2/3} S_0^{1/2} \qquad Q = V_0 R^2\left(\theta - \frac{\sin 2\theta}{2}\right) \qquad (10.20)$$

For a given n and slope S_0, we may plot these two relations versus y/D in Fig. 10.6b. There are two different maxima, as follows:

$$V_{\max} = 0.718 \frac{\alpha}{n} R^{2/3} S_0^{1/2} \quad \text{at} \quad \theta = 128.73° \quad \text{and} \quad y = 0.813D$$

$$\qquad\qquad (10.21)$$

$$Q_{\max} = 2.129 \frac{\alpha}{n} R^{8/3} S_0^{1/2} \quad \text{at} \quad \theta = 151.21° \quad \text{and} \quad y = 0.938D$$

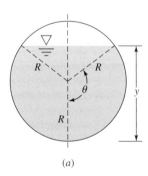

(a)

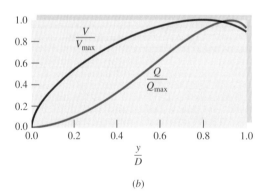

Fig. 10.6 Uniform flow in a partly full circular channel: (a) geometry; (b) velocity and flow rate versus depth.

(b)

As shown in Fig. 10.6b, the maximum velocity is 14 percent more than the velocity when running full, and similarly the maximum discharge is 8 percent more. Since real pipes running nearly full tend to have somewhat unstable flow, these differences are not that significant.

10.3 Efficient Uniform-Flow Channels

The engineering design of an open channel has many parameters. If the channel surface can erode or scour, a low-velocity design might be sought. A dirt channel could be planted with grass to minimize erosion. For nonerodible surfaces, construction and lining costs might dominate, suggesting a cross section of minimum wetted perimeter. Nonerodible channels can be designed for maximum flow.

The simplicity of Manning's formulation (10.19) enables us to analyze channel flows to determine the most efficient low-resistance sections for given conditions. The most common problem is that of maximizing R_h for a given flow area and discharge. Since $R_h = A/P$, maximizing R_h for given A is the same as minimizing the wetted perimeter P. There is no general solution for arbitrary cross sections, but an analysis of the trapezoid section will show the basic results.

Consider the generalized symmetric trapezoid of angle θ in Fig. 10.7. For a given side angle θ, the flow area is

$$A = by + \beta y^2 \qquad \beta = \cot \theta \tag{10.22}$$

The wetted perimeter is

$$P = b + 2W = b + 2y(1 + \beta^2)^{1/2} \tag{10.23}$$

Eliminating b between (10.22) and (10.23) gives

$$P = \frac{A}{y} - \beta y + 2y(1 + \beta^2)^{1/2} \tag{10.24}$$

To minimize P, evaluate dP/dy for constant A and β and set equal to zero. The result is

$$A = y^2[2(1 + \beta^2)^{1/2} - \beta] \quad P = 4y(1 + \beta^2)^{1/2} - 2\beta y \quad R_h = \tfrac{1}{2}y \tag{10.25}$$

The last result is very interesting: For any angle θ, the most efficient cross section for uniform flow occurs when the hydraulic radius is half the depth.

Since a rectangle is a trapezoid with $\beta = 0$, the most efficient rectangular section is such that

$$A = 2y^2 \qquad P = 4y \qquad R_h = \tfrac{1}{2}y \qquad b = 2y \tag{10.26}$$

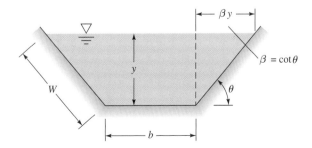

Fig. 10.7 Geometry of a trapezoidal channel section.

To find the correct depth y, these relations must be solved in conjunction with Manning's flow rate formula (10.19) for the given discharge Q.

Best Trapezoid Angle

Equations (10.25) are valid for any value of β. What is the best value of β for a given depth and area? To answer this question, evaluate $dP/d\beta$ from Eq. (10.24) with A and y held constant. The result is

$$2\beta = (1 + \beta^2)^{1/2} \qquad \beta = \cot \theta = \frac{1}{3^{1/2}}$$

or
$$\theta = 60° \tag{10.27}$$

Thus the maximum-flow trapezoid section is half a hexagon.

Similar calculations with a circular channel section running partially full show best efficiency for a semicircle, $y = \frac{1}{2}D$. In fact, the semicircle is the best of all possible channel sections (minimum wetted perimeter for a given flow area). The percentage improvement over, say, half a hexagon is very slight, however.

EXAMPLE 10.4

(a) What are the best dimensions y and b for a rectangular brick channel designed to carry 5 m³/s of water in uniform flow with $S_0 = 0.001$? (b) Compare results with a half-hexagon and semicircle.

Solution

Part (a)

From Eq. (10.26), $A = 2y^2$ and $R_h = \frac{1}{2}y$. Manning's formula (10.19) in SI units gives, with $n \approx 0.015$ from Table 10.1,

$$Q = \frac{1.0}{n} A R_h^{2/3} S_0^{1/2} \qquad \text{or} \qquad 5 \text{ m}^3/\text{s} = \frac{1.0}{0.015}(2y^2)\left(\frac{1}{2}y\right)^{2/3}(0.001)^{1/2}$$

which can be solved for
$$y^{8/3} = 1.882 \text{ m}^{8/3}$$
$$y = 1.27 \text{ m} \qquad \qquad Ans.$$

The proper area and width are
$$A = 2y^2 = 3.21 \text{ m}^2 \qquad b = \frac{A}{y} = 2.53 \text{ m} \qquad Ans.$$

Part (b)

It is constructive to see what flow rate a half-hexagon and semicircle would carry for the same area of 3.214 m².

For the half-hexagon (HH), with $\beta = 1/3^{1/2} = 0.577$, Eq. (10.25) predicts

$$A = y_{HH}^2[2(1 + 0.577^2)^{1/2} - 0.577] = 1.732y_{HH}^2 = 3.214$$

or $y_{HH} = 1.362$ m, whence $R_h = \frac{1}{2}y = 0.681$ m. The half-hexagon flow rate is thus

$$Q = \frac{1.0}{0.015}(3.214)(0.681)^{2/3}(0.001)^{1/2} = 5.25 \text{ m}^3/\text{s}$$

or about 5 percent more than that for the rectangle.

For a semicircle, $A = 3.214 \text{ m}^2 = \pi D^2/8$, or $D = 2.861$ m, whence $P = \frac{1}{2}\pi D = 4.494$ m and $R_h = A/P = 3.214/4.494 = 0.715$ m. The semicircle flow rate will thus be

$$Q = \frac{1.0}{0.015}(3.214)(0.715)^{2/3}(0.001)^{1/2} = 5.42 \text{ m}^3/\text{s}$$

or about 8 percent more than that of the rectangle and 3 percent more than that of the half-hexagon.

10.4 Specific Energy; Critical Depth

The total head of any incompressible flow is the sum of its velocity head $\alpha V^2/(2g)$, pressure head p/γ, and potential head z. For open-channel flow, surface pressure is everywhere atmospheric, so channel energy is a balance between velocity and elevation head only. Since the flow is turbulent, we assume that $\alpha \approx 1$—recall Eq. (3.77). The final result is the quantity called *specific energy E,* as suggested by Bakhmeteff [1] in 1913:

$$E = y + \frac{V^2}{2g} \tag{10.28}$$

where y is the water depth. It is seen from Fig. 10.8 that E is the height of the *energy grade line* (EGL) above the channel bottom. For a given flow rate, there are usually two states possible, called *alternate states,* for the same specific energy. There is also a minimum energy, $E_{\min}$, which corresponds to a Froude number of unity.

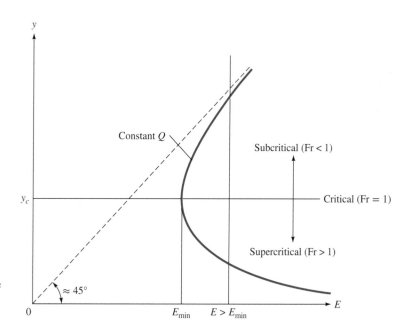

Fig. 10.8 Illustration of a specific energy curve. The curve for each flow rate Q has a minimum energy corresponding to critical flow. For energy greater than minimum, there are two *alternate* flow states, one subcritical and one supercritical.

Rectangular Channels

Consider the possible states at a given location. Let $q = Q/b = Vy$ be the discharge per unit width of a rectangular channel. Then, with q constant, Eq. (10.28) becomes

$$E = y + \frac{q^2}{2gy^2} \qquad q = \frac{Q}{b} \qquad \text{(10.29)}$$

Figure 10.8 is a plot of y versus E for constant q from Eq. (10.29). There is a minimum value of E at a certain value of y called the *critical depth*. By setting $dE/dy = 0$ at constant q, we find that E_{min} occurs at

$$y = y_c = \left(\frac{q^2}{g}\right)^{1/3} = \left(\frac{Q^2}{b^2 g}\right)^{1/3} \qquad \text{(10.30)}$$

The associated minimum energy is

$$E_{min} = E(y_c) = \tfrac{3}{2} y_c \qquad \text{(10.31)}$$

The depth y_c corresponds to channel velocity equal to the shallow-water wave propagation speed C_0 from Eq. (10.10). To see this, rewrite Eq. (10.30) as

$$q^2 = gy_c^3 = (gy_c)y_c^2 = V_c^2 y_c^2 \qquad \text{(10.32)}$$

By comparison it follows that the critical channel velocity is

$$V_c = (gy_c)^{1/2} = C_0 \qquad \text{Fr} = 1 \qquad \text{(10.33)}$$

For $E < E_{min}$ no solution exists in Fig. 10.8, and thus such a flow is impossible physically. For $E > E_{min}$ two solutions are possible: (1) large depth with $V < V_c$, called *subcritical*, and (2) small depth with $V > V_c$, called *supercritical*. In subcritical flow, disturbances can propagate upstream because wave speed $C_0 > V$. In supercritical flow, waves are swept downstream: Upstream is a zone of silence, and a small obstruction in the flow will create a wedge-shaped wave exactly analogous to the Mach waves in Fig. 9.18c. The angle of these waves must be

$$\mu = \sin^{-1}\frac{c_0}{V} = \sin^{-1}\frac{(gy)^{1/2}}{V} = \sin^{-1}\left(\frac{1}{\text{Fr}}\right) \qquad \text{(10.34)}$$

The wave angle and the depth can thus be used as a simple measurement of supercritical flow velocity.

Note from Fig. 10.8 that small changes in E near E_{min} cause a large change in the depth y, by analogy with small changes in duct area near the sonic point in Fig. 9.7. Thus critical flow is neutrally stable and is often accompanied by waves and undulations in the free surface. Channel designers should avoid long runs of near-critical flow.

The Water Channel Compressible Flow Analogy

The simple water wave expression of Eq. (10.34), $\sin \mu = 1/\text{Fr}$, can be extended into a general, often qualitative, analogy between gas dynamics and water channel flow [21, Chap. 11]. The analogy is derived from small-disturbance theory and has the results

Froude number is analogous to Mach number.

Water depth is analogous to gas density.

Water depth squared is analogous to gas pressure.

Hydraulic jumps are analogous to gas shock waves.

Both experiments and CFD results have exploited this analogy [37, 38]. A further result is that small-disturbance channel flow is equivalent to a fictitious gas with a specific heat ratio $k = 2.0$. However, for larger disturbances, such as shock waves, the numerical results differ and, oddly, are more accurate for $k = 1.4$ than for $k = 2.0$. A few examples are assigned here as Probs. P10.85, P10.88, and P10.91.

EXAMPLE 10.5

A wide rectangular clean-earth channel has a flow rate $q = 50$ ft³/(s · ft). (a) What is the critical depth? (b) What type of flow exists if $y = 3$ ft?

Solution

Part (a)

The critical depth is independent of channel roughness and simply follows from Eq. (10.30):

$$y_c = \left(\frac{q^2}{g}\right)^{1/3} = \left(\frac{50^2}{32.2}\right)^{1/3} = 4.27 \text{ ft} \qquad \textit{Ans. (a)}$$

Part (b)

If the actual depth is 3 ft, which is less than y_c, the flow must be *supercritical*. *Ans. (b)*

Nonrectangular Channels

If the channel width varies with y, the specific energy must be written in the form

$$E = y + \frac{Q^2}{2gA^2} \qquad (10.35)$$

The critical point of minimum energy occurs where $dE/dy = 0$ at constant Q. Since $A = A(y)$, Eq. (10.35) yields, for $E = E_{min}$,

$$\frac{dA}{dy} = \frac{gA^3}{Q^2} \qquad (10.36)$$

But $dA = b_0 \, dy$, where b_0 is the channel width at the free surface. Therefore, Eq. (10.36) is equivalent to

$$A_c = \left(\frac{b_0 Q^2}{g}\right)^{1/3} \qquad (10.37a)$$

$$V_c = \frac{Q}{A_c} = \left(\frac{gA_c}{b_0}\right)^{1/2} \qquad (10.37b)$$

For a given channel shape $A(y)$ and $b_0(y)$ and a given Q, Eqs. (10.37) have to be solved by trial and error or by Excel iteration to find the critical area A_c, from which V_c can be computed.

By comparing the actual depth and velocity with the critical values, we can determine the local flow condition.

$$y > y_c, \; V < V_c: \quad \text{subcritical flow (Fr} < 1)$$
$$y = y_c, \; V = V_c: \quad \text{critical flow (Fr} = 1)$$
$$y < y_c, \; V > V_c: \quad \text{supercritical flow (Fr} < 1)$$

Note that V_c is equal to the speed of propagation c of a shallow-water wave in the channel and is dependent upon the depth, as in Fig. 10.4a. For a rectangular channel, $c = (gy)^{1/2}$.

Critical Uniform Flow: The Critical Slope

If a critical channel flow is also moving uniformly (at constant depth), it must correspond to a *critical slope* S_c, with $y_n = y_c$. This condition is analyzed by equating Eq. (10.37a) to the Chézy (or Manning) formula:

$$Q^2 = \frac{gA_c^3}{b_0} = C^2 A_c^2 R_h S_c = \frac{\alpha^2}{n^2} A_c^2 R_h^{4/3} S_c$$

or $\qquad S_c = \dfrac{n^2 g A_c}{\alpha^2 b_0 R_{hc}^{4/3}} = \dfrac{n^2 V_c^2}{\alpha^2 R_{hc}^{4/3}} = \dfrac{n^2 g}{\alpha^2 R_{hc}^{1/3}} \dfrac{P}{b_0} = \dfrac{f}{8} \dfrac{P}{b_0}$ $\qquad$ (10.38)

where α^2 equals 1.0 for SI units and 2.208 for BG units. Equation (10.38) is valid for any channel shape. For a wide rectangular channel, $b_0 \gg y_c$, the formula reduces to

Wide rectangular channel: $\qquad S_c \approx \dfrac{n^2 g}{\alpha^2 y_c^{1/3}} \approx \dfrac{f}{8}$

This is a special case, a reference point. In most channel flows $y_n \neq y_c$. For fully rough turbulent flow, the critical slope varies between 0.002 and 0.008.

EXAMPLE 10.6

The 50° triangular channel in Fig. E10.6 has a flow rate $Q = 16$ m³/s. Compute (a) y_c, (b) V_c, and (c) S_c if $n = 0.018$.

Solution

Part (a)

This is an easy cross section because all geometric quantities can be written directly in terms of depth y:

$$P = 2y \csc 50° \qquad A = y^2 \cot 50°$$
$$R_h = \tfrac{1}{2} y \cos 50° \qquad b_0 = 2y \cot 50° \qquad (1)$$

The critical flow condition satisfies Eq. (10.37a):

$$gA_c^3 = b_0 Q^2$$

or $\qquad g(y_c^2 \cot 50°)^3 = (2y_c \cot 50°) Q^2$

$$y_c = \left(\frac{2Q^2}{g \cot^2 50°}\right)^{1/5} = \left[\frac{2(16)^2}{9.81(0.839)^2}\right]^{1/5} = 2.37 \text{ m} \qquad Ans. (a)$$

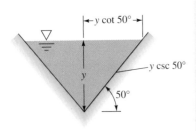

E10.6

Part (b)

With y_c known, from Eqs. (1) we compute $P_c = 6.18$ m, $R_{hc} = 0.760$ m, $A_c = 4.70$ m^2, and $b_{0c} = 3.97$ m. The critical velocity from Eq. (10.37b) is

$$V_c = \frac{Q}{A_c} = \frac{16 \text{ m}^3/\text{s}}{4.70 \text{ m}^2} = 3.41 \text{ m/s} \qquad \text{Ans. (b)}$$

Part (c)

With $n = 0.018$, we compute from Eq. (10.38) a critical slope:

$$S_c = \frac{gn^2P}{\alpha^2 R_h^{1/3} b_0} = \frac{9.81(0.018)^2(6.18)}{1.0(0.760)^{1/3}(3.97)} = 0.00542 \qquad \text{Ans. (c)}$$

Frictionless Flow over a Bump

A rough analogy to compressible gas flow in a nozzle (Fig. 9.12) is open-channel flow over a bump, as in Fig. 10.9a. The behavior of the free surface is sharply different according to whether the approach flow is subcritical or supercritical. The height of the bump also can change the character of the results. For frictionless two-dimensional flow, sections 1 and 2 in Fig. 10.9a are related by continuity and momentum:

$$V_1 y_1 = V_2 y_2 \qquad \frac{V_1^2}{2g} + y_1 = \frac{V_2^2}{2g} + y_2 + \Delta h$$

Eliminating V_2 between these two gives a cubic polynomial equation for the water depth y_2 over the bump:

$$y_2^3 - E_2 y_2^2 + \frac{V_1^2 y_1^2}{2g} = 0 \qquad \text{where } E_2 = \frac{V_1^2}{2g} + y_1 - \Delta h \qquad (10.39)$$

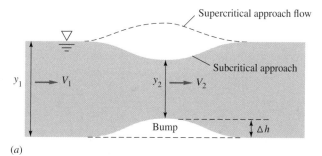

Fig. 10.9 Frictionless two-dimensional flow over a bump: (a) definition sketch showing Froude number dependence; (b) specific energy plot showing bump size and water depths.

This equation has one negative and two positive solutions if Δh is not too large. Its behavior is illustrated in Fig. 10.9b and depends on whether condition 1 is on the upper or lower leg of the energy curve. The specific energy E_2 is exactly Δh less than the approach energy E_1, and point 2 will lie on the same leg of the curve as E_1. A subcritical approach, $\text{Fr}_1 < 1$, will cause the water level to decrease at the bump. Supercritical approach flow, $\text{Fr}_1 > 1$, causes a water level increase over the bump.

If the bump height reaches $\Delta h_{max} = E_1 - E_c$, as illustrated in Fig. 10.9b, the flow at the crest will be exactly critical (Fr = 1). If $\Delta h > \Delta h_{max}$, there are no physically correct solutions to Eq. (10.39). That is, a bump too large will "choke" the channel and cause frictional effects, typically a hydraulic jump (Sec. 10.5).

These bump arguments are reversed if the channel has a *depression* ($\Delta h < 0$): Subcritical approach flow will cause a water level rise and supercritical flow a fall in depth. Point 2 will be $|\Delta h|$ to the right of point 1, and critical flow cannot occur.

EXAMPLE 10.7

Water flow in a wide channel approaches a 10-cm-high bump at 1.5 m/s and a depth of 1 m. Estimate (a) the water depth y_2 over the bump and (b) the bump height that will cause the crest flow to be critical.

Solution

Part (a)   First check the approach Froude number, assuming $C_0 = \sqrt{gy}$:

$$\text{Fr}_1 = \frac{V_1}{\sqrt{gy_1}} = \frac{1.5 \text{ m/s}}{\sqrt{(9.81 \text{ m/s}^2)(1.0 \text{ m})}} = 0.479 \quad \text{(subcritical)}$$

For subcritical approach flow, if Δh is not too large, we expect a depression in the water level over the bump and a higher subcritical Froude number at the crest. With $\Delta h = 0.1$ m, the specific energy levels must be

$$E_1 = \frac{V_1^2}{2g} + y_1 = \frac{(1.5)^2}{2(9.81)} + 1.0 = 1.115 \text{ m} \qquad E_2 = E_1 - \Delta h = 1.015 \text{ m}$$

This physical situation is shown on a specific energy plot in Fig. E10.7. With y_1 in meters, Eq. (10.39) takes on the numerical values

$$y_2^3 - 1.015 y_2^2 + 0.115 = 0$$

There are three real roots: $y_2 = +0.859$ m, $+0.451$ m, and -0.296 m. The third (negative) solution is physically impossible. The second (smaller) solution is the *supercritical* condition for E_2 and is not possible for this subcritical bump. The first solution is correct:

$$y_2(\text{subcritical}) \approx 0.859 \text{ m} \qquad\qquad\qquad Ans. (a)$$

The surface level has dropped by $y_1 - y_2 - \Delta h = 1.0 - 0.859 - 0.1 = 0.041$ m. The crest velocity is $V_2 = V_1 y_1/y_2 = 1.745$ m/s. The Froude number at the crest is $\text{Fr}_2 = 0.601$. Flow downstream of the bump is subcritical. These flow conditions are shown in Fig. E10.7.

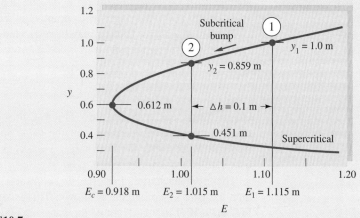

E10.7

Part (b)   For critical flow in a wide channel, with $q = Vy = 1.5$ m²/s, from Eq. (10.31),

$$E_{2,min} = E_c = \frac{3}{2}y_c = \frac{3}{2}\left(\frac{q^2}{g}\right)^{1/3} = \frac{3}{2}\left[\frac{(1.5 \text{ m}^2/\text{s})^2}{9.81 \text{ m/s}^2}\right]^{1/3} = 0.918 \text{ m}$$

Therefore, the maximum height for frictionless flow over this particular bump is

$$\Delta h_{max} = E_1 - E_{2,min} = 1.115 - 0.918 = 0.197 \text{ m}$$ *Ans.* (b)

For this bump, the solution of Eq. (10.39) is $y_2 = y_c = 0.612$ m, and the Froude number is unity at the crest. At critical flow the surface level has dropped by $y_1 - y_2 - \Delta h = 0.191$ m.

Flow under a Sluice Gate   A sluice gate is a bottom opening in a wall, as sketched in Fig. 10.10a, commonly used in control of rivers and channel flows. If the flow is allowed free discharge through the gap, as in Fig. 10.10a, the flow smoothly accelerates from subcritical (upstream) to critical (near the gap) to supercritical (downstream). The gate is then

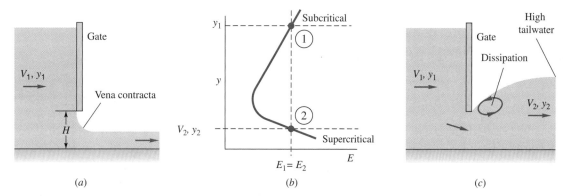

Fig. 10.10 Flow under a sluice gate passes through critical flow: (a) free discharge with vena contracta; (b) specific energy for free discharge; (c) dissipative flow under a drowned gate.

analogous to a converging–diverging nozzle in gas dynamics, as in Fig. 9.12, operating at its *design condition* (similar to point *H* in Fig. 9.12*b*).

For free discharge, friction may be neglected, and since there is no bump ($\Delta h = 0$), Eq. (10.39) applies with $E_1 = E_2$:

$$y_2^3 - \left(\frac{V_1^2}{2g} + y_1\right)y_2^2 + \frac{V_1^2 y_1^2}{2g} = 0 \qquad (10.40)$$

Given subcritical upstream flow (V_1, y_1), this cubic equation has only one positive real solution: supercritical flow at the same specific energy, as in Fig. 10.10*b*. The flow rate varies with the ratio y_2/y_1; we ask, as a problem exercise, to show that the flow rate is a maximum when $y_2/y_1 = \frac{2}{3}$.

The free discharge, Fig. 10.10*a*, contracts to a depth y_2 about 40 percent less than the gate's gap height, as shown. This is similar to a free *orifice* discharge, as in Fig. 6.39. If *H* is the height of the gate gap and *b* is the gap width into the paper, we can approximate the flow rate by orifice theory:

$$Q = C_d H b \sqrt{2gy_1} \qquad \text{where} \qquad C_d \approx \frac{0.61}{\sqrt{1 + 0.61H/y_1}} \qquad (10.41)$$

in the range $H/y_1 < 0.5$. Thus a continuous variation in flow rate is accomplished by raising the gate.

If the tailwater is high, as in Fig. 10.10*c*, free discharge is not possible. The sluice gate is said to be *drowned* or partially drowned. There will be energy dissipation in the exit flow, probably in the form of a drowned hydraulic jump, and the downstream flow will return to subcritical. Equations (10.40) and (10.41) do not apply to this situation, and experimental discharge correlations are necessary [3, 19]. See Prob. P10.77.

10.5 The Hydraulic Jump

In open-channel flow a supercritical flow can change quickly back to a subcritical flow by passing through a hydraulic jump, as in Fig. 10.5. The upstream flow is fast and shallow, and the downstream flow is slow and deep, analogous to the normal shock wave of Fig. 9.8. Unlike the infinitesimally thin normal shock, the hydraulic jump is quite thick, ranging in length from 4 to 6 times the downstream depth y_2 [20].

Being extremely turbulent and agitated, the hydraulic jump is a very effective energy dissipator and is a feature of stilling-basin and spillway applications [20]. Figure 10.11 shows the jump formed in a laboratory open channel. It is very important

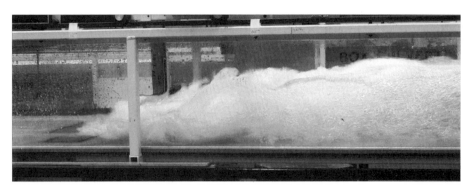

Fig. 10.11 Hydraulic jump in a laboratory open channel. Note the extreme, dissipative turbulence in the downstream flow. Data are given in Prob. P10.94. (*Courtesy of Prof. Hubert Chanson, University of Queensland.*)

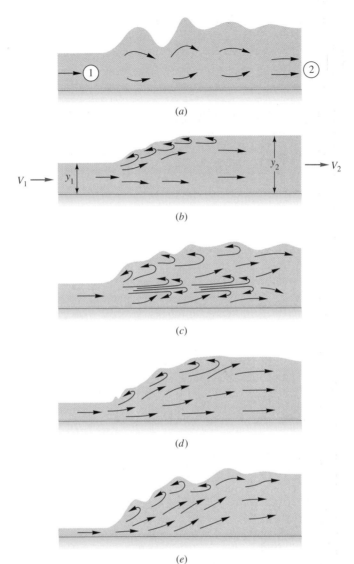

Fig. 10.12 Classification of hydraulic jumps: (*a*) Fr = 1.0 to 1.7: undular jump; (*b*) Fr = 1.7 to 2.5: weak jump; (*c*) Fr = 2.5 to 4.5: oscillating jump; (*d*) Fr = 4.5 to 9.0: steady jump; (*e*) Fr > 9.0: strong jump.
Source: Adapted from U.S. Bureau of Reclamation, "Research studies on stilling Basins, Energy Dissipators, and Associated Appurtenances," Hydraulic Lab, Rep., Hyd-399, June 1, 1995.

that such jumps be located on specially designed aprons; otherwise the channel bottom will be badly scoured by the agitation. Jumps also mix fluids very effectively and have application to sewage and water treatment designs.

Classification

The principal parameter affecting hydraulic jump performance is the upstream Froude number $Fr_1 = V_1/(gy_1)^{1/2}$. The Reynolds number and channel geometry have only a secondary effect. As detailed in Ref. 20, the following ranges of operation can be outlined, as illustrated in Fig. 10.12:

$Fr_1 < 1.0$:	Jump impossible, violates second law of thermodynamics.
$Fr_1 = 1.0$ to 1.7:	Standing-wave or *undular jump* about $4y_2$ long; low dissipation, less than 5 percent.

Fr_1 = 1.7 to 2.5:   Smooth surface rise with small rollers, known as a *weak jump;* dissipation 5 to 15 percent.

Fr_1 = 2.5 to 4.5:   Unstable, *oscillating jump;* each irregular pulsation creates a large wave that can travel downstream for miles, damaging earth banks and other structures. Not recommended for design conditions. Dissipation 15 to 45 percent.

Fr_1 = 4.5 to 9.0:   Stable, well-balanced, *steady jump;* best performance and action, insensitive to downstream conditions. Best design range. Dissipation 45 to 70 percent.

Fr_1 > 9.0:   Rough, somewhat intermittent *strong jump,* but good performance. Dissipation 70 to 85 percent.

Further details can be found in Ref. 20 and Ref. 2, Chap. 15.

Theory for a Horizontal Jump

A jump that occurs on a steep channel slope can be affected by the difference in water-weight components along the flow. The effect is small, however, so the classic theory assumes that the jump occurs on a horizontal bottom.

You will be pleased to know that we have already analyzed this problem in Sec. 10.1. A hydraulic jump is exactly equivalent to the strong fixed wave in Fig. 10.4b, where the change in depth δy is not neglected. If V_1 and y_1 upstream are known, V_2 and y_2 are computed by applying continuity and momentum across the wave, as in Eqs. (10.7) and (10.8). Equation (10.9) is therefore the correct solution for a jump if we interpret C and y in Fig. 10.4b as upstream conditions V_1 and y_1, respectively, with $C - \delta V$ and $y + \delta y$ being the downstream conditions V_2 and y_2, respectively, as in Fig. 10.12b. Equation (10.9) becomes

$$V_1^2 = \tfrac{1}{2}gy_1\,\eta(\eta + 1) \tag{10.42}$$

where $\eta = y_2/y_1$. Introducing the Froude number $Fr_1 = V_1/(gy_1)^{1/2}$ and solving this quadratic equation for η, we obtain

$$\boxed{\frac{2y_2}{y_1} = -1 + (1 + 8\,Fr_1^2)^{1/2}} \tag{10.43}$$

With y_2 thus known, V_2 follows from the wide-channel continuity relation:

$$V_2 = \frac{V_1 y_1}{y_2} \tag{10.44}$$

Finally, we can evaluate the dissipation head loss across the jump from the steady flow energy equation:

$$h_f = E_1 - E_2 = \left(y_1 + \frac{V_1^2}{2g}\right) - \left(y_2 + \frac{V_2^2}{2g}\right)$$

Introducing y_2 and V_2 from Eqs. (10.43) and (10.44), we find after considerable algebraic manipulation that

$$\boxed{h_f = \frac{(y_2 - y_1)^3}{4y_1 y_2}} \tag{10.45}$$

Equation (10.45) shows that the dissipation loss is positive only if $y_2 > y_1$, which is a requirement of the second law of thermodynamics. Equation (10.43) then requires that $Fr_1 > 1.0$; that is, the upstream flow must be supercritical. Finally, Eq. (10.44) shows that $V_2 < V_1$ and the downstream flow is subcritical. All these results agree with our previous experience analyzing the normal shock wave.

The present theory is for hydraulic jumps in wide or rectangular horizontal channels. For the theory of prismatic or sloping channels see advanced texts [for example, 2, Chaps. 15 and 16].

EXAMPLE 10.8

Water flows in a wide channel at $q = 10$ m³/(s · m) and $y_1 = 1.25$ m. If the flow undergoes a hydraulic jump, compute (a) y_2, (b) V_2, (c) Fr_2, (d) h_f, (e) the percentage dissipation, (f) the power dissipated per unit width, and (g) the temperature rise due to dissipation if $c_p = 4200$ J/(kg · K).

Solution

Part (a) The upstream velocity is

$$V_1 = \frac{q}{y_1} = \frac{10 \text{ m}^3/(\text{s} \cdot \text{m})}{1.25 \text{ m}} = 8.0 \text{ m/s}$$

The upstream Froude number is therefore

$$Fr_1 = \frac{V_1}{(gy_1)^{1/2}} = \frac{8.0}{[9.81(1.25)]^{1/2}} = 2.285$$

From Fig. 10.12 this is a weak jump. The depth y_2 is obtained from Eq. (10.43):

$$\frac{2y_2}{y_1} = -1 + [1 + 8(2.285)^2]^{1/2} = 5.54$$

or $\quad y_2 = \tfrac{1}{2}y_1(5.54) = \tfrac{1}{2}(1.25)(5.54) = 3.46 \text{ m}$ *Ans. (a)*

Part (b) From Eq. (10.44) the downstream velocity is

$$V_2 = \frac{V_1 y_1}{y_2} = \frac{8.0(1.25)}{3.46} = 2.89 \text{ m/s} \qquad \textit{Ans. (b)}$$

Part (c) The downstream Froude number is

$$Fr_2 = \frac{V_2}{(gy_2)^{1/2}} = \frac{2.89}{[9.81(3.46)]^{1/2}} = 0.496 \qquad \textit{Ans. (c)}$$

Part (d) As expected, Fr_2 is subcritical. From Eq. (10.45) the dissipation loss is

$$h_f = \frac{(3.46 - 1.25)^3}{4(3.46)(1.25)} = 0.625 \text{ m} \qquad \textit{Ans. (d)}$$

Part (e) The percentage dissipation relates h_f to upstream energy:

$$E_1 = y_1 + \frac{V_1^2}{2g} = 1.25 + \frac{(8.0)^2}{2(9.81)} = 4.51 \text{ m}$$

Hence $\qquad$ Percentage loss $= (100) \dfrac{h_f}{E_1} = \dfrac{100(0.625)}{4.51} = 14$ percent $\qquad$ *Ans. (e)*

Part (f) The power dissipated per unit width is

$$\text{Power} = \rho g q h_f = (9800 \text{ N/m}^3)[10 \text{ m}^3/(\text{s} \cdot \text{m})](0.625 \text{ m})$$
$$= 61.3 \text{ kW/m} \qquad \qquad \text{\textit{Ans. (f)}}$$

Part (g) Finally, the mass flow rate is $\dot{m} = \rho q = (1000 \text{ kg/m}^3)[10 \text{ m}^3/(\text{s} \cdot \text{m})] = 10{,}000 \text{ kg/(s} \cdot \text{m)}$, and the temperature rise from the steady flow energy equation is

$$\text{Power dissipated} = \dot{m} c_p \, \Delta T$$

or $\qquad\qquad$ 61,300 W/m $= [10{,}000 \text{ kg/(s} \cdot \text{m)}][4200 \text{ J/(kg} \cdot \text{K)}]\Delta T$

from which

$$\Delta T = 0.0015 \text{ K} \qquad\qquad \text{\textit{Ans. (g)}}$$

The dissipation is large, but the temperature rise is negligible.

10.6 Gradually Varied Flow[3]

In practical channel flows both the bottom slope and the water depth change with position, as in Fig. 10.3. An approximate analysis is possible if the flow is gradually varied, as is the case if the slopes are small and changes not too sudden. The basic assumptions are

1. Slowly changing bottom slope.
2. Slowly changing water depth (no hydraulic jumps).
3. Slowly changing cross section.
4. One-dimensional velocity distribution.
5. Pressure distribution approximately hydrostatic.

The flow then satisfies the continuity relation (10.1) plus the energy equation with bottom friction losses included. The two unknowns for steady flow are velocity $V(x)$ and water depth $y(x)$, where x is distance along the channel.

Basic Differential Equation

Consider the length of channel dx illustrated in Fig. 10.13. All the terms that enter the steady flow energy equation are shown, and the balance between x and $x + dx$ is

$$\frac{V^2}{2g} + y + S_0 \, dx = S \, dx + \frac{V^2}{2g} + d\left(\frac{V^2}{2g}\right) + y + dy$$

or $\qquad\qquad\qquad \dfrac{dy}{dx} + \dfrac{d}{dx}\left(\dfrac{V^2}{2g}\right) = S_0 - S \qquad\qquad\qquad (10.46)$

where S_0 is the slope of the channel bottom (positive as shown in Fig. 10.13) and S is the slope of the EGL (which drops due to wall friction losses).

---

[3]This section may be omitted without loss of continuity.

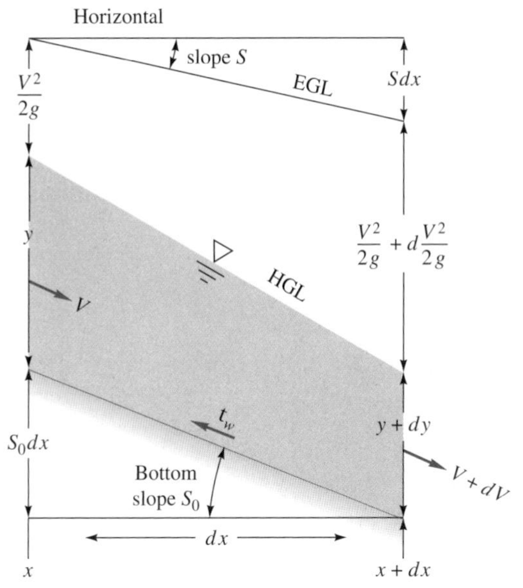

Fig. 10.13 Energy balance between two sections in a gradually varied open-channel flow.

To eliminate the velocity derivative, differentiate the continuity relation:

$$\frac{dQ}{dx} = 0 = A\frac{dV}{dx} + V\frac{dA}{dx} \tag{10.47}$$

But $dA = b_0\,dy$, where b_0 is the channel width at the surface. Eliminating dV/dx between Eqs. (10.46) and (10.47), we obtain

$$\frac{dy}{dx}\left(1 - \frac{V^2 b_0}{gA}\right) = S_0 - S \tag{10.48}$$

Finally, recall from Eq. (10.37) that $V^2 b_0/(gA)$ is the square of the Froude number of the local channel flow. The final desired form of the gradually varied flow equation is

$$\boxed{\frac{dy}{dx} = \frac{S_0 - S}{1 - \mathrm{Fr}^2}} \tag{10.49}$$

This equation changes sign according to whether the Froude number is subcritical or supercritical and is analogous to the one-dimensional gas dynamic area-change formula (9.40).

The numerator of Eq. (10.49) changes sign according to whether S_0 is greater or less than S, which is the slope equivalent to uniform flow at the same discharge Q:

$$\boxed{S = S_{0n} = \frac{f}{D_h}\frac{V^2}{2g} = \frac{V^2}{R_h C^2} = \frac{n^2 V^2}{\alpha^2 R_h^{4/3}}} \tag{10.50}$$

where C is the Chézy coefficient. The behavior of Eq. (10.49) thus depends on the relative magnitude of the local bottom slope $S_0(x)$, compared with (1) uniform flow,

$y = y_n$, and (2) critical flow, $y = y_c$. As in Eq. (10.38), the dimensional parameter α^2 equals 1.0 for SI units and 2.208 for BG units.

Classification of Solutions   It is customary to compare the actual channel slope S_0 with the critical slope S_c for the same Q from Eq. (10.38). There are five classes for S_0, giving rise to 12 distinct types of solution curves, all of which are illustrated in Fig. 10.14:

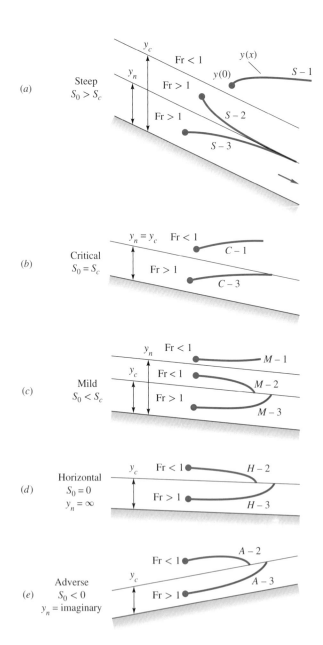

Fig. 10.14 Gradually varied flow for five classes of channel slope, showing the 12 basic solution curves.

Slope class	Slope notation	Depth class	Solution curves
$S_0 > S_c$	Steep	$y_c > y_n$	S-1, S-2, S-3
$S_0 = S_c$	Critical	$y_c = y_n$	C-1, C-3
$S_0 < S_c$	Mild	$y_c < y_n$	M-1, M-2, M-3
$S_0 = 0$	Horizontal	$y_n = \infty$	H-2, H-3
$S_0 < 0$	Adverse	$y_n =$ imaginary	A-2, A-3

The solution letters S, C, M, H, and A obviously denote the names of the five types of slopes. The numbers 1, 2, 3 relate to the position of the initial point on the solution curve with respect to the normal depth y_n and the critical depth y_c. In type 1 solutions, the initial point is above both y_n and y_c, and in all cases the water depth solution $y(x)$ becomes even deeper and farther away from y_n and y_c. In type 2 solutions, the initial point lies between y_n and y_c, and if there is no change in S_0 or roughness, the solution tends asymptotically toward the lower of y_n or y_c. In type 3 cases, the initial point lies below both y_n and y_c, and the solution curve tends asymptotically toward the lower of these.

Figure 10.14 shows the basic character of the local solutions, but in practice, of course, S_0 varies with x, and the overall solution patches together the various cases to form a continuous depth profile $y(x)$ compatible with a given initial condition and a given discharge Q. There is a fine discussion of various composite solutions in Ref. 2, Chap. 9; see also Ref. 22, Sec. 12.7.

Numerical Solution

The basic relation for gradually varied flow, Eq. (10.49), is a first-order ordinary differential equation that can be easily solved numerically. For a given constant-volume flow rate Q, it may be written in the form

$$\frac{dy}{dx} = \frac{S_0 - n^2 Q^2/(\alpha^2 A^2 R_h^{4/3})}{1 - Q^2 b_0/(g A^3)} \tag{10.51}$$

subject to an initial condition $y = y_0$ at $x = x_0$. It is assumed that the bottom slope $S_0(x)$ and the cross-sectional shape parameters (b_0, P, A) are known everywhere along the channel. Then one may solve Eq. (10.51) for local water depth $y(x)$ by any standard numerical method. The author uses an Excel spreadsheet for a personal computer. Step sizes Δx may be selected so that each change Δy is limited to no greater than, say, 1 percent. The solution curves are generally well behaved unless there are discontinuous changes in channel parameters. Note that if one approaches the critical depth y_c, the denominator of Eq. (10.51) approaches zero, so small step sizes are required. It helps physically to know what type of solution curve (M-1, S-2, or the like) you are proceeding along, but this is not mathematically necessary.

EXAMPLE 10.9

Let us extend the data of Example 10.5 to compute a portion of the profile shape. Given is a wide channel with $n = 0.022$, $S_0 = 0.0048$, and $q = 50$ ft^3/(s · ft). If $y_0 = 3$ ft at $x = 0$, how far along the channel $x = L$ does it take the depth to rise to $y_L = 4$ ft? Is the 4-ft depth position upstream or downstream in Fig. E10.9a?

Solution

In Example 10.5 we computed $y_c = 4.27$ ft. Since our initial depth $y = 3$ ft is less than y_c, we know the flow is supercritical. Let us also compute the normal depth for the given slope S_0 by setting $q = 50$ ft^3/(s · ft) in the Chézy formula (10.19) with $R_h = y_n$:

$$q = \frac{\alpha}{n} A R_h^{2/3} S_0^{1/2} = \frac{1.486}{0.022} [y_n (1 \text{ ft})] y_n^{2/3} (0.0048)^{1/2} = 50 \text{ ft}^3/(\text{s} \cdot \text{ft})$$

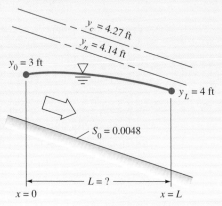

$y_c = 4.27$ ft

$y_n = 4.14$ ft

$y_0 = 3$ ft

$y_L = 4$ ft

$S_0 = 0.0048$

$L = ?$

$x = 0$ $x = L$

E10.9a

Solve for: $y_n \approx 4.14$ ft

Thus both $y(0) = 3$ ft and $y(L) = 4$ ft are less than y_n, which is less than y_c, so we *must* be on an S-3 curve, as in Fig. 10.14a. For a wide channel, Eq. (10.51) reduces to

$$\frac{dy}{dx} = \frac{S_0 - n^2 q^2/(\alpha^2 y^{10/3})}{1 - q^2/(gy^3)}$$

$$\approx \frac{0.0048 - (0.022)^2 (50)^2/(2.208 y^{10/3})}{1 - (50)^2/(32.2 y^3)} \qquad \text{with } y(0) = 3 \text{ ft}$$

The initial slope is $y'(0) \approx 0.00494$, and a step size $\Delta x = 5$ ft would cause a change $\Delta y \approx (0.00494)(5 \text{ ft}) \approx 0.025$ ft, less than 1 percent. We therefore integrate numerically with

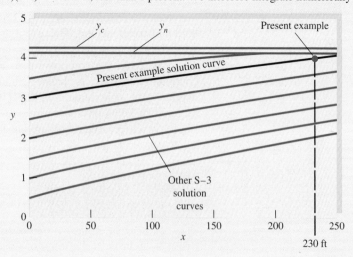

y_c

y_n

Present example

Present example solution curve

y

Other S–3 solution curves

x

E10.9b

230 ft

$\Delta x = 5$ ft to determine when the depth $y = 4$ ft is achieved. Tabulate some values:

x, ft	0	50	100	150	200	230
y, ft	3.00	3.25	3.48	3.70	3.90	4.00

The water depth, still supercritical, reaches $y = 4$ ft at

$$x \approx 230 \text{ ft downstream} \qquad\qquad Ans.$$

We verify from Fig. 10.14a that water depth does increase downstream on an S-3 curve. The solution curve $y(x)$ is shown as the bold line in Fig. E10.9b.

For little extra effort we can investigate the entire family of S-3 solution curves for this problem. Figure E10.9b also shows what happens if the initial depth is varied from 0.5 to 3.5 ft in increments of 0.5 ft. All S-3 solutions smoothly rise and asymptotically approach the uniform flow condition $y = y_n = 4.14$ ft.

Approximate Solution for Irregular Channels

Direct numerical solution of Eq. (10.51) is appropriate when we have analytical formulas for the channel variations $A(x)$, $S_0(x)$, $n(x)$, $b_0(x)$, and $R_h(x)$. For natural channels, however, cross sections are often highly irregular, and data can be sparse and unevenly spaced. For such cases, civil engineers use an approximate method to estimate gradual flow changes. Write Eq. (10.46) in finite-difference form between two depths y and $y + \Delta y$:

$$\Delta x \approx \frac{E(y + \Delta y) - E(y)}{(S_0 - S_{avg})} \quad \text{where } E = y + \frac{V^2}{2g} \qquad (10.52)$$

Average values of velocity, slope, and hydraulic radius are estimated between the two sections. For example,

$$V_{avg} \approx \frac{1}{2}[V(y) + V(y + \Delta y)]; \; R_{h,\,avg} \approx \frac{1}{2}[R_h(y) + R_h(y + \Delta y)]; \; S_{avg} \approx \frac{n^2 V_{avg}^2}{\alpha^2 R_{h,\,avg}^{4/3}}$$

Again, computation can proceed either upstream or downstream, using small values of Δy. Further details of such computations are given in Chap. 10 of Ref. 2.

EXAMPLE 10.10

Repeat Example 10.9 using the approximate method of Eq. (10.52) with a 0.25-foot increment in Δy. Find the distance required for y to rise from 3 ft to 4 ft.

Solution

Recall from Example 10.9 that $n = 0.022$, $S_0 = 0.0048$, and $q = 50$ ft³/(s-ft). Note that $R_h = y$ for a wide channel. Make a table with y varying from 3.0 to 4.0 ft in increments of 0.25 ft, computing $V = q/y$, $E = y + V^2/(2g)$, and $S_{avg} = [n^2 V^2/(2.208 y^{4/3})]_{avg}$:

y, ft	V (ft/s) $= 50/y$	$E = y + V^2/(2g)$	S	S_{avg}	$\Delta x = \Delta E/(S_0 - S)_{avg}$	$x = \Sigma\Delta x$
3.0	16.67	7.313	0.01407	—	—	0
3.25	15.38	6.925	0.01078	0.01243	51	51
3.5	14.29	6.669	0.00842	0.00960	53	104
3.75	13.33	6.511	0.00669	0.00756	57	161
4.0 ft	12.50 ft/s	6.426 ft	0.00539	0.00604	69 ft	230 ft

Comment: The accuracy is excellent, giving the same result, $x = 230$ ft, as the Excel spreadsheet numerical integration in Example 10.9. Much of this accuracy is due to the smooth, slowly varying nature of the profile. Less precision is expected when the channel is irregular and given as uneven cross sections.

Some Illustrative Composite-Flow Transitions

The solution curves in Fig. 10.14 are somewhat simplistic, since they postulate constant-bottom slopes. In practice, channel slopes can vary greatly, $S_0 = S_0(x)$, and the solution curves can cross between two regimes. Other parameter changes, such as $A(x)$, $b_0(x)$, and $n(x)$, can cause interesting composite-flow profiles. Some examples are shown in Fig. 10.15.[4]

Figure 10.15*a* shows a transition from a mild slope to a steep slope in a constant-width channel. The initial M-2 curve must change to an S-2 curve farther down the steep slope. The only way this can happen physically is for the solution curve to pass smoothly through the critical depth, as shown. The critical point is mathematically *singular* [2, Sec. 9.6], and the flow near this point is generally *rapidly,* not gradually, varied. The flow pattern, accelerating from subcritical to supercritical, is similar to a converging–diverging nozzle in gas dynamics. Other scenarios for Fig. 10.15*a* are impossible. For example, the upstream curve cannot be M-1, for the break in slope would cause an S-1 curve that would move away from uniform steep flow.

Figure 10.15*b* shows a mild slope that suddenly changes to an even milder slope. The approach flow is assumed uniform, and the break in slope makes its presence known upstream. The water depth moves smoothly along an M-1 curve until it exactly merges, at the break point, with a uniform flow at the new (milder) depth y_{n2}.

Figure 10.15*c* shows a steep slope that suddenly changes to a less steep slope. Note for both slopes that $y_n < y_c$. Because of the supercritical ($V > V_c$) approach flow, the break in slope cannot make its presence known upstream. Thus, not until the break point does an S-3 curve form, and then this profile proceeds smoothly to uniform flow at the new (higher) normal depth.

Figure 10.15*d* shows a steep slope that suddenly changes to a mild slope. Various cases may occur, possibly beyond the ability of this author to describe. The two cases shown depend on the relative magnitude of the mild slope. If the downstream depth y_{n2} is shallow, an M-3 curve will start at the break and develop until the local supercritical flow is just sufficient to form a hydraulic jump up to the new normal depth. As y_{n2} increases, the jump moves upstream until, for the "high" case shown, it forms on the steep side, followed by an S-1 curve that merges into normal depth y_{n2} at the break point.

---

[4]The author is indebted to Prof. Bruce Larock for clarification of these transition profiles.

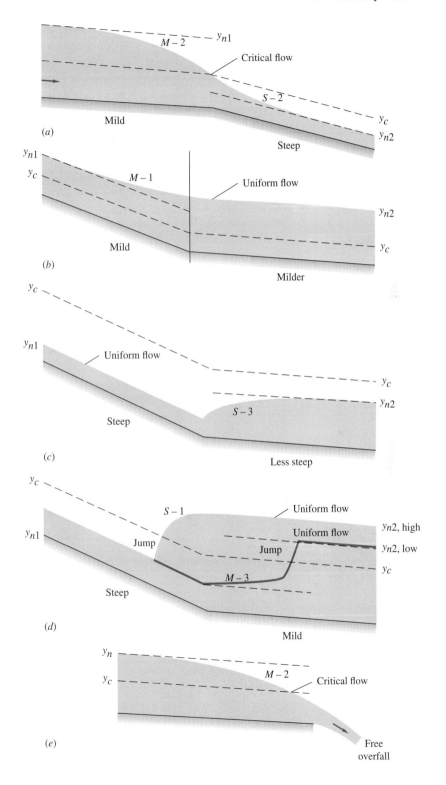

Fig. 10.15 Some examples of composite-flow transition profiles.

Figure 10.15*e* illustrates a *free overfall* with a mild slope. This acts as a *control section* to the upstream flow, which then forms an M-2 curve and accelerates to critical flow near the overfall. The falling stream will be supercritical. The overfall "controls" the water depths upstream and can serve as an initial condition for computation of $y(x)$. This is the type of flow that occurs in a weir or waterfall, Sec. 10.7.

The examples in Fig. 10.15 show that changing conditions in open-channel flow can result in complex flow patterns. Many more examples of composite-flow profiles are given in Ref. 2, pp. 229–233.

10.7 Flow Measurement and Control by Weirs

A *weir*, of which the ordinary dam is an example, is a channel obstruction over which the flow must deflect. For simple geometries the channel discharge Q correlates with gravity and with the blockage height H to which the upstream flow is backed up above the weir elevation (see Fig. 10.16). Thus a weir is a simple but effective open-channel flowmeter. We used a weir as an example of dimensional analysis in Prob. P5.32.

Figure 10.16 shows two common weirs, sharp-crested and broad-crested, assumed to be very wide. In both cases the flow upstream is subcritical, accelerates to critical near the top of the weir, and spills over into a supercritical *nappe*. For both weirs the discharge q per unit width is proportional to $g^{1/2}H^{3/2}$ but with somewhat different coefficients. The short-crested (or thin-plate) weir nappe should be *ventilated* to the

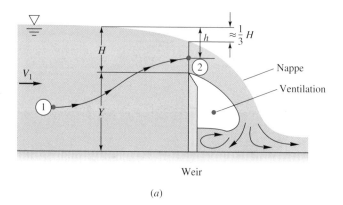

(*a*)

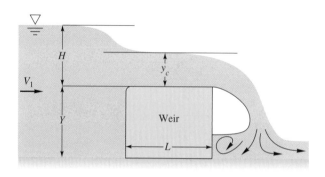

Fig. 10.16 Flow over wide, well-ventilated weirs: (*a*) sharp-crested; (*b*) broad-crested.

(*b*)

atmosphere; that is, it should spring clear of the weir crest. Unventilated or drowned nappes are more difficult to correlate and depend on tailwater conditions. (The spillway of Fig. 10.11 is a sort of unventilated weir.)

A very complete discussion of weirs, including other designs such as the polygonal "Crump" weir and various contracting flumes, is given in the text by Ackers et al. [23]. See Prob. P10.122.

Analysis of Sharp-Crested Weirs

It is possible to analyze weir flow by inviscid potential theory with an unknown (but solvable) free surface, as in Fig. P8.71. Here, however, we simply use one-dimensional flow theory plus dimensional analysis to develop suitable weir flow rate correlations.

A very early theoretical approach is credited to J. Weisbach in 1855. The velocity head at any point 2 above the weir crest is assumed to equal the total head upstream; in other words, Bernoulli's equation is used with no losses:

$$\frac{V_2^2}{2g} + H - h \approx \frac{V_1^2}{2g} + H \qquad \text{or} \qquad V_2(h) \approx \sqrt{2gh + V_1^2}$$

where h is the vertical distance down to point 2, as shown in Fig. 10.16a. If we accept for the moment, without proof, that the flow over the crest draws down to $h_{min} \approx H/3$, the volume flow $q = Q/b$ over the crest is approximately

$$q = \int_{crest} V_2 \, dh \approx \int_{H/3}^{H} (2gh + V_1^2)^{1/2} \, dh$$

$$= \frac{2}{3} \sqrt{2g} \left[\left(H + \frac{V_1^2}{2g} \right)^{3/2} - \left(\frac{H}{3} + \frac{V_1^2}{2g} \right)^{3/2} \right]$$

Normally the upstream velocity head $V_1^2/(2g)$ is neglected, so this expression reduces to

Sharp-crested theory: $$q \approx 0.81 (\tfrac{2}{3})(2g)^{1/2} H^{3/2} \qquad (10.53)$$

This formula is functionally correct, but the coefficient 0.81 is too high and should be replaced by an experimentally determined discharge coefficient.

Analysis of Broad-Crested Weirs

The broad-crested weir of Fig. 10.16b can be analyzed more accurately because it creates a short run of nearly one-dimensional critical flow, as shown. Bernoulli's equation from upstream to the weir crest yields

$$\frac{V_1^2}{2g} + Y + H \approx \frac{V_c^2}{2g} + Y + y_c$$

If the crest is very wide into the paper, $V_c^2 = gy_c$ from Eq. (10.33). Thus we can solve for

$$y_c \approx \frac{2H}{3} + \frac{V_1^2}{3g} \approx \frac{2H}{3}$$

This result was used without proof to derive Eq. (10.53). Finally, the flow rate follows from wide-channel critical flow, Eq. (10.32):

Broad-crested theory: $q = \sqrt{gy_c^3} \approx \dfrac{1}{\sqrt{3}}\left(\dfrac{2}{3}\right)\sqrt{2g}\left(H + \dfrac{V_1^2}{2g}\right)^{3/2}$ (10.54)

Again we may usually neglect the upstream velocity head $V_1^2/(2g)$. The coefficient $1/\sqrt{3} \approx 0.577$ is about right, but experimental data are preferred.

Experimental Weir Discharge Coefficients

Theoretical weir flow formulas may be modified experimentally as follows: Eliminate the numerical coefficients $\frac{2}{3}$ and $\sqrt{2}$, for which there is much sentimental attachment in the literature, and reduce the formula to

$$Q_{\text{weir}} = C_d b\sqrt{g}\left(H + \frac{V_1^2}{2g}\right)^{3/2} \approx C_d b\sqrt{g}H^{3/2}$$ (10.55)

where b is the crest width and C_d is a dimensionless, experimentally determined *weir discharge coefficient,* which may vary with the weir geometry, Reynolds number, and Weber number. Many data for many different weirs have been reported in the literature, as detailed in Ref. 23.

An accurate (± 2 percent) composite correlation for wide ventilated sharp crests is recommended as follows [23]:

Wide sharp-crested weir: $C_d \approx 0.564 + 0.0846\,\dfrac{H}{Y}$ for $\dfrac{H}{Y} \leq 2$ (10.56)

The Reynolds numbers $V_1 H/\nu$ for these data vary from 1 E4 to 2 E6, but the formula should apply to higher Re, such as large dams on rivers.

The broad-crested weir of Fig. 10.16b is considerably more sensitive to geometric parameters, including the surface roughness ε of the crest. If the leading-edge nose is rounded, $R/L \geq 0.05$, available data [23, Chap. 7] may be correlated as follows:

Round-nosed broad-crested weir: $C_d \approx 0.544\left(1 - \dfrac{\delta^*/L}{H/L}\right)^{3/2}$ (10.57)

where $\dfrac{\delta^*}{L} \approx 0.001 + 0.2\sqrt{\varepsilon/L}$

The chief effect is due to turbulent boundary layer displacement-thickness growth δ^* on the crest as compared to upstream head H. The formula is limited to $H/L < 0.7$, $\varepsilon/L \leq 0.002$, and $V_1 H/\nu > 3$ E5. If the nose is round, there is no significant effect of weir height Y, at least if $H/Y < 2.4$.

If the broad-crested weir has a sharp leading edge, thus commonly called a *rectangular* weir, the discharge may depend on the weir height Y. However, in a certain range of weir height and length, C_d is nearly constant:

Sharp-nosed broad-crested weir: $C_d \approx 0.462$ for $0.08 < \dfrac{H}{L} < 0.33$

and $0.22 < \dfrac{H}{Y} < 0.56$ (10.58)

Surface roughness is not a significant factor here. For $H/L < 0.08$ there is large scatter (± 10 percent) in the data. For $H/L > 0.33$ and $H/Y > 0.56$, C_d increases up to 10 percent due to each parameter, and complex charts are needed for the discharge coefficient [19, Chap. 5].

EXAMPLE 10.11

A weir in a horizontal channel is 1 m high and 4 m wide. The water depth upstream is 1.6 m. Estimate the discharge if the weir is (a) sharp-crested and (b) round-nosed with an unfinished concrete broad crest 1.2 m long. Neglect $V_1^2/(2g)$.

Solution

Part (a)

We are given $Y = 1$ m and $H + Y \approx 1.6$ m, hence $H \approx 0.6$ m. Since $H \ll b$, we assume that the weir is "wide." For a sharp crest, Eq. (10.56) applies:

$$C_d \approx 0.564 + 0.0846\,\frac{0.6 \text{ m}}{1 \text{ m}} \approx 0.615$$

Then the discharge is given by the basic correlation, Eq. (10.55):

$$Q = C_d b \sqrt{g} H^{3/2} = (0.615)(4 \text{ m})\sqrt{(9.81 \text{ m/s}^2)}(0.6 \text{ m})^{3/2} \approx 3.58 \text{ m}^3/\text{s} \qquad Ans.\ (a)$$

We check that $H/Y = 0.6 < 2.0$ for Eq. (10.56) to be valid. From continuity, $V_1 = Q/(by_1) = 3.58/[(4.0)(1.6)] = 0.56$ m/s, giving a Reynolds number $V_1 H/\nu \approx 3.4$ E5.

Part (b)

For a round-nosed broad-crested weir, Eq. (10.57) applies. For an unfinished concrete surface, read $\varepsilon \approx 2.4$ mm from Table 10.1. Then the displacement thickness is

$$\frac{\delta^*}{L} \approx 0.001 + 0.2\sqrt{\varepsilon/L} = 0.001 + 0.2\left(\frac{0.0024 \text{ m}}{1.2 \text{ m}}\right)^{1/2} \approx 0.00994$$

Then Eq. (10.57) predicts the discharge coefficient:

$$C_d \approx 0.544\left(1 - \frac{0.00994}{0.6 \text{ m}/1.2 \text{ m}}\right)^{3/2} \approx 0.528$$

The estimated flow rate is thus

$$Q = C_d b \sqrt{g} H^{3/2} = 0.528(4 \text{ m})\sqrt{(9.81 \text{ m}^2/\text{s})}(0.6 \text{ m})^{3/2} \approx 3.07 \text{ m}^3/\text{s} \qquad Ans.\ (b)$$

Check that $H/L = 0.5 < 0.7$ as required. The approach Reynolds number is $V_1 H/\nu \approx 2.9$ E5, just barely below the recommended limit in Eq. (10.57).

Since $V_1 \approx 0.5$ m/s, $V_1^2/(2g) \approx 0.012$ m, so the error in taking total head equal to 0.6 m is about 2 percent. We could correct this for upstream velocity head if desired.

Other Thin-Plate Weir Designs

Weirs are often used for flow measurement and control of artificial channels. The two most common shapes are a rectangle and a V notch, as shown in Table 10.2. All should be fully ventilated and not drowned.

Table 10.2a shows a full-width rectangle, which will have slight end-boundary-layer effects but no end contractions. For a thin-plate design, the top is approximately

Table 10.2 Thin-Plate Weirs for Flow Measurement

Thin-plate weir	Flow-rate correlation
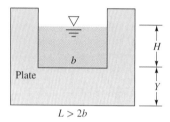 (a) Full-width rectangle.	$Q \approx \left(0.564 + 0.0846\,\dfrac{H}{Y}\right) bg^{1/2}H^{3/2}$
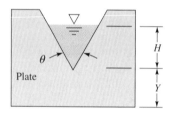 $L > 2b$ (b) Rectangle with side contractions.	$Q \approx 0.581\,(b - 0.1H)g^{1/2}H^{3/2} \quad H < 0.5Y$
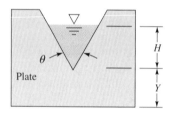 (c) V notch.	$Q \approx 0.44 \tan\dfrac{\theta}{2}\,g^{1/2}H^{5/2} \quad 20° < \theta < 100°$

sharp-crested, and Eq. (10.56) should give adequate accuracy, as shown in the table. Since the overfall spans the entire channel, artificial ventilation may be needed, such as holes in the channel walls.

Table 10.2b shows a partial-width rectangle, $b < L$, which will cause the sides of the overfall to contract inward and reduce the flow rate. An adequate contraction correction [23, 24] is to reduce the effective weir width by $0.1H$, as shown in the table. It seems, however, that this type of weir is rather sensitive to small effects, such as plate thickness and sidewall boundary layer growth. Small heads ($H < 75$ mm) and small slot widths ($b < 30$ cm) are not recommended. See Refs. 23 and 24 for further details.

The V notch, in Table 10.2c, is intrinsically interesting in that its overfall has only one length scale, H—there is no separate "width." The discharge will thus be proportional to $H^{5/2}$, rather than a power of $\frac{3}{2}$. Application of Bernoulli's equation to the triangular opening, in the spirit of Eq. (10.52), leads to the following ideal flow rate for a V notch:

V notch: $$Q_{ideal} = \frac{8\sqrt{2}}{15} \tan\frac{\theta}{2}\,g^{1/2}H^{5/2} \qquad (10.59)$$

where θ is the total included angle of the notch. The actual measured flow is about 40 percent less than this, due to contraction similar to a thin-plate orifice. In terms of an experimental discharge coefficient, the recommended formula is

$$Q_{V\text{ notch}} \approx C_d \tan \frac{\theta}{2} g^{1/2} H^{5/2} \qquad C_d \approx 0.44 \qquad \text{for} \qquad 20° < \theta < 100° \qquad (10.60)$$

for heads $H > 50$ mm. For smaller heads, both Reynolds number and Weber number effects may be important, and a recommended correction [23] is

$$\text{Low heads, } H < 50 \text{ mm:} \qquad C_{d,V\text{ notch}} \approx 0.44 + \frac{0.9}{(\text{Re We})^{1/6}} \qquad (10.61)$$

where $\text{Re} = \rho g^{1/2} H^{3/2}/\mu$ and $\text{We} = \rho g H^2/Y$, with Y being the coefficient of surface tension. Liquids other than water may be used with this formula, as long as $\text{Re} > 300/\tan(\theta/2)^{3/4}$ and $\text{We} > 300$.

A number of other thin-plate weir designs—trapezoidal, parabolic, circular arc, and U-shaped—are discussed in Ref. 25, which also contains considerable data on broad-crested weirs. See also Refs. 29 and 30.

EXAMPLE 10.12

A V notch weir is to be designed to meter an irrigation channel flow. For ease in reading the upstream water-level gage, a reading $H \geq 30$ cm is desired for the design flow rate of 150 m³/h. What is the appropriate angle θ for the V notch?

Solution

- *Assumptions:* Steady flow, negligible Weber number effect because $H > 50$ mm.
- *Approach:* Equation (10.60) applies with, we hope, a notch angle $20° < \theta < 100°$.
- *Property values:* If surface tension is neglected, no fluid properties are needed. Why?
- *Solution:* Apply Equation (10.60) to the known flow rate and solve for θ:

$$Q = \frac{150 \text{ m}^3/\text{h}}{3600 \text{ s/h}} = 0.0417 \frac{\text{m}^3}{\text{s}} \geq C_d \tan\left(\frac{\theta}{2}\right) g^{1/2} H^{5/2} = 0.44 \tan\left(\frac{\theta}{2}\right)\left(9.81 \frac{\text{m}}{\text{s}^2}\right)^{1/2} (0.3 \text{ m})^{5/2}$$

$$\text{Solve for } \tan\left(\frac{\theta}{2}\right) \leq 0.613 \quad \text{or} \quad \theta \leq 63° \qquad \qquad Ans.$$

- *Comments:* An angle of 63° will create an upstream head of 30 cm. Any angle less than that will create an even larger head. Weir formulas depend primarily on gravity and geometry. Fluid properties such as (ρ, μ, Y) enter only as slight modifications or as correction factors.

Backwater Curves

A weir is a flow barrier that not only alters the local flow over the weir but also modifies the flow depth distribution far upstream. Any strong barrier in an open-channel flow creates a *backwater curve*, which can be computed by the gradually varied flow theory of Sec. 10.6. If Q is known, the weir formula, Eq. (10.55), determines H and hence the water depth just upstream of the weir, $y = H + Y$, where

Y is the weir height. We then compute $y(x)$ upstream of the weir from Eq. (10.51), following in this case an M-1 curve (Fig. 10.14c). Such a barrier, where the water depth correlates with the flow rate, is called a channel *control point*. These are the starting points for numerical analysis of floodwater profiles in rivers [26].

EXAMPLE 10.13

A rectangular channel 8 m wide, with a flow rate of 30 m³/s, encounters a 4-m-high sharp-edged dam, as shown in Fig. E10.13a. Determine the water depth 2 km upstream if the channel slope is $S_0 = 0.0004$ and $n = 0.025$.

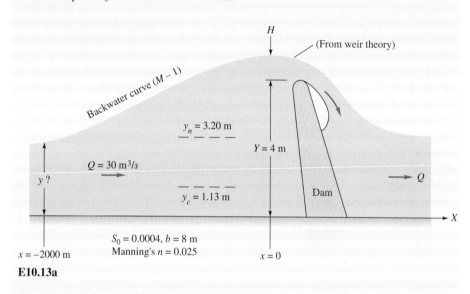

E10.13a

Solution

First determine the head H produced by the dam, using sharp-crested full-width weir theory, Eq. (10.56):

$$Q = 30 \text{ m}^3/\text{s} = C_d b g^{1/2} H^{3/2} = \left(0.564 + 0.0846 \frac{H}{4 \text{ m}}\right)(8 \text{ m})(9.81 \text{ m/s}^2)^{1/2} H^{3/2}$$

Since the term $0.0846H/4$ in parentheses is small, we may proceed by iteration to the solution $H \approx 1.59$ m. Then our initial condition at $x = 0$, just upstream of the dam, is $y(0) = Y + H = 4 + 1.59 = 5.59$ m. Compare this to the critical depth from Eq. (10.30):

$$y_c = \left(\frac{Q^2}{b^2 g}\right)^{1/3} = \left[\frac{(30 \text{ m}^3/\text{s})^2}{(8 \text{ m})^2(9.81 \text{ m/s}^2)}\right]^{1/3} = 1.13 \text{ m}$$

Since $y(0)$ is greater than y_c, the flow upstream is subcritical. Finally, for reference purposes, estimate the normal depth from the Chézy equation (10.19):

$$Q = 30 \text{ m}^3/\text{s} = \frac{\alpha}{n} b y R_h^{2/3} S_0^{1/2} = \frac{1.0}{0.025}(8 \text{ m}) y_n \left(\frac{8 y_n}{8 + 2 y_n}\right)^{2/3} (0.0004)^{1/2}$$

By trial and error, solve for $y_n \approx 3.20$ m. If there are no changes in channel width or slope, the water depth far upstream of the dam will approach this value. All these reference values $y(0)$, y_c, and y_n are shown in Fig. E10.13b.

Since $y(0) > y_n > y_c$, the solution will be an M-1 curve as computed from gradually varied theory, Eq. (10.51), for a rectangular channel with the given input data:

$$\frac{dy}{dx} \approx \frac{S_0 - n^2 Q^2/(\alpha^2 A^2 R_h^{4/3})}{1 - Q^2 b_0/(gA^3)} \qquad \alpha = 1.0 \qquad A = 8y \qquad n = 0.025 \qquad R_h = \frac{8y}{8 + 2y} \qquad b_0 = 8$$

Beginning with $y = 5.59$ m at $x = 0$, we integrate backward to $x = -2000$ m. For the Runge-Kutta method, four-figure accuracy is achieved for $\Delta x = -100$ m. The complete solution curve is shown in Fig. E10.13b. The desired solution value is

At $x = -2000$ m: $\hspace{4cm} y \approx 5.00$ m $\hspace{4cm}$ *Ans.*

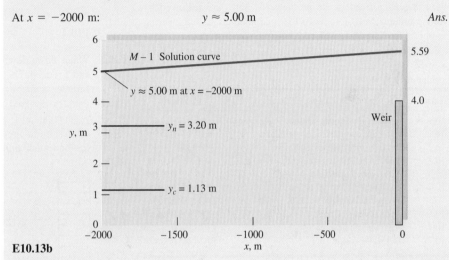

E10.13b

Thus, even 2 km upstream, the dam has produced a "backwater" that is 1.8 m above the normal depth that would occur without a dam. For this example, a near-normal depth of, say, 10 cm greater than y_n, or $y \approx 3.3$ m, would not be achieved until $x = -13,400$ m. Backwater curves are quite far-reaching upstream, especially in flood stages.

Summary

This chapter has introduced open-channel flow analysis, limited to steady, one-dimensional flow conditions. The basic analysis combines the continuity equation with the extended Bernoulli equation including friction losses.

Open-channel flows are classified either by depth variation or by Froude number, the latter being analogous to the Mach number in compressible duct flow (Chap. 9). Flow at constant slope and depth is called uniform flow and satisfies the classical Chézy equation (10.19). Straight prismatic channels can be optimized to find the cross section that gives maximum flow rate with minimum friction losses. As the slope and flow velocity increase, the channel reaches a *critical* condition of Froude number unity, where velocity equals the speed of a small-amplitude surface wave in the channel. Every channel has a critical slope that varies with the flow rate and roughness. If the flow becomes supercritical (Fr > 1), it may undergo a hydraulic jump to a greater depth and lower (subcritical) velocity, analogous to a normal shock wave.

The analysis of gradually varied flow leads to a differential equation (10.51) that can be solved by numerical methods. The chapter ends with a discussion of the flow over a dam or weir, where the total flow rate can be correlated with upstream water depth.

Problems

Most of the problems herein are fairly straightforward. More difficult or open-ended assignments are labeled with an asterisk. Problems labeled with a computer icon 💻 may require the use of a computer. The standard end-of-chapter problems P10.1 to P10.128 (categorized in the problem list here) are followed by word problems W10.1 to W10.13, fundamentals of engineering exam problems FE10.1 to FE10.7, comprehensive problems C10.1 to C10.7, and design projects D10.1 and D10.2.

Problem Distribution

Section	Topic	Problems
10.1	Introduction: Froude number, wave speed	P10.1–P10.10
10.2	Uniform flow: the Chézy formula	P10.11–P10.36
10.3	Efficient uniform-flow channels	P10.37–P10.47
10.4	Specific energy: critical depth	P10.48–P10.58
10.4	Flow over a bump	P10.59–P10.68
10.4	Sluice gate flow	P10.69–P10.78
10.5	The hydraulic jump	P10.79–P10.96
10.6	Gradually varied flow	P10.97–P10.112
10.7	Weirs and flumes	P10.113–P10.123
10.7	Backwater curves	P10.124–P10.128

Introduction: Froude number, wave speed

P10.1 The formula for shallow-water wave propagation speed, Eq. (10.9) or (10.10), is independent of the physical properties of the liquid, like density, viscosity, or surface tension. Does this mean that waves propagate at the same speed in water, mercury, gasoline, and glycerin? Explain.

P10.2 Water at 20°C flows in a 30-cm-wide rectangular channel at a depth of 10 cm and a flow rate of 80,000 cm³/s. Estimate (a) the Froude number and (b) the Reynolds number.

P10.3 Narragansett Bay is approximately 21 (statute) mi long and has an average depth of 42 ft. Tidal charts for the area indicate a time delay of 30 min between high tide at the mouth of the bay (Newport, Rhode Island) and its head (Providence, Rhode Island). Is this delay correlated with the propagation of a shallow-water tidal crest wave through the bay? Explain.

P10.4 The water flow in Fig. P10.4 has a free surface in three places. Does it qualify as an open-channel flow? Explain. What does the dashed line represent?

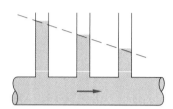

P10.4

P10.5 Water flows down a rectangular channel that is 4 ft wide and 2 ft deep. The flow rate is 20,000 gal/min. Estimate the Froude number of the flow.

P10.6 Pebbles dropped successively at the same point, into a water channel flow of depth 42 cm, create two circular ripples, as in Fig. P10.6. From this information estimate (a) the Froude number and (b) the stream velocity.

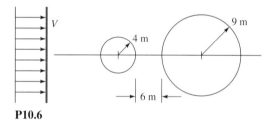

P10.6

P10.7 Pebbles dropped successively at the same point, into a water channel flow of depth 65 cm, create two circular ripples, as in Fig. P10.7. From this information estimate (a) the Froude number and (b) the stream velocity.

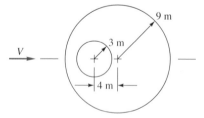

P10.7

P10.8 An earthquake near the Kenai Peninsula, Alaska, creates a single "tidal" wave (called a *tsunami*) that propagates southward across the Pacific Ocean. If the average ocean depth is 4 km and seawater density is 1025 kg/m³, estimate the time of arrival of this tsunami in Hilo, Hawaii.

P10.9 Equation (10.10) is for a single disturbance wave. For *periodic* small-amplitude surface waves of wavelength λ and period T, inviscid theory [8 to 10] predicts a wave propagation speed

$$c_0^2 = \frac{g\lambda}{2\pi} \tanh \frac{2\pi y}{\lambda}$$

where y is the water depth and surface tension is neglected. (a) Determine if this expression is affected by the Reynolds number, Froude number, or Weber number. Derive the limiting values of this expression for (b) $y \ll \lambda$ and (c) $y \gg \lambda$. (d) For what ratio y/λ is the wave speed within 1 percent of limit (c)?

P10.10 If surface tension Y is included in the analysis of Prob. P10.9, the resulting wave speed is [8 to 10]

$$c_0^2 = \left(\frac{g\lambda}{2\pi} + \frac{2\pi Y}{\rho\lambda} \right) \tanh \frac{2\pi y}{\lambda}$$

(a) Determine if this expression is affected by the Reynolds number, Froude number, or Weber number. Derive the limiting values of this expression for (b) $y \ll \lambda$ and (c) $y \gg \lambda$. (d) Finally, determine the wavelength λ_{crit} for a minimum value of c_0, assuming that $y \gg \lambda$.

Uniform flow: the Chézy formula

P10.11 A rectangular channel is 2 m wide and contains water 3 m deep. If the slope is 0.85° and the lining is corrugated metal, estimate the discharge for uniform flow.

P10.12 (a) For laminar draining of a wide, thin sheet of water on pavement sloped at angle θ, as in Fig. P4.36, show that the flow rate is given by

$$Q = \frac{\rho g b h^3 \sin \theta}{3\mu}$$

where b is the sheet width and h its depth. (b) By (somewhat laborious) comparison with Eq. (10.13), show that this expression is compatible with a friction factor $f = 24/\text{Re}$, where $\text{Re} = V_{\text{av}}h/\nu$.

P10.13 A large pond drains down an asphalt rectangular channel that is 2 ft wide. The channel slope is 0.8 degrees. If the flow is uniform, at a depth of 21 in, estimate the time to drain 1 acre-foot of water.

P10.14 The Chézy formula (10.18) is independent of fluid density and viscosity. Does this mean that water, mercury, alcohol, and SAE 30 oil will all flow down a given open channel at the same rate? Explain.

P10.15 The painted-steel channel of Fig. P10.15 is designed, without the barrier, for a flow rate of 6 m³/s at a normal depth of 1 m. Determine (a) the design slope of the channel and (b) the reduction in total flow rate if the proposed painted-steel central barrier is installed.

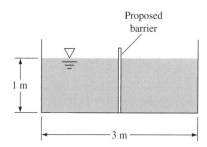

P10.15

P10.16 Water flows in a brickwork rectangular channel 2 m wide, on a slope of 5 m/km. (a) Find the flow rate when the normal depth is 50 cm. (b) If the normal depth remains 50 cm, find the channel width which will triple the flow rate. Comment on this result.

P10.17 The trapezoidal channel of Fig. P10.17 is made of brickwork and slopes at 1:500. Determine the flow rate if the normal depth is 80 cm.

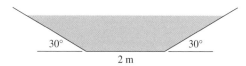

P10.17

P10.18 A V-shaped painted steel channel, similar to Fig. E10.6, has an included angle of 90°. If the slope, in uniform flow, is 3 m per km, estimate (a) the flow rate, in m³/s and (b) the average wall shear stress. Take $y = 2$ m.

P10.19 Modify Prob. P10.18, the 90° V channel, to let the surface be clean earth, which erodes if the average velocity exceeds 6 ft/s. Find the maximum depth that avoids erosion. The slope is still 3 m per km.

P10.20 An unfinished concrete sewer pipe, of diameter 4 ft, is flowing half-full at 39,500 U.S. gallons per minute. If this is the normal depth, what is the pipe slope, in degrees?

P10.21 An engineer makes careful measurements with a weir (see Sec. 10.7) that monitors a rectangular unfinished concrete channel laid on a slope of 1°. She finds, perhaps with surprise, that when the water depth doubles from 2 ft 2 inches to 4 ft 4 inches, the normal flow rate more than doubles, from 200 to 500 ft³/s. (a) Is this plausible? (b) If so, estimate the channel width.

P10.22 For more than a century, woodsmen harvested trees in Skowhegan, ME, elevation 171 ft, and floated the logs down the Kennebec River to Bath, ME, elevation 62 ft, a distance of 72 miles. The river has an average depth of 14 ft and an average width of 400 ft. Assuming uniform flow and a stony bottom, estimate the travel time required for this trip.

P10.23 It is desired to excavate a clean-earth channel as a trapezoidal cross section with $\theta = 60°$ (see Fig. 10.7). The expected flow rate is 500 ft³/s, and the slope is 8 ft per mile. The uniform flow depth is planned, for efficient performance, such that the flow cross section is half a hexagon. What is the appropriate bottom width of the channel?

P10.24 A rectangular channel, laid out on a 0.5° slope, delivers a flow rate of 5000 gal/min in uniform flow when the depth is 1 ft and the width is 3 ft. (a) Estimate the value of Manning's factor n. (b) What water depth will triple the flow rate?

P10.25 The equilateral-triangle channel in Fig. P10.25 has constant slope S_o and constant Manning factor n. If $y = a/2$, find an analytic expression for the flow rate Q.

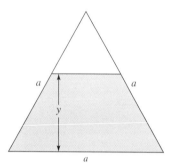

P10.25

P10.26 In the spirit of Fig. 10.6b, analyze a rectangular channel in uniform flow with constant area $A = by$, constant slope, but varying width b and depth y. Plot the resulting flow rate Q, normalized by its maximum value Q_{max}, in the range $0.2 < b/y < 4.0$, and comment on whether it is crucial for discharge efficiency to have the channel flow at a depth exactly equal to half the channel width.

P10.27 A circular corrugated-metal water channel has a slope of 1:800 and a diameter of 6 ft. (a) Estimate the normal discharge, in gal/min, when the water depth is 4 ft. (b) For this condition, calculate the average wall shear stress.

P10.28 A new, finished-concrete trapezoidal channel, similar to Fig. 10.7, has $b = 8$ ft, $y_n = 5$ ft, and $\theta = 50°$. For this depth, the discharge is 500 ft³/s. (a) What is the slope of the channel? (b) As years pass, the channel corrodes and n doubles. What will be the new normal depth for the same flow rate?

P10.29 Suppose that the trapezoidal channel of Fig. P10.17 contains sand and silt that we wish not to erode. According to an empirical correlation by A. Shields in 1936, the average wall shear stress τ_{crit} required to erode sand particles of diameter d_p is approximated by

$$\frac{\tau_{crit}}{(\rho_s - \rho)g\,d_p} \approx 0.5$$

where $\rho_s \approx 2400$ kg/m³ is the density of sand. If the slope of the channel in Fig. P10.17 is 1:900 and $n \approx 0.014$, determine the maximum water depth to keep from eroding particles of 1-mm diameter.

P10.30 A clay tile V-shaped channel, with an included angle of 90°, is 1 km long and is laid out on a 1:400 slope. When running at a depth of 2 m, the upstream end is suddenly closed while the lower end continues to drain. Assuming quasi-steady normal discharge, find the time for the channel depth to drop to 20 cm.

P10.31 An unfinished-concrete 6-ft-diameter sewer pipe flows half full. What is the appropriate slope to deliver 50,000 gal/min of water in uniform flow?

P10.32 Does half a V-shaped channel perform as well as a full V-shaped channel? The answer to Prob. 10.18 is $Q = 12.4$ m³/s. (Do not reveal this to your friends still working on P10.18.) For the painted-steel half-V in Fig. P10.32, at the same slope of 3:1000, find the flow area that gives the same Q and compare with P10.18.

P10.32

P10.33 Five sewer pipes, each a 2-m-diameter clay tile pipe running half full on a slope of 0.25°, empty into a single asphalt pipe, also laid out at 0.25°. If the large pipe is also to run half full, what should be its diameter?

P10.34 A brick rectangular channel with $S_0 = 0.002$ is designed to carry 230 ft³/s of water in uniform flow. There is an argument over whether the channel width should be 4 or 8 ft. Which design needs fewer bricks? By what percentage?

P10.35 In flood stage a natural channel often consists of a deep main channel plus two floodplains, as in Fig. P10.35. The floodplains are often shallow and rough. If the channel has the same slope everywhere, how would you analyze this situation for the discharge? Suppose that $y_1 = 20$ ft, $y_2 = 5$ ft, $b_1 = 40$ ft, $b_2 = 100$ ft, $n_1 = 0.020$, and $n_2 = 0.040$, with a slope of 0.0002. Estimate the discharge in ft³/s.

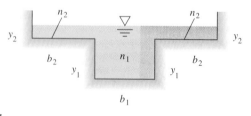

P10.35

P10.36 The Blackstone River in northern Rhode Island normally flows at about 25 m^3/s and resembles Fig. P10.35 with a clean-earth center channel, $b_1 \approx 20$ m and $y_1 \approx 3$ m. The bed slope is about 2 ft/mi. The sides are heavy brush with $b_2 \approx 150$ m. During Hurricane Carol in 1954, a record flow rate of 1000 m^3/s was estimated. Use this information to estimate the maximum flood depth y_2 during this event.

Efficient uniform-flow channels

P10.37 A triangular channel (see Fig. E10.6) is to be constructed of corrugated metal and will carry 8 m^3/s on a slope of 0.005. The supply of sheet metal is limited, so the engineers want to minimize the channel surface. What are (a) the best included angle θ for the channel, (b) the normal depth for part (a), and (c) the wetted perimeter for part (b)?

P10.38 For the half-Vee channel in Fig. P10.32, let the interior angle of the Vee be θ. For a given value of area, slope, and n, find the value of θ for which the flow rate is a maximum. To avoid cumbersome algebra, simply plot Q versus θ for constant A.

P10.39 A trapezoidal channel has $n = 0.022$ and $S_0 = 0.0003$ and is made in the shape of a half-hexagon for maximum efficiency. What should the length of the side of the hexagon be if the channel is to carry 225 ft^3/s of water? What is the discharge of a semicircular channel of the same cross-sectional area and the same S_0 and n?

P10.40 Using the geometry of Fig. 10.6a, prove that the most efficient circular open channel (maximum hydraulic radius for a given flow area) is a semicircle.

P10.41 Determine the most efficient value of θ for the V-shaped channel of Fig. P10.41.

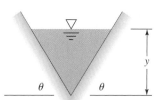

P10.41

P10.42 It is desired to deliver 30,000 gal/min of water in a brick-work channel laid on a slope of 1:100. Which would require fewer bricks, in uniform flow: (a) a V channel with $\theta = 45°$, as in Fig. P10.41, or (b) an efficient rectangular channel with $b = 2y$?

P10.43 Determine the most efficient dimensions for a clay tile rectangular channel to carry 110,000 gal/min on a slope of 0.002.

P10.44 What are the most efficient dimensions for a half-hexagon cast iron channel to carry 15,000 gal/min on a slope of 0.16°?

P10.45 Calculus tells us that the most efficient wall angle for a V-shaped channel (Fig. P10.41) is $\theta = 45°$. It yields the highest normal flow rate for a given area. But is this a sharp or a flat maximum? For a flow area of 1 m^2 and an unfinished-concrete channel with a slope of 0.004, plot the normal flow rate Q, in m^3/s, versus angle for the range $30° \leq \theta \leq 60°$ and comment.

P10.46 It is suggested that a channel that reduces erosion has a parabolic shape, as in Fig. P10.46. Formulas for area and perimeter of the parabolic cross section are as follows [7, p. 36]:

$$A = \frac{2}{3} bh_0; \quad P = \frac{b}{2}\left[\sqrt{1 + \alpha^2} + \frac{1}{\alpha}\ln(\alpha + \sqrt{1 + \alpha^2})\right]$$

$$\text{where} \quad \alpha = \frac{4 h_0}{b}$$

For uniform flow conditions, determine the most efficient ratio h_0/b for this channel (minimum perimeter for a given constant area).

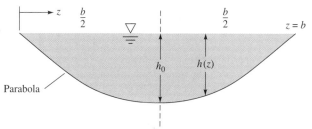

P10.46

P10.47 Calculus tells us that the most efficient water depth for a rectangular channel (such as Fig. E10.1) is $y/b = 1/2$. It yields the highest normal flow rate for a given area. But is this a sharp or a flat maximum? For a flow area of 1 m^2 and a clay tile channel with a slope of 0.006, plot the normal flow rate Q, in m^3/s, versus y/b for the range $0.3 \leq y/b \leq 0.7$ and comment.

Specific energy: critical depth

P10.48 A wide, clean-earth river has a flow rate $q = 150$ ft^3/(s · ft). What is the critical depth? If the actual depth is 12 ft, what is the Froude number of the river? Compute the critical slope by (a) Manning's formula and (b) the Moody chart.

P10.49 Find the critical depth of the brick channel in Prob. P10.34 for both the 4- and 8-ft widths. Are the normal flows subcritical or supercritical?

P10.50 A pencil point piercing the surface of a rectangular channel flow creates a wedgelike 25° half-angle wave, as in Fig. P10.50. If the channel surface is painted steel and the depth is 35 cm, determine (a) the Froude number, (b) the critical depth, and (c) the critical slope for uniform flow.

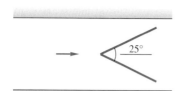

P10.50

P10.51 An unfinished concrete duct, of diameter 1.5 m, is flowing half-full at 8.0 m³/s. (*a*) Is this a critical flow? If not, what is (*b*) the critical flow rate, (*c*) the critical slope, and (*d*) the Froude number? (*e*) If the flow is uniform, what is the slope of the duct?

P10.52 Water flows full in an asphalt half-hexagon channel of bottom width *W*. The flow rate is 12 m³/s. Estimate *W* if the Froude number is exactly 0.60.

P10.53 For the river flow of Prob. P10.48, find the depth y_2 that has the same specific energy as the given depth $y_1 = 12$ ft. These are called *conjugate depths*. What is Fr_2?

P10.54 A clay tile V-shaped channel has an included angle of 70° and carries 8.5 m³/s. Compute (*a*) the critical depth, (*b*) the critical velocity, and (*c*) the critical slope for uniform flow.

P10.55 A trapezoidal channel resembles Fig. 10.7 with *b* = 1 m and *θ* = 50°. The water depth is 2 m, and the flow rate is 32 m³/s. If you stick your fingernail in the surface, as in Fig. P10.50, what half-angle wave might appear?

P10.56 A 4-ft-diameter finished-concrete sewer pipe is half full of water. (*a*) In the spirit of Fig. 10.4*a*, estimate the speed of propagation of a small-amplitude wave propagating along the channel. (*b*) If the water is flowing at 14,000 gal/min, calculate the Froude number.

P10.57 Consider the V-shaped channel of arbitrary angle in Fig. P10.41. If the depth is *y*, (*a*) find an analytic expression for the propagation speed c_0 of a small-disturbance wave along this channel. [*Hint:* Eliminate flow rate from the analyses in Sec. 10.4.] If *θ* = 45° and the depth is 1 m, determine (*b*) the propagation speed and (*c*) the flow rate if the channel is running at a Froude number of 1/3.

P10.58 For a half-hexagon channel running full, find an analytic expression for the propagation speed of a small-disturbance wave travelling along this channel. Denote the bottom width as *b* and use Fig. 10.7 as a guide.

Flow over a bump

P10.59 Uniform water flow in a wide brick channel of slope 0.02° moves over a 10-cm bump as in Fig. P10.59. A slight depression in the water surface results. If the minimum water depth over the bump is 50 cm, compute (*a*) the velocity over the bump and (*b*) the flow rate per meter of width.

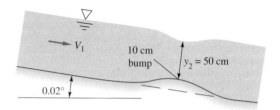

P10.59

P10.60 Water, flowing in a rectangular channel 2 m wide, encounters a bottom bump 10 cm high. The approach depth is 60 cm, and the flow rate 4.8 m³/s. Determine (*a*) the water depth, (*b*) velocity, and (*c*) Froude number above the bump. *Hint:* The change in water depth is rather slight, only about 8 cm.

P10.61 Modify Prob. P10.59 as follows: Again assuming uniform subcritical approach flow (V_1, y_1), find (*a*) the flow rate and (*b*) y_2 for which the flow at the crest of the bump is exactly critical ($Fr_2 = 1.0$).

P10.62 Consider the flow in a wide channel over a bump, as in Fig. P10.62. One can estimate the water depth change or *transition* with frictionless flow. Use continuity and the Bernoulli equation to show that

$$\frac{dy}{dx} = -\frac{dh/dx}{1 - V^2/(gy)}$$

Is the drawdown of the water surface realistic in Fig. P10.62? Explain under what conditions the surface might rise above its upstream position y_0.

P10.63 In Fig. P10.62 let $V_0 = 1$ m/s and $y_0 = 1$ m. If the maximum bump height is 15 cm, estimate (*a*) the Froude number over the top of the bump and (*b*) the maximum depression in the water surface.

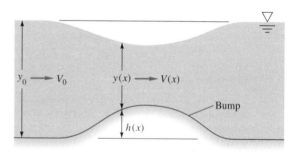

P10.62

P10.64 For the rectangular channel in Prob. P10.60, the Froude number over the bump is about 1.37, which is 17 percent less than the approach value. For the same entrance conditions, find the bump height Δ*h* that causes the bump Froude number to be 1.00.

P10.65 Program and solve the differential equation of "frictionless flow over a bump," from Prob. P10.62, for entrance conditions $V_0 = 1$ m/s and $y_0 = 1$ m. Let the bump have the convenient shape $h = 0.5h_{max}[1 - \cos(2\pi x/L)]$, which simulates Fig. P10.62. Let $L = 3$ m, and generate a numerical solution for $y(x)$ in the bump region $0 < x < L$. If you have time for only one case, use $h_{max} = 15$ cm (Prob. P10.63), for which the maximum Froude number is 0.425. If more time is available, it is instructive to examine a complete family of surface profiles for $h_{max} \approx 1$ cm up to 35 cm (which is the solution of Prob. P10.64).

***P10.66** In Fig. P10.62, let $V_o = 5.5$ m/s and $y_o = 90$ cm. (a) Will the water rise or fall over the bump? (b) For a bump height of 30 cm, determine the Froude number over the bump. (c) Find the bump height that will cause critical flow over the bump.

P10.67 Modify Prob. P10.63 so that the 15-cm change in bottom level is a *depression*, not a bump. Estimate (a) the Froude number above the depression and (b) the maximum change in water depth.

P10.68 Modify Prob. P10.65 to have a supercritical approach condition $V_0 = 6$ m/s and $y_0 = 1$ m. If you have time for only one case, use $h_{max} = 35$ cm (Prob. P10.66), for which the maximum Froude number is 1.47. If more time is available, it is instructive to examine a complete family of surface profiles for 1 cm $< h_{max} <$ 52 cm (which is the solution to Prob. P10.67).

Sluice gate flow

***P10.69** Given is the flow of a channel of large width b under a sluice gate, as in Fig. P10.69. Assuming frictionless steady flow with negligible upstream kinetic energy, derive a formula for the dimensionless flow ratio $Q^2/(y_1^3 b^2 g)$ as a function of the ratio y_2/y_1. Show by differentiation that the maximum flow rate occurs at $y_2 = 2y_1/3$.

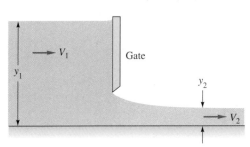

P10.69

P10.70 A periodic and spectacular water release, in China's Henan province, flows through a giant sluice gate. Assume that the gate is 23 m wide, and its opening is 8 m high. The water depth far upstream is 32 m. Assuming free discharge, estimate the volume flow rate through the gate.

P10.71 In Fig. P10.69 let $y_1 = 95$ cm and $y_2 = 50$ cm. Estimate the flow rate per unit width if the upstream kinetic energy is (a) neglected and (b) included.

***P10.72** Water approaches the wide sluice gate of Fig. P10.72 at $V_1 = 0.2$ m/s and $y_1 = 1$ m. Accounting for upstream kinetic energy, estimate at the outlet, section 2, the (a) depth, (b) velocity, and (c) Froude number.

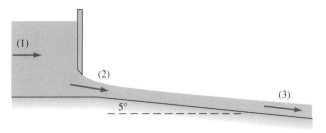

P10.72

P10.73 In Fig. P10.69, let $y_1 = 6$ ft and the gate width $b = 8$ ft. Find the gate opening H that would allow a free-discharge flow of 30,000 gal/min under the gate.

P10.74 With respect to Fig. P10.69, show that, for frictionless flow, the upstream velocity may be related to the water levels by

$$V_1 = \sqrt{\frac{2g(y_1 - y_2)}{K^2 - 1}}$$

where $K = y_1/y_2$.

P10.75 A tank of water 1 m deep, 3 m long, and 4 m wide into the paper has a closed sluice gate on the right side, as in Fig. P10.75. At $t = 0$ the gate is opened to a gap of 10 cm. Assuming quasi-steady sluice gate theory, estimate the time required for the water level to drop to 50 cm. Assume free outflow.

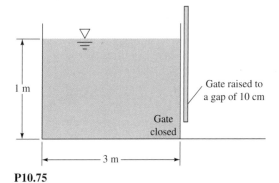

P10.75

P10.76 Figure P10.76 shows a horizontal flow of water through a sluice gate, a hydraulic jump, and over a 6-ft sharp-crested weir. Channel, gate, jump, and weir are all 8 ft wide unfinished concrete. Determine (a) the flow rate in ft³/s and (b) the normal depth.

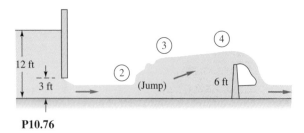

P10.76

P10.77 Equation (10.41) for sluice gate discharge is for free outflow. If the outflow is *drowned*, as in Fig. 10.10c, there is dissipation, and C_d drops sharply, as shown in Fig. P10.77, taken from Ref. 2. Use this data to restudy Prob. 10.73, with $H = 9$ in. Plot the estimated flow rate, in gal/min, versus y_2 in the range 0.5 ft $< y_2 <$ 5 ft.

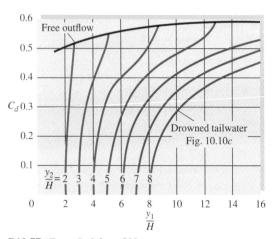

P10.77 *(From Ref. 2, p. 509.)*

P10.78 In Fig. P10.69, free discharge, a gate opening of 0.72 ft will allow a flow rate of 30,000 gal/min. Recall $y_1 = 6$ ft and the gate width $b = 8$ ft. Suppose that the gate is drowned (Fig. P10.77), with $y_2 = 4$ ft. What gate opening would then be required?

The hydraulic jump

P10.79 Show that the Froude number downstream of a hydraulic jump will be given by

$$\text{Fr}_2 = 8^{1/2}\,\text{Fr}_1/[(1 + 8\,\text{Fr}_1^2)^{1/2} - 1]^{3/2}$$

Does the formula remain correct if we reverse subscripts 1 and 2? Why?

P10.80 Water flowing in a wide channel 25 cm deep suddenly jumps to a depth of 1 m. Estimate (a) the downstream Froude number; (b) the flow rate per unit width; (c) the critical depth; and (d) the percentage of dissipation.

P10.81 Water flows in a wide channel at $q = 25$ ft^3/(s · ft), $y_1 = 1$ ft, and then undergoes a hydraulic jump. Compute y_2, V_2, Fr$_2$, h_f, the percentage of dissipation, and the horsepower dissipated per unit width. What is the critical depth?

P10.82 Downstream of a wide hydraulic jump the flow is 4 ft deep and has a Froude number of 0.5. Estimate (a) y_1, (b) V_1, (c) Fr$_1$, (d) the percentage of dissipation, and (e) y_c.

P10.83 A wide-channel flow undergoes a hydraulic jump from 40 to 140 cm. Estimate (a) V_1, (b) V_2, (c) the critical depth, in cm, and (d) the percentage of dissipation.

*P10.84 Consider the flow under the sluice gate of Fig. P10.84. If $y_1 = 10$ ft and all losses are neglected except the dissipation in the jump, calculate y_2 and y_3 and the percentage of dissipation, and sketch the flow to scale with the EGL included. The channel is horizontal and wide.

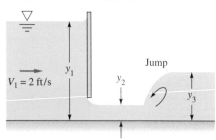

P10.84

P10.85 The analogy between a hydraulic jump and a normal shock equates Mach number and Froude number, air density and water depth, air pressure and the square of the water depth. Test this analogy for Ma$_1$ = Fr$_1$ = 4.0 and comment on the results.

P10.86 A *bore* is a hydraulic jump that propagates upstream into a still or slower-moving fluid, as in Fig. P10.86, on the Sée-Sélune channel, near Mont Saint Michel in northwest France. The bore is moving at about 10 ft/s and is about one foot high. Estimate (a) the depth of the water in this area and (b) the velocity induced by the wave.

P10.86 Tidal bore on the Sée-Sélune river channel in northwest France. *(Courtesy of Prof. Hubert Chanson, University of Queensland.)*

P10.87 A *tidal bore* may occur when the ocean tide enters an estuary against an oncoming river discharge, such as on the Severn River in England. Suppose that the tidal bore is 10 ft deep and propagates at 13 mi/h upstream into a river that is 7 ft deep. Estimate the river current in kn.

*__P10.88__ Consider supercritical flow, $Fr_1 > 1$, down a shallow flat water channel toward a wedge of included angle 2θ, as in Fig. P10.88. By the compressible flow analogy, hydraulic jumps should form, similar to the shock waves in Fig. P9.132a. Using an approach similar to Fig. 9.20, develop and explain the equations that could be used to find the wave angle β and Fr_2.

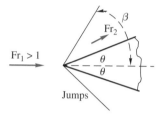

P10.88

P10.89 Water 30 cm deep is in uniform flow down a 1° unfinished concrete slope when a hydraulic jump occurs, as in Fig. P10.89. If the channel is very wide, estimate the water depth y_2 downstream of the jump.

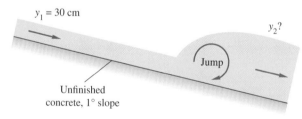

P10.89

P10.90 For the gate/jump/weir system sketched in Fig. P10.76, the flow rate was determined to be 379 ft³/s. Determine (a) the water depths y_2 and y_3, and (b) the Froude numbers Fr_2 and Fr_3 before and after the hydraulic jump.

*__P10.91__ Follow up Prob. P10.88 numerically with flow down a shallow, flat water channel 1 cm deep at an average velocity of 0.94 m/s. The wedge half-angle θ is 20°. Calculate (a) β; (b) Fr_2; and (c) y_2.

P10.92 A familiar sight is the circular hydraulic jump formed by a faucet jet falling onto a flat sink surface, as in Fig. P10.92. Because of the shallow depths, this jump is strongly dependent on bottom friction, viscosity, and surface tension [35]. It is also unstable and can form remarkable noncircular shapes, as shown in the website <http://web.mit.edu/jeffa/www/jump.htm>.

P10.92 A circular hydraulic jump in a kitchen sink. *(Courtesy of Prof. Hubert Chanson, University of Queensland.)*

For this problem, assume that two-dimensional jump theory is valid. If the water depth outside the jump is 4 mm, the radius at which the jump appears is $R = 3$ cm, and the faucet flow rate is 100 cm³/s, find the conditions just upstream of the jump.

P10.93 Water in a horizontal channel accelerates smoothly over a bump and then undergoes a hydraulic jump, as in Fig. P10.93. If $y_1 = 1$ m and $y_3 = 40$ cm, estimate (a) V_1, (b) V_3, (c) y_4, and (d) the bump height h.

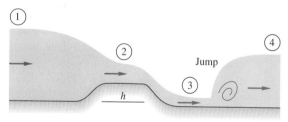

P10.93

P10.94 In Fig. 10.11, the upstream flow is only 2.65 cm deep. The channel is 50 cm wide, and the flow rate is 0.0359 m³/s. Determine (a) the upstream Froude number, (b) the downstream velocity, (c) the downstream depth, and (d) the percent dissipation.

P10.95 A 10-cm-high bump in a wide horizontal water channel creates a hydraulic jump just upstream and the flow pattern in Fig. P10.95. Neglecting losses except in the jump, for the case $y_3 = 30$ cm, estimate (a) V_4, (b) y_4, (c) V_1, and (d) y_1.

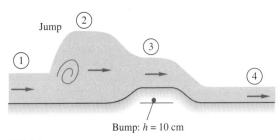

P10.95

P10.96   For the circular hydraulic jump in Fig. P10.92, the water depths before and after the jump are 2 mm and 4 mm, respectively. Assume that two-dimensional jump theory is valid. If the faucet flow rate is 150 cm^3/s, estimate the radius R at which the jump will appear.

Gradually varied flow

P10.97   A brickwork rectangular channel 4 m wide is flowing at 8.0 m^3/s on a slope of 0.1°. Is this a mild, critical, or steep slope? What type of gradually varied solution curve are we on if the local water depth is (a) 1 m, (b) 1.5 m, and (c) 2 m?

P10.98   A gravelly earth wide channel is flowing at 10 m^3/s per meter of width on a slope of 0.75°. Is this a mild, critical, or steep slope? What type of gradually varied solution curve are we on if the local water depth is (a) 1 m, (b) 2 m, or (c) 3 m?

P10.99   A clay tile V-shaped channel of included angle 60° is flowing at 1.98 m^3/s on a slope of 0.33°. Is this a mild, critical, or steep slope? What type of gradually varied solution curve are we on if the local water depth is (a) 1 m, (b) 2 m, or (c) 3 m?

P10.100   If bottom friction is included in the sluice gate flow of Prob. P10.84, the depths (y_1, y_2, y_3) will vary with x. Sketch the type and shape of gradually varied solution curve in each region (1, 2, 3), and show the regions of rapidly varied flow.

P10.101   Consider the gradual change from the profile beginning at point a in Fig. P10.101 on a mild slope S_{01} to a mild but steeper slope S_{02} downstream. Sketch and label the curve $y(x)$ expected.

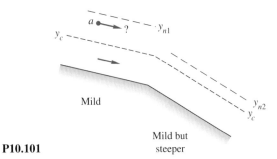

P10.101

*P10.102   The wide-channel flow in Fig. P10.102 changes from a steep slope to one even steeper. Beginning at points a and b, sketch and label the water surface profiles expected for gradually varied flow.

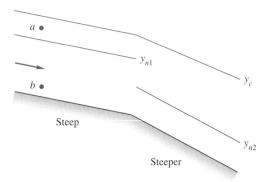

P10.102

P10.103   A gravelly rectangular channel, 7 m wide and 2 m deep, is flowing at 75 m^3/s on a slope of 0.013. (a) Is this on a mild, critical, or steep curve? (b) Approximately how many meters downstream will the gradually varied solution reach the normal depth?

P10.104   The rectangular-channel flow in Fig. P10.104 expands to a cross section 50 percent wider. Beginning at points a and b, sketch and label the water surface profiles expected for gradually varied flow.

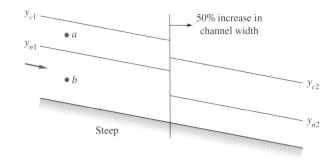

P10.104

P10.105   In Prob. P10.84 the frictionless solution is $y_2 = 0.82$ ft, which we denote as $x = 0$ just downstream of the gate. If the channel is horizontal with $n = 0.018$ and there is no hydraulic jump, compute from gradually varied theory the downstream distance where $y = 2.0$ ft.

P10.106   A rectangular channel with $n = 0.018$ and a constant slope of 0.0025 increases its width linearly from b to $2b$ over a distance L, as in Fig. P10.106. (a) Determine the variation $y(x)$ along the channel if $b = 4$ m, $L = 250$ m, the initial depth is $y(0) = 1.05$ m, and the flow rate is 7 m³/s. (b) Then, if your computer program is running well, determine the initial depth $y(0)$ for which the exit flow will be exactly critical.

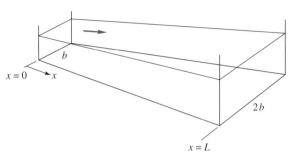

P10.106

P10.107 A clean-earth wide-channel flow is climbing an adverse slope with $S_0 = -0.002$. If the flow rate is $q = 4.5$ m³/(s · m), use gradually varied theory to compute the distance for the depth to drop from 3.0 to 2.0 m.

P10.108 Water flows at 1.5 m³/s along a straight, riveted-steel 90° V-shaped channel (see Fig. P10.41, $\theta = 45°$). At section 1, the water depth is 1.0 m. (a) As we proceed downstream, will the water depth rise or fall? Explain. (b) Depending upon your answer to part (a), calculate, in one numerical swoop, from gradually varied theory, the distance downstream for which the depth rises (or falls) 0.1 m.

P10.109 Figure P10.109 illustrates a free overfall or *dropdown* flow pattern, where a channel flow accelerates down a slope and falls freely over an abrupt edge. As shown, the flow reaches critical just before the overfall. Between y_c and the edge the flow is rapidly varied and does not satisfy gradually varied theory. Suppose that the flow rate is $q = 1.3$ m³/(s · m) and the surface is unfinished concrete. Use Eq. (10.51) to estimate the water depth 300 m upstream as shown.

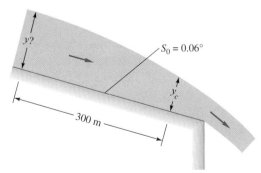

P10.109

P10.110 We assumed frictionless flow in solving the bump case, Prob. P10.65, for which $V_2 = 1.21$ m/s and $y_2 = 0.826$ m over the crest when $h_{max} = 15$ cm, $V_1 = 1$ m/s, and $y_1 = 1$ m. However, if the bump is long and rough, friction may be important. Repeat Prob. P10.65 for the same bump shape, $h = 0.5h_{max}[1 - \cos(2\pi x/L)]$, to compute conditions (a) at the crest and (b) at the end of the bump, $x = L$. Let $h_{max} = 15$ cm and $L = 100$ m, and assume a clean-earth surface.

*P10.111** The Rolling Dam on the Blackstone River has a weedy bottom and an average flow rate of 900 ft³/s. Assume the river upstream is 150 ft wide and slopes at 10 ft per statute mile. The water depth just upstream of the dam is 7.7 ft. Calculate the water depth one mile upstream (a) for the given initial depth, 7.7 ft; and (b) if flashboards on the dam raise this depth to 10.7 ft.

P10.112 The clean-earth channel in Fig. P10.112 is 6 m wide and slopes at 0.3°. Water flows at 30 m³/s in the channel and enters a reservoir so that the channel depth is 3 m just before the entry. Assuming gradually varied flow, how far is the distance L to a point in the channel where $y = 2$ m? What type of curve is the water surface?

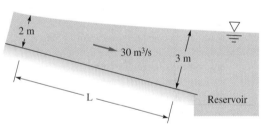

P10.112

Weirs and flumes

P10.113 Figure P10.113 shows a channel contraction section often called a *venturi flume* [23, p. 167] because measurements of y_1 and y_2 can be used to meter the flow rate. Show that if losses are neglected and the flow is one-dimensional and subcritical, the flow rate is given by

$$Q = \left[\frac{2g(y_1 - y_2)}{1/(b_2^2 y_2^2) - 1/(b_1^2 y_1^2)} \right]^{1/2}$$

Apply this to the special case $b_1 = 3$ m, $b_2 = 2$ m, and $y_1 = 1.9$ m. (a) Find the flow rate if $y_2 = 1.5$ m. (b) Also find the depth y_2 for which the flow becomes critical in the throat.

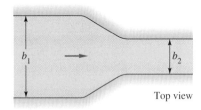

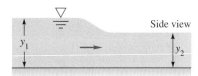

P10.113

P10.114 For the gate/jump/weir system sketched in Fig. P10.76, the flow rate was determined to be 379 ft³/s. Determine the water depth y_4 just upstream of the weir.

P10.115 Gradually varied theory, Eq. (10.49), neglects the effect of *width* changes, db/dx, assuming that they are small. But they are not small for a short, sharp contraction such as the venturi flume in Fig. P10.113. Show that, for a rectangular section with $b = b(x)$, Eq. (10.49) should be modified as follows:

$$\frac{dy}{dx} \approx \frac{S_0 - S + [V^2/(gb)](db/dx)}{1 - \mathrm{Fr}^2}$$

Investigate a criterion for reducing this relation to Eq. (10.49).

P10.116 A Cipolletti weir, popular in irrigation systems, is trapezoidal, with sides sloped at 1:4 horizontal to vertical, as in Fig. P10.116. The following are flow-rate values, from the U.S. Dept. of Agriculture, for a few different system parameters:

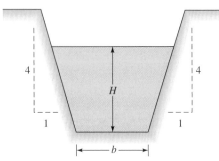

P10.116

H, ft	0.8	1.0	1.35	1.5
b, ft	1.5	2.0	2.5	3.5
Q, gal/min	1620	3030	5920	9740

Source: *U.S. Dept of Agriculture.*

Use this data to correlate a Cipolletti weir formula with a reasonably constant weir coefficient.

P10.117 A popular flow-measurement device in agriculture is the *Parshall flume* [33], Fig. P10.117, named after its inventor, Ralph L. Parshall, who developed it in 1922 for the U.S. Bureau of Reclamation. The subcritical approach flow is driven, by a steep constriction, to go critical ($y = y_c$) and then supercritical. It gives a constant reading H for a wide range of tailwaters. Derive a formula for estimating Q from measurement of H and knowledge of constriction width b. Neglect the entrance velocity head.

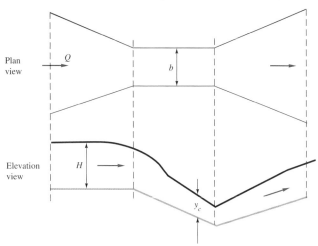

P10.117 The Parshall flume

P10.118 Using a Bernoulli-type analysis similar to Fig. 10.16a, show that the theoretical discharge of the V-shaped weir in Fig. P10.118 is given by

$$Q = 0.7542g^{1/2} \tan \alpha \, H^{5/2}$$

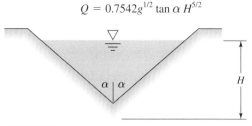

*P10.118

P10.119 Data by A. T. Lenz for water at 20°C (reported in Ref. 23) show a significant increase of discharge coefficient of V-notch weirs (Fig. P10.118) at low heads. For $\alpha = 20°$, some measured values are as follows:

H, ft	0.2	0.4	0.6	0.8	1.0
C_d	0.499	0.470	0.461	0.456	0.452

Determine if these data can be correlated with the Reynolds and Weber numbers vis-à-vis Eq. (10.61). If not, suggest another correlation.

P10.120 The rectangular channel in Fig. P10.120 contains a V-notch weir as shown. The intent is to meter flow rates between 2.0 and 6.0 m³/s with an upstream hook gage

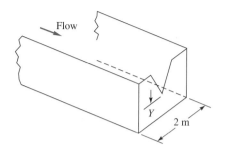

P10.120

set to measure water depths between 2.0 and 2.75 m. What are the most appropriate values for the notch height Y and the notch half-angle α?

P10.121 Water flow in a rectangular channel is to be metered by a thin-plate weir with side contractions, as in Table 10.2b, with $L = 6$ ft and $Y = 1$ ft. It is desired to measure flow rates between 1500 and 3000 gal/min with only a 6-in change in upstream water depth. What is the most appropriate length for the weir width b?

P10.122 In 1952 E. S. Crump developed the triangular weir shape shown in Fig. P10.122 [23, Chap. 4]. The front slope is 1:2 to avoid sediment deposition, and the rear slope is 1:5 to maintain a stable tailwater flow. The beauty of the design is that it has a unique discharge correlation up to near-drowning conditions, $H_2/H_1 \leq 0.75$:

$$Q = C_d b g^{1/2}\left(H_1 + \frac{V_1^2}{2g} - k_h\right)^{3/2}$$

where $C_d \approx 0.63$ and $k_h \approx 0.3$ mm

The term k_h is a low-head loss factor. Suppose that the weir is 3 m wide and has a crest height $Y = 50$ cm. If the water depth upstream is 65 cm, estimate the flow rate in gal/min.

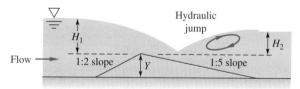

P10.122 The Crump weir [23, Chap. 4]

*P10.123 Water in a 20-ft-wide rectangular channel, flowing at 120 ft³/s and a depth of 10 ft, is to be metered by a rectangular weir with side contractions, as in Table 10.2b. Suggest some appropriate design values of b, Y, and H to match the table conditions for this weir.

Backwater curves

P10.124 Water flows at 600 ft³/s in a rectangular channel 22 ft wide with $n \approx 0.024$ and a slope of 0.1°. A dam increases the depth to 15 ft, as in Fig. P10.124. Using gradually varied theory, estimate the distance L upstream at which the water depth will be 10 ft. What type of solution curve are we on? What should be the water depth asymptotically far upstream?

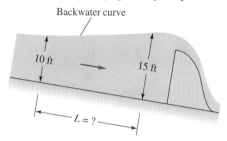

P10.124

P10.125 The Tupperware dam on the Blackstone River is 12 ft high, 100 ft wide, and sharp-edged. It creates a backwater similar to Fig. P10.124. Assume that the river is a weedy-earth rectangular channel 100 ft wide with a flow rate of 800 ft³/s. Estimate the water depth 2 mi upstream of the dam if $S_0 = 0.001$.

P10.126 Suppose that the rectangular channel of Fig. P10.120 is made of riveted steel and carries a flow of 8 m³/s on a slope of 0.15°. If the V-notch weir has $\alpha = 30°$ and $Y = 50$ cm, estimate, from gradually varied theory, the water depth 100 m upstream.

P10.127 A clean-earth river is 50 ft wide and averages 600 ft³/s. It contains a dam that increases the water depth to 8 ft, to provide head for a hydropower plant. The bed slope is 0.0025. (a) What is the normal depth of this river? (b) Engineers propose putting flashboards on the dam to raise the water level to 10 ft. Residents a half mile upstream are worried about flooding above their present water depth of about 2.2 ft. Using Eq. (10.52) in one big half-mile step, estimate the new water depth upstream.

P10.128 A rectangular channel 4 m wide is blocked by a broad-crested weir 2 m high, as in Fig. P10.128. The channel is horizontal for 200 m upstream and then slopes at 0.7° as shown. The flow rate is 12 m³/s, and $n = 0.03$. Compute the water depth y at 300 m upstream from gradually varied theory.

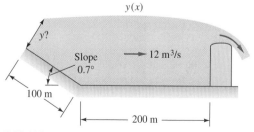

P10.128

Word Problems

W10.1   Free-surface problems are driven by gravity. Why do so many of the formulas in this chapter contain the *square root* of the acceleration of gravity?

W10.2   Explain why the flow under a sluice gate, Fig. 10.10, either is or is not analogous to compressible gas flow through a converging–diverging nozzle, Fig. 9.12.

W10.3   In uniform open-channel flow, what is the balance of forces? Can you use such a force balance to derive the Chézy equation (10.13)?

W10.4   A shallow-water wave propagates at the speed $c_0 \approx (gy)^{1/2}$. What makes it propagate? That is, what is the balance of forces in such a wave motion? In which direction does such a wave propagate?

W10.5   Why is the Manning friction correlation, Eq. (10.16), used almost universally by hydraulics engineers, instead of the Moody friction factor?

W10.6   During horizontal channel flow over a bump, is the specific energy constant? Explain.

W10.7   Cite some similarities, and perhaps some dissimilarities, between a hydraulic jump and a gas dynamic normal shock wave.

W10.8   Give three examples of rapidly varied flow. For each case, cite reasons why it does not satisfy one or more of the five basic assumptions of gradually varied flow theory.

W10.9   Is a free overfall, Fig. 10.15e, similar to a weir? Could it be calibrated versus flow rate in the same manner as a weir? Explain.

W10.10 Cite some similarities, and perhaps some dissimilarities, between a weir and a Bernoulli obstruction flowmeter from Sec. 6.12.

W10.11 Is a bump, Fig. 10.9a, similar to a weir? If not, when does a bump become large enough, or sharp enough, to be a weir?

W10.12 After doing some reading and/or thinking, explain the design and operation of a *long-throated flume*.

W10.13 Describe the design and operation of a *critical-depth flume*. What are its advantages compared to the venturi flume of Prob. P10.113?

Fundamentals of Engineering Exam Problems

The FE Exam is fairly light on open-channel problems in the general (morning) session, but this subject plays a big part in the specialized civil engineering (afternoon) exam.

FE10.1   Consider a rectangular channel 3 m wide laid on a 1° slope. If the water depth is 2 m, the hydraulic radius is
(*a*) 0.43 m, (*b*) 0.6 m, (*c*) 0.86 m, (*d*) 1.0 m, (*e*) 1.2 m

FE10.2   For the channel of Prob. FE10.1, the most efficient water depth (best flow for a given slope and resistance) is (*a*) 1 m, (*b*) 1.5 m, (*c*) 2 m, (*d*) 2.5 m, (*e*) 3 m

FE10.3   If the channel of Prob. FE10.1 is built of rubble cement (Manning's $n \approx 0.020$), what is the uniform flow rate when the water depth is 2 m?
(*a*) 6 m³/s, (*b*) 18 m³/s, (*c*) 36 m³/s, (*d*) 40 m³/s, (*e*) 53 m³/s

FE10.4   For the channel of Prob. FE10.1, if the water depth is 2 m and the uniform flow rate is 24 m³/s, what is the approximate value of Manning's roughness factor n?
(*a*) 0.015, (*b*) 0.020, (*c*) 0.025, (*d*) 0.030, (*e*) 0.035

FE10.5   For the channel of Prob. FE10.1, if Manning's roughness factor $n \approx 0.020$ and $Q \approx 29$ m³/s, what is the normal depth y_n?
(*a*) 1 m, (*b*) 1.5 m, (*c*) 2 m, (*d*) 2.5 m, (*e*) 3 m

FE10.6   For the channel of Prob. FE10.1, if $Q \approx 24$ m³/s, what is the critical depth y_c?
(*a*) 1.0 m, (*b*) 1.26 m, (*c*) 1.5 m, (*d*) 1.87 m, (*e*) 2.0 m

FE10.7   For the channel of Prob. FE10.1, if $Q \approx 24$ m³/s and the depth is 2 m, what is the Froude number of the flow?
(*a*) 0.50, (*b*) 0.77, (*c*) 0.90, (*d*) 1.00, (*e*) 1.11

Comprehensive Problems

C10.1   February 1998 saw the failure of the earthen dam impounding California Jim's Pond in southern Rhode Island. The resulting flood raised temporary havoc in the nearby village of Peace Dale. The pond is 17 acres in area and 15 ft deep and was full from heavy rains. The breach in the dam was 22 ft wide and 15 ft deep. Estimate the time required for the pond to drain to a depth of 2 ft.

C10.2   A circular, unfinished concrete drainpipe is laid on a slope of 0.0025 and is planned to carry from 50 to 300 ft³/s of runoff water. Design constraints are that (1) the water depth should be no more than three-fourths of the diameter and (2) the flow should always be subcritical. What is the appropriate pipe diameter to satisfy these requirements? If no commercial pipe is exactly this calculated size, should you buy the next smallest or the next largest pipe?

C10.3   Extend Prob. P10.72, whose solution was $V_2 \approx 4.33$ m/s. (*a*) Use gradually varied theory to estimate the water depth 10 m downstream at section (3) for the 5° unfinished concrete slope shown in Fig. P10.72. (*b*) Repeat your calculation for an *upward* (adverse) slope of 5°. (*c*) When you find that part (*b*) is impossible with gradually varied theory, explain why and repeat for an adverse slope of 1°.

C10.4   It is desired to meter an asphalt rectangular channel of width 1.5 m, which is designed for uniform flow at a depth of 70 cm and a slope of 0.0036. The vertical sides of the channel are 1.2 m high. Consider using a thin-plate rectangular weir, either full or partial width (Table 10.2*a,b*) for this purpose. Sturm [7, p. 51] recommends, for accurate correlation, that such a weir have $Y \geq 9$ cm and $H/Y \leq 2.0$. Determine the feasibility of installing such a weir that will be accurate and yet not cause the water to overflow the sides of the channel.

C10.5   Figure C10.5 shows a hydraulic model of a *compound weir,* one that combines two different shapes. (*a*) Other than measurement, for which it might be poor, what could be the engineering reason for such a weir? (*b*) For the prototype river, assume that both sections have sides at a 70° angle to the vertical, with the bottom section having a base width of 2 m and the upper section having a base width of 4.5 m, including the cut-out portion. The heights of lower and upper horizontal sections are 1 m and 2 m, respectively. Use engineering estimates and make a plot of upstream water depth versus Petaluma River flow rate in the range 0 to 4 m³/s. (*c*) For what river flow rate will the water overflow the top of the dam?

C10.6   Figure C10.6 shows a horizontal flow of water through a sluice gate, a hydraulic jump, and over a 6-ft sharp-crested weir. Channel, gate, jump, and weir are all 8 ft wide unfinished concrete. Determine (*a*) the flow rate, (*b*) the normal depth, (*c*) y_2, (*d*) y_3, and (*e*) y_4.

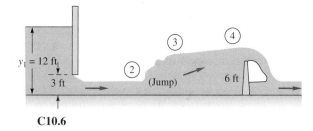

C10.6

C10.5 (*Courtesy of the U.S. Army Corps of Engineers Waterways Experiment Station.*)

C10.7 Consider the V-shaped channel in Fig. C10.7, with an arbitrary angle θ. Make a continuity and momentum analysis of a small disturbance $\delta y \ll y$, as in Fig. 10.4. Show that the wave propagation speed in this channel is independent of θ and does *not* equal the wide-channel result $c_0 = (gy)^{1/2}$.

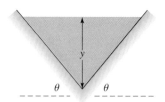

C10.7

Design Projects

D10.1 A straight weedy-earth channel has the trapezoidal shape of Fig. 10.7, with $b = 4$ m and $\theta = 35°$. The channel has a constant bottom slope of 0.001. The flow rate varies seasonally from 5 up to 10 m³/s. It is desired to place a sharp-edged weir across the channel so that the water depth 1 km upstream remains at 2.0 m $\pm$ 10 percent throughout the year. Investigate the possibility of accomplishing this with a full-width weir; if successful, determine the proper weir height Y. If unsuccessful, try other alternatives, such as (a) a full-width broad-crested weir or (b) a weir with side contractions or (c) a V-notch weir. Whatever your final design, cite the seasonal variation of normal depths and critical depths for comparison with the desired year-round depth of 2 m.

D10.2 The Caroselli Dam on the Pawcatuck River is 10 ft high, 90 ft wide, and sharp edged. The Coakley Company uses this head to generate hydropower electricity and wants *more* head. They ask the town for permission to raise the dam higher. The river above the dam may be approximated as rectangular, 90 ft wide, sloping upstream at 12 ft per statute mile, and with a stony, cobbled bed. The average flow rate is 400 ft³/s, with a 30-year predicted flood rate of 1200 ft³/s. The river sides are steep until 1 mi upstream, where there are low-lying residences. The town council agrees the dam may be heightened if the new river level near these houses, during the 30-year flood, is no more than 3 ft higher than the present level during average flow conditions. You, as project engineer, have to predict how high the dam crest can be raised and still meet this requirement.

References

1. B. A. Bakhmeteff, *Hydraulics of Open Channels,* McGraw-Hill, New York, 1932.
2. V. T. Chow, *Open Channel Hydraulics*, Blackburn Press, Caldwell, NJ, 2009.
3. M. H. Chaudhry, *Open Channel Flow*, 2d ed., Springer, New York, 2007.
4. R. Srivastava, *Flow Through Open Channels*, Oxford University Press, New York, 2008.
5. H. Chanson, *The Hydraulics of Open Channel Flow,* 2d ed., Elsevier, New York, 2004.
6. J. O. Akan, *Open Channel Hydraulics*, Butterworth-Heinemann, Woburn, MA, 2006.
7. T. W. Sturm, *Open Channel Hydraulics,* McGraw-Hill, New York, 2001.
8. J. Pedlosky, *Waves in the Ocean and Atmosphere: Introduction to Wave Dynamics*, Springer, New York, 2003.
9. L. H. Holthuijsen, *Waves in Oceanic and Coastal Waters*, Cambridge University Press, New York, 2007.
10. M. K. Ochi, *Ocean Waves: The Stochastic Approach*, Cambridge University Press, London, 2008.
11. G. Masselink, M. Hughes, and J. Knight, *Introduction to Coastal Processes and Geomorphology*, 2d ed., Routledge, New York, 2011.
12. M. B. Abbott and W. A. Price, *Coastal, Estuarial, and Harbor Engineers Reference Book,* Taylor & Francis, New York, 1994.
13. P. D. Komar, *Beach Processes and Sedimentation,* 2d ed., Pearson Education, Upper Saddle River, NJ, 1998.
14. W. Yue, C.-L. Lin, and V. C. Patel, "Large Eddy Simulation of Turbulent Open Channel Flow with Free Surface Simulated by Level Set Method," *Physics of Fluids*, vol. 17, no. 2, Feb. 2005, pp. 1–12.
15. J. M. Robertson and H. Rouse, "The Four Regimes of Open Channel Flow," *Civ. Eng.,* vol. 11, no. 3, March 1941, pp. 169–171.
16. R. W. Powell, "Resistance to Flow in Rough Channels," *Trans. Am. Geophys. Union,* vol. 31, no. 4, August 1950, pp. 575–582.
17. R. Manning, "On the Flow of Water in Open Channels and Pipes," *Trans. I.C.E. Ireland,* vol. 20, 1891, pp. 161–207.

18. "Friction Factors in Open Channels, Report of the Committee on Hydromechanics," *ASCE J. Hydraul. Div.,* March 1963, pp. 97–143.

19. E. F. Brater, H. W. King, J. E. Lindell, and C. Y. Wei, *Handbook of Hydraulics,* 7th ed., McGraw-Hill, New York, 1996.

20. U.S. Bureau of Reclamation, "Research Studies on Stilling Basins, Energy Dissipators, and Associated Appurtenances," *Hydraulic Lab. Rep.* Hyd-399, June 1, 1955.

21. P. A. Thompson, *Compressible-Fluid Dynamics,* McGraw-Hill, New York, 1972.

22. R. M. Olson and S. J. Wright, *Essentials of Engineering Fluid Mechanics,* 5th ed., Harper & Row, New York, 1990.

23. P. Ackers et al., *Weirs and Flumes for Flow Measurement,* Wiley, New York, 1978.

24. M. G. Bos, J. A. Replogle, and A. J. Clemmens, *Flow Measuring Flumes for Open Channel Systems,* American Soc. Agricultural and Biological Engineers, St. Joseph, MI, 1991.

25. M. G. Bos, *Long-Throated Plumes and Broad-Crested Weirs,* Springer-Verlag, New York, 1984.

26. D. H. Hoggan, *Computer-Assisted Floodplain Hydrology and Hydraulics,* 2d ed., McGraw-Hill, New York, 1996.

27. R. Jeppson, *Open Channel Flow: Numerical Methods and Computer Applications,* CRC Press, Boca Raton, FL, 2010.

28. R. Szymkiewicz, *Numerical Modeling in Open Channel Hydraulics,* Springer, New York, 2010.

29. R. Baban, *Design of Diversion Weirs: Small Scale Irrigation in Hot Climates,* Wiley, New York, 1995.

30. H. Chanson, *Hydraulic Design of Stepped Cascades, Channels, Weirs, and Spillways,* Pergamon Press, New York, 1994.

31. D. Kampion and A. Brewer, *The Book of Waves: Form and Beauty on the Ocean*, 3d ed., Rowman and Littlefield, Lanham, MD, 1997.

32. L. Mays, *Water Resources Engineering,* Wiley, New York, 2005.

33. D. K. Walkowiak (ed.), *Isco Open Channel Flow Measurement Handbook*, 5th ed., Teledyne Isco, Inc., Lincoln, NE, 2006.

34. H. Chanson, "Photographic Observations of Tidal Bores (Mascarets) in France," Hydraulic Model Report CH71/08, The University of Queensland, 2008, 104 pages.

35. E. J. Watson, "The Spread of a Liquid Jet over a Horizontal Plane," *J. Fluid Mechanics*, vol. 20, 1964, pp. 481–499.

36. Z. Arendze and B. W. Skews, "Experimental and Numerical Study of the Hydraulic Analogy to Supersonic Flow," *South African Institution of Mechanical Engineering R&D Journal*, vol. 24, 2008, pp. 9–15.

37. T. J. Mueller and W. L. Oberkampf, "Hydraulic Analog for the Expansion Deflection Nozzle," *AIAA Journal*, vol. 5, 1967, pp. 1200–1202.

Wind turbines will play a large role in our energy future. The photo shows a 100 kW HAWT, installed in 2011 at the Fisherman's Memorial State Camp Ground in Narragansett, Rhode Island. It is programmed to generate 100 kW in winds from 13 to 25 m/s and supplies half the electricity needed for the camp's 18,000 annual visitors. Wind energy is good, but expensive. This turbine cost more, just to install, than it will recover in power savings over its 20-year life span. [*Photo courtesy of F. M. White*]

Chapter 11
Turbomachinery

Motivation. The most common practical engineering application for fluid mechanics is the design of fluid machinery. The most numerous types are machines that *add* energy to the fluid (the pump family), but also important are those that *extract* energy (turbines). Both types are usually connected to a rotating shaft, hence the name *turbomachinery.*

The purpose of this chapter is to make elementary engineering estimates of the performance of fluid machines. The emphasis will be on nearly incompressible flow: liquids or low-velocity gases. Basic flow principles are discussed, but not the detailed construction of the machines.

11.1 Introduction and Classification

Turbomachines divide naturally into those that add energy (pumps) and those that extract energy (turbines). The prefix *turbo-* is a Latin word meaning "spin" or "whirl," appropriate for rotating devices.

The pump is the oldest fluid energy transfer device known. At least two designs date before Christ: (1) the undershot-bucket waterwheels, or *norias,* used in Asia and Africa (1000 B.C.) and (2) Archimedes' screw pump (250 B.C.), still being manufactured today to handle solid–liquid mixtures. Paddlewheel turbines were used by the Romans in 70 B.C., and Babylonian windmills date back to 700 B.C. [1].

Machines that deliver liquids are simply called *pumps,* but if gases are involved, three different terms are in use, depending on the pressure rise achieved. If the pressure rise is very small (a few inches of water), a gas pump is called a *fan;* up to 1 atm, it is usually called a *blower;* and above 1 atm it is commonly termed a *compressor.*

Classification of Pumps

There are two basic types of pumps: positive-displacement and dynamic or momentum-change pumps. There are several billion of each type in use in the world today.

Positive-displacement pumps (PDPs) force the fluid along by volume changes. A cavity opens, and the fluid is admitted through an inlet. The cavity then closes, and the fluid is squeezed through an outlet. The mammalian heart is a good example, and many mechanical designs are in wide use. References 35–38 give a summary of PDPs. A brief classification of PDP designs is as follows:

A. Reciprocating
   1. Piston or plunger
   2. Diaphragm
B. Rotary
   1. Single rotor
      a. Sliding vane
      b. Flexible tube or lining
      c. Screw
      d. Peristaltic (wave contraction)
   2. Multiple rotors
      a. Gear
      b. Lobe
      c. Screw
      d. Circumferential piston

All PDPs deliver a pulsating or periodic flow as the cavity volume opens, traps, and squeezes the fluid. Their great advantage is the delivery of any fluid regardless of its viscosity.

Figure 11.1 shows schematics of the operating principles of seven of these PDPs. It is rare for such devices to be run backward, so to speak, as turbines or energy extractors, the steam engine (reciprocating piston) being a classic exception.

Since PDPs compress mechanically against a cavity filled with liquid, a common feature is that they develop immense pressures if the outlet is shut down for any reason. Sturdy construction is required, and complete shutoff would cause damage if pressure relief valves were not used.

Dynamic pumps simply add momentum to the fluid by means of fast-moving blades or vanes or certain special designs. There is no closed volume: The fluid increases momentum while moving through open passages and then converts its high velocity to a pressure increase by exiting into a diffuser section. Dynamic pumps can be classified as follows:

A. Rotary
   1. Centrifugal or radial exit flow
   2. Axial flow
   3. Mixed flow (between radial and axial)
B. Special designs
   1. Jet pump or ejector (see Fig. P3.36)
   2. Electromagnetic pumps for liquid metals
   3. Fluid-actuated: gas lift or hydraulic ram

We shall concentrate in this chapter on the rotary designs, sometimes called *rotodynamic pumps*. Other designs of both PDP and dynamic pumps are discussed in specialized texts [for example, 3, 31].

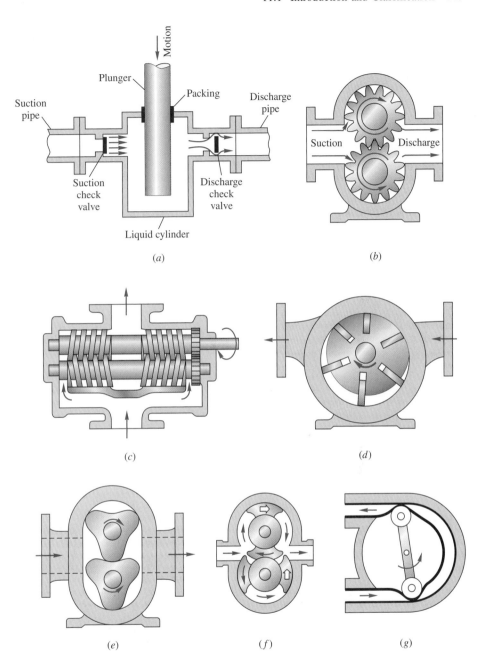

Fig. 11.1 Schematic design of positive-displacement pumps: (*a*) reciprocating piston or plunger, (*b*) external gear pump, (*c*) double-screw pump, (*d*) sliding vane, (*e*) three-lobe pump, (*f*) double circumferential piston, (*g*) flexible-tube squeegee.

Dynamic pumps generally provide a higher flow rate than PDPs and a much steadier discharge but are ineffective in handling high-viscosity liquids. Dynamic pumps also generally need *priming;* if they are filled with gas, they cannot suck up a liquid from below into their inlet. The PDP, on the other hand, is self-priming for most applications. A dynamic pump can provide very high flow rates (up to 300,000 gal/min) but usually with moderate pressure rises (a few atmospheres). In contrast,

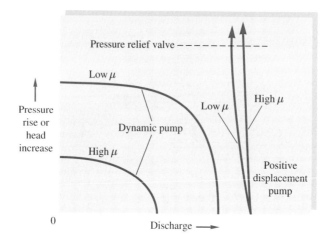

Fig. 11.2 Comparison of performance curves of typical dynamic and positive-displacement pumps at constant speed.

a PDP can operate up to very high pressures (300 atm) but typically produces low flow rates (100 gal/min).

The relative *performance* (Δp versus Q) is quite different for the two types of pump, as shown in Fig. 11.2. At constant shaft rotation speed, the PDP produces nearly constant flow rate and virtually unlimited pressure rise, with little effect of viscosity. The flow rate of a PDP cannot be varied except by changing the displacement or the speed. The reliable constant-speed discharge from PDPs has led to their wide use in metering flows [35].

The dynamic pump, by contrast in Fig. 11.2, provides a continuous constant-speed variation of performance, from near-maximum Δp at zero flow (shutoff conditions) to zero Δp at maximum flow rate. High-viscosity fluids sharply degrade the performance of a dynamic pump.

As usual—and for the last time in this text—we remind the reader that this is merely an introductory chapter. Many books are devoted solely to turbomachines: generalized treatments [2 to 7], texts specializing in pumps [8 to 16, 30, 31], fans [17 to 20], compressors [21 to 23], gas turbines [24 to 26], hydropower [27, 28, 29, 32], and PDPs [35 to 38]. There are several useful handbooks [30 to 32], and at least two undergraduate textbooks [33, 34] have a comprehensive discussion of turbomachines. The reader is referred to these sources for further details.

11.2 The Centrifugal Pump

Let us begin our brief look at rotodynamic machines by examining the characteristics of the centrifugal pump. As sketched in Fig. 11.3, this pump consists of an impeller rotating within a casing. Fluid enters axially through the *eye* of the casing, is caught up in the impeller blades, and is whirled tangentially and radially outward until it leaves through all circumferential parts of the impeller into the diffuser part of the casing. The fluid gains both velocity and pressure while passing through the impeller. The doughnut-shaped diffuser, or *scroll,* section of the casing decelerates the flow and further increases the pressure.

The impeller blades are usually *backward-curved,* as in Fig. 11.3, but there are also radial and forward-curved blade designs, which slightly change the output pressure.

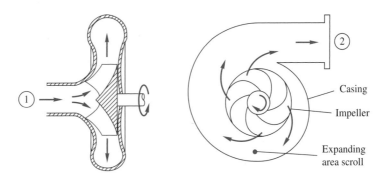

Fig. 11.3 Cutaway schematic of a typical centrifugal pump.

The blades may be *open* (separated from the front casing only by a narrow clearance) or *closed* (shrouded from the casing on both sides by an impeller wall). The diffuser may be *vaneless,* as in Fig. 11.3, or fitted with fixed vanes to help guide the flow toward the exit.

Basic Output Parameters

Assuming steady flow, the pump basically increases the Bernoulli head of the flow between point 1, the eye, and point 2, the exit. From Eq. (3.73), neglecting viscous work and heat transfer, this change is denoted by *H:*

$$H = \left(\frac{p}{\rho g} + \frac{V^2}{2g} + z\right)_2 - \left(\frac{p}{\rho g} + \frac{V^2}{2g} + z\right)_1 = h_s - h_f \qquad (11.1)$$

where h_s is the pump head supplied and h_f the losses. The net head *H* is a primary output parameter for any turbomachine. Since Eq. (11.1) is for incompressible flow, it must be modified for gas compressors with large density changes.

Usually V_2 and V_1 are about the same, $z_2 - z_1$ is no more than a meter or so, and the net pump head is essentially equal to the change in pressure head:

$$H \approx \frac{p_2 - p_1}{\rho g} = \frac{\Delta p}{\rho g} \qquad (11.2)$$

The power delivered to the fluid simply equals the specific weight times the discharge times the net head change:

$$P_w = \rho g Q H \qquad (11.3)$$

This is traditionally called the *water horsepower.* The power required to drive the pump is the *brake horsepower*[1]

$$bhp = \omega T \qquad (11.4)$$

where ω is the shaft angular velocity and *T* the shaft torque. If there were no losses, P_w and brake horsepower would be equal, but of course P_w is actually less, and the *efficiency* η of the pump is defined as

$$\eta = \frac{P_w}{bhp} = \frac{\rho g Q H}{\omega T} \qquad (11.5)$$

---

[1]Conversion factors may be needed: 1 hp = 550 ft · lbf/s = 746 W.

The chief aim of the pump designer is to make η as high as possible over as broad a range of discharge Q as possible.

The efficiency is basically composed of three parts: volumetric, hydraulic, and mechanical. The *volumetric efficiency* is

$$\eta_v = \frac{Q}{Q + Q_L} \tag{11.6}$$

where Q_L is the loss of fluid due to leakage in the impeller casing clearances. The *hydraulic efficiency* is

$$\eta_h = 1 - \frac{h_f}{h_s} \tag{11.7}$$

where h_f has three parts: (1) *shock* loss at the eye due to imperfect match between inlet flow and the blade entrances, (2) *friction* losses in the blade passages, and (3) *circulation* loss due to imperfect match at the exit side of the blades.

Finally, the *mechanical efficiency* is

$$\eta_m = 1 - \frac{P_f}{\text{bhp}} \tag{11.8}$$

where P_f is the power loss due to mechanical friction in the bearings, packing glands, and other contact points in the machine.

By definition, the total efficiency is simply the product of its three parts:

$$\eta \equiv \eta_v \eta_h \eta_m \tag{11.9}$$

The designer has to work in all three areas to improve the pump.

Elementary Pump Theory

You may have thought that Eqs. (11.1) to (11.9) were formulas from pump *theory*. Not so; they are merely definitions of performance parameters and cannot be used in any predictive mode. To actually *predict* the head, power, efficiency, and flow rate of a pump, two theoretical approaches are possible: (1) simple one-dimensional flow formulas and (2) complex computer models that account for viscosity and three-dimensionality. Many of the best design improvements still come from testing and experience, and pump research remains a very active field [39]. The last 10 years have seen considerable advances in *computational fluid dynamics* (CFD) modeling of flow in turbomachines [42], and at least eight commercial turbulent flow three-dimensional CFD codes are now available.

To construct an elementary theory of pump performance, we assume one-dimensional flow and combine idealized fluid velocity vectors through the impeller with the angular momentum theorem for a control volume, Eq. (3.59).

The idealized velocity diagrams are shown in Fig. 11.4. The fluid is assumed to enter the impeller at $r = r_1$ with velocity component w_1 tangent to the blade angle β_1 plus circumferential speed $u_1 = \omega r_1$ matching the tip speed of the impeller. Its absolute entrance velocity is thus the vector sum of w_1 and u_1, shown as V_1. Similarly, the flow exits at $r = r_2$ with component w_2 parallel to the blade angle β_2 plus tip speed $u_2 = \omega r_2$, with resultant velocity V_2.

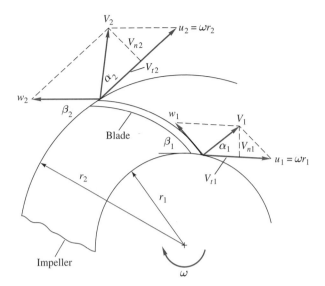

Fig. 11.4 Inlet and exit velocity diagrams for an idealized pump impeller.

We applied the angular momentum theorem to a turbomachine in Example 3.18 (Fig. 3.15) and arrived at a result for the applied torque T:

$$T = \rho Q(r_2 V_{t2} - r_1 V_{t1}) \tag{11.10}$$

where V_{t1} and V_{t2} are the absolute circumferential velocity components of the flow. The power delivered to the fluid is thus

or

$$\boxed{\begin{aligned} P_w &= \omega T = \rho Q(u_2 V_{t2} - u_1 V_{t1}) \\ H &= \frac{P_w}{\rho g Q} = \frac{1}{g}(u_2 V_{t2} - u_1 V_{t1}) \end{aligned}} \tag{11.11}$$

These are the *Euler turbomachine equations,* showing that the torque, power, and ideal head are functions only of the rotor-tip velocities $u_{1,2}$ and the absolute fluid tangential velocities $V_{t1,2}$, independent of the axial velocities (if any) through the machine.

Additional insight is gained by rewriting these relations in another form. From the geometry of Fig. 11.4

$$V^2 = u^2 + w^2 - 2uw \cos \beta \qquad w \cos \beta = u - V_t$$

or

$$uV_t = \tfrac{1}{2}(V^2 + u^2 - w^2) \tag{11.12}$$

Substituting this into Eq. (11.11) gives

$$H = \frac{1}{2g}[(V_2^2 - V_1^2) + (u_2^2 - u_1^2) - (w_2^2 - w_1^2)] \tag{11.13}$$

Thus the ideal head relates to the absolute plus the relative kinetic energy change of the fluid minus the rotor-tip kinetic energy change. Finally, substituting for H from its definition in Eq. (11.1) and rearranging, we obtain the classic relation

$$\frac{p}{\rho g} + z + \frac{w^2}{2g} - \frac{r^2 \omega^2}{2g} = \text{const} \qquad (11.14)$$

This is the *Bernoulli equation in rotating coordinates* and applies to either two- or three-dimensional ideal incompressible flow.

For a centrifugal pump, the power can be related to the radial velocity $V_n = V_t \tan \alpha$ and the continuity relation

$$P_w = \rho Q (u_2 V_{n2} \cot \alpha_2 - u_1 V_{n1} \cot \alpha_1) \qquad (11.15)$$

where

$$V_{n2} = \frac{Q}{2\pi r_2 b_2} \qquad \text{and} \qquad V_{n1} = \frac{Q}{2\pi r_1 b_1}$$

and where b_1 and b_2 are the blade widths at inlet and exit. With the pump parameters r_1, r_2, β_1, β_2, and ω known, Eq. (11.11) or Eq. (11.15) is used to compute idealized power and head versus discharge. The "design" flow rate Q^* is commonly estimated by assuming that the flow enters exactly normal to the impeller:

$$\alpha_1 = 90° \qquad V_{n1} = V_1 \qquad (11.16)$$

We can expect this simple analysis to yield estimates within ± 25 percent for the head, water horsepower, and discharge of a pump. Let us illustrate with an example.

EXAMPLE 11.1

Given are the following data for a commercial centrifugal water pump: $r_1 = 4$ in, $r_2 = 7$ in, $\beta_1 = 30°$, $\beta_2 = 20°$, speed $= 1440$ r/min. Estimate (*a*) the design point discharge, (*b*) the water horsepower, and (*c*) the head if $b_1 = b_2 = 1.75$ in.

Solution

Part (a)

The angular velocity is $\omega = 2\pi$ r/s $= 2\pi(1440/60) = 150.8$ rad/s. Thus the tip speeds are $u_1 = \omega r_1 = 150.8(4/12) = 50.3$ ft/s and $u_2 = \omega r_2 = 150.8(7/12) = 88.0$ ft/s. From the inlet velocity diagram, Fig. E11.1a, with $\alpha_1 = 90°$ for design point, we compute

$$V_{n1} = u_1 \tan 30° = 29.0 \text{ ft/s}$$

whence the discharge is

$$Q = 2\pi r_1 b_1 V_{n1} = (2\pi)\left(\frac{4}{12}\text{ ft}\right)\left(\frac{1.75}{12}\text{ ft}\right)\left(29.0\,\frac{\text{ft}}{\text{s}}\right)$$

$$= (8.87 \text{ ft}^3/\text{s})(60 \text{ s/min})\left(\frac{1728}{231}\text{ gal/ft}^3\right)$$

$$= 3980 \text{ gal/min} \qquad \qquad Ans. (a)$$

(The actual pump produces about 3500 gal/min.)

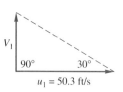

V_1

90°   30°

$u_1 = 50.3$ ft/s

E11.1a

Part (b)

The outlet radial velocity follows from Q:

$$V_{n2} = \frac{Q}{2\pi r_2 b_2} = \frac{8.87 \text{ ft}^3/\text{s}}{2\pi(\frac{7}{12}\text{ft})(\frac{1.75}{12}\text{ft})} = 16.6 \text{ ft/s}$$

This enables us to construct the outlet velocity diagram as in Fig. E11.1b, given $\beta_2 = 20°$. The tangential component is

$$V_{t2} = u_2 - V_{n2}\cot\beta_2 = 88.0 - 16.6\cot 20° = 42.4 \text{ ft/s}$$

$$\alpha_2 = \tan^{-1}\frac{16.6}{42.4} = 21.4°$$

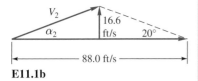

E11.1b

The power is then computed from Eq. (11.11) with $V_{t1} = 0$ at the design point:

$$P_w = \rho Q u_2 V_{t2} = (1.94 \text{ slugs/ft}^3)(8.87 \text{ ft}^3/\text{s})(88.0 \text{ ft/s})(42.4 \text{ ft/s})$$

$$= \frac{64,100 \text{ ft}\cdot\text{lbf/s}}{550 \text{ ft}-\text{lbf/(s}-\text{hp)}} = 117 \text{ hp} \qquad \text{Ans. (b)}$$

(The actual pump delivers about 125 water horsepower, requiring 147 bhp at 85 percent efficiency.)

Part (c)

Finally, the head is estimated from Eq. (11.11):

$$H \approx \frac{P_w}{\rho g Q} = \frac{64,100 \text{ ft}\cdot\text{lbf/s}}{(62.4 \text{ lbf/ft}^3)(8.87 \text{ ft}^3/\text{s})} = 116 \text{ ft} \qquad \text{Ans. (c)}$$

(The actual pump develops about 140-ft head.) Improved methods for obtaining closer estimates are given in advanced references [for example, 7, 8, and 31].

Effect of Blade Angle on Pump Head

The simple theory just discussed can be used to predict an important blade-angle effect. If we neglect inlet angular momentum, the theoretical water horsepower is

$$P_w = \rho Q u_2 V_{t2} \qquad (11.17)$$

where

$$V_{t2} = u_2 - V_{n2}\cot\beta_2 \qquad V_{n2} = \frac{Q}{2\pi r_2 b_2}$$

Then the theoretical head from Eq. (11.11) becomes

$$H \approx \frac{u_2^2}{g} - \frac{u_2\cot\beta_2}{2\pi r_2 b_2 g}Q \qquad (11.18)$$

The head varies linearly with discharge Q, having a shutoff value u_2^2/g, where u_2 is the exit blade-tip speed. The slope is negative if $\beta_2 < 90°$ (backward-curved blades) and positive for $\beta_2 > 90°$ (forward-curved blades). This effect is shown in Fig. 11.5 and is accurate only at low flow rates.

The measured shutoff head of centrifugal pumps is only about 60 percent of the theoretical value $H_0 = \omega^2 r_2^2/g$. With the advent of the laser-doppler anemometer, researchers can now make detailed three-dimensional flow measurements inside pumps and can even animate the data into a movie [40].

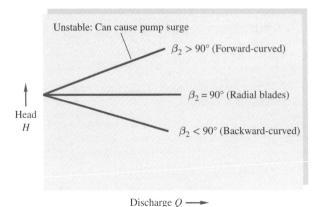

Fig. 11.5 Theoretical effect of blade exit angle on pump head versus discharge.

The positive slope condition in Fig. 11.5 can be unstable and can cause pump *surge,* an oscillatory condition where the pump "hunts" for the proper operating point. Surge may cause only rough operation in a liquid pump, but it can be a major problem in gas compressor operation. For this reason a backward-curved or radial blade design is generally preferred. A survey of the problem of pump stability is given by Greitzer [41].

11.3 Pump Performance Curves and Similarity Rules

Since the theory of the previous section is rather qualitative, the only solid indicator of a pump's performance lies in extensive testing. For the moment let us discuss the centrifugal pump in particular. The general principles and the presentation of data are exactly the same for mixed flow and axial flow pumps and compressors.

Performance charts are almost always plotted for constant shaft rotation speed n (in r/min usually). The basic independent variable is taken to be discharge Q (in gal/min usually for liquids and ft^3/min for gases). The dependent variables, or "output," are taken to be head H (pressure rise Δp for gases), brake horsepower (bhp), and efficiency η.

Figure 11.6 shows typical performance curves for a centrifugal pump. The head is approximately constant at low discharge and then drops to zero at $Q = Q_{max}$. At this speed and impeller size, the pump cannot deliver any more fluid than Q_{max}. The positive slope part of the head is shown dashed; as mentioned earlier, this region can be unstable and can cause hunting for the operating point.

The efficiency η is always zero at no flow and at Q_{max}, and it reaches a maximum, perhaps 80 to 90 percent, at about $0.6Q_{max}$. This is the *design flow rate Q^** or *best efficiency point* (BEP), $\eta = \eta_{max}$. The head and horsepower at BEP will be termed H^* and P^* (or bhp*), respectively. It is desirable that the efficiency curve be flat near η_{max}, so that a wide range of efficient operation is achieved. However, some designs simply do not achieve flat efficiency curves. Note that η is not independent of H and P but rather is calculated from the relation in Eq. (11.5), $\eta = \rho gQH/P$.

As shown in Fig. 11.6, the horsepower required to drive the pump typically rises monotonically with the flow rate. Sometimes there is a large power rise beyond the

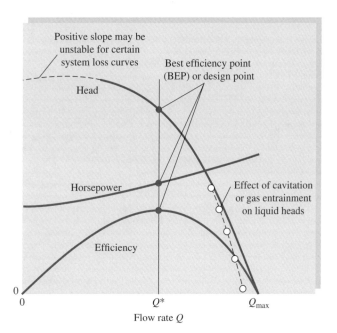

Fig. 11.6 Typical centrifugal pump performance curves at constant impeller rotation speed. The units are arbitrary.

BEP, especially for radial-tipped and forward-curved blades. This is considered undesirable because a much larger motor is then needed to provide high flow rates. Backward-curved blades typically have their horsepower level off above BEP ("nonoverloading" type of curve).

Measured Performance Curves

Figure 11.7 shows actual performance data for a commercial centrifugal pump. Figure 11.7a is for a basic casing size with three different impeller diameters. The head curves $H(Q)$ are shown, but the horsepower and efficiency curves have to be inferred from the contour plots. Maximum discharges are not shown, being far outside the normal operating range near the BEP. Everything is plotted raw, of course [feet, horsepower, gallons per minute (1 U.S. gal = 231 in^3)] since it is to be used directly by designers. Figure 11.7b is the same pump design with a 20 percent larger casing, a lower speed, and three larger impeller diameters. Comparing the two pumps may be a little confusing: The larger pump produces exactly the same discharge but only half the horsepower and half the head. This will be readily understood from the scaling or similarity laws we are about to formulate.

A point often overlooked is that raw curves like Fig. 11.7 are strictly applicable to a fluid of a certain density and viscosity, in this case water. If the pump were used to deliver, say, mercury, the brake horsepower would be about 13 times higher while Q, H, and η would be about the same. But in that case H should be interpreted as feet of *mercury,* not feet of water. If the pump were used for SAE 30 oil, *all* data would change (brake horsepower, Q, H, and η) due to the large change in viscosity (Reynolds number). Again this should become clear with the similarity rules.

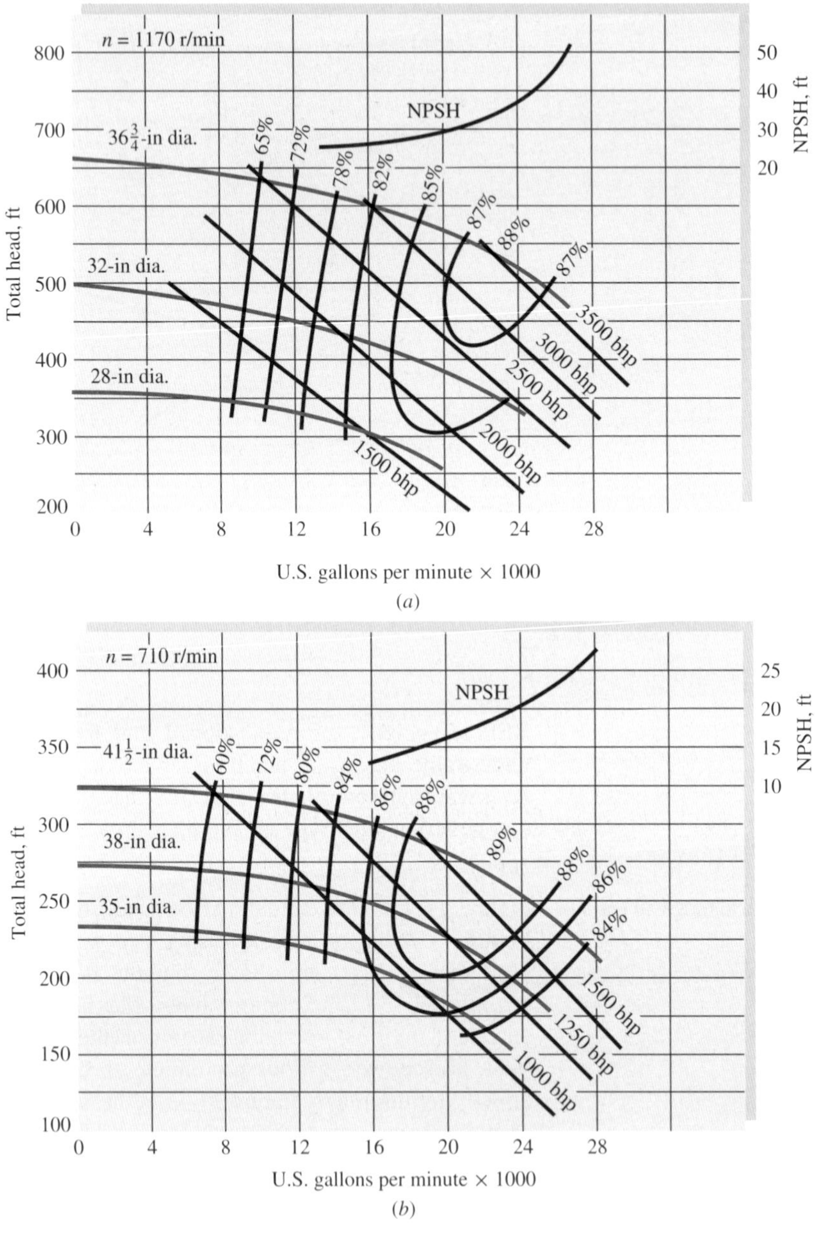

Fig. 11.7 Measured-performance curves for two models of a centrifugal water pump: (*a*) basic casing with three impeller sizes; (*b*) 20 percent larger casing with three larger impellers at slower speed. (*Courtesy of Ingersoll-Rand Corporation, Cameron Pump Division.*)

Net Positive-Suction Head

In the top of Fig. 11.7 is plotted the *net positive-suction head* (NPSH), which is the head required at the pump inlet to keep the liquid from cavitating or boiling. The pump inlet or suction side is the low-pressure point where cavitation will first occur. The NPSH is defined as

$$\text{NPSH} = \frac{p_i}{\rho g} + \frac{V_i^2}{2g} - \frac{p_v}{\rho g} \tag{11.19}$$

where p_i and V_i are the pressure and velocity at the pump inlet and p_v is the vapor pressure of the liquid. Given the left-hand side, NPSH, from the pump performance curve, we must ensure that the right-hand side is equal or greater in the actual system to avoid cavitation.

If the pump inlet is placed at a height Z_i above a reservoir whose free surface is at pressure p_a, we can use Bernoulli's equation to rewrite NPSH as

$$\text{NPSH} = \frac{p_a}{\rho g} - Z_i - h_{fi} - \frac{p_v}{\rho g} \tag{11.20}$$

where h_{fi} is the friction head loss between the reservoir and the pump inlet. Knowing p_a and h_{fi}, we can set the pump at a height Z_i that will keep the right-hand side greater than the "required" NPSH plotted in Fig. 11.7.

If cavitation does occur, there will be pump noise and vibration, pitting damage to the impeller, and a sharp dropoff in pump head and discharge. In some liquids this deterioration starts before actual boiling, as dissolved gases and light hydrocarbons are liberated.

Deviations from Ideal Pump Theory

The actual pump head data in Fig. 11.7 differ considerably from ideal theory, Eq. (11.18). Take, for example, the 36.75-in-diameter pump at 1170 r/min in Fig. 11.7a. The theoretical shutoff head is

$$H_0(\text{ideal}) = \frac{\omega^2 r_2^2}{g} = \frac{[1170(2\pi/60) \text{ rad/s}]^2 [(36.75/2)/(12) \text{ ft}]^2}{32.2 \text{ ft/s}^2} = 1093 \text{ ft}$$

From Fig. 11.7a, at $Q = 0$, we read the actual shutoff head to be only 670 ft, or 61 percent of the theoretical value (see Prob. P11.24). This is a sharp dropoff and is indicative of nonrecoverable losses of three types:

1. *Impeller recirculation loss,* significant only at low flow rates.
2. *Friction losses* on the blade and passage surfaces, which increase monotonically with the flow rate.
3. *"Shock" loss* due to mismatch between the blade angles and the inlet flow direction, especially significant at high flow rates.

These are complicated three-dimensional flow effects and hence are difficult to predict. Although, as mentioned, numerical (CFD) techniques are becoming more important [42], modern performance prediction is still a blend of experience, empirical correlations, idealized theory, and CFD modifications [45].

EXAMPLE 11.2

The 32-in pump of Fig. 11.7a is to pump 24,000 gal/min of water at 1170 r/min from a reservoir whose surface is at 14.7 lbf/in^2 absolute. If head loss from reservoir to pump inlet is 6 ft, where should the pump inlet be placed to avoid cavitation for water at (a) 60°F, $p_v = 0.26$ lbf/in^2 absolute, SG = 1.0 and (b) 200°F, $p_v = 11.52$ lbf/in^2 absolute, SG = 0.9635?

Solution

Part (a) For either case read from Fig. 11.7a at 24,000 gal/min that the required NPSH is 40 ft. For this case $\rho g = 62.4$ lbf/ft^3. From Eq. (11.20) it is necessary that

$$\text{NPSH} \le \frac{p_a - p_v}{\rho g} - Z_i - h_{fi}$$

or

$$40 \text{ ft} \le \frac{(14.7 - 0.26 \text{ lbf/in}^2)(144 \text{ in}^2/\text{ft}^2)}{62.4 \text{ lbf/ft}^3} - Z_i - 6.0$$

or

$$Z_i \le 27.3 - 40 = -12.7 \text{ ft} \qquad\qquad Ans. \ (a)$$

The pump must be placed at least 12.7 ft below the reservoir surface to avoid cavitation.

Part (b) For this case $\rho g = 62.4(0.9635) = 60.1$ lbf/ft^3. Equation (11.20) applies again with the higher p_v:

$$40 \text{ ft} \le \frac{(14.7 - 11.52 \text{ lbf/in}^2)(144 \text{ in}^2/\text{ft}^2)}{60.1 \text{ lbf/ft}^3} - Z_i - 6.0$$

or

$$Z_i \le 1.6 - 40 = -38.4 \text{ ft} \qquad\qquad Ans. \ (b)$$

The pump must now be placed at least 38.4 ft below the reservoir surface. These are unusually stringent conditions because a large, high-discharge pump requires a large NPSH.

Dimensionless Pump Performance

For a given pump design, the output variables H and brake horsepower should be dependent on discharge Q, impeller diameter D, and shaft speed n, at least. Other possible parameters are the fluid density ρ, viscosity μ, and surface roughness ε. Thus the performance curves in Fig. 11.7 are equivalent to the following assumed functional relations:[2]

$$gH = f_1(Q, D, n, \rho, \mu, \varepsilon) \qquad \text{bhp} = f_2(Q, D, n, \rho, \mu, \varepsilon) \qquad (11.21)$$

This is a straightforward application of dimensional analysis principles from Chap. 5. As a matter of fact, it was given as an exercise (Example 5.3). For each function in Eq. (11.21) there are seven variables and three primary dimensions (M, L, and T); hence we expect $7 - 3 = 4$ dimensionless pi groups, and that is what we get. You can verify as an exercise that appropriate dimensionless forms for Eqs. (11.21) are

$$\frac{gH}{n^2 D^2} = g_1\left(\frac{Q}{nD^3}, \frac{\rho n D^2}{\mu}, \frac{\varepsilon}{D}\right)$$

$$\frac{\text{bhp}}{\rho n^3 D^5} = g_2\left(\frac{Q}{nD^3}, \frac{\rho n D^2}{\mu}, \frac{\varepsilon}{D}\right) \qquad (11.22)$$

---

[2]We adopt gH as a variable instead of H for dimensional reasons.

The quantities $\rho n D^2/\mu$ and ε/D are recognized as the Reynolds number and roughness ratio, respectively. Three new pump parameters have arisen:

$$\text{Capacity coefficient } C_Q = \frac{Q}{nD^3}$$

$$\text{Head coefficient } C_H = \frac{gH}{n^2 D^2} \qquad (11.23)$$

$$\text{Power coefficient } C_P = \frac{\text{bhp}}{\rho n^3 D^5}$$

Note that only the power coefficient contains fluid density, the parameters C_Q and C_H being kinematic types.

Figure 11.7 gives no warning of viscous or roughness effects. The Reynolds numbers are from 0.8 to 1.5×10^7, or fully turbulent flow in all passages probably. The roughness is not given and varies greatly among commercial pumps. But at such high Reynolds numbers we expect more or less the same percentage effect on all these pumps. Therefore it is common to assume that the Reynolds number and the roughness ratio have a constant effect, so that Eqs. (11.23) reduce to, approximately,

$$C_H \approx C_H(C_Q) \qquad C_P \approx C_P(C_Q) \qquad (11.24)$$

For geometrically similar pumps, we expect head and power coefficients to be (nearly) unique functions of the capacity coefficient. We have to watch out that the pumps are geometrically similar or nearly so because (1) manufacturers put different-sized impellers in the same casing, thus violating geometric similarity, and (2) large pumps have smaller ratios of roughness and clearances to impeller diameter than small pumps. In addition, the more viscous liquids will have significant Reynolds number effects; for example, a factor-of-3 or more viscosity increase causes a clearly visible effect on C_H and C_P.

The efficiency η is already dimensionless and is uniquely related to the other three. It varies with C_Q also:

$$\eta \equiv \frac{C_H C_Q}{C_P} = \eta(C_Q) \qquad (11.25)$$

We can test Eqs. (11.24) and (11.25) from the data of Fig. 11.7. The impeller diameters of 32 and 38 in are approximately 20 percent different in size, and so their ratio of impeller to casing size is the same. The parameters C_Q, C_H, and C_P are computed with n in r/s, Q in ft^3/s (gal/min $\times$ 2.23 $\times$ 10^{-3}), H and D in ft, $g = 32.2$ ft/s^2, and brake horsepower in horsepower times 550 ft · lbf/(s · hp). The nondimensional data are then plotted in Fig. 11.8. A dimensionless suction head coefficient is also defined:

$$C_{HS} = \frac{g(\text{NPSH})}{n^2 D^2} = C_{HS}(C_Q) \qquad (11.26)$$

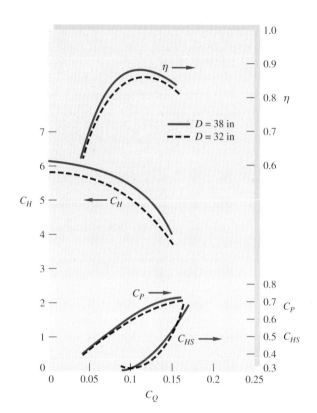

Fig. 11.8 Nondimensional plot of the pump performance data from Fig. 11.7. These numbers are not representative of other pump designs.

The coefficients C_P and C_{HS} are seen to correlate almost perfectly into a single function of C_Q, while η and C_H data deviate by a few percent. The last two parameters are more sensitive to slight discrepancies in model similarity; since the larger pump has smaller roughness and clearance ratios and a 40 percent larger Reynolds number, it develops slightly more head and is more efficient. The overall effect is a resounding victory for dimensional analysis.

The best efficiency point in Fig. 11.8 is approximately

$$C_{Q*} \approx 0.115 \qquad C_{P*} \approx 0.65$$

$$\eta_{max} \approx 0.88 \tag{11.27}$$

$$C_{H*} \approx 5.0 \qquad C_{HS*} \approx 0.37$$

These values can be used to estimate the BEP performance of any size pump in this geometrically similar family. In like manner, the shutoff head is $C_H(0) \approx 6.0$, and by extrapolation the shutoff power is $C_P(0) \approx 0.25$ and the maximum discharge is $C_{Q,max} \approx 0.23$. Note, however, that Fig. 11.8 gives no reliable information about, say, the 28- or 35-in impellers in Fig. 11.7, which have a different impeller-to-casing-size ratio and thus must be correlated separately.

By comparing values of $n^2 D^2$, nD^3, and $n^3 D^5$ for two pumps in Fig. 11.7, we can see readily why the large pump had the same discharge but less power and head:

	D, ft	n, r/s	Discharge nD^3, ft³/s	Head n^2D^2/g, ft	Power $\rho n^3 D^5/550$, hp
Fig. 11.7a	32/12	1170/60	370	84	3527
Fig. 11.7b	38/12	710/60	376	44	1861
Ratio	—	—	1.02	0.52	0.53

Discharge goes as nD^3, which is about the same for both pumps. Head goes as n^2D^2 and power as n^3D^5 for the same ρ (water), and these are about half as much for the larger pump. The NPSH goes as n^2D^2 and is also half as much for the 38-in pump.

EXAMPLE 11.3

A pump from the family of Fig. 11.8 has $D = 21$ in and $n = 1500$ r/min. Estimate (a) discharge, (b) head, (c) pressure rise, and (d) brake horsepower of this pump for water at 60°F and best efficiency.

Solution

Part (a)

In BG units take $D = 21/12 = 1.75$ ft and $n = 1500/60 = 25$ r/s. At 60°F, ρ of water is 1.94 slugs/ft³. The BEP parameters are known from Fig. 11.8 or Eqs. (11.27). The BEP discharge is thus

$$Q^* = C_{Q*}nD^3 = 0.115\,(25\text{ r/s})(1.75\text{ ft})^3 = (15.4\text{ ft}^3/\text{s})\left(448.8\,\frac{\text{gal/min}}{\text{ft}^3/\text{s}}\right) = 6900\text{ gal/min}$$

Ans. (a)

Part (b)

Similarly, the BEP head is

$$H^* = \frac{C_{H*}n^2D^2}{g} = \frac{5.0(25)^2(1.75)^2}{32.2} = 300\text{-ft water}$$

Ans. (b)

Part (c)

Since we are not given elevation or velocity head changes across the pump, we neglect them and estimate

$$\Delta p \approx \rho gH = 1.94(32.2)(300) = 18{,}600\text{ lbf/ft}^2 = 129\text{ lbf/in}^2$$

Ans. (c)

Part (d)

Finally, the BEP power is

$$P^* = C_{P*}\rho n^3D^5 = 0.65(1.94)(25)^3(1.75)^5$$

$$= \frac{323{,}000\text{ ft}\cdot\text{lbf/s}}{550} = 590\text{ hp}$$

Ans. (d)

EXAMPLE 11.4

We want to build a pump from the family of Fig. 11.8, which delivers 3000 gal/min water at 1200 r/min at best efficiency. Estimate (a) the impeller diameter, (b) the maximum discharge, (c) the shutoff head, and (d) the NPSH at best efficiency.

	Solution

Part (a) 3000 gal/min $= 6.68$ ft³/s   and 1200 r/min $= 20$ r/s. At BEP we have

$$Q* = C_{Q*}nD^3 = 6.68 \text{ ft}^3/\text{s} = (0.115)(20)D^3$$

$$D = \left[\frac{6.68}{0.115(20)}\right]^{1/3} = 1.43 \text{ ft} = 17.1 \text{ in} \qquad\qquad Ans. (a)$$

Part (b)   The maximum Q is related to $Q*$ by a ratio of capacity coefficients:

$$Q_{max} = \frac{Q*C_{Q,max}}{C_{Q*}} \approx \frac{3000(0.23)}{0.115} = 6000 \text{ gal/min} \qquad\qquad Ans. (b)$$

Part (c)   From Fig. 11.8 we estimated the shutoff head coefficient to be 6.0. Thus

$$H(0) \approx \frac{C_H(0)n^2D^2}{g} = \frac{6.0(20)^2(1.43)^2}{32.2} = 152 \text{ ft} \qquad\qquad Ans. (c)$$

Part (d)   Finally, from Eq. (11.27), the NPSH at BEP is approximately

$$\text{NPSH*} = \frac{C_{HS*}n^2D^2}{g} = \frac{0.37(20)^2(1.43)^2}{32.2} = 9.4 \text{ ft} \qquad\qquad Ans. (d)$$

Since this is a small pump, it will be less efficient than the pumps in Fig. 11.8, probably about 85 percent maximum.

Similarity Rules

The success of Fig. 11.8 in correlating pump data leads to simple rules for comparing pump performance. If pump 1 and pump 2 are from the same geometric family and are operating at homologous points (the same dimensionless position on a chart such as Fig. 11.8), their flow rates, heads, and powers will be related as follows:

$$\frac{Q_2}{Q_1} = \frac{n_2}{n_1}\left(\frac{D_2}{D_1}\right)^3 \qquad \frac{H_2}{H_1} = \left(\frac{n_2}{n_1}\right)^2\left(\frac{D_2}{D_1}\right)^2$$

$$\frac{P_2}{P_1} = \frac{\rho_2}{\rho_1}\left(\frac{n_2}{n_1}\right)^3\left(\frac{D_2}{D_1}\right)^5 \qquad\qquad\qquad (11.28)$$

These are the *similarity rules,* which can be used to estimate the effect of changing the fluid, speed, or size on any dynamic turbomachine—pump or turbine—within a geometrically similar family. A graphic display of these rules is given in Fig. 11.9, showing the effect of speed and diameter changes on pump performance. In Fig. 11.9a the size is held constant and the speed is varied 20 percent, while Fig. 11.9b shows a 20 percent size change at constant speed. The curves are plotted to scale but with arbitrary units. The speed effect (Fig. 11.9a) is substantial, but the size effect (Fig. 11.9b) is even more dramatic, especially for power, which varies as D^5. Generally we see that a given pump family can be adjusted in size and speed to fit a variety of system characteristics.

Strictly speaking, we would expect for perfect similarity that $\eta_1 = \eta_2$, but we have seen that larger pumps are more efficient, having a higher Reynolds number and lower roughness and clearance ratios. Two empirical correlations are recommended for

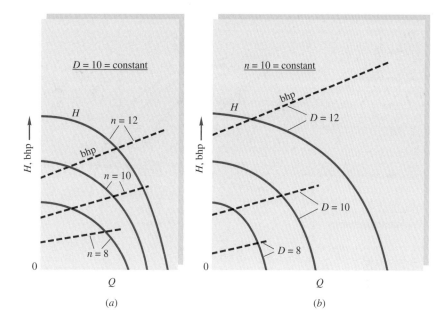

Fig. 11.9 Effect of changes in size and speed on homologous pump performance: (*a*) 20 percent change in speed at constant size; (*b*) 20 percent change in size at constant speed.
Source: Courtesy of Vickers Inc., PDN/PACE Division.

maximum efficiency. One, developed by Moody [43] for turbines but also used for pumps, is a size effect. The other, suggested by Anderson [44] from thousands of pump tests, is a flow rate effect:

Size changes [43]:
$$\frac{1 - \eta_2}{1 - \eta_1} \approx \left(\frac{D_1}{D_2}\right)^{1/4} \tag{11.29a}$$

Flow rate changes [44]:
$$\frac{0.94 - \eta_2}{0.94 - \eta_1} \approx \left(\frac{Q_1}{Q_2}\right)^{0.32} \tag{11.29b}$$

Anderson's formula (11.29*b*) makes the practical observation that even an infinitely large pump will have losses. He thus proposes a maximum possible efficiency of 94 percent, rather than 100 percent. Anderson recommends that the same formula be used for turbines if the constant 0.94 is replaced by 0.95. The formulas in Eq. (11.29) assume the same value of surface roughness for both machines—one could micropolish a small pump and achieve the efficiency of a larger machine.

Effect of Viscosity

Centrifugal pumps are often used to pump oils and other viscous liquids up to 1000 times the viscosity of water. But the Reynolds numbers become low turbulent or even laminar, with a strong effect on performance. Figure 11.10 shows typical test curves of head and brake horsepower versus discharge. High viscosity causes a dramatic drop in head and discharge and increases in power requirements. The efficiency also drops substantially according to the following typical results:

μ/μ_{water}	1.0	10.0	100	1000
η_{max}, %	85	76	52	11

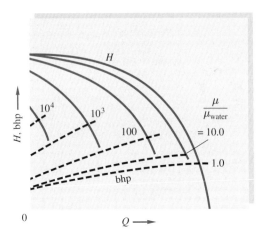

Fig. 11.10 Effect of viscosity on centrifugal pump performance.

Beyond about $300\mu_{water}$ the deterioration in performance is so great that a positive-displacement pump is recommended.

11.4 Mixed- and Axial-Flow Pumps: The Specific Speed

We have seen from the previous section that the modern centrifugal pump is a formidable device, able to deliver very high heads and reasonable flow rates with excellent efficiency. It can match many system requirements. But basically the centrifugal pump is a high-head, low-flow machine, whereas there are many applications requiring low head and high discharge. To see that the centrifugal design is not convenient for such systems, consider the following example.

EXAMPLE 11.5

We want to use a centrifugal pump from the family of Fig. 11.8 to deliver 100,000 gal/min of water at 60°F with a head of 25 ft. What should be (a) the pump size and speed and (b) brake horsepower, assuming operation at best efficiency?

Solution

Part (a)

Enter the known head and discharge into the BEP parameters from Eq. (11.27):

$$H^* = 25 \text{ ft} = \frac{C_{H*}n^2D^2}{g} = \frac{5.0n^2D^2}{32.2}$$

$$Q^* = 100,000 \text{ gal/min} = 222.8 \text{ ft}^3/\text{s} = C_{Q*}nD^3 = 0.115nD^3$$

The two unknowns are n and D. The algebra is quite simple, so we don't really need Excel. Solve for n in the Q^* equation and substitute into the H^* equation:

$$n = \frac{222.8}{0.115\,D^3} = \frac{1937}{D^3}; \quad 25 = \frac{5.0D^2}{32.2}\left(\frac{1937}{D^3}\right)^2 = \frac{582,840}{D^4}, \quad \text{or: } D^4 = 23,314$$

$$\text{Solve for} \quad D = 12.4 \text{ ft} \quad n = 1.03 \text{ r/s} = 62 \text{ r/min} \qquad Ans. (a)$$

Part (b)   The most efficient horsepower is then, from Eq. (11.27),

$$\text{bhp*} \approx C_{P*}\rho n^3 D^5 = \frac{0.65(1.94)(1.03)^3(12.4)^5}{550} = 720 \text{ hp} \qquad Ans. \ (b)$$

The solution to Example 11.5 is mathematically correct but results in a grotesque pump: an impeller more than 12 ft in diameter, rotating so slowly one can visualize oxen walking in a circle turning the shaft.

Other dynamic pump designs provide low head and high discharge. For example, there is a type of 38-in, 710 r/min pump, with the same input parameters as Fig. 11.7b, which will deliver the 25-ft head and 100,000 gal/min flow rate called for in Example 11.5. This is done by allowing the flow to pass through the impeller with an axial-flow component and less centrifugal component. The passages can be opened up to the increased flow rate with very little size increase, but the drop in radial outlet velocity decreases the head produced. These are the mixed-flow (part radial, part axial) and axial-flow (propeller-type) families of dynamic pump. Some vane designs are sketched in Fig. 11.11, which introduces an interesting new "design" parameter, the specific speed N_s or N_s'.

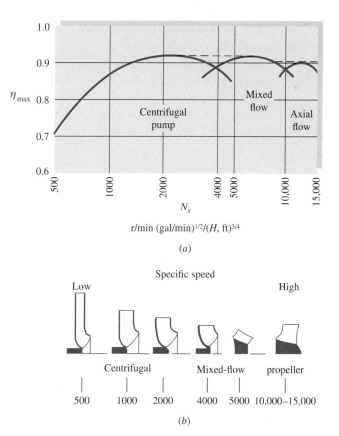

Fig. 11.11 (a) Optimum efficiency and (b) vane design of dynamic pump families as a function of specific speed.

The Specific Speed

Most pump applications involve a known head and discharge for the particular system, plus a speed range dictated by electric motor speeds or cavitation requirements. The designer then selects the best size and shape (centrifugal, mixed, axial) for the pump. To help this selection, we need a dimensionless parameter involving speed, discharge, and head but not size. This is accomplished by eliminating the diameter between C_Q and C_H, applying the result only to the BEP. This ratio is called the *specific speed* and has both a dimensionless form and a somewhat lazy, practical form:

Rigorous form:

$$N'_s = \frac{C_{Q*}^{1/2}}{C_{H*}^{3/4}} = \frac{n(Q*)^{1/2}}{(gH*)^{3/4}}$$

(11.30a)

Lazy but common:

$$N_s = \frac{(\text{r/min})(\text{gal/min})^{1/2}}{[H(\text{ft})]^{3/4}}$$

(11.30b)

In other words, practicing engineers do not bother to change n to revolutions per second or $Q*$ to cubic feet per second or to include gravity with head, although the latter would be necessary for, say, a pump on the moon. The conversion factor is

$$N_s = 17{,}182N'_s$$

Note that N_s is applied only to BEP; thus a single number characterizes an entire family of pumps. For example, the family of Fig. 11.8 has $N_s' \approx (0.115)^{1/2}/(5.0)^{3/4} = 0.1014$, $N_s = 1740$, regardless of size or speed.

It turns out that the specific speed is directly related to the most efficient pump design, as shown in Fig. 11.11. Low N_s means low Q and high H, hence a centrifugal pump, and large N_s implies an axial pump. The centrifugal pump is best for N_s between 500 and 4000, the mixed-flow pump for N_s between 4000 and 10,000, and the axial-flow pump for N_s above 10,000. Note the changes in impeller shape as N_s increases.

Suction Specific Speed

If we use NPSH rather than H in Eq. (11.30), the result is called *suction-specific speed:*

Rigorous:

$$N'_{ss} = \frac{nQ^{1/2}}{(g\ \text{NPSH})^{3/4}}$$

(11.31a)

Lazy:

$$N_{ss} = \frac{(\text{r/min})(\text{gal/min})^{1/2}}{[\text{NPSH (ft)}]^{3/4}}$$

(11.31b)

where NPSH denotes the available suction head of the system. Data from Wislicenus [4] show that a given pump is in danger of inlet cavitation if

$$N'_{ss} \geq 0.47 \qquad N_{ss} \geq 8100$$

In the absence of test data, this relation can be used, given n and Q, to estimate the minimum required NPSH.

Axial-Flow Pump Theory

A multistage axial-flow geometry is shown in Fig. 11.12a. The fluid essentially passes almost axially through alternate rows of fixed *stator* blades and moving *rotor* blades. The incompressible flow assumption is frequently used even for gases because the pressure rise per stage is usually small.

The simplified vector diagram analysis assumes that the flow is one-dimensional and leaves each blade row at a relative velocity exactly parallel to the exit blade angle. Figure 11.12b shows the stator blades and their exit velocity diagram. Since the stator is fixed, ideally the absolute velocity V_1 is parallel to the trailing edge of the blade. After vectorially subtracting the rotor tangential velocity u from V_1, we obtain the velocity w_1 relative to the rotor, which ideally should be parallel to the rotor leading edge.

Figure 11.12c shows the rotor blades and their exit velocity diagram. Here the relative velocity w_2 is parallel to the blade trailing edge, while the absolute velocity V_2 should be designed to smoothly enter the next row of stator blades.

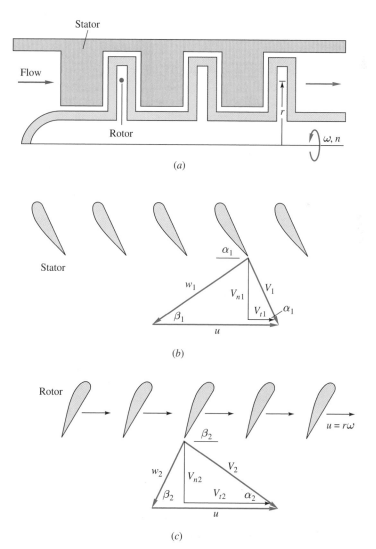

Fig. 11.12 Analysis of an axial-flow pump: (*a*) basic geometry; (*b*) stator blades and exit velocity diagram; (*c*) rotor blades and exit velocity diagram.

The theoretical power and head are given by Euler's turbine relation (11.11). Since there is no radial flow, the inlet and exit rotor speeds are equal, $u_1 = u_2$, and one-dimensional continuity requires that the axial-velocity component remain constant:

$$V_{n1} = V_{n2} = V_n = \frac{Q}{A} = \text{const}$$

From the geometry of the velocity diagrams, the normal velocity (or volume flow) can be directly related to the blade rotational speed u:

$$u = \omega r_{av} = V_{n1}(\cot \alpha_1 + \cot \beta_1) = V_{n2}(\cot \alpha_2 + \cot \beta_2) \qquad (11.32)$$

Thus the flow rate can be predicted from the rotational speed and the blade angles. Meanwhile, since $V_{t1} = V_{n1} \cot \alpha_1$ and $V_{t2} = u - V_{n2} \cot \beta_2$, Euler's relation (11.11) for the pump head becomes

$$gH = uV_n(\cot \alpha_2 - \cot \alpha_1)$$

$$= u^2 - uV_n(\cot \alpha_1 + \cot \beta_2) \qquad (11.33)$$

the preferred form because it relates to the blade angles α_1 and β_2. The shutoff or no-flow head is seen to be $H_0 = u^2/g$, just as in Eq. (11.18) for a centrifugal pump. The blade-angle parameter $\cot \alpha_1 + \cot \beta_2$ can be designed to be negative, zero, or positive, corresponding to a rising, flat, or falling head curve, as in Fig. 11.5.

Strictly speaking, Eq. (11.33) applies only to a single streamtube of radius r, but it is a good approximation for very short blades if r denotes the average radius. For long blades it is customary to sum Eq. (11.33) in radial strips over the blade area. Such complexity may not be warranted since theory, being idealized, neglects losses and usually predicts the head and power larger than those in actual pump performance.

Performance of an Axial-Flow Pump

At high specific speeds, the most efficient choice is an axial-flow, or propeller, pump, which develops high flow rate and low head. A typical dimensionless chart for a propeller pump is shown in Fig. 11.13. Note, as expected, the higher C_Q and lower C_H compared with Fig. 11.8. The head curve drops sharply with discharge, so a large system head change will cause a mild flow change. The power curve drops with head also, which means a possible overloading condition if the system discharge should suddenly decrease. Finally, the efficiency curve is rather narrow and triangular, as opposed to the broad, parabolic-shaped centrifugal pump efficiency (Fig. 11.8).

By inspection of Fig. 11.13, $C_{Q*} \approx 0.55$, $C_{H*} \approx 1.07$, $C_{P*} \approx 0.70$, and $\eta_{max} \approx 0.84$. From this we compute $N_s' \approx (0.55)^{1/2}/(1.07)^{3/4} = 0.705$, $N_s = 12,000$. The relatively low efficiency is due to small pump size: $d = 14$ in, $n = 690$ r/min, $Q* = 4400$ gal/min.

A repetition of Example 11.5 using Fig. 11.13 would show that this propeller pump family can provide a 25-ft head and 100,000 gal/min discharge if $D = 46$ in and $n = 430$ r/min, with bhp $= 750$; this is a much more reasonable design solution, with improvements still possible at larger-N_s conditions.

Pump Performance versus Specific Speed

Specific speed is such an effective parameter that it is used as an indicator of both performance and efficiency. Figure 11.14 shows a correlation of the optimum efficiency of a pump as a function of the specific speed and capacity. Because the

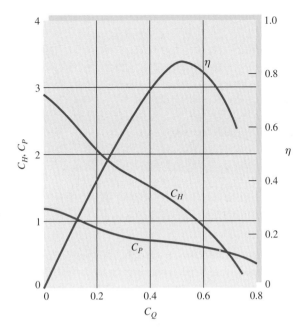

Fig. 11.13 Dimensionless performance curves for a typical axial-flow pump, $N_s = 12{,}000$. Constructed from data given by Stepanoff [8] for a 14-in pump at 690 r/min.

dimensional parameter Q is a rough measure of both size and Reynolds number, η increases with Q. When this type of correlation was first published by Wislicenus [4] in 1947, it became known as *the* pump curve, a challenge to all manufacturers. We can check that the pumps of Figs. 11.7 and 11.13 fit the correlation very well.

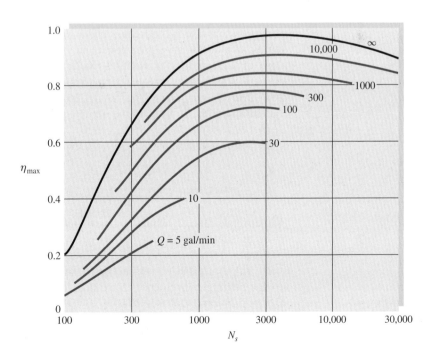

Fig. 11.14 Optimum efficiency of pumps versus capacity and specific speed. *(Adapted from Refs. 4 and 31.)*

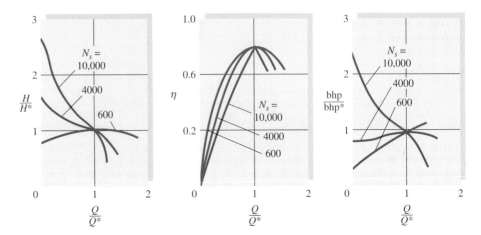

Fig. 11.15 Effect of specific speed on pump performance curves.

Figure 11.15 shows the effect of specific speed on the shape of the pump performance curves, normalized with respect to the BEP point. The numerical values shown are representative but somewhat qualitative. The high-specific-speed pumps ($N_s \approx 10,000$) have head and power curves that drop sharply with discharge, implying overload or start-up problems at low flow. Their efficiency curve is very narrow.

A low-specific-speed pump ($N_s = 600$) has a broad efficiency curve, a rising power curve, and a head curve that "droops" at shutoff, implying possible surge or hunting problems.

The Free Propeller

The propeller-style pump of Fig. 11.12 is enclosed in a duct and captures all the approach flow. In contrast, the *free propeller,* for either aircraft or marine applications, acts in an unbounded fluid and thus is much less effective. The analog of propeller-pump pressure rise is the free propeller *thrust* per unit area ($\pi D^2/4$) swept out by the blades. In a customary dimensional analysis, thrust T and power required P are functions of fluid density ρ, rotation rate n (rev/s), forward velocity V, and propeller diameter D. Viscosity effects are small and neglected. You might enjoy analyzing this as a Chap. 5 assignment. The NACA (now the NASA) chose (ρ, n, D) as repeating variables, and the results are the accepted parameters:

$$C_T = \text{thrust coefficient} = \frac{T}{\rho n^2 D^4} = \text{fcn}(J), J = \text{advance ratio} = \frac{V}{nD}$$

$$C_P = \text{power coefficient} = \frac{P}{\rho n^3 D^5} = \text{fcn}(J), \eta = \text{efficiency} = \frac{VT}{P} = \frac{JC_T}{C_P} \quad (11.34)$$

The advance ratio, J, which compares forward velocity to a measure proportional to blade tip speed, has a strong effect upon thrust and power.

Figure 11.16 shows performance data for a propeller used on the Cessna 172 aircraft. The thrust and power coefficients are small, of $\mathcal{O}(0.05)$, and are multiplied by 10 for plotting convenience. Maximum efficiency is 83 percent at $J = 0.7$, where $C_T^* \approx 0.040$ and $C_P^* \approx 0.034$.

There are several engineering methods for designing propellers. These theories are described in specialized texts, both for marine [60] and aircraft [61] propellers.

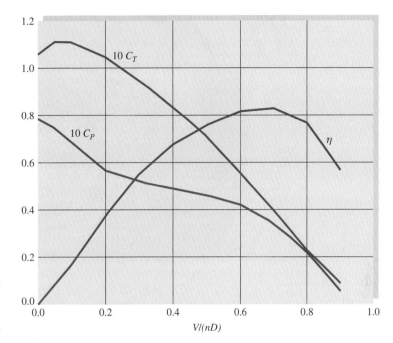

Fig. 11.16 Performance data for a free propeller used on the Cessna 172 aircraft. Compare to Fig. 11.13 for a (ducted) propeller pump. The thrust and power coefficients are much smaller for the free propeller.

Computational Fluid Dynamics

The design of turbomachinery has traditionally been highly experimental, with simple theories, such as in Sec. 11.2, only able to predict trends. Dimensionless correlations, such as Fig. 11.15, are useful but require extensive experimentation. Consider that flow in a pump is three-dimensional; unsteady (both periodic and turbulent); and involves flow separation, recirculation in the impeller, unsteady blade wakes passing through the diffuser, and blade roots, tips, and clearances. It is no wonder that one-dimensional theory cannot give firm quantitative predictions.

Modern computer analysis can give realistic results and is becoming a useful tool for turbomachinery designers. A good example is Ref. 56, reporting combined experimental and computational results for a centrifugal pump diffuser. A photograph of the device is shown in Fig. 11.17a. It is made of clear Perspex, so that laser measurements of particle tracking velocimetry (LPTV) and doppler anemometry (LDA) could be taken throughout the system. The data were compared with a CFD simulation of the impeller and diffuser, using the grids shown in Fig. 11.17b. The computations used a turbulence formulation called the k-ε model, popular in commercial CFD codes (see Sec. 8.9). Results were good but not excellent. The CFD model predicted velocity and pressure data adequately up until flow separation, after which it was only qualitative. Clearly, CFD is developing a significant role in turbomachinery design [42, 45].

11.5 Matching Pumps to System Characteristics

The ultimate test of a pump is its match with the operating system characteristics. Physically, the system head must match the head produced by the pump, and this intersection should occur in the region of best efficiency.

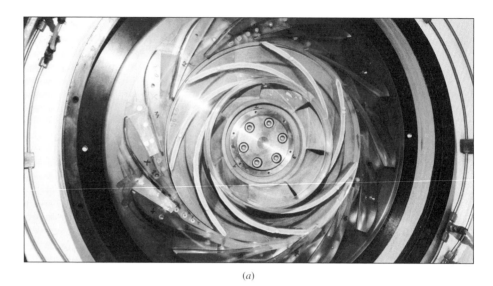

(a)

Impeller

Fig. 11.17 Turbomachinery design now involves both experimentation and computational fluid dynamics (CFD): (a) a centrifugal impeller and diffuser; (b) a three-dimensional CFD model grid for this system. *Sources: (a) courtesy of K. Eisele et al., "Flow Analysis in a Pump Diffuser: Part 1, Measurements: Part 2, CFD," Journal of Fluids Eng. Vol. 119, December 1997, pp. 967–984/American Society of Mechanical Engineers (b) From K. Eisele et al., "Row Analysis in a Pump Diffuser: Part I Measurements; Part 2, CFD," J. Fluids Eng., vol. 119, December 1997, pp. 967–984. by permission of the American Society of Mechanical Engineers.*

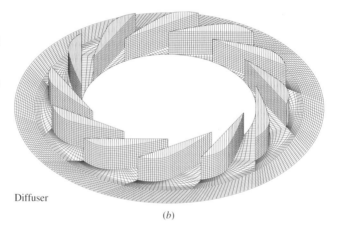

Diffuser

(b)

The system head will probably contain a static elevation change $z_2 - z_1$ plus friction losses in pipes and fittings:

$$H_{sys} = (z_2 - z_1) + \frac{V^2}{2g}\left(\sum \frac{fL}{D} + \sum K\right)$$

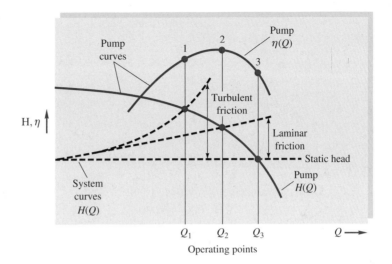

Fig. 11.18 Illustration of pump operating points for three types of system head curves.

where $\Sigma\, K$ denotes minor losses and V is the flow velocity in the principal pipe. Since V is proportional to the pump discharge Q, the equation represents a system head curve $H_s(Q)$. Three examples are shown in Fig. 11.18: a static head $H_s = a$, static head plus laminar friction $H_s = a + bQ$, and static head plus turbulent friction $H_s = a + cQ^2$. The intersection of the system curve with the pump performance curve $H(Q)$ defines the operating point. In Fig. 11.18 the laminar friction operating point is at maximum efficiency while the turbulent and static curves are off design. This may be unavoidable if system variables change, but the pump should be changed in size or speed if its operating point is consistently off design. Of course, a perfect match may not be possible because commercial pumps have only certain discrete sizes and speeds. Let us illustrate these concepts with an example.

EXAMPLE 11.6

We want to use the 32-in pump of Fig. 11.7a at 1170 r/min to pump water at 60°F from one reservoir to another 120 ft higher through 1500 ft of 16-in-ID pipe with friction factor $f = 0.030$. (a) What will the operating point and efficiency be? (b) To what speed should the pump be changed to operate at the BEP?

Solution

Part (a)

For reservoirs the initial and final velocities are zero; thus the system head is

$$H_s = z_2 - z_1 + \frac{V^2}{2g}\frac{fL}{D} = 120\text{ ft} + \frac{V^2}{2g}\frac{0.030(1500\text{ ft})}{\frac{16}{12}\text{ ft}}$$

From continuity in the pipe, $V = Q/A = Q/[\frac{1}{4}\pi(\frac{16}{12}\text{ ft})^2]$, and so we substitute for V to get

$$H_s = 120 + 0.269Q^2 \qquad Q \text{ in ft}^3/\text{s} \tag{1}$$

Since Fig. 11.7a uses thousands of gallons per minute for the abscissa, we convert Q in Eq. (1) to this unit:

$$H_s = 120 + 1.335Q^2 \qquad Q \text{ in } 10^3 \text{ gal/min} \tag{2}$$

We can plot Eq. (2) on Fig. 11.7a and see where it intersects the 32-in pump head curve, as in Fig. E11.6. A graphical solution gives approximately

$$H \approx 430 \text{ ft} \qquad Q \approx 15,000 \text{ gal/min}$$

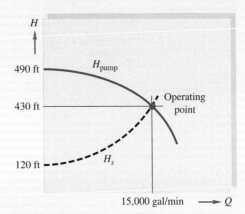

E11.6

The efficiency is about 82 percent, slightly off design.

An analytic solution is possible if we fit the pump head curve to a parabola, which is very accurate:

$$H_{\text{pump}} \approx 490 - 0.26Q^2 \qquad Q \text{ in } 10^3 \text{ gal/min} \tag{3}$$

Equations (2) and (3) must match at the operating point:

$$490 - 0.26Q^2 = 120 + 1.335Q^2$$

or
$$Q^2 = \frac{490 - 120}{0.26 + 1.335} = 232$$

$$Q = 15.2 \times 10^3 \text{ gal/min} = 15,200 \text{ gal/min} \qquad\qquad Ans.\ (a)$$

$$H = 490 - 0.26(15.2)^2 = 430 \text{ ft} \qquad\qquad Ans.\ (a)$$

Part (b)   To move the operating point to BEP, we change n, which changes both $Q \propto n$ and $H \propto n^2$. From Fig. 11.7a, at BEP, $H^* \approx 386$ ft; thus for any n, $H^* = 386(n/1170)^2$. Also read $Q^* \approx 20 \times 10^3$ gal/min; thus for any n, $Q^* = 20(n/1170)$. Match H^* to the system characteristics, Eq. (2):

$$H^* = 386\left(\frac{n}{1170}\right)^2 \approx 120 + 1.335\left(20\,\frac{n}{1170}\right)^2 \qquad\qquad Ans.\ (b)$$

which gives $n^2 < 0$. Thus it is impossible to operate at maximum efficiency with this particular system and pump.

Pumps Combined in Parallel

If a pump provides the right head but too little discharge, a possible remedy is to combine two similar pumps in parallel, sharing the same suction and inlet conditions. A parallel arrangement is also used if delivery demand varies, so that one pump is used at low flow and the second pump is started up for higher discharges. Both pumps should have check valves to avoid backflow when one is shut down.

The two pumps in parallel need not be identical. Physically, their flow rates will sum for the same head, as illustrated in Fig. 11.19a. If pump A has more head than pump B, pump B cannot be added in until the operating head is below the shutoff head of pump B. Since the system curve rises with Q, the combined delivery Q_{A+B} will be less than the separate operating discharges $Q_A + Q_B$ but certainly greater than

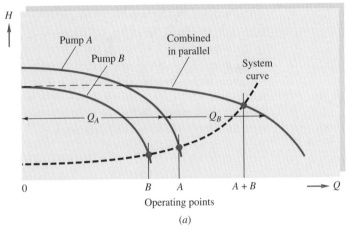

(a)

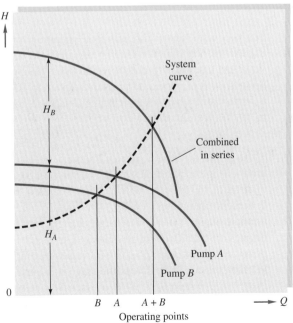

Fig. 11.19 Performance and operating points of two pumps operating singly and (a) in parallel or (b) in series.
Source: Copyright United Technologies Corporation 2008. Used with permission.

(b)

either one. For a very flat (static) curve two similar pumps in parallel will deliver nearly twice the flow. The combined brake horsepower is found by adding brake horsepower for each of pumps A and B at the same head as the operating point. The combined efficiency equals $\rho g(Q_{A+B})(H_{A+B})/(550 \text{ bhp}_{A+B})$.

If pumps A and B are not identical, as in Fig. 11.19a, pump B should not be run and cannot even be started up if the operating point is above its shutoff head.

Pumps Combined in Series

If a pump provides the right discharge but too little head, consider adding a similar pump in series, with the output of pump B fed directly into the suction side of pump A. As sketched in Fig. 11.19b, the physical principle for summing in series is that the two heads add at the same flow rate to give the combined performance curve. The two need not be identical at all, since they merely handle the same discharge; they may even have different speeds, although normally both are driven by the same shaft.

The need for a series arrangement implies that the system curve is steep, that is, it requires higher head than either pump A or B can provide. The combined operating point head will be more than either A or B separately but not as great as their sum. The combined power is the sum of brake horsepower for A and B at the operating point flow rate. The combined efficiency is

$$\frac{\rho g(Q_{A+B})(H_{A+B})}{550 \text{ bhp}_{A+B}}$$

similar to parallel pumps.

Whether pumps are used in series or in parallel, the arrangement will be uneconomical unless both pumps are operating near their best efficiency.

Multistage Pumps

For very high heads in continuous operation, the solution is a multistage pump, with the exit of one impeller feeding directly into the eye of the next. Centrifugal, mixed-flow, and axial-flow pumps have all been grouped in as many as 50 stages, with heads up to 8000 ft of water and pressure rises up to 5000 lbf/in^2 absolute. Figure 11.20 shows a section of a seven-stage centrifugal propane compressor that develops 300 lbf/in^2 rise at 40,000 ft^3/min and 35,000 bhp.

Compressors

Most of the discussion in this chapter concerns incompressible flow—that is, negligible change in fluid density. Even the pump of Fig. 11.7, which can produce 600 ft of head at 1170 r/min, will increase standard air pressure only by 46 lbf/ft^2, about a 2 percent change in density. The picture changes at higher speeds, $\Delta p \propto n^2$, and multiple stages, where very large changes in pressure and density are achieved. Such devices are called *compressors*, as in Fig. 11.20. The concept of static head, $H = \Delta p/\rho g$, becomes inappropriate, since ρ varies. Compressor performance is measured by (1) the pressure ratio across the stage p_2/p_1 and (2) the change in stagnation enthalpy $(h_{02} - h_{01})$, where $h_0 = h + \frac{1}{2}V^2$ (see Sec. 9.3). Combining m stages in series results in $p_{\text{final}}/p_{\text{initial}} \approx (p_2/p_1)^m$. As density increases, less area is needed: note the decrease in impeller size from right to left in Fig. 11.20. Compressors may be either of the centrifugal or axial-flow type [21 to 23].

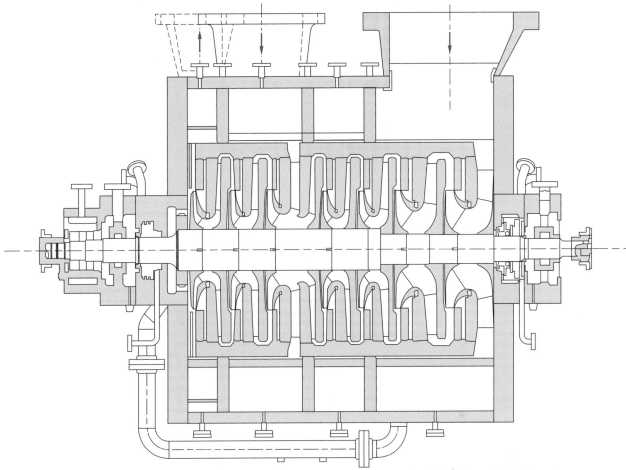

Fig. 11.20 Cross section of a seven-stage centrifugal propane compressor that delivers 40,000 ft^3/min at 35,000 bhp and a pressure rise of 300 lbf/in^2. Note the second inlet at stage 5 and the varying impeller designs.
Source: Courtesy of DeLavai-Stork V.OF., Centrifugal Compressor Division.

Compressor efficiency, from inlet condition 1 to final outlet f, is defined by the change in gas enthalpy, assuming an adiabatic process:

$$\eta_{\text{comp}} = \frac{h_f - h_{01}}{h_{0f} - h_{01}} \approx \frac{T_f - T_{01}}{T_{0f} - T_{01}}$$

Compressor efficiencies are similar to hydraulic machines ($\eta_{\text{max}} \approx 70$ to 80 percent), but the mass flow range is more limited: on the low side by compressor *surge,* where blade stall and vibration occur, and on the high side by *choking* (Sec. 9.4), where the Mach number reaches 1.0 somewhere in the system. Compressor mass flow is normally plotted using the same type of dimensionless function formulated in Eq. (9.47): $\dot{m}(RT_0)^{1/2}/(D^2 p_0)$, which will reach a maximum when choking occurs. For further details, see Refs. 21 to 23.

EXAMPLE 11.7

Investigate extending Example 11.6 by using two 32-in pumps in parallel to deliver more flow. Is this efficient?

Solution

Since the pumps are identical, each delivers $\frac{1}{2}Q$ at the same 1170 r/min speed. The system curve is the same, and the balance-of-head relation becomes

$$H = 490 - 0.26(\tfrac{1}{2}Q)^2 = 120 + 1.335Q^2$$

or $\qquad Q^2 = \dfrac{490 - 120}{1.335 + 0.065} \qquad Q = 16{,}300 \text{ gal/min} \qquad\qquad Ans.$

This is only 7 percent more than a single pump. Each pump delivers $\frac{1}{2}Q = 8130$ gal/min, for which the efficiency is only 60 percent. The total brake horsepower required is 3200, whereas a single pump used only 2000 bhp. This is a poor design.

EXAMPLE 11.8

Suppose the elevation change in Example 11.6 is raised from 120 to 500 ft, greater than a single 32-in pump can supply. Investigate using two 32-in pumps in series at 1170 r/min.

Solution

Since the pumps are identical, the total head is twice as much and the constant 120 in the system head curve is replaced by 500. The balance of heads becomes

$$H = 2(490 - 0.26Q^2) = 500 + 1.335Q^2$$

or $\qquad Q^2 = \dfrac{980 - 500}{1.335 + 0.52} \qquad Q = 16.1 \times 10^3 \text{ gal/min} \qquad\qquad Ans.$

The operating head is $500 + 1.335(16.1)^2 = 845$ ft, or 97 percent more than that for a single pump in Example 11.5. Each pump is operating at 16.1×10^3 gal/min, which from Fig. 11.7a is 83 percent efficient, a pretty good match to the system. To pump at this operating point requires 4100 bhp, or about 2050 bhp for each pump.

Gas Turbines

Some modern devices contain both pumps and turbines. A classic case is the *gas turbine,* which combines a compressor, a combustion chamber, a turbine, and, often, a fan. Gas turbines are used to drive aircraft, helicopters, Army tanks, and small electric power plants. They have a higher power-to-weight ratio than reciprocating engines, but they spin at very high speeds and require high-temperature materials and thus are costly. The compressor raises the inlet air to pressures as much as 30 to 40 times higher, before entering the combustion chamber. The heated air then passes through a turbine, which drives the compressor. The airflow then exits to provide the thrust and is generally a supersonic flow.

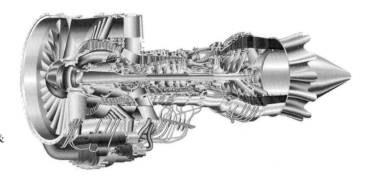

Fig. 11.21 Cutaway view of a Pratt & Whitney 6000 turbofan aircraft engine. *(Copyright United Technologies Corporation 2008. Used with permission.)*

Fan LPC HPC Combustor HPT LPT Exhaust

The example illustrated in Fig. 11.21 is a Pratt & Whitney 6000 turbofan aircraft engine. The large entrance fan greatly increases the airflow into the engine, some of which bypasses the compressors. The central flow enters a low-pressure (LPC) and a high-pressure (HPC) compressor and thence into the combustor. After combustion, the hot, high-velocity gases pass through a high-pressure turbine (HPT), which drives the HPC, and a low-pressure turbine (LPT), which separately drives both the LPC and the fan. The exhaust gases then create the thrust in the usual momentum–exchange manner. The engine shown, designed for shorter airline flights, has a maximum thrust of 24,000 lbf.

11.6 Turbines

A turbine extracts energy from a fluid that possesses high head, but it is fatuous to say a turbine is a pump run backward. Basically there are two types, reaction and impulse, the difference lying in the manner of head conversion. In the *reaction turbine,* the fluid fills the blade passages, and the head change or pressure drop occurs within the impeller. Reaction designs are of the radial-flow, mixed-flow, and axial-flow types and are essentially dynamic devices designed to admit the high-energy fluid and extract its momentum. An *impulse turbine* first converts the high head through a nozzle into a high-velocity jet, which then strikes the blades at one position as they pass by. The impeller passages are not fluid-filled, and the jet flow past the blades is essentially at constant pressure. Reaction turbines are smaller because fluid fills all the blades at one time.

Reaction Turbines

Reaction turbines are low-head, high-flow devices. The flow is opposite that in a pump, entering at the larger-diameter section and discharging through the eye after giving up most of its energy to the impeller. Early designs were very inefficient because they lacked stationary guide vanes at the entrance to direct the flow smoothly into the impeller passages. The first efficient inward-flow turbine was built in 1849 by James B. Francis, a U.S. engineer, and all radial- or mixed-flow designs are now called *Francis turbines.* At still lower heads, a turbine can be designed more compactly with purely axial flow and is termed a *propeller turbine* [52]. The propeller may be either fixed-blade or adjustable (Kaplan type), the latter being complicated mechanically but much

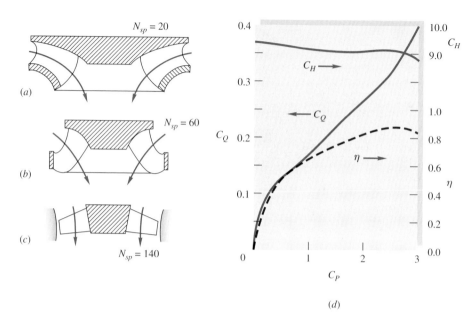

Fig. 11.22 Reaction turbines: (*a*) Francis, radial type; (*b*) Francis mixed-flow; (*c*) propeller axial-flow; (*d*) performance curves for a Francis turbine, $n = 600$ r/min, $D = 2.25$ ft, $N_{sp} = 29$.

more efficient at low-power settings. Figure 11.22 shows sketches of runner designs for Francis radial, Francis mixed-flow, and propeller-type turbines.

Idealized Radial Turbine Theory

The Euler turbomachine formulas (11.11) also apply to energy-extracting machines if we reverse the flow direction and reshape the blades. Figure 11.23 shows a radial turbine runner. Again assume one-dimensional frictionless flow through the blades. Adjustable inlet guide vanes are absolutely necessary for good efficiency. They bring the inlet flow to the blades at angle α_2 and absolute velocity V_2 for minimum "shock" or directional-mismatch loss. After vectorially adding in the runner tip speed $u_2 = \omega r_2$, the outer blade angle should be set at angle β_2 to accommodate the relative velocity w_2, as shown in the figure. (See Fig. 11.4 for the analogous radial pump velocity diagrams.)

Application of the angular momentum control volume theorem, Eq. (3.59), to Fig. 11.23 (see Example 3.18 for a similar case) yields an idealized formula for the power P extracted by the runner:

$$P = \omega T = \rho\omega Q(r_2 V_{t2} - r_1 V_{t1}) = \rho Q(u_2 V_2 \cos\alpha_2 - u_1 V_1 \cos\alpha_1) \quad (11.35)$$

where V_{t2} and V_{t1} are the absolute inlet and outlet circumferential velocity components of the flow. Note that Eq. (11.35) is identical to Eq. (11.11) for a radial pump, except that the blade shapes are different.

The absolute inlet normal velocity $V_{n2} = V_2 \sin\alpha_2$ is proportional to the flow rate Q. If the flow rate changes and the runner speed u_2 is constant, the vanes must be adjusted to a new angle α_2 so that w_2 still follows the blade surface. Thus adjustable inlet vanes are very important to avoid shock loss.

Power Specific Speed

Turbine parameters are similar to those of a pump, but the dependent variable is the output brake horsepower, which depends on the inlet flow rate Q, available head H,

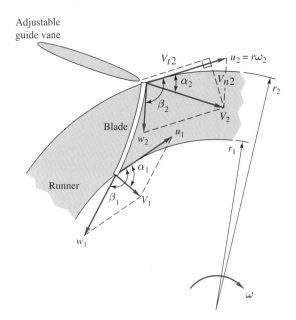

Fig. 11.23 Inlet and outlet velocity diagrams for an idealized radial-flow reaction turbine runner.

impeller speed n, and diameter D. The efficiency is the output brake horsepower divided by the available water horsepower $\rho g Q H$. The dimensionless forms are C_Q, C_H, and C_P, defined just as for a pump, Eqs. (11.23). If we neglect Reynolds number and roughness effects, the functional relationships are written with C_P as the independent variable:

$$C_H = \frac{gH}{n^2 D^2} = C_H(C_P) \qquad C_Q = \frac{Q}{nD^3} = C_Q(C_P) \qquad \eta = \frac{\text{bhp}}{\rho g Q H} = \eta(C_P) \qquad (11.36)$$

where

$$C_P = \frac{\text{bhp}}{\rho n^3 D^5}$$

Figure 11.22d shows typical performance curves for a small Francis radial turbine. The maximum efficiency point is called the *normal power,* and the values for this particular turbine are

$$\eta_{\max} = 0.89 \qquad C_{P*} = 2.70 \qquad C_{Q*} = 0.34 \qquad C_{H*} = 9.03$$

A parameter that compares the output power with the available head, independent of size, is found by eliminating the diameter between C_H and C_P. It is called the *power specific speed:*

Rigorous form:

$$N'_{sp} = \frac{C_P^{*1/2}}{C_H^{*5/4}} = \frac{n(\text{bhp})^{1/2}}{\rho^{1/2}(gH)^{5/4}} \qquad (11.37a)$$

Lazy but common:

$$N_{sp} = \frac{(\text{r/min})(\text{bhp})^{1/2}}{[H\,(\text{ft})]^{5/4}} \qquad (11.37b)$$

For water, $\rho = 1.94$ slugs/ft^3 and $N_{sp} = 273.3 N'_{sp}$. The various turbine designs divide up nicely according to the range of power specific speed, as follows:

Turbine type	N_{sp} range	C_H range
Impulse	1–10	15–50
Francis	10–110	5–25
Propeller:		
Water	100–250	1–4
Gas, steam	25–300	10–80

Note that N_{sp}, like N_s for pumps, is defined only with respect to the BEP and has a single value for a given turbine family. In Fig. 11.22d, $N_{sp} = 273.3(2.70)^{1/2}/(9.03)^{5/4} = 29$, regardless of size.

Like pumps, turbines of large size are generally more efficient, and Eqs. (11.29) can be used as an estimate when data are lacking.

The design of a complete large-scale power-generating turbine system is a major engineering project, involving inlet and outlet ducts, trash racks, guide vanes, wicket gates, spiral cases, generator with cooling coils, bearings and transmission gears, runner blades, draft tubes, and automatic controls. Some typical large-scale reaction turbine designs are shown in Fig. 11.24. The reversible pump-and-turbine design of Fig. 11.24d requires special care for adjustable guide vanes to be efficient for flow in either direction.

The largest (1000-MW) hydropower designs are awesome when viewed on a human scale, as shown in Fig. 11.25. The economic advantages of small-scale model testing are evident from this photograph of the Francis turbine units at Grand Coulee Dam.

Impulse Turbines

For high head and relatively low power (that is, low N_{sp}) not only would a reaction turbine require too high a speed but also the high pressure in the runner would require a massive casing thickness. The impulse turbine of Fig. 11.26 is ideal for this situation. Since N_{sp} is low, n will be low and the high pressure is confined to the small nozzle, which converts the head to an atmospheric pressure jet of high velocity V_j. The jet strikes the buckets and imparts a momentum change similar to that in our control volume analysis for a moving vane in Example 3.9 or Prob. P3.51. The buckets have an elliptical split-cup shape, as in Fig. 11.26b. They are named *Pelton wheels,* after Lester A. Pelton (1829–1908), who produced the first efficient design.

In Example 3.10 we found that the force per unit mass flow on a single moving vane, or in this case a single Pelton bucket, was $(V_j - u)(1 - \cos \beta)$, where u is the vane velocity and β is the exit angle of the jet. For a single vane, as in Example 3.10, the mass flow would be $\rho A_j(V_j - u)$, but for a Pelton wheel, where buckets keep entering the jet and capture all the flow, the mass flow would be $\rho Q = \rho A_j V_j$. An alternative analysis uses the Euler turbomachine equation (11.11) and the velocity diagram of Fig. 11.26c. Noting that $u_1 = u_2 = u$, we substitute the absolute exit and inlet tangential velocities into the turbine power relation:

$$P = \rho Q(u_1 V_{t1} - u_2 V_{t2}) = \rho Q\{uV_j - u[u + (V_j - u)\cos \beta]\}$$

or

$$P = \rho Q u(V_j - u)(1 - \cos \beta) \tag{11.38}$$

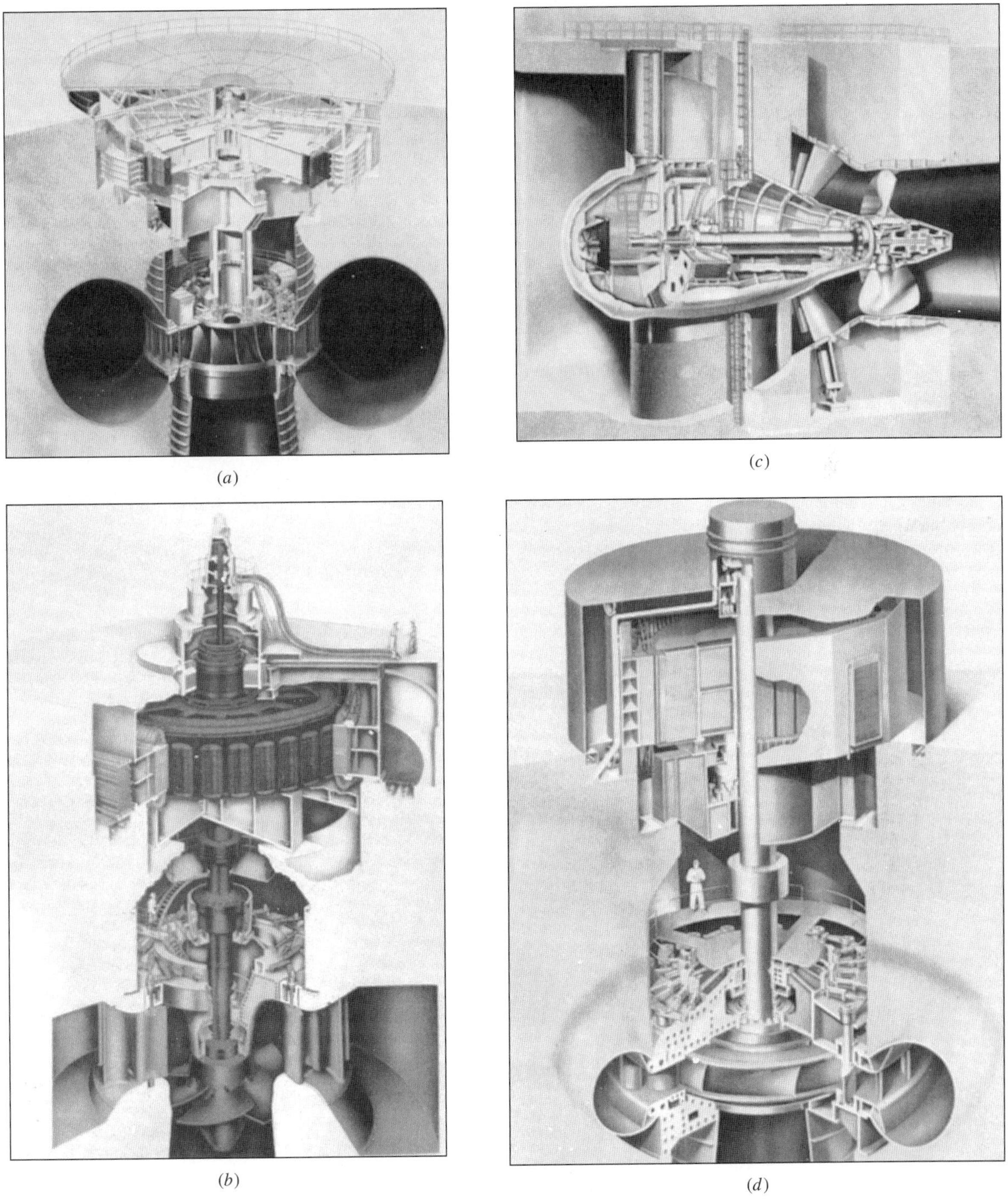

(a)

(c)

(b)

(d)

Fig. 11.24 Large-scale turbine designs depend on available head and flow rate and operating conditions: (*a*) Francis (radial); (*b*) Kaplan (propeller); (*c*) bulb mounting with propeller runner; (*d*) reversible pump turbine with radial runner. *(Courtesy of Voith Siemens Hydro Power.)*

Fig. 11.25 Interior view of the 1.1-million hp (820-MW) turbine units on the Grand Coulee Dam of the Columbia River, showing the spiral case, the outer fixed vanes ("stay ring"), and the inner adjustable vanes ("wicket gates"). *(Courtesy of Voith Siemens Hydro Power.)*

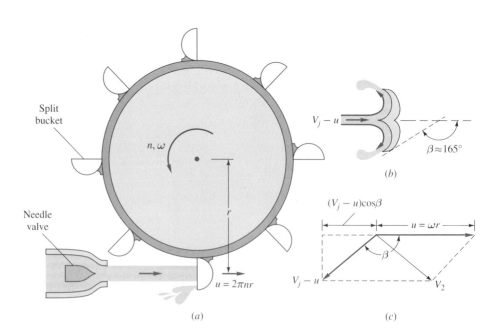

Fig. 11.26 Impulse turbine:
(*a*) side view of wheel and jet;
(*b*) top view of bucket;
(*c*) typical velocity diagram.

where $u = 2\pi nr$ is the bucket linear velocity and r is the *pitch radius,* or distance to the jet centerline. A bucket angle $\beta = 180°$ gives maximum power but is physically impractical. In practice, $\beta \approx 165°$, or $1 - \cos \beta \approx 1.966$ or only 2 percent less than maximum power.

From Eq. (11.38) the theoretical power of an impulse turbine is parabolic in bucket speed u and is maximum when $dP/du = 0$, or

$$u^* = 2\pi n^* r = \tfrac{1}{2}V_j \tag{11.39}$$

For a perfect nozzle, the entire available head would be converted to jet velocity $V_j = (2gH)^{1/2}$. Actually, since there are 2 to 8 percent nozzle losses, a velocity coefficient C_v is used:

$$V_j = C_v(2gH)^{1/2} \quad 0.92 \le C_v \le 0.98 \tag{11.40}$$

By combining Eqs. (11.36) and (11.40), the theoretical impulse turbine efficiency becomes

$$\boxed{\eta = 2(1 - \cos \beta)\phi(C_v - \phi)} \tag{11.41}$$

where

$$\boxed{\phi = \frac{u}{(2gH)^{1/2}} = \text{peripheral velocity factor}}$$

Maximum efficiency occurs at $\phi = \tfrac{1}{2}C_v \approx 0.47$.

Figure 11.27 shows Eq. (11.41) plotted for an ideal turbine ($\beta = 180°$, $C_v = 1.0$) and for typical working conditions ($\beta = 160°$, $C_v = 0.94$). The latter case predicts $\eta_{max} = 85$ percent at $\phi = 0.47$, but the actual data for a 24-in Pelton wheel test are somewhat less efficient due to windage, mechanical friction, backsplashing, and nonuniform bucket flow. For this test $\eta_{max} = 80$ percent, and, generally speaking, an impulse turbine is not quite as efficient as the Francis or propeller turbines at their BEPs.

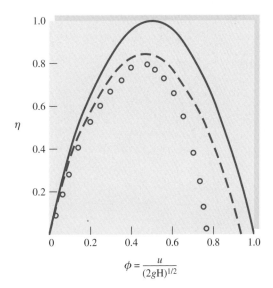

Fig. 11.27 Efficiency of an impulse turbine calculated from Eq. (11.41): solid curve = ideal, $\beta = 180°$, $C_v = 1.0$; dashed curve = actual, $\beta = 160°$, $C_v = 0.94$; open circles = data, Pelton wheel, diameter = 2 ft.

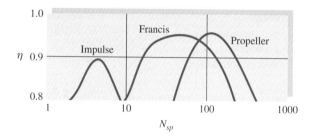

Fig. 11.28 Optimum efficiency of turbine designs.

Figure 11.28 shows the optimum efficiency of the three turbine types, and the importance of the power specific speed N_{sp} as a selection tool for the designer. These efficiencies are optimum and are obtained in careful design of large machines.

The water power available to a turbine may vary due to either net head or flow rate changes, both of which are common in field installations such as hydroelectric plants. The demand for turbine power also varies from light to heavy, and the operating response is a change in the flow rate by adjustment of a gate valve or needle valve (Fig. 11.26a). As shown in Fig. 11.29, all three turbine types achieve fairly uniform efficiency as a function of the level of power being extracted. Especially effective is the adjustable-blade (Kaplan-type) propeller turbine, while the poorest is a fixed-blade propeller. The term *rated power* in Fig. 11.29 is the largest power delivery guaranteed by the manufacturer, as opposed to *normal power,* which is delivered at maximum efficiency.

For further details of design and operation of turbomachinery, the readable and interesting treatment in Ref. 33 is especially recommended. The feasibility of micro-hydropower is discussed in Refs. 27, 28, and 46.

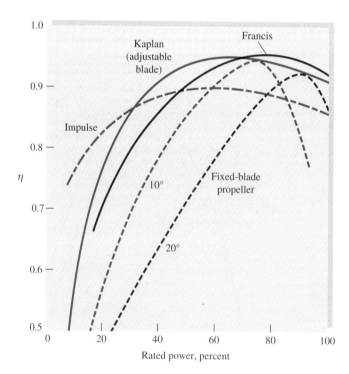

Fig. 11.29 Efficiency versus power level for various turbine designs at constant speed and head.

EXAMPLE 11.9

Investigate the possibility of using (a) a Pelton wheel similar to Fig. 11.27 or (b) the Francis turbine family of Fig. 11.22d to deliver 30,000 bhp from a net head of 1200 ft.

Solution

Part (a)

From Fig. 11.28, the most efficient Pelton wheel occurs at about

$$N_{sp} \approx 4.5 = \frac{(\text{r/min})(30{,}000 \text{ bhp})^{1/2}}{(1200 \text{ ft})^{1.25}}$$

or
$$n = 183 \text{ r/min} = 3.06 \text{ r/s}$$

From Fig. 11.27 the best operating point is

$$\phi \approx 0.47 = \frac{\pi D(3.06 \text{ r/s})}{[2(32.2)(1200)]^{1/2}}$$

or
$$D = 13.6 \text{ ft} \qquad \textit{Ans. (a)}$$

This Pelton wheel is perhaps a little slow and a trifle large. You could reduce D and increase n by increasing N_{sp} to, say, 6 or 7 and accepting the slight reduction in efficiency. Or you could use a double-hung, two-wheel configuration, each delivering 15,000 bhp, which changes D and n by the factor $2^{1/2}$:

Double wheel: $\quad n = (183)2^{1/2} = 260 \text{ r/min} \qquad D = \dfrac{13.6}{2^{1/2}} = 9.6 \text{ ft} \qquad \textit{Ans. (a)}$

Part (b)

The Francis wheel of Fig. 11.22d must have

$$N_{sp} = 29 = \frac{(\text{r/min})(30{,}000 \text{ bhp})^{1/2}}{(1200 \text{ ft})^{1.25}}$$

or
$$n = 1183 \text{ r/min} = 19.7 \text{ r/s}$$

Then the optimum power coefficient is

$$C_{P*} = 2.70 = \frac{P}{\rho n^3 D^5} = \frac{30{,}000(550)}{(1.94)(19.7)^3 D^5}$$

or
$$D^5 = 412 \qquad D = 3.33 \text{ ft} = 40 \text{ in} \qquad \textit{Ans. (b)}$$

This is a faster speed than normal practice, and the casing would have to withstand 1200 ft of water or about 520 lbf/in² internal pressure, but the 40-in size is extremely attractive. Francis turbines are now being operated at heads up to 1500 ft.

Wind Turbines

Wind energy has long been used as a source of mechanical power. The familiar four-bladed windmills of Holland, England, and the Greek islands have been used for centuries to pump water, grind grain, and saw wood. Modern research concentrates on the ability of wind turbines to generate electric power. Koeppl [47] stresses the potential for propeller-type machines. See also Refs. 47 to 51.

Some examples of wind turbine designs are shown in Fig. 11.30. The familiar American multiblade farm windmill (Fig. 11.30*a*) is of low efficiency, but thousands are in use as a rugged, reliable, and inexpensive way to pump water. A more efficient design is the propeller mill in Fig. 11.30*b*, similar to the pioneering Smith-Putnam 1250-kW two-bladed system that operated on Grampa's Knob, 12 mi west of Rutland, Vermont, from 1941 to 1945. The Smith-Putnam design broke because of inadequate blade strength, but it withstood winds up to 115 mi/h and its efficiency was amply demonstrated [47].

The Dutch, American multiblade, and propeller mills are examples of *horizontal-axis wind turbines* (HAWTs), which are efficient but somewhat awkward in that they require extensive bracing and gear systems when combined with an electric generator. Thus a competing family of *vertical-axis wind turbines* (VAWTs) has been proposed to simplify gearing and strength requirements. Figure 11.30*c* shows the "eggbeater" VAWT invented by G. J. M. Darrieus in 1925. To minimize centrifugal stresses, the twisted blades of the Darrieus turbine follow a *troposkien* curve formed by a chain anchored at two points on a spinning vertical rod. The Darrieus design has the advantage that the generator and gearbox may be placed on the ground for easy access. It is not as efficient, though, as a HAWT, and, furthermore, it is not self-starting. The largest Darrieus device known to the writer is a 4.2 MW turbine, 100 m in diameter, at Cap Chat, Québec, Canada.

The four-arm Dutch-type windmill in Fig. 11.30*d* is found throughout Europe and the Middle East and dates back to the 9th century. In the Netherlands, they are primarily used to drain lowlands. The mill in the photo was built in 1787 to grind corn. It is now a Rhode Island tourist attraction.

Idealized Wind Turbine Theory

The ideal, frictionless efficiency of a propeller windmill was predicted by A. Betz in 1920, using the simulation shown in Fig. 11.31. The propeller is represented by an *actuator disk,* which creates across the propeller plane a pressure discontinuity of area A and local velocity V. The wind is represented by a streamtube of approach velocity V_1 and a slower downstream wake velocity V_2. The pressure rises to p_b just before the disk and drops to p_a just after, returning to free-stream pressure in the far wake. To hold the propeller rigid when it is extracting energy from the wind, there must be a leftward force F on its support, as shown.

A control-volume–horizontal-momentum relation applied between sections 1 and 2 gives

$$\sum F_x = -F = \dot{m}(V_2 - V_1)$$

A similar relation for a control volume just before and after the disk gives

$$\sum F_x = -F + (p_b - p_a)A = \dot{m}(V_a - V_b) = 0$$

Equating these two yields the propeller force:

$$F = (p_b - p_a)A = \dot{m}(V_1 - V_2) \tag{11.42}$$

(a)

(c)

Fig. 11.30 Wind turbine designs:
(a) the American multiblade farm
HAWT; (b) a modern three-blade,
750 kW HAWT on a wind farm in
Plouarzel, France *(courtesy of
Hubert Chanson)*; (c) The Darrieus
VAWT *(courtesy of National
Research Council Canada)*; (d) a
four-blade Dutch-type windmill,
built in 1787 in Jamestown, Rhode
Island *(courtesy of F. M. White)*.

(b)

(d)

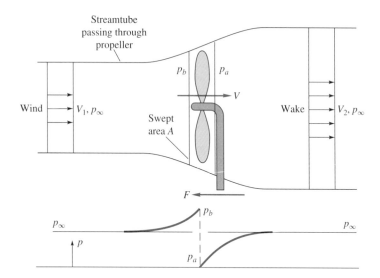

Fig. 11.31 Idealized actuator disk and streamtube analysis of flow through a windmill.

Assuming ideal flow, the pressures can be found by applying the incompressible Bernoulli relation up to the disk:

From 1 to b: $$p_\infty + \tfrac{1}{2}\rho V_1^2 = p_b + \tfrac{1}{2}\rho V^2$$

From a to 2: $$p_a + \tfrac{1}{2}\rho V^2 = p_\infty + \tfrac{1}{2}\rho V_2^2$$

Subtracting these and noting that $\dot{m} = \rho A V$ through the propeller, we can substitute for $p_b - p_a$ in Eq. (11.42) to obtain

$$p_b - p_a = \tfrac{1}{2}\rho(V_1^2 - V_2^2) = \rho V(V_1 - V_2)$$

or $$V = \tfrac{1}{2}(V_1 + V_2) \tag{11.43}$$

Continuity and momentum thus require that the velocity V through the disk equal the average of the wind and far-wake speeds.

Finally, the power extracted by the disk can be written in terms of V_1 and V_2 by combining Eqs. (11.42) and (11.43):

$$P = FV = \rho A V^2(V_1 - V_2) = \tfrac{1}{4}\rho A(V_1^2 - V_2^2)(V_1 + V_2) \tag{11.44}$$

For a given wind speed V_1, we can find the maximum possible power by differentiating P with respect to V_2 and setting equal to zero. The result is

$$P = P_{\text{max}} = \tfrac{8}{27}\rho A V_1^3 \qquad \text{at } V_2 = \tfrac{1}{3}V_1 \tag{11.45}$$

which corresponds to $V = 2V_1/3$ through the disk.

The maximum available power to the propeller is the mass flow through the propeller times the total kinetic energy of the wind:

$$P_{\text{avail}} = \tfrac{1}{2}\dot{m}V_1^2 = \tfrac{1}{2}\rho A V_1^3$$

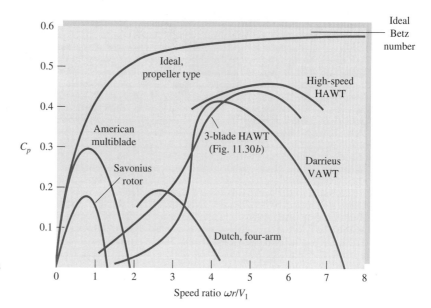

Fig. 11.32 Estimated performance of various wind turbine designs as a function of blade-tip speed ratio. *(From Ref. 53.)*

Thus the maximum possible efficiency of an ideal frictionless wind turbine is usually stated in terms of the *power coefficient:*

$$C_P = \frac{P}{\frac{1}{2}\rho A V_1^3} \tag{11.46}$$

Equation (11.45) states that the total power coefficient is

$$C_{p,\text{max}} = \tfrac{16}{27} = 0.593 \tag{11.47}$$

This is called the *Betz number* and serves as an ideal with which to compare the actual performance of real windmills.

Figure 11.32 shows the measured power coefficients of various wind turbine designs. The independent variable is not V_2/V_1 (which is artificial and convenient only in the ideal theory) but the ratio of blade-tip speed ωr to wind speed. Note that the tip can move much faster than the wind, a fact disturbing to the laity but familiar to engineers in the behavior of iceboats and sailing vessels. The Darrieus has the many advantages of a vertical axis but has little torque at low speeds (see Fig. 11.32) and also rotates more slowly at maximum power than a propeller, thus requiring a higher gear ratio for the generator. The Savonius rotor (Fig. 6.29b) has been suggested as a VAWT design because it produces power at very low wind speeds, but it is inefficient and susceptible to storm damage because it cannot be feathered in high winds.

As shown in Fig. 11.33, there are many areas of the world where wind energy is an attractive alternative, such as Ireland, Greenland, Iceland, Argentina, Chile, New Zealand, and Newfoundland. Robinson [53] points out that Australia, with only moderate winds, could generate half its electricity with wind turbines. Inexhaustible and available, the winds, coupled with low-cost turbine designs, promise a bright future for this alternative.

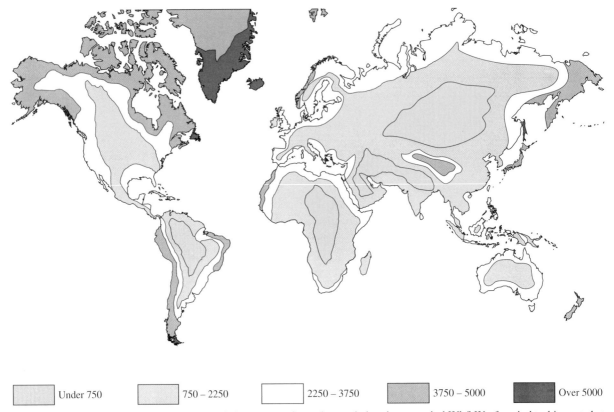

| Under 750 | 750 – 2250 | 2250 – 3750 | 3750 – 5000 | Over 5000 |

Fig. 11.33 World availability of land-based wind energy: estimated annual electric output in kWh/kW of a wind turbine rated at 11.2 m/s (25 mi/h).
Source: D. F. Warne and P. G. Calnan, "Generation of Electricity from lhe Wmd," IEE Rev., vol. 124, no. 11R, November 1977, pp. 963–985.

With fossil fuel limited, and increasing worry about global warming, the prospects for wind power are assured. Global wind speed data by Archer and Jacobsen [62] show that harnessing a modest fraction of available wind energy could supply *all* of the earth's electricity needs. No one expects that to happen, but the American Wind Energy Association [59] projects that 20 percent of America's power could be wind generated by the year 2030.

Up until 2010, the United States had the most wind-power capacity in the world, but China has recently taken over first place, as shown in the following table.

Country	Capacity in 2012, GW	Percent of world total
China	75.6	26.8
United States	60.0	21.2
Germany	31.3	11.1
Spain	22.8	8.1
India	19.6	6.9
Rest of the world	73.2	25.9
TOTALS:	**282.5**	**100.0**

Since China's installations are generally less breezy, the United States actually leads in total annual wind energy generated, 120 terawatt-hours to 73 for China. The growth in wind energy generation is excellent, but 283 GW is still only 2.5 percent of total world energy needs. Most of the future growth will probably be land-based, because of the high costs of construction, transmission, and maintenance of offshore wind turbines. In the United States, emphasis has shifted to localized turbines, due to the high cost of transmission lines from isolated wind farms. For example, three separate large (1.5 MW) turbines are now being proposed for the writer's small seaside village. In general, costs will be high, and the political debate fractious, but the future of wind energy seems bright.

New Developments in Wind Turbine Technology

Wind turbines are a large "green" part of our energy future, but wind energy, especially on offshore locations, is expensive compared to fossil-fuel power plants. The chief burden is the cost of manufacturing and installing the turbines. The U.S. Department of Energy states that offshore wind power is the most expensive of the large-scale systems.

Leases have been granted for offshore turbines near Cape Cod, Rhode Island, and Delaware. The Cape Wind project is proposing an initial cost, to the ground-based utility, of 19 ¢/kWh. The proposal from the Rhode Island project, Deepwater Wind, calls for 24 ¢/kWh. Since electric generation by fossil-fuel plants cost about 8 ¢/kWh, the environmental benefits of wind turbines, with no CO_2 or SO_2 pollution, are balanced by greatly increased costs to the consumer.

There are many proposals to lessen wind power costs. Here we list three.

1. *Floating offshore turbines.* This avoids the problem of imbedding towers in deeper water and allows putting the system farther from shore. For example, a 2300 kW floating turbine was installed recently off the coast of Norway.

2. *Replacing a giant onshore HAWT with an array of small VAWTs.* Today's massive horizontal-axis propellers, with diameters as large as 100 meters, cost more to install than many small, shorter vertical-axis turbines. The vertical array would have generators on the ground and thus be easier to access. However, many, perhaps hundreds, of the smaller turbines would be required. This idea is best suited for remote locations.

3. *Tethered shrouded-balloon turbines.* A buoyant, ring-shaped shroud, with a turbine inside, can be deployed at high altitudes, where winds are two to three times higher.

Figure 11.34 shows an experimental design by Altaeros Energies, Inc. The shroud also helps draw in more wind than a free propeller. Installation costs are less. For the test in Fig. 11.34, the turbine at 350 ft produced twice as much power compared to ground level. In 2014 a large Altaeros balloon turbine was purchased by the city of Fairbanks, Alaska.

Summary

Turbomachinery design is perhaps the most practical and most active application of the principles of fluid mechanics. There are billions of pumps and turbines in use in the world, and thousands of companies are seeking improvements. This chapter has

Fig. 11.34 An experimental 35-ft-diameter buoyant-ring high-altitude wind turbine. Tested in Limestone, Maine, at an altitude of 350 ft. [*Image courtesy of Altaeros Energies*]

discussed both positive-displacement devices and, more extensively, rotodynamic machines. With the centrifugal pump as an example, the basic concepts of torque, power, head, flow rate, and efficiency were developed for a turbomachine. Nondimensionalization leads to the pump similarity rules and some typical dimensionless performance curves for axial and centrifugal machines. The single most useful pump parameter is the specific speed, which delineates the type of design needed. An interesting design application is the theory of pumps combined in series and in parallel.

Turbines extract energy from flowing fluids and are of two types: impulse turbines, which convert the momentum of a high-speed stream, and reaction turbines, where the pressure drop occurs within the blade passages in an internal flow. By analogy with pumps, the power specific speed is important for turbines and is used to classify them into impulse, Francis, and propeller-type designs. A special case of reaction turbine with unconfined flow is the wind turbine. Several types of windmills were discussed and their relative performances compared.

Problems

Most of the problems herein are fairly straightforward. More difficult or open-ended assignments are labeled with an asterisk. Problems labeled with a computer icon 💻 may require the use of a computer. The standard end-of-chapter problems P11.1 to P11.108 (categorized in the problem list here) are followed by word problems W11.1 to W11.10, comprehensive problems C11.1 to C11.8, and design project D11.1.

Problem Distribution

Section	Topic	Problems
11.1	Introduction and classification	P11.1–P11.14
11.2	Centrifugal pump theory	P11.15–P11.21
11.3	Pump performance and similarity rules	P11.22–P11.41
11.3	Net positive-suction head	P11.42–P11.44
11.4	Specific speed: mixed- and axial-flow pumps	P11.45–P11.62
11.5	Matching pumps to system characteristics	P11.63–P11.73
11.5	Pumps in parallel or series	P11.74–P11.81
11.5	Pump instability	P11.82–P11.83
11.6	Reaction and impulse turbines	P11.84–P11.99
11.6	Wind turbines	P11.100–P11.108

Introduction and classification

P11.1 Describe the geometry and operation of a human peristaltic PDP that is cherished by every romantic person on earth. How do the two ventricles differ?

P11.2 What would be the technical classification of the following turbomachines: (*a*) a household fan, (*b*) a windmill, (*c*) an aircraft propeller, (*d*) a fuel pump in a car, (*e*) an eductor, (*f*) a fluid-coupling transmission, and (*g*) a power plant steam turbine?

P11.3 A PDP can deliver almost any fluid, but there is always a limiting very high viscosity for which performance will deteriorate. Can you explain the probable reason?

P11.4 Figure P11.4 shows the impeller on a common device which, when operating, turns at up to 300,000 r/min. Can you guess what it is and offer a description?

P11.4 [*Image provided by Sigma-Aldrich Corporation.*]

P11.5 What type of pump is shown in Fig. P11.5? How does it operate?

P11.6 Figure P11.6 shows two points a half-period apart in the operation of a pump. What type of pump is this [13]? How does it work? Sketch your best guess of flow rate versus time for a few cycles.

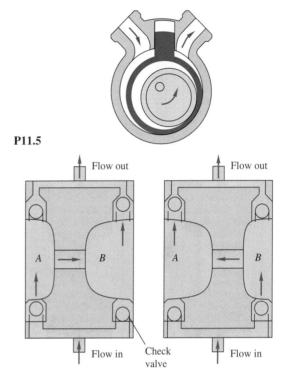

P11.5

P11.6

P11.7 A piston PDP has a 5-in diameter and a 2-in stroke and operates at 750 r/min with 92 percent volumetric efficiency. (*a*) What is its delivery, in gal/min? (*b*) If the pump delivers SAE 10W oil at 20°C against a head of 50 ft, what horsepower is required when the overall efficiency is 84 percent?

P11.8 A Bell and Gossett pump at best efficiency, running at 1750 r/min and a brake horsepower of 32.4, delivers 1050 gal/min against a head of 105 ft. (*a*) What is its efficiency? (*b*) What type of pump is this?

P11.9 Figure P11.9 shows the measured performance of the Vickers model PVQ40 piston pump when delivering SAE 10W oil at 180°F ($\rho \approx 910$ kg/m^3). Make some general observations about these data vis-à-vis Fig. 11.2 and your intuition about the behavior of piston pumps.

P11.10 Suppose that the pump of Fig. P11.9 is run at 1100 r/min against a pressure rise of 210 bar. (*a*) Using the measured displacement, estimate the theoretical delivery in gal/min. From the chart, estimate (*b*) the actual delivery and (*c*) the overall efficiency.

P11.11 A pump delivers 1500 L/min of water at 20°C against a pressure rise of 270 kPa. Kinetic and potential energy changes are negligible. If the driving motor supplies 9 kW, what is the overall efficiency?

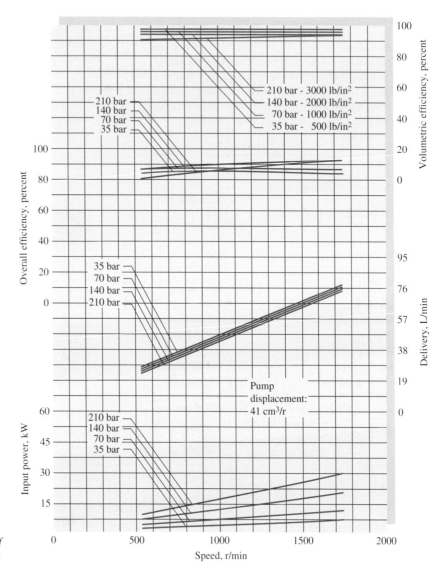

P11.9 Performance of the model PVQ40 piston pump delivering SAE 10W oil at 180°F. (*Courtesy of Vickers Inc., PDN/PACE Division.*)

P11.12 In a test of the centrifugal pump shown in Fig. P11.12, the following data are taken: $p_1 = 100$ mmHg (vacuum) and $p_2 = 500$ mmHg (gage). The pipe diameters are $D_1 = 12$ cm and $D_2 = 5$ cm. The flow rate is 180 gal/min of light oil (SG = 0.91). Estimate (*a*) the head developed, in meters, and (*b*) the input power required at 75 percent efficiency.

P11.13 A 3.5 hp pump delivers 1140 lbf of ethylene glycol at 20°C in 12 seconds, against a head of 17 ft. Calculate the efficiency of the pump.

P11.14 A pump delivers gasoline at 20°C and 12 m³/h. At the inlet $p_1 = 100$ kPa, $z_1 = 1$ m, and $V_1 = 2$ m/s. At the exit $p_2 = 500$ kPa, $z_2 = 4$ m, and $V_2 = 3$ m/s. How much power is required if the motor efficiency is 75 percent?

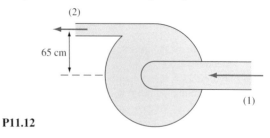

P11.12

Centrifugal pump theory

P11.15 A lawn sprinkler can be used as a simple turbine. As shown in Fig. P11.15, flow enters normal to the paper in the center and splits evenly into $Q/2$ and V_{rel} leaving each nozzle. The arms rotate at angular velocity ω and do work on a shaft. Draw the velocity diagram for this turbine. Neglecting friction, find an expression for the power delivered to the shaft. Find the rotation rate for which the power is a maximum.

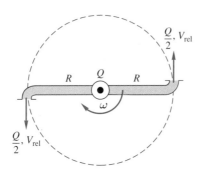

P11.15

P11.16 The centrifugal pump in Fig. P11.16 has $r_1 = 15$ cm, $r_2 = 25$ cm, $b_1 = b_2 = 6$ cm, and rotates *counterclockwise* at 600 r/min. A sample blade is shown. Assume $\alpha_1 = 90°$. Estimate the theoretical flow rate and head produced, for water at 20°C, and comment.

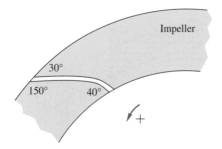

P11.16

P11.17 A centrifugal pump has $d_1 = 7$ in, $d_2 = 13$ in, $b_1 = 4$ in, $b_2 = 3$ in, $\beta_1 = 25°$, and $\beta_2 = 40°$ and rotates at 1160 r/min. If the fluid is gasoline at 20°C and the flow enters the blades radially, estimate the theoretical (a) flow rate in gal/min, (b) horsepower, and (c) head in ft.

P11.18 A jet of velocity V strikes a vane that moves to the right at speed V_c, as in Fig. P11.18. The vane has a turning angle θ. Derive an expression for the power delivered to the vane by the jet. For what vane speed is the power maximum?

P11.19 A centrifugal pump has $r_2 = 9$ in, $b_2 = 2$ in, and $\beta_2 = 35°$ and rotates at 1060 r/min. If it generates a head of 180 ft, determine the theoretical (a) flow rate in gal/min and (b) horsepower. Assume near-radial entry flow.

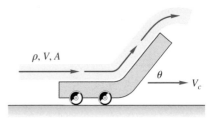

P11.18

P11.20 Suppose that Prob. P11.19 is reversed into a statement of the theoretical power $P_w \approx 153$ hp. Can you then compute the theoretical (a) flow rate and (b) head? Explain and resolve the difficulty that arises.

P11.21 The centrifugal pump of Fig. P11.21 develops a flow rate of 4200 gal/min of gasoline at 20°C with near-radial absolute inflow. Estimate the theoretical (a) horsepower, (b) head rise, and (c) appropriate blade angle at the inner radius.

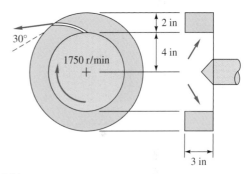

P11.21

Pump performance and similarity rules

P11.22 A 37-cm-diameter centrifugal pump, running at 2140 r/min with water at 20°C, produces the following performance data:

Q, m³/s	0.0	0.05	0.10	0.15	0.20	0.25	0.30
H, m	105	104	102	100	95	85	67
P, kW	100	115	135	171	202	228	249

(a) Determine the best efficiency point. (b) Plot C_H versus C_Q. (c) If we desire to use this same pump family to deliver 7000 gal/min of kerosene at 20°C at an input power of 400 kW, what pump speed (in r/min) and impeller size (in cm) are needed? What head will be developed?

P11.23 When pumping water, (a) at what speed should the 11-in Bell and Gossett centrifugal pump of Prob. P11.8 be run, at best efficiency, to deliver 800 gal/min? Estimate the resulting (b) head, and (c) brake horsepower.

P11.24 Figure P11.24 shows performance data for the Taco, Inc., model 4013 pump. Compute the ratios of measured shutoff head to the ideal value U^2/g for all seven impeller sizes. Determine the average and standard deviation of this ratio and compare it to the average for the six impellers in Fig. 11.7.

P11.25 At what speed in r/min should the 35-in-diameter pump of Fig. 11.7b be run to produce a head of 400 ft at a discharge of 20,000 gal/min? What brake horsepower will be required? *Hint:* Fit $H(Q)$ to a formula.

P11.26 Would the smallest, or the largest, of the seven Taco, Inc. pumps in Fig. P11.24 be better (a) for producing, near best efficiency, a water flow rate of 600 gal/min and a head of 95 ft? (b) At what speed, in r/min, should this pump be run? (c) What input power is required?

P11.27 The 11-in Bell and Gossett pump of Prob. P11.8 is to be scaled up to provide, at best efficiency, a head of 250 ft and a flow rate of 3000 gal/min. Find the appropriate (a) impeller diameter; (b) speed in r/min; and (c) horsepower required.

P11.28 Tests by the Byron Jackson Co. of a 14.62-in-diameter centrifugal water pump at 2134 r/min yield the following data:

Q, ft^3/s	0	2	4	6	8	10
H, ft	340	340	340	330	300	220
bhp	135	160	205	255	330	330

What is the BEP? What is the specific speed? Estimate the maximum discharge possible.

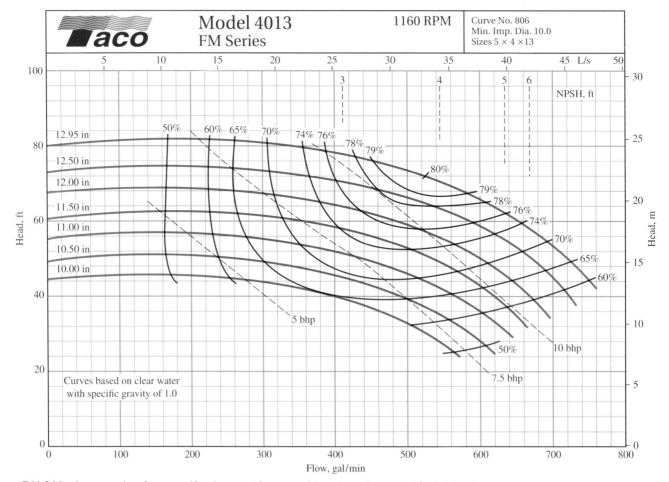

P11.24 Performance data for a centrifugal pump. (*Courtesy of Taco, Inc., Cranston, Rhode Island.*)

P11.29 If the scaling laws are applied to the pump of Prob. P11.28 for the same impeller diameter, determine (a) the speed for which the shutoff head will be 280 ft, (b) the speed for which the BEP flow rate will be 8.0 ft³/s, and (c) the speed for which the BEP conditions will require 80 hp.

P11.30 A pump, geometrically similar to the 12.95-in model in Fig. P11.24, has a diameter of 24 in and is to develop 30 hp at BEP when pumping *gasoline* (not water). Determine (a) the appropriate speed, in r/min; (b) the BEP head, in ft; and (c) the BEP flow rate, in gal/min.

P11.31 A centrifugal pump with backward-curved blades has the following measured performance when tested with water at 20°C:

Q, gal/min	0	400	800	1200	1600	2000	2400
H, ft	123	115	108	101	93	81	62
P, hp	30	36	40	44	47	48	46

(a) Estimate the best efficiency point and the maximum efficiency. (b) Estimate the most efficient flow rate, and the resulting head and brake horsepower, if the diameter is doubled and the rotation speed increased by 50 percent.

P11.32 The data of Prob. P11.31 correspond to a pump speed of 1200 r/min. (Were you able to solve Prob. P11.31 without this knowledge?) (a) Estimate the diameter of the impeller. [*Hint:* See Prob. P11.24 for a clue.] (b) Using your estimate from part (a), calculate the BEP parameters C_Q^*, C_H^*, and C_P^* and compare with Eqs. (11.27). (c) For what speed of this pump would the BEP head be 280 ft?

P11.33 In Prob. P11.31, the pump BEP flow rate is 2000 gal/min, the impeller diameter is 16 in, and the speed is 1200 r/min. Scale this pump with the similarity rules to find (a) the diameter and (b) the speed that will deliver a BEP water flow rate of 4000 gal/min and a head of 180 ft. (c) What brake horsepower will be required for this new condition?

P11.34 You are asked to consider a pump geometrically similar to the 9-in-diameter Taco pump of Fig. P11.34 to deliver 1200 gal/min at 1500 r/min. Determine the appropriate (a) impeller diameter, (b) BEP horsepower, (c) shutoff head, and (d) maximum efficiency. The fluid is kerosene, not water.

P11.35 An 18-in-diameter centrifugal pump, running at 880 r/min with water at 20°C, generates the following performance data:

Q, gal/min	0.0	2000	4000	6000	8000	10,000
H, ft	92	89	84	78	68	50
P, hp	100	112	130	143	156	163

Determine (a) the BEP, (b) the maximum efficiency, and (c) the specific speed. (d) Plot the required input power versus the flow rate.

P11.36 The pump of Prob. P11.35 has a maximum efficiency of 88 percent at 8000 gal/min. (a) Can we use this pump, at the same diameter but a different speed, to generate a BEP head of 150 ft and a BEP flow rate of 10,000 gal/min? (b) If not, what diameter is appropriate?

P11.37 Consider the two pumps of Problems P11.28 and P11.35. If the diameters are not changed, which is better for delivering water at 3000 gal/min and a head of 400 ft? What is the appropriate rotation speed for the better pump?

P11.38 A 6.85-in pump, running at 3500 r/min, has the following measured performance for water at 20°C:

Q, gal/min	50	100	150	200	250	300	350	400	450
H, ft	201	200	198	194	189	181	169	156	139
η, %	29	50	64	72	77	80	81	79	74

(a) Estimate the horsepower at BEP. If this pump is rescaled in water to provide 20 bhp at 3000 r/min, determine the appropriate (b) impeller diameter, (c) flow rate, and (d) efficiency for this new condition.

P11.39 The Allis-Chalmers D30LR centrifugal compressor delivers 33,000 ft³/min of SO_2 with a pressure change from 14.0 to 18.0 lbf/in² absolute using an 800-hp motor at 3550 r/min. What is the overall efficiency? What will the flow rate and Δp be at 3000 r/min? Estimate the diameter of the impeller.

P11.40 The specific speed N_s, as defined by Eqs. (11.30), does not contain the impeller diameter. How then should we size the pump for a given N_s? An alternate parameter is the *specific diameter*, D_s, which is a dimensionless combination of Q, gH, and D. (a) If D_s is proportional to D, determine its form. (b) What is the relationship, if any, of D_s to C_{Q*}, C_{H*}, and C_{P*}? (c) Estimate D_s for the two pumps of Figs. 11.8 and 11.13.

P11.41 It is desired to build a centrifugal pump geometrically similar to that of Prob. P11.28 to deliver 6500 gal/min of gasoline at 20°C at 1060 r/min. Estimate the resulting (a) impeller diameter, (b) head, (c) brake horsepower, and (d) maximum efficiency.

Net positive-suction head

P11.42 An 8-in model pump delivering 180°F water at 800 gal/min and 2400 r/min begins to cavitate when the inlet pressure and velocity are 12 lbf/in² absolute and 20 ft/s, respectively. Find the required NPSH of a prototype that is 4 times larger and runs at 1000 r/min.

P11.43 The 28-in-diameter pump in Fig. 11.7a at 1170 r/min is used to pump water at 20°C through a piping system at 14,000 gal/min. (a) Determine the required brake horsepower. The average friction factor is 0.018. (b) If there is 65 ft of 12-in-diameter pipe upstream of the pump, how far below the surface should the pump inlet be placed to avoid cavitation?

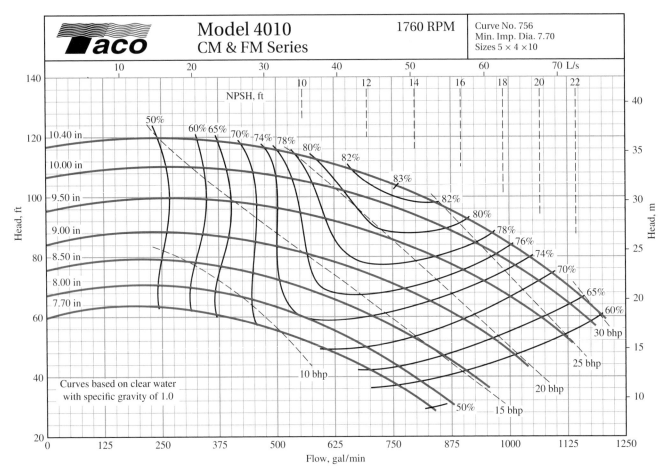

P11.34 Performance data for a family of centrifugal pump impellers. *(Courtesy of Taco, Inc., Cranston, Rhode Island.)*

P11.44 The pump of Prob. P11.28 is scaled up to an 18-in diameter, operating in water at best efficiency at 1760 r/min. The measured NPSH is 16 ft, and the friction loss between the inlet and the pump is 22 ft. Will it be sufficient to avoid cavitation if the pump inlet is placed 9 ft below the surface of a sea-level reservoir?

Specific speed: mixed- and axial-flow pumps

P11.45 Determine the specific speeds of the seven Taco, Inc., pump impellers in Fig. P11.24. Are they appropriate for centrifugal designs? Are they approximately equal within experimental uncertainty? If not, why not?

P11.46 The answer to Prob. P11.40 is that the dimensionless "specific diameter" takes the form $D_s = D(gH^*)^{1/4}/Q^{*1/2}$, evaluated at the BEP. Data collected by the author for 30 different pumps indicate, in Fig. P11.46, that D_s correlates well with specific speed N_s. Use this figure to estimate

the appropriate impeller diameter for a pump that delivers 20,000 gal/min of water and a head of 400 ft when running at 1200 r/min. Suggest a curve-fitted formula to the data. *Hint:* Use a hyperbolic formula.

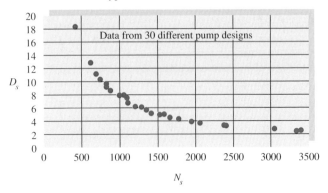

P11.46 Specific diameter at BEP for 30 commercial pumps.

P11.47 A pump must be designed to deliver 6 m³/s of water against a head of 28 m. The specified shaft speed is 20 r/s. What type of pump do you recommend?

P11.48 Using the data for the pump in Prob. P11.8, (a) determine its type: PDP, centrifugal, mixed-flow, or axial-flow. (b) Estimate the shutoff head at 1750 r/min. (c) Does this data fit on Fig. 11.14? (d) What speed and flow rate would result if the head were increased to 160 ft?

P11.49 Data collected by the author for flow coefficient at BEP for 30 different pumps are plotted versus specific speed in Fig. P11.49. Determine if the values of C_Q^* for the three pumps in Probs. P11.28, P11.35, and P11.38 also fit on this correlation. If so, suggest a curve-fitted formula for the data.

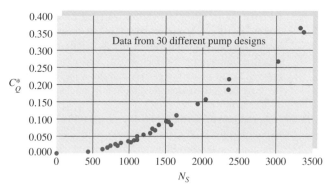

P11.49 Flow coefficient at BEP for 30 commercial pumps.

P11.50 Data collected by the author for power coefficient at BEP for 30 different pumps are plotted versus specific speed in Fig. P11.50. Determine if the values of C_P^* for the three pumps in Prob. P11.49 also fit on this correlation. If so, suggest a curve-fitted formula for the data.

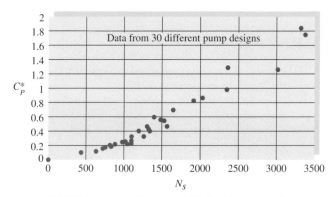

P11.50 Power coefficient at BEP for 30 commercial pumps.

P11.51 An axial-flow blower delivers 40 ft³/s of air that enters at 20°C and 1 atm. The flow passage has a 10-in outer radius and an 8-in inner radius. Blade angles are $\alpha_1 = 60°$ and $\beta_2 = 70°$, and the rotor runs at 1800 r/min. For the first stage compute (a) the head rise and (b) the power required.

P11.52 An axial-flow fan operates in sea-level air at 1200 r/min and has a blade-tip diameter of 1 m and a root diameter of 80 cm. The inlet angles are $\alpha_1 = 55°$ and $\beta_1 = 30°$, while at the outlet $\beta_2 = 60°$. Estimate the theoretical values of the (a) flow rate, (b) horsepower, and (c) outlet angle α_2.

P11.53 Figure P11.46 is an example of a centrifugal pump correlation, where D_s is defined in the problem. From data in the literature, we can suggest the following correlation for axial-flow pumps and fans:

$$D_s \approx \frac{130}{N_s^{0.485}} \qquad \text{for } N_s > 8000$$

where N_s is the *dimensional* specific speed, Eq. (11.30b). Use this correlation to find the appropriate size for a fan that delivers 24,000 ft³/min of air at sea-level conditions when running at 1620 r/min with a pressure rise of 2 inches of water. *Hint:* Express the fan head in feet of *air*, not feet of water.

P11.54 It is desired to pump 50 ft³/s of water at a speed of 22 r/s, against a head of 80 ft. (a) What type of pump would you recommend? Estimate (b) the required impeller diameter and (c) the brake horsepower.

P11.55 Suppose that the axial-flow pump of Fig. 11.13, with $D = 18$ in, runs at 1800 r/min. (a) Could it efficiently pump 25,000 gal/min of water? (b) If so, what head would result? (c) If a head of 120 ft is desired, what values of D and n would be better?

P11.56 Determine if the Bell and Gossett pump of Prob. P11.8 (a) fits the three correlations in Figs. P11.46, P11.49, and P11.50. (b) If so, use these correlations to find the flow rate and horsepower that would result if the pump is scaled up to $D = 24$ in but still runs at 1750 r/min.

P11.57 Performance data for a 21-in-diameter air blower running at 3550 r/min are as follows:

Δp, in H₂O	29	30	28	21	10
Q, ft³/min	500	1000	2000	3000	4000
bhp	6	8	12	18	25

Note the fictitious expression of pressure rise in terms of water rather than air. What is the specific speed? How does the performance compare with Fig. 11.8? What are C_Q^*, C_H^*, and C_P^*?

P11.58 Aircraft propeller specialists claim that dimensionless propeller data, when plotted as (C_T/J^2) versus (C_P/J^2), form a nearly straight line, $y = mx + b$. (a) Test this hypothesis for the data of Fig. 11.16, in the high efficiency range $J = V/(nD)$ equal to 0.6, 0.7, and 0.8. (b) If successful, try this straight line to predict the rotation rate, in r/min, for a propeller with $D = 5$ ft, $P = 30$ hp, $T = 95$ lbf, and $V = 95$ mi/h, for sea level standard conditions. Comment.

P11.59 Suppose it is desired to deliver 700 ft³/min of propane gas (molecular weight $= 44.06$) at 1 atm and 20°C with a single-stage pressure rise of 8.0 in H_2O. Determine the appropriate size and speed for using the pump families of (a) Prob. P11.57 and (b) Fig. 11.13. Which is the better design?

P11.60 Performance curves for a certain free propeller, comparable to Fig. 11.16, can be plotted as shown in Fig. P11.60, for thrust T versus speed V for constant power P. (a) What is striking, at least to the writer, about these curves? (b) Can you deduce this behavior by rearranging, or replotting, the data of Fig. 11.16?

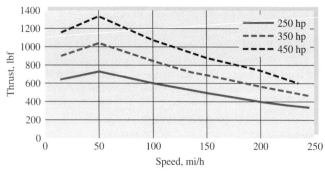

P11.60

P11.61 A mine ventilation fan, running at 295 r/min, delivers 500 m³/s of sea-level air with a pressure rise of 1100 Pa. Is this fan axial, centrifugal, or mixed? Estimate its diameter in ft. If the flow rate is increased 50 percent for the same diameter, by what percentage will the pressure rise change?

P11.62 The actual mine ventilation fan discussed in Prob. P11.61 had a diameter of 20 ft [Ref. 20, p. 339]. What would be the proper diameter for the pump family of Fig. 11.14 to provide 500 m³/s at 295 r/min and BEP? What would be the resulting pressure rise in Pa?

Matching pumps to system characteristics

P11.63 A good curve-fit to the head vs. flow for the 32-in pump in Fig. 11.7a is

$$H \text{ (in ft)} \approx 500 - (2.9\text{E}{-}7) Q^2 \quad Q \text{ in gal/min}$$

Assume the same rotation rate, 1170 r/min, and estimate the flow rate this pump will provide to deliver water from a reservoir, through 900 ft of 12-in pipe, to a point 150 ft above the reservoir surface. Assume a friction factor $f = 0.019$.

P11.64 A leaf blower is essentially a centrifugal impeller exiting to a tube. Suppose that the tube is smooth PVC pipe, 4 ft long, with a diameter of 2.5 in. The desired exit velocity is 73 mi/h in sea-level standard air. If we use the pump family of Eqs. (11.27) to drive the blower, what approximate (a) diameter and (b) rotation speed are appropriate? (c) Is this a good design?

*P11.65 An 11.5-in-diameter centrifugal pump, running at 1750 r/min, delivers 850 gal/min and a head of 105 ft at best efficiency (82 percent). (a) Can this pump operate efficiently when delivering water at 20°C through 200 m of 10-cm-diameter smooth pipe? Neglect minor losses. (b) If your answer to (a) is negative, can the speed n be changed to operate efficiently? (c) If your answer to (b) is also negative, can the impeller diameter be changed to operate efficiently and still run at 1750 rev/min?

P11.66 It is proposed to run the pump of Prob. P11.35 at 880 r/min to pump water at 20°C through the system in Fig. P11.66. The pipe is 20-cm-diameter commercial steel. What flow rate in ft³/min will result? Is this an efficient application?

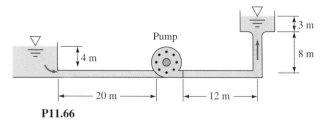

P11.66

P11.67 The pump of Prob. P11.35, running at 880 r/min, is to pump water at 20°C through 75 m of horizontal galvanized iron pipe. All other system losses are neglected. Determine the flow rate and input power for (a) pipe diameter $= 20$ cm and (b) the pipe diameter found to yield maximum pump efficiency.

P11.68 A popular small aircraft cruises at 230 km/h at 8500 ft altitude. It weighs 2200 lbf, has a 180-hp engine, a 76-in-diameter propeller, and a drag-area $C_D A \approx 5.6$ ft². The propeller data in Fig. P11.68 is proposed to drive this aircraft. Estimate the required rotation rate, in r/min, and power delivered, in hp. [NOTE: Simply use the coefficient pairs. The actual advance ratio is too high.]

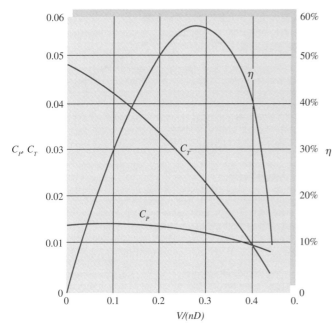

P11.68

P11.69 The pump of Prob. P11.38, running at 3500 r/min, is used to deliver water at 20°C through 600 ft of cast iron pipe to an elevation 100 ft higher. Determine (a) the proper pipe diameter for BEP operation and (b) the flow rate that results if the pipe diameter is 3 in.

P11.70 The pump of Prob. P11.28, operating at 2134 r/min, is used with 20°C water in the system of Fig. P11.70. (a) If it is operating at BEP, what is the proper elevation z_2? (b) If $z_2 = 225$ ft, what is the flow rate if $d = 8$ in.?

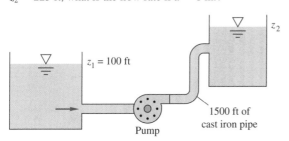

P11.70

P11.71 The pump of Prob. P11.38, running at 3500 r/min, delivers water at 20°C through 7200 ft of horizontal 5-in-diameter commercial steel pipe. There are a sharp entrance, sharp exit, four 90° elbows, and a gate valve. Estimate (a) the flow rate if the valve is wide open and (b) the valve closing percentage that causes the pump to operate at BEP. (c) If the latter condition holds continuously for 1 year, estimate the energy cost at 10 ¢/kWh.

P11.72 Performance data for a small commercial pump are as follows:

Q, gal/min	0	10	20	30	40	50	60	70
H, ft		75	75	74	72	68	62	47	24

This pump supplies 20°C water to a horizontal $\frac{5}{8}$-in-diameter garden hose ($\varepsilon \approx 0.01$ in) that is 50 ft long. Estimate (a) the flow rate and (b) the hose diameter that would cause the pump to operate at BEP.

P11.73 The Bell and Gossett pump of Prob. P11.8, running under the same conditions, delivers water at 20°C through a long, smooth, 8-in-diameter pipe. Neglect minor losses. How long is the pipe?

Pumps in parallel or series

P11.74 The 32-in pump in Fig. 11.7a is used at 1170 r/min in a system whose head curve is H_s (ft) $= 100 + 1.5Q^2$, with Q in thousands of gallons of water per minute. Find the discharge and brake horsepower required for (a) one pump, (b) two pumps in parallel, and (c) two pumps in series. Which configuration is best?

P11.75 Two 35-in pumps from Fig. 11.7b are installed in parallel for the system of Fig. P11.75. Neglect minor losses. For water at 20°C, estimate the flow rate and power required if (a) both pumps are running and (b) one pump is shut off and isolated.

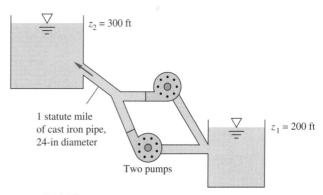

P11.75

P11.76 Two 32-in pumps from Fig. 11.7a are combined in parallel to deliver water at 60°F through 1500 ft of horizontal pipe. If $f = 0.025$, what pipe diameter will ensure a flow rate of 35,000 gal/min for $n = 1170$ r/min?

P11.77 Two pumps of the type tested in Prob. P11.22 are to be used at 2140 r/min to pump water at 20°C vertically upward through 100 m of commercial steel pipe. Should they be in series or in parallel? What is the proper pipe diameter for most efficient operation?

P11.78 Consider the axial-flow pump of Fig. 11.13, running at 4200 r/min, with an impeller diameter of 36 in. The fluid is propane gas (molecular weight 44.06). (*a*) How many pumps in series are needed to increase the gas pressure from 1 atm to 2 atm? (*b*) Estimate the mass flow of gas.

P11.79 Two 32-in pumps from Fig. 11.7*a* are to be used in series at 1170 r/min to lift water through 500 ft of vertical cast iron pipe. What should the pipe diameter be for most efficient operation? Neglect minor losses.

P11.80 Determine if either (*a*) the smallest or (*b*) the largest of the seven Taco pumps in Fig. P11.24, running in series at 1160 r/min, can efficiently pump water at 20°C through 1 km of horizontal 12-cm-diameter commercial steel pipe.

P11.81 Reconsider the system of Fig. P6.62. Use the Byron Jackson pump of Prob. P11.28 running at 2134 r/min, no scaling, to drive the flow. Determine the resulting flow rate between the reservoirs. What is the pump efficiency?

Pump instability

P11.82 The S-shaped head-versus-flow curve in Fig. P11.82 occurs in some axial-flow pumps. Explain how a fairly flat system loss curve might cause instabilities in the operation of the pump. How might we avoid instability?

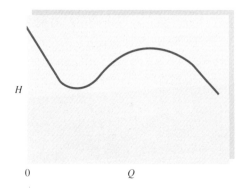

P11.82   0   *Q*

P11.83 The low-shutoff head-versus-flow curve in Fig. P11.83 occurs in some centrifugal pumps. Explain how a fairly flat system loss curve might cause instabilities in the operation of the pump. What additional vexation occurs when two of these pumps are in parallel? How might we avoid instability?

Reaction and impulse turbines

P11.84 Turbines are to be installed where the net head is 400 ft and the flow rate 250,000 gal/min. Discuss the type, number, and size of turbine that might be selected if the generator selected is (*a*) 48-pole, 60-cycle ($n = 150$ r/min) and (*b*) 8-pole ($n = 900$ r/min). Why are at least two turbines desirable from a planning point of view?

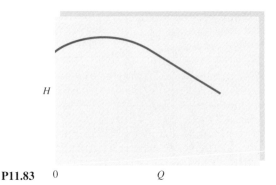

P11.83   0   *Q*

P11.85 For a high-flow site with a head of 45 ft, it is desired to design a single 7-ft-diameter turbine that develops 4000 bhp at a speed of 360 r/min and 88-percent efficiency. It is decided first to test a geometrically similar model of diameter 1 ft, running at 1180 r/min. (*a*) What likely type of turbine is in the prototype? What are the appropriate (*b*) head and (*c*) flow rate for the model test? (*d*) Estimate the power expected to be delivered by the model turbine.

P11.86 The Tupperware hydroelectric plant on the Blackstone River has four 36-in-diameter turbines, each providing 447 kW at 200 r/min and 205 ft³/s for a head of 30 ft. What type of turbine are these? How does their performance compare with Fig. 11.22?

P11.87 An idealized radial turbine is shown in Fig. P11.87. The absolute flow enters at 30° and leaves radially inward. The flow rate is 3.5 m³/s of water at 20°C. The blade thickness is constant at 10 cm. Compute the theoretical power developed.

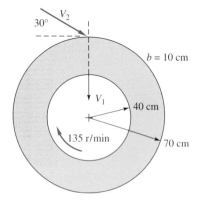

P11.87

P11.88 Performance data for a very small ($D = 8.25$ cm) model water turbine, operating with an available head of 49 ft, are as follows:

Q, m³/h	18.7	18.7	18.5	18.3	17.6	16.7	15.1	11.5
RPM	0	500	1000	1500	2000	2500	3000	3500
η	0	14%	27%	38%	50%	65%	61%	11%

(a) What type of turbine is this likely to be? (b) What is so different about these data compared to the dimensionless performance plot in Fig. 11.22d? Suppose it is desired to use a geometrically similar turbine to serve where the available head and flow are 150 ft and 6.7 ft³/s, respectively. Estimate the most efficient (c) turbine diameter, (d) rotation speed, and (e) horsepower.

P11.89 A Pelton wheel of 12-ft pitch diameter operates under a net head of 2000 ft. Estimate the speed, power output, and flow rate for best efficiency if the nozzle exit diameter is 4 in.

P11.90 An idealized radial turbine is shown in Fig. P11.90. The absolute flow enters at 25° with the blade angles as shown. The flow rate is 8 m³/s of water at 20°C. The blade thickness is constant at 20 cm. Compute the theoretical power developed.

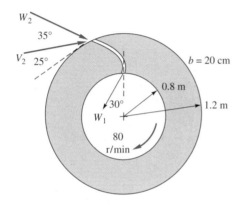

P11.90

P11.91 The flow through an axial-flow *turbine* can be idealized by modifying the stator–rotor diagrams of Fig. 11.12 for energy absorption. Sketch a suitable blade and flow arrangement and the associated velocity vector diagrams.

P11.92 A dam on a river is being sited for a hydraulic turbine. The flow rate is 1500 m³/h, the available head is 24 m, and the turbine speed is to be 480 r/min. Discuss the estimated turbine size and feasibility for (a) a Francis turbine and (b) a Pelton wheel.

P11.93 Figure P11.93 shows a cutaway of a *cross-flow* or "Banki" turbine [55], which resembles a squirrel cage with slotted curved blades. The flow enters at about 2 o'clock and passes through the center and then again through the blades, leaving at about 8 o'clock. Report to the class on the operation and advantages of this design, including idealized velocity vector diagrams.

P11.94 A simple cross-flow turbine, Fig. P11.93, was constructed and tested at the University of Rhode Island. The blades were made of PVC pipe cut lengthwise into three 120°-arc pieces. When it was tested in water at a head of 5.3 ft and a flow rate of 630 gal/min, the measured power output was 0.6 hp. Estimate (a) the efficiency and (b) the power specific speed if n = 200 r/min.

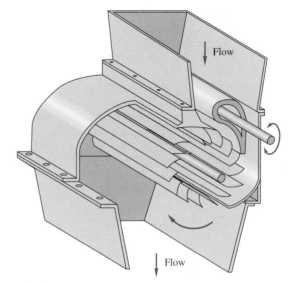

P11.93

*P11.95 One can make a theoretical estimate of the proper diameter for a penstock in an impulse turbine installation, as in Fig. P11.95. Let L and H be known, and let the turbine performance be idealized by Eqs. (11.38) and (11.39). Account for friction loss h_f in the penstock, but neglect minor losses. Show that (a) the maximum power is generated when $h_f = H/3$, (b) the optimum jet velocity is $(4gH/3)^{1/2}$, and (c) the best nozzle diameter is $D_j = [D^5/(2fL)]^{1/4}$, where f is the pipe friction factor.

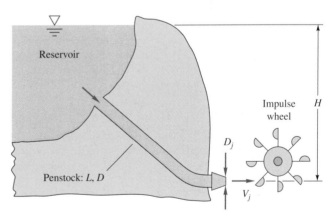

P11.95

P11.96 Apply the results of Prob. P11.95 to determine the optimum (a) penstock diameter and (b) nozzle diameter for a head of 330 m and a flow rate of 5400 m³/h with a cast iron penstock of length 600 m.

P11.97 Consider the following nonoptimum version of Prob. P11.95: $H = 450$ m, $L = 5$ km, $D = 1.2$ m, $D_j = 20$ cm. The penstock is concrete, $\varepsilon = 1$ mm. The impulse wheel diameter is 3.2 m. Estimate (*a*) the power generated by the wheel at 80 percent efficiency and (*b*) the best speed of the wheel in r/min. Neglect minor losses.

P11.98 Francis and Kaplan turbines are often provided with *draft tubes,* which lead the exit flow into the tailwater region, as in Fig. P11.98. Explain at least two advantages in using a draft tube.

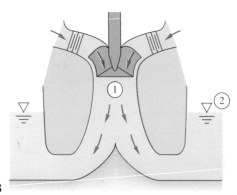

P11.98

P11.99 Turbines can also cavitate when the pressure at point 1 in Fig. P11.98 drops too low. With NPSH defined by Eq. (11.20), the empirical criterion given by Wislicenus [4] for cavitation is

$$N_{ss} = \frac{(\text{r/min})(\text{gal/min})^{1/2}}{[\text{NPSH (ft)}]^{3/4}} \geq 11,000$$

Use this criterion to compute how high $z_1 - z_2$, the impeller eye in Fig. P11.98, can be placed for a Francis turbine with a head of 300 ft, $N_{sp} = 40$, and $p_a = 14$ lbf/in^2 absolute before cavitation occurs in 60°F water.

Wind turbines

P11.100 The manufacturer of the wind turbine in the chapter-opener photo claims that it develops exactly 100 kW at a wind speed of 15 m/s. Compare this with an estimate from the correlations in Fig. 11.32.

P11.101 A Darrieus VAWT in operation in Lumsden, Saskatchewan, that is 32 ft high and 20 ft in diameter sweeps out an area of 432 ft^2. Estimate (*a*) the maximum power and (*b*) the rotor speed if it is operating in 16 mi/h winds.

P11.102 An American 6-ft-diameter multiblade HAWT is used to pump water to a height of 10 ft through 3-in-diameter cast iron pipe. If the winds are 12 mi/h, estimate the rate of water flow in gal/min.

P11.103 Only a mile from the wind turbine in the chapter-opener photo is a 100-ft-high, 23-ft-diameter HAWT, in Fig. P11.103. It is rated at 10 kW and provides one-half of the electricity for the Salty Brine State Beach bathhouse. From the data in Fig. 11.32, at a wind velocity of 20 mi/h, estimate (*a*) the maximum power developed, and (*b*) the rotation speed, in r/min.

P11.103 [*Rhode Island Department of Environmental Management*]

P11.104 The controversial Cape Cod Wind Project proposes 130 large wind turbines in Nantucket Sound, intended to provide 75 percent of the electric power needs of Cape Cod and the Islands. The turbine diameter is 328 ft. For an average wind velocity of 14 mi/h, what are the best rotation rate and total power output estimates for (*a*) a HAWT and (*b*) a VAWT?

P11.105 In 2007, a wind-powered-vehicle contest, held in North Holland [64], was won with a design by students at the University of Stuttgart. A schematic of the winning three-wheeler is shown in Fig. P11.105. It is powered by a shrouded wind turbine, not a propeller, and, unlike a sailboat, can move directly into the wind. (*a*) How does it work? (*b*) What if the wind is off to the side? (*c*) Cite some design questions you might have.

P11.106 Analyze the wind-powered-vehicle of Fig. P11.105 with the following data: turbine diameter $D = 6$ ft, power coefficient (Fig. 11.32) = 0.3, vehicle $C_D A = 4.5$ ft^2, and turbine rotation 240 r/min. The vehicle moves directly into a head wind, $W = 25$ mi/h. The wind backward thrust on the turbine is approximately $T \approx C_T (\rho/2) V_{rel}^2 A_{turbine}$, where V_{rel} is the air velocity relative to the turbine, and $C_T \approx 0.7$. Eighty percent of the turbine power is delivered by gears to the wheels, to propel the vehicle. Estimate the sea-level vehicle velocity V, in mi/h.

P11.107 Figure 11.32 showed the typical *power* performance of a wind turbine. The wind also causes a *thrust* force that must be resisted by the structure. The thrust coefficient C_T of a wind turbine may be defined as follows:

$$C_T = \frac{Thrust\ force}{(\rho/2)\ AV^2} = \frac{T}{(\rho/2)\ [(\pi/4)D^2]\ V^2}$$

Values of C_T for a typical horizontal-axis wind turbine are shown in Fig. P11.107. The abscissa is the same as in Fig. 11.32. Consider the turbine of Prob. P11.103. If the

wind is 20 mi/h and the rotation rate 115 r/min, estimate the bending moment about the tower base.

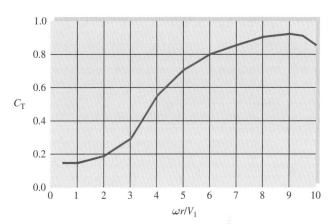

P11.107 Thrust coefficient for a typical HAWT.

P11.108 To avoid the bulky tower and impeller and generator in the HAWT of the chapter-opener photo, we could instead build a number of Darrieus turbines of height 4 m and diameter 3 m. (*a*) How many of these would we need to match the HAWT's 100 kW output for 15 m/s wind speed and maximum power? (*b*) How fast would they rotate? Assume the area swept out by a Darrieus turbine is two-thirds the height times the diameter.

P11.105

Word Problems

W11.1 We know that an enclosed rotating bladed impeller will impart energy to a fluid, usually in the form of a pressure rise, but how does it actually happen? Discuss, with sketches, the physical mechanisms through which an impeller actually transfers energy to a fluid.

W11.2 Dynamic pumps (as opposed to PDPs) have difficulty moving highly viscous fluids. Lobanoff and Ross [15] suggest the following rule of thumb: D (in) $> 0.015\nu/\nu_{water}$, where D is the diameter of the discharge pipe. For example, SAE 30W oil ($\approx 300\nu_{water}$) should require at least a 4.5-in outlet. Can you explain some reasons for this limitation?

W11.3 The concept of NPSH dictates that liquid dynamic pumps should generally be immersed below the surface. Can you explain this? What is the effect of increasing the liquid temperature?

W11.4 For nondimensional fan performance, Wallis [20] suggests that the head coefficient should be replaced by FTP/$(\rho n^2 D^2)$, where FTP is the fan total pressure change. Explain the usefulness of this modification.

W11.5 Performance data for centrifugal pumps, even if well scaled geometrically, show a decrease in efficiency with decreasing impeller size. Discuss some physical reasons why this is so.

W11.6 Consider a dimensionless pump performance chart such as Fig. 11.8. What additional dimensionless parameters might modify or even destroy the similarity indicated in such data?

W11.7 One parameter not discussed in this text is the *number of blades* on an impeller. Do some reading on this subject, and report to the class about its effect on pump performance.

W11.8 Explain why some pump performance curves may lead to unstable operating conditions.

W11.9 Why are Francis and Kaplan turbines generally considered unsuitable for hydropower sites where the available head exceeds 1000 ft?

W11.10 Do some reading on the performance of the *free propeller* that is used on small, low-speed aircraft. What dimensionless parameters are typically reported for the data? How do the performance and efficiency compare with those for the axial-flow pump?

Comprehensive Problems

C11.1 The net head of a little aquarium pump is given by the manufacturer as a function of volume flow rate as listed below:

Q, m³/s	H, mH₂O
0	1.10
1.0 E-6	1.00
2.0 E-6	0.80
3.0 E-6	0.60
4.0 E-6	0.35
5.0 E-6	0.0

What is the maximum achievable flow rate if you use this pump to move water from the lower reservoir to the upper reservoir as shown in Fig. C11.1? *Note:* The tubing is smooth with an inner diameter of 5.0 mm and a total length of 29.8 m. The water is at room temperature and pressure. Minor losses in the system can be neglected.

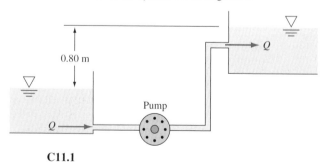

C11.1

C11.2 Reconsider Prob. P6.62 as an exercise in pump selection. Select an impeller size and rotational speed from the Byron Jackson pump family of Prob. P11.28 to deliver a flow rate of 3 ft³/s to the system of Fig. P6.62 at minimum input power. Calculate the horsepower required.

C11.3 Reconsider Prob. P6.77 as an exercise in turbine selection. Select an impeller size and rotational speed from the Francis turbine family of Fig. 11.22d to deliver maximum power generated by the turbine. Calculate the turbine power output and remark on the practicality of your design.

C11.4 The system of Fig. C11.4 is designed to deliver water at 20°C from a sea-level reservoir to another through new cast iron pipe of diameter 38 cm. Minor losses are $\Sigma K_1 = 0.5$ before the pump entrance and $\Sigma K_2 = 7.2$ after the pump exit. (a) Select a pump from either Fig. 11.7a or 11.7b, running at the given speeds, that can perform this task at maximum efficiency. Determine (b) the resulting flow rate, (c) the brake horsepower, and (d) whether the pump as presently situated is safe from cavitation.

C11.5 For the 41.5-in water pump of Fig. 11.7b, at 710 r/min and 22,000 gal/min, estimate the efficiency by (a) reading it directly from Fig. 11.7b; and (b) reading H and bhp and then calculating efficiency from Eq. (11.5). Compare your results.

C11.6 An interesting turbomachine [58] is the *fluid coupling* of Fig. C11.6, which circulates fluid from a primary pump rotor and thus turns a secondary turbine on a separate shaft. Both rotors have radial blades. Couplings are common in

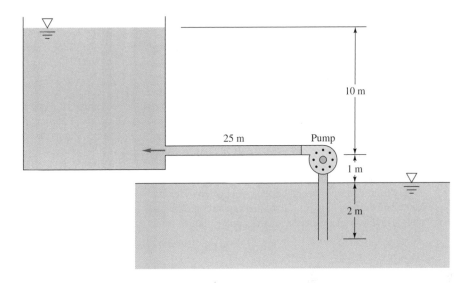

C11.4

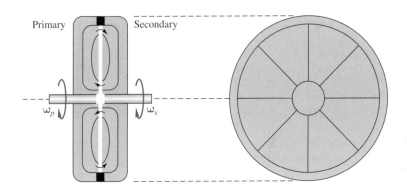

C11.6

all types of vehicle and machine transmissions and drives. The *slip* of the coupling is defined as the dimensionless difference between shaft rotation rates, $s = 1 - \omega_s/\omega_p$. For a given volume of fluid, the torque T transmitted is a function of s, ρ, ω_p, and impeller diameter D. (*a*) Nondimensionalize this function into two pi groups, with one pi proportional to T. Tests on a 1-ft-diameter coupling at 2500 r/min, filled with hydraulic fluid of density 56 lbm/ft³, yield the following torque versus slip data:

Slip, s	0%	5%	10%	15%	20%	25%
Torque T, ft-lbf	0	90	275	440	580	680

(*b*) If this coupling is run at 3600 r/min, at what slip value will it transmit a torque of 900 ft-lbf? (*c*) What is the proper diameter for a geometrically similar coupling to run at 3000 r/min and 5 percent slip and transmit 600 ft-lbf of torque?

C11.7 Report to the class on the *Cordier method* [63] for optimal design of turbomachinery. The method is related to, and greatly expanded from, Prob. P11.46 and uses both software and charts to develop an efficient design for any given pump or compressor application.

C11.8 A *pump-turbine* is a reversible device that uses a reservoir to generate power in the daytime and then pumps water back up to the reservoir at night. Let us reset Prob. P6.62 as a pump-turbine. Recall that $\Delta z = 120$ ft, and the water flows through 2000 ft of 6-in-diameter cast iron pipe. For simplicity, assume that the pump operates at BEP (92%) with $H^*_p = 200$ ft and the turbine operates at BEP (89%) with $H^*_t = 100$ ft. Neglect minor losses. Estimate (*a*) the input power, in watts, required by the pump; and (*b*) the power, in watts, generated by the turbine. For further technical reading, consult the URL www.usbr.gov/pmts/hydraulics_lab/pubs/EM/EM39.pdf.

Design Project

D11.1 To save on electricity costs, a town water supply system uses gravity-driven flow from five large storage tanks during the day and then refills these tanks from 10 P.M. to 6 A.M. at a cheaper night rate of 7 ¢/kWh. The total resupply needed each night varies from 5 E5 to 2 E6 gal, with no more than 5 E5 gallons to any one tank. Tank elevations vary from 40 to 100 ft. A single constant-speed pump, drawing from a large groundwater aquifer and valved into five different cast iron tank supply lines, does this job. Distances from the pump to the five tanks vary more or less evenly from 1 to 3 mi. Each line averages one elbow every 100 ft and has four butterfly valves that can be controlled at any desirable angle. Select a suitable pump family from one of the six data sets in this chapter: Figs. 11.8, P11.24, and P11.34 plus Probs. P11.28, P11.35, and P11.38. Assume ideal similarity (no Reynolds number or pump roughness effects). The goal is to determine pump and pipeline sizes that achieve minimum total cost over a 5-year period. Some suggested cost data are

(a) Pump and motor: $2500 plus $1500 per inch of pipe size
(b) Valves: $100 plus $100 per inch of pipe size
(c) Pipelines: 50¢ per inch of diameter per foot of length

Since the flow and elevation parameters vary considerably, a random daily variation within the specified ranges might give a realistic approach.

References

1. D. G. Wilson, "Turbomachinery—From Paddle Wheels to Turbojets," *Mech. Eng.,* vol. 104, Oct. 1982, pp. 28–40.
2. D. Japikse and N. C. Baines, *Introduction to Turbomachinery,* Concepts ETI Inc., Hanover, NH, 1997.
3. E. S. Logan and R. Roy (eds.), *Handbook of Turbomachinery,* 2d ed., Marcel Dekker, New York, 2003.
4. G. F. Wislicenus, *Fluid Mechanics of Turbomachinery,* 2d ed., McGraw-Hill, New York, 1965.
5. S. L. Dixon and C. Hall, *Fluid Mechanics and Thermodynamics of Turbomachinery*, 7th ed., Butterworth-Heinemann, Burlington, MA, 2013.
6. W. W. Peng, *Fundamentals of Turbomachinery*, Wiley, New York, 2007.
7. S. A. Korpela, *Principles of Turbomachinery*, Wiley, New York, 2011.
8. A. J. Stepanoff, *Centrifugal and Axial Flow Pumps,* 2d ed., Wiley, New York, 1957.
9. J. Tuzson, *Centrifugal Pump Design,* Wiley, New York, 2000.
10. P. Girdhar and O. Moniz, *Practical Centrifugal Pumps,* Elsevier, New York, 2004.
11. L. Bachus and A. Custodio, *Know and Understand Centrifugal Pumps*, Elsevier, New York, 2003.
12. J. F. Gülich, *Centrifugal Pumps*, Springer, New York, 2010.
13. R. K. Turton, *Rotodynamic Pump Design,* Cambridge University Press, Cambridge, UK, 2005.
14. I. J. Karassik and T. McGuire, *Centrifugal Pumps,* 2d ed., Springer-Verlag, New York, 1996.
15. V. L. Lobanoff and R. R. Ross, *Centrifugal Pumps: Design and Application,* 2d ed., Elsevier, New York, 1992.
16. H. L. Stewart, *Pumps,* 5th ed. Macmillan, New York, 1991.
17. A. B. McKenzie, *Axial Flow Fans and Compressors: Aerodynamic Design and Performance,* Ashgate Publishing, Brookfield, VT, 1997.
18. A. J. Wennerstrom, *Design of Highly Loaded Axial-Flow Fans and Compressors,* Concepts ETI Inc., Hanover, NH, 2001.
19. F. P. Bleier, *Fan Handbook: Selection, Application, and Design,* McGraw-Hill, New York, 1997.
20. R. A. Wallis, *Axial Flow Fans and Ducts,* Wiley, New York, 1983.
21. H. P. Bloch, *A Practical Guide to Compressor Technology,* 2d ed., McGraw-Hill, New York, 2006.
22. P. C. Hanlon, *Compressor Handbook*, McGraw-Hill, New York, 2001.
23. Ronald H. Aungier, *Axial-Flow Compressors: A Strategy for Aerodynamic Design and Analysis,* ASME Press, New York, 2003.
24. H. I. H. Saravanamuttoo, G. F. C. Rogers, H. Cohen, and Paul Straznicky, *Gas Turbine Theory*, 6th ed., Pearson Education Canada, Don Mills, Ontario, 2008.
25. P. P. Walsh and P. Fletcher, *Gas Turbine Performance,* ASME Press, New York, 2004.
26. M. P. Boyce, *Gas Turbine Engineering Handbook,* 4th ed., Gulf Professional Publishing, Burlington, MA, 2011.
27. Fluid Machinery Group, Institution of Mechanical Engineers, *Hydropower,* Wiley, New York, 2005.
28. Jeremy Thake, *The Micro-Hydro Pelton Turbine Manual,* Intermediate Technology Pub., Colchester, Essex, UK, 2000.
29. L. Rodriguez and T. Sanchez, *Designing and Building Mini and Micro Hydro Power Schemes*, Practical Action Publishing, Warwickshire, UK, 2011.
30. Hydraulic Institute, *Hydraulic Institute Pump Standards Complete,* 4th ed., New York, 1994.
31. P. Cooper, J. Messina, C. Heald, and I. J. Karassik (eds.), *Pump Handbook,* 4th ed., McGraw-Hill, New York, 2008.
32. J. S. Gulliver and R. E. A. Arndt, *Hydropower Engineering Handbook,* McGraw-Hill, New York, 1990.

33. R. L. Daugherty, J. B. Franzini, and E. J. Finnemore, *Fluid Mechanics and Engineering Applications,* 9th ed., McGraw-Hill, New York, 1997.

34. R. H. Sabersky, E. M. Gates, A. J. Acosta, and E. G. Hauptmann, *Fluid Flow: A First Course in Fluid Mechanics,* 4th ed., Pearson Education, Upper Saddle River, NJ, 1994.

35. J. P. Poynton, *Metering Pumps,* Marcel Dekker, New York, 1983.

36. Hydraulic Institute, *Reciprocating Pump Test Standard,* New York, 1994.

37. T. L. Henshaw, *Reciprocating Pumps,* Wiley, New York, 1987.

38. J. E. Miller, *The Reciprocating Pump: Theory, Design and Use,* Wiley, NewYork, 1987.

39. D. G. Wilson and T. Korakianitis, *The Design of High Efficiency Turbomachinery and Gas Turbines,* 2d ed., Pearson Education, Upper Saddle River, NJ, 1998.

40. S. O. Kraus et al., "Periodic Velocity Measurements in a Wide and Large Radius Ratio Automotive Torque Converter at the Pump/Turbine Interface," *J. Fluids Engineering,* vol. 127, no. 2, 2005, pp. 308–316.

41. E. M. Greitzer, "The Stability of Pumping Systems: The 1980 Freeman Scholar Lecture," *J. Fluids Eng.,* vol. 103, June 1981, pp. 193–242.

42. R. Elder et al. (eds.), *Advances of CFD in Fluid Machinery Design,* Wiley, New York, 2003.

43. L. F. Moody, "The Propeller Type Turbine," *ASCE Trans.,* vol. 89, 1926, p. 628.

44. H. H. Anderson, "Prediction of Head, Quantity, and Efficiency in Pumps—The Area-Ratio Principle," in *Performance Prediction of Centrifugal Pumps and Compressors,* vol. 100127, ASME Symp., New York, 1980, pp. 201–211.

45. M. Schobeiri, *Turbomachinery Flow Physics and Dynamic Performance,* Springer, New York, 2004.

46. D. J. Mahoney (ed.), *Proceedings of the 1997 International Conference on Hydropower,* ASCE, Reston, VA, 1997.

47. G. W. Koeppl, *Putnam's Power from the Wind,* 2d ed., Van Nostrand Reinhold, New York, 1982.

48. P. Jain, *Wind Energy Engineering*, McGraw-Hill, New York, 2010.

49. D. Wood, *Small Wind Turbines: Analysis, Design, and Application*, Springer, New York, 2011.

50. E. Hau, *Wind Turbines: Fundamentals, Technologies, Application, Economics,* 2d ed., Springer-Verlag, New York, 2005.

51. R. Harrison, E. Hau, and H. Snel, *Large Wind Turbines,* Wiley, New York, 2000.

52. R. H. Aungier, *Turbine Aerodynamics: Axial-Flow and Radial-Flow Turbine Design and Analysis,* ASME Press, New York, 2006.

53. M. L. Robinson, "The Darrieus Wind Turbine for Electrical Power Generation," *Aeronaut. J.,* June 1981, pp. 244–255.

54. D. F. Warne and P. G. Calnan, "Generation of Electricity from the Wind," *IEE Rev.,* vol. 124, no. 11R, November 1977, pp. 963–985.

55. L. A. Haimerl, "The Crossflow Turbine," *Waterpower,* January 1960, pp. 5–13; see also *ASME Symp. Small Hydropower Fluid Mach.,* vol. 1, 1980, and vol. 2, 1982.

56. K. Eisele et al., "Flow Analysis in a Pump Diffuser: Part 1, Measurements; Part 2, CFD," *J. Fluids Eng.,* vol. 119, December 1997, pp. 968–984.

57. D. Japikse and N. C. Baines, *Turbomachinery Diffuser Design Technology,* Concepts ETI Inc., Hanover, NH, 1998.

58. B. Massey and J. Ward-Smith, *Mechanics of Fluids,* 7th ed., Nelson Thornes Publishing, Cheltenham, UK, 1998.

59. American Wind Energy Association, "Global Wind Energy Market Report," URL: <http://www.awea.org/pubs/documents/globalmarket2004.pdf>.

60. J. Carlton, *Marine Propellers and Propulsion,* 3d ed., Butterworth-Heinemann, New York, 2012.

61. M. Hollmann, *Modern Propeller and Duct Design,* Aircraft Designs, Inc., Monterey, CA, 1993.

62. C. L. Archer and M. Z. Jacobson, "Evaluation of Global Wind Power," *J. Geophys. Res.-Atm.,* vol. 110, 2005, doi:10.1029/2004JD005462.

63. M. Farinas and A. Garon, "Application of DOE for Optimal Turbomachinery Design," Paper AIAA-2004-2139, AIAA Fluid Dynamics Conference, Portland, OR, June 2004.

64. C. Crain, "Running Against the Wind," *Popular Science,* March 2009, pp. 69–70.

Appendix A
Physical Properties of Fluids

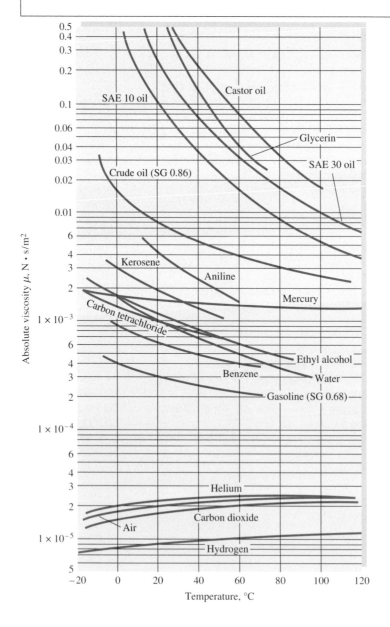

Fig. A.1 Absolute viscosity of common fluids at 1 atm.

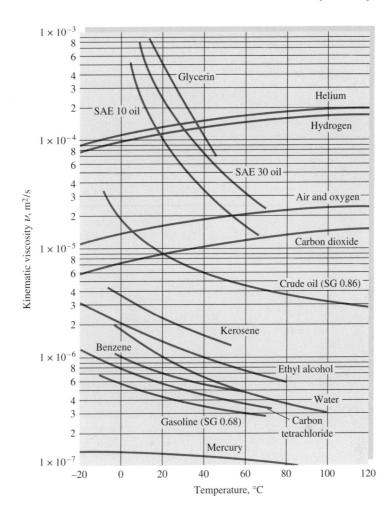

Fig. A.2 Kinematic viscosity of common fluids at 1 atm.

Table A.1 Viscosity and Density of Water at 1 atm

T, °C	ρ, kg/m³	μ, N·s/m²	ν, m²/s	T, °F	ρ, slug/ft³	μ, lb·s/ft²	ν, ft²/s
0	1000	1.788 E−3	1.788 E−6	32	1.940	3.73 E−5	1.925 E−5
10	1000	1.307 E−3	1.307 E−6	50	1.940	2.73 E−5	1.407 E−5
20	998	1.003 E−3	1.005 E−6	68	1.937	2.09 E−5	1.082 E−5
30	996	0.799 E−3	0.802 E−6	86	1.932	1.67 E−5	0.864 E−5
40	992	0.657 E−3	0.662 E−6	104	1.925	1.37 E−5	0.713 E−5
50	988	0.548 E−3	0.555 E−6	122	1.917	1.14 E−5	0.597 E−5
60	983	0.467 E−3	0.475 E−6	140	1.908	0.975 E−5	0.511 E−5
70	978	0.405 E−3	0.414 E−6	158	1.897	0.846 E−5	0.446 E−5
80	972	0.355 E−3	0.365 E−6	176	1.886	0.741 E−5	0.393 E−5
90	965	0.316 E−3	0.327 E−6	194	1.873	0.660 E−5	0.352 E−5
100	958	0.283 E−3	0.295 E−6	212	1.859	0.591 E−5	0.318 E−5

Suggested curve fits for water in the range $0 \le T \le 100$°C:

$$\rho(\text{kg/m}^3) \approx 1000 - 0.0178\,|T°C - 4°C|^{1.7} \pm 0.2\%$$

$$\ln \frac{\mu}{\mu_0} \approx -1.704 - 5.306z + 7.003z^2$$

$$z = \frac{273\ \text{K}}{T\ \text{K}} \qquad \mu_0 = 1.788\ \text{E}{-}3\ \text{kg/(m·s)}$$

Table A.2 Viscosity and Density of Air at 1 atm

T, °C	ρ, kg/m³	μ, N·s/m²	ν, m²/s	T, °F	ρ, slug/ft³	μ, lb·s/ft²	ν, ft²/s
−40	1.52	1.51 E−5	0.99 E−5	−40	2.94 E−3	3.16 E−7	1.07 E−4
0	1.29	1.71 E−5	1.33 E−5	32	2.51 E−3	3.58 E−7	1.43 E−4
20	1.20	1.80 E−5	1.50 E−5	68	2.34 E−3	3.76 E−7	1.61 E−4
50	1.09	1.95 E−5	1.79 E−5	122	2.12 E−3	4.08 E−7	1.93 E−4
100	0.946	2.17 E−5	2.30 E−5	212	1.84 E−3	4.54 E−7	2.47 E−4
150	0.835	2.38 E−5	2.85 E−5	302	1.62 E−3	4.97 E−7	3.07 E−4
200	0.746	2.57 E−5	3.45 E−5	392	1.45 E−3	5.37 E−7	3.71 E−4
250	0.675	2.75 E−5	4.08 E−5	482	1.31 E−3	5.75 E−7	4.39 E−4
300	0.616	2.93 E−5	4.75 E−5	572	1.20 E−3	6.11 E−7	5.12 E−4
400	0.525	3.25 E−5	6.20 E−5	752	1.02 E−3	6.79 E−7	6.67 E−4
500	0.457	3.55 E−5	7.77 E−5	932	0.89 E−3	7.41 E−7	8.37 E−4

Suggested curve fits for air:

$$\rho = \frac{p}{RT} \qquad R_{\text{air}} \approx 287\ \text{J/(kg·K)}$$

Power law:
$$\frac{\mu}{\mu_0} \approx \left(\frac{T}{T_0}\right)^{0.7}$$

Sutherland law:
$$\frac{\mu}{\mu_0} \approx \left(\frac{T}{T_0}\right)^{3/2}\left(\frac{T_0 + S}{T + S}\right) \qquad S_{\text{air}} \approx 110.4\ \text{K}$$

with $T_0 = 273$ K, $\mu_0 = 1.71$ E−5 kg/(m·s), and T in kelvins.

Table A.3 Properties of Common Liquids at 1 atm and 20°C (68°F)

Liquid	ρ, kg/m³	μ, kg/(m · s)	Υ, N/m*	p_v, N/m²	Bulk modulus K, N/m²	Viscosity parameter C†
Ammonia	608	2.20 E−4	2.13 E−2	9.10 E+5	1.82 E+9	1.05
Benzene	881	6.51 E−4	2.88 E−2	1.01 E+4	1.47 E+9	4.34
Carbon tetrachloride	1590	9.67 E−4	2.70 E−2	1.20 E+4	1.32 E+9	4.45
Ethanol	789	1.20 E−3	2.28 E−2	5.7 E+3	1.09 E+9	5.72
Ethylene glycol	1117	2.14 E−2	4.84 E−2	1.2 E+1	3.05 E+9	11.7
Freon 12	1327	2.62 E−4	—	—	7.95 E+8	1.76
Gasoline	680	2.92 E−4	2.16 E−2	5.51 E+4	1.3 E+9	3.68
Glycerin	1260	1.49	6.33 E−2	1.4 E−2	4.35 E+9	28.0
Kerosene	804	1.92 E−3	2.8 E−2	3.11 E+3	1.41 E+9	5.56
Mercury	13,550	1.56 E−3	4.84 E−1	1.1 E−3	2.85 E+10	1.07
Methanol	791	5.98 E−4	2.25 E−2	1.34 E+4	1.03 E+9	4.63
SAE 10W oil	870	1.04 E−1‡	3.6 E−2	—	1.31 E+9	15.7
SAE 10W30 oil	876	1.7 E−1‡	—	—	—	14.0
SAE 30W oil	891	2.9 E−1‡	3.5 E−2	—	1.38 E+9	18.3
SAE 50W oil	902	8.6 E−1‡	—	—	—	20.2
Water	998	1.00 E−3	7.28 E−2	2.34 E+3	2.19 E+9	Table A.1
Seawater (30‰)	1025	1.07 E−3	7.28 E−2	2.34 E+3	2.33 E+9	7.28

*In contact with air.

†The viscosity–temperature variation of these liquids may be fitted to the empirical expression

$$\frac{\mu}{\mu_{20°C}} \approx \exp\left[C\left(\frac{293\,\text{K}}{T\,\text{K}} - 1\right)\right]$$

with accuracy of ±6 percent in the range $0 \leq T \leq 100°C$.

‡Representative values. The SAE oil classifications allow a viscosity variation of up to ±50 percent, especially at lower temperatures.

Table A.4 Properties of Common Gases at 1 atm and 20°C (68°F)

Gas	Molecular weight	R, m²/(s² · K)	ρg, N/m³	μ, N · s/m²	ν, m²/s	Specific-heat ratio	Power-law exponent n*
H_2	2.016	4124	0.822	9.05 E−6	1.08 E−04	1.41	0.68
He	4.003	2077	1.63	1.97 E−5	1.18 E−04	1.66	0.67
H_2O	18.02	461	7.35	1.02 E−5	1.36 E−05	1.33	1.15
Ar	39.944	208	16.3	2.24 E−5	1.35 E−05	1.67	0.72
Dry air	28.96	287	11.8	1.80 E−5	1.49 E−05	1.40	0.67
CO_2	44.01	189	17.9	1.48 E−5	8.09 E−06	1.30	0.79
CO	28.01	297	11.4	1.82 E−5	1.56 E−05	1.40	0.71
N_2	28.02	297	11.4	1.76 E−5	1.51 E−05	1.40	0.67
O_2	32.00	260	13.1	2.00 E−5	1.50 E−05	1.40	0.69
NO	30.01	277	12.1	1.90 E−5	1.52 E−05	1.40	0.78
N_2O	44.02	189	17.9	1.45 E−5	7.93 E−06	1.31	0.89
Cl_2	70.91	117	28.9	1.03 E−5	3.49 E−06	1.34	1.00
CH_4	16.04	518	6.54	1.34 E−5	2.01 E−05	1.32	0.87

*The power-law curve fit, Eq. (1.27), $\mu/\mu_{293K} \approx (T/293)^n$, fits these gases to within ±4 percent in the range $250 \leq T \leq 1000$ K. The temperature must be in kelvins.

Table A.5 Surface Tension, Vapor Pressure, and Sound Speed of Water

T, °C	Y, N/m	p_v, kPa	a, m/s
0	0.0756	0.611	1402
10	0.0742	1.227	1447
20	0.0728	2.337	1482
30	0.0712	4.242	1509
40	0.0696	7.375	1529
50	0.0679	12.34	1542
60	0.0662	19.92	1551
70	0.0644	31.16	1553
80	0.0626	47.35	1554
90	0.0608	70.11	1550
100	0.0589	101.3	1543
120	0.0550	198.5	1518
140	0.0509	361.3	1483
160	0.0466	617.8	1440
180	0.0422	1002	1389
200	0.0377	1554	1334
220	0.0331	2318	1268
240	0.0284	3344	1192
260	0.0237	4688	1110
280	0.0190	6412	1022
300	0.0144	8581	920
320	0.0099	11,274	800
340	0.0056	14,586	630
360	0.0019	18,651	370
374*	0.0*	22,090*	0*

*Critical point.

Table A.6 Properties of the Standard Atmosphere

z, m	T, K	p, Pa	ρ, kg/m³	a, m/s
−500	291.41	107,508	1.2854	342.2
0	288.16	101,350	1.2255	340.3
500	284.91	95,480	1.1677	338.4
1000	281.66	89,889	1.1120	336.5
1500	278.41	84,565	1.0583	334.5
2000	275.16	79,500	1.0067	332.6
2500	271.91	74,684	0.9570	330.6
3000	268.66	70,107	0.9092	328.6
3500	265.41	65,759	0.8633	326.6
4000	262.16	61,633	0.8191	324.6
4500	258.91	57,718	0.7768	322.6
5000	255.66	54,008	0.7361	320.6
5500	252.41	50,493	0.6970	318.5
6000	249.16	47,166	0.6596	316.5
6500	245.91	44,018	0.6237	314.4
7000	242.66	41,043	0.5893	312.3
7500	239.41	38,233	0.5564	310.2
8000	236.16	35,581	0.5250	308.1
8500	232.91	33,080	0.4949	306.0
9000	229.66	30,723	0.4661	303.8
9500	226.41	28,504	0.4387	301.7
10,000	223.16	26,416	0.4125	299.5
10,500	219.91	24,455	0.3875	297.3
11,000	216.66	22,612	0.3637	295.1
11,500	216.66	20,897	0.3361	295.1
12,000	216.66	19,312	0.3106	295.1
12,500	216.66	17,847	0.2870	295.1
13,000	216.66	16,494	0.2652	295.1
13,500	216.66	15,243	0.2451	295.1
14,000	216.66	14,087	0.2265	295.1
14,500	216.66	13,018	0.2094	295.1
15,000	216.66	12,031	0.1935	295.1
15,500	216.66	11,118	0.1788	295.1
16,000	216.66	10,275	0.1652	295.1
16,500	216.66	9496	0.1527	295.1
17,000	216.66	8775	0.1411	295.1
17,500	216.66	8110	0.1304	295.1
18,000	216.66	7495	0.1205	295.1
18,500	216.66	6926	0.1114	295.1
19,000	216.66	6401	0.1029	295.1
19,500	216.66	5915	0.0951	295.1
20,000	216.66	5467	0.0879	295.1
22,000	218.60	4048	0.0645	296.4
24,000	220.60	2972	0.0469	297.8
26,000	222.50	2189	0.0343	299.1
28,000	224.50	1616	0.0251	300.4
30,000	226.50	1197	0.0184	301.7
40,000	250.40	287	0.0040	317.2
50,000	270.70	80	0.0010	329.9
60,000	255.70	22	0.0003	320.6
70,000	219.70	6	0.0001	297.2

Appendix B
Compressible Flow Tables

Table B.1
Isentropic Flow
of a Perfect Gas,
$k = 1.4$

Ma	p/p_0	ρ/ρ_0	T/T_0	A/A^*	Ma	p/p_0	ρ/ρ_0	T/T_0	A/A^*
0.00	1.0000	1.0000	1.0000	∞	2.10	0.1094	0.2058	0.5313	1.8369
0.10	0.9930	0.9950	0.9980	5.8218	2.20	0.0935	0.1841	0.5081	2.0050
0.20	0.9725	0.9803	0.9921	2.9635	2.30	0.0800	0.1646	0.4859	2.1931
0.30	0.9395	0.9564	0.9823	2.0351	2.40	0.0684	0.1472	0.4647	2.4031
0.40	0.8956	0.9243	0.9690	1.5901	2.50	0.0585	0.1317	0.4444	2.6367
0.50	0.8430	0.8852	0.9524	1.3398	2.60	0.0501	0.1179	0.4252	2.8960
0.60	0.7840	0.8405	0.9328	1.1882	2.70	0.0430	0.1056	0.4068	3.1830
0.70	0.7209	0.7916	0.9107	1.0944	2.80	0.0368	0.0946	0.3894	3.5001
0.80	0.6560	0.7400	0.8865	1.0382	2.90	0.0317	0.0849	0.3729	3.8498
0.90	0.5913	0.6870	0.8606	1.0089	3.00	0.0272	0.0762	0.3571	4.2346
1.00	0.5283	0.6339	0.8333	1.0000	3.10	0.0234	0.0685	0.3422	4.6573
1.10	0.4684	0.5817	0.8052	1.0079	3.20	0.0202	0.0617	0.3281	5.1210
1.20	0.4124	0.5311	0.7764	1.0304	3.30	0.0175	0.0555	0.3147	5.6286
1.30	0.3609	0.4829	0.7474	1.0663	3.40	0.0151	0.0501	0.3019	6.1837
1.40	0.3142	0.4374	0.7184	1.1149	3.50	0.0131	0.0452	0.2899	6.7896
1.50	0.2724	0.3950	0.6897	1.1762	3.60	0.0114	0.0409	0.2784	7.4501
1.60	0.2353	0.3557	0.6614	1.2502	3.70	0.0099	0.0370	0.2675	8.1691
1.70	0.2026	0.3197	0.6337	1.3376	3.80	0.0086	0.0335	0.2572	8.9506
1.80	0.1740	0.2868	0.6068	1.4390	3.90	0.0075	0.0304	0.2474	9.7990
1.90	0.1492	0.2570	0.5807	1.5553	4.00	0.0066	0.0277	0.2381	10.7188
2.00	0.1278	0.2300	0.5556	1.6875					

Table B.2 Normal Shock Relations for a Perfect Gas, $k = 1.4$

Ma_{n1}	Ma_{n2}	p_2/p_1	$V_1/V_2 = \rho_2/\rho_1$	T_2/T_1	p_{02}/p_{01}	A_2^*/A_1^*
1.00	1.0000	1.0000	1.0000	1.0000	1.0000	1.0000
1.10	0.9118	1.2450	1.1691	1.0649	0.9989	1.0011
1.20	0.8422	1.5133	1.3416	1.1280	0.9928	1.0073
1.30	0.7860	1.8050	1.5157	1.1909	0.9794	1.0211
1.40	0.7397	2.1200	1.6897	1.2547	0.9582	1.0436
1.50	0.7011	2.4583	1.8621	1.3202	0.9298	1.0755
1.60	0.6684	2.8200	2.0317	1.3880	0.8952	1.1171
1.70	0.6405	3.2050	2.1977	1.4583	0.8557	1.1686
1.80	0.6165	3.6133	2.3592	1.5316	0.8127	1.2305
1.90	0.5956	4.0450	2.5157	1.6079	0.7674	1.3032
2.00	0.5774	4.5000	2.6667	1.6875	0.7209	1.3872
2.10	0.5613	4.9783	2.8119	1.7705	0.6742	1.4832
2.20	0.5471	5.4800	2.9512	1.8569	0.6281	1.5920
2.30	0.5344	6.0050	3.0845	1.9468	0.5833	1.7144
2.40	0.5231	6.5533	3.2119	2.0403	0.5401	1.8514
2.50	0.5130	7.1250	3.3333	2.1375	0.4990	2.0039
2.60	0.5039	7.7200	3.4490	2.2383	0.4601	2.1733
2.70	0.4956	8.3383	3.5590	2.3429	0.4236	2.3608
2.80	0.4882	8.9800	3.6636	2.4512	0.3895	2.5676
2.90	0.4814	9.6450	3.7629	2.5632	0.3577	2.7954
3.00	0.4752	10.3333	3.8571	2.6790	0.3283	3.0456
3.10	0.4695	11.0450	3.9466	2.7986	0.3012	3.3199
3.20	0.4643	11.7800	4.0315	2.9220	0.2762	3.6202
3.30	0.4596	12.5383	4.1120	3.0492	0.2533	3.9483
3.40	0.4552	13.3200	4.1884	3.1802	0.2322	4.3062
3.50	0.4512	14.1250	4.2609	3.3151	0.2129	4.6960
3.60	0.4474	14.9533	4.3296	3.4537	0.1953	5.1200
3.70	0.4439	15.8050	4.3949	3.5962	0.1792	5.5806
3.80	0.4407	16.6800	4.4568	3.7426	0.1645	6.0801
3.90	0.4377	17.5783	4.5156	3.8928	0.1510	6.6213
4.00	0.4350	18.5000	4.5714	4.0469	0.1388	7.2069
4.10	0.4324	19.4450	4.6245	4.2048	0.1276	7.8397
4.20	0.4299	20.4133	4.6749	4.3666	0.1173	8.5227
4.30	0.4277	21.4050	4.7229	4.5322	0.1080	9.2591
4.40	0.4255	22.4200	4.7685	4.7017	0.0995	10.0522
4.50	0.4236	23.4583	4.8119	4.8751	0.0917	10.9054
4.60	0.4217	24.5200	4.8532	5.0523	0.0846	11.8222
4.70	0.4199	25.6050	4.8926	5.2334	0.0781	12.8065
4.80	0.4183	26.7133	4.9301	5.4184	0.0721	13.8620
4.90	0.4167	27.8450	4.9659	5.6073	0.0667	14.9928
5.00	0.4152	29.0000	5.0000	5.8000	0.0617	16.2032

Table B.3 Adiabatic Frictional
Flow in a Constant-Area Duct
for $k = 1.4$

Ma	$\bar{f}L/D$	p/p^*	T/T^*	$\rho^*/\rho = V/V^*$	p_0/p_0^*
0.00	∞	∞	1.2000	0.0000	∞
0.10	66.9216	10.9435	1.1976	0.1094	5.8218
0.20	14.5333	5.4554	1.1905	0.2182	2.9635
0.30	5.2993	3.6191	1.1788	0.3257	2.0351
0.40	2.3085	2.6958	1.1628	0.4313	1.5901
0.50	1.0691	2.1381	1.1429	0.5345	1.3398
0.60	0.4908	1.7634	1.1194	0.6348	1.1882
0.70	0.2081	1.4935	1.0929	0.7318	1.0944
0.80	0.0723	1.2893	1.0638	0.8251	1.0382
0.90	0.0145	1.1291	1.0327	0.9146	1.0089
1.00	0.0000	1.0000	1.0000	1.0000	1.0000
1.10	0.0099	0.8936	0.9662	1.0812	1.0079
1.20	0.0336	0.8044	0.9317	1.1583	1.0304
1.30	0.0648	0.7285	0.8969	1.2311	1.0663
1.40	0.0997	0.6632	0.8621	1.2999	1.1149
1.50	0.1361	0.6065	0.8276	1.3646	1.1762
1.60	0.1724	0.5568	0.7937	1.4254	1.2502
1.70	0.2078	0.5130	0.7605	1.4825	1.3376
1.80	0.2419	0.4741	0.7282	1.5360	1.4390
1.90	0.2743	0.4394	0.6969	1.5861	1.5553
2.00	0.3050	0.4082	0.6667	1.6330	1.6875
2.10	0.3339	0.3802	0.6376	1.6769	1.8369
2.20	0.3609	0.3549	0.6098	1.7179	2.0050
2.30	0.3862	0.3320	0.5831	1.7563	2.1931
2.40	0.4099	0.3111	0.5576	1.7922	2.4031
2.50	0.4320	0.2921	0.5333	1.8257	2.6367
2.60	0.4526	0.2747	0.5102	1.8571	2.8960
2.70	0.4718	0.2588	0.4882	1.8865	3.1830
2.80	0.4898	0.2441	0.4673	1.9140	3.5001
2.90	0.5065	0.2307	0.4474	1.9398	3.8498
3.00	0.5222	0.2182	0.4286	1.9640	4.2346
3.10	0.5368	0.2067	0.4107	1.9866	4.6573
3.20	0.5504	0.1961	0.3937	2.0079	5.1210
3.30	0.5632	0.1862	0.3776	2.0278	5.6286
3.40	0.5752	0.1770	0.3623	2.0466	6.1837
3.50	0.5864	0.1685	0.3478	2.0642	6.7896
3.60	0.5970	0.1606	0.3341	2.0808	7.4501
3.70	0.6068	0.1531	0.3210	2.0964	8.1691
3.80	0.6161	0.1462	0.3086	2.1111	8.9506
3.90	0.6248	0.1397	0.2969	2.1250	9.7990
4.00	0.6331	0.1336	0.2857	2.1381	10.7187

Table B.4 Frictionless Duct Flow with Heat Transfer for $k = 1.4$

Ma	T_0/T_0^*	p/p^*	T/T^*	$\rho^*/\rho = V/V^*$	p_0/p_0^*
0.00	0.0000	2.4000	0.0000	0.0000	1.2679
0.10	0.0468	2.3669	0.0560	0.0237	1.2591
0.20	0.1736	2.2727	0.2066	0.0909	1.2346
0.30	0.3469	2.1314	0.4089	0.1918	1.1985
0.40	0.5290	1.9608	0.6151	0.3137	1.1566
0.50	0.6914	1.7778	0.7901	0.4444	1.1141
0.60	0.8189	1.5957	0.9167	0.5745	1.0753
0.70	0.9085	1.4235	0.9929	0.6975	1.0431
0.80	0.9639	1.2658	1.0255	0.8101	1.0193
0.90	0.9921	1.1246	1.0245	0.9110	1.0049
1.00	1.0000	1.0000	1.0000	1.0000	1.0000
1.10	0.9939	0.8909	0.9603	1.0780	1.0049
1.20	0.9787	0.7958	0.9118	1.1459	1.0194
1.30	0.9580	0.7130	0.8592	1.2050	1.0437
1.40	0.9343	0.6410	0.8054	1.2564	1.0777
1.50	0.9093	0.5783	0.7525	1.3012	1.1215
1.60	0.8842	0.5236	0.7017	1.3403	1.1756
1.70	0.8597	0.4756	0.6538	1.3746	1.2402
1.80	0.8363	0.4335	0.6089	1.4046	1.3159
1.90	0.8141	0.3964	0.5673	1.4311	1.4033
2.00	0.7934	0.3636	0.5289	1.4545	1.5031
2.10	0.7741	0.3345	0.4936	1.4753	1.6162
2.20	0.7561	0.3086	0.4611	1.4938	1.7434
2.30	0.7395	0.2855	0.4312	1.5103	1.8860
2.40	0.7242	0.2648	0.4038	1.5252	2.0451
2.50	0.7101	0.2462	0.3787	1.5385	2.2218
2.60	0.6970	0.2294	0.3556	1.5505	2.4177
2.70	0.6849	0.2142	0.3344	1.5613	2.6343
2.80	0.6738	0.2004	0.3149	1.5711	2.8731
2.90	0.6635	0.1879	0.2969	1.5801	3.1359
3.00	0.6540	0.1765	0.2803	1.5882	3.4245
3.10	0.6452	0.1660	0.2650	1.5957	3.7408
3.20	0.6370	0.1565	0.2508	1.6025	4.0871
3.30	0.6294	0.1477	0.2377	1.6088	4.4655
3.40	0.6224	0.1397	0.2255	1.6145	4.8783
3.50	0.6158	0.1322	0.2142	1.6198	5.3280
3.60	0.6097	0.1254	0.2037	1.6247	5.8173
3.70	0.6040	0.1190	0.1939	1.6293	6.3488
3.80	0.5987	0.1131	0.1848	1.6335	6.9256
3.90	0.5937	0.1077	0.1763	1.6374	7.5505
4.00	0.5891	0.1026	0.1683	1.6410	8.2268

Table B.5 Prandtl-Meyer Supersonic Expansion Function for $k = 1.4$

Ma	ω, deg	Ma	ω, deg	Ma	ω, deg	Ma	ω, deg
1.00	0.00	3.10	51.65	5.10	77.84	7.10	91.49
1.10	1.34	3.20	53.47	5.20	78.73	7.20	92.00
1.20	3.56	3.30	55.22	5.30	79.60	7.30	92.49
1.30	6.17	3.40	56.91	5.40	80.43	7.40	92.97
1.40	8.99	3.50	58.53	5.50	81.24	7.50	93.44
1.50	11.91	3.60	60.09	5.60	82.03	7.60	93.90
1.60	14.86	3.70	61.60	5.70	82.80	7.70	94.34
1.70	17.81	3.80	63.04	5.80	83.54	7.80	94.78
1.80	20.73	3.90	64.44	5.90	84.26	7.90	95.21
1.90	23.59	4.00	65.78	6.00	84.96	8.00	95.62
2.00	26.38	4.10	67.08	6.10	85.63	8.10	96.03
2.10	29.10	4.20	68.33	6.20	86.29	8.20	96.43
2.20	31.73	4.30	69.54	6.30	86.94	8.30	96.82
2.30	34.28	4.40	70.71	6.40	87.56	8.40	97.20
2.40	36.75	4.50	71.83	6.50	88.17	8.50	97.57
2.50	39.12	4.60	72.92	6.60	88.76	8.60	97.94
2.60	41.41	4.70	73.97	6.70	89.33	8.70	98.29
2.70	43.62	4.80	74.99	6.80	89.89	8.80	98.64
2.80	45.75	4.90	75.97	6.90	90.44	8.90	98.98
2.90	47.79	5.00	76.92	7.00	90.97	9.00	99.32
3.00	49.76						

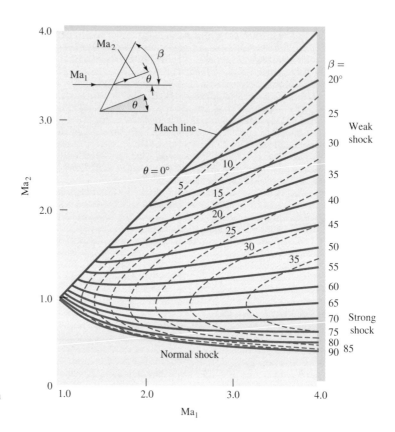

Fig. B.1 Mach number downstream of an oblique shock for $k = 1.4$.

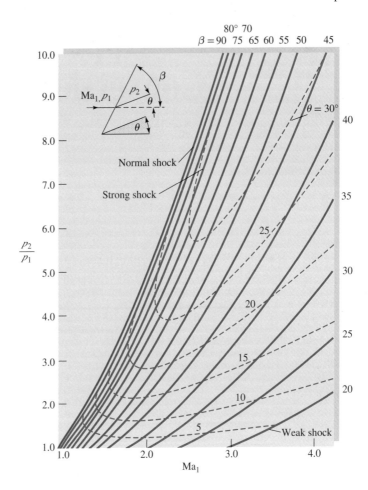

Fig. B.2 Pressure ratio downstream of an oblique shock for $k = 1.4$.

Appendix C
Conversion Factors

During this period of transition there is a constant need for conversions between BG and SI units (see Table 1.2). Some additional conversions are given here. Conversion factors are given inside the front cover.

Length	Volume
1 ft = 12 in = 0.3048 m 1 mi = 5280 ft = 1609.344 m 1 nautical mile (nmi) = 6076 ft = 1852 m 1 yd = 3 ft = 0.9144 m 1 angstrom (Å) = 1.0 E−10 m	1 ft^3 = 0.028317 m^3 1 U.S. gal = 231 in^3 = 0.0037854 m^3 1 L = 0.001 m^3 = 0.035315 ft^3 1 U.S. fluid ounce = 2.9574 E−5 m^3 1 U.S. quart (qt) = 9.4635 E−4 m^3 1 barrel = 42 U.S. gal = 0.15899 m^3
Mass	**Area**
1 slug = 32.174 lbm = 14.594 kg 1 lbm = 0.4536 kg 1 short ton = 2000 lbm = 907.185 kg 1 tonne = 1000 kg 1 U.S. ounce = 0.02835 kg	1 ft^2 = 0.092903 m^2 1 mi^2 = 2.78784 E7 ft^2 = 2.59 E6 m^2 1 acre = 43,560 ft^2 = 4046.9 m^2 1 hectare (ha) = 10,000 m^2
Velocity	**Acceleration**
1 ft/s = 0.3048 m/s 1 mi/h = 1.466666 ft/s = 0.44704 m/s 1 kn = 1 nmi/h = 1.6878 ft/s = 0.5144 m/s 1 kn = 1.1508 mi/h	1 ft/s^2 = 0.3048 m/s^2
Mass flow	**Volume flow**
1 slug/s = 14.594 kg/s 1 lbm/s = 0.4536 kg/s	1 gal/min = 0.002228 ft^3/s = 0.06309 L/s 1 × 10^6 gal/day = 1.5472 ft^3/s = 0.04381 m^3/s 1 ft^3/s = 0.028317 m^3/s

Pressure	Force
$1\ \text{lbf/ft}^2 = 47.88\ \text{Pa}$	$1\ \text{lbf} = 4.448222\ \text{N} = 16\ \text{oz}$
$1\ \text{lbf/in}^2 = 144\ \text{lbf/ft}^2 = 6895\ \text{Pa}$	$1\ \text{kgf} = 2.2046\ \text{lbf} = 9.80665\ \text{N}$
$1\ \text{atm} = 2116.2\ \text{lbf/ft}^2 = 14.696\ \text{lbf/in}^2 =$	$1\ \text{U.S. (short) ton} = 2000\ \text{lbf}$
$\quad 101{,}325\ \text{Pa}$	$1\ \text{dyne} = 1.0\,\text{E}{-}5\ \text{N}$
$1\ \text{inHg (at } 20°\text{C}) = 3375\ \text{Pa}$	$1\ \text{ounce (avoirdupois) (oz)} = 0.27801\ \text{N}$
$1\ \text{bar} = 1.0\ \text{E5 Pa}$	$1\ \text{poundal} = 0.13826\ \text{N}$
$1\ \text{torr} = (1/760)\text{atm} = 133.32\ \text{Pa} = 2.7845\ \text{lbf/ft}^2$	

Energy	Power
$1\ \text{ft}\cdot\text{lbf} = 1.35582\ \text{J}$	$1\ \text{hp} = 550\ \text{ft}\cdot\text{lbf/s} = 745.7\ \text{W}$
$1\ \text{Btu} = 252\ \text{cal} = 1055.056\ \text{J} = 778.17\ \text{ft}\cdot\text{lbf}$	$1\ \text{ft}\cdot\text{lbf/s} = 1.3558\ \text{W}$
$1\ \text{kilowatt hour (kWh)} = 3.6\ \text{E6 J}$	
$1\ \text{calorie} = 4.1868\ \text{J}$	
$1\ \text{therm} = 1\ \text{E5 Btu} = 1.0551\ \text{E8 J}$	

Specific weight	Density
$1\ \text{lbf/ft}^3 = 157.09\ \text{N/m}^3$	$1\ \text{slug/ft}^3 = 515.38\ \text{kg/m}^3$
	$1\ \text{lbm/ft}^3 = 16.0185\ \text{kg/m}^3$
	$1\ \text{g/cm}^3 = 1000\ \text{kg/m}^3$

Viscosity	Kinematic viscosity
$1\ \text{slug/(ft}\cdot\text{s)} = 47.88\ \text{kg/(m}\cdot\text{s)}$	$1\ \text{ft}^2\text{/h} = 0.000025806\ \text{m}^2\text{/s}$
$1\ \text{poise (P)} = 1\ \text{g/(cm}\cdot\text{s)} = 0.1\ \text{kg/(m}\cdot\text{s)}$	$1\ \text{stokes (St)} = 1\ \text{cm}^2\text{/s} = 0.0001\ \text{m}^2\text{/s}$

Temperature scale readings

$$T_F = \tfrac{9}{5}T_C + 32 \qquad T_C = \tfrac{5}{9}(T_F - 32) \qquad T_R = T_F + 459.69 \qquad T_K = T_C + 273.16$$

where subscripts F, C, K, and R refer to readings on the Fahrenheit, Celsius, Kelvin, and Rankine scales, respectively.

Specific heat or gas constant*	Thermal conductivity*
$1\ \text{ft}\cdot\text{lbf/(slug}\cdot°\text{R)} = 0.16723\ \text{N}\cdot\text{m/(kg}\cdot\text{K)}$	$1\ \text{Btu/(h}\cdot\text{ft}\cdot°\text{R)} = 1.7307\ \text{W/(m}\cdot\text{K)}$
$1\ \text{Btu/(lbm}\cdot°\text{R)} = 4186.8\ \text{J/(kg}\cdot\text{K)}$	

*Although the absolute (Kelvin) and Celsius temperature scales have different starting points, the intervals are the same size: 1 kelvin = 1 Celsius degree. The same holds true for the nonmetric absolute (Rankine) and Fahrenheit scales: 1 Rankine degree = 1 Fahrenheit degree. It is customary to express temperature differences in absolute temperature units.

Appendix D
Equations of Motion in Cylindrical Coordinates

The equations of motion of an incompressible newtonian fluid with constant μ, k, and c_p are given here in cylindrical coordinates (r, θ, z), which are related to cartesian coordinates (x, y, z) as in Fig. 4.2:

$$x = r \cos \theta \qquad y = r \sin \theta \qquad z = z \tag{D.1}$$

The velocity components are v_r, v_θ, and v_z. Here are the equations:
Continuity:

$$\frac{1}{r}\frac{\partial}{\partial r}(r v_r) + \frac{1}{r}\frac{\partial}{\partial \theta}(v_\theta) + \frac{\partial}{\partial z}(v_z) = 0 \tag{D.2}$$

Convective time derivative:

$$\mathbf{V} \cdot \nabla = v_r \frac{\partial}{\partial r} + \frac{1}{r} v_\theta \frac{\partial}{\partial \theta} + v_z \frac{\partial}{\partial z} \tag{D.3}$$

Laplacian operator:

$$\nabla^2 = \frac{1}{r}\frac{\partial}{\partial r}\left(r \frac{\partial}{\partial r}\right) + \frac{1}{r^2}\frac{\partial^2}{\partial \theta^2} + \frac{\partial^2}{\partial z^2} \tag{D.4}$$

The r-momentum equation:

$$\frac{\partial v_r}{\partial t} + (\mathbf{V} \cdot \nabla) v_r - \frac{1}{r} v_\theta^2 = -\frac{1}{\rho}\frac{\partial p}{\partial r} + g_r + \nu\left(\nabla^2 v_r - \frac{v_r}{r^2} - \frac{2}{r^2}\frac{\partial v_\theta}{\partial \theta}\right) \tag{D.5}$$

The θ-momentum equation:

$$\frac{\partial v_\theta}{\partial t} + (\mathbf{V} \cdot \nabla) v_\theta + \frac{1}{r} v_r v_\theta = -\frac{1}{\rho r}\frac{\partial p}{\partial \theta} + g_\theta + \nu\left(\nabla^2 v_\theta - \frac{v_\theta}{r^2} + \frac{2}{r^2}\frac{\partial v_r}{\partial \theta}\right) \tag{D.6}$$

The z-momentum equation:

$$\frac{\partial v_z}{\partial t} + (\mathbf{V} \cdot \nabla) v_z = -\frac{1}{\rho}\frac{\partial p}{\partial z} + g_z + \nu\nabla^2 v_z \tag{D.7}$$

The energy equation:

$$\rho c_p\left[\frac{\partial T}{\partial t} + (\mathbf{V} \cdot \nabla)T\right] = k\nabla^2 T + \mu[2(\varepsilon_{rr}^2 + \varepsilon_{\theta\theta}^2 + \varepsilon_{zz}^2) + \varepsilon_{\theta z}^2 + \varepsilon_{rz}^2 + \varepsilon_{r\theta}^2] \tag{D.8}$$

where

$$\varepsilon_{rr} = \frac{\partial v_r}{\partial r} \qquad\qquad \varepsilon_{\theta\theta} = \frac{1}{r}\left(\frac{\partial v_\theta}{\partial \theta} + v_r\right)$$

$$\varepsilon_{zz} = \frac{\partial v_z}{\partial z} \qquad\qquad \varepsilon_{\theta z} = \frac{1}{r}\frac{\partial v_z}{\partial \theta} + \frac{\partial v_\theta}{\partial z} \tag{D.9}$$

$$\varepsilon_{rz} = \frac{\partial v_r}{\partial z} + \frac{\partial v_z}{\partial r} \qquad \varepsilon_{r\theta} = \frac{1}{r}\left(\frac{\partial v_r}{\partial \theta} - v_\theta\right) + \frac{\partial v_\theta}{\partial r}$$

Viscous stress components:

$$\tau_{rr} = 2\mu\varepsilon_{rr} \qquad\qquad \tau_{\theta\theta} = 2\mu\varepsilon_{\theta\theta} \qquad\qquad \tau_{zz} = 2\mu\varepsilon_{zz}$$

$$\tau_{r\theta} = \mu\varepsilon_{r\theta} \qquad\qquad \tau_{\theta z} = \mu\varepsilon_{\theta z} \qquad\qquad \tau_{rz} = \mu\varepsilon_{rz} \tag{D.10}$$

Angular velocity components:

$$2\omega_r = \frac{1}{r}\frac{\partial v_z}{\partial \theta} - \frac{\partial v_\theta}{\partial z}$$

$$2\omega_\theta = \frac{\partial v_r}{\partial z} - \frac{\partial v_z}{\partial r} \tag{D.11}$$

$$2\omega_z = \frac{1}{r}\frac{\partial}{\partial r}(rv_\theta) - \frac{1}{r}\frac{\partial v_r}{\partial \theta}$$

Estimating Uncertainty in Experimental Data

Uncertainty is a fact of life in engineering. We rarely know any engineering properties or variables to an extreme degree of accuracy. The *uncertainty* of data is normally defined as the band within which one is 95 percent confident that the true value lies. Recall from Fig. 1.7 that the uncertainty of the ratio μ/μ_c was estimated as ±20 percent. There are whole monographs devoted to the subject of experimental uncertainty, so we give only a brief summary here.

All experimental data have uncertainty, separated into two causes: (1) a *systematic* error due to the instrument or its environment and (2) a *random* error due to scatter in repeated readings. We minimize the systematic error by careful calibration and then estimate the random error statistically. The judgment of the experimenter is of crucial importance.

Here is the accepted mathematical estimate. Suppose a desired result P depends upon a single experimental variable x. If x has an uncertainty δx, then the uncertainty δP is estimated from the calculus:

$$\delta P \approx \frac{\partial P}{\partial x}\delta x$$

If there are multiple variables, $P = P(x_1, x_2, x_3, \ldots x_N)$, the overall uncertainty δP is calculated as a root-mean-square estimate [4]:

$$\delta P = \left[\left(\frac{\partial P}{\partial x_1}\delta x_1\right)^2 + \left(\frac{\partial P}{\partial x_2}\delta x_2\right)^2 + \cdots + \left(\frac{\partial P}{\partial x_N}\delta x_N\right)^2\right]^{1/2} \tag{E.1}$$

This calculation is statistically much more probable than simply adding linearly the various uncertainties δx_i, thereby making the unlikely assumption that all variables simultaneously attain maximum error. Note that it is the responsibility of the experimenter to establish and report accurate estimates of all the relevant uncertainties δx_i.

If the quantity P is a simple power-law expression of the other variables, for example, $P = \text{Const } x_1^{n_1}x_2^{n_2}x_3^{n_3}\ldots$, then each derivative in Eq. (E.1) is proportional to P and the relevant power-law exponent and is inversely proportional to that variable.

If $P = \text{Const } x_1^{n_1} x_2^{n_2} x_3^{n_3} \ldots$, then

$$\frac{\partial P}{\partial x_1} = \frac{n_1 P}{x_1}, \frac{\partial P}{\partial x_2} = \frac{n_2 P}{x_2}, \frac{\partial P}{\partial x_3} = \frac{n_3 P}{x_3}, \ldots$$

Thus. from Eq. (E.1),

$$\frac{\delta P}{P} = \left[\left(n_1 \frac{\delta x_1}{x_1}\right)^2 + \left(n_2 \frac{\delta x_2}{x_2}\right)^2 + \left(n_3 \frac{\delta x_3}{x_3}\right)^2 + \cdots\right]^{1/2} \qquad (E.2)$$

Evaluation of δP is then a straightforward procedure, as in the following example.

EXAMPLE

The so-called dimensionless Moody pipe friction factor f, plotted in Fig. 6.13, is calculated in experiments from the following formula involving pipe diameter D, pressure drop Δp, density ρ, volume flow rate Q, and pipe length L:

$$f = \frac{\pi^2}{8} \frac{D^5 \Delta p}{\rho Q^2 L}$$

Measurement uncertainties are given for a certain experiment: $D = 0.5$ percent, $\Delta p = 2.0$ percent, $\rho = 1.0$ percent. $Q = 3.5$ percent, and $L = 0.4$ percent. Estimate the overall uncertainty of the friction factor f.

Solution

The coefficient $\pi^2/8$ is assumed to be a pure theoretical number, with no uncertainty. The other variables may be collected using Eqs. (E.1) and (E.2):

$$U = \frac{\delta f}{f} = \left[\left(5\frac{\delta D}{D}\right)^2 + \left(1\frac{\delta \Delta p}{\Delta p}\right)^2 + \left(1\frac{\delta \rho}{\rho}\right)^2 + \left(2\frac{\delta Q}{Q}\right)^2 + \left(1\frac{\delta L}{L}\right)^2\right]^{1/2}$$

$$= [\{5(0.5\%)\}^2 + (2.0\%)^2 + (1.0\%)^2 + \{2(3.5\%)\}^2 + (0.4\%)^2]^{1/2} \approx 7.8\% \quad Ans.$$

By far the dominant effect in this particular calculation is the 3.5 percent error in Q, which is amplified by doubling, due to the power of 2 on flow rate. The diameter uncertainty, which is quintupled, would have contributed more had δD been larger than 0.5 percent.

References

1. I. Hughes and J. Hase, *Measurements and their Uncertainties*, Oxford University Press, New York, 2010.
2. H. W. Coleman and W. G. Steele, *Experimentation and Uncertainty Analysis for Engineers*, 3d ed., Wiley, New York, 2009.
3. S. E. Serrano, *Engineering Uncertainty and Risk Analysis*, Hydroscience Inc., Toms River, NJ, 2011.
4. S. J. Kline and F. A. McClintock, "Describing Uncertainties in Single-Sample Experiments," *Mechanical Engineering*, January, 1953, pp. 3–9.

Answers to Selected Problems

Chapter 1

P1.2	5.7 E18 kg; 1.2 E44 molecules
P1.6	$\{\alpha\} = \{L^{-1}\}$
P1.8	$\sigma \approx 1.00\ My/I$
P1.10	Yes, all terms are $\{ML/T^2\}$
P1.12	$\{B\} = \{L^{-1}\}$
P1.14	$Q = \text{Const } B\ g^{1/2}H^{3/2}$
P1.16	All terms are $\{ML^{-2}T^{-2}\}$
P1.18	$V = V_0 e^{-mt/K}$
P1.20	(b) 2080
P1.24	(a) 41 kPa; (b) 0.65 kg/m^3
P1.26	$W_{air} = 0.71$ lbf
P1.28	$\rho_{wet} = 1.10$ kg/m^3, $\rho_{dry} = 1.13$ kg/m^3
P1.30	$W_{1\text{-}2} = 21$ ft · lbf
P1.32	(a) 76 kN; (b) 501 kN
P1.34	(a) $\rho_1 = 5.05$ kg/m^3; (b) $\rho_2 = 2.12$ kg/m^3 (ideal gas)
P1.36	(b) $\rho \approx 628$ kg/m^3
P1.38	$\tau = 1380$ Pa, $Re_L = 28$
P1.40	Approximately 25 N · m per meter
P1.42	$T \approx 539°C$
P1.44	$\mu \approx 0.040$ kg/m · s
P1.46	(d) 3.0 m/s; (e) 0.79 m/s; (f) 22 m/s
P1.48	$F \approx (\mu_1/h_1 + \mu_2/h_2)AV$
P1.50	(a) Yes; (b) $\mu \approx 0.40$ kg/(m · s)
P1.52	$P \approx 73$ W
P1.54	$M \approx \pi\mu\Omega R^4/h$
P1.56	$\mu = 3M \sin \theta/(2\pi\Omega R^3)$
P1.58	$\mu = 0.040$ kg/(m · s), last 2 points are *turbulent* flow
P1.60	39,500 Pa
P1.62	28,500 Pa
P1.64	$D > 5$ mm
P1.66	$F = 0.014$ N
P1.68	$h = (Y/\rho g)^{1/2} \cot \theta$
P1.70	$h = 2Y \cos \theta/(\rho g W)$
P1.72	$z \approx 4800$ m
P1.74	8.6 km
P1.76	(b) $\beta_{steam} \approx 262$ kPa
P1.78	(a) 25°C; (b) 4°C
P1.80	Ma = 1.20
P1.82	$y = x \tan \theta + $ constant
P1.86	Approximately 5.0 percent

Chapter 2

P2.2	$\sigma_{xy} = -289$ lb/ft^2, $\tau_{AA} = -577$ lb/ft^2
P2.4	Approximately 100 degrees
P2.6	(a) 26.9 ft; (b) 30.0 in; (c) 10.35 m; (d) 13,100 mm
P2.8	Approximately 2.36 E6 Pa
P2.10	10,500 Pa
P2.12	8.0 cm
P2.14	$h_1 = 6.0$ cm, $h_2 = 52$ cm
P2.16	(a) 1885 lbf/ft^2; (b) 2165 lbf/ft^2
P2.18	1.56
P2.20	14 lbf
P2.22	0.94 cm
P2.24	$p_{sealevel} \approx 115$ kPa, $m_{exact} = 5.3$ E18 kg
P2.28	(a) 454 ft
P2.30	(a) 29.6 kPa; (b) K = 0.98
P2.32	22.6 cm
P2.34	$\Delta p = \Delta h[\gamma_{water}(1 + d^2/D^2) - \gamma_{oil}(1 - d^2/D^2)]$
P2.36	25°
P2.38	$p_A = 219$ kPa
P2.40	$p_B = 17.6$ lbf/in^2
P2.42	$p_A - p_B = (\rho_2 - \rho_1)gh$
P2.44	(a) 171 lb/ft^2; (b) 392 lb/ft^2; manometer reads friction loss
P2.46	1.45
P2.48	(a) 132 kPa; (b) 1.38 m

P2.50   (a) 220 ft; (b) 110,000 lbf

P2.52   (a) 38,400 lbf; (b) 5.42 ft from A

P2.56   16.08 ft

P2.58   0.40 m

P2.60   (a) Approximately 62,000 lbf

P2.62   10.6 ft

P2.64   1.35 m

P2.66 $F = 1.18$ E9 N, $M_C = 3.13$ E9 N · m counterclockwise, no tipping

P2.68   18,040 N

P2.70   0.79 m

P2.72 $M_A = 32,700$ N · m

P2.74 $H = R[\pi/4 + \{(\pi/4)^2 + 2/3\}^{1/2}]$

P2.76   (a) 239 kN; (c) 388 kN · m

P2.78   (b) $F_{AB} = 4390$ N, $F_{CD} = 4220$ N

P2.80 $\theta > 77.4°$

P2.82 $F_H = 97.9$ MN, $F_V = 153.8$ MN

P2.84   (a) $F_V = 2940$ N; $F_H = 6880$ N

P2.86 $P = 59$ kN

P2.88 $F_H = 176$ kN, $F_V = 31.9$ kN, yes

P2.90 $F_V = 22,600$ N; $F_H = 16,500$ N

P2.92 $F_{one\ bolt} \approx 11,300$ N

P2.94   Forces on each panel are equal.

P2.96 $F_H = 110$ kN , $F_V = 279$ kN

P2.98 $F_H = 245$ kN, $F_V = 51$ kN

P2.100 $F_H = 0, F_V = 297$ kN

P2.102 (a) 238 kN; (b) 125 kN

P2.104 5.0 N

P2.106 $D \approx 2.0$ m

P2.108 (a) 0.0427 m; (b) 1592 kg/m^3

P2.110 (a) 14.95 N, SG = 0.50

P2.112 (a) 39 N; (b) 0.64

P2.114 0.636

P2.116 (a) Yes; (b) Yes; (c) 3.51 in

P2.118 6.14 ft

P2.120 34.3°

P2.122 $a/b \approx 0.834$

P2.124 6850 m

P2.126 3130 Pa (vacuum)

P2.128 Yes, stable if $S > 0.789$

P2.130 Slightly unstable, MG = −0.007 m

P2.132 Stable if $R/h > 3.31$

P2.134 (a) unstable; (b) stable

P2.136 $MG = L^2/(3\pi R) − 4R/(3\pi) > 0$ if $L > 2R$

P2.138 2.77 in deep; volume = 10.8 fluid ounces

P2.140 $a_x = −4.9$ m^2/s (decelerating)

P2.142 (a) 16.3 cm; (b) 15.7 N

P2.144 (a) $a_x \approx 319$ m/s^2; (b) no effect, $p_A = p_B$

P2.146 Leans to the right at $\theta = 27°$

P2.148 (a) backward; (b) forward

P2.150 5.5 cm; linear scale OK

P2.152 (a) 224 r/min; (b) 275 r/min

P2.154 552 r/min

P2.156 420 r/min

P2.158 10.57 r/min

Chapter 3

P3.2 $\mathbf{r}$ = position vector from point O

P3.4 $V = 4.38$ m/s

P3.6 $Q = (2b/3)(2g)^{1/2}[(h + L)^{3/2} − (h − L)^{3/2}]$

P3.8   (a) 5.45 m/s; (b) 5.89 m/s; (c) 5.24 m/s

P3.10   (a) 3 m/s; (b) 18 m/s; (c) 5 cm/s out

P3.12 $\Delta t = 46$ s

P3.14 $dh/dt = (Q_1 + Q_3 − Q_2)/(\pi d^2/4)$

P3.16 $Q_{top} = 3U_0 b\delta/8$

P3.18 $V_3 = 14.7$ m/s (out)

P3.20   (a) 7.8 mL/s; (b) 1.24 cm/s

P3.22   (a) 0.06 kg/s; (b) 1060 m/s; (c) 3.4

P3.24 $h = [3Kt^2 d^2/(8 \tan^2 \theta)]^{1/3}$

P3.26 $Q = 2U_0 bh/3$

P3.28   (a) 0.131 kg/s; (b) 115 kPa

P3.30   (a) Ma$_1 = 1.00$; (b) $T_2 = 216$ K

P3.32 $V_{hole} = 6.1$ m/s

P3.34 $V_2 = 4660$ ft/s

P3.36 $U_3 = 6.33$ m/s

P3.38 $V = V_0 r/(2h)$

P3.40   500 N to the left

P3.42 $F = (p_1 − p_a)A_1 − \rho_1 A_1 V_1^2[(D_1/D_2)^2 − 1]$

P3.44 $F = \rho U^2 Lb/3$

P3.46 $\alpha = (1 + \cos \theta)/2$

P3.48 $V_0 \approx 2.27$ m/s

P3.50   102 kN

P3.52   8.65 lbf

P3.54   163 N

P3.56   (a) 18.5 N to left; (b) 7.1 N up

P3.58   40 N

P3.60   2100 N

P3.62   3100 N

P3.64   980 N

P3.66   8800 N

P3.70   91 lbf

P3.72   Drag ≈ 4260 N

P3.74 $F_x = 0, F_y = −17$ N, $F_z = 126$ N

P3.76   (a) 1670 N/m; (b) 3.0 cm; (c) 9.4 cm

P3.80 $F = (\rho/2)gb(h_1^2 − h_2^2) − \rho h_1 b V_1^2(h_1/h_2 − 1)$

P3.82   25 m/s

P3.84   23 N

P3.86   274 kPa

P3.88 $V = \zeta + [\zeta^2 + 2\zeta V_j]^{1/2}, \zeta = \rho Q/2k$

P3.90 $dV/dt = g$

P3.92 $dV/dt = gh/(L + h)$

P3.94 $V_{jet} = 23.7$ ft/s

P3.96 $d^2Z/dt^2 + 2gZ/L = 0$

P3.100   (a) 507 m/s and 1393 m; (b) 14.5 km

P3.102 $h_2/h_1 = -\frac{1}{2} + \frac{1}{2}[1 + 8V_1^2/(gh_1)]^{1/2}$

P3.104 $\Omega = (-V_e/R) \ln (1 - \dot{m}t/M_0)$

P3.106 $F = (\pi/8) \rho D^2 V^2$

P3.108   (a) $V = V_0/(1 + CV_0t/M)$, $C = \rho bh(1 - \cos \theta)$

P3.110 $F_{\text{bolts}} = 1340$ lbf

P3.112   (a) 10.3 kg/s; (b) 760 kPa

P3.114   (a) $V_2 = 9.96$ m/s; (b) $h = 40$ cm

P3.116 $X = 2[h(H - h)]^{1/2}$

P3.120   (a) 0.495 ft³/s; (b) 12.3 ft³/s

P3.122 $h_{\max} = 25.4$ cm

P3.126   (a) 0.197 ft³/s; (b) 0.089 ft³/s

P3.130   104 kPa (gage)

P3.132 $Q = 127$ cm³/s

P3.134   (a) 15 m; (b) 25 mm

P3.136   0.037 kg/s

P3.140   5.93 m (subcritical); 0.432 m (supercritical)

P3.142 $t_0 = [2(\alpha - 1)h_0/g]^{1/2}$, $\alpha = (D/d)^4$

P3.144   Approximately 294 gal/min

P3.150 $T_0 = -305 \mathbf{k}$ N · m

P3.154 $T_B = 40$ ft-lbf

P3.156   2.44 kg/s

P3.158 $P = \rho Q\omega R V_n(\cot \alpha_1 + \cot \alpha_2)$

P3.160 $\mathbf{T}_B = -2400 \mathbf{k}$ N · m

P3.162   197 hp; max power at 179 r/min

P3.164 $\mathbf{T}_0 = \rho Q V_w (R + L/2) \mathbf{k}$

P3.166 $Q_0 = 2.5$ m³/s; $T_0 = 23.15°$C

P3.168 $\Delta T \approx 0.7°$F

P3.170   (a) 699 kJ/kg; (b) 7.0 MW

P3.172   8.7 m

P3.174   (a) 410 hp; (b) 540 hp

P3.176   97 hp

P3.178   8.4 kW

P3.180   112 hp

P3.182   3.2°C/s

P3.184   76.5 m³/s and 138 m³/s

Chapter 4

P4.2   (a) $du/dt = (2V_0^2/L)(1 + 2x/L)$

P4.4   (b) $a_x = (U_0^2/L)(1 + x/L)$; $a_y = (U_0^2/L)(y/L)$

P4.6   (b) $a_x = 16 x$; $a_y = 16 y$

P4.8   (a) $0.0196 U^2/L$; (b) at $t = 1.05 L/U$

P4.10   (b) $\mathbf{a} = 8 \, \mathbf{r}$

P4.12   If $\upsilon_\theta = \upsilon_\phi = 0$, $\upsilon_r = r^{-2}$ fcn (θ, ϕ)

P4.14 $\upsilon_\theta =$ fcn(r) only

P4.16   (a) Yes, continuity is satisfied.

P4.18 $\rho = \rho_0 L_0/(L_0 - Vt)$

P4.20 $\upsilon = \upsilon_0 =$ const, $\{K\} = \{L/T\}$, $\{a\} = \{L^{-1}\}$

P4.22 $v_r = -B r/2 + f(z)/r$

P4.24   (b) $B = 3v_w/(2h^3)$

P4.28   (a) Yes; (b) Yes

P4.30   (a, b) Yes, continuity and Navier-Stokes are satisfied.

P4.32 $f_1 = C_1 r$; $f_2 = C_2/r$

P4.36 $C = \rho g \sin \theta/(2\mu)$

P4.40 $T = T_w + (\mu U^2/3k)(1 - y^4/h^4)$

P4.48 $\psi = U_0 r \sin \theta - V_0 r \cos \theta + $ const

P4.50   (a) Yes, ψ exists.

P4.52 $\psi = -4Q\theta/(\pi b)$

P4.54 $Q = ULb$

P4.60   Irrotational, $z_C = H - \omega^2 R^2/(2g)$

P4.62 $\psi = Vy^2/(2h) + $ const

P4.66 $\psi = -K \sin \theta/r$

P4.68   (a) Yes, a velocity potential exists.

P4.70 $V \approx 2.33$ m/s, $\alpha \approx -16.5°$

P4.72   (a) $\psi = -0.0008 \, \theta$; (b) $\phi = -0.0008 \ln(r)$

P4.74 $\psi = B r \sin \theta + B L \ln r + $ const

P4.76   Yes, ψ exists.

P4.78 $y = A r^n \cos(n\theta) + $ const

P4.80   (a) $w = (\rho g/2\mu)(2\delta x - x^2)$

P4.82   Obsessive result: $\upsilon_\theta = \Omega R^2/r$

P4.84 $\upsilon_z = (\rho gb^2/2\mu) \ln (r/a) - (\rho g/4\mu)(r^2 - a^2)$

P4.86 $Q = 0.0031$ m³/(s · m)

P4.88 $\upsilon_z = U \ln (r/b)/[\ln (a/b)]$

P4.90   (a) 54 kg/h; (b) 7 mm

P4.92 $h = h_0 \exp[-\pi D^4\rho gt/(128\mu LA_0)]$

P4.94 $v_\theta = \Omega R^2/r$

P4.96   (a) 1130 Pa

Chapter 5

P5.2   Prototype $V = 22.8$ mi/h

P5.4 $V = 1.55$ m/s, $F = 1.3$ N

P5.6   (a) 1.39; (b) 0.45

P5.8   Ar $= gH^3(\Delta\rho)^2/\mu^2$

P5.10   (a) $\{ML^{-2}T^{-2}\}$; (b) $\{MLT^{-2}\}$

P5.12   St $= \mu U/(\rho gD^2)$

P5.14   One possible group is hL/k.

P5.16   Stanton number $= h/(\rho Vc_p)$

P5.18 $Q\mu/[(\Delta p/L)b^4] = $ const

P5.20   One possible group is $\Omega D/U$.

P5.22 $\Omega D/V = $ fcn$(N, H/L)$

P5.24 $F/(\rho V^2 L^2) = $ fcn$(\alpha, \rho VL/\mu, L/D, V/a)$

P5.26   (a) Indeterminate; (b) $T = 2.75$ s

P5.28 $\delta/L = $ fcn$[L/D, \rho VD/\mu, E/(\rho V^2)]$

P5.30 $\dot{m}(RT_o)^{1/2}/(p_oD^2) = $ fcn(c_p/R)

P5.32 $Q/(bg^{1/2}H^{3/2}) = $ const

P5.34 $k_{\text{hydrogen}} \approx 0.182$ W/(m · K)

P5.36   (a) $Q_{\text{loss}}R/(A\Delta T) = $ constant

P5.38 $d/D = $ fcn$(\rho UD/\mu, \rho U^2D/Y)$

P5.42   Halving m increases f by about 41 percent.

P5.44   (a) $\{\sigma\} = \{L^2\}$

P5.48 $F \approx 0.17$ N; (doubling U quadruples F)

P5.50   Approximately 2000 lbf (on earth)

P5.52   (a) 0.44 s; (b) 768,000

P5.54	Power $\approx$ 7 hp	P6.74	$L = 205$ m
P5.56	$F_{air} \approx 25$ N/m	P6.76	$Q = 15$ m^3/h or 9.0 m^3/h
P5.58	$V \approx 2.8$ m/s	P6.78	$Q = 25$ m^3/h (to the left)
P5.60	(b) 4300 N	P6.80	$Q = 0.905$ m^3/s
P5.62	(a) $\omega = 14.4$ r/min	P6.82	(a) 10.9 m^3/h; (b) 100 m^3/h
P5.64	$\omega_{aluminum} = 0.77$ Hz	P6.84	$D \approx 0.104$ m
P5.66	(a) $V = 27$ m/s; (b) $z = 27$ m	P6.86	(a) 3.0 m/s; (b) 0.325 m/m; (c) 2770 Pa/m
P5.68	(b) Approximately 1800 N	P6.88	About 17 passages
P5.70	$F = 87$ lbf (extrapolated)	P6.90	$H = 36$ in
P5.72	About 44 kN (extrapolated)	P6.92	(a) 1530 m^3/h; (b) 6.5 Pa (vacuum)
P5.74	Prototype moment = 88 kN · m	P6.94	$a = 18.3$ cm
P5.76	Drag = 107,000 lbf	P6.96	(b) 12,800 Pa
P5.78	Weber no. $\approx$ 100 if $L_m/L_p = 0.0090$	P6.98	Approximately 128 squares
P5.80	(a) 1.86 m/s; (b) 42,900; (c) 254,000	P6.100	4.85 m^3/h
P5.82	561 kN	P6.102	(a) 5.55 hp; (b) 5.31 hp with 6° cone
P5.84	$V_m = 39$ cm/s; $T_m = 3.1$ s; $H_m = 0.20$ m	P6.104	Approximately 34 kPa
P5.88	At 340 W, $D = 0.109$ m	P6.106	$Q = 0.0296$ ft^3/s
		P6.108	(a) $K \approx 9.7$; (b) $Q \approx 0.48$ ft^3/s

Chapter 6

		P6.110	840 W
P6.2	(a) Yes	P6.112	$Q = 0.0151$ ft^3/s
P6.4	(a) 106 m^3/h; (b) 3.6 m^3/h	P6.114	Short duct: $Q = 6.92$ ft^3/s
P6.6	(a) hydrogen, $x = 43$ m	P6.116	$Q = 0.027$ m^3/s
P6.8	(a) −3600 Pa/m; (b) −13,400 Pa/m	P6.118	$\Delta p = 131$ lbf/in^2
P6.10	(a) From A to B; (b) $h_f = 7.8$ m	P6.120	$Q_1 = 0.0281$ m^3/s, $Q_2 = 0.0111$ m^3/s, $Q_3 = 0.0164$ m^3/s
P6.12	$\mu = 0.29$ kg/m · s	P6.122	Increased ε/d and L/d are the causes
P6.14	$Q = 0.0067$ m^3/h if $H = 50$ cm	P6.124	$Q_1 = -2.09$ ft^3/s, $Q_2 = 1.61$ ft^3/s, $Q_3 = 0.49$ ft^3/s
P6.16	19 mm	P6.126	$\theta_{opening} = 35°$
P6.18	4.3 m^3/h	P6.128	$Q_{AB} = 3.47$, $Q_{BC} = 2.90$, $Q_{BD} = 0.58$, $Q_{CD} = 5.28$,
P6.20	4500 cc/h		$Q_{AC} = 2.38$ ft^3/s (all)
P6.22	$F = 4.0$ N	P6.130	$Q_{AB} = 0.95$, $Q_{BC} = 0.24$, $Q_{BD} = 0.19$, $Q_{CD} = 0.31$,
P6.24	(a) 0.019 m^3/h, laminar; (b) $d = 2.67$ mm		$Q_{AC} = 1.05$ ft^3/s (all)
P6.26	(a) $D_2 = 5.95$ cm	P6.132	$2\theta = 6°$, $D_e = 2.0$ m, $p_e = 224$ kPa
P6.28	$\Delta p = 65$ Pa	P6.134	$2\theta = 10°$, $W_e = 8.4$ ft, $p_e = 2180$ lbf/ft^2
P6.30	(a) 19.3 m^3/h; (b) flow is up	P6.136	(a) 25.5 m/s, (b) 0.109 m^3/s, (c) 1.23 Pa
P6.32	(a) flow is up; (b) 1.86 m^3/h	P6.138	46.7 m/s
P6.36	(a) 0.029 lbf/ft^2; (b) 70 ft/s	P6.140	333 Pa
P6.38	5.72 m/s	P6.142	$Q = 18.6$ gal/min, $d_{reducer} = 0.84$ cm
P6.42	16.7 mm	P6.144	(a) $h = 58$ cm
P6.44	$h_f = 10.4$ m, $\Delta p = 1.4$ MPa	P6.146	(a) 0.00653 m^3/s; (b) 100 kPa
P6.46	46 hp/mi	P6.148	(a) 1.58 m; (b) 1.7 m
P6.48	238,000 barrels/day	P6.150	$\Delta p = 27$ kPa
P6.50	(a) −4000 Pa/m; (b) 50 Pa; (c) 46 percent	P6.152	$D = 4.12$ cm
P6.52	$p_1 = 2.38$ MPa	P6.154	106 gal/min
P6.54	$t_{drain} = [4WY/(\pi D^2)][2h_0(1 + f_{av}L/D)/g]^{1/2}$	P6.156	$Q = 0.924$ ft^3/s
P6.56	(a) 2680 lbf/in^2; (b) 5300 hp	P6.158	(a) 49 m^3/h; (b) 6200 Pa
P6.58	80 m^3/h		
P6.60	(a) Not identical to Haaland	**Chapter 7**	
P6.62	204 hp		
P6.64	$Q = 19.6$ m^3/h (laminar, Re = 1450)	P7.2	This is probably helium.
P6.66	(a) 56 kPa; (b) 85 m^3/h; (c) $u = 3.3$ m/s at $r = 1$ cm	P7.4	(a) 4 μm; (b) 1 m
P6.70	$Q = 31$ m^3/h	P7.6	$H = 2.5$ (versus 2.59 for Blasius)
P6.72	$D \approx 9.2$ cm	P7.8	Approximately 0.073 N per meter of width
		P7.12	Does not satisfy $\partial^2 u/\partial y^2 = 0$ at $y = 0$

P7.14 $C = \rho v_0/\mu = \text{const} < 0$ (wall suction)

P7.16   (a) F = 181 N; (b) 256 N

P7.18   (a) 3.41 m/s; (b) 0.0223 Pa

P7.20 $x \approx 0.91$ m

P7.22   (a) y = 3.2 mm

P7.24 $h_1 = 9.2$ mm; $h_2 = 5.5$ mm

P7.26 $F_a = 2.83 F_1$, $F_b = 2.0 F_1$

P7.28   (a) $F_{\text{drag}} = 2.66 N^2(\rho\mu L)^{1/2}U^{3/2}a$

P7.30   Predicted thickness is about 10 percent higher

P7.32 $F = 0.0245 \rho v^{1/7} L^{6/7} U_0^{13/7} \delta$

P7.34   45 percent

P7.36   7.2 m/s = 14 kn

P7.38   (a) 7.6 m/s; (b) 6.2 m/s

P7.40   L = 3.51 m, b = 1.14 m

P7.42   (a) 5.2 N/m

P7.44   Accurate to about ±6 percent

P7.46 $\varepsilon \approx 9$ mm, U = 11.1 m/s = 22 kn

P7.48   Separation at x/L = 0.158 (1 percent error)

P7.50   Separation at $\theta \approx 2.3$ degrees

P7.52   (a) $\text{Re}_b = 0.84 < 1$; (b) 2a = 30 mm

P7.54 $z^* = T_0/[B(n+1)]$, n = g/(RB) − 1

P7.56   (a) 14 N; (b) crosswind creates a very large side force

P7.60   Tow power = 140 hp

P7.62   Square side length ≈ 0.83 m

P7.64 $\Delta t_{1000-2000m} = 202$ s

P7.68   69 m/s

P7.70   40 ft

P7.72   (a) L = 6.3 m; (b) 120 m

P7.74   About 130 mi/h

P7.76   (a) 343 hp

P7.78   28,400 hp

P7.80 $\theta = 72°$

P7.82   (a) 46 s

P7.84   V = 9 m/s

P7.86   Approximately 2.9 m by 5.8 m

P7.88   (a) 62 hp; (b) 86 hp

P7.90 $V_{\text{overturn}} \approx 145$ ft/s = 99 mi/h

P7.94   (a) 100 mi/h; (b) 88 mi/h

P7.96 $\Omega_{\text{avg}} \approx 0.21 \, U/D$

P7.98   (b) $h \approx 0.18$ m

P7.100   (a) 73 mi/h; (b) 79 mi/h

P7.104   29.5 knots

P7.106   1130 m²

P7.108 $\Delta x_{\text{ball}} \approx 13$ m

P7.110 $\Delta y \approx 1.9$ ft

P7.114 $V_{\text{down}} \approx 25$ m/min; $V_{\text{up}} \approx 30$ m/min

P7.116   (a) 87 mi/h; (b) 680 hp

P7.118   (a) 27 m/s; (b) 360 m

P7.120 $(L/D)_{\text{max}} = 21$; $\alpha = 4.8°$

P7.122   (a) 6.7 m/s; (b) 13.5 m/s = 26 kn

P7.124 $\Omega_{\text{crude theory}} \approx 340$ r/s

P7.126   Approximately 850 ft

Chapter 8

P8.2 $\Gamma = \pi\Omega(R_2^2 − R_1^2)$

P8.4   No, 1/r is not a proper two-dimensional potential

P8.6 $\psi = B r^2 \sin(2\theta)$

P8.8 $\Gamma = 4B$

P8.10   (a) 1.27 cm

P8.12 $\Gamma = 0$

P8.14   Irrotational outer, rotational inner; minimum $p = p_\infty − \rho\omega^2R^2$ at r = 0

P8.16   (a) 0.106 m to the left of A

P8.18   From afar: a single source 4m

P8.20   Vortex near a wall (see Fig. 8.17b)

P8.22   Stagnation flow toward a bump

P8.24 $C_p = −\{2(x/a)/[1 + (x/a)^2]\}^2$, $C_{p,\text{min}} = −1.0$ at x = a

P8.26   (a) 8.75 m; (b) 27.5 m on each side

P8.28   Creates a source in a square corner

P8.30   r = 25 m

P8.32 $m_2 = 40$ m²/s

P8.34   Two stagnation points, at $x = \pm a/\sqrt{3}$

P8.36 $U_\infty = 12.9$ m/s, 2L = 53 cm, $V_{\text{max}} = 22.5$ m/s

P8.40   1.47 m

P8.42   111 kPa

P8.44   K = 3.44 m²/s; (a) 218 kPa; (b) 205 kPa *upper,* 40 kPa *lower*

P8.46 $F_{\text{1-bolt}} = 5060$ N

P8.50   h = 3a/2, $U_{\text{max}} = 5U/4$

P8.52 $V_{\text{boat}} = 10.4$ ft/s with wind at 58°

P8.54 $F_{\text{parallel}} = 6700$ lbf, $F_{\text{normal}} = 2700$ lbf, power ≈ 560 hp (very approximate)

P8.60   This is Fig. 8.18a, flow in a 60° corner

P8.62   Stagnation flow near a "bump"

P8.66 $\lambda = 0.45m/(5m + 1)$ if $U = Cx^m$

P8.68   Flow past a Rankine oval

P8.70   Applied to wind tunnel "blockage"

P8.72   Adverse gradient for x > a

P8.74 $V_{B,\text{total}} = (8K\mathbf{i} + 4K\mathbf{j})/(15a)$

P8.78   Need an infinite array of images

P8.82   (a) 4.5 m/s; (b) 1.13; (c) 1.26 hp

P8.84   (a) 0.21; (b) 1.9°

P8.86   (a) 26 m; (b) 8.7; (c) 1600 N

P8.88   (a) 11.1; (b) 0.56

P8.92   (a) 0.77 m; (b) V = 4.5 m/s at $(r, \theta) = (1.81, 51°)$ and (1.11, 88°)

P8.94   Yes, they are orthogonal

P8.96   (a) $0.61 \, U_\infty^2/a$

P8.98   Yes, a closed teardrop shape appears

P8.100   V = 14.1 m/s, $p_A = 115$ kPa

P8.102   (a) 1250 ft; (b) 1570 ft (crudely)

Chapter 9

P9.2   (a) $V_2 = 450$ m/s, $\Delta s = 515$ J/(kg · K); (b) $V_2 = 453$ m/s, $\Delta s = 512$ J/(kg · K)

P9.4   (a) +372 J/(kg · K)

P9.6   (a) 381 K
P9.8   410 K
P9.10   (a) 0.80
P9.12   (a) 2.13 E9 Pa and 1460 m/s; (b) 2.91 E9 Pa and 1670 m/s; (c) 2645 m/s
P9.14   Approximately 1300 m/s
P9.18   Ma ≈ 0.24
P9.20   (a) 41 kPa; (b) 421 m/s; (c) 1.27
P9.22   (a) 267 m/s; (b) 286 m/s
P9.24   (b) at Ma ≈ 0.576
P9.28   (b) 232 K
P9.30   Deviation less than 1 percent at Ma = 0.3
P9.32   (a) 141 kPa; (b) 101 kPa; (c) 0.706
P9.34   (a) 3.74 cm
P9.36   (a) 0.142 kg/s
P9.40   (a) 0.192 kg/s
P9.42   (a) Ma = 0.90, T = 260 K, V = 291 m/s
P9.44 V_e = 5680 ft/s, p_e = 15.7 psia, T_e = 1587°R, thrust = 4000 lbf
P9.46   (a) 0.0020 m^2
P9.48   (a) 313 m/s; (b) 0.124 m/s; (c) 0.00331 kg/s
P9.50   (a) 0.0970 kg/s
P9.52   (a) 5.9 cm^2; (b) 773 kPa
P9.54   (a) Ma$_2$ = 0.513
P9.56   At about A_1 ≈ 24.7 cm^2
P9.58   (a) 3.50
P9.60   Upstream: Ma = 1.92, V = 585 m/s
P9.62 C = 19,100 ft/s, V_{inside} = 15,900 ft/s
P9.64   (a) 4.0 cm^2; (b) 325 kPa
P9.66 h = 1.09 m
P9.68 p_{atm} = 92.6 kPa; max flow = 0.140 kg/s
P9.70   119 kPa
P9.72 D ≈ 9.3 mm
P9.74   0.191 kg/s
P9.76 Δt_{shocks} ≈ 23 s; $\Delta t_{choking\text{-}stops}$ ≈ 39 s
P9.78   Case A: 0.071 kg/s; B: 0.068 kg/s
P9.80 A^* = 2.4 E-6 ft^2 or D_{hole} = 0.021 in
P9.82 V_e = 110 m/s, Ma$_e$ = 0.67 (yes)
P9.84   (a) 0.96 kg/s; (b) 0.27; (c) 435 kPa
P9.86 V_2 = 107 m/s, p_2 = 371 kPa, T_2 = 330 K, p_{02} = 394 kPa
P9.88   (a) 12.7 m
P9.90   (a) 0.030; (b) 16.5 lbf/in^2
P9.92   (a) 14.46 m
P9.96   (a) 128 m; (b) 80 m; (c) 105 m
P9.98   (a) 430; (b) 0.12; (c) 0.00243 kg/h
P9.100   0.345 kg/s
P9.102   Flow is choked at 0.56 kg/s
P9.104 p_{tank} = 190 kPa
P9.106   about 91 s
P9.108   Mass flow drops by about 32 percent
P9.112   (b) 129 kPa
P9.114   (a) 2.21; (b) 779 kPa; (c) 1146 K

P9.116   V$_{plane}$ < 2640 ft/s
P9.118 V = 204 m/s, Ma = 0.6
P9.120 P is 3 m ahead of the small circle, Ma = 2.0, T_{stag} = 518 K
P9.122 β = 23.13°, Ma$_2$ = 2.75, p_2 = 145 kPa
P9.124   (a) 1.87; (b) 293 kPa; (c) 404 K; (d) 415 m/s
P9.126   (a) 2.11
P9.128 δ_{wedge} ≈ 15.5°
P9.132   (a) p_A = 18.0 psia; (b) p_B = 121 psia
P9.134   Ma$_3$ = 1.02, p_3 = 727 kPa, ϕ = 42.8°
P9.136   (a) h = 0.40 m; (b) Ma$_3$ = 2.43
P9.138 p_r = 21.7 kPa
P9.140   Ma$_2$ = 2.75, p_2 = 145 kPa
P9.142   (a) Ma$_2$ = 2.641, p_2 = 60.3 kPa; (b) Ma$_2$ = 2.299, p_2 = 24.1 kPa
P9.144   (a) 10.34 degrees
P9.146   (a) 2.385; (b) 47 kPa
P9.148   (a) 4.44; (b) 9.6 kPa
P9.150   (a) α = 4.10°; (b) drag = 2150 N/m
P9.152   Approximately 53 lbf
P9.156   (a) C_L = 0.139; C_D = 0.0146

Chapter 10

P10.2   (a) Fr = 2.69
P10.4   These are piezometer tubes (no flow)
P10.6   (a) Fr = 3.8; (b) $V_{current}$ = 7.7 m/s
P10.8 Δt_{travel} = 6.3 h
P10.10 λ_{crit} = $2\pi(\Upsilon/\rho g)^{1/2}$
P10.14   Flow must be fully rough turbulent (high Re) for Chézy to be valid
P10.16   (a) 2.27 m^3/s
P10.18   (a) 12.4 m^3/s; (b) about 22 Pa
P10.20   0.0174 or 1.0°
P10.22 S_0 = 0.00038 (or 0.38 m/km)
P10.24   (a) n ≈ 0.027; (b) 2.28 ft
P10.28   (a) 0.00106
P10.30 Δt ≈ 32 min
P10.32 A = 4.39 m^2, 10 percent larger
P10.34   If b = 4 ft, y = 9.31 ft, P = 22.62 ft; if b = 8 ft, y = 4.07 ft, P = 16.14 ft
P10.36 y_2 = 3.6 m
P10.38   Maximum flow at θ = 60°
P10.42   The two are equally efficient.
P10.44   Hexagon side length b = 2.12 ft
P10.46 h_0/b ≈ 0.49
P10.48   (a) 0.00634; (b) 0.00637
P10.50   (a) 2.37; (b) 0.62 m; (c) 0.0023
P10.52 W = 2.06 m
P10.54   (a) 1.98 m; (b) 3.11 m/s; (c) 0.00405
P10.56   (a) 7.11 ft/s; (b) 0.70
P10.58   (a) 0.0033; (b) 0.0016
P10.60 y_2 = 0.679 m; V_2 = 3.53 m/s
P10.64 Δh = 15.94 cm

P10.66   (b) 1.39

P10.70   2600 m^3/s

P10.72   (a) 0.046 m; (b) 4.33 m/s; (c) 6.43

P10.76   (a) 379 ft^3/s

P10.78 $H \approx 1.01$ ft

P10.80   (a) 0.395

P10.82   (a) 1.46 ft; (b) 15.5 ft/s; (c) 2.26; (d) 13 percent; (e) 2.52 ft

P10.84 $y_2 = 0.82$ ft; $y_3 = 5.11$ ft; 47 percent

P10.86   (a) 1.18 ft; (b) 4.58 ft/s

P10.88   (a) 2.22 m^3/s/m; (b) 0.79 m; (c) 5.17 m; (d) 60 percent; (e) 0.37 m

P10.90   (a) $y_2 = 1.83$ ft; $y_3 = 7.86$ ft

P10.92 $y_1 = 1.71$ mm; $V_1 = 0.310$ m/s

P10.94   (a) 5.32; (b) 0.385 m/s; (c) 18.7 cm

P10.96 $R \approx 4.92$ cm

P10.98   (a) steep S-3; (b) S-2; (c) S-1

P10.106 No entry depth leads to critical flow

P10.108 Approximately 6.6 m

P10.110 (a) $y_{crest} \approx 0.782$ m; (b) $y(L) \approx 0.909$ m

P10.112 M-1 curve, with $y = 2$ m at $L \approx 214$ m

P10.114 11.5 ft

P10.120 $Y = 0.64$ m, $\alpha = 34°$

P10.122 5500 gal/min

P10.124 M-1 curve, $y = 10$ ft at $x = -3040$ ft

P10.126 At $x = -100$ m, $y = 2.81$ m

P10.128 At 300 m upstream, $y = 2.37$ m

Chapter 11

P11.6   This is a diaphragm pump.

P11.8   (a) 86 percent

P11.10   (a) 12 gal/min; (b) 12 gal/min; (c) 87 percent

P11.12   (a) 11.3 m; (b) 1520 W

P11.14   1870 W

P11.16 $Q \approx 7100$ gal/min; $H \approx 38$ m

P11.18 $V_{vane} = (1/3)V_{jet}$ for max power

P11.20   (a) 2 roots: $Q = 7.5$ and 38.3 ft^3/s; (b) 2 roots; $H = 180$ ft and 35 ft

P11.22   (a) BEP = 92 percent at $Q = 0.20$ m^3/s

P11.26   (a) Both are fine, the largest is more efficient.

P11.28   BEP at about 6 ft^3/s; $N_s \approx 1430$, $Q_{max} \approx 12$ ft^3/s

P11.30   (a) 640 r/min; (b) 75 ft

P11.32   (a) $D \approx 15.5$ in; (c) $n \approx 2230$ r/min

P11.34   (a) 11.5 in; (b) 28 hp; (c) 100 ft; (d) 78 percent

P11.36   (a) No; (b) 24.5 in at 960 r/min

P11.38   (a) 18.5 hp; (b) 7.64 in; (c) 415 gal/min; (d) 81 percent

P11.40   (a) $D_s = D(gH*)^{1/4}/Q*^{1/2}$

P11.42   NPSH$_{proto} \approx 23$ ft

P11.44   No cavitation, required depth is only 5 ft

P11.46 $D_s \approx C/N_s$, $C = 7800 \pm 7$ percent

P11.48   (b) Approximately 130 ft

P11.52   (a) 6.56 m^3/s; (b) 12.0 kW; (c) 28.3°

P11.54   (a) 21 in; (b) 490 bhp

P11.56   (a) $D = 5.67$ ft, $n = 255$ r/min, $P = 700$ hp; (b) $D = 1.76$ ft, $n = 1770$ r/min, $P = 740$ hp

P11.58   (b) Approximately 2500 r/min

P11.60   (b) No.

P11.62 $D = 18.7$ ft, $\Delta p = 1160$ Pa

P11.64   (a) 15.4 in; (b) 900 r/min

P11.66   720 ft^3/min, non-BEP efficiency 78 percent

P11.68   (a) 4.8 in; (b) 6250 r/min

P11.70   (a) 212 ft; (b) 5.8 ft^3/s

P11.72   (a) 10 gal/min; (b) 1.3 in

P11.74   (a) 14.9; (b) 15.9; (c) 20.7 kgal/min (all)

P11.76 $D_{pipe} \approx 1.70$ ft

P11.78   Approximately 10 stages

P11.80   Both pumps work with three each in series, the largest being more efficient.

P11.84   Two turbines: (a) $D \approx 9.6$ ft; (b) $D \approx 3.3$ ft

P11.86 $N_{sp} \approx 70$, hence Francis turbines

P11.88   (a) Francis; (c) 16 in; (d) 900 r/min; (e) 87 hp

P11.90 $P \approx 800$ kW

P11.94   (a) 71 percent; (b) $N_{sp} \approx 19$

P11.96   (a) 0.45 m; (b) 0.17 m

P11.100 About 5.7 MW

P11.102 $Q \approx 29$ gal/min

P11.104 (a) 69 MW

P11.106 Approximately 15 mi/h

P11.108 (a) About 15 Darrieus turbines

Index

D

N

W